HANDBOOK OF RESEARCH ON SCIENCE EDUCATION

Building on the foundation set in Volume I—a landmark synthesis of research in the field—Volume II is a comprehensive, state-of-the-art new volume highlighting new and emerging research perspectives.

Features of Volume II
- International range of authors who are the most prominent scholars in the field
- Overarching attention to research paradigms and their relationship to learning theory, research design, data collection, data analysis
- Coverage of both global issues (such as policy) and the teaching and learning of specific disciplines
- Balanced treatment of research on teaching and research on learning

The contributors, all experts in their research areas, represent the international and gender diversity in the science education research community. The volume is organized around six themes: theory and methods of science education research; science learning; culture, gender, and society and science learning; science teaching; curriculum and assessment in science; and science teacher education. Each chapter presents an integrative review of the research on the topic it addresses—pulling together the existing research, working to understand the historical trends and patterns in that body of scholarship, describing how the issue is conceptualized within the literature, how methods and theories have shaped the outcomes of the research, and where the strengths, weaknesses, and gaps are in the literature.

Providing guidance to science education faculty and graduate students and leading to new insights and directions for future research, the *Handbook of Research on Science Education,* Volume II is an essential resource for the entire science education community.

Norman G. Lederman is Professor and Chair, Department of Mathematics and Science Education, Illinois Institute of Technology, USA.

Sandra K. Abell (deceased) was MU Curators Professor of Science Education, University of Missouri, USA. A renowned researcher and author nationally and internationally, she was named a fellow of the American Association for the Advancement of Science (AAAS), the American Educational Research Association (AERA), and the National Science Teachers Association (NSTA) and received numerous awards for her teaching and mentoring of students.

HANDBOOK OF RESEARCH ON SCIENCE EDUCATION

Volume II

Edited by

Norman G. Lederman

Sandra K. Abell

NEW YORK AND LONDON

First published 2014
by Routledge
711 Third Avenue, New York, NY 10017

and by Routledge
2 Park Square, Milton Park, Abingdon, Oxon OX14 4RN

Routledge is an imprint of the Taylor & Francis Group, an informa business

© 2014 Taylor & Francis

Library of Congress Cataloging-in-Publication Data

Handbook of research on science education / edited by Sanda K. Abell and Norman G. Lederman.
   p. cm.
 1. Science—Study and teaching—Research.   I. Abell, Sandra K.   II. Lederman, Norman G.
 Q181.H149 2006
 507.1—dc22

ISBN: 978-0-415-62937-9 (hbk)
ISBN: 978-0-415-62955-3 (pbk)
ISBN: 978-0-203-09726-7 (ebk)

Typeset in Times
by Apex CoVantage, LLC

Printed and bound in the United States of America by Sheridan Books, Inc. (a Sheridan Group Company).

Dedication

Volume I of this *Handbook* grew from conversations between Sandi and Naomi Silverman, who at that time was at Lawrence Erlbaum Associates, Inc. Sandi then reached out to me to serve as a co-editor. Sandi's influence on the research preceding and following the publication of Volume I was strong and continues to be as strong and visionary as ever. Consequently, it would be a crime not to include Sandi as co-editor for Volume II. Sandi and I were already discussing this new volume prior to the time of her unfortunate passing. Throughout Sandi's career, she was an excellent scholar in the area of teacher education, among other areas, a strong mentor (I think one of her PhD students described her as the master of tough love), global leader in science education, and a role model for us all. She had the perfect balance of theory and practice that many of us only aspire to develop. Personally, I always respected Sandi's work, but I also could always rely on her honesty and integrity when it related to my work and a wide variety of other professional and personal topics. I miss Sandi greatly, and it is my sincerest hope that Volume II of the *Handbook of Research on Science Education* will help continue her legacy, not that her legacy needs any additional help. We miss you, Sandi!!

Contents

Section IV. Science Teaching
Section Editor: Jan H. van Driel

Section V. Curriculum and Assessment in Science
Section Editor: Paul Black

Preface

This volume builds on the foundation presented in Volume I. Volume I will remain in print, as what is provided here builds on but does not simply repeat what was previously published. This volume consists of updated chapters from Volume I. These chapters are not repetitions of previous chapters, and overlap only exists where necessary to understand current and emerging trends in the field. Most of the chapters have been written by chapter authors from the previous volume, but some new authors have also been included. Since the publication of Volume I, Taylor & Francis and I have been surveying members of the science education community about topics omitted from Volume I or those topics needing expansion or reduction. In response, this volume also includes numerous chapters, written by prominent scholars, on topics of critical importance to researchers and theoreticians in science education.

As with Volume I, the contributors to this volume are experts in their research areas and represent the international and gender diversity in the science education research community. The volume is organized around six themes: theory and methods of science education research; science learning; diversity and equity in science learning; science teaching; curriculum and assessment in science; and science teacher education. Each chapter presents an integrative review of the research on the topic it addresses—pulling together the existing research, working to understand the historical trends and patterns in that body of scholarship, and describing how the issue is conceptualized within the literature, how methods and theories have shaped the outcomes of the research, and where the strengths, weaknesses, and gaps are in the literature.

Each of the aforementioned sections was organized and monitored by a section editor prominent in the field, who reviewed each manuscript and integrated the evaluations by at least two external reviewers. Finally, the overall sets of chapters were reviewed by myself as the primary editor for the *Handbook*. To this end, the compilations of chapters were thoroughly peer reviewed.

Since the publication of Volume I, research on teaching and learning in science has remained a highly active area of study. Our continued quest to improve science teaching and learning has been further fueled, in recent years, by the proliferation of international comparisons and the emergence of numerous standards for teaching and learning throughout the world. The primary goal continues to be scientific literacy, but how this construct is defined has been changing, and perspectives on how it is achieved are equally varied. The continued emergence of the learning sciences has altered researchers' perspectives on the interpretation of classroom practice, classroom environments, and student learning. This is reflected in the expanded section on Science Learning edited by **Richard Lehrer**.

In-depth discussions of theory and methods of science education research were not provided in the previous volume. A separate section, edited by **David F. Treagust**, on these perspectives has been added as the opening section to the *Handbook* in an effort to create an overall perspective from which to interpret what follows. The section addresses both qualitative and quantitative perspectives, and there is no intended prominence or favor given to one approach versus another. There is intentionally not a separate chapter on mixed-methods research, but the authors of both the qualitative and quantitative chapters have addressed the mixed-methods perspective.

In response to reviewers and growing emphasis within the science education community, the section on diversity and equity in science learning, under the editorship of **Cory A. Buxton and Okhee Lee**, has been significantly expanded and enhanced. In particular, much more attention is given to indigenous knowledge and English language learners. A separate chapter on inquiry teaching has been added to the science teaching section, which is edited by **Jan H. van Driel**. In addition, there are now new chapters in the curriculum and assessment in science section, edited by **Paul Black**, on socioscientific issues and precollege engineering education. The section on science teacher education, edited by **J. John Loughran**, primarily consists of enhanced and updated chapters from Volume I. As you would expect, the emphasis on the nature and development of pedagogical content knowledge remains a strong theme.

At the end of the Preface for the previous *Handbook*, Sandi and I included a section titled "The Future of Science Education." In this section, we provided some suggested guidelines for researchers to consider related to our overall purpose of improving teaching and learning, keeping an open mind with respect to alternative theoretical perspectives, grounding our research in the *real world*, and communicating our research to teachers. The two former guidelines need not be repeated here, but I would like to return to the latter two. I think Sandi would agree with this decision.

Science education and education in general is an applied field. I know some would like to hold on to the importance of theoretical research that may or may not have applications in the future. After all, some research that seems quite theoretical now may be of practical use in a decade. Realistically speaking (given the constraints within which we operate and the mandate of the public), somewhere along the way our research and our research-derived suggestions must be grounded in the *real world* of teachers and students. Our research must address the concerns of teachers and students, and it must be applicable in our school systems and society. To have any warrant, our research must address questions of educational importance. Each chapter contains a section addressing the implications of its topic. We need to think carefully about the meaning of these sections and not let them fall into the category of an article section that must be included. We continue to have a problem with the gap between research and practice. I have heard this since I was a PhD student. We need to work more on communicating our research to teachers and policy makers. All too often, our meetings and journals are set up so we are only speaking with other researchers. On a personal level, when I attend National Association for Research in Science Teaching or other research meetings and present my work on nature of science, the audience is very interested in my research design, data analysis, and conclusions, and there is very little interest in or time to discuss how I actually teach people about nature of science. When I attend NSTA or other practitioner-oriented meetings, the audience is primarily interested in what I actually do with students and teachers and not as interested in the specifics of research design and data analysis. You certainly notice a similar pattern in articles printed in "teacher" journals and "researcher" journals. The problem is multifaceted, but we must continue to work on communicating our research to teachers. It is our responsibility.

This *Handbook of Research on Science Education* is written for researchers, and it will be read almost exclusively by researchers. It would not be the best choice for a preservice or inservice teaching strategies course. We need to make the conscious effort to translate what is presented in the pages of this *Handbook* into a form that is readily understandable and usable by teachers, with the ultimate goal of helping their students. It is not often talked about, but we must work on developing our pedagogical content knowledge for teacher education.

Acknowledgments

Serving as a volume editor can be as labor intensive as one wants to make it. However, there is always a variety of important tasks that would not be completed without significant help. I want to thank Dionysius Gnanakkan, research assistant at Illinois Institute of Technology, for all his help related to substantive editing, clerical editing, formatting of chapters, and the development and application of the *Handbook* database. Because of Dion's extensive knowledge of science education and science education research, his assistance exceeded what could be expected from a general editor. This *Handbook* could not have come to fruition without his help. I hope he doesn't graduate too soon!

Section I

Theory and Methods of Science Education Research

SECTION EDITOR: DAVID F. TREAGUST

1

Paradigms in Science Education Research

DAVID F. TREAGUST, MIHYE WON, AND REINDERS DUIT

Why Discuss Research Paradigms?

From the nature of science studies, science education researchers are familiar with Thomas Kuhn's (1962) theory of paradigm shifts. Kuhn's main focus was on scientific inquiry and the scientific community, not on social or educational research, but his term "paradigm" provides a convenient reference point to talk about different sets of beliefs, values, and methodologies in educational research (Schwandt, 2001). A paradigm in educational research is recognized as a worldview that sets the value of research and asks such questions as (Guba & Lincoln, 1994): What is counted as social knowledge, action, and meaning? What are the main goals of educational research? What are the roles of educational researchers? How do we carry out our research projects? As Anderson (1998) notes, "How you see the world is largely a function of where you view it from" (p. 3). Consequently, the research paradigms guide the researchers throughout the empirical research process, from setting the research purpose to selecting data collection methods to analyzing the data and reporting the findings.

Despite their importance, research paradigms are rather hidden from plain view, especially for novice educational researchers. Many introductory research methods books do not extensively talk about research paradigms and philosophical backgrounds, except for the procedural differences between quantitative and qualitative research (Creswell, 2012; Fraenkel, Wallen, & Hyun, 2012; Punch, 2005; Wiersma & Jurs, 2005). Rather, they focus on "practical" aspects of data collection and analysis—that is, step-by-step how-to procedures, such as how to phrase survey questions, how to use statistical packages, or how to conduct effective interviews. In such discussions of the research process, educational researchers view their studies mainly in terms of technicalities, without recognizing the worldviews that shape and validate their knowledge claims (Kincheloe & Tobin, 2009). The fact that many people conduct studies without seriously considering

research paradigms may be interpreted as the practical aspects of identifying a research paradigm not being as paramount as some researchers believe (Bryman, 2008). Some researchers even regard discussion of paradigms as a purely philosophical exercise, a remnant of the paradigm wars in the 1980s and 1990s (Morgan, 2007). A seminal article published by Gage (1989, written as though it was 2009) described the situation of the paradigm wars from a vantage point of 20 years hence. As discussed in this article, positivist and post-positivist research flourished in the 1980s and was later challenged by alternative paradigms, namely those of an interpretivist and critical nature. Much of what Gage wrote about has turned out to be what occurred in practice. However, initial antagonism of proponents of one paradigm toward another appears to have been somewhat moderated with the development and use of mixed-methods research (Bryman, 2008) and the wider acknowledgement of the contributions that research from different paradigms brings to the education community (Bredo, 2009).

Nevertheless, in recent years, we have witnessed some heated discussion on the diversity of research paradigms and what it means in the practice of educational research (Moss et al., 2009). Many education philosophers and researchers have found that the education research guidelines and policies published in 2002 in the United States by the National Research Council and by other research funding organizations dogmatically promote a certain type of research studies under the banner of evidence-based, *agree scientific research. These educational authors believe that it is dangerous to have such a limited view on what "other" types of research could contribute to establishing better education. (For more detailed discussion of this issue, please refer to the journals *Educational Researcher* in 2002 [volume 31, issue 8] and 2009 [volume 38, issues 6–7] and *Qualitative Inquiry* in 2004 [volume 10, issue 1].)

Without an analytical understanding of each research paradigm, it is easy to misjudge the quality and the value of research studies and miss the opportunities to learn from them (Moss et al., 2009). In the education community and the science education community in particular, there is a tendency to ignore/dismiss research studies in other research paradigms (Kincheloe & Tobin, 2009). Post-positivists may think that interpretivist studies are anecdotal and not methodically rigorous enough, and critical theory studies are too politically oriented. Interpretivists may regard that post-positivist studies are superficial or limiting. Critical theorists may consider that post-positivist studies are exacerbating educational inequality. Yet there is great need to have an open mind to learn from the differences (Maxwell, 2004; Moss et al., 2009). The philosophical and practical diversity in the education research community not only supports building more balanced knowledge in education (St. Pierre, 2002) but also makes ways for more comprehensive research efforts with common goals (Bredo, 2009).

In this chapter, we outline three research paradigms and describe how each paradigm is realized in various research studies in science education and conclude with a discussion of the pragmatic approaches taken by mixed-methods researchers. This is not an attempt to pin research studies on one category of paradigm or another. Rather, by describing how different paradigms play out in the science education research field, we attempt to reflect on our own research practices and facilitate a dialogue across paradigms among science education researchers. While there are many different categorizations and boundary drawings of research paradigms (Clandinin & Rosiek, 2007; Lincoln & Guba, 2000; Moss et al., 2009; Taylor, Taylor, & Luitel, 2012), we have used the categories of positivist/post-positivist, interpretivist, and critical theory and illustrated the characteristics of each paradigm in relation to one another. We intentionally did not use the common categories of quantitative and qualitative research in this chapter because they could be misleading—as if paradigm is limited to the choice of data collection methods. As mentioned, we believe a research paradigm is much more encompassing than the choice of data types.

Positivist/Post-Positivist Research Paradigm

Philosophical Backgrounds of Positivist Research

Positivism is understood as "any approach that applies scientific method to the study of human action" (Schwandt, 2001, p. 199). Following the empirical science tradition, positivist researchers assert that in order to make a meaningful knowledge claim, research studies should be firmly supported by *logical reasoning and empirical data* that are self-evident and verifiable (Schwandt, 2001). Many science education researchers may find this ideology of positivism familiar because it is well integrated within Western academic culture—such as viewing objective, scientific, logical, evidence-based research as the

most desirable form of research (Howe, 2009; Kincheloe & Tobin, 2009). In contemporary discourse, however, positivism carries some negative implications due to its link to naïve realism, and modified forms of positivism are quite prevalent and influential in the education field. Next, we present post-positivism as a variation of positivism (logical empiricism) rather than as a counterpart of positivism.

Different from positivists, post-positivists do admit that our culture, personal value systems, and other surroundings influence our perception of the world in both positive and negative ways (Phillips & Burbules, 2000)—positive because it guides what to look for and how to make a reasonable, logical explanation but negative because it may lead to tunnel vision, limiting our understanding of the phenomenon in the truest form. Because of the negative influence of our prejudices, we cannot be sure whether our knowledge claims really reflect the truth. Yet this does not mean that the truth does not exist or that the truth does not matter. For example, a group of teachers may personally prefer a didactic teaching method based on their experience. Their reluctance to recognize alternative teaching methods, however, does not mean that there could be certain teaching methods that are more effective and yield better outcomes with students. Here, the role of post-positivist researchers is, as objective investigators, to systematically approach the truth as best as they can. Rather than simply relying on prior experiences, the researchers endeavor to collect comprehensive empirical data methodically and compare the different teaching methods objectively. By conducting a systematic empirical inquiry, post-positivist researchers believe that they can reach close to the truth and are able to inform the people of interest (teachers, policy makers, parents, students, etc.) in order to help make wise decisions, for example, on a new educational program or educational improvement plans (in this case, informing teachers which teaching method is better).

Examples of Post-Positivist Research

Similar to research in the natural sciences or psychology, the post-positivist tradition focuses on seeking a scientific causal or at least a correlational explanation—for example, the effectiveness of a new teaching method on students' achievement, the relationship of students' family background and their attitudes toward schooling, or the influence of students' perceptions toward science on their academic performance. Naturally, post-positivist researchers regularly adopt comparative experimental designs or survey designs to find a causal or correlational explanation. To help readers understand the distinct characteristics of post-positivist research, we introduce three research studies from the science education literature.

Kihyun Ryoo and Marcia Linn (2012) followed this post-positivist research tradition and investigated the effectiveness of an educational program in terms of students' conceptual achievement through pre- and posttests. This study resembles much of an experiment report in the natural sciences. The authors conservatively designed their study in advance, strictly followed the research protocols, and methodically elaborated the research procedures in the report to convince the readers that they fulfilled the quality standards of the post-positivist experimental design. At the beginning of their report, they posed their research question, "How do dynamic visualizations, compared to static illustrations, improve middle school students' understanding of energy transformation in photosynthesis?" The researchers divided students into an experimental group with dynamic visualization and one control group with static visualization. While the researchers did put the effort in making the experimental education program attractive (in this case, dynamic visualization), they tried to make the control and experimental conditions similar as much as possible, except for the instruction materials (that is, independent variable of dynamic versus static visualization). To equalize those two conditions, the researchers adopted a few measures: they selected two teachers with similar teaching experience (5 years); within each teacher's class, the students were randomly assigned to two groups after a pretest; the students went through identical lessons and assessments except for the visualization modes; and the number of students was large enough to make analytical claims based on statistics (200 students in total). After the lesson and assessments, the researchers categorized the students' written answers based on an assessment rubric to decide on the improvements of students' understanding of the concept. Once the data were in, the researchers used a set of statistical packages to analyze the data and backed up their research findings using various sources of data and triangulation. In order to convince the reader that procedures had been followed faithfully, the researchers provided an extensive explanation of the research procedures with statistical significance, internal validity, and external validity of the study. After the data analysis, the researchers informed the readers of the educational implications of the findings and the limitations of the study, such as where the results can and cannot be generalized to and possible ways to increase the educational effects for further studies.

Another post-positivist study by Sunitadevi Velayutham, Jill Aldridge, and Barry J. Fraser (2011) examined the affective domain. The researchers developed a survey instrument to measure students' motivation and self-regulation in science learning. Based on a literature review, the researchers identified a few key components that reportedly influence students' motivation in science learning, such as learning goal orientation, task value, self-efficacy, and self-regulation. Here, we notice the researchers' firm belief that extensive utilization of previous research studies is the effective way to make a reliable instrument to measure students' perception of themselves (Jaeger, 1997). They painstakingly identified the possible factors and wrote the questionnaire items, because the wording of the questions is regarded as being very important to obtaining the corresponding response. They conducted a pilot study and interviewed some teachers and students. The interviews were not a substantial part of the study but were used to check whether students' responses in the survey matched with what they said in their interviews. After the confirmation, the researchers distributed the survey to a large number of students (1,360 students in 78 classes). The students were the data source, and any personal connection with them was neither necessary nor desirable to make an unbiased, scientific claim. After the data collection, the researchers ran a series of statistical analyses to validate the instrument. With the numbers neatly organized in a table format, the researchers methodically claimed that their survey instrument has internal consistency reliability, concurrent validity, and predictive validity. They also claimed that they took stringent measures to safeguard themselves against methodical biases during their study. The researchers concluded the report with possible uses of the instrument for future studies.

Another research domain that lends itself to a post-positivist research paradigm includes studies that assess national standards or competencies of learning. National standards have been introduced worldwide (Waddington, Nentwig, & Schanze, 2007) and, for the evaluation of these standards, quantitative measures have been developed and evaluated for the various competencies addressed (DeBoer, 2011). These competencies include understanding and application of science concepts, principles and views of the nature of science, and also the competences to evaluate and judge the role of science knowledge in understanding key problems of society and lifeworld. In Germany, Julia Holstenbach, Hans Fischer, Alexander Kauertz, Jürgen Mayer, Elke Sumfleth, and Maik Walpuski (2011) developed a model of these competencies that is theoretically based and empirically validated by a test composed of items allowing large-scale assessment. The model includes the following areas of competence: (1) science knowledge, (2) knowledge about science, (3) communication, and (4) evaluation and judgment. The work draws on earlier work on evaluation and judgment competence in the field of biology education by Eggert and Bögeholz (2006), who presented a theoretically based competence model for decision making in the area of sustainable development. This work discusses the difficult task of developing instructional settings and materials to guide students in achieving the complex competencies addressed.

Common Features of Post-Positivist Research

Common research topics. The primary concern of positivist/post-positivist research is to provide a rational explanation for a variety of educational phenomena, but it is often linked with a scientific test for effectiveness or efficiency of a teaching program or educational system—in other words, investigating what works and why it works for evidence-based educational practice (Feuer, Towne, & Shavelson, 2002). Studies that typically are within a post-positivist paradigm include intervention studies as seen in Ryoo and Linn's (2012) study and other educational software studies such as the one by van Borkulo, van Joolingen, Savelsbergh, and de Jong (2012); large-scale assessment studies such as No Child Left Behind (NCLB) in the United States (Dee & Jacob, 2011) and the National Assessment Program—Literacy and Numeracy (NAPLAN) in Australia (Dulfer, Polesel, & Rice, 2012); and international comparison studies such as the Trends in International Mathematics and Science Study (TIMSS; Thomson, Hillman, & Wernert, 2012) and the Programme for International Student Assessment (PISA; Organisation for Economic Cooperation and Development, 2010).

Common research designs. Based on logical empiricism, post-positivists painstakingly focus on establishing formal research designs and data that can self-evidently explain what is happening within education programs/systems and why. In order to make their knowledge claim more scientific and generalizable to other educational systems, post-positivists may adopt various research designs but frequently choose experiments (Ryoo & Linn, 2012) or large-scale surveys (Velayutham et al., 2011). For such research designs, researchers adopt comprehensive sampling strategies (e.g., stratified, systematic, or cluster sampling) to represent the target population, and they endeavor to control the variables (e.g., dependent, independent, or confounding variables) in various ways to establish a clear causal relationship (Porter, 1997). They also spend a significant amount of time methodically developing a quantitative instrument or rubric to record the research participants' understanding, perceptions, or behaviors (Jaeger, 1997). The general standards of quantitative study, such as reliability, internal and external validity, and statistical precision, are faithfully attended to (Cohen, Manion, & Morrison, 2011). While qualitative data may be collected for such research designs through interviews, observations, or students' essays, the data are converted into numbers to correspond to preset categories (Ryoo & Linn, 2012) or used to support or elaborate on the quantitative data as a form of triangulation (Velayutham et al., 2011).

Role of the researcher in relation to the participants. Like natural scientists, post-positivist education researchers aim to be unbiased, knowledgeable experts who contemplate an educational phenomenon at a distance (Schwandt, 2001). The researchers primarily rely on the previously established body of knowledge, their intellectual reasoning power, and their impartiality to the study to make knowledge claims (Moss et al., 2009). Their personal values/beliefs or their involvement with the research participants may damage the objectivity of the study, and post-positivist researchers strive not to become too involved with the participants to proceed with the study fairly. In Ryoo and Linn's (2012) study, the researchers were not directly involved in teaching the students themselves; rather, they were outsiders who sat in class to check the intervention protocols and collect the necessary data. They did not try to build any personal connection with the participating students. Similarly, for the studies of Velayutham and colleagues (2011) and of Holstenbach and colleagues (2011), the same basic relationship was established between the researchers and the participants, with no personal attachment with the participants.

Because of the limited connections with the participants, the ethical obligations of the post-positivist researchers to the researched are seemingly straightforward. They follow the ethical guidelines outlined by the Institutional Review Board or Ethics Committee (see, for example, the ethics approval process of the American Educational Research Association, 2011, and the Australian Association for Research in Education, 2005, or similar institutional departments). These guidelines involve voluntary participation, informing participants about the research procedures in advance, being sure to avoid physical and psychological harm to the participants, safeguarding the anonymity of the participants, and reporting the data honestly (Fraenkel et al., 2012).

Common quality standards. While many researchers characterize positivism/post-positivism in terms of rigorous research methods and verifiable data (Kincheloe & Tobin, 2009), D.C. Phillips (2005) argues that researchers in this tradition value not just the methods but also how the overall case is made. He explains that a research study should be firmly based on objective, comprehensive data, but the arguments of the study should also be meticulously structured to present the main argument convincingly. Robert Floden (Moss et al., 2009) focuses on the connection of the research study to the research community and to the established body of knowledge and lists three important criteria to judge the quality of research in this tradition: (a) clear definition of concepts/constructs that are employed in the study; (b) strong, logical reasoning throughout the research process—from literature review to interpretation of the empirical data to drawing of its conclusions; and (c) significant contribution of the study findings to educators or policy makers.

Common Report Styles: Most post-positivist researchers follow the traditional scientific research report format: starting from the literature review, research problem/questions, research design, data analysis, and discussion of research findings, and finishing with limitations and educational implications. The flow of the report is logically organized to demonstrate how scientifically the study was conducted. The procedures are elaborately described to enable replications. The report is frequently written in a passive voice or third-person narrative, such as "the data were collected" rather than "I collected the data," to give an impersonal, objective tone.

Interpretivist Research Paradigm

Philosophical Backgrounds of Interpretivist Research

Interpretivism emerged as the reaction against the prevalent "scientific" positivism research. Different from positivists and their search for the objective, generalizable truth of the world, interpretivists focus on the *localized meanings of human experience*. Stemming from the relativist ontology and constructivist epistemology, the researchers in this tradition focus on the fact that people construct their understanding based on their experiences, culture, and context. Even one simple action of shaking hands could be interpreted differently—as pleasant, too formal, or repulsive—depending on the social convention, location, time, and company. Likewise, when an educational program is introduced, a young, enthusiastic, personable Ms. Alison may interpret and implement it differently from an experienced, charismatic Mr. Buckley. Consequently, the "proven" effects of the educational program may have little relevance to the students in Ms. Alison's class because of the local educational context. Thus, interpretivist researchers are scornful of the positivists' effort to gloss over the specifics to generalize their research findings. They argue that measuring and generalizing human understanding and behaviors—as in positivist studies—do not tell the more important part of human action—the situated meanings that people make out of such social, educational interactions. Researchers in the interpretivist tradition thus do not overly claim generalizability of their findings into other situations, because people's meanings and intentions are contextual, temporal, and particular. While academic researchers often feel the urge to make generalizable knowledge claims—that could go beyond the immediate context of the study to be widely applicable to address the situation at hand—interpretivists aim to describe in detail people's lived experiences (Dewey, 1925/1981) regarding educational phenomena. If the audience of the study finds the researcher's interpretation plausible, informative, or thought provoking, the research is regarded as worthwhile (Wolcott, 2009).

Researching people's localized, subjective interpretation of social phenomena, however, involves multiple layers of complication. For example, how do we know researchers identified the true local meanings? Understanding people's lived experience is not the same as interviewing and transcribing every word into a research paper. Researchers need to interpret what the research participants have shared with them, and the participants would share only what they want to share with the researchers. Based on researchers' own personal, social, and cultural experiences, the information from the participants could be interpreted quite differently. In order for researchers to claim that they have a good understanding of the educational phenomenon or of the participants' lived experiences, they usually spend an extended period of time with the participants, build rapport, empathize with the participants to make better sense of the situation, and review their own interpretation with the participants and against the literature. While the interpretivist researchers strive to examine their own values and experiences to establish better understanding of the situation by conducting member checks, audit trails, and other means (Guba & Lincoln, 1989; Merriam, 2009), the researchers do not claim that their knowledge claim is a complete or the right one but that it is a sensible interpretation of the situation.

The subjectivity issue becomes more complicated when considering the audience of the research report. When interpretivist researchers describe their understanding of the educational phenomenon and of the research participants, the audience has to reinterpret the research findings. Based on the readers' lived experience, the meaning drawn from the research report would be different. Aware of the multiple levels of subjectivity—from the social interaction to the research participants, from the research participants to the researcher, and from the researcher to the audience—the researchers in this tradition often offer "thick descriptions" of the situation to communicate the researchers' interpretation (Geertz, 1973).

Examples of Interpretivist Research

Similar to researchers in anthropology, science education researchers in the interpretivist paradigm set out to examine in some detail the way that individuals—be they teachers, students, administrators, or parents—develop an understanding of their experiences and activities. Consequently, researchers spend much time studying participants and collecting large amounts of (mostly) qualitative data from observations, interviews, descriptive narratives, and the like. Interpretivist studies vary widely in the amount of structure, the length of time, and the level of engagement of the researchers with the participants. The following examples provide some evidence of the variety of interpretivist studies.

An example of a more methodical interpretivist research position is one by David Treagust, Roberta Jacobowitz, James J. Gallagher, and Joyce Parker (2001). The study explored how a middle school teacher used assessment embedded within her teaching the topic of sound. Jim Gallagher had studied ethnographic research methods under Fred Erickson and had been influential in disseminating interpretivist research methods in science education through national and international contacts. During an academic leave, Treagust joined Gallagher in conducting this case study and regularly went to the research site—a Grade 8 science class with 23 students—to explore how the teacher "incorporated assessment tasks as an integral part of her teaching about the topic of sound" (p. 140). Despite the fact that one of the co-authors (Jacobowitz) was the teacher of the class, the rest of the researchers made minimal interference of the classroom activities. After 3 weeks of intensive observations of science class and interviews with the teacher and the students, the researchers combed through the data to identify how the assessment strategies were used and contributed to or detracted from learning the sound concepts of the lessons. Consistent with the qualitative research design espoused by Erickson (1986, 2012), analysis of the data enabled the development of five assertions that focused on the embedded assessment tasks. Each of the assertions was supported by detailed data from the classroom observations, as well as interviews and analysis of materials produced by the students during the lessons. The research showed

> that nearly every activity had an assessment component integrated into it, that students had a wide range of opportunities to express their knowledge and understanding through writing tasks and oral questioning, and that individual students responded to and benefited from the different assessment techniques in various ways.
>
> (p. 137)

Taking a more philosophical perspective, Beth Warren, Cynthia Ballenger, Mark Ogonowski, Ann Rosebery, and Josiane Hudicourt-Barnes (2001) at the Cheche Konnen Center illustrated how Haitian immigrant elementary school children develop scientific discourse in relation to their everyday interactions. The science education researchers in the sociocultural tradition often regard science as a discourse of a scientific community and science learning as crossing borders or gaining control of multiple discourses (C.W. Anderson, 2007). Warren and her colleagues, however, argued that children's everyday discourse and a scientific one are not dichotomous but are in a continuum. Using detailed descriptions of students' and scientists' interactions, the researchers in this study support their points. One of the episodes in the study was about Jean-Charles. He was a Haitian immigrant student who spoke Haitian Creole (known not to contain technical, scientific, abstract terms) as his first language. The researchers had known the student and the class for a considerably long time, and they were able to describe the usual modes of Jean-Charles's interactions with his peers, how it took a long time for him to speak about his ideas, how his drawings were admired by others, and so forth. In analyzing a class dialogue on metamorphosis, the researchers dissected the meaning of each student's sentences—both literal and contextual meanings in which they were understood by the members of the class—and how the casual language use and the class environment contributed to the sense making of the metamorphosis of insects in relation to the human growth. In analyzing an interview with Jean-Charles, the researchers discovered how the use of his everyday language helped the young child to distinguish growth and transformation in a unique way. Questioning the value of dichotomy between everyday language and scientific language, the researchers concluded that educators need to observe more deeply and carefully how the students' negotiation of meanings could help their scientific sense making.

Heidi B. Carlone (2004) conducted an ethnographic case study, entering the field with a research question: How do students, especially girls, make sense of science and being a good science participant in a reform-based physics class? The focus is on the female students' experiences—the meanings they build from the instruction and the local culture within which they operate. Science learning is understood not as a cognitive activity but as a sociocultural activity that integrates students' identities, discourses, and values. Different from post-positivist researchers, Carlone actively sought to get to know the students and spent much time in their naturalistic setting—the physics classroom. Six weeks may not be regarded as a long enough time to call this study an ethnography, but she stayed at school as a participant observer and collected an extensive data set utilizing ethnographic practices—as did Treagust and colleagues (2001). She took field notes in class, talked with students informally and in interviews, collected students' documents, and interviewed the teacher and school administrators. Any verbal or behavioral data were entered into the data set. She might have had an initial research design, but as she was accumulating data, she redirected the research to follow up on the preliminary results of data analysis. Instead of summarizing students' responses to the interview questions, Carlone endeavored to portray the participants' experiences, values, and ways of thinking through their own words and actions. She allocated an extensive portion of the paper to demonstrate the subtle way the participants' experiences are integrated into their way of communicating by directly quoting them. Because of the thick description of the situation, readers feel as if they are sitting in the classroom or seeing through the participants' minds. In conclusion, rather than giving a definite answer to the research question, Carlone shows the complexities in implementing an inclusive science curriculum for diverse students and calls for more nuanced understanding of students' participation in science learning.

Interpretivist studies in German physics classrooms by Reinders Duit and his colleagues involved an examination of nonlinear systems, which play a significant role in contemporary science but are seldom discussed in school science. A research and development program investigated the educational significance of this new topic, and explorative studies were carried out to find out which ideas of nonlinear systems may be taught to Grade 10 students. In one of the major studies, 25 students worked in small groups and tried to investigate key features of simple chaotic systems. The work in three groups was video-documented. Using a methodological approach fusing conceptual change and a discourse perspective allowed descriptions and analyses of students' learning trajectories both in terms of conceptual change and in terms of minute shifts of students' language games (Duit, Roth, Komorek, & Wilbers, 1998). The studies were carried out within the framework of a theoretical model for instructional planning, the Model of Educational Reconstruction (Duit, Gropengießer, Kattmann, Komorek, & Parchmann,

2012). This model shares major features of design-based research (Cobb, Confrey, diSessa, Lehrer, & Schauble, 2003). In the first steps of investigating whether a topic so far not included in the curriculum should be taught and may be taught in ordinary classroom settings, the results show how interpretive research designs are powerful. In this instructional program, the analytical and empirical (interpretive) research concerning the educational significance of the topic in question (understanding nonlinear systems) and the empirical (qualitative) research on the means to teach the new topic in schools resulted in a preliminary teaching and learning sequence. In addition, insights into the fine structure of analogy use were gained that in subsequent interpretive studies resulted in a model of analogy use. Briefly summarized, the studies resulted in preliminary ideas on teaching key issues of nonlinear systems and provided new insights in the fine structure of analogy use, partly challenging the predominating cognitive science approaches (Duit, Roth, Komorek, & Wilbers, 2001). Finally, another related exploratory study resulted in a "heuristic" model of analogy use (Wilbers & Duit, 2005), explaining why analogies provided by teachers often fail to achieve their intended aim.

Common Features of Interpretivist Research

Common research topics. Interpretivist studies focus on the cultures (Carlone, 2004), language use (Warren, Ballenger, Ogonowski, Rosebery, & Hudicourt-Barnes, 2001), classroom interactions (Gallas, 1995; Paley, 1981; Treagust et al., 2001), and lived experiences of students, teachers, scientists, and community members (Wong, 2002). Through the researcher's empathic identification with the participants and through reflection on the beliefs and values of the researcher and the society, researchers aim to understand the research participants' meaning making around science teaching and learning. Even when a new educational intervention program is implemented, the researchers in this tradition highlight the dynamic interactions between the program and the local contexts, and consider how the local participants interact with and understand the new program (Erickson & Gutierrez, 2002). The interpretivists do not expect that their research results could be readily or directly translated into general science education policies or strategies (Bryman, 2012).

Common research designs. As an interpretivist research study is perceived as a sense-making process for the researchers involved, the research design itself can evolve as illustrated by the studies by Duit and colleagues (2001), which is consistent with grounded theory. As the researchers immerse themselves in the situation, they get to know the "prominent" research questions better, develop a clearer focus, and may change the research design accordingly. The evolving research design is not something that is frowned upon, as in post-positivist research, but a natural process of interpretivist research. Interpretivist researchers tend to adopt qualitative research designs, such as case study, ethnography, narrative, and phenomenological

research. The qualitative data collection methods tend to be interviews, observations, and document analysis. To capture the everyday experiences of the research participants, studies usually occur in naturalistic settings rather than experimental comparative settings as in post-positivist studies.

Role of the researcher in relation to the participants. Within the interpretivist paradigm, researchers do not aim to claim objectivity attained by disinterested, unbiased researchers. Because interpretivists believe that meanings are not pregiven but are co-created through hermeneutic dialogues (Schwandt, 2000), researchers often aim to study by engaging with the activities of the research participants (Clandinin & Rosiek, 2007; Guba & Lincoln, 2005; Wolcott, 2009). As the sense maker and narrator of the situation under study, the researcher may solicit the views of the research participants and sometimes seeks immersion in the situation to experience it him/herself. Because of the close relationship with the participants, researchers are obligated to consider many ethical issues beyond the Institutional Review Board guidelines, such as how to draw a boundary between the stories that are intriguing to readers and the stories that are too personal to pry into or too consequential to report, or how much to honor the participants' willingness to share their stories when they do not fully grasp the meaning of participating in a research project (Clark & Sharf, 2007; Einarsdottir, 2007; Etherington, 2007; Jones & Stanley, 2008).

Common quality standards. Interpretivist researchers admit that the quality of research depends on the skills, sensitivity, and integrity of the researcher because research itself is a sense-making process. Frederick Erickson (Moss et al., 2009) categorizes the criteria to judge quality interpretivist research study into two areas: the technical aspects and the educational imagination. Technical aspects involve: (a) prolonged, meaningful interaction in the field; (b) careful, repeated sifting through the data; (c) reflective analysis of the data; and (d) clear, rich reporting. However, interpretivists focus more on the substance than on the methodical rigor by itself, and that is what Erickson meant by educational imagination. One of the criteria most interpretivist researchers uphold is crystallization (Denzin & Lincoln, 2011). Like a clear crystal that casts multiple colors, the researchers endeavor to create a strong image of the lived experiences of the participants through comprehensive deliberation and persuasive presentation (p. 5). As a general guideline for interpretivist research studies, Tracy (2010) offers eight criteria: a worthy, relevant, significant topic; rich data and appropriate theoretical construct; researcher's reflexivity and transparency in value and biases; credible data through thick description and respondents' validation; aesthetic representation of findings; significant contribution in theory and practice; ethical; and meaningful coherence of study. Interestingly enough, a few of these criteria sound very similar to the post-positivist quality standards listed earlier.

Common report styles. The most distinctive feature of interpretivist studies is that the data are qualitative, much of which is thick description of the situation (individuals, contexts, or events). Lengthy transcripts or rich, verbal descriptions of a situation often characterize interpretivist research. The report could take the form of a traditional empirical study with literature review, methods description, and data analysis (Carlone, 2004). Or it could take a narrative format of describing a daily procedure of a schoolteacher or children's discussion in class (Gallas, 1995, 1997; Paley, 1981). In such narrative reports, researchers do not make a long validity claim or methodological justification; they simply describe what they have done and explain why. Yet the writing is not an easy task for interpretivist researchers. It is "endlessly creative and interpretive" (Denzin & Lincoln, 2011, p. 14). Researchers often ask questions such as: How much contextual description is enough for the readers? How much analysis and how much description are adequate? Through whose voice is the story told? (Wolcott, 2009). The rich description of research participants' lived experience needs to be artfully woven into researchers' interpretations, and the researchers' writing ability (or storytelling ability) is counted critical. Interpretivist researchers do not regard their interpretation of the situation as the absolute truth, so they tend not to provide the final words (or conclusions) of the study (Wolcott, 2009).

However, in science education research journals, the extent of this thick description is often limited by the page requirements of the journal, and only short episodes can be reported. Depending on who reviews such work, these abbreviated thick descriptions or dialogues can be seen as not meeting the necessary criteria. In addition, many research reports lack the detailed description of how the researchers selected the participants, why they chose to focus on certain aspects or data collection methods, what they did to ensure the quality of data analysis, and how they considered alternative interpretations. Yet, in recent years, sociocultural, interpretivist research studies appear more frequently in major science education journals such as *Journal of Research in Science Teaching* and *Science Education* (Carter, 2007; Hammond & Brandt, 2004). *Cultural Studies in Science Education* publishes articles with this particular focus and has greatly widened the scope of work that is designed to better understand science as a cultural practice. Research studies in this tradition aim to integrate students' cognition with the context (Hammond & Brandt, 2004).

Critical Theory[1] Research Paradigm

Philosophical Backgrounds of Critical Theory Research

Similar to interpretivist researchers, critical theory researchers acknowledge that people's values, ideas, and facts are shaped by social, political, cultural, economic, gender, and ethnic experiences. Critical theory researchers, however, put more focus on *the inequality and the power dynamics* in human interactions because they understand that all ideas and social interactions are "fundamentally mediated by power relations" (Kincheloe & McLaren, 2005, p. 304). This tradition could be traced back to Marxism in terms of the exploration of unequal power relationships and power struggles. They view that "social reality is not always what it should or could be," but the social arrangements make people feel comfortable with the status quo (Kincheloe & McLaren, 2005). Academia contributes to such social arrangements by making people develop false consciousness to believe the existing body of knowledge is neutral and scientific (rather than a tool to serve a certain group of people), effectively preventing people from questioning the status quo (Kincheloe & Tobin, 2009). Clandinin and Rosiek (2007) observe that the critical theory researchers believe that "large scale social arrangements conspire not only to physically disempower individuals and groups but also to epistemically disempower people" (p. 47).

Because the social narrative is conceptualized that way, researchers strive to examine the current social values and roles in historical and cultural contexts and problematize many taken-for-granted ideas for the benefit of socially marginalized people, such as: Is science learning or educational reform really beneficial for everyone (Barton & Osborne, 2001; Eisenhart, Finkel, & Marion, 1996)? Why don't ethnic minority students or female students participate in school science as much as their white male counterparts (Lee, 2002; Noddings, 1998)? Isn't there something that inherently discourages them from learning science at school (Aikenhead & Jegede, 1999; Allen & Crawley, 1998; Brickhouse, Lowery, & Schultz, 2000; Harding, 1991)?

By asking such philosophical questions, researchers in this tradition focus on uncovering the unequal power relationship in societies and institutions. They aim not just to expand the knowledge of the society but to contribute to transform the society and emancipate the disempowered people (Kincheloe, 2003). Carter (2007) argued, "science education should not only work toward a deeper understanding of our planetary systems but also toward the explicit goals of creating a more just, equitable, and sustainable world" (p. 175). Researchers ask themselves, "If the society or science education is not open, democratic and equal, what should we do to change, as teacher, educational researcher, and concerned community member?" (Bouillion & Gomez, 2001; Elmesky & Tobin, 2005; Fusco, 2001; Roth & Desautels, 2002; Tan & Barton, 2008). In order to enact changes in the lives of the socially, economically, and historically marginalized people, they often go into the low-income, ethnic-minority-neighborhood schools and become involved in some type of an action project.

Examples of Critical Theory Research

Critical theory research studies may look quite different from more "traditional" research studies in terms of their

(1) critique of the social discourse/structure; (2) orientation toward social action and change; (3) explicit analysis on the researchers' identities, values, and intentions; and (4) experimental way of writing research reports (Kincheloe, 2003). The first two studies discussed (by Bouillion & Gomez and by Elmesky & Tobin) illustrate how science education researchers attempted to change how schooling or social research is done. They first pointed out the limitations of the status quo and then enacted alternative ways. Their primary goal was not only to observe but also to change the situation and empower the students and their community for the betterment of the people involved. The third study (by Tan & Barton) was conducted in the same vein as the first two, but this study may look very similar to an interpretivist study in terms of the authors' defense of research methods, presentation of results, and interpretations. The last study (by Eisenhart) is a critical autoethnographic study in which the author conveys her own experience and reflections as "data." The author made clear that her critical interpretation of the social phenomena was socially and politically motivated. These studies follow different research methods and reporting styles. Despite the difference, we put them in this critical research tradition because of their explicit focus on challenging the inequality of the status quo and the commitment toward social change (Maulucci, 2012).

Lisa Bouillion and Louis Gomez (2001) conducted an action-oriented, transformative research study at an elementary school in a low-income urban neighborhood in Chicago, Illinois. Instead of following the traditional school learning model, the researchers along with the teachers at the school implemented a science project in which science was taught beyond the school walls and promoted the school–community partnership. The project was called the Chicago River Project. As students recognized illegally dumped garbage was a major community problem, they investigated the environmental issues scientifically in terms of river pollution and water safety. They shared the results with other community members through writing. They organized a series of actions to change the situation. The project was not just one of interesting school activities for the teachers and students. It was their own community problem that they found intimately relevant and in need of action. As the project evolved, the researchers not only collected data for the research report, they also helped the students and teachers make the action project successful. The researchers aimed to change the existing practice of science teaching at the school and to break down several existing power relations or boundaries through the study: between students and science as they become users and producers of scientific knowledge with the help from local community activist-scientists; between teachers and students as students' ideas were purposefully incorporated into the activity planning and execution; between education researchers and schoolteachers as they became equal contributors in the collaborative project; and between students and the city council as the students'

persistent effort persuaded the city to act on behalf of the community. While the research report may look similar to a qualitative study, a major goal of this study was to effect a change in the community and the identity of students and teachers within their learning environments.

In conventional educational research, students are often the ones who supply data for the research project by filling out questionnaires, answering competency tests, or responding to interview questions, while researchers design, execute, and analyze the study. Rowhea Elmesky and Kenneth Tobin (2005) conducted a study trying to change the power imbalance in the research process. Instead of following the conventional model of objectifying students' ideas, Elmesky and Tobin involved students as the collaborative researchers rather than as subjects. Elmesky and Tobin framed their research study as an alternative to the status quo educational research in American inner-city (low-income, ethnic-minority neighborhood) schools. They started their study by questioning the effectiveness or the true intention of educational programs in improving the scientific literacy of students in socially marginalized communities. Because they saw that the cultural deficit view on the marginalized is oppressive and hegemonic, the researchers adopted a research method that would value the students' cultural resources and empower them. Following the model of Joe Kincheloe and Shirley Steinberg (1998), the researchers recruited high school students as collaborative researchers so as to equip them with critical research skills and to challenge the conventional role of students as the researched. The students were not only provided with multiple research opportunities to reflect on their own ideas and their school life, but they also worked as a resource to shed a new light on the ways to appreciate their culture and educate how to teach in low-income-neighborhood schools. When presenting their research project, the researchers used a transcript format (as if they were research participants) for their interpretation of students and sometimes they used a research narrative format (as if they were the authoritative researchers). The mixed formats of presenting their interpretations gave the impression that they were just telling their version of the stories, not the authoritative interpretation.

Edna Tan and Angela Barton (2008) started their study in a similar tone to Elmesky and Tobin's by critiquing the implementation of the American national initiative for scientific literacy. Tan and Barton argued that the current education initiatives focus on the test scores and marginalize low-income, ethnic-minority students by framing them as "problem" or "failure" and by depriving them of learning opportunities to make meaningful personal connections to science. After a discussion of a feminist stance on the global knowledge economy, the researchers carefully described how two sixth-grade ethnic-minority girls from a low-income-neighborhood school negotiated their identities through various school science activities and their interactions with the teacher and peers. While the researchers adopted the format of an ethnographic case study in analyzing and presenting the students' interactions, they did so to problematize the status quo in school science and education research.

Within the frame of critical autoethnographic, reflective research, Margaret Eisenhart (2000) told her own story of publishing a book on women's participation in various venues of science. At the beginning of the paper, she explicitly mentioned that her story is not value neutral—rather, it is positioned with certain values and purpose. She intended to critically reflect on how she, as an established academic, conceptualizes and practices science education research, and how the larger sociocultural discourse shapes or constrains her practice. Retelling her story in two parts, she straightforwardly described why she wanted to investigate various science-related activities in which women were successfully participating and how she designed a multiple-case study, including a case of the pro-choice and pro-life activist groups' use of science. She portrayed that the participants in the pro-choice and pro-life groups were highly educated, politically charged, and strongly committed to learn and use science, but their use of science was "unsophisticated" and "divisive" (p. 48). In the second part of her story, she described a series of encounters with strong discouragement to include the story of the pro-choice and pro-life groups in the book. Publishers and reviewers adamantly noted that those groups' stories did not add anything new or valuable to the book. Initially, she blamed her inability to write persuasive, convincing arguments and tried to revise the writing. However, from the fear of not being able to publish the book, she conformed to the expectation of the publisher and the society. Eisenhart later reflected on the reason people isolated the pro-choice and pro-life groups' stories, how the invisible boundary of what's counted as scientific activities played a role in their omission, and what she could have done differently. In the paper, Eisenhart continuously reminded the reader what she was doing and why—for example, why she constructed her story in a more academically conventional way and how placing the blame for what happened to the larger social discourse eased her guilty conscience when relating to her co-author. This reflective, honest piece of writing leads us to reconsider the social meaning of what we do in the research process in a new light.

Common Features of Critical Theory Research

Common research topics. While a large portion of science education studies focuses on the technical aspects of how to teach science better, critical theory researchers concentrate on the political and historical aspects of education and educational inequality, seeking to challenge the status quo. The obvious topic for the critical researchers is investigating multiple, subtle ways to discourage or marginalize the participation of socially disadvantaged people in schooling or science. For example, Sandra Harding (1991) questioned how science and science education are framed in our society and how they have systematically

discouraged women's participation and contribution. Allen and Crawley (1998) investigated how school science excludes the worldview of Native American students and the elders and how it prevents their successful learning. Barton and her colleagues (Barton, 1998; Barton & Osborne, 1998; Barton & Yang, 2000) investigated how families in a homeless shelter were dissuaded from succeeding in school science.

Common research designs. The designs of critical theory research are often very similar to those of interpretivist studies, but with more explicit emphasis on larger social ideologies and power relationships. Critical theory researchers believe that empirical research and its data, no matter how rigorous the research methods are, cannot escape the dominant narrative of the society (Kincheloe, 2003). Because of this limitation, researchers in this tradition try to be critical of researchers' own assumptions and their relationship with the researched. Interpretivist researchers often display reflexivity in their relation with the research participants in terms of their values and experiences in understanding the participants. Critical theory researchers, on the other hand, show their reflexivity in terms of power dynamics between the researchers and the researched and even what the research participants have shared as their experiences. In critical ethnography, "[researchers] will be listening through the person's story to hear the operation of broader social discourses shaping that person's story of their experience" (Clandinin & Rosiek, 2007, p. 55). Listening to people's stories is a way to uncover the larger social discourse and false consciousness to enlighten the public.

Another common research design is participatory action research that actively addresses the inequalities in school and community. Researchers go into a low-income neighborhood and involve students and community members to recognize the issue of the community and take actions to change situations and their identities. Studies by Bouillion and Gomez (2001) and by Elmesky and Tobin (2005) could be examples.

Role of the researcher. The main goal of research is not expanding the body of knowledge but challenging and transforming the society and institution for the betterment of the people involved. Rather than distant, unbiased scholars, the critical theory researchers claim they are enlightened intellectuals and activists, working for social justice and for the people who are socially and politically disempowered (Fine, Weis, Weseen, & Wong, 2000).

Common quality standards. Because critical theory researchers are skeptical of unbiased research through rigorous methodical measures, they do not provide a set of guidelines on how to ascertain quality research. Rather, they argue that by explicitly discussing the biases of researchers and societies, they are conducting more "objective" research studies because they are not operating under any "hidden agenda" or exacerbating social inequality. However, they highly value the democratic procedures in research (e.g., egalitarian relationship with research participants, democratic decision making, and shared contributions to study) and the social impact of the study in transforming society (e.g., greater understanding of the society, the empowerment of the participants, and prompting or enacting changes in social/personal practices) (G. Anderson, Herr, & Nihlen, 1994; Greenwood & Levin, 1998; Griffiths, 1998).

Common report styles. Because they are consciously problematizing what is given or conventional, critical theory researchers intentionally do not follow the traditional fabric of research report. They experiment with the reporting of the study, such as adopting a performance or writing the story as a fiction (Flores-González, Rodriguez, & Rodriguez-Muniz, 2006). Some social-action-oriented research studies could be regarded as less methodically rigorous, thus not meeting the criteria of many academic journals. Consequently, to address this potential concern, many critical theory researchers adopt less radical, more traditional forms of ethnographic research reports, such as those by Barton (1998) and by Eisenhart (2000).

Paradigmatic or Pragmatic Research in Science Education

Science education researchers, like any other social science researchers, strive to establish the credibility and validity of their studies. Locating their studies within a particular research tradition or paradigm gives researchers philosophical, methodological, and practical guidelines to design and conduct a persuasive and convincing research project. In the preceding pages, we have described three research traditions and identified relevant studies that illustrate post-positivist, interpretivist, and critical theory paradigms in terms of the underlying epistemological, ontological, and methodological differences. We aimed to show how a research paradigm frames research effort by conditioning the research topics to be studied, the research designs used, the role of the researcher in relation to the participants, the common quality standards, and the common report styles presented. As we noted in the introduction to this chapter, we do not distinguish between different paradigms on the basis of whether the data are qualitative or quantitative, even though there is a tendency for post-positivist researchers to use mainly quantitative data and for interpretivist and critical theory researchers to use qualitative data extensively.

However, some science education researchers might wonder why we have not included mixed-methods approach as a research paradigm. Many contemporary research studies have both quantitative and qualitative data, and they may not seem to fit nicely into any specific research paradigm. Mixed-methods researchers (e.g., Creswell, 2012; Morgan, 2007) are not committed to any particular perspective on the nature of knowledge or reality, and they believe that dichotomizing quantitative and qualitative is not only unproductive but fallacious (Ercikan & Roth, 2006). They even question the practical value of research paradigms. David Morgan (2007), for example, claims that when designing and executing research projects, researchers tend to focus on practical aspects of research design and methods rather than worldviews or paradigms. Evaluative educational researchers, on the other hand, focus on diverse stakeholders' demands (Greene, 2008). No matter the worldview of the researchers, they are obligated to adopt various research approaches to satisfy the demands of diverse stakeholders (e.g., large-scale statistical analysis for policy makers or contextual vignettes for parents of students' welfare programs). Other mixed-methods researchers claim that the mixed use of quantitative and qualitative data enables a thorough triangulation of the findings and makes stronger knowledge claims (Creswell, 2012; Mathison, 1988; Reeves, 1997). Philosophically, though, Bryman (2012) regards this mixed-methods approach as qualitative researchers' practical attempts to establish themselves in a post-positivist-dominated academic world without committing themselves too much to the interpretivists' research paradigm. Others (e.g., Greene, 2008) focus on the practical problem-solving approach and the dynamic interplay of theory and practice in this tradition and list John Dewey's (1938/1991) pragmatism as their philosophical framework.

Given the circumstances, the authors of this chapter had a dilemma: whether to regard mixed methods as a separate research paradigm or as a research design. As Bryman (2008) notes, combining different research methods is an area in which researchers still have different views. While many post-positivist researchers welcome such adjustment as a way to increase the validity of research findings, interpretivist researchers are rather critical of such approaches. Denzin and Lincoln (2011), for example, regard it as a remnant of positivist legacies that relies on numbers as scientific evidence, resisting acknowledging the value of interpretivist qualitative studies and the political issue of what counts as evidence. Next, we list a few studies that adopt mixed-methods approaches to help readers recognize the similarities and differences between paradigmatic research studies and mixed-methods research studies.

Using an overtly described two-phase, sequential mixed-methods study, Sedat Ucar, Kathy Cabe Trundle, and Lawrence Krissek (2011) examined the effects of an intervention with preservice teachers at various educational levels in terms of their conceptual understanding. Following inquiry-based instruction using archived, online data about tides, a total of 79 preservice teachers completed a questionnaire, and subsequently a subset of 29 participants was interviewed. From the qualitative and quantitative data, the authors described and measured the impact of the intervention. The manner in which the quantitative and qualitative data were analyzed was described in detail, including reliability and trustworthiness measures. The findings were presented as a response to the research questions and discussed in relation to previous literature, with implications made for teacher education and future research.

As an example of another clearly described mixed-methods study, Liesl Hohenshell and Brian Hand (2006) investigated whether differences in student performance on science tests was a direct result of the implementation of a science writing program when the students in Grades 9 and 10 were learning cell biology. In this "mixed-method, quasi-experimental [study] . . . with a non-random sample" (p. 267), the researchers investigated the students' performance and explored students' perceptions of the writing activities using a survey and semistructured interviews. The authors emphasized the complementary role of quantitative and qualitative methods by using the quantitative results to document science achievement while using the qualitative data to enhance their interpretation of any findings arising from the quantitative data. The data interpretation was presented separately for the quantitative and qualitative analyses, as were the initial results. In drawing five assertions arising from the study, the authors integrated the analysis of the quantitative and qualitative data.

In a similar manner, Renee Clary and James Wandersee (2007) used a concurrent mixed-methods research design to investigate whether an integrated study of petrified wood could help students gain an improved geobiological understanding of fossilization, geologic time, and evolution. The researchers adopted Creswell's QUAL and QUAN approaches "to cross validate, confirm or corroborate the findings" (p. 1016). A survey about petrified wood was used pre- and postinstruction in a quasi-experimental setting, with the treatment class receiving the integrated petrified wood instruction. In addition to the quantitative data from the survey, qualitative data were collected from the content analysis of students' free responses on the survey as well as from the discussion board feedback and researchers' field notes. Some of the qualitative data were later quantified. Although there were quantitative and qualitative data from this investigation, the qualitative data were used to support the findings from the quantitative data. The students who experienced the integrated petrified wood instruction showed greater knowledge about aspects of petrified wood and geologic time; geochemistry of fossilization remained problematic for both groups.

Vaughan Prain and Bruce Waldrip (2006) conducted research with a group of teachers and their Year 4 through 6 students when they engaged with multiple representations of the same science concepts in electrical circuits and collisions and vehicle safety. Using "a mixed-methods approach entailing collection and analysis of both quantitative and qualitative data within the same study, including triangulation of different data sources"

(p. 1848), the authors identified teachers' and students' practices and beliefs in using multimodal representations of science concepts. Based on survey responses from 20 teachers and their students, 6 teachers and their classes were selected for a case study of their classroom practice with a multimodal focus. The data included classroom observations and interviews with students when they were involved in classroom activities. Two science classes were observed. While these two teachers used various modes to engage students, the researchers observed that the teachers were not systematic in developing students' knowledge integration and their effective use of different modes. Students who demonstrated conceptual understanding were those who recognized the relationships between modes.

So what are the differences and what are the commonalities between these examples of overtly mixed-methods studies compared to those studies we have described based on a specific paradigm? From this review, what becomes evident to us is that mixed methods often involve an intervention and its evaluation, and mixed-methods researchers essentially work within an unstated post-positivist paradigm. They use quantitative and qualitative data in a complementary manner as far as possible. However, as we noted in the introduction of this chapter, we acknowledge that the development and use of mixed methods has, to a certain degree, moderated the antagonism between researchers working in different paradigms (Bryman, 2008). Jennifer Greene (2008) writes,

> A mixed-methods way of thinking is an orientation toward social inquiry that actively invites us to participate in dialogue about multiple ways of seeing and hearing, multiple ways of making sense of the social world, and multiple standpoints on what is important and to be valued and cherished.
>
> (p. 20)

Greene believes that "the mixed-methods approach to social inquiry has the potential to be a distinctive methodology within the honoured traditions of social science. . . because it embraces multiple paradigm traditions" (p. 20). If readers are interested in further discussions about the character and value of research paradigms and mixed-methods research, please further refer to Greene's paper.

In this chapter, we have reviewed how three well-known research paradigms are presented or practiced in science education research in recent years. The landscape of conducting research within these paradigms has gradually changed over the years, and in the concluding section, we have indicated how once-incommensurable paradigmatic positions have been embraced in mixed-methods research approaches. In the years ahead, we can imagine that approaches to research will continuously evolve to incorporate new issues and ideas. We hope our review can contribute to productive discussion of science education researchers across different paradigms, including pragmatic research with mixed methods.

Acknowledgments

We would like to thank Bruce Waldrip and John Staver, who carefully and critically reviewed this chapter. We hope that we have done justice to their critiques and constructive suggestions.

Note

1. Critical theory studies include several research traditions, such as feminism, postcolonialism, poststructuralism, emancipatory/participatory, postmodernism, etc.

References

Aikenhead, G.S., & Jegede, O.J. (1999). Cross-cultural education: A cognitive explanation of a cultural phenomenon. *Journal of Research in Science Teaching, 36*(3), 269–287.

Allen, N.J., & Crawley, F.E. (1998). Voices from the bridge: Worldview conflicts of Kickapoo students of science. *Journal of Research in Science Teaching, 35*(2), 111–132.

American Educational Research Association. (2011). Code of ethics. *Educational Researcher, 40*(3), 145–156.

Anderson, C.W. (2007). Perspectives on science learning. In S.K. Abell & N.G. Lederman (Eds.), *Handbook of research on science education* (pp. 3–30). Mahwah, NJ: Lawrence Erlbaum Associates.

Anderson, G. (1998). *Fundamentals of educational research* (2nd ed.). London: Routledge.

Anderson, G., Herr, K., & Nihlen, A.S. (1994). *Studying your own school: An educator's guide to qualitative practitioner research.* Thousand Oaks, CA: Corwin Press.

Australian Association for Research in Education. (2005). *Annotated bibliography—Ethics in educational research.* Retrieved June 2013, from www1.aare.edu.au/pages/static/aareethc.htm

Barton, A.C. (1998). Teaching science with homeless children: Pedagogy, representation, and identity. *Journal of Research in Science Teaching, 35*(4), 379–394.

Barton, A.C., & Osborne, M.D. (1998). Marginalized discourses and pedagogies: Constructively confronting science for all. *Journal of Research in Science Teaching, 35*(4), 339–340.

Barton, A.C., & Osborne, M.D. (2001). Introduction. *Teaching science in diverse settings: Marginalized discourses and classroom practice.* New York: Peter Lang Publishing, Inc.

Barton, A.C., & Yang, K. (2000). The culture of power and science education: Learning from Miguel. *Journal of Research in Science Teaching, 37*(8), 871–889.

Bouillion, L.M., & Gomez, L.M. (2001). Connecting school and community with science learning: Real world problems and school–community partnerships as contextual scaffolds. *Journal of Research in Science Teaching, 38*(8), 878–898.

Bredo, E. (2009). Comments on Howe: Getting over the methodology wars. *Educational Researcher, 38*(6), 441–448. doi:10.3102/0013189x09343607

Brickhouse, N.W., Lowery, P., & Schultz, K. (2000). What kind of a girl does science? The construction of school science identities. *Journal of Research in Science Teaching, 37*(5), 441–458.

Bryman, A. (2008). The end of paradigm wars? In P. Alasuutari, L. Bickman, & J. Brannen (Eds.), *SAGE handbook of social research methods* (pp. 12–26). Thousand Oaks, CA: Sage.

Bryman, A. (2012). *Social research methods* (4th ed.). Oxford: Oxford University Press.

Carlone, H.B. (2004). The cultural production of science in reform-based physics: Girls' access, participation, and resistance. *Journal of Research in Science Teaching, 41*(4), 392–414.

Carter, L. (2007). Sociocultural influences on science education: Innovation for contemporary times. *Science Education, 92*(1), 165–181. doi:10.1002/sce.20228

Clandinin, D.J., & Rosiek, J. (2007). Mapping a landscape of narrative inquiry: Borderland spaces and tensions. In D.J. Clandinin (Ed.), *Handbook of narrative inquiry: Mapping a methodology* (pp. 35–75). Thousand Oaks, CA: Sage.

Clark, M.C., & Sharf, B.F. (2007). The dark side of truth(s): Ethical dilemmas in researching the personal. *Qualitative Inquiry, 13*(3), 399–416. doi:10.1177/1077800406297662

Clary, R.M., & Wandersee, J.H. (2007). A mixed methods analysis of the effects of an integrative geobiological study of petrified wood in introductory college geology classrooms. *Journal of Research in Science Teaching, 44*(8), 1011–1035. doi:10.1002/tea.20178

Cobb, P., Confrey, J., diSessa, A., Lehrer, R., & Schauble, L. (2003). Design experiments in educational research. *Educational Researcher, 32*(1), 9–13.

Cohen, L., Manion, L., & Morrison, K. (2011). *Research methods in education* (7th ed.). London: Routledge.

Creswell, J.W. (2012). *Educational research: Planning, conducting, and evaluating quantitative and qualitative research* (4th ed.). Boston: Pearson.

DeBoer, G.E. (2011). The globalization of science education. *Journal of Research in Science Teaching, 48*(6), 567–591. doi:10.1002/tea.20421

Dee, T.S., & Jacob, B. (2011). The impact of No Child Left Behind on student achievement. *Journal of Policy Analysis and Management, 30*(3), 418–446.

Denzin, N.K., & Lincoln, Y.S. (2011). Introduction: The discipline and practice of qualitative research. In N.K. Denzin & Y.S. Lincoln (Eds.), *SAGE handbook of qualitative research* (4th ed., pp. 1–19). Thousand Oaks, CA: Sage.

Dewey, J. (1925/1981). Experience and nature. In J.A. Boydston (Ed.), *John Dewey: The later works, 1925–1953* (Vol. 1). Carbondale, IL: Southern Illinois University Press. (Reprinted from: 1997).

Dewey, J. (1938/1991). Logic: The theory of inquiry. In J.A. Boydston (Ed.), *John Dewey: The later works, 1925–1953* (Vol. 12). Carbondale, IL: Southern Illinois University Press.

Duit, R., Gropengießer, H., Kattmann, U., Komorek, K., & Parchmann, I. (2012). The model of educational reconstruction—A framework for improving teaching and learning science. In D. Jorde & J. Dillon (Eds.), *Science education research and practice in Europe: Retrospective and prospective* (pp. 13–38). Rotterdam, the Netherlands: Sense Publishers.

Duit, R., Roth, W.M., Komorek, M., & Wilbers, J. (1998). Conceptual change cum discourse analysis to understand cognition in a unit on chaotic systems: Towards an integrative perspective on learning in science. *International Journal of Science Education, 20*(9), 1059–1073. doi:10.1080/0950069980200904

Duit, R., Roth, W.M., Komorek, M., & Wilbers, J. (2001). Fostering conceptual change by analogies—between Scylla and Charybdis. *Learning and Instruction, 11*(4), 283–303. doi:10.1016/S0959-4752(00)00034-7

Dulfer, N., Polesel, J., & Rice, S. (2012). *The experience of education: The impacts of high stakes testing on school students and their families.* Sydney, Australia: Whitlam Institute, University of Western Sydney.

Eggert, S., & Bögeholz, S. (2006). Göttinger Modell der Bewertungskompetenz—Teilkompetenz "Bewerten, Entscheiden und Reflektieren" für Gestaltungsaufgaben nachhaltiger Entwicklung [The Göttingen Model of evaluation and judgment competence—evaluating, deciding, and reflecting in the area of sustainable development]. *Zeitschrift für Didaktik der Naturwissenschaften, 12,* 177–197.

Einarsdottir, J. (2007). Research with children: Methodological and ethical challenges. *European Early Childhood Education Research Journal, 15*(2), 197–211. doi:10.1080/13502930701321477

Eisenhart, M. (2000). Boundaries and selves in the making of science. *Research in Science Education, 30*(1), 43–55.

Eisenhart, M., Finkel, E., & Marion, S. (1996). Creating conditions for scientific literacy: A re-examination. *American Educational Research Journal, 33*(2), 261–295.

Elmesky, R., & Tobin, K.G. (2005). Expanding our understandings of urban science education by expanding the roles of students as researchers. *Journal of Research in Science Teaching, 42*(7), 807–828. doi:10.1002/tea.20079

Ercikan, K., & Roth, W.-M. (2006). What good is polarizing research into qualitative and quantitative? *Educational Researcher, 35*(5), 14–23. doi:10.3102/0013189X035005014

Erickson, F. (1986). Qualitative methods in research on teaching. In M.C. Wittrock (Ed.), *Handbook of research on teaching* (3rd ed., pp. 119–161). New York: MacMillan.

Erickson, F. (2012). Qualitative research methods for science education. In B.J. Fraser, K.G. Tobin, & C.J. McRobbie (Eds.), *Second international handbook of science education* (Vol. 2, pp. 1451–1469). Dordrecht, the Netherlands: Springer.

Erickson, F., & Gutierrez, K. (2002). Comment: Culture, rigor, and science in educational research. *Educational Researcher, 31*(8), 21–24. doi:10.3102/0013189x031008021

Etherington, K. (2007). Ethical research in reflexive relationships. *Qualitative Inquiry, 13*(5), 599–616. doi:10.1177/1077800407301175

Feuer, M.J., Towne, L., & Shavelson, R.J. (2002). Scientific culture and educational research. *Educational Researcher, 31*(8), 4–14. doi:10.3102/0013189x031008004

Fine, M., Weis, L., Weseen, S., & Wong, L. (2000). For whom?: Qualitative research, representations, and social responsibilities. In N.K. Denzin & Y.S. Lincoln (Eds.), *Handbook of qualitative research* (2nd ed., pp. 107–131). Thousand Oaks, CA: Sage.

Flores-González, N., Rodriguez, M., & Rodriguez-Muniz, M. (2006). From hip-hop to humanization: Batey Urbano as a space for Latino youth culture and community action. In S. Ginwright, P. Noguera, & J. Cammorota (Eds.), *Beyond resistance! Youth activism and community change* (pp. 175–196). New York: Routledge.

Fraenkel, J.R., Wallen, N.E., & Hyun, H.H. (2012). *How to design and evaluate research in education* (8th ed.). New York: McGraw-Hill.

Fusco, D. (2001). Creating relevant science through urban planning and gardening. *Journal of Research in Science Teaching, 38*(8), 860–877.

Gage, N.L. (1989). The paradigm wars and their aftermath: A "historical" sketch of research on teaching since 1989. *Educational Researcher, 18*(7), 4–10.

Gallas, K. (1995). *Talking their way into science: Hearing children's questions and theories, responding with curricula.* New York: Teachers College Press.

Gallas, K. (1997). *Sometimes I can be anything: Power, gender, and identity in a primary classroom.* New York: Teachers College Press.

Geertz, C. (1973). *The interpretation of cultures.* New York: Basic Books.

Greene, J.C. (2008). Is mixed methods social inquiry a distinctive methodology? *Journal of Mixed Methods Research, 2*(1), 7–22. doi:10.1177/1558689807309969

Greenwood, D.J., & Levin, M. (1998). *Introduction to action research: Social research for social change.* Thousand Oaks, CA: Sage.

Griffiths, M. (1998). *Educational research for social justice: Getting off the fence.* Philadelphia: Open University Press.

Guba, E.G., & Lincoln, Y.S. (1989). *Judging the quality of fourth generation evaluation.* London: Sage.

Guba, E.G., & Lincoln, Y.S. (1994). Competing paradigms in qualitative research. In N.K. Denzin & Y.S. Lincoln (Eds.), *Handbook of qualitative research* (pp. 105–117). Thousand Oaks, CA: Sage.

Guba, E.G., & Lincoln, Y.S. (2005). Paradigmatic controversies, contradictions, and emerging confluences. In N.K. Denzin & Y.S. Lincoln (Eds.), *SAGE handbook of qualitative research* (3rd ed., pp. 191–215). Thousand Oaks, CA: Sage.

Hammond, L., & Brandt, C. (2004). Science and cultural process: Defining an anthropological approach to science education. *Studies in Science Education, 40*(1), 1–47. doi:10.1080/03057260408560202

Harding, S. (1991). *Whose science? Whose knowledge? Thinking from women's lives.* Ithaca, NY: Cornell University Press.

Hohenshell, L., & Hand, B. (2006). Writing-to-learn strategies in secondary school cell biology: A mixed method study. *International Journal of Science Education, 28*(2–3), 261–289. doi:10.1080/09500690500336965

Holstenbach, J., Fischer, H., Kauertz, A., Mayer, J., Sumfleth, E., & Walpuski, M. (2011). Modellierung der Bewertungskompetenz in den Naturwissenschaften zur Evaluation der Nationalen Bildungsstandards [Modeling the evaluation and judgment competence in science to evaluate national educational standards]. *Zeitschrift für Didaktik der Naturwissenschaften, 17,* 261–287.

Howe, K.R. (2009). Positivist dogmas, rhetoric, and the education science question. *Educational Researcher, 38*(6), 428–440. doi:10.3102/0013189X09342003

Jaeger, R.M. (1997). Survey research methods in education. In R.M. Jaeger (Ed.), *Complementary methods for research in education* (2nd ed., pp. 449–476). Washington, DC: American Educational Research Association.

Jones, M., & Stanley, G. (2008). Children's lost voices: Ethical issues in relation to undertaking collaborative, practice-based projects involving schools and the wider community. *Educational Action Research, 16*(1), 31–41. doi:10.1080/09650790701833089

Kincheloe, J.L. (2003). Critical research in science education. In B.J. Fraser & K.G. Tobin (Eds.), *International handbook of science education* (Vol. 2, pp. 1191–1205). Dordrecht, the Netherlands: Springer.

Kincheloe, J.L., & McLaren, P. (2005). Rethinking critical theory and qualitative research. In N.K. Denzin & Y.S. Lincoln (Eds.), *Handbook of qualitative research* (3rd ed., pp. 303–342). Thousand Oaks, CA: Sage.

Kincheloe, J.L., & Steinberg, S.R. (1998). Students as researchers: Critical visions, emancipatory insights. In S.R. Steinberg & J.L. Kincheloe (Eds.), *Students as researchers: Creating classrooms that matter* (pp. 2–19). London: Falmer Press.

Kincheloe, J.L., & Tobin, K.G. (2009). The much exaggerated death of positivism. *Cultural Studies of Science Education, 4,* 513–528. doi:10.1007/s11422–009–9178–5

Kuhn, T.S. (1962). *The structure of scientific revolution.* Chicago: University of Chicago Press.

Lee, O. (2002). Promoting scientific inquiry with elementary students from diverse cultures and languages. *Review of Research in Education, 26,* 23–69.

Lincoln, Y.S., & Guba, E.G. (2000). Paradigm controversies, contradictions, and emerging confluences. In N.K. Denzin & Y.S. Lincoln (Eds.), *Handbook of qualitative research* (2nd ed., pp. 163–188). Thousand Oaks, CA: Sage.

Mathison, S. (1988). Why triangulate? *Educational Researcher, 17*(2), 13–17.

Maulucci, M.S.R. (2012). Social justice research in science education: Methodologies, positioning, and implications for future research. In B.J. Fraser, K.G. Tobin, & C.J. McRobbie (Eds.), *Second international handbook of science education* (Vol. 1, pp. 583–594). Dordrecht, the Netherlands: Springer.

Maxwell, J.A. (2004). Reemergent scientism, postmodernism, and dialogue across differences. *Qualitative Inquiry, 10*(1), 35–41. doi:10.1177/1077800403259492

Merriam, S.B. (2009). *Qualitative research: A guide to design and implementation.* San Francisco: Jossey-Bass.

Morgan, D.L. (2007). Paradigms lost and pragmatism regained: Methodological implications of combining qualitative and qualitative methods. *Journal of Mixed Methods Research, 1*(1), 48–76. doi:10.1177/2345678906292462

Moss, P.A., Phillips, D.C., Erickson, F.D., Floden, R.E., Lather, P.A., & Schneider, B.L. (2009). Learning from our differences: A dialogue across perspectives on quality in education research. *Educational Researcher, 38*(7), 501–517. doi:10.3102/0013189X09348351

Noddings, N. (1998). Perspectives from feminist philosophy. *Educational Researcher, 27*(5), 17–18. doi:10.3102/0013189X027005017

Organisation for Economic Cooperation and Development. (2010). *PISA 2009 results: What students know and can do: Student performance on reading mathematics and science* (Vol. 1). Paris, France: OECD Publishing.

Paley, V. G. (1981). *Wally's stories*. Cambridge, MA: Harvard University Press.

Phillips, D. C. (2005). The contested nature of empirical educational research (and why philosophy of education offers little help). *Journal of Philosophy of Education, 39*(4), 577–597. doi:10.1111/j.1467-9752.2005.00457.x

Phillips, D. C., & Burbules, N. C. (2000). *Postpositivism and educational research*. Lanham, MD: Rowman & Littlefield Publishers.

Porter, A. C. (1997). Comparative experiments in educational research. In R. M. Jaeger (Ed.), *Complementary methods for research in education* (2nd ed., pp. 523–544). Washington, DC: American Educational Research Association.

Prain, V., & Waldrip, B. (2006). An exploratory study of teachers' and students' use of multi-modal representations of concepts in primary science. *International Journal of Science Education, 28*(15), 1843–1866. doi:10.1080/09500690600718294

Punch, K. F. (2005). *Introduction to social research: Quantitative and qualitative approaches* (2nd ed.). London: Sage.

Reeves, T. (1997). Educational paradigms. In C. R. Dills & A. J. Romiszowski (Eds.), *Instructional development paradigms* (pp. 163–178). Englewood Cliffs, NJ: Educational Technology Publications.

Roth, W.-M., & Desautels, J. (2002). Science education as/for sociopolitical action: Charting the landscape. In W.-M. Roth & J. Désautels (Eds.), *Science education as/for sociopolitical action* (pp. 1–16). New York: Peter Lang.

Ryoo, K., & Linn, M. C. (2012). Can dynamic visualization improve middle school students' understanding of energy in photosynthesis? *Journal of Research in Science Teaching, 49*(2), 218–243. doi:10.1002/tea.21003

Schwandt, T. A. (2000). Three epistemological stances for qualitative inquiry: Interpretivism, hermeneutics, and social constructionism. In N. K. Denzin & Y. S. Lincoln (Eds.), *Handbook of qualitative research* (2nd ed., pp. 189–214). Thousand Oaks, CA: Sage.

Schwandt, T. A. (2001). *Dictionary of qualitative inquiry* (2nd ed.). Thousand Oaks, CA: Sage.

St. Pierre, E. A. (2002). Comment: "Science" rejects postmodernism. *Educational Researcher, 31*(8), 25–27. doi:10.3102/0013189x031008025

Tan, E., & Barton, A. C. (2008). Unpacking science for all through the lens of identities-in-practice: The stories of Amelia and Ginny. *Cultural Studies of Science Education, 3*(1), 43–71. doi:10.1007/s11422-007-9076-7

Taylor, P. C., Taylor, E., & Luitel, B. C. (2012). Multi-paradigmatic transformative research as/for teacher education: An integral perspective. In B. J. Fraser, K. G. Tobin, & C. J. McRobbie (Eds.), *Second international handbook of science education* (Vol. 1, pp. 373–387). Dordrecht, the Netherlands: Springer.

Thomson, S., Hillman, K., & Wernert, N. (2012). *Monitoring Australian Year 8 student achievement internationally: TIMSS 2011*. Camberwell, Victoria: Australian Council of Educational Research Ltd.

Tracy, S. J. (2010). Qualitative quality: Eight "big-tent" criteria for excellent qualitative research. *Qualitative Inquiry, 16*(10), 837–851. doi:10.1177/1077800410383121

Treagust, D. F., Jacobowitz, R., Gallagher, J. L., & Parker, J. (2001). Using assessment as a guide in teaching for understanding: A case study of a middle school science class learning about sound. *Journal of Research in Science Teaching, 85*(2), 137–157.

Ucar, S., Trundle, K. C., & Krissek, L. (2011). Inquiry-based instruction with archived, online data: An intervention study with pre-service teachers. *Research in Science Education, 41*(2), 261–282. doi:10.1007/s11165-009-9164-7

van Borkulo, S. P., van Joolingen, W. R., Savelsbergh, E. R., & de Jong, T. (2012). What can be learned from computer modeling? Comparing expository and modeling approaches to teaching dynamic systems behavior. *Journal of Science Education and Technology, 21*(2), 267–275. doi:10.1007/s10956-011-9314-3

Velayutham, S., Aldridge, J., & Fraser, B. J. (2011). Development and validation of an instrument to measure students' motivation and self-regulation in science learning. *International Journal of Science Education, 33*(15), 2159–2179. doi:10.1080/09500693.2010.541529

Waddington, D., Nentwig, P., & Schanze, S. (2007). *Making it comparable: Standards in science education*. Münster, Germany: Waxmann.

Warren, B., Ballenger, C., Ogonowski, M., Rosebery, A. S., & Hudicourt-Barnes, J. (2001). Rethinking diversity in learning science: The logic of everyday sense-making. *Journal of Research in Science Teaching, 38*(5), 529–552.

Wiersma, W., & Jurs, S. G. (2005). *Research methods in education: An introduction* (8th ed.). Boston: Pearson.

Wilbers, J., & Duit, R. (2005). Post-festum and heuristic analogies. In P. J. Aubusson, A. G. Harrison, & S. M. Richie (Eds.), *Metaphors and analogy in science education* (Vol. 32, pp. 1073–1098). Dordrecht, the Netherlands: Springer.

Wolcott, H. F. (2009). *Writing up qualitative research* (3rd ed.). Thousand Oaks, CA: Sage.

Wong, E. D. (2002). To appreciate variation between scientists: A perspective for seeing science's vitality. *Science Education, 86*(3), 386–400.

2

Quantitative Research Designs and Approaches

Hans E. Fischer, William J. Boone, and Knut Neumann

Introduction

The main aim of science education research is to improve science learning. In order to do so, as researchers, we need to understand the complex interplay of teaching and learning in science classrooms. If science instruction is to be improved, it is not enough to understand how people learn about a particular topic. In the reality of the classroom, a tremendous number of variables affect the teaching and learning of science. This includes variables on (1) the individual level, such as students' prior knowledge, (2) the classroom level, such as the teachers' content knowledge, and (3) the system level, such as school funding (Fischer et al., 2005). However, research is about evidence. Therefore, many established and necessarily oversimplified models of teaching and learning science must be iteratively refined in order to account for increasingly more specific variables on the respective levels. And the quality of evidence is of particular importance.

On the one hand, qualitative research seeks to improve science education through developing an understanding of the complexity of the teaching and learning of science, often starting with highly selected and isolated cases. On the other hand, quantitative research often is characterized by investigating commonalities across all teaching and learning of science. Both qualitative and quantitative communities have particular rules for estimating the quality of evidence in their field. As one approach to the question of evidence, researchers have to answer the decisive question: "Cui bono?" What does the researcher want to investigate, to whom are the results addressed, and what are the consequences when the results are applied and put into practice? Research results can be used for different levels of decision making. Here again, we can identify three different levels of variables describing and influencing teaching and learning at schools: (1) the level of individual teaching and learning processes, including knowledge, competencies, beliefs, motivation, and interest, (2) the classroom level including teacher and student activities and the quality

of instruction as a measure of those activities, and (3) the system level, including system conditions of schools and larger social units. For research in science education, the quality of in-class instruction and, to a lesser extent, the quality of out-of-class instruction are the main focus. However, we want to inform first and foremost teachers and policy makers how they can improve and/or control the quality of instruction and the output of the educational system. Teachers want to know how to support students so that they can increase their abilities individually or improve the quality of lessons to increase the average ability of a class; the principals and also regular teachers want to know how to support the science faculty in comparison with other schools. Also, policy makers want to know how to allocate resources most efficiently in order to increase educational achievement across their district, state, or nation in relation to the development of economic and social affairs.

To perform quantitative studies, one has to start with a research question, including the operational definitions of variables and the purpose of the study. The results of investigating each of the levels of the educational system and the research-based conclusions should be of a kind that other researchers can rely on; and such conclusions should also be a base for extending their research.

Trustworthiness of Evidence

Many issues must be addressed as one seeks to ensure the trustworthiness of research results. As researchers, we have to be aware of the manifoldness of variables and conditions that possibly influence research quality. For instance, it appears to be easy to compare the average achievement of two classes in one school. But without taking into account issues such as the classes' average pre-knowledge, reading ability, socioeconomic background, and cognitive abilities, mismeasurement is possibly too large for drawing conclusions of certainty. This is true for quantitative as well as for theory-based qualitative studies that are addressed in this chapter. For a description of grounded theory- and design-based research, see chapter 3 in this handbook. For example, the ability of a participant to express scientific features in a certain language or preknowledge about a specific scientific concept might influence the participant's responses in a semistructured interview. Theory-based qualitative researchers should also consider these factors even in case studies in order to produce reliable interpretations of the observed dialogs between teachers and students or between students in classroom activities. Therefore, in the first step, we have to think very carefully about possible confounding variables and possible influences of such variables on assessment, motivation, or other categories with regard to the focus of the investigation. All in all, the question of trustworthiness and generalizability of research results has to be answered to address the different ways in which the aforementioned stakeholders consider the results of research for improving teacher education and research. Additionally, knowing about the confounding variables means understanding the limitations of the study and aids the interpretation of the research results. With regard to teacher education, it is abundantly clear how important it is to communicate and to teach content in a way that reflects the state of the art in teaching by referring to empirically evident results. Researchers should be able to tell future teachers how to increase the probability of high-quality teaching. Often enough, teacher education cannot refer to empirically based results; this therefore reproduces intuitive beliefs and myths. For example, a great amount of time is spent on teaching future teachers about students' everyday conceptions or misconceptions, although there is little evidence that such teachers' knowledge is beneficial for students' learning and thus for improvement in science instruction. In fact, a recent study comparing teaching and learning physics in Finland and Germany shows that Finish teachers know less about misconceptions than do German teachers, but their students learn significantly much more than do German students (Olszewski, 2010; Olszewski, Neumann, & Fischer, 2009). Despite these and other findings that knowing about misconceptions is not as important for high-quality teaching (Hammer, 1996), there are a multitude of studies on students' misconceptions, and some universities have advocated that the knowledge about misconceptions in all sciences is important for a science teacher (e.g., New York Science Teacher, 2013). This begs the question of whether misconceptions are as important as what science educators have considered and whether training on knowing misconceptions might be a waste of learning time in science teacher education. As authors, we believe that this leads to the natural conclusion that in science teacher education, teacher educators should teach only or at least mostly those content areas that can be trusted from the standpoint of the commonly agreed-on rules of the research community. But sadly, this perspective has not always been applied. For example, in a meta-analysis of inquiry-based science teaching, Furtak,

Seidel, Iverson, and Briggs (2012) started with about 5,800 studies. After excluding papers in a first step using criteria—such as studies not in English, outcome variables not about science achievement, studies not published in peer-reviewed journal, data not provided in the paper—Furtak and colleagues found that only 59 papers remained. After criteria of good research practices—such as prepost design, two-group, cognitive outcome measures, and effect size calculations—were applied in further selection, only 15 papers from the 5,800 studies remained. After asking some authors of the excluded articles for data and additional calculations, Furtak and colleagues found that 22 of the excluded studies could be included in their meta-analysis. In another meta-analysis, Ruiz-Primo, Briggs, Shepard, Iverson, and Huchton (2008) analyzed the impact of innovations in physics education. They started with more than 400 papers and found that only 51 papers that reported the studies could be used for a quantitative synthesis of the effects. Profound meta-analyses such as these are excellent examples of applied trustworthiness. They make clear that the standards of the research community need to be applied to studies to be able to use the published results for further research.

Obtaining Evidence

One of the main problems of research in science education in general is to classify different types of cognition. The direct sensory experience of human beings is generally incomplete and not dependable because of the restricted sensitivity range of different types of our organs of perception. Everyday communication and other social interactions rely on agreed-on common knowledge and intuition, which is fuzzy by nature, to be applicable and trustworthy in social interaction and can even be wrong. At least, as researchers, we are not able to guarantee the correctness of such communication and interaction to a certain extent. If we are not sure, we can ask experts about their opinions. However, experts' opinions can be mistaken, and their reasoning, even if it is based on certain logical systems and rules, can be based on false premises. To avoid mistakes and to obtain trustworthy conclusions, we have to use scientific methods and procedures that are agreed on by researchers and experts and that allow more trustworthy statements than those based on a few experts' opinions. Studies must be linked to the whole range of relevant past studies and conducted using scientific methods and utilizing quality criteria. Therefore, planning and performing a study must include a theoretical model with regard to relevant past work, rigorous sampling, well-elaborated instrument construction that involves piloting of the instruments, adequate experiment design, up-to-date psychometrics, carefully captured data, and rigorous interpretation of results. Within the research community, these criteria and the process must again be discussed and agreed on. Doing so will then allow for estimating the quality of the results of all investigations, and this will also provide implications for further research and practice.

The necessary agreement in a community of researchers requires publicity and discussion such as what has taken place with regard to nature of science (e.g., Lederman, 2006, 2007; Lederman, Abd-El Khalick, Bell, & Schwartz, 2002; Osborne, Collins, Ratcliffe, Millar, & Duschl, 2003) or professional knowledge of science teachers (e.g., Magnusson, Krajcik, & Borko, 1999; Park & Oliver, 2008; cf. Gess-Newsome & Lederman, 1999). Also, it is important in science education that researchers be able to replicate studies. In natural sciences, replication and public discussion are indispensable parts of evaluating the trustworthiness of scientific investigations. We suggest that national and international associations for science education should allow and support publishing and reporting of replications of research in their journals and at conferences.

Obviously, empirical research can never be a method of proving anything (Popper, 1959). The results have to be discussed and interpreted, but conclusions are tentative and open to revision. Therefore, it is necessary that all published work include a detailed description of the project data, with a clear explanation of the process of constructing the respective measures and the analysis of the measures. Raw data must be available on demand.

Theory and Evidence

In the field of science education, research attempts have been made to utilize theories or models to evaluate and describe the quality of what is taking place in teaching in the classroom. Of great importance is the use of theories or models to serve as guides to research investigations and to allow for the development and use of consistent methodologies (Ditton, 2000; Neumann, Kauertz, & Fischer, 2012). Attempts to identify and describe quality of instruction and its components were already undertaken in the 1960s—mostly as observational studies in which classroom instruction was observed and criteria identified regarding what was thought to be the teaching by a high-quality teacher. These attempts were followed by extensive research programs on teacher effectiveness in the late 1960s and throughout the 1970s. This type of research—oftentimes termed "process-product research"—investigated relations between characteristics of good teachers (or good teaching) as components of the process-outcomes such as student achievement, which is viewed as a product. In the late 1970s and 1980s, researchers attempted to systematize the results of teacher effectiveness research in an effort to establish more comprehensive models of instructional quality; such research was mainly composed of meta-analyses. One shortfall in these efforts was not explaining instructional outcomes. This void was apparent as the TIMSS study attempted to investigate instruction and to relate instructional characteristics to students' achievements. One factor fueling this shift was that video analysis of lessons had become technically possible. Video analyses allowed researchers to record and analyze classroom instruction in an extensive and thorough manner in multiple iterations. This led to a further refinement of models of instructional quality as more complex methodologies became available for capturing and researching the complex reality of the classroom (cf. Neumann et al., 2012). This brief review of the history of research of quality of science instruction highlights the importance of building a study on previous research in order to advance a field.

Building a research study on a sound theoretical framework is indispensable for obtaining clear and relevant results. There must be a linkage between theory and research experiments—theory informs and provides a framework for experiments, and research findings allow acceptance, modification, or total rejection of the theoretical model used. The essence of research in science education is to find regular patterns in social situations, which in our case refers to teaching and learning sciences. In the end, researchers should be able to conclude that a certain educational activity or setting most likely results in the intended learning process, student behavior, or increase of competences. If a newly developed theoretical model is not tested, it does not permit generalization to other cases.

As already described, building theoretical models of aspects of teaching and learning science at school has to take into account multiple variables, the interdependencies of variables, and hierarchically ordered system structures. Perhaps it is not surprising that controlling as many influencing variables of classroom settings as possible is absolutely necessary when researchers wish to reach conclusions with regard to the impact of changes in teaching and learning recommended by some science educators. The effect of a newly developed unit, for example, for quantum mechanics, surely depends on design and strategy of presenting the subject matter adequately regarding its scientific content and structure. But this is not enough. The scientific content taught at schools is not identical with that taught at universities because the learners at schools and universities are dissimilar in so many ways that teachers have to think about the teaching and learning process specifically suited for the recipients. For example, the academic content structure of a unit is moderated by features of the teacher's personality, his or her pedagogical content knowledge, students' socioeconomic background, the structure of student–teacher interactions in the classroom, and, in particular, students' cognitive abilities. This holds true for every description of learning and teaching processes and for every intervention aiming to change teaching practice. Consistent with the idea of science instruction as a complex system, it should be obvious that an adequate model is needed to describe as many influences as possible on the teaching and learning processes. Clausen (2000) suggested three critical aspects for developing and validating a theory (or model) for assessing instructional quality: selection of representative constructs (variables of theoretical models), formulation of hypothetical correlations (structure models), and the development of adequate indicators for operationalization (measuring models; Fischer & Neumann, 2012, p. 118).

Quantitative Research: Theoretical and Methodological Considerations

As discussed in the preceding section, strong research has to be built on strong theory; the stronger the theoretical framework, the stronger the research. The theoretical framework should be based on a synthesis of previous research studies and new ideas regarding unknown and/or innovative influences and variables. In quantitative research, a theoretical framework is oftentimes presented as a model, that is, a conglomerate of variables and relations between these variables. The model identifies the variables that are assessed or surveyed respectively through an empirical study. Depending on the theoretical framework and the particular research questions, the empirical study may utilize one of a number of different designs. In addition to selecting a research design, the sampling of participants of the study is a major consideration of quantitative research. Sample size and sample composition (e.g., what type of students are to be studied) are tightly connected to the theoretical framework, the respective research design, and the proposed analysis procedures. For example, classical approaches, such as an analysis of variance (ANOVA), require a smaller sample size than do structural equation models (SEM).

Sample Size and Effect Size

There are, however, some general guidelines for estimating a sample size. A sample size of 20 students per combination of grouping variables is commonly considered the minimum, and group sizes of 40 students are typically recommended. If two different treatments are to be compared under control of the effect of gender, one group of 20 female and one group of 20 male students are required per treatment. However, in this example, the minimum sample size of 20 students per each of the four groups requires at least a large effect size ($f > .4$) for drawing conclusions. The recommended sample size of 40 students per group would allow for identifying medium effect sizes ($f > .25$); for identifying small effect sizes ($f > .1$), a sample size of 400 per group would be required. Note that these sample sizes are unique to this example, as the sample size depends on many factors related to the design of a study. If, for example, random assignment of students to treatment or control groups is not possible, then whole classes are sampled instead. That means that instead of a minimum of 20 students per group, 20 classes per group would be required for sound conclusions about the effect of the teaching strategy under investigation. All considerations regarding the design, sampling, and procedures of analysis should be based on a theoretical framework, that is, the research questions and the expected findings (i.e., tested hypotheses). If the conclusions are expected to only extend to selected ninth graders in New York City, the sample will need to be composed of exactly that—selected ninth graders from New York City. In order to be able to extend the conclusions to the population of students across the whole United States, a representative sample for U.S. students (i.e., a sample of particularly large size) is required.

Criteria of Trustworthiness

In principle and irrespective of whether researchers are performing theory-based qualitative research or quantitative research, four criteria of trustworthiness of data and results must be clarified: objectivity, reliability, validity, and significance. Important features of research design and the goal of research instrumentation can be derived from formulating the purpose of the study as precisely as possible, identifying the levels of the analysis, considering all possible confounding variables, and utilizing these four criteria of trustworthiness.

Objectivity refers to the reduction or, at best, the elimination of any external influences on a measurement or an observation. The idea of objectivity was already expressed by Francis Bacon at the beginning of the 17th century (Bacon, 1904), who demanded researchers avoid becoming four so-called idols: the Idols of the Tribe (*Idola tribus*), who do not accept human senses as human baseline for scientific descriptions; the Idols of the Cave (*Idola specus*), who are the specific perspective of an individual caused by his or her education, socialization, and individual life experience; the Idols of the Market (*Idola fori*), which can be translated as acting as socially desired; and the Idols of the Theatre (*Idola theatri*), which refer to dogmata and ideologically guided principles. We suggest that observations and results shall be verifiable independently of subjective influences (intersubjectivity). It is often helpful if researchers can consider to perform, evaluate, and interpret objectively. Objectivity in quantitative research is possible when well-established rigorous steps of performance standardization (e.g., scripts for classroom videos, detailed manuals to administrate a test), psychometrics (e.g., ensuring the marking of items along a variable is maintained over time), statistics (e.g., routine computation of effect size, addressing the hierarchical nature of educational data), and interpretation are utilized. Within the realm of qualitative studies, the issue of objectivity is more difficult to address, for it is not possible to distinguish easily between an observer and a participant.

Reliability refers to the error of a measurement. To explain the true value T, we have to consider different error types. First of all, there is random error E, for example, variation in the subject's attention, ambiguous answers, disturbances of classroom settings from the outside, mistakes during data entry, errors in data coding, and so on. Because random error will have an influence on the reliability and validity of a measurement, the measurement has to be conducted and data have to be processed as carefully as possible. The second type of error is systematic error. Systematic errors stem, for example, from social desirability. A systematic error does not undermine reliability. So, if X is an observed value (e.g., an average value of performance in biology of a certain sample), the true value T can be expressed as $T = X + E + S$ where E denotes the random error and S the systematic error. Reliability is typically expressed as the percentage of variance of the true value related to the total variance of a measure. In case of qualitative analyses such as categorizations or interpretations of specific situations, typical measures of reliability include interrater reliability (Gwet, 2012) or intraclass correlation (ICC; Shrout & Fleiss, 1979).

Grounded theory assumes that, for example, a teaching-learning situation in a biology lesson can be interpreted without a theoretical assumption at the beginning of the study; instead, a parallel process of constructing an interpretation and a theoretical model of the situation are utilized during data capturing (Glaser & Strauss, 1967). A similar idea ("objective hermeneutics") was considered in German-speaking countries in the late 1970s and refers mainly to the work of Oevermann, Allert, Konau, and Krambeck (1979). These researchers refer to scientific criteria in which reliability is the expression of the interpretation process of a group of experts interpreting a situation. The agreement of the experts on one interpretation in the end is seen as an expression of person reliability as well as item reliability (Breuer & Reichertz, 2002; Oevermann, Allert, Konau, & Krambeck, 1987; Strauss & Corbin, 2008) and therefore must be documented precisely.

A central aspect of quantitative research is to measure constructs such as students' science achievement or students' interest in science; and, not surprisingly, the reliability of the measures obtained through achievement tests or questionnaires is of particular importance. Typically a Cronbach's alpha (or coefficient α) is used to provide information about the consistency with which a given set of items measures the same construct. High to perfect reliability is indicated by values of Cronbach's alpha between .7 and 1.0. Cronbach's alpha is typically lower than that when there is only a small correlation among the items of a test or questionnaire, indicating that the items correctly measure the underlying theoretical construct (e.g., intelligence or competence) only to a small extent. As is the case with any measurement, Cronbach's alpha and thus the reliability of the overall score may be improved by adding more items to the test or questionnaire or by removing items of low quality.

As for reliability of test scores, it often is observed that the reliability (i.e., Cronbach's alpha) is much lower for pretest scores than for posttest scores of intervention studies. This is not necessarily considered as bad, because a test designed to assess student learning should represent students' preknowledge and—to a larger extent—what students should learn as a result of the intervention.

Validity is a very important commonly evaluated category for evaluating the trustworthiness of all kinds of qualitative or quantitative observations. An instrument that measures something is called "valid" if it measures what it is supposed to measure. To evaluate validity, first of all, as researchers, we have to ask if the design and the instruments of our observation or measurement correspond with our theoretical construct or at least our theoretical assumptions (e.g., if our theory predicts a particular item ordering from easy to difficult, if the theory matches what is observed in the instrument's use, and if our instruments and our design can detect specific characters of the construct with high accuracy). There are different types of validity, some of which are briefly outlined in the following sections.

Content validity can only be discussed in the context of a theoretical framework as a matter of semantic accordance of the measuring instrument and the theoretical assumptions or theoretical construct (Haynes, Richard, & Kubany, 1995). All different aspects of the construct should be represented in the instruments. If the professional knowledge of science teachers to be validated contains, for example, three elements—content knowledge (CK), pedagogical content knowledge (PCK), and pedagogical knowledge (PK)—they have to be each theoretically described and given an operational definition that can be a starting point for the construction of the three corresponding test instruments. If the theoretical model contains, for example, the assumption of CK, PCK, and PK being three independent dimensions of professional knowledge, the researcher needs to consider a three-dimensional model.

Criterion validity is also known as **concurrent validity** and **prognostic validity**. Concurrent validity compares the test results with a criterion assessed at the same time. For example, a student tells an interviewer that he or she is not able to solve physics tasks about force. To validate the student's statement, the interviewer administers to the student a short, previously validated test on force such as one on parts of the force concept inventory (Hestenes, Wells, & Swackhamer, 1992). For prognostic validity, the criterion is assessed at a later date; for example, high school examination results of individuals can be compared with their success at university.

Construct validity considers, in essence, if and how a theoretical construct or model correlates with the results measured by an instrument that purports to measure the construct. If, for example, the construct of physics competency is operationalized to be measured by a test, the test must demonstrate how its items measure the construct. To approach construct validity, researchers usually determine the correlation between the results of their test instrument and those of other instruments that also purport to measure the same construct. In order to achieve construct validity, content validity is a necessary precondition. To check if a test can validly measure the operationalized form of a construct, for example, pedagogical content knowledge in chemistry (PCK-Ch), researchers can compare the results measured by the instrument with those by another previously used test that also claims to test PCK-Ch administered to the same sample at the same time. If the correlation is high, both instruments are valid (convergent validity) and the probability that they both measure PCK-Ch increases. On the contrary, researchers can compare the results of one instrument using chemistry teachers and mathematics teachers and expect only low correlation (discriminant validity) between the results of the two samples. If this is the case, the probability that the test validly measures the PCK of chemistry teachers increases.

To assess the quality of a measurement, researchers need both reliability and validity criteria if objectivity is asserted.

> Sociological theorists often use concepts that are formulated at rather high levels of abstraction. These are quite different from the variables that are in the stock-in-trade of empirical sociologists. (. . .) The problem of bridging the gap between theory and research is then seen as one of measurement error.
>
> (Blalock, 1968, pp. 6–12)

This is the basic idea of theory-guided measurement—there is a true value (e.g., of motivation or performance in chemistry), and a measurement should be able to make a statement about the level of probability that the true value can be expressed as the observed value corrected by the error: T = X + E (where X is observed, E is error).

If T is the estimated true value, S is a systematic error, and objectivity, as a precondition, is given, then measurements can be characterized roughly as shown in Figure 2.1.

Further procedures of empirical measures and calculations, such as criteria that confront non-normal distributed data, are described in this chapter. A detailed description of further procedures and criteria of trustworthiness can be found in Field (2005) or Shavelson and Towne (2002).

Significance refers to the trustworthiness of results obtained through procedures of data reduction. As quantitative research usually involves consideration of larger samples, procedures of data reduction are very important in analyzing data and obtaining results that can be used to answer research questions. For example, as researchers, we examine the relation between two variables in terms of correlation and want to claim that the two variables are correlated with each other at a medium level. Then we would have to obtain a measure that informs us—on the basis of the data we have collected—as to how sure we can be that there is in fact a correlation between the two variables or whether it may be that we were mistaken in concluding that there is a correlation.

In test theory, four possible cases with respect to testing a hypothesis through empirical data can be differentiated: (1) the hypothesis is in fact true and the data confirm the hypothesis; (2) the hypothesis is true, but the data suggest the hypothesis be rejected; (3) the hypothesis is false, but the data confirm the hypothesis; and (4) the hypothesis is false and the data suggest the hypothesis be rejected. Case 3, in which a false hypothesis is falsely accepted, is called error of the first kind. This is a case researchers typically try to avoid. For example, if a new science curriculum is falsely found to be more effective than the traditional curriculum, it may not be useful for student learning of science. Thus, in quantitative research, a researcher wants to ensure that a hypothesis is only accepted if the chance for it being false is small. The error of the first kind is sometimes also referred to as alpha error because alpha in test theory is used to denote the probability that a false hypothesis is erroneously accepted as true based on the data. What is considered an acceptable value for the alpha error is determined by the researcher and the community. For example, as students are not expected to know much about what they are supposed to learn, many of the items in the pretest are not correctly answered by the students, who may attempt to answer them by guessing. Students may randomly know the answers to some individual items of a test but do not yet have a coherent understanding of the domain. As such, when piloting an instrument, the sample should include

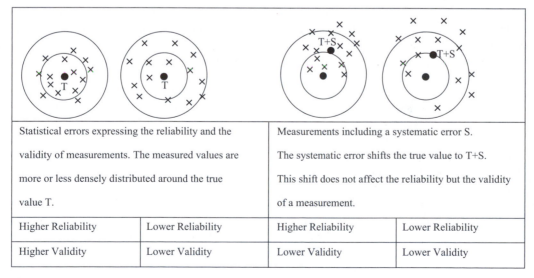

Statistical errors expressing the reliability and the validity of measurements. The measured values are more or less densely distributed around the true value T.		Measurements including a systematic error S. The systematic error shifts the true value to T+S. This shift does not affect the reliability but the validity of a measurement.	
Higher Reliability	Lower Reliability	Higher Reliability	Lower Reliability
Higher Validity	Lower Validity	Lower Validity	Lower Validity

Figure 2.1 Different scenarios of reliability and validity.

students across different ability levels in the pretest prior to and the posttest after instruction.

These criteria of the alpha error apply in principle to all kinds of measurement, and as quantitative (and qualitative) research builds on the measurement of various constructs, they also apply to research in general. However, these criteria must be individually adapted or expanded depending on the concrete designs, samples, and methods of analysis. Typically, in science education, only an alpha error level of less than 5 percent is considered acceptable.

Designs, Samples, and Methods of Analysis

One important decision following the establishment of a strong theoretical framework as well as the identification of research questions and hypotheses based on that framework is the choice of an appropriate research design. There are a multitude of research designs and categorizations of research designs. One principal categorization divides research designs into experimental and non-experimental designs.

Experimental designs are those set-ups in which at least one group is "treated" in a particular manner and the expected outcomes are compared to data and measures collected from a control group that receives a different treatment. To identify the effect of a treatment is not easy. Besides designing the treatment as carefully as possible, the control group is often taken as it appears in the field. For example, researchers want to measure the impact of teachers' process-oriented sequencing of a physics lesson on student learning in a study in which the research team trains the teachers. The researchers have to design a lesson for the teachers in the experimental group including classroom management and so on and provide or even construct learning material for their students. The teachers of the control group have to be supported in the same way on all aspects of the lesson planning except for sequencing the lesson. Otherwise, the researchers are not able to decide if the measured effect is a result of the treatment.

Non-experimental research designs typically include studies that seek to identify (1) characteristics of a population and (2) relations between such characteristics. This would, for example, include a study that researches college freshmen's interest in science and how that interest is related to students' choice of their master's degree specialization.

Another design classification addresses the differences between descriptive, correlative, and experimental studies. Descriptive studies are thought to mainly aim to describe particular characteristics within a population, correlative studies seek to identify correlations among such characteristics, and experimental studies aim to establish causal relations between at least one independent and one dependent variable. Other research design classifications are differentiated based on sampling (e.g., cross-sectional and longitudinal studies). Irrespective of design classification, a selected research design for a project should be one that lends the researchers to address the research questions

and hypotheses. Both research questions and hypotheses emerge from previous research and science education theory. Design and methodological choices should be made with the research questions and hypotheses in mind. However, recent methodological developments allow for better research designs, resulting in more trustworthy findings. Specific considerations that arise from these developments are discussed in the following section.

Specific Methodological Considerations

In quantitative research, statistical procedures play a central role. If the theoretical framework is fixed and the research questions and hypotheses are formulated, then a research design has to be chosen. Depending on the area of research, different designs are employed to obtain evidence to answer the specific research questions. However, before answering the research questions, the data obtained—usually data from a large sample of participants—need to be analyzed by means of statistical procedures. That is, the full set of information—as represented by every single answer of every single participant to every single question in all the instruments utilized in the study—needs to be reduced to the actual information in which the researchers are interested. This is how statistical procedures help quantitative researchers. For example, if 50 treatment-group students receive teaching on mechanics in everyday contexts and the same number of students in a control group receives regular teaching, then both have to answer the same test, for example, the Force Concept Inventory (FCI), a 30-item test instrument. The full data set contains a unique identifier for each student, the group the student belonged to, and the student's answer to each of the 30 items. In the first step, typically the Rasch measure (e.g., Granger, 2008; Wright, 1995) is calculated for each student. Then a t-test is applied in order to determine whether students from the treatment group had a higher measure than did students from the control group in order to find out how sure we, as researchers, can be about our findings. But what if the t-test gave us a false positive? What if we were not allowed to actually use the t-test? Certainly, the t-test cannot be applied if we only had two students in each group. In fact, statistical procedures come with certain requirements that need to be checked.

Central Requirements of Statistical Procedures

One of the central requirements of statistical procedures is normal distribution of the measures such as the students' scores on the FCI test in the example. Another requirement is the linearity of measures. That is that students not only can be ranked by their measures, indicating that those with a measure of 2.0 logits had a higher ability than a student with a measure of 1.0 logit, but that the increase in the measure from 1.0 logit to 2.0 logits corresponds to the same increase in the knowledge about mechanics as the increase of a measure from 0 logit to 1.0 logit. For a long time, researchers have been concerned about the normal distribution of measures (which usually is a sound assumption) and have neglected the consideration of the linearity of measures. Linearity can, in part, be considered an appraisal of the accuracy of the measurements over the full range of the instruments (for an in-depth discussion of this issue, see Neumann, Neumann, & Nehm, 2011). However, more recently, the work of Georg Rasch (1960), a Danish mathematician, has received increasing and deserved attention, as the Rasch analysis allows researchers to obtain linear measures from ordinal scores such as test scores or sum scores from Likert scales. A more complete treatment of Rasch analysis follows later in this chapter. In a similar way, researchers in science education have begun to use other methodologies developed in, for example, educational psychology or educational research that can help ensure that the results obtained through statistical procedures capture the complexity of the teaching and learning about science inside and outside of the classroom.

Obtaining Linear Measures and Rasch Analysis

Up to this point in our chapter, we have described the necessary considerations and requirements for conducting science education research. In this section, we present, as an example, details of how Rasch measurement theory can be utilized by science education researchers in the course of investigations utilizing instrumentation such as tests and survey questionnaires. Many examples of the application of statistical techniques (e.g., ANOVA, regression, correlation) have been presented in the science education literature. However, here we concentrate on detailing selected aspects of applying the Rasch theory because this theory provides measures of the quality needed for statistical analysis. Core themes of earlier sections of our chapter are revisited in our discussion about the Rasch method.

Rasch measurement techniques were developed by the Danish mathematician George Rasch (1960) and greatly expanded by the University of Chicago's Benjamin Wright in his books *Best Test Design* (Wright & Stone, 1979) and *Rating Scale Analysis* (Wright & Masters, 1982).

Rasch and Wright noticed that raw test data (e.g., scores for an answer and dichotomous and partial credit) and raw rating scale data are ordinal. This means that, among many implications, the use of parametric statistics to evaluate raw ordinal data violates assumptions of such statistical tests. Additional problems involve (1) the weakness of quality control with regard to data quality and instrument functioning, (2) an inability to express how an individual student performed on a test (or the attitude expressed on a survey) with respect to instrument items, and (3) the inability to track development of students over time in detail with a single scale.

Rasch analysis is now being utilized worldwide to (1) guide and facilitate the development of rigorous measurement instruments, (2) express student performance with respect to item difficulty, (3) compute linear student measures that can be used for parametric tests, and (4) develop alternative forms of tests and survey questionnaires (multimatrix design), which can be linked (e.g., Kolen & Brennan, 2004; Neumann, Viering, Boone, & Fischer, 2013).

Rasch analysis is not simply the application of the Rasch model in a computer program, but it is also about thinking of what it means to measure. When Rasch measurement is utilized, there is frequent reflection on and the assessment of many pieces of evidence for reaching a conclusion, for example, the overall functioning of an instrument.

To determine the quality of evidence in a field, one requirement is to be able to evaluate the quality of the measurement instruments utilized to collect data. Rasch measurement provides a multitude of techniques by which instrument functioning can be gauged. For those who have utilized Rasch measurement, it is abundantly clear that the steps taken to evaluate instrument functioning greatly parallel the steps taken by biologists, physicists, and other scientists as they create laboratory instruments.

Measurement Error and Validity

Let us first begin with the issue of reliability. It is common in the field of science education that a researcher computes reliability as a way of attempting to evaluate, to some degree, the quality of results collected with an instrument. There are a number of pitfalls in the computation of a Cronbach's alpha or a Kuder-Richardson formula (KR-8, -20, or -21), as is detailed in Smith, Linacre, and Smith, 2003 (pp. 198–204):

> Reliability was originally conceptualized as the ratio of the true variance to the observed variance. Since there was no method in the true score model of estimating the SEM a variety of methods (e.g., KR-20, Alpha) were developed to estimate reliability without knowing the SEM. In the Rasch model it is possible to approach reliability the way it was originally intended rather than using a less than ideal solution.

Thus, when Rasch analysis is used, improved reliability can be computed rather than utilizing other methods to estimate the reliability without taking into account the standard error of measurement. An additional problem in the computation of an alpha involves raw data, which are nonlinear, and a well-known ceiling effect of indices such as alpha. There are also additional weaknesses in the traditional computation of an alpha in science education studies that involve the lack of investigation of both the reliability of test items and the reliability of persons, for example, in the use of reliability indices such as Cronbach's alpha (e.g., Clauser & Linacre, 1999; Linacre, 1997). When Rasch analysis is used, there are reliabilities computed for persons and items.

Rasch measurement provides a number of indices and techniques by which instrument quality and trustworthiness can be assessed. Some examples involve item fit and person fit assessed through mean square residual (MNSQ) criteria (e.g., Smith, 1986, 1991, 1996). Item fit can be thought of as a technique by which one can identify items that may not lie on the same measurement scale of the variable as the majority of items (items not part of a construct), and person fit can be used to identify idiosyncratic responses to the test (or survey questionnaire) by the respondents (e.g., poorly performing students who unexpectedly give correct answers to very difficult items on a test). Misfitting items may need to be removed from an instrument, and misfitting students have to be excluded from the analysis because they may not be those for which useful measures can or should be computed. Rasch analysis also includes indices such as person separation/person strata and item separation/item strata (e.g., Fisher, 1992), which can be used to evaluate additional aspects of instrument functioning.

We now consider the topic of measurement error that impacts the trustworthiness of data collected with instruments and the trustworthiness of statistical results. In any laboratory in which data are collected, the scientist is acutely aware of the possible errors in each measurement. And the scientist will know that the error is not necessarily the same for each measure taken. The issue of measurement error in science education has been almost entirely ignored for many years. When a Rasch analysis is conducted, measurement errors are computed for each respondent and each item. When science education researchers review the errors of respondent measures, they will soon understand a number of errors they themselves have been making. For example, a test taker who has earned a perfect raw score on a test will have a much larger Rasch error of measurement than another test taker who has only correctly answered half of the test items. This difference in error can be understood by reasoning that a perfect score does not reveal how much more the test taker knows. The test taker with the perfect score could have been presented with 10 more very difficult items and have correctly answered all, some, or none of these items. This is similar to the full-scale deflection of a needle on a 12-volt voltmeter when it is known that the voltage is higher than 12 volts and that it could be 12.5 volts or 1,000 volts. Numerous articles in science education have presented details that further discuss the computation of Rasch item/person error and the use of error in Rasch measurement for analysis of data (e.g., Granger, 2008; Wright, 1995).

In earlier sections of this chapter, we discuss the important issue of considering what a researcher wants to investigate. The question might seem to be a simple one, but it is not trivial. With regard to Rasch measurement, the question becomes: Does an instrument measure what is needed to be measured, and how well does the instrument measure? When Rasch measurement is used, great care is taken to define the variable of interest and to define what different examples of the variable would be as the researcher moves from one end of the variable's range to the other. In Figure 2.2, we present a common tool used by those applying Rasch analysis to the development of a

1	4	76	5	2	3	8

Less difficult   More difficult

Figure 2.2 Example for a latent variable defined by eight items (numbered 1 to 8).

measurement device. And we provide the predicted location and order of eight biology test items.

When one understands what it means to measure and what is needed for a good measurement tool, be it a ruler, a thermometer, or a knowledge test, it should make sense that the variable being measured by a survey or test should be measured by items along a range of levels of the variable. This means, in the case of a test, that there should be items that range from easy to difficult. In the case of an attitudinal survey questionnaire with a rating scale of agreement, there should be items that range from "easier to agree with" to items that are "more difficult to agree with." In our example, the gaps between the test items will mean that some respondents who differ in their traits (e.g., ability or attitude in the case of a survey) as variables being measured cannot be distinguished or differentiated (e.g., a student John may have an ability level just above that of item 6, while a student Paul may have an ability level just below the portion of the trait measured by item 5).

By utilizing the Rasch idea of how items measure a variable, a researcher is able to avoid using an instrument inappropriately for the goal of the study or avoid utilizing an existing instrument for which the researcher may not have clearly defined a range of values of the variable being measured to distinguish and differentiate respondents. Without consideration of a single variable and the range of levels along one variable, a new instrument may fall short of measurement precision, often to the extent that it makes no sense to attempt any statistical analysis.

As presented in Figure 2.2, the identification of items that measure a variable (which items fall on the line) clearly involves content validity; and the prediction of item ordering and spacing along a variable (where items fall on the line) involves construct validity.

Differential Item Functioning

In addition to considering construct validity by predicting the order and spacing of items along the measurement scale of a variable using a guiding theory, Rasch analysis provides many analytical techniques by which construct validity can be evaluated, the most common of which is perhaps the investigation of differential item functioning (DIF) conducted with Rasch analysis. DIF, in essence, involves being able to compare whether the manner in which items of a test (or a survey questionnaire) define the variable in the same way as a function of the participants' attributes across all groups, including subgroups or comparison groups. If an item defines the variable in a different manner, it may mean that this item does not measure the construct (or the defined variable) in the same manner across the groups. Identification of such an item may mean that the item needs to be removed from a measurement instrument, but such an item can often be of great interest for the researcher in that the item often reveals some differences between comparison subgroups of respondents. The work of Brown, Unsworth, and Lyons (2009) provided a good example of the use of these and other Rasch measures in the Rasch evaluation of construct validity of a measurement instrument.

As detailed in the first part of this chapter, of immense importance to science education researchers is the hierarchical structure of school systems. There are for researchers a number of models that can be used to provide guidance for conducting studies on school systems. One such example was the study conducted by the Consortium on Chicago School Research (CCSR) in which hierarchical linear modeling (HLM), Rasch analysis, and other statistical techniques were utilized to facilitate an analysis of a large school system (see Bryk & Raudenbush, 1992; Kapadia, Coca, & Easton, 2007).

Scales of Person Measure and Variable

In science education research, we have argued that science educators should be able to provide meaningful and accurate guidance to teachers, policy makers, and researchers to improve and/or control the quality of instruction or the output of the educational system. Rasch analysis provides meaningful guidance to teachers, policy makers, and researchers. Since Rasch analysis (in the case of tests and survey questionnaires) facilitates the computation on the same scale of a person measure (that can be placed on the same scale on the variable) and an item measure (that can be placed on same scale of the variable), it is possible to express the relation between person measures and item measures (see Figure 2.3). In Figure 2.3, we provide

a Wright map, in which person measures are plotted on the left side and item measures on the right side of the map. Each item is identified with the phrase Q Item Number (e.g., Q5). Items higher up on the Wright map are more difficult items.

The importance of such a Wright map is that not only is the distribution of person measures presented on a linear measurement scale of the variable (e.g., ability of the students) but also that of the item measures is presented on the same linear measurement scale of the variable. This enables the performance of each student (or group of students) to be expressed in light of which item (or items) the student(s) would be predicted to have correctly answered or not answered. For example, to make use of this map to study gender differences, the average measures or means of the males and females on the test have to be marked. To understand which items the typical male could do, we simply draw a horizontal line from the average measure of the males across the Wright map. Those items below the male line are those items a typical male would be predicted to have correctly answered, but not those items above the line. This technique allows explaining the meaning of a measure. Now one is able to understand what the performance means (what a test taker or a group of test takers can or cannot do).

An additional way this Wright map can be used can best be understood by drawing a horizontal line from the average measure of female test takers and then evaluating the items between the line for the males and the line for the females. Those items that fall between the two lines are the items that describe the differences observed between the two groups. It may be that *t*-test results have shown a statistically significant difference between the average male and female measures. However, now it is possible to explain what the meaning of the difference between the two groups is by interpreting and comparing items that are correctly answered and those predicted to be correctly answered in relation to different individuals and different groups. The meaning of the difference between groups can be detailed in terms of what students can and cannot do and how they differ. Versions of such Wright maps have been widely used in Australia for a number of decades, and such Wright maps are now often used to write parent reports (e.g., Family Report, 2012) and to compare different groups in science education research (e.g., Kauertz & Fischer, 2006; Neumann et al., 2011; Neumann et al., 2013). Boone, Staver, and Yale's (2014) book has two chapters on detailed discussion of Wright maps. Boone and Scantlebury (2006) and Boone, Townsend, and Staver (2011) also described the use of Rasch analysis for science education research and discussed Wright maps in particular. Wright maps have also been frequently used in medical fields to communicate instrument validity as well as patient measures (Stelmack et al., 2004).

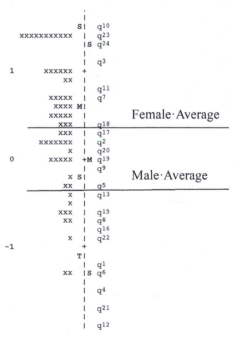

Figure 2.3 Wright map of person measures and item difficulty ordered on one scale.

Hierarchical Structure of Data

Another characteristic of researching teaching and learning in real classrooms (beyond the sheer complexity of variables) is the hierarchical structure of data. Every part of a school system contains many variables that are dependent on each other. For example, it is well known that student learning (i.e., the increase in the scores on a test of student competence in a domain) depends on cognitive ability. But what if students with a lower cognitive ability have, for example, difficulties in processing complex diagrams? Naturally, if a teacher uses the same complex diagrams in two different classes, the students in one class—a larger number of whom exhibit a lower average cognitive ability—will, on average, learn less compared to the students in the other class. However, the pertinent issue is that although in both classes the students with a lower cognitive ability will learn less, there are fewer students with a low cognitive ability in the class with a higher average cognitive ability. This will not become apparent when both classes are compared.

The bottom line is that in order to capture such complex relations between various factors on the individual level and the aggregate level (i.e., the classroom or school system), more complex procedures than t-tests or ANOVA are required. Although ANOVA allows for accounting for variables on the classroom level, it does not allow for modeling the effect of a classroom variable that the variable has on another variable on the individual level. For example, if a teacher alters his/her teaching style by presenting specific, less complex diagrams to students with lower cognitive abilities, the students may learn better and this learning may in turn affect the overall correlation between their cognitive abilities and their learning outcomes. One method to account for such a complex situation is the method of hierarchical linear modeling (HLM). In addition to utilizing HLM, two other related analysis techniques, structural equation models (SEM) and path analysis, are also of importance for the rigorous analysis of data in science education research. There is one particularly important aim of quantitative science education research for researchers to consider. That is to describe the complex situation in classrooms and how variables are correlated with each other and to identify the nature of the relation between such information. If two variables such as student achievement and student interest are correlated, is it that one affects the other? Will a higher interest lead to better achievement, or is it the other way around and a higher achievement leads to more interest? Or is it that both, achievement and interest, progress alongside each other as specific features of the teacher–student interaction mediates or moderates both, depending on a third variable (e.g., students' self-efficacy)? In the discussion section of papers, it is oftentimes pointed out how correlation may not be mistaken as indicating causal relations and that identifying causal relations requires experimental designs. In fact, with path analysis or its more sophisticated variant, structural equation modeling (SEM), it becomes possible

to specify the directions of relations in a model and to test the validity of the model against a given data set.

A variety of methodologies (many new or further developed) address quantitative science education research. Examples of such methodologies include Rasch analysis, video analysis, hierarchical linear modeling, and structural equation modeling. These methodologies and their potential for quantitative science education research are discussed in the following sections.

Quantitative Approaches in Science Education Research

As discussed earlier in this chapter, three major areas of research in science education may be identified: (1) research on evaluating science teaching strategies, including any kind of research that evaluates different approaches for enhancing student learning (e.g., students' knowledge, interest or skills); (2) research on classroom-based learning, including research on any kind of learning processes with regard to science in larger groups such as science field trips; and (3) research on how people learn about science, including research on constructs related to learning (e.g., interest in science or beliefs about science related to subjects/individuals).

Evaluating Strategies of Science Teaching

Research in science education very often concerns the investigation of changes in outcome variables such as students' achievement, interest, or motivation. However, if the focus is on (1) evaluating different ways of teaching science and/or (2) more precisely evaluating strategies to foster improvement in science achievement, interest, or motivation of different groups (which require group comparisons), different research designs than the ones described previously are required. These designs are commonly referred to as experimental or quasi-experimental designs. In such designs, instruments are needed to assess changes in students' achievement, interest, or motivation as a result of treatment or intervention. The instruments need to be administered to students before and after students are taught according to a particular strategy (an approach commonly referred to as a pre-post design). Using such a design, the effect of the particular teaching strategy on students' achievement may be investigated. However, the problem of using a simple pre-post design is that it does not provide conclusive evidence that the change in students' achievement is related to the new teaching strategy. It might be that the achievement change may be the result of other teaching strategies. In order to obtain evidence for the conclusion that the observed change in student achievement is in fact due to teaching with a particular strategy, a second group of students is required. This second group needs to be taught with a different strategy or, at the minimum, have received regular instruction. Another teaching strategy, instead of regulation instruction, is usually preferred as it can rule out alternative explanations for students' potential improvement, for example, a novelty effect. Therefore, evaluation of teaching strategies—that is, any strategies that foster increase in any science learning-related variables, including soft skills such as interest or motivation—requires more sophisticated experimental designs than a pre-post design.

In experimental designs, students should ideally be randomly assigned to one of the groups that are compared to each other (usually at least one treatment and one control group). Consequently, these designs are referred to as randomized experimental designs. Such randomization should be a goal of a study using experimental designs, as randomization is expected to rule out effects of differences—in cognitive abilities and any other variables—that may affect the results of the study. Randomization obviously requires a large enough sample size, and in some cases it is either not possible or not feasible to randomly assign students to treatment and control groups. In this case, the variables expected to influence the variables targeted for assessment need to be controlled. This means added variables should be assessed as well and included in an analysis to determine their effects. We find that these added variables are very often not addressed in science education studies when the limitations of a study are discussed.

When randomization is not possible, we suggest a strategy is to sample a large enough group of students to rule out particular unwanted influences. We cannot provide exact numbers for study sample sizes, but the sample size would have to be large enough to allow for the assumption that the distribution of the variables—that may cause unwanted influences confounding the results on an analysis—is similar in both groups. Experimental designs that do not use randomized samples are also commonly referred to as quasi-experimental designs.

Procedures of data analysis in experimental designs typically include a variety of analyses of variance (ANOVA), where the grouping variable serves as the independent variable. As discussed earlier, in the case of just one dependent variable (e.g., change in student achievement) and just two different values of the independent (grouping) variable (i.e., one treatment and one control group), an ANOVA yields the same results as does a t-test. One strength of the ANOVA approach to analysis is, however, that it allows for more than one independent variable, which may be considered as in the case of experimental pre-post designs and in longitudinal studies. ANOVA is also applicable as repeated measures ANOVA. In addition to the grouping variable that distinguishes students from treatment and control groups, there may be other grouping variables such as gender. The so-called analysis of covariance (ANCOVA), moreover, allows for adding continuous variables such as students' cognitive abilities or interests that are not of primary interest, known as covariates. ANCOVA is a general linear model to combine regression and ANOVA to control the effects of the covariates. An ANCOVA adjusts the dependent variable (e.g., students'

competence) as if all comparison groups are equal on the covariates (Best & Kahn, 2006).

Investigating Classroom Instruction

As science education research aims at improving instruction, even if a randomized experimental design cannot be applied to obtain evidence of how teaching works in different classrooms with different teachers, the starting point for estimating the sample size is the number of theoretical parameters for distinguishing the teachers. If, for example, gender is the only parameter, the researcher needs at least 20 male and 20 female teachers. Every additional parameter requires 20 more individuals. For example, the teacher effectiveness research shows that although a particular teaching strategy may have been found to work with one group of students, the strategy may not work with another group, as a variety of characteristics of teachers, students, and instruction affects the learning outcomes. Because many strategies have been found to only work with a particular group of students such as high or low achievers, there are nuances in selecting a sample size and a research design that are impacted by a particular group of students (e.g., high achievers). One example of this issue involves the influence of students' socioeconomic status (SES). SES has been found to influence students' mathematics achievement (Prenzel, 2004, p. 251). Accordingly, on average, 16.8% of variance in students' mathematics achievement was found to be explained by their SES across participating countries in the Programme for International Student Assessment (PISA). In Germany's case, SES accounted for an above-average variance in students' mathematics achievement at 21.1% (Prenzel, 2004, p. 275). As a consequence, SES must be controlled in studies investigating instructional quality and be included as a moderator or mediator when analyzing the effects of instructional characteristics on student achievement. Also, any other factors such as political, organizational, or institutional conditions must be controlled as well, as these may influence instruction, student achievement, or the relation between the two. That is, in order to improve instruction as a whole, it is of utmost importance to understand the complex processes in regular classrooms and how they are affected by different characteristics of students, teachers, and the classroom environment, as well as other factors such as funding of the schools.

At present, little is known about the complex processes of instruction and how such processes are affected by framework characteristics such as those mentioned. As a consequence, it is not yet possible to detail and describe a full-blown theoretical framework of classroom teaching and learning from previous research with respect to instructional quality. For example, the effect of certain aspects of professional knowledge of teachers on the quality of lessons is not known, nor is the kind of content knowledge teachers should learn at universities for best practice in schools. Certainly, knowing more about the interdependencies between teaching and learning would definitely lead to a more precise formulation of goals for teacher education and would result in a more effective use of the limited learning time of future teachers at universities. Some examples of quality criteria that should be utilized to detail a theoretical framework are classroom management (Fricke, van Ackeren, Kauertz, & Fischer, 2012), cognitive activation (Baumert et al., 2010), and feedback (Hattie & Timperley, 2007).

Once the constituents of a model of professional knowledge have been established, a test instrument can be selected if one exists for the model. If appropriate instruments do not exist, as researchers, we need to validate our self-developed instruments. This is what is required whether the instruments are for tests, surveys, or video analysis. In case an instrument exists, we must consider convergent validity and discriminant validity. Therefore, we need either another instrument that was already used for the same purpose (convergent validity) or we have to choose samples of participants with different characteristics to validate our instrument by correlating the results of this sample and those of our target sample (discriminant validity). For example, in the validation of an instrument for measuring PCK of physics teachers, mathematics or English teachers should perform significantly lower than do physics teachers, and the correlation between the samples should be low, too. Ultimately, we are able to describe the professional knowledge of a certain sample of teachers in terms of the mean and variance, and we are able to compare these measures between different samples—for example, a number of schools and those schools' teachers or representative samples of two countries.

The mere description of data does not allow one to draw conclusions. Thus, the description of the quality of teacher education or the quality of teaching does not allow one to make a conclusion. To draw conclusions or to investigate directions of an effect, one needs criteria to classify instructional quality, and one must have a theory of how professional knowledge contributes to a framework of instruction quality. An example of a criterion might be measures of students' learning outcomes, including knowledge, competences, motivation, and interest (controlled for cognitive abilities and socioeconomic status). To measure outcomes, we must have appropriate tests and questionnaires. As we advance in our analysis using our selected instruments, we should be able to discriminate between low- and high-achieving classes and their teachers. In case the correlation between students' and teachers' test results is moderately significant or higher, a connection between the two can be assumed. Otherwise, we have to think about possible external influences that were not taken into account but may have influenced our data. Our point is that external influences have to be taken into consideration and have to be reflected on to improve ongoing and future research.

To answer the research question of whether our construct of PCK matters for classroom performance and students' outcomes, an experimental study should be designed to determine the direction of the effect before measuring correlation. Once the effect of PCK is known from such a study, we can proceed to investigate how teachers' PCK affects instructional quality in real classrooms. In the best situation, such studies can target a representative sample of students in a particular setting. Previous research has shown that classroom instruction follows so-called specific cultural scripts for different countries (Hiebert et al., 2003; Roth et al., 2006; Stigler & Hiebert, 1997).

To complete our discussion on the complexity of science education research and how/why this research must be improved, we wish to summarize some caveats and issues that must be considered by science education researchers. In order to capture the complex processes of classroom instruction, the use of statistical tools such as t-tests, ANOVA, or regression analyses has its limitations. In order to consider a variety of different characteristics on different aggregation levels with respect to classroom instruction (i.e., the individual level of the students, the classroom level, the level of schools, or even whole countries), we require more sophisticated procedures of analysis. This starts with the fact that in the reality of the classroom, aptitude-treatment-interaction effects (Cronbach & Snow, 1977) must be considered and taken into account—for example, individual characteristics of students that resonate with characteristics of the teacher, the school, and/or the country's school system. Procedures typically applied to the analysis of more complex instructional settings are path analysis, hierarchical linear modeling, or structural equation modeling. Some of these procedures are discussed in the following section.

Longitudinal and Cross-Sectional Panel Studies

Understanding how students learn about science is a central requirement of research for improving science education. Generally, this research is related to questions of how students proceed in making sense of a particular domain, for example, learning the energy concept (e.g., Driver, Leach, Scott, & Wood-Robinson, 1994; Duit, 1984; Lee & Liu, 2010; Liu & McKeough, 2005; Neumann et al., 2013). This research is also related to the development of concepts or learning progressions (for the energy concept, see, for example, Nordine, Krajcik, & Fortus, 2011). To analyze the development of concepts or learning progressions, students must be tracked over a long period of time. Instructional components and students' outcomes must be assessed using assessment instruments (e.g., Krajcik, Drago, Sutherland, & Merritt, 2012). As such, this research most likely utilizes longitudinal designs, which means sampling students from different points in the learning process over time (panel design). When the same instruments must be evaluated for use with students with different ages and different subsamples, the design is called cross-sectional design. However, cross-sectional studies do not produce data about cause-and-effect relationships because such studies only offer a snapshot of a single moment; and such studies do not allow tracking development over time. As a result, one weakness of cross-sectional studies is that one cannot know with certainty if students develop certain energy concepts as a consequence of the completed lessons or students' cognitive development.

Both panel and cross-sectional (also called trend studies) are observational ones. Researchers collect data about their samples without changing the environment of the study, for example, through an intervention or a selection of specific individuals. Typical research questions for panel studies focus on how students proceed in their understanding of a concept, skill, or domain based on a particular curriculum, that is, the existing or a new curriculum (cf. Neumann et al., 2013). However, panel studies come with a particular number of constraints. They require test instruments that can compare students and questionnaires that are understood in the same way by students of different ages and different cognitive development. In addition, longitudinal studies require assigning an individual ID to each student's performance at each measurement time point to allow collation of data from the different measurements. However, this procedure is prone to errors, as students may not know their mother's birth date or other dates chosen as identifiers. As a consequence, so-called "panel mortality" is increased. This particular term refers to the complete set of data measures obtained from a panel study compared to the number of theoretically possible full data measures. Common causes of missing data are students' absences due to different reasons. This issue is exacerbated when a study extends over a longer period of time (e.g., several years). This is a particularly important issue because a crucial sample size is needed at the final measurement time point (the sample must be large enough for statistical analysis). Typical procedures of analyses on students' understanding include *t*-tests, different kinds of analysis of variance (ANOVA), linear regression analyses, or combinations of these.

Given the great cost in time and money associated with longitudinal studies, it is often reasonable to carry out a cross-sectional study first, particularly when the time frame exceeds a reasonable amount of time. The time frame is determined by students' expected progression (e.g., Grades 6, 7, 8, and 9).

Based on students' (linear) measures of ability obtained through Rasch analysis, students' progression in mastering the particular concept, skill, or domain may be analyzed as a function of schooling. In a longitudinal study, typically repeated measures ANOVA are utilized. This allows for analyzing whether there are statistically significant differences in measures of students' ability depending on the time of measurement. In cross-sectional studies, typically regular ANOVA is utilized. Using ANOVA, measures of students' ability are investigated as a function of schooling (e.g., grades). With regard to independent variables (e.g., the variable that denotes the amount of schooling received or learning that has taken place respectively)—spanning a larger number of values

(i.e., when learning about science is investigated across the life span and age is utilized as an indicator of the amount of learning that has taken place), linear regression analysis should be used. In cases in which there are only two different groups for comparison with respect to measures of students' ability, the *t*-test may be used. Generally, an ANOVA with only two groups (students at the beginning and end of Grade 8) will yield the same results as in a *t*-test. Comparison of more than two groups requires the use of an ANOVA or regression analysis. In case additional variables (e.g., students' interest in science) are to be included in the analysis, two- or more-factor ANOVAs or more complex regression models may be applied (for a detailed discussion of *t*-tests, different ANOVAs, or regression analyses, see Field, 2005). It is important to note that whereas regression analysis provides information about the (linear) relation between the independent and dependent variable, ANOVA does not. ANOVA only informs the researcher about the differences between different values of the independent variable (e.g., different groups of students). The exact nature of the relation needs to be investigated through further analyses such as the use of predefined contrasts (see Field, 2005).

The intended statistical technique to analyze the data greatly impacts the procedures and details of sampling. A simple ANOVA requires a minimum of 10 persons per value of the grouping variable (e.g., Chi, 1994). However, usually a minimum of 20 persons is suggested (Bortz, 2005; Field, 2005; Linacre, 1994). In general, the sample size depends on the size of the expected effects. To resolve a medium effect ($d = .5$) for a regression of college students' semester achievement, a sample size of 34 students is required. More complex procedures naturally require a higher sample size. If, for example, Rasch analysis is to be used to obtain linear measures of students' ability, a minimum of 80 students per task is suggested, and in the case of structural equation modeling, a minimum of 50 students per variable included in the model is suggested. This provides an estimate of the required initial sample size of a longitudinal study when, for example, 10 variables are tested four times with an average panel mortality of 30%.

Analyzing Teaching and Learning Processes by Means of Video Analysis

One particular method is the analysis of lessons by means of analyzing video recordings of the lessons. Although at first glance this method may not appear to be a statistical procedure, it is tremendously useful in capturing teaching and learning about science in real classrooms. For example, in analyzing student interviews, the transcription of video recordings and their analysis were utilized in science education research as early as the 1970s. However, as technological developments have made video equipment more affordable and easier to use, it has become possible to standardize the way recordings are made and analyzed such that video analysis could be used in quantitative research (e.g., Roth et al., 2006; Stigler & Hiebert,

1999). This development was partly due to the development of the method of category-based analysis of text, including video recordings, or category-based analysis of videotapes (CBAV; for details, see Niedderer et al., 1998, 2002). However, as is often the case, the availability of a new methodology not only led to better answers regarding long-standing research questions but also resulted in the identification of new theoretical and methodological deficits. One of these theoretical deficits that became apparent from video analysis is how little is known about complex classroom processes.

Video analysis is a method that originally was developed in qualitative research. Certainly, video analysis as such is a qualitative process because a social interaction has to be interpreted. However, the development of CBAV has made video analysis available as a tool for quantitative research. CBAV provides a standardization of the process of interpretation and the introduction of measures of reliability and validity of the category systems used. Needless to say, the category system is of central importance when analyzing video data.

Video data may be considered as raw data from lessons, which, once recorded, needs to be analyzed based on a particular theoretical framework; and thereafter, it is used for developing research questions. However, before the lessons can be analyzed, they have to be recorded; the teaching and learning in the classroom needs to be captured by a video camera. This procedure involves decisions such as where to position the cameras and microphones in the classroom and how many to use. Naturally, these decisions have to be made based on an underlying theoretical framework. Even the location of the video cameras in the classroom is part of a research question. Investigation of group work requires camera locations different from those for the investigation of teacher–student interactions (for a description of different arrangements of how to video record lessons, see Fischer & Neumann, 2012). Once the actual arrangement of the recording equipment is decided on, recording guidelines have to be specified to ensure that the video recordings of different classrooms are comparable. In principle, these guidelines are supposed to ensure standardized and comparable recordings independent of the actual person doing the video recording, that is, to ensure objectivity of the findings. When video recordings are made, even the cameraperson has to be familiar with the guidelines.

Once video data have been properly recorded and processed (e.g., digitized for digital analysis utilizing computer based analysis software), the analysis can commence. The first step when analyzing video data is to decide on the detail level of the analysis. In the second step, a coding procedure has to be developed and applied to the data. Finally, in the third step, quality measures have to be determined.

Obtaining quantitative data from video analysis requires exact rules on how to observe, secure, and categorize the observable features—based on the respective theoretical framework or model. This set of rules must be applied to the observation material to obtain quantitative data in a process called coding. The set of rules is termed the coding or the category system (Mayring, 1995) that emphasizes the necessity of a sound category system. If the category system is not developed with the greatest of care, the obtained quantitative data will be rendered meaningless. Mayring (2007) differentiated between two approaches to obtain a category system: an inductive and a deductive approach. Whereas the inductive approach is of particular importance for qualitative content analysis, a deductive, theory-guided process is more appropriate for quantitative video analysis of instruction. This is because an inductive approach will allow for only a strictly qualitative analysis of video data. A deductive approach, on the other hand, will allow for a qualitative or a quantitative analysis as well as a combination of the two. A deductive approach always starts from theory, whereas a qualitative approach involves developing theoretical statements inductively during the process of data analysis. Based on theoretical considerations, the decisions on the exact research questions and hypotheses have to be made. This would include, for example, decisions about the segmentation of data or further processing of data such as transcripts of the video recordings. In the case of an analysis of teacher–student dialogs, the raw recorded data would be segmented into "turns" (e.g., teacher speaking or student speaking). To analyze students' time on tasks, segmenting the recording into "intervals" (e.g., deciding every 30 seconds whether students are on or off task) would be reasonable. A transcript can also be helpful, especially when a decision in favor of segmenting data into completed sections of interaction (so-called turns) is made. In the case of the investigation of teacher–student dialogs, it is better to identify individual turns than to analyze the interval-based situation.

When video analysis is conducted, transcription requires clear and precise rules to consider activities of interest. For example, gestures and facial expressions, as well as affective expressions or transformed everyday language or dialect, have to be carefully examined during transcription. Examples of rules for transcription are given in Mayring (2007, p. 49). Once the material has been prepared accordingly, the development of the category system itself can begin.

Development of the category system begins by identifying the theoretical constructs of relevance and operationalizing the constructs into categories. A construct may be represented by one or more categories. The construct *teacher use of media*, for example, may be represented by the categories *smart phone*, *blackboard*, *overhead projector*, or *textbook*. Each of the categories comes with a series of indicators that provide guidance as to whether the respective category should be coded. An example of an "indicator" could be *the teacher writes or draws on the blackboard* or *the teacher asks students to open their textbooks*. The key here is that the indicators have to characterize the related category as precisely and completely as possible using a potentially extensive collection of examples. Once categories and indicators are created, a coding manual should be written, thoroughly describing categories and indicators. With the coding manual, this initial version of the category system can be applied to coding real data in order to test their practicability and determine the quality measures.

In the next step, the data obtained from the coding are analyzed. In this step, investigation of the reliability of the coding is of central importance. In addition to determining the validity of data analysis, ensuring the validity of data interpretation is also needed.

In a final step, the findings, and in particular the quality measures and estimates, need to be carefully examined with respect to the formulated research questions and hypotheses and particularly to the expectations regarding quality measures. If the quality measures do not meet established requirements, that is, reliability remains unsatisfactorily low and validity cannot be established, the coding procedure needs to be refined in a new iteration of the previously described sequence of steps. A detailed discussion of quality measures is discussed in the next section. It should be emphasized that developing a coding procedure is an intense and demanding process, but for a sound video analysis, it is a mandatory step.

Although reliability, in the context of video analysis, is often a primary concern of researchers, validity is also important as a quality criterion. Reliability of the coding obtained through video analysis depends on the coders. In many ways, the human coders can be considered as the measurement instrument in video analysis. In the context of video analysis, reliability is usually determined by means of intercoder reliability. To determine intercoder reliability, selected video material has to be coded independently by different coders following the (same) coding procedure. The different codings are compared on a per-unit-of-analysis basis. Different techniques can be used to determine reliability. The simplest measure is the percentage of agreement ρ. Whereas the percentage of agreement ρ is quick to calculate, it is unfortunate that it cannot be used to consider random agreements. More sophisticated measures that are corrected for random agreement are suitable for use, for example, Cohen's κ in the case of nominal data or Goodman-Kruskal's γ in the case of ordinal data. However, there is no agreement on the cutoff values that have to be met by the above measures in order to consider intercoder reliability to be sufficient. One issue is that the criterion for sufficient reliability depends on how much interpretation is involved in the coding, that is, the level of inference inherent in a particular category. Higher inference entails higher influence of a coder's knowledge, expectations, and beliefs on the coding process. High inference is therefore tied to lower intercoder reliability. For example, when coding the addressee(s) of a teacher's communication, three mutually exclusive categories of addressees may be differentiated: individual, group, or class. These categories involve high inference because asking one student in front of the class does not necessarily indicate communication that is directed to only one individual. Different cutoff values are needed to determine whether the coding is sufficiently reliable. Typically for high-inference codings, a reliability of Cohen's $\kappa > .6$ is considered sufficient.

Video analysis can be utilized in many areas of research to obtain empirical evidence: in case studies to investigate learning processes, in experimental studies to check implementation of a treatment, or in field studies to describe characteristics of interest. As such, video analysis is a valuable tool for analyzing teaching and learning about science in very different scenarios in science education research. However, linking video analysis with data and measures from tests and questionnaires is also necessary to obtain better results for estimating the quality of observed instruction. One measure of the quality of a lesson is students' outcomes, for example, competences and interest they gained during a certain newly developed unit or other intervention. Another research aim can be to find out if teachers' professional knowledge has influenced classroom interaction and students' outcomes. In this case, to calculate correlations, linear regressions, or path analyses, a measure of quality of the different categories of the video analysis must be developed (see Fischer & Neumann, 2012; Klieme, Pauli, & Reusser, 2006; Ohle, 2010; Ohle, Fischer, & Kauertz, 2011; Seidel & Prenzel, 2006; Seidel, Prenzel, & Kobarg, 2005).

Accounting for the Complexity of Classrooms

As researchers, we always have to take into account that in studies on teaching and learning at schools, at least three different levels of organization have to be considered. For example, when analyzing the effect of teaching, we should be aware of the individual teachers and the individual students being at different levels in a teaching–learning process. From a statistical point of view when designing a study, we need at least 20 different teachers and their classes to obtain satisfying results with confidence and to calculate by means of multilevel analysis, for example, using hierarchic linear models (HLM; Hox, 2010).

Because of different contextual effects or socioeconomic backgrounds, observations within one group are in some cases not independent from each other, that is, the similarities between individuals in one group regarding one variable can be larger than the similarities between the individuals of different groups. To test the variables, we must partition the sum of squares. Because the variables are correlated, there are sums of squares that could be attributed to more than one variable; and therefore, the variables are not as independent as they are expected to be. The overlaps between the variances of the variables depend on the type of sum of squares that the researcher uses and other judgments made by the researcher. To estimate these variances of independent variables, standard methods, such as simple regressions, cannot quantify the share of the variance between groups and the total variance of all groups, but an intraclass-correlation can (Hox, 2010).

Thus, multilevel analysis is needed to appropriately analyze hierarchically organized problems, for example, hierarchical linear models (HLM), which are also known as random-coefficient or variance-component models. Objects of different order—such as individuals on the lowest level and collectives on higher levels—can be simultaneously assigned to each other, whereas the highest level embeds all lower levels. Students are embedded within classes and classes are in turn embedded within schools. The idea of a related analysis is that the achievement of students in science is dependent on parameters of the science lessons, and these parameters are influenced by conditions of the school, and so on. Ignoring the multilevel character of classroom settings is likely to produce mistakes (see Raudenbush & Bryk, 2002).

Figure 2.4 shows the student mean test scores in the assessment of a sample of two classes in one school as a standard regression with one mean and one slope coefficient and also separately for the two classes. The information differs substantially between the two ways of looking at the individual students of two different classes.

Using a multilevel analysis turns out to dissipate the variance of a distribution of the classes as a whole in different classes at different levels of the system. In this example (see Figure 2.4), the starting level can be described as a school level, or a year level, of a school; and the embedded level is the classes that can be resolved in more detail. The measure of preknowledge in physics as mean test score is plotted against the knowledge of students in the two classes of one school measured after an intervention. Now the classes can be distinguished according to the connection between both pre and post physics knowledge.

Conclusion for Modeling the Complex Teaching and Learning Processes

In line with research on science education in general, numerous attempts have been made to link investigations to theories or models for describing the quality of classroom teaching and learning in order to guide research and to allow for the development and use of consistent methodologies (Ditton, 2000; Neumann et al., 2012). As we have discussed in this chapter, building theoretical models of aspects of teaching and learning at school has to take into account multiple variables, their interdependencies, and hierarchically ordered system structures. This helps researchers control as many influencing variables of classroom settings as possible.

The effect of a newly developed instructional unit (e.g., quantum mechanics) surely depends on its adequate design and strategy in presenting the subject matter to students regarding its scientific content and structure. However, the learning outcomes of an instructional unit may also be moderated by features of the teacher's personality, his or her pedagogical content knowledge, students' socioeconomic backgrounds, the structure of student–teacher interactions in the classroom, and in particular by students' cognitive abilities and their respective preknowledge. This holds true for every description and every intervention. Following the idea of science instruction as a complex system, it is now clear that an adequate model is needed to describe most of the influences on the teaching–learning process as far as possible in order to understand the actual state of research on science education. To advance our field, investigations must carefully make use of the tools and techniques that we have outlined in this chapter—ranging from techniques (e.g., HLM), which consider the structure of educational systems, to techniques that provide linear measures (Rasch), and to the appropriate use of

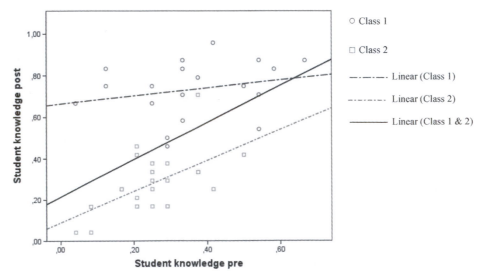

Figure 2.4 Standard regression of two classes on the relation between physics knowledge and social index. The graph for "Class 1 & 2" hides information about the sample, which is uncovered in the graphs for Class 1 and Class 2 plotted separately.

multilevel statistics. Doing so helps confidently draw conclusions from the effects of intended changes on teaching and learning in studies in science education and tell future teachers how to improve the quality of their own teaching. Often enough, there is little evidence that such teachers' knowledge is beneficial for students' learning, and teacher education cannot refer to empirically based results; this therefore reproduces intuitive beliefs and myths. With the careful use of these and other tools, advances can be made in science education research, and in turn teachers and policy makers can be informed of useful guidance for achieving high-quality science teaching and learning.

Acknowledgments

We would like to thank John Staver (Purdue University) and Bob Evans (University of Copenhagen), who carefully and critically reviewed this chapter.

References

Bacon, F. (1904). Novum organum (translated by W. Wood). In J. Devey (ed.), *The physical and metaphysical works of Lord Bacon, including the advancement of learning and novum organum* (pp. 380–567). London: Bell and Sons.

Baumert, J., Kunter, M., Blum, W., Brunner, M., Voss, T., Jordan, A., & Tsai, Y.-M. (2010). Teachers' mathematical knowledge, cognitive activation in the classroom, and student progress. *American Educational Research Journal, 47,* 133–180.

Best, J.W., & Kahn, J.V. (2006). *Research in education* (10th ed.). Needham Heights, MA: Allyn & Bacon.

Blalock, H.M. (1968). Measurement problem: A gap between the languages of theory and research. In Hubert M. Blalock, Jr., & Ann B. Blalock (Eds.), *Methodology in social research* (pp. 5–27). New York: McGraw-Hill.

Boone, W., Townsend, S., & Staver, J. (2011). Using Rasch theory to guide the practice of survey development and survey data analysis in science education and to inform science reform efforts: An exemplar utilizing STEBI self-efficacy data. *Science Education, 95*(2), 258–290.

Boone, W.J., & Scantlebury, K. (2006). The role of Rasch analysis when conducting science education research utilizing multiple-choice tests. *Science Education, 90,* 253–269.

Boone, W.J., Staver, J., & Yale, M. (2014). *Rasch Analysis in the Human Sciences.* Berlin, Germany: Springer.

Bortz, J. (2005). *Statistik für Human- und Sozialwissenschaftler: Mit 242 Tabellen* (6., vollständig überarbeitete und aktualisierte Aufl.). [Statistics for human- and social sciences: including 242 tables (6th edition, completely revised and updated)]. Berlin, Heidelberg, New York: Springer.

Breuer, F., & Reichertz, J. (2002). FQS debates: Standards of qualitative social research. *Historical Social Research, 27*(4), 258–269.

Brown, T., Unsworth, C., & Lyons, C. (2009). An evaluation of the construct validity of the developmental test of visual-motor integration using the Rasch measurement model. *Therapy Journal, 56*(6), 393–402.

Bryk, A.S., & Raudenbush, S.W. (1992). *Hierarchical linear models: Applications and data analysis methods.* Newbury Park, CA, London, New Delhi: Sage.

Chi, M. (1994). Eliciting self-explanations improves understanding. *Cognitive Science, 18*(3), 439–477. doi:10.1016/0364-0213(94)90016-7

Clausen, M. (2000). Wahrnehmung von Unterricht, Übereinstimmung, Konstruktvalidität und *Kriteriumsvalidität in der Forschung zur Unterrichtsqualität* (Dissertation). [Perceiving lessons, accordance, construct validity and criterion validity in research on quality of instruction]. Berlin: Freie Universität Berlin.

Clauser, B., & Linacre, J.M. (1999). Relating Cronbach and Rasch reliabilities. *Rasch Measurement Transactions, 13*(2), 696.

Cronbach, L., & Snow, R. (1977). *Aptitudes and instructional methods: A handbook for research on interactions.* New York: Irvington.

Ditton, H. (2000). Qualitätskontrolle und Qualitätssicherung in Schule und Unterricht: Ein Überblick zum Stand der empirischen Forschung. [Quality control and quality management for school and instruction.] In A. Helmke, W. Hornstein, & E. Terhart (Eds.), *Qualität und Qualitätssicherung im Bildungsbereich: Schule, Sozialpädagogik, Hochschule* (S. 73–92) [Quality and quality management in education: School, social pedagogy, university]. *Zeitschrift für Pädagogik, 41. Beiheft.*

Driver, R., Leach, J., Scott, P., & Wood-Robinson, C. (1994). Young people's understanding of science concepts: Implications of cross-age studies for curriculum planning. *Studies in Science Education, 24,* 75–100.

Duit, R. (1984). Learning the energy concept in school—empirical results from the Philippines and West Germany. *Physics Education, 19,* 59–66.

Family Report. (2012). *Family Report interpretive guide for Ohio achievement assessments. Ohio Department of Education, Columbus Ohio.* Retrieved April 19, 2013, from http://education.ohio.gov/Topics/Testing/Ohio-Achievement-Assessments/Family-Report-Interpretive-Guide-for-Ohio-Achievem

Field, A. (2005). *Discovering statistics using SPSS.* London: Sage Publications.

Fischer, H.E., Klemm, K., Leutner, D., Sumfleth, E., Tiemann, R., & Wirth, J. (2005). Framework for empirical research on science teaching and learning. *Journal of Science Teacher Education, 16,* 309–349.

Fischer, H.E., & Neumann, K. (2012). Video analysis as tool for understanding science instruction. In D. Jorde & J. Dillon (Eds.), *Science education research and practice in Europe* (pp. 115–140). Rotterdam: Sense Publishers.

Fisher, W., Jr. (1992). Reliability, separation, strata statistics. *Rasch Measurement Transactions, 6*(3), 238.

Fricke, K., van Ackeren, I., Kauertz, A., & Fischer, H.E. (2012). Students' perceptions of their teacher's classroom management in elementary and secondary science lessons. In T. Wubbels, J. van Tartwijk, P. den Brok, & J. Levy (Eds.), *Interpersonal relationships in education* (pp. 167–185). Rotterdam, the Netherlands: Sense Publishers.

Furtak, E.M., Seidel, T., Iverson, H., & Briggs, D. (2012). Experimental and quasi-experimental studies of inquiry-based science teaching: A meta-analysis. *Review of Educational Research, 82*(3), 300–329.

Gess-Newsome, J., & Lederman, N.G. (Eds.). (1999). *Examining pedagogical content knowledge.* Dordrecht, the Netherlands: Kluwer Academic Press.

Glaser, B.G., & Strauss, A.L. (1967). *The discovery of grounded theory: Strategies for qualitative research.* New Brunswick, NJ: Aldine Transaction.

Granger, C. (2008). Rasch analysis is important to understand and use for measurement. *Rasch Measurement Transactions, 21*(3), 1122–1123.

Gwet, K.L. (2012). *Handbook of inter-rater reliability, the definitive guide to measuring the extent of agreement among raters.* Gaithersburg, MD: Advanced Analytics, LLC.

Hammer, D. (1996). More than misconceptions: Multiple perspectives on student knowledge and reasoning, and an appropriate role for education research. *American Journal of Physics, 64,* 1316.

Hattie, J., & Timperley, H. (2007). The power of feedback. *Review of Educational Research, 77,* 81–112.

Haynes, S.N., Richard, D.C.S., & Kubany, E.S. (1995). Content validity in psychological assessment: A functional approach to concepts and methods. *Psychological Assessment, 7*(3), 238–247.

Hestenes, D., Wells, M., & Swackhamer, G. (1992). Force concept inventory. *The Physics Teacher, 30,* 141–166.

Hiebert, J., Gallimore, R., Garnier, H., Bogard Givvin, K., Hollingsworth, H., & Jacobs, J. (2003). *Teaching mathematics in seven countries:*

Results from the TIMSS 1999 video study. Retrieved February 20, 2013, from http://research.acer.edu.au/timss_video/5

Hox, J.J. (2010). *Multilevel analysis: Techniques and applications*. New York: Routledge.

Kapadia, K., Coca, V., & Easton, J.Q. (2007). *Keeping new teachers—research report, consortium on Chicago school research (CCSR)*. Chicago: Consortium on Chicago School Research (CCSR).

Kauertz, A., & Fischer, H.E. (2006). Assessing students' level of knowledge and analyzing the reasons for learning difficulties in physics by Rasch analysis. In X. Liu & W.J. Boone (Eds.), *Applications of Rasch measurement in science education* (pp. 212–246). Maple Grove, MN: JAM Press.

Klieme, E., Pauli, C., & Reusser, K. (Eds.). (2006). *Dokumentation der Erhebungs-und Auswertungsinstrumente zur schweizerisch-deutschen Videostudie "Unterrichtsqualität, Lernverhalten und mathematisches Verständnis." Teil 3: Videoanalysen (Materialien zur Bildungsforschung, Bd. 15, Deutsches Institut für internationale pädagogische Forschung). [Documentation of the instruments of the Swiss-German video study, lesson quality, learning behavior, and mathematical understanding Part 3: Video analysis (material for educational research, volume 15, German Institute for International Educational Research)]*. Frankfurt am Main: GFPF.

Kolen, M.J., & Brennan, R.L. (2004). *Test equating, scaling, and linking: Methods and practices* (2nd ed.). New York: Springer.

Krajcik, J., Drago, K., Sutherland, L.A., & Merritt, J. (2012). The promise and value of learning progression research. In S. Bernholt, P. Nentwig, & K. Neumann (Eds.), *Making it tangible—learning outcomes in science education* (pp. 261–283). Münster: Waxmann.

Lederman, N.G. (2006). Syntax of nature of science within inquiry and science instruction. In L.B. Flick & N.G. Lederman (Eds.), *Scientific inquiry and nature of science* (pp. 301–317). Dordrecht, the Netherlands: Springer.

Lederman, N.G. (2007). Nature of science: Past, present, and future. In S.K. Abell & N.G. Lederman (Eds.), *Handbook of research on science education* (pp. 831–879). Mahwah, NJ: Lawrence Erlbaum.

Lederman, N.G., Abd-El Khalick, F., Bell, R.L., & Schwartz, R. (2002). Views of nature of science questionnaire: Toward valid and meaningful assessment of learners' conceptions of nature of science. *Journal of Research in Science Teaching, 30*, 497–521.

Lee, H.-S., & Liu, O.L. (2010). Assessing learning progression of energy concepts across middle school grades: The knowledge integration perspective. *Science Education, 94*(4), 665–688. doi:10.1002/sce.20382.

Linacre, J.M. (1994). Sample size and item calibrations stability. *Rasch Measurement Transactions, 7*(4), 328.

Linacre, J.M. (1997). KR-20 or Rasch reliability: Which tells the "truth"? *Rasch Measurement Transactions, 11*(3), 580–581.

Liu, X., & McKeough, A. (2005). Developmental growth in students' concept of energy: Analysis of selected items from the TIMSS database. *Journal of Research in Science Teaching, 42*(5), 493–517.

Magnusson, S., Krajcik, J., & Borko, H. (1999). Nature, sources and development of pedagogical content knowledge for science teaching. In J. Gess-Newsome & N.G. Lederman (Eds.), *Examining pedagogical content knowledge* (pp. 95–132). Dordrecht, the Netherlands: Kluwer Academic Press.

Mayring, P. (1995). Möglichkeiten fallanalytischen Vorgehens zur Untersuchung von Lernstrategien. *Empirische Pädagogik, 9*(2), 155–171.

Mayring, P. (2007). Mixing qualitative and quantitative methods. In P. Mayring, G.L. Huber, L. Gürtler, & M. Kiegelmann (Eds.), *Mixed methodology in psychological research* (pp. 27–36). Rotterdam: Sense Publishers.

Neumann, I., Neumann, K., & Nehm, R. (2011). Evaluating instrument quality in science education: Rasch-based analyses of a nature of science test. *International Journal of Science Education, 10*(33), 1–33. doi:10.1080/09500693.2010.511297

Neumann, K., Kauertz, A., & Fischer, H.E. (2012). Quality of instruction in science education. In B. Fraser, K. Tobin, & C. McRobbie (Eds.), *Second international handbook of science education* (pp. 247–258). New York: Springer.

Neumann, K., Viering, T., Boone, W.J., & Fischer, H.E. (2013). Towards a learning progression of energy. *Journal of Research in Science Teaching, 50*(2), 162–188. doi:10.1002/tea.21061

New York Science Teacher. (2013). *Common science conceptions*. Retrieved February 2014 from http://newyorkscienceteacher.com/sci/pages/miscon/subject-index.php

Niedderer, H., Buty, C., Haller, K., Hucke, L., Sander, F., Fischer, H.E., . . . Tiberghien, A. (2002). Talking physics in labwork contexts—a category based analysis of videotapes. In D. Psillos & H. Niedderer (Eds.), *Teaching and learning in the science laboratory* (pp. 31–40). Boston: Kluwer Academic Publishers.

Niedderer, H., Tiberghien, A., Buty, C., Haller, K., Hucke, L., Sander, F., . . . Welzel, M. (1998). Category based analysis of videotapes from labwork (CBAV)—the method and results from four case studies. In *Working paper 9 from the European project labwork in science education* (Targeted Socio-Economic Research Programme, Project PL 95-2005), 51 pages.

Nordine, J., Krajcik, J., & Fortus, D. (2011). Transforming energy instruction in middle school to support integrated understanding and future learning. *Science Education, 95*(4), 670–699. doi:10.1002/sce.20423

Oevermann, U., Allert, T., Konau, E., & Krambeck, J. (1979). Die Methodologie einer "objektiven Hermeneutik" und ihre allgemeine forschungslogische Bedeutung in den Sozialwissenschaften. In H.-G. Soeffner (Hrsg.): *Interpretative Verfahren in den Sozial-und Textwissenschaften* (S. 352–434). [The methodology of an "objective hermeneutic? and its general research logical significance in social sciences. In H.-G. Soeffner (Ed.): *Interpretative methods in social sciences and text analysis*]. Stuttgart: Metzler.

Oevermann, U., Allert, T., Konau, E., & Krambeck, J. (1987). Structures of meaning and objective hermeneutics. In V. Meja, D. Misgeld, & N. Stehr (Eds.), *Modern German sociology, European perspectives: A series in social thought and cultural criticism* (pp. 436–447). New York: Columbia University Press.

Ohle, A. (2010). *Primary school teachers' content knowledge in physics and its impact on teaching and students' achievement*. Berlin: Logos.

Ohle, A., Fischer, H.E., & Kauertz, A. (2011). Der Einfluss des physikalischen Fachwissens von Primarstufenlehrkräften auf Unterrichtsgestaltung und Schülerleistung. [The impact of physics content knowledge of primary school teachers on lesson design and students' performance]. *Zeitschrift für Didaktik der Naturwissenschaften, 17*, 357–389.

Olszewski, J. (2010). *The impact of physics teachers' pedagogical content knowledge on teacher action and student outcomes* (unpublished dissertation). Essen: University of Duisburg-Essen.

Olszewski, J., Neumann, K., & Fischer, H.E. (2009). Measuring physics teachers' declarative and procedural PCK. In *Proceedings of the 7th International ESERA Conference*, Istanbul, Turkey.

Osborne, J., Collins, S., Ratcliffe, M., Millar, R., & Duschl, R. (2003). What "ideas-about-science" should be taught in school science? A Delphi study of the expert community. *Journal of Research in Science Teaching, 40*(7), 692–720.

Park, S., & Oliver, S.J. (2008). Revisiting the conceptualization of pedagogical content knowledge (PCK): PCK as a conceptual tool to understand teachers as professionals. *Research in Science Education, 38*(3), 261–284.

Popper, K.R. (1959). *The logic of scientific discovery*. London: Hutchinson.

Prenzel, M. (Ed.). (2004). *PISA 2003: Der Bildungsstand der Jugendlichen in Deutschland—Ergebnisse des zweiten internationalen Vergleichs* [PISA 2003: Student competence in Germany—Results from the second international comparison]. Münster, München, Berlin: Waxmann.

Rasch, G. (1960). *Probabilistic models for some intelligence and attainment tests* (reprint, with Foreword and Afterword by B.D. Wright, Chicago: University of Chicago Press, 1980). Copenhagen, Denmark: Danmarks Paedogogiske Institut.

Raudenbush, S.W., & Bryk, A.S. (2002). *Hierarchical linear models* (2nd ed.). Thousand Oaks, CA: Sage Publications.

Roth, K.J., Druker, S.L., Garnier, H.E., Lemmens, M., Chen, C., Kawanaka, T., . . . Gallimore, R. (2006). *Teaching science in five countries: Results from the TIMSS 1999 video study statistical analysis report.* (NCES 2006–011). U.S. Department of Education, National Center for Education Statistics. Washington, DC: U.S. Government Printing Office. Retrieved February 2014 from http://nces.ed.gov

Ruiz-Primo, M.A., Briggs, D., Shepard, L., Iverson, H., & Huchton, M. (2008). Evaluating the impact of instructional innovations in engineering education. (Evaluando el impacto de las innovaciones instruccionales en la enseñaza de la ingeniería.) In M. Duque (Ed.), *Engineering education for the XXI century: Foundations, strategies and cases* (pp. 241–274). Bogotá, Colombia: ACOFI Publications.

Seidel, T., & Prenzel, M. (2006). Stability of teaching patterns in physics instruction: Findings from a video study. *Learning and Instruction, 16*(3), 228–240.

Seidel, T., Prenzel, M., & Kobarg, M. (Eds.). (2005). *How to run a video study. Technical report of the IPN Video Study.* Münster: Waxmann.

Shavelson, R.J., & Towne, L. (Eds.). (2002). *Scientific research in education.* Washington, DC: National Academies Press.

Shrout, P.E., & Fleiss, J.L. (1979). Intraclass correlation: Uses in assessing rater reliability. *Psychological Bulletin, 86,* 420–428.

Smith, R.M. (1986). Person fit in the Rasch model. *Educational and Psychological Measurement, 46*(2), 359–372.

Smith, R.M. (1991). The distributional properties of Rasch item fit statistics. *Educational and Psychological Measurement, 51*(3), 541–565.

Smith, R.M. (1996). Polytomous mean-square fit statistics. *Rasch Measurement Transactions, 10*(3), 516–517.

Smith, R.M., Linacre, J.M., & Smith, Jr., E.V. (2003). *Journal of Applied Measurement,* guidelines for manuscripts (n.d.). Jampress. org. Retrieved April 27, 2013, from www.rasch.org/guidelines.htm. Reprinted from Guidelines for Manuscripts. *Journal of Applied Measurement, 4,* 198–204.

Stelmack, J., Szlyk, J., Stelmack, T., Babcock-Parziale, J., Demers-Turco, P., Williams, R.T., & Massof, R.W. (2004). Use of Rasch person item map in exploratory data analysis: A clinical perspective. *Journal of Rehabilitation Research and Development, 41,* 233–242.

Stigler, J.W., & Hiebert, J. (1997). Understanding and improving mathematics instruction: An overview of the TIMSS Video Study. *Phi Delta Kappa, 79*(1), 7–21.

Stigler, J. W., & Hiebert, J. (1999). *The teaching gap: Best ideas from the world's teachers for improving education in the classroom.* New York: Free Press.

Strauss, A.L., & Corbin, J. (2008). *Basics of qualitative research: Grounded theory procedures and techniques.* Thousand Oaks, CA: Sage.

Wright, B.D. (1995). Which standard error? *Rasch Measurement Transactions, 9*(2), 436.

Wright, B.D., & Masters, G.N. (1982). *Rating scale analysis: Rasch measurement.* Chicago: MESA Press.

Wright, B.D., & Stone, M.H. (1979). *Best test design: Rasch measurement.* Chicago: MESA Press.

3

Contemporary Qualitative Research

Toward an Integral Research Perspective

PETER CHARLES TAYLOR

A rather large group of individuals has taken a set of methods, devised an alternative paradigm/model/metaphysics for looking at the world, primarily utilizing those self-same methods; set about building new methods and fleshing out the repertoire; constantly adapted to changing social contexts (such as the advent of the Internet and the Web); integrated all of the best late 20th-century thinking about representation, texts, and Western authority; moved quite deliberately to make space for the margin(s) at the center(s); criticized ourselves incessantly in the interests of dealing with the field's problems, its issues, and its relationships with those whom we would study; built designs to encourage democratic practice and agency out in the fields; systematically thought through major answers to the questions that frame scientific inquiry (Lather, 2006); and set about healing the Enlightenment rift between art and science, between mind and body, between reason and spirituality, between logic and emotion, and between technical rationality and human invention. It is a rather great sweep of events, this past 25 years, and as I've tried to demonstrate, it is not over yet.

(Yvonna Lincoln, 2009, p. 8)

Since its border crossing from the social sciences around 30 years ago, qualitative research has been providing science education researchers with radically new perspectives for examining and transforming curricular policies and practices at all levels, up to and including teacher education and graduate research. However, despite the growing popularity of qualitative research, its full potential is far from being realized. There are two main reasons for this. First, qualitative research does not sit easily within the traditions of science education, especially among those who hold steadfastly to a worldview in which methods of knowledge production are regulated by the objectivity of the so-called scientific method. As a result, much qualitative research is designed to fit within this worldview as a supplement to quantitative research approaches, thereby blunting the sharp edge of its transformative potential.

A second and equally important reason concerns the nature of contemporary qualitative research, which is notorious for having evolved into a complex, chaotic, and contested field. Its complexity is due to the multiparadigmatic nature of the field. Several interacting research paradigms govern contemporary qualitative research, providing diverse theories about how to understand our relationship with reality, how to make legitimate sense of and represent our experiences, and how to act in accordance with how we value ourselves, others, and our environments. Making a coherent choice of qualitative research design principles from among this complexity can be confronting for both novice and expert researchers. Furthermore, the field is chaotic inasmuch as there is no agreed-on best taxonomy of qualitative research approaches, designs, or methods. This has given rise to a profound lack of consensus on the crucial question of how to optimize the "validity" of qualitative research, with many scholars rejecting the term and proposing alternative quality standards unique to qualitative research.

To add to the discomfit of novice researchers, the term "qualitative" is now being contested as a suitable descriptor for the field, with many arguing that the "qualitative-quantitative" distinction is well past its use-by date. How did this come to pass? The qualitative research pioneers of the 1990s raised our awareness of the narrow (and largely invisible) assumptions underpinning much of our research and began the process of contesting the privileged status of the dominant quantitative (or "scientific") perspective we had imported from the natural sciences. The resulting "qualitative versus quantitative" clash of civilizations eventually generated a more sophisticated and nuanced understanding of the philosophical foundations of educational research. Practitioners of the contrasting schools engaged in productive dialogue and began to cross-fertilize their research designs with methods from the other camp to produce "quantitative and qualitative" research designs, known more recently as "mixed-methods" research. Today, qualitative methods such as interviewing are incorporated into quantitative research designs, and qualitative research designs at times make use of quantitative methods such as questionnaires.

So when we use the adjectives "qualitative" and "quantitative," what do we actually mean in this new era of hybrid research designs? Are we distinguishing among contrasting types of data or research methods or research designs, or are we making a distinction based on something deeper, more profound, such as fundamentally different ways of producing, representing, and legitimating knowledge? For many novice researchers sorting through the plethora of textbooks on the subject, where complexity, chaos, and contestation abound, linguistic confusion begets conceptual confusion; more questions than answers tend to arise.

As an experienced practitioner of contemporary qualitative research I have the challenging task of writing a chapter that brings some order and insight to our understanding of the field while being careful not to overreach myself in a vain attempt to settle, once and for all, the complexity and contestation characterizing the discourse of its proponents. I shall, at least, endeavor to reduce the chaos. A hallmark of contemporary qualitative research is its transparency, with researchers making visible their engagement in the inquiry process. In writing this chapter, I did, in fact, engage in an interpretive process of *writing as inquiry* (Richardson, 1994) wherein I obtained "data" by sampling the vast literature on qualitative research and reflected on how, in my professional capacity as a researcher and graduate research teacher, I have helped my graduate students conceptualize the field and find productive ways of designing and conducting their inquiries. The result is, therefore, a necessarily partial account of a dynamic and emergent scholarly field.

Rather than duplicating the many textbooks on qualitative research that focus on methods of producing and processing qualitative data (oftentimes overlooking important framing assumptions), I have chosen instead to focus this chapter on the main philosophical, sociocultural, historical, and political influences shaping contemporary qualitative research and on its exciting prospects for transforming science education. In the absence of these theoretical considerations, it is highly unlikely that the transformative potential of contemporary qualitative research can be realized.

I have chosen also to use a largely expository style of writing rather than the usual narrative style that makes transparent the process of qualitative inquiries, especially the researcher's unfolding subjectivity. In making this choice, I took into account the general predilections of the audience of this handbook and the advice of my reviewers and editor. To compensate for this conservatism (some might call it "heresy"), I direct the reader to other publications in which illustrative exemplars of contemporary qualitative research writing can be found.

To untangle the linguistic and conceptual knot I refer to, it is helpful to understand the origins of qualitative and quantitative research. To this end, I start with a brief historical account.

Historical Roots of Quantitative and Qualitative Research

A succinct account of the historical emergence of qualitative research is given by David Hamilton (1994), who argues that "The epistemology of qualitative research . . . had its origins in an epistemological crisis of the late eighteenth century" (p. 63). Earlier in the 17th century, Rene Descartes's *Discourse on Method* (1637) had created the philosophical foundations of quantitative research: reasoning based on empirical objectivity and mathematical certainty, known as Cartesian absolutism. Almost 150 years later, Immanuel Kant's *Critique of Pure Reason* (1781) proposed a contrasting model of human rationality in which the mind has a central role in shaping perception and mediates our (interpretive) understanding of the natural world. Kant established the role of the investigator's subjectivity as central to his/her inquiry of natural phenomena, thereby laying the epistemological foundations for qualitative research in the social sciences.

The contrast between these two schools of thought is stark. Cartesian objectivity, which separates the observer from the observed, serves the production of universal law-like knowledge of causal relationships among naturally occurring phenomena on the basis that the material universe is strongly deterministic: given knowledge of initial conditions, the final state of affairs can be predicted with certainty. There is little room for self-determination or free will in a Cartesian worldview. Isaac Newton was embedded in the Cartesian worldview when he formulated the fundamental laws of motion of a seemingly clockwork universe. Cartesian objectivity is the *sine qua non* of the classical quantitative research model of the physical sciences.

By contrast, a Kantian perspective adds a moral dimension to human reasoning about practical matters affecting our lives, giving rise to *practical knowledge* grounded in everyday experience. A Kantian perspective is concerned with human freedom and social emancipation and focuses attention on moral decision-making in acts of self-determination. In the 19th century, neo–Kantians such as Wilhelm Dilthey helped establish qualitative research for the social sciences with an epistemological emphasis on the role of "understanding" (or *Verstehen*) and "lived experience" (or *Erlebnis*), which contrast sharply with the Cartesian concept of "explanation" (or *Erklaren*). For neo–Kantians, the observer and observed are intimately interconnected in a dialectical relationship, with one affecting the other and vice versa. Interestingly, quantum theory has a similar perspective, with the conscious mind of the observer collapsing the "probability wave function" through an act of observation (or measurement) to produce a particular physical manifestation, one of many possible realities. The paradox of the life or death of Schrodinger's Cat is a classic example. Quantum theorists propose that not only subatomic phenomena but all of life, especially human consciousness, is subject to this quantum effect (e.g., Goswami, 1993; Rossenblum & Kuttner, 2011).

In the 19th century, a neo–Kantian perspective gave rise to the emancipatory role of the social scientist as social activist working with underprivileged sections of society to empower them with the freedom and means to respond to the repressive social conditions of their lives. This emancipatory sentiment—applied research as/for social justice—flowed through into the 20th century, where it was taken up by critical social philosophers of the Frankfurt School, such as Jurgen Habermas (Habermas, 1972), and brought into the field of education by critical action researchers such as Wilfred Carr and Stephen Kemmis (e.g., Carr & Kemmis, 1986).

But the foregoing account gives a distorted version of history if the reader concludes that 20th-century social science research witnessed the demise of quantitative research and the ascendency of qualitative research. Notwithstanding successful philosophical critiques of the Cartesian/Newtonian scientific paradigm by philosophers such as Paul Feyerabend, Thomas Kuhn, Imre Lakatos, Karl Popper, Ilya Prigonone, and Stephen Toulmin, alongside critiques of the supportive Platonist and formalist philosophies of mathematics by Kurt Godel and Morris Kline, quantitative research, albeit in a modified form, retains a powerful presence in the social sciences, especially in science education. The reason for this has little to do with the intellectual merits of philosophical debate and much more to do with the pendulum swing in politics to right-wing "neoconservatism" throughout the Western world during the past 30 years (e.g., Smith, 2008).

Yvonna Lincoln (2005) provides a compelling explanation of the new era of "methodological conservatism" policed by governments and institutional (university) review boards that require "scientific evidence" of the success of their economic rationalist management policies—a model that necessarily equates greater system efficiencies, higher productivity, and increased accountability with "improved" teaching and learning outcomes. Funding for quantitative research approaches that promise to provide this scientific "proof" was prioritized in the run up to the turn of this century. Ernest House (2006) attributes this "methodological fundamentalism" to the United States federal administration, which espoused the ideological policy belief "that only randomized experiments could produce true findings," a proposition that House interprets as a thinly disguised attempt to "restore traditional authority relationships" (p. 93).

In a similar vein, postcolonial scholars warn that overt political control of social science research is reminiscent of the one-size-fits all curriculum ideology imposed by European nations on their colonies in the 19th century in an endeavor to "civilize the natives" by cultural identity and linguistic replacement "therapy" masquerading as school education (see, for example, Haarman, 2007;

Mutua & Swadener, 2004; Nhalevilo, 2013). And it is also resonant of current graduate programs in Western(ized) universities that indoctrinate students in the Cartesian/Newtonian worldview of quantitative research with little or no regard for epistemological pluralism (Paul & Marfo, 2001).

A useful way to understand the state of play of educational research today is to examine contemporary social science research textbooks. When I started teaching research classes in a graduate school of science and mathematics education in the 1980s, the main textbooks of the day (Tuckman, 1978) presented only quantitative research; the term "epistemology" was absent and the Cartesian/Newtonian worldview exercised a hegemonic stranglehold over graduate students' (and their supervisors') understanding of the nature and purpose of educational research. In metaphorical terms, the fish were largely unaware of the water in which they were swimming (e.g., Taylor & Medina, 2013).

As a transformative educator seeking to instill higher-order consciousness, I find myself in agreement with Yvonna Lincoln (2005) that developing comprehensive understanding of research epistemologies should be a core goal of graduate research education. In order to escape the hegemonic grip of the Cartesian/Newtonian worldview, especially for science educators for whom it is akin to "mother's milk," and to be able to exercise informed choice (which involves freedom to choose qualitative or quantitative research approaches), graduate students need to be epistemologically astute, that is, critically aware of the assumptions about the nature of knowledge underpinning the processes of research knowledge production.

Today, there is a large range of offerings in social science research textbooks. While some authors are concerned largely with the technicalities of implementing research methods (e.g., Creswell, 2012), others prefer a philosophical perspective that classifies research in terms of paradigms, comparing and contrasting their ontologies, epistemologies, and methodologies (e.g., Bryman, 2012; Cohen, Manion, & Morrison, 2011; Guba, 1990; Howell, 2013; Willis, 2007). The following set of four paradigms is commonplace in contemporary social science research textbooks.

Post-positivism
Interpretivism
Criticalism
Postmodernism

There is lack of consensus, however, on precisely how to map the terms "quantitative research" and "qualitative research" onto this four-paradigm taxonomy. The popular mixed-methods perspective (formerly known as "quantitative and qualitative research") suggests that qualitative research methods can be combined unproblematically with quantitative research methods. Later in the chapter, I explain that this is feasible but restrictive, as it tends to result in research designs governed by the epistemology of the post-positivist paradigm. A contrasting view, which resonates with me, is that quantitative research is governed by the epistemology of post-positivism, whereas contemporary qualitative research is affiliated with the multiple epistemologies offered by the interpretive, critical, and postmodern paradigms. This lack of consensus explains why many graduate students find the field of educational research to be incoherent and confusing. Before considering the first of the qualitative research paradigms, we shall consider, as a point of departure, the characteristics of the positivist paradigm that governs traditional quantitative research in science education.

Beyond Positivist Research

Underpinned by Descartes's philosophy of reasoning based on empirical objectivity and mathematical certainty and concerned with uncovering the law-like properties (Dilthey's *erklaren*) of the material universe, the paradigm of positivism (or empiricism) has become synonymous with "the scientific method." Quantitative research approaches that seek the elusive goal of proving causality are designed to control as much of the experimental conditions as possible (to minimize statistical variance or the "noise-to-signal" ratio). The purpose is to test the legitimacy of a carefully crafted *a priori* theory. In agricultural science, researchers compare the yield of a genetically modified crop with the yield of a standard unmodified variety. In particle physics, high-energy beams of subatomic particles are collided under rigorously controlled conditions to track their trajectories; the recent near-confirmation of the existence of the Higgs-Boson particle is an exemplar of this approach.

In the late 19th century, the successful experimental research approach of the physical sciences was imported into the social sciences to achieve, among other things, academic legitimacy for this new discipline (Schon, 1983). Classic positivist research designs for examining human behavior feature control and treatment groups, pre- and posttests, randomized sampling, and large sample sizes. They are regulated by the gold standard of objectivity embodied in various forms of validity and reliability. Social science research writers have associated the positivist paradigm with the *principle of verificationism*, which drives researchers to collect empirical (i.e., sensory) data to confirm their *a priori* hypotheses, and with the *correspondence theory of truth*, which drives researchers to claim to have discovered accurate descriptions (rather than interpretations) of reality, often labeled as an ontology of *naïve realism*.

It is easy to appreciate why science educators are attracted to positivist research when we reflect on the way science (our primary discipline) has been represented in traditional undergraduate university science curricula as objective and uncontestable facts. A perception of the implacable objectivity of science has been reinforced by didactic teaching methods, "cookbook-type" laboratory experiments, and a museum-like encounter with the end-products of scientific research rather than with the messy (inter/subjective) processes of creative discovery and consensual validation that produced them (Kuhn, 1962).

For educational researchers, a disadvantage of positivist research is that because the results have a large "grain size," they are usually insensitive to local contexts and individuals, be they a particular school or teacher or class or student; we learn nothing about the "small dots" (especially the outliers) that make up the big statistical picture of ANOVAs, regression equations, or mean scores and standard deviations. Furthermore, because quantitative research designs and methods can be unwieldy and time consuming to implement, requiring a team of specially trained academic researchers to employ them, they are seldom of use to individual teachers, thereby reinforcing the traditional *theory–practice gap* of research serving primarily the interests of academic researchers over teacher practitioners.

But perhaps the decline in the popularity of positivist research can be largely attributed to the recent rapid rise of research ethics committees (in universities, schools, state authorities) that require researchers not only to avoid harm (i.e., non-maleficence) but to make a positive contribution (i.e., beneficence) to research sites (Cohen, et al., 2011). The critical question arises as to who benefits from the research and who does not. In Western democracies, many school communities no longer regard as ethically acceptable the experimental research practice of dividing students randomly into treatment and control classes and applying a teaching innovation to the former while withholding it from the latter. A teaching innovation must be preapproved as highly likely to make a positive contribution to the curriculum, in which case an ethic of fairness dictates that it should be applied to all students in the cohort. Few parents would be pleased to have their school-aged child treated like a "lab rat" in the interest of science. As part of this *ethical turn*, democratic institutions are increasingly observing the principle of social equity. This has leveled the professional playing field, resulting in academic researchers no longer having the privileged status they once enjoyed; they can no longer necessarily expect to "command" schools to comply with their large-scale data collection wishes.

During the closing decades of the 20th century, in the social sciences the classical paradigm of positivism underwent an epistemological softening; it was retuned to better serve the interests, structures, and priorities of local communities in which educational researchers wished to work. Although post-positivism shares with its parent paradigm a philosophy of reasoning based on empirical objectivity and mathematical certainty, it has taken a step away from the scientific (moral?) high ground of proving causation and has settled for establishing the next best thing: correlation, or compelling evidence that key variables tend to co-occur (or are associated) under given circumstances. This has resulted in the deregulation of quantitative research, with a wide range of contemporary research designs: quasi-experimental designs that dispense with a control group, correlational designs that dispense with pretesting, and survey designs that dispense with sampling across time. Sampling theory now includes non-random sampling, purposive sampling, and convenience sampling, among others, and sample sizes have shrunk to as small as a single class size of, say, 25 students.

The striking feature of many post-positivist research designs is the addition of *qualitative research methods*—observational checklists, (semi-)structured interviewing—as a supplement to the primary quantitative methods, giving rise to hybrid labels such as "quantitative and qualitative research" and "mixed-methods research." Objectivity continues to serve as the gold standard, but it too has softened, with changes to the ways in which validity and reliability are optimized. Although the observer–observed dualism continues, the researcher–researched relationship is far less clinical and clear cut. It is commonplace for university researchers to work with teachers in school classrooms to facilitate improvements to teaching and learning, with teachers being empowered as co-researchers.

More than this, post-positivist research has enabled teachers themselves to adopt independent teacher-researcher roles as a core aspect of in-house professional development. For example, armed with a university-designed questionnaire that has been previously validated for obtaining measures of students' perceptions of selected aspects of the learning environment, a teacher undertakes an *action research* study for the purpose of improving a particular aspect of student learning, such as the ability to work collaboratively in small groups on an open-ended inquiry. The questionnaire provides a scholarly theoretical framework for shaping the teacher's innovative teaching approach and, when used as a post-test, generates class mean scores that provide a handy snapshot of the perceptions of the whole class. Subsequently, semistructured interviews with selected students help confirm (or perhaps disconfirm) the validity of the quantitative pattern.

In this case, the theory–practice gap has narrowed, but there is still a one-way bridge to cross, with "expert" theory being imported under the assumption of it having universal applicability regardless of the local sociocultural context. Although the teacher-researcher has much greater involvement in controlling and applying the research, this form of mixed-methods research, which is growing rapidly in popularity among science educators, serves to implement a normative theory of teaching and learning, the standards of which are embedded implicitly in the questionnaire. This normative (critical theorists would say "covert") purpose is very different from *emancipatory research* that aims to enable teachers to generate what Jean McNiff and Jack Whitehead (2011) call "living educational theory" grounded in the unique authority of teachers' own professional experiences. I am not suggesting, however, that the importation of academic theory is necessarily a weakness

of post-positivist research or that mixed-methods research serves a sinister purpose. Rather, I am arguing that this form of research, as with all research, is limited in what it can achieve and that this limitation should be recognized, especially in graduate research schools.

Interpretive Research

> Kant revived a distinction, found in Aristotle, between theoretical and practical knowledge. Theoretical knowledge refers to states of affairs whose existence can be checked, tested, and accepted. Practical knowledge . . . refers to decision making . . . Practical reasoning . . . relates, therefore, to the application of moral judgments in the realm of human action.
>
> (Hamilton, 1994 p. 63)

An intellectual revolution in the social sciences started in the United Kingdom during the 1970s to 1980s: qualitative program evaluation and qualitative case studies became prominent among scholars in the field of education and training (e.g., Hamilton, 1977; Simons, 1980; Walker, 1980). In the United States during the 1980s, Jim Gallagher (1991) introduced interpretive research into science education, drawing on the scholarship of educational anthropologist Frederick Erickson (1986), who had based his ideas on the German social science tradition of *hermeneutic-phenomenology*.

> Interpretive research is the name given to a family of approaches that includes ethnographic, qualitative, participant-observational, case study, phenomenological, symbolic interactionist, and constructivist research . . . This line of research arose over 100 years ago as an attempt by German intellectuals to distinguish between "natural sciences" and "human sciences". This distinction was viewed as necessary since humans differ from other animals and inanimate objects in their ability to make and share meaning.
>
> (Gallagher, 1991, p. 5)

The uniquely powerful feature of interpretive research is its explicit *social constructivist epistemology*, which directs science education researchers to ethnographic research methods—prolonged participant-observation, non-clinical interviewing, emergent analysis via grounded theorizing, and thick description. These qualitative methods enable interpretive researchers to construct insightful understandings of the "meaning-perspectives" (i.e., ideas, beliefs, values, worldviews) underpinning teachers' and students' classroom interactions. Interpretive researchers carefully document the context (physical, social, cultural) that shapes and, in turn, is shaped by participants' interactions, thereby generating practical knowledge of the complexity, context, and dynamics of teaching and learning.

Interpretive research arrived in science education at a fortuitous time: a "constructivist revolution" in teaching and learning was underway in the early 1990s. Constructivist theory was introduced into science curricula to create meaningful learning environments that optimized students' engagement in making sense of their experiences. Constructivist teachers experimented with radically new metaphors of knowledge production in their classrooms, focusing on the quality of students' sense-making processes. Innovative researchers adopted person-sensitive methods of interpretive research to "look into" the hearts and minds of teachers and students, producing insightful understandings of the affordances and constraints of constructivist reform in science education (e.g., Tobin, 1993).

At the same time, mathematics education was undergoing a similar epistemological revolution. Researchers from both disciplines shared their innovative development of constructivist theories of teaching and learning and the empirical outcomes of their research (e.g., Eisenhart, 1988; Wheatley, 1991). An account of the constructivist transformation of science and mathematics education is beyond the scope of this chapter, but it is important to point out that two contrasting schools emerged—personal construct theory and radical/social constructivism—which employed qualitative research in markedly different ways.

Personal construct theory researchers, working from a traditional psychology-of-learning perspective, adopted a conservative approach to curriculum reform by applying constructivist theory to the focus but not the methodology of their research. They tended to work within the classical model of science, designing innovative teaching methods to correct students' errant understandings of conventional scientific concepts (i.e., misconceptions, alternative conceptions). Their preferred research approach was quantitative: using paper-and-pencil instruments to measure the extent of students' "conceptual change," at times correlating achievement outcomes with attitude and scientific reasoning. Later, when mixed-methods research was introduced, participant observation and structured interviews helped researchers validate their quantitative analyses, which, in turn, helped them validate their measuring instruments. The valuable but subordinate role of qualitative research methods within an overarching quantitative research design remains a frequently used mixed-methods approach in science education. However, it seldom involves an interpretive perspective.

By contrast, radical/social constructivists applied constructivist theory to both the focus and methodology of their research. They focused on rethinking the fundamental assumptions of science teaching and learning, reconceptualized classroom discourse as social inquiry, and designed interpretive studies to map the processes of constructivist teaching reforms as they worked collaboratively with teacher-researchers. Interpretive researchers were not simply observing classroom life but were deeply involved in interventions designed to make a difference: to the teaching and learning experience, to the pedagogy of the curriculum, to the nature and purpose of schooling, and to society at large. As the constructivist reform agenda expanded, so did perceptions of the nature and purpose of educational research. Interpretive researchers

moved away from the value-neutral standpoint of classical quantitative research to an interventionist role driven by a moral imperative to improve the human condition, leading them to embrace critical social theory and methods that are discussed in the section on critical research.

The 1990s were an exciting time to be an interpretive researcher in science education. The constructivist revolution in teaching and research was gathering pace with high-level scholarly support available from a rapidly growing network of social science researchers across many disciplines. Pioneering science education researchers, foremost among whom was Ken Tobin, introduced advanced scholarship of interpretive research into graduate research programs, spawning many studies of the social constructivist reform of science teaching and science teacher education in colleges and universities (Taylor, Gilmer, & Tobin, 2002).

As the *reflective turn* in the social sciences became increasingly prominent, many interpretive researchers shifted their focus from an ethnographic perspective on understanding the culturally different other to the active role of their own subjectivities in constructing that understanding. Guba and Lincoln (1989) defined the term "progressive subjectivity" to indicate the importance of the emergent quality of the researcher's self-understanding and the need to make this process transparent in their research reporting. The researcher as *reflective practitioner* had arrived (Schon, 1983), giving rise to diverse communities of scholars in institutions of higher education interested in improving their own professional practices.

The field of practitioner research is known variously as *self-study research* (Lassonde, Galman, & Kosnik, 2009; Pithouse, Mitchell, & Moletsane, 2010), *participatory action research* (Reason & Bradbury, 2001), and *living theory action research* (McNiff & Whitehead, 2011), although there are other variations on these terms. Practitioner researchers draw on personal experience methods (Clandinin & Connelly, 1994), biographical methods such as life writing and autobiography (Smith, 1994), narrative inquiry methods (Chase, 2005), and auto/ethnographic methods (Reed-Danahay, 1997). As discussed in the next two sections, they also draw on critical research methods and arts-based research methods to engage in writing as critical inquiry (Richardson, 1994) and to generate evocative research texts. In the third edition of the *Handbook of Qualitative Research*, we find that Egon Guba and Yvonna Lincoln (2005) have assigned the status of paradigm to the field of practitioner research. However, I am inclined to regard practitioner research as multiparadigmatic, with its practitioners drawing on any or all of the major paradigms discussed in this chapter, as will become clear in the later section on integral research.

The scholarly status of interpretive research has been strengthened by the scholarship of naturalistic researchers (Guba & Lincoln, 1988) and contributors to the *Handbook of Qualitative Research* (Denzin & Lincoln, 2005a). Interpretive research, with its underpinning social constructivist epistemology and relativist ontology (multiple realities exist), is clearly differentiated from objectivism and various realisms of the classical positivist and post-positivist research paradigms. Norman Denzin and Yvonna Lincoln (2000) have identified three "crises" that have arisen in the field of social science research as a result of the emergence of new research paradigms. No longer is there a single best way to validate knowledge (*crisis of legitimation*) or to represent the experiences of the researcher and his/her participants (*crisis of representation*) or to enact the role of researcher (*crisis of praxis*). Each of these fundamental aspects of research depends on the governing paradigm. I shall now consider appropriate (and inappropriate) quality standards for legitimating interpretive research.

Quality Standards for Interpretive Research

Many qualitative researchers eschew validity and reliability as standards for legitimating their scholarly work, arguing that these gold standards are epistemologically irrelevant (e.g., Schwandt, 2001). As a result, a range of alternative criteria have arisen—for example, descriptive adequacy, fidelity, accuracy, comprehensiveness, plausibility, believability, authenticity, consistency, coherence (in Green, Camilli, & Elmore, 2006), or cogency, efficacy, potency, punch, and persuasiveness (Wolcott, 1990). This diversity makes it very difficult for novice researchers to know which criteria to select. For interpretive research, two complementary sets of quality standards were designed by naturalistic researchers Egon Guba and Yvonna Lincoln: *trustworthiness* and *authenticity*. These twin standards have been uniquely designed in accordance with the epistemology of social constructivism, as explained initially in *Fourth Generation Evaluation* (Guba & Lincoln, 1989) and later in the *Handbook of Qualitative Research* (Guba & Lincoln, 1994). Here I shall outline these standards before considering the popular standard of triangulation and the less well-known alternative for contemporary qualitative research, crystallization.

Trustworthiness. There are four trustworthiness criteria: *credibility, transferability, dependability,* and *confirmability*. Implementing these criteria helps ensure that researchers construct deep understandings of the meaning-perspectives of their participants, understandings that emerge from prolonged immersion in their participants' social worlds, that have been verified through "member checking," and that have been challenged by seeking evidence to disconfirm inferences arising from grounded theorizing. Importantly, trustworthiness is optimized also by researchers making visible (i) the context of participants' social worlds by means of "thick description" and (ii) the process of fieldwork inquiries by means of narrative writing in which their unfolding subjectivities are expressed in the first person (i.e., "I" and "we") voice with probabilistic reasoning (i.e., "it seems that . . .," "it appears that . . .," "it is likely that . . ."), thereby conveying the implicit uncertainty of interpretations. The availability of literary genres

(discussed later in the section on postmodern research) provides contemporary interpretive researchers with richly expressive means for writing trustworthy accounts of their inquiries.

The trustworthiness criteria address methodological issues that are "parallel to" the positivist standards of internal and external reliability and validity. Guba and Lincoln's explicit mapping of the interpretive criteria onto the positivist criteria is of great assistance to science education researchers endeavoring to make the counterintuitive epistemological border crossing from the positivist to the interpretive paradigm. However, Valerie Janesick (1994) has warned of the danger of "methodolatry" (i.e., worshipping method) that arises from focusing fixedly on methodological criteria to the extent that relationships with one's participants are distorted by the researcher's academic self-interest.

Authenticity. The second set of interpretive research standards—*fairness, ontological authenticity, educative authenticity,* and *tactical authenticity*—are unique to this paradigm and are intended to create ethically sound, empowering, and beneficial relationships between researchers and their participants. For researchers to act fairly, they need to seek a full range of perspectives across the participant group, including conflicting or contradictory views, and to represent this value pluralism in research reports. Ontological and educative authenticity are optimized by researchers actively contributing to participants' self-understandings as well as their understandings of other stakeholders outside their immediate group. Catalytic and tactical authenticity are judged by the extent to which researchers facilitate participants' roles as change agents within their local context, empowering them to develop their own standards of judgment for evaluating the efficacy of changes to their professional practice. For research designs that draw on both the interpretive and critical paradigms, the authenticity standards can be combined with critical research standards.

Although the trustworthiness and authenticity standards are of fundamental importance to interpretive research, they are not intended to serve as a prescriptive straitjacket for all interpretive research designs. Rather, they should be carefully adapted in accordance with the epistemological nuances and practical feasibility of each study.

Triangulation. Triangulation is a popular standard for mixed-methods research, but it does not necessarily serve the epistemological interests of interpretive researchers. Triangulation is a metaphor drawn from the field of engineering, in which surveyors use multiple (usually two) observation points at either end of a baseline to calculate (via the mathematics of similar triangles) the straight-line distance to a faraway object such as a mountain. In the social sciences, triangulation directs researchers to employ multiple research methods (Mathison, 1988). The classical framing assumption underpinning triangulation is that multiplicity will help achieve empirical objectivity and inferential certainty. Thus, triangulation is an automatic "weapon of choice" to optimize the validity and reliability of many contemporary mixed-methods research designs, situating them clearly in the post-positivist paradigm.

Jerry Willis (2007) argues that triangulation is not a key quality standard for qualitative research underpinned by a social constructivist epistemology (i.e., interpretive research), especially when seeking to generate deep understandings of participants' complex social realities. Triangulation tends to engage researchers in convergent thinking, that is, seeking confirming evidence (or verification) of the consistency of their participants' meaning-perspectives (i.e., beliefs, perceptions, values) while overlooking the possibility that they might be holding multiple, perhaps contradictory, perspectives. Triangulation also has a tendency to direct researchers to verify their own "etic" (or outsider) perspective rather than uncover the "emic" (or insider) perspective of the culturally different other. This problem has been detected in cultural studies of science education in which simplistic understanding of complex indigenous perspectives is "discovered" by non-indigenous researchers using structured interview protocols based largely on prior (armchair) theorizing (Abrams, Taylor, & Guo, 2013). Michelle Fine is critical of this naïve and disrespectful practice of "Othering," which I take up in the next section on critical research.

Crystallization. Interpretive research needs to be regulated by standards such as the trustworthiness and authenticity criteria that direct researchers to seek to construct multiple and contingent interpretations of participants' meaning-perspectives. In this context, Laurel Richardson (1994) argues for the metaphor of crystallization that conveys a holistic, multifaceted, and dynamic perspective when compared to the two-dimensional fixity of triangulation (based on plane geometry). Richardson favors the metaphor of the multifaceted crystal (based on light theory) that reflects externalities and refracts within itself, creating a spectrum of dynamic and colorful images. In relation to narrative research writing, crystallization values texts that provide "a deepened, complex, thoroughly partial, understanding of the topic" (p. 934). This is made possible by arts-based research genres discussed in the postmodern research section. So it seems that crystallization rather than triangulation is a better fit for interpretive research when it comes to understanding and representing the complexity of social realities.

Critical Research

Philosophy has evidenced a subversive element from its inception. Plato's Apology tells us how Socrates was condemned by the Athenian citizenry for corrupting the morals of the young and doubting the gods . . . Socrates called conventional wisdom into question. He subjected long-standing beliefs to rational scrutiny and speculated about concerns that projected beyond the existing order.

What became known as "critical theory" was built upon this legacy. . . . Interdisciplinary and uniquely experimental in character, critical theory was always concerned not merely with how things were but how they might be and should be. This ethical imperative led its primary thinkers to develop a cluster of themes and a new critical method that transformed our understanding of society.

(Bronner, 2011, pp. 1, 2)

Critical social theory and research methods entered education via the field of curriculum theorizing in the 1970s/1980s, and science educators began to embrace this approach in the 1990s. Central to the critical research paradigm is a transformative intent to promote social justice, with practitioners acting on the world to make it more democratic, fairer, more equitable, and more inclusive. A critical perspective extends the interpretive researcher's role of understanding the lived experience of the other (*verstehen*) to an advocacy (*praxis*) role of "making a difference."

In the social sciences, critical practitioners employ *ideology critique* to make visible, analyze critically, and transform social structures (normative social practices and their governing policies) that suppress the free will, dignity, and right to self-determination of individuals and minority groups—in other words, the less powerful members of society. Kincheloe (2007) calls this a process of engaging in "critical democracy." Critical practitioners develop a professional praxis for working with socially and/or economically disadvantaged communities. Their transformative goals include fostering a community's social conscience, intellectual prowess, and vision of a brighter future and facilitating the community's critical voice and strategic political skills with which to acquire resources for improving its well-being.

In the field of science education, critical researchers have embraced a range of sociocultural theories imported from the fields of philosophy, anthropology, and sociology. For more than 25 years, science educators have employed critical feminist theory to identify how girls have been disadvantaged historically by "boy-friendly" science instruction and to create gender-inclusive curricula and pedagogies. In the past decade, there has been an upsurge in cultural studies of science education, with critical researchers identifying how "First World" science curricula and research practices transmit a Western modern worldview that excludes and therefore delegitimizes the cultural capital of minority and indigenous communities by reproducing a narrow range of cultural values, beliefs, aspirations, languages, and identities (Mutua & Swadener, 2004).

A contemporary focus of critical science educators is development of "socially responsible" science curricula and pedagogies for facilitating students' higher-order critical literacy skills (Taylor, Taylor, & Chow, 2013) for participating in social decision making about the appropriate (ethical) use of science and technology in improving the human condition. Socially responsible science engages students in critical reflective thinking and critical discourse on contentious issues such as human-induced climate change, genetically modified crops, destruction of ecosystems and loss of biodiversity, and biomedical interventions, among many other issues.

For postgraduate researchers, the critical paradigm provides conceptual tools for ideology critique, self-decolonization, and visionary thinking and supports development of transformative professional practices (or praxes). An *emancipatory* interest (after Habermas; see Young, 1990) fuels the mission of critical researchers to identify and lay bare the hegemony of powerful systems of social thought and action that have colonized historically their societies and continue to maintain a powerful presence by virtue of their invisibility, such as the ideologies of scientism and "crypto-positivism" (Kincheloe & Tobin, 2009) embedded in the Western modern worldview. Adopting a critical epistemology enables postgraduate researchers, especially those from newly independent nations in Africa and Asia with multilingual indigenous populations, to explore ways in which their cultural identities may have been suppressed by culturally insensitive imported curricula, to reconceptualize their cultural identities, values, and aspirations, and to develop transformative philosophies for their future professional practice.

To help avoid hubris—the seductive tendency to occupy the higher moral ground and prescribe how others should change for the better—critical practitioners engage in *critical subjectivity*. While engaging in ideology critique, they turn a critical eye inward and examine their own belief systems, via *critical self-reflection* (or *critical reflexivity*), in order to identify their (perhaps unwitting) complicity in reproducing repressive social structures and power relationships (Brookfield, 1995). The practice of pointing the critical finger ever outward to identify external sources of repression, while insulating from critique one's "revolutionary" values, runs the danger of courting cultural narcissism (Malisa, 2010). The science education community witnessed this process in the early 1990s when constructivist revolutionaries contested established behaviorist psychology, and again, soon after, when advocates of the newly emerging interpretive research paradigm contested advocates of the entrenched classical positivist research paradigm. Both sides engaged in prolonged, impassioned, and critical finger pointing until "paradigm peace" was established, although the rapprochement will become truly universal only when advocates of both sides relinquish their hubris.

To further help avoid the hubris associated with engaging single-mindedly in "win-lose" dualistic thinking, astute critical practitioners employ *dialectical reasoning*. There are numerous forms of dialectical reasoning, but Hegel's *thesis-antithesis-synthesis* has proved to be highly productive (Osborne, 1992). From this perspective, long-standing antinomies, such as individual free will versus conformity to established social norms, are regarded as being complementary (in the sense of mutually presupposing) rather than mutually annihilating in the way we understand the interaction of matter and antimatter. In order for democratic societies to survive and thrive, it is important that neither individual entitlement nor social responsibility is privileged over the other; both must co-exist, much in the way that we understand light to have both particlelike and wavelike properties. A coherent yet vital democratic society flourishes by means of the creative energy generated by its citizens working productively with the ongoing dialectical tension between competing ideologies.

A number of contemporary qualitative researchers have integrated dialectical thinking into their research perspectives. Michelle Fine (1994) evokes a dialectical perspective when she argues for interpretive researchers to "work the self–other hyphen"; that is, to focus self-consciously on the relationship between the researcher (self) and his/her participant (other) rather than on either one alone, thereby maintaining critical awareness of the process of achieving mutual understanding: "When we construct texts collaboratively, self-consciously examining our relations with/for/despite those who have been contained as Others, we move against, we enable resistance to, Othering . . . Our work will never 'arrive' but must always struggle 'between'" (pp. 74, 75). Wolff-Michael Roth (2005) signifies the dialectical relationship between the individual and society by use of the slash ("/") in the term "auto/ethnography" and argues for "auto/ethnography" as a critical method for science educators to engage in research that critically explores cultural practices, values, and beliefs through the lens of the life history of individuals embedded in those cultures. Steinar Kvale (1996) has developed a dialectical approach to qualitative interviewing, an approach that dispenses with the classical interview method of searching for interpretive coherence in participants' meaning-perspectives and focuses instead on revealing and responding to the contradictions in their everyday lives. According to Kvale, "If social reality is in itself contradictory, the task of social science is to investigate the real contradictions of the social situation and posit them against each other" (p. 57). Dialectical thought is concerned also with new developments in the social world, not only with being but also with becoming, thereby fostering an action orientation toward changing the world—or as critical theorists call it, with praxis.

Critical practitioners maintain a critical awareness of the ever-present danger of the dialectic collapsing into a seductive singularity that resolves naively the tension in people's lives. In examining the dialectic between the dominant ideological press for social conformity and the resistant struggle for individual freedom, it can be tempting to abandon the emancipatory struggle in favor of complacency or cynicism. The challenging task for the critical practitioner, therefore, is to help maintain opportunities for dialectical thought and critical discourse associated with social change. In this regard, critical theorists are contributing to growing disquiet worldwide about the neoconservative political agenda that is reasserting the positivist research imperative (Denzin & Giardina, 2006).

Quality Standards for Critical Research

For the interpretive research paradigm, I outlined two important sets of quality standards—trustworthiness and authenticity—which support a social constructivist epistemology. Guba and Lincoln (1989) designed these (epistemic and ethical) criteria to ensure that interpretive researchers seek to establish and maintain relationships of mutual understanding and mutual benefit with their participants. The authenticity criteria are applicable also as quality standards for regulating the emancipatory work of critical researchers, ensuring that they avoid hubris and engage in *mutually empowering* relationships with their participants.

In summary, the following quality standards serve to regulate critical research and its reporting, ensuring that critical research practitioners sustain a transformative intent to establish educational policies and practices that enshrine an emancipatory interest in improving the human condition.

Ideology critique. Does the text express a critical perspective on the dominant ideologies that frame social norms and police normative social practices associated with educational policy and/or practice?

Critical subjectivity. Does the author demonstrate critical awareness of her/his own cultural history, explicate the contradictions that beset her/his professional life, and examine critically and insightfully her/his own complicity in its uncritical reproduction in the context of his/her professional practice?

Authentic relationships. Does the author demonstrate an educative relationship with his/her research participants that seeks to foster their development of critical consciousness and empowers them, in the context of their professional roles, as agents of social and cultural reconstruction?

Vision. Does the author articulate a vision for more socially just, equitable, and/or inclusive professional policies and/or practices?

Postmodern Research

> Postmodern knowledge is not simply a tool of the authorities; it refines our sensitivity to differences and reinforces our ability to tolerate the incommensurable. Its principle is not the expert's homology, but the inventor's paralogy.
> (Lyotard, 2004, p. xxv)

> The postmodern and postexperimental moments were defined in part by a concern for literary and rhetorical tropes and the narrative turn, a concern for storytelling, for composing ethnographies in new ways . . . this moment

> was shaped by a new sensibility, by doubt, by a refusal to privilege any method or theory . . . researchers continued to move away from foundational and quasi-foundational criteria . . . [toward] criteria that might prove evocative, moral, critical, and rooted in local understandings.
> (Denzin & Lincoln, 2005b, p. 3)

The 20th century witnessed the unfolding of a postmodern sensibility—the *linguistic* (or *narrative*) *turn*—especially in the arts. The literary turn was due in large part to continental philosophers such as Michel Foucault, Jacques Derrida, and Jean-Francois Lyotard. Foucault made explicit the largely hidden relationship between power and knowledge, exposing ways in which the individual mind (and thus one's social identity) is controlled by the official discourses of institutions that define the meaning of concepts such as reason and normality. He argued that these concepts should be understood not as stable and inevitable but as contingent and mutable, changing over time according to the needs of authority to control and regulate the behavior of the individual (Stokes, 2002). For the oppressed to gain power involves resisting having one's lifeworld colonized (unwittingly) by the sociocultural norms that inhere in the official discourse of the powerful other. Derrida deconstructed the structuralist myth of the fixed meaning of terms (or signifiers) in language, arguing that languages (including scientific discourse and mathematical symbol systems) are cultural systems of representation rather than deliverers of a single authoritative truth about the world (the signified). Language is differential rather than referential (Belsey, 2002).

Lyotard (2004) argued that, given the postmodern condition of postindustrial societies, the tradition of using "grand narratives" to legitimate social knowledge as overarching (or secure) truth is no longer tenable. Grand narratives (or metanarratives) comprise philosophies of history, or totalizing ideologies (or paradigms), that prescribe ethical, epistemological, and political means of legitimating knowledge production and regulating social decision-making (consensus forming) processes, driven by the seductive modernist worldview of progressively liberating humanity. They range from the emancipatory goal of neo–Marxism favored by critical social theorists to the aspirations of positivist science (or scientism) favored by many science education researchers. Lyotard's postmodern sensibility rejects the grand narrative status of all paradigms, including post-positivism, interpretivism, and criticalism (and postmodernism!): "Simplifying to the extreme, I define *postmodern* as incredulity toward metanarratives" (Lyotard, 2004, p. xxiv).

Of particular relevance to science education is Lyotard's consideration of quantum theory, fractal geometry (Mandelbrot), meta-mathematics (Godel's Incompleteness Theorem), catastrophe theory (Rene Thom), and game theory (Rapoport). He concludes that the legitimacy of knowledge generated by these forms of "postmodern science" relies not on the classical realist correspondence theory of truth, in which a perfect match is sought between nature and knowledge, but by *paralogy*. Paralogy constitutes deferring consensus (or seeking dissensus) by focusing one's inquiry on the unintelligible, counterexamples, undecidables, "fracta," conflicts of incompleteness, instabilities, anomalies, paradox, and irony and with "new rules in the games of reasoning" (Lyotard, 2004, p. 54). Lyotard draws on Wittgenstein's notion of "language games" to argue that postmodern science and narrative inquiry share the goal of searching for imaginative new insights, that this is achieved by practicing locally determined (but distinctly different) rules of reasoning, and that both tell stories in the form of "little narratives." Postmodernism promotes plurality of language games and directs incredulity at the imperialism of positivist science's claim to a privileged status in the academy.

A postmodern sensibility arose from the dissolution of the "two cultures" dichotomy separating art and science that had been perpetuated by the positivist paradigm (Snow, 1993). In the social sciences, this dissolution came to be known as the *blurred genres moment* (Denzin & Lincoln, 1994), bringing a literary look and feel to social science research, especially a focus on "developing experimental voices that expand the range of narrative strategies" (Tierney & Lincoln, 1997, p. x). The blurred genres moment is characterized by an "ideology of doubt" associated with the Derridean *crisis of representation*, which states that rather than lived experience being captured by the researcher's text, "it is created in the social text written by the researcher" (p. 11); "language produces meaning, creates social reality" (Richardson, 1994, p. 518). Central to this is the issue of voice.

Thanks to the literary turn, social science researchers have access to new literary genres such as *creative nonfiction* (Barone, 2008), *literary tales* (van Maanen, 1988), *poetic inquiry* (Prendergast, Leggo, & Sameshima, 2009), *blogs* (Runte, 2008), and *literary fiction* (Banks, 2008). In post-positivist research, writing is restricted to the classical realist genre that prescribes an objective (authorless) voice set in the past tense. In stark contrast, the multiplicity of voices expressed artfully by literary genres enhances the rhetorical power and transparency of research, greatly enriching the process of research writing as "a method of inquiry" (van Manen, 1990; Richardson, 1994).

Writing as inquiry involves generating qualitative "data texts" of lived experience. These narrative constructions embody the researcher's *ethnographic impulse* to understand deeply the other's lifeworld experience made accessible by postmodern "interviewing," which takes the form of dialogue (Gubrium & Holstein, 2003). In contrast to the semiclinical interview practices of post-positivism, the traditional boundary between interviewers and interviewees is blurred in postmodern research as both parties engage collaboratively in "good conversations," which Steiner Kvale (1996) has playfully labeled "InterViews" and which Mary Gergen (2004) recognizes as "joint constructions." Narrative constructions embody also the researcher's *auto/ethnographic impulse* to "self-dialogue"

as a means of excavating, reimagining, and reconstructing her/his culturally storied identity (Ellis, 2004). The role of imagination in reconstructing identity in narrative inquiry is explored by Theodore Sarbin (2004) and Cynthia Lightfoot (2004).

Denzin and Lincoln (2005b) describe the contemporary qualitative researcher responding to the literary turn in the "postmodern and postexperimental moment" as a *bricoleur* concerned with the aesthetics of representation as s/he stitches together narratives, stories, poems, screenplays, and the like into meaningful and significant "montages" (or wholes). For Clandinin and Connelly (2000), in narrative research, qualitative data texts (arising from fieldwork) are subjected to narrative analysis to produce research texts, a creative writing process that involves achieving balance between "authorial voice," "signature," and "audience." Donald Polkinghorne (1997) draws on Ricoeur and Bourdieu to make a case for "diachronic" research reports that portray narratively the temporal sequence of events comprising research as unfolding human action and experience. The sequencing is carefully "configured" and "smoothed" as a narrative discourse in the form of a story with a plot told by multiple voices: "In a narrative research report, researchers speak with the voice of the storyteller . . . in the first person as the teller of their own tale. Stories are told to (written for) audiences . . . The voices of the subjects who participated in the research are allowed to speak" (pp. 15–16).

Literary genres embody rationalities (or "rules of reasoning") distinctly different from the "pure cold logic" of the Cartesian/Newtonian mechanistic "regime of reason" (Pinar, 1997). One such alternative is a compelling counter-narrative proposed by Joe Kincheloe and Shirley Steinberg (1993). Drawing on physicist-philosopher David Bohm's concept of the "implicate order" of nature, consciousness, and society (Bohm & Peat, 1987), Kincheloe and Steinberg outline a system of *post-formal thinking* that comprises metaphoric, critical, reflective, dialectic, deconstructive, imaginative, relational, spiritual, emotional, holistic, and place-based modes of thinking/being/ acting. Post-formal thinking is sensitive to the dynamic, indeterminate, nonlinear, and self-transformative nature of complex living and social systems that characterize education (Davis & Sumara, 2006). In contemporary qualitative research, post-formal thinking embedded in literary genres enables researchers to explore aesthetic and emotional aspects of lived experience and construct narratives that illustrate the complexity, contingency, and emergence of social realities (Barone & Eisner, 2012).

Increasing interest in aesthetics has accelerated the expansion of *arts-based research*, an emerging field engaging contemporary social science researchers across the disciplines. Eliot Eisner (2008) explains the unique contribution of the arts to the production of knowledge in social science research: "Through art we come to feel, very often, what we cannot see directly" (p. 8); "The arts are a way of enriching our awareness and expanding our humanity" (p. 11). The *Handbook of the Arts in Qualitative Research* (Knowles & Cole, 2008) presents a collection of new genres—*literary forms, performance, visual art, new media, folk art,* and *popular art forms*—for enhancing artful representations of the process and outcomes of social science research into the human condition. Among the nondiscursive categories are visual images, dance, music, painting, and photographs. The arts have added an expressive dimension to social science research, giving rise to arts-based (educational) research approaches such as *performance ethnography* (Denzin, 2003), *evocative auto/ethnography* (Ellis, 1997), *testimonio* (Beverley, 2000), *life writing* (Smith, 1994), *ethnodrama* and *ethnotheatre* (Saldana, 2008), and *reader's theatre* (Donmoyer & Donmoyer, 2008), among many others.

Quality Standards for Postmodern Research

Postmodern social science research is a diverse and moving target with a key concern to promote pluralism and deconstruct imperialism, especially the imperialism of the classic validity standards associated with the objectivist epistemology of the positivist paradigm (Lincoln & Denzin, 1994). There is a range of quality standards for regulating writing as inquiry. Here is what some of the leading exponents of postmodern research recommend.

Authorial voice. John van Maanen (1988) argues for postmodern ethnographers to expand the range of their authorial voices beyond classical realism by adopting the literary genres of confessional and impressionistic writing, drawing on literary standards of narrative rationality such as plausibility and verisimilitude (see below). Writing should avoid the conceit of both positivism and solipsism and be judged in terms of its interest, coherence, and fidelity. The following literary devices are offered for writing impressionistic tales: textual identity, fragmented knowledge, characterization, and dramatic control (see also Taylor, 2002).

Verisimilitude. This literary standard is based on the classic French theatrical concept of *vraisemblance* and has been taken to mean that an "authentic" text draws readers into the lifeworlds of its characters because it corresponds with what readers recognize from their own experiences (Adler & Adler, 1994). For Ellis (2004), auto/ethnographic texts achieve verisimilitude inasmuch as they evoke "a feeling that the experience described is lifelike, believable, and possible" (p. 124), with the goal of broadening the researcher's and reader's perspectives, helping them understand empathically the different other and thus overcome their own self-absorption.

Pedagogical thoughtfulness. Max van Manen (1991) argues for writing that engages both researcher and reader in reflecting critically on their values and beliefs about teaching and learning in order to develop "pedagogical thoughtfulness [which] is a multifaceted and complex mindfulness toward children . . . Such pedagogical text needs to possess an inspirational quality together with a narrative structure that invites critical reflection and possibilities for insight that leads to a personal appropriation of a moral intuition" (pp. 8, 9). In developing his postmodern human science approach of "hermeneutic-phenomenology," van Manen (1990) argues that in order to engage the reader in pedagogical thoughtfulness, research writing needs to be "oriented," "strong," "rich," and "deep" if it is to display a dialogical quality.

Performative criteria. A special issue of the journal *Qualitative Inquiry* (June 2000) contains a set of articles by leading practitioner-theorists of postmodern experimental writing in which they discuss criteria for judging the quality of postmodern research writing. Denzin (2003) draws on the literary and aesthetic criteria of Carolyn Ellis, Art Bochner, and Laurel Richardson and the cultural criticism of Patricia Clough to outline a set of seven performative criteria. He values auto/ethnographic texts that "(1) unsettle, criticize, and challenge taken-for-granted, repressed meanings; (2) invite moral and ethical dialogue while reflexively clarifying their own moral positions; (3) engender resistance and offer utopian thoughts about how things can be made different; (4) demonstrate that they care, that they are kind; (5) show instead of tell, using the rule that less is more; (6) exhibit interpretive sufficiency, representational adequacy, and authentic adequacy; and (7) present political, functional, collective, and committed viewpoints" (pp. 123–124). Theoretical discussion combined with practical examples of these criteria in action can be found in Denzin and Giardina's (2008) book on the politics of evidence and Denzin's (1997) book on interpretive ethnography for the 21st century.

Integral Research

> That science is value-free is a myth, and I think that when we realize that this is the case, we do better science . . . We need to blend scientific data (what I call "science sense") with intuition, common sense, indigenous knowledge, and qualitative research, as we try to comprehend the world in which we're immersed.
>
> (Bekoff, 2009)

In the introduction to this chapter, I argued that the transformative potential of qualitative research is yet to be fully realized by science educators due to their traditional affiliation to positivism, the "mother ship" of traditional science education. Too often we resolve this conflict of interest by importing qualitative research methods into post-positivist research designs, thereby privileging the so-called gold standard of objectivity. There is a danger that such mixed-methods research designs breed epistemic blindness among novice researchers that prevents them from expanding the boundaries of science education beyond the confines of the traditional Cartesian/Newtonian worldview.

The four-paradigm taxonomy commonplace in advanced educational research textbooks—*post-positivism*, *interpretivism*, *criticalism*, *postmodernism*—provides a helpful structure for understanding important fundamental differences between quantitative research and qualitative research, differences that are grounded in paradigmatic ways of knowing, being, representing, and valuing rather than (simplistically) in contrasting types of data or methods of collection/analysis. This structure also helps us understand the broad scope of contemporary qualitative research with its interdisciplinary origins in the arts and humanities. However, this structure is not without challenge. How can we justify mixing and matching contrasting epistemologies, especially from the so-called qualitative and quantitative paradigms, given that the philosopher Thomas Kuhn (1962) defined paradigms as intrinsically incommensurable worldviews? The justification needs to be more profound than is allowed for by the simple assertion that it is pragmatically feasible.

Postmodern thinking provides us with a helpful way out of this impasse by pointing out that dualistic "either/or" reasoning is not the only or best way of creating coherent systems of thought. A fundamental problem with dualistic reasoning is its tendency to make us think in terms of binary opposites and to treat these oppositional categories as mutually exclusive, resulting in win-lose discrimination based on, for example, gender (masculine/feminine), ethnicity (White/Black), social class (rich/poor), or body shape (fat/lean)—and, in the case of educational research, paradigm preference. As I have discussed, numerous modes of reasoning are available to us, including postformal thinking, for which there is a precedent in the physical sciences in the form of dialectical reasoning about the nature of light (i.e., the visible part of the electromagnetic spectrum), allowing for the tension-filled co-existence of the oppositional metaphors of light as particles and light as waves.

For the purpose of my current argument, I shall make use of an inclusive mode of reasoning, *vision-logic*, as discussed recently by the evolutionary philosopher Ken Wilber (1999). Vision-logic draws on Western and Eastern wisdom traditions, seeking to integrate matter, mind, and spirit to generate a holistic understanding of ourselves and our connectedness to one another and to the planet that sustains us. From a vision-logic perspective, each of the paradigms comprising the current taxonomy of educational research is an integral part of a larger system, called the *integral paradigm*. The integral paradigm values absolutely the unique contribution of each and every paradigm (none is privileged) to our ultimate endeavor as educational researchers to help create curricula policies and pedagogical practices that prepare future generations for a world in growing need of its living and nonliving inhabitants being treated with ethical sensitivity (for details, see Taylor, Taylor, & Luitel, 2012). The integral paradigm is already well established in shaping scientific thinking and practice, as evidenced by the recent publication of *Integral Ecology* (Esbjorn-Hargens & Zimmerman, 2009), a textbook for ecologists and environmentalists inspired by Wilber's integral theory. The authors explain that their book:

> . . . demonstrates that there are numerous approaches to ecology and the environment—philosophical, spiritual, religious, social, political, cultural, behavioural, scientific, and psychological. Each highlights an essential component while ignoring other dimensions. To overcome this fragmentation, *Integral Ecology* provides a way to weave all approaches into an environmental mandala, an ecology of ecologies.
>
> (p. 486)

From an integral research perspective, it is less helpful to distinguish between qualitative and quantitative forms of research and more productive to think holistically about the prospective contribution of multiple research paradigms (from post-positivism to postmodernism), asking *what unique range of research questions can we address by adopting an integral research perspective?* Integral research design is in its infancy, but already graduate students in science education have successfully designed research methodologies that integrate multiple paradigms (e.g., Neumayr & Taylor, 2001; Taylor & Wallace, 2007). By way of illustrating at least one possible approach, the following are synopses of doctoral dissertations that have integrated multiple research paradigms to create *arts-based critical auto/ethnographic research* designs (see also Taylor, 2013).

Exemplar 1

Emilia is a science teacher educator at a university in Mozambique, a multicultural and multilingual Southern African nation that gained political independence from Portugal in 1975. She brought to her doctoral research a concern that science education should enable her country to embrace the modern science and technology of a rapidly globalizing world while not, at the same time, serving a neocolonial agenda of Westernization. Emilia's ambition was to develop a culturally inclusive philosophy of science teacher education that would transform her own professional practice and the practice of science teaching throughout her country. To this end, she designed an arts-based critical auto/ethnography to address two research questions: What are the prospects of creating culturally/inclusive science teacher education in Mozambique, and what obstacles need to be overcome? Her theoretical perspective combined aspects of postcolonial theory, radical constructivism, and holistic curriculum inquiry. As befits interpretive research, another research question emerged during the inquiry: How can I promote good communication in my classes and avoid impediments in communication that reduce my students to the status of things? Emilia's theoretical perspective continued developing with the inclusion of cultural theory, philosophy of science, transformative learning, deep ecology, discourse theory and semiotics, and indigenous knowledge theory.

She employed a range of qualitative research methods to excavate and interrogate her lived experience, including narrative inquiry, autobiography and student testimonials, writing as inquiry and ironic writing, logics of poetry, and metaphor. The diachronic dissertation structure reflects the unfolding process of Emilia's inquiry as she develops a decolonizing eco-pedagogy for science education (for details see Afonso-Nhalevilo, 2010.

Exemplar 2

Yuli Rahmawati is a science teacher educator at an Indonesian university and came to Australia to work on a nationally funded research project on co-teaching and co-generative dialogue in secondary school environmental science. She focused her doctoral research on the development of her own pedagogy, in particular, the emergence of her teaching identity. Yuli designed an arts-based critical auto/ethnography not only to understand deeply her (cultural and religious) teaching self but also to develop as a transformative science educator committed to education for sustainability. She employed a range of qualitative research methods, including narratives of lived experience, stories, informal interview excerpts, vignettes of observed/recalled activities, evocative images, boxed quotes, and poems. This self-study methodology allowed theoretical ideas and questions to emerge and interact throughout the inquiry, including identity theory, philosophy of science, Islamic precepts, and "green" chemistry principles. The dissertation takes the reader on a journey through Yuli's life as she reflects critically on how her teaching identity was shaped by her lived experiences since childhood. The journey continues into the present as she reconceptualizes her teaching identity in relation to her vision as a transformative science teacher educator (for details, see Rahmawati, 2012).

Exemplar 3

Sue Stack brought to her doctoral thesis a unique variety of professional experiences: industrial scientist, sculptor, journalist, and secondary school teacher of science and journalism. She also brought an inquiring mind that had long grappled with the thorny issue of the relationship between science and spirituality, especially in the context of creating an authentic and meaningful science education. For doctoral research, Sue designed an arts-based critical auto/ethnography and employed narrative inquiry; poetic, metaphoric, and fictive genres and images; dialectical reasoning' and transpersonal methods, supplemented by questionnaires, with which she excavated and interrogated her lived experiences, as well as the experiences of colleagues and students. She drew on integral and holistic theories, largely new to science education, to formulate an integral philosophy of science and spirituality, with profound implications for transforming science education. The diachronically structured dissertation evidences an ongoing interaction between emergent research questions and theoretical referents and illustrates Sue's artful engagement in writing as a method of inquiry, taking her reader with her on a deep philosophical journey to reimagine science evolving from modernist to postmodernist to integral science (for details, see Stack, 2006).

Coda

The integral paradigm has opened our doors of perception (Huxley, 1959) to exciting and powerful possibilities for the way we conceive of the interrelationship among the interpretive, critical, and postmodern research paradigms. Already doctoral researchers are occupying this multiparadigmatic research space and are conducting insightful research aimed at transforming science (and mathematics) education policies and practices. Beyond this, the integral paradigm is also challenging us to reconceptualize the relationship between qualitative and quantitative research perspectives. The popular mixed-methods approach has been a good first step in this direction. However, as I have argued, the transformative potential of contemporary qualitative research can be readily blunted by simply importing qualitative methods into post-positivist research designs. The challenge for future researchers is less about how to combine qualitative and quantitative research methods and more about how to integrate the disparate and seemingly conflicting theories of knowing, being, representing, and valuing of multiple paradigms. A key issue for these integral researchers is to ensure that appropriate quality standards are employed to regulate the research methods associated with their parent paradigms.

Acknowledgments

I thank Professor Ken Tobin, City University of New York, and Professor John Wallace, University of Toronto, who reviewed earlier drafts of this chapter and gave me very helpful advice that contributed to a more succinct style of writing and confidence to cite my own publications. I also thank Professor David F. Treagust, Curtin University, whose close editorial reading of the penultimate draft enabled me to correct some errors of fact and contributed to the wording of the subtitle of the chapter. These constructively critical peer reviewers helped to significantly improve the coherence of this chapter.

References

Abrams, E., Taylor, P. C., & Guo, C. J. (2013). Contextualizing culturally relevant science and mathematics teaching for indigenous learning. *International Journal of Science and Mathematics Education, 11*(1), 1–21.

Adler, P. A., & Adler, P. (1994). Observational techniques. In N. K. Denzin & Y. S. Lincoln (Eds.), *Handbook of qualitative research* (pp. 377–392). Thousand Oaks, CA: Sage.

Afonso-Nhalevilo, E. (2010). *Endless journeys: An autoethnographic search for culturally inclusive philosophy of science teacher education in Mozambique.* Saarbruken, Germany: VDM Publishing Group.

Banks, S. (2008). Writing as theory: In defense of fiction. In J. G. Knowles & A. L. Cole (Eds.), *Handbook of the arts in qualitative research* (pp. 155–164). Thousand Oaks, CA: Sage.

Barone, T. (2008). Creative nonfiction and social research. In J.G. Knowles & A.L. Cole (Eds.), *Handbook of the arts in qualitative research* (pp. 105–115). Thousand Oaks, CA: Sage.

Barone, T., & Eisner, E.W. (2012). *Arts based research.* Thousand Oaks, CA: Sage.

Bekoff, M. (2009). Foreword. In S. Esbjorn-Hargens & M. Zimmerman, *Integral ecology: Uniting multiple perspectives on the natural world* (pp. xix–xxxii). Boston, MA: Integral Books.

Belsey, C. (2002). *Poststructuralism: A very short introduction.* New York, NY: Oxford University Press.

Beverley, J. (2000). Testimonio, subalternity, and narrative authority. In N.K. Denzin & Y.S. Lincoln (Eds.), *The SAGE handbook of qualitative research* (2nd ed., pp. 555–565). Thousand Oaks, CA: Sage.

Bohm, D., & Peat, F.D. (1987). *Science, order, and creativity.* New York: Bantam Books.

Bronner, S.E. (2011). *Critical theory: A very short introduction.* New York, NY: Oxford University Press.

Brookfield, S.D. (1995). *Becoming a critically reflective teacher.* San Francisco, CA: Jossey-Bass.

Bryman, A. (2012). *Social research methods* (4th ed.). New York, NY: Oxford University Press.

Carr, W., & Kemmis, S. (1986). *Becoming critical: Education, knowledge and action.* London: Falmer.

Chase, S.E. (2005). Narrative inquiry: Multiple lenses, approaches, voices. In N.K. Denzin & Y.S. Lincoln (Eds.), *The SAGE handbook of qualitative research* (3rd ed., pp. 651–679). Thousand Oaks, CA: Sage.

Clandinin, D.J., & Connelly, F.M. (1994). Personal experience methods. In N.K. Denzin & Y.S. Lincoln (Eds.), *Handbook of qualitative research* (pp. 413–427). Thousand Oaks, CA: Sage.

Clandinin, D.J., & Connelly, F.M. (2000). *Narrative inquiry: Experience and story in qualitative research.* San Francisco, CA: Jossey-Bass.

Cohen, L., Manion, L., & Morrison, K. (2011). *Research methods in education* (7th ed.). Abingdon, OX: Routledge.

Creswell, J.W. (2012). *Educational research: Planning, conducting, and evaluating quantitative and qualitative research* (4th ed.). Boston, MA: Pearson Education.

Davis, B., & Sumara, D. (2006). *Complexity and education: Inquiries into learning, teaching and research.* Mahwah, NJ: Lawrence Erlbaum.

Denzin, N.K. (1997). *Interpretive ethnography: Ethnographic practices for the 21st century.* Thousand Oaks, CA: Sage Publications.

Denzin, N.K. (2003). *Performance ethnography: Critical pedagogy and the politics of culture.* Thousand Oaks, CA: Sage.

Denzin, N.K., & Giardina, M.D. (Eds.). (2006). *Qualitative inquiry and the conservative challenge.* Walnut Creek, CA: Left Coast Press.

Denzin, N.K., & Giardina, M.D. (Eds.). (2008). *Qualitative inquiry and the politics of evidence.* Walnut Creek, CA: Left Coast Press.

Denzin, N.K., & Lincoln, Y.S. (Eds.). (1994). *Handbook of qualitative research.* Thousand Oaks, CA: Sage.

Denzin, N.K., & Lincoln, Y.S. (2000). Introduction: The discipline and practice of qualitative research. In N.K. Denzin & Y.S. Lincoln (Eds.), *Handbook of qualitative research* (2nd ed., pp. 1–28). Thousand Oaks, CA: Sage.

Denzin, N.K., & Lincoln, Y.S. (Eds.). (2005a). *The SAGE handbook of qualitative research* (3rd ed.). Thousand Oaks, CA: Sage.

Denzin, N.K., & Lincoln, Y.S. (2005b). Introduction: The discipline and practice of qualitative research. In N.K. Denzin & Y.S. Lincoln (Eds.), *The SAGE handbook of qualitative research* (3rd ed., pp. 1–32). Thousand Oaks, CA: Sage.

Donmoyer, R., & Donmoyer, J.Y. (2008). Readers' theatre as a data display strategy. In J.G. Knowles & A.L. Cole (Eds.), *Handbook of the arts in qualitative research* (pp. 209–224). Thousand Oaks, CA: Sage.

Eisenhart, M.A. (1988). The ethnographic research tradition and mathematics education research. *Journal for Research in Mathematics Education, 19*(2), 99–114.

Eisner, E. (2008). Art and knowledge. In J.G. Knowles & A.L. Cole (Eds.), *Handbook of the arts in qualitative research* (pp. 3–12). Thousand Oaks, CA: Sage.

Ellis, C. (1997). Evocative autoethnography: Writing emotionally about our lives. In W.G. Tierney & Y.S. Lincoln (Eds.), *Representation and the text: Re-framing the narrative voice* (pp. 115–139). Albany: State University of New York Press.

Ellis, C. (2004). *The ethnographic I: A methodological novel about autoethnography.* Walnut Creek, CA: Altamira Press.

Erickson, F. (1986). Qualitative methods in research on teaching. In M.C. Wittrock (Ed.), *Handbook of research on teaching* (3rd ed., pp. 119–159). New York, NY: Macmillan.

Esbjorn-Hargens, S., & Zimmerman, M.E. (2009). *Integral ecology: Uniting multiple perspectives on the natural world.* Boston, MA: Integral Books.

Fine, M. (1994). Working the hyphens: Reinventing self and other in qualitative research. In N.K. Denzin & Y.S. Lincoln (Eds.), *Handbook of qualitative research* (pp. 70–82). Thousand Oaks, CA: Sage.

Gallagher, J.J. (Ed.). (1991). *Interpretive research in science education.* NARST Monograph, No 4. National Association for Research in Science Teaching. Manhattan, KS: Kansas State University.

Gergen, M. (2004). Once upon a time: A narratologist's tale. In C. Daiute & C. Lightfoot (Eds.), *Narrative analysis: Studying the development of individuals in society* (pp. 267–285). Thousand Oaks, CA: Sage.

Goswami, A. (1993). *The self-aware universe: How consciousness creates the material world.* New York, NY: Tarcher/Putnam/Penguin.

Green, J.L., Camilli, G., & Elmore, P.B. (Eds.). (2006). *Handbook of complementary methods in education research.* Mahwah, NJ: Lawrence Erlbaum.

Guba, E.G. (1990). The alternative paradigm dialog. In E.G. Guba (Ed.), *The paradigm dialog* (pp. 17–27). Newbury Park, CA: Sage Publications.

Guba, E.G., & Lincoln, Y.S. (1988). Naturalistic and rationalistic enquiry. In J.P. Keeves (Ed.), *Educational research, methodology, and measurement: An international handbook* (pp. 81–85). Sydney, Australia: Pergamon Press.

Guba, E.G., & Lincoln, Y.S. (1989). *Fourth generation evaluation.* Newbury Park, CA: Sage.

Guba, E.G., & Lincoln, Y.S. (1994). Competing paradigms in qualitative research. In N.K. Denzin & Y.S. Lincoln (Eds.), *Handbook of qualitative research* (pp. 105–117). Thousand Oaks, CA: Sage.

Guba, E.G., & Lincoln, Y.S. (2005). Paradigmatic controversies, contradictions, and emerging confluences. In N.K. Denzin & Y.S. Lincoln (Eds.), *The SAGE handbook of qualitative research* (3rd ed., pp. 191–215). Thousand Oaks, CA: Sage.

Gubrium, J.F., & Holstein, J.A. (2003). *Postmodern interviewing.* Thousand Oaks, CA: Sage.

Haarman, H. (2007). *Foundations of culture: Knowledge-construction, belief systems and worldview in their dynamic interplay.* Frankfurt, Germany: Peter Lang.

Habermas, J. (1972). *Knowledge and human interests* (J.J. Shapiro, Trans.). London: Heinemann.

Hamilton, D. (1977). *Beyond the numbers game: A reader in educational evaluation.* Basingstoke, UK: Macmillan.

Hamilton, D. (1994). Traditions, preferences, and postures in applied qualitative research. In N.K. Denzin, & Y.S. Lincoln (Eds.), *Handbook of qualitative research* (pp. 60–69). Thousand Oaks, CA: Sage.

Howell, K.E. (2013). *An introduction to the philosophy of methodology.* London: Sage.

House, E.R. (2006). Methodological fundamentalism and the quest for control(s). In N.K. Denzin & M.D. Giardina (Eds.), *Qualitative inquiry and the conservative challenge* (pp. 93–108). Walnut Creek, CA: Left Coast Press.

Huxley, A. (1959). *The doors of perception and heaven and hell.* New York, NY: Bantam Books.

Janesick, V.J. (1994). The dance of qualitative research design. In N.K. Denzin & Y.S. Lincoln (Eds.), *Handbook of qualitative research* (pp. 209–219). Thousand Oaks, CA: Sage.

Kincheloe, J.L. (2007). Critical pedagogy in the twenty-first century. In P. McLaren & J.L. Kincheloe (Eds.), *Critical pedagogy: Where are we now?* (pp. 9–42). New York, NY: Peter Lang.

Kincheloe, J.L., & Steinberg, S.R. (1993). A tentative description of post-formal thinking: The critical confrontation with cognitive thinking. *Harvard Educational Review, 63,* 296–320.

Kincheloe, J., & Tobin, K. (2009). The much exaggerated death of positivism. *Cultural Studies of Science Education, 4,* 513–528.

Knowles, J.G., & Cole, A.L. (Eds.). (2008). *Handbook of the arts in qualitative research.* Thousand Oaks, CA: Sage.

Kuhn, T.S. (1962). *The structure of scientific revolutions.* Chicago: University of Chicago Press.

Kvale, S. (1996). *InterViews: An introduction to qualitative research interviewing.* Thousand Oaks, CA: Sage.

Lassonde, C.A., Galman, S., & Kosnik, C. (Eds.). (2009). *Self-study research for teacher educators.* Rotterdam, the Netherlands: Sense Publishers.

Lightfoot, C. (2004). Fantastic self: A study of adolescents' fictional narratives, and aesthetic activity as identity work. In C. Daiute & C. Lightfoot (Eds.), *Narrative analysis: Studying the development of individuals in society* (pp. 21–37). Thousand Oaks, CA: Sage.

Lincoln, Y.S. (2005). Institutional review boards and methodological conservatism: The challenge to and from phenomenological paradigms. In N.K. Denzin & Y.S. Lincoln (Eds.), *The SAGE handbook of qualitative research* (3rd ed., pp. 165–181). Thousand Oaks, CA: Sage.

Lincoln, Y.S. (2009). "What a long, strange trip it's been . . ." Twenty-five years of qualitative and new paradigm research. *Qualitative Inquiry, 16*(1), 3–9.

Lincoln, Y.S., & Denzin, N.K. (1994). The fifth moment. In N.K. Denzin & Y.S. Lincoln (Eds.), *Handbook of qualitative research* (pp. 575–586). Thousand Oaks, CA: Sage.

Lyotard, J.F. (2004). *The postmodern condition: A report on knowledge* (G. Bennington & B. Massumi, Trans.). Minneapolis: University of Minnesota Press. (Original work published 1979)

Malisa, M. (2010). *(Anti) narcissisms and (anti) capitalisms: Human nature and education in the works of Mahatma Gandhi, Malcolm X, Nelson Mandela and Jurgen Habermas.* Rotterdam, the Netherlands: Sense publishers.

Mathison, S. (1988). Why triangulate? *Educational Researcher, 17,* 13–17.

McNiff, J., & Whitehead, J. (2011). *All you need to know about action research* (2nd ed.). Thousand Oaks, CA: Sage.

Mutua, K., & Swadener, B.B. (Eds.). (2004). *Decolonizing research in cross-cultural contexts: Critical personal narratives.* Albany, NY: State University of New York Press.

Neumayr, E., & Taylor, P.C. (2001). A cosy bedding for science education research? Ken Wilber's integral philosophy. In S. Gunn & A. Begg (Eds.), *Mind, body & society: Emerging understandings of knowing and learning* (pp. 109–116). Melbourne, Australia: Department of Mathematics and Statistics, University of Melbourne.

Nhalevilo, E.Z. de F. (2013). Rethinking the history of inclusion of IKS in school curricula: Endeavouring to legitimate the subject. *International Journal of Science and Mathematics Education, 11*(1), 23–42.

Osborne, R. (1992). *Philosophy for beginners.* New York, NY: Writers and Readers Publishing.

Paul, J.L., & Marfo, K. (2001). Preparation of educational researchers in philosophical foundations of inquiry. *Review of Educational Research, 71,* 525–547.

Pinar, W.F. (1997). Regimes of reason and the male narrative voice. In W.G. Tierney & Y.S. Lincoln (Eds.), *Representation and the text: Re-framing the narrative voice* (pp. 82–113). Albany: State University of New York Press.

Pithouse, K., Mitchell, C., & Moletsane, R. (Eds.). (2010). *Making connections: Self-study & social action.* New York, NY: Peter Lang.

Polkinghorne, D.E. (1997). Reporting qualitative research as practice. In W.G. Tierney & Y.S. Lincoln (Eds.), *Representation and the text: Re-framing the narrative voice* (pp. 3–21). Albany: State University of New York Press.

Prendergast, M., Leggo, C., & Sameshima, P. (Eds.). (2009). *Poetic inquiry: Vibrant voices in the social sciences.* Rotterdam, the Netherlands: Sense Publishers.

Rahmawati, Y. (2012). *Revealing and reconceptualising teaching identity through the landscapes of culture, religion, transformative learning, and sustainability education: A transformation journey of a science educator* (Doctoral thesis, Curtin University, Perth, Australia). Retrieved from http://espace.library.curtin.edu.au

Reason, P., & Bradbury, H. (2001). Introduction: Inquiry and participation in search of a world worthy of human aspiration. In P. Reason & H. Bradbury (Eds.), *Handbook of action research: Participative inquiry and practice* (pp. 1–14). Thousand Oaks, CA: Sage Publications.

Reed-Danahay, D.E. (Ed.). (1997). *Auto/ethnography: Rewriting the self and the social.* Oxford, UK: Berg.

Richardson, L. (1994). Writing: A method of inquiry. In N.K. Denzin & Y.S. Lincoln (Eds.), *Handbook of qualitative research* (pp. 516–529). Thousand Oaks, CA: Sage.

Rossenblum, B., & Kuttner, F. (2011). *Quantum enigma: Physics encounters consciousness* (2nd ed.). New York, NY: Oxford University Press.

Roth, W.-M. (Ed.). (2005). *Auto/biography and auto/ethnography: Praxis of research method.* Rotterdam, the Netherlands: Sense Publishers.

Runte, R. (2008). Blogs. In J.G. Knowles & A.L. Cole (Eds.), *Handbook of the arts in qualitative research* (pp. 299–312). Thousand Oaks, CA: Sage.

Saldana, J. (2008). Ethnodrama and ethnotheatre. In J.G. Knowles & A.L. Cole (Eds.), *Handbook of the arts in qualitative research* (pp. 195–207). Thousand Oaks, CA: Sage.

Sarbin, T. (2004). The role of the imagination in narrative construction. In C. Daiute & C. Lightfoot (Eds.), *Narrative analysis: Studying the development of individuals in society* (pp. 5–20). Thousand Oaks, CA: Sage.

Schon, D.A. (1983). *The reflective practitioner: How professionals think in action.* New York, NY: Basic Books.

Schwandt, T.A. (2001). *Dictionary of qualitative inquiry* (2nd ed.). Thousand Oaks, CA: Sage Publications.

Simons, H. (Ed.). (1980). *Towards a science of the singular.* Norwich, UK: University of East Anglia, Centre for Applied Research in Education.

Smith, D.G. (2008). From Leo Strauss to collapse theory: Considering the neoconservative attack on modernity and the work of education. *Critical Studies in Education, 49*(1), 33–48.

Smith, L. (1994). Biographical method. In N.K. Denzin & Y.S. Lincoln (Eds.), *Handbook of qualitative research* (pp. 286–305). Thousand Oaks, CA: Sage.

Snow, C.P. (1993). *Two cultures and the scientific revolution.* London, NY: Cambridge University Press.

Stack, S.J. (2006). *Integrating science and soul in education: The lived experience of a science teacher bringing holistic and integral perspectives to the transformation of science teaching* (Doctoral thesis, Curtin University of Technology, Perth, Australia). Retrieved from http://espace.library.curtin.edu.au

Stokes, P. (2002). *Philosophy: 100 essential thinkers.* London: Arcturus Publishing.

Taylor, E., Taylor, P.C., & Chow M.L. (2013). Diverse, disengaged and reactive: A teacher's adaptation of ethical dilemma story pedagogy as a strategy to re-engage learners in education for sustainability. In N. Mansour & R. Wegerif (Eds.), *Science education for diversity: Theory and practice* (pp. 97–117). Rotterdam, the Netherlands: Sense Publishers.

Taylor, P.C. (2002). On being impressed by college teaching. In P.C. Taylor, P.J. Gilmer & K. Tobin (Eds.), *Transforming undergraduate science teaching* (pp. 3–43). New York, NY: Peter Lang.

Taylor, P.C. (2013). Research as transformative learning for meaning-centred professional development. In O. Kovbasyuk & P. Blessinger (Eds.), *Meaning-centred education: International perspectives and explorations in higher education* (pp. 168–185). New York, NY: Routledge.

Taylor, P.C., Gilmer, P.J., & Tobin, K. (Eds.). (2002). *Transforming undergraduate science teaching: Social constructivist perspectives.* New York, NY: Peter Lang Publishing.

Taylor, P.C., & Medina, M.N.D. (2013). Educational research paradigms: From positivism to multiparadigmatic. *Journal for Meaning-Centered*

Education, 1. Retrieved from www.meaningcentered.org/journal/volume-01/educational-research-paradigms-from-positivism-to-multiparadigmatic/

Taylor, P.C., Taylor, E., & Luitel, B.C. (2012). Multi-paradigmatic transformative research as/for teacher education: An integral perspective. In B.J. Fraser, K.G. Tobin, & C.J. McRobbie (Eds.), *Second international handbook of science education* (pp. 373–387). Dordrecht, the Netherlands: Springer.

Taylor, P.C., & Wallace, J. (Eds.). (2007). *Contemporary qualitative research: Exemplars for science and mathematics educators*. Dordrecht, the Netherlands: Springer.

Tierney, W.G., & Lincoln, Y.S. (1997). Introduction: Explorations and discoveries. In W.G. Tierney & Y.S. Lincoln (Eds.), *Representation and the text: Re-framing the narrative voice* (pp. vii–xvi). Albany: State University of New York Press.

Tobin, K. (Ed.). (1993). *The practice of constructivism in science education*. Hillsdale, NJ: Lawrence Erlbaum.

Tuckman, B.W. (1978). *Conducting educational research* (2nd ed.). Chicago, IL: Harcourt Brace Jovanovich.

van Maanen, J. (1988). *Tales of the field: On writing ethnography*. Chicago, IL: University of Chicago Press.

van Manen, M. (1990). *Researching lived experience: Human science for an action sensitive pedagogy*. London, Ontario: State University of New York.

van Manen, M. (1991). *The tact of teaching: The meaning of pedagogical thoughtfulness*. Albany: State University of New York Press.

Walker, R. (1980). The conduct of educational case studies: Ethics, theory and procedures. In W.B. Dockerell & D. Hamilton (Eds.), *Rethinking educational research* (pp. 30–63). London: Hodder and Stoughton.

Wheatley, G. (1991). Constructivist perspectives on science and mathematics learning. *Science Education, 75*(1), 9–21.

Wilber, K. (1999). *The collected works of Ken Wilber: Volume 4*. Boston, MA: Shambhala.

Willis, J.W. (2007). *Foundations of qualitative research: Interpretive and critical approaches*. Thousand Oaks, CA: Sage.

Wolcott, H. (1990). On seeking—and rejecting—validity in qualitative research. In E.W. Eisner & A. Peshkin (Eds.), *Qualitative inquiry in education: The continuing debate* (pp. 121–152). New York, NY: Teachers College Press.

Young, R. (1990). *A critical theory of education: Habermas and our children's future*. New York, NY: Teachers College Press.

Section II

Science Learning

Section Editor: Richard Lehrer

4

Student Conceptions and Conceptual Change

Three Overlapping Phases of Research

TAMER G. AMIN, CAROL L. SMITH, AND MARIANNE WISER

From the 1970s onward, researchers have tried to understand the content and nature of student conceptions, how these conceptions can both hinder and contribute to learning, and how student conceptions change to resemble those of scientists. Progress in understanding student conceptions and the process of change has led to suggestions for how to design more effective instruction. The literature on student conceptions and their change is vast, as evidenced by a periodically updated bibliography containing thousands of publications (Duit, 2009). No single review can do justice to it all.

Over the years, others have reviewed many aspects of this literature. We have approached ours in an effort to complement previous contributions. Driver and Easley (1978) drew attention to the specific content of student conceptions as researchers on science learning increasingly rejected the Piagetian stage view of concept development. Smith, diSessa, and Roschelle (1993) cautioned researchers against overlooking the positive contributions of students' conceptions to the learning process. Sinatra and Pintrich (2003) reviewed the connections among metacognition, epistemology, intentional learning, and conceptual change. diSessa (2006) highlighted the disagreements over the coherence versus fragmentation of student conceptions. Scott, Asoko, and Leach (2007) contrasted cognitive and social perspectives on science concept learning. Vosniadou (2008) surveyed the broad scope of the research, which spans student learning, the philosophy and history of science, and research on topics beyond science, including mathematics and history. Mason (2007) discussed attempts to bridge cognitive and social/situated perspectives on conceptual change.

In our review, we take a broad yet loosely historical perspective. While we acknowledge diverse perspectives, we believe that a broad historical view of the field over the last three to four decades reveals some steady progress, which we characterize in terms of three distinguishable (but sometimes overlapping) phases. The first phase (the 1970s and 1980s) was united in revealing the importance of characterizing student conceptions in specific domains, thereby rejecting a domain-general view of concept development. A second phase (1990s and early 2000s) focused on understanding the process of change, recognizing that a range of diverse knowledge elements was involved. The third phase, currently underway, sees researchers increasingly adopting systemic perspectives—characterizing concepts and conceptual change and designing instruction taking into consideration the interaction of various knowledge elements at multiple levels of analysis.

In addition to outlining this three-phase picture of the history, we have a number of parallel objectives. Although we focus on research on conceptual change within science education, we also clarify contributions made by foundational research in developmental psychology and cognitive science. Moreover, while we review research conducted from a variety of perspectives, our engagement with the literature is framed within a cognitive perspective. We assume that understanding student conceptions and conceptual change requires us to posit *internal* mental representations and processes of various kinds, which interact with external representations and social processes. With regard to "bridging the cognitive and sociocultural approaches" to conceptual change, Mason (2007) asks: "Is it feasible?" We assume such bridging is feasible and that this is apparent in the research synthesis that we offer here.

Phase One—Emergence of Domain Specificity and the Importance of Qualitative Reasoning in Science

One can trace the "modern" era of conceptual change as an approach to studying science learning to several sources: widespread attention to students' misconceptions, a broad rejection of empiricism, and psychologists' disenchantment with Piaget's theory. New perspectives in psychology and philosophy of science provided science educators with theoretical frameworks for interpreting students' ideas, understanding learning processes, and designing teaching interventions, although Piaget's influence (both positive and negative) remained strong in science education at large.

On the positive side, Piaget's constructivist and "child-centered" approach prefigured the view that students bring their own ideas to science classrooms and should be constructing their own knowledge. Assimilation and accommodation as engines of conceptual development and the role of measurement and mental schemas (e.g., atomistic schemas) in constructing quantities (e.g., weight and volume; Piaget & Inhelder, 1942) are part of many contemporary views. But his account of development as a succession of stages with different logico-mathematical structures implies a "logical deficit" view of young students that had a detrimental effect on science education. He proposed that *preoperational* children's (preschoolers' and kindergartners') understanding of the physical world is perceptually bound, noncausal, and based on preconcepts; that *concrete operational* children (6- to 12-year-olds) can only reason about concrete situations; and that it is not until the *formal operational* stage (adolescence) that children can reason in a hypothetico-deductive manner and are capable of model-based reasoning and theory building and revision—that is, of scientific thinking (Inhelder, Piaget, Parsons, & Milgram, 1958). His emphasis on hypothetico-deductive reasoning as the hallmark of science missed important aspects of scientific practice such as qualitative reasoning and developing descriptive or even explanatory models (Acher, Arca, & Sanmarti, 2007; Lehrer & Schauble, 2000).

Piaget's view of concepts as sets of necessary and sufficient features, conceptual structure as mainly hierarchical, and class inclusion as essential to achieving concepts is similarly restrictive (i.e., a "classical" view of concepts). Although he related some concepts to each other (e.g., amount to weight and volume), he was essentially focusing on concepts in isolation from each other. Making conservation the cornerstone of achieving concepts of quantities and contingent on logical operations (reversibility, coordination of dimensions) distracts from the complex construction of the *content* of concepts themselves, the more *qualitative* aspects of their meaning, and how they relate to others (e.g., the concept amount of material develops in relation to the concept of material itself).

This overly logico-mathematical view of science, concepts, and learning contributed to the sharp divide that still exists between elementary school standards and curricula, on the one hand, and middle and high school ones, on the other. Perhaps overplaying the limitations of concrete operational thinking, most elementary school science education has been based on atheoretical observations and hands-on experiments (Metz, 1995). Given the centrality of self-regulation of mental structures in Piaget's theory, its focus is not which concepts are presented in what order or on the relationship among concepts themselves but on

the relationship between concepts and logical structures. Moreover, it is easy to (mistakenly) attribute logical (and therefore conceptual) changes to maturation, because Piagetian accounts of how knowledge acquisition can lead to the construction of more powerful logico-mathematical structures are somewhat obscure. In addition, the Piagetian view that elementary school children are inescapably "naïve realists" while high school students are "inescapably" capable of hypothetical reasoning is probably an important reason that the relation between conceptual content and epistemology was not initially explored.

From Domain-General Logical Structures to Domain-Specific Content Structures in Cognitive Science

Starting in the 1970s, several strands of research in psychology challenged Piaget's domain-general account of development with its focus on logical structures. While endorsing constructivism, sharing his concern for the structure of knowledge, and acknowledging that children often have very different ways to interpret the world, developmental psychologists started to question the psychological reality of broad logical structures at different stages of development. Evidence was mounting that preschoolers, although more perceptually bound than older children, can also show evidence of reasoning abilities characteristic of Piaget's concrete operational stage—e.g., distinguishing appearance from reality, expecting cause–effect relations to be mediated by unseen mechanisms, and reasoning in terms of conservation and class inclusion (see Gelman & Baillargeon, 1983). On the other hand, hallmarks of hypothetico-deductive reasoning (e.g., distinguishing theory from evidence, understanding the nature of scientific models) were found to pose major difficulties to most adults and adolescents (Grosslight, Unger, Jay, & Smith, 1991; D. Kuhn, 1989). For children of all ages, reasoning abilities are more advanced in familiar contexts (Donaldson, 1978), suggesting that reasoning involves representations of content as well as logical abilities. Moreover, Piaget's theory could not account for "decalages." If concepts such as number, amount, and weight depend on the acquisition of the same logical structures and operations, why are they not conserved at the same time?

A different line of research, on the "novice-expert shift," strengthened the view that reasoning and some aspects of knowledge structure depend on amount of knowledge in a specific domain. Some children develop extensive knowledge networks in a domain (e.g., dinosaurs), which has far-reaching effects on inference, memory, and categorization performances (Chi, Hutchinson, & Robin, 1989).

Thus there was a shift to a *continuity* view of conceptual change: Children are capable of abstract and rational reasoning from a very young age, but younger children are less likely to display advanced reasoning skills because they *know a lot less* (Carey, 1985a). Making conceptual change *content based* also makes it *domain specific*—for example, the developments of concepts about the physical and mental world are different and independent—and takes care of Piaget's decalages. The continuity view, however, encountered difficulty accounting parsimoniously for the radical qualitative differences in how younger and older children explain some phenomena (e.g., trait inheritance, matter transformations). Help came from T. Kuhn's (1962, 1977) work in the philosophy of science, which provided a framework for privileging content in conceptual change as opposed to logical structure. He viewed theories as "substantive" (rather than logical) systems and proposed that scientific concepts take their meaning from the theories of which they are part. Thus the same term (e.g., force) takes radically different meanings in different theories.

Carey (1985b) used a Kuhnian approach to explain the differences between older and younger children's reasoning as radical changes in the content and relationships of concepts. She contrasted *strong* and *weak restructuring*. In weak restructuring, concepts are enriched, superordinates and other relationships among concepts are acquired, but their core meaning stays the same. In strong restructuring, concepts change; they may differentiate, coalesce, appear, or disappear, and relations among them are fundamentally altered. Explanatory mechanisms and ontology (one's understanding of what kinds of entities there are in the world) also change. For example, Carey proposed that young children think of animals only as "behaving beings," whereas older children think of them as biological entities as well. This change includes a change in domain (young children's behavioral explanations do not apply to plants), in explanations for behaviors such as eating, and in many concepts (e.g., death) and conceptual relations.

The *theory theory* (e.g., Gopnik & Wellman, 1994) was a strong version of Carey's proposal. It highlighted the parallel between children and scientists at the level of theory (vs. conceptual) change and drew attention to young children's use of abstract entities in their explanations (e.g., "A is heavier than B because the *stuff inside is more packed*."). Cognitive scientists were also foregrounding the content, explanatory role, and domain specificity of adult concepts as they were abandoning the classical view for *explanation-based views* in which concepts are "large chunks" of knowledge that explain aspects of the world (Murphy & Medin, 1982).

In sum, cognitive psychologists were developing a new framework for understanding concepts and conceptual change. It was content based and domain specific; assumed that knowledge was organized in deeply similar ways to scientific theories; and foregrounded explanatory causal mechanisms and multiple relations among concepts. It was continuous in that it granted young children the same *kind* of concepts and conceptual organization as adults and that conceptual *content* could be traced across development. It could explain how young children's thinking could be at the same time so similar to and so different from older children's, adults,' and scientists' by proposing that concepts can radically change while the format of representation stays the same.

From Domain-General to Domain-Specific Science Learning

The shift away from a domain-general account of conceptual change found its counterpart in science education. The dominant approach to science education in previous decades had emphasized scientific inquiry and hands-on activities as sources of data from which students were expected to induce general principles, a pedagogy reinforced by Piaget's view of the child as actively constructing knowledge. Underlying this pedagogy (although at odds with Piaget's constructivism) was an *empiricist epistemology*: all knowledge derives from sensory experience and is accretive; if students are trained in the scientific method correctly, they will induce principles that get closer and closer to those of science.

In the 1970s, educators were becoming more and more aware that students of all ages evince profound difficulties with all core scientific ideas (e.g., evolution), principles (e.g., Newton's laws), and models (e.g., models of the earth) and hold beliefs incompatible with those of scientists. The ubiquity and resiliency of student misconceptions testified to the limitations of the "discovery" movement. Classroom observations showed that misconceptions do not result from faulty observations or illogical reasoning. Rather, students interpret observations and assess new ideas in light of their preinstruction conceptions. Widespread consensus developed about a *conceptual change* approach to science teaching, seeking to foster *understanding* and *adoption* of scientific ideas as new systems of interpretation. Kuhn's argument that observations are theory laden and that concepts take their meanings from each other within knowledge systems applied to science students as well (Strike & Posner, 1985). In sharp contrast to this prevalent approach, which we will call the "coherence view," diSessa (1993a) promoted a "knowledge-in-pieces" view—students interpret events in terms of isolated phenomenological primitives ("p-prims"); the goal of science education should be to reorganize those p-prims, subsuming them under scientific concepts and principles.

We refer the reader to several cogent reviews of conceptual change in science education during this period (e.g., Driver & Easley, 1978; Scott, Asoko, & Driver, 1992; Vosniadou & Brewer, 1987). We focus here on two debates: (a) the extent to which students' preconceptions were coherent and (b) the extent to which conceptual change involves transformation versus replacement. While agreeing that instruction should take students' initial ideas into account and scaffold students' understanding of scientific ideas, different theorists characterized the structure of students' ideas in different ways and proposed different instructional models.

The parallel between some students' misconceptions and early scientific ideas (e.g., Aristotelian understanding of motion) combined with the popularity of the theory theory in psychology led to the "knowledge-as-theory" view in science education (e.g., McCloskey, 1983). McCloskey made the strong claim that "people develop on the basis of their everyday experiences remarkably well articulated naïve theories of motion . . . best described as different forms of the same basic theory. [The theory] is strikingly inconsistent with the fundamental principles of classical physics. [It is] similar to [the medieval impetus theory]" (McCloskey, 1983, p. 299). Strike and Posner (1985) softened this position by acknowledging that student theories are not explicit. Adopting a Kuhnian perspective, they proposed a four-step normative model of science learning based on conceptual change as theory change: (1) Students become dissatisfied with their current conceptions, (2) new conceptions are "minimally" understood (i.e., students grasp the new conception sufficiently to want to explore it), (3) the new conception is made plausible (i.e., it explains what the old conception explained and fits with other knowledge and experience), and (4) the new conception is seen as fruitful (i.e., it has greater explanatory power or applies to more phenomena). Moreover, they proposed that conceptual change took place within *conceptual ecologies*—including anomalies, analogies, metaphors, epistemological beliefs, metaphysical beliefs, and knowledge of other areas of enquiry. While not developed empirically, this idea prefigured systemic perspectives we discuss later in this chapter.

Strike and Posner's (1985) model may not have been "Kuhnian enough," however, in the following sense. Missing is one of Kuhn's themes—theories are resistant to change because they consist of networks of interrelated concepts that give meaning to each other. Their purely epistemological and rationalist perspective only addresses why one would choose one theory over another, not how one comes or fails to understand them, and therefore ignores a paradox: In their model, students appraise their existing theory vis-à-vis candidates for replacement, something they can only do in terms of concepts they already possess. At the same time, new concepts take their meaning from the new theory. How can a new concept be meaningful before the whole theory is understood, and how can the whole theory be understood if not one concept at a time? Moreover, evaluating the relative merit of two theories requires epistemological sophistication beyond most students, many of whom have difficulty distinguishing theory from evidence and understanding the nature and function of scientific models.

Carey (1985b), Vosniadou and Brewer (1987), and their collaborators also viewed conceptual learning in science as theory change, but their levels of analysis and the epistemological issues they took into account were different from Posner and Strike's. They characterized the content and structure of children's knowledge before instruction in several domains (biology, the day/night cycle, the Earth, matter, heat/temperature), providing evidence for its theory-like nature and identifying the changes in the relations between concepts inherent to theory change. Theory theorists were constructivists in the sense that they saw children's theories as knowledge structures that were transformed by experience and instruction, not something to replace.

Other theorists (e.g., Driver, Guesne, & Tiberghien, 1985; Nussbaum & Novick, 1982; Osborne & Freyberg, 1985) also viewed children's ideas as coherent but not embedded in theories. Individual interviews, classroom observations, and teaching studies documented children's ideas in many scientific areas, including matter, force, motion, energy, and photosynthesis. Driver (1983) referred to students' ideas as "alternative frameworks" to emphasize the coherence, stability, and rationality of students' knowledge and its resistance to change.

The instructional implications of students' alternative conceptions were clear: Teachers should choose classroom activities and lessons that bring out students' own ideas and help students reflect on them. Educators disagreed, however, on whether students' ideas should be replaced by scientific ones (as advocated by Strike and Posner) or transformed into them. According to the replacement view, teachers should create explicit conflicts between students' and scientific frameworks, make scientific ideas understandable, and promote their adoption (e.g., Driver, 1983). In contrast, the transformation view promoted capitalizing on students' ideas rather than confronting them and restructuring knowledge systems by progressively integrating new pieces of information into them (Osborne & Freyberg, 1985).

Whereas the coherence view treats students' ideas as alternatives to scientific ones (although not necessarily as theories themselves), diSessa saw a profound ontological difference between students' ideas ("p-prims") and scientific theories. *Towards an Epistemology of Physics* (diSessa, 1993a) outlines a theory of knowledge development, which was, in many ways, more specific and richer than the coherence views mentioned in the previous section. It was also radically different from them in some ways but, we will argue, less so than stated in the paper and reflected in subsequent articles.

What diSessa called "naïve physics" consists of a large number of phenomenological primitives or "p-prims." P-prims are small knowledge units, intermediate between percepts and concepts. For example, the "Ohm p-prim" (which has the schematic form "an *agent* is the locus of an impetus that acts against a *resistance* to produce some sort of *result*") implies, "more resistance, less result; more effect, more result." P-prims are "minimally" abstracted from sensorimotor experiences in that they are explanatorily shallow and have limited conscious access; and their use is extremely context dependent, although they can be applied to broad ranges of phenomena. Some p-prims are domain specific, some are not.

To students, p-prims have the same "irreducibility" and explanatory force as theoretical principles do to physicists, but of course they are profoundly different from them. P-prims are weakly organized; they rarely entail one another. There is no rational necessity for applying p-prims to particular contexts. In other words, naïve physics is loosely organized, implicit, and "unreliable" knowledge. However, diSessa saw strong continuity from novice to expert. Students' ideas are not misconceptions, because they are not explicit beliefs but the product of occasional mismatches between p-prims and contexts. Teaching physics should aim at reorganizing p-prims to subsume them under theoretical principles, which form a new level of representation. As they do, p-prims lose their irreducibility to become distributed encodings of the theory. diSessa speculated that equations and verbal statements expressing the theory's laws and principles help organize the p-prims. Each p-prim plays a role in "knowing" a principle; together, they "unpack" the meaning of scientific laws and principles according to contexts.

diSessa contrasted his proposal to McCloskey's, which was not prototypical of the "knowledge-in-theory" view, let alone of the coherence approach as a whole. On epistemological grounds, he questioned attributing to students beliefs that are theoretical, universally applicable, and "false." On empirical grounds, he argued that McCloskey's evidence could be fruitfully reinterpreted in terms of p-prims. Unfortunately, this rebuttal downplayed possible commonalities of the knowledge-in-pieces and coherence views other than McCloskey's and shortchanged in-depth comparisons of various researchers' units of analysis, views of students' ontologies, epistemologies, and conceptual coherence, and of the process of conceptual change itself.

Phase One was the beginning of a paradigm shift, an exploratory phase; research focused mainly on describing the phenomena (students' ideas) that were instrumental in rejecting the old paradigm and finding appropriate frameworks to interpret them and help students develop scientific ideas. Those new frameworks embodied a domain-specific, content-based view of science learning, which still holds today. Ausubel (1968) and Novak (1977) had called attention to the importance of *students' preconceptions* and to the need to answer a number of "big questions": How does students' thinking change over time in reference to core scientific concepts? In what ways do students' existing ideas influence the assimilation of new information? Under what circumstances do "misconceptions" contribute positively to conceptual growth (Ault, Novak, & Gowin, 1988)? As they were beginning to answer those questions, education researchers were discovering that conceptual change was more complex and harder to foster than expected initially and that more sophisticated instructional models were needed.

Phase Two—Recognizing the Multiple Components of Conceptual Change

Phase Two research began to examine the process of conceptual change more closely and, in so doing, identified a variety of cognitive components operating at different levels and varying in their scope of applicability. Of particular interest were the relations between conceptual change and (a) changes in broad ontological categories, (b) increasing sophistication in epistemological beliefs, (c) the use of models and modeling, and (d) the dynamics of communication and social interaction. While there are other influences on conceptual change, we think these four components are inherent to conceptual change in ways other influences are not. We review research in each of these four strands, pointing out influences from fields outside science education as well.

Ontology

As researchers began to explore the processes of change, many noted that learning science concepts was especially difficult when it involved major ontological shifts—for example, from thinking of the Earth as a physical to astronomical object (Vosniadou, 1994), heat as hotness to exchanged energy (Wiser & Amin, 2001), or force as a property or material substance to a constraint-based interaction (Chi, 1992). Ontology became an object of study in its own right in an effort to understand sources of coherence in naïve views and resistance to change. However, researchers varied in how they characterized naïve and scientific ontologies, saw the relation between the two, and designed instruction to develop scientific ontologies. For Chi (1992), naïve and scientific ontological categories were defined in domain-general terms and were thought to be amenable to direct instruction via replacement strategies. For others, the development of ontological categories was seen as a gradual transformational process building on precursor concepts and tied to multiple domain-specific processes of theory change (Nersessian, 1989; Vosniadou, 1994; Wiser & Amin, 2001). Vosniadou (1994) also proposed that ontological and epistemological commitments defined a broad framework theory that constrained how students formed more specific models and theories.

Chi's influential domain-general approach rests on the assumption that concepts belong to categories and inherit the properties of the category to which they are assigned. Building on the work of Keil (1979), she viewed ontologies as broad categories (e.g., *material entities, processes*, and *mental states*) within abstract hierarchical trees and the predicates that can span terms that designate concepts in the hierarchy. She and her colleagues were especially interested in students' understandings of distinctions within the ontological category of *processes*, because many science concepts are processes, and modern science has changed the fundamental way we think about them. For example, Chi and Slotta (1993) contrasted the subcategory of *events* (time-bound, causal processes that are part of our commonsense ontology) with *constraint-based interactions* (an ontological subcategory they proposed was important in science but missing in everyday ontology). They argued that students have difficulty with many physics concepts, such as force, heat, diffusion, and natural selection, because they assign them to the wrong ontological category (e.g., *substances, properties of substances*, or *direct causal events* rather than *constraint-based interactions*). Student use of substance-based predicates such as "blocks," "contains," "moves" instead of interaction-based predicates such as "transfers," "occurs simultaneously," and "is in equilibrium" provided evidence for their claim (Slotta, Chi, & Joram, 1995).

Chi's instructional remedy involved replacement strategies: (a) First, provide *direct instruction* about the new ontological category and its general properties, and then (b) directly teach students that the concept in question is a member of the new category. Instruction also had a domain-general flavor: For example, students were taught about the new category of constraint-based interactions in the context of air expansion and liquid diffusion and then asked to apply it to learning about electric current (Slotta & Chi, 2006). Finally, to prevent students from developing a faulty ontology for the new concepts, she recommended "expunging" material-based language and analogies in both teacher explanations and texts.

In contrast, the theory-change proponents viewed the development of ontological categories as part and parcel of theory change. They assumed greater variety in the ontological categories available to the student and took a *transformation* rather than *replacement* view of change. Precursors are built on via multiple coordinated changes in content, epistemology, and representational tools. As a result, elements of the naïve ontology are not expunged but are reanalyzed, integrated, and explained within the emerging theory.

For example, Nersessian (1989) used her analysis of the development of "an inertial frame of reference" in the history of science (from medieval impetus theorists to Galileo to Newton) to inform her understanding of the structure of student ideas about force and motion and how students might be similarly led to construct an understanding of Newtonian ideas. She focused on changes in an entire conceptualization that includes multiple linked concepts. In contrast to Chi, she proposed a richer set of everyday ontological concepts (e.g., the medieval view includes categories of *place, process, motion, state, property, space*, and *body*) and argued that the construction of Newtonian ideas involves *many* ontological shifts (e.g., motion shifts from a *process* to a *state* like rest, and concepts originally conceived of as *properties* such as force, heaviness, and speed become reanalyzed as *relations*; other categories, such as *place* and *process*, are no longer important in the revised conceptualization). For her, ontological shifts are difficult not because students lack the top-level categories but because "abstract entities need to be constructed . . . that only exist in mental models. For example, a Newtonian object is a point mass moving in an idealized Euclidean space" (p. 178). Thus, just as Galileo used thought experiments and limiting case analysis to help his colleagues construct new abstract representations, so too should teachers help students develop and use a repertoire of "abstraction techniques" to bridge from their everyday intuitions to more precise quantitative models.

Wiser and Amin (2001) provided another detailed account of the ontological difficulties students face and how they should be handled from a theory change perspective. The central ontological categories they considered are heat as *hotness* versus *exchanged energy*, both domain-specific ontological categories. They argued that students' difficulty is not with understanding the energy exchanges that occur among colliding particles but in recognizing their relevance to their concept of heat. Their multipronged instructional approach, therefore, first works to *enhance* student understanding of these energy exchanges via computer modeling activities, before explicitly contrasting the scientists' definition of "heat" as "exchanged energy" with students' idea that heat is inherently hot. Rather than ignoring students' everyday concept in their teaching, they worked to help students reanalyze hotness as a perceptual rather than objective property and to see how their perceptual experiences can be explained in terms of the interaction of their perceptual system with physical variables. Like Chi, however, they regard the ontological stumbling block as important and needing explicit attention before addressing other topics in thermodynamics such as the differentiation of heat and temperature and the quantification of heat.

In contrast to these researchers, diSessa (1993b) was more skeptical about whether novices have any ontological categories or commitments, at least in the area of naïve mechanics, and if they do, whether they are that constraining. More recently, however, knowledge-in-pieces researchers have begun to theorize about the "ontological resources" of novices, and ontological classification has been reexamined from a knowledge-in-pieces perspective. We discuss this new work in our review of Phase Three research.

Epistemology

In Phase One, the focus was on highlighting *domain-specific cognitive elements* at variance with the ideas of scientists and the challenges they posed for science learning. The ways limitations in students' general *metacognitive* capabilities pose challenges for content learning were hinted at but largely unexplored. Instead, children's lack of meta-conceptual knowledge and skill was used to explain poor performance on various tasks despite substantial conceptual knowledge and reasoning skills being in place.

In Phase Two, researchers began to explore whether known developments in metacognitive capabilities (including epistemological beliefs) might be implicated in the process of conceptual change itself. The assumption was that greater understanding of the processes of knowledge construction enables the learner to become more aware of her changing conceptions and take control of the learning process. Developing greater epistemological understanding of science had long been an important, independent aim of science education, but now a new reason its development might be important emerged—promoting conceptual change itself.

As in many aspects of research on conceptual change, key terms are used in a variety of ways. Briefly, we take "metacognition" to be a broad term that encompasses more specific types of knowledge and strategies that take any aspect of cognition as an object of thought. These include thinking about concepts (metaconceptual), memory (metamemory), language (metalinguistic), diverse learning processes (memorizing, understanding), and knowledge (epistemology), among others. The last—epistemology—is particularly important to clarify because it has been seen as potentially central in the study of conceptual change. "Epistemology" refers to that aspect of metacognition that deals specifically with the nature of knowledge, including its sources, its structure, its justification, and its limits (Hofer & Pintrich, 1997; Sandoval, 2005). Metacognition (including epistemology) can also be categorized in terms of its declarative (e.g., beliefs) and strategic (e.g., monitoring, self-regulation) aspects (Brown, 1978; Flavell, 1976).

Metacognitive knowledge and strategies can be studied from early childhood, and there is a vast developmental literature examining its beginnings and transformations (see Kitchener, 1983; Kuhn, 2000, for reviews). Children's capacity for simple metacognitive reflection and monitoring is present in the preschool years but greatly expands in elementary school, when comprehension monitoring improves and learning becomes more strategic (Kuhn, 2000). In contrast, most work on epistemic cognition focuses on adolescents and adults, because it is assumed to be a "late" aspect of metacognitive development. Although even preschoolers make some distinction between "knowing" and "believing" and hence have some resources for developing epistemological beliefs about knowledge and its justification (Montgomery, 1992), schools typically present science as a "rhetoric of conclusions" (Schwab, 1964), affording little opportunity for students to develop more sophisticated epistemological views of science. Indeed, it is common for middle and high school students to have "knowledge unproblematic" views of science (Carey & Smith, 1993), with more sophisticated epistemological views only emerging in late adolescence and the college years, if at all (see Hofer & Pintrich, 1997, for review). Studies show that K–12 students think the goals of science concern simple description of what happens rather than deeper explanation (Carey, Evans, Honda, Jay, & Unger, 1989; Driver, Leach, Millar, & Scott, 1996). They think of experiments as finding out "what works" instead of as testing competing explanatory hypotheses (Carey et al., 1989; Schauble, Klopfer, & Ragavan, 1991). For them, models are concrete replicas rather than tools for developing and revising theories (Grosslight et al., 1991). Here, we review literature that explicitly connects epistemological beliefs and conceptual change.

How might epistemological beliefs impact conceptual change? First, they may *directly affect* what students pay attention to in a situation (Stathopoulou & Vosniadou, 2007a). For example, students who think science involves only *description* may be more likely to focus on isolated or salient facts, whereas those who think it involves *explanatory hypotheses and theories* may look for organizing principles and patterns of relationships. Students who think science is *certain* and *unchanging* may avoid thinking about data that conflict with their ideas, whereas students who think theories develop and change in response to disconfirming evidence may embrace such anomalies as a chance to learn something new.

Second, students' epistemological beliefs may have *indirect effects* through activating *goals*, which in turn elicit *strategies* that promote or impede learning (Stathopoulou & Vosniadou, 2007a). Some strategies might affect learning in general ways. For example, the belief in simple knowledge may activate the goal to *memorize* information, which elicits superficial processing strategies such as rote rehearsal; in contrast, the belief that knowledge is complex may activate the goal to *understand* information, eliciting deeper processing strategies (e.g., making connections, integrating ideas). Other goals and strategies may be more specific to conceptual change in science. For example, in the classic conceptual change model of Strike and Posner (1985, 1992), students need to activate goals of identifying competing claims, monitoring their intelligibility, and competitively evaluating them based on their fit with other ideas, valued epistemological standards, and new research evidence.

Finally, there may be *interactive effects*: Whether epistemological assumptions support or impede learning may depend upon instructional context. For example, a classroom that is supportive of conceptual change may mitigate the negative effects of a less favorable personal epistemology (and even serve to develop more constructivist views), while traditional learning environments may exacerbate the differences.

A number of *correlational* studies have shown links between more sophisticated epistemologies and deeper conceptual understanding in particular domains. For example, Songer and Linn (1991) found that after an innovative unit on thermodynamics, middle school students who held dynamic rather than static views of science were more likely to have differentiated heat and temperature. Stathopoulou and Vosniadou (2007b) found that 10th graders with more sophisticated epistemological views about the structure, construction, and stability of physics knowledge scored higher on the Force and Motion Conceptual Evaluation instrument after a traditionally taught physics unit. Using in-depth interviews with university physics students, Hammer (1994) found a strong relation between more constructivist epistemological beliefs (focusing on coherence, concepts, and independent effort) and deeper physics understanding. May and Etkina (2002) found that college students who started with low scores on the Force Concept Inventory and who made dramatic learning gains had more constructivist ideas about what and how they were learning and the coherence of physics knowledge (as expressed in weekly reflection journals) than a comparable group at pretest who made little gain.

Case studies and experimental designs provide stronger evidence for the causal connection between epistemology, reflection on learning, and conceptual change. Some case studies have outlined mechanisms by which epistemological views may *limit* the physics learning of otherwise capable high school or college students. For example, some students expect that science relies only on formal reasoning and therefore do not think conflicts between formal and informal reasoning need to be reconciled (e.g., Hammer, 1994; Lising & Elby, 2005). Some research has sought to understand the processes by which more sophisticated epistemologies and conceptions of learning could be developed to *support* conceptual change. For example, Sister Gertrude Hennessey designed an entire elementary school science curriculum to help students develop their ideas about many challenging science topics by engaging them in cycles of testing and revising their ideas to meet emerging classroom epistemological standards (e.g., clarity, generalizability). Students also learned to evaluate the changing status of their and others' ideas using the language of Strike and Posner's conceptual change model ("intelligibility," "plausibility," and "fruitfulness"). Her students not only developed more sophisticated constructivist epistemological views of science and learning (Hennessey, 2003; Smith, Maclin, Houghton, & Hennessey, 2000) but also used those as tools to develop greater conceptual understanding of difficult science content such as Newton's laws of motion (Beeth, 1998).

Experimental studies at the elementary, middle school, and college levels provided evidence that enriching good curricula either with written reflective self-assessments or explicit attention to epistemological issues enhanced students' metacognitive understandings and conceptual change gains compared to outcomes observed for *those same curricular experiences* without those enhancements. For example, Mason and Boscolo (2000) added "writing to learn" activities to a best-practices fourth-grade unit about plant growth, nutrition, and photosynthesis (e.g., students learned to regularly use writing to reflect on what they learned, express doubt, make predictions, and compare new explanations with previous ones). Students in the writing-to-learn class not only developed greater metaconceptual awareness of the process of conceptual change but also made more progress on conceptual understanding than a control classroom that had the same unit without the writing activities. Redish and Hammer (2009) found that a redesigned college physics course that emphasized "learning how to learn physics" (building coherence, thinking in terms of mechanisms, considering implications of assumptions) in addition to other best practices not only enhanced students' epistemological expectations but also produced better pre-post gains on the Force Concept Inventory than previous versions of the course. Finally, White and Frederiksen (1998) studied multiple classes of seventh- to ninth-grade students in which students investigated force and motion through constructing a progressive series of models using innovative software. Half the classes also engaged in repeated self-assessment (using explicit criteria related to understanding science content, process, and habits of mind), while the other half did not. Those classes with self-assessment demonstrated better gains on measures of understanding of inquiry processes and on one of two physics knowledge measures. There was also evidence students' understanding of inquiry contributed to their learning of physics content in this curricular environment.

In sum, there is a convincing body of research establishing a connection between epistemological sophistication and conceptual change. Although more needs to be learned about what aspects of epistemology are most important, under what conditions, and through what mechanisms, conceptual change is promoted by encouraging students to (a) reflect on the development of their own ideas in situations in which they are engaged in authentic knowledge-construction practices, (b) develop shared norms and epistemological standards for evaluating ideas, and (c) pay attention to anomalies or inconsistencies between formal and informal methods and work to resolve them. Most studies, however, have focused on force and motion. Concept learning in different domains may make some distinctive epistemological demands (e.g., the relation between formulas, concepts, and laws is critical for force and motion; the ideas of explanatory model and macro and micro levels of description and emergent processes may be more important for atomic-molecular theory). Exploring these potential interactions with science domain is central to the more systemic approaches considered in Phase Three.

Models and Modeling

Phase Two research also began to examine the role of models and modeling in the process of change. We consider a *model* to be a structural analog of a thing or a process. A *scientific* model is a simplified representation of a natural object or phenomenon that captures its central structural relations. A model can be internal, in the form of a *mental* model, or external, embodied in various types of representations (e.g., diagrams, three-dimensional objects). We consider *modeling* to be those processes that lead to the construction of models. An example is analogical reasoning, which involves the use of a familiar, well-understood (source) domain of knowledge as a basis for improving understanding of a less familiar (target) domain.

The 1980s saw emerging interest in models and modeling in a variety of fields. In cognitive science, it was suggested that reasoning, even logical reasoning, was grounded in analogical mental models (Johnson-Laird, 1983) and that analogical structure mapping allowed the construction of novel understanding via the transfer of relations between domains (Gentner, 1983). In history and philosophy of science, there was interest in the role of models in representing scientific theories (Giere, 1988) and modeling in novel theory construction (Nersessian, 1992). In science education, the construct of mental model was used to characterize some student conceptions, and analogies had been recognized as instructional tools for some time (see Duit, 1991, for a review).

We focus here on work characterizing the role of models and modeling in the *process* of conceptual change and instruction, tackling the following themes: (1) using visual representations and concrete situations in guiding students' construction of mental models that deepen understanding; (2) considering the appropriate level of abstraction at which to identify entry points and the appropriate sequencing of models in instruction; (3) using multiple, coordinated models that capture different aspects (both qualitative and quantitative) of scientific concepts; (4) presenting students with ready-made models versus engaging them in model construction; and (5) attending to students' epistemological sophistication as a prerequisite for and outcome of instruction using models and modeling. Our review highlights these key themes but not separately, because individual studies often addressed more than one theme.

Brown, Clement, and Minstrell (Brown & Clement, 1989; Clement, 1993; Minstrell, 1982) sought to build student understanding of Newtonian concepts using intuitive knowledge elements they called "anchoring intuitions"—for example, students' understanding of normal forces was grounded in their intuitions that a spring exerts an upward force on an object placed on it. This was an intelligible analog of the less transparent (target) situation of a table exerting a normal force on a book resting on it. But students often found the analogy between the two situations implausible. Therefore, Brown and Clement (1989) proposed using a "bridging analogy" that retained key features of the "anchoring intuition" but resembled the target situation more closely (e.g., a book on a thin, and thus slightly springy, plank of wood). The rationale for their approach was that anchoring intuitions and bridging analogies supported students' construction of analogical *explanatory* models of the target situation that incorporated key intuitions (e.g., modeling a wooden table as made of microscopic springs exerting upward forces on a book placed on it).

The work of Smith (Smith, Maclin, Grosslight, & Davis, 1997; Smith, Snir, & Grosslight, 1992) and Wiser (1995; Wiser & Amin, 2001) was based on the idea that certain concepts—for example, heat/temperature and weight/density—are differentiated in science but undifferentiated in the learner before instruction. In both cases, a learner possesses an undifferentiated perceptually based concept (i.e., "hotness" and "felt weight"), and computer-based visual representations were designed that could embody the scientific concepts and the relationships between them and be intuitively compelling. For example, the heating of an object could be represented using a variety of models, such as (a) the number of Es entering a rectangle/object from a hotplate and (b) the number of Es per molecule with numbers inside partial circles representing the molecule. The models embodied the distinction between the extensive concept of heat (total Es added) and the intensive concept of temperature ("packedness" of Es per molecule). A "grid-and-dots" model captured the extensive/intensive distinction between weight and density, with dots representing weight units, boxes representing volume units, and dots per box representing density. This model was at the center of programs that provided progressively more complex modeling possibilities embedded in investigations of density of materials, floatation, and thermal expansion. The distinct visual representations of key quantities encouraged metaconceptual discussion of the contrasting meanings of terms and the nature of models as well as simplified the quantitative aspect of the domains in question. Both approaches supported the differentiation of key concepts.

In related work, White (1995; White & Frederiksen, 1998) designed an inquiry-oriented, computer-based learning environment within which students engaged with multiple models to investigate forces and motion at different levels of abstraction. The research made the case for the value of models at an *intermediate level* of abstraction as an entry point for instruction, as well as the progressive construction of models of more complex microworlds (e.g., motion without gravity before motion with). Central to the design was building on and extending student intuitions to make sense of the motion of a dot in a simulated Newtonian microworld. Students used a joystick to impart "impulses" that changed the speed of the dot by one unit with each impulse. The speed of the dot was represented via points left in the wake of the movement of the dot. The "dot-print" representation was at an intermediate degree of abstraction in between the immediacy yet complexity of real object motion and mathematical formulations of Newton's laws. In this way, students could construct qualitative understandings and formulations of laws governing a Newtonian world that were easier to align with mathematical representations. This learning environment was successful in developing middle school students' conceptual understanding of Newtonian mechanics, as well as their inquiry and modeling skills and understanding of laws.

The research reviewed so far made use of *ready-made models* provided by researchers. Although these models were designed to be interpreted both qualitatively and quantitatively, qualitative reasoning was seen as an initial step to address problematic misconceptions to be followed by mathematization. One problem with ready-made models, noted by Wiser and Amin (2002), is that while students might understand the analog models themselves, they do not readily map them onto their existing concepts (e.g., heat/temperature) that are being targeted by instruction. A different line of research has approached science learning from the perspective that model *construction* and mathematical reasoning are central to scientific practice and so should be central to the practice of science education as well (Lehrer & Schauble, 2000; Lehrer, Schauble, Carpenter, & Penner, 2000; Lehrer, Schauble, Strom, &

Pligge, 2003). Lehrer and Schauble (2000) proposed a taxonomy of models that can be seen as a possible developmental corridor, with students progressing gradually to more abstract models over extended (multiyear) periods of time: three-dimensional microcosms (e.g., a globe), maps and other two-dimensional representations, syntactic models (e.g., probability models), and hypothetical-deductive models (e.g., kinetic model of gases).

In this model *construction* approach, students are given design or inquiry tasks driven by a goal or question. For example, in Lehrer and colleagues (2000), second graders explored the motion of objects rolling down inclined planes in the context of designing Lego cars that go down a track "as quickly" or "as slowly" as possible. As they worked, children encountered conceptual obstacles, and teachers guided the students in their attempts to solve these problems, with an emphasis on the use of inscriptions of various kinds. The conventions of representation and modeling were not taught directly but emerged over the course of student work. Lehrer and colleagues argue that presenting ready-made inscriptions or models rather than expecting students to construct these when the need arises will often result in students misunderstanding both the general representational function of the model and the specific mappings between the model and the entities it represents.

Because the scientific topics addressed in this approach are motivated by student questions that emerge during instruction, many challenging conceptual domains have not been studied from this perspective. But Lehrer and colleagues (2003) have shown how this kind of modeling instruction can drive fifth graders' differentiation of weight and density, reaching a level of understanding in a difficult domain often found challenging to middle school students. They argue that if students develop strong mathematical concepts of measure and similarity first, this can support more sophisticated modeling of physical phenomena and drive conceptual change.

One way to contrast the ready-made models versus the model-construction approach is in terms of the simplicity or complexity of the quantitative reasoning targeted and the time scale of interventions. The ready-made-models approach involves interventions on the order of months and aims to simplify quantitative reasoning, focusing instead on supporting learners in constructing deeper theoretical understanding of the domain in question, using existing mathematical knowledge. The model-construction approach, involving multiyear interventions, aims to engage students in complex quantitative reasoning that is grounded in conceptual understanding of measure. No research has explicitly evaluated the relative effectiveness of ready-made models versus model-construction approaches. While such comparison might yield interesting results, more worthwhile might be the comparison of affordances of the two approaches for future learning. We discuss this line of work on long-term learning progressions in our review of Phase Three research.

In sum, research on models and modeling made progress in highlighting the role of analogical restructuring and the strategic recruiting of intuitive knowledge in the process of conceptual change. It also drew attention to the relationship between qualitative and quantitative understanding. In addition, it attracted researchers' attention to the interplay among conceptual change, processes of model-based reasoning, and epistemological understanding about modeling. Phase Three research extends this pioneering work by developing more explicit accounts of the format and interaction of internal and external representations, social interaction, and epistemological development.

Social Interaction

Phase Two research on conceptual change also began to examine the role of social interaction in the process of conceptual change. Our review includes *only* research that has addressed social interaction processes in relation to scientific *concept* learning specifically. (See Scott et al., 2007, for a review that takes a broader perspective on social processes in science learning.) Three (complementary) perspectives are considered. Research from a *sociocultural perspective* on learning (Vygotsky, 1978; Wertsch, 1991) assumes that internalization of knowledge results from two types of social interactions: scaffolding provided to learners by those more knowledgeable and knowledge jointly constructed by peers. The goal of this research is to show that social interaction (in general) enhances concept learning and to describe the kind of scaffolding that allows students to participate in effective discourse. Research from a *discourse analysis perspective* sought to describe the details of communication occurring in these interactions that allows *convergence* among diverse ideas. In contrast, research from a *Piagetian (1995) perspective* examined the role of cognitive conflict arising from interaction between peers with different ideas in a domain, challenging the assumption that internalization was the sole mechanism by which social interactions affects conceptual change.

Research on science concept learning conducted from a sociocultural perspective emphasizes that scientific concepts are learned not through direct experience but through guidance in appropriating a way of seeing the world embedded in a symbolically constructed reality (Driver, Asoko, Leach, Mortimer, & Scott, 1994). For example, scientists think about/see/analyze the world in terms of abstract and symbolically represented theoretical concepts. Further, although they explicitly reflect on "theory," "predictions," "results" and their relations, these analytic categories are cultural constructions that are not obvious to young students. Driver and colleagues (1994) argued that through classroom discourse, students can be "scaffolded" into a scientific way of talking about (and thereby "seeing") the world.

A prominent example of research that attempted to so structure the discourse of science classrooms and examine its effects on concept learning is Herrenkohl, Palincsar, DeWater, and Kawasaki (1999). In this study, upper elementary students were assigned roles to scaffold inquiry and participation in scientific thinking practices during investigations of flotation and sinking. *Procedural* roles structured students' efficient completion of the small-group investigations and *audience* roles (e.g., questioners, commentators) focused on particular tasks (e.g., checking predictions and theories, summarizing results, and evaluating the relationship among predictions, theories, and results) during whole-group discussion. In this way, engaging in a complex task was broken up into parts, and students were encouraged to focus on the particular kinds of thinking expected of them. Analysis of transcripts of classroom conversations showed the progress students made in appropriating these roles over the 10-week unit. Moreover, pre- and posttests revealed dramatically improved conceptual understanding of floatation (that drew on an understanding of density) and better explicit understanding of predictions, theories, scientific problem solving, and how scientific ideas are evaluated.

Other sociocultural researchers have explored the effect of peer interaction on concept learning in a series of experimental studies using the hypothesis-experiment-instruction (HEI) method. In one study (Hatano & Inagaki, 1991), a control group of students was asked to select from a number of possible predictions about a physical phenomenon and was then presented with a text providing an authoritative answer. An experimental group included the additional component of asking students to discuss their predictions with one another before being presented with the correct prediction. Significantly more students in the experimental condition, which included discussion among peers, produced better-quality explanations than the control condition.

If social interaction contributes to concept learning, this connection may be mediated by the details of communication between interlocutors. During Phase Two, some researchers began to examine the details of communication, highlighting the features of communication they thought were most relevant to understanding the process of concept learning. For example, Pea (1994) suggested that concept learning is more likely to occur when interlocutors transform their understandings together as they negotiate interpretations of each other's utterances, trying to arrive at common ground. Pea also suggests that effective science concept learning will occur when learners' communication is modeled on that of scientists, involving the sharing of multiple interpretations of phenomena and requests for clarification from each other about the meaning of representations.

Other researchers adopted a similar discourse-oriented perspective on conceptual change (Duit, Roth, Komorek, & Wilbers, 1998; Roschelle, 1992), drawing on methods of conversational analysis (Garfinkel & Sacks, 1970; Goodwin & Heritage, 1990) to describe the types of *conversational moves* occurring when students engage in collaborative learning activities. For example, Roschelle

(1992) suggested that interlocutors' understanding will converge as a result of conversational moves related specifically to conceptual change (e.g., constructing representations of the key entities and processes underlying natural phenomena and coordinating metaphors to interpret the representations) and others that help establish convergence (e.g., engaging in cycles of "displaying, confirming, and repairing" meanings and applying increasingly higher standards of evidence for establishing convergence in the meanings constructed by participants). Overall, the conversational interactions seen by these researchers as relevant to conceptual change align with the audience roles of questioning and commenting that Herrenkohl and colleagues (1999) included in their intervention but focuses more on the dynamics of negotiating the interpretation of representations in contrast to Herrenkohl and colleagues' emphasis on the broader structures of participation and participant roles.

The research reviewed so far assumes that students construct novel conceptual understandings by *internalizing* knowledge provided by teachers or jointly constructed with peers. A different body of literature took as its starting point the Piagetian (Piaget, 1995) view that conceptual conflict is an important driver of knowledge change. Howe and colleagues (1992) considered the possibility that individual, *internal* constructions provoked by disagreements during interaction might be the source of change rather than joint constructions. Carefully controlled experimental studies bore out this hypothesis in the context of elementary children's collaborative inquiry into different topics, including motion down an inclined plane (Howe, Tolmie, & Rodgers, 1992). Student gains in conceptual understanding were greater when students were placed in groups with different (rather than similar) ideas about the topic. Moreover, while significant correlations were found between group-level performance and degree of agreement within a group, there was no significant correlation between within-group change and individual student gains for student groups whose members had different ideas. This research also identified domain differences, with private conflict resolution being more important in physics than in biology (Williams & Tolmie, 2000). More recent research in this tradition has begun to examine more closely the relative importance of joint and individual constructions and the interactions between group-level and individual-level mechanisms (Howe, 2009; Howe, McWilliam, & Cross, 2005). An interesting finding emerging from this literature is the connection between unresolved conflict in group interactions and long-term conceptual gains.

In sum, the research just reviewed suggests that a variety of mechanisms are at work, mediating the influence of social interaction on conceptual change. Effective concept learning in the context of social interaction seems to require carefully thought-out scaffolding of scientific discourse on the part of teachers. However, the research also suggests that we must be cautious in assuming internalization of group products as the sole mechanism of individual concept change in the context of social interaction. Individual cognitive constructions driven by group-level conflict might also be an important (if not primary) mechanism of change in some domains. Overall, research in this area suggests that there are important connections between the roles of social interaction and epistemology in conceptual change, connections that future research will need to explore.

Phase Three—Emerging Systemic Perspectives on Conceptual Change

In this final section, we highlight emerging *systemic* perspectives on conceptual change and suggest directions for future research. Some researchers use a particular approach to systemic thinking—for example, Brown and Hammer (2008) use dynamic systems theory. However, we use the term "systemic" informally to capture a tendency among researchers to understand conceptual change in terms of multiple interacting elements, often at different levels of analysis. We begin by describing attempts to understand concepts and conceptual change from various systemic perspectives, pointing out implications for instruction. Next, we describe research that has investigated instructional designs based on a systemic understanding of conceptual change.

Understanding Concepts and Conceptual Change From Systemic Perspectives

We frame our review in terms of four foundational themes in cognitive science. First, concepts are grounded in multiple image-schemas (abstractions from sensorimotor experience) and imagery (reenactments of perceptual experience). Second, the use of language and other external symbolic systems overcomes the limitations of image-schematic representations and imagery. Third, propositionally expressed concepts can be understood as language-like symbols that participate in networks of beliefs. This idea resolves some tensions among competing accounts of conceptual change. Fourth, the conceptual knowledge of young children and laypersons is sparse. But because this sparse knowledge is associated with epistemological beliefs that more specific knowledge exists, the source of which is often other people, it supports further learning. Together, these four sets of ideas reflect an increasingly systemic turn in cognitive scientists' thinking about concepts and conceptual change.

Concepts and conceptual change are grounded in perception and action. We begin by clarifying some key constructs. As these have occupied philosophers and psychologists for centuries, we will only clarify how we use them here, drawing on extended treatments of others (Barsalou, 1999; Carey, 2009; Mandler, 2004). We assume *perception* to be an automatic process, carried out by innately specified systems that provide the mind with analogical representations of the here and now, resulting in sensorimotor experience. What makes these systems perceptual is that they

automatically provide the mind with *rich* representations of entities in the outside world. We understand a *conceptual* representation to be one that can be productively combined with others, supports inferences about real and imagined entities, and can be articulated with language. Thus, a conception is accessible to different aspects of cognition. We assume that innate *perceptual* processes can generate some *conceptual* representations of objects, agency, number, and cause, referred to as "core cognition" (Carey, 2009).

The construct *image-schema* captures the idea that through repeated sensorimotor experiences and processes of selective attention, commonalities across those experiences are extracted, forming more schematic structures. Image-schemas are analogical (iconic) representations that structurally resemble the objects and events represented in perception. For example, an image-schema of containment, with the components *inside, outside,* and *a boundary separating the two,* can be abstracted from many similar experiences of putting objects in and removing them from various containers. Despite being analogical representations, image-schemas are *conceptual* in the sense clarified above. While conceptual, they are not propositional, language-like representations, with an arbitrary symbolic relationship to what they represent, but resemble their referents. However, they are not to be equated with imagery, analogical "movie-like" re-enactments of perceptions/actions in the mind's eye, invoked in the absence of the actual objects and events of the world they represent. Because imagery is unanalyzed and holistic, it cannot on its own support productive conceptual combination, inferences, and articulation with language.

There is considerable agreement on the importance of image-schematic representations, especially in *preverbal* conception (Barsalou, 1999; Carey, 2009; Mandler, 2004). However, there is disagreement regarding how image-schemas are constructed. While Mandler (2004) suggests that the processes of abstraction and selective attention are sufficient, Carey (2009) has persuasively argued that innate, core conceptual representations are needed to constrain the process of abstraction from sensorimotor representations. It has also been suggested that adult concepts, including abstract concepts, are represented in terms of multiple image-schemas. For example, Barsalou and Wiemer-Hastings (2005) have suggested that the difference between concrete and abstract concepts is not in the *format* of the concepts' representation but in complexity. They provide evidence that whereas the representations of situations or events are backgrounded in the representation of concrete concepts, they are foregrounded in the case of abstract concepts. Another proposal, based on analysis of patterns of language use, is that many abstract concepts are understood *metaphorically* in terms of image-schemas (Lakoff & Johnson, 1980, 1999). The claim is that systematic conceptual mappings exist between abstract and experiential *conceptual* domains ("conceptual metaphors")—for example, states are construed as possessions (as in "He *has* a headache"); time as a resource (as in

"Time is *running out*"). This view of abstract concepts as grounded in perception and action has also contributed to accounts of scientific concepts and model-based representations of scientific theories and reasoning (Clement, 2008; Nersessian, 2008; Thagard, 2012).

This idea that concepts are grounded in image-schemas extends to science concept learning research in Phase Three, as researchers continue use of the constructs p-prim and mental model. Most researchers drawing on the notion of p-prim treat it as an image-schema (e.g., Ke, Monk, & Duschl, 2005; Sherin, 2006), which seemed to be the intended sense in the most explicit and extended account of the construct (diSessa, 1993a). While some have used the construct without a strict image-schematic interpretation (e.g., D. Clark, 2006), we believe that it is useful to so limit the interpretation of p-prims. This emphasizes their origin in perception and action and clearly distinguishes them from other knowledge elements of different format, such as propositionally formulated beliefs. Assuming that scientific concepts are grounded in image-schematic p-prims was a key contribution of the knowledge-in-pieces view described earlier and continues to be an important assumption in much of Phase Three research, consistent with the cognitive science literature more broadly.

The notion of a mental model also continues to be used. While earlier research was not always explicit about the representational format of mental models (Gentner & Stevens, 1983), recent work has been more explicit in viewing mental models as consisting of imagistic simulations of perceived objects and events, interpreted in terms of multiple image-schemas (Clement, 2008; Nersessian, 2008). Since they are constituted by image-schemas, mental models are *conceptual* representations. Methods are now being explored to provide evidence of the format of mental models and their image-schematic and imagistic constituents, relying on the analysis of gestures and drawings used by scientists and students as they engage in creative analogical and extreme-case reasoning and thought experiment (Stephens & Clement, 2010). Another method of identifying image-schematic representations of relevance to science learning focuses on the analysis of the language of science from the perspective of the theory of conceptual metaphor (Amin, 2009; Amin, Jeppsson, Haglund, & Strömdahl, 2012; Jeppsson, Haglund, Amin, & Strömdahl, 2013).

What are the instructional implications of the assumption that scientific concepts and reasoning might be grounded in image-schemas and imagistic simulation? Because multiple image-schemas need to be activated, organized, and reorganized during science concept learning in ways that are highly sensitive to context, there is no "quick tell" in concept formation. This implies the importance of presenting concepts in *contexts of their use*. While this idea has long been a staple of "reform" science curricula, recognizing the importance of a complex, non-verbal component to concept formation indicates that this approach is not just desirable but *necessary*.

In addition, while mental models have been found to ground understanding of scientific concepts, other representational resources are needed. Since most scientific models include very abstract and often quantified entities and processes, they will need propositional symbol systems (such as language and equations) to represent them (see next subsection). Recognizing that the image-schemas and imagery that constitute mental models are shared by learners and scientists suggests that scientific models with more iconic components are likely to be more accessible entry points for instruction. For example, Lehrer and Schauble (2006) have argued that initial models based on *resemblance* are important starting points for elementary school students' modeling; with appropriate instruction, students can construct progressively more sophisticated models drawing on language or equations. Moreover, research (Wilensky & Novak, 2010; Wilensky & Reisman, 2006) has explored the use of "agent-centered modeling" in supporting understanding of emergent processes in many domains (e.g., electricity, population biology), a widely recognized instructional challenge (Chi, 2005; Perkins & Grotzer, 2005). Students first create agent-based models consisting of objects with specific properties; then they run the models on computers that use visual representations to help students "see" the consequences at another level (the emergent properties of aggregates).

A final instructional implication is based on identifying the set of conceptual metaphors that construe a given scientific concept. Once these are known, they can guide the design of visual representations that aim to foster conceptual change (Amin, 2009; Scherr, Close, McKagan, & Vokos, 2012) and guide the strategic selection of particular analogies (Amin et al., 2012; Niebert, Marsch, & Treagust, 2012). For example, Amin and colleagues (2012) argue that the Entropy As Freedom analogy is more likely to trigger the application of productive intuitive, image-schematic knowledge than Entropy As Disorder, because the former is more consistent with the conceptual metaphors conventionally used in science to construe entropy.

The picture that emerges from the literature reviewed in this subsection is that the concepts of both learners and scientists are represented in terms of multiple perception- and action-based image-schemas and their use in reasoning employs imagistic simulation. This recognizes a degree of continuity between the learner and the scientist and suggests useful entry points for instruction.

The limitations of image-schemas and imagery can be overcome with external (especially propositional) representations. Both the content and format of image-schemas and imagery are limited in the kind of conceptualizing and reasoning they support. Language and other representational tools (e.g., equations) play an important role in expanding the possibilities of the human conceptual system (A. Clark, 2008). Research in developmental psychology suggests that learning *language* can both shape the formation of conceptual categories (Mandler, 2004; Waxman & Markow, 1995) and provide a basis for the construction of novel concepts that would not be possible without language (Carey, 2009). According to Carey, a sentence first functions as a shallowly interpreted symbolic *placeholder* (e.g., "Matter is that which has weight and occupies space"), which then gets interpreted through modeling practices that draw on image-schematic and other conceptual resources. It has also been suggested that understanding conceptual development will involve understanding how language can guide cross-domain mapping (e.g., the domains of space and physical objects) and integration, using image-schemata from one domain to construct understanding in another domain (Gentner, 2003). Recent research on scientific understanding and reasoning has investigated the interactions within distributed systems of internal (mental) and external representations (e.g., diagrams, equations, language), both in characterizing scientific models (Giere, 2002) and in accounts of conceptual change in the history of science (Nersessian, 2008).

Recent work in the knowledge-in-pieces tradition in science education has been incorporating more attention to propositional representations (diSessa, 1996; Levrini & diSessa, 2008; Sherin, 2001, 2006). diSessa (1996) lists nominal facts, narratives, and committed facts (all propositional representations) as relevant to an account of the novice's understanding and reasoning about the physical world, in addition to more imagistic elements (p-prims, mental models). Nominal facts are statements appropriated from everyday discourse or formal instruction, which initially have little meaning to the learner—for example, "Temperature is proportional to average kinetic energy." Narratives are sequences of shallowly interpreted propositions that describe a sequence of events and the objects that participate in them, such as the energy transformation narrative of a falling object. Committed facts are statements interpreted more fully (e.g., "Moving something requires a force").

In a knowledge-in-pieces account of concept learning, nominal facts and shallowly interpreted narratives can be initially learned by rote but play a role in guiding the strategic application of p-prims and other resources, functioning as placeholders for conceptual change (Carey, 2009). For example, Levrini and diSessa (2008) show that high school students struggled to make sense of two definitions of proper time in special relativity across contexts, but their assumption that these definitions should lead to the same conclusions guided their construction of a more general understanding of the concept. Cheng and Brown (2010) argue for the importance of integrating linguistic and imagistic representations. They found that elementary school children who relied only on intuitive knowledge when constructing explanations about magnets across a range of situations constructed fragile and fragmented models. Notably, the one student who developed and revised an explanatory model across situations had integrated both linguistic and imagistic representations and was metacognitively aware of her model building.

Adopting the conceptual metaphor perspective, Brookes (2006; Brookes & Etkina, 2007) has proposed that many analogical models that played a role in scientific concept formation are encoded in the language of scientists as conceptual metaphors, reflecting current and defunct models. Over time, scientists develop a tacit understanding of the strengths and limits of metaphorical models and the appropriate contexts in which to reason with them. However, students may be misled by scientists' language. Indeed, Brookes and Etkina (2007) document some common and robust science misconceptions (including ontological misclassifications) that may originate in patterns of language students commonly hear. Part of the solution, they suggest, may be more care with the language used in instruction. However, given the implicit way in which metaphor pervades language, it might be more practical to have explicit discussions with students about scientific language and misleading ontological construals (Amin et al., 2012; Brookes & Etkina, 2007; Jeppsson et al., 2013).

Focusing on another type of propositional representation, Sherin (2001, 2006) provided evidence that "symbolic forms" mediate the interaction between physics equations and conceptual understanding when university physics students solve problems. Symbolic forms are pairings of conceptual schemata (many of which are image-schemas like p-prims—e.g., opposing influences) with general patterns of symbols in equations (e.g., $\square - \square$) that are used to interpret equations. Sherin (2006) suggests that use of equations can actually guide the activation, reorganization, and refinement of p-prims. More work is needed to understand how students develop these symbolic forms and the role they play in guiding the use of intuitive knowledge when using equations. Another issue for future work is the role of language in mediating between qualitative and algebraic understanding. Jeppsson and colleagues (2013) suggest that metaphorical language, in coordination with symbolic forms, plays such a mediating role. If so, one way to enhance students' construction and use of symbolic forms may be for instructors to talk aloud and model some of their processes of *interpreting* equations in the course of problem solving.

The significance of this research on the role of external representations can be appreciated in relation to the criticism in early concept learning research of the traditional practice of "leading" with definitions of new words, as that was seen as preventing students from activating meaningful conceptual resources. While valid, this critique may have led some to overlook the central role of linguistic and mathematic symbols in the construction of scientific concepts. Although the resurgence of social interactionist perspectives during Phase Two led to increased attention to student language and other forms of symbolization and inscription, the main focus was on the *discourse or inscriptional forms* themselves rather than on their interaction with internal conceptual resources. Future work will need to examine this interaction more closely.

Concepts as participants in versus constituted *by beliefs: Resolving a tension.* Earlier, we contrasted two perspectives on conceptual change: the "coherence" and "knowledge-in-pieces" perspectives. Recent developments have led to considerable convergence. However, the views continue to be contrasted in the literature, especially with regard to what concepts are taken to be. We argue that the apparent difference in how the two perspectives view concepts reflects a tension between viewing concepts as *participants in* versus *constituted by* beliefs. We suggest here that a view of concepts described by Carey (2009) helps resolve this tension and reveals considerable consensus in how coherence and knowledge-in-pieces perspectives view concepts.

We begin with some considerations on the nature of concepts relevant to the coherence versus knowledge-in-pieces debate. Earlier we clarified that image-schematic abstractions from sensorimotor experience are *conceptual* representations that support the construction of preverbal concepts. The more developed conceptual system also consists of concepts expressed propositionally. Indeed, all *scientific* concepts are of this type (as was implied in the previous subsection). Thus, our focus here will be on providing a precise characterization of what we assume a propositionally expressed concept (henceforth, "concept") to be. To Carey (2009), a concept is a language-like symbol that can participate in propositions, relating it to other symbols. On her account, characterizing the *content* of that concept involves specifying two things: (a) those processes (both external and internal) that enable the concept to *refer* to entities in the world and (b) the concept's inferential role, which is specified in terms of the network of propositions that the concept participates in. This view of concepts helps resolve the apparent tension between viewing concepts as participants in beliefs and as constituted by them. A concept per se, seen as a unitary, language-like symbol, can participate in beliefs. The idea that concepts are constituted by beliefs refers to the *content* of the concept—that is, the way the concept functions and contributes to thought is specified by its role in a network of inferences and the mechanisms that establish what entities in the world the concept picks out.

Viewing concepts in this way helps us consider more carefully the differences between coherence and knowledge-in-pieces perspectives. As discussed earlier, from a coherence perspective, concepts, even naïve ones, cannot be characterized in isolation (Chi, 2005; Smith, 2007; Vosniadou, Vamvakoussi, & Skopeliti, 2008; Wiser & Smith, 2013). A concept is understood in relation to others in terms of a network of beliefs, and conceptual change involves a set of interconnected changes leading to a different network. But conceptual change is usually envisioned as gradual because many changes in the conceptual system need to occur. What current coherence accounts add to Phase One research is that more elements are recognized as involved in the process of change—for example, domain-specific beliefs (both qualitative and

quantitative), epistemic beliefs about what constitute appropriate sources of knowledge about entities in the world, models, and beliefs about the nature and function of scientific models.

From a knowledge-in-pieces perspective, naïve conceptual knowledge is believed to be fragmented but contains many potentially useful knowledge elements. However, earlier work had not provided an account of the nature of *scientific* concepts in terms of readily available knowledge elements. The construct "coordination class" has now been put forward to address that gap (diSessa, 2002; diSessa & Sherin, 1998). A coordination class is a knowledge system with multiple constituents, including p-prims, mental models, and beliefs. Its function is not categorization per se, which diSessa and Sherin (1998) suggest has been the main function attributed to concepts by psychologists, so much as reliably picking up information about an important invariant in the world. Some but not all scientific concepts are assumed to be coordination classes—candidates are those concepts that reliably pick out quantitative information (e.g., force or velocity). Having a coordination class involves possessing a structure that can adapt to different contexts of use such that information can be extracted consistently across contexts. Coordination classes are composed of two distinct types of components that differ in function: read-out strategies (e.g., perceptual) that enable a person to identify instances of appropriate application of that class (e.g., establishing when it is appropriate to "see" force) and the causal net (a network of heterogeneous elements including p-prims, mental models, equations, and beliefs) that enable inferences that provide the desired information (e.g., the magnitude or direction of a force).

So how do the coherence and knowledge-in-pieces perspectives on concepts differ? diSessa (2002) suggests that while the knowledge-in-pieces perspective has put forward the construct of coordination class as an account of the *internal* structure of some scientific concepts, coherence views focus on networks of *relationships* between concepts within networks of beliefs. In a later review, diSessa (2006) formulated this difference in terms of the "nesting" of concepts within larger networks of beliefs. Coherence views provide accounts of scientific concepts as (tightly) constrained by the networks of beliefs that they are nested within. Although nesting is acknowledged as a feature of coordination classes (knowledge elements such as p-prims are nested within coordination classes), the constraints that arise between elements and levels are relatively weak.

We suggest that this difference dissolves in light of the distinction between a concept understood as a unitary language-like symbol and the content of a concept understood as its inferential role and the mechanisms that establish reference. Both coherence and knowledge-in-pieces proponents are really concerned with the *content* of concepts as defined above. This is clear in the case of coherence views, especially those that are explicit about being concerned about coordinated changes in networks of beliefs. Similarly, accounts of coordination classes also appeal to networks of beliefs relating concepts to each other when characterizing the causal net (e.g., the Newtonian Force coordination class includes the equation $F = ma$ (diSessa & Sherin, 1998); determining the magnitude of a force, F, implicates recognizing and determining magnitudes for m and a, which in turn can be given coordination class accounts). If we understand concepts in this way, the word "Force" or the symbol "F" (or some mental token representing both), which participates in key propositions within a causal net, *is* the scientific concept of force; it is the *content* of the scientific concept in Carey's account that corresponds to the coordination class as a whole. It is this content that tells us what entities will be picked out in the world by the concept and what inferences it would support

Carey's account is also not incompatible with the knowledge-in-pieces claim that different elements are activated in different contexts. There is no *a priori* assumption that the same knowledge elements are activated every time a given concept (understood as a unitary, language-like symbol) is used. Thus, we suggest that the emerging consensus on the learning of scientific concepts is that it involves the gradual formation of increasingly organized *networks* of heterogeneous knowledge elements, including propositional representations such as language or mathematical representations, as well as image-schematic representations.

Pointing out this deep similarity in the view of concepts adopted by coherence and knowledge-in-pieces perspectives does not deny an important difference that is often highlighted—that they adopt different assumptions regarding the degree of coherence of naïve knowledge. However, this difference is really in the *degree* of coherence in *specific domains* of knowledge. Coherence views expect that small networks of beliefs and broad ontological presuppositions can constrain knowledge construction in specific domains, especially in early childhood (possibly guided by innate constraints). But as coherence researchers increasingly appeal to multiple, heterogeneous knowledge elements in the characterization of naïve understanding, the two views look increasingly similar, especially as some knowledge-in-pieces theorists have granted the possibility that novices may have small-scale networks of interconnected beliefs (Brown & Hammer, 2008). Moreover, coherence theorists increasingly acknowledge that the network of beliefs that constitutes naïve conceptual understanding is not as well organized as initially assumed and that learning will involve a substantial process of organizing and expanding its scope of application (see Vosniadou et al., 2008; Wiser & Smith, 2013).

This consensus view of concepts has an important instructional implication—that the curriculum should foreground *relations* among concepts rather than focusing on concepts in isolation as is typical in traditional instructional units. Reorienting science curricula generally to focus on

models and modeling addresses the need to emphasize relations (Lehrer & Schauble, 2006). However, this raises central questions about how decisions about sequencing and revisiting these relations should be made in specific domains. One constraint on sequencing has depended on what relations can be directly investigated more *concretely* via experimentation and what ones have to be *inferred*. For example, as Minstrell (1984) argued some time ago, in teaching Newton's three laws, it was important to present the *second law* about the relation of force to acceleration *before* the first that asserts that no net force is needed to maintain constant velocity, because the former but not the latter could easily be demonstrated. This issue is at the heart of current curricular design studies exploring effective "pathways" for learning (Cobb, Confrey, diSessa, Lehrer, & Schauble, 2003), didactic theories (Andersson & Wallin, 2006), and work on long-term learning progressions (Wiser, Smith, & Doubler, 2012), to be discussed shortly in our review of new, systemically oriented research on instruction.

Expanding the scope of systemic thinking about conceptual change: Ontology, epistemological beliefs, modes of construal, and social interaction.   Phase Two research identified ontological classification, epistemic beliefs, and social interaction as influences on conceptual change. We revisit these influences again here, highlighting recent efforts to examine these influences in more systemic terms.

The idea that conceptual change involves a process of ontological reclassification of concepts has been criticized recently by knowledge-in-pieces proponents (Gupta, Hammer, & Redish, 2010; Hammer, Gupta, & Redish, 2011). They question whether the shift is from one static, stable ontological category to another and whether certain ontological categories, often considered absent in the novice, are in fact absent. For example, the notion of emergent processes, as in diffusion, can be found in the intuitive appreciation of the idea that while crowds can be seen as moving in some direction at a global level, specific individuals can be moving in a variety of directions. Moreover, both learners and experts classify a given concept with considerable flexibility, often straddling multiple ontological categories. In response, Slotta (2011) has argued that experts may hold *parallel* ontologies for a concept, but only under exceptional circumstances, such as in the case of wave-particle duality in modern physics. Slotta also accepts that scientists may construe an abstract concept more concretely in terms of a material substance in informal or pedagogical contexts but will not treat this way of thinking as scientifically acceptable. As Slotta (2011, p. 157) puts it, "experts can still think of electric current as 'juice' squirting through a wire but would quickly acknowledge that such a substance does not actually exist."

We find this to be an interesting debate but one that would benefit from a broader theoretical framing in terms of emerging systemic perspectives. On the one hand, there is the assumption that abstract concepts are often grounded in informal, imagistic representations (as discussed earlier). The argument that experts sometimes talk metaphorically and reason about abstract concepts such as emergent processes as if they are material substances is consistent with this assumption. On the other hand, the emerging systemic perspectives on concepts and conceptual change alert us to the need to distinguish between conceptual knowledge and metacognitive beliefs *about* that knowledge. Some resolution of the debate between stable and flexible ontological classification might be possible by acknowledging that scientists know, *metacognitively*, that energy and entropy are not material substances but still draw on substance-like metaphors when construing these concepts for particular purposes (Jeppsson et al., 2013). The distinction between *explicit* ontological stances and *implicit* ontological resources might be important if we are to understand the role of ontology in conceptual change from a systemic perspective.

The knowledge-in-pieces framework has also been extended to include epistemological elements, reflecting the systemic turn we are describing. Hammer and Elby (2002) identified many "epistemological resources" that even young children activate in learning situations. They organize them in four broad types: resources for understanding the diverse *sources of knowledge* (e.g., other people vs. direct perception), *epistemological forms* (e.g., stories, statements, pictures), *epistemological activities* (e.g., gathering information, guessing, brainstorming), and *epistemological stances* (e.g., doubt, making sense or puzzlement, acceptance). Like p-prims, these epistemological resources may be activated in different contexts. However, they are rarely activated in isolation but in networks due to mutual cuing. More recently, Elby and Hammer (2010, p. 1) put forward the idea of an *"epistemological frame"*—"a locally coherent activation of a network of resources that may look like a stable belief or theory" that can be more or less productive in a particular situation. Therefore, teachers should guide students toward more productive framing (e.g., redirect students to work on a problem by focusing on "what they know," thus shifting them from a "memorizing" to a "sense-making" frame). New frames may "emerge" by activating resources in different combinations. However, future work needs to examine how new resources may develop and change over time, including those needed for more advanced knowledge construction in science (such as the construction of coordination classes and complex scientific models). Some work on learning progressions (discussed next) does begin to address some of these issues. But more work is certainly needed.

The research just reviewed has begun to examine the separate influences of ontological classification and epistemological beliefs on conceptual change, but in more systemic terms than in Phase Two research. Recently, cognitive science research on young children and adults has begun to explore *connections* between both types of influences. Keil and colleagues (Keil, 2011; Keil, Stein, Webb, Billings, & Rozenblit, 2008) have shown that both children and adults are often ignorant of mechanistic details but have knowledge of higher-level functional patterns and principles ("modes of construal") that allow them to know what kinds of properties are likely to be causal or important for entities in different domains. For example, artifacts but not living things are likely to have a purpose (although *parts* of living things may have a purpose); color may be important for distinguishing different living things more than artifacts, while shape may be particularly important for artifacts (given reliance on function). This kind of knowledge may have ontological import, contributing to picking out different domains. Moreover, in the case of natural kind concepts, children and adults adopt an essentialist stance, in which they assume an underlying essence that causally accounts for observed characteristics without knowing the specifics of these causes. Thus, the representation of some concepts may be inherently connected to broad modes of construal and an epistemic stance in which an underlying causal essence is assumed by the learner.

These connections between early concept development and ontological and epistemological beliefs have also been related to the role of other people in the concept-learning process. Knowledge of modes of construal may support patterns of deference in a cognitive division of labor in which children as young as 4 are able to match experts with the appropriate domains of knowledge (Lutz & Keil, 2002), although still in very fragile ways. Moreover, the essentialist stance associated with natural kind concepts has been proposed as the basis for why laypeople defer to experts for more detailed accounts and the identification of instances of a concept that they do not know themselves (Carey, 2009).

There are interesting pedagogical implications of these connections among concept learning, ontological, and epistemological beliefs and the contribution of other people to individual learning. First, rather than overloading students with too many factual details, curricula should target the development of higher-level forms of knowledge that might offer needed guidance. Recent work has suggested that just such a strategy may be productive. In her cognitive analysis of the types of knowledge undergraduate students use in reasoning about familiar and novel problems about how genes cause diseases or other phenotypes, Duncan (2007) found that students frequently activated *domain-general solution frames*. These frames contained placeholders (e.g., something causes *damage* which leads to a *counterreaction*) that activated *domain-specific heuristics* (e.g., genes codes for proteins) that constrained their search for more domain-specific solutions (e.g., find the altered protein responsible for this disease). Duncan has built on these analyses (Duncan, Rogat, & Yarden, 2009) to identify important "big ideas" that should be targets for instruction in a learning progression for genetics.

Second, in earlier work on students' epistemological understandings in science, sources of knowledge were often treated as one-dimensional with reliance on *authority* at the unsophisticated end of the pole and reliance on *reasoning, inference*, based on *first-hand experimental* observation, at the other end. As Chinn, Buckland, and Samarapungavan (2011) argue in their recent review on epistemic cognition, there is increasing recognition of the importance of multiple sources (e.g., perception, introspection, memory, reasoning, testimony) that are simultaneously operative and interactive in the sophisticated learner. This type of interaction was examined by Magnusson and Palincsar (2005). In their instruction, they introduce a "second-hand investigation" text (a fictitious notebook of a scientist reporting findings of her studies) as a powerful way of helping students extend their first-hand investigations. They argue that students' initial investigations "prepare" them for engaging with this text meaningfully, while at the same time the text pushes students' investigations forward in new directions. Thus, rather than seeing learning from others and by oneself as antithetical, they are seen as synergistic and mutually supportive. Similarly, Lehrer, Schauble, and Lucas (2008) have shown that through extended modeling instruction that includes weekly research meetings to provide a carefully designed structure for social interaction in the classroom over the course of the year, sixth-grade students developed substantial epistemological sophistication and understanding of the nature of science.

The Challenges of Designing Instruction From More Systemic Perspectives

The four specific themes that have emerged recently in thinking about the systemic nature of concepts and conceptual change provide more *guidance* for designing effective instruction than the simple dictum "pay attention to," "engage," or "confront" students' prior ideas. They also deepen our understanding of what it means for both students and scientists to have a *complex conceptual ecology*, a central idea introduced in Phase One. In this section, we consider the productive insights of three newer curriculum design frameworks: knowledge-integration, learning-goals, and learning-progressions frameworks. The learning progressions framework builds on many features of the other two and offers a way of thinking about how large-scale transformations in an individual's knowledge and capacity to participate in scientific practices can be brought about that is quite different from Piaget's original developmental vision and has the potential to transform how we design and organize science standards.

Knowledge integration: Providing sufficient time and guidance to connect, differentiate, and reorganize multiple elements. If conceptual change involves coordinating changes among multiple elements in a complex knowledge network, then it follows that conceptual change will be a slow process because it takes time to add, distinguish, connect, and sort out productive from unproductive connections of these elements across multiple contexts. Linn and her colleagues provided dramatic support for this assumption in an extensive series of design studies of an

eighth-grade curriculum addressing four key topics in thermodynamics (Clark, 2006; Clark & Linn, 2003; Linn, 2008; Linn & Hsi, 2000).

According to the proponents of the knowledge-integration framework, students needed to integrate a variety of different kinds of elements (e.g., nominal and committed facts, p-prims, mental models, narratives, visualizations). Their curriculum focused on developing "intermediate" models, such as a heat-flow model, rather than atomic-molecular models. Students integrated knowledge by comparing and contrasting different situations, considering pivotal cases, looking for generalizations, making explanatory connections across topics and between principles and everyday contexts, and re-explaining "disruptive sensory experiences" in terms of more normative ideas.

They found that their full 13-week curriculum was much more effective than three more streamlined versions (10, 8, and 6 weeks) on measures calling for students to explain and articulate their reasoning across all topics (Clark & Linn, 2003). Follow-up interviews when the students were in 10th and 12th grade showed that they had not only maintained their understanding but continued to improve. Overall, they argued that knowledge integration takes more time but provides a stronger basis for transfer and continued learning. Unfortunately, the typical U.S. eighth-grade curriculum allots only 1 to 2 weeks to thermodynamics, too little time for any serious knowledge integration to occur.

Clark's (2006) case studies of individuals in the longitudinal sample provide detailed depictions of how the linkages among different ideas were changing during the 13-week curriculum and beyond and show that individual restructuring is a "messy" process. For example, Clark found that although adding ideas was easy, normatively connecting ideas was much harder. Students often invented non-normative connections and held multiple contradictory ideas. Students took different paths as they traversed the curriculum—varying not only in rate of progress and ultimate success but also in which idea was the first they understood, and which gave them the most difficulty. This finding highlights the need for the curriculum to support multiple paths and to devise methods to respond differentially to the needs of students.

Learning goals design: Identifying goals by unpacking standards and integrating content and practice in diverse "learning performances." As researchers investigated how to produce the deep interest and engagement that would make conceptual change possible, many began to consider the role that innovative project-based pedagogy might play in the process. Project-based pedagogy creates a meaningful context for learning (e.g., a driving question about a real-world problem—for example, "How can I make new stuff out of old stuff?") that students collectively work to solve, with new information and ideas introduced on a "need to know" basis. Thus, learning science content is embedded in investigations that involve students in complex knowledge-building practices (e.g., argumentation, explanation, and modeling) as part of knowledge-building communities.

Building on prior successful work implementing individual project-based units among at-risk urban youth (Geier et al., 2008; Marx et al., 2004), Krajcik, Reiser, and colleagues took on the challenge of designing a 3-year middle school project-based science curriculum (IQWST) that was integrated and coherent. To create better alignment among standards, curricular units, and assessments, they developed a Learning Goals design framework (Krajcik, McNeill, & Reiser, 2008; Nordine, Krajcik, & Fortus, 2011). "Identifying and unpacking" a coherent cluster of standards ("big ideas") that would be investigated in depth in the unit was the first step. Unpacking was needed to identify the component ideas implicit but not fully stated in the standards (e.g., definitions of key terms, relevant background knowledge). Developing "learning performances" for each standard was the second step. A critical assumption was that scientific knowledge was not just a collection of declarative statements and skills but "knowledge in use" as part of a "knowledge-building practice" (p. 7). Hence, for each main idea in the standard, they identified a set of learning performances by combining that idea with important practices (e.g., defining terms, creating models or explanations, designing investigations, making arguments based on evidence). This aspect of their design framework became very influential in later learning progressions work.

The elaborated maps of learning goals and performances then guided the curriculum-development phase and were refined through feedback from classroom trials. By the third trial for each unit, they were obtaining gain scores with large effect sizes on all their measures. Further, the recent National Field trials of the IQWST 3-year chemistry curriculum sequence provided evidence that students not only made significant progress across each unit but also were cumulatively benefiting (i.e., those who had multiple years did better on subsequent pretests and made larger improvements than those who did not; Krajcik, Sutherland, Drago, & Merritt, 2011). Thus, IQWST provided evidence of the benefits of curricular depth and coherence and responded to the concern raised by prior researchers about the poor alignment across learning goals, curricular activities, and assessments of typical middle school curricula (Kesidou & Roseman, 2002).

One reason that IQWST may have been so successful is that, like Linn's heat/temperature unit, it provided the instructional time and depth of focus to allow students to make *connections* among multiple elements in their knowledge networks and to sort out and revise those connections. It also paid attention to the *language* used in instruction, carefully introducing and discussing with students the meaning of new terms. With a focus on modeling, the curriculum encouraged students to make connections across *different levels of analysis* (e.g., macroscopic vs. nanoscopic) and to see how the same model

could explain diverse phenomena. Finally, by being organized around coherent learning goals, it focused on the kinds of "sparse knowledge" (e.g., organizing models and general principles) that may be most helpful in preparing students for further learning. It went beyond Linn's work in investigating how curricular units can build on one another to allow knowledge to become more sophisticated over time (e.g., introducing particulate models in Grade 6 to explain the material nature of gas and phase change, developing more elaborated atomic-molecular models in Grade 7 to understand and explain simple chemical reactions, etc.).

Learning progressions: Identifying productive intermediate stepping stones that bridge lower and upper anchors. Learning progressions (LPs) have been described as testable hypotheses about (relatively efficient, productive, and complete) paths[1] by which students can be led from their initial ideas and forms of reasoning (lower anchor) to a deeper understanding of important theories and concepts in modern science (upper anchor). They focus on "big ideas" (often of a disciplinary nature) that take extended time to develop and that will not "naturally" develop from interaction with the adult culture without explicit instructional support. Because the "conceptual" distance between the lower and upper anchor is so great, the path involves a number of intermediate stepping stones, many of which are not yet widely recognized as important by existing standards and curricula. Although the path is continuous, the stepping stones represent important qualitative shifts in student understanding. Those successive shifts are ordered not only in terms of increasing complexity (often captured as "levels" in an LP) but also in terms of causal import—that is, reaching one stepping stone enables students (makes them more likely) to reach the next (see Corcoran, Mosher, & Rogat, 2009; National Research Council, 2007, for reviews).

Although LPs could be developed for any big idea, including scientific practices such as modeling, most LPs focus on *disciplinary core ideas* (e.g., matter, energy, genetics, evolution, matter and energy flow in living things, celestial motion). Disciplinary core ideas are a meaningful locus for LPs, because they provide a context for integrating the development of scientific epistemology and practices with the development of specific content understanding.

In keeping with the systemic turn for analyzing concepts and conceptual change, both the lower and upper anchors and the evolving knowledge network the LPs describe have increasingly been analyzed in terms of multiple components. For example, new work in developmental psychology identifies multiple types of early knowledge elements that can be used as resources for science learning. These include some initial concepts for a given domain (e.g., object, material, weight, and size for matter; diverse types of living things, individual differences, growth and change, places where organisms live for evolution), a wide range of image-schemas possibly assembled in models, ontological assumptions (e.g., weight is heft, species are kinds), and epistemological commitments (e.g., senses are a reliable source of information; there are hidden essences) that mutually support each other. Even preschoolers are aware of multiple forms of explanation across domains (e.g., contact causality, intentional causality, causal explanations in terms of needs or purpose, explanations by analysis into parts) and are also developing mathematical competence, symbolic competence, metacognitive abilities, and epistemic understandings. What is a relevant part of the lower anchor for a given LP is not a tightly organized initial theory, but rather all the elements that will be drawn on in developing further knowledge for that LP; some are already used and partially interrelated to understand the domain, but many others are yet to be related to that domain or are only of peripheral importance. (See National Research Council, 2007, chapters 3, 5, and 6, for reviews of these foundational resources.)

The upper anchor is often characterized as a "framework of understanding" that includes multiple interrelated concepts and models, forms of symbolization, and supporting ontological and epistemological assumptions. For example, understanding atomic-molecular theory (AMT) involves understanding not only the core tenets of the theory but also how different models explain a variety of macroscopic phenomena (e.g., transmission of smell, phase change only require a particulate model, while chemical reactions require an atomic-molecular model). Such understandings rely on interpretations of matter and its behavior at the macroscopic level (e.g., material, phase change, weight, volume, density, mass) that are scientifically compatible with AMT. It also involves making an ontological distinction between atoms and molecules, understanding the nature and function of models, and having an epistemology that includes emergent properties, in order to grasp that atoms, invisible to the naked eye, can form visible matter with physical and perceptual properties they themselves do not have (Wiser & Smith, 2013). Characterizing both the upper and lower anchor, in terms of multiple related elements, contrasts with the much narrower focus of earlier conceptual change work, which focused on one or two concepts, a domain at a time.

Thinking about the upper and lower anchor as a complex knowledge network raises the challenge of how to describe what progresses in terms of productive stepping stones and achievable conceptual changes. A recent synthetic report by a large group of LP researchers concluded:

> [T]he most compelling way to characterize the successive levels of understandings we think students will proceed through if they are to reach the goals for high school science, is to frame them as a series of successively more sophisticated explanatory models that take into account more and more of the relevant phenomena and that move from naive explanations based on folk concepts and directly observable interactions to models that deal with hypothesized interactions among constructs and entities that are observed or measured only with sophisticated tools and/or inferred from their observed effects.
>
> (Rogat et al., 2011, pp. 4–5)

An advantage of organizing these stepping stones around *models* is that models integrate multiple knowledge elements (e.g., image schemas, propositional beliefs) as well as embody different ontological and epistemological commitments.

The number of intermediate models that have been recognized in recent LP work is striking because many are entirely overlooked by current standards and instruction. These break the distance between the upper and lower anchor into several more manageable steps, making it more likely to move students' knowledge networks forward while maintaining coherence. For example, at least five different intermediate models have been proposed within a K–12 matter LP—a macroscopic compositional model, a microscopic compositional model, a particle model, an atomic-molecular model, and a subatomic model based on the Bohr model. The first two are crucial in elementary school and the last three in middle and high school (Rogat et al., 2011). Similarly, Lehrer and Schauble (2012) have proposed a sequence of four increasingly complex ways elementary students can model variation, change, and ecosystems to lay a foundation for evolutionary thinking. They emphasize gradually "expanding the repertoire of student models" for variation and change through introducing *new representational means* such as annotated drawings, tables of measures, frequency displays of distribution, chance models of distribution, thus also highlighting the powerful role that student-generated *external representations* can play in helping students "get a grip" on nature and in developing student understanding of the epistemic practice of modeling.

Research results from specific LP projects are just beginning to be reported, and it will, of course, take some time to develop, revise, and test conjectures about productive stepping stones in different domains, as well as to assess the overall value of the LP approach. But already one result is clear: Elementary school children are capable of developing much more sophisticated models and understandings than is observed with traditional instruction (see Doubler et al., 2011, for matter; Lehrer & Schauble, 2012, for concepts laying the foundation for evolutionary thinking). An exciting next step will be not only to continue to clarify our understanding of knowledge growth in the elementary school years, but also to explore how learning in the middle and high school years is affected by this foundational preparation, as well as what the long term payoffs might be.

Conclusion

We have organized our review of the literature on student conceptions and conceptual change in terms of three overlapping phases of research that we believe capture broadly the progress that has been made in the field since the rejection of Piaget's stage view of development. His domain-general view of conceptual development in terms of changes in logico-mathematical structures has now been replaced by a systemic view of concepts and conceptual change involving complex interactions between various forms of knowledge: propositionally expressed beliefs of various kinds (domain specific, ontological, and epistemological) and iconic representations that help ground understanding in perception and action (image-schemas, imagery, and mental models). These knowledge elements are distributed across internal and external representations, and processes of change involve processes internal to individual learners' minds and interactions with others (including more knowledgeable individuals and peers). Future research will need to take on the challenge of improving our understanding of this complexity and fostering conceptual change through instruction that takes this understanding into account.

Note

1. The fact that learning progressions are *models or idealizations* of a relatively strategic pathway is another crucial feature that distinguishes them from the actual *individual learning trajectories* of students (described by Clark, 2006) that are much messier and include dead ends and which by their nature are particular events, not generalizations.

References

Acher, A., Arca, M., & Sanmarti, N. (2007). Modeling as a teaching learning process for understanding materials: A case study in primary education. *Science Education, 91,* 398–418.

Amin, T. G. (2009). Conceptual metaphor meets conceptual change. *Human Development, 52,* 165–197.

Amin, T. G., Jeppsson, F., Haglund, J., & Strömdahl, H. (2012). Arrow of time: Metaphorical construals of entropy and the second law of thermodynamics. *Science Education, 96*(5), 818–848.

Andersson, B., & Wallin, A. (2006). On developing content oriented theories taking biological evolution as an example. *International Journal of Science Education, 28*(6), 673–695.

Ault, C. R., Novak, J. D., & Gowin, D. B. (1988). Constructing Vee-maps for clinical interviews on energy concepts. *Science Education, 72*(4), 515–545.

Ausubel, D. P. (1968). *Educational psychology: A cognitive view.* New York: Holt, Rinehart & Winston.

Barsalou, L. W. (1999). Perceptual symbol systems. *Behavioral and Brain Sciences, 22,* 577–660.

Barsalou, L. W., & Wiemer-Hastings, K. (2005). Situating abstract concepts. In D. Pecher & R. Zwaan (Eds.), *Grounding cognition: The role of perception and action in memory, language, and thought* (pp. 129–163). Cambridge: Cambridge University Press.

Beeth, M. (1998). Teaching for conceptual change: Using status as a metacognitive tool. *Science Education, 82*(3), 343–354.

Brookes, D. T. (2006). *The role of language in learning physics.* Ph.D. Dissertation submitted to Rutgers University, New Brunswick, New Jersey.

Brookes, D. T., & E. Etkina, (2007). Using conceptual metaphor and functional grammar to explore how language used in physics affects student learning. *Physical Review Special Topics: Physics Education Research, 3*(1), 1–16.

Brown, A. (1978). Knowing when, where, and how to remember: A problem of metacognition. In R. Glaser (Ed.), *Advances in instructional psychology* (Vol. 1, pp. 77–165). Hillsdale, NJ: Lawrence Erlbaum Associates.

Brown, D., & Hammer, D. (2008). Conceptual change in physics. In S. Vosniadou (Ed.), *International handbook of research on conceptual change* (pp. 127–154). New York: Routledge.

Brown, D. E., & Clement, J. (1989). Overcoming misconceptions via analogical reasoning: Abstract transfer versus explanatory model construction. *Instructional Science, 18*(4), 237–261.

Carey, S. (1985a). Are children fundamentally different types of thinkers and learners than adults? In S. Chipman, J. Segal, & R. Glaser (Eds.), *Thinking and learning skills* (Vol. 2, pp. 485–517). Hillsdale, NJ: Erlbaum. Reprinted by Open University Press: *Open University Readings in Cognitive Development.*

Carey, S. (1985b). *Conceptual change in childhood.* Cambridge: MIT Press.

Carey, S. (2009). *The origin of concepts.* Oxford, UK: Oxford University Press.

Carey, S., Evans, R., Honda, M., Jay, E., & Unger, C. (1989). An experiment is when you try it and see if it works. *International Journal of Science Education, 11*(5), 514–529.

Carey, S., & Smith, C. (1993). On understanding the nature of scientific knowledge. *Educational Psychologist, 28*(3), 235–251.

Cheng, M.-F., & Brown, D. (2010). Conceptual resources in self-developed explanatory models: The importance of integrating conscious and intuitive knowledge. *International Journal of Science Education, 32*(17), 2367–2392.

Chi, M., Hutchinson, J., & Robin, A. (1989). How inferences about novel domain-related concepts can be constrained by structured knowledge. *Merrill-Palmer Quarterly, 35*(1), 27–62.

Chi, M. T. H. (1992). Conceptual change within and across ontological categories: Examples from learning and discovery in science. In R. Giere (Ed.), *Cognitive models of science: Minnesota studies in the philosophy of science* (pp. 129–186). Minneapolis: University of Minnesota Press.

Chi, M. T. H. (2005). Common sense conceptions of emergent processes. *Journal of the Learning Sciences, 14,* 161–199.

Chi, M. T. H., & Slotta, J. D. (1993). The ontological coherence of intuitive physics. Commentary on A. diSessa's "Toward an epistemology of physics." *Cognition and Instruction, 10*(2, 3), 249–260.

Chinn, C., Buckland, L., & Samarapungavan, A. (2011). Expanding the dimensions of epistemic cognition: Arguments from philosophy and psychology. *Educational Psychologist, 46,* 141–167.

Clark, A. (2008). *Supersizing the mind: Embodiment, action and cognitive extension.* Oxford: Oxford University Press.

Clark, D. B. (2006). Longitudinal conceptual change in students' understanding of thermal equilibrium: An examination of the process of conceptual restructuring. *Cognition and Instruction, 24*(4), 467–563.

Clark, D. B., & Linn, M. (2003). Designing for knowledge integration: The impact of instructional time. *Journal of the Learning Sciences, 12*(4), 451–493.

Clement, J. (1993). Using bridging analogies and anchoring intuitions to deal with students' preconceptions in physics. *Journal of Research in Science Teaching, 30*(10), 1241–1257.

Clement, J. (2008). *Creative model construction in scientists and students: The role of imagery, analogy and mental simulation.* Dordrecht, the Netherlands: Springer.

Cobb, P., Confrey, J., diSessa, A., Lehrer, R., & Schauble, L. (2003). Design experiments in educational research. *Educational Researcher, 32*(1), 9–13.

Corcoran, T., Mosher, F., & Rogat, A. (2009). *Learning progressions in science: An evidence based approach to reform.* Unpublished CPRE Research Report #RR-63. Teachers College, Columbia University.

diSessa, A. (1993a). Towards an epistemology of physics. *Cognition and Instruction, 10*(2/3), 105–224.

diSessa, A. (1993b). Ontologies in pieces: Response to Chi and Slotta. *Cognition and Instruction, 10*(2/3), 272–280.

diSessa, A. (1996). What do "just plain folk" know about physics? In D.R. Olson & N. Torrance (Eds.), *Handbook of education and human development* (pp. 709–730). Oxford: Blackwell.

diSessa, A. (2002). Why "conceptual ecology" is a good idea. In M. Limon & L. Mason (Eds.), *Reconsidering conceptual change. Issues in theory and practice* (pp. 29–60). Dordrecht, the Netherlands: Kluwer Academic Publishers.

diSessa, A. (2006). A history of conceptual change research: Threads and fault lines. In R. Sawyer (Ed.), *The Cambridge handbook of the learning sciences* (pp. 265–281). Cambridge, UK: Cambridge University Press.

diSessa, A., & Sherin, B. (1998). What changes in conceptual change? *International Journal of Science Education, 20*(10), 1155–1191.

Donaldson, M. (1978). *Children's minds.* Glasgow: William Collins.

Doubler, S., Carraher, D., Tobin, R., Asbell-Clarke, J., Smith, C., & Schliemann, A. (2011). *The inquiry project: Final report.* Submitted to the National Science Foundation DRK-12 Program.

Driver, R. (1983). *The pupil as scientist?* Milton Keynes, UK: Open University Press.

Driver, R., Asoko, H., Leach, J., Mortimer, E., & Scott, P. (1994). Constructing scientific knowledge in the classroom. *Educational Researcher, 23*(7), 5–12.

Driver, R., & Easley, J. (1978). Pupils and paradigms: A review of the literature related to concept development in adolescent science students. *Studies in Science Education, 5,* 61–84.

Driver, R. Guesne, E., & Tiberghien, A. (1985). *Children's ideas in science.* Philadelphia, PA: Open University Press.

Driver, R., Leach, J., Millar, R., & Scott, P. (1996). *Young children's images of science.* Buckingham, UK: Open University Press.

Duit, R. (1991). On the role of analogies and metaphors in learning science. *Science Education, 75*(6), 649–672.

Duit, R. (2009). *STCSE—Bibliography—Students and teachers conceptions and science learning.* Kiel, Germany: IPN—Leibniz Institute for Science and Mathematics Education.

Duit, R., Roth, W.-M., Komorek, M., & Wilbers, J. (1998). Conceptual change cum discourse analysis to understand cognition in a unit on chaotic systems: Towards an integrative perspective on learning in science. *International Journal of Science Education, 20*(9), 1059–1073.

Duncan, R. (2007). The role of domain specific knowledge in generative reasoning about complicated multi-level phenomena. *Cognition and Instruction, 25*(4), 271–336.

Duncan, R., Rogat, A., & Yarden, A. (2009). A learning progression for deepening students' understandings of modern genetics across the 5th to 10th grades. *Journal of Research in Science Teaching, 46*(6), 655–674.

Elby, A., & Hammer, D. (2010). Epistemological resources and framing. In L.D. Bendixen & F.C. Feucht (Eds.), *Personal epistemology in the classroom: Theory, research, and implications for practice* (pp. 409–434). Cambridge: Cambridge University Press.

Flavell, J. (1976). Metacognitive aspects of problem solving. In L. Resnick (Ed.), *The nature of intelligence* (pp. 231–236). Hillsdale, NJ: Lawrence Erlbaum Associates.

Garfinkel, H., & Sacks, H. (1970). On formal structures of practical actions. In J.C. McKinney & E.A. Tiryakian (Eds.), *Theoretical sociology* (pp. 338–366). New York: Appleton-Century-Crofts.

Geier, R., Blumenfeld, R., Marx, R., Krajcik, J., Fishman, B., Soloway, E., Jay-Chambers, J. (2008). Standardized test outcomes of students engaged in inquiry-based science curricula in the context of urban reform. *Journal of Research in Science Teaching, 45*(8), 922–938.

Gelman, R., & Baillargeon, R. (1983). A review of Piagetian concepts. In P.H. Mussen (Series Ed.) & J.H. Flavell & E.M. Markman (Vol. Eds.), *Handbook of child psychology* (4th ed., Vol. 3, pp. 167–230). New York: Wiley.

Gentner, D. (1983). Structure-mapping: A theoretical framework for analogy. *Cognitive Science, 7,* 155–170.

Gentner, D. (2003). Why we are so smart. In D. Gentner & S. Goldin-Meadow (Eds.), *Language in Mind* (pp. 195–235). Cambridge: MIT Press.

Gentner, D., & Stevens, A. (1983). *Mental models.* Hillsdale, NJ: Erlbaum.

Giere, R.N. (1988). *Explaining science: A cognitive approach.* Chicago: University of Chicago.

Giere, R.N. (2002). Scientific cognition as distributed cognition. In P. Curruthers, S. Stich, & M. Siegal (Eds.), *The cognitive basis of science* (pp. 285–299). Cambridge: Cambridge University Press.

Goodwin, C., & Heritage, J. (1990). Conversational analysis. *Annual Review of Anthropology, 19,* 283–307.

Gopnik, A., & Wellman, H.M. (1994). The theory theory. In L.A. Hirschfeld & S.A. Gelman (Eds.), *Mapping the mind* (pp. 257–293). Cambridge: Cambridge University Press.

Grosslight, L., Unger, C., Jay, E., & Smith, C. (1991). Understanding models and their use in science: Conceptions of middle and high school students and experts. *Journal of Research in Science Teaching, 28*(9), 799–822.

Gupta, A., Hammer, D., & Redish, E. (2010). The case for dynamic models of learners' ontologies in physics. *Journal of the Learning Sciences, 19,* 285–321.

Hammer, D. (1994). Epistemological beliefs in introductory physics. *Cognition and Instruction, 12*(2), 151–184.

Hammer, D., & Elby, A. (2002). On the form of a personal epistemology. B.K. Hofer & P.R. Pintrich (Eds.), *Personal epistemology: The psychology of beliefs about knowledge and knowing* (pp. 169–190). Mahwah, NJ: Erlbaum.

Hammer, D., Gupta, A., & Redish, E. (2011). On static and dynamic intuitive ontologies. *Journal of Learning Sciences, 20*(1), 163–168.

Hatano, G., & Inagaki, K. (1991). Sharing cognition through collective comprehension activity. In L.B. Resnick, J.M. Levine, & S.D. Teasley (Eds.), *Perspectives on socially shared cognition* (pp. 331–348). Washington, DC: American Psychological Association.

Hennessey, M.G. (2003). Metacognitive aspects of students' reflective discourse: Implications for intentional conceptual change teaching and learning. In G.M. Sinatra & P.R. Pintrich (Eds.), *Intentional conceptual change* (pp. 103–132). Mahwah, NJ: Erlbaum.

Herrenkohl, L.R., Palincsar, A.S., DeWater, L.S., & Kawasaki, K. (1999). Developing scientific communities in classrooms: A socio-cognitive approach. *Journal of the Learning Sciences, 8,* 451–493.

Hofer, B., & Pintrich, P. (1997). The development of epistemological theories: Beliefs about knowledge and knowing and their relation to learning. *Review of Educational Research, 67,* 88–140.

Howe, C. (2009). Collaborative group work in middle childhood: Joint construction, unresolved contradiction and the growth of knowledge. *Human Development, 52,* 215–239.

Howe, C.J., McWilliam, D., & Cross, G. (2005). Chance favors only the prepared mind: Incubation and the delayed effects of peer collaboration. *British Journal of Psychology, 96,* 67–93.

Howe, C.J., Tolmie, A., & Rodgers, C. (1992). The acquisition of conceptual knowledge in science by primary school children: Group interaction and the understanding of motion down an incline. *British Journal of Developmental Psychology, 10,* 113–130.

Inhelder, B., Piaget, J., Parsons, A., & Milgram, S. (1958). *The growth of logical thinking from childhood to adolescence.* New York: Basic Books.

Jeppsson, F., Haglund, J., Amin, T., & Strömdahl, H. (2013). Exploring the use of conceptual metaphors in solving problems on entropy. *Journal of Learning Sciences, 22(1),* 70–120.

Johnson-Laird, P. (1983). *Mental models.* Cambridge: Cambridge University Press.

Ke, J.L., Monk, M., & Duschl, R. (2005). Learning introductory quantum mechanics: Sensori-motor experience and mental models. *International Journal of Science Education, 27*(13), 1571–1594.

Keil, F. (1979). *Semantic and conceptual development: An ontological perspective.* Cambridge, MA: Harvard University Press.

Keil, F. (2011). The problem of partial understanding. *Current Trends in LSP Research: Aims and Methods Series: Linguistic Insights, 44,* 251–276.

Keil, F., Stein, C., Webb, L., Billings, V., & Rozenblit, L. (2008). Discerning the division of cognitive labor: An emerging understanding of how knowledge is clustered in other minds. *Cognitive Science: A Multidisciplinary Journal, 32*(2), 259–300.

Kitchener, K. S. (1983). Cognition, metacognition, and epistemic cognition. *Human Development, 26,* 222–232.

Kesidou, S., & Roseman, J. (2002). How well do middle school science programs measure up? *Journal of Research in Science Teaching, 39*(6), 522–549.

Krajcik, J., MacNeill, K., & Reiser, B. (2008). Learning goals driven design model: Developing curricular materials that align with national standards and incorporate project based pedagogy. *Science Education, 92*(1), 1–23.

Krajcik, J. S., Sutherland, L. M., Drago, K., & Merritt, J. (2011). The promise and value of learning progression research. In S. Bernholt, K. Neumann, & P. Nentwig (Eds.), *Making it tangible—Learning outcomes in science education* (pp. 261–284). Münster: Waxmann.

Kuhn, D. (1989). Children and adults as intuitive scientists. *Psychological Review, 96*(4), 674–689.

Kuhn, D. (2000). Theory of mind, metacognition, and reasoning. In P. Mitchell & K. Riggs (Eds.), *Children's reasoning and the mind* (pp. 301–326). Hove, UK: Psychology Press.

Kuhn, T. (1962). *The structure of scientific revolutions.* Chicago: University of Chicago Press.

Kuhn, T. (1977). *The essential tension: Selected studies in scientific tradition and change.* Chicago: University of Chicago Press.

Lakoff, G., & Johnson, M. (1980). *Metaphors we live by.* Chicago: University of Chicago Press.

Lakoff, G., & Johnson, M. (1999). *Philosophy in the flesh: The embodied mind and the challenge to Western thought.* New York: Basic Books.

Lehrer, R., & Schauble, L. (2000). Developing model-based reasoning in mathematics and science. *Journal of Applied Developmental Psychology, 21*(1), 39–48.

Lehrer, R., & Schauble, L. (2006). Scientific thinking and scientific literacy. In W. Damon, R. Lerner, K. Renninger, & I. Sigel (Eds.), *Handbook of child psychology, child psychology in practice* (pp. 156–196). New York: John Wiley & Sons.

Lehrer, R., & Schauble, L. (2012). Seeding evolutionary thinking by modeling its foundations. *Science Education, 96*(4), 701–724.

Lehrer, R., Schauble, L., Carpenter, S., & Penner, D. E. (2000). The interrelated development of inscriptions and conceptual understanding. In P. Cobb, E. Yackel, & K. McClain (Eds.), *Symbolizing and communicating in mathematics classrooms: Perspectives on discourse, tools and instructional design* (pp. 325–360). Mahwah, NJ: Erlbaum.

Lehrer, R., Schauble, L., & Lucas, D. (2008). Supporting the development of the epistemology of inquiry. *Cognitive Development, 23,* 512–529.

Lehrer, R., Schauble, L., Strom, D., & Pligge, M. (2003). Similarity of form and substance: Modeling material kind. In D. Klahr & S. Carver (Eds.), *Cognition and instruction: 25 years of progress* (pp. 39–74). Mahwah, NJ: Erlbaum.

Levrini, O., & diSessa, A. (2008). How students learn from multiple contexts: Proper time as a coordination class. *Physics Education Research, 4*(1), 1–18.

Linn, M. (2008). Teaching for conceptual change: Distinguish or extinguish ideas. In S. Vosniadou (Ed.), *International handbook of research on conceptual change* (pp. 694–722). New York: Routledge.

Linn, M., & Hsi, S. (2000). *Computers, teachers, peers: Science learning partners.* Mahwah, NJ: Erlbaum.

Lising, L., & Elby, A. (2005). The impact of epistemology on learning: A case study from introductory physics. *American Journal of Physics, 73*(4), 372–382.

Lutz, D. R., & Keil, F. C. (2002). Early understanding of the division of cognitive labor. *Child Development, 73,* 1073–1084.

Magnusson, S., & Palincsar, A. (2005). Teaching to promote the development of scientific knowledge and reasoning about light at the elementary school level. In S. Donovan & J. Bransford (Eds.), *How students learn: Science in the classroom* (pp. 421–474). Washington, DC: National Academies Press.

Mandler, J. (2004). *The foundations of mind: Origins of conceptual thought.* Oxford, UK: Oxford University Press.

Marx, R., Blumenfeld, P., Krajcik, J., Fishman, B., Soloway, E., Geier, R., & Tal, R. (2004). Inquiry-based science in the middle grades: Assessment of learning in urban systemic reform. *Journal of Research in Science Teaching, 41*(10), 1063–1080.

Mason, L. (2007). Bridging the cognitive and sociocultural approaches to research on conceptual change: Is it feasible? *Educational Psychologist, 42*(1), 1–7.

Mason, L., & Boscolo, P. (2000). Writing and conceptual change: What changes? *Instructional Science, 28,* 199–226.

May, B., & Etkina, E. (2002). College physics students' epistemological self-reflection and its relationship to conceptual learning. *American Journal of Physics, 70*(12), 1249–1258.

McCloskey, M. (1983). Naïve theories of motion. In D. Gentner & A. Stevens (Eds.), *Mental models* (pp. 299–324). Hillsdale, NJ: Erlbaum.

Metz, K. (1995). Reassessment of developmental constraints on children's science instruction. *Review of Educational Research, 65,* 93–127.

Minstrell, J. (1982). Explaining the "at rest" condition of an object. *The Physics Teacher, 20,* 10–14.

Minstrell, J. (1984). Teaching for the development of understanding of ideas: Forces on moving objects. In C. Anderson (Ed.), *AETS Yearbook: Observing science classrooms: Observing science perspectives from research and practice* (pp. 55–73). Columbus: Ohio State University.

Montgomery, D. E. (1992). Young children's theory of knowing: The development of a folk epistemology. *Developmental Review, 12,* 410–430.

Murphy, G. L., & Medin, D. L. (1982). The role of theories in conceptual coherence. *Psychological Review, 92,* 289–316.

National Research Council (NRC). (2007). *Taking science to school: Learning and teaching science in grades K–8.* Washington, DC: National Academies Press.

Nersessian, N. (1989). Conceptual change in science and science education. *Synthese, 80*(1), 163–183.

Nersessian, N. (1992). How do scientists think? Capturing the dynamics of conceptual change in science. In. R. Giere (Ed.), *Cognitive models of science* (pp. 3–44). Minneapolis: University of Minnesota.

Nersessian, N. (2008). *Creating scientific concepts.* Cambridge: MIT Press.

Niebert, K., Marsch, S., & Treagust, D. F. (2012). Understanding needs embodiment: A theory-guided reanalysis of the role of metaphors and analogies in understanding science. *Science Education, 96*(5), 849–877.

Nordine, J., Krajcik, J., & Fortus, D. (2011). Transforming energy instruction in middle school to support integrated understanding and future learning. *Science Education, 95,* 670–699.

Novak, J. D. (1977). *A theory of education.* Ithaca, NY: Cornell University Press.

Nussbaum, J., & Novick, S. (1982). Alternative frameworks, conceptual conflict, and accommodation: Towards a principled teaching strategy. *Instructional Science, 11,* 183–200.

Osborne, R., & Freyberg, P. (1985). *Learning in science: The implications of children's science.* Portsmouth, NH: Heinemann Education Books.

Pea, R. D. (1994). Seeing what we build together: Distributed multimedia learning environments for transformative communications. *Journal of the Learning Sciences, 3*(3), 285–299.

Perkins, D., & Grotzer, T. A. (2005). Dimensions of causal understanding: The role of complex causal models in students' understanding of science. *Studies in Science Education, 41,* 117–165.

Piaget, J. (1995). *Sociological studies*. London: Routledge. (Original work published 1977).

Piaget, J., & Inhelder, B. (1942). *The child's construction of quantities: Conservation and atomism*. London: Routledge and Kegan Paul.

Redish, E., & Hammer, D. (2009). Reinventing college physics for biologists: Explicating an epistemological curriculum. *American Journal of Physics, 77*(7), 629–642.

Rogat, A., Anderson, C., Foster, J., Goldberg, F., Hicks, J., Kanter, D., Krajcik, J., Lehrer, R., Resier, B., & Wiser, M. (2011). *Developing learning progressions in support of the new science standards: A RAPID Workshop Series*. CPRE. Teachers College, Columbia University.

Roschelle, J. (1992). Learning by collaborating: Convergent conceptual change. *Journal of the Learning Sciences, 2*(3), 235–276.

Sandoval, W. (2005). Understanding students' practical epistemologies and their effect on learning through inquiry. *Science Education, 89*(4), 634–656.

Schauble, L., Klopfer, L., & Ragavan, K. (1991). Students' transition from an engineering model to a science model of experimentation. *Journal of Research in Science Teaching, 28*(9), 859–882.

Scherr, R.E., Close, H.G., McKagan, S.B., & Vokos, S. (2012). Representing energy. I. Representing a substance ontology for energy. *Physical Review—Special Topics: Physics Education Research, 8*(2), 1–11.

Schwab, J. (1964). *The teaching of science as enquiry*. Cambridge, MA: Harvard University Press.

Scott, P.H., Asoko, H.M., & Driver R.H. (1992). Teaching for conceptual change: Review of strategies. In R. Duit, F. Goldberg, & H. Niederer (Eds.), *Research in physics learning: Theoretical issues and empirical studies* (pp. 310–329). Kiel, Germany: IPN—Institute for Science Education.

Scott, P., Asoko, H., & Leach, J. (2007). Student conceptions and conceptual learning in science. In S. K. Abell & N.G. Lederman (Eds.), *Handbook of research on science education* (pp. 31–54). Mahwah, NJ: Lawrence Erlbaum Associates.

Sherin, B. (2001). How students understand physics equations. *Cognition and Instruction, 19*(4), 479–541.

Sherin, B. (2006). Common sense clarified: The role of intuition knowledge in physics problem solving. *Journal of Research in Science Teaching, 43*(6), 535–555.

Sinatra, G., & Pintrich, P. (2003). The role of intentions in conceptual change learning. In G. Sinatra & P. Pintrich (Eds.), *Intentional conceptual change* (pp. 1–18). Mahwah, NJ: Erlbaum.

Slotta, J. (2011). In defense of Chi's ontological incompatibility hypothesis. *Journal of the Learning Sciences, 20*(1), 151–162.

Slotta, J.D., & Chi, M.T.H. (2006). The impact of ontology training on conceptual change: Helping students understand the challenging topics in science. *Cognition and Instruction, 24*(2), 261–289.

Slotta, J.D., Chi, M.T.H., & Joram, E. (1995). Assessing students' misclassifications of physics concepts: An ontological basis for conceptual change. *Cognition and Instruction, 13*(3), 373–400.

Smith, C. (2007). Bootstrapping processes in the development of students' commonsense matter theories. *Cognition and Instruction, 25*(4), 337–398.

Smith, C., Maclin, D., Grosslight, L., & Davis, H. (1997). Teaching for understanding: A comparison of two approaches to teaching students about matter and density. *Cognition and Instruction, 15*(3), 317–393.

Smith, C., Maclin, D., Houghton, C., & Hennessey, M.G. (2000). Sixth grade students' epistemologies of science: The impact of school science experiences on epistemological development. *Cognition & Instruction, 18*, 349–422.

Smith, C., Snir, J., & Grosslight, L. (1992). Using conceptual models to facilitate conceptual change: The case of weight-density differentiation. *Cognition and Instruction, 9*(3), 221–283.

Smith, J., diSessa, A., & Roschelle, J. (1993). Misconceptions reconceived: A constructivist analysis of knowledge in transition. *Journal of the Learning Sciences, 3*(2), 115–163.

Songer, N., & Linn, M. (1991). How do students' views of science influence knowledge integration? *Journal of Research in Science Teaching, 28*(9), 761–784.

Stathopoulou, C., & Vosniadou, S. (2007a). Conceptual change in physics and physics-related epistemological beliefs: A relationship under scrutiny. In S. Vosniadou, A. Baltas, & X. Vamvakoussi (Eds.), *Reframing the conceptual change approach in learning and instruction* (pp. 145–163). New York: Elsevier.

Stathopoulou, C., & Vosniadou, S. (2007b). Exploring the relationship between physics-related epistemological beliefs and physics understanding. *Contemporary Educational Psychology, 32*, 255–281.

Stephens, L., & Clement, J. (2010). Documenting the use of expert scientific reasoning processes by high school physics students. *Physical Review Special Topics—Physics Education Research, 6*(2). Retrieved from http://link.aps.org/doi/10.1103/PhysRevSTPER.6.020122

Strike, K.A., & Posner, G.J. (1985). A conceptual change view of learning and understanding. In L.H. West & A.L. Pines (Eds.), *Conceptual structure and conceptual change* (pp. 189–210). Orlando, FL: Academic Press, Inc.

Strike, K.A., & Posner, G.J. (1992). A revisionist theory of conceptual change. In R. Duschl & R. Hamilton (Eds.), *Philosophy of science, cognitive psychology, and educational theory and practice* (pp. 147–174). Albany: State University of New York Press.

Thagard, P. (2012). *The cognitive science of science: Explanation, discovery, and conceptual change*. Cambridge: MIT Press.

Vosniadou, S. (1994). Capturing and modeling the process of conceptual change. *Learning and Instruction, 4,* 45–69.

Vosniadou, S. (2008). Conceptual change research: An introduction. In S. Vosniadou (Ed.), *International handbook of research on conceptual change* (pp. xiii–xxviii). New York: Routledge.

Vosniadou, S., & Brewer, W.F. (1987). Theories of knowledge restructuring in development. *Review of Educational Research, 57,* 51–67.

Vosniadou, S., Vamvakoussi, X., & Skopeliti, I. (2008). The framework theory approach to the problem of conceptual change. In S. Vosniadou (Ed.), *International handbook of research on conceptual change* (pp. 3–34). New York: Routledge.

Vygotsky, L.S. (1978). *Mind in society: The development of higher psychological processes*. Cambridge, MA: Harvard University Press.

Waxman, S.R., & Markow, D.B. (1995). Words as invitations to form categories: Evidence from 12- to 13-month-old infants. *Cognitive Psychology, 29,* 257–302.

Wertsch, J.V. (1991). *Voices of the mind: A sociocultural approach to mediated action*. Cambridge, MA: Harvard University Press.

White, B.Y. (1995). The ThinkerTools project: Computer microworlds as conceptual tools for facilitating scientific inquiry. In S.M. Glynn & R. Duit (Eds.), *Learning science in the schools: Research reforming practice* (pp. 201–227). Hillsdale, NJ: Lawrence Erlbaum Associates.

White, B.Y., & Frederiksen, J. R. (1998). Inquiry, modeling, and metacognition: Making science accessible to all students. *Cognition and Instruction, 16*(1), 3–118.

Wilensky, U., & Novak, M. (2010). Teaching and learning evolution as an emergent process: The BEAGLE project. In R. Taylor & M. Ferrari (Eds.), *Epistemology and science education: Understanding the evolution vs. intelligent design controversy* (pp. 243–268). New York: Routledge.

Wilensky, U., & Reisman, K. (2006). Thinking like a wolf, sheep, or firefly: Learning biology through constructing and testing computation theories—an embodied modeling approach. *Cognition and Instruction, 24*(2), 171–209.

Williams, J.M., & Tolmie, A. (2000). Conceptual change in biology: Group interaction and the understanding of inheritance. *British Journal of Developmental Psychology, 18,* 625–649.

Wiser, M. (1995). Use of history of science to understand and remedy students' misconceptions about heat and temperature. In D.N. Perkins, J.L. Schwartz, M.M. West, & M.S. Stone (Eds.), *Software goes to school* (pp. 23–38). New York: Oxford University Press.

Wiser, M., & Amin, T. (2001). "Is heat hot?" Inducing conceptual change by integrating everyday and scientific conceptions. *Learning and Instruction, 11,* 331–355.

Wiser, M., & Amin, T. G. (2002). Computer-based interactions for conceptual change in science. In M. Limon & L. Mason (Eds.), *Reconsidering conceptual change: Issues in theory and practice* (pp. 357–387). Dordrecht, the Netherlands: Kluwer.

Wiser, M., & Smith, C. (2013). Learning and teaching about matter in the middle school years: How can the atomic-molecular theory be meaningfully introduced? In S. Vosniadou (Ed.), *International handbook of research on conceptual change* (2nd ed., pp. 177–194). New York: Routledge.

Wiser, M., Smith, C., & Doubler, S. (2012). Learning progressions as tools for curriculum development: Lessons from the Inquiry Project. In A. Alonzo & A. Gotwals (Eds.), *Learning progressions in science: Current challenges and future directions* (pp. 359–404). Rotterdam, the Netherlands: Sense Publishers.

5

Attitudes, Identity, and Aspirations Toward Science

RUSSELL TYTLER

Concerns About Student Attitudes Toward and Engagement With Science

Student attitudes toward science have received constant research attention for a number of decades, for reasons that have changed over time. Science curriculum outcomes have for many years included attitudinal outcomes alongside knowledge and skills. Curriculum innovations and activities are often premised on evoking student interest or making science "fun" (see Appelbaum & Clark, 2001, for a critique of this construct). Yet no such concern for attitudes is evident in English or history, for example. The particular interest in attitudes toward science can be traced to the challenge for science education of fulfilling two distinct roles (Millar & Osborne, 1998). Firstly, under recent and current rubrics of "science for all" (Fensham, 1985) or scientific literacy, school science is charged with preparing future citizens to engage with science in their lives, involving an appreciation of the nature of science as a distinctive and powerful way of looking at the world. This aim has inevitable dispositional implications. On the other hand, school science is charged with preparing the next generation of scientists. These dual mandates have often been taken to be in conflict—the first involving engaging students who may not necessarily be "science disposed" in activities that attract them to science and offering a perspective on how science works in the world (Ryder, 2001). The second emphasizes serious attention to foundational concepts in the science disciplines and the enlistment of students presumed science enthusiastic to future science studies and work. But are these roles fundamentally in conflict? To what extent do they imply different framings of the curriculum and, importantly for this review, different perspectives on the role of attitudes in supporting and promoting learning? From an attitudinal perspective, the two roles might be taken to imply different emphases in terms of the target of attention to attitudes, whether this relates primarily to improving learning, promoting

scientific ways of looking at the world, designing activities to maximize engagement, or enlisting students to science over the longer term.

This review will explore the relations among these different attitudinal "targets." It will pursue the following clusters of questions in relation to attitudes, with the aim of arriving at a position on attitudes and identity that can inform the deeper purposes of engagement with quality learning in science.

1. In planning school science programs, what attitudes should we focus on to develop? What are the methodological challenges in framing and measuring attitudes?
2. How do different attitudes interrelate with each other and with different aspects of student behavior and intentions? To what extent can we consider attitudes as psychological traits or as socially situated, contextually related dispositions?
3. What patterns of attitudes to and engagement with school science can be discerned, and what are their key determinants?
4. What is the nature of the identity construct, and how does it relate to attitudes to science? What does an identity focus bring to our understanding of student aspirations in relation to science?

Three key themes in the science education literature relate to attitudes, which bear on the distinctions just raised concerning the different targets of attitudinal research:

1. The relationship of attitudes to quality of learning, variously cast as a prior requirement for learning, or as a fundamental aspect of learning
2. The relationship of attitudes to engagement with science, which manifests as
   * Engagement of students in classroom science activities, as active and involved participants. In the longer term, this might be expected to result in the creation of a broadly science-friendly public.

- Longer-term commitments and participation in postcompulsory science
3. The distinction among attitudes toward science, and scientific attitudes

Representing the first theme, that of the relationship of attitudes to conceptual learning, interest in attitudes gained ground with the rediscovery that conceptual learning is fundamentally affected by student motivation—the "warming trend" in conceptual change research that argued for motivation (Pintrich, Marx, & Boyle, 1993; Sinatra, 2005) and broader personal factors including epistemological (Sinatra & Pintrich, 2002) and aesthetic responses (Wickman, 2006), as critical for student engagement with conceptual learning. Many studies treat attitudes as necessary precursors to or outcomes of science learning sequences. There is increasing interest in research that uses the identity construct to link attitudes to the nature of school science knowledge processes and structures (e.g., Schreiner & Sjøberg, 2007).

Related to the second theme, there is increasing concern about mounting evidence of a decline in student attitudes toward science across the schooling years and across time, affecting uptake into postcompulsory science courses (Tytler et al., 2008). Policy makers in most countries are increasingly looking to science and mathematics education to produce a supply of technical expertise to maintain or improve their economic edge in an increasingly technology-dependent world. There is considerable concern about student attitudes to science related to the uptake of postcompulsory STEM (science, technology, engineering, and mathematics) pathways, the "leaky pipeline" of supply of the next generation of scientific and technological expertise. This concern is evidenced by high-level reports in the United States (National Academy of Sciences: Committee on Science Engineering and Public Policy, 2005; National Commission on Mathematics and Science Teaching for the 21st Century, 2000), the UK (HM Treasury, 2006), Europe (European Commission, 2004; Osborne & Dillon, 2008), and Australia (Office of the Chief Scientist, 2012; Tytler et al., 2008).

An important distinction is that drawn by Leopold Klopfer (1971) between "attitudes toward science" and "scientific attitudes." The latter are a set of attitudes that characterize the nature of working in science, including a commitment to evidence as the basis of belief, a belief in rational argument, and skepticism toward hypotheses and claims about the material world. Scientific attitudes also include curiosity concerning aspects of the natural world. It is the first of these two constructs, "attitudes toward science," that is the major focus of this chapter and the body of research discussed here, but we will raise the question of whether, at a more fundamental level, the distinction can be maintained.

Attitudinal Constructs and Their Measurement

A variety of attitudinal constructs are explored in the psychological and science education literature, often with a lack of clarity as to how they relate to each other. Much of the literature in the psychological tradition relates to clarifying these constructs and their interrelations. Each of them has its own history of research and theoretical formulations of interrelations. In science education, these distinctions have often gone unacknowledged. The constructs related to science education include:

- exhibiting favorable attitudes toward science and scientists, which might include interest in what scientists do, perceptions of scientists and their work, valuing of the scientific enterprise, and valuing of evidence-based scientific approaches
- exhibiting favorable attitudes toward school science, either as a "liking of doing science" or in comparison to other subjects
- valuing of the evidence-based approaches characteristics of science and adopting of scientific attitudes that include objectivity, commitment to rational argumentation, persistence, or curiosity
- the enjoyment of science learning experiences, which includes the pervasive "science is fun" concept (Appelbaum & Clark, 2001), or appreciation of exploring the objects of science
- the development of interests in science and science-related activities, which might relate to short-term activities or a longer-term orientation of interest in science
- the development of an interest in or commitment to pursuing a career in science or science-related work
- a sense of self-efficacy in relation to science, the counter of which is anxiety toward science
- motivation to do science and learn science

The question arises as to which of these constructs are the most relevant for students' future lives as citizens or as scientists. In planning school science programs, which attitudes do we want to develop, and for what purposes? How might we measure these?

Measuring Attitudes Through Surveys

Research into student attitudes to science, either to establish a profile at different grade levels or to track changes due to innovation, has mostly used surveys constructed to explore a range of dimensions of student attitude. Yet questions have been raised about the validity of these surveys and the methodologies associated with their use.

A recent comprehensive review of 66 attitude instruments referred to in 150 peer-reviewed articles was conducted by Cheryl Blalock and colleagues (2008). These researchers identified four major attitude categories from the student science attitudes research: (1) attitudes toward science—"the emotional reactions of students towards science . . . interest, satisfaction, and enjoyment" (Gardner, 1975, p. 2); (2) scientific attitudes having the characteristics of "critical mindedness, respect for evidence, objectivity, open-mindedness, and questioning attitude" (Mayer & Richmond, 1982, p. 56); (3) the nature of science—"the aims of science, its epistemology, its tactics, its values, its institutional functions, its interactions with society, and its human needs" (Aikenhead, 1973, p. 540); and (4) interest in scientific-related careers.

We can see immediately that these major attitude constructs are quite different in (a) time scale—some relate to context-specific responses and others to longer-term orientations such as career intentions; (b) in their focus—on school science, on science itself, or on leisure interest; (c) in their relation to cognition—some involve appreciative understanding, for instance of the nature of science or of scientists, while others have no necessary cognitive dimension; and (d) in whether they describe a scientific attitude or an attitude toward science or school science. There is a need, in researching and drawing conclusions from attitude research, to be clear about which constructs are appropriate for which purposes.

Construct validity is one of the key issues in constructing an attitude instrument. This is essentially a question of whether each construct within the survey is grounded in a well-developed theoretical framework. Without careful attention to the meaning of what is being measured, it is likely that items sitting underneath the construct will not yield a consistent representation and that disparate items will be put together in a single scale that is theoretically indefensible (Gardner, 1975: 12). Without this assurance of a valid construct grounded in theory, there is no purpose in constructing an attitude score.

The Blalock and colleagues (2008) review established significant problems in science education with developing and using instruments meeting reliability and validity criteria. The 66 reviewed instruments were assessed against the criteria of the extent to which they were theoretically grounded, what tests had been undertaken of their reliability, the measures that had been used to establish their validity, how the dimensionality of the instrument had been used in reporting the scores, and the extent to which the instrument had been tested and developed prior to its use. Using these criteria, the authors reported that the highest-scoring instrument was that developed by Paul Germann (1988), yet this instrument has only been used in a single study. In contrast, an instrument that scored poorly on the criteria, Richard Moore and Frank Sutman's Scientific Attitude Inventory (Moore & Sutman, 1970), had been used in 13 additional studies. Blalock and colleagues demonstrated a tendency for researchers, rather than use existing, validated instruments, to each time design one anew without subjecting it to the kind of development required of a good psychometric measure. This practice has not helped the building of a defensible canon in attitude research in science education.

Other Attitude Measures

Across many studies of attitudes and attitude change in science, there have been a number of techniques used, including:

Interest inventories. The Relevance of Science Education (ROSE) study (Sjøberg & Schreiner, 2005) has received wide attention, comparing student perceptions and attitudes to science across a range of countries. ROSE included items that presented a list of topics and asked students which ones they were interested to learn about. The questionnaire responses from an English cohort were summarized by Jenkins and Pell (2006, p. 6):

> When asked what they wished to learn about, there are marked differences in the responses of boys and girls. For girls, the priorities lie with topics related to the self and, more particularly, to health, mind and well-being. The responses of the boys reflect strong interests in destructive technologies and events. Topics such as "Famous scientists and their lives" and "How crude oil is converted into other materials" are among the least popular with both boys and girls.

Such inventories can tell us a lot about comparative attitudes to different aspects of science, but on their own they do not tell us much about what may be the formative influences on these views or how they may play out in the classroom setting.

A similar but more embedded technique was used in the PISA science test (OECD, 2006), in which students were asked, for some questions, to rate their interest in finding out more about aspects of the phenomenon. These data were the subject of a special issue of the *International Journal of Science Education* (Olsen, Prenzel, & Martin, 2011).

Subject preference studies. In these studies (e.g., Jovanovic & King, 1998; Lightbody & Durndell, 1996b; Whitfield, 1980), students are asked to rank school subjects in order of preference or importance. Such scales do not establish absolute measures of attitudes. A student may, for instance, rank science low on such scales but still have a positive orientation to science.

Draw a scientist test (DAST). A frequently used probe of students' images of science involves asking them to "draw a scientist" (Chambers, 1983; Mead & Metraux, 1957). This instrument identified a range of stereotypical features students associated with scientists (Chambers, 1983; Farland-Smith, 2012), including that they were mainly white, male, eccentric, and surrounded by laboratory accouterments. The test has been used to investigate a number of influences on students' images of scientists, including age, gender, socioeconomic status (Chambers, 1983), and media effects (Steinke et al., 2007). The research has exposed an "image problem" for scientists that it is argued affects students'—especially girls'—engagement with future science studies. However, there is evidence

(Losh, Wilke, & Pop, 2008) that the instrument invites students to reproduce a stereotype rather than represent possible diversity in their views about science and scientists.

Qualitative Methodologies

A general critique of survey instruments is that they cannot accurately measure student attitudes because the statements and forced-choice responses typically reflect the researcher's ideologies rather than the students'. Ryan and Aikenhead (1992) argue that instruments should be based on data generated from student interviews. A companion criticism of attitude scales derived from questionnaire surveys, related to their interpretation, is that, while they are useful in identifying the current circumstance of student attitudes, they have not been helpful in understanding the generative mechanisms.

Flowing from these criticisms, there has recently been a growth of qualitative methodological approaches to exploring student attitudes to science. Terry Lyons (2006a), in a paper reviewing three recent, similar qualitative studies from the UK, Sweden, and Australia, points to the remarkable similarity of students' experiences of science in these countries. The studies were conducted by Britt Lindahl (Lindahl, 2007), Terry Lyons (Lyons, 2003, 2006a), and Jonathan Osborne and Sue Collins (Osborne & Collins, 2001). Lindahl's study employed a longitudinal design, following 80 Swedish students from upper elementary school to the point at which they chose their senior school subjects. While such studies of necessity have smaller samples and therefore lack the ability to identify significant variables in a psychometrically defined manner and are subject to limited generalizability, they do provide significant insights into the details and origins of attitudes to school science, more so than do quantitative methods. The following quote from Lyons's research demonstrates a reality of a student called Malcolm's response to traditional science pedagogy that would be opaque to most survey instruments.

> Malcolm: Things were presented as fact. [Teachers] never said, "this is what someone discovered," or "this is what someone thought 200 years ago." You know, they always said, "this is what happens." So they never presented it as a theory, or as something to be argued against.
>
> (Lyons, 2006a, p. 601)

Many more recent studies into student attitudes and identity in relation to science use qualitative methods. Some, such as Deborah Chetcuti's and Berita Kioko's (2012) study of Kenyan girls' attitudes to science, use a mixture of survey and interview/focus groups.

Complexities in Interpreting Attitude Constructs

In the research on student attitudes, a number of complexities make straightforward description and measurement of attitudes difficult and need to be born in mind when proposing or interpreting attitudinal research.

A distinction needs to be made between attitudes to school science and science in general. Both Lyons (2006a) and Lindahl (2007) found students who expressed strong interest in science and science-related hobbies yet were bored or frustrated with school science. Jonathan Osborne and colleagues (Osborne, Simon, & Collins, 2003) argue that attitudes toward school science are better predictors of student behavior than are attitudes toward science in general. Making a clear distinction between these discrete attitudes should enable researchers to be more clear-sighted about intervention opportunities designed to make school science more attractive to science-friendly students.

Attitudinal constructs can occur on different time scales and with different degrees of specificity. Thus, interest or enjoyment might relate to a particular episode or topic in school science, or it might relate to a more general disposition over a longer time that appears as a pervasive orientation. A distinction is made between affect as a relatively long-term trait and as a specific short-term response.

Attitudes such as interest, motivation, enjoyment, curiosity, and confidence each have different contexts in which they are applied and specific characteristics that define them. Yet they are interrelated. The question arises, then, as to which of these is particularly worthy of promotion in science education and for what purposes. Some of these constructs are not uncontroversial. The promotion of science as "fun," for instance, has been critically analyzed by Peter Applebaum and Stella Clark (2001) and argued to be a cover for the establishment of an authoritarian regime in promoting science. On the other hand, Yannis Hadzigeorgiou (2012) found that emphasizing the "wonder" of science phenomena in a ninth-grade science unit led to enhanced involvement and learning.

In investigating attitudes, researchers need to be clear about the nature of the particular construct and its relation to the research aims. Is the attitude positioned as a long-term psychological trait, or is it contextually framed and socially constituted? For instance, Renninger and Hidi (2011), in reviewing research on student interest, argue that if researchers are clear how the level or phase of interest can vary among students, then informed decisions can be made about how to best support students with little interest or those with developed interest.

> For example, if researchers focus on developed interest and conceptualize it as a trait, then they may not recognize that students' interests could be nurtured and that lack of interest could be changed and become a future interest with support from others.
>
> (2011, p. 169)

They argue a need for reciprocity among theoretical frameworks, research questions, intentions, analysis, and recommended interventions.

There are thus complexities in exploring attitudinal constructs that bear on both theoretical and methodological considerations. How attitudes are theorized determines how they are measured, how data are interpreted, and how implications for practice are framed. There is a rich history in the psychological and sociological literatures concerning how attitudes interrelate and how they relate to intentions and observable behaviors.

Models Linking Attitudinal Constructs and Orientation to Learning

Classical attitudinal research aims to determine relationships among complex interacting variables such as student behavior, motivation, and achievement. Modeling of the relationships between different attitude constructs has been a major preoccupation in the psychological literature. Structural equation modeling, exploring how latent variables interrelate using factor analysis as its basis, has been used as the basis for exploring causal links between attitude constructs and learning. A number of frequently cited models interconnect different attitude constructs with learning intentions and behaviors.

Pekrun's control value theory of achievement emotions, developed and refined in a research program spanning a number of years (Pekrun, Frenzel, Goetz, & Perry, 2007), argues that a diverse array of emotions impacts students' approach to learning. These academic emotions can be self-referenced, task-related, and social emotions and include enjoyment, hope, pride, anger, anxiety, hopelessness, and shame. They interact in complex ways with characteristics of the learning environment to influence students' motivation, learning strategies, cognitive resources, self-regulation, and academic achievement (Pekrun, Goetz, Titz, & Perry, 2002, p. 91). These authors find that "negative" emotions such as anxiety can have positive effects on learning and that some "positive" emotions can inhibit learning.

A number of models position attitude constructs as part of a person's fundamental positioning with regard to self-concepts across multiple dimensions, bringing us closer to a framing of attitudes and value positions that combine psychological and sociological features. The Eccles Expectancy-Value Model (Eccles et al., 1983) perceives students' engagement in terms of the link between valuing a task and expectancy of success. In recent years, Eccles's model, conceptualized in terms of two sets of self-perceptions—those related to *skills*, *characteristics*, and *competencies* and perceptions related to *personal values and goals* (Bøe, 2012; Brophy, 2009; Eccles, 2009)—has found its way into identity-based and STEM–related science education research (Andrée & Hansson, 2012; Aschbacher, Li, & Roth, 2010; Bøe, 2011; Bøe, Henriksen, Lyons, & Schreiner, 2011; Cerinsek, Hribar, Glodez, & Dolinsek, 2012; Hill, Corbett, & St. Rose, 2010; Lyons & Quinn, 2010; Riegle-Crumb, Moore, & Ramos-Wada, 2011). For Eccles (2009), these sets of perceptions inform an individual's expectation of success and the significance of "becoming involved in a wide range of tasks" (p. 78).

Albert Bandura's model (Bandura, 1997) emphasizes the perception of self-efficacy—the belief that one has the power to produce effects by one's actions. Bandura argued that self-efficacy is a major determinant of an individual's choice of activity and her or his willingness or motivation to expend effort. The self-efficacy construct has achieved widespread currency in the research literature as a way of explaining individuals' motivation and engagement. It has been used in studies exploring, for instance, career choice (Bandura, Barbaranelli, Caprara, & Pastorelli, 2001). In a recent UK study, Blenkinsop, McCrone, Wade, and Morris (2006) concluded that self-efficacy emerged as a result of the interaction between "socioeconomic, familial, academic and self-referent influences [operating] in concert to shape young people's career trajectories" and that young people's beliefs in their academic capabilities, rather than their actual academic achievement, "had the most direct pervasive impact on their judgments of their occupational efficacy" (Bandura in Blenkinsop et al., 2006, p. 4).

Interest is an attitudinal construct that has achieved greater prominence in the literature as linked to learning and to students' inclination to maintain science studies. Hidi and Renninger (2006) claim that interest is recognized as a critical cognitive and affective motivational variable that guides attention. They argue that despite a long history of use of the interest construct in the literature, it is only recently that it has been studied systematically. They ascribe to interest five characteristics: (1) as referring to an individual's focused engagement with particular objects or events; (2) as involving a particular relation between a person and the environment, sustained through interaction; (3) as having both cognitive and affective components; (4) that the learner may not be aware of their interest, especially if absorbed; and (5) as having a physiological/neurological basis. Hidi and Renninger's (2006) Four-Phase Model of Interest Development posits that significant interest occurs through four stages: triggered situational interest, maintained situational interest, emerging individual interest, and well-developed individual interest. All four phases are stimulated by supportive learning environments and a predisposition for students to maintain engagement with certain classes of content or activities over time. The model proposes that knowledge, affect, and value are essential components of a strong individual interest in science. We can thus see that interest in science, in its final phase, is positioned as a characterizing feature of a person's response to the subject that transcends particularities.

Azevedo (2011, 2012) has conducted longitudinal studies of hobbies of individuals such as model rocketry and amateur astronomy as paradigmatic examples of interest-driven practices. He argued the need to shift from conceptualizations of such long-term, self-motivated engagement in terms of individual interest as a topic specific engagement to a more practice-based theory based on what he calls "lines of practice." A line of practice is a distinctive, recurrent pattern of long-term engagement that reflects the intersection of individuals' deeper goals, values, and beliefs attuned to particular conditions of practice operating in hobby communities. He explores (Azevedo, 2012) the implications of this perspective for interest-driven classroom practices and the transactions among students, teachers, and the wider classroom environment. These flow from four structural and process features he identified in hobby practice: a varied material infrastructure that allowed variation in practice, participation across multiple sites, activity structural resources operating as activity templates, and collaboration and idea sharing. A key feature of interest-driven engagement in lines of practice is the capacity for individuals to tailor their activities to their existing and emerging practices.

Ainley and Ainley (2011) used responses to various attitude constructs in the PISA 2006 survey of science achievement (OECD, 2007) to investigate links among socioeconomic status, science knowledge, personal value of science, enjoyment of science, and embedded interest in particular topics in which students were asked to nominate their extent of interest in finding out about particular science-related aspects of PISA question units. Using structural equation modeling, they found strong predictive association between enjoyment of science and interest in engaging with topics and between attitudes generally and intentions. They also found evidence that personal relevance and meaning for students' lives is an important indicator of enjoyment and of both topic-specific and general interest.

The Relationship of Affect to Cognition

Ainley and Ainley's (2011) finding that knowledge and personal value combine to determine student enjoyment and interest links to sociocultural and pragmatist perspectives that see affect and value not as separate dispositions feeding into engagement with learning and knowing but as an integral part of what it is to learn and know. Affect and cognition are opposite sides of the same coin, discursively constructed as part of an effective education in science. Ainley and Ainley link their finding to Dewey's (1933) construct of "serious play." Dewey argues that learning is maximized when an activity is both playful and serious. From this perspective, the essential condition for learning is that enjoyment and focused attention of interest are both triggered by the learning activity. Learning to know and learning to value are inseparable. This links also to the notion of undivided interest in the work of Rathunde and Csikszentmihalyi (1993) and of Csikszentmihalyi's (1992) concept of "flow."

There is growing interest in the construct of aesthetic experience as expressing an essential "continuity" or mutuality between the affective and cognitive domains (Girod, Rau, & Schepige, 2003; Girod & Wong, 2002; Hobbs, 2012; Pugh & Girod, 2007). According to Dewey (1934/1980 p. 47), aesthetic experience signifies "experience as appreciative, perceiving and enjoying." Dewey's epistemology does not separate cognitive ways of knowing from affective and aesthetic understandings. Girod and colleagues (2003, p. 575) explored the role that

"aesthetics, creativity, passion, beauty and art play in the lives and learning of scientists." Wickman (2006) argues that the traditional opposition between aesthetic and value positions and conceptual work is a false dichotomy both for scientists and learners of science. Aesthetic judgments should not be seen as general dispositions separate from learned ways of understanding but as an element of culturally acquired discursive practices in science. Extending this program of research, Jakobson and Wickman (2008) showed how primary teachers of science blended aesthetic and conceptual talk in motivating and challenging elementary science students.

In this work on aesthetic understanding, we can see not only a coming together of the affective and cognitive domains but also a blending of the distinction between "attitudes toward science" and "scientific attitudes." The recognition of scientific objects as valued and scientific knowledge as valued and transformative establishes aesthetic understanding as involving a positive attitude toward science while at the same time being a core aspect of the knowledge itself. Gaining an aesthetic understanding is part of what is meant by developing a scientific attitude.

Attitudes and Subject Choice

A distinction should made between attitudes and behavior in that attitudes need not necessarily relate to the behaviors a person actually exhibits (Potter & Wetherell, 1987). For instance, a student may express interest in science but avoid publicly demonstrating it among his or her peers if they regard such an expression of intellectual interest as not being "cool." Anticipated consequences may modify the behavior so that it is inconsistent with the attitude held. Environmental education researchers have long been interested in the relationship among knowledge, attitudes, and behavior in relation to environmental action. Joe Heimlich and Nicole Ardoin (2008) have reviewed the main ideas and empirical studies in this field.

The potential disjunction between attitudes and behavior makes it problematic to associate student enrolment data directly with interest in science. Subject choice can be significantly affected by such factors as perceived structure of economic opportunities, expectations of peers and of parents, patterns of prerequisites, perceived difficulty of the subjects, and gendered expectations—all of which can be independent of a student's core attitude toward school science. Also, students who choose subjects other than science out of interest are not necessarily expressing a dislike of science but rather a greater liking or identification with other subjects.

The Landscape of Attitudes to School Science

Studies over the last few decades have identified some clearly defined features of students' attitudes to school science. We will discuss three major patterns from the literature, the first relating to a decline in positive attitudes across the years of schooling, the second relating to differences between countries, and the third relating to gender.

Age-Related Decline in Attitude

Many studies have identified a general downward trend of attitudes with age, from as early as the first year of elementary school (Murphy & Beggs, 2003; Pell & Jarvis, 2001). The trend continues and accelerates over the early years of secondary school (Breakwell & Beardsell, 1992; Goodrum, Hackling, & Rennie, 2001; Simpson & Oliver, 1985; Yager & Penick, 1986). Speering and Rennie (1996) explored the decline in interest in science across the elementary–secondary school transition, pointing out these were critical years in which dispositions to pursue science subjects and careers are formed. However, studies have also shown a decline in attitudes to schooling generally over the adolescent years (Eccles & Wigfield, 1992; Epstein & McPartland, 1976). The key question concerns the relative decline of attitudes to science compared to other subjects. Richard Whitfield's (1980) analysis of UK Institute for Educational Assessment data showed that physics and chemistry were two of the least popular subjects post–14 and that these were distinct in pupils' minds from biology. Lyons's (2006a) comparative study of interview data from England, Sweden, and Australia confirms the broad trend, and the Osborne and Collins (2001) study paints a similar picture of the differential response to the different sciences. It is clear that "attitude to school science" is not a unitary construct, given that these and other studies such as ROSE (Sjøberg & Schreiner, 2005) identify different attitudes for the different sciences and for different topics within these.

Country and Gender Patterns

In the ROSE study, which compared responses to science across a variety of countries, students were asked to respond on a four-point Likert scale to assertions such as "I like school science better than other subjects." There are two major features of data from the study. First, there is less interest in school science in more industrialized countries, judged by the simple "I like science" scale but also from scales relating to intention to pursue science studies or careers. Second, girls have a more negative attitude compared to boys, a finding that is supported by a wide range of research and that we will discuss at more length in upcoming sections.

Similar findings emerge from Yasushi Ogura's (2006) analysis of the 1999 data for the Third International Mathematics and Science Study (TIMSS). Ogura plotted their achievement scores, based on their knowledge of science concepts, against the percentage of students with high scores for positive attitudes toward science. He found a substantial negative correlation (0.496), with high-performing countries such as Korea and Japan having less than 10% of students with high attitude scores, compared to low-performing countries such as Iran, Indonesia, or the Philippines, with more than 50% of students with high attitude scores.

What is surprising here is that students in countries that were most successful in terms of knowledge outcomes, whose achievements other countries seek to emulate and that offer a traditional, well-resourced, and knowledge-focused science curriculum have the most negative attitudes to school science. Such data have caused considerable disquiet in developed countries, being linked to data showing a decline in participation in science, technology, engineering, and mathematics (STEM) subjects and careers. This essentially economic concern was discussed previously. These findings, however, raise two distinct questions—first about whether responses to attitude measures are culturally mediated, with some cultures possibly reticent to express strongly positive attitudes and second concerning the measure of "knowledge" being employed here, defined in terms of test results arguably advantaged by highly structured classroom environments.

The classroom realities implied by such findings are undoubtedly of concern to teachers, given that student attitudes to the subject inevitably strongly influence their job satisfaction. Analysis of the international TIMSS tests, however (Mullis, Martin, Foy, & Arora, 2012), shows that within any particular country, there is a positive relationship between students' extent of liking of science and their level of performance.

Are Students Positive About Science?

These trends in student attitude data showing decreasing positive attitudes to science over time and lower levels of affect in developed economies shift attention from a more basic judgment concerning whether students on the whole have positive attitudes toward their science studies. One reading of the data from the ROSE study, for instance, is that even in Norway, which is at the bottom of the attitude scale, 40% of boys and 22% of girls answer the question about liking science more than other subjects positively. Given the number of subjects competing for students' attention, the question arises as to whether the concern has been exaggerated.

The Research Council's UK survey of public attitudes to science asked people whether they thought their school science was worse than other subjects, about the same, or better. One in five young people (age 16–24) thought it worse but one in three thought it better. Likewise, a study conducted in England (Jenkins & Nelson, 2005) for the ROSE study found that 61% agreed with the proposition that school science is interesting. A decreasing percentage agreed that they liked science more than other subjects (31%) or they would like to become a scientist (21%). Previous studies have found similar levels of attitudes to school science (Assessment of Performance Unit, 1988; Research Business, 1994). A recent UK study of the public attitudes to science (Research Councils UK, 2008) based on a random sample of 2,137 individuals found that a third of young people (age 16–24) felt that their school science education had been better than other subjects, and 43% felt it had been about the same. Comparable figures for adults (age 25 or higher) were respectively 17% and 48%. The recent PISA analyses showed a relatively positive picture for the United States, with 45% of eighth-grade students indicating that they would like to study science after high school (OECD, 2007).

It should be pointed out also that the assumption that not enough students are choosing to study science has been challenged on a number of fronts, including mixed opinion on whether there is a real shortage of STEM professionals entering the workforce. A body of evidence suggests that the production of scientists is in fact healthy (Butz et al., 2003; Jagger, 2007; Lynn & Salzman, 2006; Nature Editorial, 2009; Teitelbaum, 2007). Nevertheless, regularly, there are particular shortages in science and engineering professions and arguably a shortage in STEM competencies across the workforce generally in developed economies. STEM graduates find themselves over time in a variety of professions that make use of their particular skills (Marginson, Tytler, Freeman, & Roberts, 2013). Notwithstanding these important supply-and-demand issues, the question of whether students are positively and productively engaged with school science is perhaps better viewed from the perspective that science classrooms should be inviting places for students to learn and that future citizens should emerge from their school science experience with a disposition and capacity to engage with science more broadly (Symington & Tytler, 2004).

This being said, the declining interest and participation in school science subjects over time, particularly with the physical sciences, is cause for some concern and raises questions about the underlying causes of the shift. To what extent can this be seen as a problem with the science curriculum (Lyons, 2006b) or the changing nature of youth in postindustrial societies (Schreiner & Sjøberg, 2007) or other factors? In the following section, we will explore this question of the determinants of student engagement with science as a subject of interest worth pursuing into the postcompulsory years.

What Are the Key Determinants of Student Engagement With Science?

Krogh and Andersen (2012) argue that the exploration of a broad range of variables in STEM–related science education research might provide insights into how students' "internalise [or not] science into their personal value systems" (n.p.). While classical attitudinal research in the psychology tradition focuses on relationships among intrinsic variables such as enjoyment, interest, and motivation and their impact on achievement or behavior, there is abundant evidence that socially based variables impact strongly on behavior. These variables may reasonably be extended to include students' experiences, achievements, significant relationships including family, peers, and teachers (Cerinsek et al., 2012), socioeconomic status (Christidou, 2011), and community engagements (Lamb, Annetta,

Meldrum, & Vallett, 2012). Lamb and colleagues' (2012) "science interest" survey found that "extrinsic factors such as family, community, and schools might be more influential than intrinsic attitudes toward science interest" (p. 643). Studies such as these have signaled a shift in emphasis within the literature on student response to science from the purely psychological to more contextually based sociological determinants of engagement. We will first explore a range of determinants identified in the literature, including both psychological and sociological, before introducing the construct of identity as an analytical tool to make sense of students' response to science that includes sociological as well as psychological features.

A number of studies identify a range of interacting variables that influence student engagement with science and choice of science in the postcompulsory years. Aschbacher and colleagues' (2010) research findings point to factors that may undermine otherwise interested students' efforts to achieve in science, such as gender, socioeconomic status, parents' perceptions of the value of science, and school issues (e.g., classroom climate, numerous substitute teachers). These findings challenge the possibility of there existing simple correlations between science interest and achievement and flag a need for a more socially grounded approach to studying attitudes that link personal values and the complexity of students' life circumstances with features of the epistemological and social agendas of science.

A shift away from traditional or classical psychological research approaches to the study of attitudes is identified in Saleh and Khine's (2011) edited text *Attitude Research in Science Education: Classic and Contemporary Measurements*. In this, critical perspectives on the use of attitudinal research in science education blend classical, psychologically grounded approaches with more contemporary social psychological and sociocultural approaches, asserting the need to consider the socially situated nature of attitudes. These perspectives lay the groundwork for the growing interest in identity as a construct capable of marrying the psychological with the sociological in accounting for the complex processes by which students navigate their way through encounters with science in school and in life.

Student choice of science as a subject (and STEM subjects generally) depends on multiple and interacting factors. Fouad and colleagues (2007) used a questionnaire instrument based on social cognitive career theory with students at different stages of schooling to identify key supports and barriers to choosing science. The instrument looked at student interest and aspirations in terms of the effects of interactions between personal factors and learning experiences on outcome expectations and self-efficacy. Key barriers identified were perceptions of subject difficulty (related to self-efficacy) and the presence of test anxiety. Factors that were significant predictors of choosing to take ongoing science subjects were *science interest* (which may itself represent a number of factors), *self-evaluation of science ability, parental expectation and guidance, exposure to career guidance and having goals*, and *exposure to inspirational teachers*. Teacher support and teacher expectations of success were significant supports for middle and high school students particularly.

A few studies have shown the interactions among various factors—including self-efficacy, perceived difficulty and usefulness, and parental and teacher encouragement—at different stages in schooling. Maltese (2008) undertook a complex data analysis of a large U.S. longitudinal data set that collected information over the school and college years about family demographics and background, academic support, and achievement test results in a variety of subjects. He found a complex picture, with changing students' choice into and out of STEM subjects governed by a variety of factors. These included (a) early perceived usefulness of STEM as an indicator of future degrees in STEM, (b) academic score as an important indicator of choice of subject, and (c) the perception of usefulness of science and mathematics as a positive indicator of persistence in these subjects. An emphasis in teaching on lecturing and textbooks negatively predicted persistence in science.

In an in-depth interview study of 72 high-achieving secondary students, Anna Cleaves (2005) explored the factors influencing student subject choices across time, from Year 9 to Year 11. She separated student trajectories into five distinct patterns of choice regarding persistence in STEM. In the study, she identified many of the negative attributions to school science that have been described by other researchers, such as irrelevance, boredom, and stereotypical views of scientists and their work. For some students, however, these negative experiences were not enough to deter them from a commitment to pursue further STEM studies. Interested students chose to continue in STEM study despite negative experiences of school science. Through out-of-classroom experiences, they had often gained a deeper appreciation of what a science career might look like. She concludes that to encourage students into science, it is important both to raise the profile of science and to develop students' understanding of science-related work. Cleaves interprets the self-perceptions of students through an identity framework, showing that students' perceptions of their ability, in conjunction with their life aspirations, drive the decision to opt into or out of STEM (see also Leonardi, Syngollitou, & Kiosseoglou, 1998).

Four factors stand out as the major determinant of student interest in school science: gender, early experiences, family and cultural influences, and the quality of teaching. Space only permits detailed consideration of these four, plus some consideration of career information as a determinant. More information can be found in Jonathan Osborne and colleagues' (2003) review of the field.

Gender

Numerous studies have explored the effect of gender on student attitudes to and engagement with science. There have been a number of review articles, including Renato Schibeci's (1984) extensive review of the literature and Jane Kenway and Annette Gough's (1998) review and recent meta-analyses of the literature between 1970 and 2005 (Brotman & Moore, 2008; Murphy & Whitelegg, 2006; Weinburgh, 1995). The reviews support Paul Gardner's contention that "sex is probably the most significant variable related toward pupils' attitude to science" (Gardner, 1975). Studies have been consistent in showing that boys have a persistently more positive attitude to school science than do girls. Recent work demonstrates that the pattern continues to persist (Haste, 2004; Jones, Howe, & Rua, 2000; Sjøberg & Schreiner, 2005).

The significant issue lies with attitudes to the physical sciences and engineering (OECD, 2006), where patterns of participation continue to be skewed toward boys. Despite many interventions undertaken in the 1980s and 1990s to encourage more young women into a study of science, limited headway has been made, such that Gail Jones and colleagues (2000) were forced to conclude "that the future pipeline of scientists and engineers is likely to remain unchanged" (p. 190). Adamuti-Trache and Andres (2008) describe the situation as both chronic and a matter of concern. The problem is proving trenchant, with little to show for 25 years of effort. We will explore possible reasons for this later in this chapter through the identity construct. It is also a matter of concern, because young women who choose to study science and mathematics in high school have an "increased likelihood of attending a university and a much broader range of program options at the post-secondary level" (p. 1577; Adamuti-Trache & Andres, 2008).

Jacob Blickenstaff (2005) produced a useful review of explanatory hypotheses for women's lack of engagement with science. He argues strongly against any suggestion of innate genetic differences as a causal reason for this attitudinal difference. Rather, examining other hypotheses, he suggests that the problem is complex and not amenable to simplistic solutions. Useful insights into possible causes of the disparity come from studies that focus on the context in which science is taught. For instance, the ROSE questionnaire presents 108 topics that students might like to learn about and asks respondents to rate them on a 1 ("not at all") to a 4 ("very interested") scale. There were 80 statistically significant differences, with topics that boys are more interested in headed by "explosive chemicals, how it feels to be weightless in space, how the atom bomb functions, and biological weapons and what they do to the human body" and topics girls were interested in headed by "why we dream when we are sleeping and what the dreams might mean, what we know about cancer and how we can treat it, how to perform first aid, and sexually transmitted diseases and how to be protected against them."

Thus, girls seem to be interested in a very different science curriculum compared to boys. Haussler and Hoffmann (2002) have argued that the content of interest to girls is significantly underrepresented in the curriculum. This is consistent with the findings of other research, suggesting that girls would be interested in a physics curriculum that had more human-related content (Krogh & Thomsen, 2005). A recent survey by Helen Haste and colleagues of student attitudes based on a sample of 327 14- and 15-year-old boys and 256 girls explored how their perception of science was related to their personal, social, and ethical values (Haste, Muldoon, Hogan, & Brosnan, 2008). Dividing the sample into those oriented toward science by positive responses to questions about employment in science and an expressed interest in technology, a factor analysis of the data was conducted, with four factors discriminating the sample. She called these "trust in the benefits of science," "science in my life," "ethical skepticism," and "facts and high-tech fixes." These factors were strongly gender influenced. For girls, the consideration of ethical factors was a large positive factor, while it was a negative factor for boys. The perception of the relevance of science to their lives was a large contributing factor for girls positively inclined toward science but not for other groups. Thus, girls and boys differ in what they value in a science study. Context, purpose, and implications of science matter for girls, and the traditional presentation of science as objective and value free is likely to reduce their engagement. It would seem, given that boys have a very different perspective, that offering a homogenous curriculum would be a mistake.

Early Experiences

Student interest in science at age 10 is high, with little gender difference in either interest (Murphy & Beggs, 2005; Pell & Jarvis, 2001) or aptitude (Haworth, Dale, & Plomin, 2008). Recent research suggests, however, that by age 14, for most students, interest in pursuing further science studies is largely determined. In an analysis of data from the U.S. National Educational Longitudinal Study, Robert Tai and colleagues (Tai, Qi Liu, Maltese, & Fan, 2006) showed that by age 14, students *with* expectations of science-related careers were 3.4 times more likely to earn a physical science and engineering degree than students *without* similar expectations. This effect was even more pronounced for those who demonstrated high ability in mathematics—51% being likely to undertake a STEM–related degree. Further, Tai and colleagues' analysis shows that the average mathematics achiever at age 14 with a science-related career aspiration has a substantially greater chance of completing a physical science/engineering degree (34%) than a high mathematics achiever with a nonscience career aspiration (19%). A survey by the Royal Society (2006) of 1,141 Science, Engineering, and Technology (SET) practitioners' reasons for pursuing scientific careers provides further evidence that children's experiences prior to 14 are the major determinant of any decision to pursue the study of science. The study found that 28% of respondents first started thinking about a STEM–related career before the age of 11 and a further 35% between the ages of 12 and 14. Adam Maltese and Robert Tai (2008)

analyzed interviews with 116 scientists and graduate students to find that 65% claimed interest in pursuing science prior to middle school and a further 30% during middle and high school. An interesting gender difference underpinned these interest figures, with females more likely to refer to school- or family-related interest and males tending to claim intrinsic or self-related interest in science.

An in-depth, smaller-scale, interview-based longitudinal study conducted by Britt Lindahl, who followed 70 Swedish students from Grade 5 (age 12) to Grade 9 (age 16; Lindahl, 2007), found that children's career aspirations and interest in science were largely formed by age 13. Lindahl concluded that engaging children in science becomes progressively harder beyond this age. Similar data were generated in a study by Bandura and colleagues (2001) on children's career aspirations and choices.

Studies such as these demonstrate the importance of career aspirations of young adolescents long before the age at which many make the choice about subject specialization and before they are properly apprised of the nature of work in the STEM area (Lindahl, 2007). These findings suggest that initiatives to engage school students with science would be significantly advantaged by (a) understanding what are the formative influences on student interest and career aspirations before the age of 14 and (b) aiming to foster the interest of this younger cohort of adolescents, particularly girls, in STEM–related work.

Family and Cultural Influences

Implied by the importance of early interest in science as an indicator of engagement with science in the later years is the importance of family influence on students' early attitudes and choices with regard to science. Research has also highlighted the significance of families in students' attitudes and choices in the middle years of schooling. The mechanisms by which families play a role in student interest and beliefs and participation with respect to science are complex. The literature focuses on a number of aspects, including encouraging early interest, support for scientific reasoning, supporting positive self-efficacy, and providing role models and advice.

An Australian government Youth Attitudes Survey (DEST, 2006) found that students who chose science and technology subjects reported overall higher levels of parental influence on their decision making. Haeusler and Kay (1997) found also that parental and teacher advice played a more prominent role in selection of science subjects than for other school subjects. There is some evidence (Watt, 2005) that this influence is greater in the earlier years of schooling, compared to the later years when perceived aptitude and interest are more important in driving choice.

Encouragement by families plays an important role in developing children's interest in particular aspects of science and science generally (Crowley, Callanan, Tenenbaum, & Allen, 2001; Fender & Crowley, 2007; Palmquist & Crowley, 2007; Sjaastad, 2012). Crowley and colleagues (2001), in a study of parental interactions with children in an informal science setting, argue that:

> Parents who involve children in informal science activities not only provide an opportunity for children to learn factual scientific information, but also provide opportunities for children to engage in scientific reasoning, to develop an interest to learn more about science, and to develop a sense that practicing the habits of scientific literacy is an important priority.
>
> (p. 261)

They found, however (Crowley et al., 2001), that while parents talked equally to their boy and girl children about how to approach and what to notice in museum exhibits, "the crucial step of providing an explanatory context for the experience was primarily reserved for boys" (p. 260). This gender differentiation in parent–child interaction was also found in studies by Harriet Tenenbaum and Campbell Leaper (2003), who found in a set of structured teaching activities that there was a tendency for fathers to use more cognitively demanding speech with sons than daughters, and parents were more likely to believe that science was less interesting and more difficult for daughters. Parents' beliefs significantly predicted children's interest and self-efficacy in science.

Palmquist and Crowley (2007) found that children with high levels of knowledge, "expert" about dinosaurs, were more likely to have home environments in which family members shared dinosaur interests and in which there were a variety of supporting resources. Surprisingly, in a museum visit, parents with "novice" children engaged them in more learning conversations than parents of expert children. In terms of establishing early interest, Simpkins, Davis-Kean, and Eccles (2006) employed expectancy value theory to study longitudinal links between math and science out-of-school activity participation in fifth grade and subsequent high school enrolment. They found that children's activity involvement experiences during middle childhood influence subsequent beliefs and mathematics and science enrolment patterns.

Family has been the focus of a number of studies as an influence on and a resource for improved engagement with STEM. Harackiewicz, Rozek, Hulleman, and Hyde (2012) applied motivational theory to design an intervention in which parents were supported to convey the importance of mathematics and science courses to their adolescent children. They found this simple intervention increased participation in science and mathematics in the final 2 years of high school by nearly one semester, leading them to claim that "parents are an untapped resource for increasing STEM motivation in adolescents" (p. 899).

Interpersonal relationships were found to be key in role modeling for inspiring and motivating choices into STEM education (Sjaastad, 2002). In his study of the sources of inspiration for 5,007 Norwegian STEM students, he identified different roles for parents, who help their children define themselves through conversation and support, and

teachers, who display how STEM subjects might bring fulfillment and provide positive learning experiences.

Terry Lyons (2006b) worked with high-performing year 10 students in Australia, studying their attitudes to science and backgrounds to their subject choices using a combination of questionnaire and interview data. He identified that students choosing physical science were those who had (a) supportive family relationships, (b) parents who recognized the value of formal education, and (c) family members advocating or supporting an interest in science. These students had higher levels of self-efficacy than non–physical science choosers, which he argued was important in a decision to take subjects with a reputation for difficulty. Lyons explained these findings through the construct of "cultural and social capital," which he argued was needed by students to select into STEM pathways.

Maria Adamuti-Trache and Lesley Andres (2008) draw on Pierre Bourdieu's "cultural capital" and related constructs to examine the level of influence of parents in transmitting cultural values and practices to their children, thus disposing them, or not, toward studies in STEM. Students with university-educated parents were shown to decide earlier about their career directions and were more likely to choose science subjects. It thus seems that the transmission of cultural capital is a pervasive and early influence on student pathways. For students whose parents and family contexts do not facilitate, encourage, assist, and fund academic pursuits in STEM, this can serve to prematurely restrict their choices. There is also evidence from this study that the job satisfaction of parents in STEM careers, particularly the mother, can significantly influence children's career aspirations.

Blenkinsop and colleagues (2006) argue the greater predictive power of the self-efficacy construct in occupational choice compared to other frameworks. Family socioeconomic status, they argued, had an indirect effect on young people's perceptions of their capabilities, operating through their self-efficacy. They argue that higher-status parents have higher parental aspirations, which are passed on to their children in two senses: as expectations and as belief in their capabilities and academic aspirations.

While many studies have shown that students who persist in STEM are more likely to have a higher socioeconomic-status (SES) background (see Committee for the Review of Teaching and Teacher Education, 2003; Helme & Lamb, 2007; Lamb & Ball, 1999; Thomson & De Bortoli, 2008), there continue to be questions raised about the nature of the causal link. This also raises the question of the usefulness of SES as an explanation or indicator of student participation in STEM subjects. The studies described demonstrate the importance of social capital and child–parent relations and these may provide the causal link to SES. Robert Putnam (2001, 2004) found that community-based social capital was a better indicator of improved educational outcomes than was socioeconomic status. David Grissmer and colleagues (Grissmer, Flanagan, Kawata, & Williamson, 2000) argue that this occurs through "peer effects, quality of communication and trust among families in communities, the safety of neighbourhoods, and the presence of community institutions that support achievement" (pp. 17–18).

The argument would seem to be supported by the differentially high achievement of students in Asian communities, often associated with parental support and expectations of students. Dacheng Zhao and Michael Singh (2011) explained the gap in performance in mathematics between Chinese-Australian and other Australian students in terms of differences in motivation, attributing success to effort, influence of parent help, and support. These are cultural-community norms. Esther Ho (2010) identified types of parental investment that were associated with Hong Kong students' science achievement and self-efficacy toward science. These include parent investment in cultural resources and involvement in organizing science enrichment activities from an early age.

Quality of Teaching

Quality of teaching is a difficult construct to operationalize or to measure. It has two major components: the approach to teaching and learning embedded in curriculum practices and the capabilities of the teacher in translating this into an engaging and effective pedagogy. Despite this significant caveat, a considerable body of evidence now exists that identifies quality of teaching as a major determinant of student engagement with and success in school subjects (Barber & Mourshed, 2007; Cooper & McIntyre, 1996; Darling-Hammond, 1999, 2007; Maltese & Tai, 2008; Osborne et al., 2003; Rivkin, Hanushek, & Kain, 2005; Rowe, 2003; Sanders, Wright, & Horn, 1997; Strauss & Sawyer, 1986; Wayne & Youngs, 2003; Woolnough, 1994).

A number of qualitative studies into students' perceptions of their school science classrooms and teaching and learning practices and their attitudes to these (Lindahl, 2007; Lyons, 2006a; Osborne & Collins, 2001) have provided insights into the nature and cause of student dissatisfaction with school science. Lyons (2006a) summarized student responses across the three studies thus: students complain that school science is not relevant to their lives and interests; there is too much content that is dealt with superficially and is repetitive across the elementary, middle, and high school curriculum; that there is lack of opportunity to discuss the science content or its implications or to express an opinion; that it becomes too difficult too early; and there is an overemphasis on copying notes from the board or other sources.

Students view the curriculum as dominated by a large body of content that must be learned and reproduced in exams. This has been reinforced in a number of countries through the increasing use of "high-stakes testing" as part of increasingly pervasive accountability regimes. Wayne Au's (2007) extensive meta-analysis of all relevant studies undertaken in the field of assessment led him to conclude such testing leads to a more fragmented curriculum and a transmission-dominated pedagogy. He further argues that this approach tends to lead to performance learning by students, motivated by extrinsic rewards rather than inherent interest in the subject itself.

A study led by Mihaly Csikszentmihalyi and Barbara Schneider (2000) provides insights into why such approaches fail to engage students. Their study uses the concept of "flow"—the feeling generated by total engagement with an activity. Using self-report data collected at random from students over a day, they identified the kinds of experience that are generative of "flow." They concluded that "classroom activities that facilitate flow experiences are those that are well structured, and where students are given adequate opportunities to demonstrate their skills and knowledge as autonomous individuals." One of the experiences that clearly generates the experience of "flow" for most pupils is laboratory work (Csikszentmihalyi & Schneider, 2000; Woolnough, 1994), consistent with students often nominating these activities as positive experiences in science. The failure of school science in many countries to include substantial practical laboratory work is a matter of concern.

Identifying what makes a good teacher of science has been the focus of a series of Australia-based projects at the secondary (Tobin & Fraser, 1990; Tobin, Tippins, & Gallard, 1994) and primary levels (Tytler, 2003; Tytler, Waldrip, & Griffiths, 2004). A necessary condition for quality teaching is good subject knowledge that provides a base level of confidence essential for providing high-quality feedback and scaffolding (Hattie & Timperley, 2007). Robin Alexander (2005) argues for a dialogic approach, suggesting that while "rote, recitation and expository teaching" might provide teachers with a sense of security and control, they make it less likely that the classroom will become a theatre for dealing with awkward, contingent questions which deal with issues of evidence and reasons for belief. These are exactly the kinds of interaction which Leo van Lier argues are engaging (van Lier, 1996).

The findings described strongly imply that a school science practice (a) dominated by short-term goals (b) in which science is presented through lectures with an emphasis on transmission, and (c) that lacks challenge is likely to be unappealing to students. Other research suggests that school science lacks for students a sense of purpose in terms of the major ideas, how they interrelate, and to what end should these be engaged with (Millar & Osborne, 1998; Osborne, 2008).

Career Knowledge

Lindahl (2007), in her longitudinal study of students and their aspirations, found that in the upper elementary and lower secondary years when their career aspirations were being broadly set, students had very little idea about the type and variety of work that a choice of science subjects might lead to. This lack of student knowledge about science-related work has been the broad finding of a number of studies (e.g., Blenkinsop et al. 2006; Stagg,

2007). A UK questionnaire survey of a random sample of 1,011 students at age 14 (Engineering and Technology Board, 2005) found very limited and stereotypical views of the work of engineers, technologists, and scientists.

Students identified subject teachers as the most useful source of career information, but UK research has found that teachers of science regard career information and advice as the responsibility of the careers teacher (Munro & Elsom, 2000). Yet most careers teachers come predominantly from nonscience backgrounds. Peter Stagg (2007) found that teachers were not well informed about careers in science, let alone career possibilities outside science to which a study of science might lead. There is a need to develop effective approaches, through a curriculum content focus and/or through a more coherent approach to information dissemination, that effectively inform students of career possibilities associated with science.

Sarah Blenkinsop and colleagues (2006) reported that 14- to 16-year-olds believed that direct information from someone who works in the field or a school careers teacher were more likely to have been influential than media-based information:

> People, their lives, and the work they do are the richest and most respected resource for learning about careers. Whilst a proportion of young people are attracted to science and technology for itself, many are interested first in the people (role models etc.).
>
> (Stagg, 2007, p. 4)

Consistent with this, Gayle Buck and colleagues (2008) found that, particularly for girls, role models were somebody with whom they held a "deep personal connection." To engage them with the work that scientists undertook, it was judged essential to establish a personal connection. These findings concerning the personal nature of significant information about scientists' work that constitutes effective career knowledge is consistent with work on student identity as the basis for choices concerning a science-related future.

Student Identity Work and Engagement With Science

To understand student responses to science, especially over the longer term implied by the interest in STEM participation (Marginson et al., 2013), there has been recent and increasing interest in exploring the construct of identity, which adds a sociological dimension to what, with attitudes, has been predominantly the province of the psychological literature. Identity is a construct that goes beyond short-term attitudes and responses to tasks and classroom events to instead frame aspirations and perceptions in terms of social relationships and self-processes (Lee, 2002). The identity construct entails that the self (or selves) is bounded by social structures and that

interactions with others shape the organization and content of self. An abundant, well-established identity literature in multiple disciplines, including anthropology, education, environmental education, and feminist studies (Ulriksen, Møller Madsen, & Holmegaard, 2010), has done much to bring issues around young people's identity and its relationship to their everyday lives to the fore.

The identity construct has been fruitful for making sense of the response of coherent groups such as indigenous (Aikenhead, 2006; McKinley, 2005) and gender groupings (Barton et al., 2013; Johnson, 2007) in making sense of the complex processes through which students in general frame their responses to school science and possible science futures. This involves recognition of the myriad dynamic factors that shape decisions over time in multiple contexts and particularly of the significance of "relationships with family, teachers, peers, and others, and identifying the degree of synergy, or disjuncture, experienced by young people between their everyday lives and their educational pursuit of STEM" (Tytler et al., 2008, p. 61). The identity construct has been claimed to be the "perfect candidate for the role of 'the missing link' in the . . . complex dialectic between learning and its sociocultural context" (Sfard & Prusak, 2005, p. 15).

With increased interest in the more holistic identity construct as a way into students' construction of their "science" selves and their relationships with science subjects, attitudes may play a more productive role if considered within the complex experiential landscape of students' contingent science interests, passions, and future aspirations. As Hazari, Sonnert, Sadler, and Shanahan (2010) assert: "We believe that this [identity] focus provides a basis for understanding students' long-term personal connection to physics and is a more meaningful measure than a general assessment of students' attitudes" (p. 979). Lee (2012) claims that through the lens of identity, we may gain a clearer view into students' agent-centered development and into their "sense of belonging and affiliation, and engagement with learning" (p. 35).

There is a significant history of research on the role of identity negotiation in the education-related choices of young people (Archer, Hollingworth, & Halsall, 2007; Archer, Pratt, & Phillips, 2001; Archer & Yamashita, 2003; Boaler, 1997; Connell, 1989; Francis, 2000). Many of these choices—whether to continue in school, which subjects to choose, the person I will aspire to become—impact each student's success in achieving his or her aspirations.

The Identity Construct in Science Education

Identity-related research is currently burgeoning in science education as in other disciplines. Identity theories have developed within a range of disciplinary divisions and draw on different interpretive traditions and positions on the relation of the individual to society and to agency/ structure dualities (Lee, 2012). Attempts to definitively conceptualize identity are, as a result, fraught: "everybody it seems is talking about identities, but it is not at all clear that they are talking about the same thing" (Rattansi & Phoenix, 2005, p. 98). In science education, Barton and colleagues (2013, p. 48) reflect this methodological problematic, preferring to focus on analyses of the processes of identity "work" as individuals interact over time with the complexity of their social worlds rather than treating identity as a fixed and definable entity at any point in time.

Despite this complexity, the diverse identity-related studies found in science education have in common an interest in exploring questions to do with "Is science me?" (Aschbacher et al., 2010), and assertions such as "I may be clever enough to do it" (Krogh & Andersen, 2012) and "I'm the kind of kid who needs a good teacher to get ahead" (Aschbacher et al., 2010, p. 571).

Lee's (2012) "rough guide" to the identity terrain describes how the concept has energized science educators in recent times and explores the theoretical roots of identity. He describes a number of common frameworks used by science educators, including figured worlds and practice theories (Barton et al., 2013; Varelas, Kane, & Wylie, 2011, 2012) and discursive stances (Barton, 2003; Brown, 2006). Figured worlds and practice theories lie within a critical research tradition and posit that identities are "situated achievements" and that identity can be conceived of as a verb in the sense of the work of "self" (Lee, 2012, p. 37). Lave and Wenger (1991) argue that learning involves the construction of identities and can be thought of as the "historical production, transformation, and change of persons" (pp. 51–52).

"Discursive stances" take as their starting point that language, as pre-eminent social practice, is inseparable from identity. In this tradition, identities, along with phenomena and mental states, are spoken into existence by prevailing discourses (Gee, 1996, 2004). Science education work in this tradition follows two approaches. The first treats language as a resource to be analyzed for underlying meaning—for instance, Bryan Brown's (2006) exploration of students' clusters of science sense making or Barton's (2003) stories of kids negotiating discrimination, poverty, and science. In the second approach, language in itself is the topic of scrutiny, as in Oliveira, Sadler, and Suslak's (2007) examination of the construction of expert identity through discussion.

Along with the theoretical diversity of identity research, there is also methodological diversity. Rattansi and Phoenix (2005) assert that studies of young people cannot be reliant on methodologies such as attitudinal survey research at the expense of ethnographically rich descriptions of "myriad ways . . . identities are constructed and re-worked in different social contexts" (p. 107). However, the use of large-scale survey questionnaire approaches remains both pervasive and useful for generating different types of data and for providing the basis for further studies (see Cerinsek et al., 2012; DeWitt et al., 2011; Hazari et al., 2010; Krogh & Andersen, 2012; Riegle-Crumb et al., 2011). Not surprisingly, many of the studies located are wholly or in part longitudinal, as a necessary design requirement to better understand the ongoing formative character of identity development and to track this at different points in time and place (see Aschbacher et al., 2010; Barton et al., 2013; Cerinsek et al., 2012; Hazari et al., 2010; Krogh & Andersen, 2012).

Minority Groups and Identity

The identity construct has been particularly powerful for interpreting the challenges experienced by students in minority groups such as indigenous students and ethnic minorities and girls tackling gendered conceptions of science. Glen Aikenhead (2006) argues that for indigenous students, and indeed for many mainstream students, coming to appreciate science requires an identity shift whereby they come to consider themselves as science friendly: "to learn science meaningfully is identity work" (p. 117). He argues that the persistence of traditional versions of school science, despite a history of considerable critique (of the sort described in this chapter), relates to teachers' subscription to the strong discursive traditions that underpinned their enculturation during their own schooling and undergraduate studies. In many countries with significant indigenous populations, there is widespread concern about gaps in performance in science (and other subjects) between indigenous and nonindigenous students (e.g., Thomson & De Bortoli, 2008). Aikenhead and Masakata Ogawa (2007) argue that the tendency of school science to portray scientific ways of knowing as free from value, ignoring of multiple or contested views, and transcendent of context acts to marginalize some students on the basis of their "cultural self-identities" (p. 540). Aikenhead (2001, p. 338) argues that only a small minority of students' "worldviews resonate with the scientific worldview conveyed most frequently in school science. All other students experience the single-mindedness of school science as alienating, and this hinders their effective participation in school science."

For indigenous peoples, there is a need to represent a broader range of identity futures consonant with science work. Elizabeth McKinley (2005) writes about the difficulty experienced by Maori women scientists in managing inconsistent images of themselves—as women, as Maori, as scientists. She argues that competing legacies of science, knowledge, and culture have built strong cultural stereotypes of Maori women, who describe being discriminated against, prejudged, and overlooked in their scientific roles.

Nadya Fouad and colleagues (Fouad, Byars-Winston, & Angela, 2005) found, in the U.S. context, that while race does not have an impact on students' initial career aspirations, it does affect the barriers that students encounter as they take action to fulfill those aspirations. Such barriers can include expectations of teachers, peers, or family or lack of role models. It is clear from the literature on indigenous or other minority groups' engagement with science, "choice" of subject or career can be severely constrained, depending upon factors such as prior academic performance, student cultural capital, or other resources that can be drawn on.

Angela Johnson (2007) researched barriers to U.S. science-interested minority females' continuing participation in STEM. These included lack of sensitivity to their difference, discouragement, and a sense of alienation from school science. She described how this alienation could be associated even with well-meaning practices. Even a laudable activity like asking questions of students in lectures can advantage competitive and confident white male students and cause women to feel a loss of status.

Geoffrey Cohen and colleagues (Cohen, Garcia, Apfel, & Master, 2006) have worked to address such barriers through addressing what they call "stereotypical threat"—a psychological notion. Cohen and his coworkers argue that for individuals who are members of a group who commonly are perceived to fail at science—for example, African Americans or women—what inhibits students' performance is when the individual internalizes the stereotype judgment. By conducting a small intervention to address and challenge such perceptions, this group has been able to demonstrate significant improvements in performance of underperforming minorities and women.

Gendered Identities and Science

A number of studies have contributed to our understanding of how youth respond to school science and science, technology, and the environment. Helen Haste (2004) conducted a survey of the values and beliefs about science and technology held by 704 11- to 21-year-old UK individuals. Her analysis identified four distinct groups of students: (1) the "green" who held ethical concerns about the environment, were skeptical about interfering with nature, and were predominantly girls under 16; (2) the "techno-investor" enthusiastic about technology and the beneficial effects of science, who trusted scientists and the government and were mostly male; (3) the "science oriented" interested in science and with faith in the general application of scientific ways of thinking, mostly male; and (4) the "alienated from science" who were bored with science and skeptical of its potential, predominantly female. Haste found that girls were not less interested in science or science careers than boys, but they focused on and valued different things. Girls related more strongly to "green" values associated with science (socially responsible and people-oriented aspects of science) than to the "space and hardware" aspects that often dominate communication about science. Based on these findings, she argues that the science curriculum needs to represent both these dimensions of science and to acknowledge the value aspects and ethical concerns surrounding science and its applications. However, from her later study (Haste, et al., 2008, described earlier), it seems that it will be difficult to interest boys and girls simultaneously given that girls and boys have quite conflicting responses to the inclusion of ethical values and the need for content to be contextually relevant.

Archer and colleagues' (2010) study examined possible reasons for gender imbalances in STEM participation. Their findings suggest that girls and boys have distinctly different views of science, depending on the context in which science is "done." For girls, home and primary school are perceived as settings for doing "safe" science, while the real world of science work is understood as "dangerous." Boys in this study anticipated "doing" more dangerous science at secondary school: "it's better because they trust you with more dangerous chemicals, stuff like that" (participant, Archer et al., 2010, p. 623). The significance of the Archer study lies in teasing out of "complex identity processes to reveal deep-seated, often trenchant, resistance to interventions" designed to increase young people's, and in particular girls', positive engagements with science (p. 637). The study employed feminist poststructuralist and critical sociological identity perspectives. From these standpoints, they found that "a sense of self is constructed as much through a sense of what/who one is not, as much through the sense of who/what one is" (p. 619).

Barton and colleagues' (2013) study, located within social practice theory and feminist writings on intersectionality, presents rich narrative data on girls' science identities, longitudinally exploring the nature of science identity work performed by girls in their middle school years. For instance, the research includes a focus on one girl, Chantelle, who in the beginning of the story is almost invisible in science class and aspires to be a dancer. Through joining an after-school Green Club, Chantelle initially used her interest in dance, and then video, to gradually establish herself as interested and an expert in energy conservation practices. She increasingly took on the discursive practices associated with the science of green concerns, and this opened up the possibility of reconfigured identity positioning in her science class, where she was increasingly active and influential. The researchers argue that the way girls will likely view their possible future selves in science is contingent upon their identity work being "recognised, supported, and leveraged towards expanded opportunities for engagement in science" (2013, p. 37).

The key affordance of the identity construct in this research is its focus on the positioning of students to scientific ways of thinking and acting that are central to the way they configure their lives and interest. These move beyond short-term responses implied by more psychologically oriented attitudinal constructs such as motivation, enjoyment, or earlier stages of interest.

Chantelle's case emphasizes the importance of student agency in committing to scientific discourses as part of reconfiguring the figured world of the classroom in the identity construction process. Beyond the specific focus on gendered or indigenous identities, this research speaks to the need to engage students generally in identity work in coming to reconfigure and identify with the discursive practices of science through scientific inquiry. Recent research in science education seeks to engage students in approximations of scientific practices in classrooms or other informal environments. In the work of Lehrer and

Schauble (2012) and associates (Manz, 2012) and Hubber and colleagues (Hubber, Tytler, & Haslam, 2010; Tytler, Prain, Hubber, & Waldrip, 2013), students are engaged in inquiry processes in which they take on the role of scientific knowledge production within a classroom community of practice.

Longitudinal Studies of Identity and Engagement With Science

Motivated by the science education dilemma earlier raised, DeWitt, Archer, and Osborne's (2012) longitudinal UK study drawn from the larger ASPIRES (Science Aspirations and Career Choice: Age 10–14) project, provides insights into both children's and their parents' perceptions of science. Responding to a perceived lack of research focused on children's perceptions of "science-keen peers," the study used interview data to identify the types of science discourses children and their parents may invoke to give shape to ways children (and parents) construct their own science identity. Study findings revealed a number of discourses, including the "highly visible" stereotypical "geek nerd" scientist congruent with the white male and modifying or qualifying discourses that position scientists as "clever" specialists (DeWitt et al., 2012, n.p.). These findings suggest that both discourses are likely to position those who aspire to a science career as "other" and are likely to "act against student . . . willingness to take up a science identity" (DeWitt et al., 2012, n.p.).

Aschbacher and colleagues (2010) followed an ethnically and economically diverse sample of 33 high school girls to explore the question: Why do some students interested in science during middle and early high school decide to leave the science, engineering, and medical (SEM) pipeline by the end of high school while others opt to persist? The identity theory in this study found home in the notion of communities of practice in which identity is informed by situated everyday social interactions. To better understand students' science identity trajectories, the researchers used Eccles's "expectancy theory" model to link the students' educational and career decisions to expectations of success and to the value priorities of possible career options. The attraction of this model centered on its emphasis on significant people in students' lives and their role in shaping how students "access, interpret, and evaluate their lived experiences, in turn, affecting their short- and long-term goals, attitudes, values and priorities" (Aschbacher et al., 2010, p. 566). The findings suggest that each group's diverse social "microclimates" act as shapers of students' science identities and their perceptions of their study capabilities, career options, and expected success.

Krogh and Andersen's (2012) longitudinal study focused on the dynamic and self-reflexive identity narratives of a group of Danish A-level maths students' science identity trajectories during their final secondary school years as they participated in a university mentorship program. From a hermeneutic analysis of the students' narratives, the researchers developed a model to characterize their identity trajectories, comprising four factors: identity process orientations, personal values, subject self-concept, and subject interest (see Krogh & Andersen, 2012, n.p., Table 1). These analyses highlighted "personal values" as a distinctive characteristic of the narratives. In particular, Krogh and Andersen note, "Social relationships, recognition, family, knowledge, excitement/challenge were among the core values found" (2012, n.p.).

Identity and Postmodern Youth

The task of reconciling the construction of subjectivities/identity trajectories with the value systems of science and school science is significant for contemporary youth. The circumstances of youth in postmodern societies are very different from those of previous generations in terms of education and career patterns, access to media and knowledge, and changing ways of relating. Studies of youth in transition, from adolescence to the early years of their working lives and personal relations, have identified a different landscape for conceptualizing transition and the range of subjectivities available to be negotiated by young people in their personal and working lives (Wyn, 2011; Wyn & White, 1997). Adolescence is a time when young people are first confronted by the need to construct their sense of self, creating a state of insecurity or moratorium (Head, 1985). While this angst is not a new phenomenon, it has particular significance when the choice of future options is seen to be much greater and more fluid. Contemporary youth perceive a new freedom in their choice of address, religion, social group, politics, education, profession, sexuality, lifestyle, and values (Beck & Beck-Gernsheim, 2002) compared to previous generations, when choice was much more constrained and conceptualized mainly in terms of choice of profession. Flexibility is the touchstone for postmodern youth. Helen Stokes and Johanna Wyn (2007) argue that young people at school or in work view workplaces as sites of learning and identity formation. Young people "regard adulthood as no longer a 'given', but a 'project', a 'task' or a 'journey' that demands their on going commitment" (Stokes & Wyn, 2007, p. 499).

From this perspective, the decision-making landscape that young people negotiate in deciding who they want to be, selecting their school subjects, and constructing their aspirations for a fulfilling future is complex terrain. Analysis of the bases on which young people make these choices is further complicated by that fact that the barriers that hinder young people's decision making are not always immediately apparent and will change over time and in degree as students grow and develop (Engineering and Technology Board, 2005; Fouad et al., 2007; Walker, 2007; Walker, Alloway, Dalley-Trim, & Patterson, 2006).

Camilla Schreiner (2006) studied the patterns of attitude and aspirations of secondary school students in Norway. Her analysis has a significant identity component. She administered a questionnaire that had been extensively validated to a sample of 1,204 students drawn from

53 randomly selected schools consisting of equal numbers of boys and girls. Using a cluster analysis, she identified five student types with distinct and different responses to science and to their own aspirations with respect to science. As with the Haste (2004) and Haste and colleagues (2008) studies, the categories were highly gender specific and showed different patterns of response to a range of items relating to the perceived value of school science and science and their future aspirations. On the basis of this work, Schreiner interprets the declining recruitment into STEM subjects in developed countries in terms of changing values of youth in late modern societies, consistent with the research into the values and programs of contemporary youth outlined previously, and with identity work in science education described earlier with respect to indigenous peoples, gender, and minority groups. In this case, however, the analysis draws the wider net of encompassing identity formation relating to contemporary, wealthy societies.

Schreiner and Svein Sjøberg (2007) argue that in early and late industrial countries, scientists and engineers are seen as crucial to people's lives and well-being, as part of a major national project of a progress, growth, and country-building agenda. In less-developed countries, young people have an image of science and scientists as the key to future progress and to their own futures. These values have changed, however, for youth in advanced late modern societies. These societies have a diminishing industrial base, and material needs are largely satisfied compared to those of previous generations. In this circumstance, the public perception of the role and value of the scientist and technologist is diminished. They speculate that the main reason that an increasing number of young people, especially girls, are reluctant to engage with the physical sciences is because they perceive the identities of physical scientists and engineers as incongruent with their own. Many studies (Boaler, 1997; Lightbody & Durndell, 1996a; Mendick, 2006; Walkerdine, 1990) have argued that STEM subjects and careers have a masculine image that discourages girls from developing identities connected with STEM. Schreiner and Sjøberg suggest that the identities of youth in advanced and wealthy societies are connected with late modern values such as self-realization, creativity and innovation, working with people and helping others, and making money. They argue that if this is indeed the case, then attracting more young people into STEM pathways will require transforming the images of STEM work to address these ideals. This implies a need to transform the content and practice of school STEM subjects to more explicitly represent these values.

The Identity Construct, Student Attitudes, and Aspirations Regarding Science

We have argued that the identity construct is a powerful tool for making sense of the complexities of students' engagement with science and school science and the nature of their decisions with respect to a commitment to science in the postcompulsory years and into the workplace. Given the increasing concern with the falling participation in STEM in late modern societies, the identity construct becomes particularly relevant and is replacing the more traditional "attitude" construct because of its attention to the multiple social influences that make up the complex landscape of young people's decisions about themselves and their futures.

Of course, the process of construction of identities carries with it implications for affective response to subjects, to tasks, and to classroom processes. Attitudinal research has a powerful place in making sense of and evaluating student responses to science at the micro level and across time scales within students' schooling lives. However, the usefulness of the identity construct can be seen in its attention to the multifactorial nature of these responses and particularly when looking at student engagement with science related to factors that span their lives over the schooling years and beyond. Thus, we have explored the research on identity in relation to indigenous students and girls, for both of which the ongoing identity work in relation to science has a long personal history and will continue to evolve through transitions into work and possibly over a lifetime. Longitudinal studies of identity attest to the centrality of this temporal dimension of identity construction.

This strand of research thus alerts us to the complexity of the issue of response to school science and the personal historical dimension of this. If we are to engage students in serious thinking and learning about science and in seeing for themselves a future engaged with science in some capacity, then we need to plan our school science curriculum in ways that attend to the complex and varied histories of students who attend our classes. While we cannot hope for a simple match with all students' aspirations and identity construction trajectories, the strong message is that if we are to enlist young people into science subjects or even science-friendly positions, then it will be necessary to present a richer vision of science, its values, and the work of scientists.

Acknowledgments

Thanks to Richard Lehrer and Norman G. Lederman, who reviewed this chapter.

References

Adamuti-Trache, M., & Andres, L. (2008). Embarking on and persisting in scientific fields of study: Cultural capital, gender, and curriculum along the science pipeline. *International Journal of Science Education, 30*(12), 1557–1584.

Aikenhead, G. (1973). The measurement of high school students' knowledge about science and scientists. *Science Education, 57*, 539–549.

Aikenhead, G. (2001). Students' ease in crossing cultural borders into school science. *Science Education, 85*(2), 180–188.

Aikenhead, G. (2006). *Science education for everyday life: Evidence based practice.* New York: Teachers College Press.

Aikenhead, G., & Ogawa, M. (2007). Indigenous knowledge and science revisited. *Cultural Studies of Science Education, 2*(3), 539–620.

Ainley, M., & Ainley, J. (2011). Student engagement with science in early adolescence: The contribution of enjoyment to students' continuing interest in learning about science. *Contemporary Educational Psychology, 36,* 4–12.

Alexander, R. (2005). *Towards dialogic teaching.* York, UK: Dialogos.

Andrée, L., & Hansson, L. (2012). Marketing the 'broad line': Invitations to STEM education in a Swedish recruitment campaign. *International Journal of Science Education.* Retrieved November 5, 2012, from http://dx.doi.org/10.1080/09500693.2012.695880

Applebaum, P., & Clark, S. (2001). Science! Fun? A critical analysis of design/content/evaluation. *Journal of Curriculum Studies, 33*(5), 583–600.

Archer, L., Dewitt, J., Osborne, J., Dillon, J., Willis, B., & Wong, B. (2010). "Doing" science versus "being" a scientist: Examining 10/11-year-old schoolchildren's constructions of science through the lens of identity. *Science Education, 94,* 617–639.

Archer, L., Hollingworth, S., & Halsall, A. (2007). "University's not for me—I'm a Nike person": Urban, working-class engagement young people's negotiations of "style," identity and education. *Sociology, 41*(2), 219–237.

Archer, L., Pratt, S., & Phillips, D. (2001). Working class men's constructions of masculinity and negotiations of (non)participation in higher education. *Gender and Education, 13*(4), 431–449.

Archer, L., & Yamashita, H. (2003). Theorising inner-city masculinities: "race," class, gender and education. *Gender & Education, 15*(2), 115–132.

Aschbacher, P., Li, E., & Roth, E. (2010). Is science me? High school students' identities, participation and aspirations in science, engineering, and medicine. *Journal of Research in Science Teaching, 47,* 564–582.

Assessment of Performance Unit. (1988). *Science at age 15: A review of the APU survey findings.* London: HMSO.

Au, W. (2007). High stakes testing and curricular control: A qualitative metasynthesis. *Educational Researcher, 36*(5), 258–267.

Azevedo, F. (2011). Lines of practice: A practice-centered theory of interest relationships. *Cognition and Instruction, 29*(2), 147–184.

Azevedo, F. (2012). The tailored practice of hobbies and its implication for the design of interest-driven learning environments. *The Journal of the Learning Sciences.* doi:10.1080/10508406.2012.730082

Bandura, A. (1997). *Self-efficacy: The exercise of control.* New York: W. H Freeman and Company.

Bandura, A., Barbaranelli, C., Caprara, G.V., & Pastorelli, C. (2001). Self-efficacy beliefs as shapers of children's aspirations and career trajectories. *Child Development, 72,* 187–206.

Barber, M., & Mourshed, M. (2007). *How the world's best-performing school systems come out on top.* New York: McKinsey & Company.

Barton, A., Kang, H., Tan, E., O'Neill, T., Bautista-Guerra, J., & Brecklin, C. (2013). Crafting a future in science: Tracing middle school girls' identity work over time and space. *American Educational Research Journal, 50*(1), 37–75.

Barton, A.C. (2003). *Teaching science for social justice.* New York: Teachers College Press.

Beck, U., & Beck-Gernsheim, E. (2002). *Individualization.* London: Sage Publications Ltd.

Blalock, C.L., Lichtenstein, M.J., Owen, S., Pruski, L., Marshall, C., & Toepperwein, M. (2008). In pursuit of validity: A comprehensive review of science attitude instruments. *International Journal of Science Education, 30*(7), 961–977.

Blenkinsop, S., McCrone, T., Wade, P., & Morris, M. (2006). *How do young people make choices at 14 and 16?* Slough, UK: National Foundation for Educational Research, Department for Education and Skills (DfES).

Blickenstaff, J.C. (2005). Women and science careers: Leaky pipeline or gender filter? *Gender and Education, 17*(4), 369–386.

Boaler, J. (1997). Reclaiming school mathematics: The girls fight back. *Gender and Education, 9*(3), 285–305.

Bøe, M. (2012). Science choices in Norwegian upper secondary school: What matters? *Science Education, 96,* 1–20.

Bøe, M.V., Henriksen, E.K., Lyons, T., & Schreiner, C. (2011). Participation in science and technology: Young people's achievement-related choices in late modern societies. *Studies in Science Education, 47*(1), 37–71.

Breakwell, G.M., & Beardsell, S. (1992). Gender, parental and peer influences upon science attitudes and activities. *Public Understanding of Science, 1*(2), 183–197.

Brophy, J. (2009). Connecting with the Big Picture. *Educational Psychologist, 44,* 147–157.

Brotman, J.S., & Moore, F.M. (2008). Girls and science: A review of four themes in the science education literature. *Journal of Research in Science Teaching, 45*(9), 971–1002.

Brown, B. (2006). "It isn't no slang that can be said about this stuff": Language, identity and appropriating science discourse. *Journal of Research in Science Teaching, 43,* 96–126.

Buck, G.A., Plano, V.L., Diandra, C., Pelecky, L., Lu, Y., & Cerda-Lizarraga, V. (2008). Examining the cognitive processes used by adolescent girls and women scientists in identifying science role models: A feminist approach. *Science Education, 92*(4), 688–707.

Butz, W.P., Bloom, G.A., Gross, M.E., Kelly, T.K., Kofner, A., & Rippen, H.E. (2003). *Is there a shortage of scientists and engineers? How would we know?* Santa Monica, CA: Rand Corporation.

Cerinsek, G., Hribar, T., Glodez, N., & Dolinsek, S. (2012). Which are my future career priorities and what influenced my choice of studying science, technology, engineering or mathematics? Some insights on educational choice—case of Slovenia. *International Journal of Science Education.* Retrieved September 17, 2012, from http://dx.doi.org/10.1080/09500693.2012.681813

Chambers, D. (1983). Stereotypic images of the scientist: The draw-a-scientist test. *Science Education, 67*(2), 255–265.

Chetcuti, D., & Kioko, B. (2012). Girls' attitudes towards science in Kenya. *International Journal of Science Education, 34,* 1571–1589.

Christidou, V. (2011). Interest, attitudes and images related to science: Combining students' voices with the voices of school science, teachers, and popular science. *International Journal of Environmental & Science Education, 6,* 141–159.

Cleaves, A. (2005). The formation of science choices in secondary school. *International Journal of Science Education, 27*(4), 471–486.

Cohen, G.L., Garcia, J., Apfel, N., & Master, A. (2006). Reducing the racial achievement gap: A social-psychological intervention. *Science, 313*(5791), 1307–1310.

Committee for the Review of Teaching and Teacher Education. (2003). *Australia's teachers: Australia's future, advancing innovation, science, technology and mathematics—Background data and analysis.* Canberra: Department of Education Science and Training (DEST), Commonwealth of Australia.

Connell, R.W. (1989). Cool guys, swots and wimps: The interplay of masculinity and education. *Oxford Review of Education, 15*(3), 291–303.

Cooper, P., & McIntyre, D. (1996). *Effective teaching and learning: Teachers' and students' perspectives.* Buckingham, UK, and Philadelphia: Open University Press.

Crowley, K., Callanan, M.A., Tenenbaum, H.R., & Allen, E. (2001). Parents explain more often to boys than to girls during shared scientific thinking. *Psychological Science, 12,* 258–261. doi:10.1111/1467-9280.00347

Csikszentmihalyi, M. (1992). The flow experience and its significance for human psychology. In M. Csikszentmihalyi & I. S. Csikszentmihalyi (Eds.), *Optimal experience: Psychological studies of flow in consciousness* (pp. 15–35). Cambridge: University of Cambridge.

Csikszentmihalyi, M., & Schneider, B. (2000). *Becoming adult: Preparing teenagers for the world of work.* New York: Basic Books.

Darling-Hammond, L. (1999). *Teacher quality and student achievement: A review of state policy evidence.* University of Washington: Centre for the Study of Teaching and Policy.

Darling-Hammond, L. (2007). The flat earth and education: How America's commitment to equity will determine our future. *Educational Researcher, 36*(16), 318–334.

DEST. (2006). *Youth attitudes survey: Population study on the perceptions of science, mathematics and technology study at school and career decision making.* Canberra, Australia: Department of Education Science and Training.

Dewey, J. (1933). *How we think.* Boston: DC Heath.

Dewey, J. (1934/1980). *Art as experience.* New York: Berkley.

DeWitt, J., Archer, L., & Osborne, J. (2012). Nerdy, brainy and normal: Children's and parents' constructions of those who are highly engaged with science. *Research in Science Education.* doi:10.1007/s11165-012-9315-0

DeWitt, J., Archer, L., Osborne, J., Dillon, J., Willis, B., & Wong, B. (2011). High aspirations but low progression: The science aspirations–careers paradox amongst minority ethnic students. *International Journal of Science and Mathematics Education, 9,* 243–271.

Eccles, J. (2009). Who am I and what am I going to do with my life? Personal and collective identities as motivators of action. *Educational Psychologist, 44*(2), 78–89.

Eccles, J.S., Adler, T.F., Futterman, R., Goff, S.B., Kazcala, C.M., Meece, J.L., et al. (1983). Expectations, values and academic behaviors. In T. Spence (Ed.), *Achievement and achievement motivations* (pp. 75–146). San Francisco: W. H Freeman.

Eccles, J.S., & Wigfield, A. (1992). The development of achievement-task values: A theoretical analysis. *Developmental Review, 12,* 265–310.

Engineering and Technology Board. (2005). *Factors influencing Year 9 career choices:* London: National Foundation for Educational Research.

Epstein, J.L., & McPartland, J.M. (1976). The concept and measurement of the quality of school life. *American Educational Research Journal, 13,* 15–30.

European Commission. (2004). *Europe needs more scientists: Report by the High Level Group on Increasing Human Resources for Science and Technology.* Brussels: Author.

Farland-Smith, D. (2012). Development and field test of the modified draw-a-scientist test and the draw-a-scientist rubric. *School Science and Mathematics, 112*(2), 109–116.

Fender, J.G., & Crowley, K. (2007). How parent explanation changes what children learn from everyday scientific thinking. *Journal of Applied Developmental Psychology, 28,* 189–210.

Fensham, P. (1985). Science for all: A reflective essay. *Journal of Curriculum Studies, 17*(4), 415–435.

Fouad, N., Byars-Winston, A., & Angela, M. (2005). Cultural context of career choice: Meta-analysis of race/ethnicity differences. *Career Development Quarterly, 53*(3), 223–233.

Fouad, N., Hackett, G., Haag, S., Kantamneni, N., & Fitzpatrick, M.E. (2007, August). *Career choice barriers: Environmental influences on women's career choices.* Paper presented at the Annual Meeting of the American Psychological Association Convention, San Francisco, CA.

Francis, B. (2000). The gendered subject: Students' subject preferences and discussions of gender and subject ability. *Oxford Review of Education, 26*(1), 35–48.

Gardner, P.L. (1975). Attitudes to science. *Studies in Science Education, 2,* 1–41.

Gee, J. (1996). *Social linguistics and literacies: Ideologies in discourse* (2nd ed.). London: Taylor & Francis.

Gee, J.P. (2004). Language in the science classroom: Academic social languages as the heart of school-based literacy. In E.W. Saul (Ed.), *Crossing borders in literacy and science instruction: Perspectives in theory and practice* (pp. 13–32). Newark, DE: International Reading Association/National Science Teachers Association.

Germann, P.J. (1988). Development of the attitude toward science in school assessment and its use to investigate the relationship between science achievement and attitude toward science in school. *Journal of Research in Science Teaching, 25*(8), 689–703.

Girod, M., Rau, C., & Schepige, A. (2003). Appreciating the beauty of science ideas: Teaching for aesthetic understanding. *Science Education, 87*(4), 574–587. doi:10.1002/sce.1054.

Girod, M., & Wong, D. (2002). An aesthetic (Deweyan) perspective on science learning: Case studies of three fourth graders. *The Elementary School Journal, 102*(3), 199–224.

Goodrum, D., Hackling, M., & Rennie, L. (2001). *The status and quality of teaching and learning of science in Australian schools.* Canberra, Australia: Department of Education, Training and Youth Affairs.

Grissmer, D., Flanagan, A., Kawata, J., & Williamson, S. (2000). *Improving student achievement: What state NAEP test scores tell us.* Santa Monica, CA: RAND Corporation.

Hadzigeorgiou, Y. (2012). Fostering a sense of wonder in the science classroom. *Research in Science Education, 42,* 985–1005.

Haeusler, C., & Kay, R. (1997). School subject selection by students in the post-compulsory years. *Australian Journal of Career Development, 6*(1), 32–38.

Harackiewicz, J.M., Rozek, C.S., Hulleman, C.S., & Hyde, J.S. (2012). Helping parents to motivate adolescents in mathematics and science: An experimental test of a utility-value intervention. *Psychological Science, 23*(8), 899–906.

Haste, H. (2004). *Science in my future: A study of the values and beliefs in relation to science and technology amongst 11–21 year olds.* London. Nestlé Social Research Programme.

Haste, H., Muldoon, C., Hogan, A., & Brosnan, M. (2008, Sept 11). *If girls like ethics in their science and boys like gadgets, can we get science education right?* Paper presented at the Annual Conference of the British Association for the Advancement of Science, Liverpool, UK.

Hattie, J., & Timperley, H. (2007). The power of feedback. *Review of Educational Research, 77*(1), 81–112.

Haussler, P., & Hoffmann, L. (2002). An intervention study to enhance girls' interest, self-concept, and achievement in physics classes. *Journal of Research in Science Teaching, 39*(9), 870–888.

Haworth, C.M.A., Dale, P., & Plomin, R. (2008). A twin study into the genetic and environmental influences on academic performance in science in nine-year-old boys and girls. *International Journal of Science Education, 30*(8), 1003–1025.

Hazari, Z., Sonnert, G., Sadler, P., & Shanahan, M.-C. (2010). Connecting high school physics experiences, outcome expectations, physics identity, and physics career choice: A gender study. *Journal of Research in Science Teaching, 47,* 978–1003.

Head, J. (1985). *The personal response to science.* Cambridge: Cambridge University Press.

Heimlich, J.E., & Ardoin, N.M. (2008). Understanding behavior to understand behavior change: A literature review. *Environmental Education Research, 14*(3), 215–237.

Helme, S., & Lamb, S. (2007). *Student experiences of VCE Further Mathematics.* Paper presented at the Mathematics Essential Research, Essential Practice: 30th Annual conference of the Mathematics Education Research Group of Australasia. Hobart, Tasmania, Australia.

Hidi, S., & Renninger, K.A. (2006). The four-phase model of interest development. *Educational Psychologist, 41*(2), 111–127. doi:10.1207/s15326985ep4102_4

Hill, C., Corbett, C., & St. Rose, A. (2010). *Why so few? Women in science, technology, engineering, and mathematics.* Washington, DC: AAUW.

HM Treasury. (2006). *Science and Innovation investment framework: Next steps.* London: HMSO.

Ho, E.S.C. (2010). Family influences on science learning among Hong Kong adolescents: What we learned from PISA. *International Journal of Science and Mathematics Education, 8*(3), 409–428.

Hobbs, L. (2012). Examining the aesthetic dimensions of teaching: Relationships between teacher knowledge, identity and passion. *Teaching & Teacher Education, 28*(5), 718–727. doi:10.1016/j.tate.2012.01.010

Hubber, P., Tytler, R., & Haslam, F. (2010). Teaching and learning about force with a representational focus: Pedagogy and teacher change. *Research in Science Education, 40*(1), 5–28.

Jagger, N. (2007). *Internationalising doctoral careers.* Paper presented at the Conference on The National Value of Science Education. September, University of York, York, UK.

Jakobson, B., & Wickman, P.-O. (2008). The roles of aesthetic experience in elementary school science. *Research in Science Education, 38*(1), 45–66.

Jenkins, E., & Nelson, N.W. (2005). Important but not for me: Students' attitudes toward secondary school science in England. *Research in Science & Technological Education, 23*(1), 41–57.

Jenkins, E.W., & Pell, R.G. (2006). *The relevance of science education project (ROSE) in England: A summary of findings.* Centre for Studies in Science and Mathematics Education, University of Leeds, UK.

Johnson, A.C. (2007). Unintended consequences: How science professors discourage women of color. *Science Education, 91*(5), 805–821.

Jones, G., Howe, A., & Rua, M. (2000). Gender differences in students' experiences, interests, and attitudes towards science and scientists. *Science Education, 84,* 180–192.

Jovanovic, J., & King, S.S. (1998). Boys and girls in the performance-based science classroom: Who's doing the performing? *American Educational Research Journal, 35*(3), 477–496.

Kenway, J., & Gough, A. (1998). Gender and science education in schools: A review "with attitude." *Studies in Science Education, 31,* 1–30.

Klopfer, L.E. (1971). Evaluation of learning in science. In B.S. Bloom, J.T. Hastings, & G.F. Madaus (Eds.), *Handbook of formative and summative evaluation of student learning.* London: McGraw-Hill.

Krogh, L., & Andersen, H. (2012). "Actually, I may be clever enough to do it." Using identity as a lens to investigate students' trajectories towards science and university. *Research in Science Education.* doi:10.1007/s11165-012-9285-2

Krogh, L.B., & Thomsen, P.V. (2005). Studying students' attitudes towards science from a cultural perspective but with a quantitative methodology: Border crossing into the physics classroom. *International Journal of Science Education, 27*(3), 281–302.

Lamb, R.L., Annetta, L., Meldrum, J., & Vallett, D. (2012). Measuring science interest: Rasch validation of the science interest survey. *International Journal of Science and Mathematics Education, 10,* 643–668.

Lamb, S., & Ball, K. (1999). Curriculum and careers: The education and labour market consequences of Year 12 subject choice. *Longitudinal Surveys of Australian Youth: Research Report Number 12.* Camberwell: Australian Council for Educational Research.

Lave, J., & Wenger, E. (1991). *Situated learning: Legitimate peripheral participation.* Cambridge, UK: Cambridge University Press.

Lee, J.D. (2002). More than ability: Gender and personal relationships influence science and technology involvement. *Sociology of Education, 75*(4), 349–373.

Lee, Y.J. (2012). Identity-based research in science education. In B.J. Fraser, K. Tobin, & C.J. McRobbie (Eds.), *Second international handbook of science education* (pp. 34–45). Dordrecht, the Netherlands: Springer.

Lehrer, R., & Schauble, L. (2012). Seeding evolutionary thinking by engaging children in modeling its foundations. *Science Education, 96*(4), 701–724.

Leonardi, A., Syngollitou, E., & Kiosseoglou, G. (1998). Academic achievement, motivation and future selves. *Educational Studies in Mathematics, 24,* 153–163.

Lightbody, P., & Durndell, A. (1996a). Gendered career choice: Is sex-stereotyping the cause or the consequence? *Educational Studies in Mathematics, 22*(2), 133–146.

Lightbody, P., & Durndell, A. (1996b). The masculine image of careers in science and technology—fact or fantasy. *British Journal of Educational Psychology, 66*(2), 231–246.

Lindahl, B. (2007). *A longitudinal study of Students' attitudes towards science and choice of career.* Paper presented at the 80th NARST International Conference New Orleans, Louisiana.

Losh, S., Wilke, R., & Pop, M. (2008). Some methodological issues with "draw a scientist tests" among young children. *International Journal of Science Education, 30*(6), 773–792.

Lynn, L., & Salzman, H. (2006). Collaborative advantage: New horizons for a flat world. *Issues in Science and Technology, Winter,* 74–81.

Lyons, T. (2003). *Decisions by science proficient Year 10 students about post-compulsory high school science enrolment: A sociocultural exploration.* Unpublished Ph.D. thesis, University of New England, Armidale, NSW, Australia.

Lyons, T. (2006a). Different countries, same science classes: Students' experience of school science classes in their own words. *International Journal of Science Education, 28*(6), 591–613.

Lyons, T. (2006b). The puzzle of falling enrolments in physics and chemistry courses: Putting some pieces together. *Research in Science Education, 36*(3), 285–311.

Lyons, T., & Quinn, F. (2010). *Choosing science. Understanding the declines in senior high school science enrolments.* Research report to the Australian Science Teachers Association. Armidale: University of New England, NSW, Australia. Retrieved September 8, 2012, from www.une.edu.au/simerr/pages/projects/131choosingscience.pdf

Maltese, A. (2008). *Persistence in STEM: An investigation of the relationship between high school experiences in science and mathematics and college degree completion in STEM fields.* Unpublished Ph.D. thesis, University of Virginia, Charlottesville.

Maltese, A., & Tai, R. (2008). *Eyeballs in the fridge: Sources of early interest in science.* Paper presented at the American Educational Research Association. New York, NY.

McKinley, E. (2005). Brown bodies, white coats: Postcolonialism, Maori women and science. *Discourse: Studies in the Cultural Politics of Education, 26*(4), 481–496.

Manz, E. (2012). Understanding the codevelopment of modeling practice and ecological knowledge. *Science Education, 96*(6), 1071–1105.

Marginson, S., Tytler, R., Freeman, B., & Roberts, K. (2013). *STEM: Country comparisons.* Melbourne: Australian Council of Learned Academies. Retrieved February 8, 2014, from www.acola.org.au

Mayer, V., & Richmond, J. (1982). An overview of assessment instruments in science. *Science Education, 66,* 49–66.

Mead, M., & Metraux, R. (1957). Image of the scientist among high school students: A pilot study. *Science, 126,* 384–390.

Mendick, H. (2006). *Masculinities in mathematics.* Maidenhead, UK: Open University Press.

Millar, R., & Osborne, J.F. (Eds.). (1998). *Beyond 2000: Science education for the future.* London: King's College London.

Moore, R.W., & Sutman, F.X. (1970). The development, field test and validation of an inventory of scientific attitudes. *Journal of Research in Science Teaching, 7,* 85–94.

Mullis, I.V., Martin, M.O., Foy, P., & Arora, A. (2012). *TIMSS 2011 international results in science.* Boston: International Association for the Evaluation of Educational Achievement.

Munro, M., & Elsom, D. (2000). *Choosing science at 16: The influence of science teachers and career advisers on students' decisions about science subjects and science and technology careers.* Cambridge, UK: National Institute for Careers Education and Counselling (NICEC).

Murphy, C., & Beggs, J. (2003). Children's attitudes towards school science. *School Science Review, 84*(308), 109–116.

Murphy, C., & Beggs, J. (2005). *Primary science in the UK: A scoping study. Final Report to the Wellcome Trust.* London: Wellcome Trust.

Murphy, P., & Whitelegg, E. (2006). *Girls in the physics classroom: A review of research of participation of girls in physics.* London: Institute of Physics.

National Academy of Sciences: Committee on Science Engineering and Public Policy. (2005). *Rising above the gathering storm: Energizing and employing America for a brighter economic future.* Washington, DC: Author.

National Commission on Mathematics and Science Teaching for the 21st Century. (2000). *Before it's too late.* Washington, DC: U.S. Department of Education.

Nature Editorial. (2009). A crisis of confidence. *Nature, 457*(7230), 635–635.

OECD. (2006). *Evolution of student interest in science and technology studies policy report.* Paris: Author.

OECD. (2007). *PISA 2006: Science competencies for tomorrow's world: Volume 1: Analysis.* Paris: Author.

Office of the Chief Scientist. (2012). *Health of Australian science.* Canberra: Australian Government. Retrieved February 8, 2014, from www.chiefscientist.gov.au/2012/05/health-of-australian-science-report-2/

Ogura, Y. (2006). *Graph of student attitude v student attainment.* Based on data from Martin, M.O., et al. (2000). *TIMSS 1999 international science report: Findings from IEA's repeat of the Third International Mathematics and Science Study at the eighth grade.* Chestnut Hill, MA: Boston College; National Institute for Educational Research: Tokyo.

Oliveira, A., Sadler, T., & Suslak, D. (2007). The linguistic construction of expert identity in professor–student discussions of science. *Cultural Studies of Science Education, 2,* 119–150.

Olsen, R., Prenzel, M., & Martin, R. (2011). Interest in science: A many-faceted picture painted by data from the OECD PISA study. *International Journal of Science Education, 33*(1), 1–6.

Osborne, J.F. (2008). Engaging young people with science: Does science education need a new vision? *School Science Review, 89*(328), 67–74.

Osborne, J.F., & Collins, S. (2001). Pupils' views of the role and value of the science curriculum: A focus-group study. *International Journal of Science Education, 23*(5), 441–468.

Osborne, J., & Dillon, J. (2008). *Science education in Europe: Critical reflections:* London: Nuffield Foundation.

Osborne, J., Simon, S., & Collins, S. (2003). Attitudes towards science: A review of the literature and its implications. *International Journal of Science Education, 25,* 1049–1079.

Palmquist, S.D., & Crowley, K. (2007). From teachers to testers: Parents' role in child expertise development in informal settings. *Science Education, 91*(5), 712–732.

Pekrun, R., Frenzel, A.C., Goetz, T., & Perry, R.P. (2007). The control-value theory of achievement emotions: An integrative approach to emotions in education. In P.A. Schutz & R. Pekrun (Eds.), *Emotion in education* (pp. 13–36). San Diego, CA: Elsevier Inc.

Pekrun, R., Goetz, T., Titz, W., & Perry, R.P. (2002). Academic emotions in students' self-regulated learning and achievement: A program of qualitative and quantitative research. *Educational Psychologist, 37*(2), 91–105.

Pell, T., & Jarvis, T. (2001). Developing attitude to science scales for use with children of ages from five to eleven years. *International Journal of Science Education, 23*(8), 847–862.

Pintrich, P.R., Marx, R.W., & Boyle, R.A. (1993). Beyond cold conceptual change: The role of motivational beliefs and classroom contextual factors in the process of conceptual change. *Review of Educational Research, 63*(2), 167–199.

Potter, J., & Wetherell, M. (1987). *Discourse and social psychology: Beyond attitudes and behaviour.* London: Sage Publications.

Pugh, K.J., & Girod, M. (2007). Science, art, and experience: Constructing a science pedagogy from Dewey's aesthetics. *Journal of Science Teacher Education, 18,* 9–27.

Putnam, R. (2001). Community-based social capital and educational performance. In D. Ravitich & J. Viteritti (Eds.), *Making good citizens: Education and civil society* (pp. 58–95). London: Yale University Press.

Putnam, R. (2004). *Education, diversity, social cohesion and "social capital."* Paper delivered at meeting of OECD Education Ministry—Raising the Quality of Learning for All. Dublin, Ireland: March 18.

Rathunde, K., & Csikszentmihalyi, M. (1993). Undivided interest and the growth of talent: A longitudinal study of adolescents. *Journal of Youth and Adolescence, 22*(4), 385–405.

Rattansi, A., & Phoenix, A. (2005). Rethinking youth identities: Modernist and postmodernist frameworks. *Identity: An International Journal of Theory and Research, 5*(2), 97–123.

Renninger, K., & Hidi, S. (2011). Revisiting the conceptualization, measurement, and generation of interest. *Educational Psychologist, 46*(3), 168–184.

Research Business, The. (1994). *Views of science among students, teachers and parents.* London: Institution of Electrical Engineers.

Research Councils UK. (2008). *Public attitudes to science 2008: A survey.* London: Department for Innovation, Universities and Skills.

Riegle-Crumb, C., Moore, C., & Ramos-Wada, A. (2011). Who wants to have a career in science or math? Exploring adolescents' future aspirations by gender and race/ethnicity. *Science Education, 95,* 458–476.

Rivkin, S., Hanushek, E.A., & Kain, J. (2005). Teachers, schools, and academic achievement. *Econometrics, 73*(2), 417–458.

Rowe, K. (2003). *The importance of teacher quality.* Paper presented to the Australian Council for Educational Research Conference, Melbourne, Australia.

Royal Society, The. (2006). *Taking a Leading role.* London: Author.

Ryan, A., & Aikenhead, G. (1992). Students' preconceptions about the epistemology of science. *Science Education, 76*(6), 559–580.

Ryder, J. (2001). Identifying science understanding for functional scientific literacy. *Studies in Science Education, 36,* 1–42.

Saleh, I.M., & Khine, M.S. (Eds.). (2011). *Attitude research in science education: Classic and contemporary measurements.* Charlotte, NC: Information Age Publishing.

Sanders, W., Wright, S.P., & Horn, S. (1997). Teacher and classroom context effects on student achievement: Implications for teacher evaluation. *Journal of Personnel Evaluation in Education, 11*(1), 57–67.

Schibeci, R.A. (1984). Attitudes to science: An update. *Studies in Science Education, 11,* 26–59.

Schreiner, C. (2006). *Exploring a ROSE-garden: Norwegian youth's orientations towards science seen as signs of late modern identities.* Oslo: University of Oslo.

Schreiner, C., & Sjøberg, S. (2007). Science education and youth's identity construction—two incompatible projects? In D. Corrigan, J. Dillon, & R. Gunstone (Eds.), *The re-emergence of values in the science curriculum* (pp. 231–247). Rotterdam: Sense Publishers.

Sfard, A., & Prusak, A. (2005). Telling identities: In search of an analystic tool for investigating learning as a culturally shaped activity. *Educational Researcher, 34,* 14–22.

Simpkins, S.D., Davis-Kean, P.E., & Eccles, J.S. (2006). Math and science motivation: A longitudinal examination of the links between choices and beliefs. *Developmental Psychology, 42*(1), 70–83. doi:10.1037/

Simpson, R.D., & Oliver, J.S. (1985). Attitude toward science and achievement motivation profiles of male and female science students in grades six through ten. *Science Education, 69*(4), 511–526.

Sinatra, G. (2005). The "warming trend" in conceptual change research: The legacy of Paul R. Pintrich. *Educational Psychologist, 40*(2), 107–115.

Sinatra, G., & Pintrich, P. (Eds.). (2002). *Intentional conceptual change.* Mahwah, NJ: Lawrence Erlbaum.

Sjaastad, J. (2012). Sources of inspiration: The role of significant persons in young people's choice of science in higher education. *International Journal of Science Education, 34*(10), 1615–1636. doi:10.1080/09500693.2011.590543

Sjøberg, S., & Schreiner, C. (2005). How do learners in different cultures relate to science and technology? Results and perspectives from the project ROSE. *Asia Pacific Forum on Science Learning and Teaching, 6*(2), 1–16.

Speering, W., & Rennie, L. (1996). Students' perceptions about science: The impact of transition from primary to secondary school. *Research in Science Education, 26,* 283–298.

Stagg, P. (2007). *Careers from science: An investigation for the Science Education Forum:* Warwick, UK: Centre for Education and Industry (CEI).

Steinke, J., Lapinski, M., Crocker, N., Zietsman-Thomas, A., Williams, Y., Evergreen, S., & Kuchibhotia, S. (2007). Assessing media influences on middle school-aged children's perceptions of women in science using the Draw-a-Scientist Test (DAST). *Science Communication, 29*(1), 35–64.

Stokes, H., & Wyn, J. (2007). Constructing identities and making careers: Young people's perspectives on work and learning. *International Journal of Lifelong Education, 26*(5), 495–511.

Strauss, R.P., & Sawyer, E.A. (1986). Some new evidence on teacher and student competencies. *Economics of Education Review, 5*(1), 41–48.

Symington, D., & Tytler, R. (2004). Community leaders' views of the purposes of science in the compulsory years of schooling. *International Journal of Science Education, 26*(11), 1403–1418.

Tai, R. H., Qi Liu, C., Maltese, A. V., & Fan, X. (2006). Planning early for careers in science. *Science, 312,* 1143–1145.

Teitelbaum, M. (2007). *Do we need more scientists and engineers?* Paper presented at the Conference on The National Value of Science Education. University of York, York, UK.

Tenenbaum, H. R., & Leaper, C. (2003). Parent–child conversations about science: The socialization of gender inequities? *Developmental Psychology, 39*(1), 34–47.

Thomson, S., & De Bortoli, L. (2008). *Exploring scientific literacy: How Australia measures up.* Camberwell, Victoria, Australia: ACER.

Tobin, K., & Fraser, B. (1990). What does it mean to be an exemplary science teacher? *Journal of Research in Science Teaching, 27*(1), 3–25.

Tobin, K., Tippins, D. J., & Gallard, A. J. (1994). Research on instructional strategies for teaching science. In D. L. Gabel (Ed.), *Handbook of research on science teaching and learning* (pp. 45–93). New York: MacMillan.

Tytler, R. (2003). A window for a purpose: Developing a framework for describing effective science teaching and learning. *Research in Science Education, 30*(3), 273–298.

Tytler, R., Osborne, J. F., Williams, G., Tytler, K., Clark, J. C., Tomei, A., et al. (2008). *Opening up pathways: Engagement in STEM across the primary-secondary school transition. A review of the literature concerning supports and barriers to science, technology, engineering and mathematics engagement at primary-secondary transition. Commissioned by the Australian Department of Education, Employment and Workplace Relations.* Melbourne, Australia: Deakin University.

Tytler, R., Prain, V., Hubber, P., & Waldrip, B. (Eds.). (2013). *Constructing representations to learn science.* Rotterdam, the Netherlands: Sense Publishers.

Tytler, R., Waldrip, B., & Griffiths, M. (2004). Windows into practice: Constructing effective science teaching and learning in a school change initiative. *International Journal of Science Education, 26*(2), 171–194.

Ulriksen, L., Møller Madsen, L., & Holmegaard, H. T. (2010). What do we know about explanations for drop out/opt out among young people from STM higher education programmes? *Studies in Science Education, 46*(2), 209–244.

van Lier, L. (1996). *Interaction in the language curriculum.* New York: Longman.

Varelas, M., Kane, J., & Wylie, C. (2011). Young African American children's representations of self, science, and school: Making sense of difference. *Science Education, 95*(5), 824–851.

Varelas, M., Kane, J., & Wylie, C. (2012). Young black children and science: Chronotopes of narratives around their science journals. *Journal of Research in Science Teaching, 49,* 568–596.

Walker, E. (2007). The structure and culture of developing a mathematics tutoring collaborative in an urban high school. *High School Journal, 91*(1), 57–67.

Walker, K., Alloway, N., Dalley-Trim, L., & Patterson, A. (2006). Counsellor practices and student perspectives: Perceptions of career counselling in Australian secondary schools. *Australian Journal of Career Development, 15*(1), 37–45.

Walkerdine, V. (1990). *Schoolgirl fictions.* London: Verso.

Watt, H. (2005). Exploring adolescent motivations for pursuing maths-related careers. *Australian Journal of Educational and Developmental Psychology, 5*(2005), 107–116.

Wayne, A., & Youngs, P. (2003). Teacher characteristics and student achievement gains: A review. *Review of Educational Research, 73*(1), 89–122.

Weinburgh, M. (1995). Gender differences in student attitudes toward science: A meta-analysis of the literature from 1970 to 1991. *Journal of Research in Science Teaching, 32*(4), 387–398.

Whitfield, R. C. (1980). Educational research & science teaching. *School Science Review, 60,* 411–430.

Wickman, P.-O. (2006). *Aesthetic experience in science education: Learning and meaning-making as situated talk and action.* London; Mahwah, NJ: Lawrence Erlbaum Associates.

Woolnough, B. (1994). *Effective science teaching.* Buckingham, UK: Open University Press.

Wyn, J. (2011). The sociology of youth. *Youth Studies Australia, 30*(3), 34–39.

Wyn, J., & White, R. (1997). *Rethinking youth.* London: Sage.

Yager, R. E., & Penick, J. E. (1986). Perception of four age groups toward science classes, teachers, and the value of science. *Science and Education, 70*(4), 355–363.

Zhao, D., & Singh, M. (2011). Why do Chinese-Australian students outperform their Australian peers in mathematics? A comparative case study. *International Journal of Science and Mathematics Education, 9*(1), 69–87.

6

Classroom Learning Environments

Historical and Contemporary Perspectives

BARRY J. FRASER

Introduction

Because students spend a huge amount of time in classrooms—approximately 20,000 hours by the time they graduate from university (Fraser, 2001)—the quality of classroom life is important in its own right. However, despite its importance, researchers and practitioners often rely heavily and sometimes exclusively on student outcomes, especially achievement. The field of classroom learning environments provides one approach for conceptualizing, assessing, investigating, and improving what goes on in classrooms.

Furthermore, research with many tens of thousands of students around the world provides consistent and convincing evidence that the classroom environment influences students' outcomes, including achievement (Fraser, 2007, 2012). Therefore, having a positive classroom environment can be considered both a worthy end itself and a means to valuable ends (i.e., improved student outcomes).

In particular, science education researchers have contributed much to the foundations, methods, and expansion of learning environments research internationally, as well as authoring or editing most of the books in the field (Aldridge & Fraser, 2008; Fisher & Khine, 2006; Fraser, 1986; Fraser & Walberg, 1991; Khine & Fisher, 2003). This chapter describes the current state of research on learning environments using the following main sections:

- historical beginnings of the field of learning environments
- learning environment questionnaires
- past research on classroom learning environments
- emerging line of research

Historical Beginnings of the Field of Learning Environments

The historical beginnings of contemporary learning environments research usually are attributed to Herbert Walberg and Rudolf Moos, who independently pioneered the use of participant perceptions of various learning settings. Research and evaluation related to Harvard Project Physics led to the development of the Learning Environment Inventory (LEI; Anderson & Walberg, 1968; Walberg, 1979). Independently, Moos (1974) developed a scheme for classifying human environments into three dimensions (relationship, personal development, and system maintenance and change) to enable the classification and sorting of various components of any human environment. This led Moos to the development of the Classroom Environment Scale (CES; Moos, 1979; Moos & Trickett, 1974), which linked his work in other human environments to school settings. One of Moos's contributions was the insight that the same fundamental dimensions characterized diverse human environments, including hospital wards, work settings, families, and schools.

This pioneering research on learning environments in the United States soon spread to Australia. Walberg's work on evaluating Harvard Project Physics inspired other researchers to incorporate the LEI, either in its original or a modified form, in their evaluations of the Australian Science Education Project (ASEP). Fraser (1979) compared the learning environment of ASEP and conventional classrooms among a sample of 541 Grade 7 students, whereas Fraser and Northfield (1981) monitored changes during the use of ASEP materials among 17 seventh-grade classes. This research also replicated with Australian students the consistent associations between student outcomes and classroom environment reported in Walberg's studies in the United States. For example, Walberg's meta-analysis involving 17,805 students revealed that performance on a variety of student outcomes was superior in classes with higher cohesiveness, satisfaction, and goal direction and lower disorganization and friction (Haertel, Walberg, & Haertel, 1981).

Early research using the CES in Tasmania, involving 116 Grade 8 and 9 science classes, made several significant contributions to the emergence of learning environments research in Australia. First, the CES was cross-validated for use in Australia (Fisher & Fraser, 1983a). Second, interesting patterns of differences were reported between students' and teachers' perceptions of actual and preferred classroom environment (Fisher & Fraser, 1983b). In particular, both students and teachers preferred a more favorable classroom environment than the one perceived to be actually present; and teachers perceived the same classroom environment more favorably than did their students. Third, associations were established between student outcomes (attitudes and inquiry skills) and the classroom learning environment (Fraser & Fisher, 1982). Fourth, in an innovative application of learning environment ideas, Fraser and Fisher (1983) utilized a person–environment fit perspective to establish that students achieve cognitive and affective outcomes better when in their preferred classroom environment. This research not only supported the importance of the actual classroom environment for improving student outcomes but also suggested that changing actual classroom environments to better align with students' preferences also could lead to additional improvements in student outcomes.

The first major questionnaire development undertaken in the field of learning environments in Australia focused on the Individualised Classroom Environment Questionnaire (ICEQ), which grew out of awareness that both the LEI and CES assessed the environment of teacher-centered classrooms and were not ideal for student-centered, individualized, and inquiry-based settings. Its five dimensions (Personalisation, Participation, Independence, Investigation, and Differentiation) assess those dimensions that distinguish individualized classrooms from conventional ones (Fraser, 1990; Rentoul & Fraser, 1979). When the CES was used in investigating relationships between student outcomes and the nature of the classroom environment (Fraser & Fisher, 1982), it was found that scores for attitudes to science and inquiry skills were higher in classes with higher order/organization, teacher support, and innovation. As well, research revealed differences between actual and preferred perceptions and between students' and teachers' perceptions with a sample of 116 classes in Tasmania (Fisher & Fraser, 1983a). In particular, teachers perceived the same classroom environment more favorably than did their students in the same classroom (the "rose-colored glasses" phenomenon), and both students and teachers preferred a more favorable classroom environment than the one that they perceived as being actually present.

Simultaneously with this research in Australia, another program of learning environments research emerged in the Netherlands. Wubbels and his colleagues began ambitious programmatic research focusing specifically on the interaction between teachers and students in the classroom and involving use of the Questionnaire on Teacher Interaction (QTI; Wubbels & Brekelmans, 1998; Wubbels, den Brok, van Tartwijk, & Levy, 2012; Wubbels & Levy, 1993). This questionnaire is based on a model of teacher interpersonal behavior with the two dimensions of influence (dominance–submission) and proximity (opposition–cooperation). Its eight scales assess Leadership, Helping/Friendly, Understanding, Student Responsibility/Freedom, Uncertain, Dissatisfied, Admonishing, and Strict behavior.

A recent literature review (Wubbels & Brekelmans, 2012) describes some of the many past and contemporary accomplishments of this impressive and important program of research involving the QTI. As described later in this chapter, the QTI has been used in developing typologies of classroom environments in the Netherlands, the United States, and Australia. An extensive study has identified changes in teacher interpersonal behavior during the professional career, with teachers with 6 to 10 years of experience having the best relationships (in terms of exhibiting leadership and friendly and strict behaviors) with their students in terms of promoting achievement and positive attitudes (Brekelmans, Wubbels, & van Tartwijk, 2005). The research on teacher–student interaction involving use of the QTI spread to many countries including Australia (Ferguson & Fraser, 1998; Henderson, Fisher, & Fraser, 2000), Korea (Kim, Fisher, & Fraser, 2000), Brunei (Scott & Fisher, 2004), and Singapore (Goh & Fraser, 1998; Quek, Wong, & Fraser, 2005a, 2005b).

The consolidation and long-term continuation of any new field requires the establishment not only of strong research traditions but also of structures to support the field. Because the American Educational Research Association (AERA) sponsors the world's largest and most prestigious educational research conference, clearly, it was advantageous for learning environment researchers to have the opportunity to meet together and report their work in this forum. Therefore, in 1984, the AERA Special Interest Group (SIG) on Learning Environments was established. This highly successful and widely international SIG has sponsored its own program at every AERA annual meeting since 1985. In 2012, the AERA annual meeting program had 103 entries in its index under the heading "learning environments." The next landmark in the field's evolution was to establish a new journal devoted especially to learning environments research. The first issue of *Learning Environments Research: An International Journal* was published in 1998 by a leading international publisher, Springer (formally Kluwer). In 2013, this journal was in its 16th volume. More recently, a decade after the establishment of this journal, another landmark was the evolution in 2008 of a book series titled *Advances in Learning Environment Research* sponsored by Sense Publishers (Aldridge & Fraser 2008; Wubbels et al., 2012).

Learning Environment Questionnaires

A hallmark of the field of classroom learning environments is the existence of a wide range of economical and robust questionnaires that have been found to be valid and useful in many studies around the world. According to Fraser (2007), the use of these questionnaire has several advantages over the direct observation of classrooms. Defining the classroom environment in terms of the shared perceptions of the students and teachers has the dual advantage of characterizing the setting through the eyes of the participants themselves and capturing data the observer could miss or consider unimportant. Students are at a good vantage point to make judgments about classrooms because they have encountered many different learning environments and have enough time in a class to form accurate impressions. Also, even if teachers are inconsistent in their day-to-day behavior, they usually project a consistent image of the long-standing attributes of the classroom environment. Although questionnaires have numerous advantages, Tobin and Fraser (1998) advocate the combination of quantitative and qualitative methods in learning environment research.

In this section, several contemporary classroom environment questionnaires are reviewed. In particular, the Science Laboratory Environment Inventory (SLEI), Constructivist Learning Environment Survey (CLES), and What Is Happening In This Class? (WIHIC) are widely used around the world today.

Table 6.1 provides an overview of 11 historically significant or contemporary classroom learning environment questionnaires. This table shows the name of each scale in each instrument, the level (primary, secondary, higher education) for which each instrument is suited, the number of items contained in each scale, and the classification of each scale according to Moos's (1974) scheme for classifying human environments. Moos's three basic types of dimension are Relationship Dimensions (which identify the nature and intensity of personal relationships within the environment and assess the extent to which people are involved in the environment and support and help each other), Personal Development Dimensions (which assess basic directions along which personal growth and self-enhancement tend to occur), and System Maintenance and System Change Dimensions (which involve the extent to which the environment is orderly, clear in expectation, maintains control, and is responsive to change).

Science Laboratory Environment Inventory (SLEI)

Because of the importance of laboratory settings in science education, an instrument specifically suited to assessing the environment of science laboratory classes at the senior high school or higher education levels was developed (Fraser, Giddings, & McRobbie, 1995; Fraser & McRobbie, 1995). The SLEI has five seven-item scales (Student Cohesiveness, Open-Endedness, Integration, Rule Clarity, and Material Environment), and the five response alternatives are Almost Never, Seldom, Sometimes, Often, and Very Often. Typical items are "I use the theory from my regular science class sessions during laboratory activities" (Integration) and "We know the results that we are supposed to get before we commence a laboratory activity" (Open-Endedness).

The SLEI was field tested and validated simultaneously with a sample of 5,477 students in 269 classes in six different countries (the United States, Canada, England, Israel, Australia, and Nigeria) and later cross-validated with Australian students (Fisher, Henderson, & Fraser, 1997; Fraser & McRobbie, 1995). As described later in this chapter, the SLEI subsequently has been cross-validated and used in other countries such as the United States with 761 high school biology students (Lightburn & Fraser, 2007), Korea with 439 high school students (Fraser & Lee, 2009), and Singapore with 1,592 Grade 10 chemistry students (Wong & Fraser, 1996). The replicated validity, usefulness, and versatility of the SLEI suggest that other researchers and practitioners around the world can use it with confidence for various purposes.

Constructivist Learning Environment Survey (CLES)

Taylor, Fraser, and Fisher (1997) developed the CLES to assist researchers and teachers to assess the degree to which a particular classroom's environment is consistent with a constructivist epistemology and to assist teachers to reflect on their epistemological assumptions and reshape their teaching practice. The CLES has 35 items, with five response alternatives ranging from Almost Never to Almost Always, which assess Personal Relevance, Uncertainty of Science, Critical Voice, Shared Control, and Student Negotiation. Typical items are "I help the teacher to decide what activities I do" (Shared Control) and "Other students ask me to explain my ideas" (Student Negotiation). Taylor and colleagues (1997) reported sound validity for the use of the CLES with both Australian and American students.

Later, as noted below, the CLES was cross-validated in science classes with 1,079 students in 59 classes in Texas (Nix, Fraser, & Ledbetter, 2005), 739 Grade K–3 students in Miami (Peiro & Fraser, 2009), 1,081 students in 50 classes in Australia, 1,879 students in 50 classes in Taiwan (Aldridge, Fraser, Taylor, & Chen, 2000), 1,083 Korean students in 24 classes (Kim, Fisher, & Fraser, 1999), and 1,864 South African students in 43 classes (Aldridge, Fraser, & Sebela, 2004).

What Is Happening In This Class? (WIHIC)

The WIHIC is the most widely used learning environment questionnaire in the world today. It combines modified versions of salient scales from a range of existing questionnaires with additional scales that accommodate contemporary educational concerns (e.g., equity and constructivism). The original 90-item, nine-scale version was refined by both statistical analysis of data from 355 junior high school science students and extensive interviewing of students about their views of their classroom environments in general, the wording and salience of individual items, and their questionnaire responses (Fraser, Fisher, & McRobbie, 1996). Analysis of data from an Australian sample of 1,081 students in 50 classes and a Taiwanese

TABLE 6.1
Overview of Scales Contained in Some Classroom Environment Instruments (LEI, CES, ICEQ, CUCEI, MCI, QTI, SLEI, CLES, WIHIC, TROFLEI and COLES)

Instrument	Level	Items per scale	Scales Classified According to Moos's Scheme		
			Relationship dimensions	Personal development dimensions	System maintenance and change dimensions
Learning Environment Inventory (LEI)	Secondary	7	Cohesiveness Friction Favoritism Cliqueness Satisfaction Apathy	Speed Difficulty Competitiveness	Diversity Formality Material Environment Goal Direction Disorganization Democracy
Classroom Environment Scale (CES)	Secondary	10	Involvement Affiliation Teacher Support	Task Orientation Competition	Order and Organization Rule Clarity Teacher Control Innovation
Individualised Classroom Environment Questionnaire (ICEQ)	Secondary	10	Personalization Participation	Independence Investigation	Differentiation
College and University Classroom Environment Inventory (CUCEI)	Higher education	7	Personalization Involvement Student Cohesiveness Satisfaction	Task Orientation	Innovation Individualization
My Class Inventory (MCI)	Elementary	6–9	Cohesiveness Friction Satisfaction	Difficulty Competitiveness	
Questionnaire on Teacher Interaction (QTI)	Secondary/ Primary	8–10	Leadership Helpful/Friendly Understanding Student Responsibility and Freedom Uncertain Dissatisfied Admonishing Strict		
Science Laboratory Environment Inventory (SLEI)	Upper Secondary/ Higher Education	7	Student Cohesiveness	Open-Endedness Integration	Rule Clarity Material Environment
Constructivist Learning Environment Survey (CLES)	Secondary	7	Personal Relevance Uncertainty	Critical Voice Shared Control	Student Negotiation
What Is Happening In this Class? (WIHIC)	Secondary	8	Student Cohesiveness Teacher Support Involvement	Investigation Task Orientation Cooperation	Equity
Technology-Rich Outcomes-Focused Learning Environment Inventory (TROFLEI)	Secondary	10	Student Cohesiveness Teacher support Involvement Young Adult Ethos	Investigation Task Orientation Cooperation	Equity Differentiation Computer Usage
Constructivist-Oriented Learning Environment Survey (COLES)	Secondary	11	Student Cohesiveness Teacher Support Involvement Young Adult Ethos Personal Relevance	Task Orientation Cooperation	Equity Differentiation Formative Assessment Assessment Criteria

sample of 1,879 students in 50 classes (Aldridge & Fraser, 2000; Aldridge, Fraser, & Huang, 1999) led to a final form of the WIHIC containing seven eight-item scales (Student Cohesiveness, Teacher Support, Involvement, Investigation, Task Orientation, Cooperation, and Equity). Frequency response alternatives range from Almost Never to Very Often. Typical items are "I discuss ideas in class" (Involvement) and "I work with other students on projects in this class" (Cooperation).

Using a sample of 3,980 high school students from Australia, Britain, and Canada, confirmatory factor analysis supported the seven-scale *a priori* structure of the WIHIC (Dorman, 2003). All items loaded strongly on their own scale, although model fit indices revealed a degree of scale overlap. The factor structure was found to be invariant for country, grade level, and gender. Overall, this study strongly supported the international applicability of the WIHIC as a valid measure of classroom psychosocial environment. Subsequently, in another study using multitrait-multimethod modeling, Dorman (2008) reported further evidence supporting the validity of actual and preferred forms of the WIHIC.

The WIHIC has been cross-validated in many studies in numerous countries. For example, English-language versions of the WIHIC have been cross-validated with 1,077 Grade 4 through 7 students in South Africa (Aldridge, Fraser, & Ntuli, 2009), 1,021 students in India (Koul & Fisher, 2005), 2,310 Grade 10 students in Singapore (Chionh & Fraser, 2009), 1,404 students in Canada and Australia (Zandvliet & Fraser, 2004, 2005), 1,434 middle school students in New York (Wolf & Fraser, 2008), and 924 Grade 8 and 10 students in Florida (Helding & Fraser, 2013). As well, the WIHIC has been translated into other languages and validated with 543 Grade 8 students in Korea (Kim, Fisher, & Fraser, 2000), 1,879 junior high school students in Taiwan (Aldridge et al., 1999), 763 college students in the United Arab Emirates (MacLeod & Fraser, 2010), and 594 secondary students in Indonesia (Fraser, Aldridge, & Adolphe, 2010).

Table 6.2 lists 22 studies that have involved the use of the WIHIC in various countries and in various languages. The first four studies are examples of crossnational research. The next six studies involved the use of WIHIC in English in Singapore, India, Australia, and South Africa, although the study by Chua, Wong, and Chen (2011) in Singapore involved a bilingual version of the WIHIC in both Chinese and English. The 10th and 11th studies involved the use of the WIHIC, respectively, in the Korean language and in the Indonesian language in Indonesia. The next two studies involved the use of an Arabic translation of the WIHIC in the United Arab Emirates. The last eight entries in Table 6.2 are all studies that involved the use of the WIHIC in the United States, including three studies in California, one study in New York, and four studies in Florida. Although the four studies in Miami all involved the use of an English-language version of the WIHIC, it is noteworthy that three of them

offered students the option of responding to a version of the WIHIC in either Spanish or English. For each study involving the WIHIC in Table 6.2, details are provided not only of the country and language involved but also the size of and nature of the sample. In this table, it also is noted that every study reported evidence to support the factorial validity and internal consistency reliability of the WIHIC. Finally, the last column of Table 6.2 identifies the unique contributions of each study.

The seven scales of the WIHIC have been included along with three new scales (namely, Differentiation, Computer Usage, and Young Adult Ethos) to form the Technology-Rich Outcomes-Focused Learning Environment Inventory (TROFLEI; Aldridge, Dorman, & Fraser, 2004; Aldridge & Fraser, 2008). Based on an Australian sample of 2,317 students in 166 classes, Aldridge and Fraser (2008) reported strong factorial validity and internal consistency reliability for the TROFLEI. Aldridge and colleagues (2004) used multitrait-multimethod modeling with TROFLEI responses from a sample of 1,249 students, of whom 772 were from Western Australia and 477 were from Tasmania. When the 10 TROFLEI scales were used as traits and the actual and preferred forms of the instrument as methods, the results supported the TROFLEI's construct validity and sound psychometric properties, as well as indicating that the actual and preferred forms share a common structure. The TROFLEI recently was translated, validated, and used in Turkey with a sample of 980 Grade 9 through Grade 12 students, as well as the English-language version being used with 130 Grade 9 through Grade 12 students in the United States (Welch, Cakir, Peterson, & Ray, 2012). For both actual and preferred forms and for both Turkey and the United States, the TROFLEI exhibited sound reliability and factorial validity when confirmatory factor analysis was used. The strong cross-cultural validity of this newer instrument, based on comprehensive studies in Australia, Turkey, and the United States, supports its confident future use by other researchers.

The Constructivist-Oriented Learning Environment Survey (COLES) incorporates numerous scales from the WIHIC into an instrument that is designed to provide feedback as a basis for reflection in teacher action research. In constructing the COLES, Aldridge, Fraser, Bell, and Dorman (2012) were especially conscious of the omission in all existing classroom environment questionnaires of important aspects related to the assessment of student learning. The COLES incorporates six of the WIHIC's seven scales (namely, Student Cohesiveness, Teacher Support, Involvement, Task Orientation, Cooperation, and Equity) while omitting the WIHIC's Investigation scale. Like the TROFLEI, the COLES also includes the scales of Differentiation and Young Adult Ethos. In addition, the COLES includes the Personal Relevance scale from the CLES (the extent to which learning activities are relevant to the student's everyday out-of-school experiences). The two new COLES scales related to assessment are

TABLE 6.2

Overview of Studies That Involved the Use of the What Is Happening In This Class? (WIHIC) Questionnaire

Reference(s)	Country(ies)	Language(s)	Sample(s)	Factorial Validity & Reliability	Associations with Environment for:	Unique Contributions
Aldridge, Fraser, & Huang (1999); Aldridge & Fraser (2000)	Australia Taiwan	English Mandarin	1,081 (Australia) & 1,879 (Taiwan) junior high science students in 50 classes	√	Enjoyment	Mandarin translation Combined quantitative and qualitative methods
Dorman (2003)	Australia UK Canada	English	3,980 high school students	√	NA	Confirmatory factor analysis substantiated invariant structure across countries, grade levels, and sexes.
Fraser, Aldridge, & Adolphe (2010)	Australia Indonesia	English Bahasa	567 students (Australia) and 594 students (Indonesia) in 18 secondary science classes	√	Several attitude scales	Differences were found between countries and sexes.
Zandvliet & Fraser (2004, 2005)	Australia Canada	English	1,404 students in 81 networked classes	√	Satisfaction	Involved both physical (ergonomic) and psychosocial environments
Chionh & Fraser (2009)	Singapore	English	2,310 grade 10 geography & mathematics students	√	Achievement Attitudes Self-esteem	Differences between geography and mathematics classroom environments were smaller than between actual and preferred environments.
Khoo & Fisher (2008)	Singapore	English	250 working adults attending computer education courses	√	Satisfaction	Adult population Males perceived more trainer support and involvement but less equity.
Chua, Wong, & Chen (2011)	Singapore	Chinese & English	1,460 Grade 9 in 50 Chinese language classes	√	NA	Bilingual instrument Compared students with teachers and male students with female students
Koul & Fisher (2005)	India	English	1,021 science students in 31 classes	√	NA	Differences in classroom environment according to cultural background
Dorman (2008)	Australia	English	978 secondary school students	√	NA	Multitrait-multimethod modeling validated actual and preferred forms
Aldridge, Fraser, & Ntuli (2009)	South Africa	English	1,077 Grade 4–7 students	√	NA	Preservice teachers undertaking a distance-education program used environment assessments to improve teaching practices
Kim, Fisher, & Fraser (2000)	Korea	Korean	543 Grade 8 science students in 12 schools	√	Attitudes	Korean translation Sex differences in WIHIC scores

(Continued)

TABLE 6.2 (Continued)

Reference(s)	Country(ies)	Language(s)	Sample(s)	Factorial Validity & Reliability	Associations with Environment for:	Unique Contributions
Wahyudi & Treagust (2004)	Indonesia	Indonesian	1,400 lower-secondary science students in 16 schools	√	NA	Indonesian translation Urban students perceived greater cooperation and less teacher support than did suburban students.
MacLeod & Fraser (2010)	UAE	Arabic	763 college students in 82 classes	√	NA	Arabic translation Students preferred a more positive actual environment.
Afari, Aldridge, Fraser, & Khine (2013)	UAE	Arabic	352 college students in 33 classes	√	Enjoyment Academic efficacy	Arabic translation Use of games promoted a positive classroom environment.
den Brok, Fisher, Rickards, & Bull (2006)	California, USA	English	665 middle-school science students in 11 schools	√	NA	Girls perceived the environment more favorably.
Martin-Dunlop & Fraser (2008)	California, USA	English	525 female university science students in 27 classes	√	Attitude	Very large increases in learning environment scores for an innovative course
Ogbuehi & Fraser (2007)	California, USA	English	661 middle-school mathematics students	√	Two attitude scales	Used three WIHIC & three CLES scales Innovative teaching strategies promoted task orientation.
Wolf & Fraser (2008)	New York, USA	English	1,434 middle school science students in 71 classes	√	Attitudes Achievement	Inquiry-based laboratory activities promoted cohesiveness and were differentially effective for males and females.
Pickett & Fraser (2009)	Florida, USA	English	573 Grade 3–5 students	√	NA	Mentoring program for beginning teachers was evaluated in terms of changes in learning environment in teachers' school classrooms.
Allen & Fraser (2007)	Florida, USA	English Spanish	120 parents and 520 Grade 4 & 5 students	√	Attitudes Achievement	Involved both parents and students Actual-preferred differences were larger for parents than students.
Robinson & Fraser (2013)	Florida, USA	English Spanish	78 parents and 172 kindergarten science students	√	Achievement Attitudes	Kindergarten level Involved parents Spanish translation Relative to students, parents perceived a more favorable environment but preferred a less favorable environment.
Helding & Fraser (2013)	Florida, USA	English Spanish	924 students in 38 Grade 8 & 10 science classes	√	Attitudes Achievement	Spanish translation Students of NBC teachers had more favorable classroom environment perceptions.

Formative Assessment (the extent to which students feel that the assessment tasks given to them make a positive contribution to their learning) and Assessment Criteria (the extent to which assessment criteria are explicit so that the basis for judgments is clear and public).

For a sample of 2,043 Grade 11 and 12 students from 147 classes in nine schools in Western Australia, data analysis supported the sound factorial validity and internal consistency reliability of both actual and preferred versions of the COLES. A noteworthy methodological feature of this study was that the Rasch model was used to convert data collected using a frequency response scale into interval data suitable for parametric analyses. Interestingly, when analyses were performed separately for raw scores and Rasch scores, Aldridge and colleagues (2012) found that the differences between the validity results (e.g., reliability, discriminant validity, and ability to differentiate between classrooms) were negligible. It is noteworthy that the COLES has been used successfully by teachers in action research aimed at improving their classroom environments (Aldridge et al., 2012).

Other Questionnaires

Working specifically in the Catholic school sector, Dorman, Fraser, and McRobbie (1995) and colleagues developed and validated the Catholic School Classroom Environment Questionnaire. Interestingly, use of this questionnaire revealed a difference between the rhetoric and the reality of classroom environments in Catholic schools (Dorman, Fraser, & McRobbie, 1997).

Fisher and Waldrip developed the Cultural Learning Environment Questionnaire (CLEQ) to assess culturally sensitive factors in students' learning environments (Fisher & Waldrip, 1997, 1999). The scales are called Gender Equity, Collaboration, Deference, Competition, Teacher Authority, Modelling, and Congruence. This questionnaire was used later in modified form to investigate the beliefs of 475 trainee teachers enrolled at the University of Brunei Darussalam (Dhindsa & Fraser, 2004) and to identify sex and age differences in the perceptions of 912 Grade 8 students in Brunei (Dhindsa & Fraser, 2011).

Although the LEI is historically significant, it is no longer used in contemporary learning environment research. However, the My Class Inventory (MCI), a simplified version of the LEI for children aged 8 to 12 years, is still used today because of its unusually low reading level. The MCI, which has only five scales and simplified wording, has been validated in Australia (Fisher & Fraser, 1981) and Texas (Scott Houston, Fraser, & Ledbetter, 2008). Also it has been modified, cross-validated, and used with large samples of 1,565 lower-secondary students in Brunei (Majeed, Fraser, & Aldridge, 2002), 2,835 Grade 4 through 6 students in Washington State (Sink & Spencer, 2005), and 1,512 Grade 5 students in Singapore (Goh & Fraser, 1998).

The WEBLEI (Web-Based Learning Environment Instrument) was designed by Chang and Fisher (2003) to quantify Australian students' perceptions of their learning environments in a tertiary institution in which the entire course was offered online. The WEBLEI measures students' perceptions of Access, Interaction, Response, and Results. In another study (Chandra & Fisher, 2009), the course was offered in a blended environment to Australian students in a high school. Whereas courses in a university environment are generally delivered through sophisticated software, in this instance, the course was delivered using a teacher-developed website. Therefore, the items in the WEBLEI were amended to suit the setting.

Past Research on Classroom Learning Environments

The subsections that follow (1) identify several common lines of past learning environment research (namely, evaluation of educational innovations, associations between classroom environment and student outcomes, and practical attempts to improve classrooms) and review past learning environment research in (2) Asia, (3) North America and (4) African and Arab countries, and (5) emerging lines of research (namely, links between educational environments, cross-national studies, and typologies of classroom environments).

Common Lines of Past Classroom Environment Research

Classroom environment instruments have been used as a valuable source of process criteria in the evaluation of educational innovations. For example, in an early evaluation of the Australian Science Education Project, ASEP students perceived their classrooms as being more satisfying and individualized and having a better material environment relative to a comparison group (Fraser, 1979). In evaluating computer-assisted learning (Fraser & Teh, 1994), a group of students using micro-PROLOG-based computer-assisted learning had much higher scores for achievement (3.5 standard deviations), attitudes (1.4 standard deviations), and classroom environment (1.0–1.9 standard deviations) than did a comparison group. Other examples of this application of learning environment assessments include evaluating the use of anthropometry activities in high school science (Lightburn & Fraser, 2007), inquiry-based computer-assisted learning (Maor & Fraser, 1996), and outcomes-focused education (Aldridge & Fraser, 2008).

The strongest tradition in past classroom environment research has involved investigation of associations between students' cognitive and affective learning outcomes and their perceptions of psychosocial characteristics of their classrooms. In particular, the meta-analysis mentioned previously revealed more favorable student outcomes in classes with more cohesiveness, satisfaction, and goal direction and less disorganization and friction (Haertel et al., 1981). Relationships between outcome measures and classroom environment perceptions have been reported for a variety of cognitive and affective outcome measures, a variety of classroom environment instruments, and a variety of samples (ranging across numerous countries and grade levels). For example, McRobbie and Fraser (1993) used the SLEI in an investigation of associations between student outcomes and classroom environment among 1,594 senior high school chemistry students in 92 classes. Simple, multiple, and canonical correlation analyses were conducted separately for two units of analysis (student scores and class means) and separately with and without control for general ability. Past research was replicated in that the nature of the science laboratory classroom environment (especially integration between theory classes and laboratory work) accounted for appreciable proportions of the variance in both cognitive and affective outcomes beyond that attributable to general ability. Science educators wishing to enhance student outcomes in science laboratory settings are likely to find useful the result that both cognitive and attitude outcomes were enhanced in laboratory classes in which the laboratory activities were integrated with the work in nonlaboratory classes.

Although many past learning environment studies have employed techniques such as multiple regression analysis, fewer have used multilevel analysis, which takes cognizance of the hierarchical nature of classroom setting (i.e., students within intact classes are more homogeneous than a random sample of students). When Wong, Young, and Fraser (1997) used a sample of 1,592 Grade 10 students in 56 chemistry classes to investigate associations among three student attitude measures and a modified version of the SLEI, most of the statistically significant results from the multiple regression analyses were replicated in the Hierachical Linear Model (HLM) analyses, as well as being consistent in direction. Another study employing HLM in investigating outcome–environment associations was reported by Goh, Young, and Fraser (1995).

Teachers have used feedback information based on assessment of students' actual and preferred classroom learning environment as a basis for guiding practical improvements in their classroom environments. The five-step procedure used in past research involves (1) assessment, (2) feedback, (3) reflection and discussion, (4) intervention, and (5) reassessment (Fraser, 1999b). This technique has been applied successfully in case studies in Australia (Aldridge & Fraser, 2008; Fraser & Fisher, 1986; Yarrow, Millwater, & Fraser, 1997), South Africa (Aldridge, Fraser, & Sebela, 2004), and the United States (Sinclair & Fraser, 2002).

Learning Environments Research in Asia

Collaboration between Korean and Australian science education researchers involved the translation, validation, and use of the CLES (Kim, Fisher, & Fraser, 1999) with 1,083 science students in 12 schools, as well as the use of WIHIC and QTI (Kim et al., 2000) with a sample of 543 Grade 8 science students in the same 12 schools.

This study paved the way for later learning environment research in Korea by cross-validating a Korean-language version of three well-established questionnaires, as well as replicating past studies of associations between student outcomes and the nature of Korean science classroom environments.

Kim's research in Korea was followed up by Lee. In addition to using and cross-validating a Korean-language version of the QTI (Lee, Fraser, & Fisher, 2003), Lee also translated and validated a Korean-language version of the SLEI (Fraser & Lee, 2009) with a sample of 440 Grade 10 and 11 students in 13 classes. As well as replicating past findings of outcome–environment associations, interesting differences were found between the learning environment perceptions of science students in three different streams (science-independent, science-oriented, and humanities). Teacher–student interactions in Korean senior high school science classrooms reflected the general image of the youth–elder relationship in society, as well as the senior high school's unique nature—portraying a scene of "directing teachers and obeying students."

While working in Brunei Darussalam, Scott undertook the translation and validation of a Malay version of the QTI with 3,104 science students in 136 classrooms. Statistical analyses revealed that this Malay version of the QTI for these Malay-speaking primary school students in Brunei was indeed valid and reliable. When associations between students' perceptions of their teachers' interpersonal behaviors and their end-of-year results on an external science examination were investigated, students' perceptions of cooperative behaviors were positively correlated while submissive behaviors were negatively correlated with their achievement (den Brok, Fisher, & Scott, 2005; Scott & Fisher, 2004).

In contrast to Scott's use of a Malay-language version of a learning environment questionnaire in Brunei, Majeed used a modified English-language version of the My Class Inventory (MCI) with 1,565 students from 81 classes. As well as cross-validating the MCI for use in Brunei, Majeed and colleagues (2002) reported sex differences in students' perceptions, as well as associations between student satisfaction and positive classroom environments.

Koul and Fisher cross-validated English versions of the QTI and WIHIC in Jammu, India, among 1,021 students from 31 classes. It was found that Kashmiri students perceived their classroom environments more positively than did students from other cultural groups (Koul & Fisher, 2005).

Indonesian educators were involved in the translation and cross-validation of questionnaires in the Indonesian language and the beginning of traditions of learning environment research in that country. Margianti undertook research involving an Indonesian version of the WIHIC with a large sample of 2,498 university students in 50 classes (Margianti, Aldridge, & Fraser, 2004). Student achievement was better when lecturers emphasized classroom involvement and equity, and attitudes were more positive when there was more teacher support, involvement, task orientation, and equity. Another study in Indonesia involved the use of the WIHIC among 1,188 lower-secondary students in 72 science classes in Kalimantan Selatan (Wahyudi & Treagust, 2004). As well as cross-validating the WIHIC and reporting significant differences between actual and preferred classroom environments, these researchers identified differences in classroom environments according to locality. Students in rural schools held less favorable perceptions than students in urban and suburban schools for all WIHIC scales. Students in urban and suburban schools generally perceived their classroom environments similarly, with the exception that students in urban schools perceived more cooperation and less teacher support than did students in suburban schools. Also, in Indonesia, Fraser, Aldridge, and Soerjaningsih (2010) validated an Indonesian version of the QTI with 422 university students.

Singaporean educational researchers have made numerous and important contributions to the field of learning environments. Using a locally developed questionnaire that drew ideas from existing instruments, Teh and Fraser (1994, 1995) used learning environment criteria in the evaluation of computer-assisted learning among a sample of 671 secondary students in 24 classes. More recently, Khoo and Fraser (2008) cross-validated an adapted version of the WIHIC with a sample of 250 working adults, who reported higher satisfaction in classes with more teacher support, involvement, and task orientation.

Working specifically with final-year chemistry students (1,592 students in 28 classes), Wong and Fraser (1996) reported the first major study in Singapore into associations between students' attitudes to science and the perceived classroom learning environment. For this study, the original SLEI was modified to form the Chemistry Laboratory Environment Inventory (CLEI). Strong and statistically significant attitude–environment associations (especially for the environment scales of integration and rule clarity) were confirmed through multilevel analysis (Wong et al., 1997). In a later study involving 497 chemistry students responding to both the CLEI and the QTI, Quek and colleagues (2005a, 2005b) not only replicated the existence of attitude–environment associations but also reported significant differences in classroom environment perceptions according to the students' sex and stream (i.e., gifted vs. nongifted).

Other large-sample collaborative studies in Singapore have involved the adaptation, validation, and application of well-known learning environment questionnaire. For example, relationships between psychosocial climate and student achievement and attitudes were established for 1,512 primary school students using both multiple-regression analysis (Goh & Fraser, 1998) and multilevel analysis (Goh et al., 1995). Both the MCI and QTI were adapted and used. When Chionh and Fraser (2009) used the WIHIC among 2,310 Grade 10 students in 75 classes,

they found large differences between actual and preferred learning environment scores. Also, better examination scores were found in classrooms with more student cohesiveness, whereas self-esteem and attitudes were more favorable in classrooms with more teacher support, task orientation, and equity.

Learning Environments Research in North America

Numerous learning environment questionnaires originally developed in Australia have been modified and cross-validated with large samples of science students in the United States. For example, the WIHIC has been cross-validated with 655 middle school students in California (den Brok et al., 2006), 525 university students in California (Martin-Dunlop & Fraser, 2008), 573 primary school students in Florida (Pickett & Fraser, 2009), and 1,434 middle school physical science students in New York (Wolf & Fraser, 2008). The SLEI has been cross-validated with 761 high school biology students in Florida (Lightburn & Fraser, 2007), and the CLES has been cross-validated with 1,079 students in 59 classes in North Texas (Nix et al., 2005) and 739 Grades K–3 students in Florida (Peiro & Fraser, 2009). Peiro's research with the CLES also involved its translation into the Spanish language.

As well as replicating findings from past research concerning empirical links between positive classroom environments and improved student outcomes, the studies referred to provided good examples of the use of learning environment scales as criteria of effectiveness in the evaluation of educational programs and teaching methods. For example, these studies included evaluations of the use of anthropometric activities (Lightburn & Fraser, 2007), an innovative science course for prospective primary teachers (Martin-Dunlop & Fraser, 2008), an innovative teacher development program (Nix & Fraser, 2010; Nix et al., 2005), an instructional intervention for early childhood children based on constructivist principles (Peiro & Fraser, 2009), and inquiry-based activities for middle school science students (Wolf & Fraser, 2008).

Although the evaluation of teacher professional development programs often involves surveying participant teachers' opinions and satisfaction related to various aspects of a program, Pickett and Fraser (2009) argue that the litmus test of the success of any professional development program is the extent of changes in teaching behaviors and ultimately student outcomes in the participating teachers' school classrooms. Their evaluation of a 2-year mentoring program in science for beginning elementary school teachers is unique in that it drew on the field of learning environments in evaluating this program in terms of participants' classroom teaching behavior as assessed by their school students' perceptions of their classroom learning environments. As well, students' attitudes to and achievement in science were assessed. Changes over a school year were monitored for a sample of seven beginning Grade 3 through 5 teachers in the southeastern United States and their 573 elementary school students. Data analyses supported the sound factorial validity of the WIHIC, while the use of MANOVA and effect sizes supported the efficacy of the mentoring program in terms of some improvements over time in the classroom learning environment and students' attitudes and achievement (Pickett & Fraser, 2009).

For the first time in any study, parents' perceptions were utilized in conjunction with students' perceptions in investigating science classroom learning environment among Grade 4 and 5 science students in south Florida (Allen & Fraser, 2007). The WIHIC was modified for young students and their parents and administered to 520 students and 120 parents. Both students and parents preferred a more positive classroom environment than the one perceived to be actually present, but effect sizes for actual–preferred differences were appreciably larger for parents than for students. With a sample of 78 parents and their 172 kindergarten science students in Miami, Robinson and Fraser (2013) used a simplified Spanish version of the WIHIC to reveal that, relative to students, parents perceived a more favorable classroom environment but preferred a less favorable environment.

Unique research in Canada focused simultaneously on the psychosocial and physical environments of networked classrooms (Zandvliet & Fraser, 2004, 2005). Whereas the psychosocial environment was assessed with the WIHIC, ergonomic evaluations were made of the physical environment (e.g., workspace and visual environments). For a sample of 1,404 students (which included Australian students as well as Canadians), classroom psychosocial environment was significantly and directly associated with students' satisfaction with their learning, but no direct associations were found between student satisfaction and measures of the physical classroom environment. However statistically significant associations emerged between physical and psychosocial learning environment variables in classrooms using new information technologies. These associations suggested a model of educational productivity for learning environments in technology-rich classrooms.

Learning Environments Research in African and Arab Countries

Research on classroom learning environments has slowly begun to take root in Africa. Nigerian researchers developed and used questionnaires for investigating learning environments in science laboratory classes (Fraser, Okebukola, & Jegede, 1992) and the role of sociocultural beliefs in hindering learning in science classroom environments (Jegede, Fraser & Okebukola, 1994). Also in Nigeria, use of scales from the CLES and ICEQ in a study of 1,175 agricultural science students in 50 classes from 20 schools (Idiris & Fraser, 1997) revealed low levels of classroom student-centeredness and student negotiation.

In South Africa, a national curriculum reform involving outcomes-based education stimulated the development and use of new learning environment instruments for monitoring the development of outcomes-based learning environments. At the classroom level, Aldridge, Laugksch, Seopa, and Fraser (2006) developed the OBLEQ (Outcomes-Based Learning Environment Questionnaire) in the North Soto language and validated it with a sample of 2,638 Grade 8 science students from 50 schools in the Limpopo Province. At the school level, Aldridge, Laugksch and Fraser (2006) developed a South African version of the School-Level Environment Questionnaire and validated it with a sample of 403 teachers. The study revealed differences between teachers' perceptions of actual and preferred school environment and also that teachers who had been involved in outcomes-based education perceived their school environments differently from teachers who had not been involved.

In another study in South Africa, Aldridge, Fraser, and Sebela (2004) adapted the English version of the CLES for use among teachers and their 1,864 students in 43 classes who were attempting to change classroom environments to a more constructivist orientation. Not only did their study yield a validated and widely applicable questionnaire for future use, but also it involved case studies of teachers' successful and not-so-successful attempts to change their classroom environments during a 12-week intervention period. Also in South Africa, Aldridge and colleagues (2009) investigated 31 inservice teachers who were undertaking a distance-education program and who administered a primary school version of the WIHIC in the IsiZulu language to 1,077 Grade 4 through 7 learners in the KwaZulu-Natal province. Different teachers were able to use feedback from the WIHIC with varying degrees of success in their attempts to improve their classroom environments.

Apparently, learning environment research has been virtually nonexistent in the Arabic-speaking world, perhaps partly because of the unavailability of any validated questionnaires in the Arabic language. Recently, MacLeod and Fraser (2010) pioneered the painstaking translation and comprehensive validation of an Arabic version of the WIHIC with a sample of 763 college students in 82 classes in the United Arab Emirates. As well as providing a useful and valid learning environment questionnaire for future use by researchers and practitioners in Arabic-speaking countries, MacLeod and Fraser reported that students would prefer their classroom environments to be more positive for all dimensions assessed. In another study involving a translation of WIHIC into Arabic, Afari and colleagues reported that the use of mathematics games promoted a positive classroom environment among a sample of 352 college students in 33 classes (Afari et al., 2013).

Emerging Lines of Research

Although most individual studies of educational environments in the past have tended to focus on a single environment, there is potential in simultaneously considering the links between and the joint influence of two or more environments. Several studies have investigated whether the nature of the school-level environment influences or transmits to what goes on in classrooms (i.e., the classroom-level environment). In South Africa, Aldridge, Laugksch, and Fraser (2006) used a school environment instrument with 50 secondary school science teachers from 50 different schools, together with a classroom environment questionnaire based on the WIHIC with the 2,638 Grade 8 students in the 50 classes of these 50 teachers. Although there emerged a small number of interesting specific relationships (e.g., schools encouraging teachers to be innovative was related to the extent to which students perceived more outcomes-based pedagogy in their classrooms), overall, the school environment did not have a strong influence on what happens in classrooms. When Dorman and colleagues (1997) administered a classroom environment instrument to 2,211 students in 104 classes and a school environment instrument to the 208 teachers of these classes, only weak associations between classroom environment and school environment were reported. For example, classroom individualization was greater in school environments with more affiliation and less work pressure. Although school rhetoric often would suggest that the school ethos would be transmitted to the classroom level, it appears that classrooms are somewhat insulated from the school as a whole.

Using secondary analysis of a large database from a Statewide Systemic Initiative (SSI) in the United States, Fraser and Kahle (2007) examined the effects of several types of environments on student outcomes. Over three years, nearly 7,000 students in 392 middle school science and mathematics classes in 200 different schools responded to a questionnaire that assesses class, home, and peer environments as well as student attitudes. Students also completed an achievement measure. Rasch analyses allowed comparison across student cohorts and across schools. Findings confirmed the importance of extending research on classroom learning environments to include the learning environments of the home and the peer group. Although all three environments accounted for statistically significant amounts of unique variance in student attitudes, only the class environment (defined in terms of the frequency of use of standards-based teaching practices) accounted for statistically significant amounts of unique variance in student achievement based partly on public release items from the National Assessment of Educational Progress (Fraser & Kahle, 2007).

Science education research that crosses national boundaries offers much promise for generating new insights. Aldridge and colleagues (1999) reported a cross-national learning environment study involving six Australian and seven Taiwanese science education researchers in working together. The WIHIC was administered to 50 junior high school science classes in each of Taiwan (1,879 students) and Australia (1,081 students).

An English version of the questionnaire was translated into Chinese, followed by an independent back translation of the Chinese version into English by team members who were not involved in the original translation. Qualitative data, involving interviews with teachers and students and classroom observations, were collected to complement the quantitative information and to clarify reasons for patterns and differences in the means in each country.

The scales of Involvement and Equity had the largest differences in means between the two countries, with Australian students perceiving each scale more positively than did students from Taiwan. Data from the questionnaires were used to guide the collection of qualitative data. Student responses to individual items were used to form an interview schedule that was used to clarify whether items had been interpreted consistently by students and to help to explain differences in questionnaire scale means between countries. Classrooms were selected for observations on the basis of the questionnaire data, and specific scales formed the focus for observations in these classrooms. The qualitative data provided valuable insights into the perceptions of students in each of the countries, helped to explain some of the differences in the means between countries, and highlighted the need for caution when interpreting differences between the questionnaire results from two countries with cultural differences (Aldridge & Fraser, 2000). Similar cross-national research involving the use of the CLES in Taiwan and Australia was reported by Aldridge and colleagues (2000), whereas cross-national research in Indonesia and Australia was reported by Fraser, Aldridge, and Adolphe (2010).

The creation and empirical investigation of typologies of classroom learning environments has been pursued in a handful of past studies. Using the CES in the United States among a sample of 200 junior-high and high school classrooms, Moos (1978, 1979) identified five clusters that describe five learning environment orientations: control, innovation, affiliation, task completion, and competition. Using the QTI with samples of students in both the Netherlands and the United States led to the identification of eight distinct interpersonal profiles: directive, authoritative, tolerant–authoritative, tolerant, uncertain–tolerant, uncertain–aggressive, repressive, and drudging (Brekelmans, Levy, & Rodriguez, 1993; Wubbels, Brekelmans, den Brok, & van Tartwijk, 2006). Based on a large-scale administration of the QTI to 6,148 Grade 8 through 10 science students from four Australian states and their 283 teachers, Rickards, den Brok, and Fisher (2005) reported that the eight types found for Dutch and American teachers only partly applied to the Australian context. Whereas some profiles were less common in Australia, others were more common. Two new types (namely, flexible and cooperative–supportive) were unique to the Australian sample.

Working in Turkey with a Turkish translation of the WIHIC, den Brok, Telli, Cakiroglu, Taconis, and Tekkaya (2010) created learning environment profiles for a sample of 1,474 high school biology students in 52 classes. The six distinct classroom profiles that emerged were self-directed learning, task-orientated cooperative learning, mainstream, task-orientated individualized, low-effective learning, and high-effective learning. The most common profile was the mainstream classroom, for which all WIHIC scales had medium–high scores. Based on sample of 4,146 Australian students from 286 Grade 8 through 13 classes, Dorman, Aldridge, and Fraser (2006) used the 10-scale TROFLEI to develop a classroom typology with five relatively homogeneous groups of classes: exemplary, safe and conservative, nontechnological teacher-centered, contested technological, and contested nontechnological. The authors recommended more frequent use of cluster analysis to achieve greater parsimony in analyzing classroom environment data.

Conclusion

Through their research on classroom learning environments, science education researchers have contributed much to the field's growth and international expansion and have generated numerous insights. First, researchers have stimulated greater awareness that, because measures of learning outcomes cannot provide a complete picture of the educational process, researchers, evaluators, and practitioners need to pay more attention to classroom learning environments. Second, science educators have developed, validated, and cross-validated a range of robust and economical instruments that are used widely around the world for assessing classroom environments. Third, these researchers have contributed to our knowledge base about how to improve student outcomes through creating positive classroom environments. Fourth, evaluation studies have frequently demonstrated the value of including classroom environment dimensions as process criteria of effectiveness in evaluating a host of educational programs, innovations, and teaching methods. Last but not least, science education researchers have created new structural foundations to support the field's continuation: the AERA Special Interest Group on Learning Environments, *Learning Environments Research: An International Journal*, and a book series called *Advances in Learning Environments Research*.

Much has been achieved, but still much is left to be done in the future. Although learning environments research has flourished in Australia, Asia, and the United States, work in African and Arab countries has only just begun, and limited learning environments research has been undertaken in Europe or the Spanish-speaking world. Researchers have contributed to the combination of quantitative and qualitative data-collection methods in learning environment research (Fraser, 1999a; Tobin & Fraser, 1998), but there is considerable scope for the development of new methods and the wider use of established methods for qualitative studies. Some teachers have used learning environment questionnaires successfully in guiding their practical attempts to improve

their classroom environments (Aldridge et al., 2012), but teachers' uptake of learning environment ideas and their use of classroom environment questionnaires generally have been disappointing worldwide. Similarly, the widespread inclusion of learning environment ideas in preservice and inservice teacher education programs remains an elusive goal.

Acknowledgments

Thanks to Rebekah Nix and Angela Wong, who reviewed this chapter.

References

Afari, E., Aldridge, J. M., Fraser, B. J., & Khine, M. S. (2013). Students' perceptions of the learning environment and attitudes in game-based mathematics classrooms. *Learning Environments Research, 16,* 131–150.

Aldridge, J. M., Dorman, J. P., & Fraser, B. J. (2004). Use of multitrait-multimethod modelling to validate actual and preferred forms of the Technology-Rich Outcomes-Focused Learning Environment Inventory (TROFLEI). *Australian Journal of Educational and Developmental Psychology, 4,* 110–125.

Aldridge, J. M., & Fraser, B. J. (2000). A cross-cultural study of classroom learning environments in Australia and Taiwan. *Learning Environments Research, 3,* 101–134.

Aldridge, J. M., & Fraser, B. J. (2008). *Outcomes-focused learning environments: Determinants and effects.* Rotterdam, the Netherlands: Sense Publishers.

Aldridge, J. M., Fraser, B. J., Bell, L., & Dorman, J. P. (2012). Using a new learning environment questionnaire for reflection in teacher action research. *Journal of Science Teacher Education, 23,* 259–290.

Aldridge, J. M., Fraser, B. J., & Huang, I. T.-C. (1999). Investigating classroom environments in Taiwan and Australia with multiple research methods. *Journal of Educational Research, 93,* 48–62.

Aldridge, J. M., Fraser, B. J., & Ntuli, S. (2009). Utilising learning environment assessments to improve teaching practices among in-service teachers undertaking a distance education programme. *South African Journal of Education, 29,* 147–170.

Aldridge, J. M., Fraser, B. J., & Sebela, M. P. (2004). Using teacher action research to promote constructivist learning environments in South Africa. *South African Journal of Education, 24,* 245–253.

Aldridge, J. M., Fraser, B. J., Taylor, P. C., & Chen, C.-C. (2000). Constructivist learning environments in a cross-national study in Taiwan and Australia. *International Journal of Science Education, 22,* 37–55.

Aldridge, J. M., Laugksch, R. C., & Fraser, B. J. (2006). School-level environment and outcomes-based education in South Africa. *Learning Environments Research, 9,* 123–147.

Aldridge, J. M., Laugksch, R. C., Seopa, M. A., & Fraser, B. J. (2006). Development and validation of an instrument to monitor the implementation of outcomes-based learning environments in science classrooms in South Africa. *International Journal of Science Education, 28,* 45–70.

Allen, D., & Fraser, B. J. (2007). Parent and student perceptions of the classroom learning environment and its association with student outcomes. *Learning Environments Research, 10,* 67–82.

Anderson, G. L., & Walberg, H. J. (1968). Classroom climate group learning. *International Journal of Educational Sciences, 2,* 175–180.

Brekelmans, M., Levy, J., & Rodriguez, R. (1993). A typology of teacher communication style. In Th. Wubbels & J. Levy (Eds.), *Do you know what you look like? Interpersonal relationships in education* (pp. 46–55). London: Falmer Press.

Brekelmans, M., Wubbels, Th., & van Tartwijk, J. (2005). Teacher–student relationships across the teaching career. *International Journal of Educational Research, 43,* 55–71.

Chandra, V., & Fisher, D.L. (2009). Students' perceptions of a blended web-based learning environment. *Learning Environments Research, 12,* 31–44.

Chang, V., & Fisher, D. (2003). The validation and application of a new learning environment instrument for online learning in higher education. In M.S. Khine & D. Fisher (Eds.), *Technology-rich learning environments: A future perspective* (pp. 1–20). Singapore: World Scientific.

Chionh, Y.H., & Fraser, B.J. (2009). Classroom environment, achievement, attitudes and self-esteem in geography and mathematics in Singapore. *International Research in Geographical and Environmental Education, 18,* 29–44.

Chua, S.L., Wong, A.F.L., & Chen, D.-T. (2011). The nature of Chinese language classroom learning environments in Singapore secondary schools. *Learning Environments Research, 14,* 75–90.

den Brok, P., Fisher, D., Rickards, T., & Bull, E. (2006). Californian science students' perceptions of their classroom learning environments. *Educational Research and Evaluation, 12*(1), 3–25.

den Brok, P., Fisher, D.L., & Scott, R.H. (2005). The importance of teacher interpersonal behaviour for student attitudes in Brunei primary science classes. *International Journal of Science Education, 27,* 765–779.

den Brok, P., Telli, S., Cakiroglu, J., Taconis, R., & Tekkaya, C. (2010). Learning environment profiles of Turkish secondary biology students. *Learning Environments Research, 13,* 187–204.

Dhindsa, H.S., & Fraser, B.J. (2004). Culturally-sensitive factors in teacher trainees' learning environments. *Learning Environments Research, 7,* 165–181.

Dhindsa, H.S., & Fraser, B.J. (2011). Culturally sensitive factors in the learning environment of science classrooms in Brunei Darussalam. *The Open Education Journal, 4,* 90–99.

Dorman, J.P. (2003). Cross-national validation of the What Is Happening In This Class? (WIHIC) questionnaire using confirmatory factor analysis. *Learning Environments Research, 6,* 231–245.

Dorman, J.P. (2008). Use of multitrait-multimethod modelling to validate actual and preferred forms of the What Is Happening In This Class? (WIHIC) questionnaire. *Learning Environments Research, 11,* 179–193.

Dorman, J.P., Aldridge, J.M., & Fraser, B.J. (2006). Using students' assessment of classroom environment to develop a typology of secondary school classrooms. *International Education Journal, 7,* 909–915.

Dorman, J., Fraser, B., & McRobbie, C. (1995). Associations between school-level environment and science classroom environment in secondary schools. *Research in Science Education, 25,* 333–351.

Dorman, J.P., Fraser, B.J., & McRobbie, C.J. (1997). Classroom environment in Australian Catholic and government secondary schools. *Curriculum and Teaching, 12*(1), 3–14.

Ferguson, P.D., & Fraser, B.J. (1998). Changes in learning environment during the transition from primary to secondary school. *Learning Environments Research, 1,* 369–383.

Fisher, D.L., & Fraser, B.J. (1981). Validity and use of My Class Inventory. *Science Education, 65,* 145–156.

Fisher, D., & Fraser, B. (1983a). Validity and use of Classroom Environment Scale. *Educational Evaluation and Policy Analysis, 5,* 261–271.

Fisher, D.L., & Fraser, B.J. (1983b). A comparison of actual and preferred classroom environment as perceived by science teachers and students. *Journal of Research in Science Teaching, 20,* 55–61.

Fisher, D.L., Henderson, D., & Fraser, B.J. (1997). Laboratory environments and student outcomes in senior high school biology. *American Biology Teacher, 59,* 214–219.

Fisher, D.L., & Khine, M.S. (Eds.). (2006). *Contemporary approaches to research on learning environments: Worldviews.* Singapore: World Scientific.

Fisher, D.L., & Waldrip, B.G. (1997). Assessing culturally sensitive factors in learning environments of science classrooms. *Research in Science Education, 27,* 41–48.

Fisher, D.L., & Waldrip, B.G. (1999). Cultural factors of science classroom learning environments, teacher–student interactions and student

outcomes. *Research in Science and Technological Education, 17,* 83–96.

Fraser, B. (1979). Evaluation of a science-based curriculum. In H. Walberg (Ed.), *Educational environments and effects: Evaluation, policy, and productivity* (pp. 218–234). Berkeley, CA: McCutchan.

Fraser, B. (1986). *Classroom environment.* London, UK: Croom Helm. (Reprinted by Routledge in 2012.)

Fraser, B.J. (1990). *Individualised classroom environment questionnaire.* Melbourne, Australia: Australian Council for Educational Research.

Fraser, B.J. (1999a). "Grain sizes" in learning environment research: Combining qualitative and quantitative methods. In H.C. Waxman & H.J. Walberg (Eds.), *New directions for teaching practice and research* (pp. 285–296). Berkeley, CA: McCutchan.

Fraser, B.J. (1999b). Using learning environment assessments to improve classroom and school climates. In H.J. Freiberg (Ed.), *School climate: Measuring, improving and sustaining healthy learning environments* (pp. 65–83). London: Falmer Press.

Fraser, B.J. (2001). Twenty thousand hours: Editor's introduction. *Learning Environments Research, 4,* 1–5.

Fraser, B.J. (2007). Classroom learning environments. In S.K. Abell & N.G. Lederman (Eds.), *Handbook of research on science education* (pp. 103–124). Mahwah, NJ: Lawrence Erlbaum.

Fraser, B.J. (2012). Classroom learning environments: Retrospect, context and prospect. In B.J. Fraser, K.G. Tobin, & C.J. McRobbie (Eds.), *Second international handbook of science education* (pp. 1191–1239). New York: Springer.

Fraser, B.J., Aldridge, J.M., & Adolphe, F.S.G. (2010). A cross-national study of secondary science classroom environments in Australia and Indonesia. *Research in Science Education, 40,* 551–571.

Fraser, B.J., Aldridge, J.M., & Soerjaningsih, W. (2010). Instructor–student interpersonal interaction and student outcomes at the university level in Indonesia. *The Open Education Journal, 3,* 32–44.

Fraser, B.J., & Fisher, D.L. (1982). Predicting student outcomes from their perceptions of classroom psychosocial environment. *American Educational Research Journal, 19,* 498–518.

Fraser, B.J., & Fisher, D.L. (1983). Use of actual and preferred classroom environment scales in person–environment fit research. *Journal of Educational Psychology, 75,* 303–313.

Fraser, B., & Fisher, D. (1986). Using short forms of classroom climate instruments to assess and improve classroom psychosocial environment. *Journal of Research in Science Teaching, 23,* 387–413.

Fraser, B., Fisher, D., & McRobbie, C. (1996, April). *Development, validation, and use of personal and class forms of a new classroom environment instrument.* Paper presented at the annual meeting of the American Educational Research Association, New York, NY.

Fraser, B.J., Giddings, G.J., & McRobbie, C.J. (1995). Evolution and validation of a personal form of an instrument for assessing science laboratory classroom environments. *Journal of Research in Science Teaching, 32,* 399–422.

Fraser, B.J., & Kahle, J.B. (2007). Classroom, home and peer environment influences on student outcomes in science and mathematics: An analysis of systemic reform data. *International Journal of Science Education, 29,* 1891–1909.

Fraser, B.J., & Lee, S.S.U. (2009). Science laboratory classroom environments in Korean high schools. *Learning Environments Research, 12,* 67–84.

Fraser, B., & McRobbie, C. (1995). Science laboratory classroom environments at schools and universities: A cross-national study. *Educational Research and Evaluation, 1,* 289–317.

Fraser, B., & Northfield, J. (1981). *A study of ASEP in its first year of availability.* Canberra: Australian Curriculum Development Centre.

Fraser, B., Okebukola, P., & Jegede, O. (1992). Assessment of the learning environment of Nigerian science laboratory classes. *Journal of the Science Teachers Association of Nigeria, 27*(2), 1–17.

Fraser, B., & Teh, G. (1994). Effect sizes associated with micro-PROLOG-based computer-assisted learning. *Computers and Education: An International Journal, 23,* 187–196.

Fraser, B., & Walberg, H. (Eds.). (1991). *Educational environments: Evaluation, antecedents and consequences.* Oxford, UK: Pergamon Press.

Goh, S. C., & Fraser, B. J. (1998). Teacher interpersonal behaviour, classroom environment and student outcomes in primary mathematics in Singapore. *Learning Environments Research, 1,* 199–229.

Goh, S. C., Young, D. J., & Fraser, B. J. (1995). Psychosocial climate and student outcomes in elementary mathematics classrooms: A multi-level analysis. *Journal of Experimental Education, 64,* 29–40.

Haertel, G. D., Walberg, H. J., & Haertel, E. H. (1981). Socio-psychological environments and learning: A quantitative synthesis. *British Educational Research Journal, 7,* 27–36.

Helding, K. A., & Fraser, B. J. (2013). Effectiveness of NBC (National Board certified) teachers in terms of learning environment, attitudes and achievement among secondary school students. *Learning Environments Research, 16,* 1–21.

Henderson, D., Fisher, D. L., & Fraser, B. J. (2000). Interpersonal behavior, learning environments and student outcomes in senior biology classes. *Journal of Research in Science Teaching, 37,* 26–43.

Idiris, S., & Fraser, B. (1997). Psychosocial environment of agricultural science classrooms in Nigeria. *International Journal of Science Education, 19,* 79–91.

Jegede, O., Fraser, B., & Okebukola, P. (1994). Altering socio-cultural beliefs hindering the learning of science. *Instructional Science, 22,* 137–152.

Khine, M. S., & Fisher, D. (Eds.). (2003). *Technology-rich learning environments: A future perspective.* Singapore: World Scientific.

Khoo, H. S., & Fraser, B. J. (2008). Using classroom psychosocial environment in the evaluation of adult computer application courses in Singapore. *Technology, Pedagogy and Education, 17,* 53–67.

Kim, H. B., Fisher, D. L., & Fraser, B. J. (1999). Assessment and investigation of constructivist science learning environments in Korea. *Research in Science and Technological Education, 17,* 239–249.

Kim, H. B., Fisher, D. L., & Fraser, B. J. (2000). Classroom environment and teacher interpersonal behaviour in secondary science classes in Korea. *Evaluation and Research in Education, 14,* 3–22.

Koul, R. B., & Fisher, D. L. (2005). Cultural background and students' perspectives of science classroom learning environment and teacher interpersonal behaviour in Jammu, India. *Learning Environments Research, 8,* 195–211.

Lee, S. S. U., Fraser, B. J., & Fisher, D. L. (2003). Teacher–student interactions in Korean high school science classrooms. *International Journal of Science and Mathematics Education, 1,* 67–85.

Lightburn, M. E., & Fraser, B. J. (2007). Classroom environment and student outcomes among students using anthropometry activities in high-school science. *Research in Science and Technological Education, 25,* 153–166.

MacLeod, C., & Fraser, B. (2010). Development, validation and application of a modified Arabic translation of the What Is Happening In This Class? (WIHIC) questionnaire. *Learning Environments Research, 13,* 105–125.

Majeed, A., Fraser, B. J., & Aldridge, J. M. (2002). Learning environment and its associations with student satisfaction among mathematics students in Brunei Darussalam. *Learning Environments Research, 5,* 203–226.

Maor, D., & Fraser, B. J. (1996). Use of classroom environment perceptions in evaluating inquiry-based computer assisted learning. *International Journal of Science Education, 18,* 401–421.

Margianti, E. S., Aldridge, J. M., & Fraser, B. J. (2004). Learning environment perceptions, attitudes and achievement among private Indonesian university students. *International Journal of Private Higher Education.* Retrieved March 10, 2006, from www.xaiu.com/xaiujournal

Martin-Dunlop, C., & Fraser, B. J. (2008). Learning environment and attitudes associated with an innovative course designed for prospective elementary teachers. *International Journal of Science and Mathematics Education, 6,* 163–190.

McRobbie, C. J., & Fraser, B. J. (1993). Associations between student outcomes and psychosocial science environment. *Journal of Educational Research, 87,* 78–85.

Moos, R. H. (1974). *The social climate scales: An overview.* Palo Alto, CA: Consulting Psychologists Press.

Moos, R. H. (1978). A typology of junior high and high school classrooms. *American Educational Research Journal, 15,* 53–66.

Moos, R. H. (1979). *Evaluating educational environments: Procedures, measures, findings, and policy implications.* San Francisco: Jossey-Bass.

Moos, R. H., & Trickett, E. J. (1974). *Classroom environment scale manual.* Palo Alto, CA: Consulting Psychologists Press.

Nix, R. K., & Fraser, B. J. (2010). Using computer-assisted teaching to promote constructivist practices in teacher education. In B. A. Morris & G. M. Ferguson (Eds.), *Computer-assisted teaching: New developments* (pp. 93–115). Hauppauge, NY: Nova Science Publishers.

Nix, R. K., Fraser, B. J., & Ledbetter, C. E. (2005). Evaluating an integrated science learning environment using the Constructivist Learning Environment Survey. *Learning Environments Research, 8,* 109–133.

Ogbuehi, P. I., & Fraser, B. J. (2007). Learning environment, attitudes and conceptual development associated with innovative strategies in middle-school mathematics. *Learning Environments Research, 10,* 101–114.

Peiro, M. M., & Fraser, B. J. (2009). Assessment and investigation of science learning environments in the early childhood grades. In M. Ortiz & C. Rubio (Eds.), *Educational evaluation: 21st century issues and challenges* (pp. 349–365). Hauppauge, NY: Nova Science Publishers.

Pickett, L. H., & Fraser, B. J. (2009). Evaluation of a mentoring program for beginning teachers in terms of the learning environment and student outcomes in participants' school classrooms. In A. Selkirk & M. Tichenor (Eds.), *Teacher education: Policy, practice and research* (pp. 1–15). Hauppauge, NY: Nova Science Publishers.

Quek, C. L., Wong, A. F. L., & Fraser, B. J. (2005a). Teacher–student interaction and gifted students' attitudes toward chemistry in laboratory classrooms in Singapore. *Journal of Classroom Interaction, 40*(1), 18–28.

Quek, C. L., Wong, A. F. L., & Fraser, B. J. (2005b). Student perceptions of chemistry laboratory learning environments, student–teacher interactions and attitudes in secondary school gifted education classes in Singapore. *Research in Science Education, 35,* 299–321.

Rentoul, A., & Fraser, B. (1979). Conceptualization of enquiry-based or open classroom learning environments. *Journal of Curriculum Studies, 11,* 233–245.

Rickards, T., den Brok, P., & Fisher, D. L. (2005). The Australian science teacher: A typology of teacher-student interpersonal behaviour in Australian science classes. *Learning Environments Research, 8,* 267–287.

Robinson, E., & Fraser, B. J. (2013). Kindergarten students' and parents' perceptions of science classroom environments: Achievement and attitudes. *Learning Environments Research, 16,* 1–17, *16*(2), 151–167.

Scott, R. H., & Fisher, D. L. (2004). Development, validation and application of a Malay translation of an elementary version of the Questionnaire on Teacher Interaction (QTI). *Research in Science Education, 34,* 173–194.

Scott Houston, L., Fraser, B. J., & Ledbetter, C. E. (2008). An evaluation of elementary school science kits in terms of classroom environment and student attitudes. *Journal of Elementary Science Education, 20,* 29–47.

Sinclair, B. B., & Fraser, B. J. (2002). Changing classroom environments in urban middle schools. *Learning Environments Research, 5,* 301–328.

Sink, C. A., & Spencer, L. R. (2005). My Class Inventory—Short Form as an accountability tool for elementary school counsellors to measure classroom climate. *Professional School Counseling, 9,* 37–48.

Taylor, P. C., Fraser, B. J., & Fisher, D. L. (1997). Monitoring constructivist classroom learning environments. *International Journal of Educational Research, 27,* 293–302.

Teh, G., & Fraser, B. J. (1994). An evaluation of computer-assisted learning in terms of achievement, attitudes and classroom environment. *Evaluation and Research in Education, 8,* 147–161.

Teh, G., & Fraser, B. (1995). Development and validation of an instrument for assessing the psychosocial environment of computer-assisted learning classrooms. *Journal of Educational Computing Research, 12,* 177–193.

Tobin, K., & Fraser, B. (1998). Qualitative and quantitative landscapes of classroom learning environments. In B.J. Fraser & K.G. Tobin (Eds.), *The international handbook of science education* (pp. 623–640). Dordrecht, the Netherlands: Kluwer.

Wahyudi, & Treagust, D.F. (2004). The status of science classroom learning environments in Indonesian lower secondary schools. *Learning Environments Research, 7,* 43–63.

Walberg, H.J. (Ed.). (1979). *Educational environments and effects: Evaluation, policy and productivity.* Berkeley, CA: McCutchan.

Welch, A.G., Cakir, M., Peterson, C., & Ray, C.M. (2012). A cross-cultural validation of the Technology-Rich Outcomes-Focussed Learning Environment Inventory (TROFLEI) in Turkey and the USA. *Research in Science and Technological Education, 30,* 49–63.

Wolf, S.J., & Fraser, B.J. (2008). Learning environment, attitudes and achievement among middle-school science students using inquiry-based laboratory activities. *Research in Science Education, 38,* 321–341.

Wong, A.F.L., & Fraser, B.J. (1996). Environment–attitude associations in the chemistry laboratory classroom. *Research in Science and Technological Education, 14,* 91–102.

Wong, A.F.L., Young, D.J., & Fraser, B.J. (1997). A multilevel analysis of learning environments and student attitudes. *Educational Psychology, 17,* 449–468.

Wubbels, Th., & Brekelmans, M. (1998). The teacher factor in the social climate of the classroom. In B.J. Fraser & K.G. Tobin (Eds.), *International handbook of science education* (pp. 565–580). Dordrecht, the Netherlands: Kluwer.

Wubbels, Th., & Brekelmans, M. (2012). Teacher–students relationships in the classroom. In B.J. Fraser, K.G. Tobin, & C.J. McRobbie (Eds.), *Second international handbook of science education* (pp. 1241–1255). New York: Springer.

Wubbels, Th., Brekelmans, M., den Brok, P., & van Tartwijk, J. (2006). An interpersonal perspective on classroom management in secondary classrooms in the Netherlands. In C. Evertson & C. Weinstein (Eds.), *Handbook of classroom management: Research, practice, and contemporary issues* (pp. 1161–1191). Mahwah, NJ: Lawrence Erlbaum Associates.

Wubbels, Th., den Brok, P., van Tartwijk, J., & Levy, J. (Eds.). (2012). *Interpersonal relationships in education: An overview of research.* Rotterdam, the Netherlands: Sense Publishers.

Wubbels, Th., & Levy, J. (Eds.). (1993). *Do you know what you look like? Interpersonal relationships in education.* London: Falmer Press.

Yarrow, A., Millwater, J., & Fraser, B.J. (1997). Improving university and primary school classroom environments through preservice teachers' action research. *International Journal of Practical Experiences in Professional Education, 1*(1), 68–93.

Zandvliet, D.B., & Fraser, B.J. (2004). Learning environments in information and communications technology classrooms. *Technology, Pedagogy and Education, 13,* 97–123.

Zandvliet, D.B., & Fraser, B.J. (2005). Physical and psychosocial environments associated with networked classrooms. *Learning Environments Research, 8,* 1–17.

7

Learning Science Outside of School

Léonie J. Rennie

Opportunities for learning science outside of school make a significant contribution to science education. The 2006 PISA survey demonstrated that exposure to science-related extracurricular activities has positive relationships "not only to student performance, but also to students' attitudes towards learning and their belief in their own abilities" (OECD, 2012, p. 4). Dabney and colleagues (2012) surveyed 6,556 university students and found that participation in out-of-school-time science activities was strongly related to career interest in Science, Technology, Engineering, and Mathematics (STEM). When asked why they studied science, 726 Australian and New Zealand citizens with at least a bachelor's degree in science ranked "Science-based television programs" 5th, "science books or magazines" 8th, and "a science center or museum" 10th (Venville, Rennie, Hanbury, & Longnecker, 2013). The highest-ranked reasons for doing science were "I was interested in science" and "I was good at science," confirming the importance of students' attitudes and beliefs in their ability to do science.

What out-of-school resources are used by today's youth? For the 2012 Wellcome Trust Monitor in the UK (Clemence, Gilby, Shah, Swiecicka, & Warren, 2013), 460 randomly sampled young people aged 14 to 18 years were asked about exposure to science in everyday life. More than half (57%) had visited at least one science-related attraction in the previous year, including a zoo or aquarium (33%), science museum (25%), nature reserve (17%), science discovery center (8%), working laboratory (6%), planetarium (3%), and science festival (2%). Young people were likely to visit outdoor attractions with their families and indoor attractions in school groups. About half of young people consulted a factual science book or read a science fiction book at least once a year. The earlier Wellcome Trust Monitor (Butt, Clery, Abeywardana, & Phillips, 2010) reported similar results and also that 98% of young people used the Internet for other than work purposes, mainly for computer games (70%), watching a broadcast (46%), or downloading information (65%). Two thirds watched television for more than 10 hours a week, but only 30% watched news daily and 18% listened to radio news every day. The U.S. Science and Engineering Indicators 2012 (National Science Board, 2013) reported that in 2010, the primary sources of information about science and technology for 18- to 24-year-olds were the Internet (65%) and television (24%).

Based on this information, research in this chapter is reviewed in three clusters: museums and other institutions with an educational focus, community-organized activities targeting families, and media. Implications are then drawn for continuing research, educational practice, and policy. Preference is given to research published since 2007 that advances the field by addressing gaps identified in my earlier review (Rennie, 2007a), exploring issues that were problematic, and pursuing new methods and directions. To frame the review, concepts that relate to learning in out-of-school settings and the term "informal" are revisited, because the literature suggests that their use remains contentious, unresolved, and often confusing.

What Is Meant by Learning Outside of School?

Learning occurs when the meaning people make of their experiences results in change, which may be cognitive, affective, psychomotor, social, or cultural and, although not necessarily visible, can be inferred through behavioral change in the learner. Learning is personalized, contextualized, and cumulative (Rennie, 2007a). These characteristics have particular salience when considering learning outside of school, because out-of-school contexts usually involve a degree of volition, so individuals' unique backgrounds and experiences and the choices they make about the nature of their activities can bring about very different learning outcomes. The nature of these outcomes is also influenced by the sociocultural context of those activities. Falk and Dierking's Contextual Model of Learning (Falk & Dierking, 2000) continues to be a useful conceptual underpinning for research in this area (Phipps, 2010). Many out-of-school science-related activities, such as museum visits or excursions, are of short duration, so the impact of those experiences may come later; thus the cumulative nature of learning becomes an important factor when evaluating the contribution of out-of-school experiences to learning in science.

What Is Meant by Informal Learning, Free Choice, and Informal Science Education?

The Informal Science Education Ad Hoc Committee of the National Association for Research in Science Teaching determined that learning in out-of-school contexts means "learning that is self-motivated, voluntary, guided by the learner's needs and interests, learning that is engaged in throughout his or her life" (Dierking, Falk, Rennie, Anderson, & Ellenbogen, 2003, p. 109). Use of the term "informal learning" is discouraged because "if learning is an ongoing, cumulative process that occurs from experience in a range of settings, it does not make sense to try to distinguish it as formal or informal" (Rennie, 2007a, p. 126). Rather, the setting might be described as formal or informal, usually in terms of whether there is a formal curriculum (as in classrooms) or a formal structure (as in a docent-led museum visit, for example).

The term "free choice," coined by Falk and Dierking (Falk, 2001), is used to describe the learning that occurs when the learner chooses what, how, where, and with whom to learn. Different circumstances may prevail in the same environment to make opportunities for learning less or more free choice, such as students completing a worksheet on a guided visit to a zoo compared to being able to wander wherever they wished. "Informal" can be used more generically to describe the learning setting, but it is not an appropriate term to describe learning.

Because of the diversity of nonschool environments in which science learning can occur, "informal science education" remains in use as a catch-all term for science-related activities that are not part of a formal, assessable curriculum offered by an educational institution. A voluntary visit to a natural history museum, playing a computer game with science-related content, a guide-led tour of an industrial facility, or doing a science project in an after-school program might all be described as informal science education.

The important message about terminology is that wherever research is done and whatever conditions apply to what, where, how, and with whom learners are given opportunity to learn, researchers should make clear the meaning of the terms they use. The outcomes of their research can then be integrated meaningfully with other research findings and thus contribute to the expanding body of knowledge in this field.

Research on Learning Science Outside of School

The last decades have seen increased funding for research, expanded diversity in the outlets for its promulgation, and an upsurge of publications in print and online, particularly in the United States and Europe. Significant recent research compilations include *In Principle, In Practice: Museums as Learning Institutions* (Falk, Dierking, & Foutz, 2007), which illuminates contemporary perspectives on learning and the theoretical bases of research in museums and similar institutions. The National Research Council in the United States supported a major consultative program that culminated in two publications, *Learning Science in Informal Environments: People, Places, and Pursuits* (Bell, Lewenstein, Shouse, & Feder, 2009), a synthesis of research in the field, and its companion *Surrounded by Science: Learning Science in Informal Environments* (Fenichel & Schweingruber, 2010), to bring those findings to practitioners. Although the editors pointed out that the primary source of information was the United States, these volumes are a valuable addition to the field. In 2011, the *International Journal of Science Education* established a second strand—*Part B: Communication and Public Engagement*—focused on research in the informal sector.

The Wellcome Trust commissioned two reports on learning science in informal settings in the UK (Falk, Osborne, Dierking, Dawson, Wenger, & Wong, 2012; Lloyd, Neilson, King, & Dyball, 2012). These reports, together with the Wellcome Trust's reflections on them (Matterson & Holman, 2012), critically examine how the field views itself and its aims and carries out its research and evaluation. A comprehensive, aggregator website, Informalscience.org, funded by the National Science Foundation (NSF) and managed by the Center for Advancement of Informal Science Education (CAISE), demonstrates the increased activity, worldwide, in interest, research, and communication about science, with a dominant theme of nonschool learning in science.

Approaches to Research Into Learning Science Outside of School

There may be differences in *what* is learned about science outside of school compared to inside school, but the *processes* of learning are similar. Indeed, many of the theoretical frameworks and methods used to research learning outside of school are borrowed from other disciplines, as recorded in historical overviews of research in the field (Bell et al., 2009; Falk & Dierking, 1995; Falk et al., 2012; Hein, 1998; Martin, 2007; McManus, 1992; Phipps, 2010; Rennie, 2007a). Over the years, there has been a shift in focus and a refinement of methods. Hein (1998) suggested in his review that visitor studies began in 1884, and most early studies were concerned with the educational value of museums. The 1960s saw a rapid expansion of research focusing on exhibit evaluation, as fundamental work in evaluation methodology associated with the post–*Sputnik* development of school science curricula was appropriated into the museum context. Exhibit evaluation remains a focus for research because of the importance of maintaining a positive visitor experience. Rennie (2007a) described the development of visitor studies and how, as the dominant learning theories moved from behaviorist to constructivist epistemologies and then included a greater focus on sociocultural perspectives, changes in research methods and approaches to data collection followed.

Falk and colleagues (2012) carried out a thorough search and review of international literature in informal science education published between 1980 and 2011. More than half of the 553 peer-reviewed articles identified were published in the three main science education journals (*Science Education*, the *International Journal of Science Education*, and the *Journal of Research in Science Teaching*) and the remainder spread over more than 200 other journals. A social constructivist theoretical framework was most common, one "that sees learning as a product of a process of deliberate and discursive interactions with others—interactions which then enable the individual to construct new understandings and mental models of the world" (Falk et al., 2012, p. 37). Research methods used were described as qualitative (34%), quantitative (17%), and mixed method (13%). Another 13% were classified as literature review or theoretical.

Phipps (2010) analyzed 85 articles published in the three journals mentioned during 1997 through 2007. She found an increasing focus on sociocultural compared to behaviorist views of learning and classified 9% of articles as behaviorist, 32% as constructivist, and 38% as sociocultural, with some overlap among these three. Fourteen of the articles used Falk and Dierking's (2000) Contextual Model of Learning as their framework. Data collection methods used in the 72 empirically based articles varied with setting and participants and were classified as observations, interviews, surveys, and written artifacts. Data analysis included both descriptive and inferential statistical analyses and several qualitative methods, such as developing taxonomies based on coding interviews and observations and discourse analysis. Phipps (2010) tabulated three data collection methods (surveys, observations, and interviews) against theoretical underpinnings (labeled behaviorism, constructivism, Contextual Model of Learning, and socioculturalism) to demonstrate that the research methods were influenced by the chosen conceptual framework.

Falk and colleagues (2012) identified 31 distinct research contexts among 553 published articles. The dominant contexts were science museums (67 articles); electronic media, excluding television (55); science and discovery centers (51); and general rather than science-specific museums (51). The dominant targets were teachers and students in schools, with a third of articles focusing on young people aged 16 or under. Visitors to museums were the subject of 91 articles and family groups 48. Very few articles dealt with ethnic minorities, females, and low-income groups. As the 85 articles reviewed by Phipps (2010) were a subset of those reviewed by Falk and colleagues (2012), her conclusions are similar. Nearly two thirds focused on learning in museums and other public settings, with the remainder divided between learning science in everyday life and community programs. Clearly, noninstitutional opportunities for informal science education are under-researched, possibly leading to a bias in findings. Also under-researched are the learning and engagement of minority and disadvantaged groups, females, and adults (Falk et al., 2012; Lloyd et al., 2012).

Research into learning outside of school has explored a diversity of learning outcomes, most commonly affective outcomes such as interest, enjoyment, and motivation, and cognitive outcomes relating to specific areas of science and its processes. Three examples of frameworks that attempt to account for this breadth are the six learning strands approach taken by Bell and colleagues (2009); the CAISE *Framework for Evaluating Impacts of Informal Science Education Projects* (Friedman, 2008), which identified six categories relating to impact on learning in STEM: awareness, knowledge, or understanding of STEM concepts, processes, or careers; engagement or interest in STEM concepts, processes, or careers; attitudes toward STEM-related topics or capabilities; behavior resulting from experience; skills based on experience; and other (to capture unique projects); and Hooper-Greenhill (2007) described the Generic Learning Outcomes (GLO), namely increases in knowledge and understanding; increases in skills; change in attitudes and values; evidence of enjoyment, inspiration, and creativity; and evidence of activity, behavior, and progression.

In the following review, clustered under museums, community-organized activities, and media, outcomes considered as impacting science learning will include cognitive, affective, psychomotor, and social dimensions.

Learning Science In and From Museums

The term "museum" is used generically in this chapter to include science museums and science centers, aquariums, botanic and zoological gardens, environmentally based interpretive centers, and planetariums. All of these institutions have an educational focus in their mission statement, and all fit within the definition of "museum" according to Article 03–3 of The Statutes of the International Council of Museums (http://icom.museum/who-we-are/the-organisation/icom-statutes/3-definition-of-terms.html#sommairecontent). Rennie's (2007a) overview of the history and changing roles of museums and learning from them demonstrated that although the outcomes of visits to museums and similar institutions are variable, depending on the personal, social, and physical contexts of the visit, learning does occur. However, it is not easy to measure, and much early research failed to find measurable impacts from a visit. This created a problem for museums that needed to justify their public and/or private funding.

People who doubted the learning value of museum visits usually invoked one or more of three myths: that playing and learning cannot occur at the same time; that if learning occurs, it must happen at the museum; and that what people learn is predictable and therefore easily measurable (Rennie, 2007a). An understanding of the nature of play, particularly for children, and remembering that learning is personal, contextualized, and cumulative enables the rapid debunking of these myths and also gives insight into just how difficult research into the learning outcomes from visits might be. Not only are the outcomes often unexpected and frustratingly unique, making measurement difficult, they are often delayed. Contexts are variable, and their parameters interwoven and complex. Collecting meaningful data, particularly from visitors more concerned with pursuing their own agendas than helping researchers with theirs, is also fraught, because the act of measurement can result in changed behaviors and confound what is being measured.

Rennie and Johnston (2007) documented the difficulties of research in museums and concluded that research designs must be "sufficiently broad based to capture a range of impacts, some trivial, some amazingly complex, and some that become evident well after the visit" (p. 72). Further, several data collection methods are often required to capture the range of visitor outcomes from a learning experience (see also Falk & Storksdieck, 2005). In the context of evolving conceptual and theoretical models to underpin research (Astor-Jack, Whaley, Dierking, Perry, & Garibay, 2007; Martin, 2007), the sharing of research questions so that the outcomes might be triangulated more easily, more effort being given to conduct longer-term studies (Anderson, Storksdieck, & Spock, 2007), and better understanding of how to cope with the complexity of museum research (Allen et al., 2007), there has been continued progress in understanding the impacts of the visit experience.

Science Museums and Science Centers

Much of the research into learning science outside of school takes place in science and natural history museums and science centers. These places experience a high rate of visitation, with an estimated 95 million visits made to the 600 member institutions of the Association of Science-Technology Centers in 2011 (ASTC, 2012). Nearly one sixth of these visitors were school groups, but extensive outreach programs contact far more school students. School excursions are considered in a later section, because the context is markedly different from a voluntary visit. Research focusing on family visits will also be considered separately. This section provides a general overview of research in science museums and science centers.

Historically, science museums differed from science centers because they were essentially collections based, whereas science centers displayed purpose-built exhibits, most of which enabled sensory engagement by visitors, often with reciprocal interactivity. This distinction has blurred as traditional museums included more opportunities for visitor interactivity, particularly with increasing use of technology. The original goals of the science museum were conservation, collection, research, and training, but the current generation of science-technology centers has just one mission: public education (Friedman, 2010). Without the collections and curators of traditional museums, science centers have the freedom to focus on education rather than conservation. Since the Exploratorium and Ontario Science Center opened in 1969, in an era of expanding interest in learner-centered science education, these hands-on, interactive venues have assumed a significant place in the world of informal science education.

Unlike many traditional museums, science centers rarely have endowments and rely on external funding, so remaining financially viable is an increasing concern. Visitor attraction becomes an implicit part of their agenda, which risks compromising the espoused educational mission. Another concern for museums is the digital revolution and the necessity (and cost) to join it. Digital connectivity tools, such as the Internet and smart phones, that allow people to choose when, where, and from whom they wish to learn, have led to what Semper (2007) called "the deinstitutionalization of education—a state of affairs in which individual institutions in a particular location lose their unique status as educational providers" (p. 148). This raises myriad questions for such institutions, the central theme being how to remain relevant, vibrant, and interesting, pressuring them to demonstrate accountability, impact, and a quality visitor experience.

Demonstrating impact requires credible empirical evidence, but often that is not available. For example, the UK government commissioned an evaluation of publicly funded science centers to assess whether they represented good value for money. Frontier Economics (2009) found that, although science centers were focused on the government's science and society objectives, their value for money could not be assessed because there was "insufficient evidence on the long-term outcomes of science centers or comparator programs" (p. 2). They recommended that funded organizations should provide data of better quality and that science centers should be encouraged to collect similar types of information to assist comparability. In response, the UK Association for Science and Discovery Centers (2010) advocated that their members use a set of common performance indicators, including quantitative measures of impact (such as visitation and demographics) and short surveys of questions mapped onto the GLO conceptual framework. Although this approach has appeal because of its simplicity and low cost, no results seem to be available.

Longitudinal studies can provide compelling data relating to the impact of science centers, but they are expensive and time consuming. The few studies that claim to be long term tend to be over months rather than years. An exception is Falk and Needham's (2011) study over a decade of the California Science Center. Since its opening in 1998, 45% of the Los Angeles population had visited the center, and visitors were very positive about the benefits derived, particularly for their children. Falk and Needham found strong evidence that this science center "contributes to science learning, interests, and behaviors of a large subset of the L.A. community" (p. 11). Importantly, there was a strong indication that visits reinforced and extended visitors' knowledge rather than added "new" knowledge. This is consistent with evidence from other research (for example, Rennie & Williams, 2006a) and underscores the importance of these places in continuing the process of lifelong learning for adults.

Science Exhibit(ion)s and the Visitor Learning Experience

Rennie (2007a) discussed two criticisms of science centers. First, they were accused of promoting fun and enjoyment, spectacle, and entertainment rather than education in science. However, the experience of learning is enjoyable, and if visitors are encouraged to engage in meaningful activities because they are having fun, then learning is a likely outcome. The second criticism is more problematic. Science centers were censured for portraying science as factual, uncontroversial, and without ethical dimensions rather than as a means of building understanding through a fallible, distinctly human process. If science is portrayed as fixed, authoritative, and unproblematic, then science museums and science centers are missing opportunities to enhance visitors' understanding of science, its processes, and its sociocultural context. However, exhibitions that portray risk and uncertainty and try to provoke visitors to think critically about science must represent complex ideas that may confuse and frustrate visitors.

Tlili, Cribb, and Gewirtz (2006) interviewed 10 staff at two science centers in England to explore how science was presented. Staff recognized the need to attract visitors and that science needed to be accessible and entertaining to attract them. Tlili and colleagues (2006) pointed out that "official science" had to be "mediated, re-inflected, and re-interpreted in science centers" (p. 203) and identified that science was mediated in six ways: science as relevant to everyday life, as personal, as fun, as doing, as a route into the public sphere, and as multicultural. They concluded that science centers ease the distance between the lived experiences of visitors and those of scientists "by more or less directly representing official science as a socially relevant, human, potentially enjoyable, and contestable set of socio-cultural practices" (p. 224).

At the heart of this issue is that science as it is used and understood in the world of scientists is not readily understood by most audiences. People are active consumers of information, not passive recipients of science knowledge. Layton, Jenkins, Macgill, and Davey (1993) found that people selectively filter science information that is relevant to their concern; they deconstruct and then reconstruct it into a form that is meaningful and useful to them. In a similar way, the science that is to be conveyed via an exhibit(ion) must be deconstructed and then reconstructed into a version that has meaning for the intended audience. The concept "museographic transposition" describes the transposition of what is considered learned knowledge into the knowledge that is to be presented in an exhibition (Simonneaux & Jacobi, 1997).

Using the model of museographic transposition, Mortensen (2010) undertook a retrospective analysis of an immersive exhibit on animal adaptations to darkness. She demonstrated how scientific knowledge was deconstructed into a set of reference knowledge, then reconstructed in the context of various curatorial constraints in building the exhibit. This interplay between reference knowledge and constraints determined how the knowledge was eventually displayed to the visitor. Mortensen (2011) then investigated visitors' responses to this immersive exhibit using a praxeological approach, which linked the exhibit environment with what visitors do within it. Full interpretation of this exhibit required visitors to assume the role of a cave beetle inside a dark cave; however, many visitors did not realize this. Mortensen concluded that immersive exhibits built as metaphors needed to make that metaphor explicit, advising visitors of their intended participatory role and giving hints on how to play it. Using a hot air balloon exhibit, Achiam (2013, nee Mortensen) showed how a praxeological, didactic approach could be used to create a template for the design of exhibits: a way to deconstruct and reconstruct the science knowledge in the context of the exhibit as an educational environment.

Laherto (2012) also argued for a more theoretical approach to exhibition development. He suggested merging a model for developing science teaching and learning sequences in the classroom (Duit, cited in Laherto, 2012) with a model focusing on how visitors make sense of their exhibit experience in a free-choice environment (Stocklmayer & Gilbert, 2002). Laherto was realistic about the time and cost involved to engage research to the extent suggested in his "ideal case." Nevertheless, the thoughtful combination of models from different fields of science education is a rare attempt to bring the fields more closely together.

Rennie (2013) likened the museographic transposition process to creating science stories: selecting which parts of official science to portray, then packaging and presenting the chosen science information (or story) as an exhibit(ion) that the intended audience can understand and interpret according to their own needs and experience. Rennie (2013) illustrated how exhibition "stories" are interpreted by contrasting visitors' responses to entirely different exhibitions; a *Body Worlds* exhibition (Pedretti, 2012) and a traditional museum and a science center (Rennie & Williams, 2006b). Although visitors expressed enjoyment at all venues, their experiences were clearly different and different stories were evoked. The plastinates in *Body Worlds* elicited emotional responses from visitors, and stories communicated were very personal (Jagger, Dubek, & Pedretti, 2012). In contrast, the traditional museum and science center offered friendly and comfortable interpretations of science, and few visitors were challenged to think beyond what they already knew. Rennie (2013) argued that, because they had different stories to tell and told them in different ways, there was no basis for saying one exhibition was "better" than the other. She discussed the challenges and constraints faced by exhibit designers, particularly if science is to be presented as both process and product. Fundamentally, however, if exhibit(ion)s are to be designed to promote learning, they must provoke engagement from visitors, a two-way dialogue that can communicate the science story desired to be told.

Other studies have looked at the educational consequences of exhibit design. Afonso and Gilbert (2007a) used observations followed by interviews to analyze the outcomes of visitors' use of two kinds of interactive exhibits: those described by Stocklmayer and Gilbert (2002) as exemplars of phenomena (such as the Bernoulli ball) and those based on analogies (such as a black hole exhibit comprising a funnel with a spiraling ball). They found that visitors' evaluations of exhibits were based on entertainment value, educative value, or ease of use. Exhibits that were easily related to everyday situations were more educationally successful than those that were not, because many visitors failed to recognize the underpinning concepts of exhibits that exemplified phenomena or were unable to identify the source and/or target of an analogy-based exhibit. In these cases, misconceptions rather than understanding of the concepts portrayed often resulted. Afonso and Gilbert (2007b) analyzed the descriptions of 87 exhibits designed to demonstrate acoustics, determining that only 7 were based on analogies with good potential for causal understanding of the concepts, 39 were exemplars of phenomena with low educational value, and the remainder were merely technology-based applications of the science. These authors pleaded for more collaboration with scientists to improve the conceptual representation of exhibits to promote visitor understanding.

Characteristics of exhibits that affected visitors' use of them were explored in several studies. Hohenstein and Tran (2007) examined the effect of simplifying labels in a science museum and adding a question designed to provoke thought. Although the nature of conversations changed, with more open-ended questions asked among visitors and more explanation, the effect varied with the nature of the exhibit. A study of visitors' responses to broken exhibits (Kollmann, 2007) revealed a negative impact; however, some visitors reported as broken exhibits that they could not operate because of poor design. This is reminiscent of Allen's (2004) concept of "immediate apprehendability" in good exhibit design: It should be obvious what one has to do to engage effectively.

A practical contribution to the monitoring of exhibit effectiveness is an assessment tool proposed by Barriault

and Pearson (2010). The Visitor Engagement Framework comprises seven observable visitor behaviors divided into three levels: Initiating Behaviors (visitors do the activity or watch others), Transition Behaviors (visitors repeat the activity, express positive emotion in response to engagement), and Breakthrough Behaviors (visitors refer to past experiences while engaging, seek and share information, are engaged and involved). High levels of breakthrough behaviors are expected if an exhibit promotes learning. Barriault and Pearson demonstrated that observing visitors in a science center, plotting behavior frequencies, and redesigning exhibits accordingly could increase the rate of breakthrough behaviors.

Dioramas are static exhibits, described by Reiss and Tunnicliffe (2011) as "a careful positioning of a number of museum objects in a naturalistic setting" (p. 447). Natural history dioramas are usually designed to tell a biological and/or ecological story. Because physical features (such as water and rocks) can be included, plants and animals are presented in context, offering different learning opportunities to plants and animals displayed individually. Research with dioramas exploring what visitors learn must take into account what visitors bring to the experience. The naming of animals or other features based on visitors' own knowledge dominates their conversations, but if their interest is captured, more thoughtful observations and interpretation can follow. Tunnicliffe and Scheersoi (2010) used data collected from visitors' spontaneous conversations as they viewed dioramas, postviewing interviews, and children's drawings of their favorite diorama to identify a four-stage response to the dioramas: "identify–interest–interpret–investigate." These inquiry-based discussions can raise emotions as visitors build their own narratives about the display and develop them into powerful learning experiences, particularly for younger visitors if adults or docents are available to scaffold thinking to a higher level (Reiss & Tunnicliffe, 2011). Piqueras, Wickman, and Hamza (2012) explained how a teacher used questions to scaffold preservice teachers' learning by focusing on salient features of a diorama, prompting closer observation and further reasoning as they interpreted the story displayed.

Using Technology in Museums

The incorporation of technology into museum exhibits has had variable success. Computers and interactive screens may provide a technologically interactive experience, but if they are not socially interactive, co-participation and collaboration are limited, preventing the co-construction of knowledge (Heath, vom Lehn, & Osborne, 2005). However, with sufficient space around the screen, the individual user can gather an audience, creating a shared experience. Meisner and colleagues (2007) recorded the action and talk of people gathered around computer-based energy exhibits, describing them as "performances," arguing that they supplemented conversation and created shared engagement and, potentially, science learning. They encouraged exhibit design to facilitate this kind of co-participation by using multiple interfaces, large screens, and spaces for observers.

Louw and Crowley (2013) probed the use of gigapixel imaging technology to create very large, explorable images that "allow users to seamlessly move from full views to extreme close-ups that reveal details hidden in layers of resolution that often exceed one billion pixels" (p. 89), enabling viewers to observe scientifically by manipulating the image as they wish. The authors described ongoing research into how providing visitors with an interactive experience using gigapixel images of normally inaccessible specimens created opportunities for scientific observation and interpretation, thus enlivening the visitor experience of what might otherwise be inert museum collections.

Portable audio-phones are commonplace for static exhibitions in various museums and heritage sites. Although they offer easily digestible information at a touch, earphones may isolate visitors from others. New digital technologies are more amenable to sharing a learning experience. Mobile devices, such as tablets and smart phones, are being used as aids to exhibit interpretation by providing "just in time" guidance relating to exhibits, links to social media, and bookmarks to be followed up later. Ucko (2013) suggested that these devices "augment reality" within real science center settings.

Digital games can complement particular exhibits. The Maryland Science Center designed *Planetaria*, an app game about astrobiology to promote interaction with a permanent exhibit titled *Life Beyond Earth*. Children can download the free app to their mobile device, answer quiz questions, and work with content cards to earn "astrobucks" to spend at the Center's shop. A pre-post, quasi-experimental summative evaluation with 24 9- to 11-year-olds (Flagg, 2012) found that the game was engaging and educational, and children believed that it assisted their learning, but success and enjoyment varied with usability. Fears that game players would ignore the exhibit in favor of the game were not realized, suggesting that the game increased accessibility to the exhibit's content and enhanced learning outcomes.

Hillman, Weilenmann, and Jungselius (2012) reported how young people visiting a traditional natural museum and a science center documented their visit by using smart phones to photograph or video-record exhibits and themselves and their friends using exhibits and then shared the results. Pictures were uploaded to social networks, often modified by photo-software apps, where they were commented on by friends. Video-records were uploaded to YouTube, stimulating active conversations. Hillman and colleagues (2012) considered that these activities expanded the reach of the museum and enriched the visitor's own experience.

During a field trip to a history museum, Charitonos, Blake, Scanlon, and Jones (2012) investigated groups of ninth-grade students interacting with artifacts and tweeting about their experiences. Students collected evidence relating to assigned activities using smart phones, with the aim of making a back-in-classroom presentation about their experiences. Analysis of the Twitter streams revealed groups to be differentially on task, but in interview, students referred to sharing ideas, reading other students' tweets, and incorporating these into their own meaning making. Pierroux, Krange, and Sem (2011) used a Web platform enabling students to use smart phones to obtain information about art exhibits and blog about their experiences at a Norwegian museum. Multimodal blog entries made during the visit could be shared with the teacher and classmates, and subsequent reworking at school resulted in reflective assignments informed by the interpretations of others. Pierroux and colleagues (2011) believed this digital process resonated with the young people and helped bridge the gap between school and museum. Charitonos and colleagues (2012) noted that social media enabled students to slip between individual/social and offline/online interfaces, to share an "interconnected opinion space" (p. 815) that was not restricted to the visit but could be "archived" for future use. These authors suggested further studies to test their conclusions that social and mobile technologies used as learning tools improved students' impressions, participation, and enthusiasm during the field trip, thus shaping their collective experience.

Zoos, Aquariums, Botanic Gardens, and Planetariums

Zoos, aquariums, and botanic gardens are a major source of out-of-school learning in the natural and earth sciences. They have particular appeal because they feature living organisms, and modern institutions endeavor to display plants and animals in contexts closely resembling their natural habitats. Interpretive nature centers have similarities to these institutions but, being based in the actual habitat, are able to highlight ecological features of the environment. Geological and paleontological sites may not focus on living organisms, but they enable visitors to experience phenomena that have environmental significance.

These institutions play a significant role in conveying messages about conservation and the environment. Part of the vision of the World Zoo and Aquarium Conservation Strategy states, "The educational role of zoos and aquariums will be socially, environmentally and culturally relevant, and by influencing people's behaviour and values, education will be seen as an important conservation activity" (World Association of Zoos and Aquariums, 2005, p. 35). The aims of the International Association of Botanic Gardens (IABG) include the conservation of plants through cultivation and other means and habitat conservation by cooperation between IABG and other relevant bodies (www.bgci.org/index.php?option=com_content&id=1530&print=1). However, research assessing success in communicating environmental and conservation messages reveals that these do not rank highly on visitors' agendas.

Zoo visitors enjoy viewing the animals, learning about them, having a picnic, attending talks, using the kiosk, and viewing a special event or display. However, relaxing and enjoying being with their family and friends were more important than learning about nature and how to help conservation activities (Crilley, 2011). Perdue, Stoinski, and Maple (2012) found that visitors attending a live presentation at an orangutan exhibit stayed longer and scored higher on questions about the conservation messages than visitors experiencing no presentation. A video presentation had similar stay time but less knowledge retention than the live presentation. Although the same information was available in signage, visitors with no presentation retained less information about conservation.

Clayton, Fraser, and Saunders (2009) interviewed 206 adults at a zoo, finding that visitors came to enjoy themselves rather than learn, but when they thought they had learned something, they were more likely to express concern for and connection with the animals. Clayton and colleagues also recorded viewing time and signage reading for 1,207 visitors and conversations for 1,891 visitors at three zoos. More than 77% were in family groups, only 27% of visitors looked at interpretative signs, and time spent varied with the animal. About half of the comments recorded were descriptive, simply stating a fact about or drawing attention to the animal. Other common comments reflected curiosity and a positive response to or making connections between the animal and humans. Family groups were more likely to use the animals to teach each other. The authors concluded that zoos are places that can increase visitors' concern for animals, but there was no indication that visitors were learning about conservation, and they could only do so if they read the signs. Pre-post measures of attitudes toward marine sustainability used by Wyles and colleagues (2013) indicated that leisure visitors to a UK aquarium became more conscious of threats to sustainability, particularly if they were given focused information. The challenge is to provide visitors with an appropriate mix of information and entertainment.

According to Myers, Saunders, and Birjulin (2004), zoos provide visitors with rich and positive emotional experiences, an important outcome because emotion is a central component of meaning making. The long-term influences of zoos on attitudes and behavior were examined by Smith, Weiler, and Ham (2011), who suggested that paying attention to the animals and what they do distracts visitors, reducing their focus on messages about conservation. L. Smith and colleagues concluded that more research on long-term behaviors was needed. Lindemann-Matthies and Kamer (2006) found that zoo visitors who used touch tables as well as having access to signage learned more about the biology, ecology, and conservation of bearded vultures than those who did not use the touch table, and they also were more satisfied with the information provided to them. Learning persisted for 2 months after the visit, but the authors noted that zoo rangers were available to assist interpretation at the touch tables by

explaining features and background information, and this also enhanced learning.

Opportunities to touch organisms add an element of physical interactivity at zoos and aquariums that can lead to higher-level thinking. Kisiel, Rowe, Vartabedian, and Kopczak (2012) explored families' scientific reasoning during interactions at aquarium touch tanks. Beyond activities such as identification and gathering information about organisms, Kisiel and colleagues (2012) identified the broad categories of making claims, challenging claims, and confirmation activities, each of which move beyond the simple naming of species or repeating information and can be described as scientific reasoning. Attendants thought the touch tanks provided opportunities for promoting stewardship and respect for marine species but made little effort to support visitors in scientific thinking. There was also no signage to assist this kind of learning. In further research, Rowe and Kisiel (2012) described "the debrief," which follows touching or close observation of an organism. The debrief is stimulated by a comment from the toucher or a question from an observer enabling family members to build explanations and interpretations, make and test predictions, and practice scientific thinking. Again, Rowe and Kisiel observed that attendants missed many opportunities to use debriefing to scaffold learning.

In perhaps the most comprehensive recent research into zoos and aquariums, Falk, Reinhard, and colleagues (2007) conducted a 3-year study over 12 member institutions of the Association of Zoos and Aquariums (AZA) to understand the impact of these institutions on visitors. The extensive data collections, with samples of various sizes, involved pre- and postvisit surveys about visit motivation and personal meaning mapping, cognitive and affective exit surveys relating to messages (such as conservation), a tracking study, and a long-term impact study in which visitors responded to questions about their visit by phone or email up to 11 months after their visit. Overall, the findings were positive, suggesting visitors' elevated awareness of their role in environmental and conservation action, their enhanced belief in the educational importance of zoos and aquariums, and that they gained a stronger connection to nature. This study was criticized on methodological grounds by Marino, Lilienfeld, Malamud, Nobis, and Broglio (2010). Reading this critique and Falk, Heimlich, Vernon, and Bronnenkant's (2010) rebuttal throws into relief many of the difficulties faced by researchers endeavoring to measure impact on visitors in such institutions and explains approaches taken to ameliorate some of those difficulties.

School field trips tend to include zoos and aquariums rather than botanical gardens and arboretums, possibly because students are thought to consider plants passive and boring, whereas animals "do things" and are more interesting. Nevertheless, places that grow plants can contribute to learning about botany, biology more generally, ecology, and conservation. Visitors may take guided walks or wander freely, students on field trips may have other information sessions, such as handling plants, observing them closely, even gardening, and watching videos. Sanders (2007) attempted to reestablish the worth of botanical gardens as important informal science education environments. She collected data in botanic gardens in three countries, reporting on 75 elementary children's written and drawn responses some months after their visit. Sanders found that children liked "secret places," such as secluded areas, the greenhouses, and experiencing plants, particularly the large, rare, or unique plants. She reiterated that botanic gardens are places for exploration and "being" and argued for more research on their contribution to children's learning. The passivity of plants enhances their value in helping children develop the skills of observation but, as Eberbach and Crowley (2009) explained, children need considerable scaffolding to help them think about the meaning of what they see and to learn to observe carefully enough to support scientific reasoning.

A review by Lelliott and Rollnick (2010) of 35 years of research into astronomy education revealed that students—and many teachers—have difficulty understanding the "big ideas" related to astronomy, such as the seasons, gravity, the solar system, and size and scale. The authors suggested that manipulating physical models is helpful to learning, and there is a need to develop good teaching sequences, particularly to counter alternative conceptions developed from "informal sources of information (such as television)" (p. 1791) and the poor quality of available teaching resources. Although only 7 of the 103 reviewed studies were conducted in a science center or museum, most science centers have some exhibits illustrating the effects of gravity and other astronomical phenomena, so there is opportunity for further research, particularly in terms of visitors' use of models. Lelliott's own research (2008) found that students visiting a planetarium and a radio astronomy observatory improved their knowledge, either incrementally or, if they already had prior knowledge, by restructuring it. Science centers and planetariums are well placed to provide quality astronomy education, and Lelliott recommended that astronomy presentations should focus on a limited number of concepts around big ideas.

Learning on Family Visits

Families are a major segment of museum visitors, and research has focused on intrafamily social interaction and teaching behaviors. Parent–child interaction varies with the age of children and at different kinds of exhibits. Because the family group exists before and after the visit, families tend to visit with their own agenda, frequently using the museum as a context for learning rather than a source of particular content. Through subsequent references to their visit experiences, family learning is continued after the visit and is an important part of children's learning about science (Rennie, 2007a).

Research into family discourse indicates that parents endeavor to complement their child's perceived needs. Palmquist and Crowley (2007) examined how parents talked to children aged 5 to 7 years who were "expert" or "novice" in their knowledge of dinosaurs. In dyads, expert children talked more than parents, who, by remaining silent, missed opportunities to challenge or assist new learning. In contrast, parents talked more than novice children and engaged them in learning conversations. The metacognitive approach taken by Thomas and Anderson (2013) revealed that parents held definite views about how they and their children think and learn based on experiences in contexts outside of the museum. These views determined how they interacted with their 8- to 15-year-old children at a motion track exhibit. In a study of 40 families of Mexican descent, Siegel, Esterly, Callanan, Wright, and Navarro (2007) observed that parents were more directive of their children at home on a structured task and more collaborative in similar but open-ended activities in a museum, regardless of the child's age.

Other research has investigated ways to assist children's inquiry-related behavior. Szechter and Carey's (2009) research with 20 parent–child dyads at a science center found that parents' "learning talk" included describing evidence, giving directions, providing explanations, connecting with past experience, and making predictions. They talked more about the exhibits than did children, but children initiated engagement more often. More time was spent at exhibits designed to support experimentation and choice to encourage prolonged engagement (rather than demonstrate a single phenomenon), where parents elicited more predictions from their children and children were more likely to describe evidence and give directions.

Gutwill and Allen (2010) developed family games for use with science exhibits, focusing on two inquiry skills: asking questions or making a plan to begin an investigation and making observations, interpretations, or explanations during or after an investigation. The "juicy question game" required families to pose a questions then work collaboratively to answer it. The "hands-off game" allowed any family member to call "hands off" and have everyone else listen to a discovery or question proposed by the caller. Both games increased the quantity and quality of scientific inquiry demonstrated among families compared to families who had an interactive tour of the exhibits. Families using the juicy question game also outperformed families who were free to explore the exhibits as they wished. The success of this game was attributed to coaching in the target skills and the collaboration it engendered. Gutwill and Allen (2012) had similar findings when they repeated the study with students in school field trips. The juicy question game resulted in more inquiry activity, explained in terms of everyone being required to participate, the collaborative framing of the questions, and the explicit interpretation phase. Chaperones also became more deeply involved.

Young children's exploratory behavior with interactive exhibits seems to be facilitated when others offer procedural assistance rather than explanations about how things work (Fender & Crowley, 2007). Van Schijndel, Franse, and Raijmakers (2010) encouraged parents to "coach" their 4- to 6-year-old children's behavior at interactive exhibits using appropriate scaffolding, and this resulted in a higher quality of exploratory behavior. Based on additional research with 2- to 3-year-old children, Van Schijndel, Singer, Van der Maas, and Raijmakers (2010) warned against assuming that the level of young children's hands-on exploration predicts their level of learning about the activity.

McClafferty and Rennie (2012) observed 145 3- to 6-year-old children at a science center using a multicomponent exhibit, where children cranked handles or turned wheels to move balls around the components. Children's cognitive understanding about how the exhibit worked was assessed by interview, using a photograph of the exhibit to stimulate recall, and a correlation of .53 was found between children's age and level of understanding. However, video recordings of 12 children revealed no relationship between their level of understanding and the nature of their activity or the length of interaction time. McClafferty and Rennie recommended caution in attributing understanding from level of exploration or time spent interacting and emphasized the need for more than one kind of data to provide complementary information about children's experiences. Sanford's (2010) exploration of 493 families interacting with 25 museum exhibits led to similar conclusions. She employed three common indicators of learning during a visit: time spent, nature of engagement, and interpretative talk about the exhibits. Low correlations among these indicators demonstrated the need to use multiple measures.

Museums provide opportunities for learning about science in a sociocultural context, and this is reflected in how families structure their learning experiences. Leinhardt and Knutson (2006) reviewed conversations between visitors and their grandchildren and suggested that the intergenerational conversations were likely to involve grandparents in storytelling, as co-learners or teachers, and as modelers of appropriate social interactions. Ash and colleagues (2007) used a dialogical approach to analyze how 20 Spanish-speaking and English-speaking families used "everyday" words to convey science meaning and further their scientific understanding of marine biology exhibits. They emphasized that learning science is not just a cognitive task but a product of social and cultural practice. Zimmerman, Reeve, and Bell (2010) focused on what epistemic resources (knowledge types) families brought to make meaning of their interaction with biological exhibits. Videotaping, observational field notes, and pre- and postvisit interviews were used to document the entire visit of experienced family visitors to a science center. The authors found that families combined science knowledge brought by individual members, information from exhibit signage, and other, sometimes nonbiological, cultural knowledge from everyday activities, such as school, television, hobbies, and jobs, as analogies or metaphors to make sense of exhibit content. Parents encouraged transfer talk to scaffold and guide children's observations and understanding. A significant finding was the combination of knowledge from everyday experience with scientific knowledge to make sense of the biological exhibits, a hybrid discourse that is used for problem solving and sense making in everyday life.

Briseño-Garzón and Anderson (2012) used a sociocultural approach in 20 case studies of Latin American family groups who frequently visited a Mexican science center. Families are strong social groups for Latin Americans and are the basis for all learning activities, including moral and religious development. Data were collected and analyzed in Spanish, and the findings indicated that not only are museum visits used for cognitive and affective learning experiences, "but also are contexts where the co-construction and reaffirmation of socio-cultural identities occur through the social exchanges of the family members" (p. 196). The authors suggested that Latino visitors to museums outside of Latin America could benefit from more exhibits designed for family interaction. It is also likely that using the home language of minorities in other countries would similarly encourage visitation and quality participation by such visitors.

Spaces designed for young children can provide links to outside activities. For example, children's play areas in a zoo that simulated natural environments encouraged families to express interest in visiting other natural environments (Oxarart, Monroe, & Plate, 2013). To make their museum more family friendly, Dockett, Main, and Kelly (2011) involved 40 children aged between 6 months and 6 years and their families in the design of a new play/learning space for children. Data were collected by children showing their favorite places and taking photographs; talking with children as they played, constructed, drew, or painted; and 18 children's journals about their museum experiences. As well as the significance of family members, themes identified included the importance of real objects; children's use of imagination, creativity, and pretense; their sense of humor; physical space of the museum; its social context; connections with children's lives; and engaging with the cultural messages of the museum. Children's ideas were considered in redesigning the space, resulting in more places that encouraged family play, small "pods" into which children could climb, and places to display children's drawings and photos, thus increasing connection with children's own lives. So far, no evidence of the effects of this redesign is available.

Trends in Visitor Studies

Observing visitors remains the most common approach to collecting data in museum research and exhibit(ion) evaluation because learning is associated with time spent "paying attention" to exhibits and their labels and interacting with others. The considerable diversity in collecting observational data was reduced by Serrell (1998, 2010), who argued that greater uniformity in approaches to visitor timing and tracking would result in more useful outcomes. She created a database of tracking-and-timing studies, suggested new metrics for analyzing and interpreting these data, and established parameters to assess the success of particular exhibits by comparison across similar others. Building on Serrell's (1998) contribution, Yalowitz and Bronnenkant (2009) added an exposition and guide about the techniques for observing visitor activity in museums. Handheld devices and appropriate software now available for collecting and analyzing these kinds of data provide greater consistency and efficiency in visitor studies. Moussouri and Roussos (2013) used the GPS facility of smart phones to track family visitors through a zoo. They found that educationally motivated families visited only exhibit areas, but entertainment-motivated families spent considerable time in nonexhibit areas. This technology offers insights into visitor behavior, but knowing where visitors go and how long they spend there does not describe what they are doing. Although observation with digital devices is possible, ethical issues relating to privacy must be considered.

Another research use of digital media is netnography, a technique based on ethnography used to analyze data available in people's online communications. The ethical issues of using people's texts as data without seeking permission are usually explained in terms of the information being in the public sphere and removing identifying information. Goulding, Saren, and Lindridge (2013) analyzed relevant content from seven blogging sites to investigate how visitors to von Hagens' *Body Worlds* exhibitions described their experiences. Five explanatory themes were identified in visitors' comments: the body as spectacle, the body and mortality salience, the commodified body, the body as machine, and dehumanizing the human body. Their findings report little about visitors' learning but a great deal about personal responses. This technique has potential in examining visitors' responses to exhibitions but is limited to what people choose to reveal rather than responding to targeted questions from the researcher.

The notion of "identity" has become a focus in research exploring participation in informal science education. Identity concerns how one construes oneself in terms of what one knows, enjoys, and can do; it expresses continuity between one's construal of what one did in the past, does in the present, and will do in the future. Identities are formed through interacting and identifying with significant others (such as parents, teachers, peers); they determine one's choices and behaviors and can be modified through interaction with others and artifacts. Identities are situated and multiple; people's motivations and therefore their behavior varies according to circumstances.

Identity-related motivations are likely to be influential in voluntary activities, because they guide individual choices about what to participate in, how, and with what outcomes. The concept of identity offers an avenue through which visitor behavior can be understood in ways

that may assist institutions to effect improvements in visitors' experience. Further, if people with similar identity-related motivations can be grouped together, findings can be reported in ways that may aid comparison across institutions and contribute meaningfully to a database of research evidence. Based on considerable research about the concept of identity as a means of understanding the visit experience, Falk (2006, 2009, 2011) has described seven clusters of identity-related motivations—explorers, facilitators, professional/hobbyists, experience seekers, rechargers, respectful pilgrims, and affinity seekers—titles that are descriptive of the motivational needs and roles engendered by the underlying identities (Falk, 2011, p. 153). Although the dominant motivations of many visitors can be ascribed to one of these clusters, many others are better described as multidominant, so the clusters are not exclusive.

Identity-related motivations were a focus in the zoo and aquarium study by Falk, Reinhard, and colleagues (2007; see also Falk, Heimlich, & Bronnenkant, 2008), who found that visitors arrived "with specific identity-related motivations and these motivations directly impact how they conduct their visit and what meaning they derive from their experience" (p. 3). Different patterns of profiles were found at different institutions. Dawson and Jensen (2011) criticized the use of identity-related motivations as a means of visitor segmentation, arguing the need to acknowledge the complexity and change over time of individuals' unique motivations and ideas and the interwoven sociocultural variables that influenced these changes. Falk (2011) restated that the visitor experience is complicated and that an identity-motivations approach is just one means of trying to understand it. Jensen, Dawson, and Falk (2011) noted the importance of drawing on theoretically informed models and the need for mixed-method approaches to improve explanatory power in the field of visitor studies. More research using identity-related motivation that is cognizant of its strengths and limitations is needed to establish whether and how its use can assist institutions to improve the visit experience.

Rowe and Nickels (2011) used the AZA tool, developed by Falk, Reinhard, and colleagues (2007), to explore visitors' identity-related motivations over three informal education settings; an aquarium, a science center, and a boat-based eco-tour. The tool was easy to use and analyze, and it provided a more nuanced description of visitors but failed to discriminate among nearly half of them, confirming that many people come with multiple motivations. Acknowledging that the instrument had since been revised to be more discriminative, Rowe and Nickels suggested that "our theoretical understanding that identity is situated, dynamic, and sometimes contradictory has outpaced our instruments and techniques for documenting identity . . . [current instruments] tend to operationalize identity in terms of either demographic variables or more or less fixed personal characteristics rather than as emergent properties of complex systems of interactions among active agents, cultural tools, and contexts" (p. 173). Thinking of motivation as "identity-related transactions" with people, places, and objects (Paris & Mercer, 2002, as cited by Rowe & Nickels, 2011) that have a direct bearing on people's performances of self might help to clarify motivation and identity and suggest ways of developing more inclusive measures that assist understanding of current audiences and reach new ones.

Learning on Trips Outside the Classroom

The value of taking students outside of the classroom to observe and experience science-related phenomena and processes and to participate in activities not easily offered within the school building has long been recognized. For example, 87% of UK teachers responding to a survey "greatly agreed" that out-of-school trips could "be one of the most valuable educational activities," and 54% greatly agreed that they wished they could do more (QA Research, 2008, p. 10). Syntheses of research on school trips reveal that their educational effectiveness in terms of complementing the science learning at school depends on the teachers who lead them (DeWitt & Storksdieck, 2008; Rennie, 2007a; Rowell, 2012).

Notable similarities in teachers' perceptions of field trips to a museum in the United States, a science center in Canada, and a planetarium in Germany were reported by Anderson, Kisiel, and Storksdieck (2006). Most teachers believed that field trips were valuable experiences and that pre- and postvisit activities were important, but few teachers used them effectively. Logistical barriers to be overcome included costs and fitting field trips into their busy curriculum. Being able to demonstrate curricular fit was viewed as justification for overcoming the difficulties associated with organizing the trip, yet paradoxically, few teachers planned and implemented strategies to ensure that the trip was effectively integrated into the curriculum, even though they knew what should be done. Museum educators recognize the importance of curriculum fit and endeavor to map their exhibits to local curriculum goals, as shown by Rowell's (2012) analysis of the programs of 12 Canadian institutions. Rowell noted the paradox that museum program developers wished to create innovative, interesting experiences but felt constrained by the need for curriculum fit, whereas most teachers gave more attention to the affective outcomes of a visit than the cognitive curriculum outcomes and did little to ensure that students' experiences linked back to school.

Studies of guided field trips to natural history museums in Israel (Tal, Bamberger, & Morag, 2005; Tal & Morag, 2007) found that guides typically used a knowledge-transmission approach in dealing with students, but teachers rarely participated in ways that would help students to engage thoughtfully or require them to make links with everyday experiences. Indeed, teachers had very limited involvement in planning or participation in the field trip experience. After similar findings relating to students' visits to three museums and a zoo, Bamberger and Tal (2008)

argued for more teacher participation in structuring the visit experience by in-class preparation, active participation during the visit, and follow-up postvisit activities back at school. Similarly, Faria and Chagas (2012) observed that guide-directed visits in a Portugal aquarium resulted in limited interactions among students, teachers, and aquarium resources, with teachers essentially passive spectators. Further, the teachers' agenda was limited; they did little to scaffold students' learning and had planned no pre- or postvisit tasks.

The significance of the teacher's agenda for a field trip and its implementation was illustrated by Davidson, Passmore, and Anderson (2010), who compared the outcomes of two seventh-grade class visits to a zoo. Teacher A had vague expectations apart from the students enjoying the trip, whereas Teacher V explicitly incorporated the trip into her science curriculum about endangered animals. In class, Teacher A's transmissive approach to teaching contrasted with Teacher V's student-centered pedagogical approach that encouraged group work and the development of student independence. Pre- and postvisit activities were completed in this class, and students had clear goals for their task at the zoo. In both classes, an important aspect for students was socializing with their friends, but the learning outcomes matched the teachers' approaches to the visit. Compared to students in Teacher A's class, students in Teacher V's class demonstrated considerable learning, well remembered 3 months after the visit. Although for both classes the zoo educators made presentations about conservation, this had very little effect on students' activities, an outcome attributed to their different agendas: having fun in Teacher A's class and learning about endangered animals in Teacher V's class.

Agendas are important determinants of visit outcomes. Anderson, Piscitelli, and Everett (2008) demonstrated how the agendas of children aged 6 to 8 years conflicted with those of the docents. Potential conflicts related to content (child wishing to tell his story and the docent wishing to talk about the exhibit), mission (children wishing to see dinosaurs but the docent wanting to escort children through the galleries), and time (child wishing to continue exploration but the docent needing to move on). Anderson and colleagues argued that agenda conflict has the potential to affect children's experience and their learning. While adults have the power to negotiate their agenda with docents, considerable skill is required to listen to children and negotiate their wishes to maximize outcomes.

Agenda conflict draws attention to the pedagogical skills of docents and museum educators whose educational work is to mediate learning through the institution's exhibits, particularly as there is considerable diversity in their educational background and they frequently have a range of roles (Rowell, 2012; Tran, 2008). Tran and King (2007) investigated the content and pedagogical knowledge of museum educators and considered this a basis for increased professionalization of their roles as mediators rather than tellers of knowledge. Ash, Lombana, and

Alcala (2012) described research in which museum educators were encouraged to reflect on and transform their roles from content deliverers to scaffolders of learning, collaboratively sharing their knowledge with visitors. Such research endorses the potential of docents' contributions to effective visit outcomes.

Bamberger and Tal (2008) interviewed a total of 50 sixth- to eighth-grade students who visited one of three museums or a zoo to investigate the visit experience. They categorized outcomes as content oriented (science content knowledge, concrete experience, connecting knowledge), social oriented (relating to student–student interactions and guide–student interactions, which could be positive or negative), and interest oriented (personal relevance, emotional engagement, willingness to revisit, enriching experience). Outcomes differed in the different environments: For example, the live animals in the guide-led zoo visit stimulated more learning talk and outcomes that were more meaningful to students than at the other institutions, where the exhibits and stuffed animals allowed more active engagement but with less direction. Bamberger and Tal (2007) found that the degree of choice students experienced in museum visits affected both the nature of engagement and learning. No choice usually involved students being given information with little personal interaction; free choice resulted in considerable social interaction, but without clear purpose for any activity; limited choice, such as doing worksheets with some choice, structured students' activity, scaffolded their learning, and encouraged deeper engagement and relevant interactions. Interestingly, in all situations, students made connections with their life experience even though it was rarely referred to by guides, teachers, or worksheets. In a different study, Tal (2012) arranged for two teachers to take their sixth-grade classes with several parents to an ecological garden. Students participated in groups of four to five with an adult in a free-choice, family-like visit to the garden. Tal found that the students were very engaged, asked questions, and reflected on what they observed and, according to their teachers, demonstrated considerable learning and other positive social and affective outcomes. Tal suggested this kind of trip as a useful way to promote meaningful learning in out-of-school settings.

In other studies exploring choice, Wilde and Urhahne (2008) designed matched open-ended and closed-ended worksheet tasks relating to birds and fishes for able fifth-graders visiting a natural history museum. There were knowledge gains, which declined slightly over a month, and the closed tasks were more enjoyable and motivating than the open tasks, possibly because they were easier and less time consuming. Stavrova and Urhahne (2010) modified a docent-led tour in an energy gallery to include more group work, more active participation, and closed- rather than open-ended questions on an accompanying worksheet. Surveys comparing the outcomes between the original and modified tour for eighth- and ninth-grade students found that while both demonstrated knowledge gains, those in the modified tour were more motivated and interested.

Using Falk and Dierking's (2000) Contextual Model of Learning and Kisiel's (2003) analysis of worksheets for school visits, Mortensen and Smart (2007) derived an approach to worksheet design. They suggested that worksheets should be low density (to allow for personal exploration and social interaction), contain cues to assist orientation, be flexible with regard to site for completion, emphasize group work and observation rather than reading, have a high level of choice, employ a variety of response formats, and emphasize concepts not facts, and the cognitive level should match learners' ages and development. Mortensen and Smart had teachers use an existing Chaperone's Guide, focused on the local curriculum and fitting their criteria as a "free-choice" group worksheet, to lead groups of fourth graders around five exhibitions. Groups using the guide had higher levels of curriculum goal conversation, addressed a greater number of curriculum goal categories, and had more opportunities for learning.

Structure in visits to a German zoo was explored by Randler, Kummer, and Wilhelm (2012), who divided a total of 845 fifth and sixth graders into four experiences. A control group's visit was unstructured, a second group was led by a zoo guide, and two groups worked in small groups during their visit, one with a teacher-centered summary and the other with peer tutoring. Knowledge tests were given before the zoo visit, the day after, and 6 weeks later. All treatment groups scored higher than the control group. The zoo-guide group scored highest immediately after the visit, but the group-work with teacher summary scored best 6 weeks later. Randler and colleagues concluded that learner-centered approaches are valuable provided students are used to working in groups. Dohn's (2013) study of 12th-grade biology students during a structured day-long visit to a Danish zoo found that students enjoyed hands-on involvement during group experiments, socializing with their classmates, and the novelty of the setting. These factors provided a motivating experience for students finding schoolwork "monotonous."

The importance of discourse, particularly questioning, as a mode of learning was explored by DeWitt and Hohenstein (2010a, 2010b). They examined talk among students aged 9 to 12 years during a visit to a science museum in the UK or the United States and in their classrooms during follow-up lessons. Student talk reflected both cognitive and affective engagement with the exhibition or with classwork content at school, and talk was predominantly cooperative, but there was a higher level of such talk in the museum setting, where more open-ended questions were included. Driscoll and Lownds (2007) described a "wonder wall" in a children's garden on which young children posted questions from their activities. Questions either sought basic information (50%) or implied "wonderment" (50%), seeking explanations to increase understanding. All questions were answered by garden educators. The authors recommended this approach as a nonthreatening way for children to ask questions and enhance their learning, as well as providing feedback to educators.

Research about field trips continues; a sample has been referred to here and recent studies using digital media were noted earlier. In sum, the research has confirmed and built on the outcomes of earlier reviews. The need for previsit, during-visit, and postvisit instruction and guidance by the teacher continues to be emphasized by researchers. Effective outcomes flow from trips that are well planned, involving communication between teachers and educators at the site to be visited, clear goals for which students feel ownership, and sufficient structure to scaffold rather than stifle students' engagement and learning. However, there is considerable evidence that many teachers lack the skills to make the most of out-of-school opportunities for learning (Anderson et al., 2006; Griffin, 2012; Morag & Tal, 2012; Rennie, 2011; Rowell, 2012), and this lack of skills impacts students' learning outcomes.

Supporting Teachers' Use of Out-of-School Resources for Science

Assisting teachers to make effective use of out-of-school resources requires building self-confidence in both their science content knowledge and pedagogical knowledge and developing the skills needed to support students' learning in informal contexts. Research has explored the potential of including informal science education as part of preservice teaching programs, and many museums have formed partnerships with universities for this purpose. A survey by Phillips, Finkelstein, and Wever-Frerichs (2007) of 524 informal science institutions in the United States found that, in addition to offering programs for students, 59% offered professional development programs for teachers, more than a third of which were associated with preservice teachers. Most aimed at increasing teachers' content knowledge and/or improving their pedagogical knowledge. Gupta and Adams (2012) described different kinds of long-running programs in three countries that gave preservice teachers opportunities to work within museum environments, and McGinnis and colleagues (2012) synthesized research on using informal science education in teacher preparation. Both studies identified benefits that included increased confidence and interest relating to science, gains in science content knowledge, and exposure to teaching in different contexts using different strategies. These experiences clearly support preservice teachers' skill development, but an inherent challenge is for them to transfer the skills gained to teaching science in school and to organizing effective field trips.

Many inservice teachers, even those who have well-developed content and pedagogical knowledge, also need support to enable them to use informal avenues for science learning effectively. Phillips and colleagues (2007) found that 42% of informal science institutions they surveyed offered resources to assist teachers to connect their science curriculum with the experiences available during a school field trip. This is a widely used means of outreach, but research evidence suggests that many teachers require guidance to make use of these materials (Rowell, 2012). DeWitt and Osborne (2007) suggested a framework to advise museum educators on ways to support teachers, including pre- and postvisit activities, and ways to ensure the museum visit tied into school science. A research-based guide for elementary teachers was provided by Melber (2008) to ensure their field trips are engaging for students and learning outcomes enhanced.

Some programs aimed to help teachers plan and implement successful field trips. Tal and Morag (2009) worked with five preservice and inservice teachers, offering support as they developed activities for and reflected upon their teaching experiences in an outdoor ecological garden as a means of addressing their lack of confidence, building their pedagogical knowledge, and recognizing the importance of careful preparation. Griffin (2012) described a formal course for preservice teachers and a professional development for inservice teachers. Both focused on integrating school–museum learning before, during, and after the visits and developing skills for self-directed learning in students. Teachers' ability to conduct successful field trips was enhanced by giving them a museum experience in a supportive, collaborative environment, enabling them to realize the importance of developing a clear understanding of purpose for the visit and giving a sense of ownership and choice to students.

Long-term collaborations between museums and schools can be effective but take time to develop. Kisiel (2010) used a community-of-practice approach to analyze a formal collaboration between an aquarium and a nearby elementary school. School classes had free access to the aquarium and aquarium educators visited the school to conduct lessons. Problems relating to curriculum content, time pressures, and miscommunication between teachers and aquarium educators diminished as they began to understand each other's circumstances and explore how their interaction could be complementary, and by the second year, the relationship had progressed to a successful collaboration as the two communities of practice overlapped, assisted by the aquarium education coordinator, who acted as a broker between the two communities. Rahm (2012) described how a science center acted as a source of materials and support for schools to participate in a robotics program; however, the intentions of the program were not congruent with the realities of the school, particularly the demands on time, and the program closed after 4 years. Rahm used activity theory to uncover the tensions and contradictions in how the program functioned and suggested that co-constructed programs pursuing shared objectives are necessary for effective school–museum partnerships. Rowell (2012) also advocated activity theory as a means to analyze museum programs for schools because its emphasis on collaborative transformation could help untangle the complex network of relationships among museum educators, school students and teachers, and their communities.

Science in the Community and Family Life

A range of community-organized sources of science learning is available for young people, including citizen science programs, after-school science and science clubs, science fairs and competitions, science festivals and similar events, and science theater and other performances. Space constraints preclude attention being given in this chapter to formally structured activities often related to schooling, such as after-school science (see Afterschool Alliance, 2011) and science fairs (see Bencze & Bowen, 2009), or those not specifically targeting youth, such as citizen science (see Dickinson & Bonney, 2012). Instead, this section focuses on informal science activities associated with family life.

Science in Everyday Activities

Although science is implicit in most of children's activities at home, including play, hobbies, and chores, little is recognized as science and, apart from school homework, connections with science at school are rarely made. Zimmerman and Bell (2012) interviewed 13 fourth- and fifth-grade students about 36 different activities engaged in at home, in school, in the community, and media based. They found that students saw connections to science across their everyday activities but had different definitions of science. Those seeing more science included the use of technology and products of science, like electricity. Others included as science anything associated with knowledge building, or learning something new through inquiry. Children with science-related hobbies saw connections to science in many of their daily activities. Zimmerman (2012) explored how science was learned via one girl's home-based and hobby activities, particularly animal care, from fourth to seventh grade. The girl participated in biology-related science practices as she became an expert on hamsters through observation, feeding, handling of the animals, and researching information about them. Although perceiving herself and wishing to be recognized as an animal person, she did not wish to be perceived as a science person because she found her activity-poor science classes boring. The significance of youth's desire to be recognized in ways they consider important to them problematizes the potential overlap between science at school and science elsewhere. Developing a science identity is a complex negotiation of sense of self, sense of science, the ways science is used and supported in family life (Aschbacher, Li, & Roth, 2010), and also in other community-based activities (McCreedy & Dierking, 2013).

To assist parents to do science-related activities with children, Riedinger (2012) listed strategies they could use when taking children to informal science institutions. Helping children observe closely, ask open-ended questions, test their ideas, and modeling interest and enthusiasm

are appropriate for any kind of family activity. Luke and McCreedy (2012) reported on a museum program designed to assist parents in underserved communities to become more engaged in their 5- to 10-year-old children's education. The program included science learning opportunities involving parent, teacher, and child at school or the museum; collaborative activities at home for parents and children; and developing spaces, such as gardens, in the community or at school for parents, teachers, and children to come together. Luke and McCreedy found that parents gained resources and opportunities to engage with their children and their child's schooling and more comfort with science. The program gave parents and teachers tools to break down barriers such as power differentials between school and home, easing discomfort parents felt in assisting with their child's schoolwork.

Science Festivals and Performances

Students attend science festivals with their families or peers. Science festivals are diverse, public events that promote science, such as lectures, debates, and various science-related activities, held in a variety of venues and usually over a period of time, such as a weekend or a week. Bultitude, McDonald, and Custead (2011) reviewed the characteristics of a range of international science festivals, noting significant diversity in how they are organized, their target audience, and types of activities included.

There is a trend toward increasing the evaluation efforts associated with science festivals, but most is informal and internal, particularly when the budget is small. Data are usually collected about the number and demographics of participants and the quality of events in terms of whether attendees enjoyed them, found them interesting and/or inspiring, and believed they had learned something new. For example, nearly 83% of those responding to evaluation survey forms for the 2012 British National Science and Engineering Week claimed to have learned something new, and 59% thought they would continue to talk about science and engineering after the event (British Science Association, 2012). Bultitude and colleagues (2011) pointed out that more focused evaluation able to be shared among organizers would be beneficial. They found no work relating to the measurement of long-term outcomes of participation in science festival events.

Bultitude and Sardo (2012) interviewed participants attracted to three events in England: *Physics in the Field*, held as part of a family festival where physics experiments were demonstrated over three days; *BioBlitz*, a 30-hour event for scientists and volunteers to identify species at a particular site; and *Guerilla Science*, where young science communicators took science to a music festival over three afternoons and evenings. Children were interviewed only at the first two events. Two thirds of the 60 interviewees had not come specifically for the science part of the event, tending to view it as combining enjoyment with science content. People enjoyed the informality of the surroundings and the opportunities to meet "real" scientists, and many were able to re-engage with science. Bultitude and Sardo concluded such events offered good opportunities to reach audiences, including children, who generally professed little interest in science.

Science performances have been a means of communicating science for more than three centuries, with scientists such as Michael Faraday demonstrating their current discoveries to entranced audiences (Walker, 2012). Hodder (2011) noted a revival over the last three decades with scientist-as-performer presentations now common in science centers as well as on stage and as part of science festivals. Hodder noted that "telling stories of science" was a theme through all kinds of performance: single, group, or as part of an exhibition. Hall, Foutz, and Mayhew (2012) described a café scientifique program in New Mexico, guided by Youth Leadership Teams. Given that youth are a demographic group difficult to access, with many interests and activities competing for their time, this initiative presented considerable challenges, and the procedure has been continually modified based on feedback. Youth prefer less formal presentations with a high level of interactivity. Using a matched control-treatment group design with a sample of almost 400, Hall and colleagues found that participation in the program positively influenced interest in science and science careers and knowledge about scientists and science in their daily lives, as well as self-efficacy and cognitive competence toward science.

Zimmerman and Bell (2012) discussed how youth's participation in science-related activities and practices provided "assets" or resources for future learning of science. Archer and colleagues (2012) explored family relationships with science, uncovering perspectives ranging from "proscience" to science as peripheral or irrelevant. Children in families that facilitated their science interests and aspirations by supporting them with science-related experiences and activities could more easily identify with science and consider STEM careers. Such families were mainly "middle-class," and Archer and colleagues described them as having economic and "science-related capital." In contrast, children pursuing a science interest individually, without active family support, were more likely to fall out of science. Family relationships with science are complex and intertwined with social class, culture, and other variables but are strongly associated with children's science aspirations and identities (Archer et al., 2012).

Learning Science From Media

People use television, film, radio, books, and the Internet as entertainment. They access events and issues of interest to them and use social media to communicate with peers and others. The use of mobile digital devices is now nearly ubiquitous, particularly for adolescents. The "smart" phone is also a camera, a TV, a radio, a computer, a GPS, a library for music and video, and a console for games. Traditional divisions of media are collapsing as visual and broadcast media, computer games, and the printed word become available for download to a digital device. However, for convenience in this section, learning science from media outside the classroom is reviewed in three sections: visual, print, and digital.

Visual Media

Despite its potential, recent research on science learning from media outside of school is hard to find. In a synthesis paper on television, Dhingra (2012) argued that the building of science knowledge and its use should be central to how science stories are told. She identified four genres of science-related stories on television: stories relating to citizen science (mainly news), documentaries, educational programs for children, and drama. She summarized research in each genre to demonstrate that television can be an effective learning tool, but "learning about the learning of television viewers is complex" (p. 1136). Dhingra pointed out that children's views about what they perceive to be scientific or not and attributes of their background will contribute to how they construct science based on their viewing experience.

Other research demonstrates how this occurs. Orthia and colleagues (2012) used focus groups to investigate the perceptions of young adults watching a science-rich episode of *The Simpsons*. Their responses varied widely; some saw no science at all, while others saw a range of interpretations. Orthia and colleagues attributed this variability to viewers using their own background experiences to fill gaps in the storyline, thus "concretizing" their own views about science. Barnett and colleagues (2006) showed that students can develop misconceptions from incorrect science in science fiction films used in class, suggesting not only that teachers lack the appropriate skills to help students critique the science they see, but in viewing television and films outside of school, such misconceptions are likely to result.

The representation of science and scientists in media is of interest because role models are important for young people considering careers (Steinke, 2013); however, scientists rarely appear in fictional television. Dudo and colleagues (2011) analyzed the occupations of 2,868 characters appearing in selected primetime television programs with a storyline. Over the period 2000 to 2008, only 1% were scientists, most were "good" rather than not, and most were White males. Long and colleagues (2010) examined how scientists were portrayed in 14 television programs, including drama, cartoons, educational, and situation comedy, that they considered popular with children aged 12 to 14 years. Scientists were usually Caucasian, intelligent, and unmarried; further, male scientists had a greater presence, both in terms of numbers and number of scenes in which they appeared, and were more likely to be portrayed as independent and violent. However, males and females had similar status as scientists, there was a general absence of gender-stereotyped characteristics, and scientists were usually portrayed as less nerdy than they have been in the past. This is consistent with Steinke's (2013) synthesis of research on the representation of female scientists in the mass media, concluding that, over time, portrayals have become less stereotyped, but females are still under-represented and there is an increased focus on attractiveness, compared to earlier portrayals of scientists as male, unattractive, and geeky. Steinke acknowledged the complexity of factors that interact to determine career choice but suggested that the inclusion and positive portrayal of females in STEM careers may assist students to consider science as a profession. A cautious note comes from Bergman's (2012) exploration of the representation of three women scientists in crime fiction in literature, television, and film. Despite being recognized as highly intelligent, skilled in their fields, and loving their work, women were often treated like children or objects of sexual desire by their co-workers. These less desirable aspects of their workplace question their value as good role models for young girls pondering science careers.

Print Media

Print media remain a significant source of science information outside of school. Apart from science textbooks designed for their use, students may read about science in fiction and nonfiction books, journals, magazines, newspapers, and brochures or pamphlets, as well as on the Internet. For young readers, books like the *Horrible Science* series can teach about science in a positive but seemingly irreverent way (A. Bell, 2011). Afonso and Gilbert (2013) reviewed 193 popular chemistry books in English and Portuguese from 80 publishers, with content ranging from chemistry experiments to do at home, the use of chemistry in other fields, and biographies of chemists to chemistry in everyday life. By asking undergraduates to read some of the books, Afonso and Gilbert found that ease of reading and comprehension were assisted by illustrations, analogies, detailed explanations, clear structure, and giving practical examples.

Access to scientific information via any medium requires the conversion of unfamiliar terminology and concepts into a language that is accessible to the intended audience. Rennie (2007b) showed how "scientists' science" is converted to science news stories for public consumption and how front-page nature articles were charged with social, emotional, and political values. Readers require not only skills to make sense of written language but abilities to filter out the implicit value positions and determine the validity of the science presented. Vestergård (2011) found more than half of journal articles relating to climate change in Danish newspapers contained inaccuracies, and about a tenth confused the source of information. Such inaccuracies suggest that misconceptions may arise for young people who lack the skills and experience to read critically.

A group of specialists on science in the media was convened by McClune and Jarman (2010) to identify the fundamental elements that enabled the critical reading of news reports. They identified knowledge of science, methods of inquiry, and the scientific enterprise; knowledge of writing and language; knowledge about journalistic practices, the nature of news, and the characteristics of newspaper reports; skills in reading and critical thinking; and attitudes such as curiosity and self-confidence. Young people need assistance to develop these abilities. Jarman, McClune, Pyle, and Braband (2012) examined the images related to news stories about science and identified a range of potential misinterpretations that could arise from poorly prepared diagrams, figures, and graphs. They developed lists of "learning intentions" that might be used for students of different ages and urged that that critical interpretation of news reports be part of their school education. McClune and Jarman (2010) warned, "the primary purpose of media is not to educate, rather to inform, interpret, persuade, frequently to entertain, and, crucially, to make profit for its proprietors or at least to ensure economic viability" (p. 748). The principles in this quotation are generalizable to all kinds of mass media. School-aged students have almost unlimited access to media outside of school, and the evidence suggests that most need assistance to learn to deal critically with media stories.

Digital Media

Young people are prodigious users of digital media. Hsi (2007, pp. 1513–1514) described the attributes of "digital kids" who, in using computers and mobile devices for playing games and social networking, also search for information, build their skills and knowledge, voluntarily spend time becoming digitally fluent, and multitask with multiple devices. They take on different identities and roles, co-construct a social reality and establish norms for participation, take ownership of media creations and online expression, consume multimedia created by others to engage in two-way literacies in the cultural production of knowledge, and work on complex problems that require distributed teams to solve. Hsi discussed the theoretical perspectives used to conceptualize the nature of learning in these digital environments, focusing on the aspects of social networking, game play, and online identity development and the means by which data can be collected. She noted that research is challenged by the everyday rather than in-school nature of digital activities and the difficulty of measuring educational progress when there are no shared educational goals. Not surprisingly, studies of learning outside of school supported by digital technologies are harder to find than studies of technology supporting in-school learning.

Computer games, originally designed for fun more than four decades ago, are now designed for broader purposes. The term "serious games" is sometimes used for games developed for learning and behavior change rather than entertainment. Learning is most effective when computer games are active, experiential, situated, problem-based, and provide immediate feedback (Boyle, Connolly, & Hainey, 2011). Annetta (2008) argued that serious games requiring "the use of logic, memory, problem-solving, critical thinking skills, visualization, and discovery" (p. 231) assist students to learn the media literacies required in the 21st century.

A review by Connolly, Boyle, MacArthur, Hainey, and Boyle (2012) of computer games used in education found more than 7,000 papers, but most described game potentials rather than research into game outcomes, and few examined serious games. The few that did confirmed that outcomes were both positive and negative. Researchers tended to use survey or quasi-experimental approaches to examine positive outcomes in terms of knowledge acquisition and content understanding in games for learning and looked for affective and motivational outcomes in entertainment games. These authors concluded that "to encourage the use of games in learning beyond simulations and puzzles, it is essential to develop a better understanding of the tasks, activities, skills and operations that different kinds of game can offer and examine how these might match desired learning outcomes" (p. 672).

Role-playing and simulation games are popular, and when game playing involves others, learning and thinking can become social activities (Gee, 2007). Well-designed role-playing games afford students a virtual "apprenticeship," or situated learning experiences otherwise inaccessible to them. Krajcik and Mun (this volume) describe how virtual environments allow students access to authentic contexts in which they can collect data, solve problems, and build models, all important skills for learning science. Research suggests that learning can result from digital games in a supportive educational environment, but if played in leisure time, potential learning would likely depend on the nature of the concepts presented in games and providing players with reasons to transfer learning to new situations. There are numerous video games, or apps, available for mobile phones that are well designed and engaging and have the potential for learning science concepts. For example, the aim of the strategy game *Plague Inc.* is to design a disease to infect everybody on the planet (E. Smith, 2012), but the players have the potential to learn about the spread of disease and about disease prevention. These are games played avidly (not only by youth), but it is difficult to find research that has measured learning in their use outside of school.

Portable, wireless-connected mobile devices open up opportunities for "a continuity of the learning experience across different environments," described by Chan and colleagues (2006, p. 6) as "seamless learning," and much research is required to illuminate this field. A review of 54 papers by Wong and Looi (2011) revealed considerable variation in terminology (including what were considered as formal or informal learning settings) and dimensions of learning considered in research. Little research has been conducted in informal settings, and most of that concerns field trips, as noted earlier. A longitudinal exploration by Song, Wong, and Looi (2012) of elementary students' learning about life cycles in a goal-based program in Singapore incorporated in-class instruction, a field trip to a farm, and follow-up activities. Each student was given 24/7 use of a smart phone, which Song and colleagues characterized as a "learning hub," to mediate a seamless experience between the contexts of school, home, and the farm. Instructions and worksheets were tailored for the smart phone, which students also used for taking photos, animated sketching, and Web searching. Students could choose what life cycles to study, how they researched them, and how they presented their work, thus demonstrating how the mobile learning environment enables personalized learning, not only in content but in where the learning takes place. Wong and Looi (2011) described this as "cross-time and cross-location" (p. 2369) constructivist learning. Wong (2012) summed up this notion with these words: "Mediated by technology, a seamless learner should be able to explore, identify and seize boundless opportunities that her daily living spaces may offer to her, rather than always being inhibited by externally defined learning goals and resources" (p. E22).

Schuck and Aubusson (2010) explored the educational implications of interactive websites and social networking that allow the sharing of ideas and participation in virtual worlds. Like Hsi (2007) and others, they recognized the need to view these avenues for learning as legitimate activity and re-vision school education accordingly. Chan and colleagues (2006) speculated on the time it may take for one-to-one technology-enhanced learning to become common in schools. They suggested that the pervasive use of mobile devices may be a tipping point in shifting the way students learn inside and outside of schools, because they cross the boundaries between formal and informal environments. Whatever ways new technologies are used in formal schooling, change is likely to be slow, and more immediate effects will occur outside of school. Assessing outcomes presents new challenges for researchers not only in terms of how learning occurs but the potential for misleading and mislearning. Brossard and Scheufele (2013) warned that the communication of balanced science stories via the Internet can be affected by the tone of social comments on blogs and Twitter. They stressed the need for rigorous empirical research on how best to communicate science online in an era in which online social communication can impact the public view of science.

Implications for Research, Practice, and Policy

The contribution to learning and participation in STEM attributable to informal science education legitimizes the continuation of research in this field. The progress made over the last decades has marked the maturity of the field and bestowed belief in the significance of its findings, but there are still gaps and opportunities for consolidation and cooperation among the various providers.

Implications for Research Into Learning Outside of School

Research has shown that the nature of the impact from out-of-school activities is variable, but the attributes that result in science learning outcomes have become clearer. One attribute relates to the context that makes engagement meaningful. Learning from any science-related experience is most likely when young people's engagement is purposeful and prolonged or revisited, such as by discussing with family and friends—in person or online—enabling the experience to be remembered, rehearsed, and reflected on. If learning outside of school is to complement the science curriculum in school, students need sufficient structure to prepare them for active but enjoyable participation in the out-of-school experience and consolidating activities back in the classroom. Research exploring the teacher's contribution in the context of school trips to institutions and the contribution of docents, guides, or museum educators continues to show a diversity of outcomes related to the nature of the teacher's agenda and how well it is put into practice. If docents and/or teachers provide students with scaffolding at the right time, higher-level cognitive learning is more likely to result. Having teachers and museum educators work more collaboratively to support student learning has become a research focus but remains a challenge.

A second attribute relates to meaningful communication. Despite progress in understanding how meaning is made from engagement in science-related activities outside of school, there remain avenues to explore. Several times in this chapter, the metaphor of story was used to explain how science is translated into a format (an exhibit, TV program, news report) that can be understood by its intended audience. The required transposition of science content is difficult and highlights the need for clear definitions of purpose and audience and for evaluation of the effectiveness of communication.

A recurring thread is the need for an effective means to assess outcomes. Establishing impact may have implications for funding, for example, to continue support for an activity, or to choose between alternative methods of delivering a program. In June 2012, a Summit on Assessment of Informal and Afterschool Science Learning was convened by the Board on Science Education at the National Academies, in cooperation with the Harvard Program in Education, Afterschool and Resiliency. Consensus among the commissioned papers was that the important outcomes related to engagement, content knowledge, and skills and that two levels of assessment might be advisable: a level that gave a broad picture and a more fine-grained approach that could capture the specifics of particular programs. Several frameworks (Friedman, 2008; GLO; P. Bell et al., 2009) were referenced, but the nature of outcomes, outcome indicators, and evidence to support them remain to be articulated for many out-of-school experiences in science. Steps toward the wider use of effective outcome measures will advance the field.

Much of the research mentioned in this chapter has examined specific aspects of informal science education in a particular context of out-of-school learning. Less common is research in which the focus has been on the linking of or collaboration between different kinds of venues for informal science education or even among institutions of the same kind. An important but neglected perspective is that all of these sources, as part of the same societal infrastructure, are working toward the same goals. Their various aims have considerable overlap: to stimulate interest in and educate the populace about science. The two interlinked reports commissioned by the Wellcome Trust (Falk et al., 2012; Lloyd et al., 2012) took the opportunity of reviewing a countrywide field to explore such a perspective. They found that nearly two thirds of providers saw their work as supporting formal learning through links to the national curriculum, stimulating an interest in science, and/or providing professional development for teachers. Even so, using the analogy of a community ecology for the entire science education system in the UK, including schools, Falk and colleagues discovered that, in essence, this diverse range of institutions operated at the individual level; few had reciprocal interactions. The data revealed that between the formal and informal communities, there was often poor understanding of the roles and capabilities of and even disrespect for the members of one community for the other. Falk and colleagues (2012) concluded that providers of informal learning experiences needed to conceptualize themselves as parts of "a complex, interconnected system" and become "more reflective and evidence-based in its practice, helping it to acquire more sophisticated models of science, the value of science, how science is learned and what makes science interesting and engaging" (p. 17). Both reports gave comprehensive recommendations to implement steps to build a stronger and common identity among providers of science education. The Wellcome Trust's reflections on the reports (Matterson & Holman, 2012) generally supported these directions, noting "limitations of the [informal] community on the use of theory and research, its need to garner evidence more effectively and its need to become more professional in its sharing of knowledge and expertise" (p. 7).

The research reported in this chapter suggests that these reflections are relevant more widely than only in the UK. Within each community, a publicly accessible database of providers would facilitate productive links between formal and informal institutions and organizations. A systematic approach to evaluation of the impacts of the informal sector could build a consolidated, more effective base of evidence that could be used to support advocacy, as most informal providers require funding for the continuation of their activities. A research agenda that highlights the closing of gaps might assist in reaching those presently underserved and hard-to-reach groups in the informal sector.

Implications for Practice and Policy

It is time to set aside differences between learning in school and out, time to break down this artificial divide in the learning of science. Experiencing science outside of school provides the "science-based capital" (Archer et al. 2012) or "assets" (Zimmerman & Bell, 2012) for future science learning and participation. Building bridges between the two sectors is a productive approach to improving STEM understanding for students at school and in later life. Stocklmayer, Rennie, and Gilbert (2010) explored models for the relationship between the formal and informal sector and, using Moje, Collazo, Carillo, and Marx's (2001) notion of a third space between the cultural worlds of school and community that could bridge these boundaries, suggested that the most hopeful but still challenging relationship would be that "the formal sector integrates the capabilities of the informal sector into its everyday working, thus creating a "third space" for science education" (p. 29). From an extensive review, Stocklmayer and colleagues distilled the factors that were found to encourage learning in the informal sector (p. 25) and suggested ways these aspects might gradually be incorporated into school science and thus fill up the third space. Recognizing that formal schooling systems are resistant to change, these authors argued for a holistic approach driven by the school system as the only practical solution. They also noted the role that will be played by new technologies in permeating the boundaries between learning in formal and informal contexts.

Digital media, including the Internet, allow for ubiquitous communication, threatening the need for educational institutions like schools and museums to be sources of knowledge about science (and other things). The use of portable devices encourages social interaction within and beyond the museum visit. Ucko (2013) discussed the future of science centers within this changing environment, and his arguments have salience in all kinds of museums. Strengths of these institutions reside in their "capacity to create meaningful, socially-mediated learning experiences that cannot be readily duplicated online, at home, or at school" (p. 23). These places have authentic, frequently large objects, experiences can be immersive, access to scientists and engineers and their research is possible, and the growing number of "maker" and "tinkerer" spaces often reside in museums. Ucko (2013) is optimistic: "Taking advantage of these affordances and approaches will strengthen the role of science centers in their communities, helping them to occupy a vital niche in the expanding STEM learning ecology" (p. 28). The future will tell how well technology will be incorporated into museum environments and how effectively it is used to cut across or at least connect the formal and informal sectors.

Does connecting the sectors mean that we need a unified theoretical base? Sfard (1998) explained that "theories of learning, like all scientific theories, come and go" (p. 4), and this is evident in research into learning outside of school. Sfard illustrated two metaphors for learning by mapping an acquisition metaphor against a participation metaphor. The former concerns learning from an individual perspective, regarding the individual as an acquisitor or recipient of knowledge, whereas the latter looks more to the communal building of knowledge, in which the individual is a participant or apprentice. Research in the out-of-school field reflects these metaphors, with key words such as "conception," "meaning," "sense," "development," and "construction" representing the individual as a recipient of learning and key words such as "situatedness," "context," "social mediation," "discourse," and "communication" representing the learner as participant in the learning process. Sfard argued against the separation of these two metaphors and the notion of them as competing perspectives; instead, she argued for a peaceful co-existence. Despite their ontological discrepancies, both have strengths and both have something to contribute to research. Further, argued Sfard (1998), "our work is bound to produce a patchwork of metaphors rather than a unified, homogeneous theory of learning" (p. 12). So is it with learning in science outside of school.

The reviews of research papers by Falk and colleagues (2012) and Phipps (2010), together with the chapter in the first edition of this handbook (Rennie, 2007a), reveal a variety of approaches to research in this field. Apart from the sociocultural and constructivist perspectives that dominate, newer to the field are activity theory (Rahm, 2012), identity theory (Falk, 2006), netnography (Goulding et al., 2013), and the use of GPS to track visitors (Moussouri & Roussos, 2013). It is difficult to integrate the findings into one coherent, unified body of work, because researchers have come from different perspectives. Perhaps this is not important; it is likely that a more complete but not unified picture of learning in this diverse field is possible and perhaps even desirable by using more than one theoretical approach. It is more important in research and its reporting to state one's theoretical position or perspective than to argue about whether it is formal or informal. Further, clarifying the purpose of the research and how learning is defined within it are interdependent with the theoretical perspective that underpins the research. Although Phipps (2010) noted that 96% of the articles she reviewed could be placed within a theoretical framework, she found that "Many authors were not explicit in their definition of learning or the theoretical underpinnings of their studies. The theoretical underpinnings of a number of studies were artfully hidden in the phrasing of the research question, or the framing of the conclusion" (p. 17). Artful or not, some researchers have been lax about ensuring that the theoretical underpinnings to their work, the research questions, and the research design, including data collection and analysis, are explicitly coherent and that the threads that link these facets of research are clearly articulated. The provision of this information is critical to assist readers to understand the stance taken by researchers, how their results were interpreted, and the credibility of the outcomes.

Acknowledgments

Thanks to Richard Lehrer, John Gilbert, and Susan Stocklmayer, who reviewed this chapter.

References

Achiam, M. F. (2013). A content-oriented model for science exhibit engineering. *International Journal of Science Education, Part B: Communication and Public Engagement, 3*(3), 214–232. doi:10.1080/21548455.2012.698445

Afonso, A. S., & Gilbert, J. K. (2007a). Educational value of different types of exhibits in an interactive science and technology center. *Science Education, 91*(6), 967–987.

Afonso, A. S., & Gilbert, J. K. (2007b). The nature of exhibits about acoustics in science and technology centers. *Research in Science Education, 38*(5), 633–651.

Afonso, A. S., & Gilbert, J. K. (2013). The role of "popular" books in informal chemistry education. *International Journal of Science Education, Part B: Communication and Public Engagement, 3*(1), 77–99.

Afterschool Alliance. (2011). *STEM learning in Afterschool: An analysis of impacts and outcomes*. Retrieved from www.afterschoolalliance.org/STEM-Afterschool-Outcomes.pdf

Allen, S. (2004). Designs for learning: Studying science museum exhibits that do more than entertain. *Science Education, 88*(Suppl. 1), S17–S33.

Allen, S., Gutwill, J., Perry, D. L., Garibay, C., Ellenbogen, K., Heimlich, J. E., . . . Klien, C. (2007). Research in museums: Coping with complexity. In J. H. Falk, L. D. Dierking, & S. Foutz (Eds.), *In principle, in practice: Museums as learning institutions* (pp. 229–245). Walnut Creek, CA: AltaMira Press.

Anderson, D., Kisiel, J., & Storksdieck, M. (2006). Understanding teachers' perspectives on field trips: Discovering common ground in three countries. *Curator: The Museum Journal, 49*(3), 365–386.

Anderson, D., Piscitelli, B., & Everett, M. (2008). Competing agendas: Young children's museum field trips. *Curator: The Museum Journal, 51*(3), 253–273.

Anderson, D., Storksdieck, M., & Spock, M. (2007). Understanding the long-term impacts of museum experiences. In J. H. Falk, L. D. Dierking, & S. Foutz (Eds.), *In principle, in practice: Museums as learning institutions* (pp. 197–215). Walnut Creek, CA: AltaMira Press.

Annetta, L. A. (2008). Video games in education: Why they should be used and how they are being used? *Theory Into Practice, 47*(3), 229–239.

Archer, L., DeWitt, J., Osborne, J., Dillon, J., Willis, B., & Wong, B. (2012). Science aspirations, capital, and family habitus: How families shape children's engagement and identification with science. *American Educational Research Journal, 49*(5), 881–908.

Aschbacher, P. R., Li, E., & Roth, E. J. (2010). Is science me? High school students' identities, participation and aspirations in science, engineering, and medicine. *Journal of Research in Science Teaching, 47*(5), 564–582.

Ash, D., Crain, R., Brandt, C., Loomis, M., Wheaton, M., & Bennett, C. (2007). Talk, tools, and tensions: Observing biological talk over time. *International Journal of Science Education, 29*(12), 1581–1602.

Ash, D. B., Lombana, J., & Alcala, L. (2012). Changing practices, changing identities as museum educators: From didactic telling to scaffolding in the ZPD. In E. Davidsson & A. Jakobsson (Eds.), *Understanding interactions at science centers and museums* (pp. 23–44). Rotterdam, the Netherlands: Sense Publishers.

Association for Science and Discovery Centres (ASDC). (2010). *Assessing the impact of UK science and discovery centres: Towards a set of common indicators*. Bristol, UK: Author. Retrieved from www.sciencecentres.org.uk

Association of Science-Technology Centers (ASTC). (2012). *2011 science center and museum statistics*. Washington, DC: Author.

Astor-Jack, T., Whaley, K. L. K., Dierking, L. D., Perry, D. L., & Garibay, C. (2007). Investigating socially-mediated learning. In J. H. Falk, L. D. Dierking, & S. Foutz (Eds.), *In principle, in practice: Museums as learning institutions* (pp. 217–228). Walnut Creek, CA: AltaMira Press.

Bamberger, Y., & Tal, T. (2007). Learning in a personal context: Levels of choice in a free choice learning environment in science and natural history museums. *Science Education, 91*(1), 75–95.

Bamberger, Y., & Tal, T. (2008). Multiple outcomes of class visits to natural history museums: The students' view. *Journal of Science Education and Technology, 17,* 274–284.

Barnett, M., Wagner, H., Gatling, A., Anderson, J., Houle, M., & Kafka, A. (2006). The impact of science fiction film on student understanding of science. *Journal of Science Education and Technology, 15*(2), 179–191.

Barriault, C., & Pearson, D. (2010). Assessing exhibits for learning in science centers: A practical tool. *Visitor Studies, 13*(1), 90–106.

Bell, A. (2011). Science as "horrible": Irreverent deference in science communication. *Science as Culture, 20*(4), 491–512.

Bell, P., Lewenstein, B., Shouse, A. W., & Feder, M. A. (Eds.). (2009). *Learning science in informal environments: People, places, and pursuits*. Washington, DC: National Academies Press.

Bencze, J. L., & Bowen, G. M. (2009). A national science fair: Exhibiting support for the knowledge economy. *International Journal of Science Education, 31*(18), 2459–2483.

Bergman, K. (2012). Girls just wanna be smart? The depiction of women scientists in contemporary science fiction. *International Journal of Gender, Science and Technology, 4*(3). Retrieved from http://genderandset.open.ac.uk/index.php/genderandset/article/viewFile/224/438

Boyle, E. A., Connolly, T. M., & Hainey, T. (2011). The role of psychology in understanding the impact of computer games. *Entertainment Computing, 2,* 69–74.

Briseño-Garzón, A., & Anderson, D. (2012). "My child is your child"; Family behavior in a Mexican science museum. *Curator: The Museum Journal, 55*(2), 179–201.

British Science Association. (2012). *Evaluation report: National Science & Engineering Week 2012*. Retrieved from www.britishscienceassociation.org/national-science-engineering-week/archive/evaluation-reports

Brossard, D., & Scheufele, D. A. (2013). Science, new media, and the public. *Science, 339,* 40–41.

Bultitude, K., McDonald, D., & Custead, S. (2011). The rise and rise of science festivals: An international review of organised events to celebrate science. *International Journal of Science Education, Part B: Communication and Public Engagement, 1*(2), 165–188.

Bultitude, K., & Sardo, A. M. (2012). Leisure and pleasure: Science events in unusual locations. *International Journal of Science Education, 34*(18), 2775–2795.

Butt, S., Clery, E., Abeywardana, V., & Phillips, M. (National Centre for Social Research). (2010). *Wellcome Trust Monitor Survey report (September 2009 updated November 2012)*. London: Wellcome Trust.

Chan, T.-W., Roschelle, J., Hsi, S., Kinshuk, Sharples, M., Brown, T., . . . Hoppe, U. (2006). One-to-one technology-enhanced learning: An opportunity for global research collaboration. *Research and Practice in Technology-Enhanced Learning, 1*(1), 3–29. Retrieved from http://telearn.archives-ouvertes.fr/docs/00/19/06/32/PDF/A132_Chan-et-al2006_OneToOne.pdf

Charitonos, K., Blake, C., Scanlon, E., & Jones, A. (2012). Museum learning via social and mobile technologies: (How) can online interactions enhance the visitor experience? *British Journal of Educational Technology, 43*(5), 802–819.

Clayton, S., Fraser, J., & Saunders, C. D. (2009). Zoo experiences: Conversations, connections, and concern for animals. *Zoo Biology, 28,* 377–397.

Clemence, M., Gilby, N., Shah, J., Swiecicka, J., & Warren, D. (Ipsos MORI). (2013). *Wellcome Trust Monitor: Wave 2*. London: Wellcome Trust.

Connolly, T.M., Boyle, E.A., MacArthur, E., Hainey, T., & Boyle, J.M. (2012). A systematic literature review of empirical evidence on computer games and serious games. *Computers & Education, 59,* 661–686.

Crilley, G. (2011). Visitor expectations and visit satisfaction at zoos. In W. Frost (Ed.), *Zoos and tourism: Conservation, education, entertainment?* (pp. 171–185). Bristol, UK: Channel View Publications.

Dabney, K.P., Tai, R.H., Almarode, J.T., Miller-Friedmann, J.L., Sonnert, G., Sadler, P.M., & Hazari, Z. (2012). Out-of-school time science activities and their association with career interest in STEM. *International Journal of Science Education, Part B: Communication and Public Engagement, 2*(1), 63–79.

Davidson, S.K., Passmore, C., & Anderson, D. (2010). Learning on zoo field trips: The interaction of the agendas and practices of students, teachers, and zoo educators. *Science Education, 94*(1), 122–141.

Dawson, E., & Jensen, E. (2011). Towards a contextual turn in visitor studies: Evaluating visitor segmentation and identity-related motivations. *Visitor Studies, 14*(2), 127–140.

DeWitt, J., & Hohenstein, J. (2010a). Supporting student learning: A comparison of student discussion in museums and classrooms. *Visitor Studies, 13*(1), 41–66.

DeWitt, J., & Hohenstein, J. (2010b). An investigation into teacher–student talk in two settings. *Journal of Research in Science Teaching, 47*(4), 454–473.

DeWitt, J., & Osborne, J. (2007). Supporting teachers on science-focused school trips: Towards an integrated framework of theory and practice. *International Journal of Science Education, 29*(6), 685–710.

DeWitt, J., & Storksdierk, M. (2008). A short review of school field trips: Key findings from the past and implications for the future. *Visitor Studies, 11*(2), 181–197.

Dhingra, K. (2012). Science stories on television. In K. Tobin, B.J. Fraser, & C. McRobbie (Eds.), *Second international handbook of science education* (Vol. 2, pp. 1135–1146). Dordrecht, the Netherlands: Springer.

Dickinson, J.L., & Bonney, R. (Eds.). (2012). *Citizen science: Public participation in environmental research.* New York: Cornell University Press.

Dierking, L.D., Falk, J.H., Rennie, L., Anderson, D., & Ellenbogen, K. (2003). Policy statement of the "Informal Science Education" Ad Hoc Committee. *Journal of Research in Science Teaching, 40*(2), 108–111.

Dockett, S., Main, S., & Kelly, L. (2011). Consulting young children: Experiences from a museum. *Visitor Studies, 14*(1), 13–33.

Dohn, N.B. (2013). Upper secondary students' situational interest: A case study of the role of a zoo visit in a biology class. *International Journal of Science Education, 35*(16), 2732–2751.

Driscoll, E.A., & Lownds, N.K. (2007). The garden wonder wall: Fostering wonder and curiosity on multi-day garden field trips. *Applied Environmental Education and Communication, 6,* 105–112.

Dudo, A., Brossard, D., Shanahan, J., Scheufele, D.A., Morgan, M., & Signorielli, N. (2011). Science on television in the 21st century: Recent trends in portrayals and their contributions to public attitudes toward science. *Communication Research, 38*(6), 754–777.

Eberbach, C., & Crowley, K. (2009). From everyday to scientific observation: How children learn to observe the biologist's world. *Review of Educational Research, 79*(1), 39–68.

Falk, J.H. (Ed.). (2001). *Free-choice science education: How we learn science outside of schools.* New York: Teachers College Press.

Falk, J.H. (2006). An identity-centered approach to understanding museum learning. *Curator: The Museum Journal, 49*(2), 151–166.

Falk, J.H. (2009). *Identity and the museum visitor experience.* Walnut Creek, CA: Left Coast Press.

Falk, J.H. (2011). Contextualizing Falk's identity-related visitor motivation model. *Visitor Studies, 14*(2), 141–157.

Falk, J.H., & Dierking, L.D. (1995). *Public institutions for personal learning: Establishing a research agenda.* Washington, DC: American Association of Museums.

Falk, J.H., & Dierking, L.D. (2000). *Learning from museums: Visitor experiences and the making of meaning.* Walnut Creek, CA: AltaMira Press.

Falk, J.H., Dierking, L.D., & Foutz, S. (Eds.). (2007). *In principle, in practice: Museums as learning institutions.* Walnut Creek, CA: AltaMira Press.

Falk, J.H., Heimlich, J.E., & Bronnenkant, K. (2008). Using identity-related visit motivations as a tool for understanding adult zoo and aquarium visitor's meaning making. *Curator: The Museum Journal, 51*(1), 55–80.

Falk, J.H., Heimlich, J.E., Vernon, C.L., & Bronnenkant, K. (2010). Critique of a critique: Do zoos and aquariums promote attitude change in visitors? *Society and Animals, 18,* 415–419.

Falk, J.H., & Needham, M.D. (2011). Measuring the impact of a science center on its community. *Journal of Research in Science Teaching, 48*(1), 1–12.

Falk, J.H., Osborne, J., Dierking, L., Dawson, E., Wenger, M., & Wong, B. (2012). *Analysing the UK science education community: The contribution of informal providers.* London: Wellcome Trust.

Falk, J.H., Reinhard, E.M., Vernon, C.L., Bronnenkant, K., Heimlich, J.E., & Deans, N.L. (2007). *Why zoos and aquariums matter: Assessing the impact of a visit to a zoo or aquarium.* Silver Spring, MD: Association of Zoos and Aquariums.

Falk, J.H., & Storksdieck, M. (2005). Using the contextual model of learning to understand visitor learning from a science center exhibition. *Science Education, 89,* 744–778.

Faria, C., & Chagas, I. (2012). Investigating school-guided visits to an aquarium: What roles for science teachers? *International Journal of Science Education, Part B: Communication and Public Engagement, 3*(2), 159–174.

Fender, J.G., & Crowley, K. (2007). How parent explanation changes what children learn from everyday scientific thinking. *Journal of Applied Developmental Psychology, 28,* 189–210.

Fenichel, M., & Schweingruber, H.A. (2010). *Surrounded by science: Learning science in informal environments.* Washington, DC: National Academies Press.

Flagg, B. (2012). *Summative evaluation of "PlanetMania" mobile app in Maryland Science Center's "Life Beyond Earth" exhibit.* [Multimedia Research]. Maryland Science Center (Research Report No. 13–001). Retrieved from http://informalscience.org/evaluation/ic-000-000-003-551/_Summative_Evaluation_of_PlanetMania_Mobile_App_in_Maryland_Science_Center_s_Life_Beyond_Earth_Exhibit_

Friedman, A. (Ed.). (2008). *Framework for evaluating impacts of informal science education projects.* Retrieved from http://informalscience.org/documents/Eval_Framework.pdf

Friedman, A.J. (2010). The evolution of the science museum. *Physics Today, 63*(10). Retrieved from http://scitation.aip.org/content/aip/magazine/physicstoday/article/63/10/10.1063/1.3502548

Frontier Economics. (2009). *Assessing the impact of science centres in England: A report prepared for the BIS.* London: Author. Retrieved from sciencecentres.org.uk/govreport/docs/impact_of_science_centres.pdf

Gee, J.P. (2007). *What video games have to teach us about learning and literacy* (2nd ed.). New York: Palgrave Macmillan.

Goulding, C., Saren, M., & Lindridge, A. (2013). Reading the body at von Hagen's "Body Worlds." *Annals of Tourism Research, 40,* 306–330.

Griffin, J. (2012). Exploring and scaffolding learning interactions between teachers, students and museum educators. In E. Davidsson & A. Jakobsson (Eds.), *Understanding interactions at science centers and museums* (pp. 115–128). Rotterdam, the Netherlands: Sense Publishers.

Gupta, P., & Adams, J.D. (2012). Museum–university partnerships for preservice science education. In K. Tobin, B.J. Fraser, & C. McRobbie (Eds.), *Second international handbook of science education* (Vol. 2, pp. 1147–1162). Dordrecht, the Netherlands: Springer.

Gutwill, J.P., & Allen, S. (2010). Facilitating family group inquiry at science museum exhibits. *Science Education, 94*(4), 710–742.

Gutwill, J.P., & Allen, S. (2012). Deepening students' scientific inquiry skills during a science museum field trip. *Journal of the Learning Sciences, 21*(1), 130–181.

Hall, M. K., Foutz, S., & Mayhew, M. A. (2012). Design and impacts of a youth-directed café scientifique program. *International Journal of Science Education, Part B: Communication and Public Engagement, 3*(2), 175–198.

Heath, C., vom Lehn, D., & Osborne, J. (2005). Interaction and interactives: Collaboration and participation with computer-based exhibits. *Public Understanding of Science, 14*(1), 91–101.

Hein, G. E. (1998). *Learning in the museum.* London: Routledge.

Hillman, T., Weilenmann, A., & Jungselius, B. (2012). *Creating live experiences with real and stuffed animals: The use of mobile technologies in museums.* Paper presented at the Dream Conference, Denmark. Retrieved from www.dreamconference.dk/wp-content/uploads/2012/03/Hillman.pdf

Hodder, P. (2011). Science as theatre: A New Zealand history of performances and exhibitions. *Journal of Science Communication, 10*(2), A01. Retrieved from http://jcom.sissa.it

Hohenstein, J., & Tran, L. U. (2007). Use of questions in exhibit labels to generate explanatory conversation among science museum visitors. *International Journal of Science Education, 29*(12), 1557–1580.

Hooper-Greenhill, E. (2007). *Museums and education: Purpose, pedagogy, performance.* New York: Routledge.

Hsi, S. (2007). Conceptualizing learning from the everyday activities of digital kids. *International Journal of Science Education, 29*(12), 1509–1529.

Jagger, S. L., Dubek, M. M., & Pedretti, E. (2012). "It's a personal thing": Visitors' responses to Body Worlds. *Museum Management and Curatorship, 27*(4), 357–374.

Jarman, R., McClune, B., Pyle, E., & Braband, G. (2012). The critical reading of the images associated with science-related news reports: Establishing a knowledge, skills and attitudes framework. *International Journal of Science Education, Part B: Communication and Public Engagement, 2*(2), 103–129.

Jensen, E., Dawson, E., & Falk, J. H. (2011). Dialog and synthesis: Developing consensus in visitor research methodology. *Visitor Studies, 14*(2), 158–161.

Kisiel, J. (2003). Teachers, museums and worksheets: A closer look at the learning experience. *Journal of Science Teacher Education, 14*(1), 3–21.

Kisiel, J. (2010). Exploring a school–aquarium collaboration: An intersection of communities of practice. *Science Education, 94*(1), 95–121.

Kisiel, J., Rowe, S., Vartabedian, M. A., & Kopczak, C. (2012). Evidence for family engagement in scientific reasoning at interactive animal exhibits. *Science Education, 96*(6), 1047–1070.

Kollmann, E. K. (2007). The effect of broken exhibits on the experiences of visitors at a science museum. *Visitor Studies, 10*(2), 178–191.

Laherto, A. (2012). Informing the development of science exhibitions through educational research. *International Journal of Science Education, Part B: Communication and Public Engagement, 3*(2), 121–143.

Layton, D., Jenkins, E., Macgill, S., & Davey, A. (1993). *Inarticulate science? Perspectives on the public understanding of science and some implications for science education.* Nafferton, UK: Studies in Education Ltd.

Leinhardt, G., & Knutson, K. (2006). Grandparents speak: Museum conversations across generations. *Curator: The Museum Journal, 49*(2), 235–252.

Lelliott, A., & Rollnick, M. (2010). Big ideas: A review of astronomy education research 1974–2008. *International Journal of Science Education, 32*(13), 1771–1799.

Lelliott, A. D. (2008). *Learning about astronomy: A case study exploring how grade 7 and 8 students experience sites of informal learning in South Africa.* Retrieved from http://wiredspace.wits.ac.za/handle/10539/4480

Lindemann-Matthies, P., & Kamer, T. (2006). The influence of an interactive educational approach on visitors' learning in a Swiss zoo. *Science Education, 90*(2), 296–315.

Lloyd, R., Neilson, R., King, S., & Dyball, M. (2012). *Review of informal science learning.* London: Wellcome Trust.

Long, M., Steinke, J., Applegate, B., Lapinski, M. K., Johnson, M. J., & Ghosh, S. (2010). Portrayals of male and female scientists in television programs popular among middle school-age children. *Science Communication, 32*(3), 356–382.

Louw, M., & Crowley, K. (2013). New ways of looking and learning in natural history museums: The use of gigapixel imaging to bring science and publics together. *Curator: The Museum Journal, 56*(1), 87–104.

Luke, J. J., & McCreedy, D. (2012). Breaking down barriers: Museum as broker of home/school collaboration. *Visitor Studies, 15*(1), 98–113.

Marino, L., Lilienfeld, S. O., Malamud, R., Nobis, N., & Broglio, R. (2010). Do zoos and aquariums promote attitude change in visitors? A critical evaluation of the American zoo and aquarium study. *Society and Animals, 18,* 126–138.

Martin, L. (2007). An emerging research framework for studying free-choice learning and schools. In J. H. Falk, L. D. Dierking, & S. Foutz (Eds.), *In principle, in practice: Museums as learning institutions* (pp. 247–259). Walnut Creek, CA: AltaMira Press.

Matterson, C., & Holman, J. (2012). *Informal science learning review: Reflections from the Wellcome Trust.* London: Wellcome Trust.

McClafferty, T. P., & Rennie, L. J. (2012). Look and learn: Young children's behaviour at an interactive exhibit. In E. Davidsson & A. Jakobsson (Eds.), *Understanding interactions at science centers and museum* (pp. 129–145). Rotterdam, the Netherlands: Sense Publishers.

McClune, B., & Jarman, R. (2010). Critical reading of science-based news reports: Establishing a knowledge, skills and attitudes framework. *International Journal of Science Education, 32*(6), 727–752.

McCreedy, D., & Dierking, L. D. (2013). *Cascading influences: Long-term impacts of informal STEM experiences for girls.* Philadelphia: Franklin Institute.

McGinnis, J. R., Hestness, E., Riedinger, K., Katz, P., Marbach-Ad, G., & Dai, A. (2012). Informal science education in formal science teacher preparation. In K. Tobin, B. J. Fraser, & C. McRobbie (Eds.), *Second international handbook of science education* (Vol. 2, pp. 1097–1108). Dordrecht, the Netherlands: Springer.

McManus, P. M. (1992). Topics in museums and science education. *Studies in Science Education, 20,* 157–182.

Meisner, R., vom Lehn, D., Heath, C., Burch, A., Gammon, B., & Reisman, M. (2007). Exhibiting performance: Co-participation in science centres and museums. *International Journal of Science Education, 29*(12), 1531–1555.

Melber, L. M. (2008). *Informal learning and field trips: Engaging students in standards-based experiences across the K–5 curriculum.* Thousand Oaks, CA: Corwin Press.

Moje, E. B., Collazo, T., Carillo, R., & Marx, R. W. (2001). "Maestro, what is quality?" Language, literacy and discourse in project-based science. *Journal of Research in Science Teaching, 38,* 469–495.

Morag, O., & Tal, T. (2012). Assessing learning in the outdoors with the Field Trip in Natural Environments (FiNE) framework. *International Journal of Science Education, 34*(5), 745–777.

Mortensen, M. F. (2010). Museographic transposition: The development of a museum exhibit on animal adaptations to darkness. *Éducation & Didactique, 4*(1), 119–137.

Mortensen, M. F. (2011). Analysis of the educational potential of a science museum learning environment: Visitors' experience with and understanding of an immersion exhibit. *International Journal of Science Education, 33*(4), 517–545.

Mortensen, M. F., & Smart, K. (2007). Free-choice worksheets increase students' exposure to curriculum during museum visits. *Journal of Research in Science Teaching, 44*(9), 1389–1414.

Moussouri, T., & Roussos, G. (2013). Examining the effect of visitor motivation on observed visit strategies using mobile computer technologies. *Visitor Studies, 16*(1), 21–38.

Myers, O. E., Jr., Saunders, C. D., & Birjulin, A. A. (2004). Emotional dimensions of watching zoo animals: An experience sampling study building on insights from psychology. *Curator: The Museum Journal, 47*(3), 299–321.

National Science Board. (2013). *The science and engineering indicators 2012*. Arlington, VA: National Science Foundation. Retrieved from www.nsf.gov/statistics/seind12/pdf/c07.pdf

OECD. (2012, July). Are students more engaged when schools offer extracurricular activities? *PISA in Focus, 2012/7*, 4.l. Retrieved from www.oecd.org/edu/pisa%20in%20focus%20n18%20(eng)-v05.pdf

Orthia, L.A., Dobos, A.R., Guy, T., Kan, S.Z., Keys, S.E., Nekvapil, S., & Ngu, D.H. (2012). How do people think about the science they encounter in fiction? Undergraduates investigate responses to science in *The Simpsons*. *International Journal of Science Education, Part B: Communication and Public Engagement, 2*(2), 149–174.

Oxarart, A.L., Monroe, M.C., & Plate, R.R. (2013). From play areas to natural areas: The role of zoos in getting families outdoors. *Visitor Studies, 16*(1), 82–94.

Palmquist, S., & Crowley, K. (2007). From teachers to testers: How parents talk to novice and expert children in a natural history museum. *Science Education, 91*(5), 783–804.

Pedretti, E. (2012). The medium is the message: Unravelling visitors' views of Body Worlds and the story of the heart. In E. Davidsson & A. Jakobsson (Eds.), *Understanding interactions at science centers and museums* (pp. 45–61). Rotterdam, the Netherlands: Sense Publishers.

Perdue, B.M., Stoinski, T.S., & Maple, T.L. (2012). Using technology to educate visitors about conservation. *Visitor Studies, 15*(1), 16–27.

Phillips, M., Finkelstein, D., & Wever-Frerichs, S. (2007). School site to museum floor: How informal science institutions work with schools. *International Journal of Science Education, 29*(12), 1489–1507.

Phipps, M. (2010). Research trends and findings from a decade (1997–2007) of research on informal science education and free-choice science learning. *Visitor Studies, 13*(1), 3–22.

Pierroux, P., Krange, I., & Sem, I. (2011). Bridging contexts and interpretations: Mobile blogging on art museum field trips. *MedieKultur Journal of Media and Communication Research, 50*, 30–47.

Piqueras, J., Wickman, P.-O., & Hamza, K.M. (2012). Student teachers' moment-to-moment reasoning and the development of discursive themes. In E. Davidsson & A. Jakobsson (Eds.), *Understanding interactions at science centers and museums* (pp. 79–96). Rotterdam, the Netherlands: Sense Publishers.

QA Research. (2008). *"Out of school" trips research*. Retrieved from www.nationalforest.org/document/visitor/Industry/Out_of_school_trips_national_research_findings.pdf

Rahm, J. (2012). Activity theory as a lens to examine project-based museum partnerships in robotics: Tools, challenges and emergent learning opportunities. In E. Davidsson & A. Jakobsson (Eds.), *Understanding interactions at science centers and museums* (pp. 147–171). Rotterdam, the Netherlands: Sense Publishers.

Randler, C., Kummer, B., & Wilhelm, C. (2012). Adolescent learning in the zoo: Embedding a non-formal learning environment to teach formal aspects of vertebrate biology. *Journal of Science Education and Technology, 21*, 384–391.

Reiss, M.J., & Tunnicliffe, S.D. (2011). Dioramas as depictions of reality and opportunities for learning in biology. *Curator: The Museum Journal, 54*(4), 447–459.

Rennie, L.J. (2007a). Learning science outside of school. In S.K. Abell & N.G. Lederman (Eds.), *Handbook of research on science education* (pp. 125–167). Mahwah, NJ: Lawrence Erlbaum Associates.

Rennie, L.J. (2007b). Values in science portrayed in out-of-school contexts. In D. Corrigan, D. Gunstone, & J. Dillon (Eds.), *The re-emergence of values in science education* (pp. 197–212). Rotterdam, the Netherlands: Sense Publications.

Rennie, L.J. (2011). Blurring the boundary between the classroom and the community: Challenges for teachers' professional learning. In D. Corrigan, J. Dillon, & R. Gunstone (Eds.), *The professional knowledge base of science teaching* (pp. 13–29). Dordrecht, the Netherlands: Springer.

Rennie, L.J. (2013). The practice of science and technology communication in science museums. In J.K. Gilbert & S. Stocklmayer (Eds.), *Communication and engagement in the informal sector: Issues and dilemmas* (pp. 197–211). London: Routledge.

Rennie, L.J., & Johnston, D.J. (2007). Research on learning from museums. In J.H. Falk, L.D. Dierking, & S. Foutz (Eds.), *In principle, in practice: Museums as learning institutions* (pp. 57–73). Walnut Creek, CA: AltaMira Press.

Rennie, L.J., & Williams, G.F. (2006a). Communication about science in a traditional museum: Visitors' and staff's perceptions. *Cultural Studies of Science Education, 1*, 791–820. Retrieved from www.springerlink.com/content/b4k4082561696l18/

Rennie, L.J., & Williams, G.F. (2006b). Adults' learning about science in free-choice settings. *International Journal of Science Education, 28*, 871–893.

Riedinger, K. (2012). Family connections: Family conversations in informal learning environments. *Childhood Education, 88*(2), 125–127.

Rowe, S., & Kisiel, J.A. (2012). Family engagement at aquarium touch tanks—exploring interactions and the potential for learning. In E. Davidsson & A. Jakobsson (Eds.), *Understanding interactions at science centers and museums* (pp. 63–77). Rotterdam, the Netherlands: Sense Publishers.

Rowe, S., & Nickels, A. (2011). Visitor motivations across three informal education institutions: An application of the identity-related visitor motivation model. *Visitor Studies, 14*(2), 162–175.

Rowell, P.M. (2012). *Perspectives on programs for schools in science centres and museums*. Edmonton: Centre for Mathematics, Science and Technology Education, University of Alberta.

Sanders, D.L. (2007). Making public the private life of plants: The contribution of informal learning environments. *International Journal of Science Education, 29*(10), 1209–1228.

Sanford, C. (2010). Evaluating family interactions to inform exhibit design: Comparing three different learning behaviors in a museum setting. *Visitor Studies, 13*(1), 67–89.

Schuck, S., & Aubusson, P. (2010). Educational scenarios for digital futures. *Learning, Media and Technology, 35*(3), 293–305.

Semper, R. (2007). Science centers at 40: Middle-aged maturity or midlife crisis? *Curator: The Museum Journal, 50*(1), 147–150.

Serrell, B. (1998). *Paying attention: Visitors and museum exhibitions*. Washington, DC: American Association of Museums.

Serrell, B. (2010). *Paying more attention to paying attention*. Retrieved from www.informalscience.org/perspectives/blog/paying-more-attention-to-paying-attention

Sfard, A. (1998). On two metaphors for learning and the dangers of choosing just one. *Educational Researcher, 27*(2), 4–13.

Siegel, D.R., Esterly, J., Callanan, M.A., Wright, R., & Navarro, R. (2007). Conversations about science across activities in Mexican-descent families. *International Journal of Science Education, 29*(12), 1447–1466.

Simonneaux, L., & Jacobi, D. (1997). Language constraints in producing prefiguration posters for a scientific exhibition. *Public Understanding of Science, 6*(4), 383–408.

Smith, E. (2012). Mobile game of the week—Plague Inc. *International Business Times*, October 12. Retrieved from www.ibtimes.co.uk/articles/393735/20121012/mobile-game-week-plague-inc-android-ios.htm

Smith, L., Weiler, B., & Ham, S. (2011). The rhetoric versus the reality: A critical examination of the zoo proposition. In W. Frost (Ed.), *Zoos and tourism: Conservation, education, entertainment?* (pp. 59–68). Bristol, UK: Channel View Publications.

Song, Y., Wong, L.-H., & Looi, C.-K. (2012). Fostering personalized learning in science inquiry supported by mobile technologies. *Education Technology Research & Development, 60*(4), 679–701.

Stavrova, O., & Urhahne, D. (2010). Modification of a school programme in the Deutsches Museum to enhance students' attitudes and understanding. *International Journal of Science Education, 32*(17), 2291–2310.

Steinke, J. (2013). Portrayals of female scientists in the mass media: End times for a media history paradigm. *The International Encyclopedia of Media Studies*. Retrieved from http://onlinelibrary.wiley.com/doi/10.1002/9781444361506.wbiems070/full

Stocklmayer, S. M., & Gilbert, J. K. (2002). New experiences and old knowledge: Towards a model for the public awareness of science. *International Journal of Science Education, 24,* 835–858.

Stocklmayer, S. M., Rennie, L. J., & Gilbert, J. K. (2010). The roles of the formal and informal sectors in the provision of effective science education. *Studies in Science Education, 46,* 1–44.

Szechter, L. E., & Carey, E. J. (2009). Gravitating toward science: Parent–child interactions at a gravitational-wave observatory. *Science Education, 93*(5), 846–858.

Tal, R., Bamberger, Y., & Morag, O. (2005). Guided school visits to natural history museums in Israel: Teachers' roles. *Science Education, 89*(6), 920–935.

Tal, T. (2012). Imitating the family visit: Small-group exploration in an ecological garden. In E. Davidsson & A. Jakobsson (Eds.), *Understanding interactions at science centers and museums* (pp. 193–206). Rotterdam, the Netherlands: Sense Publishers.

Tal, T., & Morag, O. (2007). School visits to natural history museums: Teaching or enriching? *Journal of Research in Science Teaching, 44*(5), 747–769.

Tal, T., & Morag, O. (2009). Reflective practice as a means for preparing to teach outdoors in an ecological garden. *Journal of Science Teacher Education, 20*(3), 245–262.

Thomas, G. P., & Anderson, D. (2013). Parents' metacognitive knowledge: Influences on parent–child interactions in a science museum setting. *Research in Science Education, 43*(3), 1245–1265.

Tlili, A., Cribb, A., & Gewirtz, S. (2006). What becomes of science in a science centre? Reconfiguring science for public consumption. *The Review of Education, Pedagogy, and Cultural Studies, 28,* 203–228.

Tran, L. U. (2008). The work of science museum educators. *Museum Management and Curatorship, 23*(2), 135–153.

Tran, L. U., & King, H. (2007). The professionalization of museum educators: The case of science museums. *Museum Management and Curatorship, 22*(2), 131–149.

Tunnicliffe, S. D., & Scheersoi, A. (2010). Natural history dioramas: Dusty relics or essential tools for biology learning? In A. Filippoupoliti (Ed.), *Science exhibitions: Communication and evaluation* (pp. 186–216). Edinburgh, Scotland: MuseumsEtc.

Ucko, D. A. (2013). Science centers in a new world of learning. *Curator: The Museum Journal, 56*(1), 21–30.

Van Schijndel, T. J. P., Franse, R. K., & Raijmakers, M. E. J. (2010). The Exploratory Behavior Scale: Assessing young visitors' hands-on behavior in science museums. *Science Education, 94*(5), 794–809.

Van Schijndel, T. J. P., Singer, E., Van der Maas, H. L. J., & Raijmakers, M. E. J. (2010). The effects of a sciencing program on young children's exploratory play in the sandpit. *European Journal of Developmental Psychology, 7*(5), 603–617.

Venville, G., Rennie, L., Hanbury, C., & Longnecker, N. (2013). Scientists reflect on why they chose to study science. *Research in Science Education.* doi:10.1007/s11165-013-9352-3

Vestergård, G. L. (2011). From journal to headline: The accuracy of climate science news in Danish high quality newspapers. *Journal of Science Communication, 10*(2), A03. Retrieved from http://jcom.sissa.it/archive/10/02/Jcom1002(2011)A03/

Walker, G. J. (2012). Science shows: Past, present and future. *The Informal Learning Review, 116,* 4–7.

Wilde, M., & Urhahne, D. (2008). Museum learning: A study of motivation and learning achievement. *Journal of Biological Education, 42*(2), 78–83.

Wong, L.-H. (2012). A learner-centric view of mobile seamless learning. *British Journal of Educational Technology, 43*(1), E19–E23.

Wong, L.-H., & Looi, C.-K. (2011). What seams do we remove in mobile-assisted seamless learning? A critical review of the literature. *Computers & Education, 57*(4), 2364–2381.

World Association of Zoos and Aquariums. (2005). *Building a future for wildlife—the world zoo and aquarium conservation strategy.* Retrieved from www.waza.org/files/webcontent/1.public_site/5.conservation/conservation_strategies/building_a_future_for_wildlife/wzacs-en.pdf

Wyles, K. J., Pahl, S., White, M., Morris, S., Cracknell, D., & Thompson, R. C. (2013). Towards a marine mindset: Visiting an aquarium can improve attitudes and intentions regarding marine sustainability. *Visitor Studies, 16*(1), 95–110.

Yalowitz, S. S., & Bronnenkant, K. (2009). Timing and tracking: Unlocking visitor behavior. *Visitor Studies, 12*(1), 47–64.

Zimmerman, H. T. (2012). Participating in science at home: Recognition work and learning in biology. *Journal of Research in Science Teaching, 49*(5), 597–630.

Zimmerman, H. T., & Bell, P. (2012). Where young people see science: Everyday activities connected to science. *International Journal of Science Education, Part B: Communication and Public Engagement.* doi:10.1080/21548455.2012.741271

Zimmerman, H. T., Reeve, S., & Bell, P. (2010). Family sense-making practices in science center conversations. *Science Education, 94*(3), 478–505.

8

Teaching Learning Progressions

An International Perspective

Per-Olof Wickman

This chapter reviews how science education has been approached and developed in Europe within the discipline of didactics. It particularly reviews science didactics in Germany, the Netherlands, France, and Sweden with regard to how teachers can better support students' learning progressions in science. The research schools selected represent well-developed systematic models to support teachers' selection of content and ways of teaching with this aim. They are all comparatively recent, and concrete examples are given to show how these models have been used and are developed further. The different schools do not simply represent competing models but can be seen as complementary, emphasizing various aspects that all are important for teachers.

Didactics as the Professional Science of Teachers

Anyone from an English-speaking country who has visited a European science education institution or conference outside Britain has come across *Didaktik, didactiques*, or similar constructs. In the English language, this word is mainly known as a derogative adjective. In Europe, however, this is the name of an academic discipline, usually translated to *didactics* in English. Here *didactic* means "having to do with the discipline didactics." The term originates from the Greek *didaskein*, which means to teach or educate. Didactics originates in Central Europe and can be traced back to 17th-century curriculum reforms in Germany (Knecht-von Martial, 1985).

Today the discipline is unique to teacher education and the teacher profession. In many European countries, didactics is recognized as the professional science of teachers (cf. Schneuwly, 2011; Seel, 1999; Wickman, 2012a). Professionally, didactics plays a similar role to teachers as that of medicine to physicians or engineering to engineers. An interesting comparison can be made between the establishment of the discipline of didactics in Europe and

Lee Shulman's (1987) efforts in the United States of trying to formulate what the unique expertise and knowledge base of teachers are (Fensham, 2003). However, one crucial difference is that didactics is not merely an effort to define teachers' knowledge base but is an effort to develop an academic discipline at teacher education institutions.

The difference between the United States and Europe is often described as a difference between a curriculum tradition and a didactics tradition (Fensham, 2003; Riquarts & Hopmann, 1995). Generally, in the United States, research on subject content came to be largely lost in educational research during the 1900s (Shulman, 1986). In the didactics tradition, on the other hand, a connection was built between content and pedagogy during the same period through different systematic efforts of developing analytic instruments to support teachers' professional decisions. Didactic analysis starts in an analysis of content to be taught. To the curriculum tradition, teaching and learning in the classroom was the end of a long chain of decisions starting from the needs of society, implemented in the classroom, and to be followed up with standardized testing. There was little room for teachers making decisions on the content, especially as researchers were busy trying to find teacher-proof reforms, which would reduce the gap between the intended and the learned curriculum caused by inefficient teaching (Eryaman & Riedler, 2010).

Of course this is a simplification. The development of didactics has not been straightforward anywhere in Europe, in the haphazard political field of education, where there always seems to be a crisis that needs to be quickly remedied without consulting practicing teachers or researchers in didactics. After World War II, didactics has had to withstand strong influences from the curriculum tradition (Riquarts & Hopmann, 1995). Also, globalized testing seems to have favored less trust in teacher professionalism. For example, Sweden has introduced more detailed national standards and also nationwide testing in science in compulsory school as a response to declining school results in the PISA and TIMSS studies. Finland, on the other hand, which repeatedly has come out on top in the PISA, has continued with its high dependence on teacher professionalism, still with very open standards and with no national testing of compulsory school students (Sahlberg, 2011).

However, even when teachers have been granted significant freedom to decide content, strong teaching traditions nevertheless reduce the options available to them. An important aim for didactic research is thus to make teachers critically aware that there are other options than those suggested by local tradition. Seen in this way, a pluralism of teaching traditions is a resource to draw on.

The differences aside, today science education research and science didactics research share many common interests across the Atlantic. Content issue debates today are livelier in North America than ever, through research on curriculum emphases (Duschl, 2008; Roberts, 1982), scientific literacy and science for everyday life (Aikenhead, 2006; Linder, Östman, Roberts, Wickman, Erickson, & MacKinnon, 2011; Roberts & Bybee, 2014; Roth & Calabrese Barton, 2004), learning about the epistemology and nature of science (Duschl & Jiménez-Aleixandre, 2012; Lederman, 2014), socioscientific issues (Sadler, 2009) and argumentation on science-related issues (Erduran & Jiménez-Aleixandre, 2007). Still, in a policy statement by Duncan and Rivet (2013) in *Science* magazine regarding the new U.S. national standards, selection of content is a matter of finding student learning progressions that will produce the correct learning of the science curriculum. Duncan and Rivet (2013) do not mention scientific literacy or socioscientific issues. Scientists and students are mentioned repeatedly but teachers only once as a possible obstacle to reform. Teachers' knowledge and current practice are not advanced as resources to build on for curriculum reform.

The Field of Didactic Inquiry

The central questions of didactics are "*What* content is to be taught?", "*How* is this content going to be taught?", and "*Why* teach this content and *why* with these methods?" Didactics thus has a critical stance in supporting teachers' choices of content and methods, beyond what state requirements prescribe as the given content. Teachers should not just be able to choose and practice appropriate methods to teach a certain given content but also be able to understand which content should be selected within the frames given by society and the circumstances set by their school and their students, and the actual content that results as learning through the teaching of certain content in certain ways with certain students (Wickman, 2012a). The why-question emphasizes the need for rationality; teachers should be able to give reasons publicly for their choices, not only in meeting students and parents but also as experts in the public debate on curriculum issues. This is why a science of didactics is needed, and this is the primary purpose of didactics: to share such systematic

grounds for choices beyond established prescriptions and traditions. This idea is similar to Shulman's (1986, p. 13) rendering of teachers' professionalism:

> The professional holds knowledge, not only of how—the capacity for skilled performance—but of what and why. The teacher is not only a master of procedure but also of content and rationale, and capable of explaining why something is done.

Teachers should be first authorities on the rationales and consequences of choosing certain content and methods. This is particularly important in a democratic society, in which they make these decisions with other stakeholders and in which these stakeholders need to be informed by teachers on didactic questions.

Traditionally, didactics is understood as dealing with the system of the so-called didactic triangle, that is, the relationship among the teacher, the student(s), and the content. How the students and the teacher jointly enact the content is critical for the education of students (Hudson & Meyer, 2011; Sensevy, 2011), not just with regard to the knowledge and skills learned but also for their learning of values (Östman, 1994, 1996; Wickman, 2006). A professional teacher is the orchestrator of the relationship of the didactic triangle, from the curriculum and its texts through teaching to students' learning (Ligozat, 2011; cf. Cuban, 1992). In these processes, teachers enact a *transposition* (Chevallard, 2007; Tiberghien, 2007) of the curriculum through planning and all the bit-by-bit choices as part of classroom transactions with the students and the setting. In the classroom, the didactic relationships of the triangle must be within bounds of the *zone of proximal development* (ZPD), defined as

> . . . the distance between the actual development level [of the child] as determined by independent problem solving and the level of potential development as determined through problem solving under adult guidance or in collaboration with more capable peers.
> (Vygotsky, 1978, p. 86)

Learning progressions can be defined as the pathways "by which children can bridge their starting point and the desired end point" (National Resource Council, 2007, p. 214). Such progressions are beyond learning and also require a teacher. Approaching the didactic triangle and its transposition through the ZPD highlights the necessity of clarifying, on the one hand, students' starting points and, on the other hand, to which end point teachers (and peers) can take students and what roles are ascribed to students and teachers, respectively, in such a progression.

The ZPD will be used as a tool in this review to inquire into how different didactic models have been used to support teachers in their work. The ZPD can be understood in more or less individualistic or social terms. Sfard (1998) used the two metaphors *acquisition* and *participation* to illustrate this difference. Formulated in more social and actional terms rather than just from an individual and mental understanding, the ZPD does not merely concern the acquisition of knowledge by the learner but a visible process of changed participation situated within *communities of practice* (Wenger, 1998). So as to avoid restricting my review to only one perspective, the ZPD will be discussed along this whole range.

Teaching is a complex transactional process that cannot be fully reconstructed from official documents, research, or planning but depends on what happens in the classroom. However, rendering of the teacher's job only within the system of the didactic triangle risks overlooking the fact that what is happening among the actors of the didactic triangle is not set in a vacuum (Hudson & Meyer, 2011). The professional teacher needs to consider how the material, social, and institutional conditions for teaching interact with choices of content and methods (Ligozat, 2011; Seel, 1999). At the same time, "[t]o conduct a piece of research scholars must necessarily narrow their scope, focus their view, and formulate a question far less complex than the form in which the world presents itself in practice. This holds for any piece of research; there are no exceptions" (Shulman, 1986, p. 6).

For these reasons, we need to constantly remind ourselves that the teacher's work cannot be reduced just to theories. Didactics is usually referred to as a *science* rather than an *art*. Still, the discipline has preserved the close relationship between theory and action orientation, understanding theory as an underdetermination of what it means to be a teacher (Jank & Meyer, 2003). Theory has to be understood in relation to practice, and so didactics as the professional science of teachers needs a strong emphasis on teaching as an art (cf. May, 1993). Didactics researchers therefore also need to do research on how theory can best interact with teachers' practice and decision making and thus modify theory in interaction with teachers (Lijnse & Klaassen, 2004; Parchmann et al., 2006; Wickman, 2012a).

The Science Subject Content From the Didactics Point of View

To science education research, the science content is as central to any inquiry into teaching and learning as it is to didactics. The discipline of science didactics would not make sense without an inquiry into the subject content, just as teaching without content is inconceivable. Nevertheless, to didactics, the content of specific school disciplines is not, as a matter of course, taken as derived merely from the corresponding academic subjects. In many European countries, this is reflected by the name of the school subject, especially in primary school, which is not *science* but *nature studies* or similar names that transcend science (Hansen & Olson, 1996; Wickman, Liberg, & Östman, 2012). In Sweden, for example, content in the subjects dealing with science in compulsory school traditionally have included elements such as everyday appliances, use of natural resources, health, ethics, and nature relations

(see also Fensham, 2003, p. 151). According to such an understanding, the aims are not primarily concerned with making students understand science proper but rather with contributing to the *Bildung* of the growing person. The question is rather how the science content chosen can contribute to the *Bildung* or growth of the person as a whole.

In many European countries, didactics has a close coupling to *Bildung* (Duit, Gropengießer, Kattmann, Komorek, & Pachmann, 2012). The German concept of *Bildung* has origins almost as old as those of didactics. Its current usage primarily can be traced to the 19th century (Biesta, 2002; Peukert, 2002). *Bildung* means *formation* or *constitution*, and just like these English words, *Bildung* deals both with the process of becoming and its result as a state of being (a related usage of formation is to be found in *formative assessment*). It is based on an idea of becoming human by cultivation of one's dispositions in a way that is true to those dispositions but also to the development of society. *Bildung* in this way does not only mean being a well-informed citizen but also encompasses the formation of values and of moral and aesthetic judgments. In the 19th century, these ideals of *Bildung* came to be restricted to the upper classes and Latin schools and typically associated with conservative notions of morality and taste (Wickman et al., 2012). However, already at the birth of didactics in the 17th-century curriculum reforms, education also encompassed natural history and was aimed at what today may be called *Bildung* for all (Knecht-von Martial, 1985). John Amos Comenius, one of the founders of didactics, in his *Didactica Magna* (1633–1638), maintained that didactics is based on *omnes omnia docere*—that is, teaching everything to everyone (Riquarts & Hopmann, 1995).

Bildung or allgemeine Bildung (generic *Bildung*) still has a strong position and association with didactics. It now usually is adopted in the original more inclusive sense as an aim for all students and school subjects (Hansen & Olson, 1996). It is often also given a more critical meaning, in which the relationship to other areas of knowledge (e.g., technology and society) and to values is examined (Hansen & Olson, 1996). For example, a standard text in science teacher education in Scandinavian countries is Svein Sjøberg's (2011) book titled *Science as allgemeine Bildung—a critical subject didactics*, which analyzes what science subject matter belongs to the allgemeine *Bildung* of the citizen today.

Bildung can be related to *scientific literacy* (Wickman et al., 2012). Scientific literacy is not easily defined, but it usually encompasses competencies that are closely related to ideals of using scientific knowledge for personal and societal aims beyond the science pipeline (Roberts & Bybee, 2014). In encompassing questions of decision making, scientific literacy also necessarily includes values and moral judgments (Östman & Almqvist, 2011; Zeidler, 1984; Zeidler & Sadler, 2011).

Today a distinction often is made between *general didactics* and *subject didactics*. The discipline *science education* in Europe is an instance of subject didactics and may be translated to *subject didactics of science* or simply *science didactics.* Helmut Seel (1999) and Bernard Schneuwly (2011) have discussed the problems of the relationship between general and subject didactics. Didactics necessarily deals with content, and science is one such content. At the same time, didactics associates content with *Bildung*, and there is no necessary connection just to the academic science subjects but also to engineering, ethics, agriculture, medicine, outdoor education, sustainable development, philosophy of science, and so forth. Moreover, there are also more general principles when choosing content and how to teach, beyond science, on which the professional teacher depends.

There is no easy solution to this matter for teacher education. Didactics is often split into the disciplines *general didactics* and different disciplines of *subject didactics.* The irony of this solution is that an informed critical discussion of content may be lost from both disciplines. General didactics concerns more general principles with little emphasis on the transposition of a specific content for teaching. At the same time, science didactics, dominated by teachers trained in academic science, risks transforming science didactics into science education as known from the curriculum tradition, in which content is taken for granted and not critically discussed from a *Bildung* perspective.

In this regard, the development of *comparative didactics* in France offers a fruitful alternative (Caillot, 2007). In France, subject content is understood in an inclusive sense as the school subject, the academic subject, and what surrounds it (e.g., philosophy, history, and science in society). Within each subject area, theoretical concepts are forged, which should be developed with the aim of supporting didactic situations and the understanding of didactic phenomena of a certain subject. At the same time, these concepts have proven to have validity beyond certain school subjects. For example, the concepts of *didactic transpositions* and *didactic contract* (see following sections), developed in mathematics didactics, have had great use in other school subjects including science (Tiberghien, 2007; Tiberghien, Vince, & Gaidioz, 2009). This is the program of comparative didactics: to arrange meetings between didacticians from different subjects, to critically compare the methods and concepts they use for mutual benefit (Caillot, 2007).

Some European Orientations in Didactics

In Germany, there is a tradition of working with *didactic models* and *didactic analysis.* These two concepts are closely related. A didactic model is based on assumptions about how didactic theory and practice can fruitfully interact, and it is used for didactic analysis of preparation and realization of didactic action (teaching and learning)—that is, for what in current parlance is often called didactic design (Ruthven, Laborde, Leach, & Tiberghien, 2009).

Different basic theoretical assumptions result in different suggestions for action (Blankertz, 1975). I here draw on these two notions in reviewing didactics.

A number of orientations have developed in Europe to support didactic decisions in teaching science. I will here review four major schools from Germany, the Netherlands, France, and Sweden. They are chosen because they draw on somewhat different but overlapping assumptions and because all permit didactic analysis based on comprehensive and systematic didactic models. By adopting the concept of ZPD and communities of practice, a common framework is adopted to examine how the various models support teachers' analysis and enactment of a transposition of content for progression. The rationale for the order in which schools are presented is a gradual transition from modeling the ZPD as a conceptual distance to one in which it is approached as the bridging of practices.

The Model of Educational Reconstruction in Germany

A widely used didactic model in German science education is the *model of educational (didactic) reconstruction* (MER; Duit et al., 2012). The aim of MER is to scaffold the design of teaching-learning sequences that support students' learning and understanding of science. MER is used by researchers to construct units, which are presented to teachers, and to explicate to teachers why the units have been designed in a particular way and what this means for teacher action. Its basic theoretical assumptions draw on conceptual change and social constructivism (Komorek & Duit, 2004). Of central concern are students' conceptions, which are used as "points to start from and mental instruments to work with in further learning" (Duit et al., 2012, p. 20). At the same time, MER is specifically aimed at avoiding "one-sidedness" in curriculum, either in terms of science content structures or of students' conceptions (Duit, Komorek, & Wilbers, 1997). Here the idea of *Bildung* as conceived by the German educator Wolfgang Klafki (1958, 1969) in his didactic analysis plays a critical role (Duit et al., 2012).

Klafki's (1958, 1969) didactic analysis encompasses five didactic questions (as translated in Duit et al., 2012, p. 17):

1. What is the more general idea that is represented by the content of interest? What basic phenomena or basic principles, what general laws, criteria, methods, techniques, or attitudes may be addressed in an exemplary way by dealing with the content?
2. What is the significance of the referring content or the experiences, knowledge, abilities, and skills to be achieved by dealing with the content in students' actual intellectual life? What is the significance the content should have from a pedagogical point of view?
3. What is the significance of the content for students' future life?

4. What is the structure of the content if viewed from the pedagogical perspectives outlined in questions 1 through 3?

5. What are the particular cases, phenomena, situations, or experiments that allow making the structure of the referring content interesting, worth questioning, accessible, and understandable for the students?

This is a *Bildung*-oriented analysis asking how certain already-established content could be chosen and presented in a way that is not only understood by students but also useful to them in their *Bildung* for current and future life. According to the social constructivist theoretical orientation of the MER, it is supplemented by an assumption of how students' intellectual and attitudinal preconditions (e.g., interests, preconceptions) and their sociocultural preconditions (e.g., norms of society) influence choice of aims, content, and methods and media of instruction. The design has to take equal notice of the science content to be learned (in the sense of scientific literacy or *Bildung*) as to the cognitive and affective variables of students linked to the content (Duit, Komorek, & Wilbers, 1997).

The process of educational reconstruction utilizes turns of three nested components: (1) analysis of content structure, (2) construction of instruction, and (3) empirical investigations on learning processes. It starts from a clarification of science subject matter through analyses of textbooks, curricula, research reports, and so forth regarding how the topics of the content are connected and are exemplars of more general ideas and the current and future meaning they may have for students and society (Komorek & Duit, 2004). It encompasses an empirical and literature investigation into students' perspectives and conceptions on the subject matter area. These steps are used to construct a clarification of basic (elementary) concepts to be taught and learned in relation to the whole. In this way, the content is said to be *elementarized* but also *contextualized* (Duit et al., 2012).

In many cases, this initial step is followed by *teaching experiments* before the successive try-out of the unit in cycles in the classroom for the completion of its conceptual structure and final outline (Komorek & Duit, 2004). The model is a way of taking into account that an academic science structure may not simply be transferred directly into a teaching sequence but that the content structure of the unit has to be made by taking into consideration the wider societal and personal significance of the content as well as the possible learning trajectories of students.

The teaching experiment is useful to this end. It originates from work by Leslie Steffe and colleagues in mathematics education (see Steffe & Thompson, 2000) and has been adopted for use in science education (see Komorek & Duit, 2004). The teaching experiment is derived from the clinical interviews of Piaget but is organized as a learning situation for the interviewee. The interviewer takes the role of one who is interested in inquiring into the students' ideas and finding ways of developing them. Often the "interview" lasts for several sessions in which interventions are tried out to develop the students' conceptions. The interviews can be carried out with single students or with a couple of students to examine how a community of learners can support learning (Komorek & Duit, 2004; Riemeier & Gopengießer, 2008). In this way, the learning experiment is used as a powerful tool to supplement and render the MER process more efficient.

Typically, the content structures as learning process are formulated in terms of the role of analogies and the relationship between students' everyday knowledge and scientific knowledge (Duit et al., 1997). For example, Tanja Riemeier and Harald Gopengießer (2008) used teaching experiments to find out ninth-grade students' conceptions of cell division prior to interviews and how they change due to interventions with different analogies. The researchers used, for instance, the analogy of dividing a chocolate bar to make students see that cell division alone cannot result in plant growth but that also enlargement is required.

MER offers a way "to analyse critically and investigate whether a certain science content is worth teaching and learning and may be achieved by the learner" (Duit et al., 1997). The assumption of MER is that content is mainly conceptual and analogical and along constructivist notions that learning ultimately is the construction of concepts used to make sense of the world. Teaching and learning starts in already-acquired concepts and ends in the concepts acquired through teaching and learning. A tool to make the ZPD visible is the teaching experiment, in which it is operationalized as how the teacher, through metaphors and analogical reasoning, can support students' everyday understanding and explaining to be successively developed into more scientific ones. It is emphasized, however, that this progression is mainly one of conceptual growth rather than one of radical conceptual exchange. Students' conceptions are not foremost approached as hurdles but as resources to build on for the teacher (Duit et al., 2012). However, except for acknowledging the role of students in supporting each other's conceptual learning, learning originally was not examined as the transformation of participation in communities of practice.

Using Context in Germany

With regard to the conceptual emphasis of MER, influences from the German movement of *Chemistry in Context* (ChiK) has been important (Duit et al., 2012) for incorporating the idea of communities of practice and also how emphasizing important aspects of the relevance of the concepts as part of different contexts, beyond analogies, in organizing teaching units. ChiK has the two-fold aim of improving secondary chemistry teaching and learning and of supporting teacher collaboration and cooperation between science educators and teachers. Such cooperative reform efforts of teachers and science educators are described as a symbiotic implementation to build strong and continuous *communities of learners* (Parchmann et al., 2006).

The expertise of researchers and teachers is respected, and participation means professional development for both groups. Related approaches are to be found in the German program *Physics in Context* (Duit et al., 2012) and in similar programs for chemistry in the Netherlands (see next sections).

Because there is a great diversity of German chemistry curricula and variable sets of conditions for teachers, there is not one best way to teach ChiK. In line with a German didactics tradition of finding exemplary content and methods rather than best practice, ChiK tries to find a general common framework to start from and use it to produce exemplary units and teaching materials. These are then used in trials and revised so that they can be used successfully by teachers in different conditions (Parchmann et al., 2006). In extension, these exemplary units have been used to devise whole curricula and so have transformed the program into an established part of the curriculum (Demuth, Gräsel, Parchmann, & Ralle, 2008).

Just like MER, ChiK is based on constructivist learning theories, and contexts are important means to situate chemistry in student-oriented ways, which at the same time enable students to develop a more systematic understanding of chemistry (Parchmann et al., 2006). Contexts have three functions in the project: (1) they are the source of questions that should produce a demand for basic chemistry concepts through the exercise of certain scientific activities (e.g., research, experimentation, communication); (2) they should provide a motive for active learning; and (3) they should support the learning of application of knowledge (e.g., in decision making) but also its transfer between units. Contexts are drawn from daily life, from societal issues, and from science proper (Parchmann et al., 2006).

The results suggest that the units have been well received by teachers and students and that they are successfully adapted to local circumstances. The variety of teaching methods used by teachers has increased, as has student participation. The largest problem concerns the central question of content. The units do not support the "abstraction" of general basic chemistry concepts as expected (Parchmann et al., 2006, p. 1055). The student-oriented approach can easily "lead to a feeling of getting lost in the context" (Ibid., p. 1041). It is thus as if the teachers have difficulties in supporting students in seeing how scientific concepts (e.g., regarding matter and particles) can be used in dealing with contexts (e.g., food, fuels).

Using Contexts in the Netherlands

Efforts in connecting contexts and concepts have been made also by Astrid Bulte, Hanna Westbroek, Onno de Jong, and Albert Pilot (2006) and colleagues from a curriculum-reform program in chemistry education at the secondary level in the Netherlands. Initially, their primary aim was that of using context to improve students' conceptual understanding (Bulte, 2007). However, to remedy

the problems of connecting concepts and context, the focus tended to shift from context as a setting for conceptual learning toward understanding context as practice, in which concepts and activities are valued because they are part of practice (Westbroek, Klaassen, Bulte, & Pilot, 2010). A basic principle for choosing content in terms of such contexts is that the context should reflect an authentic practice involving chemistry and that this practice presents a problem, which creates a *need to know* for students. The road to this change in the relationship between context and concepts is reported in Bulte and colleagues (2006) and Bulte (2007).

Bulte and colleagues (2006) and Bulte (2007) refer to three consecutive didactic models (called *frameworks*), which were used by the researchers in finding contexts for three successive sequences, which students would find worthwhile and that would promote learning chemistry conceptually as well as practically. All of these sequences dealt with contexts of analyzing the quality of surface water in the neighborhood to see if it was good enough for specific functions (e.g., drinking).

According to Bulte and colleagues (2006), Sequence 1 was developed using the same framework as ChiK and was divided into three phases. First, the students were told that they were going to judge water quality during the next five lessons and were then asked questions to help them see what they needed to know to analyze water quality in relation to specific functions. This first phase was supposed to assist students in understanding the kind of problems that the context involved. In the next phase, they were taught more general conceptual knowledge about accuracy of measurement. Finally, the students had to solve a problem applying the conceptual knowledge. Although students enjoyed the conceptual phase, they were not capable of applying it in dealing with the problem. The students were not able to judge the usefulness of the concepts taught, because the second part was not contextualized from the students' perspective of relevance and need to know in relation to solving the problem. Only the expert, already familiar with the use of the general concepts, could see the point of them before inquiry.

Building on Piet Lijnse and Kees Klaassen (2004), Bulte and colleagues (2006) argue that there has to be an improved progression in the sequence so that each step makes the students see the point of learning the content of the next step in a way that furthers them in the direction of solving the problem (Bulte et al., 2006). Lijnse and Klaassen (2004) use examples from physics to illustrate how sequences can be developed with a wide range of aims, from physical theory and the nature of physics to generic skills such as problem solving. Referring to work by Hans Freudenthal (1991) in mathematics education, they (2004) reason that science teaching entails a *guided reinvention* of science that students can participate in:

> That means that, for them [students], the concepts to be
> reinvented will function for a particular purpose, and

that the reasons for their construction and acceptance are directly derived from that functioning. [. . .] Knowledge is (guidedly) constructed for a certain purpose. And it is accepted by those who construct it to the extent that it functions productively for that purpose.

(Lijnse and Klaassen, 2004, p. 540)

In this comparison with mathematics education, Lijnse and Klaassen (2004) refer to the reinvention as one in which the science teacher guides students in *scientificalizing* their world. Central to their approach is a practical problem that the students see the point of solving. The sequence as a whole is built around such motives, in which there is a global content-related motive connected through a series of content-related local motives. That the motive is *content related* means that the students see that science is needed to solve the problem.

As the kind of need to know and progression of the didactic model of Lijnse and Klaassen (2004) apparently was lacking in Sequence 1, it was adjusted along these lines in an altered Sequence 2 (Bulte et al., 2006). Now the problems given to the students were changed to create a stronger need to know. In its first phase, students not only had to clarify what the context was all about but also discuss what they already knew about it. In the second phase, students had to bring their own surface water samples to produce water that they could drink. Through an analysis in the third phase, they then had to examine the water to see whether it was clean enough to drink. In this third phase, the concepts related to accuracy of measurement were integrated to answer this question. Hence, students were not just supposed to examine the water to see if it was good enough for drinking but also make it drinkable.

However, in Sequence 2, a new hurdle was encountered. The activity of finding a way to purify the water disrupted learning about water quality; the teachers and students became heavily involved in distillation and filtration. This reorientation meant that a new set of concepts concerning purifying water dominated activities instead of the functional analysis of water quality. The need to know was directed away from the intended context (Bulte, 2007; Bulte et al., 2006).

The experiences from the two first trial sequences are reminiscent of those from ChiK of getting lost in context and losing sight of the intended concepts. In the first sequence, students could not apply the abstract concepts first learned when later given a context. Students did not see what they needed to know in the abstract conceptual phase for later use in the inquiry phase, which was not yet known to them. Concepts cannot be used as ready-made sets directly from science but need to be transformed for new purposes (Jenkins, 2002; Layton, Jenkins, Macgill, & Davey, 1993). Bruno Latour (1987) has shown how this also applies in society, in which scientific results need years of transformation to become useful technology in society.

In the second sequence, this unproductive abstract phase of clarifying the concepts related to accuracy of measurement was abandoned. Instead, techniques for making clean water took supremacy over techniques for judging the quality of the water. From a practical perspective, a good technique for purifying water makes a technique for analyzing the water quality secondary and obsolete in terms of making water good enough to drink, as the technique for purifying water guarantees the quality in the first place. As is well known from cybernetics, there are many different ways (practically as well as conceptually) of producing the same outcome. Various kinds of mechanical or electronic computers may be used to produce the same answer to arithmetic problems (Wickman et al., 2012).

To resolve the problems, activity theory (e.g., Van Aalsvoort, 2004) was applied to a third model and its corresponding third sequence (Bulte, 2007; Bulte et al., 2006). *Context* was now redefined into *practice.* This change was motivated because practice does not define just a certain situation (e.g., water quality) but also specific kinds of actions and the knowledge needed to perform these actions (the professional practice of assessing water quality; see also Gilbert, Bulte, & Pilot, 2011; Prins, Bulte, & Pilot, 2011). Apart from activity theory, Sequence 3 also builds on strengthening its content-related motive as defined by Lijnse and Klaassen (2004). The idea is that an existing authentic practice is used to select content to guarantee the close connection between knowledge and action. At the same time, this content is adapted and sequenced so that it gives students a sense of content-related purpose that orients them in gaining the conceptual and procedural knowledge of the practice. There is a focus on the functionality of the scientific content taught for the activities of the practice in which students are involved and for the practice into which they are initiated. For this reason, there has to be a consistent distinction between *student functions* and *teacher functions* of each episode of the sequence. This didactic model is said to build on finding an instructional version of an authentic practice (Bulte et al., 2006).

In Sequence 3, the four-phase unit of Sequence 2 was adapted accordingly (Bulte et al., 2006). Students were now first asked to find out by imitating authentic practice (in a simplified way) how professionals judge water quality. This first phase involved an orientation so that the purposes, general procedures, and students' roles were clear to them, giving students a need to know. The aim was to create an instructional version of authentic practice, which does not serve to turn students into experts but that can be used as a guiding principle to learn some concepts valued by society and how these concepts functions in society. Students were given a case of analyzing the quality of two actual alternative water supplies, in which a decision had to be made. The subsequent three phases were very similar to those of Sequence 2, with the important exception that students now were not supposed to make the water drinkable. Results showed that in the first two phases of the sequence, students' need to know now created a flow of activities in which only some further fine-tuning was needed and that students acquired the requested knowledge. However, students did not see the point of expressing more general rules for how to judge water quality (Bulte et al., 2006).

Further analysis of the third didactic model can be found in additional publications (e.g., Prins, Bulte, & Pilot, 2011; Prins, Bulte, Van Driel, & Pilot, 2008; Westbroek et al., 2010). The take-home message from these Dutch studies may be formulated in terms of the ZPD and of communities of practice. To support the progression of the students, the teacher needs to arrange for a renewed need to know in each phase so as to create a continuous need for further content. The teacher models these phases from authentic practices so as to support the need for relevant concepts and actions while at the same time adapting them to where students are at each phase. Central to this is the notion that the practice is not there merely to give students emotional desire to participate but as an "advanced organizer" in terms of Ausubel (1968), which helps the students see what they need to know and do (Westbroek et al., 2010). The full meaning of need to know is thus that it supports students in bridging the ZPD. However, it is not fully clear what the role of the student and the teacher is in this initiation of the student into the practice, even though the importance of differentiating between student and teacher function is emphasized. Few examples are given of actual interactions between teachers and students.

Part of this project also meant to introduce this model of teaching science with teachers (Stolk, de Jong, Bulte, & Pilot, 2011). Here the teachers engaged in building an exemplary teaching sequence using the didactic model. Nevertheless, the teachers had difficulties in seeing how the model applied to the exemplary unit and also more widely. It was as if the teachers conflated their traditional practice of trying to motivate their students emotionally with the more content-oriented and inclusive idea of need to know and their traditional lab work with the open inquiry of authentic practice. This tended to disrupt the flow between the different phases of the units. Here it is as if another authentic practice intervenes, namely the teachers' and students' traditional classroom practice. The context-based chemistry units introduced do not build on teachers' current practice. Suggestions for how to make teachers' current practice continuous with the new model in the learning process of teachers are not given. Teachers' learning is modeled as building on repetition, their "understanding of the context-based model, and their ability to teach and design a context-based unit" (Stolk et al., 2011, p. 373).

Further research is needed regarding the principles for choosing content using this didactic model. Content is analyzed primarily in terms of so-called authentic practices. *Authentic practice* is intended mainly to mean established professional practices applying or producing chemistry knowledge (Bulte et al., 2006; Gilbert et al., 2011; Westbroek et al., 2011). Mundane practices, in which the need for scientific knowledge is less well defined, are not easily included. Such diffuse practices encompass a major part of the content in learning for everyday use (e.g., as a consumer, in personal life), for socioscientific issues, or for questions related to decision making. Both of these knowledge emphases constitute important content of the original science in context movement (Parchmann et al., 2006). It would be interesting to investigate how such contexts could be made more supportive to conceptual learning within a model of contexts as practices.

In a wider content perspective, the bigger question of selecting and sequencing content for more general overarching progression, beyond single units and for whole science classes or for school science as a whole, is the next challenge. What does progression look like when the structural relationship of concepts (everyday and scientific), which apparently in themselves do not organize students' learning, is thrown overboard? Bulte and colleagues (2006) used a hypothetical example to illustrate what it might look like in a specific case. Gilbert and colleagues (2011) discuss this further by arguing for how certain practices may be connected to certain mental models and how such mental models could be developed and transferred between practices. The reported research illustrates how the progression of practices is not merely a theoretical question but also an empirical one that needs to be based on how progressions are received and adopted by teachers and students. It is one of the most important challenges in giving legitimacy to context-based science education.

Didactic Transposition in France

French didactics (*didactique*) emphasizes the intimate relationship of the student, the teacher, and the content (often referred to as the *piece of knowledge at stake*) as envisioned by the system of the didactic triangle (Sensevy, 2011) and how it is sociohistorically embedded and what this setting as a whole means for the curriculum taught and learned (Chevallard, 2007; Ligozat, 2011). The origin of French didactics is quite recent, emanating from curriculum reforms that began in the 1960s in mathematics and science. Those in mathematics education were especially successful, most likely because of its intimate contact with teacher education (Caillot, 2007) but also because of the genius of Guy Brousseau (1997), a mathematics teacher who, in concert with academia, developed a didactic model (called a *didactic theory* in France; in this case *the theory of didactic situations in mathematics*) in mathematics for primary school. Brousseau's work has been seminal also for other school subjects, including science, and so some of its main ideas are worth mentioning. It has been built on by others and transformed during the years, although many of its main ideas prevail in recognizable form.

Central to Brousseau's (1997) thinking is the idea that teaching as situated in the classroom makes up a whole, including the student, the teacher, the social relationships, and material conditions. Such a whole is called a *situation*, and the didactic model concerns how to order such situations to produce a progression, which entails the devolution of the piece of knowledge at stake from the teacher to the students through the situation (Brousseau, 1997). The situation is typically based on a game, in which both the teacher and the students should be winners in the end, resulting in the students learning the piece of knowledge at stake. Through the situation, knowledge is transposed from the academic discipline of mathematics so as to be useful to students in playing a winning strategy in the game. Characteristic of Brousseau's model is its didactic teacher orientation.

The game starts in a so-called *adidactic situation* that is successively turned into a *didactic situation. Adidactic* means that the rules of such an initial situation can be easily understood by the students and that the game can be played by the students without the piece of knowledge at stake. This adidactic situation can be seen as setting up a community of practice in which students can solve the problems independently, without the support of the teacher. A typical game would be the race from 1 to 20. The student teams take turns and can add either 1 or 2 in each turn. The team first to reach the number 20 is the winner. Students soon discover that also 17 is a winning number (Brousseau, 1997). The team first to reach 17 wins regardless of whether the other team chooses to add 1 or 2 in the next turn. Starting in such an adidactic situation and a game is to see that the students can take part in the actions of the classroom community and that they see that there is something that they can get better at. The game is there to link the intentions of the participants in the practice with a certain structure of doing things. If you understand the rules of the game, you at the same time understand the intentions of the other players (cf. Sensevy, 2012; Wickman, 2012c).

The development of the adidactic situation into the didactic situation entails that the students come to see that they need more knowledge to play the game better. Here students are entering the zone of proximal development in which the teacher is needed for students to gain this new piece of knowledge, which is disciplinary knowledge. Students learn how to use mathematics to improve their playing of the game. The piece of knowledge at stake so is devolved by the teacher to the student to accomplish this. Typically the teacher is reticent in this transposition. The students are not simply told how the piece of knowledge can be used to play the game better, but the teacher asks the students for arguments and rationales for their suggestions of how to improve the game, and these suggestions are evaluated rationally or empirically in such a way that the students can explain the new strategy of playing the game using mathematics (Sensevy, 2011). Through the practice of playing a game, the students are introduced to the new practice of mathematics, in which there are not just trial and error but patterns and proof. This way of thinking can be adapted to transpositions in other subjects and to science.

Hence, according to this didactic model, the content is not only in the hands of the teacher and the students but very much in the situation as a whole and the course the game played takes. This needs to be carefully monitored by the teacher and is analyzed through the concepts of *didactic contract* and *milieu.* Describing the changing sets of conditions of the classroom is a description of the milieu and how it is changing through the situation. How this milieu is played out in the joint action of the students and the teacher is the didactic contract that develops. A didactic contract can be understood as a set of norms, rules, and habits of action, which functions as a common background and which the students and teacher jointly draw on and also renegotiate to proceed with the game and the situation of a the milieu (Sensevy, 2011). It constitutes the background against which the intentions of participants are made publicly available (Sensevy, 2012).

However, before any sequence of adidactic or didactic situations can be designed, a careful didactic analysis of the didactic transposition of the content from its place of origin to school is needed (Chevallard, 2007). Knowledge is not given directly from the academic discipline of mathematics in such a way that it can be used directly without change or adaptation to the new milieu of school, either for the adidactic or didactic situations. At the same time, to be useful, knowledge cannot be invented de novo in school. The teacher and the curriculum designer need to argue for how knowledge taken from academia or other institutions in society can legitimately be built up and transformed, or, in the language used, *transposed* to be useful to students. Andrée Tiberghien (2007) describes how such transpositions in science may follow two different routes to gain legitimacy.

The type I transposition of Tiberghien (2007) concerns science content that draws on a well-defined community of practice in which the knowledge has meaning, as is the case for science subject matter and knowledge on scientific inquiry. Through its relation to an academic community that is respected in society, the transposition of content accrues legitimacy. At the same time, the content needs to be transposed to its new use in such a way that it can live in the community of practices of the school. Although the same terms may be used in school as by scientists, they are not identical. This means that the transposition is not just a question of how but also of what. Also, science from vocational practices such as medicine, agriculture, and so forth can be given legitimacy and be transposed along these principles.

The type II transposition of Tiberghien (2007) deals with more complex transpositions in which the knowledge cannot be clearly pinpointed to one community in society and in which several communities of practice typically are involved. Such content concerns, for example, socioscientific issues. Teachers should be given assistance from a group consisting of representatives of different referent knowledge communities and stakeholders to make transpositions. In a first step, representative information and situations from different stakeholders are selected. In a second step, a further transposition is made through an epistemological, ethical, moral, and historical analysis into elements of the curriculum. It is important that these transpositions do not turn the classroom merely into a public space of debate, with the risk that parents and society will not give it legitimacy because the instructional role of the curriculum is lost.

Although French didactics originates in mathematics education, there are applications in science education. One example is the *two-world model*, which was developed to inform the teaching designs in upper secondary school physics. It is based on socioconstructivist notions, especially those of Vygotsky, that learning is a process of internalization of what first occurs on a social plane and that this internalization is mediated through language (Ruthven et al., 2009; Sensevy, Tiberghien, Santini, Laubé, & Griggs, 2008). Physics knowledge is approached as primarily involving modeling relationships of the material world. It is subsumed that modeling is not just the way physicists make sense of the material world in physics but also that it is a basic human process of sense making of material phenomena and it is also used spontaneously by students in everyday life (Tiberghien, 1994, 2000). Whenever people explain, interpret, or make predictions about the material world, modeling activity is involved. In this two-world model, there are the relationships between the objects and events of the material world and the theories and models used to explain, interpret, and predict those objects and events as part of physics knowledge as well as part of everyday knowledge. Links can also be established between physics and everyday knowledge. Hence there are potential relationships among all four categories of knowledge: physics theories/models, physics objects/events, everyday theories/models, and everyday objects/events (Ruthven et al., 2009).

As is evident, this theory of the epistemology and of learning physics is also an idea of how to make a transposition of content from physics to school. It specifically deals with the type I transpositions of Tiberghien (2007). So as not to transgress the ZPD, the physics content needs to be devolved to the students in steps drawing on students' everyday theories/models and objects/events. To accomplish this, two tools for didactic analysis have been developed. First, the *knowledge distance tool* is used to guide the overall framing and sequencing of the teaching content. Second, the *modeling relations tool* orients the design of the finer details of specific activities (Ruthven et al., 2009).

The *knowledge distance tool* is used to give a detailed map of the physics to be taught and students' existing knowledge. It deals with the starting points and end points of developing ZPDs in the classroom. It is described in the four categories of knowledge and the relationships among them. The relations of students' existing knowledge are mapped using assessments from prior instruction and also using the research literature. A list is made of the relationships between the world of theories/models and the world of objects/events not yet known by the student so that they can be the focus of the teaching design (Ruthven et al., 2009).

The *modeling relations tool* helps make clear the types of relations and their content that the student should establish within and between worlds as part of a specific sequence (Ruthven et al., 2009). One unusual feature of this model is that it means that no relationship between worlds is taken for granted, but it makes them explicit targets for design. It is thus not just assumed that conceptual change means the wholesale exchange of one explanatory model for another. For example, it is rare in science education that care is taken to see that students can describe the objects and events in the way physicists do before they are introduced to the model supposed to explain the events (Sensevy et al., 2008). In introducing mechanics in Grade 10, students are asked to describe the objects that act on a stone suspended on an elastic string. They are also asked to give the objects on which the stone is acting. In this way, new usage of the words *objects* and *act* are introduced. From their everyday use of words, students are not familiar with this use of the concept of action, in which nothing is changing (the stone is just hanging there on the string). Most students come to see that the string is an object acting on the stone. However, it is harder to consider the earth as an object acting in this way. In similar ways, students are also becoming familiar with recognizing the relevant *system,* which is the focus of physicist modeling activities. In a similar manner, students are given the problem of a ball after it has left a throwing hand but still is moving upward and in which they need to distinguish between the *direction of action* and the *direction of motion,* that they are different things to a physicist involved in Newtonian mechanics (Sensevy et al., 2008).

A further development of these ideas in French didactics is the Joint Action Theory in Didactics (JATD; Ligozat & Schubauer-Leoni, 2010; Sensevy, 2010; Sensevy, Mercier, & Schubaur-Leoni, 2000; Sensevy, Mercier, Schubauer-Leoni, Ligozat, & Perrot, 2005), which has also been adopted to analyze the transcripts from the two-world physics project (Tiberghien & Sensevy, 2012). This model is influenced by the ideas of the French-speaking didactics community, but it also has pragmatist influences, especially from John Dewey and George Herbert Mead (Sensevy, 2011). Its emphasis on joint action means that didactic action must be understood from the system of the didactic triangle, how the content is transacted through the joint actions of teaching and learning (Sensevy, 2011). Some concepts of JATD have already been treated earlier: for example, how the didactic contract can be understood against a common background of classroom norms and of seeing objects, events, and actions in similar ways. Learning physics means that the students jointly with the teacher develop a common background, which means learning a certain thought style through learning to talk like a physicist together with the teacher (see the earlier example of using the terms *object* and *action* in new ways; Sensevy et al., 2008).

Jérôme Santini (2009) has used JATD to make a didactic analysis of earth science in French fifth-grade classes. In his study, three concepts were used to analyze the relationship between, on the one hand, the *learning game*, which is played out in the classroom, and the *epistemic game*, on the other hand, which is the competence targeted with the learning game. This didactic situation can be compared to a didactic transposition of type I (Tiberghien, 2007) and a two-world analysis for a teaching sequence (Tiberghien et al., 2009), in which the learning game starts in student experiences and advances toward the problem solving and language usage of the earth scientist. Santini (2009) analyzed this transposition in four different classes adopting the three concepts of *knowledge density, knowledge specificity*, and *knowledge distance*. Knowledge density is an analysis of the range of knowledge offered in the game. For example, a sequence asking students to give reasons for descriptions they make is denser than one that only asks them to give descriptions. Knowledge specificity increases as more scientifically specialized concepts are used. Teachers may, for example, use more everyday words instead of more scientifically specialized concepts. Knowledge distance is a description of the range of various actions needed from students and supported by the teacher in the learning game to make students master the epistemic game. Comparing these three variables with outcomes (e.g., through pre- and posttests) makes it possible to link differences of student performances with the practices of classrooms and to the efficiencies not only with regard to ways of teaching but also in relation to how the content is organized (see also Tiberghien & Sensevy, 2012, for applications of these concepts to mechanics).

Florence Ligozat (2011) has used JATD to analyze the transactions between curriculum materials and teachers' classroom practices. Along with Gérard Sensevy's (2010) use of the ideas of Ludwik Fleck (1979), Ligozat posits that there are professional thought styles characterizing communities of teachers and that form habits or customs along which suggestions for design in the curriculum materials are interpreted into practical action in classrooms. She, for example, demonstrates how one Swiss teacher hands over a large responsibility to students to find out for themselves, and how such practice is embedded in the socioconstructivist understanding shared by the curriculum materials and the thought style of the teachers. Paradoxically, this shared socioconstructivist understanding does not enable the teachers to see their own critical epistemic role in supporting students in bridging the ZPD. Ligozat argues that reform efforts need to consider carefully how the (1) curriculum materials, (2) teachers' thought styles, and (3) teachers' more idiosyncratic interpretive schemes can be made to fruitfully interact to support curriculum reform. Ligozat (2011) and colleagues are now using this three-fold approach to support curriculum reform in primary science in the Geneva region.

Through the two types of transpositions of Tiberghien (2007) and their formulation in relation to type I transpositions in physics as a relationship between theories and models in two worlds, or more generally and in Brousseau's terms as a relationship between a learning game and an epistemic game, French didactics has come to make increasingly didactically powerful models of the ZPD. These involve the conceptual distance between the models used by students and by scientists as well as how the teacher deals with knowledge distance through knowledge density and specificity through joint action in developing the competence of the targeted science community of practice. The concepts of the didactic contract and the milieu support this model by offering a didactic analysis of the didactic teaching-learning situation as a whole, also including its social and material transactional aspects. Further development is needed to study how these approaches oriented to model well-developed science practices and communities can be used to constitute progression also for primary school science (Ligozat, 2011), type II transpositions, and uses of science that are not easily situated within professional practices but more concern everyday uses of science for citizenship and *Bildung*.

Practical Epistemologies in Sweden

In Sweden, science didactics originates in science teacher education in the period from the 1970s to the early 1990s, when the first doctoral theses in the field were defended. The early research, to a large extent, was inspired by American constructivists drawing on the work of Piaget—for example, by Robert Karplus (Karplus & Thier, 1967), Joseph Novak (1977; Ausubel, Novak, & Hanesian, 1978) and Rosalind Driver (Driver & Easley, 1978). These early Swedish studies (e.g., Andersson, 1976; Helldén, 1992; Pedersen, 1992) typically examined students' misconceptions or alternative frameworks and how these could be changed through teaching and innovations such as the notion of interaction in physics (Karplus & Thier, 1967) or concept maps (Novak, 1990), although there were important exceptions (e.g., Staberg, 1992, who studied gender issues in science education). In Sweden, this research already from the beginning came to be defined as science didactics and became part of science teacher education curricula.

During the 1990s and the first decade of the new millennium, the individualist constructivist understanding of science education came under scrutiny in a debate that very much paralleled the debate in North America (e.g., Kelly, Carlsen, & Cunningham, 1993; Lemke, 1990). As a result, science education came to include also socioconstructivist and sociocultural perspectives. Roger Säljö and Kerstin Bergqvist (1997), for example, in an influential study, demonstrated how the school uptake of child-centered constructivist ideas risked leaving children without the teacher support they needed to make sense of lab work.

Another important development was represented by Leif Östman (1994), who argued that science education could not just be understood as conceptual and cognitive learning, it also meant socialization of students and so also the learning of values and morals. Together with North American scholars (Roberts & Östman, 1998), it was demonstrated how learning science also involves collateral messages, called *companion meanings*, which means that students apart from the scientific curriculum aims also learn ways to be and about their own place in relationship to nature and to science. In his dissertation, Östman (1995) constructed a didactic model of analyzing content selection from a *Buildung* and scientific literacy perspective. These models *inter alia* expanded on Douglas Roberts's (1982) knowledge emphases to also include value content in a discursive sense, that is, as inclusions and exclusions of possible messages to students (see Wickman, et al., 2012).

Here I review one specific Swedish approach to didactic modeling related to sociocultural and pragmatic theory frameworks, namely that of *practical epistemologies* (Wickman, 2004; Wickman & Östman, 2002a). The idea is to offer a framework that permits didactic analysis from a teacher's interest, which means distinguishing units of analysis that can be experienced and transacted by the teacher in action together with the students. An important pragmatic idea was also that the didactic analysis of content of classrooms should not *a priori* assume that science education is only about conceptual change but also about the transformation of the values and the habits of the person as a whole in relation to the setting. Central for this approach are John Dewey's (1929/1958, 1938/1997) notions of *inquiry* and *continuity,* further explicated next. Also, the later Ludwig Wittgenstein's (1967) ideas on language have been influential. Both these philosophers share a situated and sociohistorical understanding of communication with many socioculturally oriented thinkers (Rogoff, 1990; Wickman, 2006).

Practical epistemologies should be understood as the actual epistemologies used in talk and action by teachers and students together in the classroom in proceeding with teaching and learning. It is the epistemology of the transacting persons in a community and not of a lone mind. Epistemology deals with the problem of what knowledge is and how we get it (Grayling, 1996). From a didactic empirical point of view, this question is about the relationship between how students learn and what they learn (i.e., what becomes known). Epistemologies are thus seen as something that develops through shared actions and their consequences in the classroom. It is largely an empirical question to examine how the various practical epistemologies that may develop in classrooms support the learning of science in the widest sense, also including values and the embodied transformation of the person as a whole.

Studying practical epistemology means a teacher's perspective and thus a didactic approach (Wickman, 2004). The teacher is interested in how the transactions with the students and with the material conditions of the classroom influence the direction learning takes for students—that is, what students are afforded to learn through the classroom arrangements and if this learning is the knowledge aimed for. The focus is on the conditions that can be changed by the teacher and not on every cause for a situation. Studying practical epistemologies is a way to support the choices teachers make in planning and evaluating the teaching. Learning and knowledge are here analyzed as they are experienced by the teacher, that is, as talk and action developing and being transformed in the classroom. It is only through mutual talk and action that the teacher can transact with students and assess how they progress. In line with Richard Rorty's (1991) understanding of epistemology, a practical epistemology approach does not "view knowledge as a matter of getting reality right, but as a matter of acquiring [situated] habits of action for coping with reality" (p. 1). Studying learning as practical epistemologies is about studying how the transactions that occur in the classroom influence the transformation of habits (Wickman, 2004, 2006). Ultimately more systematic knowledge and values only become evident as habits— that is, as habitual patterns of talking about and acting towards objects, actions, and events in various situations.

Basic to practical epistemology is John Dewey's *empirical method of inquiry* and his *principle of continuity* (Wickman, 2012c). According to this didactic model, any classroom scientific inquiry conducive to learning starts in a classroom practice or activity in which students already can act and talk competently to accomplish certain purposes (they can be seen by the teacher to have functioning habits that they can draw on). The start and end of learning and teaching progressions according to this understanding is how a practice in which students already can act competently can be improved by introducing new ways of talking and acting from a scientific practice and so transforming the well-known activity into a more scientific one, meaning one in which students better can use science in their lives (Wickman & Ligozat, 2011). In this way, the familiar and more scientific practices are said to be made *continuous.* To accomplish this, it is essential that the students continually can see the purposes of what they are doing, first of the familiar activity and eventually also of the more scientific activity.

The purposes of the familiar activity are called *proximate purposes*, because these are chosen by the teacher to be close to the students' understanding at the beginning of their inquiry. The purposes of the more scientific activity have a more final role and are therefore called *ultimate purposes*, as they do not first make sense to the students in terms of action but only ultimately, when they have carried out the inquiry in full together with the teacher to learn this new content (Johansson & Wickman, 2011). The inquiry that belongs to the proximate purposes can be solved independently by the students, whereas that of the ultimate purposes cannot but needs the scaffolding of the teacher to be accomplished. Together, the proximate purposes and ultimate purposes can thus be seen as a description of the ZPD, and these two *organizing purposes* can be used by the teacher to *organize* and assess teaching and learning progressions in the classroom (Wickman, 2012a).

The function of the proximate purpose of the first inquiry activity in which students take part in is thus not merely to help the teacher access what students already know but, more importantly, to help students understand *what it is that's going on* in the classroom (cf. Goffman, 1974) so that they can act and thus learn purposefully (i.e., give students agency). First, when they understand what is going on (the purpose), can they share what they know, because then they understand what it is that is relevant and not relevant knowledge to share and ask for together with other students and the teacher to make the activity proceed according to purpose. A proximate purpose that helps students in this way is said to give them an *end in view* (Dewey 1938/1997; Johansson & Wickman, 2011). That the students have an end in view operationally means that they can use first-hand knowledge from their own experience, that they can use words they know well, and that they can anticipate what are relevant contributions and questions to fulfill the purpose. If the students do not understand what the purpose is, they are left guessing what might be important and less important in the situation or trying to remember everything (i.e., rote learning). Every intelligent inquiry requires that the participants see the purpose of what they are doing as part of what is going on. This is a discursive understanding of meaning, in which meaning is already part of certain habits and customs, that is, culturally embedded systematic ways of including and excluding certain ways of being, acting, and talking (cf. Cherryholmes, 1988; Goffman, 1974).

The ultimate purposes are introduced gradually by the teacher to support the proximate activity with its proximate purposes. Typically, scientific concepts or methods of the more scientific ultimate activity are introduced by the teacher to meliorate the proximate activity. At the same time, the classroom practice as a whole is transformed slowly also with regard to its purposes, because the scientific concepts and methods offer new distinctions and thus new ways of doing things. The scientific activity and its ultimate purpose through its new language use, artifacts, and methods open up new inquiries and new distinctions and procedures that were not known to the students before. In this way, students learn new habits of talking and acting that incorporate science knowledge as part of new inquiries.

When the teacher sees that the students can use the new scientific ways (e.g., a new scientific concept or method) to deal with the proximate purposes in a way that is in line also with handling the ultimate purposes, the two kinds of organizing purposes are said to have become *continuous*,

which means that the students, according to Dewey's (1938/1997, p. 35) principle of continuity, use prior experiences to deal with current experience in a way that is conducive to purpose and that changes their future ways of dealing with similar inquiries.

It should be noted that giving proximate purposes, which give students an end in view and which become continuous with ultimate purposes, is typical of a any good lesson and is used by many good teachers more or less spontaneously, although they do not use the terms to describe what they are doing. These terms therefore can function as part of a didactic model for didactic analysis of already-established teaching and learning practices to meliorate them.

Annie-Maj Johansson and Wickman (2011) give an example of a physics lesson in a Swedish Grade 5 class (12-year-old students) in which the proximate purpose is for the whole class to discuss together with the teacher why we have tires on our cars. The ultimate purpose is that they should understand how friction facilitates or impedes motion. It is obvious during the discussion that the inquiry into why we have tires on our cars gives students an end in view. Students use experiences from home and from an earlier experiment with a toy car with a rubber-band motor that they observed moving with and without tires. Students also use their everyday language to describe how the tires affect the way cars move but also how the tires solve other problems, for example, that without tires, the rims of the car and the road would be destroyed. Although the teacher and the students together have an engaging discussion dealing with the proximate purpose, the teacher has difficulties in making this discussion continuous to the physics concepts and explaining what is about friction and about other problems with tires, such as not destroying the road (Johansson & Wickman, 2011). The teacher never relates the ordinary experiences and language use of students as part of the proximate purpose to how the terms *friction* and *motion* are related and used for the ultimate purposes of physics. On the whole, the ultimate purpose stays opaque and is never realized by the teacher as a new practice together with the students. The ZPD between this proximate purpose and the ultimate purpose was not seen to be bridged by the students in the conversation between the teacher and the students. In supporting such continuity, teachers need to be aware of how to make different semiotic resources and various kinds of multimodal representations already familiar to the students continuous in communication with increasingly scientific representations and their use in inquiry.

In explaining how, this continuity could be accomplished, Johansson and Wickman (2011) relate to a study by Peter Hubber, Russell Tytler, and Filocha Haslam (2010) of a school development program in Australia in which the researchers introduced learning support through multimodal semiotic resources. Although Hubber and colleagues (2010) do not relate to the concepts of organizing purposes, they have a pragmatic interest in understanding how students' and science's semiotic resources can be made continuous and how inquiries can be formulated in such a way that they give students "a need to know" (cf. Bulte et al., 2006) and so a purpose. The specific case here related to concerns a unit introducing the concept of force in a Year 7 class. In this case, proximate purposes were introduced in steps, which, through novel, more scientific multimodal semiotic resources gradually were made continuous with the already familiar language use of students, which they used to deal with the proximate purpose.

The teacher first told the students to mold a lump of Plasticine. Students then had to describe to the others in class what they did to their lump of Plasticine to reshape it. Gestures also played an important role in this communication, both for students and for teachers in re-presenting what had been done. Both of these were familiar activities using familiar language, which the students easily saw the purpose of. The proximate purposes of these activities (molding the Plasticine and describing what they did in words) thus worked as ends in view, because the students could be seen to use their first-hand knowledge from their own experience, they could use words they knew well, and they could anticipate what were relevant contributions and questions to fulfill the purpose. The teacher then gradually introduced the ultimate purpose of being able to describe force as either *push* or *pull*. The teacher listed on the board all the words students used to describe what they did to the Plasticine (*stretch*, *carve*, etc.) under the two headings of push and pull, thus showing them how their descriptions could be simplified through the use of these words. The teacher also showed them how these words could be categorized as either push or pull by representing these two words with different gestures with her hands. The teacher then introduced the meaning of *force* as either the push or pull on an object (Hubber et al., 2010). In this sequence, the scientific concepts were introduced by the teacher to meliorate the description of what the students did to their lump of Plasticine. Most importantly, the teacher could follow and assess how the students in action used the semiotic resources of the two language-games to make them continuous. After this sequence, the unit described by Hubber and colleagues (2010) continued according to the same didactic model.

Organizing purposes can be seen as a way of operationalizing the ZPD as the transformation of one community of practice into another (Wickman, 2012a). In the case of science education, this means that of introducing an inquiry with a proximate purpose that works as an end in view and that is made continuous with a more scientific way of doing things. This understanding of progression means that it is not understood primarily as one of conceptual change, in which a more everyday conceptual use is replaced by scientific concepts, but rather that students' habits of talking and acting change as they learn to take part *also* in the new kind of practices. It is important that the activity with proximate purposes is not seen only as a pedagogical means of achieving the ultimate purposes.

The content for the proximate purpose should be chosen because it concerns knowledge in itself that is important learning goals. These aims typically concern more diffuse and less well-defined practices in which science can be useful together with other kinds of knowing, such as choosing tires for our cars. An important ultimate purpose is then not only to teach students about physics alone but also for students to understand when physical arguments are valid as opposed to, for instance, economic, environmental, or technical considerations.

This is a situated and discursive understanding of progression in which the teacher needs to keep track of what the students systematically include and exclude and how they make the organizing purposes continuous. It emphasizes the important role of making this progression evident to the teacher in communication between the teacher and the students in the classroom. Through students' actions, the teacher can keep track of and scaffold students' changing habits. Teaching is seen as intimately entwined with formatively assessing how students continually progress in action (Johansson & Wickman, 2011). It also means that progression is inseparable from slowly changed doings and what such doings accomplishes in relation to shared purposes (Wickman & Ligozat, 2011).

A support for monitoring how classroom activity supports the continuity of the organizing purposes is practical epistemology analysis (PEA). It starts by asking what shared purposes are developing between the students and the teacher in the classroom. It supports coding of the classroom transactions for analysis of what students are afforded to learn through the specific setting of the classroom (Wickman, 2004; Wickman & Östman, 2002a). PEA makes it possible to examine functional and dysfunctional word usages and how transactions with the teacher, among students, or with material conditions support meanings in making the organizing purposes continuous. PEA has also been used to ask more general questions about how students make sense of and learn scientific content in science classrooms (e.g., Almqvist & Östman, 2006; Hamza & Wickman, 2008, 2012, 2013; Lidar, Lundqvist, & Östman, 2006; Lundqvist, Almqvist, & Östman, 2009, 2012; Wickman & Östman, 2002b), at science exhibitions at museums (e.g., Piqueras, Hamza, & Edvall, 2008), and how values (Lundegård, 2008), such as morals (Öhman & Östman, 2007) and aesthetic experience (Arvola-Orlander & Wickman, 2011; Jakobson & Wickman, 2008; Wickman, 2006), are integral parts of learning.

Studies of aesthetic experience in classrooms (Wickman, 2006) in combination with the work of Pierre Bourdieu (1984) have contributed to methodologies for studying how interest in science is constituted through the transactions in the classroom, supporting also the development of didactic analyses of how a teacher can support engagement in science class (Anderhag, Wickman, & Hamza, under review). Related to the interest in French didactics of how students can learn to talk about objects like physicists to support their learning of explanations (Ruthven et al., 2009), Karim Hamza and Per-Olof Wickman (2009) showed how students' explanations of the workings of an electrochemical cell also involved making sense of all the details of the cell as distinguished by a chemist. In a teaching experiment akin to those employed by Komorek and Duit (2004), it was also demonstrated how a teacher could use such taxonomic distinctions to support students' learning of explanations (Hamza & Wickman, 2013).

According to a practical epistemology approach, content choice is largely an empirical problem of finding activities that make sense and engage young people and how they can be made continuous with new practices that employ scientific ways of making distinctions and that are valued by the curriculum and a democratic society. This constitutes an action-oriented approach to the problem of didactic transposition and to Klafki's (1958, 1969) question about how certain established content could be chosen and presented in a way that is not only understood by students but also useful to them in their *Bildung* for current and future life (Wickman, Liberg, & Östman, 2012; Wickman & Ligozat, 2011).

Progression is the gradual and continuous communication between the teacher and the students using the methods and languages of the two practices to improve and transform their purposes (Wickman & Ligozat, 2011). It is a question of teachers and students mutually and continuously negotiating the content. In different grades, similar content is often treated, but at various levels of refinement. Progression could then hardly be organized merely with correct science concepts or authentic scientific practice as models. It is necessary that the activities and practices that are modeled have organizing purposes that are not just steps along the way but give students meaningful participatory competencies in practices they can meaningfully be part of. How this is accomplished is not merely a theoretical question of applying the didactic model of organizing purposes but largely empirical for each particular lesson. Teachers need to try out what proximate activities and purposes give them and their students ends in view, what students bring into these proximate activities, and how they can be made continuous with the ultimate purposes in accord with the curriculum. The content and events of these activities are highly contingent on the specific experiences and transactions that meet in the classroom (Hamza & Wickman, 2008, 2013). This is not just a question about what students know, but it is also highly contingent on the existing knowledge of teachers, their manners of teaching (Munby, Cunningham, & Lock, 2000; Munby & Russell, 1992), and the teaching traditions they are part of (Gyllenpalm & Wickman, 2011; Gyllenpalm, Wickman, & Holmgren, 2010a, 2010b; Lundqvist, Almqvist, & Östman, 2012; Sund & Wickman, 2011). From a pragmatic perspective, this knowledge and these traditions are seen as valuable and necessary resources to build on in curriculum reform (Wickman, 2012b).

By analyzing what the actual consequences of changing classroom practices are for how proximate purposes function as ends in views to students and whether students can be seen to make proximate and ultimate purposes continuous, teaching sequences can be continually revised and adapted to local conditions. How this can be integrated and implemented in inservice and preservice teacher education is currently under development in a joint research project of Gothenburg University and Stockholm University (unpublished material). Crucial in this project is not to produce wholesale units for the curriculum but rather to start in teachers' current practice and discuss with researchers to what degree they can better see how proximate purposes function as ends in view and to what degree they make evident, through classroom communication, that students make the proximate and ultimate purposes continuous. This is in line with the idea that didactics is the scientific discipline concerned with improving the systematic basis supporting teachers' choices of content and methods.

Apart from building such joint progressions of teachers and students on various scientific practices and student experiences and lives, they also need to build on what teachers know and what practices they are familiar with. The ZPD cannot span a wider gap than that between the practices familiar to students and those familiar to teachers. Practical epistemologies offer a way for teachers to actively take part in developing progressions that are meaningful to them and their students. However, the study of how teachers can use practical epistemology as didactic models for didactic analysis is only in the beginning. Further research is needed to establish more generally how practical epistemologies can become useful in supporting teachers' choices for a wide range of content, situations, and students. Likewise, research on how they can support more long-term progressions over the span of many lessons has just started.

Conclusions

There is hardly one well-defined field of science didactics across European countries, as little as there is in science education more generally. Yet this relatively restricted review of some science didactic approaches in four European countries demonstrates many similarities in what a didactic approach may mean as a field for developing didactic models for didactic analysis. There are, for instance, obvious similarities between the guided reinvention of Lijnse and Klaassen (2004), the (a)didactical situations of Brousseau (1997), and the organizing purposes of Johansson and Wickman (2011). These models are based on various theoretical assumptions that influence the models developed and offered. However, ultimately, the models developed in didactics should not be judged from their theoretical basis only but on their merits for supporting teaching and learning of science in purposeful ways and in ways that we value. All models report areas of success and problems that need to be dealt with further. Here the widening in all countries of the understanding of the content of science and the ZPD as not merely conceptual but also involving action, values, contexts, and shared practices has proven to be productive in developing more useful and fruitful models for teaching science for *Bildung*.

One important axis of variation between didactic schools is between offering teachers ready-made designed sequences and starting from their own practice. Without doubt, there will always be a need for both. As pointed out by Tiberghien (2000), the design of sequences for every teaching situation in science seems to be an endless task (Tiberghien, 2000). Moreover, since there are no teacher-proof designs, in didactics such designs should better be seen as exemplars that are used to introduce teachers to didactic models for more general didactic analysis, meant to improve their decision making regarding content and teaching methods generally. The introduction of research-designed sequences to teachers and the redesign of teachers' existing practice thus can be said to work along the same lines, transferring principles from one teaching sequence to another. The results of Stolk and colleagues (2011) in the Netherlands demonstrate how teachers need support to generalize the didactic models from research designs and exemplars to their existing practice.

An important future challenge to science didactics research generally is to develop models that also can support the development of teaching and learning progressions together with teachers over longer periods of time extending over several units, courses, and years. Another one is how projects better can support teachers in taking over and developing didactic models practically so that they can use them independently for didactic analysis. The largest challenge of them all is not didactic but about policy: How can curriculum reform best be given sustained support from the institutions of which researchers and teachers are parts?

Acknowledgments

I want to thank Leif Östman and Meinert Meyer for helpfully reviewing this manuscript. Richard Lehrer, Gérard Sensevy, and the Science Education Group in Stockholm also gave supporting comments.

References

Aikenhead, G. S. (2006). *Science education for everyday life: Evidence-based practice.* New York: Teachers College Press.

Almqvist, J., & Östman, L. (2006). Privileging and artifacts: On the use of information technology in science education. *Interchange, 37*(3), 225–250.

Anderhag, P., Wickman, P.-O., & Hamza, K. M. (under review). Signs of taste for science: A methodology for studying the constitution of interest in the science classroom. Submitted to *Cultural Studies of Science Education.*

Andersson, B. (1976). *Science teaching and the development of thinking.* Gothenburg, Sweden: Gothenburg University.

Arvola-Orlander, A., & Wickman, P.-O. (2011). Bodily experiences in secondary school biology. *Cultural Studies in Science Education, 6*(3), 569–594.

Ausubel, D. P. (1968). *Educational psychology, a cognitive view.* New York: Holt, Rinehart, and Winston.

Ausubel, D. P., Novak, J. D., & Hanesian, H. (1978). *Educational psychology: A cognitive view* (2nd ed.). New York: Holt, Rinehart, and Winston.

Biesta, G. (2002). How general can *Bildung* be? Reflections on the future of a modern educational ideal. *Journal of Philosophy of Education, 36,* 377–390.

Blankertz, H. (1975). *Theorien und Modelle der Didaktik* (9 ed.). München: Juventa Verlag.

Bourdieu, P. (1984). *Distinction: A social critique of the judgement of taste.* London: Routledge.

Brousseau, G. (1997). *Theory of didactical situations in mathematics.* Dordrecht, the Netherlands: Kluwer Academic Publishers.

Bulte, A. M. W. (2007). How to connect concepts of science and technology when designing context-based science education. In C. Linder, L. Östman, & P.-O. Wickman (Eds.), *Promoting scientific literacy: Science education research in transaction. Proceedings of the Linnaeus Tercentenary Symposium* (pp. 140–147). Uppsala: Uppsala University.

Bulte, A. M. W., Westbroek, H. B., de Jong, O., & Pilot, A. (2006). A research approach to designing chemistry education using authentic practices as contexts. *International Journal of Science Education, 28,* 1063–1086.

Caillot, M. (2007). The building of a new academic field: The case of French didactiques. *European Educational Research Journal, 6,* 125–130.

Cherryholmes, C. H. (1988). *Power and criticism.* New York: Teachers College Press.

Chevallard, Y. (2007). Readjusting didactics to a changing epistemology. *European Educational Research Journal, 6*(2), 131–134.

Cuban, L. (1992). Curriculum stability and change. In P. Jackson (Ed.), *Handbook of research on curriculum* (pp. 216–247). New York: Macmillan.

Demuth, R., Gräsel, C., Parchmann, I., & Ralle, B. (2008). *Chemie im Kontext—Von der Innovation zur nachhaltigen Verbreitung eines Unterrichtskonzepts.* Münster: Waxmann.

Dewey, J. (1929/1958). *Experience and nature* (2nd ed.). New York: Dover.

Dewey, J. (1938/1997). *Experience and education.* New York: Touchstone, Simon and Schuster.

Driver, R., & Easley, J. (1978). Pupils and paradigms: A review of literature related to concept development in adolescent science students. *Studies in science education, 5,* 61–84.

Duit, R., Gropengießer, H., Kattmann, U., Komorek, M., & Parchmann, I. (2012). The model of educational reconstruction—a framework for improving teaching and learning science. In D. Jorde & J. Dillon (Eds.), *Science education research and practice in Europe* (pp. 13–37). Rotterdam, the Netherlands: Sense Publishers.

Duit, R., Komorek, M., & Wilbers, J. (1997). Studies on educational reconstruction of chaos theory. *Research in Science Education, 27,* 339–357.

Duncan, R. G., & Rivet, A. E. (2013). Science learning progressions. *Science, 339,* 396–397.

Duschl, R. (2008). Science education in 3 part harmony: Balancing conceptual, epistemic and social learning goals. *Review of Research in Education, 32,* 268–291.

Duschl, R. A., & Jiménez-Aleixandre, M. P. (2012). Epistemic foundations for conceptual change. In S. Carver & J. Shrager (Eds.), *The journey from child to scientist: Integrating cognitive development and the education sciences* (pp. 245–262). Washington: American Psychological Association (APA) Press.

Erduran, S., & Jiménez-Aleixandre, M. P. (2007). *Argumentation in science education: Perspectives from classroom-based research.* Dordrecht, the Netherlands: Springer.

Eryaman, M. Y., & Riedler, M. (2010). Teacher-proof curriculum. In C. Kridel (Ed.), *Encyclopedia of curriculum studies* (pp. 865–866). Thousand Oaks, CA: SAGE.

Fensham, P. (2003). *Defining an identity: The evolution of science education as a field of research*. Dordrecht, the Netherlands: Kluwer Academic.

Fleck, L. (1979). *Genesis and development of a scientific fact*. Chicago: University of Chicago Press.

Freudenthal, H. (1991). *Revisiting mathematics education*. Dordrecht, the Netherlands: Kluwer.

Gilbert, J. K., Bulte, A. M. W., & Pilot, A. (2011). Concept development and transfer in context-based science education. *International Journal of Science Education, 33*(6), 817–837.

Goffman, E. (1974). *Frame analysis: An essay on the organization of experience*. Boston: Northeastern University Press.

Grayling, A. C. (1996). Epistemology. In N. Bunnin & E. P. Tsui-James (Eds.), *The Blackwell companion to philosophy* (pp. 38–63). Oxford, UK: Blackwell.

Gyllenpalm, J., & Wickman, P.-O. (2011). "Experiments" and the inquiry emphasis conflation in science teacher education. *Science Education, 95*(5), 908–926.

Gyllenpalm, J., Wickman, P.-O., & Holmgren, S.-O. (2010a). Secondary science teachers' selective traditions and examples of inquiry-oriented approaches. *Nordic Studies in Science Education, 6*(1), 44–60.

Gyllenpalm, J., Wickman, P.-O., & Holmgren, S.-O. (2010b). Teachers' language on scientific inquiry: Methods of teaching or methods of inquiry? *International Journal of Science Education, 32*(9), 1151–1172.

Hamza, K. M., & Wickman, P.-O. (2008). Describing and analyzing learning in action: An empirical study of the importance of misconceptions in learning science. *Science Education, 92,* 141–164.

Hamza, K. M., & Wickman, P.-O. (2009). Beyond explanations: What else do students need to understand science? *Science Education 93*(6), 1026–1049.

Hamza, K. M., & Wickman, P.-O. (2012). Student engagement with artefacts and scientific ideas in a laboratory and a concept mapping activity. *International Journal of Science Education.* doi:10.1080/09500 693.2012.743696

Hamza, K. M., & Wickman, P.-O. (2013). Supporting students' progression in science: Continuity between the particular, the contingent, and the general. *Science Education, 97*(1), 113–138.

Hansen, K.-H., & Olson, J. (1996). How teachers construe curriculum integration: The Science, Technology, Society (STS) movement as Bildung. *Journal of Curriculum Studies, 28,* 669–682.

Helldén, G. (1992). Grundskoleelvers förståelse av ekologiska processer *Studia Psychologica et Pedagogica. Series Altera C.* Stockholm: Almqvist & Wiksell International.

Hubber, P., Tytler, R., & Haslam, F. (2010). Teaching and learning about force with a representational focus: Pedagogy and teacher change. *Research in Science Education, 40,* 5–28.

Hudson, B., & Meyer, M.A. (2011). *Beyond fragmentation: Didactics, learning, and teaching in Europe*. Opladen, Germany: Barbara Budrich.

Jakobson, B., & Wickman, P.-O. (2008). The roles of aesthetic experience in elementary school science. *Research in Science Education 38,* 45–65.

Jank, W., & Meyer, H. (2003). *Didaktische Modelle* (rev. ed.). Berlin: Cornelsen Scriptor.

Jenkins, E. (2002). Linking school science education with action. In W.-M. Roth & J. Désautels (Eds.), *Science education as/for sociopolitical action* (pp. 17–34). Oxford: Peter Lang.

Johansson, A.-M., & Wickman, P.-O. (2011). A pragmatist approach to learning progressions. In B. Hudson & M. A. Meyer (Eds.), *Beyond fragmentation: Didactics, learning, and teaching in Europe* (pp. 47–59). Leverkusen, Germany: Barbara Budrich Publishers.

Karplus, R., & Thier, H.D. (1967). *A new look at elementary school science: Science curriculum improvement study*. Chicago: Rand McNally.

Kelly, G. J., Carlsen, W. S., & Cunningham, C. M. (1993). Science education in sociocultural context: Perspectives from the sociology of science. *Science Education, 77,* 207–220.

Klafki, W. (1958). Didaktische Analyse als Kern der Unterrichtsvorbereitung. *Die deutsche Schule, 10,* 450–471.

Klafki, W. (1969). Didaktische Analyse als Kern der Unterrichtsvorbereitung. In H. Roth & A. Blumental (Eds.), *Auswahl, Didaktische Analyse* (10th ed.). Hannover, Germany: Schroedel.

Knecht-von Martial, I. 1985: *Geschichte der Didaktik. Zur Geschichte des Begriffs und der didaktischen Paradigmen*. Frankfurt am Main: R. G. Fischer.

Komorek, M., & Duit, R. (2004). The teaching experiment as a powerful method to develop and evaluate teaching and learning sequences in the domain of non-linear systems. *International Journal of Science Education, 26,* 619–633.

Latour, B. (1987). *Science in action: How to follow scientists and engineers through society*. Milton Keynes, UK: Open University Press.

Layton, D., Jenkins, E., Macgill, S., & Davey, A. (1993). *Inarticulate science? Perspectives on the public understanding of science and some implications for science education*. Driffield, UK: Studies in Education.

Lederman, N. G. (2014). Research on teaching and learning of science. In N. G. Lederman (Ed.), *Handbook of research on science education* (2nd ed.). New York: Routledge.

Lemke, J. L. (1990). *Talking science: Language, learning and values*. Norwood, NJ: Ablex Publishing Corporation.

Lidar, M., Lundqvist, L., & Östman, L. (2006). Teaching and learning in the science classroom: The interplay between teachers' epistemological moves and students' practical epistemology. *Science Education, 90*(3), 148–163.

Ligozat, F. (2011). The determinants of the joint action in didactics: The text–action relationship in teaching practice. In M. A. Meyer & B. Hudson (Eds.), *Beyond fragmentation: Didactics, learning and teaching in Europe* (pp. 157–176). Opladen, Germany: Barbara Budrich Publishers.

Ligozat, F., & Schubauer-Leoni, M.-L. (2010). The joint action theory in didactics: Why do we need it in the case of teaching and learning mathematics? In V. Durand Guerrier, S. Maury, & F. Arzarello (Eds.), *Proceedings of the Sixth Congress of the European Society for Research in Mathematics Education* (pp. 1615–1624). Lyon, France: INRP.

Lijnse, P. L., & Klaassen, K. (2004). Didactical structures as an outcome of research on teaching–learning sequences? *International Journal of Science Education, 26*(5), 537–554.

Linder, C., Östman, L., Roberts, D. A., Wickman, P.-O., Erickson, G., & MacKinnon, A. (Eds.). (2011). *Exploring the landscape of scientific literacy*. New York: Routledge.

Lundegård, I. (2008). Self, values and the world—young people in dialogue on sustainable development. In J. Öhman (Ed.), *Values and democracy in education for sustainable development—contributions from Swedish research* (pp. 123–144). Stockholm: Liber.

Lundqvist, E., Almqvist, J., & Östman, L. (2009). Epistemological norms and companion meanings in science classroom communication. *Science Education, 93*(5), 859–874.

Lundqvist, E., Almqvist, J., & Östman, L. (2012). Institutional traditions in teachers' manners of teaching. *Cultural Studies of Science Education, 7*(1), 111–127.

May, W. T. (1993). Teaching as a work of art in the medium of the curriculum. *Theory Into Practice, 32,* 210–218.

Munby, H., Cunningham, M., & Lock, C. (2000). School science culture: A case study of barriers to developing professional knowledge. *Science Education, 84,* 193–211.

Munby, H., & Russell, T. (1992). Frames of reflection: An introduction. In T. Russell & H. Munby (Eds.), *Teachers and teaching: From classroom to reflection* (pp. 1–8). London: Falmer Press.

National Research Council. (2007). *Taking science to school: Learning and teaching science in grades K–8*. Washington, DC: National Academies Press.

Novak, J. D. (1977). *A theory of education*. Ithaca, NY: Cornell University Press.

Novak, J. D. (1990). Concept maps and vee diagrams: Two metacognitive tools for science and mathematics education. *Instructional Science, 19,* 29–52.

Öhman, J., & Östman, L. (2007). Continuity and change in moral meaning-making: A transactional approach. *Journal of Moral Education, 36,* 151–168.

Östman, L. (1994). Rethinking science teaching as a moral act. *Journal of Nordic Educational Research, 14,* 141–150.

Östman, L. (1995). *Meaning and socialization: Science education as a political and environmental-ethical problem.* English summary in L. Östman, *Socialisation och mening: no-utbildning som politiskt och miljömoraliskt problem* (pp. 195–210). Stockholm: Almqvist & Wiksell.

Östman, L. (1996). Discourses, discursive meanings and socialization in chemistry education. *Journal of Curriculum Studies, 28,* 37–55.

Östman, L., & Almqvist, J. (2011). What do values and norms have to do with scientific literacy? In C. Linder, L. Östman, D.A. Roberts, P.-O. Wickman, G. Erickson, & A. MacKinnon (Eds.), *Exploring the landscape of scientific literacy* (pp. 160–175). New York: Routledge.

Parchmann, I., Gräsel, C., Bear, A., Nentwig, P., Demuth, R., Ralle, B., & Group, T. C.P. (2006). "Chemie im Kontext": A symbiotic implementation of a context-based teaching and learning approach. *International Journal of Science Education, 28,* 1041–1062.

Pedersen, S. (1992). *Om elevers förståelse av naturvetenskapliga förklaringar och biologiska sammanhang* (Vol. 31). Stockholm: Almqvist & Wiksell International.

Peukert, H. (2002). Beyond the present state of affairs: *Bildung* and the search for orientation in rapidly transforming societies. *Journal of Philosophy of Education, 36,* 421–435.

Piqueras, J., Hamza, K.M., & Edvall, S. (2008). The practical epistemologies in the museum: A study of students' learning in encounters with dioramas. *Journal of Museum Education, 33*(2), 153–164.

Prins, G. T., Bulte, A. M. W., & Pilot, A. (2011). Evaluation of a design principle for fostering students' epistemological views on models and modelling using authentic practices as contexts for learning in chemistry education. *International Journal of Science Education, 33*(11), 1539–1569.

Prins, G. T., Bulte, A. M. W., Van Driel, J. H., & Pilot, A. (2008). Selection of authentic modelling practices as contexts for chemistry education. *International Journal of Science Education, 30*(1), 1–24.

Riemeier, T., & Gropengießer, H. (2008). On the roots of difficulties in learning about cell division: Process-based analysis of students' conceptual development in teaching experiments. *International Journal of Science Education, 30,* 923–939.

Riquarts, K., & Hopmann, S. (1995). Starting a dialogue: Issues in a beginning conversation between didaktik and the curriculum traditions. *Journal of Curriculum Studies, 27,* 3–12.

Roberts, D.A. (1982). Developing the concept of "curriculum emphases" in science education. *Science Education, 66,* 243–260.

Roberts, D.A., & Bybee, R. (2014). Science and scientific literacy. In N.G. Lederman (Ed.), *Handbook of research on science education,* (2nd ed.). New York: Routledge.

Roberts, D.A., & Östman, L. (Eds.). (1998). *Problems of meaning in science curriculum.* New York: Teachers College Press.

Rogoff, B. (1990). *Apprenticeship in thinking. Cognitive development in social context.* Oxford: Oxford University Press.

Rorty, R. (1991). *Objectivity, relativism, and truth. Philosophical papers volume I* (pp. 1–17). Cambridge, UK: Cambridge University Press.

Roth, W.-M., & Calabrese Barton, A. (2004). *Rethinking scientific literacy.* New York: Routledge.

Ruthven, K., Laborde, C., Leach, J., & Tiberghien, A. (2009). Design tools in didactical research: Instrumenting the epistemological and cognitive aspects of the design of teaching sequences. *Educational Researcher, 38*(5), 329–342.

Sadler, T.D. (2009). Situated learning in science education: Socio-scientific issues as contexts for practice. *Studies in Science Education, 45*(1), 1–42.

Sahlberg, P. (2011). *Finnish lessons: What can the world learn from educational change in Finland?* New York: Teachers College Press.

Säljö, R., & Bergqvist, K. (1997). Seeing the light: Discourse and practice in the optics lab. In L.B. Resnick, R. Säljö, C. Pontecorvo, & B. Burge (Eds.), *Discourse, tools, and reasoning: Essays on situated cognition* (pp. 385–405). Berlin: Springer.

Santini, J. (2009). *Characterization of the joint elaboration of conceptual understanding and of students' performances. Volcanoes and earthquakes at Grade 5.* Paper presented at the European Conference on Educational Research, Vienna, Austria.

Schneuwly, B. (2011). Subject didactics—an academic field related to the teacher profession and teacher education. In B. Hudson & M.A. Meyer (Eds.), *Beyond fragmentation: Didactics, learning and teaching in Europe* (pp. 275–286). Leverkusen Opladen, Germany: Barbara Budrich.

Seel, H. (1999). Didaktik as the professional science of teachers. *TNTEE Publications, 2,* 85–93.

Sensevy, G. (2010). Outline of a joint action theory in didactics. In V. Durand Guerrier, S. Maury, & F. Arzarello (Eds.), *Proceedings of the Sixth Congress of the European Society for Research in Mathematics Education* (pp. 1645–1654). Lyon, France: INRP.

Sensevy, G. (2011). Overcoming fragmentation: Towards a joint action theory in didactics. In B. Hudson & M. A. Meyer (Eds.), *Beyond fragmentation: Didactics, learning, and teaching in Europe* (pp. 60–76). Leverkusen, Opladen: Barbara Budrich.

Sensevy, G. (2012). Patterns of didactic intentions, thought collective and documentation work. In G. Gueudet, B. Pepin, & L. Trouche (Eds.), *From text to 'lived' resources: Mathematics curriculum materials and teacher development* (pp. 43–57). New York: Springer.

Sensevy, G., Mercier, A., & Schubauer-Leoni, M.-L. (2000). Vers un modèle de l'action didactique du professeur, à propos de la Course à 20. *Recherches en Didactique des Mathématiques, 20*(3), 263–304.

Sensevy, G., Mercier, A., Schubauer-Leoni, M.-L., Ligozat, F., & Perrot, G. (2005). An attempt to model the teacher's action in mathematics. *Educational Studies in Mathematics, 59*(1), 153–181.

Sensevy, G., Tiberghien, A., Santini, J., Laubé, S., & Griggs, P. (2008). An epistemological approach to modeling: Case studies and implications for science teaching. *Science Education, 92*(3), 424–446.

Sfard, A. (1998). On two metaphors for learning and the danger of choosing just one. *Educational Researcher, 27*(2), 4–13.

Shulman, L.S. (1986). Those who understand: Knowledge growth in teaching. *Educational Researcher, 15,* 4–14.

Shulman, L.S. (1987). Knowledge and teaching: Foundations of the new reform. *Harvard Educational Review, 57,* 1–22.

Sjøberg, S. (2009). *Naturfag som allmenndannelse: en kritisk fagdidaktikk* [In Norwegian: *Science as allgemeine Bildung—a critical subject didactics*] (3rd ed.). Oslo: Gyldendal.

Staberg, E.-M. (1992). *Olika världar skilda värderingar—Hur flickor och pojkar möter högstadiets fysik, kemi och teknik.* Umeå: Pedagogiska institutionen, Umeå universitet.

Steffe, L. P., & Thompson, P. W. (2000). Teaching experiment methodology: Underlying principles and essential elements. In R. Lesh & A. E. Kelly (Eds.), *Research Design in Mathematics and Science Education* (pp. 267–307). Hillsdale, NJ: Erlbaum.

Stolk, M.J., de Jong, O., Bulte, A.M.W., & Pilot, A. (2011). Exploring a framework for professional development in curriculum innovation: Empowering teachers for designing context-based chemistry education. *Research in Science Education, 41,* 369–388.

Sund, P., & Wickman, P.-O. (2011). Socialisation content in schools and education for sustainable development: I. A study of teachers' selective traditions. *Environmental Education Research, 17,* 599–624.

Tiberghien, A. (1994). Modeling as a basis for analyzing teaching—learning situations. *Learning and instruction, 4,* 71–87.

Tiberghien, A. (2000). Designing teaching situations in the secondary school. In R. Millar, J. Leach, & J. Osborne (Eds.), *Improving science education: The contribution of research* (pp. 22–47). Buckingham, UK: Open University Press.

Tiberghien, A. (2007). Legitimacy and references for scientific literacy. In C. Linder, L. Östman, & P.-O. Wickman (Eds.), *Promoting scientific literacy: Science education research in transaction. Proceedings of the Linnaeus Tercentenary Symposium* (pp. 130–133). Uppsala: Uppsala University.

Tiberghien, A., & Sensevy, G. (2012). The nature of video studies in science education: Analysis of teaching and learning processes. In D. Jorde & J. Dillon (Eds.), *Science education research and practice in Europe: Retrospective and prospective* (pp. 141–179). Rotterdam, the Netherlands: Sense Publishers.

Tiberghien, A., Vince, J., & Gaidioz, P. (2009). Design-based research: Case of a teaching sequence on mechanics. *International Journal of Science Education, 31,* 2275–2314.

Van Aalsvoort, J. (2004). Activity theory as a tool to address the problem of chemistry's lack of relevance in secondary school chemical education. *International Journal of Science Education, 26*(13), 1635–1651.

Vygotsky, L. S. (1978). *Mind in society. The development of higher psychological processes.* Cambridge: Harvard University Press.

Wenger, E. (1998). *Communities of practice. Learning, meaning, and identity.* Cambridge: Cambridge University Press.

Westbroek, H. B., Klaassen, K., Bulte, A. M. W., & Pilot, A. (2010). Providing students with a sense of purpose by adapting a professional practice. *International Journal of Science Education, 32*(5), 603–627.

Wickman, P.-O. (2004). The practical epistemologies of the classroom: A study of laboratory work. *Science Education, 88*(3), 325–344.

Wickman, P.-O. (2006). *Aesthetic experience in science education: Learning and meaning-making as situated talk and action.* Mahwah, NJ: Lawrence Erlbaum Associates.

Wickman, P.-O. (2012a). Using pragmatism to develop didactics in Sweden. *Zeitschrift für Erziehungswissenschaft, 15,* 483–501.

Wickman, P.-O. (2012b). How can conceptual schemes change teaching? *Cultural Studies of Science Education, 7,* 129–136.

Wickman, P.-O. (2012c). A comparison between practical epistemology analysis and some schools in French didactics. *Education & Didactique, 6*(2), 145–159.

Wickman, P.-O., Liberg, C., & Östman, L. (2012). Transcending science: Scientific literacy and *Bildung* for the 21st century. In D. Jorde & J. Dillon (Eds.), *Science education research and practice in Europe* (pp. 39–61). Rotterdam, the Netherlands: Sense Publishers.

Wickman, P.-O., & Ligozat, F. (2011). Scientific literacy as action: Consequences for content progression. In C. Linder, L. Östman, D. A. Roberts, P.-O. Wickman, G. Erickson, & A. MacKinnon (Eds.), *Exploring the landscape of scientific literacy* (pp. 145–159). New York: Routledge.

Wickman, P.-O., & Östman, L. (2002a). Learning as discourse change: A sociocultural mechanism. *Science Education, 86*(5), 601–623.

Wickman, P.-O., & Östman, L. (2002b). Induction as an empirical problem: How students generalize during practical work. *International Journal of Science Education, 24*(5), 465–486.

Wittgenstein, L. (1967). *Philosophical investigations* (3rd ed.). Oxford, UK: Blackwell.

Zeidler, D. L. (1984). Moral issues and social policy in science education: Closing the literacy gap. *Science Education, 68,* 411–419.

Zeidler, D. L., & Sadler, T. D. (2011). An inclusive view of scientific literacy: Core issues and future directions. In C. Linder, L. Östman, D. A. Roberts, P.-O. Wickman, G. Erickson, & A. MacKinnon (Eds.), *Exploring the landscape of scientific literacy* (pp. 176–192). New York: Routledge.

Section III

Diversity and Equity in Science Learning

SECTION EDITORS: CORY A. BUXTON AND OKHEE LEE

9

Unpacking and Critically Synthesizing the Literature on Race and Ethnicity in Science Education

Eileen Carlton Parsons

I am an invisible man. . . . I am invisible, understand, simply because people refuse to see me. . . . When they approach me they see only my surroundings, themselves, or figments of their imagination—indeed, everything and anything except me. . . . You're constantly being bumped against by those of poor vision. Or again, you often doubt if you really exist. You wonder whether you aren't simply a phantom in other people's minds. . . . It's when you feel like this that, out of resentment, you begin to bump people back.

(Ellison, 1994, as cited in Parsons, Simpson, & Cooper, 2009, p. 3)

This quote is taken from Ralph Ellison's classic novel titled *The Invisible Man*, first published in its entirety in 1952. The main character and narrator in *The Invisible Man* is an unnamed African American male whose story speaks to the experiences of those who were Black and American in the United States during the time period the book was written. The protagonist described himself as being invisible, a state of being present but unacknowledged. Invisibility is confirmed in two ways in the quote.

The main character implicates the first way in which invisibility is imposed upon him in his description of how others, those empowered to decide whether they see him, approach him. Others know he is there because they bump against him, but instead of seeing him and acknowledging his presence, they use proxies to infer his existence and approximate the space that he occupies. They use the surroundings, their own life experiences, and frameworks they select to account for and make meaning of his reality. That is, the protagonist becomes that which is circumvented. The second mechanism that substantiates the character's invisibility is the need for the character to become visible by bumping back, the protagonist's attempt to compel recognition. Recognition, although compelled, is defined here as a noticing necessitated by circumstances. Though fictional in nature and written several decades ago, the protagonist's state of invisibility depicted in the quote from

The Invisible Man is analogous to the status of race and ethnicity in science education research and scholarship.

Chapter Overview

At first glance, the literature searches described in Appendix A[1] appeared to identify a large corpus of literature in science education that pertained to race and ethnicity. Upon closer scrutiny, far less than what one would imagine from research and scholarship conducted over many decades constituted the pool for this critical unpacking and synthesis of the literature, the intent of this handbook chapter. The examination of this literature, limited in scope and depth, was conducted from a critical perspective, one that aligns with critical race theory that is discussed later in the chapter, and occurred with respect to several purposes. The purposes of this handbook chapter were to (1) unpack and synthesize science education research on race and ethnicity, (2) critique this body of literature, and (3) propose recommendations for future research and scholarship. Throughout the chapter, which consists of three sections, recommendations and closing remarks, invisibility of Ellison's (1994) protagonist and its substantiation are revisited to further illuminate the status of race and ethnicity in science education.

Integral to the purposes of the chapter are how race and ethnicity are viewed. The chapter's first section presents the conceptualizations of race and ethnicity that inform the deconstruction and synthesis of the literature. The conceptualizations are borrowed from the disciplines of anthropology, history, and sociology. Race and ethnicity are treated in this chapter as context-based sociohistorical constructs that exist across space and time (Parsons & Bayne, 2012). In addition, the conceptualizations of race and ethnicity are situated in the United States, and the evolution of race and ethnicity over time are emphasized (Parsons, 2008).

The second section of the chapter addresses the first purpose, an unpacking of the science education research and scholarship on race and ethnicity. Ways in which the science education research and scholarship conducted over several decades converged and diverged guide the review. Responses to the aforementioned pertain to how race and ethnicity were constructed and treated, with secondary attention to methods and findings.

The sociological and historical view of the context-based sociohistorical constructions of race and ethnicity posited in the first section along with the conceptualizations highlighted and the methodologies mentioned in the second section provide the foundations for the critique, the second purpose of the handbook chapter. Four critiques comprise the third section: presentism, lack of conceptual clarity, individualism, and methodological myopia. The science education research and scholarship on race and ethnicity is heavily steeped in presentism, the first limitation of the reviewed literature. Presentism is a view that exclusively situates and circumscribes current conditions to the here and now (Noblit, 2013; Parsons, 2008). The neglect of the purposeful construction of race and ethnicity over time in the United States, the connection between their historical meanings and contemporary adaptations, and the resemblances of past and present outcomes (e.g., who has access to high quality science experiences) associated with race and ethnicity relate to the second limitation—lack of conceptual clarity.

Much of the science education research and scholarship on race and ethnicity did not explicitly define the constructs. When conceptualizations were present, proxies constituted them or they were rooted in frameworks that appropriately considered the individual with respect to race and ethnicity but ignored the structural and systems view of race and ethnicity. That is, the conceptualizations of race and ethnicity employed in the science education literature predominantly ignored the systemic constructions of race and ethnicity that enable them to exist across spaces and time in ways that impact, in perpetuity, the life experiences of groups and their individual members. The last critique pertains to methods employed in the science education literature on race and ethnicity. A vast majority of research conducted in the mid- to late 20th century approached race and ethnicity using quantitative methods, and these methods appeared to be undergirded by a post-positivist perspective, whereas work conducted in the latter 20th and early 21st century employed qualitative methods that seemed to be rooted in the constructivist paradigm. The use of a narrow selection of methods severely limited the potential of science education research and scholarship to impact science education with respect to equality and equity, one purported aims of science education.

Recommendations, included in the last part of the chapter, address the third purpose. Suggestions are offered for research and scholarship on race and ethnicity in science education. The recommendations propose tenets of critical race theory as possible underpinnings for ethnicity- and race-focused science education research and scholarship. The tenets, which are conceptual and methodological in nature, can alleviate the preeminence of presentism and provide conceptual clarity that balances race and ethnicity as individual, group-level, and structural and systems phenomena. Additionally, the recommendations discuss the transformative paradigm as an alternative to the either-or use of quantitative and qualitative methods and post-positivist and constructivist paradigms that have previously restricted the usefulness of science education research and scholarship on race and science in informing practice and policy.

Section I: The Evolution of Race and Ethnicity

The boundaries of the two constructs are blurry, both historically and contemporarily. For example, in current U.S. policy, one ethnic classification, Hispanic, based on language, is recognized, but it is acknowledged that the ethnic group can consist of various racial groups. Race and ethnicity were broached as related but conceptually distinct in this critical, integrative review.

Fenton (2010) described race and ethnicity as members of the same family of concepts that share noticeable family characteristics. The resemblances of descent, ancestry, or common antecedents are at their core, but they diverge in important ways at the periphery (Fenton, 2010). Although Fenton treated race and ethnicity as indistinguishable in his examination of ethnicity, Fenton's summary of the distinctions cited in the sociological and anthropological literature were relevant in this review: Race is founded on visible, physical appearance as markers of difference, and ethnicity is based on cultural identifiers as the reference point for difference. Culture, in this sense, is used broadly to include a myriad of factors like religion, customs, and traditions.

Ethnicity

A clear consensus on what is ethnicity in the U.S. context was absent in the sociological and anthropological literature. Many of the conceptualizations predicated ethnicity on ancestry and a shared culture. A shared culture was generally described as customs, traditions, and language, with self-identification and self-affiliation as elements (Nagel, 1994). These conceptualizations also historically situated ethnicity as a social identifier to position one group superior to another and to separate and distance the superior group from the inferior one. Ethnicity as the criteria for sorting individuals into various groups primarily occurred with Whites. Consequently, many scholars associated ethnicity with the differentiation of Whites, one racial group formally recognized in the U.S. census and other civic documents (Fenton, 2010; Yinger, 1985), and not with other groups (Omi & Winant, 1994). For instance, it is uncommon for Blacks to be considered an ethnic group (Omi & Winant, 1994). Other scholars linked ethnicity to immigration (Greer, 1984). In the present day, the association of ethnicity to Whites is tenuous, but ethnicity to immigrants is not.

Indigenous Native Americans and people from Britain, Ireland, and the continent of Africa largely constituted the U.S. population during the 17th, 18th, and 19th centuries. As implicated in the later section on the construction of race,

> ideas of freedom and human dignity applied to whites. The ideals of the Enlightenment simultaneously identified the "enlightened" races and the lower peoples. U.S. citizenship and civic participation were founded on a concept of white and black, of white and red and of enlightened and savage (Jacobson, 1998).
>
> (Fenton, 2010, p. 27)

The Naturalization Act of 1790 established by the first U.S. Congress was an example of how freedom, human dignity, and enlightenment were reserved for Whites. The Act declared that "all free white persons" who emigrated to the United States were entitled to the rights of citizenship (e.g., property ownership). The Act further articulated the rules for accessing such entitlements.

Between 1820 and 1920, the period of industrialization in the United States, massive numbers emigrated from southern and eastern Europe to the United States, secured work as laborers in industry, and clustered in the poorer areas of the growing industrial urban centers. The early settlers, who had formed a group identity as Anglo-Saxon and mostly Protestant in religion, labeled these newcomers as non–Anglo-Saxon and predominately Catholic. The early settlers regarded the southern and eastern Europeans as undesirables who engaged in depraved customs and traditions (Banks, 1995). Although confronted by prejudices, the European immigrants were largely given citizenship as a consequence of their physical appearance as White. They enjoyed the psychological and material benefits citizenship and civic participation entailed.

In lieu of subjugation, the end served by the construction of race, ethnicity at this time in U.S. history functioned to control contact among the early settlers and the newly arrived and to socialize the newcomers, mainly through some form of education, to be the right kind of citizen (Webb, 2006). For the southern and eastern European immigrants, challenges surfaced in reconciling polarizing positions that pertained to group identity: assimilation and incorporation into the Anglo-Saxon, Protestant way or cultural pluralism and preservation of one's cultural heritage (Omi & Winant, 1994).

The 20th century marked the conflation of ethnicity and race. As basic rights afforded to White U.S. citizens were extended to previously subjugated groups with phenotypes that differed from those of Whites, political leaders and scholars employed aspects of the ethnicity paradigm to these groups. The paradigm was used to either advance the inclusion of these groups with U.S. competitiveness and democratic ideals as justifications for their inclusion or to explain their lack of integration into society. Based on the experience of the White, European immigrants in the 17th, 18th, and 19th centuries, the inclusion of racial groups into 20th-century society was contingent on assimilation.

The White immigrants from southern and eastern Europe, the vast majority with free rather than indentured servitude status, were initially viewed upon their arrival as ethnically inferior individuals, but because they shared the phenotypes of the Anglo-Saxon settlers, the European immigrants were allotted various rights, given access to opportunities, and naturalized. In contrast, subjugated groups that differed in phenotype from the Anglo-Saxon settlers were treated as property, persistently viewed as inferior beings unworthy of basic human rights. Naturalization of these groups was illegal, and any form of citizenship was regarded as heretical. Because of their differentiated status in the United States, assimilation for European immigrants and for subjugated racial groups resulted in different consequences and outcomes (e.g., becoming culturally similar in order to integrate versus accepting property-status norms to secure second-class citizenship).

The ethnicity paradigm expected subjugated racial groups, like the White, European immigrants, to succeed through hard work without taking note that these racial groups were relegated to labor in certain domains that generated material outcomes for others, not for themselves. These racial groups were denied citizenship and its corresponding material and psychological benefits; such denial inextricably limited their access to opportunities to procure and build wealth (e.g., property, higher education legacies) that established the foundations from which every generation thereafter could build (Omi & Winant, 1994). In addition, the application of the ethnicity paradigm to subjugate racial groups ignored the continued existence of mechanisms that consistently and systematically reproduced the status quo: race-based exclusion from full participation in civic life (e.g., voting restrictions, inhibitions to educational opportunities). Consequently, in the 1960s and 1970s, racial groups—Blacks later joined by Chicanos, Indians, and Asians—rejected ethnicity and embraced race as they demanded group rights and representation in governance (Omi & Winant, 1994).

Possibly due to the increasing diversity of immigrants and because of the silencing discourse around race to be discussed later, ethnicity, including symbolic in nature (i.e., customs and traditions not practiced; Nagel, 1994), became more pervasive in the latter 20th century and into the 21st century. This shift to ethnicity was most evident in labels used by groups to self-identify; in some cases, the labels went from signification of color (e.g., Black) to identification of continent of origin (e.g., African American). Discourse in the United States used global labels to identify (e.g., Asian American), whereas some groups featured country or culture of origin (e.g., Korean American) to self-identify.

These ethnic-signifying labels highlighted the tensions between self-identification and identification ascribed by others. ". . . self-identification is not simply a matter of individual choice, but is affected by the larger societal, historical, and political constraints" (Atwater, Lance, Woodard, &

Woodard, 2013, p. 7). Whether or not an individual is a member of groups that favorably rank (e.g., positively perceived, well-represented in or dominate governance in public life) in the societal hierarchy influences how self-identification versus ascription by others translates into lived experiences. Self-identification for groups and the groups' members versus ascription by others are existent perplexities in the research and scholarship in science education.

Race

Scientific work conducted over centuries sought a genetic basis for the construct of race to support its veracity as an evidence-based, objective measure to separate human beings into identifiable groups. Research eventually showed that race was not a biological phenomenon: Any two human beings are approximately 99.9% genetically the same (Bohnam, Warshauer-Baker, & Collins, 2005). The lack of evidence for a genetic delineation of human beings into subgroups negated a biologistic view of race, but it did not prevent its continued use to organize and structure the social world.

Currently, many concede that race is a social construction that ascribes meaning to aspects of human physiognomy, that race is a human-derived relation, not a thing (Bonilla-Silva, 1999). Worth is assigned to different kinds of human bodies, and these valuations serve varied economic, political, educational, social, and cultural aims. These ascribed meanings to physical characteristics first create societal hierarchies and then position groups and their members within them (Omi & Winant, 1994). The sociological literature extensively documents, from various vantage points and perspectives, the social and historical processes to which Omi and Winant referred.

The predecessor to the U.S. contemporary construction of race emerged in Europe as part of the conquest of Ireland during the 12th century; Whites were categorized on the basis of ethnicity into inferior (e.g., Irish) and superior groups (e.g., English; Banks, 1995; Bonnet, 1998). This inferior-superior dichotomy of human worth organized reality when the English settlers encountered the indigenous peoples in what is now the United States. As the U.S. settlement grew, the demand for labor to ensure its continual growth increased. Simultaneously, condemnation of White servitude as the labor base intensified and the philosophy that the human race consisted of different species eclipsed the once-dominant belief that all human beings were of one race and one species (Watkins, 2001). Race rather than ethnicity defined groups as superior and inferior. Race was based on biological markers, physical features linked to characteristics that were used to assign value to various groups in relation to the needs of the developing nation (Bonnet, 1998; Smedley & Smedley, 2005).

In the early 1600s, a system that constructed Whites as a racial group and subordinated other groups, primarily those that differed from the Anglo-Saxon settlers in phenotype, was established. In significantly larger numbers than other groups, Blacks were subjected by Whites.

By the mid-1800s with the support of science (Gould, 1981; Jackson & Weidman, 2006), an identifiable racial ideology emerged. Physical characteristics were linked to behaviors, ability, intelligence, and the like, and these linkages were used to designate groups as superior and inferior. The racial ideology that separated human beings into superior and inferior groups organized reality in the United States such that group membership indelibly shaped the lives of group members (Manning, 1993; Smedley, 2001). Although prominently evident in the U.S. history of Blacks, this racial ideology was also operative for other groups. For example, Mexican Americans were considered naturalized citizens and classified as White in 1848, but in 1930, the economic depression era, Mexican Americans were classified into a separate category as Mexicans for the first time in the U.S. Census. This reclassification as non–White reflected Mexicans' diminishing status in society (Sheridan, 2003).

This racial ideology with Whites as the superior other with certain rights and privileges associated with being White (i.e., whiteness) has manifested in different ways throughout U.S. history. Racial apartheid in the 18th and 19th centuries; a tiered system of U.S. citizenship in the 20th century; and a 21st-century racialized underclass, impoverished people of low social status with limited and structurally (informally and formally) circumscribed political, economic, and educational influence are just a few ways in which the construct of race has persisted across time and space in the United States. This racial ideology has been challenged or championed throughout U.S. history in the form of wars, sociopolitical movements, and legislations. The racial ideology and its ramifications are cemented in U.S. history. The trademark of this racial record is a cycle of progress and retrenchment, the abrogation of progress when advances radically deviate from and threaten existent societal hierarchies (Bell, 1995).

Critical scholars contend, not to disparage the progress made but to advance the work that remains, that the U.S. racial legacy continues in contemporary times by way of modified and widely accepted configurations. One accepted configuration, documented by extensive research, is the *de facto* racial segregation in public education and the association of this segregation with distinctive patterns of resource allocation according to racial composition of schools (Ladson-Billings, 2006; Wells & Frankenberg, 2007). Public schools referred to as low minority enrollment receive higher-quality and greater quantities of resources. These modified configurations that reflect the racial history of the United States are buttressed by color blindness and, more recently, postracialism. Color blindness and postracialism seek to conceal race, make it invisible, or circumvent it, subsequently making normative the existent racial hierarchy in society.

Race neutrality, an understandably appealing notion in light of past and present injustices and brutalities that have occurred around race, is the ideal for color blindness. The logic often attributed to the ideal of race neutrality is as follows: If there is no race then its material effects will cease to exist. No race translates into no racism, no racial inequity, no racial inequality, and no racial atrocities (Ullucci & Battey, 2011). In the quest to realize race neutrality, individuals and institutions disfavor any use of race even if color blindness perpetuates and exacerbates disparities across racial lines (Lopez, 2006).

The notion of color blindness first emerged in Justice Harlan's dissent decision for the 1896 U.S. Supreme Court case *Plessy v. Ferguson,* a case that examined the constitutionality of *de jure* segregation of public accommodations. Lopez (2007) argued that the adherents of the Harlan variety of color blindness are not justified in their liberal use of it, that is, reject all uses of race. Harlan, based on his expressed sentiment in 1896 that Whites were superior in the United States in all aspects of civic life and would continue to hold such status in the future, objected to the uses of race when it would oppress the "inferior other." In the more recent past, color blindness gained popularity among the populace in the 1960s, first as a misinterpretation of Martin Luther King's *I Have a Dream* speech[2] and later as a counterresponse to policies that explicitly and intentionally recognized and considered race as a remedy to systemic, racial discrimination (Berry, 1996; Lopez, 2007). Color blindness advocates an ignoring of race with race neutrality as the goal. Similar to color blindness, race neutrality is central to postracialism, an ideology that has emerged in the 21st century. In contrast to color blindness, postracialism situates race neutrality not as an aspiration but as an achieved state.

After U.S. citizens elected as president the first individual who self-identified as African American, a postracial perspective became more prevalent. A postracial perspective contends that race is irrelevant. Cho (2009) purported that postracialism has several essential features. First, postracialism is premised on significant racial progress, an evaluation that does not consider equity and equality in *outcomes* (e.g., proportional representation that reflects U.S. demographics in science, technology, engineering, and mathematics fields). The postracial view contends that the United States has transcended issues of race, as epitomized in the election of a Black person to the highest office in the country. Second, postracialism promotes a race-neutral universalism as the solution to America's "race problem." Postracialism proponents define the U.S. race problem in terms of tensions among races, not as the systemic and structural positioning of races in civic life (e.g., who governs and controls resources). As such, the adoption of a race-neutral universalism in speech (e.g., eliminating the identification of racial groups) and in action (e.g., revocation of all race-based remedies to systemic racial disparities) alleviates racial divisiveness and discord, the race problem according to postracialism. Third, Cho purported that postracialism adheres to moral equivalence logic with an emphasis on individual rights. For example, according to the logic of moral equivalence, the systematic exclusion of a group of students

from a program is equal in social import and impact to the criteria-based denial of one individual from a program. In summary, postracialism contends that the racial progress made in the United States is sufficiently sound. Whites as overrepresented in every positive public domain like policy making and people of color as overrepresented in every negative public domain like incarceration (Mutegi, 2011) are exemplars of this racial progress.

Even though color blindness and postracialism assume different postures on the ideal of race neutrality, they serve the same ends: the concealment of race and normalization of the racial status quo. Color blindness and postracialism constrict the space, thereby making racial disparities impervious to scrutiny and subsequent action. Concealing race simply removes race from the nation's sight but does not eradicate its actual presence, the lived effects of race.

Section II: Unpacking and Synthesizing the Literature

Just as siblings from the same biological family are similar but differ in their characteristics—physical appearance, personality, and the like—race and ethnicity are closely related but distinct. Both are markers of group-level differences and both are founded on the notions of descent, ancestry, or common antecedents (Fenton, 2010). Cultural identifiers like religion and language are points of difference for ethnicity, and physical attributes are markers of difference for race. They further diverge in that group identity and inclusion are key issues for ethnicity, whereas group rights and equality are central concerns for race.

In its early formation, ethnicity was restricted to segregating Whites into subgroups of differing statuses. These statuses did not curtail citizenship and associated rights per se; however, they impacted social acceptance, a group's inclusion in the informal but valued workings of society. Such inclusion heavily depended upon a group's assimilation, becoming like the group with esteemed status. In later renditions of ethnicity, Whites remained at the center, but cultural pluralism, inclusion enhanced by a group's cultural identity, assuaged the preeminence of inclusion by assimilation. This expansion continued into the more recent past with ethnicity being applied to people of color, groups challenging ascription by others and advocating self-identification. In contrast to group identity and inclusion by way of assimilation or cultural pluralism, race emphasized group rights and equality.[3]

Race, group-level difference determined by human physiognomy imbued with meaning that structures social life, was constructed in the United States under identifiable conditions. These identifiable conditions also existed when race was applied to various groups (e.g., Mexican Americans before and after the onset of the economic depression era, Japanese Americans before and during World War II). In light of how race was constructed and under what conditions it was constructed and applied to various groups, capital as a valued medium of exchange appears central to the construct of race.[4] Throughout history to contemporary times, the sociohistorical construction of race systemically acts at the group level to increase capital and access to it for some and restrict capital and access to it for others.

When conceptualizations of ethnicity and race are given primacy, science education research and scholarship are limited. Little of the science education literature prioritized race and ethnicity in the research questions or objectives, the problem statements, and so on (see Appendix A for selection criteria for reviewed literature). For the research and scholarship for which race and ethnicity were the primary or secondary constructs of interest, either through intentional design or emergent in the course of the investigation, discernible patterns existed.

Ethnicity in Science Education Research and Scholarship

Science as universal is a widespread belief. Many view it as a body of knowledge that accurately reflects a knowable reality that exists independently of those who ascertain it. A scientific claim about reality is not influenced by the investigators' lived experiences affiliated with gender, race, ethnicity, and the like. A corollary of these universalistic presuppositions exists in science education: the comprehension of scientific knowledge and the examination of the associated educative processes are impervious to life experiences and corresponding subjectivities (e.g., personal beliefs, values, and attitudes). The universalism corollary was reproduced, largely as an unexamined assumption, without indelible disruption in the science education literature until the 1990s, the time period in which ethnicity-focused research and scholarship began to appear with some consistency. A few key pieces of scholarship questioned this universalism and provided the conceptual opening in the science education literature for ethnicity-focused research and scholarship.

In 1993, Atwater and Riley highlighted diversity in science education in their introduction of multicultural science education to the science education community. This essay opened with vignettes of the same prospective science teacher instructing in a classroom outside and inside the United States. The vignettes and subsequent discussions featured the explicit preparation of the teacher for students' descent and language, elements of ethnicity, in the international classroom and the lack thereof for the U.S. classroom. In their essay, Atwater and Riley issued a call for actions that accommodated diversity in the areas of curriculum and teaching. Although not entertained by Atwater and Riley, a critical examination of science from European and non–European perspectives was among the call. In their conceptual essays, Stanley and Brickhouse (1994), Cobern (1996), and Lemke (2001) accepted the charge and critically unpacked science, science education, and the educative processes therein.

Stanley and Brickhouse (1994) clearly articulated the universalistic view of science and discussed the use of this view to marginalize, at best, and to discount, at worst, multicultural perspectives in science education. Stanley and Brickhouse challenged the notion that the ontological physical world can account for the validity of scientific claims by deconstructing the vital role of scientists in scientific accounts, the sole mediators of scientific claims, and the homogeneity among their communities—conditions often ignored or deemphasized in universalism. Lemke (2001), in applying sociocultural theory to science education, further highlighted the implausibility of the universalistic view. Lemke described science and science education as social activities initiated, facilitated, and conducted by humans who operate from and within institutional and cultural frames. Stanley and Brickhouse's naming of the exclusionary function of the universalistic view operative in science and science education and Lemke's positioning of science and science education within sociocultural theory helped forge a conceptually legitimate space for ethnicity-focused research and scholarship in the literature. Within this space, Cobern (1996) laid a foundation from which ethnicity-focused research and scholarship could build.

Cobern (1996) challenged the dominant conceptual change approach and conceptual change research and scholarship that required individuals to "break with" understandings in order to acquire canonical scientific understandings. The understandings that students were expected to forfeit were based on values and beliefs that had force, central in individuals' thinking, and scope, personal relevance in a myriad of domains. Cobern problematized this "breaking with" and situated it within an idea borrowed from anthropology: worldview. Cobern defined worldview as a set of interrelated and coherent nonrational presuppositions upon which individuals' conceptions of reality are based and dispelled the myth that the presuppositions of science and science education are wholly rational. Cobern positioned science and science education as worldviews among many, debunking the privileged status of universalism and underscoring the significance of what it means for individuals to "break with" understandings that are based on values and beliefs of import to them as a requisite to adopting scientifically orthodox conceptions. "Breaking with" requires individuals to abandon one worldview for another, a process that closely resembles the assimilation-cultural pluralism tension emblematic of the ethnicity construct.

Even though scholarship on multicultural science education (Atwater & Riley, 1993), the myth of science as universal (Stanley & Brickhouse, 1994), the social and contextual nature of science and science education (Lemke, 2001), and worldview (Cobern, 1996) laid the foundation and provided the conceptual legitimacy for ethnicity-focused research and scholarship in science education, such work is meager. The next sections present and discuss science education research and scholarship with an ethnicity focus. The overt point of departure of the reviewed work is difference based on descent, ancestry, or common antecedents with group identification at the core.

Treatment of Ethnicity: Invisibility and Circumvention

As in the case of the main character in Ellison's (1994) *The Invisible Man*, ethnicity, when it is treated as invisible in the science education literature, is unacknowledged but present. When ethnicity is invisible, it is assumed or implied; it is present as a subtext in the study's problem statement, literature review, or conceptual framework. Ethnicity as assumed and implied is explicated in two examples from the literature. A group native to the United States is the subject of the first example and an immigrant group is featured in the second example.

An understanding of ethnicity is assumed in the many studies that do not conceptualize ethnicity but cite it in the descriptions of research contexts or include it as a factor in analysis. The quasi-experimental study conducted by Matthews and Smith (1994) is one example that further explicates the assumption of ethnicity in science education research and scholarship. Matthews and Smith examined, by way of multivariate analysis of covariance (MANCOVA), the influence of culturally relevant materials upon Native American students' science achievement, attitudes toward science, and attitudes toward scientists. They hypothesized that the culturally relevant materials would enhance the students' motivation, facilitate the connection between home science and school science beliefs, and thereby increase achievement. The presented findings, accompanied by cautionary remarks, confirmed the hypotheses. On one hand, the study insinuated difference along the lines of ethnicity in the investigation of culturally relevant materials and in the inclusion of "home science" and "tribe" in the hypotheses and analyses, respectively; on the other hand, what characterized these differences was not described or discussed, especially in relation to the culturally relevant materials. Ethnicity was an undergirding assumption of the study.

The second way in which ethnicity is unacknowledged but present is when it is implied. One example that elucidates the aforementioned is the qualitative case study of two Dominican mothers who collaborated and partnered with teachers to implement a curriculum that connected science and food (Hagiwara, Barton, & Contento, 2007). Although what ethnicity means in relation to Dominicans, the group to which the mothers claimed membership, was not articulated, the study's concepts implicated ethnicity. For example, the researchers discussed diaspora, a construct that allowed for the consideration of transnational experiences as well as those that were incongruent with practices at home, and funds of knowledge, which was defined as "the culturally based household knowledge that is essential to understanding what and how learning takes place with the cultural systems of immigrants' homes" (p. 479). Ethnicity was also implied throughout the findings, rich descriptions of how the mothers used the capital of their backgrounds and experiences (e.g., mixing of and switching between Spanish and English) to construct roles in school and school science that garnered positive recognition.

As explicated in the previous examples, ethnicity is invisible, an assumed or implied presence that is not explicitly acknowledged; this invisibility permeated decades of science education research and scholarship that involved ethnic groups. Within this corpus of literature in which ethnicity is largely invisible, ethnicity was made perceptible through circumvention, one means that made Ellison's (1994) invisible protagonist visible, in a small pool of studies. Circumvention, as connoted in the opening quote, primarily occurs in two ways. Proxies, including surroundings, are used to make meaning of that which is circumvented. Understanding that which is circumvented can also be derived from another's life experiences or through the use of frameworks that excluded the circumvented in their constructions. Hagiwara and colleagues (2007) alluded to circumvention when situating their study within the larger body of literature. They asserted that the immigrant Dominican population is under-researched as a partial consequence of being subsumed under categories like "minorities," "people of color," "Hispanics," or "Latinos." Masking, a term used to describe the version of circumvention mentioned in Hagiwara, Barton, and Contento, is illustrated in Basu's (2008) study. Distortion, the use of frameworks that do not appropriately or aptly capture the experiences of the circumvented, is another form that is demonstrated in Smith and Hausafus (1998).

In a critical ethnographic study that included the interviews of students and their family members, Basu (2008) investigated the cultivation of voice of five immigrant students. Basu's rich descriptions of the students' life histories highlighted the students' country of origin (i.e., Black Caribbean and Hispanic Caribbean) and family practices. These life histories were integrated into the findings, the students' expressions of identities as intellectuals in conceptual physics that challenged existent power dynamics in classrooms, schools, and communities. These identities and power dynamics were not grounded in ethnicity, one warranted expectation in light of the students' life histories and family practices. Instead, negative stereotypes of low-income, minority youth were the points of departure for cultivation of voice and the power dynamics the students' expressions questioned. In essence, low-income and minority appeared to serve as proxies for ethnicity. Like Basu (2008), Smith and Hausafus (1998) used minority as a proxy in their study. They also employed the status "at-risk" as a proxy in their study with Native American, African American, Asian American, Hispanic American, and Caucasian students and their mothers. In addition to circumventing ethnicity through the use of proxies, Smith and Hausafus employed a framework that other scholars have deemed ill suited for the study's research participants (Epstein & Dauber, 1991; Nieto, 1987). Smith and Hausafus's survey study investigated the relationship between the mothers' support of their children in mathematics and science and the children's scores on standardized tests. The telephone survey elicited mothers' responses about their behaviors, what was present in the physical environments of their homes, and their attitudes toward science and mathematics. The telephone survey, devised to measure parental support, reflected mainstream participation (e.g., volunteer in child's school, attend school-sponsored events). The stepwise regression analyses that used students' standardized test scores as the dependent variables showed that children had higher test scores if mothers conveyed the importance of science and mathematics in course taking and careers, set boundaries for their children, and visited science and mathematics exhibits and fairs with their children.

Conceptualization of Ethnicity

A small segment of the science education literature recognized ethnicity. In ways akin to the protagonist's bumping back in Ellison's (1994) *The Invisible Man*, the recognition seemed to be compelled by circumstances as evident in the justifications for the work. The circumstances cited in studies that recognized ethnicity included the changing demographics of the U.S. population (Brand & Glasson, 2004), obstacles in realizing the intentions of science education reform (Lee, 1997), and challenges in achieving equity (Ryu, 2012). This research and scholarship with ethnicity in the foreground attempted to conceptualize ethnicity.

In their ethnographic study of the role of preservice teachers' early life experiences in teachers' beliefs about diversity in the science classroom and their science pedagogy, Brand and Glasson (2004) conceptualized ethnicity through their use of Banks's (1988) ethnic identity typology as the backdrop for their study. This typology features the individual's rejection or acceptance of his or her ethnic group with his or her view of other groups as the evaluative standard. Even though the typology focuses on the individual, inherent in it are notions of group identifications with groups demarcated by cultural differences. Lee's (1997) critique of the model minority stereotype refined this group demarcation from a generalist category of Asian American to the ethnic groups contained therein.

In addressing the various factors that influenced science learning, Lee (1997) called attention to the various ethnic backgrounds of students classified as Asian American: "East Asians (i.e., Chinese, Filipino, Japanese, Korean), Pacific Islanders (i.e., Fijian, Guamanian, Hawaiian, Marshall Islander, Melanesian, Samoan, Tahitian, Tongan), Southeast Asians (i.e., Cambodian/Kampuchean, Hmong, Indonesian, Lao, Malayan, Singaporean, Thai, Vietnamese), and South Asians (i.e., Bangladeshi, Burmese, Asian Indian, Nepali, Pakistani, Sri Lankan)" (p. 109). Lee discussed the barriers that result from the model minority stereotype with regard to the different traditions (e.g., Confucianism, Buddhism) and cultural practices of the various groups, thereby conceptualizing through examples the ethnicity construct. Like Lee, Lehner (2007) conceptualized ethnicity by way of illustrations, but these illustrations highlighted ethnicity within the Black social group and were derived from the stories of high school students of the African Diaspora, historical descendants and present-day immigrants. Lehner's ethnographic study explicated ethnicity through the biology class experiences of a student who self-identified as a Black-Panamanian. Ryu (2012) also situated the experiences of students, in this case students identified as Korean immigrants, to conceptualize ethnicity, but Ryu further articulated ethnicity by discussing what it lacked, an accommodation of the structural aspects of being Asian in America. That is, Ryu conceptualized ethnicity by contrasting it to race.

Ryu (2012) examined the discursive participation of Korean students—how, when, and why they participate in science classroom discourses. Even though the qualitative study employed an identity lens in making sense of collected data, Ryu framed the study by deconstructing how Asian immigrants are positioned as both an ethnic and racial group in the United States. Ryu elaborated the traditions, customs, and cultural views posited in Lee's (1997) essay, indicators of ethnicity. Ryu also discussed, with regard to race, the perception of Asians as perpetual foreigners even when several generations had passed since emigrating to the United States and the discrimination they face as a consequence of this forever-foreigner status (e.g., restricted opportunities due to physical appearance).

In summary, few studies with an ethnicity focus included conceptualizations of ethnicity as a construct. Ethnicity was primarily defined through the experiences of research participants who were mostly people of color. The findings of this collection of works, which is small relative to the existent science education literature, affirmed what Stanley and Brickhouse called the myth of universalism: the ethnicity-focused work indicated that ethnicity matters.

How Ethnicity Matters in Science Education

The evolution of ethnicity situated it as a group-level phenomenon. Ethnicity captures the common views and practices of a group of individuals who share lived experiences. Conditions and experiences that consistently and systematically impenetrate the lives of individuals who are members of a social group in similar ways can coalesce in Cobern's (1996) worldview, a set of interrelated and coherent presuppositions upon which individuals' conceptions of reality are based. An unpacking of the science education literature showed that some of the ethnicity-focused research and scholarship implicated ethnicity as a group phenomenon in its framing, but the vast majority examined the experiences of individuals, insular units disconnected from a group experience. How ethnicity matters as a group-level phenomenon was most evident in research on Native Americans, the group of interest in much of the ethnicity-focused work in science education. The work of Allen and Crawley (1998) and Bang and Medin (2010) articulates the ways in which ethnicity matters in science education.

Allen and Crawley (1998) conducted an 18-month ethnographic study with the Traditional Kickapoo Band that involved students, teachers, and elders from the community. By way of individual and group interviews and observations in the science classrooms and in the villages in which the students lived, Allen and Crawley concluded that the Kickapoo students held participant-articulated worldviews that qualitatively differed from what was advanced in the science classroom. They further asserted that these differences in the nature and verification of knowledge, organization of content knowledge, instructional preferences, spatial propensities, and engagement styles were not irreconcilable and inhibitive to students' full participation in science. Bang and Medin (2010) reported findings similar to those of Allen and Crawley in their community-based participatory action research conducted with the Menominee tribe in Wisconsin. They compared the student participants' views and understanding of scientific knowledge before and after their involvement in a science curriculum jointly developed by the researchers and Menominee community. Bang and Medin found that after the science unit, the students' understanding changed from a list of facts to describing relationships among organisms that they identified by specific names. Additionally, students viewed scientific knowledge not as a body of facts separate from Native Americans but as a set of "knowledge-making activities done in school and community by Native people" (p. 1022).

The exemplar studies indicated that the traditions, customs, cultural practices, and other constitutive elements of ethnicity matter in several ways. Ethnicity is important in how it may infiltrate ontology, what aspects of reality are perceivable, and how this perceptible reality is interpreted and acted upon; epistemology, what counts as valid knowledge and how it is known; and learning, how knowledge is engaged.

Race in Science Education Research and Scholarship

Like the ethnicity-focused research and scholarship, the body of literature on race in science education was small relative to the science education literature writ large. The majority of this body of work employed racial classifications to divide samples into groups in order to examine a phenomenon in relation to group membership. From the review of the literature, this examination of phenomena with respect to group membership gained prominence in the late 1960s, a time when public schools began to desegregate in response to the 1954 U.S. Supreme Court decision that declared *de jure* segregation unconstitutional. Research on race in science education prior to the late 1960s, the period in which research focused on group membership seemed to surface, examined race in several different ways, ranging from conceptual essays that unpacked the meaning of race to empirical work that examined the effects of studying race as part of the science curriculum. Research in the present day continued to use racial classifications for comparing and contrasting groups, but the collection of literature also included investigations that explored race as a construct.

Treatment of Race

As in the case of ethnicity, race is invisible in the science education research and scholarship because it is assumed or implied in the majority of race-focused literature. This assumptive or implied status of race was evident in the treatment of race as a group identifier. Studies that employed race as a group identifier used race as a criterion in research. This approach circumvented race, primarily through the use of conceptual and theoretical frameworks that did not aptly accommodate the experiences of racial groups. Two additional approaches that emerged from unpacking the race-related literature, race as a focus of query and race as a structure, recognized race. Race as a focus of query explored the conceptualization of race and contemplated how the constructions of race were enacted in classrooms, schools, and U.S. society writ large. Research and scholarship that situated race as a structure cast race as a sociopolitical construction that maintained the racial status quo.

Race as a Focus of Query

The historical record noted the late 1800s as the official emergence of color blindness, but its impact on public discourse (e.g., silence around race) did not surface until more than a century later. Science education research in the 1940s, 1950s, and 1960s treated race as a topic and construct of inquiry.

The work in the 1940s highlighted the possible role of science education in addressing the polarizing public views around race. Some segments of society contended that race was indeed a functionally important and genetically based distinction among human beings, whereas others, naming Nazi Germany as an illustration, argued the opposite, race as a human construction devised for sociopolitical purposes. Based on the premise that "race is an expression of nature (inheritance), not nurture (learning)," Washburn (1944) proffered a middle ground between the two dominant views on race by defining racial classifications as an anatomical concept (p. 65). By tracing the history of anatomical classifications from the simple noting of physical attributes of populations in different parts of the world to describing the evolutionary history of humankind, Washburn discussed the utility of racial classification, a scheme central to the work of physical anthropologists seeking to understand human variation and information important for international relations. Washburn also discussed the limitations of racial classifications; they were unable to provide information on intelligence, language, and so forth. Washburn considered the conceptualization of race, clarification of facts, and articulation of valid uses of facts to be the areas in which science teachers could contribute. Evans and Tannenbaum (1944) further elaborated Washburn's view on the role of science teachers by describing the popular blood typing laboratory activity and using the students' findings to critique current race-related policies like the separation of blood given by White and Black donors in U.S. blood banks.

Opinion pieces on the importance of understanding what race meant in the context of the times (Boulos, 1965; McEwan, 1951; Schindelman 1946) and its inclusion in the science curriculum (Brown, 1945) followed the early 1940s emphasis on facts related to race. The 1950s ushered in an empirical approach to the study of race that reiterated the importance of addressing race in science instruction and science curriculum purported in opinion essays. These studies examined the impact of race-related instruction on the attitudes of college-age students (Solomon & Braunschneider, 1950); such systematic inquiry did not emerge at the precollege level until the early 1960s. These quasi-experimental studies, systematic queries that examine causation by manipulating the variable of interest under conditions that do not include random assignment of participants, investigated changes in White students' knowledge and attitudes before and after some type of race instruction. These studies of racial knowledge and attitudes that indicated positive changes, such as from a biologistic to a social construction view of race (Davis, 1963), were largely displaced by research that examined phenomena with respect to racial group membership; this began in the late 1960s, a period of civil unrest in the United States around rights for people of color.

Race as a Group Identifier

Race as a group identifier comprised the vast majority of race-related research in science education. Race was a procedural criterion for identifying and subdividing groups for the purposes of data analyses. Quantitative research designs and the use of statistical analyses were common among these studies. These studies portrayed race in three distinct ways: (1) race as a plausible contributing factor to outcomes of interest, (2) race as a factor in outcomes of interest, and (3) race as a differentiator in impact.

The first genre in which race was used as a group identifier explored the role of race in outcomes. The science education literature included at least three vantage points from which these explorations occurred. First, the role of race was quantitatively explored with large student samples by using standardized instruments for the purpose of developing theoretical frameworks. Simpson and Troost's (1982) research exemplified this work. In the development of a conceptual frame for examining commitment to and achievement in science, they identified variables from the literature and grouped them into three domains: self or individual, home or family, and school or classroom. Simpson and Troost discussed and examined race as a variable associated with self. Second, race was explored to validate or invalidate existing models. For instance, Welch, Walberg, and Fraser (1986) selected a large, stratified random sample from students involved in the national assessment of science and investigated a model of educational productivity with improved achievement and attitudes as the desired results. Last, the third goal associated with race was to test its appropriateness as a factor in examining phenomena. Butler's (1999) study

of race as a predictor of behavioral intention to participate in laboratory and nonlaboratory activities is an example of this last type of exploration.

Unlike the work that explored the potential usefulness of race as a factor, the second collection of studies presented race as a contributing factor in differential outcomes. These investigations of varied designs (e.g., experimental, quasi-experimental, observation) covered a diverse array of dimensions in science education but uniformly compared Whites to other racial groups. Studies examined dispositions like curiosity (Petersen & Lowery, 1972), concept-specific understandings such as conservation (Lepper, 1967) and metrics (Jones & Rowsey, 1990), and skills like critical thinking (Hill & Pettus, 1990). Other investigations targeted more global constructs such as perceptions (Huffman, Lawrenz, & Minger, 1997; Jones et al., 2007; Ledbetter, 1993), worldviews (Lee, 1999), engagement (Conwell, Griffin, & Algozzine, 1993), and attitudes toward science and science achievement (Greenfield, 1996; Muller, Stage, & Kinzie, 2001; Schibeci & Riley, 1986). Of these domains, differences in attitudes toward science and science achievement were the most heavily researched, so much so that Fleming and Malone (1983) conducted a meta-analysis in 1980. Another popular topic of investigation fell within the third genre.

The third genre that used race as a group identifier investigated the impact of instructional practices and curricula. Differential impact by race was the primary foci of these studies. In these studies, Whites were most often compared to non–Whites, a group category that included Blacks, Hispanics, and Native Americans. Some studies showed that teacher-centered or traditional instruction negatively impacted the science achievement of non–White students (von Secker & Lissitz, 1999; Wilson, Taylor, Kowalski, & Carlson, 2010). Other research reported that standards-based instruction and curricula had similar impacts for White and non–White students with a corresponding decrease in the achievement gap (Johnson, Kahle, & Fargo, 2006; Lynch, Kuipers, Pyke, & Szesze, 2005).

Race as a Structure

The term "structure" has a variety of meanings in the literature and in scholarly discourse. Here, the use aligns with Sewell's (1992) idea of structure. Structure denotes systemic mechanisms that allow, facilitate, and reify the reproduction of social life. These mechanisms can be formal (e.g., written protocols, procedures, and regulations) and officially documented, or they can be informal (e.g., unwritten etiquettes, social practices, and habit-based common understandings) and undocumented. These mechanisms can also be explicit and conscious, as is often the case when they are formalized, or they can be implicit and unconscious, as is often the case when they are informal, undocumented practices. These mechanisms can assume numerous forms and function at various levels. For example, they can be enacted as an ethos (e.g., democracy), a set of dominant assumptions that define the nature and establish the foundation of a society. They can function at the level of an institution (e.g., government, science education) that operates within a society and in policy, principle-based plans of action developed by authoritative sources that inform and direct activity. Mechanisms can operate at the level of individuals in the form of beliefs, attitudes, and dispositions. Research and scholarship in science education that broached race as a structure were scarce, but the work that existed addressed all of the previously described levels.

Race as a structuring ethos at the societal level was evident in Mutegi (2011) and Parsons (2008). The previously cited works discussed colonialism, both as the expansion of one's properties and possessions through the coercive procurement of another's as well as the exploitative and oppressive arrangements that maintain and increase the forcibly acquired assets. Mutegi, in questioning the relevancy of "science for all" reform in the United States for African Americans, described the deleterious effects of colonialism in his depiction of the political, economic, education, health, and social conditions of African Americans in the United States and people of African descent worldwide. Parsons, in positing an imperative for research involving African Americans, featured 21st-century manifestations of exploitation and oppression and their influences on the status of African Americans in science education.

Mutegi's (2011) and Parsons's (2008) position papers also implicated the structural manifestation of race as an institution, with science education research serving as the institution. Parsons argued that science education research did not adequately consider in its construction and advancement of knowledge the position of African Americans in the United States, a station that was heavily influenced by race and cultural imperialism. Additionally, Parsons, Tran, and Gomillion (2008) asserted in their mixed-methods investigation of small, racially mixed science groups that science education research and scholarship projected a distorted image of African Americans when failing to account for whiteness, an influential status that engenders favor (Fine, 2004; Kincheloe & Steinberg 1998), in research and scholarly activity (e.g., how problems and concepts are defined, researchers conducting the research). Without an adequate consideration of African Americans' historical and contemporary positions in the United States and whiteness, the vast majority of research and scholarship in science education rendered African Americans as deficient and invisible (Mutegi, 2013; Parsons, Cooper, & Simpson, 2011).

Policy was another way in which race was structurally indicted at the institutional level in the science education literature. Atwater (2000) did not label the examples provided as policy, but the examples are regarded as such here because they were the outcomes of policy. In Atwater's evaluation of equitable science education for Black Americans, Atwater described poor facilities, outdated and limited equipment, inadequate curricula and course offerings, and less qualified teachers—conditions to which the policies around funding (i.e., taxes on local property) for public schools contribute. Atwater's essay also featured the results of instructional policies and practices like ability grouping and tracking, policies and practices that are reinforced by the attitudes, beliefs, and dispositions of individuals (Oakes, 1985).

Zuniga, Olson, and Winter (2005) situated race structurally at the level of individuals in their quantitative study of science course placements of Latino students. Zuniga, Olson, and Winter found racial disparities: Latino/a students with high standardized test scores and grade point averages were disproportionately placed in lower-level science courses and their low-achieving non–Latino/a White counterparts were placed in upper-level science courses. In line with what is extensively noted in the research literature on tracking, students in the low-level courses did not subsequently enroll in other science courses even though they voiced college aspirations (Zuniga, Olson, & Winter, 2005). How race structured experience is not restricted to placement in specific academic tracks; the organizing function of race was also identified in classroom dynamics.

The last structural function of race uncovered in the science education literature was exemplified in the qualitative studies of Gilbert and Yerrick (2001), Brand, Glasson, and Green (2006), and Kurth, Anderson, and Palincsar (2002). The study conducted by Gilbert and Yerrick examined teacher and student expectations. The findings indicated that the teacher had low performance expectations for the students of color that comprised the standard-track earth science class and that students were somewhat complicit in subverting high-quality science instruction. Even though the research of Kurth, Anderson, and Palincsar included vignettes that showcased the instructor, the study highlighted sixth graders in small groups and how children enacted the histories of their families, a history that reflected discrimination, exclusion, inequality, and inequity in U.S. society. In their study, the Black female who began the science unit enthused and engaged in the investigations of density was continually marginalized in the small-group work, a marginalization that she and not her non–Black peers attributed to race. With a similar focus on students as the research participants, Brand, Glasson, and Green discussed the research participants' experiences with respect to their perceptions of teachers' stereotypes that Blacks could not do math and science.

How Race Matters in Science Education

Science education research and scholarship indicated that who has access to what and who gets what; the quality, quantity, and continuity of what is received; and the outputs and outcomes that materialize from the previously stated inputs corresponded with race—visible, physical appearance as markers of difference. A significant portion of the race-focused work, the treatment of race as a group identifier, gave primacy to outputs and outcomes. This work reported similar results with Whites positioned more positively in relation to phenomena, except for attitudes and interest for which findings were mostly inconclusive, than their counterparts often classified as minority or Black, Hispanic, and Native American. In contrast to the other approaches to race in the science education literature, these investigations that emphasized outputs and outcomes did not deliberate the historical and contemporary legacies of who has access to what and who gets what. Research and scholarship that couched race as a focus of query and race as a structure provided contexts for making sense of the differential outcomes, Whites as superior and people of color as inferior, featured in science education research and scholarship that employed race as a group identifier.

Research and scholarship on race as a focus of query entertained definitions of race and confronted how these constructions of race were manifest in society through public attitudes and subsequent policies. This early race-focused work called for the inclusion of scientific facts about race into the curriculum and the teaching of these facts by science teachers as mechanisms to alter public attitudes and public policy, the overt ways in which race mattered in U.S. society in the 1940s, 1950s, and 1960s. More than 50 years from the onset of the previously mentioned research and scholarship, a time when race is obscured and concealed, a collection of work accentuated how race consciously or unconsciously operates as an organizing schema for action at the levels of society, institutions, and individuals. This body of work contended that these actions intentionally and unintentionally maintain the existing racial hierarchies in U.S. society that were established at the founding of the nation.

Section III: Critique of the Literature

Equity and equality were typically included among the reasons for investigating race and ethnicity in science education. More often than not, the justification for such research and scholarship was what Secada (1989) called enlightened self-interest. Such work was needed to inform the development of an increasingly diverse populace. This educated populace would sustain U.S. global prominence and high quality of living. The importance of science education research and scholarship with an intentional focus on race and ethnicity was also couched in the democratic ideals proclaimed in the U.S. Declaration of Independence: All persons are created equal; they are endowed with the inalienable rights to life, liberty, and the pursuit of happiness. As a body of work, the research and scholarship in science education on race and ethnicity were compromised in advancing either the enlightened self-interest goals or democratic ones. The body of work was entrenched in presentism, lacked conceptual clarity, was ensconced in individualism, and was constricted by methodological myopia.

Presentism

Presentism is a view that detaches systemic group-level, structural conditions from history and treats them as isolated, individual occurrences that emerge in the moment (Noblit, 2013; Parsons, 2008). Presentism excises the current racial and ethnic arrangements from their historical foundations and dismisses or ignores the uninterrupted continuities from the past to present that are evident in group outcome disparities. On one hand, in light of the horrid racial and ethnic history of the United States, an acceptance and adoption of presentism is neither surprising nor condemnable. On the other hand, the acceptance, adoption, and blind adherence to presentism prevents the undesirables from the past from existing in the present. Presentism preempts critical examination; it inhibits learning from the past and using these lessons to inform what occurs in the present and what is envisioned and engineered for the future. The corpus of literature for which race and ethnicity were a primary or secondary focus did not entertain in the framing or discussion, the most straightforward ways to do so, the histories of groups and individuals studied. Countries, societies, communities, families, and individuals have histories, and these histories are integral, in obvious and oblivious ways, to present-day realities and future possibilities (Cole, 1996; Holland, 1998). To insulate and to sever the present and future from the past strips away context from which deeper and perhaps more insightful and accurate understandings can be garnered. Presentism resulted in circumvention and distortion, this chapter's characterizations of the race- and ethnicity-focused science education research and scholarship. The absence of a historical grounding for the constructs of race and ethnicity, inherent in presentism, contributed to the second limitation of the research and scholarship on race and ethnicity.

Conceptual Clarity

Greater conceptual clarity of race and ethnicity as constructs can facilitate the development of the science education literature base in these domains and enhance the usefulness of the body of literature in informing research, policy, and practice. The vast majority of the reviewed literature—race and ethnicity as assumed or implied—did not offer a conceptualization or discussion of race and ethnicity and proceeded as though a common and shared understanding existed. In the case of race, the explicit and implicit meanings as *practiced* for an overwhelmingly significant portion of the existence of the United States are that race is a naturally occurring, genetically based distinction among human beings that accounts for differential outcomes, with Whites being the more superior race. A similar parallel exists for ethnicity. Behaviors, beliefs, values, and dispositions that emanate from an immersion in customs, traditions, religion, and so on are sometimes treated as inheritable traits in lieu of developed practices; with regard to ethnicity, the developed practices of Europeans are often deemed superior. When left unexplained, biologistic understandings in lieu of social constructions devised to advance sociopolitical aims are likely to be the default for making sense of ethnicity- and race-related research findings. Explicitly defining or discussing race and ethnicity as constructs mitigates the uncritical adoption of the genetic-based conceptualizations.

Conceptualizations with greater clarity than those in the current science education literature would explicate the cores of race and ethnicity (i.e., descent, ancestry, or common antecedents of the research participants) that locate them within the same conceptual family and distinguish them in accordance with the focus of the work. Clear articulations of where race and ethnicity intersect and overlap and where they bifurcate, as exemplified in Ryu (2012), are important in using research findings to inform research, policy, and practice. Clear conceptualizations of the investigated constructs elucidate the findings such that problem identification, problem definition, and remedies in policy and practice are more congruent. For example, if a challenge is associated with racial disparities in the distribution of what Ladson-Billings and Tate (1995) called intellectual property (e.g., quality science teachers, curricula, equipment) then investing resources in instructional strategies that incorporate into science teaching the students' customs, language, traditions, and the like will be of limited effectiveness. In the previous example, inclusive instructional strategies are responses to ethnicity and are inadequate solutions to the race-based challenge, resource-distribution disparities based on difference marked by physical characteristics. One way to enhance conceptual clarity is by drawing from the research and scholarship, among them original works, in other disciplines like anthropology, history, social psychology, and sociology. Contained in these disciplines are decades of inquiry and scholarship on ethnicity and race as constructs. After race and ethnicity are clearly defined, it is important for studies and scholarship to speak to the race- and ethnic-related research, policies, and practices that reify and normalize disparities. The capabilities for the body of race- and ethnic-focused science education literature to speak to the discourses, practices, and policies within and outside the community of researchers, and scholars are bounded by individualism.

Individualism

In the United States, the individual is paramount (Parsons, 1997). This primacy of the individual is evinced in numerous facets such as the nation's Constitution and widespread beliefs like meritocracy—a member of society gets what she or he contributes to it—that comprise the country's general ethos (Harris, 1995; McNamee & Miller, 2009). Considering the centrality of individualism in the U.S. worldview in concert with the troublesome history of group conflict in the United States, the situating of race and ethnicity as individual-level phenomena in science education research and scholarship was expected. This casting of race and ethnicity as individual-level constructs often excluded a group-level and systems view, an exclusion that is problematic for informing systemic change.

Much of the race- and ethnicity-focused research and scholarship in science education examined how individuals negotiated the barriers and challenges associated with race and ethnicity and how individuals exercised agency and affordances to make the most out of a structurally constrained situation. Such foci are very important in developing a deeper understanding of race and ethnicity as lived experiences; however, when these lived experiences are disconnected from larger systems, changes are relegated to one individual at a time, an approach that is not feasible in instituting structural systemic and systemwide changes. Structural and systemic changes are achieved via group-level policies that are adapted to heterogeneity within groups by competent professionals (Parsons & Wall, 2011). Essentializing is one purported reason for what seems to be a prioritizing of individualism over needed structural and systemic change.

When groups are essentialized, they are viewed as having some unchangeable essence, some kind of inherited property that *determines* who they are (Prentice & Miller, 2007). Essentialized groups are viewed as fixed in membership and separate from others, and it is assumed that all members of the group share this connective essence to the same degree. As evident in the evolution of race in the United States, essentializing groups has been one foundation of group oppression. From a critical perspective, the indiscriminant use of essentialism to the other extreme, an exclusive focus on individuals in lieu of the historical emphasis on groups, also serves to oppress by reifying existent societal hierarchies: Group-level patterns are inadequately addressed one individual at a time. Indiscriminant uses of essentialism impede policy development and implementation by advocating a blind eye to group-related patterns. It is sometimes uncritically used with little attention to detail and, perhaps unwittingly like color blindness, constricts the space for investigation and subsequently curtails productive and positive systemic action.

In its unbridled use, the deterministic element that is at the core of what it means to essentialize, is not considered. That is, the role of environments and individuals' choices to develop, adopt, and enact beliefs, values, and so forth of which they are consciously aware are ignored when commonalities across members of a group are dismissed as essentialistic. In other instances, the deterministic element of essentialism is ascribed by powerful and authoritative others who are not members of the groups of interest to which the charge of essentialism refer. This ascription by others nullifies the groups' agency to self-identify. For example, consider science education research and scholarship on Native American tribal groups in which tribal members described, owned, and explicated the role of community in cultivating certain aspects of a worldview (Allen & Crawley, 1998; Bang & Medin, 2010; Grimberg & Gummer, 2013). Liberally used, these studies would be accused of essentializing. In this charge, the evidence against the deterministic element of essentialism (e.g., self-identification and community cultivation) is not considered, and others' ascription of essentialism is privileged over the tribal groups' definitions of themselves (e.g., ignores tribal adoption and heralding of view).

On one hand, the focus on individuals when examining race and ethnicity in science education is warranted and provides useful information for research, policy, and practice. On the other hand, an exclusive focus on individuals and the carte blanche relegation of commonalities across members that comprise a group as essentialistic hinders the development of policy. Race- and ethnicity-focused science education research and scholarship restricted to the examination of individuals insulated from the social arrangements writ large in a society undercuts public policy, developed and implemented at the level of groups, that could address the very challenges and issues that the individualistic work are devised to illuminate. These extremes, the individual severed from group arrangements in society versus group arrangements excised from experiences of individual group members, are reflected in the methodologies employed in science education, the last critique.

Methodological Myopia

Mertens (2010) defined a paradigm as a set of philosophical assumptions that underlie ways of seeing and thinking about the world and that guide ways of acting on that world. Two paradigms were prominent in the reviewed literature: post-positivist and constructivist. Research and scholarship devised to maximize objectivity, the alleviation of subjectivities and mitigation of influences outside the phenomenon of interest, and generalizability, the application of data-based claims beyond the research situation, were deemed valid designs in the earlier race- and ethnicity-focused work. Quantitative research designs dominated the race- and ethnicity-focused literature in science education. These designs were premised on the philosophical assumptions of the post-positivist paradigm: One observable reality is knowable independently of the knower and is knowable within a specified level of probability. Based upon the populations on which data-collecting instruments were developed and the perspectives reflected in the constructs studied, the observable and knowable reality mirrored the dominant group in the United States. Similar to the situation faced by Ellison's (1994) unnamed African American protagonist in *The Invisible Man*, the literature generated distorted views with respect to those who experienced race and ethnicity differently from the dominant group. A discernible line of work that sought to capture race and ethnicity from diverse perspectives emerged in the early 1990s.

In lieu of objectivity and generalizability, confirmability, tracking data and corresponding interpretations back to sources, and transferability, judging the applicability of findings to other contexts on the basis of rich descriptions of the research situation, respectively were among the quality guideposts for qualitative approaches (Guba & Lincoln, 1989). Qualitative research designs examined multiple social constructions of phenomena, a philosophical underpinning of the constructivist paradigm. These multiple constructions can be apprehended, but their apprehension is deemed inseparable from researchers'

values. Central to the investigation of these multiple constructions is the critical and reflective examination of the researchers' positions in societal configurations and the subjectivities that emerge from their positionalities (Mertens, 2010). Although cognizant of the different interpretations of reality, the corpus of literature on race and ethnicity conducted in the qualitative tradition also exclusively focused on the individual and did not consider the systemic ways in which race and ethnicity operated in the larger society and possibly impacted individuals' realities.

The use of quantitative and qualitative research designs in research and scholarship on race and ethnicity were virtually nonexistent in the science education literature. It appeared that race and ethnicity were approached in a dichotomous fashion—either quantitative research methodologies and related assumptions or qualitative research methodologies and corresponding presuppositions. Such a dichotomy unnecessarily narrows the scope of impact.

Moving Forward

Race and ethnicity were historically devised to highlight differences for the specific purpose of separating groups such that some groups were advanced over others. This advantaging of groups and disadvantaging of other groups, especially in relation to various forms of capital, became a part of the ethos of the United States and permeated its institutions and policies. In the current era, as epitomized in color blindness and postracialism, some believe that history has been contained and that contemporary times reflect a complete break from the past; past hierarchies and group disparities in outcomes that continue in the present contradict the aforementioned beliefs.

Evident in contemporary times is the cycle of progress and retrenchment replete throughout the racial and ethnic history of the United States. That is, policies diminish group disparities in outcomes for a period of time, but when these changes begin to affect existent hierarchies then policies are retracted and progress is abated. This progress and retrenchment around race and ethnicity in public life contribute to the complexities of race and ethnicity as researchable phenomena. As shown in the recount of their evolution, race and ethnicity within the context of the United States are not innocuous constructs. The very nature of race and ethnicity make it challenging and professionally risky but not insurmountable to examine them. The investigation of gender in science education is an example.

Gender is similar to race in the ways it is constructed and enacted in civic life. Like race, gender is a social construction in which worth is assigned to different kinds of human bodies, and these valuations, perpetuated through durable systems, serve varied sociopolitical aims. Unlike race and ethnicity in science education, gender operating at the level of individuals is not exclusive of a structural and systems view of gender, and essentialism is seldom lobbied against research and scholarship that position gender as a group-level phenomenon. Aspects of the work around gender in science education are informative for race- and ethnicity-focused efforts in science education.

Recommendation 1:   Critical theories should be used alone or in conjunction with other theories to frame the study of race and ethnicity. Critical theory questions the historical and existing power structures in society and their associated relations with the transformative intent to end domination and oppression. Constructivism or a sociocultural perspective served as the guiding frameworks for much of the literature reviewed for this chapter that conceptualized ethnicity. Though instrumental in elucidating the experiences of individuals or discussing group-level findings, these conceptual frameworks situated historical and contemporary power structures and relations as normative and did not critically scrutinize them. Just as an intelligible segment of the work on gender in science education is couched within critical feminist theory, the first recommendation is to employ tenets of critical race theory (CRT) in the study of race and ethnicity in science education.

Ladson-Billings and Tate (1995) introduced CRT, a theory that originated from critical legal studies in the United States, to education more than a decade ago. Although rare, tenets of CRT are not totally absent in science education research and scholarship; they have been entertained. For example, Wallace and Brand (2012) utilized ingrained racism, tenet one below, in their examination of the culturally responsive practices of two middle school science teachers and asserted that an understanding of racial inequities is essential for developing sociocultural awareness, a staple of multicultural approaches like culturally responsive pedagogy. Other premises, the CRT tenets related to methodology, also have been employed but detached from their critical foundations (Yerrick & Johnson, 2011). Parsons, Rhodes, and Brown (2011) emphasized several tenets in their critique of Yerrick and Johnson's use of CRT, and these tenets are recommended as the starting points for employing CRT in the study of race and ethnicity in science education. Although the tenets specifically name race, they are also applicable to ethnicity. The tenets are as follows (Crenshaw, Gotanda, Peller, & Thomas, 1994): (1) Racism is endemic and normal in the United States; (2) racism has contributed to the advantage and disadvantage of groups; (3) the existence and attainability of neutrality, objectivity, meritocracy, and color blindness are, at best, questionable and are, at worst, vehicles to maintain existent social hierarchies like the racial one in America; (4) a historical and contextual analysis of phenomena are imperative; (5) recognizing the experiential knowledge of people of color and their communities as valid is central to the examination of phenomena; and (6) ending all forms of domination and oppression is the goal.

According to the first premise of CRT, racism is an ingrained, ordinary part of U.S. life. It operates on the planes of consciousness and unconsciousness. The blatant, egregious forms of racism (e.g., use of negative racial epithets by official authorities) are addressed, while the more subtle, systematic forms (e.g., unequal and inequitable distribution of science education resources between high-minority- and nonminority-enrollment public schools) are accepted as routine business. This conscious and unconscious racism is enacted through whiteness as property (Harris, 1995). In brief, whiteness as property encapsulates the power of groups to define reality, to enjoy the nonmaterial and material effects of this definition, to impose this definition of reality on others, and to exclude others on the basis of this definition. Whiteness as property is one culprit for the advantaging of some groups over others that is captured in the second tenet. Whiteness as property is reified in the ideas emphasized in tenet three.

A liberal racial ideology, one that undergirds much of the racial progress in the United States, promotes equality. According to a liberal racial ideology, neutrality, objectivity, color blindness, and meritocracy are key in achieving equality. Racism is treated as an irrational, conscious, and intentional act that originates in the present and that is executed by individuals. It is not considered a rational, historically based system that is perpetuated across space and time to maintain group dominance. In line with the third premise of CRT, neutrality and color blindness buttress the existing status quo by enabling them to function as the accepted defaults. In neutrality and color blindness, race is rendered an abstract ideology instead of a social structure and a cultural representation with material effects (Bonilla-Silva, 1999; Omi & Winant, 1994). Neutralizing race by turning a blind eye to it would not alter conditions. For example, in the absence of acknowledging race, the teacher in Gilbert and Yerrick's (2001) study would still possess and act on low expectations for the racially and ethnically diverse students in his lower-track science class. Even if color became invisible, the Latino/as in the Zunga, Olson, and Winter (2005) investigation, who were disproportionately placed in lower-track science classes irrespective of performance on designated indicators, would still be assigned to lower-level science classes and their lower-achieving White counterparts would continue to be placed in the higher tracks that did not coincide with their performance. Objectivity allows the presuppositions that underlie existing hierarchies to go unexamined, and meritocracy camouflages and backgrounds the structures and systems that either facilitate and reward or hinder and invalidate efforts.

The fourth and fifth precepts of CRT relate to methodologies. Historical and contextual analyses, the focus of the fourth CRT premise, expose the roles of neutrality, objectivity, meritocracy, and color blindness in cementing and advancing the current arrangements in society. Such analyses reveal the linkages between conditions and practices in contemporary times in which the racial and ethnic intentions and goals are obscured to the historical events and periods in which systems were crafted with specific racial and ethnic intent in order to achieve clear racial and ethnic aims. CRT, in the fifth tenet, prioritizes the voices of people of color in understanding and disrupting these structures and systems that sustain White dominance. CRT elevates narratives that counter dominance and oppression, "stories that center the experiences of people of color and bring to light a reality that is often obfuscated in stories narrated by Whites" (Parsons, Rhodes, & Brown, 2011, p. 953). All the premises of CRT work toward the last tenet: the elimination of all forms of domination and oppression.

Recommendation 2: Race- and ethnicity-focused research and scholarship should not only generate knowledge but should also transform science education to become more equitable and socially just. As asserted in the methodological myopia critique of the reviewed literature, the race- and ethnicity-focused research and scholarship in science education fell within a post-positivist or constructivist paradigm. In line with the first recommendation, the use of critical theory, the second suggestion proposes the transformative paradigm as the lens for guiding thought and action. Similar to the constructivist paradigm, the transformative paradigm acknowledges multiple versions of what can be perceived as real. In contrast to the constructivist paradigm, the transformative paradigm centralizes the critical examination of what privileges one version of reality over another and stresses the deconstructive analysis of power and related issues in service to the ultimate goal of creating a more just society. Mindful of power and justice, methodologies of the transformative paradigm are varied in nature, the thrust of the third recommendation.

Recommendation 3: The either-or dichotomy and the paradigm wars about which method is more valid for what should be abandoned and breadth and depth of research findings simultaneously embraced. At present, a diverse assortment of methods is used in other disciplines to study race and ethnicity as constructs. However, the investigations in science education utilized either quantitative methods or qualitative methods; very few studies of race and ethnicity as constructs used both. The complex nature of race and ethnicity warrants more frequent uses of mixed methods. For example, qualitative methods can be used to gauge people of color and their White counterparts' multiple constructions of a phenomenon in science education; these constructions can then be quantized in a way that retains context followed by uses with large samples. Research and scholarship that utilize purpose-driven quantitative and qualitative methods in multiple phases have the capacity to unpack race and ethnicity as localized, lived experiences acting from the bottom up to alter societal conditions as well as society-level structures and cultural representations that act from the top down to circumscribe and impact individual circumstances. Research and scholarship on race and ethnicity that employ both qualitative and quantitative designs are more likely, by the very nature of their design, to generate findings of depth and breadth that will provide insights to help policy makers and practitioners tailor initiatives for specific contexts on one hand and facilitate widespread and systemic implementation on the other hand.

The science education research and scholarship that acknowledged race and ethnicity were plagued by presentism, lack of conceptual clarity, individualism, and methodological myopia. In this section, three recommendations were proposed and discussed. The recommendations—use of critical theory located in a transformative paradigm that employs multiple methods in order to create a more equitable and socially just science education enterprise—address the aforementioned critiques.

Coda

The primary goal of this chapter on race- and ethnicity-focused science education research and scholarship was to critically unpack and synthesize the existent literature. Considering the breadth and depth of literature on certain topics in science education, race and ethnicity were largely absent. In addition to highlighting their absence, the critical analysis of the science education literature featured in this chapter made explicit their invisibility. Like Ellison's (1994) protagonist in *The Invisible Man*, race and ethnicity in science education were mostly circumvented and distorted. In cases in which they were recognized, this recognition was not situated as a value in its own right, but it was a compelled recognition, an acknowledgment justified by circumstances.

Race and ethnicity as constructs are complex and contentious. These complexities and tensions could deter the science education community from engaging them. The investigation of constructs with an abundance of complexities and tensions is not unchartered territory in science education; gender is one example. Researchers and scholars do not avoid gender as a construct because of its complexities or the existing tensions (e.g., essentializing women, the group most often featured in gender studies). Instead, researchers and scholars utilize the literature in science education and other disciplines to conceptualize gender-related phenomena of interest. They conduct investigations that identify affordances among women or girls as individuals and as a group and critically examine structural constraints that impede their progress. Researchers and scholars of gender studies in science education generate knowledge that advances the understanding of issues in the field that differentially impact female participation and success in science and generate findings that promote widespread and systemic efforts that structurally transform the status of women in science (e.g., parity in degrees conferred in the life sciences). If the analogous conditions existed for race and ethnicity in science education, then just maybe an indelible impact on science education in the 21st century could be made.

Now is the time to act. The demographics of the U.S. population are shifting from a predominantly White nation-state to a nation-state in which people of color are projected to comprise the numerical majority (U.S. Census Bureau, 2012). The disparities between Whites and non–Whites are getting wider. The underclass is growing as technology becomes more central to life in the United States. The racialization of the underclass is becoming more pronounced as the numbers of people of color increase and opportunities for social mobility for these groups decrease. The demands for scientifically competent individuals increase as the pool of individuals from other countries to meet this demand decreases (National Science Board, 2012). This constriction in the pool of international candidates is accompanied by a narrowing accessibility of larger segments of the U.S. population to high-quality science educative experiences. Now is the time to engage and generate science education research and scholarship on race and ethnicity that informs and impacts future research, policy, and practice. The science education community has the capacity to engage race and ethnicity. Does the community have the will and the courage to engage in such a high-risk endeavor?

Acknowledgments

Thanks to Malcolm Butler and Julio Lopez-Ferrao for their review and comments on the initial version of this chapter.

Notes

1. Appendix A contains the criteria, rationale, and procedures for the literature search.
2. One argument that challenges the seemingly color-blind language of the speech analyzes the well-known phrase, "I have a dream that my four little children will one day live in a nation where they will not be judged by the color of their skin but by the content of their character." The argument highlights the use of the term "judged." Being judged, to make evaluative conclusions, is not synonymous with being recognized, to be acknowledged or perceived (Gotanda, 1991, 2000). The second argument emphases King's naming of racial and ethnic groups later in the speech.
3. Equality and equity are often cited together in U.S. race discussions. When the evolution of race and how it has been addressed in the United States were considered, equality rather than equity was typically the focus. Equality emphasized sameness and was commonly observed in education as treating everyone the same and providing the same experiences to everyone with little interest in sameness or equality of outcomes. Even if sameness of outcomes was achieved, equality of racial groups would remain elusive due to the differential starting points of groups. Contrary to equality in which sameness is the guiding criteria, equity is fair treatment according to some principle for the purposes of achieving a specific outcome (e.g., accessibility of high-quality science experiences). In the United States, democratic ideals often served as the guiding principles.
4. Capital is broadly defined here and encompasses three forms of capital: economic, cultural, and social (Bourdieu, 1986, 1990). Economic capital can be thought of as money and the physical assets it can purchase; this material capital is convertible and transferable from one generation to the next. Cultural capital is that which results from the possession of dispositions, behaviors, and goods valued by society. Social capital is the aggregate of resources, actual and potential, that can be mobilized for a specific purpose.

These resources result from a connection with durable networks. These networks are composed of informal and formal recognized relationships in which the members within the network share tacit understandings about the associations. Cultural and social capital, sometimes referred to as symbolic capital, are also transferrable from one generation to the next and can be used as leverage in gaining access to and obtaining economic capital and vice versa.

References

Allen, N. J., & Crawley, F. E. (1998). Voices from the bridge: Worldview conflicts of Kickapoo students of science. *Journal of Research in Science Teaching, 35*(2), 111–132.

Atwater, M. M. (2000). Equity for Black Americans in precollege science. *Science Education, 84,* 154–179.

Atwater, M. M., Lance, J., Woodard, U., & Johnson, N. H. (2013). Race and ethnicity: Powerful forecasters of science learning and performance. *Theory Into Practice, 52*(1), 6–13.

Atwater, M. M., & Riley, J. P. (1993). Multicultural science education: Perspectives, definitions, and research agenda. *Science Education, 77*(6), 661–668.

Bang, M., & Medin, D. (2010). Cultural processes in science education: Supporting the navigation of multiple epistemologies. *Science Education, 94*(6), 1008–1026.

Banks, J. (1995). The historical reconstruction of knowledge about race: Implications for transformative teaching. *Educational Researcher, 24*(2), 15–24.

Banks, J. A. (1988). *Multiethnic education: Theory and practice.* Newton, MA: Allyn and Bacon.

Basu, J. S. (2008). How students design and enact physics lessons: Five immigrant Caribbean youth and the cultivation of student voice. *Journal of Research in Science Teaching, 45*(8), 881–899.

Bell, D., Jr. (1995). *Brown v. Board of Education* and the interest convergence dilemma. In K. Crenshaw, N. Gotanda, G. Peller, & K. Thomas (Eds.), *Critical race theory: The key writings that formed the movement* (pp. 20–29). New York, NY: The New Press.

Berry, M. F. (1996). Vindicating Martin Luther King, Jr.: The road to a color-blind society. *Journal of Negro History, 1*(4), 137–144.

Bonham, V., Warshauer-Baker, E., & Collins, F. S. (2005). Race and ethnicity in the genome era: The complexity of the constructs. *American Psychologist, 60*(1), 9–15.

Bonilla-Silva, E. (1999). The essential social fact of race. *American Sociological Review, 64*(6), 899–906.

Bonnet, A. (1998). Who was White? The disappearance of non–European White identities and the formation of European racial Whiteness. *Ethnic and Racial Studies, 21*(6), 1029–1055.

Boulos, S. (1965). Teaching science and world understanding. *Science Education, 49*(2), 190–192.

Bourdieu, P. (1986). (Translated by R. Nice). The forms of capital. In J. E. Richardson (Ed.), *Handbook of theory of research for the sociology of education* (pp. 241–258). New York, NY: Greenwood Press.

Bourdieu, P. (1990). *The logic of practice.* Cambridge, UK: Polity Press.

Brand, B. R., & Glasson, G. E. (2004). Crossing cultural borders into science teaching: Early life experiences, racial and ethnic identities, and beliefs about diversity. *Journal of Research in Science Teaching, 41*(2), 119–141.

Brand, B. R., Glasson, G. E., & Green, A. M. (2006). Sociocultural factors influencing students' learning in science and mathematics: An analysis of the perspectives of African American students. *School Science and Mathematics, 106*(5), 228–236.

Brown, H. E. (1945). The influence of world events on science experiences in the elementary school. *Science Education, 29*(5), 244–249.

Butler, M. (1999). Factors associated with students' intentions to engage in science learning activities. *Journal of Research in Science Teaching, 36*(4), 455–473.

Cho, S. (2009). Post-racialism. *Iowa Law Review, 94,* 1589–1649.

Cobern, W. W. (1996). Worldview theory and conceptual change in science education. *Science Education, 85*(5), 579–610.

Cole, M. (1996). *Cultural psychology: A once and future discipline.* Cambridge, MA: Belknap Press of Harvard University Press.

Conwell, C., Griffin, S., & Algozzine, B. (1993). Gender and racial differences in unstructured learning groups in science. *International Journal of Science Education, 15*(1), 107–115.

Crenshaw, K., Gotanda, N., Peller, G., & Thomas, K. (1994). Introduction. In K. Crenshaw, N. Gotanda, G. Peller, & K. Thomas (Eds.), *Critical race theory: The key writings that informed the movement* (pp. xiii–xxxii). New York, NY: The New Press.

Davis, J. (1963). Attitude changes on fallout and race associated with special instruction in biology. *Science Education, 47*(2), 178–183.

Ellison, R. (1994). *The invisible man.* New York, NY: Random House.

Epstein, J. L., & Dauber, S. L. (1991). School programs and teacher practices of parent involvement in inner-city elementary and middle schools. *The Elementary School Journal, 91,* 289–305.

Evans, H., & Tannenbaum, H. (1994). A, AB, B, and O? *Science Education, 28*(3), 165–166.

Fenton, S. (2010). *Ethnicity.* (2nd ed.). Cambridge, UK: Polity Press.

Fine, M. (2004). Witnessing Whiteness/gathering intelligence. In M. Fine, L. Weis, L. P. Pruitt, & A. Burns (Eds.), *Off-white: Readings on power, privilege, and resistance* (2nd ed., pp. 245–255). New York, NY: Routledge.

Fleming, M. L., & Malone, M. R. (1983). The relationship of student characteristics and student performance in science as viewed by meta-analysis research. *Journal of Research in Science Teaching, 20*(5), 481–495.

Gilbert, A., & Yerrick, R. (2001). Same school, separate worlds: A sociocultural study of identity, resistance, and negotiation in a rural, lower track science classroom. *Journal of Research in Science Teaching, 38*(5), 574–598.

Gotanda, N. (1991). A critique of "Our constitution is color-blind." *Stanford Law Review, 44*(1), 1–68.

Gotanda, N. (2000). A critique of "Our constitution is color-blind." In R. Delgado & J. Stefancic (Eds.), *Critical race theory: The cutting edge* (2nd ed., pp. 35–38). Philadelphia, PA: Temple University Press.

Gould, S. J. (1981). *The mismeasure of man.* New York, NY: Norton.

Greenfield, T. A. (1996). Gender, ethnicity, science achievement, and attitudes. *Journal of Research in Science Teaching, 33*(8), 901–933.

Greer, C. (1984). The ethnic question. *Social Text, 9/10,* 119–136.

Grimberg, B. I., & Gummer, E. (2013). Teaching science from cultural points of intersection. *Journal of Research in Science Teaching, 50*(1), 12–32.

Guba, E. G., & Lincoln, Y. S. (1989). *Fourth generation evaluation.* Newbury Park, CA: Sage.

Hagiwara, S., Barton, A. C., & Contento, I. (2007). Culture, food, and language: Perspectives from immigrant mothers in school science. *Cultural Studies of Science Education, 2,* 475–515.

Harris, C. I. (1995). Whiteness as property. *Harvard Law Review, 106*(8), 1707–1791.

Hill, O., & Pettus, O. (1990). Three studies of factors affecting the attitudes of Blacks and females toward the pursuit of science and science-related careers. *Journal of Research in Science Teaching, 27*(4), 289–314.

Holland, D. (1998). *Identity and agency in cultural worlds.* Cambridge, MA: Harvard University Press.

Huffman, D., Lawrenz, F., & Minger, M. (1997). Within-class analysis of ninth-grade science students' perceptions of the learning environment. *Journal of Research in Science Teaching, 34*(8), 791–804.

Jackson, J. P., Jr., & Weidman, N. M. (2006). The origins of scientific racism. *The Journal of Blacks in Higher Education, 50,* 66–79.

Jacobson, M. F. (1998). *Whiteness of a different color: European immigrants and the alchemy of race.* Cambridge, MA: Harvard University.

Johnson, C. C., Kahle, J. B., & Fargo, J. D. (2007). Effective teaching results in increased science achievement for all students. *Science Education, 91,* 371–383.

Jones, M. G., Tretter, T., Paechter, M., Kubasko, D., Bokinsky, A., Andre, T., & Negishi, A. (2007). Differences in African-American and European-American students' engagement with nanotechnology experiences: Perceptual position or assessment artifact? *Journal of Research in Science Teaching, 44*(6), 787–799.

Jones, M. L., & Rowsey, R. E. (1990). The effects of immediate achievement and retention of middle school students involved in a metric unit designed to promote the development of estimating skills. *Journal of Research in Science Teaching, 27*(9), 901–913.

Kincheloe, J. L., & Steinberg, S. R. (1998). Addressing the crisis of Whiteness: Reconfiguring White identity in a pedagogy of Whiteness. In J. L. Kincheloe, S. R. Steinberg, N. M. Rodriguez, & R. E. Chennault (Eds.), *White reign: Deploying Whiteness in America* (pp. 3–29). New York, NY: St. Martin's Press.

Kurth, L., Anderson, C., & Palincsar, A. (2002). The case of Carla: Dilemmas of helping all students understand science. *Science Education, 86*(3), 287–313.

Ladson-Billings, G. (2006). From the achievement gap to the education debt: Understanding achievement in U.S. schools. *Educational Researcher, 35*(7), 3–12.

Ladson-Billings, G., & Tate, W. F. (1995). Toward a critical race theory of education. *Teachers College Record, 97,* 47–68.

Ledbetter, C. (1993). Qualitative comparisons of students' conceptions of science. *Science Education, 77*(6), 611–624.

Lee, O. (1997). Diversity and equity for Asian American students in science education. *Science Education, 81*(1), 107–122.

Lee, O. (1999). Science knowledge, world views, and information sources in social and cultural context: Making sense after a natural disaster. *American Educational Research Journal, 36*(2), 187–219.

Lehner, E. (2007). Describing students of the African Diaspora: Understanding micro and meso level science learning as gateways to standards based discourse. *Cultural Studies of Science Education, 2,* 441–473.

Lemke, J. (2001). Articulating communities: Sociocultural perspectives on science education. *Journal of Research in Science Teaching, 38*(3), 296–316.

Lepper, R. (1967). A cross-cultural investigation of development of selected Piagetian science concepts, social status, and reading readiness. *Journal of Research in Science Teaching, 5,* 324–337.

Lopez, I. F. H. (2006). Colorblind to the reality of race in America. *The Chronicle of Higher Education, 53,* 11. Downloaded from the *Academic OneFile.* Web. 25 May 2011.

Lopez, I. F. H. (2007). "A nation of minorities": Race, ethnicity, and reactionary colorblindness. *Stanford Law Review, 59*(4), 985–1063.

Lynch, S., Kuipers, J., Pyke, C., & Szesze, M. (2005). Examining the effects of a highly rated science curriculum unit on diverse students: Results from a planning grant. *Journal of Research in Science Teaching, 42*(8), 912–946.

Manning, K. (1993). Race, science, and identity. In G. Early (Ed.), *Lure and loathing: Essays on race, identity, and the ambivalence of assimilation* (pp. 317–351). New York, NY: Allen Lane/Penguin Press.

Matthews, C. E., & Smith, W. S. (1994). Native American related materials in elementary instruction. *Journal of Research in Science Teaching, 31*(4), 363–380.

McEwan, B. (1951). Society changes the biology teacher. *Science Education, 35*(5), 289–291.

McNamee, S. J., & Miller, R. K. (2009). *The meritocracy myth.* Lanham, MD: Rowman & Littlefield Publishers.

Mertens, D. (2010). *Research and evaluation in education and psychology: Integrating diversity with quantitative, qualitative, and mixed methods* (3rd ed.). Los Angeles, CA: Sage.

Muller, P. A., Stage, F. K., & Kinzie, J. (2001). Science achievement growth trajectories: Understanding factors related to gender and racial-ethnic differences in precollege science achievement. *American Educational Research Journal, 38,* 981–1012.

Mutegi, J. (2011). The inadequacies of "Science for All" and the necessity and nature of a socially transformative curriculum approach for African American science education. *Journal of Research in Science Teaching, 248*(3), 301–316.

Mutegi, J. (2013). "Life's first need is for us to be realistic" and other reasons for examining the sociocultural construction of race in the science performance of African American students. *Journal of Research in Science Teaching, 50*(1), 82–103.

Nagel, J. (1994). Ethnicity: Creating and recreating ethnic identity and culture. *Social Problems, 41*(1), 152–176.

National Science Board. (2012). *Science and engineering indicators 2012.* Arlington VA: National Science Foundation (NSB 12–01).

Nieto, S. (1987). Parent involvement in bilingual education: Whose responsibility is it? *NABE Journal, 11,* 189–201.

Noblit, G. (2013). Culture bound: Science, teaching, and research. *Journal of Research in Science Teaching, 50*(2), 238–249.

Oakes, J. (1985). *Keeping track: How schools structure inequality* (2nd ed.). New Haven, CT: Yale University Press.

Omi, M., & Winant, H. (1994). *Racial formation in the United States: From the 1960s to 1990s* (2nd ed.). New York, NY: Routledge.

Parsons, E.C. (1997). Black high school females' images of the scientist: Expressions of culture. *Journal of Research in Science Teaching, 34*(7), 745–768.

Parsons, E.C. (2008). Positionality of African Americans and a theoretical accommodation of it: Rethinking science education research. *Science Education, 92,* 1127–1144.

Parsons, E.C., & Bayne, G.U. (2012). Conceptualizations of context in science education research: Implications for equity. In J. Bianchini, V. Akerson, A.C. Barton, O. Lee, & A. Rodriguez (Eds.), *Moving the equity agenda forward: Equity research, practice, and policy in science education* (pp. 153–172). Dordrecht, the Netherlands: Sense Publishers.

Parsons, E.C., Cooper, J., & Simpson, J. (2011). The neglect and significance of race and culture in science education research involving Blacks in the United States: A critical review of the literature from 1997–2007. In B. Fraser, K. Tobin, & C. McRobbie (Eds.), *International handbook on science education* (pp. 569–581). New York, NY: Springer.

Parsons, E.C., Rhodes, B., & Brown, C. (2011). Unpacking CRT in *Negotiating White science. Cultural Studies of Science Education, 6,* 951–960.

Parsons, E. C., Simpson, J., & Cooper, J. (2009). Low status and positionality of African Americans: A critique of science education reform and research. In K. Tobin & W.-M. Roth (Eds.), *The world of science education: Handbook of research in North America, vol. 1* (pp. 331–351). Dordrecht, the Netherlands: Sense Publishers.

Parsons, E.C., Tran, L.U., & Gomillion, C.T. (2008). An investigation of student roles within small, racially mixed science groups: A racial perspective. *International Journal of Science Education, 30*(11), 1469–1489.

Parsons, E.C., & Wall, S. (2011). Unpacking the critical in culturally relevant pedagogy: An illustration involving African Americans and Asian Americans. In L. Scherff & K. Spector (Eds.), *Culturally relevant pedagogy: Clashes and confrontations* (pp. 15–34). New York, NY: Rowman & Littlefield Education.

Petersen, R., & Lowery, L. (1972). The use of motor activity as an index of curiosity in children. *Journal of Research in Science Teaching, 9*(3), 193–200.

Prentice, D.A., & Miller, D.T. (2007). Psychological essentialism of human categories. *Current Directions in Psychological Science, 16*(4), 202–206.

Ryu, M. (2012). "But at school . . . I became a bit shy": Korean immigrant adolescents' discursive participation in science. *Cultural Studies of Science Education.* doi:10.1007/s11422-012-9406-2

Schibeci, R.A., & Riley, J.P., III. (1986). Influence of students' background and perceptions on science attitudes and achievement. *Journal of Research in Science Teaching, 23*(3), 177–187.

Schindelman, B. (1946). Changing concepts in education. *Science Education, 30*(1), 35–36.

Secada, W. (1989). Enlightened self-interest and equity in mathematics education. *Peabody Journal of Education, 66*(2), 22–56.

Sewell, W., Jr. (1992). A theory of structure: Duality, agency, and transformation. *American Journal of Sociology, 98,* 1–29.

Sheridan, C. (2003). "Another White race": Mexican Americans and the paradox of whiteness in jury selection. *Law and History Review, 21*(1), 109–144.

Simpson, R., & Troost, K. (1982). Influences on commitment to and learning of science among adolescents. *Science Education, 66*(5), 763–781.

Smedley, A. (2001). Social origins of the idea of race. In C. Stokes, T. Melendez, & G. Rhodes-Reed (Eds.), *Race in 21st century America* (pp. 1–24). East Lansing: Michigan State University Press.

Smedley, A., & Smedley, B. (2005). Race as biology is fiction, racism as a social problem is real: Anthropological and historical perspectives on the social construction of race. *American Psychologist, 60*(1), 16–26.

Smith, E.M., & Hausafus, C. (1998). Relationship of family support and ethnic minority students' achievement in science and mathematics. *Science Education, 82*(1), 111–125.

Solomon, M.D., & Braunschneider, G.E. (1950). Relation of biological science to the social attitudes. *Science Education, 34*(2), 80–84.

Stanley, W.B., & Brickhouse, N.W. (1994). Multiculturalism, universalism, and science education. *Science Education, 78*(4), 387–398.

Ullucci, K., & Battey, D. (2011). Exposing colorblindness/grounding color consciousness: Challenges for teacher education. *Urban Education, 46*(6), 1195–1225.

U.S. Census Bureau. (2012). *Statistical abstract of the United States, 2012.* Washington, DC: Government Printing Office. Retrieved from www.census.gov/compendia/statab/cats/education.html

Von Secker, C.E., & Lissitz, R.W. (1999). Estimating the impact of instructional practices on student achievement in science. *Journal of Research in Science Teaching, 36*(10), 1110–1126.

Wallace, T., & Brand, B.R. (2012). Using critical race theory to analyze science teachers' culturally responsive practices. *Cultural Studies of Science Education, 7,* 341–374.

Washburn, S.L. (1944). Thinking about race. *Science Education, 28*(2), 65–76.

Watkins, W. (2001). Chapter 2: Scientific racism. In W. Watkins, *The White architects of Black education: Ideology and power in America: 1865–1954* (pp. 24–40). New York, NY: Teachers College Press.

Webb, L.D. (2006). *The history of American education: A great American experiment.* Upper Saddle River, NJ: Pearson-Merrill Prentice Hall.

Welch, W.W., Walberg, H.J., & Fraser, B. (1986). Predicting elementary science learning using national assessment data. *Journal of Research in Science Teaching, 23*(8), 699–706.

Wells, A., & Frankenberg, E. (2007). The public schools and the challenge of the Supreme Court's integration decision. *The Phi Delta Kappan, 89*(3), 178–188.

Wilson, C.D., Taylor, J.A., Kowalski, S.M., & Carlson, J. (2010). The relative effects and equity of inquiry-based and commonplace science teaching on students' knowledge, reasoning, and argumentation. *Journal of Research in Science Teaching, 47*(3), 276–301.

Yerrick, R., & Johnson, J. (2011). Negotiating White science in rural Black America: A case for navigating the landscape of teacher knowledge domains. *Cultural Studies of Science Education, 6,* 915–939.

Yinger, J.M. (1985). Ethnicity. *Annual Review of Sociology, 11,* 151–180.

Zuniga, K., Olson, J.K., & Winter, M. (2005). Science education for rural Latino/a students: Course placement and success in science. *Journal of Research in Science Teaching, 42*(4), 376–402.

Appendix A

The search included numerous databases like Journal Storage (*JSTOR*) and ArticlesPlus that include field-advancing literature in the sciences and social sciences. A broad search was conducted by using terms and phrases related to science education and science, technology, engineering, and mathematics; level (e.g., precollege, elementary or primary); and race and ethnicity (e.g., use of stems like ethn*). The term "minority" does not encompass Whites as a racial or ethnic group and was not included as part of the search, but the search included labels for groups commonly positioned as U.S. racial or ethnic groups (i.e., Asian American and its subgroups). Additionally, using the 5-year impact factor as a general criterion, the search included specific journals—*Journal of Research in Science Teaching, Science Education, International Journal of Science Education, Cultural Studies of Science Education, Research in Science Education, Journal of Science Teacher Education, Journal of Science Education and Technology, Research in Science & Technological Education, School Science and Mathematics, American Education Research Journal, Educational Researcher,* and *Educational Evaluation and Policy Analysis.* The references cited in the reviewed literature were examined for additional works not tagged in the previous searches. Although important, the review excluded literature on interactions among various social identifiers (e.g., gender, socioeconomic status); factors involved in these interactions are addressed in other chapters in the handbook.

10

Gender Matters

Building on the Past, Recognizing the Present, and Looking Toward the Future

Kathryn Scantlebury

Gender is shorthand to capture a diverse range of scholarship that address gender relations, identities, inequalities, differences and the cluster of experiences, identifications, discourses, histories and forms of subjectivity that intersect with the category or sign of "gender." Gender has always been, and remains, an over-determined signifier, a key word in contemporary culture, which is often called upon to perform much analytic and descriptive work.

(Dillabough, McLeod, & Mills, 2009, p. 3)

On October 9, 2012, newspapers and websites reported that the Taliban shot Malala Yousafzai, a 14-year-old Pakistani girl who campaigned for girls' education rights. In the months following the incident, Malala was transferred to Britain for her medical recovery and recuperation, and supporters began petitions to nominate her for the Nobel Peace Prize. Gender research encompasses more than "girls' education," however; the World Bank (2011) reported that girls have less access to education than boys. The five countries with the highest number of out-of-school females are Nigeria, Pakistan, India, Ethiopia, and the United States. And while girls in school have higher literacy rates than their male peers, worldwide, girls' basic literacy is lower than that of boys because fewer of them complete primary school. Malala's heroism is a reminder that gender matters.

Gender is a social construction and is constituted within society's *structural*, *symbolic*, and *individual* levels (Harding, 1986; Risman & Davis, 2013). The *structural* level examines how gender influences the division of labor within a culture, and men's labor typically has higher status compared to women's labor. For example, although more women than men teach young children, more men than women teach at the university, which has a higher status. There is a higher percentage of men teaching at the more prestigious universities, and across most disciplines, more men than women are professors (Harding, 1986).

The *symbolic* level produces conceptions of feminine and masculine and the appropriate practices for women and men, such as what occupations are "appropriate" clothing, and other characteristics. At the *symbolic* level, science is viewed as rational, logical, difficult, hard, and as disembodied knowledge. Thus science at a structural and symbolic level is masculine. In contrast, the characteristics of nurturing and caring are associated practices for teaching young children. These practices are more associated with feminine characteristics; teaching is constructed as suitable for women.

Structural and symbolic levels can impact the individual level and, in particular, the socialization process that contributes to one's identity. The gender system is hierarchical (Harding, 1986; Risman & Davis, 2013). The formation of gender establishes difference between female and male; typically female is subordinate to male. The understanding of femininity and masculinity within the three levels differs from one culture to another and over time, but within one culture, these three levels of gender are related to each other. Gender theory is also sensitive for other social categories such as ethnicity, age, socioeconomic status, religion, language proficiency, and sexuality. Despite calls from feminist science educators for a more refined gender analysis that would include these other social categories, there is little information on how these factors, along with gender, influence student achievement on international and national tests or participation patterns in science (*structural issues*). Previous research has documented how teachers' practices and instruction can mediate students' learning, but there are few recent studies that examine how teachers' pedagogical practices and student expectations are influenced by gender. Gender studies at this *symbolic* level are needed. Finally, there is limited research on how a student's gender impacts her/his learning, attitude toward science, achievement, and/or participation in science (*individual*). Although in science education, we explore issues of identity and science learning, gender is rarely, if at all, foregrounded in the research.

This chapter focuses on gender research in science education published since the review chapters by Scantlebury and Baker (2007) and Kahle and Meece (1994) in previous handbooks. Database searches were conducted using the terms "gender," "sex," "equity," "feminism," "masculinity," "queer," "heteronormative," and "science." The first section summarizes research reviews on gender and science education since Scantlebury and Baker's (2007) overview of the field. The second section examines gender and science education research from a structural perspective, focusing on results of Program for International Student Achievement (PISA) and Third International Mathematics and Science Study (TIMSS) achievement tests and attitude surveys. The third section examines sociocultural aspects and gender at the symbolic and individual levels. The final section suggests future directions for gender research in science education.

Gender and Science Education

Research in gender and science education expanded when Kelly (1978) noted a lack of empirical evidence to explain achievement differences between girls and boys on the International Association for the Evaluation of Educational Achievement (IEA) science assessments. Girls were the "missing half" in science because of their limited opportunities to learn (Kelly, 1985). While girls were "missing" or "invisible" in British science education (Kelly, 1981, 1985; Spender, 1982), Kahle and Lakes (1983) noted the "myth of equality" in U.S. classrooms, and researchers in other western countries also documented the inequity between girls' and boys' science education (Calabrese Barton & Brickhouse, 2006; Kenway, Willis, Blackmore, & Rennie, 1998; Scantlebury & Baker, 2007).

After several decades of researching and documenting the pattern of female's participation in science, identifying strategies to engage girls in science through the introduction of female role models and mentors and out-of-school programs to provide girls "tinkering" skills, Kahle and Meece (1994) critiqued the plethora of intervention programs that focused on "fixing" girls. They proposed that science education research should examine the sociocultural aspects of learning, especially in regard to the classroom climate and the formal science curriculum. More than a decade after Kahle and Meece's (1994) review, Scantlebury and Baker (2007) reported how some science education research had engaged in a broader examination of gender issues, such as heteronormativity in biology textbooks, and used queer theory to critique science teacher education. However, few studies examined how gender and other social categories influenced students' engagement in science, nor had the field taken a critical approach to science as a culture, the culture of school science, or the role of gender stereotypes in the cultural reproduction of science as a masculine endeavor.

In addition to the handbook chapters, Brotman and Moore's review (2008) analyzed articles on gender and K–12 education published from 1995 through 2006 in selected science education research journals. They grouped the articles into equity and access, curriculum and pedagogy, reconstructing the nature and culture of science, and identity. In the theme of equity and access, girls' preference to study the biological sciences and boys' preference for the physical sciences has remained a consistent, and unexplained trend (Sikora & Pokropek, 2012). The next major theme focused on revising curriculum to align with students' preferences and interests and changing pedagogical practices to engage more students in science. Modifying science curriculum had developed from different feminist perspectives, such as *"girl friendly"* or *"gender inclusive."* Girl-friendly curriculum focused on including topics that interested girls or topics that researchers and teachers thought would interest girls, such as the inclusion of women's contribution to science. Gender-inclusive curriculum integrated the science interests of girls and boys and engaged teachers in a critique of their pedagogical practices that could expose gender-biased practices toward girls and students from under-represented groups.

The fourth theme examined how gender influenced students' science identity. Identity research in science education has moved from analyzing data from a female/male binary perspective and has argued that other categories, such as one's racial/ethnic background, socioeconomic status, immigration status, language acquisition, and/or religious affiliation can also shape one's science identity. However, there are few studies that view gender as a continuum rather than a female/male binary or examine how other social categories combine with gender to influence students' identities.

While Brotman and Moore reviewed the research on K–12 education, other studies focused on issues impacting the participation of American women in science, technology, engineering, and mathematics (STEM); Hill, Corbett, & St. Rose, 2010), women of color (Ong, Wright, Espinosa, & Orfield, 2011), women in chemistry (Lorber Newsome, 2013), and women in science education (Kahle, 2011; Parsons, 2007; Scantlebury, 2014; Scantlebury, Kahle, & Martin, 2010; Venville, 2008; Wiseman & Weinburgh, 2009). Science education and feminist researchers have examined the issues impacting women's participation in science, and overall, the number and percentage of women has increased (Scantlebury & Baker, 2007). Rosser (2012) reported that qualified women continued to leave science in part because of the continual micro-inequities[1] they experienced throughout graduate school, postdoctoral positions, and/or when they enter the academy. Across disciplines, cultures, and time, common themes from women's experiences were isolation, being perceived by professors and peers as incompetent, and the struggle of balancing personal and professional goals.

The consensus from these studies was that social and environmental factors explained the under-representation of women in STEM. Moreover, there is a continued perception that males are inherently better at mathematics compared to women; thus, students' cognitive abilities rather than sociocultural factors are used to explain gender differences in science participation (Clark Blickenstaff 2005; Hill et al., 2010). Hill and colleagues (2010) suggested that small changes in the social climate of academic departments, such as a broader overview in introductory courses, integration of women into the faculty, and the retention of female faculty through "family-friendly" policies such as maternity leave and stop-the-clock tenure programs could improve the retention of women in STEM.

In the United States, Ong and colleagues (2011) reviewed more than 100 empirical studies on the participation of American women of color in postsecondary STEM education. Historically Black colleges and universities (HBCU) and women's colleges produced a disproportionate number of female, African American STEM majors because those institutions had supportive faculty, curriculum focused on real-world applications, and research opportunities for students.

Overall, women often reported being the only person of color in a research group, and to counteract the isolation, they found support through university-wide programs focused on recruitment and retention of under-represented students. The female STEM students used their networks to reject negative stereotypes, to identify with colleagues, and to acquire the skills and strategies they needed to deal with microaggressions (subtle offenses). Informal networks also provided women access to role models, mentors, and teachers. The women established support networks within their racial or ethnic groups rather than with STEM colleagues and peers. The climate in science departments remained "chilly" for women because of disinterested faculty and peers who viewed the women as incompetent or needing assistance to succeed.

The STEM fields are slowly diversifying, yet the image of a competent scientist remains male, white, and heterosexual (Hussénius & Scantlebury, 2011; Mendick & Moreau, 2013; Owens, 2009; Scantlebury, Tai, & Rahm, 2007). In order to mask their sexuality and ethnic identities, STEM women of color used their clothing and social practices (such as speech patterns) to imitate the masculine image of a scientist. However, these practices "splintered" the women's identity into STEM and "other" (Ong et al., 2011). Many women reported supportive families being critical for their continued participation in science, but the family environment could also have a negative influence. For some women, continuing their studies meant financial hardship for the family. Moreover, in order to succeed in their STEM careers, the women delayed motherhood and marriage, actions that deferred personal, parental, and familial expectations of establishing one's own family.

Managing of personal goals and obligations with a professional career is not unique to women in science, as women pursuing careers in law, business, or other disciplines in academe face similar challenges (Babcock & Laschever, 2007). But the disproportionate number of women to men in the sciences, especially the physical sciences, has meant that masculine practices continue to dominate the social climate in classrooms, laboratories, and research settings. The research examining the careers of female science educators has produced themes similar to those reported by women scientists. The female science educators offered an extensive view of the challenges and career paths they faced working at a range of institutions with every diverse academic climates. Those themes included marginalization, isolation, alienation from families, and the challenges of balancing career and family responsibilities (Kahle, 2011; Parsons, 2007; Scantlebury, 2014; Scantlebury et al., 2010; Venville, 2008; Wiseman & Weinburgh, 2009). Many of the female science educators foregrounded equity in their lived experiences and teaching and research practices and were cognizant of their presence as role models to students, teachers, and peers.

There is a continued need for researchers to examine how other social categories along with gender influence students' participation and retention in science. The review studies suggest little has changed in the daily teaching of science in K–12 education, and for many women, the sociocultural climate in science and science education remains chilly. The majority of the STEM education research examining the issues impacting women of color focused on African American women. However, given the changing demographics in the United States, with an increasing percentage of the general population having a Latin heritage, future research needs to examine the issues impacting Chicana and Latina participation in STEM. There was also limited racial diversity in the studies associated with women in science, and the other reviews did not address gender and other social categories, possibly because data are rarely collected and disaggregated in multiple ways.

Gender and Structure

Science and science education are social organizations and, as such, are gendered (Acker, 1990). Gender influences who studies, participates, and engages in science. An ongoing trend is that females are overrepresented in the biological/life sciences and males are disproportionally represented in the physical sciences (Hill et al., 2010). Previously, researchers have suggested that achievement and attitudinal differences accounted for the gendered pattern of females' and males' science participation. However, meta-analytic studies have shown minimal differences in achievement between females and males (Hyde & Linn, 2006). In the United States, Riegle-Crumb, King, Grodsky, and Muller (2012) used three national databases to examine gender differences in students' entry into physical science and engineering majors. They concluded that the larger societal structures, rather than differences between groups, explained why academically capable and qualified women chose not to enroll in physical science and/or engineering majors.

Gender devaluation, egalitarianism, and essentialism may provide some explanation for the uneven participation of women and men in science and engineering. England (2010) proposed that devaluation and egalitarianism have caused uneven changes in the gender system. While the women's movement, using an argument for egalitarianism, garnered females' access to traditional male occupations, it did not add value to female occupations. Women moved into male-dominated areas and gained status, power, and higher wages. But the movement of men from the workforce into home responsibilities or into female occupations was limited, and there was an uneven or asymmetric gender change (England, 2010).

Concurrent with the asymmetrical movement of women into male-dominated occupations was the impact of gender essentialism. Gender essentialism is the perspective that one gender has inherently different interests and is "better" at some things compared to the other. For example, women are better nurturers than men, while men are more rational and logical compared to women (Sikora & Pokropek, 2012). Sikora and Pokropek (2012) used gender essentialism in their study of high school students' science self-concept and career expectations. Using data from PISA 2006, they found approximately the same percentage of girls and boys stated an interest in a science career, but more than three times the number of boys indicated their interest in a computing, engineering, or mathematics career compared to girls. And more girls compared to boys indicated a preference for a biology, agricultural, or health career. They concluded that the structural components of gender essentialism are resistant to the usual outcome that high student performance is related to a student planning a career in science. Supposedly girls are hardworking and relate to careers in the biological and life sciences because their interests lie in working with living things, while boys are smart and more suited than girls to study the physical sciences and engineering.

Why do academically capable girls and women chose to pursue science careers in the biological and/or health sciences? Although the biological and/or health sciences may have a lesser status than the physical sciences and engineering, women can pursue their science interests working in the biological and/or health sciences without having to participate in the more masculine, hegemonic sociocultural climate in the physical sciences and engineering. The perception that men are "naturally" better at science than women continues to impact individuals' participation at the structural, symbolic, and individual levels.

International studies such as TIMSS (Gonzales et al., 2008) and PISA (Organization of Economic Cooperation and Development [OECD], 2009) provided information on student science achievement and attitudes by gender at a structural level. The patterns can provide information and direction for recommendations on the current gender issues that are impacting science education. The next section reviews two international studies that examined gender differences in students' science achievement and attitudes toward science, two studies that used the databases to examine gender issues and other attitudinal studies conducted at a national level or with a large sample size.

International Studies of Students' Science Achievement and Attitudes

Recently TIMSS (Gonzales et al., 2008) and PISA (OECD, 2009) have produced international studies on students' science achievement and attitudes. Gender differences in students' science achievement have decreased over the past few decades (Francis & Skelton, 2011; Hyde & Linn, 2006). Yet, despite calls for a more nuanced review of students' science achievement by gender and other social categories, TIMSS and PISA studies reported results only by gender. PISA provided a more detailed gender analysis compared to TIMSS by using gender as a category in a differential item functioning analysis of its test items (Le, 2009) and a secondary study that examined the performance and attitudes of 15-year-old students (OECD, 2009).

In 2007, TIMSS reported that fourth- and eighth-grade girls had higher achievement scores than boys. At the fourth grade, girls had higher scores than boys on physical and life sciences and reasoning, while boys performed better than girls on earth science questions (Louis & Mistele, 2011). In eighth grade, girls had higher scores than boys in biology and chemistry and the three cognitive domains of knowing, applying, and reasoning, while boys scored higher than girls in physics (Gonzales et al., 2008).

PISA (OECD, 2009) examined gender differences to identify inequalities, to examine student performance, and to provide an understanding of how 15-year-old students learn science. For 22 of the 30 countries, there were no gender differences in science achievement, and in countries where there was a gender difference, it was small (Francis & Skelton, 2011). PISA's science test had questions that focused on *identifying scientific issues*, *explaining phenomena scientifically*, and *using scientific evidence*. Females had significantly higher scores than males on questions related to *identifying scientific issues*, while boys scored significantly higher than girls on *explaining phenomena scientifically*. The different achievement patterns for girls and boys on PISA and TIMSS may be due to each test's different characteristics. Girls have higher literacy scores than boys, and PISA has a higher level of reading comprehension and contextual questions. In contrast, TIMMS has more factual questions and fewer interpretative questions (Kahle, 2004). The different style of questions between the two tests many account for the varying results.

The latest international science assessment tests showed no gender differences in students' science achievement. However, when the data are disaggregated and examined by content area and question type, some differences appear. In TIMSS, fourth- and eighth-grade girls had a higher mean score compared to boys, while boys had higher achievement in physics compared with girls.

For most countries, there were no gender differences on students' PISA science achievement. Patterns emerged in the different types of questions and also for different structural levels (i.e., national comparison between girls and boys versus school-level comparisons). As the student demographics of many Western countries diversify because of immigration, including other social categories, such as immigration status (that is, how long a student has studied in the country in which s/he is taking the test), first language proficiency, and socioeconomic status when analyzing students' science achievement is warranted.

Students' Attitudes Toward Science

This section begins with an examination of the research on students' attitudes toward science at international and national levels and includes studies with smaller sample sizes. OECD (2009) examined students' self-efficacy, self-concept, interest in science, enjoyment of science, motivation to learn, career intentions, awareness of environmental issues, optimism regarding environmental issues, and responsibility for sustainable development. There were no gender differences on self-concept, interest in science, enjoyment of science, and motivation to learn, but in Japan, the Netherlands, Iceland, Korea, and Taiwan, boys had higher self-efficacy compared to girls. Other research had shown that Japanese girls viewed women as having the ability, confidence, and interest to participate in science, but high school boys and college men reported women had less science ability than males and that science was not an appropriate career choice for women (Scantlebury, Baker, Sugi, Yoshida, & Uysal, 2007). Taiwanese girls had less interest in science compared to boys (Chang, Yau-Yuen, Yeung, & Cheng, 2009), and male Taiwanese science teachers viewed science as more suitable for boys and gave boys more encouragement than girls (Huang & Fraser, 2009). The influence of Japanese and Taiwanese societal attitudes that girls are not as capable as boys in science may have contributed to the lower self-efficacy of girls from these two countries.

OECD (2009) examined whether gender differences occurred between students attending single-sex schools. After the analysis was controlled for the schools' socioeconomic status, there were no gender differences between female and male students. Many successful women scientists have experienced a single-sex environment either in school or in their families (Rossiter, 2012). One recommendation is that providing girls single-sex science and/or mathematics classes would improve their participation in these fields (Hyde & Linn, 2006). However, the PISA results suggest that socioeconomic status is a stronger predictor for students' achievement, attitudes, and participation in science than learning science in a single-sex environment. But girls studying physics in single-sex schools had higher self-esteem and sense of belonging compared to girls in coeducation schools (Murphy & Whitelegg, 2006). And in the United States, ninth-grade urban boys had more positive attitudes and confidence in

science compared to girls when placed in single-sex science and mathematics classes (Brown & Ronau, 2012). The outcomes of single-sex education experiences on girls and boys warrant more study at a symbolic and individual level because situation and context influence the outcome.

Sikora and Pokropek (2012) used PISA student survey data to examine high school students' career goals and plans from 50 countries. The study used science self-concept, expectation of employment in biology, agriculture, or health, and expectation of employment in computing, engineering, or mathematics as dependent variables on the career goals and plans of high school students (Sikora & Pokropek, 2012). Students' career expectations were a combination of their perceptions of how they might cope with a future career, along with the perceived personal benefits of that career. Girls had a lower science self-concept than boys, and girls in industrial countries underestimated their science ability. Overall, nearly equal numbers of girls (27%) and boys (24%) reported an interest in a science career. However, boys were three times more likely than girls to choose a career in computing, engineering, or mathematics. Students' self-concept, science performance, or family status did not explain the gender differences between girls' and boys' career preferences.

In an international, longitudinal study of 79,000 student questions posed to scientists via a website, girls asked more questions than boys, but their interest in asking questions declined throughout their school years (Baram-Tsabari, Sethi, Bry, & Yarden, 2009). The decline in girls' asking questions was consistent across countries, but it was most significant for the United States, United Kingdom, Canada, Australia, and New Zealand. Girls' questions focused more on life science topics and boys focused on physical sciences, a pattern that has remained consistent across time, geographic region, and student age.

Various studies have showed that students' attitudes toward science have declined as they progressed through schooling. More recent attitudinal studies using gender as an analytical category were conducted with kindergarten students (Mantzicopoulos, Patrick, & Samarapungavan, 2008; Patrick, Mantzicopoulos, & Samarapungavan, 2009), middle school students, and high school students (Chang et al., 2009; Hanson, 2009; Kiran & Sungur, 2011) on topics that ranged from students' interest, enjoyment, and educational and career science aspirations to an examination of how gender and race influenced those interests and aspirations (Perry, Link, Boelter, & Leukefeld, 2012; Riegle-Crumb, Moore, & Ramos-Wada, 2011).

There were no gender differences with kindergarten children's confidence and motivation toward science (Mantzicopoulos et al., 2008). However, in another study, Patrick and colleagues (2009) reported that linguistically diverse, low socioeconomic status kindergarten students who were taught science using inquiry enjoyed science more than a comparison group that did not experience inquiry science. In the comparison group, boys liked science more than girls did. In the United States, African American girls had positive attitudes toward science, learned self-reliance, and attained a higher level of independence compared to their Latina and White peers (Hanson, 2009; Perry et al., 2012; Riegle-Crumb et al., 2011). Urban, African American, and Latin boys had lower self-esteem and academic aspirations and higher truancy rates compared with their sisters. However, African American males had the same career aspirations as White males (Perry et al., 2012).

Researchers have examined a range of attitudinal variables by gender and, in some cases, gender and other social categories. Taking a different approach to the information produced from students' science attitude surveys, Sinnes and Løken (2012) used a feminist critique to examine Project Lily's recommendations for recruiting and retaining Norwegian students into STEM majors and careers. The analysis showed that the report made three assumptions about the attitudes and perceptions of females and males. First, males and females had different values. Second, females reinforced a feminine identity through the subjects they chose to study. Third, female role models were necessary to recruit more girls and women into STEM subjects. Project Lily's report essentialized females and males through the recommendation that increasing the number of females in the physical sciences would improve sustainability and socially responsible research (Sinnes & Løken, 2012). Moreover, studies on high school students' physics identity found that female role models had no impact on girls' physics identity (Hazari, Sonnert, Sadler, & Shanahan, 2010).

As well as examining data from different social categories, the large survey data studies provided information on how gender operates at the structural level, which could impact how individuals ameliorate gender within their science identities. Across 50 countries, females continue to choose life sciences over the physical sciences. Will the current curriculum reforms aimed at incorporating engineering, technology, and mathematics into science exacerbate this difference or reduce the gap?

Nor have we examined the structural issues that continue to influence gender and science education. Gender essentialism has impacted students' participation within the sciences. Research on how to change these structural issues in the gender system may influence students' science participation patterns. Other studies could also focus from the broad definition of science to examining patterns by different science disciplines, such as chemistry, earth science, environmental science, marine science, and also various social categories.

Gender and Symbolic

Gender is a social construct that influences sociocultural practices and experiences. This section reviews the research at a symbolic level, such as how families can support participation in science. Parents may encourage children's science interests by taking them to museums or providing access to other out-of-school science activities

and experiences. Yet the gender of the child and the family's socioeconomic status and ethnicity may contribute to different levels of support. Families offering support are important to women of color in science and science education. Another consideration at the symbolic level is how gender influences science learning in different cultural settings and spaces, formal and informal, physical and discursive, and these different learning environments may provide individuals the experiences and opportunities to ascribe science into their identities.

Families

Parents and families have different science expectations for girls and boys, and these expectations vary within other social categories such as ethnicity and socioeconomic or immigrant status (Archer et al., 2012; Jovanovic & Bhanot, 2008). Parents reported providing boys more opportunities to learn science than girls, except when the experience involved caring for animals (Alexander, Johnson, & Kelley, 2012). Middle-class families established a pattern of engaging children with science activities, and if their daughters expressed an interest in science, the parents provided ongoing and sustained support. African American girls reported high parental expectations, but Latina girls noted that their parents had higher expectations for boys (Perry et al., 2012).

Postsecondary, African American, Native American, and Maori women interested in science relied on the support provided by their families, communities, and social networks (Brandt, 2007; McKinley, 2008; Ong et al., 2011). The isolation women felt in their research labs or peer groups while studying at the university was offset by connecting to their families and communities, although they described their identities as splintered or hybrid in dealing with the different sociocultural environments and expectations of family and work (McKinley, 2008; Ong et al., 2011). Families provide important support for students to engage with and continue in science. That support can vary by socioeconomic status and ethnicity, but in general, students who express interest in science also report that their families encourage that interest. There is an opportunity to examine ways schools and other entities could encourage families to connect children with science.

Learning Science in Different Spaces

An emerging theme in science education is to provide students, especially those from under-represented groups, the space to engage with science outside of a formal classroom. Changing where and how science is learned can provide students a different context to structure their science identities. For several decades, science educators have engaged girls in out-of-school science activities with the purpose of positively impacting their attitudes toward science and improving their skills (such as spatial ability and mathematical skills; Kahle & Meece, 1994). The out-of-school spaces include after-school programs or camps that are located within school buildings or elsewhere, such as museums, youth clubs, or shelters, and within the formal school structure during cogenerative dialogues.

Informal science experiences can provide students, especially girls, the opportunity to construct a unique learning space in which they can develop the practices to succeed in science. Girls constructed hybrid identities as people who learned, did, valued, and owned science after their involvement with an after-school program (Rahm, 2008). Middle school girls, who participated in a 5-day summer camp that engaged them in hands-on problem-solving activities with scientists, used the time to develop friendships, pursue leadership opportunities, and make connections between their view of science and scientists and their role in science (Farland-Smith, 2012). Out-of-school science experiences often have goals of encouraging girls to remain in science but are rarely evaluated for their long-term effect. An impact study with 14 girls, 8 years after their involvement in an after-school program, found that the girls had higher perceptions of science careers than did a comparison group of young women who had not been involved with the program. This research was one of the few longitudinal studies that examined the long-term impact of an intervention program on girls' achievement, participation, and attitudes toward science (Tyler-Wood, Ellison, Lim, & Periathiruvadi, 2012). Fiscal support is needed to support longitudinal research to examine the factors that can encourage students from under-represented groups to remain in STEM education and career pathways.

When given the opportunity, girls used spaces to share their perspectives on science and learning with each other and their teachers (Calabrese Barton, Tan, & Rivet, 2008). Urban Latina girls produced scientific artifacts such as songs, puppets, posters, and magnets as part of their science class in which they could play and enjoy their science identities while negotiating their science roles. The space allowed the girls to merge their personal experiences from home, outside of school, and the classroom while developing their science knowledge and thus incorporate science into their identities as learners.

Women of color established discursive spaces to support and talk with each other while studying in undergraduate science programs (Brandt, 2007). Out-of-school programs can provide students the discursive space to challenge the gender schema that science is a masculine field and engage in conversations with teachers, instructors, and each other about how they could incorporate science into their identities.

Cogenerative dialogues. Cogenerative dialogues are spaces with a formal school setting that can also provide students the opportunity to discuss science.

More than a decade ago, researchers introduced cogenerative dialogues (cogens) to engage urban high school students in discussions with their teachers and peers about improving science teaching and learning. Cogens provided a social space within the classroom that examined the power structures by establishing rules that all participants had an equal right to voice their perspectives and that all participants assumed individual and collective responsibility for the cogen and its outcomes (Bayne & Scantlebury, 2013).

One cogen study focused on how gender schema influenced students' science learning and/or teachers' practices. After engaging a group of African American high school girls in a series of cogens, a teacher changed her understanding of how one can "do science" to include aspects of their culture such as othermothering, with a focus on learning science and engaging with the subject (Scantlebury, 2007; Scantlebury & LaVan, 2006). Cogens that focus on how gender schema are impacting students' science learning or a cogen that considers masculinity theories in examining the context of boys' engagement with science are also examples of gender research. To date, science education researchers engaged with cogens have not used theories of masculinity to understand students' engagement with science.

Brandt's (2007) case study research of four Native American women explored their engagement with science as undergraduate students. Brandt (2007) recognized how "locations of possibility" meant that women could engage with science. However, those locations were in social settings such as study groups, academic clubs, or outside of the university rather than in lectures or laboratory classes. Several studies have shown that constructing a different space for students to engage in learning science, via out-of-school or university experiences (Brandt, 2007; Rahm, 2008; Tyler-Wood et al., 2012) or within school (Bayne & Scantlebury, 2013; Quigley, 2011; Tan & Calabrese Barton, 2008a, 2008b), can assist students in developing science identities through generating local knowledge to support student learning and improve science teaching. Future research could examine how these spaces may modify students' and teachers' gendered perceptions about science and gendered practices within more formal education settings.

Classroom discourses. Several studies used gender as an analytical category for examining classroom discussions between teachers and students. Due (2012) used gender symbolism, gender structure, and individual gender when examining students' discourse and perceptions about gender and physics. The students' discourse about physics when working in mixed and single-sex groups provided evidence of how they positioned each other and themselves as learners. Students viewed physics either masculine or gender neutral, with boys being more suited to physics than girls. Girls assumed the caretaker roles of recordkeeper and notetaker. In mixed groups, boys were viewed as the "physics authorities" and often contradicted girls who voiced their physics knowledge (Due, 2012). Boys talked more during the group work, were more likely to share incorrect information, and received more verbal support from their peers compared with girls. Several girls positioned themselves as ambitious, hardworking, and responsible physics students, but these positions were not available to boys. Boys could only position themselves as playful or irresponsible students. Students did not ask questions in case this caused their peers and teachers to infer they were not competent in physics (Due, 2012).

Two other studies, Orlander (2012) and Lundin (2014), examined the discourse between students during high school biology lessons focused on human genitals or human relationships. Both studies documented the heteronormative tone of the discussions that framed gender and sexuality as inseparable categories ascribed to woman and man. Orlander (2012) noted that students and teachers viewed value-neutral statements about human genitalia as "facts." While students gave examples connected to their lives, the discussion did not move into how emotions or feelings may impact one's biological sexual functions, and the discussion about sexuality focused on heterosexuality. In Lundin's (2014) study, during the selected lessons, students used homophobic comments and slurs to mask being uncomfortable when discussing sexuality and the physical features of a hypothetical heterosexual partner.

The discourse in science classrooms between students and teachers continues to reproduce science as a hegemonic and heteronormative domain (Lemke, 2011; Nyström, 2009). Informative studies on how pedagogical practices, curriculum choices, and engaging students in cogenerative dialogues that focus on how gender schema influence science teaching and learning could elucidate strategies to challenge the masculine and heteronormative schema that continue to dominate science classes.

Teachers' Gendered Perspectives

Several gender studies focused on science teacher background, attitudes, practices, and career trajectories. Science teachers had power and status in a school because science is constructed as being a difficult subject to teach (Nyström, 2009). However, gender-difference discourse impacted female and male teachers in different ways because science is viewed as masculine. Students and male science teachers viewed female teachers as less capable in science compared to men. Their involvement with science raised questions about their value as teachers and/or women. Conversely, male teachers were viewed as capable in science but were not attributed with the characteristics of caring and nurturing associated with teaching (Nyström, 2009).

Research on how gender impacts science teachers' identity could extend to university-level teacher educators in areas such as their teaching practices, curriculum and assessment choices, attitudes toward students, and perspectives on gender. There are no recent studies exploring these issues, nor have we examined faculty's views on how gender influences the culture of teaching, science teaching, and science education.

Teacher attitudes. Female Taiwanese science teachers had significantly higher mean scores than their male peers on *collegiality*, *professional interest*, and *gender equity*, while the male teachers had higher scores on the *principal leadership* and *staff freedom* subscales compared to the female teachers. The teachers' gender, school level, subject taught, and number of teaching years at their current school contributed to a significant difference between female and male teachers on *work pressure*. Female teachers had more positive attitudes regarding their professional relationships and felt more pressure to complete their work compared to their male colleagues. Female teachers reported that science was important for girls and boys. But the male science teachers noted that they viewed science as more suitable for boys and gave boys more encouragement than girls (Huang & Fraser, 2009).

Science teaching as a profession is hierarchical and gendered (Kreitz-Sandberg, 2013; Nyström, 2009). While teaching is a feminized profession, the teaching of science remains highly gendered. Women teachers work primarily in the lower grades and in the lower-status subjects such as general science, biology, and chemistry. More men teach physics, and they are less likely to teach young children compared to women (Banilower et al., 2013; Nyström, 2009). Although women have the qualifications to teach higher-status science subjects, such as advanced courses in science or physics, male teachers typically receive these teaching assignments (Clark Blickenstaff 2005; Nyström, 2009). Nyström (2009) reported how, in one school, female and male science teachers had sex-segregated work areas, establishing "different worlds" between the teachers. The female teachers reported discipline issues with boys who showed their disrespect by interrupting teachers, refusing to follow instructions, and framing the teachers as "unqualified, unauthorized and unskilled" (Nyström, 2009, p. 742).

Teachers also noted that over time, more girls and immigrant students enrolled in science courses, and these students had different knowledge (Nyström, 2009). Although teachers in Nyström's (2009) study noted the importance of addressing gender inequalities in the classroom, they believed that issues related to students' sexuality and ethnicity should be addressed outside of the science classroom. The focus on gender difference discourse by teachers, students, and researchers reproduced the gender inequality in science and, in some circumstances, ignored other inequalities, such as immigration status (Nyström, 2009). One area of future research could expand upon teachers' attitudes and perceptions toward teaching science to girls and boys and how those views are nuanced by other social categories.

Pedagogical approaches. Teachers using gender theory as a framework for examining classroom events and interactions recognized how unconscious gender stereotyping impacted their teaching and students' science participation (Andersson, Hussenius, & Gustafsson, 2009). The teachers identified four feminist pedagogical strategies: (1) paying attention and validating the children's science experience; (2) recognizing when children used scientific practices and engaging the students at those times; (3) remaining as a presence and allowing children to provide their explanations; (4) and asking the children challenging questions (Andersson & Gullberg, 2012). For some teachers, tensions occurred between their views about science, the production of knowledge, and pedagogical practices. Laura, a teacher in a study conducted by Zapata and Gallard (2007), focused her attention on the boys in her class to mange their behavior. Laura's unconscious practices reinforced cultural norms around gender stereotypes about students' academic abilities, attitudes, and behaviors.

If teachers are not cognizant of critical theories, such as the feminist framework by Andersson and Gullberg (2012) or Black feminist theory (Buck & Quigley, 2013; Quigley, 2011), and how to use those theories to examine their teaching, they may continue to repeat gender stereotypic practices in science classrooms that previous researchers have identified as shortchanging girls. Studies by de Groot Kim (2011) and Dyer (2011) noted that teachers had to proactively intervene in children's play and learning experiences because as early as 18 months of age, boys demanded and commandeered the available space (both inside the classroom and outside in play areas), the learning resources, and the teachers' time. Girls waited to leave the classroom, to play outside, and to gain access to toys and center resources and to their teachers.

Teachers' perceptions of students' competence and ability in science continue to influence their practices. For example, teachers restricted Latina girls' opportunities to learn science through instruction that provided students notes and required them to complete worksheets (Parker, 2014). Or teachers assigned boys who had been absent from class into groups of high-achieving Asian girls and asked the girls to "catch them up." Several of the girls expressed their frustration at being asked to "teach" the boys rather than focus on learning science (Martin, Wassell, & Scantlebury, 2013).

Teachers can unconsciously reinforce stereotypic gender roles by asking girls to assume roles as caregivers, to teach peers who have missed instruction, to act as mediators of boys' behavior, to maintain the order and neatness of the shared spaces, and to wait for science equipment and other resources. Engaging teachers in critical reflection of their practice through action research projects focused on gender or foregrounding gender in cogenerative dialogues could provide teachers the tools to critique their pedagogical practices and promote changes to those practices.

Gender and Individuals

The next section will summarize studies focused on individuals' engagement with learning science and/or as a career pathway. In particular, researchers interested in physics and gender have conducted studies with high school, undergraduate, and graduate students examining how students incorporated the schema and practices of a physics culture into their identities using gender and masculinity theory.

Gendered Identities

Feminist researchers have problematized the construction of identity as a mechanism to dismantle the discussion around different groups and thus identify inequities (Skelton & Francis, 2009. Recently, several studies have focused on how gender influences science identity for women of color (Brandt, 2007; Carlone & Johnson, 2007; Johnson, 2007; McKinley, 2008), high school students (Due, 2012; et al., 2010), and undergraduate and graduate students (Danielsson, 2012; Gonsalves, 2011, 2012; Hazari, Sadler, & Tai, 2008; Pettersson, 2011).

Kindergarten teachers and community members promoted African American girls' science learning by encouraging the girls to present stories connecting science with their home lives. The girls engaged with science using their voices and writing, which helped them achieve self-definition and self-valuation (Collins, 1991; Quigley, 2011). Teachers in an urban middle school understood the importance of recognizing their female African American students as scientists so the girls would view themselves as belonging in science. The teachers required the girls to use science equipment and to wear lab coats so the girls could connect their identity to the image of science (Buck & Quigley, 2013).

Girls interested in science performed a "restrained" femininity to produce a "feminine science identity" (Archer et al., 2012). Similar to the "top girls" in McRobbie's (2007) study of high-achieving high school students, girls with a feminine science identity were socially popular and academically successful. The girls' performativity showed a balance of interests in science, clothes, sports, and friends (Archer et al., 2012). Another group of girls was characterized as "bluestocking scientists." These girls were academically successful but not interested in feminine practices or as popular with their peers as girls with a feminine science identity (Archer et al., 2012). In various studies, girls used different strategies to identify as female and as people interested in science. They used the tools of science and accessories, such as clothing, to present as a scientist or emphasized feminine aspects of their identity combined with their science interests.

Carlone and Johnson (2007) developed a science identity model from their study of four Latina, three Native American, and four Asian American women. The model had three components: competence, performance, and recognition. Their analysis described several science identities including research scientist, altruistic scientist, and disrupted scientist. Women with a research scientist identity had engaged with science through research experiences. The women in this group received repeated recognition as research scientists through awards, fellowships, and/or scholarships. The altruistic scientists connected science knowledge to humanitarian goals and pursued their careers within medical fields. Their recognition came from the areas in which they planned to offer their help and expertise rather than from scientists or the scientific field. The disrupted scientists reported having negative experiences, such as a lack of support or discrimination. Others framed disrupted scientists as belonging to an under-represented science category that contributed to the women's perceptions that they had interrupted science trajectories. A key factor of the women's science identities depended on the recognition, both positive and negative, they received during their undergraduate and graduate studies. The women who were categorized as disrupted scientists were the most diverse from the White, masculine norm of science.

Women of color and indigenous (Maori) female scientists managed their splintered or hybrid identities by connecting with their family and communities. They also established spaces where they could negotiate their science identity with their other identities (McKinley, 2008; Ong et al., 2011). A group of Native American women established "locations of possibility" to engage with science (Brandt, 2007). However, those locations were not in a "traditional" science setting such as a laboratory but rather in other social settings such as study groups, academic clubs, or outside the university. In these venues, the women connected their identities with science.

Faculty and teachers should be aware of how competence, performance, and recognition combine to produce students' science identities. Science faculty gained students' respect by establishing spaces in their classes for science discussions (Brandt, 2007). Women established science identities through working as researchers and discussing their ideas with other scientists and peers, either in formal settings or in other arranged spaces.

Physics and Masculinity

Within physics, researchers have examined how gender and the alignment of the subject's practices with masculinity have impacted men. While feminist critiques of science illuminated the field's masculine image, the scholarship of masculinity that has evolved in the past decade has focused on men/male as a political category and documented how men are also gendered in relational contexts (Connell, 1995). Connell (1995) proposed that hegemonic masculinity legitimizes patriarchy and is heterosexual, aggressive, and competitive.

Experimental physicists constructed their work as "boys and their toys," in particular "big, high power toys, which is male thing" (Pettersson, 2011, p. 55). This discourse framed the machines as masculine and established the laboratory as a bounded space in which participants enacted a masculine culture. An aspect of that culture was the physical labor associated with building equipment to test scientific theories. The labor and work conditions in setting up and maintaining the equipment were also another reason the men gave as to why there are so few women in plasma physics. And several participants

voiced their perspective that women were not biologically capable of understanding plasma physics and viewed the research lab as gender neutral (Pettersson, 2011).

Danielsson's (2012) extensive interviews with the two male physics students elucidated that not only were they "doing gender" when studying physics and working in the lab, they were also "doing class." They valued experimental physics because it emphasized an understanding of "practical" things and was not theoretically bound with mathematics. Similar to the men in Pettersson's (2011) research, these undergraduate physics students viewed the manual labor associated with laboratory work and the mechanical skills needed to operate and repair equipment as indicative of masculine practices.

The gendering of physics, career trajectories, and the construction of gender order could explain the disparity in the number of women and men studying the subject at an advanced level (Gonsalves, 2011). Gonsalves (2012) examined how individuals and others positioned female doctoral students in physics. Carlone and Johnson's (2007) themes of competence (technical, analytical, and academic) and recognition emerged from their study of four women enrolled in a graduate physics program. Technical competence was related to fixing machines, and similar patterns were reported in Pettersson's (2011) and Danielsson's (2012) studies. The ability to build, service, and repair machines is an importance asset in the research physics laboratory and is associated with masculinity. Analytical competence referred to solving problems, while academic competence was the ability to communicate physics and understand the culture of the discipline. However, women consciously chose "gender-neutral" clothes because a feminine dress style could negate being recognized as a competent physicist.

The perception that physics is accommodating only to women who exhibit masculine or gender-neutral identities and to heterosexual men are based on cultural expectations and ideals. Girls' physics identities are influenced by discussions of the under-representation of women in science, but other experiences previously suggested to influence students' perceptions about science, such as discussing women scientists' research or inviting female scientists to speak to high school students, had no effect (Hazari et al., 2010). Multiple studies have shown that girls and women are reluctant to study physics, they attribute any success in the subject to hard work rather than to ability, they believe a physics identity implies working alone, and they do not see physics as useful in their career choices (Hazari et al., 2010; Whitelegg, Murphy, & Hart, 2007). Students interested in physics have to engage with a hegemonic masculinity that promotes competition and aggressive practices. Some females modified their voices and used clothing to disguise their femininity in order to identify as physicists. Males have refused to ask questions because this practice exhibited a lack of knowledge and thus raised doubts about their physics competence (Due, 2012). The culture of physics and how it interacts with gender impacts females and males in different ways. And while males are three times as likely as females to study physics, overall fewer students are choosing the subject. The culture of physics needs to change its practices and image so in the future more students identify with the subject.

Future Directions

Research in gender and education has evolved from a focus on issues of equity and access to difference and intersectionality and, more recently, subjectivity and identity (Dillabough et al., 2009). While science education research has continued its focus on access, difference, and identity, gender research within the field has become fused, and possibly lost, within other social categories (Kahle, in Joslin et al., 2007). McRobbie (2009) labeled the erosion of feminist research through the devaluing of its ideas and goals as disarticulation. She argued that rather than producing new goals and themes across social categories, disarticulation acted as a "dispersal strategy," to the detriment of all social groups. Feminism was no longer viewed as a place in which different subordinate groups could learn from each other and identify common political causes focused on feminist ideals (McRobbie, 2009).

As feminist and gender research in science education moves forward, we should consider the questions that are not asked. At a structural level, gender remains "two"—that is, female and male. Our international comparisons of student achievement, attitudes, and participation are examined with those analytical categories. Data are rarely reported by gender and race, socioeconomic status, immigration status, or sexuality. Yet, within these results, countries and other large structural entities could examine data comparing several categorical groups—that is, gender, race, socioeconomic status, first language acquisition, and immigrant status. While Sikora and Pokropek (2012) controlled for students' socioeconomic status, science performance, school, and country, what else could be learned if the data were studied by gender and other social categories? As the percentage of immigrant students increases in many countries, how can we learn more about gendered patterns of engagement in science if some baseline data are not collected?

While researchers have examined the labor distribution within the sciences, we have not conducted this type of analysis within science education. A recent study in the United States documented that 94% of elementary teachers and 70% of middle and 54% of high school science teachers were female, and more than 90% of teachers were white. What are the issues preventing the American science teaching workforce from diversifying? Are similar patterns evident in other countries and cultures? What are the gendered teaching patterns within the sciences? Do women and men equally teach the upper-level sciences? Who teaches science education at the college/university

level? To date, the field has not examined this last question, but research from Europe suggests that teacher education is also becoming feminized (Kreitz-Sandberg, 2013). However, preservice teachers' gender essentialist perspectives and statements are rarely challenged or discussed. As science education is reconstructed into STEM education, what research is being planned and conducted about engaging under-represented students? What steps are being taken to ensure that incorporating two fields, engineering and technology (which have a stronger masculine image than science), does not reinforce the perception that STEM is a field for white, middle-class, heterosexual males?

A large portion of research in science education is conducted at the symbolic and individual levels, yet key areas in science education research have never asked how gender or other social categories have influenced the research, the context, or the theoretical frameworks. The percentage of peer-reviewed articles with "gender or feminist or equity" as a research category in peer-reviewed science articles is less than 5% (Hussénius et al., 2013). For example, science education researchers have rarely addressed gender issues in changing students' conceptions or examining teachers' pedagogical content knowledge (Hussénius et al., 2013; Scantlebury & Martin, 2010). What knowledge would be generated through taking gender into account in the studies of students' science conceptions and the associated research of teachers' pedagogical practices to address those conceptions? How would a discussion of the nature of science be reformulated from a feminist perspective?

Since the previous review, several studies have focused on gender and physics regarding students' identity (Danielsson, 2012; Gonsalves, 2012; Hazari et al., 2010), using masculinity theories to understand the culture of physics (Pettersson, 2011), gendered discourses in high school classes (Due, 2012), curriculum and pedagogical practices (Murphy & Whitelegg, 2006; Whitelegg et al., 2007), and materialism (Götschel, 2013). Other researchers have examined issues in biology, such as heteronormative discussions of sex and sexuality in classrooms, textbooks, and curriculum (Bazzul & Sykes, 2011; Lemke, 2011; Lundin, 2014; Orlander, 2012). There is little research in the other school science subjects, such as chemistry, earth and space science, or environmental science. Feminist researchers have offered few critiques of chemistry, but these are recent and limited studies compared to the breadth and depth of research that has critiqued biology and physics (Götschel, 2013). Some teachers have viewed chemistry as more suited to girls' interests (Nyström, 2009), and as a subject it has less status than physics. Do students' perceptions about chemistry and gender reflect their teachers' ideas? What is the sociocultural climate for women in chemistry in undergraduate and research laboratories? What new perspectives on chemistry would be generated from a feminist/masculinities/postcolonial critique of the discipline?

Science education curriculum is merging and emerging as STEM, and there will be challenges in connecting the Next Generation Science Standard with under-represented (Achieve, 2013). Possibly, the expansion of science curriculum to include technology, engineering, and mathematics opens up vast possibilities in connecting these areas to students' interest and reframing the cultural practices of STEM for more inclusivity. However, engineering and technology remain highly gendered toward the masculine, and thus there is also a potential that new STEM questions, curriculum, and practices may exclude more students. How will a STEM curriculum engage all students? Since the previous review, Calabrese Barton (2008) provided one of the few studies that critiqued science education curriculum from a feminist perspective. She used examples from ecological feminism to show how women have voiced their concerns for their families and communities and improved living conditions for themselves, their families, and their neighbors. Ecological feminism is an example of a cross-disciplinary theme that also relates to human needs and concerns. These are issues that could engage all students.

The devaluing of feminism as a critical, political theory that foregrounded societal issues that impacted girls and women may have influenced science education researchers to ignore the theoretical developments in gender and feminist research. In the next section, I discuss how intersectionality, material feminism, and queer theory could provide theoretical frameworks for science education researchers to re-engage with feminism and feminist researchers to engage with science education.

Intersectionality

> When I see something that looks racist, I ask, "Where is the patriarchy in this?" When I see something that looks sexist, I ask, "Where is the heterosexism in this"? When I see something that looks homophobic, I ask, "Where is the class interest in this?"
>
>   (Matsuda, 1991, p. 1189)

Intersectionality examines a group's different social positioning, how power influences those positions, and how power differentials generate evolving and changing hierarchies. Intersectionality provides a "platform for feminist theory as a shared enterprise" (Davis, 2011, p. 46) and a discursive site in which "feminist perspectives are in critical dialogue or productive conflict with each other" (Lykke, 2010, p. 208). Most science education research is framed using one critical framework without examining the data and asking, "Where is the . . . ?"

Intersectionality notes that social categories are intertwined and impact individuals in different ways determined by power structures (Crenshaw, 1989). Using intersectionality to re-analyze data from multiple perspectives could potentially generate a productive conflict—the strategies to engage one group of students in science may advantage one group, or finding that an analogy that is effective in helping one group of students learn science marginalizes another group. Using an intersectional approach to examining their data, Riegle-Crumb and King (2010) dispelled several myths about Black students' interest in science and raised questions about why Latina and White women chose not to study physical sciences and engineering. They found men from all racial groups had higher participation in science and engineering compared to women, which explained why there were four times as many men as women in physical sciences and engineering. The study found that Black women are more likely to declare a STEM major than their White female peers, and overall Latina and White women are the least likely groups to chose physical sciences and engineering.

Lykke (2011) suggests that one useful way of using intersectionality as an analytical tool is as a nodal point, starting with the "traditional" social categories of gender, race, and class. Nodal points are temporary contexts that feminist researchers use to generate local theory. For example, an examination of science education faculty could initially begin with a gender analysis of who teaches science education and at what levels they teach—undergraduate and/or graduate students. Who prepares the teachers of young children? High school teachers? How is gender addressed in teacher education programs? Are preservice teachers asked to consider immigration status and language proficiency? What topics are prioritized in a teacher education program? What role could cogenerative dialogues play in generating local knowledge for preservice teachers, faculty, teachers, and students?

Intersectionality provides a challenge to researchers to reconsider and examine the theoretical frameworks used to analyze data and interpret the results. Education engages individuals and relies on the interactions between individuals to learn, to teach, and to generate new knowledge in science education. Intersectionality provides a theoretical framework for examining what role gender plays in the production of knowledge in science education and how that role is changed in different social contexts.

Material Feminism

> Material feminists explore the interaction of culture, history, discourse, technology, biology, and the "environment" without privileging any one of these elements.
>
>   (Alaimo & Hekman, 2009, p. 7)

Material feminism connects language and reality and incorporates both into discussions of identity (Hekman, 2010). Barad (2003) argued that researchers had granted language "too much power" and called for feminists to re-engage with matter/material. Material feminism offers a theoretical framework for science educators because it moves the theorizing and analysis from the postmodern and posthumanities approaches to social critique that focused solely on language/discourse to incorporate matter into the analysis.

Barad (2003) introduced *intra-actions*, *agential realism*, and *apparatus* when arguing the need for "making matter matter" in feminist studies. *Intra-actions* position matter as agentic and as important as discourse. The engagement of matter through *intra-actions* brings into play material-discursive practices. The implications for science education research could be in reframing studies to consider how the material, such as the physical arrangement of laboratories, laboratory equipment, and the body/embodiment of who is a scientist, influences the teaching and learning of science. *Agential realism* examined intra-actions between human and nonhuman entities in particular contexts (Barad, 2007). For science education research, this engagement of material with discursive practices promotes the opportunity for agential cuts. Barad (2007) argued that the researcher and subject are not bounded, nor is there separation between knower and subject. Rather, knower and subject are part of the same reality (Lykke, 2011). However, with agential realism, the researcher subject and the object of the research are defined and contextualized. The defined relationship between the researcher subject and the object of the research establishes a boundary. However, the boundary is not fixed but a momentary phenomenon. An agential cut occurs when the boundary is defined and used. For example, when a researcher decides to make gender the first level of data analysis, when that choice is made, the reasons establish the boundary and produce a cut. *Apparatus* emerges from the specific material-discursive practices and can construct researcher subject and the object of the research.

Science education research using sociocultural theoretical frameworks has included studies of language and discourse without taking into consideration how the material "kicks back" (Barad, 2007). Material feminism is engaged in understanding issues of agency (human and nonhuman), body, culture, discourse, and the material world and could provide a framework to restructure science education research to focus on gender issues.

Queer Theory

While education research continues to use critical theoretical frameworks, such as queer theory, to address gay, lesbian, bisexual, and transgender (GLBT) issues, science education has produced little research in the area since the last handbook review. Broadway (2011) suggested three approaches for including queer theory in science education through the curriculum, the pedagogy, and the body. Bazzul and Sykes (2011) examined the heteronormative portrayal of sex, gender, and sexuality in a high school biology textbook using queer theory, paying specific attention to the following terms: "gender, sex, sexuality, human relationships, genetics, reproduction, homosexual, heterosexual, lesbian, gay, bisexual, male, female, testosterone, estrogen, AIDS, sexually transmitted diseases, men, and women" (p. 274). Their analysis showed that the biology text promulgated a socially conservative interpretation of sex as a binary, that is, female/male and heteronormative

view of human sexuality. Further, human sexuality and reproduction are connected to heterosexual sex and hormone production. There is no discussion of other pathways such as *in vitro* fertilization or of nonheterosexuals being involved in human reproduction. The text also uses the terms "sex" and "gender" interchangeably, which is problematic in a textbook in which sex is a key concept.

Lemke (2011) critiqued the silence of biology texts regarding the complicated nature of sex and sexualities, as well as their promulgation of incorrect facts regarding these issues. But more importantly, he questions the inclusiveness, sensitivity, and awareness of science education researchers, and if the field is "secretly" heteronormative in general, our field is socially, culturally, and politically biased. Lemke (2011) asked,

> Do we choose to see science teachers as merely employees of the state, shoveling whatever beliefs and values are politically dominant over the desks of our students? Or are we as educators, by long-standing Western tradition, advocates for students and opinion-leaders in our communities?
>
> (p. 292)

While queering biology texts may be a first step, science education also needs to engage in conversations with students about the connections of emotions and feelings with biological, sexual functions. Lundin (2014) used aspects of a seven-part framework to assess heteronormative practices and language in Swedish high school biology classes. The categories included *repetition of desirability*, *dichotomization of sexes*, *differentiation of sexualities*, *hierarchy of positions*, *marginalization*, *issue making*, and *personation*. Lundin (2014) used the first four categories to analyze discussions between students and their teachers on human sexuality and reproduction. He concluded that students and teachers rarely challenged the heteronorm, nor did they discuss different sexualities such as polyamory, asexuality, and/or bisexuality perspectives or the dichotomization of the sexes. Students used homophobic comments and slurs to mask being uncomfortable in discussing sexualities, and an assignment to describe the physical features of a hypothetical partner was framed as a heterosexual relationship. National policy documents in Sweden state that teachers should engage students in discussions of identity, gender equality, relationships, love, and responsibility, but the directions and details of how to implement this policy are vague (Lundin, 2014).

Teachers may need more direction on how to inject queer into the science curriculum and pedagogy. Science education could also engage queer theory to move beyond a focus on sexuality to include desire and to challenge what we "think we know" through making the familiar strange (Fifield & Letts, 2014). Queer theory provides the framework to critique science as "entangled systems of identity politics" that science educators could examine from various stances and views, (e.g., ways of knowing, science disciplines, the public, pseudoscience; Fifield &

Letts, 2014). Analysis of curriculum and textbooks could identify the silent, the absent, and the normative. Science education research that is engaged in queering its practices could identify how pedagogy and curriculum are heterosexualized and offer examples and strategies to broaden this approach.

Social science researchers use intersectionality, material feminism, and queer theory to generate new knowledge. These theories could provide new tools for science educators to expand their research analysis and, in particular, offer direction for including gender and other social categories in future research directions.

Conclusion

Dillabough and colleagues (2009) engaged in troubling gender and education by asking if there was a field of scholarship and, if so, what were the boundaries and what scholarship defined and defended those boundaries. The theoretical developments within feminism and gender have engaged with new hierarchies, power structures, different geographies, time, policy, and practice. Yet in science education, we have few studies using feminist, masculinity, queer, or postcolonial theories to frame our research and inform out findings.

Science remains a discipline that is strongly masculine, but to date, few researchers have engaged with the theories of masculinities that may help us elucidate how that image influences males and constructs the field in strongly heteronormative ways. Broadway and Leafgren (2012) responded to research on how science education may counteract violence in schools by using masculinity theory to understand the boys' physical challenges to each other and the role of aggression in defining and establishing masculinity in schools. Moreover, the strong linking of the binaries masculine/feminine with the cultural practice of science and science education continues to need examination.

The published gender and science education research since the previous handbook has focused on the culture of science as it is taught and practiced. However, many of those studies are located within the discipline of physics. Research is needed on how gender impacts teaching and learning in other sciences, especially chemistry, and also what are the gender implications for the movement toward STEM education. The expansion of science curriculum to include technology, engineering, and mathematics opens up possibilities in connecting these areas to students' interest and in reframing the cultural practices of STEM for more inclusivity. However, engineering and technology remain highly gendered toward the masculine, and thus there is also a potential that new questions, curriculum, and practices that are incorporating these disciplines may exclude students rather than expand the diversity of people engaged in science. Looking forward to the 21st century, there are areas in science education that would benefit from a "gender gaze," as gender matters.

Acknowledgments

Thanks to Sherry Southerland and Angela Johnson for their review and comments on the initial version of this chapter.

Note

1. Micro-inequities are small devaluations that members of a subordinate group may experience that accumulate over time and contribute to disadvantage (Valian, 1998).

References

Achieve. (2013). *Next generation science standards*. Retrieved June 1, 2013, from www.achieve.org/next-generation-science-standards

Acker, J. (1990). Hierarchies, jobs and bodies: A theory of gendered organizations. *Gender & Society, 4*, 139–158.

Alaimo, S., & Hekman, S. (2009). Introduction: Emerging models of materiality in feminist theory. In S. Alaimo & S. Hekman (Eds.), *Material feminisms* (pp. 1–22). Bloomington: Indiana University Press.

Alexander, J., Johnson, J., & Kelley, J. (2012). Longitudinal analysis of the relations between opportunities to learn about science and the development of interests related to science. *Science Education, 96*, 763–786.

Andersson, K., & Gullberg, A. (2012). What is science in preschool and what do teachers have to know to empower children? *Cultural Studies of Science Education*. doi:10.1007/s11422-012-9439-6

Andersson, K., Hussenius, A., & Gustafsson, C. (2009). Gender theory as a tool for analyzing science teaching. *Teaching and Teacher Education, 25*, 336–343.

Archer, L., Dewitt, J., Osborne, J., Dillion, J., Willis, B., & Wong, B. (2012). "Balancing acts": Elementary school girls' negotiations of femininity, achievement, and science. *Science Education, 96*, 967–989.

Babcock, L., & Laschever, S. (2007). *Women don't ask*. New York: Bantam.

Banilower, E.R., Smith, P.S., Weiss, I.R., Malzahn, K.A., Campbell, K.M., & Weis, A.M. (2013). *Report of the 2012 National Survey of Science and Mathematics Education*. Chapel Hill, NC: Horizon Research, Inc.

Barad, K. (2003). Posthumanist performativity: Toward an understanding of how matter comes to matter. *Signs, 28*, 801–831.

Barad, K. (2007). *Meeting the universe halfway: Quantum physics and the entanglement of matter and meaning*. Durham, NC: Duke University Press.

Baram-Tsabari, A., Sethi, R.J., Bry, L., & Yarden, A. (2009). Asking scientists: A decade of questions analyzed by age, gender, and country. *Science Education, 93*, 131–160.

Bayne, G., & Scantlebury, K. (2013). Cogenerative dialogues as pedagogy|research in science education. In K. Irby, G. Brown, & R. Lara-Aleci (Eds.), *The handbook of educational theories* (pp. 237–247). Charlotte, NC: Information Age Publishing Inc.

Bazzul, J., & Sykes, H. (2011). The secret identity of a biology textbook: Straight and naturally sexed. *Cultural Studies of Science Education, 6*, 265–286.

Brandt, C.B. (2007). Discursive geographies in science: Space, identity, and scientific discourse among indigenous women in higher education. *Cultural Studies of Science Education, 3*, 703–730.

Broadway, F.S. (2011). Queer (v.) queer (v.): Biology as curriculum, pedagogy, and being albeit queer (v.). *Cultural Studies of Science Education, 6*, 293–304.

Broadway, F.S., & Leafgren, S. (2012). Unmasking: On violence, masculinity, and superheroes in science education. *Cultural Studies of Science Education, 7*, 719–733.

Brotman, J. S., & Moore, F. M. (2008). Girls and science: A review of four themes in the science education literature. *Journal of Research in Science Teaching, 45,* 971–1002.

Brown, S., & Ronau, R. (2012). Students' perceptions of single-gender science and mathematics classroom experiences. *School Science and Mathematics, 112,* 1–22.

Buck, G. A., & Quigley, C. (2013). Allowing our research on urban, low-SES, African American girls and science education to actively and continually rewrite itself. In J. Bianchini, V. Akerson, A. C. Barton, O. Lee, & A. Rodriguez (Eds.), *Moving the equity agenda forward: Equity research, practice, and policy in science education* (pp. 173–189). New York: Springer.

Calabrese Barton, A. (2008). Feminisms and a world not yet: Science with and for social justice. In W. M. Roth & K. Tobin (Eds.), *World of science education: North America* (pp. 409–426). Dordrecht, the Netherlands: Sense Publishers.

Calabrese Barton, A., & Brickhouse, N. (2006). Engaging girls in science. In C. Skelton, B. Francis, & L. Smulyan (Eds.), *The Sage handbook of gender and education* (pp. 221–235). London: Sage.

Calabrese Barton, A., Tan, E., & Rivet, A. (2008). Creating hybrid spaces for engaging school science among urban middle school girls. *American Educational Research Journal, 45,* 68–103.

Carlone, H. B., & Johnson, A. (2007). Understanding the science experiences of successful women of color: Science identity as an analytic lens. *Journal of Research in Science Teaching, 44,* 1187–1218.

Chang, S., Yau-Yuen, A., Yeung, A., & Cheng, M. (2009). Ninth graders' learning interests, life experiences and attitudes towards science and technology. *Journal of Science Education and Technology, 18,* 447–457.

Cheung, D. (2009). Students' attitudes toward chemistry lessons: The interaction effect between grade level and gender. *Research in Science Education, 9,* 75–91.

Clark Blickenstaff, J. (2005). Women and science careers: Leaky pipeline or gender filter? *Gender and Education, 17,* 369–386.

Collins, P. H. (1991). *Black feminist thought: Knowledge, consciousness, and the politics of empowerment.* New York: Routledge.

Connell, R. W. (1995). *Masculinities.* Los Angeles: University of California Press.

Crenshaw, K. (1989). Demarginalizing the intersections of race and sex: A Black feminist critique of antidiscrimination doctrine, feminist theory, and antiracist politics. *University of Chicago Legal Forum, 140,* 139–167.

Danielsson, A. (2012). In the physics class: Intersections of social class and gender in university physics students' identity constitutions. *Culture Studies of Science Education.* doi:10.1007/s11422–012–9421–3.

Davis, K. (2011). Intersectionality as a buzzword. In H. Lutz, M. T. H. Vivar, & L. Supik (Eds.), *Framing intersectionality: Debates on a multi-faceted concept in gender studies* (pp. 43–54). Surrey, UK: Ashgate Publishing Limited.

Dillabough, J., McLeod, J., & Mills. M. (Eds.). (2009). *Troubling gender in education.* New York: Routledge.

Due, K. (2012). Who is the competent physics student? A study of students' positions and social interaction in small-group discussions. *Cultural Studies of Science Education.* doi:10.1007/s11422-012-9441-z

Dyer, D. (2011). Block building in primary classrooms as a gender equalizer in math and science. In T. Jacobson (Ed.), *Perspectives on gender in early childhood* (pp. 179–190). St. Paul, MN: Redleaf Press.

England, P. (2010). The gender revolution: Uneven and stalled. *Gender & Society, 24,* 149–166.

Farland-Smith, D. (2012). Personal and social interactions between young girls and scientists: Examining critical aspects for identity formation. *Journal of Science Teacher Education, 23,* 1–18.

Fifield, S., & Letts, W. (2014). (Re)considering queer theories and science education. *Cultural Studies of Science Education.*

Francis, B., & Skelton, B. (2009). "The self-made self": Analysing the applicability of current key ideas for theories of gender and education. In J. Dillabough, J. McLeod, & M. Mills (Eds.), *Troubling gender in education* (pp. 11–23). New York: Routledge.

Francis, B., & Skelton, B. (2011). A feminist analysis of gender and educational achievement. In K. Van den Branden, P. Van Avermaet, & M. Van Houtte (Eds.), *Equity and excellence in education: Towards maximal learning opportunities for all students* (pp. 96–118). New York: Routledge.

Gonsalves, A. (2011). Gender and doctoral physics education: Are we asking the right questions? In L. McAlpine & C. Amundsen (Eds.), *Doctoral education: Research-based strategies for doctoral students, supervisors and administrators* (pp. 117–123). New York: Springer.

Gonsalves, A. (2012). Physics and the girly girl—there is a contradiction somewhere: Doctoral students' positioning around discourses of gender and competence in physics. *Cultural Studies of Science Education.* doi:10.1007/s11422–012–9447–6

Gonzales, P., Williams, T., Jocelyn, L., Roey, S., Kastberg, D., & Brenwald, S. (2008). *Highlights from TIMSS 2007: Mathematics and science achievement of U.S. fourth- and eighth-grade students in an international context* (NCES 2009-001). Washington, DC: National Center for Education Statistics, Institute of Education Sciences, U.S. Department of Education.

Götschel, H. (Ed.). (2013). *Transforming substance: Gender in material sciences—an anthology.* Uppsala, Sweden: University Printers, Centre For Gender Research.

de Groot Kim, S. (2011). Lessons learned early: Girls wait. In T. Jacobson (Ed.), *Perspectives on gender in early childhood* (pp. 231–246). St. Paul, MN: Redleaf Press.

Hanson, S. (2009). *Swimming against the tide: African American girls and science education.* Philadelphia: Temple University Press.

Harding, S. (1986). *The science question in feminism.* Ithaca, NY: Cornell University Press.

Hazari, Z., Sadler, P., & Tai, R. (2008). Gender differences in the high school and affective experiences of introductory college physics students. *The Physics Teacher, 46,* 423–427.

Hazari, Z., Sonnert, G., Sadler, P. M., & Shanahan, M. C. (2010). Connecting high school physics experiences, outcome expectations, physics identity, and physics career choice: A gender study. *Journal of Research in Science Teaching, 47,* 978–1003.

Hazari, Z., Tai, R., & Sadler, P. (2007). Gender differences in introductory university physics performance. *Science Education, 91,* 847–876.

Hekman, S. (2010). *Material of knowledge: Feminist disclosures.* Bloomington: Indiana University Press.

Hill, C., Corbett, C., & St. Rose, A. (2010). *Why so few? Women in science, technology, engineering and mathematics.* Washington, DC: AAUW.

Huang, S., & Fraser, B. (2009). Science teachers' perceptions of the school environment: Gender differences. *Journal of Research in Science Teaching, 46,* 404–420.

Hussénius, A., & Scantlebury, K. (2011). Witches, alchemists, poisoners, and scientists: The changing image of chemistry. In P. Gilmer, M. H. Chiu, & D. F. Treagust (Eds.), *Celebrating 100th anniversary of Marie Curie's Nobel award in chemistry in 2011* (pp. 125–137). New York: Sense Publishers.

Hussénius, A., Scantlebury, K., Andersson, K., & Gullberg, A. (2013). Ignoring half the sky: A feminist critique of science education's knowledge society. In N. Mansour & R. Wegerif (Eds.), *Science education for diversity in knowledge society.* doi:10.1007/978-94-007-4563-614. New York: Springer.

Hyde, J. S., & Linn, M. C. (2006). Gender similarities in mathematics and science. *Science, 314,* 599–600.

Johnson, A. (2007). Unintended consequences: How science professors discourage women of color. *Science Education, 91,* 805–821.

Joslin, P., Stiles, K. S., Marshall, J. S., Anderson, O. R., Gallagher, J. J., Kahle, J. B., et al. (2007). NARST: A lived history. *Cultural Studies of Science Education, 3,* 157–207.

Jovanovic, J., & Bhanot, R. (2008). Gender differences in science. In W. M. Roth & K. Tobin (Eds.), *World of science education: North America* (pp. 427–450). Dordrecht, the Netherlands: Sense Publishers.

Kahle, J.B. (2004). Will girls be left behind? Gender differences and accountability. *Journal of Research in Science Teaching, 41,* 961–969.

Kahle, J.B. (2011). Professor Lesley Parker: A science educator writ large. *Cultural Studies of Science Education, 6,* 775–781.

Kahle, J.B., & Lakes, M. (1983). The myth of equality in science classrooms. *Journal of Research in Science Teaching, 20,* 131–140.

Kahle, J.B., & Meece, J. (1994). Research on gender issues in the classroom. In D. Gabel (Ed.), *Handbook of research in science teaching and learning* (pp. 542–576). Washington, DC: National Science Teachers Association.

Kelly, A. (1978). *Girls and science: An international study of sex differences in school science achievement.* Stockholm: Almqvist & Wiksell International.

Kelly, A. (Ed.). (1981). *The missing half: Girls and science education.* Manchester, UK: Manchester University Press.

Kelly, A. (1985). The construction of masculine science. *British Journal of Sociology of Education, 6,* 133–153.

Kenway, J., Willis, S., Blackmore, J., & Rennie, L. (1998). *Answering back: Girls, boys and feminism in schools.* New York: Routledge.

Kiran, D., & Sungur, S. (2012). Middle school students' science self-efficacy and its sources: Examination of gender difference. *Journal of Science Education and Technology, 21,* 619–630.

Kreitz-Sandberg, S. (2013). Gender inclusion and horizontal gender segregation: Stakeholders: Strategies and dilemmas in Swedish teachers' education. *Gender and Education, 25,* 444–465.

Le, L. (2009). Investigating gender differential item functioning across countries and test languages for PISA science items. *International Journal of Testing, 9,* 122–133.

Lemke, J. (2011). The secret identity of science education: Masculine and politically conservative? *Cultural Studies of Science Education, 6,* 287–292.

Lorber Newsome, J. (2013). *The chemistry PhD: The impact on women's retention.* London: Royal Society of Chemistry.

Louis, R., & Mistele, J. (2011). The differences in scores and self-efficacy by student gender in mathematics and science. *International Journal of Science and Mathematics Education, 10,* 1163–1190.

Lundin, M. (2014). Inviting queer ideas into the science classroom: Studying sexual education from a queer perspective. *Cultural Studies of Science Education.*

Lykke, N. (2010). *Feminist studies: A guide to intersectional theory, methodology and writing.* London: Routledge.

Mantzicopoulos, P., Patrick, H., & Samarapungavan, A. (2008). Young children's motivational beliefs about learning science. *Early Childhood Research Quarterly, 23,* 378–394.

Martin, S., Wassell, B., & Scantlebury, K. (2013). Examining the intersections of race, ethnicity, class and gender: An analysis of research on English language learners in K–12 science education. In J. Bianchini, V. Akerson, A.C. Barton, O. Lee, & A. Rodriguez (Eds.), *Moving the equity agenda forward: Equity research, practice, and policy in science education* (pp. 81–98). New York: Springer.

Matsuda, M. (1991). Beside my sister, facing the enemy: Legal theory out of coalition. *Stanford Law Review, 43,* 1183–1192.

McKinley, E. (2008). From object to subject: Hybrid identities of indigenous women in science. *Cultural Studies of Science Education, 3,* 959–975.

McRobbie, A. (2007). Top girls? Young women and the post-feminist sexual contract. *Cultural Studies, 21,* 718–737.

McRobbie, A. (2009). *The aftermath of feminism: Gender, culture and social change.* London: Sage Publications.

Mendick, H., & Moreau, M.P. (2013). New media, old images: Constructing online representations of women and men in science, engineering and technology. *Gender and Education, 25,* 325–339.

Murphy, P., & Whitelegg, E. (2006). Girls and physics: Continuing barriers to "belonging." *The Curriculum Journal, 17,* 281–305.

Nyström, E. (2009). Teacher talk: Producing, resisting and challenging discourses about the science classroom. *Gender and Education, 21,* 735–751.

Ong, M., Wright, C., Espinosa, L., & Orfield, G. (2011). Inside the double bind: A synthesis of empirical research on undergraduate and graduate women of color in science, technology, engineering, and mathematics. *Harvard Educational Review, 81,* 172–207.

Organization for Economic Cooperation and Development (OECD). (2009). *Equally prepared for life? How 15-year-old boys and girls perform in school.* Retrieved June 30, 2012, from www.oecd.org/pisa/pisaproducts/PIF-2014-gender-international-version.pdf

Orlander, A.A. (2012). What if we were in a test tube? Students meaning making during a biology lesson about the human genitals. *Cultural Studies of Science Education.* doi:10.1007/s11422-012-9430-2

Owens, T. (2009). Going to school with Madame Curie and Mr. Einstein: Gender roles in children's science biographies. *Cultural Studies of Science Education, 4,* 929–943.

Parker, C. (2014). Multiple influences: Latinas, middle-level science, and school. *Cultural Studies of Science Education.*

Parsons, E.C. (2007). Mary Monroe Atwater: A transformative force in science education. *Cultural Studies of Science Education, 3,* 209–216.

Patrick, H., Mantzicopoulos, P., & Samarapungavan, A. (2009). Motivation for learning science in kindergarten: Is there a gender gap and does integrated inquiry and literacy instruction make a difference? *Journal of Research in Science Teaching, 46,* 166–191.

Perry, B., Link, T., Boelter, C., & Leukefeld, C. (2012). Blinded to science: Gender differences in the effects of race, ethnicity, and socioeconomic status on academic and science attitudes among sixth graders. *Gender and Education, 24,* 725–743.

Pettersson, H. (2011). Making masculinity in plasma physics: Machines, labour and experiments. *Science Studies, 24,* 47–65.

Quigley, C.F. (2011). With their help: How community members construct a congruent third space in an urban kindergarten classroom. *International Journal of Science Education, 35*(5), 837–863.

Rahm, I. (2008). Urban youths' hybrid positioning in science practices at the margin: A look inside a school–museum–scientist partnership project and an after-school science program. *Cultural Studies of Science Education, 3,* 97–121.

Riegle-Crumb, C., & King, B. (2010). Questioning a White male advantage in STEM: Examining disparities in college major. *Educational Researcher, 39,* 656–664.

Riegle-Crumb, C., King, B., Grodsky, E., & Muller, C. (2012). The more things change, the more they stay the same? Prior achievement fails to explain gender inequality in entry into STEM college majors over time. *American Educational Research Journal, 49,* 1048–1073.

Riegle-Crumb, C., Moore, C., & Ramos-Wada, A. (2011). Who wants to have a career in science or math? Exploring adolescents' future aspirations by gender and race/ethnicity. *Science Education, 95,* 458–476.

Risman, B., & Davis, G. (2013). From sex roles to gender structure. *Current Sociology.* doi:10.1177/0011392113479315

Rosser, S.V. (2012). *Breaking into the lab. Engineering progress for women in science.* New York: New York University Press.

Rossiter, M. (2012). *Women scientists in America: Forging a new world since 1972.* New York: Johns Hopkins University Press.

Scantlebury, K. (2007). Outsiders within: Urban African American girls' identity and science. In W.-M. Roth & K. Tobin (Eds.), *Science, learning, and identity: Sociocultural and cultural-historical perspectives* (pp. 121–134). New York: Sense Publishers.

Scantlebury, K. (2014). Jane Butler Kahle: Passion, determination and vision. *Cultural Studies of Science Education.*

Scantlebury, K., & Baker, D. (2007). Gender issues in science education research: Remembering where the difference lies. In S.K. Abell & N.G. Lederman (Eds.), *Handbook of research on science education* (pp. 257–286). Mahwah, NJ: Lawrence Erlbaum.

Scantlebury, K., Baker, D., Sugi, A., Yoshida, A., & Uysal, S. (2007). Avoiding the issue of gender in Japanese science education. *International Journal of Science and Mathematics Education, 5,* 415–438.

Scantlebury, K., Kahle, J.B., & Martin, S. (Eds.). (2010). *Re-visioning science education from feminist perspectives: Challenges, choices and careers.* New York: Sense Publishers.

Scantlebury, K., & LaVan, S.K. (2006). Re-visioning cogenerative dialogues as feminist pedagogy|research. *FQS: Forum Qualitative Social Research, 7*(2), 1–10.

Scantlebury, K., & Martin, S. (2010). How does she know? Re-visioning conceptual change from feminist perspectives. In W. M. Roth, *Re/structuring science education: Reuniting sociological and psychological perspectives* (pp. 173–186). New York: Springer Publishers.

Scantlebury, K., Tai, T., & Rahm, J. (2007). "That don't look like me." Stereotypic images of science: Where do they come from and what can we do with them? *Cultural Studies of Science Education, 1,* 545–558.

Sikora, J., & Pokropek, A. (2012). Gender segregation of adolescent science career plans in 50 countries. *Science Education, 96,* 234–264.

Sinnes, A., & Løken, M. (2012). Gendered education in a gendered world: Looking beyond cosmetic solutions to the gender gap in science. *Culture Studies of Science Education.* doi:10.1007/s11422-012-9433-z

Skelton, C., & Francis, B. (2009). *Feminism and "the schooling scandal."* London: Routledge.

Spender, D. (1982). *Invisible women: The schooling scandal.* London: Writers and Readers Publishing Cooperative.

Tan, E., & Calabrese Barton, A. (2008a). From peripheral to central, the story of Melanie's metamorphosis in an urban middle school science class. *Science Education, 92,* 567–590.

Tan, E., & Calabrese Barton, A. (2008b). Unpacking science for all through the lens of identities-in-practice: The stories of Amelia and Ginny. *Cultural Studies of Science Education, 3,* 43–71.

Tyler-Wood, T., Ellison, A., Lim, O., & Periathiruvadi, S. (2012). Bringing up girls in science (BUGS): The effectiveness of an afterschool environmental science program for increasing female students' interest in science careers. *Journal of Science Education and Technology, 21,* 46–55.

Valian, V. (1998). *Why so slow? The advancement of women.* Cambridge: MIT Press.

Venville, G. (2008). Ocean to outback: Léonie Rennie's contribution to science education in Australia. *Cultural Studies of Science Education, 4,* 323–334.

Whitelegg, E., Murphy, P., & Hart, C. (2007). Girls and physics: Dilemmas and tensions. In R. Pintó & D. Couso (Eds.), *Contributions from science education research* (pp. 27–36). New York: Springer Publishers.

Wiseman, K., & Weinburgh, M. H. (Eds.). (2009). *Becoming and being: Women's experience in leadership in K–16 science education communities.* New York: Springer Publishers.

World Bank. (2011). *The EdStats Newsletter,* V (1), Retrieved December 10, 2012, from http://siteresources.worldbank.org/EXTEDSTATS/Resources/3232763-1197312825215/EdStatsNewsletter22.pdf

Zapata, M., & Gallard, A. (2007). Female science teacher beliefs and attitudes: Implications in relation to gender and pedagogical practice. *Cultural Studies of Science Education, 3,* 43–71.

11

English Learners in Science Education

CORY A. BUXTON AND OKHEE LEE

A focus on high academic standards and achievement for all students has been at the heart of sweeping educational reforms since the publication of *A Nation at Risk* (National Commission on Excellence in Education, 1983). In recent years, this push for high achievement in science education has grown in both urgency and complexity as a result of four primary factors: (a) the growing cultural and linguistic diversity of the U.S. student population; (b) the persistence of testing gaps across demographic subgroups coupled with the increased accountability demands for all students following the No Child Left Behind (NCLB) Act of 2001 and the Race To The Top (RT³) initiatives that began in 2010; (c) an increase in both cognitive and linguistic demands inherent in *A Framework for K–12 Science Education* (National Research Council [NRC], 2011) and the *Next Generation Science Standards* (Achieve, 2013); and (d) a combination of evolving personal and social reasons all students need to learn challenging science, such as to make informed decisions about technologically driven problems and solutions, for career and college readiness, and as a robust context for learning valuable academic English.

In this chapter, we begin by briefly discussing each of these four factors. Then, with these factors in mind as a rationale for why all students, including English learners (ELs), need a robust understanding of science, we present a review of the current literature on teaching science to ELs. The review is organized into six topics: (a) science learning, (b) science instructional strategies, (c) science curriculum materials, (d) science assessment, (e) science teacher education, and (f) connections among homes, communities, schools, and science. Taken together, these themes point to directions for future research and practice that can support ELs, and all students, in achieving high standards.

In selecting literature to include in this review, we adhered to several basic principles to delimit our search. First, we focused primarily on research programs conducted in the United States and published as peer-reviewed journal articles (please refer to chapter 16 in this volume for a review of international literature on diversity and equity, including second-language learning, in science education). Second, we limited our search to publications that provide clear statements of research questions, clear descriptions of research methods, convincing links between the research questions and the evidence presented, and valid conclusions based on the results (Shavelson & Towne, 2002). Third, we focused on research that was not included in the first volume of this handbook published in 2007. While we have referenced some research that predates the first volume to provide context, our emphasis is on how the more recent work in this field contributes to and builds upon what we know about science education for ELs. Our goal is to connect recent findings to existing ones in ways that highlight common themes rather than to simply describe a series of studies and their conclusions.

We tried to minimize ideological bias by including research programs from multiple theoretical perspectives and methodological orientations. A major goal of this chapter is to highlight theory and practice interactions and to point the way toward practical means of improving science teaching and learning for ELs. We did not attempt to provide a complete literature review on each topic we address but rather to highlight specific research programs that seem to provide fruitful directions for improving both our understanding and our practice.

Primary Factors Central to Current Science Education Reform

The specific needs of ELs are fundamental to each of the four factors that are central to current science education reform: (a) growing student diversity, (b) persistent science testing gaps in the context of increased accountability measures, (c) the advent of the Next Generation Science Standards (NGSS), and (d) the necessity for all students to learn challenging science.

Growing Cultural and Linguistic Diversity of the U.S. Student Population

Teachers in virtually every school district in the nation have been first-hand witnesses to the steady increase of cultural and linguistic diversity in the U.S. population. According to the 2010 U.S. Census, 36% of the total U.S. population is composed of people who racially identify as non–Caucasian (referred to as racial minorities by the Census Bureau), while 45% of the population under 19 years of age (the school-aged population) is non–Caucasian (U.S. Census Bureau, 2012). Based on census trends and projections, the U.S. Census Bureau projects that by the year 2042, the total U.S. population will become majority non–Caucasian for the first time since the colonial period, while the school-aged population will become majority non–Caucasian as early as 2022.

Parallel trends can be seen in the nation's changing linguistic profile. According to the National Center for Education Statistics (NCES, 2011), 21% of the school-aged population speaks a language other than English as the primary language at home. Students with limited English proficiency (the term used by the federal government), or English learners, currently constitute 11% of public school students (5.6 million), an increase from only 5% of the student population in 1993 (NCELA, 2007). Of the 5.6 million ELs, 4.4 million of these students are Spanish speaking (U.S. Department of Education [USDOE], 2007), representing approximately 80% of the U.S. EL public school population. It is important to recognize three additional facts that sometimes get lost in these statistics. First, the 4.4 million Spanish-speaking ELs represent less than half of the approximately 10 million Latin@ students in U.S. schools, meaning that most Latin@ students are fluent English speakers. Second, while slightly more than two thirds (68%) of Latin@ students in the U.S. are of Mexican descent, the other third of Latin@ students represent a broad range of nations with highly diverse cultures and experiences. Finally, the 20% of ELs who are not Spanish speakers represent more than 400 different languages spoken in U.S. schools (Pew Research Center, 2012). Thus, while these data indicate that it is sensible to focus our attention on Spanish-speaking ELs, we must also keep in mind the needs of non–Spanish-speaking ELs as well as the needs of non–EL Latin@ students.

Further, when we consider demographic issues related to ELs, it is important to highlight the increasing diaspora of ELs into geographic regions that have not traditionally educated linguistically diverse student populations. Most notably, the 12-state Southeastern region has seen the largest percentage increase of ELs in the last decade (National Clearinghouse for English Language Acquisition [NCELA], 2012). In Georgia, for example, the number of students classified as ELs jumped from approximately 16,000 in 1995 to 73,000 in 2008, nearly a 500% increase (Pandya, Batalova, & McHugh, 2011). North Carolina and Virginia have seen similar rates of EL student growth in this time period, placing these three Southeastern states (in addition to Florida) in the top 12 states in the nation in terms of total numbers of ELs (NCELA, 2012).

Finally, despite ongoing demographic shifts, major urban school districts continue to educate the vast majority of ELs. An examination of the Common Core of Data indicates that more than half of the total EL student population is educated in the 20 largest metropolitan areas in the U.S. (NCES, 2011). Thus, the challenge of preparing teachers to meet the academic needs of ELs is both a new challenge in response to shifting demographics in some parts of the nation and a renewal of old and entrenched challenges in major urban settings.

Persistent Testing Gaps Among Demographic Subgroups and Increased Accountability

It has been well documented that U.S. students have generally not ranked favorably on international science assessments. We refer to the gaps in scores on such assessments as testing gaps rather than achievement gaps, as they measure only a limited conception of science achievement. Dating from the 1995 TIMSS assessment (Schmidt, McKnight, & Raizen, 1997), in which U.S. 4th-grade students scored within the cluster of top-performing nations, 8th-grade students only slightly above the international average, and 12th-grade students among the lowest-performing nations, such international comparisons have been used to critique science education in the United States. While the more recent administrations of TIMSS in 2003 and 2007 indicated some gains for U.S. students, especially at the eighth-grade level, older U.S. students still do not compare favorably with students in many other developed nations.

Testing gaps are even less favorable for results of the Program for International Student Assessment (PISA), which is administered to 15-year-olds and which strives to assess not only basic content knowledge but also problem solving and relevant life skills related to the academic disciplines. When assessed on applications of science, such as using scientific evidence, identifying scientific issues, and explaining phenomena scientifically, U.S. students performed in the bottom half of the international comparison in 2000, 2003, and 2006 and did not show significant improvements across the three administrations.

When disaggregated into demographic subgroups, testing gaps paint a more nuanced but still troubling picture. For example, on the National Assessment of Educational Progress (NAEP) between 1996 and 2011, testing gaps have remained largely consistent and wide for students who live in poverty, for African American students, and for Latin@ students overall. However, testing gaps on NAEP science have decreased for ELs in the same period, although gaps still remain between ELs and non–ELs (NCES, 2012a). Shaw (2009) analyzed these trends and identified specific science topics and item formats that seemed to favor either ELs or non–ELs, implying the need for greater attention to assessment development (see the science assessment section).

Additionally, although the overall Latin@ high school dropout rate has decreased markedly over the past two decades from 31% to 18%, the Latin@ EL dropout rate remains nearly unchanged at 27% (NCES, 2012b). Thus, despite the increased attention paid to closing testing gaps for demographic subgroups as required by No Child Left Behind and Race To The Top, testing gaps in science and other key academic indicators for ELs, such as high school dropout rates, have persisted and, in some cases, have increased.

Cognitive and Linguistic Demands of the Next Generation Science Standards

The challenges we have discussed so far regarding changing student demographics and persistent testing gaps for demographic subgroups including ELs are on the verge of intersecting with the new demands of the NGSS. First laid out in the conceptual framework document *A Framework for K–12 Science Education: Practices, Crosscutting Concepts, and Core Ideas* (NRC, 2011), the new standards include fundamental shifts in expectations of students (and teachers) regarding the required depth of scientific understanding. These expectations take the form of a three-part emphasis on science and engineering practices, crosscutting concepts, and disciplinary core ideas. The NGSS represents a renewed attempt to enact the *less is more* curricular approach that failed to be taken up in the state standards documents that resulted from the *National Science Education Standards* (NRC, 1996).

It has been made clear by the NRC's Framework Committee and the NGSS design team that these new standards will be more cognitively demanding for students. Successful application of the science and engineering practices (such as developing models and constructing explanations) used to understand how crosscutting concepts (such as cause and effect or structure and function) play out across a range of disciplinary core ideas (such as genetics or plate tectonics) will demand increased cognitive expectations of all students. While advanced students have long been asked to make such connections, the NGSS make it clear that such expectations will now apply to all students, including ELs and other students who have not traditionally performed well at demonstrating mastery, even using the previous generation of less cognitively demanding standards.

While the cognitive demands have been explicitly discussed in relation to the expectations of the NGSS, the accompanying linguistic demands have, thus far, received little attention (Lee, Quinn, & Valdés, 2013). In order to gain and demonstrate competence in the science and engineering practices, crosscutting concepts, and disciplinary core ideas that are at the heart of the NGSS, students will need to engage with the full range of oral and written communication skills in new and challenging ways. Students will need to read challenging science texts for purposes other than just extracting factual data. They will need to write in a variety of formats (such as science lab notebooks and engineering design reports) using the academic language of science to express complex ideas. They will need to listen carefully as others construct explanations and argue from evidence while also learning to speak in ways that allow them to successfully engage in such practices. Finally, viewing and visually representing will take on an increased importance for successfully engaging with science and engineering practices and crosscutting concepts that rely heavily on the use of models, graphs, and other image-rich modes of communication.

When taken together, the linguistic demands of the NGSS combine with the cognitive demands in ways that will challenge all students, but especially ELs, in new and perhaps unforeseen ways. At the same time, the linguistic demands of the NGSS are well aligned with the linguistic goals of the Common Core State Standards for English language arts (Lee et al., 2013). For example, the Common Core English language arts standards give an increased attention to the construction of complex texts across the content areas, an increased emphasis on how students use informational texts to build content knowledge, and the importance of developing both reading and writing skills to effectively extract and make use of evidence from text. Thus, while the challenges for ELs in meeting the new science standards appear to be great, there will also be new opportunities and new infrastructure for teachers across content areas to work together in order to support ELs in simultaneously learning science and developing language skills.

Evolving Personal and Social Reasons for All Students to Learn Challenging Science

If all students are to be engaged in challenging science learning, educators must provide reasons for this challenge that all students find meaningful. While the specter of high-stakes assessments may serve to motivate some students, it is clear from examining our current testing regimen that many students fail to find such extrinsic motivation compelling. A more intrinsic rationale for why we must improve Science, Technology, Engineering, and Mathematics (STEM) education for all students is multifaceted. Since the publishing of *Science for All Americans* (American Association for the Advancement of Science, 1990), the central tenet of that rationale has been the value of scientific literacy. As our country and our planet face challenges that can be both exacerbated and ameliorated by human actions, broad scientific literacy is essential so that collectively we can make informed decisions regarding science and technology. The nation's future will increasingly depend on today's students, including large numbers of ELs, gaining the education needed to make scientifically sound personal and public decisions.

More recently, as regional and global economic struggles seem to have eclipsed concerns about environmental challenges, the argument that science and engineering education is essential for career readiness by providing pathways to growth industry jobs in fields such as biotechnology, pharmaceuticals, and green energy has played a more central role in the rationale for science learning. Indeed, a key concern during the development of the NGSS has been the degree to which the standards actually address college and career readiness. Representatives from technical training programs, as well as from colleges and universities and K–12 education, have reviewed drafts of the standards to explicitly comment from a college and career readiness perspective. Thus, both informed decision making and preparation for employment in tomorrow's growth fields and industries may be intrinsically motivating reasons for more students, including ELs, to engage in rigorous science and technology education.

An additional rationale that may be especially salient for ELs is that content area instruction, such as science, can provide a meaningful context for English language and literacy development. At the same time, improving English skills should provide the medium for better understanding of academic content (Teachers of English to Speakers of Other Languages [TESOL], 2006). In reality, however, ELs frequently confront the demands of academic learning through a yet-unmastered language without the instructional support they need to make such learning meaningful. ELs may also be pulled out of content classes, such as science, for additional English support, which often focuses on general conversational English rather than on the academic English needed for content learning. As a result of these practices, ELs often fall behind their English-speaking peers in content area learning, the implications of which can be seen in the assessment data as well as the school dropout rates noted earlier.

Thus far, we have argued that the four primary factors that make the current wave of science education reform both essential and challenging are integrally linked to the increasing numbers of ELs in our schools. Research on how best to support ELs in science must also be contextualized within sociocultural issues and demographic variables, including race, ethnicity, gender, socioeconomic status, rural or urban contexts, and other structural features that influence education generally and science education specifically. While we allude to many of these features in this chapter, more detailed research on these topics is discussed in other chapters of this section, as well as elsewhere in the handbook.

Learning and Teaching of Science With ELs

Research on the learning and teaching of science with ELs remains a relatively young field, but it has grown substantially in the past decade. We have synthesized the research on science education with ELs into six topics that highlight what the field has learned about how ELs develop robust understanding of science while also acquiring proficiency in English language and literacy.

Science Learning and ELs

As the expectations about what it means to learn science have evolved to include more cognitively and linguistically challenging practices, such as reasoning scientifically and arguing from evidence (NRC, 2011), the field can learn from researchers who have considered the nature of the learning experiences that foster these practices for all students. At the same time, it has been well documented that ELs tend to have less access to learning experiences that support these practices than do their fluent English-speaking peers (Callahan, Wilkinson, & Muller, 2010). To better provide learning opportunities that support the development of science and engineering practices to a wider range of students, teachers need to understand the place of these practices in science learning for all of their students, including ELs.

Foundational to understanding science learning with ELs, the programmatic line of research by members of the Chèche Konnen team has involved case studies of students from African American, Haitian, and Latino backgrounds in both bilingual and monolingual classrooms. These studies have considered children's experimental reasoning in ways that look quite similar to the new recommendations of the Framework and the NGSS. The Chèche Konnen research has used open-ended tasks to frame experimentation as an exploratory process of constructing meaning from emerging variables (Rosebery, Ogonowski, DiSchino, & Warren, 2010). By asking questions about what children do as they engage in experimental tasks, what resources they draw upon as they develop and evaluate ideas, and how children's scientific reasoning corresponds to the nature of experimentation practiced by scientists, these studies have provided evidence that ELs are capable of engaging in science practices through open inquiry.

In the Chèche Konnen body of work, researchers and scholars also explicitly consider the role of language in scientific sense making by investigating how ELs' home languages and discourse styles can be used as resources to understand and gradually take ownership of the discourse patterns of scientific communities. For example, Hudicourt-Barnes (2003) demonstrated how argumentative discussion is a major feature of social interaction among Haitian adults and how this discourse pattern can then be leveraged as a resource for students as they practice argumentation in science class. More recent work by this group (Warren & Roseberry, 2011) has considered the value of viewing science learning as an intercultural process in which students and teachers negotiate the boundaries of race, culture, language, and subject matter in order to overcome the traditional inequalities that often persist in science classrooms for ELs.

By the time ELs come to school, they already possess a range of knowledge, values, and ways of looking at the world that have developed during their socialization into their families and communities that could be leveraged to support science learning (Lee & Fradd, 1998). All too often, however, these intellectual and cultural resources are undervalued because teachers do not easily recognize them as being relevant or valuable (Moje, Collazo, Carillo, & Marx, 2001). For example, in a paired study of third- through fifth-grade ELs and their teachers, Buxton and Lee (2010) and Buxton, Salinas, Mahotiere, Lee, and Secada (2013) found that ELs at all levels of English proficiency were able to provide a range of examples from home experiences that were directly connected to school science standards on topics ranging from measurement to energy transfer to the changing seasons. The majority of these students' science teachers, however, when viewing video recordings of the students discussing these science topics, were more likely to highlight linguistic or conceptual limitations than to focus on the relevant experiences that could be leveraged to support science learning. These studies conclude that recognition of ELs' academic strengths as well as limitations related to their prior knowledge is critical in enabling ELs to better gain the high-status knowledge that is valued in school science.

In the aforementioned studies, researchers make it clear that teachers can benefit from frameworks that more explicitly demonstrate both the language demands and opportunities that science learning provides to ELs. Shaw, Bunch, and Geaney (2010) developed and tested a framework to categorize the language demands of science learning. Using both functional and interactional theoretical perspectives, the researchers classified the language demands of science performance tasks into three dimensions: participant structures, communicative modes, and written genres that students must reproduce in order to be successful in academic science. Such frameworks can help to clarify how ELs learn language through science, as well as how they learn science through language.

Exploring ELs' science learning from another perspective, a body of literature highlights how the cultural beliefs and practices prevalent in some communities, including communities with sizable numbers of ELs, are sometimes discontinuous with Western scientific practices (Aikenhead, 2001; Riggs, 2005). This literature has shown that learning to recognize and value diverse views of the natural world can simultaneously promote academic achievement and strengthen ELs' cultural and linguistic identities. More specifically, the portion of this research that considers the impact of students' communication and interaction patterns on their science learning is of particular importance to how ELs can learn to reconcile their linguistic and cultural practices with those of Western science.

Brown and colleagues (Brown, 2006; Brown, Reveles, & Kelly, 2005) built on earlier studies of communication and interaction patterns among students and teachers of various cultural and linguistic backgrounds in learning science (Lee, 2004; Warren, Ballenger, Ogonowski, Rosebery, & Hudicourt-Barnes, 2001). Focusing on the notion of discursive identity as an analytical tool for understanding student learning, Brown taught two courses of high school biology and analyzed the interactions in his classroom,

detailing the cultural and linguistic moves that helped to shape individual access to the specific classroom culture he was attempting to construct. He found that while marginalized students, including ELs, were comfortable in adopting both the scientific worldview (epistemology) and the science inquiry practices he was promoting, many students expressed a great deal of difficulty and resistance toward appropriating the discursive norms of science. Brown and colleagues concluded both that science discourse serves as a potential gatekeeper that prevents some students from assimilating into the culture of science and that students' attempts to recast their discursive identities to incorporate the academic language of science should essentially be seen as a move to become multilingual, not just for ELs but for all students from marginalized groups.

When taken together, researchers on the topic of science learning and ELs have indicated that there is a range of sociocultural and sociolinguistic factors, as well as cognitive and academic factors, that influence how, when, and in what conditions ELs chose to engage (or not) in school science. If the expectation is for all students, including ELs, to learn and apply science and engineering practices, crosscutting concepts, and disciplinary core ideas of science, teachers must develop learning environments and adopt instructional strategies that acknowledge these cultural and linguistic challenges as well as the cognitive challenges that their students face in adopting a discursive identity in science. In the following section, we turn to the instructional strategies that have been shown to best support ELs in the science classroom.

Science Instructional Strategies to Support ELs

There is a long history of ELs receiving either very limited science instruction or science instruction dominated by teacher-directed, expository instruction rather than the varieties of student-directed, collaborative, and language-rich learning opportunities that have been shown to be most effective for ELs (Yore, Bisanz, & Hand, 2003). Teachers and school administrators have often presumed that science instruction (as well as other content area instruction) must wait until ELs have developed a certain level of language skills in English. However, current language standards for ELs (TESOL, 2006), as well as Common Core State Standards for English language arts (Achieve, 2013), specifically target academic language proficiency in core content areas as a central goal for all levels of English proficiency. Thus, in order not to fall behind their English-speaking peers in both content knowledge and academic language development, ELs need to develop English language and literacy skills in the context of content area instruction. Despite these needs, content area instruction and language instruction for ELs have traditionally been conceptualized as separate domains that have failed to adequately support each other (Lee, 2004).

In much of the early literature on effective science instruction with ELs, researchers highlighted the importance of engaging students in hands-on activities to make science concrete and experiential. More recently, researchers have tended to focus on the need for teachers to integrate cognitively challenging science inquiry practices with an explicit focus on academic language and literacy development in English. Finally, there is a body of research on instructional strategies in which researchers use ELs' home language and culture as an instructional support to enhance science learning.

Early research on teaching science to ELs was strongly influenced by ESOL models that included sheltered content instruction (Chamot & O'Malley, 1996). These approaches focused on the role of hands-on inquiry and concrete examples (or realia) to support comprehensible learning. It is still accepted that hands-on science provides all students, including ELs, with opportunities to practice scientific communication skills in contexts that focus on developing an understanding of science concepts while at the same time leveraging instructional approaches that are particularly beneficial to ELs (Stoddart, Solis, Tolbert, & Bravo, 2010). First, hands-on activities depend less on formal mastery of the language of instruction, reducing the linguistic burden on ELs. Second, hands-on activities promote language acquisition in the context of science knowledge and practice. Third, reporting about hands-on science encourages students to communicate their understanding in a variety of formats, including gestural, oral, pictorial, graphic, and textual. Finally, language functions, such as describing, hypothesizing, explaining, predicting, and reflecting, can develop simultaneously with hands-on science skills, such as observing, describing, explaining, predicting, estimating, representing, and inferring.

While the value of hands-on inquiry approaches continues to be an important component of science instruction for ELs, more recent literature has acknowledged that hands-on activities do not necessarily lead to conceptual understanding (NRC, 2011). Thus, a current emphasis has been on creating integrated models of instruction that promote cognitively challenging science inquiry practices while simultaneously focusing on academic language and literacy development in English. There is now broad agreement in terms of key instructional features that support robust science and language learning (Lee & Buxton, 2012).

First, there should be explicit goals for literacy development for all students embedded in science instruction, as well as explicit science learning goals (Bruna & Gomez, 2008). These language and literacy goals may include a focus on comprehension of expository science texts, language functions (e.g., explain, contrast, report) in science assignments, graphic organizers (e.g., concept maps, word walls, Venn diagrams, KWL charts), trade books, or writing prompts.

Second, science instruction should include language support strategies that are especially useful for ELs, typically identified as ESOL strategies (Fathman & Crowther, 2006). For example, teachers can guide students to comprehend and use a small number of key science vocabulary words, both content-specific and general academic terms. They can encourage students to communicate ideas using multiple modes of representation through gestural, oral, pictorial, graphic, and textual communication. They can also use language in multiple contexts (e.g., introduce, write, repeat, highlight). In recent studies and teacher resources, researchers have highlighted ways in which ESOL strategies can be used to benefit all students in science while proving especially beneficial to ELs.

Third, science instruction can make specific use of discourse strategies, such as arguing from evidence or outlining cause-and-effect relationships, that support robust science inquiry practices while also enhancing ELs' understanding of academic content through language development. Researchers have explored ways in which effective teachers of science to ELs modify classroom discourse while also maintaining the rigor of science content and processes (Brown & Spang, 2008; Buxton, Allexsaht-Snider, & Rivera, 2012). Further, general EL strategies (e.g., slowing the rate of speech, lengthening wait time, using synonyms or paraphrases of difficult language, restating main ideas, and recasting and elaborating on students' responses) can support student comprehension without diminishing the challenge of science content (TESOL, 2006).

Fourth, researchers have explored the importance of building on students' lived experiences at home and in the community and capitalizing on the students' intellectual resources to enhance science learning (Rosebery & Warren, 2008). Effective teachers ask questions that elicit students' funds of knowledge related to science topics (González, Moll, & Amanti, 2005) and use cultural artifacts and community resources in ways that are academically meaningful and culturally relevant (Rodriguez & Berryman, 2002). Examples and analogies drawn from students' lives and instructional topics that examine issues from the perspectives of multiple cultures can be of great assistance as students strive to integrate prior experiences with new academic expectations (Villegas, 2007).

Finally, researchers have highlighted students' home language as an instructional support to enhance science learning. It is important to draw a distinction between home language instruction (i.e., bilingual education) and home language support (Goldenberg, 2008). Effective teachers use various strategies, such as introducing key science vocabulary in both the home language and English; highlighting cognates as well as false cognates between English and the home language (for example, Spanish and other Romance lexicon is derived from Latin, the primary language of science); encouraging bilingual students to assist less English-proficient students in their home language as well as in English; allowing ELs to write about science ideas or experiments in their home language; and inviting family and community members to participate as local experts in classroom literacy events.

Thus, even when the teacher does not speak the home language of the students, she can still build upon and make use of students' home language. While some forms of home language support are beneficial to emergent ELs in learning science, concurrent translation seems not to be a highly effective teaching strategy, either with regard to teaching science or to developing English proficiency. For example, Luykx, Lee, and Edwards (2008) observed science teaching in a class of combined third- and fourth-grade beginning ELs with a monolingual English-speaking teacher assisted by a bilingual co-teacher. The researchers compared the classroom discourse during typical class periods when both teachers were present and during nontypical class periods when the bilingual co-teacher was absent. They concluded that the classroom language practices were based on the assumption that the two languages (English and Spanish) were essentially equivalent and neutral codes, and that science concepts were viewed as essentially independent of the language in which they were being constructed and expressed. In contrast to these assumptions, analysis of the bilingual co-teacher's attempts to translate science content from English into Spanish and the students' attempts to negotiate language barriers during class discussions about the science content demonstrated that science concepts were tightly tied to the language in which they were constructed.

Similarly, a meta-analysis by Calderón, Slavin, and Sanchéz (2011) of varied instructional strategies for supporting ELs in content area learning, ranging from bilingual instruction to English-only instruction, concluded that any given linguistic approach was less important than other key school and classroom factors. Most important factors included strong school leadership that expected high standards and outcomes for ELs; thoughtful integration of language, literacy, and content instruction, regardless of the language of that instruction; ongoing professional development focused on meeting the needs of ELs; and the presence of active parent and family support teams. Thus, while bilingual education versus English-only education has been the most hotly contested debate related to instructional strategies for supporting ELs, when it comes to content area learning, the language of instruction does not seem to be the most salient instructional feature.

Science Curriculum Materials to Support ELs

Curriculum materials play a critical role in education reform (Ball & Cohen, 1996), influencing both the content that is covered and the instructional approaches that are used in classrooms in intended and unintended ways. As federal and state standards have become more central to the goals of teaching and learning, textbooks and other curriculum materials have become the primary vehicles by which those standards are taught (Banilower et al., 2013). As researchers and curriculum developers have sought to better support teachers in using curriculum materials as intended, there has been a push toward the development of *educative curriculum materials* to help teachers more fully realize the intentions of the curriculum in promoting student understanding (Davis & Krajcik, 2005). Although curriculum projects have played a large role in science

education reforms since the Cold War and the launch of the Soviet *Sputnik* satellite (Rudolph, 2002), high-quality materials that meet current science education standards are difficult to find. For example, even though the National Science Foundation (NSF) has funded a large number of curriculum reform projects, a comprehensive evaluation of school science curricula by the NSF concluded that most existing materials did not meet the expectations of the NRC's (1996) National Science Education Standards (Kesidou & Roseman, 2002). With the arrival of the NGSS, a new generation of science curriculum materials will need to be developed, and teachers will need professional development to implement these materials in ways that support the increased cognitive and linguistic demands of the standards, as discussed earlier.

As an added challenge to providing high-quality science curricula for all students, science curriculum developers must consider how best to meet the unique learning needs of ELs. For example, NSF (1998) has long called for more "culturally and gender relevant curriculum materials" that recognize "diverse cultural perspectives and contributions so that through example and instruction, the contributions of all groups to science will be understood and valued" (p. 29). The fact that ELs are less likely to have access to such materials presents a barrier to equitable learning opportunities (Lee & Buxton, 2008). Yet efforts to develop curriculum materials that better address the needs of a culturally and linguistically diverse student population present a number of challenges.

First, there is an inadequate knowledge base of how norms, practices, and worldviews of different cultural and linguistic groups relate to the norms and practices of scientific communities (see the discussion in the previous science learning section). Where such knowledge has been collected, such as in the case of First Nations groups in Canada, instructional materials have been successfully developed and used with students from those specific cultural and linguistic groups (e.g., Aikenhead, 2001; Garza, 2011). However, in educational settings that bring together students from multiple cultural and linguistic backgrounds, it is difficult to incorporate culturally and linguistically relevant content for all students.

Second, there is the risk of fueling stereotypes, biases, and overgeneralizations about the learning needs of ELs and/or specific cultural and linguistic groups. For example, curriculum materials developed to support ELs have often highlighted the importance of fostering collaborative group environments rather than individual or competitive class structures (Tharp, 1997). While such materials may well serve the needs of many ELs as well as non–ELs, they may also reinforce a stereotype that ELs are not academically independent or competitive in ways that may disadvantage academically high-performing ELs.

Third, the development of curriculum materials that incorporate local linguistic and cultural knowledge runs counter to the current desire for more standardized materials that can be used for large-scale implementation

(Lee & Luykx, 2005). There is a tension between a desire for standardization and a wish to ensure that students have access to curriculum that reflects the people and places at a state or regional level (Buxton, 2010; Gruenewald, 2003). Thus, there is an inherent trade-off between designing materials that meet the needs of specific local contexts but have limited relevance to other settings and designing materials that can potentially be implemented across a wide range of settings but fail to account for how contexts differ.

The linguistic needs of ELs add yet another layer of complexity to the challenge of how curriculum might become more standardized to meet common goals while simultaneously becoming more differentiated to meet unique needs of ELs. Much of the research on science curriculum for ELs has taken place in urban schools in low-income neighborhoods, creating the challenge of disentangling the role that curriculum plays in supporting ELs from these other structural features of socioeconomic status (SES) and urban contexts. Some studies have involved evaluation of existing curriculum materials and the degree to which these materials meet the needs of ELs. Other studies have focused on the development of new curriculum materials that focus on hands-on, inquiry-based science as a way to promote science learning and English language development simultaneously for ELs.

For example, Lynch, Kuipers, Pyke, and Szesze (2005) examined the effect of a highly rated science curriculum unit on ELs' learning. The curriculum unit was not designed to specifically meet the needs of ELs or to support cultural or linguistic relevance; instead, it was designed for wide implementation, and all instruction was in English. Disaggregated achievement data indicated that students who worked with this curriculum outscored a comparison group who did not use the curriculum, with the exception of the ELs in the treatment. In other words, the curriculum was effective for all students except ELs.

In another example, Hampton and Rodriguez (2001) used the Full Option Science Series (FOSS) curriculum with Spanish-speaking elementary children. In this case, while the curriculum itself was not modified, the language of instruction was, with the teachers conducting half of the instruction in Spanish and half in English. After 6 weeks, students completed an open-ended written science assessment in the language of their choice. Hampton and Rodriguez found no significant difference in performance between children who chose to respond in Spanish (55% of the students) and those who chose to respond in English (45% of the students), implying that similar levels of academic language and science content knowledge were being developed in both English and Spanish through the use of the FOSS curriculum when the material was taught in both languages.

In addition to these evaluation studies of how ELs engage with pre-existing high-quality science curriculum, there are a few examples of projects that have sought to develop and test their own curriculum materials with an explicit goal of better supporting science and language learning with ELs. For example, Diane August and colleagues (August, Branum-Martin, Hagan, & Francis, 2009) designed and tested the Quality English and Science Teaching (QuEST) curriculum to simultaneously support the science knowledge and academic language development of middle-grades ELs. Building on science textbooks and workbooks that were already in use in middle schools, the QuEST curriculum involved the infusion of the 5E (engage, explore, explain, elaborate, evaluate) science inquiry model and the direct instruction of both general and topic specific academic vocabulary to the existing curriculum. The QuEST intervention also included the enhanced use of visual materials and graphic organizers, previews of science experiments for ELs, and additional scaffolding for ELs on the use of instructional conversations during science investigations. A controlled study of the QuEST intervention showed that use of the curriculum materials had a statistically significant positive effect on ELs' science knowledge and science vocabulary development.

In the most systematic curriculum research and development effort focused specifically on the needs of ELs, Lee and colleagues constructed a curriculum reflecting the evolution of the knowledge base of teaching science to ELs as well as the shifting policy contexts regarding ELs (e.g., English-only instructional policy) and science education (e.g., the rise of high-stakes testing and accountability policy). These curriculum materials, designed to support the simultaneous development of science content and academic language, then served as the foundation for a series of professional development interventions with elementary teachers. Over the years, the project developed complete science curricula for third, fourth, and fifth grades that were used to fully replace the district science curriculum in schools that participated in the interventions.

From its early stages (Fradd, Lee, Sutman, & Saxton, 2002) to its more recent iterations (Lee, Lewis, Adamson, Maerten-Rivera & Secada, 2008), the project followed a sequence of instruction from basic skills and concepts (measurement and matter) to variable global systems (the water cycle and weather) to increasingly large-scale systems (the ecosystem and the solar system). The curriculum materials for each science topic included consumable science workbooks for students, teachers' guides (including transparencies), and class sets of consumable and nonconsumable science supplies (including trade books related to the science topics in the units). All the units emphasize three domains relevant to the science learning of ELs: (a) science inquiry, progressing along a continuum from teacher-explicit instruction to student-initiated inquiry (for details, see Lee, Hart, Cuevas, & Enders, 2004), (b) integration of English language and literacy development in science instruction (for details, see Hart & Lee, 2003), and (c) incorporation of students' home language and cultural experiences in science instruction (for details, see Lee, Luykx, Buxton, & Shaver, 2007). Together, these domains mutually support students' science content and academic language development. Research on the impact of this curriculum on ELs' outcomes over a number of years, and with thousands of students, has consistently indicated increases in overall science and literacy achievement, decreases in testing gaps among demographic subgroups, and improvements on NAEP and TIMSS sample items (Lee, Deaktor, Enders, & Lambert, 2008; Lee, Mahotiere, Salinas, Penfield, & Maerten-Rivera, 2009).

When taken together, the literature on science curriculum development has shown significant progress in meeting the needs of ELs. While the early history of curricular modifications for ELs often amounted to little more than conceptually and linguistically simplified versions of existing curricula, the current generation of curricular development for supporting the learning needs of ELs has held curricular rigor as a fundamental goal. The NGSS will surely prompt a new flurry of activity in curriculum development, including consideration of how curriculum can best meet the needs of ELs as they strive to meet the rigorous goals of the NGSS. Curriculum efforts attending to the needs of ELs have and will continue to occur in tandem with assessment reforms, as we discuss in the next section.

Science Assessment and ELs

The overall body of literature on educational assessment is extensive, as is the literature on assessment with culturally diverse students. However, research that specifically focuses on science assessment with ELs is extremely limited (Buxton et al., 2012; Solano-Flores & Li, 2008). During the first decade of No Child Left Behind implementation, science was not part of most states' accountability frameworks. When science was included in statewide assessments, it was frequently omitted from the accountability measures or formulas that were used to calculate student achievement. Additionally, because assessment of ELs has tended to concentrate on basic skills in literacy and numeracy, other subject areas, including science, have typically been ignored. However, more recent reforms in science accountability policy in many states began to prompt significant changes to science assessment for all students and especially for students in high-needs demographic subgroups such as ELs. Thus, it has become increasingly important for teachers and scholars to consider how linguistic and cultural characteristics may influence measures of science learning for ELs. At the same time, it is difficult to draw conclusions about how to provide more valid and equitable science assessments for ELs, as few studies to date have directly addressed this issue, and results of those studies have been somewhat inconsistent (e.g., Lawrenz, Huffman, & Welch, 2001; Young et al., 2010).

A crucial issue in the assessment of ELs is how to address linguistic and cultural factors to ensure valid and equitable measures for all students. Assessments of science achievement require consideration of fairness to different student groups. Fairness in this context can be taken to mean "the likelihood of any assessment allowing students to show what they understand about the construct being tested" (Lawrenz et al., 2001, p. 280). There has been considerable debate about the question of cultural and linguistic biases in science assessments and how these biases might affect the validity of the assessments for ELs and other subgroups of students. While some see such biases as a serious validity threat (Solano-Flores & Li, 2008), others continue to attribute differences in academic performance across student demographic subgroups as accurate measures of differences in students' abilities or limitations based on their experiences or home environments (Young et al., 2010).

Among those who believe that cultural and linguistic bias is a serious problem in assessment, there seem to be two competing perspectives on how best to address the concern (Luykx et al., 2008). Advocates of the first position aim to increase test validity by removing cultural and linguistic biases from assessment instruments and practices (Vijver & Tanzer, 2004). In contrast, advocates of the second position claim that because cultural and linguistic biases cannot be removed, nonmainstream students' cultural beliefs and linguistic practices should be considered and incorporated throughout the assessment process (Solano-Flores & Trumbull, 2003; Trumbull & Koelsch, 2011).

Assessments of ELs should be particularly attentive to sociocultural and sociolinguistic influences that affect students' thinking and meaning making, as well as the ways in which students interpret and respond to assessment items. Students of differing cultural and linguistic backgrounds may express their ideas in ways that mask their knowledge and abilities in the eyes of teachers who are unfamiliar with the linguistic and cultural norms of students' homes and communities. While all students are shaped by numerous cultural influences, the linguistic and cultural knowledge that White, middle-class, native English-speaking students use to express their understanding is more likely to parallel the language and culture of teachers, researchers, and test developers. Thus, the backgrounds of these students are more likely to support their performance on assessments than to interfere with it.

A small but growing body of work focuses explicitly on the question of how best to assess ELs in science. Major questions remain about the form and content of assessments to best measure ELs' science learning. First, should assessments be given in English, in the home language, or bilingually? Second, what kinds of accommodations can best enable ELs to demonstrate their knowledge and abilities in science? Third, how can assessments distinguish between science knowledge and academic language proficiency (either in English or in the home language)? Each of these three questions is taken up in turn.

Language of assessment. To better address the complexities of linguistic and cultural factors in assessment,

Solano-Flores and Trumbull (2003) proposed a new paradigm to promote valid and equitable assessment of ELs. While current efforts focus on assuring test validity by attempting to eliminate the confounding effects of students' language and culture, Solano-Flores and Trumbull propose that efforts should be oriented in the opposite direction. Arguing that it is virtually impossible to construct tests that are free from cultural and linguistic influences, understanding how best to account for these inevitable influences should guide all elements of the assessment process, including test development, test review, test use, and test interpretation.

One possible approach is dual-language assessment in both the home language and the language of instruction. Assessing students' knowledge in both languages allows students a more balanced opportunity to demonstrate their content knowledge while reducing the confounding effect of language. This approach, however, presents challenges. First, ensuring the comparability of assessment instruments between two languages is complicated, raising additional issues of validity. Second, translated assessment instruments do not necessarily eliminate sources of linguistic and cultural confusion and may well introduce new ones. Third, this approach may still fail to give an accurate picture of students' content knowledge if students have not developed grade-appropriate literacy skills in the home language. This is often the case, since ELs rarely receive academic language instruction in their home language. Finally, ELs may feel peer pressure and/or pressure from teachers or school administrators to abandon their home language as a valid academic resource.

For example, in a study by Buxton and colleagues (2012), approximately 1,600 middle school students were given a bilingual English/Spanish constructed-response science assessment and were asked to read and respond to each question in the language(s) of their choice. Students were asked to indicate for each item if they read the question in English only, in Spanish only, or in both languages. Students' written responses were coded into the same three categories. Only about one third of students who spoke Spanish as their home language indicated that they read any items in Spanish or in both languages, while less than 10% of the Spanish-speaking students chose to write their responses completely or partially in Spanish. The authors concluded that even when bilingual assessments are made available, some cultural, linguistic, and academic barriers hinder their use.

Despite these challenges, the approach of dual-language assessment warrants further study and should be weighed against the threats to validity inherent in English-only assessment. Dual-language assessment has the potential to produce clearer understandings of the interactions among first and second language proficiency, students' content knowledge, and the linguistic and content demands of test items. Dual-language assessment can also shed light on the linguistic norms and policies in schools that serve large numbers of ELs (Solano-Flores, 2008).

However, dual-language assessment has so far gained little ground in policy and assessment circles in the U.S. education system.

Assessment accommodations. A range of accommodation strategies can be used to support ELs. For example, during the 2005 and 2009 NAEP science assessments, ELs were allowed the use of bilingual dictionaries, bilingual texts, subject-specific glossaries, English language dictionaries, extra time to complete assessments, having test items read aloud, permission to ask clarifying questions, and permission to dictate oral responses to a scribe (NCES, 2011). As can be seen from this list, all of the accommodations were meant to help ELs make sense of the language *as written* rather than using accommodations that would modify the actual language of the assessment. There were no accommodations such as translation of test items or avoidance of unnecessarily complex grammatical constructions, polysemic terms, or idiomatic expressions.

In a meta-analysis of testing accommodations, Kieffer, Lesaux, Rivera, and Francis (2009) examined the effectiveness and the validity of specific testing accommodations in improving the performance of ELs on large-scale assessments in mathematics and science. Effectiveness was defined in terms of whether ELs who received an accommodation outperformed ELs who did not receive the accommodation. Validity was defined in terms of whether an accommodation altered the overall construct validity of a test, measured by whether non–ELs who received an accommodation outperformed non–ELs who did not receive the accommodation. The researchers analyzed data from 11 studies on the effects of accommodations for ELs on NAEP, TIMSS, and state accountability test items in mathematics and science at fourth and eighth grades. The studies considered accommodations including extra time, dual-language questions, a Spanish version of the test, use of a bilingual dictionary, use of an English dictionary, and simplified English-language versions of test questions. Surprisingly, the results indicated that the only accommodation that consistently improved ELs' performance was providing students with English-language dictionaries. This finding raises intriguing questions about why home language supports did not yield improved test performance. One hypothesis would be that if students do not receive academic instructional support in their home language, then they will not possess the academic language skills in their first language to take advantage of home language accommodations. The results also indicated, however, that there was little evidence of threats to validity from these accommodations, implying that there is little harm in continuing to explore a wide range of possible testing accommodations for ELs, as well as studying how changes in instructional practices could result in changes in the effectiveness of testing accommodations.

In contrast to examining testing accommodations on large-scale assessments, Siegel (2007) studied accommodations for ELs on teacher-developed formative and summative assessments. Unlike large-scale assessments that attempt to contain and reduce the language factor, these classroom assessments were meant to improve written assessment items in as many ways as possible to make the items more accessible and equitable for ELs. Siegel studied two middle school life science classes that used NSF–supported science curriculum materials for a full academic year between taking a pretest and posttest. Participating students were ELs who had some proficiency in reading and writing in English, as well as non–ELs in the same classes. Siegel developed and used an equity framework for written classroom assessments based on five principles: (a) match the learning goals of the original items and the language of instruction, (b) be comprehensible for ELs both linguistically and culturally, (c) challenge students to think about difficult ideas without diluting content, (d) elicit student understanding, and (e) scaffold the use of language to support learning. Based on these five principles, 11 kinds of assessment modifications were made to support linguistic (e.g., reducing the number of words), cognitive (e.g., adding a graphic organizer), and visual (e.g., including a picture) improvements.

Results indicated that both native English speakers and ELs scored significantly higher on the modified classroom assessments. Thus, these modifications, unlike the accommodations studied in Kieffer and colleagues' analysis of standardized tests, did improve ELs' performance but also caused validity threats, in that non–ELs' performance increased as well. One possible interpretation of these findings is that the meaning of assessment items is often unclear to students, regardless of home language, and thus comprehensive assessment modifications to support student understanding are beneficial to all students. In other words, if our goal in creating assessment accommodations is for students to better understand test items, test writers should consider principles such as those developed by Siegel.

Emergent technologies offer additional possibilities for accommodations to support the assessment of ELs, as well as the potential to improve science instruction. For example, Kopriva and Sexton (2011) developed a technology-based assessment methodology called ONPAR (www.onpar.us) that is designed to minimize the distraction of construct-irrelevant text. The focus of the approach is to capture students' explanatory responses using relatively little language. Assessment items are posed using a range of linguistic supports, including multiple modalities, computer-based animation and simulation, multiple redundancies, and use of auditory supports. The ONPAR approach has been shown to improve the measurement of challenging content knowledge as well as academic language skills for ELs, while also providing teachers with tools to support their instruction of complex content in their classrooms (Kopriva, 2008).

Distinction between content and language. When ELs are assessed in English, attempts should be made to distinguish between students' science knowledge and their academic language proficiency in English. While an obvious consideration in theory, it is quite challenging in practice to avoid confounding language proficiency with science knowledge, as it is through language that students must interpret questions and demonstrate understanding (Siegel, 2007).

Studies have considered the degree to which classroom science assessments function as a measure of science knowledge or as a measure of English language proficiency. For example, Shaw (1997) used science performance assessments with two classes of ELs in a high school that was unusual in that the schools implemented bilingual education programs with extensive resources. Two bilingual teachers who had training and experience in hands-on inquiry science with ELs conducted a 4-day performance assessment task on heat energy. The assessment involved an open-ended inquiry and hands-on investigation by students working in small groups, followed by a series of written assessment items. The students' ability to demonstrate that they could develop an acceptable inquiry procedure was significantly affected by students' level of English proficiency. In contrast, students' abilities to demonstrate use of graphs, calculations, equations, data tables, and final summary questions were not significantly affected by their level of English proficiency but were significantly affected by their level of science knowledge. Shaw concluded that there was no simple answer to the question of the degree to which science assessments with ELs are measuring English language proficiency rather than or in addition to science knowledge; the answer seems to depend on the assessment task and the focus of the questions being asked.

Summary. The literature on assessing ELs' science learning has raised many interesting questions about the roles of test items and validity issues, the roles of language competence in first and second languages, the role of culture and experience, and the differences that various types of assessments might highlight. However, the research literature has provided few definitive answers to any of these questions. Studies suggest the need to develop and refine test items in both English and students' home language at the same time so that both versions are validated throughout the assessment process (Solano-Flores, 2008; Solano-Flores & Trumbull, 2003), although ELs may not make use of home language assessment items when available (Buxton et al., 2012). The studies by Kieffer and colleagues (2009) and Siegel (2007) indicate tensions between the purpose of enhancing the validity of assessments by using accommodations for ELs and the purpose of improving the performance (and presumably the learning that occurs) on assessments of all students, both ELs and non–ELs. The study by Shaw (1997) highlights the difficulty of separating content, language, and culture in science assessments with ELs. While emergent technologies may provide new supports for assessing the science learning of ELs (Kopriva, 2008), assessment will continue to be a challenging area when considering equitable science education opportunities for all students. Further, in addition to concerns about standardized assessments, the research literature does not offer sufficient guidance for classroom teachers in terms of using diagnostic, formative, and summative assessments with their ELs. Thus, assessment should be one important focus in science teacher education to support ELs, the topic we take up in the next section.

Science Teacher Education to Support ELs

As we noted at the outset of the chapter, our nation's schools will continue to educate increasing numbers of ELs, requiring that today's and tomorrow's teachers will need a new set of knowledge, skills, and dispositions, distinct from those of their predecessors, in order to provide equitable learning opportunities for all of their students. In contrast to the rapidly changing demographics in student population, the teaching profession continues to be dominated by White, female, socioeconomically middle-class teachers (Banilower et al., 2013). In 2000, Jorgenson concluded, "school districts across the United States confront an urgent shortage of minority educators, while the number of minority students in the public schools steadily increases. This imbalance is expected to worsen" (pp. 1–2), and indeed this trend has continued (Sable & Plotts, 2010).

While teachers need not share their students' ethnic, cultural, or linguistic backgrounds in order to teach effectively (Ladson-Billings, 1995), all teachers must gain an increased awareness of the cultural and linguistic knowledge that their ELs (and all their students) bring to the classroom (Garcia, Arias, Harris Murri, & Serna, 2010). Too few teachers, however, receive substantive professional development opportunities focused on how students' ethnic, cultural, and linguistic backgrounds may affect their educational experiences (Gere, Buehler, Dallavis, & Haviland, 2009). Based on the teacher professional development literature, it is clear that facilitating changes in teachers' knowledge, beliefs, and practices is a long and demanding process, not conducive to quick fixes or one-time interventions (Wayne, Yoon, Zhu, Cronen, & Garet, 2008). This is especially true when it comes to connecting students' cultural and linguistic experiences to specific content area learning objectives (Buxton, Salinas et al., 2013; Lee & Luykx, 2005). Teachers need opportunities to reflect on how these cultural and linguistic experiences may affect a student's educational experience. In short, there is a critical need for teacher education that specifically addresses teachers' beliefs and practices with regard to students' languages and cultures as related to subject areas.

Despite the growing awareness of the need to address issues of linguistic diversity, including the needs of ELs, limited progress has been made in preparing teachers to succeed in today's culturally and linguistically diverse classrooms. There are multiple challenges. First, it is difficult to conceptualize classroom practices that are both academically rigorous and equitable for all students. Second, even when teacher education does address rigor and equity simultaneously, this does not easily translate into a workable model of classroom practices that support the needs of ELs. Third, the vast majority of teachers (>80%) working with ELs continue to believe they are not adequately prepared to meet their students' learning needs, particularly in academically demanding subjects such as science, mathematics, and reading (Banilower et al., 2013). Finally, teachers often feel constrained by school accountability discourse focusing on narrow outcomes that make many teachers reluctant to deviate from traditional pedagogies (Buxton, Kayumova, & Allexsaht-Snider, 2013).

Teacher professional development to promote science as well as English language and literacy development with ELs must be multifaceted. First, in addition to ensuring that ELs acquire the language skills necessary for social communication, teachers need to promote ELs' development of general and content-specific academic language functions, such as describing, explaining, comparing, and concluding (Wong-Fillmore & Snow, 2002). Second, teachers must be able to formulate appropriate expectations about language and content learning needs depending on the student's unique situation. A high school EL who is newly arrived and has limited English proficiency and interrupted prior schooling clearly needs a different approach to both English and content area learning than either a first-grade EL or another high school EL who received strong content area schooling in her first language (Calderón et al., Slavin, & Sanchez, 2011). Finally, teachers need to be able to apply this knowledge to the teaching of general and content-specific academic language (Stoddart et al., 2010). The combination of these three knowledge sources points to the value of teaching practices that engage students at all levels of English proficiency in academic language learning, in learning activities that have multiple points of entry at varying levels of English proficiency, using multiple modes for students to display learning, and encouraging each student to participate in a manner that allows for maximum language development.

As a practical example, Buck, Mast, Ehlers, and Franklin (2005) explored the process a beginning teacher went through to establish a classroom conducive to the academic, linguistic, and social needs of middle-grades ELs learning science. The analysis of 5 months of classroom data revealed that (a) many strategies that this beginning teacher used for teaching middle-grades ELs in a mainstream classroom involved complex considerations that were not part of her teacher preparation program; (b) science learning increased for all students over time, but there were differences in learning between ELs and non–ELs; and (c) student and peer feedback proved to be effective means of enhancing growth of a beginning teacher seeking to increase her skills in teaching science to ELs.

A limited number of studies have addressed professional development efforts to help in-service teachers effectively integrate science learning with English language development for ELs. These studies range from large-scale professional development at the school or district level to intensive teacher research with small numbers of participants. A common feature is that all of these studies explicitly connect science learning with literacy development. Without gaining literacy skills, it is impossible for students to gain grade-appropriate science content knowledge. At the same time, rigorous content learning provides an authentic context for gaining academic language skills.

Stoddart, Pinal, Latzke, and Canaday (2002) have argued that inquiry-based science provides a particularly powerful instructional context for the integration of science content and second language development with ELs. Because it is often not possible to teach academic subjects to ELs in their home language while they are acquiring proficiency in English, Stoddart and colleagues developed a model (Effective Science Teaching for English Language Learners, or ESTELL) for integrating the teaching of science with second language development. They studied 24 elementary teachers during a 5-week summer professional development program. Prior to their participation, the majority of the teachers viewed themselves as well prepared to teach either science or language, but not both. After their participation, the majority of teachers believed they had improved in the domain in which they had initially felt less prepared, typically by shifting their view of the connections between these two domains.

Building on these findings, Stoddart and colleagues (2010) sought to further strengthen their professional development model by integrating the science, language, and literacy framework from their prior study with the CREDE standards for effective pedagogy (Tharp, 1997). In their ongoing work with beginning elementary science teachers, Stoddart and colleagues have documented effectiveness of this integrated model of science content and English literacy development with ELs.

In another longitudinal project targeting lower-elementary–grade students (K–2), Tong, Irby, Lara-Alecio, Yoon, and Mathes (2010) developed and tested a professional development model that focused on early English language and literacy development through science. A total of 76 teachers participated in professional development that highlighted the use of ESL strategies, such as using advance organizers, leveled questioning, shared reading, vocabulary dramatization, and story retelling, in the context of science instruction. Students in the classrooms of the 76 participating teachers were compared with students in the classrooms of teachers in the same schools who did not participate in the project. Students were assessed for language and literacy development using measures of phonemic awareness, oral language skills, and reading-related skills. Multilevel modeling indicated that the intervention produced positive and significant effects on students'

phonological awareness, oral language skills, and decoding and reading proficiency.

Finally, the ongoing work by Lee and colleagues has a long history of professional development to support elementary school teachers of ELs. In earlier work, Lee (2004) examined patterns of change in the beliefs and practices of a group of bilingual Latin@ elementary teachers as they learned to teach English language and literacy as part of science instruction throughout a 3-year professional development experience. Although teachers initially spoke in very broad and general terms about integration of science and literacy, they gradually learned to focus on specific aspects of English language and literacy in the context of science instruction.

In the more recent Promoting Science among English Language Learners (P-SELL) project, Lee and colleagues conceptualized the professional development as responses to a series of competing tensions in three categories: (a) balancing science content and inquiry, (b) supporting the content areas of English language and literacy through science, and (c) recognizing contextual features common to urban settings, and high-stakes testing and accountability (Buxton, Lee, & Santau, 2008).

Lee, Lewis, and colleagues (2008) examined 38 third-grade teachers' knowledge and practices in teaching science while supporting English language development of ELs at the end of the first year of the P-SELL project. The study examined four areas: teacher knowledge of science content, teaching science for understanding, teaching science for inquiry, and teacher support for English language development. Results indicate that teachers' knowledge and practices were generally aligned with the goals supported by the intervention. However, only a small fraction of the teachers moved beyond the explicit instruction that served as the starting point of the professional development model to exhibit stronger reform-oriented practices in science instruction (NRC, 2007, 2011) or English language and literacy development in content area instruction (TESOL, 2006).

At the conclusion of the fifth year of the P-SELL project, Lee and Maerten-Rivera (2012) examined changes in knowledge and practices of a total of 198 teachers at Grades 3 through 5. Three sets of results are noteworthy. First, the professional development intervention did result in changes in teachers' knowledge and practices in teaching science to all students, including ELs. Changes were most pronounced at the fifth-grade level, when science counted toward state accountability measures. Second, teachers generally followed the project curriculum in their teaching practices; however, many teachers fell short of the goal of reform-oriented practices in teaching science to ELs. Finally, external factors influenced the implementation and impact of the intervention, including high rates of teacher (and student) mobility and high-stakes testing and accountability policies. These external factors presented challenges to the implementation of the intervention and might have resulted in an underestimation of the efficacy of the intervention. Yet these same factors allow the results to be more generalizable, as the project teachers and schools were responding to the typical pressures common to most public school settings.

Overall, researchers who have studied professional development that supports the teaching of science to ELs indicate that educational interventions aiming to integrate the teaching of science inquiry with the teaching of academic English development typically yield positive results in changing teachers' knowledge, beliefs, and practices. These researchers also suggest that when teachers combine teaching science content with teaching academic language development with ELs, they do improve at meeting the needs of their ELs. However, many teachers fall short of the goal of reform-oriented practices in teaching science to ELs.

Connections Among Homes, Schools, and Science for ELs

The relationship between students' broad academic success and parental involvement in schooling has long been understood (Baker & Stevenson, 1986; Epstein, 1987). Recent research focused more directly on how home–school connections can be supported and whether certain types of family or community involvement might be particularly helpful to support student achievement. For example, Bloome and colleagues (2000) explored how the dominant relationship between schools and families is a school-centered model in which school-based intellectual practices are presented to parents as "best practices" that should be reinforced in the home. Instead, Bloome and colleagues advocated a community-centered model in which the cultural and intellectual practices of family, community, business, and so on are valued and accepted. These two models are not easily resolved, however, and point to tensions such as the desire of families for their children to maintain the cultural and linguistic practices of their heritage while also wanting their children to participate fully in the dominant school culture. These tensions may be especially acute for the families of ELs, in which linguistic, cultural, and familial norms and values may differ sharply from those of the mainstream school culture (Cone, Buxton, Mahotiere, & Lee, 2013). Thus, while it has long been recognized that building home and school connections is important for the academic success of ELs, in practice, this is rarely done in an effective manner.

Rodriguez, Collins-Parker, and Garza (2013) reviewed the literature on parental involvement with an eye toward implications for science teaching and learning. They proposed a model for organizing this literature around three dimensions: home environment, parents and school/community, and students and school/community. In terms of home environment, Rodriguez and colleagues found that some features that are popularly assumed to increase students' academic achievement, such as providing homework help (J. S. Lee & Bowen, 2006) and monitoring student activities (Hong & Ho, 2005), seemed to make little difference in student achievement. Other features, such as positive peer and sibling role models (Horn & Carroll, 1998) and clear familial aspirations and expectations (Hill & Tyson, 2009), were connected to improved student achievement.

Second, in terms of parental involvement in school and community, Rodriguez and colleagues (2013) point to the importance of two-way communication between parents and school personnel. When parents are unsure or reluctant about communicating with school personnel, more personal outreach on the part of school representatives, such as explicit information on how to contact teachers and personal invitations to attend school events, increases parental engagement (Sheldon & Epstein, 2005). Similarly, getting parents of ELs to volunteer in school often requires putting new structures in place to support parents' linguistic needs and to help parents feel valued through contributing in ways in which they are already competent. This allows parents to grow in confidence and perhaps volunteer in additional ways.

Finally, little of the research on parental involvement has given significant consideration to the roles of students and student agency. One exception was the study by Rodriguez, Zozakiewicz, and Yerrick (2008) in which ELs were trained as technology coaches to help teachers, peers, and family members in using and troubleshooting computers and other technology. Students who participated in this project demonstrated increased self-confidence in school and increased agency for their learning, not just in science but across content areas.

The main point that Rodriguez, Collins-Parker, and Garza highlight is that parents and their children are already playing various roles related to their schooling and exerting agency that can be linked to the goals of science education through their involvement at home, at school, and in the community. It is up to teachers and other educators to become aware of these roles and to explicitly connect existing student and parent initiative to the tasks and expectations of schooling. Doing so may support students' science achievement and promote lifelong engagement with science learning.

In the specific case of science learning with ELs, a major challenge facing many schools is the perceived disconnect between academic content, language, and practices in school science and language and practices in students' home and community. Students are more likely to engage in school science if they see it as relevant and meaningful to their lives beyond school. Students and families possess funds of knowledge from their homes and communities that can serve as resources for science learning if teachers understand and find ways to activate this prior knowledge (González et al., 2005).

Building on the belief that ELs, their parents, and their science teachers could learn from each other and share funds of knowledge related to science if they were brought together as co-learners, Buxton, Allexsaht-Snider, and

Rivera (2012) outlined a model they refer to as Steps to College through Science. This model of bilingual science workshops, held on college, technical school, and community college campuses allows parents to gain awareness of science-specific as well as general academic expectations that are placed on their children in middle and high school. It also allows students to see their parents and teachers in an unfamiliar light, as co-learners. In addition, it allows teachers to interact with parents in a science learning setting in which they are not in the role of evaluating the students' performance. After 3 years of Steps to College through Science workshops, the researchers found that parents were more involved in the school, students were more engaged in science, and teachers had higher expectations for their EL students to succeed in science.

While there has been less research to date on the topic of connecting homes, schools, and science for ELs than there has been on the other topics reviewed in this chapter, the limited research shows substantial potential for supporting home–school connections as a key component of improving science learning of ELs. Additional research in this area would seem to be warranted.

Conclusions and Implications for Practice and Future Research

We began this chapter by outlining four primary factors that are central to the current state of science education reform: (a) growing student diversity, (b) persistent science testing gaps in the context of increased accountability measures, (c) the advent of the NGSS, and (d) the necessity for all students to learn challenging science. We made the case that each of these factors is directly connected to the specific needs of ELs in our schools. We then presented a review of the current literature on teaching science to ELs, organized around six topics: (1) science learning, (2) science instructional strategies, (3) science curriculum materials, (4) science assessment, (5) science teacher education, and (6) connections among homes, schools, and science. We now conclude with brief comments regarding the implications and emergent opportunities that each of these topics provides for practice and future research.

Science Learning

ELs face a unique challenge of learning science in a language that they are still in the process of acquiring. In many educational settings, ELs are initially given intensive language instruction through ESOL or ESL programs, often at the expense of content area instruction. English language and literacy development in these programs is rarely taught in the context of grade-appropriate academic learning. When language instruction focuses on basic interpersonal communication instead of the academic language needed for content area learning, ELs are at an even greater disadvantage in terms of future academic success. As this chapter has pointed out, this traditional approach has limited ELs' opportunities to learn science. However,

the NGSS should provide new opportunities, as well as new challenges, as the increased emphasis on science and engineering practices, crosscutting concepts, and disciplinary core ideas will create language-rich and contextualized learning experiences.

Further research on science learning with ELs should support understanding the nuances in relationships between content learning and language learning. For example, what language demands and opportunities will ELs face as they engage in science and engineering practices, crosscutting concepts, and disciplinary core ideas (Lee et al., Quinn, & Valdés, 2013)? What do science teachers and language specialists need to know about language demands and opportunities to support ELs' engagement in science and engineering practices?

Science Instruction

Students of all backgrounds should be provided with academically challenging learning opportunities to explore scientific phenomena and construct scientific meanings based on their own linguistic and cultural experiences. Too often, ELs have been taught through direct instruction of basic skills, placed in low-track classes with low academic expectations, and pulled out of science classrooms to receive instruction in basic literacy and numeracy. Such practices place ELs farther and farther behind in learning science. The shift away from pull-out and toward push-in instructional models for ELs creates new opportunities for co-teaching models that have the potential to enrich science instruction for ELs.

In terms of future research, the field needs a better understanding of how (and how well) hands-on science inquiry may contribute to ELs' science learning, given the new foci of the NGSS. For example, an emphasis on modeling and argumentation may benefit from ongoing hands-on experience but may require making use of that hands-on experience in different ways. Further research should also address the question of what types of academic language development may be most useful to ELs in science and what instructional strategies best support such language development. In addition, research on how to make the best use of co-teaching, home language support, and other instructional strategies based on the classroom presence of adults besides the science teacher requires further study.

Science Curriculum

Science curriculum materials for ELs require attention at multiple levels. Such curriculum materials should be coherent, rigorous, focused on big ideas, and designed to support opportunities for students' sense making. These materials should also support the scaffolded acquisition of academic language through science. All students need to be challenged by a science curriculum that is aligned with reform-oriented practices and with the current and next generation of science standards. When teaching ELs, science curriculum materials need to take into account additional issues related to culture, language, and worldview.

There are inherent tensions in attempts to design curriculum materials to meet the needs of all students and those designed to target specific student groups such as ELs (Calabrese Barton, Tan, & O'Neill, this volume). At the same time, work by Chinn (2007) and Buxton (2010) points to new opportunities to tie students' life-wide experiences with science to the school science curriculum as new NGSS-aligned materials are developed.

In terms of further research on science curriculum with ELs, the field needs a better understanding of how the worldviews of ELs align with the norms and practices required by the NGSS. As curriculum materials are developed or modified to support the NGSS, the language demands and opportunities to support ELs (and all students) will need to be considered if we expect students to effectively communicate about new and challenging science content and practices. Furthermore, the question of place-based curriculum and local knowledge needs to be studied in relation to the more globalized curriculum push that will result from the NGSS.

Science Assessment

Given the research evidence that the validity and fairness of science assessments for ELs may be called into question due to cultural and linguistic properties of the assessments, more accurate and complete understanding of how to design science assessments and provide accommodations for ELs is needed. For example, assessment designers should consider the multiple components (e.g., item content, item context, item format, wording) that are differentially difficult for ELs rather than simply providing a standard set of accommodations for all ELs. At the same time, opportunities for a new generation of performance-based and technology-enhanced assessments aligned with the NGSS may enable ELs to more accurately show what they know and can do.

In terms of further research on science assessment with ELs, there is much we still do not know about how linguistic and cultural characteristics affect measures of science learning for ELs and how such knowledge could help the development of science assessments that would be both more valid and more equitable for all students. While high-stakes testing receives much attention, there is a simultaneous need to better understand how teacher-made formative and summative assessments can be improved to better support the educative potential of classroom assessment for ELs and all students. Finally, questions about how dual-language or multilingual assessments, as well as multimodal assessments, may both support and hinder valid and equitable assessment need to be examined.

Science Teacher Education

Teachers are the key to educational innovations and improvements, and the success of any professional development intervention relies on considering teachers' perspectives while enabling teachers to adopt reform-oriented practices. As the nation's schools become increasingly diverse culturally and linguistically, there is a growing awareness that today's teachers need a broader array of knowledge, skills, and dispositions to provide equitable learning opportunities for all students. Despite this trend, only limited progress has been made in addressing the professional development needs of teachers to better prepare them to succeed in today's culturally and linguistically diverse classrooms. Greater attention to student learning differences, however, should lead to new opportunities for teacher professional learning focused on the needs of ELs.

In terms of further research on science teacher education with ELs, the field needs a better understanding of how to support teachers in bringing together instructional strategies for rigorous academic content learning with English language development. Also, more research is needed on how professional development approaches can help teachers balance supporting ELs' academic goals with supporting ELs in the sociocultural and sociolinguistic challenges they face in school science. Research is also needed on how helping teachers deepen their own knowledge of science and language may translate into better support for their ELs' learning.

School Science and Home Connections

While the body of research on home and school connections involving ELs and science is quite limited, the research that does exist points to the value of parental engagement and suggestions for how to build stronger home–school connections. For example, supporting two-way communication about what is important for students, acknowledging that parents and students already exert agency in ways that can support students' education, and looking for ways to bring parents, teachers, and students together as co-learners all show promise for supporting ELs in science education. The NGSS, with its increased focus on college and career readiness and life-wide educational focus, should provide new opportunities to highlight the value of home–school connections for all students.

In terms of further research on connections among homes, schools, and science with ELs, the field needs to examine the range of models that can strengthen connections between teachers and the families of ELs. Researchers who study ELs should build deeper understandings of community funds of knowledge while moving away from deficit perspectives on ELs and their families. More research is needed on how to systematically engage the parents and families of ELs in science classrooms and in science activities both in and out of school. Finally, more research is needed on the role that students can play in fostering parental engagement in school science, given that it is on behalf of the students that parental engagement is sought.

Closing

The current state of knowledge about ELs in science education can be summarized by the claim that when provided with equitable learning and assessment opportunities,

ELs are capable of demonstrating high levels of science achievement, taking agency and ownership of their science learning, and developing positive attitudes toward science and potential careers in science fields. Many, if not most, of the academic difficulties faced by ELs in the science classroom are rooted in the education system itself rather than in the students, their families, or their communities. All students, especially those who have traditionally performed poorly in science, must be provided with equitable learning and assessment opportunities. States, districts, and schools should consider how they allocate material, human, and social resources to support ELs in learning rigorous science standards at the same time that they are learning English language and literacy. Only in this way will the United States be able to take full advantage of what has always been one of its greatest assets—the energy and determination of its immigrant populations.

Acknowledgments

The authors wish to thank Jerome Shaw and Rafael Lara for their review and comments on the initial version of this chapter.

References

Achieve, Inc. (2013). *Next generation science standards.* Washington, DC: Author. Retrieved from www.nextgenscience.org/next-generation-science-standards

Aikenhead, G. S. (2001). Students' ease in crossing cultural borders into school science. *Science Education, 85*(2), 180–188.

American Association for the Advancement of Science (AAAS). (1990). *Science for all Americans.* New York: Oxford University Press.

August, D., Branum-Martin, L., Hagan, E., & Francis, D. (2009). The impact of an instructional intervention on the science and language learning of middle grade English language learners. *Journal of Research on Educational Effectiveness, 2,* 345–376.

Baker, D. P., & Stevenson, D. L. (1986). Mothers' strategies for children's achievement: Managing the transition to high school. *Sociology of Education, 59,* 156–166.

Ball, D. L., & Cohen, D. K. (1996). Reform by the book: What is—or might be—the role of curriculum materials in teacher learning and instructional reform? *Educational Researcher, 25,* 6–8.

Banilower, E. R., Smith, P. S., Weiss, I. R., Malzahn, K. A., Campbell, K. M., & Weis, A. M. (2013). *Report of the 2012 national survey of science and mathematics education.* Chapel Hill, NC: Horizon Research, Inc.

Bloome, D., Katz, L., Solsken, J., Willett, J., & Wilson-Keenan, J. (2000). Interpellations of family/community and classroom literacy practices. *Journal of Educational Research, 93*(3), 155–63.

Brown, B. A. (2006). "It isn't slang that can be said about this stuff": Language, identity, and appropriating science discourse. *Journal of Research in Science Teaching, 43*(1), 96–126.

Brown, B. A., Reveles, J. M., & Kelly, G. J. (2005). Scientific literacy and discursive identity: A theoretical framework for understanding science learning. *Science Education, 89,* 779–802.

Brown, B. A., & Spang, E. (2008). Double talk: Synthesizing everyday and science language in the classroom. *Science Education, 92,* 708–732.

Bruna, K. R., & Gomez, K. (Eds.). (2008). *Talking science, writing science: The work of language in multicultural classrooms.* Mahwah, NJ: Taylor and Francis.

Buck, G. A., Mast, C., Ehlers, N., & Franklin, E. (2005). Preparing teachers to create a mainstream science classroom conducive to the needs of English language learners: A feminist action research project. *Journal of Research in Science Teaching, 42*(9), 1013–1031.

Buxton, C. (2010). Social problem solving through science: An approach to critical place-based science teaching and learning. *Equity and Excellence in Education, 43*(1), 120–135.

Buxton, C., Allexsaht-Snider, M., & Rivera, C. (2012). Science, language and families: Constructing a model of language-rich science inquiry. In J. Bianchini, V. Atkerson, A. Calabrese Barton, O. Lee, & A. Rodriguez (Eds.), *Moving the equity agenda forward: Equity research, practice and policy in science education* (pp. 241–259). New York: Springer.

Buxton, C., Allexsaht-Snider, M., Suriel, R., Kayumova, S., Choi, Y., Bouton, B., & Land, M. (2012). Using educative assessments to support science teaching for middle school English language learners. *Journal of Science Teacher Education, 24*(2), 347–366.

Buxton, C., Kayumova, S., & Allexsaht-Snider, M. (2013). Teacher, researcher and accountability discourses shaping democratic practices for science teaching in middle schools. *Democracy & Education, 21*(2).

Buxton, C., & Lee, O. (2010). Fostering scientific reasoning as a strategy to support science learning for ELLs. In D. Senal, C. Senal, & E. Wright (Eds.), *Teaching Science with Hispanic ELLs in K–16 Classrooms* (pp. 11–36). Charlotte, NC: Information Age Publishing.

Buxton, C., Lee, O., & Santau, A. (2008). Promoting science among English language learners: Professional development for today's culturally and linguistically diverse classrooms. *Journal of Science Teacher Education, 19*(5), 495–511.

Buxton, C., Salinas, A., Mahotiere, M., Lee, O., & Secada, W. G. (2013). Leveraging cultural resources through teacher reasoning: Teachers analyze second language learners' problem solving in science. *Teaching and Teacher Education, 32,* 31–42.

Calabrese Barton, A., Tan, E., & O'Neill, T. (2013). Science education in urban contexts: New conceptual tools and stories of possibilities. In N. G. Lederman & S. K. Abell (Eds.), *Handbook of research in science education* (2nd ed., pp. 246–265). New York: Routledge.

Calderón, M., Slavin, R., & Sánchéz, M. (2011). Effective instruction for English learners. *Future Child, 21*(1), 103–127.

Callahan, R., Wilkinson, L., & Muller, C. (2010). Academic achievement and course taking among language minority youth in U.S. schools: Effects of ESL placement. *Educational Evaluation and Policy Analysis, 32*(1), 84–117.

Chamot, A. U., & O'Malley, J. M. (1996). The Cognitive Academic Language Learning Approach (CALLA): A model for linguistically diverse classrooms. *The Elementary School Journal, 96*(3), 259–273.

Chinn, P. W. (2007). Decolonizing methodologies and indigenous knowledge: The role of culture, place and personal experience in professional development. *Journal of Research in Science Teaching, 44*(9), 1247–1268.

Cone, N., Buxton, C., Mahotiere, M., & Lee, O. (2013). Negotiating a sense of identity in a foreign land: Navigating public school structures and practices that often conflict with Haitian culture and values. *Urban Education.* doi:10.1177/0042085913478619

Davis, E., & Krajcik, J. (2005). Designing educative curriculum materials to promote teacher learning. *Educational Researcher, 34*(3), 3–14.

Epstein, J. (1987). Parent involvement: What research says to administrators. *Education and Urban Society, 19,* 119–136.

Fathman, A. K., & Crowther, D. T. (Eds.). (2006). *Science for English language learners: K–12 classroom strategies.* Arlington, VA: National Science Teachers Association.

Fradd, S. H., Lee, O., Sutman, F. X., & Saxton, M. K. (2002). Materials development promoting science inquiry with English language learners: A case study. *Bilingual Research Journal, 25*(4), 479–501.

Garcia, E., Arias, M. B., Harris Murri, N., & Serna, C. (2010). Developing responsive teachers: A challenge for a demographic reality. *Journal of Teacher Education, 61*(1–2), 132–142.

Garza, D. (2011). *Alaska native science: A curriculum guide.* Fairbanks, AK: Alaska Native Knowledge Network.

Gere, A. R., Buehler, J., Dallavis, C., & Haviland, V. S. (2009). A visibility project: Learning to see how preservice teachers take up culturally responsive pedagogy. *American Educational Research Journal, 46,* 816–852.

Goldenberg, C. (2008). Teaching English language learners: What the research does—and does not—say. *American Educator, 32*(2), 42–44.

González, N., Moll, L. C., & Amanti, C. (2005). *Funds of knowledge: Theorizing practices in households, communities, and classrooms.* Mahwah, NJ: Lawrence Erlbaum Associates.

Gruenewald, D. (2003). The best of both worlds: A critical pedagogy of place. *Educational Researcher, 32*(4), 3–12.

Hampton, E., & Rodriguez, R. (2001). Inquiry science in bilingual classrooms. *Bilingual Research Journal, 25*(4), 461–478.

Hart, J., & Lee, O. (2003). Teacher professional development to improve science and literacy achievement of English language learners. *Bilingual Research Journal, 27*(3), 475–501.

Hill, N. E., & Tyson, D. F. (2009). Parental involvement in middle school: A meta-analytic assessment of the strategies that promote achievement. *Developmental Psychology, 45*(3), 740–763.

Hong, S., & Ho, H.-Z. (2005). Direct and indirect longitudinal effects of parental involvement on student achievement: Second-order latent growth modeling across ethnic groups. *Journal of Educational Psychology, 97*(1), 32–42.

Horn, J. L., & Carroll, C. D. (1998). *Confronting the odds: Students at risk and the pipeline to higher education.* Washington, DC: National Center for Education Statistics.

Hudicourt-Barnes, J. (2003). The use of argumentation in Haitian Creole science classrooms. *Harvard Educational Review, 73*(10), 73–93.

Jorgenson, O. (2000). The need for more ethnic teachers: Addressing the critical shortage in American public schools. *Teachers College Record.* Date Published: September 13. Retrieved from www.tcrecord.org/Content.asp?ContentId=10551

Kesidou, S., & Roseman, J. E. (2002). How well do middle school science programs measure up? Findings from Project 2061's curriculum review. *Journal of Research in Science Teaching, 39*(6), 522–549.

Kieffer, M. J., Lesaux, N. K., Rivera, M., & Francis, D. (2009). Accommodations for English language learners on large-scale assessments: A meta-analysis on effectiveness and validity. *Review of Educational Research, 79*(3), 1168–1201.

Kopriva, R. J. (2008). *Improving testing for English language learners: A comprehensive approach to designing, building, implementing, and interpreting better academic assessments.* New York: Routledge.

Kopriva, R. J., & Sexton, U. (2011). Using appropriate assessment processes in the classroom: How to get accurate information about the academic knowledge and skills of English language learners. In M. del Rosario-Basterra, E. Trumbull, & G. Solano-Flores (Eds.), *Cultural validity in assessment: Addressing linguistic and cultural diversity.* New York: Routledge Publishers.

Ladson-Billings, G. (1995). Toward a theory of culturally relevant pedagogy. *American Educational Research Journal, 32*(3), 465–491.

Lawrenz, F., Huffman, D., & Welch, W. (2001). The science achievement of various subgroups of alternative assessment formats. *Science Education, 85*(3), 279–290.

Lee, J. S., & Bowen K. N. (2006). Parent involvement, cultural capital, and the achievement gap among elementary school children. *American Educational Research Journal, 43*(2), 193–218.

Lee, O. (2004). Teacher change in beliefs and practices in science and literacy instruction with English language learners. *Journal of Research in Science Teaching, 41*(1), 65–93.

Lee, O., & Buxton, C. A. (2008). Science curriculum and student diversity: Culture, language, and socioeconomic status. *The Elementary School Journal, 109*(2), 123–137.

Lee, O., & Buxton, C. A. (2012). Integrating science and English proficiency for English language learners. *Theory into Practice, 52*(1), 31–42.

Lee, O., Deaktor, R., Enders, C., & Lambert, J. (2008). Impact of a multi-year professional development intervention on science achievement of culturally and linguistically diverse elementary students. *Journal of Research in Science Teaching, 45*(6), 726–747.

Lee, O., & Fradd, S. H. (1998). Science for all, including students from non–English language backgrounds. *Educational Researcher, 27*(3), 12–21.

Lee, O., Hart, J., Cuevas, P., & Enders, C. (2004). Professional development in inquiry-based science for elementary teachers of diverse students. *Journal of Research in Science Teaching, 41*(10), 1021–1043.

Lee, O., Lewis, S., Adamson, K., Maerten-Rivera, J., & Secada, W. G. (2008). Urban elementary school teachers' knowledge and practices in teaching science to English language learners. *Science Education, 92*(4), 733–758.

Lee, O., & Luykx, A. (2005). Dilemmas in scaling up educational innovations with nonmainstream students in elementary school science. *American Educational Research Journal, 43,* 411–438.

Lee, O., Luykx, A., Buxton, C. A., & Shaver, A. (2007). The challenge of altering elementary school teachers' beliefs and practices regarding linguistic and cultural diversity in science instruction. *Journal of Research in Science Teaching, 44*(9), 1269–1291.

Lee, O., & Maerten-Rivera, J. (2012). Teacher change in elementary science instruction with English language learners: Results of a multi-year professional development intervention across multiple grades. *Teachers College Record, 114*(8), 1–44.

Lee, O., Mahotiere, M., Salinas, A., Penfield, R. D., & Maerten-Rivera, J. (2009). Science writing achievement among English language learners: Results of three-year intervention in urban elementary schools. *Bilingual Research Journal, 32*(2), 153–167.

Lee, O., Quinn, H., & Valdés, G. (2013). Science and language for English language learners: Language demands and opportunities in relation to Next Generation Science Standards. *Educational Researcher, 42*(4), 223–233.

Luykx, A., Lee, O., & Edwards, U. (2008). Lost in translation: Negotiating meaning in a beginning ESOL science classroom. *Educational Policy, 22*(5), 640–674.

Lynch, S., Kuipers, J., Pyke, C., & Szesze, M. (2005). Examining the effects of a highly rated science curriculum unit on diverse populations: Results from a planning grant. *Journal of Research in Science Teaching, 42*(8), 912–946.

Moje, E., Collazo, T., Carillo, R., & Marx, R. W. (2001). "Maestro, what is quality?": Examining competing discourses in project-based science. *Journal of Research in Science Teaching, 38*(4), 469–495.

National Center for Education Statistics. (2011). *The condition of education 2011* (NCES 2011–033). Washington, DC: U.S. Department of Education.

National Center for Education Statistics. (2012a). *Science 2011: National assessment of educational progress at Grade 8* (NCES 2012–465). Washington, DC: U.S. Department of Education.

National Center for Education Statistics. (2012b). *Trends in high school dropout and completion rates in the United States: 1972–2009.* Washington, DC: U.S. Department of Education.

National Clearinghouse for English Language Acquisition. (2007). *The growing numbers of limited English proficient students: 1996–2006.* Washington, DC: U.S. Department of Education Office of English Language Acquisition.

National Clearinghouse for English Language Acquisition. (2012). *The growing number of English learner students: 1995–2010.* Washington, DC: U.S. Department of Education Office of English Language Acquisition.

National Commission on Excellence in Education. (1983). *A nation at risk: The imperative for educational reform.* Washington, DC: U.S. Department of Education.

National Research Council. (1996). *National science education standards.* Washington, DC: National Academies Press.

National Research Council. (2007). *Taking science to school: Learning and teaching science in Grades K–8.* Washington, DC: National Academies Press.

National Research Council. (2011). *A framework for K–12 science education: Practices, crosscutting themes, and core ideas.* Washington, DC: National Academies Press.

National Science Foundation. (1998). *Infusing equity in systemic reform: An implementation scheme.* Washington, DC: Author.

No Child Left Behind (NCLB) Act. (2002). Public Law No. 107–110, 115 Stat. 1425.

Pandya, C., Batalova, J., & McHugh, M. (2011). *Limited English proficient individuals in the United States: Number, share, growth, and linguistic diversity.* Washington, DC: Migration Policy Institute.

Pew Research Center. (2012). *The rise of Asian Americans.* Washington, DC: Pew Social and Demographic Trends.

Race To The Top (RT³ Act of 2011, Senate Bill 844 (2011)).

Riggs, E. M. (2005). Field-based education and indigenous knowledge: Essential components of geoscience education for Native American communities. *Science Education, 89,* 296–313.

Rodriguez, A., & Berryman, C. (2002). Using sociotransformative constructivism to teach for understanding in diverse classrooms: A beginning teacher's journey. *American Educational Research Journal, 39*(4), 1017–1045.

Rodriguez, A., Collins-Parker, T., & Garza, J. (2013). Interpreting research on parent involvement and connecting it to the science classroom. *Theory Into Practice, 52*(1), 51–58.

Rodriguez, A., Zozakiewicz, C., & Yerrick, R. (2008). Students acting as change agents in culturally diverse schools. In A. J. Rodriguez (Ed.), *The multiple faces of agency: Innovative strategies for effecting change in urban school contexts* (pp. 47–72). Rotterdam, the Netherlands: Sense Publishing.

Rosebery, A. S., Ogonowski, M., DiSchino, M., & Warren, B. (2010). "The coat traps all your body heat": Heterogeneity as fundamental to learning. *Journal of the Learning Sciences, 19*(3), 322–357.

Rosebery, A. S., & Warren, B. (Eds.). (2008). *Teaching science to English language learners: Building on students' strengths.* Arlington, VA: National Science Teachers Association.

Rudolph, J. (2002). *Scientists in the classroom: The Cold War reconstruction of American science education.* New York: Palgrave.

Sable, J., & Plotts, C. (2010). *Public elementary and secondary school student enrollment and staff counts from the Common Core of Data: School year 2008–09.* Washington, DC: U.S. Department of Education National Center for Education Statistics.

Schmidt, W. H., McKnight, C. C., & Raizen, S. A. (1997). *A splintered vision: An investigation of U.S. science and mathematics education.* Dordrecht, the Netherlands: Kluwer.

Shavelson, R. J., & Towne, L. (Eds.). (2002). *Scientific research in education.* Washington, DC: National Academies Press.

Shaw, J. M. (1997). Threats to the validity of science performance assessments for English language learners. *Journal of Research in Science Teaching, 34*(7), 721–743.

Shaw, J. M. (2009). Science performance assessment and English learners: An exploratory study. *Electronic Journal of Literacy Through Science, 8*(3). Retrieved from http://ejlts.ucdavis.edu/article/2009/8/3/science-performance-assessment-and-english-learners-exploratory-study

Shaw, J. M., Bunch, G., & Geaney, E. (2010). Analyzing the language demands facing English learners on science performance assessments: The SALD framework. *Journal of Research on Science Teaching, 47*(8), 909–928.

Sheldon, S. B., & Epstein L. J. (2005). Involvement counts: Family and community partnerships and mathematics achievement. *Journal of Educational Research, 98*(4), 196–206.

Siegel, M. A. (2007). Striving for equitable classroom assessments for linguistic minorities: Strategies for and effects of revising life science items. *Journal of Research in Science Teaching, 44,* 864–881.

Solano-Flores, G. (2008). Who is given tests in what language by whom, when, and where? The need for probabilistic views of language in the testing of English language learners. *Educational Researcher, 37*(4), 189–199.

Solano-Flores, G., & Li, M. (2008). Examining the dependability of academic achievement measures for English-language learners. *Assessment for Effective Intervention, 33*(3), 135–144.

Solano-Flores, G., & Trumbull, E. (2003). Examining language in context: The need for new research and practice paradigms in the testing of English-language learners. *Educational Researcher, 32*(2), 3–13.

Stoddart, T., Pinal, A., Latzke, M., & Canaday, D. (2002). Integrating inquiry science and language development for English language learners. *Journal of Research in Science Teaching, 39*(8), 664–687.

Stoddart, T., Solis, J., Tolbert, S., & Bravo, M. (2010). A framework for the effective science teaching of English language learners in elementary schools. In D. Sunal, C. Sunal, & E. Wright (Eds.), *Teaching science with Hispanic ELLs in K–16 classrooms.* Charlotte, NC: Information Age Publishing.

Teachers of English to Speakers of Other Languages. (2006). *PreK–12 English language proficiency standards.* Alexandria, VA: Author.

Tharp, R. G. (1997). *From at-risk to excellence: Research, theory, and principles for practice.* Santa Cruz, CA: Center for Research on Education, Diversity & Excellence. Retrieved from www.cal.org/crede/pubs/researchreports.html

Tong, F., Irby, B., Lara-Alecio, R., Yoon, M., & Mathes, P. (2010). Hispanic English learners' responses to longitudinal English instructional intervention and the effect of gender: A multilevel analysis. *The Elementary School Journal, 110*(4), 542–566.

Trumbull, E., & Koelsch, N. (2011). Language-arts: Designing and using a reading assessment for learners transitioning to English-only instruction. In M. Rosario Basterra, E. Trumbull, & G. Solano-Flores (Eds.), *Cultural validity in assessment: Addressing linguistic and cultural diversity* (pp. 195–217). New York: Routledge.

U.S. Census Bureau. (2012). *Statistical abstract of the United States, 2012.* Washington, DC: U.S. Government Printing Office.

U.S. Department of Education. (2007). *Participation in education: Elementary and secondary education.* Washington, DC: Author.

Vijver, F., & Tanzer, N. (2004). Bias and equivalence in cross-cultural assessment: An overview. *European Review of Applied Psychology, 54*(2), 119–135.

Villegas, A. M. (2007). Dispositions in teacher education: A look at social justice. *Journal of Teacher Education, 58*(5), 370–380.

Warren, B., Ballenger, C., Ogonowski, M., Rosebery, A., & Hudicourt-Barnes, J. (2001). Rethinking diversity in learning science: The logic of everyday language. *Journal of Research in Science Teaching, 38*(5), 529–552.

Warren, B., & Rosebery, A. (2011). Navigating interculturality: African American male students in the science classroom. *Journal of African American Males in Education, 2*(1), 98–115.

Wayne, A. J., Yoon, K. S., Zhu, P., Cronen, S., & Garet, M. S. (2008). Experimenting with teacher professional development: Motives and methods. *Educational Researcher, 37*(8), 469–479.

Wong-Fillmore, L., & Snow, C. (2002). *What teachers need to know about language.* Washington DC: Center for Applied Linguistics.

Yore, L., Bisanz, G., & Hand, B. (2003). Examining the literacy component of science literacy: 25 years of language arts and science research. *International Journal of Science Education, 25*(6), 689–725.

Young, J. W., Steinberg, J., Cline, F., Stone, E., Martiniello, M., Ling, G., & Cho, Y. (2010). Examining the validity of standards-based assessments for initially fluent students and former English language learners. *Educational Assessment, 15*(2), 87–106.

12

Special Needs and Talents in Science Learning[1]

J. RANDY MCGINNIS AND SAMI KAHN

Every learner in science is unique with diverse abilities. Teachers as well as educational researchers have long recognized and used that understanding to varying degrees in their teaching and research. Learners in science who differ substantially in their performances from typical learner performances (physical, cognitive, or behavioral dimensions) and who need additional services and supports are the focus of this chapter. Those learners who exceed typical performances are referred to as possessing special talents; those learners who do not achieve up to the typical level are identified as having special needs. Both of these groups of learners require additional educational, social, or medical services to support them in learning and performing science. Professionals in the field of special education use the comprehensive term "exceptional learners" to refer to learners with learning and/or behavioral challenges, learners with physical or sensory impairments, and learners who are intellectually gifted or have a special talent (Hardman, Drew, & Egan, 2002; Heward, 2000). We continue use of that nomenclature to refer collectively to learners in science with special needs and talents.

Science education researchers interested in developing a knowledge base that would guide policy makers and teachers in achieving their longstanding goal of making science a discipline that all learners could learn, consider as an occupation, and apply in personal and societal decision-making processes, expressed commonly in the literature as "Science for All" (Fensham, 1985) or contemporarily as "All Standards, All Students" (Achieve, 2013a), have been attracted to studying these two groups of learners. The purpose of this chapter is to outline what is known about how exceptional learners learn science, including consideration of how the totality of science education (context, personnel, curriculum, and assessment) supports or hinders this process, and to use that understanding to make recommendations for future research directions. Included is discussion of how certain schools of thought on learning influence the research in this area.

Structurally, this chapter reviews in two parts the literature on science learning by exceptional learners. Part I focuses on the science learning population with special needs. Part II focuses on the science learning population with special talents.

Theoretical Perspectives Guiding Research on Exceptional Learners

There continues to be no one accepted theoretical model of learning that provides a grand explanation for why learners engage science in differing ways and at varying levels of achievement. Three prevailing different schools of thought on learning that have guided research on exceptional learners in science are the behavioral, developmental, and cognitive perspectives (Stefanich & Hadzegeorgiou, 2001). While the behaviorist perspective historically has dominated research by special educators in this area, a growing number of researchers, including those in science education dissatisfied with that perspective, have been drawn to more contemporary applications of cognitive science (National Research Council, 2007) that include an appreciation of social context (Rogoff, 1990). In addition, a fourth school of thought, a sociocultural perspective, also has its proponents. Consideration of these theoretical perspectives is critical due to the impact they have on researchers' question posing and interpretation of outcomes.

Behaviorist psychologists believe that learning consists of making connections between events (stimuli) and behaviors (responses). External forces, such as rewards and punishments, and drives, such as hunger, provide the learner motivation to make stronger connections between stimuli and behaviors—to learn. While the primary form of data valued in this theoretical perspective is observable behavior, theorists applying behaviorism to educational research have expanded on the theory to include hypotheses on mental states including thinking, understanding, and reasoning (Bransford, Brown, Cocking, Donovan, & Pellegrino, 2000). Behaviorists assert that instruction should be based on the identification of clear outcomes and be directed toward those outcomes. Instruction based on a behaviorist learning theory is referred to as explicit or direct instruction (Steele, 2005). Generally, classroom instruction is characterized as featuring much practice and review of skills and information until mastery is obtained. Developmental psychologists believe that the thinking of children is distinctly different from that of adults. They assert that as individuals progress through life, their thinking patterns change dramatically over short periods of time and then remain somewhat stable for an extended period. A key assumption is that rates of learning vary per individual. Developmental psychologists examine the external factors (such as science instruction) that might influence an individual's rate of intellectual maturity. A cognitive science perspective, referred to as constructivism in science education, examines mental functioning, in the individual and the social contexts, frequently by use of technology to collect biological data on the brain. It uses a multidisciplinary approach that incorporates developmental psychology, computer science, and neuroscience, as well as other fields of study. The testing of theories of teaching and learning characterizes studies in this perspective, which has dominated in science education for more than two decades and contrasts dramatically with the behaviorist perspective in educational applications except for the need for clear identification of clear instructional objectives. The sociocultural perspective is distinguished by its attention to the interaction between learners' mental functioning and their cultural, historical, and institutional settings (Wertsch & Kanner, 1992). A key assumption is that learners' mental development is the result of a complex interaction among multiple factors and not determined solely by their mental development.

Some researchers, influenced by findings from brain research, have proposed that there are disrupted brain functions in some learners that can be identified and hypothetically "rewired," producing additional compensatory activation in other brain regions (Shaywitz, 2003; Simos et al., 2002; Temple et al., 2003). However, other researchers have challenged these tenets, and no studies have been conducted that support such claims. Donald (2001) rejected the explanation that certain brain regions perform specialized operations. Instead, he stated that the mechanisms and connectivity for language are set by experience with countless interconnection points, or synapses, that connect neurons in various patterns. He concluded that learning and experience create and shape the brain's circuits, and therefore these circuits are not predetermined. Coles (2004) argued that brain researchers have misconstrued data and have drawn conclusions to justify unwarranted beliefs. Coles (2004) stated, "Dyslexia remains no more of a proven malady among a substantial percentage of beginning readers than when Glasow ophthalmologist James Hinshelwood first discussed it as 'congenital word-blindness' at the end of the 19th century" (p. 351).

Awareness of these four schools of thought assists researchers in their sense making of the reported studies on exceptional learners in science. While this scholarship area is oftentimes advocacy oriented, the observant reader will note that individual articles include reported data (either in empirical studies or summary articles) that can be inferred to reflect one of these theoretical perspectives or a blending of two or more. For example, many researchers holding a cognitive or sociocultural perspective place an emphasis on inquiry through problem posing and solving by application of scientific practices as an essential distinguishing feature of learning in science, while those taking a behaviorist perspective place emphasis on the mastery of skills and the learning of information generated by science. Likewise, the literature on inclusion may be viewed, in general, as being founded primarily on a learning perspective that places highest value on the social context and developmentalism, with some efforts made to incorporate a scientific thinking perspective.

Part I: Special Needs in Science Learning

Definitions

If education is devoted to offering opportunities for all students to gain sufficient schooling to help them make life choices and become productive members of society, it is essential that all teachers have the knowledge to make appropriate adaptations so that every student with special needs can become an active participant in the learning process. This basic statement brings to the forefront the complex nature of the issues of teaching science to students with disabilities. Because of that complexity, there has been much effort devoted recently to educate science teachers worldwide to learn how to make needed accommodations and modifications. Accommodations are services or supports that address how students access curriculum and instruction or demonstrate learning; they do not change the content or performance expectations. Modifications, on the other hand, adjust the content or performance expectations of the lesson or assessment in order to make success feasible for the learner (Nolet & McLaughlin, 2000). We use the term "adaptations" to refer to both types of adjustments collectively. Teachers need to implement a variety of adaptations in order to effectively differentiate the science curriculum for students with special needs (Finson, Ormsbee, & Jensen, 2011).

To understand the scope of the challenge, data from the U.S. school population provides one example. The United States Department of Education (National Center for Educational Statistics, 2012) indicated that 13.0% (6,432,944) of all prekindergarten through 12th-grade students (49,484,181) were identified as having some type of disability and that this percentage has remained above 13% since 2000. Of this group, most students are identified as having a specific learning disability (4.8%, or 2,375,241 students). Other commonly occurring disabilities include speech or language impairment (2.8%, or

TABLE 12.1
Students With Special Needs Served in Public Schools in the US, 2010–2011

Population Enrolled in Public Schools[1]	Percent of Students
Individuals with Disabilities	13.0
Autism	0.8
Deaf-blindness	#[2]
Developmental delay	0.8
Emotional disturbance	0.8
Hearing impairments	0.2
Intellectual disability	0.9
Multiple disabilities	0.3
Orthopedic impairments	0.1
Other health impairments[3]	1.4
Specific learning disabilities	4.8
Speech or language impairments	2.8
Traumatic brain injury	0.1
Visual impairments	0.1

[1] Total student enrollment, all grades, 49,484,181.

[2] Rounds to zero.

[3] Other health impairments include having limited strength, vitality, or alertness due to chronic or acute health problems such as a heart condition, tuberculosis, rheumatic fever, nephritis, asthma, sickle cell anemia, hemophilia, epilepsy, lead poisoning, leukemia, diabetes, attention deficit disorder, or attention deficit hyperactivity disorder.

1,344, 000 students) and other health impairments (1.4% or 692,779 students). Other less common disabilities (less than 1.0% of the total student population) include intellectual disability (0.9% or 445,358 students), autism, developmental and emotional disturbance (each, 0.8%, or 395,873 students), hearing impairment (0.2%, or 98,968 students), and orthopedic impairment, traumatic brain injury, and visual impairments (each, 0.1%, or 49,484 students). The deaf-blindness disability is the least, and the number of students rounds off to 0%. See Table 12.1.

Students with special needs are typically considered to divide into two large categories that can overlap: those with physical impairments (such as deaf-blind and orthopedic impairments) and those with cognitive, social-personal, or intellectual disabilities (such as autism and specific learning disabilities). The first category consists of individuals with physical impairments, many of whom are considered to have the cognitive, social, and intellectual capabilities to potentially become career scientists, mathematicians, or engineers. Approximately a quarter of the students with disabilities (1,608,236) would fall into this group. Approximately 22% (353,811) of these students have speech and language impairments that require minimal accommodation in a science classroom or laboratory. This group is still significantly underrepresented in the disciplines of science. Historically, members of this group that succeeded in science were persons of special talents and exceptional persistence.

The second category of students, approximately 75% of the total U.S. school-age population with disabilities, consisting of around 4,824,708 students with cognitive or social-personal disabilities, often experiences difficulty with science in secondary and postsecondary education.

Some do have potential for the highest levels of science achievement, but they need assistance to have a career in science. For the others, a reasonable goal is general science literacy as opposed to a professional career in a science field.

In higher education, the challenge becomes one of overcoming the barriers that prevent capable students with disabilities from pursuing college and entering the STEM workforce, where they are underrepresented (National Science Foundation [NSF], 2011). Transition to higher education is one roadblock. A recent study using data from the National Longitudinal Transition Study—2 found that students with autism spectrum disorder were more likely than their typical peers to major in STEM fields once in college yet have one of the lowest overall college enrollment rates among students with and without disabilities (Wei, Yu, Shattuck, McCracken, & Blackorby, 2012). Attrition throughout the higher education pipeline contributes to persons with disabilities' underrepresentation among recipients of doctorates in STEM fields (NSF, 2011). Identifying and promoting practices that encourage students with disabilities to pursue and persist in STEM is critical to ensuring more equitable representation.

Exceptional Students and Issues of Race

In a seminal report that is often cited, the *National Research Council Report on Minority Students in Special Education and Gifted Education* (National Research Council [NRC], 2002) indicated that minority students are overrepresented in U.S. special education programs. States vary widely in how they determine students with disabilities. The NRC reported the percentage of minority students in special education categories as compared to the majority population. The percentages of minority students identified with a learning disability (the largest classification of disabilities) were noted as follows: Native American and Alaska Native students 7.45%, Black students 6.49%, Hispanic students 6.44%. In comparison, the percentage was 6.02% for White students. Percentages for developmental disabilities were 2.64% for Black students and 1.28% for American Indians and Alaska Native Students. In comparison, at the extreme, the ratio for Black students being identified as developmentally delayed was 10 times higher in Alabama than in New Jersey. Emotional disability ratios were 1.45% for Black students and 1.03% for American Indians and Alaska Native students.

Based on these figures, researchers since 2002 have reported on the continuing disproportionality of the overrepresentation of minorities in U.S. special education and the underrepresentation of minorities in U.S. gifted education. A prevailing view is that the figures hold the danger of reinforcing the notion that some ethnic groups are superior to others. A number of potential factors can be generated to explain the performance of certain groups, including linguistic ability, poverty, family dysfunction, transience, and devaluing of academic achievement. As a result, one research direction taken has been to re-examine the referral/nomination process, including the identification criteria, as to its impact on minority student placement in special education (Jordan, Bain, McCallum, & Bell, 2012). Another direction taken has been to study the impact of the school context, including charter schools (Algozzine, 2005; Grant, 2005), on minority student placements in special education. The assumption made is that these are mutable circumstances. Appropriate interventions, supported as necessary by legal action that alleges equal protection violations protected by the law, can serve to lessen their damaging effects collectively on population groups (Welner, 2006).

The educational research community at times questions the labeling of students as holding special needs in science (or otherwise) by school personnel. In challenge to the research on special needs, Gray and Denicolo (1998) contested research that purported to be objective and falls in an empirical-analytic paradigm. Instead, they advocated an alternative paradigm that attempts to challenge the normalization approach to teaching learners designated as having special needs. In science education, in a study that examined the science participation in an environmental education activity by two students who were labeled by their school as learning disabled, Roth (2002) supported Mehan's (1993) argument that the placement of learners into a special-needs category resulted from how they were assessed in specific learning situations and did not convey valid information as to their attributes across situations. These findings have direct implication for science teacher education programs, which address the important topic of how teachers "code" students' behaviors in ways that reinforce who can and cannot do science (Shippen, Curtis, & Miller, 2009).

Within the field of science education, research has examined key science education documents to see to what extent, if any, they have supported science education's goal of science literacy for all, regardless of any categorization of learners' abilities (McGinnis, 2000). The primary purpose of such documents is to provide a vision of the teaching and learning of science and to provide criteria to measure progress toward that vision. For example, in the *U.S. National Science Education Standards* (National Research Council [NRC], 1996), students with special needs were viewed explicitly as participating (as fits their ability and interest) in inquiry-based science classrooms.

The new U.S. national standards for science, the Next Generation Science Standards (NGSS), assert that they promote an equitable perspective as represented in the phrase "all standards; all students" (Achieve, 2013a, p. 1). Included is an appendix that delineates the challenges and opportunities presented by the adoption of the NGSS for "non-dominant student groups" (p. 1), including students with disabilities and gifted students.

Legislation Impacting the Rights of Persons With Special Needs

In addition to considering learning theory and science education policy documents, it is also necessary for researchers in this area to be knowledgeable about how legislation impacts the educational rights of persons with special needs. It is informative in regard to the science education documents to note that Collins (1998) stated that educational policy documents were designed in a political context and were therefore "political in context, political in process, and political in intent" (p. 711). Special education in the United States found its present profile and substance through federal law, the Civil Rights Movement, and resulting court cases, as well as the evolutionary influences of politics and society (Smith, Polloway, Patton, & Dowdy, 1998). The legislation having the greatest impact on educational practice in U.S. schools was the Education for All Handicapped Children Act (1975), passed by the U.S. Congress as PL94–142 and amended and renamed in 1990 as the Individuals with Disabilities Education Act (IDEA). This law, which has since undergone several amendments and reauthorizations, requires that children with special needs be provided a free and appropriate public education (FAPE) in the least restrictive environment (LRE). The IDEA mandates that students with special needs be integrated into general education classes with typical peers to the maximum extent appropriate. The major components of this landmark legislation, which now covers students with disabilities from birth to age 21, include FAPE for all eligible students, the creation, review, and revision of an IEP (individualized education program), a guarantee of placement in the LRE, and detailed parental rights (Smith, 2005). Both the IDEA and its predecessor, statute PL 94–142, represented critical turning points for those with disabilities, as these laws addressed the issue of where students with disabilities would be educated, not simply if they would be educated. As a result of the passage of PL 94–142, many students with mild disabilities were placed in the LRE (Smith et al., 1998), while school districts offered separate classes and separate schools for those with more severe disabilities. At the time, most advocates considered this an equitable move forward because students with greater needs had previously been denied public education in any form. The Regular Education Initiative (REI) associated with PL 94–142 was viewed as a major first step in the movement to include students with special needs in typical education settings (Fuchs & Fuchs, 1994; Will, 1986), and although the term "inclusion" did not appear in the law itself, the law effectively made science (and other subjects) more accessible to students with disabilities.

The most recent reauthorization of the IDEA occurred in 2004 when the law was amended and renamed the Individuals with Disabilities Education Improvement Act (IDEA, 2004). The goal of the reauthorized law was to forge a stronger connection between special education and the general education curriculum while ensuring due process and high standards for students with disabilities (Arthaud, Aram, Breck, Doelling, & Bushrow, 2007). In addition to emphasizing planning for transition toward higher education, employment, and independence, the IDEA 2004 was promulgated to align with the No Child

Left Behind Act of 2001 (NCLB, 2002). Together, these statutes require that special education teachers be "highly qualified" in the content area they teach and that states include most students with disabilities in statewide standardized assessments with accommodations as needed. Alternative assessments must be developed for the small percentage of students who are determined to have cognitive impairments precluding participation in the standardized assessment even with accommodations. In essence, these mandates require schools to be both "equitable and excellent" (McLeskey, Waldron, & Redd, 2012, p. 1) in meeting students' needs. To ensure that students with disabilities achieve "adequate yearly progress" (AYP) and are taught by "highly qualified teachers" as required by these laws, many schools responded by including more students with disabilities in general education classes, particularly at the secondary level (McLeskey, Landers, Williamson, & Hoppey, 2012). Content areas including science have been strongly impacted by this movement. As a result of emphases on access to general education curriculum and environments, approximately 95% of the 6.5 million school-age students with disabilities are educated in regular schools, with a majority of them spending at least 80% of their day in the general classroom (U.S. Department of Education, 2011). In their survey of 137 school districts in Texas, Vannest and colleagues (2009) found that fifth-grade students with disabilities were educated in a variety of instructional settings for science, with almost all participating districts offering general education settings as an option.

Over several decades, legislation impacting persons with disabilities has evolved from the LRE to the Regular Education Initiative (Will, 1986) to full inclusion and, finally, toward full access to general education curriculum (McGuire, Scott, & Shaw, 2006). Accordingly, the questions regarding the education of students with disabilities have clearly shifted from where students are educated to what and how students are taught and assessed (Soukup, Wehmeyer, Bashinski, & Bovaird, 2007).

The U.S. Congress has passed many laws designed to deal with the rights of people with disabilities, but it has taken much time to enact and enforce them. A summary of significant U.S. legislative actions related to the education of learners with special needs includes:

1. *Sections 501, 503, and 504 of the Rehabilitation Act of 1973.* The major impact of this legislation was to prohibit federal agencies, federal contractors, and recipients of federal financial assistance from discriminating against otherwise qualified persons with disabilities solely on the basis of disability (Tucker & Goldstein, 1992).
2. *Section 02 Amendments, 1978 & 1979.* These amendments authorized federal agencies to provide grants to state units overseeing work with people with disabilities; establish and operate comprehensive rehabilitation centers; and make the remedies, procedures, and

rights of Title VI (Civil Rights Act, 1964) available to section 504 discrimination victims.
3. *Section 504 Amendment, Civil Rights Restoration Act of 1987 [CRRA].* This amendment clarified "program or activity" to mean all of the operations of a college, university, or other postsecondary institution, and that if federal financial assistance was extended to any part of an institution, all of the operations were covered.
4. *Education for All Handicapped Children Act [EAHCA], 1975.* This act required states to provide all children with disabilities with FAPE. This is the predecessor statute to the IDEA.
5. *Americans with Disabilities Act [ADA], 1990, 2008.* This sweeping legislation protects the civil rights of people with disabilities in employment, access to public services such as transportation, and access to public entities including public schools. It ensures that "reasonable accommodations" are utilized to prevent discrimination and make comparable benefits and services available to persons with disabilities as those offered to their nondisabled peers.
6. *Individuals with Disabilities Education Act [IDEA], 1997, 2004, overdue for reauthorization in 2013.* This act contains provisions concerning the rights of individuals with disabilities to receive an equivalent education and the opportunity to learn with other students of all abilities. It requires the participation of the regular classroom teacher in the IEP process and in the delivery of an equivalent education.
7. *No Child Left Behind Act [NCLB], 2002.* This legislation emphasizes accountability and requires that all students, including those with disabilities, are taught by "highly qualified teachers," are assessed to ensure "adequate yearly progress," and receive instruction informed by "scientifically based research."

Review of the Literature

For heuristic purposes, the review of the literature on special learners in science is presented in two subsections: Curriculum and Instruction and Assessment.

Curriculum and Instruction

The literature concerning curriculum and instruction in science for learners with special needs is associated with collaboration (the sharing of the teaching responsibility among educators of different professional expertise, content, and pedagogy) and with the advocacy and study of inclusion (the placement of learners with disabilities in the general classroom, including science).

COLLABORATION

Science teachers often find themselves isolated in their efforts to serve students with special needs who are placed in their classrooms (McGinnis & Nolet, 1995). Isolation makes teachers more resistant to the changes involved in including students with special needs. Perceptions that may interfere with effective collaboration can become ingrained in professional practice. Unless they are brought to the surface, they serve as persistent bottlenecks to collegiality between professionals.

Inclusion necessitates collaboration between educators who have traditionally represented dual systems of general education and special education. While there is no one standard model of collaborative service, Bauwens (1991) described three common models: teacher assistance teams, collaborative consultation, and cooperative teaching. Of the three basic models, cooperative teaching is the more frequently implemented practice in most school districts (Reeve & Hallahan, 1994). Cooperative teaching, also generically referred to as "collaboration," involves general and special educators coordinating efforts to jointly teach heterogeneous groups of students in integrated settings to meet the needs of all students (Bauwens & Hourcade, 1997).

McGinnis and Nolet (1995) reported one possible model for science teacher preparation and science instruction when the goal was for general and special educators to work collaboratively as a way of meeting the science content needs (curricular, instructional, and evaluative) of learners with disabilities. They presented a model that was designed to bridge the gap between the fields of special education and science education by focusing on the development of what McGinnis and Nolet termed "a new professional relationship between the practitioners" (p. 32). The model was built on the premise that if the needs of the student with disabilities were to be met in authentic school settings, then the focus of the collaboration between the general and the special educator should be on science content and the effective teaching of such knowledge. Differing aspects of expertise were identified for the general science educator as key science knowledge forms: facts, concepts, principles, and procedures. They also identified for special educators the pedagogy of students with special needs: designing instruction, implementing classroom management, and motivational strategies).

Research in instituting collaboration has found that the underlying belief system within a school building must be examined thoroughly before embarking on a mission of collaborative change. The building administration must embrace the theory and concept behind collaboration, support the teachers initiating such a change, and also provide structural supports that will allow the collaboration to occur (Walter-Thomas, Bryant, & Land, 1996).

Special and general educators can work collaboratively on making adaptations, using the student's IEP as a framework and reference (Golomb & Hammeken, 1996). However, research also suggests that the role of the special educator in science may be limited to a support role for students and not an authentic co-teaching role (Moin, Magiera, & Zigmond, 2009). Many teachers believe that they are skilled and accommodating and are willing to serve on IEP teams in all aspects of planning and implementation of appropriate education for students with special needs (Friend & Bursuck, 1999). However,

many teachers also believe that mechanisms are lacking to capitalize on their skills and respect their professional talents and limitations.

Zembylas and Isenbarger (2002), in a small case-study research design, examined the role of teachers' care and enthusiasm (measured qualitatively by how the teachers interacted with the learners) during science instruction of a student with special needs. They found that the combination of an activity-oriented science curriculum and a caring teaching construct (respecting their talents and strengths) was an effective approach.

INCLUSION

Mainstreaming, integration, and inclusion have all been used to describe the movement to meet the needs of learners with special needs in the general school setting. Inclusive schools are those in which students with and without special needs are educated together within one educational system (Stainback & Stainback, 1990). Research in this area is extensive. As a result, this section is presented in subsections identified by their headings.

Science as an inclusive setting. Current research on effective schools and effective classroom practices supports the integration of students with special needs into general education classes as a way of enhancing their academic performances (National Council on Disability, 2011). The literature shows, however, that this conclusion has proceeded in a nonlinear manner with several challenges that needed to be overcome.

As reported by McGinnis (2000), teachers inclined toward inclusion (a minority of all teachers) have identified science classes as especially suited for students with disabilities. These teachers identify the perceived relevance of the content, the possibility for practical experiences, and the opportunity for group learning with typical peers as the strengths of science classes for inclusion purposes (Mastropieri et al., 1998). However, this perspective does not mean that most contemporary teachers in science (or otherwise) are comfortable including students with disabilities in their classrooms (McCann, 1998; Scruggs & Mastropieri, 1994). Instead, as reported by Norman, Caseau, and Stefanich (1998), both elementary and secondary science teachers identify teaching students with special needs as one of their primary concerns.

Contrary to the teachers' misgivings, findings reported in the literature appear to support inclusion (including in science learning contexts) as a more desirable alternative than segregated instruction for students with disabilities. Ferguson and Asch (1989) found that the more time children with disabilities spent in general classes, the more they achieved as adults in employment and continuing education. This held true regardless of gender, race, socioeconomic status (SES), type of disability, or the age at which the child gained access to general education. In a review of three meta-analyses that looked at the most effective setting for educating students with special needs, Baker, Wang, and Walberg (1994) concluded that "students [with disabilities] educated in general classes do better academically and socially than comparable students in noninclusive settings" (p. 34). Their review yielded the same results regardless of the type of disability or grade level.

Regarding students with severe disabilities, Hollowood, Salisbury, Rainforth, and Palombaro (1995) found that including these students in the general education classroom was not detrimental to classmates. Other researchers found such inclusion enhanced classmates' as well as their own learning and yielded social and emotional benefits for all students, with self-esteem and attendance improving for some students considered at risk (Costello, 1991). This research, coupled with strong public press to change current models of delivery in schools, provided a strong impetus for major educational reform.

Some researchers have generated questions about serving mildly developmentally delayed students via pull-out programs because of their limited growth abilities (Epps & Tindall, 1987). Other researchers have indicated that providing adaptations within the general education classroom instead of pull-out programs may prove to be more effective (Baker & Zigmond, 1990).

Supporters of the early inclusion movement (1980s) cited such claims as basic rights of all individuals to have equal opportunity to life in a typical manner and attend school with typical peers, to participate as fully as possible (Ferguson, 1995; McNulty, Connolly, Wilson, & Brewer, 1996). Researchers claimed that all students would benefit from having students with special needs in the general classroom (Lipsky & Gartner, 1998; McLeskey & Waldron, 1996; Stainback, Stainback, & Stefanich, 1996). Mercer, Lane, Jordan, Allsopp, and Eisele (1996) found that teaching methods and strategies utilized in special education classrooms did not differ so drastically from those used in general classes. Service models that required the students to leave the classroom for prescriptive services denied the students much valuable instructional time and socialization in the general classroom (Sapon-Shevin, 1996). Wang and Reynolds (1996) reported that when students with disabilities left their class to attend resource or pull-out programs they incurred risk of being negatively labeled and stigmatized.

In meta-analyses that examined the best setting for students with special needs, Baker and colleagues (1994) and Stainback and colleagues (1996) reported that learning core subjects such as social studies, science, and mathematics is beneficial for the long-term for students with disabilities, including those with severe disabilities. These researchers and others have documented that adaptations are often needed if students with special needs are to receive instruction in the content areas. However, the expertise of the general classroom science teacher to adapt lessons for students has been identified as an area of need in professional development. Cawley (1994) reported that science teachers generally have little experience or preparation teaching students with disabilities and, in general,

special educators have little or no exposure to science education. More recently, Kahn and Lewis (2013) found in their survey of 855 U.S. science teachers that nearly one third of the study's participants had received no training in teaching science to students with disabilities, while those who did cited "on-the-job training" as the most frequent source.

Lang (1994) found that the majority of instruction deaf students receive in science is by teachers with inadequate content preparation in the discipline. Less than 5% of teachers of deaf children reported a major in the physical sciences. Lang concluded, "Although 86% of deaf students report liking science, their academic preparation is inadequate for post-secondary education" (p. 148).

In a study focused on undergraduate science teacher preparation, McGinnis (2003) reported that teacher interns (general education and special education populations collaboratively learning pedagogy) expressed differing beliefs concerning the inclusion of students with special needs in science classrooms. A significant finding was that the general education majors were more likely to support the inclusion of students with developmental delays while those majoring in special education expressed reservations. An examination of the teacher interns' epistemological perspectives of learning (cognitive based or behavioral based), as well as their perspectives on group participation in inclusion classroom settings, offered explanatory insight into their inclusion/exclusion decision making. In addition, McGinnis reported an analysis of the ways in which teacher interns modified their science lesson plans to include a hypothetical learner with a developmental delay. In the majority of instances in which interns supported the inclusion of the learner with special needs in general science lessons, the pedagogical action they took was to have others (the students' peers or a teacher's aide) rather than the science teacher provide the learner support in the classroom, typically addressing only social needs. It was rare for any intern to use the ideas recommended by the literature to meet the student's intellectual needs. McGinnis concluded,

> As a field, science educators are in moral jeopardy without a moral perspective in making decisions on the inclusion/ exclusion of students with disabilities, particularly those with developmental disabilities, in the science classroom.
> (p. 212)

In another study conducted in a higher education context, Moriarty (2007) conducted a mixed-methods study to examine inclusive pedagogy by STEM faculty at three community colleges. The goal was to identify barriers to inclusive methods in science education. One hundred fifty-one community college STEM faculty completed an online questionnaire, 11 were interviewed, and 9 were observed. Community colleges are particularly important to study as they enroll many students with disabilities in postsecondary education. Moriarty found that the community college STEM instructors used a greater variety of teaching methods than prior research of 4-year colleges indicated. The community college instructors also had awareness of the need for differentiated pedagogy, but there existed an observable gap between knowledge of pedagogy and actual implementation in the classroom.

Adaptations to facilitate inclusion and instruction of students with special needs in science. The inclusion initiative has resulted in efforts to adapt science curriculum and instruction to provide students with special needs with rich experiences that they may not receive in traditional settings. However, due to the limited science background of many general educators, adapting science curriculum can present special challenges. According to a comprehensive review of the relevant research by Scruggs and Mastropieri (1994), classroom teachers can successfully include students with disabilities in science when the following are present: administrative support, support from special educators, an accepting classroom atmosphere, effective teaching skills, student-to-student peer assistance, and disability-specific teaching skills.

When students with special needs are included for science instruction, the most commonly used approach is the content approach (Scruggs & Mastropieri, 1993). In this approach, textbooks are the primary source of curriculum and instruction. A contrasting approach is the activity-oriented approach. In this approach, the teacher may still employ direct instruction, but students are also actively engaged in the exploration of science concepts (Scruggs & Mastropieri, 1993). In the activity-oriented approach, the use of the textbook and the need for acquisition of new vocabulary is significantly decreased, and students can apply the processes of science—observation, classification, measurement, comparison, predictions, and making inferences. Activity-oriented approaches to science that address fewer topics in greater depth can be especially beneficial for students with special needs (Patton, 1995). Both content- and activity-oriented approaches can be adapted and modified to meet the diverse learning needs of students.

While general education teachers implement a wide variety of adaptations to meet student needs, they do not always find that all types of adaptations are as readily implemented as others. The most feasible adaptations centered on using positive methods and multisensory techniques that were readily integrated into daily classroom routines (Johnson & Pugach, 1990). Adaptations less favorably rated involved dealing with students individually.

Stefanich (1983) identified the attributes of teachers in effective schools that support the instruction of students with special needs: maintain a clear focus on academic goals; select instructional goals; perceive the students as able learners; implement an evaluation system based on individual student learning rather than on a comparison with other students' achievements; accurately diagnose student learning needs to foster high student achievement; prepare lessons (including adaptations) in advance; meet

students' needs in both academic achievement and socialization; be readily available to consult with students about issues and problems; attend staff development courses to continue your professional development; and keep parents informed and involved. Teachers can also play a substantial role in fostering scientific habits of mind in their students with special needs. In their instrumental cross-case study of three earth science classrooms in three high schools for deaf students, Kahn, Feldman, and Cooke (2013) found that teachers can promote the development of autonomy and inquiry in their students by actively engaging in open-ended questioning, encouraging students to collaborate, allowing students to make and correct their own mistakes, connecting science to real-world contexts and careers, and respecting the individuality of each student by not making assumptions about their abilities based on their disability.

Multimodality instruction is especially critical in helping students with disabilities gain a familiarity with the content material. Scruggs, Mastropieri, Bakken, and Brigham (1993), in presenting suggestions for teaching science lessons to students with disabilities, stated that students with disabilities are likely to encounter far fewer problems when participating in activity-oriented approaches to science education. Wood (1990) noted that strategies that lend multiple exposures to new terms and concepts enhance opportunities for all students to understand that content more fully. As result, actual examples or models are considered to be especially helpful to students with disabilities.

Curricular adaptations are often varied according to content and grade-level expectations. They can be designed for groups of students and for individual students. Booth and Ainscow (1998) suggested that one type of curricular adaptation is allowing students to participate in setting their own learning and social objectives combined with the teachers' objectives in the same areas. The students can then evaluate their progress on their goals as well as the teacher's goals. However, Stainback and colleagues (1996) warned that writing separate or varying learning outcomes for one student or small groups of students can foster a sense of isolation and separateness in the general education setting.

The process by which teachers implement adaptations. In inclusive settings, instruction can be adapted to ensure the academic success of all students (Smith et al., 1998). But to do this in content areas, such as science, a match needs to exist between the student's abilities and learning preferences and the curriculum and instructional methodologies. Stainback and colleagues (1996) stated, "Some students exhibit learned helplessness when there is not a good match between learning objectives and student attributes" (p. 14). Making adaptations for students is one way to create that match (Salisbury et al., 1994).

If teachers are given structures and supports for implementing adaptations, they will use them effectively in the general education classroom (Fuchs, Fuchs, Hamlett, Phillips, & Karns, 1995). Scott, Vitale, and Masten (1998) reported that when these support systems are in place, teachers make the necessary adaptations for students. Udvari-Solner (1996) found that when teachers decide what adaptations need to be implemented, they engage in a personal, reflective dialog with self-questioning. This leads to these same questions being posed when they meet in a group setting with other educators and parents. Parents often desire the opportunity to work collaboratively with teachers when determining appropriate adaptations for their children (National Council on Disability, 1989). This collaboration can foster positive relations between home and school.

When teachers determine if adaptations should be made, the next question to consider is, what are the goals of such adaptations? Researchers such as that by Salisbury and associates (1994) argued that curriculum adaptations should achieve two main goals: to promote positive student outcomes and to optimize the physical, social, and instructional inclusion of the student in ongoing classroom lessons and activities.

Creating an inclusive science classroom is thought to be a balance of designing an accepting environment, implementing effective instructional techniques, and adapting curriculum, materials, and instruction. Inclusive science classrooms are important for students (Patton, 1995). Organizing space and materials in science classrooms to allow access and participation by all students is an ongoing area of investigation to meet the needs of learners with special needs. The fundamental goal of this initiative, referred to as universal design or universal design for learners (UDL; Trundle, 2008), is to design environments, products, services, and resources to be usable by all people, to the greatest extent possible, without the need for adaptation or specialized design. As stated by McGinnis (2013) in a review of UDL,

> The goal of UDL is to design upfront and on-the-spot interactions, environments, products, services, and resources to be accessible by all learners, to the greatest extent possible (Hitchcock, Meyer, Rose, & Jackson, 2002; Kurtts, Matthews, & Smallwood, 2009). A hope held by many is that rigorous and systematic studies in UDL may be supported with significant resources as a way to lead to major breakthroughs in meeting the needs of students with special needs across the content areas, including science.
>
> (p. 48)

Unfortunately, the typical design for a science classroom or laboratory that has not benefited from the UDL initiative has been guided by the needs of the average able-bodied user. Therefore, it is often necessary to make major physical accommodations for students in science with significant disabilities or health impairments.

Designing and implementing curricular and instructional adaptations in the science classroom is similar to adaptations in other content areas. However, science adaptations can sometimes pose special challenges due to the nature of experiments and the materials used (Stefanich,

1994). Teachers must plan lesson adaptations in advance and anticipate difficulties that students may encounter with the materials needed or the science activity.

When teachers feel that the types of adaptations are feasible and desirable, they will use them (Ysseldyke, Thurlow, Wotruba, & Nania, 1990). In inclusive settings in which adaptations are made, all children can learn, feel a sense of belonging, and achieve their educational and social goals (Winter, 1997). However, many teachers also believe that mechanisms are lacking to capitalize on their skills and respect their professional talents and limitations.

The role of the general educator in the development, implementation, and evaluation of IEPs is a critical issue in response to compliance efforts of schools to the IDEA (Sapon-Shevin, 1996). Studies at the secondary level indicate that while the majority of general education teachers who had learners with special needs included in their classes felt successful, more than one third of them received no prior or ongoing preparation or professional development for inclusion, and less than one-half had been involved in development of the IEP (Rojewski & Pollard, 1993). Other findings indicated that teachers did willingly make specialized adaptations when the IEP teams advised them to do so and supported the teachers (Sapon-Shevin, 1996).

Mastropieri, Scruggs, and Magnusen (1999) reported the findings of several extended classroom investigations in science education that included students with special needs. In the investigations, certified teachers implemented the science instruction over extended time periods to their students (with and without disabilities). In all cases, the science curricula were adapted as necessary to support the successful participation and learning of students with disabilities. In all of the implementations, activities-based curriculum materials were used solely or in combination or comparison with textbook-based curriculum materials. Findings across all classroom implementations suggested that students with special needs learned more and reported greater enjoyment from the activities-based science curriculum. Teachers noted that during activities-oriented instruction, students appeared more motivated to learn and to participate in class and demonstrated more on-task behaviors. However, teachers also reported that activities-oriented instruction involved considerably more teacher preparation time, behavior-management skills, and organizational skills than traditional textbook instruction.

In a study by Mastropieri, Scruggs, and Butcher (1997), the purpose was to determine whether students with learning disabilities (LD) and mild mental retardation (MR) differed from typically achieving students with respect to inductive thinking on an inquiry-learning task involving pendulum motion. Twenty typically achieving students, 18 students with LD, and 16 students with MR were provided individually with guided coaching in a pre-specified sequence of steps, intended to promote induction of the association between pendulum length and pendulum motion. After the initial guided activity, 75% of the typically achieving students and 50% of the students with LD but none of the students with MR provided the correct induction. More than one fourth of the students with LD and nearly all of the students with MR required all of the prescribed coaching levers, including direct explanation of the rule. Students with LD and MR were less likely to correctly answer transfer/application questions. Therefore, the researchers concluded that to the extent that inquiry tasks are developmentally appropriate and carefully structured, learning may be more successful for students with mild disabilities. To the extent, however, that students are expected to "discover" new rules and generalizations on their own with little or no special support, learning is likely to be less successful.

Cawley, Hayden, Cade, and Baker-Kroczynski (2002) studied a science project taught to junior high school students with severe emotional disturbances or learning disabilities in the general education science classroom. The study was a small case study ($n = 16$). The outcomes of the project indicated there were no behavioral difficulties in the form of discipline referrals reported for the students with disabilities during the science class. Academic performance was measured by a districtwide science test and final grade. The authors reported that the academic success of the students with emotional disturbances or learning disabilities was comparable to the passing rate of the other students. Eleven of the 16 students in special education (69%) passed the district exam. Their pass rate was equal to the rate at which the other students passed the exam. Of note was that the researchers found that the behavior of the students with special needs posed no problem in the science class. In addition, the behavior of the other students was not affected in a deleterious way by the presence of the students with special needs. In fact, the researchers reported improvement in the behavior of the general education students: in one case, a class had 50% fewer discipline referrals than did a class that did not have any students with special needs.

McCarthy (2005) examined how 18 students with special needs (serious emotional disturbances) learned science in two different instruction environments. Students in one classroom received a traditional textbook approach to science content, whereas students in another classroom received science instruction by a hands-on, thematic approach. Over the course of instruction (8 weeks), data were collected regarding students' behavior and achievement. Results indicated that, overall, students in the hands-on instructional program performed significantly better than the students in the textbook program on two of three measures of science achievement, a hands-on assessment and a short-answer test. Of particular note was that the use of alternative assessment (the hands-on assessment) provided a nontraditional method for the students with special needs to demonstrate science content knowledge and practices. The students did not differ on a multiple-choice-format test. With regard to behavior, there were no significant differences in behavioral problems

found between the two groups of students over the course of the study.

An experimental design study by Bay, Staver, Bryan, and Hale (1992) examined the science achievement of third- and fourth-grade students ($n = 103$), some with a diagnosed special need ($n = 16$), in instruction environments that used either direct instruction or discovery learning. Two experimenter-developed assessment devices were constructed for this study, a 20-item science test and performance-based assessment procedure. All test items were read aloud to the students to control for differences in reading ability. This written test was used as a pretest, posttest, and measure of retention. The performance-based assessment, which required students to determine the variable that affects the length of time of a pendulum swing, was constructed to determine the degree to which students had generalized the scientific process learned in the lessons. The researchers found that students with typical and special needs learned equally well as measured by an immediate posttest, but students in the discovery teaching condition retained the material longer. Furthermore, students with special needs who were in the discovery condition performed better than their counterparts in the direct instruction condition on the performance-based measure. The results of this study challenged the notion that the teaching behavior typical of direct instruction systems creates the most effective learning environments for all curricular areas.

Lynch and colleagues (2007) reported on the results of a quasi-experimental study of the implementation of a science unit, Chemistry That Applies (CTA), with learners with special needs ($N = 202$) in general education classrooms. An analysis of the effect sizes for students with special needs who were taught CTA indicated they were basically the same as those obtained for the entire aggregate group, that is, small to medium effect sizes. The results supported the claims that "instruction that includes guided inquiry, hands-on science, and students working in heterogeneous lab groups can be appropriate and effective for students with special needs" (p. 219).

Mastropieri and colleagues (2006) conducted a study designed to compare quantitative outcomes associated with classwide peer tutoring that used differentiated hands-on activities versus teacher-directed instruction for students with mild disabilities. The context of the study was inclusive eighth-grade science classes. In a randomized field trial design, 13 classes ($n = 213$ students: 109 males and 104 females) that included 44 students with special needs participated in 12-week sessions. The experimental classes received units of differentiated, peer-mediated, hands-on instruction. The control classes received traditional science instruction. Results indicated that the hands-on activities done in collaborative groups statistically enhanced learning of middle school science content on posttests and on state high-stakes tests for all students. Furthermore, the students indicated that they enjoyed using the activities in science education.

In a study that examined the role of task analysis in inquiry-based science instruction, Courtade, Browder, Spooner, and DiBiase (2010) focused their attention first on the education the science teachers needed to carry out the instructional activity. After conducting professional development on task analysis, they found that the science teachers successfully mastered the skills and knowledge required and were able to apply them. Measurements indicated that all students increased inquiry skills completed independently. The researchers concluded that an advantage of using task analysis over daily skills curriculum is that it is more generalizable across content areas. Similar results regarding the use of task analysis in science education were reported by Spooner, Knight, Browder, Jimenez, and DiBiase (2011), who conducted a meta-analysis on interventions with students with severe developmental disabilities. The review looked at teaching strategies, content, and rationale for inclusion of students with severe disabilities. Their findings suggested that systematic instruction is an evidence-based practice for teaching science to students with severe developmental disabilities. Systematic instruction included task analysis for teaching chained skills and time delay for discrete skills.

A meta-analysis of the literature by Dexter, Park, and Hughes (2011) of six studies (published between 1986 and 1992) examined the effects of using graphic organizers with LD students in Grade 6 through 12 science classes. Graphic organizers (such as semantic maps and visual displays) were associated with increased vocabulary knowledge and factual comprehension. Graphic organizers also facilitate maintenance of science content learned by students with learning disabilities. Implications for practice included that "instructionally intensive" (p. 211) types of graphic organizers, such as semantic maps and semantic feature analysis, are better for immediate factual recall, while more "computationally efficient" (p. 211) graphic organizers, such as syntactic/semantic feature analysis, are better for maintenance. Also, LD students must be explicitly taught to use graphic organizers in order for them to be effective.

Assistive technology (AT) refers to "any item, piece of equipment, or product system, whether acquired commercially off the shelf, modified, or customized, that is used to increase, maintain, or improve functional capabilities of a child with a disability" (IDEA, 2004, 602.1A). The role of AT for students with disabilities cannot be understated, particularly as it relates to postsecondary success in STEM careers (Burgstahler, 2003). Common ATs range from "low tech" such as pencil grips, lined paper, and concrete manipulatives to more "high tech," including virtual manipulatives, computer-based concept mapping, augmentive and alternative communication (AAC) devices, and screen readers (Bouck, 2010). Adaptive laboratory equipment, such as audible thermometer probes, large-display digital balances, magnifying cameras, or beakers with handles, are AT that can prove to be invaluable for making science accessible for students with physical disabilities (Neely, 2007). Boyd-Kimball (2012) reports an extensive array of adaptive instructional aids that proved helpful in teaching a blind student in a nonmajors college chemistry course, including the use of magnetic letters and numbers for writing and balancing equations, and raised "puff paint" to denote Lewis Dot structures (p. 1397). In a yearlong study that examined the use of adaptive equipment that accompanied a science curriculum for students with visual impairments, the researchers found that the students' attitudes improved (Rule, Stefanich, Boody, & Peiffer, 2011).

Levy and Lahav (2012) utilized sound-based mediation to model concepts about the behavior of contained gas particles for blind students, noting that these types of complex, abstract systems are particularly difficult for visually impaired students to grasp. The authors assessed the efficacy of "listening to complexity" (L2C), which provides students with sound-based (e.g., cowbell, oboe, gong, etc.), real-time information regarding particles' speed, location, and interactions. The study involved four adults using a pre- and posttest design and reported significant learning gains on the understanding of physical system concepts. While the authors note the study limitations of a small sample size and the use of adults rather than middle school students, the target audience of this learning environment, they nonetheless present compelling evidence for the use of this emerging technology to make complex systems accessible for persons with visual impairments.

Several projects, including Creating Laboratory Access for Science Students (CLASS; Lunsford & Bargerhuff, 2006) and Disabilities, Opportunities, Internetworking, and Technology (Do-It; Burgstahler, Moore, & Crawford, 2011), document the success of interventions that make technology and equipment accessible for students with disabilities. In their longitudinal study of the Do-It program, Burgstahler and colleagues (2011) report that program participants rated the availability of adaptive hardware and software as the most valuable of the evidence-based practices employed by Do-It. All of these findings underscore the need for and the advantages of adaptive equipment for students with special needs in science education.

Virtual reality (VR) is emerging as a particularly promising AT tool for making learning opportunities, including science, accessible for students with disabilities (Jeffs, 2010). By creating virtual learning environments, these technologies create opportunities for interactive learning and "provide a variety of opportunities for the learner to have control over the learning process" (p. 253) and offer access for students whose disabilities might otherwise limit participation (Schaff, Jerome, Behrmann, & Sprague, 2005). Adamo-Villani and Wilbur (2009) describe an innovative approach to teaching science to deaf and hearing students using 3D animated interactive software called Science and Math in an Immersive Learning Environment (SMILE). SMILE is a bilingual (English and ASL) virtual learning environment that uses interactive 3D animated characters that respond to the user's input in written and spoken English as well as ASL. In SMILE, elementary students participate in a game that challenges them to build objects in the virtual environment requiring acquisition of STEM skills as well as the related ASL signs. The authors conducted formative evaluation in their pilot study of 21 elementary students (14 hearing and 7 deaf) to assess usability and fun of the system. The results suggest that the SMILE interface is a promising technology for all students, as it was highly engaging. However, learning and knowledge acquisition were not assessed in this study.

While it is clear that AT is an essential tool for promoting access and opportunities in science education, there exists a need for more robust empirical studies specifically targeting knowledge acquisition by students with disabilities utilizing various AT in order to get a clearer understanding of the learning gains that have been realized through these technological advancements and the challenges that remain.

Assessment

Assessment is a major and necessary component of education. But the assessment of students with special needs in science and elsewhere typically has led to controversy. Some believe assessment can serve as a stimulus for education reform, while others think it is a deterrent to educational programs sensitive to individual differences.

Much of the controversy swirling around educational assessment exists because groups involved have different: agendas; views on the validity and reliability of standardized assessments; concerns about how the results of assessment will impact the students being tested; concerns about how the results of assessment will be used to evaluate those giving instruction or delivering programs; concerns about how legislative bodies will use the information from assessments in funding and evaluating schools; concerns about the use of assessment in labeling and categorizing students; and concerns about whether the test(s) accurately assess the knowledge of the individuals and their ability to perform in tasks relating to qualifications.

Kohn (2001) asserted that school testing is driven by a top-down, heavy-handed, corporate-style version of school reform that threatens the basic premises of school improvement and that the current high-stakes assessment system suits the political appetite for rapid, quantifiable results (Thompson, 2001). Innovations supported by best-practice research become overlooked, particularly in communities in which the need for developmentally appropriate practice is most needed. Eisner (2001) expressed concern that when there is a limited array of areas in which assessment occurs, students whose aptitudes and interests lie in other areas become marginalized.

Science is particularly vulnerable. A way some science teachers may attempt to raise test scores is to employ utilizing practices not recommended by the Next Generation Science Standards (Achieve, 2013b)—that is, to use direct instruction to present to learners a large amount of declarative knowledge (Kohn, 2001). In the Next Generation

Science Standards' section titled "All Standards, All Students: Making Next Generation Science Standards Accessible to All Students" (Achieve, 2013a), the authors caution against the methodological limitations of large-scale, standardized tests in understanding achievement gaps among underserved groups in science. These limitations include (1) overgeneralization about achievement of highly diverse groups, (2) reinforcement of stereotypes, and (3) overlooking of interactions between variables. These limitations can readily apply to students with disabilities if educators interpreting standardized tests fail to recognize the heterogeneity among and within disability categories, hold low expectations for academic success of students with disabilities, or overlook the conflation between variables such as race, gender, and disability as exemplified by the overrepresentation of minority males in special education.

Assessment of students with disabilities is, to a large extent, guided by legislation. U.S. citizens have the right to (a) a guarantee of equal protection under the law and (b) due process when state action may adversely affect an individual. In education, constitutional rights translate into a guarantee of equal educational opportunity (not equal outcomes). Section 504 of the U.S. Rehabilitation Act of 1973 mandated that admissions tests for persons with disabilities must be validated and reflect the applicants' aptitude and achievement rather than any disabilities extraneous to what is being measured. The Education for All Handicapped Children Act (1975) PL 94–142 mandated that all children with disabilities receive a free, appropriate public education. It also mandated due process rights, responsibilities of the federal government in providing some financial assistance, and the requirement that special education services be monitored. Legal rights of students with special needs were again emphasized in the IDEA legislation. According to Welner (2006):

> The Individuals with Disabilities Act also includes rules for how culturally and linguistically diverse students should be assessed for possible special education placement. IDEA says that all students have the right to be tested in ways that are free from racial or cultural bias. Federal guidelines specify that evaluations should meet three criteria to be considered fair and nonbiased:
>
> 1. The assessment should be conducted in the student's native language;
> 2. Any evaluation material or test should be used for the specific purpose for which it was validated (designed); and
> 3. Tests should be administered by a professional with the appropriate training and expertise.
>
> (p. 60)

In addition, the passage of the Americans with Disabilities Act in 1990 (PL 101–336), continues to have many implications for education, specifically for the licensing/certification/credentialing process. This act requires that the test application process and the test itself be accessible to individuals with disabilities. Although a person may not be able to meet other requirements of the credentialing process, he or she may not be barred from attempting to pass the credentialing exam. The agency or entity administering the test must provide auxiliary aids and/or modification and may not charge the individual with a disability for the accommodations made. Accommodations that may be provided include an architecturally accessible testing site, a distraction-free space, an alternative location, test schedule variation, extended time, the use of a scribe, sign language interpreter, readers, adaptive equipment, adaptive communication devices, and modifications of the test presentation and/or response format (Thurlow, Ysseldyke, & Silverstein, 1995).

Concerning performance examinations in science, the facilities must be accessible and usable by individuals. Acquisition or modification of equipment or devices, appropriate adjustment or modifications of examinations, qualified readers or interpreters, appropriate modification in training materials and/or policies, and other similar modifications must be made for individuals with disabilities (42 USC 12/11, Section 101(9)), who must provide documentation of the disability.

Unfortunately, a long series of research has indicated a continuing lack of responsiveness by science teachers to adjust the learning environment so students with disabilities feel a sense of success and accomplishment. For example, in an examination of science grades for more than 400 students with mild disabilities in Grades 9 through 12, Cawley, Kahn, and Tedesco (1989) reported 50% to 60% of the grades were Ds or Fs.

Research has indicated that teachers should be cautious in their actions as a result of interpretations of student performance on standardized assessment instruments (Darling-Hammond, 1999). The use and interpretation of evaluation instruments is a fundamental concern in student identification for special services. Indeed, the validity and reliability of tests used for classification and placement have been repeatedly challenged (Stainback, Stainback, & Bunch, 1989). Gartner and Lipsky (1987) described these tests as "barely more accurate than a flip of the coin" (p. 372). Addressing the relative permanence of classifications based on these tests, Gartner and Lipsky reported that less than 5% of the students are declassified and returned to the general education classroom.

Most troubling in an era of standardized testing, research suggests that many students with special needs are unable to demonstrate their true level of understanding under traditional testing conditions. Specifically, several authors have noted that traditional assessments may reflect students with disabilities' delays in reading and writing rather than their full understanding of the subject matter (Cawley & Parmar, 2001; Seifert & Espin, 2012). In response, researchers such as McCarthy (2005) have advocated the use of alternative assessment strategies for learners with special needs. Alternatively, other researchers have examined inclusive science education contexts that have proven to be successful for students with special needs. Scruggs, Mastropieri, Berkely, and Graetz (2009) conducted a literature review of empirical studies of students with diverse learning needs in content-area classes. In science, explicit instruction that employed differential practice time and levels and cognitive strategies (e.g., peer tutoring and embedded strategic information) enhanced students' learning of content, which increased student performance on high-stakes tests.

Much has been written on the seemingly incongruent emphases between the IDEA's original meaning of a FAPE and the high-stakes nature of the NCLB. Kaufman and Blewett (2012) note that the definition of free, appropriate public education originally contemplated in the IDEA and interpreted in *Hendrick Hudson School District v. Rowley* (1982) emphasized access to an individualized program "reasonably calculated" to provide "educational benefit" (p. 207) has shifted to the more rigid outcome-focused requirements of adequate yearly progress (AYP) necessitated by the NCLB. In other words, Congress "has shifted its focus from what schools do to how students perform" (Kaufman & Blewett, p. 5). This shift in emphasis has had profound impacts on the education of students with disabilities and on the schools and teachers charged with educating them, yet the overarching question of how the outcomes-based emphasis of NCLB impacts the education of students with disabilities specifically in science with regard to curriculum, assessment, and achievement remains largely unanswered. Evidence of the impact of high-stakes testing on students with disabilities in contexts not specific to science suggests mixed results (Katsiyannis, Zhang, Ryan, & Jones, 2007), with studies demonstrating positive effects such as increased availability of testing accommodations (Lazarus, Thurlow, Lail, & Christensen, 2009) and negative results including increased test anxiety (Sena, Lowe, & Lee, 2007). While more students with disabilities are being included in general education classes, including science, in response to NCLB's requirements, this may amount to little more than a change in geography unless accompanied by thoughtful, individualized supports. Access to curriculum does not guarantee opportunity for achievement unless paired with "(a) assessments and curricular materials that are accessible to every student, (b) the use of research-based instruction consistent with individual need and ability, and (c) sufficient material and human resources to deliver the instruction and to assess student learning" (Hardman & Dawson, 2008, p. 7). This begs the question of whether, post–NCLB, the multitude of benefits conferred by inclusion of students with disabilities in general science classrooms are trumped, or at least challenged, *if* an educational system is unable to maintain the individualized educational approach promised by the IDEA. More research is needed to identify specific impacts of high-stakes testing environments on students with disabilities and their teachers in post–NCLB science classrooms.

Conclusions

The Next Generation Science Standards (Achieve, 2013a) promote as a key commitment the need to provide all students in science with challenging learning opportunities appropriate to their abilities and talents. Many students who are capable of high performance in science are labeled as students with disabilities because of low performance or limitations in other areas not related to reasoning in science. Science teachers must be prepared to recognize these differences and respond to the unique learning needs of each student. Evidence indicates that both practicing and prospective science teachers note inadequacy of their preparation to make instructional adjustments for students with disabilities.

Other limitations are evidenced when students receive instruction in science primarily from special educators, including time allocated to science, delivery of science through textbook teaching as the primary mode of instruction, and limited teacher knowledge of the science content. In learning contexts in which universal design predominates, research suggests that learners with special needs in science are able to learn without significant adaptations. In general, accommodations found consistently to improve the learning of all students are teaching through multimodality instructional approaches, allowing students opportunities to resubmit and improve assignments, and willingness to collaborate with other educators about ways to better serve the needs of individual students. Modifications that allow students with disabilities opportunities to share what they have learned in both formative and summative assessments (that are required in legislation) result in improved student participation and commitment in the learning process.

There is no substantive empirical evidence that students with special needs process information differently than other students do. Instead, findings from a wide range of studies on learners' engagement in science show that students with mild disabilities, in particular, are capable of high-level disciplinary engagement with scientific concepts and procedures if they are supported appropriately (NRC, 2007). Effective teaching of students with special needs must be grounded in interaction between the learner and the learning environment, making efforts to understand the cognitive processing that occurs. Findings from research on student performance indicate that teachers who use greater variety in their teaching and take time to get to know their students are more effective with all students, regardless of ability.

Future Research Directions

A perennial question for the U.S. courts (as new legislation covering the educational rights of persons with disabilities is enforced) is the extent and degree of responsibility educators have in accommodating the educational needs of students with disabilities. Globally, there continues to exist an uncertainty as to how to accommodate students with special needs in science education. While the universal design learning initiative shows promise in meeting the needs of all students in science, more research is needed in this area. Research that documents the extent and efficacy of science curriculum, instruction, science teacher education context, and assessment of students with special needs continues to be urgently needed.

Other, more specific research questions to investigate include: How have teachers (with data disaggregated by school level and by science discipline) included students with special needs (with data disaggregated by type of disability and personal characteristics) in the general science classroom? What has been the outcome of such efforts across multiple dimensions (e.g., class ecology, curriculum and instruction, and assessment)? What types of teacher professional development throughout the teacher professional continuum have been designed to prepare teachers to teach students with special needs, and what influence have those experiences had on the teachers' practices? What outcomes are associated with the differing approaches to teaching science to learners with special needs, and to what extent do these outcomes align with local and high-stakes assessment requirements? What sense do teachers make of adaptations for learners with special needs in science, and how does their perception of their school culture influence such understandings and actions? What strategies assist teachers to make adaptations for learners with special needs in the science classroom? From the general classroom teacher's perspective, what mechanisms and strategies would support them in contributing productively at meetings for learners with special needs in their science classrooms? How are the various collaboration models between the general science teacher and the special educator enacted in school environments? To what extent and limitation do the various models benefit learners with special needs to learn for understanding as well as to perform on assessment tasks (traditional as well as alternative)? From the perspective of learners with special needs, how do they access the general curriculum in science? And, from a systems perspective, how can we identify and foster talents in science for students with disabilities via curriculum, instruction, and assessment? We wonder what new insights in research in special needs might emerge if researchers posed such questions and used a broad array of theoretical paradigms.

Part II: Special Talents in Science

George DeBoer, in *A History of Ideas in Science Education* (1991), pointed out that in the field of science education, particularly in regard to the U.S. context, a long-standing barrier to meeting the unique needs of learners with special talents was sensitivity by educators to avoid charges of favoritism. Spurred by concerns for national security in the post–World II period, the American Association for the Advancement of Science (AAAS) Cooperative Committee argued that, by not recognizing the special abilities in talented learners, science education was committing a double error: (a) not addressing the unique educational needs of such individuals and (b) not developing a national resource that was in high demand (DeBoer, 1991). While the record since that period has not been an unqualified success for learners with special talents in science, progress has occurred.

Learners with special talents in science previously have been referred to as "gifted." Contemporary labels seek to describe this group of learners by placing a greater focus on "creativity," "extraordinary abilities," or "talents" (i.e., observable performances in situated events, context, and domain specific activities) rather than sole reliance on superior test-taking performances (academic or IQ examinations; Sternberg, 2001). Maker (1993) described such a learner as a problem solver who

> enjoys the challenge of complexity and persists until the problem is solved . . . [and who is capable of] a) creating a new or more clear definition of an existing problem, b) devising new and more efficient or effective methods, and c) reaching solutions that may be different from the usual, but are recognized as being effective, perhaps more effective, than previous solutions.
>
> (p. 71)

Tannenbaum (1997) proposed two types of talented individuals: performers and producers. Performers are those who excel at "staged artistry" or "human services" (p. 27); producers excel at contributing "thoughts" and "tangibles" (p. 27). Other theoreticians, such as Piirto (1999), placed attention, especially in precollegiate education, on precocity (the ability to easily do those things typically seen in older learners) as a hallmark of the talented. Sternberg (2007) added to the discussion of the talented learners that cultural origins and contexts should be considered when identifying giftedness in order to reflect the diversity of culturally valued competencies throughout the world. In 2011, the National Association for Gifted Children defined gifted students as individuals that demonstrate outstanding aptitude (exceptional ability to learn or reason) or competence (documented performance or achievement in the top 10% of the population in one or more areas).

As a result of the multiple views of researchers, policy makers, and education professionals interested in education for the talented, between 3% and 15% of the student population can be identified as fitting into this category of learners (Hardman et al., 2002). However, as pointed out by Gilbert and Newberry (2007), there is no evidence based on longitudinal studies that such an identification is a fixed personal characteristic. Whitmore and Maker (1985) and Willard-Holt (1998) investigated talented learners in the population with special needs (visual, hearing, physical, and learning disabilities population) and suggested that a similar percentage (3% to 15%) would apply to the identification of the talented in that group of learners as well.

Legislation Impacting the Rights of Talented Learners in Science

In contrast to U.S. legislation that mandates educational services for learners with special needs, learners with talents in science (or any subject areas) have no such legal entitlement. Accordingly, funding for talented learners in science is a state and local issue. The U.S. federal Gifted and Talented Children's Act of 1978 and the 1993 Javits Gifted and Talented Education Act provided definitions of talented learners as well as some funding to support a national research center, demonstration programs, and activities for leadership personnel throughout the United States (Gallagher, 1997). At this time (February, 2014), the Talent Act, a proposed amendment to the Elementary and Secondary Education Act (ESEA) to support high-ability and high-achieving students, is under consideration by Congressional committees to determine whether it will be sent to the full Senate or House for a vote. If passed, the Talent Act will revise the accountability and assessment systems to report performance of top students on state report cards, require schools to include gifted students in their Title II funding, increase professional development for teachers of gifted students, and emphasize research and best practices (Stephens, 2011). Nevertheless, the inconsistent record of supporting gifted education through legislation has led some advocates to assert that U.S. policy has compromised excellence for the sake of equity (Gallagher, 2002). The National Science Board's (2010) report titled *Preparing the Next Generation of STEM Innovators: Identifying and Developing Our Nation's Human Capital* suggests that "the dual goals of raising the floor of base-level performance and elevating the ceiling for achievement are not mutually exclusive," but rather, equity and excellence are "mutually reinforcing" (p. 10). Recommendations in the report for supporting gifted education include providing opportunities for quality STEM experiences and training for gifted students and their teachers, broadening talent assessments and identification, and creating supportive networks for all gifted students in STEM.

The U.S. Department of Education's (1993) definition of the talented is:

1. Children and youth with outstanding talent perform or show the potential for performing at remarkably high levels of accomplishment when compared with others of their age, experience, or environment.
2. These children and youth exhibit high performance capability in intellectual, creative, and/or artistic areas, possess an unusual leadership capacity, or excel in specific academic fields. They require services or activities not ordinarily provided by the schools.
3. Children and youth with outstanding talents are present in all cultural groups, across all economic strata, and in all areas of human endeavor. (p. 3)

Globally, the legal entitlement for educational services for the talented varies greatly, with countries such as the

Republic of Korea that passed such a law in 2000, while others, at most, have no legal entitlements but have set up school environments within existing schools and in separately defined schools for students considered talented in science.

Review of the Literature

For heuristic purposes, the review of the literature on talented learners in science is presented in two subsections: Curriculum and Instruction and Identification of Talented Science Learners.

Curriculum and Instruction

The basic principles of education for the talented have been identified as acceleration of content delivery, selective grouping of the learners, and enrichment of the curriculum (VanTassel-Baska, 2003). Research in the study of curriculum and instruction for talented learners in science has examined two intervention models: a specialized administrative model (enrolling only talented learners) and a general education model (differentiation of instruction for all ability groups). Other studies have sought to document and understand the perspectives of all the stakeholders (administrators, teachers, learners, and parents) concerned with science education for the talented.

INTERVENTION MODELS

Researchers have sought to understand the impact of special programs in science, such as accelerated summer experiences or specialized school science courses, designed to meet the needs of talented learners. Lynch (1992) examined the effectiveness of an accelerated summer program in science (biology, chemistry, and physics) at Johns Hopkins University that taught talented learners (ages 12–16) a year of content in 3 weeks. The study extended over 6 years and included 905 learners. Lynch found that the summer program effectively prepared the learners to accelerate in science content and that the learners also benefited by beginning high school sciences earlier than regularly allowed. In a similar line of investigation, Enersen (1994) surveyed a sample of talented secondary students ($N = 161$) who had attended high school summer science residencies and found that their attitude toward science increased by participation. In a follow-up survey, most students reported that they were studying or working in scientific fields (no difference between genders). Bass and Ries (1995) investigated the scientific reasoning abilities of talented students in a high school's gifted education program. The researchers designed a data collection strategy that used analogous problems and questions to measure understanding of basic scientific concepts and skills. They determined that the talented learners did not uniformly benefit from the experience; their performances varied on measures that documented their ability to solve different kinds of scientific problems.

Jones (1997) reported on a 6-year precollegiate intervention program designed to prepare academically talented, lower-socioeconomic minority learners for college. The Young Scholars Program at Ohio State University transformed the way agriculture was presented to the learners. Success was measured in achievement and in career interest. In a series of evaluation studies that measured the curricular impact on elementary-level talented learners in science, Boyce, VanTassel-Baska, Burruss, Sher, and Johnson, (1997) and VanTassel-Baska, Bass, Ries, Poland, and Avery (1998) reported that problem-based learning and integration of disciplines in science benefited talented learners as measured by increased motivation, enhanced process skills, and greater ability to make intra- and interdisciplinary connections. In an exploratory study that sought to understand how a sample of talented secondary learners displayed domain-relevant skills possessed by experts in disciplinary content knowledge, Fehn (1997) found that the talented learners in science varied most widely among his sample in critical abilities (interpretation, evaluation for bias, and synthesis). The talented science learners who had previous experience with primary sources in history performed better than did those with no experience. Fehn speculated that this finding had strong implications for the teaching of talented science learners not only the history curriculum but in all instructional contexts that required such skills.

Renzulli, Baum, Hebert, and McCluskey (1999) reported on the problems of underachievement by highability learners. The researchers presented a new perspective and advocated a strategy to increase success for such learners. *Type III Enrichment*, an educational experience for the talented, encouraged learners to take on the role of actual investigators by studying problems of their choice. The learners were responsible for carrying out their investigations using appropriate methods of inquiry and presenting their findings to an audience. More than 80% of the learners showed gain in the areas of achievement, effort, attitude, self-regulated behavior, and positive classroom behavior.

Another intervention model that researchers have examined is the general education model in which talented learners in science share the experience with other learners. In a study that examined the impact of mixed-ability classes for science learning in secondary schools, Hacker and Rowe (1993) reported negative results. They found that the mixed-ability class resulted in deteriorations in the quality of classroom interactions of both high- and lowability learners. However, in a study that investigated the differentiation practices of a sample of Scottish secondary science teachers, in which differentiation was defined as teaching individual students in a class at different paces and in different ways, Simpson and Ure (1994) reported evidence of success. Success resulted when teachers shared with their learners (of varying abilities, including the talented) the management of their learning, promoted the belief that achievement can improve, used a wide range of information and support, identified a range of needs, and gave and received continuous feedback.

Scott, Mortimer, and Aguiar (2006) have reported on small case classroom studies of "talk" or discourse in the science classroom in which they suggested that talented learners benefit (as measured by their involvement in class discussions and in their expressed motivation in science) particularly when the teacher moves from an initiation, response, evaluation (I-R-E) discourse pattern to a more interactive/dialogic communicative approach that uses an initiation, response, prompt, response, prompt (I-R-P-R-P . . .) discourse pattern.

Park and Oliver (2009), in a qualitative research study, looked at the responses of three high school teachers to the specific challenges of teaching science to gifted students. Through classroom observations, semistructured interviews, review of lesson plans, teachers' written reflections, students' work samples including assessments, and researchers' field notes, the researchers determined that gifted students bring certain challenges to the classroom, including "(a) asking challenging questions, (b) being impatient with the pace of others/getting easily bored, (c) having perfectionist traits/having a fear of failure, (d) disliking routine, drills, and busywork, (e) being critical of others, and (f) being aware of being different from others" (p. 339). Teachers responded to gifted students' special needs through "(a) instructional differentiation, for example, thematic units, (b) variety in instructional mode and/or students' products, (c) student grouping strategies and peer tutoring, (d) individualized support, (e) strategies to manage challenging questions, (f) strategies to deal with the perfectionism, and (g) psychologically safe classroom environments" (p. 342). The researchers concluded that teachers have an increased instructional load due to the unique needs of gifted students. As teachers become more aware of gifted students' cognitive and affective characteristics, they are more receptive to implementing instructional adaptations to meet students' particular needs. "Both pre and inservice teacher education programs should provide opportunities for teachers to research or analyze their students in terms of reasoning types, learning styles, motivation, characteristics, and interests" (p. 348).

In a novel study that explored the gifted styles of students who have disabilities (termed "twice exceptional = 2Es"), Sumida (2010) developed a checklist for identifying gifted learning characteristics of primary children in Japan with and without mild developmental disabilities in science with the goal of helping teachers to identify and nurture gifts in science class. The sample consisted of 86 children from eight primary schools; 50% had learning disabilities (LD), attention deficit/hyperactivity disorder (ADHD), and high-functioning autism (HA). The students were observed using a 60-item checklist that included attitudes, thinking, skills, and knowledge/understanding. Using factor analysis, Sumida identified three "gifted styles" in science: (1) Spontaneous style; (2) Expert style; (3) Solid style. Students with LD/ADHD/HA were found to display the Spontaneous style (high originality, creativity, surprising questions), while nondisabled students

displayed Solid style (general science competence). There was a low number of Expert style in both groups. Sumida made two recommendations based on the study's findings. The first recommendation was that students with Expert style profiles (with and without disabilities) should be given challenging tasks in areas of their strength to raise self-esteem. A second recommendation was that there should be an increased use of technology with such students in science education to allow for more sophisticated use of data as well as expanded informal science opportunities.

Overall, as reported by VanTassel-Baska (2003) and continuing to the present day, a comprehensive review of the literature (primarily descriptive reports of practice) suggests that instruction may benefits talented learners in science when there is a focus on:

- concepts (as opposed to memorization of facts)
- inquiry (in which the learner takes on the role of active investigator)
- higher-order thinking (evaluating information and modeling authentic scientific thinking)
- metacognition and self-regulation (in which learners are self-directed and take the lead in setting agendas)
- product and audience (the learners produce authentic products and report to a genuinely interested audience)
- variety and pacing (use of a variety of teaching strategies and the use of a rapid teaching pace, particularly when introducing new material)

PERSPECTIVES OF TALENTED LEARNERS, PARENTS, AND SCHOOL PERSONNEL

In addition to researchers' interest in examining the impact of intervention models, they have investigated the perspectives of talented learners, their parents, and school personnel along a range of topics. Lynch (1990) investigated credit and placement issues for talented learners in science following accelerated summer studies in science and mathematics. She reported that while the learners and their parents appreciated the acceleration, their schools were less receptive. Schools had practical concerns about how to incorporate the summer credits into existing academic programs and appropriate course placements for the learners.

Cross and Coleman (1992) documented by survey methodology the perspectives of a high school sample ($N = 100$) of talented learners in science. The key finding was that the learners felt restrained by the pace of instruction and the science content of their science courses. They expressed frustration with the lecture-memorization instructional strategy and desired to be more challenged academically.

The attitudes toward science of talented upper elementary students in Singapore were studied by Caleon and Subramaniam (2008) using a survey design. They found that the above-average and gifted students reported more positive attitudes than average-ability students. Among all students, boys, as compared to girls, expressed more positive views toward science.

A study conducted by Miedijensky and Tal (2009) suggested embedded assessment incorporating self- and peer assessment can be a powerful strategy for promoting learning for gifted students in science. The researchers used a qualitative methodology to investigate how gifted students perceive the model of Embedded Assessment for Learning (EAfL) in project-based science (PBS) courses. The study conducted in Israel was premised upon the idea that gifted students should be assessed using tools that reflect their special capabilities. EAfL includes continuous self- and peer assessment throughout the learning units. Eighty-six junior high students in the study took part in six 1-year science courses for the gifted. The researchers used an interpretative methodology that included open-ended response questionnaires and semistructured interviews to understand students' views on assessment. The researchers reported positive impacts of EAfL on the students' views of assessment and learning. Students' views of assessment shifted from traditional perceptions of assessment as summative, quantitative, and done by the teacher to the view that assessment is an integral part of their science work and learning process. Students reported that self-assessment and peer assessment promoted learning, enhanced motivation, and improved social relationships throughout their science projects.

Identification of Talented Science Learners

The identification and description of learners who would be considered talented in science has been of interest to the research community. Brandwein (1955) wrote a widely read and influential book, *The Gifted Student as Future Scientist*, which, along with presenting ideas for increasing the number of talented students in science, began the contemporary conversation on the identification of talented learners in science.

School districts' reliance on aptitude tests to select for talented science learners has drawn the interest of investigators. Jarwan and Feldhusen (1993) studied the procedures used in selecting talented learners for state-supported residential high schools for mathematics and science. The researchers used both quantitative and qualitative research designs. They determined that the learners' home school adjusted grade point average was the best predictor of first- and second-year grade point averages. Their performance on the Scholastic Aptitude Test (SAT) was the second-best predictor. Most significantly, they determined that statistical prediction was superior to professional prediction by interview or ratings of learner portfolio files. In addition, they identified by examination of enrollment data that African American and Latino learners were underrepresented.

In an effort to move forward the discussion of the identification of talented students in science, Taber (2007) in *Science Education for Gifted Learners* and other contributors (including J. Gilbert and M. Newberry) proposed a new way of thinking about the identification of such learners. They place a spotlight on determining a number of the learner's characteristics, including scientific curiosity, cognitive abilities, meta-cognitive abilities, and leadership. Based on a holistic analysis of such listed characteristics (i.e., not expecting necessarily any talented learner to exhibit all the characteristics at any one time across engagement with the science curriculum), they argue that the identification process may be more productive. As stated by Gilbert and Newberry (2007, p. 17),

> We suggest that, rather, than relying completely on the results of tests that are not valid for this purpose, a better way forward would be to base the school science curriculum *for all pupils* on what is known about how giftedness is exercised. Those students who react most positively to such curriculum will therefore be encouraged and supported to demonstrate their giftedness throughout their school careers rather than being identified from test results taken at certain stages.

Conclusions

Researchers' attention has been drawn to understanding how talented learners in science can be assisted to perform to the best of their abilities in science. A limited number of studies have investigated what talented learners have gained academically from participation in specific science programs and what perceptions talented learners express about science and their schooling. Limited findings suggest that talented science learners benefit from learning situations that decrease the focus on memorization of information and increase opportunities for problem solving and inquiry.

While the current research in science education has not determined which of two types of intervention model is more effective for talented learners (acceleration or enhancement), available evidence suggests that both types of models offer benefits and challenges that call for further exploration. Summer science acceleration programs for the talented have resulted in measurable academic and attitudinal gains.

There continues to be a paucity of research concerning the instructional and learning process for learners with special needs who also have special talents. One limitation is a lack of legal entitlement for students with special needs who meet or exceed academic proficiency requirements. Additional services to address their talents are often ascertained as a general classroom issue without the same type of IEP reporting requirements as those identified with academic learning deficiencies.

Researchers have examined possible ways to identify talented science learners. The limited research in this area suggests that complete reliance on aptitude tests is not warranted and that other measures should be considered. The trend is to move beyond testing of cognitive abilities and to include a broader examination of learner characteristics shown to impact performance in science learning, including scientific curiosity and metacognitive abilities.

Future Research Directions

Due to the limited nature of research in science for talented learners, research is urgently needed in key areas. Recommended specific research questions include: What happens to the talented female learners in science as they proceed through their educational programs (mixed-ability and high-ability groupings)? What happens to the talented learners in science with special needs as they proceed through their educational programs (mixed-ability and high-ability groupings)? What are the attributes of talented programs in science that could be instituted in science programs for the general population? What happens to the talented learners in science from different cultural backgrounds or living in poverty as they proceed through their educational programs (mixed-ability and high-ability groupings)? And what relationship, if any, exists between the identification of talented learners in science and the types of outcomes that the talented programs in science are designed to achieve?

Concluding Thoughts

There is continuing tension on the research of exceptional learners in science. A major contributing factor is the tendency for special education and science education researchers to emphasize preferentially different theoretical views on learning and teaching. Special education researchers' widespread and continuing use of behaviorism as a theoretical lens in research is recognized as being in conflict with science education researchers' more common use of cognitive and sociocultural views of learning and teaching, frequently referred to as social constructivism (Steele, 2005). Science educators' strong commitment to engaging learners in authentic scientific practices of science, such as those articulated in the recent release of the Next Generation Science Standards (i.e., problem posing and evidence-based problem solving; Achieve, 2013b), as opposed to a primary focus on skill and information acquisition that is more easily taught and measured, contributes to the differences between these two fields of educational research. As result, researchers in this area who seek cohesion will find that need unmet.

Compounding the epistemological disagreement among researchers interested in understanding the learning in science by exceptional learners is the unique role of legislation in regulating the education of exceptional learners. A clear consequence of the legislative involvement is that a preponderance of researchers have focused their attention on pressing issues of curriculum and instruction within the legal and administrative contexts of schools. The hope is that future research on exceptional learners in science will be expanded to address more fundamental questions of learning theory, especially as new emphasis is placed on both students with special needs and students with talent in STEM education worldwide.

Acknowledgments

The authors wish to thank Janice Koch for her review and comments on the initial version of this chapter.

Note

1. The authors of this chapter acknowledge the contributions of Gregory P. Stefanich, who was a co-author of this chapter in the 2007 edition of the *Handbook of Research on Science Education*.

References

Achieve, Inc. (2013a). *Diversity and equity in the Next Generation Science Standards (NGGS): "All standards, all students."* Retrieved from www.nextgenscience.org/sites/ngss/files/Appendix%20D%20Diversity%20and%20Equity%20-%204.9.13.pdf

Achieve, Inc. (2013b). *The Next Generation Science Standards.* Retrieved from www.nextgenscience.org/

Adamo-Villani, N., & Wilbur, R. (2009). Two novel technologies for accessible math and science education. *IEEE Multimedia, 15*(4), 38–46.

Algozzine, B. (2005). Restrictiveness and race in special education: Facts that remain difficult to ignore anymore. *Learning Disabilities: A Contemporary Journal, 3,* 64–69.

Americans With Disabilities Act. (1990). Washington, DC: United States Department of Justice, Civil Rights Division.

Arthaud, T. J., Aram, R. J., Breck, S. E., Doelling, J. E., & Bushrow, K. M. (2007). Developing collaboration skills in pre-service teachers: A partnership between general and special education. *Teacher Education and Special Education, 30*(1), 1–12.

Baker, E., Wang, M., & Walberg, H. (1994). The effects of inclusion on learning. *Educational Leadership, 52*(4), 33–35.

Baker, J. M., & Zigmond, N. (1990). Are regular education classes equipped to accommodate students with learning disabilities? *Exceptional Children, 56,* 515–526.

Bass, G. M., & Ries, R. R. (1995, April). *Scientific understanding in high-ability school students: Concepts and process skills.* Paper presented at the annual meeting of the American Educational Research Association, San Francisco, CA.

Bauwens, J. (1991, March). *Blueprint for cooperation teaching.* Symposium conducted at the meeting of the Special Education Conference, Cedar Rapids, IA.

Bauwens, J., & Hourcade, J. (1997, April). *Cooperative teaching; Portraits of possibilities.* Paper presented at the Annual Convention of the Council for Exceptional Children, Salt Lake City, UT.

Bay, M., Staver, J. R., Bryan, T., & Hale, J. B. (1992). Science instruction for the mildly handicapped: Direct instruction versus discovery teaching. *Journal of Research in Science Teaching, 29*(6), 555–570.

Booth, T., & Ainscow, M. (Eds.). (1998). *From them to us: An international study of inclusion in education.* London: Routledge.

Bouck, E. C. (2010). Technology and students with disabilities: Does it solve all the problems? In F. E. Obiakor, J. P. Bakken, & A. F. Rotatori (Ed.), *Current issues and trends in special education: Research, technology, and teacher preparation (Advances in SPECIAL EDUCATION, Volume 20;* pp. 91–104). Bingley, United Kingdom: Emerald Group Publishing Limited.

Boyce, L. N., VanTassel-Baska, J., Burruss, J. D., Sher, B. T., & Johnson, D. T. (1997). A problem-based curriculum: Parallel learning opportunities for students and teachers. *Journal for the education of the gifted, 20,* 363–379.

Boyd-Kimball, D. (2012). Adaptive instructional aids for teaching a blind student in a nonmajors college chemistry course. *Journal of Chemical Education, 89,* 1395–1399.

Brandwein, P. (1955). *The gifted student as future scientist: The high school student and his commitment to science.* New York: Harcourt Brace.

Bransford, J.D., Brown, A.L., Cocking, R.R., Donovan, M.S., & Pellegrino, J.W. (2000). *How people learn: Brain, mind, experience, and school.* Washington, DC: National Academies Press.

Burgstahler, S. (2003). The role of technology in preparing youth with disabilities for postsecondary education and employment. *Journal of Special Education Technology, 18*(4), 7–19.

Burgstahler, S., Moore, E., & Crawford, L. (2011). *2011 Report of the Access STEM/Access Computing/DO-IT Longitudinal Transition Study (ALTS).* Retrieved from www.washington.edu/doit/Stem/tracking4.html

Caleon, I.S., & Subramaniam, R. (2008). Attitudes towards science of intellectually gifted and mainstream upper primary students in Singapore. *Journal of Research in Science Teaching, 45*(8), 940–954.

Cawley, J., Hayden, S., Cade, E., & Baker-Kroczynski, S. (2002). Including students with disabilities into the general education science classroom. *Exceptional Children, 68*(4), 423–435.

Cawley, J., & Parmar, R. (2001). Literacy proficiency and science for students with learning disabilities. *Reading and Writing Quarterly, 17,* 105–125.

Cawley, J.F. (1994). Science for students with disabilities. *Remedial and Special Education, 15,* 67–71.

Cawley, J.F., Kahn, H., & Tedesco, A. (1989). Vocational education and students with learning disabilities. *Journal of Learning Disabilities, 22,* 630–634.

Civil Rights Act. (1964). *Civil right act of 1964.* Retrieved from www.ourdocuments.gov/doc.php?doc=97

Coles, G. (2004). Danger in the classroom: "Brain glitch" research and learning to read. *Phi Delta Kappan, 85,* 344–351.

Collins, A. (1998). National education standards: A political document. *Journal of Research in Science Teaching, 35,* 711–727.

Costello, C. (1991). *A comparison of student cognitive and social achievement for handicapped and regular education students who are educated in integrated versus a substantially separate classroom.* Unpublished doctoral dissertation, University of Massachusetts, Amherst.

Courtade, G.R., Browder, D.M., Spooner, F., & DiBiase, W. (2010). training teachers to use an inquiry-based task analysis to teach science to students with moderate and severe disabilities. *Education and Training in Autism and Developmental Disabilities, 2010, 45*(3), 378–399.

Cross, T.L., & Coleman, L.J. (1992). Gifted high school students' advice to science teachers. *Gifted Child Today, 15*(5), 25–26.

Darling-Hammond, L. (1999). *Teaching for high standard, what policymakers need to know and be able to do.* Washington, DC: United States Department of Education.

DeBoer, G.E. (1991). *A history of ideas in science education: Implications for practice.* New York: Teachers College Press.

Dexter, D.D., Park, Y.J., & Hughes, C.A. (2011). A meta-analytic review of graphic organizers and science instruction for adolescents with learning disabilities: Implications for the intermediate and secondary science classroom. *Learning Disabilities Research & Practice, 26*(4), 204–213.

Donald, M. (2001). *A mind so rare: The evolution of human consciousness.* New York: Cambridge University Press.

Education for All Handicapped Children Act of 1975, Pub. L. No. 94–142. 20 U.S.C. 1400 et seq. (1975).

Eisner, E.W. (2001). What does it mean to say a school is doing well? *Phi Delta Kappan, 82,* 367–372.

Enersen, D.L. (1994). Where are the scientists? Talent development in summer programs. *Journal of Secondary Gifted Education, 5*(2), 23–26.

Epps, S., & Tindall, G. (1987). The effectiveness of differential programming in serving students with mild handicaps: Placement options and instructional programming. In M.C. Wang, M.C. Reynolds, & H.J. Walberg (Eds.), *Handbook of special education: Research and practice: Vol. 1. Learner characteristics and adaptive education* (pp. 231–248). New York: Pergamon Press.

Fehn, B. (1997, March). *Historical thinking ability among talented math and science students: An exploratory study.* Paper presented at the annual meeting of the American Educational Research Association, Chicago, IL.

Fensham, P.J. (1985). Science for all. *Journal of Curriculum Studies, 17,* 415–435.

Ferguson, D.L. (1995). The real challenge of inclusion: Confessions of a "rabid inclusionist." *Phi Delta Kappan, 77,* 281–287.

Ferguson, P., & Asch, A. (1989). Lessons from life: Personal and parental perspectives on school, childhood, and disability. In D. Bicklen, A. Ford, & D. Ferguson (Eds.), *Disability and society* (pp. 108–140). Chicago: National Society for the Study of Education.

Finson, K.D., Ormsbee, C.K., & Jensen, M.M. (2011). *Differentiating science instruction and assessment for learners with special needs, K–8.* Thousand Oaks, CA: Corwin.

Friend, M., & Bursuck, W.D. (1999). *Including students with special needs: A practical guide for classroom teachers.* Boston: Allyn and Bacon.

Fuchs, D., & Fuchs, L.S. (1994). Inclusive school movement and radicalization of special education reform. *Exceptional Children, 60,* 294–309.

Fuchs, L.S., Fuchs, D., Hamlett, C.L., Phillips, N., & Karns, K. (1995). General educator's specialized adaptations for students with learning disabilities. *Exceptional Children, 61,* 440–459.

Gallagher, J.J. (1997). Issues in the education of gifted students. In N. Clangelo & A.D. Davis (Eds.), *Handbook of gifted education* (2nd ed.; pp. 27–42). Boston: Allyn and Bacon.

Gallagher, J.J. (2002). *Society's role in educating gifted students: The role of public policy* [Monograph]. Storrs, CT: National Research Center on the Gifted and Talented. (ERIC Document Reproduction Service No. ED 476370)

Gartner, A., & Lipsky, D.K. (1987). Beyond special education: Toward a quality system for all students. *Harvard Educational Review, 57,* 367–395.

Gilbert, J.K., & Newberry, M. (2007). The characteristics of the gifted and exceptionally able in science. In K.S. Taber (Ed.), *Science education for gifted learners* (pp. 15–31). New York: Routledge.

Golomb, K., & Hammeken, P. (1996). Grappling with inclusion confusion? *Learning, 24*(4), 48–51.

Grant, P.A. (2005). Restrictiveness and race in special education: Educating all learners. *Learning Disabilities: A Contemporary Journal, 3*(1), 70–74.

Gray, D.E., & Denicolo, P. (1998). Research in special needs education: Objective or ideology? *British Journal of Special Education, 25,* 140–145.

Hacker, R.G., & Rowe, M.J. (1993). A study of the effects of an organizational change from streamed to mixed-ability classes upon science classroom instruction. *Journal of Research in Science Teaching, 30,* 223–231.

Hardman, M.L., & Dawson, S. (2008). The impact of federal public policy on curriculum and instruction for students with disabilities in the general classroom. *Preventing School Failure, 52*(2), 5–11.

Hardman, M.L., Drew, C.J., & Egan, M.W. (2002). *Human exceptionality: Society, school, and family.* Boston: Allyn & Bacon.

Heward, W.L. (2000). *Exceptional children: An introduction to special education* (6th ed.). Upper Saddle River, NJ: Merrill.

Hitchcock, C., Meyer, A., Rose, D., & Jackson, R. (2002). Providing new access to the general curriculum: Universal design for learning. *Teaching Exceptional Children, 35,* 8–17.

Hollowood, T., Salisbury, C., Rainforth, B., & Palombaro, M. (1995). Use of instructional time in classrooms serving students with and without severe disabilities. *Exceptional Children, 61,* 242–253.

Individuals With Disabilities Education Act of 1990. 20 U.S.C. 1400–1485.

Individuals With Disabilities Education Act Amendments of 1997, PL 105–17, 20 U.S.C. 1400-et seq., 105th Congress, 1st session.

Individuals With Disabilities Education Improvement Act. (2004). P.L. 108–446, 118 Stat. 2647.

Jarwan, F.E., & Feldhusen, J. (1993). *Residential schools of mathematics and science for academically talented youth: An analysis of admission programs.* Collaborative Research Study (CRSS, 93304). Storrs,

CT: University of Connecticut, National Research Center on Gifted and Talented.

Jeffs, T.L. (2010). Virtual reality and special needs. *Themes in Science and Technology Education, 2*(1–2), 253–268.

Johnson, L.J., & Pugach, M.C. (1990). Classroom teacher's views of intervention strategies for learning and behavior problems: Which are reasonable and how frequently are they used? *Journal of Special Education, 24*(1), 69–84.

Jones, L.S. (1997). Opening doors with informal science: Exposure and access for underserved students. *Science Education, 81*, 663–677.

Jordan, K.R., Bain, S.K., McCallum, R.S., & Bell, S.M. (2012). Comparing gifted and non-gifted African American and Euro-American students on cognitive and academic variables using local norms. *Journal for the Education of the Gifted, 35*, 241–258.

Kahn, S., Feldman, A., & Cooke, M.L. (2013). Signs of autonomy: Facilitating independence and inquiry in deaf science classrooms. *Journal of Science Education for Students with Disabilities,17*(1), 13–35.

Kahn, S., & Lewis, A.R. (2013, January). *Survey on teaching science to K–12 students with disabilities: Teacher preparedness and attitudes.* Paper presented at the annual meeting of the Association for Science Teacher Education, Charleston, SC.

Katsiyannis, A., Zhang, D., Ryan, J.B., & Jones, J. (2007). High-stakes testing and students with disabilities: Challenges and promises. *Journal of Disability Policy Studies, 18*, 160–167.

Kaufman, A.K., & Blewett, E. (2012). When good enough is no longer good enough: How the high stakes nature of the No Child Left Behind Act supplanted the Rowley definition of a free appropriate public education. *Journal of Law & Education, 41*(1), 5–23.

Kohn, A. (2001). A practical guide to rescuing our schools. *Phi Delta Kappan, 82*, 358–362.

Kurtts, S.A., Matthews, C.E., & Smallwood, T. (2009). (Dis)solving the differences: A physical science lesson using universal design. *Intervention in school and clinic, 44*, 151–159.

Lang, H.G. (1994). *Silence of the spheres: The deaf experience in the history of science.* Westport, CT: Bergan and Garvey.

Lazarus, S.S., Thurlow, M.L., Lail, K.E., & Christensen, L. (2009). A longitudinal analysis of state accommodations policies twelve years of Change, 1993–2005. *Journal of Special Education, 43*(2), 67–80.

Levy, S.T., & Lahav, O. (2012). Enabling people who are blind to experience science inquiry learning through sound-based mediation. *Journal of Computer Assisted Learning, 28*, 499–513.

Lipsky, D.K., & Gartner, A. (1998). Taking inclusion into the future. *Educational Leadership, 56*(2), 78–82.

Lunsford, S.K., & Bargerhuff, M.E. (2006). A project to make the laboratory more accessible to students with disabilities. *Journal of Chemical Education, 83*, 407–409.

Lynch, S. (1990). Credit and placement issues for the academically talented following summer studies in science and mathematics. *Gifted Child Quarterly, 34*, 27–30.

Lynch, S. (1992). Fast-paced high school science for the academically talented: A six-year perspective. *Gifted Child Quarterly, 36*, 147–154.

Lynch, S., Taymans, J., Watson, W.A., Ochsendorf, R.J., Pyke, C., & Szesze, M.J. (2007). Effectiveness of a highly rated science curriculum unit for students with disabilities in general education classrooms. *Exceptional Children, 73*(2), 202–223.

Maker, C.J. (1993). Creativity, intelligence, and problem solving: A definition and design for cross-cultural research and measurement related to giftedness. *Gifted Education International, 9*(2), 68–77.

Mastropieri, M.A., Scruggs, T.E., & Butcher, K. (1997). How effective is inquiry learning for students with mild disabilities? *Journal of Special Education, 31*(2), 199–211.

Mastropieri, M.A., Scruggs, T.E., & Magnusen, M. (1999). Activities-oriented science instruction for students with disabilities. *Learning Disability Quarterly, 22*(4), 240–249.

Mastropieri, M., Scruggs, T.E., Mantziopoulos, P., Sturgeon, A., Goodwin, L., & Chung, S. (1998). "A place where living things affect and depend on each other": Qualitative and quantitative outcomes associated with inclusive science teaching. *Science Education, 82*, 163–179.

Mastropieri, M.A., Scruggs, T.E., Norland, J.J., Berkeley, S., McDuffie, K., Tornquist, E.H., & Connors, N. (2006). Differentiated curriculum enhancement in inclusive middle school science: Effects on classroom and high-stakes tests. *Journal of Special Education, 40*(3), 130–137.

McCann, W.S. (1998). *Science classrooms for students with special needs.* Washington, DC: Office of Educational Research and Improvement. (ERIC Document Reproduction Service No. ED433185)

McCarthy, C.B. (2005). Effect of thematic-based, hands-on science teaching versus a textbook approach for students with disabilities. *Journal of Research in Science Teaching, 42*(3), 245–263.

McGinnis, J.R. (2000). Teaching science as inquiry for students with disabilities. In J. Minstrell & E.H. VanZee (Eds.), *Inquiring into inquiry/learning and teaching in science* (pp. 425–433). Washington, DC: American Association for the Advancement of Science.

McGinnis, J.R. (2003). The morality of inclusive verses exclusive settings: Preparing teachers to teach students with mental disabilities in science. In D. Zeidler (Ed.), *The role of moral reasoning on socio-scientific issues and discourse in science education* (pp. 196–215). Boston: Kluwer Academic Publishers.

McGinnis, J.R. (2013). Teaching science to learners with special needs. Special issue, diversity and equity in science education (O. Lee & C. Buxton, Eds.), *Theory into Practice, 52*(1), 43–50.

McGinnis, J.R., & Nolet, V.W. (1995). Diversity, the science classroom, and inclusion: A collaborative model between the science teacher and the special educator. *Journal of Science for Persons with Disabilities, 3*, 31–35.

McGuire, J.M., Scott, S.S., & Shaw, S.F. (2006). Universal design and its applications in educational environments. *Remedial and special education, 27*(3), 166–175.

McLeskey, J., Landers, E., Williamson, P., & Hoppey, D. (2012). Are we moving toward educating students with disabilities in less restrictive settings? *Journal of Special Education, 46*(3), 131–140.

McLeskey, J., & Waldron, J.L. (1996). Responses to questions teachers and administrators frequently ask about inclusive school programs. *Phi Delta Kappan, 78*, 150–156.

McLeskey, J., Waldron, N.L., & Redd, L. (2012). A case study of a highly effective, inclusive elementary school. *Journal of Special Education.* Retrieved from http://sed.sagepub.com/content/early/2012/03/23/0022466912440455

McNulty, B.A., Connolly, T.R., Wilson, P.G., & Brewer, R.D. (1996). LRE policy: The leadership challenge. *Remedial and Special Education, 17*, 158–167.

Mehan, H. (1993). Beneath the skin and between the ears: A case study in the politics of representation. In S. Chaiklin & J. Lave (Eds.), *Understanding practices: Perspectives on activity and content* (pp. 241–268). Cambridge, UK: Cambridge University Press.

Mercer, C.D., Lane, H.B., Jordan, L., Allsopp, D.H., & Eisele, M.R. (1996). Empowering teachers and students with instructional choices in inclusive settings. *Remedial and Special Education, 17*, 226–236.

Miedijensky, S., & Tal, T. (2009). Embedded assessment in project-based science courses for the gifted: Insights to inform teaching all students. *International Journal of Science Education, 31*(18), 2411–2435.

Moin, L.J., Magiera, K., & Zigmond, N. (2009). Instructional activities and group work in the US inclusive high school co-taught science class. *International Journal of Science and Mathematics Education, 7*, 677–697.

Moriarty, M.A. (2007). Inclusive pedagogy: Teaching methodologies to reach diverse learners in science instruction. *Equity & Excellence in Education, 40*(3), 252–265.

National Association for Gifted Children. (2011). *Redefining gifted for a new century: Shifting the paradigm* [Position Paper]. Retrieved from www.nagc.org/index2.aspx?id=6404

National Center for Educational Statistics. (2012). Table 48. *Children 3 to 21 years old served under Individuals with Disabilities Education Act, Part B, by type of disability: Selected years, 1976–77 through 2010–11.* Retrieved from http://nces.ed.gov/programs/digest/d12/tables/dt12_048.asp

National Council on Disability. (1989, September). *The education of students with disabilities: Where do we stand?* A report to the President and Congress of the United States. Washington, DC: Author.

National Council on Disability. (2011, September). *A letter to Secretary Duncan regarding forthcoming NCLB waivers.* Retrieved from www.ncd.gov/publications/2011/September192011

National Research Council. (1996). *National science education standards.* Washington, DC: National Academies Press.

National Research Council. (2002). *National Research Council on Minority Students in Special Education and Gifted Education.* Washington, DC: National Adacemies Press.

National Research Council. (2007). *Taking science to school: Learning and teaching science in Grades K–8.* Washington, DC: National Academies Press.

National Science Board. (2010). *Preparing the next generation of STEM innovators: Identifying and developing our nation's human capital.* Retrieved from www.nsf.gov/nsb/publications/2010/nsb1033.pdf

National Science Foundation. (2011). *Broadening participation in America's STEM workforce.* Committee on Equal Opportunities in Science and Engineering Biennial Report to Congress 2009–2010. Retrieved from www.nsf.gov/od/oia/activities/ceose/reports/2009-2010_CEOSEBiennialReportToCongress.pdf

Neely, M. B. (2007). Using technology and other assistive strategies to aid students with disabilities in performing chemistry lab tasks. *Journal of Chemical Education, 84*(10), 1697.

No Child Left Behind Act of 2001, Pub. L. No. 107–110, 115 Stat. 1425 (2002).

Nolet, V., & McLaughlin, M. J. (2000). *Accessing the general curriculum: Including students with disabilities in standards-based reform.* Thousand Oaks, CA. Corwin Press.

Norman, K., Caseau, D., & Stefanich, G. (1998). Teaching students with disabilities in inclusive science classrooms: Survey results. *Science Education, 82,* 127–146.

Park, S., & Oliver, J. S. (2009). The translation of teachers' understanding of gifted students into instructional strategies for teaching science. *Journal Science Teacher Education, 20,* 333–351.

Patton, J. R. (1995). Teaching science to students with special needs. *Teaching Exceptional Children, 27*(4), 4–6.

Piirto, J. (1999). *Talented children and adults* (2nd ed.). Upper Saddle, NJ: Merrill/Prentice Hall.

Reeve, P. T., & Hallahan, D. P. (1994). Practical questions about collaboration between general and special educators. *Focus on Exceptional Children, 26*(7), 1–11.

Renzulli, J. S., Baum, S. M., Hebert, T., & McCluskey, K. W. (1999). Reversing underachievement through enrichment. Reclaiming children and youth. *Journal of Emotional and Behavioral Problems, 7,* 217–223.

Rogoff, B. (1990). *Apprenticeship in thinking: Cognitive development in social context.* New York: Oxford University Press.

Rojewski, J. W., & Pollard, R. R. (1993). A multivariate analysis of perceptions held by secondary academic teachers toward students with special needs. *Teacher Education and Special Education, 16,* 330–341.

Roth, W.-M. (2002, April). *Constructing dis/ability in science.* Paper presented at the annual meeting of the National Association for Research in Science Teaching, New Orleans, LA.

Rule, A. C., Stefanich, G. P., Boody, R. M., & Peiffer, B. (2011). Impact of adaptive materials on teachers and their students with visual impairments in secondary science and mathematics classes. *International Journal of Science Education, 33*(6), 865–887.

Salisbury, C., Mangino, M., Petrigala, M., Rainforth, B., Syryca, S., & Palombaro, M. (1994). Promoting the instructional inclusion of young children with disabilities in the primary grades. *Journal of Early Intervention, 18,* 311–322.

Sapon-Shevin, M. (1996). Full inclusion as a disclosing tablet: Revealing the flaws in our present system. *Theory Into Practice, 35*(1), 35–41.

Schaff, J., Jerome, M., Behrmann, M., & Sprague, D. (2005). Science in special education: Emerging technologies. In D. Edyburn, K. Higgins, & R. Boone, (Eds.), *Handbook of special education technology and practice* (pp. 643–660). Whitefish Bay, WI: Knowledge by Design.

Scott, B. J., Vitale, M. R., & Masten, W. G. (1998). Implementing instructional adaptations for students with disabilities in inclusive classrooms. *Remedial and Special Education, 19*(2), 106–119.

Scott, P., Mortimer, E., & Aguiar, O. (2006). The tension between authoritative and dialogic discourse: A fundamental characteristic of meaning making interactions in high school science lessons. *Science Education, 90*(4), 605–631.

Scruggs, T. E., & Mastropieri, M. A. (1993). Successful mainstreaming in elementary science classes: A qualitative study of three reputational cases. *American Research Journal, 31,* 785–811.

Scruggs, T. E., & Mastropieri, M. A. (1994). Current approaches to science education: Implications for mainstream instruction of students with disabilities. *Remedial and Special Education, 14*(1), 15–24.

Scruggs, T. E., Mastropieri, M. A., Bakken, J. P., & Brigham, F. J. (1993). Reading vs. doing: The relative effects of textbook-based and inquiry-oriented approaches to science education in special education classrooms. *Journal of Special Education, 27,* 1–15.

Scruggs, T. E., Mastropieri, M. A., Berkely, S., & Graetz, J. E. (2009). Do special education interventions improve learning of secondary content? A meta-analysis. *Remedial and Special Education, 31,* 437–449.

Seifert, K., & Espin, C. (2012). Improving reading of science text for secondary students with learning disabilities: Effects of text reading, vocabulary learning, and combined instruction. *Learning Disabilities Quarterly, 35*(4), 236–247.

Sena, J. D. W., Lowe, P. A., & Lee, S. W. (2007). Significant predictors of test anxiety among students with and without learning disabilities. *Journal of Learning Disabilities, 40*(4), 360–376.

Shaywitz, S. E. (2003). *Overcoming dyslexia: A new and complete science-based program for reading problems at any level.* New York: Knopf.

Shippen, M. E., Curtis, R., & Miller, A. (2009). A qualitative analysis of teachers' and counselors' perceptions of overrepresentation of African Americans in special education: A preliminary study. *Teacher Education & Special Education, 32*(3), 226–238.

Simos, P. G., Fletcher, J. M., Bergman, J. I., Breier, B. R., Foorman, E. M., & Castillo, R. N. (2002). Dyslexia-specific brain activation profile becomes normal following successful remedial training. *Neurology, 58,* 1203–1213.

Simpson, M., & Ure, J. (1994). *Studies of differentiation practices in primary and secondary schools. Interchange No. 30.* Scotland, UK: Scottish Office Education Department, Edinburgh, Research and Intelligence Unit.

Smith, T. E., Polloway, E., Patton, J. R., & Dowdy, C. A. (1998). *Teaching students with special needs in inclusive settings* (2nd ed.). Boston: Allyn and Bacon.

Smith, T. E. C. (2005). IDEA 2004: Another round in the reauthorization process. *Remedial and Special Education, 26*(6), 314–319.

Soukup, J. H., Wehmeyer, M. L., Bashinski, S. M., & Bovaird, J. (2007). Classroom variables and access to the general education curriculum of students with intellectual and developmental disabilities. *Exceptional Children, 74,* 101–120.

Spooner, F., Knight, V., Browder, D., Jimenez, B., & DiBiase, W. (2011). Evaluating evidence-based practice in teaching science content to students with severe developmental disabilities. *Research & Practice for Persons With Severe Disabilities, 36*(1–2), 62–75.

Stainback, S., & Stainback, W. (1990). *Understanding and conducting qualitative research.* Dubuque, IA: Council for Exceptional Children.

Stainback, W., Stainback, S., & Bunch, G. (1989). Introduction and historical background. In S. Stainback, W. Stainback, & M. Forest (Eds.), *Educating all students in the mainstream of regular education* (pp. 3–14). Baltimore, MD: Brookes.

Stainback, W., Stainback, S., & Stefanich, G. (1996). Learning together in inclusive classrooms: What about curriculum? *Teaching Exceptional Children, 28*(3), 14–19.

Steele, M. M. (2005, April 30). Teaching students with learning disabilities: Constructivism or behaviorism? *Current Issues in Education* [On-line], *8*(10). Retrieved from http://cie.ed.asu.edu/volume8/number10/

Stefanich, G. (1983). The relationship of effective schools research to school evaluation. *North Central Association Quarterly, 53,* 343–349.

Stefanich, G. (1994). Science educators as active collaborators in meeting the educational needs of students with disabilities. *Journal of Science Teacher Education, 5*(2), 56–65.

Stefanich, G., & Hadzegeorgiou, Y. (2001). Nature of the learner: Implications for teachers from the constructivist perspective. *Science teaching in inclusive classrooms: Theory & foundations* (pp. 23–43). National Science Foundation (Grant Numbers HRD-953325 and HRD 9988729).

Stephens, K. R. (2011). Federal and state response to the gifted and talented. *Journal of Applied School Psychology, 27*(4), 306–318.

Sternberg, R. J. (2001). Giftedness as developing expertise: A theory of the interface between high abilities and achieved excellence. *High Ability Students, 12*(2), 159–79.

Sternberg, R. J. (2007). Cultural concepts of giftedness. *Roeper Review, 29*(3), 160–165.

Sumida, M. (2010). Identifying twice-exceptional children and three gifted styles in the Japanese primary science classroom. *International Journal of Science Education, 32*(15), 2097–2111.

Taber, K. (Ed.). (2007). *Science education for gifted learners.* New York: Routledge.

Tannenbaum, A. J. (1997). The meaning and making of giftedness. In N. Colangelo & A. D. Davis (Eds.), *Handbook of gifted education* (2nd ed.; pp. 27–42). Boston: Allyn and Bacon.

Temple, E., Deutsch, G. K., Poldrack, R. A., Miller, S. L., Tallal, P., & M. M. Merzenich (2003). Neural deficits in children with dyslexia ameliorated by behavioral remediation: Evidence from functional MRI. *Proceedings of the National Academy of Sciences, USA, 110,* 2860–2865.

Thompson, S. (2001). The authentic standards movement and its evil twin. *Phi Delta Kappan, 82,* 358–362.

Thurlow, M. L., Ysseldyke, J. E., & Silverstein, B. (1995). Testing accommodations for students with disabilities. *Remedial and Special Education, 16*(5), 260–270.

Trundle, K. G. (2008). Inquiry-based science instruction for students with disabilities. In *Science as inquiry in the secondary setting* (pp. 79–85). Arlington, VA: NSTA Press.

Tucker, B. P., & Goldstein, B. A. (1992). *Legal rights of persons with disabilities, an analysis of federal law.* Horsham, PA: LRP Publications.

Udvari-Solner, A. (1996). Examining teacher thinking: Constructing a process to design curricular adaptations. *Remedial and Special Education, 17,* 245–254.

U.S. Department of Education. (1993). *National excellence: A case for developing America's talent.* Washington, DC: Office of Education Research and Improvement, U.S. Department of Education.

U.S. Department of Education. (2011). *30th annual report to Congress on the implementation of the Individuals with Disabilities Education Act, 2008.* Washington, DC: Office of Special Education and Rehabilitative Services, U.S. Department of Education.

Vannest, K. J., Mason, B. A., Brown, L., Dyer, N., Maney, S., & Adiguzel, T. (2009). Instructional settings in science for students with disabilities: Implications for teacher education. *Journal of Science Teacher Education, 20*(4), 353–363.

VanTassel-Baska, J. (2003). Implementing innovative curricular and instructional practices in classrooms and schools. In J. VanTassel-Baska & C. Little (Eds.), *Content-based curriculum for high-ability learners* (pp. 355–375). Waco, TX: Prufrock Press.

VanTassel-Baska, J., Bass, G., Ries, R., Poland, D., & Avery, L. D. (1998). A national study of science curriculum effectiveness with high ability students. *Gifted Child Quarterly, 42*(4), 200–211.

Walter-Thomas, C., Bryant, M., & Land, S. (1996). Planning for effective co-teaching: The key to successful inclusion. *Remedial and Special Education, 17,* 255–264.

Wang, M. C., & Reynolds, M. (1996). Progressive inclusion: Meeting new challenges in special education: Bringing inclusion into the future. *Theory Into Practice, 35*(1), 20–25.

Wei, X., Yu, J. W., Shattuck, P., McCracken, M., & Blackorby, J. (2012). Science, technology, engineering, and mathematics (STEM) participation among college students with an autism spectrum disorder. *Journal of Autism and Developmental Disorders,* 1–8. doi:10.1007/s10803-012-1700-z

Welner, K. (2006). Legal rights: The overrepresentation of culturally and linguistically diverse students in special education. *Teaching Exceptional Children, 38,* 60–62.

Wertsch, J., & Kanner, B. (1992). A sociocultural approach to intellectual development. In R. Sternberg & C. Berg (Eds.), *Intellectual development* (pp. 328–349). New York: Cambridge University Press.

Whitmore, J. R., & Maker, C. J. (1985). *Intellectual giftedness in the disabled persons.* Rockville, MD: Aspen.

Will, M. C. (1986). Educating children with learning problems: A shared responsibility. *Exceptional Children, 52*(5), 411–415.

Willard-Holt, C. (1998). Academic and personality characteristics of gifted students with cerebral palsy: A multiple case study. *Exceptional Children, 65,* 37–50.

Winter, S. (1997). "SMART" planning for inclusion. *Childhood Education, 73,* 212–218.

Wood, K. (1990). Meaningful approaches to vocabulary development. *Middle School Journal, 21*(4), 22–24.

Ysseldyke, J. E., Thurlow, M., Wotruba, J., & Nania, P. (1990). Instructional arrangements: Perceptions for general education. *Teaching Exceptional Children, 22*(4), 4–7.

Zembylas, M., & Isenbarger, L. (2002). Teaching science to students with learning disabilities: Subverting the myths of labeling through teachers' caring and enthusiasm. *Research in Science Education, 32*(1), 55–79.

13

Science Education in Urban Contexts

New Conceptual Tools and Stories of Possibilities

ANGELA CALABRESE BARTON, EDNA TAN, AND TARA O'NEILL

More than 50% of the world's population lives in urban centers. In Latin America, more than 80% of the population lives in urban communities. China's urban population has doubled since 1990, shifting from one quarter to one half of the population living in urban centers (Zhang, 2007). According to the Census Bureau in the United States, 60% of the U.S. population lives in urbanized areas of more than 200,000 people, with an additional 21% living in urbanized clusters (U.S. Census Bureau, 2010). Thus, the majority of youth in the United States and around the world live and attend schools in urban centers.

The equity issues in urban science education in cities are broad and challenging. In many countries (i.e., Thailand, China, and Vietnam), city schools are more highly resourced than their suburban and rural counterparts, having greater access to a range of instructional supports through museums, universities, and other institutions. Cities are also home to the most diverse populations per capita. Human and cultural diversity and access to resources—cities' greatest strengths—also serve to accentuate some of our world's greatest urban challenges. Historical practices such as apartheid, redlining, and other forms of marginalization have led to de facto segregation in cities, and local and national approaches to school funding have led to fundamentally inequitable schooling outcomes across race, social class, and language in city schools. A recent study of equity issues in science education in South Africa (Ramnarain, 2011) suggests that postapartheid middle-class migration to the suburbs has yielded achievement and resource gaps between urban and suburban science classrooms that parallel the stark inequalities in the United States. These inequalities also reflect the sociocultural position of groups within society. Semli and Mehta (2012) highlight the issues science teachers in Arusha, Tanzania, are struggling with: overcrowding, lack of resources, teachers with minimal science content knowledge, and devaluing students' and teachers' indigenous science knowledge. Although the

authors do not explicitly frame their study as one in the urban context, Arusha is the financial and cultural capital of the region and a major multiethnic city.

In the United States, these challenges have been under great scrutiny over the past decade. As the Council of Great City Schools in the United States reports, urban education, more than any other institution in the United States, has been singled out as a failure and is under enormous pressure to produce results (Council of Great City Schools, 2011). As illustrated in the preceding paragraph, this phenomenon is not unique to the United States (see Pink & Noblit, 2008), although the contexts and contributing factors and thus research foci differ (Luke, 2008). In North America and the UK, the focus is on the postindustrial city, sociodemographic diversity, and stratification in schooling outcomes. In developing economies such as Tanzania, Zimbabwe, and regions in South Asia, there is an emphasis on the need for compulsory education and greater accessibility across classes and ethnics. These educational structures must confront the complex negotiation of culture and systems (Luke, 2008).

In addition to the general focus on urban education, there is a global focus on low levels of success in science education, as measured by standardized and internationalized test scores, along with low levels of enrollment and graduation rates among students who attend the poorest city schools (Council of Great City Schools, 2011; Pink & Noblit, 2008). However, to classify urban education writ large as a failure in the United States and elsewhere and to speak of urban education as a homogenous experience for all who participate obfuscates the inequalities as well as the pitfalls and possibilities of education in urban contexts. All schools in an urban context are not the same, and neither are the students or their experiences in these schools. In New York City, the world-renowned Bronx High School of Science (a select science-focused public high school) sits just blocks from a much-denigrated neighborhood high school. Both are public schools in an urban context; however, they posses distinctly different reputations and provide vastly different educational experiences and opportunities. Society, as a whole, has significantly different impressions of the kinds of students who attend each of these schools and the expectations we hold for them.

What Is Urban Science Education?

This question is crucial to any discussion of urban science education. As our points suggest, the narratives that permeate urban science education simplify the issues in racially and socioeconomically charged and problematic ways.

An urban area is characterized foremost by population density. According to the U.S. Census Bureau, the term "urban" refers to a "territory, population, and housing units located within an urbanized area (UA) or an urban cluster (UC), which has: a population density of at least 1,000 people per square mile; and surrounding census blocks with an overall density of at least 500 people per square mile" (U.S. Census Bureau, 2010).

However, population density is only one of the fibers that make up the tapestry of urban centers. Urban centers are characterized by a complex ecology of population density, economic and cultural resources, politics, and geography. Urban education, according to Milner (2012), "speaks to the size and density of a particular locale; the broader environments, outside of school factors such as housing, poverty, and transportation are directly connected to what happens inside of the school" (p. 559). In the vast majority of cities around the world, these ecologies are particularly complex, giving rise to stark inequalities that continue to grow both in the developing and developed worlds and for which "urban schools" have come to be known. "The inequitable distribution of resources, the underachievement of, and the disproportionate representation of racially, culturally, ethnically, and linguistically diverse students in special needs, provides evidence of how far we have to go to realize a more just and equitable education for all of our students" (Griner, 2012, p. 2).

The term "urban" has been misappropriated by researchers, teachers, communities, and policy makers (particularly in Western countries) to reference (1) students from nondominant backgrounds (e.g., low-income/high-poverty youth and youth from underrepresented minority populations) and (2) particular school-based challenges (e.g., truancy, lack of motivation, lack of parental involvement). As noted by several scholars, this view of urban and urban education is deficit oriented, focusing on the problems and the perceived shortcomings of students, families, and teachers (Milner, 2012; Tan & Calabrese Barton, 2012). When researchers equate urban education exclusively with research on the limited academic success of youth from nondominant backgrounds, it positions these youth as "inferior others" (Mutegi, 2013, p. 82). This stance promotes the erroneous view that all urban youth in public schools are minority, low-income, and substandard students and that

White people or non-dominant people with economic means do not live in cities or attend urban schools. It neglects the rich heterogeneity that makes up urban spaces. Moreover, this view of "urban" fails to account for the capital provided by the diverse social, geographical, and cultural contexts of which cities are made. Nonetheless, the inequalities starkly present in urban education demand attention on how and why students from nondominant backgrounds disproportionately receive low-quality educational experiences.

We argue that the field of science education needs *conceptual tools* for critically unpacking the ways in which urban contexts shape science education and repositioning our collective view of urban science education as spaces of possibility rather than a collection of deficits. While we recognize urban education and urban science education as global issues, the focus on "urban education" has been most pronounced in the literature from the Western world (i.e., the United States, Canada, and the UK). In this chapter, we present a review of a subset of urban science education–focused articles that enable us to frame and delve deeply into a set of conceptual tools that show promise in research and development work in urban science education—their development, purpose, affordances, and constraints. While we examined a broader set of literature than is presented here, we limited our review to those manuscripts that offer such conceptual tools and explicitly addressed the ways in which the urban contexts matter. That a study took place in an urban context was not enough to be considered in this review.

The majority of the articles reviewed appear in the two main peer-reviewed journals (*Journal of Research in Science Teaching* and *Science Education*) since 2002. We also include articles from *Cultural Studies of Science Education*, *International Journal of Science Education*, and other top-tier, multidisciplinary-focused research journals (*American Education Research Journal*, *Journal of the Learning Sciences*, *Urban Education*, *Journal of Curriculum Studies*, and *Teachers College Record*).

Our chapter takes the following shape. First, we present a critical stance on urban science education in order to frame the challenges and possibilities of science education in urban contexts. We use this framing to raise questions that can guide the field in reframing the deficit construct of urban education and in making sense of science education in urban contexts. We then address these questions and highlight key conceptual tools using a small but exemplary set of manuscripts before offering recommendations for research and policy.

Reframing Urban Science Education: Urban Education as Sites of Possibility

Similar to urban education, the literature has constructed urban science education as a problem in need of fixing. It is a place where diversity is a challenge to be overcome (Rosebery, Ogonowski, DiSchino, & Warren, 2010) and where resources are lacking (Oakes, 1990). Dominating this literature, the media and state and federal policy discussions are "urban schools"–based statistics and stories of children who "differ" from the norm because of culture, race, class, linguistic background, and/or their families' formal schooling backgrounds.

These data clearly matter in how they foreground stark inequalities and their impact on the opportunities children have to learn science (Gutiérrez & Orellana, 2006). Such data help us understand why it is a potential problem that the majority of beginning teachers in underresourced urban schools in the United States are White, monolingual, female, middle class, and from rural and suburban communities (Clotfelter, Ladd, & Vigdor, 2005). They provide context for understanding why hiring and retaining good science teachers in urban schools is a persistent and acute problem (Oakes , Lipton, Anderson, & Stillman, 2012), with a 50% turnover rate of qualified and effective beginning science teachers in the United States (Ingersoll & Smith, 2004).

The inequities under which these schools operate are, in part, a result of inequitable fiscal and policy initiatives. Most urban schools serve disproportionately high levels of students living at or below the poverty line, yet these same districts receive the fewest per-pupil expenditure dollars, with noted intradistrict gaps (Council of Great City Schools, 2011). The largest 65 urban school systems educate 14% of U.S. public school children even though these districts make up less than one half of 1% of the nation's 17,000 school districts (Council of Great City Schools, 2011). This 14% represents close to one third of the nation's African American and English language learners and one fourth of the nation's Hispanic students and poor students, meaning that what happens in urban schools in the United States deeply affects these populations (Meyer, Carl, & Cheng, 2010, p. 4). In the United States, under recent policy initiatives, such as No Child Left Behind and Race to the Top, science has been sidelined in urban schools in favor of math and English language arts, creating inequalities in educational opportunities in science. Higher teacher turnover rates coupled with the low priority of science in the current testing climate appear to signify paltry to nonexistent science education opportunities. With such inequalities, it should not be shocking that achievement gaps for urban students and especially for urban students from nondominant groups continue to grow (NAEP, 2009). Given the framing of urban education and urban schools in the research literature and popular media, it is also not surprising that the term "urban" in science education circles has become a proxy for "poor and non-dominant."

While such harsh realities mark the science education experiences for many urban youth, these are not the only stories that can be told. In this chapter, we take an antideficit stance, recasting some of the unique characteristics of urban settings typically viewed as challenges into legitimate resources that can enrich science teaching and learning in the urban classroom. Based on these resources, we highlight three conceptual tools—place, funds of knowledge, and identity-in-practice—that should be used to frame possibilities in urban science education. The following questions guide the remainder of our review:

- What stories of possibilities are present in the research literature on the place of urban science education?
- What do these stories of possibilities teach us regarding teaching, learning, and methodological approaches?
- What are the recommendations for potentially new and continuing lines of research?

Stories of Possibilities

In this section, we present stories of possibilities that showcase data that offer productive directions for research, teaching, and learning in science education in urban settings and that develop and leverage conceptual tools for making visible the elements of possibility. In telling these narratives, three tool sets that capture the research findings focused on science education in urban settings and appropriate an antideficit lens emerge. These tool sets are (1) the *place* of urban science education, (2) *funds of knowledge* and cultural practices as sources of meaningful teaching and learning, and (3) *identity* work and lasting interest. These tool sets emerged from a broader landscape depicting rigorous science in urban classrooms. They are presented in this sequence to clearly illustrate their interconnecting threads and cumulative potential in brokering for a robust science education for urban youth. First, we present each of the tool sets, highlighting the literature and the conceptual tool(s). Second, we present a discussion across the themes, highlighting the connections among the hows and whys of the conceptual tools in facilitating rigorous science engagement for urban youth, especially as we consider their use across stakeholders.

Tool Set 1: Place

Science education in urban contexts is unique because of the complex interplay of people, history, politics, and language as well as built and ecological systems. Specifically, we view place as a geohistorical and sociocultural phenomenon, capturing the idea that places are dynamically shaped and experienced by the multitude of narratives that describe them (Gruenewald & Smith, 2008; Lim, 2010; Lim & Calabrese Barton, 2010). A focus on place, therefore, calls attention to the physical settings, human activities, and human psychological processes or meanings rooted in the place (Relph, 1976). As these dimensions intersect through activity and over time, people develop a *sense of place*, or their own unique and living sense of being in and with place. A focus on place, therefore, does not ignore the stark inequalities experienced in science education by urban youth but rather dynamically positions inequalities within the politics of participation and oppression that operate within the networked, relational, and territorial place of cities.

A sense of place, in order to be utilized productively in learning science, needs to be recognized as relevant and valued. Tzou, Scalone, and Bell (2010) describe how places are constructed *by* and *for* youth as they engage in science learning in both formal and informal environments. In particular, the authors highlight what happens when youths' sense(s) of place challenge the ways in which dominant culture positions them in oppressive ways. Using case studies of youth engaged in informal environmental science programs, Tzou and colleagues (2010) illustrate the rich personal narratives of place that youth bring with them to learning science and the ways in which these narratives shape how they engage science. One of the examples presented in the paper poignantly captures how contradictions in youths' sense of place and that which is assumed by authoritative others can actively position youth as outsiders to science. In this example, they tell of what happened when an after-school club, populated primarily by Mexican American youth, visited a city farm as part of their scientific investigation of urban ecology. Upon their arrival at the farm, the youth were greeted in Spanish by one of the (White) men in charge. There was an assumption made by the man that all of the youth spoke Spanish and preferred to be addressed in Spanish. The youth were tasked in Spanish with moving manure from compost to farm plot by wheelbarrow, despite the fact that their visit was to learn about the role of the farm in urban ecology. While engaged in this task, they noticed others at the garden were stringing plots, planting, and doing other activities less physically demanding. As their teachers noted, the youth were given the most difficult and "stinkiest" jobs, reinscribing the "dominant cultural-historical narrative that links Mexicans to doing hard labor" (p. 112).

Assumptions of place made by the farm leaders actively positioned the youth in ways that shaped their learning possibilities. As this example illustrates, the negative consequences are great when students' sense of place is assumed and/or not valued. How does an explicit focus on the urban place shape students' engagement and learning in science? In what follows, we examine studies that highlight the possibilities (and tensions) emergent in organizing science instruction around the urban place and the realities and assumptions therein. There are two main conceptual tools within the broader tool of *place* that we highlight below: (1) organizing around knowledge of place and (2) organizing around attachments to place.

Knowledge of place.   The first conceptual tool is "knowledge of place." By knowledge of place, we mean a core understanding of students' sense of place and how it informs curriculum and pedagogy and how students take these up as they engage in science. Knowledge of place is grounded in the literature in sense of place. This tool helps us think about how students' grounding place shapes their engagement and learning in science and how it is possible to leverage this understanding for meaningful teaching and learning. As a tool, knowledge of place addresses how the ways in which students frame the intersections of the physical, social, and cultural settings and how this shapes activity over time. We distinguish between curriculum and pedagogy based on topics of place. If our students live near a park, we will study the park. However, what is it about the park that matters to students, how, and why? This is the essence of this tool.

Urban children's knowledge of place and their relationship with that place are powerful sources of sense making in science in both formal (Lim & Calabrese Barton, 2006) and informal science learning environments (Buxton, 2010). Next we present two studies that explicitly invoke a focus on knowledge of place for organizing science instruction.

The first study we examine is Buxton's (2010) study of the impact of the Social Problem Solving through Science project (SPSS) on middle school youth. With a more pronounced emphasis on social justice than many of the school-based studies, we see how a focus on place allows for innovative approaches to leveraging students' funds of knowledge and contexts in powerful and transformative ways. The SPSS project engaged middle school–aged youth in the study of local environmental challenges with implications for human health and well-being both globally and locally. Through a series of inquiry-based investigations on water health and safety at an urban seaside nature center, the students studied environmental risk factors related to water. One of the outcome projects was for students to create and share "public service announcements" in the form of posters to educate their peers, family, and community members about one of the public health topics they had studied.

Using both critical pedagogy and place-based perspectives, the study shows how, when a sense of place is taken as the core of the curriculum, middle school–aged youth transform both their understanding of their place in the world and also their science knowledge in the study of local environmental challenges, with implications for human health. This blending of conceptual tools is important. As Buxton (2010) notes, "While place based pedagogy asks students to better understand their local environmental context, it does not have a history of unpacking the power dynamics or political history that has largely determined who lives where and with access to what resources" (p. 124). At issue here is how a teacher can leverage a pedagogy of place to foreground the students' (and teacher's) relationship with their place as integral to science learning—in how their context and location matter when it comes to interpreting and understanding the natural world.

Lim and Calabrese Barton (2006) provide insight into how knowledge of place shaped engagement in school science learning. Unlike the Buxton study, which focused more on how a focus on knowledge of place transforms student learning, this study focuses more on the pedagogical tensions emergent in such practice and how these tensions can lead to unanticipated moments of possibility. Their study explores urban youths' sense of place and the use of their sense of place in an urban middle school (Grade 6–8) environmental statistics classroom in New York City. Using a combination of participatory observations, interviews, mapping, autophotography, content-based think-alouds, and the collection of students' class work, the authors analyze how the youths' sense of place impacted class investigations during two environmental science units: the Pigeons Study and the Playground Study. The goal of the Pigeon Study unit was for students to recognize the different color morphs of pigeons and to statistically analyze the pigeon population in the school's neighborhood. The goal of the Playground Study was for students to study existing playgrounds in the school's neighborhood in order to design their own playgrounds, taking into consideration the types of materials they would use that would make their playground fun, aesthetically pleasing, and safe.

While there are multiple aspects of this study, there are two findings we find to be particularly salient. First, across these two units, students expressed a sense of place in science class along four dimensions: "(1) a mix of the cognitive with the affect, (2) drawn from several sources, (3) operationalized interdimensionally, and (4) contextualized in ways that made it both subjective and personal" (p. 117). Second, valuing and leveraging students' sense of place in the context of school science nurtures a dynamic learning environment and creates opportunities to learn "content science" (p. 31).

A good example of the ways in which sense of place shapes sense making in science is presented in the authors' discussion of the Pigeon Study. During the unit, while the students were outside observing collections of pigeons, a student asked, "Can pigeons be racist?" (p. 127). This question is interesting for three reasons. First, the asking of this one question embodies all four dimensions along which the authors observed students expressing their sense of place. The student's attempt to make sense of the pigeons in his neighborhood and his everyday experiences as a young Latino invited his peers and teacher into his sense-making efforts. The students grappled with data from their field trip during which they observed that pigeons of different morphs gathered together and did not observe any segregating behavior among the different morphs. Second, the teacher's response to this question is important to note. Rather then dismissing the question, or worse, making fun of it, the teacher replied to the whole class, "Ah . . . That is a big question . . . I mean what is racism?" (p. 127). In so doing, the teacher, in that moment, both valued and leveraged that student's sense of place and sparked a dynamic class discussion. The student's question provided an opportunity for the class to revisit and review what they had observed and to rethink the meanings of their observations in a new way. Though initially most of the students in the class argued that pigeons could be racist, they were forced to reconsider that conjecture when one of their classmates pointed out that during their observations, they had not seen the pigeons separate themselves by color or other identifiable characteristics. When the students' sense of place was leveraged through questioning, it not only helped the student's personal sense making but also benefited the whole class with an engaging learning opportunity.

Attachments to place.   The second conceptual tool is attachments to place. The mechanisms by which place shapes learning are shaped by the ways in which urban youth are *rooted in place*. The psychological, social, and physical connections to place are not only sources of knowledge as discussed above but also critical leverage points if the *nature of the connection* is made evident (Endreny, 2010; Rose & Calabrese Barton, 2012). The nature of the attachments is framed by how students connect to place. These can be emotional attachments, but these can also be economic, familial, or community attachments. Next we examine two studies that trace how attachments to place provide a substantive basis for science learning in ways that enrich understanding.

In the first study, we look at the importance of recognizing emotional attachments and the role they play in curriculum enactments. Endreny (2010) reports on a partnership between a university earth science department and a northeastern postindustrial city school system. The teacher-researcher sought to determine how a unit on watersheds might transform student learning if students were to investigate the watershed where their school is located. While the goals of this unit and research focus more on student understanding of science concepts than on the emotional attachments and meaning that are referred to as sense of place, this unit still fits within the place-based education continuum. She reports that most of the students "came to understand that their watershed was part of an urban environment where water drains from the surrounding land into a body of water" and "how urban land use affects water quality" (p. 510). The author also reports that the majority of students did not learn concepts "that were only taught through lessons within the classroom walls" (p. 515).

Endreny argues that place-based science education in urban contexts supports students in developing scientific understanding by leveraging an *emotional attachment* to place. She suggests that place-based education does more than focus on the geographical or natural features of the phenomenon under investigation (in her case, the local watershed) but that these features are made salient to students because they also integrate the "diverse meanings that place holds for the instructor, the students and the community" and "teaches by authentic experiences such as field work or in an environment that strongly evokes that place" (p. 516). For example, diverse perspectives and forms of expertise were incorporated through teacher and parent stories about the watershed from when they were children, as well as visits to the watershed as families.

In the second study, we look at a more complex interaction grounded in place: how students' economic and community concerns shape how they engage with and solve a socioscientific problem. This example involves youth in a community club–based after-school program focused on green energy and the environment (Rose & Calabrese Barton, 2012). In this study, researchers examined how youth constructed decisions on whether to support their city's plan to build a new hybrid power plant. Using critical sociocultural perspectives on learning and qualitative case study, the authors illustrate how two youth navigated a controversial community issue (i.e., building a hybrid power plant) and how they leveraged local resources, scientific and otherwise, in defining the problem from their perspective and eventually coming to a resolution (i.e., crafting a final position statement in regard to building a new power plant).

Just before the beginning of a unit on alternative energies, the city's electric company sent a letter to all city residents informing them of the need to close the city's existing coal-burning power plant due to changes in emissions standards. Unfortunately, this plant was also responsible for 69% of the city's electricity. As such, the electric company proposed building a new hybrid power plant and asked for feedback from the community. The after-school instructors used this opportunity as a vehicle for engaging the students in a 4-month investigation into whether their city should build a new hybrid power plant. During this unit, students surveyed adult residents regarding their opinions about the proposed power plant, researched and tested forms of alternative energy (i.e., wind, solar), studied the electric company's hybrid power plant proposal, and researched the environmental impacts of both the old and the proposed power plant.

Findings from this study indicate that the scientific knowledge youth brought with them (e.g., causes and functions of climate change, air pollution, and asthma) and acquired over the course of the investigation influenced how they made sense of the issue. However, their knowledge was deeply connected to a range of personal and public place-negotiated discourses that influenced how they defined the issue and why it mattered to them. In particular, it was through how they framed their range of knowledge and experiences that they were able to recognize the multidimensional nature of the problem and propose complex solutions resonant with the science they understood.

For example, Jeremy, a seventh grader, understood the need for "a step up" from the old power plant. The new plant would be "cleaner and more efficient" and would "produce less CO_2," and produce more electricity with less harm to the environment. And while the design was not perfect—he worried that the plant would still rely on coal for 70% of its electrical production and that burning coal does emit CO_2 and other harmful emissions—he strongly espoused the need for the new jobs a new plant might provide for his city, which suffers from high unemployment. In building his argument, he leveraged the statements of professional scientists and data he collected

from experiments he conducted. Jeremy's reasonings were based in both his scientific understanding and his multilayered personal, political, and public perspectives of place. He positions himself a part of his place in how he asserts, if opponents to the plant "say they want less coal, then I will say we are working towards it" (Rose & Calabrese Barton, 2012, p. 553).

This study reveals how *critical connections to place shape how and why youth engage science, and the roles they play in science.* Youth made sense of broader scientific content and problems by foregrounding economic concerns—whether it be making electricity affordable or creating jobs. That these youth live in an economically depressed city and in lower-income families that have experienced job loss is important to how they connect with the broader scientific investigation. In particular, these youth leverage their expertise of both place and energy-related issues to reposition science as engaging and connected to the community for a local audience and to reposition themselves in science (i.e., Jeremy making himself a partner of the electric company).

Tool set 1 summary. Across these studies, we see the importance of two conceptual tools: knowledge of place and attachments to place. A person's sense of place plays a vital role in determining what expertise and experiences are leveraged when deciding on a course of action. These studies indicate that youths' engagement with place as a part of learning and doing science is central to productive disciplinary engagement. Their scientific understandings, alongside their capacity to navigate the physical and social spaces of their community, constitutes expertise that they leverage to make meaning of new science content, apply that content to their everyday lives, and share their knowledge of issues with community members.

Tool Set 2: Funds of Knowledge

The previous conceptual tools examined the complex and dynamic construct of place and the ways in which place shapes engagement in the learning environment. This next set of tools homes in on one aspect of place: the funds of knowledge that youth develop in community and their role in student science learning and engagement. Learning science is a long-term process of becoming a legitimate participant and involves learning the discourses and practices of science (Lave & Wenger, 1991). For students for whom science represents different ways of knowing, talking, or doing than are prevalent in their life experiences, figuring out how to negotiate the multiple texts, discourses, and knowledge available within the learning community can be a challenging undertaking (Moje, Collazo, Carillo, & Marx, 2001; Rosebery et al., 2010).

Funds of knowledge are defined by researchers Luis Moll, Cathy Amanti, Deborah Neff, and Norma González (1992) "to refer to the historically accumulated and culturally developed bodies of knowledge and skills essential for household or individual functioning and well-being"

(p. 133). Funds of knowledge are posited as repositories of valuable resources or "accumulated bodies embodied knowledge of households" (Moll et al., 1992, p. 133) that can be strategically tapped as a foundation for more sophisticated content-based learning. Studies of youth in urban contexts and their funds of knowledge and discourses have been of growing interest in science education. These studies reveal new possibilities for engaging youth in science, with a particular focus on youth from nondominant backgrounds.

We specifically separate funds of knowledge from place. Knowledge of and attachment to place highlight the importance of how and why youth may view particular topics or investigations with particular lenses—how does my place matter to me? Funds of knowledge speak more specifically to the rich cultural and cognitive resources that youth bring to classrooms by virtue of their experiences, over time, in their families and community. As a conceptual tool, funds of knowledge ask teachers and researchers to position themselves not as experts but as learners with their students.

There are three specific ways in which funds of knowledge serves as tools in building possibilities for productive science teaching and learning in science in urban settings.

First, youth from urban contexts have a rich store of funds of knowledge and local practices reflective of their cultural and linguistic backgrounds and their local communities. These cultural knowledges and practices of youth have been framed as distinct from science knowledge and practice. However, the studies we present next illustrate the powerful ways in which they function as important tools in building community among learners, breaking down normative practices in the classroom that "consciously or unconsciously function to create inequitable spaces within classrooms" and supporting consequential learning in science (Emdin, 2010, p. x; see also Tan & Calabrese Barton, 2007, 2008, & 2010; Zimmerman, 2012).

Second, when teachers have profound understandings of students' cultural backgrounds, they are able to engage pedagogical practices that foster full and authentic engagement by their students, with particular attention to those students for whom success in school science has been most elusive. When students are provided with opportunities to leverage cultural practices in support of developing scientific knowledge and practice, they engage in higher-level scientific reasoning and participate productively in scientific inquiry (Calabrese Barton & Tan, 2009; Upadhyay, 2005, 2010; Varelas & Pappas, 2006).

Third, classroom communities are robust and complex spaces encompassing a variety of funds of knowledge and their attendant discourses, whether recognized or not. Designing instructional encounters with how students' lived experiences intersect with these discourses creates continuous and multiple possibilities for seeing the world scientifically (Rosebery & Warren, 2008; Varelas et al., 2010). In what follows, we first illustrate how funds of knowledge shape how and why students engage in science

and the role that knowledge of students' funds of knowledge can play in instructional design.

Youths' funds of knowledge and cultural practices. In the 2002 review of the literature on urban science education, a section was devoted to the importance of developing students' funds of knowledge in science learning. As noted in that review, the research on this topic that occurred prior to 2002 highlighted primarily sources and areas of knowledge that were parts of the cultural toolkits that youth bring to learning science. Published research since 2002 continues this line of thought but with a stronger focus on discourse in which these funds are situated and in which the meaning of such knowledge and its associated practices take shape. Next we present three studies that examine the possibilities created for learning when students' funds of knowledge are recognized as discourse and practice in the classroom.

In our own work, we have tried to elucidate how the approach to using funds of knowledge as a core conceptual tool for understanding student learning provides nuanced insight into how and why urban youth engage in science (Basu & Calabrese Barton, 2007; Calabrese Barton & Tan, 2009). In both of these studies, we draw on qualitative methodologies to investigate the connections between the funds of knowledge that students from lower-income, urban settings bring to science learning and the development of a sustained interest in science. In the first of these studies, we examined closely the science experiences of a group of youth in after-school science (Basu & Calabrese Barton, 2007). Presenting the stories of three youth in depth, we attempted to situate our claims regarding the students' funds of knowledge in context, adding both depth and rigor to our analysis. We found that youth developed a sustained interest in science when their funds of knowledge became an integral part of how and why they engaged in after-school science. In particular, we noted that when the students' science experiences connected with how they viewed their future and when the science activities supported students' sense of agency for enacting these views, they maintained an interest in science over the course of middle school. Important were both cultural and social funds of knowledge, including enacting practices that linked home and school, such as taking things apart and putting them back together, and elevating the importance of social relationships in doing science.

In another study, Moje and her colleagues (Moje et al., 2004) analyze the "intersections and disjunctures between everyday (home, community, peer group) and school funds of knowledge and Discourse (Gee, 1990) that frame the school-based, content area literacy practices" of middle school youth (p. 39). The study was conducted over more than 5 years, among 30 Latino/a youth in Detroit, Michigan. What the study reveals is that there were clear patterns in both the connections that students made between their everyday funds of knowledge and science and the ways in which youth leveraged their funds of knowledge toward learning science. The authors highlight four core areas of knowledge: family, community, peer groups, and popular culture. As the authors illustrate these funds, they also carefully link these funds to their attendant discourses and point out the ways in which the funds and discourses are connected and/or disconnected from the science classroom. For example, in discussing funds associated with work in the home, Moje and colleagues (2004) describe how youth learn to carefully observe activities in the home such as different cooking procedures and from these observations develop important insights into scientific phenomena:

> During a lesson on complete and incomplete combustion, a seventh-grade girl used the frying of tortillas to explain her argument that smoke was not white, as the teacher had claimed, but black . . . Had the teacher heard this whispered comment, he could have used Tana's knowledge of the "black stuff " produced in burning to clarify his point and to extend the discussion on combustion.
>
> (p. 53)

In addition to providing sources of knowledge for scientific phenomenon, Moje also reveals how funds of knowledge position the importance of multiple discourses as central to knowing and doing science. Citing the example of youth experiences with familial jobs in "dry-cleaning establishments, construction sites, and auto plants, all industries with direct connections to community air- and water-quality issues," the authors make the argument that knowledge of family work in these areas fosters an awareness of the "economic and social consequences of scientific activity," making talk about science more complex (p. 52).

In the third study, we focus more closely on cultural practices as critical funds of knowledge for learning and engagement. The value of non-dominant students' funds of knowledge and associated cultural practices in urban classrooms is also a core tenet of Emdin's (2010) work with high school inner-city youth. Different from Moje and colleagues (2004), who take the stance that funds of knowledge reflect areas of knowledge, this study looks at hip-hop as a source of knowledge (see Hogg, 2011, for an elaboration on this distinction). Emdin (2010) makes a compelling case for the close connection between hip-hop culture and that of science and advocates for the deliberate embracing of the former (replete with its attendant sets of actions and behaviors) into urban science classrooms. As he describes it, hip-hop as a culture beckons to those who have been marginalized by societal norms, who are often plagued with poverty and oppressed by racism—the profile of the majority of non-dominant students in urban schools. Alienated from mainstream school and science discourse, non-dominant youth gather agentically under the banner of hip-hop. Emdin argues that the "passion students have for hip-hop should be ignited within conventional educational settings" (p. 2), given that many of the practices students employ as committed participants of hip-hop culture, such as memorizing lyrics and debate, are also tools that can belong in a science classroom.

Using the example of cogenerative dialogues in science as related to rap cypher in hip-hop, Emdin draws out the similarities between the two practices: all voices heard, democratic turn-taking to talk, cogeneration of an action plan to improve qualities of a shared community. The youth Emdin works with are skilled participants of rap cypher—where rappers stand in a supportive circle to recite raps, share ideas, and encourage one another to further the field of rap. By inviting the youth from a high school with a health science profession focus and another high school serving as a suspension center to engage in cogenerative dialogues with science teachers and science education researchers (replicating the core structures of a rap cypher), Emdin reports that the youth were able to candidly examine their experiences in science and reasons for their lack of interest. The youth from both institutions commented on feeling alienated from science as it should be—a subject with hands-on activities. These dialogues led to suggestions and plans, coconstructed by students and teachers, on how to change the science curriculum to better address student interests and concerns. During cogenerative dialogues, youth also generated analogies between science concepts and the happenings in hip-hop culture. For example, youth related the phenomenon of electron gain or loss by an atom to how hip-hop rap stars gain or lose fans based on their commercial success. While those who are not intimately part of hip-hop culture may question the value of such an analogy, Emdin argues that for hip-hop youth, the ability to leverage cultural knowledge in the science classroom not only gives them more impetus to engage with the science content, such connections also have enduring effects in the youths' developing positive relationships with science and school.

Teachers' leveraging funds of knowledge towards meaningful learning. The research literature indicates that new teachers often take positions teaching youth from much different backgrounds from their own. New teachers—the majority of whom are White, monolingual, and female—are more likely to begin working in hard-to-staff school districts having high proportions of students of color, poor students, and English language learners (Cochran-Smith & Zeichner, 2005). Contrasts between the lived experiences of students and their families and those of classroom teachers may inhibit the development of intellectual and affective connections between school and students' out-of-school lives (Bouillion & Gomez, 2001; Buck & Skilton-Sylvester, 2005). Especially at risk are students from nondominant households and those at urban schools. Inexperienced in teaching and unfamiliar with the out-of-school lives of their students, new teachers may be especially at risk of failing to elicit, recognize, or effectively leverage students' knowledge and skills in ways that are productive and allow for a fluidity of movement across borders (García & Guerra, 2004). This further obscures the potential utility of students' funds of knowledge to support science learning.

Thus, the studies that have highlighted the role of the classroom teachers in eliciting and validating students' cultural resources and the potentially positive affective, participatory, and academic outcomes offer critical insights into more equitable science instruction. Below we look at three manuscripts, which take up how teachers design for the integration of students' funds of knowledge in the classroom.

In the first of these studies, Upadhyay (2006) describes a fourth-grade teacher's enactment of a life and environment science curriculum in her urban classroom. In sharing her own lived experiences and allowing students to bring their own funds of knowledge to bear on science lessons, the teacher helped students "to make sense of science, embrace science learning, and feel welcome in a new environment" (Upadhay, 2006, p. 107). In this study, Upadhay (2006) reported on a case study of Jane, a White, female science teacher in her 50s, who was purposeful in soliciting for and harnessing urban students' funds of knowledge and everyday experiences in her elementary science classroom. Upadhyay's study points out that it is equally important to pay attention to the teacher's lived experiences and knowledges as well. For Jane, her personal experiences with limited science instruction when she was a student, attending public school in Germany where she was an outsider, having lived in countries with other first languages apart from English, and watching her daughter struggle with science all led to her crafting a science teaching philosophy in which "students have to have a part of guiding the lessons . . . [as] that allows them to take risks and own the lesson" (p. 106). Here is a White, female teacher who has encountered marginalization and experienced what it means to be a member of a diverse community, who has personally struggled with science as a learner, and who appreciates the value of science and the importance of having opportunities to do science. As a result, Jane values and practices inclusive teaching, firm in her belief that her ethnically diverse students have "so many different experiences, ideas, views, and knowledge that I should use them in my teaching . . . [as] a "tool that [can] enhance my own learning as well as other students' learning of science" (p. 102).

Inviting students to be a part of the curriculum translated into Jane actively asking students for their daily encounters relevant to the science topic under investigation. For example, while learning about nutrition, Jane positioned students as "food scientists." She asked for students' questions and everyday observations about food choices made by family members and to critique the choices adult family members made in feeding their babies. Upadhyay reported a high level of student enthusiasm and participation in which dialogue and heteroglossia were clearly evident, with teacher Jane skillfully weaving students' funds of knowledge and questions into scientific inquiry. Key concepts such as nutritional value of different

food sources and the complex connections between lifestyle and dietary changes were discussed. This case study stressed the importance of recognizing students' funds of knowledge as a legitimate knowledge base for learning science concepts and making connections between science, students' everyday lived experiences, and their future life choices.

Next, we highlight a study that looks at the use of drama among early elementary school children in their study of two integrated science-literacy units focused on matter and forests (Varelas et al., 2010). The authors pose the question: What are "the possibilities and challenges that arise as children and teachers engaged in scientific knowing through such experiences" (Varelas et al., 2010, p. 306)? In particular, the researchers were interested in what they call the "togetherness of dramatizing" (p. 306), or how the teacher and her students' dramatization fostered scientific discourse.

The authors raise several important points. Reminding the reader that all learning and action is mediated, they show us how new understandings of the particulate nature of matter among young people emerges collaboratively and interactionally. They show us how drama—how being able to use one's whole body as a tool to imagine science—supported multimodal sense making, allowing for greater opportunities to negotiate ambiguity around concepts and communicating meaning. That these children were exploring ideas that were, according to the national science standards, several grade levels above expectation, makes these findings seem particularly salient. Additionally, the dramatic enactments of the scientific ideas under investigation operated on what the authors refer to as "multiple mediated levels": as "material objects that moved through space, as social objects that negotiated classroom relationships and rules, and as metaphorical objects that stood in for water molecules in the various states of matter or for entities in a food web" (p. 320).

In the third of these studies, O'Neill (2010) describes a 3-year teacher action research study focused on supporting students in developing ownership in the science classroom. O'Neill (2010) presents two vignettes to illustrate how students fostered ownership in the school science setting, how this supported students' engagement in science class, and how specific "ownership structures" supported students' cultivation of ownership. These vignettes make evident the role of a teacher recognizing and leveraging students' funds of knowledge in fostering spaces of student ownership in the science classroom and how these spaces led to increased student engagement and learning outcomes.

An example of this is found in the vignette of Sneaker Boy, a student who began his seventh-grade year identifying as a "bad kid" who believed he got "kick[ed] out of stuff for stupid things because the teachers hated [him]" (p. 13). Given his previous poor academic experiences in school science and his distrust of teachers, Sneaker Boy was reluctant to engage in science class. However, the classroom had been designed around a number of "ownership structures." These were physical locations in the classroom that were meant to create "a clear expectation for students to engage and interact with each other, the teacher, and the physical space in order to create a shared learning environment" (p. 12). One of these structures was the class zoo. This was a collection of shelves on a wall of the classroom that held fish, turtle tanks, and other animals students brought in to share with their class. Sneaker Boy had a general affinity for all animals and took great interest in the maintenance and care of the class zoo.

At the beginning of the school year, during science class Sneaker Boy rarely engaged with the content being studied and often looked as though he could not wait for the bell to ring. However, during lunch and after school, the most likely place to find Sneaker Boy was in the science classroom either caring for the class zoo or instructing his peers on how to care for the animals. O'Neill found that Sneaker Boy was able to position himself as an animal expert, effectively becoming her teacher. How O'Neill and Sneaker Boy collectively activated his funds of knowledge shifted his authority in the classroom and increased his access to material and nonmaterial resources for doing science.

This shift in authority was an important precursor to Sneaker Boy's increased engagement during science class. Toward the middle of the school year during a science lesson on bacteria, Sneaker Boy discovered that he was able to connect the content of the science lesson to his work with the class zoo. While the teacher was lecturing on different types of bacteria, he raised his hand as if to ask a question. When called upon, Sneaker Boy began to "interject his knowledge [of bacteria] not as a question or as an interesting statement but as a voice of authority, almost taking on a co-teaching role" (p. 14). The shift in authority created via interaction in connection with the class zoo had, over time, altered the culture of the classroom such that the teacher was not the only science content authority. This shift in classroom culture is significant because it opens opportunities for students' meaningful participation in science, promotes students' generation of positive identities in relation to science practice and content, and presents students with extended opportunities of their own making to demonstrate their science understanding and connection of the content to their lives.

Extending the arc of science through cultural heterogeneity in the classroom. Over the last few decades, contrasting traditions have emerged with respect to the relationship between scientific knowledge and children's culturally based understandings, practices, and experiences. The discontinuity tradition highlights the disjunctures between the students' worlds and school science and presents children's ways of knowing and talking as potential impediments to robust learning. Studies on funds of knowledge and discourse challenge the discontinuity tradition by focusing on how children make ongoing connections to scientific content matter through their everyday discourses (Warren & Ogonowksi, 2005). A continuous stance toward children's ideas, experiences, and ways of talking and knowing requires teachers to engage in revealing the competencies that children bring with them to learning. The purpose of instruction thus becomes to develop more robust scientific understanding through refinement of students' prior knowledge and experiences rather than through their replacement.

For example, Rosebery and Warren (2008) illustrate how youth from nondominant backgrounds have repertoires of cultural practices that are highly relevant to doing science. These resources constitute part of the cultural identity of the classroom and can be leveraged toward developing a kind of practice in science that attends to both the discipline and the home. They show us how, in bilingual classrooms, students often imagine themselves a part of science and of the scientific phenomenon they are trying to understand, even when they feel marginalized by norms and practices of school science. Instead of expecting students to "cross over" into the culture of school science, where one's primary discourse is viewed as discontinuous with that of school science or mathematics, the process of acculturation should attend to how outside discourses productively transform a community.

The authors note that children are sophisticated consumers of schooling. Many get the idea that to do well, you have to "play the school science game" (Rosebery & Warren, 2008, p. 109). Yet, especially for children whose ways of exploring the world, whose words, meanings and ways of knowing do not align with the normative practices of schooling, learning science becomes an inauthentic endeavor. Having opportunities to play with science, to imagine oneself a part of the phenomenon or in a what-if scenario, and to actively position oneself as a part of science create transformative possibilities for significant science thinking and doing. Calabrese Barton, Tan, and Rivet (2008) also note that being playful in science, by taking on the identities of others to role play scientific thinking, creates a safer classroom space for testing out ideas. They further note that these moments of role playing also activate a broader expanse of real and symbolic resources for doing science, including peer enthusiasm and epistemological authority, resources not often available to youth who may feel marginal to school science. These kinds of expanded outcomes speak directly to the pathways for learning science, but they also speak to the outcomes. Succeeding in science involves a careful merging of knowing, being, and doing in the classroom, a complex interweaving impossible to capture on paper and pencil exams.

Rosebery, and colleagues' (2010) study is another excellent example of how the varied discourse of youth is both "a necessary and generative, although often underdeveloped or unrecognized, aspect of learning and teaching" science (p. 326). Whether recognized or not, the heterogeneity of discourse is always present in the classroom. Providing spaces to allow students to make thinking visible through their own discourses intentionally broadened the discourses allowed in the classroom, providing new spaces for teachers to recognize when ideas needed to be further explored and for students to analytically create meaningful personal and scientific connections.

Rosebery and colleagues (2010) analyze children's discourse in a third- and fourth-grade classroom during a series of lessons focused on heat transfer and the particulate nature of matter. They illustrate how discussions around heat transfer and matter, which were both planned and emergent of the lived experiences children brought to the classroom, provided space for reinterpreting understandings and practices through the "eyes and language of the Second Law [of thermodynamics]" (p. 337). Their work was built around three pedagogical values: first, that classrooms must be "provisioned . . . with scientific tools, materials, and activities" to allow for emergent and planned encounters around scientific ideas to happen (p. 351). Second, the allowable discourse space in the science classroom needed to purposefully invite and value a wide range of talk, including the scientific and the myriad other ways of knowing children bring to understanding their worlds. Third, analytic work that crossed scientific and everyday worlds should be encouraged as valid inquiry. By enacting these values, the researchers show how teachers and students collaboratively create and sustain heterogeneous encounters with science. In one example, the authors describe how the students in the classroom leveraged personal, everyday, and science resources to build a more robust understanding of heat transfer. The students in the classroom had been investigating the second law of thermodynamics and doing various experiments, such as putting ice in bags by the window of the classroom. One day, the teacher asked the students to use the second law to explain why they wear coats in the winter. The teacher reported that the conversation was stilted, and then the fire alarm went off unexpectedly. Children went outside without coats and began to talk among themselves about why they were getting cold, what was happening to their body heat, and what they might do to stay warm. The authors explain what happened:

> Prior to the fire drill, they said things like "Because it is cold" and "To stay warm because it's windy and cold." These responses were based in their everyday knowledge of ways to respond to the reality of winter in New England. After the fire drill, however, their thinking about coats was infused with the Second Law, aspects of which they used to frame causal explanations (i.e., "Because your blood is warm blooded and the warm goes into the coat," "When you zip [your jacket] all the way up to the top it traps um the warmness in you," "When you go outside your body heat flows out of you but when you put a coat on it acts as a stopper for the body heat and it traps it."
>
> (p. 339)

The authors argue that the experience during the fire drill "brought the Second Law to life in a way that neither the words of the law alone nor their prior experience with

cold had. Here, their experience and the Second Law made contact, each giving shape to the other's potential meaning" (p. 335). This example highlights how, for students themselves, science is not something bounded in the classroom. Rather, science is relevant and key to making sense of everyday experiences, such as feeling cold without a coat because of haste mandated in a fire drill. Science teachers should both seize and create such opportunities to engage in heteroglossia (Bakhtin, 1981), where everyday experiences are validated as legitimate text in the science classroom alongside canonic scientific discourse.

Tool set 2 summary. These studies highlight the rich resources in cultural knowledge, practice, and discourse that can and should be employed in the science classroom. They make the case that urban youth are not so impoverished in possessing the tools to learn science, as most assume them to be. These studies provide insight into how the urban context matters in terms of the complex heterogeneity of people and histories and how a teacher might recognize and draw upon those in teaching science. These studies also provide us with a glimpse of the possibilities of what robust science urban youth can engage in if they are empowered to do so, when their funds of knowledge, interests, and talents are rightfully respected and actively recruited ass valid tools for learning science.

In our summary, we would be remiss if we did not include a careful critique levied on how funds of knowledge are taken up vis-à-vis discussions of cultural capital in academic spaces. Rios-Aguilar and colleagues (Rios-Aguilar, Kiyama, Gravitt, & Moll, 2011) raise the question, "Are funds of knowledge for the poor and forms of capital for the rich?" (p. 163). These authors argue that these constructs are differentially applied to youths and their cultural knowledge and experience based upon "social class and the privileges associated with them" (p. 179). They further argue that this matters because it shapes how the education community frames what and why it means to activate these knowledge, discourses, and practices toward educational attainment. This is not so much a critique of the Funds Of Knowledge (FOK) research as much as it is an imperative to advance the development of FOK to attend to the "specific mechanisms in which activation/mobilization of social and cultural capital and funds of knowledge occur" for youth from lower-income backgrounds. We see some work done along these lines in the studies discussed (Calabrese Barton & Tan, 2009; Rosebery et al., 2010), but more work should be done in this area.

Tool Set 3: Identities-in-Practice and Identity Work

Science has long been deemed the domain of White, middle-class males (e.g., Sadker, Sadker, & Zittleman, 2009). Urban youth or inner-city youth, of which a large percentage are non-dominant and poor, often do not identify with science (e.g., Brickhouse & Potter, 2001; Emdin,

2010; Fordham, 1993). Thus, in addition to the science achievement gap between White and non-dominant youth, there is also an *identity gap* that needs to be addressed. Alongside conceptual understanding and content mastery, attention needs to be paid to students' identity construction (Wenger, 1998) so as to elucidate how non-dominant students make sense of themselves and science as they engage in scientific experiences.

Despite two decades of sustained science education reform efforts enacted under the banner of "science for all," professionals in the Science, Technology, Engineering, and Mathematics (STEM) fields still remain largely White. The percentage of African Americans in STEM professions has increased by a mere 2 to 3% in the last 30 years (National Science Board, 2012). In 2011, African Americans received just 7% of STEM–related bachelor degrees, 4% of masters, and 2% of doctorates (Kaba, 2013), while Latino/as, at 4%, are the most underrepresented ethnic group in STEM professions. At the K–12 level, science education is plagued with the "leaky pipeline" phenomenon in which the number of students who drop out of science classes increases with each successive year (Chapa & De La Rosa, 2006; Gandara, 2006). It has also been shown that, for African American youth, their sense of self as African American students in relation to a particular discipline (i.e., science or mathematics) is related to their achievement (Chavous et al., 2003). For some non-dominant youth, to do well in school means one is guilty of "acting White" (Fryer, 2006). It is likely that doing well in science can cause a non-dominant youth to be similarly judged. Taking into consideration the traditional culture of canonical science with its specialized scientific language, youth, and especially non-dominant youth, have to be convinced that there is a net gain in the trade-off they are required to make to be successful in science—namely forgoing everyday self- and community-affirming practices for the distant culture of science (Gee, 2004).

Identities-in-practice is a fundamental tool for supporting students' engagement and investment in science education. Researchers such as Brickhouse, Lowery, and Schultz (2000) have pointed out that students need to see themselves in science before being persuaded to engage with the subject matter. We need to be concerned about youth's identity development in science, asking such questions as "Who is successful in science?," "Who do I become when I engage in science?," and "Can I see myself enjoying science and pursuing science?" In short, what is the relationship between doing science and who students are and who they want to be? Before students can be motivated to learn science, they have to develop identities that are congruent with science.

Identities-in-practice are authored or constructed in practice, within activity systems or figured worlds (Holland, Lachicotte, Skinner, & Cain, 2001). When youth are learning about science content knowledge in a classroom, they are also learning about the rules and norms of science, what counts as scientific, who is valued in

science, and what one needs to be able to do to be deemed successful in science. Through engaging in identity work via the actions they take and the relationships they form, youth position themselves as particular types of people in science through time and space. The reception of one's identity work by others in the figured world (e.g., peers, science teacher) highlights its highly dialectic nature. That one is also a concurrent member of other figured worlds while a science student (e.g., basketball player, girl, band member, African American) further shows the complexity of identity work, as competing expectations about who one can and should be from figured worlds jostle against one another. Such interactions can result in tensions like "acting White."

We focus on four papers in this section, each reporting on how the identity work of non-dominant youth in the urban context served as a tool for supporting or deterring students' engagement in a given science learning context. Two of the studies take place in the formal science classroom, one in an after-school science context and one that traverses both formal and informal science spaces.

Varelas, Kane, and Wylie (2011) reported on how 25 young African American students in the first, second, and third grades constructed identities as they engaged in reform-based science. The students in their study had opportunities to participate in scientific inquiry through various activities and discussions. They also kept science journals with drawings and notes. The authors used these journals as identity artifacts to engage the children in a series of conversations. They sought to uncover how young African American students construct representations of themselves vis- à -vis scientific practice and scientists in an effort to pinpoint the salient aspects of science engagement that matter for these students as they engaged in inquiry-based science as promoted by the National Science Education Standards.

There were clear gender differences in how the young students talked about identities in science. For a majority of girls, the authors found that the students conflated identities of a typical good student with being good in science. When asked to imagine themselves as scientists and what it means to be successful in scientific endeavors, many girls referenced school behavioral norms. To be a scientist, to be good in science means one works hard, pays attention, does not misbehave, and is nice to other students and the teacher. The authors conclude that these students do not distinguish between "doing school" and "doing science" as they engage in both aspects in the classroom and in their daily lives. While scientists and certain scientific practices may share similar characteristics also priced in doing school (e.g., hard work, civil behavior, honesty), they are not unique to the practice of science. Three times as many girls as boys also viewed literary dimensions such as writing and reading as features of science. The authors highlight the troubling finding that girls are the ones who internalized school behavioral norms as science norms. Good behavior, obedience, and careful writing are school norms that are explicitly rewarded and possibly most tangible for students who are seeking teacher approval in establishing membership. Varelas and her colleagues (2011) rightly caution against the danger of equating being good at "doing school" to "doing science," since many critical scientific practices require one to ask questions and try novel ways to solve problems, practices that are antithetical to obedience and "falling in line." This is especially perturbing given the low representation of girls and women in higher-level science courses and in STEM professions.

The boys, on the other hand, were much less likely to intertwine teacher-sanctioned school norms with doing science. Boys the authors interviewed cited important science disciplinary practices such as being creative, coming up with "cool inventions," and figuring things out as distinguishing features of being a scientist. Some students of both sexes also voiced aspects of teaching, caring, and building tools as identifiers of science and scientists. Half of the students, including both girls and boys, associated "smartness" with being a scientist, which they elaborated as possessing a large knowledge base. Thus, a scientist is someone who knows a lot of information. Related to this point, several students talked about how they have to work hard when talking about themselves in science but not when talking about scientists in general. This alludes to students' ideas that scientists may be people who are inherently smart without exerting much effort. Finally, students identified with different forms of capital—social, symbolic, and cultural—that can be gained through science.

This study points to the possibilities for productive science identity work among African American youth, when teachers support students in teasing out the social norms and practices that shape schooling. The authors found that the youth in their study form identities in response to the ways in which they conflate doing school (non–subject-specific academic practices) with doing science, doing school science (science-specific practices endorsed by science teacher) with doing science, to science discipline–specific practices. The overemphasis on behavioral norms and authoritarian teacher positioning often distort students' ideological framings of science, especially since science values competing characteristics such as innovation and flexibility. Such institutional narratives of good behavior and what it means to be successful in school science can inadvertently steer non-dominant students away from the pursuit of science. This is especially so if science educators and teachers want to make inroads with both the quality and longevity of science participation and achievement among non-dominant students. This study provides insight into how to work against this trend.

The dominant role of institutional narratives is also apparent in the study by Calabrese Barton, Kang, Tan, O'Neill, Bautista-Guerra, and Brecklin (2013). The authors presented longitudinal, 3-year ethnographic case studies on the identity work and identity trajectories of

two African American middle school girls, Diane and Chantelle, across different figured worlds (school, after school, home) in which they engaged in science. They are interested in what non-dominant girls do—in terms of their identity work as manifested in actions, relationships, power dynamics, and recognition—to author themselves in or out of science. The authors situate this study on the premise that identity work can be better captured and understood through locating identity traces, key events of identity authoring that carry meaning over space and time, and have enduring effects on a girl's science identity trajectory.

Diane's case highlighted the complex contradictions in her science identity work. As an African American girl in a large middle school experiencing student-body segregation and racial tensions, Diane was also one of the few African American students placed on the high-ability track in seventh grade. Despite the fact that Diane was deeply engaged in science both in and out of school and enacted many scientific practices key to authentic inquiry across these spaces, her interests and authentic participation in science were not recognized by either her seventh-grade science teacher or her peers. Nobody remembered that Diane was the one who won the rocket competition (ascribing the victory, instead, to a boy). Diane's teacher, a genuinely caring teacher who has won awards for her teaching at the local and state levels, was surprised at Diane's grades for science when she made As. While the authors showed how Diane's careful engagement in science tasks led to a deeper understanding of subject matter as compared to one of the star students, Diane's achievements in science were invisible to the other members and to the authority figure (teacher) in the science classroom. While she attended a weekly lunch science club run by her science teacher in the seventh grade, she dropped out of science club after one of her friends moved away and the rest of the members were either White or Asian girls. Instead of attending science club, Diane spent the lunch hour socializing with her other African American friends who were not in her track.

Diane's case highlights three issues pertinent to science education for non-dominant youth: (1) Even in an inquiry-based science classroom where student and science centered practices are enacted, what is valued as successful by the teacher can still be traditional forms of behavioral codes instead of authentic science practices; (2) stereotyping of student ability, whether intentional or not, can still occur despite traditional achievement markers such as good grades; and (3) student membership in conflicting figured worlds forces them to choose between opportunities in science and other salient worlds.

On the other hand, Chantelle's case is more clearly a "story of possibility." Her case showed the transference and cross-leveraging of positive identity work across figured worlds in ways that reinforced and stabilized her emerging science identities, gaining much momentum for her science identity trajectory. Initially a quiet girl who only joined an after-school community-based science club (Green Club) because her friend invited her, Chantelle's subsequent active participation at Green Club allowed her to author the identity of a green energy science expert at the local community youth club. This positive identity work was supported by her ability to use her talents in dance and choreography as legitimate resources to create Green Club science artifacts. The authors describe a short movie Chantelle and two peers made that documented the process of a light bulb audit in their middle school. The girls changed 50 incandescent light bulbs to compact fluorescent ones, explaining the savings in terms of both carbon emissions and dollars. Chantelle took an active leadership role in directing, editing, selecting music, and choreographing dance sequences for this documentary. The authors argue that Chantelle's initial foray into making the documentary because of her artistic talents opened up more opportunities for her to engage in science. More importantly, Chantelle was able to negotiate for opportunities to showcase her light bulb audit movie in school, once in a workshop format to the student government body and another in her own science class, in conjunction with Earth Day. In both presentations, Chantelle engaged her audience in conversation and led the discussions, a marked departure from her typical "quiet girl" identity in science class. Her identity as a green energy expert was reified and acknowledged across figured worlds.

Looking across these cases, the authors point out how traces of identity over time and space can configure different identity trajectories through the de/stabilization of identities. Such de/stabilization of identities is a result of how one's identity work is recognized (or not) and valued (or not) by salient members of the figured world. Diane's social figured world (with her African American peers) conflicted with her science lunch club figured world. Chantelle's Green Club figured world had porous boundaries that encouraged her use of artistic talents to do science. Her school and classroom boundaries were also porous, in that she was allowed to share her science artifacts and position herself as a green energy expert to her peers in school. In addition to whether the girls' resources in one figured world could gain currency in another, the authors also point out that resources take on meaning and "become points of social negotiation and symbolic representations of critical identity work" (p. 67).

The final study by Rahm, Martel-Reny, and Moore (2010) examined the roles informal science programs play in the lives of urban youth. Presenting cases of three student participants in two different informal science learning environments, the authors argue that youth were motivated to engage and learn science because the learning goals and expected outcomes extended beyond knowledge acquisition. Indeed, the cases reveal that the youth found the after-school science experiences meaningful because they enabled them to imagine their possible future selves in science. Equally, and perhaps maybe more importantly, in these informal science spaces, the youth were able to

view their participation through a broader lens of success because the programs and their instructors did.

The study examines two different informal science learning programs, one focused on girls ages 9 through 12 and another focused on lower-income youth ages 13 through 18. What the two programs had in common was that they supported youths' engagement in positive identity work as they began to experience what it meant to be scientific and successful. The flexible structures of these programs encouraged urban youth who otherwise had few opportunities to engage deeply with science to "test the waters" on their own terms and redefine for themselves what it means to do science. While it was important in these science learning spaces for student to in fact learn science process and content, the outcomes used to assess that learning ranged from evaluation of student work and presentations to observations of their moods, behaviors, attitudes, engagement levels, peer interactions, evaluations of shifts in their science identity, and the extent to which youth developed a sense of belonging.

The study also revealed that how youth engage in science meaningfully and productively differed. Take for example, the case of Rosine, a student who was initially "ambivalent about the program and especially its focus on science" (Rahm, Martel-Reny, and Moore, 2005, p. 286). For Rosine, science engagement is meaningful when it is hands on, when she can take part in activities, has the freedom to be curious, and feels like she is learning something new. The authors explain how upon completion of a group science fair project on rockets, Rosine expressed pride in being able to not only explain the parts of a rocket and what they do but also have the opportunity to build and test a model rocket and to be able to demonstrate a rocket launch as part of their science fair presentation. She later referred to her work on the science fair as "interesting, amazing and magnificent" and also said that she would still like to learn more about rockets and "to get the difficult words" (Rahm et al., 2005, p. 286).

What is important to note in the story of Rosine is that what made this particular science experience meaningful was not winning a prize, getting an A, or scoring well on a test. What was meaningful to her was developing the skills to support her curiosities so that she and her teammates could be the directors of their own learning. Instead of merely being positioned as a learner, Rosine was supported to "try on" a scientific identity, inventing and experimenting with rocket design. It was meaningful to her that she and her team could construct and test a model rocket and explain how it works. What was also meaningful about this experience is that it left her wanting more. The rocket project was not something simply to be completed. It was an activity to engage in and learn from. The most significant learning outcome from this project is that Rosine, a student who almost did not take part in the after-school program for fear of the science, ended the rocket project wanting to know more of the science and expecting more of herself. Rosine saw both who she is (a successful rocket model builder) and who she could be, in science.

Rahm and her colleagues posit that these informal science programs appealed to urban youth because through these flexible modes of participation largely determined by youth themselves, the process of doing science—what it means to do science and how the processes by which doing science unfold—opened up possibilities for urban youth in the arena of science. As both their particular interests and ways of participation were valued by the informal programs, a dynamic learning environment was fostered and the youth expected more of themselves. Youth began to identify positively with science, and some started to contemplate possible futures in science (e.g, Kamila). These informal programs were able to help the youth redefine who can do science and broaden what it means to be scientific, thus opening a new world of possibilities.

Tool set 3 summary. The critical roles student identities-in-practice play in science learning are made clear in the three studies discussed in this section. These studies point out how student science learning and achievement are ineluctably linked to their ongoing and concurrent identity work. Students' experiences, struggles, successes, and failures in school science are not mere reflections on their interest, competence, and aptitude (or lack thereof) in science; they are also labels that signify who students are and can be (or not) in science. Paying attention to how students and the science community (including peers and teachers) ascribe labels to themselves and one another is important, for such identifying acts can have enduring effects on students' current and future engagement with science. While the studies in this section presented stories of African American students, they also were cautious in not essentializing African American students or African American female students. Instead, the authors presented detailed and nuanced findings on the complexity and dialectical nature of the students' identity work in science. The studies show that if we want to encourage and support their participation and achievement in science for non-dominant youth in urban schools, then attending to their identity work in science class is equally as critical as focusing on their science conceptual understanding. They also highlight the vital role identity work *reception* plays in whether a student becomes recognized as a "science person," regardless of the students' grades in science.

Looking Across the Conceptual Tools

The three themes discussed—place, funds of knowledge, and identities-in-practice—offer conceptual tools essential for moving forward with antideficit and antiessentializing approaches for the teaching and learning of science in urban contexts. Next we discuss the ways in which these tools offer two core affordances for moving forward in productive ways in designing science education in urban settings by opening up how we think about the outcomes of science education and in our own positioning along the insider–outsider continuum of urban settings. We also look at the constraints of these conceptual tools and offer directions for next steps.

Affordances

It is a strength that research on science education in urban contexts draws upon different conceptual frames (primarily sociocultural views of learning, social practice theories, and narrative/discourse perspectives). Such different but complementary perspectives can offer us a more robust understanding of student learning and engagement in science in urban contexts and its connections to the design of the learning environment. From these different lenses, the studies presented provide us with a set of conceptual tools for reimagining science education in urban contexts through the lens of possibilities.

All three of these conceptual tools help us see the importance of movement across boundaries—school, home, community, peer groups. They also show us how youth actively break down the binaries such as school/not school and science/not science that define their lives in science education. What these tools help us to see is "what" might "move" across boundaries. In terms of place (knowledge of and attachments to), we can see how relationships to place move in how meaning is given to topics of investigation and the nature of the inquiry itself. In terms of funds of knowledge, experience and the emergent knowledge and values of that experience move across boundaries and the role this knowledge might play in positioning youth as experts in an aspect of science. In terms of identities-in-practice and identity work, it is practices and artifacts that move, shaping how individuals engage in science and their reasons for doing so, as well as how they are recognized by others for what they know and can do.

Thus, together, these conceptual tools offer us a way to both expand our lenses for framing learning outcomes as well as the pathways to learning. The current education policy climate focuses attention almost exclusively on student achievement in individual subject areas. Achievement scores in discrete subject areas, tightly aligned with content standards, remain the gold standard for documenting the impact science education has on learners. As noted by others (e.g., Bell, Lewenstein, Shouse, & Feder, 2009; Carlone, Haun-Frank, & Webb, 2011), this narrow framing overlooks other crucial indicators of learning, including identity work, forms of engagement, and culturally based knowledge and practices. Though achievement scores offer a form of evidence for student learning, they reveal only a narrow slice of it. While they may give us some indication of what students know from a content perspective, they tell us little about what students can do with that information, what they understand science to be, or the mechanisms by which students come to engage in meaningful science learning and to see themselves as a part of science. Compelling evidence suggests that opening up avenues to bridge knowledge frameworks and positioning individuals as particular kinds of experts within communities expands student learning opportunities (Gresalfi, Martin, Hand, & Greeno, 2008; Nasir, Rosebery, Warren, & Lee, 2006).

Studies reviewed in this chapter reveal that the successes observed in informal science learning environments are, in part, because outcomes such as science identity development (i.e., I am an oceanographer who loves to dance with the dolphins) and novel forms of participation that merge cultural practices with the scientific (e.g., choreographer of an artistic scientific documentary) are recognized as important forms of learning and achievement in informal settings in ways they are not in traditional settings (Calabrese Barton & Tan, 2010; Fusco, 2001; Nasir et al., 2006). This is not surprising given the much wider berth of flexibility informal science programs enjoy without the constraints of testing. However, much as we agree with the need for and celebrate the successes of such rigorous and inclusive informal science programs as those described in this chapter, the real gate-keeping of youths' advancement in a science trajectory resides within the portals of school science. Encouragingly, there is emerging evidence that when formal school science is designed to elicit these broader outcomes as a part of the learning process, students who have historically been unsuccessful in school science become successful as indicated by standard measures (Varelas et al., 2010).

Expanding the lens of what we recognize as indicators of students' potential for science learning and science learning outcomes aids in the process of disrupting the framing of school success. For example, although Native Hawaiians and Pacific Islanders have a long history of scientific and mathematical exploration and STEM understanding in connection with voyaging and environmental sustainability (Kanahele, 1986), the predominant narrative is that Native Hawaiian and Pacific Islander youth, particularly those from low-income backgrounds living in urban areas, have a poor understanding of and limited interest in science and STEM careers. This narrative is primarily based on student performance on national assessments such as the 2011 NAEP, where the majority of students scoring "basic" and "below basic" were of Native Hawaiian or Pacific Islander descent and/or from low-income families (nces. ed.gov/nationsreportcard/pdf/stt2011/2012467HI8.pdf-2012-04-27; nces.ed.gov/nationsreportcard/pdf/main2011/2012459.pdf-2011-10-31). However, research has shown how indigenous "values and epistemological orientations for approaching and understanding the natural world" have "integrity in the contemporary practice of science" (Bang & Medina, 2010, p. 8). Despite geographic location (i.e., Honolulu, New York City, Los Angeles, etc.), youth from nondominant backgrounds in an urban context encounter a similar deficit narrative. However, as demonstrated by the articles highlighted, in spaces where cultural knowledge and lived experiences are valued and leveraged for science learning, in "moving beyond the lenses of summative statistics" (Rahm et al., 2005, p. 283), these same youth

demonstrate positive learning outcomes such as increased engagement, positive shifts in science identity and views of themselves in relation to science and STEM careers, and improved levels of science discourse (using both everyday and science terminology) with both peers and teachers (Calabrese Barton & Tan, 2010).

The urban context offers a living intersection of geography, history, culture, and other critical dimensions that provide youth with a wealth of social and cultural capital that enriches their learning and engagement with science. What these conceptual tools help us see is that the possibilities for reframing urban science education through place reside, in part, in working with teachers to position themselves as a part of or inside the urban ecology rather than outside it. Relph (1976) first proposed the insideness–outsideness dialectic to illustrate how one's sense of place exists as "a full range of possible awareness, from simple recognition for orientation, through the capacity to respond empathetically to the identities of different places, to a profound association with places as cornerstones of human existence and individual identity" (p. 63). The salient point here is that the insideness–outsideness dialectic suggests that the "essence" of developing a relationship with and a view of place—a sense of place—"lies in how one positions self in a place" (Lim & Calabrese Barton, 2010, p. 331, emphasis added). In schools, teachers and students are rarely asked to identify with place. The very notion that one can position oneself as inside or outside of place stands in stark contrast to the driving norm in science education, where a focus is placed on standardization through testing and curriculum. Indeed, a push away from place has been the hallmark of reform of the past decade.

For example, Rosebery and colleagues (2010), in their study of heteroglossia, provide a rich account for how the children's experiences with cold weather and family and peer talk about how to stay warm in cold weather actively positioned them as producers of complex ideas about heat transfer. However, the teacher needed to leverage this knowledge and thoughtfully elicit their experiences through imaginative dialog. In another example by Emdin (2010), we see how the place of urban hip-hop culture, when made a part of the science class, positioned youth with authority in class, a position denied many of the students when their love of hip-hop was viewed as outside of science.

Building future science education research in urban contexts around these conceptual tools enables us as science education researchers and educators to see the stories of possibility. This is powerful because changing our focus from the deficit lens traditionally presented in urban science research to a focus on possibilities provides us with examples of success we can learn from and build on. This is not to say that we should ignore the stark inequities that exist for students and educators in urban context. On the contrary, we need to address these inequities by learning from the stories of success such as those presented in this

TABLE 13.1
Affordances of Tools

Theme	Tools	Key points	Cross-cutting points
Place	Knowledge of place Place attachment	Local experience and relationship shape engagement with science	• Movement across boundaries • Breaking down binaries • Harnessing diverse science-related expertise and points of interest • Recruit and deepen youths' everyday connections with science • Make visible and strengthen youths' continued impetus to engage with science
Funds of knowledge	Youth have a rich store of funds of knowledge and local practices reflective of their cultural and linguistic backgrounds and their local communities.	Valuing heteroglossia opens up more legitimate entry points for youth to engage with science and strengthen the connections between science and the everyday.	
Identity work over time	We can observe identity in practice through (a) representations of self in practice, (b) identity artifacts, and (c) recognition work.	Identity shapes how one engages in science, reasons for and opportunities to engage in science, and in positioning.	

chapter and develop tools and strategies to generate more stories of possibility (see Table 13.1).

Constraints and Moving Forward

We note that the vast majority of studies are ethnographic accounts of science education in urban contexts, and the field would benefit from more action-oriented and design-based research to advance change. The studies highlighted in this chapter (being representative of research in the field as a whole) have centrally focused on issues of equity and diversity. They are also primarily ethnographic in nature. Ethnography is a clear choice for documenting local settings in rich detail with in-depth focus on individuals, resources, tools, actions, and interactions and discourses. However, to move research on science education in urban contexts beyond reporting and into spaces of action, more diverse methodologies are needed. While much has been learned from the literature on science education in urban contexts in the last decade, as we move forward, the focus of our work must continue to build on these lessons and engage in new and complementary methodologies and approaches for conducting research that account for cultural variation in coming to know and be and the role of place in science learning need to be developed.

We suggest that more attention should also be paid to (1) the development of tools, procedures, and analytic approaches that enable researchers to see and account for variation in ways of knowing and being in the classroom in context-sensitive ways; (2) research designs that seek out more and different populations of students to push back against the stereotype that urban = African American and/or Hispanic and that seek out a diversity of experiences (including program design and learning environment) and their role in how students author science identities with, through, and for meaning making in science; (3) develop interdisciplinary and diverse collaborations to allow for debate within projects regarding interpretive outcomes;

and (4) research that moves beyond documentation of failure into action taking, drawing upon local strengths.

Additionally, a series of questions emerges from the studies discussed in this chapter that the field of urban science education would be well served to study using the expanded array of research designs and focuses outlined.

First, what does science education in urban contexts look like from a global perspective? As made evident in this chapter, review of the literature reveals a distinctly Western perspective of science education in urban contexts. As part of an effort to seek out more diverse student populations and diversity of experiences, we recommend more studies that focus urban science education in a global context. There is much to be learned from gaining a greater understanding of the state of urban science education around the world. For example, in Thailand, many government schools in urban centers are generally considered to be stronger than competing private schools and suburban and rural government and private schools. What creates this dynamic? What lessons can be learned in the structure and function of urban schools in other parts of the world to support action-based reform in U.S. urban contexts?

Second, what pedagogical actions and classroom or curriculum structures support the incorporation of place and students' sense of place in urban science learning environments (both formal and informal)? As indicated from the literature highlighted in this chapter, students display higher levels of science content understanding and application, positive science identity development, and increased levels of engagement when they are able to leverage their understanding of place and sense of place in connection with science learning. In an effort to move this research beyond reporting and into a space of action, we suggest that the lessons learned from this literature be used to develop tools, procedures, and analytic approaches that aid science educators in creating science learning spaces that intentionally value and leverage students' understanding of place and sense of place.

Last, what is required to create school science learning environments that value a more expansive set of learning outcomes, and how can these expansive sets of learning outcomes be included in our overall all assessment of student and teacher performance in urban settings? Standardized tests and similar gauges of student performance are going to continue to be a part of the reality of our educational system. However, the structure and nature of these assessments is in constant flux. If we, as a science education community, truly want to gauge what is being gained in formal and informal science learning environments, we must be willing to look beyond simple content acquisition. If our goal nationally is to significantly increase the number of students pursuing STEM careers, we need students to develop more than a strong base of content understanding. We need them to be able to integrate knowledge and ideas from multiple content areas and be able to apply that knowledge in meaningful way. Above all, we must support students developing a sense of self in science and STEM. As such, we encourage research in how expanded learning outcomes can be valued as vital assessment tools in formal learning environments so that our assessment models show a more complete picture of what is being gained and accomplished than is provided by the current myopic structure of school testing.

Conclusions

The narratives around urban science education have typically been deficit focused—schools lack material and human resources, students (typically non-dominant) are low performing and "at risk." However, as Gee (2004) reminds us, "'[a]t risk,' doesn't need to mean any more than that you don't need another bad learning experience" (p. 74). We hope that the three sets of conceptual tools presented in this chapter—place, funds of knowledge, and identities-in-practice/identity work—will enable science teachers and educators to uncover and create good learning experiences for all youth, including youth who reside in urban spaces.

Acknowledgments

The authors wish to thank Gail Seiler and Randy Yerrick for their review and comments on the initial version of this chapter.

References

Bakhtin, M.M. (1981). Discourse in the novel. In M. Holquist (Ed.), *The dialogic imagination: Four essays by M.M. Bakhtin* (C. Emerson & M. Holquist, Trans., pp. 259–428). Austin: University of Texas Press.

Bang, M., & Medina, D. (2010). Cultural processes in science education: Supporting the navigation of multiple epistemologies. *Science Education, 94*(6), 1008–1026.

Basu, S.J., & Calabrese Barton, A. (2007). Urban students' sustained interest in science. *Journal of Research in Science Teaching, 44*(3), 466–489.

Bell, P., Lewenstein, B., Shouse, A.W., & Feder, M.A. (Eds.). (2009). *Learning science in informal environments: People, places, and pursuits.* Washington, DC: National Academies Press.

Bouillion, L., & Gomez, L. (2001). Connecting school and community with science learning: Real world problems and school-community partnerships as contextual scaffolds. *Journal of Research in Science Teaching, 38*, 878–898.

Brickhouse, N., Lowery, P., & Schultz, K. (2000). What kind of a girl does science? The construction of a school science identity. *Journal of Research in Science Teaching, 37*, 441–458.

Brickhouse, N., & Potter, J. (2001). Young women's scientific identity formation in an urban context. *Journal of Research in Science Teaching, 38*, 965–980.

Buck, P., & Skilton-Sylvester, P. (2005). Preservice teachers enter urban communities: Coupling funds of knowledge research and critical pedagogy in teacher education In N. González, L.C. Moll, & C. Amanti (Eds.), *Funds of knowledge: Theorizing practices in households, communities and classrooms* (pp. 213–232). Mahwah, NJ: Lawrence Erlbaum.

Buxton, C. (2010). Social problem solving through science: An approach to critical place-based science teaching and learning. *Equity and Excellence in Education, 43,* 120–135.

Calabrese Barton, A., Kang, H., Tan, E., O'Neill, T., Bautista-Guerra, C., & Brecklin, C. (2013). Crafting a future in science: Tracing middle school girls' identity work over time and space. *American Education Research Journal, 50*(1), 37–75.

Calabrese Barton, A., & Tan, E. (2009). Funds of knowledge, discourses and hybrid space. *Journal of Research in Science Teaching, 46*, 50–73.

Calabrese Barton, A., & Tan, E. (2010). We be burnin': Agency, identity and learning in a green energy program. *Journal of the Learning Sciences, 19*(2), 187–229.

Calabrese Barton, A., Tan, E., & Rivet, A. (2008). Creating hybrid spaces for engaging school science among urban middle school girls. *American Education Research Journal, 45*, 68–103.

Carlone, H.B., Haun-Frank, J., & Webb, A. (2011). Assessing equity beyond knowledge- and skills-based outcomes: A comparative ethnography of two fourth-grade reform-based science classrooms. *Journal of Research in Science Teaching, 48*, 459–485.

Chapa, J., & De La Rosa, B. (2006). The problematic pipeline: Demographic trends and Latino participation in graduate science, technology, engineering, and mathematics programs. *Journal of Hispanic Higher Education, 5*(3), 203–221.

Chavous, T., Bernat, D., Schmeelk-Cone, K., Caldwell, C., Kohn-Wood, L., & Zimmerman, M. (2003). Racial identity and academic attainment among African American adolescents. *Child Development, 74*, 1076–1090.

Clotfelter, C., Ladd, H., & Vigdor, J. (2005). Who teaches whom? Race and the distribution of novice teachers. *Economics of Education Review, 24*, 377–392.

Cochran-Smith, M., & Zeichner, K. (2005). *Studying teacher education: The report of the AERA panel on research and teacher education.* Washington, DC: American Education Research Association.

Council of Great City Schools. (2011). *Pieces of the puzzle: Full Report.* Washington, DC: Council of Great City Schools.

Emdin, C. (2010). Affiliation and alienation: Hip-hop, rap, and urban science education. *Journal of Curriculum Studies, 42*(1), 1–25.

Endreny, A.H. (2010). Urban 5th graders' conceptions during a place-based inquiry unit on watersheds. *Journal of Research in Science Teaching, 47*, 501–517. doi:10.1002/tea.20348

Fordham, S. (1993). Those loud Black girls: (Black) women, silence, and gender "passing" in the academy. *Anthropology and Education Quarterly, 24*(1), 3–32.

Fryer, R. (2006). Acting White: The social price paid by the best and brightest minority students. *Education Next, 6*(1). Retrieved from http://educationnext.org/actingwhite/

Fusco, D. (2001). Creating relevant science through urban planning and gardening. *Journal of Research in Science Teaching, 38*(8), 860–877.

Gandara, P. (2006). Strengthening the academic pipeline leading to careers in math, science, and technology for Latino students. *Journal of Hispanic Higher Education, 5*(3), 222–237.

García, S. B., & Guerra, P. L. (2004). Deconstructing deficit thinking: Working with educators to create more equitable learning environments. *Education and Urban Society, 36*(2), 150–168.

Gee, J. P. (1990). *Social linguistics and literacies: Ideology in discourses.* London: Falmer.

Gee, J. P. (2004). *Situated language and learning.* London: Routledge.

Gresalfi, M. S., Martin, T., Hand, V., & Greeno, J. G. (2008). Constructing competence: An analysis of student participation in the activity systems of mathematics classrooms. *Educational Studies in Mathematics, 70,* 49–70.

Griner, A. (2012). *Addressing the achievement gap and disproportionality through the use of culturally responsive teaching practices urban education.* doi:10.1177/0042085912456847

Gruenewald, D. A., & Smith, G. A. (Eds.). (2008). *Place-based education in the global age: Local diversity.* New York: Erlbaum.

Gutiérrez, K., & Orellana, M. (2006). The problem of English learners: Constructing genres of difference. *Research in the Teaching of English, 40,* 502–507.

Hogg, L. (2011). Funds of knowledge: An investigation of coherence within the literature. *Teaching and Teacher Education, 27,* 666–677.

Holland, D., Lachicotte, W. J., Skinner, D., & Cain, C. (2001). *Identity and agency in cultural worlds.* Cambridge: Harvard University Press.

Ingersoll, R. M., & Smith, T. M. (2004). Do teacher induction and mentoring matter? *NASSP Bulletin, 88,* 28–40.

Kaba, A. J. (2013). Black Americans, gains in science and engineering degrees, and gender. *Sociology Mind, 3*(1) 67–82. Retrieved from http://works.bepress.com/amadu_kaba/50

Kanahele, G. (1986). *Kū Kanaka, stand tall: A search for Hawaiian values.* Honolulu: University of Hawai'i Press.

Lave, J., & Wenger, E. (1991). *Situated learning: Legitimate peripheral participation.* New York: Cambridge University Press.

Lim, M. (2010). Historical consideration of place. *Cultural Studies of Science Education, 5,* 899–909.

Lim, M., & Calabrese Barton, A. (2006). Science learning and a sense of place in an urban middle school. *Cultural Studies of Science Education, 1,* 107–142.

Lim, M., & Calabrese Barton, A. (2010). Exploring insideness in urban children's sense of place. *Journal of Environmental Psychology, 30,* 328–337.

Luke, A. (2008). Urban education dystopia: 2050. In W. Pink & G. Noblit (Eds.), *International handbook of urban education* (pp. 1177–1186). New York: Springer-Verlag.

Meyer, R., Carl, B., & Cheng, H. (2010). *Accountability and performance in secondary education in Milwaukee public schools.* Volume II of the Senior Urban Education Research Fellowship Series. Washington DC: Great Council of City Schools.

Milner, H. R. (2012). But what is urban education? *Urban Education, 47,* 556.

Moje, E., Collazo, T., Carillo, R., & Marx, R. W. (2001). "Maestro, what is 'quality?'": Language, literacy, and discourse in project-based science. *Journal of Research in Science Teaching, 38*(4), 469–498.

Moje, E. B., Ciechanowski, K. M., Kramer, K., Ellis, L., Carrillo, R., & Collazo, T. (2004). Working toward third space in content area literacy: An examination of everyday funds of knowledge and discourse. *Reading Research Quarterly, 39*(1), 38–70.

Moll, L. C., Amanti, C., Neff, D., & González, N. (1992). Funds of knowledge for teaching: Using a qualitative approach to connect homes and classrooms. *Theory Into Practice, 31*(2), 132–141.

Mutegi, J. (2013). Life's first need is for us to be realistic and other reasons for examining the sociocultural construction of race in the science performance of African American students. *Journal of Research in Science Teaching, 50,* 82–103.

Nasir, N. S., Rosebery, A., Warren, B., & Lee, C. D. (2006). Learning as a cultural process: Achieving equity through diversity. In K. Sawyer (Ed.), *Cambridge handbook of the learning sciences* (pp. 489–504). New York: Cambridge University Press.

National Assessment of Educational Progress (NAEP). (2009). *The nation's report card: 2009.*

National Center for Education Statistics. (2011). *Nation's Report Card.* Retrieved from nces.ed.gov/nationsreportcard/pdf/stt2011/2012467HI8.pdf-2012-04-27; nces.ed.gov/nationsreportcard/pdf/main2011/2012459.pdf-2011-10-31. Washington, DC: U.S. Department of Education.

National Science Board. (2012). *Science and engineering indicators 2012.* Arlington, VA: Author.

Oakes, J. (1990). *Multiplying inequalities: The effects of race, social class, and tracking on opportunities to learn mathematics and science.* Santa Monica, CA: Rand.

Oakes, J., Lipton M., Anderson L., & Stillman J. (2012). *Teaching to change the world* (4th ed.). Columbus, OH: McGraw Hill.

O'Neill, T. (2010). Fostering spaces of student ownership in middle school science. *Equity & Excellence in Education, 43*(1), 6–20.

Pink, W., & Noblit, G. (2008). *International handbook of urban education.* New York: Springer-Verlag.

Rahm, J., Martel-Reny, M. P., & Moore, J. C. (2005). The role of after-school and community science programs in the lives of urban youth. *School Science and Mathematics, 105*(6), 283–291.

Rahm, J., Martel-Reny, M. P., & Moore, J. C. (2010). The role of after-school and community science programs in the lives of urban youth. *School Science and Mathematics, 105*(6), 283–291.

Ramnarain, U. (2011). Equity in science at South African schools: A pious platitude or an achievable goal? *International Journal of Science Education, 33*(10), 1353–1371.

Relph, E. (1976). *Place and placelessness.* London: Pion Limited.

Rios-Aguilar, C., Kiyama, J. M., Gravitt, M., & Moll, L. C. (2011). Funds of knowledge for the poor and forms of capital for the rich? A capital approach to examining funds of knowledge. *Theory and Research in Education, 9*(2), 163–184.

Rose, S., & Calabrese Barton, A. (2012). Should Great Lakes City build a new power plant? How youth navigate complex socioscientific issues. *Journal of Research in Science Teaching, 49*(5), 541–567.

Rosebery, A., Ogonowski, M., DiSchino, M., & Warren, B. (2010). "The coat traps all your body heat": Heterogeneity as fundamental to learning. *Journal of the Learning Sciences, 19*(3), 322–357.

Rosebery, A. S., & Warren, B. (Eds.). (2008). *Teaching science to English language learners.* Arlington, VA: NSTA Press.

Sadker, D., Sadker, M., & Zittleman, K. (2009). *Still failing at fairness: How gender bias cheats girls and boys in school and what we can do about it.* New York: Scribner.

Semli, L., & Mehta, K. (2012). Science education in Tanzania: Challenges and policy responses. *International Journal of Educational Research, 53,* 225–239.

Tan, E., & Calabrese Barton, A. (2007). From peripheral to central, the story of Melanie's metamorphosis in an urban middle school science class. *Science Education, 92*(4), 567–590.

Tan, E., & Calabrese Barton, A. (2008). Unpacking science for all through the lens of identities-in-practice. *Cultural Studies of Science Education, 3,* 43–71.

Tan, E., & Calabrese Barton, A. (2010). Transforming science learning and student participation in 6th grade science: A case study of an urban minority classroom. *Equity & Excellence in Education, 43*(1), 38–55.

Tan, E., & Calabrese Barton, A. (2012). *Empowering math and science education in urban contexts.* Chicago: University of Chicago Press.

Tzou, C., Scalone, G., & Bell, P. (2010). The role of environmental narratives and social positioning in how place gets constructed for and by youth. *Equity and Excellence in Education, 43*(1), 105–119.

Upadhyay, B. (2006). Using students' lived experiences in an urban science classroom: An elementary school teacher's thinking. *Science Education, 90,* 94–110.

Upadhyay, B. R. (2005). Practicing reform-based science curriculum in an urban classroom: A Hispanic elementary school teacher's thinking and decisions. *School Science and Mathematics, 105*(7), 343–351.

Upadhyay, B. R. (2010). Teaching science for empowerment in an urban classroom: A case study of a Hmong teacher. *Equity and Excellence in Education, 42*(2), 217–232.

U.S. Census Bureau. (2010). *2010 census: Urban and rural classification.* Retrieved from www.census.gov/geo/www/ua/urbanruralclass.html

Varelas, M., Kane, J. M., & Wylie, C. D. (2011). Young African American children's representations of self, science, and school: Making sense of difference. *Science Education, 95*(5), 824–851.

Varelas, M., & Pappas, C. C. (2006). Intertextuality in read-alouds of integrated science-literacy units in primary classrooms: Opportunities for the development of thought and language. *Cognition & Instruction, 24,* 211–259.

Varelas, M., Pappas, C. C., Tucker-Raymond, E., Kane, J., Hankes, J., Ortiz, I., et al. (2010). Drama activities as ideational resources for primary-grade children in urban science classrooms. *Journal of Research in Science Teaching, 47,* 302–325.

Warren, B., & Ogonowski, M. (2005). "Everyday" and "scientific": Rethinking dichotomies in modes of thinking and science learning. In R. Nemirovsky, A. S. Rosebery, J. Solomon, & B. Warren (Eds.), *Everyday matters in science and mathematics* (pp. 119–148). Mahwah, NJ: Lawrence Erlbaum.

Wenger, E. (1998). *Communities of practice: Learning, meaning, and identity.* New York: Cambridge University Press.

Zhang, T. (2007). Urban development patterns in China: New, renewed, and ignored urban spaces. In Y. Song (Ed.), *Urbanization in China: Critical issues in an era of rapid growth.* Cambridge, Lincoln *Institute of Land Use Policy,* 3–27.

Zimmerman, H. (2012). Participating in science at home: Recognition work and learning in biology. *Journal of Research in Science Teaching, 49,* 597–630.

14

Rural Science Education

New Ideas, Redirections, and Broadened Definitions

J. Steve Oliver and Georgia W. Hodges

Introduction

At the conclusion of the first chapter on rural science education (Oliver, 2007a) for the previous *Handbook of Research on Science Education*, a question was posed to readers in this way: "where do we leave the question of technology and its potential to bring universal access to knowledge to all persons regardless of location?" (p. 366). As one of the current authors (JSO) concluded the research for the first chapter, that question seemed to be the most important one looming in the future for rural science education. As we began to think of structures and themes that have now formed the backbone of the new chapter, the many possibilities of how technologies could impact (and were impacting) the educative lives of rural science students across the United States and around the world again emerged as a highly visible and potentially transformative issue. In our present day, the number of schools that are isolated from the Internet and its huge cache of knowledge resources is diminishing rapidly.

Though we like to complain about the fact that cell phone calls are sometimes dropped when traveling through remote areas, the inhabited land of the world is rapidly becoming enveloped by the service areas of the companies offering cellular phone service. And though this issue is not the same as the number of schools that have access to the Internet through computers, it is perhaps more important. The presence of cell phones in the pocket of almost every person must change our perception of isolation or remoteness as an educational variable of importance for rural communities. A great majority of all school students, in the United States and elsewhere, are in possession of increasingly "smart" phones that provide powerful portals to the Web and all of the knowledge found there. As Caterina Fake, the cofounder of the photo-sharing service Flickr, was quoted in a 2013 interview in *The Atlantic*: "The computers people have are no longer on their desks, but in their hands, and that is probably the transformative feature of the technology. These computers are with you, in the world" (Madrigal, 2013). As the parallel realizations of ubiquitous smart phones and massive online open courses (MOOC), to name just two examples, make access to knowledge and learning so widespread, a serious reconsideration of what is educationally unique about rural schools is required.

As the previous *Handbook* was being published in 2007, final preparations for the presentation of the first e-reader, the Kindle, were being made. Since that time, and with even greater flair, the Apple iPad was released for sale in 2010. However, both of these devices are becoming platforms for the secondary science textbook. And though this may seem like good news to the students who lugged backpacks, the best news is that the textbook is finally becoming an interactive learning device that can be connected to all of the knowledge bases of the Internet. And though there will likely always be financial issues to consider, the challenges presented by distance that have restricted access to science for the remote rural school student will drop away for good. But our reconsideration of what it means to discuss rural science education will not be sufficient if the notions of place and context are also lost from our discussion.

The idea that technology will abate the distance is not the only issue of importance among the research of recent years related to rural science education. In this chapter, we have identified four major themes around which subsections of the chapter have been constructed within an overall framework that puts particular emphasis on the exploration of social justice and diversity. Stretching across and touching on all of these themes are the attributes of science teaching in rural and small schools that emerge from the research literature. With that said, the first theme is a synthesis of the scholarship regarding the nature and identification of rural schools, with particular interest in two interrelated components of that theme. New scholarship in a variety of fields, perhaps most importantly rural sociology, has elaborated new schemes for identifying rural places and thus allowing for more reliable identification of rural schools. This is closely linked to and encapsulated by the debate about how the nature of rural places should shape the research and scholarship conducted there. In turn, a secondary debate examines how science teaching specifically should be shaped by the nature of the place in which rural schooling takes place. Second, as a link to the chapter from the previous *Handbook*, a number of recent research reports in rural science education will be considered in detail to examine how the themes of learner, teacher, technology, community, and context impact how the scholarship of rural science teaching has moved forward to evoke an emphasis on social justice and diversity. The third theme relates to the issue of technology as a force of change for rural schools. The focus will be on both globalization and also how technology is impacting the teaching and learning of science in rural schools. The fourth theme deals with the recruitment of science teachers to small and rural school districts. As a complementary issue, this section will also, to a lesser degree, examine research on the retention of science teachers in those districts. Finally, we will conclude and share the apparent implications for research into science in rural and small schools.

Looking Deeper for a Definition of Rural

The study of rural science education has in recent times been hampered by the difficulty of validly identifying what is and what is not a rural school. The challenge of representing the characteristics of a school that qualifies it for inclusion under the label of rural is reflected in the challenges of consistently applying the label of rural to any given place. Shortall and Warner (2012) described the ease of distinction in an earlier time: "until the mid-1900s, the distinction between urban and rural areas was relatively obvious and easy to study. The rural economy was distinctive because of its reliance on primary industries, especially agriculture . . ." (p. 3). It is this notion of being able to recognize a rural place, the *we'll know it when we see it* characteristic, that is at the heart of the difficulty that scholars have in creating a categorization of rural that can be widely applied in research. The problem is not one of agreement about what constitutes a rural place or school. In all too many examples, the description of the school provided by the research ends with only the report of population size, the distance to the nearest metropolitan area, or simply the researchers' application of the label "rural" to the site (Coladarci, 2007; Oliver, 2007a).

History and the myth of rural places. In its most idealized form, the *we'll know it when we see it* characteristics date back to popular culture ideas of rural utopia from a previous period. The tradition of the rural idyll has been a major factor in the work of rural science education since at least the 19th century. In her 1962 article "The Myth of Agrarianism in Rural Educational Reform, 1890–1911," Keppel described the widespread belief in the rural idyll in terms of the Acadian myth in which humans live in lovely pastoral settings completely in harmony with nature. Even with the recognition among rural educators and reformers of the severe limitations for this myth as a reasonable description of the late-19th-century farm, it still held sway. In the writings of the early 1900s, the rural myth was given added emphasis by two powerful arguments. One of those is directly relevant to our cause of understanding rural science education and the other only indirectly. It was common for authors to describe horrible living conditions and multiple forms of degradation for anyone who moved to the city to find work. Phrases like "the vortex of sin and corruption, lowest depths of degradation, and half-fed, half-clothed people worked as slaves" (Keppel, 1962) were used to describe life in cities. More subtle characterizations continue to appear in the literature today but extend through a second point that puts emphasis on how the study of rural schooling must include the study of the environment, and thus the science of the place in which the rural students and teachers live. It is the second point that makes the most direct and powerful connection across the many years of study of rural science education. This second point of emphasis described science as the activity that would revolutionize farming and all aspects of life in the rural setting in terms of knowledge and attitude. Keppel quoted the president of Illinois Normal University from a 1911 address putting science knowledge clearly at the head of factors improving the life of the farmer:

> If the farmer, as he trudges down the corn rows under the June sun, sees only clods and weeds and corn, he leads an empty and barren existence. But if he knows of the work of the moisture in the soil and air . . . of the mysterious chemistry of the sunbeam . . . of the bacteria in the soil laboratory; he then knows that he is no mere toiler, he is marshaling the hosts of the universe and upon his skill of generalship depends the life of nations."
>
> (cited in Keppel, 1962, p. 106)

It was in this spirit that educational reform, with emphasis on science, was seen as a savior and thus "in the first decade of the twentieth century rural people turned to . . . education to heal the ills of rural society" (Keppel, 1962, p. 106). Already in place to fulfill this need was the Nature Study curriculum (Comstock, 1939), which is considered to be one of the very first formal science curricula for the elementary school (Underhill, 1941). The Nature Study curriculum materials consisted of pamphlets that were mailed to the subscribing schools and described the natural history of an organism or examined a natural phenomenon while also addressing attitude and emotional issues related to this bit of science. Ultimately, the study of more formal science won out over Nature Study (Keppel, 1962), but the "glorification of farming as a way of life" continued.

The importance of this debate, which is the nature of rural schooling, for our current-day understanding of the nature of rural science education, is not just found in its existence as an interesting artifact of long-ago debates. The tension over the appropriate characterization of rural science education continues to this day. Brown and Schafft (2011) describe how the rural mystique is alive and well in conceptualizations of rural life when they write:

> The mystique is composed of treasured or almost sacred elements. It is an idealized form of community that stands in contrast to urban life. It is the antithesis of the modern urban world, somehow more moral, virtuous, and simple.
>
> (p. 10)

Beyond this point, concerns have been expressed throughout the literature of rural science education of the importance of making connections between schools and communities. Curricula with the primary goal of helping students learn science in the context of their rural places has been promoted by some (Avery, 2013). Other researchers point to the recognition of the uniqueness of rural schools while forwarding reform efforts that ensure the standards-based nature of the new directions. For instance, the Appalachian Rural Systemic Initiative (Henderson & Royster, 2000) created an emphasis on "the development of a skilled and committed leadership for mathematics and science program(s)" that has resulted in district teams that "now have a 'standards-based vision' of mathematics and science instruction" (p. 10) that provides direction for reform efforts.

Defining rural education for today. As a concluding gesture to his long editorship of the *Journal of Research in Rural Education*, Coladarci (2007) provided a very thoughtful reflection on the means by which researchers might improve "the yield of rural education research." In keeping with the statements by essentially all rural education researchers, he points to the lack of definition of rural as an initial major stumbling block. After briefly examining several definitions, he concluded that "Difference, notwithstanding, there is the recurring assertion that the purest definition of rural entails a population fewer than 2,500" (p. 2).

This idea that a number of people within a locality can be used as the primary defining characteristic of rural falls within what Brown and Schafft (2011) refer to as the "location or place approach to defining rural" (p. 4). In a more general sense, this form of definition relies on "a particular kind of socio-geographic place that is distinguished by certain attributes . . . such as population size or dependence on farming" (p. 4). Coladarci (2007) succinctly described his concern about the use of "a population of fewer than 2,500" as a defining characteristic when he wrote that use of this figure alone "leaves a lot to be desired" (p. 2). But the use of numbers as a defining feature of rural places is pervasive throughout the literature, and other researchers, and certainly other government agencies, come up with different numbers. For instance, Shortall and Warner (2012) are in agreement with Coladarci in their interpretation of how U.S. government agencies define rural—using

the 2,500 population number—but they report that in England and Wales, "settlements of ten thousand or less are defined as rural" (p. 8), while those in Scotland must be under 3,000 or those in Northern Ireland must be under 4,500 to receive the rural label. Coladarci (2007) went on to elaborate how the definition of rural places is the product of recognizing what is *left over* after the more recognizable categorizes in the definition of place have been taken. Shortall and Warner (2012) gave complete support to his contention. They wrote:

> In the US, rural is the residual; in other words, urban is defined, and what is not urban is rural. Nonmetropolitan/rural areas are those that are not metropolitan urban areas.
>
> (p. 8)

As these scholars collectively point out, the use of numbers to categorize a place as rural will always come up short due to the other factors that go unaccounted for in that model. In creating a categorical model, the statistical definition inherent in the delineation of its categories "presumes similarities that do not exist" (Shortall & Warner, 2012, p. 9). To make this point even more emphatically, Shortall and Warner (2012) use the example of proximity as an addition to description. If a rural place is adjacent to an urban area, it will quite likely be extremely different from a rural area that is remote from urban centers. In keeping with these ideas, Hoggart (1990) has suggested that the lack of clarity in the assumptions through which researchers label places as rural is theoretically untenable and that "the designation 'rural', no matter how defined, does not provide an appropriate abstraction" (p. 246). Hoggart believed that the differentiation of rural and urban must be based in and "take account of their very different structural circumstances" (p. 245). And it is to this exact point that Coladarci (2007) addressed the most pointed aspects of his reflection. He wrote: "the problem in my view is that rural education researchers . . . typically fail to describe the context of their research in sufficient detail" (p. 2). It is clear that concerns held in common between these scholars are very similar. Speaking further to the problematic aspects of these concerns, Coladarci (2007) wrote:

> Why is this a problem? It is a problem because cursory descriptions of context in rural education research preclude the clear and informed interpretation of results from an individual study, the meaningful synthesis of results across studies, and ultimately, the accumulation of reliable knowledge about rural education.
>
> (p. 2)

One possible source of resolution to this problem comes from Brown and Schafft (2011) with their description of a multidimensional approach to defining rural. The model consists of four dimensions and is based in the vision that rural areas exist as "places where people live, work, and visit and as spatially delimited natural environments" (p. 5). The four distinguishing dimensions, which are described with considerable detail in Brown and Schafft (2011), are based on traits labeled as (a) demographic and ecological, (b) economic, (c) institutional, and (d) sociocultural. In this way, Brown and Schafft (2011) constructed a model in which to define rural "in terms of what [these places] are and what they are not, in terms of their intrinsic characteristics, or as a critique of urban" (p. 5). In this manner, the four dimensions also establish a framework about which the rural science education researcher can provide descriptions of the rural context to such a degree that the nature of its specific rurality can be established within the work of scholarship. Most importantly, the creation of this description according to the accepted model will allow for the interpretation, synthesis, and accumulation of knowledge learned from research into rural schools (Coladarci, 2007). As we shall see in the next section, not all researchers agree with this type of multidimensional scheme. But as we will also address in a subsequent section, the issues of social justice and diversity in rural science education do in many ways mirror the issues of rural identity.

Methodology and rural science education research. As the year 2002 began, the reauthorization of the Elementary and Secondary Act, as shaped by the Bush administration and approved by the U.S. Congress under the title No Child Left Behind (NCLB), created a new federal mandate for the reform of educational practice in the United States. This new approach to federal funding for public schools required the assessment of all students' subject matter learning by way of standardized tests. But further, this renewal of the federal statute "exalts scientific evidence as the key driver of education policy and practice" (Feuer et al., 2002, p. 4). Close study of the revised law has shown that it contains 111 references to "scientifically based research" and the "unmistakable theme" that educational research will need to be based in randomized controlled experiments if it is to form a basis of policy (Feuer et al., 2002). The use of true scientific experiments as a methodology in educational research has been the basis of long debate, but to have research methodology written into law, in the words of Feuer and colleagues (2002), can be quite startling to academic researchers.

> . . . but surprise turns to anxiety when the law appears to instruct them on methodology and to tie public funding of research to specific modes of inquiry.
>
> (Feuer et al., 2002, p. 5)

It seems clear that it was, at least in part, this sense of "surprise turning to anxiety" that stimulated Howley, Theobald, and Howley's (2005) response in the *Journal of Research in Rural Education* to the Arnold, Newman, Gaddy, and Dean (2005) article regarding "the condition of rural education research." Arnold and colleagues published an investigation of rural education research that had examined the abstracts of nearly 500 manuscripts found using ERIC and PsycINFO. These abstracts were classified

based on how the research could be fitted into one of two categories of rural education research. According to the article, an effort was made to distinguish those abstracts that described an apparent intent to develop understanding of rural schooling from those that reported research conducted in rural sites but without an "apparent intent to investigate a rural education issue or explain how rurality influences some aspect of schooling" (Arnold et al., 2005, p. 2). Science education–related articles fit within the "instruction" subcategory and numbered six within the *understanding rural education* category with an additional five manuscripts in the *rural context only*. This small number of research articles dealing with rural science education is not surprising and is consistent with reports worldwide.

At the outset, Arnold and colleagues (2005) made it clear that rigorous research is the standard by which all judgments will be characterized. And though in a later response to a critique of this article, Arnold (2005) seems to disavow this statement, originally they wrote that rural education research is "driven by a belief that there is a quality inherent in rural communities and schools that should be preserved" and that this viewpoint has not been established by "rigorous research" (p. 1). And so it was not surprising that the authors quickly turned their focus to identifying which of the rural education research articles identified were founded on rigorous research. This identification was based on the researchers' use of the methodologies through which, in the view of Arnold and his colleagues, rigorous research can be accomplished. The authors expressed disappointment with the small number of studies that are focused on "identifying causal relationships between interventions and outcomes with higher degrees of certainty" (p. 10). Though they make a statement in support of the value of "nonexperimental research or observational studies," this valuing seems somewhat disingenuous when the authors revealed how they judge *quality* of research. Using a scale labeled the "Quality of Research criteria developed by McREL" (Mid-Continent Research for Education and Learning), Arnold and his co-authors proceeded to evaluate 222 of the original set of articles. The criteria that make up the "quality" assessment are described by eight measures of validity (Arnold et al., 2005) that are used in quantitative research in which statistical tests establish significance of results. Subsequent to the publication of this article, many articles published were aimed at addressing issues of research quality in light of the new emphasis on scientific educational research. Arnold and colleagues (2005) seem to conjoin quality and rigor in a manner similar to what Floden described (Moss et al., 2009) regarding a different discussion: "this dialogue uses quality and rigor as though they were interchangeable terms" (p. 505). In the current literature on education research, quality and rigor are distinguished in a variety of ways. Using criteria from the recent research literature (Moss et al., 2009), there would apparently be agreement that Arnold and colleagues (2005) were on track in their efforts to identify quality when they differentiated research that has an apparent intent to examine a research question that would create understanding of rural education (Moss et al., 2009).

In the absence of any randomized controlled experiments, the authors identified 106 articles that used a "comparative research design to investigate a rural education problem" (p. 10). Using tables and text in the article (see, for instance, p. 11 of the article), it seems clear that experimental research is on a separate plateau high above other comparative research, which is divided among three lesser labels: higher quality, medium quality, and lower quality.

Ultimately, Arnold and his colleagues (2005) concluded that

> In many cases, the researchers expected to observe change or rural/nonrural differences, but when higher-quality research methods are evident, changes and differences were not detected. These observations lead us to question what is generally accepted as being known about rural education and suggest that the research areas identified in this section need conceptual refinement around rural research questions and more rigorous study.
>
> (p. 15)

And with that statement, Arnold and colleagues (2005) seem to have come full circle, casting doubt on all research previously done on rural education. Thus we turn to the reply.

The response by Howley and colleagues, Theobald, and Howley (2005) to Arnold's negative evaluation of rural education research castigated the review as both misplaced and misbegotten. Further, Howley and colleagues (2005) established their response within a place-based research tradition of the rural education research community. They wrote:

> Arnold and colleagues' review takes as a given that the rural education research of most worth identifies 'the causes of different student outcomes' (p. 9). Such a mission might reasonably guide research in a field that doesn't take context as the principal defining condition. We might as well *not have* rural education research, nor rural education for that matter, that fails to center itself on rural cultures and ways of engaging in life.
>
> (p. 1)

In place of Arnold and colleagues' perspective, Howley and colleagues (2005) ask of educational research a set of questions arising from differing outlooks.

> Rural education research simply *must ask* what sort of schooling rural kids are getting, why they are getting it, who benefits and who gets injured in the process, and by what mechanisms.
>
> (p. 3)

And ultimately, it is the concept of "critique" that, for Howley and his co-authors, constitutes the primary action of research proper. For these authors, "critique in the academic sense refers to the exercise of careful judgment, especially in extended discussion" (p. 3). And so this exercise of careful judgment intersects with the doing of

this form of social science in a deliberate examination of "doubt." They continue: "Doubt sponsors critique; doubt is intuitive—a stance toward claims and appearances; critique is part of the method for dealing with doubt. So is good science . . ." (p. 3). (For an extension of this discussion of the nature of critique, see Howley, 2009.)

In his somewhat sardonic response to Howley and colleagues, Arnold (2005) expressed disappointment at the lack of stimulus for further discussion. He expressed the opinion that nothing from their retort would "further the conversation about future directions for rural education research" (p. 1). Arnold (2005) suggested that confirmation bias is more important in Howley and colleagues' (2005) acceptance of research findings than the examination of the total set of published reports. Arnold succinctly states the case in this way: "The belief that rural communities and schools should be preserved should not trump scholarly integrity" (2005, p. 1).

Each group of scholars, in their ordered replies, attempted to keep the discussion away from the specific issue of research methodology and design. For instance, Howley and colleagues (2005) wrote:

> Rural meanings are the raison d'etre, the motive for the best rural education research. This answer to our question might suggest—wrongly—to some readers a qualitative turn, but we're not dealing with overall methods or specific issues of research design.
>
> (p. 1)

Ultimately, Arnold rejects the Howley and colleagues (2005) response as "jumping the shark" (in reference to a low moment when it became evident that the TV show *Happy Days* had passed its prime) but, like Howley and colleagues, takes the opportunity to add a bit of intrigue. Howley and colleagues (2005) originally challenged Arnold and colleagues to own up to an ulterior motive. Howley linked the work of Arnold and colleagues tightly to the agenda of the U.S. Department of Education's (USDOE) Institute for Education Sciences (IES) and used this linkage to suggest that Arnold and colleagues were, at best, forwarding the message of the agency that pays their bills. But not to be outdone, Arnold (2005) retorts that intrigue is also present on the Howley and colleagues side of the street and returns the accusation with regard to their association with the Appalachian Collaborative Center for Learning, Assessment and Instruction in Mathematics (ACCLAIM). As it turns out, intrigue is not at all uncommon with regard to the debate concerning the promotion of and detraction from scientifically based educational research.

In the fall of 2012, a series of articles identified and examined a possible subterfuge regarding the use of randomized control trials (RCT) in educational research. At the center of the issue was the supposed reticence of educational researchers to adopt randomized experimental design-based research methodologies. A set of four articles appeared in the October 2012 issue of the journal *Educational Researcher*, and though this issue was not directed at rural education research, it is illuminating with regard to the importance of the "scientific research" debate to rural education research. In the original article, Skidmore and Thompson (2012) described different versions of a single graph that had been used to show the cumulative frequency of educational research studies using RCT or possible RCT (PRCT) research designs between 1950 and 2000. In the graph, originally published in an article by Petrosino and colleagues (2000), the cumulative frequency of educational research studies using RCT or PRCT methodologies was shown to have increased over time, and there were more educational research studies using RCTs or PRCTs than in other fields identified in this comparison (i.e., criminology, social policy, and psychology). However, this graph was altered when reproduced in another publication (Cook, 2001). The altered graph was used by then director of the USDOE IES program in a variety of presentations in the first years that IES was in existence and in the first years of NCLB. The problem was that the altered graph had changed the labels of the bottom line from Criminology to Education. The cumulative frequency of the education research studies using RCT/PRCTs was incorrectly ranked fourth among the four. Thus, whereas educational researchers were in fact doing more RCT/PRCT research studies than the comparison fields, we were represented as doing the fewest. There are many questions that could arise out of this foul-up, but two are of particular importance. First, did this representation damage the reputations of educational researchers given that the director of IES was using the incorrect graph in presentations? The various authors involved in the four articles published in one issue of *Educational Researcher* do not all agree, but it is hard to see, however, how it did not damage the already delicate reputation (Labaree, 2005) of educational scholars. But second, and most important for the purposes of this chapter, were even the correct versions of these graphs a germane representation of the data? Robinson (2012) questioned the use of cumulative frequency as an indicator of worth. He produced a different graph that, rather than showing the cumulative frequency across years, again showed the frequency of RCT/PRCT studies, but rather than as a continuous line graph, now grouped within 5-year time intervals. The revised graph shows that the number of RCT/PRCT educational research studies peaked in 1975 and has been declining in each 5-year period since. This same trend was evidenced in each of the disciplinary fields that constituted the comparison of the original graph. But then with even greater importance, he asked this question: "We have no reason to believe the four fields have equal amounts of research, so why compare them?" (p. 172). Cumulative frequency was simply not an appropriate representation of the activity of educational researchers with regard to researchers in other fields. Why compare them at all?

The only research that can impact a field like rural science education is that which asks serious questions of importance to that field. In the research vernacular of this time, those serious questions must be informed by and grow out of a theoretical framework based in the relevant research literature. But this theoretical framework must have a complementary epistemological framework that allows the researcher to pose and answer the question of "how can we know?" (Oliver, 2007b). The debate between Arnold and colleagues (2005) and Howley and colleagues (2005) should point out to researchers that there is a wide range of approaches to educational research regarding rural science education. But there are equally wide disagreements about the appropriateness of these approaches. Grounding research in a theoretical framework constructed around "place" is an accepted practice among rural education researchers regardless of federal policy. But most importantly, researchers must ask important questions that help illuminate how rural science education can be made better for the students and teachers who are the consumers and providers of it. Research methodology alone cannot add the needed illumination.

The Changing Demographics of Rural Education

In both the developing and industrialized countries of the world, there has been an ongoing migration of people toward cities (Brown & Schafft, 2011). And though the proportion of a given country's population living in cities in the more developed parts of the world is greater than in the less-developed parts, the United Nations has projected that even the less-developed nations "will surpass the 50% urban threshold by 2019" (Brown & Schafft, 2011, p. 3). As these authors point out, the population change of rural areas is often due to several pervasive factors. Often most immediately noticeable to families is the out-migration of the young. But often there is a selectivity factor in this out-migration that has huge impact on the community. Research by Domina (2006) shows that "rural net out-migration at young adult ages was highly selective of the better educated individuals" (as cited in Brown & Schafft, p. 115). Although rural populations may receive a boost by in-migration, two of the most common types have dramatically different impacts on schools. Retirement in-migration usually has no effect on schools' student populations but will likely have the benefit of providing extra revenue to the coffers directly by way of taxes paid or indirectly through money spent in the community. The second type of in-migration, international in-migration, to rural communities has also dramatically increased in recent times in some areas of the rural United States. In particular, demographic statistics show that "for Latinos the period between 1990 and 2008 is marked by steady increases in the total number living in nonmetropolitan areas" (Brown & Schafft, 2011, p. 125). Many of these Latino individuals are international immigrants who arrive in the rural areas with entire families and typically as limited English proficient (LEP). Brown and Schafft go on to report that "between 1990 and 2000 alone, Latino populations tripled in size in the South and doubled in size in the

Midwest, creating both new opportunities and new challenges for rural receiving communities" (p. 126). Further, the in-migration of Latino families often comes as a result of large numbers of new jobs that become available within a locality. These jobs are usually characterized as requiring low skill and providing low pay and thus create a "boomtown" phenomenon as these workers arrive and take jobs in "construction, agricultural production, rug manufacture and leather tanning, and in particular, animal slaughtering and processing" (Brown & Schafft, 2011, p. 139). As the local demographics are impacted by this influx of new individuals, the fact that families often come as whole groups means that schools are impacted in powerful ways. Communities must find means to support the schooling needs of students for whom every language-based communication may be a major problem. In places where little attention may have previously been paid to issues of multicultural education, diversity, and social justice, these issues can suddenly take on paramount importance. As an example characteristic of this day and time, the potential to impact the rural/small school's overall performance on standardized test scores can be very great. As Brown and Schafft (2011) wrote:

> Given that educational outcomes are heavily influenced by family and community context, and in particular socioeconomic status, many rural schools with large low-income student populations may therefore face particular challenges. Small school size may also affect assessment since changes in student scores from year to year at the aggregate level may be more sensitive to random variation in factors over which schools may have little or no control, such as changing student demographics (Goetz, 2005) associated with the arrival of new student populations including English Language Learners who may disproportionately underperform in academic assessments.
>
> (p. 67)

No doubt, in these rural communities, there will be great levels of concern about the performance of the schools and their teachers and administrators. As Boyd (1978) wrote more than 35 years ago, "If there is one proposition about curriculum politics that is clear, it is that the school curriculum becomes an issue in communities and societies that are undergoing significant change" (p. 582). And though there is an ongoing need to conduct educational research in rural sites around the globe, the issues that arise in localities experiencing rapidly changing school population demographics suggest a special need for educational research highly focused on the education of the children found there. Briefly we will turn to the status of science in rural schools in the United States where baseline data are readily available.

Educational Statistics of the Rural Schools in the United States

The size of the population found in the typical rural locality of the United States, like countries around the globe, is shrinking. In concert with this diminished human population is a reduction in the number of schools and school districts serving the educational needs of children. Boyd (1978) reported that between 1950 and 1978, the number of school districts in the United States dropped from more than 80,000 to fewer than 17,000. By the 2003 to 2004 academic year, this number had dropped further to about 14,000 (Provasnik et al., 2007). Approximately 10 million U.S. students attend the rural schools that make up about 55% of these school districts but account for only about 31% of the total number of schools (Brown & Schafft, 2011). "Of students attending rural schools, well over one-third go to schools with 400 or fewer students, and over 90 percent attend schools of 800 students or fewer" (p. 62).

Science achievement in the rural schools of the United States, as measured by the National Assessment of Educational Progress (NAEP; Provasnik et al., 2007), is remarkably constant across grade levels measured by the assessment. At the fourth-grade level, 32% of rural students scored at or above the Proficient level on the science items of the 2005 NAEP assessment. When added to the 42% of students at the Basic level, this total of 74% of students scoring above basic accomplishment greatly exceeds that of the city school counterparts. No statistical difference can be found in these data between science accomplishments of rural students compared to their suburban peers (Provasnik et al., 2007).

At the eighth-grade level, the comparison for rural students with the city and suburban students continues to hold up though the total proportion of rural students achieving at the Basic or higher level for science has diminished from 74% at the elementary level to 63% in middle school. Again at the 12th-grade level, the pattern continued to hold true with regard to comparisons with city and suburban peers, but now the overall proportion of students who achieved at the Basic or higher level in science has fallen to 54% for the rural students (Provasnik et al., 2007).

Though not unique among the countries of the world, the U.S. immigration patterns of the past 25 years have caused changes in the demographic patterns of rural America. These patterns are affecting the schools and the education of children in those rural places. We will return to this issue in a later section when we consider the attrition, satisfaction, and recruitment of science teachers to school districts in the United States and in other countries. In the next section, we attempt to characterize a small number of studies that focus on issues of social justice and diversity and that represent a new wave of research approaches in rural science education.

Students, Social Justice, and Rural Science

The identification of rural schools is very complex and often carried out in a manner that does not result in a reproducible characterization. The use of superficial categories is particularly problematic. And this is a problem, as Coladarci (2007) pointed out, because in the absence of a deep description from which a substantial characterization of the school/place as rural is built, users of that scholarship cannot form "clear and informed interpretations" of the findings or create meaningful syntheses to compare those results to findings that emerge from research at other sites/schools. The problem arises from the complexity of the characterization required. But it is a parallel complexity that also presents a stumbling block in the teaching of children. Lee and Buxton (2013) stated this concern as follows:

> [T]he demographic subgroups typically used to categorize students in schools are not fixed or natural characteristics, but rather social constructions . . . [such that] all of these dimensions of identity—race, ethnicity, gender, culture, language, special needs, social class, religion, family, and community—are complex, shifting, social and political fields and that the interplay among these dimensions adds further layers of complexity to questions of diversity and equity.
>
> (p. 1)

In this chapter, we have used Mensah's (2013) definition of teaching for social justice and diversity as a lens for examining scholarship. She wrote, "To teach science for diversity and equity, the science teacher must embrace beliefs that each child has a right to learn science, should be given free access to science, is empowered by knowing science, and can benefit from opportunities to advance themselves educationally within science" (p. 66). We will examine four different studies that look at how equity, diversity, and social justice can be fostered in rural school contexts. Those studies will individually point to the importance of learners, teachers, technology, community, and contexts as factors in understanding how to foster diversity, equity, and social justice.

The first consideration is about the learners. A number of recently published research studies in rural science education examine the knowledge that students bring to school but that arose from out-of-school sources. Lloyd (2010), for instance, found that each member of a group of rural students with whom she worked on an extracurricular club activity had funds of knowledge that are or could be relevant to school as well as out-of-school science learning. These funds of knowledge that were possessed by the students ranged from knowledge of electronics to knowledge of farming and a variety of things in between. In total, she identified 13 different sources for these funds of knowledge with several (i.e., knowledge of farming and of farmers' markets) being described as uniquely rural. Ultimately Lloyd (2010) concluded that

> These funds of knowledge can be utilized to improve the accessibility of the science instruction or assessments . . . Recognizing that rural students . . . may have common core funds of knowledge could be an important step towards understanding why standardized testing and curricula do not equally serve all students. This realization could have broad implications across the standards

movement, and could serve to push teachers, curriculum designers and test writers to critique the assumption that there can be a "one-size-fits all" type of assessment or curriculum.

(p. 158)

Supporting students to enter science learning doors that are already partly open due to the prior experiences encapsulated by their funds of knowledge is one way that science can be opened to all students.

Avery and Kassam (2011) used a counterpoint between "knowing that" and "knowing how" based on the critical pedagogy of Gruenewalde in order to examine how students would find examples of science and engineering outside of the school. Using the ancient concept of phronesis, the anchoring of learning in experience, these researchers advocated the implementation of an "approach that positions rural children's funds of knowledge at the epicenter of their science education" (p. 2). In their study, Avery and Kassam (2011) provided cameras to students and gave them instructions to find and photograph examples of science and engineering in their "home and local environment." All of the students were successful in their searches, and family members were important sources of information in the students' quest to find these examples. However, only 1 of the 20 students who participated could make explicit connections between the science and engineering in the photographs and science learning in the classroom. These finding suggested an ongoing need for teachers as organizers/leaders for student educative experiences, but it also points to these students' ability to recognize science within the local context. Connecting schooling to a local context can also be a function of community.

As Schafft, Alter, and Bridger (2006) wrote: "Although the mandate of the school is centered on provision of education, the reality is that rural schools take on multiple social, cultural, and economic development roles that are likely to only become more important as rural economies continue to change" (p. 3). Among those social and cultural concerns is the "provision of education" so as to best accomplish equitable outcomes among their student populations. In their study of a small rural community in central Pennsylvania, Schafft, Alter, and Bridger (2006) found that an investment by the local government to bring advanced communications and computer technology to a school district can have a profound impact on both the schools and communities. According to these authors, after gaining these new technologies, "Students are offered educational opportunities previously unheard of in resource-limited rural districts, with a broader goal of community development—enhancing both the integration of the school and community, and the economic development of the area" (Schafft et al., 2006, p. 2). The researchers presented results that suggest that the infusion of technology resulted in a greater recognition of the needs of all children in the district, an increase in self-esteem of those students, and a recognition by many members of the community that they were not just "hillbillies." This became an issue of social justice within the school district as it was recognized that "within a low-resource community, concerted efforts were made so that the benefits of the initiative would directly accrue across broad swaths of the community, including those members who, for social or economic reasons, would ordinarily be excluded" (Schafft et al., 2006, p. 8).

The school–community linkage, however, may play out quite differently in schools in differently localities. In Nigeria, Okebukola, Owolabi, and Okebukola (2013) found that the requirement of teaching science to students of the primary grades in their mother tongue failed to be carried out in urban schools more often than in rural schools. An investigation of this phenomenon showed that between primary grade 1 and primary grade 3, the percentage of time that science was taught in a mother tongue language diminished from 62% to 27% in the urban school context. In contrast, the teachers of the rural school taught science in the mother tongue 93.6% of the time in primary grade 1 and dropped to 84.6% of the time in primary grade 3. For these authors, this is clearly an issue of social justice as they state: "Language of delivery of science through classroom discourse or presentation through textbooks is, therefore, a key determinant of concept formation and mastery because children tend to comprehend in the language to which they have greatest familiarity" (Okebukola et al., 2013, p. 63). But the situation is complicated by the fact that the rural classes tend to be composed of students who use a common mother tongue in contrast to the urban classrooms in which students from a variety of backgrounds may be brought together. The situation is further complicated by the fact that later in the academic life of the students, science will be shifted to English-language instruction for all students, and the urban teachers may be thinking ahead in terms of how to best prepare their students. The fact that the reform to teach in the mother tongue was inspired by an effort to "move from an education system inherited from the colonialists to a more transformative and culturally relevant education which takes into account African values, linguistics, and sociocultural backgrounds" (Okebukola et al., 2013, p. 62) can get lost in the pragmatic issues of schools.

The study of teachers of the rural science students is also of great importance in understanding the educative process, particularly as it relates to the efforts to implement culturally relevant and effective science instruction. Mensah (2009) studied science teachers in two high schools of a rural predominantly Black school district in the southeastern United States. Her motivation was based in research showing that the number of Black teachers is declining and that context of schools is a major factor in this decline. Though the number of Black teachers may be declining, the number of Black students, as well as students of other racial and ethnic nonmajority groups, is increasing. Mensah (2009), using stories of personal and professional development, constructed this report of the

significance of the teachers' efforts as being based in their love for science and their own "content-specific expertise." But the motivation for the job was also based in the teachers' beliefs about "an obligation to teach science, a community connection, and a desire for students to learn science in ways that connect to their daily lives" (p. 48). Their view of teaching as a profession is inseparable from their desire for students to be knowledgeable users of science within real-world examples.

Finally, we consider the issue of context and rural science education as presented by Carlone, Kimmel, and Tschida (2010). These scholars make the case that science education has for too long been focused on individuals and how individuals learn. The authors expressed concern about "the overly narrow consideration of what counts as relevant context in most of the science education literature" (p. 448). Their motivation in this endeavor was to create understanding of "why we have the kind of science education we have, why reform is difficult, and why reform happens in unexpected places through novel means and methods" (p. 448) and point to rural science education as an area particularly in need of this study. Their study of the Horizon Elementary magnet school for mathematics, science, and technology, where place-based science (i.e., farming-related science) is used as a cornerstone of the science curriculum, presents a study of context in which character education and science education operate in a connected sphere as factors of a network of practice that existed prior to creation of the school. The authors found that the enactment of the curriculum at this school is a product of its context and cannot be divorced from it. Thus the teaching of science is unique not only to the physical environment but also to the cultural and political environment. These factors impact all schools, but given the local significance of and the means used to promote the Horizon school in the public eye, they are particularly important.

As a group, these studies provide linkages among the research in rural science education but also insight into the future of that research. There is profound insight to be gained by increasing understanding about how students, teachers, communities, and contexts intersect in the act of producing an agency for education in which people, working alone and in groups, continue to seek the best ways to educate children.

Technology, Globalization, STEM Education, and Rural Places

Over the last 25 years, through vast improvements in technology as well as increased educational accomplishment throughout the countries of the world, the phenomenon of globalization has come to represent the interconnectivity and integration of the peoples of the world. Metaphors for this connectedness of civilization of the Earth, such as the "global village" and the "flat world," are utilized by economists, scientists, policy makers, and educators to inform policy as it relates to new visions of worldwide educational, political, and economic landscapes (Friedman, 2005). As Legrain (2002) explained, "Our lives are becoming increasingly intertwined with those of distant people and places around the world-economically, politically, and culturally. These links are not always new, but they are more pervasive than ever before" (p. 4). U.S. President Barak Obama added an emphatic declarative point when he stated,

> In a 21st-century world, where jobs can be shipped wherever there's an Internet connection, where a child born in Dallas is now competing with a child in New Delhi, where your best job qualification is not what you do, but what you know, education is no longer just a pathway to success: it's a prerequisite for success.
>
> (Obama, 2009)

And certainly, this aspect of international integration and interconnectedness of people and their knowledge is highly related to science, technology, and education in those fields. As Stewart (2012) asserted, "the future of the economy, jobs, and other national challenges is always unpredictable, but a good education is the best tool we have to prepare the next generation of Americans for the rapidly changing world" (p. 31). As we considered technology in rural places, we delimited our examination to Canada, Australia, China, Finland, and the United States, five industrialized countries where exceptional Science, Technology, Engineering, and Mathematics (STEM) education takes place, as evidenced by achievement scores on comparative assessments. Across these countries, as a function of globalization, low-skill jobs have diminished while knowledge-based jobs (i.e., jobs that require significant educational attainment in a specific area) have increased. For example, the U.S. job landscape has experienced a pronounced shift away from blue-collar, low-skill jobs, which have decreased, as a proportion of total employment, from 56% in 1969 to 39% in 1999. Meanwhile, professional and technical jobs increased, again as a proportion of total employment, from 23% to 33% during the same interval (Levy & Murnane, 2004). The effect of a shifting job landscape is more pronounced in rural places where the closing of one industrial plant may disrupt and possibly end the economy of a small town. As the economies of our civilizations "flatten," how does this impact the people, schools, and science education of rural places? Has globalization increased opportunities in rural places academically? To consider these questions, we will examine scholarship related to school-based science achievement in rural places as well as the development and implementation of technology-based STEM education interventions in rural places.

Achievement in Rural Places

Throughout the first decade and a half of the 21st century, educational opportunity has increased greatly throughout the world. One example, labeled the Education for All initiative, has resulted from nations of the world uniting behind the goal of providing universal primary education in every country. For example in sub–Saharan Africa, school attendance rolls have increased by more than 33 million children from 2000 to 2008 (UNESCO, 2010). Some of these gains have resulted in wake-up calls in nations whose scores on international science comparisons previously had them leading by large measures. Amid this context, we will explore research related to rural schooling with particular emphasis on examining rural places, rural science teachers, and exemplars in STEM education in rural places.

U.S. college completion rates. As more students attend colleges, researchers have begun to examine issues associated with degree attainment. For example, in 2007, 42% of rural high school graduates attended 4-year colleges, an increase from 35% in 2003 (Snyder & Dillow, 2010). These data support the claim that there is more access to higher education for rural students today than in the recent past. However, this increased access does not always translate into degree attainment. In fact, some scholars (e.g., Maltzan, 2006) have found diminished rates of degree persistence among rural students attending college. Factors such as family economic difficulties, first-generation college student status, and inadequate academic preparation are linked to decreased persistence in college. In addition, researchers (Byun, Irvin, & Meece, 2012; Provasnik et al., 2007) have found that rural students are less likely to graduate from 4-year college than nonrural students are.

Yan (2002) identified socioeconomic status (SES), number of science courses taken, and type of institution first attended as factors affecting student persistence in college. Further, other research suggests that the typical high school for rural students makes them more likely to have experienced a narrow curriculum (Irvin, Hannum, Farmer, de la Varre, & Keane, 2009; Provasnik et al., 2007) absent the college preparatory courses and advanced-placement options characteristic of the curriculum available to their suburban and urban peers. Byun and colleagues (2012) utilized logistic regression modeling to identify characteristics of youth attending 4-year colleges and factors associated with their subsequent graduation. They utilized data gathered by the National Educational Longitudinal Survey to create a comparison of rural and urban youth who attended 4-year colleges. Byun and colleagues found that rural youth who attended college were more likely to be White than were their urban peers (85% vs. 65%). Rural students were less likely to have a parent who had graduated from a 4-year university than were their urban peers (38% vs. 50%) and less likely to have been raised in a household in which family income surpassed $50,000, compared to urban peers (38% vs. 49%).

These studies suggest that factors inherent in some rural communities do have an impact on rural students' success in college, especially in the United States. Research that is based in countries other than the United States demonstrates some of these findings as well. Finland and China, in particular, serve as exemplars of expanding educational opportunities for all students, regardless of sociological context. The following discussion of Finland, China, and Canada highlights the expansion of educational opportunities to students spanning each country.

Finland: An exemplar in equity. Stewart (2012) asserted that schools were pivotal in shifting Finland from a rural, poor, and timber- and agriculture-based economy to a modern technologically based economy. In 1970, only 40% of Finnish students graduated from high school. By the end of the first decade of the 21st century, Finland could brag of a world-class educational system that ranked second in science, fifth in math, and third in reading on the 2009 Programme for International Student Assessment (PISA). The dramatic shift was attributed to a variety of changes but to three in particular. In the 1960s, Finland had implemented a common school for all students (Grades 1–9) such that all students were tasked with a newly designed curriculum that was notable for both its rigor and comprehensive coverage (Sahlberg, 2010). Second, Finland shifted teacher preparation to the university, where individuals were trained to differentiate instruction, develop pedagogical content knowledge, and diagnose student learning difficulties. This change resulted in teaching becoming, in Finland, a sought-after profession (Sahlberg, 2010). Remarkably, there are no countrywide external assessments, yet equity abounds as scores within Finland vary by less than 5% across the student population, when scored internationally by tests such as the PISA and Trends in International Mathematics and Science Study (TIMMS). Scholars contend that the factors driving positive school change within Finland are due to the unmatched teaching workforce. Finland provides a model of education that varies significantly from that of other countries by the lack of standardized testing. Finland serves as an exemplar for expanding educational opportunity equitably, without relying on standardization of curriculum or vast accountability schemes to do so.

China: An exemplar in access and technology. In 1988, China enacted a law that required 9 years of basic education for each young person. In a related shift, the number of students in higher education had expanded from 8 million in 2000 to an expected 45 million in 2015 (Yang, 2008). During this time of rapid educational expansion, vast disparities between urban and rural education emerged. In addition, these rural places were unable to recruit qualified teachers in special subject areas such as English and STEM courses. The difficulty of recruiting rural teachers was related most significantly to teachers' working and living conditions, extreme teacher workloads, poor transportation, limited professional learning, and lower salaries than those of city teachers (McQuaide, 2009).

In an effort to provide universal education to rural places, the Chinese government implemented the Distance Education Project for Rural Schools (DEPRS) beginning in 2003. The DEPRS provided computers, high-speed Internet, satellite television, a DVD player, and DVDs to 37,500 rural junior high schools. In addition to the media tools, Chinese Central Television aired various education programs, and Web-based educational programs were provided by the Ministry of Education supplemented with teacher training materials. Regional education officials provided guidance related to the implementation of each of the learning tools (McQuaide, 2009).

In 2007, researchers reported that more than 100 million rural school students were utilizing the new materials. Chinese universities conducted two evaluations to measure the impact of DEPRS on student learning. Findings indicate that education in rural places was improved through this vast initiative as evidenced by decreased teacher shortages and increased access to various course offerings (McQuaide, 2009).

Canada: An exemplar in curriculum integration and a professional, satisfied workforce. Canada's public educational system is characterized by elementary, junior high, and high schools within a decentralized system. Specifically, education is overseen by 10 provinces and three territories, with no federal involvement. In international comparisons, Canada consistently ranks in the top 10 in math, science, and reading on international assessments. Within the rural, prairie province of Alberta, a region characterized by high poverty rates and large numbers of students who are English language learners (ELLs), the province was outscored only by Finland on the 2006 PISA. The Alberta Minister of Education David Hancock had led a transition in the educational locus that shifted emphasis toward higher-order thinking that focuses on students' use of data to analyze and solve problems in STEM subjects (Jahnukainen, 2011). Alberta teachers were heavily involved in the reform design, which rebuilt the K–12 curriculum and assessments in every subject. Practicing teachers then were given the autonomy to implement the curriculum as they saw fit in the classroom. The Albertans attribute their success to their teacher workforce, which is paid significantly more than the American teaching workforce, experiences greater autonomy to develop its own professional goals, and utilizes action research to assess its effectiveness.

Collectively, these countries highlight a range of successful strategies that have improved educational opportunities for students across the entire country but particularly in rural places. As the United States has sought to find success in reform by implementing more standardization in curriculum and in assessment, other countries, notably Finland and Canada, have continued to seek increased educational success and equity with minimal standardization. A common theme throughout those countries is the important role of the teacher and the status associated with the profession of teaching. At a later point in the chapter, we will return to this theme and examine research related to the retention of science teachers in these rural areas (particularly in the United States). The next section of the chapter, however, explores the actual implementation of technology-based teaching and learning within specific rural places.

Distance Education in Rural Places

Within rural schools and other rural education outlets (i.e., libraries, etc.), technology is reshaping educational access. Scholars find that access by way of broadband Internet and cell phones (Avery, 2013) continues to vary widely by location, yet the use of technology to access knowledge and other resources continues to gain traction. Though access is not yet universal in 2014, that day seems close.

Countries around the world have increased their utilization of distance learning for the purpose of broadening access to education. This is true across industrialized and developing nations. For example, the countries of Indonesia, Nigeria, India, Tanzania, and Zimbabwe are each notable for their utilization of distance education both to recruit individuals for the teaching profession and to train those persons who choose (or who are chosen) to become teachers. Other countries utilize distance education to provide professional learning opportunities to inservice teachers (McQuaide, 2009).

During the first years of the 21st century, online education has experienced exponential growth as more than 700,000 U.S. K–12 students utilized virtual schools in 2005 through 2006 (Picciano & Seaman, 2009). Advocates of online distance education (ODE) asserted that successful utilization of this virtual school platform would improve the educational experiences of students by providing individualized, learner-focused interventions needed to become productive, 21st-century workers. Educators in rural areas conceptualize ODE as an avenue to provide increased course options for students. For example, students who attend small, rural schools in Canada are less likely to complete advanced-placement coursework (Barbour & Mulcahy, 2006) due to lack of course availability and interest. Hodges (2010) found course availability of higher-level STEM courses to be more limited than in all other core subjects in their study of four rural schools districts. Specifically, only one county school out of four offered any advanced-placement courses in the STEM fields. To combat this inequity, multiple rural schools have implemented various ODE options to increase access. In rural places, ODE faces particular difficulties, as rural students are accustomed to attentive teachers who are personally involved in their education (Irvin et al., 2009).

In Australia, researchers (Lyons, Cooksey, Panizzon, Parnell, & Pegg, 2006) found that implementation of ODE in rural schools was more difficult than in urban and suburban schools due to limited online access, resources, professional development, and access to technical support. Tytler, Symington, Darby, Malcolm, and Kirkwood (2011) identified school size and isolation of rural schools as factors related to high-quality professional learning. However, these scholars found that the relatively small size of schools in their study promoted the creation of a learning community among teachers.

Collectively, these examples highlight the tensions faced in utilizing ODE in various nations. Technological competencies of school staff and faculty, equitable access to learning for students, and schooling in remote locations remain issues that technology may help diminish.

Another approach to using distance education is through partnerships and collaborations between universities and school districts. In 2002, the National Science Foundation (NSF) launched the Math and Science Partnership program with the explicit purpose of connecting school improvement efforts between colleges/universities and K–12 schools. Three examples we highlight below were chosen for their apparent success impacting science teaching and learning in rural places. In each case, the collaboration caused the formation of a professional learning community (PLC).

1. North Cascades and Olympic Science Partnership (NCOSP)

This partnership, between Western Washington University and 26 targeted rural school districts, began with the explicit goal of improving STEM education through reform of the curricula and engagement with the community. A case study of one rural school in northwest Washington State became an exemplar in which representatives from each grade level in the K–5 school had release time during the school day to strategically plan STEM instructional interventions. This school system implemented the Full Option Science System (FOSS) kits and required *all* teachers to utilize at least one FOSS kit per year. The PLC then adapted to the needs of the teachers and began developing meaningful student learning assessments to be utilized in conjunction with the science learning materials. The PLC followed up by implementing a science fair that would feature student work and promote community engagement throughout the small and rural schools. Within this school, improvement in student proficiency on the state science test increased by 19.7% over the 3 years (Hamos et al., 2009).

2. Institute for Chemistry Literacy Through Computational Science (ICLCS)

This partnership targeted 118 rural districts in Illinois as part of a collaboration with the University of Illinois at Urbana/Champaign with the explicit goal of developing teacher leaders in chemistry to move forward an agenda of improving student achievement. One case study that resulted from this partnership described an innovative plan that implemented a program called Virtual Professional Learning Community (VPLC) to reach rural high school chemistry teachers living in Illinois. Twenty-four of the 100 teachers that participated in this VPLC taught in schools in which they were the sole science teacher. The project utilized Moodle to partner Illinois university faculty and practicing teachers in these rural places.

The technology utilized tracked more than 44,000 logins and 16,000 postings during the 23-month project. The project utilized a randomized control research design that revealed a 45% improvement on a standardized measure by the students of teachers who participated in the VPLC (Hamos et al., 2009).

3. Vertical Teaming: Professional Learning— Minimizing Effects of Isolation

Another intervention strategy used to improve science teaching and learning in rural schools is vertical teaming of teachers and other school district stakeholders. Gilmer (2010) identified various states (Oklahoma, South Dakota, and Colorado) as rural areas that implement vertical teaming. Gilmer asserted that "vertical teaming offers science teachers a greater ability to communicate with other district teachers, share ideas and learn about local resources and feel connected both to the larger scientific discipline as well as the educational community" (p. 2). Gilmer (2010) tested this hypothesis in rural Florida from Grades 3 through 12. Gilmer created 29 vertical teams that consisted of preservice teachers, a participant from elementary, middle, and high school, and a practicing scientist. Findings from the research indicated that there was improved curriculum planning at the school sites, increased individual science content understanding, greater integration of process skills into the classroom due to an increased understanding of scientific inquiry, and increased amount of environmental research performed by students in these rural places (Gilmer, 2010).

Summary

Collectively across these studies, the logistics involved in the conveyance methods of professional learning and remote content delivery vary significantly within each rural school context. Teachers and/or providers of professional development must often travel great distances in order to collaborate in traditional face-to-face professional learning. In like manner, providing students access to otherwise unavailable courses though a technological venue seems quite appealing, but its impact has not been widely tested.

In other contexts, these partnerships utilized technology in varying capacities to increase collaboration, in effect "flattening the earth." As Internet-based charter schools and universities continue to shift to online teaching and learning, the implementation of these approaches to teach science in rural settings deserves serious effort in research to better understand enactment in these novel educational contexts. We must create deep understandings of the fine details of technology-related actions that lead to success. With unparalleled access to technology, we must recognize that the instruction of science in rural schools will shift in ways that may not be predictable. We recognize this as a cautionary tale and are reminded of the rush to replace teachers with movies and television in the 1960s and 1970s (Rudolph, 2002). In many

of those earlier implementations, one teacher on a screen was intended to replace a large number of teachers who were actually present in the classrooms with the children. But the computer technologies of this day and of the near future do have the promise of being able to replace the minimal libraries of many small schools with endless online libraries whose offerings do not differ from those of the greatest universities. Textbooks are moving to virtual forms that can be accessed with tablets and that are also supplemented by dynamic representations or places for students to construct those representations. We must continue to find ways to understand how these technologies will impact student learning as well as the teaching profession. As we turn toward an examination of science teacher recruitment and retention in rural schools, we must also consider how technology as a shaper of student learning experiences will also impact teacher mobility.

Addressing Equity Through Teacher Recruitment, Retention, and Attrition

As numerous studies (Dobbie, 2011; MetLife Foundation Issue Brief, 2008) have identified, teacher quality is the most important variable affecting student achievement. We must consider how to attract and retain highly qualified teachers for the often difficult-to-staff science classrooms of rural schools. Thoughtful policy interventions and innovative curricula fail without good teachers. During this time of globalization as countries aim to create innovation-oriented, science- and technology-driven economies, the type of teacher and the associated skill set desired varies significantly from 20 years ago (Stewart, 2012). Within rural contexts throughout the world, the difficulty of adequately staffing science classrooms in schools is pronounced, as evidenced by scholarship from Australia (Plunkett & Dyson, 2011), China (Asia Society, 2010), Canada, and the United States (Ingersoll & Perda, 2010). We recognize that the challenges associated with staffing any school with highly qualified science teachers are multidimensional; as such, we will examine staffing issues in general while addressing the enduring question, *What is the impact of the rural context on teacher recruitment, retention, attrition, and migration?* Educational research scholars have attempted to understand teacher recruitment, attrition, retention, and migration (Ingersoll & Perda, 2009), while others have identified and examined various personal and environmental factors correlated with teacher turnover (Boe, Cook, & Sunderland, 2008; Horng, 2009; Liu, 2009).

During the 21st century, as educational research has transitioned to a global conversation (see, for instance, Paine & Zeichner, 2012; UNESCO Institute for Statistics, 2006), questions related to the importance of teacher quality, equitable educational access, and measured outcomes of student achievement are being asked around the globe. Thus, this review is focused on teacher staffing in light of the powerful economic and social forces in this age of accountability and globalization.

Teacher Recruitment: An International Perspective on Successful Teacher Recruitment Strategies

The education and recruitment of a STEM workforce, prepared for employment in the 21st century, has received considerable attention from stakeholders, politicians, and scholars across the globe. Undergirding each of these recruitment strategies is the creation of a professional environment in which teachers are equipped and supported to meet the needs of a specific country within a specific *context*. The scholarship of Carlone and colleagues (2010) utilized Nespor's "networks of practice" to examine the happenings within a school context. Carlone and her colleagues asserted that "Considering science education in the context of globalization means that we must analytically peel back the walls of the classroom, to view it as what Nespor (1997) called 'a knot in a web of practices that stretch into complex systems beginning and ending outside the [classroom]'" (p. 448). We will examine these rural exemplars against a global backdrop.

Strategic Recruitment Efforts in Rural Places

Throughout the world, within rural settings, factors such as remote location, lower salaries, and smaller student populations often change the working conditions of STEM teachers as compared to peers who teach in larger, more accessible schools. The use of financial incentives, homegrowing teachers, and alternative certification pathways have emerged as main avenues utilized to recruit STEM teachers to rural settings.

Financial incentives. Across the globe, a few countries with large rural populations offer financial incentives to teachers who will agree to teach in those rural places (McGaw, 2010). Included in that list are policy makers from the United States, UK, Kenya, and China who have attempted this tactic in order to recruit high-quality applicants to rural schools and other difficult-to-staff places. Compelling evidence as to the efficacy of such programs has emerged from China and the Free Teacher Education (FTE) program that the government implemented to address the unequal distribution of teachers in rural China. The FTE program provides economic incentives to students to attend six of the elite "normal" universities in China in exchange for a 10-year commitment to teach in their home province. The FTE program provides a tuition waiver, free housing, and a monthly stipend for all students chosen to participate (Wang & Gao, 2013). Zhou (2010, cited in Wang & Gao, 2013) examined the career trajectory plans of 1,800 of the FTE students and found that more than 80% of these students planned to break their contract. Similarly, it was found that 78% of prospective teachers in this program aspired to work in elite urban schools rather than in rural schools due to lower pay, decreased access to professional tools, and geographic isolation. Wang and Gao (2013) conducted in-depth interviews with 19 students who highlighted the financial inequities of teaching in rural settings as well as other career hindrances. Teachers produced by this program expressed opinions that the rural places were "a waste of talent" and that "anyone could teach there" (p. 70). These authors highlighted the need for recruitment plans to include a commitment to equity as well as the need to outline a social justice framework as a component of the call to teach in rural places in China. Overall, students chose the FTE program due to the status obtained by attending a top-tier normal university, not necessarily due to the financial assistance. Variations on this example extend beyond the borders of China.

Homegrowing teachers. A different variant on the scheme just described has the same intent: recruitment of teachers to return to the areas of (or like that of) their upbringing. The driving factor, however, in this new variant is local rather than regional/national in nature. When a local community or district specifically becomes involved to encourage individuals from their locality to enter teaching, these programs are colloquially known as "homegrowing."

In an effort to diminish local consequences of teacher shortages, many rural school districts began to create some version of homegrowing, a concept suggested by multiple researchers (Collins, 1999; Darling-Hammond, 2003; Monk, 2007). Goodpaster, Adedokun, and Weaver (2012) examined the lived experiences of six rural STEM teachers. Each of these teachers identified the strong interpersonal relationships they had developed within the community as "double-edged swords" that benefited and challenged them as teachers at various times. These benefits and challenges are very well illustrated in a study by Hodges (2010), whose findings were mixed regarding homegrown teachers as well. In one school in this study of rural science teacher retention, the arrival of two homegrown science teachers was correlated with improved test scores on high school graduation tests, where student aggregated success went from less than 50% passing to more than 90% passing in 3 years (Hodges, Oliver, & Tippins, 2013). However, in an adjacent county, a homegrown STEM teacher was described by the principal as "impossible to remove, regardless of performance" due to the connections he had developed during his 50 years in the county. His supervisor described him as perpetuating the status quo: "he was raised in these schools and he refuses to raise the bar" (Hodges, 2010). Reininger (2012) quantified this tension as she found an inequitable sorting of teachers across schools by examining data from the National Education Longitudinal Study (NELS). Her study demonstrated that teachers are more likely than other college graduates to return *home* to live. Beyond this finding, the analysis of the NELS data indicated that difficult-to-staff schools are often lower-performing schools; as such, homegrowing teachers may require caution in its enactment to avoid perpetuating inequalities.

Science Teacher Attrition in Rural Places

The issue of teacher attrition is also an important consideration with regard to staffing issues faced by rural and small schools. Research findings suggest that attrition rates for science teachers and special education teachers surpass those of other educational fields (Borman & Dowling, 2008; Guarino, Santibanez, & Daley, 2006). According to the National Science Foundation's Government Performance and Results Act (GPRA) NSF GPRA Strategic Plan, created prior to the onset of the economic downturn of 2008, the labor market for trained scientists has continued to increase dramatically, while the number of people receiving degrees in scientific fields has continued to decrease. Strunk and Robinson (2006) suggested that these statistics support the need to increase wages for science teachers. In a like vein, Henke, Zahn, and Carroll (2001) found that novice teachers who majored in STEM fields were less likely than teachers who had majored in education to still be teaching after 3 years in the profession.

In 2009, Ingersoll and Perda reported that approximately 223,000 science teachers were teaching in America's schools. More than 35,000 of these individuals were new hires for their current school in that school year. The majority (53%) had migrated to their current school from another school; but 32% were new to teaching and 15% had returned to teaching after having been out of the profession for some period of time. Of those individuals new to science teaching, 6,200 had graduated from universities in the United States with qualifications for certification to teach science, with an additional 4,900 entering teaching as delayed entrants with full qualifications but no teaching experience. Ingersoll and Perda, using data from the 1999 to 2000 academic year, found large variations in reported teacher shortages across the nation. Their studies indicated that 14% of schools who searched for a teacher of the physical sciences reported difficulty in filling that position compared to 13% of schools searching for a teacher of the biological sciences. Although other subject areas have similar challenges in terms of the number of needed teachers, other fields did not experience the difficulty replacing those who have left. In the sciences, teacher retirement accounted for only 12% to 14% of the attrition across all five cycles of the School and Staffing Survey (SASS) and Teacher Follow-up Survey (TFS) from 1988 to 2004. However, job changing and dissatisfaction with the career accounted for more than 25% of the turnover of science teachers (Ingersoll & Perda, 2009). Ingersoll and Perda summarized the SASS data to assert that there were plenty of certified science teachers, but there were not enough people willing to teach. And this situation has certainly changed again in the most recent times due to budget cuts to schools combined with increased class size that have diminished demand in many areas of the country.

Analysis of the SASS data indicated that rural high schools, with their smaller student bodies, average 50% fewer teachers than nonrural schools. Given the number of science teachers within a given rural school, the possibility of being required to teach an out-of-field science course or to have multiple preparations is increased. For example, Hodges and colleagues (2013), in an in-depth qualitative study of 10 rural STEM teachers, found that each of these teachers had to prepare to teach multiple subjects across the school day, with some teaching a different subject every class period of the day. This type of workload requirement is certainly linked to teacher attrition given its established links to teacher career dissatisfaction (Goodpaster et al., 2012).

An in-depth examination of science teacher turnover in Australia highlights similar issues related to career dissatisfaction. Lyons and colleagues (2006) conducted a large-scale national study that utilized a variety of analytical strategies to examine teacher turnover throughout the country. The authors found that science teachers in provincial (rural) areas were demonstrated to have significantly higher annual turnover rates than were teachers in other areas. It was also reported that the difficulty in filling vacant science teaching positions in rural areas was higher when compared with staffing in metropolitan schools across all disciplines. Three of the main tensions highlighted by science teachers in rural places were related to dissatisfaction with their teaching load as well as their professional development opportunities. In Australia, science teachers in rural areas were twice as likely, and those in "remote" areas were about three times as likely, as those in metropolitan areas to teach a science subject in which they are not highly qualified. In addition, science teachers in provincial and remote areas demonstrated a significantly higher unmet need than teachers in metropolitan areas for professional development opportunities. Specifically, the rural Australian science teachers identified needs for help with teaching targeted groups of students (e.g., gifted and talented, indigenous, and special needs). In contrast, teachers in metropolitan schools had a lower level of unmet needs for every professional development and resource item (e.g., laboratory consumables) included in the survey.

Forming linkages between small rural school districts and higher education institutions is also a means to deal with the problem of science teacher recruitment. The U.S. Government Accountability Office (GAO, 2004) surveyed rural and nonrural school superintendents and found that small rural districts were less likely than larger districts to establish partnerships with higher education institutions for the purpose of linking teacher education specifically to jobs in their school districts.

Across the body of research on science teacher attrition, there is a compounding effect related to recruitment and attrition issues in rural places as administrators face difficulties with recruitment of science teachers. The total equation is greater than the sum of the parts. As countries throughout the world address teacher recruitment and attrition using new and hopefully more comprehensive models of teacher career development, we must find ways to balance the uniqueness of each rural school within a larger framework of equitable schooling.

Conclusions and Implications

Looking ahead, the greatest looming specter seems to be that some future version of *common standards* and the high-stakes standardized tests that follow on their implementation will completely remove a teacher's ability to support her students' science content learning by relating it to the context and the environment in which those students live. Brown and Schafft (2011) make this case in this way:

> Although rural schools have traditionally had strong community ties and are seen as being sensitive to local cultures and responsive to local needs, the emphasis on standardized testing may have the effect of narrowing the focus of education to satisfying testing requirements. As test scores become ever more concretized proxies for educational achievement, and accountability revolves increasingly around the state test, there is a danger that rural education will become de-linked from students' needs and desires, their families, and the communities in which they reside.
>
> (p. 67)

As pointed out by Lloyd (2010) and others cited previously, we must move away from the idea of a one-size-fits-all mentality for schoolchildren in science. Efforts to create schools that have a central focus on equity and social justice are dependent on this realization.

The existence of standards for the rural school is not new. In 1938, Slacks (considering only U.S. schools) reported that most states had prepared courses of study for the rural schools and that one important purpose of those courses of study was to "set a standard of work" (p. 160). Slacks also reported that in 1938, there were approximately 153,000 one-teacher schools in the United States, and it was to those rural/small schools to which he was directing his attention. The big difference is that in Slacks's time, the existence of the attendant assessments, along with their manner of registering a link between student achievement and teacher effectiveness, was not part of the picture of rural school standards. In 1938, what Boyd (1978) called the "*hallowed* principle of local control of education" (p. 579) was still strongly entrenched in the rural areas of the United States. Around the world, the U.S. system of school governance was the exception and not the norm. Many, perhaps most, other countries have a centralized system through which a national ministry of education has the helm for all schools. Corresponding to this style of oversight, schools throughout entire nations use identical curricula and assessments. Whether the U.S. direction continues to align with this international norm or diverge back toward traditional norms remains to be seen.

In parallel with this ongoing movement toward a unified curriculum is the similar, though more limited in scope, movement in research methodology. The great commonality of these movements is the impact of federal funding agencies. In the former case, the intervention comes through legislation regarding standards and thus curricula and, as a result, has an impact on all public school teachers and students. In the latter, the impact comes as a result of the restricted availability of funding from governmental foundations and granting agencies for researchers and developers being related to the required use of certain methodologies for research design. Although Schneider (Moss et al., 2002) has written that "It seems to me that one point of consensus within the education research community is a sense that high-quality research can take multiple approaches" (p. 507), this magnanimous view seems at odds with the disparate opinions presented earlier by a few prominent researchers in rural education. The answer to the question of "What constitutes high-quality educational research in rural education?" will not be represented by a singular statement or even a statement that community stakeholders agree with the appropriateness of multiple approaches. It cannot be overstated how important these parallel issues of standards and methodology are to both rural schools and the researchers who attempt to provide understanding of the activities that happen within them.

And finally we return to the issue of computer and mobile phone technologies and their power to transform the education of rural children in science. There can be no doubt that the questions posed in the 2007 version of this chapter are still of great importance, but at this moment, most rural schools continue to have libraries, textbooks, and formal classrooms bounded by walls and to exist within structures found in rural places. The isolation from knowledge will diminish, but the isolation from places will continue. Access to greater wells of knowledge will change how people think about their rural locality, but as Caterina Fake explained, the mobility of the new technologies will be the hallmark of their transformative power (Madrigal, 2013). And perhaps it is the use of the new mobile technologies that will come to us in the form of next-generation smart phones and other as-yet-unknown devices that will allow us to once again learn science within the context of our local rural place. Perhaps it is these devices that will allow for rural science teachers and their students to connect teaching and learning to recognizable, relevant, and locally important phenomena, events, and environments. And hopefully, the politicians of the future, enlightened by education professionals, will enable those teachers to implement schooling so that the potential of all children can be equitably realized through both adaptive technologies for instruction and assessment and also the recognition of the importance of learning within place.

Acknowledgments

The authors wish to thank Leanne Avery and Debra Panizzon for their review and comments on the initial version of this chapter.

References

Arnold, M. L. (2005). Jump the shark: A rejoinder to Howley, Theobald, and Howley. *Journal of Research in Rural Education, 20*(20), 1–2.

Arnold, M. L., Newman, J. H., Gaddy, B. B., & Dean, C. B. (2005). A look at the condition of rural education research: Setting a difference for future research. *Journal of Research in Rural Education, 20*(6). Retrieved from http://jrre.psu.edu/articles/20-6.pdf

Asia Society. (2010). *Meeting the challenge: Preparing Chinese language teachers for American schools.* New York: Author.

Avery, L. M. (2013). Rural science education: Valuing local knowledge. *Theory Into Practice, 52*(1), 28–35.

Avery, L. M., & Kassam, K.-A. (2011). *Phronesis:* Children's local rural knowledge of science and engineering. *Journal of Research in Rural Education, 26*(2), 1–18. Retrieved from http://jrre.psu.edu/articles/26-2.pdf

Barbour, M., & Mulcahy, D. (2006). An inquiry into retention and achievement differences in campus based and web based AP courses. *Rural Educator, 27,* 8–12.

Boe, E., Cook, L., & Sunderland, R. (2008). Teacher turnover: Examining exit attrition, teaching area transfer, and school migration. *Exceptional Children, 75*(1), 7–31.

Borman, G., & Dowling, M. (2008). Teacher attrition and retention: A meta-analytic and narrative review of the research. *Review of Educational Research, 78,* 367–409.

Boyd, W. L. (1978). The changing politics of American curriculum policy making. *Review of Educational Research, 48*(4), 577–628.

Brown, D. L., & Schafft, K. A. (2011). *Rural people and communities in the 21st century: Resilience and transformation.* Cambridge, UK: Polity Press.

Byun, S. Y., Irvin, M. J., & Meece, J. L. (2012). Predictors of bachelor's degree completion among rural students at four-year institutions. *Review of Higher Education, 35*(3), 463–484.

Carlone, H. B., Kimmel, S., & Tschida, C. (2010). A rural math, science, and technology elementary school tangled up in global networks of practice. *Cultural Studies in Science Education, 5,* 447–476.

Coladarci, T. (2007, May 24). Improving the yield of rural education research: An editor's swan song. *Journal of Research in Rural Education, 22*(3). Retrieved from http://jrre.psu.edu/articles/22-3.pdf

Collins, T. (1999). *Attracting and retaining teachers in rural areas* (ED438152). Charleston, WV: Eric Clearinghouse on Rural Education and Small Schools. (ERIC Document Reproduction Service No.ED438152).

Comstock, A. B. (1939). *Handbook of nature study.* Ithaca, NY: Cornell University Press.

Cook, T. D. (2001). Sciencephobia: Why education researchers reject randomized experiments. *Education Next, 1,* 62–68.

Darling-Hammond, L. (2003). Keeping good teachers: Why it matters, what leaders can do? *Educational Leadership, 60*(8), 6–13.

Dobbie, W. (2011, July). *Teacher characteristics and student achievement: Evidence from Teach for America.* Harvard University. Retrieved from http://blogs.edweek.org/edweek/teacherbeat/teacher characteristicsjuly2011.pdf

Domina, T. (2006). What clean break? Education and nonmetropolitan migration patterns, 1984–2004. *Rural Sociology, 71*(3), 373–398.

Feuer, M. J., Towne, L., & Shavelson, R. J. (2002). Scientific culture and educational research. *Educational Researcher, 31*(8), 4–14.

Friedman, T. L. (2005). *The world is flat: A brief history of the twenty-first century.* New York: Farrar, Strauss, and Giroux.

GAO (U.S. Government Accountability Office). (2004, September). *No Child Left Behind Act: Additional assistance and research on effective strategies would help small rural districts.* GAO-04-909. Retrieved from www.gao.gov/assets/250/244228.pdf

Gilmer, P. J. (2010). Vertical teaming: K–12 teachers engaged in scientific research in rural settings. *Rural Educator, 31*(3), 1–6.

Goodpaster, K. P. S., Adedokun, O. A., & Weaver, G. C. (2012). Teachers' perceptions of rural STEM teaching: Implications for rural teacher retention. *Rural Educator, 33*(3), 9–22.

Guarino, C. M., Santibanez, L., & Daley, G. A. (2006).Teacher recruitment and retention: A review of the recent empirical literature. *Review of Educational Research, 76,* 173–208.

Hamos, J., Bergin, K., Maki, D., Perez, L., Prival, J., Rainey, D., Rowell, G., & VanderPutten, E. (2009). Opening the classroom door: Professional learning communities in the math and science partnership program. *Science Educator, 18*(2), 14–25.

Henderson, S. A., & Royster, W. C. (2000, March 14). The Appalachian rural systemic initiative: Improving science and mathematics student achievement in economically disadvantaged rural counties in central Appalachia through a school-based teacher partner approach. *Education Policy Analysis Archives, 8*(17). Retrieved from http://epaa.asu.edu/ojs/article/view/408/531

Henke, R., Zahn, L., & Carroll, C. (2001). *Attrition of new teachers among recent college graduates: Comparing occupational stability among 1992–1993 college graduates who taught and those who worked in other occupations.* Washington, DC: National Center for Education Statistics.

Hodges, G. W. (2010). *The intersection of science teacher retention, attrition, and migration with accountability reform in rural Georgia.* Dissertation from the University of Georgia.

Hodges, G. W., Oliver, J. S., & Tippins, D. (2013). A study of highly qualified science teachers' career trajectory in the deep, rural South: Examining a link between deprofessionalization and teacher dissatisfaction. *School Science and Mathematics, 113*(6), 263–274.

Hoggart, K. (1990). Let's do away with rural. *Journal of Rural Studies, 6*(3), 245–257.

Horng, E. (2009). Teacher tradeoffs: Disentangling teachers' preferences for working conditions and student demographics. *American Educational Research Journal, 46*(3), 690–717.

Howley, C. (2009). Critique and fiction: Doing science right in rural education research. *Journal of Research in Rural Education, 24*(15). Retrieved from http://jrre.psu.edu/articles/24-15.pdf

Howley, C. B., Theobald, P., & Howley, A. (2005). What rural education research is of most worth? A reply to Arnold, Newman, Gaddy, and Dean. *Journal of Research in Rural Education, 20*(18), 1–6.

Ingersoll, R., & Perda, D. (2010). Is the supply of mathematics and science teachers sufficient? *American Education Research Journal, 47*(3), 563–594.

Ingersoll, R. M., & Perda, D. (2009, March). The mathematics and science teacher shortage: Fact and myth. CPRE Research Report #RR-62. Retrieved from www.cpre.org/images/stories/cpre_pdfs/math%20 science%20shortage%20paper%20march%202009%20final.pdf

Irvin, M., Hannum, W., Farmer, T., de la Varre, C., & Keane, J. (2009). Supporting online learning for advanced placement students in small rural schools: Conceptual foundations and intervention components of the facilitator preparation program. *The Rural Educator, 31*(1), 29–36.

Jahnukainen, M. (2011). Different strategies, different outcome? The history and trends of the inclusive and special education in Alberta (Canada) and in Finland. *Scandinavian Journal of Educational Research, 55*(5), 489–502.

Keppel, A. M. (1962). The myth of agrarianism in rural educational reform, 1890–1914. *History of Education Quarterly, 2*(2), 100–112.

Labaree, D. F. (2005). Progressivism, schools and schools of education: An American romance. *Paedagogica Historica, 41*(1 & 2), 275–288.

Lee, O., & Buxton, C. A. (2013). This issue. *Theory Into Practice, 52*(1), 1–5.

Legrain, P. (2002). [Book review] Open world, the truth about globalization. *Economist, 365,* 79.

Levy, F., & Murnane, R. J. (2004). *The new division of labor: How computers are creating the next job market.* Princeton, NJ: Princeton University Press.

Liu, L. (2009). Effective management of quality distance training: Case study of the summer training project held by China Ministry of Education. *China Educational Technology, 268*(5), 55–58.

Lloyd, E. M. (2010). *Eliciting and utilizing rural students' funds of knowledge in the service of science learning: An action research study.* Unpublished dissertation, University of Rochester, Rochester, NY.

Lyons, T., Cooksey, R., Panizzon, D., Parnell, A., & Pegg, J. (2006). *Science, ICT and mathematics education in rural and regional Australia: The SiMERR National Survey.* Canberra: Department of Education, Science and Training. Retrieved from www.une.edu.au/simerr/pages/resources_publications.php

Madrigal, A. (2013, March). Look smarter. *The Atlantic.* Retrieved from www.theatlantic.com/magazine/archive/2013/03/look-smarter/309234/

Maltzan, T.L. (2006). *Rurality and higher education: Implications for identity and persistence.* Doctoral dissertation, the Ohio State University.

McGaw, B. (2010). President's report: Transforming school education. *Dialogue, 29*(1). Retrieved from Academy of Social Sciences in Australia at www.assa.edu.au/publications/dialogue/2010_Vol29_No1.pdf

McQuaide, S. (2009). Making education equitable in rural China through distance learning. *International Review of Research in Open and Distance Learning, 10*(1). Retrieved from www.irrodl.org/index.php/irrodl/article/view/590/1177

Mensah, F.M. (2009). A portrait of Black teachers in science classrooms. *The Negro Educational Review, 60*(1–4), 39–51.

Mensah, F.M. (2013). Theoretically and practically speaking, what is needed in diversity and equity in science teaching and learning? *Theory Into Practice, 72,* 66–72.

MetLife Foundation Issue Brief. (2008). *What keeps teachers in the classroom? Understanding and reducing teacher turnover.* Retrieved from http://all4ed.org/reports-factsheets/what-keeps-good-teachers-in-the-classroom-understanding-and-reducing-teacher-turnover/

Monk, D. (2007). Recruiting and retaining high-quality teachers in rural areas. *The Rural Educator, 17*(1), 155–174.

Moss, P.A., Phillips, D.C., Erickson, F.D., Floden, R.E., Lather, P.A., & Schneider, B.L. (2009). Learning from our differences: A dialogue across perspectives on quality in educational research. *Educational Researcher, 38*(7), 501–517.

Nespor, J. (1997). *Tangled up in schools: Politics, space, bodies, and signs in the educational process.* Mahwah, NJ: Lawrence Erlbaum.

Obama, B. (2009, March 10). President Obama's remarks to the Hispanic Chamber of Commerce. Retrieved from www.nytimes.com/2009/03/10/us/politics/10text-obama.html

Okebukola, P.A., Owolabi, O., & Okebukola, F.O. (2013). Mother tongue as default language of instruction in lower primary science classes: Tension between policy prescription and practice in Nigeria. *Journal of Research in Science Teaching, 50*(1), 62–81.

Oliver, J.S. (2007a). Rural science education. In S.K. Abell & N.G. Lederman (Eds.), *Handbook on Research on Science Education* (pp. 345–369). Mahwah, NJ: Lawrence Erlbaum.

Oliver, J.S. (2007b). Rural science education research and the frameworks that give it form. *The Rural Educator, 28*(3), 1–3.

Paine, L., & Zeichner, K. (2012). The local and the global in reforming teaching and teacher education. *Comparative Education Review, 56*(4), 569–585.

Petrosino, A., Boruch, R.F., Rounding, C., McDonald, S., & Chalmers, I. (2000). The Campbell Collaboration Social, Psychological, Educational and Criminological Trials Register (C2-SPECTR) to facilitate the preparation and maintenance of systematic reviews of social and educational interventions. *Evaluation and Research in Education, 14,* 206–219.

Picciano, A.G., & Seaman, J. (2009). *K–12 online learning: A 2008 follow-up of the survey of U.S. School District Administrators.* Newburyport, MA: Sloan Consortium.

Plunkett, M., & Dyson, M. (2011). Becoming a teacher and staying one: Examining the complex ecologies associated with educating and retaining new teachers in Rural Australia. *Australian Journal of Teacher Education, 36*(1), 31–47.

Provasnik, S., Kewal Ramani, A., Coleman, M.M., Gilbertson, L., Herring, W., & Xie, Q. (2007). *Status of education in rural America* (NCES 2007–040). Washington, DC: National Center for Education Statistics, Institute of Education Sciences, U.S. Department of Education.

Reininger, M. (2012). Hometown disadvantage? It depends on where you're from: Teachers' location preferences and the implications for staffing schools. *Educational Evaluation and Policy Analysis, 34*(2), 127–145.

Robinson, D.H. (2012). The strange case of the changing graph: Much ado about nothing? *Educational Researcher, 41*(5), 171–173.

Rudolph, J. (2002). *Scientists in the classroom: The Cold War reconstruction of American science education.* New York: MacMillan.

Sahlberg, P. (2010, April). *Key drivers of educational performance in Finland.* Presentation at the International Perspectives on U.S. Education Policy and Practice symposium, Washington, DC. Retrieved from Asia Society at http://asiasociety.org/education/learning-world/what-accounts-finlands-high-student-achievement-rate

Schafft, K.A., Alter, T.R., & Bridger, J.C. (2006). Bringing the community along: A case study of a school district's information technology rural development initiative. *Journal of Research in Rural Education, 21*(8). Retrieved from http://jrre.psu.edu/articles/21-8.pdf

Shortall, S., & Warner, M.E. (2012). Rural transformations: Conceptual and policy issues. In M. Shucksmith, D.L. Brown, S. Shortall, J. Vergunst, & M.E. Warner (Eds.), *Rural transformations and rural policies in the US and UK.* Retrieved from site.ebrary.com/lib/ugalib/docDetail.action?docID=10

Skidmore, S.T., & Thompson, B. (2012). Propagation of misinformation about frequencies of RFTs/RCTs in education: A cautionary tale. *Educational Researcher, 41*(5), 163–170.

Slacks, J.R. (1938). *The rural teacher's work.* Boston: Ginn and Company.

Snyder, T.D., & Dillow, S.A. (2010). *Digest of education statistics 2009.* Washington, DC: National Center for Education Statistics, Institute of Education Sciences, U.S. Department of Education.

Stewart, V. (2012). *A world-class education: Learning from international models of excellence and innovation.* Alexandria, VA: Association for Supervision & Curriculum Development.

Strunk, K., & Robinson, P. (2006). Oh won't you stay. A multi-level analysis of the difficulties in retaining highly qualified teachers. *Peabody Journal of Education, 81*(4), 65–94.

Tytler, R., Symington, D., Darby, L., Malcolm, C., & Kirkwood, V. (2011). Discourse communities: A framework from which to consider professional development for rural teachers of science and mathematics. *Teaching and Teacher Education, 27*(5), 871–879.

Underhill, O.E. (1941). *The origins and development of elementary school science.* Chicago: Scott Foresman.

UNESCO. (2010). *Education for All global monitoring report: Reaching the marginalized.* Paris: UNESCO; and Oxford, UK: Oxford University Press.

UNESCO Institute for Statistics. (2006). *Teachers and educational quality: Monitoring global needs for 2015* (Vol. 253). Montreal, Quebec, Canada: UNESCO Institute for Statistics.

Wang, D., & Gao, M. (2013). Educational equality or social mobility: The value conflict between preservice teachers and the free teacher education program in China. *Teaching and Teacher Education, 32,* 66–74.

Yan, W. (2002). *Postsecondary enrolment and persistence of students from rural Pennsylvania.* Harrisburg, PA: Centre for Rural Pennsylvania.

Yang, R. (2008). Transnational higher education in China: Contexts, characteristics and concerns. *Australian Journal of Education, 52*(3), 272–286.

15

Culturally Responsive Science Education for Indigenous and Ethnic Minority Students

Elizabeth McKinley and Mark J. S. Gan

Introduction

Since the writing of the last chapter in the previous handbook (McKinley, 2007), educational research continues to be concerned with indigenous and minority students' access, participation, and achievement in science education. The underrepresentation of indigenous and some ethnic minority students in secondary science education is a major social and economic disadvantage for these communities and a major challenge for science educators in industrial countries. The reason for this is that the lack of participation and achievement by these communities is perceived as being particularly urgent as they strive for a highly skilled workforce specifically in science-based subjects to build their knowledge-based economies. Identified as a "barrier" to this goal is that the number of students being educated in science, technology, engineering, and mathematics (STEM) subjects has fallen (Ezeife, 2003). There are two forces at work here: The numbers of students in science courses from groups who have historically participated has diminished, and the demographics of First World nations' move toward greater proportions of indigenous and ethnic minority students. In essence, science education research is faced with questions regarding how it can increase the uptake of science-based subjects by students who have previously been excluded from participating in them and, to a large extent, participating in many of their benefits.

The construction of the "problem" as a lack of participation and achievement brings into stark relief the two strands that will flow through this chapter. The first strand is that of a "practical" framework that focuses on a country's potential STEM workforce and what needs to be done to increase the number of people in a given population to take up knowledge-based, resource-based, and industrial employment. Viewing these issues within this framework tends to "solutions" that are pragmatic, short term, and patchwork like in which strategies are added to currently established approaches. The philosophical

underpinnings of this approach are located in questions about the nature of equity and excellence. While the concepts are very complex and there are several definitions (see Jordan, 2010), there is a tendency in this framework to under-theorize the roles of politics and power—ideas of particular importance to science education researchers of indigenous and other ethnic minority students (see, for example, Aikenhead & Michell, 2011; Stewart, 2010). The significant and increasing volume of literature on equity and excellence has begun to bring indigenous students into the frame without addressing indigenous researchers' concerns (see, for example, Heymann & Cassola, 2012). The equity and excellence framework is mostly operationalized and translated through the context and practice of school accountability. Schools are driven to ask questions related to their classroom practice, such as, "How do we increase the participation and success in science education for indigenous and ethnic minority students?" and seek answers in relation to their pedagogies and, to a lesser extent, curriculum.

The second strand in this chapter focuses on a broader view of *student success* that encompasses the complex interaction of family, social, cultural, educational, economic, and political contexts. Led in particular by indigenous researchers, this strand contests the characterization of success evident in the first strand, which mainly lies in achievement. Arguments within this view are based on the nature of knowledge and the importance of cultural identity to indigenous and ethnic minority communities. Although little or nothing has changed from the indigenous research point of view forwarded in the earlier chapter (McKinley, 2007), there is still a pervasiveness of unresolved concerns—the devaluation and destruction of people's cultures, languages, beliefs, and values have all affected and continue to affect indigenous people's well-being. For example, Richards and Scott (2009) argue that a policy of cultural genocide in Canada led to the establishment of residential schools administered by religious groups, which resulted in catastrophic intergenerational disruptions in parenting capabilities, self-worth, cultural self-identity, and the use of indigenous languages. The direct legacy of this, they argue, is a disproportionate frequency of dysfunctional families, chronic poverty, youth suicide, criminal incarceration, and barriers to educational access and success. These broad historical circumstances are echoed in other countries (see Cajete, 1994; McIntosh & Mulholland, 2011). The resulting effects from such circumstances in each society can become significant barriers, including deep-seated psychological ones, for access, participation, and achievement in school (and postsecondary) science programs for indigenous and minority students and contribute to students' negative experiences.

It is important to note that these two strands in the science education research literature are not completely separate. While the two identified strands of work come from different philosophical traditions, they operate within the same schooling context that brings them together, jostling for space and leverage under the prevailing conditions of the day. If we largely accept the social institution of schooling, then both strands face complex resolutions. The equity and excellence approach is faced with questions regarding teacher education, pedagogy, and curriculum. For example, "What cultural literacy should science teachers develop (pedagogy and curriculum) to empower their own competence in supporting indigenous and ethnic students in learning science?" Furthermore, as the chapter will show, there are a number of strongly held beliefs concerning the nature of science and indigenous knowledge and the nature of indigenous and minority students and their families and communities that are perceived to be obstacles to increasing student achievement and creating conditions for teachers to change practice. One of the challenges for an "equity and excellence" approach is how it can support the culture, language, and identity of students in science education. The second identified strand is also faced with challenges. Educational solutions that address complex social, cultural, economic, and political ideals require significant societal shifts. One solution that has been identified in indigenous communities has involved the establishment of indigenous-language education, including the establishment of indigenous-language science curricula, which has been discussed in other places and will not be rehearsed extensively here (see for example, McKinley, 1996, 2007; Stewart, 2010). The establishment of indigenous-language schools has occurred historically (see Deyhle & Comeau, 2009) and is again being used as a means to establish more control over schooling outcomes by indigenous communities. This solution in itself, as practiced in New Zealand, has a number of problems associated with it, including that of indigenous science language and content development (Stewart, 2012). In dominant-language schooling, other solutions and issues present. These include educating science teachers (preservice and inservice) to be able to respond in alternative ways of engaging families and communities (e.g., develop

cultural literacy); to encourage them to become aware of themselves as practitioners mediated by sociocultural experiences (e.g., become culturally responsive); and to recognize and draw on the abilities and practices of indigenous and minority children's experiences in the classroom (e.g., draw on prior experiences/funds of knowledge).

The meeting and crossing of the strands do create some uneasy alliances and tensions that get played out in policy and classrooms. However, the purpose of the chapter is not to set up two oppositional positions and make a judgment about which is better and for whom. We wish to convey some of the complexity of the situation. Recent times have shown there has been an expansion in science education research on "culture," and particularly its inclusion in pedagogy, and it is now appearing in New Zealand, Canada, the United States, Australia, Peru, Finland, Taiwan, the Pacific Islands (e.g., Fiji, Samoa, Tonga), Papua New Guinea, Indonesia, and other places (see McKinley & Stewart, 2009).

This chapter will begin with briefly examining the nature of equity and excellence debates and how these position schooling success for indigenous and ethnic minority students. The importance of this debate to science education is the pervasiveness of the accountability-driven policies that come with the framework and are brought to bear in nearly all aspects of schooling in industrial nations. Equity and excellence, at first glance, seemingly support cultural outcomes, but the "promise" embedded in the theory is mostly deferred and rarely if ever realized. The ideal of equality, for a number of indigenous communities particularly, is enshrined in settler treaties (such as the Treaty of Waitangi in New Zealand) and includes the promise of being equal as indigenous (e.g., Māori—in other words, the promise of "being" in schools and classrooms. The next section in this chapter will briefly outline the debates on the place and role of indigenous knowledge (IK) in the science curriculum. The two positions in this debate, commonly referred to in the field as "universalism" and "multiculturalism," are philosophical positions on the nature of knowledge. They emerge from debates on the nature of science knowledge and contribute to discussions on what knowledge should be included in the curriculum. The terrain of the debate is well worn, but we will show there are attempts to theorize an "in-between" path between what appear to be more extreme positions. The section that follows examines "culture" in school science and how we understand this concept. And finally, we describe, through reviewing empirical studies, the growing importance of pedagogical relationship studies in science classrooms and how this impacts shaping science learning for indigenous and minority students. In particular, we build on the literature to argue for the need to move toward a cultural perspective that is situated in the science classroom with a focus on teacher–student relationships and taking into consideration the indigenous and minority community's worldviews in the science curriculum. We conclude with a discussion on some potential avenues for future research.

Equity, Excellence, and Indigenous and Ethnic Minority Students

It has long been an axiom of democratic societies that all students should receive and achieve a high standard of education, irrespective of their income, social, or other group membership. Yet there has been a long history of students being educated differently within the same school system according to their class, ethnic, or racial background. One of the best illustrations of this counter-intuitive phenomenon is Jeannie Oakes's (2005) examination of educational developments in the United States showing the ways in which inequality of education along class, ethnic, and racial lines was explained and accommodated against a prevailing principle of equality. The debates over student achievement and social justice continue to be dominated by the implementation of schooling improvement programs via various forms of legislation, such as Race to the Top. The pervasive school reform movement has brought with it social justice frameworks to understand how schools, states, and countries are responding to access, participation, and achievement for all students. We wish to briefly explore this widespread (at least among Western industrial nations) and inescapable paradigm, and how it relates to indigenous and minority students and the goals of their communities.

The current dominance of educational policy in Western countries on inequity at the level of educational output has translated into schools focusing on educational achievement and equality of opportunity (for detailed discussions, see Branden, Avermaet, & Houtte, 2011; Luke, Green, & Kelly, 2010). In turn, this brings a focus on the individual and the schooling conditions that affect academic achievement. While there is nothing to exclude the notion of equality of results for students with differing backgrounds under current policy, reaching this ideal depends on what sort of outcome the system produces. In other words, stakeholders need to ask how we assess the success of the system in reaching equality of outcome and how communities (including schools) define success for the individual students. This is recognized in the following example.

A social justice framework proposed by philosopher Nancy Fraser is currently being used in schools with indigenous students in Australia (Woods, Dooley, Luke, & Exley, 2014) and with minority students in the UK (Ainscow, Dyson, Goldrick, & West, 2012). Fraser (2010) argues that to gain parity of participation there needs to be a dismantling of institutionalized obstacles that prevent some people from participating as full partners. The obstacles identified are economic structures that deny people the resources they need, institutionalized hierarchies of cultural value that deny them the requisite standing, and decision rules that deny them an equal voice in public deliberations and democratic decision making. All three injustices violate Fraser's principle of participatory parity. These participatory dimensions of social justice have been used with regard to research being carried out in evaluating school reform programs and the progress and performance of schools and their indigenous and minority students. Woods and colleagues (2012) are using Fraser's framework to research in schools that serve Australian indigenous and minority students. Their position in relation to outcomes is stated as:

> [. . .] we begin from a philosophical and political commitment to the more equitable redistribution of resources, knowledge, credentials and access to educational pathways for students from linguistic/cultural minority and working class backgrounds. [. . .] we argue that the recognition of these students and their communities' lifeworlds, values, knowledge and experiences in the curriculum, and in classroom teaching and learning relations is both a means and an end: a means towards improved achievement according to conventional measures, and an end goal for reform and revision of mainstream curriculum knowledge and what is made to count as valued knowledge and practice.
>
> (Woods et al., 2014, p. 1)

Of importance here is that the authors renounce the inclusion of indigenous communities in schools as a technical exercise, to perceive the child as separate from their wider location in the home, culture, language, and community. Furthermore, they reject the single investment in learning relationships to include curriculum and, implicitly, its orientation. Through rejecting an approach of working with an individual child within the confines of the classroom and working to exclude that which impinges from the "outside," the researchers offer a counter-narrative within the schooling reform paradigm that does not bend to the challenge of equity paradigms being a continuation of colonial projects.

However, much of the equity and excellence work leaves an important question unanswered. A significant concern in the "evidence-based" approach to equity and excellence has been centered on the strengths and limits of standardized testing. One particular concern of relevance to this chapter is the omission of any reference to indigenous and ethnic minority students' identity in achieving at school. In New Zealand, the "output" of identity is defined. New Zealand's policy on Māori education (Ministry of Education, 2008) states that schools, while meeting academic achievement targets, must also have the goal of "Māori succeeding as Māori." The phrase is a reminder to all schools that success for Māori students is defined as having access, participation, achievement, and learning in Māori identity, language, knowledge, and values in their school curriculum. It creates an expectation that all curriculum areas will place some focus on cultural achievements, notwithstanding the debates within the science education research literature as to whether "cultural knowledge" has a place in science education and to what extent cultural beliefs and values can be expressed. However, the same culturally defined expectations with respect to student success do not exist in other countries' educational administrations (state, province, or national). Researchers in the United States suggest the No Child Left Behind Act and ensuing policies focus too much on high-stakes standardized tests that have disproportionately affected indigenous and minority students (Chappell & Cahnmann-Taylor, 2013). The traditional academic measures used in this approach do not address the broader goals and outcomes indigenous and ethnic minority communities wish for their students unless they are specified clearly, and even then sufficient resources do not always follow to attend to what is needed.

The main criticism then becomes that the equity and excellence paradigm can be interpreted differently, with possible alternatives of either supporting or not supporting the inclusion of indigenous and minority languages, cultures, knowledge, and values in schooling (for example, see Ainscow et al., 2012; Luke et al., 2010). Indigenous and ethnic minority students and their communities do not want to leave this outcome up to chance—they are searching for more certainty. While there is general understanding that the presence of racism, poverty, and adverse health affect student learning outcomes, science teachers can influence indigenous and ethnic minority students' marginalization in their classrooms. This contesting of science curriculum knowledge and the experience of indigenous and ethnic minority student learning in science classrooms forms part of the basis for the debates that we highlight in the next section. For a number of science education researchers, the inclusion of indigenous knowledge, in particular, in the curriculum challenges the basis of the discipline and can present a challenge to science researchers' professional identity. The debate, which can be fierce, is not new, and the following section seeks to present a summary of the issues and examine any movement with respect to positions.

Contesting Knowledge in Science Education

Debates about the nature of knowledge in the school science curriculum continue to be highly contentious but still a central issue in the relationship between culture and science education. Much of the work has been covered in the previous chapter (McKinley, 2007) and been reviewed in publications in the intervening years (see McKinley & Stewart, 2009, 2012). In this section, we will briefly summarize the nature of the debates and indicate what movement, if any, has occurred since 2007 and at the same time suggest where the influence of this debate is situated in the more prolific research currently being carried out in the field, namely in theorizing and researching practice on culturally responsive pedagogies in science education.

Universalism and Multiculturalism

The core epistemological debate that affects science education involves that between proponents of universal and multicultural views of science. An example of this debate can be found in a special issue (Issue 1) of *Science Education* in 2001. Broadly, universalism conceives science as governed by a single set of rules that is culture free. The important characteristic of the universalism argument is that it *denies* difference (McKinley & Stewart, 2009).

Protagonists argue that science (sometimes referred to as Western modern science or WMS) is a system of knowledge that is the most powerful knowledge available to humanity. Taken to its extreme, the universalist position is politically objectionable to many cultures, as it infers science knowledge belongs to Westernized industrial nations. Not only does this position ignore the contributions to science from many cultures around the world, it also hides the extent to which science has been complicit in the West's ascendancy to its current position (McKinley, 2001).

In contrast, multicultural science is viewed as socially and culturally constructed and, as such, recognizes difference (Aikenhead & Elliott, 2010; Lee & Luykx, 2006; Ogawa, 1995). Multiculturalists advocate the importance of ethnoscience, highlighting the value of what has become known as "traditional ecological knowledge" (TEK) in supporting environmental processes and human needs. This knowledge is argued to be relevant to the advancement of Western scientific and technological fields. Besides recognizing the scientific and technological contributions of other cultures, a multicultural view suggests that there are multiple ways of understanding our natural world, and these alternative worldviews may be compatible or incompatible with the scientific worldview. The justification of a multicultural science is drawn from principles of moral justice as well as antiracism. While a multicultural view values both WMS and alternative views of the natural world, the literature indicates researchers differ in the level of emphasis in the approach—from arguing for a radical transformation of the nature and practice of science to including multiple voices and ways of knowing characteristic of underrepresented participants (e.g., Harris & Mercier, 2006) to more moderate views that consider the integration of different worldviews with that of Western modern science (e.g., Aikenhead, 2006). Van Eijick and Roth (2007) accept both frameworks but argue that each framework is incompatible with the other and can only be understood as one-sided expressions of a diversity of human understanding. They suggest that scientific knowledge transcends the local and has little use in local contexts (other than its own).

There is some evidence that despite not finding resolutions, the heat has gone from the debate. In a more recent special issue of *Cultural Studies of Science Education* (CSSE) in 2008 (Issue 3), the format used was a forum of open review, encouraging authors and reviewers to engage in conversations about contentious issues. This enabled reviewers and authors greater opportunities for teasing out the debates and grounding them in practice and experience, and as a result, the responses have become more complex and conciliatory. This special issue partly typifies a shift and perhaps maturity in the debate through the inclusion of more diverse research perspectives and contexts than in traditional science education research. In his editorial, Tobin (2008, p. 536) commented that the intent for the journal was to "resis[t] a tendency to seek closure on issues," describing CSSE as "an emerging hybrid field." While Tobin refers here to the dialogue taking place between diverse views of the reviewers and authors in the journal resulting in hybrid formations of ideas, the notion of hybridity or third space has begun to gain some ascendancy in the field in other ways.

Cultural Hybridity and Third Space

More recently, science educational researchers (e.g., Roth, 2009) have drawn from postcolonial theory, and particularly Bhabha (2004), to theorize and circumscribe a third space in science education. Some researchers have used it to describe how teachers, students, and others in school settings establish new forms of participation that bring together the first space of school science with the second space of the home/culture to create a third space that is inclusive of both in the form of hybrid knowledge. This third or hybrid space draws attention to the different knowledge, discourses, and relationships that influence science learning, allowing for a collective construction of new knowledge, discourses, and identities (Moje et al., 2004; Roth, 2009). Moje, Collazo, Carillo, and Marx (2001) proposed three different but interrelated views on third space as "a bridge, a navigational space, or a space for critical understandings of the relationships between science and students' 'everyday worlds'" (p. 54). In doing so, the authors suggest that teachers and students value and build on the resources they have brought from family, community, and peers as well as popular culture resources to create better ways to succeed within the school setting.

Other researchers conceptualize third space as a theoretical tool to investigate identity. For example, Zembylas and Avraamidou (2008) argue that the notion of hybridity provides science educators with a theoretical tool to unpack and understand the issues of identity (e.g., of science learners). In this work, "hybridity" is defined as the creation of transcultural forms of experiences as a result of colonization, draws attention to the nature of identity as fluid rather than "fixed," and acknowledges the contextual influence of social, historical, and political practices on identity formation. Indeed, the co-construction of hybrid identities constitutes a third space, bringing to the fore the interests, power relations, and discursive practices as sites for further dialogue and critique. A key observation by the authors is that inquiries in the third space are not without tensions and contradictions, offering in-between spaces for problematization or "disturbing the normality within which pedagogical relations are conducted" (Zembylas & Avraamidou, 2008, p. 991). This concept of "ambivalent spaces" (Bhabha, 2004) is illustrated in Adams, Luitel, Afonso, and Taylor's (2008) narrative of three teacher educators' personal reflections on their hybrid cultural identities as enacted within a third space. A common theme in this work is that contradictions exist between self (hybrid identities) and a dominant culturally decontextualized local science education. The potential conflict between students' cultural experiences and background and what is taught in school science needs to be resolved before meaningful science learning can take place. They propose that

the way forward is to create a dialogic space in the science classroom that engages students in co-constructing an understanding of science that incorporates their cultural knowledge and the way of living within their community.

Another line of research that employs the third space looks at the interaction between science educators and their community. The growing attention to global sustainability of humans and the environment points to the need for developments in scientific knowledge and problem-solving skills that will help address the pressing challenges of not only addressing human needs such as finding clean, renewable energy sources or feeding an increasing world population but also ensuring that the earth's life-support systems are conserved (Carter, 2007). This drive to understand the complex interactions between nature and society has provided the impetus for science educators and researchers to view indigenous knowledge systems and ways of living as inclusive and collaborative (involving teachers, students, and the local community). Studies that investigate this notion of dialogical inquiry have moved away from the dichotomy between Eurocentric and indigenous knowledge systems and adopted the postcolonial concepts of third space and hybridity (see, for example, Taylor, 2006a, 2006b; Zembylas & Avraamidou, 2008). According to Wallace (2004), the third space "is an abstraction of a space/time location in which neither the speaker's meaning nor the listener's meaning is the 'correct' meaning, but in which the meaning of the utterance is hopeful for either co-construction of interpretation or new hybrid meanings" (p. 908). The third space provides a common and open platform for the ongoing negotiation of meanings while at the same time recognizing the rich cultural experiences and worldviews that students and teachers bring to the classroom (Roth, 2009).

An example of this is Glasson, Mhango, Phiri, and Lanier's (2010) in-depth interviews with Malawian farmers on their traditional agricultural practices. Glasson and colleagues (2010) were able to draw connections between the indigenous way of living of these African elders and the practices relevant to the field of sustainability science to co-construct a science education curriculum. Using a third-space framework, the authors argued for creating a dialogic space that allows for bringing science educators and Malawian elders together in order to negotiate on how best to include in the science curriculum the practical indigenous knowledge held by the Malawian elders as well as what sustainability science education can offer for the community. A dialogic space was created in which the Malawian farmers considered the issue of sustainable agriculture by bringing together Western agricultural practices (such as the use of synthetic fertilizers) and indigenous farming practices (growing crops under msangu trees and using the leaves to act as natural fertilizers) to make decisions about the choice of farming practices. At the same time, by inquiring and listening carefully to how the elders explain the use of indigenous knowledge in farming, the authors were able to work within the third space to understand and reflect on the importance of the local knowledge held by the Malawian farmers and how this can be used as a pedagogical resource to support students learning science within the same community.

Besides conceptualizing the third space as a collective pedagogical tool for identifying and developing deeper understandings of the relationships between science and students' worldviews, researchers have also examined the third space for generating new knowledge, what anthropologists call "cultural production" (Carlone & Johnson, 2012; Eisenhart, 2001). For example, Calabrese Barton, Tan, and Rivet (2008) observed the use of sanctioned and unsanctioned resources and identities by a group of urban middle school girls to create hybrid spaces for participation and deeper engagement in their science classrooms. The authors found that these spaces allowed the girls to engage deeply in science on their own terms, in which new forms of authority and positionality were actively negotiated and enacted, while at the same time maintaining social status and relational authority among their peers. It is the blending of students' self-identities and their social world that generated and legitimized new forms of participation, opening up opportunities to tap the repertoire of resources available to all the students in the classroom.

The use of third space and hybridity in relation to indigenous knowledge and communities is more accepted in some quarters than others. Schech and Haggis (2000) call it a "linguistic space" wherein flourishes richly hybridized languages and fluid cultural identities. Roth (2009) broadly agrees and encourages us to first understand then move away from "the problematic nature of difference as constructed by researchers, official discourses and reigning ideologies." He argues that we should

> no longer celebrate the third spaces in which our students are said to cobble together new forms of culture, but come to understand that our everyday cultural practices are themselves forms of bricolage that continuously produce and reproduce difference in a mêlée of forms and content where difference comes to brush up against itself.
>
> (Roth, 2009, p. 20)

In Roth's view, there is neither purity nor impurity, only the continual process of mixing. However, Kincheloe and Steinberg (2008) state, "many advocates of indigenous knowledge resent the use of the term hybridity and find it inappropriate in indigenous studies" (pp. 143–144). The main argument here is that hybridity is seen to be a continuing or neocolonizing act on indigenous peoples and their knowledge. The authors understand the political sentiments but do not see the stated positions as incompatible. Māori scholar Hirini Moko Mead (2003) likens mātauranga Māori (Māori knowledge) to the nursery rhyme "Humpty Dumpty," saying that when Humpty Dumpty fell, "the whole being was shattered and broken into pieces—some have been destroyed, some hidden and others just waiting to be reconstructed" (p. 306). He goes on to say, "Efforts are being made to reassemble Humpty Dumpty, but the task has become difficult because meanwhile Humpty is

changing and continues to grow and expand despite being shattered and scattered" (p. 306). The point he makes is that indigenous knowledge should not be an archive of information, static and unchanging, but a tool for thinking. It will change (as it should), but it need not be incorporated into other knowledge without a trace—indigenous knowledge is firmly entwined with customary ideas and values that are more constant.

Understanding Language and Identity in Science Education Research

Students often come to the science classroom with prior knowledge, cultural norms, and practices that are incongruent with those of school science (Atwater, 1994; Solano-Flores & Nelson-Barber, 2001). A main concern for science educators and teachers is the danger of subscribing to a teaching and learning theory that ignores or undermines the cultural languages and identities that students bring to the classroom. The research literature on indigenous and ethnic minority students and their communities in relation to languages in particular is both similar and different. For example, the literature on indigenous languages in science education focuses on language revitalization, survival, and translations, whereas for many ethnic minority communities, the focus concerns the acquisition of English as a second (or more) language. However, there are some concerns that overlap such as both groups acquiring a scientific language. This section begins with briefly reviewing literature on the identity tension for ethnic groups—an identity that is "inherited" and one that is "sociocultural." This will be followed by reviewing the literature on a sociolinguistic approach to indigenous and ethnic minority groups in science education. In particular, it highlights the tensions present for many of these students in crossing borders to learning science language. Finally, we review the use of indigenous languages in science education and the tensions created in trying to establish science education as a vehicle for support.

Modern indigenous and ethnic minority groups inevitably grapple with their conflicting sense of self (McKinley, 2005; Stewart, 2010; Webber, McKinley, & Hattie, 2013). The research on language and identity in science education takes two paths. Stewart (2010) argues indigenous peoples face a dichotomy. First, indigeneity and ethnicity are viewed as *inherited*. From this point of view, cultures are viewed as deterministic and essentialist. This means the people who identify with each culture are seen to have defined behaviors (e.g., "Māori" or indigenous learning styles), and the groups are seen as being internally homogeneous (e.g., Māori all think alike) and separate from one another. Second, a *situational* understanding of indigeneity and ethnicity views groups as being governed by their sociocultural relationship to others. Cultural differences in students seen in deficit terms have been criticized for being deterministic and simplistic (Gutierrez & Rogoff, 2003) and leading to assumptions of fixed characteristics, generalization of learning styles, and overly stereotypical notions of individuals within particular ethnic groups

(Carlone & Johnson, 2007). The importance of inheritance and kinship as integral parts of indigenous and other ethnic groups' identity is unquestioned, so while not being wrong, it is an inadequate explanation on its own. A situational understanding has been criticized for understating the social and cultural constraints on an individual's ethnic choices. This is where identity choices are made on the basis of their "use value," such as whether learning an indigenous language "will get you a job" (May, 2001). This situational or instrumentalist view of identity is one that has some appeal in a climate of accountability and rational choice theory, as drivers of identity are measured by value in the marketplace. This can be seen in later sections of the chapter in which there is increased research on being "culturally responsive" in science teaching. More extreme approaches that have little regard for cultural identity tend to value the economic worth of culture exclusively, with resultant losses of smaller cultures and their languages seen as collateral damage. This is the danger for indigenous communities in particular.

From a sociolinguistic perspective, culturally rich language practices often denote cultural affiliation and serve as markers of cultural membership (Brown, 2013). The transition from a vernacular discourse to science discourse involves acquiring a new science language, as well as appropriating the cultural norms that are associated with the dominant science discourse. The types of interactions and discourse that are expected of students in scientific inquiry may be less familiar to some students than to others (Buxton, 2005; Lemke, 1990; Moje et al., 2001). The science student is faced with the learning challenge of developing a clear understanding of the science phenomenon and its associated discourse and, at the same time, adopting the identity relationships associated with using science discourse. Students who are unable to reconcile this language-identity challenge may suffer learning problems as a result of this identity conflict (Cupane, 2011; Gilbert & Yerrick, 2001). Brown (2013) contends that the reasons for learning problems are twofold—the first reason stems from the *cultural discontinuity position* while the second points to the difficulties in mastering the science language. Recent research indicates that there are differential levels of continuity between the home culture of students and the culture of school science (Lee, 2005; Reveles & Brown, 2008). A significant challenge for students' adopting the classroom science discourse involves resolving the implicit identity conflicts associated with their home culture and the culture of school science. Teachers need to be aware of the potential cultural conflicts that language presents and provide explicit instructional support to help students make the "appropriation of science discourse more comfortable and less symbolic of cultural affiliation" (p. 227). From another perspective, acquiring the science language can be daunting for some students and act as a barrier to their conceptualization. The argument here is that students' ability to develop a scientific cognition is directly influenced by their use of vernacular language resources and, thus, the access to and

availability of the culture of science classroom discourse (Lemke, 1990; Warren, Ballenger, Ogonowski, Rosebery, & Hudicourt-Barnes, 2001). Brown (2011) proposes an intervention framework for science teachers, which he calls "disaggregating instruction," incorporating students' everyday language to introduce concepts and then provide explicit instruction on the new language and opportunities to use their new science language through formative assessment activities. In disaggregating instruction, science instruction is taught by separating instruction into both a conceptual teaching component and a science language component. First, students are introduced to the science idea or concept by using the language that they are familiar with. This is seen as an important step in reducing students' anxiety (intimidation and frustration about grappling with the new scientific language) and leveraging the cultural familiarity that a common language brings for the students. Second, new science language is introduced after the basic tenets of the science idea are taught. Third, students are instructed to use their new science language to explain science phenomena through formative assessment activities. This approach has the potential to improve students' understanding and reduce their discomfort in learning science.

Further research by Lee and her colleagues proposes a framework of "instructional congruence" that focuses on articulating academic disciplines with students' cultural and linguistic experiences to develop congruence between the two domains (Lee, 2002, 2004; Lee & Fradd, 1998). They argue that teachers need to provide explicit instruction about the rules and norms of classroom science discourse as well as make visible students' everyday knowledge, the relationship between students' knowledge and academic tasks, and the transition between the experiences and practices of their home and community and those of Western modern science. The study involved elementary students from culturally and linguistically diverse backgrounds in a large urban school district in the United States. Teachers attend a series of workshops that advocate a scaffolding teaching approach consisting of moving progressively from more explicit to more student-centered instruction, encouraging the students to gradually take ownership and responsibility of their own learning. The results show the positive impact of this 3-year professional development implementation and indicate that the intervention was overall effective in promoting achievement and equity with students from diverse background (Lee, Deaktor, Enders, & Lambert, 2008). This study also points to the need for extensive support for elementary teachers in terms of science content, content-specific teaching strategies, and literacy skills, as well as support for English language learners in learning science and incorporating students' home language and culture into science instruction.

As noted in the previous edition (McKinley, 2007), the survival of indigenous languages in particular is perilous. The political act of education, including science education, has become a vehicle for survival of many indigenous languages to a greater or lesser extent, creating a number of complex issues. For example, Stewart (2010) explores the trajectory of kura kaupapa Māori (Māori medium schooling, known as KKM) in New Zealand that was introduced more than 30 years ago. While the difficulties of establishing a technical language in the Māori language in order to carry out the science curriculum have been discussed elsewhere (McKinley, 1996; McKinley & Keegan, 2008), Stewart's work interrogates and critiques science education in the KKM movement. This work moves the philosophical debates regarding IK, science knowledge, use of Māori language in science, and educational policy to another level. Aikenhead and Michell (2011) provide an example from Canada of what gets lost in translation between English and Indigenous languages. They argue that when Indigenous-language speakers express themselves in English, they are often unable to convey exactly what they mean—a meaning originally constructed in their own language. They take the English phrase "Indigenous knowledge":

> The noun "knowledge" does not translate easily into most Indigenous languages, in part because English is a noun-rich linguistic system while Indigenous languages are verb-rich. When translated into English, the corresponding Indigenous expression for "knowledge" often results in something like "ways of living" or "ways of being." Thus, it is appropriate to adopt the more authentic phrase "ways of living in nature" in place of "knowledge of nature." The phrase "scientific knowledge" fits the context of Eurocentric thinking, whereas the expression "ways of living in nature" generally fits an Indigenous context, although different communities may prefer different wording.
>
> (Aikenhead and Michell, 2011, p. 65)

As with all languages, there are words in each language that cannot be translated into another.

When translating science into an indigenous (and possibly other) language, there are two schools of thought—the instrumental and the romantic ideologies—that parallel the ethnicity debate (Stewart, 2010). The "instrumentalist" approach is one in which language is seen as a tool for transforming ideas into new linguistic patterns, whereas the "romantic" approach is one in which language is seen to be inextricably linked with a person's being. The instrumental position becomes dominant through "implementational cascades" (Stewart, 2010, p. 115), in which governments devolve responsibility to individual contractors that strive to meet outputs. It has been dominant during early stages in the development of Māori-medium curricula and schooling in New Zealand (see McKinley, 1996; McKinley & Keegan, 2008). Striking the balance between these positions of being practical but keeping hold of the language and protocols of culture means a far more nuanced language policy in indigenous-language led science education (for extended comment, see Stewart, 2012).

Culturally Responsive Science Teaching and Learning

While most researchers recognize that culture plays an important role in the teaching and learning of science (Aikenhead, 1996; Gutierrez & Rogoff, 2003; Lee, 2002), there is less consensus on the conceptualization of "culture" in school science instruction and how it is understood and applied by educators in classroom practices. One exception can be seen in Alaska with the Alaskan Native Knowledge Network (ANKN), in which the Alaska Standards for Culturally Responsive Schools (www.ankn.uaf.edu/publications/standards.html) have been written and accepted by various governing bodies. These standards have been developed by Alaskan Native educators "to provide a way for schools and communities to examine the extent to which they are attending to the educational and cultural well-being of the students in their care" and cover students, educators, curriculum, schools, and communities. They are set up as an evaluative framework against which schools, educators, and communities can measure achievement. While these standards are not specific to science education, the standards are intended to be applied across any curriculum area. These, in conjunction with many Native Alaskan and other researchers in science and mathematics education (e.g., Kawagley, 2006; Kawagley & Barnhardt, 2007) and the resources they have produced, suggest there is some support for teachers and leaders to meet the standards.

This section will show the difficulties that arise from this lack of clarity in defining "culture" and the different notions connected with the assumptions or theoretical underpinnings drawn to frame and interpret the cultural approaches to teaching and learning of science in the classroom. The first part of this section examines the various conceptualizations of culture in science education research and provides examples of how these cultural views are incorporated into different theoretical frameworks to explicate culturally responsive science teaching in schools (see Carlone, Johnson, & Eisenhart in this volume for a discussion on culture). This is followed by a discussion of the challenges and barriers that science teachers face when trying to implement this approach to engage their students. The final part of the section draws on the current research evidence to comment on the implications of culturally responsive science pedagogy for supporting indigenous science education.

Conceptions of Culture in Science Education Research

One line of research that draws on developmental psychology and anthropology conceptualizes a cultural view of teaching and learning as a dichotomy of two idealized developmental pathways: individualistic—focusing individual identity, independence, self-fulfillment, and standing out—and collectivistic or sociocentric—focusing on group identity, interdependence, social responsibility, and fitting in (Greenfield, Keller, Fuligni, & Maynard, 2003). The two cultural pathways are often viewed as in conflict when there is a mismatch between what is valued in the classroom as compared to what is valued at home or the community the student comes from. For example, the Bridging Cultures Project study by Greenfield, Quiroz, and Raeff (2000) found that there are tensions between home cultures and school cultural expectations and between parents and teachers, particularly on aspects such as individual versus family accomplishment, praise versus criticism, cognitive versus social skills, and oral expression versus respect for authority. These deep cultural values/orientations shape parents' as well as teachers' beliefs, expectations, and behaviors of children and schooling. Greenfield and colleagues (2000) argue the two divergent cultural priorities placed on students mean that teachers need to understand and mediate the learning process not only in relation to cognitive demands but to cultural demands as well. Bridging between home and school culture thus provides an underlying cultural approach for teachers to support learners who come from different cultural background.

A similar line of research builds on a cultural anthropological perspective of learning science, whereby teaching science is a form of cultural transmission and the way science learning takes place is viewed as culture acquisition (see Cobern & Aikenhead, 1998; Wolcott, 1991). In this research, science can be seen as a subculture of Western or Euro-American culture, and the prevalent influence of Western culture gives rise to a subculture of science—Western modern science (WMS). Previous research has shown that the dominant discourse in school science is closely aligned to WMS, with the goal of cultural transmission of the subculture of science and cultural transmission of the country's dominant culture (Stanley & Brickhouse, 1994). A cultural transmission view suggests that students have to negotiate the cultural borders between their indigenous subcultures and the subculture of science, resulting in differential effects on learning science. Enculturation occurs when the subculture of science harmonizes with a student's everyday culture and science instruction supports the student's view of the world (Hawkins & Pea, 1987). On the other hand, assimilation takes place when the subculture of science is at odds with a student's worldview, and science instruction causes students to adopt new ways of knowing at the expense of their own indigenous culture and experiences (Jegede, 1995).

Attempts to engage non–Western students in the subculture of science are challenging for science teachers. Students who are capable of negotiating the transitions between their everyday worlds and the subculture of science without having to assimilate or acculturate (a process of intercultural borrowing or adaptation of attractive content or aspects of another culture and incorporating them into one's indigenous culture) science's cultural baggage are seen as more successful learners in science (Aikenhead, 1996, 1997). Those who struggle to negotiate the cultural borders will require explicit instructional support in order to traverse from the subcultures of their peers and family into the subcultures of science and school science. This is aptly captured by the metaphor "border crossing" (Giroux, 1992), which suggests that there are domains of knowledge specific to various cultural contexts and that excursions from one way of knowing to another can occur

in science learning. Aikenhead (2006) proposed that teachers make border crossings explicit for students; facilitate these border crossings; promote discourse so that students, not just the teacher, are talking science; substantiate and build on the legitimacy of students' personally and culturally constructed ways of knowing; and teach the knowledge, skills, and values of Western science in the context of its societal roles (e.g., social, political, economic, etc.).

In crossing cultural borders, students are challenged to become consciously aware of their pre-existing beliefs and life experiences as related to their own racial and ethnic identities. As students assimilate new subcultures, they may experience collateral learning in which they experience cognitive conflict with their existing belief system (Aikenhead & Jegede, 1999). Jegede (1995, p. 117) defined collateral learning as "an accommodative mechanism for the conceptual resolution of potentially conflicting tenets within a person's cognitive structure." Four types of collateral learning were proposed: parallel, dependent, simultaneous, and secured. At one end of the continuum, parallel collateral learning is said to occur when students hold conflicting concepts in long-term memory. Secured collateral learning, at the other end, occurs when there is conscious interaction between conflicting schemata. Simultaneous collateral learning occurs when both sets of concepts are learned at the same time and they reinforce each other. Dependent collateral learning involves an amalgamation of ideas.

The collateral learning model has been applied to research studies as a framework to further our understanding about border crossing in science learners (Aikenhead & Jegede, 1999). For example, Herbert (2008) investigated the nature of a class of 12- to 17-year-old students' responses to a cross-cultural science unit designed to help students to build bridges between their traditional practices and beliefs and Western science concepts. The bridge-building strategy involves eliciting students' personal views or prior knowledge about a scientific phenomenon (contextualized within the topic of health-related traditional principles and practices) and instructing them to make explicit comparisons with conventional science concepts. Prompts or cues were provided to elicit either personal explanations or Western science explanations. From a comparison of pretest and posttest responses of the students' explanations, it was evident that the nature of students' prior knowledge impacted their final responses, suggesting that the ease of border crossing is mediated by the students' capacity to identify differences in the two cultural knowledge systems (traditional and Western science), their capacity to talk about their interpretations or science explanations as "the other half" (Herbert, 2008, p. 990), and their capacity to negotiate and resolve the conflicts that arise when there is incongruence between their prior knowledge and the scientific concepts presented. The researcher concluded that the bridge-building pedagogy facilitated student entry into the Western science world through secured, dependent, and parallel collateral learning.

Culturally Responsive Science Pedagogies (CRSP)

Researchers focusing on implementing culturally responsive teaching in science classrooms have benefited and built on the pioneering works such as Ladson-Billings (1994), Geneva Gay (2000), and Ana Maria Villegas and Tamara Lucas (2002). According to Ladson-Billings (1995), culturally relevant pedagogy proposes to produce students who are academically successful, demonstrate cultural competence, and can both understand and be critical of sociopolitical issues. Three pedagogical principles characteristic of teacher-enacted culturally relevant pedagogy include teacher conceptions of self and others, teacher-structured social relations, and teacher conceptions of knowledge. A key tenet of Ladson-Billings's framework (1995) is the focus on "cultural competence," which means that teachers need to support students in maintaining their community and heritage ways with language and other cultural practices in the process of gaining access to dominant ones. Likewise, Gay (2000) proposed that when culturally responsive teaching is situated within the lived experiences and frames of reference of students, they are more personally meaningful, have higher interest and appeal, and are learned more easily and thoroughly. According to Gay (2002), the employment of cultural characteristics, experiences, and perspectives of students acts as a conduit for effective teaching. In order for this to occur, teachers must (a) develop a cultural diversity knowledge base, (b) develop ethnic and cultural diversity content in the curriculum, (c) foster a learning environment in which caring and cultural scaffolding occur, (d) support cross-cultural communications, and (e) acquire knowledge and skills to respond to students from a variety of cultures in the delivery of instruction (p. 106). From a teacher education perspective, Villegas and Lucas (2002) posit that teacher educators should adopt a framework that focuses on the following six characteristics of a culturally responsive teacher: (a) recognize that their students may see the world differently than they do and accept that worldviews are not universal but are influenced by each person's individual, social, and cultural experiences, (b) show affirming attitudes toward students of diverse backgrounds and view their differences as resources for learning, (c) see themselves as agents of change who are responsible for and capable of identifying inequitable school practices and challenge them, (d) understand and embrace constructivist views of teaching and learning, (e) know their students well, and (f) use what they know about their students to support their learning through practices such as engaging all students in the construction of knowledge, building their interests and strengths while stretching them beyond what they already know (p. 21).

A number of studies have examined culturally responsive pedagogy in classroom settings (e.g., Morrison, Robbins, & Rose, 2008; Young, 2010) and in subject-specific domains, including literacy (e.g., Cheesman & De Pry, 2010), mathematics (e.g., Gay, 2009), and science

(e.g., Klump & McNeir, 2005; Lewthwaite & McMillan, 2007; Lewthwaite, McMillan, Renaud, Hainnu, & MacDonald, 2010). Aikenhead (2006) has provided an extensive review of teachers' orientation in relation to implementing a humanistic curriculum in science education and examples of cross-cultural teaching as cultural border crossing. Lee and Luykx (2006) reviewed and synthesized a large number of studies on the impact of culturally congruent science instruction on nonmainstream students' science achievement and learning experiences. In general, the majority of the studies on culturally responsive science pedagogy (CRSP) relied on ethnographic research and the collection of teachers' and students' own narratives of their classroom experiences.

Challenges and Barriers in Culturally Responsive Science Pedagogies

Taken together, the studies on CRSP offer several key findings. First, teachers need to acknowledge the degrees of cultural differences between students' cultural self-identities and the culture of their science classroom and take a proactive approach in helping students negotiate this cross-cultural classroom environment (Boutte, Kelly-Jackson, & Johnson, 2010). Furthermore, in order for teachers to engage in CRSP, they need more knowledge about the nature of science, epistemology, and knowledge and cultural competency within indigenous communities (Brayboy & Castagno, 2008; Meyer & Crawford, 2011). For example, Wallace and Brand (2012) examined the beliefs and practices of two effective middle school science teachers deemed culturally responsive by their administrator. The study addressed the main issue of teachers' critical awareness of societal constructions of difference or characterization of race in teaching African American students. Both grounded theory and critical race theory were used to analyze the teachers' beliefs and practices. The results indicate that teachers' beliefs and practices were informed by their critical awareness of social constraints imposed on their African American students' identities. Teachers' background experiences were found to provoke a critical awareness of societal constructions of race, influencing their teaching philosophies and helping inform their perceptions of students' needs and behaviors. The authors suggest that sociocultural awareness builds trust and creates learning environments that engage and motivate students to participate in science learning activities in the classroom.

A second key finding about studies on CRSP is that there are pervasive challenges facing teachers who are attempting to change their current practices into a culturally responsive approach (Aikenhead, 2006). Teachers who do not share the same cultural background and experiences as their students may struggle to understand them in relation to culture, race, and ethnicity and their commitment to teach in a culturally responsive matter. For example, Atwater, Freeman, Butler, and Draper-Morris (2010) examined two preservice science teachers' understandings of "Other" students' (non-dominant group) cultures, races, and ethnicities and the ways they respond to the "Other" students' needs in their science classrooms. The findings indicate that the two teachers did not acknowledge or understand that there are relationships among and within race, class, and responsive science teaching. The authors argued that teachers need opportunities to reflect on these cultural constructs and their interrelationships with teaching, especially in the design of science teacher preparation programs.

Sleeter (2012) argues that neoliberal school reforms, ideas that promote personal responsibility through individual choice within markets, reverse the empowering learning that culturally responsive pedagogy has the potential to support. The reasons offered for the marginalization of culturally responsive pedagogy include (a) persistent faulty and simplistic conceptions of what it is, (b) too little research connecting its use with student achievement, and (c) elite and White fear of losing national and global hegemony. There is a tendency to view culturally responsive pedagogy as *cultural celebration* that is disconnected from academic learning. This limited view results in educators, parents, or policy makers interpreting culturally responsive pedagogy as learning about other cultural traditions as an end itself rather than learning to teach challenging academic knowledge and skills through cultural processes and knowledge students bring to the classroom. Moreover, teachers may assume culture to be a fixed and homogenous characteristic of individuals who belong to a group and that students who are group members identify with that conception, thereby engaging in essentializing culture. This results in teachers who do not necessarily enact a robust conception of culturally responsive pedagogy. In light of these problems, there is a need for much more systematic research that links culturally responsive pedagogy with its impact on student learning and teacher professional development in culturally responsive pedagogy with improved student outcomes.

A third key finding about studies on CRSP is that successful implementation of CRSP is characterized by drawing teachers' attention to *relationships, partnerships, and apprenticeships.* Johnson (2011) carried out a longitudinal study of two middle-school science teachers who participated in a professional development program based on the transformative professional development model (TPD). The TPD framework was developed using Ladson-Billings's (1995) three propositions of culturally responsive pedagogy and includes three main components: (a) the development of student conceptual understanding through culturally relevant science and effective teaching methods, (b) a focus on building relationships between teachers and their colleagues, teachers and students, and teachers and university faculty members, and (c) creation of positive school and classroom climate (Johnson & Marx, 2009). A key finding of this study is that both teachers understood the importance of building mutual respect and valued teacher–student relationships. This finding was consistent with other research, such as the Te Kotahitanga program.

Te Kotahitanga is a New Zealand Ministry of Education–funded research and development initiative designed to improve educational outcomes of Māori students and used in a number of NZ secondary schools since 2001 (Bishop, Berryman, Powell, & Teddy, 2007; Bishop, Berryman, Tiakiwai, & Richardson, 2003). Teacher effectiveness for Māori students has depended on teachers' ability to form and maintain effective relationships with them. Further, it is the type of relationships developed between the teacher and Māori students that were the most crucial factor in mediating their engagement and learning in schools (Hynds et al., 2011).

Rogers and Jaime (2010) conducted semistructured interviews with five Native community members to identify practical ways to support the development of culturally responsive teachers. Through in-depth narratives, three themes were identified: (a) learning from the community, (b) transforming thinking through discomfort, and (c) gaining awareness of positive values. In this study, the researchers were able to build a collaborative partnership with Native community members (cultural insiders) and developed a set of expectations for responsive non–Native educators to help guide planning and facilitation of field experiences, professional development, and future research. The key message is that "emerging culturally responsive educators must strive to learn from community members, to step outside of their comfort zones, and to notice the unique, positive aspects of Native culture while acknowledging the needs for their own continued, career-long learning" (Rogers & Jaime, 2010, p. 198).

Experiential learning is seen as an important element in CRSP for promoting science teachers to experience for themselves indigenous culture, language, and cross-cultural science teaching (Higgins, 2009; Sutherland & Henning, 2009). With greater understanding of indigenous knowledge and culture, a teacher has more ways to recognize students' cultural resources. Andrea Belczewski (2009) describes her experiences collaborating and learning alongside First Nations people, with a focus on self-reflection to decolonize her thinking and teaching practice in order to make science education relevant, meaningful, and respectful for First Nations students. Belczewski, who is White and comes from an education background in Western modern science, grappled with the challenges to teach science that is practical, relevant, and inclusive for Mi'kmaq and Maliseet (First Nations) students in her classroom. Feedback from her students prompted her to self-reflect and to look for answers to questions such as "Is who I am as a White person synonymous with colonialism and do I perpetuate assimilative practices in the classroom? How do I feel about incorporating cultural content in courses and will I ever know cultural content well enough to present it, or by doing so am I patronizing people and their culture?" (Belczewski, 2009, p. 194). An opportunity to work alongside First Nations youths and instructors on science camps within their home communities further allowed Belczewski to experience first-hand the need to work on decolonizing not only the content in science learning but that of her thinking as well—a process of personal transformation that included explicit pedagogy changes. For example, there is greater awareness of creating "a safe environment for honest dialogues" (p. 198) in the science classroom and a conscious effort to value and incorporate students' perspectives and ways of knowing in the learning process while at the same time recognizing and acknowledging the rich cultural knowledge they bring to the classroom. Thus, being reflective and engaging personally with her students' communities (with a decolonizing view toward her teaching practices and self) provided Belczewski with a deeper understanding and appreciation for First Nations people and their culture and ways of knowing. This, in turn, heightened her own epistemologies, opened her thinking to other worldviews, and drew her closer to knowing and valuing her students.

Using Funds of Knowledge as
Resource Pedagogies

The concept of funds of knowledge is based on the recognition that an individual's experiences within the family or community yield knowledge that is useful, powerful, and transferable (Gonzalez & Moll, 2002; Gonzalez, Moll, & Amanti, 2005). Funds of knowledge are "historically and culturally developed bodies of knowledge and skills" (Moll, Amanti, Neff, & Gonzalez, 1992, p. 133) that are useful in drawing connections between home and school culture and open up opportunities for explicit and purposeful use of students' ways of being and experiences as resources for teaching and learning. In short, students' lives outside of the classroom serve as a resource for their classroom-based science learning (Roth & Tobin, 2007). Seiler (2013) argued for an alternative view of culture in science education, suggesting moving away from a dichotomy between discontinuous and continuous perspectives, which Carlone and Johnson (2012) referred to as the cultural difference tradition. Instead, she proposed an articulation of science classrooms as cultural spaces that are porous, emergent, and can support cultural fluidity. Seen from this new cultural lens, science researchers and teachers are encouraged to shift their attention from identifying cultural conflicts in the classroom and other normative ways to respond to indigenous students to the cultural resources that students acquire through participation in their homes and communities and how their use can bring about reproduction of culture or production of new cultural forms. This cultural conception invokes new metaphors—funds of knowledge and third space, which have the potential to change teachers' conceptual orientations and teaching practices.

Taking a resource-rich view challenges the deficit views that blame students and explains failure in terms of poor motivation, low interest, and low ability levels of students (Chigeza, 2011). According to Chigeza (2011), cultural resources include (a) cultural disposition—a student's pattern of behaviors created as a result of cultural

experiences, (b) community cultural wealth—an array of cultural knowledge, skills, abilities, and contacts possessed by a student's community, and (c) cultural capital—a student's acquired skills, awards, knowledge, and forms of language. Creating culturally responsive pedagogies can be achieved by helping students use their existing cultural resources in new, productive, and meaningful ways.

Researchers have begun using the concept of funds of knowledge to investigate science learning in the classroom that respect, value, and leverage on students' cultural backgrounds and practices. For example, Calabrese Barton and Tan (2009) examined the different types of funds of knowledge and discourse sixth-grade students brought into science classrooms. A design experiment was set up to understand how better to help the teacher in supporting students' strategic use of funds of knowledge and discourse to enhance their learning experiences in science. Through detailed analysis of lessons designed to elicit students' funds of knowledge, transcripts of student dialogues and focus group interviews, 4 categories (family funds, community funds, peer culture, and popular culture) with 15 subcategories of key discourse threads were identified. The adapted science unit activities stimulated students in using their own funds of knowledge, opening up opportunities for multiple ways of participating in the science learning community. The dialogic platform gave students the confidence to bring in nontraditional funds for discussion, where the dominant school science discourse is challenged and renegotiated, creating a hybrid space for repositioning the students to view their funds of knowledge as legitimate, relevant, and applicable to school science. Besides fostering active participation and meaningful use of funds of knowledge, the hybrid spaces are seen as valuable learning moments in which transformative physical (student as narrative/positional authority given the familiarity of the place), political (student empowered to lead and participate), and pedagogical (student as co-planner of lessons) changes occur.

McLaughlin and Calabrese Barton (2012) examined preservice teachers' uptake and understanding of funds of knowledge in the elementary science classroom. The preservice teachers' understanding of funds of knowledge are documented and described in terms of how they recognize, interpret, and react to what they learn from and about students. The sources of funds of knowledge that preservice teachers notice students as having mapped largely onto Moje and colleagues' (2004) categories—organisms, locations, activities, and popular culture. These student resources were interpreted through a utility lens, by their perceived usefulness in supporting classroom activities, including behavioral and learning outcomes. Most preservice teachers considered students' funds of knowledge as a prompt (a potential "hook") to engage students in class, while a smaller group of teachers saw the funds of knowledge as helping students in meaning making in science and recognizing students as being more knowledgeable peers. Although students' funds of knowledge were predominantly seen as productive resources for teaching and learning, some teachers expressed doubts about students' funds of knowledge in relation to being insufficient in number or scope to support learning science as well as incongruent with scientific explanations. These teachers were able to describe positive approaches to better support these students in the classroom.

Place-based funds of knowledge offer teachers a rich resource for providing opportunities to help indigenous students connect science and society and to focus more on real-world issues based in students' lives and communities (Kawagley & Barnhardt, 2007). Place-based teaching is a situated approach that recognizes and leverages local knowledge about people and their environment to engage students in problem solving, experiential learning, cross-cultural and trans-disciplinary learning, and service learning such as outreach to the community (Lim & Calabrese Barton, 2006; Smith, 2007). Chinn (2012) has provided a comprehensive review of place-based and culture-based programs and their impacts on supporting teacher expertise and agency. A key finding is that professional development that prepares science teachers to locate science learning in their students' lives and communities increases teacher agency and empowers them to contextualize lessons and to teach in ways that are meaningful and relevant to diverse learners.

Future Directions

The field of indigenous and ethnic minority science education research is fraught with conundrums, tensions, and contradictions because of the specific contexts necessary to work with the communities and the complexity that such contexts present. When papers report on "ethnic minority students," the reader needs to be fully cognizant that the groupings are neither homogenous nor easy to understand from an external point of view. One key may be the country in which the research is being carried out, but even then there are nuances to grasp. For example, in the UK, ethnic minority groups are identified as including Black Caribbean, Pakistani, Bangladeshi, Indian, and Chinese. But at the same time, the reader is directed to note the differences in the achievement between immigrant and British Black Caribbean, Pakistani, and Bangladeshi and the "other" ethnic minority students such as Indian and Chinese (DeWitt et al., 2011). The identification of other ethnic minority groups and indigenous students is similarly problematic and confusing to outsiders (see Abrams, Taylor, & Guo, 2013; McKinley, 2007). For example, the grouping of Asian Americans and Pacific Islanders in the United States includes both indigenous groups (native Hawaiians) and immigrant Pacific Island groups, such as Samoans and Tongans (Pang, Han, & Pang, 2011). Not only are the categorizations constantly moving according to country, but the surrounding contexts (e.g., state of the language, ways knowledge is constructed, colonizing countries) and the experiences of the groups can differ markedly, too. However, this complexity should not deter researchers from working in the field. The point is not

finding a consensus or a universal definition of what constitutes each of these groups—identity understandings will always be locally driven—but that the inclusion of the communities (over a wide range of influences) has been shown to be influential in student academic success (Clinton & Hattie, 2013).

There is a need to promote more equitable relationships and interactions between Indigenous communities and the academy. Educators and scholars working within the "interface" of both indigenous knowledge and the Western epistemological system ought to consider the four requirements: respect, relevance, reciprocity, and responsibility (Kirkness & Barnhardt, 1991)—respect the cultural integrity of indigenous people, make learning relevant to their ways of knowing, offer reciprocal teaching and learning relationships that build on the cultural background of the students, and empower them to exercise responsibility over their own lives. These four Rs may act as discursive norms for building positive relationships and better understanding and embracing indigenous ways of knowing. Norms of interaction are not only relevant in knowledge sharing with indigenous communities but are also important for establishing dialogic or dialectical learning environments in the science classrooms that facilitate making students' worldview visible and determining how best to engage them using the cultural resources for meaningful science learning. Furthermore, increased school connections with local communities will result in a greater involvement in science and science education (see Sutherland & Henning, 2009). This objective will bring with it further research opportunities in how partnerships between schools and local indigenous and/or ethnic minority communities are formed and work in the context of science education learning.

What accountability frameworks have highlighted in science education research, as they have in other areas, are the methodological and practical challenges of measuring equity and excellence outcomes. Ultimately science education must be assessed by evaluating its capacity to cope with diversity and be judged on its ability to achieve both equity and excellence. As shown in this review, the notion of success or excellence is what gives rise to the conflict. Although achievement gaps reflect ongoing inequality, the usual studies of achievement that compare subgroups of students by selecting quantitative outcomes fall short of telling the whole story of educational equity or inequity and the goal of excellence. In current discourse, achievement data are foregrounded to the possible detriment of other factors. While standardized tests currently used do provide necessary information about student performance and equity within and across the schools, not all qualities for which schools should be held accountable can or should be measured by achievement grades. Factors such as culture, language, family–school relations, student engagement, motivation, and family aspirations, among others, are also very important in influencing educational success. Science learning occurs in a cultural context, as we have shown in the chapter, and it is, fundamentally, a socially mediated process. One pressure the accountability system has on indigenous and ethnic minority students is the individualism the system promotes. This is not unexpected. The student body is heterogeneous from an academic point of view, and each student should be stimulated to make the best of her or his capabilities. But in order to determine accountability, one needs to ask, "Accountable to whom?" Returning to Fraser (2010), she argues that when it comes to practice (such as schools), accountability should be explored through three interacting dimensions: distribution, recognition, and representation. Who gets what? Who is treated in what way? Who can do what? These can open questions such as: How are educational opportunities, resources, and outcomes in science education distributed between individuals and across groups? Who has the power to make decisions and how far can learners and their families shape what happens to them? But Woods and colleagues (2014) suggest that accountability must be partnered with both responsibility and commitment. McCarty (2009, p. 26) promotes an "authentic accountability" plan that includes measurements of achievement (including locally developed indicators), highlights relationships between schools and communities, and views communities as important stakeholders in their children's education and involves them in decision making, among other ideas. While some education systems (e.g., New Zealand) work on accountability at the local level, with every school having its own parent-elected governance structure, other countries' systems are more hierarchical and layered (e.g., United States), and accountability tends to reside in structures more removed from the local school. Accountability is a highly contested issue but a very important one for indigenous communities in particular and one that has yet to be fully explored in relation to science education.

This chapter has shown there has been a surge in research on culturally responsive science pedagogies. This work has been largely driven by the current accountability frameworks in schools, particularly in industrialized countries. The culturally responsive research in science education classrooms serves two purposes. First, it brings a resolution to the question of how to respond to the situation of indigenous and ethnic minority students' "underachievement" in science education without the need to engage in deep and meaningful ways with the excluded communities. There has been a realization of an unwitting tendency for science teachers, who are mainly drawn from ethnic groups outside indigenous and ethnic minorities, to focus on authoritative views of science education and to center on the assumptions and points of view that dominate the thinking. The second purpose, again unintentionally, is to domesticate the knowledge of others—to make indigenous knowledge "fit" prevailing views of science and to bring it under the control of others. These approaches leave open the possibility of a misunderstanding by teachers (and others) of indigenous and ethnic minority

students by recognizing culture and language as mere iconography. While there is a view that the culturally responsive response weakens the radical potential from an indigenous community point of view (see McKinley, 2001, for discussion), the CRSP research is currently a strong thread in this field.

The increase in interest in CRSP implies that there are a number of research avenues to investigate. First, research is needed to identify ways to support teachers and students to better leverage the funds of knowledge that each brings to the science classroom. We think "third space" research has potential to contribute to CRSP in our understanding of how to do this. An important area of research involves how teachers and students from diverse backgrounds make use of their linguistic and cultural experiences as intellectual resources in learning science and how they attempt to overcome the tensions and challenges that may arise when these resources are found to be discontinuous with the way science is defined and taught in the classroom. In a recent paper, Nam, Roehrig, Kern, and Reynolds (2013) researched the culturally relevant science teaching perceptions and practices of U.S. teachers in American Indian classrooms and found they were limited in what IK topics they could choose from. Another finding was that teachers who position themselves as learners with and build strong relationships with their indigenous and ethnic minority students are more likely to have stronger culturally responsive practices in their classrooms. A number of questions that could be pursued in future work include: Does culturally relevant pedagogy support indigenous and ethnic minority students to learn science? If so, how? And what can be done to help teachers become more skilled in practicing culturally relevant science teaching? Little work exists on finding out what students bring to the science classroom. Second, developing teachers' culturally responsive pedagogies must arise from the actions of an entire school system rather than from classroom teachers alone (Aikenhead, 2011). The school system should actively support teachers to build a cultural perspective on teaching science and involve the community in helping create a collaborative learning environment, which will not only enrich the school science content but also promote a cultural shift of school science that facilitates more responsive science teaching (Bang, Medin, Washinawatok, & Chapman, 2010).

Increasingly, indigenous communities (and possibly, to a lesser extent, ethnic minority communities) will assert their right to direct, not just inform, research programs in science and science education and develop their potential as partners of science and education. For example, the New Zealand Ministry of Education, acting as agent for the government, has signed 32 partnership education plans with Iwi (tribal groupings) with 10 more Iwi in negotiation (Ministry of Education, 2010). These plans form the basis for ongoing partnerships and developments that align both government and Iwi priorities. This is an exciting development and is a potential avenue of research that is only beginning to be articulated. What would a science curriculum look like if we viewed partnership seriously? What would educational success look like? What would accountability look like under the same conditions? It is important that science education research establish strong links with indigenous communities in particular—it is the only way to gain true sustainability of any programs in school and student success that are meaningful to all.

Acknowledgments

The authors wish to thank Mei-hung Chiu and Sarah Tolbert for their review and comments on the initial version of this chapter.

References

Abrams, E., Taylor, C.T., & Guo, C.J. (2013). Editorial: Contextualizing culturally relevant science and mathematics teaching for indigenous students. *International Journal of Science and Mathematics Education, 11*, 1–21.

Adams, J., Luitel, B.C., Afonso, E., & Taylor, P.C. (2008). A cogenerative inquiry using postcolonial theory to envisage culturally inclusive science education. *Cultural Studies of Science Education, 3*, 999–1019.

Aikenhead, G.S. (1996). Science education: Border crossing into the subculture of science. *Studies in Science Education, 27*, 1–52.

Aikenhead, G.S. (1997). Toward a First Nations cross-cultural science and technology curriculum. *Science Education, 81*, 217–238.

Aikenhead, G.S. (2006). *Science education for everyday life: Evidence-based practice.* New York: Teachers College Press.

Aikenhead, G.S. (2011). Towards a cultural view on quality science teaching. In D. Corrigan, J. Dillon, & R. Gunstone (Eds.), *The professional knowledge base of science teaching* (pp. 107–127). New York: Springer.

Aikenhead, G.S., & Elliott, D. (2010). An emerging decolonizing science education in Canada. *Canadian Journal of Science, Mathematics and Technology Education, 10*, 321–338.

Aikenhead, G.S., & Jegede, O.J. (1999). Cross-cultural science education: A cognitive explanation of a cultural phenomenon. *Journal of Research in Science Teaching, 36*, 269–287.

Aikenhead, G.S., & Michell, H. (2011). *Bridging cultures: Indigenous and scientific ways of knowing nature.* Toronto: Pearson Education Canada.

Ainscow, M., Dyson, A., Goldrick, S., & West, M. (2012). *Developing equitable education systems.* London: Routledge.

Atwater, M.M. (1994). Research on cultural diversity in the classroom. In D.L. Gabel (Ed.), *Handbook of research on science teaching and learning* (pp. 558–576). New York: Macmillan.

Atwater, M.M., Freeman, T.B., Butler, M.B., & Draper-Morris, J. (2010). A case study of science teacher candidates' understandings and actions related to the culturally responsive teaching of "other" students. *International Journal of Environmental & Science Education, 5*(3), 287–318.

Bang, M., Medin, D., Washinawatok, K., & Chapman, S. (2010). Innovations in culturally-based science education through partnerships and community. In M. Khine & I. Saleh (Eds.), *New science of learning: cognition, computers and collaboration in education* (pp. 569–592). New York: Springer.

Belczewski, A. (2009). Decolonizing science education and the science teacher: A White teacher's perspective. *Canadian Journal of Science, Mathematics and Technology Education, 9*(3), 191–202.

Bhabha, H.K. (2004). *The location of culture.* London: Routledge.

Bishop, R., Berryman, M., Powell, A., & Teddy, L. (2007). *Te Kotahitanga: Improving the educational achievement of Māori students in mainstream education Phase 2: Towards a whole school approach*

(Report to the Ministry of Education). Wellington, NZ: Ministry of Education.

Bishop, R., Berryman, M., Tiakiwai, S., & Richardson, C. (2003). *Te Kotahitanga: The experiences of Year 9 and 10 Māori students in mainstream classrooms.* Wellington, NZ: Ministry of Education.

Boutte, G., Kelly-Jackson, C., & Johnson, G.L. (2010). Culturally relevant teaching in science classrooms: Addressing academic achievement, cultural competence, and critical consciousness. *International Journal of Multicultural Education, 12*(2), 1–20.

Branden, K., Avermaet, P., & Houtte, M. (2011). *Equity and excellence in education: Towards maximal learning opportunities for all students.* New York: Routledge.

Brayboy, B.M.J., & Castagno, A.E. (2008). How might Native science inform "informal science learning"? *Cultural Studies of Science Education, 3*(3), 731–750.

Brown, B.A. (2011). Isn't that just good teaching? Disaggregate instruction and the language identity dilemma. *Journal of Science Teacher Education, 22*(8), 679–704.

Brown, B.A. (2013). The language-identity dilemma: An examination of language, cognition, identity, and their associated implications for learning. In J.A. Bianchini, V.L. Akerson, A. Calabrese Barton, O. Lee, & A.J. Rodriguez (Eds.), *Moving the equity agenda forward: Equity research, practice, and policy in science education* (pp. 223–239). New York: Springer.

Buxton, C. (2005). Creating a culture of academic success in an urban science and math magnet high school. *Science Education, 89*(3), 392–417.

Cajete, G. (1994). *Look to the mountain: An ecology of indigenous education.* Durango, CO: Kivaki Press.

Calabrese Barton, A., & Tan, E. (2009). Funds of knowledge and discourses and hybrid space. *Journal of Research in Science Teaching, 46*, 50–73.

Calabrese Barton, A., Tan, E., & Rivet, A. (2008). Creating hybrid spaces for engaging school science among urban middle school girls. *American Education Research Journal, 45*, 68–103.

Carlone, H.B., & Johnson, A. (2007). Understanding the science experiences of successful women of color: Science identity as an analytic lens. *Journal of Research in Science Teaching, 44*, 1187–1218.

Carlone, H.B., & Johnson, A. (2012). Unpacking "culture" in cultural studies of science education: Cultural difference versus cultural production. *Ethnography and Education, 7*(2), 151–173.

Carter, L. (2007). Sociocultural influences on science education: Innovation for contemporary times. *Science Education, 92*(1), 165–181.

Chappell, S.V., & Cahnmann-Taylor, M. (2013). No child left with crayons: The imperative of arts-based education and research with language "minority" and other minoritized communities. *Review of Educational Research, 37*(1), 255–280.

Cheesman, E., & De Pry, R. (2010). A critical review of culturally responsive literacy instruction. *Journal of Praxis in Multicultural Education, 5*(1), 83–99.

Chigeza, P. (2011). Cultural resources of minority and marginalised students should be included in the school science curriculum. *Cultural Studies of Science Education, 6*(2), 401–412.

Chinn, P. (2012). Developing teachers' place-based and culture-based pedagogical content knowledge and agency. In B. Fraser, C. McRobbie, & K. Tobin (Eds.), *Second international handbook of science education* (pp. 323–334). New York and London: Springer.

Clinton, J., & Hattie, J. (2013). New Zealand students' perceptions of parental involvement in learning and schooling. *Asia Pacific Journal of Education, 33*(3), 324–337.

Cobern, W.W., & Aikenhead, G.S. (1998). Cultural aspects of learning science. In B.J. Fraser & K.G. Tobin (Eds.), *International handbook of science education* (pp. 39–52). Dordrecht, the Netherlands: Kluwer Academic.

Cupane, A.F. (2011). Towards an understanding of the role of language in the science classroom and its association with cultural identity development in the context of Mozambique. *Cultural Studies of Science Education, 6*(2), 435–440.

DeWitt, J., Archer, L., Osborn, J., Dillon, J., Willis, B., & Wong, B. (2011). High aspirations but low progression: The science aspirations-careers paradox amongst minority ethnic students. *International Journal of Science and Mathematics Education, 9,* 243–271.

Deyhle, D., & Comeau, K. G. (2009). Connecting the Circle in American Indian Education. In J. A. Banks (Ed.), *The Routledge international companion to multicultural education* (pp. 265–275). New York: Routledge.

Eisenhart, M. (2001). Changing conceptions of culture and ethnographic methodology: Recent thematic shifts and their implications for research on teaching. In V. Richardson (Ed.), *Handbook of research on teaching* (pp. 209–225). Washington, DC: American Educational Research Association.

Ezeife, A. N. (2003). Using the environment in mathematics and science teaching: An African and Aboriginal perspective. *International Review of Education, 49,* 319–342.

Fraser, N. (2010). *Scales of justice.* New York: Columbia University Press.

Gay, G. (2000). *Culturally responsive teaching: Theory, research, and practice.* New York: Teachers College Press.

Gay, G. (2002). Preparing for culturally responsive teaching. *Journal of Teacher Education, 53,* 106–116.

Gay, G. (2009). Preparing culturally responsive teachers. In B. Greer, S. Mukhopadhyay, S. Nelson-Barber, & A. B. Powell (Eds.), *Culturally responsive mathematics education* (pp. 65–84). New York: Routledge.

Gilbert, A., & Yerrick, R. (2001). Same school, separate worlds: A sociocultural study of identity, resistance, and negotiation in a rural, lower track science classroom. *Journal of Research in Science Teaching, 38,* 574–598.

Giroux, H. A. (1992). *Border crossings: Cultural workers and the politics of education.* New York: Routledge.

Glasson, G. E., Mhango, N., Phiri, A., & Lanier, M. (2010). Sustainability science education in Africa: Negotiating indigenous ways of living with nature in the third space. *International Journal of Science Education, 32*(1), 125–141.

Gonzalez, N., & Moll, L. C. (2002). Cruzando el puente: Building bridges to funds of knowledge. *Educational Policy, 16*(4), 623–641.

Gonzalez, N., Moll, L. C., & Amanti, C. (2005). *Funds of knowledge: Theorizing practices in households, communities, and classrooms.* Mahwah, NJ: Lawrence Erlbaum.

Greenfield, P. M., Keller, H., Fuligni, A., & Maynard, A. (2003). Cultural pathways through universal development. *Annual Review of Psychology, 54,* 461–490.

Greenfield, P. M., Quiroz, B., & Raeff, C. (2000). Cross-cultural conflict and harmony in the social construction of the child. In S. Harkness, C. Raeff, & C. M. Super (Eds.), *Variability in the social construction of the child* (pp. 93–108). New Directions in Child Development, No. 87. San Francisco: Jossey-Bass.

Gutierrez, K. D., & Rogoff, B. (2003). Cultural ways of learning: Individual traits or repertoires of practice. *Educational Researcher, 32*(5), 19–25.

Harris, P., & Mercier, O. (2006). Te Ara Putaiao. In M. Mulholland (Ed.), *State of the Māori Nation.* Auckland, NZ: Reed Publishing.

Hawkins, J., & Pea, R. D. (1987). Tools for bridging the cultures of everyday and scientific thinking. *Journal of Research in Science Teaching, 24*(4), 291–307.

Herbert, S. (2008). Collateral learning in science: Students' responses to a cross-cultural unit of work. *International Journal of Science Education, 30*(7), 979–993.

Heymann, J., & Cassola, A. (Eds.). (2012). *Lessons in educational equality.* New York: Oxford University Press.

Higgins, M. (2009). *Shared horizons: A dialogue between Indigenous and Western science.* Unpublished thesis proposal, Lakehead University, Thunder Bay, ON.

Hynds, A., Sleeter, C., Hindle, D., Savage, C., Penetito, W., & Meyer, L. (2011). Te Kotahitanga: A case study of a repositioning approach to teacher professional development for culturally responsive pedagogies. *Asia Pacific Journal of Teacher Education, 39*(4), 339–351.

Jegede, O. (1995). Collateral learning and the eco-cultural paradigm in science and mathematics education in Africa. *Studies in Science Education, 25,* 97–137.

Johnson, C. (2011). The road to culturally relevant science: Exploring how teachers navigate change in pedagogy. *Journal of Research in Science Teaching, 48*(2), 170–198.

Johnson, C. C., & Marx, S. (2009). Transformative professional development: A model for urban science education reform. *Journal of Science Teacher Education, 20*(2), 113–134.

Jordan, W. J. (2010). Defining equity: Multiple perspectives to analyzing the performance of diverse learners. *Review of Research in Education, 34,* 142–178.

Kawagley, A. (2006). *A Yupiaq worldview: A pathway to ecology and spirit.* Long Grove, IL: Waveland Press.

Kawagley, A., & Barnhardt, R. (2007). *Education indigenous to place: Western science meets native reality.* Retrieved May 31, 2013, from www.ankn.uaf.edu/curriculum/Articles/BarnhardtKawagley/EIP.html

Kincheloe, J., & Steinberg, S. (2008). Indigenous knowledges in education: Complexities, dangers, and profound benefits. In N. K. Denzin, Y. S. Lincoln, & L. T. Smith (Eds.), *Handbook of critical and indigenous methodologies* (pp. 135–156). Thousand Oaks, CA: Sage.

Kirkness, V. J., & Barnhardt, R. (1991). First Nations and higher education: The four R's—respect, relevance, reciprocity, responsibility. *Journal of American Indian Education, 30*(3), 1–15.

Klump, J., & McNeir, G. (2005). *Culturally responsive practices for student success: A regional sampler.* Retrieved April 16, 2013, from www.ode.state.or.us/opportunities/grants/saelp/culturallynwrel.pdf

Ladson-Billings, G. (1994). *The dreamkeepers: Successful teachers of African American children.* San Francisco: Jossey-Bass.

Ladson-Billings, G. (1995). But that's just good teaching! The case for culturally relevant pedagogy. *Theory Into Practice, 34,* 159–165.

Lee, O. (2002). Science inquiry for elementary students from diverse backgrounds. In W. G. Secada (Ed.), *Review of research in education* (pp. 23–69). Washington, DC: American Educational Research Association.

Lee, O. (2004). Teacher change in beliefs and practices in science and literacy instruction with English language learners. *Journal of Research in Science Teaching, 41,* 65–93.

Lee, O. (2005). Science education with English language learners: Synthesis and research agenda. *Review of Educational Research, 75,* 491–530.

Lee, O., Deaktor, R., Enders, C., & Lambert, J. (2008). Impact of a multiyear professional development intervention on science achievement of culturally and linguistically diverse elementary students. *Journal of Research in Science Teaching, 45*(6), 726–747.

Lee, O., & Fradd, S. H. (1998). Science for all, including students from non-English-language backgrounds. *Educational Researcher, 27,* 12–21.

Lee, O., & Luykx, A. (2006). *Science education and student diversity: Synthesis and research agenda.* New York: Cambridge University Press.

Lemke, J. (1990). *Talking science: Language, learning, and values.* Norwood, NJ: Ablex.

Lewthwaite, B., McMillan, B., Renaud, R., Hainnu, R., & MacDonald, C. (2010). Combining the views of "both worlds": Science education in Nunavut Piqusiit Tamainik katisugit. *Canadian Journal of Educational Administration and Policy, 98,* 1–71.

Lewthwaite, G., & McMillan, B. (2007). Combing the views of both worlds: Perceived constraints and contributors to achieving aspirations for science education in Qikiqtani. *Canadian Journal of Science, Mathematics and Technology Education, 7,* 355–376.

Lim, M., & Calabrese Barton, A. (2006). Science learning and a sense of place in an urban middle school. *Cultural Studies of Science Education, 1,* 107–142.

Luke, A., Green, J., & Kelly, G. J. (2010). Introduction: What counts as evidence? *Review of Research in Education, 34,* vii–xvi.

May, S. (2001). *Language and minority rights.* Essex, UK: Pearson Education Limited.

McCarty, T. L. (2009). The impact of high-stakes accountability policies on Native American learners: Evidence from research. *Teaching Education, 20*(1), 7–29.

McIntosh, T., & Mulholland, M. (Eds.). (2011). *Māori and social issues*. Wellington, NZ: Huia Publishers.

McKinley, E. (1996). Towards an indigenous science curriculum. *Research in Science Education, 26*(2), 155–67.

McKinley, E. (2001). Cultural diversity: Masking power with innocence. *Science Education, 85*(1), 74–76.

McKinley, E. (2005). Brown bodies, white coats: Postcolonialism, Māori women and science. *Discourse: Studies in the Cultural Politics of Education, 26*(4), 481–496.

McKinley, E. (2007). Postcolonialism, indigenous students and science education. In S. K. Abell & N. G. Lederman (Eds.), *International handbook of research in science education* (pp. 199–226). Mahwah, NJ: Lawrence Erlbaum.

McKinley, E., & Keegan, P. J. (2008). Curriculum and language in Aotearoa New Zealand: From science to pūtaiao. *L1—Educational Studies in Language and Literature, 8*(1), 135–147.

McKinley, E., & Stewart, G. M. (2009). Falling into place: Indigenous science education research in the Pacific. In S. Ritchie (Ed.), *World of science education, Vol. 2. Handbook of research in Australasia* (pp. 49–65). Rotterdam, the Netherlands: Sense Publishers.

McKinley, E., & Stewart, G. M. (2012). Out of place: Indigenous knowledge (IK) in the science curriculum. In B. Fraser, C. McRobbie, & K. Tobin (Eds.), *Second international handbook of science education* (pp. 541–554). New York and London: Springer.

McLaughlin, D. S., & Calabrese Barton, A. (2012). Preservice teachers' uptake and understanding of funds of knowledge in elementary science. *Journal of Science Teacher Education, 24*(1), 13–36.

Mead, H. M. (2003). *Tikanga Māori*. Wellington, NZ: Huia Publishers.

Meyer, X., & Crawford, B. A. (2011). Teaching science as a cultural way of knowing: Merging authentic inquiry, nature of science, and multicultural strategies. *Cultural Studies in Science Education, 6*(3), 525–547.

Ministry of Education. (2008). *Ka Hikitia—Managing for success: The Māori education strategy 2008–2012*. Wellington, NZ: Author.

Ministry of Education. (2010). *Ngā Haeata Mātauranga*. Retrieved July 16, 2013, from www.educationcounts.govt.nz/publications/series/5851/75954/organisational-success

Moje, E., Collazo, T., Carillo, R., & Marx, R. W. (2001). "Maestro, what is 'quality?'": Language, literacy, and discourse in project-based science. *Journal of Research in Science Teaching, 38*(4), 469–498.

Moje, E., McIntosh Ciechanowski, K., Kramer, K., Ellis, L., Carrillo, R., & Collazo, T. (2004). Working toward third space in content area literacy: An examination of everyday funds of knowledge and discourse. *Reading Research Quarterly, 39*(1), 38–70.

Moll, L. C., Amanti, C., Neff, D., & Gonzalez, N. (1992). Funds of knowledge for teaching: Using a qualitative approach to connect homes and classrooms. *Theory Into Practice, 31*(2), 132–141.

Morrison, K. A., Robbins, H. A., & Rose, D. G. (2008). Operationalizing culturally relevant pedagogy: A synthesis of classroom-based research. *Equity and Excellence in Education, 41*(4), 433–452.

Nam, Y., Roehrig, G., Kern, A., & Reynolds, B. (2013). Perceptions and practices of culturally relevant science teaching in American Indian classrooms. *International Journal of Science and Mathematics Education, 11*, 143–167.

Oakes, J. (2005). *Keeping track: How schools structure inequality* (2nd ed.). New Haven, CT, & London: Yale University Books.

Ogawa, M. (1995). Science education in a multi-science perspective. *Science Education, 79*, 583–593.

Pang, V., Han, P., & Pang, J. (2011). Asian American and Pacific Islander students equity and the achievement gap. *Educational Researcher, 40*(8), 378–389.

Reveles, J., & Brown, B. (2008). Discursive identity and science teaching: Teachers emphasizing student identity in science instruction. *Science Education, 92*(5), 1015–1041.

Richards, J., & Scott, M. (2009). *Aboriginal education: Strengthening the foundations*. Ottawa, ON: Canadian Policy Research Networks.

Rogers, C. A., & Jaime, A. M. (2010). Listening to the community: Guidance from Native community members for emerging culturally responsive educators. *Equity and Excellence in Education, 43*(2), 188–201.

Roth, W.-M. (Ed.). (2009). *Science education from people for people: Taking a stand(point)*. New York: Routledge.

Roth, W.-M., & Tobin, K. (Eds.). (2007). *Science, learning, identity: Sociocultural and cultural historical perspectives*. Rotterdam, the Netherlands: Sense Publishers.

Schech, S., & Haggis, J. (2000). *Culture and development: A critical introduction*. Oxford: Blackwell Publications.

Seiler, G. (2013). New metaphors about culture: Implications for research in science teacher preparation. *Journal of Research in Science Teaching, 50*(1), 104–121.

Sleeter, C. E. (2012). Confronting the marginalization of culturally responsive pedagogy. *Urban Education, 47*(3), 562–584.

Smith, G. A. (2007). Place-based education: Breaking through the constraining regularities of public school. *Environmental Education Research, 13*(2), 189–207.

Solano-Flores, G., & Nelson-Barber, S. (2001). On the cultural validity of science assessments. *Journal of Research in Science Teaching, 38*(5), 553–573.

Stanley, W. B., & Brickhouse, N. W. (1994). Multiculturalism, universalism, and science education. *Science Education, 78*(4), 387–398.

Stewart, G. M. (2010). *Good science? The growing gap between power and education*. Rotterdam, the Netherlands: Sense Publishers.

Stewart, G. M. (2012). Achievements, orthodoxies and science in Kaupapa Māori schooling. *New Zealand Journal of Educational Studies, 47*(2), 51–63.

Sutherland, D., & Henning, D. (2009). Ininiwi-Kiskānītamowin: A framework for long-term science education. *Canadian Journal of Science, Mathematics and Technology Education, 9*(3), 173–190.

Taylor, P. E. (2006a). Toward culturally inclusive science classrooms. *Cultural Studies of Science Education, 1*, 189–195.

Taylor, P. E. (2006b). Cultural hybridity and third space science classrooms. *Cultural Studies of Science Education, 1*, 201–208.

Tobin, K. G. (2008). Contributing to the conversation in science education. *Cultural Studies in Science Education, 3*, 535–540.

Van Eijick, M., & Roth, W. M. (2007). Keeping the local local: Recalibrating the status of science and traditional ecological knowledge (TEK) in science education. *Science Education, 6*, 926–947.

Villegas, A. M., & Lucas, T. (2002). *Educating culturally responsive teachers: A coherent approach*. Albany: SUNY Press.

Wallace, C. S. (2004). Framing new research in science literacy and language use: Authenticity, multiple discourses, and the "third space." *Science Education, 88*, 901–914.

Wallace, T., & Brand, B. R. (2012). Using critical race theory to analyze science teachers' culturally responsive practices. *Cultural Studies of Science Education, 7*(2), 341–374.

Warren, B., Ballenger, C., Ogonowski, M., Rosebery, A., & Hudicourt-Barnes, J. (2001). Rethinking diversity in learning science: The logic of everyday sense-making. *Journal of Research in Science Teaching, 38*, 1–24.

Webber, M., McKinley, E., & Hattie, J. (2013). The importance of race and ethnicity: An exploration of New Zealand Pākehā, Māori, Samoan and Chinese adolescent identity. *New Zealand Journal of Psychology, 42*(1), 43–54.

Wolcott, H. F. (1991). Propriospect and the acquisition of culture. *Anthropology and Education Quarterly, 22*, 251–273.

Woods, A., Dooley, K., Luke, A., & Exley, B. (2014). School leadership, literacy and social justice: The place of local school curriculum planning and reform. In I. Bogotch & C. Shields (Eds.), *International Handbook of Educational Leadership and Social (In)Justice* (pp. 509–520). New York: Springer.

Young, E. (2010). Challenges to conceptualizing and actualizing culturally relevant pedagogy: How viable is the theory in classroom practice? *Journal of Teacher Education, 61*(3), 248–260.

Zembylas, M., & Avraamidou, L. (2008). Postcolonial foldings of space and identity in science education: Limits, transformations, prospects. *Cultural Studies of Science Education, 3*, 977–998.

Section IV

Science Teaching

Section Editor: Jan H. van Driel

16

General Instructional Methods and Strategies

David F. Treagust and Chi-Yan Tsui

Science teachers use a multiplicity of instructional methods and strategies when teaching science classes in K–12 schools and tertiary institutions. These strategies range from primarily didactic or teacher-centered to those that are primarily student-centered or learner-centered. This situation remains unchanged in the digital age when computer and network technologies have become ubiquitous; however, this simplistic dichotomy of student- or teacher-centeredness has become somewhat blurred and has taken on new meanings. Since the previous publication of this chapter (Treagust, 2007), there have been many changes in science, human societies, and science education, resulting in a new crisis in science and science education in the Western or developed countries (e.g., Gluckman, 2011; Hilton, 2010; McKinsey & Company, 2012; Sjøberg & Schreiner, 2010; Tytler, 2007). For example, the crisis in Australia was fourfold as reviewed by Tytler in 2007:

> There is the shortage of skilled science professionals in the workplace in Australia and the shift in momentum of science-based development to developing countries, considerable evidence of student disenchantment with school science in the middle years, and a growing concern with a current and looming shortage of qualified teachers of science.
>
> (p. ix)

These changes have necessitated a major revision of the original chapter in the previous *Handbook*. Since the 1980s, scientists and science educators in the UK and the United States have called for better public understanding of science and reforms in school science to promote scientific literacy or science for all students based on five major arguments—economic, utilitarian, democratic, cultural, and moral (Driver, Leach, Millar, & Scott, 1996)—which have since significantly impacted the directions of science education in other Western or developed countries. For example, these arguments or their variants for learning school science are adopted by Australian and New Zealand science educators in arguing for improving school science education for all students with different interests and career aspirations (Gluckman, 2011; Tytler, 2007). Moreover, U.S. science educators and other experts have worked together to explore the intersections of science education and 21st-century skills in order to improve school science teaching and learning for skills required for employment in the contemporary world (Hilton, 2010). We believe that these five arguments for scientific literacy to promote public understanding of science continue to impact what and how to teach science in the 21st century in ways to make school science more relevant to students and thus increase their interest and engagement in learning science. In particular, from a global perspective, we believe that the democratic argument for science education is becoming increasingly more important in empowering citizens in many developing countries for improving democracy and social justice (e.g., Young, 2008).

Indeed, the last few decades have seen more public concern for emerging socioscientific issues around the world such as sustainable forests, gene technology, and pollution problems (e.g., Robottom, 2012; Tytler, 2007). The cause of action against these socioscientific issues is often based on citizens' understanding of the science and technology behind these issues—for example, the action of environmental groups in China (Shapiro, 2012). This participatory democracy has both currency and relevancy for today's students, many of whom are concerned about equity and social justice, and therefore, the democratic argument can be a motivator for their learning of science. Moreover, students' knowledge of science can empower them to participate in discussion and debate or make informed decisions associated with issues that affect their lives (Venville & Dawson, 2010).

As in the original chapter of this *Handbook* (Treagust, 2007), instructional methods and strategies in this new chapter are organized in terms of the amount of direct control teachers have over their implementation. In rewriting and updating this chapter, our consideration was to organize the review of the latest relevant literature so the chapter can provide readers with a general picture of pedagogical research in science education. This chapter is intended to be a continuum of the original chapter and not a repetition of the content thereof. At the same time, readers can locate more information about the latest research relevant to this review by the cited references. We intend to frame the discussion as far as possible in international contexts in line with the latest trend of science education toward globalization (e.g., Chiu & Duit, 2011). However, our limited knowledge of the literature about the status of science education in non–English-speaking countries has constrained our review in this direction.

Teaching and learning in this digital age are often assumed to be more student-centered when digital technologies become more commonly available and affordable to learners in their schools and homes. Research has shown that inquiry-based teaching approaches—an umbrella term for a repertoire of methods and strategies with more emphasis on student-centeredness than teacher-centeredness—are found to be most useful in teaching science in schools (see a review in Tytler, 2007).

The term "teachers" in the context of control of learning can now be extended to mean curriculum designers, educational courseware or games designers, and other educationalists involved in implementing learning programs in different educational settings. This chapter reviews the literature with a focus on five of the original six general instructional methods and strategies as in the original chapter (Treagust, 2007) with slightly different headings that reflect the recent changes in these topics—demonstrations, explanations, questioning, scientific reasoning, and representational learning. These five topics are interconnected and overlap with one another in ways that show the complexity of teaching science at all levels of education. The increasingly important impact of digital technologies and online learning environments is obvious in many of the cited examples of research on teaching science. The review of the topic "group learning and cooperative leaning" in the original chapter is not included in this chapter; however, these forms of student-centered learning continue to play important roles in science education in the 21st century.

Four theoretical considerations given in the original chapter (Treagust, 2007) continue to have major but slightly different influences on instructional methods and strategies used in science classes in the 21st century. The first theoretical consideration is the acknowledgment that learners construct their own individual understanding and that this can be promoted by specially designed instruction. In recent years, sociocultural and discursive views have become increasingly popular in science education (e.g., Jaipal, 2010; Marquez, Izquierdo, & Espinet, 2006; Tytler, Symington, Darby, Malcolm, & Kirkwood, 2011). However, we caution that science teachers should not over-emphasize contextualization and students' participation in classroom learning to the extent that their acquisition of the content of science is being discounted. According to Sfard's (1998) two metaphors of learning, both participation in the sociocultural milieu of the classroom and individual construction of knowledge are important. Indeed, there have been recent discussions and debates among educational psychologists as to whether "minimally guided instruction" is "less effective than direct-guided instruction for science learning" (Duschl & Hamilton, 2010, p. 81). Accordingly, some researchers argue for using instruction based on authentic learning situated within social and collaborative contexts to parallel the contexts within which scientific knowledge is developed and modified. On the other hand, others argue for using direct-guided approaches to support the efficiency of information search and retrieval because of the nature of human cognitive architecture (i.e., huge long-term memory and limited working memory capacities).

The second theoretical consideration is that the canonical content of the science to be learned in school is acknowledged as a problematic issue (e.g., Fensham, 2001; Fensham, Gunstone, & White, 1994). Science educators argued that student understanding of science should go beyond learning of science content and should also be about science itself or nature of science, as well as the relationship between science and society (e.g., Driver et al., 1996; Aikenhead, 2006). There has also been a debate on what canonical science content should be included to increase student interest and engagement for all students (i.e., scientific literacy) and, at the same time, cater for those in the important minority who aspire to become scientists (Aikenhead, 2006; Fensham, 2009; Tytler, 2007).

The third theoretical consideration that pervades the instructional methods and strategies discussed in this new chapter continues to be the promise that teaching of science aims at enhancing student metacognition, which in turn might lead to corresponding improvements in cognitive learning for conceptual understanding of science (e.g., Hennessey, 2003; Thomas, 2012; Zohar & Dori, 2012). Strategies shown in previous research to be of value in developing metacognitive capabilities (e.g., concept maps, POEs, etc.) are still useful and are often technology enhanced in today's teaching and learning of science. As shown by the review in this chapter, the teaching of science is now more focused on learning how to learn science or develop metacognitive skills that regulate the cognitive process in learning science rather than just learning science (e.g., Gluckman, 2011; National Research Council, 2007; Zohar & Dori, 2012).

The fourth theoretical consideration is the realization that the teaching methods and strategies reviewed in this chapter are based on evidence from a plethora of previous studies or are evidence based. Science teachers can try out these methods and strategies in the form of action research to further their teaching as they examine, implement, and evaluate their teaching using the various analytical frameworks designed by researchers. The best practice in science education at all levels is evidence-based or theoretically informed methods and strategies. Moreover, best practice requires that these strategies be aligned with the intended objectives and assessment methods based on clearly designed rubrics that explicitly state the intended learning outcomes. The assessment results can then be used for further improvement of the practice (e.g., Bodzin & Beerer, 2003; Braaten & Windschitl, 2011; Chin, 2006; Luft, 1999).

Each section that follows starts with the key theoretical and empirical issues of learning identified in the literature that underpin each type of instructional method or approach. This is then followed by some examples of research to illustrate the effectiveness or otherwise of each instructional method or approach. This short review introduces the latest scenarios of general instructional methods and strategies in science education. Further, the issues from existing research are intended to help readers to re-evaluate the status of these methods and strategies, to ask new questions, and to spark new directions in research and practice.

Demonstrations

Demonstrations in teaching science are a less expensive or a safer way of providing students with experiences of laboratory experimental work, which, for more than a century, has played a central and distinctive role in teaching school science in which students benefit from the laboratory activities (e.g., Fensham, 1990; Hofstein & Lunetta, 2004; White, 1996). Although the use of demonstrations in teaching science may not serve all the main goals of laboratory work such as learning skills and concepts, developing cognitive abilities, and understanding nature of science and attitudes, it does serve to motivate students' learning by increasing their interest and engagement in the science classroom from high schools to universities (e.g., Lazarowitz & Tamir, 1994; Milne & Otieno, 2007; Schmidt, Bohn, Rasmussen, & Sutherland, 2012; White, 1996). With the availability of digital technologies in schools, classroom teachers and university professors/instructors are increasingly using interactive computer activities or video clips from the Internet as part of their demonstrations in teaching science (e.g., Ai-Lim Lee, Wong, & Fung, 2010; Chang, Chen, Lin, & Sung, 2008; Chittleborough, Mocerino, & Treagust, 2007; Johnson, Trout, Brekke, & Luedecke, 2004).

Traditionally presented laboratory or classroom demonstrations can provide colorful, surprising, or dramatic effects, such as burning a piece of magnesium ribbon before a junior class of science, which increases their interest and engagement by motivating them to learn. However, such demonstrations may not necessarily help students develop an understanding of the particular concept being demonstrated as intended by the teacher because the students lack the necessary theoretical background, pay attention only to the surface features, or fail

to piece together what they observe for understanding. Also, they have no opportunities to test their ideas and to ask their teacher questions during passive demonstrations or for other reasons (e.g., Crouch, Fagen, Callan, & Mazur, 2004; Mancuso, 2010; Roth, McRobbie, Lucas, & Boutonné, 1997). Over the years, much effort has been made to design better classroom or laboratory demonstrations to address these shortcomings in various science disciplines such as physics (e.g., Crouch et al., 2004), biology (e.g., Kelley, 2010), chemistry (e.g., Keeratichamroen, Dechsri, Panijpan, & Ruenwongsa, 2010), and food science (e.g., Schmidt et al., 2012). One exemplar is the demonstrations used in the United States for fostering teaching in the Science, Technology, Engineering and Mathematics (STEM) Education Initiative (Schmidt et al., 2012). This set of food science demonstrations greatly increased interest and engagement of students from elementary through university classrooms. Accordingly, these food demonstrations are successful in engaging students in their learning because they are familiar to the students, relevant to public awareness about food and health, and interdisciplinary (chemistry, microbiology, engineering and so on). They also are appealing in a sensory way because students can eat the food after the demonstrations.

To make the passive, traditionally presented classroom or laboratory demonstrations more cognitively engaging, researchers developed predict-observe-explain activities (POEs; Gunstone, 1995; White & Gunstone, 1992) in the 1980s, which can be a very useful way to juxtapose demonstrations with explanations (e.g., Kearney, Treagust, Yeo, & Zadnik, 2001; Liew & Treagust, 1995). Thirty years on, the latest literature shows that POEs or their modified forms are still powerful and cognitively engaging for conceptual change learning across different levels of education and subject areas and are often technology based (e.g., Bonello & Scaife, 2009; Costu, Ayas, & Niaz, 2010; Ruiz-Primo, Li, Tsai, & Schneider, 2010). In particular, when using POEs in teaching based on demonstrations, teachers can include discrepant events (e.g., a floating bowling ball) that are very powerful ways to engage students, stimulate their interest, motivate them to challenge their own misconceptions, and therefore promote understanding and higher-order thinking skills (e.g., Gonzalez-Spada, Birriel, & Birriel, 2010; Herrington & Scott, 2011).

Among the different demonstrations, research has shown that computer-based simulations are useful cognitive tools for conceptual learning (e.g., Horwitz, 2013; Liu, Tsui, & Treagust, 2013; Riopel, Potvin, & Vázquez-Abad, 2009). Computer-based simulations enable students to experience by visualizing scientific phenomena such as plate tectonic drift, biological evolution, or molecular structure and reactivity that are all beyond human experiential limits (Kozma & Russell, 1997). For example, evolution by natural selection can be taught via computer-based simulation as in Horwitz's (2013) study on teaching 10-year-old students in the United States. Horwitz used an interactive computer game, *Evolution Readiness*, that features a virtual greenhouse, a virtual field, and virtual ecosystems with which students can be guided to explore the process of evolution of organisms by natural selection. Another example is Chang and colleagues' (2008) simulation-based teaching about optical lenses in secondary school physics in Taiwan. The computer simulation system features five categories of learning support for students: "(1) providing background knowledge; (2) helping learners to formulate experiment prompting; (3) helping learners to conduct experiments; (4) helping learners to interpret data; and (5) helping learners to regulate their learning process" (Liu et al., 2013, p. 276). In both studies, extensive learning supports of various kinds are provided in the computer-based learning environments, and learning outcomes are positive and encouraging.

Explanations

Teaching for understanding in science classrooms always involves both descriptions and explanations of scientific phenomena: Descriptions provide pieces of information, not necessarily related, whereas explanations connect between and among pieces of information (Horwood, 1988). Students often view teacher explanations as teaching that goes beyond what can be observed "either through establishing a causal link between a cause and an outcome or by describing an empirically derived generalization" (Driver et al., 1996, p. 139). Whereas science explanations are theory and evidence driven, use the correct scientific terms, and include analogical models, teacher explanations differ in rigor, length, and detail in varying degrees in explaining "how" and "why" (Treagust & Harrison, 2000). Some science educators recently debated whether scientific explanations differ from scientific arguments (Berland & McNeill, 2012; Osborne & Patterson, 2011, 2012). Moreover, teacher explanations are sometimes open ended, including human agency and raising new related questions in addition to answering the previous questions. In the late 1990s, Treagust and his colleagues (e.g., Treagust, Chittleborough, & Mamiala, 2003; Treagust & Harrison, 2000) highlighted the importance of teachers' effective explanations in the science classroom and how expert teachers can tailor their classroom explanations to effectively communicate and share the knowledge of scientists with students of varying abilities and at different levels. A review of the literature indicates that many studies have since been conducted in the area of explanations in science classrooms around the world (e.g., Besson, 2010; Braaten & Windschitl, 2011; Geelan, 2012; Treagust et al., 2003; Zacharia, 2005). Generally, teacher explanations use analogy, anthropomorphism, and teleology but avoid using tautological explanations (Geelan, 2012). Apart from using teacher explanations, teachers can also encourage students to generate explanations in collaboration with their peers or with their teacher during classroom discussions (e.g., Braaten &

Windschitl, 2011; Dawes, 2004; Hamza & Wickman, 2009; Ruiz-Primo et al., 2010). It is noteworthy that students have difficulties learning those causal explanations, very common in science classroom teaching, that involve the cause-effect relationships in phenomena. As pointed out by Besson (2010), physics teachers "focus on equilibrium or steady state situations, using formal explanations and functional relationships between physical quantities at a given instant," whereas physics students require causal explanations of phenomena using "causal reasoning based on a logical and chronological linear sequence of one cause-one effect chains" (p. 252). We revisit this later in the section on reasoning.

On analyzing the exemplary explanations by the late Richard Feynman, Treagust and Harrison (2000) suggested an explanatory framework for guiding teachers to construct effective explanations in educational settings that take into account balanced science content, appropriate educational context, student factors, and teacher factors for "transforming scientific knowledge into student-friendly explanations," which is "surprisingly complex because effective explanations need to be customized for each audience" (p. 1167). Their work called for more research on teachers' pedagogical content knowledge (PCK; Shulman, 1987), which has since made a significant impact on how classroom explanations could be better constructed and used in instruction. For example, Braaten and Windschitl (2011) further developed these ideas about developing explanations from theory to practice in U.S. schools. Accordingly, three common uses of explanations in science education are (1) explanation as explication, (2) explanation as causation, and (3) explanation as justification. Braaten and Windschitl also proposed an explanatory tool for advancing science teachers' and students' classroom explanations and moving them from "what" to "how" and to "why" in explaining the natural phenomena of science.

In today's classroom, science teachers are increasingly using verbal or written language alongside visualizations in their classroom explanations (e.g., Geelan, 2012). Given that verbal language is still a major vehicle for explanations in the classroom, what Ogborn, Kress, Martin, and McGillicuddy (1996) identified—regarding the central role of using language in classroom explanations for understanding science—remains useful for today's science teachers. Osborne and colleagues considered classroom explanations of science as analogous to stories and summarized four roles of language in meaning making while explaining science in the classroom: (1) creating differences, (2) constructing entities, (3) transforming knowledge, and (4) putting meaning into matter (see Treagust, 2007). Their work on classroom explanations is consistent with research on instruction using language and discursive practices (e.g., Halliday & Martin, 1993; Lemke, 1990), as well as Vygotskian sociocultural perspectives in science classrooms (e.g., Hodson & Hodson, 1998; Howe, 1996; Jones, Rua, & Carter, 1998; Panofsky, John-Steiner, &

Blackwell, 1990). Indeed, in their classroom explanations, science teachers are also using gestures, actions, simulations, symbols, physical models, and so on, which we consider as external representations, as well as using digital technologies (e.g., Gilbert & Treagust, 2009; Treagust & Tsui, 2013). Explanations are related to other instructional methods and strategies discussed in this chapter.

As pointed out by some researchers (e.g., Braaten & Windschitl, 2011; Geelan, 2012), more research on using explanations in science instruction needs to be conducted to further improve classroom learning in the 21st century when explanations in science become an important part of the science curriculum around the world. For example, many UK schools are using scientific explanations and ideas about science (nature of science) as two major parts of the school science curriculum (Millar, 2006, 2011; Ratcliffe & Millar, 2009). Furthermore, there seems to be a dearth of studies on teacher explanations in the area of biology education. Some recent examples in this area can be found in Treagust and Tsui (2013).

Questioning

The latest literature about teacher questioning (e.g., Chin, 2006, 2007; Chin & Osborne, 2008, 2010a; Harris & Williams, 2007; Levy Nahum, Ben-Chaim, Azaiza, Herskovitz, & Zoller, 2010) indicates that questioning continues to play a central role in students' meaningful and inquiry-based learning in today's science classrooms. Some recent studies (e.g., Chin & Osborne, 2010a; Zoller & Levy Nahum, 2012) also show that the discursive and sociocultural instructional practices such as wait time (Slavin, 2009), dialogic patterns (e.g., Lemke, 1990), and checking student understanding in classroom discourse (e.g., Mortimer & Scott, 2000) are still relevant in the science classroom in the 21st century.

Over the past decades, research has indicated that questioning during classroom teaching is often unproductive without students thinking before answering or being given sufficient wait time (Slavin, 2009), which is important in instruction when teachers pursue higher-cognitive-level learning in their students (e.g., Chin, 2006; Tobin, 1987). Classroom discourse is shaped by the way teachers use questioning methods and strategies. For better meaning making, questioning has to go beyond the triadic dialogue initiation-response-evaluation (IRE) or initiation-response-and-feedback (IRF) pattern in which the teacher asks questions, calls on students to answer them, and then evaluates and comments on their answers. In analyzing such discourse, Lemke (1990) suggested more useful classroom dialogues other than the traditional triadic dialogue—student-questioning dialogue, teacher–student duolog, teacher–student debate, true dialogue, and cross-discussion. Some 20 years later, the dominant discursive patterns in most of today's science classrooms still appear to be more or less like the IRE or IRF patterns in which students are conditioned to provide single correct answers

to teachers' or textbooks' questions (e.g., Chin & Osborne, 2008; Geelan, 2012; Zoller & Levy Nahum, 2012).

Teachers asking questions that stimulate higher-level thinking by students has been shown to be significant in improving the quality of classroom discourse (e.g., Mercer & Littleton, 2007). Further, teachers' questioning needs to be flexible in accommodating students' contributions and responses in the classroom discourse (e.g., Chin, 2006; Mortimer & Scott, 2000). From Vygotskian and neo-Vygotskian (Vygotsky, 1978; Wertsch, 1991) sociocultural perspectives, learning that involves higher mental functioning in an individual first develops on the social or intermental plane and then becomes internalized on the intramental plane as personal knowledge of science. Classroom talk can, therefore, mediate the development of meanings and understandings between teachers and students and individuals' learning of science concepts (Mortimer & Scott, 2000). Such mediation can also be interpreted in terms of Vygotsky's notion of "verbal thought" or "verbal thinking" (Stierer & Maybin, 1993, pp. 47–48) that concept formation of an individual depends on using verbal language as a functional tool for internalizing the thinking concerned. Mortimer and Scott (2000) argued that a teacher's ability to manage classroom discourse that can support students' development of knowledge and meaning making is part of the teacher's "pedagogical subject expertise, which frequently passes unnoticed in analyzing teaching practice" (Shulman, 1986, p. 141). They expanded upon the triadic dialogic pattern to a form of teacher intervention as he or she regulates and guides the classroom discourse and developed the "'flow of discourse' analytical framework" (p. 126) for analyzing classroom talk so as to improve classroom teaching.

Among recent studies, Christine Chin's (Chin, 2006; Chin & Osborne, 2008, 2010a) research on questioning-based classroom discourse best illustrates the key role of questioning in the science classroom for more meaningful constructivist-based and inquiry-based classroom learning of science. Building on Mortimer and Scott's (2000) framework, Chin (2006) developed a questioning-based discourse analytical framework by further expanding the classical IRF discursive pattern to discursive moves (I-, R- or F-move). While responding (R-move) to their teacher's questions (I-move), students engage in cognitive processes of learning the intended scientific content of a lesson through the processes of "hypothesizing, recalling, observing, evaluating, explaining, deducing, and predicting" (Chin, 2006, p. 1325). Chin's analytical framework proposed four types of teachers' useful feedback such that their F-move is closely aligned to the I-move: (1) affirming and reinforcing correct responses followed by further exposition and direct instruction; (2) accepting correct responses followed by further questioning and extending the student's conceptual thought; (3) explicitly correcting incorrect responses followed by direction instruction; and (4) evaluating or neutrally commenting on incorrect response followed by further questioning to challenge the student. It is important for the teacher to shift the questioning-based classroom teaching from an *authoritative discourse* to a *dialogic discourse* (Scott, 1998) through discursive moves and turns of utterances (e.g., teachers' or students' question, answer, statement, or comment; Chin, 2007; Mortimer & Scott, 2000; Scott, 1998). Both discourses can be pedagogically useful for classroom learning, as Chin (2006) argued, "(w)hile dialogic discourse allows students to argue and justify their ideas, the authoritative discourse also has its place in the classroom, particularly when the already constructed shared knowledge needs to be emphasized" (p. 1317).

In exploring how to improve school science curriculum by including the teaching of the ideas of science or nature of science, Osborne, Collins, Ratcliffe, Millar, and Duschl (2003) found that questioning is one of nine major themes that should be taught in schools to allow students to test their understanding of science in a cyclic process of questioning and seeking answers and that this way of learning can be extended to other subject areas. At the secondary level, as Chin and Osborne (2008) put it, students posing their own questions in the classroom is "a first step towards filling their knowledge gaps and resolving puzzlements . . . to articulate their current understanding of a topic, to make connections with other ideas, and also to become aware of what they do or do not know" (p. 2). In higher education, ongoing reforms have been taking place to move from teacher-centered teaching to student-centered teaching in which students' questioning ability is becoming fundamental to develop critical reasoning, and the process of scientific enquiry (e.g., Pedrosa-de-Jesus, da Silva Lopes, Moreira, & Watts, 2012; Seker & Komur, 2008; Shinohara, 2006). In reality, the recent literature shows that in the contemporary science classroom, teachers seldom provide opportunities for students to ask questions, and when they do ask, their questions are mostly factual, procedural, or closed ended, not useful for conceptual learning (Chin & Osborne, 2008). It is crucial that teachers encourage students to ask good thinking questions that are a potential resource for teaching and learning science. Student questioning in the science classroom helps students in their knowledge construction, discussion and debate, self-evaluation/monitoring of understanding, and development of interest and motivation, as well as argumentation (Chin & Osborne, 2008, 2010b). Accordingly, teachers can also use student-generated questions for diagnosing students' understanding, evaluating their higher-order thinking, stimulating further inquiry of the topic being taught via investigations or projects for informing future teaching, and developing reflective classroom practice. Therefore, as Chin and Osborne's (2008) literature review showed, teachers can explicitly teach students questioning skills to improve their performance in science-related tasks (e.g., reading science texts, formulating research questions for projects, learning in cooperative groups, and asking higher-level questions).

Overall, as a general instructional strategy, questioning in classroom teaching continues to play a very important role in determining the quality of discourse in both face-to-face classroom teaching as well as in increasingly common computer and network learning environments from K–12 to higher education (e.g., Almeida & de Souza, 2010; Angeli & Valanides, 2008; Harris & Williams, 2007; Pedrosa-de-Jesus et al., 2012). On reviewing recent research, Pedrosa-de-Jesus and colleagues (2012) argued that university professors' questioning competences should become a central focus of current reforms in higher education in the 21st century. Questioning as an instructional strategy may now take on new meanings in in-class or out-of-class learning in which questioning and responding to questions are much more interactive because of digital technologies such as online environments (e.g., Angeli & Valanides, 2008). Much work is needed for advancing the research on instruction based on questioning as a useful classroom pedagogy in the digital age.

Scientific Reasoning

In this section, we focus our review on instruction based on scientific reasoning, but the review also is related to other sections on explanations, questioning, and representational learning in this chapter. Although somewhat synonymous to thinking and problem solving, reasoning per se refers to directed cognitive processes of working on some tasks that involve deduction and induction (Mayer & Wittrock, 2012). To educational psychologists, deductive reasoning is to draw specific, logically valid conclusions from evidence going from the general to the specific, whereas inductive reasoning is to draw reasonable general conclusions from evidence of specific facts or observations going from the specific to the general (Sternberg & Williams, 2002). Not only is scientific reasoning fundamental to problem solving and discovery in scientific research, it is also useful beyond the scientific context such as decision making and general problem solving in real-life situations (Moore & Rubbo, 2012). Reasoning skills and argumentative skills are also key elements of scientific literacy for all students and are usually displayed in the social context of the classroom (Simon, Erduran, & Osborne, 2006).

Since the 1970s, science educators (e.g., Karplus, 1977; Lavoie, 1999; Lawson, 2000) have called for the use of instructional practices that emphasize reasoning in school science, and the learning cycle approach was one important way of teaching reasoning. The original learning cycle was first developed by Atkin and Karplus (1962) for teaching scientific reasoning from Piagetian perspectives (Karplus, 1977). The learning cycle is an instructional model based on an inquiry-based learning that promotes critical thinking, active learning, and meaningful learning (Marek, Laubach, & Pedersen, 2003). It consists of three basic phases: (1) the *exploration* phase that provides students with the experience to explore objects and events (e.g., by doing experiments) under the guidance and support of the teacher; (2) the *concept development* phase in which the students and/or teacher develop the concept from the data through classroom discussions involving explanations and questioning that physically and mentally engage students in developing the concept; and (3) the *conceptual expansion* phase in which the student is given the opportunities (e.g., additional experiments or field studies) to explore the usefulness and application of the concept. In a study on students' learning of reasoning with the learning cycle model, Musheno and Lawson (1999) classified students into three types of reasoners of increasing sophistication: empirical-inductive reasoners, transitional reasoners, and hypothetico-deductive reasoners. Lawson, Oehrtman, and Jensen (2008) argued that hypothetico-deductive reasoning in the form of "If/and/then/therefore pattern" (p. 405) plays an important role in scientific practices that involves hypotheses, planned tests, predictions, results, and conclusions; and therefore, hypothetico-deductive reasoning is important for student understanding of nature of science.

Over the past decades, science teachers have been using research-based, coordinated, and coherent sequencing of lessons, particularly learning cycles among other instructional models, to engender students' development of scientific reasoning and problem solving in science education (Bybee, 2009). As reported by Bybee, the Biological Science Curriculum Study (BSCS) 5E learning cycle—developed and extended from Atkin and Karplus's (1962) original learning cycle—has been commonplace in science instruction. Since the late 1980s, the 5E instructional model has been used in the development of new curricular materials and professional development experiences (Bybee, 2009). The improved learning cycle instructional model, commonly referred to as the BSCS 5Es, or simply the 5Es, consists of the five phases instead of three: engagement, exploration, explanation, elaboration, and evaluation, which were explained by Bybee as follows:

> Each phase has a specific function and contributes to the teacher's coherent instruction and to the learners' formulation of a better understanding of scientific and technological knowledge, attitudes, and skills. The model frames a sequence and organization of programs, units, and lessons. Once internalized, it also can inform the many instantaneous decisions that science teachers must make in classroom situations.
>
> (p. 2)

According to Bybee (2009), the 5Es learning cycle instructional methods and strategies have been extensively used at all level of science education. Some recent examples using the 5E method in science education include the teaching of the concept of osmosis (Carlsen & Marek, 2010); health education for preventing HIV/AIDS (Basta & Barman, 2008); promoting students' learning of genetics (Dogru-Atay & Tekkaya, 2008); learning about Newton's first law of motion (McCarthy, 2005); and various professional development programs for science teachers (e.g., Ates, 2005; Bell & Odom, 2012; Tural, Akdeniz, & Alev, 2010). In Australia, the 5Es have been used extensively in a program called Primary Connections to increase the quality of science teaching in primary classrooms. Research has demonstrated that the program improves teachers' confidence, self-efficacy, and practice, as well as the status of science within schools (Hackling, 2006).

Traditional textbook or didactic approaches to science learning provide information and challenge students to think deductively by reasoning from cause to effect, which contrasts with the way that many scientists, such as geneticists, inductively reason and learn in their research work from effect to cause (Horwitz & Christie, 2000). Interactive computer-based activities designed to support students' learning of genetics, such as *BioLogica* (Concord Consortium, 2001), have been found to promote student scientific reasoning (Tsui & Treagust, 2003, 2013). As explained by Buckley and Quellmatz (2013), the tasks in *BioLogica* activities required reasoning from cause to effect (i.e., prediction), from effect to cause (i.e., explanation), and reasoning in both directions. These are in fact predict-observe-explain activities (POEs) we discuss in the section on explanations. In Tsui and Treagust's (2013) case studies, the students from both Perth and Hong Kong found it more difficult to reason from effect to cause (i.e., explanation) than from cause to effect (i.e., prediction) when reasoning with Mendelian genetics in their investigations using *BioLogica*. These findings have implications for improving the teaching of scientific reasoning.

Scientific reasoning has now become one of the most important cornerstones of science education after several decades of reforms (e.g., American Association for the Advancement of Science, 1999; National Research Council, 2007; Tytler, 2007). Whereas some science educators advocate the explicit teaching of scientific reasoning to students so they can understand how scientists think and reason, others argue that scientific reasoning is also useful beyond the scientific contexts for solving problems and making effective decisions in real-life situations (e.g., Moore & Rubbo, 2012). However, scientific reasoning within the canonical content of science is often beyond the capabilities of most schoolchildren, who lack the domain-specific knowledge. For example, Millar (2011) argued that children who lack the domain-specific knowledge should be taught reasoning in a learning progression through three types of reasoning based on phenomena, relationships, and models, as suggested by Driver and colleagues (1996):

> a progression in children's thinking from phenomenon-based reasoning (largely descriptive), to relationship-based reasoning (using the idea of a variable and focusing on interactions between observable variables), to model-based reasoning (in which a model or theory is held in mind as distinct from the observables it is being used to explain).
>
> (Millar, 2011, p. 181)

We believe that Driver and colleagues' three-stage learning progression is still relevant in the 21st century when scientific literacy becomes the major purpose of teaching school science. As we discuss elsewhere in this chapter, model-based reasoning is central to scientific practices. Notwithstanding the huge number of learning cycle methods being used for teaching reasoning at all educational levels, many of these methods may not match the lessons' intellectual demands with students' reasoning skills and their declarative knowledge (Lawson, 2010). For example, as Lawson pointed out, some teachers use descriptive learning cycles—which require students to explore nature and simply identify patterns and/or make observations without generating possible explanations—but not the more useful hypothesis-driven and enquiry-based learning cycles in which students can generate and test their hypotheses using their reasoning skills. More teacher education is needed in this area.

As digital technology continues to further revolutionize how teachers teach and how students learn scientific reasoning, there has been an explosive increase in the use of computer and network technologies in instruction based on the 5Es cycle approach (e.g., Liu, Peng, Wu, & Lin, 2009; Turkmen, 2006). The teaching of scientific reasoning in terms of the learning cycle approach continues to be popular at today's universities around the world and predominantly through online learning systems (e.g., Ates, 2005; Moore & Rubbo, 2012; Tural et al., 2010). There has also been a gradual shift from Piagetian stage-based reasoning for individual understandings of the canons of science to sociocultural, socioscientific, or evidence-based reasoning in real-life contexts beyond the canonical science content (e.g., Furberg & Ludvigsen, 2008; Robottom, 2012; Simonneaux & Simonneaux, 2009). Perhaps science teachers should pay attention to Russ, Coffey, Hammer, and Hutchison's (2009) portrayal of scientists: "Scientists do not believe ideas by authority; they believe ideas because of the evidence and arguments that support them" (p. 877). We argue that teaching scientific reasoning based on evidence using real-life contexts related to human affairs can be both motivating and relevant to the needs of modern society—that is, to educate students to become scientifically literate and informed citizens who are able to participate in democratic societies, as well as to inculcate in students the awareness of social justice. Research agendas on these issues associated with teaching scientific reasoning continue to beckon in the 21st century.

Representational Learning

We review a group of instructional methods and strategies based on representations rather than direct experience of a phenomenon for the sake of safety, emotional impact, accessibility, or clarity. According to Ainsworth and Lowe (2012), these representations are "'second-hand' accounts of the phenomenon using one or more specific types of information" (p. 2833). External representations (e.g., text, pictures, gestures, animations, etc.) used in instruction are intended to engender students' understanding through their construction of internal representations or mental models (Johnson-Laird, 1983) of phenomena.

The different external representations used for teaching and learning of science over the past decades have been extensively researched and documented, promising in many ways to improve students' cognitive and affective outcomes despite the associated limitations. From our perspectives, the variety of external representations in the science education literature across a range of content areas fall into the following major categories overlapping with one or more other categories to varying degrees:

(1) *analogies* (e.g., Dagher, 1994; Treagust, Harrison, & Venville, 1998) and *metaphors* (e.g., Aubusson, Harrison, & Ritchie, 2006; Martins & Ogborn, 1997);
(2) *visualization* (e.g., Gilbert, Reiner, & Nakhleh, 2008);
(3) *models and model-based learning* (e.g., Buckley, 2000; Clement & Rae-Mamirez, 2008; Gilbert, 2004; Gilbert & Boulter, 1998);
(4) *multilevel representations* (e.g., Chandrasegaran, Treagust, & Mocerino, 2011; Gilbert & Treagust, 2009);
(5) *multimodal representations* (e.g., Waldrip & Prain, 2012; Waldrip, Prain, & Carolan, 2010); and
(6) *multiple external representations (MERs)*[1] (Ainsworth, 1999; de Jong et al., 1998; Treagust & Tsui, 2013; Tsui & Treagust, 2003).

Analogies and Metaphors

Both analogies and metaphors are linguistic devices used in science and other areas (Gilbert, 2004). An analogy is a process for identifying similarities between different concepts—the familiar concept or the source is called the analog and the unfamiliar one the target (Glynn, 1991). Analogical thinking "requires knowledge to be represented in an explicit form so that systematic comparisons can be made between the source and target" (Holyoak & Thagard, 1995, p. 37). According to Holyoak and Thagard, one of the great historical scientific analogies was the analogy between light and sound first proposed by Christiaan Huygens in 1678 in support of his wave theory of light. The wave theory was eclipsed for more than a century by Newton's particle theory until the early 19th century, when the wave theory was revived by Thomas Young and Augustin Fresnel. Another example was the mapping in Charles Darwin's analogy in 1859 between natural and artificial selection. These scientific analogies have played important roles in discovery, development, evaluation, and exposition in scientific progress in human history (for a list of great scientific analogies, see Holyoak & Thagard, 1995, pp. 186–188).

A metaphor, the second linguistic device, simply means "the temporary assumption that one thing is *another* thing," for example, "the sun is a furnace" (Gilbert, 2004, p. 124) or the beginning verse of Carl Sandberg's poem: "The fog comes on little cat feet . . ." (Holyoak & Thagard, 1995, p. 220). Thus, a metaphor is similar to an analogy, but its source and target are in different domains; and although a metaphor is often a linguistic expression, it is an intelligent way of thinking that can be used for indirect communication to evoke different emotional reactions (e.g., amusement, disgust, love, and other reactions; Holyoak & Thagard, 1995).

Teachers' use of analogies and metaphors, in one or several forms of representation, has been an important line of research into learning of abstract science concepts, reasoning and problem solving, and learning for conceptual change (e.g., Dagher, 1994; Duit, 1991; Harrison & Treagust, 2000a; Zheng, Yang, Garcia, & McCadden, 2008) as well as in instructional strategies to engender interest, motivation, and understanding (e.g., BouJaoude & Tamim, 2008; Glynn, 1991; Harrison & Treagust, 1994; Martins & Ogborn, 1997; Venville & Treagust, 1996). In the new millennium, the use of analogies and metaphors in classroom instruction continues to be popular from K–12 schools to higher education and is often used in tandem with digital technology. Some recent studies include teaching analogical reasoning in classrooms of young children (e.g., Haglund, Jeppsson, & Andersson, 2012; Zheng et al., 2008), the use of metaphors by upper secondary and tertiary students in learning protein functions (e.g., Rundgren, Hirsch, & Tibell, 2009), and the use of analogies in teacher education (e.g., Oliva, Azcarate, & Navarrete, 2007).

Despite their pedagogical values, analogies are "double-edged swords" (Glynn, 1991, p. 227), which, when not used cautiously, may lead to miscomprehension and misdirection. To address teachers' inappropriate use of textbook analogies that were unhelpful for student understanding, Treagust and colleagues (1998) developed a teaching model called FAR—referring to focus, action, and reflection—whereby teachers overtly direct students' attention to the similarities and dissimilarities of the analog and target concepts. The FAR approach is still a useful instructional strategy for explicitly teaching about the "principle of analogy" in the science classroom (Gilbert et al., 2008, p. 21). We discuss these issues further in a later section on models and model-based learning.

Visualizations

Science teachers are increasingly using visual representations (e.g., photos, drawings, graphs, videos etc.), together with PowerPoint and alongside verbal representations in today's classrooms well-equipped with digital technology facilities (e.g., Adams, 2012). In terms of external representations and internal representations (mental models), "visualization" has two meanings (Gilbert et al., 2008): as a process or a verb to understand "the meaning attributed to an internal representation" (p. 2) or as an external representation of an object or a noun—"a visualization is something that is in the public realm" (p. 2).

On the one hand, science educators argue for using visual representations with appropriate pedagogical purposes and at different representational levels (the macro,

submicro, and symbolic) to develop students' visualization skills for learning science (e.g., Gilbert, 2008). On the other hand, cognitive and computational scientists explain that visual representations, such as diagrams, group together relevant information indexed by two-dimensional locations but sentential representations of group relevant information indexed in a single sequence (e.g., Larkin & Simon, 1987; Underwood, 1997). Therefore, learners find it easier to search the data structure in a visual representation, recognize the relevant information, and draw inferences from the target information than they can do in a piece of writing representing the same information.

Recent studies of the various instructional methods using visualization in science education can be found in Gilbert and colleagues (2008), Phillips, Norris, and Macnab (2010), and Treagust and Tsui (2013). It is important for teachers to become critically aware that visual representations, if not appropriately designed and implemented, may result in student difficulties and misconceptions—for example, learning difficulties are usually attributed to the characteristics of learners, representation, pedagogy, and context associated with the visual representations (Eilam, 2013). Science educators should be informed by these research findings in terms of the benefits and costs of using visual representations in designing learning materials and in their instructional practices.

Models and Model-Based Learning

This section overlaps substantially with most of the methods and strategies in the section about representations. Among the diversity in scientific practices, scientists' work invariably involves building and refining models of the world that instantiate powerful scientific ideas and theories—whose subsequent development, changes, and revisions over time through model-based reasoning have resulted in the ever-progressing advances in science and technology in human history (Lehrer & Schauble, 2006). A model in science can be viewed as "a representation of a phenomenon initially produced for a specific purpose" (Gilbert, Boulter, & Elmer, 2000, p. 11). In science education, model-based learning is generally about the process of formation and subsequent development of learners' mental models of scientific phenomena (Buckley, 2000). A mental model (an internal representation of a real or fictional state of a scientific phenomenon) is usually built on the spot in response to specific learning situations—for which the learner has no available schemas to fit the situation—in order to deeply understand and reason about that phenomenon (Bucciarelli & Cutica, 2012; Buckley, 2012a). Accordingly, the learner's mental models are subsequently evaluated, revised, or rejected; and when such models are deemed useful by the learner, they become routinized or permanent through cognitive or physical practice as schemas for future learning situations.

Numerous typologies of models have been suggested by science educators (e.g., Gilbert et al., 2000; Harrison & Treagust, 2000b; see Treagust, 2007). Of more relevance to instruction are the *consensus models*, models generally accepted by the scientists (e.g., Boyle's law), the *teaching models* used by teachers in teaching, and *expressed models* that are those models expressed, or communicated to or interpreted by others, through different modes of expression such as language, drawings, or in textbooks or scientific writing (Coll & Lajium, 2011; Gilbert, 2004). Harrison and Treagust recommended that science teachers "model scientific modelling to their students, encourage the use of multiple models in science lessons, progressively introduce sophisticated models, systematically present in-class models using the focus, action, and reflection (FAR) guide, and socially negotiate all model meanings" (p. 1011).

Instruction based on models and modeling can cognitively engage students in their learning in that modeling involves mapping some elements of the model's source (e.g., a snake biting its tail or any everyday/prior experiences) onto those of its target (e.g., benzene's ringed molecular structure as postulated by Friedrich Kekulé in 1865). Models are used as a bridge by means of analogy for three major purposes in science education: (1) to create simpler forms of objects/concepts, (2) to enable visualization for learning concepts/phenomena, and (3) to explain concepts/phenomena (Coll & Lajium, 2011; Duit, 1991). There is a general consensus that models and modeling are central to understanding in science education (e.g., Coll & Lajium, 2011; Gilbert, 2004). According to a more recent review by Buckley (2012b), instruction based on model-based learning supports the development of the evolution of learners' mental models whose accuracy and completeness the learners build, extend, elaborate, and improve in ways similar to what scientists do in their scientific practices. Such instruction can be used in formal or informal learning settings with didactic to discovery methods and strategies as well as tactics over different periods of instruction.

Multimodal Representations

Science education research focused on using several modes of representations, that is, using multimodal representations, in designing and implementing instruction in science, is now more evident in the literature (e.g., Gillen, Littleton, Twiner, Staarman, & Mercer, 2008; Jaipal, 2010; Marquez et al., 2006; Waldrip et al., 2010). In teaching students how to think and act scientifically, teachers can integrate the multimodal discourses of science in classroom teaching for which different modes of representations serve different purposes in reasoning, scientific inquiry, and knowledge construction as argued by Waldrip and colleagues (2010). According to Waldrip's team, mathematical, verbal, and graphic modes can be used individually and in coordinated ways for supporting student learning a science discipline. Again, the advent of digital technology has provided unprecedented interactive technology-mediated learning environments using several modes of representations in ways consistent with the evolution of

science as a discipline. We discuss this issue again in a later section on multiple external representations.

Some studies in this area showed that instruction based on multimodal representations is useful for supporting primary science classrooms with interactive whiteboards or electronic smart boards (Gillen et al., 2008), for student learning in reading scientific texts in middle schools (Alvermann & Wilson, 2011), and for teacher education as a metacognitive tool and analytical tool for discourse analysis in science teacher education (Jaipal, 2010). The latest development in multimodal research can be found in Tytler, Prain, Hubber, and Waldrip (2013), which focused on "student-generated representational work through sequences of representational challenges accompanied by negotiation and refinement of the produced representation" (p. 3). The area of research on multimodal representations overlaps substantially with the work on visualization, multilevel representations, and multiple representations in this chapter.

Multilevel Representations

Johnstone (1991) argued that science in general and chemistry in particular is difficult to learn because scientific knowledge can be represented at three levels, two of which are not observable to the learners; this "triangle of thought" (p. 78) consisting of the macro, the submicro, and the symbolic as the apices was originally based on the "conceptual tripod" (p. 78) representing three big ideas in chemistry (structure, bonding, and energy) during the curriculum reforms of the 1960s in the UK. According to Johnstone, physics also has three similar levels: "the macro, the invisible (e.g., force, reactions, electrons) and the symbolic (maths, formulae etc.)" and in biology, too, there are "the macro (plants or animals), the micro (cells) and the biochemical (DNA etc.)" (p. 78). Thus, Johnstone (1991) critiqued that most science teachers simultaneously used the triangle of multilevel thought in their teaching without being aware of the demands on their students. Over half of a century that followed, Johnstone's multilevel thinking has spawned numerous studies in chemistry teaching (e.g., Chandrasegaran, Treagust, & Mocerino, 2009; Cook, Wiebe, & Carter, 2008; Gilbert & Treagust, 2009; Treagust et al., 2003) and some studies on biology teaching (e.g., Buckley & Quellmatz, 2013; Marbach-Ad & Stavy, 2000). It appears that what Johnstone critiqued about science teachers' use of the triangle of thought in teaching chemistry some 20 years ago is still an issue in teaching chemistry, as pointed out by Johnstone's (2009) book review. There is a need for further investigation in this area.

Multiple External Representations (MERs)

Learners are likely to benefit when information is presented in more than one representation because (1) specific information can best be conveyed in a particular representation, (2) several representations can be more useful in displaying a variety of information, and (3) problem-solving expertise depends on the problem solver's different representations of the same domain (de Jong et al., 1998). This general claim about learning from more than one representation was based on numerous studies in a variety of domains including computational science, mathematics, physics, chemistry, accidentology, economics, and clinical medicine as documented in van Someren, Reimann, Boshuizen, and de Jong's (1998) *Learning with Multiple Representations*. Paivio's (1986) dual coding theory—that humans have separate channels for processing visual and verbal representations—has also provided an important theoretical rationale for using both verbal and visual representations in teaching science to enhance learning.

Ainsworth (1999) proposed a functional taxonomy of multiple external representations (MERs) that has significantly impacted research in using multiple representations in instruction. Accordingly, multiple external representations (MERs) of knowledge—when co-deployed (i.e., when two or more external representations are simultaneously used) in teaching and learning—can serve three basic pedagogical functions in supporting learning (to complement, to constrain, and to construct):

> The first function is to use representations that contain complementary information or support complementary cognitive processes. In the second, one representation is used to constrain possible (mis)interpretations in the use of another. Finally, MERs can be used to encourage learners to construct a deeper understanding of a situation.
>
> (p. 134)

Over the last decade, the notion of multiple representations, commonly used as a theoretical framework in many studies on mathematics education, has also influenced pedagogical research across different disciplines of science, for example, in physics (e.g., Bryan & Fennell, 2009; Dufresne, Gerace, & Leonard, 1997; Guelman, De Leone, & Price, 2009; Nguyen & Rebello, 2011) and also in chemistry (e.g., Linenberger & Bretz, 2012; Madden, Jones, & Rahm, 2011), biology (e.g., Neibert, Riemeier, & Gropengiesser, 2013; Schwartz & Brown, 2013; Tsui & Treagust, 2003, 2007; Yarden & Yarden, 2013), and earth science (e.g., Atchison et al., 2012; McNeal, Miller, & Herbert, 2008). However, there are the costs and benefits of using more than one representation in instruction that must not be overlooked (Ainsworth, 1999, 2006).

We believe that Ainsworth's (1999) pedagogical functions of multiple external representations (MERs) can be a useful theoretical framework for conceptualizing instruction based on co-deploying multiple external representations such as analogies, metaphors, visualizations, or models in various combinations across different content areas and contexts in teaching science. In our recent work (Treagust & Tsui, 2013), we attempted to seek a unifying theoretical model that could show how these seemingly disparate external representations can be harnessed for improving higher-order learning in biology, such as reasoning and problem solving, as well as for constructing learners' internal representations or mental models (Johnson-Laird, 1983) of their understanding. We also believe that this theoretical model can be extended to other science disciplines or science in general and developed into a similar theoretical model or models for analyzing teaching with MERs. We recommend more research be conducted in this area.

Teachers' PCK and Representational Competence

Instruction based on more than one external representation (e.g., multimodal, multilevel or multiple representations) may overload students with too much information because of their limited short-term memory according to the cognitive load theory (Sweller, 1994). It follows that effective instruction based on representations is dependent on teachers' pedagogical content knowledge (PCK; Shulman, 1987)—their appropriate selection and use of teaching models and modeling strategies with analogies, metaphors, diagrams, pictures, simulations, and so on in their teaching, as well as their knowledge about the limitations of the teaching models that can enhance student understanding of the scientific models (Coll & Lajium, 2011). This kind of PCK is also known as teachers' representational competence useful for effective instruction in various science disciplines (e.g., Halverson & Friedrichsen, 2013; Kozma & Russell, 2005; Madden et al., 2011). Teacher educators should focus more on developing pre- and inservice teachers' PCK, including their representational competence for using various external representations in their teaching.

Teaching Science in the 21st Century

From the review of various general instructional method and strategies, it is obvious that in the second decade of the 21st century, science educators are facing more challenges than ever before. As we state at the beginning of this chapter, there have been many changes in science, human societies, and science education, resulting in a new crisis in science and science education in the Western or developed countries in Europe, the United States, and Australasia. Three pressing perennial problems also are challenging science education at school level around the world, as Gilbert (2010) rightly pointed out:

(1) "the increasing intellectual isolation of science from the other subjects in the school curriculum";

(2) "how to accommodate a 'science education for citizenship', and one that is relevant to the needs of all students, in a curriculum which has traditionally been focused on . . . a preparation to be a scientist/ engineer"; and

(3) "a consequence of the exponentially increasing gap between the phenomena in which science is currently interested and what science education seems able to address."

(p. v)

There has also been an ongoing debate on whether school science intersects with some generic or domain-general skills required by employment in the 21st-century workforce. The 21st-century skills, for example, the five skills deemed important by U.S. science educators and other experts—*adaptability, complex communities/social skills, nonroutine problem-solving skills, self-management/self-development,* and *systems thinking* (for a definition of each, see Hilton, 2010, p. 2)—can be matched against the science curriculum standards (Schunn, 2009). Similar policy initiatives on improving 21st-century education have also been proposed in other countries, for example, in the UK (Millar, 2006), Australia (Tytler, 2007), New Zealand (Gluckman, 2011), and Canada (Orpwood, Schmidt, & Hu, 2012). The major challenge for science teachers is that they have to teach science to all students for scientific literacy and, at the same time, teach the canonical content of science to the elite minority who aspire to become scientists or to pursue science-related careers. It is important for science teachers to bear in mind that "[t]he goal of science education is not knowledge of a body of facts and theories but a progression towards key ideas which enable understanding of events and phenomena of relevance to students' lives" (Harlen, 2010, p. 2). They also need to consider some local issues within their educational settings and contexts, such as inclusivity considerations (e.g., gender, ethnic, or ability factors) as well as language problems.

The Internet has now become an important resource in education with its roles in electronic communications and as a content information library, as well as its increasingly influential current development as a means of collaboration for knowledge sharing; for example, online learning, Web-based collaborative tools, and the use of mobile devices were the most significant trends of the year 2011 (Brown & Green, 2011). Accordingly, many students on university campuses use mobile devices with global positioning, Web browsing, video capture, and other functions that could be used as learning tools. The new Web 2.0—open-architecture World Wide Web technologies also represent a paradigm shift—enhances creativity and facilitates information sharing and collaborative knowledge building through such technologies as blogs, wikis, podcasts, Twitter, and social networking (Bednar & Coperland, 2012). All these are substantially changing the way people work, play, and interact in the digital age. New developments in virtual learning environments, electronic whiteboards, smart phones, and new educational software tools are significantly changing the landscape of teaching and learning from preschools and K–12 schools to universities around the world (Adams, 2012). However, despite the rhetoric of many researchers' promises, claims, and justifications for the positive outcomes in using digital technology in school settings, some critics argue that "schools often fail to make sustained 'best use' of digital technology" (Selwyn, 2011, p. 22).

In a meta-analysis of science teaching in Australia, Sweden, and England to understand the declines in interest and enrolments in high school and university science, Lyons (2006) identified three themes in the many science classrooms: (1) transmissive pedagogy, (2) decontextualized content, and (3) unnecessary difficulty of school science. Unfortunately, the widespread use of digital technology in instruction in these countries has not substantially improved science education in terms of engendering students' interest, motivation, and understanding so that there is not much change in the status of science education discussed at the beginning of this chapter. According to Selwyn's (2011) review of "schools technology" (p. 22) in England, Ethiopia, Estonia, Singapore, New Zealand, Australia, France, Austria, and some other countries, many teachers continued to passively deliver information through interactive whiteboards, virtual learning environments, and other managed learning systems; and students' in-school use of digital technology was restricted to "cut-and-pasting" of online material downloaded from search engines such as Google into their assignment writings.

To improve teaching science in the 21st century, science educators should caution that good teaching in the predigital age should not be superseded by technology-based instruction; rather, they should carefully examine how technology can be harnessed to enhance student learning, interest, and motivation. In particular, we believe that even when online and Web-based teaching is becoming increasingly common in higher education around the world, the traditional face-to-face instruction—in which the teachers and students can interact nondigitally with a human touch—should be considered an indispensable part of quality university education. In the review in this chapter, we highlight representational learning as a comprehensive portmanteau repertoire, which we claim could encompass most instructional methods and strategies based on representations science teachers can use in teaching. As we argue in our recent work (Treagust & Tsui, 2013), there is a need for a unifying framework to conceptualize the pedagogical functions of the multiple representations when they are co-deployed in classroom or virtual learning environments. Representational learning is closely associated with digital technology use in contemporary science instruction from preschool and K–12 to higher education. We concur with the view of Ainsworth and Lowe (2012) that the quality of the learning experience provided by the new possibilities of representations is more important than these representations per se because technological sophistication and novelty do not necessarily lead to effectiveness in enhancing learning; and that much more research is needed for improving the quality of teaching and learning using desirable new technological *opportunities* for representational learning but not just new technological *possibilities*.

Summary

As is apparent from the work reviewed in this chapter, a wide variety of instructional methods and strategies can be used in teaching science, ranging from those that are more teacher-centered to those that are more student-centered. Each of the six groups of instructional methods and strategies is supported by a growing body of theory. Further, a reasonable quantity of research has been conducted with these methods and strategies to provide some evidence for their effectiveness in enhancing student learning and opportunities for student learning from K–12 schools to universities. We have also added a new section on teaching science in the 21st century and discussions on some issues associated with the widespread and expanding use of digital technology in science education. In particular, we highlight representational learning as a potentially all-encompassing repertoire of instructional approaches based on representations and discuss the associated possibilities and problems. We believe that none of the approaches reviewed in this chapter by themselves should be seen as a panacea to improve science learning, but each method or strategy can be part of a successful science teacher's instructional repertoire.

Acknowledgments

We would like to thank Grady Venville and Gregory Kelly, who carefully and critically reviewed this chapter. We hope that we have done justice to their critiques and constructive suggestions.

Note

1. The use of the term "multiple representations" or "multiple external representations" (MERs) in this chapter refers exclusively to Ainsworth's (1999) work unless stated otherwise.

References

Adams, C. (2012). PowerPoint and the pedagogy of digital media technologies. In M. Orey, S. A. Jones, & R. M. Branch (Eds.), *Educational media and technology yearbook: Volume 36, 2011* (pp. 139–154). New York: Springer.

Aikenhead, G. S. (2006). *Science education for everyday life: Evidence-based practice.* New York: Teachers College Press.

Ai-Lim Lee, E., Wong, K. W., & Fung, C. C. (2010). How does desktop virtual reality enhance learning outcomes? A structural equation modeling approach. *Computers & Education, 55*(4), 1424–1442.

Ainsworth, S. (1999). The functions of multiple representations. *Computers & Education, 33*(2/3), 131–152.

Ainsworth, S. (2006). DeFT: A conceptual framework for considering learning with multiple representations. *Learning and Instruction, 15*(3), 183–198.

Ainsworth, S., & Lowe, R. (2012). Representational learning. In N. M. Seel (Ed.), *Encyclopedia of the sciences of learning* (pp. 2832–2835). Boston: Springer US.

Almeida, P., & de Souza, F. N. (2010). Questioning profiles in secondary science classrooms. *International Journal of Learning and Change, 4*(3), 237–251.

Alvermann, D. E., & Wilson, A. A. (2011). Comprehension strategy instruction for multimodal texts in science. *Theory Into Practice, 50*(2), 116–124.

American Association for the Advancement of Science. (1999). *Science for all Americans: A project 2061 report on literacy goals in science, mathematics, and technology.* Retrieved from www.project2061.org/publications/sfaa/online/intro.htm

Angeli, C., & Valanides, N. (2008). Examining the effects of electronic mentoring prompts on learners' scientific reasoning skills in a text-based online conference for a science education course. *Science Education International, 19*(4), 357–369.

Atchison, C. L., Stredney, D., Irving, K. E., Toomey, R. S., Price, A., Kerwin, T., . . . Reed, P. J. (2012). Overcoming physical barriers to provide cave and karst field experiences through the multiple representation of virtual reality. *Abstracts with Programs—Geological Society of America, 44*(7), 513–513.

Ates, S. (2005). The effectiveness of the learning-cycle method on teaching DC circuits to prospective female and male science teachers. *Research in Science & Technological Education, 23*(2), 213–227.

Atkin, J. M., & Karplus, R. (1962). Discovery or invention? *The Science Teacher, 29,* 45–51.

Aubusson, P. J., Harrison, A. G., & Ritchie, S. M. (Eds.). (2006). *Metaphor and analogy in science education.* Dordrecht, the Netherlands: Springer.

Basta, T. B., & Barman, C. R. (2008). An application of the learning cycle in health education: HIV/AIDS prevention. *American Journal of Health Education, 39*(4), 245–247.

Bednar, A. K., & Coperland, N. L. (2012). Enlisting the collaboration of the educational technology professional community to develop a knowledge management system of the field: edu-techKNOWiki. In M. Orey, S. A. Jones, & R. M. Branch (Eds.), *Educational media and technology yearbook: Volume 36, 2011* (pp. 81–89). New York: Springer.

Bell, C. V., & Odom, A. L. (2012). Reflections on discourse practices during professional development on the learning cycle. *Journal of Science Teacher Education, 23*(6), 601–620.

Berland, L. K., & McNeill, K. L. (2012). For whom is argument and explanation a necessary distinction? A response to Osborne and Patterson. *Science Education, 96*(5), 808–813.

Besson, U. (2010). Calculating and understanding: Formal models and causal explanations in science, common reasoning and physics teaching. *Science & Education, 19*(3), 225–257.

Bodzin, A. M., & Beerer, K. M. (2003). Promoting inquiry-based science instruction: The validation of the science teacher inquiry rubric (STIR). *Journal of Elementary Science Education, 15*(2), 39–49.

Bonello, C., & Scaife, J. (2009). PEOR—engaging students in demonstrations. *Journal of Science and Mathematics Education in Southeast Asia, 32*(1), 62–84.

BouJaoude, S., & Tamim, R. (2008). Middle school students' perceptions of the instructional value of analogies, summaries and answering questions in life science. *Science Educator, 17*(1), 72–78.

Braaten, M., & Windschitl, M. (2011). Working toward a stronger conceptualization of scientific explanation for science education. *Science Education, 95*(4), 639–669.

Brown, A., & Green, T. (2011). Issues and trends in instructional technology: Lean times, shifts in online learning, and increased attention to mobile devices. In M. Orey, S. A. Jones, & R. M. Branch (Eds.), *Educational media and technology yearbook: Volume 36* (pp. 67–80). New York: Springer.

Bryan, A. J., & Fennell, D. B. (2009). Wave modelling: A lesson illustrating the integration of mathematics, science and technology through multiple representations. *Physics Education, 44*(4), 403–410.

Bucciarelli, M., & Cutica, I. (2012). Mental models in improving learning. In N. M. Seel (Ed.), *Encyclopedia of the sciences of learning* (pp. 2213–2216). Boston: Springer US.

Buckley, B. C. (2012a). Model-based learning. In N. M. Seel (Ed.), *Encyclopedia of the sciences of learning* (pp. 2300–2303). Boston: Springer US.

Buckley, B. C. (2012b). Model-based teaching. In N. M. Seel (Ed.), *Encyclopedia of the sciences of learning* (pp. 2312–2315). Boston: Springer US.

Buckley, B. C., & Quellmatz, E. S. (2013). Supporting and assessing complex biology learning with computer-based simulations and representations. In D. F. Treagust & C.-Y. Tsui (Eds.), *Multiple representations in biological education* (pp. 247–267). Dordrecht, the Netherlands: Springer.

Buckley, C. B. (2000). Interactive multimedia and model-based learning in biology. *International Journal of Science Education, 22*(9), 895–935.

Bybee, R. W. (2009). *The BSCS 5E instructional model and 21st century skills.* Paper prepared for the Workshop on Exploring the Intersection of Science Education and the Development of 21st Century Skills. Retrieved from http://sites.nationalacademies.org/DBASSE/BOSE/DBASSE_080127

Carlsen, B., & Marek, E. A. (2010). Why do athletes drink sports drinks? A learning cycle to explore the concept of osmosis. *Science Teacher, 77*(9), 48–52.

Chandrasegaran, L. A., Treagust, D. F., & Mocerino, M. (2009). Emphasizing multiple levels of representation to enhance students' understandings of the changes occurring during chemical reactions. *Journal of Chemical Education, 86*(12), 1433–1436.

Chandrasegaran, L. A., Treagust, D. F., & Mocerino, M. (2011). Facilitating high school students' use of multiple representations to describe and explain simple chemical reactions. *Teaching Science, 57*(4), 13–20.

Chang, K., Chen, Y., Lin, H., & Sung, Y. (2008). Effects of learning support in simulation-based physics learning. *Computers & Education, 51*(4), 1486–1498.

Chin, C. (2006). Classroom interaction in science: Teacher questioning and feedback to students' responses. *International Journal of Science Education, 28*(11), 1315–1346.

Chin, C. (2007). Teacher questioning in science classrooms: Approaches that stimulate productive thinking. *Journal of Research in Science Teaching, 44*(6), 815–843.

Chin, C., & Osborne, J. (2008). Students' questions: A potential resource for teaching and learning science. *Studies in Science Education, 44*(1), 1–39.

Chin, C., & Osborne, J. (2010a). Students' questions and discursive interaction: Their impact on argumentation during collaborative group discussions in science. *Journal of Research in Science Teaching, 47*(7), 883–908.

Chin, C., & Osborne, J. (2010b). Supporting argumentation through students' questions: Case studies in science classrooms. *Journal of the Learning Sciences, 19*(2), 230–284.

Chittleborough, G. D., Mocerino, M., & Treagust, D. F. (2007). Achieving greater feedback and flexibility using online pre-laboratory exercises with non-major chemistry students. *Journal of Chemical Education, 84*(5), 884–884.

Chiu, M.-H., & Duit, R. (2011). Globalization: Science education from an international perspective. *Journal of Research in Science Teaching, 48*(6), 553–566.

Clement, J. J., & Rae-Mamirez, M. A. (Eds.). (2008). *Model based learning and instruction in science.* Dordrecht, the Netherlands: Springer Science + Business Media B. V.

Coll, R. K., & Lajium, D. (2011). Modeling and the future of science learning. In M. S. Khine & I. M. Saleh (Eds.), *Models and modeling: Cognitive tools for scientific enquiry* (pp. 4–21). Dordrecht; New York: Springer.

Concord Consortium. (2001, October). *BioLogica.* Retrieved from http://biologica.concord.org

Cook, M., Wiebe, E., & Carter, G. (2008). The influence of prior knowledge on viewing and interpreting graphics with macroscopic and molecular representations. *Science Education, 92*(5), 848.

Costu, B., Ayas, A., & Niaz, M. (2010). Promoting conceptual change in first year students' understanding of evaporation. *Chemistry Education Research and Practice, 11*(1), 5–16.

Crouch, C. H., Fagen, A. P., Callan, J. P., & Mazur, E. (2004). Classroom demonstrations: Learning tools or entertainment? *American Journal of Physics, 72,* 835–838.

Dagher, Z. R. (1994). Does the use of analogies contribute to conceptual change? *Science Education, 78*(6), 601–614.

Dawes, L. (2004). Talk and learning in classroom science. *International Journal of Science Education, 26,* 677–695.

de Jong, T., Ainsworth, S., Dobson, M., Van der Hulst, A., Levonen, J., Reimann, P., . . . Swaak, J. (1998). Acquiring knowledge in science and mathematics: The use of multiple representations in technology based learning environments. In M. W. V. Someren, P. Reimann, H. P. A. Boshuizen, & T. D. Jong (Eds.), *Learning with multiple representations* (pp. 9–40). London: Elsevier.

Dogru-Atay, P., & Tekkaya, C. (2008). Promoting students' learning in genetics with the learning cycle. *Journal of Experimental Education, 76*(3), 259–280.

Driver, R., Leach, J., Millar, R., & Scott, P. (1996). *Young people's images of science.* Buckingham/Philadelphia: Open University Press.

Dufresne, R. J., Gerace, W. J., & Leonard, W. J. (1997). Solving physics problems with multiple representations. *The Physics Teacher, 35,* 270–275.

Duit, R. (1991). On the role of analogies and metaphors in learning science. *Science Education, 75*(6), 649–672.

Duschl, R., & Hamilton, R. (2010). Learning science. In R. E. Mayer & P. A. Alexander (Eds.), *Handbook of research on learning and instruction* (pp. 78–107). New York: Routledge.

Eilam, B. (2013). Possible constraints of visualization in biology: Challenges in learning with multiple representations. In D. F. Treagust & C.-Y. Tsui (Eds.), *Multiple representations in biological education* (pp. 55–73). Dordrecht, the Netherlands: Springer.

Fensham, P. J. (1990). Practical work and the laboratory in science for all. In E. Hegarty-Hazel (Ed.), *The student laboratory and the science curriculum* (pp. 291–311). London; New York: Routledge.

Fensham, P. J. (2001). Science content as problematic issues for research. In H. Behrendt, H. Dahncke, R. Duit, W. M. Komorek, A. Kross, & P. Reiska (Eds.), *Research in science education—past, present and future* (pp. 27–41). Dordrecht, the Netherlands: Kluwer.

Fensham, P. J. (2009). Real world contexts in PISA science: Implications for context-based science education. *Journal of Research in Science Teaching, 46*(8), 884–896.

Fensham, P. J., Gunstone, R. F., & White, R. T. (Eds.). (1994). *The content of science: A constructivist approach to its teaching and learning.* London; Washington, DC: Falmer Press.

Furberg, A., & Ludvigsen, S. (2008). Students' meaning-making of socio-scientific issues in computer mediated settings: Exploring learning through interaction trajectories. *International Journal of Science Education, 30*(13), 1775–1799.

Geelan, D. (2012). Teacher explanations. In B. J. Fraser, K. Tobin, & C. J. McRobbie (Eds.), *Second international handbook of science education* (pp. 987–999). Dordrecht, the Netherlands: Springer.

Gilbert, J. (2008). Visualization: An emerging field of practice and enquiry in science education. In J. K. Gilbert, M. Reiner, & M. Nakhleh (Eds.), *Visualization: Theory and practice in science education* (pp. 3–24). London: Springer.

Gilbert, J., Boulter, C. J., & Elmer, R. (2000). Positioning models in science education and in design and technology education. In J. Gilbert & C. J. Boutler (Eds.), *Developing models in science education* (pp. 3–17). Dordrecht: the Netherlands: Kluwer.

Gilbert, J. K. (2004). Models and modelling: Routes to more authentic science education. *International Journal of Science and Mathematics Education, 2*(2), 115–130.

Gilbert, J. K. (2010). Preface. In L. M. Phillips, S. P. Norris, & J. S. Macnab (Eds.), *Visualization in Mathematics, Reading, and Science Education* (pp. v–vii). Dordrecht, the Netherlands: Springer.

Gilbert, J. K., & Boulter, C. J. (1998). Learning science through models and modelling. In B. J. Fraser (Ed.), *International handbook of science education* (pp. 53–66). Dordrecht, the Netherlands: Kluwer.

Gilbert, J. K., Reiner, M., & Nakhleh, M. (Eds.). (2008). *Visualization: Theory and practice in science education.* New York: London: Springer.

Gilbert, J. K., & Treagust, D. F. (Eds.). (2009). *Multiple representations in chemical education.* Dordrecht, the Netherlands: Springer.

Gillen, J., Littleton, K., Twiner, A., Staarman, J. K., & Mercer, N. (2008). Using the interactive whiteboard to resource continuity and support multimodal teaching in a primary science classroom. *Journal of Computer Assisted Learning, 24*(4), 348–358.

Gluckman, P. (2011). *Looking ahead: Science education for the twenty-first century.* Wellington, New Zealand: Office of the Prime Minister

Office's Science Advisory Committee. Retrieved from www.pmcsa. org.nz/wp-content/uploads/Looking-ahead-Science-education-for-the-twenty-first-century.pdf

Glynn, S.M. (1991). Explaining science concepts: A teaching-with-analogies model. In M. Shawn, S.M. Glynn, R.H. Yeany, & B.K. Britton (Eds.), *The psychology of learning science* (pp. 219–240). Hillsdale, NJ: Lawrence Erlbaum Associates.

Gonzalez-Spada, W.J., Birriel, J., & Birriel, I. (2010). Discrepant events: A challenge to students' intuition. *Physics Teacher, 48*(8), 508–511.

Guelman, C.B., De Leone, C., & Price, E. (2009, July). *The influence of tablet PCs on students' use of multiple representations in lab reports.* Paper presented at the Physics Education Research Conference 2009. Ann Arbor, MI.

Gunstone, R. (1995). Constructive learning and the teaching of science. In B. Hand & V. Prain (Eds.), *Teaching and learning in science: The constructivist classroom* (pp. 3–20). Sydney: Harcourt Brace.

Hackling, M. (2006). *Primary connections: A new approach to primary science and to teacher professional learning.* Retrieved from http://research.acer.edu.au/research_conference_2006/14

Haglund, J., Jeppsson, F., & Andersson, J. (2012). Young children's analogical reasoning in science domains. *Science Education, 96*(4), 725–756.

Halliday, M.A.K., & Martin, J.R. (1993). *Writing science: Literacy and discursive power.* London: Falmer.

Halverson, K.L., & Friedrichsen, P. (2013). Learning tree thinking: Developing a new framework of representational competence. In D.F. Treagust & C.-Y. Tsui (Eds.), *Multiple representations in biological education* (pp. 185–201). Dordrecht, the Netherlands: Springer.

Hamza, K.M., & Wickman, P.-O. (2009). Beyond explanations: What else do students need to understand science? *Science Education, 93*(6), 1026–1049.

Harlen, W. (Ed.). (2010). *Principle and big ideas of science education.* Hatfield, UK: Association for Science Education. Retrieved from http://cmaste.ualberta.ca/en/Outreach/~/media/cmaste/Documents/Outreach/IANASInterAmericasInquiry/PrinciplesBigIdeasInSciEd.pdf

Harris, D., & Williams, J. (2007). Questioning "open questioning" in early years science discourse from a social semiotic perspective. *International Journal of Educational Research, 46*(1), 15–15.

Harrison, A.G., & Treagust, D.F. (1994). Science analogies. *Science Teacher, 61*(4), 40–43.

Harrison, A.G., & Treagust, D.F. (2000a). Learning about atoms, molecules, and chemical bonds: A case study of multiple-model use in grade 11 chemistry. *Science Education, 84,* 352–381.

Harrison, A.G., & Treagust, D.F. (2000b). A typology of school science models. *International Journal of Science Education, 22*(9), 1011–1026.

Hennessey, M.G. (2003). Metacognitive aspects of students' reflective discourse: Implications for intentional conceptual change teaching and learning. In G.M. Sinatra & P.R. Pintrich (Eds.), *Intentional conceptual change* (pp. 103–132). Mahwah, NJ: Lawrence Erlbaum Associates.

Herrington, D., & Scott, P. (2011). Get in the game with team density. *Science Teacher, 78*(4), 58–61.

Hilton, M. (2010). *Exploring the intersection of science education and 21st century skills: A workshop summary.* Retrieved from www.nap.edu/catalog.php?record_id=12771#toc

Hodson, D., & Hodson, J. (1998). From constructivism to social constructivism: A Vygotskian perspective on teaching and learning science. *School Science Review, 79*(289), 33–41.

Hofstein, A., & Lunetta, V.N. (2004). The laboratory in science education: Foundations for the twenty-first century. *Science Education, 88*(1), 28–54.

Holyoak, K.J., & Thagard, P. (1995). *Mental leaps: Analogy in creative thought.* Cambridge, London: MIT Press.

Horwitz, P. (2013). Evolution is a model: Why not teach it that way? In D.F. Treagust & C.-Y. Tsui (Eds.), *Multiple representations in biological education* (pp. 129–145). Dordrecht, the Netherlands: Springer.

Horwitz, P., & Christie, M.A. (2000). Computer-based manipulatives for teaching scientific reasoning: An example. In M.J. Jacobson &

R.B. Kozma (Eds.), *Innovations in science and mathematics education: Advanced design for technologies of learning* (pp. 163–191). Hillsdale, NJ: Lawrence Erlbaum Associates.

Horwood, R.H. (1988). Explaining and description in science teaching. *Science Education, 72*(1), 41–49.

Howe, A.C. (1996). Development of science concepts within a Vygotskian framework. *Science Education, 80*(1), 35–51.

Jaipal, K. (2010). Meaning making through multiple modalities in a biology classroom: A multimodal semiotics discourse analysis. *Science Education, 94*(1), 48–72.

Johnson, L.H., Trout, L.B., Brekke, J.C., & Luedecke, O.L. (2004). Hands-on, demonstration, and videotape laboratories for non-science majors in a food science course: Achievement, attitude, and efficiency. *Journal of Food Science Education, 3*(1), 2–7.

Johnson-Laird, P.N. (1983). *Mental models: Towards a cognitive science of language, inferences, and consciousness.* Cambridge: Cambridge University Press.

Johnstone, A.H. (1991). Why is science difficult to learn? Things are seldom what they seem. *Journal of Computer Assisted Learning, 7,* 75–83.

Johnstone, A.H. (2009). Book review: Multiple representations in chemical education. *International Journal of Science Education, 31*(16), 2271–2273. doi:10.1080/09500690903211393

Jones, M.G., Rua, M.J., & Carter, G. (1998). Science teachers' conceptual growth within Vygotsky's zone of proximal development. *Journal of Research in Science Teaching, 35*(9), 967–985.

Karplus, R. (1977). Science teaching and the development of reasoning. *Journal of Research in Science Teaching, 14*(2), 169–175.

Kearney, M., Treagust, D.F., Yeo, S., & Zadnik, M.G. (2001). Student and teacher perceptions of the use of multimedia supported predict-observe-explain tasks to probe understanding. *Research in Science Education, 31*(4), 589–615.

Keeratichamroen, W., Dechsri, P., Panijpan, B., & Ruenwongsa, P. (2010). The tapioca bomb: A demonstration to enhance learning about combustion and chemical safety. *Teaching Science, 56*(1), 39–41.

Kelley, R.L. (2010). Worms in the college classroom: More than just a composting demonstration. *Journal of College Science Teaching, 39*(3), 52–55.

Kozma, R., & Russell, J. (2005). Students becoming chemists: Developing representational competence. In J.K. Gilbert (Ed.), *Visualization in science education* (pp. 121–146). Dordrecht, the Netherlands: Springer.

Kozma, R.B., & Russell, J. (1997). Multimedia and understanding: Expert and novice responses to different representations of chemical phenomenon. *Journal of Research in Science Teaching, 34*(9), 949–968.

Larkin, J.H., & Simon, H.A. (1987). Why a diagram is (sometimes) worth ten thousand words. *Cognitive Science, 11,* 65–99.

Lavoie, D.R. (1999). Effects of emphasizing hypothetico-predictive reasoning within the science learning cycle on high school student's process skills and conceptual understandings in biology. *Journal of Research in Science Teaching, 36*(10), 1127–1147. doi:10.1002/(sici)1098-2736(199912)36:10<1127::aid-tea5>3.0.co;2-4

Lawson, A., Oehrtman, M., & Jensen, J. (2008). Connecting science and mathematics: The nature of scientific and statistical hypothesis testing. *International Journal of Science and Mathematics Education, 6*(2), 405–416. doi:10.1007/s10763-007-9108-5

Lawson, A.E. (2000). The generality of hypothetico-deductive reasoning: Making scientific thinking explicit. *American Biology Teacher, 62*(7), 482–495.

Lawson, A.E. (2010). Basic inferences of scientific reasoning, argumentation, and discovery. *Science Education, 94*(2), 336–364.

Lazarowitz, R., & Tamir, P. (1994). Research on using laboratory instruction. In L. Gabel (Ed.), *Handbook of research on science teaching and learning* (pp. 94–128). New York: Praeger Publishers.

Lehrer, R., & Schauble, L. (2006). Cultivating model-based reasoning in science education. In R.K. Sawyer (Ed.), *The Cambridge handbook of the learning sciences* (pp. 371–387). Cambridge: Cambridge University Press.

Lemke, J.L. (1990). *Talking science: Language, learning, and values.* Norwood, NJ: Ablex Publishing Corporation.

Levy Nahum, T., Ben-Chaim, D., Azaiza, I., Herskovitz, O., & Zoller, U. (2010). Does STES-oriented science education promote 10th-grade students' decision-making capability? *International Journal of Science Education, 32*(10), 1315–1336.

Liew, C.W., & Treagust, D.F. (1995). A predict-observe-explain teaching sequence for learning about students' understanding of heat and expansion of liquids. *Australian Science Teachers Journal, 4*(1), 68–71.

Linenberger, K.J., & Bretz, S.L. (2012). Generating cognitive dissonance in student interviews through multiple representations. *Chemistry Education Research and Practice, 13*(3), 172–178.

Liu, T.-C., Peng, H., Wu, W.-H., & Lin, M.-S. (2009). The effects of mobile natural-science learning based on the 5E learning cycle: A case study. *Educational Technology & Society, 12*(4), 344–358.

Liu, Y., Tsui, C.-Y., & Treagust, D.F. (2013). Roles of computer-based simulations in conceptual change learning of school science. In C.B. Lee & D. Jonassen (Eds.), *Fostering conceptual change with technology: Asian perspectives* (pp. 261–286). Singapore: Cengage Learning Asia Pte Ltd.

Luft, J.A. (1999). Rubrics: Design and use in science teacher education. *Journal of Science Teacher Education, 10*(2), 107–121.

Lyons, T. (2006). Different countries, same science classes: Students' experiences of school science in their own words. *International Journal of Science Education, 28*(6), 591–613.

Madden, S.P., Jones, L.L., & Rahm, J. (2011). The role of multiple representations in the understanding of ideal gas problems. *Chemistry Education Research and Practice, 12*(3), 283–293.

Mancuso, V.J. (2010). *Using discrepant events in science demonstrations to promote student engagement in scientific investigations: An action research study.* Unpublished PhD Thesis, University of Rochester, New York. Retrieved from http://search.proquest.com/docview/8814 56335?accountid=10382 Eric database

Marbach-Ad, G., & Stavy, R. (2000). Students' cellular and molecular explanations of genetic phenomena. *Journal of Biological Education, 34*(4), 200–205.

Marek, E.A., Laubach, T.A., & Pedersen, J. (2003). Preservice elementary school teachers' understandings of theory based science education. *Journal of Science Teacher Education, 14*(3), 147–159.

Marquez, C., Izquierdo, M., & Espinet, M. (2006). Multimodal science teachers' discourse in modeling the water cycle. *Science Education, 90*(2), 202–226.

Martins, I., & Ogborn, J. (1997). Metaphorical reasoning about genetics. *International Journal of Educational Research, 19*(6), 48–63.

Mayer, R.E., & Wittrock, M.C. (2012). Problem solving. In P.A. Alexander & P.H. Winne (Eds.), *Handbook of educational psychology* (2nd ed., pp. 287–303). Hoboken, NJ: Taylor & Francis.

McCarthy, D. (2005). Newton's first law: A learning cycle approach. *Science Scope, 28*(5), 46–49.

McKinsey & Company. (2012). *Education to employment: Designing a system that works.* Retrieved from http://mckinseyonsociety.com/downloads/reports/Education/Education-to-Employment_FINAL.pdf

McNeal, K.S., Miller, H.R., & Herbert, B.E. (2008). The effect of using inquiry and multiple representations on introductory geology students' conceptual model development of coastal eutrophication. *Journal of Geoscience Education, 56*(3), 201–211.

Mercer, N., & Littleton, K. (2007). *Dialogue and the development of children's thinking: A sociocultural approach.* London; New York: Routledge.

Millar, R. (2006). "Twenty first century science": Insights from the design and implementation of a scientific literacy approach in school science. *International Journal of Science Education, 28*(13), 1499–1521.

Millar, R. (2011). Reviewing the national curriculum for science: Opportunities and challenges. *Curriculum Journal, 22*(2), 167–185.

Milne, C., & Otieno, T. (2007). Understanding engagement: Science demonstrations and emotional energy. *Science Education, 91*(4), 523–553.

Moore, C.J., & Rubbo, L.J. (2012). Scientific reasoning abilities of non-science majors in physics-based courses. *Physical Review Special Topics—Physics Education Research, 8*(1), 010106–010101.

Mortimer, E., & Scott, P. (2000). Analysing discourse in the science classroom. In R. Millar, J. Leach, & J. Osborne (Eds.), *Improving science education: The contribution of research* (pp. 125–142). Buckingham UK; Philadelphia, PA: Open University Press.

Musheno, B.V., & Lawson, A.E. (1999). Effects of learning cycle and traditional text on comprehension of science concepts by students at differing reasoning levels. *Journal of Research in Science Teaching, 36*(1), 23–37.

National Research Council. (2007). *Taking science to school: Learning and teaching science kindergarten to eighth grade.* Washington, DC: National Academies Press. Retrieved from www.nap.edu

Neibert, K., Riemeier, T., & Gropengiesser, H. (2013). The hidden hand that shapes conceptual understanding: Choosing effective representations for teaching cell division and climate change. In D.F. Treagust & C.-Y. Tsui (Eds.), *Multiple representations in biological education* (pp. 293–310). Dordrecht, the Netherlands: Springer.

Nguyen, D.-H., & Rebello, S.N. (2011). Students' difficulties with multiple representations in introductory mechanics. *US–China Education Review, 8*(5), 559–569.

Ogborn, J., Kress, G., Martin, I., & McGillicuddy, K. (1996). *Explaining science in the classroom.* Buckingham, UK: Open University Press.

Oliva, J.M., Azcarate, P., & Navarrete, A. (2007). Teaching models in the use of analogies as a resource in the science classroom. *International Journal of Science Education, 29*(1), 45–66.

Orpwood, G., Schmidt, B., & Hu, J. (2012). *Competing in the 21st century skills race.* Canadian Council of Chief Executives. Retrieved from www.ceocouncil.ca/wp-content/uploads/2012/07/Competing-in-the-21st-Century-Skills-Race-Orpwood-Schmidt-Hu-July-2012-FINAL.pdf

Osborne, J., Collins, S., Ratcliffe, M., Millar, R., & Duschl, R. (2003). What "ideas-about-science" should be taught in school science? A Delphi study of the expert community. *Journal of Research in Science Teaching, 40*(7), 692–720.

Osborne, J., & Patterson, A. (2012). Authors' response to "For whom is argument and explanation a necessary distinction? A response to Osborne and Patterson" by Berland and McNeill. *Science Education, 96*(5), 814–817.

Osborne, J.F., & Patterson, A. (2011). Scientific argument and explanation: A necessary distinction? *Science Education, 95*(4), 627–638.

Paivio, A. (1986). *Mental representation and dual coding approach.* New York: Oxford University Press.

Panofsky, C.P., John-Steiner, V., & Blackwell, P.J. (1990). The development of scientific concepts and discourse. In L.C. Moll (Ed.), *Vygotsky and education: Instructional implications and applications of sociohistorical psychology* (pp. 252–267). Cambridge: Cambridge University Press.

Pedrosa-de-Jesus, H., da Silva Lopes, B., Moreira, A., & Watts, M. (2012). Contexts for questioning: Two zones of teaching and learning in undergraduate science. *Higher Education: The International Journal of Higher Education and Educational Planning, 64*(4), 557–571.

Phillips, L.M., Norris, S.P., & Macnab, J.S. (Eds.). (2010). *Visualization in mathematics, reading, and science education.* Dordrecht, the Netherlands: Springer.

Ratcliffe, M., & Millar, R. (2009). Teaching for understanding of science in context: Evidence from the pilot trials of the "Twenty First Century Science" courses. *Journal of Research in Science Teaching, 46*(8), 945–959.

Riopel, M., Potvin, P., & Vázquez-Abad, J. (2009). *Utilisation des technologies pour la recherche en éducation scientifique* [Utilisation of technologies for research in science education]. Québec, Canada: Les Presses de l'Université Laval.

Robottom, I. (2012). Socio-scientific issues in education: Innovative practices and contending epistemologies. *Research in Science Education, 42*(1), 95–107.

Roth, W.-M., McRobbie, C.J., Lucas, K.B., & Boutonné, S. (1997). Why may students fail to learn from demonstrations? A social practice perspective on learning in physics. *Journal of Research in Science Teaching, 34,* 509–533.

Ruiz-Primo, M.A., Li, M., Tsai, S.-P., & Schneider, J. (2010). Testing one premise of scientific inquiry in science classrooms: Examining students' scientific explanations and student learning. *Journal of Research in Science Teaching, 47*(5), 583–608.

Rundgren, C.-J., Hirsch, R., & Tibell, L.A. (2009). Death of metaphors in life science? A study of upper secondary and tertiary students' use of metaphors in their meaning-making of scientific content. *Asia-Pacific Forum on Science Learning and Teaching, 10*(1), 21–21.

Russ, R.S., Coffey, J.E., Hammer, D., & Hutchison, P. (2009). Making classroom assessment more accountable to scientific reasoning: A case for attending to mechanistic thinking. *Science Education, 93*(5), 875–891. doi:10.1002/sce.20320

Schmidt, S.J., Bohn, D.M., Rasmussen, A.J., & Sutherland, E.A. (2012). Using food science demonstrations to engage students of all ages in science, technology, engineering, and mathematics (STEM). *Journal of Food Science Education, 11*(2), 16–22.

Schunn, C. (2009). *Are 21st century skills found in science standards?* Paper presented at the Workshop on Exploring the Intersection of Science Education and the Development of 21st Century Skills, New York. Retrieved from www7.nationalacademies.org/bose/Schunn.pdf

Schwartz, R., & Brown, M. (2013). Understanding photosynthesis and cellular respiration: Encouraging a view of biological nested systems. In D.F. Treagust & C.-Y. Tsui (Eds.), *Multiple representations in biological education* (pp. 203–223). Dordrecht, the Netherlands: Springer.

Scott, P. (1998). Teacher talk and meaning making in science classrooms: A Vygotskian analysis and review. *Studies in Education, 32,* 45–80.

Seker, H., & Komur, S. (2008). The relationship between critical thinking skills and in-class questioning behaviours of English language teaching students. *European Journal of Teacher Education, 31*(4), 389–402.

Selwyn, N. (2011). *Schools and schooling in the digital age: A critical analysis.* New York: Routledge.

Sfard, A. (1998). On two metaphors for learning and the danger of just choosing one. *Educational Researcher, 27*(2), 4–13.

Shapiro, J. (2012). *China's environmental challenges.* Malden, MA: Polity.

Shinohara, F. (2006). Innovative methods in science education in Japan—strategic methods on smooth transition from upper secondary school to the university. *Journal of Science and Mathematics Education in Southeast Asia, 29*(1), 98–117.

Shulman, L.S. (1986). Those who understand: Knowledge growth in teaching. *Educational Researcher, 15*(2), 4–14.

Shulman, L.S. (1987). Knowledge and teaching: Foundation of the new reform. *Harvard Educational Review, 57*(1), 1–22.

Simon, S., Erduran, S., & Osborne, J. (2006). Learning to teach argumentation: Research and development in the science classroom. *International Journal of Science Education, 28*(2), 235–260.

Simonneaux, L., & Simonneaux, J. (2009). Students' socio-scientific reasoning on controversies from the viewpoint of education for sustainable development. *Cultural Studies of Science Education, 4*(3), 657–687.

Sjøberg, S., & Schreiner, C. (2010). *The ROSE project: An overview and key findings.* Retrieved from http://folk.uio.no/sveinsj/ROSE-overview_Sjoberg_Schreiner_2010.pdf

Slavin, R.E. (2009). *Educational psychology: Theory into practice* (9th ed.). Boston: Pearson.

Sternberg, R.J., & Williams, W.M. (2002). *Educational psychology.* Boston: Allen & Bacon.

Stierer, B., & Maybin, J. (1993). *Language, literacy and learning in educational practice: A reader.* Clevedon, UK: Open University.

Sweller, J. (1994). Cognitive load theory, learning difficulty, and instructional design. *Learning and Instruction, 4,* 295–312.

Thomas, G. (2012). Metacognition in science education: Past, present and future considerations. In B.J. Fraser, K. Tobin, & C.J. McRobbie (Eds.), *Second international handbook of science education* (pp. 131–144). Dordrecht, the Netherlands: Springer.

Tobin, K. (1987). The role of wait time in higher cognitive level learning. *Review of Educational Research, 57*(1), 69–95.

Treagust, D.F. (2007). General instructional methods and strategies. In S.K. Abell & N.G. Lederman (Eds.), *Handbook of research on science education* (pp. 373–391). Mahwah, NJ: Lawrence Erlbaum.

Treagust, D.F., Chittleborough, G.D., & Mamiala, T.L. (2003). The role of sub-microscopic and symbolic representations in chemical explanations. *International Journal of Science Education, 25*(11), 1353–1369.

Treagust, D.F., & Harrison, A.G. (2000). In search of explanatory frameworks: An analysis of Richard Feynman's lecture "Atoms in Motion." *International Journal of Science Education, 22*(11), 1157–1170.

Treagust, D.F., Harrison, A.G., & Venville, G.J. (1998). Teaching science effectively with analogies: An approach for preservice and inservice teacher education. *Journal of Science Teacher Education, 9*(2), 85–101.

Treagust, D.F., & Tsui, C.-Y. (Eds.). (2013). *Multiple representations in biological education.* Dordrecht, the Netherlands: Springer.

Tsui, C.-Y., & Treagust, D.F. (2003). Genetics reasoning with multiple external representations. *Research in Science Education, 33*(1), 111–135.

Tsui, C.-Y., & Treagust, D.F. (2007). Understanding genetics: Analysis of secondary students' conceptual status. *Journal of Research in Science Teaching, 44*(2), 205–235.

Tsui, C.-Y., & Treagust, D.F. (2013). Secondary students' understanding of genetics using BioLogica: Two case studies. In D.F. Treagust & C.-Y. Tsui (Eds.), *Multiple representations in biological education* (pp. 269–292). Dordrecht, the Netherlands: Springer.

Tural, G., Akdeniz, A.R., & Alev, N. (2010). Effect of 5E teaching model on student teachers' understanding of weightlessness. *Journal of Science Education and Technology, 19*(5), 470–488.

Turkmen, H. (2006). What technology plays supporting role in learning cycle approach for science education. *Turkish Online Journal of Educational Technology—TOJET, 5*(2), 7–7.

Tytler, R. (2007). *Re-imagining science education: Engaging students in science for Australia's future* (Australian Education Review 51). Camberwell, Victoria: Australian Council of Educational Research.

Tytler, R., Prain, V., Hubber, P., & Waldrip, B. (Eds.). (2013). *Constructing representations to learn in science.* Rotterdam, the Netherlands: Sense Publishers.

Tytler, R., Symington, D., Darby, L., Malcolm, C., & Kirkwood, V. (2011). Discourse communities: A framework from which to consider professional development for rural teachers of science and mathematics. *Teaching and Teacher Education: An International Journal of Research and Studies, 27*(5), 871–879.

Underwood, J. (1997). If a picture is worth a thousand words, what is the value of two? *Journal of Information Technology for Teacher Education, 6*(1), 3–8.

van Someren, M.W., Reimann, P., Boshuizen, H.P.A., & de Jong, T. (Eds.). (1998). *Learning with multiple representations.* London: Pergamon.

Venville, G.J., & Dawson, V. (2010). The impact of an argumentation intervention on Grade 10 students' conceptual understanding of genetics. *Journal of Research in Science Teaching, 47*(8), 952–977.

Venville, G.J., & Treagust, D.F. (1996). The role of analogies in promoting conceptual change in biology. *Instructional Science, 24,* 295–320.

Vygotsky, L.S. (1978). *Mind in society: The development of higher psychological processes.* Cambridge, MA: Harvard University Press.

Waldrip, B., & Prain, V. (2012). Learning from and through representations in science. In B.J. Fraser, K. Tobin, & C.J. McRobbie (Eds.), *Second international handbook of science education* (Vol. 40, pp. 145–154). Dordrecht, the Netherlands: Springer.

Waldrip, B., Prain, V., & Carolan, J. (2010). Using multi-modal representations to improve learning in junior secondary science. *Research in Science Education, 40*(1), 65–80.

Wertsch, J.V. (1991). *Voices of the mind: A sociocultural approach to mediated action.* London: Harvester Wheatsheaf.

White, R.T. (1996). The link between the laboratory and learning. *International Journal of Science Education, 18*(7), 761–774.

White, R.W., & Gunstone, R. (1992). *Probing understanding.* London: Palmer Press.

Yarden, H., & Yarden, A. (2013). Learning and teaching biotechnological methods using animations. In D.F. Treagust & C.-Y. Tsui (Eds.), *Multiple representations in biological education* (pp. 93–108). Dordrecht, the Netherlands: Springer.

Young, M. (2008). From constructivism to realism in the sociology of the curriculum. In G.J. Kelly, A. Luke, & J. Green (Eds.), *Review of research in education: What counts as knowledge in educational settings, disciplinary knowledge, assessment, and curriculum* (Vol. 32, pp. 1–28). Thousand Oaks, CA: Sage.

Zacharia, Z.C. (2005). The impact of interactive computer simulations on the nature and quality of postgraduate science teachers' explanations in physics. *International Journal of Science Education, 27*(14), 1741–1767.

Zheng, Z.R., Yang, W., Garcia, D., & McCadden, P.E. (2008). Effects of multimedia and schema induced analogical reasoning on science learning. *Journal of Computer Assisted Learning, 24*(6), 474–482.

Zohar, A., & Dori, Y.J. (Eds.). (2012). *Metacognition in science education: Trends in current research.* Dordrecht, the Netherlands: Springer.

Zoller, U., & Levy Nahum, T. (2012). From teaching to KNOW to learning to THINK in science education. In B.J. Fraser, K. Tobin, & C.J. McRobbie (Eds.), *Second international handbook of science education* (pp. 209–229). Dordrecht, the Netherlands: Springer.

17

Discourse Practices in Science Learning and Teaching

Gregory J. Kelly

The field of science education has become increasingly interested in understanding the nature and relationship of discourse processes and social practices in instructional settings. This chapter begins by providing a rationale for the study of discourse in science education research. Theoretical perspectives and methodological approaches for researching discourse in science education are reviewed. Discourse studies include consideration of social languages, speech genres, contextualization, paralinguistic communication, interactional contexts, and the role of language in social practice. Studies of discourse in science education reviewed in this chapter were organized into four broad categories. These categories are not mutually exclusive and overlap across a number of dimensions. The first group examines how access to science and identity with science and school are constructed and positioned through interaction. These studies focus on issues of equity and student diversity and are often set in urban and other multicultural educational settings. A second set of studies considers discourse practices across multiple learning contexts. These studies investigate different forms of science instruction and student engagement and include inquiry approaches, group work, and project-based learning. A third set of studies treats argumentation as a discourse practice for students and teachers in science education. The fourth category concerns the discourse of teaching and teacher education. Given the nature of discourse processes in educational events, any given study can be characterized multiple ways. For example, a study of student identity through engagement in an urban community-based science project might fit into any of the four categories used in this review. After reviewing the current knowledge of discourse practices in science education, the chapter concludes by proposing topics, methods, and audiences for future research directions.

Rationale for Discourse Studies

Discourse is central to the ways communities collectively construct norms and expectations, define common

knowledge for the group, build affiliation, frame disciplinary knowledge, and invite or limit participation. In short, educational events are constructed through discourse. Through the everyday practices of educational events, learning opportunities are supported or constrained by how participants make choices about how to communicate, interact, attend, and contribute to group processes. In science classrooms, the ways that teachers talk science, frame communicative norms, and engage students in the range of semiotics of the relevant discipline construct the nature of the scientific knowledge and practices available to be learned (Kelly, 2007). As communication and interpretation of this range of semiotic meanings are integral to teaching and learning, the study of discourse becomes most relevant to researchers interested in understanding how access to science is interactionally accomplished in educational settings. Furthermore, education systems in many countries are becoming increasingly multicultural and multilingual, reflecting changes in societies. Such cultural diversity provides many opportunities for developing mutual understanding and awareness across cultural differences. Yet this diversity can pose challenges for science teaching and learning, where differences in knowledge, expectations, and communication styles may vary among members. Science in its many forms often has unique linguistic features that differ from the ways of being, speaking, and interaction common among students' other discourse communities (Brown, Reveles, & Kelly, 2005). A number of studies of discourse practices identify how the linguistic features of science pose challenges to learners.

Interactional contexts are constructed through discourse in various settings. Research on discourse processes in science education has examined how knowledge and practice are communicated in different settings and how research processes themselves entail uses of discourse. Studies of discourse include examination of everyday talk and action in ongoing teaching and learning events, interviews of participants, and written texts in their various forms, and as such, each research method lends itself to particular research questions.

The study of social processes in schools has the advantage of considering the actual work of participants as they construct everyday life in science classrooms. As this work occurs in naturalistic settings and is made available to analysts through participation as researchers, it offers the possibility of the study of educational events as they are constructed in real time. As a result, the study of naturally occurring discourse in education provides ways of understanding the communication and uptake of conceptual knowledge, distribution of power, definitions of roles, and ways that affiliation and identity are constructed among participants.

Discourse analysis can also be applied to the study of interviews. Often, educational researchers are interested in talking with participants in a given study about relevant research topics. However, such interviews are also discourse events, with norms and expectations, rules for interchanges, and contextualization through paralinguistic communication (Lemke, Kelly, & Roth, 2006; Mishler, 1986; Russ, Lee, & Sherin, 2012). Treating interviews as discourse events, where meaning is constructed among individuals and relevant artifacts and contextualization are taken into account, can lead to differences in what knowledge is made available by participants and interviewers alike. This suggests careful consideration of how meaning is constructed through the moment-to-moment turns of the interview conversation rather than taking the interviewee's comments at face value and as representative of extant knowledge. Thus, the discourse practices of the interview itself can be the subject of study.

Written texts can also be analyzed from a discourse point of view. Science textbooks, written products of students, and representations of scientific knowledge in its many forms can be analyzed with a variety of textual analyses. Thus, discourse analytic research methods provide a set of tools to research the ways that teaching and learning, identity development, and patterns of power and control are constructed in educational settings.

Theoretical and Methodological Considerations for Studying Discourse

Discourse is typically defined as language in use, or a stretch of language larger than a sentence or clause (Cameron, 2001; Jaworski & Coupland, 1999). As discourse entails more than the ideational communication; the broader contexts of social groups, cultural practices, and interpersonal goals need to be taken into consideration when deciphering meaning in interactional contexts. Social norms, expectations, and practices are constructed through discourse processes over time and in turn shape ways that discourse is evoked in each instance, thus instantiating the symbiotic relationship of discourse and sociocultural practices. Hence, discourse is embedded in social

knowledge, practice, power, and identity (Fairclough, 1995). In each instance of use, discourse is constructed among people in some context, with some history, projections of future actions, and ideological commitments. Such histories, assumptions, and commitments, while similarly constructed through cultural practices, play a role in the meaning derived from the social accomplishment of the discourse event. Therefore, discourse analysis generally focuses on more than the moment-to-moment use of language to consider broader patterns over time and the ways that such use is embedded in cultural practices and ideological commitments. Fairclough (1992) identified three dimensions of discourse analysis: analysis of text, analysis of text production, and social analysis of the discursive events, conditions, and consequences for participants. Therefore, the study of discourse processes in science education should properly include a definition of discourse as using language in social contexts. As Gee (2001) argued, discourse is connected to social practices, "ways of being in the world . . . forms of life which integrate words, acts, values, beliefs, attitudes, and social identities as well as gestures, glances, body positions, and clothes" (p. 526). For the purposes of this review, I shall leave the definition of discourse broad and consider a range of studies that encompass the many epistemological, ideological, and social dimensions of language use (Kelly, 2007).

Scientific discourse includes unique features, derived from the highly specialized nature of the epistemic communities constructing these discourse processes and practices. In professional and educational settings, scientific discourse is characterized by multiple modes of semiotic communication, including spoken, written, representational, inscriptional, and symbolic, among others. Studies of scientific practice *in situ* have identified the importance of discourse practices in constructing scientific knowledge (Knorr-Cetina, 1999). From the sensemaking banter of investigations to inscriptions of events to the formalization of text in publications in specialized genres, scientific communities dedicate considerable time to the production of spoken, written, and symbolic discourse (Bazerman, 1988; Kelly, Carlsen, & Cunningham, 1993; Latour & Woolgar, 1986). This range of varied semiotic forms is often alien to science students' ways of communicating in other aspects of their lives. This may pose challenges to learners of science, as the unique linguistic forms of science include passive voice and conditionals, technical vocabulary, interlocking taxonomies, abstraction and nominalization, and complex symbols and notational systems (Halliday & Martin, 1993). Studies of classroom discourse have documented that science is constructed through talk and action in ways often alienating to students, leaving the impression that science is difficult, reserved for cognitive elites, and regimented (Lemke, 1990).

Discourse analysis refers to the study of language in use. To examine the range and types of communicative situations of discourse in science education, analysts have sought to understand how uses of discourse are situated both in social practice and over time. Social practices, norms for interacting, and expectations about communicative demands are tied to the ways that language is used. Discourse analysis thus often considers how discourse is shaped by the norms and expectations of the communicative events. This suggests the need for ethnographic and other research approaches that seek to understand broader cultural patterns of activity governing the uses of discourse (Gee & Green, 1998; Gumperz, 2001). Such studies consider the micro-moments of interaction, the meso-level construction of practices through multiple interactions, and the macro-level analysis of cultural practices, thus acknowledging the importance of ways specific interactions are shaped by cultural norms and expectations. Spoken communication occurs through both verbal and nonverbal channels. To understand meaning in interactional contexts, discourse analysis needs to consider pitch, stress, intonation, pause structures, physical orientation, proxemic distance, and eye gaze, among other paralinguistic features of talk.

This chapter is an update from a previous handbook chapter (Kelly, 2007) and thus focuses primarily on recent publications in science education discourse. The review is limited to studies that specifically examine how the form, function, and/or interactional aspects of language are used in an explicit manner. Generally, this means that studies that self-identify as explicitly related to language, literacy, and discourse are more likely to be included in the review.

Across the range of both substantive topics of research and various educational settings, a number of communicative issues have been observed. Typically, discussion in science classrooms is directed by teacher talk, which often closely follows science textbooks. Such talk in the interactional context of whole-class discussion falls into a pattern of teacher initiation, student response, and teacher evaluation (IRE; Lemke, 1990; Mehan, 1979). This pattern of talk has implications for what is made available to learn, how the particular science discipline is positioned, and how students develop their identity with science. Educational reformers have argued for a more expansive range of interactional contexts that includes opportunities for an active role of students in classroom conversations. Programs include situating learning in scientific practices, project-based activities, reasoning through socioscientific issues, and inquiry investigations. Such varied contexts offer expanded opportunities to learn science and different aspects of science but also impose new communicative demands on students. To address the range of communicative situations, Mortimer and Scott (2003) proposed a model to examine five important dimensions of classroom discourse: teaching purpose, science content, communicative approach, patterns of discourse, and teacher interventions. This model helps understand the nature of discourse events and provides a basis for designing teacher

education with a focus on the centrality of discourse for science learning.

Discourse Processes and Practices in Science Education

Studies of discourse have become a prominent research tradition in science education, with an ever-expanding number of studies and perspectives. Educational reform has progressively shifted to views about the importance of language and social practice in learning science. The conceptual and epistemic goals of such reform in science education suggest the need to develop and examine the linguistic repertoire of students. From the point of view of discourse studies, learning entails being able to communicate with members of a group in an effective manner, be seen as competent, and achieve personal and social goals (Kelly, 2011). As students come to learn science concepts and engage in scientific practices, they develop more expansive ways of speaking, listening, and interpreting the discourse of science and can be viewed as communicatively competent with members of a relevant community. Such a view is consistent with sociohistorical learning theories that consider how cultural tools, signs, and symbols mediate social interaction as a basis for learning (Vygotsky, 1978).

A range of studies has investigated the uses of discourse in science education. In this chapter, I review four applications of discourse analysis to the study of science education: identity and access, discourse practices in multiple learning contexts, argumentation as discourse practice, and teaching and teacher education. One important research tradition centers on issues of access and equity. In the United States and throughout the world, there is a concern regarding differential privileging of certain discourse practices in schooling. Students from backgrounds with linguistic repertoires different than that of school and science may face obstacles to success in science fields. As discourse not only communicates the disciplinary knowledge and practices but also is the basis for identity and affiliation, increasingly studies of equity in science education have been drawn to the uses of discourse. Another research approach is emerging around the discourse practices involved in science learning, epistemology, and epistemic practices. Research in this area examines how knowledge is represented, evoked, positioned, and taken up in educational settings, and includes an emphasis not only on the knowledge and practices of science but also on the epistemic practices involved in the construction of what counts as science in schooling (Kelly, McDonald, & Wickman, 2012). These studies often investigate contexts in which students are expected to take an active role in learning, whether it be through inquiry science, project-based learning, or in a nonschool setting. A third research approach considers argumentation and explanation. Argument often refers to the uses of evidence to persuade an audience of a thesis. Explanation in science is a complex notion that includes consideration of the purposes of science, the nature of current knowledge, the audience, and the specific linguistic features of science. Each of these has unique linguistic forms and social purposes. Finally, a number of scholars examine how the discourse of teaching and teacher education need to be considered for developing ways of engaging students in the knowledge and practices suggested in educational reform.

Constructing Access and Identity Through Discourse Processes

A central concern for science educators has been student access to scientific knowledge, given the differences in register between scientific discourse and everyday ways of speaking, knowing, and being. This concern for equity in science has led to studies of the ways that scientific concepts are constructed in different contexts of use. Scientific communities create social languages or discourses with particular features, often emerging out of the needs of professional work (Bazerman, 1988) and within unique linguistics features (Halliday & Martin, 1993). Taking on a scientific discourse includes building an identity with the discipline and members of the local discourse community, which can be alienating for some students (Brown, 2006), as their everyday way of speaking and interacting is often not valued in educational settings. Thus, students from language backgrounds that differ from that spoken by scientists and science teachers face more serious learning challenges than students whose discourse background matches that of science teachers. To address the variation in discourse practices across communities, studies of educational equity need to account for language variation, specific forms of scientific discourse that pose problems for learners, potential contributions from students' cultural knowledge, and ways that affiliation and identity are constructed through language use. Such studies include considerations of multicultural learning communities and the ways that discourse is hybridized through different ways of speaking, acting, and being.

To improve student participation in and affiliation with science, some educational reformers have sought to develop students' identities by introducing science seen as relevant to the students. Barton and Tan (2010) examined the relationship of agency and identity among students in a voluntary after-school program focused on Green Energy Technology in the City (GET City). The study drew from figured worlds by considering how the affordances and constraints, tasks and discourses, symbols and significances of the activities were constructed by the students and others in the setting. The education program positioned the students to serve as "community science experts" regarding urban heat islands. This study demonstrated how students constructed hybrid discourses through the students' agency and activity (see also, Barton & Tan, 2009) to build understanding of their local environment. Hybrid discourses refer to the mixture of two social languages separated by social differentiation occurring within an encounter (Bakhtin, 1981). This construct has been found useful in studies of science education discourse where different discourses emerge as relevant to the local situation. For example, the relevance of hybridity for developing a more socially just school science was investigated by Hanrahan (2006), who applied critical discourse analysis to the interactions in an Australian secondary school. By providing a contrast in teaching approaches and applying critical discourse analysis to how subjectivities were shaped and constrained by the social structures of the school experience (p. 12), Hanrahan provided evidence for how one teacher was able to construct access-enhancing discourse, thus facilitating student talk, participation, and learning. The results of the study showed how teacher communication was decisive for student engagement, science learning, and development of student identity. Kamberelis and Wehunt (2012) assessed the potential of hybrid discourses for science learning by considering how such discourses are constructed through the shifting relations and power among students working in small groups and a whole-class conversation. The students worked on a standard owl pellet laboratory and created a written report of the results of this dissection. By examining the multiple discourses in the construction of the students' identities, the study identifies how the students were able to draw in language and ways of speaking from popular culture to make sense of science activity and find ways to make such activities manageable. Hybridization was not always the result of multiple discourses in classrooms. Bellocchi and Ritchie (2011) found in a secondary chemistry class that during lessons, students' everyday discourse did not become hybridized with chemical discourse; rather, such hybridization occurred through analogy-writing activities.

Urban schools in the United States present challenges for student learning. Such schools often are underresourced, face teacher attrition, and suffer from the pedagogy of poverty. These schools often have students with varied language backgrounds and classrooms with many speakers of English as a second language. Such contexts have led researchers, teachers, and educational reformers to consider a range of pedagogical innovations. Brown and Spang (2008) examined the developing discursive identity in a fifth-grade classroom in Detroit, Michigan, with a 99% African-American student population. The classroom used a method called "directed discourse" to develop "students with a conceptual and linguistic repertoire" (p. 712). A key feature of this approach is the use of double talk in which the teacher makes science accessible through reworking and rephrasing of ideas to communicate the science in different ways. Bridging science talk and that of the participating students was also addressed by Varelas, Pappas, Kane, Arsenault, Hankes, & Cowan (2008). This study took a sociocultural perspective to consider the discourses of science and that of the "life-world" of the students. Working in six urban classrooms and focusing on students' conceptions of matter, the study found that the use of ambiguous objects encouraged debate. These ambiguous objects, such as a bag of shaving cream, encouraged the students to debate the state of matter and led them to reason about the science, thus deriving meaning from the initial confusion.

Studies of discourse in urban settings also included the ways that classroom interaction develops identity. Varelas, Kane, and Wylie (2012) examined the narratives of figured worlds for 30 Black elementary students, Grades K–2. The study considered student representation of knowledge in science journals. The authors drew from Bakhtin's (1981) idea of chronotopes (use of space and time in students' work) to analyze how students saw themselves as scientists and with science. The creation of the journals and conversations around the journal entries helped develop confident and hopeful science identities for the students. The results showed how these students constructed positive ways to view "their selves relative to science and scientists" (p. 592) through the chronotopic arrangements in their narratives. Barton, Tan, and Rivet (2008) demonstrated how the issue of identity and building affiliation and participation was important to a teacher in an urban middle school classroom. This longitudinal case study considered how girls came to develop hybrid discourses as they created science artifacts, played with identities, and negotiated new roles. The study identified how the girls in the class were able to draw on out-of-school resources to construct hybrid discourses, which allowed for greater affiliation. Ash (2008) also drew from Bakhtin and considered the important role of hybrid discourses for urban middle school students. The study took into consideration the varied participant structures of the classrooms including "research rotations" (team work on research topics), "crosstalk" (whole-class synthesis around emerging ideas), "benchmark lesson" (whole class where content ideas were introduced), "jigsaw" (small-group work for students to teach each other), and "dilemma" (whole class and small group to solve ecological dilemma). Besides analysis of classroom discourse, guided clinical interviews were employed to assess student understanding. The results identified how students were able to appropriate the biological principle of adaptation, although with variations in understanding, through uses of everyday and scientific discourses. Olitsky, Flohr, Gardner, and Billups (2010) offered a different approach in a number of ways. They designed a collaborative research experience that included urban high school students and chose to focus on why some students did not achieve academically or develop identity with school science even when they were well prepared to do so. Through extensive ethnographic video analysis and cogenerative dialogues, the research team found that classroom structures that allowed students to build social and symbolic capital (e.g., helping a peer) facilitated participation in science-related activities, while external motivation (e.g., grades) was not sufficient to overcome the students' perceived risks of participating in science.

Other studies identified ways that race and linguistic repertoires influenced how students were able to engage with science. For example, Brown (2006) studied how participation in discursive practices of science presents cultural costs for marginalized students. While serving as the teacher in an urban high school where he developed intimate knowledge of the students, Brown used focus-group interviews to examine students' diverse views of science and their experiences in school science. He found that students faced cultural costs when learning how to participate in scientific epistemology, practices, and discourse. These students needed to become bicultural to engage in these practices, thus appropriating some new ways of being into their repertoire of discursive registers. The issue of cultural costs for students participating in science is central to comparative set of case studies presented by Reveles and Brown (2008). Across two cases (in an urban school with primarily African-American students and a suburban school with a large Spanish-speaking and English-learner student population), these authors identified the need for students to contextually shift their discourse practices in ways similar to code switching in order to negotiate the science of their respective classroom cultures. One teacher used metadiscourse (talk about science talk) to help students make connections across events and science topics. This strategy was designed to build academic practices across subject matter and provide students ways of developing academic identities. The second teacher helped students shift from everyday understanding to learning to engage in scientific discourse around classifying in biology by providing students access to scientific terminology.

Issues of access and identity surfaced in other studies concerned with equity in science education. While small-group work has been shown to open up some possibilities for student participation, studies of the discourse processes of small-group interactions point to a number of problems. Although lectures, even when peppered with IRE sequences, pose constraints to students, small-group discussions also pose problems for learners. Issues around variations in students' status, race, class, and gender surface as relevant in such contexts. Gomes, Mortimer, and Kelly (2011) examined how the construction of inclusion and exclusion of particular students was a complex web of multiple meanings and variation in ways of participating. The study took place in secondary chemistry classrooms in Brazil using a sociocultural approach that examined the details of small-group conversation. The study showed how gender, ethnic group, and social class were insufficient to explain the construction of inclusion or exclusion from group work. Rather, some students' agency led to taking on leadership roles based on a core set of beliefs about school as a means of social ascent. A study by Parsons, Tran, and Gomillion (2008) presents a contrast. This study considered how a supposed color-blind philosophy and dysconsciousness (accepting inequality and exploitation) among eighth-grade students in a rural school led to the privileging of European-American students. The research approach considered the roles taken up in group work (leading, supporting, challenging) and showed how European-American students were more likely to take up important roles when working with African-American students of similar academic ability. Parsons and colleagues (2008) identified how "Whiteness" was evoked to attain leadership roles and recommended a consideration of race when assigning students to small groups.

Inquiry-oriented approaches often include student work in small groups (Kelly, in press). Such interactional settings pose different language demands than teacher lectures or various forms of direct instruction. The shift in science education reform (National Research Council, 1996, 2011) toward developing knowledge and experience with scientific practices requires that students learn through engagement, heavily dependent on discourse processes. These new language demands pose new challenges for students learning science in a second language. One central educational challenge is to design effective assessments that lead to improved instructional approaches for these students (Duran, 2008). The challenges of developing new assessments that take into consideration the language demands of inquiry science was investigated by Shaw, Bunch, and Geaney (2010). This study examined three performance assessments designed for fifth-grade students. Through textual analysis, the researchers considered the language demands of the assessments and how these might pose challenges to English learners. The emerging analytical framework considered the participant structures (whole class, small group, pair, individual), the communicative modes (interpersonal, interpretive, presentational), and the written texts and genres (experimental accounts, science explanations, science reports, science persuasion, and narrative). This framework offers science teachers and designers of assessments ways of considering the language demands and how to measure student knowledge given their varied language backgrounds.

Studies of equity and identity have surfaced a number of important dimensions of access to science that depend on language use and associated cultural practices. These studies make visible the constraints to improving participation. By drawing on discourse analysis, a new set of opportunities emerges for the field. To improve access to science, research on equity may need to make stronger ties with developing trends in the field around learning, epistemic practices, and teacher education. Building affiliation and participation are important steps for increasing equity, yet as these studies have shown, much more needs to be done. The links from discourse and social practice to access to science need to be made throughout the science education system and most particularly in teacher education.

Discourse Practices Across Multiple Learning Contexts

The study of discourse has also been viewed as important for student engagement, including inquiry approaches and student-led group work in laboratory settings. A number of instructional strategies have been developed and enhanced to provide students with opportunities to engage in the discourse and cultural practices of science. These include focusing on the epistemic practices and conceptual understandings of science, teaching science as inquiry, using project-based learning, learning through group work, and learning in everyday life settings.

Studies of student learning suggest that features of scientific discourse are not mastered as received knowledge through didactic instruction but rather through participation as a member of a group in a discourse community. Students learn meanings of scientific terms through engagement in discourse and practices (Kelly et al., 2012). A number of studies have sought to examine meaning as constructed in use by students in activity. One set of studies has emerged from Wickman and Östman and their colleagues (Lidar, Almqvist, & Östman, 2010; Wickman & Östman, 2002). These studies are based in a "practical epistemology analysis" that considers meaning in use and how students fill in conceptual gaps when encountering unfamiliar discursive situations. Hamza and Wickman (2008) analyzed Swedish upper secondary students' talk while working on an electrochemical cell. They considered the various encounters students had with unknown situations and found that misconceptions were either neutral or generative for furthering the scientific activity rather than impeding learning as previously thought. The focus on practical meaning as enacted by participants in interaction also has methodological implications for research in science education—the need to examine ways that meaning is made through discourse in specific contexts of use. Jakobsson, Mäkitalo, and Säljö (2009) sought to understand how students make sense of the greenhouse effect in the context of conversations around global warming. In contrast to previous survey and interview studies, these researchers set the locus of meaning in the context of student small-group work in which they were asked to address contradictory claims about the Earth's future temperature. Through analysis of the students' discourse, the analysts were able to document the struggles students had with the conceptual knowledge, particularly as related to the differences between the natural and anthropogenic greenhouse effect and what counted as a greenhouse gas. These results differ markedly from previous studies that sought to assess individual students' knowledge as if it were pre-existing and independent of the research elicitation context.

The relationship of epistemic practices and students' engagement in discourse was examined in two recent studies. Manz (2012) examined how third-grade students came to engage in epistemic practices supported by the use of modeling. In this study, the students were involved in the study of a local ecosystem adjacent to their school. The modeling activity was aimed at developing student participation in model making, making claims with models, and understanding the entailments of the models. Through the extended curriculum, the students engaged with a number of disciplinary concepts through the uses of models in this way. Manz drew from interviews and videotape of classwork and found that students' discourse demonstrated that modeling practice made visible objects and relations in the ecosystem, supported deepening of students' disciplinary understanding, and served as a scaffold for further uses of modeling. Oliveira, Akerson, Colak, Pongsanon, and Genel (2012) considered how teachers' discourse features and practices communicated explicit and implicit meanings about the epistemology of science. By examining the uses of hedges and boosters in two classrooms (kindergarten and fourth grade), the study showed how differential uses of qualifiers led to differences in illocutionary uptake. For example, hedged comments from the teacher suggested tentativeness and uncertainty as "acceptable features of scientific meaning making" (p. 677). The study showed how typical misconceptions about science as certain and static are communicated through choices in descriptors used by teachers. This suggests that implicit meanings about the nature of science are communicated through the ways that discourse is enacted in classrooms.

Another learning context involved the use of inquiry in science classrooms. Inquiry entails seeking knowledge of the natural, designed, or social world. Learning through inquiry often involves engaging students in scientific practices using language such as posing questions, providing explanations, communicating results, evaluating inferences, and critiquing ideas (Kelly, in press). As these practices are heavily language dependent, discourse analysis provides a way to consider how opportunities for learning are constructed in education events and how the merits of educational practice can be accessed. Inquiry instruction often includes students working with material objects to derive conclusions based on evidence. The processes of discovering how to make inferences, draw conclusions, and communicate results are interactionally accomplished through discourse. Thus, student reasoning can be viewed as a social process, highly dependent on the types of discourse moves available in their sociolinguistic repertoire (Kelly, 2011).

Such inquiry approaches seek to engage students in a range of discourses and discourse modes including written and spoken language, mathematics, inscriptions, and gestures (Airey & Linder, 2009). For example, Crawford (2005) considered how fifth-grade students could be viewed as communicatively competent by displaying knowledge in different modes in an inquiry task. The study identified how the spoken, written, and visual (e.g., graphs, diagrams) need to be considered by teachers and analysts to get a full understanding of how student knowledge is manifest through engagement practices. Use of representational practices in science must be learned as students come to understand how to employ language and signs and symbols. Danish and Phelps (2011) studied how mediating factors fostered kindergarten and first-grade students learning to represent knowledge. In this case, the students were asked to create storyboards about how honeybees collect nectar. The analysis of the student practices and how these practices changed

through an intervention focused on inquiry and representational practices regarding collection of nectar. The results show student improvement in understandings about the structure, behavior, and function of the honeybee activity and also how to represent and assess representations of the science ideas. To achieve these results, the teachers spent a great deal of time on task requirements, discussions of science content, and ways such content could be represented. Thus, the storyboards were the product of multiple discourse practices and also became the subject of discussion through comment and critique among students.

Multimodal interactions among young learners (5- and 6-year-old children) were the focus of a study by Siry, Ziegler, and Max (2012), which occurred in Luxembourg. These authors took the perspective of science as discourse-in-interaction to consider how students made meaning of lessons centered on water. Students' discursive practices were coconstructed among participants and emergent in the specific conversations around water. Through these practices, science was talked into being by the participants through multimodal interactions that included verbal, gestural, and relevant material resources. This importance of the uses of gesture in discourse was emphasized by Givry and Roth (2006), who proposed a new conception of conceptions to shift away from viewing students' conceptions as in the mind to "linguistic structures made available" (p. 1087) in public discursive spaces. Through a detailed study of interaction in French upper secondary physics classrooms, they propose to treat conceptions as a unit of analysis composed of talk, gesture, and salient semiotic resources in the local setting. Multimodal discourse analysis was also found useful in other secondary school contexts. Jaipal (2010) identified how different modalities for communication enhanced students' understanding of chemosynthesis. This was accomplished by a Canadian biology teacher through multimodal representations that communicated the epistemological, presentational, orientational, and organizational meanings of the scientific knowledge. Other studies such as that of Maeng and Kim (2011) investigated modalities of science teaching practice and students' pedagogical subject positioning. This study occurred in middle school in Korea and considered the communication of science in this predominantly teacher-directed classroom. This study identified the discourse code and discourse register as important for meaning making.

Studies of discourse processes have shifted the focus of scientific inquiry to include the importance of communication in the construction, critique, and refinement of scientific knowledge. Issues of scientific method, epistemic practices, and engagement with science can be investigated through the study of discourse practices constructed in local settings (Kelly, 2008). Furthermore, many interventions and implementations of inquiry approaches to science instruction include an emphasis on argument, explanation, and uses of evidence, all of which entail learning about the discourse practices of science. Ford and Wargo (2012) make the case for developing dialogic teaching that includes both conceptual and epistemic aspects of understanding. They argued that understanding a scientific idea entails using the idea to explain natural phenomena, understanding where this idea sits in a range of alternatives, and understanding the criteria for which various ideas are adjudicated in science by considering the relative explanatory success. Drawing from studies of natural selection, Ford and Wargo demonstrated how and what students understand are connected to the ways that disciplinary knowledge and practices are framed through instructional conversations. The importance of such epistemic framing was evidenced in a study by Tang, Coffey, Elby, and Levin (2010), who applied discourse analysis to show how the steps of a supposed scientific method limited students' thinking when compared to a more open, authentic set of inquiry practices. Much like the study by Manz (2012), these studies demonstrated that learning disciplinary knowledge in robust ways included learning of relevant epistemic practices.

Project-based science provided the context for analysis of inquiry discussions in a study by Alozie, Moje, and Krajcik (2010). The study examined how embedded features in the project-based curriculum could support science discussions. In particular, the curriculum focused on four discussion practices: making knowledge explicit, asking questions and providing nonevaluative follow-up, supporting student communication, and discussion norms. Across a range of data sources in two urban, 10th- and 11th-grade biology classes, Alozie and colleagues (2010) found that time restraints, a push to cover curriculum topics, and testing limited the teachers' abilities to encourage student–student interactive discourse. Rather, and in spite of the project-based approach and support provided, the teachers had difficulty engaging students in the abstract disciplinary concepts and connecting to the students' everyday discourse. The study called for a thorough approach to reform that includes specific work on developing the students' and teachers' abilities to engage in science discussions.

Small-group discussions offer interactional contexts in which students are often asked to engage in disciplinary discourse. A review of 94 studies of small-group discussions by Bennett, Hogarth, Lubben, Campbell, and Robinson (2010) identified four effective engagement strategies in science discourse. Such groups were specifically constituted to offer divergent views on the topic at hand, included some training in how to manage group work, had leaders with inclusion discourse styles, and offered students specific ways to engage in specialized discourse, such as argumentation. Across the studies, the authors found that single-sex groups function more purposefully than mixed groups do.

Discourse processes involving science occur in many diverse contexts across settings. While classroom discourse occurs in different contexts, a number of out-of-school settings are also important for science learning. Zimmerman, Reeve, and Bell (2010) created an "everyday

expertise framework" for considering the learning interactions across planes of meaning, including the individual, social, and cultural influences on sense making during museum visits. In this study, they considered how 15 families moved through a science center and examined the interactions of the participants with each other, the artifacts available to them, and extant knowledge brought to bear on the meaning-making conversations around biology. The study identified a number of science-related (e.g., perceptual talk about biological processes, fact talk about specific topics) and not–science-related sense-making processes (e.g., prior experiences, hobbies). The families used these processes as epistemic resources for developing meaning in the science center. While the study by Zimmerman and colleagues (2010) considered families visiting a science center, DeWitt and Hohenstein (2010) considered students visiting different science museums (in London and New York) as part of classroom activities. They noted the importance of considering the pre- and postvisit discussions for understanding the meaning that can be made by the visiting students at the museums. To address this issue, they considered the types of discourse patterns found for each of the four classes in each of the two settings, classroom and science museum. They considered both the extent of the use of the triadic dialogue (initiation-response-evaluation; see Lemke, 1990) and the range and type of teacher questions. They found that in both settings, teachers generally did not vary much from the use the triadic dialogue, tended to dominate the conversations, and often posed task-related procedural questions or questions seeking a faculty response. Despite this overall trend, there was a higher proportion of nontriadic dialogue and more inviting questions in the museum settings. The study identified the importance of understanding the discourse patterns in multiple contexts and the ways the museum setting may be able to introduce interactional sequences in which teachers can vary from the patterned ways of talking often found in classrooms.

These studies of epistemic practice, inquiry, and project-based learning in multiple settings are developing knowledge about contexts that foster student discourse. These studies provide points of success and plausible directions for new curriculum development and research methods. Much work remains to be done to realize these new pedagogies on a wide scale. The arguments need to be made first with the research community that student engagement in discourse practices of science enhanced learning in demonstrable ways and then to the larger educational practitioner and policy world. Such studies would do well to connect to interests in equity and the value of integration in teacher education.

Argumentation as Discourse Practice

One central practice emerging as relevant to many pedagogical approaches is argumentation. Argumentation generally refers to the uses of evidence to persuade an audience of the merits of a position, although definitions vary and are subject to empirical investigation and theoretical discussion (Berland & Reiser, 2011; Bricker & Bell, 2008). Argumentation is particularly relevant to inquiry approaches that place emphasis on evidence and explanation. Educational programs often include asking students to build arguments in interactive settings, where supporting and defending claims relate to cognitive, social, and epistemic goals (Duschl, 2008). Across different research traditions, building an argument entails understanding genre conventions of ways of aligning data, warrants, and claims. Thus, arguments occur within a social context with conventionalized ways of using discourse. As with other forms of interaction and language use, the discourse processes of argumentation include not only verbal communication but also the uses of signs and symbols, important for communicating and critiquing scientific models, graphs, and other knowledge representations. Argumentation is thus a learned discourse practice, with particular genre conventions that determine what counts as relevant data, a valid argument, sufficient evidence, and so forth (Kelly, Regev, & Prothero, 2008). As such, argumentation occurs when the merits of a claim or claims are in question, and thus differs from explanation, where the phenomenon is not in doubt and an understanding of a causal mechanism is sought (Osborne & Patterson, 2011). Argumentation is one of many discourse practices employed in science and science education and needs to be framed as a practice with these particular genre conventions (Berland & Hammer, 2012; McDonald & Kelly, 2012).

Since the review in the previous edition of this handbook (Kelly, 2007), there have been a large number of studies of argumentation across many contexts in science education. A thorough review of this literature merits a separate chapter. As I will not be able to review all studies of argumentation, I shall focus on some key systematic reviews of the literature that provide a thorough overview of the field. I also refer the reader to two recent edited volumes that treat the range of relevant topics for argumentation in science education (Erduran & Jimenez-Aleixandre, 2008; Khine, 2012).

Bricker and Bell (2008) considered the ways that argumentation has been conceptualized in science education. They drew from science studies and the learning sciences to identify ways that science education can benefit from drawing in knowledge from these other fields. They provided a critique of studies of argumentation in science education by noting the narrow uses of argumentation (often derived from the Toulmin model) and suggested the potential of broader considerations provided from outside science education. The review documented ways that argumentation is conceptualized and applied in fields such as formal logic, argumentation theory, philosophy, sociology and anthropology of science, rhetoric, and the learning sciences. The review documents three problems: (a) standpoint, questions about what counts as argumentation; (b) purpose, questions about the educational

purposes of different conceptualizations of argumentation; and (c) nonverbal modes of communication, questions about to what extent arguments are made through various inscriptions. The implications of this review suggest that science education consider a range of issues currently receiving little attention. For example, the rhetoric of science, the systematic study of persuasion in science, offers ways of clarifying the nature and uses of persuasion. In addition, the learning sciences' focus on everyday argumentation that occurs in the lives of young people can provide different understandings of what counts as evidence for students under different conditions. They conclude that argumentation can be part of science education programs that teach not only the theories and concepts of science through engagement in discourse practices but also the ways in which science gets constructed.

Many studies of argumentation in science education focus on how students come to understand and use arguments. Sampson and Clark (2008) provided a thorough and balanced review of different analytic techniques employed in science education to assess the merits and characteristics of students' arguments. The review identified a number of domain-general and domain-specific analytic frameworks underlying the methods for assessing argument and documents the constraints and affordances of each framework. The researchers considered how each framework treated the structure and content of argument and the nature of the justification. Through their analysis, they were able to distill some general patterns about how the field has conceptualized analytics to assess argument. While the various frameworks have differences in how they consider argument structure, across the studies, the researchers have found that students struggle to produce justification for claims, generate complex explanations, and develop coherence linking ideas together. Assessing the cognitive content of student arguments remains a question for the field. Sampson and Clark noted that content may include more than just the factual nature of specific claims, as these are assessed in a broader perspective comprising the overall argument. Additional criteria for cognitive and social goals include logical coherence, relevance, and explanatory power (p. 467). Regarding justification, most studies have shown that students tend to focus on the claims or assertions and neglect the relevant information related to justifying the claims put forth.

The review by Sampson and Clark (2008) noted the prominence of the Toulmin model in argumentation studies in science education but also identified a number of shortcomings of the model. Böttcher and Meisert (2011) provided a critique of studies of argumentation in science education from the perspective of a model-based view of scientific investigation. This approach is derived from philosophy of science and cognitive science and thus defines argument from this perspective: "Arguments are indicators for or against the fitting of a model according to its logical coherence or in comparison to empirical data" (p. 109). This model-based view similarly defines argumentation as a process of evaluation of competing models. The authors propose a model of model-based argumentation that includes students developing competence in arguing, understanding of arguments and argumentation, and knowledge of models and data. The review includes an extensive application of the model-based view of argumentation and compares this to the more semantic-oriented approaches of the Toulmin model. The authors make the case that the model-based view has certain advantages, such as being derived from current thinking in philosophy of science and providing students with opportunities to examine empirical data in reference to evolving scientific models.

Cavagnetto (2010) provided a review of studies of argumentation with the goal of fostering scientific literacy defined as "the ability to accurately and effectively interpret and construct science-based ideas in the popular media and everyday contexts" (p. 352). The review considered the nature of the argument activity, the emphasis of these interventions, and the science included in the argument activity. Across studies of uses of argument in science education, Cavagnetto found that studies, while often holding overlapping domains, could be classified into three orientations: understanding the interaction of science and society, immersion in learning scientific argument, and learning the structure of argument that can transferred to diverse situations. The review showed how argument-based instruction can be used to foster scientific literacy through a variety of interventions.

Learning scientific argumentation poses a problem for students and teachers. While the normative goals of developing abilities to articulate evidence and draw together lines of reasoning connect disciplinary practice with student activity, achieving such goals remains difficult. Berland and McNeill (2010) presented ways of designing supportive instructional contexts through the development of a learning progression for scientific argumentation. They view a learning progression as "a sequence of successively more complex ways of thinking about a practice or content that develop over time" (p. 766) and that "increasingly align with scientific versions of the practice" (p. 767). The proposed learning progression considers three dimensions: the instructional context, argumentation product, and argumentation process. The progression recommends an instructional context that provides support for student development of argumentation practices in general (claim, evidence, reasoning) and context-specific support grounded in the disciplinary and curriculum constraints of the relevant situation. A second way to support argumentation involves establishing norms and expectations for the classroom culture. Supporting and defending claims, posing questions, and evaluating reasoning requires a classroom culture that places value on dialectical reasoning (Kelly, 2008). Finally, Berland and McNeill (2010) make clear the need to connect spoken and written discourse. Spoken and written discourse offer different opportunities and constraints for learning about evidence use in context.

These modes of communication need to be connected to develop a culture supporting a value on evidence.

Studies of argument and argumentation are emerging areas of research in science education with much potential to develop students' conceptual and epistemic knowledge. Research has begun to specify the relationship of students' scientific knowledge with the processes of argumentation (Clark & Sampson, 2008; von Aufschnaiter et al., 2008). This connection of conceptual and epistemic goals brings together important aspects of scientific reasoning. There have been a number of interventions to support such goals, including use of the science writing heuristic (Choi, Notebaert, Diaz, & Hand, 2010), seeding discussions with online discourse software (Clark & Sampson, 2007), and using student-generated questions in group work to support effective argumentation (Chin & Osborne, 2010a, 2010b).

An emerging area related to argumentation is the development of science education programs aimed at fostering discourse among students around socioscientific issues. These programs provide situations in which science and technology are connected to issues that involve values (Walker & Zeidler, 2007). In these cases, students need to draw on knowledge of science but also consider other criteria for decision making such as ethics. While there has not been extensive discourse analysis applied to debates and arguments regarding socioscientific issues, there are some trends suggesting the need to look carefully at how issues are framed, reasoned, and debated through discourse. Kolstø (2006) studied Norwegian students' informal reasoning about the relationship of power lines and childhood leukemia. This study showed how students slotted into five different ways of making arguments around risk, precautions, and pros and cons. Nielsen (2012) applied normative pragmatics to the study of Danish secondary students' arguments about gene therapy. This approach considers the type of speech act, the argumentative indicators (e.g., "yes, but"), choices in lexicon by speakers, and scorekeeping of commitments and entitlements referenced by speakers in the conversations. The results indicated that students drew from science to identify or articulate issues and evoked science in response to previous lines of reasoning. The students' disciplinary knowledge partly determined the range and extent of their ability to engage in the socioscientific issues but was not necessarily used in deliberations. Albe (2008) drew from sociolinguistics to show the importance of French secondary students' understanding of the social and often controversial nature of scientific knowledge in its construction, not just when applied to a social controversy—in this case, the possible dangers of uses of mobile telephones. This study noted the importance of developing students' epistemological orientation and knowledge along with the conceptual and social goals of science teaching. These results are consistent with other studies that identify the range of reasons students use to makes decisions about socioscientific issues, often based on nonepistemic issues or based on epistemic issues derived from affiliation with a cause (Evagorou, Jimenez-Aleixandre, & Osborne,

2012). Such studies need also to consider the competing discourses of school science and how ways of speaking, arguing, and presenting oneself may vary across students from diverse backgrounds and sociocultural status (Ideland, Malmberg, & Winberg, 2011).

Despite the strong growth in studies of argumentation and the potential value of engaging students in such practices, a number of unresolved issues need to be addressed in the field. First, there is an ongoing debate about the nature of argument and its relationship with explanation (Berland & McNeill, 2012; Berland & Reiser, 2009; Osborne & Patterson, 2011). There are some clear differences between an explanation and an argument, although each can be integrated into effective discourse practices in science education. Such debates may require drawing from philosophy of science and analyzing the linguistic characteristics of each in various settings. Second, argumentation is one of many plausible discourse practices in science instruction (McDonald & Kelly, 2012). The range of discourse practices, how each contributes to learning, and how various discourse practices can be mutually supportive needs further elaboration. Third, analytics for argumentation are being developed. These analytics have for the most part examined arguments in the moment of interaction or end products such as writing samples. The field also needs to consider how to analyze the development of arguments over time as speakers and writers learn, develop, and potentially enhance their argumentative skills. Thus, the refinement of analytics is needed. Fourth, science has suffered from a rhetoric of conclusions (Schwab, 1960), and argumentation risks becoming viewed as only a cognitive goal without careful considerations of the epistemic and social goals needed for effective science instruction (Duschl, 2008).

Teaching and Teacher Education

Across educational settings, much of classroom life is dominated by teacher talk. While the move toward more student-centered approaches—for example, inquiry, project-based learning, and argumentation—has been advocated, there remain tensions in developing effective learning and open dialogue in science classrooms. Yet the implications for science teaching of discourse studies in science education are clear. Students need to learn science knowledge and practices by participating in meaning-making processes through engagement. While attending to a speaker is a form of processing language, and certainly learning can occur through listening to a well-articulated lecture, to fully understand and develop meaning through use requires that students use language and employ science concepts in relevant contexts (Lemke, 1990). As engaging with science includes working in a range of semiotic fields, teachers need to find ways that students are given opportunities to use words, signs, and symbols to communicate and interpret meaning in a variety of interactional contexts and settings. By providing opportunities for students to learn through speaking, listening, and using concepts in context of use, such as while engaging in scientific practices such as observing, reasoning, explaining, or providing evidence in an argument, teachers can engage students in science through active participation where learning is most likely to occur.

The study of teacher questioning has a long tradition in science education (e.g., Carlsen, 1991). Chin (2007) designed a study to examine how teachers use questions in classroom discourse to scaffold student learning of scientific knowledge. The study was set in six seventh-grade classrooms, focused on 36 lessons across the six teachers. Chin found that teachers were able to use four types of questioning leading to productive thinking among the students: Socratic questioning, verbal jigsaw, semantic tapestry, and framing. Each of these strategies provided ways for students to engage in productive discourse leading to learning gains. Oliveira (2010) sought to understand how elementary teachers facilitated science inquiry discussions. This study took a sociolinguistic perspective to examine the teachers' social understanding of questioning and changes in questioning discourse patterns. The teachers participated in professional development focused on incorporating scientific modeling, scientific inquiry, and nature of science into their classroom practices. The results of the study showed how teachers' social knowledge of questioning was improved in four ways: developing understanding of the multiple cognitive functions of questions, reframing of the teachers' views of their intentions for uses of questions, acknowledging the ways their sincerity was understood by students, and finding ways to increase student discourse through questions. The effects of the experience in the institute and the development of social knowledge led to an increased focus on student-centered questioning practices. Oliveira's implications for professional development for teachers includes not only attending to cognitive ends but also a consideration of the linguistic awareness needed to understand how questions function in classroom discourse.

Chin and Osborne (2010a) considered ways that developing students' abilities to use questions fostered argumentation. The study introduced argumentation as a way of teaching science to secondary teachers in Singapore and London. The intervention also included providing students with question stems to develop their abilities to pose questions. Analysis was done on the students' questions and arguments, following the Toulmin layout of argument. The study was able to identify the ways that the students' questions mediated productive discourse and fostered conversations around issues (puzzlements) identified through this questioning.

Learning to teach and learning from teaching involve understanding how to employ, decipher, interpret, and produce discourse in the moment-to-moment interactions of educational events. This requires not only knowledge of students, instructional strategies, and subject matter but also of how language works in conversations. Teacher education has become increasingly focused on the ways that science teachers learn to reflect on their practice and in particular how to use discourse moves to engage students in reasoning about ideas (Zembal-Saul, 2009). To enact reform in science curricula and assessment, there needs to be corresponding reform in how discourse practices are understood in teacher education. As science education reform seeks to help students understand concepts, models, and epistemic practices, teachers face the challenges of helping students engage with the subject matter in this way. Much of the research in the area of teacher education parallels studies of students and classroom discourse, such as developing ways of teaching inquiry, argumentation, and socioscientific issues and in ways that develop students' identities in science.

The importance of epistemic discourse can be taken up in studies of teacher education. For example, Windschitl, Thompson, and Braaten (2008) devised a system of heuristics for progressive disciplinary discourse (HPDD) to engage novice secondary science teachers in model-based approaches to inquiry. This teacher education program sought to introduce progressively ways that scientific models can be used for instructional purposes. Through an extensive collection of relevant data sources for the novice teachers, Windschitl and colleagues (2008) were able to document participants' evolving understanding of epistemic discourses around models, inquiry, and argument. The study showed how a "combination of mutually reinforcing experiences and the consistent infusion of elements of HPDD" (p. 359) provided conditions for the participants to restructure their thinking regarding epistemic aspects of model-based inquiry. One epistemic discourse is argumentation, which Sadler (2006) introduced in a teacher education program. He sought to emphasize the importance of discourse and uses of argument in science teaching with preservice secondary science teachers. Interestingly, the preservice teachers, to the extent to which they endorsed the uses of argumentation, viewed argumentation as a means to improve the acquisition of science content (i.e., concepts) rather than as a legitimate goal for learning. This study demonstrated the deeply engrained views favoring conceptual over epistemic and social goals for science learning among novice teachers.

Bringing about true dialogue that fosters student learning has been a goal of a number of projects concerning science teaching and teacher education. Mercer, Dawes, and Staarman (2009) examined the discourse practices of two primary school teachers as part of a larger study on teacher–student discourse. The study investigated how teachers used dialogue to explore students' current understandings, considered the learning trajectory of students, made links across events time, and modeled "ways of using talk for sharing ideas, reasoning, and developing shared understanding" (p. 353). The teachers were able to use questions to encourage student involvement, to provide interactional spaces for students to speak in pairs or groups, and make references to the temporal organization

of events. Yet despite such discursive moves, the whole-class discussions were dominated by the triadic dialogue in very traditional ways and were not able to develop interactive dialogues (cf., Mortimer & Scott, 2003). The authors advocate more explicit teacher education around the effective use of talk for learning. Loxley (2009) made a different case for developing effective teacher discourse. This study suggested the importance of developing persuasive discourse. The author noted that science education has tended to focus on students constructing knowledge from practical experiences but that they rarely have the background knowledge to engage in sense-making discourse. Through the study of three cases, Loxley found that the teachers, despite committing to developing persuasive discourse, fell into the standard pattern of focusing on mediating practical tasks and using science concepts "authoritatively as labels for objects or events" (p. 1621). The issue of developing stronger dialogue in elementary school contexts was the central issue of a focused collection on elementary science teacher education (Mikeska, Anderson, & Schwarz, 2009). Each of the studies in this series placed importance on the need for dialogue in teaching and teacher education, including developing knowledge about uses of argument, modeling, and engaging with inquiry curricula.

In order to understand how to change the interpretation and use of language in science teacher education, researchers need to document relevant current practices and uses of language. As inquiry-oriented pedagogies have been advocated in science education reform, Gyllenpalm, Wickman, and Holmgren (2010) investigated how secondary teachers in Sweden used two key terms related to inquiry: "hypothesis" and "experiment." They found that teachers often conflated technical uses of hypothesis and experiment with everyday uses of the terms, thus failing to provide students with access to the nature of science. The inaccurate use of these terms was attributed to a lack of distinction between methods of teaching and methods of inquiry. This study showed that not only are the meanings of science concepts not always accurately employed, but that meanings of supposed scientific practices are similarly ambiguous in teacher talk, thus limiting understanding of inquiry and the nature of science. Interestingly, terms such as "hypothesis" played a significant role in teacher education courses, but were rarely employed in pure science courses, even when students were involved in an inquiry event (Gyllenpalm & Wickman, 2011).

Eylon, Berger, and Bagno (2008) examined teachers' collective discourse in a professional development setting. The study is interesting as the purpose of the professional development was to enhance student-centered classroom discourse. The research focused on how the high school physics teachers learned about using a knowledge integration approach to the teaching of their students. The discourse analysis centered on the teachers' collective reflections on their teaching as part of a continuing professional development program. Changes were found in the teachers' knowledge as manifest in their reflective discourse. The teachers learned about the importance of students learning from peers, listening to students' ideas, and developing a variety of assessment strategies.

Studies of discourse in science education have generally focused on teacher talk and student small-group work. Little work has examined the study of discourse in teacher education or the study of the discourse of teacher education. Yet, across the range of studies reviewed in this chapter, many of students' opportunities to learn are mediated by teacher discourse and teacher knowledge of uses of discourse. Thus, a clear direction, begun already in works cited earlier, concerns how to develop in teachers the recognition of the importance of discourse for pedagogical practices, evaluating student knowledge, and including students in reasoning processes. Understanding uses and variations in discourse processes can become a key area for teachers concerned about students' access of science and educational opportunities.

Emerging Research Directions for Studies of Discourse Practices in Science Education

This chapter considered studies of discourse in science education settings, primarily from the year 2007 to present, as an update to a previous review (Kelly, 2007). A number of key themes emerge from this recently published research relevant to future studies of discourse practices but also to other aspects of science learning and teaching, such as studies of cognition, curriculum development, and teacher education. This review suggests that future studies focused on discourse in science education need to consider sociocultural learning theory, development of programs supporting equity in science, language use in student-led investigations, ongoing debates in science education, and refinements of research methods.

One research direction concerns the development and emerging prominence of sociocultural learning theories. Such theories place a premium on cultural knowledge, socialization, language, and learning mediated by social processes. Use of discourse theory can be useful in at least two ways. First, discourse can be viewed a normative goal. Science education programs can be designed to develop teachers' and students' abilities to engage with discourse practices in new ways, thus expanding their respective repertoires and providing access to multiple new communities. Second, discourse analysis can be employed as a means to assess the uses of language in education events and artifacts, as a set of methodological tools to assess learning. Discourse analysis provides unique tools for understanding how learning theories can be tested in educational settings. Such analysis is especially relevant to those studies examining the everyday life of people learning science in schools, museums, and other naturalist settings.

A second research direction concerns access to science and knowledge and equity in science education. Emerging from studies of equity is the clear recognition of the ways that access (or lack thereof) is interactionally accomplished through social processes, each embedded in sets of cultural norms, assumptions, and ways of being. Tied to the uses of discourse and engaging in social processes are teacher and student identities. A range of studies show how identities develop through discourse processes and practices over time. Building ways of participating and making sense of knowledge and practice occur through affiliation and identity development around how teachers and students take up and are positioned in different identity potentials (Varelas, 2012). As much of this work is constructed in and through language, attention to discourse processes in studies of equity is much needed. A focus on identity makes visible various ways in which learners, teachers, and students take on and are positioned with and against different ways of being. Emerging identities and positions taken up in social contexts have consequences for affiliation, achievement, emotional well-being, career paths, and status (Kelly, 2012).

A third direction concerns the uses of language in student-led practical investigations and experiences. Science laboratory experience and the uses of general empirical evidence (e.g., demonstration, simulations) often fail to consider the ways that science gets talked into being—that is, the ways that concepts are framed and evoked so that empirical evidence can be seen as some relevant phenomenon. Studies of epistemology and social practice identify the importance of discourse in socializing students into ways of seeing, acting, and being that come to define science in a local settings, in some point in time. A number of interesting pedagogical approaches, such as project-based learning or treating socioscientific issues pose new communicative challenges for students and teachers. Investigations are increasingly dependent on the production and interpretation of inscriptions for understanding and communicating knowledge and practices of science.

A fourth research direction concerns the role of research on discourse in informing ongoing debates about research topics in science education—each of which has unique linguistic features that can be examined through discourse analysis. For example, there is ongoing discussion about the nature of argument and explanation (Berland & McNeill, 2012; Osborne & Patterson, 2011). The nature of language in argument and explanation and the important role of audience for each are central to developing clarity in use of such practices. Similarly, issues such as the definition, interpretation, and assessment of the nature of science remain important points needing clarification (Abd-El-Khalick, 2012; Allchin, 2011; Irzik & Nola, 2011). While such debates require developing perspectives from science education and science studies (e.g., philosophy, sociology, history of science), analysis of the role of language use in assessments of instruments and interviews also need to be taken into consideration (Russ et al., 2012).

In addition to themes around emerging research directions, there are a number of implications for research methods. First, studies of discourse have shown the importance of situating specific processes in time, space, and social practice. Discourse is always contextualized and cannot be interpreted in isolation from the social setting, history of participants, sequences of topics, linguistic abilities, and cognitive framing of the event. Studies of discourse processes thus need to examine a range of interactional contexts through use of differential units of analysis (Kelly, 2014). Second, the emergence of increasing inexpensive and ubiquitous video recording and cataloguing provides new avenues for data collection, analysis, representation, archiving, and sharing. Digital records provide new possibilities for the field to develop methodologies for discourse analysis and for sharing results in new ways. Finally, discourse analysts need to consider the range of the relevant audiences for this research. The emerging digital technologies provide opportunities for expanding the range of audiences with access to the results and discourse studies. To speak to multiple audiences beyond just researchers, analysts will need to create ways of communicating knowledge about educational events and practices relevant to students, teachers, and policy analysts.

Acknowledgments

I would like to thank Beth Hufnagel and Jan H. van Driel for their helpful comments on an earlier draft of this chapter.

References

Abd-El-Khalick, F. (2012). Examining the sources for our understandings about science: Enduring conflations and critical issues in research on nature of science in science education. *International Journal of Science Education, 34,* 353–374.

Airey, J., & Linder, C. (2009). A disciplinary discourse perspective on university science learning: Achieving fluency in a critical constellation of modes. *Journal of Research in Science Teaching, 46,* 27–49.

Albe, V. (2008). When scientific knowledge, daily life experience, epistemological and social considerations intersect: Students' argumentation in group discussions on a socio-scientific issue. *Research in Science Education, 38,* 67–90.

Allchin, D. (2011). Evaluating knowledge of the nature of (whole) science. *Science Education, 95,* 518–542.

Alozie, N. M., Moje, E. B., & Krajcik, J. S. (2010). An analysis of the supports and constraints for scientific discussion in high school project-based science. *Science Education, 94,* 395–427.

Ash, D. (2008). Thematic continuities? Talking and thinking about adaptation in a socially complex classroom. *Journal of Research in Science Teaching, 45,* 1–30.

Bakhtin, M. M. (1981). *The dialogic imagination* (C. Emerson & M. Holquist, Trans.). Austin: University of Texas Press.

Barton, A. C., & Tan, E. (2009). Funds of knowledge and discourses and hybrid space. *Journal of Research in Science Teaching, 46,* 50–73.

Barton, A. C., & Tan, E. (2010). We be burnin'! Agency, identity, and science learning. *Journal of the Learning Sciences, 19,* 187–229.

Barton, A. C., Tan, E., & Rivet, A. (2008). Creating hybrid spaces for engaging school science among urban middle school girls. *American Educational Research Journal, 45,* 68–103.

Bazerman, C. (1988). *Shaping written knowledge: The genre and activity of the experimental article in science.* Madison: University of Wisconsin Press.

Bellocchi, A., & Ritchie, S. M. (2011). Investigating and theorizing discourse during analogy writing in chemistry. *Journal of Research in Science Teaching, 48,* 771–792.

Bennett, J., Hogarth, S., Lubben, F., Campbell, B., & Robinson, A. (2010). Talking science: The research evidence on the use of small group discussions in science teaching. *International Journal of Science Education, 32,* 69–95.

Berland, L. K., & Hammer, D. (2012). Framing for scientific argumentation. *Journal of Research in Science Teaching, 49,* 68–94.

Berland, L. K., & McNeill, K. L. (2010). A learning progression for scientific argumentation: Understanding student work and designing supportive instructional contexts. *Science Education, 94,* 765–793.

Berland, L. K., & McNeill, K. L. (2012). For whom is argument and explanation a necessary distinction? A response to Osborne and Patterson. *Science Education, 96,* 808–813.

Berland, L. K., & Reiser, B. J. (2009). Making sense of argumentation and explanation. *Science Education, 93,* 26–55.

Berland, L. K., & Reiser, B. J. (2011). Classroom communities' adaptations of the practice of scientific argumentation. *Science Education, 95,* 191–216.

Böttcher, F., & Meisert, A. (2011). Argumentation in science education: A model-based framework. *Science & Education, 20,* 103–140.

Bricker, L. A., & Bell, P. (2008). Conceptualizations of argumentation from science studies and the learning sciences and their implications for the practices of science education. *Science Education, 92,* 473–498.

Brown, B. A. (2006). "It isn't no slang that can be said about this stuff": Language, identity, and appropriating science discourse. *Journal of Research in Science Teaching, 43,* 96–126.

Brown, B. A., Reveles, J. M., & Kelly, G. J. (2005). Scientific literacy and discursive identity: A theoretical framework for understanding science learning. *Science Education, 89,* 779–802.

Brown, B. A., & Spang, E. (2008). Double talk: Synthesizing everyday and science language in the classroom. *Science Education, 92,* 708–732.

Cameron, D. (2001). *Working with spoken discourse.* Thousand Oaks, CA: Sage.

Carlsen, W. S. (1991). Questioning in classrooms: A sociolinguistic perspective. *Review of Educational Research, 61,* 157–178.

Cavagnetto, A. R. (2010). Argument to foster scientific literacy: A review of argument interventions in K–12 science contexts. *Review of Educational Research, 80,* 336–371.

Chin, C. (2007). Teacher questioning in science classrooms? Approaches that stimulate productive thinking. *Journal of Research in Science Teaching, 44,* 815–843.

Chin, C., & Osborne, J. (2010a). Journal of the learning supporting argumentation through students' questions: Case studies in science classrooms. *Journal of the Learning Sciences, 19,* 230–284.

Chin, C., & Osborne, J. (2010b). Students' questions and discursive interaction: Their impact on argumentation during collaborative group discussions in science. *Journal of Research in Science Teaching, 47,* 883–908.

Choi, A., Notebaert, A., Diaz, J., & Hand, B. (2010). Examining arguments generated by year 5, 7, and 10 students in science classrooms. *Research in Science Education, 40,* 149–169.

Clark, D. B., & Sampson, V. D. (2007). Personally-seeded discussions to scaffold online argumentation. *International Journal of Science Education, 29,* 253–277.

Clark, D. B., & Sampson, V. (2008). Assessing dialogic argumentation in online environments to relate structure, grounds, and conceptual quality. *Journal of Research in Science Teaching, 45,* 293–321.

Crawford, T. (2005). What counts as knowing: Constructing a communicative repertoire for student demonstration of knowledge in science. *Journal of Research in Science Teaching, 42,* 139–165.

Danish, J. A., & Phelps, D. (2011). Representational practices by the numbers: How kindergarten and first-grade students create, evaluate, and modify their science representations. *International Journal of Science Education, 33,* 2069–2094.

DeWitt, J., & Hohenstein, J. (2010). School trips and classroom lessons: An investigation into teacher–student talk in two settings. *Journal of Research in Science Teaching, 47,* 454–473.

Duran, R.A. (2008). Assessing English-language learners' achievement. *Review of Research in Education, 32,* 292–327.

Duschl, R.A. (2008). Science education in 3 part harmony: Balancing conceptual, epistemic and social learning goals. *Review of Research in Education, 32,* 1–25.

Erduran, S., & Jimenez-Aleixandre, M.P. (Eds.). (2008). *Argumentation in science education: Recent developments and future directions.* New York: Springer.

Evagorou, M., Jimenez-Aleixandre, M.-P., & Osborne, J. (2012). "Should we kill the grey squirrels?" A study exploring students' justifications and decision-making. *International Journal of Science Education, 34,* 401–428.

Eylon, B., Berger, H., & Bagno, E. (2008). An evidence-based continuous professional development programme on knowledge integration in physics: A study of teachers' collective discourse. *International Journal of Science Education, 30,* 619–641.

Fairclough, N. (1992). *Discourse and social change.* Boston: Blackwell Publishing.

Fairclough, N. (1995). *Critical discourse analysis: The critical study of language.* London: Longman.

Ford, M.J., & Wargo, B.M. (2012). Dialogic framing of scientific content for conceptual and epistemic understanding. *Science Education, 96,* 369–391.

Gee, J.P. (2001). Literacy, discourse, and linguistics: Introduction and what is literacy? In E. Cushman, E.R. Kintgen, B.M. Kroll, & M. Rose (Eds.), *Literacy: A critical sourcebook* (pp. 525–544). Boston: Bedford St. Martin's.

Gee, J.P., & Green, J.L. (1998). Discourse analysis, learning, and social practice: A methodological study. *Review of Research in Education, 23,* 119–169.

Givry, D., & Roth, W. (2006). Toward a new conception of conceptions? Interplay of talk, gestures, and structures in the setting. *Journal of Research in Science Teaching, 43,* 1086–1109.

Gomes, M.D.C., Mortimer, E.F., & Kelly, G.J. (2011). Contrasting stories of inclusion/exclusion in the chemistry classroom. *International Journal of Science Education, 33,* 747–772.

Gumperz, J. (2001). Interactional sociolinguistics: A personal perspective. In D. Schiffrin, D. Tannen, & H.E. Hamilton (Eds.), *The handbook of discourse analysis* (pp. 215–228). Malden, MA: Blackwell Publishing.

Gyllenpalm, J., & Wickman, P. (2011). The uses of the term hypothesis and the inquiry emphasis conflation in science teacher education. *Journal of Science Education, 33,* 1993–2015.

Gyllenpalm, J., Wickman, P.-O., & Holmgren, S.-O. (2010). Teachers' language on scientific inquiry: Methods of teaching or methods of inquiry? *International Journal of Science Education, 32,* 1151–1172.

Halliday, M.A.K., & Martin, J.R. (1993). *Writing science: Literacy and discursive power.* Pittsburgh, PA: University of Pittsburgh Press.

Hamza, K.M., & Wickman, P.-O. (2008). Describing and analyzing learning in action? An empirical study of the importance of misconceptions in learning science. *Science Education, 92,* 141–164.

Hanrahan, M.U. (2006). Highlighting hybridity: A critical discourse analysis of teacher talk in science classrooms. *Science Education, 90,* 8–43.

Ideland, M., Malmberg, C., & Winberg, M. (2011). Culturally equipped for socio-scientific issues? A comparative study on how teachers and students in mono- and multiethnic schools handle work with complex issues. *International Journal of Science Education, 33,* 1835–1859.

Irzik, G., & Nola, R. (2011). A family resemblance approach to the nature of science for science education. *Science & Education, 20,* 591–607.

Jaipal, K. (2010). Meaning making through multiple modalities in a biology classroom: A multimodal semiotics discourse analysis. *Science Education, 94,* 48–72.

Jakobsson, A., Mäkitalo, A., & Säljö, R. (2009). Conceptions of knowledge in research on students' understanding of the greenhouse effect: Methodological positions and their consequences for representations and knowing. *Science Education, 93,* 978–995.

Jaworski, A., & Coupland, N. (Eds.). (1999). *The discourse reader.* New York: Routledge.

Kamberelis, G., & Wehunt, M.D. (2012). Hybrid discourse practice and science learning. *Cultural Studies of Science Education, 7,* 505–534.

Kelly, G., Regev, J., & Prothero, W.A. (2008). Analysis of lines of reasoning in written argumentation. In S. Erduran & M.P. Jiménez-Aleixandre (Eds.), *Argumentation in science education: Recent developments and future directions* (pp. 137–157). New York: Springer.

Kelly, G.J. (in press). Inquiry teaching and learning: Philosophical considerations. In M. Matthews (Ed.), *International Handbook of Research in History, Philosophy and Science Teaching.* Springer.

Kelly, G.J. (2007). Discourse in science classrooms. In S.K. Abell & N.G. Lederman (Eds.), *Handbook of research on science education* (pp. 443–469). Mahwah, NJ: Lawrence Erlbaum Associates.

Kelly, G.J. (2008). Inquiry, activity, and epistemic practice. In R.A. Duschl & R.E. Grandy (Eds.), *Teaching scientific inquiry: Recommendations for research and implementation* (pp. 99–117; 288–291). Rotterdam, the Netherlands: Sense Publishers.

Kelly, G.J. (2011). Scientific literacy, discourse, and epistemic practices. In C. Linder, L. Östman, D.A. Roberts, P. Wickman, G. Erikson, & A. McKinnon (Eds.), *Exploring the landscape of scientific literacy* (pp. 61–73). New York: Routledge.

Kelly, G.J. (2012). Developing critical conversations about identity research in science education. In M. Varelas (Ed.), *Identity construction and science education research: Learning, teaching, and being in multiple contexts* (pp. 185–192). Dordrecht, the Netherlands: Springer.

Kelly, G.J. (2014). Analysing classroom activities: Theoretical and methodological considerations. In C. Bruguière, A. Tiberghien, & P. Clément (Eds.),. *Topics and Trends in Current Science Education:* 9th *ESERA Conference Selected Contributions* (pp. 353–368). Dordrecht: Springer.

Kelly, G.J., Carlsen, W.S., & Cunningham, C.M. (1993). Science education in sociocultural context: Perspectives from the sociology of science. *Science Education, 77,* 207–220.

Kelly, G.J., McDonald, S.P., & Wickman, P.-O. (2012). Science learning and epistemology. In B.J. Fraser, K. Tobin, & C.J. McRobbie (Eds.), *Second international handbook of science education* (pp. 281–291). Dordrecht, the Netherlands: Springer.

Khine, M.S. (Ed.). (2012). *Perspectives on scientific argumentation: Theory, practice and research.* Dordrecht, the Netherlands: Springer.

Knorr-Cetina, K. (1999). *Epistemic cultures: How the sciences make knowledge.* Cambridge, MA: Harvard University Press.

Kolstø, S.D. (2006). Patterns in students' argumentation confronted with a risk-focused socio-scientific issue. *International Journal of Science Education, 28,* 1689–1716.

Latour, B., & Woolgar, S. (1986). An anthropologist visits the laboratory. In B. Latour & S. Woolgard (Eds.), *Laboratory life: The construction of scientific facts* (pp. 43–90). Princeton, NJ: Princeton University Press.

Lemke, J.L. (1990). *Talking science: Language, learning and values.* Norwood, NJ: Ablex.

Lemke, J.L., Kelly, G.J., & Roth, W.-M. (2006). Forum: Toward a phenomenology of interviews. *Cultural Studies of Science Education, 1,* 83–106.

Lidar, M., Almqvist, J., & Östman, L. (2010). A pragmatist approach to meaning making in children's discussions about gravity and the shape of the earth. *Science Education, 94,* 689–709.

Loxley, P.M. (2009). Evaluation of three primary teachers' approaches to teaching scientific concepts in persuasive ways. *International Journal of Science Education, 31,* 1607–1629.

Maeng, S., & Kim, C.-J. (2011). Variations in science teaching modalities and students' pedagogic subject positioning through the discourse register and language code. *Science Education, 95,* 431–457.

Manz, E. (2012). Understanding the codevelopment of modeling practice and ecological knowledge. *Science Education, 96,* 1071–1105.

McDonald, S., & Kelly, G. J. (2012). Beyond argumentation: Sense making discourse in the science classroom. In M. S. Khine (Ed.), *Perspectives on scientific argumentation: Theory, practice and research* (pp. 265–281). Dordrecht, the Netherlands: Springer.

Mehan, H. (1979). *Learning lessons: Social organization in the classroom.* Cambridge, MA: Harvard University Press.

Mercer, N., Dawes, L., & Staarman, J. K. (2009). Dialogic teaching in the primary science classroom. *Language and Education, 23,* 353–369.

Mikeska, J. N., Anderson, C. W., & Schwarz, C. V. (2009). Principled reasoning about problems of practice. *Science Education, 93,* 678–686.

Mishler, E. G. (1986). *Research interviewing: Context and narrative.* Cambridge, MA: Harvard University Press.

Mortimer, E. F., & Scott, P. H. (2003). *Meaning making in secondary science classrooms.* Maidenhead, UK: Open University Press.

National Research Council (NRC). (1996). *National science education standards.* Washington, DC: National Academies Press.

National Research Council (NRC). (2011). *A framework for K–12 science education: Practices, crosscutting concepts, and core ideas.* Washington, DC: National Academies Press.

Nielsen, J. A. (2012). Science in discussions: An analysis of the use of science content in socioscientific discussions. *Science Education, 96,* 428–456.

Olitsky, S., Flohr, L. L., Gardner, J., & Billups, M. (2010). Coherence, contradiction, and the development of school science identities. *Journal of Research in Science Teaching, 47,* 1209–1228.

Oliveira, A. W. (2010). Improving teacher questioning in science inquiry discussions through professional development. *Journal of Research in Science Teaching, 47,* 422–453.

Oliveira, A. W., Akerson, V. L., Colak, H., Pongsanon, K., & Genel, A. (2012). The implicit communication of nature of science and epistemology during inquiry discussion. *Science Education, 96,* 652–684.

Osborne, J. F., & Patterson, A. (2011). Scientific argument and explanation: A necessary distinction? *Science Education, 95,* 627–638.

Parsons, E., Tran, L. U., & Gomillion, C. T. (2008). An investigation of student roles within small, racially mixed science groups: A racial perspective. *International Journal of Science Education, 30,* 1469–1489.

Reveles, J. M., & Brown, B. A. (2008). Contextual shifting: Teachers emphasizing students' academic identity to promote scientific literacy. *Science Education, 92,* 1015–1041.

Russ, R. S., Lee, V. R., & Sherin, B. L. (2012). Framing in cognitive clinical interviews about intuitive science knowledge: Dynamic student understandings of the discourse interaction. *Science Education, 96,* 573–599.

Sadler, T. D. (2006). Promoting discourse and argumentation in science teacher education. *Journal of Science Teacher Education, 17,* 323–346.

Sampson, V., & Clark, D. B. (2008). Assessment of the ways students generate arguments in science education: Current perspectives and recommendations for future directions. *Science Education, 92,* 447–472.

Schwab, J. (1960). The teaching of science as enquiry. In J. Schwab & P. Brandwein (Eds.), *The teaching of science* (pp. 3–103). Cambridge, MA: Harvard University Press.

Shaw, J. M., Bunch, G. C., & Geaney, E. R. (2010). Analyzing language demands facing English learners on science performance assessments: The SALD framework. *Journal of Research in Science Teaching, 47,* 909–928.

Siry, C., Ziegler, G., & Max, C. (2012). "Doing science" through discourse-in-interaction: Young children's science investigations at the early childhood level. *Science Education, 96,* 311–326.

Tang, X., Coffey, J. E., Elby, A., & Levin, D. M. (2010). The scientific method and scientific inquiry: Tensions in teaching and learning. *Science Education, 94,* 29–47.

Varelas, M. (Ed.). (2012). *Identity construction and science education research: Learning, teaching, and being in multiple contexts.* Dordrecht, the Netherlands: Springer.

Varelas, M., Kane, J. M., & Wylie, C. D. (2012). Young Black children and science: Chronotopes of narratives around their science journals. *Journal of Research in Science Teaching, 49,* 568–596.

Varelas, M., Pappas, C. C., Kane, J. M., Arsenault, A., Hankes, J., & Cowan, B. M. (2008). Urban primary-grade children think and talk science: Curricular and instructional practices that nurture participation and argumentation. *Science Education, 92,* 65–95.

von Aufschnaiter, C., Erduran, S., Osborne, J., Simon, S., Education, P., & Giessen, J. (2008). Arguing to learn and learning to argue: Case studies of how students' argumentation relates to their scientific knowledge. *Journal of Research in Science Teaching, 45,* 101–131.

Vygotsky, L. S. (1978). *Mind in society: The development of higher psychological processes* (M. Cole, V. John-Steiner, S. Scribner, & E. Souberman, Eds.). Cambridge, MA: Harvard University Press.

Walker, K. A., & Zeidler, D. L. (2007). Promoting discourse about socioscientific issues through scaffolded inquiry. *International Journal of Science Education, 29,* 1387–1410.

Wickman, P. O., & Östman, L. (2002). Learning as discourse change: A sociocultural mechanism. *Science Education, 86,* 601–623.

Windschitl, M., Thompson, J., & Braaten, M. (2008). How novice science teachers appropriate epistemic discourses around model-based inquiry for use in classrooms. *Cognition & Instruction, 26,* 310–376.

Zembal-Saul, C. (2009). Learning to teach elementary school science as argument. *Science Education, 93,* 687–719.

Zimmerman, H. T., Reeve, S., & Bell, P. (2010). Family sense-making practices in science center conversations. *Science Education, 94,* 478–505.

18

Promises and Challenges of Using Learning Technologies to Promote Student Learning of Science

JOSEPH S. KRAJCIK AND KONGJU MUN

Introduction

Why should we use technology to support students in learning science? How can technology be designed to promote student understanding of science, both core ideas and science practices? What evidence is there that the use of various technologies promotes student understanding of science?

The use of various forms of computer-based technology in science has captured the imagination of teachers, designers, and researchers since the 1980s, when desktop computers first appeared. Interactive features along with the ability to capture, display, and analyze data made computers seem ideal for engaging students in science. Students could use technology to explore various complex aspects of science, including building and visualizing complex molecules and analyzing large data sets. Visualization and interactive features became more sophisticated, and researchers used scaffolds to engage learners in complex tasks, problems solving, and model building. However, we might ask if there is evidence to support using technology in the teaching and learning of science. Even with advancements in technology, the promises of widespread use of computer technology for improving science education never materialized. Computer technologies, even with all their interactive capabilities, were not used as tools to construct knowledge. With the advent of portable technologies, including interactive tablets, the use of technologies to support student learning has once again captured the imagination of teachers and researchers across the globe. The portability of smartphones and tablets and network technologies empower designers and educators to develop electronic learning environments that make use of these new tools. The functionality of these tools to allow students to analyze data, build models, use simulations of unseen worlds, and solve complex problems has become a thrust for educational systems worldwide. The flexibility, interactive power, and networking, customization, and multiple representation capabilities of these new portable devices could help to change the structure of the science classroom. Instead of students receiving information, students could engage in constructing knowledge by building models and developing explanations using evidence.

Even with all these advances in technology, the potential to promote student learning in school will be realized when we use them in ways to support learning of ideas that can't be accomplished without them. This chapter focuses on the potential of *learning technologies* in facilitating student construction of integrated understanding of disciplinary core ideas with crosscutting concepts and science practices (National Research Council, 2012). We first describe what we mean by learning technologies, including the potential of these tools to support students in constructing integrated understanding. We also describe the central role of scaffolding in supporting students in using technology to accomplish challenging tasks. Throughout the entire chapter, we provide research and theoretical underpinnings related to the impact of learning technologies to promote student learning.

Learning Technologies

Learning technologies can involve multimedia, Web-based learning, computer-assisted learning, e-books, and other new technology that supports student learning. However, not all forms of computer applications are necessarily learning technologies. Spreadsheets, for instance, can accomplish a number of challenging tasks and, in the hands of a skilled teacher, can be used for instructional purposes and promote student learning. However, spreadsheets were not designed to facilitate learning but to organize and analyze data in tabular forms to accomplish a number of repeated analyses. To be considered a learning technology, the software application needs to be designed to promote learning (Krajcik, Blumenfeld, Marx, & Soloway, 2000). As such, learning technologies can serve as powerful cognitive tools that help learners meet important

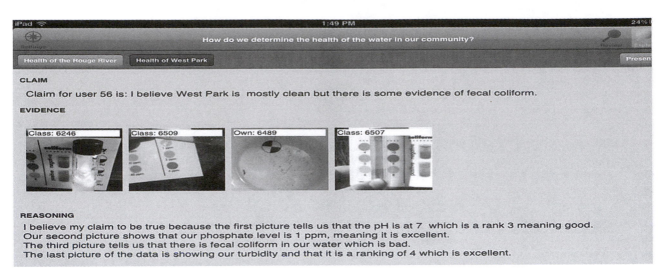

Figure 18.1 Claim, Evidence and Reasoning Window from Zydeco.

learning goals and engage in various science practices. "Educational technology" is used synonymously with "learning technology." These terms focus on the use of technology to support innovations in teaching and learning (Oliver, 2000).

Learning technologies have the potential to promote achievement of important learning goals and can help transform the science classroom into a learning environment in which students actively construct knowledge (Linn, 1998; Novak & Krajcik, 2005). The Zydeco Project (Quintana, 2012) uses iPads and other mobile devices with ubiquitous information access from cloud technologies to support students in the collection, organization, and analysis of data and the development of scientific explanations. What makes Zydeco a learning technology is that it provides support for learning the practice of constructing scientific explanations (McNeill & Krajcik, 2011). Zydeco supports students in specifying a claim, evidence to support the claim, and scientific reasoning for why the evidence that the students selected serves as evidence. Figure 18.1 shows an image from the Zydeco application in which it breaks the explanation task down into claim, evidence, and reasoning. Research suggests that Zydeco does serve as a learning technology (Kuhn et al., 2012; Quintana, 2012).

Learning technologies can support students in accessing and collecting a range of scientific data and information. They do this by allowing and supporting students to (1) use visualization, interactive, and data analysis tools similar to those used by scientists, (2) collaborate and share of information across remote sites, (3) plan, build, and test models, (4) develop multimedia documents that illustrate student understanding (Novak & Krajcik, 2004), (5) access information and data when needed, and (6) use remote tools to collect and analyze data. These features expand the range of questions that students can investigate and the variety and type of phenomena students can experience and explain. Before we launch into an examination of various learning technologies, we first describe what

we mean by integrated understanding and describe several learning principles that guide our work.

Developing Integrated Understanding

Our goal in teaching science is to help students develop integrated understandings. Integrated understanding occurs when the learner builds meaningful relationships and connections between ideas (Fortus & Krajcik, 2012; Krajcik & Czerniak, 2013; Linn & Eylon, 2011). Understanding is a function of knowledge accumulation and knowledge integration (Linn & Hsi, 2000). It is possible for students to accumulate a large number of isolated bits of information without building relationships between those pieces of knowledge, thus not being able to use that information to solve problems, make decisions, and learn more and, as such, not demonstrating in-depth and integrated understanding. It is also possible for students to possess a very limited amount of knowledge, where each piece is well integrated or connected to pieces of other knowledge. Our goal is to have students understand the core ideas of science and make numerous connections among these core ideas. Linn and Eylon (2006, 2011) define knowledge integration as the building of connections between the ideas that students bring to the classroom with the more normative ideas held by scientists. This is the fundamental principle of what it means to make use of prior knowledge. As such, because of the connections students form among prior knowledge and new ideas, integrated understanding can be used to solve problems, make decisions, explain phenomena, and learn new concepts.

Recent educational approaches emphasize the use of technology in environments in which learners engage in extended inquiry and develop knowledge and skills in the context of investigating complex and meaningful problems (Blumenfeld, Fishman, Krajcik, Marx, & Soloway, 2000; Bransford, Brown, & Cocking, 2000; Linn, 1998; Linn & Eylon, 2011). Learning environments, including those that incorporate learning technologies, should engage learners in challenging and open-ended problems to provide students with opportunities to grapple with ideas and make connections. In such environments, students develop an integrated understanding of scientific core ideas by applying and using them to explain phenomena, solve problems, and make decisions.

Theoretical Principles Guiding Our Work

The Framework for K–12 Science Education (National Research Council, 2012) prompted a new direction for science education in the United States by making use of what is known to promote the teaching and learning of science. The Framework presents a paradigm shift in science education in order to meet the demands of 21st-century society. The Framework focuses on students actively engaging in science and engineering practices, applying crosscutting concepts, and using core ideas to develop integrated understanding (National Research Council, 2012). As such, the Framework provides a valuable vision for those interested in supporting students to develop understanding that can be used for problem solving, decision making, explaining phenomena, and learning new information.

Science and engineering practices are the multiple ways of knowing and doing that scientists employ to study the natural and design world (National Research Council, 2012). They go beyond just knowing how to do science to include knowing what counts as scientific knowledge and what is needed to provide evidence for that knowledge. Table 18.1 presents a summary of the eight science and engineering practices identified by the National Research Council (NRC, 2012). While this table shows the practices in a list, science is not a linear process but rather happens more in a Web-based manner (Krajcik & Czerniak, 2013). For instance, data analysis could lead to a new question that could result in a new way of analyzing the data.

Core ideas are critical to the discipline and provide explanations for a host of phenomena. Core ideas are generative, as they are necessary to explore new phenomena and incorporate new ideas (National Research Council, 2012; Stevens, Sutherland, & Krajcik, 2009). Crosscutting concepts include broad themes like cause and effect, patterns, and systems and system models. Core ideas and crosscutting concepts offer students the conceptual tools to think about and explain phenomena. Understanding the core ideas and crosscutting concepts and engaging in the science practices help students understand the broader

TABLE 18.1
Science and Engineering Practices (NRC, 2012)

- Asking questions (for science) and defining problems (for engineering)
- Developing and using models
- Planning and carrying out investigations
- Analyzing and interpreting data
- Using mathematical and computational thinking
- Constructing explanations (for science) and designing solutions (for engineering)
- Engaging in argument from evidence
- Obtaining, evaluating, and communicating information

and deeper levels of scientific knowledge and how to make use of that knowledge (Bybee, 2011; Krajcik, 2013; National Research Council, 2012) and develop integrated understanding.

Based on situated cognition (Brown, Collins, & Duguid, 1989; Lave & Wenger, 1991), the Framework for K–12 Science Education (National Research Council, 2012) argues that students learn science content (core ideas and crosscutting concepts) using practices and, likewise, students learn the science practices through engaging with science content. Learning content in the absence of science and engineering practices provides no context, and learning science and engineering practices void of content lacks conceptual tools for students to use. Both situations lead to learners developing isolated ideas that do not support problem solving and future learning (Krajcik & Shin, 2014). To form integrated understanding, knowing and doing cannot be separated. Learning technologies can help develop such environments, as they can place students in situations in which they actively use ideas.

Learning technologies can support students in learning core ideas, crosscutting concepts, and science practices; however, to do so, learning technologies need to be designed with appropriate supports and embedded in appropriate curriculum (National Research Council, 2011). Next we describe the five major learning principles that ground our work in the use and design of learning technologies: (1) active construction, (2) situated learning, (3) cognitive tools, (4) learning goals, and (5) scaffolding that is essential in supporting students to engage in challenging tasks.

Active construction.

Research demonstrates that integrated understanding occurs when an individual actively constructs meaning based on his or her experiences and interactions in the world, while superficial learning occurs when learners passively take in information presented by the teacher, a computer, or a book (Sawyer, 2006). The growth of understanding is a continuous, developmental process that requires students to construct and reconstruct what they know from new experiences and ideas with prior knowledge and experiences (National Research Council, 2007; Smith, Wiser, Anderson, & Krajcik, 2006). Learning is not a passive process but one in which learners actively build knowledge as they explore the world in which they live, observe and interact with phenomena, seek additional evidence to support their ideas, take in new ideas and information, make connections between new and old ideas, and discuss and debate ideas with others. Learning technologies can support learning in this process. For instance, probes—discussed in what follows—allow learners to collect data that would be difficult, time consuming, or impossible to collect without their use. Using electronic probes, students can monitor the temperature change of a lake during a 24-hour period as well as how the temperature changes at different depth or with the amount of sunlight that penetrates to that depth. Multiple representations allow students to see ideas represented in different ways, helping them make connections and links to their prior ideas.

Moreover, learning complex ideas takes time and often occurs when students work on a meaningful task that forces them to synthesize and use ideas. Here again, learning technologies could be helpful. Learning technologies can allow students to interact with underlying models of scientific ideas and experience phenomena that would not be possible without their support. For instance, learning technologies allow students to visualize the world of atoms and molecules and observe what happens when the temperature changes. Learning technologies can also provide scaffolding that can support students in challenging tasks such as developing and revising models (see Barab, Hay, Barnett, & Keating, 2000; Frederiksen, White, & Gutwill, 1999; Rouse & Morris, 1986; Model-it example upcoming) and constructing explanations (see Zydeco example).

Engaging learners in science practices can support them in active construction. Various learning technologies such as probeware, modeling tools, and interactive visualization can support students engaging in and developing capability in performing science practices.

Situated learning. Research shows that the most effective learning occurs when the learning is situated in an authentic, real-world context (Lave & Wenger, 1991; National Research Council, 2007, 2012; Rivet & Krajcik, 2008; Sawyer, 2006). In some scientific disciplines, scientists, such as chemists and those in various branches of biology, conduct experiments in laboratories. Other scientists, such as astronomers and those in other fields of biology, observe the natural world and draw conclusions from their observations. Here again, learning technologies can play an important role. Various probes can help students conduct, collect, and analyze data, and students can use portable technologies to record information, including digital images and movies, in the field. Situated learning in science involves learners in experiencing phenomena as they take part in various science practices such as designing investigations, constructing explanations, collecting and analyzing data, developing models, and presenting their ideas to others. Various learning technologies can help in these areas. One of the benefits of situated learning is that students can more easily see the value and meaning of the tasks and activities they perform. When learners design their own investigation to answer a question that they helped frame, and the question is important to them and their community, they learn that science ideas can be applied to solve problems and make decisions important to them. Various technologies can help students take part in these authentic learning opportunities.

When students acquire information in a meaningful context (Blumenfeld et al., 1991; Krajcik & Czerniak, 2013) and relate it to their prior knowledge and experiences, they can form connections between the new information and the prior knowledge to develop a deep, comprehensive, and connected conceptual understanding, helping to form integrated understanding. Situated learning is based on students exploring authentic problems or issues. Students need to engage in real, meaningful problems that are important to them and that are similar to what scientists do. Developing these authentic environments, students are more likely to engage in the learning process. This doing aligns with the science and engineering practices (National Research Council, 2012). Students need to ask and investigate questions, propose explanations based on evidence, argue for their ideas, challenge those of others, and try out new ideas.

Various researchers (Krajcik & Czerniak, 2013; Linn & Eylon, 2011) make use of driving questions or key questions to create meaningful contexts. A driving/key question encompasses worthwhile content that is meaningful and anchored in a real-world situation. The driving question also organizes and drives activities by providing a context in which students can use and explore core ideas and science practices and by providing continuity and coherence across the project. For instance, a driving question such as "How can I smell something from across the room?" in which middle-level students explore and develop core ideas related to the particle nature of matter, allows students to use a variety of software tools including probes, visualizations, and modeling tools. A lack of relevancy to the science questions is a strong factor in deterring girls and minorities from science (Calabrese Barton & Tan, 2010; Calabrese Barton, Tan & Rivet, 2008). This idea of making science accessible to learners is related to Linn and Eylon's research (2006, 2011), a component of their knowledge integration framework. Making science accessible engages students in relevant contexts by connecting the science idea to a task that students might encounter in their daily lives. It goes without saying that if the tasks are not authentic and meaningful, technologies will not help to promote learning in students.

Learning technologies can help create these authentic environments by providing virtual simulations for problem solving and real-data accessibility for answering questions. For example, researchers from the Harvard Graduate School of Education developed situated learning environments using technology. One environment is *Eco-MUVE*. *EcoMUVE* is designed to support middle-level students in learning science practices through problem solving in a virtual world with multiuser virtual environments in a 3D–reality graphical world named River City (Metcalf, Dede, Grotzer, & Kamarainen, 2010). River City is a virtual world in which residents become ill. Students need to take on the role of scientists who explore what causes this illness. In River City, students control their virtual avatars to walk around the virtual town, talk to residents, and investigate and explore the environment using data collection tools (Figure 18.2). A second environment is *EcoMOBILE*. *EcoMOBILE* combines augmented reality (AR) experiences with probes to collect data during field trips (Kamarainen et al., 2013; see

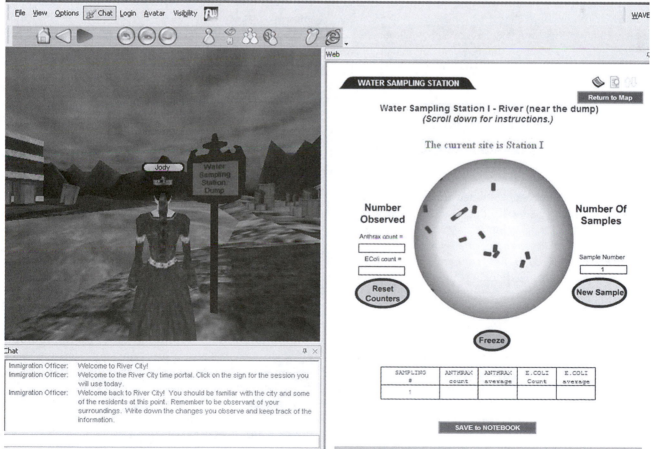

Figure 18.2 Students' avatar and virtual microscope for measuring bacteria in the water. (Metcalf, Dede, Grotzer, & Kamarainen, 2010)

details at http://ecomuve.gse.harvard.edu for *EcoMUVE* and http://ecomobile.gse.harvard.edu for *EcoMOBILE*). Both projects show how technology can provide situated learning experiences, promote students' use of science practices, and help build integrated understanding.

Cognitive tools. Research has also shown the critical role of cognitive tools in learning (Jonassen, 1995; Salomon, Perkins, & Globerson, 1991). Computer applications such as databases, spreadsheets, networks, and multimedia/ hypermedia construction can function as computer-based cognitive tools with the role of an intellectual supporter that is intended to facilitate cognitive process. With appropriate supports and instructional components, cognitive tools can amplify and expand what students can do in constructing knowledge (Jonassen, 1995). The periodic table serves as a cognitive tool for many chemists, as it summarizes a host of important ideas that chemists can apply. The chemist understands the underlying ideas and how to apply those ideas. Unfortunately, in school, the periodic table is often seen as something to memorize. However, for these various computer applications to promote learning, instruction needs to be designed around them.

Various forms of computer applications also serve as cognitive tools because they allow learners to carry out tasks not possible without the application's assistance and support. For instance, new forms of computer software allow learners to visualize complex data sets and interact with visualizations that show underlying mechanisms that explain phenomena (Edelson & Reiser, 2006; Linn & Eylon, 2011). In addition, many e-learning environments provide prompts to promote student reflection on the learning process (see example of WISE project in what follows).

Aligning technology with learning goals. Specifying learning goals is critical to promoting learning and the design of learning environments, including technology-based learning environments. The National Research Council's Committee on Science Learning: Computer Games, Simulations and Education stresses that the first step in designing computer simulations and games is developing clear learning goals (National Research Council, 2011). One of the major reasons for students not reaching the intended goals is unclear or unspecified learning goals, resulting in tasks that do not align with the objectives (Kesidou & Roseman, 2002; Krajcik, Slotta, McNeill, & Reiser, 2008). The important role that learning goals play in creating good instructional materials, including the incorporation of software applications and learning technologies, is that they guide the selection of materials, tasks, and instructions (Wilson & Berenthal, 2006).

Because the goal is for students to use what they learn to solve problems, explain phenomena, make decisions and learn more—knowledge in use—researchers recommend the construct of learning goals by blending core ideas and science practices (Krajcik, McNeill, & Reiser, 2008;

TABLE 18.2
Blending Science Practices and Core Ideas to Form Learning Goal

Science Practice	Core Idea	Learning Goal (specified as a performance)
Construct a science explanation based on evidence	Each pure substance has characteristic physical and chemical properties (for any bulk quantity under given conditions) that can be used to identify it. (Physical Science Core Idea 1, NRC 2012)	Develop a scientific explanation that different substances have different properties.

Krajcik et al., 2008; Wilson & Berenthal, 2006). This approach mirrors the suggestion in the Framework for K–12 Science Education for developing standards (National Research Council, 2012). Table 18.2 illustrates the process of blending a core idea and science practice to construct a learning goal described as a performance. This learning goal points to engaging students in tasks in which they construct explanations using evidence that different substances have different properties.

Using scaffolding in learning technologies. A critical design element for developing learning technologies is the incorporation of educational scaffolds. Scaffolding allows a teacher or a more knowledgeable peer to support and assist learners in accomplishing a challenging task—such as designing an experiment, analyzing data, or constructing a model—that would otherwise be unattainable for the learner (Collins, Brown, & Newman, 1989; Palincscar, 1998; Wood, Bruner, & Ross, 1976). Scaffolding is closely associated with Vygotsky's (1978) notion of the zone of proximal development (ZPD), the region between what tasks learners can accomplish on their own and what they could accomplish with assistance (Rogoff, 1990). Providing scaffolding support to learners helps them accomplish tasks they normally would find impossible by bringing the task within their zone of proximal development. Scaffolding in software tools can support students in accomplishing tasks that the learners could not accomplish without the scaffold (Sherin, Reiser, & Edelson, 2004). For example, a teacher may help learners by setting appropriate goals that they can achieve with some guidance, providing assistance, or breaking down a task into manageable chunks. The breakdown of explanations in the Zydeco project (described earlier) into claim, evidence, and reasoning is an example of a learning technology that offers the support necessary to successfully engage in a challenging task.

Quintana and colleagues (Quintana et al., 2004) and Kali and colleagues (Kali, Fortus, & Ronen-Fuhrmann, 2008) argue that designers need explicit methods and guidelines for designing scaffolds into software that supports different aspects of a complex learning task.

TABLE 18.3

Guidelines to Scaffold Students in Inquiry (Quintana et al., 2004)

- Guideline 1: Use representations and language that bridge learners' understanding
- Guideline 2: Organize tools and artifacts around the semantics of the discipline
- Guideline 3: Use representations that learners can inspect in different ways to reveal important properties of underlying data
- Guideline 4: Provide structure for complex tasks and functionality
- Guideline 5: Embed expert guidance about science practices
- Guideline 6: Automatically handle nonsalient, routine tasks
- Guideline 7: Facilitate ongoing articulation and reflection during the investigation

Table 18.3 summarizes the guidelines proposed by Quintana and colleagues (2004) to support students in inquiry.

As an illustration, Guideline 4, *Provide structure for complex tasks and functionality,* might consist of breaking down the construction of a scientific explanation into claim, evidence, and reasoning (McNeill & Krajcik, 2011) and include descriptions of what each of these components means. This supports learners in crafting the various components of an explanation, which is a task most learners would not be able to do without this structure. This scaffold makes the underlying reasoning around the development of an explanation transparent to learners by breaking down the complex task into manageable components—task decomposition. Quintana and colleagues (2004) argue that by making the underlying thinking more visible to learners, the learners will more easily be able to accomplish challenging tasks. This scaffolding guideline was used in the design of Zydeco, described earlier (see Figure 18.1). The task decomposition of an explanation into claim, evidence, and reasoning makes the task of writing explanations accessible to learners by bringing the task of writing explanations into their zone of approximate development. Eventually, like all scaffolds, it will need to gradually decrease in level of assistance to allow students to carry out the task on their own and promote integrated understanding (McNeill, Lizotte, Krajcik, & Marx, 2006).

Perhaps one of the most important studies that demonstrate the value of incorporating various scaffolds to support student learning is the Computer as Lab Partner (CLP) project (Linn, 1998; Linn & Eylon, 2011). The CLP curriculum engages students in learning about thermodynamics (heat energy and temperature—important core ideas) by involving students in experiments that incorporate real-time data-collection instruments (probes) and classroom discussions. Linn and colleagues conducted 10 design experiments using the CLP curriculum. These design experiments, or curriculum reformulations, provide important insights into the use of instructional scaffolds to support students in learning. Although the first three iterations of the curriculum showed positive and promising results and the addition of making predictions showed improved student performance, it wasn't until the fourth and fifth revisions, when students were prompted by the software to make predications and reconcile their predictions with their observations, that major improvements in student understanding occurred. As a result of adding these two instructional scaffolds to the learning environment, students' posttest scores improved by 250% compared to the first initial versions of the curriculum. These results provide evidence that students' knowledge was becoming more integrated.

The next major improvement in the CLP curriculum occurred in versions 8 and 9 when students were prompted to develop principles that explain the results of their experiments to describe various real-world situations. The results of the pre- and posttests, as well as student interviews, showed that the adjustment to the learning environment supported students in developing integrated understanding when appropriate scaffolds were used. It is also important to point out that Linn's (Linn & Eylon, 2011) work illustrates students engaging in various science practices in the context of learning about important science ideas. Making predictions, reconciling observations with predictions, and providing principles to make sense of the data are important science practices that scientists engage in to explore and explain phenomena.

This series of design experiments illustrates that if we want students to develop integrated understanding of important science ideas, then instructional scaffolds to help students make sense of what data means are critical. Quintana and colleagues (2004) refer to the type of scaffolding that Linn and colleagues provided as embedding expert guidance about science practices, Guideline 5 from Table 18.3. Although probes allow students to collect a range of data to explore various phenomena in the classroom, curriculum scaffolds are necessary to promote learning. This premise, that technology alone will not promote learning, will be a reoccurring theme in this chapter.

The work that Linn and her colleagues conducted demonstrates the value of iteratively refining curriculum materials and technology based upon research evidence to promote student learning. Linn's work serves as a valuable model of how to design instructional materials, including learning technologies, to promote integrated understanding.

Software Application to Promote Learning Science

Next we discuss various other software applications that support students in learning science. In our discussion, we will explain how these software tools illustrate our underlying principles. Unfortunately, the scope of this chapter will only permit covering a few key tools: electronic probes, modeling tools, visualization, and integrated e-learning environments.

Use of Electronic Probes

Perhaps one of the oldest, most ubiquitous, and valuable applications of technology in the science classroom is the use of probes—electronic sensors and software—to collect and analyze data. Probes have been used in science classrooms since the early 1980s as laboratory tools. Electronic probes attached to computers, along with associated software, allow students to collect, graph, and visualize a variety of data, including pH, force, light, distance and speed, and dissolved oxygen, to name a few. More specialized probes even allow students to collect heart rate and blood pressure data. Thus, probes in the classroom allow students to have, at their access, a suite of scientific laboratory tools. Although the use of probes is not new, more user-friendly interfaces and sophisticated software for data collection and graphing have been developed. The use of probes in the classroom, in many respects, allows learners to engage with several science practices critical to supporting students in learning science. The most salient practices include designing and carrying out investigations, analyzing and interpreting data, and computational and mathematical thinking. However, the use of probes also supports students in asking and refining questions and engaging in argumentation from evidence. Figure 18.3 shows two middle school students using probes to gather water-quality data at a local stream.

A variety of research studies supports the claim that using probes in the science classroom can facilitate learning of science concepts and relational thinking (Adams & Shrum, 1990; Kamarainen et al., 2013; Krajcik & Layman, 1992; Linn, Layman, & Nachmias, 1987; Metcalf & Tinker, 2004; Mokros & Tinker, 1987; Novak & Gleason, 2001). Novak and Gleason (2001) show how the use of probes in a project-based learning environment supports middle school student learning about water quality, chemistry, and biological concepts. Novak and Gleason (2001) created a project-based environment to allow students to explore

the driving question: "How clean is the stream behind our school?" Students used portable handheld probes to measure pH, temperature, dissolved oxygen, and conductivity (measuring amount of dissolved substances). Students collected stream data three times during the school year—during the fall, winter, and spring—and looked for patterns and relationships among the variables and for trends in the data across the three data collection points. To assess students' understanding, students created initial and final concept maps about water quality. The final concept maps portrayed rich connections among the concepts, an indication of integrated understanding. These, compared to the initial maps and the pre- and posttest results, showed substantial learning gains and an integrated and in-depth understanding of the science ideas (Krajcik & Starr, 2001; Novak & Gleason, 2001). Novak and Gleason's work illustrates the value of using probes to support student engagement in science practices and learning important science ideas.

Using probes for scientific experiments also can support students' graphing skills, design of experiments, and problem-solving skills (Linn, 1998; Linn et al., Layman, & Nachmias, 1987). One reason is that using probes affords students more time to interpret and evaluate data and redesign their experiments, because they spend less time on more routine tasks such as the collecting and recording of data (Brasell, 1987; Thornton & Sokoloff, 1990). Probes and accompanying software handle the routine tasks of recording data, and students have more time to engage in cognitive activities. As such, the use of probes in the science classroom provides an application of Quintana and colleagues' (2004) scaffolding Guideline 5: *Automatically handle nonsalient, routine tasks* (see Table 18.3).

Figure 18.3 Students using probes to collect acid and base data.

The graphing software that accompanies probes also holds many advantages. Students are able to see a graph of the data while they are collecting the data. This offers students linked multiple representations—their involvement in the phenomena and the graph. There is some evidence to suggest that seeing the data graphed immediately as students collect the data promotes learning (Brasell, 1987). The software can also show students several runs of the same experiment, providing further support for data analysis and interpretation.

With advances in technology, probes can now be used on various handheld devices. Reid-Griffin and Carter (2008) examined the potential of using portable data collection devices with selected seventh- and eighth-grade students. During data collection, students used the data analysis system that involved a graphing calculator, a temperature probe, a voltage probe, a light probe, and a motion detector to collect data for various investigations. This learning environment allowed students to learn fundamental skills in using tools for data collection, conducting investigations, and engaging in scientific discourse. Students also learned how to diagnose and correct errors and to solve problems. The authors hypothesized that using the probes would allow students to collect and analyze results immediately, without having to wait. It shortened the amount of time needed to revise and repeat their investigations when the students noticed errors in the design of investigations or in data they collected. Here, we see another example of the advantage of the computer technology handing routine tasks and, as a result, promoting learning. The efficiency of data collection with probes afforded students opportunities to maximize their learning and provided students opportunities to change their original experiments, manipulate variables, and alter their inquiry designs. Using probes attached to handheld devices allows students to collect data and explore questions that they find valuable and experience authentic science (Nicaise, Gibney, & Crane, 2000). The use of portable data collection devices supports students in doing science rather than just memorizing isolated science facts (Novak, Gleason, Mahoney, & Krajcik, 2002).

Kamarainen and her colleagues (2013) also emphasize educational benefits of using probes for understanding scientific concepts related to water quality during a field trip to a local pond. They combined handheld probes and augmented reality (AR) to further support learning by situating the data collection activities in a larger, meaningful context that connects to students' activities in the real world (Squire & Klopfer, 2007). AR is a live view of a physical environment whose elements are augmented by computer-generated sensory input such as sound, video, graphics, or GPS data and software that enables participants to interact with digitalized information embedded within the real world (Dunleavy & Dede, 2014).

Using probes in real-world situations can provide challenges in meeting learning goals. For instance, often it might not be feasible for students to collect data outside of the classroom. Another challenge students face is in deciding how to analyze and interpret the data. AR interfaces can help solve these difficulties by contextualizing the learning, providing just-in-time instruction for self-directed data collection from the real world and following feedback on the student's performance (Kamarainen et al., 2013). Additionally, AR can help students engage in social interaction, facilitate cognition, and provide individualized scaffolding (Dunleavy & Dede, 2014; Klopfer, 2008; Klopfer & Squire, 2008). Handheld probes with AR applications can scaffold students using relevant science investigation tools and media of communication (Kamarainen et al., 2013; Squire & Klopfer, 2007). Although probes and accompanying software offer many advantages for classroom teaching and learning, the roles that curriculum and instruction play in scaffolding student learning are critical (Linn, 1998; Linn & Hsi, 2000).

Dynamic Modeling Tools

Models play an important role for the acquisition, production, and distribution of scientific knowledge and for making connections between real-world phenomena and scientific theoretical explanations (Gilbert, 2004; Halloun, 2006; Koponen, 2007). The construction of models allows scientists as well as learners to visualize the microscopic world and the world of galaxies and provides causal accounts of complex phenomena. In addition, scientific models can provide descriptions and simplification of complex phenomena (Pluta, Chinn, & Duncan, 2011; Rouse & Morris, 1986) and allow scientists and learners to test out their predictions. Pluta, Chinn, and Duncan (2011) reviewed research related to model-based learning in science education and suggest that using models and modeling in science learning can support cognitive, metacognitive, social, and epistemological improvements. They also suggest that modeling tools support learning in various ways (Louca & Zacharia, 2012). Various researchers discuss the value of modeling tools to enhancing science learning (e.g., Barab et al., 2000; Barnett, Barab, & Hay, 2001; Chang, Quintana, & Krajcik, 2010; Dede, Salzman, Loftin, & Sprague, 1999; Hansen, Barnett, Makinster, & Keating, 2004; Sabelli, 1994; Stratford, Krajcik, & Soloway, 1998). Constructing models based on evidence is also one of the eight science practices in the Framework for K–12 Science Education (NRC, 2012). Dynamic modeling tools allow learners to construct and revise models to provide explanations of phenomena and test out ideas.

Model-It.
Model-It allows students to create dynamic computer models of complex science systems such as water quality, ecosystems, and systems of the body (Metcalf-Jackson, Krajcik, & Soloway, 2000). Designed especially for learners, *Model-It* provided users with various supports and an easy-to-use visual and qualitative interface to scaffold student learning. *Model-It* uses the following scaffolds (see Table 18.3) to support student learning: (1) reducing the complexity of the task

by breaking the tasks down into more manageable parts (Guideline 4: *Provide structure for complex tasks and functionality*); (2) automatic handling of routine tasks (Guideline 6: *Automatically handle nonsalient, routine tasks*; (3) including representations that learners can inspect (Guideline 2: *Use representations that learners can inspect in different ways to reveal important properties of underlying data*); and (4) using language that bridges learners' understanding (Guideline 1: *Use representations and language that bridge learners' understanding*). Students construct models to explain phenomena by building quantitative relationships between identified variables using qualitative language accompanied by detailed descriptions that explain these relationships. Building relationships using qualitative language is an example of Guideline 1: *Use representations and language that bridge learners' understanding.*

Model-It was used successfully in middle and high school science classrooms in conjunction with project-based curriculum (e.g., Fretz et al., 2002; Metcalf-Jackson et al., 2000; Spitulnik, Stratford, Krajcik, & Soloway, 1997; Stratford et al., 1998; Zhang, 2012). Key to the success of *Model-It*, however, were instructional units and the teacher, who created an environment that encouraged student conversations related to the design of the model. Studies (Fretz et al., 2002) have demonstrated that the use of *Model-It* promotes the learning of challenging science ideas. For example, Zhang (2012) showed that the use of modeling software, integrated with curriculum, supported students in developing important learning skills such as planning, testing, and evaluating.

Chemation. Chemation, a software application that runs on handheld computer devices, allows students to construct, revise, and critique 2D models of molecules and animations of chemical reactions using a flip-book style animation (Chang et al., 2010). Selecting from a limited palette of atoms, students draw molecules and show how molecules might rearrange to form new molecules during a chemical reaction. Chang and colleagues (2010) demonstrate that allowing middle school students to design animations of the particle nature of matter using *Chemation* and then engage in peer evaluation is more effective at improving student learning than just viewing or constructing the animation. Reducing complexity and embedding *Chemation* into project-based materials supported students in learning important science ideas.

The Virtual Solar System (VSS) project. VSS is an experimental astronomy course for undergraduate students. In the *VSS* course, students build their own 3D models of different features of the solar system using a virtual reality modeling language (VRML) editor. Barab and colleagues (2000) indicate that the *VSS* project was successful for learning of astronomy concepts through the construction of virtual reality (VR) model building.

Virtual reality modeling has the potential to place students in various contexts that otherwise would not be possible to visualize.

Computer modeling programs, such as *Model-It*, *Chemation*, and the *VSS Project*, are powerful learning technologies as they support students in constructing understanding through creating dynamic models that they would not otherwise be able to do in the science classroom. Such tools support students in engaging in the science practice of modeling and place the act of constructing in the hands of the learner.

Interactive Visualizations—Making Unseen Processes Visible to Learners

Technologies can present students with interactive visualizations that can permit learners to explore a range of phenomena and underlying mechanisms that they normally would be unable to do in the science classroom. Linn and Eylon (2011) describe "visualization as including interactive, computer-based animations of scientific phenomena including models and simulations" (p.12). Although dynamic visualization allows learners to see dynamic processes, interactive visualization and simulations give learners the ability to interact with the visualization by changing variables and then observing the consequence. Interactive visualization allows learners to examine and explore phenomena that are too small, too large, too fast, or too dangerous to explore. As such, interactive visualizations invite students to the world of cells and molecules, or to the galaxies. They can also explore phenomena that are too dangerous to examine, like volcanoes, or too fast, like earthquakes, or too slow to observe, like growth of an organism over time. But the power of interactive visualizations is that they can present underlying causal accounts of the phenomena that allow learners to explore what happens when variables change. Students can change a variable and observe the consequence.

Molecular Workbench. The Concord Consortium provides a variety of open-source interactive visualizations and models that teachers can incorporate into lessons. Figure 18.4 shows two images from Concord's Molecular Workbench (Pallant & Tinker, 2004; Xie & Tinker, 2006) (http://mw.concord.org/modeler/) that enable students to explore how the concentration of substances will affect the movement of substances into and out of cells. The interactive visualization helps learners construct ideas related to diffusion. Students are able to change the concentration of carbon dioxide and oxygen and then observe what happens to the concentration inside and outside a cell at the molecular level. The figure on the top shows initial concentrations of carbon dioxide and oxygen outside and inside a cell; the figure on the bottom shows the concentration after the simulation has run for a short period of time. Notice how students can observe what occurs at the molecular level and read scales at the macroscopic level. These linked representations allow learners to make inspections

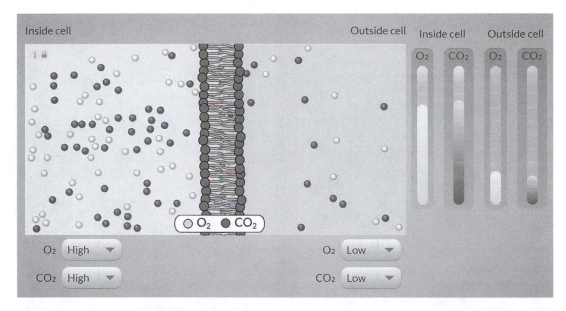

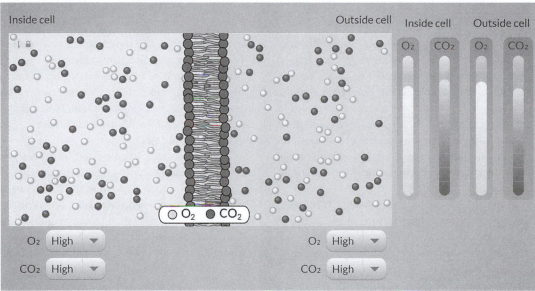

Figure 18.4 Interactive visualizations of diffusion in a cell. The image on the left shows the initial conditions inside and outside the cell, and the image on the right shows the conditions after the simulation has run for a period of time.

that promote understanding (Guideline 3: *Use representations that learners can inspect in different ways to reveal important properties of underlying data*). This linking of the dynamic, multiple, interactive visualization can help support students in building deeper understanding because of the explicit connection between molecular representations and macroscopic representations, an area in which learners typically struggle (Kozma & Russell, 1997, 2005; Stieff, 2011). However, more research is needed to study the impact of these efforts on student learning, as there is debate regarding use of dynamic simulations in classrooms (Zhang & Linn, 2011).

NetLogo. NetLogo also provides a variety of simulations and visualizations that learners can manipulate and then observe the outcomes. NetLogo, while a programmable

language, is more of a dynamic simulation that teachers can incorporate into their lessons. These interactive simulations provide unique opportunities to explore ideas from biology to physical science concepts. Figure 18.5 shows images of NetLogo (Novak & Wilensky, 2007; Wilensky, 1999). A list of NetLogo simulations can be found at http://ccl.northwestern.edu/netlogo/. Stieff (2011) used NetLogo in a chemistry curriculum, Connected Chemistry, available on the NetLogo site, to improve students' ability to move between the macroscopic world (phenomena) and the microscopic/molecular world. Although chemists freely move among the macroscopic, microscopic, and symbolic worlds, students find it challenging (Kozma & Russell, 1997; Krajcik, 1991). Stieff (2011) used animations from NetLogo and other curriculum resources to support students' representational competencies—or the

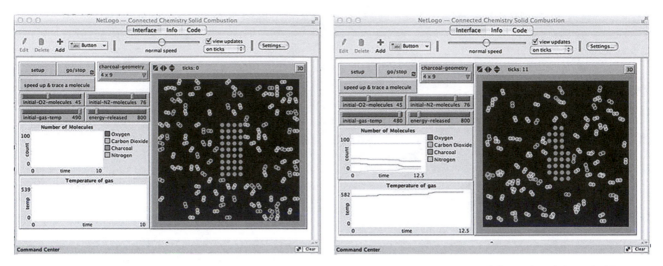

Figure 18.5 Interactive visualizations from the Connected Chemistry project showing a molecular level view of the reaction of charcoal with oxygen linked to some graphical representations of the same phenomena. The image on the left shows the initial conditions, and the image on the right shows the conditions after the simulation has run for a period of time.

capacity to move among the microscopic, symbolic, and macroscopic worlds. Figure 18.5 shows screen images from the Connected Chemistry project. The image on the left displays the initial conditions of reacting charcoal with oxygen, whereas the image on the right shows conditions after the simulations have run for a period of time. Notice how these images also contain linked, interactive visualizations. The molecular image on the left side of the window is tied to graphical representations on the right side of the window.

Although Stieff (2011) found that students who used the interactive visualization in the Connected Chemistry curriculum only demonstrated small to modest gains on summative achievement tests compared to a comparison group, this result should not be surprising, as the test materials did not assess for using representational competencies. However, analysis of Connected Chemistry students' representation use on pre- and postassessments indicates that they were significantly more likely to use submicroscopic representations of chemical systems that are consistent with teacher and expert representation use on the postassessment than they were on the preassessment. Stieff's (2011) work provides evidence that using interactive visualizations promotes students' use of representations in chemistry. It is important to point out that Stieff's visualizations were embedded in a chemistry curriculum sequence that involved the negotiating of meaning in the classroom. As we argue, technology will only be of value when it supports students in meeting important learning goals.

PhET online library of simulations. The *PhET* online library of simulations (http://phet.colorado.edu) provides easy-to-use interactive simulations for a variety of important topics in physics, chemistry, biology, and earth science. The visualization of plate tectonics allows learners to explore how plates move on the surface of the earth. Like the other visualizations discussed, the simulations are available free of charge and require minimal training to use. Students are able to change temperature, composition, and thickness of plates and observe the resulting effects. Figure 18.6 shows an image from the plate tectonics simulation in *PhET*.

PhET simulations can be used to supplement existing curriculum materials or to engage students' exploration of phenomena. However, it is up to the teacher to decide how to use the materials. The materials do come with sample student learning goals and a teacher's guide.

EcoMUVE. EcoMUVE (Multi-User Virtual Environments) is 3D virtual world simulation that places students inside the simulation and provides a situated learning experience. Students take on the identity of an avatar that allows them to explore the 3D virtual world. *EcoMUVE* has the potential to scaffold students to take part in expert practices. *EcoMUVE* is a design-centered environment that provides a problem-based learning platform that engages students in ecological issues arising over time. The environment provides students an opportunity to learn from solving problems rather than memorize events and related concepts of the ecosystem (Grotzer, Tutwiler, Dede, Kamarainen, & Metcalf, 2011).

Committee on Science Learning: Computer Games, Simulations and Education. The Committee on Science Learning (National Research Council, 2011) concluded that computer simulations have potential to promote students' engagement in various science practices and are appealing to K–12 learners, as they are immersed in digital technologies throughout the day, but the committee also reported that there are many gaps in the literature that still need further exploration with respect to simulations and

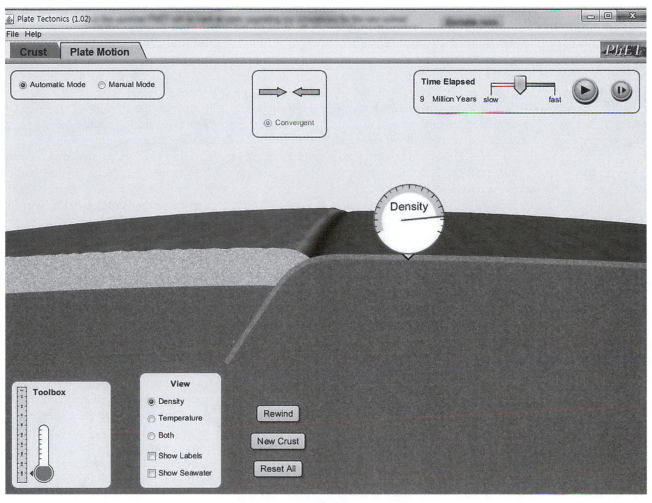

Figure 18.6 Plate tectonics simulation in PhET. (http://phet.colorado.edu)

Figure 18.7 Screenshot of EcoMUVE pond ecosystem. (http://ecomuve.gse.harvard.edu/)

games for educational purposes. Although the research on the use of simulations to promote conceptual understanding is promising (Njoo & de Jong, 1993), less evidence is available with respect to promoting student understanding of science practices. Other benefits for using simulations also exist in the literature. Researchers report that the use of virtual experimental simulations has benefits such as saving time and cost compared to conducting real experiments, providing low risk of accidents in the experiment process (Kang, Kim, & Lee, 2011; Merrill, Hammons, Vincent, Reynolds, & Tolman, 1996), and allowing students to engage in science practices (see de Jong & van Joolingen, 1998; Kang, Kim, & Lee, 2011). For example, Kang and colleagues (2011) used the Gizmos simulation (www.explorelearning.com) in high school chemistry and found that students' graphing ability and inquiry skills improved. Noh, Cha, and Kim (1999) report that engaging students in molecular animations can help to increase students' self-reliance in learning challenging tasks.

E-Learning Environments

E-learning materials have several advantages over the paper-based materials. These features include providing linked multiple interactive representations, scaffolds to support reflection and articulation, engagement in science practices, and customized learning sequences to meet individual needs.

Stieff's (2011) work illustrates how the use of visualizations can be used in curriculum materials. *The Molecular Workbench*, *NetLogo*, and *PhET* provide simulations that other designers and teachers can use in their classrooms. Other researchers are building e-learning systems in which learning materials are presented to students on a computer platform. However, teacher interactions and use of laboratory experiments are still considered important. We review four of these environments: the *Web-Based Inquiry Science Environment* (WISE; Slotta & Linn, 2009), *SimQuest* (de Jong, 2006), and two environments that Krajcik helped design and develop—*eIQWST* and the *Interactions Portal*.

Web-Based Inquiry Science Environment. The *Web-Based Inquiry Science Environment* (WISE; Slotta & Linn, 2009) takes advantage of technology to develop interactive lessons for enhancing inquiry learning and strengthening knowledge integration. *WISE* uses interactive visualizations of scientific phenomena embedded in carefully designed instructional modules to help students integrate their ideas while at the same time prioritizing the needs of teachers by focusing on learning goals. *WISE* incorporates various scaffolds to support students in learning, including an online map to help guide students through inquiry tasks and embedded assessments to provide feedback to students and teachers. The map helps students to work independently through their projects (Linn & Hsi, 2000) and can be customized depending on students' prior

experience with inquiry and their level of understanding of the inquiry question (Choi & Shin, 2009; Rose & Meyer, 2002). The interactive visualizations in *WISE* make science visible by representing unseen phenomena, such as the molecular changes that occur in chemical reactions (Zhang & Linn, 2011). *WISE* incorporates prompts to help students reflect and monitor their progress on research and evidence pages to keep track of the evidence they collected. *WISE* promotes students' engagement in science practices by providing scaffolds so that students can compare viewpoints, generate criteria for selecting fruitful ideas, use ideas to build arguments, gather evidence to support their own positions, and critique the arguments presented by their peers. Because of the various supports, *WISE* enables learners to perform opened-ended investigations and receive guidance as they perform their investigations. *WISE* is part of the Technology-Enhanced Learning in Science (TELS) Center (Linn, Lee, Tinker, Husic, & Chiu, 2006; for details about TELS, see http://telscenter.org). *WISE* units can be found at http://wise.berkeley.edu.

WISE contains several key features that capitalize on previous research conducted by Linn's research group, including ideas discussed above about the Computer as Learning Partner Project. Each *WISE* activity elicits student ideas, allows students to make predictions, includes pivotal cases that present contrasting ideas, and provides interactive visualizations. *WISE* also contains scaffolds for constructing explanations and supporting online discussion and provides supports to elicit student reflections. The *WISE* units present an excellent example of a fully integrated technology package that incorporates what is currently known about promoting the learning of science.

Bell (Bell, 2004; Linn, Davis, & Bell, 2004) used a precursor to the *WISE*, called Mildred, to engage students in debate projects such as how far can light travel, the cause of increasing frog deformities, and the threat of malaria. Using prompts to support students in argumentation, Bell's work shows that guiding students in arguing about topics they find meaningful enables students to gain a deeper understanding into the nature of science. Moreover, when students prepared to argue for both sides of a position, they more successfully distinguished among the key ideas involved in the debate.

Williams and colleagues (Williams & Linn, 2002; Williams, Montgomery, & Manokore, 2012) developed a *WISE* system to scaffold students' understanding of heredity, inherited traits, and related concepts such as cells and reproduction. A unique feature of the materials developed by Williams (Williams et al., 2012) is blending students conducting laboratory-based experiments with the online learning environment. Like other *WISE* materials, an online inquiry map is used to guide students through various activities and support interactive visualizations. Figure 18.8 shows a screenshot of the *WISE* environment. The left side of the image shows the online inquiry map for guiding students through activities and the center shows an interactive animation that enables students to trace a genotype through generations.

Figure 18.8 An image from Williams's heredity unit showing an interactive animation that enables students to trace a genotype through generations. (Williams et al., 2012)

In one of the activities, students interact with the online visualization that enables them to explore asexual and sexual reproduction and then create offspring from one or two parents. In another activity, students determine which Wisconsin fast plant trait is dominative or recessive, including determining the genotype, by examining data from growing the fast plants. Findings from middle school students using the materials suggest that significant learning gains from pretest to posttest in understanding complex topics were made; however, some students struggled to explain the importance of mitotic and meiotic divisions in transferring genetic information. Based on results, Williams and colleagues are modifying the materials. This is another example of using design experiments to improve the learning materials.

Zhang and Linn (2011) used the *WISE* system with embedded dynamic visualizations from the *Molecular Workbench* to support students in learning about chemical reactions, a core idea in physical science. However, like Chang and colleagues (Chang et al., 2010), Zhang and Linn (2011) added a construction feature to the *WISE* so that students would be challenged to draw their ideas about how the combustion of hydrogen takes place. Students drew images four times during their work—before the reaction, when it started, during the reaction, and after the reaction. The *WISE* contained features that promoted knowledge integrations, such as making predictions and reflecting on progress. Zhang and Linn compared the results of the students who generated drawings with those of students who spent more time interacting with the visualizations. Their results from the use of embedded

assessments show that the students who drew images of the process integrated more ideas about chemical reactions and made more precise interpretations of the visualization than did the group that only interacted with the visualizations. This work shows, like that of Chang and colleagues (Chang et al., 2010), that the act of constructing promotes student learning.

SimQuest. SimQuest provides various simulations for understanding scientific conceptual knowledge and learning experimental processes. Many students experience difficulties when they engage in science practices (de Jong, 2006; de Jong & van Joolingen, 1998). De Jong (2006) indicates that students need support to design experiments (e.g., what variables to choose, how many variables to change, how to state and test hypotheses); implement them (e.g., make predictions, avoid being fixated with achieving particular results rather than testing hypotheses); and interpret and present results from them (e.g., compare and visualize data, then present these appropriately). His work focuses on students' everyday problems as an important factor for engaging students in inquiry learning. He used a computer simulation program that focused on everyday problems to enhance inquiry-based learning. The *SimQuest* application allows students to change variables and perform virtual experiments. Simulation programs like *SimQuest* provided students opportunities to plan and carry out investigations. *SimQuest* provides both an example of a simulation and an authoring system for teachers and educators to create computer simulations (Van Joolingen & de Jong, 2003). E-learning

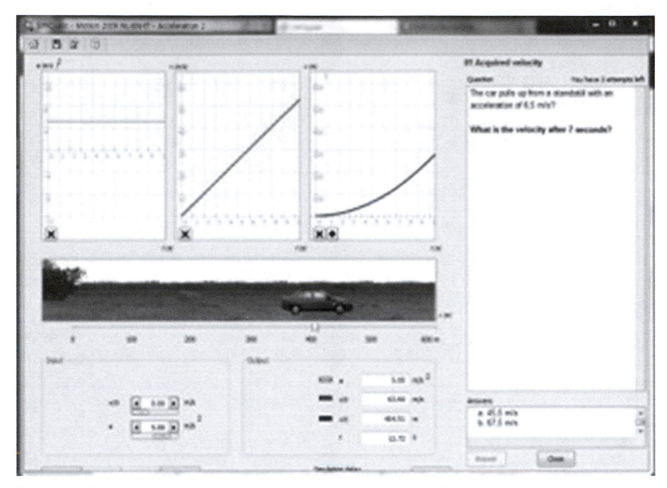

Figure 18.9 SimQuest module: simulation, graphing, data, and assessment questions for understanding velocity and distance.

environments that incorporate simulations can help students to explore hypothetical situations, to interact with a simplified version of a process or system, to change the time-scale of events, and to practice tasks and solve problems in a realistic environments without stress (Van Berkum & de Jong, 1991). This exploring, investigating, and predicting in a simulated environment supports students to develop conceptual understanding (Kang et al., Kim, & Lee, 2011; Windschitl & Andre, 1998). Figure 18.9 shows one example of a module related to movement of a car in *SimQuest*. Each module provides data, text explanation, graph illustrations, animation, and assessment questions related to the event. From this module, students can learn the relations among time, distance, and velocity.

E-learning IQWST (eIQWST). In work conducted with LeeAnn Sutherland and Namsoo Shin from the University of Michigan and David Rose from the Center for Applied Special Technologies (Shin, Sutherland, & McCall, 2011; Sutherland & Krajcik, 2007), we converted a unit from a middle school curriculum series to e-learning materials in order to engage a greater range of students. A unit on the

particle nature of matter—"*How can I smell things from a distance?*" (Krajcik, Reiser, Sutherland, & Fortus, 2012; Merritt, Shwartz, Sutherland, Van de Kerkhof, & Krajcik, 2012), from the Investigating and Question our World through Science Technologies (IQWST)—was adapted to take advantage of interactive visualizations and to incorporate various support features and scaffolds consistent with universal design for learning (Choi & Shin, 2009; Rose, Meyer, & Hitchcock, 2005).

This 8- to 10-week unit involves middle school students in answering the driving question "How can I smell things from a distance?" The unit supports students in learning one of the core ideas in science, the particle nature of matter, by experiencing and then explaining a variety of phenomena. The unit focuses on the common phenomenon of smelling odors to contextualize chemistry ideas and science practices in everyday experiences. The unit also supports students in the science practice of modeling. Students construct and revise their model of matter, both as a drawing and a written explanation of their drawing, as they experience more phenomena (Merritt & Krajcik, 2013).

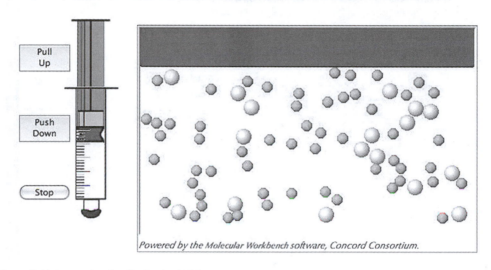

Figure 18.10 Interactive visualization in eIQWST.

The e-learning materials have several advantages over the paper-based materials. These features include providing linked multiple interactive represents and using tools to create interactive opportunities for learners to *construct and express* understanding, and they take into consideration the needs of all learners by providing *learning resources and strategies that support and challenge each learner. eIQWST* allows learners to access a multimedia glossary of terms, linked videos of phenomena that students experience, a text-to-speech function, and sentence starters and hints to support them in responding to embedded assessments. Students also benefit from a drawing tool to draw models to explain phenomena and from interactive visualization, and they are able to store their work online for future access and review. Figure 18.10 illustrates the interactive visualizations of *eIQWST*. This simulation from Concord Consortium's Molecular Workbench allows students to compress or expand a gas in the syringe by pushing it down or pulling it and then watch the change that occurs at the microscopic level.

Students experience expanding and compressing a syringe as a hands-on activity in class. The students who use *eIQWST* are additionally able to observe and interact with the simulation, where they compress and expand the syringe and observe what happens at the molecular level. Observing and interacting with the visualization allows learners to inspect the underlying model that explains

when it gets more and more difficult to push in the piston (or to expand the piston; Guideline 3: *Use representations that learners can inspect in different ways to reveal important properties of underlying data*, from Table 18.3).

Figure 18.11 shows some of the sentence starters used in *eIQWST* to support students in articulating their ideas. Sentence starters are an example of embedding expert guidance into the system, Guideline 5: *Embed expert guidance about science practices*, from Table 18.3.

Interactions Portal. Krajcik and colleagues (Damelin, Stevens, Choi, Russell, & Krajcik, 2013; Lee, McGee, Duck, Choi, & Krajcik, 2013), much like Williams and colleagues (Williams et al., 2012), designed materials delivered through a digital platform, the *Interactions Portal* on the Concord Consortium System (http://concord. org), that integrate the use of student tasks, teacher-led demos, "lab-like" experiences, computer simulations, and embedded assessments (Damelin & Koile, 2011). Like the *IQWST* and *eIQWST* materials, the *Interactions Portal* design is project based and engages students in answering the driving question: *Why do some things stick together while other things don't?* The materials focus on supporting students in developing understanding of the electrical interactions that occur among matter to provide causal accounts of why matter sticks together,

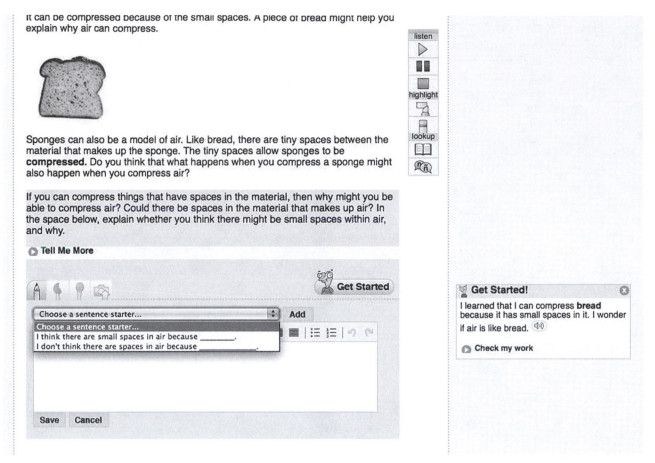

Figure 18.11 Sentence prompts in eIQWST support students in responding to embedded assessments.

a core physical science idea in the Framework for K–12 Science Education (National Research Council, 2012) and the Next Generation of Science Standards (NGSS Lead States, 2013). An additional feature of the system is that student work can be viewed and reviewed by the teacher in real time or later via electronic reports. Teachers can use these electronic reports both during class and later to provide students with more detailed feedback and to plan subsequent lessons. The materials blend physical representations, computer representations, and interactive visualizations to support students in constructing understanding. Figure 18.12 shows instructions delivered through the *Interactions Portal* for one of the tasks students complete in the classroom.

The materials also engage students in using online interactive visualizations. Figure 18.13 allows students to interact with a model at the molecular level to explain how a neutral object can be attracted to a charged object.

A key aspect of the materials is that students use computer drawing tools to construct models to illustrate their evolving understanding of electrostatic interactions. Figure 18.14 shows a student model of how charged objects, in this case a balloon, can stick to a neutral object, the wall. This model can also serve as an embedded assessment that allows the teacher to track how student understanding changes across time.

The materials for the *Interaction Project* are still in the development and pilot testing phase, but our initial

research in ninth-grade science classrooms shows that the materials are usable by teachers and students. Moreover, students report being engaged when using the materials. Tentative data indicate that student models become more sophisticated as students experience more phenomena and discuss ideas.

E-learning environments that blend interactive visualizations, embedded assessment, and physical representations and tasks—like the *Interactions Portal*, *eIQWST*, and Williams's Genetic Inheritance Module—offer the potential to engage students in learning core ideas of science and science practices. Their interactivity and multiple representations are two key features that promote student learning. Providing multiple representations like those used in *SimQuest* and other e-learning environments can support students in developing integrated understanding of challenging concepts (Eylon & Linn, 2011; Spitulnik et al., 1997). Using more than one representation is more engaging to students and can promote learning as ideas are expressed in multiple ways. Students can build integrated understandings when they build thoughtful connections among various representations (Ainsworth, 1999, 2008; Linn, 1998). In addition, graphs, tables, diagrams, flowcharts, animations, simulations, and written descriptions are part of the repertoire of engaging in science practices (Jaipal, 2009). However, a learner's ability to make scientific meaning is dependent

How can you roll a plastic bottle across a table without touching it? (1)

Have your partner hold a dry, empty plastic bottle by its cap and **rub the bottle with fur**. Be careful **not to touch the rest of the bottle**. Still holding the bottle by the cap, carefully place it on the smooth surface.

Bring your hand close to the side of the bottle without touching it (see picture).
Hint: If you touch it, you will have to start over.

1. Write your observations below.

Figure 18.12 Student task delivered through the Interaction Portal.

In some previous experiments, you have seen that neutral objects can be attracted to either positively or negatively charged objects. How can it happen? In this activity, you will use your model of atomic structure to explain how a charged balloon sticks to the wall. First, explore the simulation below.

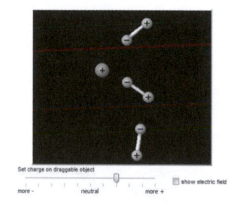

Set charge on draggable object

more −   neutral   more +   ☐ show electric field

1. What is the overall charge of the stick (with positive on one end and negative on the other end)? Explain your answer.

Figure 18.13 Interactive simulations illustrating how neutral objects can become charged.

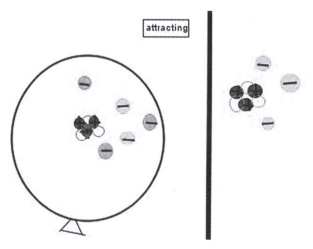

Figure 18.14 Example of a student model from the Interactions project showing why a charged object can stick to a new object

on a learner's ability to make sense of different representations, both singularly and in conjunction with text. As such, when developing e-learning environments using multiple representations, designers need to ensure that learners can grasp the connections among the various representations (Ainsworth, 1999, 2008). Scaffolding that shows how the representations are connected is important for helping students to make the cognitive links among the representations.

Teachers, however, play a significant role in e-learning environments, as they serve as facilitators of the learning and help students make sense of what is going on (Barab, Squire, & Barnett, 1999). One disappointment in using the *Interactions Portal* is that some teachers felt they did not have a role in the classroom. Williams (2008) reported the experience of one teacher who incorporated a *WISE* module into his science instruction (experienced elementary school teacher, 3-year case study) and increasing the integrated use of the technology by this teacher in years 2 and 3. She suggested that repeated opportunities for teaching experiences with the use of *WISE* made this teacher change his pedagogy (Williams, 2008). These observations point to the need for professional development in helping teachers develop teaching strategies for using these new electronic resources.

Concluding Comment

Learning technologies serve as powerful tools that can support students in learning science. As with any instructional materials, the underlying goal is to foster students toward building integrated understanding of core ideas, crosscutting concepts, and science practices. The functionality of these learning technologies for students to analyze data, build models, use simulations to interact virtually with phenomena too dangerous to do in real time, and solve complex problems can support students in constructing integrated understanding. Moreover, the flexibility, interactive power, networking capability, customization, and multiple representation capabilities of new portable devices could help to change the structure of the science classroom to engage students in constructing knowledge by building models and developing explanations using evidence. However, as we argued in the chapter, computer applications by themselves won't necessarily support learning. Computer applications need to be designed to support learning and be embedded in rich learning environments. Learning technologies embedded within a curriculum that engage learners in answering meaningful questions, that support clear and specified learning goals, and that contain scaffolds to support students in challenging tasks are essential if the potential of technology is to be realized. As such, instructional sequences that make use of learning technologies need to be planned carefully to consider learning goals and the learning context. Although research supports the use of learning technologies to help learners develop integrated understanding, more needs to be learned. Unfortunately, often the use of these technologies is short lived, and they have not spread throughout the science teaching and learning community, although there are exceptions like the use of sensors to collect data.

We described five learning principles that designers and teachers can use to guide the design of instruction when use learning technologies: (1) active construction, (2) situated learning, (3) cognitive tools, (4) learning goals, and (5) scaffolding to support students in completing challenging tasks. These learning principles suggest how to design learning environments for enhancing students' integrated understanding. From a review of the research literature and various research programs regarding the use of technology in science education, we illustrated how learning technologies support developing deeper conceptual understanding of core ideas and science practices such as collecting and analyzing data, constructing models, and using evidence to develop explanations. When teachers and designers develop and use technology around these learning principles, the technologies support students in connecting core ideas with science practices (National Research Council, 2012).

Learning technologies allow students to participate in a variety of science practices that they would not otherwise be able to do, such as building and testing dynamic models, using interactive visualizations of unseen phenomena, visualizing science principles that they cannot experience firsthand, and analyzing and visualizing complex data sets. Learning technologies allow students to ask and explore "What if . . .?" questions and provide opportunities to engage in these "What if" questions multiple times because there is not as much cost from an expense or time perspective in redoing the investigation. Additionally, unlike exploring some potentially dangerous real-world phenomena, simulations and interactive visuals are low risk with respect to safety.

We also explored computer applications and e-learning environments as examples, including probeware, modeling tools, interactive visualizations, and integrated suites. These various technology environments allow students to use tools and engage in similar activities to those scientists carry out. The examples we provided can offer guidelines for using technology for science education. However, we also need to consider the teachers' role and their ability in using technology.

Learning technologies will change the role of teachers and require that they use new teaching practices, but this does not diminish the role of the teacher in science classroom. Science teachers play a critical role, and the use of learning technologies requires their active involvement. Although designers can embed scaffolds in the technology, teachers provide additional in-the-moment scaffolding for students as they engage in challenging practices of building models, analyzing and making sense of data, and constructing evidence-based explanations.

Research is needed to explore and refine these high-level teaching practices and capabilities that are necessary for effectively supporting student learning in e-learning environments. Research that provides answers to these questions can provide new directions for science teacher education programs—both preservice and inservice programs. Not only should teacher educators and designers develop new curriculum that embeds the design principles we described in this chapter, but teachers also need to develop professional networks to share opportunities to enrich their practices and strategies for using technology effectively in science lessons.

We hope that this chapter shows that learning technologies can meet clearly specified learning goals to support the development of integrated understanding. However, technologies are only part of the story. Technologies need to be embedded in a much larger framework—curriculum, learning goals, and teacher practices. The learning goals, teacher instruction, and curriculum materials need to provide a context in which the materials are used. With this integration, learning technologies will become necessary tools in the science classroom to support students in engaging in science, experiencing phenomena and ideas that can't be accomplished without them that foster the development of integrated understanding that will allow students to solve problems, explain phenomena, and have the foundation to learn more.

References

Adams, D., & Shrum, J.W. (1990). The effects of microcomputer-based laboratory exercises on the acquisition of line graph construction and interpretation skills by high school biology students. *Journal of Research in Science Teaching, 27*(8), 777–787.

Ainsworth, S. (1999). The functions of multiple representations. *Computers & Education, 33*(2/3), 131–152.

Ainsworth, S. (2008). The educational value of multiple-representations when learning complex scientific concepts. In J.K. Gilbert, M. Reiner, & M. Nakhleh (Eds.), *Visualization: Theory and practice in science education* (pp. 191–208). London: Springer.

Barab, S.A., Hay, K.E., Barnett, M., & Keating, T. (2000). Virtual solar system project: Building understanding through model building. *Journal of Research in Science Teaching, 37*(7), 719–756.

Barab, S.A., Squire, K., & Barnett, M. (1999, May). *From teachers' fixed curricular objectives toward students' emergent practices.* Presented at the Annual Meeting of the American Educational Research Association, Montreal, Canada.

Barnett, M., Barab, S.A., & Hay, K.E. (2001). The virtual solar system project: Student modeling of the solar system. *Journal of College Science Teaching, 30*(5), 300–305.

Bell, P. (2004). Promoting students' argument construction and collaborative debate in the science classroom. In M.C. Linn, E.A. Davis, & P. Bell (Eds.), *Internet environments for science education* (pp. 115–144). Mahwah, NJ: Erlbaum.

Blumenfeld, P., Fishman, B., Krajcik, J.S., Marx, R.W., & Soloway, E. (2000). Creating useable innovations in systemic reform: Scaling-up technology-embedded project-based science in urban schools. *Educational Psychologist, 35*(3), 149–164.

Blumenfeld, P., Soloway, E., Marx, R., Krajcik, J.S., Guzdial, M., & Palincsar, A. (1991). Motivating project-based learning. *Educational Psychologist, 26*(3 & 4), 369–398.

Bransford, J., Brown, A.L., & Cocking, R. (2000). *How people learn: Brain, mind, experience and school.* Washington, DC: National Academies Press.

Brasell, H. (1987). The effect of real-time laboratory graphing on learning graphic representations of distance and velocity. *Journal of Research in Science Teaching, 24*(4), 385–395.

Brown, J.S., Collins, A., & Duguid, P. (1989). Situated cognition and the culture of learning. *Educational Researcher, 18*(1), 32–42.

Bybee, R.W. (2011). Scientific and engineering practices in K–12 classrooms: Understanding a framework for K–12 science education. *Science Teacher, 78*(9), 34–40.

Calabrese Barton, A., & Tan, E. (2010). We be burnin: Agency, identity and learning in a green energy program. *Journal of the Learning Sciences, 19*(2), 187–229.

Calabrese Barton, A., Tan, E., & Rivet, A. (2008). Creating hybrid spaces for engaging school science among urban middle school girls. *American Education Research Journal, 45*(1), 68–103.

Chang, H., Quintana, C., & Krajcik, J.S. (2010). The impact of designing and evaluating molecular animations on how well middle school students understand the particulate nature of matter. *Science Education, 94*(1), 73–94.

Choi, J., & Shin, N. (2009). Digital textbook design principles: Adapting the universal design for learning. *Journal of Educational Technology, 25*(1), 29–59.

Collins, A., Brown, J.S., & Newman, S.E. (1989). Cognitive apprenticeship: Teaching the crafts of reading, writing, and mathematics. In L.B. Resnick (Ed.), *Knowing, learning, and instruction: Essays in honor of Robert Glaser* (pp. 453–494). Hillsdale, NJ: Lawrence Erlbaum Associates.

Damelin, D., & Koile, K. (2011). Technology-enabled formative assessment in the science classroom. In P.E. Noyce & D.T. Hickey (Eds.), *New frontiers in formative assessment* (pp. 175–190). Cambridge, MA: Harvard Educational Publishing Group.

Damelin, D., Stevens, S.Y., Choi, S., Russell, R., & Krajcik, J.S. (2013, April). *Supporting student understanding of submicroscopic interactions using technology infused materials: A curriculum design study.* Paper session presented at the 86th annual international meeting of National Association for Research in Science Teaching, Rio Grande, Puerto Rico.

Dede, C., Salzman, M., Loftin, B., & Sprague, D. (1999). Multisensory immersion as a modeling environment for learning complex scientific concepts. In W. Feurzeig & N. Roberts (Eds.), *Computer modeling and simulation in science and mathematics education* (pp. 282–319). New York: Springer Verlag.

de Jong, T. (2006). Computer simulations: Technological advance in inquiry learning. *Science, 312*, 532–533.

de Jong, T., & van Joolingen, W. (1998). Scientific discovery learning with computer simulations of conceptual domains. *Review of Educational Research, 68*(2), 179–202.

Dunleavy, M., & Dede, C. (2014). Augmented reality teaching and learning. In M.J. Bishop & J. Elen (Eds.), *Handbook of research on educational communications and technology,* 4th ed., Vol. 2 (pp. 735–746). New York: Macmillan.

Edelson, D.C., & Reiser, B. (2006). Making authentic practices accessible to learners: Design challenges and strategies. In R.K. Sawyer (Ed.), *Cambridge handbook of the learning sciences* (pp. 335–354). New York: Cambridge University Press.

Fortus, D., & Krajcik, J.S. (2012). Curriculum coherence and learning progressions. In B.J. Fraser, K.G. Tobin, & C.J. McRobbie (Eds.), *Second international handbook of science education* (pp. 783–798). Dordrecht, the Netherlands: Springer.

Frederiksen, J.R., White, B.Y., & Gutwill, J. (1999). Dynamic mental models in learning science: The importance of constructing derivational links among models. *Journal of Research in Science Teaching, 36*(7), 806–836.

Fretz, E.B., Wu, H., Zhang, B., Davis, E.A., Krajcik, J.S., & Soloway, E. (2002). An investigation of software scaffolds supporting modeling practices. *Research in Science Education, 32*(4), 567–589.

Gilbert, J.K. (2004). Models and modelling: Routes to more authentic science education. *International Journal of Science and Mathematics Education, 2*(2), 115–130.

Grotzer, R., Tutwiler, S., Dede, C., Kamarainen, A., & Metcalf, S. (2011, April). *Helping students learn more expert framing of complex causal dynamics in ecosystems using EcoMUVE.* Paper presented at the National Association of Research in Science Teaching (NARST) Conference, Orlando, Florida.

Halloun, I.A. (2006). *Modeling theory in science education.* Dordrecht, the Netherlands: Springer.

Hansen, J.A., Barnett, M., Makinster, J.G., & Keating, T. (2004). The impact of three dimensional computational modeling on students' understanding of astronomy concepts: A qualitative analysis. *International Journal of Science Education, 26*(11), 65–78.

Jaipal, K. (2009). Meaning making through multiple modalities in a biology classroom: A multimodal semiotics discourse analysis. *Science Education, 94*(1), 48–72.

Jonassen, D.H. (1995). Computers as cognitive tools: Learning with technology, not from technology. *Journal of Computing in Higher Education, 6*(2), 40–73.

Kali, Y., Fortus, D., & Ronen-Fuhrmann, T. (2008). Designing learning environments to support students constructing coherent understandings. In Y. Kali, M.C. Linn, & J.E. Roseman (Eds.), *Designing coherent science education* (pp. 185–200). New York: Teachers College Press.

Kamarainen, A.M., Metcalf, S., Grotzer, T., Browne, A., Mazzuca, D.M. Tutwiler, S., & Dede, C. (2013). EcoMOBILE: Integrating augmented reality and probeware with environmental education field trips. *Computer & Education, 68*, 545–556.

Kang, M., Kim H.S., & Lee, J. (2011). The effects of flow and cognitive presence on learning outcomes in a middle school science class using Web-based simulation. *Journal of Educational Information and Media, 17*(1), 39–61.

Kesidou, S., & Roseman, J.E. (2002). How well do middle school science programs measure up? Findings from Project 2061's curriculum review. *Journal of Research in Science Teaching, 39*(6), 522–549.

Klopfer, E. (2008). *Augmented learning: Research and design of mobile educational games.* Cambridge: MIT Press.

Klopfer, E., & Squire, K.D. (2008). Environmental detectives—the development of an augmented reality platform for environmental simulations. *Education Technology Research and Development, 56*, 203–228.

Koponen, I. (2007). Models and modeling in physics education: A critical re-analysis of philosophical underpinnings and suggestions for revisions. *Science and Education, 16*(7–8), 751–773.

Kozma, R., & Russell, J. (1997). Multimedia and understanding: Expert and novice responses to different representations of chemical phenomena. *Journal of Research in Science Teaching, 34*(9), 949–968.

Kozma, R., & Russell, J. (2005). Students becoming chemists: Developing representational competence. In J.K. Gilbert (Ed.), *Visualization in science education* (pp. 121–146). Dordrecht, the Netherlands: Springer.

Krajcik, J.S. (1991). Developing students' understandings of chemical concepts. In S.H. Glynn, R.H. Yeany, & B.K. Britton (Eds.), *The psychology of learning science* (pp. 117–148). Hillsdale, NJ: Lawrence Erlbaum Associates.

Krajcik, J.S. (2013). The next generation science standards: A focus on physical science. *The Science Teacher, 80*(3), 13–24.

Krajcik, J., Blumenfeld, B., Marx, R., & Soloway. E. (2000). Instructional, curricular, and technological supports for inquiry in science classrooms. In J. Minstell & E. Van Zee (Eds.), *Inquiry into inquiry: Science learning and teaching* (pp. 283–315). Washington, DC: American Association for the Advancement of Science Press.

Krajcik, J.S., & Czerniak, C. (2013). *Teaching science in elementary and middle school classrooms: A project-based approach* (4th ed.). London: Taylor and Francis.

Krajcik, J.S., & Layman, J.W. (1992). *Research matters to the science teacher: Microcomputer–based laboratories in the science classroom.* Reston, VA: NARST. Retrieved from www.narst.org/publications/research/microcomputer.cfm

Krajcik, J.S., McNeill, K.L., & Reiser, B.J. (2008). Learning-goals–driven design model: Developing curriculum materials that align with national standards and incorporate project-based pedagogy. *Science Education, 92*(1), 1–32.

Krajcik, J., Reiser, B., Sutherland, L., & Fortus, D. (2012). *IQWST: Investigating and questioning our world through science and technology (middle school science curriculum materials).* Sangari Global Education/Active Science.

Krajcik, J.S., & Shin, N. (2014). Project-based learning. In R.K. Sawyer (Ed.), *The Cambridge handbook of the learning sciences* (2nd ed.). New York: Cambridge.

Krajcik, J.S., Slotta, J., McNeill, K.L., & Reiser, B. (2008). Designing learning environments to support students constructing coherent understandings. In Y. Kali, M.C. Linn, & J.E. Roseman (Eds.), *Designing coherent science education* (pp. 39–64). New York: Teachers College Press.

Krajcik, J., & Starr, M. (2001). Learning science content in a project-based environment. In R. Tinker & J.S. Krajcik (Eds.), *Portable technologies: Science learning in context* (pp. 103–119). Dordrecht, the Netherlands: Springer.

Kuhn, A., McNally, B., Schmoll, S., Cahill, C., Lo, W., Quintana, C., & Delen, I. (2012). *How students find, evaluate, and utilize peer-collected annotated multimedia data in science inquiry with Zydeco.* Human Factors in Computing Systems: CHI 2012 Conference Proceedings, Austin, Texas.

Lave, J., & Wenger, E. (1991). *Situated learning: Legitimate peripheral participation.* New York: Cambridge University Press.

Lee, J., McGee, S., Duck, J., Choi, S., & Krajcik, J. (2013, April). *Using interactive materials to develop high school students' understandings of how objects interact.* Paper session presented at the 86th annual international meeting of National Association for Research in Science Teaching, Rio Grande, Puerto Rico.

Linn, M.C. (1998). The impact of technology on science instruction: Historical trends and current opportunities. In B. Fraser & K. Tobin (Eds.), *International handbook of science education, part two* (pp. 265–294). Dordrecht, the Netherlands: Kluwer Academic Publishers.

Linn, M.C., Davis, E.A., & Bell, P. (Eds.). (2004). *Internet environments for science education.* Mahwah, NJ: Lawrence Erlbaum Associates.

Linn, M.C., & Eylon, B.S. (2006). Science education: Integrating views of learning and instruction. In P.A. Alexander & P.H. Winne (Eds.), *Handbook of educational psychology* (2nd ed., pp. 511–544). Mahwah, NJ: Lawrence Erlbaum Associates.

Linn, M.C., & Eylon, B.S. (2011). *Science learning and instruction: Taking advantage of technology to promote knowledge integration.* New York and London: Routledge, Taylor and Francis Group.

Linn, M.C., & Hsi, S. (2000). *Computers, teachers, peers: Science learning partners.* Mahwah, NJ: Lawrence Erlbaum Associates.

Linn, M.C., Layman, J.W., & Nachmias, R. (1987). Cognitive consequences of microcomputer-based laboratories: Graphing skills development. *Contemporary Educational Psychology, 12*(3), 244–253.

Linn, M.C., Lee, H.S., Tinker, R., Husic, F., & Chiu, J.L. (2006). Teaching and assessing knowledge integration in science. *Science, 313*(5790), 1049–1050.

Louca, L.T., & Zacharia, Z.C. (2012). Modeling-based learning in science education: Cognitive, metacognitive, social, material and epistemological contributions. *Educational Review, 64*(4), 471–492.

McNeill, K.L., & Krajcik, J.S. (2011a, March). *Claim, evidence and reasoning: Supporting middle school students in evidence-based scientific explanations.* Workshop presented at the annual national meeting of National Science Teachers Association. San Francisco, CA.

McNeill, K.L., & Krajcik, J.S. (2011b). *Supporting Grade 5–8 students in constructing explanations in science: The claim, evidence and reasoning framework for talk and writing.* New York: Pearson.

McNeill, K.L., Lizotte, D. J., Krajcik, J., & Marx, R.W. (2006). Supporting students' construction of scientific explanations by fading scaffolds in instructional materials. *Journal of the Learning Sciences, 15*(2), 153–191.

Merrill, P.F., Hammons, K., Vincent, B.R., Reynolds, P.L., & Tolman, M.N. (1996). *Computers in education.* Boston: Allyn & Bacon.

Merritt, J., & Krajcik, J.S. (2013). Supporting students in building a particle model of matter. In G. Tsaparlis & H. Sevian (Eds.), *Concepts of matter in science education* (pp. 11–46). Dordrecht, the Netherlands: Springer.

Merritt, J., Shwartz, Y., Sutherland, L. M., Van de Kerkhof, M. H., & Krajcik, J. S. (2012). Introduction to chemistry. In J. Krajcik, B. Reiser, L. Sutherland, & D. Fortus (Eds.), *IQWST: Investigating and questioning our world through science and technology* (middle school science curriculum materials). Greenwich, CT: Sangari Global Education/Active Science.

Metcalf, S. J., Dede, C. J., Grotzer, T. A., & Kamarainen, A. (2010, May). *EcoMUVE: Design of virtual environments to address science learning goals.* Paper session presented at American Educational Research Association (AERA) Conference, Denver, CO.

Metcalf, S. J., & Tinker, F. T. (2004). Probeware and handhelds in elementary and middle school science. *Journal of Science Education and Technology, 13*(1), 43–49.

Metcalf-Jackson, S., Krajcik, J. S., & Soloway, E. (2000). Model-it: A design retrospective. In M. Jacobson & R. B. Kozma (Eds.), *Innovations in science and mathematics education: Advanced designs for technologies and learning* (pp. 77–116). New York: Lawrence Erlbaum.

Mokros, J., & Tinker, R. F. (1987). The impact of microcomputer-based labs on children's ability to interpret graphs. *Journal of Research in Science Teaching, 24*(4), 369–383.

National Research Council, Duschl, R. A., Schweingruber, H. A. & Shouse, A. W. (Eds.). (2007). Taking science to school: Learning and teaching science in grades K–8. Washington, DC: National Academies Press. Retrieved from www.nap.edu/catalog.php?record_id=11625

National Research Council, Committee on Science Learning: Computer Games, Simulations, and Education, Honey, M., & Hilton M. (Eds.). (2011). *Learning science through computer games and simulations.* Washington, DC: National Academies Press. Retrieved from www.nap.edu/catalog.php?record_id=13078

National Research Council. (2012). *A framework for K–12 science education: Practices, crosscutting concepts, and core ideas.* Washington, DC: National Academies Press.

NGSS Lead States. 2013. *Next Generation Science Standards: For States, By States.* Washington, DC: The National Academies Press.

Nicaise, M., Gibney, T., & Crane, M. (2000). Toward an understanding of authentic learning: Student perceptions of an authentic classroom. *Journal of Science Education and Technology, 9*(1), 79–94.

Njoo, M., & de Jong, T. (1993). Exploratory learning with a computer simulation for control theory: Learning processes and instructional support. *Journal of Research in Science Teaching, 30*(8), 821–844.

Noh, T., Cha, J., & Kim, C. (1999). The effect of computer-assisted instruction using molecular-level animation and worksheet in high school chemistry class. *Journal of the Korean Association for Research in Science Education, 19*(1), 128–136.

Novak, A. M., & Gleason, C. (2001). Incorporating portable technology to enhance an inquiry: Project-based middle school science classroom. In R. Tinker & J. S. Krajcik (Eds.), *Portable technologies: Science learning in context* (pp. 29–26). Dordrecht, the Netherlands: Kluwer Publishers.

Novak, A. M., Gleason, C., Mahoney, J., & Krajcik, J. S. (2002). Inquiry through portable technology. *Science Scope, 26*(3), 18–21.

Novak, A. M., & Krajcik, J. S. (2004). Using technology to support inquiry in middle school science. *Science & Technology Education Library, 25,* 75–101.

Novak, A. M., & Krajcik, J. S. (2005). Using learning technologies to support inquiry in middle school science. In L. Flick & N. G. Lederman (Eds.), *Scientific inquiry and nature of science: Implications for teaching, learning and teacher education* (pp. 75–102). Dordrecht, the Netherlands: Kluwer Publishers.

Novak, M., & Wilensky, U. (2007). *NetLogo connected chemistry solid combustion model.* Retrieved from http://ccl.northwestern.edu/netlogo/models/ConnectedChemistrySolidCombustion. Evanston, IL: Center for Connected Learning and Computer-Based Modeling, Northwestern Institute on Complex Systems, Northwestern University.

Oliver, M. (2000). An introduction to the evaluation of learning technology. *Educational Technology & Society, 3*(4), 20–30.

Palincsar, S. A. (1998). Social constructivist perspectives on teaching and learning. *Annual Review of Psychology, 49*(1), 345–375.

Pallant, A., & Tinker, R. (2004). Reasoning with atomic-scale molecular dynamic models. *Journal of Science Education and Technology, 13*(1), 51–66.

Pluta, J. W., Chinn, A. C., & Duncan, R. G. (2011). Learners' epistemic criteria for good scientific models. *Journal of Research in Science Teaching, 48*(5), 486–511.

Quintana, C. (2012). Pervasive science: Using mobile devices and the cloud to support science education anytime, anyplace. *Interactions, 19*(4), 76–80.

Quintana, C., Reiser, B. J., Davis, E. A., Krajcik, J. S., Fretz, E., Duncan, R. D., Kyza, E., Edelson, D., & Soloway, E. (2004). A scaffolding design framework for software to support science inquiry. *Journal of the Learning Sciences, 13*(3), 337–386.

Reid-Griffin, A., & Carter, G. (2008). Uncovering the potential: The role of technologies on science learning of middle school students. *International Journal of Science and Mathematics Education, 6*(2), 329–350.

Rivet, A. E., & Krajcik, J. S. (2008). Contextualizing instruction: Leveraging students' prior knowledge and experiences to foster understanding of middle school science. *Journal of Research in Science Teaching, 45*(1), 79–100.

Rogoff, R. (1990). *Apprenticeship in thinking: Cognitive development in social context.* Oxford, UK: Oxford University Press.

Rose, D. H., & Meyer, A. (2002). *Teaching every student in the digital age: Universal design for learning.* Alexandria, VA: ASCD.

Rose, D. H., Meyer, A., & Hitchcock, C. (2005). *The universally designed classroom: Accessible curriculum and digital technologies.* Cambridge, MA: Harvard Education Press.

Rouse, W. B., & Morris, N. M. (1986). On looking into the black box: Prospects and limits in the search for mental models. *Psychological Bulletin, 100*(3), 349–363.

Sabelli, N. (1994). On using technology for understandings science. *Interactive Learning Environments, 4*(3), 195–198.

Salomon, G., Perkins, D. N., & Globerson, T. (1991). Partners in cognition: Extending human intelligence with intelligent technologies. *Educational Researcher, 20*(3), 2–9.

Sawyer, R. K. (2006). The new science of learning. In R. K. Sawyer (Ed.), *The Cambridge handbook of the learning sciences* (pp. 1–18). New York: Cambridge.

Sherin, B., Reiser, B., & Edelson, D. (2004). Scaffolding analysis: Extending the scaffolding metaphor to learning artifacts. *Journal of the Learning Sciences, 13*(3), 387–421.

Shin, N., Sutherland, L. M., & McCall, K. (April, 2011). *Design research of features in inquiry-based science materials.* Paper session presented at annual meeting of American Educational Research Association, New Orleans, LA.

Slotta, J. D., & Linn, M. C. (2009). *WISE science: Web-based inquiry in the classroom. Technology, education.* New York: Teachers College Press.

Smith, C. L., Wiser, M., Anderson, C. W., & Krajcik, J. S. (2006). Implications of research on children's learning for standards and assessment: A proposed learning progression for matter and the atomic molecular theory. *Measurement: Interdisciplinary Research and Perspectives, 4*(1&2), 1–98.

Spitulnik, M., Stratford, S., Krajcik, J. S., & Soloway, E. (1997). Using technology to support students' artifact construction in science. In B. Fraser & K. Tobin (Eds.), *International handbook of science education, part two* (pp. 363–382). Dordrecht, the Netherlands: Kluwer Academic Publishers.

Squire, K. D., & Klopfer, E. (2007). Augmented reality simulations on handheld computers. *Journal of the Learning Sciences, 16*(3), 371–413.

Stevens, S., Sutherland, L., & Krajcik, J. S. (2009). *The big ideas of nanoscale science and engineering.* Arlington, VA: National Science Teachers Association Press.

Stieff, M. (2011), Improving representational competence using molecular simulations embedded in inquiry activities. *Journal of Research in Science Teaching, 48*(10), 1137–1158.

Stratford, S. J., Krajcik, J., & Soloway, E. (1998). Secondary students' dynamic modeling processes: Analyzing, reasoning about, synthesizing, and testing models of stream ecosystems. *Journal of Science Education and Technology, 7*(3), 215–234.

Sutherland, L., & Krajcik, J. S. (2007). *Collaborative research: Universal design of inquiry–based middle and high school science curriculum* (NSF; DRL–0730348; 2007–2011); UM: LeeAnn Sutherland (PI) & Joe Krajcik (CoPI); CAST: David Rose (PI) & Boris Goldowsky (CoPI); EDC: Jackie Miller (PI) & June Foster (CoPI).

Thornton, R. K., & Sokoloff, D. (1990). Learning motion concepts using real-time microcomputer-based laboratory tools. *American Journal of Physics, 58*(9), 858–866.

Van Berkum, J. J. A., & de Jong, T. (1991). Instructional environments for simulations. *Education & Computing, 6*(3/4), 305–358.

Van Joolingen, W. R., & de Jong, T. (2003). SimQuest, authoring educational simulations. In T. Murray, S. Blessing, & S. Ainsworth (Eds.), *Authoring tools for advanced technology learning environments: Toward cost-effective adaptive, interactive, and intelligent educational software* (pp. 1–31). Dordrecht, the Netherlands: Kluwer.

Vygotsky, L. S. (1978). *Mind in society: The development of the higher psychological processes* (A. Kozulin, Trans.). Cambridge, MA: Harvard University Press.

Wilensky, U. (1999). *NetLogo.* http://ccl.northwestern.edu/netlogo/. Evanston, IL: Center for Connected Learning and Computer-Based Modeling, Northwestern Institute on Complex Systems, Northwestern University.

Williams, M. (2008). Moving technology to the center of instruction: How one experienced teacher incorporates a Web-based environment over time. *Journal of Science Education and Technology, 17*, 316–333.

Williams, M., & Linn, M. C. (2002). WISE inquiry in fifth grade biology. *Research in Science Education, 32*(4), 415–436.

Williams, M., Montgomery, B. L., & Manokore, V. (2012). From phenotype to genotype: Exploring middle school students' understanding of genetic inheritance in a web-based environment. *The American Biology Teacher, 74*(1), 35–40.

Wilson, M. R., & Berenthal, M. W. (2006). *Systems for state science assessment.* Washington, DC: National Academies Press.

Windschitl, M., & Andre, T. (1998). Using computer simulations to enhance conceptual change: The roles of constructivist instruction and student epistemological beliefs. *Journal of Research in Science Teaching, 35*(2), 145–160.

Wood, D., Bruner, J., & Ross, G. (1976). The role of tutoring in problem-solving. *Journal of Child Psychology and Psychiatry, 17*(2), 89–100.

Xie, Q., & Tinker, R. (2006). Molecular dynamics simulations of chemical reactions for use in education. *Journal of Chemical Education, 83*, 77.

Zhang, B. H. (2012). *Students' computer-based modeling practices and their changes: Classroom-based research with middle school science students.* Saarbrücken, Germany: LAP LAMBERT Academic Publishing.

Zhang, Z. H., & Linn, M. C. (2011). Can generating representations enhance learning with dynamic visualizations? *Journal of Research in Science Teaching, 48*(10), 1177–1198.

19

Elementary Science Teaching

Kathleen J. Roth

This chapter examines research on elementary science teaching in the last decade—from approximately 2000 through 2012.[1] This is an exciting decade to review because of huge strides in research showing what is possible in terms of supporting elementary children's scientific reasoning and understanding. Research shows, for example, that even very young students can reason in scientific ways (beyond simply describing their observations) and develop strong beginning understandings of concepts once considered too abstract for them (Duschl, Schweingruber, & Shouse, 2007).

In tandem with this research on young students' science learning, work in the area of science studies has contributed to the field of science education a more sophisticated, contemporary view of science (Barnes, Bloor, & Henry, 1996; Bricker & Bell, 2008; Simosi, 2003; Sismondo, 2004). This view of science contrasts with the archaic image of "the scientific method" and paints a much richer picture of the range of practices in science, challenging the image of scientific activity as a linear set of steps that leads unproblematically to scientific explanations. In particular, this contemporary view of science introduces aspects of science that are rarely seen embodied in science classrooms: the construction of evidence-based explanations, the centrality of model-based reasoning, discourse that is argumentation focused, and the interconnectedness of science practices and science ideas and concepts.

These bodies of knowledge about student learning and scientific practices are now driving policy initiatives that impact elementary science teaching. A new vision and standards for science education in the United States (National Research Council, 2012; Next Generation Science Standards [NGSS], 2013) reflect this new view of science and raise the expectations for elementary students' science learning. Similar shifts to more investigation-oriented science teaching are also occurring in other countries (Kim, Tan, & Talaue, 2013; Ministry of Education, 1999; National Center for Educational Research and Development, 1997; National Curriculum Board, 2009).

In contrast with this progress in research and policy, studies worldwide document that typical elementary science teaching stands in stark contrast with what we now know from research is possible and from the NGSS image of what's needed. These gaps raise important questions for research on elementary science teaching. This chapter is organized around these issues, addressing the following questions:

I.   What exists? What does typical elementary science teaching look like?
II. What kinds of science teaching and learning are needed?
III. How can research help narrow the gap between what exists and what's needed? How might identifying teaching frameworks and high-leverage teaching strategies contribute to the transformation of elementary science teaching?
IV. What does research show is possible in elementary science teaching?
V.   What are the research gaps and needed directions for research on elementary science teaching?

Boundaries of This Review: What's Included and What's Not Included?

This chapter focuses on science teaching and learning in Grades K–6 that typically includes students from 5 to 11 years of age. In some countries, this level of schooling is called primary school. There are differences across and within countries about the grade levels included in elementary or primary school. For example, in the United States, Grade 6 is sometimes in the elementary school and sometimes in middle school (Grades 6 through 8), while in some German federal states, primary school includes Grades 1 through 4 (ages 6 to 9), with Grades 5 through 9 considered lower secondary (*Sekundarstufe I*; Cortina, 2008).

Although reformers in science education call for adding technology, engineering, and mathematics to the science curriculum (STEM; National Research Council, 2012), this chapter focuses primarily on *science* teaching. A few studies in which technology or mathematics is used to support science teaching are included, but engineering is left out because of the scant research on engineering teaching at the elementary level and because research on engineering education is addressed in Chapter 36.

There is a large body of research on elementary science teaching over the past decade, and I had to be selective. To avoid overlap with other chapters in this volume, I looked only at research that included explicit attention to classroom teaching at the elementary level. For space reasons, I reluctantly removed a section about elementary science curriculum materials.[2] The key question for each candidate research report was: Does this study provide any evidence about elementary school science teaching practice and its impact on student learning? I reviewed only research reports and focused mainly on research reported in peer-reviewed journals. I looked at a variety of U.S. and international research journals, but a more thorough review was done of the U.S.–based journals, *Journal of Research in Science Teaching* and *Science Education*. Even in these journals, however, it was impossible to review every study written about elementary science teaching during this time period. In selecting studies to highlight with a fuller description in the chapter, I focused on studies that were part of a larger, longer-term program of research.

I read many excellent studies that do not appear in this chapter. For length and coherence considerations, difficult choices had to be made.

Part I. What Exists? What Does Typical Elementary Science Teaching Look Like at the Beginning of the 21st Century?

Some of most widely reported findings about elementary science teaching are about elementary science teachers rather than about the teaching. Researchers consistently find that elementary teachers lack the science content knowledge needed to teach science effectively, have little training in science-specific pedagogy (pedagogical content knowledge), and have even less training in the scientific disciplines they are expected to teach (Appleton, 2003; Dorph, Shields, Tiffany-Morales, Hartry, & McCaffrey, 2011; Fulp, 2002; Goodrum, Hackling, & Rennie, 2001; Harlen, 1997; Kidman, 2012; Smith & Neale, 1989, 1991; Smith, 1999; Stoddart, Connell, Stofflett, & Peck, 1993). There are also gaps in elementary teachers' knowledge about how to adapt science instruction to the diverse needs of students, especially English language learners (ELLs) and students from racial/ethnic groups that are underrepresented in science (Lee, Luykx, Buxton, & Shaver, 2007).

Perhaps related to teachers' weak science backgrounds, science receives much less instructional time in elementary schools compared with English language arts (ELA) and mathematics (Banilower et al., 2013). While teachers' lack of confidence to teach science may play a role in

marginalizing science in the elementary curriculum, the increasing emphasis on high-stakes testing in English language arts and mathematics clearly contributes to reducing time for science instruction in U.S. schools (Banilower, Heck, & Weiss, 2007; Carlone, Haun-Frank, & Webb, 2011; Weiss, Pasley, Smith, Banilower, & Heck, 2003). High-stakes testing plays out differently in other countries but similarly pushes teachers to cover science content rather than to provide the kinds of high-quality science teaching that research shows will support student understanding (Abd-El-Khalick et al., 2004).

When science is taught in elementary schools, it is often of low quality. The *Looking Inside the Classroom* study (Weiss et al., 2003) observed a U.S. sample of 180 K–12 science classrooms, including 55 K–5 classrooms, using a framework of teaching for understanding to judge quality (Banilower, Smith, Pasley, & Weiss, 2006; Weiss et al., 2003). At the elementary level, 58% of the lessons were rated low in quality, while only 18% were rated high. In general, lessons receiving the lowest ratings were categorized as focusing either on passive learning approaches or on activity for activity's sake. Factors that contributed to low-quality ratings included:

(1) Inadequate time and structure for sense making
(2) Inadequate time and structure for wrap-up
(3) Instruction not adapted according to students' level of understanding
(4) Teachers' questioning does not support student understanding
(5) Students' lack of intellectual engagement with important science ideas
(6) Science not portrayed as a dynamic body of knowledge

Of particular significance in light of the focus on science practices and the integration of science ideas and science practices in the Next Generation Science Standards (2013) is the finding that only 13% of elementary science lessons received high ratings in providing opportunities for students to engage in the use of scientific practices such as explanation and argumentation. In addition, Weiss and colleagues (2003) described the overarching downfall of low-quality lessons as students' lack of engagement with important science content. Elementary students often experienced lessons that did not highlight important science ideas or lessons in which they engaged in activity for activity's sake, with little or no connection to science ideas.

The problematic features of elementary science teaching identified in the *Looking Inside the Classroom* study have been supported in other research studies and in other countries (Osborne & Dillon, 2008). Some of these connections to other studies include the following:

(1) Teacher questioning and classroom discourse is right-answer focused and teacher dominated (Newton, Driver, & Osborne, 1999; Reinsvold & Cochran, 2012; Roth et al., 2006).

(2) Students lack opportunities to engage with important science ideas (Abrahams & Reiss, 2012; Mercer, Wegerif, & Dawes, 1999; Roth et al., 2006; Roth & Garnier, 2007).

(3) Many elementary teachers prioritize helping students like science rather than developing conceptual understandings (Furtak & Alonzo, 2010; Howes, Lim, & Campos, 2009).

(4) Even in classrooms where teachers are using hands-on science and inquiry-oriented curriculum materials, complex scientific thinking is seldom observed (Aschbacher & Roth, 2002), and student learning is not demonstrably better than in traditional textbook-oriented classrooms (Pine et al., 2006).

(5) There are inequities in elementary science teaching, resulting in achievement gaps among racial, ethnic, gender, and socioeconomic groups and across urban, suburban, and rural settings (Harris & Williams, 2012; Tao, Oliver, & Venville, 2013; U.S. Department of Education, 2011).

Although there are pockets of excellent elementary science teaching, the larger picture is grim. Little time is spent on science in elementary schools, and when science is taught, it does not reflect what we know from research about effective science teaching. Teachers engage students in hands-on science activities without linking those effectively to science ideas and practices. At best, we can hope that elementary teachers' desire to make science interesting for students will engage and maintain student interest and identity in science. But this is not enough to meet society's needs for science literacy.

Part II. What Kinds of Science Learning Are Needed?

What Is Possible for Young Science Learners?

The current status of elementary science teaching is not encouraging. But evidence suggests that improvements are possible. The 2007 report *Taking Science to School* (*TSTS*; Duschl et al., 2007) presents results from an in-depth review of research about young children's science learning and the implications for K–8 science education. This groundbreaking synthesis of research on learning concluded that young children bring to the science classroom rich although sometimes implicit knowledge about the natural world and how it works, and they are capable of much more sophisticated science thinking than previously assumed. "Contrary to conceptions of development held 30 or 40 years ago, young children can think both concretely and abstractly" (Duschl et al., 2007, pp. 2–3).

The *TSTS* report (Duschl et al., 2007) emphasizes the importance of both experience and instruction in enabling elementary school children to think and reason in scientific ways previously thought unattainable. Students will not naturally develop the understandings of science core ideas and crosscutting concepts or the ability to think

and reason using scientific practices and ways of knowing (Kuhn & Franklin, 2006; Roth, 2002). Instructional experiences are critical to building on what children bring to the science classroom and supporting them in their growth.

The authors of the *TSTS* report (Duschl et al., 2007) identified the following studies as providing evidence that carefully designed science instruction can support elementary[3] (K–6) students in:

- Using science practices to develop conceptual understandings (Beeth & Hewson, 1999; Hennessey, 2003; Herrenkohl & Guerra, 1998; Lehrer, Schauble, Strom, & Pligge, 2001; Raghavan, Saroris, & Glaser, 1998; Roth, 1984; Roth, Peasley, & Hazelwood, 1992; White, 1993)
- Engaging in scientific argumentation (Cornelius & Herrenkohl, 2004; Herrenkohl & Guerra, 1998; Warren et al., 2001)
- Representing data and formulating models to explain phenomena (Lehrer & Schauble, 2000, 2004)
- Generating questions and designing and conducting productive investigations (Metz, 2004; Smith, Maclin, Houghton, & Hennessey, 2000)
- Understanding the constructive, knowledge-focused nature of scientific work (Smith et al., 2000)

The report highlighted that explicit instruction is especially critical for those students who bring cultural knowledge and worldviews that contrast with scientific ways of thinking and knowing (Delpit, 1988, 2006; Duschl et al., 2007; Grimberg & Gummer, 2013; Lee, 2003, 2005). Understanding the differences between everyday thinking and scientific thinking is difficult for all students, but "it may be particularly difficult for students who have had less experience with the forms of reasoning and talk that are privileged in American middle class schools" (Duschl et al., 2007, p. 190).

Thus it is not enough to engage students in doing science activities that ask them to predict, observe, and explain. Students need to be taught not just about scientific concepts but also how scientific ways of thinking are different from everyday thinking and why they are important.

The authors of the *TSTS* report offered six broad conclusions about effective K–8 science teaching. The first two conclusions were about the science curriculum itself, calling for more coherence and depth and for a new research emphasis that identifies the progressions of learning and instruction that can support students' understanding of a few central, core science ideas. Regarding science teaching, the *TSTS* authors presented four conclusions for supporting the ambitious kinds of learning that research shows are possible for elementary students (Duschl et al., 2007):

- *Engage students in scientific practices and discourse.* Students should be supported in interacting with each other in carrying out scientific tasks using the discourse, representations, and tools of science.

- *Move beyond the scientific method.* Science should be presented as a process of building theories and models, checking them for internal consistency, and testing them empirically. There is a broad range of methods in science.
- *Use a range of instructional approaches.* The artificial dichotomy that pits teacher-directed instruction against discovery learning is not productive. A range of instructional approaches is necessary.
- *Formative assessment is an essential part of instruction.* Ongoing assessment is an integral part of instruction that can foster student learning when appropriately designed and regularly used.

The classroom teaching studies highlighted in the *TSTS* report were primarily small-scale, long-term interventions that demonstrated profound learning effects resulting from well-designed, high-quality science instruction. These studies showed that even very young elementary students can develop more sophisticated forms of scientific reasoning and conceptual understandings than was previously assumed. But few of these studies included controlled, quasi-experimental designs, and none were conducted at scale. The review in this chapter will build on the *TSTS* base by describing findings from a growing number of studies, many of which were completed after publication of the *TSTS* report. This research includes design-based studies, case studies, quasi-experimental studies, and a few scale-up, randomized controlled experiments.

What Is Needed to Help All Elementary Students Develop Rich Understandings of Science?

The *TSTS* report, taken in tandem with science studies that challenge the traditional "scientific method" model of doing science, played an important role in shaping the latest national science education reform effort in the United States—the *Framework for K–12 Science Education* (National Research Council, 2012) and the Next Generation Science Standards (2013). These documents provide a new vision for science education that is based on what is needed to prepare students to be scientifically literate citizens in the 21st century. Highlighted next are two components of the new vision that raise the bar for elementary science teaching:

Coherence

The new vision challenges the disconnected teaching of science topics, facts, and activities that characterizes much of elementary science teaching today. Elementary students typically experience distinct units, chapters, or "kits" that give teachers the flexibility of using them in any sequence both within and across grades. This has many practical advantages, but research shows that such an approach enables students to develop only fragmented bits of knowledge and little sense of what it means to really understand the big ideas of science. In this isolated-topics approach, students miss the opportunity to see science as making connections among ideas that build over time into increasingly satisfying understandings.

The *Framework* (National Research Council, 2012) describes three aspects of coherence: First, science teaching needs to help students develop their understandings over time so that they are able to build on and revise their knowledge and abilities. Well-designed learning progressions can map how students' understandings and abilities can develop across as well as within grade levels and can guide the development of instructional supports needed to enable such progress.

Second, there should be a focus on a limited number of core ideas that are connected to a limited number of crosscutting concepts. Reducing the number of details to be mastered makes room for more time to engage in scientific investigations and argumentation to build deeper, more connected understandings. Developing such understandings does not happen nearly as quickly as teachers typically presume. Students need time and compelling evidence to change their personally constructed theories, and they need time to wrestle with new ideas and to try using them in a variety of contexts before they truly make sense and become part of their way of understanding phenomena (Duschl et al., 2007; Roth, 2002).

The third aspect about coherence highlighted in the *Framework* is that "knowledge and practice must be intertwined in designing learning experiences in K–12 science education" (National Research Council, 2012, p. 11). Students should not be learning about science practices in the absence of learning about important science ideas, and students should not be learning science content ideas in the absence of using science practices.

Science Practices

Instead of presenting science as "inquiry" or as "the scientific method," the *Framework* (National Research Council, 2012) defines science in terms of eight practices that guide scientific reasoning and sense making:

1. Asking questions
2. Developing and using models
3. Planning and carrying out investigations
4. Analyzing and interpreting data
5. Using mathematics and computational thinking
6. Constructing explanations
7. Engaging in argument from evidence
8. Obtaining, evaluating, and communicating information

The focus on these eight science practices raises the bar for elementary science teaching by directly challenging the assumption that younger students should engage primarily in the practice of making observations and describing things. To develop deep conceptual understandings, elementary students at each grade level should be taught how to engage in arguing from evidence, developing and using models, planning investigations, and constructing evidence-based explanations.

Part III. How Can Research Help Narrow the Gap Between What Exists and What's Needed? Identifying Teaching Frameworks and High-Leverage Teaching Strategies to Transform Elementary Science Teaching

Research shows that it is possible to teach science and other subject matters in more ambitious ways than what exists (Donovan & Bransford, 2005; Duschl et al., 2007; Lampert, Boerst, & Graziani, 2011; Lampert & Graziani, 2009; Thompson, Windschitl, & Braaten, 2013). The *Framework for K–12 Science Education* (National Research Council, 2012) and other science education reform documents make the case that such a vision of science teaching is not only possible; it is needed in order to prepare students for the kinds of decision making and citizen responsibilities essential in an increasingly technological and scientific world. But transforming elementary science teaching from its current status to the more ambitious forms of teaching needed to achieve the goals laid out in the NGSS (and other reform documents) will require drastic changes. How can elementary teachers be supported in teaching science more ambitiously? Can research help narrow the gap between what exists and what's needed?

Identifying High-Leverage Teaching Practices and Frameworks

This chapter takes the stance that the identification of a small set of research-supported, high-leverage science teaching practices could play an important role in closing the gap between what exists and what is needed. Instead of picking and choosing from a huge array of teaching strategies, teachers would focus on learning to implement effectively a few core strategies and to become increasingly sophisticated in their use of these strategies over time.

Researchers across subject matters make a compelling case for identifying such high-leverage teaching practices (Ball, Sleep, Boerst, & Bass, 2009; Franke, Grossman, Hatch, Richert, & Schultz, 2006; Grossman et al., 2009; Grossman, Hammerness, & McDonald, 2009; Kazemi, Lampert, & Ghousseini, 2007; Sleep, Boerst, & Ball, 2007; Thompson et al., 2013; Windschitl, Thompson, Braaten, & Stroupe, 2012; Windschitl & Calabrese Barton, in press). High-leverage teaching practices are defined as:

> teaching practices in which the proficient enactment by a teacher is likely to lead to comparatively large advances in student learning. High leverage practices are those that, when done well, give teachers a lot of capability in their work.
>
> (Ball et al., 2009, pp. 460–461)

Taking this idea of high-leverage practices a step further, organizing these core science teaching strategies within a conceptual framework, model, or theory of science teaching would support teachers in using the high-leverage practices most effectively both in their planning and in the moment of teaching. To be useful in this way, the guiding framework would need to be theoretically sound, research based, and still compact enough to guide teacher thinking while planning, teaching, assessing, and reflecting. A guiding framework could become more nuanced and complete over time as teachers used it in their practice and in their various professional activities and as research continued to refine and deepen our understandings of particular teaching practices. Instead of creating across a career a longer and longer shopping list of alternative teaching strategies from which to choose, the teacher's guiding framework could be used to make reasoned decisions about which of the latest "fads" or research findings might contribute in important ways to the framework. Through this process, the framework and high-leverage teaching strategies could be elaborated and revised in a reasoned, systematic way.

Linking This Review to the Search for Frameworks and High-Leverage Science Teaching Strategies

How can this review of research inform the development of such teaching frameworks and identification of high-leverage science teaching practices? We do not yet have a research base that is focused enough on the effectiveness of specific teaching frameworks and strategies to nominate a set of high-leverage elementary science teaching strategies. Further research and research syntheses are needed, as is collaboration across research projects in science education. Therefore, this review will *not* nominate high-leverage teaching frameworks and strategies.

Instead, representative studies are described in enough detail to bring to the foreground instructional frameworks and specific teaching strategies that are part of programs/interventions shown to have a positive impact on student learning. By bringing these science teaching frameworks and practices to the fore, I provide readers with a menu of potential candidates for high-leverage teaching frameworks and teaching practices. Thus, this review will contribute to the process of identifying high-leverage practices by cataloguing those practices and teaching frameworks that have been shown to support student learning. In Part V of this chapter, I suggest how we as a research community might build on this catalogue in future research.

Part IV. What's Possible in Elementary Science Teaching?

What has research over the past decade shown is possible in elementary science teaching? What teaching frameworks and teaching strategies show promise for helping students develop deep understandings of and abilities in science? This section is the heart of the chapter, in which I present findings from a range of studies about elementary science teaching. I organize the findings into seven categories that reflect the most commonly researched aspects of elementary science teaching over the past decade. These categories highlight a point I will come back to in Part V: Few studies that I encountered focused directly and primarily on studying specific elementary science teaching practices or strategies. Instead, I found descriptions of elementary science teaching embedded within studies that focused more centrally on other important issues, such as identifying learning progressions, studying scientific discourse and argumentation in classrooms, examining elementary students' scientific reasoning and use of science practices, integrating students' language and literacy development into science instruction, identifying ways of supporting students from groups that are underrepresented in science, studying programs designed to support teacher learning, and examining the role of formative assessment in improving science teaching. These contexts became the seven categories I used to organize this section. In each of these categories, representative studies are described with a focus on the particular frameworks and teaching strategies that had a positive impact on student learning. Other studies addressing similar issues are referenced.

1. Elementary Science Teaching That Supports Students' Learning Through Learning Progressions

The past decade has seen an active line of research that is mapping K–12 student learning progressions based on empirical data. An important part of this work involves instructional interventions to examine what is possible for learners when they are given appropriate supports. At the elementary level, this exploration of science teaching includes work on learning progressions in the following areas:

- Ecology and biodiversity (Songer & Gotwals, 2012; Songer, Kelcey, & Gotwals, 2009)
- Scientific modeling (Baek, Schwarz, Chen, Hokayem, & Zhan, 2011; Bamberger & Davis, 2013; Hokayem & Schwarz, 2013; Schwarz et al., 2009; Schwarz et al., 2012)
- Carbon cycling in socio-ecological systems (Mohan, Chen, & Anderson, 2009)
- Environmental literacy (Gunckel, Mohan, Covitt, & Anderson, 2012)
- Modern genetics (Duncan, Rogat, & Yarden, 2009)
- Evolution (Catley, Lehrer, & Reiser, 2005)
- Nature of matter (Liu & Lesniak, 2006; Smith, Wiser, Anderson, & Krajcik, 2006; Smith, Wiser, & Carraher, 2010; Stevens, Delgado, & Krajcik, 2009)
- Energy (Neumann, Viering, Boone, & Fischer, 2013)
- Celestial motion (Plummer, 2009; Plummer & Krajcik, 2010)
- Buoyancy (Kennedy & Wilson, 2007)

I elaborate in this category studies related to the development of a learning progression for model-based reasoning because this program of research includes details about the teaching framework that was used to guide classroom teaching. Findings about student learning are presented first, followed by a description of the teaching framework used to achieve these outcomes.

A series of studies examined changes (before, during, and after instruction) in fifth- and sixth-grade students' abilities to use models, their metaknowledge about the use of models in science, and their understanding of concepts they are investigating through the use of models (Baek et al., 2011; Bamberger & Davis, 2013; Hokayem & Schwarz, 2013; Schwarz et al., 2009). Results show that instructional interventions helped fifth- and sixth-grade students become more sophisticated in their use of models and deepened their understandings of the concepts that they are modeling. In one study, fifth-grade students shifted from models that simply showed their observations of evaporation and condensation to more sophisticated models that explained how the phenomena occur (Schwarz et al., 2009). Students' models showed increasing attention over time to nonobservable processes, mechanisms, or components such as unseen water particles. Some students moved to the third level of modeling sophistication, explicitly drawing on prior models to extrapolate to new phenomena. Bamberger and Davis (2013) showed that sixth-grade students are able to transfer their scientific modeling practices to a new content area.

What do we learn from these studies about the science teaching frameworks or strategies that supported students' growth in model-based reasoning? While these studies focused primarily on assessing student thinking and learning, careful thought went into the development of an instructional sequence, or framework, that supported student learning about models. As summarized in Table 19.1, the instructional sequence began with an anchoring phenomenon and a key question(s) about the phenomenon. The selected phenomenon was either easily found in students' everyday lives or potentially intriguing to them. The key question(s) elicited a variety of student ideas or hypotheses about challenges that can be investigated. After a series of activities that engaged students in constructing, revising, and evaluating their models and then building a class consensus model, this consensus model was then used to predict or explain related phenomena and to assess the model's strengths and limitations.

These learning-progressions studies do not describe how teachers implemented this instructional sequence or how teachers' use of particular teaching strategies impacted student learning, but the student learning outcomes suggest that the model-based reasoning instructional model is a good candidate as a framework to guide elementary science teaching. Further research is needed to understand the usefulness of this framework for teachers and to identify "high-leverage" strategies to guide model-based reasoning.

2. Elementary Science Teaching That Supports Students' Scientific Discourse and Argumentation

The past decade has seen a great deal of research that examines classroom science discourse. Consistent across these studies is a commitment among researchers to move from the desultory pattern of classroom talk that dominates science classrooms today, with its initiation-response-evaluation

TABLE 19.1
A Model-Based Reasoning Instructional Framework

Sequence	Modeling Practices	Description
Anchoring phenomena		Introduce central questions and phenomena.
Initial models constructed	Model construction	Students create an initial model.
		Discuss purpose and nature of models.
Initial models tested/evaluated	Model evaluation	Investigate phenomena predicted/explained by the model.
Scientific ideas introduced		Science ideas related to the phenomena are introduced.
Initial models evaluated/revised	Model evaluation	Students evaluate and revise their models based on evidence and
	Model revision	introduced science ideas.
Peer evaluation conducted	Model evaluation	Students share models and give evaluative feedback.
Consensus model constructed	Model construction	Students compare models and construct consensus model.
Consensus model used to predict or explain new phenomena.	Model use	Students use the consensus model to predict or explain other related phenomena.

This table was created by drawing from multiple sources (Table 2 in Schwarz et al., 2009; Table 9.1 in Baek et al., 2011; and Appendix I in Hokayem & Schwarz, 2013) and edited to make the model more generic and compact.

TABLE 19.2
Summary of Key Features of Talk Moves in Accountable Talk

Talk Move	Description	Examples
Helping Individual Students Clarify and Share Their Own Thoughts		
Say more	Ask individual student to elaborate	Can you expand on that?
Revoice	Ask student to verify the teacher's interpretation	So let me see if I've got it right. You're saying ——?
Helping Students Orient to the Thinking of Other Students		
Restate	Ask students to restate someone else's reasoning	Can you repeat what he just said in your own words?
Helping Students Deepen Their Reasoning		
Press for reasoning	Ask students to explain their reasoning	Why do you think that?
Helping Students Engage With Others' Reasoning		
Agree or disagree	Ask students to compare their own reasoning to someone else's	Do you agree or disagree and why?
Add on	Ask students to add their own ideas	Can someone add more to this?
Use wait time	Give students time to think and answer	Take your time . . . we'll wait.

Drawn and adapted from Michaels, Shouse, & Schweingruber, 2008, p. 91, and from Chapin, O'Connor, & Anderson, 2009, pp. 12–18.

drone, toward a classroom discourse in which students' voices, ideas, and reasoning play a prominent role (Loucas, Zacharia, & Constantinou, 2011; Radinsky, Oliva, & Alamar, 2010; Roth, 2002; Shepardsom & Britsch, 2006).

But beyond this consensus about the importance of creating more student-centered classroom talk, research on science classroom discourse includes differing theoretical perspectives, differing ideas about how instruction should be organized to support more student talk, and differing purposes for engaging students in "talking science." With regard to instructional approaches, the studies fall along a continuum from those that support the explicit teaching and structuring of student talk to those that support more of an immersion approach that engages students in learning the language of science by using it in authentic inquiries, much as foreign languages are learned by being immersed in a new language culture (Cavagnetto, 2008). With regard to purposes of student-centered talk, some studies focus specifically on scientific argumentation talk, while others explore multiple purposes of classroom talk.

To represent this range of studies, this section first presents studies that focused on classroom talk in general ways and then moves to studies focused specifically on argumentation discourse. Across all studies, I highlight what is learned about instructional frameworks and teaching strategies that support student learning.

Multiple Purposes of Classroom Talk and Multiple Ways of Teaching Talk Moves in Science Classrooms

Some researchers identify multiple ways in which science classroom talk supports students' science learning. Michaels and colleagues (Chapin, O'Connor, & Anderson, 2009; Michaels, O'Connor, & Resnick, 2008; Michaels, O'Connor, Hall, with Resnick, 2002; Michaels, Shouse, & Schweingruber, 2008; Michaels, Sohmer, & O'Connor, 2004) assert that classroom talk challenges students to think about and articulate their ideas and prompts students to reflect on what they do and do not understand and that these purposes cut across subject matter areas. They developed the notion of Accountable Talk® to support all students in participating in academically productive talk in all subject areas. The Accountable Talk® teaching practices have been shown to result in rigorous academic learning for diverse populations of students across a wide range of classrooms, subject areas, and grade levels. In science, Michaels and colleagues emphasize the importance of talking explicitly with students about science-specific and common meanings of words and of engaging students in scientific argumentation. Their "talk moves" are summarized in Table 19.2.

Mercer, Dawes, Wegerif, and Sams (2004) designed and tested the Thinking Together program to help children in British primary schools understand the importance of using talk to think together and to develop their abilities to use language as a tool for thinking. Children would then apply these language tools in studying science. The focus was on Exploratory Talk, in which (Mercer et al., 2004, p. 362):

- All relevant information is shared
- All members of the group are invited to participate
- Opinions and ideas are respected and considered
- Everyone is asked to make their reasons clear
- Challenges and alternatives are made explicit and are negotiated
- The group seeks to reach agreement before making a decision or acting

In this study, 109 Year 5 students (ages 9–10) experienced the Thinking Together program, starting with five lessons focused on the teaching of generic talk skills such as critical questioning, sharing information, and negotiating a decision. The remaining seven lessons encouraged students to apply these skills to their study of the science curriculum. Children who were supported in using talk strategies were more successful on reasoning tasks than a matched, control group of children who studied the same science curriculum without the talk instruction. The authors conclude that the explicit focus on talk and meaning negotiation improved students' reasoning and scientific understanding. Similar to Michaels and colleagues, this approach emphasized generic talk strategies that can apply across subject matters.

The authors counter the critique that providing students with rules for talk constrains their thinking. Instead, the authors argue that when children agree on ground rules and then implement them, this represents a kind of freedom. In particular, the social status of individuals can be neutralized by the "rules," creating a more equitable learning environment. The authors conclude that explicit introduction to the use of language for collective reasoning supports better individual and collective reasoning.

Roth (2002) analyzed teacher and student talk in a fifth-grade classroom in a working-class, low-performing school in which the teacher-researcher (Roth) used a conceptual change model of instruction and examined what is possible when students are supported in making sense of phenomena and making connections among concepts across a school year. Examination of each student's learning across the year revealed a high level of conceptual connectedness in student thinking. For example, at the end of the school year and again a year later at the end of sixth grade, 80% of students were able to apply their knowledge of plants and photosynthesis (a fall unit) to explain a variety of novel, real-world situations. In interviews at the end of the year, the students constructed and explained coherent and reasonable concept maps showing connections between how plants get their food, how humans digest and use their food, and how matter cycles in ecosystems.

In examining the teaching that supported such learning, Roth identified different purposes of teacher talk moves at each instructional phase across a unit of study (Table 19.3).

TABLE 19.3

Purposes of Teacher and Student Talk as Observed in a Sequence of Science Lessons; (Roth, 2002)

Phase of Instruction	Observed Teacher Talk Moves
(each phase can be multiple lessons)	**Bold indicates teacher talk moves that best describe the distinct purpose(s) of each phase of instruction.**
Establish a problem and elicit initial student ideas	• **Elicits multiple student ideas** • Encourages listening to others' viewpoints • Asks for clarification or elaboration • Makes different viewpoints visible
Explore and challenge students' initial ideas: Investigate phenomena to gather evidence to support or challenge initial ideas	• Frames: "What we are trying to find out?" • **Asks for evidence from investigation to support or challenge initial ideas** • Encourages listening to others' ideas • Asks for clarification or elaboration • Makes different viewpoints visible • Encourages questioning and suggestions for gathering additional evidence • Highlights key points made by students that support or challenge initial ideas • Frames/summarizes: "Where we are and where are we going next?"
Compare scientific explanation with initial ideas	• Frames: "Where are we and what are we trying to figure out?" • **Provides scientific explanation** • **Encourages use of evidence to build arguments to support and challenge the scientific explanation and compare to students' own ideas** • Encourages students to question and reason about the scientific explanation • Challenges students to reconcile science ideas with their own ideas • Frames/summarizes: "Where are we and where are we going next?"
Apply new ideas to new situations	• Frames: "Where are we and what are we still confused about?" • **Coaches students' use of new knowledge by:** Focusing attention on scientific explanation, asking for clarification/elaboration, challenging student ideas, highlighting differing viewpoints and evidence to support • Frames/summarizes: "Where are we and what have we learned?"

Roth emphasized that in addition to talk about the science content and their observations, students benefited from explicit talk about (a) the nature of science and scientific talk, (b) students' identities and values, and (c) critiques of science from sociocultural perspectives. To support explicit talk about the nature of science, Roth helped students learn to communicate scientifically using the strategies and sentence starters shown in the BSCS Communicating in Scientific Ways classroom poster (see Table 19.4). Regarding students' identities and values, she provided opportunities to help students connect with science and explore their values. For example, she periodically asked students: "How are you feeling about yourself as a science learner?" She also engaged students in critiques of science from sociocultural perspectives. For example, students considered the case of a Native American scientist who had to dissect plants in her training, although this went against her cultural and religious beliefs: "Do scientists have to give up who they are to become scientists?"

The work of Michaels and colleagues (2002, 2004, 2008, 2012), Mercer and colleagues (2004), and Roth (2002)

addresses multiple purposes of science classroom discourse. We turn next to a focus on one specific type of classroom discourse: scientific argumentation.

Argumentation Discourse in Science Classrooms

The importance of argumentation discourse as central in learning science was highlighted in the *TSTS* research synthesis. Studies of argumentation discourse are grouped in this section in two categories[4] (Cavagnetto, 2010):

(1) Learning a language structure to learn and use scientific argument
(2) Immersion in science to learn and understand scientific argument

INTERVENTIONS THAT TEACH STUDENTS A LANGUAGE
STRUCTURE FOR SCIENTIFIC ARGUMENTATION

The interventions reviewed here approached argumentation by explicitly teaching a structure for engaging students in scientific explanation building. The most frequently used instructional structure for supporting explanation and

TABLE 19.4
BSCS Communicating in Scientific Ways

What a scientist does	Symbol	What a scientist says
1. Ask why and how questions		How come . . .? I wonder. . . . How do they know that . . .?
2. Observe		I noticed. . . . I recorded. . . . I measured. . . .
3. Organize data and observations		I see a pattern. . . . I think we could make a graph. . . . Let's make a chart. . . .
4. Think of an idea, claim, prediction, or model to explain your data and observations		My idea is. . . . I think that. . . . I think it looks like this. . . .(draws a picture)
5. Give evidence for your idea or claim		My evidence is. . . . The reason I think that is. . . .
6. Reason from evidence or models to explain your data and observations		The reason I think my evidence supports my claim is because. . . . The model shows that. . . .
7. Listen to others' ideas and ask clarifying questions		Are you saying that . . .? What do you mean when you say . . .? What is your evidence?
8. Agree or disagree with others' ideas		I agree with ____ because. . . . I disagree with _____ because. . . .
9. Add on to someone else's idea		I want to piggyback on April's idea. I want to add to what Jeremiah said.
10. Search for new ideas from other sources		We could get some new ideas from/by. . . .
11. Consider if new ideas make sense		That idea makes sense to me because. . . . That idea doesn't make sense to me because. . . .
12. Suggest an experiment or activity to get more evidence or to answer a new question		What if we . . .? We could get better evidence if we. . . .
13. Lets ideas change and grow		I think I'm changing my idea. I have something to add to my idea.

Roth, 2002 and revised 2013

TABLE 19.5
Claim, Evidence, Reasoning Framework in the Unit *What Will Survive?*

	Definition	Examples from the unit *What Will Survive?*
Claim	An answer to the question; this is a description of what happened or an identification of the critical causal factor	What happened to a native fish population when the sea lamprey was introduced? The native fish population declined because they were eaten by the sea lamprey.
Evidence	Information or data that support the claim	Evidence could include numerical data (changes in population sizes), observations (sea lamprey have millions of eggs as seen in a dissection), and facts from readings/discussion (sea lamprey eat trout).
Reasoning	A justification that shows why the data count as evidence to support the claim by including relevant background knowledge or scientific theories, or by describing the logical connections between the evidence and the claim	In explaining finch population fluctuations, students might point to data showing that finches died in a particular year and claim that the birds died of starvation, reasoning that a drought led to the death of most of the plants so the birds had no seeds to eat.

Berland & Reiser, 2009, pp. 33–34

argumentation is the claim, evidence, reasoning framework (Berland & Reiser, 2009; McNeill, 2011; Songer & Gotwals, 2012). This framework guided the development and study of the *Investigating and Questioning Our World Through Science and Technology* (IQWST) middle school curriculum. In a study of a sixth-grade IQWST unit, *What Will Survive?* (Bruozas et al., 2004), Berland and Reiser (2009) describe the claim, evidence, reasoning framework in relationship to this unit (see Table 19.5). Students who experienced this framework in the 8-week unit consistently constructed and defended explanations that were accurate and logically bound by the evidence. Students successfully articulated their ideas and providing scientifically plausible and coherent causal chains of thought. Results were not as strong in the persuasion aspect of argumentation, suggesting that instruction might need to create a more authentic need to be persuasive, such as placing students in the role of responding to and critiquing one another's arguments.

McNeill (2011) investigated the use of the claim, evidence, reasoning framework in a study of fifth graders' conceptions of explanation, argument, and evidence as they developed across a school year. The teacher in this diverse, urban classroom strove to make explicit connections between students' everyday lives and science by (a) making the structure of science visible using the claim, evidence, reasoning framework, (b) actively engaging students in academic discourse by creating meaningful roles for students, and (c) engaging students in metalevel analysis to help them compare/contrast everyday knowledge and discourse with scientific knowledge and discourse.

Across a school year, the study focused on seven argumentation-focused lessons related to classroom investigations. The following teacher moves were observed in these lessons:

(1) Discussing the claim, evidence, reasoning framework
(2) Modeling and critiquing examples of arguments
(3) Connecting to everyday arguments
(4) Providing students with feedback on their arguments
(5) Engaging students in peer critique of their arguments
(6) Debating arguments as a whole class

The teacher used all of these strategies but used most consistently Strategy 1 and Strategy 4. With this support, students' writing showed increased focus on argumentation across the school year, with 100% of the students' explanations in Lesson 7 and 88% of the students' writing on the end-of-year assessment being characterized as constructing an argument. At the beginning of the year, in contrast, most students provided information text only (55%), with only 28% developing an argument.

These studies show the impact of explicit teaching about the claim, evidence, reasoning structure on students' explanation construction. The successes of this strategy with diverse students makes it a good candidate as a useful conceptual framework for teachers and as a set of high-leverage teaching practices.

INTERVENTIONS THAT IMMERSE STUDENTS IN SCIENCE
TO LEARN AND UNDERSTAND SCIENTIFIC ARGUMENT

In this section, I highlight two intervention studies that immerse students in argumentation discourse without emphasizing an explicit structure for how to talk and argue in scientific ways.

Rosebery, Ogonowski, DiSchino, and Warren (2010) look at classroom talk from a sociocultural perspective, emphasizing the importance of students' varied life experiences as central to science learning. Instead of viewing students from underrepresented groups through a deficit lens, they argue that the learning of all students is limited when heterogeneity of experience, knowledge, and culture goes unrecognized in classrooms. A key teaching approach that supports this view is called *science talk*. This is not a structure that teaches students how to talk in scientific ways. Instead, it creates space for students to think about, share, and explore ideas without worrying about right or wrong. In this format, students have quite a bit of control over the discussion, determining the range and flow of ideas and exploring their emerging understandings of the question or phenomenon.

In one study of this approach, Rosebery and colleagues (2010) showed how the varied life experiences of the children emerged as central to learning in a third- to fourth-grade urban classroom. During a study of heat transfer and the particulate nature of matter, science talks were embedded in a sequence of 18 lessons, and the study unpacks the various ways in which students' ideas and experiences shaped their thinking and the unfolding instruction.

It is not easy to provide a summary of the instructional framework in this study because the instruction was largely responsive to students' ideas and classroom events. This is not to say that the unit of study was unplanned. The design team selected a clear focus on core ideas about heat transfer and the particulate nature of matter in relationship to evaporation and melting, and progress toward scientific understandings of these ideas guided curriculum decisions. Knowing that this was challenging content that many believe cannot be understood by students this young, the design team planned specific phenomena for students to observe and explain (ice cubes in a baggie, wrapping ice cubes in a winter coat) and strategies for presenting new science ideas (poster with statement of second law of thermodynamics and computer simulations of the behavior of molecules). But as the unit progressed, the teacher took opportunities to build on classroom events and student ideas that emerged in science talks.

A key event illustrates the value of privileging students' experiences as resources for understanding scientific ideas. After being introduced to the second law of thermodynamics, students participated in a science talk addressing the question: "Why do we wear coats in winter?" The children initially had little to say but were interrupted by a fire alarm, resulting in students going outside into the chilly weather without their coats. After this experience, the conversation took off as students now had a way of visualizing "body heat" leaving their warm bodies into the cold December air. The student talk that emerged provided opportunities for the teacher to highlight three conceptual threads: (a) Heat flows from one object to another, (b) heat flows from objects at higher temperatures to objects at lower temperatures, and (c) it is possible to stop or greatly reduce the flow of heat, in this case with a coat. This highlights the central importance in this instructional model of being responsive to student ideas and experiences.

The student learning results in this study are remarkable. Students responded to test items about the particulate nature of matter and heat transfer, some of which were constructed by the design team and some taken from standardized achievement tests, including an eighth-grade item from the Massachusetts Comprehensive Assessment System. Mean percentage correct across the questions for all students was 90%. Ninety-five percent of the students answered the third- to fourth-grade TIMSS item correctly (international average for fourth graders is 47%), and 80% of the students answered the eighth-grade item correctly (MA state average for eighth graders is 67%). These results communicate the power of teaching that makes room for students' heterogeneity of ideas and experiences, and they suggest that this kind of learning can occur without explicit teaching about how to construct scientific explanations. However, this kind of teaching demands much from the teacher, who in this case was supported by a design team of researchers.

In another discourse immersion approach, Varelas and colleagues (2008) studied six teachers of Grades 1 through 3 as they implemented a unit about matter that provided rich opportunities for argumentation. As in the Rosebery and colleagues (2010) study, there was a focus on fostering open-ended conversations that "celebrate explanations and reasoning rather than just 'the correct answer'" (Varelas et al., 2008, p. 70). Children's ideas were privileged, and knowledge was seen as emerging from student–student and student–teacher interactions.

The matter unit had clear learning goals about the states of matter (solid, liquid, gas), changes of state, and the water cycle, and it was organized around seven read-aloud children's information books. In between read-alouds, children engaged in a variety of hands-on explorations. Children also wrote and drew in their science journals throughout the unit. A class mural of their evolving ideas about matter was created, and they kept track of their ideas via an ongoing class semantic map. At the end of the unit they created their own illustrated information book on a topic of their choice. Clearly this is a literacy- and language-rich learning environment. How does argumentation discourse emerge in this context?

Analysis focused on Lesson Seven in which students sorted everyday objects into solids, liquids, and gases and recorded their decisions on a data chart. The ambiguous objects in this activity (shaving cream, bar of soap) evoked conflict and debate among the children, creating a stimulus for reasoning and argumentation as they sorted the objects. The discourse analysis of this lesson paints a rich picture of these young students' theorizing, their ability to attend to ideas from different sources, and their engagement in arguing and debating ideas. In their arguments, they used knowledge from the readings as well as evidence from investigations. Although not all students sorted the objects in scientifically correct ways by the end of the lesson, the authors conclude that these young students were explaining, reasoning, theorizing, and debating ideas.

What does the study tell us about effective elementary teaching frameworks and strategies? The teachers in this study regularly used the following teaching strategies as they responded to student thinking:

- Summarizing what the students were saying
- Repeating or paraphrasing what a child shared
- Encouraging children to think of reasons behind their choices
- Encouraging children to debate and explain to each other
- Manipulating objects in particular ways to open up new ways for students to look at them
- Challenging student ideas

This list of teaching strategies shares some similarities with the talk moves in Accountable Talk® (Table 19.2;

Michaels & O'Connor, 2012; Michaels et al., 2002; Michaels, Shouse, & Schweingruber, 2008) and in the BSCS Communicating in Scientific Ways chart (Table 19.4; Roth, 2002; Roth et al., 2011). A difference is that these teachers were not teaching the children explicitly how to think and talk scientifically. Instead, they allowed students to talk and then guided student thinking with questioning and suggestions. Students were free to think without worrying about being right or wrong and possibly without being constrained by science language rules.

3. Elementary Science Teaching That Supports Scientific Reasoning and Use of Science Practices

The *Framework for K–12 Science Education* (National Research Council, 2012) and the *Next Generation Science Standards* (2013) emphasize the importance of engaging students in using scientific reasoning and practices. What do we know about how elementary science teachers can support students in using scientific reasoning and practices to understand core ideas and crosscutting concepts and to understand the nature of science? This section highlights three different instructional approaches. The first engages students in scientific reasoning by immersing them in authentic scientific activity without focusing explicitly on particular science practices. The next approach teaches explicitly about the nature of science in ways that go beyond specific science practices and considers instead the tentative, subjective, and culturally and socially embedded nature of science. The third approach involves explicit teaching about specific science practices. Examples from this third approach will address six of the eight science practices described in the *Framework* (National Research Council, 2012), and these are presented in the order that they are described in the *Framework* report, with one exception. The practice of using mathematics and computational thinking is presented in partnership with the practice of developing and using models. Few studies examine the use of mathematics in elementary science teaching, but mathematics was central in one line of research about modeling. Two practices are omitted here because they are addressed in other sections of this chapter (see Part IV-2 for studies of the argumentation practice and IV-4 for studies about the practice of obtaining, evaluating, and communicating scientific knowledge).

Elementary Science Teaching as Immersion in Scientific Reasoning

We begin with a line of research that challenges some of the assumptions in the *Framework for K–12 Science Education*. Hammer and colleagues (Hammer, Goldberg, & Fargason, 2012; Hammer, Russ, Mikeska, & Scherr, 2008) take a strongly student-centered view that engages students in authentic scientific reasoning and inquiry. They do not advocate teaching students how to do specific science practices or teaching explicitly about the nature of science. Instead, they take seriously the capabilities that

students bring to the science classroom and argue that we can build on those strengths by engaging and supporting students in the pursuit of true scientific inquiry. There are two fundamental ideas in this responsive view of teaching—the importance of recognizing students' competencies and experience, and the importance of engaging students with authentic scientific inquiry.

This responsive teaching approach stands in contrast with standards-based curricula that are learning-goal driven, starting with a clear definition of specific learning goals and then organizing instruction as a largely planned sequence of experiences that support student understanding of the intended ideas and practices. This planning, Hammer argues, makes it difficult to engage students in science as "real" inquiry, that is, inquiry in which students can pose their own questions, have their own ideas, and pursue investigations to explore those ideas. In authentic inquiry, unanticipated questions and ideas are expected to arise. But if the learning sequence is preset, the teacher loses the option to pursue productive but unanticipated student thinking, and students quickly learn that school science is a game of figuring out what the teacher wants you to say rather than trying to figure out answers to questions about the world.

Hammer and colleagues (2012) use one teacher's explorations of ideas about energy and motion with her third-grade students to illustrate the characteristics of a responsive teaching approach as well as to demonstrate the power of the approach as revealed by students' engagement in a variety of scientifically productive ways of thinking and reasoning. Responsive teaching starts with a productive launching question or task ("What could we do to get this toy car moving?"). The teacher's role is to support student engagement with that question or task, listen carefully to students' thinking, and identify productive directions to support their scientific thinking.

This teaching approach puts a lot of responsibility in the hands of the teacher, and Hammer and colleagues (2010) propose ways to support teachers in teaching responsively. They suggest that curriculum materials can anticipate different possibilities that might emerge in student thinking in response to particular launching questions. This anticipatory work can then be used to construct a menu of possible activities to help teachers choose and plan where to go next based on what they hear from their students.

Elementary Science Teaching to Support Students' Understanding of the Nature of Science

Another body of research considers ways in which elementary science teaching can support students in understanding universal aspects of the scientific endeavor. These include but go beyond the science practices defined in the *Framework* (National Research Council, 2012) and the *Next Generation Science Standards* (2013), teaching students about the nature of science (NOS): (a) Scientific knowledge is both reliable and tentative; (b) no single scientific method exists, but there are shared characteristics of scientific approaches, such as scientific explanations being supported by empirical evidence; (c) creativity plays a role in the development of scientific knowledge; (d) there is a relationship between theories and laws; (e) there is a relationship between observations and inferences; (f) although science strives for objectivity, there is always an element of subjectivity in the development of scientific knowledge; and (g) social and cultural contexts also play a role in the development of scientific knowledge (National Science Teachers Association, 2000).

The literature describes two main approaches to teaching about the nature of science. Explicit approaches teach ideas about the nature of science as learning goals, while implicit approaches assume that engagement in scientific inquiry practices will improve students' NOS understandings. Recent research provides empirical support for an explicit approach that adds reflective components to inquiry-oriented instruction (Akerson & Abd-El-Khalick, 2003; Akerson, Abd-El-Khalick, & Lederman, 2000). Khishfe and Abd-El-Khalick (2002) involved sixth-grade students in reflecting on certain elements of NOS after their participation in inquiry investigations. The researchers found that this explicit reflective approach was more effective than an implicit inquiry-oriented approach in enhancing the students' understandings of the nature of science. Yacoubian and BouJaoude (2010) found similar results in their study of sixth-grade Lebanese students. In a variation on this instructional design, Hardy, Kloetzer, Moeller, and Sodian (2010) compared two fourth-grade classrooms in Germany. One class received an extended unit on the nature of science before studying about floating and sinking, while the other class experienced the same floating and sinking unit without any emphasis on the nature of science. The students who experienced explicit teaching about the NOS demonstrated a higher average level of evidence-based reasoning.

These examples of teaching about the nature of science suggest that explicit NOS reflection connected with inquiry-based activities is more effective than implicit approaches.

Elementary Science Teaching to Support Students in Using Particular Scientific Practices

ASKING QUESTIONS

The *Framework for K–12 Science Education* (National Research Council, 2012) emphasizes the importance of students developing the ability to ask scientific questions. They should understand the nature of questions that science can and cannot answer, the role of questioning in scientific knowledge building, and the importance of asking questions of the texts they read, the phenomena they observe, and the conclusions they draw from model-building work or scientific investigations.

Few studies of elementary science teaching focus solely on scientific questioning, but one study that focused specifically on student development of inquiry questions examined two ways in which teachers negotiated the inquiry question to be investigated in fifth-grade classrooms (Cavagnetto,

Hand, & Norton-Meier, 2010). Students in two classrooms worked in small groups to brainstorm questions about the big ideas they were studying (light and color in one class, aquatic biomes in the other) and then categorized their questions as either *nice to know*, *need to know*, or *essential to the big idea*. The teacher visited each group and pushed students to justify why their questions were necessary to learn about the big idea. In one approach, individual groups then chose a question to investigate and planned and carried out their investigations. In another approach, the class reviewed questions nominated by the groups and selected one question that all groups then investigated.

The results showed no significant differences between these two instructional variations. Instead, the negotiation structure used in both approaches—*nice to know, need to know, essential for understanding the big idea*—productively supported student self-assessment and peer review that led to selection of inquiry questions that were consistent with the main ideas of the units of study. This study contributes an instructional approach that supports students in constructing appropriate scientific questions that contribute to their knowledge growth.

DEVELOPING AND USING MODELS/USING MATHEMATICS AND COMPUTATIONAL THINKING

Model-based reasoning, which involves constructing, revising, applying, and defending models of the natural world, characterizes the core work of science (Lehrer & Schauble, 2012). Classroom science teaching typically represents science as "the scientific method"—a straightforward, linear process of making and testing predictions that results in conclusions that summarize the patterns in the data but fall short of providing explanations (Windschitl, Thompson, & Braaten, 2008). Model-based reasoning, in contrast, involves the continual testing and revising of models by "evaluating hypotheses that make sense within the context of a potentially explanatory model" (Windschitl et al., 2008, p. 948). Models are conceptual tools that help build explanations, and they are theories that are used to "generate plausible hypotheses, new conceptions, new predictions at any point in the inquiry" (Windschitl et al., 2008, p. 948). In contrast to this rich image of scientific modeling, models in school science are typically limited to static artifacts (diagrams, 3-D models, etc.) that are used to present science ideas in interesting ways rather than as tools for thinking.

Some researchers exploring model-based reasoning in elementary classrooms were referenced in Part IV-1 (learning progressions). In this section, I highlight recent work in the productive line of research on modeling conducted by Lehrer and Schauble (2000, 2002, 2004, 2005, 2006, 2012). Their work is also of interest because of the ways they engage young students in using mathematical and computational thinking in their model-building work.

Lehrer and Schauble's work focuses mainly on engaging elementary students in modeling about growth, change, and variability in living systems. Lehrer and Schauble have worked with students across Grades 1 through 5, providing important insights about what both younger and older students are capable of accomplishing when provided appropriate instructional supports. What are the key features of these instructional supports? At a broad level, the instructional approach is student centered, creating the intellectual space, resources, and time for students to generate their own questions and models and to design and pursue investigations to support model-building work. The data-modeling approach allows students to struggle with the challenges and messiness of figuring out the best ways to make sense of phenomena and data. But as with other successful efforts in supporting such student-generated inquiry (e.g., Metz, 2011), thoughtful scaffolding is built into the instructional design and the teaching.

One key aspect of this scaffolding is a sequence of activities that begins with the investigation of real systems and with initial models that are highly analogical with the real-world systems (Lehrer & Schauble, 2004, 2012). For example, students study an untended area of the playground and work simultaneously with models that are very similar to the "real thing" such as a terrarium or compost bin. Over time, the goal shifts toward helping students interact with increasingly symbolic and mathematical models. First graders might engage in the following sequence: (a) draw pictures at different points in a plant's life cycle, (b) create a sequence of photocopied silhouettes of Wisconsin Fast Plants that have been pressed at different stages of growth, (c) organize quantitative measurements of the plant's height arranged to show growth over time, and (d) create graphs of these measurements (Lehrer & Schauble, 2000). The symbolic challenge increases as students work on successive data representations.

Six instructional design principles guide the data-modeling activities (titles italicized below are from Lehrer and Schauble, 2012, pp. 716–720; descriptions are my summaries).

1. *Learning in depth.* Students conduct repeated investigations of a system (e.g., a particular ecosystem) over time. Their growing knowledge of the system enables them to ask increasingly sophisticated questions.
2. *Posing questions.* Students pose questions that can be investigated. Teachers support revisions and orient students toward the most fruitful questions.
3. *Comparative study.* Students compare similar systems, which stimulates new questions and investigations.
4. *Arranging conditions of investigation.* Students design ways to pursue their questions.
5. *Inventing measures.* Students invent ways of measuring.
6. *Inscribing and representing nature.* Students create representations of their systems using reduction (selecting features to highlight) and amplification (showing hidden features).

This instructional approach differs from other examples of responsive teaching highlighted in this chapter (Hammer et al., 2012; Rosebery et al., 2010) in the careful sequencing of increasingly symbolic and mathematical modeling activities, the student invention of measures, the emphasis on comparative study, and the repeated investigation and representation of the same system. As in any form of responsive science teaching, model-based reasoning approaches are challenging to enact. For many elementary teachers, a model-based reasoning approach contradicts their understanding of how science is done.

PLANNING AND CARRYING OUT INVESTIGATIONS

Engaging students in planning and carrying out their own investigations supports their understanding of how scientific inquiry can both describe and explain the natural world. Kathleen Metz (2004, 2011) explores the capabilities of young elementary students in planning and carrying out investigations to explore their own questions. In a study of two first-grade classes taught by Ms. Poirier, she found that by the end of the school year, all but one pair of students were able to describe their own investigations—what they had done and why—and to identify limitations of their investigations. In describing strategies to address those limitations, half of the students went beyond phenomena-based reasoning to relation-based reasoning. In addition, many students went beyond a single cause-and-effect relationship to identify other possible factors and to generate plans to investigate those factors. These students' understandings are surprisingly sophisticated given previous research showing that much older students rely on more modest forms of relationship-based reasoning (Driver, Leach, Millar, & Scott, 1996) and that seventh-grade students have a "try it and see what happens" orientation (Carey, Evans, Honda, Jay, & Unger, 1989).

What do we learn from this study about the instruction that enables such powerful learning? Similar to Lehrer and Schauble's curriculum design work, Metz marries carefully planned curriculum design with a student-centered context in which the teacher is responsive to students' emerging investigation questions and ideas while providing extensive scaffolding across time. The teacher highlighted in the 2011 study used curriculum modules designed by Metz; each module targeted one domain that served as the focus of inquiry for an entire school year (Metz, 2002a, 2002b). In Year 1 the focus was on botany and in Year 2 the focus was on animal behavior. Five design principles guided the development of students' scientific inquiry (italicized titles are from Metz, 2011, pp. 58–62; the descriptions are my summaries):

1. *Reflect the robust goal structure of scientific inquiry, teaching science processes and methods as instruments in the context of their application.* Metz describes the "absurdity" of teaching science process skills or practices in the absence of students' curiosity about a question or problem. She foregrounds questions that motivate inquiry, while science practices are instruments that serve the interest driving the inquiry.
2. *Scaffold relatively rich knowledge of the domain, emphasizing the big ideas that transcend domain.*

Like Lehrer and Schauble, Metz emphasizes the importance of students becoming deeply knowledgeable about the domain under study. This contrasts with the typical practice of moving rather quickly from one science topic to the next.

3. *Use rich domain knowledge to empower inquiry and vice versa.* Consistent with the *Next Generation Science Standards'* call to intertwine content knowledge and science practices, Metz (2011, p. 60) states, "Robust domain knowledge is intimately connected with robust inquiry and vice versa. Indeed, only from the conjunction of the two can one appreciate the status of scientific knowledge and how scientific knowledge advances."

4. *Manipulate cognitive demand by adjusting the social unit responsible for the inquiry and the degree to which inquiry is well structured.* The cognitive load for the individual student is less when the whole class works together under the guidance of the teacher and is the most demanding when students work independently in pairs. Metz advocates a gradual move from well-structured, teacher-guided investigations done by the whole class to ill-structured investigations taken on by the whole class and finally to children's independence in designing and carrying out investigations.

5. *Build knowledge and responsibility to the point at which academically homogeneous dyads assume responsibility for their own investigations.* Metz advocates for homogeneous dyads that allow for collaboration and sharing of the intellectual load while maximizing each child's responsibility and control.

Metz attributes the demonstrated competence of students in Ms. Poirier's classroom to the knowledge and insights that students bring to instruction, the instruction that supported further development of their initial thinking, and a curriculum design "that fostered the students' personal investment in taking their ideas, claims, and methods as critical objects of thought." She highlighted, in particular, the importance of the development of students' domain knowledge (Metz, 2011, p. 106).

In contrast to Metz's overarching design principles, Harris, Phillips, and Penuel (2012) examined specific teacher moves in a context in which fifth graders were generating inquiry questions and designing their own investigations related to defining the optimum habitat for isopods. In the *Isopod Habitat Challenge* unit (12 weeks), students shared their ideas and questions about isopods, then participated in a teacher-guided investigation, and finally carried out student-generated investigations to answer their own questions. The study focused on specific teacher moves: *eliciting*, *revoicing*, *connecting*, and *building upon* students' science ideas and questions.

Three case study teachers all succeeded in eliciting student ideas and questions, following suggestions provided in the curriculum materials. But they differed in their "next-step" moves. The teacher whose students scored lowest on a test of ability to develop investigable questions tended to acknowledge student contributions and move on. In contrast, a more successful teacher made the following kinds of moves (Harris et al., 2012, p. 780):

a. Involved students in clarifying their own thinking and exploring others' perspectives
b. Invited students to help each other think through ideas and questions
c. Encouraged students to ask questions of each other
d. Gave clear feedback when recognizing student thinking
e. Modeled her own thinking about what students were saying

In addition to these strategies, the third teacher, whose students were most successful:

f. Engaged students directly to help refine their ideas and questions
g. Connected their findings and ideas to those of others
h. Actively worked with students to ensure that their questions and procedures were feasible

This study suggests the importance of developing tools and routines to support teachers in responding to student thinking. Harris and colleagues (2012) point to the need for specific discourse moves to support students' design and implementation of investigations.

ANALYZING AND INTERPRETING DATA

Few studies focus specifically on how students analyze and interpret data. One study, however, provides fascinating insights about students' predictions, observations, interpretations, and generalizations about anomalous data. Chinn and Malhotra (2002) studied fourth, fifth, and sixth graders who made predictions, observed phenomena that allowed room for different assessments of what actually happened, and responded to questions about their interpretations and generalizations. For example, students predicted and then observed whether a dropped heavy object or a dropped lighter object of the same size would hit the floor first. Students had difficulty making the correct observations, but the pattern of their mistakes contradicts the commonly held assumption that students will observe what they predict they will observe. While students who made the correct prediction also made the correct observation, students with incorrect predictions were able to make observations that contradicted their prediction. Importantly, students who made the correct observation were also highly likely to interpret their observations correctly, while students who made inaccurate observations did not. The authors conclude that students should be taught explicitly about the following aspects of observation (Chinn & Malhotra, 2002, p. 342):

a. Observations can be biased, and one should use techniques that minimize biases.

b. Even when events are the same, there can be slight differences in measurements.

c. One should expect effects in quantitative proportion to their causes.

CONSTRUCTING EXPLANATIONS

Explanations are central in science. To understand the world, scientists develop explanations about phenomena that are useful in predicting future events and in making sense of past events (National Research Council, 2012). Engaging students in constructing explanations of phenomena helps them understand how scientific knowledge is created while also deepening their understandings of science facts, concepts, and theories (Beyer & Davis, 2008).

Several researchers examining explanation building in elementary classrooms draw from Toulmin's (1958) argumentation framework, focusing in particular on how the structure of claim, evidence, and reasoning can be helpful in teaching students how to construct explanations (Beyer & Davis, 2008; McNeill & Krajcik, 2007, 2008; McNeill, Lizotte, Krajcik, & Marx, 2006; Songer & Gotwals, 2012; Zembal-Saul, 2009). Using this framework, teachers help students understand the importance of supporting claims with evidence, of using data in scientific reasoning, of defending and evaluating claims in light of evidence, and of accounting for disconfirming evidence (Abell, Anderson, & Chezem, 2000; McNeill & Krajcik, 2008). Studies using this framework to support argumentation discourse were described in Part IV-2.

In one study of explanation construction in urban fourth-, fifth-, and sixth-grade classrooms, students experienced a sequence of three 8-week curricular units related to ecology, each of which contained a set of activities that culminated in guided explanation construction using the claim, evidence, reasoning framework (see Table 19.5; Songer & Gotwals, 2012). There were strong content and practice learning results across all three grade levels. Even the younger students were able to make significant progress from pretest to posttest in their ability to fuse content knowledge with explanation construction.

In another study in this line of research, Songer, Shah, and Fick (2013) focused more on the teachers' talk moves related to use of the claim, evidence, reasoning framework. Observations of fourth- and fifth-grade teachers revealed their use of up to five different verbal descriptions of the meaning of evidence, which were revisited multiple times. Researchers concluded that the teacher plays a crucial role in supporting explanation construction by clarifying meanings and repeatedly coming back to key definitions.

ENGAGING IN ARGUMENT FROM EVIDENCE

See Part IV-2.

OBTAINING, EVALUATING, AND COMMUNICATING INFORMATION

The *Framework for K–12 Science Education* (National Research Council, 2012) focuses attention on the importance of helping students learn to read scientific texts and to communicate scientific ideas clearly in a variety of written forms. Studies focusing on the development of these language and literacy capabilities are described in Part IV-4. Studies related to communication through classroom discourse are reviewed in Part IV-2.

Another important issue related to obtaining and evaluating information is the question: When and how should students obtain canonical science ideas? There is wide agreement that a variety of sources and strategies can be used to introduce science ideas, including children's informational books (Varelas & Pappas, 2006) and simulations (Schwarz, 2009). There is also consensus that new science ideas should not be presented as a first step in an instructional model. Most research interventions use instructional models, such as the BSCS 5E Instructional Model (Bybee & Landes, 1988; Bybee et al., 2006) or variants of it that focus first on eliciting students' ideas and then on engaging students in explorations of phenomena to test out their own ideas before any science ideas are presented. Beyond this apparent consensus, there are differing viewpoints about when to "tell." Researchers following a model-based reasoning approach advocate waiting until after students have constructed initial models, gathered empirical evidence, and revised their models based on their investigations (Schwarz, 2009). Students are then ready for new ideas to inform and revise their models. In a responsive teaching model (Hammer et al., 2012), the teacher makes decisions about when to introduce new science ideas, waiting to see how much the students can do on their own before introducing science concepts. In contrast, the literature-rich approach described by Varelas, Pappas, and Rife (2006; see Part IV-4) allows for many science ideas to be made available to students throughout the inquiry process through the use of science information books.

4. Elementary Science Teaching That Supports Students' Language and Literacy Development

Integration of science with language and literacy development is appealing to science educators for two reasons. First, as noted in Part I, science instructional time is scarce (Banilower et al., 2013). Integrating science with literacy instruction is a way to create more time for science by simultaneously addressing literacy and science learning goals. Second, teachers have increasing numbers of English language learners in their classrooms. Integrating science and literacy is a way to help these students be successful in science by supporting their language learning needs.

Integrating Literacy and Science

There is a large research base about ways to integrate reading and writing as a part of scientific inquiry in elementary classrooms (Cervetti et al., 2012; Cervetti & Barber, 2008; Fang & Wei, 2010; Guthrie, Anderson, Alao, & Rinehart, 1999; Guthrie & Cox, 2001; Guthrie et al., 2004; Guthrie, McRae, Coddington, Klauda, Wigfield, & Barbosa, 2009; Guthrie, McRae, & Klauda, 2007; Hand, 2008; Howes et al., 2009; Palincsar & Magnusson, 2001; Pappas, Keifer, & Levstik, 2006; Romance & Vitale, 1992, 2001, 2011, 2012; Varelas & Pappas, 2006; Varelas, Pappas, & Rife, 2006; Varelas et al., 2008; Varelas et al., 2010; Yore, Bisanz, & Hand, 2003). Two approaches to integrating science and literacy are prominent in recent research on elementary science teaching (Stoddart, Pinal, Latzke, & Canaday, 2002[5]): (a) an interdisciplinary approach in which content/processes in one domain are used to support learning in another and (b) an integrated approach in which the two domains are fully intertwined, with an equal emphasis on learning goals in both domains. Work by Varelas and colleagues (2006) represents an interdisciplinary approach, while the Science IDEAS approach (Romance & Vitale, 2011, 2012) is an example of a fully integrated program.[6]

AN INTERDISCIPLINARY APPROACH: LITERATURE-RICH SCIENCE INQUIRY

Varelas and colleagues (2006) studied a second-grade urban classroom in which students experienced language-rich science instruction. Read-aloud texts played a prominent role in science instruction, but the teacher's goal was not to teach students to be better readers. Instead, her goal was to engage students as agents in their own science thinking who can move back and forth among various kinds of "texts." The researchers defined "texts" as including first-hand observations of phenomena, ideas presented in the read-aloud books and other sources, each other's writing/drawing, prior discourse in the classroom, and specific and generalized events that students bring into the conversation.

In a 6-week unit about states of matter and the water cycle, students listened to the teacher read children's information books, engaged in hands-on investigations, wrote in their science journals, participated in small-group literature circles using other information books, and constructed illustrated books as a culminating activity. In this literacy-rich environment, students used various texts to think, reason, talk, and write/draw about evaporation, condensation, and boiling in scientific ways. Although their ideas were not always matched to canonical science ideas, they had multiple, complex, sometimes speculative and tentative ways of making sense of phenomena and were able to theorize about these processes, drawing from multiple "texts."

What was the teacher doing in this kind of dialogic, responsive, and language-rich science teaching? One thing the teacher, Amy, was NOT doing was providing specific frameworks, steps, guidelines, or rules to guide students in their explorations of various "texts." Instead, she "orchestrated collaborative, dialogically-oriented discourse practices so that children had many opportunities to offer their own ideas, comments, and questions, upon which Amy and peers could contingently respond" (Varelas et al., 2006, p. 638). The students engaged in sense making through "inquiry language acts" (Lindfors, 1999).

Closer analysis revealed that the teacher made specific teaching moves that positioned her as a member of the classroom sense-making community (rather than the typical teacher-as-authority) and as a leader of the community who stimulated, encouraged, and guided student thinking:

- She was the most frequent initiator of connections between hands-on explorations and prior discourse.
- She explicitly invited theory building: "Any ideas why this one's foggy and this one isn't?" "How does a cloud get on the can?"
- She made the most frequent references to prior discourse, offering opportunities for children to express their understandings and attempt to make meaning of developing ideas.
- She read the information books to the students.
- She paraphrased students' ideas.
- She made suggestions to help children see phenomena in more scientifically accepted ways.

Amy was not trying to teach reading comprehension in science, although it can be argued that her approaches may have supported that goal. Her focus was on using the information books, writing activities, and classroom talk to support students' reasoning about phenomena.

Compared with other teaching approaches, such as the approach in Science IDEAS described next, Amy's teaching is also less focused on teaching students explicit structures to guide their reasoning and less focused on assuring that every student ends with an accurate canonical understanding of evaporation, boiling, and condensation. Instead, the focus is on providing a rich array of "texts" to stimulate student thinking and on guiding students to make increasingly sophisticated connections among these texts.

FULL INTEGRATION: SCIENCE IDEAS

In contrast to Varelas and colleagues' interdisciplinary approach (2006), the Science IDEAS program represents a full integration of literacy and science teaching. Developed by Romance and Vitale (2011), this approach has six basic elements that focus on the central goals of developing in-depth understandings of core science concepts and improving reading comprehension (http://scienceideas.org/SI_Model/Model_6Basics.html).

(a) Hands-on science activities are connected to the other Science IDEAS elements.
(b) Reading comprehension activities use a knowledge-based reading comprehension strategy that guides student access of prior knowledge when reading and has students summarize what is being read.
(c) Concept-mapping tasks challenge students to show relationships among the concepts.
(d) Students write to develop and organize science concepts learned from lesson activities.
(e) Application activities challenge students to link science concepts to everyday events.

(f) Prior knowledge/cumulative review strategies activate prior knowledge and summarize developing knowledge.

Integrated science/literacy time blocks (1.5–2 hours daily) include the six types of activities listed. These activity sequences give students multiple supports to help them develop a deep understanding about a core science concept or set of related concepts and to improve their reading comprehension. The program identifies specific teaching strategies or procedures for each activity type. For example, to activate prior knowledge, teachers query students about what they know, write correct answers on the white board, and respond orally to incorrect responses. During cumulative reviews, teachers select representative activities to be considered during the review, remind students of these activities, and question students about them.

A 6-year longitudinal evaluation of Science IDEAS was carried out in elementary schools, Grades 3 through 8, in a large urban district in Florida. Twelve schools used Science IDEAS, teaching the curriculum daily for a 90-minute science/reading block. Twelve similar schools used the district reading and science curriculum materials, teaching reading and science separately. Controlling for pretests, analyses showed significantly higher scores for students in the IDEAS group at the end of eighth grade on both the science and reading comprehension assessments.

Which of the array of teaching strategies in Science IDEAS enabled this growth? As with many studies, we can look only at the package of teaching approaches embedded in the program and assume that teachers' use of the entire set of strategies contributed to the learning outcomes. It would be useful to know, however, whether particular strategies—for example, the procedures for activating prior knowledge and guiding cumulative reviews—were more predictive of student learning than others. As another example, did the reading comprehension strategies contribute to both science learning and reading comprehension?

The instructional framework and teaching strategies guiding the Science IDEAS program contrasts with the Varelas and colleagues approach (2006), with the IDEAS program providing specific structures for teaching students explicit strategies to improve their reading comprehension while the Varelas approach (2006) immersed students in a language-rich environment in which they were challenged to explore science inquiry questions. These contrasting cases create a conundrum. The two approaches use different instructional frameworks and teaching strategies, but there is evidence in both cases of powerful student learning outcomes. How does this help us identify high-leverage teaching practices in science? Does this suggest that more research is needed to better compare the two approaches, or does it acknowledge that there can be a variety of effective approaches? In the latter case, this might argue for the development of multiple sets of high-leverage practices guided by different goals and theoretical stances.

Supporting English Language Learners and Students

Looking specifically at programs designed to support English language learners, Lara-Alecio and colleagues (2012) developed and studied an intervention to improve the science and English reading achievement of fifth-grade English language learners in an urban district in Texas. The intervention included a professional development sequence, scripted lesson plans, and strategies for teaching language and reading in science.

In a quasi-experimental study, students in the experimental group outperformed control-group peers receiving the same amount of instructional time on multiple measures. The experimental intervention produced higher academic achievement in both science and reading as reflected in districtwide, standards-based measures, with larger effect sizes in science than in reading. On standardized state tests, a larger percentage of treatment-group students performed above the state passing standards on four out of five science benchmark tests and on three out of four reading benchmark tests. The results show the positive effects of integrating literacy with science instruction for both science and literacy outcomes for English language learners.

What does this study tell us about potential high-leverage teaching strategies for ELLs? As with many intervention studies, we know only that the package of professional development, lesson plans organized on a 5E model, and teaching strategies was effective. In this case, there was a rather lengthy list of teaching strategies made explicit to teachers (see Table 19.6). It is interesting that the most scripted strategies focus on language development. From this list, the authors underscore the importance of implementing direct and explicit vocabulary instruction within content area instruction for ELLs. Additional research is needed to identify if any of these strategies qualify as high-leverage science teaching practices.

Across the past decade, Lee and colleagues have produced a line of research examining ways to support English language learners and their teachers. Because of the focus in this chapter on science teaching practices, the studies of most interest here are those that included analyses of teachers' practice (Lee, Penfield, & Maerten-Rivera, 2009; Santau, Secada, Maerten-Rivera, Cone, & Lee, 2010).

The Lee and colleagues 2009 study was a fidelity-of-implementation study and thus held promise for helping us better understand which aspects of the science teaching predicted student learning. Each of 35 third-grade teachers was videotaped while using project-developed curriculum materials to teach one lesson in the fall (measurement unit) and one lesson in the spring (water cycle). Four aspects of reform-based teaching practice were coded on a five-point scale: (1) teachers' content knowledge accuracy, (2) use of

TABLE 19.6
Teaching strategies to support English Language Learners

Instruction Phase	Strategies	Details of Scripted Strategies
Warm up	Daily Oral and Written Language in Science (DOWLS)	**DOWLS protocol:** Students respond to science-related prompt or scenario in writing and orally
Engage activity	Teacher demonstrates a science concept and connects to previous work.	
Explore activity	Students explore science concepts through hands-on science activities.	
Explain activity	• Direct instruction in vocabulary • Content Area Reading in Science for English Literacy and Language Acquisition (CRISELLA) • Interaction with science software that explains concepts through animation or simulations	**CRISELLA protocol:** • Before reading, direct instruction of vocabulary • Partner reading; scripted comprehension questions • Students reread to increase fluency, comprehension • Teacher reviews, clarifying any misconceptions • Teacher models academic science language • Teacher encourages use of complete sentences • Students enter vocabulary in science journal glossary
Evaluate activity	Written and Academic oral language Vocabulary development in English in Science (WAVES)	**WAVES protocol:** In daily science journals, students: • Record predictions and observations • Illustrate and label diagrams • Organize information using two-dimensional figures • Record vocabulary in glossary section • Develop writing skills; perspective-based writing
Elaborate activity	Students apply knowledge in new activities.	

strategies to help students understand science, (3) use of strategies to engage students in science inquiry, and (4) use of strategies to support English language development. Unfortunately, perhaps due to measurement problems, none of the variables related to teacher reform-based practices predicted student achievement. Thus, a connection between student learning and teaching practices was not established in this study.

Another study by Lee's group (Santau et al., 2010) examined third-, fourth-, and fifth-grade teachers' practice during the fall and the spring in their first year in the professional development program as they implemented project-developed curriculum. Both in the fall (pre) and in the spring (post), teachers' videotaped lessons were scored on a five-point scale for teachers' content knowledge, teachers' practices supporting science understanding, and teachers' practices supporting English language development. On average, teachers' practice was scored a "3"—within "bounds of acceptability" but falling short of reform-oriented practice, with little evidence of change from fall to spring (Santau et al., 2010, p. 2024). The authors noted that teachers appeared to be implementing the curriculum as written without supplementing it with the strategies to scaffold students' reasoning and language development that had been emphasized in the professional development.

As in the Lara-Alecio and colleagues study (2012), this intervention introduced teachers to a rather long list of teaching strategies to support English language learners in learning both science and the English language. In contrast with the strategies detailed by Lara-Alecio and colleagues (2012), Lee and colleagues did not provide specific sequences of teacher moves (such as the DOWLS,

CRISELLA, and WAVES sequences in the Lara-Alecio and colleagues study [2012]; Table 19.6). Instead, they presented in the professional development (PD) a philosophical orientation and rationale for adapting instruction to meet the needs of ELLs, embedded specific strategies in the curriculum materials, and discussed additional strategies to use with ELLs during instruction. No framework was described that might help teachers organize these lists to guide their planning and teaching. In addition, this study did not examine the relationship of the teaching to student learning. Thus, these studies of teachers' practice provide few insights about how we might identify key (high-leverage) strategies for supporting both science learning and English language development. However, evidence from Lee and colleagues' studies that focused on ELL students' learning provide more insights about possible high-leverage teaching strategies (see Part IV-5a).

5. Elementary Science Teaching That Supports Students From Underrepresented Groups

Research over the past decade has explored the slogan "science for all" and its implications for elementary science teaching. Studies in this area examine how science teaching often fails students from cultural, racial, socioeconomic, and language groups that are underrepresented in science (e.g., Carlone et al., 2011; Kurth, Anderson, & Palincsar, 2002). They also explore ways that science teaching can address the needs of all students, with a focus on the needs of students from underrepresented groups who are not achieving in science at the levels of white, middle- and upper-class students and who often dissociate themselves from science. How can we close the achievement gaps between dominant and underrepresented groups (U.S. Department of Education, 2011)? How can all students feel welcome and participate fully in classroom science communities?

Many of the studies in this area delve deeply into the experiences of students in science classrooms, analyzing ways in which both traditional and reform-based inquiry science teaching are unintentionally inequitable (e.g., Carlone et al., 2011; Kurth et al., 2002) as well as ways in which students from nondominant cultures and communities are able to succeed in science and identify with science (e.g., Hudicourt-Barnes, 2003; Radinsky et al., 2010; Rosebery et al., 2010; Tan & Barton, 2008b; Varelas, Kane, & Wylie, 2012). For the purpose of this review, these *learning-focused* studies were examined for insights they might provide about the teaching approaches that support students from underrepresented groups. Of particular interest, however, are *teaching-focused* studies that examine those aspects of teaching that address the needs of all students (e.g., Barton & Tan, 2009; Grimberg & Gummer, 2013; Lee, Buxton, Lewis, & LeRoy, 2006; Reveles, Cordova, & Kelly, 2004; Upadhyay, 2006).

Looking across these learning- and teaching-focused studies, there are differences in theoretical frameworks and learning goals. While all of these frameworks value engaging students in scientific investigations and building on students' home and cultural knowledge and experiences, some put inquiry front and center while others move issues of student agency, funds of knowledge, and identity to the foreground. Those foregrounding inquiry take the stance that improving the quality of inquiry-oriented science teaching will improve the learning of *all* science students. Others assert that good inquiry science teaching is not enough; it needs to be disrupted in important ways. In particular, science instruction needs to take seriously the diverse cultures, languages, and experiences of students and include them as central and fundamental in science teaching; in addition to supporting the learning of science concepts and practices, science teaching needs to promote students' sense of agency and identity in science. The studies also vary in pedagogical orientations from more structured 5E-oriented instructional models in an inquiry-focused approach to more responsive instructional models. The studies described next are organized in four categories to highlight the commonalities and differences in the theoretical frameworks and teaching strategies found to be successful in supporting students from underrepresented groups.

Inquiry Science Teaching for All

In a study of student learning conducted by Lee and colleagues (2006), an inquiry-focused framework and ELL teaching strategies guided the design of a teaching intervention that was implemented in ethnically and racially diverse urban elementary classrooms with large numbers of English language learners. In pre-post interviews, 25 third- and fourth-grade students were asked to design an investigation to solve a problem relating surface area to the rate of evaporation. The interviewed students came from six elementary schools using the inquiry framework curriculum materials; they represented various ability levels, English language competence, and demographic groups. The study found that students from all demographic groups showed substantial pre-post gains in understanding control of variables and in providing evidence to support their claims, with the gains being more pronounced for ELLs, girls, and low-achieving students.

What teaching framework and/or teaching strategies contributed to these learning outcomes? The program's framework had two main conceptual foundations: (a) an inquiry framework with five phases of inquiry (questioning, planning, implementing, concluding, reporting) and (b) a steady transition from highly scaffolded, teacher-explicit inquiry work to more student-initiated inquiry. More scaffolded support at the beginning was deemed important in helping students, especially those from underrepresented groups, to understand the language, practices, and norms of science. In addition to this grounding in inquiry science, the instructional materials and professional development provided strategies and activities to foster the development of English literacy skills by embedding expository writing activities and reading comprehension passages in the curriculum (see Table 19.7). Finally, the instructional approach built on students' prior linguistic and cultural experiences; for example, metric units were used in addition to English units, activities took place in a variety of group formations, student prior knowledge was activated, and the teacher guides included science terms in Spanish and Haitian Creole. In this regard, the curriculum sought to integrate students' home languages and cultures in science instruction. The teaching strategies supported by the curriculum materials and PD are summarized in Table 19.7. We do not have data to assess which of these might be considered as high-leverage practices.

Funds of Knowledge, Hybrid Spaces, Heterogeneity

Research evidence suggests that the learning of all students is limited when students' diverse experiences, knowledge, and cultures go unrecognized in science classrooms. In contrast, researchers assert that science teaching for all students is improved when teachers listen to their students beyond the traditional scope of science instruction and bring students' ways of knowing and experiences into a central role in science teaching. This goes far beyond eliciting students' prior knowledge at the beginning of a lesson or unit or acknowledging students' cultural experiences to make them feel welcome in science. Instead, students' heterogeneity of cultures, experiences, and language is fundamental to the science learning of all students in the classroom (Rosebery et al., 2010).

Barton and Tan (2009) use the language of *funds of knowledge* and *hybrid spaces* to describe the goals of a sixth-grade unit on food and nutrition to support the learning

TABLE 19.7
Key Supports and Strategies to Promote Science and Language Learning for ELLs

Component	Science Supports and Strategies	Language and Literacy Supports and Strategies
Curriculum Materials		
Teacher's guide	• Moves from teacher-explicit to student-initiated science inquiry • Connects use of key science ideas to explain phenomena • Scaffolds students' scientific inquiry and understanding	• Presents vocabulary in English, Spanish, Haitian Creole • Suggests science writing prompts, trade books, literature • Suggests strategies to promote literacy development • Provides graphics
Student booklet	• Key science concepts are emphasized • After each inquiry activity, science background information is provided	• Introduces key vocabulary in the beginning • Provides opportunities to use vocabulary in various settings • Uses graphic materials extensively • Provides science terms in Spanish and Haitian Creole • Highlights strategies to foster general literacy • Includes reading comprehension activity in each lesson • Describes science academic language functions
Professional Development		
Face-to-face PD	• Examine science content, hands-on activities, common student misconceptions, potential learning difficulties in each lesson • Discuss how to move away from teacher-explicit instruction to more student-initiated activity	• Strategies for developing general literacy for all students: Activation of prior knowledge, comprehension of expository science texts, academic language functions, scientific genres of writing, graphic organizers, multiple forms of representation, writing prompts • Strategies to provide language support for ELLs Use realia, use hands-on activities, use multiple modes of representation, introduce key vocabulary at beginning, practice use of vocabulary in variety of contexts, use language in multiple contexts • Strategies to provide linguistic scaffolding for ELLs Recognize levels of proficiency, adjust language load (slow down, enunciate), communicate at or slightly above students' levels of communicative competence

of African-American (45%) and Hispanic (55%) students in a low-income, economically depressed urban school. They emphasize the importance of the diverse funds of knowledge that students bring from membership and experiences in their out-of-school worlds. Funds of knowledge are defined as historically accumulated cultural knowledge, skills, and resources that students bring from their homes (Moll, Amanti, Neff, & Gonzalez, 1992). A central teacher role is to "recruit" (p. 52) these student funds of knowledge and use them in prominent and productive ways in teaching science. Using these student funds of knowledge, the teacher can create a hybrid space in the classroom in which traditionally marginalized knowledge and ways of talking/thinking coalesce with more academic, scientific knowledge and ways of knowing to "destabilize and expand the boundaries of official school Discourse" (Barton & Tan, 2009, p. 52). In this framework, the goal of enriching and empowering youths' lives is privileged; this contrasts with Rosebery and colleagues' (2010) foregrounding of science learning goals.

In the Barton and Tan study (2009), a small group of sixth-grade students participated with the teacher and researchers in planning aspects of the science curriculum. Students were asked about how food and nutrition is meaningful in their lives, about their experiences with food and nutrition, and about what they thought their peers needed to know about this topic. The students proposed instructional activities, three of which were enacted in the curriculum:

comparing fast-food restaurants, participating in a healthiest-snack-for-$2 competition, and making and sharing healthy appetizers. Another teacher-developed activity that proved productive in bringing "home discourses" into the classroom was a homework assignment to interview a family member about a favorite home salad recipe. These activities stand in contrast with the kinds of scientific investigations promoted in the National Research Council's *Framework* (2012). The analysis of the enacted food and nutrition unit, taught by Mr. M., focuses on how students drew from family, community, peer, and popular culture funds of knowledge and how the classroom became a hybrid space in which these funds of knowledge played roles just as important as the scientific knowledge and ways of knowing.

In terms of student learning in Mr. M's classes, the level of student engagement, completion of homework assignments, and grades on unit assignments was remarkable in comparison with typical performance. All his students (five sections) completed the two major assignments with passing grades; this differed from other units in which students were often called to task for not turning in work. In addition, more students participated in class discussions, including those who were previously less engaged or silent, and students selected items from this unit to include in their end-of-year sixth-grade portfolio more than any other science unit, demonstrating a level of care and commitment to this work.

What do we learn about the teaching within this framework? Barton and Tan (2009) highlight that the content and teaching of the unit were heavily based on the students' nontraditional funds of knowledge. In comparison with the Rosebery and colleagues (2010) study, in which the curriculum made room for *unplanned* activities to draw in students' heterogeneous experiences, the food and nutrition unit *planned* activities that went beyond those clearly identifiable as "science" activities to include those that stretch the bounds of science by making connections to students' home and community lives and experiences. Many activities in this unit were planned to stimulate and bring in kinds of talk and experiences that might traditionally be regarded as distracting from the science storyline of a unit.

Culturally Responsive Teaching

A number of studies examine science teaching that is guided by a culturally responsive framework (Grimberg & Gummer, 2013; Johnson, 2011; Morrison, Robbins, & Rose, 2008; Tsurusaki, Barton, Tan, Koch, & Contento, 2013). Culturally responsive teaching is instruction that "makes sense to students who are not members of, or assimilated into, the dominant social group" (Klug & Whitfield, 2003, p. 151). In a review of research, Morrison and colleagues (2008) identified three key features of culturally responsive pedagogy: (1) Teachers have high academic expectations for students but not at the expense of losing their cultural identity, (2) students are supported in developing positive ethnic and cultural identities, and (3) students develop the ability to understand and critique societal issues and inequities.

Grimberg and Gummer (2013) examined culturally relevant pedagogy in their work with teachers in 25 K–8 schools near or on American Indian reservations in Montana. In a 2-year professional development program, they engaged teachers in examining the intersection of three cultures: tribal culture, the culture of the science classroom, and the culture of science. Three intertwined goals guided the professional development: (1) to deepen teachers' knowledge of the tribes, (2) to model teaching methods congruent with cultural practices of the tribes, and (3) to enhance teachers' science content knowledge. The program built on the assumption that teachers need to help learners cross cultural borders among the various cultures to which they belong by identifying intersection points between science and students' cultures.

Results of a quasi-experimental study showed that teachers in the treatment group changed both their beliefs about their ability to use culturally responsive approaches and their teaching practices, resulting in a positive impact on student learning. No significant changes in practices or beliefs were found in the comparison group of teachers. Treatment teachers spent more time on the teaching practice of making connections between science topics, students' real-life issues, and hands-on activities, and this practice predicted student learning. For example, the study

of accelerated motion was connected to arrow making and throwing, and ideas about vectors were connected to community festivals and storytelling by community elders. Notably, of the six variables examined in this study, only the two variables that relate closely to the notion of cultural intersection—teachers' beliefs about equitable practices and teachers' practice of connecting science and community—predicted the increase in student science test scores. This provides strong empirical evidence that the teaching practice of connecting science ideas to students' cultural backgrounds might be among a set of high-leverage teaching practices.

Agency and Identity as Learning Goals

In culturally responsive teaching, the concepts of agency and identity take on central importance. Drawing from sociocultural analyses of science teaching, researchers conclude that it is not enough to engage students in reform-based science teaching and to produce students who know and can do science. To address the needs of *all* students, science teaching must also attend to students' identity development (Archer, et al., 2010; Carlone et al., 2011). In addition, equitable classrooms cultivate among students a sense of ownership and agency (Barton & Tan, 2009; Tan & Barton, 2008a, 2008b).

A study of reform-based science teaching in two fourth-grade classrooms (Carlone et al., 2011) found that although students in both classrooms developed similar levels of science understanding and attitudes toward science, there were inequities in terms of students' affiliation with science. In one classroom, a group of fourth-grade African-American and Latina girls expressed clear disaffiliation with science ("They are the science people. We aren't like them."), despite the fact that they showed evidence of understanding the science as well as, or in one case better than, their classmates.

What led to this disaffiliation? The teaching in both of these classrooms exemplified many aspects of reform-based, inquiry-oriented science teaching. However, the teachers differed in how they enacted students' sharing of science ideas. In one class, students shared ideas by taking turns to state their individual ideas, while in the other class students were obligated to interact, exchange ideas, and work toward shared understandings. The researchers conclude that the turn-taking structure contributed to student disaffiliation with science and that we need to reframe what counts in science classrooms, including a new focus on whether and to what extent students identify with scientific activity in the classroom (Cobb, Gresalfi, & Hodge, 2009; Gresalfi & Cobb, 2006).

To support the codevelopment of scientific understandings and academic identity, a third-grade teacher, Mr. Cordova, built into his curriculum—across subject areas—an ongoing metacognitive discourse about the actions of inquirers in different disciplines (Reveles et al., 2004). At the beginning of the year, he engaged students in exploring questions such as: What do readers do? What do mathematicians do? What do scientists do? These initial explorations were revisited throughout the year as students became more sophisticated in their understandings of what scientists do and why. This work supported students in reformulating their identities in relationship to science and other subject matter areas. Students' identity reformulation was also supported by the teacher's validation of the identities that students brought to the classroom. From this case study, the authors conclude with two key points:

- Analysis of the cognitive dimensions of classroom discourse needs to coexist with considerations of the identity formulation among student and teacher participants.
- If all students . . . are to have equitable access to science knowledge, it . . . becomes necessary to create scientific learning opportunities that are in congruence with the unique knowledge and understanding that these students bring to the classroom (Reveles et al., 2004, pp. 1140–1141).

6. Examining the Role of Teacher Learning Programs in Improving Science Teaching and Learning

Those who work to support teacher learning at the preservice, induction, and inservice levels are often forced by time and institutional constraints to make difficult choices about which aspects of science teaching to emphasize in their work with teachers. This has resulted in a number of studies that examine science teacher learning and practice within particular, focused frameworks. That is, they don't attempt to "do it all" but focus instead on a subset of key ideas and strategies. This is consistent with recommendations from scholars for teacher education experiences that are carefully crafted around coherent conceptual frameworks (Bransford, Darling-Hammond, & LePage, 2005; Darling-Hammond, Hammerness, Grossman, Rust, & Shulman, 2005).

While many science professional development programs have a broad focus on supporting teachers in teaching science through inquiry (Czerniak, Beltyukova, Struble, Haney, & Lumpe, 2006; Johnson, Kahle, & Fargo, 2007; Lakshmanan, Heath, Perlmutter, & Elder, 2011; Lee, Deaktor, Enders, & Lambert, 2008[7]; Lumpe, Czerniak, Haney, & Beltyukova, 2012) and have demonstrated evidence of positive impact on teachers and/or students, this review highlights teacher learning programs that are guided by more constrained frameworks, which I refer to as framework-driven programs. These framework-driven programs can make important contributions to our thinking about identifying a smaller set of high-leverage science teaching practices and organizing them into useful and meaningful conceptual frameworks for teachers. These framework-driven programs are examples of how some researchers are, in effect, making their best bets about high-leverage frameworks and practices and testing them out. The distinction I make here between broad inquiry-focused programs and framework-driven programs is somewhat artificial but one that I hope might help readers consider the advantages and difficulties of attempting to define frameworks that tackle in-depth work on a subset of teaching practices for elementary science teachers.

Consistent with the goals of this chapter, I focus on describing each framework in terms of the particular teaching framework and strategies that teachers are learning to use within preservice or inservice teacher learning programs. I do not detail how each program was organized to support teachers in developing the knowledge and abilities to enact the particular teaching strategies.

Framework 1: Teaching Science as Argument

Zembal-Saul (2009) developed and studied a program that organized elementary science preservice teacher education around evidence and argument. This choice of emphasis is in line with the focus in the *Next Generation Science Standards* (2013) on engaging students in using science practices, one of which is argumentation from evidence.

This framework clearly delimits what will be covered in this program, focusing on selected aspects of scientific inquiry: (a) using an argument structure to guide class discussion, (b) reasoning publicly about the development of claims from evidence and the evaluation of claims on the basis of evidence, and (c) engaging authentically with the language of science. Making meaning of science concepts is at the center of this curriculum, but what counts as meaningful understanding is evidence-based explanations informed by interactions with phenomena, existing scientific knowledge, and argumentation.

Preservice teachers in this program learn to use an argument structure derived from Toulmin (1958)—claims, evidence, and justification. Teachers use a child-friendly version of the Toulmin framework, the KLEW chart, to map argument development with children. The mapping process engages elementary students in articulating what they think they know from prior knowledge and experience (K), the claims they are negotiating (i.e., what they are learning; L), the evidence upon which the claims are based (E), and the new testable questions they are interested in pursuing (i.e., wonderings; W). Using this argumentation framework, preservice teachers are guided in learning to plan and teach in six planning phases (see Table 19.8, left column). Planning and teaching strategies within these six categories are tightly linked to the claim, evidence, justification argumentation framework for building explanations (Table 19.8, right column).

Framework 2: Modeling-Centered Inquiry

Schwarz (2009) used another scientific practice, the development and use of models, as the organizing framework in her work with preservice teachers. She worked to deepen preservice teachers' knowledge about modeling-centered inquiry, reformulated their views of effective science teaching to include modeling-centered inquiry, and developed their pedagogical content knowledge and teaching practices using tools such as technology simulations, frameworks, and reform-based curriculum materials.

TABLE 19.8
Teaching Science as Argument: Teaching Framework Foci and Teaching Strategies

Framework Foci	Planning and Teaching Strategies
Science concept: overarching explanation	• Identify the scientific explanation that students will construct.
Prior knowledge	• Identify student prior knowledge and assess how students' ideas might assist or interfere with understanding science ideas.
Data collection: sequencing investigations	• Engage students with phenomena and collection of data that will help them construct claims. • Sequence investigations to support construction of the argument.
Data representation: data analysis	• Engage students in organizing and representing data to identify patterns.
Coordinating claims and evidence: weighing alternatives, negotiating meaning	• Ask questions to help students identify patterns in the data. • Provide materials to help students resolve discrepancies in their observations or interpretations. • Ask questions to assist students in comparing/contrasting claims. • Ask questions to assist students in negotiating a scientifically accurate argument from evidence.
Testable questions: predictions	• Provide opportunities for students to use their explanation to predict and test related interactions with the phenomena. • Provide opportunities for students to pursue new questions that arise from the investigation.

To support preservice teachers in making modeling central in their science teaching, Schwarz developed a coherent and compact instructional framework to guide teachers' work with students. This modeling framework, EIMA (engage-investigate-model-apply), was adapted from the BSCS 5E instructional model (Bybee & Landes, 1988; Bybee et al., 2006). The phases of this framework are described by Schwarz as:

(a) Engaging students in the topic and eliciting their prior ideas
(b) Helping students investigate the topic, phenomena, or ideas, with high priority for data collection and analysis of those data into patterns
(c) Helping students create models or explanations and comparing and reconciling those models and explanations with those from the scientific community
(d) Asking students to apply those models or explanations to novel situations

In one variation of her science methods course, Schwarz added a curriculum analysis focus, using AAAS Project 2061 Instructional Analysis Criteria (Kesidou & Roseman, 2002; Stern & Roseman, 2004). She notes that adding this component shifted the course from a focus on modeling-centered inquiry toward more general principles of effective teaching found in the Project 2061 criteria. She found that the large number of curriculum analysis criteria diluted the course emphasis and that preservice teachers' use of those criteria for analysis and lesson planning was disappointing. This finding supports the notion of focusing in depth on a limited set of high-leverage teaching practices.

Framework 3: Student Thinking and
Science Content Storyline Lenses
Roth, and colleagues (2011) developed and studied a videocase-based, analysis-of-practice professional development program for inservice teachers that focused teachers' attention on analyzing, planning, and teaching science through two lenses: the Student Thinking Lens and the Science Content Storyline Lens. To identify this focus for the program, the Science Teachers Learning from Lesson Analysis (STeLLA) program developers drew from research to select a small set of ideas that showed high potential for improving teacher learning, teaching practice, and student learning within a 1-year PD program. The 1-year limitation recognized elementary teachers' limited time for science professional development while still providing enough time (88.5 total hours of PD) for substantial change in teachers' knowledge and practices. To impact teaching and learning significantly within this 1-year period, it was assumed that the substance of the program would need to be tightly focused on a few ideas and teaching strategies addressed in depth.

Table 19.9 depicts the conceptual framework that guided the STeLLA program. The Science Content Storyline Lens focused attention on how the science ideas in a science lesson or unit are sequenced and linked to one another and to lesson activities to help students construct a coherent "story" that makes sense to them. Many times, teachers present accurate science content and engage students in hands-on activities, but these ideas and activities are not woven together to tell or reveal a coherent story (Roth et al., 2006). The STeLLA Science Content Storyline Lens was brought to life for teachers through a set of nine teaching strategies to support the development of a coherent storyline (see Table 19.9).

The decision to include the Student Thinking Lens was influenced by the extensive body of research that explores students' ideas about natural phenomena, the role student ideas can play in teachers' science teaching, the importance of attending to student ideas and cultures in supporting science learning of students from groups underrepresented in science, and research showing that teachers do not typically focus on students' ideas in their planning, teaching, and analyses of teaching (van Es &

TABLE 19.9
STeLLA Conceptual Framework: The Two Lenses

Student Thinking Lens	Science Content Storyline Lens
Strategies to Reveal, Support, and Challenge Student Thinking	**Strategies to Create a Coherent Science Content Storyline**
1. Ask questions to elicit student ideas and predictions.	A. Identify one main learning goal.
2. Ask questions to probe student ideas and predictions.	B. Set the purpose with a focus question and/or goal statement.
3. Ask questions to challenge student thinking.	C. Select activities that are matched to the learning goal.
4. Engage students in interpreting and reasoning about data and observations.	D. Select content representations matched to the learning goal and engage students in their use.
5. Engage students in constructing explanations and arguments.	E. Sequence key science ideas and activities appropriately.
6. Engage students in using and applying new science ideas in a variety of ways and contexts.	F. Make explicit links between science ideas and activities.
7. Engage students in making connections by synthesizing and summarizing key science ideas.	G. Link science ideas to other science ideas.
8. Engage students in communicating in scientific ways.	H. Highlight key science ideas and focus question throughout.
	I. Summarize key science ideas.

Sherin, 2002). Eight teaching strategies that reveal, support, and challenge student thinking are highlighted in the STeLLA conceptual framework.

The initial study of this program in a quasi-experimental design (Roth et al., 2011) revealed that the following aspects of science teaching predicted student learning: (1) teacher science content knowledge, (2) teacher ability to analyze science teaching about student thinking, and (3) teacher classroom use of four Science Content Storyline teaching strategies:

(a) lesson activities match the learning goal
(b) students use, modify, or create content representations matched to the learning goal
(c) science content ideas are explicitly linked to activities
(d) science content ideas are linked to other content ideas

A randomized, controlled study with a larger number of teachers is now underway (Roth, Taylor, Wilson, & Landes, 2013), with initial results showing a similar impact on teachers' science content knowledge and pedagogical content knowledge. With a larger sample size, the study should be able to detect additional relationships between particular teaching strategies and student learning. Those teaching strategies that predict student learning will make excellent candidates as potential high-leverage science teaching practices.

Other Frameworks
Other important and innovative alternative frameworks and theoretical approaches should be considered in thinking about effective methods for supporting elementary science teaching. For example, there are frameworks that focus on culturally responsive teaching practices that draw on students' diverse discourses and funds of knowledge (Barton, Gunckel, Covitt, & McLaughlin, 2007; LaVan, 2006; Moore, 2008). In one such approach, Moore (2008) focuses on agency, identity, and social justice as a framework in her work with preservice teachers. Akerson and colleagues (Akerson, Buzzelli, & Donnelly, 2010; Akerson

& Hanuscin, 2007; Akerson & Volrich, 2006) use a nature-of-science framework in working with preservice and inservice elementary teachers. In one study (Akerson & Volrich, 2006), they documented a preservice teacher's success in teaching explicitly about the nature of science during her internship in a first-grade classroom. Other productive frameworks foreground developing teachers' pedagogical design capacity (Davis & Smithey, 2009) or developing teachers' expertise in working with a particular instructional model (Gunckel, 2011). Heller et al. (2012) studied three PD programs that shared a framework focused on deepening teachers' understanding of specific science content knowledge in combination with analysis of learner thinking about that content and analysis of teaching strategies for helping learners understand that content. Within this common framework, the three programs varied in the types of activities that supported teachers' exploration of the framework: (a) analysis of cases, (b) analysis of student work, or (c) metacognitive analysis. Across all three groups, teachers' and students' scores on science tests were well beyond those of controls, and effects were maintained a year later. Student achievement also improved significantly for English language learners in both the study year and follow-up, and treatment effects did not differ based on sex or race/ethnicity. Among other findings, this study suggests the power of a framework that integrates science content learning with analysis of student learning and teaching strategies matched to that same content.

The evidence from these framework-driven studies demonstrates the potential power of focusing in depth on particular aspects of science teaching. Particularly intriguing are findings that preservice and first-year teachers who learned about these frameworks were able, even as beginners, to teach science in ways aligned with reform-based visions. Avraamidou and Zembal-Saul (2010) documented two of these first-year "well-started beginners." Both of these teachers engaged their students in investigations and in using practices such as making predictions, collecting and recording data, and constructing generalizations. One of these teachers successfully supported her students in using the claim, evidence, justification frame-work. Gunckel (2011) reports a case study of a preservice teacher who in her first science teaching experience was successful in using the inquiry-application instructional model (I-AIM) in her science teaching. And Akerson and Volrich (2006) succeeded in supporting a preservice teacher in engaging first graders in thinking about important aspects of the nature of science. What is striking about these studies is that (a) even beginning teachers were able to implement reform-based teaching in meaningful ways and (b) these teachers' thinking about their practice was in line with their actual practice. This potentially speaks to the power of a framework-focused approach.

At the end of her 2009 article, Schwarz poses a question quite relevant to the search for productive frameworks and high-leverage practices: "In considering all of these research-based frameworks and theoretical approaches, which may have the largest productive impact for preservice teachers and in what manner?" (p. 741). This chapter is designed to prompt thinking about this question.

7. Examining the Role of Formative Assessment in Improving Science Teaching and Learning

Ruiz-Primo and Furtak's study (2007) of teachers' informal assessment practices is among the few reviewed for this chapter that examined closely teachers' use of a set of teaching strategies and then linked those specific teacher moves to student learning. The study focused on teachers' use of strategies to informally assess student learning while teaching and to use that knowledge to support student learning. The authors proposed a framework that shifts from the typical initiation-response-evaluation (IRE) pattern of student–teacher interaction (Cazden, 2001) to a pattern that fosters assessment conversation. Their proposed ESRU model begins with the teacher eliciting (E) followed by a student response (S). The teacher then recognizes (R) the student response (revoicing, rephrasing) and uses (U) the student response to help the student reach learning goals. Examples of specific teacher moves that could be used to elicit, recognize, and use students' response are provided in Table 19.10.

Three teachers (one elementary sixth-grade teacher and two middle school teachers) were observed teaching the first four investigations in a unit about properties of matter (mass, volume, density, sinking and floating). The curriculum materials were constructivist and inquiry based (*Foundation Approaches to Science Teaching*; Pottenger & Young, 1992). Videotapes of lessons across time were coded to identify how teachers interacted with students. Student learning data were collected to allow for analysis of the relationship between the teaching strategies used and student learning.

Results showed that the sixth-grade elementary teacher conducted more assessment conversations than the two middle school teachers and that the characteristics of her assessment conversations were more consistent with the ESRU model. Although all students performed similarly on a unit pretest, students in the classroom with the most assessment conversations (elementary sixth grade) outperformed students in the middle school seventh- and eighth-grade classrooms. This suggests that better informal assessment strategies might better support student learning. It is interesting to note that the middle school teachers had stronger science backgrounds than the elementary school teacher. This suggests that content knowledge alone may not be a sufficient precursor to conducting effective informal formative assessment. The authors conclude that the ESRU questioning patterns might help teachers distinguish between asking questions for the purpose of recitation and asking questions for the purpose of eliciting student ideas and improving student learning.

Part V. What Are the Research Gaps and Needed Directions for Research on Elementary Science Teaching?

How can future research help narrow the huge gap between what exists and what's needed to support deep and meaningful understandings of science? How can this body of research inform practice? This review of research on elementary science teaching was organized to highlight the range of science teaching frameworks and strategies that have demonstrated effectiveness in supporting students'

TABLE 19.10
Selected Examples of Strategies for ESRU Cycles

Eliciting	Recognizing	Using
Conceptual—*Teacher asks students to:* • Provide definitions • Apply, relate, compare, contrast concepts • Compare/contrast others' ideas Epistemic—*Teacher asks students to:* • Compare/contrast observations, data, or procedures • Use and apply known procedures • Make predictions • Interpret data, patterns	*Teacher:* • Clarifies/elaborates student response • Repeats/paraphrases student's words • Revoices student's words • Captures/displays student responses/explanations	*Teacher:* • Asks students to elaborate (why, how) • Compares/contrasts student responses and pushes for alternative explanations • Promotes debating and discussion among students' ideas • Helps students achieve consensus • Helps relate evidence to explanations • Makes connections to previous learning

Adapted from Ruiz-Primo & Furtak, 2007

science learning or identity in science. As argued in Part III, this cataloging of science teaching frameworks and teaching practices serves as a first step in a research agenda focused on identifying a smaller set of high-leverage practices and instructional frameworks to guide elementary teachers. Such a research agenda acknowledges the practical needs of elementary teachers, who typically have limited science backgrounds and who are responsible for teaching multiple subject areas, leaving limited time to focus on improving their science teaching. This proposed agenda also recognizes the stark contrast between current elementary science teaching practice and the kinds of teaching that make it possible for students from both dominant and underrepresented groups in science to be meaningfully engaged in using science practices to deepen their understandings of science concepts, to understand and appreciate scientific ways of knowing and communicating, and to see themselves as competent science learners. It is my assertion that research can play an important role in transforming elementary science teaching by identifying a limited number of high-leverage science teaching strategies that are organized into a coherent set that is guided by a compact conceptual framework, model, or theory that teachers can realistically use to guide their decision making, both while planning and in the moment of teaching.

The descriptions of representative studies in this review underscore that the science education research community has a wealth of knowledge to inform the identification of core teaching strategies and frameworks. As a community, we are testing out various instructional frameworks and teaching strategies and learning much about what is possible in terms of student learning. The teaching approaches that are having an impact are challenging, "ambitious" forms of teaching that are organized around different instructional frameworks or models (Lampert, Beasley, Ghousseini, Kazemi, & Franke, 2010; Windschitl, Thompson, & Braaten, 2011). Each of these approaches foregrounds a particular set of teaching strategies, such as strategies for constructing scientific explanations, for eliciting and responding to student ideas, for constructing and revising models, for bringing students' cultural experiences into the science classroom, for developing students' English language competency, and for integrating language arts and science. How can elementary teachers make sense of the sometimes competing models we investigate and the long list of teaching strategies coming out of our research studies? What are the next steps we might take as a research community to identify a set of high-leverage teaching practices that will make it feasible for elementary teachers to teach science effectively for all of their students? I suggest five possible next steps, while expecting readers to have additional ideas about how we might proceed.

First, we can look across our research studies (starting with this review) to identify teaching practices or strategies that are common across studies, even studies operating from different theoretical or instructional frameworks. For example, there seems to be consensus that it is important

for teachers to elicit students' ideas and experiences, at least as a starting point in exploring a new phenomenon or content area. Meta-analyses can also be helpful in this process (e.g., Schroeder, Scott, Tolson, Huang, & Lee, 2007).

Second, we can clearly articulate differences in our frameworks and theoretical stances and design research studies to explore those differences. For example, this review suggests that while there is a shared commitment to eliciting and using student ideas, there are differences about the degree to which science instruction should unfold in response to students' ideas and theories (e.g., Hammer, Russ, Mikeska, & Scherr, 2008; Hammer, Goldberg, & Fargason, 2012; Rosebery et al., 2010) versus maintaining a coherent, learning goal–driven sequence (Krajcik, McNeill, & Reiser, 2008; Roth et al., 2011). There are also differences about the role of real-life applications and connections to students' home, culture, and community lives. Should instruction begin with applications to students' lives (Barton & Tan, 2009) or with engagement with interesting or puzzling phenomena? Are applications to students' lives a way of giving students practice in applying science ideas in new contexts (Roth et al., 2011), or should applications to students' lives be foregrounded throughout any unit of study (Barton & Tan, 2009)? We can also clarify our differences in thinking about when and how new science ideas are most effectively introduced to students.

Third, we can explore further what it takes to help teachers be well-started beginners. Studies by Avraamidou and Zembal-Saul (2010), Gunckel (2011), and Akerson and Volrich (2006) demonstrate that preservice teachers' experiences in framework-focused teacher education programs can enable them to implement important aspects of reform-based science teaching in their first teaching experiences. As a field, we would benefit from more studies like these that engage preservice or beginning teachers in thinking about science teaching in terms of a specific framework that is supported by a limited number of related teaching strategies that are explored in depth and then implemented in student teaching, internship experiences, and the beginning years of teaching. This kind of work would represent an important first step in thinking about a continuum of science teacher learning across a career.

Fourth, we can use the power of video images of elementary science teaching to work toward stronger shared understandings among researchers. For example, a recently completed proof-of-concept study, Tying Words to Images of Science Teaching (TWIST), demonstrated the feasibility of using a research community consensus-building process to develop an instrument that supports researchers in analyzing videos of classroom teaching consistently across projects by providing a "words-to-images" tool that matches words (via a coding manual) to images of science teaching (via consensus-coded lesson videos; Gardner, Stuhlsatz, & Roth, 2013).

Finally, we will benefit from more studies that are designed to focus on better understanding the impact of particular teaching strategies and approaches. For this review, I found many studies in which the teaching was described in broad, general terms only, usually because the focus of the study was, quite appropriately, on student learning. What I am now suggesting is that researchers add to their research agenda studies that focus on smaller sets of teaching strategies and their relationships to student learning. Both qualitative and quasi-experimental/experimental designs would make important contributions in our search for high-leverage teaching practices. Qualitative findings from a number of studies described in this review, for example, highlighted the importance of:

- explicitly teaching students about science argumentation, explanation, and discourse structures (McNeill, 2011; McNeill et al., 2007, 2008; Michaels, O'Connor, & Resnick, 2008; Michaels, Shouse, & Schweingruber, 2008; Roth, 2002; Songer & Gotwals, 2012; Varelas et al., 2008; Zembal-Saul, 2009)
- coherence over time (Krajcik et al., 2008; Lehrer & Schauble, 2012; Metz, 2011; Wiser, Smith, & Doubler, 2012)
- making students' backgrounds, knowledge, and experiences central (Barton & Tan, 2009; Carlone et al., 2011; Grimberg & Gummer, 2013; Lee, Maerten-Rivera, Buxton, Penfield, & Secada, 2009; Rosebery et al., 2010)

Quasi-experimental and experimental designs cited in this review used hierarchical linear modeling (HLM) analyses to identify the following teaching strategies that predict student learning:

- making connections among science topics, students' real-life issues, and hands-on activities (Grimberg & Gummer, 2013)
- having students complete activities by carrying out investigations themselves rather than watching a teacher demonstration and by participating in class discussions before and after the investigation (Fogleman, McNeill, & Krajcik, 2011)
- developing a coherent science content storyline in which (Roth et al., 2011)
  - lesson activities match the learning goal
  - students use, modify, or create content representations matched to the learning goal
  - science content ideas are explicitly linked to activities
  - science content ideas are linked to other content ideas

There are also largely neglected areas of research on elementary science teaching. Notably scarce are studies examining engineering and the use of mathematics in science, both of which are emphasized in the *National Research Council Framework* (2012) and the *Next Generation Science Standards* (2013). There are also few studies investigating systemwide supports and constraints for elementary science teaching. A few case studies of elementary teachers bring to light the need for attending more to teachers' larger institutional and policy contexts. For example, Smith and Southerland (2007) point out the sometimes contradictory messages that teachers receive about science education reform from their interactions with the standards, the mandated curriculum, and end-of-level district tests. Carlone, Haun-Frank, and Kimmel (2010) spotlight the dilemma of strong, science-enthusiast elementary teachers who nevertheless felt seriously constrained by federal and local accountability demands. If we hope to change the status of elementary science teaching, we need strategies for effectively supporting teachers in reconciling their science teaching goals with the realities of their teaching contexts.

Another gap in our research is the relatively small number of large-scale quasi-experimental and experimental studies investigating elementary science teaching practices. These studies are not a panacea. Sometimes such studies show no effects on student learning, so we learn nothing about the potential power of particular teaching strategies embedded within them (Borman, Boydston, Lee, Lanehart, & Cotner, 2009; Borman, Gamoran, & Bowdon, 2008; Pine et al., 2006). Other times we learn only about positive impacts on student learning and do not benefit from HLM analyses that identify specific teaching practices that predict that student learning (Granger, Bevis, Saka, & Southerland, 2010), or the measures of student learning are so distal from the curriculum or professional development (e.g., high-stakes achievement tests) that impact on student learning is not detected (Shymansky, Yore, & Anderson, 2004). However, when the intervention focuses clearly on a subset of targeted teaching strategies and the research design examines relationships between the use of teaching strategies and student learning, we can gain important insights about potentially high-leverage teaching practices.

This review provides a map of the territory of elementary science teaching that the research community has investigated over the past decade. The map is full of promising data and a variety of possible routes that can take us from current elementary science teaching practices to new visions of what is possible. Future research can focus on developing more coherent understandings of core, effective elementary science teaching practices that can be used to provide elementary teachers with a clear pathway to begin moving toward more ambitious forms of science teaching.

Notes

1. Previous *Handbook* chapters provide a review of the earlier history of research on elementary science teaching (Appleton, 2007; Gabel, 1994).
2. The removed text about elementary science curriculum materials is available from the author, kroth@bscs.org.
3. I removed citations for studies that investigated learning by students in grades 7 and 8. Interestingly, more than half of the K–6 citations listed by *TSTS* involved sixth-grade students (Beeth, Hennessey, Khishfe, Raghavan, Smith, White). The Herrenkohl, Lehrer, Metz, Roth, and Warren citations involved younger students.

4. Cavagnetto also identified a third category of argumentation discourse, *Understanding the interaction between science and society to learn scientific argument.* Studies using this approach in elementary classrooms were not found in this review.

5. These authors report a third type of literacy and science integration that is common in classrooms but not present in the research literature: a thematic approach in which science and literacy are taught separately but connected by an overarching theme.

6. Another fully integrated approach is enacted in the *Seeds of Science, Roots of Reading* curriculum materials (Cervetti, Barber, Dorph, Pearson, & Goldschmidt, 2012). For further information about this curricular program, write to the author for a section on curriculum materials that appeared in an earlier draft of this chapter (kroth@bscs.org).

7. The professional development program developed and studied by Lee and colleagues could also be considered a framework-driven program. Because this program included both a broad science inquiry focus and a focus on language development, we might consider the language-science inquiry connection as a framework that teachers can use to guide their teaching. On the other hand, the focus on both science inquiry and the needs of English language learners resulted in a rather long list of teaching strategies (see Table 8). So this framework might be viewed as increasing the territory to be covered (to literacy, not just science), rather than focusing in deeply on selected parts of the territory.

References

Abd-El-Khalick, F., BouJaoude, S., Duschl, R., Lederman, N.G., Mamlok-Naaman, R., Hofstein, A., Niaz, M., Treagust, D., & Tuan, H.-L. (2004). Inquiry in science education: International perspectives. *Science Education, 88,* 397–419.

Abell, S.K., Anderson, G., & Chezem, J. (2000). Science as argument and explanation: Exploring concepts of sound in third grade. In J. Minstrell & E. Van Zee (Eds.), *Inquiring into inquiry learning and teaching in science* (pp. 65–79). Washington, DC: American Association for the Advancement of Teaching.

Abrahams, I., & Reiss, M.J. (2012). Practical work: Effectiveness in primary and secondary schools in England. *Journal of Research in Science Teaching, 49*(8), 1035–1055.

Akerson, V.L., & Abd-El-Khalick, F. (2003). Teaching elements of nature of science: A yearlong case study of a fourth grade teacher. *Journal of Research in Science Teaching, 40,* 1025–1049.

Akerson, V.L., Abd-El-Khalick, F., & Lederman, N.G. (2000). Influence of a reflective explicit activity-based approach on elementary teachers' conceptions of nature of science. *Journal of Research in Science Teaching, 32,* 295–317.

Akerson, V.L., Buzzelli, C.A., & Donnelly, L.A. (2010). On the nature of teaching nature of science: Preservice early childhood teachers' instruction in preschool and elementary settings. *Journal of Research in Science Teaching, 47*(2), 213–233.

Akerson, V.L., & Hanuscin, D.L. (2007). Teaching nature of science through inquiry: Results of a 3-year professional development program. *Journal of Research in Science Teaching, 44*(5), 653–680.

Akerson, V.L., & Volrich, M.L. (2006). Teaching nature of science explicitly in a first-grade internship setting. *Journal of Research in Science Teaching, 43*(4), 377–394.

Appleton, K. (2003). How do beginning primary school teachers cope with science? Toward an understanding of science teaching practice. *Research in Science Education, 33,* 1–25.

Appleton, K. (2007). Elementary science teaching. In S.K. Abell & N.G. Lederman (Eds.), *Handbook of research on science education* (pp. 493–535). Mahwah, NJ: Lawrence Erlbaum Associates.

Archer, L., Dewitt, J., Osborne, J., Dillon, J., Willis, B., & Wong, B. (2010). "Doing" science versus "being" a scientist: Examining 10/11-year-old schoolchildren's constructions of science through the lens of identity. *Science Education, 94,* 617–639.

Aschbacher, P.R., & Roth, E.J. (2002). *What's happening in the elementary inquiry science classroom and why? Examining patterns of practice and district factors affecting science reforms.* Paper presented in a Symposium: Policy Levers for Urban Systemic Mathematics and Science Reform: Impact Studies From Four Sites at the Annual Meeting of the AERA, New Orleans, LA.

Avraamidou, L., & Zembal-Saul, C. (2010). In search of well-started beginning science teachers: Insights from two first-year elementary teachers. *Journal of Research in Science Teaching, 47*(6), 661–686.

Baek, H., Schwarz, C., Chen, J., Hokayem, H., & Zhan, L. (2011). Engaging elementary students in scientific modeling: The MoDeLS fifth-grade approach and findings. In M.S. Khine & I.M. Saleh (Eds.), *Models and modeling in science education* (pp. 195–218). New York, NY: Springer.

Ball, D.L., Sleep, L., Boerst, T.A., & Bass, H. (2009). Combining the development of practice and the practice of development in teacher education. *The Elementary School Journal, 109*(5), 458–474.

Bamberger, Y.M., & Davis, E. (2013). Middle-school science students' scientific modeling performances across content areas and within a learning progression. *International Journal of Science Education, 35*(2), 213–238.

Banilower, E.R., Heck, D.J., & Weiss, I.R. (2007). Can professional development make the vision of the standards a reality? The impact of the National Science Foundations' local systemic change through teacher enhancement initiative. *Journal of Research in Science Teaching, 44,* 375–395.

Banilower, E.R., Smith, P.S., Pasley, J.D., & Weiss, I.R. (2006). The state of K12 science teaching in the United States: Results from a national observation survey. In D. Sunal & E. Wright (Eds.), *The impact of state and national standards on K–12 teaching.* Greenwich, CT: Information Age Publishing.

Banilower, E.R., Smith, P.S., Weiss, I.R., Malzahn, K.A., Campbell K.M., & Weis, A.M. (2013). *Report of the 2012 National Survey of Science and Mathematics Education.* Chapel Hill, NC: Horizon Research, Inc.

Barnes, B., Bloor, D., & Henry, J. (1996). *Scientific knowledge: A sociological analysis.* Chicago, IL: University of Chicago Press.

Barton, A., Gunckel, K., Covitt, B., & McLaughlin, D. (2007, July). *Considering students' strengths: Helping elementary preservice teachers take account of students' resources in planning and teaching science lessons.* Poster presented at the Center for Curriculum Materials in Science Knowledge Sharing Institute, Washington, DC.

Barton, A.C., & Tan, E. (2009). Funds of knowledge and discourses and hybrid space. *Journal of research in science teaching, 46*(1), 50–73.

Beeth, M.E., & Hewson, P.W. (1999). Learning goals in an exemplary science teacher's practice: Cognitive and social factors in teaching for conceptual change. *Science Education, 83*(6), 738–760.

Berland, L.K., & Reiser, B.J. (2009). Making sense of argumentation and explanation. *Science Education, 93*(1), 26–55.

Beyer, C., & Davis, E.A. (2008). Fostering second-graders' scientific explanations: A beginning elementary teacher's knowledge, beliefs, and practice. *Journal of the Learning Sciences, 17*(3), 381–414.

Borman, G., Gamoran, A., & Bowdon, J. (2008). A randomized trial of teacher development in elementary science: First-year achievement effects. *Journal of Research on Educational Effectiveness, 1,* 237–264.

Borman, K., Boydston, T., Lee, R., Lanehart, R., & Cotner, B. (2009, March). *Improving elementary science instruction and student achievement: The impact of a professional development program.* Paper presented at the annual meeting of the Society for Research on Educational Effectiveness, Washington, D.C.

Bransford, J., Darling-Hammond, L., & LePage, P. (2005). Introduction. In L. Darling-Hammond & J. Bransford (Eds.), *Preparing teachers for a changing world: What teachers should learn and be able to do* (pp. 1–39). San Francisco, CA: Jossey-Bass.

Bricker, L.A., & Bell, P. (2008). Conceptualizations of argumentation from science studies and the learning sciences and their implications for the practices of science education. *Science Education, 92,* 473–498.

Bruozas, M., Finn, L.E., Tzou, C., Hug, B., Kuhn, L., & Reiser, B.J. (2004). Struggle in natural environments: What will survive? In J. Krajcik & B.J. Reiser (Eds.), *IQWST: Investigating and questioning our world through science and technology*. Evanston, IL: Northwestern University.

Bybee, R.W., & Landes, N.M. (1988). What research says about the new science curriculum (BSCS). *Science and Children, 25*, 35–39.

Bybee, R.W., Taylor, J.A., Gardner, A., Van Scotter, P., Powell, J.C., Westbrook, A., et al. (2006). *The BSCS 5E instructional model: Origins and effectiveness*. Colorado Springs, CO: BSCS.

Carey, S., Evans, R., Honda, M., Jay, E., & Unger, C. (1989). "An experiment is when you try it and see if it works:" A study of junior high school students' understanding of the construction of scientific knowledge. *International Journal of Science Education, 11*, 514–529.

Carlone, H.B., Haun-Frank, J., & Kimmel, S.C. (2010). Tempered radicals: Elementary teachers' narratives of teaching science within and against prevailing meanings of schooling. *Cultural Studies of Science Education, 5*, 941–965.

Carlone, H.B., Haun-Frank, J., & Webb, A. (2011). Assessing equity beyond knowledge- and skills-based outcomes: A comparative ethnography of two fourth-grade reform-based science classrooms. *Journal of Research in Science Teaching, 48*(5), 459–485.

Catley, K., Lehrer, R., & Reiser, B. (2005). *Tracing a proposed learning progression for developing understanding of evolution*. Paper commissioned for the Committee on Test Design for K–12 Science Achievement. Center for Education, National Research Council. Washington, DC.

Cavagnetto, A.R. (2008). Factors influencing the implementation of the science writing heuristic in two elementary science classrooms. In B. Hand (Ed.), *Science inquiry, argument, and language: A case for the science writing heuristic* (pp. 37–52). Rotterdam, the Netherlands: Sense.

Cavagnetto, A.R. (2010). Argument to foster scientific literacy: A review of argument interventions in K–12 science contexts. *Review of Educational Research, 80*, 336–371.

Cavagnetto, A.R., Hand, B.M., & Norton-Meier, L. (2010). The nature of elementary science discourse in the context of the science writing heuristic approach. *International Journal of Science Education, 32*(4), 427–449.

Cazden, C.B. (2001). *Classroom discourse: The language of teaching and learning*. Portsmouth, NH: Heinemann.

Cervetti, G.N., & Barber, J. (2008). Text in hands-on science. In E.H. Hiebert & M. Sailors (Eds.), *Finding the right texts: What works for beginning and struggling readers* (pp. 89–108). New York, NY: Guilford.

Cervetti, G.N., Barber, J., Dorph, R., Pearson, P.D., & Goldschmidt, P.G. (2012). The impact of an integrated approach to science and literacy in elementary school classrooms. *Journal of Research in Science Teaching, 49*(5), 631–658.

Chapin, S.H., O'Connor, C., & Anderson, N.C. (2009). *Classroom discussions: Using math talk to help students learn*. Sausalito, CA: Scholastic Math Solutions.

Chinn, C.A., & Malhotra, B.A. (2002). Children's responses to anomalous scientific data: How is conceptual change impeded? *Journal of Educational Psychology, 94*, 327–343.

Cobb, P., Gresalfi, M., & Hodge, L.L. (2009). An interpretive scheme for analyzing the identities that students develop in mathematics classrooms. *Journal for Research in Mathematics Education, 40*, 40–68.

Cornelius, L.L., & Herrenkohl, L.R. (2004). Power in the classroom: How the classroom environment shapes students' relationships with each other and with concepts. *Cognition and Instruction, 22*(4), 389–392.

Cortina, A. (Ed.). (2008). *The education system of the Federal Republic of Germany*. Reinbek, Germany: Rowohlt Verlag.

Czerniak, C.M., Beltyukova, S., Struble, J., Haney, J.J., & Lumpe, A.T. (2006). Do you see what I see? The relationship between a professional development model and student achievement. In R.E. Yager (Ed.), *Exemplary science in Grades 5–8: Standards-based success stories* (pp. 13–43). Arlington, VA: NSTA Press.

Darling-Hammond, L., Hammerness, K., Grossman, P., Rust, F., & Shulman, L. (2005). The design of teacher education programs. In L. Darling-Hammond & J. Bransford (Eds.), *Preparing teachers for a changing world: What teachers should learn and be able to do* (pp. 390–441). San Francisco, CA: Jossey-Bass.

Davis, E., & Smithey, J. (2009). Beginning teachers moving toward effective elementary science teaching. *Science Education, 93*(4), 745–770.

Delpit, L.D. (1988). The silenced dialogue: Power and pedagogy in educating other people's children. *Harvard Educational Review, 28*(3), 280–299.

Delpit, L.D. (2006). *Other people's children: Cultural conflict in the classroom*. New York, NY: W.W. Norton.

Donovan, S., & Bransford, J.D. (2005). *How students learn: Science in the classroom*. Washington, DC: National Academies Press.

Dorph, R., Shields, P., Tiffany-Morales, J., Hartry, A., & McCaffrey, T. (2011). *High hopes—few opportunities: The status of elementary science education in California*. Sacramento, CA: Center for the Future of Teaching and Learning at WestEd.

Driver, R., Leach, J., Millar, R., & Scott, P. (1996). *Young people's images of science*. Buckingham, England: Open University Press.

Duncan, R., Rogat, A.D., & Yarden, A. (2009). A learning progression for deepening students' understandings of modern genetics across the 5th–10th grades. *Journal of Research in Science Teaching, 46*(6), 655–674.

Duschl, R., Schweingruber, H., & Shouse, A. (2007). *Taking science to school: Learning and teaching science in grades K–8*. Washington, DC: National Academies Press.

Fang, Z., & Wei, Y. (2010). Improving middle school students' science literacy through reading infusion. *Journal of Educational Research, 103*, 262–273.

Fogleman, J., McNeill, K.L., & Krajcik, J. (2011). Examining the effect of teachers' adaptations of a middle school science inquiry-oriented curriculum unit on student learning. *Journal of Research in Science Teaching, 48*(2), 149–169.

Franke, M., Grossman, P., Hatch, T., Richert, A., & Schultz, K. (2006, April). *Using representations of practice in teacher education*. Paper presented at the annual meeting of the American Educational Research Association, San Francisco, CA.

Fulp, S.L. (2002). *2000 national survey of science and mathematics education: Status of elementary school science teaching*. Chapel Hill, NC: Horizon Research.

Furtak, E.M., & Alonzo, A.C. (2010). The role of content in inquiry-based elementary science lessons: An analysis of teacher beliefs and enactment. *Research in Science Education, 40*(3), 425–449.

Gabel, D.L. (1994). *Handbook of research on science teaching and learning*. New York, NY: Macmillan.

Gardner, A., Stuhlsatz, M., & Roth, K.J. (2013, April). *Video analysis of science teaching: Developing a shared "words-to-images" analytical tool*. Paper presented at the annual international meeting of the National Association for Research in Science Teaching, San Juan, Puerto Rico.

Goodrum, D., Hackling, M., & Rennie, L. (2001). *The status and quality of teaching and learning of science in Australian schools*. Department of Education, Training, and Youth Affairs, Commonwealth of Australia, Canberra, Australia.

Granger, E.M., Bevis, T.H., Saka, Y., & Southerland, S.A. (2010, March). *Large scale, randomized cluster design study of the relative effectiveness of reform-based and traditional/verification curricula in supporting student science learning*. Paper presented at the annual meeting of the National Association for Research in Science Teaching, Philadelphia, PA.

Gresalfi, M.S., & Cobb, P. (2006). Cultivating discipline-specific dispositions as a critical goal for pedagogy and equity. *Pedagogies, 1*, 49–57.

Grimberg, B.I., & Gummer, E. (2013). Teaching science from cultural points of intersection. *Journal of Research in Science Teaching, 50*(1), 12–32.

Grossman, P., Compton, C., Igra, D., Ronfeldt, M., Shahan, E., & Williamson, P. (2009). Teaching practice: A cross-professional perspective. *Teachers College Record, 111*(9), 2055–2100.

Grossman, P., Hammerness, K., & McDonald, M. (2009). Redefining teaching, re-imagining teacher education. *Teachers and Teaching: Theory and Practice, 15*(2), 273–289.

Gunckel, K. L. (2011). Mediators of a preservice teacher's use of the inquiry-application instructional model. *Journal of Science Teacher Education, 22*(1), 79–100.

Gunckel, K. L., Mohan, L., Covitt, B. A., & Anderson, C. W. (2012). Addressing challenges in developing learning progressions for environmental science literacy. In A. C. Alonzo & A. W. Gotwals (Eds.), *Learning progressions in science: Current challenges and future directions* (pp. 39–76). Boston, MA: Sense Publishers.

Guthrie, J. T., Anderson, E., Alao, S., & Rinehart, J. (1999). Influences of concept-oriented reading instruction on strategy use and conceptual learning from text. *Elementary School Journal, 99*, 343–366.

Guthrie, J. T., & Cox, K. E. (2001). Classroom conditions for motivation and engagement in reading. *Educational Psychology Review, 13*, 283–302.

Guthrie, J. T., McRae, A., Coddington, C. S., Klauda, S. L., Wigfield, A., & Barbosa, P. (2009). Impacts of comprehensive reading instruction on diverse outcomes of low- and high-achieving readers. *Journal of Learning Disabilities, 42*, 195–214.

Guthrie, J. T., McRae, A., & Klauda, S. (2007). Contributions of concept-oriented reading instruction to knowledge about interventions for motivation in reading. *Educational Psychologist, 43*, 237–250.

Guthrie, J. T., Wigfield, A., Barbosa, P., Perencevich, K. C., Taboada, A., Davis, M. H., et al. (2004). Increasing reading comprehension and engagement through concept-oriented reading instruction. *Journal of Educational Psychology, 96*, 403–423.

Hammer, D., Goldberg, F., & Fargason, S. (2012). Responsive teaching and the beginnings of energy in a third grade classroom. *Review of Science, Mathematics and ICT Education, 6*(1), 51–72.

Hammer, D., Russ, R., Mikeska, J., & Scherr, R. (2008). Identifying inquiry and conceptualizing students' abilities. In R. Duschl & R. Grandy (Eds.), *Teaching scientific inquiry: Recommendations for research and implementation* (pp. 138–156). Rotterdam, the Netherlands: Sense Publishers.

Hand, B. (2008). *Science inquiry, argument, and language: A case for the science writing heuristic.* Rotterdam, the Netherlands: Sense.

Hardy, I., Kloetzer, B., Moeler, K., & Sodian, B. (2010). The analysis of classroom discourse: Elementary school science curricula advancing reasoning with evidence. *Educational Assessment, 15*, 197–221.

Harlen, W. (1997). Primary teachers' understanding in science and its impact in the classroom. *Research in Science Education, 27*, 323–337.

Harris, C. J., Phillips, R. S., & Penuel, W. R. (2012). Examining teachers' instructional moves aimed at developing students' ideas and questions in learner-centered science classrooms. *Journal of Science Teacher Education, 23*, 769–788.

Harris, D., & Williams, J. (2012). The association of classroom interactions, year group and social class. *British Educational Research Journal, 38*(3), 373–397.

Heller, J. I., Daehler, K. R., Wong, N., Shinohara, M., & Miratrix, L. W. (2012). Differential effects of three professional development models on teacher knowledge and student achievement in elementary science. *Journal of Research in Science Teaching, 49*(3), 333–362.

Hennessey, M. G. (2003). Probing the dimensions of metacognition: Implications for conceptual change teaching-learning. In G. M. Sinatra & P. R. Pintrich (Eds.), *Intentional conceptual change* (pp. 105–132). Mahwah, NJ: Lawrence Erlbaum Associates.

Herrenkohl, L. R., & Guerra, M. R. (1998). Participant structures, scientific discourse, and student engagement in fourth grade. *Cognition and Instruction, 16*(4), 433–475.

Hokayem, H., & Schwarz, C. (2013). Engaging fifth graders in scientific modeling to learn about evaporation and condensation. *International Journal of Science and Mathematics Education.* Published online first, January 16, 2013.

Howes, E. V., Lim, M., & Campos, J. (2009). Journeys into inquiry-based elementary science: Literacy practices, questioning, and empirical study. *Science Education 93*(2), 189–217.

Hudicourt-Barnes, J. (2003). The use of argumentation in Haitian Creole science classrooms. *Harvard Educational Review, 73*(1), 73–93.

Johnson, C. C. (2011). The road to culturally relevant science: Exploring how teachers navigate change in pedagogy. *Journal of Research in Science Teaching, 48*(2), 170–198.

Johnson, C. C., Kahle, J. B., & Fargo, J. D. (2007). A study of the effect of sustained, whole-school professional development on student achievement in science. *Journal of Research in Science Teaching, 44*(6), 775–786.

Kazemi, E., Lampert, M., & Ghousseini, H. (2007). *Conceptualizing and using routines of practice in mathematics teaching to advance professional education.* Report to the Spencer Foundation. Chicago, IL: Spencer Foundation.

Kennedy, C. A., & Wilson, M. (2007). *Using progress variables to interpret student achievement and progress.* BEAR Report Series, 2006–12–01. Berkeley, CA: University of California.

Kesidou, S., & Roseman, J. E. (2002). How well do middle school science programs measure up? Findings from Project 2061's curriculum review. *Journal of Research in Science Teaching, 39*(6), 522–549.

Khishfe, R., & Abd-El-Khalick, F. (2002). Influence of explicit and reflective versus implicit inquiry-oriented instruction on sixth graders' view of nature of science. *Journal of Research in Science Teaching, 39*, 551–578.

Kidman, G. (2012). Australia at the crossroads—A review of school science practical work. *EURASIA Journal of Mathematics, Science and Technology Education, 8*(1), 35–47.

Kim, M., Tan, A. L., & Talaue, F. T. (2013). New vision and challenges in inquiry-based curriculum change in Singapore. *International Journal of Science Education, 35*(2), 289–311.

Klug, B., & Whitfield, P. (2003). *Widening the circle: Culturally relevant pedagogy for American Indian children.* New York, NY: Routledge.

Kuhn, D., & Franklin, S. (2006). The second decade: What develops (and how) In W. Damon, R. M. Lerner, D. Kuhn, & R. S. Siegler (Eds.), *Handbook of child psychology, volume 2, cognition, perception, and language* (6th ed., pp. 954–994). Hoboken, NJ: Wiley.

Krajcik, J. S., McNeill, K. L., & Reiser, B. L. (2008). Learning-goals-driven design model: Developing curriculum materials that align with national standards and incorporate project-based pedagogy. *Science Education, 92*(1), 1–32.

Kurth, L. A., Anderson, C. W., & Palincsar, A. S. (2002). The case of Carla: Dilemmas of helping *all* students to understand science. *Science Education, 86*(3), 287–313.

Lakshmanan, A., Heath, B. P., Perlmutter, A., & Elder, M. (2011). The impact of science content and professional learning communities on science teaching efficacy and standards-based instruction. *Journal of Research in Science Teaching, 48*(5), 534–555.

Lampert, M., Beasley, H., Ghousseini, H., Kazemi, E., & Franke, M. (2010). Using designed instructional activities to enable novices to manage ambitious mathematics teaching. In M. K. Stein & L. Kucan (Eds.), *Instructional explanations in the disciplines* (pp. 129–144). New York, NY: Springer Science+Business Media.

Lampert, M., Boerst, T., & Graziani, F. (2011). Organization resources in the service of school-wide ambitious teaching practice. *Teachers College Record, 113*(7), 1361–1400.

Lampert, M., & Graziani, F. (2009). Instructional activities as a tool for teachers' and teacher educators' learning. *Elementary School Journal, 109*(5), 491–509.

Lara-Alecio, R., Tong, F., Irby, B. J., Guerrero, C., Huerta, M., & Fan, Y. (2012). The effect of an instructional intervention on middle school English learners' science and English reading achievement. *Journal of Research in Science Teaching, 49*(8), 987–1011.

LaVan, S.-K. (2006, April). *Culturally-adaptive practices.* Paper presented at the annual meeting of the National Association for Research in Science Teaching, San Francisco, CA.

Lee, O. (2003). Equity for linguistically and culturally diverse students in science education: A research agenda. *Teachers College Record, 105*(3), 465–489.

Lee, O. (2005). Science education with English language learners: Synthesis and research agenda. *Review of Educational Research, 75*(4), 491–530.

Lee, O., Buxton, C., Lewis, S., & LeRoy, K. (2006). Science inquiry and student diversity: Enhanced abilities and continuing difficulties after an instructional intervention. *Journal of Research in Science Teaching, 43*, 607–636.

Lee, O., Deaktor, R., Enders, C., & Lambert, J. (2008). Impact of a multiyear professional development intervention on science achievement of culturally and linguistically diverse elementary students. *Journal of Research in Science Teaching, 45*(6), 726–747.

Lee, O., Luykx, A., Buxton, C., & Shaver, A. (2007). The challenge of altering elementary school teachers' beliefs and practices regarding linguistic and cultural diversity in science education. *Journal of Research in Science Teaching, 44*(9), 1269–1291.

Lee, O., Maerten-Rivera, J., Buxton, C., Penfield, R., & Secada, W. G. (2009). Urban elementary teachers' perspectives on teaching science to English language learners. *Journal of Science Teacher Education, 20*(3), 263–286.

Lee, O., Penfield, R., & Maerten-Rivera, J. (2009). Effects of fidelity of implementation on science achievement gains among English language learners. *Journal of Research in Science Teaching, 46*(7), 836–859.

Lehrer, R., & Schauble, L. (2000). Model-based reasoning in mathematics and science. In R. Glaser (Ed.), *Advances in instructional psychology, Vol. 5* (pp. 101–159). Mahwah, NJ: Erlbaum.

Lehrer, R., & Schauble, L. (Eds.). (2002). *Investigating real data in the classroom: Expanding children's understanding of math and science.* New York, NY: Teachers College Press.

Lehrer, R., & Schauble, L. (2004). Modeling natural variation through distribution. *American Educational Research Journal, 41*(3), 635–680.

Lehrer, R., & Schauble, L. (2005). Developing modeling and argument in elementary grades. In T. Romberg, T. Carpenter, & F. Dremock (Eds.), *Understanding mathematics and science matters* (pp. 29–53). Mahwah, NJ: Erlbaum.

Lehrer, R., & Schauble, L. (2006). Cultivating model-based reasoning in science education. In R. K. Sawyer (Ed.), *Handbook of the learning sciences* (pp. 371–387). New York, NY: Cambridge University Press.

Lehrer, R., & Schauble, L. (2012). Seeding evolutionary thinking by engaging children in modeling its foundations. *Science Education, 96*(94), 701–724.

Lehrer, R., Schauble, L., Strom, D., & Pligge, M. (2001). Similarity of form and substance: Modeling material kind. In D. Klahr and S. Carver (Eds.), *Cognition and instruction: 25 years of progress* (pp. 39–74). Mahwah, NJ: Lawrence Erlbaum Associates.

Lindfors, J. W. (1999). *Children's inquiry: Using language to make sense of the world.* New York, NY: Teachers College Press.

Liu, X., & Lesniak, K. (2006). Progression in children's understanding of the matter concept from elementary to high school. *Journal of Research in Science Teaching, 43*(3), 320–347.

Loucas, T. L., Zacharia, Z. C., & Constantinou, C. P. (2011). In quest of productive modeling-based learning discourse in elementary school science. *Journal of Research in Science Teaching, 48*(8), 919–951.

Lumpe, A., Czerniak, C., Haney, J., & Beltyukova, S. (2012). Beliefs about teaching science: The relationship between elementary teachers' participation in professional development and student achievement. *International Journal of Science Education, 34*(2), 153–166.

McNeill, K. L. (2011). Elementary students' views of explanation, argumentation, and evidence, and their abilities to construct arguments over the school year. *Journal of Research in Science Teaching, 48*(7), 793–823.

McNeill, K. L., & Krajcik, J. (2007). Middle school students' use of appropriate and inappropriate evidence in writing scientific explanations. In M. Lovett & P. Shah (Eds.), *Thinking with data* (pp. 233–265). New York, NY: Taylor & Francis.

McNeill, K. L., & Krajcik, J. (2008). Scientific explanations: Characterizing and evaluating the effects of teachers' instructional practices on student learning. *Journal of Research in Science Teaching, 45*(1), 53–78.

McNeill, K. L., Lizotte, D. J., Krajcik, J., & Marx, R. W. (2006). Supporting students' construction of scientific explanations by fading scaffolds in instructional materials. *Journal of the Learning Sciences, 15*(2), 153–191.

Mercer, N., Dawes, L., Wegerif, R., & Sams, C. (2004). Reasoning as a scientist: Ways of helping children to use language to learn science. *British Education Research Journal, 30*, 359–377.

Mercer, N., Wegerif, R., & Dawes, L. (1999). Children's talk and the development of reasoning in the classroom. *British Educational Research Journal, 25*(1), 95–111.

Metz, K. E. (2002a). *Children doing science: Investigation of animal behavior.* Unpublished science curriculum module for grades 1–3. University of California, Berkeley.

Metz, K. E. (2002b). *Children doing science: Investigation of plants.* Unpublished science curriculum module for grades 1–3. University of California, Berkeley.

Metz, K. E. (2004). Children's understanding of scientific inquiry: Their conceptualization of uncertainty in investigations of their own design. *Cognition and Instruction, 22*(2), 219–290.

Metz, K. E. (2011). Disentangling robust developmental constraints from the instructionally mutable: Young children's reasoning about a study of their own design. *Journal of the Learning Sciences, 20*, 50–110.

Michaels, S., & O'Connor, C. (2012). *Talk science primer.* Cambridge, MA: TERC.

Michaels, S., O'Connor, C., Hall, M., with Resnick, L. B. (2002). *Accountable Talk: Classroom conversation that works.* (CD-ROM set). Pittsburgh, PA: University of Pittsburgh.

Michaels, S., O'Connor, C., & Resnick, L. (2008). Reasoned participation: Accountable Talk® in the classroom and in civic life. *Studies in Philosophy and Education, 27*(4), 283–297.

Michaels, S., Shouse, A. W., & Schweingruber, H. A. (2008). *Ready, set, science! Putting research to work in K–8 science classrooms.* Washington, DC: National Academies Press.

Michaels, S., Sohmer, R. E., & O'Connor, M. C. (2004). Classroom discourse. In H. Ammon, N. Dittmar, K. Mattheier, & P. Trudgill (Eds.), *Sociolinguistics: An international handbook of the science of language and society* (2nd ed., pp. 2351–2366). New York, NY: Walter de Gruyter.

Ministry of Education. (1999). *Curriculum outline for "nature science and living technology."* Taipei, Taiwan: Ministry of Education. (In Taiwanese).

Mohan, L., Chen, J., & Anderson, C. W. (2009). Developing a multi-year learning progression for carbon cycling in socio-ecological systems. *Journal of Research in Science Teaching, 46*(6), 675–689.

Moll, L. C., Amanti, C., Neff, D., & Gonzalez, N. (1992). Funds of knowledge for teaching. *Theory Into Practice, 31*, 132–141.

Moore, F. M. (2008). Agency, identity and social justice education: Preservice teachers' thoughts on becoming agents of change in urban elementary science classrooms. *Research in Science Education, 38*(5), 589–610.

Morrison, K. A., Robbins, H. H., & Rose, D. G. (2008). Operationalizing culturally relevant pedagogy: A synthesis of classroom-based research. *Equity and Excellence in Education, 41*(4), 433–452.

National Center for Educational Research and Development. (1997). *Public educational curricula and goals.* Beirut, Lebanon: Author. (In Lebanese.)

National Curriculum Board. (2009). *Shape of the Australian Curriculum: Science.* Retrieved from www.acara.edu.au/verve/_resources/Australian_Curriculum_-_Science.pdf

National Research Council. (2012). *A framework for K–12 science education: Practices, crosscutting concepts, and core ideas.* Washington, DC: National Academies Press.

National Science Teachers Association. (2000). *NSTA position statement: The nature of science.* Retrieved from http://www.nsta.org/about/positions/natureofscience.aspx

Neumann, K., Viering, T., Boone, W. J., & Fischer, H. J. E. (2013). Towards a learning progression of energy. *Journal of Research in Science Teaching, 50*(2), 162–188.

Newton, P., Driver, R., & Osborne, J. (1999). The place of argumentation in the pedagogy of school science. *International Journal of Science Education, 21*(5), 553–576.

Next Generation Science Standards. (2013). www.nextgenscience.org/

Osborne, J., & Dillon, J. (2008). *Science education in Europe: Critical reflections.* A report to the Nuffield Foundation. London, England: Kings College.

Palincsar, A. S., & Magnusson, S. J. (2001). The interplay of first-hand and second-hand (text-based) investigations to model and support the development of scientific knowledge and reasoning. In S. M. Carver & D. Klahr (Eds.), *Cognition and instruction: Twenty-five years of progress* (pp. 151–187). Mahwah, NJ: Erlbaum.

Pappas, C. C., Keifer, B. Z., & Levstik, L. S. (2006). *An integrated language perspective in the elementary school: An action approach.* Boston, MA: Pearson Education.

Pine, J., Aschbacher, P., Roth, E., Jones, M., McPhee, C., Martin, C., Phelps, S., Kyle, T., & Foley, B. (2006). Fifth graders' science inquiry abilities: A comparative study of students in hands-on and textbook curricula. *Journal of Research in Science Teaching, 43*(5), 467–484.

Plummer, J. D. (2009). Early elementary students' development of astronomy concepts in the planetarium. *Journal of Research in Science Teaching, 46*(2), 192–209.

Plummer, J. D., & Krajcik, J. (2010). Building a learning progression for celestial motion: Elementary levels from an earth-based perspective. *Journal of Research in Science Teaching, 47*(7), 768–787.

Pottenger, F., & Young, D. (1992). *FAST 1: The local environment.* Manoa, HI: Curriculum Research and Development Group, University of Hawaii.

Radinsky, J., Oliva, S., & Alamar, K. (2010). Camila, the earth, and the sun: Constructing an idea as shared intellectual property. *Journal of Research in Science Teaching, 47*(6), 619–642.

Raghavan, K., Sartoris, M., & Glaser, R. (1998). Why does it go up? The impact of the MARS curriculum as revealed through changes in student explanations of a helium balloon. *Journal of Research in Science Teaching, 35*(5), 547–567.

Reinsvold, L. A., & Cochran, K. R. (2012). Power dynamics and questioning in elementary science classrooms. *Journal of Science Teacher Education, 23,* 745–768.

Reveles, J. M., Cordova, R., & Kelly, G. J. (2004). Science literacy and academic identity formulation. *Journal of Research in Science Teaching, 41*(10), 1111–1144.

Romance, N., & Vitale, M. (1992). A curriculum strategy that expands time for in-depth elementary science instruction by using science-based reading strategies: Effects of a year-long study in Grade four. *Journal of Research in Science Teaching, 29*(6), 545–554.

Romance, N., & Vitale, M. (2001). Implementing an in-depth expanded science model in elementary schools: Multi-year findings, research issues, and policy implications. *International Journal of Science Education, 23,* 272–304.

Romance, N., & Vitale, M. (2011, March). *An interdisciplinary model for accelerating student achievement in science and reading comprehension across grades 3–8: Implications for research and practice.* Paper presented at the annual meeting of the Society for Research in Educational Effectiveness, Washington, DC.

Romance, N. R., & Vitale, M. R. (2012). Expanding the role of K–5 science instruction in educational reform: Implications of an interdisciplinary model for integrating science and reading. *School Science and Mathematics, 112*(8), 506–515.

Rosebery, A. S., Ogonowski, M., DiSchino, M., & Warren, B. (2010). "The coat traps all your body heat": Heterogeneity as fundamental to learning. *Journal of the Learning Sciences, 19*(3), 322–357.

Roth, K. (1984). Using classroom observations to improve science teaching and curriculum materials. In C. W. Anderson (Ed.), *Observing science classrooms: Perspective from research and practice* (pp. 77–102). Columbus, OH: ERIC.

Roth, K. J. (2002). Talking to understand science. In J. Brophy (Ed.), *Social constructivist teaching: Affordances and constraints. Advances in research on teaching* (vol. 9, pp. 197–262). New York, NY: JAI Press.

Roth, K. J., Druker, S. D., Garnier, H. E., Lemmens, M., Chen, C., Kawanaka, T., Rasmussen, D., Trubacova, S., Warvi, D., Okamoto, Y., Gonzales, P., Stigler, J., & Gallimore, R. (2006). *Teaching science in five countries: Results from the TIMSS 1999 video study* (NCES 2006–011). Washington, DC: National Center for Education Statistics. Retrieved from http://nces.ed.gov/timss

Roth, K. J., & Garnier, H. (2007). How five countries teach science. *Educational Leadership, 64*(4), 16–23.

Roth, K. J., Garnier, H., Chen, C., Lemmens, M., Schwille, K., & Wickler, N. I. Z. (2011). Videobased lesson analysis: Effective science PD for teacher and student learning. *Journal of Research in Science Teaching, 48*(2), 117–148.

Roth, K. J., Peasley, K., & Hazelwood, C. (1992). *Integration from the student perspective: Constructing meaning in science.* Elementary subjects series No. 63. East Lansing, MI: Center for Learning and Teaching for Elementary Subjects.

Roth, K. J., Taylor, J., Wilson, C., & Landes, N. M. (2013, April). *Scale-up study of a videocase-based lesson analysis PD program: Teacher and student science content learning.* Proceedings CD of the annual conference of the National Association for Research in Science Teaching, Rio Grande, Puerto Rico.

Ruiz-Primo, M. A., & Furtak, E. M. (2007). Exploring teachers' informal formative assessment practices and students' understanding in the context of scientific inquiry. *Journal of Research in Science Teaching, 44*(1), 57–84.

Santau, A. O., Secada, W., Maerten-Rivera, J., Cone, N., & Lee, O. (2010). US urban elementary teachers' knowledge and practices in teaching science to English language learners: Results from the first year of a professional development intervention. *International Journal of Science Education, 32*(15), 2007–2032.

Schroeder, C. M., Scott, T. P., Tolson, H., Huang, T.-Y., & Lee, Y.-H. (2007). A meta-analysis of national research: Effects of teaching strategies on student achievement in science in the United States. *Journal of Research in Science Teaching, 44*(10), 1436–1460.

Schwarz, C. (2009). Developing preservice elementary teachers' knowledge and practices through modeling centered scientific inquiry. *Science Education, 93*(4), 720–744.

Schwarz, C. V., Reiser, B. J., Acher, A., Kenyon, L., & Fortus, D. (2012). MoDeLS: Challenges in defining a learning progression for scientific modeling. In A. Alonzo & A. W. Gotwals (Eds.), *Learning progressions in science: Current challenges and future directions* (pp. 101–138). Rotterdam, the Netherlands: Sense Publishers.

Schwarz, C. V., Reiser, B. J., Davis, E. A., Kenyon, L., Acher, A., Fortus, D., Shwartz, Y. H., Hug, B., & Krajcik, J. (2009). Developing a learning progression for scientific modeling: Making scientific modeling accessible and meaningful for learners. *Journal of Research in Science Teaching, 46*(2), 141–165.

Shepardson, D. P., & Britsch, S. J. (2006). Zones of interaction: Differential access to elementary science discourse. *Journal of Research in Science Teaching, 43*(5), 443–466.

Shymansky, J. A., Yore, L. D., & Anderson, J. O. (2004). Impact of a school district's science reform effort on the achievement and attitudes of third- and fourth-grade students. *Journal of Research in Science Teaching, 41*(8), 771–790.

Simosi, M. (2003). Using Toulmin's *Framework* for the analysis of everyday argumentation: Some methodological considerations. *Argumentation, 17,* 185–202.

Sismondo, S. (2004). *An introduction to science and technology studies.* Malden, MA: Blackwell.

Sleep, L., Boerst, T., & Ball, D. (2007). *Learning to do the work of teaching in a practice-based methods course.* Atlanta, GA: NCTM Research Pre-Session.

Smith, C., Maclin, D., Houghton, C., & Hennessey, M. G. (2000). Sixth-grade students' epistemologies of science: The impact of school science experiences on epistemological development. *Cognition and Instruction, 18*(3), 349–422.

Smith, C. L., Wiser, M., Anderson, C. W., & Krajcik, J. (2006). Implications of research on children's learning for standards and assessment: A proposed learning progression for matter and the atomic molecular theory. *Measurement: Interdisciplinary Research and Perspectives, 14*(1&2), 1–98.

Smith, C.L., Wiser, M., & Carraher, D.W. (2010). *Using a comparative, longitudinal study with upper elementary school students to test some assumptions of a learning progression for matter*. Paper presented at the annual conference of the National Association for Research in Science Teaching, Philadelphia, PA.

Smith, D., & Neale, D.C. (1989). The construction of subject matter knowledge in primary science teaching. *Teaching and Teacher Education, 5,* 1–20.

Smith, D., & Neale, D.C. (1991). The construction of subject matter knowledge in primary science teaching. *Advances in Research on Teaching, 2,* 187–243.

Smith, D.C. (1999). Changing our teaching: The role of pedagogical content knowledge in elementary science. In N. Lederman & J. Guess-Newsome (Eds.), *Examining pedagogical content knowledge* (pp. 163–198). Dordrecht, the Netherlands: Kluwer.

Smith, L.K., & Southerland, S.A. (2007). Reforming practice or modifying reforms? Elementary teachers' response to the tools of reform. *Journal of Research in Science Teaching, 44*(3), 396–423.

Songer, N.B., & Gotwals, A.W. (2012). Guiding explanation construction by children at the entry points of learning progressions. *Journal of Research in Science Teaching, 49*(2), 141–165.

Songer, N.B., Kelcey, B., & Gotwals, A.W. (2009). How and when does complex reasoning occur? Empirically driven development of a learning progression focused on complex reasoning about biodiversity. *Journal of Research in Science Teaching, 46*(6), 610–631.

Songer, N.B., Shah, A.M., & Fick, S. (2013). Characterizing teachers' verbal scaffolds to guide elementary students' creation of scientific explanations. *School Science and Mathematics, 113*(7), 321–332.

Stern, L., & Roseman, J.E. (2004). Can middle-school science textbooks help students learn important ideas? Findings from Project 2061's curriculum evaluation study: Life science. *Journal of Research in Science Teaching, 41*(6), 538–568.

Stevens, S.Y., Delgado, C., & Krajcik, J.S. (2009). Developing a hypothetical multi-dimensional learning progression for the nature of matter. *Journal of Research in Science Teaching, 47*(6), 687–715.

Stoddart, T., Connell, M., Stofflett, R., & Peck, D. (1993). Reconstructing elementary teacher candidates' understanding of mathematics and science content. *Teaching and Teacher Education, 9,* 229–241.

Stoddart, T., Pinal, A., Latzke, M., & Canaday, D. (2002). Integrating inquiry science and language development for English language learners. *Journal of Research in Science Teaching, 39*(8), 664–687.

Tan, E., & Barton, A.C. (2008a). From peripheral to central, the story of Melanie's metamorphosis in an urban middle school science class. *Science Education, 92*(4), 567–590.

Tan, E., & Barton, A.C. (2008b). Unpacking science for all through the lens of identities-in-practice: The stories of Amelia and Ginny. *Cultural Studies of Science Education, 3,* 43–71.

Tao, Y., Oliver, M., & Venville, G. (2013). A comparison of approaches to the teaching and learning of science in Chinese and Australian elementary classrooms: Cultural and socioeconomic complexities. *Journal of Research in Science Teaching, 50*(1), 33–61.

Thompson, J., Windschitl, M., & Braaten, M. (2013). Developing a theory of ambitious early-career teacher practice. *American Educational Research Journal, 50*(3), 574–615.

Toulmin, S. (1958). *The uses of argument*. Cambridge, UK: Cambridge University Press.

Tsurusaki, B.K., Barton, A.C., Tan, E., Koch, P., & Contento, I. (2013). Using transformative boundary objects to create critical engagement in science: A case study. *Science Education, 97*(1), 1–31.

Upadhyay, B.R. (2006). Using students' lived experiences in an urban science classroom: An elementary school teacher's thinking. *Science Education, 90,* 94–110.

U.S. Department of Education. (2011). *Science 2009: National assessment of educational progress at grades 4, 8, and 12*. Washington, DC: Institute of Education Sciences, National Center for Education Statistics.

van Es, E.A., & Sherin, M.G. (2002). Learning to notice: Scaffolding new teachers' interpretations of classroom interactions. *Journal of Technology and Teacher Education, 10*(4), 571–596.

Varelas, M., Kane, J.M., & Wylie, C.D. (2012). Young black children and science: Chronotopes of narratives around their science journals. *Journal of Research in Science Teaching, 49*(5), 568–596.

Varelas, M., & Pappas, C.C. (2006). Intertextuality in read-alouds of integrated science-literacy units in primary classrooms: Opportunities for the development of thought and language. *Cognition and Instruction, 24,* 211–259.

Varelas, M., Pappas, C.C., Kane, J.M., Arsenault, A., Hankes, J., & Cowan, B.M. (2008). Urban primary-grade children think and talk science: Curricular and instructional practices that nurture participation and argumentation. *Science Education, 92*(1), 65–95.

Varelas, M., Pappas, C.C., & Rife, A. (2006). Exploring the role of intertextuality in concept construction: Urban second-graders make sense of evaporation, boiling, and condensation. *Journal of Research in Science Teaching, 43,* 637–666.

Varelas, M., Pappas, C.C., Tucker-Raymond, E., Kane, J., Hankes, J., Ortiz, I., Keblawe-Shamah, N. (2010). Drama activities as ideational resources for primary-grade children in urban science classrooms. *Journal of Research in Science Teaching, 47*(3), 302–325.

Warren, B., Ballenger, C., Ogonowski, M., Rosebery, A.S., & Hudicourt-Barnes, J. (2001). Rethinking diversity in learning science: The logic of everyday sense-making. *Journal of Research in Science Teaching, 38*(5), 529–552.

Weiss, I.R., Pasley, J.D., Smith, P.S., Banilower, E.R., & Heck, D.J. (2003). *Looking inside the classroom: A study of K–12 mathematics and science education in the United States*. Chapel Hill, NC: Horizon Research, Inc.

White, B. (1993). Thinkertools: Causal models, conceptual change, and science instruction. *Cognition and Instruction, 10,* 1–100.

Windschitl, M., & Calabrese Barton, A. (in press). Rigor and equity by design: Locating a set of core practices for the science education community. *Handbook of research on teaching*. American Educational Research Association.

Windschitl, M., Thompson, J., & Braaten, M. (2008). Beyond the scientific method: Model-based inquiry as a new paradigm of preference for school science investigations. *Science Education, 92*(5), 941–967.

Windschitl, M., Thompson, J., & Braaten, M. (2011). Ambitious pedagogy by novice teachers? Who benefits from tool-supported collaborative inquiry into practice and why. *Teachers College Record, 113*(7), 1311–1318.

Windschitl, M., Thompson, J., Braaten, M., & Stroupe, D. (2012). Proposing a core set of instructional practices and tools for teachers of science. *Science Education, 96,* 878–903.

Wiser, M., Smith, C., & Doubler, S. (2012). Learning progressions as tool for curriculum development: Lessons from the Inquiry Project. In A. Alonzo & A. Gotwals (Eds.), *Learning progressions in science: Current challenges and future directions* (pp. 359–404). Rotterdam, the Netherlands: Sense Publishers.

Yacoubian, H.A., & BouJaoude, S. (2010). The effect of reflective discussions following inquiry-based laboratory activities on students' views of nature of science. *Journal of Research in Science Teaching, 47*(10), 1229–1252.

Yore, L., Bisanz, G.L., & Hand, B. (2003). Examining the literacy component of science literacy: 25 years of language arts and science research. *International Journal of Science Education, 25*(6), 689–725.

Zembal-Saul, C. (2009). Learning to teach elementary school science as argument. *Science Education, 93*(4), 687–719.

20

Interdisciplinary Science Teaching

Charlene M. Czerniak and Carla C. Johnson

Although the topic of curriculum integration has been around for more than 100 years, it has gained considerable momentum recently with the emergence of STEM (science, technology, engineering, and mathematics) education initiatives in the United States and new standards in science, mathematics, and reading (e.g., Common Core State Standards Initiative, 2012; Standards for Mathematical Practice and *Framework for K–12 Science Education* [National Research Council, 2012]). Integration is a pivotal component in the Framework for K–12 Science Education, which includes scientific and engineering practices, crosscutting concepts, and disciplinary core ideas. The science and engineering practices clearly encourage integration of science with engineering, technology, and literacy (e.g., discourse, reading, and writing). Within the dimensions of the framework are integration of mathematical skills, technological literacies, and the role of society in the realm of science.

Similarly, other key reform efforts in the United States including the Common Core State Standards Initiative (2012), college and career readiness (Achieve, 2013), and Partnership for 21st Century Skills (n.d.) have argued that an interdisciplinary approach to K–12 education is needed. Thus, the observed movement toward integration is more grounded in policy than ever before.

Arguably, the common method of schooling is organized in an artificial manner, as disciplinary content is taught in isolation as academic coursework in K–12 schools. The real world, in contrast, is integrated by nature, and an interdisciplinary approach provides authentic contexts for learning (e.g., Petrie, 1992; Ronis, 2007; Roth, 1993). Thus, an interdisciplinary approach should make learning more relevant.

Support is growing for integration of content areas, as interdisciplinary approaches enable students to gain critical thinking and problem-solving skills, as well as to develop a general core of knowledge necessary for success in the future (Carnegie Council on Adolescent Development, 1989; Partnership for 21st Century Skills, n.d.). Curriculum integration advocates speak of the numerous advantages of integration in helping students form deeper understandings, see big-picture concepts, make curriculum relevant to students, build connections among central concepts, and become interested and motivated in school (Berlin, 1994; Berlin & White, 2012; George, 1996; Mason, 1996; Morrison & McDuffie, 2009; Venville, Rennie, & Wallace, 2004). Additionally, with the rapid growth of technological tools that can be utilized in the classroom, there is increased desire internationally to integrate technology within science education (Harrison, 2011; Jimoyiannis, 2010; Johnson & Saylor, 2013).

Advocates of curriculum integration also assert that integration is anchored in psychology and human development. In defining constructivism, Brooks and Brooks (1993) said that deep understanding is formed when students make connections between prior knowledge and new experiences. Meaningful learning occurs when they see relationships among ideas. Cohen (1995), who used the term *thematic teaching*, said that it is supported by brain research, and Beane (1996) said that people process information through patterns and connections rather than through fragmented snippets.

With the recent focus on various forms of STEM education internationally (e.g., Breiner, Harkness, Johnson, & Koehler, 2012; Williams, 2011), the literature on integrated approaches is growing. However, educators attempting to implement an integrated curriculum, both in the United States and abroad, continue to encounter barriers to enactment (e.g., Lebeaume, 2011; Venville, Wallace, Rennie, & Malone, 2002). In this chapter, a brief history of interdisciplinary science teaching is presented with a focus on the emergence of integration in new standards and STEM education initiatives. Some topics of discussion in this context include defining integration and STEM education, the role of integration in school curriculum, advantages and disadvantages associated with integration, and potential challenges to implementing an integrated curriculum. These topics are critical to the understanding and implementation of integration and also present areas for future research that can help elucidate the value of integrated approaches.

The Debate: Disciplinary or Interdisciplinary?

Justification can be found in the literature to support both teaching science as a standalone subject and integrating science with other disciplines. Academic scholars have traditionally structured knowledge within the major disciplines recognizable today (science, mathematics, social sciences, and language arts). Some academics believe that academic disciplines are a powerful way to organize knowledge. For instance, Gardner and Boix-Mansilla (1994) said that academic disciplines "constitute the most sophisticated ways yet developed for thinking about and investigating issues that have long fascinated and perplexed thoughtful individuals. . . . [and] they become, when used relevantly, our keenest lenses on the world" (pp. 16–17).

In contrast, others (e.g., Perkins, 1991) considered academic disciplines "artificial partitions with historical roots of limited contemporary significance." Mason (1996) described present-day school curriculum as moribund—a retrogradation to the factory system in which students proceed down a hallway to the next class. Mason pointed out that, while our factories today have changed, our schools remain out of sync with society and real life, where knowledge and skills are not separated.

Recently, the impetus for integration of the science curriculum with other disciplines has been the observed decline of critical thinking and problem-solving skills, as well as other 21st-century skills necessary to compete in the workforce of the future. As Mason (1996) discussed, many school systems are not preparing students to be successful. Many national reports have also called for transforming the curriculum at the school level to be more integrated, including the Carnegie Foundation's (2009) report, *Opportunity Equation*, which recommended focus on "new designs for schools and systems to deliver mathematics and science learning more effectively."

Several arguments have been presented to support the need for integration, including the need for creating authentic contexts for learning to engage more learners and improve student performance in secondary school (Hargreaves, Earl, Moore, & Manning, 2001). Further, McBride and Silverman (1991) summarized literature on integration of science and mathematics dating to the early 1900s and concluded with four primary reasons for integrating the subjects:

1. Science and mathematics are closely related systems of thought and are naturally correlated in the physical world.
2. Science can provide students with concrete examples of abstract mathematical ideas that can improve learning of mathematics concepts.
3. Mathematics can enable students to achieve deeper understanding of science concepts by providing ways to quantify and explain science relationships.
4. Science activities illustrating mathematics concepts can provide relevancy and motivation for learning mathematics. (pp. 286–287)

Rennie, Venville, and Wallace (2012a) proposed four generalizations regarding the nature and purpose of integration found in STEM curricula. First, there are a variety of forms of integration. Second, integration requires a significant investment of effort to move away from the traditional, discipline-centric approach of school curriculum. Third, integration focuses on real-world concepts tied to personal interests and experiences of students. Last, the greater the emphasis on integration, the more student centered the learning environment. Given these generalizations, it is clear that considerable change in traditional learning environments is necessary to successfully implement an integrated approach.

Historical Context

Although disciplinary knowledge has been developed for centuries and shapes the basis for exploring a particular area of knowledge, integration of subject areas has been discussed for more than a hundred years. Berlin (1994) noted that since the early 1900s, the School Science and Mathematics Association has published numerous articles on the topic. In 1903, as Moore was retiring as president of the American Mathematical Society, he provided momentum to the reform efforts of that time by devoting part of his presidential address to mathematics in secondary education. He called for "the unification of pure and applied mathematics" and "the correlation of the different subjects," (in Moore, 1967). Beane (1996) summarized several historical references to integration during the Progressive Era in U.S. education, in Kilpatrick's work in the 1920s, Hopkins's efforts in 1937, and writings of John Dewey in the 1930s. A 1927 third-grade integrated unit on the study of boats on the Hudson River in New York is outlined in Cremin's (1964) book. The word *integration* first appeared in Education Index in 1936 (Beane, 1996).

Hurley (1999) summarized several additional periods in U.S. history in which integration was used: the core curriculum in the 1940s and 1950s, the curriculum improvement projects in the 1960s and 1970s, the science-technology-society (STS) movement in the 1980s and 1990s, the middle school movement, and, most recently, the national standards established by various professional organizations.

For science education, the curriculum improvement projects of the post–*Sputnik* era were a particularly important period in history during which curriculum integration took a foothold. Numerous curriculum projects were developed with the intent to integrate science and mathematics (Lehman, 1994). Examples of projects (and contemporary offshoots) designed to integrate the curriculum include the Minnesota Mathematics and Science Project (1970), Unified Science and Mathematics for Elementary Schools Project (1973), Nuffield Foundation Science Teaching Project (1967), Lawrence Hall of Science's (1984) Great Explorations in Math and Science Project (GEMS), Fresno Pacific College's Activities That Integrate Mathematics and Science (AIMS Educational Foundation, 1986, 1987), and the University of Chicago's Teaching Integrated Mathematics and Science Project (TIMS; Institute for Mathematics and Science Education, 1995).

Middle School and Early Childhood Education Movements

Curriculum integration is a cornerstone of efforts aimed at creating schools focused on the developmental needs of students. The National Association for the Education of Young Children (NAEYC, 1987) and the Association for Middle Level Education, formerly known as the National Middle School Association (NMSA), organizations specializing in instructional practices appropriate for the education of young children and young and early adolescents, respectively, publish numerous materials to guide teachers in the selection and use of materials for young children and adolescents. Curriculum integration is stressed in various NAEYC reports (Copple & Bradekamp, 2009), and the NMSA book titled *A Middle School Curriculum: From Rhetoric to Reality* (Beane, 1993, 1997) argued for integration around personal and social concerns that interest adolescents and young adults. *This We Believe* (National Middle School Association, 2010) argued for developmentally responsive middle schools in which curriculum is challenging, integrative, and exploratory. Numerous NMSA resources have supported curriculum integration (Beane, 1997; Brazee & Capelluti, 1995; Erb, 2001; Nesin & Lounsbury, 1999; Smith, 2001; Stevenson & Carr, 1993), and the *Middle School Journal* has devoted considerable space to articles on curriculum integration (e.g., see the January 2009 issue).

Integration in the Context of Standards

For more than a decade, almost all national reform efforts have emphasized connections among subject areas (National Council for the Social Studies [NCSS], 2010; National Council of Teachers of English, 1996; National Council of Teachers of Mathematics [NCTM], 2000; National Research Council [NRC], 2012; National Science Teachers Association [NSTA], 1996; Rutherford & Ahlgren, 1990). Drake and Burns (2004) argued that integrated curriculum helped teachers cover standards. But, for many reasons, including the fact that individual states across the United States each develop and implement their own academic standards, integration has failed to be included in any coordinated manner. This is expected to change with the adoption of the Common Core Standards in Mathematics (CCSM) and English Language Arts (CCSE), which were rolled out in 2011. For example, the

CCSE included "an integrated model of literacy" with focus on content area literacy for college and career readiness (p. 4). Additionally, the CCSM recommended acquisition of many practices also included in science, such as problem solving, argumentation, reasoning, and modeling. Heitin (2013) notes that interdisciplinary thematic units help teachers cover requirements in the Common Core.

The *Framework for K–12 Science Education* (NRC, 2012) is an organizing document for the Next Generation Science Standards (2013). Twenty-six states led the development of these standards, and most states in the United States are expected to adopt the new guide to science education. The Framework presents an even more explicit and intentional integration of science with mathematics and includes engineering as a new context for learning important science, technological, and mathematical skills and content. Science and engineering practices that anchor the Framework include asking questions, defining problems, modeling, planning and conducting investigations, analyzing and interpreting data, using mathematics and computational thinking, constructing explanations and solutions, developing argumentation, and communicating findings. Clearly, these practices require students to use skills from engineering, communication (literacy), and mathematics to engage in science inquiry. Nargund-Joshi and Liu (2013) argue that the Next Generation Science Standards, which include a focus on integrating engineering and science practices, crosscutting concepts, and core disciplinary ideas, provide new opportunities to integrate across the curriculum, and they present a framework for interdisciplinary science inquiry around these standards.

Moreover, the focus on integration in U.S. standards is reflective of growing support both nationally and internationally. Wei (2009) argued that integration beyond science subjects, where other disciplines are included in the teaching of science, is necessary to meet the goal of scientific literacy in China. Curriculum reform in China was driven by needs to increase the relevance of schooling to children's lives and to emphasize an inquiry approach to learning (Wei, 2009).

Integration, or thematic instruction, is often used as a key idea in school reform efforts. The Biological Science Curriculum Study (BSCS) group (1994) identified 10 common reform strands and found that thematic instruction is one of the common elements of reform. For example, Crane (1991) described a restructured high school science curriculum focused on the four themes of change, interactions, energy, and patterns. Similarly, Greene (1991) described a science-centered reform at the elementary school level.

In the early 1990s, the NSTA's (1992) *Scope, Sequence and Coordination* project recommended replacing traditional high school discipline curricula with 4 years of integrated science. In 1996, NSTA published a position statement on interdisciplinary learning in grades preK–4 that represented the thinking of members of a variety of professional organizations (NCTM, NCTE, International

Reading Association [IRA], NSTA, NCSS, Speech Communication Association, and Council for Elementary Science International) that met to develop guidelines for integrating curriculum. This position statement addressed some of the matters raised by Berlin and White (1994), because it focused on ways of learning and knowing, process and thinking skills, content knowledge, attitudes and perceptions, and teaching strategies.

An increased emphasis on integration existed prior to the current standards movement in the United States. *Science for All Americans* (Rutherford & Ahlgren, 1990) stated, "The alliance between science and mathematics has a long history, dating back centuries. Science provides mathematics with interesting problems to investigate, and mathematics provides science with powerful tools to use in analyzing them" (pp. 16–18). The *National Science Education Standards* (NRC, 1996) maintained, "Curricula often will integrate topics from different subject-matter areas—such as life and physical sciences—from different content standards—such as life sciences and science in personal and social perspectives—and from different school subjects—such as science and mathematics, science and language arts, or science and history" (p. 23). Its Science Teaching Standards chapter noted, "Schools must restructure schedules so that teachers can use blocks of time, interdisciplinary strategies and field experiences to give students many opportunities to engage in serious scientific investigation as an integral part of their science learning" (p. 44). The chapter on Science Education Content Standards stated,

> The standard for unifying concepts and processes is presented for grades K–12, because the understanding and abilities associated with major conceptual and procedural schemes need to be developed over an entire education, and the unifying concepts and processes transcend disciplinary boundaries.
>
> (p. 104)

NCTM (2000) said, "School mathematics experiences at all levels should include opportunities to learn about mathematics by working on problems arising in contexts outside of mathematics. These connections can be to other subject areas and disciplines as well as to students' daily lives" (p. 65). The new Common Core State Standards Initiative (2012) has a similar emphasis.

Elementary educators viewed the whole-language movement in the 1990s as a way to integrate across content areas (Willis, 1992). Others advocated the use of language arts strategies to help teachers develop science literacy (Akerson, 2001; Dickinson & Young, 1998). Dickinson and Young (1998) commented that science and language arts goals are complementary, and language arts can provide the tools for science inquiry.

Some educators have claimed that technology serves as a catalyst for integration across the curriculum (Berger, 1994), and more-recent studies suggest that technology has enhanced integration between science and mathematics by

facilitating collaboration, providing real-world contexts for problem solving, removing limits on instructional time, and offering students opportunities to apply knowledge to real problems (Fogarty, 1991; Pang & Good, 2000). Increased use of mobile technologies creates opportunities for teachers to integrate the curriculum around real-world questions (Krajcik & Czerniak, 2014).

Transforming Science Teacher Education

Typically, teacher education programs have not focused on integrated science teaching repertoires. Hurley (2003) said that although there have been appeals for integrated approaches for years, only in the last decade have integrated methods courses been offered at universities. Findings from Hurley's (2003) study of the presence, value, and reasoning behind universities offering integrated science and mathematics methods courses revealed influences such as state and national standards, program reorganization, constructivist reforms, and research on their decision to integrate.

Teacher education programs have adopted integrated approaches to preparing future teachers. Akerson (2001) discussed how educators have implemented integrated curricular ideas into their methods courses at universities in an effort to help teachers meet the state and national standards. Integration is now more prevalent in university courses and even college degrees (e.g., Beane, 1996; Berlin & White, 2012).

Defining Integration and STEM

Despite the plea for integration, many have argued that few empirical research studies support the assertion that integrated approaches are more effective than traditional, discipline-based teaching. A summary of 423 articles from the 1991 Wingspread conference on integration found that 99 were related to theory and research and only 22 were research-based articles (Berlin, 1994). Lederman and Niess (1997) echoed concerns that research at that time was almost nonexistent to support the use of integrated instruction or thematic curriculum. Czerniak, Weber, Sandmann, and Ahern (1999) summarized literature on integration of science and mathematics with other subject areas and concluded that few empirical studies exist even to support the notion that an integrated curriculum is any better than a well-designed traditional curriculum.

At the fundamental level, a common definition of integration does not seem to exist that can be used as a basis for designing, carrying out, and interpreting results of research. Stinson, Harkness, Meyer, and Stallworth (2009) investigated 33 middle school teachers' understandings of integration and found that few had common characterizations of integration.

Earlier, Davison, Miller, and Metheny (1995) had appealed for a definition of integration, stating, "Few educators would argue about the need for an interwoven, cross-disciplinary curriculum, but to many, the nature of the integration in many interdisciplinary projects is not readily apparent. A more pervasive problem is that integration means different things to different educators." (p. 226). A few years earlier, Hurley (2001, 2003) had also concluded after a comprehensive study that an agreed-on definition of integration could not be found.

Despite Davison and colleagues' (1995) request for clarification, this elusiveness is evident in the sheer number of words used to convey integration: interdisciplinary, multidisciplinary, transdisciplinary, thematic, integrated, connected, nested, sequenced, shared, webbed, threaded, immersed, networked, blended, unified, coordinated, and fused. Lederman and Niess's (1997) editorial in *School Science and Mathematics* explained that many educators use the terms *integrated*, *interdisciplinary*, and *thematic* synonymously, which only compounded the confusion and limited the ability to research the topic adequately.

Berlin and White (1992) reported that a group of 60 scientists, mathematicians, science and mathematics educators, teachers, curriculum developers, educational technologists, and psychologists assembled at a conference funded by the National Science Foundation (NSF) were unable, after 3 days of deliberation, to reach a consensus on the definition of integration of science and mathematics. The group proposed an operational definition: "Integration infuses mathematical methods in science and scientific methods into mathematics such that it becomes indistinguishable as to whether it is mathematics or science" (p. 341).

Historical references to integration (Hopkins, 1937, as cited in Beane, 1996) defined integration as problem-centered, integrated knowledge. Beane (1996) used four characteristics to define integration: (a) curriculum that is organized around problems and issues that are of personal and social significance in the real world, (b) use of relevant knowledge in the context of topic without regard for subject lines, (c) knowledge used to study an existing problem rather than for a test or grade-level outcome, and (d) emphasis placed on projects and activities with real application of knowledge and problem solving. He maintained that other forms of integrated curriculum (such as parallel disciplines or multidisciplinary curricula) still focus on separate content areas and, therefore, are not fully integrated.

Drake (1998) compared integration to a continuum, including multidisciplinary, interdisciplinary, and transdisciplinary approaches, with the level of integration scaling from across each format. Fogarty (1991) presented a 10-step continuum ranging from within a discipline to across a discipline. Applebee, Adler, and Flihan (2007) posited integration ranged from correlated, shared, and reconstructed forms. Rennie, Venville, and Wallace (2012b) argued definitions of integration evolved from the focus on school subjects as the starting point to beginning with real-world issues and problems as the driver for integration. In other words, integration is more driven today by social constructs rather than academic disciplines.

To distinguish between *integration* and other terms, Lederman and Niess (1997) defined integration as a blending of science and mathematics to the point that the separate parts are indiscernible. The metaphor of tomato soup was used: The tomatoes cannot be distinguished from the water or other ingredients in the soup. They defined *interdisciplinary* as a blending of science and mathematics in which connections are made between the subjects, but the two subjects remain identifiable. The metaphor used is chicken noodle soup, where you can still distinguish the broth, chicken, and noodles. (Earlier, Jacobs, 1989, had described interdisciplinary as "a knowledge view and curriculum approach that consciously applies methodology and language from more than one discipline to examine a central theme, issue, problem, topic, or experience.") Lederman and Niess (1997) defined *thematic* as a unifying topic used to transcend traditional subject boundaries.

More recently, Rennie and colleagues (2012b) argued a theoretical frame for integrated learning is anchored by three lenses: integrated, discipline-based, and sources-of-knowledge. The integrated lens examines "skills such as a students' ability to transfer ideas from one context to another, the application of understandings to practical contexts, and students' general motivation and perception of the relevance of their school work." The discipline-based lens focuses on traditional disciplinary conceptual knowledge. The sources-of-knowledge lens examines "how students access knowledge in order to make key learning decisions."

For some people, the acronym STEM connotes integration of the four disciplines. In fact, many people think STEM is merely a shorthand way of referring to the individual disciplines represented by the acronym. In the Breiner and colleagues (2012) study of higher education faculty in a large urban research university, more respondents held the second definition (STEM as a collective way to say the individual disciplines) rather than integrated STEM.

STEM education gained renewed interest with recent global policy initiatives. Williams (2011) reviewed the landscape of STEM and presented an argument for proceeding with caution due to the origin of STEM movements coming from primarily noneducational rationales and most often tied to economic prosperity. STEM originally emerged from the policy arena and work by the NSF in the United States, which first used SMET (science, mathematics, engineering, and technology) before choosing STEM as the acronym for the collective curricular areas (Sanders, 2009; Teaching Institute for Excellence, 2010).

Since the term STEM was coined, it has been adopted by stakeholders in education at various levels (Breiner et al., 2012). National programs focused on STEM have been established globally, including in the UK and South Africa. Much like in the United States, they lack coordination but are supported by substantial governmental funding (Williams, 2011). In the United States, the publication of *Rising Above the Gathering Storm* (Committee on Prospering in the Global Economy of the 21st Century, 2007) and use of STEM in the context of college success, economic development, and national security by the White House and other subcommittees has placed it in the spotlight for funding and focus. Despite the attention, many groups have various conceptions of STEM, including those shaped by educational, political and societal, and personal influences (Breiner et al., 2012; Johnson, 2013a). STEM as integration of subjects used to solve real-world problems (e.g., Labov, Reid, & Yamamoto, 2010; Sanders, 2009) is the definition identified by most who are engaged in STEM reform through the New Media Consortium.

Arguably, the lack of common definitions for integration and STEM is a result of the variety of approaches to each that have resulted without coordination and outlets for communication of ideas. Rennie and colleagues (2012b) used the analogy of integration being like "a large umbrella sheltering a multitude of related practices" as a means to represent the variety of forms integration has taken. Thus, due to the broad range of ways integration is implemented, a common definition is nearly impossible. Therefore, it may be necessary to further define forms of integration (e.g., multidisciplinary, interdisciplinary) and begin to create common understandings of each. It is fortuitous that the Next Generation Science Standards (2013) include a focus on integration of engineering and mathematics. This, combined with continued funding of STEM initiatives internationally, will provide the field with multiple opportunities to further define and research the effectiveness of integration.

Integrated Curriculum Design

Educators espousing integration have provided a variety of curriculum design options, ranging from the merging of two academic subjects to the creation of project-based schools (Christensen, Horn, & Johnson, 2011; Venville et al., 2002). Beane (1995) argued that curriculum integration must have social meaning and, therefore, design begins with "problems, issues and concerns posed by life itself" (p. 616). The notion of organizing science and mathematics curriculum around projects as a relevant way to connect science, mathematics, and events outside of the classroom had been a consensus of the NSF–sponsored Wingspread conference (Berlin & White, 1992).

In Australia, Venville, Wallace, Rennie, and Malone (1998) identified technology-based projects, competitions, and local community projects as forms of curriculum integration. Project-based and problem-based learning have emerged as approaches that allow for curriculum integration, because their key features (driving questions, student engagement in investigations, communities of learners collaborating together, use of technology, and creation of artifacts) are congruent with the way scientists do their work in the real world (Krajcik & Czerniak, 2014) and can be implemented in a variety of curricular settings. Rakow and Vasquez (1998) stated, "Project-based integration may be the most authentic form of cross-curricular integration because it involves students in real-world learning experiences. In project-based integration, students investigate

real issues in real contexts." Capraro and Slough (2008) and Basham, Koehler, and Israel (2011) argued that integral to STEM school philosophy is an interdisciplinary STEM curriculum, utilizing problem-based and project-based strategies to deliver instruction. A number of studies in the urban schools in the United States show student achievement gains in a project-based science environment (Geier et al., 2008; Marx et al., 2004; Rivet & Krajcik, 2004; Schneider, Krajcik, Marx, & Soloway, 2002). Additionally, Brears, Tutor, and MacIntyre (2011) researched the use of problem-based learning in New Zealand and found that this integrated teaching approach supported "collaborative inquiry and reflective practice."

Jacobs (1989) is well known for her work on science and mathematics curriculum integration. She presented a continuum of curriculum design options that moves from discipline-based to parallel disciplines, multidisciplinary, and interdisciplinary units or courses, integrated day, and complete program integration. Underhill's (1995) editorial illustrated six perspectives on science and mathematics integration that echoed some of the alternatives presented in Jacobs's (1989) continuum: math and science are disjointed; there is some overlap between science and math; math and science are the same; math is a subset of science; science is a subset of math; and there is major overlap between science and mathematics.

Davison and colleagues (1995) identified five different models of integration: discipline specific (i.e., two or more branches of science, integrating life and chemical science), content specific (combining related objects from several disciplines, combining mathematics with science), process (using skills such as collecting data, analyzing data, and reporting results to examine real-life situations), methodological (i.e., the learning cycle model as a good way to solve problems in science), and thematic (selecting a theme, such as sharks, and teaching academic concepts around the theme). Projects such as AIMS and GEMS are commercial examples of curricula that focus on integrating science and mathematics by using process skills such as observing, classifying, and analyzing (Roebuck & Warden, 1998).

A similar continuum of integration for science and mathematics, ranging from independent mathematics, mathematics focus, balanced mathematics and science, science focus, and independent science was developed by Lonning and DeFranco (1997) and Lonning, DeFranco, and Weinland (1998). They suggested that readers should ask two questions when planning an integrated curriculum: "What are the major mathematics and science concepts being taught in the activity?" and "Are these concepts worthwhile? That is, are they key elements in the curricula and meaningful to students?" (p. 214). Likewise, Huntley (1998) presented a mathematics and science continuum on which both ends of the spectrum represent separate subject area teaching, and the center represents integration of the two subjects. However, Huntley extended the Lonning and DeFranco model by emphasizing that the center point, integration, occurs only when science and mathematics are dealt with in a synergistic fashion. Francis (1996) had previously proposed a connections matrix that integrated mathematics and science standards to integrate the curriculum.

Hurley (2001) conducted a study to determine the types of integration that have historically been used and found five major types of integration: sequenced (science and mathematics are planned and taught one preceding the other); parallel (science and mathematics are planned and taught together); partial (the subjects are taught separately as well as integrated); enhanced (one of the subjects is the major discipline being taught, and the other is added to enhance the other); and total (science and mathematics are taught equally together). She found that no form of integration ever totally dominated in any period of history from the 1940s to 1990s.

STEM integration, in which science, technology, engineering, and mathematics are included in the curriculum within science or across multiple content areas, has grown with the enactment of STEM policy and subsequent funding in the United States (Johnson, 2013a). For example, STEMx is a consortium of 13 states in the United States that are involved in STEM education, including integrated STEM programs and schools. Thus, it is evident that there are implications for integrated curriculum development in these STEM schools.

Empirical Evidence and STEM Integration

Most of the historical literature on curriculum integration up until the last few years could be characterized as "testimonials," "how-tos," or "unit/activity ideas." For example, a thematic approach is used in all K–8 classrooms in which teachers report student excitement and teachers' cooperative spirit (Peters, Schubeck, & Hopkins, 1995). Descriptions abound of integrated methods, units, and processes used with preservice and inservice teachers, undergraduate coursework, and K–12 students (e.g., Deeds, Allen, Callen, & Wood, 2000; Francis & Underhill, 1996; McDonald & Czerniak, 1998; Sandmann, Weber, Czerniak, & Ahern, 1999; Stuessy, 1993).

In the last decade, a greater amount of research-based literature has surfaced focusing on integration. Concerned with the lack of empirical evidence supporting integration of science and mathematics, Hurley (2001) used mixed methodology to review 31 studies with reported outcomes conducted between 1935 and 1997. She used study effect meta-analytic methods to review the quantitative aspects of these studies, and she used grounded theory to analyze the qualitative portions. Hurley's review found quantitative evidence favoring integration and qualitative evidence revealing existence of multiple forms of integration. Most of the published empirical research studies on integration reviewed in her chapter support integration. A number of K–12 studies sustain the notion that integration helps students learn, motivates students, and helps build problem-solving skills. Studies regarding teachers' reactions to integration focus on teacher beliefs and attitudes, subject matter knowledge, and obstacles faced when implementing integrated approaches.

Student Achievement and Affective Gains

Meier, Nicol, and Cobbs (1998) stated, "Without evidence that integration will produce improved student performance in mathematics and science, little change can be expected" (p. 439). This call for research that provides evidence of student performance using integration has been met somewhat in the last few years.

Greene (1991) reported that students' achievement scores significantly improved after a yearlong restructuring to connect science to all subject areas. Seventy-eight percent of students had improved National Assessment of Educational Progress scores in science, exceeding the nationwide figures. Teachers and principals also reported success with educationally disadvantaged students and indicated that real-world integration accelerated the rate of language acquisition for bilingual students. Stevenson and Carr (1993) reported increased student interest and achievement in integrated instruction. A Canadian study of integration in ninth-grade science found impact on student learning (Ross & Hogaboam-Gray, 1998). Similarly, Vars (1991) and Beane (1995) reported that interdisciplinary programs produced higher standardized achievement scores than did separate-subject curriculum. These authors also acknowledged that interdisciplinary curriculum is frequently embedded in other reforms, such as block scheduling and multi-age grouping, and therefore, separating the effects of integration and those of other reform strategies is difficult.

McGehee (2001) described the development of a problem-solving framework for interdisciplinary units used with minority students in a northern Arizona summer academy and found evidence of student success based on artifacts from student projects. Vitale and Romance (2011) found that an integrated approach produced significantly higher achievement on Iowa Tests of Basic Skills in reading and science for children in first and second grades. Romance and Vitale (2012) reported reading and science achievement gains for a program that integrated science and reading. Similarly, Johnson and Fargo (in press) conducted a longitudinal study of the integration of science and literacy with English language learners and found that the integrated approach resulted in significant gains for students on state science assessments. Earlier, Zwick and Miller (1996) had found that American Indian students using an outdoor-based integrated science curriculum outperformed their peers using a traditional curriculum on the California Achievement Test 85 (CAT).

Studies examining student gains when using curriculum improvement projects or commercial integrated curriculum have conveyed positive results. Shann (1977) explored the effect of the Unified Science and Mathematics for Elementary Schools program and noted an increase in students' content knowledge and problem-solving skills, as well as in students' self-worth, socialization ability, and excitement for learning. Goldberg and Wagreich (1989) reported increased academic achievement in the TIMS program. Similarly, Berlin and Hillen's (1994) report increased cognitive, motivational, and attitudinal outcomes for fourth, fifth, and sixth graders using the AIMS program.

More recently, Sondergeld, Milner, Coleman, and Southern (2011) conducted a study of a STEM enrichment program for middle school students from a large, urban school district. Findings revealed that students who participated in the STEM integrated program realized statistically significant growth on state assessments of science and mathematics, compared to comparison students from the same district.

A number of older studies focused on affective gains when using integrated curricula. Friend (1985) reported that students exhibited appreciation of science as a result of an integrated mathematics/science program. McComas (1993) and Bragow, Gragow, and Smith (1995) confirmed that thematic units had a positive impact on student attitudes and interest in school. Barab and Landa (1997) stated that when focused on a problem students believed was worth solving, interdisciplinary units motivated students to learn. Integrated science and reading instruction was also found to impact motivation (Guthrie, Wigfield, & VonSecker, 2000).

In Hurley's (2001) comprehensive study of integrated curriculum, small student achievement effect sizes were found for both science and mathematics in studies from the 1930s to 1950s, and medium effect sizes were found for studies in the 1960s and 1970s (mostly curriculum improvement projects). Small effect sizes were found for studies published in the 1980s and 1990s. Student achievement effects were higher for science than for mathematics in integrated courses, especially when mathematics was used to enhance science or when the two subjects were totally integrated. Student achievement effects were higher for mathematics when mathematics was planned in sequence with science, but the subjects were taught separately—first mathematics and then science. Qualitative analyses found positive evidence for integration, attendance, student enthusiasm, and student engagement.

Hurley's meta-analyses of each type of integration on student achievement revealed differences. Sequential instruction resulted in positive effect sizes for science and mathematics, with mathematics effect sizes being larger. Parallel (but separate) integration had negative effect sizes for both science and mathematics, indicating that students achieved more in traditional instruction. Partially integrated and partially separate integration had small positive effects for science and mathematics. Enhanced instruction had medium positive effect size for science and small effect sizes for mathematics. Total integration of science and mathematics had a large effect size for science and a small effect size for mathematics.

It may be more difficult to flesh out effectiveness of integration on college-age students because of the limited number of integrated programs in universities, but McComas and Wang (1998) summarized a few studies of college-age students that demonstrated greater achievement or interest in science when it was presented as an integrated program rather than a traditional sequence.

Teacher Knowledge and Attitudes

A number of studies have examined teachers' knowledge of and attitudes toward using integrated strategies. Lehman and McDonald (1988) studied the perceptions of preservice teachers toward integrated mathematics and science and found that preservice teachers had a greater familiarity with integration than did practicing teachers, and mathematics teachers were concerned about not covering the curriculum if they used an integrated approach. Studies on integrated teacher education methods courses at the university level can be found at both the preservice and inservice level, but the findings are mixed toward the effectiveness of integration on teacher learning.

Preservice teachers. Morrison and McDuffie (2009) examined the impact of integrated science and mathematics methods coursework, in which assigned projects included both science and mathematics content, as well as common problem-solving and other necessary skills. Findings revealed that the 46 preservice participants gained desired skills and content knowledge, enhanced by the integrated nature of the course. Additionally, participants articulated plans to implement integrated pedagogy in their own classrooms.

Despite a few newer studies focused on learning outcomes in preservice teacher education related to integration, most work in this area has been based on anecdotal examinations rather than outcome measures. For example, Berlin and White (2012) found in a longitudinal study of attitudes and perceptions of preservice teachers in an integrated science and mathematics teacher education program that participants demonstrated significant positive growth in dispositions related to intent to implement an integrated approach to teaching science and mathematics.

Many years earlier, Lonning and DeFranco (1994) and Haigh and Rehfeld (1995) had both reported findings from integrated science and mathematics methods coursework as having positive impacts on attitudes of students who were enthusiastic about the courses. Briscoe and Stout (1996) described the integration of math and science through a problem-centered methods course. Using data from qualitative analyses, the authors described problems preservice teachers had with problem solving, but it is unclear whether or how these problems were different from problems preservice teachers have in separate mathematics and science methods courses. Kotar, Guenter, Metzger, and Overholt (1998) described a teacher education model for curriculum integration that they used at California State University, Chico, but provided no evidence about the effectiveness of the model. Conversely, Stuessy and Naizer (1996) report gains in reflection and problem solving after students completed an integrated mathematics and science methods course.

In a study of a team-taught middle-level mathematics and science methods course, Koirala and Bowman (2003) found that preservice teachers appreciated the emphasis on integration and had better understanding of integration. An absence of integration was sometimes found because some science and mathematics concepts did not lend themselves to integration. As a result, students were frustrated at the tension between subjects. Further, preservice teachers at some middle schools seldom taught in an integrated fashion in their methods field experiences or student teaching, and they tended to lose their appreciation for integration. In contrast, Hart (2002) studied preservice teachers' beliefs and practice after participating in an integrated mathematics/science methods course and found that beliefs and teachers' reported classroom teaching behaviors were consistent with program and reform goals.

Frykholm and Glasson (2005) conducted a study of prospective secondary science and mathematics teachers who participated in an integrated science and mathematics methods course that included focus on connecting the two disciplines. The study revealed tension for participants who were uncomfortable with their level of content knowledge of the additional discipline. However, with additional support in planning curriculum and opportunities to collaborate with each other, participants successfully implemented integrated instruction during their student teaching experiences.

Hurley (2003) studied methods course offerings and found that most universities said their integrated science and mathematics methods courses were summer courses, grant-funded projects, or experimental. Few universities had integrated courses at the time of the study, but several had integrated science and mathematics master's degree programs. Hurley's (2003) study found that universities surveyed reported successes included teachers' gaining science and mathematics concepts and reasoning, positive preservice teacher attitudes and enthusiasm, improvement in higher-order thinking skills in science, improved teacher reflectivity, and success in connecting theory to practice. Failures and challenges included difficulties in communication among teaching partners, reduced higher-order thinking skills in math, teachers' lack of content knowledge to integrate, influence of supervising teachers in field experiences, mathematics attitudes transferring to science, concern about coverage of curriculum, and challenges with enacting reforms.

Inservice teachers. Few studies on inservice teacher education have focused on teacher knowledge or pedagogical skill. More commonly, studies have reported teacher beliefs and attitudes. Again, findings are mixed regarding the effectiveness of integrated strategies.

In one of the few studies on teacher knowledge and instructional skill, Basista, Tomlin, Pennington, and Pugh

(2001) evaluated an integrated professional development program and found significant gains in understanding of content and confidence to implement integrated science and mathematics in their teaching. Similarly, Basista and Mathews (2002) discovered that a professional development program for middle-grades science and mathematics teachers (intensive summer institute, academic year support, and administrator workshops) increased teachers' content and integration knowledge, increased pedagogical knowledge and implementation, increased administrator awareness of science and mathematics standards, and helped support teachers as they implemented practices during the school year. Teachers in a collaborative professional development project that integrated science with mathematics using language arts and technology displayed increased levels of competence and confidence in using technology to teach science and mathematics (Cleland, Wetzel, Zambo, Buss, & Rillero, 1999).

Marbach-Ad and McGinnis (2008) conducted a study of elementary and middle school teachers who had participated in a preservice teacher education program focused on integration of science and mathematics. The study consisted of a follow-up survey 1 to 2 years following graduation. Findings revealed that nearly all of the responding teachers (90% in Round 1, 96% in Round 2) indicated that their pedagogy included making connections to mathematics in their science instruction.

Differential effects were found on students depending on how the teacher implemented integrated curriculum and instruction. Waldrip (2001) found that primary teachers perceived that they implemented integration in their classrooms, but the actual level of implementation influenced the students' learning. Use of a science theme without strong connections to language and mathematics was less effective, whereas strong connections to other subject areas helped students attain a deeper level of understanding.

To a greater extent, the research on inservice teachers has focused on their beliefs, attitudes, and perceived barriers of integration. Watanabe and Huntley (1998) reported that mathematics and science educators in an NSF–funded project had many of the same beliefs about integration as did other classroom teachers. The middle-level mathematics and science teachers thought that connecting mathematics and science helps students with tangible examples of mathematics, that math helps students become familiar with science relationships, and that connections provide relevancy and incentive for students. Teachers in the Maryland project saw some barriers to integrated instruction, including the conflict over time in the school day and coverage of content, students not desiring to see connections between the subjects, teachers' lack of subject matter knowledge in both subjects, and teachers feeling uncomfortable with teaching the subject for which they were not originally prepared or certified.

Likewise, Keys (2003) reported that, despite holding similar beliefs, elementary teachers used integration to compensate for lack of knowledge to teach science, whereas secondary teachers did not consider integration because it limited the amount of time needed to cover the curriculum. Wieseman and Moscovici (2003) and Venville and colleagues (2002) also described the challenges that inservice teachers face when implementing interdisciplinary approaches in the United States and abroad.

Czerniak, Lumpe, and Haney (1999) found that K–12 teachers generally had positive beliefs concerning the use of thematic units, but negative attitudes toward integration also existed. In general, K–12 teachers believed that thematic units in the classroom have the ability to foster student excitement and interest in learning science. Although some teachers believed that integration can make science more meaningful to students because students see connections between the sciences and other subject areas, others were concerned that thematic units would "water down" the curriculum. Teachers were concerned that using thematic units would be time consuming and difficult, especially because they believed integrated curriculum materials were not abundant. The teachers specified that a number of variables would be needed (but unlikely to be available) to help them use thematic units (resources including funding, curriculum materials, supplies, and equipment; staff development; less emphasis on testing and assessment; team teaching; administrative support; and a course of study that stressed integration). Although not surprising, it was revealed that teachers of lower grade levels had greater intentions to implement thematic units in their classrooms than did teachers of upper grade levels.

A study conducted even earlier among 400 schools in Missouri discovered differences among rural and low-socioeconomic-status (SES) schools regarding curriculum integration (Arredondo & Rucinski, 1996). They found that a high percentage of rural, low–SES schools were not involved in any type of curriculum integration. In schools where there was a high use of integrated curriculum, teachers reported greater involvement in decision-making processes—perhaps indicating their involvement in school reform efforts.

Educators are cognizant of the need for professional development support for in-service teachers to enable integration to happen. Lee, Chauvot, Plankis, Vowell, and Culpepper (2011) reported on the development of an online master's program through iSMART (Integration of Science, Mathematics, and Reflective Teaching) in the state of Texas. The authors argued the need for three unique characteristics for effective online programs to support integration including:

1. A cohort approach. Science and mathematics teachers work together participating in the meaning-making process and (re)defining science and mathematics integration in practice.
2. The courses are designed with equal amount of asynchronous and synchronous instruction.
3. Teacher educators and cohort teachers share a similar trajectory as members of the community of practice.

Barriers to Curriculum Integration

As mentioned previously, critics of integration purport that an insignificant amount of evidence exists to support the assertion that integrated approaches are more effective than teaching traditional, separate subjects. Several research studies have supported this claim. St. Clair and Hough (1992) had stated that few studies at the time supported an assertion that interdisciplinary curriculum results in student achievement gains. Later, Merrill's (2001) study found no significant achievement gains in high school students exposed to an integrated technology, mathematics, and science curriculum. However, Pang and Good (2000) argued implementation of integration is influenced by contextual factors that can have a direct impact on teacher and student outcomes.

George (1996) summarized assertions about integration not corroborated by research at that time:

1. Addresses the real-life concerns of students better than traditional curriculum
2. Presents greater opportunities for problem solving
3. Promotes students' independent learning
4. Offers more effective involvement with the environment and society
5. Provides more opportunities for student involvement in planning the curriculum along with the teacher
6. Allows teachers more opportunity to be "facilitators of learning"
7. Permits learning in greater depth; makes deeper connections
8. Presents students with opportunities to capitalize on prior learning more effectively
9. Allows for more application of curriculum outcomes to real life
10. Supplies more concrete experiences for slower learners or more enrichment opportunities for more able students
11. Encourages greater transfer or retention of learned information
12. More effectively rejuvenates and energizes career teachers with new experiences
13. Helps provide greater achievement, personal development, or harmonious group citizenship

Newer studies have provided some of the evidence lacking in 1996. For example, student achievement gains have been shown for science and literacy when the subjects were integrated (Romance & Vitale, 2012; Vitale & Romance, 2011). Similarly, research summarized about project-based work shows achievement gains on standardized tests (Krajcik & Czerniak, 2014).

In Australia, issues such as the grammar of schooling and the emphasis on discipline-based schooling have made integration challenging (Venville et al., 2002). From a theoretical perspective, Lederman and Niess (1997) commented that research on integrated instruction at that time seemed to demonstrate that science and mathematics instruction were severely restricted, because concepts included were narrowed to a specific framework. Evidence of this, they stated, were the disappointing achievement results associated with the science-technology-society (STS) approach. They argued that each discipline possesses unique conceptual, procedural, and epistemological differences that cannot be addressed through an integrated approach and, thus, they suggested that connections be made among topics with each subject area retaining its own identity.

Roth's (1994) experience teaching a fifth-grade unit around the theme of 1492 had supported Lederman and Niess's assertions. Roth's experiences were frustrating, because the science content was confined to the theme, and attempts to integrate science into the theme often distorted and diminished the science content she hoped to teach. Davison and colleagues (1995) had asked the following questions in reference to concerns about integration of mathematics and science:

1. To what extent can these integration efforts represent bona fide integration of science and mathematics?
2. To what extent has the integration of science and mathematics been merely cosmetic? (p. 226).

Mason (1996) listed a number of logistical problems considered to be disadvantages for using integrated strategies. For instance, mathematics concepts are sequential, and adding mathematics concepts as bits and pieces in the curriculum could confuse students if they lack prerequisite knowledge and skills. In other words, adding mathematics here and there for the sake of integrating might leave wide gaps in subject matter and student understanding. Additionally, Mason described a typical example of integration at the elementary school level, such as "the rain forest," and argued that students were typically asked to graph the number of endangered species. He cast doubt on the value of making dozens of graphs. Mason also asserted that many teachers, in an effort to force integration, trivialized the content. For example, "A poem about photosynthesis may not help one understand photosynthesis as a process, or poetry as a genre" (p. 266). Gardner and Boix-Mansilla's (1994) prior work supported Mason's assertion. They stated that prerequisite skills are often needed before students can use an integrated curriculum, and schools typically do not have time both to teach skills and to put them in an integrated curriculum.

Thus, if integration becomes contrived and formed around trivial themes, children may not have prerequisite background. Roebuck and Warden (1998) declared that few curriculum materials at the time used the content of science or mathematics as a focus of integration. Lonning and DeFranco (1997) maintained that integration was justified only when connecting science and mathematics concepts enhanced the understanding of the subject areas. To avoid a shallow curriculum that lacks meaning, they suggested that some concepts and skills are better taught separately. They advised that teachers should avoid forced integration.

Obstacles to Enacting Integrated Units

One of the true tests of any educational idea is that it can be successfully implemented in schools. McBride and Silverman (1991) cautioned that a number of problems must be addressed before integrated instruction becomes commonplace:

1. In most schools, students formally encounter the science and mathematics curricula organized and taught as separate subjects.
2. More instructional time is required to teach mathematics concepts through science concepts.
3. Classroom management can be more complicated when students are engaged in integrated science and mathematics activities than when they are solely engaged in whole-class mathematics instruction.
4. Many teachers do not have science materials to utilize in mathematics instruction.
5. Few teachers have access to or are aware of curriculum materials that integrate science and mathematics.

Meier and colleagues (1998) also pointed out a number of barriers to integration: the content barrier (science and mathematics topics do not always integrate well and sometimes leave gaps in what is taught for one of the subjects), teacher knowledge barrier (secondary teachers prepared in one subject; state licensure often is not integrated; elementary teachers have limited subject matter knowledge to know how to integrate), teacher belief barrier (inservice teachers think the curriculum is already crowded; preservice teachers do not know about integrated curriculum; and math teachers are less likely to integrate than science teachers), school structure barriers (schedules; different teachers without common planning time; tracking students; supplies/materials), and assessment and curriculum barriers (standardized tests cover separate subjects, do not measure higher-order thinking skills associated with integration).

Lehman (1994) discovered that, in spite of positive perceptions about integration, teachers' views do not carry over into their practice. Teachers often believed they had no time to add integrated ideas to an already overcrowded curriculum, and they were not aware of integrated resources. Similarly, Watanabe and Huntley (1998) reported that, although teachers in the Maryland Collaborative for Teacher Preparation had positive attitudes about connecting science and mathematics, some had problems enacting the curriculum. Some teachers were concerned with the amount of time it took to infuse integration into an already crammed curriculum. To counter the content coverage concern, Beane (1995) maintained that the separate subject curriculum was already too dense and not everything was being covered. He argued that curriculum integration allowed the most important and powerful ideas in the discipline to surface. Pang and Good (2000) mentioned that the current U.S. curriculum was already fragmented and unfocused, and therefore, any attempts to integrate a coherent content would be difficult.

Concerns about time may be related to the structure of the school day—especially in high schools, where the organization does not allow time or structure to integrate (Jacobs, 1989; Morrison & McDuffie, 2009; Venville et al., 1998). Unless teachers team teach (an approach popular in middle schools), they rarely have opportunity to work with other teachers outside of their discipline (Mason, 1996). Block scheduling has been seen as a format that allows for reforms such as integration (Canady & Rettig, 1996; Johnson, 2003).

In summarizing Lynn A. Steen's presentation at the 1991 Wingspread conference, Berlin (1994) cited inadequate teacher preparation as one cause for lack of integration. Steen declared that few science teachers, with maybe the exception of chemistry and physics teachers, have enough mathematical background to integrate advanced mathematics with science, and few mathematics teachers would be able to teach even one science subject area. Similarly, Lehman (1994) stated that less than 50% of 221 preservice and inservice teachers surveyed believed they had sufficient content background to integrate science and mathematics. Mason (1996) suggested that many teachers do not know how to create integrated curriculum, and, thus, teacher education may be one problem contributing to the limited implementation of integrated curriculum (Roebuck & Warden, 1998). Generally, preservice teachers have not taken integrated classes in their general studies, and they do not experience integrated methods. As a result, they do not know how to integrate across the curriculum (Mason, 1996). Even now, in most states, teachers (especially secondary teachers) are licensed in specific disciplines and, therefore, do not possess knowledge to integrate with other subject areas.

Student assessment is viewed as an impediment to enacting an integrated curriculum since standardized tests measure, for the most part, disciplinary knowledge (Berlin & White, 1992; Mason, 1996). Although the standards movement (NCSS, 2010; NCTE/IRA, 1996; NCTM, 2000; NRC, 1996) moved along disciplinary lines, they encouraged integration. The Common Core takes one step forward by requiring integration of reading with science, for example. Standardized tests, however, will need to integrate ideas, or national trends will likely fail to support integration.

Finally, a few studies indicate that curriculum integration poses difficulties for teachers that might impact the quality of instruction. McGehee (2001) summarized problems that occurred among instructors teaching together and found that instructors needed to work out issues among themselves (i.e., some dominating lectures and separating their subject area). Hurley (2001) discovered

that integration of science and mathematics took more time, was a challenge to teachers, and resulted in less time being spent on mathematics. She also observed that integrated courses developed by classroom teachers were less effective in impacting student achievement than were commercially designed curriculum materials.

Most recently, Basham and colleagues (2011) found that STEM schools also encounter barriers to implementing integrated STEM instruction. The most formidable challenge was the use of pacing guides by the school district, which the school was mandated to follow, leaving little time for planned project- and problem-based integrated units. Other issues were the lack of time for teachers to collaborate and need for professional development support for new teachers.

Conclusion

A number of implications can be drawn from this literature review. There are implications for research needed on integration. Additionally, the implications provide foci for science educators to provide leadership in clarifying issues, challenging basic assumptions, and solving problems associated with integrating science with other subject areas. In spite of a plethora of literature about the benefits of curriculum integration and some research studies to support this belief, additional research would be useful to verify these benefits and determine whether the results can be used to inform school-based practice.

More research is needed on integration. We cited some studies regarding achievement gains resulting from an integrated studies (i.e., when literacy/language arts is integrated with science and project-based learning). However, we found few studies about effective models of preparing teachers to deliver integrated instruction. With the upcoming demands of integration across STEM disciplines and other subject areas such as literacy, social studies, and arts (e.g., Next Generation Science Standards and Common Core), undoubtedly there is an increased need for more research in the area of integration. Particularly, we found no empirical research on integration of engineering and science. The inclusion of engineering practices in the Next Generation Science Standards (2012) will provide many opportunities for research on integration, teacher preparation, and integrated curriculum.

There continues to be a lack of consensus regarding the definition of integration. Models presented in the October 1998 special issue of *School Science and Mathematics* provided a catalyst for this discussion, but the debate continued into the 21st century (Hurley 2001, 2003; Nargund-Joshi & Liu, 2013; Pang & Good, 2000). Elucidation of definitions may help science educators eliminate confusion when discussing curriculum and instructional approaches that endeavor to integrate curriculum. Moreover, a clear-cut theoretical framework could provide the stimulus for the design and completion of further research regarding the impact of integrated curriculum.

A few STS and project-based curricula (e.g., Investigating & Questioning our World Through Science & Technology, IQWST [http://sangariglobaled.com/iqwst/]) focus on issues as a means to integrate across the curriculum and make science relevant to real life. IQWST integrates science with mathematics, engineering, and literacy (discourse during inquiry, reading for information, and writing of conclusions). Some integrated curricula, particularly commercial curricula, concentrate on skills (such as 21st-century skills) and give little attention to using science or mathematics content as the curricula's central focus. Thus, the implication is that educators continue to search for good curriculum materials that provide sufficient, high-quality science and mathematics content. With the growing use of mobile technologies in schools, teachers have greater ability to make the science curriculum relevant to students' lives by integrating it with other subjects. More research is needed to explore the benefits of integrated curriculum materials and the use of mobile technologies to integrate the curriculum.

Problems regarding the structure of the school day need to be overcome before integration becomes commonplace in schools. In the United States, schools turned to block scheduling as a way to provide teachers, particularly at the middle, junior, and high school levels, with larger portions of time to teach (Canady, 1995; Canady & Rettig, 1996). The block schedule typically provides a 90-minute segment of time rather than the traditional 45- or 50-minute class periods, and this format may give teachers the necessary time to integrate the curriculum.

Hurley (2003) identified some benefits of teacher education models designed to prepare teachers to integrate the curriculum but also noted that integrated methods courses are atypical. A few studies support curriculum integration in professional development models (Basista et al., 2001; Basista & Mathews, 2002; Johnson & Saylor, 2013). To better prepare preservice and inservice teachers to design and implement integrated units, they must be familiar with state and national reform recommendations, receive instruction in the integration of science and mathematics, learn about integrated curriculum resources, and learn to use technology tools that support integration. It is also important that teachers experience courses in which team teaching is used so they have a better understanding of the collaborative processes necessary to enact integrated strategies (Lehman, 1994; Mason, 1996).

The pressure of high-stakes standardized tests continues to be a limiting factor in implementing an integrated curriculum, and No Child Left Behind legislation may only exacerbate the problem. Some recent studies suggest that an integrated curriculum would help teachers implement the demands of standards and testing (e.g., Romance and Vitale, 2012). However, since most standardized tests examine content separately, educators mistrust whether the knowledge and skills learned in an integrated fashion would transfer to these tests. One may conclude that for integration to be widely accepted in a standards environment, either standardized tests need to measure knowledge and skills associated with learning in an integrated manner or integrated units developed commercially and by teachers need to contain assessments consistent with those in the standards and on high-stakes tests.

It is paradoxical that despite the interest in integrated approaches over the last 100 years, most standards today for each discipline remain separate (e.g., NCSS, 2010; NCTE/IRA, 1996; NCTM, 2000; NRC, 2011; Next Generation Science Standards, 2013). If progress is to be made in moving integrated instruction into the mainstream, discussions need to occur among leaders of professional organizations to establish standards for integrating content areas. This discussion has begun with the Common Core (2012), and time will tell how widespread integration of mathematics and literacy become in science.

Finally, Pang and Good (2000) perhaps best summarized the challenges surrounding attempts to integrate across the curriculum and the need for additional research,

> These issues suggest that integration of mathematics and science is one of the most daunting tasks educators face. There is no magic formula for completing the task except collaborative efforts among various disciplines and personnel. The more communication is opened about successes and failures of integration, the more significant progress can be made toward identifying what teachers are expected to teach and students are expected to learn through integrated curricula. In order to help all students become more scientifically and mathematically literate, a goal most reform documents advocate, more focused attention about integration of curriculum and instruction is necessary.
>
> (p. 78)

Acknowledgments

Thanks to Kathleen Roth and Leonie J. Rennie for reviewing this chapter.

References

Achieve. (2013). College and career readiness. Retrieved from www.achieve.org/college-and-career-readiness

AIMS Educational Foundation. (1986). *Activities integrating math and science.* Fresno, CA: Author.

AIMS Educational Foundation. (1987). *Math + science: A solution.* Fresno, CA: Author.

Akerson, V.L. (2001). Teaching science when your principal says, "Teach language arts." *Science and Children, 38*(7), 42–47.

Applebee, A.N., Adler, M., & Flihan, S. (2007). Interdisciplinary curricula in middle and high school classrooms: Case studies of approaches to curriculum and instruction. *American Educational Research Journal, 44*(4), 1002–1039.

Arredondo, D.E., & Rucinski, T.T. (1996). Integrated curriculum: Its use, initiation and support in Midwestern schools. *Mid-Western Educational Researcher, 9*(2), 37–44.

Barab, S.A., & Landa, A. (1997). Designing effective interdisciplinary anchors. *Educational Leadership, 54*(6), 52–58.

Basham, J.D., Koehler, C.M., & Israel, M. (2011). Creating a "STEM for All" environment. In C.C. Johnson (Ed.), *Secondary STEM educational reform* (pp. 1–24). New York, NY: Palgrave MacMillan.

Basista, B., & Mathews, S. (2002). Integrated science and mathematics professional development programs. *School Science and Mathematics, 102*(7), 360–370.

Basista, B., Tomlin, J., Pennington, K., & Pugh, D. (2001). Inquiry-based integrated science and mathematics professional development program. *Education, 121*(3), 615–624.

Beane, J. (1995). Curriculum integration and the disciplines of knowledge. *Phi Delta Kappan, 76,* 616–622.

Beane, J. (1996). On the shoulders of giants! The case for curriculum integration. *Middle School Journal, 28,* 6–11.

Beane, J.A. (1993). *A middle school curriculum: From rhetoric to reality.* Columbus, OH: National Middle School Association.

Beane, J.A. (1997). *Curriculum integration: Designing the core of democratic education.* New York, NY: Teachers College Press.

Berger, C.F. (1994). Breaking what barriers between science and mathematics? Six myths from a technological perspective. In D.F. Berlin (Ed.), *NSF/SSMA Wingspread conference: A network for integrated science and mathematics teaching and learning* (pp. 23–27). Bowling Green, OH: School Science and Mathematics Association.

Berlin, D. (1994). The integration of science and mathematics education: Highlights from the NSF/SSMA Wingspread conference plenary papers. *School Science and Mathematics, 94*(1), 32–35.

Berlin, D., & White, A. (1992). Report from the NSF/SSMA Wingspread conference: A network for integrated science and mathematics teaching and learning. *School Science and Mathematics, 92*(6), 340–342.

Berlin, D., & White, A. (1994). The Berlin-White integrated science and mathematics model (BWISM). *School Science and Mathematics, 94*(1), 2–4.

Berlin, D., & White, A. (2012). A longitudinal look at attitudes and perceptions related to the integration of mathematics, science, and technology education. *School Science and Mathematics, 112*(1), 20–30.

Berlin, D.F., & Hillen, J.A. (1994). Making connections in math and science: Identifying student outcomes. *School Science and Mathematics, 94*(6), 283–290.

Bragow, D., Gragow, K.A., & Smith, E. (1995). Back to the future: Toward curriculum integration. *Middle School Journal, 27,* 39–46.

Brazee, E.N., & Capelluti, J. (1995). *Dissolving boundaries: Toward an integrative curriculum.* Columbus, OH: National Middle School Association.

Brears, L., Tutor, S., & MacIntyre, B. (2011). Preparing teachers for the 21st century using PBL as an integrating strategy in science and technology education. *Design and Technology Education, 16*(1), 36–46.

Breiner, J., Harkness, M., Johnson, C.C., & Koehler, C. (2012). What Is STEM? A discussion about conceptions of STEM in education and partnerships. *School Science and Mathematics, 112,* 3–11.

Briscoe, C., & Stout, D. (1996). Integrating math and science through problem centered learning in methods courses: Effects on prospective teachers' understanding of problem solving. *Journal of Elementary Science Education, 8*(2), 66–87.

Brooks, J.G., & Brooks, M.G. (1993). *In search of understanding: The case for constructivist classrooms.* Alexandria, VA: Association for Supervision and Curriculum Development.

BSCS. (1994). *Innovations in science education survey instrument.* Colorado, Springs, CO: Author.

Canady, R. (1995). *Block scheduling: A catalyst for change in high schools.* Princeton, NJ: Eye on Education.

Canady, R., & Rettig, M. (1996). *Teaching in the block: Strategies for engaging active learners.* Princeton, NJ: Eye on Education.

Capraro, R.M., & Slough, S.W. (2008). *Project-based learning: An integrated science, technology, engineering, and technology (STEM) approach.* Rotterdam, the Netherlands: Sense.

Carnegie Council on Adolescent Development, Task Force on Education of Young Adolescents. (1989). *Turning points: Preparing American youth for the 21st century: The report of the task force on education of young adolescents.* Washington, DC: Carnegie Council on Adolescent Development.

Carnegie Foundation. (2009). *The opportunity equation: Transforming mathematics and science education for citizenship and the global economy.* New York, NY: Institute for Advanced Study.

Christensen, C.M., Horn, M.B., & Johnson, C.W. (2011). *Disrupting class: How disruptive innovation will change the way the world learns* (Vol. 98). New York, NY: McGraw-Hill.

Cleland, J.V., Wetzel, K.A., Zambo, R., Buss, R.R., & Rillero, P. (1999). Science integrated with mathematics using language arts and technology: A model for collaborative professional development. *Journal of Computers in Mathematics and Science Teaching, 18*(2), 157–172.

Cohen, P. (1995). Understanding the brain: Educators seek to apply brain research. *ASCD Education Update, 37*(7), 1, 4–5.

Committee on Prospering in the Global Economy of the 21st Century. (2007). *Rising above the gathering storm.* Retrieved from www.nap.edu/catalog/11463.html

Common Core State Standards Initiative. (2012). *Standards for mathematical practice.* Retrieved from www.corestandards.org/Math

Copple, C., & Bradekamp, S. 2009. *Developmentally appropriate practice in early childhood programs serving children from birth through age 8.* Washington, DC: National Association for the Education of Young Children.

Crane, S. (1991). Integrated science in a restructured high school. *Educational Leadership, 49*(2), 39–41.

Cremin, L. (1964). *The transformation of the school.* New York, NY: Vintage Press.

Czerniak, C.M., Lumpe, A.T., & Haney, J.J. (1999). Teachers' beliefs about thematic units in science. *Journal of Science Teacher Education, 10*(2), 123–145.

Czerniak, C.M., Weber, W., Sandmann, A., & Ahern, J. (1999). A literature review of science and mathematics integration. *School Science and Mathematics, 99*(8), 421–430.

Davison, D.M., Miller, K.W., & Metheny, D.L. (1995). What does integration of science and mathematics really mean? *School Science and Mathematics, 95*(5), 226–230.

Deeds, D.G., Allen, C.S., Callen, B.W., & Wood, M.W. (2000). A new paradigm in integrated math and science courses: Finding common ground across disciplines. *Journal of College Science Teaching, 30*(3), 178–183.

Dickinson, V.L., & Young, T.A. (1998). Elementary science and language arts: Should we blur the boundaries? *School Science and Mathematics, 98*(6), 334–339.

Drake, S.M. (1998). *Creating integrated curriculum: Proven ways to increase student learning.* Thousand Oaks, CA: Corwin.

Drake, S.M., & Burns, R.C. (2004). *Meeting standards through integrated curriculum.* Alexandria, VA: ASCD.

Erb, T.O. (2001). *This we believe . . . And now we must act.* Westerville, OH: National Middle School Association.

Fogarty, R. (1991). Ten ways to integrate curriculum. *Educational Leadership, 49*(2), 61–65.

Francis, R., & Underhill, R.G. (1996). A procedure for integrating math and science units. *School Science and Mathematics, 96*(3), 114–119.

Francis, R.W. (1996). Connecting the curriculum through the national mathematics and science standards. *Journal of Science Teacher Education, 7*(1), 75–81.

Friend, H. (1985). The effect of science and mathematics integration on selected seventh grade students' attitudes toward and achievement in science. *School Science and Mathematics, 85*(6), 453–461.

Frykholm, J., & Glasson, G. (2005). Connecting science and mathematics instruction: Pedagogical content knowledge for teachers. *School Science and Mathematics, 105*(3), 127–141.

Gardner, H., & Boix-Mansilla, V. (1994). Teaching for understanding within and across the disciplines. *Educational Leadership, 51,* 14–18.

Geier, R., Blumenfeld, P.C., Marx, R.W., Krajcik, J.S., Fishman, B., Soloway, E., & Clay-Chambers, J. (2008). Standardized test outcomes for students engaged in inquiry-based science curricula in the context of urban reform. *Journal of Research in Science Teaching, 45*(8), 922–939.

George, P.S. (1996). The integrated curriculum: A reality check. *Middle School Journal, 28,* 12–19.

Goldberg, H., & Wagreich, P. (1989). Focus on integrating science and math. *Science and Children, 26*(5), 22–24.

Greene, L.C. (1991). Science-centered curriculum in elementary school. *Educational Leadership, 49,* 42–51.

Guthrie, J.T., Wigfield, A., & VonSecker, C. (2000). Effects of integrated instruction on motivation and strategy use in reading. *Journal of Educational Psychology, 92*(2), 331–341.

Haigh, W., & Rehfeld, D. (1995). Integration of secondary mathematics and science methods courses: A model. *School Science and Mathematics, 95*(5), 240–247.

Hargreaves, A., Earl, L., Moore, S., & Manning, S. (2001). *Learning to change: Teaching beyond subjects and standards.* San Francisco, CA: Jossey-Bass.

Harrison, M. (2011). Supporting the T and the E in STEM: 2004–2010. *Design and Technology Education, 16*(1), 17–25.

Hart, L.C. (2002). Preservice teachers' beliefs and practice after participating in an integrated content/methods course. *School Science and Mathematics, 102,* 4–14.

Heitin, L. (2013). *In Common Core, teachers see interdisciplinary opportunities.* Retrieved from: www.edweek.org/tm/articles/2013/03/13/ccio_interdisciplinary_units.html

Huntley, M.A. (1998). Design and implementation of a framework for defining integrated mathematics and science education. *School Science and Mathematics, 98*(6), 320–327.

Hurley, M.M. (1999). *Interdisciplinary mathematics and science: Characteristics, forms, and related effect sizes for student achievement and affective outcomes.* Unpublished doctoral dissertation. University at Albany, State University of New York.

Hurley, M.M. (2001). Reviewing integrated science and mathematics: The search for evidence and definitions from new perspectives. *School Science and Mathematics, 101*(5), 259–268.

Hurley, M.M. (2003). *The presence, value, and reasoning behind integrated science and mathematics methods courses.* A paper presented at the annual meeting of the National Association for Research in Science Teaching, Philadelphia, PA.

Institute for Mathematics and Science Education. (1995). *Teaching integrated mathematics and science (TIMS).* Chicago, IL: Author.

Jacobs, H.H. (1989). *Interdisciplinary curriculum: Design and implementation.* Alexandria, VA: Association for Supervision and Curriculum Development.

Jimoyiannis, A. (2010). Designing and implementing an integrated technological pedagogical science knowledge framework for science teachers' professional development. *Computers & Education, 55*(3), 1259–1269. doi:10.1016/j.compedu.2010.05.022

Johnson, C. (2003). Bioterrorism is real-world science: Inquiry-based simulation mirrors real life. *Science Scope, 27*(3), 19–23.

Johnson, C.C. (2013a). Conceptualizing integrated STEM education – Editorial. *School Science and Mathematics Journal, 113*(8).

Johnson, C.C., & Fargo, J.D. (in press). A study of the impact of transformative professional development (TPD) on Hispanic student performance on state-mandated assessments of science. *Science Education.*

Johnson, C.C., & Saylor, L. (2013). Bring your own laptop (BYOL): The journey of a large middle school into the 21st century. *Journal for Computing Teachers, 9*(1), 1–7.

Keys, P. (2003). *Teachers bending the science curriculum.* Paper presented at the annual meeting of the National Association for Research in Science Teaching, Philadelphia, PA.

Koirala, H.P., & Bowman, J.K. (2003). Preparing middle level preservice teachers to integrate mathematics and science: Problems and possibilities. *School Science and Mathematics, 103*(3), 145–154.

Kotar, M., Guenter, C.E., Metzger, D., & Overholt, J.L. (1998). Curriculum integration: A teacher education model. *Science and Children, 35*(5), 40–43.

Krajcik, J., & Czerniak, C.M. (2014). *Teaching science to children: A project-based science approach.* New York, NY: Routledge.

Labov, J.B., Reid, A.H., & Yamamoto, K.R. (2010). Integrated biology and undergraduate science education: A new biology education for the twenty-first century? *CBE Life Science Education, 9,* 10–16.

Lawrence Hall of Science. (1984). *Great explorations in math and science (GEMS).* Berkeley, CA: Author.

Lebeaume, J. (2011). Integration of science, technology, engineering, and mathematics: Is this curricular revolution really possible in France? *Design and Technology Education, 16*(1), 47–52.

Lederman, N.G., & Niess, M.L. (1997). Integrated, interdisciplinary, or thematic instruction? Is this a question or is it questionable semantics? *School Science and Mathematics, 97*(2), 57–58.

Lee, M.M., Chauvot, J., Plankis, B., Vowell, J., & Culpepper, S. (2011). Integrating to learn and learning to integrate: A case study of an online master's program on science-mathematics integration for middle school teachers. *Internet and Higher Education, 14,* 191–200.

Lehman, J.R. (1994). Integrating science and mathematics: Perceptions of preservice and practicing elementary teachers. *School Science and Mathematics, 94*(2), 58–64.

Lehman, J.R., & McDonald, J.L. (1988). Teachers' perceptions of the integration of mathematics and science. *School Science and Mathematics, 88*(8), 642–649.

Lonning, R.A., & DeFranco, T.C. (1994). Development and implementation of an integrated mathematics/science preservice elementary methods course. *School Science and Mathematics, 94*(1), 18–25.

Lonning, R.A., & DeFranco, T.C. (1997). Integration of science and mathematics: A theoretical model. *School Science and Mathematics, 97*(4), 212–215.

Lonning, R.A., DeFranco, T.C., & Weinland, T.P. (1998). Development of theme-based, interdisciplinary, integrated curriculum: A theoretical model. *School Science and Mathematics, 98*(6), 312–319.

Marbach-Ad, G., & McGinnis, J.R. (2008). To what extent do reform prepared upper elementary and middle school science teachers maintain their beliefs and intended instructional actions as they are inducted into schools? *Journal of Science Teacher Education, 19,* 157–182.

Marx, R.W., Blumenfeld, P.C., Krajcik, J.S., Fishman, B., Soloway, E., Geier, R., & Tal, R.T. (2004). Inquiry-based science in the middle grades: Assessment of learning in urban systemic reform. *Journal of Research in Science Teaching, 41*(10), 1063–1080.

Mason, T.C. (1996). Integrated curricula: Potential and problems. *Journal of Teacher Education, 47*(4), 263–270.

McBride, J.W., & Silverman, F.L. (1991). Integrating elementary/middle school science and mathematics. *School Science and Mathematics, 91*(7), 285–292.

McComas, W.F. (1993). STS education and the affective domain. In R.E. Yager (Ed.), *What research says to the science teacher, 7: The science, technology, and society movement* (pp. 161–168). Washington, DC: National Science Teachers Association.

McComas, W.F., & Wang, H.A. (1998). Blended science: The rewards and challenges of integrating the science disciplines for instruction. *School Science and Mathematics, 98*(6), 340–348.

McDonald, J., & Czerniak, C.M. (1998). Scaling sharks. *School Science and Mathematics, 98*(7), 397–399.

McGehee, J.J. (2001). Developing interdisciplinary units: A strategy based on problem solving. *School Science and Mathematics, 101*(7), 380–389.

Meier, S.L., Nicol, M., & Cobbs, G. (1998). Potential benefits and barriers to integration. *School Science and Mathematics, 98*(8), 438–447.

Merrill, C. (2001). Integrating technology, mathematics, and science education: A quasi-experiment. *Journal of Industrial Teacher Education, 38*(3), 45–61.

Minnesota Mathematics and Science Project. (1970). Minneapolis: Minnesota School Mathematics and Science Center.

Moore, E. H. (1967). On the foundations of mathematics. *Mathematics Teacher, 60,* 360–374. A reprint of his 1902 retiring presidential address to the American Mathematical Society, originally published in *Science* (1903), 402–424.

Morrison, J., & McDuffie, A. R. (2009). Connecting science and mathematics: Using inquiry investigations to learn about data collection, analysis, and display. *School Science and Mathematics, 109*(1), 31–44.

Nargund-Joshi, V., & Liu, X. (2013). *Understanding meanings of interdisciplinary science inquiry in an era of Next Generation Science Standards.* A paper presented at the annual meeting of the National Association for Research in Science Teaching, Rio Grande, Puerto Rico.

National Association for the Education of Young Children. (1987). *Developmentally appropriate practice in early childhood programs serving children from birth through age 8.* Washington, DC: Author.

National Council for the Social Studies. (2010). *National curriculum and standards for social studies.* Washington, DC: Author.

National Council of Teachers of English and the International Reading Association. (1996). *Standards for the English language arts.* Urbana, IL: Author.

National Council of Teachers of Mathematics. (2000). *Principles and standards for school mathematics.* Reston, VA: Author.

National Middle School Association. (2010). *This we believe.* Columbus, OH: Author.

National Research Council. (1996). *National science education standards.* Washington, DC: National Academies Press.

National Research Council. (2012). *A framework for K–12 science education.* Washington, DC: National Academies Press.

National Science Teachers Association. (1992). *The content core.* Washington, DC: Author.

National Science Teachers Association. (1996). NSTA board endorses new position statement on interdisciplinary learning, PreK–grade 4. *NSTA Reports!, 6,* 8.

Nesin, G., & Lounsbury, J. (1999). *Curriculum integration: Twenty questions—with answers.* Atlanta: Georgia National Middle School Association.

Next Generation Science Standards. (2013). Retrieved from www.nextgenscience.org/next-generation-science-standards

Nuffield Foundation Science Teaching Project. (1967). London, England: Longmans.

Pang, J. S., & Good, R. (2000). A review of the integration of science and mathematics: Implications for further research. *School Science and Mathematics, 100*(2), 73–82.

Partnership for 21st Century Skills. (n.d.). Retrieved from http://p21.org/

Perkins, D. (1991). Educating for insight. *Educational Leadership, 49,* 4–8.

Peters, T., Schubeck, K., & Hopkins, K. (1995). A thematic approach: Theory and practice at the Aleknagik school. *Phi Delta Kappan, 76,* 633–636.

Petrie, H. G. (1992). Interdisciplinary education: Are we faced with insurmountable opportunities? *Review of Research in Education, 18,* 299–333.

Rakow, S. J., & Vasquez, J. (1998). Integrated instruction: A trio of strategies. *Science and Children, 35*(6), 18–22.

Rennie, L., Venville, G., & Wallace, J. (2012a). *Integrating science, technology, engineering, and mathematics.* New York, NY: Routledge.

Rennie, L., Venville, G., & Wallace, J. (2012b). *Knowledge that counts in a global community: Exploring the contribution of integrated curriculum.* New York, NY: Routledge.

Rivet, A. E., & Krajcik, J. S. (2004). Achieving standards in urban systemic reform: An example of a sixth grade project-based science curriculum. *Journal of Research in Science Teaching, 41*(7), 669–692.

Roebuck, K. I., & Warden, M. A. (1998). Searching for the center on the mathematics-science continuum. *School Science and Mathematics, 98*(6), 328–333.

Romance, N. R., & Vitale, M. R. (2012). Expanding the role of K–5 science instruction in educational reform: Implications of an interdisciplinary model for integrating science and reading. *School Science and Mathematics, 112*(8), 506–515.

Ronis, D. L. (2007). *Problem-based learning for math and science: Integrating inquiry and the internet.* Thousand Oaks, CA: Corwin.

Ross, J. A., & Hogaboam-Gray, A. (1998). Integrated mathematics, science, and technology: Effects on students. *International Journal of Science Education, 20*(9), 1119–1135.

Roth, K. J. (1994). Second thoughts about interdisciplinary studies. *American Educator, 18*(1), 44–48.

Roth, W. M. (1993). Problem-centered learning for the integration of mathematics and science in a constructivist laboratory: A case study. *School Science and Mathematics, 93*(3), 113–122.

Rutherford, J., & Ahlgren. (1990). *Science for all Americans.* New York, NY: Oxford University Press.

Sanders, M. (2009). STEM, STEM education, STEM mania. *Technology Teacher, 68*(4), 20–26.

Sandmann, A., Weber, W., Czerniak, C., & Ahern, J. (1999). Coming full circuit: An integrated unit plan for intermediate and middle grade students. *Science Activities, 36*(3), 13–20.

Schneider, R. M., Krajcik, J., Marx, R. W., & Soloway, E. (2002). Performance of students in project-based science classrooms on a national measure of science achievement. *Journal of Research in Science Teaching, 39*(5), 410–422.

Shann, M. H. (1977). Evaluation of an interdisciplinary, problem-solving curriculum in elementary science and mathematics. *Science Education, 61*(4), 491–502.

Smith, C. (2001). Addressing standards through curriculum integration. *Middle School Journal, 33*(2), 5–6.

Sondergeld, T. A., Milner, A. R., Coleman, L. J., & Southern, T. (2011). Lessons from the field: Examining the challenges and successes of a mathematics and science program using acceleration and enrichment for gifted urban middle school students. In C. C. Johnson (Ed.), *Secondary STEM educational reform* (pp. 193–195). New York, NY: Palgrave MacMillan.

St. Clair, B., & Hough, D. L. (1992). *Interdisciplinary teaching: A review of the literature.* (ERIC Document Reproduction Service No. 373 056).

Stevenson, C., & Carr, J. (1993). *Integrated studies: Dancing through walls.* New York, NY: Teachers College Press.

Stinson, K., Harkness, S. S., Meyer, H., & Stallworth, J. (2009). Mathematics and science integration: Models and characterizations. *School Science and Mathematics, 109*(3), 153–161.

Stuessy, C. L. (1993). Concept to application: Development of an integrated mathematics/science methods course for preservice elementary teachers. *School Science and Mathematics, 93*(2), 55–62.

Stuessy, C. L., & Naizer, G. L. (1996). Reflection and problem solving: Integrating methods of teaching mathematics and science. *School Science and Mathematics, 96*(4), 170–177.

Teaching Institute for Excellence in STEM. (2010). *What is STEM Education?* Retrieved from www.tiesteach.org/stem-education.aspx

Underhill, R. (1995). Editorial. *School Science and Mathematics, 95*(5), 225.

Unified Science and Mathematics for Elementary Schools Project. (1973). Newton, MA: Educational Development Center.

Vars, G. F. (1991). Integrated curriculum in historical perspective. *Educational Leadership, 49,* 14–15.

Venville, G., Rennie, L. J., & Wallace, J. (2004). Decision making and sources of knowledge: How students tackle integrated tasks in science, technology and mathematics. *Research in Science Education, 34*(2), 115–135. doi:10.1023/B:RISE.0000033762.75329.9b

Venville, G., Wallace, J., Rennie, L. J., & Malone, J. (1998). The integration of science, mathematics, and technology in a discipline-based culture. *School Science and Mathematics, 98*(6), 294–302.

Venville, G. J., Wallace, J., Rennie, L. J., & Malone, J. A. (2002). Curriculum integration: Eroding the high ground of science as a school subject? *Studies in Science Education, 37*(1), 43–83.

Vitale, M. R., & Romance, N. R. (2011). Adaptation of a knowledge-based instructional intervention to accelerate student learning in science and early literacy in grades one and two. *Journal of Curriculum and Instruction, 5*(2), 79–93.

Waldrip, B. (2001). Primary teachers' views about integrating science and literacy. *Investigating: Australian Primary & Junior Science Journal, 17*(1), 38–41.

Watanabe, T., & Huntley, M. A. (1998). Connecting mathematics and science in undergraduate teacher education programs: Faculty voices from the Maryland Collaborative for Teacher Preparation. *School Science and Mathematics, 98*(1), 19–25.

Wei, B. (2009). In search of meaningful integration: The experiences of developing integrated science curricula in junior secondary schools in China. *International Journal of Science Education, 31*(2), 259–277.

Wieseman, K. C., & Moscovici, H. (2003). Stories from the field: Challenges of science teacher education based on interdisciplinary approaches. *Journal of Science Teacher Education, 14*(2), 127–143.

Williams, P. J. (2011). STEM education: Proceed with caution. *Design and Technology Education, 16*(1), 26–35.

Willis, S. (1992, November). Interdisciplinary learning: Movement to link the disciplines gains momentum. *ASCD Curriculum Update, 1*–8.

Zwick, T., & Miller, K. (1996). A comparison of integrated outdoor education activities and traditional science learning with American Indian students. *Journal of American Indian Education, 35*(2), 1–9.

21

High School Biology Curricula Development

Implementation, Teaching, and Evaluation
from the 20th to the 21st Century

REUVEN LAZAROWITZ

This chapter is divided into two sections. The first part provides a description of the high school biology curricula taught in the 20th century and presents the factors that, in the author's opinion, have contributed to the creation of these different study programs, based on the rationale described by Tyler (1966). The development of high school biology curricula during the past century will be depicted on the basis of two assumptions: one, that there is a high correlation among biology research, biology content structure, and biology high school curricula; and two, that new high school curricula in biology were affected by changes in society's daily life, in the high school student populations, research in science education in biology, and learning theories and pedagogy. All of these changes required modifications in the education of preservice and inservice biology teachers; the latter issue is beyond the scope of this chapter. This section includes a short report based on selected studies of formative and summative evaluations, which investigated the implementation of the new programs in teaching biology in high school.

The second section encompasses several subjects investigated in teaching and learning biology that have had an impact on students' achievement in the cognitive, affective, and psychomotor domains. Because the new biology curricula emphasize the teaching of concepts and principles, the subjects were selected according to their relation to the "unifying themes in biology" (Schwab, 1963, p. 31), the seven levels of biological organization (Schwab, 1963, pp. 15, 16, 17), and the "fundamentals themes" in Nuffield Biology (Nuffield Foundation, 1966, p. 1). This section concludes with suggestions as to what kinds of curricula, learning materials in biology, and types of studies we need in order to address the issues of student heterogeneity in our schools, as well as their needs, interests, and abilities, in order for them to master the knowledge and skills needed to cope with our highly scientific and technological society.

Tyler's Rationale for Curriculum Development

Based on Tyler's Rationale for Curriculum Development, the concept of a course of study can be defined as a sequence of planned science topics to be taught in relation to a specific subject matter, for a particular age group of students, accompanied by recommendations as to what to teach in the classroom and laboratory. The planned curriculum recommends several textbooks written according to its organization, with suggested modes of instruction, learning, evaluation, and grading of students.

In 1960, Tyler published a monograph titled *Basic Principles of Curriculum and Instruction*, which was later revised by Madaus and Stufflebeam (1989). The study grew out of the problems brought on by the Depression, one of which was the great increase in the number of youth attending high school (many of whom would have preferred to go to work but were unable to find employment; Tyler, 1966). The motivation of the study was an attempt to define three key points with respect to qualitative education:

1. *Clarification of purpose*, which included (a) selection of learning experiences, (b) the organization of these experiences, and (c) the assessment of progress toward the attainment of the school's objectives.
2. *A program's objectives should be clarified through* the learner's studies and studies of contemporary life.
3. *Objectives should then be screened through* (a) the school's philosophy of education, (b) theories of learning, and (c) suggestions from subject matter specialists.

Four divisions of curriculum inquiry were outlined:

1. What educational purposes should the school seek to attain?
2. What educational experiences can be provided that are likely to help attain these objectives?

3. How can these educational experiences be effectively organized?
4. How can we determine whether these objectives are being met? (Tyler, 1966)

Tyler's Rationale for Curriculum Development (1966) served as a tool for analyzing high school biology curricula developed in the 20th century.

Section I: A Description of the High School Biology Curricula of the 20th Century

The Content-Oriented Curriculum in Biology

The first science study program, which we refer to as "the content-oriented curriculum," prevailed from the beginning of the 20th century until the 1960s. It was characterized by its content structure sequence. The sequence of the science topics reflected the syllabi of the courses taught at the university level (DeHart Hurd, 1961) and represented the patterns and processes used in science research at that time and the content knowledge structure (CKS) of any particular science as it was known.

In the field of biology, the main body of knowledge included major topics such as invertebrates and vertebrates in zoology, lower and higher plants in botany, and the structure of the human body. Each organism was presented in sequence as to its morphology, anatomy, physiology, growth, development, and reproduction. Various aspects of their relationships with the environment were mentioned together within a classification approach. Each organism was introduced with a short description of the cell structure and function. This information could be found at the beginning of each textbook. Microbiology, genetics, ecology, and evolution were complementary subjects. The main biology research was aimed at learning about organisms and their classification, with the appropriate physiology aspects as far as the current knowledge in chemistry and physics permitted. This was the biology CKS of the curriculum, which was reflected in the textbooks. The textbooks depicted a sequence of cells from unicellular to multicellular organisms at different levels of sophistication.

Research in Biology That Affected the CKS

The research in cell theory, for instance, was based on a sequence of technology developments, starting with the development of microscopes and what they allowed people to see. Zacharias Janssen built the first simple microscope with only one set of lenses in 1590. Following this, in 1670 Anton van Leeuwenhoek developed a microscope that could magnify objects as much as 270 times, enabling him to see bacteria, protozoa, sperm cells, red blood cells, and yeast cells. In 1665, Robert Hooke, who was a physicist, put two sets of lenses together, thus building a compound microscope. He examined a thin piece of cork and found that it was built of walled structures; he named these empty boxes "cells." Based on these earlier technologies, in 1831, Robert Brown found that in living plant cells, small spherical structures could be detected, and he decided to call these nuclei. In 1838, Matthias Schleiden concluded that all plants are composed of cells. During the same period, Theodor Schwann, while studying animal tissues, came to the conclusion that animals are also built of cells. One can see that there is a strong correlation between the technologies developed at that time and the possibility of more sophisticated research in biology. Thus, already in the 19th century, a reciprocal impact existed between research in science and technological development. Any separation between the two, thereafter, has been artificial and the result of people's decisions alone.

Another factor that had great influence on the development of the science of biology's content structure was the advances in maritime technologies that made possible the great global expeditions led by two scientists: (a) Carolus Linnaeus (1707–1778), a Swedish botanist and zoologist who firmly established the binomial system of plant and animal nomenclature in the 1750s; and (b) Charles Darwin (1809–1882), a naturalist who while on the ship *Beagle* traveled around the world between 1831 and 1836 and collected a vast number of specimens of skeletons and creatures. On his return, and based on his collections, he made public a notebook, which contained his observations on the changes of species. *Origin of Species,* published in 1859, had an enormous effect on human thought. This was the most significant book of the 19th century (Alexander, 1953, p. 204). Consequently, the research conducted by biologists helped them develop theories on the sequence of evolution of plants and animals and their classification, anatomy, physiology, reproduction, and genetics. One may say that all of this research was primarily based on the two monumental works published by Linnaeus and Darwin. It also formed the biological sciences content knowledge (SCK) structure that existed until the 1960s. This SCK was the foundation of the science programs taught at universities and in high school science classes, and all of the textbooks students in both places used reflected it.

Content-Oriented Curriculum and Methods of Instruction

The modes of instruction used in this type of curriculum, the first generation of the high school curriculum, were primarily expository. Teachers lectured and asked questions, while students had to listen and sometimes were allowed to answer. Student–student interactions in the learning process or any process of inquiry rarely occurred. One may therefore conclude that listening and memorization skills were emphasized rather than skills of learning, or seeking for knowledge, exchanging ideas, taking responsibility, and the like. This was a teacher-centered instructional activity in which students remained passive. In the late 1980s, Shulman (1987) defined the subject matter of the curriculum as content knowledge (CK). The

Grade

* The Cell Theory   9th

* Invertebrates: Morphology, Anatomy, Physiology, Reproduction   9th

* Vertebrates: Morphology, Anatomy, Physiology, Reproduction   10th

* Human Body: Morphology, Anatomy, Physiology, Reproduction   10th

* Botany: lower Plants and Higher Plants   9th

* Microbiology   9th - 10th

* Genetics   11th

* Ecology   11th

* Evolution   12th

* Classification of Plants and Animals   11th - 12th

Weekly time-table

Grade	Classroom	Laboratory
9th and 10th	2 periods	1 period
11th and 12th	3 periods	2 periods

All students in 9th and 10th grades learned Biology
In 11th and 12th grades – only those students who chose to study boilogy for the matriculation examinations.

Figure 21.1 The content knowledge structure in biology and high school biology curriculum as it was used in Europe and Israel 1930–1970.

nature of laboratory work was essentially aimed at proving what had already been learned (Lazarowitz & Tamir, 1994). Evaluation and grading procedures were based on tests with open questions in which students were asked to write their answer in a narrative mode; few tests used multiple-choice questions. The questionnaires referred mainly to the cognitive levels of knowledge and understanding. Higher cognitive levels such as application, analysis, synthesis, and evaluation were mostly ignored. Most of the examinations and tests were assessed in a summative approach and used only for grading purposes.

In Figure 21.1, the structure of the content-oriented curriculum in biology, as it was used in many countries, is presented with its suggested sequence of the subjects to be taught in high school (Grades 9–12), as was customary from 1900 to 1965. Whereas in the United States biology was taught in Grade 10 only, with electives in the 11th and 12th grades, in Europe and Israel, biology was taught in 9th to 12th grades, depending on the schools' structures, their curriculum, and students' choice in what science subject to be assessed on in their matriculation examinations.

The Inquiry-Oriented Curriculum in Biology

In the late 1960s, a second generation of high school curriculum was developed, which we call *inquiry-oriented*. It was based on the concept of inquiry as suggested and developed in the book by Schwab and Brandwein (*The Teaching of Science as Enquiry*, 1962; see also *Inquiry* by Gagne, 1963; Rutherford, 1964). This approach had its roots in the educational and philosophical theories developed in the monumental manuscripts written by Dewey (*The Theory of Inquiry,* 1938) and by Bruner (*The Act of Discovery,* 1961). These theories were incorporated into Schwab's book

Biology Teachers' Handbook (1963), which can be considered the foundation for all inquiry-oriented curricula, the Biological Sciences Curriculum Study (BSCS) textbooks, and the Invitations to Inquiry.

New High School Science Curricula

What was the trigger for the development of these new curricula? There was, and still is, a tendency to explain it by the fact that the satellite *Sputnik* had been launched by the Russians in the early 1960s, causing the United States to feel inferior for not having been the first country to launch a satellite. As a result, the Americans began an inquiry to find out why they had lost the race into space. They concluded that the high school science curricula did not reflect the knowledge of sciences as they had been known to scientists in the 1960s and were not being taught in the same way as science was practiced. Scientists and educators attempted to explain that the lack of updated science curricula and inadequate methods of instruction were responsible for the American "inferiority," and consequently there was a dearth of high school graduates who were well versed in the sciences. Indeed, there was a shortage of students in the science faculties, which resulted in a lack of scientists. This, together with a scarcity in research funds, led to a reduction in the numbers of researchers in the sciences and applied technology. Politicians and educators called for radical changes in high school science curricula, and adequate budgets were allocated by the American federal government for the development of satisfactory science curricula, in order to solve this problem. Can we say that *Sputnik* was the only factor behind the radical changes, which occurred in the second generation of high school science curricula, or were there additional reasons for these changes? The answer lies in scientific research.

Science Curricula, Technology, and Societal Issues

This chapter cannot refer to the societal issues following World War II without touching on their effect on Americans. In the United States, the aftermath of World War II saw an enormous change in students' attitudes toward the sciences and technology because of what they thought was the misuse of technology during the war. In the postwar period, they felt that the achievements of science and technology were not being used to solve social problems or to improve the lives of people living under low economic conditions. It is possible that the students' sensitivity had a significant influence on their decision about whether to study science.

Another issue that arose in the 1960s was that scientists and science educators tried to separate science from its technological applications. This trend had a huge impact on the new science curricula, which did not include any aspects of technology. This issue was addressed later in the third generation of curriculum, the problem-oriented one, where this unnatural separation between science and technology was corrected.

The Impact of Chemistry and Physics on Research in Biology

Chemistry and physics played major roles in biology research from the 1940s to the 1960s and later. Two main developments contributed to the changes in the biology CKS: One was based on biology research and the other was based on the use of advanced technology developed in chemistry (working with labeled atoms) and physics (the development of the electronic microscope). Until the late 1930s, radioactive isotopes were not commonly used to probe physiological processes below the macromolecular level. Developments in biochemistry enabled scientists to use labeled isotopes and to track the path of atoms in molecules of amino acids, proteins, nucleic acids, fats, and sugars, and more. Thus a new window of knowledge was opened, laying the foundation for molecular biology.

An example from the research in plant physiology can illustrate the impact of the use of an isotope. This example is adequate for the high school curriculum, since it can demonstrate to students how research is advancing by giving a historical view of the new methods used in the laboratory. The process of photosynthesis, until the 1940s, was taught as a process in which the chlorophyll in green plants, in the presence of light energy, liberates free oxygen and produces sugar from water and carbon dioxide. The source of the oxygen was explained to be the CO_2 molecule, which is broken down to liberate the oxygen and the carbon, and together with the molecule of water formed the skeleton of the sugar molecule. The chemical equation was very simple:

$$6CO_2 + 12H_2O \rightarrow C_6H_{12}O_6 + 6O_2 + 6H_2O.$$

It was only around 1939 when biochemists were able to add the isotope O^{18} to water and carbon dioxide, to label water H_2O^{18} and CO_2^{18}, that they were able to demonstrate that the oxygen released in photosynthesis came from water, whereas the carbohydrate that was formed contained the O from CO_2. This finding was further proved by the Hill reaction, where Hill showed that isolated chloroplasts or even fragments of them, when illuminated, can liberate oxygen from water while the hydrogen is transferred instead to the carbon dioxide, to some artificial acceptor added to the system (e.g., ferricyanide, quinone, coenzyme1):

$$2Fe^{3+} + H_2O \xrightarrow{\text{light, chloroplast}_s} 2Fe^{2+} + 2H^+ + 1/2O_2$$

(Harder, Schumacher, Firbas, & von Denffer, 1965, p. 256).

In the 1950s, the path of carbon in the photosynthesis process was described and the DNA model was suggested. The electron microscope enabled scientists to see cell ultrastructures, and organelles and membranes were more accurately described in their distinct molecular parts.

Consequently, the metabolic paths of proteins, amino acids, sugars, and fats in the cell were depicted as well, and step by step, all of the physiological processes that occur in cells were described at the molecular level, parallel to the description of all of the ultrastructures, achieved with the help of the electron microscope. These two methods—labeled atoms and electron microscopy—technological in nature, when combined, made possible sophisticated biological research, changing the face of biology CKS in the middle of the 20th century. The use of advanced technology in biological research has clearly shown the strong, inseparable relationship between science and technology. At the macro level, studies in ecology integrated with mathematical optimal methods in the framework of the ecosystem added new dimensions to field studies.

The Development of the Biological Sciences Curriculum Study in the United States

The newly accumulated body of knowledge induced changes in the corpus of the biology CKS, and scientists started to present it, using seven levels of biological organization (LBO). The seven LBO are molecular, cellular, tissue and organs, organisms, societal, communal, and biome. Unity is highest at the molecular level, is common to all living creatures, and diminishes toward the last level, the biome. In contrast, diversity is lowest at the molecular level and increases through the levels, reaching the highest order of diversity at the biome level.

Figure 21.2 presents the new biology CKS in accordance with scientific research in the 1960s, together with its relationship to the cognitive learning demands of high school students.

The changes in biology CKS led to changes in curricula, and the three versions of the Biological Sciences Curriculum Study (BSCS, 1968) represent the classical

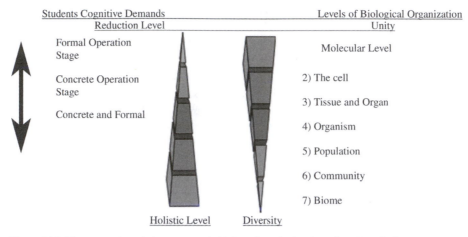

Figure 21.2 The content knowledge structure in biology from the inquiry-oriented curriculum.

examples of the second generation of high school science curricula. All three versions that were developed around the seven LBO required an inquiry mode of learning and teaching. Each version emphasized the seven LBO at different levels of depth and sophistication:

a. BSCS, *Biological Science: An Inquiry into Life—The Yellow Version* (1968), emphasized developmental and evolutionary aspects of biology. In this respect, this curriculum was the closest version to the content-oriented curriculum, and it is therefore understandable that it was the one most adopted by schools and teachers in the United States and other countries.

b. BSCS, *Biological Science: Molecules to Man—The Blue Version* (1968), emphasized molecular biology. It was the most revolutionary curriculum in that period.

c. BSCS, *High School Biology—The Green Version* (1968), which emphasized the ecological aspects the most, was primarily adopted by rural schools in the United States and agricultural high schools in other countries.

Figure 21.3 displays the comparative characteristics of the CKSs emphasized by the two generations (content-oriented and inquiry-oriented) of high school curricula.

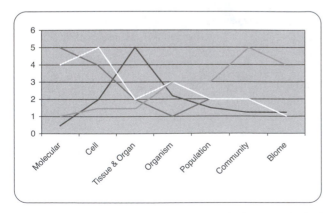

Figure 21.3 The seven levels of biological organization as emphasized in BSCS–inquiry curricula vs. traditional content-oriented curriculum. (Schwab, 1963, pp. 15, 16, 17)

In addition, other texts were developed: (a) a textbook for low academic achievers, titled *Biological Science: Patterns and Processes* (1966; the text was minimal and the experiments were integrated within the text), and (b) BSCS: *Interaction of Experiments and Ideas* (BSCS, 1970). This textbook was written in a purely inquiry mode; the experiments were integrated into the text and presented research problems in biology in a manner that required students to suggest solutions and ideas and to perform experiments in order to find answers. The textbook was developed for use in the 11th and 12th grades.

The Pedagogical Approach in the BSCS Textbooks

The content knowledge component of the BSCS textbooks emphasized the teaching of concepts and principles in biology, including a new concept, inquiry. Teachers were asked to create classroom learning environments in which students had "to search and seek" for knowledge, using the reasoning procedure and inquiry skills of scientists in their research. Students were required to use skills such as problem identification, formulation of hypotheses, planning and experimenting, collection of data and results, analysis of the results, planning, and designing and reading graphs and tables based on the results. Students were asked to draw conclusions and infer, in the hope that in this manner they would be able to identify new problems to be researched. Educators and sociologists hoped that students would use these acquired skills in their daily lives as an objective method of solving personal and societal issues. Unfortunately, no studies were carried out to establish if skills mastered in science were successfully transferred and used in daily life.

Summary of the Inquiry-Oriented Curricula

Following the *Sputnik* crisis and increased scientific research in biology, the science community was able to suggest new curricula. National committees consisting of scientists, educators, science supervisors, and science teachers were convened and asked for their input. The new curricula were expected to present the new achievements in sciences, and it was hoped that the committee members would be able to suggest methods of instruction and learning that would reflect the way science was carried out, researched, and studied.

Students were not required to perform pure research but only to use inquiry skills in their learning (Rutherford, 1964; Schwab, 1963). In investigations carried out in the laboratory, students were not compelled to discover new facts unknown to science but to seek existing knowledge in an explorative mode of learning. Later in the 1980s, Shulman (1987) called this component of any curriculum the "pedagogical content knowledge" (PCK), which was added to the content knowledge part.

The three BSCS versions were predicated on the seven levels of biological organization as presented in Fig. 20.2 and the "Unifying Themes in Biology" (Schwab, 1963, p. 31):

1. Change of living things through time: evolution
2. Diversity of type and unity of pattern in living things
3. The genetic continuity of life
4. The complementarities of organisms and their environment
5. The biological factors of behavior
6. The complementarities of structure and function
7. Regulation and homeostasis: preservation of life in the face of change
8. Science as inquiry
9. The history of biological conceptions

The Implementation of the BSCS in the United States and Evaluation Studies

The changes in biology CKS since the 1950s have had an enormous influence on high school curricula, biology education, and teaching and learning strategies. These changes required formal and summative evaluation studies, which in turn required new modes of assessment and grading as well as new tests. These tests were aimed at evaluating academic achievement; mastery of skills in the cognitive, affective, and psychomotor domains; and attitudes and classroom learning environment, to name a few areas. The years 1960 to 1975 represent one of the most active phases in biology education in the United States. The cooperation among biology scientists in colleges and universities, science educators, and high school biology teachers reached a high level that was unknown until then.

The new biology curricula, comprising all the versions of the BSCS, additional learning material that had been developed, the second course, and the biology teachers' handbook were used in schools all over the United States. BSCS materials were used in inservice and preservice courses in the education of high school biology teachers. DeHart Hurd (1978) called this period "the Golden Age of biological education" in the United States. Between the years 1959 and 1975, some 15 million high school students learned biology through one of the available BSCS programs. In the academic year of 1970 to 1971, 50% of the high school student population (of the 2,729,306 who

learned biology) studied using a BSCS variant (DeHart Hurd, 1978, p. 42). The massive implementation of this new curriculum required evaluation studies, which were carried out by graduate students for their M.Sc. and Ph.D. degrees and by science educators in the United States and all over the world. In his chapter, DeHart Hurd (1978) reviewed this vast mass of studies on the implementation of the BSCS programs, as well as general studies in biology education, and succeeded in condensing all of the findings under a large number of sections.

In the present chapter, limited as we are in space, it is impossible to present all of the findings, but we strongly suggest reading the original chapter on the golden age of biology education, which includes two sections. The first one prepares the reader by providing the information needed to relate to the studies and consists of the following parts: new programs and student enrollments; growth of research in biological education; selection of investigations for review, analysis, and organization of investigations; the conceptual base for biology teaching; and developing interpretative theories. This section introduces readers to the development process and rationale of the BSCS curricula, as well as to how the studies were selected for the review.

The second section presents the nature of the studies reviewed, such as comparative analysis of learning outcomes among students enrolled in BSCS courses and those who took conventional biology programs, students' achievements, changed attitudes, inquiry skills acquired, and subject matter mastered by the methods of pre- and posttesting. The basic assumption was that teachers who adopted the BSCS textbooks and understood the goals of the theories would assimilate them, would master the required teaching behaviors, and would teach according to the inquiry mode. However, studies clearly indicated that this was not the case. Gallagher (1967) found that the individual teacher interpretation of the new method of teaching biology by inquiry actually directed their behavior in the classroom. The other studies reviewed in the second section compared BSCS with other biology curricula, teaching by inquiry, students' attitudes, the use of BSCS textbooks, students learning biology, the appropriate grade level for teaching biology, biology teachers and their education and behavior, learning conditions, the laboratory and the teaching of inquiry method, student–teacher interaction in the laboratory, and evaluation studies on the BSCS implementations in Australia, Israel, and other countries. The studies' results did not show a clear picture of the superiority of one curriculum or one method of teaching over another curriculum and mode of instruction. We can assume that the expectations of the newly implemented educational theories embedded in the BSCS program were high because of the enthusiasm.

This huge wave of studies had its advantages and disadvantages. The advantages were the immense number of studies, which provided a multitude of findings and thus helped build a body of knowledge related to the development and implementation of new curricula and the BSCS learning materials, including all of the issues related to these processes.

BSCS Curricula, Academic Achievement, and Mastery of Inquiry Skills

What might be the reasons for the fact that the studies that investigated the implementation of BSCS programs reported contradictory results? For one, numerous research projects were carried out by graduate students who were fulfilling the requirements needed to obtain their degrees, so the studies were of a one-time nature, without any continuity or sequence that could encompass connected variables and amass results that might build a body of knowledge. A complete list of results on a set of related tested variables may portray a picture in which one result may compensate for another one. The sporadic selection of the problems to be investigated simultaneously in many places actually inhibited the possibility that each science education center would specialize in the study of one variable, laterally and in depth—for example, the study of science teacher education for teaching in an inquiry mode from all possible angles and points of view was not conducted. When a new curriculum is implemented, the list of variables to be studied can be very long: students' learning, achievement and mastery of skills, and so on. Studies were not replicated in order to ensure more reliability than that of a single study's results. Tamir and Jungwirth (1975) suggested that longitudinal studies are needed when comparative research is carried out. When one variable alone is studied, there is a danger of ignoring other variables that may have a lateral impact on understanding and interpreting the results. For instance, while investigating a certain school population—both high and low achievers—for its academic achievement, mastery of skills, and attitudes while using any BSCS program, one might ignore other characteristics, such as cognitive stages, learning styles, learning environments, and students' preferences, choices, and needs.

Comparative Studies in Science Education

Students. A problematic issue in any comparative study is how to compare the academic achievements of two different groups of students. For instance, how do we weigh one group of students who learned in a BSCS program (group *a*) against another group that learned biology traditionally (group *b*)? From the beginning, group *a* is at a disadvantage. It must learn a new topic by a new method; group *b* has to learn the new topic only, since its members are accustomed to the traditional method of teaching and learning. The assumption that, by learning a new topic in an inquiry method, students will simultaneously master the knowledge and the inquiry skills needed to study the new topic is questionable and is not founded on research. Therefore, one cannot expect that group *a* will do better than group *b*. In the optimal situation, the two groups may well achieve the same level. In their book *The Jigsaw Classroom*, Aronson, Stephan, Sikes, Blaney, and Snapp (1978) suggested that when we want to investigate the

academic achievement of students who learn in a cooperative small-groups method compared with students learning in an expository mode, we have to take care that the students should first master the needed skills of helping behavior and learning cooperatively. Only then can they learn the new topic and can their achievements be compared with those who learned by a traditional method.

Teachers. The issue of teachers is another important variable when one investigates their impact on students learning a new curriculum such as the BSCS programs. One cannot circulate an instrument on teachers' attitudes or investigate their impact on students' achievement while ignoring the teachers' past education, knowledge of science, personalities (openness vs. closeness), personal interpretations of a new CKS, and new theories and strategies of teaching, learning, and assessment as well as their attitudes toward the new method in whose development they were not involved. A single teacher cannot be an agent of change in his/her school without the cooperation of the other teachers, the principal, and other school officials or without being involved in setting the teaching timetable.

Teachers cannot be asked to introduce new curricula or new teaching strategies in their classrooms without being involved in one way or another in developing them and in the issues of the implementation process itself (from the pedagogical, educational, and administrative points of view) before they start to use them. The danger of imposing a new curriculum on teachers from top to bottom is that this will push them back from their third stage, the impact stage in their professional development in which they can focus on students' needs by adapting teaching modes to their learning styles. Thrusting a new curriculum onto teachers may shunt them back to the self-stage (survival), in which they focus on their personal problems, classroom management and discipline, teaching a lesson, and student–teacher interaction. Such a situation invites objections, resistance, antagonism, and failure (Bethel & Hard, 1981; Fuller, 1969).

Teachers' knowledge of the classroom learning environment (learning settings) and their understanding and knowledge of the nature of their student population were also ignored in most studies, and only one variable was investigated. The interrelationships between the variables, whether constant, independent, or dependent, must be taken into account when explanations and interpretations are made. This can be done only when a chain of consecutive studies on interrelated variables is carried out and a whole picture is constructed based on a set of study results in one science education center. Otherwise, we get broken and unrelated pieces of information that cannot contribute to the construction of a body of knowledge on a particular subject.

The Nuffield Project in Biology in the United Kingdom

The Nuffield curriculum in biology featured particular characteristics based on a different philosophical approach, which was used because of the structure of the English school system (Nuffield Foundation, 1966). The English school system consists of three parts: elementary school (1st to 5th grades), high school (6th to 10th grades), and sixth lower and upper forms (11th and 12th grades). In this chapter we refer only to the high school level. The biology curriculum was updated with the CKS of the 1960s and 1970s as then known to scientists. It had several major characteristics: It was divided into five parts for the five high school grades and two additional advanced courses for the sixth-form students who had chosen to study biology for their matriculation examinations. The sequence of the textbooks for every grade was as follows:

Nuffield Biology Text 1. Introducing Living Things (6th grade)
Text II. Life and Living Processes (7th grade)
Text III. The Maintenance of Life (8th grade)
Text IV. Living Things in Action (9th grade)
Text V. The Perpetuation of Life (10th grade)

The structure of the course centered around 11 fundamental themes, which recur repeatedly throughout the 5 years (Nuffield Foundation, 1966, p. 1):

1. Cycles of matter and energy
2. Structure and function
3. Interaction of organism and environment
4. Integration and homeostasis
5. Replication
6. Variation
7. Adaptation
8. Natural selection
9. Classification
10. Man
11. Mathematical relationships and experiments

Time allotment: During the first 2 years: two single periods per week. During the remaining 3 years: three periods per week (one double and one single)

Instructional Strategy

The synopsis of the course clearly indicates that the books were divided into five parts: The first two parts can be regarded as introductory, and the remaining three constitute the next intermediate phase. The introductory phase is characterized by a broad general approach to the subject. In the intermediate phase, the treatment becomes more quantitative, with greater emphasis on experimentation and reasoning.

The learning material was written according to the expected cognitive stage of the pupils in each grade. In this way, the sophistication level of the learning material increased with the grade age. In addition, each chapter was written as a sequence of texts integrated with experiments. Accordingly, the text included concepts and principles in biology, introduced facts, and raised problems that had to be solved by the performance of an experiment.

The experiment results provided answers, which, in turn, led to a new problem, which had to be solved. The activities ensured that no one could skip a text or omit performing an experiment, because the two were interconnected. Teachers and the students were requested to follow the suggested sequence.

The pedagogical approach used in the textbooks ensured that the inquiry mode of learning accompanied the learning process. Each student textbook was provided with a teacher's handbook in which, for every chapter, additional scientific information, experiments, and suggested modes of instruction were available. Thus, teachers had the needed accurate science knowledge for any particular subject and were encouraged to add more experiments to their curriculum, if time was available. They were allowed to choose the teaching strategy that matched their students' needs, their cognitive stage, and the subject being taught.

Sixth Lower and Upper Forms (11th and 12th Grades)

For the students who studied biology for their matriculation examinations, advanced courses were available based on two textbooks: 1. *Teachers' Guide to the Laboratory Guides, Volume I.* a) Maintenance of the organism; b) Organisms and populations; and *Volume II.* a) The developing organism; b) Control and coordination in organisms (Nuffield Advanced Science, 1970). The units covered all of the biological levels of organization and illustrated the major concepts and principles in biology, such as structure and function, organisms and their environment, processes of physiology and behavior, the genetic and evolutionary continuity of life, matter and energy cycles, homeostasis, and the development and uniqueness of the individual. In both textbooks, biological subjects and problems were presented to students, who were asked to perform inquiry experiments in the laboratory.

The sequence in each subject was composed of four components: (a) principles, where items of information were presented, leading to a biological problem; (b) teaching procedure with associated materials; (c) practical problems related to the investigated subject; and (d) questions and answers, in which student–student and student–teacher interactions occur. Experimental results led to the need to read biology texts, in which more problems were raised in order to be solved. The inquiry mode of learning and performing experiments transformed the class (no more than 12 students are in a sixth-form class) into a small group of learners who led discussions among themselves or with the teacher. The teacher never lectured, but rather constituted a source with whom to exchange ideas and to consult, and from whom to receive support during the process of inquiry and learning.

The goals of the advanced courses were to learn rather than to be taught, to understand rather than amass information, and to find out rather than be told (Nuffield Advanced Science, 1970, p. VI).

The Adaptation of the BSCS, Yellow Version, in Israel

The inquiry-oriented curriculum project was implemented in Israel between 1964 and 1970. *BSCS: Biological Science; An Inquiry into Life* (BSCS, 1968) was translated and adapted for Israeli high schools by a team of 25 biology teachers under the leadership of Professors Alexandra Poljakoff-Mayber, Clara Chen, and Ehud Yungwirth at the Department of Biology of the Hebrew University in Jerusalem, and Professor Haim Adomi from the Oranim Teachers College in Kiryat Tivon.

The CKS in biology of that period as presented in the seven levels of biological organization had raised several questions regarding pedagogical aspects of instruction. Since biology is taught in the United States in 10th grade only as an introductory course, its adaptation in Israel and Europe raised a series of problems, among them the fact that biology in the latter two countries is taught in Grades 9 through 12. Following the implementation of the CKS, one of the main problems was the higher level of the learning material, especially the requirements in biochemistry knowledge, which ninth-grade students, on the one hand, were required to assimilate. On the other hand, for 11th and 12th graders, the need for learning material at a higher level quickly became apparent. The two main questions were: (a) What should be the appropriate sequence of the LBO to be taught in the 9th, 10th, 11th, and 12th grades, respectively, since we know that all of the students in Grades 9 and 10 learn biology but very few will continue to study advanced courses in biology in Grades 11 and 12? and (b) What are the appropriate LBO to be taught to a certain grade, when we have to match students' cognitive stages with the cognitive demands required by the learning material? Since we cannot expand on this issue in this chapter, we only mention the fact that young students who were still in the cognitive concrete operational stage found the content of the levels of biological organization at the reduced level very difficult. For them, probably the most adequate levels are the holistic ones, whereas for the students in Grades 11 and 12, the reduced levels suited their cognitive stage. This problem requires a separate debate on how to match learning material to students' cognitive development, age, grades, learning theories, and learning styles.

The Implementation of the BSCS Curriculum in Israel

The teachers who implemented the BSCS chapters in their classes provided feedback that was used for the content validation process. Names of the plants and the animals were replaced by those of Israeli endemic organisms. Formative evaluation was carried out during the 2 years of the implementation process by Tamir and Jungwirth (1975). The formative evaluation and the feedback provided by the teachers served for the revision of the translation and adaptation of the learning material. Based on the experience of 25 teachers in their classrooms, inservice training courses were organized in four areas of the country in which teachers who wanted to adopt the new curriculum in their schools participated. The courses were led by university biology professors, their role being to update the participants in biology content knowledge, and by teams of biology teachers from the original group of the 25 teachers, as their pedagogical and didactic experience gained during the first 2 years of implementation (in instructional modes, the integration of the learning in the classroom with the performance of the experiments in the laboratory, assessment, evaluation, and grading procedure) was practical guidance for the novices. This course of action was based on Francis Fuller's (1969) findings that the implementation of a new curriculum or a new method of instruction will be successfully carried out if schoolteachers are the agents of change rather than external factors. Teachers tend to trust their colleagues rather than experts on learning theories and strategies of instruction and assessment, evaluation, and grading.

The inservice training course was organized in the following manner. During the first meetings, the professors and the teachers from the original group, who presented the new curriculum, were the most active participants, and the novices were passive. Thereafter, the latter began to participate actively by preparing lessons from the BSCS units, peer teaching, and performing experiments, followed by discussions regarding the implementation process in their classes. In addition, conducting laboratories as well as issues of evaluation, assessing, and grading were discussed. By the end of the course, the biology professors and the original group of teachers were in the background while the participating teachers took over all the activities. Only teachers who participated in these inservice training courses, which lasted almost 2 months during the summer vacation, and took two more short courses of 2 weeks each during the academic year (during the Hanukah and Passover breaks), were allowed to join the new curriculum in biology, to implement it in their schools and have their students take the BSCS matriculation examination at the end of 12th grade. Furthermore, these teachers were provided with weekly (in five different locations) additional training sessions, at which time they heard lectures on new topics in biology and feedback on the matriculation exams. The teachers shared experiences and participated in didactical and pedagogical discussions about how to teach new topics in biology or any other issues. Teachers expressed satisfaction that opportunities were provided in which they could enrich their knowledge, exchange ideas, listen, and find that they were not alone with their problems. This enabled them to seek solutions together. Later on, the Ministry of Education and Culture developed a method to recompense these teachers with an increase in their salaries according to the number of inservice courses in which they participated. It should be mentioned that almost 8 years passed until the entire population of biology teachers joined the BSCS curriculum and that during these years, two curricula in high school biology and two kinds of matriculation examinations were in use. The stipulation required of the biology teachers who wanted to introduce the inquiry curriculum into their classes was their active participation in the inservice training courses and the school principals' agreement to provide an adequate laboratory schedule, equipment, biological and chemical materials, and the aid of a laboratory technician. This long period of transition ensured the successful implementation process of the Inquiry Biology-Oriented Curriculum in Israel under the leadership of Professor Tamir and his colleagues. This was a process that the teachers chose to undertake on their own and was based on learning, experience, and support and was not imposed on them.

Consequently, there was a need to translate several chapters from the *Interaction of Experiments and Ideas* (BSCS, 1970) for use in the 11th and 12th grades. For low academic achievers in Grades 9 and 10, *Biological Science: Patterns and Process* (BSCS, 1966) was translated and adapted as well.

The Inquiry Matriculation Examinations in Biology in Israel

The new inquiry-oriented curriculum in biology required a new approach to examining students. Rather than testing for the memorization of facts and information, students were assessed on the application and mastery of inquiry skills, on higher cognitive skills such as critical thinking, problem solving, and affective skill such as responsibility in the learning process (Lazarowitz, 2000).

The matriculation examinations had four parts:

1. *A written test* (3 hours) assessed by the Ministry of Education, comprising three sections:
   a. Thirty multiple-choice questions to assess students' knowledge of the seven levels of biological organization, aimed at evaluating them on the six cognitive levels (Bloom, 1956): knowledge and understanding (low cognitive levels) and application, analysis, synthesis, and evaluation (higher cognitive levels)
   b. Six to nine open-ended questions in which students were required to demonstrate knowledge of plant and animal physiology by relating an inquiry approach to the questions. Students were meant to answer the questions in a way that would show their mastery of the inquiry skills.
   c. An "unseen" section in which students were required to analyze a portion of a real research paper published in Israel, using the inquiry skills mastered in the classrooms and laboratory practical work
2. *Laboratory work.* Performance of an unknown experiment in which students had to identify a researchable problem in biology, based on a written question. Students were required to suggest a hypothesis and an experiment to be performed in order to prove the hypothesis. Following the examiner's approval, students performed the experiment; collected data, which had to be put in tables and graphs; and analyzed

the results. Students then wrote a summation in which they demonstrated biological knowledge in physiology and mastery of practical and inquiry skills in laboratory work.
3. *The identification of an unknown plant,* in which they described the structures of the flowers, stem, leaves, roots, fruits, and seeds and, by using a taxonomic key book, found the scientific names of the family, genera, and species to which the plant belongs.
4. *An ecology project.* Students selected a biology subject to be investigated during 1 year of field observations that were reported in a portfolio. It was assumed that students choosing a subject and studying outdoors would develop learning responsibility, along with skills of observation, data collection, and care for the environment. As a consequence, students decided on what scientific topics and data they would examine. This reduced to the minimum the anxiety factor during the oral examination. It was also expected that their motivation would increase and that they would develop positive attitudes toward nature and the environment.

Summary of the Inquiry-Oriented Curriculum Implementation

In the content-oriented curriculum, the emphasis was on the sequence of biological knowledge that reflected the evolutionary and classification research in biology. The emphasis in the inquiry-oriented biology curriculum was on updating the content knowledge based on the seven levels of biological organization, from the molecular to the biome, reflecting biochemistry, biophysics, and ecological and ecosystems research in modern biology. An additional emphasis was given to the pedagogical aspects in which the pure inquiry mode of learning was recommended.

Research in biology led to changes in the CKS in biology as a subject matter, which in turn triggered modifications in the structure of the biology curriculum based on the seven levels of biological organization. Parallel to the changes in the CK and changes in the biology curriculum, changes in the nature of the student population and society occurred, too. These transformations required developments in learning theories, instructional strategies, and methods of learning, evaluation, and assessment. All these have enabled teachers to test not only students' academic achievements but also their mastery of inquiry skills, attitudes toward science, and understanding of the process of science, and their cognitive, affective, psychomotor, and social skills, which were assessed in the classroom and in practical laboratory work (Lazarowitz, 2000; Lazarowitz & Tamir, 1994; Tamir, 1974; Tamir & Glassman, 1971; Tamir & Jungwirth, 1975).

Inquiry Curricula and Heterogeneous Student Population

Were the BSCS programs and other curricula of the 1960s and 1970s suitable for the whole student population, which became more and more heterogeneous? What are the characteristics of a heterogeneous student population? We know that students differ in their cognitive operational stages, abilities, learning styles, preferences, choices, interests, and needs.

Although the inquiry curricula were updated in relation to the subject matter and asked for an inquiry mode in teaching and learning, they were not made suitable for a heterogeneous student population. In order for all students to function in a scientific and technological society, they had to be able to take a democratic stand on societal issues based on literacy and not on prejudices, naïve knowledge, and misconceptions. Moreover, it had to be recognized that only a small portion of students aspire to an academic career; the majority need an academic education in order to find a job in the market. The inquiry-oriented curricula did not address these issues, and a call for developing a curriculum to lead educators and students into the 21st century went out. Science curricula of the 1960s and 1970s represented distinct, well-defined disciplines.

In his paper, *The Crisis in Biology Education,* Yager (1982) noted that most curricula of the 1970s, the BSCS programs, the Human Science Program, or HSP (BSCS), the Outdoor Biology Instructional Strategies, or OBIS (Lawrence Hall of Science), the Biomedical Interdisciplinary Curriculum Project, or BICP, and others were challenged regarding their appropriateness. The public was concerned about the inclusion of sensitive subjects such as sex, reproduction, social issues, and evolution, since these were the topics relevant to the students' needs. Yager (1982) mentioned that biology teachers were used to relying for the majority of their teaching on textbooks, which determined the content of their classes and directed their teaching. Biology teachers did not make curriculum decisions related to the biology programs to be used in their classrooms, and the act of selecting a textbook itself was a significant educational reform for them.

Biology Textbooks Used in High Schools

Three major textbooks were in used in high schools in the United States: *Modern Biology* (Otto & Moon, 1965 used by 40%) and the *Yellow and Green Versions* (BSCS, also used by 40%). In other countries, the books used were translations of the BSCS versions in an adapted form or books written locally that used an inquiry approach. Regarding the instructional strategies practiced in the classrooms, Yager (1982) remarked that teaching science by inquiry, a major goal stated by the BSCS in the 1960s, was rarely observed in the classrooms. In the classroom, teachers tended to emphasize information related to the terminology and definitions, whereas the nature of the laboratory work was demonstrations and confirmation, which was contradictory to the principles of investigation and inquiry. Biology in the school program did not relate to applications, to current issues, to individual students' needs, or to career awareness. The teachers' main concern was with the academic preparation of students, not with

other aspects later raised by Yager and Hofstein (1986). In his paper, Yager (1982) stated that the optimal state of biological education would also include the need to relate to human adaptation, the inquiry process, decision making, values, and ethical and moral considerations of biosocial problems. These issues, he felt, are as important as biology content knowledge. Other aspects he mentioned were teaching and learning settings (individualized and cooperative work), new modes of testing and evaluation, and the use of biology to interpret personal and social problems and issues. The inclusion of human welfare and progress in biology teaching is also of great importance. Finally, Yager wrote that one has to see science education in a continuum of change, like science itself. All of these aspects should be reflected in "a curriculum problem oriented, flexible and culturally as well as biologically valid" (Yager, 1982, p. 332). Therefore, it was decided to call the third generation of biology curricula the problem-oriented curriculum. This new approach has been leading us into the new millennium.

The Problem-Oriented Curriculum in Biology

Since the 1990s, new approaches in science curricula have been started, and we now present examples of how Yager's ideas were implemented in the third generation of biology curriculum in Israel. Student populations are heterogeneous in terms of learning styles, cognitive stages, abilities, choices, preferences, and needs. In the high school student population here, we have two very well-defined, main groups studying biology. In Grades 10 through 12, only 15% of the students continue to study biology at the three- and five-point levels for the matriculation exams. This follows their participation in an integrated course given in a thematic approach that includes some aspects of science, technology, and society (STS) in junior high school in Grades 7 and 8. Eighty-five percent of high school students do not continue to study any science or technology subjects after Grade 9. With these students in mind, Harari's report (1989) recommended that every student in high school who does not choose to study a science should be provided with science and technology literacy embedded with societal aspects. It was assumed that science and technology have a reciprocal influence, and both have an impact on human life and society, the computer being one example of this. In order to produce citizens who are literate in science and technology, the goals of the curricula should give greater emphasis to societal issues and not concentrate only on preparing students for academic careers. The nature of a desired science curriculum that can fulfill students' needs was defined by Yager and Hofstein (1986). The four main goals were presented in their paper under the title *Features of a quality curriculum for school science:*

1. Emphasis on science as preparation for further academic study of a discipline has been a major focus of curricula of the past.

2. Major concerns in science are seen as a means of encountering and resolving current societal problems.
3. Means for attending to the personal needs of students.
4. Means of approaching greater awareness of career potential in science, technology and related fields, suggesting goals that may be far more important than the traditional goal of academic preparation for future courses.

(Yager & Hofstein, 1986, p. 134)

Therefore, the problem-oriented curricula in biology called for a differential approach. First, it advocated a flexible curriculum, which answers the first goal in Yager and Hofstein's paper (1986). This curriculum may consist of many independent learning units from which teachers choose the units that are most appropriate for their goals, the ones they prefer to teach, and those that meet students' preferences, interests, and needs. Sometimes students can participate in this process. Any sequence of several units studied can provide the students with an entire biological picture. Each learning unit can be replaced from time to time, and each unit can be updated, so the need to change the entire curriculum at once no longer exists. This approach was suggested for students who would be taking the matriculation examination in biology at the end of 12th grade (about 15% of the high school population). Second, it recognized the need for a curriculum for the remaining 85% of students that would address Yager's other three goals: science as relevant to societal problems and students' needs and awareness of professional career potential while learning sciences. This curriculum was built of independent units, written in a thematic content of biology, chemistry, physics, and technology with societal aspects, thus having a flavor of the STS approach. Therefore, only science and technology subjects, which could have a common background and could be integrated, were selected.

Matriculation Exams and Learning Units

The following curriculum was offered to the students who wanted to take the matriculation examination in biology. For Grade 10, the following units (called basic topics) were offered:

1. Communication, regulation, and coordination in plants and animals
2. Microorganisms
3. Reproduction systems in plants, animals, and the human body
4. Processes and metabolism in the cell
5. The organism and the environment
6. Transport and mediation systems in plants and animals
7. Darwin and theories on the origin of species and evolution

Teachers and students were allowed to choose three out of seven learning units to be studied during the academic year.

The following units were offered to Grade 11 and 12 students according to their level of matriculation examinations. Learning units for the three-point academic level (basic topics) were:

1. Heredity
2. Energy transformation in living creatures
3. Any two learning units not chosen in 10th grade, bringing the studies to a total of four units.

At the three-point academic level, the matriculation examinations were aimed at assessing students on (a) quantitative treatment of data, (b) attainment and use of inquiry laboratory skills, and (c) classification and identification of plants and animals and mastery of knowledge of the four learning units. Learning units for the five-point academic level (extended topics) were:

1. Heredity
2. Regulation and mechanisms of plant development
3. Photosynthesis
4. Microorganisms
5. Cell communication
6. Physiological systems in animals: respiration and secretion

The matriculation examinations were aimed at assessing students on (a) quantitative treatment of data, (b) an ecology project, (c) plant identification and classification, (d) inquiry laboratory work, (e) mastery of knowledge of three out of the six units, and (f) two learning units not chosen in Grade 10.

Curriculum Offered to Students Not Taking a Science Discipline

This curriculum was built around learning units, their role being to provide students with scientific and technological literacy and mastery of skills in the cognitive, affective, and psychomotor domains. The units were written using a thematic approach, integrating biology, chemistry, physics, and societal aspects based on the STS approach (Bybee, 1987). About 20 units were developed, and teachers and students chose 5 of them to be studied in Grades 10, 11, and 12. Each unit was structured so that it could be taught in 30 to 45 periods (two periods in the classroom and one in the lab). We present four of them here.

Human Health and Science

These learning units developed by Huppert, Simchoni, and Lazarowitz (1992) included health science subjects. The course was developed based on studies in which it was found that high school students (12 to 16 years old, girls and boys) were interested in learning subjects related to their bodies, everyday life, food, health, and the environment (Baird, Lazarowitz, & Allman, 1984; Lazarowitz & Hertz-Lazarowitz, 1979; and Bybee, 1987, who included human health and diseases in his list of the most important societal issues).

The Human Health and Science subunits were written in an STS approach for a 2-year biology course, three periods per week, to be used by comprehensive high school students. The learning material consisted of five modules: (a) Human Energy Expenditure, (b) Organ Transplantation, (c) Human Reproduction, (d) Diseases of Modern Civilization, and (e) Addictive Substances. Each module included the relevant biology content and physiological processes, and aspects of chemistry, physics, and technology applications, which included moral and ethical issues. The various ways of learning included laboratory work, recorded lectures, reprints of articles in science journals, computer simulations, classroom and group discussions, and films. Each module contained two learning units.

Two units from different modules are presented here to illustrate the ways in which STS was integrated:

Module 1. Human Energy Expenditure.
Learning Unit B: The Fat and the Slim

STS topics	Descriptions
Biology:	Digestions and absorption. Sugar metabolism
Chemistry:	Structure of sugars and fats.
Cholesterol Physics:	Heat and temperature. Energy in food
Technology:	Recording metabolic rates. Modern agriculture technology
Society:	Obesity. Anorexia nervosa. Dietary habits. Malnutrition

Module 2. Organ Transplantation.
Learning Unit A: The Heart

STS topics	Descriptions
Biology:	The cardiovascular system. Cardiovascular diseases
Biochemistry:	Neuro-hormones
Physics:	Blood pressure. Electrical activity of the heart
Technology:	Electrocardiogram. Artificial pacemakers. Heart surgery. Coronary angioplasty. Artificial heart
Society:	Organ donors. Religious, ethical, moral, and scientific rules for determination of death

A detailed description of the modules, subunits, learning topics, learning activities, assessments procedures, formative evaluation, and discussions regarding the development and implementation problems as well as the educational values of teaching biology in an STS approach may be found in Huppert, Simchoni, and Lazarowitz (1992).

Ionizing Radiation: Uses and Biological Effects

The learning unit Ionizing Radiation: Uses and Biological Effects (Nachshon, 2000) was written in a thematic and STS approach and included related subjects: (a) the physics-chemistry of ionizing radiation—the particle radiation of alpha and beta rays, electromagnetic radiation, gamma and X-ray radioactive phenomena and background radiation; (b) biological aspects—the effects of radiation on different levels of biological organization: the molecules (DNA molecules), organelles, cell, tissues, and organisms; (c) the technological aspects—radioisotopes as energy and radiation sources, the food industry, science research, the range of medical uses of X-ray photography and computerized tomography (CT); and (d) societal aspects and issues—uses of ionizing radiation for human needs, the use of radioisotopes for diagnosis and treatment in nuclear medicine, the use of nuclear power for electricity (advantages and disadvantages), and the use of this energy as possible weapons of mass destruction, the process of mutation, and the relationship between cancer and damage repair mechanisms and ionizing radiation's immediate effects and long-term effects, which may affect cell life cycles. The implementation and evaluation in Grades 10 and 11 revealed that students' fluency and elaboration on ideas were higher while they learned in cooperative groups rather than as individuals. One third of the students asked higher-order questions, and the questions of the other students were mainly on the knowledge and comprehension levels. Half of the students were interested in the physics of ionizing radiation and activities aimed at developing creative thinking. Students preferred to learn the subjects in the thematic mode, in group activities, and most of them mentioned the importance of the diversity in instructional strategies that were used. The academic achievement of students in control groups, who learned chemistry and physics subjects in a disciplinary approach, was significantly lower, whereas the achievement of those who studied the subjects in the STS mode was higher. All students mentioned that learning about nuclear and ionizing radiation and their uses for human needs in a thematic approach and STS mode helped them to overcome their fears, which had been based on a lack of knowledge and prejudice (Nachshon & Lazarowitz, 2002).

Microorganisms

This learning unit was written in the STS approach in Arabic and Hebrew for ninth-grade Israeli and Arab students (Khalil, 2002a, 2002b, 2007; Khalil et al., 2009). The learning unit was structured around two main biological principles: the unity of life in the world and the relationship between structure and function. The problems raised in the unit were concerned with health issues, environment, microorganisms, and drainage canalization between neighborhood villages. This unit enabled us to investigate achievement in the cognitive and affective domains as well as attitudes toward the preservation of the environment and understanding and peace between people who live close to each other. The following topics were included in the learning unit: microorganisms and their structure, the physiological processes, microorganisms' role in the food web, carbon and nitrogen cycles, the food industry, the environment, and the level of the health of society. The unit helped students to master practical skills in laboratory work and to develop scientific thinking and problem-solving skills. The learning tasks included individual and small-group instructional settings, utilizing a variety of teaching and learning methods in the classroom and laboratory. Students read scientific essays, watched videos, played group games, went on group field trips, visited food industries, and searched for information from different sources (e.g., the Internet and libraries). The learning unit was introduced to the students in a manner designed to raise their motivation. It was practical, was connected with daily life, and dealt with societal issues. In this way the relationship among science, technology, environment, and society was emphasized. It was assumed that students would develop positive attitudes and be able to judge objectively the problems involved in the preservation of the environment while understanding the important role of microorganisms in the life cycle. The outcomes in the cognitive and affective domains were obtained by analysis of students' portfolios written while they studied in the classroom, in the laboratory, and during the execution of their homework. The results showed that students gained in their academic achievement, developed positive attitudes toward the environment, and understood the role that people have in preserving nature and its relation to peace (Khalil & Lazarowitz, 2002).

Section II: Biology Textbooks and High School

In his paper, Yager (1982) stated that the existing biology curriculum was textbook centered and inflexible, and only biological validity was considered. Biological information was given in the context of the logic and structure of the discipline. While citing others, Yager mentioned that biology as it appeared in the school program was pure in the sense that few applications for it were presented, and it did not focus on individual students' needs and paid little attention to current issues and career awareness (Harms & Yager, 1981; Yager, Hofstein, & Lunetta, 1981). Citing the NSF Status Studies of 1976, Yager (1982) stated, "Biology in the school program can be characterized by one word, textbooks." The biology textbook determined the content to be taught, the order, the examples, and the applications of the content, which directed and controlled the teaching strategies. Teachers had faith in textbooks and used them 90% of the time. Teachers did not make curricular decisions about the biology programs in their classrooms, and one of their major involvements was in the "initial choice of the textbook."

Yager (1980) pointed out the need for new learning materials, which can be adapted to local situations, including new instructional strategies and models of implementation. As mentioned previously, Yager's (1982) remarks were the impetus for the development of the biology

problem-oriented curricula and the learning units, geared toward students studying for biology matriculation exams or students anxious to acquire scientific and technological literacy. The learning materials in the learning units were written in an experimental mode in order to attend to the issues raised by Yager (1982) and Yager and Hofstein (1986). The learning units (textbooks) comprised a flexible and differential biology curriculum for diverse student populations. They had specific content based on the "unifying themes in biology" (Schwab, 1963), but at different levels of depth and sophistication. Teachers and students were able to choose the learning units, which included integrative topics in sciences and technology embedded with societal issues, designed to raise students' awareness of academic and professional careers and to help them master the cognitive and affective skills that they would need. Teachers were able to decide what kind of instructional strategies, learning settings, modes of assessment, evaluation, and grading to use. The textbook remained the center of teachers' instruction and students' learning, and it is interesting to compare past studies that related to the role of textbooks with recent investigations that looked into the reasons behind teachers' choice of learning units that they made when making their curricular decisions, following the adoption of the biology problem-oriented curriculum.

Biology Teachers' Perceptions of the Textbooks' Role

An analysis of 22 high school biology textbooks carried out by Rosenthal (1984) revealed that between 1963 and 1983, the awareness of societal issues decreased. Nevertheless, when compared with other texts, Rosenthal mentioned that BSCS textbooks were preferential in both quantity and quality in terms of their treatment of science and society. In general, she noted that biology textbooks tended to avoid questions of ethics and values and that the interdisciplinary nature of problems was neglected. Although between the 1960s and 1970s there was an effort to make the biology textbooks relevant to students' personal and social needs, there was, nonetheless, a decline in the emphasis on societal issues. Understanding the relationships between science and society is necessary in order for citizens to be able to make decisions and deal with problems in an effective and constructive manner, which is so necessary in a highly scientific and technological society (Aikenhead, 1980). Biology teachers themselves are divided over how much attention to allocate to societal issues (Rosenthal, 1984). DiGisi and Willett (1995) reported that biology teachers modified their use of textbooks according to the academic level of the biology class they taught. They expected that students with higher academic levels would learn from classroom instruction and independent reading, and they understood that those with low academic levels rely only on what is taught in the classroom. Their main observation was that "biology teachers viewed both reading and inquiry activities as important to learning biology, but they appeared unsure of how to incorporate reading comprehension strategies into their science instruction" (DiGisi & Willett, 1995, p. 123). In a study conducted by German, Haskins, and Auls (1996), laboratory manuals in biology were evaluated as to how well they promoted the basic and integrated science process skills that are involved in scientific inquiry. They found that in some manuals there are some efforts to integrate science process skills, but in general they require students to use their knowledge and experience by asking questions, solving problems, investigating natural phenomena, and suggesting answers and generalizations.

Thus the issues raised by Yager (1982) regarding the role of textbooks and how teachers use them in their instruction are still valid today. In their paper, Stern and Roseman (2004) mentioned that the textbooks they analyzed were updated in terms of the scientific content knowledge and full of declarations regarding the cognitive goals to be mastered by the learners but were very lacking in the inclusion of the products of the research in science education; in other words, they were in need of didactic pedagogical knowledge of how to use the content in a variety of teaching and learning strategies and learning settings. The question arises as to whether teachers can make curricular decisions choosing the learning unit and the topic to be taught and decide upon what strategies to use so that the curriculum fits their personality as well as the students' pedagogical needs. Because schools and teachers "are still relying on textbooks as the primary source of the classroom curriculum, which strongly influence students' learning through their impact on the teachers," Stern and Roseman (2004) assumed that "curriculum material can and should play an important role in improving teaching and learning." In their opinion, textbooks that score high on the PCK, according to their criteria, should assist teachers in selecting the content and adapting the relevant pedagogical knowledge, and that this discernment and judgment will be reflected in their teaching.

Reasons for Choosing Textbooks and Their Selection

What are teachers' perceptions of the textbooks and their reasons for selecting them for their classrooms? In two studies, teachers were asked about their reasons for choosing learning units for preparing students for the matriculation exams and the criteria for their selection. In her study, Agrest (2003) found that biology teachers tended to choose the subjects for the matriculation exams primarily from the basic learning units, presented in descending order: Organisms and their Environment; The Cell; Heredity; Transport and Mediation Systems in Plants and Animals; Microorganisms; Reproduction Systems in Plants, Animals, and the Human Body; Energy Transformation in Living Creatures; Evolution; Communication, Regulation, and Co-ordination in Organisms. The expanded learning units chosen, in descending order, were: Physiological Systems in Animals: Respiration and Secretion; Heredity; Photo-synthesis; Microorganisms; Regulation

and Mechanisms of the Plant Development; and Cell Communication. While the main concerns of the scientists regarding the learning units were with regard to the scientific content and the methods of scientific thinking, most of the teachers' concerns were focused on the pedagogical aspects.

In a second study, Wagner-Gershgoren (2004) clustered the teachers' criteria for choosing and evaluating biology textbooks into three groups:

1. Scientific content: The teachers attributed the highest degree of importance to the quality of the scientific content (including considerations of being up to date; precision, reliability, and trustworthiness; organization of the information; clear explanations; innovation; relevancy to the individual and daily life; interest; and quotes from studies and articles).
2. Technical aspects: The teachers attributed the highest degree of importance to the format of the book (language, aesthetics, morphological organization of the material, color and formatting of the text).
3. Didactic aspects: The teachers attributed the highest degree of importance to illustrations and organization of data (illustrations, pictures, graphs, flow charts, and schemes and tables).

All of the considerations were presented in descending order of importance.

Teaching Concepts and Principles in Biology

One of the main goals emphasized in biology curricula is the teaching of concepts and principles. When we analyze the "unifying themes in biology" (Schwab, 1963, p. 31), we find that this is a list of concepts presented in a set of biological principles. The main and ultimate expected result of any effective biology teaching and learning is the students' mastery of and ability to use biology concepts and principles in their learning. In his paper, Yager (1982, p. 331) stated that a "closer look at biology textbooks reveals some important generalizations, and typical textbooks emphasize new words or concepts, often as many as 30 on a single page." A typical science textbook for middle or high school, according to DeHart Hurd, Robinson, Connell, and Ross (1981), includes 2,500 new words. This amount is nearly double the number of new words required from a person of the same age when he or she is learning a foreign language. In science education literature, we see studies on concept formation, concept mapping, conceptual change, misconceptions, and so on. Because these studies are reviewed in other chapters, we refer here to how a concept is taught and formed in biology.

Concepts and Names

What is the definition of a concept? Is there a distinction between the word *concept* and a name of an object? Are "new words" equivalent to the word *concept*? When can we refer to a word as a concept and when we do refer to it as a principle? Confusion often exists in the use of all of these terms. When we talk and teach about a specific amino acid, sugar, starch, chloroplasts in the green cell of a leaf, mitochondria, a specific tissue of plants or animals, organelles in a cell, an organ, a specific system within an organism, or an organism or the human body, it may be that these are "new names" for our students, a new language. Yet these new words represent objects, which can be seen, either with the help of a microscope, in a picture, or with our eyes; we can check and measure them; we can depict their characteristics or learn about their proprieties by performing chemical and other laboratory experiments. We can use our senses to learn about them, and, therefore, they are objects to which we can give names, and consequently, they are not concepts. We can learn about these objects, can classify and organize them into groups such as amino acids, organelles, cells, families genera and species, or name specific physiological processes performed by these objects or substances, respiration, photosynthesis, reproduction, and so on. These are the concepts learned, and they include names of objects, which were investigated, and their specific structures, properties, characteristics, and physiological processes were identified, learned, and grouped. Each group can be given a specific name due to common characteristics of its members, which represents a mental activity. At the same time, each group is different from another group, inasmuch as they differ in their characteristics. Facts are elicited through the use of discriminative mental activity, as a result of which a new grouping will form under a different umbrella and be given a different concept name. Accordingly, these are not concrete or abstract concepts. They are objects, which can be studied and their characteristics learned. There are objects for which we need technological aids in order to see and learn about them and others that require the use of our senses, but they continue to be real at the concrete level. Students master the new words, the new language, based on experience, and they proceed to deal with and learn about them as well as use related concepts.

Models of Teaching Biological Concepts

According to Novak (1965), in order to understand a given discipline, one must do more than just memorize statements that summarize the concepts in a topic. Students have to find out how the concepts were derived and elaborated in order to meaningfully understand them so they can grasp the discipline structure. In other words, Novak understood concepts to be generalizations of aspects of the physical or biological biome, which are composed of individual facts and emotional experiences, such as the concept of osmosis or evolution, which represent a group of related facts that stand for a composite of knowledge (Novak, 1965). Concept formation, according to Novak (1965), goes through several steps: (a) experience a student stores as cognitive information; (b) storage of affective information; (c) and the processing of all of the

information. A detailed psychological description of the formation of concepts can be found in Novak's (1965) paper, and readers are invited to study this article.

According to Koran (1971), in biology, concepts represent natural objects such as mammals, invertebrates, amino acids, and autotrophs and events such as dehydration, synthesis, oxidation, and reduction. We can add physiological processes such as respiration, photosynthesis, and reproduction. When we use the term *amino acid,* it is understood that we are not referring to a single object but to a class of objects or to groups. Koran distinguished along a continuum between the concept of all amino acids and a specific amino acid. Each amino acid has COOH and NH_2 at the opposite ends of the molecule, and between them each amino acid has a different chemical structure. We can group under the concept of amino acid any compound that shows this chemical structure; a specific amino acid is a fact or object that can be studied and its characteristics learned (Koran, 1971). In the process of concept formation, two distinct activities are involved. When we group all of the organic compounds, which have at their opposite ends the chemical structures COOH and NH_2, under the name of amino acids, we are generalizing. However, when we distinguish between these molecules and a molecule of sugar, which does not possess COOH and NH_2, we are undertaking a discriminative mental activity (Mechner, 1965). These two mental activities of generalization and discrimination are the major components of concept formation. Providing adequate examples of what a concept includes is as important as providing examples of what it does not include, according to Koran (1971).

Koran, Koran, Baker, and Moody (1978), and Koran, Koran, and Baker (1980) provided many more examples of concept formation in different fields of biology, together with models of teaching using the inductive and deductive modes of instruction and learning.

Concepts and Teaching Biology

Concepts, accordingly, do not represent concrete entities but are created in the human mind, following a learning process, and are, therefore, abstract. It is obvious that we, as teachers, usually start teaching first by presenting the concept, which requires an abstract operational activity, which immediately breaks down the communication between the teacher and the students. We do not have a common language with the students, because as far as they are concerned, we are speaking a "new language" with which they have not had any prior experience. Following the introduction, we proceed to present the objects or to perform an experiment, which are at the level of a concrete operational activity. Although the direction of the learning process as depicted (the deductive approach) is adequate for students who are in a formal cognitive stage and who can cope with this mode of instruction, most students are in the concrete cognitive stage, and the opposite direction is more appropriate for them. First, they have to be introduced to the object, learn about its characteristics, or perform an experiment in order to accumulate information and knowledge about it. Only then can we introduce the names of all the information mastered under the name of the concept, which represents all of the learning activities that have just occurred (the inductive approach). Topics, which are at the reduction level, such as molecules of glucose or macromolecules of starch, for example, since they are names of objects, can be taught by the inductive approach. Starch (an object) can be seen and its characteristics can be learned, being an object that is well known to students from their daily life experiences. Afterward we can relate to its components, the molecules (a concept) of glucose (an object), and as such the deductive approach is desirable. This is the way scientists investigate a phenomenon.

For instance, only after using a microscope and finding out that all organisms are built of microstructures did they refer to some common characteristics of the "cell" concept. The microstructure, the cell, represents an entire organism; when grouped together, the cells represent a structure, the tissue of an organism. Once having made these observations, scientists realized that every unicellular organism or any group of cells that form a tissue have a specific structure and perform a specific physiological activity, and that a relationship exists between the two. With this deduction, the basic principle in biology of structure and function emerged. Scientists can and do communicate among themselves using the word *cell,* without the necessity of explaining again and again all the knowledge related to this concept, because all of them know what the concept "cell" means. In essence, a concept such as a cell is an economical way of communication among people who have a common background of experience and knowledge, following a process of learning.

This is not the situation that may exist between the teacher and his/her students. The teacher has all the knowledge behind a concept, whereas for the students this is a new word, and they first have to attain this knowledge in order to be able to use the new concept. Thus, when the teacher starts to teach by first presenting the concepts to be learned by the students, instead of creating learning settings in which the learners will come into concrete contact with the objects to be studied, by observing, measuring and experimenting, perceiving and conceptualizing, they generally lose their audience. Nonetheless, even when these two steps, perception and conceptualization, are experienced in the correct sequence, students may still not attain the knowledge and grasp the concept. They must be taken through a third step—application. Here learners have to show that they can use the new knowledge in a new learning situation. Only then can we say that learning has occurred. This learning process can be illustrated as follows.

First Step: Perception
This is a concrete learning process. The teacher presents a biological problem that can be solved by making observations regarding objects or by performing an experiment.

Students collect information and data and construct their knowledge.

Second Step: Conceptualization
This is a formal (mental) learning activity. Students and the teacher hold class discussions, using the knowledge mastered in the perception step, and by discrimination and generalizing mental activities, they summarize the accumulated information under one name. For example, if the problem investigated is how plants nurture and they learn about the structure of leaves and perform experiments with chlorophyll, sugars, glucose, starch, solar energy, and so on, they can group all of this acquired knowledge under the concept name of photosynthesis.

Third Step: Application
Students receive variegated leaves (the leaves have areas with chlorophyll that are green and areas without chlorophyll that are albino). The question posed is: Can we find starch in both areas? In order to find an answer, students have to use their knowledge regarding the role of chlorophyll, solar energy, and the production of starch in a new situation. Depending on how their students resolve the question, the teacher will know if their students mastered the knowledge.

Learning Difficulties in Biology
The CKS of the high schools' biology curricula is based on the seven LBO. This organization of the biological content is logical from the evolutionary point of view and represents areas of research and instruction. The concepts and principles presented in most of the LBO require students to be in the formal operational stage of learning and thinking in order to successfully cope with them. In their studies, Johnstone and Mahmoud (1980), Steward (1982), Finely, Steward, and Yaroch (1982), and Friedler, Amir, and Tamir (1987) reported that several biological topics were identified by their level of difficulty in terms of instruction by teachers, as well as the difficulty students encountered while learning these subjects. The concepts were water transport in organisms, osmosis and osmoregulation, the chemistry of respiration and photosynthesis, energy cycles (ATP, ADP), cell respiration, protein synthesis, mitosis and meiosis, enzyme structure and function, the chromosome theory of heredity, and Mendel's laws of genetics and multiple alleles. According to Klinckman (1970), the LBO might be one of the reasons for these difficulties. Young learners and less academically able students may be able to achieve higher scores if they study biology topics that lie within the levels of organisms, population, and community (holistic subjects). Conversely, they may encounter substantial difficulties in learning concepts related to molecules, cells, tissues, and organs. Another reason for their problems in understanding may be the abstract level of concepts such as photosynthesis, respiration, enzyme activity, dominance and codominance, and sex linkage.

Learning Biology and Students' Cognitive Stages

Students' ability to deal with formal concepts in a meaningful manner was found to be correlated with their cognitive operational stage. This assumption was supported by Shemesh and Lazarowitz (1989) in a study with students (ages 15 to 16). These researchers found that, following lessons on the respiratory system, results showed a positive correlation between students' cognitive stages and their achievements, and that only learners at the concrete cognitive stage made errors. Lawson and Thomson (1988) investigated students' misconceptions about natural phenomena. They hypothesized that in order to overcome their mistaken beliefs, learners must be made aware of scientific knowledge and must be able to generate the logical relationships among the evidence and alternative conceptions. The results indicated that the reasoning ability of seventh-grade students, who were assessed by having them write an essay on principles of genetic and natural selection, was the main factor related to the number of misconceptions held. These two studies indicate that relationships do exist between achievement in biology and students' mastery of formal cognitive stages. Students found to be at the concrete cognitive stage were not able to go beyond the given data in a problem situation, and the inferences they drew, even when they remembered all the necessary facts, were directly related to what they had actually observed. It seems that the lack of formal reasoning skills constrained these students' capacity to encode formal concepts and to process complex information. Only a few students at the formal cognitive stage were able to meet the high criteria of relational or extended abstract responses (Shemesh & Lazarowitz, 1989).

As such, the main question asked is, can we teach biological concepts to high school students at any age, or should one delay teaching them until they reach the appropriate formal cognitive stage, when we assume that learners will be able to cope with the concepts? To answer this question, we will relate to several studies. The study by Lazarowitz and Penso (1992) looked at students (ages ranged from 17.5 to 18.5) who were given a test, which included 18 multiple-choice questions. In order to identify difficulties in learning biology and to locate the mistakes made by students in the process of choosing the correct item, they were asked to justify their choice. Their justifications were compared with a justification key prepared by the researchers. This is a method that provides teachers with a remedial teaching tool and helps students analyze their answers and master the correct knowledge. The remedial teaching can take place when the evaluated tests are returned to the students and both they and the teacher engage in a constructivist mode of learning. Students can realize that the test is used not only to give grades (as a punishment tool) but as a learning process from which all can profit. It was also determined that students can overcome test anxiety and develop positive attitudes toward the teacher, the subject matter, and, consequently, the learning process, when their justifications are compared against a justification key. All of the details of the study procedure and the biological content of the questions, the answers, and the analysis can be found in the researchers' paper (Penso & Lazarowitz, 1992).

In another study, Lawson and Worsnop (1992) reported that teaching a learning unit to high school students on the topics of evolution and natural selection yielded the following results: The instruction did not produce an overall shift toward a belief in evolution; reflective reasoning skill was significantly related to the students' initial scientific beliefs and to gains in declarative knowledge but not significantly related to changes in students' viewpoints. One of the difficulties in teaching evolution in high school is the fact that we can neither illustrate nor concretize the evolutionary process in the laboratory. In order to overcome this obstacle, Ron and Lazarowitz (1995) conducted a study among 12th-grade students in which the topic of evolution was taught in an instructional mode of cooperative groups. The topics learned were Lamarck's, Darwin's, and neutral theories; punctuated equilibria; genetics diversity; natural selection; specialization; and phylogenesis. The results showed that students' academic achievement was higher than that of the control group. The explanation for this was based on the fact that cooperative learning facilitates students' verbal interaction and construction of the knowledge, based on group products. Can ninth-grade students identified as being in the concrete operational stage learn the concept of pH, which requires formal operational ability? In their study, Witenoff and Lazarowitz (1993) found that when the laboratory worksheets according to which students performed the experiments are restructured according to Farmer and Farrell's (1980, p. 64) suggestions and taught in cooperative groups, they achieved significantly higher grades than the control group. It can be seen that when the cognitive operational stages of students are identified and the learning material restructured in order to fit their cognitive stage and learning style, they can succeed. Identifying students' cognitive stages not only provides additional independent variables but also helps teachers analyze the learning difficulties their students encounter and adjust the learning material, the instructional methods, and the learning environment to their needs and thus facilitate successful outcomes. Biology teaching and learning in classrooms and in the lab present many opportunities for evaluation and grading procedures, in addition to the use of classical tests following the instruction of a unit (Lazarowitz, 2000; Lazarowitz & Tamir, 1994).

Evaluation and Grading

Finally, we relate to the issue of students' evaluation and grading. A single study performed by Welicker and Lazarowitz (1995) is presented. A learning unit on the Cardiovascular System with Health Aspects was implemented in 10th-grade classes, and through the learning experiences in the classroom and laboratory work, a multidimensional learning environment was created. Students were able to demonstrate a variety of competencies, which were observed by the teachers and evaluated with the use of a multidimensional performance assessment instrument. This instrument served as a tool for an authentic evaluation of students' abilities and mastery of inquiry, psychomotor, and teamworking skills. The multidimensional evaluation system, which was used during the process of teaching and learning in the classrooms and laboratory work, was shown to be a qualitative and dynamic tool of assessment and may provide teachers with an alternative performance evaluation in addition to summative tests.

Morals, Ethics, and Human Values in Biology Education

The need to relate to morals, ethics and values while teaching students in biology was mentioned by Bybee, Harms, Ward, and Yager (1980) and Anderson (2003). In 1976, Gottlieb noted that public school teachers do not relate to these issues while teaching science. Should science teachers address ethics, morals, and human values as part of their educational role, in addition to teaching subjects like genetics, genetic engineering, the human genome, molecular biology, topics in ecology and population issues—subjects that have today an important role in society? Can citizens with no scientific knowledge and its connection to morals, ethics, and human values react to those issues raised in a democratic society, while they did not practice in their past any kind of discussion based on evidence and not on prejudices? These questions were raised by Dreyfus (1995, p. 215), who wrote that "teachers must try to present facts in their wider perspective of some biological principles, such as those of studies on behavior and ecology. This will enable students to develop the eclectic values of an educated member of society." Conner (2000, p. 22) noted the importance of including "bio-ethical issues in order to provide opportunities for students to be prepared to respond to issues in adult life by giving them experience in discussing personal, social and ethical dilemmas related to science and technology." Science classrooms are environments in which, in addition to reason, intuition and emotion are valued (Bryant, 2002; Bryant & Baggott la Velle 2003).

In a study carried out by Lazarowitz and Bloch (2005), the issue of morals, ethics, and human values served as the main goal of investigation. While teaching genetics, genetic engineering, molecular genetics, human heredity, and evolution to high school students, the following questions were asked:

1. Are high school biology teachers aware of the social dilemmas while teaching subjects in genetics?
2. What are the subjects in genetics that, in the teacher's opinion, should be taught in high school?
3. Do these subjects include societal issues (values, morals, and ethics)?
4. What are the reasons given by the teachers in favor of or against including societal issues in their classes of genetics, molecular genetics, genetic engineering, and evolution?

5. Do teachers differ in their opinions as to their awareness of these issues due to their years of teaching experience, gender, or religious faith?

The analysis of the results yielded four main categories: (a) genetic population, (b) molecular genetics, (c) genetic engineering, and (d) societal issues: values, morals, and ethical implications. Additional categories were practical issues, general scientific subjects and pedagogical issues.

The results related to question 2 showed that out of 125 responses, most of them belong to scientific categories. The number in parenthesis, which follows a category, indicates how many times it was mentioned. Genetics population (76 items, 60%); molecular genetics (24 items, 19%); and genetic engineering (18 items, 14%). Only seven items (6%) were found to be related to the societal implications category. Topics primarily emphasized were genetic diseases, Mendel principles, sex determination, and blood types in basic genetics and population categories. In the second category, genetic engineering and application of medicine and agriculture were emphasized. Only three teachers mentioned the seven items in the societal implication category.

While teachers were willing to add ethical subjects, they preferred specialists to deal with genetic counseling and subjects like limits acceptable or prohibited regarding the genetic engineering issue. On scientific and practical subjects, they were ready to add topics to their instruction; however, there was a tendency to refer the societal issues to others.

When teachers were required to add to their curriculum the topic of cystic fibrosis disease (CFd) and what subjects they will integrate, they mentioned 43 items on the scientific field and only 5 related to the societal area. This topic is not in their curriculum and is not found in the textbook they used. The majority of the teachers did not find it necessary or simply did not consider it their role to relate to the societal aspects of the problem. It remains to be determined if teachers lack sensitivity to societal issues or do not regard it their role as science teachers to include values and ethical aspects. One might recognize the need of including these aspects in teacher education.

The teachers were concerned with the scientific content and the ethical aspects of human cloning, including the Dolly experience and charlatans and dictators who could use biotechnology for their purposes.

Significant differences were found between the most experienced teachers and the other teachers in all four categories. Teachers with more years of teaching experience tended to provide more items in the four categories. One might expect that novice teachers would provide more items on basic genetics, molecular biology and genetic engineering, due to the fact that they had recently concluded their university studies, but this was not the case.

As a general conclusion, the results of this study indicate that among the teachers, there was a medium to low level of awareness of societal issues, and the main emphasis is on the "pure" by scientific subjects taught for the matriculation exams. Most of the teachers did not include societal issues in their classes as a planned part of their curriculum, but if students raised these issues, the teachers claimed to address them.

Citing Watson (2000, p. 3), who wrote "knowledge would liberate mankind from superstition," one may add that liberation from ignorance, prejudices, and poverty will not necessarily predict that circumstances cannot repeat themselves in the future. One may ask if it is the role of the universities to offer college courses on societal issues and bio-ethics (morals, ethics, and values) not only in the philosophy departments but in science and technology, too. The pre- and inservice courses for science teachers who teach genetics, evolution, and related topics should include opportunities to discuss these issues in class (Muller-Hill, 1998). The roles of teachers at all levels should not be based solely on "dry" knowledge but should also address societal issues in open discussions, giving every student the opportunity to take a stand on science and technology developments. Only then we will be able to say that educating through the teaching of science and technology can be relevant to students' needs as future citizens of our society. Knowledge cannot be neutral; it can only be human.

Conclusions

In this chapter, I preferred to make a historical summary of the achievements made during the second half of the 20th century in the development, implementation, and teaching of biology curricula in high schools all over the world and to pay tribute to the modern science educators who contributed so much to our field. The inquiry mode of teaching and learning; the study of cognitive skills and cognitive stages, conceptual change and formation; and the learning settings of individual, cooperative, and computer-assisted learning developed during the 20th century, to mention just a few, are milestones pointing the way toward the new century. In the 21st century, we have to grapple with the issue of teaching sciences to a heterogeneous student population in order to spread scientific and technology literacy and enable these young men and women to participate in a continually evolving society. Only by appreciating and knowing the past can one look to the future.

The reader, then, in my opinion, after reading this chapter will have a basic understanding of where research on science education has been and the directions in which it may be going.

Having said this, I point out to the reader that there are several reviews that present the topics investigated in teaching biology, some of them in specific chapters in this book and others I now mention briefly. The interested readers may look at Lawson (1988), who mentioned the research aimed at improving biology teaching. Lawson found that two major theories dominated these studies. The first, proposed by Ausubel, is a theory of verbal learning on ways students acquire specific biological concepts, and the second is Piaget's developmental theory, which focuses on ways students acquire and use general scientific reasoning patterns. The research on laboratory practical work was summarized by Lazarowitz and Tamir (1994). The research studies on teaching biology in cooperative small groups were reviewed by Lazarowitz (1995a, 1995b) and by Lazarowitz and Hertz-Lazarowitz (1998).

The topics of concept mapping in biology from different angles, the nature of biology knowledge, misconceptions in biology, language, analogy, and biology, concept circle diagramming as a knowledge mapping tool, and more topics are presented in *Mapping Biology Knowledge* by Fisher, Wandersee, and Moody (2000).

Recommendations

As we embark on the 21st century, it is becoming clear that biology curricula should serve not only the students who are pursuing academic careers but also the remainder of students, who are the majority (almost 85%) and whose needs are different.

A differential approach in developing biology curricula, which will provide an answer to our student populations who differ so much in their needs, must be adopted. It is imperative to integrate all of the findings of our research in science education, in textbooks, in preservice and inservice courses in a more rigorous way, so that teachers will have the tools for the instructional process to help students enjoy and profit from the learning of science and technology. If we want to be relevant to students' needs as future citizens who will have to function in a highly scientific and technological society, then an integration of the sequence of topics to be taught and learned with a new pedagogical and didactical approach should be developed, implemented, and evaluated. The pedagogical and didactical approach should include a variety of instructional strategies and learning settings. The issue of ethics and values cannot be ignored and should be integrated into textbooks and the education of biology teachers. The results of a study by Lazarowitz and Bloch (2005) have shown that teachers, while teaching genetics, genetics engineering, molecular biology, and evolution topics, are primarily concerned with the CKS and much less with the aspects of ethics, morals, values, and societal issues, which derive from scientific research and daily life. In this troubled world, one may ask if it is not the educational role of teachers at all levels, from K to 12th grade and in the universities, to address these issues while teaching the sciences and technology, biology in particular. These new approaches are opening new frontiers for science education research in the 21st century and becoming more relevant to a heterogeneous high school student population.

Acknowledgments

Thanks to Anton Lawson, James Wandersee, and Jan H. van Driel, who reviewed this chapter.

References

Agrest, B. (2003). *How do biology teachers choose to teach certain topics in a high school biology curriculum without compulsory parts?* Unpublished Ph.D. dissertation, Hebrew University of Jerusalem, Israel.

Aikenhead, G. S. (1980). *Science in social issues: Implications for teaching.* Ottawa: Science Council of Canada.

Alexander, G. (1953). *General biology* (6th ed.). New York: Barnes & Noble.

Anderson, S. L. (2003). Teaching today's students how to examine ethical issues and be more actively involved in the learning process. *Journal of Academic Publishers, 1*(2), 189–198.

Aronson, E., Stephan, C., Sikes, J., Blaney, N., & Snapp, M. (1978). *The jigsaw classroom.* Beverly Hills, CA: Sage.

Baird, J. H., Lazarowitz, R., & Allman, V. (1984). Science choices and preferences of middle and secondary school students in Utah. *Journal of Research in Science Teaching, 21*(1), 47–54.

Bethel, J. L., & Hard, M. S. (1981). *The study of change: Inservice teachers in a National Science Foundation Environmental Science Education Program.* Paper presented at the American Research Association Conference, Los Angeles, CA.

Biological Sciences Curriculum Study (BSCS). (1966). *Biological science: Patterns and process.* New York: Rinehart & Winston.

Biological Sciences Curriculum Study (BSCS). (1968). *1. Biological science and inquiry into life* (Yellow version). New York: Harcourt, Brace & World; *2. Molecules to man* (Blue version), New York: Houghton-Mifflin; *3. High school biology* (Green version). New York: Rand McNally.

Biological Sciences Curriculum Study (BSCS). (1970). *Interaction of experiments and ideas* (2nd ed.). Englewood Cliffs, NJ: Prentice Hall.

Bloom, B. S. (1956). *Taxonomy of educational objectives: The classification of educational goals.* London: Longmans.

Bruner, J. S. (1961). The act of discovery. *Harvard educational review.*

Bryant, J. A. (2002, May 17). Why I believe that all biology degrees study should include a module in bioethics. *Times Higher Education Supplement,* 14.

Bryant, J. A., & Baggott la Velle, L. M. (2003). A bioethics course for biology and science education students. *Journal of Biological Education, 37*(2), 91–95.

Bybee, R. W. (1987). Science education and science-technology-society (STS) theme. *Science Education, 71*(5), 667–683.

Bybee, R. W., Harms, N., Ward, B., & Yager R. (1980). Science society and science education. *Science Education, 64*(3), 377–395.

Conner, N. L. (2000). Societal issues: Recommendations for teaching in science and technology. *Pacific Asian Education, 12*(1), 19–30.

DeHart Hurd, P. (1961). *Biological education in American secondary schools (1890–1960).* Baltimore, MD: Waverly Press.

DeHart Hurd, P. (1978). The golden age of biological education 1960–1975. In W. V. Mayer (Ed.), *BSCS, Biology teacher's handbook* (3rd ed., pp. 28–96). New York: John Wiley & Sons.

DeHart Hurd, P., Robinson, J. T., Connell, M. C., & Ross, N. R. (1981). *The status of middle and junior high school science: Vol. 2. Technical report.* Louisville, CO: Biological Sciences Curriculum Study.

Dewey, J. (1938). *The theory of inquiry.* New York: Holt, Rinehart & Wiston.

DiGisi, L. L., & Willett, J. B. (1995). What high school biology teachers say about their textbooks use: A descriptive study. *Journal of Research in Science Teaching, 32*(2), 123–142.

Dreyfus, A. (1995). Biological knowledge as a prerequisite for the development of values and attitudes. *Journal of Biological Education, 29*(3), 215–219.

Farmer, W. A., & Farrell, M. A. (1980). *Systematic instruction in science for the middle and high school years.* Reading, MA: Addison Wesley.

Finely, F., Steward, J., & Yaroch, L. (1982). Teachers' perception of important and difficult science content. *Science Education, 66*(4), 531–538.

Fisher, M. K., Wandersee, H. J., & Moody, E. D. (2000). *Mapping biology knowledge.* Dordrecht, the Netherlands: Kluwer Academic.

Friedler, Y., Amir, R., & Tamir, P. (1987). High school students' difficulties in understanding osmosis. *International Journal of Science Education, 9*(5), 541–551.

Fuller, F. F. (1969). Concerns of teachers: A development conception. *American Educational Research Journal, 6*(2), 207–226.

Gagne, R. M. (1963). The learning requirements for inquiry. *Journal of Research in Science Teaching, 1,* 144–153.

Gallagher, J. J. (1967). Teacher variation in concept presentation in BSCS curriculum program. *BSCS Newsletter,* January 8–19, pp. 1–39.

German, P. J., Haskins, S., & Auls, S. (1996). Analysis of nine high school biology laboratory manuals: Promoting scientific inquiry. *Journal of Research in Science Teaching, 33*(5), 475–499.

Gottlieb, S. F. (1976). Teaching ethical issues in biology. *The American Biology Teacher,* March, 148–149.

Harari, M. (1989). *Report #1, internationalization of higher education: Effecting institutional change in the curriculum and campus ethos.* Center for International Education, California State University, Long Beach, CA.

Harder, R., Schumacher, W., Firbas, F., & von Denffer, D. (1965). *Strasburger's textbook of botany.* London: Longmans.

Harms, N. C., & Yager, R. E. (1981). *What research says to the science teacher* (Vol. 3). Washington, DC: U.S. Government Printing Office.

Huppert, J., Simchoni, D., & Lazarowitz, R. (1992). Human health and science. A model for an STS high school biology course. *The American Biology Teacher, 54*(7), 395–400.

Johnstone, A. H., & Mahmoud, N. A. (1980). Isolating topics of high perceived difficulty in school biology. *Journal of Biological Education, 14*(2), 163–166.

Khalil, M. (2002a). *Microorganisms, a STS learning unit.* Haifa, Israel: Israel Science Teaching Center and the R&D Institute, IIT, Technion.

Khalil, M. (2002b). *a. Microorganisms, a STS learning unit. b. Teachers' handbook.* Haifa, Israel: Israel Science Teaching Center and the R&D Institute, IIT, Technion.

Khalil, M. (2007). Teaching the microorganisms learning unit: Academic achievements and attitudes toward environment and peace of 9th grade students. *Journal of Stellar Peacemaking, 2*(2), 1–26.

Khalil, M., & Lazarowitz, R. (2002, April). *Developing a learning unit on the science-technology-environment-peace-society mode. Students' cognitive achievements and attitudes toward peace.* Annual Meeting of the National Association of Research in Science Teaching (NARST), New Orleans, LA.

Khalil, M., Lazarowitz, R., & Hertz-Lazarowitz, R. (2009). A conceptual model, the six mirrors of the classroom and its application to teaching and learning about microorganisms. *Journal of Science Education and Technology, 18,* 85–100.

Klinckman, E. (1970). *Biology teachers' handbook.* New York: John Wiley & Sons.

Koran, J. J., Jr. (1971). Concepts and concept-formation in the teaching of biology. *The American Biology Teacher,* October, 405–408.

Koran, J. J., Jr., Koran, M. L., & Baker, S. D. (1980). Differential response to cueing and feedback in the acquisition of an inductively presented biological concept. *Journal of Research in Science Teaching, 17*(2), 167–172.

Koran, J. J., Jr., Koran, M. L., Baker, S. D., & Moody, K. W. (1978, October). *Concept formation in science instruction: What does research tell us?* The Science Council, Alberta Teachers Association and the National Science Teachers Association, Banff, Alberta, Canada.

Lawson, A. E. (1988). A better way to teach biology. *The American Biology Teacher, 50*(5), 266–277.

Lawson, A. E., & Thompson, L. D. (1988). Formal reasoning ability and misconceptions concerning genetics and natural selection. *Journal of Research in Science Teaching, 25*(9), 733–746.

Lawson, A. E., & Worsnop, W. A. (1992). Learning about evolution and rejecting a belief in special creation: Effects of reflective reasoning skill, prior knowledge, prior belief and religious commitment. *Journal of Research in Science Teaching, 29*(2), 143–166.

Lazarowitz, R. (1995a). Learning science in cooperative modes in junior- and senior-high school: Cognitive and affective outcomes. In E.J. Pedersen & D.A. Digby (Eds.), *Cooperative learning and secondary schools: Theory, models and strategies* (pp. 185–227). New York: Garland Press.

Lazarowitz, R. (1995b). Learning biology in cooperative investigative groups. In E.J. Pedersen & D.A. Digby (Eds.), *Cooperative learning and secondary schools: Theory, models and strategies* (pp. 341–363). New York: Garland Press.

Lazarowitz, R. (2000). Research in science, content knowledge structure and secondary school curricula. *Israel Journal of Plant Sciences, 48*(3), 229–238.

Lazarowitz, R., & Bloch, I. (2005). Awareness to societal issues among high school biology teachers teaching genetics. *Journal of Science Education and Technology, 14*(5/6), 437–457.

Lazarowitz, R., & Hertz-Lazarowitz, R. (1979). Choices and preferences of science subjects by junior high school students in Israel. *Journal of Research in Science Teaching, 16*(4), 317–323.

Lazarowitz, R., & Hertz-Lazarowitz, R. (1998). Cooperative learning in the science curriculum. In B.J. Fraser & K.G. Tobin (Eds.), *International handbook of science education* (pp. 449–471). Dordrecht, the Netherlands: Kluwer Academic.

Lazarowitz, R., & Penso, S. (1992). High school students' difficulties in learning biology concepts. *Journal of Biological Education, 26*(3), 215–223.

Lazarowitz, R., & Tamir, P. (1994). Research on using laboratory instruction in science. In D. Gabel (Ed.), *Handbook of research in science teaching and learning* (Vol. 3, pp. 94–128). New York: Macmillan.

Madaus, G.F., & Stufflebeam, D.L. (Eds.). (1989). *Tyler's rationale for curriculum development*. Boston: Kluwer Academic.

Mechner, F. (1965). Science education and behavioral technology. In R. Glaser (Ed.), *Teaching machines and programmed learning, 11: Data and directions* (pp. 441–507). Washington, DC: National Education Association.

Muller-Hill, B. (1998). *Murderous science, elimination by scientific selection of Jews, Gypsies and others in Germany, 1933–1945*. Plainview, NY: Cold Spring Harbor Laboratory Press.

Nachshon, M. (2000). *Ionizing radiation. The biological effects and uses*. Haifa, Israel: Israel Science Teaching Center and the R&D Institute, IIT, Technion.

Nachshon, M., & Lazarowitz, R. (2002, April). *Ionizing radiation, uses and effects. A thematic module for 11th grade students: Academic achievements and creativity*. Presented at the Annual Meeting of the National Association of Research in Science Teaching (NARST), New Orleans, LA.

Novak, J.D. (1965). A model for the interpretation and analysis of concept formation. *Journal of Research in Science Education, 3*, 72–83.

Nuffield Advanced Science. (1970). *Biological science: 1. Teachers' guide to the laboratory guides Volume I. a). Maintenance of the organism; b) Organisms and populations; and Volume II. a) The developing organism; b) Control and co-ordination in organisms.* Harmondsworth, UK: Penguin Books.

Nuffield Foundation. (1966). *Synopsis of the Nuffield Biology Course.* London: Longmans/Penguin Books, Biological Science.

Otto, J.H., & Moon, T.J. (1965). *Modern biology*. Holt, Rinehart and Winston.

Ron, S., & Lazarowitz, R. (1995, April). *Learning environment and academic achievement of high school students who learned evolution in a cooperative mode*. Paper presented at the annual meeting of the National Association for Research in Science Teaching, NARST, San Francisco, CA.

Rosenthal, D.B. (1984). Social issues in high school biology textbooks: 1963–1983. *Journal of Re-search in Science Teaching, 21*(8), 819–831.

Rutherford, F.J. (1964). The role of inquiry in science teaching. *Journal of Research in Science Teaching, 2*, 80–84.

Schwab, J.J. (1963). *Biology teachers' handbook*. New York: John Wiley & Sons.

Schwab, J.J., & Brandwein, P.F. (1962). *The teaching of science as enquiry*. Cambridge, MA: Harvard University Press.

Shemesh, M., & Lazarowitz, R. (1989). Pupils' reasoning skills and their mastery of biological concepts. *Journal of Biological Education, 23*(1), 59–63.

Shulman, L.S. (1987). Knowledge and teaching: Foundation of the new reform. *Harvard Educational Review, 57*, 1–22.

Stern, L., & Roseman, E.J. (2004). Can middle school science textbooks help students learn important ideas? *Journal of Research in Science Teaching, 41*(6), 538–568.

Steward, J.H. (1982). Difficulties experienced by high school students when learning basic Mendelian genetics. *The American Biology Teacher, 44*(2), 80–84.

Tamir, P. (1974). An inquiry-oriented laboratory examination. *Journal of Educational Measurement, 11*, 23–25.

Tamir, P., & Glassman, F. (1971). A laboratory test for BSCS students—a progress report. *Journal of Research in Science Teaching, 8*, 332–341.

Tamir, P., & Jungwirth, E. (1975). Students' growth and trends developed as a result of studying BSCS biology for several years. *Journal of Research in Science Teaching, 12*, 263–280.

Tyler, R.W. (1966). Dimensions in curriculum development. *Phi Delta Kappan, 48*, 25–28.

Wagner-Gershgoren, I. (2004). *The development and validity of a model to set criteria for the choice and evaluation of biology textbooks.* Unpublished Ph.D. dissertation, Israel Institute of Technology, Technion, Haifa, Israel.

Watson, D.J. (2000). *A passion for DNA: Genes, genomes and society. Five days in Berlin*. Plainview, NY: Cold Spring Harbor Laboratory Press.

Welicker, M., & Lazarowitz, R. (1995, April). *Performance tasks and performance assessment of high school students studying primary prevention of cardiovascular diseases*. Paper presented at the Annual Meeting, NARST, San Francisco, CA.

Witenoff, S., & Lazarowitz, R. (1993). Restructuring laboratory worksheets for junior high school biology students in the heterogeneous classroom. *Research in Science and Technological Education, 11*(2), 225–239.

Yager, R.E. (1980). *Analysis of current accomplishments and needs in science education*. Columbus, OH: ERIC/SMEAC Clearinghouse for Science, Mathematical, and Environmental Education, Columbus State University.

Yager, R.E. (1982). The crisis in biology education. *The American Biology Teacher, 44*(6), 328–336, 368.

Yager, R.E., & Hofstein, A. (1986). Features of a quality curriculum for school science. *Journal of Curriculum Studies, 18*, 133–146.

Yager, R.E., Hofstein, A., & Lunetta, V.N. (1981). Science education attuned to social issues: Challenge for the 80s. *The Science Teacher, 48*(9), 12–13.

22

Teaching Physics

Reinders Duit, Horst Schecker, Dietmar Höttecke, and Hans Niedderer

A deliberate subject-specific view is employed in the present chapter. We attempt to provide an overview of research on teaching and learning physics—in particular from the perspective of what is special in this domain as compared to biology, chemistry, and earth science. We would like to point to two issues where physics education appears to be special already in this introduction.

First, according to the bibliography on constructivist-oriented research on teaching and learning science by Duit (2009), about 53% of the studies documented were carried out in the domain of physics, 18% in the domain of biology, and 28% in the domain of chemistry. There are various reasons for this dominance of physics in research on teaching and learning. One major reason appears to be that physics learning includes difficulties that are due to the particular nature of physics knowledge. We just mention the abstract and highly idealized kind of physics (mathematical) modeling. Research on students' conceptions has shown that most pre-instructional (everyday) ideas students bring to physics instruction are in stark contrast to the physics concepts and principles to be achieved—from kindergarten to tertiary level. Quite often students' ideas are incompatible with physics views (Wandersee, Mintzes, & Novak, 1994). This also holds for students' more general patterns of thinking and reasoning (Arons, 1984).

Second, physics clearly is the domain that is greeted with the lowest interests of students among the sciences. This is true in particular for girls (Sjøberg & Schreiner, 2010). It appears that again the nature of physics mentioned is at least partly responsible for these findings. Students, especially girls, perceive physics not only as very abstract, complicated, and difficult but also as counterintuitive and incomprehensible.

The review presented draws on European views of science education, more precisely, continental European views—with German views somewhat predominating. On the one hand, the issue of scientific literacy (see Chapter 25) is discussed from a position including the German idea of Bildung with its emphasis on issues that are beyond "functional" scientific literacy (Bybee, 1997). On the other hand, European ideas of Didaktik (Fischler, 2011; Westbury, Hopmann, & Riquarts, 2000) are used to analyze the particular role of designing the content structure of physics instruction in such a way that it meets students' perspectives (e.g., pre-instructional conceptions and interests) and the aims of instruction.

After describing the framework of our analyses, we discuss major fields of research on teaching physics. The emphasis is on issues that are special for this field. In the subsequent section, research on three content domains—the electric circuit, the force concept, and atomic physics—is reviewed. These three topics allow us to discuss major learning difficulties and major attempts to improve learning that are particularly relevant for physics instruction. Finally, we summarize major concerns and desiderata of physics education research.

Framework

The Interdisciplinary Nature of Physics Education as a Research Domain

As illustrated in Figure 22.1, physics education research is interdisciplinary in nature. Several reference domains are needed to meet the challenges of investigating and analyzing the key issues of teaching and learning physics. To begin with, there is a close partnership among physics, biology, and chemistry education, as expressed, for example, in the European Science Education Research Organization (ESERA). Philosophy and history of physics provide frameworks that allow identifying what usually is called the "nature of science" in the literature (see Chapter 28). Hence, these domains play a major role in discussing what is special in physics and therefore also what is special in teaching and learning physics. But also social sciences, especially pedagogy and psychology, are

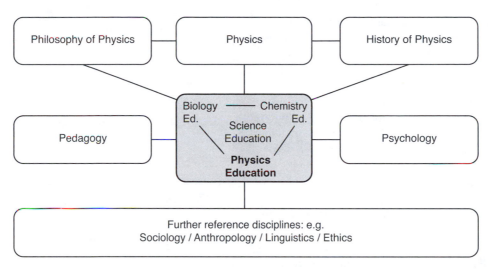

Figure 22.1 Reference and partner disciplines of physics education.

essential reference domains. Research and development that aim at improving practice have to address issues of physics as a specific way of knowing as well as general issues of learning. This is the position underlying the present review.

The German Didaktik Tradition

The European Science Education Research Association (ESERA) declares in its constitution: "Where ever the English phrase 'Science Education' appears in this document, it has a meaning equivalent to 'didactique des sciences' in French, 'Didaktiken der Naturwissenschaften' in German, 'Didáctica de las Ciencias' in Spanish, or the equivalent in other European languages." At least in continental Europe, the term Didaktik is widely used— however, with a number of slightly or more significantly different meanings. The tradition that has developed in the German-speaking countries has been rather influential, at least in continental European countries.

The meaning of the German term Didaktik should not be associated with the Anglo-Saxon meaning of didactical. Whereas the latter primarily denotes issues of educational technology, Didaktik stands for a multifaceted view of planning and performing instruction that is based on the German conception of Bildung. This term shares certain features of scientific literacy but also includes particular views of the aims of schooling and instruction (Westbury et al., 2000). Fischler (2011, p. 34) argues, "Bildung also claims to help students withstand the challenges of their future life, but by a general preparedness that is not simply acquired knowledge and skills." In addition, he claims that possessing knowledge clearly is part of Bildung. Yet knowledge framed by Bildung is meant to support an individual's development and his or her general relation to the world.

A literal translation of Bildung is *formation* (e.g., Westbury, 2000, p. 24). In fact, Bildung is viewed as a process. Bildung stands for the formation of the learner as a whole person, that is, for the development of the personality of the learner. Bildung hence does not only include the achievement of domain-specific knowledge but also the formation of what may be called "cross-curricular competencies" (including competencies allowing rational thinking and various social competencies). There is an emphasis on these cross-curricular competencies that stand for a well-educated personality. The meaning of Didaktik is based on the conception of Bildung. It concerns the analytical process of transposing (or transforming) human knowledge (the cultural heritage) like domain-specific knowledge into knowledge for schooling that contributes to the formation (Bildung) of young people. In the French Didactique tradition, the idea of transposing human knowledge into knowledge for schooling also plays a significant role. The term employed is *Transposition Didactique* (Chevallard, 2007). However, it needs to be taken into account that the German *Didaktik* and the French *Didactique* positions share major features, but there are also significant differences (Hopmann, 2007).

During the second half of the 20th century, the idea of Bildung was strongly promoted by Martin Wagenschein (Jung, 2012). Influenced by educational philosophers like Theodor Litt, Wagenschein assumed that a deeply rooted understanding of nature may arise in every child. He fostered the notion that students develop their own ideas and concepts while being engaged with natural phenomena. A student should become aware of the constructive character of science. According to this perspective, doing physics changes not only views of nature but also the self-concept of a learner or a physicist. Thus, learning physics involves critical reflections on nature and on oneself.

Fensham (2001) claims that many attempts to improve science teaching and learning (e.g., based on constructivist perspectives) put a strong emphasis on improving the way science is taught (i.e., focus on the improvement of teaching methods and media). He argues that science content itself should be regarded as problematic—that also the content structure for instruction should be given attention. In addition, he is of the opinion that the Didaktik tradition allows such an improvement of instruction by developing a content structure for instruction that addresses students' learning needs and capabilities as well as the aims of instruction.

Briefly put, the content structure *of* a certain domain (e.g., the energy concept) has to be transformed into a content structure *for* instruction. The two structures are substantially different. As mentioned briefly, the abstract and highly idealized kind of physics modeling and physics concepts are responsible for particular teaching and learning difficulties. The physics content structure of a certain topic may not be directly transferred into a content structure for instruction. Later in this chapter we discuss this problem by analyzing teaching and learning difficulties for (a) the simple electric circuit, (b) the force concept, and (c) models of the atom. It will be illustrated that the content structure for instruction has to be not only simplified (in order to make it accessible for students) but also enriched by putting it into contexts that make sense for the learners. Two phases of this process can be differentiated. The first may be called *elementarization*. It leads to a set of elementary key features of the content under consideration. For the energy concept, the following elementary ideas may result: conservation, transformation, transfer, and degradation. On the basis of this set of elementary ideas, the content structure for instruction is constructed. It is a key claim of the Didaktik tradition that both processes *elementarization* and *construction of the content structure for instruction* are intimately interrelated. Duit, Gropengießer, Kattmann, Komorek, and Parchmann (2012) call the whole process Educational Reconstruction (for an example for the use of the model, see Duit, Komorek, & Wilbers, 1997).

The essence of the content analysis outlined in Figure 22.2 may be illustrated by a set of questions comprising the Didaktische Analyse proposed by the German educator Klafki (1969; see also Fensham, 2001):

(1) What is the more general idea that is represented by the content of interest? What basic phenomena or basic principles, what general laws, criteria, methods, techniques, or attitudes may be addressed in an exemplary way by dealing with the content?

(2) What is the significance of the content for students' actual and future life?

(3) What is the structure of the content if viewed from the pedagogical perspectives outlined in questions 1 and 2?

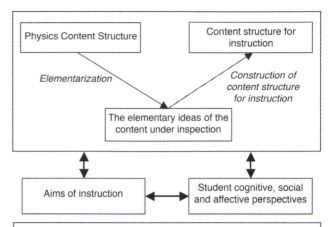

Figure 22.2 Educational reconstruction of physics content structure.

(4) What are particular cases, phenomena, situations, experiments that make the structure of the referring content interesting, worth questioning, accessible, and understandable for the students?

The conception of Educational Reconstruction outlined in Figure 22.2 adds to Klafki's set of questions the idea of a fundamental interplay of all variables of instruction, namely the *aims*, the *content*, the *teaching and learning methods*, and the *media*, which is also a key figure of thought in the German Didaktik tradition (Heimann, Otto, & Schulz, 1969). In the process of instructional planning, this fundamental interplay has to be taken into account. It has also to be regarded that students' perspectives are a key point of reference for construction of the content structure for instruction and for developing the phases of instruction and the methods, materials, and media used.

In a nutshell, the German Didaktik tradition as well as similar traditions in other European countries critically takes the content issue into account. It is a key assumption that a content structure has to be developed that addresses students' pre-instructional perspectives. At the same time, the learning environment has to be designed in such a way that students may develop an understanding of the content in question. Improving instruction includes both critical analysis and reconstruction of content and development of supportive learning environments.

Clearly, major ideas of Shulman's (1987) approach of content-specific pedagogical knowledge are in accordance with the European Didaktik tradition. However, whereas Shulman puts strong emphasis on teacher competencies, the Didaktik tradition has also developed strategies for taking the content issue seriously in instructional planning (Pasanen, 2009).

In completing the discussion of the European Didaktik tradition, commonalities and differences of the Anglo-Saxon curriculum tradition and the European Didaktik tradition will be briefly outlined. Westbury (2000) concludes that the two positions are complementary. The curriculum tradition is embedded within a pragmatic philosophical position. According to this tradition, the focus is on *how* things are enacted, while the Didaktik tradition predominantly focuses on the *why*. However, the still rapidly growing globalization of science education research and development seems to enrich the national traditions (Duschl, Maeng, & Sezen, 2011) without significantly losing key national characteristics (Chiu & Duit, 2011).

Major Fields of Research

As detailed in what follows, we provide a brief overview of major fields of research. From the extended variety of fields in which physics education researchers are working, we selected those that are in our view the most significant ones. Many research papers did not focus on physics education in particular but took a broader scope on science education. Nevertheless, research in the general field of science education matters for the narrower field of physics education in a multitude of ways. Thus, the following chapters focus on physics education without ignoring research in science education as far as relevant for physics education.

Aims of Instruction

The international school achievement studies TIMSS (in the 1990s, Third International Mathematics and Science Study; now Trends in International Mathematics and Science Study) and PISA (Programme for International Student Assessment) have had a strong impact on the discussion about proper aims of instruction, in particular for lower secondary education (cf. the discussion on scientific literacy in Chapter 26). Science is seen as a major factor influencing the daily lives of individuals as well as economic progress in technology-based societies (e.g., Beaton et al., 1996, p. 7). In order to make sensible use of technological means, to find a place in a technology-based economy, and to participate in political processes about technology-related decisions, citizens need a certain amount of physics understanding, as physics forms major foundations for domains like information technology and energy production.

The PISA consortium has agreed on a notion of scientific literacy that consists of understanding basic scientific concepts, familiarity with scientific thinking and processes, and the ability to apply this knowledge in concrete situations (OECD, 1999). Students should be able to identify issues that can be understood by applying scientific knowledge, to draw conclusions from scientific investigations, and to assess the scope of scientific findings. As these competencies apply for all citizens, they have to be targeted during the *obligatory* phase of science education.

Looking at *upper secondary*–level physics education, with its mostly *voluntary* participation in advanced

physics courses, Schecker, Fischer, and Wiesner (2004) see three major contributions of physics teaching to the goals of higher education:

- *Deeper general education* (*Allgemeine Bildung*; e.g., reflection of the specificities of the modern physics conceptions of the world, in contrast to other worldviews)
- *Introduction to advanced scientific practices* (physics as a paradigmatic science)
- *Preparation for university studies* in science and technology (e.g., sustainable knowledge of standard physics practices in experimenting and modeling)

While some countries, like the United States, have a long tradition of science education standards, several European countries, like Germany, started to work on the formulation of expected learning outcomes as reactions to results of the PISA studies. Bernholt, Neumann, and Nentwig (2012) present an overview of the global situation. Recent frameworks and standards call for more coherence in science teaching along a limited number of basic concepts. An expert committee set up by the American National Research Council, or NRC (2012) proposes seven "cross-cutting concepts," like *system* or *scale*, and four disciplinary "core ideas" for physics (*matter, motion, energy*, and *waves*). Yet there is no international consensus on which basic ideas or concepts are to be chosen. The German national physics standards, for example, name *energy, interaction, matter*, and *system* for the lower secondary curriculum (KMK, 2005). While the selections of basic concepts only partly overlap, the appeal is clear: Physics should not be taught as a sequence of content domains but as a body of comprehensive ideas and practices. Content domains keep their relevance, while basic concepts and physics-related methods of inquiry can serve as guiding ideas across contents. Duschl (2012), in similar sense, speaks of a "second dimension." Foundations for curriculum development are, for example, given in AAAS (1993), NRC (1996), KMK (2005), and NRC (2012). Compared to the American tradition with its pragmatic and optimistic view of science as a means for social progress (the NRC Framework for K–12 Science Education names "appreciation of the beauty and wonder of science" as an overarching goal; NRC, 2012, p. 1), the Didaktik view as outlined strongly emphasizes the contribution of scientific knowledge to the formation of students' personalities. Students have to decide about the extent to which they integrate scientific thinking into their world views. This belongs to the process of *Bildung*. It includes the critical reflection of problematic outcomes of the scientific enterprise.

Learning About Nature of Physics and Nature of Science

There is a wide agreement among science education researchers about the relevance of the nature of science (NOS) for teaching and learning science as well as physics in particular and the development of scientific literacy (e.g., Osborne, 2007; Chapter 30 of the present handbook). The acronym NOS points to insights from history, philosophy, and sociology of science. Some researchers separate NOS from scientific inquiry (Lederman & Lederman, 2011). While the first notion indicates particular characteristics of scientific knowledge, the latter addresses the manner in which scientists develop knowledge in science (epistemology).

There are good reasons to take account of historical and epistemological aspects in physics teaching (McComas, 1998). They range from a better understanding of physics concepts (e.g., Galili & Hazan, 2000) to students' participation in critical discourse about socioscientific issues (SSI). Liu, Lin, and Tsai (2011) have shown that students who hold beliefs about scientific knowledge as changing and tentative are more likely to recognize the complexity of SSI. They take multiple perspectives and question omniscient authority in the decision-making process.

Some key elements of a proper understanding of NOS are (e.g., Lederman & Lederman, 2011) the distinction of observation and inference, the distinction of theory and law, the empirical basis of science and the crucial role of observation, the theory-ladenness and subjectivity of knowledge in science, science as a human enterprise, and the tentativeness of scientific knowledge. Nevertheless, consensus lists of what to teach and how to teach NOS have not been established until today. Additionally, there is a danger that any NOS guideline might easily be misinterpreted by teachers as knowledge to be passed on to students in a declarative manner (Clough, 2007). Matthews (2012) points out that the various existing lists are lacking aspects of the history of science. A distortion of science compared to historical depictions might therefore be an undesirable consequence. Allchin (2011) alludes to the important role of experts and their trustworthiness in science, which has to be taken into account for teaching informed judgment and decision making. Thus, the fact has to be considered that physics is a discourse among experts within a community of experts and beyond. Teaching NOS under such a perspective is shifting from a list of tenets toward the development of capabilities for a critical appraisal of the trustworthiness of experts.

Heering and Höttecke (2014) analyze recent research in history, philosophy, and sociology of science with an emphasis on physics. They conclude that developments in these domains have not yet been sufficiently considered. In school physics, teaching knowledge is still misrepresented as a result of a linear process but not as a result of a multitude of different kinds of knowledge generation. It is, for example, underestimated that experimenting in physics bears multiple relations with theoretical ideas and is closely connected to the construction of new apparatus and materials (see also the section about practical work in this chapter).

Physics is distinguished from other natural sciences by its high level of abstraction, idealization, and the predominant role of mathematics. The complexity of natural or technical phenomena is strongly reduced in order to enable quantitative predictions. For this purpose, physics produces its own prototypical phenomena in laboratory settings, often called "effects." A basic assumption of physics is that nature is inherently organized and that the order of nature is essentially accessible to humans. Galilei even asserted that the book of nature is written in the language of mathematics (cf. Galilei, 1832). Real-world phenomena are usually influenced by complex and multiple parameters. Instead, physics phenomena have to be prepared, idealized, reduced, or even "cleaned" in order to enable deliberate manipulations. It is, for instance, almost impossible to calculate the path of a leaf falling from a tree. On the other hand, it is rather easy to measure or predict precisely the motion and path of a feather falling freely in an evacuated tube. Physics thinking does not originate from the minute observation of the world around us but from a reconstruction of certain aspects of this world under theoretical perspectives. The role of mathematics comprises the development of models and predictions. Moreover, during the course of the historical development of physics, the meaning of what counts as an explanation has changed by the use of mathematics (Gingras, 2001). While in the 17th and 18th centuries, explaining meant to specify a mechanical mechanism involved in the production of a phenomenon, in the aftermath of this development, mathematical and geometrical ideas were considered sufficient (e.g., Newton's idea of a force acting at a distance without an idea of a mechanical mechanism). Nevertheless, such a high degree of decontextualization, abstraction, idealization, and mathematization in physics is one of the major reasons for the problems many students have with learning physics (see also the section about students' interests and gender issues in this chapter).

During the last three or four decades, an extensive body of literature about NOS has been published. Critical overviews of research on students' and teachers' views on NOS (Hodson, 2009; Höttecke, 2001; Lederman, 1992) and research methods (Deng, Chen, Tsai, & Chai, 2011) are available. There is evidence that neither students nor science teachers possess an adequate understanding of NOS. Students' epistemological beliefs can be characterized as naïve-empiristic: They tend to understand scientific theories as ever-lasting truths, derived from precise observations and experiments free of any theoretical considerations. Creative speculation and theory-laden construction are not taken into account (Köller, Baumert, & Neubrand, 2000). Furthermore, physics teachers appropriately reflect neither the nature of physics nor the role of mathematics in physics (Mulhall & Gunstone, 2008). Clough (2006) points to the fact that teachers possessing an adequate understanding of NOS are a necessary but not a sufficient condition for their students' gains in this field.

Teaching and learning NOS has to be regarded as a cognitive outcome (Abd-El-Khalick, Bell, & Lederman, 1998). Teachers therefore have to plan instructional activities explicitly in order to support students' reflections on important NOS issues (e.g., Abd-El-Khalick & Lederman, 2000). Teachers should confront learners with their own deeply held beliefs about science in general and about physics in particular. However, teachers do not feel competent in the domain of NOS (Abd-EI-Khalick et al., 1998). Even if they hold adequate beliefs in NOS, their actual teaching will not necessarily be affected. There is a gap between the key objectives regarding NOS presented in educational standards and the preambles of science curricula on the one hand and how physics is actually portrayed in textbooks and in teaching practice on the other (Kircher, Girwidz, & Häußler, 2000, p. 38). NOS is hardly taught explicitly (Widodo, 2004, pp. 121) or considered in assessments and physics exams. Teachers do not regard NOS as an explicit objective of their teaching (Abd-EI-Khalick et al., 1998), and they are lacking pedagogical content knowledge in this domain (Höttecke & Silva, 2011).

Abd-El-Khalick and colleagues (1998) thus strongly argue for including more NOS elements in teacher training and teaching. McComas's book (1998) gives examples of how to introduce students and teachers to epistemological issues. Matthews (1994) stresses the historical and philosophical perspectives in teaching science. Learning about physics may be supported by a variety of activities (Clough, 2006). Among them are stories brought forward by the teacher that raise questions about science and physics in particular (e.g., Klassen, 2009), historical vignettes and short narratives (Roach & Wandersee, 1995), case studies possibly enriched with replicas of historical apparatus (e.g., Höttecke, Henke, & Rieß, 2012), and case studies of contemporary research, inquiry-based learning, research apprenticeship programs, or explicitly epistemology-based physics courses (Meyling, 1997). Black-box activities might draw students' attention to NOS issues and allow for critical reflections on knowledge generation in physics. To give an example: A wooden box is equipped with several mirrors and sealed by a teacher. Students then use flashlights to shine light into the box through various slots in the side walls. The mirrors inside are constructed in a way that enables reflections of light in particular ways. The students finally have to conjecture how the black box is constructed inside but are not allowed to open it. The activity facilitates reflections, for instance, on the nature of atomic physics, where evidence, inferences, and conclusions have to be coordinated in coherent ways, while atoms themselves can not be observed directly.

Conceptual Change

Constructivist views of conceptual change have been the dominating perspectives of research on teaching and learning science since the 1980s (Duit, Treagust, & Widodo, 2013; Mintzes, Wandersee, & Novak, 1997; Vosniadou, 2012; see also Chapter 1)—including social constructivist perspectives. A problem-solving perspective on teaching

TABLE 22.1

Number of Publications on Students' Ideas in the Bibliography by Duit (2009). In Parentheses: Predominant Concepts.

Biology—total	**782**
Chemistry—total	**1,271**
Physics—total	**2,379**
—mechanics (force)	813
—electricity (el. circuit)	519
—optics	245
—particle model	249
—thermal physics (heat/temp.)	243
—energy	187
—astronomy (earth in space)	126
—quantum physics	81
—sound	49
—nonlinear systems (chaos)	30
—magnetism	26
—relativity	8

and learning physics that addresses slightly different facets was provided by Maloney (1994). Both research perspectives have been rather influential in developing new teaching and learning approaches that deliberately take students' pre-instructional views, beliefs, and conceptions into account (for proposals on teaching and learning physics, see Arons, 1997; Redish, 2003; Viennot, 2001, 2003).

As mentioned, physics is the domain in which most research studies on investigating students' conceptions and on conceptual change have been carried out. Table 22.1 presents the number of studies documented in the bibliography by Duit (2009). It is evident that there is a particular emphasis on mechanics and electricity—with a strong focus on the force concept or the (simple) electric circuit, respectively. Clearly, these subdomains are somewhat over-researched. On the other hand, the number of studies about conceptual change in the domain of modern physics is rather limited. More details on research findings in the domains of electricity, mechanics, and atomic physics are given in what follows. General findings of research on conceptual change are reported elsewhere in the present handbook (Chapter 1). The particular difficulty of conceptual change in the process of learning physics appears to be that usually students' pre-instructional ideas about physics concepts and phenomena are deeply rooted in their everyday experiences and are therefore in stark contrast to the physics conceptions. Radical idealization and decontextualization, the reduction to pure phenomena accompanied by the particular mathematical modeling, appears to be a major hurdle for students to understand physics concepts and principles. Furthermore, in quantum physics and relativity, the physics perspective is incomprehensible in principle from everyday-world perspectives. Interestingly, this also holds for the classical particle view, which is introduced in early school grades. Also here, the world of particles is fundamentally different from the world of our everyday experiences.

Viewed from the perspective of scientific literacy (e.g., Osborne, 2007; see Chapter 25), understanding physics includes understanding physics concepts and principles on the one hand and physics processes as well as views of the nature of physics on the other. As argued in the previous section, these views *about* physics are not only essential features of scientific literacy, but they are also essential in understanding physics concepts and principles. Looking at teaching and learning physics from a conceptual change perspective should therefore include conceptual changes on the level of concepts and principles and on the level of processes and views of the nature of physics as well. Research has shown that also students' ideas of processes (like modeling) or views of the nature of physics are "naïve" in the same sense as their views of phenomena and concepts (Treagust, Chittleborough, & Mamiala, 2002). A multiple conceptual change view has to be employed. Treagust and Duit (2012), for instance, distinguish an epistemological and an ontological perspective of conceptual change as well as affective versus social aspects and learner characteristics.

Learning Progressions

Learning progressions have more recently gained significant attention, initially within the science education community in the United States, later internationally. They describe "successively more sophisticated ways of reasoning within a content domain that follows one another as students learn" (Smith, Wiser, Anderson, Krajcik, & Coppola, 2004, p. 5). Learning progressions describe a learner's shift over time toward more expert-like understanding. But the learning progression movement goes far beyond the mere attention on identifying and empirically testing efficient learning pathways. It is also driven by quite general attempts toward more efficient teaching and learning sequences. In a sense, a framework is developing that provides orientation for attempts toward more qualified general strategies for science instruction and teacher education as well. The learning progression approach shares major concerns with other approaches, taking the development of student knowledge over long periods into account (Duschl et al., 2011), such as *Teaching and Learning Sequences* (Méheut & Psillos, 2004) or *Learning Process Studies* (Duit, Goldberg, & Niedderer, 1992; Niedderer, Budde, Giry, Psillos, & Tiberghien, 2007). In physics, a large number of *learning process* studies (or teaching and learning sequences) are available, ranging from "classical" topics like the simple electric circuit to key ideas and theories of modern physics (including relativity theory, quantum theory, and nonlinear systems; see Duit, 2009). The number of *learning progression* studies on physics topics so far is limited. Major studies published concern topics like *force and motion* (Alonzo & Steedle, 2009), *matter and atomic-molecular theory* (Smith, Wiser, Anderson, & Krajcik, 2006; Stevens, Delgado, & Krajcik, 2009), and *energy* (Neumann, Viering, Boone, & Fischer, 2012).

Students' Interests and Gender Issues

International comparative studies reveal that girls' achievements and interests in physics compared to those of boys are substantially lower (Keeves & Kotte, 1996; Sjøberg & Schreiner, 2010). The same does not hold for science in general, as the PISA 2006 survey indicates. Gender differences on the overall science scale were found to be small—in particular, if compared to the variances within each gender (OECD, 2009).

However, there are significant gender-related differences between countries concerning students' interests in becoming scientists in the future. While attitudes toward science and technology among adults and adolescents are mainly positive, girls in the wealthier countries are significantly more skeptical about career choices in the sciences than boys are (Sjøberg & Schreiner, 2010). Within the sciences, physics is usually the domain that is greeted with the lowest interest, in particular by girls.

It appears that students' views of physics play a crucial role for the development of interest in physics. Science in general and physics in particular is seen as a male domain (Baker, 1998; Harding, 1996). Stadler, Benke, and Duit (2000) argue that girls and boys hold different (tacit) notions of what it means to understand physics. Girls do not assume a concept to be understood until they can relate it to a broader (even nonscientific) context. Boys, in contrast, seem to be more pragmatic. They tend to regard physics as valuable in itself and appreciate the internal coherence of the body of physics knowledge more than girls do. Students generally associate physics with difficulty, masculinity, and heteronomy (Kessels, Rau, & Hannover, 2006). Compared to girls', it appears that boys' attitudes toward physics and their notions of understanding physics are closer to how we have characterized physics as a highly abstract, idealized, and even decontextualized discipline.

Research has shown that emotional factors play an essential role in learning science. Conceptual change, for instance, will not be successful if it would be merely based on "cold cognition" (Pintrich, Marx, & Boyle, 1992). A study on teaching introductory electricity (Laukenmann et al., 2003) proved that positive emotions promote achievement. Kroh and Thomsen (2005) argue that teaching and learning methods have to take students' cognitive and affective variables into account. They show that giving students responsibility for their own learning has a positive influence on their attitudes toward physics and their self-conceptions.

It is likely that the development of interests in physics and career choices are mediated by students' self-perception and identity. Students' physics identity (a sense of self with respect to physics) is influenced by their interests and desires to learn in this domain, their experiences of competence, their beliefs about performance required for coping with physical problems, and recognition by others (Hazari, Sonnert, Sadler, & Shanahan, 2010). Physics identity is positively related to the fulfillment of intrinsic needs by learning physics. On the other hand, desires for free personal time and collaboration with others are negatively related to physics identity (Hazari et al., 2010, p. 992). While positive outcome expectations like intrinsic fulfillment have a tendency to meet the physics identities of male students, negatively related outcome expectations have been shown to be closer to the identities of female students. Moreover, girls compared to boys hold lower self-efficacy beliefs in the domain of physics.

Hannover and Kessels (2004) explain gender differences in physics with a self-to-prototype matching theory: Students compare their self-views against assumed prototypical students who like (e.g., the "intelligent boy" as a stereotype) or disapprove of physics (e.g., "attractive girls"). The theory assumes that a school subject like physics is portrayed and represented by peers. If a student's self-view matches the favorite-subject-prototype, this will lead to a higher preference of physics as a subject.

Career choices toward or away from physics are often rooted in experiences students make during high school physics. According to an international study of women in physics (Ivie & Guo, 2006), most female physicists reported that they became attracted to physics and made a choice for a corresponding career during secondary school. A serious problem seems to be that high school physics teachers underestimate the gender problem in physics teaching. Zohar (2005) asserts that almost two thirds of the teachers in her study did not see gender issues as a problem requiring action.

In order to improve the situation, several studies have been carried out to contextualize physics in order to support girls' meaning making of physics content. Instructional materials addressing girls' interests such as the human body and issues of social relevance significantly enhance girls' interests and achievements (Baker, 1998; Häußler & Hoffmann, 2002; Reid & Skryabina, 2003). Such approaches have also proven successful for boys. Research has revealed that physics should be taught in an encouraging way to enhance the self-confidence of girls. Collaborative work in single-sex groups improves interests and achievements of girls as well as of boys (Baker, 1998; Häußler & Hoffmann, 2002). Further on, physics teachers might positively influence students' physics identities by focusing on conceptual understanding, making multiple real-world connections, getting students to take on expert roles in physics teaching (e.g., teaching others), and counter-balancing stereotypes of physics as a one-dimensional pursuit (Hazari et al., 2010).

Practical Work

There is wide agreement among science education researchers that practical work is of great importance for teaching and learning and allows for the promotion of several educational goals. Students learn scientific content and experience how to connect theory and practice in science. They test knowledge claims and develop problem-solving, process, and social skills as well as scientific reasoning skills. There is a widespread belief that motivation, interest in science, and development of personality are affected in positive ways by doing practical work in physics education.

On the other hand, high expectations on students' practical work as a means for an enhancement of conceptual understanding, motivation, and interest appear to lack warrant. Lunetta (1998) asserts a considerable mismatch among goals, behavior, and learning outcomes in the school science laboratory. Tiberghien, Veillard, Le Maréchal, Buty, and Millar (2001) analyzed laboratory tasks in seven European countries. Labsheets from upper secondary schools as well as from university show striking similarities across the subjects physics, biology, and chemistry: Actions with objects and observables dominate and are largely unrelated to theoretical issues, like testing a hypothesis. However, there are some specifics for physics. Almost all physics tasks aimed at finding out or supporting relationships among physics quantities, using lab apparatus, and processing data.

Hopf (2007) presents evidence that the effect of practical work on students' learning in physics is surprisingly rather weak. A crucial factor seems to be that experiments in physics teaching should not be isolated events in a lesson but properly prepared and discussed together with students. Results and observations have to be debated thereafter in order to support meaning making of what has been done (e.g., Tesch & Duit, 2004).

Nevertheless, practical work plays a major role in physics classes. A considerable amount of time is devoted to experiments with a certain emphasis on teacher demonstration (Tesch & Duit, 2004). Teachers generally appreciate the role of experiments but usually guide their students strictly. Strong guidance of lab activities has often been criticized as cookbook-style or verification labs (e.g., Clough, 2006; Hofstein & Kind, 2012). Niedderer and colleagues (2002) analyzed videotapes from lab work to assess the amount of students' talking physics during lab work. Results show that students often use lab sheets like recipes, without thinking and talking physics. A pure inductivist idea of physics might be conveyed in this way.

It often happens instead that students do not really know what is the purpose of an experimental procedure they are following or what the data they are collecting really mean (e.g., Hofstein & Kind, 2012). Teachers too often do not consider whether their students understand what they are doing when they do practical work (Gallagher & Tobin, 1987). Jonas-Ahrend (2004) reports that the educational purpose and relationship between students' experimentation and their learning is hardly considered by physics teachers. Thus, it is not surprising that lab work is hardly ever reflected by the students in terms of NOS. Research therefore has indicated that students only have a limited understanding of the nature and purposes of experimentation in science. Solomon, Scott, and Duveen (1996) point out, for instance, that fewer than half of the students in their study were able to relate theory to the experiment they had carried out. Buffler, Lubben, and Ibrahim (2009) show that students with a NOS profile dominated by a belief that the laws of nature are to be discovered are more likely to have a view of the nature of scientific measurement as "true" values. Heinicke and Heering (2012) are reporting research results about physics students' ideas of measurement. While more than 80% of the 31 students in a written survey supported taking multiple measurements, only 4 of the 13 working groups these students composed actually did take repetitions during their own practical work. Students who believe that scientific theories are inventions and constructed from observations that are then validated through further experimentation are more likely to have a view that is underpinned by the uncertain nature of scientific evidence. Learning to deal with uncertainty has been indicated as an important objective for achieving scientific literacy (e.g., Ryder, 2001). Concerning the current situation in science teaching instead, Hofstein and Kind (2012, p. 192) conclude that "practical work meant manipulating equipment and materials, but not ideas."

Chinn and Malhotra (2002) point to the fact that the cognitive operations of students performing practical work and scientists in their laboratories are rather different. In scientific research, experimentation is a multifaceted activity with many possible relationships between experimentation and observation on the one hand and inference and theory development on the other. Accordingly, instructional sequences should be more strongly oriented to the epistemic practices of science (e.g., Duschl, 2000). Discussions, debates, and arguments about what counts as evidence deserve a more prominent role. The general role of metacognitive activities should be more greatly appreciated (Hofstein & Kind, 2012). This holds for science instruction in general and for physics instruction specifically.

Students do practical work with real apparatus in the physics lab. They also work with computer-based tools. Both ways of teaching and learning physics allow for active engagement with physics phenomena. In up-to-date teaching strategies, the two modes are gradually integrated (Goldberg & Bendall, 1995; Laws, 1997; Schecker, 1998). Redish (2003) describes the relevant teaching methods together with available resources.

Multimedia

Cognitive tools (in contrast to digital resources, cf. Chapter 17 in this volume) for physics instruction can be placed in different categories:

- *Microcomputer-based laboratories (MBL)*: probes, interfaces, and software for online data acquisition, evaluation, and graphing (Sokoloff, Thornton, & Laws, 2012; Tinker, 1996).
- *Content-specific interactive tools*, like *simulation programs*, in which learners vary the parameters and explore the behavior of physical systems on the basis of a given mathematical model (numerous packages

are available for all domains of physics; e.g., *physlets*; Christian & Belloni, 2003) or *interactive screen experiments*, in which students interact with digitized multimedia representations of a real experiments (Kirstein & Nordmeier, 2007).
- *Microworlds*: learners can set up their own simulation settings interactively by combining given object-like building blocks, like lenses and screens, on a virtual optics bench (e.g., Goldberg & Bendall, 1995; Interactive Physics, 2014).
- *Model-building systems*: students generate a quantitative model describing the behavior of a system (e.g., the motion of bodies) either by filling in a set of equations (*Modellus*; Araujo, Veit, & Moreira, 2008) or by constructing a computer-based concept map while the software generates the equations (*Stella;* Schecker, 1998; van Borkulo, van Joolingen, Savelsbergh, & de Jong, 2012).
- *General tools*: spreadsheets with tables and graphs
- *Targeted tools*: tools for analyzing digitized motion videos (Beichner, 1996)

Multimedia packages like *Coach* (Heck, Kedzierska, & Ellermeijer, 2009) integrate tools from several of these categories.

The effectiveness of multimedia tools in physics education has become a major field of empirical research. Redish, Saul, and Steinberg (1996) found significant positive effects of MBL-based tutorials in teaching mechanics. Schecker (1998) reports that the use of model-building systems has a positive effect on semiquantitative reasoning about force and motion. A review of the literature on teaching and learning with the computer (Urhahne, Prenzel, Davier, Senkbeil, & Bleschke, 2000) draws a positive picture for science. However, the effects should not be overestimated (Sharma et al., 2010). There is general agreement that the learning effects of multimedia in science education crucially depend on the instructional approach into which the materials are embedded (Bryan, 2006; Linn, Songer, Lewis, & Stern, 1993). White and Frederiksen (1998) integrate a motion and force microworld into a comprehensive inquiry approach that brings together the learning of mechanics with the acquisition of metacognitive skills. Students' investigations go through a cycle of questions, predictions, experiments, modeling, and applications. The microworld enables them to model their ideas, create their own experiments, and make measurements in simulated worlds.

Teaching Physics in Three Domains

As discussed in various places before, teaching and learning physics have proven to be rather difficult. In the following, we will analyze three standard topics of physics instruction. We will discuss the *physics concepts* involved, summarize what is known about *students' ideas* of these concepts, and present *instructional designs* provided in the literature. First, we will show that even for a seemingly rather undemanding topic, namely, the simple electric circuit, severe learning difficulties occur that are rather difficult to address in instructional settings. Second, teaching and learning a fundamental physics concept, namely force, are inspected. This has proven a challenging concept up to university level. Finally, we turn to the domain of atomic physics with a focus on concepts of "modern" physics.

Teaching the Simple Electric Circuit

Electricity is one of the physics domains in which a large number of research studies are available, with a particular emphasis on simple electric circuits (Table 22.1). It becomes rather obvious that even simple electric circuits are not simple either for primary and secondary or for tertiary students (Duit & von Rhöneck, 1998). Most studies on teaching and learning key concepts of the simple electric circuit have been carried out in the 1980s and 1990s (Duit, 2009). However, there are still some studies on the simple electric circuit carried out. Usually they investigate the effect of certain instructional interventions such as the use of "conflict maps" (Tsai, 2003) or the effect of "real and virtual experimentation" (Zacharia, 2007).

Physics Concepts

The simplest circuit of all is presented in Figure 22.3. A bulb is connected to a battery. The same topological structure holds for all kinds of "sources" and "consumers."

The following issues allow predictions of whether the circuit will properly work.

(1) *Connecting conditions. Source* and *consumer* have two connection points each; they have to be connected by *conductors* in such a way that the two connecting wires do not have direct contact (no *short circuit*). The *voltages* printed on source and consumer need to be (nearly) the same, otherwise the consumer will not work properly or will be destroyed. Note that voltage is simply a connecting condition. All the students need to know that (a) the higher the voltage, the stronger the effect and (b) voltages greater than some 20 volts are dangerous for humans. It is interesting to note that for safely dealing with electric

devices in daily life, knowledge about the connecting conditions is sufficient.

(2) *Current flow.* Usually the current flow view, as indicated by the two arrows in Figure 22.3, is seen as an essential part of theoretically framing the electric circuit. There is a closed current flow, such as a flow of electrically charged particles. The intensity of current is the same all over the circuit. In introductory physics instruction, the particular nature of electric charge usually is not discussed any further. Such a restriction is appropriate, since the strength of an electric current only depends on the source and the electric resistance of the various components that constitute the circuit. There is another essential feature of the current flow that deserves attention in instruction. The charged flowing particles may not be viewed as moving independently from one another. Rather, the whole electric circuit constitutes a coupled system like the links of a bicycle chain (Härtel, 1982). Whenever the current flow is changed at a certain spot of the circuit, the current changes at any other spot.

(3) *Simultaneous current and energy flows.* It is important to enrich the current flow view by the view of energy flow. If a current is flowing in the circuit of Figure 22.3, the bulb glows. Hence energy is transported from the battery to the bulb. Therefore every current flow is accompanied by an energy flow. Whereas the electric current flows through all parts of the circuit, the location of an energy flow is more demanding. Two different views are recommendable, namely to locate an energy flow in the electromagnetic field *around* the wires or *within* the wires. In any case, energy flow and current flow are fundamentally different in two regards. First, the energy flow is fast (nearly the speed of light), whereas the speed of charged particles (like electrons) is less than a few millimeters per second. Second, the current flow in an electric circuit is closed, while energy is running through the circuit. Either on the path to the consumer or on the way back, energy and current flow in opposite directions.

The sketch of different levels of theoretical framing for the simple electric circuit presented earlier has revealed that the simple electric circuit is not so simple and easy to conceptualize also from the physics point of view. The "elementary ideas" of the simple electric circuit may appear simple to experts in physics. However, research findings on students' conceptions and learning processes, presented next, show that too-simple ideas may deeply mislead students in their attempts to understand the electric circuit.

Students' Ideas

The following overview, to a certain extent, draws on the review by Duit and von Rhöneck (1998).

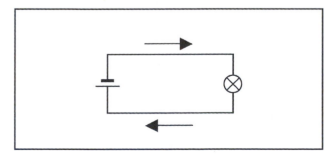

Figure 22.3 The simple electric circuit.

(1) *Everyday meanings of current.* Everyday talk about electricity is markedly different from physics talk. The meanings of words for current, for instance, are—at least in English and most major European languages—closer to the meaning of energy than to current as used in physics. Misunderstandings in class will be likely if these differences are not taken into consideration.

(2) *Consumption of current.* Already students at elementary level establish a causal connection between the battery and the bulb and explain that there is an agent moving from the battery to the bulb. The agent may be called electricity or electric current. It may be stored in the battery and is consumed in the bulb. Hence, children have problems to think about electric currents in terms of conservation. A considerable number of children think that one wire between battery and bulb suffices and that the second wire simply serves the purpose to increase the current to the bulb. Some students believe that two different kinds of currents, called "plus" and "minus" current, travel from both sides of the battery to the bulb. According to this view, there is a clash of the two currents produced in the bulb that causes the light ("clashing current," Osborne, 1983) or a sort of chemical reaction (Duit & von Rhöneck, 1998). The idea of consumption of current is commonly held even by students beyond elementary level. Research has shown that it is very difficult to change this idea; it is hardly affected by formal science education. It appears that the everyday meanings of current at least partly are responsible for the dominance of the consumption conception.

(3) *Causal reasoning.* There are several studies (e.g., Tiberghien, 1984) showing that students employ causal reasoning in the following sense. The battery supplies "something (causal agent) which permits the bulb to lit. This causal agent, called by children electricity or electric current moves from the battery to the light bulb and is consumed at the light bulb" (Tiberghien, 1984, p. 122).

(4) *Local and sequential reasoning.* Many students focus upon one point of the circuit and ignore what is happening elsewhere. A systemic view of the current flow, as described, is usually missing. An example of such local reasoning is the view that the battery delivers a constant current, independent of the circuit that is connected to the battery. Another variant of local reasoning may be called "sequential reasoning." A number of students analyze a circuit in terms of "before" and "after" current passes a certain point. If, for instance, in the simple circuit of Figure 22.3 a resistor is put into the connection leading from the battery to the bulb, students correctly predict that the bulb shines less brightly. But if the resistor is put into the other connection leading back to the battery, many students think that in this case the bulb shines as brightly as before, because only the current leading back is influenced by the additional resistor.

(5) *Current and voltage.* Voltage has proven to be a particularly difficult concept for students across different age levels. Before instruction, voltage is usually related to the "strength of the battery" (or another source) or is viewed as the intensity of force or current. Usually considerable progress in this view after instruction is lacking. Many students still have severe difficulties to differentiate between the two concepts.

(6) *Learning processes.* Many studies (e.g., Shipstone et al., 1988) have shown that success of physics instruction in developing students' ideas about the electric circuit toward the physics view is rather limited. Most of these data draw on pre-/posttest designs. However, there are also studies that follow the learning processes in detail. It becomes obvious that learning pathways students follow are very complicated. There are forward and backward movements, there are parallel developments, and there are dead-end streets (Duit & von Rhöneck, 1998; Niedderer & Goldberg, 1995; Scott, 1992).

Teaching Approaches

A substantial number of studies have been carried out investigating possibilities to guide students from their ideas to the physics concepts of the electric circuit. Basically, the same kinds of approaches as used in other science domains have been also employed here. There are attempts to support conceptual change by particularly designed multimedia learning environments and by a number of constructivist-oriented teaching and learning settings. It appears that such attempts usually (but not always) have proven superior compared to more "traditional" kinds of physics instruction. Still, the success often is disappointingly limited. There is, however, one exception. Almost all students, after appropriate experiences with electric circuits, are convinced that two wires are necessary to make the consumer work.

Students' pre-instructional conceptions of the electric circuit are—as outlined—in stark contrast to the referring physics concepts. Often new teaching and learning strategies start with elicitation of students' ideas and with establishing their experiences in question. Students carry out experiments (e.g., with batteries and bulbs) and develop and exchange their views of the phenomena investigated. From such a basis, the teacher tries to guide students toward the physics view. Challenging students' ideas is often a crucial period, as cognitive conflicts play a certain role. Cognitive conflict strategies, though successful in a number of cases, bear a number of difficulties (Vosniadou & Ioannides, 1998). The most important is that it is often difficult for students to experience the conflict. It may also happen that elicitation and long discussions of students' pre-instructional views may strengthen just these views. Therefore, also in the domain of electricity, various approaches have been developed that attempt to avoid cognitive conflicts. These approaches usually start from students' ideas that are mainly in accordance with the physics view and attempt to guide students from this kernel of conformity to the physics view via a continuous pathway. One such strategy Grayson (1996) calls "concept substitution." Instead of challenging students' views of current consumption, she provides the following reinterpretation: The view that *something* is consumed is not wrong at all—if seen in terms of energy as outlined: Energy is actually flowing from the battery to the bulb while current is flowing. Energy is "consumed," or transformed into heat and light (degradation).

Most instructional sequences toward understanding the basic concepts of the electric circuit start with introducing the concept of electric current (often conceptualized as flow of electrons or other charged particles). An alternative teaching and learning sequence is presented by Psillos, Koumaras, and Tiberghien (1988). They introduce voltage (which is usually viewed as a rather difficult concept) first.

Briefly summarized, understanding the simple electric circuit has proven rather difficult for students in school and at tertiary level also. It appears that these difficulties are at least partly due to the fact that students' ideas are deeply rooted in certain everyday experiences (predominantly everyday speech about electricity, current, and electric circuits) and that these conceptions are not adequately addressed in instruction. The case of teaching and learning about electric circuits also shows that instruction may support "false" ideas. In general, the limited success of conceptual change approaches points to the issue that the content structure for instruction has to be carefully developed in a process called Educational Reconstruction (Figure 22.2). Also, seemingly simple topics need substantially deep understanding of the physics "behind" that simple topic.

Teaching Mechanics

Within the domains of school physics, mechanics has the most substantial body of empirical research on students' conceptions (Table 22.1). There are various proposals for teaching approaches and a variety of multimedia tools. Nevertheless, mechanics remains one of the most difficult domains to teach and to learn. "Force" and "velocity" are subsumed by everyday interpretations of motion phenomena that differ substantially from physics concepts.

Physics Concepts

The concepts of classical mechanics are *displacement, velocity, acceleration, force*, and *momentum. Mechanical energy (kinetic* and *potential energy, work*) belongs to the intersection between mechanics and thermodynamics. Mechanics is canonized by Newton's three laws. In the physics classroom, they are often presented in a truncated version (see 1, 2, 3). We present this version to contrast it with a formulation that really expresses the conceptual core of the three laws ($1*, 2*, 3*$):

(1) If there is no force acting on a body, it remains in its state of motion—"inertia."
(2) The (resultant) force acting on a body is proportional to the body's mass and acceleration ($F = m\,a$).
(3) To each force exerted on a body ("action"), there is an equal but opposite force ("reaction").

Many students reproduce Newton's laws in similar phrases without really understanding their conceptual content. $F = m\,a$ is probably the best known and least understood equation in school physics. Students often consider $F = m\,a$ (Newton's universal resultant force) as just another force like $F = m\,g$ (the specific single force of gravity).

A sound way of expressing Newton's ideas that takes into account the learning difficulties caused by the upper formulations is:

($1*$) The motion of a body can only be changed by forces acting from outside. If no change of the state of motion occurs, then either the vector sum of the single forces acting on the body is zero or there are no single forces at all.
($2*$) The state of motion of a body is described by its momentum p. In order to change momentum, a resultant force has to act over a certain time interval ($\Delta p = F \cdot \Delta t$).
($3*$) Forces result from the interaction of bodies. Whenever a body A exerts a force on another body B, then B simultaneously exerts an equal but opposite force on A ($F_{A\rightarrow B} = -F_{B\rightarrow A}$).

Although the problems of teaching mechanics cannot be solved simply by using proper wordings, the second set of laws is much more likely to support students' understanding. Formulation $1*$ counters a misunderstanding that Newton's first law is only true in the absence of *any* force. Formulation $2*$ stresses that a particular amount of time is needed during which a force changes a body's state of motion. Formulation $3*$ underlines the interaction of bodies. It avoids the term "reaction," which students often confuse with a "counterforce" on body A (e.g., Viennot, 1979).

Students' Ideas

Driver, Squires, Rushworth, and Wood-Robinson (1994, p. 149) summarize the empirical findings about students' ideas on force and motion in these statements:

"• if there is motion, there is a force acting;
• if there is no motion, there is no force acting;
• there cannot be a force without motion;
• when an object is moving, there is a force in the direction of its motion;

- a moving object stops when its force is used up;
- a moving object has an own force within it which keeps it going;
- motion is proportional to the force acting;
- a constant speed results from a constant force."

One can add:

- Friction is no "real" force but a resistance to motion.
- Objects at rest or nonactive objects (like tables or roads) do not exert forces.
- Objects in circular motion "sense" a centrifugal force (independent from the system of reference).

These findings have been confirmed in empirical studies all over the world. They form the body of intuitive mechanics.

Research on students' ideas in mechanics was stimulated by Warren's book "Understanding Force" (1979). From a physicist's perspective, Warren worked out the inherent difficulties and the conceptual stepping stones—sometimes caused by imprecise instruction. Warren developed a set of test items for university beginners that were also used in several follow-up studies with younger students (see Figure 22.4 for an example). He showed that many students failed to solve seemingly simple problems.

Viennot (1979) expanded on the question of how students conceptualize mechanics alternatively. She claimed that students' spontaneous reasoning was consistent and could be formed into an intuitive law of force in which "force" depends on velocity v (instead of acceleration a). Viennot found a coexistence between the idea of "force" as an interaction force impressed on a body and a "supply of force" stored in a body.

McCloskey (1983) drew parallels between students' "intuitive physics" and medieval *impetus theory* based on the idea that force impressed on an object can somehow be stored in the body and is later used up for keeping up its motion. Students' *impetus* reasoning is very resistant to instruction. It leads to wrong predictions of the path of moving objects, like a cannon ball traveling in a straight line before the impetus is used up, so that it falls down

vertically. Students even use *impetus* ideas when they are asked to drop a ball on a target on the ground while they are running.

Jung, Wiesner, and Engelhard (1981) worked out that students conceptualize *inertia* as a sort of lameness—a resistance to motion that has to be overcome by force. It is often associated with static friction. For students, "force" has a polyvalent meaning that integrates facets of the physics concepts of energy, momentum, and Newtonian force, comparable to the ambivalent meaning of "force" in physics up to the mid-1850s.

A controversial issue is whether students' intuitive physics forms a systematic and coherent scheme—a sort of "alternative theory" (e.g., Viennot, 1979). diSessa (1988) strongly opposes this notion. He argues that students' knowledge consists of single loosely connected phenomenological primitives like "force as mover" or "more effort begs more result." According to diSessa, the transition to scientific understanding involves a major structural change toward systematization. In contrast, Vosniadou (2002) argues on the basis of patterns in students' responses that they construct their own narrow but coherent explanatory frameworks in mechanics. Chi, Slotta, and de Leeuw (1994) propose to organize students' thinking along ontological categories: In students' minds, "force" belongs to the category "matter" (something that can be stored), while it should be reassigned to the "constrained-based interaction" category. Jung and colleagues (1981) claim that it is more effective to address students' general categories of reasoning than to address specific alternative conceptions. Such categories are:

- functional descriptions of motion—in contrast to seeking the *cause* of motion
- relationships and *interactions* between bodies—in contrast to the *properties* of bodies

Research on students' understanding of mechanics culminated in the 1980s and has since reached a high degree of consensus. There are standardized instruments to assess students' reasoning:

- Force Concept Inventory (FCI; Hestenes, Wells, & Swackhamer, 1992; revised version in Mazur, 1997)
- Force and Motion Conceptual Evaluation (FMCE; Thornton & Sokoloff, 1998)
- Test of Understanding Graphs in Kinematics (TUGK; Beichner, 1994)

The FCI is the most widely used test on understanding mechanics. Its revised version contains 30 items. The sets of multiple-choice answers contain—besides the attractor—four distractors, each addressing a specific misconception of motion and forces. There has been a long discussion about the reliability of the FCI for diagnosing students' conceptions (starting with Huffman & Heller, 1995; see also Stewart, Griffin, & Stewart, 2007). Recent

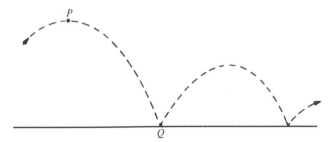

Figure 22.4 Diagram from a tutorial test on student ideas of forces (Warren, 1979, p. 34). Students are asked to draw arrows for the forces on a ball in P and Q. Most students assume a "force" in the direction of motion instead of a (resultant) force in the direction of the change of motion (in P vertically downward).

research on learning progression (see earlier) has tried to define and assess levels of understanding mechanics by ordered multiple-choice items. Alonzo and Steedle (2009) found a lack of consistency in students' answers. They varied with the context into which the items were embedded. It is therefore difficult to obtain reliable estimates of levels of learning progression (Alonzo & Steedle, 2009, p. 418).

Teaching Approaches

In the literature, there are numerous studies under various perspectives for the teaching of mechanics in general and the force concept in particular. The following section starts with a contribution from a subject matter point of view and then focuses on teaching strategies building on the knowledge about students' (alternative) ideas and on curricula that passed empirical evaluation studies.

Discussions about new approaches for teaching mechanics intensified in the 1980s and 1990s when assessments in curriculum development projects had revealed deeply rooted problems of students' understanding force and motion. Warren (1979, p. 13) points out that the Newtonian system of mechanics should in the physics perspective be fully developed in terms of "real" forces. A "real" force can be attributed to a concrete body in a definable interaction, which is subject to a recognizable law, such as gravitational forces caused by a planet or elastic forces caused by a deformed ball. Imaginary forces ("pseudo" forces) like centrifugal force would only confuse students.

Minstrell (1992) reports about positive effects of high school mechanics courses, in which students are explicitly asked to express their intuitive ideas about force and motion. The students' ideas are then juxtaposed with the physics concepts. A similar strategy is presented by Schecker and Niedderer (1996) under the term "contrastive teaching." After introducing Newton's laws, the teacher poses an open-ended problem like "investigate forces in collisions." Students then make statements like "a force is transferred from body A to body B"—even though they know the nominal Newtonian definition of force. This elicitation of students' own ideas (Driver & Oldham, 1986) helps to contrast their intuitive views with the scientific notion of force. Clement (1993) shows how students' intuitive ideas can be used as starting points ("anchors") for teaching sequences that lead to a proper understanding of related Newtonian concepts by way of "bridging analogies." Camp and Clement (1994) present a series of student activities helping them to overcome known learning obstacles.

Hake (1998) carried out a meta-analysis of studies done with the Force Concept Inventory or FCI (6,000 students involved). He found that so-called interactive-engagement courses score higher than traditional teacher-centered methods. Interactive engagement can be effectively supported by multimedia. Sokoloff and colleagues (2012) have developed activity-based mechanics curricula that center around computer-based labs with a range of new sensors, interfaces, and software. In a collaborative learning environment, the approach leads to a considerable increase of understanding kinematics (Thornton, 1992). Motion in sports (like high jumping) can be analyzed by digital video tools like Videograph (c.f. Beichner, 1996). The active construction of virtual microworlds from a given set of building blocks (bodies, springs, ropes, etc.) is another means to prompt students to explore mechanics phenomena (software package: Interactive Physics, 2014). Doerr (1997) presents a curriculum unit that integrates experimentation as well as simulation with *Interactive Physics*. Sadaghiani (2012) found a positive impact of using multimedia learning modules on understanding mechanics in introductory physics courses in university.

The following two curricular teaching approaches are based on design research: In a long-term program, Wilhelm, Tobias, Waltner, Hopf, and Wiesner (2012) have constructed, evaluated, and refined a teaching sequence for lower secondary school. The course considers research on students' conceptions as well as an alternative content structure of mechanics. Two-dimensional motion is discussed right from the start, and Newton's second law is introduced similar to formulation 2* (see earlier). There is empirical evidence for substantial learning effects. Tiberghien, Vince, and Gaidioz (2009) also stress the importance of designing usable teaching approaches that can be shared with practitioners. In a collaborative project of researchers and teachers, a teaching sequence for upper secondary mechanics was developed that focuses on distinguishing and at the same time relating the world of objects and events (e.g., measurements of forces) with the world of theories and models (e.g., Newton's laws).

Teaching Atomic Physics

Teaching atomic physics concerns an introduction to various views of the microworld ranging from simple particle models to quantum mechanical views. Many research studies are available on students' views and the conceptual change processes concerning the particle model. Also, a substantial number of studies on quantum views have been carried out (cf. Table 22.1). For both domains, it turns out that students' everyday conceptions are in stark contrast to the science views. This is already true for the simple particle model that is part of every introductory physics course. The microscopic world of the particles is different from the world of objects in lifeworld dimensions. Attempts to make the microscopic world understandable by introducing analogies to everyday-world features usually lead to major misunderstandings. Students, for instance, tend to view particles as if they were objects of the life-world and hence attach lifeworld features like color or temperature to particles (Duit, 1992; Scott, 1992).

The clash between everyday world views and physics conceptions is even more fundamental for quantum views of the microscopic world. A number of quantum features in principle appear to be inconceivable from everyday-world thinking. Examples are the particle and wave dualism (Bohr's idea of complementarity) and Heisenberg's uncertainty principle, leading, for instance, to the consequence that it is not possible to know both speed and location of a particle with unlimited precision.

Concerning models of the atom, younger students tend to have naïve realistic views. The majority see models more or less as copies of reality (Harrison & Treagust, 1996; Treagust et al., 2002). It appears that in lower secondary science teaching, there is not much development of such views toward awareness of the model character of atoms (Knote, 1975). However, there seems to be a progression in upper secondary physics instruction. Bethge (1992) found in pre-university physics courses that many students differentiated between model (of an atom) and reality. Learning science concepts and principles should include developing students' views about the nature of science (see earlier). Proper understanding of particle models and models of the atom develop only if the general character of models in physics is properly considered as well (Mikelkis-Seifert & Fischler, 2003).

Models of the Atom in Physics and Students' Ideas

The interplay between two different views—the particle view and the continuum view—characterizes scientific ideas of substance and atoms. Already the Greek philosophers held both views about the constitution of matter (Samburski, 1975, general introduction). Matter was either seen as consisting of tiny particles, called atoms, or as a continuous "something" that fills space and is indefinitely divisible. The basic particle view was further elaborated in the 18th and 19th centuries, culminating in statistical mechanics. After 1900, various atomic models were developed that propose different structures of positive and negative charges with respect to particle and continuum. Scientific views of the atom have grown over centuries.

In the following, we look at key stages in the development of atomic physics together with students' understandings or misunderstandings.

(1) *Atom as a ball.* In 1808, Dalton published his book, *A New System of Chemical Philosophy*, in which he viewed atoms as tiny balls (excerpts reprinted in Samburski, 1975). Each element had its own kind of atoms. This hypothesis was suited to explain fundamental empirical laws about weights in chemical reactions. Later in the 19th century, Boltzmann's theory of statistical mechanics was also based on atoms as balls. However, in this case the atoms were merely conceptualized as being mass points without any other features.

Students hold similar conceptions. In a study with 48 students (Grades 8 to 10), Harrison and Treagust (1996) found that more than 50% of students saw the shape of atoms as "balls or spheres," and the texture of atoms as "most like a hard polystyrene sphere."

(2) *The planetary model of the atom.* A most influential model was developed by Bohr in analogy to the system of planets revolving around the sun. The electrons (planets) are travelling in orbits around a nucleus. The orbits are derived under quantum assumptions.

The planetary model is still taught in science instruction. Often, it is the only model of so-called modern atomic physics students learn. About half of the students in lower secondary as well as the majority in upper secondary and in university actually see the atom as a planetary system, with a nucleus being surrounded by moving electrons (Fischler & Lichtfeldt, 1992; Harrison & Treagust, 1996; Knote, 1975). As the idea of electrons circulating round the nucleus provides a powerful mental model by drawing the analogy with the solar system, it has proven to be very resistant against teaching more advanced models (Bethge, 1992; Fischler & Lichtfeldt, 1992; Mashhadi, 1995; Müller & Wiesner, 2002; Taber, 2001).

(3) *The probability density conception of the atom.* This model is based on Born's interpretation of the Schrödinger equation. In this conception, the psi-function can be used to predict the probability of finding the electron in a certain distance from the nucleus: The larger the distance, the smaller is the probability. Studies have shown that students have difficulties understanding this view (Bethge, 1992; Mashhadi, 1995).

At least in the United Kingdom and in Germany, there is a tradition to teach quantum atomic physics beyond the Bohr model in upper secondary school. In these teaching approaches, students typically construct intermediate conceptions of a quantum atomic model (Bethge, 1992; Mashhadi, 1995; Petri & Niedderer, 1998). One of these models conceptualizes probability as smeared orbits (Figure 22.5).

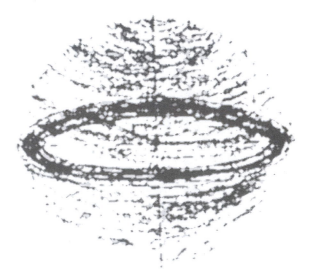

Figure 22.5 Smeared orbits model. (Petri & Niedderer, 1998)

A number of students at university level also appear to hold such ideas (Müller & Wiesner, 2002).

A more concrete interpretation of the probability density model is given in Herrmann's (1995) electron cloud model. This model consists of a nucleus and an electron cloud as a charge cloud surrounding the nucleus, its density calculated by the Schrödinger ψ function. The cloud collapses when a measurement is made and the electron localizes. Studies (Budde, Niedderer, Scott, & Leach, 2002; Niedderer & Deylitz, 1999) show that the electron cloud representation (Herrmann speaks of "electronium"; Herrmann & Job, 2006) is easier to learn than the idea of probability density. If both models are offered, students prefer the electronium model, and about 90% of them use it in the posttest and in interviews. This result corresponds with Harrison and Treagust (1996), who found that 76% of their students preferred space-filling models.

Teaching Approaches
For the discussion of teaching approaches, we focus on advanced atomic physics in pre-university instruction and on approaches that were evaluated. *Gedankenexperimente* (thought experiments) or computer simulations to introduce the concepts of quantum physics, such as the "preparation" of samples of equal particles or the new view of "measurement," play a significant role in several approaches. In the following, a brief overview is presented.

Fischler's (1999) approach starts with electron diffraction experiments and their interpretation. The experiments surprise students and catch their attention. Mechanistic interpretations of electrons are avoided. In a treatment–control group design, Fischler and Lichtfeldt (1992) found that about 20% of the students in the experimental group developed satisfactory conceptions about quantum principles, whereas none of the students in the control group (starting from experiments with photons) reached that level. Also, Müller (2003) found positive effects on understanding by introducing a more modern quantum model of the atom and by abandoning the planetary model.

In a number of approaches, major emphasis is put on explaining basic phenomena and interesting technical applications of quantum physics. Niedderer's approach (Niedderer & Deylitz, 1999) aims at understanding the size and spectra of atoms, chemical bonding, and the spectra of solids. An evaluation study (Niedderer & Deylitz, 1999) showed that—apart from problems with understanding the mathematics of Schrödinger's equation—most goals of conceptual understanding could be reached with reasonable success. As mentioned, a majority of students preferred the "electron cloud" model to the "probability density" model.

Escalada, Rebello, and Zollman (2004) analyze objects like LEDs and fluorescent lamps and fluorescent and phosphorescent materials, as well as the tunneling microscope. Potential energy diagrams are used to explain these materials. In the "visual quantum mechanics" approach, the emphasis lies on conceptual understanding and visualization instead of mathematical formalisms. Zollman, Rebello, and Hogg (2002) found that hands-on activities, computer visualization programs, and constructivist pedagogy enabled the students to build mental models that allowed them to explain their observations.

Ke, Monk, and Duschl (2005) studied teaching introductory quantum physics with Taiwanese university students at different levels. After revisiting earlier approaches (Budde et al., 2002; Fischler & Lichtfeldt, 1992), they suggest distinguishing between earlier quantum models, transitional wave mechanics, and probabilistic wave mechanics. In their study, the more capable students hold all three views and are able to switch among them in different contexts. These students can also tell the differences between the views.

In a study with students at the end of upper secondary schools in Greece, Tsaparlis and Papaphotis (2009) tried to achieve conceptual change from early quantum theory to modern orbital views of the atom, thus following an earlier suggestion of Kalkanis, Hadzidaki, and Stavrou (2003) for a radical change toward quantum mechanics concepts. Both papers assume that misconceptions or hybrid conceptions "arise because of inability of many students to separate the conceptual frameworks of classical and quantum physics, producing epistemological obstacles to the acquisition of the required knowledge" (Tsaparlis & Papaphotis, 2009). Results show that for many students, the Bohr model is still very prominent in the written tests, which were done after secondary school and before the teaching interviews. However, after the teaching interviews, students' ideas for the atomic model had changed to more intermediate models (6 out of 17) and quantum mechanics models (11 out of 17). So conceptual change was partially successful.

Briefly summarized, research has shown that students' understanding of particle models and quantum models of the atom may be substantially improved by approaches that are oriented toward constructivist conceptual change views of teaching and learning. However, the success rate is still limited. Much more research-based development is necessary for both domains. It appears that the views of the *Didaktik* tradition (see the idea of Educational Reconstruction in Figure 22.2) may help in further improving the existing approaches. The content structure for instruction—seen from that perspective—has to be developed by taking into account (a) physics views of particles and atoms, (b) physics views of the nature of particles and atoms, (c) students' views of particles and atoms as well as of the nature of the models provided, and (d) also the aims of teaching particles and atoms. It appears that by adopting the *Didaktik* tradition, the purpose of teaching and learning particle views, and especially quantum physics views of the atoms from scientific literacy perspectives should also be further clarified.

Outlook: Desiderata for Physics Education Research

In order to improve physics teaching and learning, various changes in the present state of practice are necessary. Most changes are relevant not only for physics instruction but also for science instruction in general. However, they have to be specifically designed for the particular content structure and the content-specific pedagogical issues of physics teaching. Other necessary changes are specific for physics instruction, in particular those concerning emphases of the content taught. In the following, we outline major concerns that we consider to be of particular interest in the field of physics education.

General Concerns

Teachers' Thinking About Instruction and Their Teaching Practices

Teachers, of course, are the key players in education reforms (Anderson & Helms, 2001). Research has shown (a) that many teachers are not well informed about research findings on teaching and learning, (b) their views about "good" physics instruction are rather topic dominated, their beliefs on teaching and learning are rather transmissive than constructive, and (c) in educational practice, there appears to be still a dominance of teacher-centered instruction. It is essential that teachers' thinking about instruction include all the facets addressed in the Didaktik tradition (Figure 22.2). In terms of Shulman's (1987) perspective, there should be a balance between content aspects *and* content-specific pedagogical issues in teacher thinking. Instructional planning should include considerations of content issues as well as of issues of how students may be able to learn particular content.

More research is needed especially concerning the following two issues (see Chapter 44 on teacher professional development for more details):

- To investigate how teachers become interested in and familiarize themselves with research findings, how their views about teaching and learning physics might be improved (Gräsel & Parchmann, 2004), and whether their instructional practices improve accordingly (Bertram & Loughran, 2012). Here issues of conceptual change discussed earlier come into play. Changing deeply rooted views (here teachers' views) has proved to be a long-lasting process.
- In order to enhance the efficacy of instruction in physics education, more evidence is needed about the current practices of teaching physics. Until today, only a few studies allow deep insight into physics classrooms

(e.g., by analyzing videos; Brückmann & Knierim, 2008; Roth & Garnier, 2006; Seidel & Prenzel, 2006). More studies on the regular practice of physics instruction are needed.

Aims and Standards

The present-day discussion on scientific literacy is focused on the use of physics knowledge for the enhancement of active citizenship in general and for understanding daily-life concerns as well as for making better and well-informed decisions in socioscientific issues in particular. The concept of Bildung adds the idea of forming the learners' personalities. Further research is needed on whether the actual conceptions of scientific literacy are sound and can be put into practice. Otherwise they will remain ambitious visions. A broad spectrum of research methods has to be employed, including historical and hermeneutical studies on various views of scientific literacy in different domains including physics and in different cultural environments. Evidence about the impact of physics content and process knowledge on understanding daily life issues and active citizenship is still limited. The same holds for empirical studies on students' capabilities to achieve the envisioned facets of scientific literacy.

Standards make the more general conceptions of scientific literacy explicit. They have been a key concern for a number of countries since the 1990s (e.g., in the United States and Canada); in other countries (like Germany; Schecker & Parchmann, 2007), this is a more recent issue. A comprehensive overview of the international situation for science, with 18 country reports, is given in Waddington, Nentwig, and Schanze (2007). DeBoer (2011) summarizes the current practices and recommends the development of global standards with a common core of competencies but also giving space for each country to specify goals.

Standards usually serve two related functions: to provide a framework for defining key issues of scientific literacy and to facilitate the construction of test measures that make it possible to determine the extent the various competencies stated are reached in practice. The assessment of learning outcomes is closely bound to the standards discourse under the aspects of monitoring and accountability (c.f., Bernholt et al., 2012).

Standards as well as the assessment of learning outcomes should be based on explicit models of the structure and development of competence. Such models are, for instance, used in the Swiss HarmoS project for the development of standards (Labudde, Nidegger, Adamina, & Gingings, 2012) and in the German evaluation of the national science standards (Kremer et al., 2012).

More empirical research is needed in these areas:

- to model the development of students' competency structures in a longitudinal perspective

- to develop scenarios assessing competencies under complex demands, going beyond multiple-choice questionnaires—even if that should not be feasible in large-scale assessments

Content, Processes, and Views About the Nature of Science

As outlined, the importance of process skills, knowledge about knowledge generation in physics, and adequate views about nature of science in general and nature of physics in particular play only limited roles in physics teachers' perspectives on teaching. Teachers are gatekeepers of any curricular innovation. The same holds for teaching physics as a process or the focus on NOS. Therefore, it has to be considered how physics teachers can be encouraged and supported regarding these curricular objectives. Since we know that science teachers' views of NOS too often are as problematic as those of their students, ways of developing physics teachers' content knowledge as well as their pedagogical content knowledge in this field have to be designed and evaluated.

More research has to be done about the interplay of understanding physics content on the one hand and process skills as well as views of NOS on the other. Even though science education researchers agree on the general idea that understanding NOS is necessary for informed citizenship, the effects have hardly been explored in detail. We are still lacking evidence of which kinds of NOS knowledge support informed decision making in which kind of context. Even though there is some evidence that adequate epistemological beliefs relate to learning strategies, this relation has been hardly under scrutiny in the domain of physics. Finally, the influences of history and philosophy of science in physics instruction as well as of inquiry-based learning on understanding NOS should be researched in more detail.

Holistic Research and Development

Research has shown that the outcomes of instruction (e.g., achievement and interests) are not due simply to single, isolated factors of the instructional arrangement but to an intimate interplay of several factors (Baumert & Köller, 2000; Oser & Baeriswyl, 2001). It does not make much sense to change just one factor to improve physics instruction (e.g., introducing multimedia learning environments, new exiting experiments, or innovative teaching methods). The idea of Educational Reconstruction (Figure 22.2) may provide a framework for designing instruction that more systematically takes into account the essential interplay of central factors determining instructional outcomes. Design-based research, like the work of Wilhelm and colleagues (2012), appears to be an appropriate strategy for the implementation of comprehensive research-based conceptions for teaching physics. More long-term projects are needed that evaluate the large bodies of specific findings about teaching and learning in many subdomains of physics for the design and testing of successful teaching strategies (as already proposed in Lijnse, 1995). So far, there is more "research in pieces" than there are coherent curricular R&D programs.

Physics-Specific Concerns

Physics instruction in school covers a certain canon of content that is quite similar all over the world. Interestingly, most topics of this canon concern rather "old" physics, namely physics of the 19th century. Physics of the 20th century or even current research plays a certain role only in the upper secondary levels. Most teaching approaches for quantum physics and relativity (Table 22.1) are suited only for rather gifted students of the tertiary level. Serious attempts to make more recent physics thinking about matter, space, and time accessible also for younger or less gifted students have to be intensified. Some studies in the field of nonlinear systems have shown that this is possible (Duit et al., 1997; Stavrou, Duit, & Komorek, 2008). There is the certain irony that schools appear to be reluctant to take care of this issue, whereas popular science books on modern physics are booming. There are good ideas for the elementarization of modern physics (see "Teaching Atomic Physics"), but there is more research to be done on the *learning outcomes* of these approaches (e.g., Zhu & Singh, 2012).

Acknowledgments

We would like to thank Andrée Tiberghien and Onno de Jong, who carefully and critically reviewed this chapter.

References

AAAS—American Association for the Advancement of Science. (1993). *Project 2061—Benchmarks for scientific literacy.* New York: Oxford University Press.

Abd-El-Khalick, F., Bell, R.L., & Lederman, N.G. (1998). The nature of science and instructional practice: Making the unnatural natural. *Science Education, 82,* 417–436.

Abd-El-Khalick, F., & Lederman, N.G. (2000). Improving science teachers' conceptions of nature of science: A critical review of the literature. *International Journal of Science Education, 22*(7), 665–701.

Allchin, D. (2011). Evaluating knowledge of the nature of (whole) science. *Science Education, 95*(3), 518–542.

Alonzo, A.C., & Steedle, J.T. (2009). Developing and assessing a force and motion learning progression. *Science Education, 93*(3), 389–421.

Anderson, R.D., & Helms, J.V. (2001). The ideal of standards and the reality of schools: Needed research. *Journal of Research in Science Teaching, 38,* 3–16.

Araujo, I.S., Veit, E.A., & Moreira, M.A. (2008). Physics students' performance using computational modelling activities to improve kinematics graphs interpretation. *Computers & Education, 50*(4), 1128–1140.

Arons, A. (1984). Students' patterns of thinking and reasoning. *The Physics Teacher, 22,* 21–26; 89–93; 576–581.

Arons, A. (1997). *Teaching introductory physics.* New York: Wiley.

Baker, D.R. (1998). Equity issues in science education. In B.J. Fraser & K.G. Tobin (Eds.), *International handbook of science education* (pp. 869–895). Dordrecht, the Netherlands: Kluwer Academic Publishers.

Baumert, J., & Köller, O. (2000). Unterrichtsgestaltung, verständnisvolles Lernen und multiple Zielerreichung im Mathematik- und Physikunterricht der gymnasialen Oberstufe [Instructional planning, mindful learning and the achievement of multiple goals in mathematics and physics instruction at upper secondary level]. In J. Baumert & O. Köller (Eds.), *TIMSS/III. Dritte Internationale Mathematik- und Naturwissenschaftsstudie. Volume 2* (pp. 271–315). Opladen, Germany: Leske+Budrich.

Beaton, A. E., Martin, M. O., Mullis, I. V. S., Gonzalez, E. J., Smith, T. A., & Kelly, D. A. (1996). *Science achievement in the middle school years. IEA's Third International Mathematics and Science Study (TIMSS).* Boston: Boston College—Center for the Study of Testing, Evaluation, and Educational Policy.

Beichner, R. J. (1994). Testing student interpretation of kinematik graphs. *American Journal of Physics, 62,* 750–762.

Beichner, R. J. (1996). The impact of video motion analysis on kinematics graph interpretation skills. *American Journal of Physics, 64,* 1272–1278.

Bernholt, S., Neumann, K., & Nentwig, P. (Eds.). (2012). *Making it tangible—learning outcomes in science education.* Münster: Waxmann.

Bertram, A., & Loughran, J. (2012). Science teachers' views on CoRes and PaPeRs as a framework for articulating and developing pedagogical content knowledge. *Research in Science Education, 42,* 1027–1047.

Bethge, T. (1992). Vorstellungen von Schülerinnen und Schülern zu Begriffen der Atomphysik [Students' ideas about concepts of atomic physics]. In H. Fischler (Ed.), *Quantenphysik in der Schule* (pp. 88–113). Kiel, Germany: IPN—Leibniz Institute for Science Education.

Brückmann, M., & Knierim, B. (2008). Teaching and learning processes in physics instruction—chances of videotape classroom studies. In S. Mikelskis-Seifert, U. Ringelband, & M. Brückmann (Eds.), *Four decades of research in science education—from curriculum development to quality improvement* (pp. 191–219). Münster: Waxmann.

Bryan, J. (2006). Technology for physics instruction. *Contemporary Issues in Technology and Teacher Education, 6*(2), 230–245.

Budde, M., Niedderer, H., Scott, P., & Leach, J. (2002). The quantum atomic model 'Electronium': A successful teaching tool. *Physics Education, 37*(3), 204–210.

Buffler, A., Lubben, F., & Ibrahim, B. (2009). The relationship between students' views of the nature of science and their views of the nature of scientific measurement. *International Journal of Science Education, 31*(9), 1137–1156.

Bybee, R. (1997). *Achieving scientific literacy: From purposes to practices.* Portsmouth, NH: Heinemann Publishing.

Camp, C., & Clement, J. (1994). *Preconceptions in mechanics. Lessons dealing with students' conceptual difficulties.* Dubuque, IA: Kendall/Hunt.

Chevallard, Y. (2007). Readjusting didactics to changing epistemology. *European Educational Research Journal, 6*(2), 131–134.

Chi, M. T. H., Slotta, J. D., & de Leeuw, N. (1994). From things to processes: A theory of conceptual change for learning science concepts. *Learning and Instruction, 4,* 27–43.

Chinn, C. A., & Malhotra, B. A. (2002). Epistemologically authentic inquiry in schools: A theoretical framework for evaluating inquiry tasks. *Science Education, 86*(2), 175–218.

Chiu, M.-H., & Duit, R. (2011). Globalization: Science education from a global perspective—Editorial. *Journal of Research in Science Teaching, 48*(6), 553–566.

Christian, W., & Belloni, M. (Eds.). (2003). *Physlet? Physics: Interactive illustrations, explorations, and problems for introductory physics.* Prentice Hall, NJ: Addison-Wesley.

Clement, J. (1993). Using bridging analogies and anchoring intuitions to deal with students' preconceptions in physics. *Journal of Research in Science Teaching, 30,* 1241–1257.

Clough, M. P. (2006). Learners' responses to the demands of conceptual change: Considerations for effective nature of science instruction. *Science Education, 15,* 463–494.

Clough, M. P. (2007). Teaching the nature of science to secondary and post-secondary students: Questions rather than tenets. *The Pantaneto Forum,* Issue 25, January. Retrieved from www.pantaneto.co.uk/issue25/clough.htm (December 2012).

DeBoer, G. E. (2011). The globalization of science education. *Journal of Research in Science Teaching, 48*(6), 567–591.

Deng, F., Chen, D.-T., Tsai, C.-C., & Chai, C. S. (2011). Students' views of the nature of science: A critical review of research. *Science Education, 95*(6), 961–999.

diSessa, A. A. (1988). Knowledge in pieces. In G. Forman & P. B. Pufall (Eds.), *Constructivism in the computer age* (pp. 49–90). Hillsdale, NJ: Erlbaum.

Doerr, H. M. (1997). Experiment, simulation and analysis: An integrated instructional approach to the concept of force. *International Journal of Science Education, 19*(3), 265–282.

Driver, R., & Oldham, V. (1986). A constructivist approach to curriculum development in science. *Studies in Science Education, 13,* 105–122.

Driver, R., Squires, A., Rushworth, P., & Wood-Robinson, V. (1994). *Making sense of secondary science—Research into children's ideas.* London, UK: Routledge.

Duit, R. (1992). Teilchen- und Atomvorstellungen [Conceptions of particles and atoms]. In H. Fischler (Ed.), *Quantenphysik in der Schule* (pp. 201–204) Kiel, Germany: IPN—Leibniz Institute for Science Education.

Duit, R. (2009). *Bibliography—STCSE (students' and teachers' conceptions and science education).* Kiel: Leibniz Institute for Science and Mathematics Education. Retrieved from www.ipn.uni-kiel.de/aktuell/stcse/stcse.html (Dec. 2012)

Duit, R., Goldberg, F., & Niedderer, H. (1992). *Research in physics learning: Theoretical issues and empirical studies.* Kiel: IPN—Leibniz Institute for Science Education.

Duit R., Gropengießer H., Kattmann U., Komorek M., & Parchmann, I. (2012). The model of educational reconstruction—A framework for improving teaching and learning science. In D. Jorde & J. Dillon (Eds.), *The world of science education: Science education research and practice in Europe* (pp. 13–47). Rotterdam, the Netherlands: Sense Publishers.

Duit, R., Komorek, M., & Wilbers, J. (1997). Studies on educational reconstruction of chaos theory. *Research in Science Education, 27,* 339–357.

Duit, R., Treagust, D., & Widodo, A. (2013). Teaching science for conceptual change: Theory and practice. In S. Vosniadou (Ed.), *International handbook of research on conceptual change* (pp. 487–503). New York, London: Routledge.

Duit, R., & von Rhöneck, Ch. (1998). Learning and understanding key concepts of electricity. In A. Tiberghien, E. L. Jossem, & J. Barojas (Eds.), *Connecting research in physics education.* Boise, Ohio: ICPE—International Commission on Physics Education, ICPE Books. Retrieved from http://web.archive.org/web/20130105145245/www.physics.ohio-state.edu/~jossem/ICPE/C2.html (Jan. 2014)

Duschl, R. (2000). Making the nature of science explicit. In R. Millar, J. Leach, & J. Osborne (Eds.), *Improving science education. The contribution of research* (pp. 187–206). Buckingham, Philadelphia: Open University Press.

Duschl, R. (2012). The second dimension—Crosscutting concepts. *The Science Teacher, 79*(2), 34–38.

Duschl, R., Maeng, S., & Sezen, A. (2011). Learning progressions and teaching sequences: A review and analysis. *Studies in Science Education, 47,* 123–182.

Escalada, L. T., Rebello, S., & Zollman, D. A. (2004). Student explorations of quantum effects in LEDs and luminescent devices. *The Physics Teacher, 42,* 173–179.

Fensham, P. (2001). Science content as problematic—issues for research. In H. Behrendt, H. Dahncke, R. Duit, W. Gräber, M. Komorek, A. Kross, & P. Reiska (Eds.), *Research in science education—past, present, and future* (pp. 27–41). Dordrecht, the Netherlands: Kluwer Academic Publishers.

Fischler, H. (1999, March). Introduction to quantum physics—development and evaluation of a new course. In D. Zollman (Ed.), *Research on teaching and learning quantum mechanics* (pp. 32–40). Papers presented at the annual meeting of the National Association for Research in Science Teaching. Retrieved from http://web.phys.ksu.edu/papers/narst/QM_papers.pdf (Jan. 2014)

Fischler, H. (2011). Didaktik—An appropriate framework for the professional work of science teachers? In D. Corrigan, J. Dillon, &

R. Gunstone (Eds.), *The professional knowledge base of science teaching* (pp. 31–50). Dordrecht, the Netherlands: Springer.

Fischler, H., & Lichtfeldt, M. (1992). Modern physics and students' conceptions. *International Journal of Science Education, 14*, 181–190.

Galilei, G. (1832, reprint). Il Saggiatore. In *Opere di Galileo Galilei*, Vol. 2 (p. 13). Milano: Bettoni.

Galili, I., & Hazan, A. (2000). The influence of an historically oriented course on students' content knowledge in optics evaluated by means of facets-schemes analysis. *American Journal of Physics Supplement, 68*(7), 3–14.

Gallagher, J.J., & Tobin, K. (1987). Teacher management and student engagement in high school science. *Science Education, 71*, 535–555.

Gingras, Y. (2001). What did mathematics do to physics? *History of Science, 29*, 383–416.

Goldberg, F., & Bendall, S. (1995). Making the invisible visible: A teaching and learning environment that builds on a new view of the physics learner. *American Journal of Physics, 63*, 978–991.

Gräsel, C., & Parchmann, I. (2004). Implementationsforschung—oder: der steinige Weg Unterricht zu verändern [Implementation research—the stony path towards changing instruction]. *Unterrichtswissenschaft, 32*(3), 196–214.

Grayson, D. (1996). Improving science and mathematics learning by concept substitution. In D. Treagust, R. Duit, & B. Fraser (Eds.), *Improving teaching and learning in science and mathematics* (pp. 152–161). New York: Teachers College Press.

Hake, R.R. (1998). Interactive-engagement versus traditional methods: A six-thousand-student survey of mechanics test data for introductory physics courses. *American Journal of Physics, 66*, 64–74.

Hannover, B., & Kessels, U. (2004). Self-to-prototype matching as a strategy for making academic choices. Why high school students do not like math and science. *Learning and Instruction, 14*, 51–67.

Harding, J. (1996). Science as a masculine strait-jacket. In L.H. Parker, L.J. Rennie, & B. Fraser (Eds.), *Gender, science and mathematics* (pp. 3–16). Dordrecht, the Netherlands: Kluwer Academic Publishers.

Harrison, A.G., & Treagust, D.F. (1996). Secondary students' mental models of atoms and molecules: Implications for teaching chemistry. *Science Education, 80*, 509–534.

Härtel, H. (1982). The electric circuit as a system. A new approach. *European Journal of Science Education, 4*(1), 45–55.

Häußler, P., & Hoffmann, L. (2002). An intervention study to enhance girls' interest, self-concept and achievement in physics classes. *Journal of Research in Science Teaching, 39*(9), 870–888.

Hazari, Z., Sonnert, G., Sadler, P.M., & Shanahan, M.-C. (2010). Connecting high school physics experiences, outcome expectations, physics identity, and physics career choice: A gender study. *Journal of Research in Science Teaching, 47*(8), 978–1003.

Heck, A., Kedzierska, E., & Ellermeijer, T. (2009). Design and implementation of an integrated computer working environment for doing mathematics and science. *Journal of Computers in Mathematics and Science Teaching, 28*(2), 147–161.

Heering, P., & Höttecke, D. (2014). Historical-investigative approaches in science teaching. In M.R. Matthews (Ed.), *International handbook of research in history, philosophy and science teaching* (pp. 1473–1502). Dordrecht, the Netherlands: Springer.

Heimann, P., Otto, G., & Schulz, W. (1969). *Unterricht, Analyse und Planung* [Instruction: Analysis and planning]. Hannover, Germany: Schroedel.

Heinicke, S., & Heering, P. (2012). Discovering randomness, recovering expertise: The different approaches to the quality in measurement of Coulomb and Gauss and of today's students. *Science & Education, 22*, 483–503.

Herrmann, F. (1995). A critical analysis of the language of modern physics. In C. Bernardini, C. Tarsitani, & M. Vicentini (Eds.), *Thinking physics for teaching* (pp. 287–294). New York: Plenum Press.

Herrmann, F., & Job, G. (2006). *The Karlsruhe physics course, Vol. 3, reactions, waves, atoms, 134*. Retrieved from www.physikdidaktik. uni-karlsruhe.de/kpk/english/KPK_Volume_3.pdf (June 2013)

Hestenes, D., Wells, M., & Swackhamer, G. (1992). Force concept inventory. *The Physics Teacher, 30*, 141–158.

Hodson, D. (2009). *Teaching and learning about science. Language, theories, methods, history, traditions and values*. Rotterdam, the Netherlands: Sense Publishes.

Hofstein, A., & Kind, P.M. (2012). Learning in and from science laboratories. In B.J. Fraser, K.G. Tobin, & C.J. McRobbie (Eds.), *Second international handbook of science education* (pp. 189–207). Dordrecht, the Netherlands: Springer.

Hopf, M. (2007). *Problemorientierte Schülerexperimente* [Problem-based practical work of students]. Berlin: Logos-Verlag.

Hopmann, S. (2007). Restrained teaching: The common core of Didaktik. *European Educational Research Journal, 6*(2), 109–124.

Höttecke, D. (2001). Die Vorstellungen von Schülern und Schülerinnen von der "Natur der Naturwissenschaften" [Students' beliefs on the nature of science]. *Zeitschrift für Didaktik der Naturwissenschaften, 7*, 7–23.

Höttecke, D., Henke, A., & Rieß, F. (2012). Implementing history and philosophy in science teaching—strategies, methods, results and experiences from the European Project HIPST. *Science & Education, 21*(9), 1233–1261.

Höttecke, D., & Silva, C.C. (2011). Why implementing history and philosophy in school science education is a challenge—an analysis of obstacles. *Science & Education, 20*(3–4), 293–316.

Huffman, D., & Heller, P. (1995). What does the force concept inventory actually measure? *The Physics Teacher, 33*, 138–143.

Interactive Physics. (2014). Canton, MI: Design Simulation Technologies.

Ivie, R., & Guo, S. (2006). Women physicists speak again. American Institute of Physics Report. Retrieved from www.aip.org/statistics/reports/women-physicists-speak-again (Jan. 2014)

Jonas-Ahrend, G. (2004). *Physiklehrervorstellungen zum Experiment im Physikunterricht* [Teachers' beliefs about practical work in physics teaching]. Berlin: Logos.

Jung, W. (2012). Philosophy of science and education. *Science & Education*. doi:10.1007/s11191–012–9497-x

Jung, W., Wiesner, H., & Engelhard, P. (1981). *Vorstellungen von Schülern über Begriffe der Newtonschen Mechanik* [Students' ideas about concepts of Newtonian Mechanics]. Bad Salzdetfurth, Germany: Franzbecker.

Kalkanis, G., Hadzidaki, P., & Stavrou, D. (2003). An instructional model for a radical conceptual change towards quantum mechanics concepts. *Science Education, 87*(2), 257–280.

Ke, J.-L., Monk, M., & Duschl, R. (2005). Learning introductory quantum physics: Sensori-motor experiences and mental models. *International Journal of Science Education, 27*(13), 1571–1594.

Keeves, J.P., & Kotte, D. (1996). Patterns of science achievement: International comparisons. In L.H. Parker, L.J. Rennie, & B. Fraser (Eds.), *Gender, science and mathematics* (pp. 77–94). Dordrecht, The Netherlands: Kluwer Academic Publishers.

Kessels, U., Rau, M., & Hannover, B. (2006). What goes well with physics? Measuring and altering the image of science. *British Journal of Educational Psychology, 76*(4), 761–780.

Kircher, E., Girwidz, R., & Häußler, P. (2000). *Physikdidaktik* [Didactics of physics]. Braunschweig/Wiesbaden, Germany: Friedrich Vieweg & Sohn.

Kirstein, J., & Nordmeier, V. (2007). Multimedia representation of experiments in physics. *European Journal of Physics, 28*(3), S115–S126.

Klafki, W. (1969). Didaktische Analyse als Kern der Unterrichtsvorbereitung [Educational analysis as core issue of instructional planning]. In H. Roth & A. Blumental (Eds.), *Auswahl, Didaktische Analyse* (pp. 5–34). Hannover, Germany: Schroedel.

Klassen, S. (2009). The construction and analysis of a science story: A proposed methodology. *Science & Education, 18*, 401–423.

KMK—Ständige Konferenz der Kultusminister der Länder in der Bundesrepublik Deutschland (Hrsg.). (2005). *Bildungsstandards im Fach Physik für den Mittleren Bildungsabschluss*. Köln: Wolters Kluwer.

Knote, H. (1975). Zur Atomvorstellung bei Dreizehn- bis Fünfzehnjährigen [Thirteen to fifteen year old students' conceptions of the atom]. *Der Physikunterricht, 4,* 86–96.

Köller, O., Baumert, J., & Neubrand, J. (2000). Epistemologische Überzeugungen und Fachverständnis im Mathematik- und Physikunterricht [Epistemological beliefs and content knowledge in mathematics and physics instruction]. In J. Baumert et al. (Eds.), *TIMSS—Mathematisch-naturwissenschaftliche Bildung am Ende der Sekundarstufe II* [TIMSS—mathematics and science literacy at the end of upper secondary school] (pp. 229–270). Opladen, Germany: Leske & Budrich.

Kremer, K., Fischer, H.E., Kauertz, A., Mayer, J., Sumfleth, E., & Walpuski, M. (2012). Assessment of standards-based learning outcomes in science education: Perspectives from the German project ESNaS. In S. Bernholt, K. Neumann, & P. Nentwig (Eds.), *Making it tangible—learning outcomes in science education* (pp. 201–218). Münster: Waxmann.

Kroh, L.B., & Thomsen, P.V. (2005). Studying students' attitudes towards science from a cultural perspective but with a quantitative methodology: Border crossing into the physics classroom. *International Journal of Science Education, 27,* 281–302.

Labudde, P., Nidegger, C., Adamina, M., & Gingings, F. (2012). The development, validation, and implementation of standards in science education: Chances and difficulties in the Swiss project HarmoS. In S. Bernholt, K. Neumann, & P. Nentwig (Eds.), *Making it tangible—learning outcomes in science education* (pp. 255–280). Münster: Waxmann.

Laukenmann, M., Bleicher, M., Fuß, S., Gläser-Zikuda, M., Mayring, P., & v. Rhöneck, C. (2003). An investigation of the influence of emotional factors on learning in physics instruction. *International Journal of Science Education, 25,* 489–507.

Laws, P.W. (1997). Promoting active learning based on physics education research in introductory physics courses (Millikan Lecture 1996). *American Journal of Physics, 65,* 14–21.

Lederman, N.G. (1992). Students' and teachers' conceptions of the nature of science: A review of research. *Journal of Research in Science Teaching, 29*(4), 331–359.

Lederman, N.G., & Lederman, J.S. (2011). The development of scientific literacy. A function of interactions and distinctions among subject matter, nature of science, scientific inquiry, and knowledge about scientific inquiry. In C. Linder, L. Östman, D.A. Robert, P.-O. Wickman, G. Erickson, & A. MacKinnon (Eds.), *Exploring the landscape of scientific literacy* (pp. 127–144). New York, London: Routledge.

Lijnse, P.L. (1995). "Developmental research" as a way to an empirically based "didactical structure" of science. *Science Education, 79*(2), 189–199.

Linn, M.C., Songer, N.B., Lewis, E.L., & Stern, J. (1993). Using technology to teach thermodynamics: Achieving integrated understanding. In D.L. Ferguson (Ed.), *Advanced educational technologies for mathematics and science* (pp. 5–60). Berlin: Springer.

Liu, S.-Y., Lin, C.-S., & Tsai, C.-C. (2011). College students' scientific epistemological views and thinking patterns in scocioscientific decision-making. *Science Education, 95*(3), 597–517.

Lunetta, V.N. (1998). The school science laboratory: Historical perspectives and contexts for contemporary teaching. In K. Tobin & B. Fraser (Eds.), *International handbook of science education. Part I* (pp. 249–264). Dordrecht, the Netherlands: Kluwer Academic Publishers.

Maloney, D.P. (1994). Research on problem solving: Physics. In D. Gabel (Ed.), *Handbook of research on science teaching and learning* (pp. 327–354). New York: Macmillan Publishing Company.

Mashhadi, A. (1995). Students' conceptions of quantum physics. In G. Welford, J. Osborne, & P. Scott (Eds.), *Research in science education in Europe* (pp. 254–266). London, UK: Falmer.

Matthews, M.R. (1994). *Science teaching—the role of history and philosophy of science.* London: Routledge.

Matthews, M.R. (2012). Changing the focus: From nature of science to features of science. In M.S. Khine (Ed.), *Advances in nature of science research* (pp. 3–26). Dordrecht, the Netherlands: Springer.

Mazur, E. (1997). *Peer instruction: A user's manual.* Upper Saddle River, NJ: Prentice Hall.

McCloskey, M. (1983). Intuitive physics. *Scientific American, 284*(4), 114–122.

McComas, W.F. (Ed.). (1998). *The nature of science in science education rationales and strategies.* Dordrecht, the Netherlands: Kluwer Academic Publishers.

Méheut, M., & Psillos, D. (2004). Teaching-learning sequences. Aims and tools for science education research. *International Journal of Science Education, 26*(5), 515–535.

Meyling, H. (1997). How to change students' conceptions of the epistemology of science. *Science & Education, 6,* 397–416.

Mikelkis-Seifert, S., & Fischler, H. (2003). Die Bedeutung des Denkens in Modellen bei der Entwicklung von Teilchenvorstellungen—Stand der Forschung und Entwurf einer Unterrichtskonzeption [On the role of thinking in terms of models when developing particle ideas—state of research and a draft of an instructional approach]. *Zeitschrift für Didaktik der Naturwissenschaften, 9,* 75–88.

Minstrell, J. (1992). Facets of students' knowledge and relevant instruction. In R. Duit, F. Goldberg, & H. Niedderer (Eds.), *Research in physics learning: Theoretical issues and empirical studies* (pp. 110–128). Kiel, Germany: IPN—Institute for Science Education.

Mintzes, J.J., Wandersee, J.H., & Novak, J.D. (Eds.). (1997). *Teaching science for understanding—a human constructivist view.* San Diego, CA: Academic Press.

Mulhall, P., & Gunstone, R. (2008). Views about physics held by physics teachers with differing approaches to teaching physics. *Research in Science Education, 38,* 435–462.

Müller, R. (2003). *Quantenphysik in der Schule* [Quantum physics in high school]. Berlin: Logos.

Müller, R., & Wiesner, H. (2002). Teaching quantum mechanics on an introductory level. *American Journal of Physics, 70,* 200–209.

Neumann, K., Viering, T., Boone, W.J., & Fischer, H.E. (2012). Towards a learning progression of energy. *Journal of Research in Science Teaching.* doi:10.1002/tea.21061

Niedderer, H., Budde, M., Giry, D., Psillos, D., & Tiberghien, A. (2007). Learning process studies. In R. Pintó & D. Couso (Eds.), *Contributions from science education research* (pp. 451–463). Dordrecht, the Netherlands: Springer.

Niedderer, H., Buty, C., Haller, K., Hucke, L., Sander, F., Fischer, H.E., v. Aufschnaiter, S., & Tiberghien, A. (2002). Talking physics in labwork contexts—a category based analysis of videotapes. In D. Psillos & H. Niedderer (Eds.), *Teaching and learning in the science laboratory* (pp. 31–40). Dordrecht, the Netherlands: Kluwer Academic Publishers.

Niedderer, H., & Deylitz, S. (1999, March). Evaluation of a new approach in quantum atomic physics in high school. In D. Zollman (Ed.), *Research on teaching and learning quantum mechanics* (pp. 23–27). Papers presented at the annual meeting of the National Association for Research in Science Teaching (NARST). Retrieved from http://web.phys.ksu.edu/papers/narst/QM_papers.pdf) (The textbook is available from www.idn.uni-bremen.de/pubs/Niedderer/1998-QAP-Skript-engl.pdf [Jun. 2013]).

Niedderer, H., & Goldberg, F. (1995). Lernprozesse beim elektrischen Stromkreis [Learning processes in case of the electric circuit]. *Zeitschrift für Didaktik der Naturwissenschaften, 1,* 73–86.

NRC—National Research Council. (1996). *National science education standards.* Washington, DC: National Academies Press.

NRC—National Research Council. (2012). *A framework for K–12 science education: Practices, crosscutting concepts, and core ideas.* Washington, DC: National Academies Press.

OECD—Organization for Economic Cooperation and Development. (1999). *Measuring student knowledge and skills—a new framework for assessment.* Paris: OECD Publications.

OECD—Organization for Economic Coordination and Development. (2009). *Equally prepared for life? How 15-year-old boys and girls perform in school.* Retrieved from www.oecd-ilibrary.org/education/equally-prepared-for-life_9789264064072-en (Feb. 2014).

Osborne, J. (2007). Science education for the twenty first century. *Eurasia Journal of Mathematics, Science, and Technology Education, 3*(3), 173–184.

Osborne, R. (1983). Towards modifying children's ideas about electric current. *Research in Science and Technology Education, 1*, 73–82.

Oser, F. K., & Baeriswyl, F. J. (2001). Choreographies of teaching: Bridging instruction to learning. In V. Richardson (Ed.), *Handbook of research on teaching* (pp. 1031–1065). Washington, DC: American Educational Research Association.

Pasanen, P. (2009). Subject matter didactics as a central knowledge base for teachers, or should it be called pedagogical content knowledge? *Pedagogy, Culture & Society, 17*(1), 29–39.

Petri, J., & Niedderer, H. (1998). A learning pathway in high-school level quantum physics. *International Journal of Science Education, 20*, 1075–1088.

Pintrich, P. R., Marx, R. W., & Boyle, R. A. (1992). Beyond cold conceptual change: The role of motivational beliefs and classroom contextual factors in the process of conceptual change. *Review of Educational Research, 63*, 167–199.

Psillos, D., Koumaras, P., & Tiberghien, A. (1988). Voltage presented as a primary concept in an introductory teaching sequence on DC circuits. *International Journal of Science Education, 10*(1), 29–43.

Redish, E. F. (2003). *Teaching physics.* New York: Wiley.

Redish, E. F., Saul, J. M., & Steinberg, R. N. (1996). On the effectiveness of active-engagement microcomputer-based laboratories. *American Journal of Physics, 65*, 45–54.

Reid, N., & Skryabina, E. A. (2003). Gender and physics. *International Journal of Science Education, 25*, 509–536.

Roach, L. E., & Wandersee, J. H. (1995). Putting people back into science: Using historical vignettes. *School Science and Mathematics, 95*(7), 365–370.

Roth, K., & Garnier, H. (2006). What science teaching looks like: An international perspective. *Science in the Spotlight, 64*(4), 16–23.

Ryder, J. (2001). Identifying science understanding for functional scientific literacy. *Studies in Science Education, 36*, 1–44.

Sadaghiani, H. R. (2012). Controlled study on the effectiveness of multimedia learning modules for teaching mechanics. *Physical Review Special Topics—Physics Education Research, 8.* doi:10.1103/PhysRevSTPER.8.010103

Samburski, S. (1975). *Physical thought. From the pre-Socratics to the quantum physicists—an anthology.* New York: Pica Press.

Schecker, H. (1998). Integration of experimenting and modeling by advanced educational technology: Examples from nuclear physics. In K. Tobin & B. Fraser (Eds.), *International handbook of science education. Part I* (pp. 383–398). Dordrecht, the Netherlands: Kluwer Academic Publishers.

Schecker, H., Fischer, H. E., & Wiesner, H. (2004). Physikunterricht in der gymnasialen Oberstufe [Physics instruction in upper secondary]. In H. E. Tenorth (Ed.), *Kerncurriculum Oberstufe* (pp. 148–234). Weinheim, Germany: Beltz.

Schecker, H., & Niedderer, H. (1996). Contrastive teaching: A strategy to promote qualitative conceptual understanding of science. In D. Treagust, R. Duit, & B. Fraser (Eds.), *Improving teaching and learning in science and mathematics* (pp. 141–151). New York: Teachers College Press.

Schecker, H., & Parchmann, I. (2007). Standards and competence models—the German situation. In D. Waddington, P. Nentwig, & S. Schanze (Eds.), *Making it comparable—standards in science education* (pp. 147–164). Münster: Waxmann.

Scott, P. H. (1992). Pathways in learning science: A case study of the development of one student's ideas relating to the structure of matter. In R. Duit, F. Goldberg, & H. Niedderer (Eds.), *Research in physics learning: Theoretical issues and empirical studies* (pp. 203–224). Kiel, Germany: IPN—Leibniz-Institute for Science Education.

Seidel, T., & Prenzel, M. (2006). Stability of teaching patterns in physics instruction: Findings from a video study. *Learning and Instruction, 16*(3), 228–240.

Sharma, M. D., Johnston, I. D., Johnston, H., Varvell, K., Robertson, G., Hopkins, A., Stewart, C., Cooper, I., & Thornton, R. (2010). Use of interactive lecture demonstrations: A ten year study. *Physical Review Special Topics—Physics Education Research, 6.* doi:10.1103/PhysRevSTPER.6.020119

Shipstone, D. M., von Rhöneck, C., Jung, W., Karrqvist, C., Dupin, J. J., Joshua, S., & Licht, P. (1988). A study of secondary students' understanding of electricity in five European countries. *International Journal of Science Education, 10*, 303–316.

Shulman, L. S. (1987). Knowledge and teaching: Foundations of a new reform. *Harvard Educational Review, 57*(1), 1–22.

Sjøberg, S., & Schreiner, C. (2010). *The ROSE project. An overview and key findings.* Oslo: University of Oslo. Retrieved from www.ils.uio.no/english/rose/publications/english-pub.html (Dec. 2010)

Smith, C., Wiser, M., Anderson, C., Krajcik, J., & Coppola, B. (2004). *Implications of research on children's learning for assessment: Matter and atomic molecular theory.* Paper commissioned by the Committee on Test Design for K–12 Science Achievement. Washington, DC: Center for Education. National Research Council.

Smith, C. L., Wiser, M., Anderson, C. W., & Krajcik, J. (2006). Implications of research on children's learning for standards and assessment: A proposed learning progression for matter and the atomic molecular theory. *Measurement: Interdisciplinary Research and Perspectives, 4*(1–2), 1–98.

Sokoloff, D. R., Thornton, R. K., & Laws, P. W. (2012). *RealTime physics. Active learning laboratories. Module 1 Mechanics.* Hoboken, NJ: Wiley.

Solomon, J., Scott, L., & Duveen, J. (1996). Large-scale exploration of pupils' understanding of the nature of science. *Science Education, 80*(5), 493–508.

Stadler, H., Benke, G., & Duit, R. (2000). Do boys and girls understand physics differently? *Physics Education, 35*(6), 417–422.

Stavrou, D., Duit, R., & Komorek, M. (2008). A teaching and learning sequence about the interplay of chance and determinism in nonlinear systems. *Physics Education, 43*, 417–422.

Stevens, S. Y., Delgado, C., & Krajcik, J. (2009). Developing a hypothetical multi-dimensional progression for the nature of matter. *Journal of Research in Science Teaching, 47*(6), 687–715.

Stewart, J., Griffin, H., & Stewart, G. (2007). Context sensitivity in the force concept inventory. *Physical Review Special Topics—Physics Education Research, 3.* doi:10.1103/PhysRevSTPER.3.010102

Taber, K. S. (2001). When the analogy breaks down: Modeling the atom on the solar system. *Physics Education, 36*, 222–226.

Tesch, M., & Duit, R. (2004). Experimentieren im Physikunterricht— Ergebnisse einer Videostudie [Experiments in physics education— results of a video-study]. *Zeitschrift für Didaktik der Naturwissenschaften, 10*, 51–69.

Thornton, R. K. (1992). Enhancing and evaluating students' learning of motion concepts. In A. Tiberghien & H. Mandl (Eds.), *Physics and learning environments* (pp. 265–283). Berlin, Germany: Springer.

Thornton, R. K., & Sokoloff, D. R. (1998). Assessing student learning of Newton's laws: The force and motion conceptual evaluation and the evaluation of active learning laboratory and lecture curricula. *American Journal of Physics, 66*(4), 338–351.

Tiberghien, A. (1984). Critical review on the research aimed at elucidating the sense that notions of temperature and heat have for the students aged 10 to 16. *Twenty years of research on physics education. Proceedings of the first international workshop.* La Londe les Maures.

Tiberghien, A., Veillard, L., Le Maréchal, J.-F., Buty, C., & Millar, R. (2001). An analysis of labwork tasks used in science teaching at upper secondary school and university levels in several European countries. *Science Education, 85*(5), 483–508.

Tiberghien, A., Vince, J., & Gaidioz, P. (2009). Design-based research: Case of a teaching sequence on mechanics. *International Journal of Science Education, 31*(17), 2275–2314.

Tinker, R. (Ed.). (1996). *Microcomputer based labs: Educational research and standards.* New York: Springer.

Treagust, D., Chittleborough, G., & Mamiala, T.L. (2002). Students' understanding of the role of scientific models in learning science. *International Journal of Science Education, 24*, 357–368.

Treagust, D., & Duit, R. (2012). Conceptual change learning and teaching. In G. Venville & V. Dawson (Eds.), *The art of teaching science* (pp. 41–59). Sydney: Allen & Unwin.

Tsai, C.C. (2003). Using a conflict map as an instructional tool to change student alternative conceptions in simple series electric circuits. *International Journal of Science Education, 25*(3), 307–327.

Tsaparlis, G., & Papaphotis, G. (2009). High-school students' conceptual difficulties and attempts at conceptual change: The case of basic quantum chemical concepts. *International Journal of Science Education, 31*(7), 895–930.

Urhahne, D., Prenzel, M., Davier, M.V., Senkbeil, M., & Bleschke, M. (2000). Computereinsatz im naturwissenschaftlichen Unterricht—Ein Überblick über die pädagogisch-psychologischen Grundlagen und ihre Anwendung [Computers in science education—an overview of pedagogical and psychological foundations and their applications]. *Zeitschrift für Didaktik der Naturwissenschaften, 6*, 157–186.

van Borkulo, S.P., van Joolingen, W.R., Savelsbergh, E.R., & de Jong, T. (2012). What can be learned from computer modeling? Comparing expository and modeling approaches to teaching dynamic systems behavior. *Journal of Science Education and Technology, 21*, 267–275.

Viennot, L. (1979). Spontaneous reasoning in elementary dynamics. *European Journal of Science Education, 1*, 205–221.

Viennot, L. (2001). *Reasoning in physics. The part of common sense.* Dordrecht, the Netherlands: Kluwer Academic Publishers.

Viennot, L. (2003). *Teaching physics.* Dordrecht, the Netherlands: Kluwer Academic Publishers.

Vosniadou, S. (2002). On the nature of naïve physics. In M. Limon & L. Mason (Eds.), *Reconsidering conceptual change: Issues in theory and practice* (pp. 61–76). Dordrecht, the Netherlands: Kluwer Academic Publishers.

Vosniadou, S. (2012). Reframing the classical approach to conceptual change: Preconceptions, misconceptions and synthetic models. In B. Fraser, K. Tobin, & C. McRobbie (Eds.), *Second international handbook of science education* (pp. 119–130). Dordrecht, the Netherlands: Springer.

Vosniadou, S., & Ioannides, C. (1998). From conceptual change to science education: A psychological point of view. *International Journal of Science Education, 20*, 1213–1230.

Waddington, D., Nentwig, P., & Schanze, S. (Eds.). (2007). *Making it comparable—standards in science education.* Münster: Waxmann.

Wandersee, J.H., Mintzes, J.J., & Novak, J.D. (1994). Research on alternative conceptions in science. In D. Gabel (Ed.), *Handbook of research on science teaching and learning* (pp. 177–210). New York: Macmillan.

Warren, J.W. (1979). *Understanding force.* London, UK: Murray.

Westbury, I. (2000). Teaching as reflective practice: What might Didaktik teach Curriculum? In I. Westbury, S. Hopmann, & K. Riquarts (Eds.), *Teaching as reflective practice: The German Didaktik tradition* (pp. 15–39). New York, London: Routledge.

Westbury, I., Hopmann, S., & Riquarts, K. (Eds.). (2000). *Teaching as reflective practice: The German Didaktik tradition.* Mahwah, NJ: Erlbaum.

White, B.Y., & Frederiksen, J. (1998). Inquiry, modeling, and metacognition: Making science accessible to all students. *Cognition and Instruction, 16*(1), 3–118.

Widodo, A. (2004). *Constructivist oriented lessons.* Frankfurt: Peter Lang.

Wilhelm, T., Tobias, V., Waltner, C., Hopf, M., & Wiesner, H. (2012). Einfluss der Sachstruktur auf das Lernen Newtonscher Mechanik [The influence of content structure on learning Newtonian mechanics]. In H. Bayrhuber et al. (Eds.), *Formate Fachdidaktischer Forschung* (pp. 237–258). Münster: Waxmann.

Zacharia, Z.C. (2007). Comparing and combining real and virtual experimentation—an effort to enhance students' conceptual understanding of electric circuits. *Journal of Computer Assisted Learning, 23*(2), 120–132.

Zhu, G., & Singh, C. (2012). Improving students' understanding of quantum measurement. ii. Development of research-based learning tools. *Physical Review Special Topics—Physics Education Research, 8.* doi:10.1103/PhysRevSTPER.8.010118

Zohar, A. (2005). Physics teachers' knowledge and beliefs regarding girls' low participation rates in advanced physics classes. *International Journal of Science Education, 27*(1), 61–77.

Zollman, D.A., Rebello, N.S., & Hogg, K. (2002). Quantum mechanics for everyone: Hands-on activities integrated with technology. *American Journal of Physics, 70*, 252–259.

23

The Many Faces of High School Chemistry

ONNO DE JONG AND KEITH S. TABER

The first part of this chapter deals with two general themes in modern high school chemistry education. First, we consider studies of attempts to make chemistry more meaningful to students by using *contexts*. These contexts can be taken from students' interests, from society, or from professional practices. Second, we discuss studies of characteristics of *models* in chemistry and chemical education, especially their presentation from three related perspectives: macroscopic, submicroscopic, and symbolic.

In the second part of this chapter, the theme of models is further elaborated for two difficult core topics at school level: *chemical reactions* (especially at junior high level) and *chemical bonding* (especially at senior high level). For both topics, students' main conceptual difficulties are discussed. They are conceptualized in terms of three interrelated factors: the student, the chemistry content, and the teacher/textbook. Studies of approaches designed to support students overcoming learning difficulties are reviewed.

The final part of this chapter deals with a look to the *near future of chemical education*, concisely focusing on directions for new research and coherent innovations in chemistry education. Suggestions for priority areas for further research and curriculum development are offered at several places.

Contexts in Chemistry Education

Domains of Origin

One of the most promising contributions abolishing curriculum content isolation is the use of relevant and meaningful contexts for teaching chemistry topics (Bennett & Holman, 2002). The concept of "context" is a "container" concept—that is, it can be defined in several ways. In general, contexts are often considered as situations in which chemistry or other science concepts, processes, and so on can help communicate meaning to students. This definition can be expanded by the notion

that contexts can also be described as practices that help students give meaning to activities in the high school lab, such as inquiry and designing. Gilbert (2007) has elaborated the nature of contexts in chemistry education and suggested the use of contexts that are based on physical settings, together with their cultural justifications, and that are taught from a sociocultural perspective on learning. Contexts can be classified by looking at the domain of origin (cf. Van Aalsvoort, 2004). The following distinction can be made:

i) Contexts taken from the *personal domain* are important because high schools should contribute to the personal development of students by connecting science and technology with their everyday lives. For instance, the issue of clothes and what they are made of can be linked to fibers, threads, fabrics, their applications, and the relationship among properties and structure of materials and chemical substances (Campbell et al., 1994).

ii) Contexts taken from the *social and society domain* are important because high schools should be preparing students for their roles as responsible citizens who are able to participate in debates on science and technology and their impact on social issues. For instance, the contexts of public discussions about low-fat and low-carbohydrate diets can be used to promote learning about carbohydrates and fats in chemistry and to foster students' competency in reflecting upon the use of chemistry-related information in everyday life (Marks, Bertram, & Eilks, 2008).

iii) Contexts taken from the *professional practice domain* are relevant because high schools should prepare students for their coming role as professional workers in public or private areas. For instance, the practice of (bio)chemistry analysts can be related to investigations of the quality of surface water, including the use of (bio)chemistry concepts and procedures for determining the presence of (non)acceptable substances (Van Aalsvoort, 2004).

iv) Contexts taken from the *scientific and technological domain* are relevant because high schools should contribute to the development of scientific and technological literacy of students. For instance, the context of modeling drinking water treatment can be used to foster students' epistemological view on models and modeling (Prins, Bulte, & Pilot, 2011).

Relationship Between Contexts and Concepts

Contexts and concepts can be related in multiple ways. For instance, the context of the greenhouse effect can be linked with several concepts, such as the chemistry concept of gas reactions and the physics concepts of infrared radiation and heat. Conversely, one concept can be related to several contexts, for instance, the concept of tap water can be linked with a personal/societal context as well as a chemistry context. Note that the meaning of a concept can vary with the related context. For instance, in a personal/societal context, tap water is considered pure because it looks clear and it is safe to drink (according to the requirements of the law), but in a chemistry context, tap water is not defined as pure because it contains other substances.

Another kind of relationship between contexts and concepts is the sequence of presentation in teaching. This order can vary, and, for that reason, the function of contexts can also vary (see Table 23.1). In quite traditional approaches in the context-based teaching of chemistry, two functions of contexts are dominant. First, contexts are presented as illustrations of concepts that already have been taught, especially in the case of abstract concepts. Second, contexts are presented to offer the possibility to students of applying their knowledge of a concept. For instance, at the end of a series of lessons about acids and bases, students can be asked what type of solution they would use at home to apply to a wasp sting (George & Lubben, 2002). In more modern approaches, two other functions of contexts are emphasized. First, contexts are presented as

the starting point or rationale for teaching concepts. For instance, at the beginning of teaching a topic, students can be asked to write a short story on an experience they have had related to the topic (George & Lubben, 2002). Second, these contexts not only have an orienting function but can also enhance motivation for learning new concepts. In some recent approaches, both orders of presentation of contexts are combined. For instance, an introductory context on the water-absorbing capacity of a diaper can be linked to relevant organic chemistry concepts, while thereafter the acquired knowledge can be applied in a follow-up context of fire-resistant materials (Stolk, De Jong, Bulte, & Pilot, 2011).

Teachers' Views on Context-Based Chemistry Teaching

Although nearly every chemistry teacher has his or her personal opinion about the value of context-based teaching, only a few studies have explored teachers' views in a systematic way. Some of these studies are reviewed in the following paragraphs.

Bennet, Gräsel, Parchmann, and Waddington (2005) reported on teachers' views by comparing two groups of British chemistry teachers. The first group of teachers had experience teaching a particular context-based course, namely Salters Advanced Chemistry (SAC). The other group of teachers had experience teaching conventional chemistry courses only, but it was known that most of them were familiar with the SAC materials. The results of the study showed that, in general, both groups agreed that context-based teaching had positive effects on students' motivation and interest and that students taught by this approach would be more likely to go to university to study chemistry. Both groups also agreed that students enrolled in a context-based course would be better able to study independently but would find it more demanding to study chemistry. However, the results also indicated differences in views between the two groups. The conventional-course teachers were unconvinced that the context-based course delivered the concepts in sufficient depth. In contrast, the SAC teachers believed that their course did indeed cover the concepts adequately and that there were significant advantages in using the context-based approach as a good foundation for further study at the university.

In another study of teachers' views, Marks and colleagues (2008) found that German chemistry teachers reported a very active and motivating learning atmosphere when they were involved in context-based lessons. These results correspond with the outcomes of a similar British study reported by Millar (2006).

In general, studies of teachers' views showed that chemistry teachers have positive thoughts about the influence of context-based teaching on students' interest, but they think differently about the impact on students' learning outcomes. Research on this impact is addressed in the next subsection.

TABLE 23.1
Trends in Context-Based Approaches and Functions of Contexts

Context-based approach	Dominant function of context
Quite traditional	
* Contexts follow concepts	* Illustration of concepts
	* Application of conceptual knowledge
More modern	
* Contexts precede concepts	* Orientation on topics
	* Motivation for learning topics
Quite recent	
* Contexts precede concepts and (other) contexts follow them	* All functions given above

Vignette

In a senior high school class, students conduct an experiment on the liquid-absorbing capacity of a disposable diaper. This experiment functions as an introductory context for learning about structure–property relationship in polymers. Later on, in an inservice course for teachers, the teacher reports on the use of this context as follows: *"That diaper was full of water (. . .). I could not get it out of the diaper. But there was a very strong boy who tried to squeeze it out. He squeezed too hard, and the filling squirted out of the diaper. However, he did not get the water out. From that moment, that diaper passed from hand to hand, and they were deeply involved."*

This observation of a classroom event is taken from a study by Stolk, De Jong, Bulte, and Pilot (2011) and shows the motivating power of an introductory context.

Effects of Context-Based Chemistry Teaching on Students' Understanding and Motivation

It is not easy to come to a unanimous judgment about effects of context-based chemistry teaching on students' learning outcomes and motivation.

Some studies indicated that there is no advantage of context-based courses in terms of the development of students' understanding. For instance, Ramsden (1997) compared the effects of a context-based course and a more traditional course to British high school students' understanding of key chemistry concepts. Her study indicated that there is no difference in levels of understanding of concepts such as element and compound, chemical reaction, and the periodic table. However, other studies reported some advantages to students in context-based courses in terms of their understanding. For instance, Barker and Millar (2000) undertook a comparative study of British high school students enrolled in a context-based course or a conventional course. They found a slight advantage in students' development of an understanding of chemical bonding and thermodynamics among students in the context-based course. Nevertheless, they also reported the tenacity of a number of misunderstandings among students of both groups.

Some studies have also looked at effects on students' motivation. The comparative study of Ramsden (1997), dealing with British high school chemistry students, showed some benefits associated with a context-based approach in terms of stimulating students' interest in chemistry. Vaino, Holbrook, and Rannikmäe (2012) reported that students from Estonian high schools were much more willing to engage with context-based chemistry modules than with more traditional materials.

A meta-analysis of 17 studies, from eight different countries, on the effects of context-based (and science, technology, society [STS]) approaches was reported by Bennett, Lubben, and Hogarth (2007). They reviewed studies of approaches that use contexts as the starting point for the development of scientific ideas. Their in-depth systematic review findings indicated that context-based/STS approaches resulted in improved student motivation and fostered positive attitudes toward science in general. The review results also showed that the understanding of scientific ideas developed is comparable to that of conventional approaches.

In conclusion, the outcomes of context-based science teaching are positive from an affective development perspective, but they are somewhat disappointing from a cognitive development point of view. A comparison between context-based approaches and traditional approaches has methodological limitations. It may be that the conceptual learning outcomes of context-based approaches are of a qualitatively different kind: For instance, students may learn concepts more deeply. Another potential factor may be the difficulty of effectively implementing connections between contexts and underlying concepts that are meaningful for students. For instance, Parchmann and colleagues (2006) found that, although students became aware of the relevance of chemistry in everyday life and societal issues, they sometimes experienced a sense of getting lost in the context. This result suggests that contexts can be too general and broad to be effectively applicable.

Four-Phase Model of Context-Based Chemistry Teaching

Two relevant examples of context-based curriculum projects are the German project Chemie im Kontext (ChiK; Gräsel, Nentwig, & Parchmann, 2005) and the Dutch project New Chemistry (NC) (Driessen & Meinema, 2003). In both projects, university experts and teachers worked together in learning communities to transform a curricular framework, developed by the experts and derived from theories and relevant empirical data, into teaching and learning practice. The communities focused on the development, implementation, and evaluation of units for a range of chemistry topics.

In the ChiK project, these units usually fit a four-phase model of teaching (Parchmann et al., 2006). In the introductory phase, a context is introduced to students by using authentic material, often from media such as newspapers and TV clips. A relevant context can be the traffic-related issue of developing hydrogen cars for the near future. This is likely to fit students' interest and allows possibilities for students to investigate aspects of the context in a scientific way. In the next phase of curiosity and planning, students identify questions concerning the given context, for which they want to find answers, and they make plans regarding how to address these questions. The focus is on what chemistry can contribute to clarify the issue. The teacher helps structure the questions and give suggestions about how to carry out the investigations. Subsequently, in the phase of elaboration, teachers guide the students when they undertake the necessary inquiry to find answers to their questions, for instance, by exploring types and function of fuel cells. The results are presented and discussed.

TABLE 23.2
Four-Phase Model of Context-Based Chemistry Teaching

Phase of context-based teaching	Aim of the phase
Phase 1	
* Offering an introductory context	* Orienting students to the unit
	* Motivating students to become involved
Phase 2	
* Structuring meaningful questions	* Inducing a need to know
* Suggesting search procedures	* Preparing students for finding answers
Phase 3	
* Guiding students' inquiry	* Extending students' knowledge of chemistry
* Guiding presentations and discussions	* Communicating this knowledge
Phase 4	
* Supporting students' reflections	* Deepening students' knowledge
* Suggesting a follow-up context	* Inducing a need to apply

Finally, in the phase of deepening and connecting, students reflect on the presented results, perhaps by discussing future possibilities, and they apply their knowledge, possibly by studying the use of energy in other contexts.

In the NC project, a quite similar multiphased teaching model is used (Bulte, Westbroek, De Jong, & Pilot, 2006). In the introductory phase of orientation and motivation, a context is introduced that motivates students to become involved in the unit, such as an investigation of the water-absorbing capacity of disposable diapers. In the following phase, students become aware that their existing knowledge is insufficient to answer questions that are raised by the context given, such as explaining the surprisingly large amount of water uptake by the diaper. Subsequently, in the phase of extending knowledge, students look for answers by studying relevant underlying concepts in their chemistry textbook and other sources of information. For instance, students may seek information about the structure of water-absorbing materials and properties of constituent polymers. The teachers guide the presentation and discussion of the results. Finally, in the phase of reflection and application, students reflect on what they have learned and apply their knowledge of chemistry concepts they have studied previously, such as by investigating super-absorbent polymers in the context of fire-resistant materials.

Although there are slight differences between the two teaching models, the core of the models can be combined; the result is given in Table 23.2.

Models: Chemical Phenomena, Chemical Concepts, and the Molecular Realm

There are many kinds of models relevant to chemistry teaching and learning (Harrison & Treagust, 2000b). Developing models is a major part of the scientific enterprise (Develaki, 2007; Rosenblueth & Wiener, 1945). In forming a chemistry curriculum (or preparing a textbook), there is usually a process of both selecting and simplifying those scientific models that are considered important and accessible at the educational level concerned, and the presentation of models in chemistry curriculum/textbooks has been criticized for failing to offer authentic current or historical scientific models (Justi & Gilbert, 2000).

Moreover, it is well recognized that the intended curriculum does not always become the enacted curriculum (Keys, 2005). Teachers may offer distorted versions of curricular models, and this may occur inadvertently (perhaps due to limited teacher subject knowledge), regretfully (e.g., due to pressures to complete scheduled teaching in limited contact time), or deliberately—for example, where the teacher judges the need to mediate between a formal model that is considered too difficult for a particular class and what is judged likely to be suitable as target knowledge for those learners (cf. Figure 23.1).

Teachers use a range of teaching models including physical models: computer simulations, simplified diagrams, and various figures of speech, such as simile and analogy.

Very commonly, teachers draw upon the social world as a source of familiar comparisons for the rather unfamiliar properties of submicroscopic entities (Dagher & Cossman, 1992; Talanquer, 2007). Atoms are said to like to "share" electrons; molecules may be said to "want" to break free of the crowd and get some personal space during evaporation; or electrons may be said to behave like people on buses—preferring to sit next to an empty seat where possible rather than sitting next to another electron. Even some technical terms retain traces of anthropomorphism: "electrophiles," "nucleophilic substitution," "hydrophobic," "chemical affinity," and so on. Sometimes similes or analogies become so familiar among chemists and chemistry teachers that we may not even notice we are using them. The example of "sharing" electrons in covalent bonding is one example; the idea that electrons "spin" is another.

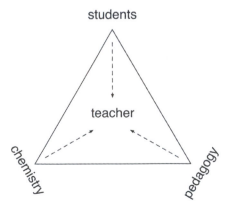

Figure 23.1 Teaching decisions are informed by the teacher's knowledge of the subject matter, the learners, and pedagogic principles. (After Taber, 2000)

The Nature of Models

Scientific models may be developed as part of the process of scientific work itself, developed—at least initially—as thinking tools, and so judged successful if they suggest fruitful hypotheses and productive paths for empirical work, allowing further progress to be made. Simulations may play a similar role—whether carried out as thought experiments in the minds of scientists (Brown, 1991; Gilbert, 2007) or modeled in some kind of computer (analog or digital).

Teaching is often about taking something unfamiliar and introducing it to learners by showing how, in some respects, the unfamiliar thing or idea is somewhat like something we already know about. That is, teachers develop (or adopt from other teachers) teaching models that they consider accessible to learners as a means of mediating between formal curriculum models and students' existing knowledge and understanding (Harrison, 2001).

Learners' Notions of Models and Modeling

This general strategy of looking to make the unfamiliar familiar fits well with the constructivist approach to thinking about teaching and learning. However, students may lack the epistemological sophistication to understand the nature of the models, analogies, and similes that we so readily use in teaching. So when showing learners a structural model of a molecule or arrangement of atomic cores in a crystal, it is quite likely that students will consider that the "real" thing is just the same, only a lot smaller. This may be particularly problematic when we are modeling the submicroscopic scale of matter where our physical models are attempts to represent some key aspects of a molecular world that is quite unlike the things of common experience.

In teaching, we often present series of quite incompatible models that, if taken literally (as students may often do), cannot all be valid, leading to confusion and commonly a sense that in chemistry we teach things we know are wrong, only to later dismiss and replace them as students progress through the subject. Examples would include what we understand by "acid" or "oxidation" or "metal," and in particular when we teach about atomic and molecular structure and bonding (discussed in more detail below). This can be frustrating for learners, and if we are going to teach through models (which is surely inevitable in chemistry), we must also teach *about* models and modeling so learners appreciate the purposes, natures, and limitations of the models they are introduced too. The importance of teaching learners about the nature and role of modeling as part of science education is increasingly being recognized in curriculum development and reform—for example in the United States (NRC, 2012), England (QCA, 2007) and Australia (ACARA, 2012).

There is now a great deal of work exploring teaching and learning with analogies (Haglund & Jeppsson, 2012; Harrison & Coll, 2008; Mozzer & Justi, 2011). It is

important to point out which features of an analogue are not to be carried over to a target (Taber, 2001b), as well as stressing those that are. In many ways, the same advice should be adopted when we use other types of models in our chemistry teaching as well.

Anthropomorphism in Chemistry Learning

The tendency to describe the world of atoms and molecules as if such entities are actors in a tiny social world is almost ubiquitous in chemistry teaching. Teachers often find it a successful strategy: Learners do tend to remember the stories of heartbreak on the atomic dance floor and seem to relate to notions of atoms that are driven to fill their shells, and find both cooperative (i.e., sharing) and more aggressive (i.e., electron transfer) ways to do this.

Such narratives seem to be effective ways of initially making the abstract world of molecules and ions accessible to learners, but in many cases students seem to retain these social descriptions of molecular behavior long after being taught more abstract formal models, and often it is the social accounts that are most readily brought to mind. There are important questions about whether and when the teacher's use of "weak" anthropomorphism (as a means to help students get an initial grasp on an abstract idea) tends to lead to a stronger form of anthropomorphism in which these social accounts are adopted as satisfactory explanations so that learners are less open to the more authentic scientific accounts they meet later (Taber & Watts, 1996). Clement (2008) argues that the most useful models have explanatory power, and it seems sensible for teachers to make clear to students when ideas are only meant as introductory analogies and to seek to move student thinking on as soon as possible.

The Centrality of Substance and the Epistemic Significance of Particles

Certain concepts within a discipline can be considered central in the sense that they provide structure for whole areas of knowledge—Fensham (1975) referred to them as "big concepts." Other concepts may be important from a pedagogic perspective because they act as "threshold" concepts (Park & Light, 2008) that learners must master in making progress toward understanding the big concepts of the subject. For students to begin to appreciate some key ("big") chemical concepts (such as chemical reactions and chemical bonding) that are used to make sense of much of the subject, they need to already have an understanding of the basic particle theory—for instance, that apparently continuous matter is quantized, being composed of myriad tiny "particles"—something that is not intuitively obvious.

Chemistry is a science that is primarily concerned with substances, a notion that can only be fully appreciated from within the framework of the discipline. Substances are often considered to be fundamental types of matter, of which pure samples can in principle be obtained. In terms

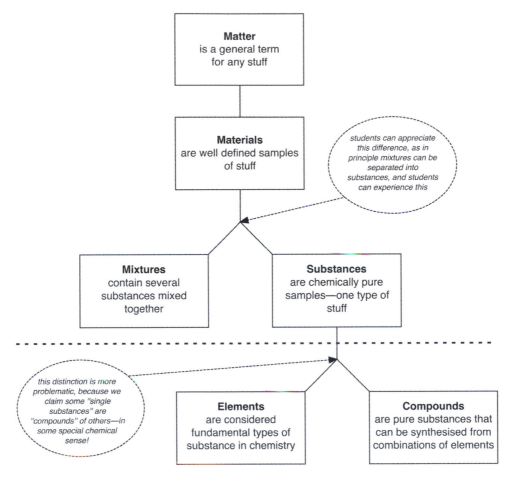

Figure 23.2 Fundamental distinctions that are important in teaching chemistry. (After Taber, 2012b)

of the internal logic of the subject discipline, teaching about this substance–mixture distinction should precede teaching about elements and compounds, as suggested in Figure 23.2. Yet in everyday life, outside of the chemistry classroom, nearly all of the materials that youngsters are familiar with are more complex than substances, often being mixtures (e.g., alloys, the air, fruit juice) or composites of various kinds (e.g., wood, milk, rocks).

In effect, we have *a conceptual model* here that is assumed as the basis of chemistry and much chemistry teaching: the various everyday materials found around us can be considered to be mixtures or composites of the more basic special types of material called substances. This conceptual model underpins the teaching of a subject that, in many curriculum contexts, initially ignores the majority of materials learners encounter in their everyday lives outside the laboratory and instead asks students to learn about substances that most learners will never directly encounter anywhere *but* in the teaching laboratory.

Substance is a threshold concept needed to make sense of chemical reactions (see later in this chapter) as changes in which some substances are changed into different substances. There is a sense in which the compound water contains or incorporates *the element* hydrogen, even though it certainly does not contain *the substance* hydrogen as that sample of hydrogen no longer existed once it reacted to form water. Hydrogen, the element, is considered to have some kind of essence that is retained in all its compounds, allowing the element hydrogen to be parts of many substances, each with its own unique set of chemical and physical properties. The "particle" models of matter that are ubiquitous in chemistry teaching are arguably essential to make good sense of the most fundamental concepts of the subject (substance and chemical change).

The Centrality of Particle Models in Learning Chemistry

For the chemist, models of the world at the submicroscopic scale of molecules, ions, and electrons do useful explanatory work, because the properties of those "particles" (i.e., the molecules, ions, electrons, etc.) are understood to interact to give rise to structures at the phenomenological macroscopic level, so they lead to the emergent properties that can be observed. This has long been a metaphysical premise of chemistry, but with the advent of nanoscience, it is increasingly being demonstrated by empirical studies (Sadownik & Ulijn, 2010; Stoddart, 2012). The interactions are therefore very important in this explanatory scheme, and thus the notion of chemical bonding (considered later in the chapter) and its significance as part of an academic course in chemistry.

So, for example, a solid may be hard because this is an emergent property, at the macroscopic level of phenomena, of the system of "particles"—the structure that emerges when the "particles" interact. It is neither helpful nor meaningful to consider the individual submicroscopic particles as "hard." The particle theory is useful because it offers explanations of bench-level phenomena in terms of the *rather different* properties of the conjectured submicroscopic particles from which matter is considered to be composed.

"Particle" as Analogy

The "particles" of particle theory are *particles by analogy*, but unlike the particles of everyday phenomena, and the billiard balls to which they are often compared, they do not necessarily have precise location in space (for example) or discrete edges. So we may "map" out the "location" of electrons in terms of probability distributions and electron density diagrams and consider that atoms overlap so that two of these "particles" may occupy the same space (in a way two billiard balls do not). Molecules and ions do not have bounded surfaces (even if for simplicity we sometimes represent them as if they do) but rather become increasingly more tenuous over extended distances.

These features are in sharp contrast to the familiar particles—granules of salt or sugar, grains of sand, and so forth—that are part of the common experience of learners and that therefore provide a fairly poor model of the nature of the theoretical entities that are being conjectured when chemists think of particles at the molecular scale. Although students often accept our teaching about everything being made of tiny particles, they very commonly misunderstand the particle model (Adbo & Taber, 2009; Johnson & Papageorgiou, 2010)—as we would expect from the constructivist notion that new meaningful learning can only occur by building upon existing understandings.

Common Misunderstanding 1: Misjudging Scale

A common misunderstanding of teaching is that the particles being referred to are the specks and grains and granules that are directly perceptible. This is perhaps not such a serious misconception (except that it may reinforce the second learning difficulty, to be described next), in that *if* students can accept this general principle, it is only a matter of shifting the degree of granularity to persuade students that we are talking about a much smaller scale beyond the limits of the most powerful (optical) microscopes.

Common Misunderstanding 2: Misjudging Type

More serious, however, is the very common misunderstanding that the particles being presented in chemistry lessons are just like familiar particles, but a great deal smaller. This might be a useful starting point (i.e., an opportunity to "anchor" a new idea in the learner's existing conceptual structure), but students are likely to think they have understood the teaching while completely missing the most important point that these "particles" have quite different properties than those we are familiar with at the phenomenological level.

Learners who acquire this idea will tend to invoke circular reasoning when using the particle models to produce explanations of phenomena (Taber, 2001a). This is shown in Figure 23.3. So, for example, if a learner thinks that butter is made up of a great many "butter" particles that are soft (because butter is soft), she may seek to then suggest that butter is soft *because* it is made of soft particles. This misses the key feature of the scientific model (that macroscopic properties emerge from the interactions of entities with quite different properties) and results in tautological explanations based on such notions as, for example, glass is made up of transparent particles; wax particles melt easily; copper particles are conductors; and so on. In many of these cases, the chemical bonding between the individual submicroscopic entities is a core part of the scientific explanation for how the macroscopic properties emerge, but the learners' explanation completely ignores this when

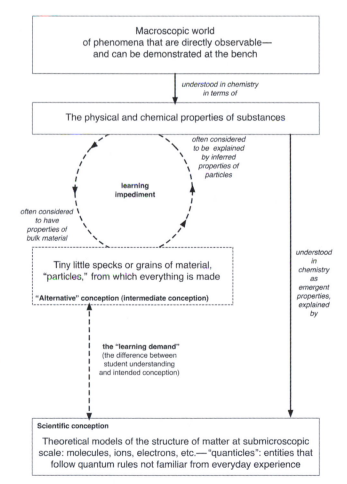

Figure 23.3 A common student misconception of the nature of submicroscopic particles invoked in chemistry lessons.

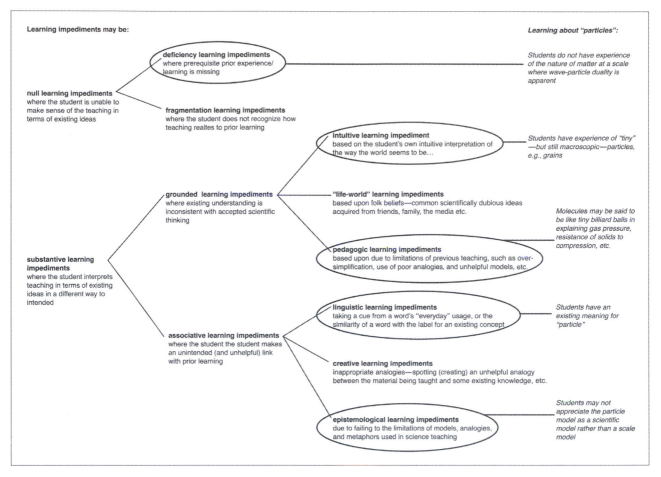

Figure 23.4 Student learning about particles can readily lead to alternative conceptions.

they assume that the property of the bulk material simply reflects the properties of the individual particles from which it is made.

The vast literature on students' "misconceptions" (Duit, 2009; Taber, 2009c) suggests teaching-learning can readily go wrong (Gilbert, Osborne, & Fensham, 1982): It is a complex system that readily admits "learning impediments" (cf. Bachelard, 1940/1968). Indeed, analysis of what is involved in effective teaching for understanding suggests a range of different types of learning impediment may occur when teaching is not well matched to the specifics of a learner's existing conceptual frameworks (Taber, 2005)—and in any class, all learners bring their own idiosyncratic prior learning. The present case offers an amalgam of potential difficulties (see Figure 23.4).

Mediating the Multiple Meanings of Chemistry

Some decades ago, Johnstone (1991) suggested that one reason science was difficult for students was that students are commonly presented with explanations that involve being asked to think about very different types of things at the same time. He suggested that in chemistry, students were asked to consider the macroscopic (tangible and visible "macrophenomena"), the submicroscopic (molecules

and ions), and the symbolic (such as formulae equations). Johnstone illustrated his point with a simple figure showing a triangle with the three apices labeled as "macro," "submicro," and "symbolic" (the basis for Figure 23.8) and argued that rather than teaching being focused at one apex or even along one side of the triangle, it often happened inside the triangle, where students were expected to cope with all three domains of meaning at once. Jensen (1995) developed a similar argument but distinguished between submicroscopic structure at the molecular and electronic levels and considered three dimensions of composition and structure, energy, and time (see Figure 23.5).

Johnstone's (1989) key point related to the demands made upon learners when teaching required learners to think about the three domains at once, something that was informed by consideration of the limitations of information processing within the human cognitive system. Often chemistry teaching starts from an observable phenomenon and then explains this in terms of atomic structure, intermolecular interactions, and the like, accompanied by a summary of the process in terms of chemical formulae or other symbolic representations. So the learner is asked to hold in mind the phenomenon, the theoretical model, and the formal representation at the same

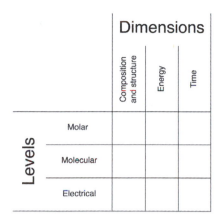

Figure 23.5 Jensen's grid setting out the logical structure of chemistry. (After Jensen, 1995, p. 680)

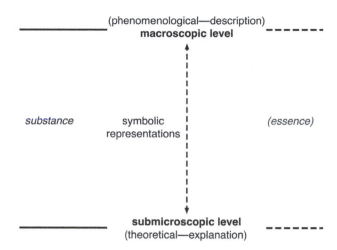

Figure 23.6 Mediating the multiple meanings of chemical discourse.

time—potentially overloading working memory (Baddeley, 2003; Tsaparlis, 1994).

Much of our more advanced teaching needs to be of this kind, and given time, learners can "chunk" related information so that complex material can be more readily mentipulated as a single chunk of information. However, at the introductory level, it makes sense to first teach students about a range of chemical phenomena that can be observed and systemized *prior to* introducing the particle theory at all. This reflects the historical development of the subject and is equivalent to a "natural history stage" (Driver & Erickson, 1983) of chemistry teaching in which we focus on classifying substances and their reactions—and introducing suitable concepts for the classes discovered: metals, acids, and so on. As Johnstone (1991) pointed out, there is considerable chemistry that can be taught and learned at the macroscopic level.

Students should be given time to acquire and consolidate chemical concepts linked to the phenomenological (macroscopic) level and to therefore also build up a wide range of explananda to motivate an appreciation of the value of a broad explanatory scheme before a particle model is introduced. Too often in teaching science subjects, students are offered explanations that answer questions they are not yet in a position to pose, and a period of exploring chemistry at the macroscopic level can offer intellectual motivation for then considering a theory of matter at the submicroscopic level. Chemistry at the macroscopic level needs to be represented symbolically if we are to communicate it through the specialized forms of representation used in the subject. So we have technical names for substances ("ammonia," "hydrochloric acid," etc.) and we use word equations to represent the changes we observe when substance react (or dissolve, or melt, etc.). There are many other aspects to the symbolic representations we use in chemistry—for example, standard diagrams of apparatus set-ups, and graphs. A key subset of the symbolic representations used in chemistry allows us to bridge *between* the macroscopic phenomena and the theoretical models posited at the submicroscopic

scale (see Figure 23.6). So when the chemistry teacher writes formulae such as H_2O or NaCl, there is a valuable ambiguity in what is represented. Representations such as these might refer to *either* (a) substances that may be observed and manipulated at the bench (i.e., at macroscopic scale) or (b) the molecules and ions that are part of the theoretical models of matter at submicroscopic scale.

This ambiguity offers an important affordance in discussing chemistry, as we frequently use these symbolic representations as a bridging device to mediate between the macroscopic descriptions and the submicroscopic explanations (Taber, 2009b). So "hydrogen" can mean either the substance or the molecules from which we consider the substance to be composed, and this can even help us with the notion that an element can be considered to have an essence it retains in its compounds—the sense in which there is hydrogen "in" the compound water even though it is a completely different substance with different properties.

This issue has been discussed in more detail elsewhere (Taber, 2009b), but the key points are that:

i) a major subset of the formal symbolic representations we use in chemistry can refer to both substances and "quanticles" (submicroscopic entities such as molecules, etc.)

ii) this is valuable because it allows chemists and chemistry teachers to readily shift between the changes in substance they work with and the submicroscopic models used to explain those changes

iii) but it also provides a potential area of confusion for learners if they are not sure when a representation is being used to refer to a substance or a molecule (or ions, etc.)

iv) therefore in teaching we should be very explicit in specifying when we are referring to the macroscopic level of substance and when to refer to theoretical models at the submicroscopic level, so learners can spot how we use this specialized language to shift our focus between these domains of meaning.

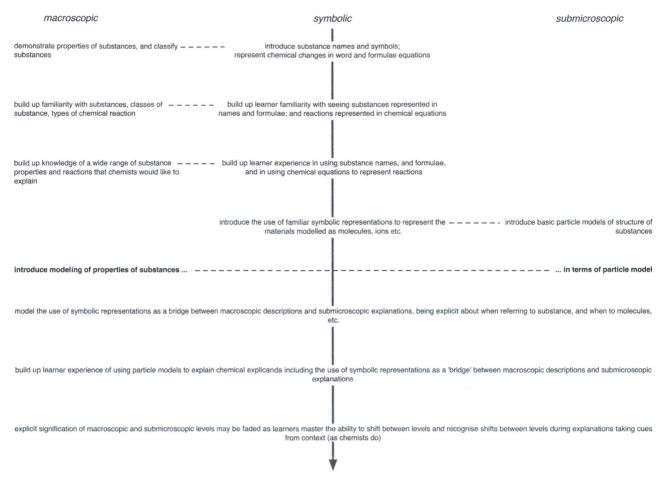

Figure 23.7 Progression in teaching learners to think like a chemist.

Having various ways to represent information is found to support learning. The forms of symbolic representation used in chemistry should be taught both because they are important in an authentic chemistry education and because ultimately they do useful work in making sense of learning to use chemical concepts. However, it is important to pace the introduction of new material over extended periods of time so that new learning can be consolidated before it is considered available for supporting further learning (see Figure 23.7).

Introducing Multiple Meanings of Chemical Reactions

Multiple Meanings

Many chemistry topics can be viewed or taught from three potential perspectives that are mutually related (Figure 23.8). The macroscopic perspective (hereinafter: macro domain) mainly focuses on substances and phenomena that can be observed, smelled, and so on. The submicroscopic perspective (hereinafter: submicro domain) mainly focuses on particle models for describing, explaining, and predicting properties of substances and characteristics of processes. The symbolic perspective mainly focuses on symbols, formulae, equations, ionic

drawings, and the like. The use of this three-cornered relationship of domains of meaning (Johnstone, 1993) plays a more dominant role in chemistry than in the other natural sciences. The triangle of meanings has been adopted by many chemistry educators, curriculum designers, and researchers, but it is also adapted in several ways. Based on a review of chemistry education literature, Talanquer (2011) reported an overview of some adaptations. For instance, macro meanings can be split up into meanings of experienced phenomena and meanings of macro models of these phenomena such as the concepts of pH and concentration. Submicro meanings can be distinguished into meanings about one single particle and meanings about clusters of many particles. Finally, symbolic meanings can be specified as meanings of symbolic systems such as element letters and word equations and meanings of algebraic systems such as formulas and graphs. Despite all these possible refinements, Johnstone's basic triangle will be used in the present section for presenting chemistry teaching and learning issues.

In introductory chemical education, the central core content deals with the topic of chemical reactions. In primary schools, if this topic is introduced, students only have to learn the macro meaning in terms of conversions of substances. High school students should also learn the

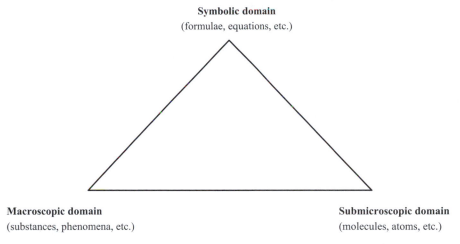

Figure 23.8 The triangle of meanings.

submicro meaning in terms of the rearrangement of particles (molecules, atoms, ions) and the intended meaning of symbolic representations in terms of reaction equations (words, iconic drawings, formulas). These students also should become able to switch mentally between these meanings in an adequate and flexible way.

This section addresses studies of students' conceptual difficulties related to chemical reactions that can be considered to proceed to completion, taking place in one direction. Difficulties in understanding reversible reaction types are treated elsewhere, including problems with understanding the nature of equilibrium reactions and factors influencing the equilibrium position (Van Driel & Graeber, 2002) and specific reaction types such as acid–base reactions (Drechsler & Schmidt, 2005) and redox reactions (De Jong & Treagust, 2002). The present section also offers explanations of the reported difficulties by analyzing three interrelated factors: the student, the chemistry content, and the teacher/textbook. Courses aiming at preventing and responding to students' difficulties are discussed. Suggestions for improving the teaching of chemical reactions are also presented.

Student Learning Difficulties

In the last two decades, numerous articles on students' difficulties in understanding multiple meanings of chemical reactions have been published. The following list of important recurrent difficulties has been compiled from studies and reviews by Ahtee and Varjola (1998), Chandrasegaran, Treagust, and Mocerino (2007), Cheng and Gilbert (2009), Kern, Wood, Roehrig, and Nyachwaya, (2010), Löfgren and Helldén (2009), and Krnel, Watson, and Glazar (1998).

Recurrent difficulties with the *macro meaning* are:

- Students may fail to recognize a process as a chemical change through lack of sufficient knowledge of substance identity. For instance, students may interpret the product of a chemical change as a mixture in which the original substances still persisted.

- Students may believe that during chemical changes, substances are displaced without any change of their properties. This is illustrated by students who think that parts of burning wood are driven off as smoke.

- Students tend to interpret chemical reactions as a process of modification—that is, chemical changes are seen as physical or biological changes, for instance, rusting of iron is considered aging of iron. Properties of substances are seen as changing, whereas the substances themselves remain the same. For instance, students may believe that the only change consists of a change of color or that the black coating formed on a piece of copper metal during heating represents black or burnt copper.

- Students may interpret chemical changes as a transmutation of a given substance into another substance or into energy. This is demonstrated by students who believe that burned steel wool has been turned into carbon.

- Students sometimes seem unaware of the interactive role of "invisible" (gaseous) reactants or products. For instance, students may believe that the mass of a rusty nail is the same as the nail before rusting.

- Students may believe that chemical changes always imply the involvement of only two substances that are combined and form a third substance. For instance, they do not consider grape juice that has become wine as an example of chemical change.

Recurrent difficulties with the *macro meaning ↔ submicro meaning* are:

- Students often hold the view that molecules or atoms are in substances like raisins in a raisin cake instead of thinking that substances are composed of molecules or atoms. In other words, they think that particles are additional to the substance.

- Students often attribute a number of features from the macro domain to individual molecules or atoms, but this ignores how the macro features emerge as a result of interactions between systems of molecules or atoms (see earlier). For instance, they may attribute the color of a substance to particles, such as the idea that individual atoms of copper are reddish-brown, and individual copper ions in aqueous solutions are blue. They may also believe that atoms of iron and chlorine become green when iron powder is added to dilute hydrochloric acid.

- Conversely, students may attribute features from the micro domain to substances by considering substances as if they were the same as particles. For instance, they may think that the substance of magnesium (instead of the particles) has a charge of +2 and may use expressions like "substances form bonding" and "substances give up and receive electrons."
- Even when students have knowledge of atoms and molecules, they may fail to invoke atoms and molecules as explanatory constructs of observed chemical phenomena. For instance, students may explain the "disappearance" of the wax of a burning candle by using intuitive ideas rather than using particle concepts learned in school.

Recurrent difficulties with the *submicro meaning* ↔ *symbolic meaning* are:

- Students may have difficulties in understanding the meaning of stoichiometric coefficients and subscripts of formulas. A typical example: students may consider $3H_2$ as a series of six linearly linked atoms.
- Students tend to interpret the formulas of compounds from an additive rather than from an interactive perspective. This is shown by students who were able to balance the reaction equation $N_2 + H_2 \rightarrow NH_3$ in a correct way but, when drawing this equation, they draw a diatomic molecule of nitrogen and, at some distance, a series of six atoms of hydrogen.
- Students may consider balancing reaction equations as mainly mathematical manipulations of symbols without much insight in the submicro meaning. For instance, students tend to change the value of the subscripts in formulas of reactants or products instead of changing the value of coefficients.
- Even when students are able to correctly balance simple chemical equations, they may fail to provide particulate drawings that are consistent with the notation of these equations, particularly in correctly translating the subscripts and coefficients of chemical formulas.
- Students may not properly interpret equations of reactions between ionic compounds in solution when these equations consist of molecular formulas. For instance, regarding the reaction between dilute nitric acid and aqueous sodium hydroxide, students tend to think that sodium and nitrate ions react to produce sodium nitrate molecules.

In conclusion, important student difficulties concern interpreting observable chemical phenomena as transformations of substances. Other student difficulties include

giving descriptions and explanations of these transformations in terms of rearrangements of particles and interpreting and writing formula reaction equations. An overall student difficulty concerns switching mentally among the three domains of meaning.

Vignette

In a junior high school class, a chemistry teacher puts a burning piece of wood in a glass with water. The burning stops.

The teacher asks: *How is that possible?*
Student #1 answers: *We do not understand, burning should go on because there is oxygen in the water, as we know because fish live in water.*
The teacher responds: *But there is not enough oxygen in the water.*
Student #2 argues: *We know that water is H_2O, so, one third of water is oxygen, whereas air consists of oxygen for one fifth only . . . so, teacher, how is that possible?*

In this vignette, student #2 compares water and air as providers of oxygen for a burning process. However, the student interprets the formula of water in an additive rather than from an interactive way: H_2O is seen as H_2 and O. This way of reasoning demonstrates a common difficulty in understanding symbolic representations.

Explanatory Analysis of Students' Conceptual Difficulties

The reported difficulties in understanding chemical change can be explained by analyzing three interrelated factors: the student, the chemistry content, and the teacher/textbook. This analysis is concisely addressed below.

i) The *student factor*. The initial knowledge of students, based on daily life experiences and expressed in everyday language, is often not very fruitful for interpreting chemical phenomena. For instance, students may have ideas that parts of burning wood are driven off as smoke and believe that the black coating formed on a piece of copper metal during heating represents black or burnt copper. Students consider their already existing conceptions, often deeply rooted in their everyday lives, as more reliable than the new conceptions. They prefer to use superficial everyday-life events for explaining chemical changes instead of using chemical models (Hesse & Anderson, 1992). Besides, students also have a lack of sufficient real experiences of different phenomena to be able to decide whether a particular phenomenon can be classified as a chemical change or not (Nelson, 2002). Finally, students tend to pay little attention to submicro models for giving meaning to the complex conventions of chemical symbols. This can foster students' alternative conceptions of formula subscripts and coefficients and will contribute to conceiving balancing reaction equations as mainly mathematical manipulations of symbols.

ii) The *chemistry content factor*. Many school chemistry concepts are abstract and do not fit students' intuitive ideas. Such concepts are difficult to understand because they require formal reasoning and knowledge of models as representations of phenomena and the particulate nature of matter. This is not easy for many students, who tend to see, for instance, molecules and atoms as "minima naturalia," that is, the "Aristotle" conception of small existing particles, instead of modern theoretical model concepts (De Vos & Verdonk, 1985). Chemical reactions are defined not only as conversions of substances but also as rearrangements of atoms including the breaking and forming of chemical bonds. However, many students find it difficult to mentally jump from the macro meaning of chemical reactions to the submicro meaning and reverse because they consider these domains of meaning disconnected (Solsona, Izquierdo, & De Jong, 2003).

iii) The *teacher/textbook factor*. In many teaching practices and textbooks, the topic of chemical reactions is often considered predominantly in terms of submicro and symbolic meanings (cf. De Jong & Van Driel, 2004). This will hinder students from connecting these meanings properly with those in the macro domain. It will also promote the tendency among students to consider chemical reactions as very formal processes. Teachers are not always aware of students' alternative conceptions. For instance, De Jong, Ahtee, Goodwin, Hatzinikita, and Koulaidis (1999) found that prospective chemistry teachers were not very familiar with current students' difficulties in understanding combustion in a macro domain. Textbook authors are also not always aware of students' alternative conceptions. For instance, students' intuitive idea that the color of a substance corresponds with the color of the individual particles is enhanced by many textbooks showing colored pictures, such as yellow sulfur atoms. The subject matter expertise of teachers and textbook authors can also function as a source of students' difficulties. Teachers as school chemistry experts are very able to move mentally among the three domains of meaning easily and almost automatically. As a consequence, when teaching, they often do not pay much attention to highlighting the mutual relationship explicitly and repeatedly (Gabel, 1999). However, students as novice learners are not familiar at all with this relationship and encounter difficulties in connecting the three domains. Moreover, in chemistry classrooms, teachers tend to use expert language, such as shortened expressions, that may evoke confusion among students, such as using the expression "copper is formed" without indicating explicitly if this statement refers to the substance copper, the type of atoms, or the type of ions (De Jong, Acampo, & Verdonk, 1995).

In conclusion, this analysis of the three connected factors can contribute to developing a deeper insight into the complex background of students' difficulties in understanding chemical reactions and, perhaps, many other topics in high school chemistry.

Modern Approaches to Teaching Chemical Reactions

The reported students' conceptual difficulties have been found among students who have been taught in mainly traditional chemistry courses. Efforts to prevent and to respond to these difficulties have led to a series of chemistry courses based on modern perspectives on teaching and learning chemistry. Studies of five exemplars of courses focusing on the topic of chemical reactions are given next.

- A course that included three phases of the *learning cycle*, namely explication, concept introduction, and concept application, was investigated by Cavallo, McNeely, and Marek (2003). They reported on the development of understanding among 60 junior high school students with respect to the three domains of meaning of chemical reactions. Findings indicated significant positive shifts in understanding. A minority (about 20%) of the students, however, showed persistent conceptual difficulties, especially regarding the difference between chemical change and physical change and the relationship between atoms and substances.

- A course that introduced a teaching strategy based on the *conceptual change perspective*, or confronting students with "chemical events" that evoke cognitive conflicts because of existing everyday conceptions, was investigated by Nieswandt (2001). She reported on the development of understanding among 81 junior high school students with respect to macroscopic features of substances and chemical reactions (with particular emphasis on combustion). Results showed a significant "erosion" of students' everyday conceptions in favor of scientific conceptions. A minority (about 25%) of the students, however, only developed "mixed" conceptions consisting of everyday conceptions and chemistry explanations.

- A course that incorporated a *context-based* teaching approach by presenting chemistry concepts within the context of everyday events was investigated by Barker and Millar (1999). They reported on the development of understanding among 250 senior high school students with respect to the conservation of mass in closed- and open-system chemical reactions. Data indicated that students' reasoning improved steadily as the course progressed. Nevertheless, a minority of the students retained misunderstandings about the conservation of mass in both closed systems (23%) and open systems (29%), especially for reactions including gases.

- A course that included a *constructivist view* on learning by taking students' own conceptions into account was investigated by Jaber and BouJaoude (2012). They reported on the development of understanding among a group of 46 junior high school students with respect to macro-, submicro-, and symbolic meanings of chemical reactions. The study included an experimental/control group design. The control group (22 students) was subject to lessons that taught for conceptual understanding, but without explicit attention to the epistemological nature of chemistry. Conversely, the experimental group (24 students) used the same lesson materials in terms of content while being explicitly introduced to an epistemic discourse paying additional attention to the interrelations between macro-submicro-symbolic meanings. Findings indicated that the majority of the experimental group developed adequate conceptual and relational understanding of chemical reactions, as compared to approximately half of the students in the control group. Despite the relative good learning gains in the experimental group, a minority (21%) of this group did not acquire sufficient understanding of chemical reactions.
- A course designed from a *mix of perspectives*, namely conceptual change, context-led, and constructivist, was investigated by Solomonidou and Stavridou (2000). They reported on the development of understanding among 168 junior high school students with respect to macroscopic features of substances and various chemical reactions. Results showed significant positive shifts in understanding. A minority (percentage not given) of the students, however, did not change their "concrete substance" idea toward the "unknown substance plus properties" scheme and the "inert mixture" concept toward the "interaction between substances" concept.

Some of the reported studies addressed only macroscopic features of chemical reactions (Barker & Millar, 1999; Nieswandt, 2001; Solomonidou & Stavridou, 2000), whereas others also covered submicro and symbolic features (Cavallo et al., 2003; Jaber & BouJaoude, 2012). All studies reported a positive development of students' understanding, but all of them also indicated conceptual difficulties despite the use of modern course designs and teaching strategies. This raises the question: What causes the persistency of the reported difficulties in these courses?

To answer this question, knowledge of the teaching-learning processes in the classroom could be helpful. Unfortunately, these reported studies only focused on learning outcomes, by using written questionnaires, sometimes combined with some interviews, in the context of pretest/(repeated) posttest designs. As a consequence, they did not provide insight in relevant learning processes. However, in a study of a constructivist course, Laverty and McGarvey (1991) not only used a pretest/posttest design and questionnaires but also other instruments, such as audio records of lessons and classroom observations This

study offered a better insight into students' struggle for understanding. The researchers reported how students designed their own diagrammatic representations for the effect of heat on copper carbonate, why some of them mistook this decomposition for burning in air, and how they debated to find the best representation for the decomposition. In an older but still influential study of a constructivist course, De Vos and Verdonk (1985) also analyzed audiotaped classroom discussions. They found that junior high school, students were able to develop primitive particle models of matter in the context of a chemical reaction, for example, for explaining the appearance of the brilliant yellow line, consisting of glittering tiny crystals in a continuous motion, when lead nitrate and potassium iodide were placed in opposite positions in a petri dish filled with water.

In conclusion, more in-depth investigations and longitudinal studies are needed to get a better "ecologically" valid insight into the factors and conditions that hinder or facilitate the development of students' conceptions of the multiple meanings of chemical reactions.

A Curriculum Dilemma: Early or Late Introduction of the Submicro Meaning of Chemical Reactions

The five reported studies dealt with courses in which the choice for a particular general teaching strategy is reported but in which the issue of an early or late introduction of particle models for understanding the submicro meaning of chemical reactions is hardly discussed. Nevertheless, this curriculum issue is the subject of an old but still ongoing debate in chemical education.

Several scholars have proposed a delayed introduction of molecules and atoms because, according to them, students should first build up suitable practical experience through exploring a variety of phenomena (e.g., Ahtee & Varjola, 1998; Tsaparlis, Kolioulis, & Pappa, 2010). However, others have shown that students did not "naturally" have a concept of substance identity, in a scientific sense, that allowed them to recognize chemical change in a proper way (e.g., Johnson, 2000; Stavridou & Solomonidou, 1998). For instance, although many courses introduced the burning of substances in an early stage, students experienced a lot of difficulties in recognizing and understanding this event as a chemical reaction (Watson, Prieto, & Dillon, 1997). Johnson (2002) even found that students began to accept the idea of substances changing into other substances only after a teaching unit in which atoms had been introduced. The model of atoms and changes in bonding was not the explanation for the idea of chemical change, but the means by which chemical change was acknowledged. On the other hand, premature introduction of the concepts of molecules and atoms was not suggested, because this approach may not enable students to consider particles as fruitful concepts for explaining chemical reactions and may induce many difficulties in the submicro domain. For instance, García Franco and

Taber (2009) explored how lower secondary school students explain physical and chemical changes commonly met in school science. They found that students generally used the notion of particles, although most of their particle-based explanations reflected alternative conceptions that have been reported in previous studies (see some previous subsections).

In conclusion, a curriculum strategy of early introduction and regular application of the submicro meaning of chemical reactions is not of itself sufficient to support the desired progression in thinking with particle models. The studies reported in this subsection do raise the question: How could chemistry education escape from this content-related dilemma of the curriculum structure?

A Possible "Way Out": Introducing a Meso Domain of Meaning

A possible "way out" from the content-related dilemma of the curriculum structure is recently reported by Meijer (2011). From the literature, he concluded that the mental task of jumping between the macro domain and the submicro domain is very hard for many students. He referred to Millar (1990) when stating that breaking down the macro-submicro jump into smaller steps could support students' understanding. In other words, introducing intermediate (meso) domains might be functional in the learning of macro-submicro thinking. This idea can be considered as an extension of the usual triangle of meaning into a tetrahedron of meanings (see Figure 23.9). Meijer (2011) has elaborated this perspective by reporting a conceptual analysis of macro-submicro thinking in terms of structure-property relations and scales of meso domains. He clarified this issue by using the example of bread. This material can be defined as a final fixed form of dough. By zooming deeper into dough, it is possible to distinguish certain meso structures, such as walls of gas holes, threads, granules embedded in networks, and entangled long molecules. These meso structures are related to properties such as the elasticity of gas holes. In general, a material has a

specific property that is not caused by a single structure but is caused by the interactions between all substructures at the lower scale.

This conceptual scheme was used as a guide for designing some context-led constructivist modules for high school students. They were asked to explore structure–property relations for three kind of materials: gluten-free organic material (bread), fire-resistant material (bulletproof jackets), and unbreakable ceramic material (crockery; Meijer, Bulte, & Pilot, 2009, 2013). The teaching of the modules was accompanied by an explorative study of students' learning (Meijer, 2011). The findings showed that students were able to acquire macro-submicro thinking using structure-property relations. However, students did not easily grasp the scales of meso levels below 10^{-5} m. Two reasons were found for this problem: (1) metaphors, related to the macro domain in students' materials and in discourses, both used as a tool to increase the understanding of the submicro domain, hindered the conceptual development of students, and (2) the scaling of structures was also a problem for students.

In conclusion, further research is required to get a deeper insight into the most effective content-/context-related curriculum structure for supporting students to really understand the relationship between macro meanings and submicro meanings of chemical reactions.

Introducing Multiple Meanings of Chemical Bonding

The ("Imaginary") Nature of Chemical Bonding

Chemical bonding has long been recognized as a "big" concept area in chemistry (Fensham, 1975). Chemical bonding can stand as a paradigm case for common difficulties in teaching and learning chemistry, because learning about chemical bonding involves meeting and making sense of a sequence of scientific models, each of which concerns theoretical entities (atoms, electrons, molecules, ions, orbitals, etc.) that are conjectured to exist at a scale many orders of magnitude below what can be directly observed by learners. Unlike the topic of chemical reactions, discussed earlier, chemical bonding does not relate to a specific set of identifiable chemical phenomena that are observable at the macroscopic level; rather, bonding is a core part of the explanatory schemes invoked to explain a great many different features of actual phenomena (such as melting temperature or solubility in a solvent).

This makes chemical bonding more abstract and so inherently more difficult for many learners. Models of chemical bonding should only be introduced once learners are familiar with the macroscopic descriptions of chemical phenomena we wish these models to explain (see Figure 23.7). An example is offered in Table 23.3 that sets out how we move from observing some white material in a melting-point tube to classifying the material as a sample of a substance "with" ionic bonding.

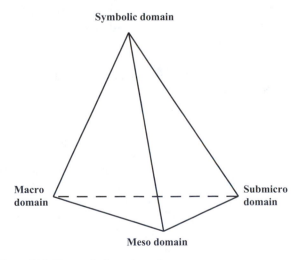

Figure 23.9 The tetrahedron of meanings.

TABLE 23.3
Inferring Bonding From Observations of Phenomena: The Example of Melting-Point Determination

Stage	Account	Notes
Observation	White opaque/translucent grain becomes transparent and loses shape: appears to have surface attaching to inside of tube.	On heating a small sample in a melting-point apparatus.
Chemical description	The sample melts.	Observations linked to a standard (theoretical) category of change
Evaluation	The substance has a "high" melting temperature.	This relies on an understanding of the apparatus and auxiliary observations (of a thermometer) that can be interpreted quantitatively. The sample is assumed to represent any pure sample of the same substance (i.e., observation is generalizable).
Inference	The substance may have ionic bonding (considering its initial appearance, and the high melting temperature).	Coordination of observations and interpretation at the macroscopic level are used to assign the substance to a category based on features of the submicroscopic structure posited within a theoretical model.

We may talk of this piece of metal as having metallic bonding or of that grain of salt as having ionic bonding, but in doing so we are transgressing the macroscopic/submicroscopic distinction and talking, for example, of metallic bonding *as if* it is a property of the metal, when actually it is a theoretical construct that is part of the explanation of the observed properties. Teachers need to be careful not to take shortcuts in moving through the kinds of processes illustrated in Table 23.3 but rather help learners to move through the different stages from observation to conceptualization—first as description and then in terms of explanatory concepts.

Teaching Bonding as a Progression of Models

Learners will generally meet a series of different models of chemical bonding of increasing sophistication, and these models may not always be consistent. It is important, therefore, to present these various models as just that, models, rather than "the way things are" (see the earlier section on models). This perspective can be introduced, when a particle model is first taught, on the basis that what is being described is so small that we cannot directly see what is going on, and therefore we have to build up models that might explain what we know and suggest hypotheses we can test through experiments. As learning progresses through the increasingly sophisticated models that are introduced, then students can be presented with an increasingly sophisticated account of *the nature of* these models *as models*, in parallel with their learning about the models themselves. As the teaching of this topic inevitably involves working with multiple models of the structure of matter, it can be used as a context for teaching about this important aspect of the nature of science.

There have now been quite a range of studies investigating students' learning about chemical bonding, and a number of reviews of this area are available (Levy Nahum, Mamlok-Naaman, Hofstein, & Taber, 2010; Özmen, 2004;

Ünal, Çalık, Ayas, & Coll, 2006), as well as recommendations on teaching the topic area (Levy Nahum, Mamlok-Naaman, Hofstein, & Krajcik, 2007; Taber, 2001a, 2012a). Here, some of the key issues raised by this research will be considered.

The Immaterial Nature of Chemical Bonding

A key feature of chemical bonding is that it is understood as due to forces between different "quanticles": binding atoms into molecules, ions into lattices, molecules into solids and liquids, and so forth. For learners to appreciate this, it is important that when basic particle theory is first introduced, the "particles" are presented as having some inherent (but not absolute) ability to attract each other (Johnson, 2012). Research suggests that students may consider bonding between particles as being due to a kind of glue. In part, such references may simply be the limitations of available language, and in some cases such statements are meant metaphorically. However, sometimes students do seem to explicitly suggest that bonds are made of *some kind of material* that connects the particles. It is likely that a number of factors encourage this:

- Our teaching models often comprise roughly spherical balls, either (visibly) glued together or connected with sticks or springs. If the models are interpreted too literally, they may be understood to imply something similar (i.e., material linkage) occurs at the submicroscopic level.
- The lack of familiarity with the nature of matter at the submicroscopic scale means that learners rely upon their understanding of how things are at more familiar scale—*generally* we need to glue, rivet, weld, materials together. (There are examples in which we "bond" materials using their inherent adhesive properties that might offer more suitable analogies.)

- It is documented (Andersson, 1990) that in learning particle models of matter, learners commonly pass through a stage in which they conceptualize the particles (that are meant to be the matter at the scale represented) as embedded in matter—of the material itself or in terms of having air between particles—so learners at this stage may readily consider other material to be available to form the bonding.

- References to "bonds" may imply material entities rather than an interaction or process (bonding), and it has sometimes been suggested that the term "bond" itself should be avoided, although that might be difficult given its ubiquity in chemistry (Pauling, 1960). Where students learn that "*everything* is made of tiny particles," then that can seem to imply that bonds must be made of particles, like everything else.

Teaching learners from the start that the "particles," from which matter is made up at a scale well below what is directly visible, have an inherent stickiness raises the question of mechanism but may help avoid students' developing alternative conceptions about bonds as material links. For much of secondary level, the notion that bonding is primarily an electromagnetic ("electrical") effect should suffice. Research has often found that many learners may fail to appreciate this, suggesting it should be emphasized more in teaching.

The Nature of Atomic Structure

The introduction of atomic structure as a notion represents a major shift in modeling matter at submicroscopic level. Amorphous particles previously considered much like ball bearings or billiard balls are now presented as something quite different and indeed largely "empty space"—a nuclear atom in which nearly all the mass is located in a tiny volume at the center, and tenuous electrons orbit at (relatively) vast distances from the nucleus. This shift from seeing the "particles" from which matter is said to be composed as *atomos*, fundamental and indivisible, to more complex entities that not only have structure but are themselves composed of even more fundamental particles (nucleons, electrons) presents a major challenge in chemistry teaching (Taber, 2003). There is a clear issue relating to whether this new account can supplement previous teaching or will be seen by learners as *replacing* earlier flawed teaching. This complication may have been previewed if students have met the topic of thermal expansion prior to being taught about atomic structure. Often teaching about how some key properties of solids (rigidity and regular shapes, for example) depend upon the close packing of the constituent particles is followed by being taught about thermal expansion of solids in terms of increases in the separations of those same particles: Those rigid solids are now said to be composed of well-spaced particles that cannot be in contact because they vibrate about their lattice positions.

From the expert perspective, there is no real contradiction here, as the nature of contact at the submicroscopic scale cannot be taken to have our familiar everyday meaning. Contact is understood in terms of electrical fields (and quantum rules) and not in terms of two discrete surfaces becoming adjacent to each other. However, such an understanding is not going to be immediately available to the learner asked to use seemingly contrary explanations, and many retain the notion of ball-like particles but invoke thermal expansion *of the particles themselves* to explain the changes at the macroscopic scale (cf. Figure 23.3).

A fundamental feature of the model of atomic structure needed to support chemistry teaching about chemical bonding (and some other important topics such as shapes of molecules, patterns of ionization energy, reaction mechanisms, etc.) is that the atom is bound by the electrical attraction between the positively charged nucleus and the negatively charged electrons, which repel each other. However, there are clear limitations to this level of description. On an electrical basis, there is no reason the neutrons would be bound in to the nucleus, and indeed good reasons to reject the notion that all the positively charged protons will be collected together at one location. That learners often fail to raise this objection suggests that they are not primarily conceptualizing the structure in electrical terms.

The basic electrical model also fails to explain why electrons are found in "shells" that moreover have the same maximum occupancy regardless of the nuclear charge, nor why electrons often seem to be found in pairs (bonding pairs, nonbonding pairs). Given the significance of quantum rules, there is a question over whether we should teach something of this idea from early in chemistry education. Traditionally, quantum mechanics has been considered an advanced topic, and any treatment that was incorporated in introductory chemistry at school level would clearly only offer a very partial account of these ideas. Yet there is a potential research theme here, regarding both (1) the extent to which some notions of there being quantum rules applying to electronic arrangements in atomic/molecular systems are inherently any more difficult or abstract than other ideas already taught at this level and (2) whether the increase in subject difficulty necessitated by introducing additional abstract notions at this point in learning might actually be justified by the increased potential for making otherwise arbitrary principles seem part of a more coherent account.

Basic Models of Bonding

If we adopt a basic model of the structure of matter consisting at submicroscopic scale of particles that form into various configurations due primarily to electrical (or electromagnetic) interactions, then we can describe most types of bonding in terms of arrangements of atomic cores (nuclei and their associated "inner" shells of electrons) and sufficient valence electrons to maintain electrical neutrality (Taber, 2012a). We can use this model to describe increasingly complex types of bonding interaction. So, for example, in teaching about solid structures, the main types of structures (in terms of increasing complexity, arguably a sensible teaching order) would be

- Metals: a lattice arrangement of a single type of atomic core, with delocalized electrons moving around the lattice
- Covalent crystals: a repeating pattern of atomic cores, with localized pairs of electrons around particular cores, or between cores
- Ionic lattice: valence electrons arranged around individual cores that are attracted into a regular lattice due to their net charges
- Molecular solids (and also liquids): discrete arrangements of a small number of cores with localized pairs of electrons around particular cores or between cores (i.e., molecules) that are then attracted together due to secondary interactions between the charges within these discrete molecules

This order reflects increasing complexity from the perspective of the discipline of chemistry, but research is indicated to explore how sequencing influences the "learning demand" (Leach & Scott, 2002) from the students' perspectives. The approach described here is, however, broadly consistent with the research-based scheme described by Levy Nahum, Mamlok-Naaman, Hofstein, and Krajcik (2007) that starts from "the principles that are common to all types of chemical bonds."

This approach leads to four main types of bonding: between delocalized electrons and the lattice of cations (cores), or metallic bonding; pairs of negative electrons between positive cores, or covalent bonding; attractions between ions of different charges, or ionic bonding; and attractions between neutral molecules due to the asymmetrical charge distributions within them, often called intermolecular forces. When described in these terms, it may not seem surprising that the latter type of intermolecular interaction tends to be weaker than the others. However, all these interactions can be understood as primarily

electrical attractions and so fundamentally the same type of interaction. It is also important to teach that although we tend to think of bonding as being about attractions, the repulsions are equally important, as the actual structures represent an equilibrium situation in which the various forces acting balance out.

These descriptions of different types of bonding refer to *models* of how we understand the "particles" to configure, and in practice most substances do not seem to match these ideal cases. No compound is known with what is considered "pure" ionic bonding, where the actual electron distribution in the structure is thought to reflect undistorted discrete ions being attracted together. Although pure covalent bonds are considered to exist (in elements, for example), the inductive effect means that not all bonds between atomic cores of the same elements can be considered completely covalent (e.g., the CC bond in CH_3. COOH). Many compounds have polar bonds in which the bonding electrons are asymmetrically located between atomic cores. And there is a continuum from the completely symmetrical covalent bond to the asymmetric polar bond to the ions distorted through the directional influence of other ions to the ideal case of a pure ionic lattice. Most metals are considered to show a degree of covalent character in their bonds, and in aromatic "covalent compounds' such as benzene, there is a possibility of increasing the extent of delocalization across increasing number of atomic cores, ultimately leading to graphite, which is a conductor and in effect has metallic (delocalized pi) bonding in the plane of the covalent (sigma) bonded framework. This situation is reflected in Figure 23.10, which suggests that most real bonds fall within the triangle rather than at its apices.

Understanding the more subtle features of bonding types involves going beyond the basic "cores + valence electrons" model (and the associated shells model of atomic structure) to consider an orbital model of atoms, molecules, and ions, probably only suitable for learners who are already familiar and comfortable with the more

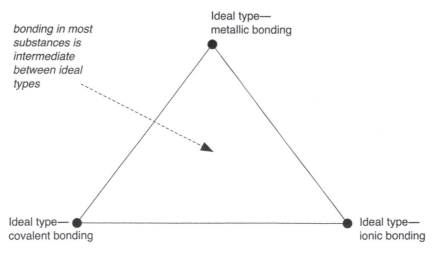

Figure 23.10 Commonly taught bonding models represent ideal types that are not generally found in nature.

basic models of structure and bonding. The orbital-level model need not be seen as completely inconsistent with what has been taught before *as long as* earlier teaching has presented the less complex ideas *as models* rather than as accounts of how matter actually "is."

Student Learning Difficulties

As suggested, there have been many learning difficulties identified in this topic that have been reviewed elsewhere (Levy Nahum et al., 2010; Özmen, 2004; Ünal et al., 2006). Here, two examples will be discussed in detail, prefaced by some general observations. It is likely that common teaching approaches, including the use of particular teaching models (especially when presented without their status as teaching models being made clear), must be considered as at least contributing factors in the widespread learning problems reported. Within science education more generally, we find that student alternative conceptions may often be linked directly to experiences and learning outside the classroom. Yet in the case of chemical bonding, it is clear that learners do not come to class with intuitive understandings of bonding (it is not something they can directly experience), and it is unlikely that many children are exposed to much extracurricular discourse about chemical bonding in their family and social lives.

That is not to say that learning difficulties in this topic are *only* due to problematic teaching—for the understanding of complex abstract concepts is believed to draw at least indirectly upon our stock of intuitions of how the world works, which are themselves based on our direct experiences of the world. Learners will inevitably seek to make sense of new teaching in terms of available ideas that already make sense to them, and the models and metaphors offered by teachers may be especially influential.

The Octet Framework

While research has reported a range of different common alternative conceptions relating to bonding concepts, many common student ideas derive from a particular alternative conceptual framework known as the octet framework (Taber, 1998a). The core feature is an alternative conception that atoms seek to fill their electron shells (or obtain octets of electrons). This principle seems to have originated as an inappropriate overinterpretation of the "octet rule," which suggests that most stable ionic and molecular structures involve atomic centers being surrounded by the same electronic configurations as found in the noble gases (see Figure 23.11). The octet rule is a useful heuristic, although as a "rule of thumb" it has many exceptions and suggests that atomic/molecular structures are inherently

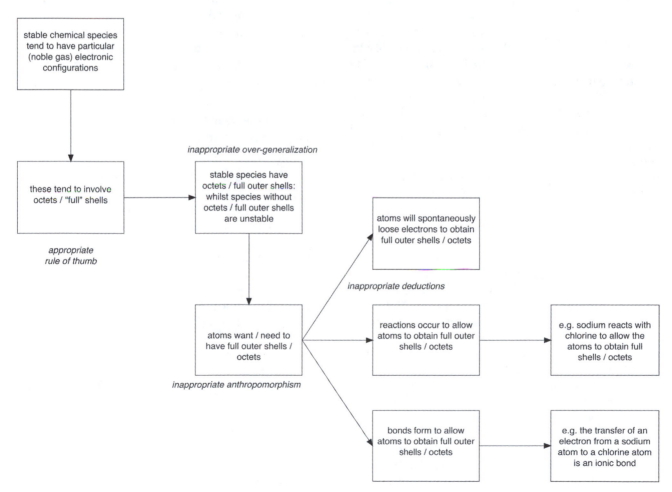

Figure 23.11 The development of the "octet" alternative conceptual framework.

stable or unstable, without regard to context. Yet stability is a relative notion: So a sodium cation can be considered relatively stable when in a lattice or when hydrated, but an isolated sodium atom is more stable as a neutral atom than when its outer electron is pulled away to be separated from the ion. For many students, however, an octet structure or full outer shell implies a stable species, be that structure Na^+, C^{4+}, Na^{7-}, Cl^{11-}, or even an excited chlorine atom with an inner-shell electron promoted to fill the outer shell (Taber, 2009a).

Given this starting point, many students assume not only that atoms will spontaneously ionize to obtain full outer shells but also that chemical reactions take place to allow atoms to fill their shells through forming bonds. Often there is an assumption of initial atomicity, so methane will be more stable than carbon and hydrogen because forming the compound allows *the atoms* to fill their shells—that is, it is assumed that the reactants are in the form of isolated carbon atoms and hydrogen atoms rather than structures that already have noble gas electronic structures.

The metaphor of covalent bonding as "sharing" electrons supports this way of thinking (as electrons shared "count" for both atoms), and often ionic bonding is associated with a hypothetical electron transfer event from an isolated metal atom to an isolated nonmetal atom. This reinforces a "molecular" conceptualization of ionic solids as comprising ion pairs bound by an ionic bond (electron transfer) and only attracted together in the ionic lattice by "just forces" due to electrical charges. This is at odds with the recommended teaching approach that bonding should be presented as primarily an electrical attraction. The misconception that ionic bonding results from electron transfer between atoms is supported by many school-level textbooks. This scheme does not seem to be questioned by many learners even when they have prepared sodium chloride themselves by neutralization and evaporation— that is, from reagents that clearly already contain the ions that will be bonded together in the product.

The octet framework is not only scientifically incorrect, but it also impedes progression in learning. Starting from the notion that bonds form to let atoms fill their shells, usually by sharing or transferring electrons, learners go on to develop further alternative conceptions (e.g., ion pairs remain bonded when salts dissolve) and develop obstacles to learning more advanced ideas (cf. Figure 23.4). Students find ways to either fit metallic and hydrogen bonds into the scheme or discount them as genuine forms of bonding. Bond polarity may be accepted as a secondary effect but seen as a subclass of covalent bonding rather than an intermediate category (at odds with Figure 23.10). Compounds such as SF_6 or even the more familiar sulfates cause problems because they do not fit the octet rule (Taber, 1998a).

Ideas linked to the octet framework and notions of atoms actively seeking to fill their shells seem to be commonly adopted by learners, and once acquired, they seem to be especially tenacious (Coll & Treagust, 2003). Moreover,

at least vestiges of such ideas remain in the thinking of teachers (Taber & Tan, 2011), suggesting that the alternative framework is in effect being taught by one generation of learners to the next when some of them become teachers themselves.

Adopting Orbital Models

A second specific area of difficulty appears to be adopting orbital models of atomic and molecular structure. Again, a wide range of alternative conceptions and learning difficulties has been reported (Taber, 2005). One clear problem here is having adopted the "shell" model of atomic structure as a precise description rather than a model at one level of simplification. Learners will commonly come across a range of ways of describing and modeling atomic and molecular structures (atomic and molecular orbitals, energy levels, electron density distributions, etc.) that cannot be seen as consistent unless appreciated as models of different facets of something complex and abstract. Studies show how progress in acquiring these ideas may be slow (Harrison & Treagust, 2000a; Petri & Niedderer, 1998) as well as how previous learning may seem to act as a barrier to progression.

Given that even some academic chemists and chemistry educators (Sánchez Gómez & Martín, 2003; Scerri, 2000) question the precise status of some of the orbital and related models that are represented in the curriculum, it is inappropriate to teach these as accounts of how matter is actually structured rather than as models chemists have developed to help understand evidence from their experimental work.

Looking to the Near Future of Chemical Education

Directions for New Research

Research into teaching and learning chemistry is an active and vibrant field (Gilbert, De Jong, Justi, Treagust, & Van Driel, 2002). Some potentially fruitful directions for this research in the near future are:

- Studies of carefully designed multimedia that are properly embedded in an overall teaching approach. Overviews of the present state of the art are given by Tortosa (2012) and Chiu and Wu (2009).
- Research and development of more "green" chemistry teaching, such as teaching with a strong focus on environmental issues and chemistry for sustainability. Overviews of the present state of the art are given by Karpudewan, Ismael, and Roth (2012) and Feierabend, Jokmin, and Eilks (2011).
- Studies of student learning progressions (Alonzo & Gotwals, 2012), preferably undertaken in comparable ways in different curriculum contexts
- Explorations of the potential for supporting conceptual integration between chemistry learning and learning in physics, biology, and technology—for instance,

in the field of nanochemistry and nanotechnology (cf. Ambrogi, Caselli, Montalti, & Venturi, 2008; Blonder & Sakhnini, 2012)

- Development of a broader range of research perspectives and techniques applied to exploring chemistry teaching and learning—for instance, more phenomenological studies, the use of lesson study (Allen, Donham, & Tanner, 2004) or design-based research (Kortland & Klaassen, 2010), and the application of repertory grid type techniques (Taber, 1994)

Much research is now being conceptualized as having as it focus *chemistry* education: research that "can and does play a role in addressing the current shortcomings in the curriculum for, and in the teaching and learning of, the ideas that constitute the subject of chemistry" (Gilbert, Justi, Van Driel, De Jong, & Treagust, 2004, p. 12). Many important themes are common in teaching the sciences, but increasingly researchers are identifying with chemistry education research (CER) as a distinct subfield and investigating specific issues and problems that relate to the particular (and perhaps often the particulate) nature of chemistry as a teaching subject. Some of these specific themes have been highlighted in this chapter. Research is needed to explore how best to coordinate teaching about models and modeling so it supports learning of the scientific and curriculum models.

One particular feature of chemistry education is the extent to which learners develop alternative conceptions in areas in which they have not had direct personal experience. If common student alternative conceptions do not derive from direct experience with the relevant phenomena, nor from "folk theories" that have currency in social discourse, then it seems likely that such conceptions develop due to the way in which our teaching interacts with more general aspects of a learner's cognition.

Interestingly, research into how conceptions can derive from implicit domain-general knowledge elements—a "knowledge-in-pieces" perspective (Smith, diSessa, & Roschelle, 1993)—is already quite familiar in PER (physics education research) if less well developed in CER, where there is well-established work based around the idea of p-prims (phenomenological primitives; diSessa, 2008; Hammer, 1996). As implicit knowledge elements, these p-prims do not relate to particular domains of thought but rather are part of the general apparatus that channels how we classify and make sense of our perceptions of the world.

This perspective has not had as much attention in CER, but where it has been applied, it has seemed to have potential to be fruitful (Taber & Tan, 2007). From the knowledge-in-pieces perspective, students' conceptions are constructed by drawing on their repertoires of available *implicit* knowledge elements: a new phenomenon or a new idea presented in teaching activates what seems the most appropriate available elements and comes to be understood accordingly.

For example, commonly, when considering how removing an electron from an atom changes the system (e.g., in studying patterns of ionization energies), students apply (1) an inappropriate "sharing-out" notion, that the force "given out" by the nucleus will now be shared among fewer electrons, so they will now be held more tightly and so become harder to remove (Taber, 1998b), but also (2) a "closer-is-stronger" pattern when considering the ease with which electrons from different shells can be removed from an atom, which *does* support learning about the scientific model. The knowledge-in-pieces perspective could offer greater potential to help channel the construction of student conceptions, as it may then be possible to sequence teaching and adopt language and teaching models that best engage the most productive p-prims to support the construction of particular chemical concepts.

Coherent Innovations in Chemistry Education

Innovations in chemical education should be developed and implemented in a more coherent way than is currently the case. This requires the fine-tuning of at least the following components of innovations:

i) The development and implementation of experimental instructional materials and student courses based on new insights into teaching and learning chemical topics, especially with respect to a substantiated content structure for introducing the multiple meanings of many chemical concepts

ii) The development and implementation of courses for chemistry teachers, to help them to acquire sufficient knowledge of new topics and appropriate competence to teach in ways that are congruent with the new approaches (cf. Stolk, Bulte, De Jong, & Pilot, 2012)

iii) The design and execution of in-depth and longitudinal studies. The purpose of this research can be twofold. From a theoretical point of view: to develop a better understanding of teaching and learning processes and outcomes with respect to particular chemistry. From a practical point of view: to develop guidelines for high school and college courses and courses of teacher preparation in chemical education that are informed by research.

The integration of these three innovative steps implies an important challenge for the near future of chemical education.

References

ACARA. (2012). *Chemistry*. Sydney: Australian Curriculum, Assessment and Reporting Authority.

Adbo, K., & Taber, K. S. (2009). Learners' mental models of the particle nature of matter: A study of 16-year-old Swedish science students. *International Journal of Science Education, 31*, 757–786.

Ahtee, M., & Varjola, I. (1998). Students' understanding of chemical reaction. *International Journal of Science Education, 20*, 305–316.

Allen, D., Donham, R., & Tanner, K. (2004). Approaches to biology teaching and learning: Lesson study—building communities of learning among educators. *Cell Biology Education, 3*, 1–7.

Alonzo, A. C., & Gotwals, A. W. (Eds.). (2012). *Learning progressions in science: Current challenges and future directions.* Rotterdam, the Netherlands: Sense Publishers.

Ambrogi, P., Caselli, M., Montalti, M., & Venturi, M. (2008). Make sense of nanochemistry and nanotechnology. *Chemistry Education Research & Practice, 9*, 5–10.

Andersson, B. (1990). Pupils' conceptions of matter and its transformations (age 12–16). *Studies in Science Education, 18*, 53–85.

Bachelard, G. (1940/1968). *The philosophy of no: A philosophy of the scientific mind.* New York: Orion Press.

Baddeley, A. (2003). Working memory: Looking back and looking forward. *Nature Reviews Neuroscience, 4*, 829–839.

Barker, V., & Millar, R. (1999). Students' reasoning about chemical reactions: What changes occur during a context-based post-16 chemistry course? *International Journal of Science Education, 21*, 645–665.

Barker, V., & Millar, R. (2000). Students' reasoning about basic chemical thermodynamics and chemical bonding: What changes occur during a context-based post-16 chemistry course? *International Journal of Science Education, 22*, 1171–1200.

Bennett, J., Gräsel, C., Parchmann, I., & Waddington, D. (2005). Context-based and conventional approaches to teaching chemistry: Comparing teachers' views. *International Journal of Science Education, 27*, 1521–1547.

Bennett, J., & Holman, J. (2002). Context-based approaches to the teaching of chemistry: What are they and what are their effects? In J. K. Gilbert, O. De Jong, R. Justi, D. F. Treagust, & J. H. Van Driel (Eds.), *Chemical education: Towards research-based practice* (pp. 165–184). Dordrecht, the Netherlands: Kluwer Academic Publishers.

Bennett, J., Lubben, F., & Hogarth, S. (2007). Bringing science to life: A synthesis of the research evidence on the effects of context-based and STS approaches to science teaching. *Science Education, 91*, 347–370.

Blonder, R., & Sakhnini, S. (2012). Teaching two basic nanotechnology concepts in secondary schools by using a variety of teaching methods. *Chemistry Education Research & Practice, 13*, 500–516.

Brown, J. R. (1991). *Laboratory of the mind: Though experiments in the natural sciences.* London: Routledge.

Bulte, A., Westbroek, H., De Jong, O., & Pilot, A. (2006). A research approach to designing chemistry education using authentic practices as contexts. *International Journal of Science Education, 28*, 1063–1086.

Campbell, B., Lazonby, J., Millar, R., Nicolson, P., Ramsden, J., & Waddington, D. (1994). Science: The Salters' approach—a case study of the process of large scale curriculum development. *Science Education, 78*, 415–447.

Cavallo, A. M. L., McNeely, J. C., & Marek, E. A. (2003). Eliciting students' understanding of chemical reactions using two forms of essay questions during a learning cycle. *International Journal of Science Education, 25*, 583–603.

Chandrasegaran, A. L., Treagust, D. F., & Mocerino, M. (2007). The development of a two-tier multiple-choice diagnostic instrument for evaluating secondary school students' ability to describe and explain chemical reactions using multiple levels of representation. *Chemistry Education Research and Practice, 8*, 293–307.

Cheng, M., & Gilbert, J. K. (2009). Towards a better utilization of diagrams in research into the use of representative levels in chemical education. In J. Gilbert & D. Treagust (Eds.), *Multiple representations in chemical education* (pp. 55–73). Dordrecht, the Netherlands: Springer.

Chiu, M.-H., & Wu, H.-K. (2009). The roles of multimedia in the teaching and learning of the triplet relationship in chemistry. In J. K. Gilbert & D. Treagust (Eds.), *Multiple representations in chemical education* (pp. 251–283). Dordrecht, the Netherlands: Springer.

Clement, J. (2008). The role of explanatory models in teaching for conceptual change. In S. Vosniadou (Ed.), *International handbook of research on conceptual change* (pp. 417–452). New York: Routledge.

Coll, R. K., & Treagust, D. F. (2003). Investigation of secondary school, undergraduate, and graduate learners' mental models of ionic bonding. *Journal of Research in Science Teaching, 40*, 464–486.

Dagher, Z., & Cossman, G. (1992). Verbal explanations given by science teachers: Their nature and implications. *Journal of Research in Science Teaching, 29*, 361–374.

De Jong, O., Acampo, J., & Verdonk, A. H. (1995). Problems in teaching the topic of redox reactions: Actions and conceptions of chemistry teachers. *Journal of Research in Science Teaching, 32*, 1097–1110.

De Jong, O., Ahtee, M., Goodwin, A., Hatzinikita, V., & Koulaidis, V. (1999). An international study of prospective teachers' initial teaching conceptions and concerns: The case of teaching "combustion." *European Journal of Teacher Education, 22*, 45–59.

De Jong, O., & Treagust, D. F. (2002). The teaching and learning of electrochemistry. In J. K. Gilbert, O. De Jong, R. Justi, D. F. Treagust, & J. H. Van Driel (Eds.), *Chemical education: Towards research-based practice* (pp. 317–337). Dordrecht, the Netherlands: Kluwer Academic Publishers.

De Jong, O., & Van Driel, J. (2004). Exploring the development of student teachers' PCK of multiple meanings of chemistry topics. *International Journal of Science and Mathematics Education, 2*, 477–491.

De Vos, W., & Verdonk, A. H. (1985). A new road to reactions, part 1. *Journal of Chemical Education, 62*, 238–240.

Develaki, M. (2007). The model-based view of scientific theories and the structuring of school science programmes. *Science & Education, 16*, 725–749.

diSessa, A. A. (2008). A bird's-eye view of the "pieces" vs. "coherence" controversy (from the "pieces" side of the fence). In S. Vosniadou (Ed.), *International handbook of research on conceptual change* (pp. 35–60). New York: Routledge.

Drechsler, M., & Schmidt, H.-J. (2005). Upper secondary school students' understanding of models used in chemistry to define acids and bases. *Science Education International, 16*, 39–53.

Driessen, H. P. W., & Meinema, H. A. (2003). *Chemistry between context and concept: Designing for renewal.* Enschede, the Netherlands: SLO.

Driver, R., & Erickson, G. (1983). Theories-in-action: Some theoretical and empirical issues in the study of students' conceptual frameworks in science. *Studies in Science Education, 10*, 37–60.

Duit, R. (2009). *Bibliography—students' and teachers' conceptions and science education.* Kiel, Germany: Leibnitz Institute for Science and Mathematics Education. Retrieved from www.ipn.uni-kiel.de/aktuell/stcse/stcse.html

Feierabend, T., Jokmin, S., & Eilks, I. (2011). Chemistry teachers' views on teaching "climate change"—An interview case study from research-oriented learning in teacher education. *Chemistry Education: Research & Practice, 11*, 85–91.

Fensham, P. J. (1975). Concept formation. In D. J. Daniels (Ed.), *New movements in the study and teaching of chemistry* (pp. 199–217). London: Temple Smith.

Gabel, D. (1999). Improving teaching and learning through chemistry education research: A look to the future, *Journal of Chemical Education, 76*, 548–554.

Garcia Franco, A., & Taber, K. (2009). Secondary students' thinking about familiar phenomena: Learners' explanations from a curriculum context where "particles" is a key idea for organizing teaching and learning. *International Journal of Science Education, 31*, 1917–1952.

George, J., & Lubben, F. (2002). Facilitating teachers' professional growth through their involvement in creating context-based materials in science. *International Journal of Educational Development, 22*, 659–672.

Gilbert, J. K. (2007). Visualization: A metacognitive skill in science and science education. In J. K. Gilbert (Ed.), *Visualization in science education* (pp. 9–27). Dordrecht, the Netherlands: Kluwer Academic Publishers.

Gilbert, J. K., De Jong, O., Justi, R., Treagust, D. F., & Van Driel, J. H. (Eds.). (2002). *Chemical education: Research-based practice.* Dordrecht, the Netherlands: Kluwer Academic Publishers.

Gilbert, J. K., Justi, R., Van Driel, J. H., De Jong, O., & Treagust, D. F. (2004). Securing a future for chemical education. *Chemistry Education: Research & Practice, 5*, 5–14.

Gilbert, J. K., Osborne, R. J., & Fensham, P. J. (1982). Children's science and its consequences for teaching. *Science Education, 66*, 623–633.

Gräsel, D., Nentwig, P., & Parchmann, I. (2005). Chemie im Kontext: Curriculum development and evaluation strategies. In J. Bennett, J. Holman, R. Millar, & D. Waddington (Eds.), *Evaluation as a tool for improving science education* (pp. 53–66). Münster, Germany: Waxmann.

Haglund, J., & Jeppsson, F. (2012). Using self-generated analogies in teaching of thermodynamics. *Journal of Research in Science Teaching, 49,* 898–921.

Hammer, D. (1996). Misconceptions or p-prims: How may alternative perspectives of cognitive structure influence instructional perceptions and intentions? *Journal of the Learning Sciences, 5,* 97–127.

Harrison, A.G. (2001). How do teachers and textbook writers model scientific ideas for students? *Research in Science Education, 31,* 401–435.

Harrison, A.G., & Coll, R.K. (Eds.). (2008). *Using analogies in middle and secondary science classrooms.* Thousand Oaks, CA: Corwin Press.

Harrison, A.G., & Treagust, D.F. (2000a). Learning about atoms, molecules, and chemical bonds: A case study of multiple-model use in grade 11 chemistry. *Science Education, 84,* 352–381.

Harrison, A.G., & Treagust, D.F. (2000b). A typology of school science models. *International Journal of Science Education, 22,* 1011–1026.

Hesse, J.J., & Anderson, C.W. (1992). Students' conceptions of chemical change. *Journal of Research in Science Teaching, 29,* 277–299.

Jaber, L., & BouJaoude, S. (2012). A macro-micro-symbolic teaching to promote relational understanding of chemical reactions. *International Journal of Science Education, 34,* 973–998.

Jensen, W.B. (1995). *Logic, history and the teaching of chemistry.* Keynote lecture, given at the 57th Annual Summer Conference of the New England Association of Chemistry Teachers. Monograph. Sacred Heart University, Fairfield, CT.

Johnson, P.M. (2000). Children's understanding of substances, part 1: Recognizing chemical change. *International Journal of Science Education, 22,* 719–737.

Johnson, P.M. (2002). Children's understanding of substances, part 2: Explaining chemical change. *International Journal of Science Education, 24,* 1037–1054.

Johnson, P.M. (2012). Introducing particle theory. In K.S. Taber (Ed.), *Teaching secondary chemistry* (2nd ed., pp. 49–73). London: Association for Science Education/Hodder Education.

Johnson, P., & Papageorgiou, G. (2010). Rethinking the introduction of particle theory: A substance-based framework. *Journal of Research in Science Teaching, 47,* 130–150.

Johnstone, A.H. (1989). Some messages for teachers and examiners: An information processing model. In Assessment Subject Group Trust (Ed.). *Assessment of chemistry in schools* (Vol. Research in Assessment VII, pp. 23–39). London: Royal Society of Chemistry Education Division.

Johnstone, A.H. (1991). Why is science difficult to learn? Things are seldom what they seem. *Journal of Computer Assisted Learning, 7,* 75–83.

Johnstone, A.H. (1993). The development of chemistry teaching. *Journal of Chemical Education, 70,* 701–705.

Justi, R., & Gilbert, J.K. (2000). History and philosophy of science through models: Some challenges in the case of "the atom." *International Journal of Science Education, 22,* 993–1009.

Karpudewan, M., Ismael, Z., & Roth, W.-M. (2012). The efficacy of a green chemistry laboratory-based pedagogy: Changes in environmental values of Malaysia pre-service teachers. *International Journal of Science and Mathematics, 10,* 497–529.

Kern, A.L., Wood, N.B., Roehrig, G.H., & Nyachwaya, J. (2010). A qualitative report of the ways high school chemistry students attempt to represent a chemical reaction at the atomic/molecular level. *Chemistry Education Research and Practice, 11,* 165–172.

Keys, P.M. (2005). Are teachers walking the walk or just talking the talk in science education? *Teachers and Teaching, 11,* 499–516.

Kortland, K., & Klaassen, K. (Eds.). (2010). *Designing theory-based teaching-learning sequences for science education* Utrecht, The Netherlands: CDBeta Press.

Krnel, D., Watson, R., & Glazar, S.A. (1998). Survey of research related to the development of the concept of "matter." *International Journal of Science Education, 20,* 257–289.

Laverty, D.T., & McGarvey, J.E.B. (1991). A "constructivist" approach to learning. *Education in Chemistry, 28,* 99–102.

Leach, J., & Scott, P. (2002). Designing and evaluating science teaching sequences: An approach drawing upon the concept of learning demand and a social constructivist perspective on learning. *Studies in Science Education, 38,* 115–142.

Levy Nahum, T., Mamlok-Naaman, R., Hofstein, A., & Krajcik, J. (2007). Developing a new teaching approach for the chemical bonding concept aligned with current scientific and pedagogical knowledge. *Science Education, 91,* 579–603.

Levy Nahum, T., Mamlok-Naaman, R., Hofstein, A., & Taber, K.S. (2010). Teaching and learning the concept of chemical bonding. *Studies in Science Education, 46,* 179–207.

Löfgren, L., & Helldén, G. (2009). A longitudinal study showing how students use a molecule concept when explaining everyday situations. *International Journal of Science Education, 31,* 1631–1655.

Marks, R., Bertram, S., & Eilks, I. (2008). Learning chemistry and beyond with a lesson plan on potato crisps, which follows a socio-critical and problem-oriented approach to chemistry lessons—a case study. *Chemistry Education Research and Practice, 9,* 267–276.

Meijer, M. (2011). *Macro-meso-micro thinking with structure-property relations for chemistry education—an explorative design-based study.* Utrecht, Netherlands: Utrecht University (Ph.D. thesis). Retrieved from igitur-archive.library.uu.nl/dissertations/2011-0627-200510/Uindex.html

Meijer, M., Bulte, A., & Pilot, A. (2009). Structure-property relations between macro and micro representations: Relevant meso-levels in authentic tasks. In J. Gilbert & D. Treagust (Eds.), *Multiple representations in chemical education* (pp. 195–213). Dordrecht, the Netherlands: Springer.

Meijer, M., Bulte, A., & Pilot, A. (2013). Macro-micro thinking with structure-property relations: Integrating "meso-levels" in secondary education. In G. Tsaparlis & H. Sevian (Eds.), *Concepts of matter in science education* (pp. 419–436). Dordrecht, the Netherlands: Springer.

Millar, R. (1990). Making sense: What use are particles to children? In P. Lijnse, P. Licht, W. de Vos, & A. Waarlo (Eds.), *Relating macroscopic phenomena to microscopic particles* (pp. 283–293). Utrecht, the Netherlands: CDß Press.

Millar, R. (2006). Twenty-first-century science: Insights from the design and implementation of a scientific literacy approach in school science. *International Journal of Science Education, 28,* 1499–1521.

Mozzer, N.B., & Justi, R. (2011). Students' pre- and post-teaching analogical reasoning when they draw their analogies. *International Journal of Science Education, 34,* 429–458.

Nelson, P. (2002). Teaching chemistry progressively: From substances, to atoms and molecules, to electrons and nuclei. *Chemistry Education Research and Practice, 3,* 215–228.

Nieswandt, M. (2001). Problems and possibilities for learning in an introductory chemistry course from a conceptual change perspective. *Science Education, 85,* 158–179.

NRC (National Research Council Committee on Conceptual Framework for the New K–12 Science Education Standards). (2012). *A framework for K–12 science education: Practices, crosscutting concepts, and core ideas.* Washington, DC: National Academies Press.

Özmen, H. (2004). Some student misconceptions in chemistry: A literature review of chemical bonding. *Journal of Science Education and Technology, 13,* 147–159.

Parchmann, I., Gräsel, D., Baer, A., Nentwig, P., Demuth, R., Ralle, B., & the ChiK Project Group. (2006). "Chemie im Kontext": A symbiotic implementation of a context-based teaching and learning approach. *International Journal of Science Education, 28,* 1041–1062.

Park, E.J., & Light, G. (2008). Identifying atomic structure as a threshold concept: Student mental models and troublesomeness. *International Journal of Science Education, 31,* 233–258.

Pauling, L. (1960). *The nature of the chemical bond and the structure of molecules and crystals: An introduction to modern structural chemistry* (3rd ed.). Ithaca, NY: Cornell University Press.

Petri, J., & Niedderer, H. (1998). A learning pathway in high school-level quantum atomic physics. *International Journal of Science Education, 20,* 1075–1088.

Prins, G., Bulte, A., & Pilot, A. (2011). Evaluation of a design principle for fostering students' epistemological views on models and modeling using authentic practices as contexts for learning in chemistry education. *International Journal of Science Education, 33,* 1539–1569.

QCA. (2007). *Science: Programme of study for key stage 3 and attainment targets.* London: Qualifications and Curriculum Authority.

Ramsden, J.M. (1997). How does a context-based approach influence understanding of key chemical ideas at 16+? *International Journal of Science Education, 19,* 697–710.

Rosenblueth, A., & Wiener, N. (1945). The role of models in science. *Philosophy of Science, 12,* 316–321.

Sadownik, J.W., & Ulijn, R.V. (2010). Dynamic covalent chemistry in aid of peptide self-assembly. *Current Opinion in Biotechnology, 21,* 401–411.

Sánchez Gómez, P.J., & Martín, F. (2003). Quantum versus "classical" chemistry in university chemistry education: A case study of the role of history in thinking the curriculum. *Chemistry Education: Research & Practice, 4,* 131–148.

Scerri, E.R. (2000). Have orbitals really been observed? *Journal of Chemical Education, 77,* 1492–1494.

Smith, J.P., diSessa, A.A., & Roschelle, J. (1993). Misconceptions reconceived: A constructivist analysis of knowledge in transition. *Journal of the Learning Sciences, 3,* 115–163.

Solomonidou, C., & Stavridou, H. (2000). From inert object to chemical substance: Students' initial conceptions and conceptual development during an introductory experimental chemistry sequence. *Science Education, 84,* 382–400.

Solsona, N., Izquierdo, M., & De Jong, O. (2003). Exploring the development of students' conceptual profiles of chemical change. *International Journal of Science Education, 25,* 3–12.

Stavridou, H., & Solomonidou, C. (1998). Conceptual reorganization and the construction of the chemical reaction concept during secondary education. *International Journal of Science Education, 20,* 205–221.

Stoddart, J.F. (2012). Editorial: From supramolecular to systems chemistry: Complexity emerging out of simplicity. *Angewandte Chemie International Edition, 51,* 12902–12903.

Stolk, M., Bulte, A., De Jong, O., & Pilot, A. (2012). Evaluating a professional development framework to empower chemistry teachers to design context-based education. *International Journal of Science Education, 34,* 1487–1508.

Stolk, M., De Jong, O., Bulte, A., & Pilot, A. (2011). Exploring a framework for professional development in curriculum innovation: Empowering teachers for designing context-based chemistry education. *Research in Science Education, 41,* 369–388.

Taber, K.S. (1994). *Can Kelly's triads be used to elicit aspects of chemistry students' conceptual frameworks?* Paper presented at the British Educational Research Association Annual Conference, Oxford. Retrieved from www.leeds.ac.uk/educol/documents/00001482.htm

Taber, K.S. (1998a). An alternative conceptual framework from chemistry education. *International Journal of Science Education, 20,* 597–608.

Taber, K.S. (1998b). The sharing-out of nuclear attraction: Or I can't think about physics in chemistry. *International Journal of Science Education, 20,* 1001–1014.

Taber, K.S. (2000). *The CERG lecture 2000: Molar and molecular conceptions of research into learning chemistry: Towards a synthesis.* Paper presented at the Variety in Chemistry Teaching 2000. Retrieved from www.leeds.ac.uk/educol/documents/00001551.htm

Taber, K.S. (2001a). Building the structural concepts of chemistry: Some considerations from educational research. *Chemistry Education: Research and Practice in Europe, 2,* 123–158.

Taber, K.S. (2001b). When the analogy breaks down: Modelling the atom on the solar system. *Physics Education, 36,* 222–226.

Taber, K.S. (2003). The atom in the chemistry curriculum: Fundamental concept, teaching model or epistemological obstacle? *Foundations of Chemistry, 5,* 43–84.

Taber, K.S. (2005). Learning quanta: Barriers to stimulating transitions in student understanding of orbital ideas. *Science Education, 89,* 94–116.

Taber, K.S. (2009a). College students' conceptions of chemical stability: The widespread adoption of a heuristic rule out of context and beyond its range of application. *International Journal of Science Education, 31,* 1333–1358.

Taber, K.S. (2009b). Learning at the symbolic level. In J.K. Gilbert & D.F. Treagust (Eds.), *Multiple representations in chemical education* (pp. 75–108). Dordrecht, the Netherlands: Springer.

Taber, K.S. (2009c). Progressing Science Education: Constructing the scientific research programme into the contingent nature of learning science. Dordrecht, the Netherlands: Springer.

Taber, K.S. (2012a). Developing models of chemical bonding. In K.S. Taber (Ed.), *Teaching secondary chemistry* (2nd ed., pp. 103–136). London: Association for Science Education/Hodder Education.

Taber, K.S. (2012b). Key concepts in chemistry. In K.S. Taber (Ed.), *Teaching secondary chemistry* (2nd ed., pp. 1–47). London: Association for Science Education/Hodder Education.

Taber, K.S., & Tan, K.C.D. (2007). Exploring learners' conceptual resources: Singapore A level students' explanations in the topic of ionization energy. *International Journal of Science and Mathematics Education, 5,* 375–392.

Taber, K.S., & Tan, K.C.D. (2011). The insidious nature of "hard core" alternative conceptions: Implications for the constructivist research programme of patterns in high school students' and pre-service teachers' thinking about ionization energy. *International Journal of Science Education, 33,* 259–297.

Taber, K.S., & Watts, M. (1996). The secret life of the chemical bond: Students' anthropomorphic and animistic references to bonding. *International Journal of Science Education, 18,* 557–568.

Talanquer, V. (2007). Explanations and teleology in chemistry education. *International Journal of Science Education, 29,* 853–870.

Talanquer, V. (2011). Macro, submicro, and symbolic: The many faces of the chemistry "triplet." *International Journal of Science Education, 33,* 179–195.

Tortosa, M. (2012). The use of microcomputer based laboratories in chemistry secondary education: Present state of the art and ideas for research-based practice. *Chemistry Education: Research & Practice, 13,* 161–171.

Tsaparlis, G. (1994). Blocking mechanisms in problem solving from the Pascual-Leone's M-space perspective. In H.-J. Schmidt (Ed.), *Problem solving and misconceptions in chemistry and physics* (pp. 211–226). Dortmund, Germany: International Council of Associations for Science Education.

Tsaparlis, G., Kolioulis, D., & Pappa, E. (2010). Lower-secondary introductory chemistry course: A novel approach based on science-education theories, with emphasis on the macroscopic approach, and the delayed meaningful teaching of the concepts of molecule and atom. *Chemistry Education Research and Practice, 11,* 107–117.

Ünal, S., Çalık, M., Ayas, A., & Coll, R.K. (2006). A review of chemical bonding studies: Needs, aims, methods of exploring students' conceptions, general knowledge claims and students' alternative conceptions. *Research in Science & Technological Education, 24,* 141–172.

Vaino, K., Holbrook, J., & Rannikmäe, M. (2012). Stimulating students' intrinsic motivation for learning chemistry through the use of context-based learning modules. *Chemistry Education Research and Practice, 13,* 410–419.

Van Aalsvoort, J. (2004). Activity theory as a tool to address the problem of chemistry's lack of relevance in secondary school chemical education. *International Journal of Science Education, 26,* 1635–1651.

Van Driel, J.H., & Graeber, W. (2002). The teaching and learning of chemical equilibrium. In J.K. Gilbert, O. De Jong, R. Justi, D.F. Treagust, & J.H. Van Driel (Eds.), *Chemical education: Towards research-based practice* (pp. 271–292). Dordrecht, the Netherlands: Kluwer Academic Publishers.

Watson, R., Prieto, T., & Dillon, J.S. (1997). Consistency of students' explanations about combustion. *Science Education, 81,* 425–443.

24

Earth System Science Education

Nir Orion and Julie Libarkin

This chapter is dedicated to the memory of Vic Mayer, a pioneer of Earth Systems Science education (1933–2011).

Introduction

Earth System Science (ESS) encompasses the array of disciplines that are concerned with understanding how the Earth's systems, including its atmosphere, hydrosphere, biosphere, and geosphere, function and interact. The challenge of ESS education is to help students recognize how processes that operate on the planet interact to generate the physical and biological diversity that is so unique to Earth. Even more challenging, this understanding must operate over diverse spatial and temporal scales.

Orion and Ault (2007) made several persuasive arguments about the uniqueness of Earth science and the value of teaching it in schools. The scientific nature of Earth science coupled with its tangible, real-world characteristics makes Earth science particularly helpful for teaching scientific inquiry that can be transferred to other sciences. At the same time, Earth and space sciences uniquely consider the role of time, both through predictive inquiry that considers the future and retrospective inquiry that considers the nature of Earth's past. Orion and Ault (2007) recognized the value of Earth science beyond classroom science, arguing that environmental insight is important for all citizens who are expected to make decisions about policy and lives intertwined with a changing planet. The current chapter is a natural extension of this earlier work, expanding the discussion to take a more holistic view of the system of processes that interact to affect Earth and its inhabitants.

The Earth sciences are both similar to and distinct from other fields of science. Earth science serves as a concrete context for better understanding of basic concepts from physics, chemistry, and biology, and hence all sciences share many common challenges. For example, using operational definitions, thinking in terms of direct and inverse proportions, and overcoming pervasive misconceptions about energy, motion, particulate matter, inheritance, and adaptation are common across sciences (Driver, Guesne, & Tiberghien, 1985; Driver, Squires, Rushworth, &

Wood-Robinson, 1994; Wandersee, Mintzes, & Novak, 1994). The readily accessible context of the planet helps introduce young adolescents to features of scientific reasoning such as observing, hypothesizing, and drawing conclusions from evidence. At the same time, learning about the Earth sciences presents distinctive challenges and opportunities not observed in other scientific disciplines. These challenges include the discontinuous nature of the long-term geologic record, the dynamic complexities inherent to Earth systems operating over many scales of time and space, and the uncertainties that are inescapable when predicting the nature of Earth's future.

This chapter focuses on the Earth systems aspect of the Earth sciences. Earth System Science, or ESS, is the field of study concerned with understanding the Earth as a system, including understanding individual systems (such as geosphere, hydrosphere, or atmosphere) and how these systems interact and influence one another. This includes recognition that Earth systems are continuously changing, that systems must be understood over both time and space, and that processes that influence Earth systems do so across many scales, from micro to planetary, and over time scales from milliseconds to millennia. Ultimately, ESS works toward a more holistic view of Earth and Earth processes. Increasingly, scientists are recognizing the role that Earth sciences and the environment play in the progression of phenomena categorized as "physical" or "biological" or "chemical." For example, geneticists are learning that genes can be turned on and off by the characteristics of the physical world; this has significant implications for understanding processes like evolution. Similarly, physicists cannot ignore the planet on which they work and engage in cross-disciplinary research (e.g., geophysics, biophysics) that explicitly incorporates Earth systems. The different fields of science are becoming increasingly enmeshed, with the Earth serving as the context in which all other sciences function outside of the computer model and the laboratory. Interdisciplinary fields like biogeochemistry and climate science operate from a fundamental recognition that the planet has its own set of rules through which it operates and that human society is inextricably intertwined with Earth processes.

ESS recognizes that interdisciplinary scholarship is necessary to solve basic environmental problems. Much as geophysics provided the interdisciplinary foundation for our modern understanding of plate tectonics, ESS is providing the complex and nuanced view of Earth systems our society needs to navigate successfully into the future. The ESS perspective recognizes a planet that is made up of interacting systems, including the human system (part of the biosphere), that fundamentally impact each other through processes that bridge the once separate domains of Earth, ocean, and atmospheric science. Understanding how these systems interact is essential as we move into a world in which climate change, coastal eutrophication, and natural hazards are increasingly important to human life and society. As such, understanding how the Earth system operates, as well as how it interacts with human societies, is of ever-increasing importance.

We designed this chapter to provide readers with an overview of ESS education, with careful attention to providing international examples of what we could find in the English published literature of the last 7 years, since the writing of the previous volume of this handbook. The chapter is organized in alignment with backward design (Wiggins & McTighe, 2005) such that we first introduce the goals for ESS instruction, review the status of assessment and research on ESS teaching and learning, and discuss curriculum—including unique challenges and a well-studied example. This is followed by a discussion of the challenges to ESS instruction and a research agenda that we believe targets both urgent needs and gaps in current work.

Goals of Earth System Science Education

The purpose of learning Earth science has become a topic of intense discussion and publication in the past decade (e.g., LaDue & Clark, 2012). Documents related to Earth science "literacy" focus on conceptions, attitudes, and skills, often with the intent of defining constructs necessary for effective decision making by an educated citizenry. The theoretical background for Earth systems education as well as its implication for schools was first introduced more than two decades ago (Mayer, 1991; Mayer & Fortner, 1995). However, "Earth System Science" is explicitly included as a major idea in the very recently published Next Generation Science Standards (NGSS; Achieve, Inc., 2013). While prior documents include the concept of Earth systems, standards for understanding are generally couched in reference to specific systems, such as the atmosphere or oceans, or with reference to human impacts on systems. We include here discussion of goals relevant to ESS from the variety of standards documents currently in use.

Standards for Primary, Secondary, and Public Understanding

Standards for science education exist in most nations across the globe. In the United States, recent innovations have resulted in the explicit inclusion of ESS content and philosophical underpinnings within science education standards. Development of the NGSS was recently completed (Achieve, Inc., 2013); while the basic ideas articulated in standards established in 1996 (National Research Council, 1996) are still present in some form, ESS is now explicitly mentioned in the NGSS as a disciplinary core idea. Other important aspects of ESS, such as causality, are also explicitly described and valued at the national level within the United States. These standards emerge primarily from the science education community focused on precollege education, although scientists were explicitly invited to comment on both drafts and published versions of the standards. In many ways, these standards represent best practice for collaborations between scientists and science educators.

The framework for U.S. science standards articulates a set of seven cross-cutting themes, all of which are certainly relevant to ESS instruction. This framework also articulates three concepts considered to be core ideas in Earth and space science, plus a suite of component concepts. We have organized each core/component idea appropriate to ESS relative to one or more of the larger cross-cutting themes and also propose other big ideas that perhaps should be considered more explicitly in global ESS instruction (see Table 24.1).

Communities in the United States have developed four documents that relate to Earth systems literacy and specifically to essential principles for understanding Earth science, ocean science, atmospheric science, and climate science (links to all four documents can be found at http://eo.ucar.edu/asl/). These documents emerge primarily from the scientific community generally engaged with college, K–12, teacher, or public understanding of science. The extent to which these documents reflect an Earth systems or holistic perspective varies; some, like the Earth science literacy principles, are descriptions of very specific concepts related to a single field, while others, like the climate literacy principles, offer broad discussion of processes that fall at the nexus of Earth system interactions.

LaDue and Clark (2012) synopsized these four sets of literacy principles to identify common themes across the documents. Five concepts appeared in at least three principles and represent what might be called core ideas for ESS literacy. This list should be considered a living document that should change as the field of ESS evolves in response to new challenges and research.

1. Exploration of Earth systems occurs through observations, scientific reasoning, and modeling.
2. Earth systems involve complex interactions among rock, water, air, and life.
3. Earth systems are continuously changing.

TABLE 24.1
Synthesis of Important Ideas for Earth System Science Instruction From the NGSS and Principles Documents

NGSS Earth's Systems Disciplinary Core Ideas and Crosscutting Themes*	Relevant NGSS Crosscutting Themes*	Related Themes from Principles Documents**
ESS2.A: Earth Materials and Systems	Patterns in Earth material location and development; Stability and change in Earth systems over space and time	Earth systems involve complex interactions among rock, water, air, and life; Earth systems are continuously changing.
ESS2.B: Plate Tectonics and Large-Scale System Interactions	Patterns in tectonic processes; patterns in interactions between Earth systems; stability and change in plate tectonics over space and time	Earth systems are continuously changing.
ESS2.C: The Roles of Water in Earth's Surface Processes	Patterns in water location and landscape change; stability and change in fresh and salt water at Earth's surface over space and time	Earth systems are continuously changing.
ESS2.D: Weather and Climate	Patterns in weather and climate, including relationships; stability and change in weather and climate over space and time	Earth systems are continuously changing.
ESS3.D: Global Climate Change	Patterns in climate, including relationships to human activities; stability and change in climate over space and time	Earth systems are continuously changing; humans are inextricably interconnected to the geosphere, hydrosphere, and atmosphere.

From ideas in *NGSS (www.nextgenscience.org) and **LaDue and Clark (2012)

4. Humans are inextricably interconnected to the geosphere, hydrosphere, and atmosphere.
5. The biosphere depends on and affects the hydrosphere, the atmosphere, and the geosphere.

Some of these ideas are similar to ideas postulated in the NGSS as important concepts for the precollege community to understand. Note that the first concept relates to the *practice* of Earth System Science, and the remaining four concepts relate to the *nature* of Earth System Science. These five concepts coupled with ideas identified in the NGSS (Achieve, Inc., 2013) provide a useful foundation from which Earth System Science education can proceed (see Table 24.1).

The Status of Research and Assessment in Earth System Science Education

Research into how well people understand ESS as well as the impact of experience and instruction on ESS literacy has a long history, albeit one that considers Earth science concepts in isolation rather than as a collective whole (e.g., Francek, 2013). This research initially emerged from within the science education community, although a new, broad community of interdisciplinary scholars looking at questions in ESS education has emerged from scholars housed in geoscience, environmental science, communications, psychology, learning science, and other communities. As a consequence, grasping the full breadth of research and assessment in ESS education requires consideration of cross-disciplinary literatures. This is both a blessing and a curse for scholars in ESS education; drawing upon multiple fields of inquiry produces rich understanding of learning not possible when scholarship is isolated to a single domain, while at the same time research published

in diverse journals is difficult to identify. We attempt here to provide an overview of literature relevant to ESS education representing the most recent work published since the last edition of this handbook. This includes brief review of those studies that have been published in the past 5 years; reviews of earlier studies are cited to provide readers with links to the significant prior literature. For simplicity, we have focused our discussion on three areas: *conceptual understanding, the affective domain*, and *assessment in ESS education*. We end this section with discussion of next steps needed to move beyond research into practice.

Conceptual Understanding

The past decade has seen a surge in research of students' alternative conceptions about Earth's spheres, such that unique patterns are beginning to emerge. The long history of research into student alternative conceptions has been reviewed extensively by other authors, and we encourage readers to refer to these works (Ault, 1994; Cheek, 2010; Francek, 2013; King, 2008; Orion & Ault, 2007). The following synopsis focuses not on specific alternative conceptions but rather on overarching generalizations evident when studies are viewed holistically and from the vantage of interacting processes working within and across spheres—that is, conceptions related to ESS specifically.

Conceptual understanding of ESS materials, contexts, and processes provides insight into the alternative conceptions students bring into the classroom. Research indicates that alternative conceptions present in elementary students can persist into secondary and even college classrooms, suggesting that some ideas are quite resistant to instruction or that ESS instruction is inadequate to address these conceptions. Francek (2013) recently reviewed hundreds of documented alternative conceptions in geoscience, including a discussion of those ideas that persist across age levels. For example, absolute time and the concept of "deep time" are difficult for many people, young children through teachers, to understand. Interestingly, explicit studies of systems understanding were sparse, suggesting that additional work related to the ESS understanding of students is needed. This review, coupled with earlier work (i.e., Ault, 1994; Cheek, 2010; King, 2008; Orion & Ault, 2007), suggests that the ESS community is well situated in the first-stage foundational work of identifying student ideas and is now ready to move into more holistic analysis of the origin, characteristics, and instructional relevance of ideas as well as how ideas are integrated within an individual's ESS model. Readers interested in the current state of Earth and related conceptual understanding research are strongly encouraged to consult Francek (2013) and earlier reviews.

Some ESS education researchers have already begun to consider alternative conceptions beyond the simple existence of nonscientific ideas and their persistence despite Earth-related instruction. Studies into ontological understanding, essentially the ways in which students categorize phenomena, suggest that students at many levels do not necessarily recognize that the Earth is itself a system that is continually changing (e.g., Libarkin & Kurdziel, 2006; Raia, 2008). Similarly, studies into the ability of students to think at a systems level, to recognize that processes interact to form complex patterns, generally find that systems-level thinking is beyond many precollege and college-level students (Ben-Zvi-Assaraf & Orion, 2010a; McNeal, Miller, & Herbert, 2008; Sibley, 2005). This work speaks directly to the goals of ESS instruction articulated by both science educators and scientists— understanding that the Earth is changeable is one of the most important concepts in ESS, as is recognition that change occurs because of very specific causes, and that the Earth is a complex system housing myriad complex processes.

ESS is also unique from other sciences in that ESS requires both prediction of outcomes of active processes and retrodiction of ancient processes that resulted in present-day observable patterns. Retrodictive reasoning about the Earth is intimately tied to systems thinking (Kali, Orion, & Eylon, 2003; Lawton, 2001), requiring that students recognize that multiple events can interact to produce often surprising results. Likely because of its limited utility in other sciences, retrodiction is often left out of discussions of scientific reasoning (Sibley, 2009). At the same time, scholars agree that retrodictive reasoning is a necessary component of effective ESS instruction (Pyle, 2008), although curricula that engage students in retrodiction are relatively rare. Certainly, precollege students are able to perform retrodictive reasoning about complex evolutionary and geologic data (Libarkin & Schneps, 2012; Thomson & Chapman Beall, 2008), as well as about complex global systems (Sunderlin, 2009). A better understanding of the Earth system overall can result from simple retrodictive exercises (Sunderlin, 2009).

Researchers are also finding that, as in other disciplines, students can hold multiple alternative conceptions about ESS concepts at the same time, often while simultaneously holding a scientific understanding (e.g., Clark, Libarkin, Kortz, & Jordan, 2011; Dickerson, Callahan, Van Sickle, & Hay, 2005; Sexton, 2012). This dichotomy of scientific and nonscientific notions may itself parallel the differences between traditional Earth science instruction (focused on isolated ideas) and ESS instruction (focused on interactions between larger domains).

Some scholars have suggested that alternative conceptions of phenomena that are not directly observable, either because of large spatial scales (e.g., plate motion) or long periodicities (e.g., macroevolution of dinosaurs), may result not from within the student but rather from our instructional materials themselves. For example, (Clark, et al., 2011) provide evidence that the most common visualization in geoscience, the U.S. Geological Surveys schematic for teaching about plate tectonics, contains elements that both confuse and reinforce alternative conceptions about the geosphere. The vast time scales associated with geologic events add to the complexity of understanding ESS phenomena, with many people simply unable to develop conceptual frameworks needed to understand deep time events that impact multiple spheres at once (Catley & Novick, 2009; Teed & Slattery, 2011).

The Affective Domain

Recent studies indicate that Earth scientists recognize the common importance in understanding, valuing, and behaving responsibly toward the Earth. These studies include development of attitudinal surveys (e.g., Jolley, Lane, Kennedy, & Frappé-Sénéclauze, 2012; Libarkin, 2001), investigation of student perceptions of fieldwork (e.g., Boyle et al., 2007; Kern & Carpenter, 1984; Orion & Ault, 2007; Stokes & Boyle, 2009; Yunker, Orion, & Lernau, 2011), and general discourse about the importance of the affective domain in geoscience instruction (McConnell & Van Der Hoeven Kraft, 2011).

Libarkin (2001) and Jolley and colleagues (2012) created new questions and modified existing attitudes toward science and nature-of-science instruments in their studies of college student attitudes and understanding of the nature of science. Both studies found that generating questions targeting the specific subject matter (i.e., earth, oceans) being taught in courses was a useful approach to measuring student affect. This work identified aspects of courses, such as inquiry, that seemed to relate to better student attitudes, although additional studies considering the role of course design on student affect about the Earth and ESS is needed.

Other scholars (e.g., Boyle et al., 2007; Stokes & Boyle, 2009) have asked questions about the role of fieldwork in student affect. Fieldwork is perhaps one of the hallmarks of ESS and certainly geologic instruction and is considered to be important for building positive attitudes about

Earth and related sciences, particularly among student geoscientists. In general, studies of the impact of fieldwork on student affect suggest that fieldwork can lessen negative attitudes, particularly toward the unknown, and can strengthen positive attitudes already in existence. Interestingly, Stokes and Boyle (2009) found that interdisciplinary experiences related to the area of study but not necessarily related to the scientific enterprise had strong, positive influences on student attitudes. This suggests that teaching ESS rather than isolated science (i.e., geoscience) in the field, and particularly linking individual ideas to the larger cohesive Earth and human system, might improve both conceptual and affective characteristics simultaneously.

A dualism between cognition and affect has emerged from several studies of earth systems education at the elementary level (Ben-Zvi-Assaraf & Orion, 2010a; Yunker, Orion & Lernau, 2011), the junior high level (Ben-Zvi-Assaraf & Orion, 2009; Orion, Ben-Menacham, & Shur, 2008) and the high school level (Orion & Bassis, 2008; Orion & Cohen, 2007). Orion (2007) suggests that the earth systems approach to education should emphasize both the development of thinking skills and affective responses (i.e., emotional intelligence). The development of thinking processes and connections between students and their physical (natural and nonnatural) environment need to be considered simultaneously. The relationship with the immediate environment begins with authentic questions that are related to the students themselves and enhance their awareness and insight regarding their environment. Later, the students can experience their environment through activities that are based on intake of stimuli of all the senses. Orion (2007) suggested the earth systems approach can serve as a holistic framework for the "science for all" paradigm and claimed that a genuine reform in science education should also include two additional holistic components: a holistic learning environment (outdoors, lab, computer, and classroom) component and holistic cognition-emotions learning component.

McConnell and Van Der Hoeven Kraft (2011) provide a persuasive argument for better inclusion of affective research in studies of the impact of instruction on student understanding of Earth and embedded systems. For example, they point out that one of the reasons we teach nonscientists about the Earth is to engender better decision making and that decision making depends in part on a person's feelings. This argument, coupled with the limited studies on student affect around ESS and related fields, suggests that better understanding of affect and decision making, and particularly the impact of instruction on these, would be useful companions to curricular reform.

Assessment in ESS Education

Assessment of literacy in Earth-related fields has a long history in precollege settings and has gained the growing attention of college-level researchers in the past decade. This assessment has predominantly focused on Earth science as a domain, with recent developments recognizing the broader context implied by considering the Earth as a system. Considering its broadest meaning, assessment involves the measurement of individual ability through qualitative or quantitative approaches. Open-ended interviews can provide deep understanding of how an individual constructs meaning about the world. At the other extreme, close-ended questionnaires allow measurement of many individuals simultaneously. To be effective, each approach requires very careful development of a research design aligned with specific questions as well as acknowledgement of the limitations of each data-collection and related analytical technique. The interdisciplinary nature of scholars looking into ESS education means that different research paradigms will be evident in papers asking similar questions. This requires, then, that ESS education researchers must become fluent in the meaning of validity and reliability for multiple communities.

High-stakes testing in Earth science has a long history in the United States, most noticeably in New York, where the Earth Science Regents Exam has been in place since the late 1800s. The development of questions for use on the Regents Exams is well organized and revolves around a community of teachers and scientists working collaboratively to develop, vet, and revise high-quality questions. This ensures that the exams have a generally high level of validity and reliability and hence are likely good measures of student understanding of ESS as well as constructs intertwined with ESS, such as graph-reading ability. While originally focused on traditional Earth science constructs (e.g., the rock cycle), the Regents Exam has expanded to include concepts inherent to systems thinking in an Earth context, including feedback, retrodiction, and large-scale phenomena like climate change.

In higher education, low-stakes tests of student understanding are becoming common outside the normative context of semester testing. The move to implement concept inventories (CIs), multiple-choice tests that purport to use student conceptions as incorrect response options, has emerged from within science disciplines as a mechanism for measuring student conceptual understanding and learning in response to instruction. Although predominantly used in higher education, the first CI was used in secondary schools (Treagust, 1986), and conceptions-based tests of learning in elementary and secondary classrooms are now experiencing broad dissemination through the Internet (e.g., http://assessment.aaas.org/). While other sciences have seen the development of many CIs that are unrelated to one another and that may or may not be properly developed and validated, research rather than instructional quality instruments are becoming available across the Earth and space sciences (e.g., Bardar, Prather, Brecher, & Slater, 2006; Libarkin & Anderson, 2006). This includes the development of a community of scholars working together to build a common pool of questions organized around the major spheres of the Earth (Libarkin, Ward, Anderson, Kortemeyer, & Raeburn, 2011). Many concept inventories in science are reviewed by Libarkin (2008), while the role of concept inventories in assessing learning is discussed in Libarkin, Jardeleza, and McElhinny (2014). We note that concept inventories represent a broad class of tests with a wide variety of validities and reliabilities, and readers should carefully consider these when choosing an assessment for use in research.

The Geoscience Concept Inventory (GCI) is a bank of test items that continues to grow and include new authors (Libarkin et al., 2011; http://geoscienceconceptinventory. wikispaces.com/). The bank now includes items developed by nearly 20 authors and organized around the major spheres (geosphere, biosphere, hydrosphere, atmosphere). Although it is not quite a decade old, scholars have already published a number of studies that use the GCI to assess learning. Several of these originate with the GCI's original authors (e.g., Libarkin & Anderson, 2005, 2006). Other studies focus on specific topics, such as geologic time (Teed & Slattery, 2011), or consider the impact of different types of instruction on student learning (e.g., McConnell et al., 2006). Researchers have used the GCI to investigate the conceptual understanding of preservice teachers (e.g., Petcovic & Ruhf, 2008) as well as college students, in a range of settings from traditional classrooms to the field, and to non–English-speaking populations (e.g., Spanish; Llerandi Roman, 2007). The GCI has also been used as a purely cognitive measure (e.g., Kelemen & Rosset, 2009) and has been shown to correlate very strongly with expert behavior (Hambrick et al., 2012). The GCI has the same limitations inherent to any multiple-choice instrument, specifically that questions must be carefully designed and validated for each population being studied. While good quantitative instruments make measurement of large populations efficient, understanding the origins and nuances of an individual's ideas can only be achieved through qualitative (i.e., survey, interview) methods.

Measurement of affective variables specifically related to ESS is less well developed than studies of conceptual understanding, although several instruments do exist. Libarkin (2001) developed a Likert-scale measure of student attitudes toward and conceptions of Earth science that has been used in affective studies of students in a variety of disciplines, including atmospheric science (Parker, Krockover, Eichinger, & Lasher-Trapp, 2008) and preservice elementary education (Bickmore, Thompson, Grandy, & Tomlin, 2009). Jolley, Lane, Kennedy, and Frappé-Sénéclauze (2012) developed a Likert-scale measure of perceptions of Earth and ocean science courses that was embedded in similar work emerging from other disciplines. Studies using these two instruments have identified both affective shifts in students as the result of instruction (e.g., Libarkin, 2001) as well as affective responses that appear to be unmoved by the classroom experience (Jolley, Lane, Kennedy, & Frappé-Sénéclauze, 2012). Future researchers are challenged to identify those experiences that appear to move student attitudes and perceptions about ESS, as well as to develop valid and reliable measures that can provide insight into other noncognitive variables, such as valuing of ESS-specific resources.

Studies of ESS Instruction in Practice

While academic research is valuable and interesting in its own right, moving from purely intellectual questions to practical applications is the outcome we ultimately need to achieve. In ESS education, this means conceptualizing how research findings can find meaning in the formal classroom, in informal educational settings, and in considering how best to communicate to the general public. Here, we provide an overview of many studies that have moved beyond basic academic studies and into practical investigation of real efforts to build ESS literacy.

There is a growing movement within the science education community that puts forth the development of environmental insights as one of the central purposes of science education (Orion & Ault, 2007). Orion and Fortner (2003) suggested that the implementation of the Earth systems approach might serve as an effective learning tool for the development of this environmental insight. The Earth systems approach is a holistic framework for Earth sciences and science curricula that emphasizes the study of the cyclic pattern of the transformation of matter and energy among the four Earth systems: geosphere, hydrosphere, atmosphere, and biosphere. The study of cycles such as the rock cycle, the water cycle, the food chain, and the carbon cycle emphasizes relationships among subsystems through the transfer of matter and energy based on the laws of conservation. Such natural cycles are being discussed within the context of their influence on people's daily lives rather than being isolated to scientific disciplines. The Earth systems approach also connects the natural world and technology: Technology transforms the raw materials that originate from Earth systems.

An important part of the educational effectiveness of the Earth systems approach depends on the systems thinking abilities of its learners. Systems thinking is a higher-order thinking skill required for the understanding of variety of scientific, technological, and social domains. In the last two decades, there has been a growing interest in the understanding of the cognitive aspects of systems thinking abilities. A review of the literature identified many studies that tried to characterize systems thinking and that emerge from a variety of disciplines (cf. Ben-Zvi-Assaraf & Orion, 2005a; Ben-Zvi-Assaraf & Orion, 2010b; Booth-Sweeney, 2000; Booth-Sweeney & Sterman, 2007; Draper, 1993; Emery, 1992; Faughnan & Elson, 1998; Fordyce, 1998; Frank, 2000; Goldstone & Wilensky, 2008; Graczyk, 1993; Hmelo-Silver, Marathe, & Liu, 2007; Hmelo-Silver & Pfeffer, 2004; Jacobson & Wilensky, 2006; Kim, 1999; Lesh, 2006; Lewis, 1998; Mandinach, 1989; Ossimitz, 2000; Senge, 1998; Steed, 1992; Ullmer, 1986; Verhoeff, Waarlo, & Boersma, 2008; Wilensky & Resnick, 1999). Common characteristics among these studies include dynamic thinking, network thinking, and temporal thinking, although some differences are clearly evident. These differences emerge primarily as a function of the discipline to which a specific system relates (e.g., technological systems, Earth systems, social systems, biological systems) and the different foci of the research (e.g., management, training, cognitive research, education).

Finally, a central feature of all ESS instruction must be a recognition that the places from which learners originate and in which learning is embedded influence the learning process. This is particularly true for domains explicitly focused on the natural world, such as geoscience, bioscience, and environmental science. At its core, place-based education recognizes that environment and culture are intertwined and utilizes this connection to engage students in learning about science. The emotional attachments that can arise from interaction with specific places generates a "sense of place" that can translate to greater attention and effective out-of-doors instruction and ultimately changes in an individual's environmental and sustainability behaviors (e.g., Israel, 2012; Semken & Butler Freeman, 2008). At its richest, place-based instruction is multidisciplinary, encourages engagement within the community, and is inherently experiential (Woodhouse & Knapp, 2000). In the geosciences, content may be accessed through interactions with landscapes as well as human interactions with specific places (Rossbacher, 2002). As the movement to engage students more deeply with the natural world has flourished, place-based approaches to curriculum, instruction, and teacher professional development have become widespread in K–12 and informal settings (Gruenewald & Smith, 2007; Sobel, 2004), and are becoming more common at the collegiate level (Miele & Powell, 2010; Zeichner, 2010).

The Status of ESS Education

For whatever reason, the Earth sciences have generally received less attention in school curriculum than the other sciences (physics, chemistry, biology). In recent years, the importance of Earth sciences has received growing acknowledgement, as citizens of the world are being called on to face environmental issues (e.g., climate change, drought, water pollution) that impact how humans live. Considering the Earth as a system as is required in ESS instruction necessitates that students understand systems and engage in systems thinking. In this section, we consider a long-standing research project working toward greater systems thinking among students as an example of ESS education research.

The Unique Learning and Teaching Challenges of Earth Systems Science

Teaching and learning about Earth System Science is becoming increasingly valued in a world in which a changing planet is having dramatic effects on human society. Despite becoming more removed from direct interaction with the planet as technology has become more advanced (e.g., www.michigan.gov/nochildleftinside), we cannot become completely isolated from large-scale natural hazards or from global climate change. We also cannot become removed from our dependence on the planet for food, mineral resources, and energy.

Understanding ESS requires acknowledgement that all of the Earth's spheres are interconnected, that processes occurring on Earth's surface are inextricably intertwined with the atmosphere, with the oceans, and, over enough time, even with the Earth's deep interior. ESS teaching and learning are challenged by the need for students to be able to think about and across three different time periods (past, present, future), recognize fundamental characteristics of unique spheres while also recognizing how spheres at different scales interact and influence each other, work with nonlinear processes and concepts, including negative and positive feedback in systems, and generate conclusions from the uncertain evidence inherent to the geologic record and models of future Earth.

Orion and Ault (2007) reviewed the contribution of multiple domains to Earth science education, particularly in precollege settings. They identified distinctive features of the Earth sciences according to their usefulness in relation to curriculum design, framing the scope of research about teaching and learning Earth sciences, and promoting science for all. For example, presumably from learning Earth sciences, students acquire an intellectually honest understanding of change through Earth's history and across many temporal and spatial scales. Developing a sense of scale is a distinctive feature of learning Earth sciences. This concept of scale functions both psychologically and epistemologically. Psychologically, scale may present obstacles to perception and insight. Epistemologically, extrapolation of Earth processes in time and space is a characteristic of deep thinking about Earth processes. The geologic time scale encompasses durations and changes vastly beyond the scale of human lifetimes; for example, forecasts of global climate change must wrestle with problems of sampling and modeling on scales that range from mere meters to the planetary. According to their analysis, Orion and Ault (2007) highlighted distinctive features of the Earth sciences, all of which are important when thinking about ESS:

1. *The historical approach to scientific inquiry* pioneered by Charles Lyell and Charles Darwin. This approach is exemplified by Darwin's account of the reefs around coral atolls of the Pacific. These islands act as a sampling distribution across space and through time of what happens to a volcanic island as it rises and subsides over immense, unwitnessed durations. Earth scientists must retrodict the processes that result in the reefs as seen today.

2. The recognition that *complex systems act over the Earth as whole* (e.g., the several "spheres": hydrosphere, geosphere, atmosphere, and their interaction with the biosphere, including the anthroposphere), as well as analysis of their subsystems on more regional and local scales.

3. *The conceptualization of phenomena through time and across space and at scales from atomic to planetary.* The concept of "deep time," both as a theoretical construct and as exemplified by the construction of the geologic timescale, is central to Earth systems thinking.

4. *The need for visual representations* to convey Earth systems phenomena as well as high demands placed upon spatial reasoning. For example, spatial concepts are inherent to geologic and contour maps as well as three-dimensional models of Earth's dynamic processes, such as ocean currents and storms.

5. *The integration across scales of solutions to problems.* Recognizing the ways in which a single phenomenon can have impacts at different spatial scales is required for deep understanding of Earth science. For example, the validation of meteor impact hypotheses with evidence gathered across scales from mineral crystal to regional topography is an excellent example of the need to work across multiple scales at once.

6. *Retrospective scientific thinking and retrodictive reasoning* are unique to Earth and space sciences. To unravel processes that took place millions of years ago, Earth and space scientists have developed a distinctive way of thinking that involves retrospection. Geological inquiry applies knowledge of present-day processes in order to draw conclusions about the nature of the materials, processes, and environments in the past.

The recent publication of the NGSS (Achieve, Inc., 2013) and the increase in attention to individual Earth systems as well as overarching ESS provides a hopeful foundation for revision of how we approach ESS instruction in classrooms. At the same time, standards do not always have the hoped-for impact; Kumar (2013) notes that reforms to Earth science instruction in response to standards developed in the 1990s never completely materialized. Some significant challenges to ensuring that ESS instruction experiences reform in the K–12 system include the inclusion of ESS on state science assessments, the hiring of teachers with strong ESS backgrounds, and explicit classroom time devoted to ESS instruction across grade levels. Collaboration among scientists, teacher educators, and school systems will be necessary if the promise of the NGSS for ESS is to be realized.

An Example of Curricular Research—ESS in Israel

The Earth science education group of Weizmann Institute, Israel, working under the leadership of the first author, has conducted an in-depth, longitudinal study of curricula that encourage systems thinking skills over the last decade. This study includes a series of three independent studies with 8th-grade (13–14 years old) junior high students (Ben-Zvi-Assaraf & Orion, 2005a, 2005b, 2010b), 4th-grade (9–10 years old) elementary students

(Ben-Zvi-Assaraf and Orion, 2010a), and 11th- to 12th-grade (16–18 years old) high school students (Orion & Bassis, 2008). The extensive investigation of this set of curricula, conducted over many years, is an example of ESS education and research in practice that can serve as an exemplar for other scholars.

The three studies were based on an Earth systems curriculum that was developed and modified to align with each age level and specific national standards. All three programs consisted of three components: inquiry-based, learner-centered, and integration of the lab, outdoor, computer, and classroom learning environments. The elementary and the junior high program, ranging from 30 to 45 hours exclusive of field trips, were implemented as part of a "Science for All" curriculum with a focus on the water cycle and systems thinking skills. The high school program includes about 400 teaching hours and focuses on learning about Earth systems and interrelationships, such as biogeochemical cycles in the context of plate tectonics; higher-order thinking skills related to cyclic and dynamic thinking; environmental problems in the context of Earth systems; and independent investigation of an Earth system.

Although the three programs differ in terms of target student age, content, extent of instructional time, and cognitive demands on students, they share several common characteristics that are important for student development of systems thinking and recognition of the broader societal importance of ESS understanding. This includes use of authentic questions that students can explore, motivation of students to deal with abstract chemical or physical concepts in the context of Earth systems, significant inquiry-based learning, and use of real-world phenomena to provide meaningful context. Through this work, students were encouraged to develop environmental insight based on an understanding of the systemic and cyclic mechanisms that govern our planet (Orion, 1993, 2002); this insight often emerged in response to knowledge-integration activities, such as concept maps or drawings, that required students to identify systems, create relationships, and organize concepts into a framework of connections.

The extent to which these curricular interventions encouraged the development of system thinking skills was investigated using a mixed-methods approach that combined qualitative and quantitative data sources from both students and teachers (Table 24.2).

Qualitative data were used to explore students' learning performances in their natural context and to better understand student cognitive abilities. Quantitative data were used in order to check correlation and causality between variables. The teachers' perspectives, including their views on the activities, served as secondary data sources. A suite of research tools was developed and modified for each age range; the complexity of these instruments illustrates the complex nature of ESS education research (Table 24.2). Students completed assessments measuring their ability to engage in systems thinking, ability to develop an evidence-based action plan, understanding of

TABLE 24.2
Learning Goals and Assessments Exemplar Curricular Study

Learning Goal	Assessment	Data Type	Population*
Dynamic thinking ability	Dynamic Thinking Questionnaire (DTQ)	Likert	E, J, H
Cyclic thinking ability	Cyclic Thinking Questionnaire (CTQ)	Likert	E, J, H
Ask effective questions for development of an evidence-based action plan	Factory Problem Solving (FPS) Inventory	Open-ended text	J, H
Recognize environmental influences on action plan	Dead Sea Problem Solving (DSPS) Inventory	Open-ended text	H
Ability to make and transfer generalizations	"My system" inventory	Drawing or concept map	H
Understand movement of matter and energy within and between systems	Transformation of Matter Inventory	Open-ended text	H
Understanding of processes and relationships in the subsurface	Hidden Dimension (HiDi) Inventory	Augmented drawing and open-ended text	H
Understanding of Earth systems	The Repertory-Grid	Interviews	E, J
Understanding of water in nature	Water drawings	Interviews	E, J
Engaged learning	Zoom-in observation	Observation	E, J, H
Systems thinking ability	Field trip reports	Open-ended text and images	E, J, H
Not applicable	Teacher perspectives	Open-ended	E, J, H

*E = elementary school, J = junior high school, H = high school

environmental influences on that plan, ability to generalize and transfer systems understanding, and understanding of the movement of matter and energy within and between systems. A detailed assessment explored student understanding of processes and relationships beneath Earth's surface by asking students questions about an ecological image (Figure 24.1).

Student field trip reports were also collected and analyzed to measure students' ability to identify the components and the processes of a system.

Figure 24.1 Hidden Dimension (HiDi) Inventory.

Students were interviewed before, during, and after the learning experience to gauge changes in their knowledge of Earth systems, with a particular focus on water for the elementary and junior high students. Students were also observed during the implementation of the curricula to provide a measure of learner engagement. Finally, teachers were interviewed weekly to provide an additional opinion about student engagement and efficacy of the curriculum.

Taken together, these studies provided invaluable insight into the impact of traditional and innovative curricula on student understanding of ESS. Two important outcomes emerged from this work: (1) recognition that the traditional junior high and high school science instruction had minimal impact on the development of systems thinking skills and (2) the development of the System Thinking Hierarchic (STH) multilayered model.

Traditional Science Learning and the Development of Systems Thinking Skills
Most of the students involved in these studies entered the 11th grade with very low levels of cyclic and dynamic thinking skills. In fact, dynamic thinking among 11th-grade students (before studying the ESS program) is just somewhat higher than that of 8th-grade students, and the cyclic thinking skills of both age groups are very similar. In addition, the system thinking abilities of fourth- and eighth-grade students are quite similar.

These data suggest that science studies in 7 years of schooling from the 4th grade till 11th grade contribute very little to the development of systems thinking skills among students. Furthermore, since the sample of each of the three studies represents a very large population of Israeli students, two conclusions follow: Maturity is a variable that has only small influence on the development

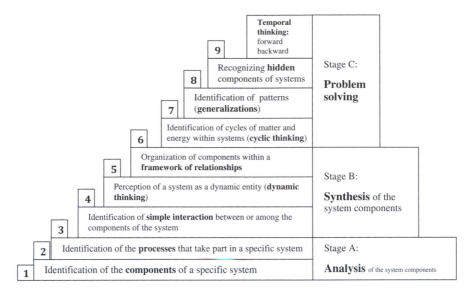

Figure 24.2 The System Thinking Hierarchic (STH) model.

of a cyclic thinking ability; and traditional learning in K–12 contributes very little to the development of system thinking skills among students. The second conclusion in particular warrants further consideration, especially as systems thinking and ESS gain importance in schooling standards (e.g., Achieve, Inc., 2013).

The Systems Thinking Hierarchic (STH) Multilayered Model

A hierarchic and pyramidal systems thinking structure emerged from data analysis in all of the studies (Ben-Zvi-Assaraf & Orion, 2010a, 2010b; Orion & Bassis, 2008). After instruction, almost all of the students were able to analyze the components and processes of the system; many fewer students could identify cycles of matter and energy, understand subsurface processes, or think backward and forward in time (Figure 24.2).

Students seem to move through three stages in their development as systems thinkers. At the Analysis Ability Stage, students are able to recognize components and processes in a system. Development of the ability to identify simple relationships among a few variables and the ability to represent a system as a network of variables and processes (cyclic thinking) occurs as students move into the Synthesis Ability Stage. At the final stage, Problem Solving, students are able to identify patterns within a system, to generalize across systems, and to transform a system forward (prediction) and backwards (retrodiction) in time. These identified stages are very well aligned with other research (e.g., Evagorou, Korfiatis, Nicolaou, & Constantinou, 2009). In addition, the student learning outcomes realized here are well aligned with the learning goals discussed earlier in this chapter. Although those goals were developed within the United States, the strong alignment of these outcomes in Israel with desired outcomes in the United States suggests that

this or a similar curriculum could be transferred effectively. For example, the ability to recognize patterns in a system, as well as the ability to understand how systems change over time (prediction and retrodiction) are themes identified here that are identified as cross-cutting themes within the NGSS. ESS education might be the ideal venue for building stronger international collaborations and ties.

However, the current STH model ignores a very important component of system thinking, which is the ability to identify feedback loops in a system (Ossimitz, 2000). This aspect does not appear in this review, since no attention was paid to this ability within any of the studies even at the high school level. This important ability should be tested in future studies. Moreover, it can serve as a prediction for the STH model, since according to the hierarchic nature of this model, it should be located at the higher levels of the abilities pyramid.

The Earth Systems Approach for Development of Systems Thinking Skills

Investigating Earth systems contributes to a significant improvement in the systems thinking abilities of students. Moreover, triangulation across studies indicates that the development of systems thinking skills occurs when links between components of the curriculum serve as a concrete model of a natural system, students actively engage in organizing and graphically representing knowledge, and instruction focuses on specific cycles (e.g., water) and processes (e.g., tectonic plate movement) of particular importance to ESS. The absence of one of these components impedes the development of systems thinking and, as a result, does not lead to meaningful learning. The incorporation of inquiry, outdoor learning, and knowledge integration activities each played important roles in student development; any one of these was insufficient for effective learning. These together provided opportunities for meaningful learning that manifests itself in long-term memory of episodes (Orion, 1993; Yunker, Orion, & Lernau, 2011).

As for the teacher, it seems that in order to create formative instruction, the teacher has to be aware of the importance of their role as instructor and mediator. Instruction that leads to the development of thinking skills requires a teacher who can identify the learner's characteristics and his/her cognitive strength and weakness, encourage students in the difficult task of processing the material on their own, and help students to shift from absorbers of information to processors of information into knowledge.

This example of an ESS curriculum that has undergone years of development, implementation, assessment, and revision provides insight into the potential value of ESS instruction for learners who need to gain the ability to engage in systems thinking. The significant classroom time required for implementation of these activities in Israel may be prohibitive elsewhere. We wonder how much time needs to be spent engaging students in inquiry, outdoor experiences, and knowledge integration before lasting effects on systems thinking might be observed.

Technology-Mediated Learning

In addition to the lab and field experiences used heavily in the Israeli curriculum just described, technology can play an important role in student learning about ESS. The influence of technology on student learning must be considered given the significant technological advances that have influenced both scientific and educational settings in recent years. We provide a brief review of relevant research related to technology-mediated learning of ESS; this review is meant to be illustrative of the potential of technology rather than exhaustive.

Laboratories enhanced by technology or completely embedded in virtual worlds are considered within the research literature: virtual field trips (e.g., Hurst, 1998; Stainfield, Fisher, Ford, & Solem, 2000), simulations (e.g., Jackson, 1997; Wang & Reeves, 2006), three-dimensional virtual environments (Pettit & Wu, 2008; Russell, Davies, & Totten, 2008), and specific technologies (e.g., Google Earth; Patterson, 2007). Although the existence of these studies indicates that Earth science learning is occurring in technology-mediated settings, much of this work lacks detailed research evidence that would allow for the drawing of specific conclusions about the value of technology in lab settings for Earth systems learning.

At the same time, a few studies are providing evidence that some technologies can improve student learning. Russell and colleagues (2008) provide evidence that use of 3D virtual environments offers students socially mediated learning experiences about the natural world that would not otherwise be available to many students, particularly those in urban settings. This work uses technology to generate social interactions, known to enhance learning in the context of Earth science. Patterson (2007) employed geographic information system (GIS) based technology, specifically Google Earth, in seventh-grade classrooms to enhance student ability to think critically about problems in geology and geography. This work suggests that critical thinking can be enhanced when the tools being used have a low technology barrier; that is, when learners can learn how to use technology quickly enough to allow attention to be predominantly focused on the underlying concepts being mediated by technology. Finally, Sanchez (2012) considered the role of visuospatial training in student ability to learn about the Earth. In this work, students played video games and then engaged in learning about plate tectonics; half of the study participants engaged in games that required visuospatial skill, while the other half engaged nonvisuospatial games. The domain-specific impact of this game play was interesting—visuospatial game players experienced both increased visuospatial skill and greater facility at learning about plate tectonics than their counterparts. This finding suggests that technology that enhances domain-general skills, like visuospatial skill, can have impacts on domain-specific learning. This is particularly important for ESS, where many domains and skills from those domains must come together to help learners understand the spatial, temporal, and physical characteristics of ESS processes.

Challenges for Moving Forward With ESS Education

As noted, Earth systems concepts are given much less attention in the precollege and undergraduate curriculum than the more traditional sciences of physics, chemistry, and biology, yet the major challenges facing society are fundamentally related to the Earth system. This disconnect between educational need and practice perhaps arises from an educational system that focuses on providing students with a solid foundation of information before allowing students to think independently. This is reflected in standards that focus on details rather than on principles and is evident throughout all levels of education and across countries. Certainly, society is ill prepared to address environmental issues threatening our economic, agricultural, and urban systems, and we argue that society will continue to be woefully unprepared to deal with issues like climate change and sustainable energy until we give ESS equal educational footing.

Understanding Earth System Science requires integrated, systems thinking. Reasoning at a systems level is not something that tends to come easily or that is taught in our schools. Research has shown that students often view the Earth and its environs as static and unchanging, or that change occurs without any underlying purpose or cause. Some of this likely arises from the lack of explicit attention paid to concepts that are nearly intuitive to scientists yet that are mysterious to students. While attempts have been made to build curricular interventions that make the causality of Earth phenomena clear, most instruction in

ESS still focuses on characteristics of the Earth rather than underlying overarching principles. This issue is clearly articulated by Kumar (2013) in describing the challenge to reforming Earth-related instruction in U.S. schools. In addition, the lack of teacher education in Earth, ocean, space, or similar sciences in the United States is extremely problematic. The new NGSS, with a strong focus on Earth and space science, may change the landscape for teacher education and provide new opportunities for ESS teaching and learning in K–12 schools.

The political challenges to teaching ESS need to be considered seriously as we develop best practices for ESS instruction and move forward with a research agenda for ESS education research. Perhaps more than other disciplines, ESS deals with concepts that have broad societal impacts economically, politically, and socially. ESS instruction dealing with water pollution, for example, must recognize that solutions proposed by science may be at odds with solutions that align with economic proposals. Issues such as climate change that have broad global and temporal reach are even more intertwined with how people respond to and engage with science that sits at the edge of controversy.

Finally, embracing the "science for all" paradigm requires that science instruction be accessible to everyone. This includes nontraditional students, comprising at least those students with disabilities and students from groups traditionally less likely to access education. For college-level instruction, older students returning to school in the face of a changing work environment present unique challenges not faced in earlier generations. While little work has been done on ensuring educational access for all, we are encouraged by efforts that take advantage of new technologies, as well as the seeming openness of the Earth science community to equality in education (Atchison & Martinez-Frias, 2012).

A Proposed Research Agenda for the Next Decade

ESS education research at the beginning of the second decade of the 21st century has many strengths. We have a solid understanding of the alternative conceptions that students are bringing into the Earth science classroom and are beginning to pinpoint instructional strategies that are most effective for student learning. Earth science educators recognize the importance of diverse learning environments for students, including the value of outdoors, laboratory, classroom, and computer learning experiences for building an informed population. This informed populace is expected to then make decisions about how humans should and should not interact with the Earth system, as well as decisions about steps that must be taken to mitigate serious alterations to Earth processes, such as climate change, that result from human activities. A research agenda for the next decade should focus in on this decision-making process; very little of the work being done by geoscience

education researchers addresses questions about the relationship between learning of concepts, often the focus of Earth scientists, and the ability to make decisions about Earth–human interactions. Here, we might consider closer interactions with the surprisingly distinct environmental education community, a community that focuses specifically on human impacts on Earth. ESS education adds an important layer to that conversation, considering in addition the impact of the planet on human society.

Effective future research in ESS education should consider all of the variables that are known to be important for decision making about the Earth system. While some work has considered the role that educational interventions play in changing how students support decisions about complex topics (e.g., Grace, 2009), ESS education has still not fully begun to ask questions about real-world impacts. For example, we know that people make decisions about the environment that are not always grounded in a rational understanding of science (Bell & Lederman, 2003). Decision making in the face of severe weather, such as whether to leave your home as a hurricane approaches, involves complex interactions among knowledge, affect, economics, and societal restrictions. As natural disasters have played a larger role in global discourse, largely made possible through the nearly instantaneous real-time news and video feeds of the Internet, ESS education has become increasingly important and clearly inadequate. The challenge of future research is to consider how to move ESS instruction into greater prominence within our formal educational systems and informal efforts and to investigate the best practices available for generating a global community well positioned to act in the face of another Hurricane Katrina, Pacific tsunami, or dramatic sea ice melt due to climate change.

In light of these growing global needs, we propose that the community focus on work that can build connections between real-world decision making and what happens in the classroom or other educational setting. In particular, we encourage high-quality research grounded in valid and reliable approaches that focus on:

1. *Environmental insight:* As already mentioned, systems thinking skills are crucial for the development of environmental insight. Very little research has considered the relationship of systems thinking ability to environmental insight, including the mechanisms that can engage and assist students in becoming better systems thinkers. Exploring the influence of systems thinking on the development of environmental insight is thus suggested as a practical research agenda. In addition, the meaning of being an environmentally insightful citizen generally focuses on environmental literacy and decision making. The conceptualization of what it means to be an effective decision maker around environmental issues is a particularly fruitful area for future research. This would include merging research pathways in multiple disciplines (e.g., ESS education,

geoscience education, environmental economics, etc.) to build a deeper and broader understanding of fruitful environmental insight among the general public.

2. *Training of ESS education researchers:* Earth System Science is by its very nature interdisciplinary across natural and some social sciences, and researchers looking into education and learning similarly span many disciplines. As a consequence, the most effective ESS education researchers are those scholars who are able to transcend disciplinary boundaries and move seamlessly between different fields of inquiry. For example, a scholar investigating the impact of formal ESS education on decision-making processes of the general public would need to be well versed in concepts and research norms from the Earth System Science, formal science education, public understanding of science, and decision-making fields. These fields are themselves interdisciplinary, potentially calling upon scholarship in Earth sciences, education, psychology, learning science, social science, communication, and beyond. Training new researchers with the fluidity to move across disciplinary boundaries is a grand challenge that faces many fields, and certainly something that requires investigation for ESS education. At the very least, we need evidence-based training opportunities for scholars to expand our understanding of how people perceive, learn about, and understand Earth systems, and we need to consider how we can more effectively value interdisciplinary scholarship that belongs in many traditional departments. A well-trained next generation of scholars is absolutely necessary if we are to meet the pressing need for building learning experiences that enhance environmental insight and decision-making ability. Practically, we suggest exploration of the factors that influence the development of systems thinking skills among precollege students and university students and the implementation of the ESS approach within schools and universities. The STH model could serve as a powerful working hypothesis for this mission. That model was developed on the basis of a small local sample of students of one culture who used specific learning materials, and there is a great need to test and refine this preliminary model and its research tools within broader contexts and to expand it to university students as well.

3. *Conceptual understanding:* The significant research on conceptual understanding among K–12 and college students, teachers, and the general public provides strong evidence for the presence or absence of understanding of specific core ideas in the Earth and related sciences. At the same time, the relative dearth of research into ESS understanding points toward a new direction for conceptual understanding research. As discussed earlier, traditional Earth science instruction focuses on isolated ideas. As we move toward the ESS instruction called for in the NGSS and other

documents, we must start to ask questions about how well learners understand and can reason about interacting processes and systems. This becomes uniquely important when asking questions about how well individuals are equipped to make decisions about human impacts on the complex Earth system.

4. *Decision making:* Decision making about human–Earth interactions is perhaps the most important research direction driving science today. Environmental decision making has roots in many fields, from environmental economics to education. The role of ESS education in decision-making research has until now been quite limited, although work is beginning to emerge that asks tantalizing questions about how people make decisions in the face of Earth phenomena (e.g., Drost, 2013). Investigation of the mechanisms people use to make decisions about the Earth, both in terms of human impacts on the planet and planetary impacts on humans, is needed to understand how to engender effective decision making among our citizenry. While the formal education system focuses most closely on content understanding (e.g., National Research Council [NRC], 1996), the ultimate goal of science education beyond production of new scientists is the development of a scientifically literate public who can make informed decisions about the world (e.g., Hazen & Trefil, 2009; Rutherford & Ahlgren, 1991). This recommendation aligns with our observation that the research base on affective outcomes of ESS instruction is limited; decision making and emotional responses are often tied together.

5. *Expertise research:* In order to provide effective educational experiences for ESS students, we must first understand what it means to be an Earth system scientist. This includes study of Earth system scientists in traditional fields, such as geoscience and atmospheric science, as well as those working on the cutting edge of new fields such as biogeochemistry and climate change. Expertise research sets the stage for reconsideration of the curriculum used to train new Earth system scientists and perhaps even the goals of ESS education overall. In addition, ESS is inherently interdisciplinary. Interdisciplinary fields bring with them a host of challenges related to the need for individuals to cross boundaries, for institutions to evaluate work in new ways, and for communities to recognize the value of and reward, individuals asking nontraditional questions and using techniques borrowed from other fields (American Association for the Advancement of Science, 2012; Andre & Frochot, 2013).

6. *New technology:* Technological advances in how we interact with and learn about the world are overwhelming and ever changing. Technology-enhanced interactions with the Earth are becoming increasingly common, from programs that allow easy visualization of broad temporal and spatial patterns (e.g., Google Earth) to smart phone applications (e.g., Google app

Field Trip) and smart glasses (e.g., Google Glass) that annotate the world on the move. Within the classroom, massively open online courses (MOOCs) have taken the world of higher education by storm. These free offerings, open essentially to anyone with Internet access, are becoming a new bandwagon to which many international institutions are tethering themselves. While research into the efficacy of online education, free-choice learning, mobile apps, and general technology can certainly inform technology development, these new innovations call for researchers to build high-quality investigations of how students engage with, learn from, and navigate through the variety of technologies that are intended to enhance our understanding of and decision making about the planet.

Acknowledgments

We thank our many colleagues both within and outside our labs for many years of fruitful discussions and collaboration that have culminated in the ideas presented here. We also thank Karen McNeal and Kristen St. John for reviews of an earlier version of this chapter.

References

Achieve, Inc. on behalf of the twenty-six states and partners that collaborated on the NGSS. (2013). *The next generation science standards.* Retrieved June 15, 2013, from www.nextgenscience.org

American Association for the Advancement of Science. (2012). *Facilitating interdisciplinary research and education: A practical guide.* Retrieved June 15, 2013, from www.aaas.org/report/facilitating-interdisciplinary-research-and-education-practical-guide

Andre. J.C., & Frochot, C. (2013). Problems arising in evaluation of interdisciplinary scientific research for innovation. *International Journal of Innovation Science, 5*(2), 103–12.

Atchison, C., & Martinez-Frias, J. (2012). Inclusive geoscience instruction. *Nature Geoscience, 5*(6), 366–366.

Ault, C.R. (1994). Research on problem solving. In D.L. Gabel (Ed.), *Handbook of research on science teaching and learning* (pp. 269–283). New York: MacMillian Publishing.

Bardar, E.M., Prather, E.E., Brecher, K., & Slater, T.F. (2006). Development and validation of the Light and Spectroscopy Concept Inventory. *Astronomy Education Review, 5*(2), 103.

Bell, R.L., & Lederman, N.G. (2003). Understandings of the nature of science and decision making on science and technology based issues. *Science Education, 87*(3), 352–377.

Ben-Zvi-Assaraf, O., & Orion, N. (2005a). The development of system thinking skills in the context of Earth System education. *Journal of Research in Science Teaching, 42*, 1–43.

Ben-Zvi-Assaraf, O., & Orion, N. (2005b). A study of junior high students' perceptions of the water cycle. *Journal of Geosciences Education, 53*, 366–373.

Ben-Zvi-Assaraf, O., & Orion, N. (2009). a design based research of an earth systems based environmental curriculum. *Eurasia Journal of Mathematics, Science & Technology Education, 5*(1), 47–62.

Ben-Zvi-Assaraf, O., & Orion, N. (2010a). System thinking skills at the elementary school level. *Journal of Research in Science Teaching, 47*, 540–563.

Ben-Zvi-Assaraf, O., & Orion, N. (2010b). Four case studies and six years later: Developing system thinking skills in junior high School and sustaining them over time. *Journal of Research in Science Teaching, 47*, 1253–1280.

Bickmore, B.R., Thompson, K.R., Grandy, D.A., & Tomlin, T. (2009). Science as storytelling for teaching the nature of science and the science-religion interface. *Journal of Geoscience Education, 57*(3), 178–190.

Booth-Sweeney, L. & Sterman, J.D. (2000). Bathtub dynamics: Initial results of a systems thinking inventory. *System Dynamics Review, 16*(4), 249–286. Retrieved February 28, 2014 from http://web.mit.edu/jsterman/www/Bathtub%20Dynamics.pdf

Booth-Sweeney, L., & Sterman, J.D. (2007). Thinking about systems: Student and teacher conceptions of natural and social systems. *System Dynamics Review, 23*, 285–312.

Boyle, A., Maguire, S., Martin, A., Milsom, C., Nash, R., Rawlinson, S., & Conchie, S. (2007). Fieldwork is good: The student perception and the affective domain. *Journal of Geography in Higher Education, 31*(2), 299–317.

Catley, K.M., & Novick, L.R. (2009). Digging deep: Exploring college students' knowledge of macroevolutionary time. *Journal of Research in Science Teaching, 46*(3), 311–332.

Cheek, K.A. (2010). Commentary: A summary and analysis of twenty-seven years of geoscience conceptions research. *Journal of Geoscience Education, 58*(3), 122–134.

Clark, S.K., Libarkin, J.C., Kortz, K.M., & Jordan, S.C. (2011). Alternative conceptions of plate tectonics held by nonscience undergraduates. *Journal of Geoscience Education, 59*(4), 251–262.

Dickerson, D., Callahan, T.J., Van Sickle, M., & Hay, G. (2005). Students' conceptions of scale regarding groundwater. *Journal of Geoscience Education, 53*, 374–380.

Draper, F. (1993). A proposed sequence for developing system thinking in a grades 4–12 curriculum. *System Dynamic Review, 9*(2), 207–214.

Driver, R., Guesne, E., & Tiberghien, A. (Eds.). (1985). *Children's ideas in Science.* Philadelphia: Open University Press.

Driver, R., Squires, A., Rushworth, P., & Wood-Robinson, V. (1994). Making sense of secondary science: Research into children's ideas. New York: Routledge.

Drost, R. (2013). Memory and decision making: Determining action when the sirens sound. *Weather, Climate, and Society, 5*(1), 43–54.

Emery, R.E. (1992). Parenting in context: Systemic thinking about parental conflict and its influence on children. *Journal of Consulting and Clinical Psychology, 60*, 909–912.

Evagorou, M., Korfiatis, K., Nicolaou, C., & Constantinou, C, (2009). An investigation of the potential of interactive simulations for developing system thinking skills in elementary school: A case study with fifth graders and sixth graders. *International Journal of Science Education, 31*, 655–674.

Faughnan, J.G., & Elson, R. (1998). Information technology and the clinical curriculum: Some predictions and their implications for the class of 2003. *Academic Medicine, 73*, 766–769.

Fordyce, D. (1998). The development of system thinking in engineering education: An interdisciplinary model. *European Journal of Engineering Education, 13*, 283–292.

Francek, M. (2013). A compilation and review of over 500 geoscience misconceptions. *International Journal of Science Education, 35*(1), 31–64.

Frank, M. (2000). Engineering systems thinking and systems thinking. *Systems Engineering, 3*, 63–168.

Goldstone, R.L., & Wilensky, U. (2008). Promoting transfer complex systems principles. *Journal of the Learning Sciences, 17*, 465–516.

Grace, M. (2009). Developing high quality decision making discussions about biological conservation in a normal classroom setting. *International Journal of Science Education, 31*(4), 551–570.

Graczyk, S.L. (1993). Get with the system: General system theory for business officials. *School Business Affairs, 59*, 16–20.

Gruenewald, D.A., & Smith, G.A. (2007). *Place-based education in the global age: Local diversity.* Ann Arbor, MI: Lawrence Erlbaum Associates.

Hambrick, D.Z., Libarkin, J.C., Petcovic, H.L., Baker, K.M., Elkins, J., Callahan, C.N., Rench, T., Turner, S., & Ladue, N.D. (2012). A test of the circumvention-of-limits hypothesis in scientific problem solving: The case of geological bedrock mapping. *Journal of Experimental Psychology. General, 141*, 397–403.

Hazen, R.M., & Trefil, J. (2009). *Science matters: Achieving scientific literacy.* New York: Random House.

Hmelo-Silver, C.E., Marathe, S., & Liu, L. (2007). Fish swim, rocks sit, and lungs breathe: Expert–novice understanding of complex systems. *Journal of the Learning Sciences, 16*, 307–331.

Hmelo-Silver, C.E., & Pfeffer, M.G. (2004). Comparing expert and novice understanding of a complex system from the perspective of structures, behaviors, and functions. *Cognitive Science, 28*, 127–138.

Hurst, S.D. (1998). Use of "virtual" field trips in teaching introductory geology. *Computers and Geosciences, 24*(7), 653–658.

Israel, A.L. (2012). Putting geography education into place: What geography educators can learn from place-based education, and vice versa. *Journal of Geography, 111*(2), 76–81. doi:10.1080/0022134 1.2011.583264

Jackson, D.F. (1997). Case studies of microcomputer and interactive video simulations in middle school earth science teaching. *Journal of Science Education and Technology, 6*(2), 127–141.

Jacobson, M.J., & Wilensky, U. (2006). Complex systems in education: Scientific and educational importance and implications for the learning sciences. *Journal of the Learning Sciences, 15*(1), 11–34.

Jolley, A., Lane, E., Kennedy, B., & Frappé-Sénéclauze, T.-P. (2012). SPESS: A new instrument for measuring student perceptions in Earth and ocean science. *Journal of Geoscience Education, 60*(1), 83–91.

Kali, Y., Orion, N., & Eylon B. (2003). Effect of knowledge integration activities on students' perception of the Earth's crust as a cyclic system. *Journal of Research in Science Teaching, 40*, 545–565. doi:10.1002/tea.10096

Kelemen, D., & Rosset, E. (2009). The human function compunction: Teleological explanation in adults. *Cognition, 111*(1), 138–143.

Kern, E.L., & Carpenter, J.R. (1984). Enhancement of student values, interest and attitudes in earth science through a field-oriented approach. *Journal of Geological Education, 32*(5), 299–305.

Kim, D.H. (1999). Introduction to system thinking. Westford, MA: Pegasus Communications, Inc.

King, C. (2008). Geoscience education: An overview. *Studies in Science Education, 44*(2), 187–222.

Kumar, M. (2013). New K–12 science education standards may face implementation challenges. *EOS, 94*(18), 166–167.

LaDue, N.D., & Clark, S.K. (2012). Educator perspectives on earth system science literacy: Challenges and priorities. *Journal of Geoscience Education, 60*(4), 372–383.

Lawton, J. (2001). Earth system science. *Science, 292*(5524), 1965.

Lesh, R. (2006). Modeling students modeling abilities: The teaching and learning of complex systems in education. *The Journal of the Learning Sciences, 15*, 45–52.

Lewis, J.P. (1998). *Mastering project management: Applying advanced concepts of system thinking, control and evaluation, resource allocation.* New York: McGraw-Hill.

Libarkin, J. (2008). *Concept inventories in higher education science.* Commissioned paper for the Board on Science Education of the National Academies. Retrieved from http://blogs.ethz.ch/didacbiol/files/2012/07/BOSE-Conf-2008-Libarkin.pdf

Libarkin, J.C. (2001). Development of an assessment of student conception of the nature of science. *Journal of Geoscience Education, 49*(5), 435–442.

Libarkin, J.C., & Anderson, S.W. (2005). Assessment of learning in entry-level geoscience courses: Results from the Geoscience Concept Inventory. *Journal of Geoscience Education, 53*(4), 394.

Libarkin, J.C., and Anderson, S.W. (2006). The geoscience concept inventory: application of Rasch analysis to concept inventory development in higher education. In X. Liu and W. Boone (Eds.), *Applications of Rasch measurement in science education* (pp. 45–73). Maple Grove, MN: JAM Press.

Libarkin, J.C., Jardeleza, S.E., & McElhinny, T.L. (2014). The role of concept inventories in course assessment. In V. Tong (Ed.), *Geoscience: Research-enhanced education in universities* (pp. 275–297), New York: Springer.

Libarkin, J.C., & Kurdziel, J.P. (2006). Ontology and the teaching of earth system science. *Journal of Geoscience Education, 54*(3), 408.

Libarkin, J.C., & Schneps, M.H. (2012). Elementary children's retrodictive reasoning about earth science. *International Electronic Journal of Elementary Education, 5*(1), 47–62.

Libarkin, J.C., Ward, E.M.G., Anderson, S.W., Kortemeyer, G., & Raeburn, S.P. (2011). Revisiting the Geoscience Concept Inventory: A call to the community. *GSA Today, 21*, 26–28.

Llerandi Roman, P.A. (2007). *The effects of a professional development geoscience education institute upon secondary school science teachers in Puerto Rico* (Ph.D.). Purdue University, United States—Indiana. Retrieved from http://search.proquest.com.proxy2.cl.msu.edu/docview/304840730/abstract/13C82EBE1B71CB667CC/15?accountid=12598

Mandinach, E.B. (1989). Model-building and the use of computer simulation of dynamic systems. *Journal of Educational Computing Research, 5*, 221–243.

Mayer, V.J. (1991). Framework for earth systems. *Education Science Activities, 28*, 8–9.

Mayer, V.J., & Fortner, R.W. (Eds.). (1995). *Science is a study of earth: A resource guide for science curriculum restructure.* Columbus: Ohio State University Research Foundation.

McConnell, D.A., Steer, D.N., Owens, K.D., Borowski, W., Dick, J., Foos, A., & Heaney, P.J. (2006). Using concepts to assess and improve student conceptual understanding in introductory geoscience courses. *Journal of Geoscience Education, 54*(1), 61–68.

McConnell, D.A., & Van Der Hoeven Kraft, K.J. (2011). Affective domain and student learning in the geosciences. *Journal of Geoscience Education, 59*(3), 106–110. doi:10.5408/1.3604828

McNeal, K.S., Miller, H.R., & Herbert, B.E. (2008). The effect of using inquiry and multiple representations on introductory geology students' conceptual model development of coastal eutrophication. *Journal of Geoscience Education, 56*(3), 201–211.

Miele, E.A., & Powell, W.G. (2010). Science and the city: Community cultural and natural resources at the core of a place-based, science teacher preparation program. *Journal of College Science Teaching, 40*(2), 40–44.

National Research Council (NRC). (1996). *National science education standards.* Washington, DC: National Academies Press.

Orion, N. (1993). A model for the development and implementation of field trips as an integral part of the science curriculum. *School Science & Mathematics, 93*, 6.

Orion, N. (2002). An earth systems curriculum development model. In V. Mayer (Ed.), *Global science literacy* (pp. 159–168). Dordrecht, the Netherlands: Kluwer.

Orion, N. (2007). A holistic approach for science education for all. *Eurasia journal for mathematics, science and technology education, 3*, 99–106.

Orion, N., & Ault, C. (2007). Learning earth sciences. In S. Abell & N.G. Lederman (Eds.), *Handbook of research on science teaching and learning* (pp. 653–688). Mahwah, NJ: Lawrence Erlbaum Associates.

Orion, N., & Bassis, T. (2008). *Characterization of high school students' system thinking skills in the context of earth systems.* National Association for Research in Science Teaching, (NARST) Symposium, Baltimore, MD.

Orion, N., Ben-Menacham, O and Shur, Y. (2008). Raising scholastic achievement in minority-reached classes through earth systems teaching. *Journal of Geosciences Education, 55*, 469–477.

Orion, N. & Cohen, C. (2007). A design-based research of an oceanography module as a part of the Israeli high school earth sciences program. *Journal of Geographie und ihre Didaktik, 4*, 246–259.

Orion, N., & Fortner, R.W. (2003). Mediterranean models for integrating environmental education and earth sciences through earth systems education. *Mediterranean Journal of Educational Studies, 8*(1), 97–111.

Ossimitz, G. (2000). *Teaching system dynamics and systems thinking in Austria and Germany.* Proceedings of the 18th International Conference of the System Dynamics Society, Bergen, Norway.

Parker, L.C., Krockover, G.H., Eichinger, D.C., & Lasher-Trapp, S. (2008). Ideas about the nature of science held by undergraduate atmospheric science students. *Bulletin of the American Meteorological Society, 89*(11), 1681–1688.

Patterson, T.C. (2007). Google Earth as a (not just) geography education tool. *Journal of Geography, 106*(4), 145–152.

Petcovic, H., & Ruhf, R. (2008). Geoscience conceptual knowledge of preservice elementary teachers: Results from the Geoscience Concept Inventory. *Journal of Geoscience Education, 56*(3), 251–260.

Pettit, C., & Wu, Y. (2008). A virtual knowledge world for natural resource management. In C. Pettit, W. Cartwright, I. Bishop, K. Lowell, D. Pullar, & D. Duncan (Eds.), *Landscape analysis and visualisation* (pp. 533–550). Heidelberg: Springer Berlin. Retrieved from http://link.springer.com/chapter/10.1007/978-3-540-69168-6_26

Pyle, E.J. (2008). A model of inquiry for teaching earth science. *Electronic Journal of Science Education, 12*(2). Retrieved from http://ejse.southwestern.edu/article/view/7770

Raia, F. (2008). Causality in complex dynamic systems: A challenge in earth systems science education. *Journal of Geoscience Education, 56*, 81–94.

Rossbacher, L. (2002). Geologic column: Knowing a place. *Geotimes, 47*, 48.

Russell, D., Davies, M., & Totten, I. (2008). GEOWORLDS: Utilizing Second Life to develop advanced geosciences knowledge. In *2008 Second IEEE International Conference on Digital Games and Intelligent Toys Based Education* (pp. 93–97). Presented at the 2008 Second IEEE International Conference on Digital Games and Intelligent Toys Based Education, Banff, AB, Canada. doi:10.1109/DIGI?.2008.50

Rutherford, F.J., & Ahlgren, A. (1991). *Science for all Americans* (2nd ed.). New York: Oxford University Press.

Sanchez, C.A. (2012). Enhancing visuospatial performance through video game training to increase learning in visuospatial science domains. *Psychonomic Bulletin & Review, 19*(1), 58–65.

Semken, S., & Butler Freeman, C.B. (2008). Sense of place in the practice and assessment of place-based science teaching. *Science Education, 92*(6), 1042–1057.

Senge, P.M. (1998). "Fifth discipline": Review and discussion. *System Practice and Action Research, 11*(3) 259–273.

Sexton, J.M. (2012). College students' conceptions of the role of rivers in canyon formation. *Journal of Geoscience Education, 60*(2), 168–178.

Sibley, D. (2009). A cognitive framework for reasoning with scientific models. *Journal of Geoscience Education, 57*(4), 255–263.

Sibley, D.F. (2005). Visual abilities and misconceptions about plate tectonics. *Journal of Geoscience Education, 53*, 471–477.

Sobel, D. (2004). *Place-based education: Connecting classrooms and communities.* Great Barrington, MA: The Orion Society.

Stainfield, J., Fisher, P., Ford, B., & Solem, M. (2000). International virtual field trips: A new direction? *Journal of Geography in Higher Education, 24*(2), 255–262.

Steed, M. (1992). Stella, a simulation construction kit: Cognitive processes and educational implications. *Journal of Computers in Mathematics and Science, 11*, 39–52.

Stokes, A., & Boyle, A.P. (2009). The undergraduate geoscience fieldwork experience: Influencing factors and implications for learning. *Geological Society of America Special Papers, 461*, 291–311.

Sunderlin, D. (2009). Integrative mapping of global-scale processes and patterns on "imaginary Earth" continental geometries: A teaching tool in an earth history course. *Journal of Geoscience Education, 57*(1), 73–81.

Teed, R., & Slattery, W. (2011). Changes in geologic time understanding in a class for preservice teachers. *Journal of Geoscience Education, 59*(3), 151–162.

Thomson, N., & Chapman Beall, S. (2008). An inquiry safari: What can we learn from skulls? *Evolution: Education and Outreach, 1*(2), 196–203.

Treagust, D.F. (1986). Evaluating students' misconceptions by means of diagnostic multiple choice items. *Research in Science Education, 16*, 199–207.

Ullmer, E.J. (1986). Work design in organizations: Comparing the organizational elements models and the ideal system approach. *Educational Technology, 26*(4), 12–18.

Verhoeff, R.P., Waarlo, A.J., & Boersma, K.T. (2008). Systems modeling and the development of coherent understanding of cell biology. *International Journal of Science Education, 30*, 543–568.

Wandersee, J.H., Mintzes, J.J., & Novak, J.D. (1994). Research on alternative conceptions in science. in D.L. Gabel (Ed.), *Handbook of research on science teaching and learning* (pp. 177–210). New York: MacMillian.

Wang, S.K., & Reeves, T.C. (2006). The effects of a web-based learning environment on student motivation in a high school earth science course. *Educational Technology Research and Development, 54*(6), 597–621.

Wiggins, G.P., & McTighe, J. (2005). *Understanding by design* (2nd ed.). Alexandria, VA: Association for Supervision & Curriculum Development.

Wilensky, U., & Resnick, M. (1999). Thinking in levels: A dynamic systems approach to making sense of the world. *Journal of Science Education and Technology, 8*, 3–19.

Woodhouse, J., & Knapp, C. (2000). *Place-based curriculum and instruction.* ERIC Document Reproduction Service No. EDO-RC-00–6.

Yunker, M., Orion, N., & Lernau, H. (2011). Merging playfulness with the formal science curriculum in an outdoor learning environment. *Children, Youth and Environments, 21*(2), 271–293.

Zeichner, K. (2010). Rethinking the connections between campus courses and field experiences in college- and university-based teacher education. *Journal of Teacher Education, 61*(1–2), 89–99.

25

Environmental Education

JUSTIN DILLON

Introduction

The publication of the first ever *International Handbook of Research on Environmental Education* (Stevenson, Brody, Dillon, & Wals, 2013) is recognition that the field has matured and should now be seen as separate from, albeit inextricably linked to, science education. Scholars can choose to submit their work to a number of journals exclusively devoted to publishing research in environmental education at both international and national levels, whereas for many years there was only one (the *Journal of Environmental Education*—first published in 1969). The major science education journals increasingly publish research in environmental education (mainly as individual studies but sometimes as special issues; see, for example, Russell & Dillon, 2010), and the European Science Education Research Association (ESERA) and the National Association for Research in Science Teaching (NARST) both recognize the field through their special interest groups and their conference strands. In the first edition of this *Handbook*, Paul Hart suggested that among the reasons for this expansion in the field were "increasingly more pervasive and global environmental issues, changing societal expectations, and educational reform" (2007, p. 689). This chapter builds on some of the ideas developed by Hart as well as developing the line of thinking William Scott and I began in the editorial for a special issue of the *International Journal of Science Education* (*IJSE*; Dillon & Scott, 2002) that focused on "perspectives on environmental education-related research in science education."

The strong identity of environmental education within and beyond science education hides the fact that the term continues to be contested and that its boundaries are rather fuzzy. Some indication of this fuzziness can be gleaned from the summary of the focus of the NARST environmental education strand: "Ecological education; experiential education; education for sustainable development; indigenous science" (NARST, 2013). Those descriptors

recognize the history of the field, its links with other aspects of outdoor education, and its rather uneasy relationship with issues such as sustainability and indigenous (or traditional ecological) knowledge.

In the *IJSE* special issue editorial, Scott and I suggested a shift in the emphasis of science education:

> Perhaps we should focus on helping learners deal with the sheer complexity and splendour of the environment as well as looking to use the local environment as a vehicle for developing understanding of the more mundane aspects of the science curriculum—in other words, shift from seeing "environment" as a focus for the consideration of science concepts to seeing a science education as one which, properly, seeks to help students understand environmental issues in the context of their lives, and their lives in the context of environmental issues.
> (Dillon & Scott, 2002, p. 1112)

Since that editorial was written, it has become clearer how science education could evolve to "help students understand environmental issues in the context of their lives." Part of the answer lies in acknowledging the growing concerns about the unsustainability of our existing lifestyles—an issue that will concern future generations as well as ourselves.

What is presented here may also be viewed as the latest in a series of reviews of environmental education research (Dillon, 2003; Hart, 2003, 2007; Hart & Nolan, 1999; Hines, Hungerford, & Tomera, 1986/1987; Iozzi, 1981; Marcinkowski, 2003; Posch, 1993; Reid & Nikel, 2003; Rickinson, 2001, 2003; Sauvé & Berryman, 2003; Williams, 1996). However, there is one contextual issue that needs to be mentioned immediately. It almost goes without saying that environmental discourses permeate our lives. Any extreme of weather is automatically linked rightly or wrongly to global warming; anything we buy is likely to have some indication of how "eco-friendly" or "organic" it is or how its packaging can be recycled; anyone standing

TABLE 25.1
Discourses of the Environment

Environment as nature . . .	*to be appreciated, respected, preserved*: dualistic, Cartesian interpretation; humans are removed from nature
Environment as a resource . . .	*to be managed:* Judeo-Christian view (book of Genesis)—this is our collective biophysical heritage and we must sustain it as it is deteriorating and wasting away
Environment as a problem . . .	*to be solved:* the biophysical environment, the life-support system is threatened by pollution and degradation. We must learn to preserve its quality and restore it (problem-solving skills emphasized)
Environment as a place to live . . .	*to know and learn about, to plan for, to take care of:* day-to-day environment—characterized by its human, sociocultural, technological, and historical components
Environment as the biosphere . . .	*in which we all live together, in the future:* "Spaceship Earth" (Fuller) and Gaia (Lovelock)—self-regulating organism
Environment as a community project . . .	*in which to get involved*
Environment of a human collectivity . . .	*a shared living place, political concern, the focus of critical analysis*: solidarity, democracy, and personal and collective involvement in order to participate in the evolution of the community

(Sauvé, 1996)

for political office displays their attitudes to environmentalism openly whether they be ally or critic. As such, environmental education has a sociopolitical undertone—and, accordingly, research in the field, as Hart noted in 2007, invariably has a political dimension, whether it be implicit or explicit.

What Is Meant by the "Environment"?

Before getting into the historical development of environmental education, it is worth considering a key term—the "environment." The relationship between the "environment" and sustainable development is particularly important if we are to make sense of how environmental education and science education relate to sustainability (an issue that is returned to later in the chapter). These issues affect both researchers *and* practitioners, as we shall see.

Lucie Sauvé (1996) summarizes different ways of conceptualizing the environment and indicates how they are related (see Table 25.1). Sauvé's taxonomy makes it easier to see how a science teacher, a geography teacher, a warden of an environmental education center, and the head of education at a natural history museum might have quite different perspectives on the environment that might affect what and how they teach, particularly in relation to sustainability, values, and knowledge.

What Sauvé's analysis does is identify a number of philosophical positions that allow us to understand why "environmental education" continues to be a contested term. These different discourses explain, to a degree, why environmental education research and practice have the political dimension mentioned earlier.

A Historical Dimension

As environmental education has developed so much since the 1960s, it is important to set current developments in a historical context. As Jo-Anne Ferreira (2013) puts it:

> Examining the historical in our present ways of thinking and ways of doing in environmental education allows us

to ask new questions of our work. To answer these questions, however, involves us approaching environmental education not as a quasi-religious cause but rather as a body of knowledge in and through which governmental relations of power operate. At stake are some firmly and fondly held beliefs about the world and about our role as educators.

(pp. 67–68)

As it is with cell phones, it is hard to imagine a time when the quality of the environment did not occupy our thoughts on a frequent basis. As a species with a long agrarian history, it might be hard to imagine how so many of us have lost touch with the countryside, but, with increasing urbanization and industrialization, that is what appeared to happen during the first half of the 20th century in a number of countries. The resulting shifts in our understandings of and relationship with the natural world have had a number of consequences, many of which provide the focus of environmental education practitioners and researchers.

The beginnings of the environmental movement (which can be seen as a response to our disconnection) can be traced to the time of the publication of Rachel Carson's *Silent Spring* (Carson, 1962). Over the next 50 years, a new public vocabulary emerged such that most English-speaking people would be familiar with terms such as "pollution," "ozone layer," "global warming," and "climate change," even if they might be less familiar with "habitat" and "biodiversity." To what extent this new understanding can be attributed to environmental education in either the formal or the informal sector is, hard to divine. However, much current research in the field focuses on what people know, how we can "improve" their knowledge, what are the links between what people know and what they do in terms of environmentally friendly actions, and what policy initiatives can help the public to engage with their local environment more frequently. More recently, as Hart (2007) noted, environmental education researchers have come to address issues concerning identity, place, culture, sustainable development, and sustainability.

Until relatively recently, John Disinger's claim that the "first known use of the term environmental education occurred at a 1948 conference" (1984, p. 109) was generally accepted as the correct genealogy (see, for example, McCrea, n.d.). However, elements of Disinger's account do not appear to be correct. He attributes the first use of the term to "Thomas Pritchard, at that time Deputy Director of The Nature Conservancy in Wales" (Disinger, 1984, p. 109; his source was a personal communication from J.J. Kirk dated December 13, 1983). However, the Nature Conservancy was not established in the UK until 1949, so it is unlikely that Pritchard was its representative in 1948.

Kate Moss Gamblin (2012) discovered, via the International Union for Conservation of Nature (IUCN) library, that Pritchard was not listed as a delegate to the conference, and in the notes about the contributors to *Insights into Environmental Education* (Martin & Wheeler, 1975), Pritchard is described as joining the Nature Conservancy in 1967. Indeed, writing in 1975, Pritchard himself states that "In the early days it was called conservation education (the term environmental education was not used until the mid-sixties)" (Pritchard, 1975, p. 177).

Perhaps a more reliable source than Disinger is Keith Wheeler who, in writing on "the genesis of environmental education," identifies a number of progenitors including Darwin, Rousseau, Le Play, and Geddes (Wheeler, 1975). Wheeler notes that "the history of environmental education reflects the many attitudes toward both 'environment' and 'education' found in society, now and in the past" (p. 2). This point is as valid now as it was back in 1975.

The first use of the term "environmental education," in the UK at least, was in 1965 at an education conference at Keele University (Wheeler, 1975). Participants at another UK conference, this time in Leicester, recommended the formation of a Society for Environmental Education, "thereby allowing the various factions within the emergent Society to work together toward teaching for the betterment of the environment as they could not all agree to each using the methods of 'environmental studies'" (p. 9).

Wheeler ponders why it took so long for the environment to become part of everyday discourse. His answer is that "like all revolutions, the environmental one began only after numerous uncontrollable pressures for change had built up to the point where they could be held back no longer" (1975, p. 13). Wheeler traces the trigger of the environmental revolution in the UK to a series of lectures by an ecologist, Sir Frank Fraser Darling, broadcast on the BBC, titled *Wilderness and Plenty*, after which "almost overnight the environment became a topic debated on chat shows, pronounced upon by pop stars and even [inspiring] the TV drama series, *Doomwatch*" (p. 13).

In the United States, environmental concerns had been the topic of much debate for many years and certainly since the early 1900s. James Swan (2010) recalls the moment when environmental education began its rise to prominence in the United States:

> [I]n 1969, inspired by the international movement building toward Earth Day in 1970, a group of faculty and students at the University of Michigan met in a seminar to envision a new direction for shaping educational policy about the environment. The name for this new educational thrust became "Environmental Education."
>
> (p. 3)

The group defined the purpose of environmental education in terms of the need "to develop a citizenry which is knowledgeable concerning the biophysical environment and its associated problems, aware of how to help resolve these problems, and motivated to do so" (Stapp et al., 1970, p. 30).

In 1970, the United States became the first country to pass environmental education legislation. President Richard Nixon signed into law the National Environmental Education Act, which established the Office of Environmental Education. However, funding for the Act only lasted until 1975, and it was repealed in 1981 as part of a budget reconciliation bill. The U.S. Congress returned to the topic in 1990, and the National Environmental Education Act was signed into law by President George H.W. Bush later in the same year. The Act mandates that the Environmental Protection Agency make environmental education a priority.

What happened to environmental education and, later, environmental education research in its early years is hinted at by Swan's (2010) comment:

> There is little argument about the need for environmental education and action nearly four decades later. The big issue, then and now, is how to effectively educate and motivate people to care about ecology so their concern translates into appropriate action. The role of psychology in creating ecological harmony is crucial, and both then, and now, it is not nearly as clear as we might hope for.
>
> (p. 3)

Toward a Global Movement

The global nature of environmental problems led to the United Nations (UN) taking a number of initiatives, ostensibly on behalf of the broader international community. The first ever UN Conference on the Human Environment was held in Stockholm, Sweden, in 1972. The subsequent Stockholm Declaration included a list of 21 Principles, including one that specifically identified a role for education:

> Education in environmental matters, for the younger generation as well as adults, giving due consideration to the underprivileged, is essential in order to broaden the basis for an enlightened opinion and responsible conduct by individuals, enterprises and communities in protecting and improving the environment in its full human dimension. It is also essential that mass media of communications avoid

contributing to the deterioration of the environment, but, on the contrary, disseminates information of an educational nature on the need to project and improve the environment in order to enable man to develop in every respect.

(UNEP, 1972)

Three years later, an International Workshop on Environmental Education was held in Belgrade (in what was then Yugoslavia). The subsequent Belgrade Charter filled in some of the detail missing from the Stockholm Declaration. It described the goal of environmental education as being

[t]o develop a world population that is aware of, and concerned about, the environment and its associated problems, and which has the knowledge, skills, attitudes, motivations and commitment to work individually and collectively towards solutions to current problems, and the prevention of new ones.

(UNESCO, 1975)

Six objectives were also identified: awareness, knowledge, attitudes, skills, evaluation ability, and participation. Participation was explained as being necessary "to help individuals and social groups develop a sense of responsibility and urgency regarding environmental problems to ensure appropriate action to resolve those problems" (UNESCO, 1975).

A subsequent meeting, 2 years later, in Tbilisi (in the then USSR) led to another declaration. The 1977 Tbilisi Declaration of the UNESCO/UNEP Intergovernmental Conference on Environmental Education "together with two of the recommendations of the Conference constitutes the framework, principles, and guidelines for environmental education at all levels—local, national, regional, and international—and for all age groups both inside and outside the formal school system" (UNESCO, 1978).

The Tbilisi Declaration contained much more detail about the goals and the philosophy underpinning environmental education and noted that one of its basic aims

is to succeed in making individuals and communities understand the complex nature of the natural and the built environments resulting from the interaction of their biological, physical, social, economic, and cultural aspects, and acquire the knowledge, values, attitudes, and practical skills to participate in a responsible and effective way in anticipating and solving environmental problems, and in the management of the quality of the environment.

(UNESCO, 1978)

While the notion of "making" people "understand" might jar with modern sensibilities about teaching and learning, the holistic view of environmental education that emerges from the Declaration is one that still resonates with much environmental education practice found around the world today.

The subsequent basic aim appears to take a much more socially critical approach to environmental education:

A further basic aim of environmental education is clearly to show the economic, political, and ecological interdependence of the modern world, in which decisions and actions by different countries can have international repercussions. Environmental education should, in this regard, help to develop a sense of responsibility and solidarity among countries and regions as the foundation for a new international order which will guarantee the conservation and improvement of the environment.

(UNESCO, 1978)

Documents such as the Tbilisi Declaration are invariably written by a group of people with differing views—"the many attitudes towards both 'environment' and 'education' found in society, now and in the past" (Wheeler, 1975, p. 2)—so we should not be surprised to see some element of incongruity or disjuncture.

The Declaration also addressed the links between development and the environment, noting that "Special attention should be paid to understanding the complex relations between socio-economic development and the improvement of the environment" (UNESCO, 1978). The Declaration made it clear that educational actions, on their own, would not be effective:

To make an effective contribution towards improving the environment, educational action must be linked with legislation, policies, measures of control, and the decisions that governments may adopt in relation to the human environment.

(UNESCO, 1978)

These visions of what environmental education might look like differ substantially from earlier ideas that emerged from earlier, science-focused conferences such as the 1968 UNESCO Biosphere Conference (Goodson, 1983) and the 1970 Australian Academy of Science conference (Evans & Boyden, 1970).

Swan's comments discussed earlier, looking back to the early days of environmental education, look rather narrow when compared with the statements found in the Tbilisi Declaration. Swan (2010) argued that the "big issue" was "how to effectively educate and motivate people to care about ecology so their concern translates into appropriate action" (p. 3). Whereas Swan saw psychology playing a crucial role "in creating ecological harmony" (p. 3), the writers of the Tbilisi Declaration seemed to have seen a role for a number of the social sciences.

Annette Gough, who has studied the history of environmental education, notes that "the foundational discourses of environmental education are "man-made" discourses at least two levels—because of the absence of women in their formulation and because of the modernist science that separates "man" and "nature" and associates "woman" with "nature" (Gough, 2013a, p. 16). These discourses persisted for some time and still influence aspects of environmental education research and practice. Swan's view represents an associated discourse, one that sees people as the problem and education as the solution—if only we could find the right bit of knowledge to change people's attitudes and subsequent behaviors. The impact of that discourse on environmental education research is discussed in the following section.

Tracing the Development of Environmental Education Research

Gough (2013a) notes that "much of the earliest research in environmental education in the United States took the form of positivist inquiries which worked from the premise that the key goal of environmental education is the acquisition of responsible environmental behavior" (p. 17; see, for example, Hungerford & Volk, 1990; Ramsey, Hungerford, & Volk, 1992). Gough also argues that the researchers grounded their studies in behavioral and social psychology (see, for example, Marcinkowski, 1993). These methodological approaches dominated the field until early in the early 1990s when, in a seismic moment, Ian Robottom and Paul Hart severely criticized them as being inappropriate and reductionist (Robottom & Hart, 1993). One indicator of the influence that quantitative approaches had on the field is that the most cited paper published in the *Journal of Environmental Education* is still "Analysis and Synthesis of Research on Responsible Environmental Behavior: A Meta-Analysis" (Hines, Hungerford, & Tomera, 1987)—the traditions of behavioral and social psychological approaches are still extant.

Robottom and others have continued to critique the traditional approaches. Robottom (2003) identified a key problem with the positivist approach to environmental education as follows:

> Environmental issues do not fundamentally consist of objectively existing facts that are more usually the concern of science and science education. If it is recognised that environmental issues actually consist of differences of opinion among human beings about the appropriateness of certain environmental actions, then it can be seen that environmental issues are best understood within a social discourse rather than a scientific discourse.
>
> (p. 34)

Partly in response to the domination of positivist research, a number of academics developed new methods and methodologies for carrying out research on very different visions of what counts as appropriate research:

> These are very different visions of research in environmental education from the simple focus on changing behaviors. They recognize that behavior change reflects non-linear rather than linear theories of knowledge. Linear epistemologies strive for one coherent knowledge system, are underpinned by assumptions of universality, foundation, homogeneity, monotony and clarity, and consider unknowns, or conflicting knowings, as "not-yet-resolved-but-in-principle-resolvable"

imperfections (Bauman, 1993, p. 8). In contrast, achieving behavior change relates more with non-linear theories of knowledge which "accept unknowns as well as plurality, dissent and conflicting knowledge claims as central and inevitable components to understanding knowledge construction, deconstruction and reconstruction processes" (Ward, 2002, p. 29).

> (Gough, 2013a, p. 18)

One of the most highly cited papers in the field is "Mind the Gap: Why Do People Act Environmentally and What Are the Barriers to Pro-Environmental Behavior?" by Anja Kollmuss and Julian Agyeman (2002). After examining the most influential and commonly used analytical frameworks including the early U.S. linear progression models, and while acknowledging that they all have some validity, they argue that "the question of what shapes pro-environmental behavior is such a complex one that it cannot be visualized through one single framework or diagram" (Kollmuss & Agyeman, 2002, p. 239). Kollmuss and Agyeman (2002) then:

> analyze the factors that have been found to have some influence, positive or negative, on pro-environmental behavior such as demographic factors, external factors (e.g. institutional, economic, social and cultural) and internal factors (e.g. motivation, pro-environmental knowledge, awareness, values, attitudes, emotion, locus of control, responsibilities and priorities).
>
> (p. 239)

Kollmuss and Agyeman (2002) point out that attempts to develop a model that tries to incorporate a myriad of factors might be neither feasible nor useful. They identify possible barriers to positive influence on pro-environmental behavior, arguing that "old habits form a very strong barrier that is often overlooked in the literature on pro-environmental behavior" (p. 257).

Critical Approaches to Environmental Education

The substantial body of research evidence built up over the last few decades of the 20th century has been used to inform a number of interventions, including policies and curriculum materials. Regula Kyburz-Graber has summarized some of these educational responses to environmental problems, such as:

- promoting individual behavioral change through improving educational strategies and research (for example, Hungerford & Volk, 1990; Sia, Hungerford, & Tomera, 1985/1986; Zelezny, 1999)
- enhancing environmental awareness through environmental literacy, usually closely linked to natural science literacy (for example, Volk & McBeth, 1997)
- enhancing nature–human relationship and ecological awareness through nature experience (for example, Bögeholz, 2006; Chawla, 1998)

- promoting action competence through action-oriented learning (for example, Bolscho & Michelsen, 1999; Jensen & Schnack, 1997)
- promoting ethical reflection and awareness of cultural contexts and diversity (for example, Greenwood & McKenzie, 2009; Jickling, 2004a, 2004b)
- educating for becoming critical through transformative and critical education (e.g. O'Donoghue & McNaught, 1991; Robottom, 1987; Robottom & Hart, 1993; Stapp, 1974; Wals, 1993)

(adapted from Kyburz-Graber, 2013, pp. 23–24)

Taking a similar line to that of Kollmuss and Agyeman, Kyburz-Graber noted that the natural science–based approaches to promoting attitudinal and behavioral change were criticized because they "are simplifications and do not form adequate approaches to the multilayered challenge of environmental problems" (p. 24). She advocates socioecological approaches that involve critical reflection on real-life situations involving the interface of the social and natural sciences (Kyburz-Graber, Rigendinger, Hirsch Hadorn, & Werner Zentner, 1997a, 1997b). The key aspects of the socioecological approaches are:

- questioning the nature of natural and social sciences and its interfaces
- questioning the ways knowledge is produced, reflected, disseminated, and continuously interpreted
- inquiring the interfaces between sciences and social questions (1997b, p. 25)

This critical approach to environmental education is designed to encourage:

> young people to explore social issues in the real world by questioning values, perceptions, conditions and opinions. While doing this, they look behind and beyond the norms of social boundaries and critically question what is generally understood as "objective" scientific facts.
>
> (Kyburz-Graber, 1999, pp. 416)

This "critical" approach to environmental education has become one of the dominant paradigms in the field (see, for example, Tseverini, 2011). In the previous edition of this *Handbook*, Hart noted that this critical approach was particularly influential outside the United States, but he also noted some critique at the turn of the century from some academics that a critical approach might simply be offering another orthodoxy. Hart (2007) argues that

> if viewed as a means of self-reflection and social scrutiny without particular ends, then environmental education researchers may in fact be engaged in methodological debates that are more characteristic of poststructuralist than critical forms of educational inquiry, involving more sophisticated philosophical arguments about social constructions of social science research.
>
> (p. 699)

Recent Trends and Developments in the Field

Hart (2007) provides a thorough summary of the state of environmental education research in terms of its geographical and methodological diversity. He also makes a strong case as to why science education researchers should attend to research issues in environmental education. Since the publication of the first version of this *Handbook*, a substantial number of studies have been published, particularly in the major science education journals, that indicate the increasing overlap between science and environmental education in terms of ontology and epistemology. From an ontological point of view, the three themes that seem to be most common are socioscientific issues, environmental science literacy, and climate change.

Socioscientific Issues

A number of papers have reported on studies in which environmental issues have provided a context for the discussion of sociocultural issues. Oliveira and colleagues (2012) note that "[w]hile environmental argumentation has recently received much attention from science educators, little consideration has been given to how personal identities and social relationships can either support or constrain student argumentation" (p. 896). Using rhetorical and sociocultural analysis of oral discourse, the authors examined how students engaged with problematic scenarios involving animals and the environment. The main implication of Oliveira and colleagues' (2012) study is that it

> highlights the need for educators to pay closer attention to specific textual elements in the design of environmental dilemmas (types of prompts used, decision-makers' identities, statements of intentionality and outcome, moral complexity, values of nature, and social representation or cultural images of animals) in order to foster an appropriate and productive sociocultural classroom context for rational and reasoned environmental argumentation to take place without the constraints of unexpected social complications.
>
> (p. 896)

Levine Rose and Calabrese Barton (2012) examined the experiences of two middle-school students who were participants in an after-school program. The issue facing the students, in their 13-week program, was whether their city should build a new hybrid power plant. The study used critical sociocultural perspectives on learning and qualitative case study. The authors found that not only did the students' scientific knowledge influence how they engaged with the issues, "but their knowledge was deeply connected to a range of personal and public discourses that influenced how they defined the issue and why it mattered to them" (Levine Rose & Calabrese Barton, 2012):

> In particular, it was through how they framed their range of knowledge and experiences that they were able to

recognize the multi-dimensional nature of the problem and propose complex solutions resonant with the science they understood.

(p. 541)

Tomas and colleagues (2011) examined the attitudinal impact of hybridized writing about a socioscientific issue. Using a triangulation mixed-methods study, the authors studied how 152 14- to 15-year-olds developed their understanding of biosecurity as they took part in an online science-writing project. The students' task was to produce a series of hybridized scientific narratives ("BioStories") that integrated scientific information with narrative storylines. The authors concluded that the students developed "more positive attitudes toward science and science learning, particularly in terms of the students' interest and enjoyment" (Tomas et al., 2011, p. 878).

Castano (2008) examined the use of socioscientific discussions to improve 9- to 10-year-old Colombian girl students' understanding of the interrelation between species and the environment. Using a mixed-methods study, Castano (2008) found that "students who had the opportunity to discuss socioscientific dilemmas gave better definitions for scientific concepts and made better connections between them, their lives and Nature than students who did not" (p. 565). The author concludes that students should do more than simply construct scientific knowledge and that they would benefit from engaging in "discussions and decision-making related to the social and moral implications of the application of Science in the real world" (p. 565; see also Evagorou, Jimenez-Aleixandre, & Osborne, 2012; Ideland, Malmberg, & Winberg, 2011).

Castano advocates that research on students' engagement with socioscientific issues should take place in a range of different cultural contexts. Lee and Grace (2012) report on a cross-contextual study that involved comparing 12- to 13-year-old Chinese students' decisions made on avian flu. The students came from two different contexts, and the research involved them using a prescribed decision-making framework. Lee and Grace (2012) found differences between students in the two settings in terms of "their reasoning perspectives, evidence perceived to be useful to gather, decision-making criteria, and postactivity decisions" (p. 787).

Environmental Science Literacy

Reflecting a recent trend in science education, Gunckel and colleagues (2012) outline a learning progression for water in environmental systems for students in elementary through high school grades. Working from students' accounts of "water and substances in water moving through atmospheric, surface, and soil/groundwater systems, including human-engineered components of these systems" (Gunckel et al., p. 843), the authors identified four levels of achievement in student reasoning:

Levels 1 and 2 force-dynamic accounts explain movement of water as interactions between natural tendencies of water and countervailing powers. Level 3 incomplete

school science accounts put events in order and trace water and substance along multiple pathways that include hidden and invisible components. Only Level 4 qualitative model-based accounts include driving forces and constraining factors to explain or predict where water and substances in water move in given situations. The majority of high school students on average provide accounts between levels 2 and 3.

(843)

In terms of using the environment as a context for developing students' thinking, Bodzin (2011) investigated the impact of a geospatial information technology (GIT)-supported science curriculum. Working with five 13- to 14-year-olds' (eighth-grade) earth and space science classes in one urban middle school, Bodzin (2011) found that:

content knowledge about environmental issues associated with LUC and spatial thinking skills involved with aerial and remotely sensed (RS) imagery interpretation increased for all learners. In most content and skill area clusters, effect sizes were larger for *lower* and *middle* track learners than for *upper* track learners. Achievement for spatial thinking items increased for all ability level tracks.

(p. 281)

Vasconcelos (2012) reports some success when using problem-based learning as part of an environmental education program.

There is increasing interest in links among science, environment, and health education in terms of the school curriculum and among researchers. Mallya and colleagues (2012) studied a group of 12- to 13-year-olds living in a poor area of New York City who were participating in an innovative program—the Choice, Control and Change (C3) science curriculum. The authors reported that their eight case-study students "began to view their worlds with a more critical mindset and to devise ways to transform themselves and the conditions of their own and others' lives" (Mallya et al., 2012, p. 244). Specifically, the authors, using the term "science agency," reported that the students could "(1) critically analyze the conditions of their food environment, (2) purposefully make healthier choices, and (3) expand the food and activity options available to themselves and others" (p. 244).

The growth of eco-schools, particularly in Europe, has been studied by a number of researchers. Boeve-de Pauw and Van Petegem (2011) examined the effect of Flemish eco-schools on student environmental knowledge, attitudes, and affect. Their study involved 1,287 10- to 12-year-olds from 59 schools (38 eco-schools and 21 control schools). Using multivariate multilevel regression analyses, Boeve-de Pauw and Van Petegem (2011) found that "eco-schools mainly influence their students' environmental knowledge; they do not influence environmental affect" (p. 1513).

Involving students in long-term, community-based, environmental science projects is increasingly common. Ebenezer and colleagues (2011) worked with 125 9th- through 12th-grade students who, over a period of 3 years, reported an increase in their fluency with innovative technologies. The authors claim that the study "points to the correlation between the development of IT fluency and ability levels to engage in scientific inquiry based on respective competencies" (Ebenezer et al., 2011, p. 94).

Noting that "Social justice education is undertheorized in science education" (Dimick, 2012, p. 990), Dimick (2012) describes a student empowerment framework for conceptualizing teaching and learning social justice science education in classroom settings. The author uses the framework to analyze a case study of a U.S. high school environmental science class in which the teacher and students created environmental action projects that were relevant to their community (see also Ruiz-Mallen, Barraza, Bodenhorn, de la Paz Ceja-Adame, & Reyes-García, 2010).

Climate Change

The growing scientific consensus about the anthropomorphic impact on climate change is not reflected in public opinion in many countries. The issue is complicated in some parts of the world by issues of public trust in scientists and policy makers. Education is seen as one possible solution, and researchers have provided evidence that might help to devise suitable strategies.

Kirkeby Hansen (2010) surveyed Norwegian students' knowledge about the greenhouse effect and the effects of the ozone layer as they finished compulsory education in 1989, 1993, and 2005. The main finding was that "more pupils confuse the greenhouse effect with the effects of the ozone layer. At the same time, specific knowledge about the greenhouse effect is improving" (Kirkeby Hansen, 2010, p. 397). Studies have looked at school and college students as well as at pre- and inservice teachers.

Sternäng and Lundholm (2011) investigated 14-year-old Chinese students' interpretations of climate change from a moral perspective. All the participants were studying at "green schools" in the Beijing area. Using semi-structured group interviews and taking account of both cognitive and situational aspects, the researchers found that

> [T]he students conceptualise the solutions to mitigating climate change in relation to two different stances. That is, they contextualise the problems and solutions by addressing the individual, where the individual is either "myself" or "someone else." The different notions of the individual become crucial as the students' views and considerations for the environment, as well as society, change according to the different contexts. From a moral point of view, the students seem quite unaware of their varying consideration for others, the environment and society.
>
> (Sternäng & Lundholm, 2011, p. 1131)

Based on previous research findings, Svihla and Linn (2012) designed a middle school inquiry intervention, based on interactive visualizations, that was aimed at preparing students to make informed decisions and develop their understanding about global climate change. Based on the findings of a student pretest, a greater focus was placed on energy transfer and transformation. The researchers reported "improved comprehension of the visualizations resulting in better understanding of energy transfer ($n = 67$)." A second iteration "improved understanding of energy transformation ($n = 109$) by adding pivotal cases, reducing deceptive clarity, and emphasizing distinguishing of ideas" (Svihla & Linn, 2012, p. 651). Svihla and Linn (2012) argue that

> [F]ocusing student investigations in the second version allowed students to make more normative, personally relevant decisions related to their energy use. These iterative refinements reflected knowledge integration principles and offer guidance for designers of inquiry units.
>
> (p. 651)

McNeill and Houle Vaughn (2012) investigated the impact of a 4- to 6-week urban ecology curriculum on students from three different urban high schools in the United States. Using a mixed-methods approach, the researchers found that

> [A]t the beginning of the curriculum, the majority of students believed that climate change was occurring; yet, they had limited conceptual understandings about climate change and were engaged in limited environmental actions. By the end of the curriculum, students had a significant increase in their understanding of climate change and the majority of students reported they were now engaged in actions to limit their personal impact on climate change.
>
> (McNeill & Houle Vaughn, 2012, p. 373)

McNeill and Houle Vaughn (2012) argue that "These findings suggest that believing a scientific theory (e.g. climate change) is not sufficient for critical science agency; rather, conceptual understandings and understandings of personal actions impact students' choices" (p. 373).

In a comparative study, Skamp and colleagues (2013) worked with high school students in Australia ($n = 500$) and England ($n = 785$). The students were asked about their beliefs about the effectiveness of various specific actions in reducing global warming, as well as their self-reported willingness to take those actions. In both countries, students "were less inclined to act than their beliefs in the effectiveness of the actions might warrant, although the extent of this disparity varied between different actions" (Skamp et al., 2013, p. 191).

Striking a contrary, methodological note, Jakobsson and colleagues (2009) argue that

> students' knowledge of complex multidisciplinary phenomena [such as global warming] may be particularly ill-suited to conventional questionnaire types of testing.

When following students' project work in school over a long period, many of the misunderstandings reported in the literature do not appear [because] the appropriation and use of scientific language when discussing complex socioscientific issues is a gradual process. When observing the language and mediational means students use over time, it is obvious that they are able to identify and use central distinctions in their interactions.

(p. 978)

Turning now to studies of pre- and inservice teachers, Lambert and colleagues (2012) developed a "Knowledge of Global Climate Change" (KGCC) instrument designed to assess elementary science methods students' knowledge of science concepts and climate change. Working with 149 U.S. participants, the researchers studied the impact of infusing climate change education into their courses. As well as more traditional teaching approaches,

> students were required to complete a climate change guided-research project. The first component of the project included viewing and analyzing the evidence that Al Gore used to support his explanations for climate change in the film, *An Inconvenient Truth.*
> (Lambert et al., 2012, p. 1170)

Lambert and colleagues (2012) reported that not only did students increase their knowledge of climate change and develop more interest and confidence in learning about climate change, they also "completed the course with more positive views on the nature of science and climate change" (p. 1170).

Arslan and colleagues (2012) also developed a three-tier, multiple-choice "atmosphere-related environmental problems diagnostic test" (AREPDiT) to assess preservice teachers' misconceptions about global warming, greenhouse effect, ozone layer depletion, and acid rain. Working with 256 preservice teachers, the researchers found that "a majority of the respondents demonstrated limited understandings about atmosphere-related environmental problems and held six common misconceptions" (Arslan et al., 2012, p. 1667).

Lombardi and Sinatra (2012) examined undergraduate college students' perceptions about the plausibility of human-induced climate change. The students, who had enrolled in an introductory science class on global climate change, completed measures (pre- and post-) of their (a) understanding of distinctions between weather and climate, (b) knowledge of deep time, and (c) plausibility perceptions of human-induced climate change. The study found that:

> [G]reater knowledge of deep time and increased plausibility perceptions of human-induced climate change provide significant explanation of variance in students' understanding of weather and climate distinctions. Furthermore, students achieve significantly increased understanding of weather and climate, even with brief instruction.
> (p. 201)

Ratinen (2013), using a mixed-method study, examined Finnish primary student teachers' understanding of the greenhouse effect using open-ended and closed-form questionnaires. Perhaps not surprisingly, Ratinen (2013) found that the student teachers' knowledge and understanding was "incomplete and even misleading" (p. 929).

Lombardi and Sinatra (2013), working with pre- and inservice teachers, focused not just on participants' knowledge of weather and climate but also how they felt about human-induced climate change. The researchers found that

> Teachers' topic emotions (anger and hopelessness) were significant predictors of plausibility perceptions, with more anger associated with lesser plausibility and greater hopelessness associated with higher plausibility. Decisiveness—an urgent desire to reach closure—was also significantly related to plausibility perceptions with greater decisiveness associated with reduced plausibility perceptions.
> (p. 167)

Interestingly, inservice secondary teachers who were not currently teaching about climate change "exhibited greater anger and decisiveness" (p. 167) than did the pre- and inservice teachers who were teaching about climate change.

Learning in the Natural Environment

A number of reviews have focused on a particular aspect of environmental education that is highly relevant to science education—learning in the natural environment (learning outside the classroom). Rickinson and colleagues (2004) critically examined 150 pieces of research on outdoor learning published in English between 1993 and 2003. The review looked at studies involving three domains: elementary-, high school- and undergraduate-level learners; fieldwork and outdoor visits; outdoor adventure education and school grounds/community projects. The authors concluded that

> [S]ubstantial evidence to indicate that fieldwork, properly conceived, adequately planned, well taught and effectively followed up, offers learners opportunities to develop their knowledge and skills in ways that add value to their everyday experiences in the classroom.
> (p. 5)

The majority of the literature reviewed tends to be located in science or geography education (see, for example, Fields, 2009; Judson, 2011; Kim & Tan, 2013; Luehmann, 2009).

Rickinson and colleagues (2004) concluded that that "fieldwork can have a positive impact on long-term memory due to the memorable nature of the fieldwork setting" (p. 5). Another key issue was the possibility of a synergy between affective and cognitive experiences:

> Effective fieldwork, and residential experience in particular, can lead to individual growth and improvements in social skills. More importantly, there can be reinforcement

between the affective and the cognitive, with each influencing the other and providing a bridge to higher order learning.

(p. 5)

Findings such as these provide strong evidence for broadening science education pedagogy to include experiences beyond the classroom and laboratory. However, despite the substantial evidence of the potential beneficial impacts on a diverse range of educational outcomes, Rickinson and colleagues (2004) noted that "there is evidence that the amount of fieldwork that takes place in the UK and in some other parts of the world is severely restricted, particularly in science" (p. 5). A number of reasons have been put forward to explain why teachers may be reluctant to take students outside, including excessive health and safety procedures, time constraints, and a crowded curriculum. Rickinson and colleagues noted some gaps in the literature, such as the relatively low number of studies that address the needs and experience of particular groups (e.g., girls) or students with specific educational needs.

Malone's (2008) review of evidence on "the role of learning outside the classroom for children's whole development from birth to eighteen years" concludes that "by experiencing the world beyond the classroom children":

- achieve higher results in knowledge and skill acquisition
- increase their physical health and motor skills
- socialize and interact in new and different ways with their peers and adults
- show improved attention and enhanced self-concept, self-esteem, and mental health
- change their environmental behaviors for the positive, along with their values and attitudes; and their resilience to be able to respond to changing conditions in their environment (pp. 5–6)

To some extent, Malone's (2008) conclusions are colored by the dominant research paradigm—that is, behavioral and social psychology. For many years, as has been discussed, research focused almost exclusively on knowledge, attitudes, and behaviors, so Malone's (2008) review tended to pick up on findings which reflect that focus. Such studies are still being carried out (see, for example, Boyes & Stanisstreet, 2012; Nisiforou & Charalambides, 2012; Oerke & Bogner, 2013; Taskin 2009). However, Malone's (2008) review (which looked at more than 100 studies) drew on a range of research: quantitative, qualitative, mixed-method, action/participatory research, and literature reviews. Malone (2008) concludes that the review supports:

a general hypothesis that learning outside the classroom has a significant impact on children's learning and is supportive of healthy child development in the cognitive domain (children's learning), physical domain (children's physical experiences), social (children's social interaction) emotional (children's emotional well-being) and personal domains (children's responses).

(p. 13)

Whittington (2006) utilized an unusual approach to evaluating the impact of an outdoor experience. She studied a group of adolescent girls on a 23-day canoe expedition that was part of an all-female wilderness program in Maine, United States. The girls were interviewed twice following the expedition, 4 to 5 months afterward and after 15 to 18 months. Whittington (2006) used a range of data-collection methods, including a "focus group, public presentation, parent surveys, journal entries, and other written materials created by the participants" (p. 205). The experience empowered the participants to challenge what Whittington (2006) described as "conventional notions of femininity in diverse ways" such as:

1) perseverance, strength, and determination; 2) challenging assumptions of girls' abilities; 3) feelings of accomplishment and pride; 4) questioning ideal images of beauty; 5) increased ability to speak out and leadership skills; and 6) building significant relationships with other girls.

(p. 205)

A number of studies have focused on students' experiences and subsequent memories of learning outside the classroom (see, for example, Williams & Dixon, 2013). Dierking and Falk (1997) reported that 96% of a group of children and adults ($n = 128$) could recall field trips taken during their early years at school. A comparative study of high school students compared 11 Californian schools that used an environmentally focused curriculum with a group that taught a more standard curriculum. The students in the environmentally focused schools scored higher in 72% of the academic assessments (reading, science, math, attendance rates, and grade point averages) than did students in the other schools (State Education and Environment Roundtable, 2000).

The impact of fieldwork on students' attitudes has been studied by a number of researchers. In an attempt to compare approaches, Eaton (2000) aimed "to determine whether an outdoor education experience would have a more positive impact on the cognitive achievement and environmental attitudes of junior-level students than in a traditional classroom setting" (p. ii). The study's participants were from six classes that attended a half-day program in beaver ecology at an outdoor and environmental education center. A comparison group of six classes was taught similar content in traditional classrooms. Eaton reported that the outdoor center students "made a greater contribution to cognitive learning compared to the classroom programme" (p. iii). Surprisingly, though, Eaton (2000) found that neither context appeared to have an impact on environmental attitudes. Other studies have found that fieldwork has impacted on attitudes. Nundy (1998, 1999a, 1999b), who looked at the role and effectiveness of residential fieldwork on U.K. elementary school students, reported an interaction between cognitive and affective impacts:

> Residential fieldwork is capable not only of generating positive cognitive and affective learning amongst students, but this may be enhanced significantly compared to that achievable within a classroom environment.
>
> (Nundy, 1999a, p. 190)

Similar results have been reported in Australia. Maller's (2005) study involved a postal survey of 500 urban Melbourne primary schools as well as more in-depth research in 12 schools and interviews with seven "key industry informants" (for example, an education officer, an architect, and a community garden manager). Maller (2005) reported that "hands-on contact with nature in primary school, regardless of the type, is an important means of connecting children with nature and can play a significant role in cultivating positive mental health and wellbeing" (p. 16). Maller's take-home message was that

> [H]ands-on contact with nature experienced via sustainability education is not only essential for protecting the environment, but it also appears to be a means of cultivating community and enhancing the mental health and wellbeing of children and adults alike.
>
> (Maller, 2005, pp. 21–22)

Randler and colleagues (2005) studied two classes of students aged 9 to 11 who were taught about amphibians. Half of the students also took part in outdoor conservation work in which they encountered amphibians. This group of students "performed significantly better on achievement tests" and they "expressed high interest and well-being and low anger, anxiety, and boredom" (p. 43). Feelings of "boredom and anxiety correlated negatively with residualized achievement scores" (p. 43). The authors concluded that biodiversity teaching should "(a) focus on a small number of species, (b) start in primary schools, (c) take place outdoors, and (d) be linked with classroom teaching" (p. 43; see also Tran, 2011).

Much of the work reported here tends to report on the positive outcomes of learning in the natural environment—few studies report negative impacts. What has not been examined in any depth is why some schools and teachers tend to promote learning outside the classroom and others do not (see Dillon & Dickie, 2012).

Environmental Education, Sustainable Development, and Sustainability

Back in the late 1970s, environmental educators noted a need to consider the links between development and the environment. As was mentioned, more than 30 years ago, the writers of the Tbilisi Declaration noted that "Special attention should be paid to understanding the complex relations between socio-economic development and the improvement of the environment" (UNESCO, 1978). Since then, notions of sustainability and sustainable development have emerged, and this section considers the relationship between sustainable development and science education through a critical discussion of scholarly work that focuses on education for sustainable development (ESD).

Sustainable Development

Sustainable development traces its intellectual origins to the Utilitarianism espoused by Bentham (1789) and John Stuart Mill (1861). The term was first used in forestry management in the 19th century (Disinger 1990; Fettis & Ramsden; 1995; Rauch, 2002), and its origins date from a system of forest cultivation in which the volume of trees cut never exceeded the natural potential for regrowth. Pinchot imported the utilitarian/sustainable development idea from Europe to the United States through the founding of the U.S. National Forest Service in 1905.

The term "sustainable development" rose to prominence following the publication of a report (entitled *Our Common Future*) by the Brundtland Commission (World Commission on Environment and Development, 1987). Brundtland defined the term as follows: "Development that meets the needs of the present without compromising the ability of future generations to meet their own needs" (ibid.). *Our Common Future* adopts a dualistic, Cartesian view that sees the environment as a global resource to be developed and managed for sustainable profit and nature as something to be revered and respected for the enjoyment and survival of human beings, thus:

> [T]he environment does not exist as a sphere separate from human actions, ambitions and needs and attempts to defend it in isolation from human concerns have given the very word "environment" a connotation of naivety in some political circles . . .
>
> (p. 6)

One of the main achievements of *Our Common Future* was that it formally recognized the strong link that exists between development and the environment: "The environment is where we all live; and development is what we all do in attempting to improve our lot within that abode. The two are inseparable" (p. 6).

The contestation emerges because, for some, sustainable development is, as Pawley (2000) sees it, a political fudge-word combining opposing positions by proposing a third. Sustainable development is also problematic for people uncomfortable with a utilitarian framework. The focus of the Brundtland Report seems to be on how to make development last rather than the nonhuman environment. As Sachs (1995) puts it, "sustainable development calls for the conservation of development, not for the conservation of nature" (p. 343). This conflict of interests is, perhaps, best illustrated in this extract from *Our Common Future*: "What is needed is an era of new economic growth—growth that is forceful and at the same time socially and environmentally sustainable" (WCED, 6).

Jickling (1999) has described the contradictions inherent in conceptualizations of the term sustainable development as "doublethink." He notes that ordinary citizens increasingly accept contradictory meanings for the same term and accept both. The generalizability of the idea of sustainability can, according to Jickling, mask issues of cultural identities, respect, social justice, nature relations, and the tensions between intrinsic and instrumental values.

Stables refers to such terms as paradoxical compound policy slogans although Scott and Gough (2003) argue that having distinctive perspectives can bring distinct learning opportunities provided that educators and others do not foreclose the issue by advocating their preferred view to the exclusion of others. Sadly, the history of environmental education and education for sustainability is that advocacy of one position against all others is the norm rather than the exception. The United Nations launched a Decade for ESD that began in 2005 and finished in 2014. It has to be said that even at the end of the decade, considerable uncertainty continues as to the purpose, role, and structure that ESD might have in national education programmed (see, for example, Tal, 2008).

One of the main areas of contestation in arguments about environmental education and ESD concerns the purpose of education. When sustainable development becomes the "something" that education should be "for" as a number of environmental educators have argued (see, for example, Tilbury, 1995), several issues are raised. Foster (2001), for example, argues that:

> The relation between education and sustainability cannot be an external, still less an instrumental one . . . Learning to understand the natural world and the human place in it can only be an active process through which our sense of what counts as going with the grain of nature is continually constituted and recreated. This process cannot have its agenda set to subserve sustainability criteria which it actually makes meaningful.
>
> (2001, p. 153)

Other criticisms of the term "education for sustainable development" were encapsulated by Sauvé during an online colloquium (Online Colloquium, 1998). Sauvé argued against moves to reshape education such that sustainable development becomes the ultimate goal of human development with education as instrumental—a line of argument foursquare with Foster's, although viewed from a distinctive perspective. Despite criticisms such as Sauvé's and Foster's, the phrase is now firmly rooted in international discourse.

UNESCO, which was instrumental in promoting environmental education in its early years, appears to have taken an uncritical stance toward ESD, which has come in for some criticism. Jickling (1999) is highly critical of Hopkins's "determinist" position outlined in the proceedings of a major UNESCO conference on ESD held in Thessaloniki in 1997. In reply to Hopkins's assertion that "education should be able to cope with determining and implanting these broad guiding principles [of sustainability] at the heart of ESD" (Hopkins, 1998, p. 172), Jickling (1999) responded by arguing that

> When highlighted in this way, most educators find such statements a staggering misrepresentation of their task. Teachers understand that sustainable development, and even sustainability, are normative concepts representing the views of only segments of our society. And, teachers know that their job is primarily to teach students how to think, not what to think.
>
> (p. 469)

Jickling (1999) goes on to argue that "if there is to be a future for sustainability within education, we must begin to recognise the educational limitations of the deterministic manifestations of the sustainability agenda" (p. 470) and warns that:

> Unfortunately, the mantra of sustainability has conditioned many to believe that this term carries unconditional or positive values. Yet critical thought depends on transient elements in ordinary language, the words and ideas that reveal assumptions and worldviews, and the tools to mediate differences between contesting value systems.
>
> (p. 472)

Jickling (1999) also described his concerns over the lack of educational philosophical analysis in environmental education and the use of education as a tool for the advancement of sustainable development "if education is trying to get people to think for themselves then education 'for' anything is inconsistent and should be rejected" (Jickling, 1999 p. 7).

The End of Environmental Education?

From the time that the Brundtland Commission popularized the term "sustainable development," environmental education as a field has sought to clarify its relationship with and its potential contribution to the concept. Following the Thessaloniki Declaration (UNESCO-EPD, 1997) promoting the concept of "education for sustainability" (EFS—which rather quickly became "education for sustainable development"—ESD—as the UN decided to focus on sustainable development [process] rather than sustainability [outcomes]), many (for example, Knapp, 1998) wondered whether this shift in language, promoted as it was by a significant cultural institution, spelled the beginning of the end for environmental education, as an idea and a practice, particularly through a loss of identify. In only 2 of the 29 statements made in the Declaration was the term "environmental education" used. One of these references suggested that environmental education be referred to as education for environment and sustainability. The argument advanced in support of this was that it might be politically advantageous, but it demonstrated how easily environmental education had been replaced by more fashionable rhetoric within UNESCO. Smyth (1998), while understanding these concerns, argued that:

If environmental education . . . takes a genuinely holistic view of environment, as originally intended, and develops for people the prospect of a better life in a richer, less threatened, more dependable world, then it may simply be at the end of the beginning and equipped for the future with a clearer vision which will sustain it and carry it forward.

(p. 15)

The nature of the relationship between environmental education and sustainable development engaged a wide range of interested academics (Ashley, 2005; Gurevitz, 2000; Hesselink, van Kempen, & Wals, 2000; Manjengwa et al., 1999; McKeown & Hopkins, 2003; Sauvé, Brunelle, & Berryman, 2005; Summers, Childs, & Corney, 2005; Summers, Corney, & Childs, 2003; Taylor, Nathan, & Coll, 2003; Wals & Jickling, 1999).

Two accounts of the EE–ESD relationship are particularly instructive. Hesselink and colleagues (2000) canvassed the views of 50 experts from 25 countries. The authors summarized responses as reflecting four perspectives:

i) EE—as part of ESD
ii) ESD—as part of EE
iii) ESD and EE—overlapping
iv) ESD as a stage in the evolution of the idea of EE

They noted that the most popular representation was the last of these [iv]. Each of these perspectives might seem legitimate from different vantage points.

The second account of note is that of McKeown and Hopkins (2003), who analyzed three "historically important documents"—two of which have been discussed: the Belgrade Charter (from 1975), the Tbilisi Declaration (from 1977), and Agenda 21 (from 1992). Their analysis was complemented by interviews with leaders involved in the development of the first two documents. McKeown and Hopkins (2003) argued that the essence of environmental education was that it "focused on the impact of humans on the natural environment" in order to priorities "environmental protection and improved resource use" (with less emphasis on social, economical, and political concerns; 2003, p. 119). They then argued (p. 119) that ESD, in contrast, is much broader, being characterized (from Agenda 21, Chapter 36) by four major thrusts:

• improving the quality of and access to basic education
• reorienting existing education to address sustainable development
• developing public understanding and awareness
• training

If this broader view involves a shift in focus "from environmental protection . . . to addressing the needs of both environment and society," as McKeown and Hopkins (2003, pp. 119–120) assert, then it seems that this is not a view that is congruent with Hesselink and

colleagues' (2000) respondents' favored perspective [iv], which supports the idea that ESD is evolving to something quite different from environmental education. Rather, it seems to argue for perspective [i] in their schema, that is, that environmental education is part of the broader church of ESD—a point also made by Scott and Gough (2003, pp. 53–55) in their setting out of "nine categories of interest which capture . . . a range of different focuses and objectives of those who espouse and promote environmental learning."

From a science education viewpoint, perspective [i] is helpful in that it conserves a role for the science curriculum within ESD while recognizing that there is clearly more to it than this; for example, children in schools still need to be taught the science of the carbon cycle, but a school that *just* taught that knowledge—and not the *social* science of understanding and dealing with the complexities and uncertainties of rapid climate change—might be thought to be failing in its responsibilities to the young—and to the future. Usefully, perspective [i] is a position that mirrors the reality that there is a role for science education in educating about (in the broadest sense of the word) sustainable development—but it is not the only role.

However, just seeing environmental education as one of many components of ESD is to miss an important point, which is the need for interconnection between ideas if we are to make sense of the world and what we teach about it. For example, a school that addresses the science of rapid climate change and its possible social implications in separate curriculum slots, never bringing them together, would miss an important opportunity to develop rounded perspectives (Greig, Pike, & Selby, 1987; Pike & Selby, 1995; Selby, 2001; Sterling, 2001, 2005) and could hardly be said to be allowing students to experience ESD. This is a prominent example of what Symons (2000) claims has dogged environmental education since its early days:

In the developed world, the environmental movement has been largely the province of the white middle classes. This may be because, by concentrating on endangered species in faraway lands and on "invisible" problems like the destruction of the ozone layer, it has failed to connect with the concerns of people for whom the most pressing environmental issues are cold, damp housing, alienating, noisy streets; lack of access to the facilities they need; or in some cases fear of leaving their homes in case of bullying or racist attacks.

(p. 24)

Arguing for a more holistic view of environmental education, she argues that:

Environmental education (both at school and government level) often focuses on personal responsibility and changes in individual lifestyle, rather than on exploring the structures within which we all live, which have a far more fundamental impact on the environment than do our individual actions.

(2000: 25)

She provides an anecdote that well illustrates a potential gap between well-meaning teacher intentions and students' needs:

> Teachers sometimes suggest that to empower children, they prefer to explore with them environmental problems which they, as children, can do something to change. At the end of a workshop that I ran about sustainability for Year 6 pupils from several different schools, I asked them to form groups to make action plans which would build on the work we had done. Adults with the groups were keen for concrete action such as recycling or developing a wildlife area but interestingly, the children themselves were quite resistant to these suggestions. The group with no adult present decided to go back to school and ask their teacher if, as part of their next topic on "Our Planet," they could learn more about where resources such as plastic, aluminium and wood, come from and what processes they go through. They recognised that without sufficient information to deconstruct where the real problem lies they could not make decisions about the personal and structural changes needed for long-term solutions.
>
> (2000, pp. 24–25)

So, children might be more cautious in trying to develop their knowledge about sustainability than might their teachers (and possibly those who write the curriculum, the textbooks, and the educational CDs).

In the Report of the World Summit on Sustainable Development (WSSD), education was seen as "critical for promoting sustainable development" (United Nations, 2002, p. 61). The extremely brief education section within the report focuses mainly on development issues of infrastructure, access and enrolment, gender equity, health issues (particularly AIDS), integration of informational technology, and literacy aimed across communities. UNESCO envisaged a strong role for science education to bridge what it sees as five gaps between science and education for sustainable development, lying between:

- what science knows and the extent to which this knowledge is incorporated into the policy-making process
- what science knows and the content of the school curricula being taught at primary, secondary, and tertiary levels throughout the world
- the knowledge and information available through science and what people are being told through the mass media
- the pace dictated by the timeframe of research and the persistence of scientific uncertainties, and the need to inject the best knowledge available immediately into policy making, education, and public information
- the language used by scientists and that understandable and usable by the many nonspecialists groups that are the main actors in human society

Criticisms of Environmental Education Research

In criticizing the notion of "thinking globally; acting locally," Noel Gough (2013a), using Wagner's (1993) terms, identifies some of the "blind spots and blank spots" that, he says, "configure the "collective ignorance" of Western-enculturated environmental education researchers as we struggle to enact defensible ways of thinking globally" (Gough, 2013a, p. 28). Gough asks, "How can we think globally *without* enacting some form of epistemological imperialism?" His answer is that it might involve:

> a process of constructing transcultural "spaces" in which scholars from different localities collaborate in reframing and decentering their own knowledge traditions and negotiate trust in each other's contributions to their collective work. For those of us who work in Western knowledge traditions, a first step must be to represent and perform our distinctive approaches to knowledge production in ways that authentically demonstrate their localness. We might not be able to speak—or think—from outside our own Eurocentrism, but we can continue to ask questions about how our specifically Western ways of "acting locally" (in the production of knowledge) might be performed *with* other local knowledge traditions.
>
> (Gough, 2013a, p. 28)

Gough's point is that by engaging in the process of coproducing global knowledge in transcultural spaces, "the limits *and strengths* of the local knowledge tradition we call Western science [can be made] increasingly visible" (see also Harvester & Blenkinsop, 2010).

Other critics of environmental education include Saylan and Blumstein (2011), who argue that:

> Environmental education has failed to bring about the changes in attitude and behavior necessary to stave off the detrimental effects of climate change, biodiversity loss, and environmental degradation that our planet is experiencing at an alarmingly accelerating rate.
>
> (p. 1)

The real failure, Saylan and Blumstein (2011) argue, "lies with our political institutions that have succumbed to the influence (and money) of lobbyists, business leaders [. . .] and even ourselves, for failing to exercise our collective power to change the world" (p. 174).

Conclusions

The evidence suggests that environmental education research has shifted from a predominantly applied-science, positivistic orientation that focused almost exclusively on environmental knowledge, attitudes, and behaviors (Hart & Nolan, 1999; Rickinson, 2001). It is generally accepted that a focus on looking for the right bit of knowledge to cause individual behavior change does not do justice to the complexity of human beings. As Stern (2000) puts it, "[e]nvironmentally significant behavior is dauntingly complex, both in its variety and in its causal influences" (p. 421).

New paradigms emerged in Australia, Canada, the UK, South Africa, and parts of continental Europe. A more socially critical approach began to take account of the need to see the contextual and political factors affecting people's lives (Robottom, 1987). Problems have also emerged with defining what actually counts as the "best" behavior. As a result, research agendas have shifted to include a focus on learning (Rickinson, 2001). Environmental education research now recognizes that individuals' worldviews and belief systems influence their understanding and interpretation of environmental issues and mediate their environmental behaviors. Some researchers focus on the central role of engagement in terms of its contribution to an individual's intellectual and emotional engagement in socioecological issues.

Methodologically, environmental education research has moved on from being dominated by logical positivism, and a number of post-positivist methodologies emerged in the 1970s and 1980s. The field has embraced a range of approaches including positivist, interpretivist/constructivist, critical, and feminist/postmodernist perspective. Qualitative approaches including narrative inquiry, participatory research, and post-structuralist approaches are increasingly common. The field is stronger because of its diversity.

There has been increasing interest in the relationship between worldviews and individual identity. Identities are not now seen as being formed; rather, they shift depending on contexts such that we are constructed by our history, geography, and culture. As such, the re-emergence of place-based approaches offers new avenues for research (see, for example, Duhn, 2012; Payne & Wattchow, 2009; Semken & Freeman, 2008).

This review of the environmental education research is partial. Other authors would draw on different sources, make different points, and draw different conclusions. It is, however, an attempt to convey a sense that the field merits study and has something to offer science education. It is an emerging and developing field that finds itself at the very heart of issues that influence our daily lives in ways that many of us never imagined some decades ago.

Acknowledgments

Thanks to Nir Orion and Jan H. van Driel, who reviewed this chapter.

References

Arslan, H.O., Cigdemoglu, C., & Moseley, C. (2012). A three-tier diagnostic test to assess pre-service teachers' misconceptions about global warming, greenhouse effect, ozone layer depletion, and acid rain. *International Journal of Science Education, 34*(11), 1667–1686.

Ashley, M. (2005). Tensions between indoctrination and the development of judgment: The case against early closure. *Environmental Education Research, 11*(2), 187–197.

Bauman, Z. (1993). *Postmodern ethics.* Oxford: Blackwell.

Bodzin, A. M. (2011). The implementation of a geospatial information technology (GIT)-supported land use change curriculum with urban middle school learners to promote spatial thinking. *Journal of Research in Science Teaching, 48,* 281–300.

Boeve-de Pauw, J., & Van Petegem, P. (2011). The effect of Flemish eco-schools on student environmental knowledge, attitudes, and affect. *International Journal of Science Education, 33*(11), 1513–1538.

Bögeholz, S. (2006). Nature experience and its importance for environmental knowledge, values and action: Recent German empirical contributions. *Environmental Education Research, 12*(1), 65–84.

Bolscho, D., & Michelsen, G. (Eds.). (1999). *Methoden der Umweltbildungsforschung.* Opladen: Leske + Budrich.

Boyes, E., & Stanisstreet, M. (2012). Environmental education for behaviour change: Which actions should be targeted? *International Journal of Science Education, 34*(10), 1591–1614.

Carson, R. (1962). *Silent spring.* New York: Houghton-Mifflin.

Castano, C. (2008). Socio-scientific discussions as a way to improve the comprehension of science and the understanding of the interrelation between species and the environment. *Research in Science Education, 38*(5), 565–587.

Chawla, L. (1998). Significant life experiences: A review of research on sources of environmental sensitivity. *Journal of Environmental Education, 29*(3), 11–21.

Dierking, L.D., & Falk, J.H. (1997). School field trips: Assessing their long-term impact. *Curator, 40,* 211–218.

Dillon, J. (2003). On learners and learning in environmental education: Missing theories, ignored communities. *Environmental Education Research, 9*(2), 215–226.

Dillon, J., & Dickie, I. (2012). *Learning in the natural environment: Review of social and economic benefits and barriers.* Natural England Commissioned Reports, Number 092. London: Natural England. Retrieved from http://publications.naturalengland.org.uk/publication/1321181

Dillon, J., & Scott, W. (2002). Perspectives on environmental education–related research in science education. *International Journal of Science Education, 24,* 1111–1117.

Dimick, A.S. (2012). Student empowerment in an environmental science classroom: Toward a framework for social justice science education. *Science Education, 96,* 990–1012.

Disinger, J. (1984). Environmental education research news. *The Environmentalist, 4,* 109–112.

Disinger, J. (1990). Environmental education for sustainable development? *Journal of Environmental Education, 21*(4), 3–6.

Duhn, I. (2012). Making "place" for ecological sustainability in early childhood education. *Environmental Education Research, 18*(1), 19–29.

Eaton, D. (2000). Cognitive and affective learning in outdoor education. *Dissertation Abstracts International—Section A: Humanities and Social Sciences, 60,* 10–A, 3595.

Ebenezer, J., Kaya, O.N., & Ebenezer, D.L. (2011). Engaging students in environmental research projects: Perceptions of fluency with innovative technologies and levels of scientific inquiry abilities. *Journal of Research in Science Teaching, 48,* 94–116.

Evagorou, M., Jimenez-Aleixandre, M. P., & Osborne, J. (2012). Should we kill the grey squirrels? A study exploring students' justifications and decision-making. *International Journal of Science Education, 34*(3), 401–428.

Evans, J., & Boyden, S. (Eds.). (1970). *Education and the environmental crisis.* Canberra, Australia: Australian Academy of Science.

Ferreira, J.-A. (2013). Transformation, empowerment and the governing of environmental conduct: Insights to be gained from a "history of the present" approach. In R.B. Stevenson, M. Brody, J. Dillon, & A.E.J. Wals (Eds.), *International handbook of research in environmental education* (pp. 63–68). New York: Routledge.

Fettis, G.C., & Ramsden, M.J. (1995). Sustainability—what is it and how should it be taught? *ENTRÉE' 95 Proceedings,* 81–90.

Fields, D.A. (2009). What do students gain from a week at science camp? Youth perceptions and the design of an immersive, research-oriented astronomy camp. *International Journal of Science Education, 31*(2), 151–171.

Foster, J. (2001). Education as sustainability. *Environmental Education Research, 7*(2), 153–165.

Goodson, I.F. (1983). *School subjects and curriculum change.* London/ Sydney: Croom Helm.

Gough, A. (2013a). The emergence of environmental education research. In R.B. Stevenson, M. Brody, J. Dillon, & A.E.J. Wals (Eds.), *International handbook of research in environmental education* (pp. 13–22). New York: Routledge.

Gough, N. (2013b). Thinking globally in environmental education. In R.B. Stevenson, M. Brody, J. Dillon, & A.E.J. Wals (Eds.), *International handbook of research in environmental education* (pp. 33–44). New York: Routledge.

Greenwood, D.A., & McKenzie, M. (Eds.). (2009). Context, experience and the socioecological: Inquiries into practice. *Canadian Journal of Environmental Education, 14*(1), n.p.

Greig, S., Pike, G., & Selby, D. (1987). *Earthrights education as if the planet really mattered.* London: World Wildlife Fund.

Gunckel, K.L., Covitt, B.A., Salinas, I., & Anderson, C.W. (2012). A learning progression for water in socio-ecological systems. *Journal of Research in Science Teaching, 49,* 843–868.

Gurevitz, R. (2000). Affective approaches to environmental education: Going beyond the imagined worlds of childhood? *International Journal of Science Education, 24,* 645–660.

Hart, P. (2003). Reflections on reviewing educational research: (Re) searching for value in environmental education. *Environmental Education Research, 9*(2), 241–256.

Hart, P. (2007). Environmental education. In S.K. Abell & N.G. Lederman (Eds.), *Handbook of research on science education* (pp. 689–726). New York: Routledge.

Hart, P., & Nolan, K. (1999). A critical analysis of research in environmental education. *Studies in Science Education, 34,* 1–69.

Harvester, L., & Blenkinsop, S. (2010). Environmental education and ecofeminist pedagogy: Bridging the environmental and the social. *Canadian Journal of Environmental Education, 15,* 120–134.

Hesselink, F., van Kempen, P.P., & Wals, A.E.J. (2000). *ESDebate: International on-line debate on education for sustainable development.* Gland, Switzerland: IUCN.

Hines, J.M., Hungerford, H.R., & Tomera, A.N. (1987). Analysis and synthesis of research on responsible environmental behavior: A meta-analysis. *Journal of Environmental Education, 18*(2), 1–8.

Hopkins, C. (1998). The content of education for sustainable development. In M.J. Scoullos (Ed.), *Environment and society: Education and public awareness for sustainability; proceedings of the Thessaloniki International Conference.* Paris: Unesco.

Hungerford, H.R., & Volk, T.L. (1990). Changing learner behavior through environmental education. *Journal of Environmental Education, 21*(3), 8–21.

Ideland, M., Malmberg, C., & Winberg, M. (2011). Culturally equipped for socio-scientific issues? A comparative study on how teachers and students in mono- and multiethnic schools handle work with complex issues. *International Journal of Science Education, 33*(13), 1835–1859.

Iozzi, L.A. (1981). *Research in environmental education 1971–1980* (ED214762). Columbus, OH: ERIC Clearinghouse for Science, Mathematics, and Environmental Education.

Jakobsson, A., Mäkitalo, Å., & Säljö, R. (2009). Conceptions of knowledge in research on students' understanding of the greenhouse effect: Methodological positions and their consequences for representations of knowing. *Science Education, 93,* 978–995.

Jensen, B.B., & Schnack, K. (1997). The action competence approach in environmental education. *Environmental Education Research, 3*(2), 163–178.

Jickling, B. (1999). Education for sustainability: A seductive idea, but is it enough for my grandchildren? In Blanken, ir. H. (Ed.), *NME met een duurzaam perspectief, essaybundel bij de slotconferentie NME Extra Impuls 1996–1999* (pp. 34–38) *(EE in a sustainable perspective, a collection of essays in the context of the final conference of the program Extra Impulse EE 1996–1999).* Amsterdam: NCDO.

Jickling, B. (2004a). Making ethics an everyday activity: How can we reduce the barriers? *Canadian Journal of Environmental Education, 9*(1), 11–28.

Jickling, B. (Ed.). (2004b). *Canadian Journal of Environmental Education, 9*(1).

Judson, E. (2011). The impact of field trips and family involvement on mental models of the desert environment. *International Journal of Science Education, 33*(13), 1455–1472.

Kim, M., & Tan, H.T. (2013). A collaborative problem-solving process through environmental field studies. *International Journal of Science Education, 35*(3), 357–387.

Kirkeby Hansen, P.J. (2010). Knowledge about the greenhouse effect and the effects of the ozone layer among Norwegian pupils finishing compulsory education in 1989, 1993, and 2005—What now? *International Journal of Science Education, 32*(3), 397–419.

Knapp, D. (1998). The Thessaloniki Declaration—the beginning of the end for environmental education. *Environmental Communicator, 28*(2), 2–14.

Kollmuss, A., & Agyeman, J. (2002). Mind the gap: Why do people act environmentally and what are the barriers to pro-environmental behavior? *Environmental Education Research, 8*(3), 239–260.

Kyburz-Graber, R. (1999). Environmental education as critical education: How teachers and students handle the challenge. *Cambridge Journal of Education, 29*(3), 415–432.

Kyburz-Graber, R. (2013). Socio-ecological approaches to environmental education and research: A paradigmatic response to behavioral change orientations. In R.B. Stevenson, M. Brody, J. Dillon, & A.E.J. Wals (Eds.), *International handbook of research in environmental education* (pp. 23–32). New York: Routledge.

Kyburz-Graber, R., Rigendinger, L., Hirsch Hadorn, G., & Werner Zentner, K. (1997a). *Sozio-ökologische Umweltbildung.* Hamburg: Krämer.

Kyburz-Graber, R., Rigendinger, L., Hirsch Hadorn, G., & Werner Zentner, K. (1997b). A socio-ecological approach to interdisciplinary environmental education in senior high schools. *Environmental Education Research, 3*(1), 17–28.

Lambert, J.L., Lindgren, J., & Bleicher, R. (2012). Assessing elementary science methods students' understanding about global climate change. *International Journal of Science Education, 34*(8), 1167–1187.

Lee, Y.C., & Grace, M. (2012). Students' reasoning and decision making about a socioscientific issue: A cross-context comparison. *Science Education, 96,* 787–807.

Levine Rose, S., & Calabrese Barton, A. (2012). Should Great Lakes City build a new power plant? How youth navigate socioscientific issues. *Journal of Research in Science Teaching, 49,* 541–567.

Lombardi, D., & Sinatra, G.M. (2012). College students' perceptions about the plausibility of human-induced climate change. *Research in Science Education, 42*(2), 201–217.

Lombardi, D., & Sinatra, G.M. (2013). Emotions about teaching about human-induced climate change. *International Journal of Science Education, 35*(1), 167–191.

Luehmann, A.L. (2009). Students' perspectives of a science enrichment programme: Out-of-school inquiry as access. *International Journal of Science Education, 31*(13), 1831–1855.

Maller, C. (2005). Hands-on contact with nature in primary schools as a catalyst for developing a sense of community and cultivating mental health and wellbeing. *Eingana, 28,* 16–21.

Mallya, A., Mensah, F.M., Contento, I.R., Koch, P.A., & Barton, A.C. (2012). Extending science beyond the classroom door: Learning from students' experiences with the *Choice, Control and Change (C3)* curriculum. *Journal of Research in Science Teaching, 49,* 244–269.

Malone, K. (2008). *Every experience matters: An evidence based research report on the role of learning outside the classroom for children's whole development from birth to eighteen years.* Report commissioned by Farming and Countryside Education for UK Department Children, School and Families. Wollongong, Australia: University of Wollongong.

Manjengwa, J., et al. (1999). *Environmental education*. Harare, Zimbabwe: Open University Press.

Marcinkowski, T. (1993). A contextual review of the "quantitative paradigm" in EE research. In R. Mrazek (Ed.), *Alternative paradigms in environmental education research* (pp. 29–78). Troy, OH: North American Association for Environmental Education.

Marcinkowski, T. (2003). Commentary on Rickinson's "Learners and learning in environmental education: A critical review of the evidence" (*EER* 7(3)), *Environmental Education Research, 9*(2), 181–213.

Martin, G.C., & Wheeler, K. (Eds.). (1975). *Insights into environmental education*. London: Oliver and Boyd.

McCrea, E.J. (n.d.). *The roots of environmental education: How the past supports the future*. Retrieved from http://cms.eetap.org/repository/moderncms_documents/History.Final.20060315.1.1.pdf

McKeown, R., & Hopkins, C. (2003). EE does not equal ESD: Defusing the worry. *Environmental Education Research, 9*(1), 118–128.

McNeill, K.L., & Houle Vaughn, M. (2012). Urban high school students' critical science agency: Conceptual understandings and environmental actions around climate change. *Research in Science Education, 42*(2), 373–399.

Moss Gamblin, K. (2012). Personal communication. July 9, 2012.

National Association for Research in Science Teaching (NARST). (2013). *NARST strand descriptions*. Retrieved from www.narst.org/about/strands.cfm

Nisiforou, O., & Charalambides, A.G. (2012). Assessing undergraduate university students' level of knowledge, attitudes and behaviour towards biodiversity: A case study in Cyprus. *International Journal of Science Education, 34*(7), 1027–1051.

Nundy, S. (1998). *The fieldwork effect: An exploration of fieldwork at KS2*. Unpublished PhD thesis, University of Southampton.

Nundy, S. (1999a). The fieldwork effect: The role and impact of fieldwork in the upper primary school. *International Research in Geographical and Environmental Education, 8,* 190–198.

Nundy, S. (1999b). Thoughts from the field: In their own words . . . *Horizons, 4,* 20–22.

O'Donoghue, R., & McNaught, C. (1991). Environmental education: The development of a curriculum through "grass-roots" reconstructive action. *International Journal of Science Education, 13*(4), 391–404.

Oerke, B., & Bogner, F.X. (2013). Social desirability, environmental attitudes, and general ecological behaviour in children. *International Journal of Science Education, 35*(5), 713–730.

Oliveira, A.W., Akerson, V.L., & Oldfield, M. (2012). Environmental argumentation as sociocultural activity. *Journal of Research in Science Teaching, 49,* 869–897.

Online Colloquium. (1998). *The future of environmental education in a postmodern world*. Whitehorse, Canada: Yukon College.

Pawley, D. (2000). Sustainability: A big word with little meaning. *Independent,* 11 July. Retrieved from www.audacity.org/Resourcing%20the%20future.htm

Payne, P.G., & Wattchow, B. (2009). Phenomenological seconstruction, slow pedagogy, and the corporeal turn in wild environmental/outdoor education. *Canadian Journal of Environmental Education, 14,* 15–32.

Pike, G., & Selby, D. (1995). *Reconnecting: From national to global curriculum*. Guildford, UK: World Wide Fund for Nature UK.

Posch, P. (1993). Research issues in environmental education. *Studies in Science Education, 21,* 21–48.

Pritchard, T. (1975). World environmental education: The role of the IUCN. In G.C. Martin & K. Wheeler (Eds.), *Insights into environmental education* (pp. 177–194). London: Oliver and Boyd.

Ramsey, J.M., Hungerford, H.R., & Volk, T.L. (1992). Environmental education in the K–12 curriculum: Finding a niche. *Journal of Environmental Education, 23*(2), 35–45.

Randler, C., Ilg, A., & Kern, J. (2005). Cognitive and emotional evaluation of an amphibian conservation program for elementary school students. *Journal of Environmental Education, 37,* 43–52.

Ratinen, I.J. (2013). Primary student-teachers' conceptual understanding of the greenhouse effect: A mixed methods study. *International Journal of Science Education, 35*(6), 929–955.

Rauch, F. (2002). The potential of education for sustainable development for reform in schools. *Environmental Education Research, 8*(1), 43–51.

Reid, A., & Nikel, J. (2003). Reading a critical review of evidence: Notes and queries on research programmes in environmental education. *Environmental Education Research, 9*(2), 149–165.

Rickinson, M. (2001). Special issue: Learners and learning in environmental education: A critical review of the evidence. *Environmental Education Research, 7*(3), 208–320.

Rickinson, M. (2003). Reviewing research evidence in environmental education: Some methodological reflections and challenges. *Environmental Education Research, 9*(2), 257–271.

Rickinson, M., Dillon, J., Teamey, K., Morris, M., Choi, M.Y., Sanders, D., & Benefield, P. (2004). *A review of research on outdoor learning*. Preston Montford, Shropshire, UK: Field Studies Council.

Robottom, I. (Ed.). (1987). *Environmental education: Practice and possibility*. Geelong, Victoria: Deakin University Press.

Robottom, I. (2003). Communities, environmental issues and environmental education research. *Education Relative A L'Environnement: Regards; Recherches; Reflexion, 4,* 77–97.

Robottom, I., & Hart, P. (1993). *Research in environmental education. Engaging the debate*. Geelong, Victoria: Deakin University Press.

Ruiz-Mallen, I., Barraza, L., Bodenhorn, B., de la Paz Ceja-Adame, M., & Reyes-García, V. (2010). Contextualising learning through the participatory construction of an environmental education programme. *International Journal of Science Education, 32*(13), 1755–1770.

Russell, C., & Dillon, J. (Eds.). (2010). *Canadian Journal of Science, Mathematics, and Technology Education, 10*(1). Special Issue on Environmental Education in Science, Mathematics, and Technology Education.

Sachs, W. (1995). Global ecology and the shadow of development. Retrieved from www.laucksfoundation.org/public_html/lauckswebpage/reprints/131.pdf

Sauvé, L. (1996). Environmental education and sustainable development. *Canadian Journal of Environmental Education, 1,* 7–35.

Sauvé, L., & Berryman, T. (2003). Researchers and research in environmental education: A critical review essay on Mark Rickinson's report on learners and learning. *Environmental Education Research, 9*(2), 167–180.

Sauvé, L., Brunelle, R., & Berryman, T. (2005). Influence of the globalized and globalizing sustainable development framework on national policies related to environmental education. *Policy Futures in Education, 3*(3), 271–283.

Saylan, C., & Blumstein, D.T. (2011). *The failure of environmental education [and how we can fix it]*. Berkeley and Los Angeles: University of California Press.

Scott, W., & Gough, S. (2003). *Sustainable development and learning. Framing the issues*. London: RoutledgeFalmer.

Selby, D. (2001). The signature of the whole: Radical interconnectedness and its implications for global and environmental education. *Encounter. Education for Meaning and Social Justice, 14*(1), 5–16.

Semken, S., & Freeman, C.B. (2008). Sense of place in the practice and assessment of place-based science teaching. *Science Education, 92,* 1042–1057.

Sia, A.P., Hungerford, H.R., & Tomera, A.N. (1985/1986). Selected predictors of responsible environmental behaviour. *Journal of Environmental Education, 17*(2), 31–40.

Skamp, K., Boyes, E., & Stanisstreet, M. (2013). Beliefs and willingness to act about global warming: Where to focus science pedagogy? *Science Education, 97,* 191–217.

Smyth, J. (1998). Environmental education—the beginning of the end or the end of the beginning? *Environmental Communicator, 28*(4), 14–16.

Stapp, W. (1974). Historical setting of environmental education. In W.B. Stapp, A.E.J. Wals, & S.L. Stankorb (Eds.), *Environmental education for empowerment. Action research and community problem solving* (pp. 41–49). Dubuque, IA: Kendall/Hunt Publishing Company.

Stapp, W., et al. (1970). The concept of environmental education. *Education Digest, 35*(7), 8–10.

State Education and Environment Roundtable (SEER). (2000). *The effects of environment-based education on student achievement* [online]. Retrieved from www.seer.org/pages/research/CSAPII2005.pdf

Sterling, S. (2001). *Sustainable education: Re-visioning learning and change.* Dartington: Green Books Ltd.

Sterling, S. (2005). *LinkingThinking: New perspectives on thinking and learning for sustainability.* Perthshire, Scotland: WWF Scotland.

Stern, P. (2000). Toward a coherent theory of environmentally significant behavior. *Journal of Social Issues, 50*(3), 65–84.

Sternäng, L., & Lundholm, C. (2011). Climate change and morality: Students' perspectives on the individual and society. *International Journal of Science Education, 33*(8), 1131–1148.

Stevenson, R. B., Brody, M., Dillon, J., & Wals, A. E. J. (Eds.). (2013). *International handbook of research in environmental education.* New York: Routledge.

Summers, M., Childs, A., & Corney, G. (2005). Education for sustainable development in initial teacher training: Issues for interdisciplinary collaboration. *Environmental Education Research, 11*(5), 623–647.

Summers, M., Corney, G., & Childs, A. (2003). Teaching sustainable development in primary schools: An empirical study of issues for teachers. *Environmental Education Research, 9*(3), 327–346.

Svihla, V., & Linn, M. C. (2012). A design-based approach to fostering understanding of global climate change. *International Journal of Science Education, 34*(5), 651–676.

Swan, J. A. (2010). Transpersonal psychology and the ecological conscience. *Journal of Transpersonal Psychology, 42*(1), 2–25.

Symons, G. (2000). Commitment to sustainable development: A rationale for the curriculum? *Primary Teaching Studies, 11*(2), 23–29.

Tal, T. (2008). Learning about agriculture within the framework of education for sustainability. *Environmental Education Research, 14*(3), 273–290.

Taskin, O. (2009). The environmental attitudes of Turkish senior high school students in the context of postmaterialism and the new environmental paradigm. *International Journal of Science Education, 31*(4), 481–452.

Taylor, N., Nathan, S., & Coll, R. K. (2003). Education for sustainability in regional New South Wales, Australia: An exploratory study of some teachers' perceptions. *International Research in Geographical and Environmental Education, 12*(4), 291–311.

Tilbury, D. (1995). Environmental education for sustainability: Defining the new focus of environmental education in the 1990s. *Environmental Education Research, 1*(2), 195–212.

Tomas, L., Ritchie, S. M., & Tones, M. (2011). Attitudinal impact of hybridized writing about a socioscientific issue. *Journal of Research in Science Teaching, 48,* 878–900.

Tran, N. E. (2011). The relationship between students' connections to out-of-school experiences and factors associated with science learning. *International Journal of Science Education, 33*(12), 1625–1651.

Tseverini, I. (2011). Towards an environmental education without scientific knowledge: An attempt to create an action model based on

children's experiences, emotions and perceptions about their environment. *Environmental Education Research, 17*(1), 53–67.

UNESCO-EPD. (1997). *Declaration of Thessaloniki.* (UNESCO Publication No. EPD-97/CONF.401/CLD.Z). Paris: Author.

United Nations. (2002). *Report of the World Summit on Sustainable Development.* Johannesburg, South Africa, 26 August–4 September 2002. New York: United Nations.

United Nations Educational, Scientific, and Cultural Organization (UNESCO). (1975). *The Belgrade Charter. A global framework for environmental education.* Retrieved from www.envir.ee/orb.aw/class=file/action=preview/id=1011467/The%2BBelgrade%2BCharter.pdf

United Nations Educational, Scientific, and Cultural Organization (UNESCO). (1978). *Intergovernmental Conference on Environmental Education: Tbilisi (USSR), 14–26 October 1977. Final Report.* Paris: Author.

United Nations Environment Program (UNEP). (1972). *Declaration of the United Nations Conference on the Human Environment.* Retrieved from www.unep.org/Documents.Multilingual/Default.Print.asp?documentid=97&articleid=1503

Vasconcelos, C. (2012). Teaching environmental education through PBL: Evaluation of a teaching intervention program. *Research in Science Education, 42*(2), 219–232.

Volk, T., & McBeth, W. (1997). *Environmental literacy in the United States.* Washington, DC: North American Association for Environmental Education.

Wagner, J. (1993). Ignorance in educational research: Or, how can you *not* know that? *Educational Researcher, 22*(5), 15–23.

Wals, A. E. J. (1993). Critical phenomenology and environmental education research. In R. Mrazek (Ed.), *Alternative paradigms in environmental education research* (pp. 153–174). Troy, OH: North American Association for Environmental Education.

Wals, A. E. J., & Jickling, B. (1999). Process-based environmental education: Setting standards without standardizing. In B. B. Jensen, K. Schnack, & V. Simovska (Eds.). *Critical environmental and health education.* Copenhagen: Royal School of Educational Studies.

Ward, M. (2002). Environmental management: Expertise, uncertainty, responsibility. In E. Janse van Rensburg, J. Hattingh, H. Lotz-Sisitka, & R. O'Donoghue (Eds.), *Environmental education, ethics and action in Southern Africa* (pp. 28–35). Pretoria, South Africa: Human Sciences Research Council.

Wheeler, K. (1975). The genesis of environmental education. In G. C. Martin & K. Wheeler (Eds.), *Insights into environmental education* (pp. 2–20). London: Oliver and Boyd.

Whittington, A. (2006). Challenging girls' constructions of femininity in the outdoors. *Journal of Experiential Education, 28,* 205–221.

Williams, D. R., & Dixon, P. S. (2013). Synthesis of research between 1990 and 2010: Impact of garden-based learning on academic outcomes. *Review of Educational Research, 83*(2), 211–235.

Williams, M. (Ed.). (1996). *Understanding geographical and environmental education: The role of research.* London: Cassell.

World Commission on Environment and Development (WCED). (1987). *Our common future.* Oxford, UK: Oxford University Press.

Zelezny, L. (1999). Educational interventions that improve environmental behaviors: A meta-analysis. *Journal of Environmental Education, 31*(1), 5–14.

26

From Inquiry to Scientific Practices in the Science Classroom

Barbara A. Crawford

Overview

In preparing this chapter on inquiry/scientific practices in the science classroom, the main focus is on recently published peer-refereed journal articles and chapters in handbooks, together with seminal articles in the literature on science teaching and learning. Recent findings are juxtaposed with historical works to better understand how we can support children in understanding (a) how to do inquiry, (b) how to use inquiry to develop deep understandings of science concepts, (c) what science is and what science is not, and, (d) how to think critically. The chapter begins with a discussion of the confusion surrounding the meaning of inquiry in science classrooms, and the variations of classroom inquiry that appear in the literature. For the purposes of this chapter, the author uses the phrase *teaching science as inquiry* to include both the pedagogy and the learning outcomes of inquiry, the pedagogy being the method of engaging students in designing and carrying out investigations and the learning outcomes referring to learning science subject matter by engaging in these investigations, in addition to learning "about" the nature of scientific inquiry. Related to learning "about" the nature of scientific inquiry, there is overlap with the learner developing understandings of nature of science.

> Important to this view of inquiry are the following student outcomes: appreciating the diverse ways in which scientists conduct their work; understanding the power of observations; knowledge of and ability to ask testable questions, make hypotheses; use various forms of data to search for patterns, confirm or reject hypotheses; construct and defend a model or argument; consider alternate explanations, and gain an understanding of the tentativeness of science, including the human aspects of science, such as subjectivity and societal influences.
> (Crawford, 2007, p. 614)

In combining historical views by Dewey and Schwab with modern views of authors of the new U.S. K–12

Framework (National Research Council [NRC], 2012) and Next Generation Science Standards (NGSS Lead States, 2013), the following definition is offered: *Teaching science as inquiry involves engaging students in using critical thinking skills, which includes asking questions, designing and carrying out investigations, interpreting data as evidence, creating arguments, building models, and communicating findings in the pursuit of deepening their understanding by using logic and evidence about the natural world.*

The chapter traces the history of emphasis on inquiry in K–12 science classrooms in the United States, as well as in countries around the world. In addition, the question of whether classroom inquiry is different or the same as inquiry done by scientists is addressed. Empirical evidence related to teachers' views and knowledge and classroom practices and models of how to support prospective and practicing teachers are presented. Benefits to students and challenges for teachers related to teaching science as inquiry are discussed. The chapter concludes with implications and proposed future research directions.

Confusion About the Meaning of Inquiry in Classrooms

Inquiry has a long history in science education reform documents, advocating that teachers use inquiry strategies that involve children in asking scientifically valid questions, setting up investigations, collecting and analyzing data, and coming to some conclusion based on the data collected. Most conversations about reform-based science teaching include the word "inquiry." Yet there is much disagreement about what inquiry teaching actually entails. Further, "Science educators continue to debate the place of inquiry in the teaching of science" (Duschl, Schweingruber, & Shouse, 2007, p. 12).

The author remembers presenting an early research study on teaching science as inquiry at a conference of the Worldwide Organization for Improving Science Teaching and Learning Through Research (NARST). The study documented and analyzed a prospective science teacher's journey into using inquiry to teach science (Crawford, 1999). After the presentation and just as the questions began, Dr. Sandra K. Abell leaped up from her chair, pointed her finger in the air, and asked, "Just what is it? What do you mean by inquiry?" Therein ensued a lively discussion and debate among the members of the audience. This kind of debate and discussion has continued into the 21st century.

In the 1990s, educational reforms in the United States positioned inquiry as the central organizing theme in science teaching. (See *National Science Education Standards* [NRC, 1996]). Despite this renewed interest, Bybee (2000) stated,

> The idea of teaching science as inquiry has a rather long history in science education. There is an equally long history of confusion . . . and . . . its implementation in the classroom. In short, we espouse the idea and do not carry out the practice.
>
> (p. 20)

Today, inquiry in the science classroom is advocated and expected yet surprisingly rare and enigmatic. More than a decade into the 21st century, many researchers claim that inquiry is not very commonly observed and most certainly is not the central organizing theme in most science classrooms in the United States (e.g., Capps & Crawford, 2012). Other countries, such as Singapore, have reported a similar state of affairs related to the status of science inquiry teaching (e.g., Kim & Tan, 2011). When observers look into many science classrooms, teachers are still delivering science concepts and principles through primarily lecture mode, and their students will likely, but not always, be passively listening and taking notes. If the lesson involves a laboratory experience, students will likely run through the procedures, step by step, in order to verify a known result. The laboratory lesson may resemble the kind of tightly structured, traditional science teaching practice found in many classrooms of the last century. Many science educators can list and describe what is *not* inquiry, yet there remains a great deal of confusion about how to precisely characterize what *is inquiry* and what it means to teach science as inquiry and all the ramifications.

In the early 1990s, there were concerted efforts to clearly define inquiry. Yet during the last two decades, many researchers lamented the lack of agreement about what inquiry entails (e.g., Barrow, 2006; Minstrell & van Zee, 2000). Multiple meanings and interpretations have been put forth, leaving many teacher educators and teachers, as well as researchers, in a quandary. Like others, Barrow (2006) called for a consensus to be reached among teacher educators. In the early 1990s, there were concerted efforts to clearly define inquiry. Minstrell (2000) provided a list of characteristics of inquiry teaching, including developing habits of the mind, motivating students, using hands-on and minds-on activities to study particular phenomena, and student-generated questions.

Today, there still remains confusion swirling around inquiry related to classroom instruction. At the turn of the 21st century, Wheeler (2000) pointed out the inconsistencies of meaning; "inquiry" is an *elastic* word, stretched and twisted to fit people's differing worldviews (p. 14). Anderson (2002) recognized different uses of the term "inquiry" and highlighted three articulated in the *NSES* (NRC, 1996). Several years later Anderson declared, "[I]nquiry is an *imprecise* word . . . it has different meanings in varied contexts, and is hard to guess what particular meaning a given speaker has in mind when the word is used" (2007, p. 808). Three uses of "inquiry" in science classrooms will be addressed in this chapter (modified from Anderson, 2002): (1) *scientific inquiry* (the various ways in which scientists study the natural world): (2) *inquiry learning* (a process by which children acquire knowledge of science concepts and learn about nature of science); and (3) *inquiry teaching* (broadly defined as the pedagogy by which teachers engage students in inquiry.

Myths of Inquiry in Science Classrooms

Numerous myths and misconceptions are identified in the literature. The term "inquiry" appeared frequently in the *NSES* (NRC, 1996, 2000), yet there was still little resolution about what the term meant. Anderson claimed the third use, "inquiry teaching," to be the most ill defined construct of the three.

Myths about inquiry as attributed to the *NSES* (NRC, 1996) include:

> Myth 1: All science subject matter should be taught through inquiry.
> Myth 2: True inquiry occurs only when students generate and pursue their own questions.
> Myth 3: Inquiry teaching occurs easily through use of hands-on or kit-based instructional materials.
> Myth 4: Student engagement in hands-on activities guarantees that inquiry teaching and learning are occurring.
> Myth 5: Inquiry can be taught without attention to subject matter.
>
> (p. 36)

Clearly, one of the most misguided notions of inquiry in classrooms is that inquiry means *exactly* the same as students having hands-on experiences. This is an inaccurate simplification of inquiry in the classroom and overlooks the basic need for a process to seek an explanation for a driving question. Further, "hands-on experience is important but does not guarantee meaningfulness" (American Association for the Advancement of Science [AAAS], 1993, p. 319). The Horizon Classroom Observation Protocol identifies "hands-on activity for activity's sake" as poor teaching (Horizon Research Corporation, Inc., 1999). A teacher erroneously concluded that if a student holds something or draws a picture holding a crayon, this would constitute "hands-on science" (personal communication, Czerniak, May 2013). Therefore, one myth is that, if a student is involved in hands-on activity, there is evidence that inquiry teaching and learning is taking place.

Another myth is that inquiry is devoid of science. In other words, inquiry can be used/taught without attention to subject matter (NRC, 2000, p. 36). A third myth involves the notion that open inquiry is the ultimate goal for all classrooms. "Holding open inquiry as the purest form of classroom inquiry and suggesting it is an ideal for which science teachers should strive is a myth" (Settlage, 2007, p. 464). For researchers and teacher educators, these myths are important to recognize and discount.

Researchers often define teaching science as inquiry in slightly differently ways. Furtak and co-authors (2012) called attention to the fact that "[T]he different terms used to describe inquiry sometimes refer to the amount of guidance provided by the teacher (e.g., discovery learning) and other times refer to the cognitive activities of the student [e.g., model-based inquiry]" (p. 324). The dual issues of (a) the amount of teacher direction and (b) the quality of the cognitive activities are important to consider when assessing the nature of the teaching of science as inquiry experience in a particular classroom. Many researchers have moved on from debating whether inquiry is "good" to researching the characteristics of inquiry instruction present in the classroom. Many researchers now focus on answering how inquiry can be successfully enacted in a wide variety of schools. Barriers, both external (classroom context and school culture) and internal (teacher knowledge, beliefs, and views), to inquiry in classrooms have been examined, and these have implications for preservice and inservice teacher education. These issues will be discussed later in this chapter.

Presently, researchers, teacher educators, and policy makers in the United States are striving to articulate more clearly what it means to engage children in inquiry in a science classroom—in other words, to address Dr. Sandra Abell's question, "What *is* it?" The author uses the phrase *teaching science as inquiry* in this chapter to include teachers using a pedagogical approach that supports their students in learning about scientific inquiry and

in developing knowledge of science concepts and nature of science through an inquiry process. Learning *about* scientific inquiry involves both the "doing" of inquiry (practices) and learning *about* the "nature of scientific inquiry" as content. Teaching students to "do" inquiry involves engaging students in asking scientific questions, designing and carrying out investigations, interpreting data, developing models and explanations, and communicating and using arguments to defend these explanations. In answering scientific questions posed by the teacher or her students, and *with the expert guidance of the teacher*, the student makes sense of observations, the text in a book, images on a computer screen, or the data gathered during an investigation. A student figures out something for her- or himself and connects this with scientific views. In an inquiry classroom, students engage in generating and evaluating scientific explanations of the natural world as they participate in scientific practices and discussion. At the heart of inquiry is the learner grappling with data and using evidence and logic to make sense of some event or phenomenon in a social, collaborative environment (NGSS Lead States, 2013; NRC, 1996, 2000). Through teaching science as inquiry, teachers can facilitate diverse children, those from populations traditionally underrepresented in the sciences, in learning how to *think scientifically*.

Variations of Inquiry in Science Classrooms

In striving to untangle the many meanings of inquiry, it seems intuitive that in all cases, there should be a central question that leads to investigation and exploration. Beyond the presence of a question, there are nuances of inquiry teaching and learning. Some of the different variations include: (a) project-based, (b) problem-based, (c) authentic science, (d) citizen science, and (e) model-based inquiry. See Table 26.1. These variations are described in what follows.

Project-based science. In the mid- to late 1990s, researchers described an instructional approach called project-based science (PBS). PBS involves the learner in active construction of science concepts and principles through carrying out investigations in collaboration with others. PBS emphasizes four features: a "driving

TABLE 26.1
Variations of Teaching Science as Inquiry

Variation	Key Components	Expectation
Project-Based	Driving question, collaboration, use of new technology, authentic artifacts	Students carry out meaningful investigations as a means of learning science facts and principles
Problem-Based	Solving complex real-world questions	Students increase abilities to solve problems; develop intrinsic motivation and self-directed learning
Authentic Science	Science practices aligning closely with the work of scientists; meaningful, real data for others	Students gain an understanding of the nature of scientific inquiry and appreciate aspects of nature of science
Citizen Science	Collaboration between scientists and volunteers; teachers help students follow protocols in collecting scientific data	Students contribute data to scientists, who then analyze the data as part of a real scientific investigation
Model-Based Inquiry	Generation, testing, and revision of scientific models	Students learn how to reason about data and phenomena by using models; invent models, use them, and evaluate them

question," an investigation, collaboration, and use of technological tools (i.e., Krajcik & Czerniak, 2014). Marx and colleagues (1994) defined PBS as "project-based science focuses on student-designed inquiry that is organized by investigations to answer driving questions, includes collaboration among learners and others, the use of new technology, and the creation of authentic artifacts that represent student understanding" (p. 341). A key aspect is the cognitive emphasis on students carrying out meaningful investigations in order to learn science. Over the past 20 years, research associated with PBS has evolved from a theoretical framing based in cognitive psychology (Blumenfeld et al., 1991) to teachers' views and support through professional development (PD); Connor, Capps, Crawford, & Ross, 2013; Marx et al., 1994), teachers' enactments in classrooms (e.g., Crawford, Krajcik, & Marx, 1999; Krajcik et al., 1998; Polman, 2000; Schneider, Krajcik, & Blumenfeld, 2005), assessing impact on student learning (Schneider, Krajcik, Marx, & Soloway, 2002), and most recently to design of assessments and educative curricular materials (Krajcik, McNeill, & Reiser, 2007).

Problem-based learning. A commonly held view of problem-based learning (PBL) is that of a method to foster learning in science classrooms by using complex, real-world problems. PBL has its roots in medical education (e.g., Schmidt, 1983). The learner is presented with a problem to solve, which in the case of medicine may be a patient's illness. In a PBL classroom, the teacher uses a real-world problem to introduce students to related science concepts and to motivate children to learn science in an active and cooperative learning environment. PBL often introduces students to a problem before they necessarily have in-depth knowledge for solving it (Drake & Long, 2009). Problems are typically complex, and students are asked to work in groups to work out a solution. The expectation is that students' abilities to solve problems will increase as their content knowledge grows. Kolodner and colleagues (2003) defined PBL "as a cognitive apprenticeship approach that focuses on learning from problem-solving experience and promotes learning of content and practices at the same time" (p. 497). PBL involves students in learning science concepts by addressing real-world problems, gathering needed scientific information, and reflecting on experiences.

Authentic science. Authentic science is a variation of inquiry teaching that aligns closely with the work of scientists, as contrasted with traditional school science laboratory exercises (commonly called "labs"). An everyday definition of the word "authentic," from the Merriam-Webster Online Dictionary is, *not false or imitation: actual, real and genuine.* Traditional science labs are often contrived, and students already know the answer. By engaging students in authentic science, it is assumed that students will learn more about the practices of science (NRC, 2012). Roth (1995) presented an example

of authentic science in a high school physics classroom. Crawford (2000) provided empirical evidence that students, through their own voices, valued the authenticity of a classroom investigation. Students appreciated that they themselves were not trained scientists, yet they believed they could contribute meaningful, real data for others (Crawford, 2000). One might view scientists' laboratories as the most authentic of all settings for teaching about scientific inquiry or the ways in which science is conducted. In translating practices of science into classrooms, it is hoped that students will gain an understanding of the nature of scientific inquiry, as well as appreciate aspects of nature of science (Schwartz & Crawford, 2004). Woolnough (2000) viewed students' research projects as authentic science, and he found evidence that projects developed core skills, especially problem-solving ones, and communication and interpersonal skills. Roth and Calabrese-Barton (2004) viewed science as a way in which laypeople use knowledge in their daily lives, and they proposed a model of learning that connects scientific literacy to participatory action. Braund and Reiss (2006) proposed an evolutionary model for authentic science. They advocated that out-of-school experiences can supplement students' authentic in-school experiences and claimed that informal learning experiences could serve to enhance traditional school science laboratories.

Citizen science. Citizen science involves collaboration between scientists and volunteers, who collect data for scientists' use (Cohn, 2008). Used in a classroom, one would assume that by participating in citizen science projects, children can learn about scientific practices, the nature of scientific inquiry, as well as science subject matter. In citizen science, teachers help students follow protocols in collecting scientific data. Students contribute data to scientists, who then analyze the data as part of a real scientific investigation. Studies have been conducted to determine the feasibility of scientists actually using the student-collected data by comparing accuracy of data collected by children and experts (i.e., Galloway, Tudor, & Vanderhaegen, 2006). It is not clear that all classroom-based citizen science projects actually produce usable data for scientists. More importantly, in the case of school science, the citizen science inquiry experience should be a point of focus for students and teachers, beyond the authentic data collected for scientists. Citizen science projects are rapidly increasing in number, yet there appears to be limited research on the impact on science knowledge or attitudes, particularly in classrooms (see Brossard, Lewenstein, & Bonney, 2005).

Model-based inquiry. In model-based inquiry (MBI), the learner is involved in the generation, testing, and revision of scientific models (e.g., Passmore & Stewart, 2002; Passmore, Stewart, & Cartier, 2009; Schwarz, 2009). Children engaged in MBI learn how to reason about data and phenomena by using models. One version of MBI includes five epistemic features of scientific knowledge: that it is testable, revisable, explanatory, conjectural, and generative (Windschitl, Thompson, & Braaten, 2008). The goal of MBI in the classroom is to help children learn how to develop defensible explanations of the way the world works. Children propose a model and test it by trying to see the best fit with observations of the natural world. Through engagement in MBI, children should come to understand science concepts, as well as the practice of modeling and argumentation. This kind of teaching demands that a teacher hold a deep understanding of science subject matter and proficiency in supporting children in discussions of data interpretation, model building, and argumentation.

Justification for Inquiry as a Central Focus of Classroom Teaching

Adding to the confusion related to the use of inquiry in science teaching, a few researchers claim that teaching science as inquiry may not benefit students and, in fact, may be detrimental to their learning. In a study that stirred a great deal of debate, researchers claimed inquiry has a negative effect on learning (Kirschner, Sweller, & Clark, 2006). The researchers defined inquiry instruction as teachers acting in a "hands-off" fashion as students carry out investigations through discovery, in a totally self-guided manner. Kirschner and colleagues (2006) concluded teachers should not use inquiry approaches in the classroom. Rather, teachers should use a directed instructional approach coupled with very structured investigations resembling verification-style laboratory activities. Some researchers refuted the claim made by Kirschner's group that inquiry-based teaching does not foster learning. "Kirschner and colleagues have indiscriminately lumped together several distinct pedagogical approaches—constructivist, discovery, problem-based, experiential, and inquiry-based—under the category of minimally guided instruction" (Hmelo-Silver, Duncan, & Chinn, 2007, p. 99). Asserting that Kirchner and colleagues had conflated inquiry learning (IL) and PBL with discovery learning, Hmelo-Silver and co-authors (2007) argued that Kirschner's group had failed to recognize the highly scaffolded nature of these approaches. In another argument weighing the benefits and detriments of inquiry teaching and learning, Mayer (2004) stated, "My thesis . . . is that there is sufficient research evidence to make any reasonable person skeptical about the benefits of discovery learning—practiced under the guise of cognitive constructivism or social constructivism—as a preferred instructional method" (p. 14). Mayer addressed the problem of confounding constructivist teaching (related to inquiry) with pure discovery methods and cautioned that research does not support immersing children in "pure discovery" and underlined the importance of empirical evidence in advocating or negating one teaching approach over another.

Despite some skeptics and an ongoing debate, many science educators remain steadfast in their advocacy for using inquiry in classrooms as a central teaching approach. In general, it appears that teaching science as inquiry is useful in providing a vehicle for facilitating several advocated learning outcomes. But one must be cautious in accepting this conclusion, in that researchers define inquiry and assess student learning in different ways. One must look critically at a particular researcher's definition of inquiry and how the researcher assesses and tracks student learning. In a recent meta-analysis, Furtak and colleagues (2012) concluded, "the results of this meta-analysis affirm this argument that engaging students in guided inquiry contexts does lead to learning gains when contrasted with comparison groups featuring traditional lessons or unstructured student-led activities" (p. 324). Clarity related to various pedagogical approaches is vitally important. Advocates for using inquiry claim the following benefits for students.

1. *Inquiry aligns with how people learn science.* Bybee and Van Scotter (2007) highlighted benefits to learners in this excerpt:

> Research has been conducted on how students learn . . . 1) Students come in with preconceptions of how the world works; 2) Competence in science includes factual knowledge, a conceptual framework, and a way to organize information; and 3) Students can control their own learning through setting goals and monitoring their progress.
>
> (p. 46)

Cognitive science research suggests learning is an active process occurring within the learner and involves building of understanding that is dependent on prior experiences of the learner (i.e., Bransford, Brown, & Cocking, 1999; Driver, Squires, Rushworth, & Wood-Robinson, 1994). Engaging students in inquiry gives them opportunity to actually get the wrong answer, which, in turn, facilitates learning. "Thus knowing why the wrong answer is wrong can help secure a deeper and stronger understanding of why the right answer is right" (NRC, 2012, p. 44).

2. *There is a national need for inquirers and engineers.* In the 1960s, Schwab noted the importance of preparing students to be knowledgeable consumers of science, as well as potentially becoming new scientists.

> What our teachers need to teach is determined, first, by the fact that our national need is a dual one. There is need for an increasing number of fluid inquirers and original engineers. There is also need for a voting and supporting republic of non-scientists who understand the work scientists do. This dual need in turn creates a dual clientele within the schools—those who are, potentially, consumers of scientific knowledge and those whose potential interest and special competences distinguish them as possible makers of that knowledge.
>
> (1960, p. 184)

Throughout the last century and in present day, the United States has stressed the importance of producing more young scientists and engineers as a desired education goal. Equally important is preparing young people to be scientifically literate and consumers of science.

3. *Inquiry is a means to understanding how science is done.* Developing in students an understanding of the core concepts of science and an appreciation that science is a way of knowing about the world have been persistent goals for science educators for many decades. Unfortunately, these goals have yet to be attained for *all*, or even the majority of learners. Bybee and Van Scotter (2007) highlighted the importance of children doing work similar to that of scientists.

> To understand science, students need to do science by participating in activities, completing projects, investigating questions, and discussing interactive readings. As they model how scientists do their work, students develop a better understanding of the process of scientific inquiry.
>
> (p. 46)

Bransford, Brown, and Cocking (1999) claimed that inquiry facilitates students in acquiring (a) a deep foundation of factual knowledge, (b) an understanding of the facts and ideas in the context of a conceptual framework, and (c) an ability to organize knowledge for retrieval of information. In addition, engaging students in inquiry can help students learn to take control of their own learning by defining learning goals and monitoring their progress in achieving them (pp. 10–13).

4. *Inquiry is a means to develop in young people an interest in science.* An important goal of science education is to motivate *all* children in learning science and to instill in them a desire to learn more science and to engage in further inquiry. It is well recognized that during certain formative years (ages 10–14), many students in the United States lose interest in science. Schwab (1960) recognized the benefit of engaging children in first-hand research on their motivation. "The classroom which rests most firmly on the uncertainties, doubts, and difficulties of first-hand reports of investigation is one most likely to evoke his competence and interest" (pp. 191–192). In recent years, projects funded by the National Science Foundation (NSF) have aimed to develop ways to engage diverse students in inquiry. For example, in 2008 the NSF funded the inquiry-based Fossil Finders project. This project features an authentic scientific investigation, and it provides opportunity for teachers and diverse children to contribute and interpret data on Devonian fossils. The scientific research site is in upstate New York; however, proximity to the research site is not necessary, as fossils are sent to classrooms across the country. In turn, paleontologists collaborate with students to use classroom data in determining the nature of the ancient past

environment at this site and changes of populations of organisms in the Devonian Period (Crawford, Ross, & Allmon, 2014). Educational studies provided empirical evidence that children ages 10 through 14, in particular those from populations underrepresented in the sciences, highly valued the authentic aspect of identifying and measuring fossils; these students clearly want to help and work with real scientists (Conner et al., 2013; Goldfisher et al., 2014). Additionally, the Fossil Finders project facilitates diverse students in learning about science as a way of knowing and bridging science learning in the classroom with learning in a child's home (Meyer & Crawford, 2011).

5. *Inquiry is an important means to understanding that science itself is changing.* It is widely acknowledged it is virtually impossible to keep up with all newly discovered science content. As we progress into the 21st century, we are experiencing an explosion of new discoveries. In this situation, one needs to learn how to be a critical consumer of science, and this requires understanding how scientific inquiry is conducted. Schwab (1958) articulated this rationale many years ago.

> The formal reason for a change in present methods of teaching the sciences lies in the fact that science itself has changed. A new view concerning the nature of scientific inquiry now controls research. "Science," to quote Eugene Rabinowitch, "is in such rapid development that it has acquired an essentially dynamic outlook. It looks at its facts, concepts, and laws as a temporary and rapidly changing codex, reflecting the momentary state of affairs."
>
> (p. 374)

6. *Inquiry addresses the need for citizens to be able to make decisions related to controversial societal problems.* Researchers (e.g., Duschl et al., 2007; Sadler, Barab, & Scott, 2007) point to the use of inquiry as a useful context for teaching and learning science and in supporting students' abilities to make informed decisions later in life. Many researchers point to the controversial and scientifically demanding debates currently in the forefront of politics and everyday living.

> At no time in history has improving science education been more important than it is today. Major policy debates about such topics as cloning, the potential of alternative fuels, and the use of biometric information to fight terrorism require a scientifically informed citizenry as never before in the nation's history.
>
> (Duschl et al., 2007, p. 1)

The need for members of society as a whole to develop an understanding of science concepts and principles, as well as how science is conducted, is justification for why young adults should develop an understanding of scientific inquiry.

How Inquiry Is Conceptualized Within the Literature

Tracing the History of Inquiry in Science Classrooms in the United States

From Dewey to inquiry to science practices. The following is a brief history of inquiry in science classrooms in the United States, from the early 20th century to the present. From viewing the education literature over the past 100 years, it is clear that inquiry in classrooms is not a new idea. The closer one looks into the history of education, the more one sees the same kind of emphasis on teaching the duality of science. More than 100 years ago, John Dewey espoused that if science is taught only as a well-established body of facts, opportunity to engage children in learning how to think scientifically will be missed. Dewey (1910) stated, "Science is more than a body of knowledge to be learned, there is a process or method to learn as well" (p. 14). Dewey (1910) cautioned, "Science teaching has suffered because science has been so frequently presented just as so much ready-made knowledge, so much subject-matter of fact and law, rather than as the effective method of inquiry into any subject-matter" (p. 124). Dewey thought many teachers placed too much emphasis on facts and not enough emphasis on how to think about the way science works. Thus, more than 100 years ago, Dewey recommended inclusion of inquiry in the science classroom.

In *How We Think* (1910, 1937), Dewey presented learner traits for what he termed reflective thinking that relate to inquiry. Those traits included (1) defining the problem, (2) noting conditions associated with the problem, (3) formulating a hypothesis for solving the problem, (4) elaborating the value of various solutions, and (5) testing the ideas to see which provide the best solution for the problem. Dewey later created a six-step model that became the basis for the Commission on Secondary School Curriculum (1937) titled S*cience in Secondary Education*. In this model, the teacher (1) presents an experience in which the students feel thwarted and sense a problem; (2) helps the students identify and formulate the problem; (3) provides opportunities for students to form hypotheses and tries to establish a relationship between the perplexing situation and previous experiences; (4) allows students to try various types of experiments, including imaginary, pencil-and-paper, and concrete experiments to test the hypothesis; (5) suggests tests that result in acceptance or rejection of the hypothesis; and (6) asks the students to devise a statement that communicates their conclusions and expresses possible actions.

The Soviet Union's successful lunching of the satellite *Sputnik* in October 1957 served as a turning point in the history of science education in the United States. Many people in the United States government, and scientists, called for improvements to science education. Post–*Sputnik* frenzy during the "space race" resulted in a flurry of new science curricula funded by the NSF. These curricula aimed to engage children in science processes as the new way for teachers to teach science. Joseph Schwab (1960) recommended that science be taught through inquiry, because this would serve the learner in later life.

> If a student is to keep rapport with the changing face of science when he is no longer a student, he must be freed as far as possible from the need for schools and schooling.
> (p. 186)

Schwab (1960) envisioned teachers helping students become learners of science by developing in them habits of mind that positioned students for their future learning as adults.

During the 1960s, a collection of newly designed curricula developed in discipline-based curriculum committees (i.e., Biological Sciences Curriculum Study [BSCS]) emphasized how teachers can support students in using inquiry to learn science content. More laboratory exercises were included in these 1960s curricula than previously. Although these laboratory exercises were designed to be open ended and inquiry based, they were highly structured and targeted at learning academic science. During this decade, textbooks drove science instruction (Yager, 2000), and some characterize this decade as one of generating "teacher-proof" curricula.

In the late 1960s, 1970s, and 1980s, studies were conducted on these early efforts to promote inquiry in classrooms. One study funded by the National Science Foundation involved a synthesis of various research findings (Project Synthesis) on the status of science education (Harms & Yager, 1981). Part of this synthesis included a study focused specifically on teachers' responses to inquiry curricula (Welch, Klopfer, Aikenhead, & Robinson, 1981). The study revealed a lack of clarity by teachers and science educators about the meaning of inquiry, as well as differences in teachers' beliefs about teaching science as inquiry versus actual classroom practices. There was evidence many teachers perceived significant difficulties in teaching science as inquiry. Teachers reported various constraints including classroom management, state requirements, limited resources and materials, and the fact that teachers did not feel confident that inquiry methods worked better than traditional approaches (Welch et al., 1981). Years ago, many teachers were simply not convinced an inquiry approach was the best for their students. In today's world, it is important to consider these historical findings related to inquiry when contemplating how to support contemporary teachers in actualizing new curricula and standards related to inquiry. Further, it is important to compare and contrast approaches that were *not* successful with those that appear more promising.

In the late 1980s and early 1990s, United States policy documents lifted teaching science as inquiry to a high visibility level. *Science for All Americans* (AAAS, 1989) advocated the inquiry-related goal of students developing habits of mind. These habits of mind included use of logic and mathematics. The *Atlas of Scientific Literacy* (AAAS, 1993) provided several strands that mapped inquiry concepts in the *Benchmarks for Scientific Literacy* (AAAS, 1993). AAAS pointed out that more imagination and inventiveness are involved in scientific inquiry than many people realize. In *Science for All Americans*, the authors stated that in science, sooner or later, strict logic and empirical evidence win out (AAAS, 1989, chapter 1).

> In addition scientific inquiry, far from a rigid set of steps, has more flexibility than the linear method commonly depicted in textbooks as "*the scientific method.*" It is much more than just "doing experiments," and it is not confined to laboratories.
>
> (AAAS, 1989, chapter 1)

Soon afterward, the *National Science Education Standards* (NRC, 1996) made clear that inquiry was the desired overarching goal of teaching science in the United States. "Learning science is something students do, not something that is done to them" (NRC, 1996, p. 20). These documents described inquiry as a way of thinking that goes beyond simply making more and more observations and organizing these observations.

A focus on children acquiring scientific habits of mind was reiterated in the addendum to the 1996 NSES document, *Inquiry and the National Science Education Standards* (NRC, 2000). "Inquiry is in part a state of mind—that of inquisitiveness" (NRC, 2000, p. xii). These standards documents targeted certain critical-thinking skills, including mathematical and logical skills, that are essential tools for both formal and informal learning and for anyone participating in today's society.

As we entered the 21st century, Anderson (2002) proposed there were three main areas of dilemmas that affected the implementation of inquiry: technical dilemmas, political dilemmas, and cultural dilemmas. Several researchers explored ways to ameliorate these situations. Bybee made reference to John Dewey in Minstrell and van Zee's (2000) edited book. Bybee noted that Rutherford in 1964 recognized the need for teachers to understand nature of science, "Until science teachers acquire a rather thorough grounding in the history and philosophy of the sciences they teach, this kind of understanding will elude them, in which event not much progress toward the teaching of science as inquiry can be expected" (p. 84—found on p. 28). Bybee also noted that in Project Synthesis (1981) the science education community used the term "inquiry" in a variety of ways, including the general categories of inquiry as content and inquiry as way to frame instruction. "Although teachers made positive statements about the value of inquiry, they often felt more responsible for teaching facts, "things which show up on tests," "basics," and "structure and the work ethic" (Bybee, 2000, found on p. 29). Finally, Wheeler (2000) described the three faces of inquiry (see pp. 14–19 in Minstrell &

van Zee, 2000), and described how an effective teacher uses inquiry.

> Good teachers recognize the ways materials and curiosity relate, and help students as they tentatively or bullishly try to connect their own questions to ways of "finding out." Good teachers also work with children to "make sense" of what they find and construct arguments that seem convincing to others in their scientific community.
>
> (p. 16)

An important idea is that inquiry should be thought of not only as a teaching approach but also as content to be learned. Wheeler (2000) stated, "Inquiry has a meta-content character that demands its presence while all the other content is being learned" (p. 18).

As mentioned earlier in this chapter, many reform-based curricula of the 1980s, 1990s, and early 21st century incorporated a focus on inquiry within their materials. Developing inquiry-based curriculum goes hand in hand with supporting teachers in teaching science as inquiry. For example, the BSCS has a long history of advocating an inquiry approach. Since the late 1980s, the BSCS 5E Instructional Model has been a central feature in the majority of BSCS texts and programs (Bybee et al., 2006). The 5E Instructional Model, commonly referred to as the 5Es, consists of phases: (1) Engagement, (2) Exploration, (3) Explanation, (4) Elaboration, and (5) Evaluation. The 5E Instructional Model has greatly influenced the teaching and learning of science throughout the United States. Although there have been many dissertations and reports, there is limited empirical evidence published in peer-reviewed journals comparing the BSCS 5E Instructional Model to alternative approaches (e.g., Akar, 2005; Atay & Tekkaya, 2008).

Not surprising, but important to note, is the reality that when students are afforded school laboratory experiences, the amount of student initiative varies greatly with the amount of teacher direction. Schwab (1960) identified three possible levels of inquiry in the laboratory: (1) structured inquiry, in which the teacher gives the question and provides the laboratory techniques used to investigate the question; (2) guided inquiry, in which the teacher gives the question but not the procedures; and, (3) open inquiry, in which the teacher allows students to choose both the question and the procedure. This range, from highly structured to open inquiry, is viewed as a continuum (see NRC, 2000). Sadeh and Zion (2009) viewed a school experience as being that of "open inquiry" when students pose the research question and they either create or choose the laboratory techniques based on their mastery of scientific reasoning skills.

With a renewed focus on teachers enacting inquiry-based pedagogy, there was need for research to track progress of inquiry teaching and learning in classrooms. Keys and Bryan (2001) recognized that "Today's reform rhetoric has revived the concept of inquiry as representing the essence of science education" (p. 631). Keys and Bryan (2001) proposed a new direction for education research, in four domains: (a) teacher beliefs about inquiry, (b) the teacher knowledge base for implementing inquiry, (c) teacher inquiry practices, and (d) student science learning from teacher-designed, inquiry-based instruction.

Shifting From Inquiry to Science Practices

As discussed earlier, a historical view of inquiry in the science classroom reveals three faces—children doing inquiry, children learning core science concepts through inquiry, and children learning the nature of scientists' inquiry. In historically tracing inquiry throughout the years, the most recent iteration of classroom inquiry in the United States occurs in the new K–12 Framework (NRC, 2012) and Next Generation Science Standards (NGSS Lead States, 2013). Authors of the K–12 Framework addressed the inconsistencies of various views of inquiry in the past. In the K–12 Framework, the term "inquiry" actually appears only a few times, related to engaging students in doing inquiry, inquiry as a pedagogy, or teaching about what scientists do (scientific inquiry). Striving to rebrand inquiry, the term "science practices" is used throughout the document.

> We use the term "practices" instead of a term such as "skills" to emphasize that engaging in scientific investigation requires not only skill but also knowledge that is specific to each practice. . . . part of our intent in articulating the practices in Dimension 1 is to better specify what is meant by inquiry in science and the range of cognitive, social, and physical practices that it requires.
>
> (p. 30)

The call for engaging students in science practices is combined with a call to engage students in the practices of engineering (NRC, 2012).

Not unlike researchers and philosophers in the 20th century (i.e., John Dewey, Joseph Schwab), authors of the 21st-century K–12 Framework place an emphasis on immersing children in investigations as the centerpiece for learning science. The K–12 Framework strongly emphasizes that students experience designing and carrying out investigations in order to learn about what scientists do, as well as the epistemology of science (NRC, 2012).

> As in all inquiry-based approaches to science teaching, our expectation is that students will themselves engage in the practices and not merely learn about them secondhand.
>
> (p. 30)

As we view 21st-century science education standards from a historical perspective, the thrust to engage students in doing science reminds us of ideas put forth by philosophers, curriculum developers, and educators of the past century. So, we might ask, what is different about the K–12 Framework and the NGSS use of the term "science practices" compared with inquiry in the *NSES* "essential features"? Is this just another way to rethink what it means to teach science as inquiry?

In the first few pages of the K–12 Framework (NRC, 2012, p. 3), the first dimension, Science and Engineering Practices, includes eight practices: (1) asking questions (for science) and defining problems (for engineering), (2) developing and using models, (3) planning and carrying out investigations, (4) analyzing and interpreting data, (5) using mathematics and computational thinking, (6) constructing explanations (for science) and designing solutions (for engineering), (7) engaging in argument from evidence, and (8) obtaining, evaluating, and communicating information.

A comparison of these science practices with teaching inquiry in earlier reform documents is shown in Table 26.2. One distinguishing feature of the new K–12 Framework and NGSS is a greater emphasis on scientific modeling and argumentation. The new documents propose a shift from simply having students form and test hypotheses to testing and revising theoretically grounded explanatory models. The idea involves students going beyond experiencing inquiry by interpreting and evaluating data as evidence to developing arguments, explanations, and models. Yet this emphasis on engaging in argumentation is not entirely a new one. For example, Abell and colleagues (2000) envisioned elementary

TABLE 26.2
Comparing Inquiry in NSES and Practices in the K–12 Framework

NSES (NRC, 1996, 2000) Essential Features of Inquiry	K–12 Framework (NRC, 2012) Science and Engineering Practices
Learners are engaged by scientifically oriented questions	Asking questions (for science) and defining problems (for engineering)
	Developing and using models
	Planning and carrying out investigations
Learners give priority to evidence, which allows them to develop and evaluate explanations that address scientifically oriented questions	Analyzing and interpreting data
	Using mathematics and computational thinking
Learners give priority to evidence, which allows them to develop and evaluate explanations that address scientifically oriented questions	Constructing explanations (for science) and designing solutions (for engineering)
Learners evaluate their explanations in light of alternative explanations, particularly those reflecting scientific understanding	Engaging in argument from evidence
Learners communicate and justify their proposed explanations	Obtaining, evaluating, and communicating information

teachers supporting children in learning science in this way: "the active quest for information and for production of new ideas characterizes inquiry-based science classrooms" (p. 65). Abell and co-authors (2000) recognized that, although elementary classrooms may have moved beyond traditional instruction to hands-on instruction, this does not necessarily mean that it is inquiry instruction. More than a decade ago, these authors described inquiry as argument and explanation. Duschl and co-authors characterized the goal of classroom science, "for students to become proficient in science . . . 1) know, use, and interpret scientific explanations of the natural world; 2) generate and evaluate scientific evidence and explanations; 3) understand the nature and development of scientific knowledge; and 4) participate productively in scientific practices and discourse" (Duschl et al., 2007, p. 2).

Another distinguishing feature of the K–12 Framework and NGSS, as compared with historical writings about teaching science as inquiry, is the focus on *integration*. The K–12 Framework emphasizes that learning about science and engineering involves teachers providing students opportunity to learn about the "integration of the knowledge of scientific explanations (i.e., content knowledge) and the practices needed to engage in scientific inquiry and engineering design" (NRC, p. 11). The vision is that teachers design learning environments in a range of classrooms in which the notions of science core concepts, crosscutting concepts, and science practices are intertwined.

Following this shift in goals, it is necessary that teacher educators consider changing the manner in which they prepare new teachers. Yet it is important to remember the historical research revealing constraints to teaching science as inquiry, as reported by teachers in the 1960s and 1970s (Welch et al., 1981). Change may require transformed experiences for teachers. Otherwise, we may find ourselves with rhetoric but no positive movement towards actual reform-based teaching in classrooms. Transformation will require different experiences and expectations for science teachers. (See the discussion of barriers later in this chapter.)

Overview of Recent Views of Inquiry Around the World

Inquiry is a prominent theme in countries other than the United States (Hasson & Yarden, 2012).

> Such an emphasis on authentic scientific inquiry and on conducting investigations appears as a major theme in science education documents also in Europe (European Commission, 2007), Australia (Australian Curriculum Assessment and Reporting Authority [ACARA], 2012), Israel (i.e., Israeli Ministry of Education, 2005, 2011), and elsewhere.
>
> (p. 1296)

In Finland, Lavonen and Laaksonen (2009) analyzed the PISA 2006 Scientific Literacy Assessment data to determine factors contributing to the high performance by Finnish students. Given that Finnish schoolchildren score consistently at or near the top of international assessments, it is interesting to explore the influence of teaching approaches. Predictors of success included Finnish teachers providing practical work in classrooms and opportunity for students to draw conclusions. It is noteworthy that teacher education programs contributed to the success of these students.

In an international science education symposium, science educators from several countries responded to questions about how different countries frame inquiry. These insights were later published in a multiauthored article (Abd-El-Khalick et al., 2004). Introductory remarks presented inquiry as both an approach for children to learn science concepts and a means and an end.

In Lebanon, BouJaoude assessed whether and to what extent inquiry was addressed in the new educational plan created by the Lebanese government in 1994. Four areas were assessed: (a) the knowledge of science, (b) the investigative nature of science, (c) science as a way of thinking, and (d) interaction of science, technology, and society. Results indicated 12% of the Lebanese curriculum dealt with the investigative nature of science. Yet although the curriculum emphasized the investigative nature of science, it did not mean this stance is being implemented. The study reported most instruction in Lebanon resembles traditional instruction due to a variety of factors.

In the United States, Lederman noted that teachers should not only focus students on doing inquiry, but they should also help students understand *about* the nature of scientific inquiry as content. Knowledge of inquiry can contribute to scientific literacy. Lederman cautioned that some states in the United States have not included inquiry in their standards. Overall, there is currently significant attention given to inquiry in classrooms. However, students may not learn about inquiry simply by doing it (teaching inquiry needs to be made explicit).

In Israel, Mamlok-Naaman and Hofstein studied the enactment of laboratory activities as a way for students in a classroom to experience inquiry. Teachers reported the importance of PD for supporting them in carrying out these activities. Students reported the labs to be beneficial. It was noted that a great deal of money and resources are required for successful implementation, and a long-term commitment is required on the part of the government and teachers.

In Venezuela, Niaz studied the relationship among inquiry, constructivism, and NOS. Findings included: (a) There is often disagreement between the relationship of these concepts, as in Venezuela concerning the secondary school curriculum; (b) the present national curriculum in Venezuela does not provide a concept of inquiry but instead presents a list of goals that conflates inquiry, NOS, and process skills; and (c) curricular materials contribute to lack of inquiry discussion (e.g., the lesson concerning atomic structure omitting historical development of theory).

In Australia, state documents do not use word "inquiry" but rather the word "investigate," and science teaching and learning are largely focused on investigating. Yet most of these investigations remain teacher directed. As reported by Treagust (Abd-El-Khalick et al., 2004), materials and people power do not seem to be an impediment to teachers conducting inquiry in secondary school. Instead, the main constraint appears to be teachers' lack of confidence to teach science in this way.

In Taiwan, Tuan explained, "[F]or the Taiwanese, philosophy of science is Taoism; "inquiry" refers to people's experiences with nature rather than their proactive exploration of nature." (Abd-El-Khalick et al., 2004, p. 410). Chinese thinking (as opposed to Western thinking) is influential. Inquiry is a search for truth, and few Taiwanese educators have questioned this definition of inquiry. In 1999, new curricula based on the U.S. document, NSES, changed the definition of inquiry. These new curricula shifted from using investigations from the science laboratory to everyday life. The government changed the nature of the standardized test to reflect more inquiry, yet teachers still feel pressured to teach in traditional ways in order that students do well on both types of tests. Another constraint reported by Taiwanese teachers is that of not enough time.

In summary, many countries emphasize teaching science as inquiry in policy documents, yet there remain differences in definition. Some countries have demonstrated successful student outcomes through teaching science as inquiry. Yet it appears there are many classrooms across the world in which this kind of teaching is not happening for various reasons (lack of confidence, pressure to teach in traditional ways due to high-stakes testing, and need for more PD).

Authentic Scientific Inquiry Versus Classroom Inquiry

The question that must be asked, Is classroom inquiry different or the same as inquiry done by professionally trained scientists? Many researchers acknowledge that the nature of inquiry that takes place in a scientist's laboratory differs to a certain degree from school science inquiry (e.g., Abd-El-Khalick et al., 2004). Yet schoolchildren can learn how to construct models much like a scientist does in developing explanations (Bybee, 2006; Driver et al., 1994; Passmore & Stewart, 2002). Scientific inquiry has been referred to (in NSES) as "the diverse ways in which scientists study the natural world and propose explanations based on evidence derived from their work" (NRC, 1996, p. 23). Scientific inquiry can also be thought of as science practiced by scientists (AAAS, 1993; Chinn & Malhotra, 2002). Inquiry includes systematic and sophisticated analyses of data and conclusions informed from a body of literature that builds on complex science principles. Scientific methods differ from one scientific discipline to another, depending on the question asked by the

scientist. Yet there are commonly recognized components of scientific inquiry (AAAS, 1989).

> Scientific inquiry is more complex than popular conceptions would have it. It is, for instance, a more subtle and demanding process than the naive idea of "making a great many careful observations and then organizing them."
> (Chapter 1: "The Nature of Science")

Children may never be able to carry out scientific inquiry to a full extent in a classroom. The first issue is that children clearly do not have the technical expertise or depth of subject matter knowledge held by professional scientists. Thus, the developmental level of children related to science subject matter needs to be considered in planning inquiry lessons. A second issue is that authentic scientific research and classroom inquiry have different goals.

Despite the differences in goals and level of sophistication, some researchers claim that carrying out authentic scientific inquiry is quite possible in a science classroom, though with some caveats (e.g., Alberts, 2000; Bybee, 2006; Crawford, 2000; Roth, 1995). The new U.S. K–12 Framework and NGSS advocate students engage in practices used by scientists and engineers, such as modeling, developing explanations or solutions, and engaging in argumentation, with a focus on data and evidence much like scientists examine and evaluate their own ideas and critique those of others. Some goals of scientific inquiry overlap with classroom goals, and these are important to consider. For example, Bybee's (2006) description of the way scientists work and think, "How scientists know and explain the natural world and what they mean by explanation and knowledge are both directly related to the processes, methods and strategies by which they develop and propose explanations" (p. 2), is very appropriate for classroom science. Yet science textbooks often promote the misconception that science is done in a prescribed, linear manner with a set number and order of steps (i.e., *the* scientific method). As stated in *Science for All Americans* (AAAS, 1989), one goal of teaching science as inquiry is to use a model of scientific thinking to support children in learning how to think. Many aspects of scientific thinking are attainable and appropriate as goals for children in classrooms. Scientific thinking involves use of evidence and logic. Duschl and colleagues (2007) proposed fostering this kind of thinking for children.

Other science education scholars and scientists have weighed in on the differences and similarities between classroom inquiry and scientists' inquiry. For example, Alberts (2000) explained, "what I mean by teaching science as inquiry is, at a minimum allowing students to conceptualize a problem that was solved by a scientific discovery, and then forcing them to wrestle with possible answers to the problem before they are told the answer" (p. 4). Alberts (2000) elaborated on the feasibility and importance of fostering children's curiosity. "The state of mind is inquisitiveness—having the curiosity to ask "Why" and "How" (p. 7). Alberts (2000) offered his view:

> Maintaining children's initial curiosity about the world requires making them confident that they can use the methods of inquiry to find answers for their questions . . . It is not enough to encourage students to inquire. They must also have many opportunities to obtain the diverse set of skills needed for repeated success in such experiences.
>
> (Alberts, 2000, p. 8)

As compared with an inquiry approach that engages students in asking and answering questions, traditional science instruction often asks students to engage in rote memorization and regurgitation of facts. In contrast, inquiry gives students opportunity to grapple with data and construct possible answers. On the one hand, scientists' science is not exactly the same as classroom science in its sophistication and use of elaborate equipment, scope, and duration. On the other hand, classroom inquiry can resemble many aspects of a scientist's inquiry. A reasonable goal of classroom science teachers includes helping students learn how to think in similar ways to that of scientists, do the kinds of work of scientists do, and develop insight into tenets of nature of science (see NGSS Lead States, 2013).

Theoretical Frameworks Related to Research on Inquiry in Classrooms

Theories of learning underpin the teaching of science as inquiry, including that of conceptual change theory (Posner, Strike, Hewson, & Gertzog, 1982; Strike & Posner, 1982). Conceptual change theory has been used by researchers to design inquiry instruction for science classrooms and for framing research on teachers' views, understandings, and enactment of inquiry in classrooms. The theory links ideas about knowledge, curriculum materials, and student epistemology. Specifically: (a) Conceptual knowledge is taught and learned in school, (b) curriculum materials can influence instruction and have unique effects on student concept development, and (c) students' prior conceptions interact with curriculum materials, facilitating new learning and/or conceptual change.

Sociocultural theory arises from the field of educational psychology. This view of learning considers the situated nature of the learning process as a defining feature. Lev Vygotsky explored human mental development, and his work is a seminal part of the development of cognitive science. Translations of Vygotsky's writings provide readers with a view of learning in a social context. Central to Vygotsky's sociocultural theory is the principle that a student internalizes higher-order cognitive functions from social interaction with more competent others (Vygotsky, 1978, pp. 52–57). In other words, learning is a socially mediated process. In using sociocultural theory, researchers interpret the inquiry activities by studying how students engage with others in the context of the classroom.

Community of practice is another theoretical framework used by researchers to describe teaching science as inquiry and as a way to understand a vibrant, productive, inquiry classroom (Lave & Wenger, 1991). Classrooms are complex, dynamic environments in which children and teachers participate in a variety of intersecting communities: social, school, and scientific. In using a community-of-practice conceptual framework, the focus is shifted from the individual child to groups of learners and how learners participate with others. Conceptual change theory, sociocultural theory, and community-of-practice theoretical frameworks will be revisited in the section on professional development.

Taken together, conceptual change theory recognizes the importance of a person's prior experiences and conceptions; sociocultural theory recognizes the impact of social interaction on learning; and a community of practice is a way to understand how groups of learners participate in a classroom. These theories of learning can contribute to framing research on how teachers and students use inquiry in classrooms.

Teacher and Student Roles in an Inquiry-Based Classroom

Teacher Roles

The teacher remains the central factor influencing creation of an inquiry-based classroom, whether the mode of inquiry is structured, guided, or open. In all modes, the teacher plays a critical role in realizing these designs. Even if an intervention is composed of carefully specified curriculum materials (e.g., Blumenfeld et al., 1991; Singer, Marx, Krajcik, & Clay Chambers, 2000), the teacher plays a key role in how the instructional materials are enacted. Driver (1989) posited that a teacher's philosophy and view of learning shape the roles the teacher takes on in the classroom. Driver acknowledged that "minimally guided discovery learning" does not work with children and that no genuine constructivist teacher should expect it to work in the 21st century.

The effective classroom teacher designs and adapts instructional materials and orchestrates the classroom to support children in learning how to carry out scientific practices and in understanding the nature of scientific inquiry. Identified roles of an expert inquiry-based teacher include that of motivator, diagnostician, guide, innovator, experimenter, researcher, modeler, mentor, collaborator, and learner. See Crawford (2000) for details of multiple roles.

McNeil (2009) studied the nature of teachers' roles in the context of an 8-week chemistry curriculum. The curriculum supported students in constructing scientific arguments. Case studies were developed from videotapes, questionnaires, and pre- and posttests, collected from six teachers and 568 students. Teachers' definitions of argumentation influenced the level of learning gains, indicating that the way in which teachers use innovative curricula is important.

Taber (2010) claimed that, rather than a focus on whether a teacher uses a teacher-centered or a student-centered approach, it would be better to focus on the interactions between the teacher and students. Thus, a teacher can structure activities and scaffold learning while checking for student understanding. Open-ended, minimally guided, and discovery learning modes do not necessarily equate with a modern constructivist approach. Constructivist pedagogy involves guiding students toward accepted scientific knowledge in ways that take into account students' beginning knowledge and ways of making sense of science.

Student Roles

An important issue has been raised that not only does a teacher need to adopt new roles in reform-based classrooms, but a student's role needs to be redefined as well. One goal of teaching science as inquiry is that of students taking ownership of and responsibility for their own learning. Historically, students have taken on passive roles in many classrooms, aligned with teacher-directed, lecture-style instruction. What should students be doing in an inquiry-based classroom? What roles and responsibilities should students adopt to expedite their growth as independent and critical thinkers?

Schwab (1960) noted the importance of a student taking on the role of and responsibility for being a "learner of science." Schwab (1960) explained, "He needs to develop the competences and the habits required to read and learn for himself. This need will require us to test that most cherished fantasy of the teacher—that students truly learn only with our help" (p. 186).

However, many students who are successful in a traditional science classroom feel threatened and uneasy in taking on new roles in an inquiry-focused classroom. The hesitancy of students to take on different roles has been identified in several studies. For example, Trautmann and colleagues (2004) documented that some students who excel in traditional instruction may not be willing to take risks or ownership in reform-based instruction.

Metacognition is one's ability to think about his or her own learning. Assisting students in becoming metacognitive is a very important goal associated with teaching science as inquiry. Being metacognitive depends on a student taking an active role in his or her own learning (White & Frederiksen, 2000). When pursuing an answer to a driving question, a student can learn to focus on the problem and about connections with various aspects of inquiry, including gathering and interpreting data, answers to the question based on evidence, evaluating alternative explanations, and critically reviewing these components. Metacognition can help students to be systematic and thorough during the course of an investigation (Blumenfeld et al., 1991). Researchers White and Frederiksen (1998) claimed that developing metacognition in students through scaffolded inquiry, reflection, and generalization can make scientific inquiry accessible to a wide range of students, including young and lower-achieving students. Teachers can grow as well through the use of inquiry, scaffolding, metacognition, and reflection.

Teachers' Use of Inquiry in Classrooms

During the period immediately following publication of the NSES (NRC, 1996, 2000), there was renewed interest in conducting research on teaching science as inquiry in classrooms. Researchers designed studies of teachers' knowledge, beliefs, and views of inquiry; how teachers carried out inquiry practices in the classroom; challenges and constraints; and impact on students' learning and views of science. An assumption of this research is that teachers do not change their current practice of teaching science as a *rhetoric of facts* to teaching *science as inquiry* without having a deep understanding of the nature of scientific inquiry.

Teacher Knowledge, Beliefs, and Views

Studying the relationship among teachers' knowledge, beliefs, and views and their implications for classroom practice is prominent in the literature. Although beliefs are complex and considered by many to be a messy construct (i.e., Pajares, 1992), they likely play an important role in whether a teacher intends to and/or actually carries out the practice of teaching science as inquiry. Beliefs are, according to Philipp (2007):

> Psychologically held understandings, premises, or propositions about the world that are thought to be true. Beliefs are more cognitive, are felt less intensely, and are harder to change than attitudes. Beliefs might be thought of as lenses that affect one's view of some aspect of the world or as dispositions toward action.
>
> (p. 259)

Following are some representative studies of the impact of teachers' beliefs on their classroom practices, related specifically to inquiry. Roehrig and Luft (2004) identified constraints that affect teachers' enactment of inquiry-based instruction, such as content knowledge, teaching beliefs and concerns about management and students. To investigate teachers' beliefs, Wallace and Kang (2004) designed a multiple case study of six experienced high school teachers. They investigated teachers' beliefs about (1) what is successful science learning, (2) what are the purposes of laboratory in science teaching, and (3) how inquiry is implemented in the classroom. Beliefs about successful science learning were linked to beliefs about use of the school laboratory and teaching inquiry. For example, two teachers who believed that successful science learning was deep conceptual understanding used mainly verification labs to illustrate these concepts, and they used inquiry as an isolated problem-solving experience. One other teacher believed that successful science learning was enculturation into scientific practices, and this teacher used inquiry-based labs extensively to teach the practices of science.

Kang (2007) conducted a phenomenographic study to ascertain the extent of beginning science teachers' views and understandings and those of instructors in an alternative teacher certification program (ATCP). Participants were four beginning science teachers and two faculty members involved in teaching science methods courses. Data included semistructured interviews, classroom observations, field notes, written materials, and interviews with each faculty member. Results showed that the beginning teachers held incomplete views of inquiry-based teaching, and their views differed from those of their instructors.

Crawford (1999) examined one prospective high school teacher's ability to create an inquiry-based classroom in order to explore the feasibility of a novice teacher carrying out this complex kind of teaching. The case study examined this teacher's beliefs about science and teaching, how she engaged her students in inquiry, and factors that helped or hindered her ability. Data included classroom observations and videos, written observations of lessons, audiotapes of conversations, lesson plans, written reflections, and teacher interviews. There was evidence students gained ownership of their own learning to some degree. A number of factors appeared to contribute to success: prior research experience, volunteering in project-oriented classrooms, clear vision of unit goals, strong relationship with mentor teacher, collaboration with experts outside the classroom, and reflection on practice. Implications included importance of exploring teachers' beliefs, need for teachers to experience authentic investigations, learning models of teaching inquiry, support in planning long-term units, and reflection on teaching practice.

Keys and Bryan (2001) proposed an agenda on beliefs, knowledge, and roles of teachers, that researchers "collect vital data on teacher beliefs, knowledge, practices, and student learning from teacher-designed inquiry instruction, especially in diverse settings" (p. 642). Of course, the fact that a teacher may hold beliefs congruent with inquiry does not necessarily mean this teacher will intend to carry out this kind of pedagogy or will be successful in carrying it out.

Ireland and colleagues (2011) used a phenomenographic research method to uncover 20 elementary school teachers' conceptions of inquiry teaching. The researchers defined inquiry as involving students in learning in their own way by drawing on direct experience, fostered by the teacher and active engagement in experiences. Data consisted of interviews. Three kinds of conceptions were reported: (a) the experience-centered conception in which teachers focused on providing interesting sensory experiences to students, (b) the problem-centered conception in which teachers focused on engaging students with challenging problems, and (c) the question-centered conception in which teachers focused on helping students ask and answer their own questions.

Investigating the relationship between three teachers' perceptions of nature of science (NOS) and inquiry teaching practices, Atar (2011) collected Views of Nature of Science–form C (VNOS-C), online postings, interviews, email, lesson plans, and videos of inquiry lessons. Improving teachers' conceptions of NOS appeared to positively impact use of inquiry practices—teachers with more sophisticated NOS views conducted less structured inquiry and more student-centered activities. However, teachers who did not possess adequate content knowledge were reluctant to change their teaching practices.

Breslyn and McGinnis (2011) examined the question, How does exemplary secondary science teachers' discipline (biology, chemistry, earth science, or physics) influence their conceptions, enactment, and goals for inquiry-based teaching and learning? Participants included 60 national board-certified science teachers. Researchers employed mixed-methods, using portfolio texts and interviews to assess enactment and views of inquiry. The discipline in which these teachers taught was found to be a major influence on conceptions and enactment of inquiry. The classroom context did not appear to be as large a factor as the structure of the discipline.

In a recent study, Windschitl and Thompson (2012) studied the effectiveness of a teacher education program designed to enhance prospective teachers' knowledge of inquiry, in particular their understandings of models and modeling. Data sources included observations, student artifacts, informal interviews, and questionnaires. Participants included 21 prospective secondary science teachers with undergraduate degrees in science, all in a secondary methods course. While prospective teachers could talk about models in a sophisticated way, they had a difficult time creating models themselves. Further, these prospective teachers viewed models as being separate from the process of inquiry.

In summary, it seems reasonable to continue to explore teachers' knowledge and beliefs and expect that these play an important part in teachers' intentions and/or abilities to successfully design and carry out inquiry-based teaching.

Evidence of Actual Classroom Practices

It is important to ascertain not only the nature of teachers' beliefs and knowledge but also the nature of teachers' intentions and actual classroom practices regarding inquiry. Following publication of the NSES (NRC, 1996), researchers Keys and Kennedy (1999) examined the teaching practice of an elementary teacher with 11 years of experience. Two years prior to the study, the teacher was involved in a science and math education reform project. The school was located in a low to middle socioeconomic status (SES) area. The classroom included 26 children of varying demographics. A case study method and participant-observer technique was used; data included field notes during lessons, informal interviews, and transcripts of three formal interviews. Four main themes were revealed: (1) The teacher planned instruction to explore questions that arose in context naturally from science activities, (2) the teacher helped students take responsibility, (3) the teacher supported children in constructing explanations and concepts from data, and (4) the teacher provided opportunities for students to apply scientific knowledge. Major challenges included lack of time, the challenge of turning questions back onto students, and teaching mandated concepts difficult to teach through inquiry.

Crawford (2000) documented and examined the beliefs and practices of an experienced rural public high school science teacher to determine how this teacher created an inquiry-based classroom environment. The researcher collected data for more than a year. The report focused on 20 students in an ecology class. Data included teacher interviews, notes of informal conversations, videotapes of classroom and field trips, interviews of eight randomly selected students, student products, and an end-of-year anonymous student questionnaire. Key characteristics emerged: (a) situating instruction in authentic problems, (b) grappling with data, (c) collaboration of students and teacher, (d) connecting students with the community, (e) the teacher modeling behaviors of a scientist, and (f) fostering students in taking ownership of their own learning. Crawford identified 10 different teacher roles. Roles of students varied as well, with some roles typically reserved for teachers being occupied by students.

Given the varied characteristics of the two classrooms described earlier, one an elementary classroom and one a secondary classroom, and the uniqueness of each teacher's background, particular school setting, and student populations, it is difficult to generalize the findings of two case studies to other classrooms in the United States and countries around the world. *Context* is important. Different contexts may likely result in different outcomes. Yet descriptive and interpretive studies such as these are vital in understanding all the complexities involved when a teacher strives to carry out teaching science as inquiry in light of high-stakes testing and state and national mandates. Large-scale quantitative studies may not provide the same in-depth view into a single classroom.

In a recent case study that took place over 2 years, Maskiewicz and Winters (2012) reported longitudinal observations of one elementary teacher's fifth-grade classroom (children ages 11–12 years). The authors presented empirical evidence that shifted from focusing on the teacher to focusing on the classroom context, including the students. Findings indicated students can have a substantive and generative influence on the nature and form of inquiry carried out by a teacher in any given year. Context is important. And change in students from one year to the next is a component of the context.

Moving beyond studying a single teacher or single classroom, an example of a study specifically focused on argumentation strategies is one conducted in Great Britain (Osborne, Erduran, & Simon, 2004). Researchers tracked 12 junior high school teachers and students in classrooms during 2 years to determine the nature and quality of the classroom discourse related to argumentation. Fogleman, McNeill, and Krajcik (2011) examined 19 teachers' use of an inquiry-oriented middle school science curriculum. Using hierarchical linear modeling, researchers aimed to determine the influence of a teacher's curricular adaptations on student learning. Data included curriculum surveys, videotape observations, and pre- and posttests from 1,234 students. Two variables significantly predicted student learning: teacher experience and amount of student initiation during instruction. Teachers who had taught the inquiry-oriented curriculum before had greater student gains. Students who completed investigations had greater learning gains as compared with students whose teachers used demonstrations or carried out the inquiry themselves. Implications include (1) it takes time for teachers to effectively implement innovative science curriculum and (2) it is important that students actively engage in inquiry investigations.

McNeill (2009) studied the enactment by six middle-level teachers of an 8-week chemistry-based unit. The curriculum focused on students constructing arguments using an adapted version of Toulmin's model of argumentation. A total of 568 middle school students participated in the study. Data included videotaped classroom lessons, student pre- and posttests, and teacher questionnaires. Findings revealed a significant teacher effect on students' learning about scientific explanations, evidence, reasoning, and content knowledge. The teacher who defined scientific explanation differently than in the curriculum had the lowest student gains in terms of scientific explanation. The study highlighted that different teachers carry out reform-based curricula in different ways, something curriculum designers need to take into account.

In summary, it is important to investigate the actual inquiry practices of teachers in their classrooms over several lessons and even over multiple years, in addition to assessing teachers' beliefs and knowledge. The studies discussed illustrate the importance of researchers moving into the classroom to determine what is happening, with all the complexities of individual student abilities and predispositions, classroom physical structures, school culture, and community. Different classrooms provide very different contexts.

Evidence of Student Learning

Reform documents of the last two decades (AAAS, 1989, 1993; NGSS Lead States, 2013; NRC, 1996) are explicit in stating that a teaching practice in which science is taught only as a body of facts, using primarily lecture modes, stressing vocabulary-driven drill-practice and using only teacher-centered ways versus student-centered approaches, is simply not effective for all students. It is important that science instruction be accessible to diverse students, including those children from populations historically underrepresented in sciences. "Science is for *all* students [and] that learning science is an active process, and that school science [should] reflect the intellectual and cultural traditions that characterize the practice of contemporary science" (NRC, 1996, p. 19).

The bottom line is the need to answer questions about student learning. In what ways does teaching science as inquiry enhance students' learning and views of science? What is the evidence that children learn better in an inquiry-based classroom than in a traditional classroom? These questions are especially relevant for children who are academically unsuccessful in traditional science classrooms. So, what do students do, and what do they learn in an inquiry-based classroom?

Two representative studies addressing the critical importance of assessment include Champagne and colleagues (2000) and Duschl (2003). Champagne and co-authors listed two major forms of inquiry (scientific inquiry as practiced by scientists and science-related practices by scientifically literate adults and students) and three forms of science-related inquiry (archival investigation, experimentation, and laboratory investigation). The authors advocated that performance standards must be set through a conversation between teachers and the school district. Duschl (2003) described a framework that included use of strategies that engage students in thinking about the structure and communication of scientific knowledge. Further, assessment of inquiry should focus on three integrated domains: (1) epistemic, including the abilities involved in the processes of science and the knowledge structures and criteria used in science to make critical judgments; (2) conceptual, including the conceptual frameworks that students are expected to develop and their alternative conceptions; and (3) social, referring to the representation and communication frameworks that students use.

Various studies assessing student learning in an inquiry-based classroom have focused on the nature of the students (diverse populations or those with disabilities), classroom locality (urban or rural or suburban), use of technology, or a comparison of traditional with various forms of inquiry, or some combination of these. Representative studies are described next.

In a meta-analysis, Shymansky, Kyle, and Alport (2006) analyzed the effects of new science curricula on student performance. The study included 105 experimental studies involving more than 45,000 students and a total of 27 different new science curricula. Results indicated students exposed to new science curricula performed better than students in traditional courses in general achievement, analytic skills, process skills, and related skills. In addition, those students exhibited more positive attitudes towards science. A recent study focused on children's written scientific explanations and the possible link between the quality and students' performance on assessment (Ruiz-Primo, Li, Tsai, & Schneider, 2010). Researchers found some evidence of a connection but limited opportunities in classrooms.

Two studies focusing on a problem-based learning (PBL) approach include Peterson and Treagust (1998) and Drake and Long (2009). Peterson and Treagust (1998) studied prospective teachers and emphasized the use of a pedagogical reasoning process. Working in small groups,

participants worked for a period of 6 weeks to solve a problem. The study followed two randomly selected participants. Findings revealed each prospective teacher considered and developed their knowledge base and pedagogical reasoning in areas that were relevant to their current understanding of teaching and learning. Drake and Long (2009) conducted a study comparing children in the fourth grade (ages 9–10 years old) as they learned about electricity through either a PBL approach or direct/experiential instruction. Data sources included pre- and post-test measures of content knowledge, Draw-a-Scientist test, student interviews, and classroom observations. PBL classroom children demonstrated significantly higher learning gains and had fewer stereotypical views of scientists, viewed themselves as scientists, and were able to list more problem-solving strategies and resources than did comparison students.

In a British study, students in a high school computer course used a Web-based learning environment to find answers to questions (Hsu, Hwang, Chuang, & Chang, 2012). Student learning gains in the selected-resource network were greater than in the open-resource network. In this study, low-achieving students in particular made excellent progress in using problem-solving skills.

An urban setting was the focus of the following two studies by Kahle, Meece, and Scantlebury (2000) and Marx and colleagues (2004). In the first study, Kahle and co-authors investigated Ohio's Statewide Systemic Initiative (SSI), Project Discovery. Data included group-administered questionnaires and achievement tests specifically designed for Ohio's SSI. Teachers who frequently used standards-based teaching practices positively influenced urban, African-American students' science achievement and attitudes, especially that of boys. Additionally, teachers' involvement in the PD was positively related to reported use of standards-based teaching practices. Marx and colleagues assessed the impact of an inquiry-based science initiative in the context of an urban systemic reform. In this study, there were reported gains from sixth grade to eighth grade. There was no reported control or comparison group; therefore, gains could have been attributed to maturation. Although findings offer support for using inquiry-based approaches in urban settings, the study revealed important cautions; this kind of teaching is not without hurdles, particularly in an urban setting.

In a study of 18 kindergarten children (5–6 years old), Samarapungavan, Patrick, and Mantzicopoulos (2011) conducted a study focused on in the context of the Science Literacy Project (SLP). Science was taught twice a week. The six SLP units (two NOS units, three biology-based units, and one motion unit) were implemented for a total of 20 weeks. Researchers measured students' growth in knowledge and changes, if any, in motivation, as compared with a control group of students. Results indicated that children in the SLP classrooms made substantial gains in subject matter and processes of inquiry and showed a higher interest in and competence for engaging in science than the comparison group did. Authors claimed these results refuted the claim held by some people that young children cannot engage in inquiry.

There is limited research on the effects of inquiry instruction on diverse learners and learners with disabilities. Four selected studies include those by Cuevas and colleagues (2005), Lynch and colleagues (2005), McCrathy (2005), and Lee, Buxton, Lewis, and LeRoy (2006). Cuevas and co-authors (2005) investigated the impact of an intervention on elementary-level diverse students' gains in inquiry skills. The study site was a large urban school district in the southeastern United States with a varied demographic population. Participants included seven elementary-level teachers selected on their effectiveness of teaching science. Units focused on measurement and matter (Grade 3) and the water cycle and weather (Grade 4). Students demonstrated a statistically significant improvement in abilities to design procedures, record results, and develop a conclusion after instruction. Significant differences were not observed in abilities to create a problem statement or how students would use materials to carry out investigations. Low-achieving students exhibited dramatic gains as compared with high-achieving students. Limitations included a small sample size, lack of a control group, and few details of the instruction.

Lynch and co-authors investigated the impact of a Michigan curriculum on middle-level students' chemistry understandings. Participants were eighth-grade teachers in 10 schools (including comparison classrooms). Teachers routinely attended PD sessions on use of reform-based strategies. The curriculum used a guided inquiry approach with diverse students. A quasi-experimental design was used, and an ethnographic portion tracked four students. Data included classroom videotapes. Teachers were asked to teach the same curriculum standards. Findings indicated statistically significant improved performance for students in project classrooms related to achievement, basic engagement, and goal orientation.

McCrathy (2005) compared hands-on science teaching (not strictly inquiry as defined in this chapter) versus textbook instruction for students with disabilities. Demographically, the students came from variable backgrounds. Two special education teachers taught approximately 16 lessons on matter during 8 weeks. Data included three pre- and posttests, one multiple-choice, one short-answer, and one hands-on test. Students involved in hands-on instruction performed significantly better on short-answer and hands-on posttests, with no significant difference between groups on the multiple-choice test. This finding is important related to appropriate assessments used in an inquiry-based classroom.

Lee and colleagues (2006) studied students of diverse backgrounds and abilities to engage in science inquiry. Students were selected based on teachers' perceptions of students, whether students were high or low achievers. The intervention had a greater impact on the inquiry abilities of older students as well as those students from diverse backgrounds.

Two studies assessing student learning in classrooms using PBS include those by Schneider and colleagues (2002) and Geier and colleagues (2008). Schneider and co-authors (2002) compared classrooms of similar White middle-class students nationally and provided evidence of PBS students attaining equal or better achievement than students in traditional classrooms. This finding suggests that teachers should not be skeptical of using inquiry approaches in a high-stakes testing environment. Geier and co-authors (2008) studied the effect of PBS curriculum on middle-level students' learning situated in a large urban reform effort. Participants included two cohorts of seventh and eighth graders, who received instruction in the project units, as compared with the remainder of the district population. Positive findings included increases in science content understandings and process skills over their peers and significantly higher pass rates on the statewide test. There was also evidence of reducing the achievement gap typically experienced by urban African-American boys.

Sadeh and Zion (2009) compared the influence of open versus guided inquiry and defined "dynamic inquiry" as instruction that emphasizes aspects of change, intellectual flexibility, and critical thinking. Student participants were divided into two groups: guided- and open-inquiry learning approaches. Each group was followed for 2 years. Data included interviews, students' inquiry summary papers, logbooks, and reflections. Open-inquiry students demonstrated significantly higher levels of performances in the criteria "changes during inquiry" and "procedural understanding." There was no significant difference in the criteria "learning as a process" and "affective points of view."

Several studies aimed to compare inquiry versus traditional instruction related to impact on student learning. Four selected studies include those of Turpin and Cage (2004), Pine and colleagues (2006), Wilson and colleagues (2010), and Blanchard and colleagues (2010).

In the first study, Turpin and Cage (2004) studied classrooms of teachers using an integrated activity-based science curriculum versus traditional science instruction. Researchers selected three schools in northern Louisiana in the United States as experimental classrooms and four schools as comparison sites. Teachers using integrated curriculum involved students in labs twice a week. Instruments used included the Iowa Test of Basic Skills (ITBS), the Science Process Skills Test, and Serve Science Attitude Survey. Results included significantly higher ITBS and Science Process Skills posttest scores in the integrated activity-based classrooms. However, posttest science attitude means were not significantly different. There was no information on the exact nature of the instruction used by two groups of classrooms.

In the second study, Pine and colleagues (2006) compared students in classrooms using hands-on versus textbook curricula. In this large-scale study, participants included 1,000 fifth-grade students from 41 classrooms. Assessments included a 65-question short-answer cognitive abilities test to determine basic aptitude in areas of literacy, mathematics, and figure analysis and a 25-item test with questions drawn from the 1995 Third International Math and Science Study tests (TIMSS). Researchers found no significant difference between students who used hands-on curriculum and those students using the textbook for both tests.

In the third study, Wilson and co-authors (2010) used a randomized, experimental designed study to compare effectiveness of inquiry-based (organized around the BSCS 5E Instructional Model) versus traditional instruction of the same unit. Fifty-eight students (14–16 years old) were randomly assigned to one of two groups. The same teacher taught both groups of students with the same learning goals. Three outcomes were measured: scientific knowledge, scientific reasoning through application of models, and construction and critique of scientific explanations. Inquiry-based-group students demonstrated significantly higher levels of achievement those in the traditional classroom. Students receiving inquiry-based instruction reached significantly higher levels of achievement in reform-based practices of scientific knowledge, reasoning, and argumentation than did students in traditional classrooms. This effect was consistent across a range of learning goals (knowledge, reasoning, and argumentation) and time frames (immediately following the instruction and 4 weeks later).

In the fourth study, Blanchard and colleagues (2010) designed a quantitative study to compare the efficacy of guided-inquiry–based instruction to more traditional, verification laboratory instruction on learning content, procedures, and nature of science. The sample included 1,700 students in classrooms of 12 middle school teachers and 12 high school teachers. Instruction for both groups included a week-long, laboratory-based forensics unit. Data included pre-, post-, and delayed posttests, the results of which were analyzed through a Hierarchical Linear model (HLM). Students in an inquiry-based laboratory unit had significantly higher posttest scores, including higher scores, more growth, and better long-term retention at both the high school and middle school levels when compared to students in traditional classrooms.

In a rare synthesis of the inquiry literature, Minner, Levy, and Century (2010) analyzed the inquiry-based research published from 1984 to 2002. The study is limited in that research after 2002 is not included in the synthesis. Minner and colleagues (2010) reported, "various findings across 138 analyzed studies indicate a clear, positive trend favoring inquiry-based instructional practices, particularly instruction that emphasizes student active thinking and drawing conclusions from data" (p. 474). One factor determining selection of articles was sufficient information to clearly determine the presence or absence of inquiry-based science instruction, as operationally defined for this project. Research designs of the majority of studies were quasi-experimental, experimental, and qualitative. Research focused primarily on K–12 classrooms with a regular classroom teacher; however, there was limited

knowledge of training and preparation of the teachers. Fifty-one percent of the studies showed positive effects of inquiry-based instruction on content learning and retention. Thirty-three percent of the studies showed mixed impacts and 14% showed no impact. The authors noted that although the evidence is not completely positive, those students who engaged in instruction that involved generating questions, designing experiments, collecting data, and drawing conclusions exhibited enhanced content learning.

In summary, some studies of student learning lack adequate descriptions of the nature of the classroom instruction, the context, the students, and how the author operationally defined inquiry-based science instruction. Yet there appears to be ample evidence that teaching science as inquiry can positively impact a student's learning of science concepts and principles and understanding the nature of scientific inquiry.

Teacher Education and Professional Development

As noted in the previous section, there are identified challenges to a teacher's success in carrying out practices aligned with inquiry. The ability to teach science as inquiry depends on prospective teachers having reform-based education experiences and practicing teachers having experiences that foster developing a belief that this kind of teaching is important and possible. In addition, supporting teachers in learning how to enact inquiry cannot be based purely on theoretical ideas. Instead, modeling how inquiry can be carried out must be clearly situated in the reality of the classroom; a complex system composed of the teacher or teachers; the diverse learners, their backgrounds, cultures, and prior knowledge; the school administration; and parents and community members. Further, there are varied expectations of an individual school, a school district, state, and country that may be perceived by teachers to be in direct conflict with using an inquiry-based approach. A meeting of academia's ivory tower and the trenches of actual classrooms is a necessity if the promise of reform-based instruction is ever to be realized in science classrooms.

Prospective Teachers and Teacher Education

Research on the practice of teaching science as inquiry has important implications for preservice teacher education. First, it is important to carefully define the pedagogy of inquiry for new teachers and offer multiple examples of inquiry-based teaching approaches grounded in classroom practice. These examples should be specific to prospective teachers' grade level and discipline. Second, there is evidence prospective teachers benefit from authentic science experiences in developing a clear image of what science is and how science works (e.g., Windschitl, 2003, 2004). These authentic experiences need to be coupled with opportunities for reflection on what it means to teach science as inquiry (Schwartz, Lederman, & Crawford, 2004; Zembal-Saul, Krajcik, & Blumenfeld, 2002). Reform-based teacher education programs should assist new teachers in carrying out high-quality inquiry teaching in classrooms and not serve simply as replicas of past teacher education programs. Changes will need to be made in current teacher education programs, yet it is not totally clear from the literature which changes are the most critical.

One might ask the question, Are most prospective teachers even capable of carrying out sophisticated inquiry-based approaches in science classrooms? To what extent should teacher educators expect prospective teachers to design and carry out this kind of instruction? Using a case study method, Crawford (1999) examined a new high school biology teacher's ability to create an inquiry-based classroom. The researcher acknowledged this prospective teacher was something of an anomaly among other Master's degree students in the same program, and few other prospective teachers tried to design and carry out inquiry-based units. The case study offers promise that some prospective teachers are capable of this kind of instruction if key factors and challenges are addressed. Carrying out inquiry-based instruction hinges on a variety of factors. It is important to examine teachers' beliefs, develop opportunities for engaging in authentic science investigations, provide models of teaching science as inquiry, support teachers in planning long-term units, and give multiple opportunities to prospective teachers to reflect on their emerging practice.

In a later study, Crawford (2007) explored five prospective teachers' views and implementation of inquiry-based instruction over the course of a 1-year internship. An assumption of the study was that the nature of a capstone student teaching placement greatly influences a prospective teacher's success in trying out reform-based pedagogies. The study took place in a clinical-immersion professional development school (PDS). In this study, the mentor teachers and the university professor co-taught the methods courses. The mentor teachers were very familiar with the inquiry-focused philosophy that underpinned the preservice teacher program, considering the PDS setting as a near best-case scenario. Even so, only one of the five interns successfully created and carried out inquiry-rich lessons in his classroom. Crawford concluded the most critical factors influencing a prospective teacher's intentions to teach science as inquiry are (a) a view of what science is and (b) a belief that this kind of teaching is effective and possible.

Forbes and Davis (2010) studied prospective teachers' abilities to adapt existing science curriculum materials in planning inquiry-oriented science lessons. Researchers used the essential features of inquiry (NRC, 2000) to define inquiry-based science teaching and pedagogical design capacity (PDC) as a framework to study prospective teachers' abilities to use curricular materials. The study aimed to fill a gap in the research related to learning how prospective teachers use curriculum materials, particularly related to reform-based, inquiry teaching. Not surprisingly, the extent to which the curriculum materials aligned with inquiry-based teaching impacted the abilities of prospective teachers to adapt the materials and develop inquiry-oriented lessons.

Windschitl and Thompson (2012) reported findings of a study of prospective secondary teachers' (21 in total) understandings of scientific models and model-based inquiry. Researchers sought to learn how to support prospective teachers' knowledge of the epistemic roles that models, theory, and argument have in inquiry and how this connects with abilities to plan model-based lessons. Previous experiences shaped these prospective teachers' abilities to use theoretical models as a foundation for their investigations. While students could talk about models in sophisticated ways, they had a difficult time creating models themselves. Additionally, these teachers held a simplistic view of "the scientific method." These findings identified some of the challenges prospective teachers will likely have in teaching their future students about how scientists build and use models as part of scientific inquiry, an important aspect of the new K–12 Framework and NGSS.

Lustick (2009) examined the impact of an authentic science inquiry learning experience on 15 secondary prospective teachers' understandings of inquiry. The researcher used mixed methods and an action research method. The scientific question posed was, "How can peak autumn color in New England be determined?" The project aimed to support teachers' understandings of inquiry. Unfortunately, the authors concluded the intervention failed to achieve its learning goals.

Two recent studies of prospective elementary teachers include those of Leonard, et al., (2009) and Yoon, Joung, and Kim (2011). Leonard et al. (2009) determined the importance of conceptions and a supportive environment to early childhood/elementary prospective teachers' abilities to carry out inquiry-based practices. In a study of 16 Korean prospective elementary teachers' knowledge of inquiry teaching, Yoon, Joung, and Kim (2011) identified several difficulties encountered in designing and carrying out inquiry lessons. These areas involved developing children's own ideas, guiding children in designing valid experiments, and scaffolding children in data interpretation and discussion. In addition, these prospective teachers held incomplete understandings of hypothesis and lacked confidence in their science content knowledge.

Providing empirical data on how to support prospective teachers in designing inquiry classrooms that engage children in thinking like a scientist, Talanquer, Tomanek, and Novodvorsky (2013) conducted a qualitative analysis of 43 prospective teachers' evaluations of assessment evidence. In general, these prospective teachers paid more attention to process skills associated with designing an investigation versus scientific practices of analyzing data and generating conclusions. Given NGSS's emphases on eight scientific practices, these findings have implications for restructuring experiences for prospective science teachers. Assessing student understanding by attending to student thinking is a critical component of teacher learning in a reform-based science teacher preparation program.

Studying how prospective teachers perceived inquiry, in the context of their practicum experiences, Fazio, Melville, and Bartley (2010) collected data on 34 participants. Questionnaires and interviews were collected over three semesters. Many prospective teachers reported not observing many examples of inquiry in their practicum but believed that if the context were different, they could teach inquiry. Participants perceived many barriers in their practicum and reported that most of their cooperating teachers thought inquiry meant "open inquiry." For the most part, they did not feel supported by their mentor teachers. The researchers highlighted the need to better understand practicum environments and prospective teachers' beliefs.

From the studies of prospective teachers' understandings and abilities to teach science as inquiry, it is clear there are many challenges and hurdles to overcome. Besides focusing on the nature of science methods courses, practicum placements, and student teaching, many teacher educators have raised concerns about prospective teachers' experiences in their undergraduate science coursework. These undergraduate experiences may be in direct contrast to inquiry approaches. To address this issue, Nugent and colleagues (2012) compared two undergraduate courses focused on geosciences. One course was a traditional education course and the other a field-based geosciences course. In this quasi-experimental-designed study, researchers examined the influence of geosciences fieldwork on prospective teachers' knowledge of subject matter, of inquiry, and of attitudes and confidence. Findings revealed that field experiences in the geosciences using an inquiry approach enhanced student learning, inquiry skills, and attitudes to a greater extent than the traditional education content course did.

Inservice Teachers and Professional Development

Taken by themselves, development of new curricula and policy documents that promote use of inquiry pedagogy do not guarantee teachers will either use new curricular materials in the designed way or adopt new teaching approaches. One might compare teaching science as inquiry to a three-legged stool. One leg is innovative inquiry-based curricula, a second leg is an inquiry-based pedagogical model, and the third leg of the stool is effective teacher PD. Teacher PD remains a critical element related to what extent teachers enact inquiry-based pedagogy in science classrooms. Surprisingly, a recent review of the literature revealed few empirical studies published in major peer-reviewed journals that focused *specifically* on science inquiry PD up to the time of the review (Capps, Crawford, & Constas, 2012).

Two representative studies focused on PD of teachers of lower grades. Brand and Moore (2011) studied the effects of a 3-year-long PD program on 30 K–5 teachers' use of inquiry, addressing the issue that inquiry is often not evident in elementary classrooms. Data sources included interviews and semantic maps. Participants met in grade-level groups to read about inquiry and plan units; they enacted planned lessons and reflected upon their enactment. Researchers reported that by front-loading teachers' needs (time, support, resources, and ownership), teachers moved toward more inquiry-based teaching. A key factor included substantial time for teachers to participate in the PD.

Lee (2011) studied the impact of inquiry-focused PD on primary teachers in Hong Kong. PD was conducted in two different schools. Science concepts addressed were electricity and expansion and contraction of air. The researcher used two measures of teachers' growth—pedagogical content knowledge (PCK) and subject matter knowledge (SMK). Data included notes from lesson planning and team evaluation meetings, classroom observations, teacher journals, and teacher questionnaires. Teachers reported continual concern about their SMK even though they seemed to improve in this area. Concerns led to lack of confidence to carry out inquiry-based lessons. Conclusions included the elusiveness of PCK of inquiry.

Representative studies of teachers in upper grades include those of Schneider and colleagues (2005), Wee and colleagues (2007), Jones and Eick (2009), Breslyn and McGinnis (2011), and Capps and Crawford (2012).

Schneider and co-authors (2005) addressed the problem that when teachers strive to teach science as inquiry by enacting reform-based curricula, the fidelity of the innovative curriculum can be an issue. Teachers had access to carefully designed inquiry-based materials (in this case PBS), yet different teachers carried out the instruction in different ways. Well-designed curricular materials are important but not sufficient in supporting teachers. Robust PD is recommended.

Wee and colleagues (2007) examined whether a PD program changed four teachers' ideas about inquiry and their teaching. ENVISION was based on environmental science issues. PD sessions included a preinstitute workshop, 4-week summer institute, site visits, and an academic-year workshop. Inquiry was presented in three ways: environmental research, environmental monitoring/field studies, and investigative labs/models. Data included lesson profiles, open-response assessments, site-visit observations and reports, and concept maps. Findings included (1) implementing inquiry-based activities in the classroom had little/no impact on teachers' ideas about inquiry and (2) the PD program assisted teachers in designing and implementing inquiry-based activities and increased understanding of inquiry, but classroom activities did not reflect a high level of understanding. Overall, the authors asserted these kinds of PD sessions can provide knowledge and assistance, but it is clear there remains difficulty in assisting teachers in attaining high levels of inquiry in their classrooms. See also Lotter and colleagues (2007) for similar results in changing a teacher's core concepts of teaching.

Jones and Eick (2009) studied two sixth-grade teachers (students ages 11–13) in the context of using two different inquiry kit–based curricula. Each was considered excellent and connected to national standards fostering teaching science as inquiry. Data included interviews, participant journals, a focus group, and classroom observations. After initial difficulties, both teachers enjoyed working with the kits, learned subject matter along with their students, and tried new pedagogical strategies. Interestingly, the teacher previously categorized as using open inquiry moved toward more teacher-centered instruction. The other teacher moved from primarily teacher-centered instruction toward more student-centered instruction. One teacher altered the curriculum in order to deal with time constraints and comfort level, thus possibly altering the quality and the nature of the inquiry. Implications included need for more PD opportunities.

Breslyn and McGinnis (2011) used a situative perspective (Brown, Collins, & Duguid, 1989) to investigate science teachers' use of inquiry. Results indicted that use of inquiry is dependent on the context of the science discipline and, to a lesser extent, the classroom context. In their study of exemplary secondary science teachers, the discipline in which teachers taught was found to be a major influence on conceptions and inquiry enactment. Based on the findings, Breslyn and McGinnis (2011) suggested it may be effective to offer more discipline-specific examples of inquiry.

Capps and Crawford (2013) tracked growth in 20 upper elementary and middle-level teachers' knowledge of earth science and views of inquiry and nature of science. Using a quasi-experimental designed study of the impact of authentic knowledge and views, comparison teachers taught similar concepts to the same grade-level students, but they did not participate in the PD, nor did they use project lessons or materials. Project teachers had statistically significant greater gains in subject matter knowledge and views of inquiry and nature of science as compared with comparison teachers. Project teachers experienced a relatively short-term yet intensive PD experience (6 consecutive days, 10 hours/day) of lessons, fieldwork, and group discussions, one that combined science inquiry and opportunity to learn subject matter in the context of an authentic investigation. There were many opportunities for project teachers to reflect on their current practice and new experiences in a collaborative setting. The findings are promising, because they suggest that short-term yet intensive PD can support teachers in subject matter knowledge and views. The study highlighted the importance of reflection in fostering teacher change.

Summarizing these studies of PD, important factors include connecting with teachers' needs, their science discipline, opportunities for reflection, and substantial time needed for teachers to travel on their journey of learning how to teach science as inquiry.

Barriers to Teachers Enacting Inquiry Pedagogy

A number of challenges have been reported over the last decade or more related to teachers' intentions to teach inquiry and constraints that deter teachers from carrying out inquiry teaching. Keys and Kennedy (1999) cited lack of time, the challenge of teachers in turning questions back onto students, and the constraint of having to teach mandated concepts that are difficult to teach through inquiry. Classroom management issues are often cited as barriers. Harris and Rooks (2010) described five interconnected management areas that need to be addressed when managing an inquiry-oriented K–8 science classroom. The NSF–funded program, Cornell Science Inquiry Partnership Program, placed doctoral students as teaching fellows in New York State schools (Trautmann, MaKinster, & Avery, 2004). The fellows worked with classroom teachers in creating and implementing inquiry-based lessons. Researchers revealed several challenges identified by the experienced teachers: (1) state curricula and high-stakes testing, (2) time constraints, (3) student expectations and abilities, and (4) teachers' fear of the unknown. The teaching fellows positively influenced the classroom teachers' willingness to engage in inquiry-based lessons.

Despite innovative PD programs targeted at using inquiry pedagogy, and although teachers may desire to engage their students in inquiry, it is important to recognize barriers that may be insurmountable. This chapter does not directly address policy issues, and it important not to blame teachers for lack of reform-based classroom practices. Institutional and social barriers may discourage teachers striving to implement inquiry-based pedagogy. Songer, Lee, and Kam (2001) explored the barriers to technology-rich inquiry pedagogy in urban science classrooms. Besides those related to technology, challenges to inquiry pedagogy included those teachers cannot control: inadequate space and materials, inadequate time, large class sizes, high student and teacher mobility, and limited instructional freedom (Songer et al., 2001). Ten years earlier, Haberman (1991) identified similar barriers in urban classrooms.

The reality is that various barriers may negate the promising influence of PD and innovative teacher education programs. There exist specific expectations of an individual school, a school district, state, and country, including the current frenzy of high-stakes testing, which teachers may perceive as in direct conflict with using an inquiry-based approach. School administrators and local, state, and national policies may create power relationships that discourage teachers from using creativity and innovations in teaching (Au, 2007). These contextual factors may make change in classroom practice virtually impossible for many teachers. The risk may be perceived as too high in comparison to benefits. Researchers should continue to explore the impact of policy issues and classroom context and take a hard look at classroom conditions that may prevent instructional innovations from becoming a reality. Further, science education researchers need to do a better job of communicating research findings to all stakeholders and help bridge research findings to teaching practice, and, as mentioned, to policy.

Strengths, Weaknesses, and Gaps in the Literature

One issue identified in this chapter is the fact that researchers have varied views of what it means to teach science as inquiry. An effort has been made in this chapter to trace the history of inquiry and to identify various meanings. However, an even more thorough and complete synthesis could prove very useful. A study that aims to clarify and categorize the various research studies connected with teaching science as inquiry and that synthesizes findings across various views of inquiry would be extremely helpful.

Many researchers, teacher educators, and curricular designers advocate teaching science as inquiry in classrooms. Yet there have been and remain some critics of this way of teaching (e.g., Kirschner, Sweller, & Clark, 2006). Despite these critics and the recognized difficulties associated with teaching in this way, there appears to be sufficiently strong evidence to support using this kind of pedagogy in classrooms. (i.e., Minner et al., 2010; Schroeder, Scott, Tolson, Huang, & Lee, 2007; Shymansky et al., 1983).

As shown in many of the empirical studies reviewed in this chapter, there are important benefits of teaching science as inquiry for children with high needs, low performance, low language skills, and from populations generally underrepresented in the sciences. Research studies of large student populations have demonstrated inquiry-based approaches as effective (i.e., Geier et al., 2008; Marx et al., 2004; Pine et al., 2006). A number of studies have taken place in the context of urban reform and have indicated the successful application of inquiry techniques on a large scale. The superiority of inquiry-based techniques to meet a variety of educational goals has been supported by results from numerous studies involving inquiry-based and traditional classes. Several studies have demonstrated support for inquiry-based instruction as more effective than traditional techniques in teaching a variety of specific science concepts (Lee et al., 2006; Thacker, Kim, Trefz, & Lea, 1994; Wilson et al., 2010). There is also empirical evidence that inquiry-based approaches are more effective than other approaches in reducing the achievement gap between different groups of students (Cuevas et al., 2005; Lee et al., 2006; Lynch et al., 2005).

One area of continued concern is the lack of empirical research on effective PD and teacher education programs published in highly refereed journals specifically targeted at inquiry learning and teaching across different grade levels, contexts, and disciplines (see Capps & Crawford, 2012; Crawford et al., 2013). Studies need to go beyond descriptions of prospective and practicing teachers' PD programs. Researchers and teacher educators need confidence in the systematic analyses of data and robust evidence of underlying factors of success or failure of different PD features. In addition, needed are more studies in diverse classrooms on how children learn and take on identities as science learners. With publication of NGSS (NGSS Lead States, 2013), we now move into a new era of reform in the United States related to teaching science/engineering practices, disciplinary core ideas, crosscutting concepts, and the integration of all of these. More empirical studies are needed to identify components of effective curricula and features of programs that are critical in making the vision a reality in science classrooms. The kind of teaching required to carry out this sophisticated and integrated instruction goes beyond what is currently asked of teachers. The reality is, what was envisioned in the past (AAAS, 1989; Dewey, 1910; NRC 1996; Schwab, 1960) is currently *not happening* in most science classrooms.

It is with the utmost respect for the professional science teacher that the author acknowledges the teacher as an agent of change. It is important to be clear that highlighting the teacher as the central factor in shifting from primarily a traditional to a more inquiry/practices-oriented classroom in no way is meant as pejorative against teachers. Anyone who has tried to create these kinds of classrooms in the current political climate like in the United States—a country steeped in an accountability system of high-stakes standardized testing and varied resources depending on the school—understands the complexity of the situation. Conditions that may dissuade teachers from using reform-based teaching approaches include state-mandated curricula that run counter to reform-based teaching and administrators who rate teachers solely on student performances as measured by high-stakes assessments. The impact of context on whether a teacher intends to and successfully enacts teaching science as inquiry includes various situations encountered in one's community, school, and classroom. "[T]he situations teachers face in their daily work provide important and underappreciated influences on teaching practice and on student learning" (Kennedy, 2010, p. 593). It would be helpful to reexamine the issues science teachers themselves identify as being problematic.

As a classroom teacher for 17 years in three different public schools, the author has first-hand knowledge of the realities of administrative and parental pressures, high-stakes testing, and enormous challenges in teaching children of a wide range of abilities, languages, and cultures. Yet also apparent are the tangible benefits from immersing children in asking and answering their own scientific questions and allowing children freedom to make mistakes, question, grapple with data, and figure things out for themselves (e.g., Crawford et al., 1999).

Conclusions, Implications, and Future Research

In conclusion, the aim of this chapter was to help clarify for the reader the issues and evidence surrounding inquiry in science classrooms. There is consensus among most science educators that the time for change in the way science is taught has arrived. Yet the fact remains that little change is taking place in our classrooms. Research indicates that inquiry-based science instruction has the potential to move learners in the direction of independent and critical thinking. But there are many obstacles to successfully teaching in this manner, not the least of which is the continued confusion over terms. Whether you call it inquiry or practices of science or something else, the central theme remains the same: learner-constructed and -articulated science understandings based on logic and evidence as crucial components of a desired educational strategy in our future science classrooms. Certainly, one goal should focus on providing the motivation and support necessary, including changes in policy, to help a teacher be successful in engaging students in science practices in her classroom.

Of course, many questions and problems remain. Inertia favors the status quo. It will take considerable resources to make such a significant change take place. Future research will vigorously examine inquiry teaching with the goal of facilitating a change from lecture-driven instruction to a classroom environment that empowers a child and facilitates his or her intellectual development as a critical thinker.

Suggestions for future research questions could include but are not limited to the following. How can science curricula be designed to support children in feasibly learning how to carry out scientific practices and learning about how scientists think? What kinds of authentic science investigations are possible in classrooms? How can undergraduate science courses be redesigned to help prospective teachers understand inquiry/practices and nature of science? Is it possible to structure student teaching experiences such that the experience will sustain changes in prospective teachers' beliefs about teaching science practices, disciplinary core ideas, and crosscutting concepts? What typically happens to teachers' beliefs in the first years of teaching? What kinds of mentoring programs are most effective for beginning teachers in helping them create inquiry-steeped classrooms? What are the key roadblocks, and how can teachers navigate these roadblocks? What are features of effective PD programs for supporting practicing teachers in teaching children what science is, and what science is not? How can we help teachers and students become metacognitive in learning and teaching science? What kinds of strategies are most influential with English-language-learning children to help them learn about scientific practices and nature of science? How can high-stakes assessments be redesigned to encourage teachers in striving to teach science as inquiry/practices versus "teaching to the test"? How can research findings related to teaching science as inquiry shape future policy?

This review and synthesis of research related to teaching science as inquiry has important implications for teachers, curriculum designers, teacher educators, and policy makers. Teachers report students seem to be disengaged with school, especially as students move up into higher grades. There is ample evidence that classroom-based inquiry science can be beneficial to student learning and to developing positive attitudes toward life-long science learning. There is potential to push the boundaries of what is possible. But teachers need to understand ways of and feel confident in scaffolding students in various aspects of scientific inquiry/practices, including learning how to reason. Inquiry can motivate students, because the answer is not obvious; it allows students to travel down unknown paths and in unknown directions. Many criticize the nature of undergraduate science teaching, which contributes to a cycle of new teachers experiencing non–inquiry-based science classes and then delivering uninspiring teaching in their K–12 classrooms. Thus, many are calling for changes at the university level. Current reforms can also benefit those who will not become scientists but will be well-informed, contributing citizens and consumers of science.

We are at an important crossroads in science education with the recent publication in the United States of the NGSS. There is renewed interest in producing a greater number of highly qualified teachers. These new teachers will be expected to facilitate *all* children in carrying out and understanding science practices, disciplinary core ideas, and crosscutting concepts and the integration of these. These ways of teaching are sophisticated and challenging. Classrooms are complex. Challenges for teachers will be great in the years to come. Yet the potential for helping children learn how to think critically, to use data as evidence, and to develop arguments, build models, and evaluate these in light of evidence will be equally great. Supporting teachers (prospective and practicing) in teaching science as inquiry requires substantial resources and attention to research-based effective programs. We need to look to the past, to understand that simply creating policy documents and new curricula, *without attention to robustly supporting teachers*, will not necessary change the way we traditionally teach science. Science teacher education programs need to change as well. PD programs for practicing teachers need to be designed with attention to the context of schools, teachers' backgrounds and beliefs, and grade level and culture of students. And we need to pay attention to policy issues and remove the roadblocks that prevent change from happening.

By transforming traditional science classrooms to be inquiry focused and student centered, we (researchers, educators, curriculum developers, and policy makers) have the opportunity to position *all* our children to become critical thinkers and consumers of science in the 21st century.

Acknowledgments

Thank you to Julianne Wenner for expert help in identifying research articles and for conversations about teaching science as inquiry in the classroom. Also, thank you to Charlene Czerniak and Carolyn Wallace for reviewing this chapter.

References

Abd-El-Khalick, F., BouJaoude, S., Duschl, R., Lederman, N. G., Mamlok-Naaman, R., Hofstein, A., Niaz, M., et al. (2004). Inquiry in science education: International perspectives. *Science Education, 88*(3), 397–419.

Abell, S. K., Anderson, G., & Chezem, J. (2000). Science as argument and explanation: Exploring concepts of sound in third grade. In J. Minstrell & E. van Zee (Eds.), *Inquiring into inquiry learning and teaching in science* (pp. 65–79). Washington, DC: American Association for the Advancement of Science.

Akar, E. (2005). Effectiveness of 5E Cycle on students' understanding of acid-based concepts. A thesis submitted to the graduate school of natural and applied science. Middle East Technical University. Ankara, Turkey. Retrieved from https://etd.lib.metu.edu.tr/upload/12605747/index

Alberts, B. (2000). Some thoughts of a scientist on inquiry. In J. Minstrell & E. van Zee (Eds.), *Inquiring into inquiry learning and teaching in science* (pp. 3–13). Washington, DC: American Association for the Advancement of Science.

American Association for the Advancement of Science (AAAS). (1989). *Science for all Americans.* Washington, DC: Author. Retrieved from www.project2061.org/publications/bsl/online/index.php?chapter=1

American Association for the Advancement of Science (AAAS). (1993). *Project 2061 atlas of scientific literacy, Volumes 1 and 2.* Retrieved January 26, 2013, from www.project2061.org/publications/atlas/default.htm

Anderson, R. D. (2002). Reforming science teaching? What research says about inquiry. *Journal of Science Teacher Education, 13*(1), 1–12.

Anderson, R. D. (2007). Inquiry as an organizing theme for science curricula. In S. K. Abell & N. G. Lederman (Eds.), *Handbook of research on science education* (pp. 807–830). Mahwah, NJ: Lawrence Erlbaum Associates.

Atar, H. Y. (2011). Investigating the relationship between teachers' nature of science conceptions and their practice of inquiry science. *Asia-Pacific Forum on Science Learning and Teaching, 12*(2), 1–26.

Atay, D. P., & Tekkaya, C. (2008). Promoting students' learning in genetics with the learning cycle. *The Journal of Experimental Education, 76*(3), 259–280.

Au, W. (2007). High stakes testing and curricular control: A qualitative metasynthesis. *Educational Researcher, 36*(5), 258–267.

Barrow, L. (2006). A brief history of inquiry: From Dewey to standards. *Journal of Science Teacher Education, 17,* 265–278.

Blanchard, M. R., Southerland, S. A., Osborne, J. W., Sampson, V. D., Annetta, L. A., & Granger, E. M. (2010). Is inquiry possible in light of accountability? A quantitative comparison of the relative effectiveness of guided inquiry and verification laboratory instruction. *Science Education, 94,* 577–616.

Blumenfeld, P., Soloway, R., Marx, R., Krajcik, J., Guzdial, M., & Palincsar, A. (1991). Motivating project-based learning: Sustaining the doing, supporting the learning. *Educational Psychologist, 26,* 369, 398.

Brand, B. R., & Moore, S. J. (2011). Enhancing teachers' application of inquiry-based strategies using a constructivist sociocultural professional development model. *International Journal of Science Education, 33*(7), 889–913.

Bransford, J. D., Brown, A. L., & Cocking, R. R. (Eds.). (1999). *How people learn: Brain, mind, experience, and school.* Washington, DC: National Academies Press.

Braund, M., & Reiss, M. (2006). Towards a more authentic science curriculum: The contribution of out-of-school learning. *International Journal of Science Education. 28*(12), 1373–1388.

Breslyn, W., & McGinnis, J. R. (2011). A comparison of exemplary biology, chemistry, earth science, and physics teachers' conceptions and enactment of inquiry. *Science Education, 96,* 48–77.

Brossard, D., Lewenstein, B., & Bonney, R. (2005). Scientific knowledge and attitude change: The impact of a citizen science project. *International Journal of Science Education, 27*(9), 1099–1121.

Brown, J. S., Collins, A., & Duguid, P. (1989). Situated cognition and the culture of learning. *Educational Researcher, 18*(1), 32–42.

Bybee, R., Taylor, J., Gardner, A., Van Scotter, P., Powell, J., Westbrook, A., & Landes, N. (2006). *The BSCS 5E instructional model: Origins and effectiveness.* A Report prepared for the office of science education National Institutes of Health. Colorado Springs, CO: BSCS.

Bybee, R. W. (2000). Teaching science as inquiry. In J. Minstrell & E. van Zee (Eds.), *Inquiring into inquiry learning and teaching in science* (pp. 20–46). Washington, DC: American Association for the Advancement of Science.

Bybee, R. W. (2006). Scientific inquiry and science teaching. In L. Flick & N. G. Lederman (Eds.), *Scientific inquiry and nature of science* (pp. 1–14). Dordrecht, the Netherlands: Springer Publishers.

Bybee, R. W., & Van Scotter, P. (2007). Reinventing the science curriculum. *Educational Leadership, 64*(4), 43–47.

Capps, D. K., & Crawford, B. A. (2012). Inquiry-based instruction and teaching about nature of science: Are they happening? *Journal of Science Teacher Education.* doi:10.1007/s10972-012-9314-z

Capps, D. K., & Crawford, B. A. (2013). Inquiry-based professional development: What does it take to support teachers in learning about inquiry and nature of science? *International Journal of Science Education, 35*(12), 1947–1978.

Capps, D. K. Crawford, B. A., & Constas, M. (2012). A review of empirical literature on inquiry professional development: Alignment with best practices and a critique of the findings. *Journal of Science Teacher Education, 23*(3), 291–318.

Champagne, A. B., Kouba, V. L., & Hurley, M. (2000). Assessing inquiry. In J. Minstrell & E. van Zee (Eds.), *Inquiring into inquiry learning and teaching in science* (pp. 447–470). Washington, DC: American Association for the Advancement of Science.

Chinn, C., & Malhotra, B. (2002). Epistemologically authentic inquiry in schools: A theoretical framework for evaluating inquiry tasks. *Science Education, 86*(2), 175–218.

Cohn, J. (2008). Citizen science: Can volunteers do real research? *BioScience, 58*(3), 192–197.

Conner, T., Capps, D. K., Crawford, B. A., & Ross, R. M. (2013). Engage all of your students using project-based learning. *Science Scope, 36*(7), 62–67.

Crawford, B. A. (1999). Is it realistic to expect a preservice teacher to create an inquiry-based classroom? *Journal of Science Teacher Education, 10,* 175–194.

Crawford, B. A. (2000). Embracing the essence of inquiry: New roles for science teachers. *Journal of Research in Science Teaching, 37,* 916–937.

Crawford, B. A. (2007). Learning to teach science as inquiry in the rough and tumble of practice. *Journal of Research in Science Teaching, 44*(4), 613–642.

Crawford, B. A., Capps, D. K., van Driel, J., Lederman, N. G., Lederman, J., Luft, J., Wong, S., Tan, A., Lim, S., Loughran, J., & Smith, K. (2013). Learning to teach science as inquiry: Developing an evidence-based framework for effective teacher professional development. In C. Bruguiére, A. Tiberghien, & P. Clément (Eds.), *Topics and trends in current science education Vol. I.* (pp. 193–212). Dordrecht, the Netherlands: Springer.

Crawford, B. A., Krajcik, J. S., & Marx, R. W. (1999). Elements of a community of learners in a middle school science classroom. *Science Education, 83,* 701–723.

Crawford, B. A., Ross, R., & Allmon, W. (2014). Fossil finders: Using fossils to teach about evolution, inquiry and nature of science. Retrieved from http://fossilfinder.coe.uga.edu/

Cuevas, P., Lee, O., Hart, J., & Deaktor, R. (2005). Improving science inquiry with elementary students of diverse backgrounds. *Journal of Research in Science Teaching, 42,* 337–357.

Dewey, J. (1910). Science as subject matter and as method. *Science,* 121–127.

Dewey, J. (1971). *How we think.* Chicago: Henry Regnery Company. Originally published in 1910.

Drake, K. N., & Long, D. (2009). Rebecca's in the dark? A comparative study of problem-based learning and direct instruction/experiential learning in two 4th-grade classrooms. *Journal of Elementary Science Education, 21*(1), 1–16.

Driver, R. (1989). The construction of scientific knowledge in school classrooms. In R. Miller (Ed.), *Doing science: Images of science in education* (pp. 83–107). New York: Routledge.

Driver, R., Squires, A., Rushworth, P., & Wood-Robinson, V. (1994). *Making sense of secondary science: Children's ideas in science.* London and New York: Routledge.

Duschl, R. A. (2003). Assessment of inquiry. In J. M. Atkin & J. E. Coffey (Eds.), *Everyday assessment in the science classroom* (pp. 41–59). Arlington, VA: National Science Teachers Association Press.

Duschl, R. A., Schweingruber, H. A., & Shouse, A. W. (2007). *Taking science to school: Learning and teaching science in grades K–8.* Washington, DC: National Academies Press.

Fazio, X., Melville, W., & Bartley, A. (2010). The problematic nature of the practicum: A key determinant of pre-service teachers' emerging inquiry-based science practices. *Journal of Science Teacher Education, 21*(6), 665–681.

Fogleman, J., McNeill, K. L., & Krajcik, J. (2011). Examining the effect of teachers' adaptations of a middle school science-oriented curriculum on student learning. *Journal of Research in Science Teaching, 48*(2), 149–169.

Forbes, C. T., & Davis, E. (2010). Curriculum design for inquiry: Preservice elementary teachers' mobilization and adaptation of science curriculum materials. *Journal of Research in Science Teaching, 47*(7), 820–839.

Furtak, E., Siedal, T., Iverson, H., & Briggs, D. (2012). Experimental and quasi-experimental studies of inquiry-based science teaching: A Meta-analysis. *Review of Educational Research, 82*(3), 300–329.

Galloway, A., Tudor, M., & Vanderhaegen. (2006). The reliability of citizen science: A case study of Oregon white oak stand surveys. *Wildlife Society Bulletin, 34*(5), 1425–1429.

Geier, R., Blumenfeld, P., Marx, R., Krajcik, J., Fishman, B., Soloway, E., & Clay-Chambers, J. (2008). Standardized test outcomes for students engaged in inquiry based science curriculum in the context of urban reform. *Journal of Research in Science Teaching, 45*(8), 922–939.

Goldfisher, D., Crawford, B. A., Capps, D., & Ross, R. (2014). Fossils, inquiry, and the English language learners. *Science Scope.*

Haberman, M. (1991). The pedagogy of poverty versus good teaching. *Phi Delta Kappan, 73,* 290–294.

Harms, M. C., & Yager, R. E. (1981). *What research says to the science teacher. Vol. 3.* Arlington, VA: National Science Teachers Association.

Harris, C., & Rooks, D. (2010). Managing inquiry-based science: Challenges in enacting complex science instruction in elementary and middle school. *Journal of Science Teacher Education, 21*(2), 227–240.

Hasson, E., & Yarden, A. (2012). Separating the research question from the laboratory techniques: Advancing high-school biology teachers' ability to ask research questions. *Journal of Research in Science Teaching, 49*(10), 1296–1320.

Hmelo-Silver, C., Duncan, R., & Chinn, C. (2007). Scaffolding and achievement in problem-based and inquiry learning: A response to Kirschner, Sweller, and Clark (2006). *Educational Psychologist, 42*(2), 99–107.

Horizon Research Corporation, Inc. (1999). *Local systemic change core evaluation data collection manual.* Chapel Hill, NC: Author.

Hsu, C.-K., Hwang, G.-J., Chuang, C.-W., & Chang, C.-K. (2012). Effects on learners' performance of using selected and open network resources in a problem-based learning activity. *Journal of Educational Technology, 43*(4), 606–623.

Ireland, J., Watters, J., Brownlee, J., & Lupton, M. (2011). Elementary teacher's conceptions of inquiry teaching: Messages for teacher development. *Journal of Science Teacher Education, 23*(2), 1–17.

Jones, M. T., & Eick, C. J. (2009). Implementing inquiry kit curriculum: Obstacles, adaptations, and practical knowledge development in two middle school science teachers. *Science Education, 91*(3), 492–513.

Kahle, J., Meece, J., & Scantlebury, K. (2000). Urban African-American middle school science students: Does standards-based teaching make a difference? *Journal of Research in Science Teaching, 37*(9), 1019–1041.

Kang, N. H. (2007). Learning to teach science: Personal epistemologies, teaching goals, and practices of teaching. *Teaching and Teacher Education, 24,* 478–498.

Kennedy, M. M. (2010). Attrition and the quest for teacher quality. *Educational Researcher, 39*(8), 591–598.

Keys, C. W., & Bryan, L. (2001). Co-constructing inquiry-based science with teachers: Essential research for lasting reform. *Journal of Research in Science Teaching, 38*(6), 631–645.

Keys, C. W., & Kennedy, V. (1999). Understanding inquiry science teaching in context: A case study of an elementary teacher. *Journal of Science Teacher Education, 10,* 315–333.

Kim, M., & Tan, A.-L. (2011). Rethinking difficulties of teaching inquiry-based practical work: Stories from elementary pre-service teachers. *International Journal of Science Education, 33*(4), 465–486.

Kirschner, P. A., Sweller, J., & Clark, R. E. (2006). Why minimal guidance during instruction does not work: An analysis of the failure of constructivist, discovery, problem-based, experiential, and inquiry-based teaching. *Educational Psychologist, 41,* 75–86.

Kolodner, J., Camp, P., Crismond, D., Fasse, B., Gray, J., Holbrook, J., Puntambekar, S., & Ryan, M. (2003). Problem-based learning meets case-based reasoning in the middle-school science classroom: Putting learning by design into practice. *Journal of the Learning Sciences, 12*(4), 495–547.

Krajcik, J., Blumenfeld, P., Marx, R., Bass, K., Fredricks, J., & Soloway, E. (1998). Inquiry in project based-science classrooms. *Journal of the Learning Sciences, 7*(3&4), 313–350.

Krajcik, J., & Czerniak, C. (2014). *Teaching science in elementary and middle school children science: A project-based science approach* (4th ed.). New York: Routledge.

Krajcik, J., McNeill, K., & Reiser, B. (2007). Learning-goals-driven design model: Developing curriculum materials that align with national standards and incorporate project-based pedagogy. *Science Education.* doi:10.1002/sce.20240

Lave, J., & Wenger, E. (1991). *Situated learning: Legitimate peripheral participation.* New York: Cambridge University Press.

Lavonen, J., & Laaksonen, S. (2009). Context of teaching and learning school science in Finland: Reflections on PISA 2006 results. *Journal of Research in Science Teaching, 46*(8), 922–944.

Lee, O., Buxton, C., Lewis, S., & LeRoy, K. (2006). Science inquiry and student diversity: Enhanced abilities and continuing difficulties after an instructional intervention. *Journal of Research in Science Teaching, 42,* 921–946.

Lee, Y. (2011). Enhancing pedagogical content knowledge in a collaborative school-based PD program for inquiry-based science teaching. *Asia-Pacific Forum on Science Learning and Teaching, 12*(2), 1–30.

Leonard, J., Boakes, N., & Moore, C. M. (2009). Conducting science inquiry in primary classrooms? Case studies of two preservice teachers' inquiry-based practices. *Journal of Elementary Science Education, 21*(1), 27–50.

Lotter, C., Harwood, W. S., & Bonner, J. J. (2007). The influence of core teaching conceptions on teachers' use of inquiry teaching practices. *Journal of Research in Science Teaching, 44,* 1318–1347.

Lustick, D. (2009). The failure of inquiry: Preparing science teachers with an authentic investigation. *Journal of Science Teacher Education, 20*(6), 583–604.

Lynch, S., Kuipers, J., Pyke, C., & Szesze, M. (2005). Examining the effects of a highly rated science curriculum unit on diverse students: Results from a planning grant. *Journal of Research in Science Teaching, 42,* 921–946.

Marx, R., Blumenfeld, P., Krajcik, J., & Soloway, E. (1994). Enacting project-based science. *The Elementary School Journal, 97*(4), Special Issue: Science (Mar., 1994), 341–358.

Marx, R. W., Blumenfeld, P. C., Krajcik, J., Blunk, M., Crawford, B., Kelly, B., & Meyer, K. (1994). Enacting project-based science: Experiences of four middle grade teachers. *Elementary School Journal, 94*(5), 499–516.

Marx, R. W., Blumenfeld, P. C., Krajcik, J. S., Fishman, B., Soloway, E., Geier, R., & Revital, T. T. (2004). Inquiry-based science in the middle grades: Assessment of learning in urban systemic reform. *Journal of Research in Science Teaching, 41*(10), 1063–1080.

Maskiewicz, A. C., & Winters, V. A. (2012). Understanding the co-construction of inquiry practices: A case study of a responsive teaching environment. *Journal of Research in Science Teaching, 49,* 429–464.

Mayer, R. E. (2004). Should there be a three-strikes rule against pure discovery learning? The case for guided methods of instruction. *American Psychologist, 59,* 14–19. doi:10.1037/0003-066X.59.1.14

McCrathy, C. (2005). Effects of thematic based, hands on science teaching versus a textbook approach for students with disabilities. *Journal of Research in Science Teaching, 42,* 245–263.

McNeil, K. (2009). Teachers' use of curriculum to support students in writing scientific arguments to explain phenomena. *Science Education, 93*(2), 233–268.

Meyer, X. S., & Crawford, B. A. (2011). Teaching science as a cultural way of knowing: Merging authentic inquiry, nature of science, and multicultural strategies. *Cultural Studies in Science Education. 6*(3), 525–547. doi:10.1007/s11422-011-9318-6

Minner, D. D., Levy, A. J., & Century, J. (2010). Inquiry-based science instruction—what is it and does it matter? Results from a research synthesis years 1984 to 2002. *Journal of Research in Science Teaching, 47,* 474–496.

Minstrell, J. (2000). Implications for teaching and learning inquiry: A summary. In J. Minstrell & E. van Zee (Eds.), *Inquiring into inquiry learning and teaching in science* (pp. 471–496). Washington, DC: American Association for the Advancement of Science.

Minstrell, J., & van Zee, E. H. (Eds.). (2000). *Inquiring into inquiry learning and teaching in science.* Washington, DC: American Association for the Advancement of Science.

National Research Council (NRC). (1996). *National science education standards.* Washington, DC: National Academies Press.

National Research Council (NRC). (2000). *Inquiry and the national science education standards.* Washington, DC: National Academies Press.

National Research Council (NRC). (2012). *A framework for K–12 science education: Practices, crosscutting concepts, and core ideas.* Washington, DC: National Academies Press.

NGSS Lead States. (2013). *Next generation science standards: For states, by states.* Washington, DC: National Academies Press.

Nugent G., Toland, M., Levy, R., Kunz, G., Harwood, D., Green, D., & Kitts, K. (2012). The impact of an inquiry-based geoscience field course on preservice teachers. *Journal of Science Teacher Education, 23*(5), 503–529.

Osborne, J., Erduran, S., & Simon, S. (2004). Enhancing the quality of argumentation in school science. *Journal of Research in Science Teaching, 41*(10), 994–1020.

Pajares, F. (1992). Teachers' beliefs and educational research: Cleaning up a messy construct. *Review of Educational Research, 62*(3), 307–332.

Passmore, C. M., & Stewart, J. (2002). A modeling approach to teaching evolutionary biology in high schools. *Journal of Research in Science Teaching, 39,* 185–204.

Passmore, C. M., Stewart, J., & Cartier, J. (2009). Model-based inquiry and school science: Creating connections. *School Science and Mathematics, 109*(7), 394–402.

Peterson, R., & Treagust, D. (1998). Learning to teach primary science through problem-based learning. *Science Education, 82*(2), 215–237.

Philipp, R. A. (2007). Mathematics teachers' beliefs and affect. In F. K. Lester (Ed.), *Second handbook of research on mathematics teaching and learning* (Vol. 2, pp. 257–315). Charlotte, NC: Information Age Publishing.

Pine, J. P., Aschbacher, P. A., Roth, E., Jones, M., McPhee, C., Martin, C., Phelps, S., Kyle, T., & Foley, B. (2006). Fifth graders' science inquiry abilities: A comparative study of students in textbook and inquiry curricula. *Journal of Research in Science Teaching, 45*(5), 467–484.

Polman, J. (2000). *Designing project-based science: Connecting learners through guided inquiry.* Williston, VT: Teachers College Press.

Posner, G., Strike, K., Hewson, P., & Gertzog, W. (1982). Accommodation of a science concept: Toward a theory of conceptual change. *Science Education, 66*(2), 211–227.

Roehrig, G. H., & Luft, J. (2004). Constraints experienced by beginning secondary science teachers in implementing scientific inquiry lessons. *International Journal of Science Education, 26*(1), 3–24.

Roth, W. M. (1995). *Authentic school science: Knowing and learning in open-inquiry laboratories.* Dordrecht, the Netherlands, and Boston: Kluwer Academic Publishers.

Roth, W. M., & Calabrese-Barton, A. (2004). *Rethinking scientific literacy.* New York: RoutledgeFalmer.

Ruiz-Primo, M. A., Li, M., Tsai, S.-P., & Schneider, J. (2010). Testing one premise of scientific inquiry in science classrooms: Examining students' scientific explanations and student learning. *Journal of Research in Science Teaching, 47*(5), 583–608.

Sadeh, I., & Zion, M. (2009). The development of dynamic inquiry performances within an open inquiry setting: A comparison to guided inquiry setting. *Journal of Research in Science Teaching, 46*(10), 1137–1160.

Sadler, T., Barab, S., & Scott, B. (2007). What do students gain by engaging in socioscientific inquiry? *Research in Science Education, 37*(4), 371–391.

Samarapungavan, A., Patrick, H., & Mantzicopoulos, P. (2011). What kindergarten students learn in inquiry-based science classrooms. *Cognition and Instruction, 29*(4), 416–470.

Schmidt, H. G. (1983). Problem based learning: Rationale and description. *Medical Education, 17,* 11–16.

Schneider, R., Krajcik, J., & Blumenfeld. (2005). Enacting reform-based science materials: The range of teacher enactments in reform classrooms. *Journal of Research in Science Teaching, 42*(3), 283–312.

Schneider R. M., Krajcik, J., Marx, R., & Soloway, E. (2002). Performance of students in project-based science classrooms on a national measure of science achievement. *Journal of Research in Science Teaching, 39*(5), 410–422.

Schroeder, C., Scott, T., Tolson, H., Huang, T.-Y., & Lee, Y.-H. (2007). A meta-analysis of national research: Effects of teaching strategies on student achievement in science in the United States. *Journal of Research in Science Teaching, 44*(10), 1136–1160.

Schwab, J. J. (1958). The teaching of science as inquiry. *Bulletin of the Atomic Scientists, 14,* 374–380.

Schwab, J. J. (1960). Inquiry, the science teacher, and the educator. *The School Review, 68*(2), 176–195.

Schwartz, R., & Crawford, B. A. (2004). Authentic scientific inquiry as a context for teaching nature of science: Identifying critical elements for success. In L. Flick & N. G. Lederman (Eds.), *Scientific inquiry and nature of science: Implications for teaching, learning, and teacher education* (pp. 331–356). Dordrecht, the Netherlands: Kluwer Publishing Co.

Schwartz, R. S., Lederman, N. G., & Crawford, B. A. (2004). Developing views of nature of science in an authentic context: An explicit approach to bridging the gap between nature of science and scientific inquiry. *Science Education, 88,* 610–645.

Schwarz, C. (2009). Developing preservice elementary teachers' knowledge and practices through modeling centered scientific inquiry. *Science Education, 93,* 720–744.

Settlage, J. (2007). Demythologizing science teacher education: Conquering the false ideal of open inquiry. *Journal of Science Teacher Education, 18*(4), 461–467.

Shymansky, J.A., Kyle, W.C., & Alport, J.M. (1983). The effects of new science curricula on student performance. *Journal of Research in Science Teaching, 20*(5), 387–404.

Singer, J., Marx, R., Krajcik, J., & Clay Chambers, J. (2000). Constructing extended inquiry projects: Curriculum projects for science education reform. *Educational Psychologist, 35*(3), 165–178.

Songer, N., Lee, H., & Kam, R. (2001, April). *Technology-rich inquiry science in urban classrooms: What are the barriers to inquiry pedagogy?* A paper presented at the 2001 Annual Meeting of the American Educational Research Association (AERA), Seattle, WA.

Strike, K., & Posner, G. (1982). Conceptual change and science teaching. *European Journal of Science Education, 4*(3), 231–240.

Taber, K.S. (2010). Constructivism and direct instruction as competing instructional paradigms: An essay review of Tobias and Duffy's constructivist instruction: Success or failure? *Education Review, 13*(8), 1–44. Retrieved from www.edrev.info/essays/v13n8index.html

Talanquer, V., Tomanek, D., & Novodvorsky, I. (2013). Assessing students' understanding of inquiry: What do prospective science teachers notice? *Journal of Research in Science Teaching, 50*(2), 189–208.

Thacker, B., Kim, E., Trefz, K., & Lea, S. (1994). Comparing problem solving performance of physics students in inquiry-based and traditional introductory physics courses. *American Journal of Physics, 62*(7), 627–633.

Trautmann, N., MaKinster, J., & Avery, L. (2004, April). *What makes inquiry so hard? (And why is it worth it?)* Paper presented at the annual meeting of the National Association for Research in Science Teaching, Vancouver, BC.

Turpin, T., & Cage, B.N. (2004). The effects of an integrated, activity-based science curriculum on student achievement, science process skills, and science attitudes. *Electronic Journal of Literacy through Science, 3*, 1–17. Retrieved from http://ejlts.ucdavis.edu/article/2004/3/3

Vygotsky, L. (1978). *Mind in society: The development of higher mental processes.* Cambridge, MA: Harvard University.

Wallace, C.W., & Kang, N. (2004). An investigation of experienced secondary science teachers' beliefs about inquiry: An examination of competing belief sets. *Journal of Research in Science Teaching, 41*, 936–960.

Wee, B., Shepardson, D., Fast, J., & Harbor, J. (2007). Teaching and learning about inquiry: Insights and challenges in professional development. *Journal of Science Teacher Education, 18*(1), 63–89.

Welch, W., Klopfer, L., Aikenhead, G., & Robinson, J. (1981). The role of inquiry in science education: Analysis and recommendations. *Science Education, 65,* 33–50.

Wheeler, G.F. (2000). In J. Minstrell & van Zee, E. (Eds.), *Inquiring into inquiry learning and teaching in science* (pp. 471–496). Washington DC: American Association for the Advancement of Science.

White, B., & Frederiksen, J. (1998). Inquiry, modeling, and metacognition: Making science accessible to all students. *Cognition and Instruction, 16*(1), 3–118.

White, B., & Frederiksen, J. (2000). An approach to making scientific inquiry accessible to all. In J. Minstrell & E. van Zee (Eds.), *Inquiring into inquiry learning and teaching in science* (pp. 331–370). Washington, DC: American Association for the Advancement of Science.

Wilson, C.D., Taylor, J.A., Kowalski, S.M., & Carlson, J. (2010). The relative effects and equity of inquiry-based and commonplace science teaching on students' knowledge, reasoning, and argumentation. *Journal of Research in Science Teaching, 47*(3), 276–301.

Windschitl, M. (2003). Inquiry projects in science teacher education: What can investigative experiences reveal about teacher thinking and eventual classroom practice? *Science Education, 87*(1), 112–143.

Windschitl, M. (2004). Folk theories of "inquiry:" How preservice teachers reproduce the discourse and practices of an atheoretical scientific method. *Journal of Research in Science Teaching, 41*(5), 481–512.

Windschitl, M., & Thompson, J. (2012). Transcending simple forms of school science investigation? The impact of preservice instruction on teachers' understandings of model-based inquiry. *American Educational Research Journal, 43*(4), 783–835.

Windschitl, M., Thompson, J., & Braaten, M. (2008). Beyond the scientific method: Model-based inquiry as a new paradigm of preference for school science investigations. *Science Education, 92,* 941–967.

Woolnough, B. (2000). Authentic science in schools? An evidence-based rationale. *Physics Education, 35*(4), 293–300.

Yager, R. (2000). The history and future of science education reform. *The Clearing House, 74*(1), 51–54.

Yoon, H.-G., Joung, Y.J., & Kim, M. (2011). The challenges of science inquiry teaching for pre-service teachers in elementary classrooms: Difficulties on and under the scene. *Research in Science Education, 42*(3), 589–608.

Zembal-Saul, C., Krajcik, J., & Blumenfeld, P. (2002). Elementary student teachers' science content representations. *Journal of Research in Science Teaching, 39*(6) 443–463.

Section V

Curriculum and Assessment in Science

SECTION EDITOR: PAUL BLACK

27

Scientific Literacy, Science Literacy, and Science Education

Douglas A. Roberts and Rodger W. Bybee

This chapter updates and extends an earlier review and analysis of the *scientific literacy* concept as a feature of school science education literature and practice over the past half century (Roberts, 2007). Unlike the 2007 review, this one is not intended to be a comprehensive survey of what is happening globally in countries where scientific literacy is being advanced. Instead, the focus is on presenting a methodology for detecting indicators of change in the way scientific literacy is being embraced as a major goal for school science programs. To that end, we have selected examples of policy and policy-oriented documents from Australia, Canada, England, and the United States, as well as the upcoming (2015) Programme for International Student Assessment (PISA) science assessment.

The 2007 review drew attention to the widespread—indeed, virtually worldwide—popularity of *scientific literacy* in recent decades as an umbrella term to represent overall educational objectives for school science programs. Referring to the appeal the term has had for the profession, one observer has characterized its rise of popularity over 50 years as "triumphal progress" (Feinstein, 2011). The term *science literacy* has become increasingly common also, especially in the United States. The status and usage of this term has grown steadily since all publications of Project 2061 of the American Association for the Advancement of Science (AAAS) began using the term exclusively. As discussed in more detail in what follows, the original review dubbed these two terms, respectively, Vision II and Vision I of the scientifically literate person.

In the nearly 10 years since the material was assembled and analyzed for the 2007 review, there have been indicators that scientific literacy is slowing its triumphal progress and losing the "worldwide cachet" it seemed to enjoy in earlier decades (McEneaney, 2003). In particular, there seems to be a withdrawal from Vision II in favor of Vision I. In the United States, for example, the 1996 document *National Science Education Standards* (National Research Council [NRC], 1996) is virtually built around Vision II scientific literacy as a backbone concept. By

contrast, in the 2012 document *A Framework for K–12 Science Education: Practices, Crosscutting Concepts, and Core Ideas* (National Research Council, 2012), the terms *scientific literacy* and *science literacy* do not appear to play a significant role. As discussed in what follows, the 2012 NRC document lacks Vision II opportunities for students to grasp how the application of scientific knowledge and practices bear on socioscientific issues. In fact, that limitation is part of the charge to the committee that developed the document.

It is our contention that the limited presence of Vision II in the NRC Framework, and the subsequent (inevitable) decreased emphasis in the new standards for U.S. science education, is an example (one of several) that suggests a trend toward withdrawal of professional commitment to Vision II of scientific literacy at this time. Following this brief introduction, the chapter unfolds in the following way:

- A restatement of the characteristics of Vision I and Vision II
- Two curriculum arrangements that provide opportunities to learn (OTL) for Vision II
- The significance of discourse: SSI (The Socio-Scientific Issues Project) sets an example
- Reduction of Vision II in the new U.S. *Framework for K–12 Science Education*
- Reduction of Vision II in the framework for Assessment of Science in PISA 2015
- The many perspectives and broad scope of Vision II
- Whither science education? Tentative explanations and implications

Science Literacy Is Not the Same as Scientific Literacy

As the title of this chapter suggests, both scientific literacy and science literacy, as curriculum concepts, have close connections to school science education research and practice at this time. However, the terms and concepts as currently used in our profession are not interchangeable. To be sure, it seemed they were when both began to appear in the literature at about the same time, in the 1950s. Since that time, much has happened to the concepts and practices the two terms represent. The distinctions between the two are crucially important for understanding the current situation as we perceive it.

Two Visions, Two Purposes for Science Education

The earlier review (Roberts, 2007) proposed that two broad, overall *visions* of the meaning of scientific literacy can be distilled from the detailed science education literature that has developed since the 1950s. Each vision embodies a broadly different image of the scientifically literate individual, and each provides the basis of a different orientation for school science education that would nurture and develop the individual in that direction. Vision I, so named because the image of student as novice scientist was probably the earliest guide used to plan precollegiate school science, offers a blueprint for science education that introduces students systematically to the scientific enterprise itself. This is very much a "foundational" (Osborne, 2007b) or "Solid Foundation" (Roberts, 1982) orientation to the purpose of school science—that is, mastering what is needed to study more advanced science in future. Vision I looks inward at science, to build curriculum from its rich and well-established array of techniques and methods, habits of mind, and well-tested explanations for the events and objects of the natural world. Literacy, in this view, is within science—general familiarity and fluency within the discipline, based on mastering a sampling of the language, products, processes, and traditions of science itself. As we understand the analysis by Norris and Phillips (2003), this would be a "fundamental sense" of scientific literacy. Historically, the reform curricula of the *Sputnik* era were consistent with a Vision I orientation.

Vision II, developed later in the history of school science, begins by looking outside science to build curriculum that illuminates how science permeates and interacts with many areas of human endeavor and life situations. These societal issues and individual life situations usually include political, economic, and ethical considerations. This view is sometimes called science for citizenship, concentrating on matters of more obvious personal and social relevance to students than preparing to grasp more demanding science they might or might not study. The slogan "science for all" represents a viewpoint that all students need some introduction to citizen science, including such matters as environmental quality, resource use, personal health, and decision making about complex socioscientific issues. According to Vision II thinking, what counts as scientific literacy is learning how science fits appropriately with such personal and societal perspectives for a more complete grasp of the issues. This is what we understand as the "derived" sense of scientific

literacy in the analysis by Norris and Phillips (2003). In Vision II classrooms, students learn how the discourse of resolving issues and making decisions differs from and complements the explanatory discourse of science itself. Historically, the term *scientific literacy* has been used to refer to this more inclusive vision. The term continues to be used, for example, in Canada, Australia, and England, in PISA, and in some science education programs such as Socio-Scientific Issues (SSI) in the United States. As a curriculum term, *scientific literacy* typically incorporates a large number of diverse school science objectives associated with personal and societal issues. Thus scientific literacy is aligned with such movements as environmental education; Science, Technology, and Society (STS); Science, Technology, Society, and Environment (STSE); Socio-Scientific Issues (SSI); and, as well, any other educational and curricular efforts that systematically link an understanding of the scientific enterprise to socioscientific issues.

The Two Visions and Their Terminology Exemplified

The most important feature for distinguishing between Vision I and Vision II is the overarching purpose for which a student is to learn scientific meaning—especially whether there is consideration of personal and societal perspectives as mentioned above. Recently, Vision I is most notably associated with AAAS Project 2061 and with the term *science literacy*. In Vision I, the reason for learning science is presumed to be self-evident, essentially. Science has been a powerful instrument for understanding the natural world. The defining instance of Vision I, in our view, is the AAAS Project 2061 characterization as it appears in the project's flagship in-house publication *Science for All Americans*. The overarching purpose for learning science is found next in the fourth bullet—namely that science is the preferred and sufficient way to think about situations that have personal and societal components.

The scientifically literate person is one who:

- is aware that science, mathematics, and technology are interdependent enterprises with strengths and limitations,
- understands key concepts and principles of science,
- is familiar with the natural world and recognizes both its diversity and unity, and
- uses scientific knowledge and scientific ways of thinking for individual and social purposes.

(American Association for the Advancement of Science, 1989, p. 4)

In the more readily available version of *Science for All Americans* (Rutherford & Ahlgren, 1991), published a bit later by Oxford University Press, this definition was not changed. However, the term *scientific literacy* was changed to *science literacy* throughout the volume. The latter term has been used consistently in all Project 2061 documents published since that time. Whatever else the name change accomplished, it gave Project 2061 philosophy and publications a distinctive brand in science education—free from the potential confusion arising from the morass of scientific literacy definitions.

Vision II is exemplified by the following remarkably different characterization of a scientifically literate person, as embodied in an ongoing research and development project in England called Twenty First Century Science.

We would expect a scientifically literate person to be able to:

- appreciate and understand the impact of science and technology on everyday life,
- take informed personal decisions about things that involve science, such as health, diet, use of energy resources,
- read and understand the essential points of media reports about matters that involve science,
- reflect critically on the information included in, and (often more important) omitted from, such reports, and
- take part confidently in discussions with others about issues involving science.

(Twenty First Century Science, retrieved February 9, 2013: www.nuffieldfoundation. org/twenty-first-century-science)

Notice that the fourth point in the Project 2061 characterization concentrates attention on but one perspective on a situation—the scientific perspective—as the way to think about issues associated with "individual and social purposes." In other words, by default (since no other perspective is mentioned), students are encouraged to understand situations as a scientist does. By contrast, in the Twenty First Century Science characterization, there is a clear implication that other perspectives are appropriate and necessary as well to understand such situations.

Opportunity to Learn (OTL) Vision II: Sample Curriculum Arrangements

The original purpose for defining and clarifying scientific literacy had to do with providing appropriate school science for students who were not inclined to pursue pre-professional science studies of the type we have been designating Vision I. In short, Vision II would be a different kind of curriculum for the students Klopfer (1969) referred to as the "SL stream," where SL stands for scientific literacy. (Klopfer estimated that the SL stream would include 90% of school students, an estimate consistent with that of many other authors.) Obviously, such an arrangement implies labeling students and, potentially, segregating them, which can have educational disadvantages. Yet the persistent dilemma for science teachers is simply that the SL stream of students is more often than not being taught in the same classroom as students who are quite comfortable with early science specialist training (Klopfer's PS or "potential scientist" stream). Contrariwise, some of the attention to scientific literacy has been animated by a concern—expressed by the slogan "science for all"—that all students, including the potential scientist group, should have some grounding in discussing issues through personal and societal perspectives that are part of Vision II. (All students are in fact future citizens.) This section explores two curricular arrangements that provide opportunities to learn science according to Vision II without losing the advantages of Vision I for the "potential scientist" group.

A Separate SL Course: Twenty First Century Science

An ongoing project, drawing in large part on the groundbreaking report titled *Beyond 2000* (Millar & Osborne, 1998), tackled this problem head-on in England. Millar (2006) comments thus: "Many curricula, the report argues, attempt to achieve both purposes—with the pre-professional training emphasis invariably coming to have a dominant and distorting influence on the whole" (p. 1505). In the Twenty First Century Science project, the two purposes have been separated or "unhooked" from each other for a part of every student's time, in the following way.

The first of the 10 recommendations in *Beyond 2000* states: "The science curriculum from [age] 5 to 16 should be seen primarily as a course to enhance general 'scientific literacy'" (Millar & Osborne, 1998, p. 9). The curricular arrangement to accomplish this goal is anticipated in the second recommendation: "At Key Stage 4 [North American grades 9–10], the structure of the science curriculum needs to differentiate more explicitly between those elements designed to enhance 'scientific literacy', and those designed as the early stages of a specialist training in science, so that the requirement for the latter does not come to distort the former" (Millar & Osborne, 1998, p. 10). A special course on scientific literacy (SL) was developed with structure and content that was characterized earlier in this chapter as a defining instance of Vision II. The course would be required of all students before they complete their compulsory or General Certificate of Secondary Education (GCSE) schooling (15- and 16-year-olds), taking up half of their science time (science is 20% of the curriculum). Options would be provided for the other half to accommodate diversified interests in future general and applied science study.

The first pilot study of the project began in September 2003. There are several very thorough descriptions of the design, intent, and content of the special SL course (e.g., Millar, 2006, 2010, 2012; Osborne, 2007b). These also report on developing research about the impact of the project, which has been substantial. To the best of our knowledge, the SL course in the Twenty First Century Science project is the only one of its kind.

Incorporating Opportunity to Learn for Both Vision I and II

A different curricular arrangement used to provide opportunities to learn both visions gives equal status to Visions I and II according to their overall educational purpose. The technique for doing so is to systematically embed the learning of science subject matter in different learning contexts, so that students learn both at the same time. Science curriculum revision that recognizes this approach has been underway in Canada for more than a decade. Canada does not have a national curriculum. Jurisdiction over educational matters resides with the governments of the 10 provinces and 3 territories. Most recently, science curriculum revision has been stimulated by a nationwide "framework" (Council of Ministers of Education, Canada [CMEC], 1997) to which provincial ministers of education subscribed in hopes of providing common ground and more consistency in learning outcomes for school science across the country. The framework "is guided by the vision that all Canadian students, regardless of gender or cultural background, will have an opportunity to develop scientific literacy" (p. 4). Scientific literacy (SL) is defined as "an evolving combination of the *science-related* attitudes, skills, and knowledge students need to develop *inquiry, problem-solving,* and *decision-making abilities,* to become lifelong learners, and to maintain a sense of wonder about the world around them" (p. 4, italics added to stress the intended links between context and science subject matter).

The definition is made operational by specifying four "foundation statements," one each for skills, knowledge, and attitudes, and a fourth for "science, technology, society, and the environment (STSE)" (CMEC, 1997, p. 6). According to the document, acquisition of science-related skills, knowledge, and attitudes "is best done through the study and analysis of the interrelationships among science, technology, society, and the environment (STSE)" (p. iii). Implicit in that statement, and more explicit in several provincially mandated curricula based on it, are two important features of the meaning of SL. First, the "science-related skills, knowledge, and attitudes" specified in the respective foundation statements for those three areas are to be developed through the STSE situations and challenges comprising the fourth. That is, the expectation is that curricula, instructional materials, and teachers will provide opportunities for students to learn about STSE interrelationships at the same time they are learning science subject matter, skills, and attitudes. This simultaneous learning is envisioned as happening through contextual communication and learning, in which units of science subject matter are organized to stress one of three "broad areas of emphasis":

- a science inquiry emphasis, in which students address questions about the nature of things, involving broad exploration as well as focussed investigations [this is an emphasis on the nature of science, thus acknowledging the importance of Vision I];
- a problem-solving emphasis, in which students seek answers to practical problems requiring the application of their science knowledge in new ways [this is an emphasis on science and technology, thus a mixture of Visions I and II];

- a decision-making emphasis, in which students identify questions or issues and pursue scientific knowledge that will inform the question or issue [this is an emphasis on socio-scientific issues, thus stressing Vision II]."
(CMEC, 1997, p. 8)

Second, although this is not stated explicitly in the document, these three areas of emphasis correspond to an Aristotelian distinction among three different human purposes for discourse, namely seeking warranted knowledge, making beautiful and useful things, and arriving at defensible decisions. Here, we shall use the terms *theoria, techne,* and *praxis,* respectively, to identify the three. A different pattern of reasoning—and therefore a different classroom discourse—is characteristic of each, and the skill set associated with each emphasis is identified accordingly. Hence SL is operationally defined as the student's grasp of not only the way science itself permeates human affairs across this broad trilogy of purposes but also how the relationship of science is different for each. (Predating the publication of the Pan-Canadian framework, this organization of a science curriculum policy was implemented in the province of Alberta, as described by Roberts, 1995).

The Significance of Discourse: The Socio-Scientific Issues Program (SSI) Sets an Example

The trilogy of *theoria, techne,* and *praxis* is based on acknowledging that a different kind of discourse is appropriate to the three different ends in view, each expressing a different domain of human purpose. Three corresponding patterns of reasoning are appropriate for the three domains.

- A *theoretical* reasoning pattern is appropriate when one intends to establish warranted knowledge. Scientific reasoning and scientific activity aim for this end in view. The discourse is epistemic.
- A *technological* reasoning pattern is appropriate when one intends to design and produce useful and beautiful things—a bridge, a building, a symphony, a sculpture. Reasoning patterns in engineering, architecture, and the arts aim for this end in view. The discourse is procedural and productive, heavily slanted toward designing and testing "what works."
- A *practical* reasoning pattern is appropriate when one intends to arrive at defensible value-laden decisions that impact other people. This discourse includes personal and societal perspectives that can be, for example, economic, political, ethical, and moral in character. This pattern is an essential part of scientific literacy just because most science-related events and issues have an impact on people. The discourse is deliberative.

The extent to which a school science classroom is providing opportunities to learn about Vision I or Vision II can be gauged by the presence or absence of one or more of these three reasoning patterns and the different discourses associated with them. In short, no discourse means no opportunities to learn or, as Kelly (2011) has pointed out, students need to *experience* and *practice* these discourses if they are to learn and comprehend them.

Needed: Opportunities to Learn a Different Discourse

Theoretical and technological discourses are probably the most familiar to science teachers. Yet Osborne cautions as follows, regarding theoretical discourse (scientific reasoning), the most familiar one.

> The correlate of the argument that learning science means learning to talk science is that learning to reason scientifically means asking students to reason scientifically. In the case of empirical work, observation of science lessons in England indicated that much of the time spent on practical work is devoted to carrying out the practical procedures themselves. . . . [I]f we want our students to develop the ability to think critically about scientific evidence, then we must offer them that opportunity.
>
> (Osborne, 2007b, pp. 178–179)

If this lack of opportunities to learn is the case for the familiar discourse of scientific reasoning (and we agree that it is, in many classrooms), imagine the bleak situation with respect to technological (e.g., engineering) discourse and the even more bleak prospects for the least familiar of the three, namely practical discourse. It is also the most inclusive and complex of the three, and its absence or misrepresentation in socioscientific contexts is arguably the most serious threat to the survival of Vision II. (See Gauthier, 1963, for a widely respected classic treatment of practical reasoning. Closer to the present concern, see Orpwood, 1998, for an analysis and example of practical reasoning in the context of science curriculum policy debate.)

Taking Discourse Seriously: The Socio-Scientific Issues Program

Typically, practical reasoning discourse includes some combination of such personal and societal perspectives as ethical, legal, political, and moral considerations. A robust research and development program in this area (considerably more modern than Aristotle) has been underway with a steady stream of publications for more than a decade: the Socio-Scientific Issues (SSI) program undertaken by Dana Zeidler, Troy Sadler, and their colleagues. There is not space to describe the significance of the contributions this program is making to science education in general and to Vision II scientific literacy in particular (but see Zeidler's chapter in the current volume). We wish to focus here on the nature of discourse development and the qualities of the discourse to which students become accustomed in the SSI program.

In describing the foundations of the program, Zeidler and Sadler (2011) point out the significance of multiple perspectives thus (italics original).

> In positioning *perspectives* as an aspect of socio-scientific reasoning, we suggest that exploring issues from the vantage of different perspectives constitutes a critical component of the thoughtful negotiation of SSI. The goal for student practice would be to move from conceptualizing SSI only from one's own personal framework toward the ability to analyze issues and potential solutions from diverse perspectives.
>
> (Zeidler & Sadler, 2011, p. 186)

Elsewhere they raise a caution about a typical alternative.

> When educators want to use real world issues related to science as vehicles for engaging students in meaningful learning experiences, they ought not attempt to distill the science and discard other elements of the issues which may be seen as beyond the boundaries of traditional science.
>
> (Sadler & Zeidler, 2009, p. 912)

Sadler (2009) has described how the SSI program relates to *situated learning* (see, e.g., Lave & Wenger, 1991) by characterizing the nature of socioscientific issues as presenting

> ill-structured problems [that] do not have single correct answers . . . Socio-scientific issues also tend to be controversial . . . because of their connections to society. Issues that have the potential to affect the lives of individuals with competing perspectives and priorities generate both interest and controversy. . . . These issues can be informed by scientific data and theory, but they are also subject to economic, social, political and/or ethical considerations.
>
> (Sadler, 2009, p. 11)

Sadler also situates SSI in the chaos of scientific literacy definitions thus: "Ryder's (2001) analysis of 'functional scientific literacy' provides an empirically derived description of the kinds of Discourses expected of communities of practice engaged in the negotiation and resolution of SSI" (Sadler, 2009, p. 12).

How the 2012 U.S. *Framework for K–12 Science Education* Withdraws From Vision II

We focus on this United States document for two reasons. (a) It is current and is very much a part of science education in the United States at this time. Also (b) it provides an opportunity to demonstrate a theoretical framework and methodology for stimulating discussion of the differences between Visions I and II as drivers of science education policy and the potential impacts of making a choice between them.

It seems clear that removing personal and societal perspectives from classroom consideration would seriously weaken the central meaning of Vision II. Yet consider the following.

> There is an important, and often unquestioned, assumption about achieving . . . the ability to apply scientific knowledge in life situations. . . . "If an individual knows enough science, he or she will apply that knowledge in life situations." Stated another way, there is an assumption that scientific knowledge directly influences personal decisions and behaviours.
>
> (Bybee & McCrae, 2011, p. 8)

Jon Miller, whose work on measuring scientific literacy still enjoys a certain cachet in the United States and internationally, has asserted this view repeatedly (see Miller, 2000, or Roberts, 2007, pp. 760–762, for a more extensive discussion of Miller's work). Such a "stripping down" of Vision II is not unusual in practice, especially when science teachers feel pressed for time and search for something to leave out of a crowded curriculum. As a matter of policy, however, we want to be quite clear that this represents a choice of Vision I over Vision II—not simply the hope that Vision II goals can be accomplished through Vision I practice. Instead, this choice eliminates a vital part of Vision II, namely an understanding of practical reasoning about science-related personal and societal issues.

Marginalizing Practical Reasoning in Science Education

The position that a scientific perspective is sufficient for understanding and dealing with science-related issues is not new, of course. (See the earlier discussion of the AAAS definition of science literacy.) *A Framework for K–12 Science Education: Practices, Crosscutting Concepts, and Core Ideas* (National Research Council, 2012) reveals that such a choice has been made deliberately. The document specifies (p. 13) that "the social, behavioral, and economic sciences are not fully addressed" in this science education document. Rather, "many of the topics related to the social, behavioral, and economic sciences are incorporated into curricula of courses identified as social studies and may be taught from a humanities perspective." Compared to the previous *National Science Education Standards* (National Research Council, 1996), the new NRC Framework—which is the foundation for the NGSS (Next Generation Science Standards, released in the spring of 2013)—has made a very important shift from the central role of Vision II in the 1996 document (cf. Roberts 2007, pp. 747–748). One indicator of the changes in the new *Framework* document is that the terms *science literacy* and *scientific literacy* are mentioned only in a token way. A second indicator is a stress on both theoretical and technological discourse patterns, but no mention of personal and societal perspectives (hence, no practical reasoning) in the treatment of socioscientific issues and decision making about science-related situations. The "Disciplinary Core Ideas" that touch on science-society issues in the document do not include personal and societal perspectives. The area in which one would expect

to find these is the five Core and Component Ideas in Engineering, Technology, and Applications of Science, starting on p. 201. The Core idea titled "Influence of Engineering, Technology, and Science on Society and the Natural World" is at least suggestive that personal and societal perspectives might be included, but instead treats socioscientific matters and issues rather dismissively as by-products of the work of science and technology.

It is worth displaying in full the "Definitions of Science, Technology, and Applications of Science" from p. 202 (bold type original, our italics, with our comments interspersed).

> **"Technology** is any modification of the natural world made to fulfill human needs or desires."
>
> **"Engineering** is a systematic and often iterative approach to designing objects, processes, and systems to meet human needs and wants."
>
> **Comment:** *For both definitions, a technological reasoning pattern is appropriate as part of the opportunities to learn about technology.*
>
> **"An application of science** is any use of scientific knowledge for a scientific purpose, whether to do more science . . ."
>
> **Comment:** *So far this is using a theoretical reasoning pattern.*
>
> ". . . to design a new process, product, or medical treatment, to develop a new technology . . ."
>
> **Comment:** *Those four—design a new process, product, treatment, or technology—would arise from using a technological reasoning pattern.*
>
> ". . . or to predict the impacts of human actions."
>
> **Comment:** *This is not practical reasoning: "Predicting the impacts" is not the same as deliberating over a socioscientific issue, including considerations that fall within perspectives other than scientific and technological.*

This document is an example of withdrawing from Vision II by "purifying" science education policy through purging the attention to personal and societal perspectives. By staying strictly with scientific and engineering aspects of the issues, this document does precisely what Sadler and Zeidler (2009, p. 912) warned about, as mentioned earlier: "they ought not attempt to distill the science and discard other elements of the issues which may be seen as beyond the boundaries of traditional science."

The inclusion of engineering along with "pure" science is a noteworthy achievement because technological reasoning is being stressed in addition to theoretical reasoning, consistent with the widespread adoption of STEM as shorthand for the current title of integrated school science: science, technology, engineering, and mathematics. The justification for including engineering is shown, in part, by this statement:

> Scientists and engineers often work together in realms, especially in new fields, such as nanotechnology or

synthetic biology and blur the lines between science and engineering. Students should come to understand these interactions and at increasing levels of sophistication as they mature. Their appreciation of the interface of science, engineering, and society should give them deeper insights into local, national, and global issues.

(National Research Council, 2012, p. 203)

The Discourse of Public Engagement With Science: Science Insiders and Science Outsiders

Feinstein (2011) has developed a provocative critique of scientific literacy/science literacy (he makes no distinction) in which he "examines . . . the very specific notion that science education can help people solve personally meaningful problems in their lives, directly affect their material and social circumstances, shape their behavior, and inform their most significant practical and political decisions" (Feinstein, 2011, p. 169). The thrust of his argument is that there is an "empirical vacuum" around this notion—that is, "our field has produced very little evidence" about how people actually use science in this way. Nevertheless,

I suggest that we do not need to abandon the . . . vision of a competent citizenry that can cope with science-related real-life challenges. . . . We do need to examine how people actually use science in daily life and . . . pay attention to research on public engagement with science.

(Feinstein, 2011, p. 170)

Feinstein analyzes some examples of the use of science in everyday life that have "the potential to transform our notions of science literacy" (e.g., Layton, Jenkins, Macgill, & Davey (1993), and Roth and Lee (2002). These are examples of actual empirical studies of the usefulness (or not) of science education for understanding everyday problems and events. They lead in a direction "relatively novel in the context of science education, [but] not new to social research. In particular, they echo some of the central findings from another field: public engagement with science" (Feinstein, 2011, p. 177). Engagement with science, he contends, is simply the connection between

science and lived experience. It is . . . the act of *an outsider* [italics added]. People do not engage with science by removing themselves from their own social contexts and asking, "what would a scientist do?" They do not, for the most part, seek to become *scientific insiders* [italics added]. They remain anchored outside of science, reaching in for bits and pieces that enrich their understanding of their own lives.

(Feinstein, 2011, p. 180)

Feinstein concludes his argument with significant recommendations.

I propose that science literate people are *competent outsiders* [italics original] with respect to science: people who have learned to recognize the moments when

science has some bearing on their needs and interest and to interact with sources of scientific expertise in ways that help them achieve their own goals. [Thus] the pursuit of science literacy is not *incidentally* but *fundamentally* about identifying relevance. . . . The idea of the competent outsider also draws attention to the fact that we are currently doing something very different: producing *marginal insiders*. These are students who have sat through a long parade of concepts and theories. . . . A small number will go on to be real scientific insiders, but for most, this glimpse is all they will get. As I observed at the outset of this essay, there is little evidence that such abridged familiarity with science translates into everyday competence.

(Feinstein, 2011, pp. 180–181, italics original)

Feinstein's critique echoes and sharpens the concerns we have expressed, following Bybee and MacRae (2011), about the assumption that knowing science (in the Vision I sense) will automatically enable students to deal with Vision II situations. (Alas, in Feinstein's essay there is some confusion about the two visions, but that is immaterial to our purpose here.) We find it surprising that Feinstein makes no mention of Twenty First Century Science or the Socio-Scientific Issues Project, both of which can be seen to be doing just what he suggests—that is, teaching students to use the kind of "outsider" discourse and skills associated with effective public engagement with science.

PISA 2015: Gradual Withdrawal From Vision II

Originating in 1997, and well known to science educators around the world, the Programme for International Student Assessment (PISA) represents an ongoing commitment by member countries of the Organisation for Economic Co-Operation and Development (OECD) to monitor educational outcomes in reading, mathematics, and science. PISA tests 15-year-old students in participating countries once every 3 years. The three domains rotate between major and minor emphasis in the assessments. Reading was the major emphasis in 2000, and mathematics was the emphasis in 2003. In 2006, science was the major domain.

The previous review (Roberts, 2007) and this update are both concerned only with the conceptualization of scientific literacy (SL) inherent in the science assessment. The conceptualization of SL initially adopted for PISA stated: "Scientific literacy is the capacity to use scientific knowledge, to identify questions and to draw evidence-based conclusions in order to understand and help make decisions about the natural world and the changes made to it through human activity" (OECD, 1999, p. 60). The meaning of and the purpose for including particular phrases in the definition, such as *scientific knowledge* and *evidence-based conclusions*, are elaborated in the OECD documents and, as well, in two very informative papers by Harlen (2001a, 2001b).

The following points about the conceptualization paraphrase Harlen (2001b).

- This conceptualization of SL is about what learners should achieve in terms of their needs as citizens—"understanding that will improve their future lives" (Harlen, 2001b, p. 87). This suggests a view that future scientists also need such understanding.
- The roots of SL are in school experience, even though it can be "developed throughout life" (Harlen, 2001b, p. 87), a point that recognizes the significance of informal science education.
- SL is not equated with vocabulary, but connotes "general competence or being 'at ease' with scientific ways of understanding" (Harlen, 2001b, p. 87). This also suggests a broader, different kind of understanding than suggested by knowing how to "do science."
- A key feature of a student's SL is skillfulness at relating evidence to claims: how evidence is used and collected in science, "what makes some evidence more dependable than other, what are its shortcomings, and where it can and should be applied" (Harlen, 2001b, p. 87).
- This SL conceptualization contextualizes scientific knowledge and scientific thinking in relation to problems, issues, and situations "in the real world" (Harlen, 2001b, p. 91)—thus students can apply what they learn in laboratory settings to nonschool settings.

Assessments based on this conceptualization of SL were conducted in 2000 and 2003 (OECD, 2003, p. 133).

Preparing for PISA 2006 presented an opportunity to revise the science framework, as this was the first time science would be a major domain. The Science Forum and the Science Expert Group, the former responsible for advising and the latter responsible for developing specific aspects of the framework, revised the 2000/2003 framework. The 2006 background, rationale, and conceptualization of SL are described in *Assessing Scientific, Reading, and Mathematical Literacy* (OECD, 2006).

In the 2006 PISA, scientific literacy referred to an individual's

- scientific knowledge and use of that knowledge to identify questions, to acquire new knowledge, to explain scientific phenomena, and to draw evidence-based conclusions about science-related issues
- understanding of the characteristic features of science as a form of human knowledge and inquiry

- awareness of how science and technology shape our material, intellectual, and cultural environments
- willingness to engage in science-related issues and with the ideas of science as a reflective citizen

The conceptualization for SL in 2006 was maintained for 2009 and 2012 assessments of PISA. The 2006 conceptualization is clearly specifying Vision II as the basis for PISA. From the beginning, the PISA project has concentrated on assessment within life situations. The 2006, 2009, and 2012 frameworks emphasized and strengthened that intention.

Science again will be a major domain for PISA 2015. A new framework was prepared for PISA 2015 (OECD, 2013) and the conception of SL as the central construct for that assessment was reviewed and revised. Following is a definition of SL for PISA Science 2015.

Scientific literacy is the ability to engage with science-related issues and with the ideas of science as a reflective citizen. A scientifically literate person, therefore, is willing to engage with science-related issues in reasoned discourse about science and technology, which requires the competencies to:

1. Explain phenomena scientifically:
   - recognize, offer and evaluate explanations for a range of natural and technological phenomena
2. Understand scientific enquiry:
   - recognize, describe and evaluate the design, practices and conduct of scientific enquiry
3. Interpret scientific evidence:
   - analyze and evaluate scientific information, claims, and arguments in a variety of representations and draw appropriate conclusions

Contrasts among 2000, 2006, and 2015 conceptions of SL are subtle but notable. For purposes of comparison, competencies are presented in Table 27.1.

We propose that scientific literacy, as expressed in Vision II, has reduced emphasis in 2015 compared to both 2000 and 2006. The basis for this proposal can be seen in the sets of competencies. Note, for example, that in PISA 2000 and 2006 science, there was a clear emphasis on the identification of scientific questions and the use of scientific knowledge (2000) or evidence (2006). In contrast, the 2015 framework gives greater emphasis to understanding scientific inquiry, and interpreting scientific evidence.

TABLE 27.1
SL Competencies 2000 to 2015

2000 Competencies for Scientific Literacy	2006 Competencies for Scientific Literacy	2015 Competencies for Scientific Literacy
• Use scientific knowledge	• Identify scientific issues	• Explain phenomena scientifically
• Identify questions	• Explain phenomena scientifically	• Understand scientific inquiry
• Draw evidence-based conclusions	• Use scientific evidence	• Interpret scientific evidence

The 2015 definition of scientific literacy has deeper and broader clarification of procedural and epistemic knowledge. It seems these changes shifted emphasis to understanding the internal processes of science, away from the application of scientific knowledge to situations external to science. The shift is toward the AAAS definition of "science literacy" presented earlier in this chapter as a defining instance of Vision I.

Citizens encounter science not in its pure form but in personal, local, and global contexts and life situations. This view is consistent with Vision II of scientific literacy. The 2015 framework for PISA science has very elaborate discussions of three variations of scientific knowledge: (1) content knowledge, (2) procedural knowledge, and (3) epistemic knowledge. These dimensions of scientific knowledge are the basis for the three competencies. While the discussions of scientific knowledge have been clarified and deepened, it seems that the application of scientific knowledge in life situations has been de-emphasized as a basic construct for scientific literacy and by extension for PISA Science 2015.

The Many Perspectives and Broad Scope of Vision II

The several examples of withdrawal from Vision II have shown a reduced emphasis on the "nonscientific" perspectives on issues, such as the personal and societal perspectives. In this section, we review how Vision II developed—that is, how those perspectives became a part of an orientation to school science. There is a more complete history of this aspect of scientific literacy (SL, for purposes of this section) in the earlier review (Roberts, 2007).

The early historical development of the term *SL* shows a remarkable diversity of definitions. A useful starting point for making sense of this apparent chaos is to examine SL according to the logic of educational slogans. That is, the term was introduced in professional science education literature as a slogan—a way to rally support for re-examining the purposes of school science in the United States' postwar period of the 1950s (see, e.g., Hurd, 1958). At first, the SL discussion was primarily (although not entirely) on behalf of curriculum planning for the "90% of students" who are not "potential scientists" and who should therefore experience a "scientific literacy stream" (Klopfer, 1969). It was, in other words, a serious effort to establish the meaning of an alternative to Vision I.

From Slogan to Accommodating Multiple Definitions

Slogans don't help professional science educators get on with their research and the practical work of specifying policy, planning programs, organizing teaching, and designing assessment. Definitions are needed instead. Between the late 1950s and the early 1980s, a very substantial amount of science education literature in North America contained analyses and views about the definition of SL. This is a characteristic feature of the logic of educational slogans. That is, slogans must be interpreted; thus anyone moving (in the logical sense) from slogan to definition provides his or her own interpretation—within reasonable bounds. It is therefore not at all surprising that definitions appeared in abundance and in considerable variety.

Several authors attempted to consolidate the definitions of this era into a synthesis that represented the meaning of SL by accommodating the contributions of the science education community. Three illustrative papers are selected, all based on the work of science education authors in the United States (see Bybee, 1997, chapters 3 and 4, for a more extensive review and analysis of the accommodating character of the American literature of this era), including the statements of professional associations such as the (U.S.) National Science Teachers Association (NSTA).

In 1966, Milton Pella and his colleagues in the Scientific Literacy Center at the University of Wisconsin in Madison reported a study of the "referents" authors had made to SL. On the basis of a comprehensive literature analysis, they identified 100 papers for further analysis and characterized SL with a composite picture based on six referents:

> The scientifically literate individual presently is characterized as one with an understanding of the basic concepts in science, nature of science, ethics that control the scientist in his [sic] work, interrelationships of science and society, interrelationships of science and the humanities, [and] differences between science and technology.
>
> (Pella, O'Hearn, & Gale, 1966, p. 206)

Building on Pella's analysis and continuing the theme of accommodation/consolidation, 8 years later Michael Agin expressed the following concern. "Many individuals use the term 'scientific literacy' but fail to give it an adequate meaning . . . A frame of reference should be established to help consolidate and summarize the many definitions" (Agin, 1974, p. 405). Agin used Pella's six categories to organize his own framework, drawing on even more literature (much of it post–1966) to embellish the categories by adding "selected dimensions" from among "the concerns and opinions of scientists and science educators" (Agin, 1974, p. 407).

An exhaustive example of seeking accommodation in the literature of this time is the doctoral study by Lawrence Gabel (1976). Gabel developed a theoretical model of SL based for the most part on statements of or suggestions about science education objectives related to interpretations of SL. His model expanded (refined, actually) Pella's six categories to eight, which constituted one dimension of a matrix. The other dimension included the six major categories of cognitive objectives and three categories of affective objectives from Bloom's taxonomies. Gabel reported that from the literature he was able to find examples for all but 16 of the 72 cells in this matrix (Gabel, 1976, p. 92). He provided examples of the missing ones himself to complete a consolidated picture of all of the possible objectives associated with SL—which, of course, is why it is a theoretical model, despite its substantial empirical basis for 56 of the cells (the complete matrix is shown in Gabel, 1976, p. 93). Thus did SL become an umbrella concept with the varied, composite meaning that ultimately gave Vision II its broad sweep. The aim of all this effort was to develop a concept that was comprehensive enough to guide curriculum making for all students and that also accommodated the thinking of the science education community of the time.

A related but slightly different approach to analyzing the history of SL is to start with significant events in the educational history and culture of science education, especially the changing societal demands on the curriculum. The purpose of this approach is to understand how events have made a difference in science education policy statements over time, with specific reference to SL. DeBoer (1991, chapter 6) provides an excellent example of such analysis in the United States. (See also Bybee & DeBoer, 1994; Matthews, 1994, chapter 3). Along the same conceptual and methodological lines, Jenkins (1990) has developed an account of the evolution of the SL concept in England.

Returning about a decade later to the historical events approach, DeBoer (2000) used as the significant event for his analysis the mid-1990s onset of standards-based reform efforts in the United States. He presents nine summary statements of science education goals that represent "a wide range of meanings of scientific literacy" (DeBoer, 2000, p. 591), essentially echoing Gabel's finding of a quarter century earlier to the effect that SL has now come to mean one, all, or some combination of the major goals to which science educators subscribe. DeBoer comments as follows, in a manner somewhat reminiscent of the initial intent of the SL slogan: "The one specific thing we can conclude is that scientific literacy has usually implied a broad and functional understanding of science for general education purposes and not preparation for specific scientific and technical careers" (DeBoer, 2000, p. 594).

Reflections on the Accommodation Approach

There is something comforting about a historical synthesis of definitions for an educational slogan such as SL. One gets a sense that despite the diversity of its definitions, SL did after all express a unity of purpose and meaning for science education by the beginning of the 1980s. In one sense, that is accurate. The focus of SL in the science education literature shifted from an image of curriculum appropriate solely for non–science-oriented students to aspects of science education appropriate for all students.

However, varied use of the term *SL* and definitional activity did not cease. Bybee (1997) points out that during the 1980s, in the United States, "the term [SL] began to take on a symbolic value distinct from its past conceptual

development because individuals used it in a variety of ways" (Bybee, 1997, p. 59). This resulted in a renewed increase in the definitional literature. It also shifted the meaning back to a distinction between Vision I and Vision II. Pressure for proliferation came from the need for the original Vision II to meet a variety of challenges to science education worldwide during the 1980s. Fensham (1992) offers the example that many countries had begun retaining a higher percentage of young people in school for a longer time. As these students reached senior levels of schooling, it became increasingly imperative to pay attention to a curriculum in science that made provision for a "scientifically literate citizenry" as well as a "scientifically based work force" (Fensham, 1992, pp. 793–795). (The reader can refer to Bybee, 1997, and DeBoer, 2000, for accounts of further elaboration of the SL concept into the 1990s.)

Whither Science Education? Tentative Explanations and Implications

It is obvious that the overall character of science education is significantly affected by the choice of one vision or another of scientific literacy. One way to keep that educational image broad and general is to use a composite definition of the type developed by Pella and his colleagues, as presented earlier. A second possibility is to make provision for all students to experience Vision II in a separate required course, as the Twenty First Century Science project has done in England.

It seems to us that more concern was being expressed about the clarity of SL at the time of the earlier review chapter (Roberts, 2007) than is now apparent. In particular, the need to counterbalance the influence of Vision I and make school science education more relevant and accessible was a clear aim. The review was used as part of the discussion material for a major research conference on scientific literacy held in May 2007 at Uppsala University, Sweden, during a celebration of the 300th birthday of Carolus Linnaeus. Twenty distinguished science educators from around the world made presentations of their research and agreed to a Statement of Concern about the condition of science education worldwide, including the following points (Linder, Östman, & Wickman, 2007, p. 1):

- Many students find little of interest in science and actually express an active dislike of it
- Compared to other subjects, science is seen as a transmission of facts of little relevance and more difficult than other school subjects
- School experience leads to loss of interest in science and technology as career possibilities, and only a mildly positive sense of their social importance.

The presentations and discussion over the 2 days of the symposium ranged across many aspects of the potential of Vision II to counteract the aforementioned concerns. The book published as a result of the symposium consists of 18 chapters prepared by 34 authors from 10 different countries (Linder et al., 2011). Some presentations were not elaborated for publication in the book but are available in the published *Proceedings* (Linder, Östman, & Wickman, 2007). Osborne's contribution in the *Proceedings* underscored the need to counterbalance Vision I as follows:

> Transforming the pedagogy of school science is [a] major challenge. . . . [S]uch pedagogy is a consequence of two features—one is a collective culturally embedded notion of what it means to teach science . . . [and] an assessment system which overwhelmingly values the reproduction of factual information as the best measure of a knowledge and understanding of science. . . . Politicians need to realise that the values embedded in those systems are resulting in an experience of school science which leads to the very effect that most concerns them—the flight of contemporary youth from school science.
>
> (Osborne 2007a, pp. 109–110).

Four Possible Reasons One Might Use Vision I as the Default

The impact of a "vision" of scientific literacy—how one *envisions* the individual as a result of his or her science education—cannot be overestimated. A vision, in the sense we are using the term, is a highly significant—indeed, controlling—part of a curriculum policy image (Roberts, 2011), which, in turn, has the potential to affect every aspect of curriculum, course development, and implementation by teachers. In that long cascade of events, there are many spots where Vision I can exert its powerful grip on school science and assume its "rightful" place as the default image for science education. Here we advance tentative explanations for the reduced emphasis on Vision II, arising from our review.

1. Vision II might be rejected not necessarily on its own terms but because curriculum decisions are increasingly in the hands of bureaucrats rather than professional science educators. Bureaucrats tend to be focused primarily on accountability; Vision I measures are not as complex as those for Vision II.

Fensham (2012) has called attention to the increased role played by bureaucrats, as opposed to experts, in monitoring the accountability of school systems, teachers, and curriculum reform. He illustrates the shift, based on five case studies of science education in Australia, noting "the rise in a number of countries of a market view of education, and of science education in particular, accompanied by demands for public accountability via simplistic auditing measures" (Fensham, 2012, p. 1).

2. Vision II might be seen as simply too broad to be taught as school science. In this view, personal and societal considerations are more appropriate for social studies, and school science should be restricted to "science-like" perspectives.

The withdrawal from personal and societal perspectives in science curriculum policy is apparent in both the 2015 PISA definition of SL and in the character of the 2012 *Framework* document prepared for the United States. This explanation derives further support from two quarters. First, In the AAAS definition of SL, one of the statements describing a scientifically literate person is this: "uses scientific knowledge and scientific ways of thinking for individual and social purposes" (p. 546 this chapter). This is a hallmark of Vision I, and AAAS publications have influenced many state and local curriculum policies in the United States and elsewhere. Second, as noted earlier, there is a common assumption (cf. Jon Miller's work, especially Miller, 2000) that knowing science is sufficient for dealing with matters of personal and societal significance.

3. Vision II requires that teachers master new content, a very different teaching style, and a familiarity and comfort level with a different kind of discourse (practical reasoning) than the classroom discourses to which they are accustomed.

Difficulties in learning to teach according to the discourse required for Vision II are of several types. Clark and colleagues (2011) describe a South African project to implement a Vision II course using a chemistry unit that had been rewritten to focus on mining. They identify two different kinds of problems encountered by the teachers. First, the teachers themselves, and their students as well, knew nothing about the real world of mining, despite its economic and cultural importance in South Africa. Second, the need to hold discussions was foreign to them as science teachers—the common view that there really is nothing to discuss in a typical science classroom. In a similar vein, Millar (2006) reported the following after the first 2 years (one cycle) of the Twenty First Century Science project: "Key challenges identified are the language and reasoning demands in looking critically at public accounts of science, and the classroom management of more open discussion about science-related issues" (p. 1499).

4. Vision II might not be recognized as a viable curriculum model. Leaders in the statement of science education policy or programs hold Vision I as the dominant (and exclusive) model and thus either reject or do not recognize Vision II as an option.

In the 1950s and 1960s, the dominant model for curriculum reform was located in the conceptual and procedural foundations of science disciplines, as interpreted by writers such as Bruner (1960). In the history of that era, the leaders of curriculum projects in the United States (e.g., PSSC, BSCS, CHEM STUDY, ESCP, SCIS) were scientists who by nature of their education and experience embraced Vision I (Rudolph, 2002) as the basis for reforms. In this historical example, Vision I was, by the perception of these leaders, the default model for curriculum reform.

The Potential Effects of Overemphasizing One Vision

Science curriculum history is littered with examples of throwing out the baby with the bathwater. Major changes in science curriculum have been due to changes in curriculum orientation from Vision I to Vision II and vice versa. (An example is the academic influence on science course changes in the late 1950s and early 1960s, which completely discredited Vision II.) Of course there have been changes to subject matter as well, but the change of vision is more remarkable. When a curriculum vision changes, for whatever reason, the rhetoric usually cries out "Stop doing *any of that*, and start doing *all of this!*" Neither Vision I nor Vision II is immune from this possibility. The introduction of some of the so-called alphabet courses—notably PSSC Physics—is the most recent example of shifting from Vision II to Vision I. The development of the STS movement is probably the most telling example of a shift from Vision I to Vision II.

Vision I programs run the risk of including situation-oriented material (such as personal and social perspectives on a science-related issue) in a token fashion, only as a source for motivating students in lessons. By the same token (pardon the pun), Vision II programs run the risk of paying insufficient attention to science. Aikenhead (1994) presents an analysis of materials development, research, and teaching approaches in STS according to eight categories that show different blends of science content and attention to situations, or "STS content" (Aikenhead, 1994, pp. 55–56). At one extreme is "Motivation by STS Content," described as "Traditional school science, plus a mention of STS content in order to make a lesson more interesting. Not normally taken seriously as STS instruction. . . . Students are not assessed on the STS content." At the other extreme is "STS Contents," described thus: "A major technology or social issue is studied. Science content is mentioned but only to indicate an existing link to science. . . . Students are not assessed on pure science content to any appreciable degree." There is a message here, as well as an analytical scheme, about what can happen in implementation efforts involving both Vision II and Vision I.

Roth and Lee (2002, 2004) and Roth and Barton (2004) have pushed Vision II to the extreme by redefining SL as "collective praxis"—as if there is no such thing as "individual" SL. All of their case studies, so far as we can determine, are based on teaching science through the same single context: personal and social perspectives. There is a comment in a "Coda" (Roth & Lee 2004, p. 288) that "Much research remains to be done to study the forms distributed and situated cognition take in the approach we propose." Indeed. More research is also needed on whether and how well students can shift from one context to another as appropriate in different situations. For example, suppose students learn about a community's river water chemistry in the context of personal and social perspectives on science. Would that inhibit, contribute to, or have no effect on their understanding of appropriate features of scientific inquiry and/or the history and nature of science—such as the system-theory character of ecological inquiry? We submit that more research is needed to answer questions of this sort. To be sure, we have substantial research on the impacts of teaching science within a single context or curriculum emphasis (e.g., the research on learning about the nature of science, about STS, etc.). The point here is about multiple contexts and how those affect learners, therefore feeding back implications for the way SL is defined in curriculum policies and implemented in instructional materials. There are risks to students' education in overemphasizing either Vision II or Vision I.

Concluding Remarks

Our review suggests to us there is more need than ever to develop ways to balance science literacy (Vision I) and scientific literacy (Vision II) in science education programs that can successfully meet the needs of all students. Surely we as a profession have seen enough examples of overemphasizing one vision at the expense of the other. The Twenty First Century Science project in England has shown how an overall, systemic solution can provide for the two major functions of school science. It truly is a systemic problem, too, in the sense that neither vision will accommodate both functions. This project could provide a template for other strategies, perhaps more suited to other educational systems. In any event, the focus has to be on the science education needs of the students, not the ideological purity or attractiveness of a vision that fits the needs of only a fraction of the students to be served.

Acknowledgments

We acknowledge the help of Justin Dillon and Gregory Kelly, who gave us useful reviews of this chapter.

References

Agin, M. L. (1974). Education for scientific literacy: A conceptual frame of reference and some applications. *Science Education 58*, 403–415.

Aikenhead, G. (1994). What is STS science teaching? In J. Solomon & G. Aikenhead (Eds.), *STS education: International perspectives on reform* (pp. 47–59). New York: Teachers College Press.

American Association for the Advancement of Science. (1989). *Science for all Americans*. Washington, DC: Author.

Bruner, J. S. (1960). *The process of education*. New York: Vintage Books.

Bybee, R. W. (1997). *Achieving scientific literacy: From purposes to practices*. Portsmouth, NH: Heinemann.

Bybee, R.W., & DeBoer, G.E. (1994). Research on goals for the science curriculum. In D.L. Gabel (Ed.), *Handbook of research on science teaching and learning* (pp. 357–387). New York: Macmillan Publishing Company.

Bybee, R., & MacRae, B. (2011). Scientific literacy and student attitudes: Perspectives from PISA 2006 science. *International Journal of Science Education, 33,* 7–26.

Clark, J., Case, J.M., Davies, N., Sheridan, G., & Toerien, R. (2011). "Struggling up Mount Improbable": A cautionary (implementation) tale of a Vision II scientific literacy curriculum in South Africa. In C. Linder, L. Östman, D.A. Roberts, P.-O. Wickman, G. Erickson, & A. MacKinnon (Eds.), *Exploring the landscape of scientific literacy* (pp. 272–287). New York: Routledge.

Council of Ministers of Education, Canada (CMEC). (1997). *Common framework of science learning outcomes K to 12: Pan-Canadian protocol for collaboration on school curriculum for use by curriculum developers.* Toronto, ON: Author. ISBN 0-88987-111-6.

DeBoer, G.E. (1991). *A history of ideas in science education: Implications for practice.* New York: Teachers College Press.

DeBoer, G.E. (2000). Scientific literacy: Another look at its historical and contemporary meanings and its relationship to science education reform. *Journal of Research in Science Teaching, 37,* 582–601.

Feinstein, N. (2011). Salvaging science literacy. *Science Education, 95,* 168–185. doi:10.1002/sce.20414

Fensham, P.J. (1992). Science and technology. In P.W. Jackson (Ed.), *Handbook of research on curriculum* (pp. 789–829). New York: Macmillan Publishing Company.

Fensham, P.J. (2012). The science curriculum; the decline of expertise and the rise of bureaucratise. *Journal of Curriculum Studies.* doi:10.1080/00220272.2012.737862

Gabel, L.L. (1976). *The development of a model to determine perceptions of scientific literacy.* Doctoral dissertation. The Ohio State University, Columbus, Ohio.

Gauthier, D.P. (1963). *Practical reasoning: The structure and foundations of prudential and moral arguments and their exemplification in discourse.* Oxford, UK: Clarendon Press.

Harlen, W. (2001a). The assessment of scientific literacy in the OECD/PISA project. In H. Behrendt, H. Dahncke, R. Duit, W. Gräber, M. Komorek, & A. Kross (Eds.), *Research in science education—past, present, and future* (pp. 49–60). Dordrecht, the Netherlands: Kluwer Academic Publishers.

Harlen, W. (2001b). The assessment of scientific literacy in the OECD/PISA project. *Studies in Science Education, 36,* 79–104.

Hurd, P.D. (1958). Science literacy for American schools. *Educational Leadership, 16,* 13–16.

Jenkins, E.W. (1990). Scientific literacy and school science education. *School Science Review, 71*(256), 43–51.

Kelly, G.J. (2011). Scientific literacy, discourse, and epistemic practices. In C. Linder, L. Östman, D.A. Roberts, P.-O. Wickman, G. Erickson, & A. MacKinnon (Eds.), *Exploring the landscape of scientific literacy* (pp. 61–73). New York: Routledge.

Klopfer, L.E. (1969). Science education in 1991. *The School Review, 77,* 199–217.

Lave, J., & Wenger, E. (1991). *Situated learning: Legitimate peripheral participation.* Cambridge, UK: Cambridge University Press.

Layton, D., Jenkins, E.W., Macgill, S., & Davey, A. (1993). *Inarticulate science? Perspectives on the public understanding of science and some implications for science education.* Nafferton, Driffield, East Yorkshire, UK: Studies in Education Ltd.

Linder, C., Östman, L, Roberts, D.A., Wickman, P.-O., Erickson, G., & MacKinnon, A. (Eds.). (2011). *Exploring the landscape of scientific literacy.* New York: Routledge.

Linder, C., Östman, L., & Wickman, P.-O. (Eds.). (2007). *Promoting scientific literacy: Science education research in transaction.* Uppsala, Sweden: Uppsala University.

Matthews, M.R. (1994). *Science teaching: The role of history and philosophy of science.* New York: Routledge.

McEneaney, E.H. (2003). The worldwide cachet of scientific literacy. *Comparative Education Review, 47*(2), 217–237.

Millar, R. (2006). Twenty First Century Science: Insights from the design and implementation of a scientific literacy approach in school science. *International Journal of Science Education, 28*(13), 1499–1521.

Millar, R. (2010). Increasing participation in science beyond GCSE: The impact of Twenty First Century Science. *School Science Review, 91*(337), 67–73.

Millar, R. (2012). Rethinking science education: Meeting the challenge of "science for all". *School Science Review, 93*(345), 21–30.

Millar, R., & Osborne, J. (Eds.). (1998). *Beyond 2000: Science education for the future.* London: King's College London, School of Education. Retrieved from www.nuffieldfoundation.org/beyond-2000-science-education-future

Miller, J.D. (2000). The development of civic scientific literacy in the United States. In D.D. Kumar & D.E. Chubin (Eds.), *Science, technology, and society: A sourcebook for research and practice* (pp. 21–47). New York: Kluwer Academic/Plenum Publishers.

National Research Council. (1996). *National science education standards.* Washington, DC: National Academies Press.

National Research Council. (2012). *A framework for K–12 science education: Practices, crosscutting concepts, and core ideas.* Washington, DC: National Academies Press.

Norris, S.P., & Phillips, L.M. (2003). How literacy in its fundamental sense is central to scientific literacy. *Science Education, 87,* 224–240.

OECD. (1999). *Measuring student knowledge and skills: A new framework for assessment.* Paris: OECD.

OECD. (2003). *The PISA 2003 assessment framework: Mathematics, reading, science and problem solving knowledge and skills.* Paris: OECD.

OECD. (2006). *The PISA 2006 assessment framework for science, reading and mathematics.* Paris: OECD.

OECD. (2013). *PISA 2015 draft science framework.* Paris: OECD. Retrieved from www.oecd.org/pisa/pisaproducts

Orpwood, G. (1998). The logic of advice and deliberation: Making sense of science curriculum talk. In D.A. Roberts & L. Östman (Eds.), *Problems of meaning in science curriculum* (pp. 54–70). New York: Teachers College Press.

Osborne, J. (2007a). Engaging young people with science: Thoughts about future direction of science education. In C. Linder, L. Östman, & P.-O. Wickman (Eds.), *Promoting scientific literacy: Science education research in transaction* (pp. 105–112). Uppsala, Sweden: Uppsala University.

Osborne, J. (2007b). Science education for the twenty first century. *Eurasia Journal of Mathematics, Science & Technology Education 3*(3), 173–184.

Pella, M.O., O'Hearn, G.T., & Gale, C.W. (1966). Referents to scientific literacy. *Journal of Research in Science Teaching, 4,* 199–208.

Roberts, D.A. (1982). Developing the concept of "curriculum emphases" in science education. *Science Education, 66,* 243–260.

Roberts, D.A. (1995). Junior high school science transformed: Analysing a science curriculum policy change. *International Journal of Science Education, 17,* 493–504.

Roberts, D.A. (2007). Scientific literacy/science literacy. In S.K. Abell & N.G. Lederman (Eds.), *Handbook of research on science education* (pp. 729–780). Mahwah, NJ: Lawrence Erlbaum Associates.

Roberts, D.A. (2011). Competing visions of scientific literacy: The influence of a science curriculum policy image. In C. Linder, L. Östman, D.A. Roberts, P.-O. Wickman, G. Erickson, & A. MacKinnon (Eds.), *Exploring the landscape of scientific literacy* (pp. 11–27). New York: Routledge.

Roth, W.-M., & Barton, A.C. (2004). *Rethinking scientific literacy.* New York: RoutledgeFalmer.

Roth, W.-M., & Lee, S. (2002). Scientific literacy as collective praxis. *Public Understanding of Science, 11,* 33–56.

Roth, W.-M., & Lee, S. (2004). Science education as/for participation in the community. *Science Education, 88,* 263–291.

Rudolph, J. L. (2002). *Scientists in the classroom*. New York: Palgrave.

Rutherford, F. J., & Ahlgren, A. (1991). *Science for all Americans*. New York: Oxford University Press.

Ryder, J. (2001). Identifying science understanding for functional scientific literacy. *Studies in Science Education, 36*, 1–44.

Sadler, T. D. (2009). Situated learning in science education: Socioscientific issues as contexts for practice. *Studies in Science Education 45*(1), 1–42.

Sadler, T. D., & Zeidler, D. L. (2009). Scientific literacy, PISA, and socioscientific discourse: Assessment for progressive aims of science education. *Journal of Research in Science Teaching, 46*(8), 909–921.

Twenty-First Century Science. www.nuffieldfoundation.org/twenty-first-century-science

Zeidler, D. L., & Sadler, T. D. (2011). An inclusive view of scientific literacy. In C. Linder, L. Östman, D. A. Roberts, P.-O. Wickman, G. Erickson, & A. MacKinnon (Eds.), *Exploring the landscape of scientific literacy* (pp. 176–192). New York: Routledge.

28

The History of Science Curriculum Reform in the United States

George E. DeBoer

AAAS Project 2061

There have been several recognizable periods of science curriculum reform in the United States since the middle of the 19th century. The first were the efforts by mid- to late 19th-century scientists to increase the intellectual rigor of science study by placing students in direct contact with natural phenomena and having them reason through the patterns and relationships they observed instead of learning by book study alone, often through rote memorization of what they read. These efforts culminated in the 1893 report of the Committee of Ten of the National Educational Association, chaired by chemist and Harvard President Charles Eliot. That was followed by a long period of Progressive-Era reforms, which lasted most of the first half of the 20th century. Then came the period of National Science Foundation (NSF) funded curriculum projects of the 1950s and 1960s, which lasted a much shorter time but whose effects are still being felt today. Then, in reaction to the highly discipline-focused and intellectually rigorous curriculum materials of the 1950s and 1960s, there was a wave of more socially responsive materials focused on environmental awareness, personal relevance, and the relationship between science and society. And then, beginning in the early 1980s, a report by the Commission on Excellence in Education, *A Nation at Risk,* stimulated an era of standards-based reform, which we are in the midst of today.

In part, these shifts were influenced by changing values in the broader society, and what was thought of as important in education changed to match the new societal vision. For example, Progressive-Era reforms took place during a time of heightened social activism in the United States—first with efforts to educate and Americanize large numbers of immigrants and then to rebuild the country after the Great Depression. Similarly, the call for renewed rigor in the curriculum and the introduction of standards-based accountability was helped along by

Reagan-era conservatism and broad-based societal concerns about U.S. international competiveness. Sometimes specific events and occurrences, such as the launching of the earth-orbiting satellite, *Sputnik,* by the Soviet Union, hastened the direction of change.

To some extent, shifts also occurred because reform movements often lead to excess, as promoters become uncritically zealous and the contradictions and weaknesses of the movements become evident. This was certainly the case for progressive education as it devolved by mid-20th century into an anti-intellectual life-adjustment education. And some would argue that it was true for the reforms of the 1950s and 1960s, as its highly intellectual approach focused on the content and methods of the disciplines and almost completely ignored the practical social relevance of science or the importance of student interest. This created a curriculum that proved too difficult and uninteresting for many students and too intellectually abstract for the tastes of education leaders who had come of age during a more activist time. The more socially relevant and humanistic approaches of the 1970s (environmental education, open schools, values education, science-technology-society approaches) were a brief response to that highly intellectual treatment of the curriculum in the 1960s (DeBoer, 1991; Rudolph & Meshoulam, in press), but those humanistic approaches in turn quickly gave way to calls for a more rigorous approach to education in *A Nation at Risk* at the same time that attitudes shifted in the broader society as well.

But it is important to point out that curriculum development is not just a cyclical process. Society's values may shift between a focus on the individual and social activism,[1] and this may influence what our educational goals are, but we do find out more about how students learn, and we do develop more effective ways of engaging students with important science content. This is possible in part because of an underlying commitment to a set of educational goals that are remarkably stable even as our thinking about their relative importance and how to accomplish them shifts over time. First is the commitment to teaching students the facts and principles of the physical world so that they can understand and appreciate natural phenomena; second is for students to understand the various ways that science is done; and third is for students to develop the ability to think rationally about the physical world. Given these ongoing commitments, it is possible for educators to focus on new approaches to science teaching that lead to more meaningful engagement by students with natural phenomena and the science ideas that explain those phenomena.

This chapter provides a brief historical summary of curriculum reform in the United States from the middle of the 19th century to the present and some of the factors that influenced that development. It should be read along with the entry by J. Myron Atkin and Paul Black in the 2007 edition of this handbook.

From Bookwork to Lab Work

During the mid to late 19th century, some of the most vocal advocates for improving the teaching of science in the schools were the scientists themselves. These scientists placed a great deal of emphasis on teaching students how science was done and engaging them in the logic of scientific thinking. For example, Thomas Huxley and Herbert Spencer believed that science teaching should be based on direct experience with the physical world rather than on the words of teachers or textbooks. It was students' direct contact with the objects and phenomena of nature that would make science a unique subject in the curriculum and would justify its presence as a disciplinary subject.

As Huxley put it:

> The great peculiarity of scientific training, that in virtue of which it cannot be replaced by any other discipline whatsoever, is this bringing of the mind directly into contact with fact, and practising the intellect in the completest form of induction; that is to say, in drawing conclusions from particular facts made known by immediate observation of Nature.
>
> (Huxley, 1899, p. 126)

Spencer argued that the laboratory would help students to draw cause-and-effect relationships from their explorations of natural phenomena, what he called "judgment."

> No acquaintance with the meaning of words, can give the power of forming correct inferences respecting causes and effects. The constant habit of drawing conclusions from data, and then of verifying those conclusions by observation and experiment, can alone give the power of judgment correctly.
>
> (Spencer, 1864, p. 88)

The study of science also provided "moral" discipline. Moral discipline included the development of independence of thought, perseverance, sincerity, and a willingness

to abandon any preconceived notion that proved to be incorrect. Words alone, as Spencer explained, increased one's dependence on authority:

> Such and such are the meanings of these words, says the teacher or the dictionary. So and so is the rule in this case, says the grammar. By the pupil these dicta are received as unquestionable. His constant attitude of mind is that of submission to dogmatic teaching. And a necessary result is a tendency to accept without inquiry whatever is established. Quite the opposite is the attitude of mind generated by the cultivation of science. By science, constant appeal is made to individual reason. Its truths are not accepted upon authority alone; but all are at liberty to test them.
>
> (Spencer, 1864, p. 89)

When late-19th-century scientists argued the value of science in the school curriculum, they wanted students to experience the logic of scientific investigation. They believed that observing and experimenting on the natural world would reveal patterns that would lead to general principles, and thinking through the cause-and-effect relationships would help students develop their rational intelligence.

There was theoretical support for these ideas from the newly developing field of psychology. For example, the view that observing the world would naturally lead to the formation of concepts about the world could be found in the writings of early psychologists such as William James. James believed that through a sequence of experiences, changes occur in the brain to form more complex ideas or "associations." In his popular *Talks to Teachers*, a series of essays published in 1899 based on lectures he had given throughout the 1890s, James said, "The laws of association govern . . . all the trains of our thinking. . . . Whatever appears in the mind must be *introduced*; and when introduced, it is as the associate of something already there" (James, 1899, p. 29).

James, however, also believed that the most that psychology offered teachers were some broad general principles and insights regarding human behavior. In his words:

> you make a great, a very great mistake, if you think that psychology, being the science of the mind's laws, is something from which you can deduce definite programmes and schemes and methods of instruction for immediate schoolroom use. Psychology is a science, and teaching is an art; and sciences never generate arts directly out of themselves.
>
> (James, 1899, p. 5)

The Committee of Ten

The scientists' attitudes about how science should be taught culminated in the work and final report of the Committee of Ten, chaired by Harvard University President Charles Eliot and assembled in 1892 by the National Education Association to make recommendations regarding the school curriculum that would enable a smoother transition from high school to college. The subject areas that were selected for discussion were those that had "disciplinary" value, that is, the ability to develop the intellect, not those having primarily "informational" or commercial utility. Charles Eliot's background as a chemist, his interest in the school science curriculum, and his prestige as president of Harvard University had much to do with the sciences being included among the subjects considered to have disciplinary value. Regarding the extensive conference reports that the scientists prepared, Eliot said:

> They ardently desired to have their respective subjects made equal to Latin, Greek, and Mathematics in weight and influence in the schools; but they knew that educational tradition was adverse to this desire, and that many teachers and directors of education felt no confidence in these subjects as disciplinary material. Hence the length of these reports.
>
> (NEA, 1893, p. 13)

Botany and zoology were to involve direct observations of nature to help students "form the habit of investigating carefully and of making clear, truthful statements, and to develop in them a taste for original investigation" (NEA, 1893, p. 142). Students would be asked to make detailed sketches and drawings of specimens, usually beginning with amoeba and ending with mammals in zoology, and starting with green algae and ending with dicotyledons in botany. Observations of structures were to be linked to a study of relevant functions. It was recommended that the high school courses in botany and zoology should be laboratory based with 3 days a week spent in direct observation and 2 days in discussions of those observations, including organized lectures and quizzing. No textbooks, except for reference books and laboratory guides, were to be used; only physiology would be taught primarily from a textbook because opportunities for experimental work in that field were limited.

The Conference on Physics, Chemistry, and Astronomy recommended that study of the physical sciences should start in the elementary grades and be taught by means of experiments carried out by the pupils. Half the work was to be quantitatively based laboratory work. Students were not expected to "discover" the laws of physics on their own but to be guided by the teacher, who would help them interpret the results of their laboratory work. The students were to be involved in determining the properties of objects and the nature of phenomena through measurements and calculations, and they were to be involved in the verification of physical laws so they would have direct evidence of their validity (NEA, 1893).

In 1902, Alexander Smith, associate professor of chemistry at the University of Chicago, and Edwin Hall, professor of physics at Harvard University, published a book titled *The Teaching of Chemistry and Physics in the Secondary School* (Smith & Hall, 1902), in which the authors reflected on many of the recommendations of the Committee of Ten. Smith and Hall believed that students should

carry out genuine inquiries in the laboratory that would lead to meaningful understanding of disciplinary content and an appreciation for independent discovery. The verification of chemical and physical principles would make the abstract principles more vivid, would make students remember them longer, and would provide evidence of the experimental basis for the principle being learned. Using the laboratory for independent discovery would increase interest on the part of students and foster a scientific habit of thought.

Hall (1894) agreed with the Committee of Ten's science conferences that quantitatively based laboratory work should begin in grammar school:

> Some years ago a body of educational leaders declared themselves in favor of teaching physics by means of experiments involving exact measurement and weighing by the pupils in grammar-schools. . . . The author at first expressed . . . the opinion that grammar-school physics must be lecture-table physics, an hour or two a week devoted by the teacher to the performance and discussion of simple experiments in the presence of the pupils. But the advocates of the lecture-table method of science-teaching cannot claim for it the disciplinary advantage and the power of bringing the pupil into close quarters with physical facts and laws, that belong to a properly-conducted course of laboratory work by the pupils themselves.
>
> (Hall, 1894, p. xx)

In his textbook in elementary physics, Hall used an inductive approach in which students began with an experiment and then were led to a conclusion about the scientific principle that was revealed by the experiment rather than using the experiments as illustrations of the principle. But he also recognized the limitations of this approach. As he put it:

> It can hardly be said for the [inductive] method that it teaches the art of making discoveries,—that art is as difficult to teach as the art of getting rich,—but it has a tendency to keep the pupil in a more active, self-dependent state of mind than the [verification] method, and in particular it prevents in a large measure that state of bias, or preconception, in the performance of experiments, which is so dangerous not merely to accuracy of observations but to mental rectitude.
>
> (pp. iii–vii)

In summary, scientists in the late 19th century argued that science should be included in the school curriculum as a prestigious subject with "disciplinary" value. For that to happen, science courses needed to be more than informational and useful. Scientists were especially opposed to rote memorization of the facts of science. This was a reaction to what they considered to be an outmoded teaching practice that viewed the development of the memory as a primary goal of education. Instead, to have disciplinary value, science courses had to lead to greater intellectual power. The argument scientists put forward was that the study of science could develop students' inductive reasoning through direct observation and careful consideration of the events and processes of nature. The scientists struggled with the appropriate amount of independence that students should have when conducting investigations and cautioned against assuming that students could discover scientific principles on their own, but they also cautioned against telling students what they were verifying in advance. Students should at least have the freedom to look for relationships and then be asked to say what it was that they had found out. The focus was on personal intellectual development, with little if any reference to the useful or practical nature of education in society. Nor was much thought given to how knowledge might be organized in the minds of the students. The science disciplines had their structure and inductive logic, and students would come to know science through their direct observation and exploration of the world and the guidance of a knowledgeable teacher. Recommendations regarding the science curriculum were based on personal insights of scientists gained from their experience with the teaching of science, not from any organized program of educational research as we know it today.

From Empiricism to Progressivism

Soon after the turn of the 20th century, a major shift began to take place in how science teaching was viewed by educators. In particular, social relevance began to take precedence over personal intellectual development. Among sociologists, education was thought to have instrumental value that would prepare students for life in a democratic society. Textbooks of the first half of the 20th century reflected these social values. To convince a wider population of students to attend and stay in school, textbook writers included topics they thought would be more interesting and useful to students, and science textbooks began to feature practical home and industrial applications, such as how a heating system or car engine worked.

Proposals for a practical and socially oriented curriculum were formally laid out by the NEA's Commission on the Reorganization of Secondary Education (CRSE) in 1918. The Commission identified seven "Cardinal Principles" that should guide the development of the school curriculum: (1) health, (2) command of fundamental processes, (3) worthy home-membership, (4) vocation, (5) citizenship, (6) worthy use of leisure, and (7) ethical character (NEA, 1918). With few exceptions, these principles guided educational thinking for nearly four decades.

A number of studies showed that the practical aim was popular among science teachers in the early years of the 20th century (Caldwell, 1909; Downing, 1915; Hunter, 1910), with more than half of the teachers who responded listing "practical science" among the most important aims of science teaching by 1915.

The practical approach, however, was not without controversy. John Coulter, for example, who had been a member of the Conference on Natural History of the Committee of Ten and a professor at the University of Chicago, thought that focusing on only those things within the experience of students was too limiting: "That our science teaching should consist only in explaining to a student what he encounters in his own experience, is to limit his life, rather than to enrich it by extending his horizon" (Coulter, 1915, p. 99). Hanor Webb (1915) said, "I am sure that the great body of the science teachers of our Nation will have little patience with those who hold the 'fundamentals' up to ridicule. Well balanced people recognize the necessity of a foundation for every structure" (Webb, 1915, pp. 681–682). Robert Bradbury (1915), head of the Department of Science in the Southern High School in Philadelphia, who later authored a popular textbook in chemistry himself, criticized the way the new practical approach was being applied in chemistry:

> They begin with a hundred pages of formal chemistry given in a purely didactic way. This portion is a kind of highly condensed and abstract grammar of chemical science and is apparently offered in the hope that the students will be able to apply the principles in the work that follows. The remaining pages are devoted to such subjects as lime, cement, pottery, inks, electric furnaces, pigments, etc. In fact, the books are, to all intents and purposes, elementary chemical technologies . . . We should firmly grasp the fact that in changing from chemistry to technology, we are deserting knowledge of proved permanent worth to deal in information whose chief characteristic is the evanescence of its value.
>
> (Bradbury, 1915, pp. 785–786)

To satisfy a range of tastes, textbook writers like Bradbury combined frequent references to personal, industrial, and commercial applications with basic ideas from the sciences and the scientific method. *A First Book in Chemistry*, published by Bradbury in 1922, blends chemical principles, historical episodes, industrial applications, connections to other areas of science, and factual evidence and logical reasoning in support of scientific claims. Basic principles of chemistry related to atoms and molecules, acid and base reactions, ionization, and the law of multiple proportions are presented early in the book in the context of the most common chemical elements. This is followed by a discussion of periodicity and a series of chapters on families of elements, their properties, and the properties and industrial applications of compounds of those elements. The author engages students through rhetorical questioning and a line of reasoning that is generally easy to follow, although the presentation of information tends to be encyclopedic, and sometimes the logical arguments that justify conclusions seem to be presented too succinctly for high school students to follow. But most students choosing to take a course in high school chemistry would have been introduced to the fundamentals of chemistry, their technological applications, and links to other areas of science.

Similarly, Robert Millikan and Henry Gale's *Elementary Physics* was used widely in secondary schools in the 1930s and 1940s. Millikan was a highly regarded physicist from the California Institute of Technology who had won the 1923 Nobel Prize in Physics for measuring the charge of an electron, and Gale was a professor of physics at the University of Chicago. Their text presents basic physics concepts about fluids, force and motion, work and heat, electricity and magnetism, sound and wave motion, light, and electronics and radiation in a didactic style. Along with basic principles of elementary physics, the text includes many industrial and everyday applications of physics, and each unit is introduced with a brief historical episode. The historical accounts, however, stand alone and are not integrated into the content of the chapters.

The approach is largely informational; the authors do little to engage the readers either by asking them to think through the logic and evidence behind physical principles or by inserting rhetorical questions in the text to keep their attention. On the other hand, at the end of each chapter, the authors do ask a number of thought-provoking conceptual questions. For example, from the chapter on change of state: "Would fanning produce a feeling of coolness (a) if the face were perfectly dry? (b) if the air around us were perfectly saturated? Why?" (Millikan & Gale, 1941, p. 246). And from the chapter on force and motion: "If the earth were to cease rotating on its axis, would bodies on the equator weigh more or less than they do now? Explain" (p. 129). These are not questions whose answers can be found in the textbook, and they are not quantitative problems that can be solved simply by plugging numbers into a formula; instead they require an application of the basic principles presented in the text.

Another textbook that was popular in the first half of the 20th century was *Modern Biology*. The book was first published as *Biology for Beginners* by Truman Moon in 1921. Subsequent editions of *Modern Biology* were authored by Moon, Mann, and Otto; Otto and Towle; and finally Albert Towle by himself until the 2002 edition. The continuous line of authorship was broken when John Postlethwait and Janet Hobson then took over authorship. The book has followed a similar format throughout its history and still enjoys widespread use today.

Early chapters present basic principles of biology followed by a chapter-by-chapter description of each classification of organisms, beginning with microorganisms, plants, and finally ending with humans. The 1956 edition (Moon, Mann, & Otto, 1956) covers basic ideas about cell structure, cell metabolism, growth and reproduction, principles of heredity, and Mendelian genetics. The phylogenetic presentation strongly suggests a progressive evolutionary development of organisms, but only a single chapter toward the end of the book, *The Changing World of Life*, addresses the topic of change over time directly. In apparent recognition of objections that might result from anti-evolutionists, the text never uses the term "evolution," although it does discuss "natural selection"

and most of the other key elements of Darwin's theory. Evidence for change over time is organized by fossil evidence, homologous structures, vestigial organs, evidence from embryology, physical similarities between species, geographical distribution, results of breeding, and experiments in plant and animal genetics. Along with the detailed coverage of each type of organism and the basic principles of biology, the text also includes many personal, industrial, and commercial applications, and considerable time is devoted to ecosystem interactions, humans' role in maintaining natural environments, and human health. The style is informational and descriptive and somewhat encyclopedic in nature, with large numbers of terms to memorize.

Students are introduced to the nature of science in an early chapter in which they are told that science requires attitudes of open-mindedness, careful judgment, healthy curiosity, belief that natural events have natural causes, and a concern for human welfare. They also learn that there is not just one single scientific method but a variety of approaches that differ according to the type of investigation being conducted. And as late as 1956, the stated goals of the course still included many of the ideas laid out in the NCRE's Cardinal Principles in 1918:

- To answer questions about life and living things
- To acquire scientific attitudes and methods
- To understand the basic principles of life
- To aid the conservation program
- To improve our general health standards
- To increase outdoor recreation
- To acquaint you with some of the outstanding biologists
- To introduce worthwhile hobbies (e.g., bird hikes)
- To improve daily life (seeding and fertilizing lawns, spraying insect pests, protecting food from spoilage, etc.)
- To introduce biological occupations (food industries, medical, agriculture, forestry, bacteriology; Moon, Mann, & Otto, 1956, pp. 9–11)

As the 1956 edition of *Modern Biology* demonstrates, by mid-century, the emphasis on applied and practical education was still strong.

Much of the theoretical support for the social and practical value of education came from the writing of John Dewey and other Progressive-Era thinkers. For the most part, this support was based on social and philosophical arguments. For example, in comparing his new socially oriented psychology with earlier ideas, Dewey said, "Earlier psychology regarded mind as a purely individual affair" (Dewey, 1990/1900). "It was forgotten that the maximum appeal, and the full meaning in the life of the child, could be secured only when the studies were presented, not as bare external studies, but from the standpoint of the relation they bear to the life of society" (p. 100). Regarding the practical importance of knowledge, he argued that both concrete experience with the world and reasoning with abstract principles needed to be applied to actual problems. In his words:

> The controversy in educational theory and practice was between those who relied more upon the sense element in knowledge, upon contact with things, upon object-lessons, etc., and those who emphasized abstract ideas, generalizations, etc.—reason, so called . . . In neither case was there any attempt to connect either the sense training or the logical operations with the problems and interests of the life of practice. Here again an educational transformation is indicated if we are to suppose that our psychological theories stand for any truths of life.
>
> (pp. 101–102)

Dewey was wary of using educational research to draw general conclusions about educational practice, preferring a more pragmatic approach that dealt with specific situations, similar to what James had recommended in his *Talks to Teachers* in 1899. Dewey argued, for example, that insights about education should come from an analysis of "what the gifted teacher does intuitively," not by "transforming isolated scientific findings into 'rules of action' that would give 'unquestionable authenticity and authority to a specific procedure to be carried out in the school room" (Dewey, p. 15, cited by Linn, Songer, & Eylon, 1996, p. 446).

From Social Relevance to the Nature of Science: The Development of the National Science Foundation-Funded Curriculum Projects

By the middle of the 20th century, national organizations such as the National Society for the Study of Education began to argue that *all* of the objectives of science instruction, including knowledge of scientific phenomena, understanding of concepts and principles, skill in the scientific method, and positive science attitudes should be taught so that they would *function* in the lives of students. "Life adjustment" became more important than understanding organized content itself.

> The information learned must result in altered thinking and in altered behavior. It must make the pupil (and later, the adult) more intelligent and readier for adequate *adjustment* (italics added) whenever that information is relevant to life situations.
>
> (National Society for the Study of Education, 1947, p. 26)

Speaking specifically of chemistry:

> Associated with the strength inherent in the organization of chemistry as a subject are certain pitfalls. One of the most crucial is the tendency to look upon the organization as the important item per se. In doing this we may seem to present chemistry content as something to be memorized

and may forget that it is only a framework which gives direction to growth . . .

> (National Society for the Study of Education, 1947, p. 201)

The U.S. Office of Education, along with many state departments of education, supported the development of life-adjustment education as a way of continuing a national commitment to democratic education for all. The U.S. Commissioner of Education, John Studebaker, appointed a National Commission on Life Adjustment Education for Youth in 1947 and again in 1950 to promote the concept. In most of these life-adjustment programs, democratic living, personal and social growth, and human relationships were considered more important than the organized disciplinary content of science, mathematics, English, history, and languages for all but the college-bound students (U.S. Office of Education, 1951).

The programs that were developed in the name of life-adjustment education were often so lacking in traditional academic content that they became easy targets for critics. For example, Mortimer Smith (1954) said that social skills should not take the place of intellectual training and the cultivation of intelligence. It should be the challenge of schools to teach *all* students the knowledge, values, and modes of thought of our cultural heritage, not just the small percentage that planned to continue their studies in college. According to Arthur Bestor (1953), the primary job of schools was the deliberate training of disciplined intelligence, and the vehicles for developing intelligence were the academic disciplines.

By the 1950s, with support from the recently established National Science Foundation (NSF), scientists through their professional scientific societies began to discuss ways to bring renewed intellectual vigor to the school science programs. The launching by the Soviet Union of its earth-orbiting satellite *Sputnik* in 1957 was the tipping point that convinced the U.S. government to provide massive financial support to these initiatives. What followed were two decades of unprecedented federal involvement in education and the development of an approach to science teaching that was focused on the logical structure of the disciplines as understood by the scientific community and on the experimental nature of science, not on the personal and social growth of students that had characterized science education in the first half of the century (DeBoer, 1991; Rudolph & Meshoulam, in press).

This was the first time since the late 19th century that scientists had taken such a prominent role in curriculum development. Whereas the major goal of 19th-century scientists had been to argue for the place of science as a true disciplinary study in the school curriculum, the goal of the curriculum developers in the mid-20th century was to provide a more accurate and up-to-date presentation of the structure of scientific knowledge through the organized disciplines and a more accurate representation of the nature of scientific investigation, something they believed had been given too little attention in recent years.

Physics

In physics, the Physical Sciences Study Committee (PSSC), chaired by Jerrold Zacharias, physics professor at MIT, began work on a new course in high school physics. The objective was to include more ideas from modern physics, provide more in-depth coverage of fewer topics, organize the content around broad unifying themes, and reduce the number of technological applications (PSSC, 1960). The brief descriptions of physical laws in the existing texts and especially the accounts of how those laws applied in everyday life were replaced by a conceptually more sophisticated account of the development of physics that tried to tell the story of physics as a human intellectual activity. The course was written by a team of scientists and science teachers during the summer of 1957 and pilot tested and revised over the next 3 years.

Chemistry

In chemistry, two high school courses were developed by the American Chemical Society (ACS). The first was the chemical bond approach (CBA). According to Strong (1962), speaking about the new course:

> Chemistry, through most of its history, has been largely descriptive. In the last sixty years, however, there has been an extensive development of theory in chemistry. These two aspects of modern chemistry—the descriptive and the theoretical—provide a possibility for acquainting students with science as a process of inquiry that interrelates the mental and the experimental.
>
> (Strong, 1962, p. 44)

A major goal of the CBA course was to introduce students to logical thinking in chemistry. Students would be expected to use chemical theory to explain observations they made in the laboratory (Chemical Bond Approach, 1962).

In 1963, ACS introduced a second course aimed at a wider audience than the CBA course. *Chemistry: An Experimental Science* was developed by the Chemical Education Material Study (1963). One goal of the new course was to further reduce the number of topics covered in chemistry by organizing the presentation around a set of core ideas that represented the central principles of the discipline:

> A reduction in the total number of topics covered would make possible a deeper penetration on narrower fronts. As a result the students' grasp of chemistry and of the nature of scientific reasoning and experimentation might be vastly improved.
>
> (Merrill & Ridgway, 1969, p. 113)

Another goal was to give students a more authentic view of the nature of chemistry as an experimental science. This would be accomplished by using the laboratory to show that theory derives from experiment and that "the ultimate 'authority' in science is natural phenomena, not the teacher or the textbook" (Merrill & Ridgway, 1969,

p. 29). These same words were used by late-19th-century scientists, who also argued that science should be taught through the authority of nature, not the authority of teacher or text (see, for example, Spencer, 1864, p. 89).

The course was outlined by the steering committee in the spring of 1960, written by teams of writers that summer, and field tested in schools over the next several years.

Biology

In biology, the American Institute of Biological Sciences formed the Biological Sciences Curriculum Study (BSCS) in 1959 under the direction of Arnold Grobman at the University of Colorado. As with the other disciplines, biologists were concerned that the content of the existing courses was out of date, that it was being presented as disconnected fragments of information rather than as an integrated, conceptual whole that could be used to explain a range of natural phenomena, and that the courses did not accurately portray the essential character of scientific inquiry. They felt that existing textbooks treated biology as a set of stable facts and principles without giving adequate attention to the historical development of the subject or the changing nature of scientific knowledge and that there was too much emphasis on memorization of factual material and not enough on deeper understanding of biological concepts.

BSCS produced three versions of the course: the Blue (molecular) version (BSCS, 1963a), the Yellow (cellular) version (BSCS, 1963b), and the Green (ecological) version (BSCS, 1963c). As with the other science fields, one of the most noticeable changes in the biology texts was the greatly diminished reference to personal, industrial, and commercial applications. The new courses took a structure-of-the-disciplines approach, with little mention of how the science had application to the world in which students lived. There was also a much greater focus on the nature of scientific investigation and discovery. This was done primarily through the laboratory material, but efforts were also made to reflect the nature of science in the text materials. In *A Word to the Student* in the 1963 edition of BSCS's *Molecules to Man* (the Blue version), the authors were explicit that their goal was to help students understand the nature of science as a vigorous interaction of facts and ideas:

> The facts of biology will not be presented to you as a series of foregone conclusions. Nor will theories be presented as though they were facts. Instead, we have attempted to present biology as an adventure in ideas, in which the ideas refer to specific observations and experiments about living things.
>
> (p. ix)

Following these initial efforts in physics, chemistry, and biology, additional courses were developed with NSF support in earth science, physical science, and elementary science (see DeBoer, 1991). Like the earlier courses, these later courses tended to be activity oriented, focused on the way science was done and on broad conceptual themes. In elementary science, *Science—A Process Approach* (American Association for the Advancement of Science, 1967) taught specific processes of science such as observing, classifying, measuring, and predicting while deemphasizing the mastery of science facts. *Elementary Science Study* (Educational Development Center, 1969) emphasized independent exploration by students, and the *Science Curriculum Improvement Study* (1970) utilized the "learning cycle" developed by Robert Karplus.

The primary impetus for the reforms was the university scientists' desire to provide a logical and more rigorous structure to the presentation of science, in part to provide a smoother transition between high school and college. Theoretical support for these initiatives came from a number of sources. In biology, Joseph Schwab, who had been involved in efforts to redesign the general education program in science at the University of Chicago since the early 1930s, brought many of his ideas about reforming the undergraduate curriculum to school science when he joined the BSCS steering committee in 1959 (Rudolph, 2008). Schwab was appointed chair of the Teacher Preparation Committee and later authored the BSCS *Biology Teachers' Handbook* (Schwab, 1963).

Schwab was particularly interested in teaching students *about* scientific inquiry. His interest in scientific inquiry went beyond simply having students become familiar with and practicing the general process of scientific investigation; he also wanted students to be familiar with the diverse modes of scientific inquiry and to understand why a scientist might choose one approach to studying a problem over another. He wanted students to appreciate that scientific knowledge is constructed theory, not something given and certain, and that scientists make choices about what they study, what theoretical framework they choose to work within, and what data they collect. He proposed that students could learn about the nature of scientific investigation by reading and discussing original scientific papers that represented the different ways of doing research as well as by conducting investigations themselves (Schwab, 1962). It was an intellectually sophisticated approach to teaching and learning science and one that fit well with the aspirations of the university scientists who were leading the reform efforts. (See DeBoer, in press, for a discussion of Schwab's contributions to science education, both at the undergraduate and school level.)

Another source of support for the reform initiatives came from cognitive psychologist Jerome Bruner. In 1960, Bruner published *The Process of Education*, a report of the Woods Hole Conference, a 1959 meeting of 35 scientists, scholars, and educators funded by the National Academy of Sciences to discuss the new developments taking place in science and mathematics education and to provide guidance for future developments. Among the participants were psychologists who were involved in such areas of research as intelligence, learning, memory,

thinking, and motivation and representing a variety of perspectives including the behavioral, the Gestalt, and the developmental perspective of Jean Piaget. Bruner noted how unusual it was for scientists and psychologists to be working together: "Strange as it may seem, this was the first time psychologists have been brought together with leading scientists to discuss the problems involved in teaching their various disciplines" (Bruner, 1960, p. xix). The group was particularly interested in how the scientists were attempting to give students a sense of the fundamental ideas and structure of the disciplines. As Bruner (1960) put it:

> The main objective of this [curriculum development] work has been to present subject matter effectively—that is, with due regard not only for coverage but also for structure. The daring and imagination that have gone into this work and the remarkable early successes it has achieved have stimulated psychologists who are concerned with the nature of learning and the transmission of knowledge.
>
> (p. 2)

Bruner (with Goodnow & Austin) had published *A Study of Thinking* in 1956 and helped found the Center of Cognitive Studies at Harvard in 1960. As such, Bruner was one of the early contributors to the cognitive revolution in psychology and one of the early proponents of the value of cognitive studies applied to education. In particular, Bruner believed that logically organized science content could be learned and remembered more effectively than content that was presented without a logical structure. In his view, the structure that defined the science disciplines as organized by scientists was a structure that could be learned in some form by school students as well. This attitude made him particularly sympathetic to the curriculum development efforts of the scientists who had built their reform efforts around that belief.

In addition to the discussions of disciplinary structure, participants also considered other topics that could be included in the research agendas of psychologists and educational researchers. These included discovery learning, general and specific transfer, readiness for learning, intuitive and analytical thinking, and motives for learning (Bruner, 1960). Prominent on the list of topics was Piaget's developmental theories presented by his colleague Barbel Inhelder.

Bruner's summary of the Woods Hole discussions in effect laid out an agenda for research on the relationship between curriculum development and the emerging field of cognitive psychology, which influenced the direction of curriculum research in the years ahead. But that research was still to come. During the 1950s and 1960s, changes in the curriculum were not based on empirical research as we know it today but rather on the experience, insights, and intuitions of the scientists who led the reform efforts and their desire to create a logically coherent treatment of their subject matter as they understood it.

Neo-Progressivism: A Social Conscience Re-emerges

The new NSF–funded texts provided a more authentic and accurate portrayal of science, both as process and as product. However, as already noted, unlike the Progressive-Era texts, the new science textbooks included very few illustrations of industrial products, manufacturing practices, or applications of science to the everyday lives of students, and the abstract nature of the materials often made it difficult for students to make their own connections to their life experiences. Curriculum developers paid attention to the structure of knowledge and how that structure might be understood by students, but they paid little attention to issues of student interest or personal relevance.

By the late 1960s and early 1970s, the country's focus again shifted toward social needs and problems. Legislation was passed in an effort to ensure equality of educational opportunity for all citizens regardless of race, gender, or physical handicap; federal funding was used to support compensatory education programs in both urban and rural communities where there was a high level of poverty; and social critics offered suggestions for humanizing social institutions. In 1972, Title IX of the Education Amendments of 1972 was passed, barring federal financial assistance to any education program that discriminated on the basis of sex. In 1973, Congress passed Section 504 of the Vocational Rehabilitation Act (Pfeiffer, 2002), which barred discrimination against people with disabilities. In science education, the term "scientific literacy" was used to describe an education that was relevant to students' lives and that focused on socially important issues (DeBoer, 2000). There was a growing interest in environmental studies, values education, humanistic approaches to education, and open classrooms. Bybee (1979) argued that ecology could become an organizing theme for science education. Moon and Brezinski (1974) said that environmental education was "fast become a major focal point of the decade" (p. 371).

The calls for intellectual rigor, for excellence, and for disciplinary study that had been made in the 1950s and 1960s were rarely heard. Many science educators who had been skeptical of the curriculum reformers' emphasis on the structure of the disciplines and abstract nature of the courses pointed to the failure of these courses to meet the new challenges of education (Hurd, 1970). To these critics, the science curriculum should be relevant to the lives of a broad range of students, not just those planning careers in science, and the methods of instruction should demonstrate a concern for the ability and interests of each individual student. This sensitivity to individual differences was seen in the widespread popularity of individualized and personalized instructional programs (see, for example, Duane, 1973, www.ed.gov/technology/draft-netp-2010/individualized-personalized-differentiated-instruction) and in the expanded opportunities for student choice in course selection. The increased attention to student interest and renewed focus on social relevance led Diane Ravitch (1983) to refer to the educational emphasis of the 1970s as the "new progressivism."

One noteworthy science curriculum development project of the 1970s was Project Physics (1970), which presents high school physics as a humanistically oriented course viewed from a historical and cultural perspective (Holton, 2003). Many of the topics are the same as those taught in more traditional courses and in the PSSC physics course—motion, motion in the heavens, mechanics, light and electromagnetism, models of the atom, and nuclear physics—but in Project Physics they are presented developmentally through the experiments and discoveries of historical figures. By presenting physics historically, the course illustrates both the methods of scientific investigation and the key findings resulting from those investigations. In addition to providing examples of scientific work, the text includes explicit statements about the nature of scientific investigation. For example:

> The general cycle of observation, hypothesis, deduction, test, modification, etc., so skillfully demonstrated by Galileo in the seventeenth century commonly appears in the work of scientists today. Though there is no such thing as *the* scientific method, some form of this cycle is almost always present in scientific research.
>
> (Project Physics, 1970, chapter 2, p. 59)

This innovative text was used successfully throughout the 1970s and 1980s.

In elementary science, the Full Option Science System (FOSS) was developed at the Lawrence Hall of Science, initially as a program for the visually impaired and funded by NSF in 1976. The program was started in response to the Education for All Handicapped Children Act (1975) but is now geared to all elementary school students (see De Lucchi & Malone, 2011). Later, the American Chemical Society published *ChemCom: Chemistry in the Community* (1988), which teaches basic ideas of chemistry in the context of issues affecting students' lives and communities.

The reforms of the 1970s were driven almost completely by the social concerns that emerged during that decade, not because of new developments in educational or psychological research. As in the first half of the century, personal and social relevance and attention to student interest were seen by many as the most important determiners of the goals of science education.

Standards-Based Reform

By the early 1980s, following a decade of increased attention to the personal and social relevance of the curriculum, U.S. policy makers were becoming concerned about low and declining test scores in science. This was especially troublesome given that the United States was also lagging economically compared with other countries that were thriving, especially Germany and Japan. Only 25 years earlier, a similar national security crisis had arisen with the launching of *Sputnik* in 1957. Then, as in the 1980s, policy makers were quick to link national security to a perceived lack of rigor in the educational program. In the 1950s, it prompted passage of the National Defense Education Act (1958) less than a year after the *Sputnik* launch, as well as a massive infusion of federal funds into the development of new curriculum materials in science and mathematics. In both the 1950s and 1980s, increased rigor in the education system was seen as the remedy for these national security concerns.

A Nation at Risk

One response to this perceived national security crisis in the 1980s was the establishment of the National Commission on Excellence in Education (NCEE) by the U.S. Department of Education to make a critical assessment of the American educational system. The commission's 1983 report, *A Nation at Risk*, was a call to mobilize the efforts of the federal government, states, and local school districts to raise the level of competence of American students in all academic areas, but especially in science and mathematics. The commission recommended a return to a more traditional academic focus and more disciplined effort on the part of students. In high school, all students would learn the "new basics," including English, mathematics, science, social studies, computer science, and two years of foreign language for college-bound students (NCEE, 1983).

The commission recommended that schools adopt measurable academic standards; that textbooks be upgraded to assure more rigorous content; and that university scientists be called on to help. In science, students should be introduced to "(a) the concepts, laws, and processes of the physical sciences; (b) the methods of scientific inquiry and reasoning; (c) the applications of scientific knowledge to everyday life; and (d) the social and environmental implications of scientific and technological development" (NCEE, 1983, p. 25). Textbooks should be chosen by states and school districts on the basis of their ability to present rigorous and challenging material clearly, and textbook publishers should be required to furnish evaluation data on the material's effectiveness.

The vision was of an academically educated society, a common culture, rigorous academic standards, and accountability through standardized tests of achievement to be administered at major transition points from one level of schooling to the next. Even though the commission recommended that the tests be administered as part of a system of standardized testing that would be national in scope but controlled at the state and local levels, the idea of any kind of public, measurable, standards-based accountability at the national level was new and radical.

The commission's use of the word "standard" to describe benchmarks for judging performance and holding state and local educators publically accountable set the stage for how education would be organized and assessed during the next three decades. Earlier reforms had been primarily about the "what and how" of teaching, that is, the knowledge that was considered most important and the best ways to teach it, not about measuring outcomes. Standards-based reform was different because the precise knowledge statements and their link to assessment offered a way of systematically organizing and keeping track of what gets taught and learned. It is the power of standards to unify the various parts of the educational system around these precise learning expectations that makes standards-based reform unique. In the end, of course, the success of a standards-based approach must also be judged by the content of those standards, how they are organized, and the teaching methods the standards support. Standards are not just a way to organize and manage a system, even though that is a large part of their appeal.

Educating Americans for the 21st Century

Also in 1983, the Commission on Precollege Education in Mathematics, Science and Technology of the National Science Board, the advisory board to the National Science Foundation, issued its report, *Educating Americans for the 21st Century* (National Science Board, 1983). Much as the National Commission on Excellence in Education had done, they argued that the educational system had undergone a period of neglect, resulting in unacceptably low performance levels in science and mathematics, and as the NCEE had done, they too recommended the development of national goals and curricular frameworks, local responsibility for meeting the goals, and a system of objective measurement to monitor progress.

The Commission made it clear that states and local school districts should implement the standards to leave room for variation in curriculum development at the local level. "This should not be construed as a suggestion for the establishment of a national curriculum; rather these are guides that state and local officials might use in developing curricula for local use" (National Science Board, 1983, p. 41). "No one course of study is appropriate for all students and all teachers in all schools in all parts of the country. . . . Various parts of the Nation must develop their total curriculum and revise it repeatedly to keep it suitable for students and teachers" (p. 92).

Science for All Americans

The first substantive response to the call for a comprehensive statement of what everyone should know and be able to do in science came from Project 2061 of the American Association for the Advancement of Science (AAAS). *Science for All Americans* (AAAS, 1990) presented concepts and skills in science, mathematics, technology, and the social sciences that all citizens should know to be able to participate effectively in modern society. In addition to core ideas in these content areas, *Science for All Americans* (SFAA) also made suggestions regarding the nature of science, mathematics, and the designed world; historical perspectives; common themes having to do with systems, models, constancy and change, and issues of scale; as well as scientific habits of mind.

Criteria that were used in selecting content included (1) the utility of the content for employment, personal decision making, and intelligent participation in society, (2) the intrinsic historical or cultural significance of the knowledge, (3) the potential to inform one's thinking about the enduring questions of human meaning, and (4) the value of the content for a child's life at the present time and not just for the future (AAAS, 1990). The content in *Science for All Americans* represented a view from the scientific community about what was important for everyone to know to be considered science literate. The attention to both personal intellectual development and practical knowledge and skills is evident in these statements.

There were also recommendations regarding pedagogy. Influenced by the cognitivist perspective and the results of research on learning, the authors of *Science for All Americans* said that to achieve understanding, "people have to construct their own meaning regardless of how clearly teachers or books tell them things" (AAAS, 1990, p. 198). The student does this by connecting new information to what he or she already knows. The authors argued that knowledge is remembered best if it is connected with other ideas and encountered in a variety of contexts. When new ideas do not fit within a student's existing knowledge framework, restructuring of existing ideas becomes necessary. This is done by providing students with experiences through which they can see how the new information helps them make better sense of the world. Other pedagogical approaches to support conceptual understanding included asking students to apply new ideas in novel situations and having students express ideas publically to obtain feedback from their peers, allowing time to reflect on the feedback they received, and having the chance to make adjustments and try again.

In addition, sound teaching should begin with

> questions and phenomena that are interesting and familiar to students, not with abstractions or phenomena outside their range of perception, understanding, or knowledge. Students need to get acquainted with the things around them—including devices, organisms, materials, shapes, and numbers—and to observe them, collect them, handle them, describe them, become puzzled by them, ask questions about them, argue about them, and then to try to find answers to their questions.
>
> (AAAS, 1990, p. 201)

It was recommended that the content and methods of science be taught together:

> In science, conclusions and the methods that lead to them are tightly coupled. Science teaching that attempts solely to impart to students the accumulated knowledge of a field leads to very little understanding and certainly not to the development of intellectual independence and facility . . .

Science teachers should help students to acquire both scientific knowledge of the world and scientific habits of mind at the same time.

> (AAAS, 1990, pp. 201, 203)

Science for All Americans also recognized that doing science was a social activity that incorporates human values such as curiosity, creativity, imagination, skepticism, and the absence of dogmatism, all of which should be acknowledged as important in the conduct of science and taught as part of the science curriculum. Science teaching should encourage students to raise questions about what is being studied, help them frame their questions clearly enough to begin to look for answers to those questions, and support the creative use of imagination. It should promote the idea that one's evidence, logic, and claims should be questioned and that experiments needed to be subjected to replication. Students should be encouraged to ask: How do we know? What is the evidence? Are there alternative explanations? *Science for All American*s makes clear that science is a way of extending understanding and not a body of unalterable truth. It also suggests that teachers and textbooks should not be viewed primarily as purveyors of truth. Because science ideas are often revised, an open mind is needed when considering scientific claims.

Finally, to appreciate the special modes of thought of science, mathematics, and technology, students should experience the kinds of thinking that characterize those fields: "To understand [science, mathematics, and technology] as ways of thinking and doing, as well as bodies of knowledge, requires that students have some experience with the kinds of thought and action that are typical of those fields" (AAAS, 1990, p. 200).

The National Governors' Conference

Along with this initial effort by Project 2061 to describe in considerable detail what everyone should know in science and suggestions on how it might be effectively taught, the idea of using standards for public accountability also gained momentum on the political front. In September 1989, President George H. W. Bush met with the state governors in Charlottesville, Virginia, to discuss a national agenda for education. At this meeting the president and the governors agreed to establish clear national performance goals and strategies to ensure U.S. international competitiveness as recommended in *A Nation at Risk*. The goals, announced in 1990, included making sure that all students would be able to demonstrate competence in core subjects (U.S. Department of Education, 1991).

It was recommended that content standards in each of five core subject areas and tests to measure achievement of that content would be developed in conjunction with a National Education Goals Panel. The tests would be national but voluntary and tied to national standards. To ensure public accountability, school districts would be required to issue report cards on results to provide clear (and comparable) information on how schools were doing.

The President's proposals called for Congress to authorize the National Assessment of Educational Progress (NAEP) "regularly to collect state-level data in grades four, eight and twelve in all five core subjects, beginning in 1994" (U.S. Department of Education, 1991, p. 4).

Benchmarks for Science Literacy

In 1989, Project 2061 began working with six school districts to develop curriculum models to implement the vision in *Science for All Americans*. At that time a "strand" group began mapping logical progressions of ideas through four grade bands (K–2, 3–5, 6–8, and 9–12), appropriate to the developmental level of the students at each grade band. With President Bush's declaration in his *America 2000* report (U.S. Department of Education, 1991) that standards "will be developed . . . for each of the five core subjects," the focus at Project 2061 shifted from the school-based curriculum models to a transformation of the mapped ideas into "benchmarks" for each grade band. By 1993 that work was complete and in print, and *Benchmarks for Science Literacy* (AAAS, 1993) became the first national content standards document in science (Atkin, Bianchini, & Holthuis, 1997, p. 168).

Then, in 1991, to officially address the specific charge from the National Goals Panel to establish content standards in the academic areas, the U.S. Department of Education and the National Science Foundation funded the National Research Council (NRC) to create national standards in science. In the words of the NRC: "Science education standards provide criteria to judge progress toward a national vision of learning and teaching science" (NRC, 1996, p. 12). In addition to drawing on the content statements in *Science for All Americans* and *Benchmarks for Science Literacy*, the NRC took a strong position with respect to inquiry as pedagogy. In its "Call to Action," the NRC said that the *Standards* "emphasize a new way of teaching and learning about science that reflects how science itself is done, emphasizing inquiry as a way of achieving knowledge and understanding *about* the world" (p. ix).

Reactions to National Standards

In June 1993 the American Educational Research Association (AERA) sponsored an invitational conference to explore the implications of the new standards-based accountability movement. Most of the papers were critical of what was seen as a move toward a national curriculum and toward greater federal control over education. The fear was that aligning national tests (even though voluntary) to national goals would lead to a national curriculum (Zumwalt, 1995). Although some felt there were likely to be advantages to having a national curriculum, there were many concerns that such centralization would take control away from local communities, which, it was argued, had the best insights into what was important for their own students to know. There were also concerns that common goals and accountability through testing would lead to a narrowing of the curriculum, a deskilling of teachers, a focus on external academic knowledge, and a move toward a more teacher-directed instructional style with little opportunity for student exploration or discovery (Kellaghan & Madaus, 1995; McNeil, 1995).

But in spite of these reservations by educators, in 1994 President Clinton signed the Improving America's Schools Act (IASA), which required states to develop challenging content standards for what students should know in mathematics and language arts. States were required to use performance standards to establish a benchmark for improvement referred to as "adequate yearly progress" (AYP). All schools were required to show continuous progress or face possible consequences, such as having to offer supplemental services or school choice options to students. The act made standards-based accountability the law of the land.

The IASA played a very significant role in how the standards movement developed because it moved the emphasis legislatively away from national standards and voluntary national testing to a state-by-state system of standards setting and accountability. It also provided the basis for the No Child Left Behind Act of 2001.

No Child Left Behind

Consistent with a move toward state-level standard setting and accountability through testing, on January 8, 2002, President George W. Bush signed into law the No Child Left Behind Act of 2001 (NCLB), a bill to again extend and revise the Elementary and Secondary Education Act of 1965. The changes in this legislation over the 1994 IASA reauthorization are significant because the new law emphasized even greater public accountability, with funding tied directly to meeting expectations.

NCLB required states to build assessment systems to track the achievement of students in their state against a common set of state-derived standards. By the 2005 to 2006 school year, states were required to test students annually in reading and mathematics between Grades 3 and 8 using statewide tests and to test students at least once during grades 10 through 12; by the 2007 to 2008 school year, students also had to be tested in science at three grade levels. Every 2 years, states were required to administer the mathematics and reading tests of the National Assessment of Educational Progress (NAEP) to a sample of students in Grades 4 and 8. This allowed states to check the rigor of their own tests and to make comparisons across states. The law also required schools, school districts, and states to disaggregate the average test score results for major racial and ethnic groups, income groups, students with disabilities, and students with limited English proficiency.

Commission on Mathematics and Science Education

During the first decade of the 21st century, the idea of using content standards to define what all students should know in science and to organize curriculum and assessment around those statements became a widely accepted approach to improving science education. There was even growing interest in revisiting the idea of common standards across states. In 2007, a Commission on Mathematics and Science Education was established by the Carnegie Corporation of New York and the Institute for Advanced Study and charged with "assessing the current state of math and science in the United States and developing actionable recommendations for the country to fully prepare American students in mathematics and science so that every student has the opportunity for a productive adult life in our rapidly changing world" (Carnegie Corporation of New York and the Institute for Advanced Study, 2009, p. iv). In its 2009 report, *The Opportunity Equation: Transforming Mathematics and Science Education for Citizenship and the Global Economy*, the commission took the position that there should be common standards that states could choose to adopt as their own, along with common assessments, so that educational efforts across the country could be concentrated on the development of instructional strategies, curriculum materials, and teacher education programs that are focused on the core ideas that all students should know. According to the commission, compared to existing state standards, these standards should be fewer in number, more clearly related to what students needed to know to succeed in college and the world of work, and aim higher in terms of intellectual challenge (Carnegie Corporation of New York and the Institute for Advanced Study, 2009).

Common Standards for K–12 Education

In 2008, the National Research Council of the National Academies issued a report, *Common Standards for K–12 Education*, which summarized the findings of two workshops, one on the current state of standards-based reform efforts at the state level and the second on possibilities for establishing common standards across the states. The report acknowledged that standards-based reform had become "the central framework guiding state education policy and practice" (p. 7). But the report also concluded that the vision of standards-based reform had not yet been met. The vision was that the entire system of curriculum, instruction, teacher preparation, professional development, and assessment would be aligned to the content standards, which in turn would produce coherence in the educational system and concentrate efforts on the goals for teaching and learning that were elaborated in those standards (see, for example, *Blueprints for Reform*, AAAS, 1998, for a discussion of how reform of various parts of the educational enterprise might be organized around content standards). One reason for this lack of success, according to the NRC report, is that for teachers and administrators to be asked to use a standards-based accountability model to improve instruction, they would also need the time and expertise to analyze and use the data that are generated, and as is well known, that time is often not available. Also, if education reform is going to be built around a set of state-level content standards, all

of those state standards would need to clearly and consistently reflect what is considered most important for all students to know. But this has not been the case. Instead, according to the NRC report, there is considerable variation from state to state, and state standards as they are written do not always adequately reflect the complexity of knowledge and how knowledge progresses, so that what is identified as important to know and what is tested are often discrete skills and factual knowledge rather than complex ideas (NRC, 2008, p. 32–33).

A Framework for K–12 Science Education

Following the recommendation of the Carnegie Commission on Mathematics and Science Education that common standards be created, a Committee on a Conceptual Framework for New K–12 Science Education Standards was formed at the National Research Council and charged with developing "a framework that articulates a broad set of expectations for students in science" (p. 1). In their report, published in 2012, it was argued, first, that a new framework was needed in science education because "new understandings in both science and in teaching and learning science have developed since the last comparable effort at the national scale" (NRC, 2012, p. 8) and, second, the movement toward common standards in mathematics and language arts provides an opportunity to do something comparable in science.

The stated goal of the new framework was

> to ensure that by the end of 12th grade, all students have some appreciation of the beauty and wonder of science; possess sufficient knowledge of science and engineering to engage in public discussions on related issues; are careful consumers of scientific and technological information related to their everyday lives; are able to continue to learn about science outside school; and have the skills to enter careers of their choice, including (but not limited to) careers in science, engineering, and technology.
> (NRC, 2012, p. 1)

The committee argued that because of a lack of coherence across the grades, because of a focus on breadth over depth, and a failure to "provide students with engaging opportunities to experience how science is actually done," these goals are not currently being met (NRC, 2012, p. 1).

The goal of the NRC's framework was to move science education toward a more coherent vision of science teaching and learning in three ways: (1) The first was to select and organize science content around learning progressions, that is, increasingly more sophisticated treatments of core ideas beginning in elementary school and running through the high school years. (2) The second was to focus on a smaller number of core ideas to encourage deeper coverage of the ideas that are taught. In the words of the committee: "Reductions of the sheer sum of details to be mastered is intended to give time for students to engage in scientific investigations and argumentation and to achieve depth of understanding of the core ideas presented" (NRC, 2012, p. 11). (3) The third way the framework attempted to achieve greater coherence was to emphasize that science content knowledge and the practices needed to engage in scientific inquiry and engineering design should be integrated when designing learning experiences (NRC, 2012).

This NRC framework served to guide the development of the Next Generation Science Standards (NGSS) by Achieve, Inc. (NGSS Lead States, 2013). NGSS is uniquely organized around learning performance statements that combine science content knowledge, common themes, and science practices. The expectation of NGSS is that if assessments can be developed that require students to demonstrate their disciplinary knowledge, knowledge of cross-cutting content, and the ability to engage in science practices at the same time, this will move the educational system toward a more integrated and coherent approach to teaching and learning in science.

Impact of Standards on Curriculum Development

It has been more than 20 years since *Benchmarks for Science Literacy* (AAAS, 1993) was published and somewhat less than that for most of the state standards documents in science. It is important to point out that as with earlier reform efforts, standards-based reform did not have a basis in empirical research. Specification of outcomes and the focus on public accountability was based on a theory of action, but as applied to the educational system, it had not been previously explored empirically. (For additional discussion of the history of the standards movement and its potential for impact on the educational system, see DeBoer, 2006; Weiss, 2006.)

One thing we do know is that it has been difficult for national publishers to target their materials to standards because of the variety of standards and range of topics across states. If anything, the proliferation of state standards has led commercial publishers to include even more content in textbooks so that multiple states can be accommodated without targeting a separate version of the textbook to each state. Besides the materials that are developed by commercial publishers, NSF has also funded the development of materials aligned with national standards, but there has generally been a rather loose interpretation of what "aligned" means, so that there has been very little tightening of the scope of topics across those materials either.

Nor has there been a clearly identifiable approach to curriculum writing during the past 20 years. Unlike the Progressive-Era texts, which emphasized practical applications, or the reform textbooks of the 1950s and 1960s, which emphasized the structure of the disciplines and scientific inquiry, the current standards-era texts take many different approaches. Some curriculum developers have blamed federal education legislation (NCLB) for the lack of concerted efforts in science curriculum development

because the legislation shifted attention away from science and toward math and English language arts, especially at the elementary level (De Lucci & Malone, 2011). At all levels, teachers are wary of trying new approaches if they don't have compelling evidence that those approaches will improve their students' scores on standardized tests.

A study conducted by AAAS Project 2061 on nine complete middle school science programs (each program encompassing physical, life, and earth science materials spanning several grades) found that none of the major textbooks presented science in a way that could be expected to lead to understanding on the part of students. They concluded:

> Programs only rarely provided students with a sense of purpose for the units of study, took account of student beliefs that interfere with learning, engaged students with relevant phenomena to make abstract scientific ideas plausible, modeled the use of scientific knowledge so that students could apply what they learned in everyday situations, or scaffolded student efforts to make meaning of key phenomena and ideas presented in the programs.
> (Kesidou & Roseman, 2002, p. 522)

They also found that "none of the major textbook publishers provided a coherent approach to content" (Kali, Koppal, Linn, & Roseman, 2008).

Between 2000 and 2002, Horizon Research, Inc. conducted a study to find out what science instruction looks like in the nation's classrooms. With respect to alignment with content standards, they found that 60% of the lessons they observed focused on science content found in the national standards and that the content was taught at the appropriate grade level. But they also found that "almost two-thirds of K–12 science lessons are low in quality, falling short in key areas such as intellectual engagement, sense-making, teacher questioning, and classroom culture" (Banilower, Smith, Weiss, & Pasley, 2006, p. 117). Moreover, they found no relationship between lesson quality and alignment of the content to national standards. The lessons that were aligned to the standards were no more likely to receive high ratings on their teaching-for-understanding framework than lessons that were not aligned to standards.

One science curriculum development project of the past decade that was directly influenced by the standards movement is a comprehensive middle school project led by researchers at the University of Michigan and Northwestern University, and funded by NSF. The project is Investigating and Questioning Our World Through Science and Technology (IQWST). IQWST is aligned to national standards, focuses on big ideas in science, and teaches the practices of scientific inquiry along with science content. IQWST materials employ research-based practices that have been shown to promote students' science learning (Krajcik, McNeill, & Reiser, 2007). Students have experience "working with models, constructing scientific explanations, engaging in argumentation and debate, analyzing data gathered either from students' own investigations or captured within complex datasets, and presenting ideas to peers" (www.umich.edu/~hiceweb/iqwst/). Additional information about the project can be found on the IQWST website.

In spite of generally pessimistic findings about the effects of standards-based reform on curriculum development, programs such as IQWST do provide hopeful signs that standards-based reform could have the positive effects that were anticipated. But, in general, when we look at the larger picture of curriculum development in the United States, it is difficult to see that the standards-era reforms have had the effect that was initially intended.

New Directions in Curriculum Development

As we have seen, most reforms in science education have been driven by societal concerns and shifts in how the social and personal relevance of the curriculum are viewed compared to the disciplinary structure and intellectual rigor of the curriculum. Historically, empirical research has played a relatively small part in these reform efforts. Curriculum materials were typically written with a particular educational philosophy, goal, or purpose in mind and then revised after a period of use based on feedback from teachers in the field. In an excellent review published in the *Review of Educational Psychology,* Linn, Songer, and Eylon (1996) describe three periods in the history of science education based on the degree of interaction between groups concerned with science education—including scientists, science teachers, education researchers, and psychologists. According to the authors, it was not until after 1975, during what they call the partnership period, that collaboration among experts from these several perspectives began to take place (p. 445). Since then, and especially during the past two decades, there has been a significant increase in collaborative curriculum research.

Most curriculum materials, however, still are not what most educational researchers would call research based. Currently, the majority of science textbooks in the United States are produced by a small number of commercial publishers, which are generally considered to be market driven rather than research based. In their 2013 national study of science and mathematics classrooms, Horizon Research, Inc. (HRI) found that 78% of elementary school, 89% of middle school, and 83% of high school science texts are published by three major commercial textbook publishers. An additional 11% of the elementary school science texts are published by a fourth publisher, the publisher of the FOSS materials (Banilower, et al., 2013, p. 93). In contrast, NSF–funded materials, which tend to be more research based, are used in only 10% of elementary classrooms, 6% of middle school classrooms, and 3% of high school classrooms (p. 95). Research based or not, HRI also found that teachers generally give textbooks high marks, with 71% of elementary school teachers, 76% of middle school teachers, and 76% of high school teachers rating their science textbooks as "good," "very good," or "excellent" (p. 96).

In spite of these generally high ratings given by teachers, many curriculum researchers see room for improvement, and NSF and the U.S. Department of Education through its Institute of Education Sciences (IES) continue to fund research-based curriculum development efforts. In the final section of this chapter, I touch briefly on seven promising ideas that could lead to the further improvement of science curriculum materials. As you will see, some of these ideas have been around for a long time, and some are relatively new, but all of them offer productive areas of research that can contribute to the improvement of the science curriculum and the teaching and learning of science for all. Throughout this discussion, I make the assumption that science education will continue to operate in a standards-based environment for some time to come.

Seven promising areas for curriculum research:

1. The Content of the Curriculum
2. The Organization of Knowledge: Learning Progressions
3. Conceptual Change
4. Situated Learning
5. Metacognition
6. Affective Responses
7. Cognitive Tools and Learning Technologies

The Content of the Curriculum

Most of the work of curriculum researchers over the past several decades has focused on *how* people learn, but, as Seymour Papert has said, "I anticipate a widening of focus from how people learn to include more study of what they learn" (Papert, 2006). Therefore, a productive area of research will be to identify and apply clear criteria that can be used for selecting content. A start was made in the NRC *Framework for K–12 Science Education* by identifying ideas that are generative, that is, ideas that can be presented in a progressively more sophisticated way from elementary school through high school. We might also systematically investigate how particular science ideas can help students understand everyday phenomena and events that are reported in the popular media, which may then stimulate a lifelong desire to learn.

One particular issue that needs to be addressed with respect to the content of the curriculum is the issue of specification. In the recent calls for new standards, it was suggested that we need "fewer" standards, as well as standards that are clearer and higher (Carnegie Corporation of New York and the Institute for Advanced Study, 2009). This is not a new suggestion; in fact we can find references to trimming material from the curriculum throughout the 20th century. The suggestion has typically been to teach "big ideas" rather than disconnected facts and principles of science. What is not addressed is that the big ideas then need to be unpacked into a network of sub ideas for them to provide useful guidance for curriculum development. What are the mental models we expect students to have and how extensive should those mental models be? Which big ideas require including the mechanisms of action that explain relevant phenomena? How much detail is needed when describing those mechanisms? Which ideas need a mathematical treatment for them to be well understood? Topical themes by themselves do not reveal the level of complexity needed for students to make sense of those themes. Clarification and elaboration of the big ideas is an area of research that is needed and would be of great benefit to curriculum developers.

To make progress in this area, it is important that researchers from the philosophical and cultural traditions contribute to these discussions about what the content of the curriculum should be. In a number of European countries, the goal of education has traditionally been the intellectual growth and cultivation of the individual in society, or what is referred to as *Bildung* (Bruford, 1975). *Bildung* involves the lifelong shaping of an individual's full humanity through identification with the culture, including the ability for self-reflection and critique of the status quo. According to Duschl and colleagues (2011), curriculum developers in this tradition "eschew psychological tenets of learning in favour of disciplinary epistemological and philosophical structures that initiate and offer learners a framework for formative development" (p. 1). It will be productive to pay attention to ideas from this tradition as well. The new *International Handbook of Research in History, Philosophy and Science Teaching* is an excellent source of ideas about specific aspects of scientific knowledge that deserve attention (Matthews, in press).

The Organization of Knowledge: Learning Progressions

Science educators have always been interested in how science content is organized and sequenced for students. Typically, this has been done by selecting topic categories from the disciplinary fields and sequencing them in a logical order. The conceptual sophistication of the presentation has followed basic understandings about human development, usually beginning with concrete observable objects and events close to the learner's experience and delaying the more abstract ideas until adolescence. During the 1960s-era reforms, efforts were made to organize content more thematically so that the number of concepts could be reduced. The idea of a "spiral curriculum," in which topics were introduced and then revisited at a higher level of sophistication throughout a student's schooling, was proposed by Bruner in *The Process of Education* (1960). The first standards documents—*Benchmarks for Science Literacy* (AAAS, 1993) and the *National Science Education Standards* (NRC, 1996)—identified with even greater precision the specific science ideas that were appropriate to each grade band and that could be developed across grade bands. AAAS Project 2061 then published two volumes of the *Atlas of Science Literacy* (AAAS, 2001/2007), which were visual displays of the vertical connections (from grade band to grade band) as well as horizontal links

between the specific ideas listed in *Benchmarks*. The mapping was based on the logical development of ideas (e.g., learn that molecules are made of atoms before learning about the internal structure of atoms and how that structure affects how atoms interact with each other to form molecules), the age appropriateness of each idea, and the published research on how students learn—both in general and with respect to specific topics.

Recently, efforts have been focused on building on that initial work through empirical research to identify "learning progressions" (Duschl, Maeng, & Sezen, 2011), what Project 2061 had called "progressions of student understanding" (AAAS, 1996, p. 305). These learning progressions are model pathways of learning that are developmentally appropriate and typically defined by a lower and an upper anchor to represent the starting and expected end points of understanding in a particular area, along with intermediate stepping stones to be targeted along the way. Learning progressions are intended to represent a progressively more sophisticated understanding of disciplinary content knowledge along with more sophisticated ways of thinking about, representing, and using that knowledge.

The reason for selecting and organizing curriculum materials and instruction around learning progressions is to break out of the pervasive mode of instruction that presents science as unconnected units of instruction (Duschl, et al., 2011) or even worse, "as a disconnected series of decontextualized facts" (Sawyer, 2006a, p. 578) and, instead to present science as a coherent, integrated whole (see Roseman, Linn, & Koppal, 2008, for a discussion of curricular coherence). The challenge for researchers who work in this area is, first, to identify topics that are "generative," that is, that lend themselves to a progressively more sophisticated treatment throughout the school years, and, second, to demonstrate empirically that a particular ordering of ideas is in fact effective in providing students with a coherent understanding of science.

Conceptual Change

Today, more than ever before, science educators recognize that students come to the classroom with existing ideas, some that are correct, others that are incorrect, and still others that are partially correct but incomplete. Sometimes students have parts of a correct interpretation of the world in place with only a few incorrect or missing pieces; other times they have fully formed ideas about the world that are inconsistent with the way the science community understands the world. Sometimes the incorrect or partially formed ideas make useful stepping stones to more sophisticated thinking, and sometimes they do not, but what is most important is that regardless of the ideas students have—correct, incorrect, or partially formed— the ideas they have must be the beginning of new learning. This has led to calls by researchers to embed findings from misconception research into textbooks, and at least some textbook writers are now paying attention to that advice. What makes this a particularly productive aspect of student thinking for curriculum developers to pay attention to is that even just knowing what misconceptions students might have is apparently useful to teachers. As diSessa says, "The very general constructivist heuristic of paying attention to naïve ideas seems powerful, independent of the details of conceptual change theory. Interventions that merely teach teachers about naïve ideas have been surprisingly successful" (diSessa, 2006, p. 276). Research on student misconceptions is ongoing and continues to be a productive source of insights into student thinking and understanding (see, for example, DeBoer, Herrmann-Abell, et al., 2008; DeBoer, Lee, & Husic, 2008; Herrmann-Abell & DeBoer, 2011).

Situated Learning

Efforts to motivate students by giving them useful tasks to perform, by making what they learn relevant in their everyday lives, and giving them problems to solve that allow them to apply their knowledge are not new. This was a particularly important feature of science education during most of the first half of the 20th century. Many Progressive-Era educators advocated the use of meaningful projects in the classroom as a way to motivate students. Today, the use of genuine problems that are similar to those that scientists might solve or that reflect the nature of tasks that might be conducted in the real world is referred to as situated learning (Greeno, 2006).

Project-based learning is one form of situated learning (Krajcik & Blumenfeld, 2006), and design-based learning is another (Kolodner et al., 2003). According to Krajcik and Blumenfeld (2006), "In project-based learning, students engage in real, meaningful problems that are important to them and that are similar to what scientists, mathematicians, writers, and historians do" (p. 318). In design-based learning,

> students learn by attempting to achieve design challenges. For example, students have designed miniature vehicles and their propulsion systems to learn about forces, motion, and Newton's laws, and they have designed ways to manage the erosion on barrier islands to learn about erosion, water currents, and the relationship between people and the environment.
>
> (Kolodner, 2006, pp. 228–229)

The main idea behind situated learning is that students are more likely to engage in learning tasks when they can create their own designs, when they attempt to answer questions that are important to them, and when there is a tangible product that is the outcome of their efforts. The research challenge is to identify projects and designs that both interest students and provide contexts for science learning.

Metacognition

Researchers are now finding that learning is more effective when learners verbalize their developing knowledge

(NRC, 2000). According to Sawyer, "In many cases, learners don't actually learn something until they start to articulate it—in other words, while thinking out loud, they learn more rapidly and deeply than studying quietly" (Sawyer, 2006b, p. 12). This has led curriculum developers to embed activities in their materials to provide opportunities for students to express their ideas in the classroom. Metacognition also has a self-monitoring aspect in which students are asked to reflect on what they are learning and what they know now that they didn't know before they started the lesson or unit. Two NRC publications, *Taking Science to School* (NRC, 2007) and *How People Learn* (NRC, 2000), include discussions of ongoing research in the area of metacognition.

Affective Responses

We usually don't pay much attention to affective responses in education, although we know they can be very important determinants of student learning. As Bransford and colleagues (2006) point out:

> Though informational resources are important in any learning ecology, affective and motivational resources are also important because they may mediate effort, attention, and a desire to engage in learning. We need a better understanding of the intertwining of affective, relational, and communicative aspects of learning interaction. How do emotional responses mediate learning, and how do they emerge from learning?
>
> (p. 29)

Schwab (1954) used the Freudian concept of *Eros*—the psychic energy that motivates humans to create and be productive—to describe the source of affective responses in students. *Eros* is the energy that "drives students' desire to learn what is placed in front of them and supplies them with a love of knowledge that makes them want to learn throughout their lifetime" (see DeBoer, in press). Schwab believed that *Eros* could be nurtured in an educational setting through classroom discussion. To him, discussion was the embodiment of the intellectual skills that define a liberal education and a way to draw upon interpersonal relationships between student and teacher that are characterized by liking and respect. For both student and teacher, the liking and respect come from shared participation in a problem of genuine interest. When done well, classroom discussion stimulates a love of learning that can last a lifetime. The research question to ask is what conditions lead to the generation of such a desire to learn, both for now and for a lifetime.

Cognitive Tools and Learning Technologies

Finally, increased computing power is now bringing the promise of information technologies closer to realization. Handheld devices are proliferating at a rapid rate, and more and more science content is being made available online. There is growing interest on the part of the research community in using these technologies to study student learning and to help students learn. The *International Journal of Computer Supported Collaborative Learning*, for example, publishes research on the nature, theory, and practice of computer-supported learning.

Learning technologies are powerful aids to instruction because they can be used to enable students to access data on the World Wide Web, employ graphing and visualization tools to observe and investigate patterns in data, expand collaboration with others by way of electronic networks, and produce multimedia artifacts (Krajcik, Slotta, McNeill, & Reiser, 2008).

Commitments to use technology to improve science education are evident in a number of curriculum development efforts, including those at the Technology Enhanced Learning in Science Center (TELS) at the University of California at Berkeley and the SimScientists program at WestEd. TELS uses WISE (the Web-based Inquiry Science Environment) as their platform for designing online activities (Slotta & Linn, 2009). WISE provides "cognitive hints, embedded reflection notes and assessments, and online discussions, as well as software tools for activities such as drawing, concept mapping, diagramming, and graphing" (http://telscenter.org/technology/wise). SimScientists is a suite of research and development projects that focuses on the roles that simulations can play in instruction and assessment. The goals of the program are "to bring together the latest research findings and best practices from model-based reasoning, cognition and learning, e-learning design, intelligent tutoring and educational measurement to design and test innovative ways of supporting student learning and instructional practice in middle school science" (http://simscientists.org/about/index.php). These examples represent just some of the ways that learning technologies are having an impact on the design and delivery of science instruction.

Summary

From this overview of the history of science curriculum development in the United States and some promising ideas for going forward, a number of themes emerge. First, historically there has been a strong commitment to teaching and learning the content of science, even when other values such as social relevance compete. That has always been the case for college-bound students and, more often than not, for all students, college bound or not. There has also been a strong commitment to teaching the nature of science and the logic of scientific reasoning even though its form and justification have changed from time to time. All these goals are played out in the context of preparing students for productive engagement in life in a democratic society. This constancy of fundamental values has enabled educators to stay focused on a common core of educational goals and to explore ways to improve the education in science for all students.

We have also been fortunate to have a broad base of well-intentioned scientists, curriculum researchers, educational theorists, and policy makers who have sought ways to link an appreciation for the content and methods of science to the present and future lives of students. The details of what educators have valued and the pedagogical tools that have been available to them have shifted over time, but most curriculum materials have been written with a clear sense of purpose and strategy for accomplishing that purpose consistent with our core values.

We have also been fortunate to have forceful critics of the goals of the science curriculum in general and of textbooks in particular. There have been and continue to be multiple perspectives on the details of what and how to teach, which keeps discourse lively and motivates new theories and arguments about the curriculum. The challenge for all of us is to continue to think about how the curriculum can be used to improve the teaching and learning in science for all.

Note

1. In his discussion of cycles of history, Arthur Schlesinger, Jr. (1986) argues that after prolonged periods of social activism, societies typically tire of it and retreat to a focus on individual well-being, which after a time leads back again to a period of renewed social activism.

References

American Association for the Advancement of Science (AAAS). (1967). *Science—A process approach.* New York, NY: Xerox Division, Ginn & Company.

American Association for the Advancement of Science (AAAS). (1990). *Science for all Americans.* New York, NY: Oxford University Press. (Published in 1989 by AAAS)

American Association for the Advancement of Science (AAAS). (1993). *Benchmarks for science literacy.* New York, NY: Oxford University Press.

American Association for the Advancement of Science (AAAS). (1998). *Blueprints for reform.* New York, NY: Oxford University Press.

American Association for the Advancement of Science (AAAS). (2001/2007). *Atlas of science literacy.* Washington, DC: Author.

American Chemical Society. (1988). *ChemCom: Chemistry in the community.* Dubuque, IA: Kendall Hunt.

Atkin, J. M., Bianchini, J., & Holthuis, N. (1997). The different worlds of Project 2061. In S. Raizen & E. Britton (Eds.), *Bold ventures: Volume 2. Case studies of innovation in science education* (pp. 131–245). Dordrecht, the Netherlands: Kluwer.

Atkin, J. M., & Black, P. (2007). History of science curriculum reform in the United States and the United Kingdom. In S. K. Abell & N. G. Lederman (Eds.), *Handbook of research in science education* (pp. 781–806). Mahwah, NJ: Lawrence Erlbaum.

Banilower, E. R., Smith, P. S., Weiss, I. R., Malzahn, K. A., Campbell, K. M., & Weis, A. M. (2013). Report of the 2012 national survey of science and mathematics education. Chapel Hill, NC: Horizon Research, Inc.

Banilower, E. R., Smith, P. S., Weiss, I. R., & Pasley, J. D. (2006). The status of K-12 science teaching in the United States: Results from a national observation study. In D. W. Sunal & E. L. Wright (Eds.), *The impact of state and national standards on K-12 science teaching* (pp. 83–112). Greenwich, CT: IAP.

Bestor, A. (1953). *Educational wastelands: The retreat from learning in our schools.* Urbana, IL: University of Illinois Press.

Biological Sciences Curriculum Study. (1963a). *Biological science: An inquiry into life* (BSCS Yellow Version). New York, NY: Harcourt, Brace & World.

Biological Sciences Curriculum Study. (1963b). *Biological science: Molecules to man* (BSCS Blue Version). Boston, MA: Houghton Mifflin.

Biological Sciences Curriculum Study. (1963c). *High school biology* (BSCS Green Version). Chicago, IL: Rand McNally.

Bradbury, R.H. (1915). Recent tendencies in high school chemistry. *School Science and Mathematics, 15,* 782–793.

Bradbury, R.H. (1922). *A first book in chemistry.* New York, NY: Appleton.

Bransford, J.D., Barron, B., Pea, R.D., Meltzoff, A., Kuhl, P., Bell, P., Stevens, R., Schwartz, D.L., Vye, N., Reeves, B., Roschelle, J., & Sabelli, N. (2006). Foundations and opportunities for an interdisciplinary science of learning. In R.K. Sawyer (Ed.), *The Cambridge handbook of the learning sciences* (pp. 19–34). New York, NY: Cambridge University Press.

Bruford, W.H. (1975). *The German tradition of self-cultivation: Bildung from Humboldt to Thomas Mann.* London: Cambridge University Press.

Bruner, J. (1960). *The process of education.* New York, NY: Vintage.

Bruner, J., Goodnow, J., & Austin, G. (1956). *A study of thinking.* New York, NY: Wiley.

Bybee, R. (1979). Science education and the emerging ecological society. *Science Education, 63,* 95–109.

Caldwell, O. (1909). An investigation of the teaching of biological subjects in secondary schools. *School Science and Mathematics, 9,* 581–597.

Carnegie Corporation of New York and the Institute for Advanced Study. (2009). *The opportunity equation: Transforming mathematics and science education for citizenship and the global economy.* A report of the Commission on Mathematics and Science Education. New York, NY: Author.

Chemical Bond Approach. (1962). *Chemical systems.* St. Louis: McGraw Hill.

Chemical Education Material Study. (1963). *Chemistry: An experimental science.* San Francisco, CA: Freeman.

Coulter, J. (1915). The mission of science in education. *School Science and Mathematics, 15,* 93–100.

DeBoer, G. (1991). *A history of ideas in science education: Implications for practice.* New York: Columbia University Teachers College Press.

DeBoer, G. (2000). Scientific literacy: Another look at its historical and contemporary meanings and its relationship to science education reform. *Journal of Research in Science Teaching, 37*(6), 582–601.

DeBoer, G. (2006). History of the science standards movement in the United States. In D.W. Sunal & E.L. Wright (Eds.), *The impact of state and national standards on K–12 science teaching* (pp. 7–49). Charlotte, NC: Information Age Publishing.

DeBoer, G. (in press). Joseph Schwab: His work and his legacy, a biographical essay. In M.R. Matthews (Ed.), *International handbook of research in history, philosophy and science teaching.* New York, NY: Springer.

DeBoer, G. E., Herrmann-Abell, C. F., Gogos, A., Michiels, A., Regan, T. & Wilson, P. (2008). Assessment linked to science learning goals: Probing student thinking through assessment. In J. Coffey, R. Douglas, & C. Stearns (Eds.). *Assessing student learning: Perspectives from research and practice* (pp. 231–252). Arlington, VA: NSTA Press.

DeBoer, G. E., Lee, H. S. & Husic, F. (2008). Assessing integrated understanding of science. In Y. Kali, M. C. Linn, & J. E. Roseman (Eds.). *Coherent science education: Implications for curriculum, instruction, and policy* (pp.153–182). New York, NY: Columbia University Teachers College Press.

De Lucchi, L., & Malone, L. (2011). The effect of educational policy on curriculum development. In G.E. DeBoer (Ed.), *The role of public policy in K–12 science education* (pp. 355–394). Charlotte, NC: Information Age Publishing.

Dewey, J. (1900/1990). *The school and society.* Chicago, IL: University of Chicago Press. (Originally published in 1900)

diSessa, A. (2006). A history of conceptual change research: Threads and fault lines. In R.K. Sawyer (Ed.), *The Cambridge handbook of the learning sciences* (pp. 265–281). New York, NY: Cambridge University Press.

Downing, E. (1915). Some data regarding the teaching of zoology in secondary schools. *School Science and Mathematics, 15,* 36–43.

Duane, J.E. (1973). *Individualized instruction: Programs and materials.* Englewood, NJ: Educational Technology Publications.

Duschl, R.A., Maeng, S., & Sezen, A. (2011). Learning progressions and teaching sequences: A review and analysis. *Studies in Science Education, 47*(2) 123–182.

Elementary and Secondary Education Act of 1965, 20 U.S.C. § 6301 *et. seq.* (1965).

Educational Development Center. (1969). *Elementary science study.* Manchester, MO: Webster Division, McGraw-Hill.

Goals 2000: Educate America Act, 20 U.S.C. § 5801 *et. seq.* (1994).

Greeno, J.G. (2006). Learning in activity. In R.K. Sawyer (Ed.), *The Cambridge handbook of the learning sciences* (pp. 79–96). New York, NY: Cambridge University Press.

Hall, E.H. (1894). *Elementary lessons in physics: Mechanics (including hydrostatics) and light.* New York, NY: Henry Holt. Available at http://archive.org/stream/elementarylesson00halliala#page/n3/mode/2up

Herrmann Abell, C.F. & DeBoer, G.E. (2011). Using distractor-driven standards-based multiple-choice assessments and Rasch modeling to investigate hierarchies of chemistry misconceptions and detect structural problems with individual items. *Chemical Education Research and Practice, 12,* 184–192.

Holton, G. (2003). The Project Physics course, then and now. *Science and Education, 12,* 779–786.

Hunter, G. (1910). The methods, content and purpose of biologic science in the secondary schools of the U.S. *School Science and Mathematics, 10,* 1–10, 103–111.

Hurd, P. (1970). *New directions in teaching secondary school science.* Chicago, IL: Rand McNally.

Huxley, T. (1899). *Science and education.* New York, NY: Appleton.

Improving America's Schools Act of 1994, 20 U.S.C. § 8001 *et. seq.* (1994).

Kali, Y., Koppal, M., Linn, M.C., & Roseman, J.E. (2008). In Y. Kali, M.C. Linn, & J.E. Roseman (Eds.), *Designing coherent science education: Implications for curriculum, instruction, and policy* (pp. xvi). New York, NY: Teachers College Press.

Kellaghan, T., & Madaus, G. (1995). National curricula in European countries. In L. McNeil (Ed.), *The hidden consequences of a national curriculum* (pp. 79–118). Washington, DC: American Educational Research Association.

Kesidou, S., & Roseman, J.E. (2002). How well do middle school science programs measure up? Findings from Project 2061's curriculum review study. *Journal of Research in Science Teaching, 39*(6) 522–549.

Kolodner, J.L. (2006). Case-based reasoning. In R.K. Sawyer (Ed.), *The Cambridge handbook of the learning sciences* (pp. 225–242). New York, NY: Cambridge University Press.

Kolodner, J.L., Camp, P.J., Crismond, D., Fasse, B., Gray, J., Holbrook, J., Puntambekar, S., & Ryan, M. (2003). Problem-based learning meets case-based reasoning in the middle-school classroom: Putting learning by design into practice. *Journal of the Learning Sciences, 12*(4), 495–547.

Krajcik, J.S., & Blumenfeld, P.C. (2006). Project-based learning. In R.K. Sawyer (Ed.), *The Cambridge handbook of the learning sciences* (pp. 317–333). New York: Cambridge University Press.

Krajcik, J.S., McNeill, K.L., & Reiser, B.J. (2007). Learning-goals-driven design model: Developing curriculum materials that align with national standards and incorporate project-based pedagogy. *Science Education, 92*(1), 1–32.

Krajcik, J.S., Slotta, J.D., McNeill, K.L., & Reiser, B.J. (2008). Designing learning environments to support students' integrated understanding. In Y. Kali, M.C. Linn, & J.E. Roseman (Eds.), *Designing coherent science education* (pp. 39–64). New York, NY: Teachers College Press.

James, W. (1899). *Talks to teachers on psychology: And to students on some of life's ideals.* New York, NY: Henry Holt. Available at www.gutenberg.org/files/16287/16287-h/16287-h.htm

Linn, M.C., Songer, N.B., & Eylon, B.-S. (1996). In R. Calfee & D. Berliner (Eds.), *Handbook of educational psychology* (pp. 438–490). New York, NY: Macmillan.

Matthews, M.R. (in press). *International handbook of research in history, philosophy and science teaching.* New York, NY: Springer.

McNeil, L. (1995). Local reform initiatives and a national curriculum: Where are the children? In L. McNeil (Ed.), *The hidden consequences of a national curriculum* (pp. 13–46). Washington, DC: American Educational Research Association.

Merrill, R., & Ridgway, D. (1969). *The CHEM study story.* San Francisco, CA: Freeman.

Millikan, R.A., & Gale, H.G. (1941). *New elementary physics.* Boston, MA: Ginn.

Moon, T.J. (1921). *Biology for beginners.* New York, NY: Henry Holt. Available at https://archive.org/details/biologyforbegin00moongoog

Moon, T.J., & Brezinski, B. (1974). Environmental education from a historical perspective. *School Science and Mathematics, 74,* 371–374.

Moon, T.J., Mann, P.B., & Otto, J.H. (1956). *Modern biology.* New York, NY: Holt.

National Commission on Excellence in Education (NCEE). (1983). *A nation at risk: The imperative for educational reform.* Washington, DC: U.S. Department of Education.

National Defense Education Act of 1958. 1 U.S.C. § 101, 72 Stat. 1581 (1958).

National Education Association (NEA). (1893). *Report of the committee on secondary school studies.* Washington, DC: U.S. Government Printing Office.

National Education Association (NEA). (1918). *Cardinal principles of secondary education: A report of the commission on the reorganization of secondary education* (U.S. Bureau of Education, Bulletin No. 35). Washington, DC: U.S. Government Printing Office.

National Research Council (NRC). (1996). *National science education standards.* Washington, DC: National Academies Press.

National Research Council (NRC). (2000). *How people learn: Brain, mind, experience, and school. Report of the Committee on Developments in the Science of Learning.* J.D. Bransford, A.L. Brown, & R.R. Cocking (Eds.). Washington, DC: National Academies Press.

National Research Council (NRC). (2007). *Taking science to school: Learning and teaching in grades K–8. Report of the committee on science of learning, kindergarten through eighth grade.* R.A. Duschl, H.A. Schweingruber, & A.W. Shouse (Eds.). Washington, DC: National Academies Press.

National Research Council (NRC). (2008). *Common standards for K–12 education.* Washington, DC: National Academies Press.

National Research Council (NRC). (2012). *A framework for K–12 science education. Report of the committee on a conceptual framework for new K–12 science education standards.* Washington, DC: National Academy Press.

National Science Board. (1983). *Educating Americans for the 21st century: A report to the American people and the National Science Board.* Washington, DC: National Science Foundation.

National Society for the Study of Education. (1947). *Science education in American schools: Forty-Sixth Yearbook of the NSSE.* Chicago, IL: University of Chicago Press.

NGSS Lead States. (2013). *Next generation science standards: For states, by states.* Washington, DC: The National Academies Press.

No Child Left Behind Act of 2001, 20 U.S.C. § 6301 *et seq.* (2002).

Papert, S. (2006). Afterword: After how comes what. In R.K. Sawyer (Ed.), *The Cambridge handbook of the learning sciences* (pp. 581–586). New York, NY: Cambridge University Press.

Pfeiffer, D. (2002). Signing the Section 504 rules: More to the story. *Ragged Edge Online, Issue 1.* Retrieved December 6, 2010, from www.ragged-edge-mag.com/0102/0102ft6.html

Physical Sciences Study Committee (PSSC). (1960). *Physics.* Boston, MA: D.C. Heath.

Project Physics. (1970). *The project physics course.* New York, NY: Holt, Rinehart, and Winston.

Ravitch, D. (1983). *The troubled crusade.* New York, NY: Basic Books.

Roseman, J.E., Linn, M.C., & Koppal, M. (2008). Characterizing curriculum coherence. In M.C. Linn, J.E. Roseman, & Y. Kali (Eds.), *Designing coherent science education: Implications for curriculum, instruction, and policy* (pp. 13–38). New York, NY: Teachers College Press.

Rudolph, J.L. (2008). The legacy of inquiry and the Biological Science Curriculum Study, in R.W. Bybee (Ed.), *BSCS: Measuring our success—the first 50 years of BSCS.* Dubuque, IA: Kendall/Hunt.

Rudolph, J.L., & Meshoulam, D. (in press). Science education in American high schools. In H.R. Slotten (Ed.), *Oxford encyclopedia of American scientific, medical, and technological history.* New York, NY: Oxford University Press.

Sawyer, R.K. (2006a). Conclusion: The schools of the future. In R.K. Sawyer (Ed.), *The Cambridge handbook of the learning sciences* (pp. 567–580). New York, NY: Cambridge University Press.

Sawyer, R.K. (2006b). Introduction: The new science of learning. In R.K. Sawyer (Ed.), *The Cambridge handbook of the learning sciences* (pp. 1–16). New York, NY: Cambridge University Press.

Schlesinger, A.M., Jr. (1986). *The cycles of American history.* Boston, MA: Houghton Mifflin.

Schwab, J.J. (1954). Eros and education: A discussion of one aspect of discussion. *Journal of General Education, 8,* 54–71.

Schwab, J.J. (1962). The teaching of science as enquiry. In J.J. Schwab & P.F. Brandwein (Eds.) *The teaching of science* (pp. 1–103). Cambridge, MA: Harvard University Press.

Schwab, J.J. (1963). *Biology teachers' handbook.* New York, NY: John Wiley and Sons.

Science Curriculum Improvement Study. (1970). *Science Improvement Curriculum Study (SCIS).* Chicago, IL: Rand McNally.

Slotta, J.D., & Linn, M.C. (2009). *WISE Science: Web-based inquiry in the classroom.* New York, NY: Teachers College Press.

Smith, A., & Hall, E. (1902). *The teaching of chemistry and physics in the secondary school.* New York, NY: Longmans, Green.

Smith, M. (1954). *The diminished mind.* Chicago, IL: Regnery.

Spencer, H. (1864). *Education: Intellectual, moral, and physical.* New York, NY: Appleton.

Strong, L. (1962). Chemistry as a science in the high school. *The School Review, 70,* 44–50.

Title IX of the Education Amendments of 1972. 20 U.S.C. §§ 1681–1688 *et seq.*

U.S. Department of Education. (1991). *America 2000: An education strategy sourcebook.* Washington, DC: Author.

U.S. Office of Education. (1951). *Life adjustment for every youth.* Washington, DC: U.S. Government Printing Office.

Webb, H. (1915). Is there a royal road to science? *School Science and Mathematics, 15,* 679–685.

Weiss, I.R. (2006). A framework for investigating the influence of the national science standards. In D.W. Sunal & E.L. Wright (Eds.), *The impact of state and national standards on K–12 science teaching* (pp. 51–79). Charlotte, NC: Information Age Publishing.

Zumwalt, K. (1995). What's a national curriculum anyway? In L. McNeil (Ed.), *The hidden consequences of a national curriculum* (pp. 1–12). Washington, DC: American Educational Research Association.

29

Scientific Practices and Inquiry in the Science Classroom

Jonathan Osborne

Summary

This chapter explores the arguments for teaching science through inquiry that have been made in science education. Beginning with Schwab, it looks at how such arguments have overemphasized the act of empirical inquiry and lacked a more detailed understanding of the epistemic and procedural aspects of this core scientific activity. Drawing on work from the history and philosophy of science, and those working in science studies, it seeks to show how more recent understandings of science have led to teaching a model of science that sees science as consisting of a set of science practices. It argues that the process of empirical inquiry cannot exist in isolation from the theories that it seeks to test, the analysis and interpretation of the data, and the arguments required to resolve conflicting interpretations. Moreover, such a model of science demands that students be taught explicitly not only domain-specific content knowledge but a body of basic procedural and epistemic knowledge that is essential to engage in the critical evaluation of any scientific activity or report. Furthermore, the learning of science is an activity that must not be confused with the doing of science—activities that have very different goals—and the reading, writing, and talking of science matter as much to the learning of science as engaging in empirical inquiry does.

Introduction

The one distinguishing feature of science in the public mind it is that is an act of inquiry into the material[1] world. Not surprisingly, many have sought to make this a central feature of how science is taught. Indeed, as long ago as 1759, Edmund Burke wrote that (Burke, 1909):

> I am convinced that the method of teaching which approaches most nearly to the method of investigation, is incomparably the best; . . . it tends to set the reader himself in the track of invention, and to direct him into those paths in which the author has made his own discoveries.
>
> (p. 12)

Not surprisingly, drawing on the analogy that the best way to learn a new skill such as playing a musical instrument, pitching a baseball, or driving a car is to practice that activity, the natural inclination has been to argue that learning science is best done through providing students the opportunity to engage in scientific inquiry in the classroom as often as possible. For instance, H.E. Armstrong, the most well-known English proponent of this approach, argued for what he termed the "heuristic method" that "involves placing our students as far as possible in the attitude of the discoverer—using methods that involve their *finding out*,[2] instead of being merely told about things" (Armstrong, 1902).

Similar notions were to be articulated 90 years later in the National Science Education Standards (National Academy of Science, 1995). This document argued that teaching science called for more than teaching science as a process and the specific skills of observing, experimenting, and inferring. In its place it offered a vision of science teaching in which "inquiry is central to science learning" in which

> students describe objects and events, ask questions, construct explanations, test those explanations against current scientific knowledge, and communicate their ideas to others. They identify their assumptions, use critical and logical thinking, and consider alternative explanations. In this way, students actively develop their understanding of science by combining scientific knowledge with reasoning and thinking skills.
>
> (p. 23)

In one sense, such an argument is seductively attractive. It offers a conception of learning science that embodies the practice of science itself. But it is flawed in two ways. The first flaw made by the proponents of inquiry lies in

Ryle's distinction between "knowing how" and "knowing that" (Ryle, 1949). Learning science through a process of inquiry does develop an extensive knowledge of the procedures required to produce new scientific knowledge—for example, "knowing how." Some of this is what Polyani defined to be "tacit knowledge" (Polyani, 1958). What it does not develop, unless explicitly taught, is knowledge of the rules, standard procedures, and ways of minimizing error that are required to produce data that can be trusted to be both accurate and precise ("knowing that"). What is more, missing from Ryle's distinction is the component "knowing why"—that is, a knowledge of how these procedures justify our belief in science's claim to know and the constructs and values that are commonly used in science—what might be termed "epistemic knowledge." Imre Lakatos, an eminent philosopher of science, once memorably commented that "most scientists tend to understand little more *about* science than fish about hydrodynamics" (Lakatos, 1970, p. 148). Kuhn (1962), too, noted that practicing scientists rarely engage in reflection on what they do. Scientists are trained through extended apprenticeship in communities of practice in which the justification for what they do and why they do it is essentially tacit and its epistemic justification rarely discussed.

More fundamentally, the emphasis on teaching science through inquiry reflects a confusion of goals. The goal of science is to develop new knowledge of the material world. Science seeks to answer the fundamental question of "What is nature like?" Regardless of the specific science, answers to this ontological question always begin with observation—the sun rises in the east, sets in the west; stars circle the Earth once every 24 hours; each individual looks like their parents. Observations in their turn, however, generate the causal question of "Why does it happen?" It is these questions that engenders the scientists' imagination, the construction of models, and the production of explanatory hypotheses. Such ideas must then be tested against the data to answer the third question—the epistemic question of "How do we know?" and "How can we be certain?" Answering these questions enables the scientist to make claims to *new* knowledge.

The goal of science education, however, is fundamentally different. It seeks not to create new knowledge but rather to help students understand a body of existing, consensually agreed and well-established *old* knowledge. The flaw in the argument for inquiry-based teaching of science has been a conflation of the *doing* of science with the *learning* of science (Chinn & Malhotra, 2003; Roth, 1995) when, in reality, the two are activities distinguished by their *differing* goals. And it is this difference in goals that makes the activity of science education *fundamentally different* from the activity of science. In particular, the goal of learning science is to comprehend the major features of the scientific landscape, to appreciate the intellectual achievement these ideas represent, and to understand how such knowledge has been derived. To suggest that inquiry, the major methodological tool of the scientist, can also be the major procedure for learning science is to make a category error akin to suggesting that learning to understand and appreciate music can only be achieved through playing an instrument—leaving no role for the education of the critic or music lover who has never played. Rather, a knowledge and understanding of science is best acquired through applying our knowledge and understanding of how humans learn (Bransford, Brown, & Cocking, 2000; Donovan & Bransford, 2005) rather than a knowledge of how people do science—an activity about which there is little consensus anyway (Alters, 1997). Thus, given the fundamental differences in the goals and intentions of the activity of science when compared to the activity of science education, the argument that science is best learned through inquiry is simply a non sequitur.

The basic premise of this chapter then is "that 'to know science' is a statement that one knows not only *what* a phenomenon is, but also *how* it relates to other events, *why* it is important and *how* this particular view of the world came to be" (Osborne, 2010, p. 67). Any science education that offers students only a conceptual understanding of science without explaining how we know what we know or why we believe what we do leaves students without any knowledge for the epistemic basis of belief. Indeed, as Norris (1997) argues,

> To ask of other human beings that they accept and memorize what the science teacher says, without any concern for the meaning and justification of what is said, is to treat those human beings with disrespect and is to show insufficient care for their welfare. It treats them with disrespect, because students exist on a moral par with their teachers, and therefore have a right to expect from their teachers reasons for what the teachers wish them to believe. It shows insufficient care for the welfare of students, because possessing beliefs that one is unable to justify is poor currency when one needs beliefs that can reliably guide action.
>
> (p. 252)

Fundamentally, one of the major contributions that science has made to contemporary culture is building a commitment to evidence as the basis of belief; in so doing, the scientific tradition has promoted rationality, critical thinking, and objectivity and that ideas should be judged not by personal or social interest but by how the world is (Kitcher, 2001; Matthews, 1995). Yet, to this day, such perspectives still meet considerable opposition (Kitcher, 2010).

Without question, students must be taught the content of science—"the what we know" and "why it happens." The concern here, though, is with what account we should give of how science works; how is it that scientists come to know what they know and what are the major constructs that guide what they do. Clearly there is a considerable overlap between content and process, as the two are deeply interrelated. But just as language only has meaning in the context of its use (Wittgenstein, 1961), it will be argued that many of the epistemic beliefs and constructs that guide the activity of science only have meaning when students are asked to engage in selected scientific practices. While the function of asking students to engage in inquiry undoubtedly has value for illustrating specific phenomena, it has more value when it is used to develop a knowledge of the content, procedures or epistemic criteria and constructs that are a feature of science. And while such activity will only be, at best, an approximation of scientific practice and a partial account, its function should enable the student to experience the intellectual engagement and satisfaction that science can offer. Perhaps, more importantly, it will help to build a deeper functional understanding of science that is required by the scientifically literate individual. To achieve the latter goal, it is important that there is a reflection on practice with clearly defined goals for the procedural and epistemic knowledge such practice seeks to build.

Teaching Science as Inquiry

As indicated previously, the leading English proponent of inquiry based teaching was H. E. Armstrong. The conception of how science should be taught is best captured in the lesson notes of Charles Browne, one of his early disciples.

Teaching Principles: Simple guidance—suggestion mainly by questions, no telling. Teacher's attitude one of co-enquirer. Must not be an authority. If a fact or data has to be given, it should be obtained from a book, and the authority quoted, thus lead to right use of books—for checking up and enlarging experience. It enables the teacher more easily to assume the role of co-inquirer as much as he wants the boys to do.[3]

Such teaching required lessons to begin with a question generated by an observation—as in the following example. Here the teacher, Van Praagh—a later disciple of Armstrong and an influential contributor to the Nuffield science teaching projects of the 1960s—shows his students that copper goes black when heated. Then he asks his students, "Why does copper go black when it is heated? What could this be and why?" The response his question generates is the production of several theories.

Smith says "I think it is soot from the flame." "Good idea." I write on the board "Smith's theory—the black stuff is soot." "He may be right," I say. "Any other ideas?" "Yes, sir" says Robinson, "I think it's an impurity driven out of the copper by heat." So Robinson's theory goes on the board too. "I know what it is," says Solly whose older brother is in the Fifth form. "If you know, you will have to prove you are right—we'll add it to our theories." Solly's theory: "the black stuff is formed by the air acting on the copper." "How shall we decide who is right? I ask. I get them to suggest three experiments to test the three theories.

(Van Praagh, 2003)

Such ideas were highly influential on the U.K. Nuffield Projects, where it was argued that this kind of approach

enabled students to be "a scientist for a day" and experience the thrill of discovery. While there was no coherent pedagogic philosophy articulated by this set of projects, time and again, the guides insist that the teacher must not give the game away but should allow the pupils to find out for themselves. The problem with this form of pedagogy is that students are aware that the experiments have been rigged to produce the appropriate result (Nott & Smith, 1995) and that, rather than advance ideas that are likely to be "wrong," the exercise becomes a process of making the "right guess," reducing the experience to one of "What's supposed to happen?" (Stevens, 1978; Wellington, 1981).

In the American context, a more sophisticated approach was developed by Joseph Schwab, who chaired the development of the materials for the Biology Sciences Curriculum Studies Science (BSCS) project. He extended and elaborated the rationale for an approach to the teaching of science as inquiry (Schwab, 1962). Schwab saw the goal of teaching science through inquiry as an "inquiry into inquiry" rather than a means of learning science. The BSCS texts were committed, from their inception, to what Schwab, called a "radical departure [from] conventional patterns" by embedding all content as an invitation to inquiry (Schwab, 1962, p. 39). An analysis of the published text would suggest that, at least in print, this objective was realized. More than 50% of the text was dedicated to helping students approach investigative problems—a feature that the most recent edition of the BSCS Human Approach biology text sustains (Chiappetta & Fillman, 2007).

Schwab's ideas were remarkably prescient for the time, advancing as he did the notion of "static inquiry" (undertaking the solution of routine problems) and "fluid inquiry" as a process of responding to perceived anomalies in theoretical accounts—ideas that bear strong parallels to Kuhn's normal and revolutionary science. What Schwab offered science education was a rationale for why engaging in inquiry was important in learning science—to provide some insight into how we know what we know. And, unlike those who were to argue for the importance of a process-based approach, Schwab saw process and content as deeply interrelated. Moreover, each of the sciences had its own structure that differentiated it from other sciences. Indeed, Schwab (1962) argued that all inquiry in science was discipline specific, "guided by a prior conceptual structure, specifically the current theories and concepts governing the phenomenon in question" (Rudolph, 2003). Each was to be presented as a "fragments of narrative of enquiry" (Rudolph, 2003, p. 270) in which knowledge was to "be imparted, not as truths out of nowhere but as conclusions from evidence" (p. 270) and deliberations about "alternatives and their consequences" (p. 270)—points that sound very similar to those of scholars who argue for the value of argumentation in science education (Driver, Newton, & Osborne, 2000; Duschl & Osborne, 2002).

However, in his writings, Schwab (1962) did attempt to present a description of the epistemic and procedural constructs that govern scientific inquiry but limited it to the "kind of conclusion, kind of data, and mode of verification" that are intrinsic to science. All sciences, Schwab argued, were reliant on a set of classificatory schema (taxonomic knowledge), measurement science that he described as "simple, quickly describable patterns of inquiry" (p. 86), causal science that seeks to show how one entity in a "system of mutually interacting and mutually determined parts acts as a concerted whole" (p. 89), and analogical science that is the attempt to explain by inventing mechanisms not directly accessible to observation. The latter form of reasoning required the development of models and theories. Thus Schwab's work can and should be seen as an attempt to define the knowledge bases required for scientific reasoning and address the lack of an explicit recognition that science depends on a body of procedural and epistemic knowledge.

However, Schwab's work only managed to identify in general terms the epistemic constructs that are the foundation of scientific reasoning. Likewise, his work did not recognize that participating in inquiry required a body of procedural knowledge of specific constructs intrinsic to inquiry such as the notion of an independent/dependent variable, types of error, reliability and validity, and more. Thus, in that he failed to identify sufficiently the forms and features of the knowledge on which scientific reasoning depended, his work lacked the insights necessary to build a deeper picture of what it means to reason scientifically, leaving the problem of what kind of knowledge science should seek to develop unresolved.

To his credit, however, Schwab did not conflate the doing of science with the learning of science. Schwab drew a distinction between presenting science as a product of the process of inquiry from using inquiry for learning and teaching, arguing that the inquiry curriculum was "by no means the only version nor necessarily the most desirable version in all schools for all students" (Schwab, 1962, p. 71). The conception that a major function of inquiry is to build meta-level knowledge of the process was a feature of the 1996 U.S. National Science Education Standards. In the explanatory volume published 4 years later, it argued that "inquiry encompasses not only the ability to engage in inquiry but an understanding of inquiry and how inquiry results in scientific knowledge" (National Research

Council, 2000, p. 13). However, the distinction between learning *about* inquiry and learning *through* inquiry was not made, and the document gives the strong impression that inquiry is the recommended form of pedagogy.

The National Science Education Standards of 1996 provide an elaborate list of the abilities necessary to do scientific inquiry. Indeed, these look remarkably similar to the list of eight practices to be found in the recently published *Framework for K–12 Science Education* (National Research Council, 2012) shown in Table 29.1.

The obvious question that must then be asked is, in what sense are these different? How is the notion of teaching science through inquiry any different from asking students to engage in scientific practices? The answer to this question, it will be argued, comes from a greater clarity of goals both about what students should experience and what students should learn.

The first problem with the teaching of science through inquiry has been the lack of a commonly accepted definition of what it means to teach science *through* inquiry. For many teachers and for many students, the notion of inquiry has been conflated with the idea that inquiry requires students to handle, investigate, and ask questions of the material world. Hence, any activity that is of a "hands-on" nature can be considered to fulfill the basic requirement of this pedagogic approach. In this form, inquiry is seen not as a means of developing a deeper understanding of the nature of scientific inquiry but rather as an end in itself serving the pedagogic function of illustrating or verifying the phenomenological account of nature offered by the teacher (Abd-El-Khalick et al., 2004). The result is that the goals of engaging in inquiry have been conflated with the goals of practical or laboratory work. Most laboratory work primarily serves an illustrative function (Wellington, 1998; Woolnough & Allsop, 1986). As Millar (1998) argues,

> In a teaching context, producing the phenomenon is also a kind of ritualised display of the power of scientific knowledge involved. The event implicitly proclaims: "see, we (that is the scientific community as embodied in the teacher) know so much about this that we can get the event to happen, reliably and regularly, before your very eyes!" The less likely the event, the more powerful this is. Practical tasks carried out by the students are really

TABLE 29.1

A Comparison of the Abilities to Do Scientific Inquiry (National Research Council, 2000) With the Set of Scientific Practices Found in the Framework for K–12 Science Education

Fundamental Abilities Necessary to do Scientific Inquiry (Grades 5–8)	Scientific Practices
• Identify questions that can be answered through scientific investigations	1. Asking questions and defining problems
• Design and conduct a scientific investigation	2. Developing and using models
• Use appropriate tools and techniques to gather, analyze, and interpret scientific data	3. Planning and carrying out investigations
• Develop descriptions, explanations, predictions, and models using evidence	4. Analyzing and interpreting data
• Think critically and logically to make the relationship between evidence and explanations	5. Using mathematical and computational thinking
• Recognize and analyze alternative explanations and predictions	6. Constructing explanations and designing solutions
• Communicate scientific procedures and explanations	7. Engaging in argument from evidence
• Use mathematics in all aspects of scientific enquiry	8. Obtaining, evaluating, and communicating information

"auto-demonstrations," so they carry the even stronger implicit message that "our understanding and consequent control of materials and events, is so good that I (the teacher) don't even have to do it for you but you can do it yourself."

(p. 26)

Thus, in the eyes of many teachers, the primary goal of engaging in inquiry is not to develop a deeper understanding of the whole process of inquiry—the acts that are listed in Table 29.1—but to provide a means of supporting their rhetorical task of persuading their students of the validity of the conceptual account of nature that they offer. If there is an alternative focus, it tends to be on the performance of the skills required to do inquiry—and then predominantly on the manipulative skills for successful experimentation (knowing how)—rather than the analysis and interpretation of the data or an understanding about inquiry and its role in science (knowing that or knowing why). At its worst, the product is cookbook laboratory exercises in which students simply follow a series of instructions to replicate the phenomenon. So the answer to the question posed about what are the problems of teaching science through inquiry is not so much one of its conception but rather one of its articulation and communication. What is lacking within science education is a professional language that defines and communicates the categories of activity that students should experience—that is a workable classification of educational practice. Bowker and Leigh Star (1999) show how the introduction of such systems in other professions, like nursing, has enabled comparability across sites, made specific activity visible, and provided a structure and control of the activity so that there is some consistency across sites. In short, that a reserved language that discriminates and communicates important concepts is an important factor in contributing to the professionalization of practice.

The Nature of Practice in Science

The notion of science as a set of practices has emerged from the work of the science historians, philosophers, cognitive scientists, and sociologists over the past 40 years. The key turning point was the work of Kuhn (1962), who showed that science was undertaken by a community of scientists whose work was dominated by a set of values and normative criteria—some of which were socially negotiated—that is, this community of practitioners engaged in specific, consensually agreed-on practices. The body of work that followed has illuminated how science is actually done, both in the short term (e.g., studies of activity in a particular laboratory or a program of study) and historically (e.g., studies of laboratory notebooks, published texts, eyewitness accounts; Collins & Pinch, 1993; Conant, 1957; Geison, 1995; Latour & Woolgar, 1986; Pickering, 1995; Traweek, 1988). Seeing science as a set of practices has shown that theory development,

reasoning, and testing are components of a larger ensemble of activities that include networks of participants and institutions (Latour, 1999; Longino, 2002), specialized ways of talking and writing (Bazerman, 1988), modeling using either mechanical and mathematical models or computer-based simulations (Nercessian, 2008), making predictive inferences, constructing appropriate instrumentation, and developing representations of phenomena (Latour, 1986; Lehrer & Schauble, 2006a).

In what sense is this different from the account offered by philosophers such as Popper, Lakatos, or Hempel? The project of philosophy has been to provide a normative account of the rules and values that govern the activity of science—essentially one of identifying the meta-level procedures that govern how science functions. One description is the pervasive notion of the scientific method as asking a question, developing a testable hypothesis, and then engaging in empirical inquiry to see if the data do or do not confirm the hypothesis. It is not the focus of this chapter to explain why the notion of a singular scientific method is simply an idealized and partial view of what some scientists do. Suffice it to say that Popper's contribution was to identify that the goal of an experiment was not confirmation of a hypothesis but merely to show that the hypothesis was not falsifiable. The problem for science education is that there is no singular philosophical description of the epistemic rules and norms that govern science that could readily form the basis of a simplified or vulgar account that might be offered to students. Indeed, there are increasing arguments that each of the sciences has distinct norms, values, and epistemic criteria such that the philosophy of biology (Mayr, 2004) is distinct from the philosophy of chemistry (Baird, Scerri, & McIntyre, 2006), which is distinct from the philosophy of physics, for example (Cartwright, 1983)—and it is the philosophy of physics that has framed much of the work on the philosophy of science.

Despite this problem, science educators have managed to show that there does exist a consensus among the many divergent groups around a basic set of features of the nature of science. One approach has been to identify the features that are common to curricula across the globe (McComas & Olson, 1998); another was to conduct a Delphi study of the community that found consensus around eight principles (Osborne, Ratcliffe, Collins, Millar, & Duschl, 2003). However, probably the most well-known is the work of Lederman (2007) and Abd-El-Khalick, Waters, and Le (2008), who, drawing on a large body of scholarship in the history, philosophy, and sociology of science, have argued for a list of 7 to 10 domain-general features that apply across all sciences. These are the ideas that science is empirically based, that scientific knowledge relies on inferences, is creative, dominated by theoretical and disciplinary commitments, subject to change, that there is no singular scientific method, that there is a distinction between a scientific law and a theory, and that scientific knowledge is a socially negotiated, culturally embedded product. One of the goals of science education, then, should be to "provide learners with ample opportunities to construct, re-construct and consolidate their own internally consistent frameworks about the epistemological foundations of science" (Abd-El-Khalick, 2012, p. 360)—epistemological foundations that are captured by such lists. Moreover, the advocates for these lists of the basic tenets of the nature of science make the important point that any understanding of this nature will only develop if such features are explicitly addressed (Abd-el-Khalick & Lederman, 2000; Lederman, 2007).

Yet this approach has been subject to a number of critiques (Allchin, 2011; Duschl & Grandy, 2013; Matthews, 2012). The first is that the activity of science is much more complex and nuanced than any such generalized list can ever capture. As a consequence, proponents of such lists are forced into devising ersatz pedagogic exercises whose relation to science is not clear. One such exercise, for instance, involves a cardboard tube and pulling strings whose connections within the tube cannot be seen. Students are then asked to construct a representational model of their interconnections, and the goal of the exercise is to exemplify that this is an analogue for the activity of science itself in which scientists are forced into constructing models and representations for entities that are not directly observable.

The second criticism is that such understandings are better developed in "the context of a case study that is sufficiently complex, on the one hand, yet also clearly delineated (concrete and detailed) on the other." Thus, "NOS instruction . . . needs to engage students in problem solving and decision making in context-rich case studies" (Allchin, 2011, p. 520). Allchin's argument is that there is "no evidence that mere recall or comprehension of such NOS tenets is adequate for applying them effectively in context." (p. 523) Rather, "NOS understanding needs to be *functional*[4], not declarative." (p. 523) What this means is that students' understanding of the epistemic basis of science needs to be developed in the context of rich, contemporary case studies of science and that one goal of science education should be to develop a broad understanding of scientific practice and how scientists establish credibility for the claims that they advance. In short, what do scientists *have to do* to establish reliable knowledge (Ziman, 1979)? A particular telling criticism is that the lists of NOS tenets disregard the role of criticism and peer review—the central core mechanism that the scientific community uses to establish credibility. In addition, they make little reference to the role of motivation, funding, cognitive biases, or fraud—all of which are elements required for a functional understanding of science that could help students to identify bad as well as good science (Goldacre, 2008). Such knowledge can only be developed through examining specific examples of scientific practice. Goldacre argues, for instance, that one of the most important epistemic features of science to understand is the role of the double-blind trial in justifying medical claims that are of

central concern to the majority of the public. Understanding a double-blind trial requires an understanding of how control-of-variables strategy enables science to advance causal claims. If he is right, then understanding what this strategy is and why it justifies belief is an essential element of any science education.

How then does a focus on the practices that scientist engage in begin to address these criticisms? The answer here lies in the fact that a focus on what scientists do enables the construction of a model of science that captures some fundamental features of science. The source of this model has emerged from empirical psychological studies of practice and normative philosophical studies of what scientist do. From such studies, Klahr and Dunbar (1993) concluded that the practice of science involves three main "processes,"[5] which they refer to as *hypothesizing*, *experimentation*, and *evidence evaluation*. The term "process" used by Klahr and Dunbar does not refer to the standard use within science education of a set of cognitive operations or skills. Rather, Klahr and Dunbar (1993) describe "processes" as the work conducted in "phases of an inquiry" and as "problem spaces." Their main intent given by the use of their terminology is to convey the idea that science requires a "process" of activity requiring reasoning that leads to the solution of three "problems" (developing hypotheses, generating data to test the hypotheses, and evaluating and coordinating evidence to draw a conclusion), and that these processes happen in phases. This description of science resembles Popper's (1972) separation of *conjecture* and *refutation* of scientific hypotheses but adds a third aspect, evidence evaluation. Klahr and colleagues (Klahr, Fay, & Dunbar, 1993), however, did not develop their model on philosophical grounds. Rather, their model of *science discovery as dual search* (SDDS) was presented as an account of their empirical findings when observing subjects and the reasoning they used to solve simulated scientific inquiry tasks in psychological experiments. In other words, Klahr et al.'s model arose from their *observations* that their subjects solved scientific problems by engaging in three principal forms of activity. Rather than a philosophical argument that reflected underlying normative principles, this conception of science was a product of empirical observation of university students and schoolchildren, the youngest being children in elementary schools, actually doing science.

What is of interest is that Giere and colleagues (Giere, Bickle, & Maudlin, 2006) provide a similar model from a philosophical perspective that also suggests three phases of inquiry as a structure for scientific reasoning. This model, however, has been derived from philosophical case studies of authentic science, such as Crick and Watson's development of the DNA model, and explains how science works *in principle*. Such a normative account describes the set of actions embodied in scientific practice, how science should be conducted, and the values that participants in the scientific community share. The distinction between Giere and colleagues' (2006) philosophical account and

Klahr et al.'s (1993) psychological account is that, whereas the Giere's et al.'s (2006) model emphasizes the reasons and the criteria that scientists advance for their judgments, Klahr et al.'s (1993) emphasizes the cognitive act or reasoning itself and its primary function that both Giere et al. (2006) and Nersessain (2002) see to be the construction of explanatory models of the material world.

The fact that a group of philosophers and a group of psychologists—that is, scholars from two distinct disciplines—independently arrived at similar models is significant, implying that there is some underlying structure to scientific activity. Taken together, these two models suggest that scientific reasoning has three distinct "phases of activity"—experimenting (the activity of investigating the material world), hypothesis generation (the activity of developing explanations and solutions of what is observed and found), and evidence evaluation (the activity of evaluating both the data and the theories and models offered as explanations)—that are identified by the nature of the specific types of problems to be solved, governed by a set of normative criteria set by the scientific community, and draw on distinctive forms of reasoning such as deduction, induction, and abduction. Figure 29.1 offers a diagrammatic representation of this structure.

In what sense, though, are these spheres of activity fundamental to science and helpful to science education? The answer is that they are a necessary consequence of the fundamental question that science begins with "What is nature like?" Thus one of the key primary practices that scientists engage in is the asking of questions. This form of activity constitutes part of what is represented by the left side of Figure 29.1. Observations, in their turn, however, generate a causal question of "Why does it happen?" Such a question engenders the scientists' creative imagination, the construction of models, and the production of explanatory hypotheses— the element of activity that is represented by the right side of Figure 29.1. Such ideas must then be tested. The testing of ideas requires the design of empirical investigations and the collection and analysis of data. Such

data and the methodological procedures enable scientists to answer the questions "How do we know?" and "How can we be certain?" However, achieving consensus and establishing the validity of such claims is reliant on argument and evidence evaluation.

Evidence evaluation is necessary, as a recent transformation within science has been the recognition that data are theory laden (Hanson, 1958). Hence, the belief that data are objective and beyond doubt is no longer tenable. Instead, science has been forced into a position in which observations of the material world can, in certain circumstances, no more be trusted prima facie than the ideas such data may or may not support. Hence, the critical evaluation of the quality of any data set is as important to the experimenter as it is to the theoretician. From a philosophical perspective, evaluation and critique are necessary, as experiments do not give definitive answers as to whether a scientific theory is true or false (Hempel, 1962; Quine, 1951). In science, there are "experimenters" who work predominantly in the spaces of experimentation and evaluation but draw on the work of theoreticians, who develop models and hypotheses that form the theoretical premises of their investigation. Conversely, there are "theoreticians" who work predominantly in the space of hypothesis generation but draw on the critical evaluation of their colleagues and the data produced by the "experimenters" to evaluate the validity of their theories. Thus, all scientists, whatever their disciplinary identity may be, are forced to engage in evaluation. Many scientists, of course, do not fall into either of these groups but, in their research, move fluidly among the three spaces.

Moreover, these spheres of activity are not self-evident. That is, someone coming new to science would not necessarily recognize these three problem spaces as the key features of the work of the scientist. Studies of young children (Driver, Leach, Millar, & Scott, 1996; Klahr & Carver, 1995; Millar, Lubben, Gott, & Duggan, 1995; Schauble, Klopfer, & Raghavan, 1991) reveal that students often see science differently. Schauble and colleagues (1991) identified that much of the investigatory work was

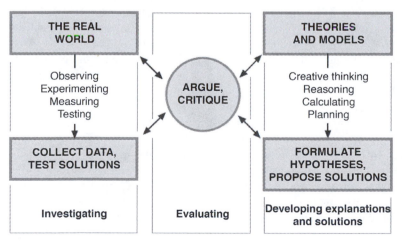

Figure 29.1 A model of scientific activity; combining Klahr and Dunbar (1988) and Giere et al. (2006).

conceptualized in terms of an "engineering frame," in which the children do not set out to test ideas but instead to test a design (i.e., change variables to achieve "best" or optimal conditions). Another study (Kind, Kind, Adamson, & Barmby, 2009) has demonstrated that students recognize the activity required for hypothesizing and experimentation more readily than that required for the evaluation of evidence. The pre-eminence given by school science to the collection of data and "hands-on" experience simply reinforces the logical positivist perspective of science that sees observational statements as the infallible premises of all deductions. As a corollary, there are number of consequences. First, students fail to build an understanding that *data can be fallible* and open to equivocation. Second, school science fails to develop an understanding that science is more about *developing explanatory hypotheses* and *constructing explanatory models* than it is about obtaining data. This is not to argue that experimentation and "hands-on" inquiry are not important aspects of the learning of science. Experience with the domain of phenomena is essential to give meaning to the concepts and theories of science, but the fundamental purpose is to construct links with the domain of ideas. For, as Harré (1984) has argued, "theories are the crowning glory of science" and scientists whose names exist in perpetuity—Darwin, Einstein, Wegner, Maxwell, Copernicus, Newton, and so on—are all recognized for their theoretical contribution. Third, it fails to show the importance and necessity *of evaluation and argumentation*[6] to the resolution of uncertainty that is intrinsic to all scientific activity.

The Centrality of Critique

Why is engaging in argumentation and critique so central to all science? As Ford (2008) has argued, its significance lies in the fact that the construction of knowledge is dependent on a "dialectic between *construction* and *critique*"[7] in which "critique motivates authentic construction of knowledge" (p. 404). Ford's (2008) view is that the critical spirit of science is founded first on a belief that any new claims to knowledge must be interpreted in the light of the data presented and the knowledge that any inference may be flawed; hence, scientists know that the explicit connections must be scrutinized critically; and third, that this process results in reliable knowledge. Ford's insight is the recognition that critique has a similar role to play in the learning of science as well.

One theoretical justification for the significance of critique is offered by the growing body of research that would suggest that scientific reasoning is fundamentally probabilistic (Howson & Urbach, 2006; Oaksford & Chater, 2007). From this perspective, scientific reasoning is best seen as an inference to the best explanation. This means that the rhetorical task confronting the scientist is not solely one of convincing other scientists of why their scientific account is correct but also one of convincing them of why alternative theoretical accounts are wrong (Szu & Osborne, 2011). Constructing knowledge is not so much a product

of conceptual change in which one conception is replaced by another (Posner, Strike, Hewson, & Gerzog, 1982) but rather a process of weighing alternatives and evaluating the balance of probabilities between two competing beliefs. Shifting the balance of beliefs is reliant not on the credibility of a single idea (Belief A) but rather on the ratio between the strength of evidence for Belief A when compared to an alternative (Belief B): in short, an assessment of which idea is more probable. Even examples such as the duality of the wave and particle model for light are simply testimony to the idea that there is evidence for both beliefs and the exact nature of light is unresolved—that is, the probability remains equal. As Bragg famously stated, "God runs electromagnetics by wave theory on Monday, Wednesday, and Friday, and the Devil runs them by quantum theory on Tuesday, Thursday, and Saturday." As Oaksford and Chater (2007) argue in most cases, "scientific inference is irremediably uncertain" (p. 76) and wave–particle duality is simply an acknowledgment of the inherent uncertainty. Obvious other examples are the ability to predict earthquakes, the determination of the age of the Earth, or the possible effect of rising CO_2 levels on mean global temperatures. Granted, there are cases in which the argument for the new theory is overwhelming, such as Maxwell's derivation of the speed of light from the constants in the electric and magnetic field theories, but most new ideas in science are initially tentative speculations and highly uncertain. A natural response to such uncertainty is to consider an idea not in isolation but as one whose validity must be assessed by conducting a probabilistic evaluation of its likelihood. Indeed, science has evolved standard methods for resolving measurement error and establishing the boundaries within which the most likely answer will be found—and a knowledge of such procedures is part of what I choose to term "procedural knowledge."

Evidence that critique is an essential part of human learning can be found in many instances, such as the work of Johnson on the history of the development of one specific engineering product—ABS braking (Johnson, 2009). In her historical account of the development of this technology, Johnson (2009) shows how it was knowledge sharing that was essential to the process of its development. Those who did not contribute any knowledge to the community, predominantly American engineers, simply did not have the information necessary to make a good judgment about the Bayesian likelihood ratio, and the outcome was that they lost the race to develop this technology to their European counterparts. Similar arguments can be made about Crick and Watson's development of their model for DNA. The critical pieces of information were as much evidence of why their and others' initial proposed structures were wrong as was the evidence from Rosalind Franklin's X-ray crystallography photograph suggesting that the structure was a helix.

Why critique is important to scientific learning then can be understood by considering the process as being metaphorically akin to weighing the two competing ideas—proposition A and proposition B. Initially, evidence might suggest they are of equal merit. Imagine then that good exposition, in the absence of critique, raises the credibility of A such that the weight of evidence for this proposition is twice as strong as the evidence for idea B. In the presence of critique, however, the credibility of the evidence for the alternative proposition B is halved as well. The ratio of credible evidence for A with respect to B now becomes four times as strong, leading to a more secure and enduring understanding. That this is so is confirmed by a series of studies demonstrating that the opportunity to engage in critique leads to enhanced conceptual knowledge when compared with students who are not provided with such an opportunity (Ames & Murray, 1982; Hynd & Alvermann, 1986; Schwarz, Neuman, & Biezuner, 2000). Critique is not something, therefore, that is peripheral to scientific practice or science learning but is central to it. And, just as critique and argument are core features of the practice of science, these empirical studies suggest that they are also essential features of human learning. Why then the virtual absence of critique and critical thinking from science education, both past and present? An absence that at least explains Rogers's comment that "we should not assume that mere contact with science, which is so critical, will make students think critically" (Rogers, 1948, p. 7).

Why Practice?

How will a focus on asking students to participate in scientific practice improve science education? Gutierrez and Rogoff (2003) argue that learning involves the development of "repertoires of practice". However, it is not the primary function of school science education to train students to do science. Engaging in practice only has value if (a) it helps students to develop a deeper and broader understanding of what we know, how we know, and the epistemic and procedural constructs that guide its practice; (b) if it is a more effective means of developing such knowledge; and (c) it presents a more authentic picture of the endeavor that is science. Currently, there is little evidence that science education is achieving such goals. For instance, in their extensive observational survey of the teaching of science and mathematics in the United States, Weiss and colleagues (2003) found only "14 percent of lessons nationally having a climate of intellectual rigor, including constructive criticism and the challenging of ideas" (p. 54). In what follows, it is argued that engaging students in scientific practices will make cognitive demands of a form that science education rarely does and that asking students to engage in practice can improve the quality of their learning.

Asking Questions

The ability to ask good thinking questions is an important component of scientific literacy, as the goal of making individuals critical consumers of scientific knowledge

(Millar & Osborne, 1998) requires such facility. Fundamentally, however, questions drive the need for explanation and are the engine that drives all scientific research. Only by engaging in such a practice can students begin to understand the importance of the driving question to any scientific research. Engaging in this practice will require opportunities to ask questions of what they observe and to refine their notion of what makes a good scientific question. The value of students' questions for learning has been emphasized by several authors (e.g., Biddulph, Symington, & Osborne, 1986; Chin & Osborne, 2008; Fisher, 1990; Penick, Crow, & Bonnsteter, 1996). Questions raised by students activate their prior knowledge, focus their learning efforts, and help them elaborate on their knowledge (Schmidt, 1993). The act of "composing questions" helps students to attend to content, main ideas, and checking if content is understood (Rosenshine, Meister, & Chapman, 1996). More importantly, knowing what the question is gives meaning to science. Textbooks, for instance, are full of explanations but rarely begin by explicating the question that they are seeking to answer (Ford, 2006), leading one acerbic student to comment that "the problem with science is that it gives answers to questions you have never asked." The point here is not that every activity has to be driven by a question but rather that it is questions that give meaning to science. Making those more explicit is an important tool in helping students to understand what science seeks to achieve.

Developing and Using Models

A second practice that is key to science is the construction of models. Models are needed in science because science deals with things too large to imagine, such as the inside of a volcano, the solar system, or the phases of the moon (Gilbert & Boulter, 2000). Conversely, models are also needed to represent things that are too small to see, such as a cell, the inside of the human body, or the atom itself (Harrison & Treagust, 2002). Young children will begin by constructing simple physical models or diagrammatic representations (Ainsworth, Prain, & Tytler, 2011) but then, at higher grades, models become more abstract and more reliant on mathematics. However, although some models are simply representational, such as the Bohr model of the atom or a model of a cell, other models can explain or enable generative predictions. Thus the bicycle chain model of an electric circuit not only explains why the electric light comes on instantaneously, it also explains why, if the chain is broken, no light will come on. A more complex example is Maxwell's mathematical model of electric and magnetic fields that correctly predicted the existence of electromagnetic waves travelling at the speed of light. As Lehrer and Schauble argue, "modeling is a form of disciplinary argument" that students must "learn to participate in over a long and extended period of practice" (Lehrer & Schauble, 2006b, p. 182).

Evidence would suggest that there are significant pedagogical benefits of having students construct their own models. For instance, using an inquiry-oriented physics curriculum with four middle school classes that required students to create their own models of force and motion produced a significant improvement of students' understanding of modeling *and* of the science content (Schwarz & White, 2005). Likewise, Acher, Arca, and Sanmarti (2007) have found that it is possible to engage elementary students both in the construction of models and in reflection on their meaning. Further evidence for the value of engaging students in modeling can be found in the work of Stewart and colleagues (2005), Wilensky and Reisman (2006), Windschitl and colleagues (2008), and Lehrer and Schauble (2012). An important point made by all of these authors is that the goal of engaging students in modeling is not just one of developing their understanding of the concepts of science. Rather, it is to develop a form of metaknowledge about science—that is, a knowledge of specific features of science and its guiding constructs, such as a hypothesis, theory, or observation, *and* their role in contributing to how we know what we know—essentially, what might be termed epistemic knowledge. For instance, asking students to construct models helps them to understand that the epistemic project of science is not the construction of a picture that accurately depicts every aspect of nature, but of a map that captures some certain features better than others, just as the Google satellite map highlights different features from the two-dimensional plan map.

Constructing Explanations

The construction of explanations, a third practice, makes similar demands to that of modeling. Many explanations in science are reliant on the construction of models so that the two practices are deeply interrelated. Commonly, students are the recipients of many explanations provided by teachers, but rarely are they asked to construct explanations for phenomena themselves (McRobbie & Thomas, 2001; Weiss, Pasley, Sean Smith, Banilower, & Heck, 2003). Yet work in cognitive science has demonstrated the value for learning of asking students to construct explanations. For instance, in a study conducted by Chi and colleagues (1989), eight college students were asked to explain to another what they understood from reading statements from three examples taken from a physics text. The four students who were more successful at solving problems at the end of the chapter (averaging 82% correct in the posttest) were the ones who had spontaneously generated a greater number of self-explanations (15.3 explanations per example). In contrast, the four students who were less successful achieved only 46% on the posttest and had generated only 2.8 explanations per example. Similar findings emerged from a later study with 14 eighth-grade students in which the focus this time was on declarative knowledge of the functioning of the valves in the heart (Chi, De Leeuw, Chiu, & Lavancher, 1994). Notably, the improvement for the students required to generate explanations was more significant for the more complex questions used to test understanding. Chi et al. 1989 or 1994? postulate the reason that asking students to engage in explanation is effective is that, having articulated an incorrect explanation, further reading of ensuing sentences (which always present the correct information) ultimately lead to the generation of a contradiction that will produce conflict. The outcome of such conflict will require metacognitive reflection and self-repair by the student if resolution is to occur. Other evidence for the cognitive value of asking students to engage in the construction of explanations can be found in the work of McNeill and colleagues (2006), who showed that providing supports for students' written explanations led to significant learning gains. Likewise, Asterhan and Schwarz (2009) showed that students who received a short instructional intervention on natural selection and were then asked to construct explanations collaboratively for certain evolutionary phenomena in dyads while engaging in dialectical argumentation achieved larger learning gains than did students who did not.

Engaging in Argument From Evidence

The argument for a fourth practice—engaging in argument from evidence—has been made substantively already. For this practice, too, there is also a growing body of empirical evidence that points to improvements in conceptual learning when students engage in argumentation (Asterhan & Schwarz, 2007; Mercer, Dawes, Wegerif, & Sams, 2004; Sampson & Clark, 2009; Zohar & Nemet, 2002). For instance, Mercer and colleagues (2004) found that students who were asked to engage in small-group discussions significantly outperformed a group of control students in their use of extended utterances and verbal reasoning, features that are rare in formal science education (Lemke, 1990). Significant improvements were also produced in their nonverbal reasoning and understanding of science concepts. Another study by Zohar and Nemet (2002) with two classes of 16- to 17-year-old students studying genetics required students to engage in argumentative discourse about the appropriate answer to specific problems. Compared to a control group, the frequency of students who used biological knowledge appropriately (53.2% versus 8.9%) was significantly higher (Zohar & Nemet, 2002).

Again, a major goal of asking students to engage in argumentation must be to develop meta-knowledge of science. Foremost must be that all claims to know in science have to be argued for. From the idea that all objects fall with the same acceleration (in the absence of air resistance) to the idea that climate change is an anthropogenic effect, all claims require justification, drawing on a body of data and warrants that show its relevance. Sources of error may be models that are flawed or data that are unreliable or fallible. The degree of confidence we hold in any idea is dependent on the minimization of error and the accumulation of a body of evidence over time. Nothing is held to be infallible. Rather, there are only degrees of certainty. The second goal must be to demonstrate that there are a range of forms of argument used in science that may be abductive[8] (inferences to the best possible explanation), such as Darwin's arguments for the theory of evolution; hypothetico-deductive, such as Pasteur's predictions about the outcome of the first test of his anthrax vaccine; or simply inductive generalizations archetypally represented by "laws." Moreover, arguments are necessary in all spheres of activity (Figure 29.1), as there may be different experimental designs, alternative models, or contested interpretations of any data set, each with their competing merits. From an educational perspective, the value of asking students to engage in argumentation is that it demands the higher-order cognitive competencies of evaluation, synthesis, and comparison and contrast (Ford & Wargo, 2011).

Planning and Carrying Out Investigations

A functional understanding of the nature of science also requires students to be able to "evaluate the design, practices and conduct of scientific enquiry" (OECD, 2012). Indeed, the Programme for International Student Assessment (PISA) assessment framework sees this as one of the three key competencies of the scientifically literate individual. Such a competency is best developed by asking students to engage in the practice of designing empirical investigations to test hypotheses. Yet evidence would suggest that this rarely happens. For instance, in a detailed study of two Grade 8 classrooms, Watson and colleagues (2004) found that the quantity and quality of discussion surrounding their empirical enquiry was low, concluding that

> The main factor that seemed to be militating against the development of argumentation in the current study was the routinized nature of the practical activity. For the most part, students and teachers seemed to view scientific inquiry as learning to carry out a set of fixed procedures, which they were not expected to justify, and which could be used over and over again in the same ways in different inquiries.
>
> (p. 40)

Watson and colleagues (1999) also developed a typology of six different forms of investigation: classifying and identifying; fair testing; pattern seeking; exploring; investigating models; and making things or developing systems. Yet in a survey that collected descriptions of 1,000 investigations from 42 elementary schools and 13 junior high schools, 50% were "fair tests" in elementary schools and 82% in lower secondary schools. The exposure to such a limited set of forms of empirical enquiry will not develop an understanding of the broad repertoire of practice with which experimental scientists engage. Moreover, as Schauble and colleagues (Schauble, Klopfer & Raghavan, 1991) have found, many young children approach experimentation with an "engineering frame" of finding the best outcome rather than one of establishing causality. Consequently, they "search unsystematically and incompletely,

fail to control extraneous variables, distort evidence to preserve favored theories, and make logical errors in interpreting patterns of data" (p. 862). Even more simplistic ideas can be found in the work of Driver and colleagues (1996), where the function of experimentation was seen as one of "doing experiments and finding out things." Schauble and colleagues (1991) conclude that only practice and explicit instruction will help students build an understanding of appropriate models of scientific inquiry necessary for the kind of functional literacy that is required to make students critical consumers of scientific knowledge (Millar & Osborne, 1998).

Analyzing and Interpreting Data

Observation and empirical enquiry produce data. Data do not wear their meaning on their sleeves. First, data may suffer from either systematic or random errors such that some values are simply outliers and should be eliminated from any data set. Second, there may be systematic errors in the data set. A good contemporary example of the latter is the tendency to publish only positive findings for drug trials and not the negative findings—what is known as publication bias. As a consequence, the evidence for the efficacy of a drug can appear significantly better than it is in reality,[9] and the consequences can be so serious that lives are lost.

In any sixth-grade science class, you can observe students measuring the boiling point of water. But to what end? As an exercise to ascertain a value that has already been determined much more accurately by others, its purpose is highly questionable (Collins & Pinch, 1993). As an activity to develop students' facility with a thermometer, it too has little value given that it takes little skill to read a digital thermometer. However, given that students' readings may vary considerably, the much more interesting question is, How can we resolve the uncertainty? What methods exist and which of these are appropriate in this context? Since there are plural answers to the latter question, its resolution requires the application of a body of domain-specific procedural knowledge that serves as the warrants to justify the most appropriate result.

While confirmatory laboratory experiments in which the data set reinforces the account offered by the teacher have a rhetorical value—effectively providing the evidence that warrants the account proffered by the teacher of science—there has to be room in the teaching of science for data sets that are ambiguous and where the meaning is less than self-evident. A plot, for instance of breath rate against pulse rate as in Figure 29.2, shows a general trend, but four differing interpretations are offered (Goldsworthy, Watson, & Wood-Robinson, 2000). Being able to justify which is the best requires procedural knowledge of why there is error in measurement, the concept of outliers, and the need to summarize the main features of the data.

The PISA framework for the 2015 assessment (OECD, 2012) sees the competency to "interpret data and evidence scientifically" as another of the three core competencies

Is there a pattern between people's pulse rate and the number of breaths they take each minute? Some pupils investigated this. Their scatter graph is shown below.

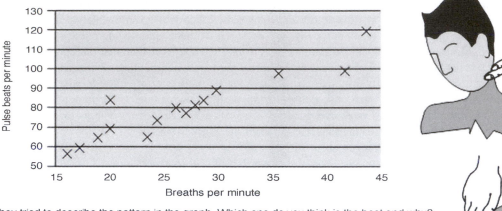

They tried to describe the pattern in the graph. Which one do you think is the best and why?

A. Jenny had the most breaths and she also had the highest pulse rate
B. All the people with a high breath rate had a high pulse rate
C. The higher your breathing rate, the higher your pulse rate
D. On the whole, those people with a higher breath rate had a higher pulse rate

Figure 29.2 Data question involving error and uncertainty.

of a scientifically literate person. Such a competency can only be developed by asking students to either gather their own sets of data or use secondary data sets and then establish and justify the best interpretation.

Using Mathematical and Computational Thinking

Another characteristic feature and practice of science is the use of mathematical and computational thinking. Science education often delays the mathematization of scientific ideas. Rather, there is a belief that it is more appropriate to develop a qualitative understanding of ideas and that too much early attention may develop an algorithmic facility but no deep understanding of science. The consequence is that "science curricula within the 5 to 16 age range appear to be seeking to manage without mathematics, or at least to function on as little as possible" (Orton & Roper, 2000, p. 146). As Orton and Roper (2000) argue, the lack of mathematics in the curriculum gives an impression of science that is "somewhat dishonest." Gill (1996) argues that "biology teachers should stop telling themselves (and their students) that biology doesn't need mathematics" such that they arrive at college with a false impression and are taken aback.

Mathematics and computational thinking *are* central to science, enabling the representation of variables, the symbolic representation of relationships, and the prediction of outcomes. As such, mathematics supports the description of the material world, enabling systematic representation that is the foundation of all scientific modeling and the clear communication of meaning. Thus mathematics serves pragmatic functions as a tool—that is, both a communicative function, as one of the languages of science,

and a structural function—which allows for logical deduction. Mathematics and numerical representation are the basis of all measurement in science. Numerical data have formalized ways of representation that enable the identification of a result in which there is more confidence (mean, mode, and median) and ways of showing variation using a range of tables, charts, or stem-and-leaf plots. Moreover, there is a body of research conducted in the learning sciences that shows that it is possible for young children to appropriate a range of mathematical resources that help formalize their interpretation and representation of their data. For instance, in an extensive program of work over 15 years (Lehrer & Schauble, 2006a, 2012), Lehrer and Schauble (2004) have shown how students learned to "read" shapes of distributions as signatures of prospective mechanisms of plant growth and conducted sampling investigations to represent repeated growth (Lehrer & Schauble, 2004).

For too many teachers of science, however, mathematics is not seen as something that is central and core to the practice of science. Many, perhaps, operate with the vaccination model of mathematics, much as they do with literacy—that it is not their responsibility to educate students in the mathematics (or the literacy) required to understand science. And if students have not been vaccinated, there is little that they, the teacher, can do. But if the use of mathematics in science is not a core feature of what happens in classrooms, the nature of science will be misrepresented. Natural language is very limited in its ability to describe continuous variation, shape, and the interrelationships of structure, form, and function—all aspects that are foci of science. Rather, science depends on a synergy of semiotic signs—symbols to represent elements, quantities, and units; graphs and charts to summarize relationships, frequencies, and patterns; tables to summarize numerical data; and mathematics to express relationships (Kress, Jewitt, Ogborn, Jon, & Tsatsarelis, 2001; Lemke, 1998). Avoiding the opportunity to use mathematical forms and representations *is a failure* to build students' competency to make meaning in science. Hence, opportunities to engage in the practice of mathematical and computational thinking are essential experiences in the teaching and learning of science. Yet again, there is a meta-level aspect to such a practice beyond developing competency in the use of mathematics in science. Students need to see for themselves that mathematics is an essential tool for the representation and analysis of data and for expressing relationships between quantities.

Obtaining, Evaluating, and Communicating Information

This practice, the eighth practice in the Framework for the K–12 standards, is one that is core to all science. Literacy is not some kind of adjunct to science—it is *constitutive of science itself* (Norris & Phillips, 2003). And just as there can be no houses without walls, there can be no science without reading and writing. Indeed, contrary to the popular image that perceives the major practice of science to be one of "doing experiments," Tenopir and King (2004) found that engineers and scientists spend more than 50% of their time engaged in reading and writing science. Similar points can be found in the work of Postman and Weingartner (1971) when they argue,

> Almost all of what we customarily call "knowledge" is language, which means that the *key to understanding a subject is to understand its language* [emphasis added]. . . This means, of course, that every teacher is a language teacher: teachers, quite literally, have little else to teach, but a way of talking and therefore seeing the world.
>
> (Postman & Weingartner, 1971)

Contemporary scholarship argues that it is the sociocultural practices that define any group, and a large element of these are carried out through the specific discourse practices of the community (Gee, 1996; Pickering, 1995; Wenger, 1998), through its conferences and its journals and *through its languages*. In short, writing and arguing are core activities for *doing* science (Jetton & Shanahan, 2012; Lemke, 1990). Indeed, as Norris and Phillips (2003) point out, the fundamental sense of literacy in science is the ability of an individual to construct meaning through interaction with the multiple forms of semiotic communication that are used *within* the discipline of science. Indeed, the five major communicative activities of science can be seen as writing science, talking science, reading science, "doing"[10] science, and representing scientific ideas—an idea that is represented by Figure 29.3.

The major point that Figure 29.3 makes is that the "doing of science" is only one of five forms of activity to

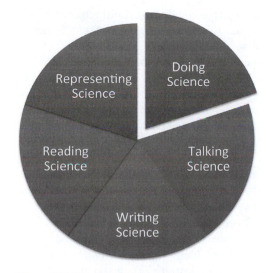

Figure 29.3 The major activities of science.

engage in science. Does, therefore, the "doing of science" deserve such a pre-eminent place?

To offer its students some kind of insight into the activity of science, science education must provide its students the opportunity to experience and practice a broad range of discursive and literate activities and scaffold students in the specific forms of disciplinary literacy required (Pearson, Moje, & Greenleaf, 2010; Shanahan & Shanahan, 2008). For, as the work of numerous systemic functional linguists has pointed out, the forms of communication within a discipline, while reliant on basic literacy, are often specific *to* the discipline (Fang, 2006; Halliday & Martin, 1993; Lemke, 1990; Martin & Veel, 1998; Schleppegrell & Fang, 2008). This body of work has led Shanahan and Shanahan (2008) and Jetton and Shanahan (2012) to argue for the concept of "disciplinary literacy" that they see as the ability to decode and interpret more complex forms of organization, to recognize the nature and function of genres specific to the discipline, and to use author intent within the discipline as a frame for a critical response.

The importance of developing students' disciplinary literacy skills in science classes has recently come to the fore in the American educational arena with the advent of the Common Core State Standards for English Language Arts and Literacy in Science (CCSS-ELA; Common Core State Standards Initiative, 2010). By including literacy standards to accompany science-content standards for each K–12 grade level, the creators of the CCSS-ELA have acknowledged the recommendation of numerous researchers: that language should play a more prominent role in science instruction (Bazerman, 1998; Halliday & Martin, 1993; Lemke, 1990; Norris & Phillips, 2003; Pearson et al., 2010; Wellington & Osborne, 2001).

The notion that there is such a thing as disciplinary literacy can be seen in the extensive vocabulary demands posed by science (Merzyn, 1987; Yore, 1991). Indeed, Merzyn (1987) has argued that there are more new terms introduced in a high school science textbook than in its foreign language counterpart. Furthermore, the real challenge posed by the language of science is not only the domain-specific vocabulary but also the use of "academic language"—the form of language that is used to attain "conciseness, achieved by avoiding redundancy; using a high density of information-bearing words, ensuring precision of expression; and relying on grammatical processes to compress complex ideas into few words" (Snow, 2010, p. 450).

Yet, traditionally, science teachers have not paid much attention to text (Wellington & Osborne, 2001), operating rather on the notion that there is nothing particularly distinctive about the genres in which science is communicated. This peripheral view of literacy creates a scenario in which science teachers lack the knowledge about "the vital role [that] literacy plays in enhancing rather than replacing science learning" (Pearson et al., 2010, p. 462) and, thus, teachers fail to mentor students in the necessary literate practices (Barton, Heidema, & Jordan, 2002).

For teachers of science, who are deeply steeped in academic language and its use, the difficulties posed by reading or producing science texts are not self-evident. For students, on the other hand, both the technical and academic language of science are often unfamiliar and not part of their identity (Brown, 2004). Moreover, research has shown that the transition to reading more discipline-specific language registers alienates students from disadvantaged or low-SES backgrounds (Fang, 2005; Schleppegrell & Fang, 2008; Snow, 2008), as many of them have not been exposed to either the features of academic language or the appropriate use of such vocabulary.

Empirical evidence that students—even ones educated to a high level in school science—lack the facility to construe appropriate meaning in scientific texts comes from the work of Norris and Phillips. In a series of studies stretching over a decade, Norris and Phillips have shown the lack of competency that students have in determining the appropriate meaning of a range of texts (Norris & Phillips, 1994; Norris, Phillips, & Korpan, 2003; Phillips & Norris, 1999). Such data would suggest that students have not been taught how to interpret and read texts in a critical fashion—that is, in a manner that would enable them to identify the epistemic constructs on which the text relies (Schleppegrell, 2004). For instance, as much as the scientist and the science teacher would like language in science to have a one-dimensional technical fixity of meaning, words have their limits. Thus science is forced into the use of analogy. Light is like a wave, clouds are like mirrors, atoms are like mini solar systems, demanding the question, In what sense are these likenesses valid and in what sense do they fail? Moreover, science texts misrepresent science. The vast majority provide nonfiction accounts of factual information, fail to state what question is being answered, explain why such a question might be important, and represent the production of scientific knowledge as process rather than a product of reasoning from evidence. The consequence is that such texts "reinforce the

representation of scientists as knowers of facts, not producers of knowledge claims" (Ford, 2006, p. 228).

The Goals of Engaging in Practice

As has been argued consistently in this chapter so far, the goal of asking students to engage in practice is not to build their competency with practice. That may be a secondary benefit. Such a notion would see practice as simply a skill. Practices are more than skills, though, as they are reliant on a body of knowledge that is specific to each practice. The primary purpose of engaging in practice is to develop students' knowledge and understanding required by that practice, how that practice contributes to how we know what we know, and how that practice helps to build reliable knowledge. The answer to the question of how we know (knowing how) is reliant on a developing a body of procedural knowledge or concepts of evidence (Gott & Duggan, 2008). Developing a knowledge and understanding of such meta-level concepts such as the control-of-variables strategy must form part of the goal of engaging in practice. Likewise, "knowing why" such strategies are important requires a body of epistemic knowledge that is essential to understand the basis of belief in science. What then are the elements of procedural and epistemic knowledge that matter in any school science education?

Procedural Knowledge

Gott and Murphy (1987) were the first to argue against seeing investigation or inquiry simply as a "process skill." Instead, they sought to define inquiry as an "activity." Within such an "activity," they argued, students made use of both *conceptual* and *procedural* understanding. The latter was a knowledge and understanding of scientific procedures, or "strategies of scientific enquiry," such as "holding one factor constant and varying the other" when controlling variables (p. 13). This insight had emerged from an analysis of their results in which the research team had found that much of the variation in student performance on tasks could not be explained solely on the basis of an absence of appropriate conceptual knowledge—for example, the lack of a suitable model of the system being investigated. Rather, it was accounted for by "procedural failures," caused by students not holding the necessary procedural knowledge. This finding led them to the conclusion that "the major influence on performance on this task is the availability to the child of certain relevant items of knowledge" and that "carrying out a scientific investigation, then, is primarily a display of understanding, and not of skill" (Gott & Murphy, 1987, p. 244).

As a consequence, Gott and Murphy (1987) argued for the explicit teaching of procedural knowledge, suggesting that "we must accept the need to develop an explicit underpinning [procedural] knowledge structure in the same way that we have developed such a structure for conceptual elements of the curriculum" (p. 52). Developing this notion in a later paper, Gott and Mashiter (1991) explicitly presented *procedural knowledge* as the "missing element" that could form the basis of a theoretical response to Millar and Driver's (1987) question of "what develops" in the process approach. As such, it offered a new theoretical perspective that made the scientific reasoning required for empirical enquiry and critique knowledge based rather than skill based.

Procedural knowledge is not, however, a new concept, having been introduced in psychology by Ryle (1949) decades earlier to describe the difference between "knowing how" and "knowing that." Ryle (1949), however, had used the notion of procedural knowledge in a more general manner to refer to tacit skill-based knowledge. Gott and colleagues' (Gott & Duggan, 2008; Gott & Murphy, 1987) notion, in contrast, is a much more specific articulation of the knowledge of procedures and methods required *by scientists* to test hypotheses and gather experimental data. Evidence of the importance of procedural knowledge in scientific reasoning has come from many research studies. One important study was the Procedural and Conceptual Knowledge in Science (PACKS) project that sought to identify what knowledge students actually apply when solving practical investigative tasks (Millar et al., 1995). This research used written items to probe students' procedural knowledge and compared their performance with that on the investigative tasks. Correlation was high, indicating that what was tested in the written items accounted for 50% or more of the variance in practical tasks. The research also revealed "misconceptions" among students about scientific methodology. Another important outcome of the study was to identify levels of understanding from simple to advanced procedural knowledge (Lubben & Millar, 1996) thereby answering Millar and Driver's question of what develops. Thus the work of Gott and his colleagues (Gott, Duggan, & Roberts, 2008; Gott & Murphy, 1987) identified a body of knowledge over and beyond domain-specific conceptual knowledge required for scientific reasoning. More recently, they have elaborated the notion of procedural knowledge as "concepts of evidence"—the constructs that are necessary to collect and analyze data (Gott, Duggan, & Roberts, 2008).

An even more recent version of what constitutes procedural knowledge is offered by the draft framework for the PISA 2015 science assessment (OECD, 2012), where procedural knowledge is defined as a knowledge of:

- Concepts of measurement, such as quantitative [measurements], qualitative [observations], the use of a scale, categorical and continuous variables
- Ways of assessing and minimizing uncertainty such as repeating and averaging measurements
- Mechanisms to ensure the replicability (closeness of agreement between repeated measures of the same quantity) and accuracy of data (the closeness of agreement between a measured quantity and a true value of the measure)
- The concepts of variables

- Common ways of abstracting and representing data using tables, graphs, and charts and their appropriate use
- The control-of-variables strategy and its role in experimental design, randomized controlled trials in avoiding confounded findings and identifying possible causal mechanisms
- The nature of an appropriate design for a given scientific questions, like experimental, field based, or pattern seeking

Nevertheless, although procedural knowledge offers an interesting alternative to the process skill paradigm, there remains one substantive problem. This is the argument that all knowledge involved in scientific reasoning is *either* conceptual *or* procedural. While such knowledge does answer the questions of "knowing that" and "knowing how," it fails to answer the question of "knowing why" such procedures are necessary.

Epistemic Knowledge

Knowing why the practices and procedures of science produce reliable knowledge requires epistemic knowledge. For while generating a scientific hypothesis requires content knowledge, less evident, however, is the finding of research (Reiner & Gilbert, 2000) that suggests that epistemic knowledge or resources also play crucial roles in its production. Experimentation, similarly, is not just a matter of knowing *how* to get reliable data—which is a procedural issue—but also *why* reliability and validity are important—which is an epistemic issue. It is true that sometimes one phase of activity may be solved without involving all types of knowledge. Klahr (2000), for instance, has shown that his subjects generated correct hypotheses to a problem without considering any experimental data. But scientific reasoning is never dependent solely on *one* type of knowledge.

Over the past two decades, science educators have been wrestling with how to incorporate epistemic knowledge into the curriculum. The movement to address the nature of science specifically (Lederman, 1992, 2007; Matthews, 1989) can be seen as one attempt to incorporate aspects of epistemic knowledge. Likewise, Millar and Osborne's (1998) notion of "ideas about science" or the more generic term "how science works" are other formulations of what is a distinct body of knowledge *about science itself.* Coupled with empirical evidence suggesting that such knowledge is perceived as a significant element of any science education (Osborne, Ratcliffe, Collins, Millar, & Duschl, 2003), such arguments have led to conceptualizing epistemic knowledge as a more prominent feature of contemporary curricula. The current version of the English national curriculum (Qualifications and Curriculum Authority, 2007) includes a specific component titled "How Science Works," while the framework for the common standards in science education outlines eight scientific practices that should be an essential element of K–12 science education

(National Research Council, 2012), though notably this document does not define specific elements of epistemic knowledge.

The PISA framework for 2015 (OECD, 2012) goes further in that it does incorporate epistemic knowledge that is seen as consisting of two components—(a) a knowledge of the constructs and defining features essential to the process of knowledge building in science and (b) the role of these constructs in justifying the knowledge produced by science. The proposed constructs and defining features of science are a knowledge of:

- The nature of scientific observations, facts, hypotheses, models, and theories
- The purpose and goals of science (to produce explanations of the material world) as distinguished from technology (to produce an optimal solution to human need), what constitutes a scientific or technological question and appropriate data
- The values of science, such as a commitment to publication, objectivity, and the elimination of bias
- The nature of reasoning used in science, such as deductive, inductive, inference to the best explanation (abductive), analogical, model base

The features of the second component—a knowledge of their role in justifying the knowledge produced by science—are a knowledge of:

- How scientific claims are supported by data and reasoning in science
- The function of different forms of empirical enquiry in establishing knowledge, their goal (to test explanatory hypotheses or identify patterns), and their design (observation, controlled experiments, correlational studies)
- The function of a scientific hypothesis in enabling a testable prediction
- How measurement error affects the degree of confidence in scientific knowledge
- The use and role of physical, system, and abstract models and their limits
- The role of collaboration and critique and how peer review helps to establish confidence in scientific claims
- The role of scientific knowledge, along with other forms of knowledge, in identifying and addressing societal and technological issues such as the prevention of disease, the supply of sufficient water, food and energy, and climate change

Such a list can only ever be partial and open to debate. Nevertheless, it performs the important function of identifying and pointing toward specific aspects of knowledge that should be a product of asking students to engage in scientific practice. The research of Metz (2008), Lehrer and Schauble (2012), and Smith and colleagues (2000) has demonstrated that students are able to participate in the cognitive, social, and epistemic practices in ways that

were not thought possible before. However, developing an educated populace that is functionally scientifically literate does require the community engaged in science education to define what bodies of knowledge should be an essential outcome of that process.

In what sense then is the specification of procedural and epistemic knowledge different from lists of domain-general, consensus-based heuristics? The problem with the approach that seeks to establish a set of domain-general, consensus-based heuristics about the nature of science as an outcome of science education is that, although such lists do define a salient body of knowledge, they are too broad and insufficiently tied to a rich context that might exemplify specific epistemic and procedural effects. The only way of testing any understanding of such tenets is by asking a specific question about specific contexts and, given their broad nature, it is difficult to develop what might be an appropriate assessment of understanding. The initial attempts to define what constitutes procedural and epistemic knowledge offered here and by others go some way to putting some flesh on the bare bones and help to define what kind of performance might be attained by the end of formal education. They are, however, only initial proposals and stand for others to critique and advance.

Curriculum design in this context might be better done if it adopted the approach advocated by Wiggins and McTighe (2004), who argue what kind of performance might we expect at the end of such an educative process as the basis for beginning any curriculum planning. The broad generality of the consensus-based heuristics about the nature of science provide little guidance. What kind of performance would generate an understanding of the requirement that "scientific theories are well-established, highly substantiated, internally consistent systems of explanation" (Abd-El-Khalick, 2012, p. 358)? Rather, as Allchin (2011) points out, surveying a set of news items and asking what kind of procedural and epistemic understanding of science would be necessary to understand contemporary newspaper reports about science does produce a list of 41 specific features about observation and reasoning, methods of investigation, history and creativity, the human context, the culture and values of those working in science, the social interaction among the scientists, the cognitive processes, and economics and funding. This lists includes features such as the role of systematic study, the consideration of alternative explanations, blind and double-blind trials, replication and sample size, error and uncertainty, collaboration, the motivation for doing science, the role of peer review, the possibility of fraud or misconduct, sources of funding, and more. Clearly no contemporary science education has the time to develop a knowledge of all these features of practice. The point, however, is that it is by engaging in practice and reflecting on the specific features of practice that students can develop at least some of these understandings. Assessment can then seek to investigate whether students are capable of identifying the salient features that should be considered in making a judgment about the validity and implications of similar, contextually situated research reports.

If we are to build on "students' emerging capacities for representation, model-building, and casual reasoning," as Duschl and Grandy (2013) argue, then it is necessary to have some plan of the structure we hope to build and its constituent elements. Otherwise practice without clear, well-specified goals is blind, while broad goals without details are little more than statements of aspiration, providing little guidance for how they should be operationalized or exemplified in the classroom.

The important point, though, is that the practices discussed in this chapter are not simply a feature of laboratory work. Rather, they are pervasive across all aspects of science, and it is difficult to imagine a single lesson of science that would not raise an opportunity to highlight one of these practices. To examine their function in laboratory work, any kind of empirical activity needs to be preceded by a dialogic exploration of the nature of the question being investigated, the appropriate design of any form of empirical enquiry, a consideration of the salient variables for an investigation of this nature, whether the inquiry requires variables to be controlled, the choice of measuring instrument or instruments, how many data need to be collected, and then how many times measurements should be taken to ensure reliability. Such an approach would require students to work with each other, possibly in teams, to consider the choices that are available and engage in argumentation to resolve any differences they may have in interpreting the data.

Another way of approaching the epistemic goals that are a feature of science could be through a requirement that all students should undertake a minimum of one historical or contemporary case study of science a year. As Allchin (2011) points out, historical case studies provide an opportunity to examine how scientists can err, the nature of radical conceptual change and uncertainty, and the role of cultural context and potential bias in scientific ideas. Case studies need to set a social context. Why, for instance, was it natural to believe that the Earth is the center of the universe, that the continents do not move, or that heavier things fall faster? In short, why does the idea being proposed appear radical? What occurred to make the idea ultimately acceptable, how long did it take, and what convinced people of its validity? The shortage of suitable materials to support such forms of inquiry that existed 20 years ago (Bybee et al., 1991; Duschl, 1994) still exists today. In addition, the lack of exploration of the history and epistemology of the subject in the education of those who would be teachers of science means that there is a paucity of professional expertise.

Ultimately, however, serious consideration of the teaching of scientific practices and procedural and epistemic knowledge will require such aspects to become a feature of summative assessment. An extensive body of literature indicates that high-stakes testing has a powerful impact on classroom instruction. In a review of this literature prepared for the U.S. Department of Education, Hannaway and Hamilton (2008) found that standards and accountability policies lead teachers to focus on particular subject areas and types of instructional practices. In addition, they found that teachers focused on skills specific to assessment and testing procedures. Thus, teaching about scientific practices will only come to be valued if students' understanding of the practices and procedural and epistemic knowledge are tested and engaging students in undertaking scientific practices is an effective vehicle to support their learning. Assessment of students' understanding of practice, procedural, and epistemic knowledge gives a key message that such outcomes matter.

Conclusion

To this date, however, teaching about science and developing students' epistemic and procedural knowledge has remained more talked about than taught. The argument of this chapter has been that teaching science through practices offers a fresh way of resolving some of the pitfalls of the past. Fifteen years ago, I and others wrote (Millar & Osborne, 1998):

> In focusing on the detail, we have lost sight of the major ideas that science has to tell. To borrow an architectural metaphor, it is impossible to see the whole building if we focus too closely on the individual bricks. Yet, without a change of focus, it is impossible to see whether you are looking at St Paul's Cathedral or a pile of bricks, or to appreciate what it is that makes St Paul's one the world's great churches. In the same way, an over concentration on the detailed content of science may prevent students appreciating why Dalton's ideas about atoms, or Darwin's ideas about natural selection, are among the most powerful and significant pieces of knowledge we possess.
>
> (p. 2013)

Analogies, however, are deceptive. The mistake here was to think that it would be sufficient to give students a vision of what St. Paul's Cathedral or science looks like. In the case of science, we must also give them some experience, understanding, and insight into how it was constructed—that is, the practices that justify our belief in the scientific worldview, and, in so doing, develop a deeper understanding of the nature of science itself.

Notes

1. Throughout this chapter, the phrase "material world" is used to refer to all natural phenomena and living organisms.
2. Author's original emphasis.
3. These notes can be found in the Christ's Hospital Archive, Horsham, Sussex.
4. Author's emphasis.
5. We use the word "process" here as it is the word used by Khlar and Dunbar—although later we will characterize these as "practices." While the distinction may be subtle, it is important for reasons we will explain later.

6. The term "argumentation" is used here to refer to the process of constructing or critiquing an argument.

7. Emphasis added.

8. Abductive arguments are also known as retroductive arguments.

9. Ben Goldacre offers an excellent discussion of this issue in a TED talk (www.ted.com/talks/ben_goldacre_what_doctors_don_t_know_about_the_drugs_they_prescribe.html).

10. In one sense, any of these activities could be said to be "doing science." In this chapter, the term "doing science" is used to refer to the act of engaging in empirical inquiry.

References

Abd-El-Khalick, F. (2012). Examining the sources for our understandings about science: Enduring conflations and critical issues in research on nature of science in science education. *International Journal of Science Education, 34*(3), 353–374.

Abd-El-Khalick, F., BouJaoude, S., Duschl, R., Lederman, N. G., Mamlok-Naaman, R., Hofstein, A., . . . Tuan, H.-l. (2004). Inquiry in science education: International perspectives. *Science Education, 88*(3), 397–419.

Abd-El-Khalick, F., & Lederman, N. G. (2000). Improving science teachers' conceptions of the nature of science: A critical review of the literature. *International Journal of Science Education, 22*(7), 665–702.

Abd-El-Khalick, F., Waters, M., & Le, A. P. (2008). Representations of nature of science in high school chemistry textbooks over the past four decades. *Journal of Research in Science Teaching, 45*(7), 835–855.

Acher, A., Arca, M., & Sanmarti, N. (2007). Modeling as a teaching learning process for understanding materials: A case study in primary education. *Science Education, 91*(3), 398–418.

Ainsworth, S., Prain, V., & Tytler, R. (2011). Drawing to learn in science. *Science, 333,* 1096–1097.

Allchin, D. (2011). Evaluating knowledge of the nature of (whole) science. *Science Education, 95*(3), 518–542.

Alters, B. J. (1997). Whose nature of science? *Journal of Research in Science Teaching, 34*(1), 39–55.

Ames, G. J., & Murray, F. B. (1982). When two wrongs make a right: Promoting cognitive change by social conflict. *Developmental Psychology, 18,* 894–897.

Armstrong, H. E. (1902). The heuristic method of teaching. *School Science and Mathematics, 1*(8), 395–401.

Asterhan, C. S. C., & Schwarz, B. B. (2007). The effects of monological and dialogical argumentation on concept learning in evolutionary theory. *Journal of Educational Psychology, 99*(3), 626–639.

Asterhan, C. S. C., & Schwarz, B. B. (2009). Argumentation and explanation in conceptual change: Indications from protocol analyses of peer-to-peer dialog. *Cognitive Science, 33*(3), 374–400.

Baird, D., Scerri, E., & McIntyre, L. (Eds.). (2006). *Philosophy of chemistry: Synthesis of a new discipline.* Dordrecht: Springer.

Barton, M. L., Heidema, C., & Jordan, D. (2002). Teaching Reading in Mathematics and Science. *Educational Leadership, 60*(3), 24–28.

Bazerman, C. (1988). *Shaping written knowledge.* Madison: University of Wisconsin Press.

Bazerman, C. (1998). Emerging perspectives on the many dimensions of scientific discourse. In J. R. Martin & R. Veel (Eds.), *Reading science* (pp. 15–28). London: Routledge.

Biddulph, F., Symington, D., & Osborne, R. (1986). The place of children's questions in primary science education. *Research in Science and Technological Education, 4,* 77–88.

Bowker, G. C., & Leigh Star, S. (1999). *Sorting things out: Classification and its consequences.* Cambridge: MIT Press.

Bransford, J. D., Brown, A. L., & Cocking, R. R. (2000). *How people learn: Brain, mind & experience in school.* Washington, DC: National Academy of Sciences.

Brown, B. (2004). Discursive identity: Assimilation into the culture of science and its implications for minority students. *Journal of Research in Science Teaching, 41*(8), 810–834.

Burke, E. (1909). *On taste. On the sublime and beautiful. Reflections on the French Revolution. A letter to a noble lord.* New York: Collier.

Bybee, R. W., Powell, J. C., Ellis, J. D., Giese, J. R., Parisi, L., & Singleton, L. (1991). Integrating the history and nature of science and technology in science and social studies curriculum. *Science Education, 75*(1), 143–155.

Cartwright, N. (1983). *How the laws of physics lie.* Oxford: Clarendon Press.

Chi, M., Bassok, M., Lewis, M. W., Reimann, P., & Glaser, R. (1989). Self-explanations: How students study and use examples in learning to solve problems. *Cognitive Science, 13,* 145–182.

Chi, M., De Leeuw, N., Chiu, M. H., & Lavancher, C. (1994). Eliciting self-explanations improves understanding. *Cognitive Science, 18,* 439–477.

Chiappetta, E. L., & Fillman, D. A. (2007). Analysis of five high school biology textbooks used in the United States for inclusion of the nature of science. *International Journal of Science Education, 29*(15), 1847–1868.

Chin, C., & Osborne, J. F. (2008). Students' questions: A potential resource for teaching and learning science. *Studies in Science Education, 44*(1), 1–39.

Chinn, A. C., & Malhotra, A. B. (2003). Epistemologically authentic inquiry in schools: A theoretical framework for evaluating inquiry task. *Science Education, 86*(2), 175–218.

Collins, H., & Pinch, T. (1993). *The golem: What everyone should know about science.* Cambridge: Cambridge University Press.

Common Core State Standards Initiative. (2010). *Common core state standards for English language arts and literacy in history/social studies & science.* Retrieved from www.corestandards.org/

Conant, J. (1957). *Harvard case histories in experimental science* (Vol. 1 & 2). Cambridge, MA: Harvard University Press.

Donovan, S., & Bransford, J. D. (2005). *How students learn science in the classroom.* Washington, DC: National Academies Press.

Driver, R., Leach, J., Millar, R., & Scott, P. (1996). *Young people's images of science.* Buckingham: Open University Press.

Driver, R., Newton, P., & Osborne, J. F. (2000). Establishing the norms of scientific argumentation in classrooms. *Science Education, 84*(3), 287–312.

Duschl, R. (1994). Research on the history and philosophy of science. In D. L. Gabel (Ed.), *Handbook of research on science teaching and learning* (pp. 443–465). New York: MacMillan.

Duschl, R., & Grandy, R. (2013). Two views about explicitly teaching nature of science. *Science and Education, 22,* 2109–2139.

Duschl, R., & Osborne, J F. (2002). Supporting and promoting argumentation discourse in science education. *Studies in Science Education, 38,* 39–72.

Fang, Z. (2005). Scientific literacy: A systemic functional linguistics perspective. *Science Education, 89*(2), 335–347.

Fang, Z. (2006). The language demands of science reading in middle school. *International Journal of Science Education, 28*(5), 491–520.

Fisher, R. (1990). *Teaching children to think.* London: Simon and Shuster.

Ford, D. J. (2006). Representations of science within children's trade books. *Journal of Research in Science Teaching, 43*(2), 214–235. doi:10.1002/tea.20095

Ford, M. J. (2008). Disciplinary authority and accountability in scientific practice and learning. *Science Education, 92*(3), 404–423.

Ford, M. J., & Wargo, B. M. (2011). Dialogic framing of scientific content for conceptual and epistemic understanding. *Science Education, 96*(3), 369–391.

Gee, J. (1996). *Social linguistics and literacies* (2nd ed.). London: Taylor & Francis.

Geison, J. (1995). *The private science of Louis Pasteur.* Princeton, NJ: Princeton University Press.

Giere, R., Bickle, J., & Mauldin, R. F. (2006). *Understanding scientific reasoning* (5th ed.). Belmont, CA: Thomson Wadsworth.

Gilbert, J., & Boulter, C. (Eds.). (2000). *Developing models in science education.* Dordrecht, the Netherlands: Kluwer.

Gill, P. (1996). Focus: Can we count on biology? *Journal of Biological Education, 30*(3), 159–160.

Goldacre, B. (2008). *Bad science.* London: Harper Collins.

Goldsworthy, A., Watson, R., & Wood-Robinson, V. (2000). *Developing understanding in scientific enquiry.* Hatfield: Association for Science Education, UK.

Gott, R., Duggan, S., & Roberts, R. (2008). *Concepts of evidence.* School of Education, University of Durham, UK.

Gott, R., & Mashiter, J. (1991). Practical work in science—a task-based approach. In B.E. Woolnough (Ed.), *Practical science: The role and reality of practical work in school science* (pp. 53–66). Milton Keynes: Open University Press, UK.

Gott, R., & Murphy, P. (1987). *Assessing investigation at ages 13 and 15. Assessment of performance unit science report for teachers: 9.* London: Department of Education and Science.

Gutierrez, K., & Rogoff, B. (2003). Cultural ways of learning: Individual traits or repertoires of practice. *Educational Researcher, 32*(5), 19–25.

Halliday, M.A.K., & Martin, J.R. (1993). *Writing science: Literacy and discursive power.* London: Falmer Press.

Hannaway, J., & Hamilton, L. (2008). *Accountability policies: Implications for school and classroom practices.* Washington, DC: Urban Institute/ RAND.

Hanson, N.R. (1958). *Patterns of discovery.* Cambridge, UK: Cambridge University Press.

Harré, R. (1984). *The philosophies of science: An introductory survey* (2nd ed.). Oxford: Oxford University Press.

Harrison, A.G., & Treagust, D.F. (2002). A typology of school science models. *International Journal of Science Education, 22*(9), 1011–1026.

Hempel, C.G. (1962). Deductive-nomological vs. statistical explanation. *Minnesota Studies in the Philosophy of Science, 3,* 98–169.

Howson, C., & Urbach, P. (2006). *Scientific reasoning: A Bayesian approach* (3rd ed.). Chicago: Open Court.

Hynd, C., & Alvermann, D. E. (1986). The role of refutation text in overcoming difficulty with science concepts. *Journal of Reading, 29*(5), 440–446.

Jetton, T.L., & Shanahan, C.H. (2012). *Adolescent literacy in the academic disciplines: General principles and practical strategies.* New York: Guilford Press.

Johnson, Ann. (2009). *Hitting the brakes: Engineering design and the production of knowledge.* Durham, NC: Duke University Press.

Kind, P. M., Kind, V., Adamson, H., & Barmby, P. (2009). *Scientific argumentation, epistemic beliefs and attitudes—a quantitative correlational study of 14–15 year old students.* Paper presented at the Biennial Conference of the European Science Education Research Association, Istanbul, Turkey.

Kitcher, P. (2001). *Science, truth and democracy.* Oxford: Oxford University Press.

Kitcher, P. (2010). The climate change debates. *Science, 328*(5983), 1230–1234.

Klahr, D. (2000). *Exploring science: The cognition and development of discovery processes.* Cambridge, MA: Bradford.

Klahr, D., & Carver, S. M. (1995). Scientific thinking about scientific thinking. *Monographs of the Society for Research in Child Development, 60*(4), 137–151.

Klahr, D., & Dunbar, K. (1988). Dual space search during scientific reasoning. *Cognitive Science: A Multidisciplinary Journal, 12*(1), 1–48.

Klahr, D., Fay, A.L., & Dunbar, K. (1993). Heuristics for scientific experimentation: A developmental study. *Cognitive Psychology, 24*(1), 111–146.

Kress, G., Jewitt, C., Ogborn, J., & Tsatsarelis, C. (2001). *Multimodal teaching and learning: The rhetorics of the science classroom.* London: Continuum Books.

Kuhn, T.E. (1962). *The structure of scientific revolutions.* Chicago: University of Chicago Press.

Lakatos, I. (1970). Falsification and the methodology of scientific research programmes. In I. Lakatos & A. Musgrave (Eds.), *Criticism and the growth of knowledge* (pp. 91–196). Cambridge: Cambridge University Press.

Latour, B. (1986). Visualization and cognition: Drawing things together. *Knowledge and Society, 6,* 1–40.

Latour, B. (1999). *Pandora's hope: Essays on the reality of science studies.* Cambridge, MA. Harvard University Press.

Latour, B., & Woolgar, S. (1986). *Laboratory life: The construction of scientific facts* (2nd ed.). Princeton, NJ: Princeton University Press.

Lederman, N. G. (1992). Students' and teachers' conceptions of the nature of science: A review of the research. *Journal of Research in Science Teaching, 29,* 331–359.

Lederman, N. G. (2007). Nature of science: Past, present and future. In S. Abell & N. G. Lederman (Eds.), *Handbook of research on science education* (pp. 831–879). Mahwah, NJ: Lawrence Erlbaum.

Lehrer, R., & Schauble, L. (2004). Modeling natural variation through distribution. *American Educational Research Journal, 41*(3), 635–679. doi:10.3102/00028312041003635

Lehrer, R., & Schauble, L. (2006a). Cultivating model-based reasoning in science education. In R. K. Sawyer (Ed.), *The Cambridge handbook of the learning sciences* (pp. 371–387).

Lehrer, R., & Schauble, L. (2006b). Scientific thinking and science literacy. In W. Damon, R. M. Lerner, & N. Eisenberg (Eds.), *Handbook of child psychology* (pp. 153–196). New York: Wiley.

Lehrer, R., & Schauble, L. (2012). Seeding evolutionary thinking by engaging children in modeling its foundations. *Science Education, 96*(4), 701–724.

Lemke, J. (1990). *Talking science: Language, learning and values.* Norwood, NJ: Ablex Publishing.

Lemke, J. (1998). *Teaching all the languages of science: Words, symbols, images and actions.* Retrieved from http://academic.brooklyn.cuny. edu/education/jlemke/papers/barcelon.htm

Longino, H. E. (2002). *The fate of knowledge.* Princeton, NJ: Princeton University Press.

Lubben, F., & Millar, R. (1996). Children's ideas about the reliability of experimental data. *International Journal of Science Education, 18*(8), 955–968.

Martin, J.R., & Veel, R. (1998). *Reading science.* London: Routledge.

Matthews, M. (1989). A role for history and philosophy in science teaching. *Interchange, 20*(2), 3–15.

Matthews, M. (1995). *Constructivism and New Zealand science education.* Auckland, New Zealand: Dunmore Press.

Matthews, M. (2012). Changing the focus: From nature of science to features of science. In M. S. Khine (Ed.), *Advances in nature of science research* (pp. 3–26). Dordrecht, the Netherlands: Springer.

Mayr, E. (2004). *What makes biology unique? Considerations on the autonomy of a scientific discipline.* Cambridge. Cambridge University Press.

McComas, W.F., & Olson, J. K. (1998). The nature of science in international science education standards documents. In W.F. McComas (Ed.), *The nature of science in science education: Rationales and strategies* (pp. 41–52). Dordrecht, the Netherlands: Kluwer.

McNeill, K., Lizotte, D., Krajcik, J., & Marx, R. (2006). Supporting students' construction of scientific explanations by fading scaffolds in instructional materials. *Journal of the Learning Sciences, 15*(2), 153–191.

McRobbie, C., & Thomas, G. (2001). *They don't teach us to explain, they only tell us other people's explanations.* Paper presented at the European Association for Research on Learning, Freiburg, Switzerland.

Mercer, N., Dawes, L., Wegerif, R., & Sams, C. (2004). Reasoning as a scientist: Ways of helping children to use language to learn science. *British Education Research Journal, 30*(3), 359–377.

Merzyn, G. (1987). The language of school science. *International Journal of Science Education, 9*(4), 483–489.

Metz, K.E. (2008). Narrowing the gulf between the practices of science and the elementary school classroom. *Elementary School Journal, 109*(2), 138–161.

Millar, R. (1998). Rhetoric and reality: What practical work in science education is *really* for. In J. Wellington (Ed.), *Practical work in school science: Which way now?* (pp. 16–31). London: Routledge.

Millar, R., & Driver, R. (1987). Beyond processes. *Studies in Science Education, 14,* 33–62.

Millar, R., Lubben, F., Gott, R., & Duggan, S. (1995). Investigating in the school science laboratory: Conceptual and procedural knowledge and their influence on performance. *Research Papers in Education, 9*(2), 207–248.

Millar, R., & Osborne, J. F. (Eds.). (1998). *Beyond 2000: Science education for the future.* London: King's College London.

National Academy of Science. (1995). *National science education standards.* Washington, DC: National Academies Press.

National Research Council. (2000). *Inquiry and the national science education standards.* Washington, DC: National Academies Press.

National Research Council. (2012). *A framework for K–12 science education: Practices, crosscutting concepts, and core ideas.* Washington, DC: Committee on a Conceptual Framework for New K–12 Science Education Standards. Board on Science Education, Division of Behavioral and Social Sciences and Education.

Nercessian, N. (2008). Model-based reasoning in scientific practice. In R.A. Duschl & R.E. Grandy (Eds.), *Teaching scientific inquiry: Recommendations for research and implementation* (pp. 57–79). Rotterdam, the Netherlands: Sense.

Nersessian, N. (2002). The cognitive basis of model-based reasoning in science. In P. Carruthers, S. Stich, & M. Siegal (Eds.), *The cognitive basis of science* (pp. 133–153). Cambridge: Cambridge University Press.

Norris, S. P. (1997). Intellectual independence for nonscientists and other content-transcendent goals of science education. *Science Education, 81*(2), 239–258.

Norris, S. P., & Phillips, L. (1994). Interpreting pragmatic meaning when reading popular reports of science. *Journal of Research in Science Teaching, 31*(9), 947–967.

Norris, S. P., & Phillips, L. (2003). How literacy in its fundamental sense is central to scientific literacy. *Science Education, 87,* 224–240.

Norris, S. P., Phillips, L.M., & Korpan, C.A. (2003). University students' interpretation of media reports of science and its relationship to background knowledge, interest, and reading difficulty. *Public Understanding of Science, 12,* 123–145.

Nott, M., & Smith, R. (1995). "Talking your way out of it," "rigging" and "conjuring": What science teachers do when practicals go wrong. *International Journal of Science Education, 17*(3), 399–410.

Oaksford, M., & Chater, N. (2007). *Bayesian rationality: The probalistic approach to human reasoning.* New York: Oxford University Press.

OECD. (2012). *The PISA 2015 assessment framework: Key competencies in reading, mathematics and science.* Retrieved from www.oecd.org/pisa/pisaproducts/pisa2015draftframeworks.htm

Orton, T., & Roper, T. (2000). Science and mathematics: A relationship in need of counselling? *Studies in Science Education, 35*(1), 123–153. doi:10.1080/03057260008560157

Osborne, J. F. (2010). Science for citizenship. In J.F. Osborne & J. Dillon (Eds.), *Good practice in science teaching: What research has to say* (2nd ed., pp. 46–67). Buckingham, UK: Open University Press.

Osborne, J. F., Ratcliffe, M., Collins, S., Millar, R., & Duschl, R. (2003). What "ideas-about-science" should be taught in school science? A Delphi study of the "expert" community. *Journal of Research in Science Teaching, 40*(7), 692–720.

Pearson, D., Moje, E. B., & Greenleaf, C. (2010). Literacy and science: Each in the service of the other. *Science, 328,* 459–463.

Penick, J.E., Crow, L.W., & Bonnsteter, R.J. (1996). Questions are the answers. *Science Teacher, 63,* 26–29.

Phillips, L.M., & Norris, S. P. (1999). Interpreting popular reports of science: What happens when the reader's world meets the world on paper? *International Journal of Science Education, 21,* 317–327.

Pickering, A. (1995). *The mangle of practice: Time, agency & science.* Chicago: University of Chicago Press.

Polyani, M. (1958). *Personal knowledge.* London: Routledge, Kegan & Paul.

Popper, K. (1972). *Obective knowledge: an evolutionary approach.* Oxford: Oxford University Press.

Posner, G.J., Strike, K.A., Hewson, P.W., & Gerzog, W.A. (1982). Accommodation of a scientific conception: Toward a theory of conceptual change. *Science Education, 66,* 211–227.

Postman, N., & Weingartner, C. (1971). *Teaching as a subversive activity.* Harmondsworth, UK: Penguin.

Qualifications and Curriculum Authority. (2007). *Programme of study: Science KS4.* London: UK. Qualifications and Curriculum Authority.

Quine, W.V. (1951). Main trends in recent philosophy: Two dogmas of empiricism. *The Philosophical Review, 60*(1), 20–43.

Reiner, M., & Gilbert, J.K. (2000). Epistemological resources for thought experimentation in science learning. *International Journal of Science Education, 22*(5), 489–506.

Rogers, E. M. (1948). Science in general education. In E.J. McGrath (Ed.), *Science in general education* (pp. 2–10). Dubuque, IA: Wm. C. Brown Co.

Rosenshine, B., Meister, C., & Chapman, S. (1996). Teaching students to generate questions: A review of the intervention studies. *Review of Educational Research, 66,* 181–221.

Roth, W.-M. (1995). *Authentic school science: Knowing and learning in open-inquiry science laboratories.* Dordrecht, the Netherlands: Kluwer Academic.

Rudolph, J. L. (2003). Portraying epistemology: School science in historical context. *Science Education, 87*(1), 64–79. doi:10.1002/sce.1055

Ryle, G. (1949). *The concept of mind.* London: Hutchinson.

Sampson, V., & Clark, D. (2009). The impact of collaboration on the outcomes of scientific argumentation. *Science Education, 93*(3), 448–484.

Schauble, L., Klopfer, L.E., & Raghavan, K. (1991). Students' transition from an engineering model to a science model of experimentation. *Journal of Research in Science Teaching, 28*(9), 859–882.

Schleppegrell, M. (2004). *The language of schooling: A functional linguistics perspective.* Hillsdale, NJ: Erlbaum.

Schleppegrell, M., & Fang, Z. (2008). *Reading in secondary content areas: A language-based pedagogy.* Ann Arbor: University of Michigan Press.

Schmidt, H.G. (1993). Foundations of problem-based learning: Rationale and description. *Medical Education, 17,* 11–16.

Schwab, J. J. (1962). *The teaching of science as enquiry.* Cambridge, MA: Harvard University Press.

Schwarz, B.B., Neuman, Y., & Biezuner, S. (2000). Two wrongs may make a right . . . if they argue together! *Cognition and Instruction, 18*(4), 461–494.

Schwarz, C.V., & White, B.Y. (2005). Metamodeling knowledge: Developing students' understanding of scientific modeling. *Cognition and Instruction, 23*(2), 165–206.

Shanahan, T., & Shanahan, C. (2008). Teaching disciplinary literacy to adolescents: Rethinking content area literacy. *Harvard Educational Review, 78*(1), 40–59.

Smith, C. L., Maclin, D., Houghton, C., & Hennessey, M. Ge. (2000). Sixth-grade students' epistemologies of science: The impact of school science experiences on epistemological development. *Cognition & Instruction, 18*(3), 349–422.

Snow, C. (2008). What is the vocabulary of science? In A. Roseberry & B. Warren (Eds.), *Teaching science to English language learners* (pp. 71–83). Washington, DC: NSTA Press.

Snow, C. (2010). Academic language and the challenge of reading for learning about science. *Science, 328,* 450–452.

Stevens, P. (1978). On the Nuffield philosophy of science. *Journal of Philosophy of Education, 12,* 99–111.

Stewart, J., Cartier, J.L., & Passmore, C.M. (2005). Developing understanding through model-based inquiry. In J.D. Bransford (Ed.), *How students learn science in the classroom* (pp. 515–565). Washington, DC: National Research Council.

Szu, E., & Osborne, J. F. (2011). Scientific reasoning and argumentation from a Bayesian perspective. In M.S. Khine (Ed.), *Perspectives on scientific argumentation* (pp. 55–71). Dordrecht, the Netherlands: Springer.

Tenopir, C., & King, D. W. (2004). *Communication patterns of engineers.* Hoboken, New York: Wiley.

Traweek, S. (1988). *Beamtimes and lifetimes: The world of high energy physicists.* Cambridge, MA: Harvard University Press.

Van Praagh, G. (2003). *A fire to be kindled: The global influence of Christ's hospital on science education.* Bury St. Edmunds, UK: St. Edmundsbury Press.

Watson, R., Goldsworthy, A., & Wood Robinson, C. (1999). What is not fair with investigations? *School Science Review, 80*(292), 101–106.

Watson, R., Swain, J., & McRobbie, C. (2004). Students' discussions in practical scientific enquiries. *International Journal of Science Education, 26*(1), 25–46.

Weiss, I. R., Pasley, J. D., Sean Smith, P., Banilower, E. R., & Heck, D. J. (2003). *A study of K–12 mathematics and science education in the United States.* Chapel Hill, NC: Horizon Research.

Wellington, J. (1981). What's supposed to happen, Sir? Some problems with discovery learning. *School Science Review, 63,* 167–173.

Wellington, J. (Ed.). (1998). *Practical work in school science: Which way now?* London: Routledge.

Wellington, J., & Osborne, J. F. (2001). *Language and literacy in science education.* Buckingham, UK: Open University Press.

Wenger, E. (1998). *Communities of practice: Learning, meaning and identity.* New York: Cambridge University Press.

Wiggins, G. P., & McTighe, J. (2004). *Understanding by design* (2nd ed.). Alexandria, VA: Association for Supervision and Curriculum Development.

Wilensky, U., & Reisman, K. (2006). Thinking like a wolf, a sheep, or a firefly: Learning biology through constructing and testing computational theories—an embodied modeling approach. *Cognition and Instruction, 24*(2), 171–209.

Windschitl, M., Thompson, J., & Braaten, M. (2008). Beyond the scientific method: Model-based inquiry as a new paradigm of preference for school science investigations. *Science Education, 92*(5), 941–967.

Wittgenstein, L. (1961). *Tracatus logico-philosophicus.* London: Routledge.

Woolnough, B., & Allsop, T. (1986). *Practical work in science.* Cambridge: Cambridge University Press.

Yore, L. D. (1991). Secondary science teachers' attitudes toward and beliefs about science reading and science textbooks. *Journal of Research in Science Teaching, 28*(1), 55–72.

Ziman, J. (1979). *Reliable knowledge.* Cambridge: Cambridge University Press.

Zohar, A., & Nemet, F. (2002). Fostering students' knowledge and argumentation skills through dilemmas in human genetics. *Journal of Research in Science Teaching, 39*(1), 35–62.

30

Research on Teaching and Learning of Nature of Science

Norman G. Lederman and Judith S. Lederman

Introduction

The purpose of this chapter is to update new advances in the research on the teaching and learning of nature of science since the previous *Handbook of Research on Science Education* (Abell & Lederman, 2007). As this is a new volume, the previous handbook will remain in print, and so a complete recapitulation of what was published previously is not necessary. However, some review of research considered in the previous handbook is needed to provide some context for the more recent work. Consequently, reference to some of the more influential studies and findings reported in the previous handbook chapter will be referenced, but an attempt is made not to reprint all that can be found in the first handbook. More than 7 years have passed, and it is debatable if anything new has been revealed relative to nature of science (NOS). One could say that there is more than 7 years of new research. On the other hand, little new about how students learn NOS or how it is best taught has been revealed. However, research on NOS does continue to be a vibrant area of concern. Alternatively, there has been much written that attempts to reconceptualize how NOS is viewed. Indeed, some of this reconceptualization can be found in the Next Generation Science Standards in the United States (NGSS Lead States, 2013), but how well this newly advocated view is consistent with the existing empirical research certainly warrants discussion. That said, this chapter will be organized around a conceptualization of the construct "nature of science" and how it is taught, learned, and assessed. In addition, there will be a discussion of recent trends regarding thinking about nature of science and how these trends may or may not help improve students' and teachers' understandings of nature of science.

Conceptualizing the Construct

The construct "nature of science" (NOS) has been advocated as an important goal for students studying science for more than 100 years and has continued to be advocated

as a critical educational outcome by various science education reform documents worldwide (e.g., Australia, Canada, China, New Zealand, South Africa, United Kingdom, and the United States, among others). When it comes to NOS, one is hard pressed to find rhetoric arguing against its importance as an educational outcome.

Volumes have been written arguing why NOS is an important educational objective. Simply put, understanding NOS is often defended as being a critical component of scientific literacy (Lederman & Lederman, 2011; NGSS Lead States, 2013; NSTA, 1982). For more elaborated rationales, the reader is referred to Driver, Leach, Millar, and Scott (1996) and Lederman (2007).

However, at this point, the arguments supporting NOS as an important educational outcome are primarily intuitive with little empirical support. Much like the general goal of scientific literacy, until we reach a critical mass of individuals who possess adequate understandings of NOS, we have no way of knowing whether achievement of the goal has accomplished what has been assumed. Still, students' and teachers' understandings of NOS remain a high priority for science education and science education research. As mentioned before, it has been an objective in science education (American Association for the Advancement of Science [AAAS], 1990, 1993; Klopfer, 1969; National Research Council [NRC], 1996, 2012; National Science Teachers Association [NSTA], 1982) for more than 100 years (Kimball, 1967–1968; Lederman, 1992, 2007).

With all the support NOS has in the science education and scientific community, one would assume that all stakeholders possess adequate understandings of the construct. Even though explicit statements about the meaning of NOS are provided in well-known reform documents (e.g., NRC, 1996), the pages of refereed journals and conference rooms at professional meetings are filled with a wide variety of definitions. Some would argue that the situation is direct support for the idea that there is NO agreement on the meaning of NOS and that the construct should be reconceptualized (Irzik & Nola, 2011). Others (Lederman, 1998; Lederman, Antink, & Bartos, 2014) are quick to note that the disagreements about the definition or meaning of NOS that continue to exist among philosophers, historians, and science educators are developmentally irrelevant to K–12 instruction. The issue of the existence of an objective reality as compared to phenomenal realities is a case in point. There is an acceptable level of generality regarding NOS that is accessible to K–12 students and relevant to their daily lives that can be found in the writings of the aforementioned authors and current reform documents. Moreover, at this level, little disagreement exists among philosophers, historians, and science educators. It is critically important that we not lose sight of the audience for which NOS learning outcomes are designed—that is, K–12 students. Furthermore, arguments about what characteristics of scientific knowledge should be included under the rubric of NOS tend to lose sight of the overarching purpose of these goals. It is not important what definitively constitutes NOS, but rather whether we consider what is being specified for students to know and do are considered important for the intended audience (Lederman, Bartos, & Lederman, 2014; Osborne, Collins, Ratcliffe, Millar, & Duschl, 2003).

Among the characteristics of scientific knowledge corresponding to this level of generality are that scientific knowledge is tentative (subject to change), empirically based (based on and/or derived from observations of the natural world), subjective (involves personal background, biases, and/or is theory laden), necessarily involves human inference, imagination, and creativity (involves the invention of explanations), and is socially and culturally embedded. Two additional important aspects are the distinction between observations and inferences and the functions of and relationships between scientific theories and laws. For a more detailed discussion of the aspects of NOS just mentioned, the reader is referred to Lederman (2007).

It is important to note that the aspects of NOS mentioned here are not meant as a comprehensive listing. There are other aspects that some researchers or reform documents include or delete (Abd-El-Khalick, Bell, & Lederman, 1998; Irzik & Nola, 2011; McComas, 2008; NGSS Lead States, 2013; Osborne, Collins, Ratcliffe, Millar, & Duschl, 2003; Scharmann & Smith, 1999). Any of these lists that consider what students can learn, in addition to a consideration of the characteristics of scientific knowledge, are of equal validity. Again, there is no definitive listing of the aspects of nature of science. The primary purpose here is not to emphasize one listing of aspects versus another, but to provide a frame of reference that helps delineate NOS from scientific inquiry/practices and processes of science.

At this point, it is important to note that there is an intuitive assumption held by many science educators that NOS is not a unitary construct across science disciplines.

That is, biologists, chemists, physicists, and scientists from other disciplines would have different conceptions of NOS. This is an area in which the assumption has really not been tested. However, one study does exist (Schwartz & Lederman, 2008). The subjects were 24 practicing scientists representing chemistry, life science, physics, and earth/space science. These individuals also represented a broad spectrum of research approaches (i.e., experimental, descriptive, and theoretical). Data were collected by open-ended questionnaires for NOS and scientific inquiry. Qualitative comparisons were made within disciplines and across disciplines. Although there were many differences related to nuances of research design depending on the context of an investigation, there were generally no differences in views of inquiry or NOS at the level of generality used in schools. The authors concluded that there is no need to approach NOS differently for each science discipline given the level of sophistication of K–12 students and the reality of curriculum constraints.

Finally, it is important to note that individuals often conflate NOS with science practices and/or scientific inquiry. Although these aspects of science overlap and interact in important ways, it is nonetheless important to distinguish the two. Scientific processes are activities related to collecting and analyzing data and drawing conclusions (AAAS, 1990, 1993; NRC, 1996). Certainly, both constructs are important, and inquiry and NOS, although different, are intimately related. Making a distinction between NOS and scientific inquiry is in no way meant to imply that the two constructs are distinct. Clearly they are intimately related.

Conceptualization Aside, Murkiness Remains

The conflation of NOS and scientific inquiry has plagued research on NOS from the beginning. Hence, the reader will note that many of the earlier studies (and even continuing to the present) are actually more focused on inquiry than on NOS. These studies are nevertheless included in this review since they have become an accepted part of the history of research on NOS. The definition used by these older studies for NOS is just not consistent with current usage of the construct. Again, the aspects of NOS presented here are not meant to be exhaustive. However, what is presented is directly consistent with what current reform documents state students should know about NOS and is consistent with the perspective taken by an overwhelming majority of the research literature. Still, it is important to note that one of the problems with some of the recent research and rhetoric on NOS is a return to the conflation of NOS and scientific inquiry (Allchin, 2011; NGSS Lead States, 2013). In the case of the latter, "scientific practices" has replaced what was formally called scientific inquiry.

The evolution of the "definition" of nature of science may provide a partial explanation for the continued murkiness created by some sectors of the research community. In the 1970s and early 1980s, the construct was labeled "nature of scientific knowledge." Toward the end of the 1980s the phrase was shortened to "nature of science" (probably at least partially N. G. Lederman's fault). Perhaps this change in wording has contributed somewhat to the continuing conflation of nature of science and scientific inquiry (Lederman, 2013). But as we all know, humans often do not learn from history. Matters remain confusing with the introduction of any new term such as "scientific practices" as a replacement for "scientific inquiry" within the Next Generation Science Standards (NGSS Lead States, 2013), and nature of science, unfortunately, is considered to fall at least partially under the label of scientific practices. Indeed, the relationship of NOS and scientific inquiry has been schizophrenic over the years. Within Project 2061 (AAAS, 1993), NOS is considered to be an overarching label, which includes scientific inquiry, while in the National Science Education Standards (NRC, 1996), NOS and scientific inquiry are considered to be separate, albeit related, categories of standards. Interestingly, the Next Generation Science Standards (NGSS Lead States, 2013) have placed NOS as a subset of the overarching category of scientific practices (formally scientific inquiry). So, within a time span of 20 years, we have totally reversed the relationship of NOS and scientific inquiry. This situation certainly has not helped clear the waters. In general, NOS has typically referred to characteristics of scientific knowledge that necessarily derived from the way the knowledge is constructed (i.e., scientific inquiry/practices). One performs and engages in scientific practices, but one does not "do" NOS. NOS itself can be a moving target. Perceptions of NOS have changed significantly over the past 30 years and, as a consequence, some individuals have dwelled too heavily on such differing perceptions as well as the differences in perceptions between science educators and scientists (e.g., Alters, 1997; Wong & Hodson, 2009, 2010). The recognition that our views of NOS have changed and will continue to change is not a justification for ceasing our research until total agreement is reached, or for avoiding recommendations or identifying what we think students should know. We have no difficulty including certain theories and laws within our science curricula even though we recognize that these may change in the near or distant future. What is important is that students understand the evidence for current beliefs about natural phenomena, and the same is true with NOS. Students should know the evidence that has lead to our current beliefs about NOS and, just as with "traditional" subject matter, they should realize that perceptions may change as additional evidence is collected or the same evidence is viewed in a different way.

Prior to this review, there have been four reviews of research related to the teaching, learning, and assessment of nature of science (Abd-El-Khalick & Lederman, 2000a; Lederman, 1992, 2007; Meichtry, 1992). In addition to revisiting the contents of previous reviews, this review will build on these prior works and hopefully provide some guidance for future research in the field.

For practical reasons, the research reviewed is restricted to published reports and to those studies with a primary focus on NOS. These studies have been divided into obvious thematic sections and are presented in a general chronological sequence within each section. Again, all of the studies included in previous reviews could not be presented here, but some of the more prominent and influential studies are reviewed again to provide a context for more recent investigations.

Research on Students' Conceptions

Considering the longevity of objectives related to students' conceptions of NOS, it is more than intriguing that research on NOS only began in earnest in 1961. Klopfer and Cooley (1963) developed the Test on Understanding Science (TOUS), which was, for some time, the most widely used paper-and-pencil assessment of students' conceptions. Using the TOUS and a comprehensive review of several nationwide surveys, Klopfer and Cooley (1963) concluded that high school students' understandings of the scientific enterprise and of scientists was inadequate. Early assessments of students' understandings were not limited to the United States. Mackay (1971) administered pre- and posttests to 1,203 Australian secondary students spanning Grades 7 through 10 using the TOUS instrument. He concluded that students lacked sufficient knowledge of (a) the role of creativity in science; (b) the function of scientific models; (c) the roles of theories and their relation to research; (d) the distinctions among hypotheses, laws, and theories; (e) the relationship among experimentation, models and theories, and absolute truth; (f) the fact that science is not solely concerned with the collection and classification of facts; (g) what constitutes a scientific explanation; and (h) the interrelationships among and the interdependence of the different branches of science. Similar findings resulted from the investigations of Aikenhead (1972, 1973).

During the development of the Nature of Scientific Knowledge Scale, Rubba and colleagues (Rubba, 1977; Rubba & Andersen, 1978) found that 30% of the high school students surveyed believed that scientific research reveals incontrovertible and necessary absolute truth. Additionally, most of Rubba's sample believed that scientific theories, with constant testing and confirmation, eventually mature into laws. With a sample of 102 high-ability seventh- and eighth-grade students, Rubba, Horner, and Smith (1981) attempted to assess students' adherence to the ideas that laws are mature theories and that laws represent absolute truth. The results indicated that the students, on the whole, tended to be "neutral" with respect to both of these ideas. The authors were particularly concerned about the results because the sample consisted of students who were considered to be the most capable and interested in science.

During the past three decades, a decreasing number of studies have focused attention on the assessment of students' conceptions. (Gilbert, 1991; Lederman, 1986;

Lederman & O'Malley, 1990), with no attempt to identify or test causal factors. However, a few notable studies are briefly described here to illustrate the consistency of findings across the decades of research on students' understandings. Most recently, Kang, Scharmann, and Noh (2004) examined the views of 6th-, 8th-, and 10th-grade students in South Korea. Using a multiple-choice test, the views of 1,702 students were assessed. Consistent with prior research, the South Korean students were found to have an empiricist/absolutist view of science. Zeidler, Walker, Ackett, and Simmons (2002) investigated the relationships between students' conceptions of NOS and their reactions to evidence that challenged their beliefs about socioscientific issues. A total of 82 students from 9th- and 10th-grade general science classes, 11th- and 12th-grade honors biology, physics classes, and college-level preservice teachers comprised the sample. Although the authors did not clarify how many of the students in the sample adhered to the array of beliefs presented, it was clear that a significant number of students did not understand scientific knowledge to be tentative, partially subjective, and involve creativity. Overall, there were no clear differences in the understandings of students with respect to grade level.

In an interesting departure from the usual focus of assessments of students' views, Sutherland and Dennick (2002) investigated conceptions of NOS in students with clearly different worldviews. Specifically, this research recognized that individuals from different cultures may have significantly different views of the world and humans' place in the world and that these views may impact how one views NOS. The sample consisted of 72 seventh-grade Cree students and 36 seventh-grade Euro-Canadian students. Although all assessments were done in English, a significant portion of the Cree students spoke English as well as Cree at home. Data were collected using both quantitative (Nature of Scientific Knowledge Scale) and qualitative (interviews) techniques. Although the two groups differed on various aspects of NOS, both groups held views that are considered less than adequate with respect to the following aspects of NOS: tentativeness, creativity, parsimony, unified nature of knowledge, importance of empirical testing, and amoral nature of scientific knowledge. They also found that both language and culture impacted students' views in addition to those factors that impact Western students' views. Certainly, the potential influence of world views, culture, and language may have on understandings of NOS is important in and of itself and is an area of much-needed research. However, the critical point here is that the findings in this study corroborate what has been found throughout the history of studies that simply aim to assess students' conceptions.

More recently, Walls (2012) focused on third-grade African American students, and although he found unique variations in students' conceptions, his findings were still consistent with studies from previous decades. As the longevity of research on NOS has evolved, there has been an obvious expansion beyond the borders of North America. Three particularly interesting studies of students' conceptions are mentioned here. Urhahne, Kremer, and Mayer (2011) studied 221 high school students from four "above-average" schools in Germany, specifically focusing on whether conceptions of NOS were general or context specific. Overall, there really was no definitive pattern that general understandings were different than context-specific understandings. Given the constant discussion among those investigating instructional impacts on NOS, the results here lend credence to the idea that understandings of NOS can be facilitated with general as opposed to context-dependent approaches.

Dogan and Abd-El-Khalick (2008) studied the conceptions of 2,020 10th-grade students in Turkey using a modified version of the Views of Science, Technology, and Society VOSTS (Aikenhead, Fleming, & Ryan, 1987). Students were sampled throughout the country. They found the students had the same misconceptions about NOS found in previous studies. Interestingly, they found a positive correlation between NOS understandings and parents' level of education. They also found differences between students from western Turkey and eastern Turkey. Given the unique cultural diversity in Turkey (i.e., a country that is located on two continents), this latter result lends some credence to the idea that understandings of NOS are influenced by culture.

Ibrahim, Buffler, and Lubben (2009) studied college freshmen in a South African university physics class. The sample was 179 students, and they were surveyed about their views of scientific knowledge, the origin of laws and theories, the relationship of theory and experiment, the purpose of experiments, the role of creativity in experiments, and the precedence of theoretical and experimental results. The results indicated that these students held the general misconceptions previously noted concerning NOS. Of particular interest was the finding that perceptions of experimentation are critically important for an informed view of NOS.

Overall, the emerging findings from more recent and more international studies on students' conceptions reinforce what was found decades before. Without any targeted instructional interventions, students do not possess the currently desired understandings of NOS.

Research on Teachers' Conceptions of NOS

In general, researchers turned their attention to teaching nature of science and teachers' conceptions as data emerged indicating that students did not possess what were considered adequate conceptions of NOS. The logic was simple: A teacher must possess adequate knowledge of what he/she is attempting to communicate to students.

Carey and Stauss (1968) investigated whether 17 prospective secondary science teachers being prepared at the University of Georgia possessed a philosophy of science that exhibited an understanding of NOS. The Wisconsin

Inventory of Science Processes (WISP) was used to assess NOS. In addition to attempting an initial assessment of the conceptions possessed by the preservice teachers, an attempt was made to investigate the effectiveness of a science methods course in improving such conceptions. Pretest scores on the WISP indicated that the science teachers, as a group, did not possess adequate conceptions of nature of science. Based on WISP posttest scores, it was concluded that a methods course specifically oriented toward NOS could significantly improve teachers' viewpoints.

Carey and Stauss (1970a) continued their line of research by assessing experienced teachers' conceptions of NOS. Once again, they used the WISP exam. The results were consistent with their previous study: (a) Teachers of science, in general, did not possess adequate conceptions of NOS; (b) science methods courses produce a significant pre- to posttest improvement of WISP scores, and (c) academic variables such as grade-point average, math credits, specific courses, and years of teaching experience are not significantly related to teachers' conceptions of science. They recommended that courses in the history and philosophy of science be included in teacher preparation programs.

Kimball (1968), using his own Nature of Science Scale (NOSS), compared understandings of NOS of scientists and science teachers. In no case were significant differences found between the groups. Although research focused on teachers' conceptions of NOS (with no attempts to change such conceptions) proliferated during 1950 through 1970, there have been several notable more recent assessments.

Beginning teachers' and preservice science teachers' views about scientific knowledge were described and compared by Koulaidis and Ogborn (1989). A 16-item, multiple-choice questionnaire was administered to 12 beginning science teachers and 11 preservice science teachers. The questionnaire items focused on scientific method, criteria for demarcation of science and nonscience, change in scientific knowledge, and the status of scientific knowledge. Based on their responses, the subjects were categorized into four predetermined categories of philosophical belief. The high frequency of individuals possessing eclectic views is consistent with previous research, which has indicated that teachers do not generally possess views that are consistently associated with a particular philosophical position. Overall, the authors concluded that although science teachers place value on scientific method, they see the procedures involved as contextually situated.

Using a case study approach, Aguirre, Haggerty, and Linder (1990) assessed 74 preservice secondary science teachers' conceptions of NOS, teaching, and learning. Subjects were asked to respond to 11 open-ended questions about science, teaching of science, and learning of science. Most individuals believed that science was either a body of knowledge consisting of a collection of observations and explanations or of propositions that have been proven to be correct. Subjects were evenly divided

among the "dispenser of knowledge" and "guide/mediator of understanding" conceptions of science teaching. The authors concluded that these preservice teachers (even though they all possessed undergraduate science degrees) did not possess adequate conceptions of nature of science.

Research on teachers' conceptions of NOS is not limited in focus to secondary teachers. Bloom (1989) assessed preservice elementary teachers' understanding of science and how certain contextual variables contribute to this understanding. Using a sample of 80 preservice elementary teachers (86% female) enrolled in three methods courses, Bloom administered a questionnaire that contained six questions related to knowledge of science, theories, and evolution. Additionally, a 21-item rating scale pertaining to prior experiences with science, the nature of science, science teaching, and evolution/creationism was administered. A qualitative analysis of questionnaire responses revealed that the preservice teachers believed science is people centered, with its primary purpose being for the benefit of humankind. Much confusion concerning the meaning and role of scientific theories (e.g., theories are related to belief in one's own thoughts apart from empirical observation) was also noted. Of most significance was the finding that beliefs significantly affect preservice teachers' understandings of science. In this particular case, the anthropocentric nature of the subjects' beliefs significantly influenced their conceptualizations of science, the theory of evolution, and how one would teach evolution.

Akerson, Buzzelli, and Eastwood (2012) were concerned with K–3 preservice teachers' cultural values and their perceptions of NOS. The Values Inventory, interviews, and the Views of Nature of Science–Form B VNOS–B were used to collect data. Overall, it was found that those teachers whose values were most similar to the values they perceived held by scientists possessed the best understandings of NOS. The authors concluded that if teachers see themselves as more similar to scientists, they will not see science as "alien" to themselves and will more likely be willing to teach science.

Liu and Lederman (2007) were also concerned with values as they tested the intuitive assumption that understandings of NOS may be impacted by one's worldview. The study focused on 54 preservice elementary Taiwanese teachers. Two open-ended questionnaires and corresponding interviews were used to assess the preservice teachers' worldviews and their understandings of NOS. Interviews were primarily used to ensure that the researchers' interpretation of questionnaire responses was the same as what was meant by the respondent. As expected, there was a definite pattern relating worldviews and understandings of NOS. The authors concluded that science curricula need to incorporate sociocultural perspectives and NOS.

There has been a consistent and recent increase in studies focusing, in part or completely, on international teachers' understandings. Fah and Hoon (2011) studied preservice secondary teachers in Malaysia in an effort to see if the findings largely found in North American studies applied to Malaysia. Their results were very similar to what the research community had already determined. The teachers believed scientific knowledge to be absolute, not involving subjectivity, and not a direct function of creativity. Studies like this further reinforced that the findings concerning teachers' understandings were universal.

Finally, there have been some attempts to compare understandings of U.S. preservice teachers with those of other nations. Cobern (1989) used Kimball's Nature of Science Scale (NOSS) to compare the understandings of 21 U.S. preservice science teachers with 32 preservice Nigerian teachers. Two significant differences were noted between the groups. Nigerian preservice teachers were more inclined to view science as a way to produce useful technology. This result is consistent with the findings of Ogunniyi (1982) in his study of 53 preservice Nigerian science teachers. This viewpoint is different from that typically desired in the Western hemisphere, which distinguishes theoretical from applied science. However, an applied view regarding science should not be unexpected in a developing nation. A second difference between the two samples was the Nigerians' view that scientists were nationalistic and secretive about their work.

On a much grander scale, Liang, Chen, Chen, Kaya, Adams, Macklin, and Ebenezer (2009) studied 640 preservice teachers from the United States, China, and Turkey. Data were collected using the Students' Understanding of Science and Scientific Inquiry (SUSSI). The SUSSI assessed the following aspects of NOS: understandings of observations and inferences, tentativeness, scientific laws and theories, social and cultural embeddednes, human creativity and imagination, and diverse scientific methods. In general, the preservice teachers possessed the general misunderstandings found in other studies, but they scored best on understanding that scientific knowledge is tentative and worst on understandings of the relationship between theories and laws. The Chinese subsample scored best on five of the six aspects of NOS studied. The U.S. subsample demonstrated informed views of observation and inference, while the Turkish group scored lowest in all six subscales. Overall, this large international study confirmed what had been found in studies focusing solely on North American teachers.

Teaching and Learning of Nature of Science (the Early Years: 1960–1980s)

Research on Students' Conceptions

Klopfer and Cooley (1963) developed the first curriculum designed to improve students' conceptions of NOS. The curriculum was called History of Science Cases for High Schools (HOSC). The rationale for the curriculum was that the use of materials derived from the history of science would help to convey important ideas about science and scientists. A sample of 108 geographically representative science classes, including biology, chemistry,

and physics (2,808 students in total), was used to assess the effectiveness of the HOSC curriculum as measured by the TOUS instrument. After a 5-month treatment period, students receiving the HOSC curriculum exhibited significantly greater gains on the TOUS than the control groups. In addition, HOSC students showed significant gains on the TOUS subscales (i.e., the scientific enterprise, the scientist, and the methods and aims of science) as well as on the overall test. It was concluded that the HOSC instructional approach was an effective way to improve students' conceptions of NOS. The large sample size used in this investigation gave it much credibility, and it was followed by widespread curriculum development.

Crumb (1965) compared the Physical Science Study Curriculum (PSSC) to traditional high school physics with respect to gains on the TOUS exam. The PSSC program is a laboratory-centered, experimental approach to physics that is designed to emphasize process as opposed to simply science content. Using a sample of 1,275 students from 29 high schools, Crumb found that PSSC students showed greater gains on the TOUS than students exposed to the traditional physics curriculum.

Aikenhead (1979) developed and field tested a curriculum titled Science: A Way of Knowing. The primary goals of the curriculum were to have students develop (a) a realistic, nonmythical understanding of the nature, processes, and social aspects of science; (b) a variety of inquiry skills and a realistic feeling of personal competence in the areas of interpreting, responding to, and evaluating their scientific and technological society; and (c) insight into the interaction of science and technology and, in turn, into the interaction of these with other aspects of society. Using the Science Process Inventory (Welch, 1967), Grade 11 and Grade 12 students were found to make significant pre- to posttest gains.

The findings related to the effectiveness of curriculum specifically designed to teach NOS were not all positive. Trent (1965) investigated the relative value of the PSSC course and traditional physics (as did Crumb, 1965). A sample consisting of 52 California high schools was used, and the TOUS exam was used to assess students' conceptions of science. Half of the students in the PSSC classes and half of those in traditional courses were not pretested on the TOUS, and the remaining students were. At the end of the school year, all students were given a posttest. When prior science understanding and student ability were statistically controlled, no differences were found between the students in the traditional and PSSC courses as measured by the TOUS.

Troxel (1968) compared "traditional" chemistry instruction to both CHEM Study and the Chemical Bond Approach (CBA). In theory, CHEM Study and CBA stress inquiry and are laboratory centered, which theoretically should promote better understandings of NOS. However, when teacher background in terms of teaching within the discipline, experience in teaching the course, general philosophy, and student background relative to school size were held constant, no significant differences were found in students' conceptions of NOS.

Two other studies using the 1960s curricula were conducted with Israeli high school students. Jungwirth (1970) attempted to investigate the effectiveness of the BSCS Yellow Version, which was first introduced in Israel in 1964. A total of 693 10th-grade students (from 25 schools) comprised the sample. Scores on both the TOUS and the Processes of Science Test (Biological Sciences Curriculum Study [BSCS], 1962) were used to assess students' understandings of scientific knowledge. Students were given pre- and posttests over the course of one academic year. No significant differences were found between those students studying BSCS biology and those in the comparison group. Thus, Jungwirth concluded, the curriculum was not any more effective with respect to the enhancement of students' conceptions of science. He concluded that pupil achievement in this area could best be enhanced through "redirected teacher effort and emphases."

Tamir (1972) compared the relative effectiveness of three curriculum projects with each other as well as with "traditional" instruction. Using the BSCS Yellow Version, CHEM Study, PSSC, and traditional instructional approaches, Tamir assessed changes in students' conceptions of the nature of science on the Science Process Inventory (Welch, 1967). A total of 3,500 students in Grades 9 through 12 were randomly selected from the four types of Israeli high schools (i.e., city academic, cooperation settlement, agricultural, and occupational) so as to allow comparisons among the different school types. The results indicated no significant differences among students studying any of the curriculum projects and those following traditional courses of study.

More recently, Carey, Evans, Honda, Jay, and Unger (1989) assessed the effectiveness of a unit specifically designed to introduce the constructivist view of science on seventh graders' epistemological views. All classes, in the 3-week unit, were taught by the regular teacher, and each lesson was observed by one or two research assistants. Twenty-seven of the students were randomly selected to be interviewed prior to and after being exposed to the instructional unit. In general, the preinstruction interview indicated that most students thought scientists seek to discover facts about nature by making observations and trying things out. However, postinstruction interviews showed many students understood that inquiry is guided by particular ideas and questions, and experiments are tests of ideas. In short, the instructional unit appeared to have been at least partially successful in enabling students to differentiate ideas and experiments.

There was an implicit assumption that clearly guided research that focused solely on the development of curricula and/or instructional materials. It was assumed that student conceptions could be improved if a concerted effort was made in that direction. Unfortunately, for the most part, the teacher's interpretation and enactment of the curriculum was ignored. The following statement from two of the earliest investigators of the curriculum development movement (Klopfer & Cooley, 1963) did little to establish the importance of the teacher: "The relative effectiveness of the History of Science Cases Instruction Method (a curriculum which strongly emphasized using history of science), in teaching TOUS-type understandings does *not* depend upon whether the teacher rates 'high' or 'low' in his initial understanding" (p. 45).

The implication of this statement is clear. That is, a teacher could promote understandings of certain concepts without having an adequate understanding of the concepts. Fortunately, others, such as Trent (1965), felt that the equivocal findings with respect to the effectiveness of NOS–oriented curricula could only mean that the instructional approach, style, rapport, and personality of the teacher are important variables in effective science teaching. He reasoned, if the same curriculum is effective for one teacher and ineffective for another and the variable of student ability is controlled, a significant factor must be the teacher.

Spears and Zollman (1977) assessed the influence of engagement in scientific inquiry on students' understandings of the process of science. Participants were randomly assigned to the four lecture sections and associated laboratory sections of a physics course. Data from about 50% of the original sample were used in the final analysis. The "structured" approach emphasized verification, whereas the "unstructured" approach stressed inquiry or discovery. Both approaches asked students to investigate problems related to physical principles discussed in the lectures. Beyond this point, the two approaches differed in a major way. In the "structured" laboratory, students were provided with explicit procedures with which they attempted to verify the physical principles concerned. Students in the "unstructured" laboratory, however, were free to investigate the problem in whichever way they deemed appropriate. They made their own decisions regarding what data to collect, how to collect these data, how to treat the data, and how to interpret and present their results. Data analyses indicated that there were no statistically significant differences between the adjusted scores of the two groups on the Assumptions, Nature of Outcomes, and Ethics and Goals components of the Science Process Inventory SPI Form D (Welch & Pella, 1967–1968).

Research on Teachers' Conceptions of NOS

The equivocal results concerning the effectiveness of curricula designed to improve students' conceptions of NOS, perhaps, motivated other researchers to focus their attentions on the teacher as a significant variable. In the 1960s, the distinction between implementation and enactment of a curriculum had not taken hold in the science education community. Yager & Wick (1966) selected eight experienced teachers to use an inquiry-oriented curriculum (BSCS Blue Version). All teachers utilized the same number of days of discussion, laboratories, examinations, and instructional materials. Students were pre- and posttested on the TOUS exam. Using an analysis of covariance, it was concluded that there were significant differences in students' ability to understand NOS when taught by different teachers. Further direct confirmation of the important influence of teachers upon students' conceptions came from Kleinman's (1965) study of teachers' questioning.

When one considers the influence of the individual teacher on student learning, there are at least two directions that can be pursued. One would be to study what a teacher does that impacts students' understandings of NOS. The other can be a focus on teachers' knowledge. Few would argue against the notion that a teacher must have an understanding of what he/she is expected to teach. Unfortunately, the latter was initially pursued in the research to the exclusion of attention to the former. Those studies focusing on teachers' knowledge are briefly described here. A more detailed discussion of each study can be found in the previous *Handbook* (Lederman, 2007).

Of critical importance here is that the following studies relied on two assumptions: (1) A positive relationship existed between teachers' knowledge of NOS and their students' knowledge and (2) teachers' knowledge of NOS necessarily impacted their classroom practice. Consequently, researchers interested in NOS never thought it necessary to go beyond attempts to improve teachers' knowledge of NOS. The two aforementioned assumptions arguably compromised efforts to improve students' conceptions of NOS for 30 years. It is also important to note that what researchers did to improve teachers' knowledge was poorly described and generally did not explicitly address NOS.

Carey and Stauss (1970b) had 35 prospective secondary science teachers and 221 prospective elementary teachers complete the WISP. Scores were correlated with background variables such as high school science courses, college science courses, college grade-point average, and science grade-point average. No relationship was found between either secondary or elementary teachers' conceptions of science, as measured by WISP, and any of the academic background variables. During the validation of the NOSS, Kimball (1968) noted that philosophy majors actually scored higher than either science teachers or professional scientists. He intuitively concluded that inclusion of a philosophy of science course as part of the undergraduate science major curriculum might improve the situation. Welch and Walberg (1968) did find success in a summer institute designed for 162 physics teachers at four institute sites. The teachers at all four sites showed significant gains on both the TOUS and Science Process Inventory. Unfortunately, no documentation of the specific activities at each of the various institutes was available.

Lavach (1969) attempted to expand on the success that Klopfer and Cooley (1963) had documented with a historical approach. Twenty-six science teachers participated; 11 constituted the experimental group and 15 served as the control group. The experimental group received instruction in selected historical aspects of astronomy, mechanics, chemistry, heat, and electricity. The teachers in the control group did not receive lectures or laboratories presented from a historical perspective. All teachers were pre- and posttested on the TOUS. The teachers in the experimental group exhibited statistically significant gains in their understanding of NOS. Further analysis indicated that these gains were not related to overall teaching experience, subjects taught, undergraduate major, previous inservice participation, or length of teaching experience in the same subject.

Six years later, Billeh and Hasan (1975) attempted to identify those factors that affect any increase in the understanding of NOS by science teachers. Their sample consisted of 186 secondary science teachers in Jordan. The teachers were divided into four groups: biology, chemistry, physical science, and physics. A 4-week course for the chemistry, physical science, and physics teachers consisted of lectures and demonstrations in methods of teaching science, laboratory investigations emphasizing a guided-discovery approach, enrichment activities to enhance understanding of specific science concepts, and 12 lectures specifically related to nature of science. The biology group did not receive any formal instruction on nature of science, thus establishing a reference group with which the other groups could be compared. The Nature of Science Test (NOST) was used to assess understanding of NOS. Those lectures that stressed nature of science were not oriented toward the specific content of the NOST. Each group of teachers was administered pre- and posttests on the NOST, and an analysis of covariance showed significant increases in the mean scores of the chemistry, physical science, and physics groups. The biology group did not show a significant gain, a finding consistent with Carey and Stauss (1968). A second result was that there was no significant relationship between teachers' gain scores on NOST and their educational qualifications, a finding in agreement with previous research (Carey & Stauss, 1970a; Lavach, 1969). Finally, science teaching experience was not significantly related to NOST gain scores. The conclusion that teaching experience does not contribute to a teacher's understanding of NOS was also consistent with previous research (Carey & Stauss, 1970b; Kimball, 1968; Lavach, 1969).

Riley (1979) argued that teachers' understandings of and attitudes toward science would improve as a result of first-hand, manipulative experiences and enhanced proficiency in the processes of science. Riley labeled an understanding of NOS as an "affective" outcome and attempted to teach NOS by involving teachers in "doing science." The study investigated the influence of hands-on versus nonmanipulative training in science process skills on preservice elementary teachers' understandings of NOS. The treatment had three levels: active-inquiry (hands-on), vicarious-inquiry (nonmanipulative), and control. The four 1.5-hour session treatment involved activities that focused on various science process skills, such as observing, classifying, inferring, predicting, communicating, measuring and the metric system, and using space/time relationships. The only difference between the aforementioned levels of treatment was participant involvement. Data analyses indicated that there were no significant differences between the groups' mean TOUS (Cooley & Klopfer, 1961) scores related to the treatments. As such, participants in the active-inquiry, vicarious-inquiry, and control groups did not differ in their understandings of NOS.

Akindehin (1988) argued that attempts to help science teachers develop adequate conceptions of NOS need to be *explicit* (i.e., NOS directly introduced and discussed, as opposed to just having teachers do investigations). The author assessed the influence of an instructional package, the Introductory Science Teacher Education (ISTE) package, on prospective secondary science teachers' conceptions of NOS. The package contained nine units including lectures, discussions, and laboratory sessions.

A statistically significant result was obtained for the experimental group. Out of 58 possible points on the NOSS, the mean score was 51.84. This mean score was the highest reported NOSS score among the studies reviewed here. It should be noted, however, that the author did not report the mean pretest and posttest scores. Thus, it was difficult to assess the practical significance of the gains achieved by the student teachers.

Scharmann and Harris (1992) assessed the influence of a three-week National Science Foundation NSF–sponsored summer institute on participants' understandings of NOS. The authors noted that "changes in an understanding of the nature of science can be . . . enhanced through a more indirect and applied context . . . and through a variety of readings and activities" that help participants to discuss their NOS views (p. 379). The NOSS (Kimball, 1968) was used to assess participants' understandings of the "philosophical" NOS, and an instrument developed by Johnson and Peeples (1987) was used to assess participants' "applied" understandings of NOS. During the first 2 weeks of the institute, participants were presented with biological and geological content relevant to evolutionary theory. In addition, various instructional methods and teaching approaches including lectures, small-group and peer discussions, field trips, and other inquiry-based approaches were taught and modeled by the authors. The authors noted that the "theme" of promoting participants' conceptions of NOS pervaded all the activities. However, no direct or explicit NOS instruction was used. Data analyses did not reveal significant differences between pretest and posttest mean NOSS scores. However, statistically significant differences were obtained in the case of the Johnson and Peeples (1987) instrument. The authors concluded that even though participants' conceptions of the "philosophical" NOS were not changed, their understandings of the "applied" NOS were significantly improved. Scharmann and Harris (1992) did not comment on the practical significance of the gain achieved by the participants. Out of 100 possible points for the latter instrument,

the pretest and posttest mean scores were 61.74 and 63.26, respectively.

Looking at research investigations that attempted to change teachers' conceptions from an alternative perspective can be enlightening. Overall, these studies took one of two approaches. The first approach was advocated by science educators such as Gabel, Rubba, and Franz (1977) and Rowe (1974). This approach is labeled the "implicit" approach for this review, as it suggests that an understanding of NOS is a learning outcome that can be facilitated through process skill instruction, science content coursework, and "doing science." Researchers who adopted this implicit approach utilized science process skills instruction and/or scientific inquiry activities (Riley, 1979) or manipulated certain aspects of the learning environment (Scharmann & Harris, 1992; Spears & Zollman, 1977) in their attempts to enhance teachers' NOS conceptions. Researchers who adopted the second approach to enhancing teachers' understandings of NOS (Akindehin, 1988; Billeh & Hasan, 1975; Carey & Stauss, 1968, 1970a; Jones, 1969; Lavach, 1969; Ogunniyi, 1982) utilized elements from history and philosophy of science and/or instruction focused on various aspects of NOS to improve science teachers' conceptions. This second approach is labeled the "explicit" approach for this review and was advanced by educators such as Billeh and Hasan (1975), Hodson (1985), Kimball (1968), Klopfer (1964), Lavach (1969), and Rutherford (1964).

Teaching and Learning of Nature of Science (Contemporary Years: A Shift in Perspective)

During the past 20 years, research on the teaching and learning of NOS has experienced a gradual but clear change in perspective. This change in perspective has influenced how we attempt to change the conceptions of both teachers and students.

Research on Teachers' Conceptions of NOS

The results of the initial research on NOS (which are supported by more recent investigations) may be summarized as follows: (a) Science teachers do not possess adequate conceptions of NOS, irrespective of the instrument used to assess understandings; (b) techniques to improve teachers' conceptions have met with some success when they have included either historical aspects of scientific knowledge or explicit attention to NOS; and (c) academic background variables are not significantly related to teachers' conceptions of NOS. Two underlying assumptions appear to have permeated the research reviewed thus far. The first assumption has been that a teacher's understanding of NOS affects his/her students' conceptions. This assumption is clear in all the research that focused on improvement of teachers' conceptions with no expressed need or attempt to do anything further. This rather intuitive assumption remained virtually untested, with the exception of two studies that only referred to the assumption in an ancillary manner. Unfortunately, both of these research efforts (Klopfer & Cooley, 1963; Rothman, 1969) contained significant methodological flaws. Klopfer and Cooley (1963) failed to properly monitor teachers' conceptions of NOS throughout the investigation, while Rothman (1969) created a ceiling effect by sampling only high-ability students.

The second assumption underlying the research reviewed thus far is closely related to the first. If it is assumed that teachers' conceptions of science affect students' conceptions, some method of influence must exist; naturally the influence must be mediated by teacher behaviors and classroom ecology. In short, initial research concerned with teachers' and students' conceptions of NOS assumed that a teacher's behavior and the classroom environment are necessarily and directly influenced by the teacher's conception of NOS. Although this assumption was explicitly stated by many, including Hurd (1969) and Robinson (1965), it remained an untested assumption into the early 1980s (Lederman & Zeidler, 1987).

As can be seen from the research reviewed thus far, several decades of research on NOS focused on student and teacher characteristics or curriculum development to the exclusion of any direct focus on actual classroom practice and/or teacher behaviors. The two assumptions guiding these lines of research compromised efforts to ultimately improve students' conceptions of nature of science for approximately 30 years. Although research designed to assess students' and teachers' conceptions continues to the present, there is clearly less willingness to accept the assumptions that guided earlier research, and the focus is now clearly moving toward teachers' classroom practice.

The presumed relationships between teachers' conceptions of science and those of their students as well as that between teachers' conceptions and instructional behaviors were finally directly tested and demonstrated to be too simplistic relative to the realities of the classroom (Duschl & Wright, 1989; Lederman & Zeidler, 1987; Zeidler & Lederman, 1989; among others). Duschl and Wright (1989) observed and interviewed 13 science teachers in a large urban high school. Their results convincingly indicated that the nature and role of scientific theories are not integral components in the constellation of influences affecting teachers' educational decisions. NOS was not being considered or taught to students as a consequence of perceived students' needs, curriculum guide objectives, and accountability.

Lederman and Zeidler's investigation (1987) involved a sample of 18 high school biology teachers from nine schools. The data clearly indicated that there was no significant relationship between teachers' understandings of NOS and classroom practice. Presently, several variables have been shown to mediate and constrain the translation of teachers' NOS conceptions into practice. These variables include pressure to cover content (Abd-El-Khalick, Bell, & Lederman, 1998; Duschl & Wright, 1989; Hodson, 1985), classroom management and organizational

principles (Hodson, 1993; Lantz & Kass, 1987; Lederman, 1999), concerns for student abilities and motivation (Abd-El-Khalick et al., 1998; Brickhouse & Bodner, 1992; Duschl & Wright, 1989; Lederman, 1995), institutional constraints (Brickhouse & Bodner, 1992), teaching experience (Brickhouse & Bodner, 1992; Lederman, 1995), discomfort with understandings of NOS, and the lack of resources and experiences for assessing understandings of NOS (Abd-El-Khalick et al., 1998).

More recently, Lederman (1999) attempted to finally put to rest (old habits die hard) the assumption that teachers' conceptions of NOS directly influence classroom practice. In a multiple case study involving five high school biology teachers with varying experience, Lederman collected data on teachers' conceptions of NOS and classroom practice. All teachers were former students of the author and all possessed informed understandings of NOS. Over the course of a full academic year, data were collected from questionnaires, structured and unstructured interviews, classroom observations, and instructional materials. Data were also collected on students' conceptions of NOS though questionnaires and interviews. The author was unable to find any clear relationship between teachers' conceptions and classroom practice. The two most experienced teachers (14 and 15 years' experience) did exhibit behaviors that seemed consistent with their views of NOS, but interview and lesson plan data revealed that these teachers were not attempting to teach NOS. Data from students in all teachers' classes indicated that none of the students had developed informed understandings of NOS. The results of the investigation indicated that, although the teachers possessed good understandings of NOS, classroom practice was not directly impacted. Furthermore, the importance of teachers' intentions relative to students' understandings was highlighted. Even in the classrooms that exhibited some similarity with teachers' understandings, students did not learn NOS because the teachers did not explicitly intend to teach NOS. Overall, the research was consistent with emerging findings about the relationship between teachers' understandings and classroom practice as well as the research indicating the importance of explicit instructional attention to NOS.

Although it is now clear that teachers' conceptions do not necessarily translate into classroom practice (but teachers do need to know NOS if they are expected to teach it), concern about teachers' conceptions persists. As was previously mentioned, the past 20 years have been marked by a slow but definite shift in perspective related to how we go about changing teachers' conceptions of NOS. In short, there has been a shift to more explicit and reflective instructional approaches in research related to teachers' conceptions of NOS.

In a study of preservice teachers' conceptions of NOS, Bell, Lederman, and Abd-El-Khalick (2000) looked at teachers' translation of knowledge into instructional planning and classroom practice. The subjects were 13 preservice teachers. The teachers' views of NOS were assessed with an open-ended questionnaire before and after student teaching. Throughout the student teaching experience, daily lesson plans, classroom videotapes, portfolios, and supervisors' clinical observation notes were analyzed for explicit instances of NOS in either planning or instruction. Following student teaching, all subjects were interviewed about their questionnaire responses and factors that influenced their teaching of NOS. Although all of the preservice teachers exhibited adequate understandings of NOS, they did not consistently integrate NOS into instruction in an explicit manner. NOS was not evident in these teachers' objectives, nor was any attempt made to assess students' understandings of NOS. The authors concluded that possessing an understanding of NOS is not automatically translated in a teacher's classroom practice. They further concluded that NOS must be planned for and included in instructional objectives as any other subject matter content.

Akerson, Abd-El-Khalick, and Lederman (2000) were concerned solely with developing elementary teachers' understandings of NOS and not with the translation of this knowledge into classroom practice. The subjects were 25 undergraduate and 25 graduate preservice elementary teachers enrolled in two separate methods courses. Before and after the courses, teachers' views about the empirical, tentative, subjective, creative, and social/cultural embeddedness of scientific knowledge were assessed. In addition, the preservice teachers' views on the distinction between observation/inference and between theories and laws were assessed. The courses explicitly addressed these aspects of NOS using a reflective, activity-based approach. The results indicated that explicit attention to NOS was an effective way to improve teachers' understandings of NOS. However, taken in the context of studies such as the previous one (Bell, Lederman, & Abd-El-Khalick, 2000), the authors were quick to point out that mere possession of adequate understandings will not automatically change classroom practice.

Abell, Martini, and George (2001) monitored the views of 11 elementary education majors during a science methods course. The particular context was a moon investigation in which the authors targeted the following aspects of NOS: empirically based, involves invention and explanations, and is socially embedded. Students were asked to observe the moon each day during the course and record their observations. An attempt was made by the instructors to be explicit as possible with respect to NOS. After the investigation, students realized that scientists make observations and generate patterns, but they did not realize that observations could precede or follow the development of a theory. Students were able to distinguish the processes of observing from creating explanations, but they could not discuss the role of invention in science. In various other instances, students were capable of articulating aspects of NOS but were unable to see the connection between what they learned in the activity and the scientific community. The authors recognized the importance of being explicit

in the teaching of NOS. They also recognized that their students' failure to generalize what they learned beyond the learning activities themselves to what occurs in the scientific community in general was a consequence of not making an explicit connection between what scientists do and the activities completed in class.

Abd-El-Khalick (2001) used an explicit, reflective approach to teach about NOS in a physics course designed for prospective elementary teachers at the American University of Beirut. The explicit, reflective approach is not to be confused with direct instruction or a lecture. Rather, it engages students in scientific investigations and demonstrations and then has students reflect on what they did and the implications this has for the knowledge and conclusions reached. Data were collected through pre and posttests on open-ended surveys about NOS. The author reported significant improvement in the aspects of NOS providing focus for the investigation: tentative, empirically based, theory-laden, inferential, imaginative, and creative characteristics of scientific knowledge. In addition, the relationship between theory and law, as well as the distinction between observation and inference, were investigated. The author definitely concluded that the explicit, reflective approach to instruction was successful.

The use of history of science has long been advocated as a means to improve students' conceptions of science. Lin and Chen (2002) extended this logic to a program designed to improve preservice teachers' understanding of NOS. Sixty-three prospective chemistry teachers in Taiwan were divided into experimental and control groups. The teachers in the experimental group were exposed to a series of historical cases followed by debates and discussions that highlighted how scientists developed knowledge. The historical cases were promoted as a way for these prospective teachers to teach science. Different from previous attempts to use history of science to achieve outcomes related to NOS, the historical materials explicitly addressed NOS. The results clearly showed significant improvement in understandings of NOS by the experimental group relative to the control group. In particular, teachers in the experimental group showed significant improvement of their knowledge of creativity in science, theory-bound nature of observations, and the functions of scientific theories.

Abd-El-Khalick and Akerson (2004) studied 28 preservice elementary teachers in a science methods course. In particular, they investigated the effectiveness of an explicit, reflective instructional approach related to NOS on these prospective teachers' views of various aspects of NOS. Data were collected from a combination of questionnaires, interviews, and reflection papers. As expected, participants initially held naïve views of NOS; however, over the course of the investigation, substantial and favorable changes in the preservice teachers' views were evident.

Using a combination of authentic research experiences, seminars, and reflective journals, Schwartz, Lederman, and Crawford (2004) studied changes in secondary preservice teachers' conceptions of NOS. Prior research had indicated that providing teachers with authentic research experiences did not impact understandings of NOS. Consequently, the researchers supported such research experiences with explicit attention to NOS through seminars and a series of reflective journal assignments. The participants were 13 Master of Arts in Teaching (MAT) students. Data were collected via questionnaires and interviews. Most of the interns showed substantial changes in their views of NOS. Participants identified the reflective journal writing and seminars as having the greatest impact on their views, with the actual research internship just providing a context for reflection.

Abd-El-Khalick (2005) considered the perennial recommendation that teachers should take courses in philosophy of science if we want to impact that knowledge of NOS. The sample was 56 undergraduate and graduate preservice secondary science teachers enrolled in a two-course sequence of science methods. Participants received explicit, reflective NOS instruction. Ten of the participants were also enrolled in a graduate philosophy of science course. The Views of Nature of Science—Form C (VNOS-C) was used to assess understandings of NOS at the beginning and end of the investigation. Participants were also interviewed about their written responses. Other data sources included lesson plans and NOS-specific reflection papers. Results indicated that the students enrolled in the philosophy of science course developed more in-depth understandings of NOS than those just enrolled in the science methods course. The methods course, with explicit instruction about NOS, was seen as providing a framework that the 10 students enrolled in the philosophy of science course could use to significantly benefit from the philosophy course.

Scharmann, Smith, James, and Jensen (2005) used an explicit, reflective approach to teaching NOS within the context of a secondary teaching methods course. Nineteen preservice teachers were the subjects. Overall, the authors decided that the instructional approach was successful and supported the emerging literature on the value of an explicit approach to teaching NOS.

Since the last review of research on the teaching and learning of NOS, continued efforts to improve teachers' understandings of NOS at both the elementary and secondary levels consistently document the effectiveness of an explicit and reflective teaching approach. At the elementary level, McDonald (2010) used a combination of explicit NOS instruction along with instruction on argumentation in a college-level science course to improve the conceptions of five preservice elementary teachers. The study originally had 16 preservice teachers, but complete data sets were only available from 5 of the teachers. Celik and Bayrakceken (2012) successfully used an activity-based explicit approach to teaching secondary preservice teachers about NOS. In a similar vein, Posnanski (2010) worked with 22 elementary preservice teachers during a 2-year professional development program focusing on

NOS. It was an activity-based program with explicit attention to NOS. The program was successful in developing teachers' understandings of and ability to teach NOS, but the author was concerned about the sustainability of the of the program's impact. Akerson, Buzzelli, and Donnelly (2010) worked with 14 K–3 teachers and were successful teaching NOS with an explicit and reflective approach. Of importance here is that the authors found that those preservice teachers who worked with cooperating teachers who provided support for the teaching of NOS were able to sustain a NOS focus, while those in classrooms with cooperating teachers who did not provide support were unable to maintain a NOS focus. These findings are provocative, as they raise an issue not yet prominent in the research community. Much effort has been placed on preparing preservice teachers to teach NOS, but these same teachers move into a school environment in which very few teachers address NOS. In short, there is no support for these teachers to continue stressing NOS. The situation is analogous to what we know about the impact of the differences between the values of teacher education programs and the values of the existing teaching community.

The research on developing teachers' conceptions of NOS continues to grow at all levels and in varied contexts: with elementary teachers (Abd-El-Khalick & Akerson, 2009; Akerson, Buzelli, & Donnelly, 2008; Akerson, Cullen, & Hanson, 2010; Akerson & Hanuscin, 2007; Akerson, Townsend, Donnelly, Hanson, Tira, & White, 2009), middle school teachers (Seung, Bryan, & Butler, 2009), secondary teachers (Smith & Scharmann, 2008), and elementary and secondary teachers in authentic laboratory contexts (Morrison, Raab, & Ingram, 2009; Sadler, Burgin, McKinney, Lyle, & Ponjuan, 2010). Although the variety of programs and contexts may differ, the one common element used to significantly improve teachers' conceptions of NOS is the use of an explicit and reflective approach. The research community acknowledged the importance of explicit and reflective instruction during the 1990s, and the research continues to provide support. It is important to reiterate, yet again, "explicit" does not refer to lecture, direct instruction, or a didactic (in the North American sense) approach but rather an approach that makes aspects of NOS "visible" in the classroom through discussion and hands-on activities followed by pertinent debriefing discussions.

In addition to the typical studies investigating ways to change and improve teachers' conceptions of NOS, there is a slowly emerging attention to the rationales that have been used to justify the importance of teaching NOS to K–12 students. One justification for teaching NOS has been that an understanding of NOS will contribute to informed decisions on scientifically based societal and personal issues. Bell and Lederman (2003) tested this assumption using a group of 21 highly educated individuals (i.e., individuals possessing a Ph.D.). These individuals were faculty members from various universities. Individuals completed an open-ended questionnaire, followed by an interview, designed to assess decision-making on science and technology related issues. A second questionnaire was used to assess participants' understandings of NOS, and an interview followed the completion of the questionnaire. Participants were separated into two groups based on the adequacy of their understanding of NOS. No differences were found between the two groups. Both groups used personal values, morals/ethics, and social concerns when making decisions, but NOS was not used. The authors concluded that decision making is complex, and the data did not support the assumption that an understanding of NOS would contribute prominently in one's decisions. The authors also speculated that NOS may not have been considered because individuals need to have instruction on how NOS understandings could be used in aiding the decision-making process.

Research on Students' Conceptions of NOS
It is safe to assume that teachers cannot possibly teach what they do not understand (Ball & McDiarmid, 1990). Research on the translation of teachers' conceptions into classroom practice, however, indicates that even though teachers' conceptions of NOS can be thought of as a *necessary* condition, these conceptions, nevertheless, should not be considered *sufficient* (Lederman, 1992, 2007). At least one implication for research related to NOS is apparent. Research efforts, it is argued, should "extend well beyond teachers' understandings of nature of science, as the translation of these understandings into classroom practice is mediated by a complex set of situational variables" (Lederman, 1992, p. 351). Clearly complex issues surround the possible influence of teachers' understandings of NOS on classroom practice and have yet to be resolved. It is safe to say, however, that there is general agreement among researchers concerning the strong influence of curriculum constraints, administrative policies, and teaching context on the translation of teachers' conceptions into classroom practice. In addition to investigations that assessed the relationship between teachers' conceptions and classroom practice, efforts to identify those factors that do influence students' conceptions have also been pursued.

The significance of teacher–student interactions to conceptual changes in students' views of science motivated a study with 18 high school biology teachers and 409 students (Zeidler & Lederman, 1989). In this investigation, specific attention was focused on the nature of teacher–student interactions and the specific language used. In general, when teachers used "ordinary language" without qualification (e.g., discussing the structure of an atom without stressing that it is a model), students tended to adopt a realist conception of science. Alternatively, when teachers were careful to use precise language with appropriate qualifications, students tended to adopt an instrumentalist conception. At the time, this investigation provided clear empirical support for Munby's

thesis (1976) that implicit messages embedded in teachers' language provide for varied conceptions of NOS. Most recently, Olivera, Akerson, Colak, Pongsanon, and Genel (2012) studied the language use of two elementary teachers. Drawing on semiotic theory, they found that the use of "unhedged or boosted" language (e.g., absolutely) relative to "hedged" language (e.g., maybe, could) lead to students perceiving scientific knowledge to be absolute, while "hedged" language more likely lead to a tentative view of scientific knowledge. Thus, although aspects of NOS are predominantly taught with an explicit approach, there are instances in which implicit messages are sent to students through language use.

Inclusion of history of science has often been touted as being a way to improve students' understandings of NOS. The value of history of science, however, has been held mostly as an intuitive assumption as opposed to being an idea having empirical support. Abd-El-Khalick and Lederman (2000b) assessed the influence of taking history of science courses on college students' and preservice teachers' conceptions of NOS. The subjects were 166 undergraduate and graduate students and 15 preservice secondary science teachers. All subjects were pre- and posttested with an open-ended questionnaire. A representative sample of students was also interviewed in an effort to establish face validity for the questionnaires. The results showed that most individuals entered the history of science courses with inadequate views of NOS and there was little change after completing the course. When change was noted, it was typically with respect to some explicit attention to NOS in one of the courses. In addition, there was some evidence that the preservice teachers learned more about NOS from the history of science courses than the other students did. This was attributed to the possible benefits of having entered the course with a perceptual framework for NOS provided in their science methods course. More recently, Hottecke, Henke, and Riess (2012) combined history and philosophy of science with an explicit approach to teaching NOS in high school physics classes as part of the European History, Philosphy, and Science Teaching (HIPST) Project. They used historical case studies, hands-on activities, reflective activities, role playing, and replications of historical apparatus in designing a curriculum over 2 years. This was an ambitious collaboration between scientists and teachers. Although there is not extensive empirical support for the effectiveness of the instructional approach, it is one of the few integrations of history and philosophy of science into instruction that heavily references the empirical literature.

Few studies have studied the relative effectiveness of explicit, reflective approaches to teaching NOS relative to implicit approaches with K–12 students. One such study was completed by Khishfe and Abd-El-Khalick (2002) in Lebanon. A total of 62 sixth-grade students in two intact groups ($n = 29$ & 32) experienced inquiry-oriented instruction related to energy transformation and sedimentary rocks. One group was taught with an approach that explicitly addressed the tentative, empirical, inferential, imaginative, and creative aspects of scientific knowledge, while in the other class only implicit attention to NOS was included. The same teacher taught both classes. Students' knowledge of NOS was assessed through a combination of an open-ended questionnaire and semistructured interviews. Both groups entered the investigation with naïve, and equivalent, views on the various aspects of NOS. After instruction, the implicit group showed no changes in views of NOS, while students in the explicit group all exhibited improvement in their understandings of one or more aspects of NOS. Again, this particular study is important in that it demonstrated the relative effectiveness of explicit instructional approaches with a sample of K–12 students as opposed to preservice and inservice teachers.

Science apprenticeship programs have been a popular approach to engaging high-ability students in science, with an eye on promoting their interest in future careers in science. A commonly stated goal of such apprenticeship programs is that students will develop improved conceptions of NOS. Bell, Blair, Crawford, and Lederman (2003) systematically tested this assumed benefit of an apprenticeship program. The apprenticeship program was 8 weeks long during the summer. Ten high-ability high school students (juniors and seniors) were pre and posttested on their understandings of NOS and scientific inquiry before and after the apprenticeship. Both students and their mentor scientists were interviewed after the program. Although the scientists were of the opinion that their students had learned a lot about inquiry and NOS, student data (from interviews and questionnaires) indicated that changes occurred only in students' abilities to do inquiry. The authors ultimately concluded that students' conceptions of NOS (and knowledge about inquiry) remained unchanged because there was no explicit instruction about either associated with the apprenticeship.

On the other hand, the recent review of research on the impact of research apprenticeships (Sadler, Burgin, McKinney, & Ponjuan, 2010) and an investigation of the impact of interactions with scientists on teachers (Morrison, Raab, & Ingram, 2009) indicated that improvements of NOS are found when NOS is made explicit.

Most of the research related to the impact of explicit instruction has been completed with teachers. However, in recent years there has been a clear increase of studies with K–12 students. Paraskevopoulou and Koliopoulos (2011) studied the understandings of 24 high school students in a physics class designed for students who had indicated that the natural sciences were not part of their career plans. Using an explicit and reflective approach, within instruction about the Millikan-Ehrenhaft dispute, one of the authors focused on the empirical nature of science, observation and inference, creativity, and subjectivity. Statistically significant improvements were noted on each these aspects of NOS using the VNOS—D instrument.

Yacoubian and BouJaoude (2010) studied the relative effects of using reflective discussions following an inquiry-based laboratory and implicit inquiry-based instruction. The study involved 38 sixth-grade students. Following a pretest–posttest control group design, students' understandings of NOS were determined based on an open-ended questionnaire, classroom observations, and interviews. Students in the experimental group showed improvement on the tentative nature of scientific knowledge, the empirical basis of scientific knowledge, and the social nature of science. Students in the control group did not show any improvement. This study clearly provided support for the effectiveness of an explicit teaching approach with students.

Many researchers have concerns about whether very young students can understand something as abstract as NOS. Akerson and Donnelly (2010) taught NOS explicitly to 27 K–2 students during a Saturday Science program. Instruction included contextualized and decontextualized activities, children's literature, debriefings of activities, and student-designed investigations. Using the VNOS—D to assess student understandings, the researchers found that students' knowledge increased on all aspects of NOS except cultural embeddedness and the distinction between theories and laws. Data with teachers shows that they have difficulty with cultural embeddedness and the theory and law distinction, so it is not surprising that these young students had difficulty with the same aspects. More importantly, this study showed not only that explicit instruction is effective but also that K–2 students can comprehend a variety of aspects of NOS. In a replication study, Quigley, Pongsanon, and Akerson (2010) taught 25 K–2 students NOS in Saturday Science program. The results of this investigation replicated the previously described investigation.

With older students (i.e., seventh grade), Khishfe (2008) implemented an explicit instructional approach for approximately 3 months. Instruction included various activities followed with in-depth debriefing sessions. Students' knowledge was assessed through a combination of open-ended questions and interviews. Students all held naïve views of NOS before instruction, intermediate views during instruction, and informed views by the end of instruction. Not all students exhibited the same magnitude of gain. The author proposed that students progress along a developmental scale with time.

Khishfe (2012) studied the effects of a combination of instruction on NOS and argumentation. The subjects were 219 Grade 11 students in Lebanon. The instruction included a focus on several socioscientific issues. Instruction focused around a unit on genetic engineering, with the controversial issue discussed being genetically modified foods. The treatment group was also taught how to use NOS in their arguments on the socioscientific issue. Students showed improvement in NOS understandings (i.e., tentative, subjective, and empirical) by the end of instruction. Strong correlations were found between NOS understandings and counterargument as opposed to argument and rebuttal. Given the context of socioscientific issues, the author felt that argumentation skills significantly contributed to students' understandings of NOS.

Debate still exists regarding the importance of teaching NOS embedded in science content or as a decontextualized topic. Khishfe and Lederman (2007) attempted to see if there was a difference in student learning in the two contexts. Participants in the investigation were three teachers and their students. There were six classes and 89 students in Grade 9 and 40 students in a mixed Grade 10 and 11 class. Students achieved equal understandings of NOS regardless of the integrated or nonintegrated context. The key issue here is that both treatments used an explicit approach to instruction on NOS. More research is still needed to determine if the difference in contexts is important.

Schalk (2012) developed a college-level microbiology course that used socioscientific issues to teach NOS aspects explicitly. Data were collected on 26 undergraduate students at a community college. Qualitative data were collected on students' reasoning and understandings of NOS. These data were analyzed inductively and the author found that, in addition to scientific reasoning skills, students developed an in-depth understanding that scientific knowledge is not absolute, but subject to change.

As can be expected, not all studies involving explicit instruction related to NOS have met with success (Leach, Hind, & Ryder, 2003). In this particular investigation, the explicit instructional approach was not effective in promoting improved student views.

Among the volumes of research that focus on effecting change in conceptions of NOS, a small minority of studies focus on the impact that one's conceptions of NOS have on other variables of interest. Sadler, Chambers, and Zeidler (2004) focused on how students' conceptions of NOS impacted how they interpreted and evaluated conflicting evidence on a socioscientific issue. Eighty-four high school students were asked to read contradictory reports related to global warming. A subsample of 30 students was interviewed in order to corroborate their written responses. The participants displayed a range of views on three aspects of NOS: empiricism, tentativeness, and social embeddedness. The authors claimed that how the students reacted to conflicting evidence was at least partially related to their views on NOS.

It is important to reiterate that not all of the existing research on teaching and learning of NOS could be presented here because of space considerations. An attempt was made to present the most prominent studies in terms of their impact on current research. However, the research studies that have not been included have provided findings that are consistent with what has been presented.

Assessing Conceptions of Nature of Science

Although there have been numerous criticisms of the validity of various assessment instruments over the years, students' and teachers' understandings have consistently been found lacking. This consistent finding, regardless of assessment approach, supports the notion that student and teacher understandings are not at the desired levels.

The history of the assessment of nature of science mirrors the changes that have occurred in both psychometrics and educational research design over the past few decades. The first formal assessments, beginning in the early 1960s, emphasized quantitative approaches, as was characteristic of the overwhelming majority of science education research investigations. Prior to the mid-1980s, with few exceptions, researchers were content to develop instruments that allowed for easily "graded" and quantified measures of individuals' understandings. In some cases, standardized scores were derived. Within the context of the development of various instruments, some open-ended questioning was involved in construction and validation of items. More recently, emphasis has been placed on providing an expanded view of an individual's beliefs regarding nature of science. In short, in an attempt to gain more in-depth understandings of students' and teachers' thinking, educational researchers have resorted to the use of more open-ended probes and interviews. As mentioned previously, a new critical analysis of assessment, which uses a significant and important perspective, is provided in the following chapter by Abd-El-Khalick.

Research on Nature of Science: Quo Vadis?

After more than 50 years of research related to students' and teachers' conceptions of NOS, a few generalizations can be justified. The following list is the same as the one included in the previous handbook (Lederman, 2007) because the overwhelming majority of research since 2005 has served to further reinforce and give the research community more confidence in what we had previously determined:

- K–12 students do not typically possess "adequate" conceptions of NOS.
- K–12 teachers do not typically possess "adequate" conceptions of NOS.
- Conceptions of NOS are best learned through explicit, reflective instruction as opposed to implicitly through experiences with simply "doing" science.
- Teachers' conceptions of NOS are not automatically and necessarily translated into classroom practice.
- Teachers do not regard NOS as an instructional outcome of equal status with that of "traditional" subject matter outcomes.

Although volumes of research have been completed since the 1950s, at this point in the history of research on nature of science, the research has been relatively superficial in the sense of an "input-output" model with little known about the in-depth mechanisms that contribute to change in teachers' and students' views. Even the more recent efforts that have documented the efficacy of explicit, reflective approaches (Abd-El-Khalick & Lederman, 2000a) to instruction are superficial in the sense that students and/or teachers are pre-tested and post-tested relative to an instructional activity or set of activities. The specific mechanisms of change and/or the dynamics of change have yet to be explored in depth. We simply have found out under what situations change has occurred in the desired direction. Clearly, much more work is needed before we, as a research community, can feel confident in making large-scale recommendations to teachers and professional developers.

Still Waters Run Deep

It is easy to look at the research on NOS since the last handbook and conclude that there have not been many new insights into students' and teachers' understandings of NOS, how to effectively teach NOS, and how to assess NOS. The recent research has effectively provided stronger support for what we knew about these matters in 2005. However, beneath the surface of our empirical research literature, theoretical discussions and debates have been turbulent. One must wonder if the undercurrents promise to be productive. What follows is a discussion, in no particular order, of some of the major issues currently confronting our community.

Conceptualizing the Construct

Recently there has been much conversation about how NOS is conceptualized in our professional journals and at our professional meetings. The phrase/question often heard is, "Whose NOS are we measuring?" Actually the discussion is not new, and it began with Alters (1997) and it continues today (Irzik & Nola, 2011; Wong & Hodson, 2009, 2010). In the end, the argument always rests on the voice of scientists and how what they think is important is not being heard or used. Actually, the international reform documents specifying outcomes regarding NOS have had strong input from the scientific community. More importantly, the audience for which these outcomes have been specified is consumers of science, K–12 students, not scientists. However, some would rather engage in arguments about why "lists" of outcomes or outcomes derived from others than scientists are anathema (Allchin, 2011; Irzik & Nola, 2011; Wong & Hodson 2009, 2010) instead of focusing on what is appropriate for K–12 students to know and be able to do. We need to continually remind ourselves for whom the NOS outcomes have been written. The knowledge specified is for what is considered important for the attainment of scientific literacy by the general citizenry. Yes, you can dissect the construct of NOS down to its very esoteric levels (Irzik & Nola, 2011), but doing so reveals a construct that is far too abstract and esoteric for the general public. This really is no different than why we do not expect all high school graduates to understand the most in-depth aspects of the dark reactions of photosynthesis. Relying too heavily on what scientists think is appropriate for K–12 students can be problematic. For example, Allchin (2011) and Wong and Hodson (2009) point out that scientists do not think it is important to discuss the differences between scientific theories and laws. After all, scientists do not sit around and argue about whether a colleague's work amounts to a theory or law. However, most of us have heard about or experienced debates concerning the teaching of evolution and creationism side by side in the science classroom. Such debates impact students, teachers, the general public, and even the Supreme Court of the United States. Scientific creationists proudly state that "evolution is just a theory" just as creationism is a theory. Knowing the difference between theories and laws and what constitutes a scientific theory and/or law is necessary to diffuse the creationists' claims. Again, this aspect of NOS is stressed for the general public and students, not scientists.

What Is So Bad About Lists?

Discussions about what ideas should be considered under the rubric of NOS often include concerns about lists. Some worry that lists of NOS aspects (and there are many) end up as "mantras" for students to memorize and repeat (Matthews, 2012). Others (Allchin, 2011; Clough & Olson, 2008; Irzik & Nola, 2011; Wong & Hodson, 2009, 2010) feel lists provide too simplistic a view of NOS. Lists serve an important function, as they help provide a concise organization of the often complex ideas and concepts they include. Each item on a list is just a label or symbol for a much more in-depth and detailed elaboration. If "tree" is included in a list, it is simply a referent for all the structures and processes that are involved in what is to be a "tree." The table of contents at the beginning of this book is a list, just as the index at the end of the book is. There are numerous science education reform documents that specify and delineate what students should know and be able to do (i.e., standards). These are also lists of learning outcomes, even though the standards can be as long as a paragraph. The only problem with a list is related to how it may be used. If students are asked to simply and mindlessly memorize a list, then there is a problem. But the problem is with pedagogy and not with the list. In their article concerned with conceptualizing NOS in terms of *family resemblance,* Irzik and Nola (2011) point out that they have produced a depiction of NOS that is much more informative and comprehensive than a list. However, what is presented is no different than a list. Their outcomes are formatted as a matrix as opposed to a linear format, but it is still a list. Often these "lists" are considered a product of the consensus approach to conceptualizing aspects of NOS. An excellent discussion about the consensus model and other criticisms concerning current views about NOS, discussed by Wong and Hodson (2010), among others, can be found in Abd-El-Khalick (2012). All is not lost, however; there remains support for the usefulness of lists (Abd-El-Khalick, Bell, & Lederman, 1998; McComas, 2008). Indeed, the knowledge and outcomes specified in the Next Generation Science Standards (NGSS Lead States, 2013) is a list as well.

Again, lists are a valuable tool that humans use to summarize key points or ideas. In the hands of an expert teacher, listings of desired student outcomes help guide instruction and help identify prerequisite knowledge students need to master before they can achieve a sophisticated understanding of the concept on the list. The value of a list is in how it used, but lists are not inherently good or bad.

There is one other issue when it comes to lists and consensus models. Some researchers (Duschl & Grandy, 2013) appear content to characterize "consensus-based heuristic principles" (i.e., lists) as out-of-date and too general, in contrast to "scientific practices in domain-specific contexts" as can be found in the Next Generation Science Standards (NGSS Lead States, 2013). Unfortunately, this position not only constitutes a gross misrepresentation of the views of nature of scientific knowledge represented in these "lists" but also shows a considerable lack of understanding of how these "lists" are used in actual classroom practice, and of general science pedagogy for that matter. Duschl and Grandy (2013) contend that this vision "focuses on the use of heuristic principles and domain general consensus-based statements taught in the context of lessons and activities," where by an aspect of NOS is connected to a specific activity meant for its explication. By contrast, the view of NOS undergirding the work of the researchers they criticize (Abd-El-Khalick, 2012; Lederman, Abd-El-Khalick, Bell, & Schwartz, 2002; Niaz, 2009) is one that strongly advocates NOS as an overarching instructional objective that permeates a science curriculum. The simple conception forwarded by Duschl and Grandy could only be characterized as simply poor teaching. Perhaps such inaccurate characterizations of how "lists" are used persist because many individuals fail to carefully consider the science curriculum, classroom practice, and the audience of students.

Why Can't We Agree to Disagree?

Recently, far too much discussion at professional meetings and on journal pages has focused on the lack of consensus on a definition or characterization of NOS. In short, scholars would rather argue about the need to reach consensus before an assessment of NOS can be developed. Why is NOS held to a higher standard than other content in science? How many of the concepts and ideas in science have achieved absolute consensus before we attempt to teach these ideas to students and assess what they have learned? Does every curriculum worldwide focus on the same structures of the human heart? As previously discussed, when one considers the developmental level of the target audience (K–12 students), the aspects of NOS stressed are at a level of generality that is not at all contentious. Nevertheless, if one is not willing to let go of the idea that the various aspects of NOS lack consensus and that assessment of NOS is, therefore, problematic, the "problem" is easily handled. One's performance on a NOS assessment

can simply be used to construct a profile of what the student knows/believes about scientific knowledge. In terms of the aspects of NOS to be assessed, there is no reason to require that all assessments measure the exact same understandings. If the focus is just upon the assessment of understandings that are considered to be important for scientifically literate individuals to know, then there is no reason to require an agreed-on domain of NOS aspects. Different assessments may stress, to one degree or another, different aspects of NOS. This is no different than assessing students' understandings of the human heart. Different valid and reliable assessments stress and include different structures.

Knowing Versus Doing

There has been a perennial problem with developing assessments of nature of science that is connected to the research literature. All too often, assessments include students' performance or inquiry skills/procedures within instruments on NOS. In spite of more than half a century of research on NOS, some science education researchers (e.g., Allchin, 2011) continue to conceptualize NOS as a skill as opposed to knowledge and espouse the belief that engagement in the practices of science is sufficient for developing understandings of NOS. The view that NOS is a skill, thus conflating it with scientific inquiry, minimizes the importance of understanding both of these constructs and their related characteristics and further obfuscates their associated nuances and interrelationships. Moreover, this view is not consistent with the National Science Education Standards (NRC, 1996), Benchmarks for Science Literacy (AAAS, 1993), the Framework for K–12 Science Education (NRC, 2011), and the Next Generation Science Standards (NGSS Lead States, 2013), all of which describe NOS as knowledge. Admittedly, the Next Generation Science Standards is not always clear on this matter. While focusing on scientific inquiry, the Benchmarks stress that students should develop understandings about SI beyond the ability to do SI, as this understanding is *sine qua non* to being scientifically literate, as is the case for understandings of NOS. Unfortunately, the Next Generation Science Standards (NGSS Lead States, 2013), which are derived from the Framework for K–12 Science Education, are not so clear regarding their "vision" for promoting understandings of NOS.

NOS has been a central theme underlying the goals of science education since the 1950s. The reason for this is that NOS understandings (irrespective of how these are defined at the time) are considered central to the goal of scientific literacy. While almost every other meaningful theme underlying past reform documents such as the Benchmarks for Science Literacy (AAAS, 1993), National Science Education Standards (NRC, 1996), and Framework for K–12 Science Education appear in the NGSS, the same cannot be said for NOS. Although NOS was eventually included in the NGSS, it has been trivialized as knowledge that will naturally follow the mastering of science practices, an assumption that runs contrary to the research of the past 20 years. In addition, NOS is sparingly included in any of the Performance Expectations. Consequently, regarding the teaching of NOS and the assessment of students' understandings, we may indeed be moving forward into the past.

The conflation described is inherently linked to the assumption that NOS is learned by having students DO science. That is, if students are involved in authentic scientific investigations, they will also come to an understanding about NOS. The empirical research reviewed in this handbook has consistently shown this assumption to be false. Clearly, students' ability to DO science is an important educational outcome, but it is not the same as having students reflect on what they have done and its implications for the knowledge developed. In terms of developing assessments of NOS, there must be a more concerted effort to realize that NOS is a cognitive outcome, not a "performance" outcome. Indeed, the lack of clarity in the NGSS may be promoting the continuance of the confusion about NOS and science practices (or inquiry). Quite recently, Salter and Atkins (2014) found a disconnect between measures of NOS understandings and students' ability to engage in science practices. The literature reviewed in this handbook, and the previous handbook, would have predicted such a disconnect (i.e., doing science does not necessarily result in learning of NOS). However, the authors chose to interpret their findings as meaning that current measures of NOS are not adequate to assess students' abilities in doing inquiry. They advocated that we need instruments that assess "procedural NOS." Unfortunately, "procedural" means doing science and totally ignores prior research on NOS.

Related to this last issue is that a small minority of individuals (e.g., Sandoval, 2005) who insist that students' and teachers' understandings of NOS are best assessed through observations of behavior during inquiry activities (i.e., knowledge in practice). The literature clearly documents the discrepancies that often exist between one's beliefs/knowledge and their behaviors. More concretely, if an individual believes that scientific knowledge is tentative (subject to change) and another individual believes the knowledge to be absolute/static, how would this be evident in their behavior during a laboratory activity? If a student recognizes that scientific knowledge is partly subjective, how would this student behave differently during a laboratory investigation than would a student with differing beliefs? This assessment approach only adds an unnecessary layer of inference. In the end, we must not forget that NOS is a cognitive outcome, not a behavior as some continue to insist (Allchin, 2011).

Epilogue

There is little doubt that the arguments described in this chapter will continue. At times it appears that our goal in academia is more about the debate than the purpose we are trying to accomplish. At the beginning of this chapter, the question was asked, "Why should students learn about NOS?" Our ultimate goal in science education has primarily been to have a literate citizenry, to have students develop into scientifically literate individuals. However, the relationship between scientific literacy and NOS has been made before (AAAS, 1993; NRC, 1996; NSTA; 1982, among others). Often arguments about the parameters and meaning of NOS lose sight of the ultimate goal of scientific literacy. Understanding NOS does not make a scientifically literate person by itself. Literate individuals also have a functional understanding of science content (interestingly, most consider NOS content knowledge), know how the content was developed (i.e., ability to do and know about inquiry/practices), and the ability to make informed decisions about scientifically based personal and societal issues. All of these abilities and knowledge are important. There are more than a few individuals who want to parcel out the knowledge and skills previously discussed in a different manner than it has been, but in the end we should keep our attention on what we decide is important for students to know and be able to do. For this reason, it is not at all productive to argue about what should be included under the rubric of NOS. It makes little sense to argue about whether lists are good or bad. The focus of our attention should always be on what we consider important for students and teachers and the general public to know and be able to do, not the label we use. And when we consider the knowledge and abilities to be assessed, let us not forget the audience, their emotional and cognitive developmental levels, and their needs as citizens. It is for this reason we often get into trouble: when the advice of well-meaning individuals, with little knowledge or experience with K–12 instruction, curriculum, and K–12 students, is given priority over those who have such experience and knowledge.

Acknowledgments

Thanks to William McComas and John Rudolph, who reviewed this chapter.

References

Abd-El-Khalick, F. (2001). Embedding nature of science instruction in preservice elementary science courses: Abandoning scientism, but . . . *Journal of Science Teacher Education, 12*(3), 215–233.

Abd-El-Khalick, F. (2005). Developing deeper understandings of nature of science: The impact of a philosophy of science course on preservice teachers' views and instructional planning. *International Journal of Science Education, 27*(1), 15–42.

Abd-El-Khalick, F. (2012). Examining the sources for our understandings about science: Enduring conflations and critical issues in research on nature of science in science education. *International Journal of Science Education, 34*(3), 353–374.

Abd-El-Khalick, F., & Akerson, V. (2004). Learning as conceptual change: Factors mediating the development of preservice teachers' views of nature of science. *Science Education, 88*(5), 785–810.

Abd-El-Khalick, F., & Akerson, V.L. (2009). The influence of metacognitive training on preservice elementary teachers' conceptions of nature of science. *International Journal of Science Education, 31*(16), 2161–2184.

Abd-El-Khalick, F., Bell, R. L., & Lederman, N. G. (1998). The nature of science and instructional practice: Making the unnatural natural. *Science Education, 82*(4), 417–437.

Abd-El-Khalick, F., & Lederman, N. G. (2000a). Improving science teachers' conceptions of the nature of science: A critical review of the literature. *International Journal of Science Education, 22*(7), 665–701.

Abd-El-Khalick, F., & Lederman, N. G. (2000b). The influence of history of science courses on students' views of nature of science. *Journal of Research in Science Teaching, 37*(10), 1057–1095.

Abell, S. K., & Lederman, N. G. (Eds.). (2007). *Handbook of research on science education.* Mahwah, NJ: Lawrence Erlbaum Associates.

Abell, S., Martini, M., & George, M. (2001). "That's what scientists have to do": Preservice elementary teachers' conceptions of the nature of science during a moon investigation. *International Journal of Science Education, 23*(11), 1095–1109.

Aguirre, J. M., Haggerty, S. M., & Linder, C. J. (1990). Student-teachers' conceptions of science, teaching and learning: A case study in preservice science education. *International Journal of Science Education, 12*(4), 381–390.

Aikenhead, G. (1972). The measurement of knowledge about science and scientists: An investigation into the development of instruments for formative evaluation. *Dissertations Abstracts International, 33,* 6590A. (University Microfilms No. 72–21, 423).

Aikenhead, G. (1973). The measurement of high school students' knowledge about science and scientists. *Science Education, 57*(4), 539–549.

Aikenhead, G. (1979). Science: A way of knowing. *The Science Teacher, 46*(6), 23–25.

Aikenhead, G., Fleming, R. W., Ryan, A. G. (1987). High school graduates' beliefs about science-technology-society: Methods and issues in monitoring student views. *Science Education, 71,* 145–161.

Akerson, V. L., Abd-El-Khalick, F., & Lederman, N. G. (2000). Influence of a reflective activity-based approach on elementary teachers' conceptions of nature of science. *Journal of Research in Science Teaching, 37*(4), 295–317.

Akerson, V. L., Buzzelli, C. A., & Donnelly, L. A. (2010). On the nature of teaching nature of science: Preservice early childhood teachers' instruction in preschool and elementary settings. *Journal of Research in Science Teaching, (47)*10, 213–233.

Akerson, V. L., Buzzelli, C. A., & Eastwood, J. L. (2012). Bridging the gap between preservice early childhood teachers' cultural values, perceptions of values held by scientists, and the relationships of these values to conceptions of nature of science. *Journal of Science Teacher Education, 23*(2),133–157.

Akerson, V. L., Cullen, T. A., & Hanson, D. L. (2010). Experience teachers' strategies for assessing nature of science conceptions in the elementary classroom. *Journal of Science Teacher Education, (21)*6, 723–745.

Akerson, V. L., & Donnelly, L. A. (2010). Teaching nature of science to K–2 students: What understandings can they attain? *International Journal of Science Education, 32*(1), 97–124.

Akerson, V. L., & Hanuscin, D. L. (2007). Teaching nature of science through inquiry: Results of a 3 year professional development program. *Journal of Research in Science Teaching, 44*(5), 653–680.

Akerson, V. L., Townsend, J. S., Donnelly, L. A., Hanson, D. L., Tira, P., & White, O. (2009). Scientific modeling for inquiring teachers network (SMIT'N): The influence on elementary teachers' views of nature of science, inquiry, and modeling. *Journal of Science Teacher Education, 20*(1), 21–40.

Akindehin, F. (1988). Effect of an instructional package on preservice science teachers' understanding of the nature of science and acquisition of science-related attitudes. *Science Education, 72*(1), 73–82.

Allchin, D. (2011). Evaluating knowledge of the nature of (whole) science. *Science Education, 95*(3), 518–542.

Alters, B. J. (1997). Whose nature of science? *Journal of Research in Science Teaching, 34,* 39–55.

American Association for the Advancement of Science (AAAS). (1990). *Science for all Americans.* New York: Oxford University Press.

American Association for the Advancement of Science (AAAS). (1993). *Benchmarks for science literacy: A Project 2061 report.* New York: Oxford University Press.

Ball, D. L., & McDiarmid, G. W. (1990). The subject-matter preparation of teachers. In W. R. Houston (Ed.), *Handbook of research on teacher education* (pp. 437–465). New York: Macmillan.

Bell, R. L., Blair, L., Crawford, B., & Lederman, N. G. (2003). *Journal of Research in Science Teaching, 40*(5), 487–509.

Bell, R. L., & Lederman, N. G. (2003). Understandings of the nature of science and decision making in science and technology based issues. *Science Education, 87*(3), 352–377.

Bell, R. L., Lederman, N. G., & Abd-El-Khalick, F. (2000). Developing and acting upon one's conception of the nature of science: A follow-up study. *Journal of Research in Science Teaching, 37*(6), 563–581.

Billeh, V. Y., & Hasan, O. E. (1975). Factors influencing teachers' gain in understanding of the nature of science. *Journal of Research in Science Teaching, 12*(3), 209–219.

Biological Sciences Curriculum Study (BSCS). (1962). *Processes of science test.* New York: The Psychological Corporation.

Bloom, J. W. (1989). Preservice elementary teachers' conceptions of science: Science, theories and evolution. *International Journal of Science Education, 11*(4), 401–415.

Brickhouse, N. W., & Bodner, G. M. (1992). The beginning science teacher: Classroom narratives of convictions and constraints. *Journal of Research in Science Teaching, 29,* 471–485.

Carey, R. L., & Stauss, N. G. (1968). An analysis of the understanding of the nature of science by prospective secondary science teachers. *Science Education, 52*(4), 358–363.

Carey, R. L., & Stauss, N. G. (1970a). An analysis of the relationship between prospective science teachers' understanding of the nature of science and certain academic variables. *Georgia Academy of Science,* 148–158.

Carey, R. L., & Stauss, N. G. (1970b). An analysis of experienced science teachers' understanding of the nature of science. *School Science and Mathematics, 70*(5), 366–376.

Carey, S., Evans, R., Honda, M., Jay, E., & Unger, C. (1989). An experiment is when you try it and see if it works: A study of grade 7 students' understanding of the construction of scientific knowledge. *International Journal of Science Education, 11,* 514–529.

Celik, S., & Bayrakceken, S. (2012). The influence of an activity-based explicit approach on the Turkish prospective science teachers' conceptions. *Australian Journal of Teacher Education, 37*(4), 75–95.

Clough, M. P., & Olson, J. K. (2008). Teaching and assessing the nature of science: An introduction. *Science & Education, 17*(2), 143–145.

Cobern, W. W. (1989). A comparative analysis of NOSS profiles on Nigerian and American preservice, secondary science teachers. *Journal of Research in Science Teaching, 26*(6), 533–541.

Cooley, W. W., & Klopfer, L. E. (1961). *Test on understanding science.* Princeton, NJ: Educational Testing Service.

Crumb, G. H. (1965). Understanding of science in high school physics. *Journal of Research in Science Teaching, 3*(3), 246–250.

Dogan, N., & Abd-El-Khalick, F. (2008). Turkish grade 10 students' and science teachers' conceptions of nature of science: A national study. *Journal of research in Science Teaching, 45*(10), 1083–1112.

Driver, R., Leach, J., Millar, R., & Scott, P. (1996). *Young people's images of science.* Buckingham, UK: Open University Press.

Duschl, R. A., & Grandy, R. (2013). Two views about explicitly teaching about nature of science. *Science and Education, 22*(9), 2109–2139.

Duschl, R. A., & Wright, E. (1989). A case study of high school teachers' decision making models for planning and teaching science. *Journal of Research in Science Teaching, 26*(6), 467–501.

Fah, L. Y., & Hoon, K. C. (2011). Teachers' views of the nature of science: A study on pre-service science teachers in Sabah, Malaysia. *Journal of Science and Mathematics Education in Southeast Asia, 34*(2), 262–282.

Gabel, D. L., Rubba, P. A., & Franz, J. R. (1977). The effect of early teaching and training experiences on physics achievement, attitude toward science and science teaching, and process skill proficiency. *Science Education, 61,* 503–511.

Gilbert, S. W. (1991). Model building and a definition of science. *Journal of Research in Science Teaching, 28*(1), 73–80.

Hodson, D. (1985). Philosophy of science, science and science education. *Studies in Science Education, 12,* 25–57.

Hottecke, D., Henke, A., & Riess, F. (2012). Implementing history and philosophy in science teaching: Strategies, methods, results and experiences from the European HIPST project. *Science & Education, 21*(9), 1233–1261.

Hurd, P. D. (1969). *New directions in teaching secondary school science.* Chicago: Rand-McNally.

Ibrahim, B., Buffler, A., & Lubben, F. (2009). Profiles of freshman physics students' views on the nature of science. *Journal of Research in Science Teaching, 46*(3), 248–264.

Irzik, G., & Nola, R. (2011). A family resemblance approach to the nature of science education. *Science & Education, 20*(7–8), 591–607.

Johnson, R. L., & Peeples, E. E. (1987). The role of scientific understanding in college: Student acceptance of evolution. *American Biology Teacher, 49*(2), 96–98.

Jungwirth, E. (1970). An evaluation of the attained development of the intellectual skills needed for "understanding of the nature of scientific enquiry" by BSCS pupils in Israel. *Journal of Research in Science Teaching, 7*(2), 141–151.

Kang, S., Scharmann, L., & Noh, T. (2004). Examining students' views on the nature of science: Results from Korean 6th, 8th, and 10th graders. *Science Education, 89*(2), 314–334.

Khishfe, R. (2008). The development of seventh graders' views of nature of science. *Journal of Research in Science Teaching, 45*(4), 470–496.

Khishfe, R. (2012). Relationship between nature of science understandings and argumentation skills: A role for counterargument and contextual factors. *Journal of Research in Science Teaching, 49*(4), 489–514.

Khishfe, R., & Abd-El-Khalick, F. (2002). Influence of explicit and reflective versus implicit inquiry-oriented instruction on sixth graders' views of nature of science. *Journal of Research in Science Teaching, 39*(7), 551–578.

Khishfe, R., & Lederman, N. G. (2007). Relationship between instructional context and views of nature of science. *International Journal of Science Education, 29*(8), 939–961.

Kimball, M. E. (1968). Understanding the nature of science: A comparison of scientists and science teachers. *Journal of Research in Science Teaching, 5*, 110–120.

Kleinman, G. (1965). Teachers' questions and student understanding of science. *Journal of Research in Science Teaching, 3*(4), 307–317.

Klopfer, L. E. (1964). The use of case histories in science teaching. *School Science and Mathematics, 64*, 660–666.

Klopfer, L. E. (1969). The teaching of science and the history of science. *Journal of Research in Science Teaching, 6*, 87–95.

Klopfer, L. E., & Cooley, W. W. (1963). The history of science cases for high schools in the development of student understanding of science and scientists. *Journal of Research in Science Teaching, 1*(1), 33–47.

Koulaidis, V., & Ogborn, J. (1989). Philosophy of science: An empirical study of teachers' views. *International Journal of Science Education, 11*(2), 173–184.

Lantz, O., & Kass, H. (1987). Chemistry teachers' functional paradigms. *Science Education, 71*, 117–134.

Lavach, J. F. (1969). Organization and evaluation of an inservice program in the history of science. *Journal of Research in Science Teaching, 6*, 166–170.

Leach, J., Hind, A., & Ryder, J. (2003). *Designing and evaluating short teaching interventions about the epistemology of science in high school classrooms. Science Education, 87*(6), 831–848.

Lederman, N. G. (1986). Students' and teachers' understanding of the nature of science: A reassessment. *School Science and Mathematics, 86*(2), 91–99.

Lederman, N. G. (1992). Students' and teachers' conceptions of the nature of science: A review of the research. *Journal of Research in Science Teaching, 29*(4), 331–359.

Lederman, N. G. (1998). The state of science education: Subject matter without context. *Electronic Journal of Science Education, 3*(2), December. Available at http://wolfweb.unr.edu/homepage/jcannon/ejse/lederman.html

Lederman, N. G. (1999). Teachers' understanding of the nature of science and classroom practice: Factors that facilitate or impede the relationship. *Journal of Research in Science Teaching, 36*(8), 916–929.

Lederman, N. G. (2007). Nature of science: Past, present, and future. In S. K. Abell & N. G. Lederman (Eds.), *Handbook of research on science education* (pp. 831–880). Mahwah, NJ: Lawrence Erlbaum Associates, Inc.

Lederman, N. G. (2013). A powerful way to learn. In L. Froschauer (Ed.), *A year of inquiry* . Arlington, VA: NSTA Press.

Lederman, N. G., Abd-El-Khalick, F., Bell, R. L., & Schwartz, R. S. (2002). Views of nature of science questionnaire: Toward valid and meaningful assessment of learners' conceptions of nature of science. *Journal of Research in Science Teaching, 39*(6), 497–521.

Lederman, N. G., Antink, A., & Bartos, S. (2014). Nature of science, scientific inquiry, and socio-scientific issues arising from genetics: A pathway to developing a scientifically literate citizenry. *Science and Education, 23*(2), 285–302.

Lederman, N. G., Bartos, S. A., & Lederman, J. S. (2014). The development, use, and interpretation of nature of science assessments. In M. R. Matthews (Ed.) *International handbook of research in history, philosophy and science teaching* (pp. 971-997). Dordrecht, the Netherlands: Springer Publishing.

Lederman, N. G., & Lederman, J. S. (2011). The development of scientific literacy: A function of the interactions and distinctions among subject matter, nature of science, scientific inquiry, and knowledge about scientific inquiry. In C. Linder, L. Ostman, D. A. Roberts, P. O Wickman, G. Erickson, & A. MacKinnon (Eds.), *Exploring the landscape of scientific literacy* (pp. 127–144). New York: Routledge.

Lederman, N. G., & O'Malley, M. (1990). Students' perceptions of tentativeness in science: Development, use, and sources of change. *Science Education, 74*, 225–239.

Lederman, N. G., & Zeidler, D. L. (1987). Science teachers' conceptions of the nature of science: Do they really influence teacher behavior? *Science Education, 71*(5), 721–734.

Liang, L. L. Chen, S., Chen, X., Kaya, O. N., Adams, A. D., Macklin, M., & Ebenezer, J. (2009). Preservice teachers' views about nature of scientific knowledge development: An international collaborative study. *International Journal of Science and Mathematics Education, 7*(5), 987–1012.

Lin, H. S., & Chen, C. C. (2002). Promoting preservice teachers' understanding about the nature of science through history. *Journal of Research in Science Teaching, 39*(9), 773–792.

Liu, S., & Lederman, N. G. (2007). Exploring prospective teachers' worldviews and conceptions of nature of science. *International Journal of Science Education, 29*(10), 1281–1307.

Mackay, L. D. (1971). Development of understanding about the nature of science. *Journal of Research in Science Teaching, 8*(1), 57–66.

Matthews, M. R. (2012). Changing the focus: From nature of science (NOS) to features of science (FOS). In M. S. Khine (Ed.), *Advances in nature of science research: Concepts and methodologies* (pp. 3–26). Dordrecht, the Netherlands: Springer.

McComas, W. F. (2008). Seeking historical examples to illustrate key aspects of the nature of science. *Science & Education, 17*(2–3), 249–263.

McDonald, C. V. (2010). The influence of explicit nature of science and argumentation instruction on preservice primary teachers' views of nature of science. *Journal of Research in Science Teaching, 47*(9), 1137–1164.

Meichtry, Y. J. (1992). Influencing student understanding of the nature of science: Data from a case of curriculum development. *Journal of Research in Science Teaching, 29*, 389–407.

Morrison, J. A., Raab, F., & Ingram, D. (2009). Factors influencing elementary and secondary teachers' views on the nature of science. *Journal of Research on Science Teaching, 46*(4), 384–403.

Munby, H. (1976). Some implications of language in science education. *Science Education, 60*(1), 115–124.

National Research Council (NRC). (1996). *National science education standards.* Washington, DC: National Academies Press.

National Research Council (NRC). (2012). *A framework for K–12 science education: Practices, crosscutting concepts, and core ideas.* Washington, DC: National Academies Press.

National Science Teachers Association (NSTA). (1982). *Science-technology-society: Science education for the 1980s.* (An NSTA position statement). Washington, DC: Author.

NGSS Lead States. (2013). *Next generation science standards: For states, by states.* Washington, DC: National Academies Press.

Niaz, M. (2009). *Critical appraisal of physical science as a human enterprise: Dynamics of scientific progress.* Dordrecht, the Netherlands: Springer.

Ogunniyi, M. B. (1982). An analysis of prospective science teachers' understanding of the nature of science. *Journal of Research in Science Teaching, 19*(1), 25–32.

Oliveira, A., Akerson, V. L., Colak, H., Pongsanon, K., & Genel, A. (2012). The implicit communication of nature of science and epistemology during inquiry discussion. *Science Education, 96*(4), 652–684.

Osborne, J., Collins, S., Ratcliffe, M., Millar, R., & Duschl, R. (2003). What "ideas-about-science" should be taught in school science? A Delphi study of the expert community. *Journal of Research in Science Teaching, 40*(7), 692–720.

Paraskevopoulou, E., & Koliopoulos, D. (2011). Teaching the nature of science through the Millikan-Ehrenhaft dispute. *Science & Education, 20*(10), 943–960.

Posnanski, T. J. (2010). Developing understanding of the nature of science within a professional development program for inservice elementary teachers: Project nature of elementary science teaching. *Journal of Research in Science Teaching, 47*(10), 589–621.

Quigley, C., Pongsanon, K., & Akerson, V. L. (2010). If we teach them, they can learn: Young students' views of nature of science aspects to early elementary students during an informal science education program. *Journal of Science Teachers Education, 21*(7), 887–907.

Riley, J. P., II. (1979). The influence of hands-on science process training on preservice teachers' acquisition of process skills and attitude toward science and science teaching. *Journal of Research in Science Teaching, 16*(5), 373–384.

Robinson, J. T. (1965). Science teaching and the nature of science. *Journal of Research in Science Teaching, 3*, 37–50.

Rothman, A. I. (1969). Teacher characteristics and student learning. *Journal of Research in Science Teaching, 6*(4), 340–348.

Rowe, M. B. (1974). A humanistic intent: The program of preservice elementary education at the University of Florida. *Science Education, 58*, 369–376.

Rubba, P., & Anderson, H. (1978). Development of an instrument to assess secondary school students' understanding of the nature of scientific knowledge. *Science Education, 62*, 449–458.

Rubba, P., Horner, J., & Smith, J. M. (1981). A study of two misconceptions about the nature of science among junior high school students. *School Science and Mathematics, 81*, 221–226.

Rubba, P. A. (1977). The development, field testing and validation of an instrument to assess secondary school students' understanding of the nature of scientific knowledge. *Dissertations Abstracts International, 38*, 5378A. (University Microfilms No. 78–00, 998).

Rutherford, J. F. (1964). The role of inquiry in science teaching. *Journal of Research in Science Teaching, 2*(2), 80–84.

Sadler, T. D., Burgin, S., McKinney, L., & Ponjuan, L. (2010). Learning science through research apprenticeships: A critical review of the literature. *Journal of Research in Science Teaching, 47*(3), 235–256.

Sadler, T. D., Chambers, F. W., & Zeidler, D. (2004). Student conceptualizations of the nature of science in response to a socioscientific issue. *International Journal of Science Education, 26*(4), 387–409.

Salter, I. Y., Atkins, L. J. (2014). What students say versus what they do regarding scientific inquiry. Science Education (98)1, 1–35.

Sandoval, W. A. (2005). Understanding students' practical epistemologies and their influence on learning through inquiry. *Science Education, 89*(5), 634–656.

Schalk, K. A. (2012). A socioscientific curriculum facilitating the development of distal and proximal NOS conceptualizations. *International Journal of Science Education, 34*(1), 1–24.

Scharmann, L. C., & Harris, W. M., Jr. (1992). Teaching evolution: Understanding and applying the nature of science. *Journal of Research in Science Teaching, 29*(4), 375–388.

Scharmann, L. C., & Smith, M. U. (1999). Defining versus describing the nature of science: A pragmatic analysis for classroom teachers and science educators. *Science Education, 85*(4), 493–509.

Scharmann, L. C., Smith, M. U., James, M. C., & Jensen, M. (2005). Explicit reflective nature of science instruction: Evolution, intelligent design, and umbrellaology. *Journal of Science Teacher Education, 16*(1), 27–41.

Schwartz, R., & Lederman, N. G. (2008). What scientists say: Scientists' views of nature of science and relation to science context. *International Journal of Science Education, 30*(6), 727–771.

Schwartz, R. S., Lederman, N. G., & Crawford, B. (2004). Developing views of nature of science in an authentic context: An explicit approach to bridging the gap between nature of science and scientific inquiry. *Science Education, 88*(4), 610–645.

Seung, E., Bryan, L. A., & Butler, M. B. (2009). Improving preservice middle grades science teachers' understanding of nature of science. *Journal of Science Teacher Education, 20*(2), 157–177.

Smith, M. U., & Scharmann, L. (2008). A multi-year program developing an explicit reflective pedagogy for teaching pre-service teachers the nature of science. *Science & Education, 17*(2–3), 219–248.

Spears, J., & Zollman, D. (1977). The influence of structured versus unstructured laboratory on students' understanding the process of science. *Journal of Research in Science Teaching, 14*(1), 33–38.

Sutherland, D., & Dennick, R. (2002). Exploring culture, language and perception of the nature of science. *International Journal of Science Education, 24*(1), 25–36.

Tamir, P. (1972). Understanding the process of science by students exposed to different science curricula in Israel. *Journal of Research in Science Teaching, 9*(3), 239–245.

Trent, J. (1965). The attainment of the concept "understanding science" using contrasting physics courses. *Journal of Research in Science Teaching, 3*(3), 224–229.

Troxel, V. A. (1968). *Analysis of instructional outcomes of students involved with three sources in high school chemistry.* Washington, DC: U.S. Department of Health, Education, and Welfare, Office of Education.

Urhahne, D., Kremer, K., & Mayer, J. (2011). Conceptions of the nature of science—are they general or context specific? *International Journal of Science and Mathematics Education, 9*(3), 707–730.

Walls, L. (2012). Third grade African American students' views of the nature of science. *Journal of Research in Science Teaching, 49*(1), 1–37.

Welch, W. W. (1967). *Science process inventory.* Cambridge, MA: Harvard University Press.

Welch, W. W., & Pella, M. O. (1967–1968). The development of an instrument for inventorying knowledge of the processes of science. *Journal of Research in Science Teaching, 5*(1), 64.

Welch, W. W., & Walberg, H. J. (1968). An evaluation of summer institute programs for physics teachers. *Journal of Research in Science Teaching, 5*, 105–109.

Wong, S. L., & Hodson, D. (2009). From the horse's mouth: What scientists say about scientific investigation and scientific knowledge. *Science Education, 93*(1), 109–130.

Wong, S. L., & Hodson, D. (2010). More from the horse's mouth: What scientists say about science as a social practice. *International Journal of Science Education, 32*(11), 1431–1463.

Yager, R. E., & Wick, J. W. (1966). Three emphases in teaching biology: A statistical comparison of the results. *Journal of Research in Science Teaching, 4*(1), 16–20.

Yacoubian, H. A., & BouJaoude, S. (2010). The effect of reflective discussions following inquiry-based laboratory activities on students' views of nature of science. *Journal of Research in Science Teaching, 47*(10), 1229–1252.

Zeidler, D. L., & Lederman, N. G. (1989). The effects of teachers' language on students' conceptions of the nature of science. *Journal of Research in Science Teaching, 26*(9), 771–783.

Zeidler, D. L., Walker, K. A., Ackett, W. A., & Simmons, M. L. (2002). Tangled up in views: Beliefs in the nature of science and responses to socioscientific dilemmas. *Science Education, 86*(3), 343–367.

31

The Evolving Landscape Related to Assessment of Nature of Science

Fouad Abd-El-Khalick

Introduction

The centrality, ubiquity, and longevity of nature of science (NOS) in precollege science education cannot be overstated. The goal of helping precollege students internalize informed NOS understandings has been the subject of continuous and intensive research and development efforts around the globe since the early 1950s (see Lederman & Lederman, Chapter 30, this volume). This longstanding focus will endure into the future: NOS continues to be explicitly emphasized as a prominent curricular component and instructional goal in, for example, the most recent science education reform efforts in the United States embodied in the *Next Generation Science Standards* (NGSS Lead States, 2013). Syntheses of the research literature on NOS in science education provide for a robust narrative (e.g., Abd-El-Khalick & Lederman, 2000a; Lederman, 1992, 2007). This narrative speaks to gains in student NOS understandings in response to particular instructional interventions but asserts continued frustration with the prevalence of naïve NOS conceptions among a majority of precollege students. The lack of substantial progress is attributed to science teachers' naïve NOS conceptions; systemic issues with science teacher education, including the nature of teachers' scientific education in the academy; the predominance of a culture of school science instruction that is incommensurate with scientific practice, even among teachers who seem to have internalized informed NOS understandings; a host of situational and contextual factors that mediate the translation of teachers' NOS understandings into their practice; and naïve representations of NOS in commercial science textbooks and instructional resources (Abd-El-Khalick, Waters, & Le, 2008; see Lederman & Lederman, Chapter 30, this volume). Research efforts continue to be dedicated to understanding the relative importance of the aforementioned factors and how best to mitigate their effects, and to delineating the nature and development among teachers of pedagogical content knowledge specific to teaching about NOS (Wahbeh & Abd-El-Khalick, 2013). Additionally, albeit drawing on incongruent empirical bases, debates continue about the differential impacts of instructional interventions (e.g., explicit versus implicit; integrated versus nonintegrated) on students' and teachers' NOS understandings; research also is being directed toward gauging the most effective contexts (e.g., argumentation, authentic research apprenticeships, historical case studies, inquiry-oriented experiences, socioscientific issues) and those best suited for addressing varying sets of NOS–related objectives; and vigorous discussions persist in relation to the sources that inform the construct of NOS, in addition to (re)emergent discussions about the very nature of the construct, this time from the perspective of domain-general versus domain-specific NOS understandings (see Abd-El-Khalick, 2012a, 2013). The aforementioned narrative also speaks to a multitude of assessments, which have been developed and used to gauge learners' understandings: As many as two dozen NOS–specific instruments have come into being over the past 60 years (Lederman, 2007). The latter instruments and associated assessment approaches are the *empirical* content and object of investigation of the present chapter.

A focus on NOS assessments is crucial. First, it is well known that the nature and underlying dimensions of the construct of NOS in science education have been and continue to be contested (e.g., Abd-El-Khalick, 2012a; Alters, 1997; Bianchini & Solomon, 2003; Good & Shymansky, 2001; Irzik & Nola, 2011; Smith, Lederman, Bell, McComas, & Clough, 1997; Wong & Hodson, 2010). However, in a "real" and practical sense, the *only* NOS construct (or constructs) in currency in the field of science education is the construct (or are those constructs) being assessed. Research claims and judgments related to the status of students' and teachers' NOS understandings (naïve, informed, etc.), relative impact of differing instructional interventions on learners' understandings, and differential appropriateness of one instructional context compared to another for teaching about specific NOS aspects, all rest on the construct as embodied in assessments used by science education researchers. Thus, by scrutinizing the embodiment of NOS in various assessment instruments and approaches, one aim of this chapter is to assess the extent to which the NOS research domain is "strained" given the seemingly contested nature of the target of assessment (i.e., the construct of NOS itself) and the varied perspectives regarding the ideal context(s) within which these assessments are most meaningful, as well as the goal(s) of such assessments. Second, prior reviews of NOS–related assessments (e.g., Aikenhead, 1973, 1988; Doran, Guerin, & Cavalieri, 1974; Guerra-Ramos, 2012; Lederman, 2007; Lederman, Wade, & Bell, 1998; Pearl, 1974) have compiled increasingly longer lists of NOS instruments over the decades, outlined the general domains targeted by these instruments, examined the approaches and types of items used (Likert, multiple-choice, agree/disagree, open-ended, etc.) and the implications of such use for the trustworthiness of the assessments, and/or—where applicable—gauged the instruments' psychometric properties. All these aspects are quite important; this chapter draws on the literature to update such aspects and defers to the aforementioned reviews in several respects throughout its discussions. However, the dominant narrative we are left with is that the NOS research domain is inundated by the use of a large number of different instruments, which tend to focus on differing dimensions of NOS. Thus, the narrative continues; attempts to generalize across empirical studies or undertake robust comparisons across contexts and interventions will always be undermined by instrument variance. Again, in a "real" and practical sense, the extent to which any one instrument impacts discourse within a research domain and contributes to shaping knowledge claims within that domain is determined by the extent to which the instrument is *used* in empirical investigations. Thus, another aim of this chapter is to scrutinize the *extent of use* of various NOS instruments to generate an empirical account of the landscape related to NOS assessments and the evolution of this landscape.

The Landscape of NOS Assessments

The terrain related to NOS assessment is, to say the least, unwieldy. The following section outlines the difficulties associated with taking accurate stock of NOS–specific assessments and presents an explicit set of inclusion criteria, which were used to admit NOS instruments into the present review. The next section lists these instruments, describes the frequency and timeline for their development, and characterizes their types and general features.

Difficulties With Mapping the Field and Inclusion Criteria

Accurately depicting the NOS assessment landscape is a major challenge in and of itself. To start with, NOS in science education has been the subject of wide-ranging and continuous research efforts for close to six decades. A conservative search of assessments related to NOS using Google Scholar would return several thousand entries. Additionally, a plethora of NOS assessment instruments have been developed since the early 1950s (e.g., Wilson, 1954) and continue to be developed to the present day (e.g., Hacıeminoğlu, Yılmaz-Tüzün, & Ertepınar, 2012). Nonetheless, for a number of reasons, taking accurate stock of these instruments and assessments is not as straightforward as one might assume. First, the NOS construct itself has evolved over time. For instance, in the 1950s and early 1960s, several instruments bundled the assessment of cognitive, affective, and attitudinal outcomes related to the nature of the scientific enterprise, such as the Science Attitude Questionnaire (SAQ; Wilson, 1954), *Attitudes Toward Science and Scientific Careers* (ASSC; Allen, 1959), and *Inventory of Science Attitudes, Interests, and Appreciations* (ISAIA; Swan, 1966). However, by the early 1970s, the constructs of "scientific attitudes" (e.g., skepticism, open-mindedness) and "attitudes toward science" (e.g., interest in science, attitudes toward science and scientists) were being carefully delineated as distinct from outcomes associated with covering terms, such as "understandings about science" (see Gardner, 1975; Mackay & White, 1974). Thus, depending on their authors' perspectives, literature reviews of "assessments" or "measures" of NOS–related objectives end up with differing lists of specific instruments (see Aikenhead, 1973, 1988; Doran et al., 1974; Guerra-Ramos, 2012; Hacıeminoğlu et al., 2012; Lederman, 2007; Lederman et al., 1998; Mayer & Richmond, 1982; Pearl, 1974). Second, over the years, many researchers have adapted, modified, and recombined extant NOS instruments in a variety of ways and to varying extents to examine learners' NOS understandings. For example, Abd-El-Khalick and BouJaoude (1997) and Dogan and Abd-El-Khalick (2008) slightly modified the 14 items they selected from the *Views of Science-Technology-Society* (VOSTS) instrument (Aikenhead & Ryan, 1992; Aikenhead, Ryan, & Fleming, 1989) by deleting the last three standard choices for each *VOSTS* item ("I don't understand," "I don't know enough about this subject to make a choice," and "None of these choices fits my basic viewpoint") and replacing these with a choice that allowed respondents to articulate whatever ideas they deemed were representative of their views on the target issue. The authors, however, left item stems and positions virtually intact. In comparison, Haidar (2000) developed a questionnaire that drew heavily on but substantially modified *VOSTS* items by regrouping the multiple positions associated with each item into only three positions (for similar modifications, see Kang, Scharmann, & Noh, 2005). In other cases, researchers used one subset or another of items from extant instruments (or even combined item subsets from different instruments), sometimes with slight modifications and, on occasion, with major modifications coupled with renaming the resulting "instrument." For instance, Wong,

Hodson, Kwan, and Yung (2008) used a slightly modified version of the *Views of Nature of Science–Form C* (VNOS–C) Questionnaire (Lederman, Abd-El-Khalick, Bell, & Schwartz, 2002), while Liu and Lederman (2007) adapted seven items from the *VNOS–C,* added another item, and recast the resulting instrument as the "Nature of Science Questionnaire" (p. 1287). Other instrument modifications were more involved. For instance, Rampal (1992) adapted a number of items from the *Test on Understanding Science* (TOUS; Cooley & Klopfer, 1961) "both linguistically and culturally to incorporate the popular positions teachers . . . [in the context of India] tend to take on such issues" (p. 418). Next, modified items were coupled with a set of eight open-ended questions, which focused on perceptions of scientists' areas of work, "minimum educational requisites to be a scientist," "women in science, the role of science in removing poverty and unemployment, [and] the role of the computer in current scientific research" (pp. 418–419), and the two-part instrument was named the "Views about Science and Scientists" questionnaire. The result of such modifications, both modest and elaborate, is a rather large number of instrument *variants* (see also Buffler, Lubben, & Ibrahim, 2009).

A third reason underlying the difficulty of taking accurate stock of NOS–specific assessments is that a number of researchers have developed NOS–related measures and assessments, which were specific to their purposes in the context of particular studies (e.g., among others, Abd-El-Khalick & BouJaoude, 2003; Bianchini & Solomon, 2003; Driver, Leach, Miller, & Scott, 1996; Flores, Lopez, Gallegos, & Barojas, 2000; Gess-Newsome, 2002; Guerra-Ramos, Ryder, & Leach, 2010; Lakin & Wellington, 1994; Lombrozo, Thanukos, & Weisberg, 2008; Mellado, 1997; Murcia & Schibeci, 1999; Rubba, Horner, & Smith, 1981; Ryder, Leach, Driver, 1999; Turgut, 2011; Vesterinen & Aksela, 2012; Zimmermann & Gilbert, 1998). These assessments mostly were of the semistructured or open-ended individual interview types but also included scenario-based items or interviews, convergent and open-ended questionnaires, repertory girds, learner-generated artifacts (e.g., reflective journals, diaries), and combinations of these variants. Nonetheless, most of these assessments were not developed as or intended to be formal "instruments." In many cases, efforts to establish the validity and/or reliability of these measures were limited to establishing face validity or securing feedback from reviewer panels (see Munby, 1982, for issues associated with the overreliance on such approaches in instrument validation). Additionally, other researchers did not "take up" these measures or put them to use in empirical investigations. Fourth, even though referenced in some reviews or studies, a few instruments could not be retrieved. For instance, Trembath (1972) reported on the development and use of an 18-multiple-choice-item questionnaire to assess prospective elementary teachers' NOS views. Mayer and Richmond (1982) noted that "Richardson and Showalter (1967) authored *The Abridged*

Scientific Literacy Instrument" (p. 54), which they listed among instruments designed to measure understandings of the nature of the scientific enterprise. Similarly, Walls (2012) listed the "Science Inventory" (Hungerford & Walding, 1974) in his review of NOS instruments. However, the instruments were not included in the original reports, could not be located and retrieved, were not cited in other literature, and/or were not used in other empirical studies that examined NOS–related objectives. Finally, tracking the use of some NOS measures in empirical studies was challenging because the developers did not title their instruments (e.g., Wilson, 1954), which were given slightly varied titles or labels throughout the years, while other instruments were given labels or acronyms that differed from those put forth by their originators. For example, Doran and colleagues (1974) labeled the instrument originally developed by Schwirian (1968) the "Science Support Scale" (p. 321) and used the acronym "SSS" to refer to it (p. 322). However, Schwirian (1969) had named the instrument the *Schwirian Science Support Scale* and abbreviated it as the *TRI-S* (p. 204). To provide as accurate an account as possible, this review referred to original publications of instruments for names, acronyms, domains, and other information. In case the developer(s) of an instrument did not provide an original name and/or acronym, the name provided was kept as close to the developer(s)' characterization of the measure as possible. Additionally, as evident in Table 31.1, original instrument names and acronyms were clearly distinguished—and appear italicized in the table—from those introduced at a later time by other researchers.

It could be seen that mapping the terrain related to NOS assessments in a meaningful and rigorous manner is challenging, to say the least. Thus, an explicit set of inclusion criteria was developed and applied both to admit instruments into the present examination and to count "instances of their use." First, albeit a serious limitation, only literature with full text (as compared, for example, to an abstract) available in English was consulted. Second, empirical studies published in refereed journals were admitted: Dissertations and theses, books and book chapters, conference papers and proceedings, ERIC documents, monographs, and other unpublished papers were excluded from the domain of review. The exception to this second criterion was applied to cases in which the development of a NOS instrument or the single instance of its use was not available as a refereed journal article (e.g., Korth, 1968, 1969; Lederman & Ko, 2002; Welch, 1966a). Drawing on peer-reviewed journal publications ensures the rigor of the research consulted and robustness of the conclusions drawn from the present review. Third, as noted, while it is well understood that early instruments lumped cognitive and affective NOS–related outcomes together, evidence suggests that by the early 1970s, outcomes related to scientific attitudes and attitudes toward science and scientists (including interests and appreciations) were clearly demarcated from understandings about science, scientific

TABLE 31.1
(An Incomplete) List of Nature of Science Instruments (1954–2012)

Date	Author(s)	Instrument	Abbreviation	Dimensions/categories/aspects	Items
1954	Wilson	Science Attitude Questionnaire[1]	SAQ[1]	Attitudes/perceptions toward scientists, science, and scientific products; ideas on methods, social aspects, tentativeness, and objectivity in science	26 agree/disagree
1957	Mead & Métraux	Images of Science, Scientists, and Scientific Careers[1]	ISSSC[1]	Attitudes toward scientists and scientific careers (vis-à-vis respondents' sex)	3 incomplete sentences (varied by sex) prompt essay responses
1958	Stice	*Facts About Science Test*	FAS	Attitudes/perceptions of scientists, science as an institution, and societal impacts of science	80 3-alternative multiple choice
1959	Allen	*Attitudes Toward Science and Scientific Careers*	ASSC[1]	Reciprocal impacts of science and society, the scientist, scientific work, and nature of science	95 5-point Likert (CA, A, N, D, TD)[2]
1961	Cooley & Klopfer	*Test on Understanding Science (From W)*	TOUS	Scientific enterprise, the scientist, and methods and aims of science	53 4-alternative multiple choice + 7 2-part (statement/reason)
1966	Swan	*Inventory of Science Attitudes, Interests, and Appreciations*	ISAIA	Affective outcomes related to scientific attitude, appreciations, interest, and skills	50 agree/disagree + 21 skill achievement experiences
1966	Welch	*Welch Science Process Inventory (Form D)*	SPI	Activities, assumptions, products, and ethics of science	135 agree/disagree
1967	Scientific Literacy Research Center	*Wisconsin Inventory of Science Processes*	WISP	Assumptions, activities, objectives, and products of science	93 3-alternative: Accurate, Inaccurate, Don't know/understand
1967–1968	Kimball	*Nature of Science Scale*	NOSS	Science is: driven by curiosity, empirical, reproducible, process oriented, open, dynamic, parsimonious, operational, tentative/uncertain, imposes human constructs on nature, and has no one "scientific method"	29 3-point Likert (A, N, D)[2]
1968	Schwirian	*Schwirian Science Support Scale*	TRI-S	Attitudes toward rationality, utility-arianism, universalism, individualism, and belief in progress and meliorism	40 5-point Likert (SA, A, U, D, SD)[2]
1968	Korth	*Test of the Social Aspects of Science*	TSAS	Interactions among science, technology, and society; social nature of scientific enterprise; social responsibilities of science and scientists	52 5-point Likert (SD, D, U, A, SD)[2]
1974	Aikenhead	*A Measurement of Knowledge About Science and Scientists (Project Physics: Form 1)*	KASSPP[1]	(See TOUS and SPI)	101 items (derived from *TOUS* and *SPI*)
1975	Billeh & Hasan	*Nature of Science Test*[3]	NOST	Assumptions, products, processes, and ethics of science	60, 4-alternative multiple choice
1975	Hillis	*Views of Science*	VOS[1]	Tentative NOS	40 5-point Likert (SA, A, N, D, SD)[2]
1976	Rubba	*Nature of Scientific Knowledge Scale*	NSKS	Science is amoral, creative, developmental, parsimonious, testable, and unified	48 5-point Likert (SA, A, N, D, SD)[2]
1977	Billeh & Malik	*Test on Understanding the Nature of Science*[3]	TUNS	Assumptions, processes, and ethics of science, and scientific enterprise	55 4-alternative multiple choice
1981	Cotham & Smith	*Conceptions of Scientific Theories Test*	COST	Ontological implications of theories, testing of theories, generation of theories, and theory choice	40 4-point Likert (SA, A, D, SD)[2] related to 4 theories
1982	Ogunniyi	*Language of Science*	LOS	Definitions, characteristics, formation, and function of concepts, laws, and theories	68 3-point Likert (A, D, Don't Know)[2]
1987	Johnson & Peeples	Methods and Nature of Science[1]	MaNS[1]	Theories and laws; limitations of science and observation; tentativeness; experimental methodology	15 5-point Likert + 5 items on acceptance of evolutionary theory) (SA to SD)[2]
1987	Aikenhead et al.	*Views of Science-Technology-Society*	VOSTS	Definitions (science and technology); external sociology of science (reciprocal influences of technology/science on society, and school science on society); internal sociology of science (characteristics of scientists, social construction of scientific knowledge and technology); epistemology (nature of scientific knowledge)	114 multiple choice, with 3 standard alternatives under each item: "I don't understand," "I don't know enough . . . to make a choice," and "None of these choices fits my basic viewpoint"

Year	Author(s)	Instrument name	Abbr.	NOS aspects	Format
1988	Koulaidis & Ogborn	Views about Philosophy of Science[1]	VaPS[1]	Scientific method, criteria of demarcation, patterns of growth, and status of scientific knowledge	6 2-alternative multiple choice + 23 agree/disagree statements (grouped as 10 items)
1990	Lederman & O'Malley	Views of Nature of Science–Form A[1,5]	VNOS-A	Tentative NOS	7 open-ended items + follow-up interviews
1992	Meichtry	*Modified Nature of Scientific Knowledge Scale*	MNSKS	Creative, developmental, testable, and unified NOS	32 5-point Likert (SA, A, N, D, SD)[2]
1993	Pomeroy	Beliefs about Nature of Science and Science Education[1]	BNSSE[1]	Creativity, intuition, and cultural-embeddedness in science, myth of the "scientific method" and determinism, and limitations of observation	30 5-point Likert (SA to SD)2 (+ 20 items related to beliefs about science education)
1995	Nott & Wellington	*Critical Incidents*	CI[1]	Experimental and social procedures of science; moral, ethical, and political issues related to science and scientists; limits and tentativeness of science; theory-laden NOS; and explanatory function of theories	13 classroom scenarios or events; ask teachers what would, could, and should they do in response to incidents
1997	Aldridge et al.	*Beliefs About Science and School Science Questionnaire*	BASSSQ	Processes of scientific inquiry, and certainty of scientific knowledge	20 5-point Likert (AN, S, ST, O, AA[4]) (+ 21 items related to beliefs about school science)
1998	Abd-El-Khalick et al.	*Views of Nature of Science–Form B*[5]	VNOS-B	Empirical, inferential, creative, tentative, and theory-laden NOS; and nature and relationship between theories and laws	7 (2 contextual) open-ended + follow-up interviews
2000	Abd-El-Khalick & Lederman	*Views of Nature of Science–Form C*[5]	VNOS-C	Empirical, inferential, creative, tentative, and theory-laden NOS; nature and relationship between theories and laws; lack of a single "scientific method"; social and cultural embeddedness of science	10 (3 contextual) open-ended + structured follow-up interviews
2002	Abd-El-Khalick	*Perspectives on Scientific Epistemology*	POSE	Empirical, inferential, creative, tentative, and theory-laden NOS; nature and relationship between theories and laws; generation of scientific knowledge; lack of a single "scientific method"	10 (4 contextual) open-ended + follow-up interviews
2002/ 2004	Lederman & Khishfe Lederman & Ko	*Views of Nature of Science–Form D/Form E*[5]	VNOS-D/ VNOS-E	Empirical, inferential, creative, theory-laden, and tentative NOS	7 (3 contextual) open-ended, administered as interview or survey
2005	Tsai & Liu	*Scientific Epistemological Views*[6]	SEVs	Social negotiation; invented/creative, theory-laden, and changing/tentative NOS; cultural impacts	19 5-point Likert (SA, A, N, D, SD)[2]
2006	Chen	*Views on Science and Education Questionnaire*	VOSE	Tentativeness; nature of observation; scientific methods; hypotheses, theories, and laws; imagination; validation of scientific knowledge; objectivity and subjectivity in science	69 5-point Likert (SD, D, U/NC, A, SA)[2] statements grouped in 13 items (+ 16 statement under 2 items related to science education)
2006	Liang et al.	*Student Understanding of Science and Scientific Inquiry*	SUSSI	Observation and inference; change of scientific theories; laws versus theories; social-cultural influences; and imagination and creativity in and methodology of investigation	24 5-point Likert (SD, D, U, A, SA)[2] grouped in 6 items + invitation to explain responses with examples per item
2009	Buaraphan	*Myths of Science Questionnaire*	MOSQ	Tentative, creative, theory-laden, social, and social-cultural NOS; relationship between hypotheses, theories and laws; lack of single "scientific method" and limitations of science; science and technology	14 3-point Likert (A, U, D)[2]
2012	Hacıeminoğlu et al.	*Nature of Science Instrument*	NOSI	Empirical, inferential, tentative, creative, and theory-laden NOS	13 3-point Likert (Wrong/ Do not know/Right)

[1] Instrument name or abbreviation introduced later and not presented in the original publication. Original instrument names and abbreviations are italicized.

[2] Likert scales: Completely/Strongly Agree (CA/SA), Agree (A), Neutral/Undecided (N/U), Disagree (D), Completely/Strongly Disagree (CD/SD).

[3] Overlap between the *NOST* and *TUNS* could not be determined as the instruments could not be located. Available sample items suggest some differences.

[4] This particular scale corresponds to: Almost never, Seldom, Sometimes, Often, Almost always.

[5] All forms of the *VNOS* were counted as a single instrument. Also note that the *VNOS–D* and *VNOS–E* are virtually identical instruments. Lederman and Ko (2002) slightly modified and relabeled the *VNOS–D* as *VNOS–E*, whereby the "E" is meant to signal the instrument's intended audience (i.e., elementary students) than to indicate the development of a new version of the *VNOS*.

[6] Tsai (2013, personal communication, January 13, 2013) advised that the *Pupils' Nature of Science Scale* (Huang, Tsai, & Chang, 2005) is subsumed under the *Scientific Epistemological Views* (Tsai & Liu, 2005).

knowledge, and the scientific enterprise. For instance, Gardner (1975) included the *Scientific Attitudes Inventory* (Moore & Sutman, 1970) in his literature review of studies about "attitudes to science." Akindehin (1988) used the *Nature of Science Scale* (NOSS; Kimball, 1967–1968) and *Test of Science-Related Attitudes* (TOSRA; Fraser, 1978), both of which appear as NOS–assessment instruments in some prior reviews. Akindehin, nonetheless, used the *NOSS* to measure his participants' "understandings of the nature of science" in clear contradistinction of using the *TOSRA* to assess their "science-related attitudes" (1988, p. 77). For a similar treatment of the *TOSRA* and the *Tests of Perception of Scientists and Self* (TOPOSS; Mackay & White, 1974) as instruments designed to assess affective outcomes related to attitudes toward science, the reader is referred to Laforgia (1988; also see Osborne, Simon, & Collins, 2003). To be sure, this review does *not* adopt a revisionist perspective on the history of the field. Nonetheless, there was need to strike a balance between accounting for the historical development of NOS assessments while remaining faithful to contemporaneous developments in conceptualizations of the construct of NOS in science education. Thus, instruments that purported to measure science-related attitudes and interests and other affective outcomes published after 1970 were not included as NOS instruments. In this regard, it should be noted that an examination of the literature indicates that a conflation between NOS and science process skills, while evident in a few early cases, has not been as prevalent in the literature of the 1960s and early 1970s as with the conflation between NOS and attitudinal-related outcomes. For instance, while Doran and colleagues (1974) included the *Processes of Science Test* (POST; Biological Sciences Curriculum Study, 1962) in their analysis of NOS instruments, contemporaneous reviews (e.g., Aikenhead, 1973; Mackay & White, 1974) clearly excluded the *POST* from the domain of NOS measures. A content analysis of the *POST* justifies this exclusion: Only 6 of the 40 *POST* items touch on issues invoked in contemporaneous instruments, such as the *TOUS* (Cooley & Klopfer, 1961), *Welch Science Process Inventory* (SPI; Welch, 1966b) and *Wisconsin Inventory of Science Processes* (WISP; Scientific Literacy Research Center, 1967), which clearly addressed NOS–related objectives. Additionally, an examination of the purposes for which researchers had used the *POST* (i.e., Anderson & Callaway, 1986; Anderson, DeMelo, Szabo, & Toth, 1975; Faryniarz, 1992; Orgren & Doran, 1975; Riban, 1976; Riban & Koval, 1971; Rivers & Vockell, 1987; Starr, 1972) indicates that science process skills were being measured as distinct from understandings about science. For example, the *POST* was used to assess students' "general problem solving" abilities (Rivers & Vockell, 1987, p. 408), and "ability to recognize and apply the processes of science" (Orgren & Doran, 1975, p. 17), which included recognizing appropriate tabular representations of a specific dataset and drawing conclusions from descriptions of specific experimental setups.

Thus, instruments that purported to measure instructional outcomes related to science process skills were excluded from the domain of the present review.

Fourth, as noted above, various modifications of many extant instruments abound, including the *TOUS* (e.g., Aikenhead, 1974a; Fisher & Fraser, 1980; Rampal, 1992; Welch, 1972), *VOSTS* (e.g., Bennett & Hogarth, 2009; Kang et al., 2005; Mbajiorgu & Ali, 2003; Yalvac, Tekkaya, Cakiroglu, & Kahyaoglu; 2007), *Nature of Scientific Knowledge Scale* (NSKS; Rubba, 1976, 1977; i.e., Meichtry, 1992), and *VNOS–C* (e.g., Akerson, Hanson, & Cullen, 2007; Rudge, Cassidy, Fulford, & Howe, 2013; Wong & Hodson, 2009, 2010). Nonetheless, modifications rarely entailed a substantial reconsideration or reconceptualization of the NOS models underlying the modified instruments. Additionally, in most cases, modifications of extant instruments were not coupled with rigorous efforts to reestablish the validity and/or reliability of the reconstituted measure once the integrity of original instruments was breached by selecting subsets of their items, rewording or translating these items, or altering responses for convergent items in one fashion or another. Exceptions included Aikenhead's (1974a) *A Measurement of Knowledge About Science and Scientists (Project Physics: Form 1*; KASSPP1) and Meichtry's (1992) *Modified Nature of Scientific Knowledge Scale* (MNSKS). Thus, in the overwhelming majority of cases, instrument modifications (including translating and contextualizing instruments, e.g., Dogan & Abd-El-Khalick, 2008; Haidar, 2000) were *not* considered distinct or new instruments. Instead, modifying and using an existing instrument in an empirical study was considered another instance of use of the original instrument. Finally, a few instruments have been developed to gauge relationships between learners' understandings of specific elements of NOS and other dimensions. For example, Cobern and Loving (2002) developed the "Thinking about Science" survey instrument, which aimed to assess the relationship of respondents' views of science to the economy, environment, public policy, religion, aesthetics, race and gender, and science for all, as well as epistemology. The latter dimension focused on views of the objectivity and certainty of scientific knowledge, as well as reliability of scientific methods. Using two questionnaires, Liu and Lederman (2007) aimed to describe their participants' "views of NOS and worldviews, and to explore relationships, if any, between these two domains of beliefs" (p. 1286). Similarly, Windschitl (2004) used interviews, among other data sources, to examine his participants' folk theories of inquiry, which entailed elucidating their understandings of some NOS aspects. Guerra-Ramos (2012) included the latter three instruments and approaches in her review of measures used to elicit teachers' NOS ideas. However, these studies assessed conceptions of widely agreed-upon NOS aspects targeted by other instruments with the aim of exploring relationships with conceptions of other constructs, such as inquiry and worldviews, which are clearly distinct from—albeit related—to NOS (see Lederman, 2007). These and similar instruments, thus, were not considered distinct or new instruments when it comes to assessing NOS understandings.

(An Incomplete) List of NOS Assessments: Characterizing the Landscape

The application of the aforementioned inclusion criteria to the NOS assessment landscape resulted in the list of 32 NOS–specific instruments shown in Table 31.1. In this table, it should be noted, the different *VNOS* forms (Lederman et al., 2002) are counted as a single instrument. Given the arguments presented in the preceding section, the list is justifiably and understandably incomplete: Some researchers who had developed a NOS instrument in a language other than English, translated and contextualized an existing instrument to fit their educational and/or cultural milieu, substantially modified an existing instrument to reflect certain nuances in their perspectives on NOS or educational research, or reworked one or more subcomponents of an existing instrument or instruments into a new measure or one with broader goals might find that the list in Table 31.1 is missing one or a few instruments. Nonetheless, to the extent that the explicit inclusion criteria presented are sensible, based on reasonable assumptions, and derived from a careful and critical examination of both the empirical literature and prior literature reviews, I contend that the present list is both robust and accurate. To be sure, it is difficult to imagine that including a few more instruments in the present review would alter the historical narrative, analyses, and resulting conclusions in any substantial manner.

Table 31.1 indicates that exploring and assessing NOS understandings among precollege and college students (e.g., Kang et al., 2005; Mead & Métraux, 1957; Walls, 2012; Welch, 1969; Wood, 1972) and preservice and inservice teachers (e.g., Billeh & Hasan, 1975; Yalçinoğlu &

Anagün, 2012; Zoller, Donn, Wild, & Beckett, 1991b), as well as science teacher educators and scientists (e.g., İrez, 2006; Kimball, 1967–1968; Wong & Hodson, 2010), has been a consistent and ongoing domain of interest throughout the past six decades. Each of these decades has featured the development of four to seven measures, with an average of about five NOS instruments developed per decade. Indeed, between 1954 (the year the first NOS instrument, the SAQ, was published) and 2013, there only is a single 5-year period (1969–1972) in which no new instruments were developed, compared to the two to three NOS instruments developed during all other 5-year periods and up to four instruments developed in the 5-year period from 1974 to 1978 (also see Figure 31.1).

Of the 32 instruments in Table 31.1, a small minority (4 or 12.5%) is of the open-ended generative type, where learners are asked to articulate their ideas in response to open-ended questions, scenarios, or prompts. In comparison, the overwhelming majority of instruments (28 or 87.5%) are of the forced-choice type, where respondents select an answer or indicate a preference from among a predetermined set of options. The 17 instruments using three-, four-, or five-point Likert-type items account for 61% of all forced-choice NOS assessments, with an additional 28% (8 instruments) comprising multiple-choice items and 11% (3 instruments) featuring agree/disagree type items. Most Likert-type instruments (70%, 12 instruments) use a five-point scale of the sort: strongly/completely agree, agree, undecided/neutral/no comment, disagree, and strongly/totally disagree, with the exception of the *Beliefs About Science and School Science Questionnaire* (BASSSQ; Aldridge et al., 1997; see Table 31.1). One instrument (6%) used a four-point and an additional four instruments (24%) used three-point Likert scales with a variety of descriptors, such as agree, neutral, disagree; and accurate, inaccurate, don't know/don't understand (e.g., the *WISP*).

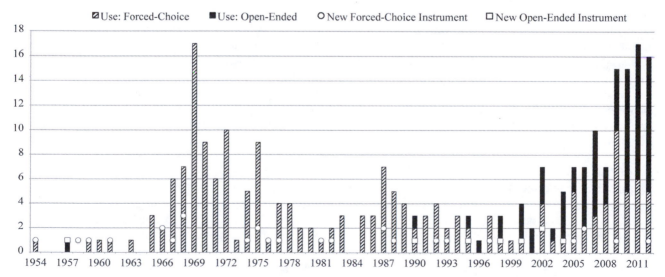

Figure 31.1 Frequency of use of forced-choice and open-ended NOS instruments in empirical studies (1954–2012).

The Evolving Landscape of NOS Assessments

An examination of the landscape of NOS assessment from a perspective focused on the number, frequency of development, and type of NOS instruments could be misleading. Indeed, data presented in the preceding section could support a number of inferences, such as that forced-choice assessments have dominated and continue to dominate the field; that the few open-ended instruments seem to have played a relatively less substantial role than forced-choice measures in gauging what learners understand about NOS; that a distinct pattern in the development of NOS assessments is lacking given that the field seems consistently preoccupied with the development of forced-choice measures—particularly of the Likert-type variety—with intermittent attempts to develop and use open-ended measures; or that the field has been and continues to be in disarray with regard to the construct of NOS as evident by the continuous development of instruments over the past six decades. Albeit consistent with the data provided in Table 31.1, such inferences, it will become evident, do not accurately capture the evolving nature of the NOS assessment field. Indeed, a very different and robust narrative emerges when the domain is examined from alternative lenses. The following sections examine the field's development from the perspective of the *use* of NOS assessments in empirical studies and explicate ways in which the alternative narrative that emerges from such examination is consistent with theoretical and conceptual advances underlying the very approaches to gauging learners' NOS understandings.

Use of NOS Assessments in Empirical Studies

While theoretical and conceptual debates about a specific definition for NOS continue or emerge at different points in time, it was argued earlier that, from a practical perspective, the only construct (or constructs) in currency in the field of science education is the NOS construct or are those constructs being assessed. Hence the significance of examining NOS assessments. Additionally, the extent to which assessments impact discourse, claims, and judgments in the field about progress, or lack thereof, toward achieving the much-desired NOS–related outcomes hinges on the extent to which these instruments are used in empirical studies. Nonetheless, the notion of "use" should not be understood as a mere quantification of an instrument's popularity. This notion is based on the assumption that researchers who opt to use a certain NOS instrument from among a number of instruments available at any one time have carefully examined these measures and (a) are in general agreement with the NOS model underlying their instrument of choice and (b) endorse the assessment approach embodied in this instrument, which they consider to be commensurate with the state of the art in terms of NOS assessment at the time of the study. It should not escape us that using a certain instrument might also be dictated, at least partially, by practical considerations. For instance, the use of an open-ended NOS assessment entails substantially more resources and effort in terms of collecting, analyzing, and interpreting data when compared to a forced-choice instrument. However, it is safe to assume that researchers would not use a NOS measure, which is incommensurate with their conceptions of the construct of NOS or which they consider would not generate a valid and reliable assessment of their participants' conceptions of this construct. In a sense, examining the use of various instruments would generate an empirical profile of the field's *collective wisdom* as it relates to NOS assessment.

A thorough review of the literature in the period from 1954 to 2013 resulted in a total of 241 empirical research studies published—with very few exceptions—in refereed journal articles, which used the instruments listed in Table 31.1. The exceptions included cases when the single use of an instrument by its developer(s) was not published as a peer-reviewed article, such as with the *Test of the Social Aspects of Science* (TSAS; Korth, 1969). The reader is reminded that, as explicated in the aforementioned inclusion criteria, use of a modified instrument in an empirical study was mostly counted as an instance of use of the original instrument (see previous discussion for the few exceptions). Nonetheless, while surely useful, the simple enumeration of instances of use would not have been sufficient to accurately depict the impact of different instruments. In particular, the use of an instrument—be it in its original or modified form—by researchers other than its original developer(s) is an important indicator of its impact. Indeed, some instruments have been used in a substantial number of studies. All these uses, however, were undertaken by the instrument developer(s). *The Scientific Epistemological Views* (SEVs) is a case in point: The *SEVs* was developed by Tsai and Liu (2005) and since then has been used in as many as eight empirical studies that were, nonetheless, undertaken by Tsai and his colleagues. Thus, while there is need to acknowledge and celebrate the work of prolific researchers, it was important to keep this limitation in mind. Secondly, longevity adds an important dimension to an instrument's impact, because it makes possible comparing investigations undertaken in different contexts over a period of time, which enable drawing meaningful and robust conclusions about the status of the field. At the same time, it was important not to overly depend on the longevity dimension given that many instruments have been in existence for substantial periods of time, which would disadvantage more recently developed instruments.

An "index of use" score was generated to account for these dimensions when examining the use of NOS instruments (see Table 31.2). This score was calculated for each instrument listed in Table 31.1 by assigning the instrument one point for each use in an empirical study undertaken by the instrument developer(s), three points for each use by researchers other than the developer(s) within the first 5 years following the instrument's publication, and five points for each use in an empirical study by other researchers beyond the

TABLE 31.2
Nature of Science Instruments Ranked by the Extent of Use in Empirical Research Studies

Instrument	Empirical studies	Used by			Index of use score[1]
		Author(s)	Others		
			≤ 5 yrs	> 5 yrs	
VNOS (Views of Nature of Science) Questionnaire		16	5	41	236
VNOS-A	Lederman & O'Malley (1990)	1	0	0	1
VNOS-B	Abd-El-Khalick & Akerson (2004); Abd-El-Khalick, Bell, & Lederman (1998); Akerson & Abd-El-Khalick (2003); Akerson, Abd-El-Khalick, & Lederman (2000); Akerson & Hanuscin (2007); Akerson & Volrich (2006); Bell, Lederman, & Abd-El-Khalick (2000)	5	0	2	15
VNOS-C	Abd-El-Khalick (2001, 2005); Abd-El-Khalick & Akerson (2009); Abd-El-Khalick & Lederman (2000b); Akçay & Koç (2009); Akerson, Hanson, & Cullen (2007); Borda, Burgess, Plog, DeKalb, & Luce (2009); Cakmakci (2012); Duncan & Arthurs (2012); Eastwood et al. (2012); Goff, Boesdorfer, & Hunter (2012); Hanuscin, Akerson, & Phillipson-Mower (2006); Howe (2007); Howe & Rudge (2005); Irez (2006, 2007); Kaya (2012); Kim & Nehm (2011); Kucuk (2008); Lederman, Schwartz, Abd-El-Khalick, & Bell (2001); Liu & Lederman (2007); Marchlewicz & Wink (2011); McDonald (2010); Nalçaci, Akarsu, Kariper (2011); Pegg & Gummer (2010); Posnanski (2010); Roehrig & Luft (2004); Russell & Aydeniz (2012); Russell & Weaver (2011); Salloum & Abd-El-Khalick (2010); Schwartz & Lederman (2002); Schwartz, Lederman, & Crawford (2004); Schwartz, Westerlund, Garcìa, & Taylor (2010); Thye & Kwen (2004); Urhahne, Kremer, & Mayer (2011); Walker & Zeidler (2007); Wong & Hodson (2009, 2010); Wong, Hodson, Kwan, & Yung (2008); Yalçinoğlu & Anagün (2012)	10	3	27	154
VNOS-D	Akerson, Buck, Donnelly, Nargund-Joshi, & Weiland (2011); Akerson, Cullen, & Hanson (2009); Akerson & Donnelly (2010); Akerson & Hanuscin (2007); Akerson & Volrich (2006); Hanuscin & Lee (2011); Leblebicioğlu, Metin, Yardimci, & Berkyürek (2011); Leblebicioğlu, Metin, Yardimci, & Cetin (2011); Metin & Leblebicioğlu (2011, 2012); Quigley, Pongsanon, & Akerson (2010, 2011)	0	2	10	56
VNOS-E	Demirbaş & Balci (2012); Walls (2012)	0	0	2	10
TOUS	Aikenhead (1974b); Anderson (1970); Broadhurst (1970); Choppin (1974); Cossman (1969); Crumb (1965); Durkee (1974); Engen, Smith, & Yager (1967–1968); Fisher (1979); Fisher & Fraser (1980); Fraser (1978); Fulton (1971a, 1971b); Ginns & Foster (1978); Glass & Yager (1970); Johnson (1972); Jones (1969); Jungwirth (1968, 1969); Jungwirth & Jungwirth (1972); Klopfer & Cooley (1963); Krockover (1971); Lavach (1969); Lowery (1967); Mackay (1971); Meyer (1969); Olstad (1969); Rampal (1992); Riley (1979); Rothman (1969); Rothman, Welch, & Walberg (1969); Tamir (1994); Tamir & Jungwirth (1975); Trent (1965); Voss (1965); Walberg (1969); Welch (1969, 1972); Welch & Rothman (1968); Welch & Walberg (1967–1968, 1970, 1972); Yager (1968); Yager & Wick (1966); Zingaro & Collette (1967–1968)	1	5	39	211
VOSTS	Abd-El-Khalick & BouJaoude (1997); Aikenhead (1987, 1997); Aikenhead, Fleming, & Ryan (1987); Ben-Chaim & Zoller (1991); Bennett & Hogarth (2009); Botton & Brown (1998); Bradford, Rubba, & Harkness (1995); Choi & Cho (2002); Dass (2005); Dogan & Abd-El-Khalick (2008); Fleming (1987, 1988); Haidar (1999, 2000); Kang, Scharmann, & Noh (2005); Kokkotas et al. (2009); Lin & Chen (2002); Marbach-Ad et al. (2009); Mbajiorgu & Ali (2003); Rubba & Harkness (1993); Walczak & Walczak (2009); Yalvac, Tekkaya, Cakiroglu, & Kahyaoglu (2007); Zoller & Ben-Chaim (1994); Zoller, Donn, Wild, & Beckett (1991a, 1991b); Zoller et al. (1990)	5	4	18	107
SPI	Aikenhead (1974b); Anderson (1970); Breedlove & Gessert (1970); Haukoos & Penick (1983, 1985, 1987); Lawrenz (1975); Lawrenz & Cohen (1985); Markle & Capie (1977); Rothman (1969); Rothman, Welch, & Walberg (1969); Spears & Zollman (1977); Tamir (1972); Tamir & Jungwirth (1975); Walberg (1969); Welch (1969, 1972, 1980); Welch & Lawrenz (1982); Welch & Pella (1967); Welch & Rothman (1968); Welch & Walberg (1967–1968, 1970, 1972)	10	4	10	72
NSKS	Chan (2005); Dienye (1987); Folmer, Barbosa, Soares, & Rocha, (2009); Güzel (2011); Lederman (1986a, 1986b); Lederman & Druger (1985); Lederman & Zeidler (1987); Lin & Chiu (2004); Lonsbury & Ellis (2002); Rubba & Andersen (1978); Sutherland & Dennick (2002); Tasar (2006); Walker & Zeidler (2007); Zeidler & Lederman (1989)	1	0	14	71
NOSS	Akindehin (1988); Andersen, Harty, & Samuel (1986); Duschl & Wright (1989); Kimball (1967–1968); Ogunniyi (1983); Scharmann (1988a, 1988b, 1989, 1994); Scharmann & Harris (1992)	1	0	9	46
WISP	Carey & Stauss (1968, 1970); Lawson, Nordland, & DeVito (1975); Leake & Hinerman (1973); Markle & Capie (1977); Simpson & Wasik (1978); Wood (1972)	0	3	4	29

(Continued)

TABLE 31.2
(Continued)

Instrument	Empirical studies	Used by Author(s)	Used by Others ≤ 5 yrs	Used by Others > 5 yrs	Index of use score[1]
FAS	Cooley & Bassett (1961); Cossman (1969); Fulton (1971a, 1971b); Glass & Yager (1970); Jacobs & Bollenbacher (1960)	0	2	4	26
POSE	Abd-El-Khalick (2002); Khishfe (2008, 2012); Khishfe & Abd-El-Khalick (2002); Seker & Welsh (2006); Yacoubian & BouJaoude (2010)	2	1	3	20
SUSSI	Fergusson, Oliver, & Walter (2012); Golabek & Amrane-Cooper (2011); Liang et al. (2008); Liang et al. (2009); Miller, Montplaisir, Offerdahl, Cheng, & Ketterling (2010); Shim, Young, & Paolucci (2010)	2	3	1	16
TRI-S	Schwirian (1968, 1969); Schwirian & Thomson (1972); Simpson, Shrum, & Rentz (1972); Spears & Hathaway (1975); Symington & Fensham (1976)	3	1	2	16
SEVs	Chai, Deng, & Tsai (2012); Huang, Tsai, & Chang (2005); Lin & Tsai (2008); Liu, Lin, & Tsai (2011); Liu & Tsai (2008); Oskay, Yilmaz, Dinçol, & Erdem (2011); Tsai (2007); Tsai & Liang (2009); Tsai & Liu (2005)	8	0	1	13
MOSQ	Buaraphan (2009a, 2009b, 2010, 2011, 2012); Buaraphan & Sung-Ong (2009); Sarkar & Gomes (2010)	6	1	0	9
MaNS	Johnson & Peeples (1987); Scharmann (1990); Scharmann & Harris (1992)	1	2	0	7
TSAS	Chrouser (1975); Korth (1969)	1	0	1	6
CI	Kim & Irving (2010); Nott & Wellington (1995, 1996, 1998)	3	1	0	6
BASSSQ	Aldridge, Taylor, & Chen (1997); İrez, Çakir, & Şeker (2011)	1	0	1	6
VOSE	Chen (2006b); Demirbas, Bozdogan, & Özbek (2012)	1	0	1	6
VOS	Barufaldi, Bethel, & Lamb (1977); Hillis (1975)	1	1	0	4
VaPS	Apostolou & Koulaidis (2010); Koulaidis & Ogborn (1988, 1989, 1995)	4	0	0	4
LOS	Ogunniyi (1982, 1983)	1	0	0	1
SAQ	Wilson (1954)	1	0	0	1
ISSSC	Mead & Métraux (1957)	1	0	0	1
ASSC	Allen (1959)	1	0	0	1
ISAIA	Swan (1966)	1	0	0	1
KASSPP1	Aikenhead (1974a)	1	0	0	1
NOST	Billeh & Hasan (1975)	1	0	0	1
TUNS	Billeh & Malik (1977)	1	0	0	1
COST	Cotham & Smith (1981)	1	0	0	1
MNSKS	Meichtry (1992)	1	0	0	1
BNSSE	Pomeroy (1993)	1	0	0	1
NOSI	Hacıeminoğlu, Yılmaz-Tüzün, & Ertepınar (2012)	1	0	0	1

[1] "Index of use score" calculated by assigning an instrument 1 point for each use in an empirical study by the instrument developer(s), 3 points for each use by other researchers within the first 5 years following the development of the instrument, and 5 points for each use by other researchers beyond the 5-year period after the instrument development.

5-year period after which the instrument was developed. The 5-year cutoff derives from the aforementioned stipulation for not disadvantaging recently developed instruments given that many NOS instruments have been in existence for substantial periods of time. Consider the *VOSTS* (Aikenhead et al., 1987) as an example. The instrument was developed in 1987 and used in a total of 27 published studies, 5 of which were undertaken by Glen Aikenhead, Reg Fleming, and/or Alan Ryan, for which it received five points. Four more studies used the *VOSTS* in the first 5 years following its development, that is, between 1987 and 1992 (Ben-Chaim & Zoller, 1991; Zoller, Donn, Wild, & Beckett, 1991a, 1991b; Zoller et al., 1990), for which it was allotted an additional 12 points. Finally, researchers other than Aikenhead and his colleagues used the *VOSTS* in 18 additional studies starting in 1993 (see Table 31.2), for which the *VOSTS* received an additional 90 points to end up with

an index of use score of 107 points. Table 31.2 lists NOS instruments ranked by their index of use score. It should be noted that uses of all forms of the *VNOS* (Lederman et al., 2002) were grouped together because the different forms share the same underlying model for NOS and approach to assessment (i.e., generic and context-based open-ended questions coupled with follow-up individual interviews) and differ only in the number, context, and phrasing of their items, which were designed to make them accessible to different populations, including science teachers and high school students (i.e., *VNOS–A , VNOS–B,* and *VNOS–C*), and elementary school students (i.e., *VNOS–D / VNOS–E*).

When examined from the use-of-instruments lens, the landscape of NOS assessment takes on different features. Most noteworthy is the observation that the seemingly large variance in assessments suggested by the proliferation of instruments over the past 60 years is *greatly* reduced. In terms of frequency of use in empirical studies, the top three instruments in Table 31.2—the *VNOS, TOUS,* and *VOSTS*—account for more than 50% of all instrument use in the past six decades. The preferential use of the *VNOS, TOUS,* and *VOSTS,* it will become evident, is closely associated with the field's evolution in terms of the different assumptions underlying approaches to assessing NOS understandings represented by each of the three instruments. Additionally, the top nine instruments in Table 31.2 account for more than 75% of all use of NOS measures: These instruments are the *VNOS* (Lederman et al., 2002), *TOUS* (Cooley & Klopfer, 1961), *VOSTS* (Aikenhead et al., 1987), *SPI* (Welch, 1966b), *NSKS* (Rubba, 1976), *NOSS* (Kimball, 1967–1968), *WISP* (Scientific Literacy Research Center, 1967), *Facts about Science Test* (FAS; Stice, 1958), and *Perspectives on Scientific Epistemology* (POSE; Abd-El-Khalick, 2002). The remaining 23 instruments account for 23% of all use in empirical studies, 17% of which were instances of use by the instruments' developers and 6% by other researchers.

Second, by employing the use of instruments as proxy for researcher sensibilities about accessing and gauging learner NOS understandings, the present approach defers judgment about available instruments to the collective of science education researchers. This approach's validity is substantiated by the fact that its outcomes resonate strongly with the conclusions of prior reviews of the domain. For instance, in their reviews of NOS assessments, Lederman (2007) and Lederman and colleagues (1998) examined the development and psychometric properties (both firsthand and by reference to other reviews) of many of the instruments being examined here. They listed all of the aforementioned nine instruments—except the *FAS,* which they considered not to address the NOS domain and which was included in the present review with qualification—as those considered to be valid and reliable measures of NOS understandings. Additionally, an examination of use in empirical studies shows that instruments that historically have been critiqued for addressing affective, attitudinal, and other outcomes deemed to be beyond the scope of the construct of NOS (see Lederman, 2007) do not seem to have played a significant role in the history of NOS assessment, as evidenced by their restricted use by researchers. The latter include instruments such as the SAQ (Wilson, 1954), ASSC (Allen, 1959), *ISAIA* (Swan, 1966), and *TRI-S* (Schwirian, 1968).

Third, a use-of-measures perspective presents a different profile in terms of the changing landscape of NOS assessment. Figure 31.1 shows instances of use of NOS measures over the past 60 years, when instruments are grouped by two broad types of items: forced-choice (i.e., agree/disagree, multiple choice, and Likert) and open-ended items. Figure 31.1 also shows the specific years when new instruments of either broad type were developed. It could be seen that between 1954 and 1998, the field was exclusively dominated by the use of forced-choice–type instruments. A substantial shift was evident in the decade from 1990 to 1999, where the use of open-ended

instruments rose sharply from virtually zero in the previous four decades to account for 27% of all empirical studies that examined learners' NOS conceptions. This trend continued to assert itself in the period from 2000 to 2012, where the use of open-ended instruments more than doubled compared to the preceding decade and came to represent 57% of all instances of use. Interestingly, the latter shift becomes even more pronounced when geographical locations of researchers are taken into account. Indeed, in the North American context where research on NOS in science education has had the deepest roots and longest-running tradition, *no* new forced-choice NOS instruments were developed during the past two decades. Researchers outside the North American context have developed *all* forced-choice instruments listed in Table 31.1 in the period from 1993 to 2012. In that sense, the shift from forced-choice, "quantitative" to more open-ended, "qualitative" approaches to NOS assessment has been rather decisive over the course of the last two decades. The implications of this shift in terms of the validity of gauging learner NOS understandings are explicated below.

The grouping of instruments into the two broad types of forced-choice and open-ended measures is useful and sheds important light on the changing nature of the field. This grouping, nonetheless, is somewhat coarse: It does not account for the unique case of the *VOSTS* (Aikenhead et al., 1987), which stands in a category of its own among forced-choice instruments. While the *VOSTS* items are of the forced-choice type, its empirically driven development process renders it unique and affords it a measure of validity that could not be claimed in the case of theoretically driven forced-choice instruments. When the development of the *VOSTS* is taken into account, a pattern of historical progression from theoretically driven forced-choice to empirically driven forced-choice to open-ended instruments becomes the most prominent feature in the landscape related to the evolution of the field of NOS assessment. The next section focuses on this progression and its underlying conceptual bases.

Evolution of Approaches to NOS Assessment

Since the outset, the development of forced-choice NOS instruments has been theoretically driven: The model for NOS underlying an instrument, the domains of the scientific enterprise targeted by the instrument, and consequently the espoused respondent positions toward issues addressed in the instrument items all were derived from some theoretical delineation or portrayal of NOS. In the case of the very first instrument, Wilson (1954) emphasized the importance of developing students' "understanding of science and the methods by which scientific knowledge has been obtained" (p. 159). Toward assessing these understandings, Wilson prepared a set of 26 statements, which became the SAQ, by drawing on "two recent books dealing with the general subject of understanding science . . . *Science and Common Sense* by James B. Conant and *The Path of Science* by C. E. Kenneth Mees" (p. 161). Similarly, the elements underlying the *SPI* were derived from "books by Beveridge, Conant, Kemeny, Lachman, Nash, and [E. B.] Wilson" and then "presented to fourteen research scientists for validity judgment" (Welch & Pella, 1967, p. 64). The latter books also were general readers about the scientific enterprise, ranging from *The Art of Scientific Investigation* (Beveridge, 1950) to a *Philosopher Looks at Science* (Kemeny, 1959) to *The Foundations of Science* (Lachman, 1960). Many authors of the books consulted by researchers to design items for early NOS instruments, such as the SAQ, *TOUS,* and *SPI,* were historians or philosophers of science or drew on these disciplines in their writings. By the late 1960s, nonetheless, many instrument developers replaced the by-proxy or secondary access to the philosophy of science with firsthand consultation of this literature. For instance, toward developing the *NOSS,* Kimball (1967–1968) noted that its underlying "theoretical model of the nature of science was developed out of extensive study on the nature and philosophy of science" and continued, "While this model was only one of many possibilities, it was consistent in its agreement with views expressed by Conant and Bronowski; and additional support . . . was found among the writings of other philosophers of science" (p. 111). The significance of Kimball's statements, in addition to illustrating the point about the shift to firsthand consultation of the philosophy of science, is their being the first to explicitly point out that assessment instruments were undergirded by a "theoretical model" of NOS, which could be "one of many possibilities." This is a crucial point to which I return shortly. By the mid-1970s, use of the philosophical literature in instrument development was firmly established. Moreover, by the late 1970s, science education researchers seemed to have started being selective about which philosophical literature they would draw on to establish their model for NOS. For instance, Ogunniyi (1982) derived his *Language of Science* (LOS) instrument items from "statements about the language of science held by Carnap (1966), Hempel (1966), Frank (1962), Kemeny (1959), Nagel (1961), Nash (1963), and Popper (1962)" (p. 26). Ogunniyi, however, made the conscious decision to exclude the work of Thomas Kuhn from among the works consulted, arguing that "although Kuhn's influence has been felt since the 1960s his effort has been mainly on the historical and socio-psychological milieu of science rather than the language of science" (p. 26). The intention here is not to be critical of Ogunniyi or his philosophical choices. What is important is the fact that NOS models underlying various instruments drew on philosophical literatures that overlapped to various extents. Thus, by design, theoretically driven NOS instruments embodied their developer(s)' selective philosophical preferences in terms of, at least, which philosophical issues and stances were included and which were excluded.

An even more involved approach was reflected in the fact that some instrument developers seem to have taken sides on certain long-lived, contemporaneous philosophical debates in their models for NOS. For instance, Pomeroy (1993) adopted what she dubbed a "nontraditional" view of science, which seems to have endorsed a constructivist view of science and scientific knowledge and suggested, among other things, that science is just another way of knowing. In accordance with the NOS model embodied in Pomeroy's BNSSE, elementary teachers held more nontraditional (considered more informed) views of science when compared to scientists, who endorsed the most traditional views (considered more naïve). Again, this observation is not intended to criticize Pomeroy's model for NOS but to indicate that hers had taken sides on controversial philosophical debates, such as that related to the relative merits or "equivalence" of scientific versus indigenous ways of knowing (see Loving, 1997). Obviously, nothing is inherently flawed in a NOS assessment embodying a theoretical model for NOS, as long as such a model is explicitly articulated and made accessible to readers. In this regard, it should be noted that several researchers did not make their NOS model and, in some cases, their very instrument, accessible to other researchers; the *NOST* (Billeh & Hasan, 1975) is a case in point. Like with the design of any assessment, a theoretical or conceptual delineation of the dimensions and attributes of the target construct is a precursor to building valid assessments. However, when theoretically driven NOS instruments are packaged as assessment tools that draw on forced-choice items, the resulting assessment approach becomes very problematic.

Discontent with forced-choice NOS instruments dates back to the early 1970s. For instance, Mackay and White (1974) criticized the use of Likert-type and multiple-choice items in several instruments, including the *TOUS* and *FAS.* Even though the authors were mostly concerned with the extent to which these instruments enable valid assessment of students' *perceptions* of scientists, their criticisms reasonably apply to accessing understandings of other NOS dimensions. Mackay and White critiqued the *TOUS*'s use of multiple-choice items because "it may be difficult to communicate to the respondent the criteria to be used in selecting the best answer" (p. 132). Moreover, they questioned the validity of responses to Likert scales because a respondent's standing on such scales "is a measure of a complex combination of his standing, of his ability to perceive the intent of the scale, and of his set to respond in a particular way" (p. 132). By the mid-1980s, these initial concerns had developed into a highly articulate critique of the validity of forced-choice, theoretically driven NOS instruments in assessing learners' conceptions. The critique had two major dimensions.

First, Aikenhead and colleagues (Aikenhead, 1988; Aikenhead et al., 1989) argued that forced-choice instruments were based on the problematic assumption that respondents' perceptions and interpretations of an instrument's items are commensurate with those of its developers. They continued that ambiguities result from assuming that respondents understand a certain item in the manner that the instrument developers *intended* for it to be understood, or that respondents would agree or disagree with a statement, select one of the alternatives furnished in a multiple-choice item, or indicate preference on a Likert scale for reasons that coincide with those of the instrument developers. Thus, the validity of these instruments is seriously threatened because of difficulties with interpreting respondent choices. Lederman and O'Malley (1990) empirically supported this position. Second, as noted, forced-choice instruments often embodied specific theoretical models for NOS. Also, items provided choices that were theoretically driven and designed with certain philosophical stances in mind, and the espoused selections or answers often reflected the developers' philosophical positions and preferences. Being of the forced-choice category, instruments ended up imposing developers' views on respondents:

> Irrespective of the choices the respondents made, they often ended up being labeled as if they firmly held coherent, consistent philosophic stances such as inductivist, verificationist or hypothetico-deductivist . . . Thus, the views that ended up being ascribed to respondents were more likely an artifact of the instrument in use than a faithful representation of the respondents' conceptions of NOS.
>
> (Lederman et al., 2002, p. 502)

Indeed, research has demonstrated that students' and teachers' NOS views are rather fluid, fragmented, lacking overarching frameworks, and sometimes outright inconsistent (e.g., Abd-El-Khalick, 2004a; Abd-El-Khalick & BouJaoude, 2003; Lederman & O'Malley, 1990). It could be seen that theoretically driven forced-choice instruments generated data that were difficult to interpret and not necessarily representative of respondents' NOS conceptions.

An additional third criticism was directed at the usefulness and meaningfulness of data garnered from theoretically driven forced-choice assessments. Aikenhead (1974b) initiated a broad critique of the meaningfulness of any conclusions about student learning when it comes to "knowledge *about* the scientific enterprise" that could be derived from quantitative instruments. He argued that the resulting aggregate data, such as total scores or gain scores on instruments, such as the *TOUS* and *SPI,* masked the "specific ideas students tended to learn" (p. 26). Such data could not address questions such as "What specific ideas have students learned? What misunderstandings have they still retained?" (p. 24). Instead, by conducting what he termed "qualitative analyses," which entailed examining student responses and performance on specific *TOUS* and *SPI* items, Aikenhead was able to discern specific NOS aspects on which students made progress as a result of engagement with instruction using the *Harvard Project Physics* course (Holton, Watson, & Rutherford, 1967).

Lederman and O'Malley (1990), Abd-El-Khalick (1998), and Lederman et al. (2002) expanded this criticism, arguing that quantitative instruments have limited usefulness. Albeit more suitable for large-scale assessments because of ease of administration and scoring, the aggregate measures that these instruments produce are generally limited to labeling respondents' views as "adequate" or "inadequate"—mostly by assigning student views cumulative numerical values—rather than elucidating and clarifying such views. Lederman (1986b) also noted that developers never clarified what numerical values constituted an "adequate" view of NOS on their instruments. Thus, the use of quantitative instruments limits the feasibility of drawing meaningful conclusions regarding the nature of learners' NOS views and/or assessing the meaningfulness and importance of any gains in understanding NOS achieved by learners as a result of various instructional interventions.

In this context, Aikenhead and his colleagues embarked on an ambitious project in the early 1980s to develop an "empirically driven" NOS instrument. The *VOSTS,* which was developed over the course of 6 years and involved thousands of Grade 11 and 12 Canadian students, is an inventory of 114 multiple-choice items, each of which comprises a statement with several reasoned viewpoints or positions. The latter were not derived from examining the philosophical literature. Instead, a student-centered process was used to develop the content and form of *VOSTS* viewpoints or positions, which were drawn from high school students' responses to open-ended items and follow-up interview questions. By substituting theoretically driven positions with student response patterns, Aikenhead and colleagues (1989) constructed an empirically based instrument, which brings a high degree of validity to *VOSTS* responses, since "the meaning that students read into the VOSTS choices tends to be the same meaning that students would express if they were interviewed" (Ryan & Aikenhead, 1992, p. 576). It should be noted that Aikenhead and colleagues never generated a scoring scheme for the *VOSTS* or used cumulative scores when reporting on *VOSTS* data. Instead, frequency and percentage distributions of respondent choices to individual items were reported and interpreted for the purpose of drawing conclusions from *VOSTS* data (e.g., Aikenhead 1987, 1997).

Empirical evidence further supported the validity of the *VOSTS.* Aikenhead (1988) investigated the degree of ambiguity associated with the use of four different response formats to assess high school students' NOS understandings. These formats were Likert-type items, student-generated paragraphs, semistructured interviews, and *VOSTS* items. He reported that Likert-type responses "offer only a guess at student beliefs, and the chances of an evaluator guessing accurately are very remote" (p. 615). The ambiguity associated with using Likert-type items was close to 80%. It is noteworthy that 56% of all NOS instruments in Table 31.1 used one or another form of Likert-type scales. Written paragraph responses generated 35 to 50% ambiguity, followed by *VOSTS* empirically derived multiple-choice items at 15 to 20% ambiguity. Semistructured interviews "offered the most lucid and accurate data" with about 5% ambiguity (p. 625). Empirically driven items, thus, far surpassed theoretically driven items in gauging respondents' NOS understandings. Following its development and dissemination, the *VOSTS* became the NOS instrument of choice for a substantial period of time. As Table 31.2 indicates, it is the third most used instrument in empirical investigations into learners' NOS understandings and continues to be used into the present, especially in the case of large-scale studies where using resource-intensive qualitative approaches (i.e., open-ended questionnaires or interviews) simply is impractical (e.g., Dogan & Abd-El-Khalick, 2008).

The next epoch in the development of NOS assessment approaches started with some dissatisfaction related to the *VOSTS*. Lederman et al. (2002) argued that, when used outside the Canadian or Western contexts, the aforementioned criticisms of forced-choice instruments would as well apply to the *VOSTS*. From the perspective of non–Canadian or non–Western respondents, *VOSTS* viewpoints, in an important sense, would impose on them a certain set of responses like with the case of other forced-choice instruments. Additionally, the *VOSTS* multiple-choice format limits the space of answers available to respondents. Indeed, Abd-El-Khalick and BouJaoude (1997) found that, when *VOSTS* items were modified to allow respondents to articulate whatever ideas they deemed to be representative of their views, participant Lebanese science teachers indicated that their positions on some issues were either not represented among or were combinations of the provided *VOSTS* positions. Some participants expressed viewpoints that were totally different from ones presented in *VOSTS* items. More importantly, the development of the next generation of NOS assessments was motivated by the demonstrated value of interviews in generating valid profiles of learners' understandings of NOS (e.g., Driver et al., 1996; Lederman & O'Malley, 1990). As Aikenhead (1988) had found, compared to other response formats, semistructured individual interviews generated the least ambiguity (about 5%) in interpreting responses to NOS–related prompts. Interviews not only help to elucidate respondents' views on issues related to NOS but also provide them with opportunities to articulate the reasoning underlying as well as the interrelationships among their views.

Lederman et al. (2002) chronicled the development of the *VNOS* instrument (Forms A, B, and C), which started as a semistructured interview protocol (Lederman & O'Malley, 1990) and developed into an open-ended questionnaire whose administration is always coupled with follow-up semistructured interviews with a subset of respondents. The detailed, follow-up interview protocol (see Abd-El-Khalick, 2004a) is intended to probe and clarify responses in order to reduce ambiguities, which might result from interpreting written responses, and ensure a high degree of congruence between researchers' interpretation and respondents' intended meaning in relation to their NOS understandings. The *VNOS* is among a very few NOS instruments whose *construct* validity has been empirically established (Bell, 1999). Its use enables researchers to avoid the threats to validity associated with the use of theoretically driven forced-choice instruments and generate expansive profiles of respondents' conceptions of several important NOS dimensions and the reasoning underlying these conceptions, thus producing more meaningful data as compared to empirically driven forced-choice instruments. While the high resource burden associated with administering the *VNOS* and analyzing the resultant data renders it less than ideal for use in large-scale studies, *VNOS* data enable pinpointing changes in respondents' NOS views and linking such changes to specific elements in instructional interventions used in empirical studies. The *VNOS* has become the most used NOS instrument (see Table 31.2).

The evolution of approaches to NOS assessment from theoretically based forced-choice instruments (e.g., *TOUS, SPI, NSKS*) to empirically based forced-choice instruments (i.e., *VOSTS*) and then to open-ended instruments (e.g., *VNOS, CI, POSE*) was based in robust conceptual arguments related to the validity and meaningfulness of these assessments, as well as supporting empirical evidence, especially the work of Aikenhead (1988). This evolution also is reflected in NOS instruments use: The pattern is most clearly evident in the use of the *TOUS, VOSTS*, and *VNOS*, which together account for 51% of the use of all instruments in empirical research studies (see Table 31.2). Figure 31.2 shows the frequency of this use

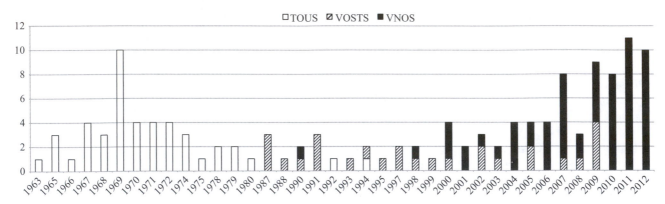

Figure 31.2 Use of the TOUS, VOSTS, and VNOS in empirical studies (1963–2012). Not shown are years in which none of the three instruments was used.

over the period from 1963—the first time the *TOUS* was used in a published study, to 2012.

Use of the *TOUS* peaked in 1969 with 10 published studies, but by the 1980s it had fallen out of favor. Since its formal introduction in 1987, the *VOSTS* dominated the field till around 2000 despite the introduction of the *VNOS–A* in 1990 (Lederman & O'Malley, 1990) and *VNOS–B* in 1998 (Abd-El-Khalick et al., 1998), as well as five other forced-choice instruments—namely, the Methods and Nature of Science (MaNS; Johnson & Peeples, 1987), Views about Philosophy of Science (VaPS; Koulaidis & Ogborn, 1988), *MNSKS* (Meichtry, 1992), BNSSE (Pomerory, 1993), and *BASSSQ* (Aldridge et al., 1997). Indeed, between 1987 and 2000, the *VOSTS* accounted for 35% of all use of NOS instruments in the field. It continues to be the forced-choice instrument of choice, especially for use in large-scale studies (e.g., Bennett & Hogarth, 2009; Dogan & Abd-El-Khalick, 2008; Kang et al., 2005). By around 2000, at the time the *VNOS–C* was introduced (Abd-El-Khalick, 1998; Abd-El-Khalick & Lederman, 2000a), use of the instrument picked up. The *VNOS* accounted for 57% of all NOS instruments use between 2000 and 2012 (see Table 31.2 and Figure 31.2). However, as Table 31.1 shows, researchers continued to develop new forced-choice instruments during the past decade. This observation invites close examination in the context of the narrative presented here about the development of NOS assessment approaches.

More Forced-Choice Instruments: Progression or Regression?

Since 2000, five new forced-choice instruments have been developed: *SEVs* (Tsai & Liu, 2005), *Views on Science and Education Questionnaire* (VOSE; Chen, 2006), *Student Understanding of Science and Scientific Inquiry* (SUSSI; Liang et al., 2006), *Myths of Science Questionnaire* (MOSQ; Buaraphan, 2009a), and *Nature of Science Instrument* (NOSI; Hacıeminoğlu et al., 2012). All five instruments, it was noted earlier, were developed outside the North American context. Indeed, no new forced-choice instruments were developed in the latter context since 1998. Close examination of these five instruments shows that they hardly provide substantially more viable alternatives than their theoretically or empirically driven forced-choice predecessors. All five instruments use Likert-type scales (see Table 31.1; note that the *SUSSI* invites respondents to explain their responses with examples), which Aikenhead (1988) had shown generated, by far, the greatest degree of ambiguity (up to 80%) compared to other response formats used in NOS assessments. Moreover, Neumann, Neumann, and Nehm (2011) articulated a number of other methodological issues associated with the use of Likert-type instruments. The issues range from whether item scores meet assumptions of normality to the meaningfulness and adequacy of calculating item means in the case of bimodal or skewed data distributions to whether "participants answered all items in a consistent

fashion, that is, whether all category options were comparably scaled by the respondent, independent of the item" (p. 1375). Consider the *MOSQ* (Buaraphan, 2009a, 2009b): This instrument's development was limited to selecting a set of 14 broad theoretically driven statements, establishing their face and content validity by a panel of researchers, and "piloting" the instrument with a small number of preservice and inservice science teachers. The *MOSQ* psychometric properties do not seem to have been explored or established, and it would not qualify as a valid and reliable instrument.

Statements on the *SEVs* also are theoretically driven, while the remaining three instruments include what could best be described as a combination of theoretically driven and by-proxy empirically driven statements. Development of statements for the *VOSE*, *SUSSI*, and *NOSI* drew on *VOSTS* items and viewpoints; student response patterns that emerged from other empirical studies, which had used open-ended tools, such as the *VNOS* and semistructured interviews; and/or results from small-scale pilot studies conducted by the instrument developers, some of which involved individual interviews. For instance, in lieu of an empirically driven process that drew on the positions of participants from the population of interest, such as that undertaken by Aikenhead and colleagues, *VOSE* items "were revised from VOSTS or generated according to statements that emerged from the pilot study and the recent literature, such as Khishfe and Abd-El-Khalick (2002), Lederman et al. (2002)" (Chen, 2006, p. 807). However, *VOSTS* viewpoints were derived in the Canadian context, and studies by Khishfe and Abd-El-Khalick (2002) and those reported by Lederman et al. (2002) were undertaken in substantially different contexts (e.g., Lebanon and the United States) from the Taiwanese context, for which the *VOSE* was intended. This concern also applies to the *SUSSI* and *NOSI*.

Development of the *SEVs*, *VOSE*, *SUSSI*, and *NOSI* involved the use of expert review panels, small-scale pilot studies coupled with follow-up individual interviews, and the establishment of the instruments' psychometric properties, mostly by the use of factor analysis techniques. Developers clearly were aware of and explicitly attempted to address the well-documented shortcomings of forced-choice theoretically driven instruments. This awareness and associated attempts surely are to be applauded. The resulting approach, however, could as well be characterized as including a set of "fixes" rather than a novel or comprehensive assessment approach that genuinely addresses issues related to forced-choice NOS instruments and the use of Likert scales. To be sure, given the meticulous, extended, large-scale, and empirical process—centered on firsthand interactions with learners from the population of interest—associated with the development of the *VOSTS*; the *SEVs*, *VOSE*, *SUSSI*, and *NOSI* are hardly an improvement. Albeit reduced to some extent by modest attempts to incorporate respondent perspectives into the development process, these instruments still are subject to validity threats entailed by assuming that respondents would select a preference on a Likert scale on any of these instruments' items for reasons that correspond with or are similar to those intended or implied by instrument developers. Additionally, the criticism related to the meaningfulness of the data generated by these forced-choice instruments still holds (Lederman et al., 2002). In this regard, these new instruments are equivalent with their older counterparts, such as the *NSKS* and *NOSS*.

These new instruments also have come under criticism from a psychometric perspective. Like most quantitative NOS instruments to date, the *SEVs*, *VOSE*, *SUSSI*, and *NOSI* were developed within the context of classical test theory. Neumann and colleagues (2011) applied item response theory (Rasch Modeling) to assess the validity, reliability, and dimensionality of the *SUSSI* (Liang et al., 2006). Neumann and colleagues (2011) reported that, first, "a construct analysis revealed that the instrument did not match published operationalizations of NOS concepts" (p. 1373). Their analyses showed that a two-dimensional Rasch model—one that accounts for NOS and the other for scientific inquiry (SI)—had a significantly better fit than the one-dimensional model underlying the *SUSSI*'s development. The two distinct dimensions, Neumann's group continued, corroborate theoretical distinctions in the literature between NOS and SI (see Abd-El-Khalick et al., 1998) and detract from the *SUSSI*'s theoretical model, which suggests the two domains are more closely aligned and could serve as a singular construct. These findings cast serious doubt on the validity of the *SUSSI*. Neumann and colleagues' (2011) work suggests that newly developed quantitative, forced-choice NOS instruments would benefit from the use of state-of-the-art item response theory to investigate their psychometric properties, including measures of validity and reliability. Based on these arguments, it could be asserted that the recent development of new forced-choice NOS instruments surely does *not* represent advancement in the field. Such development, nonetheless, speaks to the need for "quantification" of NOS understandings for purposes of investigating relationships with other important attributes and science learning outcomes. This need deserves substantial attention.

On "Context" and NOS Assessment: Issues With Inference From Actions to Beliefs

Approaches to NOS assessment, it could be seen, are of two general types. The first are generative: These ask learners to *produce responses* toward explicating and reflecting on their understandings and thinking about NOS. Generative assessments use individual interviews (e.g., Abd-El-Khalick & BouJaoude, 2003; Bianchini & Solomon, 2003; Driver et al., 1996; Lederman & O'Malley, 1990), open-ended questionnaires (e.g., Lederman et al., 2002: *VNOS*), prompts (e.g., Mead & Métraux, 1957: ISSSC), and/or scenarios (e.g., Nott & Wellington, 1995: CI). The second type includes forced-choice varieties, which ask learners to *select responses* from alternatives on multiple-choice items (e.g., Aikenhead et al., 1987: *VOSTS*; Cooley & Klopfer, 1961: *TOUS*) or *indicate a preference* on a Likert-type scale (e.g., Cotham & Smith, 1981: *COST*; Kimball, 1967–1968: *NOSS*). The preceding section spoke to the differential validity and meaningfulness of data collected as well as benefits and burdens associated with using these types of assessments. Both types, nonetheless, seem to be "susceptible" to the same factor, namely, that of "context." This factor, however, is used in two very different manners in the literature related to NOS assessment.

First, "context of assessment" is used to refer to whether and the extent to which an item, prompt, or scenario on a NOS measure is devoid of or anchored in some specific referent and the extent to which such referent is familiar, accessible, or understandable to respondents. Referents might include, among other things, a specific scientific theory or controversy, a socioscientific issue, or a context that could be typified as belonging to school science (versus authentic scientific practice), such as description of an experiment or an inquiry activity performed by students or the respondent. For example, Item #41 on the *NSKS* (Rubba, 1976) asks respondents to indicate their degree of agreement or disagreement with the statement, "Scientific theories are discovered, not created by man" (p. 5). In comparison, the *COST* provides a three-paragraph description of geological theories and then asks respondents to indicate the extent of their agreement with the statement, "Dietz and Hess didn't invent the theory of plate tectonics. They objectively derived it from the facts" (Item #2, p. 145). Clearly, both items are designed to access respondents' conceptions related to the same NOS aspect, specifically, whether scientific constructs are discovered from facts or invented to account for such facts. While the *NSKS* item stood decontextualized, the latter was anchored in a discussion of plate tectonics theory. The *COST* also purports to assess learners' familiarity with each of the theories used to contextualize its items by asking the respondent to "describe the state of your knowledge of the . . . subjects [e.g., theories or topics]" used in the questionnaire on a five-point scale from "mastery" to "no knowledge" (p. 153). Further, the *COST* asks each respondent to "estimate to what extent your responses . . . were influenced by personal convictions independent of your understanding of the subjects," again, on a five-point scale from "complete" influence to "none" (p. 153). Cotham and Smith (1981) argued that the latter information provided for additional confidence in interpreting learner responses to their context-based items. However, as with the case of the *COST*, no robust evidence currently exists about the *specific* ways in which and the extent to which context, science content knowledge, and/or background understandings or "convictions" impact the ways in which instruments provide faithful access to respondent understandings of NOS aspects and domains.

There is some evidence to suggest that context does impact responses to NOS–related items. Driver and colleagues (1996) reported that the images of science in which their participant students anchored their thinking about NOS–related interview questions impacted their expressed views. In particular, Driver and colleagues noted that students' responses differed when they thought about the familiar and proximal context of school science, as compared to the more abstract and distal context of "real" science. Nonetheless, there is need for more systematic evidence to establish and delineate these findings and gauge the extent of any associated impacts on the validity and reliability of NOS measures. Such evidence will need to draw on responses collected from the same population—as compared to drawing on a set of studies across contexts and populations as Driver and her colleagues had done—and will require the use of fully counterbalanced research designs both in terms of sequencing the prompts as well as the very content of these prompts.

Evidence related to the sensitivity of NOS views to science content knowledge has been, at best, equivocal. A host of early studies failed to establish clear or strong correlations between students' and teachers' NOS conceptions and their science content knowledge and/or science achievement (Billeh & Hasan, 1975; Carey & Stauss, 1968, 1970; Olstad, 1969; Scharmann, 1988a, 1988b; Welch & Walberg, 1972; Wood, 1972; Yager & Wick, 1966). The extent to which these findings were associated with the aforementioned problems related to the validity of the forced-choice NOS instruments used in these studies remains unclear. There is some evidence, nonetheless, to suggest that responses to NOS–related items are sensitive to the *quality* and *depth* of learners' science content understandings (as compared to the previously and often used gross measures of science content knowledge, such as grade point average or number of science credit hours). Teachers' responses to *VNOS* items is a case in point. For instance, Items #6 and #7 on the *VNOS–C* (Lederman et al., 2002, p. 509) are designed to shed light on respondents' views of the same NOS aspects, namely, the inferential, creative, and tentative NOS. Item #6 makes use of atomic theory as a context:

> Science textbooks often represent the atom as a central nucleus composed of protons (positively charged particles) and neutrons (neutral particles) with electrons (negatively charged particles) orbiting that nucleus. How certain are scientists about the structure of the atom? What specific evidence *do you think* scientists used to determine what an atom looks like?

In comparison, Item #7 uses the biological construct of species to provide such a context, while essentially asking the same question:

> Science textbooks often define a species as a group of organisms that share similar characteristics and can interbreed with one another to produce fertile offspring. How certain are scientists about their characterization of what a species is? What specific evidence *do you think* scientists used to determine what a species is?

Abd-El-Khalick (2004a) found that prospective secondary science teachers and college science students explicated differing views in relation to these two items depending on whether they had majored in physical versus biological sciences. Some respondents expressed views that could be characterized as more informed in the context of one item and ones that clearly were more naïve in the context of the other. This effect, however, mostly was observed in the case of participants who had completed advanced science courses in the physical or biological sciences and less evident in the case of those majoring, for example, in the geological sciences. Abd-El-Khalick concluded that (also see Leach, Millar, Ryder, & Séré, 2000; Ryder et al., 1999)

> For purposes of exploring college students' NOS views . . . disciplinary nuances and differences . . . need to be brought into the mix . . . researchers who aim to assess college students' NOS views have the task of further delineating and refining the specific realm and NOS aspects they aim to explore, as well as providing students with more specific contexts in their NOS assessments.
>
> (Abd-El-Khalick, 2004a, p. 417)

While there is need for more systematic research in this area, the evidence to date suggests that context—in the specific sense delineated above—matters. Given that reform efforts (e.g., AAAS, 1990; NGSS Lead States, 2013) call for developing students' understandings about the nature of the scientific enterprise writ large, it should prove very fruitful to pursue research questions about the specific ways in which learner NOS understandings are intertwined with the context in which they are learned, elicited, and assessed; the extent and feasibility of transfer from context-bound to generalized NOS understandings; and the ways in which context can facilitate or anchor as well as inform the interpretation of learner responses to various NOS measures.

Albeit much less prevalent, "context" also is used in a second, radically different sense when it comes to NOS assessment. In this second sense, some researchers argue that students' expressed ideas hardly are a faithful representation of their NOS understandings as indicated by the fact that, while engaged with the doing of science, students *are observed* to behave in ways that seem incommensurate with how they talk or write about science (e.g., Sandoval & Morrison, 2003). The implication of these findings, the argument continues, is that observing student behavior in situ or in "context," such as when they are engaged with doing inquiry activities, provides for a more valid assessment of their underlying NOS understandings (Kelly, Chen, & Crawford, 1998). Irrespective of the form that such an approach to assessment would take, it will necessarily involve inference to beliefs from actions and, thus, is apt to be problematic. Indeed, even practicing scientists do not necessarily *do* science in accordance with an articulated epistemological framework: As Kuhn (1996/1962) convincingly argued, such a framework rarely is explicated in scientific education or apprenticeships. While scientists' actions might be consistent with certain epistemological frameworks underlying the disciplinary traditions into which they were initiated, these actions might not tell much about a particular scientist's underlying epistemological beliefs. It only is during times of severe disciplinary crises, Kuhn showed, that scientists revert to explicating and examining the assumptions, rules, and frameworks underlying their practice (for a detailed discussion, see Abd-El-Khalick, 2012b).

Assessments involving inferences to beliefs from actions are based on the problematic assumption that learners' actions as they engage with *doing* science are necessarily reflective of and somehow consistent with an underlying framework on their thinking *about* science. This assumption is inconsistent with evidence indicating that students' NOS understandings often are contextual, fluid, and/or fragmented and lack overarching or consistent frameworks (Abd-El-Khalick, 2004a; Leach et al., 2000). Additionally, robust empirical evidence indicates that teachers' instructional practices—how they enact science and science instruction in their classrooms—often are incommensurate with their NOS understandings (e.g., Abd-El-Khalick et al., 1998; Lederman, 1999, 2007). More importantly, I argued (see Abd-El-Khalick, 2004c) that inferences to beliefs from actions run the risk of imposing an observer's own framework about NOS on observed behaviors, not because learners necessarily ascribe to such a framework but because observers approach the task with one or more coherent frameworks in mind (this is the theory-laden nature of observation in action!). This situation is similar to the case of forced-choice assessment instruments, which often suggested that students held some consistent NOS framework or another, which later turned out to be an artifact of the fact that instrument developers had designed these assessments with specific philosophical stances in mind (Aikenhead et al., 1987; Lederman et al., 2002).

Beyond Silence: Benchmarking "Controversial" NOS for Assessment

As noted earlier, the seeming dominant narrative in the field is one focused on a plethora of assessments and continued disagreement about the construct of NOS. Earlier, I examined the landscape of NOS assessment from a use-of-instruments lens. The examination was intended as a proxy for the collective judgment of the field about NOS measures and indicated a greatly reduced variance by virtue of differential use vis-à-vis the multitude of available instruments. This section will focus on the construct of NOS as *embodied* in these measures through a content analysis of instruments listed in Table 31.1, with the aim of gauging the extent to which the construct, as practically assessed, is contested.

A most important attribute of all NOS measures is that none embodies a covering or overarching model for NOS. This fact hardly is surprising given the very nature of scholarship in history, philosophy, sociology, and psychology of science (HPSSS; Abd-El-Khalick, 2012a). As Laudan and colleagues (1986, p. 42) put it, we currently "have no well-confirmed general picture of how science works, no theory of science worthy of general assent" (see also Rosenberg, 2005). Since the 1950s, science educators have aimed to help precollege students learn *some ideas* about the scientific enterprise and/or the development and validation of scientific knowledge, which were deemed central to a scientifically literate citizenry (Pella, O'Hearn, & Gale, 1966; Wilson, 1954). Researchers who set out to assess understandings of these ideas were keenly aware of the fact that any NOS model they had adopted toward developing their particular instrument "was only one of many possibilities" and would require some measure of consistency—though by no means complete agreement—among historians and philosophers of science (Kimball, 1967–1968, p. 111). This attribute was not explicitly acknowledged in early instruments, which outlined their domains in seemingly covering terms, such as "methods and aims of science," "assumptions of science," "science as an institution," or "activities, products, and ethics of science" (see Table 31.1). However, by the late 1960s, researchers started to explicate what is best described as an "aspects approach to NOS" (Abd-El-Khalick, 2012b), which translated into a set of descriptors signaling the NOS domains or ideas underlying the instrument at hand. The model for the *NOSS* (Kimball, 1967–1968), for instance, embodied the notions that science is driven by curiosity, empirical, reproducible, dynamic, parsimonious, tentative, imposes human constructs on nature, and is not characterized by a single "scientific method." An examination of Table 31.1 indicates that, with very few exceptions (i.e., the *NOST*, *TUNS*, and *VOSTS*), Kimball's (1967–1968) approach became commonplace, and models for NOS underlying the development of various instruments were outlined in terms of sets of NOS domains and aspects. None of these models, it should be noted, outlined an overarching framework to coherently connect and synthesize the respective domains or aspects. Below, I examine the implications of the latter, seemingly intentional omission. Toward understanding the extent to which the NOS aspects and domains targeted by various instruments were consistent across the past 60 years, a content analysis of the *individual items* for all instruments listed in Table 31.1 was undertaken. The analysis, it should be noted, did not include items that clearly were not related to NOS, such as those that addressed views of science education (*VOSE*, BNSSE), school science (*BASSSQ*), scientific inquiry (SUSSI), or acceptance of evolutionary theory (MaNS).

Analyses identified three clusters of NOS aspects. The first included an almost universal set of aspects, which were consistently addressed in the overwhelming majority of all instruments over the course of the past six decades (70–100% of instruments). These included understanding that (a) Scientific knowledge is *tentative* (changing, not certain or absolute, not to be equated with the Truth, all categories of scientific knowledge are amenable to change); (b) science is *empirical*, drawing on observations of the natural world toward developing scientific claims or adjudicating between conflicting claims; (c) scientific inquiry is *theory laden* or *theory driven:* data and observations are not inherently objective or neutral but are vulnerable to scientists' perspectives, mindsets, and theories. Data and observations do not speak for themselves: They require and are susceptible to interpretations, which are guided by scientists' perspectives and theories; (d) the development of scientific knowledge necessarily requires human *creativity*, imagination, and/or intuition, which could not be accounted for by strictly rational models of scientific discovery; (e) science is a *social* activity undertaken in the context of communities and institutions with well-defined structures and practices. The social nature of science is crucial to the production and validation of scientific knowledge, and the incorporation of such knowledge into the scientific cannon; (f) no one universal "scientific method" exists or characterizes the actual practice of scientists, and such a method does not guarantee the development of infallible claims to scientific knowledge; and (g) science is embedded in, affects, and is affected by the lager social and cultural milieu in which it is practiced. This *social and cultural embeddedness* of science also includes ideas related to the reciprocal influences of science and society (and, in some cases, technology).

The second cluster of NOS aspects was less prevalent and evident in 30 to 70% of all instruments. This cluster included ideas related to the nature of theories (e.g., role and functions of theories, theory testing, and adjudication between rival theories), nature of laws (e.g., function and epistemological status of laws), and the relationship between different types of scientific knowledge, including theories, laws, hypotheses, and/or facts. Two other aspects were focused on the distinction between scientific claims and their underlying evidence, that is, the inferential nature of scientific knowledge; and the aims of science, which often were cast in terms of contrasting utilitarian and practical perspectives on these aims with the value inherent to developing robust knowledge about, and explanations of, natural phenomena. Like the first cluster, this second set of NOS aspects could be identified in instruments throughout the past six decades, albeit not as continually addressed or revisited as with aspects in the first cluster.

The third cluster included aspects of two varieties that were much less prominent across NOS instruments. First were aspects characteristically addressed in early instruments up to the late 1960s but rarely addressed in later instruments. These include attitudes toward science, scientists, science-related careers, and products of science (especially in terms of beneficial or detrimental effects of products, such as medical technologies or nuclear weapons); perceptions of scientists (mainly focused on emphasizing that scientists were like other professionals and that being a scientist does not require inherent characteristics,

such as being objective or genius); and processes of science. The second variety received occasional emphasis across the past six decades and included defining science (sometimes in contradistinction with technology or theological knowledge); limitations of science (e.g., answering questions about the natural world or informing rather than dictating policy-related decisions); models in science; assumptions of science (e.g., consistency of patterns across natural events; nature is comprehensible through systematic, empirical study); the question of demarcation (i.e., science versus pseudoscience), ethics and morality in science; experimentation and experimental design; and a few other descriptors of science and scientific knowledge (e.g., parsimonious, unified, unique, and developmental).

The domains and aspects that cut across all or the greater majority of instruments over the past 60 years are strikingly similar to sets of NOS "consensus" lists, which currently provide the basis for research and development efforts in the field (see Lederman, Chapter 31 this volume). NOS consensus lists converge irrespective of whether researchers go about the process by analyzing HPSSS literatures (e.g., AAAS, 1990; Abd-El-Khalick et al., 1998; Hodson, 1991; NRC, 1996), empirically identifying points of agreement about NOS in global science education reform documents (McComas & Olson, 1998), or establishing agreement among "experts" (Osborne, Collins, Ratcliffe, Millar, & Duschl, 2003). Indeed, at certain levels of generality, the very understandings that were deemed desirable across analyzed instruments also were strikingly similar. In this sense, the features of the NOS construct embodied in various instruments surely are *not* nearly as divergent as they are sometimes made to be by some researchers (e.g., Alters, 1997; Rudolph, 2000; Wong & Hodson, 2010). However, this is not to say that instruments featured no disagreements about desired NOS understandings. Indeed, disagreements were evident. For instance, compared to the *VNOS* (Lederman et al., 2002), the BNSSE (Pomeroy, 1993) endorsed a relativistic perspective on the nature of scientific knowledge. Similarly, the *COST* (Cotham & Smith, 1981) would allow a more prominent role for subjective factors in choosing between rival theories compared, for instance, to the *TOUS* (Cooley & Klopfer, 1961). Such disagreements mirror continuing debates within HPSSS, which bring us back to the very point underlying the "aspects approach" to conceptualizing NOS and the aforementioned seemingly intentional—indeed, necessary—omission in terms of articulating overarching, coherent frameworks to connect various aspects outlined in the models underlying NOS instruments.

Embracing "Controversy": A Developmental Framework for Benchmarking NOS Understandings for Assessment

Starting in the late 1960s, mindful of debates within HPSSS, researchers adopted the approach of outlining a set of valued NOS aspects, coupled with an (at least, implied) argument for the pragmatic irrelevance of high-level controversies about NOS to precollege students (Abd-El-Khalick, 2012b). Most researchers and instrument developers leveraged consensus, remained *silent* on controversial issues, and did not commit to a specific philosophical stance. This approach is best exemplified in articulations of NOS in science education reform documents. For example, the AAAS (1990) and NRC (1996) documents do not take a stand on continuing debates between empiricists (e.g., van Fraassen, 1998) and realists (e.g., Musgrave, 1998) as to the ontological status of entities postulated by scientific theories, among many other issues. The ontological status of scientific entities, it should be noted, is targeted in several NOS instruments. Reform documents do not even adopt a single stance on NOS, such as constructive empiricism (van Fraassen, 1980), scientific realism (Boyd, 1983), revolutions and normal science (Kuhn, 1996/1962), sophisticated falsificationism (Lakatos, 1970), or any other well-articulated theory of science. Science educators have highlighted the resulting inherent tensions in reform documents, such as affirming that scientific knowledge is both tentative and durable (AAAS, 1990, pp. 2–3; see Good & Shymansky, 2001). What is important to emphasize is that images of NOS conveyed in reform documents are qualitatively *more* informed and accurate than those often emphasized in science textbooks (Abd-El-Khalick et al., 2008), taught by most science teachers, and endorsed by most precollege students (Lederman, 2007).

From an applied perspective, the discussed framework has enabled science educators to navigate difficulties associated with incorporating informed NOS conceptions in science curricula and instruction without being paralyzed by continuing HPSSS debates. However, major issues will continue to plague the field related to NOS assessment in terms of benchmarking the construct. More often than not, some researchers seem to misconstrue the underpinnings and logic of the self-imposed silence on controversial NOS issues and actually *take sides* on some debates, advocating certain philosophical stances. This includes, for example, advocacy for relativist perspectives on the status of scientific knowledge or empiricist/instrumentalist perspectives on the nature of scientific entities (e.g., Pomeroy, 1993). Thus, while the NOS domains and aspects often addressed in various instruments are very similar, the stances espoused by these instruments—for, at least, a subset of these NOS ideas—likely will continue to be susceptible to the instrument developers' and researchers' philosophical background, preferences, and stances.

Thus, when it comes to benchmarking NOS understandings for assessment, there is need to move the field forward by extending the current consensus framework. Researchers cannot continue to sidestep controversies by remaining silent on contested aspects of the attributes of scientific knowledge or how scientific knowledge is produced and validated. The alternative frame should remain faithful to the controversial nature of some NOS dimensions while simultaneously enabling the development and enactment of science curricula, instruction, and assessment to help students internalize images of NOS that are qualitatively more informed than the naïve portrayals of science to which they continue to hold steadfastly. Abd-El-Khalick (2012b) outlined such a framework, which continues to focus on aspects of NOS currently emphasized in reform documents and widely supported by science educators (see Chapter 31 this volume). Nonetheless, these NOS aspects would be addressed at increasing levels of depth along a *continuum* from general, simple, and unproblematic in elementary grades to a treatment that is specific, complex, and problematized/controversial in the context of teacher education (see Table 31.3 for illustrative examples). The continuum also should take learners' developmental levels into consideration. The level of generality at which NOS aspects are addressed in elementary grades would render them noncontroversial but genuinely more informed than currently prevalent naïve conceptions. Secondary school students would discuss NOS aspects with reasonable levels of sophistication that go beyond mere generalization, such as that scientific knowledge depends on empirical evidence or is tentative. All along this continuum, the interrelatedness of NOS aspects would be progressively examined with greater depth to provide learners with ample opportunities to construct, reconstruct, and consolidate their own internally consistent frameworks about the workings of science. In teacher education and professional development contexts, prospective and practicing science teachers would tackle nuanced complexities about NOS, including major debates and controversies within HPSSS. As a result, teachers would be well positioned to not only support student NOS learning but also to calibrate their teaching to the level of depth at which they address NOS and to the specific interests and abilities of their students (for a detailed discussion see Abd-El-Khalick, 2012b).

This developmental framework transforms the nature of conceptualizing and deploying NOS assessments and associated measures. Assessment developers would not only need to delineate the set of aspects or domains that underlie their assessments but also the level of depth of targeted ideas, as well as the manner in which and the sophistication with which these NOS ideas are interrelated. The framework firstly entails calibrating the level of generality at which a set of NOS ideas are noncontroversial for the *specific* learner audience in mind and the measure of agreement—or lack thereof—among HPSSS scholars, which is associated with this level of generality. For instance, there hardly is any disagreement about the idea that "observation is always selective. It needs a chosen object, a definite task, an interest, a point of view, a problem" (Popper, 1963, p. 45). As Darwin had put it in a letter to Henry Fawcett in 1861, "all observation must be for or against a point of view if it is to be of any service!" (Barlow, 1993/1958, p. 161). In this general sense, the notion that observation is *not* inherently neutral, objective, or presuppositionless is virtually noncontroversial (O'Hear, 1989), an aspect that has consistently been

TABLE 31.3

A Developmental Framework for Benchmarking NOS Understandings for Assessment: Illustrative Examples

Educational level	Examples of target NOS aspects				Level of depth
	Tentative NOS	Theory-Laden NOS	Empirical NOS	Social NOS	
College; teacher education and professional development	There are debates as to whether scientific knowledge grows by accretion (commensurable across theoretical frames) or through paradigmatic shifts (incommensurable across theoretical frames).	There are debates as to the nature and significance of the theory-ladenness of observation. Is theory-ladenness significant beyond situations in which the evidence lies at the very edge of the human perceptual apparatus and/or observational instruments?	Scientific theories are underdetermined by evidence. Debates continue about the extent to which rationality versus value judgment mediates the use of evidence in the process of theory choice in science.	Debates continue about the viability of social constructionist conceptions in accounting for science's success in the absence of "realist" conceptions. Only "miracle" can explain such success if science was not getting closer to the "true" nature of phenomena!	Specific, complex, problematized (controversial)
Secondary school	Scientific knowledge is expanded, revised, or rejected because of two fundamental reasons: (1) New evidence is brought to bear (empirical NOS), and/or (2) existing evidence is reinterpreted in light of theoretical advances (theory-laden NOS). Scientific knowledge changes in at least two fundamental ways: (1) It is expanded through accretion, and/or (2) discarded and altogether replaced with new knowledge.	Theories might determine what scientists "see" when conducting investigations through selective attention and/or influencing the interpretation of "raw" inputs from the environment. Theories are crucial to conducting scientific investigations because theories enable scientists both to choose what evidence to collect (and what evidence to disregard) and how to interpret the collected evidence.	The relationship between scientific knowledge and evidence is indirect. Theories can only be tested by comparing their consequences with empirical observations. Hypotheses do not "jump out" from evidence: Inference beyond the evidence is usually involved (creative NOS). The relationship between knowledge claims and evidence is mediated by theory (theory-laden NOS).	The social character of science contributes to its objectivity: Intersubjective critical discourse through established value-driven channels (e.g., double-blind review procedures) minimizes the subjectivities of participant scientists. Science is conducted within the context of social institutions and has established and identifiable norms.	
Elementary school	Scientific knowledge is subject to change over time.	Scientific investigations always involve theories and empirical observations.	Science demands evidence: Scientific knowledge is derived from and/or supported by observations of the natural world.	Different groups of scientists contribute to the development of scientific knowledge.	General, simple, unproblematic

emphasized in assessments and a crucial idea about NOS for secondary school students to understand. However, a developmental framework entails, secondly, that instrument developers become aware of debates or controversies associated with the ideas at hand and tailor their assessment accordingly. To continue with this example, NOS assessments should avoid taking sides in the form of commitments related to the theory-laden NOS, such as that "The course of scientific discovery resembles the process of reaching a difficult judicial decision" (Pomeroy, 1993, p. 275: BNSSE, Item 17) when working with learners at certain levels of sophistication. Science teachers, for instance, are better positioned to teach about NOS if they are, in this case, aware of the continuing debates about the nature of the relationship between theoretical commitments and empirical evidence and about the extent to which theory overrides evidence when it comes to choosing between rival theories (see Abd-El-Khalick 2012a; Curd & Cover, 1998). While similar in several respects, making judicial decisions and adjudicating between scientific theories—at least for a subset of NOS scholars—still differ in crucial ways, which are dependent on observations of the behavior of natural phenomena.

Table 31.3 provides additional illustrative examples about core NOS aspects whose assessment should be approached at different levels of generality and sophistication. It could be seen that instruments and measures designed to assess secondary science teachers' and college students' NOS understandings would need to be calibrated accordingly and create "spaces" for eliciting respondents' understanding about debates associated with and the interrelatedness of such core NOS aspects. These "spaces" could take the form of appropriate alternatives in forced-choice instruments or carefully crafted contexts, scenarios, and prompts in open-ended measures. In this sense, some level of understanding of relevant NOS debates and controversies for certain groups of audiences, especially science teachers and college students, becomes *the* espoused view underlying NOS measures. This suggested approach to NOS assessment, it should be emphasized, requires robust understandings of the *developmental appropriateness* of the various NOS ideas along a continuum, such as that outlined in Table 31.3. Currently, our understandings of such developmental appropriateness are anecdotal and informed by localized studies rather than based in a systematic body of literature. Investigating the developmental appropriates of NOS ideas along the K–16 educational ladder should prove to be a very fruitful line of research for those interested in the domain of NOS in science education in general and in the field of NOS assessment in particular.

Concluding Remarks and Moving Forward

As evident in the present review, the landscape of assessment related to NOS is much more streamlined than it is often perceived or made to be. The collective wisdom of practice reflected in the extent and patterns of use of available NOS assessments in empirical studies indicates that robust comparisons across studies, populations, and interventions are possible by virtue of the selective use in research of a rather small of number of instruments. Analyses also revealed a clear pattern for the evolution of approaches to NOS assessment from theoretically driven to empirically driven forced-choice instruments and finally to open-ended assessment approaches. This evolution carried with it substantial improvements in terms of the validity of assessments and the meaningfulness of the data generated about learners' NOS conceptions. Use, coupled with content analyses of NOS instruments developed over the past six decades, revealed wide agreement around a set of core NOS aspects and domains, which are deemed central to a robust precollege science education. Nonetheless, the very nature of HPSSS scholarship creates tensions for NOS assessment, especially around contested areas related to these core NOS aspects. Toward addressing this important tension, I argued for embracing "controversy" about NOS by adopting a developmental framework for benchmarking NOS for purposes of assessment. Additionally, I argued that context *matters* for NOS assessment and should be accounted for in related measures. However, it also was argued that approaches purporting to assess learners' views of NOS by inference from learner actions to their beliefs are very problematic.

Finally, I argued that forced-choice instruments that continue to be developed into the present despite robust theoretical arguments and empirical evidence that cast serious doubt on their validity do *not* represent an advancement in the field. The continued development of such instruments, however, reflects the need for resource-lean assessments and quantification of learners' NOS understandings for the respective purposes of use in large-scale studies and statistical examination of the interrelationship between learner NOS understandings and a host of other variables of interest. Instead of *going back* to the development and use of forced-choice instruments, the next chapter in the evolution of NOS assessment is the development of valid and reliable as well as efficient ways to quantify student responses to open-ended instruments. Abd-El-Khalick and his students have been working on the development of a rubric to "score" *VNOS–C* responses (Abd-El-Khalick, 2004b; Abd-El-Khalick, Belarmino, & Summers, 2012).

The approach capitalizes on the virtues of open-ended assessments in eliciting valid representations of respondents' NOS views and then uses detailed rubrics and decision-making trees to generate scores that reflect student understandings on a scale, which would allow valid comparisons both within and across research studies. Presently, however, the approach remains resource intensive and will continue to present challenges to large-scale studies. A possible measure to ameliorate the time and effort needed to implement this approach would be to capitalize on the emerging technologies of natural language processing to significantly reduce the load associated with the qualitative analysis and consequent scoring of learner responses to open-ended NOS instruments.

Acknowledgments

Thanks to my students John Myers and Ryan Summers for their respective help with searching the voluminous literature on NOS and examining the content of NOS instruments. Thanks also to Norman G. Lederman and Valarie Akerson, who reviewed this chapter.

References

Abd-El-Khalick, F. (1998). *The influence of history of science courses on students' conceptions of the nature of science.* Unpublished doctoral dissertation, Oregon State University, Oregon.

Abd-El-Khalick, F. (2001). Embedding nature of science instruction in preservice elementary science courses: Abandoning scientism, but . . . *Journal of Science Teacher Education, 12*(3), 215–233.

Abd-El-Khalick, F. (2002, April). *The development of conceptions of the nature of scientific knowledge and knowing in the middle and high school years: A cross-sectional study.* Paper presented at the annual meeting of the National Association for Research in Science Teaching, New Orleans, LA.

Abd-El-Khalick, F. (2004a). Over and over and over again: College students' views of nature of science. In L. B. Flick & N. G. Lederman (Eds.), *Scientific inquiry and nature of science: Implications for teaching, learning, and teacher education* (pp. 389–425). Dordrecht, the Netherlands: Kluwer.

Abd-El-Khalick, F. (2004b, April). *The relationship between students' views of nature of science and their conceptual understanding of stoichiometry: An empirical assessment.* Paper presented at the annual meeting of the American Educational Research Association, San Diego, CA.

Abd-El-Khalick, F. (2004c, April). *Assessing and influencing epistemological views: The moderate fallacies of inference to beliefs from action and influence of action on beliefs.* Paper presented at the annual meeting of the American Educational Research Association, San Diego, CA.

Abd-El-Khalick, F. (2005). Developing deeper understandings of nature of science: The impact of a philosophy of science course on preservice science teachers' views and instructional planning. *International Journal of Science Education, 27*(1), 15–42.

Abd-El-Khalick, F. (2012a). Examining the sources for our understandings about science: Enduring conflations and critical issues in research on nature of science in science education. *International Journal of Science Education, 34*(3), 353–374.

Abd-El-Khalick, F. (2012b). Nature of science in science education: Toward a coherent framework for synergistic research and development. In B. J. Fraser, K. Tobin, & C. McRobbie (Eds.), *Second international handbook of science education* (Vol. 2, pp. 1041–1060). Dordrecht, the Netherlands: Springer.

Abd-El-Khalick, F. (2013). Teaching *with* and *about* nature of science, and science teacher knowledge domains. *Science & Education, 22*(9), 2087–2107.

Abd-El-Khalick, F., & Akerson, V.L. (2004). Learning as conceptual change: Factors that mediate the development of preservice elementary teachers' views of nature of science. *Science Education, 88*(5), 785–810.

Abd-El-Khalick, F., & Akerson, V.L. (2009). The influence of metacognitive training on preservice elementary teachers' conceptions of nature of science. *International Journal of Science Education, 31*(16), 2161–2184.

Abd-El-Khalick, F., Belarmino, J., & Summers, R. (2012, March). *Development and validation of a rubric to score the views of nature of science questionnaire.* Paper presented at the annual meeting of the National Association for Research in Science Teaching, Indianapolis, IN.

Abd-El-Khalick, F., Bell, R.L., & Lederman, N.G. (1998). The nature of science and instructional practice: Making the unnatural natural. *Science Education, 82*(4), 417–436.

Abd-El-Khalick, F., & BouJaoude, S. (1997). An exploratory study of the knowledge base for science teaching. *Journal of Research in Science Teaching, 34*(7), 673–699.

Abd-El-Khalick, F., & BouJaoude, S. (2003). Lebanese middle school students' views of nature of science. *Mediterranean Journal of Educational Studies, 8*(1), 61–79.

Abd-El-Khalick, F., & Lederman, N.G. (2000a). Improving science teachers' conceptions of the nature of science: A critical review of the literature. *International Journal of Science Education, 22*(7), 665–701.

Abd-El-Khalick, F., & Lederman, N.G. (2000b). The influence of history of science courses on students' views of nature of science. *Journal of Research in Science Teaching, 37*(10), 1057–1095.

Abd-El-Khalick, F., Waters, M., & Le, A. (2008). Representations of nature of science in high school chemistry textbooks over the past four decades. *Journal of Research in Science Teaching, 45*(7), 835–855.

Aikenhead, G.S. (1973). The measurement of high school students' knowledge about science and scientists. *Science Education, 57*(4), 539–549.

Aikenhead, G.S. (1974a). Course evaluation. I: A new methodology for test construction. *Journal of Research in Science Teaching, 11*(1), 17–22.

Aikenhead, G.S. (1974b). Course evaluation. II: Interpretation of student performance on evaluative tests. *Journal of Research in Science Teaching, 11*(1), 23–30.

Aikenhead, G.S. (1987). High-school graduates' beliefs about science-technology-society. III. Characteristics and limitations of scientific knowledge. *Science Education, 71*(4), 459–487.

Aikenhead, G.S. (1988). An analysis of four ways of assessing student beliefs about STS topics. *Journal of Research in Science Teaching, 25*(8), 607–629.

Aikenhead, G.S. (1997). Student views on the influence of culture on science. *International Journal of Science Education, 19*(4), 419–428.

Aikenhead, G.S., Fleming, R.W., & Ryan, A.G. (1987). High-school graduates' beliefs about science-technology-society. I. Methods and issues in monitoring student views. *Science Education, 71*(2), 145–161.

Aikenhead, G.S., & Ryan, A.G. (1992). The development of a new instrument: "Views on Science-Technology-Society" (VOSTS). *Science Education, 76*(5), 477–491.

Aikenhead, G.S., Ryan, A., & Fleming, R. (1989). *Views on science-technology-society* (from CDN.mc.5). Saskatoon, Canada: Department of Curriculum Studies, University of Saskatchewan.

Akçay, B., & Koç, I. (2009). Inservice science teachers' views about the nature of science. *Hasan Ali Yücel Faculty of Education Journal, 11,* 1–11.

Akerson, V.L., & Abd-El-Khalick, F. (2003). Teaching elements of nature of science: A yearlong case study of a fourth grade teacher. *Journal of Research in Science Teaching, 40*(10), 1025–1049.

Akerson, V.L., Abd-El-Khalick, F., & Lederman, N.G. (2000). Influence of a reflective explicit activity-based approach on elementary teachers' conceptions of nature of science. *Journal of Research in Science Teaching, 37*(4), 295–317.

Akerson, V.L., Buck, G.A., Donnelly, L.A., Nargund-Joshi, V., & Weiland, I.S. (2011). The importance of teaching and learning nature of science in the early childhood years. *Journal of Science Teacher Education, 20,* 537–549.

Akerson, V.L., Cullen, T.A., & Hanson, D.L. (2009). Fostering a community of practice through a professional development program to improve elementary teachers' views of nature of science and teaching practice. *Journal of Research in Science Teaching, 46*(10), 1090–1113.

Akerson, V., & Donnelly, L.A. (2010). Teaching nature of science to K-2 students: What understandings can they attain? *International Journal of Science Education, 32*(1), 97–124.

Akerson, V.L., Hanson, D.L., & Cullen, T.A. (2007). The influence of guided inquiry and explicit instruction on K–6 teachers' views of nature of science. *Journal of Science Teacher Education, 18,* 751–772.

Akerson, V.L., & Hanuscin, D.L. (2007). Teaching the nature of science through inquiry: Results of a 3-year professional development programs. *Journal of Research in Science Teaching, 44*(5), 653–680.

Akerson, V.L., & Volrich, M.L. (2006). Teaching nature of science explicitly in a first-grade internship setting. *Journal of Research in Science Teaching, 43*(4), 377–394.

Akindehin, F. (1988). Effect of an instructional package on preservice science teachers' understanding of the nature of science and acquisition of science-related attitudes. *Science Education, 72*(1), 73–82.

Aldridge, J., Taylor, P., & Chen, C.C. (1997, March). *Development, validation and use of the beliefs about science and school science questionnaire (BASSSQ).* Paper presented at the annual meeting of the National Association for Research in Science Teaching, Oak Brook, IL.

Allen, H., Jr. (1959). *Attitudes of certain high school seniors toward science and scientific careers.* New York: Teachers College Press.

Alters, B.J. (1997). Whose nature of science? *Journal of Research in Science Teaching, 34*(1), 39–55.

American Association for the Advancement of Science (AAAS). (1990). *Science for all Americans.* New York: Oxford University Press.

Andersen, H.O., Harty, H., & Samuel, K.V. (1986). Nature of science, 1969 and 1984: Perspectives of preservice secondary science teachers. *School Science and Mathematics, 86*(1), 43–50.

Anderson, E.J., DeMelo, H.T., Szabo, M., & Toth, G. (1975). Behavioral objectives, science processes, and learning for inquiry-oriented instructional materials. *Science Education, 59*(2), 263–271.

Anderson, G.J. (1970). Effects of classroom social climate on individual learning. *American Educational Research Journal, 7*(2), 135–152.

Anderson, O.R., & Callaway, J. (1986). Studies of information processing rates in science learning and related cognitive variables. II: A first approximation to estimating a relationship between science reasoning skills and information acquisition. *Journal of Research in Science Teaching, 23*(1), 67–72.

Apostolou, A., & Koulaidis, V. (2010). Epistemology and science education: A study of epistemological views of teachers. *Research in Science & Technological Education, 28*(2), 149–166.

Barlow, N. (Ed.). (1993/1958). *The autobiography of Charles Darwin: 1809–1882.* New York: W.W. Norton.

Barufaldi, J.P., Bethel, L.J., & Lamb, W.G. (1977). The effect of a science methods course on the philosophical view of science among elementary education majors. *Journal of Research in Science Teaching, 14*(4), 289–294.

Bell, R.L. (1999). *Understandings of the nature of science and decision making on science and technology based issues.* Unpublished doctoral dissertation, Oregon State University, Oregon.

Bell, R.L., Lederman, N.G., & Abd-El-Khalick, F. (2000). Developing and acting upon one's conceptions of the nature of science: A follow-up study. *Journal of Research in Science Teaching, 37*(6), 563–581.

Ben-Chaim, D., & Zoller, U. (1991). The STS outlook profiles of Israeli high-school students and their teachers. *International Journal of Science Education, 13*(4), 447–458.

Bennett, J., & Hogarth, S. (2009). Would you want to talk to a scientist at a party? High school students' attitudes to school science and to science. *International Journal of Science Education, 31*(14), 1975–1998.

Beveridge, W. I. B. (1950). *The art of scientific investigation.* New York: Vintage Books.

Bianchini, J. A., & Solomon, E. R. (2003). Constructing views of science tied to issues of equity and diversity: A study of beginning science teachers. *Journal of Research in Science Teaching, 40,* 53–76.

Billeh, V. Y., & Hasan, O. E. (1975). Factors influencing teachers' gain in understanding the nature of science. *Journal of Research in Science Teaching, 12*(3), 209–219.

Billeh, V. Y., & Malik, M. H. (1977). Development and application of a test on understanding the nature of science. *Science Education, 61*(4), 559–571.

Biological Sciences Curriculum Study (BSCS). (1962). *Processes of science test.* New York: The Psychological Corporation.

Borda, E. J., Burgess, D. J., Plog, C. J., DeKalb, N. C., & Luce, M. M. (2009). Concept maps as tools for assessing students' epistemologies of science. *Electronic Journal of Science Education, 13*(2). Retrieved from http://ejse.southwestern.edu/article/view/7804

Botton, C., & Brown, C. (1998). The reliability of some VOSTS items when used with preservice secondary science teachers in England. *Journal of Research in Science Teaching, 35*(1), 53–71.

Boyd, R. N. (1983). On the current status of scientific realism. *Erkenntnis, 19,* 45–90.

Bradford, C. S., Rubba, P. A., & Harkness, W. L. (1995). Views about science-technology-society interactions held by college students in general education physics and STS courses. *Science Education, 79*(4), 355–373.

Breedlove, C. B., & Gessert, W. L. (1970). Use of an "electronic blackboard" in a physics teaching project. *School Science and Mathematics, 70*(2), 154–168.

Broadhurst, N. A. (1970). A study of selected learning outcomes of graduating high school students in south Australian schools. *Science Education, 54*(1), 17–21.

Buaraphan, K. (2009a). Preservice and inservice science teachers' responses and reasoning about the nature of science. *Educational Research and Review, 4*(11), 561–581.

Buaraphan, K. (2009b). Thai in-service science teachers' conceptions of the nature of science. *Journal of Science and Mathematics Education in Southeast Asia, 32*(2), 188–217.

Buaraphan, K. (2010). Pre-service and in-service science teachers' conceptions of the nature of science. *Science Educator, 19*(2), 35–47.

Buaraphan, K. (2011). Pre-service physics teachers' conceptions of nature of science. *US-China Education Review, 8*(2), 137–148.

Buaraphan, K. (2012). Embedding nature of science in teaching about astronomy and space. *Journal of Science Education and Technology, 21,* 353–369.

Buaraphan, K., & Sung-Ong, S. (2009). Thai pre-service science teachers' conceptions of the nature of science. *Asia-Pacific Forum on Science Learning and Teaching, 10*(1). Retrieved from www.ied.edu.hk/apfslt/

Buffler, A., Lubben, F., & Ibrahim, B. (2009). The relationship between students' views of the nature of science and their views of the nature of scientific measurement. *International Journal of Science Education, 31*(9), 1137–1156.

Cakmakci, G. (2012). Promoting pre-service teachers' ideas about nature of science through educational research apprenticeship. *Australian Journal of Teacher Education, 37*(2). Retrieved from http://ro.ecu.edu.au/ajte/vol37/iss2/8

Carey, R. L., & Stauss, N. G. (1968). An analysis of the understanding of the nature of science by prospective secondary science teachers. *Science Education, 52*(4), 358–363.

Carey, R. L., & Stauss, N. G. (1970). An analysis of experienced science teachers' understanding of the nature of science. *School Science and Mathematics, 70*(5), 366–376.

Chai, C. C., Deng, F., & Tsai, C. C. (2012). A comparison of scientific epistemological views between Mainland China and Taiwan high school students. *Asia Pacific Education Review, 13*(1), 17–26.

Chan, K. S. (2005). Exploring the dynamic interplay of college students' conceptions of the nature of science. *Asia-Pacific Forum on Science Learning and Teaching, 6*(2), 1–16.

Chen, S. (2006). Development of an instrument to assess views on nature of science and attitudes toward teaching science. *Science Education, 90,* 803–819.

Choi, K., & Cho, H. H. (2002). Effects of teaching ethical issues on Korean school students' attitudes towards science. *Journal of Biological Education, 37*(1), 26–30.

Choppin, B. H. (1974). The introduction of new science curricula in England and Wales. *Comparative Education Review, 18*(2), 196–206.

Chrouser, W. H. (1975). Outdoor vs. indoor laboratory techniques in teaching biology to prospective elementary teachers. *Journal of Research in Science Teaching, 12*(1), 41–48.

Cobern, W. W., & Loving, C. C. (2002). Investigation of preservice elementary teachers' thinking about science. *Journal of Research in Science Teaching, 39*(10), 1016–1031.

Cooley, W. W., & Bassett, R. D. (1961). Evaluation and follow-up study of a summer science and mathematics program for talented secondary school students. *Science Education, 45*(3), 209–216.

Cooley, W. W., & Klopfer, L. E. (1961). *TOUS: Test on understanding science.* Princeton, NJ: Education Testing Service.

Cossman, G. W. (1969). The effects of a course in science and culture for secondary school students. *Journal of Research in Science Teaching, 6*(3), 274–283.

Cotham, J. S., & Smith, E. L. (1981). Development and validation of the conceptions of scientific theories test. *Journal of Research in Science Teaching, 18*(5), 387–396.

Crumb, G. H. (1965). Understanding of science in high school physics. *Journal of Research in Science Teaching, 3,* 246–250.

Curd, M., & Cover, J. A. (1998). *Philosophy of science: The central issues.* New York: W. W. Norton & Co.

Dass, P. M. (2005). Understanding the nature of scientific enterprise (NOSE) through a discourse with its history: The influence of an undergraduate "history of science" course. *International Journal of Science and Mathematics Education, 3,* 87–115.

Demirbaş, M., & Balci, F. (2012). The impact of the explicit reflective approach in teaching the nature of science upon Turkish students' perceptions of science. *International Journal of Asian Social Science, 2*(8), 1255–1260.

Demirbas, M., Bozdogan, A. E., & Özbek, G. (2012). An analysis from different variables of views of pre-service science teachers in Turkey on the nature of science. *Research Journal of Recent Sciences, 1*(8), 29–35.

Dienye, N. E. (1987). The effect of inservice science education. *British Journal of In-Service Education, 14*(1), 48–55.

Dogan, N., & Abd-El-Khalick, F. (2008). Turkish grade 10 students' and science teachers' conceptions of nature of science: A national study. *Journal of Research in Science Teaching, 45*(10), 1083–1112.

Doran, R. L., Guerin, R. O., & Cavalieri, J. (1974). An analysis of several instruments measuring "nature of science" objectives. *Science Education, 58*(3), 312–329.

Driver, R., Leach, J., Millar, R., & Scott, P. (1996). *Young people's images of science.* Buckingham, UK: Open University Press.

Duncan, D. K., & Arthurs, L. (2012). Improving student attitudes about learning science and student scientific reasoning skills. *Astronomy Education Review, 11*(1). Retrieved from http://aer.aas.org/resource/1/aerscz/v11/i1/p010102_s1

Durkee, P. (1974). An analysis of the appropriateness and utilization of TOUS with special reference to high-ability students studying physics. *Science Education, 58*(3), 343–356.

Duschl, R. A., & Wright, E. (1989). A case study of high school teachers' decision making models for planning and teaching science. *Journal of Research in Science Teaching, 26*(5), 467–501.

Eastwood, J. L., Sadler, T. D., Zeidler, D. L., Lewis, A., Amiri, L., & Applebaum, S. (2012). Contextualizing nature of science instruction in socioscientific issues. *International Journal of Science Education, 34*(15), 2289–2315.

Engen, H. B., Smith, D. D., & Yager, R. E. (1967–1968). Student outcomes with rotation of teachers in secondary biology. *Journal of Research in Science Teaching, 5*, 230–234.

Faryniarz, J. V. (1992). Effectiveness of microcomputer simulations in stimulating environmental problem solving by community college students. *Journal of Research in Science Teaching, 29*(5), 453–470.

Fergusson, J., Oliver, C., & Walter, M. R. (2012). Astrobiology outreach and the nature of science: The role of creativity. *Astrobiology, 12*(12), 1143–1153.

Fisher, D. L. (1979). The impact of the inclusion of ASEP materials on some cognitive outcomes in different types of Tasmanian schools. *Research in Science Education, 9*, 111–118.

Fisher, D. L., & Fraser, B. J. (1980). Evaluating the impact of a national curriculum on content-free cognitive outcomes. *European Journal of Science Education, 2*(1), 45–59.

Fleming, R. W. (1987). High-school gradates' beliefs about science-technology-society. II. The interaction among science, technology, and society. *Science Education, 71*(2), 163–186.

Fleming, R. W. (1988). Undergraduate science students' views on the relationship between science, technology and society. *International Journal of Science Education, 10*(4), 449–463.

Flores, F., Lopez, A., Gallegos, L., & Barojas, J. (2000). Transforming science and learning concepts of physics teachers. *International Journal of Science Education, 22*(2), 197–208.

Folmer, V., Barbosa, N. B., Soares, F. A., & Rocha, J. B. T. (2009). Experimental activities based on ill-structured problems improve Brazilian school students' understanding of the nature of scientific knowledge. *Revista Electrónica de Enseñanza de las Ciencias, 8*(1), 232–254.

Fraser, B. J. (1978). Development of a test of science-related attitudes. *Science Education, 62*, 509–515.

Fulton, H. F. (1971a). An analysis of student outcomes utilizing two approaches to teaching BSCS biology. *Journal of Research in Science Teaching, 8*(1), 21–28.

Fulton, H. F. (1971b). Individualized vs. group teaching of BSCS biology. *The American Biology Teacher, 33*(5), 277–279, 291.

Gardner, P. L. (1975). Attitudes to science: A review. *Studies in Science Education, 2*(1), 1–41.

Gess-Newsome, J. (2002). The use and impact of explicit instruction about the nature of science and science inquiry in an elementary science methods course. *Science & Education, 11*, 55–67.

Ginns, I. S., & Foster, W. J. (1978). A comparison of teaching strategies and their effect on attitudes to and understanding of science. *South Pacific Journal of Teacher Education, 6*(2), 154–158.

Glass, L. W., & Yager, R. E. (1970). Individualized instruction as a spur to understanding the scientific enterprise. *The American Biology Teacher, 32*(6), 359–361.

Goff, P., Boesdorfer, S. B., & Hunter, W. (2012). Using a multicultural approach to teach chemistry and the nature of science to undergraduate non-majors. *Cultural Studies of Science Education, 7*, 631–651.

Golabek, C., & Amrane-Cooper, L. (2011). Trainee teachers' perceptions of the nature of science and implications for pre-service teacher training in England. *Research in Secondary Teacher Education, 1*(2), 9–13.

Good, R., & Shymansky, J. (2001). Nature-of-science literacy in *Benchmarks* and *Standards:* Post-modern/relativist or modern/realist? *Science & Education, 10*, 173–185.

Guerra-Ramos, M. T. (2012). Teachers' ideas about the nature of science: A critical analysis of research approaches and their contribution to pedagogical practice. *Science & Education, 21*(5), 631–655.

Guerra-Ramos, M. T., Ryder, J., & Leach, J. J. (2010). Ideas about the nature of science in pedagogically relevant contexts: Insights from a situated perspective of primary teachers' knowledge. *Science Education, 94*, 282–307.

Güzel, H. (2011). Opinions of university students about the nature of science. *World Applied Sciences Journal, 12*(7), 1005–1013.

Hacıeminoğlu, E., Yılmaz-Tüzün, O., & Ertepınar, H. (2012). Development and validation of nature of science instrument for elementary school

students. *Education 3–13: International Journal of Primary, Elementary and Early Years Education.* doi:10.1080/03004279.2012.671840

Haidar, A. H. (1999). Emirates pre-service and inservice teachers' views about the nature of science. *International Journal of Science Education, 21*(8), 807–822.

Haidar, A. H. (2000). Professors' views on the influence of Arab society on science and technology. *Journal of Science Education and Technology, 9*(3), 257–273.

Hanuscin, D. L., Akerson, V. L., & Phillipson-Mower, T. (2006). Integrating nature of science instruction into a physical science content course for preservice elementary teachers: NOS views of teaching assistants. *Science Education, 90*, 912–935.

Hanuscin, D. L., & Lee, M. H. (2011). Elementary teachers' pedagogical content knowledge for teaching the nature of science. *Science Education, 95*, 145–167.

Haukoos, G. D., & Penick, J. E. (1983). The influence of classroom climate on science process and content achievement of community college students. *Journal of Research in Science Teaching, 20*(7), 629–637.

Haukoos, G. D., & Penick, J. E. (1985). The effects of classroom climate on college science students: A replication study. *Journal of Research in Science Teaching, 22*(2), 163–168.

Haukoos, G. D., & Penick, J. E. (1987). Interaction effect of personality characteristics, classroom climate, and science achievement. *Science Education, 71*(5), 735–743.

Hillis, S. R. (1975). The development of an instrument to determine student views of the tentativeness of science. In E. J. Montague (Ed.), *Research and curriculum development in science education: Science teacher behavior and student affective and cognitive learning* (Vol. 3, pp. 34–40). Austin: University of Texas Press. (ERIC Document Reproduction Service No. ED 124 404)

Hodson, D. (1991). Philosophy of science and science education. In M. R. Matthews (Ed.), *History, philosophy, and science teaching: Selected readings* (pp. 19–32). New York: Teachers College Press.

Holton, G., Watson, F. G., & Rutherford, F. J. (1967). Harvard project physics: A progress report. *The Physics Teacher, 5*(5).

Howe, E. M. (2007). Addressing nature-of-science core tenets with the history of science: An example with sickle-cell anemia & malaria. *American Biology Teacher, 69*(8), 467–472.

Howe, E. M., & Rudge, D. W. (2005). Recapitulating the history of sickle-cell anemia research: Improving students' NOS views explicitly and reflectively. *Science & Education, 14*, 423–441.

Huang, C. M., Tsai, C. C., & Chang, C. Y. (2005). An investigation of Taiwanese early adolescents' views about the nature of science. *Adolescence, 40*(159), 645–654.

Hungerford, H., & Walding, H. (1974). *The modification of elementary methods students' concepts concerning science and scientists.* Paper presented at the annual meeting of the National Science Teachers Association.

İrez, S. (2006). Are we prepared? An assessment of preservice science teacher educators' beliefs about nature of science. *Science Education, 90*, 1113–1143.

İrez, S. (2007). Reflection-oriented qualitative approach in beliefs research. *Eurasia Journal of Mathematics, Science & Technology Education, 3*(1), 17–27.

İrez, S., Çakir, M., & Şeker, H. (2011). Exploring nature of science understandings of Turkish pre-service science teachers. *Necatibey Faculty of Education Electronic Journal of Science and Mathematics Education, 5*(2), 6–17.

Irzik, G., & Nola, R. (2011). A family resemblance approach to the nature of science for science education. *Science & Education, 20*(7), 591–607.

Jacobs, J. N., & Bollenbacher, J. K. (1960). Teaching ninth-grade biology by television. *Audiovisual Communication Review, 8*, 176–191.

Johnson, G. (1972). An integrated two year chemistry-physics course compared with consecutively taught separate courses. *Science Education, 56*(2), 143–154.

Johnson, R. L., & Peeples, E. E. (1987). The role of scientific understanding in college: Student acceptance of evolution. *American Biology Teacher, 49*(2), 96–98.

Jones, K. M. (1969). The attainment of understandings about the scientific enterprise, scientists, and the aims and methods of science by students in a college physical science course. *Journal of Research in Science Teaching, 6*(1), 47–49.

Jungwirth, E. (1968). Teaching for "understanding of science." *Journal of Biological Education, 2*(1), 39–51.

Jungwirth, E. (1969). Active understanding of the processes of science: An evaluation of certain aspects of the first two years of B.S.C.S. biology teaching in Israel. *Journal of Biological Education, 3*(1), 45–55.

Jungwirth, E., & Jungwirth, E. (1972). TOUS revisited: A longitudinal study of the development of understanding of science. *Journal of Biological Education, 6*(3), 187–195.

Kang, S., Scharmann, L. C., & Noh, T. (2005). Examining students' views on the nature of science: Results from Korean 6th, 8th, and 10th graders. *Science Education, 89,* 314–334.

Kaya, S. (2012). An examination of elementary and early childhood pre-service teachers' nature of science views. *Procedia-Social and Behavioral Science, 46,* 581–585.

Kelly, G. J., Chen, C., & Crawford, T. (1998). Methodological considerations for studying science-in-the-making in educational settings. *Research in Science Education, 28*(1), 23–49.

Kemeny, J. G. (1959). *A philosopher looks at science.* Princeton, NJ: D. Van Nostrand.

Khishfe, R. (2008). The development of seventh graders' views of nature of science. *Journal of Research in Science Teaching, 45*(4), 470–496.

Khishfe, R. (2012). Relationship between nature of science understandings and argumentation skills: A role for counterargument and contextual factors. *Journal of Research in Science Teaching, 49*(4), 489–514.

Khishfe, R., & Abd-El-Khalick, F. (2002). Influence of explicit reflective versus implicit inquiry-oriented instruction on sixth graders' views of nature of science. *Journal of Research in Science Teaching, 39*(7), 551–578.

Kim, S. Y., & Irving, K. E. (2010). History of science as an instructional context: Student learning in genetics and nature of science. *Science & Education, 19,* 187–215.

Kim, S. Y., & Nehm, R. H. (2011). Sun Young & Ross H.: A cross-cultural comparison of Korean and American science teachers' views of evolution and the nature of science. *International Journal of Science Education, 33*(2), 197–227.

Kimball, M. E. (1967–1968). Understanding the nature of science: A comparison of scientists and science teachers. *Journal of Research in Science Teaching, 5,* 110–120.

Klopfer, L. E., & Cooley, W. W. (1963). The *history of science cases for high schools* in the development of student understanding of science and scientists: A report on the HOSC instruction project. *Journal of Research in Science Teaching, 1*(1), 33–47.

Kokkotas, P., Piliouras, P., Malamitsa, K., & Stamoulis, E. (2009). Teaching physics to in-service primary schools teachers in the context of the history of science: The case of falling bodies. *Science & Education, 18,* 609–629.

Korth, W. W. (1968). *The use of history of science to promote student's understanding of the social aspects of science.* Unpublished doctoral dissertation, Stanford University, Stanford, California.

Korth, W. W. (1969, February). *Test every senior project: Understanding the social aspects of science.* Paper presented at the annual meeting of the National Association for Research in Science Teaching, Pasadena, CA. (ERIC Document Reproduction Service No. ED 028 087)

Koulaidis, V., & Ogborn, J. (1988). Use of systemic networks in the development of a questionnaire. *International Journal of Science Education, 10*(5), 497–509.

Koulaidis, V., & Ogborn, J. (1989). Philosophy of science: An empirical-study of teachers views. *International Journal of Science Education, 11*(2), 173–184.

Koulaidis, V., & Ogborn, J. (1995). Science teachers philosophical assumptions: How well do we understand them? *International Journal of Science Education, 17*(3), 273–283.

Krockover, G. H. (1971). Individualizing secondary school chemistry instruction. *School Science and Mathematics, 71*(6), 518–524.

Kucuk, M. (2008). Improving preservice elementary teachers' views of the nature of science using explicit-reflective teaching in a science, technology and society course. *Australian Journal of Teacher Education, 33*(2). Retrieved from http://ro.ecu.edu.au/ajte/vol33/iss2/1/

Kuhn, T. S. (1996). *The structure of scientific revolutions* (3rd ed.). Chicago: University of Chicago Press. (First published 1962)

Lachman, S. J. (1960). *The foundations of science.* New York: Vantage.

Laforgia, J. (1988). The affective domain related to science education and its evaluation. *Science Education, 72*(4), 407–421.

Lakatos, I. (1970). Falsification and the methodology of scientific research programmes. In I. Lakatos & A. Musgrave (Eds.), *Criticism and the growth of knowledge* (pp. 91–195). New York: Cambridge University Press.

Lakin, S., & Wellington, J. (1994). Who will teach the "nature of science"? Teachers' views of science and their implications for science education. *International Journal of Science Education, 16*(2), 175–190.

Laudan, L., Donovan, A., Laudan, R., Barker, P., Brown, H., Leplin, J., Thagard, P., & Wykstra, S. (1986). Scientific change: Philosophical models and historical research. *Synthese, 69,* 141–223.

Lavach, J. F. (1969). Organization and evaluation of an in-service program in the history of science. *Journal of Research in Science Teaching, 6,* 166–170.

Lawrenz, F. (1975). The relationship between science teacher characteristics and student achievement and attitude. *Journal of Research in Science Teaching, 12*(4), 433–437.

Lawrenz, F., & Cohen, H. (1985). The effect of methods classes and practice teaching on student attitudes toward science and knowledge of science processes. *Science Education, 69*(1), 105–113.

Lawson, A. E., Nordland, F. H., & DeVito, A. (1975). Relationship of formal reasoning to achievement, aptitudes, and attitudes in preservice teachers. *Journal of Research in Science Teaching, 4,* 423–431.

Leach, J., Millar, R., Ryder, J., & Séré, M.-G. (2000). Epistemological understanding in science learning: The consistency of representations across contexts. *Learning and Instruction, 10,* 497–527.

Leake, J. B., & Hinerman, C. O. (1973). Scientific literacy and school characteristics. *School Science and Mathematics, 73*(9), 772–782.

Leblebicioğlu, G., Metin, D., Yardimci, E., & Berkyürek, I. (2011). Teaching the nature of science in the nature: A summer science camp. *Elementary Education Online, 10*(3), 1037–1055.

Leblebicioğlu, G., Metin, D., Yardimci, E., & Cetin, P. S. (2011). The effect of informal and formal interaction between scientists and children at a science camp on their images of scientists. *Science Education International, 22*(3), 158–174.

Lederman, J. S., & Khishfe, R. (2002). *Views of nature of science, Form D.* Unpublished paper. Illinois Institute of Technology, Chicago, IL.

Lederman, J. S., & Ko, E. K. (2002). *Views of nature of science, Form E.* Unpublished paper. Illinois Institute of Technology, Chicago, IL.

Lederman, N. G. (1986a). Relating teacher behavior and classroom climate to changes in students' conceptions of the nature of science. *Science Education, 70*(1), 3–19.

Lederman, N. G. (1986b). Students' and teachers' understanding of the nature of science: A reassessment. *School Science and Mathematics, 86*(2), 91–99.

Lederman, N. G. (1992). Students' and teachers' conceptions of the nature of science: A review of the research. *Journal of Research in Science Teaching, 29*(4), 331–359.

Lederman, N. G. (1999). Teachers' understanding of the nature of science and classroom practice: Factors that facilitate or impede the relationship. *Journal of Research in Science Teaching, 36,* 916–929.

Lederman, N. G. (2007). Nature of science: Past, present, and future. In S. K. Abell & N. G. Lederman (Eds.), *Handbook of research on science education* (pp. 831–879). Mahwah, NJ: Lawrence Erlbaum.

Lederman, N. G., Abd-El-Khalick, F., Bell, R. L., & Schwartz, R. (2002). Views of nature of science questionnaire (VNOS): Toward valid and meaningful assessment of learners' conceptions of nature of science. *Journal of Research in Science Teaching, 39*(6), 497–521.

Lederman, N. G., & Druger, M. (1985). Classroom factors related to changes in students' conceptions of the nature of science. *Journal of Research in Science Teaching, 22*(7), 649–662.

Lederman, N. G., & O'Malley, M. (1990). Students' perceptions of tentativeness in science: Development, use, and sources of change. *Science Education, 74*, 225–239.

Lederman, N. G., Schwartz, R., Abd-El-Khalick, F., & Bell, R. L. (2001). Preservice teachers' understanding and teaching of nature of science: An intervention study. *Canadian Journal of Science, Mathematics and Technology Education, 1*(2), 135–160.

Lederman, N. G., Wade, P., & Bell, R. (1998). Assessing the nature of science: What is the nature of our assessments? *Science and Education, 7*, 595–615.

Lederman, N. G., & Zeidler, D. L. (1987). Science teachers' conceptions of the nature of science: Do they really influence teaching behavior? *Science Education, 71*(5), 721–734.

Liang, L. L., Chen, S., Chen, X., Kaya, O. N., Adams, A. D., Macklin, M., & Ebenezer, J. (2006, April). *Student understanding of science and scientific inquiry (SUSSI): Revision and further validation of an assessment instrument.* Paper presented at the annual meeting of the National Association for Research in Science Teaching, San Francisco, CA.

Liang, L. L., Chen, S., Chen, X., Kaya, O. N., Adams, A. D., Macklin, M., & Ebenezer, J. (2008). Assessing preservice elementary teachers' views on the nature of scientific knowledge: A dual-response instrument. *Asia-Pacific Forum on Science Learning and Teaching, 9*(1). Retrieved from www.ied.edu.hk/apfslt/v9_issue1/liang/liang3.htm

Liang, L. L., Chen, S., Chen, X., Kaya, O. N., Adams, A. D., Macklin, M., & Ebenezer, J. (2009). Preservice teachers' views about nature of scientific knowledge development: An international collaborative study. *International Journal of Science and Mathematics Education, 7*, 987–1012.

Lin, C. C., & Tsai, C. C. (2008). Exploring the structural relationships between high school students' scientific epistemological views and their utilization of information commitments toward online science information. *International Journal of Science Education, 30*(15), 2001–2022.

Lin, H. S., & Chen, C. C. (2002). Promoting preservice chemistry teachers' understanding about the nature of science through history. *Journal of Research in Science Teaching, 39*(9), 773–792.

Lin, H. S., & Chiu, H. L. (2004). Student understanding of the nature of science and their problem-solving strategies. *International Journal of Science Education, 26*(1), 101–112.

Liu, S. Y., & Lederman, N. G. (2007). Exploring prospective teachers' worldviews and conceptions of nature of science. *International Journal of Science Education, 29*(10), 1281–1307.

Liu, S. Y., Lin, C. S., & Tsai, C. C. (2011). College students' scientific epistemological views and thinking patterns in socioscientific decision making. *Science Education, 95*(3), 497–517.

Liu, S. Y., & Tsai, C. C. (2008). Differences in the scientific epistemological views of undergraduate students. *International Journal of Science Education, 30*(8), 1055–1073.

Lombrozo, T., Thanukos, A., & Weisberg, M. (2008). The importance of understanding the nature of science for accepting evolution. *Evolution: Education and Outreach, 1*, 290–298.

Lonsbury, J. G., & Ellis, J. D. (2002). Science history as a means to teach nature of science concepts: Using the development of understanding related to mechanisms of inheritance. *Electronic Journal of Science Education, 7*(2). Retrieved from http://ejse.southwestern.edu/article/view/7703/5470

Loving, C. C. (1997). From the summit of truth to its slippery slopes: Science education's journey through positivist-postmodern territory. *American Educational Research Journal, 34*(3), 421–452.

Lowery, L. F. (1967). An experimental investigation into the attitudes of fifth grade students toward science. *School Science and Mathematics, 67*, 569–579.

Mackay, L. D. (1971). Development of understanding about the nature of science. *Journal of Research in Science Teaching, 8*(1), 57–66.

Mackay, L. D., & White, R. T. (1974). Development of an alternative to Likert scaling: Tests of perceptions of scientists and self (TOPOSS). *Research in Science Education, 4*(1), 131–139.

Marbach-Ad, G., McGinnis, J. R., Dai, A. H., Pease, R., Schalk, K. A., & Benson, S. (2009). Promoting science for all by way of student interest in a transformative undergraduate microbiology laboratory for nonmajors. *Journal of Microbiology & Biology Education, 10*, 58–67.

Marchlewicz, S. C., & Wink, D. J. (2011). Using the activity model of inquiry to enhance general chemistry students' understanding of nature of science. *Journal of Chemical Education, 88*, 1041–1047.

Markle, G., & Capie, W. (1977). Assessing a competency-based physics course: A model for evaluating science courses serving elementary teachers. *Journal of Research in Science Teaching, 14*(2), 151–156.

Mayer, V. J., & Richmond, J. M. (1982). An overview of assessment instruments in science. *Science Education, 66*(1), 49–66.

Mbajiorgu, N. M., & Ali, A. (2003). Relationship between STS approach, scientific literacy, and achievement in biology. *Science Education, 87*, 31–39.

McComas, W. F., & Olson J. K. (1998). The nature of science in international science education standards documents. In W. F. McComas (Ed.), *The nature of science in science education: Rationales and strategies* (pp. 41–52). Dordrecht, the Netherlands: Kluwer.

McDonald, C. V. (2010). The influence of explicit nature of science and argumentation instruction on preservice primary teachers' views of nature of science. *Journal of Research in Science Teaching, 47*(9), 1137–1164.

Mead, M., & Métraux, R. (1957). Image of the scientist among high-school students: A pilot study. *Science, 126*, 384–390.

Meichtry, Y. J. (1992). Influencing student understanding of the nature of science: Data from a case of curriculum development. *Journal of Research in Science Teaching, 29*(4), 389–407.

Mellado, V. (1997). Preservice teachers' classroom practice and their conceptions of the nature of science. *Science & Education, 6*, 331–354.

Metin, D., & Leblebicioğlu, G. (2011). How did a science camp affect children's conceptions of science? *Asia-Pacific Forum on Science Learning and Teaching, 12*(1). Retrieved from www.ied.edu.hk/apfslt/v12_issue1/kilic/index.htm

Metin, D., & Leblebicioğlu, G. (2012). Effect of a science camp on the children's views of tentative nature of science. *Journal of Studies in Education, 2*(1). Retrieved from www.macrothink.org/journal/index.php/jse/article/view/1348

Meyer, J. H. (1969). The influence of the invitations to enquiry. *The American Biology Teacher, 31*(7), 451–453.

Miller, M. C. D., Montplaisir, L. M., Offerdahl, E. G., Cheng, F. C., & Ketterling, G. L. (2010). Comparison of views of the nature of science between natural science and nonscience majors. *CBE Life Sciences Education, 9*, 45–54.

Moore, R., & Sutman, F. (1970). The development of field test and validation of an inventory of scientific attitudes. *Journal of Research in Science Teaching, 7*, 85–94.

Munby, H. (1982). The impropriety of "panel of judges" validation in science attitude scales. *Journal of Research in Science Teaching, 19*, 617–619.

Murcia, K., & Schibeci, R. (1999). Primary student teachers' conceptions of the nature of science. *International Journal of Science Education, 21*(11), 1123–1140.

Musgrave, A. (1998). Realism versus constructive empiricism. In M. Curd & J. A. Cover (Eds.), *Philosophy of science: The central issues* (pp. 1088–1113). New York: Norton.

Nalçaci, G. Ö., Akarsu, B., & Kariper, A. I (2011). Effects of the nature of science course on science prospective teachers' knowledge and opinions. *Ahmet Kelepoðlu Journal of Education, 32*, 337–352.

National Research Council (NRC). (1996). *National science education standards.* Washington, DC: National Academies Press.

Neumann, I., Neumann, K., & Nehm, R. (2011). Evaluating instrument quality in science education: Rasch-based analyses of a nature of science test. *International Journal of Science Education, 33*(10), 1373–1405.

NGSS Lead States. (2013). *Next generation science standards: For states, by states.* Washington, DC: National Academies Press.

Nott, M., & Wellington, J. (1995). Critical incidents in the science classroom and the nature of science. *School Science Review, 76,* 41–46.

Nott, M., & Wellington, J. (1995b). Probing teachers' views of the nature of science: How should we do it and where should we be looking? In F. Finley et al. (Eds.), *Proceedings of the Third International History, Philosophy, and Science Teaching Conference* (Vol. 2, pp. 864–872). Minneapolis: University of Minnesota.

Nott, M., & Wellington, J. (1996). When the black box springs open: Practical work in school science and the nature of science. *International Journal of Science Education, 18*(7), 807–818.

Nott, M., & Wellington, J. (1998). Eliciting, interpreting and developing teachers' understandings of the nature of science. *Science & Education, 7,* 579–594.

Ogunniyi, M.B. (1982). An analysis of prospective science teachers' understanding of the nature of science. *Journal of Research in Science Teaching, 19*(1), 25–32.

Ogunniyi, M.B. (1983). Relative effects of a history/philosophy of science course on student teachers' performance on two models of science. *Research in Science & Technological Education, 1*(2), 193–199.

O'Hear, A. (1989). *An introduction to the philosophy of science.* New York: Oxford University Press.

Olstad, R.G. (1969). The effect of science teaching methods on the understanding of science. *Science Education, 53*(1), 9–11.

Orgren, J., & Doran, R.L. (1975). The effects of adopting the revised New York state regents earth science syllabus on selected teacher and student variables. *Journal of Research in Science Teaching, 12*(1), 15–24.

Osborne, J., Collins, S., Ratcliffe, M., Millar, R., & Duschl, R. (2003). What "ideas-about science" should be taught in school science? A Delphi study of the expert community. *Journal of Research in Science Teaching, 40*(7), 692–720.

Osborne, J., Simon, S., & Collins, S. (2003). Attitudes toward science: A review of the literature and its implications. *International Journal of Science Education, 25*(9), 1049–1079.

Oskay, Ö. Ö., Yilmaz, A., Dinçol, S., & Erdem, A. (2011). Determination of relationship between prospective chemistry teachers' scientific epistemological views, information commitments and online searching achievement. *Procedia Social and Behavioral Sciences, 15,* 3484–3489.

Pearl, R.E. (1974). The present status of science attitude measurement: History, theory, and availability of measurement. *School Science and Mathematics, 74*(5), 375–381.

Pegg, J., & Gummer, E. (2010). The influence of a multidisciplinary scientific research experience on teachers views of nature of science. *The Montana Mathematics Enthusiast, 7*(2 & 3), 447–460.

Pella, M.O., O'Hearn, G.T., & Gale, C.W. (1966). Referents to scientific literacy. *Journal of Research in Science Teaching, 4,* 199–208.

Pomeroy, D. (1993). Implications of teachers' beliefs about the nature of science: Comparison of the beliefs of scientists, secondary science teachers, and elementary teachers. *Science Education, 77,* 261–278.

Popper, K.R. (1963). *Conjectures and refutations: The growth of scientific knowledge.* London, UK: Routledge & Kegan Paul.

Posnanski, T.J. (2010). Developing understanding of the nature of science within a professional development program for inservice elementary teachers: Project nature of elementary science teaching. *Journal of Science Teacher Education, 21,* 589–621.

Quigley, C., Pongsanon, K., & Akerson, V.L. (2010). If we teach them, they can learn: Young students' views of nature of science aspects to early elementary students during an informal science education program. *Journal of Science Teacher Education, 21,* 887–907.

Quigley, C., Pongsanon, K., & Akerson, V.L. (2011). If we teach them, they can learn: Young students' views of nature of science during an informal science education program. *Journal of Science Teacher Education, 22,* 129–149.

Rampal, A. (1992). Images of science and scientists: A study of school teachers' views. I. Characteristics of scientists. *Science Education, 76*(4), 415–436.

Riban, D.B. (1976). Examination of a model for field studies in science. *Science Education, 60*(1), 1–11.

Riban, D.B., & Koval, D.B. (1971). An investigation of the effect of field studies in science on the learning of the methodology of science. *Science Education, 55*(3), 291–294.

Richardson, J.S., & Showalter, V. (1967). *Effects of a unified science curriculum on high school graduates.* Columbus: Ohio State University. (ERIC Document Reproduction Service No. 024 593)

Riley, J.P., II (1979). The influence of hands-on science process training on preservice teachers' acquisition of process skills and attitude toward science and science teaching. *Journal of Research in Science Teaching, 16*(5), 373–384.

Rivers, R.H., & Vockell, E. (1987). Computer simulations to stimulate scientific problem solving. *Journal of Research in Science Teaching, 24*(5), 403–415.

Roehrig, G.H., & Luft, J.A. (2004). Constraints experienced by beginning secondary science teachers in implementing scientific inquiry lessons. *International Journal of Science Education, 26*(1), 3–24.

Rosenberg, A. (2005). *Philosophy of science: A contemporary introduction* (2nd ed.). New York: Routledge.

Rothman, A.I. (1969). Teacher characteristics and student learning. *Journal of Research in Science Teaching, 6,* 340–348.

Rothman, A.I., Welch, W.W., & Walberg, H.J. (1969). Physics teacher characteristics and student learning. *Journal of Research in Science Teaching, 6,* 59–63.

Rubba, P. (1976). *Nature of scientific knowledge scale.* Bloomington: School of Education, Indiana University.

Rubba, P. (1977). *The development, field testing, and validation of an instrument to assess secondary school students' understanding of the nature of scientific knowledge.* Unpublished doctoral dissertation, Indiana University, Bloomington, IN.

Rubba, P., & Harkness, W.L. (1993). Examination of preservice and inservice secondary science teachers' beliefs about science-technology-society interactions. *Science Education, 77*(4), 407–431.

Rubba, P.A., & Andersen, H. (1978). Development of an instrument to assess secondary school students' understanding of the nature of scientific knowledge. *Science Education, 62*(4), 449–458.

Rubba, P.A., Horner, J.K., & Smith, J.M. (1981). A study of two misconceptions about the nature of science among junior high school students. *School Science and Mathematics, 81*(3), 221–226.

Rudge, D.W., Cassidy, D.P., Fulford, J.M., & Howe, E.M. (2013). Changes observed in views of nature of science during a historically based unit. *Science & Education.* doi:10.1007/s11191-012-9572-3

Rudolph, J.L. (2000). Reconsidering the "nature of science" as a curriculum component. *Journal of Curriculum Studies, 32*(3), 403–419.

Russell, C.B., & Weaver, G.C. (2011). A comparative study of traditional, inquiry-based, and research-based laboratory curricula: Impacts on understanding of the nature of science. *Chemistry Education Research and Practice, 12,* 57–67.

Russell, T., & Aydeniz, M. (2012). Traversing the divide between high school science students and sophisticated nature of science understandings: A multi-pronged approach. *Journal of Science Education and Technology.* doi:10.1007/s10956-012-9412-x

Ryan, A.G., & Aikenhead, G.S. (1992). Students' preconceptions about the epistemology of science. *Science Education, 76,* 559–580.

Ryder, J., Leach, J., & Driver, R. (1999). Undergraduate science students' images of science. *Journal of Research in Science Teaching, 36*(2), 201–219.

Salloum, S., & Abd-El-Khalick, F. (2010). A study of practical-moral knowledge in science teaching: Case studies in physical science classrooms. *Journal of Research in Science Teaching, 47*(8), 929–951.

Sandoval, W.A., & Morrison, K. (2003). High school students' ideas about theories and theory change after a biological inquiry unit. *Journal of Research in Science Teaching, 40*(4), 369–392.

Sarkar, M.A., & Gomes, J.J. (2010). Science teachers' conceptions of nature of science: The case of Bangladesh. *Asia-Pacific Forum on Science Learning and Teaching, 11*(1). Retrieved from www.ied.edu.hk/apfslt/

Scharmann, L.C. (1988a). Locus of control: A discriminator of the ability to foster an understanding of the nature of science among preservice elementary teachers. *Science Education, 72*(4), 453–465.

Scharmann, L.C. (1988b). The influence of sequenced instructional strategy and locus of control on preservice elementary teachers' understandings of the nature of science. *Journal of Research in Science Teaching, 25*(7), 589–604.

Scharmann, L.C. (1989). Developmental influences of science process skill instruction. *Journal of Research in Science Teaching, 26*(8), 715–726.

Scharmann, L.C. (1990). Enhancing the understanding of the premises of evolutionary theory: The influence of diversified instructional strategy. *School Science and Mathematics, 90*(2), 91–100.

Scharmann, L.C. (1994). Teaching evolution: The influence of peer teachers' instructional modeling. *Journal of Science Teacher Education, 5*(2), 66–76.

Scharmann, L.C., & Harris, W.M., Jr. (1992). Teaching evolution: Understanding and applying the nature of science. *Journal of Research in Science Teaching, 29*(4), 375–388.

Schwartz, R.S., & Lederman, N.G. (2002). "It's the nature of the beast": The influence of knowledge and intentions on learning and teaching nature of science. *Journal of Research in Science Teaching, 39*(3), 205–236.

Schwartz, R.S., Lederman, N.G., & Crawford, B.A. (2004). Developing views of nature of science in an authentic context: An explicit approach to bridging the gap between nature of science and scientific inquiry. *Science Education, 88*, 610–645.

Schwartz, R.S., Westerlund, J.F., Garcìa, D.M., & Taylor, T.A. (2010). The impact of full immersion scientific research experiences on teachers' views of the nature of science. *Electronic Journal of Science Education, 14*(1). Retrieved from http://ejse.southwestern.edu/article/view/7325

Schwirian, P.A. (1968). On measuring attitudes toward science. *Science Education, 52*(2), 172–179.

Schwirian, P.A. (1969). Characteristics of elementary teachers related to attitudes toward science. *Journal of Research in Science Teaching, 6*(3), 203–213.

Schwirian, P.A., & Thomson, B. (1972). Changing attitudes toward science: Undergraduates in 1967 and 1971. *Journal of Research in Science Teaching, 9*(3), 253–259.

Scientific Literacy Research Center. (1967). *Wisconsin inventory of science processes*. Madison: University of Wisconsin.

Seker, H., & Welsh, L.C. (2006). The use of history of mechanics in teaching motion and force units. *Science & Education, 15*, 55–89.

Shim, M.K., Young, B.J., & Paolucci, J. (2010). Elementary teachers' views on the nature of scientific knowledge: A comparison of inservice and preservice teachers approach. *Electronic Journal of Science Education, 14*(1). Retrieved from http://ejse.southwestern.edu/article/view/7335/5619

Simpson, R.D., Shrum, J.W., & Rentz, R. (1972). The science support scale: Its appropriateness with high school students. *Journal of Research in Science Teaching, 9*(2), 123–126.

Simpson, R.D., & Wasik, J.L. (1978). Correlation of selected affective behaviors with cognitive performance in a biology course for elementary teachers. *Journal of Research in Science Teaching, 15*(1), 65–71.

Smith, M.U., Lederman, N.G., Bell, R.L., McComas, W.F., & Clough, M.P. (1997). How great is the disagreement about the nature of science: A response to Alters. *Journal of Research in Science Teaching, 34*(10), 1101–1103.

Spears, J., & Zollman, D. (1977). The influence of structured versus unstructured laboratory on students' understanding the process of science. *Journal of Research in Science Teaching, 14*(1), 33–38.

Spears, J.D., & Hathaway, C.E. (1975). Student attitudes toward science and society. *American Journal of Physics, 43*(4), 343–348.

Starr, R.J. (1972). A study of invitations to enquiry and their effect on student knowledge of science processes. *School Science and Mathematics, 72*(8), 714–717.

Stice, G. (1958). *Facts about science test*. Princeton, NJ: Educational Testing Service.

Sutherland, D., & Dennick, R. (2002). Exploring culture, language and the perception of the nature of science. *International Journal of Science Education, 24*(1), 1–25.

Swan, M.D. (1966). Science achievement as it relates to science curricula and programs at the sixth grade level in Montana public schools. *Journal of Research in Science Teaching, 4*, 112–123.

Symington, D.J., & Fensham, P.J. (1976). Elementary school teachers' closed-mindedness, attitudes toward science, and congruence with a new curriculum. *Journal of Research in Science Teaching, 13*(5), 441–447.

Tamir, P. (1972). Understanding the process of science by students exposed to different science curricula in Israel. *Journal of Research in Science Teaching, 9*(3), 239–245.

Tamir, P. (1994). Israeli students' conceptions of science and views about the scientific enterprise. *Research in Science & Technological Education, 12*(2), 99–116.

Tamir, P., & Jungwirth, E. (1975). Students' growth as a result of studying BSCS biology for several years. *Journal of Research in Science Teaching, 12*(3), 263–279.

Tasar, M.F. (2006). Probing preservice teachers' understandings of scientific knowledge by using a vignette in conjunction with a paper and pencil test. *Eurasia Journal of Mathematics, Science and Technology Education, 2*(1), 53–70.

Thye, T.L., & Kwen, B.H. (2004). Assessing the nature of science views of Singaporean pre-service teachers. *Australian Journal of Teacher Education, 29*(2). Retrieved from http://ro.ecu.edu.au/ajte/vol29/iss2/1/

Trembath, R.J. (1972). The structure of science. *The Australian Science Teachers Journal, 18*(2), 59–63.

Trent, J. (1965). The attainment of the concept "understanding science" using contrasting physics courses. *Journal of Research in Science Teaching, 3*, 224–229.

Tsai, C.C. (2007). Teachers' scientific epistemological views: The coherence with instruction and students' views. *Science Education, 91*(2), 222–243.

Tsai, C.C., & Liang, J.C. (2009). The development of science activities via on-line peer assessment: The role of scientific epistemological views. *Instructional Science, 37*(3), 293–310.

Tsai, C.C., & Liu, S.Y. (2005). Developing a multi-dimensional instrument for assessing students' epistemological views toward science. *International Journal of Science Education, 27*(13), 1621–1638.

Turgut, H. (2011). The context of demarcation in nature of science teaching: The case of astrology. *Science & Education, 20*, 491–515.

Urhahne, D., Kremer, K., & Mayer, J. (2011). Conceptions of the nature of science—are they general or context specific? *International Journal of Science and Mathematics Education, 9*, 707–730.

van Fraassen, B.C. (1980). *The scientific image*. Oxford, UK: Oxford University Press.

van Fraassen, B.C. (1998). Arguments concerning scientific realism. In M. Curd & J.A. Cover (Eds.), *Philosophy of science: The central issues* (pp. 1064–1087). New York: Norton.

Vesterinen, V.-M., & Aksela, M. (2012). Design of chemistry teacher education course on nature of science. *Science & Education, 22*: 2193–2225. doi:10.1007/s11191-012-9506-0

Voss, B.E. (1965). "Great Experiments in Biology"—A summer program for academically talented high school students. *The American Biology Teacher, 27*(4), 257–259.

Wahbeh, N., & Abd-El-Khalick, F. (2013). Revisiting the translation of nature of science understandings into instructional practice: Teachers' nature of science pedagogical context knowledge. *International Journal of Science Education, 36*(3): 425–466. doi:10.1080/09500693.2013.786852

Walberg, H.J. (1969). Physics, femininity, and creativity. *Developmental Psychology, 1*(2), 47–54.

Walczak, M. M., & Walczak, D. E. (2009). Do student attitudes toward science change during a general education chemistry course? *Chemical Education Research, 86*(8), 985–991.

Walker, K. A., & Zeidler, D. L. (2007). Promoting discourse about socio-scientific issues through scaffolded inquiry. *International Journal of Science Education, 29*(11), 1387–1410.

Walls, L. (2012). Third grade African American students' views of the nature of science. *Journal of Research in Science Teaching, 49*(1), 1–37.

Welch, W. W. (1966a). *The development of an instrument for inventorying knowledge of the processes of science.* Unpublished doctoral dissertation, University of Wisconsin, Madison.

Welch, W. W. (1966b). *Welch science process inventory (form D).* Madison, WI: Author.

Welch, W. W. (1969). Correlates of courses satisfaction in high school physics. *Journal of Research in Science Teaching, 6,* 54–58.

Welch, W. W. (1972). Evaluation of the PSNS course. I: Design and implementation. *Journal of Research in Science Teaching, 9*(2), 139–145.

Welch, W. W. (1980). A possible explanation for declining test scores or learning less science but enjoying it more. *School Science and Mathematics, 80*(1), 22–28.

Welch, W. W., & Lawrenz, F. (1982). Characteristics of male and female science teachers. *Journal of Research in Science Teaching, 19*(7), 587–594.

Welch, W. W., & Pella, M. O. (1967). The development of an instrument for inventorying knowledge of the processes of science. *Journal of Research on Science Teaching, 5,* 64–68.

Welch, W. W., & Rothman, A. I. (1968). The success of recruited students in a new physics course. *Science Education, 52*(3), 270–273.

Welch, W. W., & Walberg, H. J. (1967–1968). An evaluation of summer institute programs for physics teachers. *Journal of Research in Science Teaching, 5,* 105–109.

Welch, W. W., & Walberg, H. J. (1970). Pretest and sensitization effects in curriculum evaluation. *American Educational Research Journal, 7*(4), 605–614.

Welch, W. W., & Walberg, H. J. (1972). A national experiment in curriculum evaluation. *American Educational Research Journal, 9*(3), 373–383.

Wilson, L. L. (1954). A study of opinions related to the nature of science and its purpose in society. *Science Education, 38*(2), 159–164.

Windschitl, M. (2004). Folk theories of "inquiry": How preservice teachers reproduce the discourse and practices of an theoretical scientific method. *Journal of Research in Science Teaching, 41*(5), 481–512.

Wong, S. L., & Hodson, D. (2009). From the horse's mouth: What scientists say about scientific investigation and scientific knowledge. *Science Education, 93,* 109–130.

Wong, S. L., & Hodson, D. (2010). More from the horse's mouth: What scientists say about science as a social practice. *International Journal of Science Education, 32*(11), 1431–1463.

Wong, S. L., Hodson, D., Kwan, J., & Yung, B. H. W. (2008). Turning crisis into opportunity: Enhancing student-teachers' understanding of nature of science and scientific inquiry through a case study of the scientific research in severe acute respiratory syndrome. *International Journal of Science Education, 30*(11), 1417–1439.

Wood, R. L. (1972). University education students' understanding of the nature and processes of science. *School Science and Mathematics, 72*(1), 73–79.

Yacoubian, H. A., & BouJaoude, S. (2010). The effect of reflective discussions following inquiry-based laboratory activities on students' views of nature of science. *Journal of Research in Science Teaching, 47*(10), 1229–1252.

Yager, R. E. (1968). Critical thinking and reference materials in the physical science classroom. *School Science and Mathematics, 68*(8), 743–746.

Yager, R. E., & Wick, J. W. (1966). Three emphases in teaching biology—a statistical comparison of results. *Journal of Research in Science Teaching, 4,* 16–20.

Yalçinoğlu, P., & Anagün, S. S. (2012). Teaching nature of science by explicit approach to the preservice elementary science teachers. *Elementary Education Online, 11*(1), 118–136.

Yalvac, B., Tekkaya, C., Cakiroglu, J., & Kahyaoglu, E. (2007). Turkish pre-service science teachers' views on science–technology–society issues. *International Journal of Science Education, 29*(3), 331–348.

Zeidler, D. L., & Lederman, N. G. (1989). The effect of teachers' language on students' conceptions of the nature of science. *Journal of Research in Science Teaching, 26*(9), 771–783.

Zimmermann, E., & Gilbert, J. K. (1998). Contradictory views of the nature of science held by a Brazilian secondary school physics teacher: Educational value of interviews. *Educational Research and Evaluation: An International Journal on Theory and Practice, 4*(3), 213–234.

Zingaro, J. S., & Collette, A. T. (1967–1968). A statistical comparison between inductive and traditional laboratories in college physical science. *Journal of Research in Science Teaching, 5,* 269–275.

Zoller, U., & Ben-Chaim, D. (1994). Views of prospective teachers versus practising teachers about science, technology and society issues. *Research in Science & Technological Education, 12*(1), 77–89.

Zoller, U., Donn, S., Wild, R., & Beckett, P. (1991a). Students' versus their teachers' beliefs and positions on science/technology/society-oriented issues. *International Journal of Science Education, 13*(1), 25–36.

Zoller, U., Donn, S., Wild, R., & Beckett, P. (1991b). Teachers' beliefs about views on selected science-technology-society topics: A probe into STS literacy versus indoctrination. *Science Education, 75*(5), 541–561.

Zoller, U., Ebenezer, J., Morley, K., Paras, S., Sandberg, V., West, C., Wolthers, T., & Tan, S. H. (1990). Goal attainment in science-technology-society (S/T/S) education and reality: The case of British Columbia. *Science Education, 74*(1), 19–36.

32

Cultural Perspectives in Science Education

Heidi B. Carlone, Angela Johnson, and Margaret Eisenhart

If research literature in science education in the past three decades has taught us anything, it is that science and science teaching and learning are cultural endeavors. A few key movements in science education set the stage for its cultural turn—science and technology studies, sociocultural theories of learning, and a push for "science for all" in reform documents of the early and mid 1990s. First, science and technology studies in the 1980s and 1990s highlighted the distinctive culture of science and scientists and emphasized science as socially and culturally constructed (Collins, 1982; Latour & Woolgar, 1986; Traweek, 1988). This body of work revealed how scientific procedures and findings are produced in the course of ongoing social relationships and work activities rather than being "found" or "discovered" in nature. It also revealed that science's fundamental practices, ways of knowing, and assumptions about the natural world are reflective of a male-dominated, Eurocentric, and middle-class context in which science practices developed (Hammond & Brandt, 2004). By identifying the values, beliefs, politics, and human relationships intertwined in the production of scientific knowledge, science and technology studies humanized science, problematizing popular perceptions of scientific knowledge as objective, neutral, and replicable, challenging the scientific method as inviolable and unbiased, and expanding the image of scientists as hyperrational, linear thinkers and usually men (Cunningham & Helms, 1998). Science educators used this work to depict science as a "foreign culture" (Aikenhead, 2006); to justify ethnographic studies of actual science practices in laboratories, classrooms, and elsewhere (Kelly, Chen, & Crawford, 1998); and to work toward new reforms of school science that emphasized its messiness, ambiguity, social embeddedness, and human nature in an effort to make it more accessible and inclusive (Cunningham & Helms, 1998).

Second, the rise of sociocultural theories of learning in the early 1990s (Brown, Collins, & Duguid, 1989; Chaiklin & Lave, 1993; Cobb, 1994; Lave & Wenger, 1991) challenged cognitive learning theories and opened the door for thinking about science learning as situated and cultural. This research drew attention to the many ways that context—including cognitive but also material, historical, and social resources—shapes the practices, activities, tools, and inscriptions of learning. This view of learning required a unit of analysis larger than the individual and pushed the field of science education beyond theories of conceptual change and constructivism. Some science education researchers working in the sociocultural tradition reframed learning as a form of gradually increased participation in authentic activities as novices or newcomers moved toward more central aspects of the scientific community of practice (Lave & Wenger, 1991). Some translated these ideas into apprenticeship programs that, for example, enabled students to learn at the "elbows" of real scientists (Barab & Hay, 2001). Others gave considerable weight to the role of social interaction, seeing it as a central rather than corollary aspect of science learning (Lemke, 1990). Science educators merged insights from science and technology studies with insights from situated learning to focus on how learners took up discipline-based practices, or the socially learned cultural traditions of science, including its discourses and representations (Lemke, 2001). Ethnographic and discourse studies of science classrooms examined disciplinary knowledge as a locally emergent and situated construction, co-created and reinforced by social practices established by classroom members over time (Kelly & Chen, 2001). More critical scholars in the sociocultural tradition pointed to the lack of consideration for human subjectivity and power relations inherent in school learning and asked hard-hitting questions like: How does science education literature account for the ways cultural processes of schooling make relevant people's positions in larger social structures? Whose interests are served by positioning science learning as an abstract, decontextualized, disembodied activity? (O'Loughlin, 1992).

The push for "science for all" in the early to mid-1990s highlighted the fact that, in North America at least, school performance and achievement in science are not equally distributed, with many students of color, indigenous students, and young women not interested and not participating in science. The publication of the National Research Council's (1996) *National Science Education Standards* elicited struggles around the meanings and goals of scientific literacy and equitable science education (Eisenhart, Finkel, & Marion, 1996; Rodriguez, 1997; Roth & Calabrese Barton, 2004). In this body of work, scholars questioned the "relevance"—or cultural appropriateness—of the science curriculum to students' interests, ideas, worldviews, lives, and futures, and also to "real" or "authentic" science (Aikenhead, 2006). Some worried that students from nondominant groups found science's practices or worldview contradictory to or in tension with their lives, identities, or future aspirations (Aikenhead, 2006). Others worried that, consistent with science and technology studies, students were being exposed to a simplified and inaccurate version of what science is. Viewing science learning as a process of cultural acquisition that may be supportive or disruptive led to a quest to reform science curriculum and teaching to be more culturally relevant to more students' lives. Scholars interested in aligning school science's practices with "real" science went in a slightly different direction, arguing for curriculum reform to promote a more accurate and nuanced approach to science education (Chinn & Malhotra, 2002). Both arguments—for a school science authentic to science and for a school science authentic to students—highlighted struggles around the meanings of science, school science, learning, and knowledge that sharpened the cultural turn in science education.

These movements—in science and technology studies, sociocultural theories of learning, and science for all—gave impetus to cultural perspectives in science education. In the last 20 years in particular, these views have gained momentum to the point that the field now has a journal of *Cultural Studies in Science Education*, founded in 2006 by Wolff-Michael Roth and Kenneth Tobin, and numerous special issues in mainstream journals have been devoted to cultural perspectives in science education (Brandt & Carlone, 2012; Calabrese Barton & Osborne, 1998; Chiu & Duit, 2011; O. Lee, 2001; Parsons & Carlone, 2013).

These theoretical approaches to understanding science and science education all rest on ideas about culture. However, there is wide variety in what researchers mean by "culture," as the term is used differently both within and across disciplines. This lack of clarity and precision is not a new problem. William Cobern and Glen Aikenhead pointed out in 1998 that "terms such as 'culture' and 'sociocultural' are found in the science education literature without a definition of what culture means in the context" (p. 39). Without clarity about what is meant by culture, theories and reforms based on it are difficult to use, apply, or evaluate.

In this chapter, we focus our attention on recent *anthropological* perspectives on culture.[1] Following Cobern and Aikenhead (1998), we argue that "cultural anthropology can provide fresh insights into familiar problems associated with students learning science" (p. 39) and culture, with "its focus on group-level, patterned behaviors and intersubjective meanings, helps us understand aspects of the human experience that stay hidden and therefore, more easily unquestioningly perpetuated, with an overemphasis on the individual" (Parsons & Carlone, 2013, p. 9). One of the first truly ethnographic studies in science education was Tobin and Gallagher's (1987) groundbreaking article titled simply *What Happens in High School Science Classrooms?* In this article, the authors examine taken-for-granted activity structures of high school science classrooms, the nature of academic work produced in the classroom, and the meanings of "curriculum" and "quality work" implied by the patterned activity structures and teachers' and students' engagement. The article was groundbreaking because it was one of the first to examine everyday practices and the taken-for-granted meanings of school science implied by them.

Anthropologists, of course, have long been focused on the concept of culture. Within anthropology, specialized definitions abound and debates continue to rage about their value and limitations. Yet in popular parlance, including among many educators, an understanding of culture as the distinctive characteristics of a socially recognized group remains widespread. Recent perspectives in anthropology challenge this classic and widely held view.

In this chapter, we will lay out—in rough historical order—a series of theoretical perspectives on what culture is and how it can be useful in studying science education. We present an overview of some insights that have arisen from these different perspectives, with a particular focus on equity and improving access for all kinds of people to high-quality science education. We intend for readers who are interested in one or more of the theoretical frameworks we describe to use this chapter as a starting point for understanding and making use of that framework. Our goal is that this chapter be of use both to those interested in various theoretical constructs of culture and to those interested in the insights into science education provided by anthropological approaches to culture.

Anthropological Perspectives on Culture

Culture, from a classic anthropological perspective, has been "defined as patterns in a way of life characteristic of a bounded social group and passed down from one generation to the next" (Eisenhart, 2001a, p. 210). Historically, anthropologists have focused on some aspect of communal life (e.g., uses of time, space, or language, beliefs and values, symbols, rituals, norms), looking for "culture as evidenced by patterns in the collective behaviors and central orientations of socially distinguishable groups" (Eisenhart, 2001a, p. 210).

Cultural Difference Theory

Cultural difference theory is one corollary of the classic definition. Cultural difference theory is based on the assumption that a group's patterned behavior emerges, over time, as a "successful adaptation to relatively stable social, economic, and political conditions" (Eisenhart, 2001a, p. 210) and "is learned through socialization in the home community" (p. 211). In this formulation of culture, a group's location in relation to larger social structures and environmental conditions gives rise to distinct patterns of behavior and thought, that is, to cultural differences. Cultural difference theory recognizes the internal integrity ("culture") of the beliefs, values, and activities of groups with differing historical, geographic, linguistic, religious, and ethnic backgrounds.

From the 1950s to the 1980s, many anthropologists of education examined the school experiences of students from culturally distinct groups. Based on fieldwork in the United States and Canada primarily, they argued that students from culturally nondominant (i.e., "nonmainstream") groups often struggled in school because they did not know or share the values, beliefs, and activities established as the norm for schools by dominant group ideals. Importantly, these researchers argued vehemently that this lack of knowledge was a "difference" but not a "deficit." Analogous to English speakers who have never encountered Spanish and thus have no means of learning how to speak or share it, culturally different children might have no means of learning how to "do school."

The implications of these findings were relatively straightforward: If teachers, parents, and students could identify the gaps and the misunderstandings the gaps created, steps could be taken to ease the transition to school for students from nondominant groups and lead them to better educational outcomes. Several prominent studies—for example, Heath (1983)—illustrated the potential in this approach.

Viewed in this way, the early version of cultural difference theory can be considered a benevolent and assimilationist approach to formal education: With attention to cultural differences, children from nonmainstream groups would have a fair chance to succeed in school and to reap the same benefits as dominant group students. While schools might make minor adjustments to accommodate culturally different students (as they do in offering English as a Second Language, for example), the nonmainstream students and their families bore most of the burden to learn and change to meet the school's requirements and expectations.

Applications of Cultural Difference Theory in Science Education Research

Cultural difference theory set the stage for science educators to think differently about reasons for science achievement gaps and the limitations of conceptual change learning theory, and to introduce a theory of science learning as a border-crossing endeavor. Beginning in the 1990s, some researchers began to argue that when children are taught formal science, they encounter a distinct culture, a culture that is more foreign to some students than others. This way of framing science teaching pushed the field to consider seriously the worldviews of students whose perspectives may conflict with formal science. Lee and Fradd (1998) point out, for example, that Western scientific values and attitudes like thinking independently, competing with peers, and making arguments based on logic and evidence rather than relying on authoritative sources are "more compatible with cultural norms of the mainstream than those of diverse cultures" (p. 17). Cobern (1996) similarly explicitly challenged the conceptual change theories of learning that ruled the day in the 1980s science education literature on grounds that they reflected an oversimplified, Western, linear view of learning and assumed that scientific conceptions were superior to other ways of knowing. His work pushed the field to consider the legitimate and useful worldviews of students whose perspectives conflict with scientific worldviews.

Aikenhead's (1996) and Aikenhead and Jegede's (1999) work similarly highlighted alternatives to psychological views of learning when they forwarded the theory of learning science as *cultural border crossing*, a process that can be unproblematic for some and difficult and disruptive for others, depending on the alignment of science culture with students' lifeworld culture. Within this framework, most students, when they enter a science classroom, are entering a new cultural milieu, with unfamiliar customs, objects, expectations, and worldview. This is true for all students but is especially true for minority or indigenous groups. For students whose everyday culture is relatively congruent with the culture they encounter in science classrooms, the border crossing is fairly smooth; this process has been called *enculturation* (Hawkins & Pea, 1987). For some students, the crossing is not so easy, and science may be taught in a way that requires them to abandon indigenous ways of knowing and replace them with a scientific way of knowing. Jegede (1995) calls this process *assimilation*. Researchers have documented three ways that students who are faced with this situation can respond: (1) assimilate, (2) resist assimilation, and (3) game the system. This third response involves finding ways to pass science class without actually learning science—for example, by following "Fatima's Rules," which include "Don't pay any attention to any information not reviewed in questions at the end of the sections," "Look for charts, tables, and bold words," and "Ask the teacher for help as soon as you're stuck" (Larson, 1995).

But, as Aikenhead (1996) argues, nondominant students do not just accept or resist. They can also learn science through *autonomous acculturation* and through *"anthropological" learning*. Autonomous acculturation takes place when instruction allows students to combine concepts from Western school science and indigenous knowledge; it is closely related to the work on funds of knowledge, which we discuss in what follows. "Anthropological" learning takes place when students enjoy and become adept at the cultural demands of school science but don't "assimilate or acculturate science's cultural baggage" (Cobern & Aikenhead, 1998, p. 43).

Phelan, Davidson, and Cao (1991) developed a useful typology in this tradition. They found that border crossings could be *smooth, managed, hazardous,* or *impossible.* Costa (1995) took this work further, identifying five categories of students based on the nature of their border crossings: "potential scientists" who cross the border smoothly; "other smart kids" who manage their crossings well; "I don't know students," whose crossings are hazardous but who nonetheless survive; "outsiders," who find the crossing virtually impossible and have no interest in pursuing it; and, most troubling, "inside outsiders," whose crossings are hindered by school policies and practices despite the students' interest in science.

Border-crossing scholarship is, in some ways, consistent with cultural difference theory, with its assumption that "without special efforts to teach 'culturally different' students the unfamiliar school culture, these students will, from the first day and through no fault of their own, have difficulty understanding what is expected of them in school" (Eisenhart, 2001a, p. 210). However, understanding science learning as a cultural border crossing privileges bridging, not necessarily replacing, students' ways of knowing with science's ways of knowing. "Students need a contextualized approach to teaching science that draws upon the cultural worlds of students and makes sense in those worlds" (Cobern & Aikenhead, 1998, p. 50). As Cobern and Aikenhead (1998) concluded in the previous edition of this handbook, science teaching should

> (1) make border crossings explicit for students, (2) facilitate these border crossings, (3) promote discourse so that *students,* not just the teacher, are talking science, (4) substantiate and build on the legitimacy of students' personally and culturally constructed ways of knowing, and (5) teach the knowledge, skills and values of Western science *in the context of* its societal roles (social, political, economic, etc.).
>
> (p. 50)

These watershed pieces of scholarship and others led science education scholars to take seriously not only the differences but also the strengths of nondominant students' cultural ways of knowing, behaving, and interacting. Another closely related branch of science education scholarship that extended cultural difference theory focuses on funds of knowledge literature (Moll, Amanti, Neff, & Gonzalez, 1992), which we discuss in the next section.

Funds of Knowledge

The cultural concept "funds of knowledge" has also been used productively in science education research. The term was defined in 1992 by anthropologists Carlos Vélez-Ibáñez and James Greenberg as a way to describe the "wide range of complex knowledge" that members of Mexican households straddling the Mexican-U.S. border needed to respond to a challenging and shifting economic and political context. "[T]hese largely rural skills, experience, technical knowledge of habitat and survival, make up the adaptive strategies that we have called funds of knowledge for much of the Arizona-Sonora Mexican population" (Vélez-Ibáñez & Greenberg, 1992, pp. 317–318). The authors argued that as U.S. Mexicans transitioned from rural to urban living and from agriculture to wage labor, "the locus of work activities moved away from the home, and the funds of knowledge required of workers became increasingly specialized" (p. 321). People became increasingly dependent on members of their own household and on clusters of households affiliated with theirs, as groups no longer held their funds of knowledge in common but instead relied on one another's particular funds of knowledge for essential activities such as "help in finding jobs, housing, and better deals on goods and services, and in dealings with institutions and government agencies" (p. 323).

Vélez-Ibáñez and Greenberg (1992) went on to argue that funds of knowledge were passed down from generation to generation not as some sort of coherent body of knowledge (as in school) but rather as a result of children being raised in the necessarily "thick" social relations this interdependence entailed. "Because Mexican children are ensconced within 'thick' multiple relations, they visit and become familiar with other households, households that contain other funds of knowledge and with whom they carry on a variety of social relationships" (p. 325). The authors argue that these funds of knowledge that children acquire at home are a rich, untapped resource available to teachers.

> We should pay greater attention to providing teachers with opportunities to learn how to incorporate the funds of knowledge from their students' households into learning modules . . . as a means to tap the vast funds of knowledge that parents have, but are seldom given the opportunity to share and express.
>
> (p. 330)

In 1992, Moll, Amanti, Neff, and Gonzalez used funds of knowledge as a tool to capitalize on "household and other community resources" among Mexican communities in Arizona (p. 132). Their goal was to use children's funds of knowledge to "organize classroom instruction that far exceeds in quality the rote-like instruction these children commonly encounter in schools" (Moll et al., 1992, p. 132). Teachers and anthropologists worked together to spend time with and interview Mexican and Mexican American families to document the households' funds of knowledge. The teachers then designed lessons that drew on these funds. One team chose to design a unit on candy. In this unit, students became a research team to explore student-generated questions, and a parent,

Mrs. Rodriguez, came into the classroom as an expert. The teacher reported,

> When Mrs. Rodriguez arrived, she became the teacher. While the candy was cooking, she talked to the class for over an hour and taught all of us not only how to make different kinds of candy but also such things as the difference in U.S. and Mexican food consumption and production, nutritional value of candy, and more. My respect and awe of Mrs. Rodriguez grew by leaps and bounds that morning.
>
> (p. 138)

Moll, Amanti, Neff, and Gonzalez (1992) showed that a funds-of-knowledge approach can result in engaging classroom activities and drawing on community members as experts. They also clarified the relationship between funds of knowledge and culture:

> Our concept of funds of knowledge is innovative, we believe, in its special relevance to teaching, and contrasts with the more general term "culture," or with the concept of a "culture-sensitive curriculum," and with the latter's reliance on folkloric displays, such as storytelling, arts, crafts, and dance performance. Although the term "funds of knowledge" is not meant to replace the anthropological concept of culture, it is more precise for our purposes because of its emphasis on strategic knowledge and related activities essential in households' functioning, development, and well-being. It is specific funds of knowledge pertaining to the social, economic, and productive activities of people in a local region, not "culture" in its broader, anthropological sense, that we seek to incorporate strategically into classrooms.
>
> (p. 139)

Although both of these research teams focused on funds of knowledge in one particular group of people, the Arizona-Sonora Mexican population, the concept of funds of knowledge has been generalized as a way to conceptualize nondominant culture as a resource for schools and to suggest ways in which the relationship between schools and nondominant communities might be changed. Science education has only recently taken up the use of funds of knowledge.

Applications of Funds of Knowledge in Science Education Research

Upadhyay (2009), for instance, in a case study of a Hmong teacher, argued that incorporating funds of knowledge into classrooms tends to increase students' enthusiasm, retention, engagement, sustained interest, and self-motivation. Further, he argued for the importance of empowering students by "including students' language and culture in the teaching and learning process" and "creating close partnerships between community and teachers" (p. 219). Upadhyay separated the student learning aspects from the empowerment and community-as-resource aspects of funds of knowledge, making separate arguments for using

funds of knowledge to improve student outcomes and *in addition* making efforts to change relationships between school and community. This separation deviates from the original argument that funds of knowledge inherently incorporate empowerment and improve school–community connections.

Despite this separation in the theoretical framing of his study, Upadhyay (2009) reunited the pedagogy and empowerment concepts in his analysis. The article is a case study of a Hmong fifth-grade teacher with a class of 19 Hmong students, seven White students, and three African Americans. Upadhyay described how the teacher incorporated Hmong funds of knowledge into science units on seasons and on environmental science. For instance, when learning about plant growth, the teacher posed the questions "Where do plants grow? What do plants need to grow? How does environment affect plant growth? What do you need to germinate seeds?" (p. 224) and had students share answers in small groups. This provided a venue for the Hmong students to talk about their daily work in their family garden plots. The teacher capitalized on this knowledge by having students design seed germination experiments that incorporated techniques their families used. On a later quiz, almost all students answered questions correctly about important science concepts, including seed germination and environmental factors affecting plant growth. Furthermore, parents supported the teachers' use of funds of knowledge in science. Upadhyay observed six different parents visiting this teacher's class and even participating in teaching, as in a dialogue he recounts where a parent posed questions to the students including "What do you see in your garden?" "What did you do before planting?" and "Why?" (p. 227).

Basu and Calabrese Barton (2007) used a funds-of-knowledge approach in their study of how poor urban middle school students developed "sustained interest" in science. Their argument was not that students brought useful funds of knowledge to school that could be used to help them learn science but that science provides useful funds of knowledge for students to pursue their visions of their own futures and that this utility sustains their science interest:

> The youth in this study had strong conceptions of the careers and lifestyles they wanted to pursue. When science assisted them in moving toward their individual goals, they expressed an ongoing interest in learning and exploring the world through science.
>
> (p. 482)

The study took place in a year-long after-school intervention and exploration program. Program themes were "invention" and "environment."

The authors defined funds of knowledge as both knowledge held in common among a large group (e.g., those living on the Arizona-Sonoran border) and knowledge held in common by a few individuals due to local circumstances (e.g., living in an extended family household). Funds of knowledge include

> the historical and cultural knowledge of a community, such as the knowledge a young person might have about animals and plants in a farming community. However, they also refer to experiences and knowledge that may be more particular to a given family within the context of a community, such as knowledge a young person might have about the care of the elderly from growing up in a family and community wherein multiple generations live in close proximity.
>
> (p. 468).

In this study, a critical ethnography, they explored the way students' funds of knowledge supported their "sustained interest" in science. They defined students with sustained interest as those who "pursued self-motivated science explorations outside the context of the classroom or used science in an ongoing way to improve, expand, or enhance an exploration or activity to which they were already deeply committed" (p. 469). They connected this sustained interest to the strategic deployment of funds of knowledge: "These 'visions of the future' fell under the category of youths' funds of knowledge because they reflected beliefs that students had about their own interests and presented goals toward which they could direct themselves by strategically building skills and knowledge" (p. 479).

The authors' focus on examining how students deployed science funds of knowledge as a way to advance their own ends, and in so doing sustained their interest in science, shifts slightly the original theory's focus on how a funds-of-knowledge approach can change the relationship between school and community. They argue that "funds of knowledge are practice—they are the cultural knowledge an individual possesses as well as *how and why they act* upon that knowledge" (p. 485) and focus less on cultural knowledge and more on how and why poor urban middle school children are able to make use of scientific funds of knowledge. The focus is helping students use science for their own aims.

Funds-of-knowledge approaches in science education include work done outside of the United States and work done outside K–12 classrooms. Cowie, Jones, and Otrel-Cass (2011) found that both teachers and students benefitted when teachers incorporated Maori cultural knowledge of mountains into a landforms unit in New Zealand. Students were more likely to develop science-related identities when their funds of knowledge were incorporated into the unit, and teachers came to understand their students better. In Uganda, in a comparison between high-performing and low-performing schools, science teachers in the high-performing schools were more likely to draw on students' funds of knowledge "as a pedagogic resource or means to induct learners into science knowledge" (Sikoyo & Jacklin, 2009, p. 720). In work focused on parents, a group of Mexican American parents of preschoolers participated in

a program to help them identify the science concepts and knowledge underlying everyday activities they engaged in with their children (Riojas-Cortez, Huerta, Flores, Perez, & Clark, 2008). After participating in the program, the parents were better able to explain those concepts to their children. In a rare funds-of-knowledge study using experimental rather than qualitative methods, a group of middle school science teachers participated in a professional development program that taught them to incorporate students' funds of knowledge, while another group, chosen at random from the original research volunteers, did not (Johnson & Fargo, 2010). The students of program participants had significantly higher test score growth in science than did students whose teachers were randomly assigned to not participate. The funds-of-knowledge literature would be greatly served by more quantitative studies like this.

The strength of the funds-of-knowledge approach is its focus on what students' communities and experiences can bring to the classroom to enrich the curriculum. This approach typically involves "conducting home visits to better understand how to bring real world experiences from different cultures into the classroom" (Johnson & Fargo, 2010, p. 45). The goal is to provide teachers with the opportunity and scaffolding to figure out how to "use diversity as a resource in the service of learning" (Nieto, 2000, p. 183), which the literature demonstrates is difficult but not impossible. In this, it "contrasts sharply with prevailing and accepted perceptions of working-class families as somehow disorganized socially and deficient intellectually" (Moll et al., 1992, p. 134). In its focus on the strengths children and parents bring to science learning, or how children can see science as useful, this approach has the potential to change not just what goes on in science classrooms but the relationship between communities and science. A funds-of-knowledge approach points its users toward concrete actions like bringing parents into decision making about the science curriculum, enabling parents and students to lead science units grounded in their funds of knowledge, and exploring ways to incorporate community and student needs and issues into the science curriculum. The funds-of-knowledge approach directs teachers toward concrete actions they can take to teach in non–deficit-based ways.

Culturally Relevant Pedagogy

How do teachers leverage students' funds of knowledge for productive and meaningful science learning? One strand of scholarship that examines this question uses culturally relevant pedagogy (CRP) as a guiding framework. In her book *The Dreamkeepers*, Ladson-Billings (1994) examined practices of successful teachers of African American children focusing on what these excellent teachers do and what it means to teach in *culturally relevant* ways. While Ladson-Billings's teachers were not formulaic, there was a decided thread running through pedagogy that could be considered culturally relevant. Specifically, culturally relevant teaching rests on three propositions: "(a) students must experience academic success; (b) students must develop and/or maintain cultural competence; and (c) students must develop a critical consciousness through which they challenge the status quo" (Ladson-Billings, 1995, p. 160). One thing that differentiates a funds-of-knowledge approach from a culturally relevant pedagogy approach is that CRP "specifically recognizes and addresses systematic power relations in the classroom and the larger social context" (Patchen & Cox-Petersen, 2008, p. 996) through its emphasis on critical consciousness. This, as we will go on to discuss, has been the least well-taken-up aspect of CRP.

Applications of Culturally Relevant Pedagogy in Science Education Research

Science educators have used ideas from culturally relevant pedagogy to describe and explain teachers' struggles to enact it (Johnson, 2011) or understand it (Chinn, 2006), to guide professional development (Buxton, Lee, & Santau, 2008; Grimberg & Gummer, 2013), to facilitate preservice teacher education (Mensah, 2011), and to illustrate what a culturally relevant *science* pedagogy (Xu, Coats, & Davidson, 2011) looks like in practice. Few studies address the *effectiveness* of successfully enacted culturally relevant instruction on students' achievement (Parsons, Travis, & Simpson, 2005) or in cultivating students' interest in science (Xu et al., 2011).

Soon after Ladson-Billings published her work on culturally relevant teaching, Lee and Fradd (1998) proposed the notion of *instructional congruence*, which is "the process of mediating the nature of academic content with students' language and cultural experiences to make such content (e.g., science) accessible, meaningful, and relevant for diverse students" (p. 12). *Cultural congruence* (or cultural relevance), they argued, emphasized students' acquisition of literacies, including academic and social discourse, but often ignored *science-specific* knowledge and habits of mind. Teachers who teach from an *instructionally congruent* framework understand their students' language and cultural experiences, scientific practices (knowing, doing, and talking science), and habits of mind (scientific values, attitudes, and worldview), and are able to relate science to students' background experiences. In other words, it is important for teachers to relate students' linguistic and cultural experiences to the classroom norms of interaction *as well as* to the specific demands of disciplinary science. Lee and Buxton (2011) offer the example of the different ways validity claims are assessed in different cultural contexts. In science's culture, knowledge claims are assessed based on evidence and theory. In other cultural contexts, validity of knowledge claims is based on authoritative sources such as teachers, parents, and textbooks. Teachers can help students understand the utility and appropriateness of different ways of evaluating knowledge claims in different cultural contexts.

The instructional congruence framework has been the basis for a range of curricular and professional development efforts that have shown generally successful changes in teacher and student practices, though these changes take time to cultivate. August, Branum-Martin, Cardenas-Hagan, and Francis (2009) tested the effectiveness of the Quality English and Science Teaching (QuEST) intervention, which was based on the instructional congruence framework and aimed at facilitating middle school teachers' abilities to improve their English language learner students' science knowledge and academic language. Students who received the QuEST intervention made statistically significant gains on posttest measures of science knowledge and vocabulary.

Okhee Lee and her colleagues have completed a number of multiyear, large-scale studies examining various outcomes of professional development based on the instructional congruence framework. A small sample of their large corpus of work includes examining students' science achievement (Lee, Deaktor, Hart, Cuevas, & Enders, 2005), teachers' pedagogical reasoning complexity about their English language learner students' problem-solving abilities in home and school contexts (Buxton, Salinas, Mahotiere, Lee, & Secada, 2013), and teachers' knowledge of science, teaching practices to support science for understanding and science for inquiry, as well as teacher support for English language development (Lee, Lewis, Adamson, Maerten-Rivera, & Secada, 2008). All studies show gains in those respective areas, but the authors note practical and methodological challenges in enacting large-scale, meaningful reform and professional development based on the ambitious instructional congruence framework in current educational contexts (e.g., high-stakes accountability climates, underresourced schools, and lack of support for enacting meaningful change).

Though there have been different emphases on, labels for, and approaches to enacting culturally relevant pedagogy, researchers generally agree that a culturally relevant science instruction leverages nonmainstream students' cultural knowledge *and* experiences and cultivates scientific literacy and learning (Johnson, 2011), but they may not necessarily agree on the role and status of students' cultural knowledge and experiences in the enactment of pedagogy and/or the learning of science (Tsurusaki, Calabrese Barton, Tan, Koch, & Contento, 2013). For example, some argue that the purpose of a culturally relevant pedagogy is to facilitate a type of bilingualism, where teachers facilitate students' fluency of the discourses of science on top of their everyday, cultural discourses (Lee, 2005). Others argue that the divide between science and students' discourse practices are not so distinct, though the continuity between them often goes unrecognized (Rosebery, Ogonowski, DiSchino, & Warren, 2010).

Most studies that address culturally relevant approaches stay fairly consistent to a cultural difference theory emphasis, focusing on the *border-crossing* aspect of learning—learning science (academic knowledge)—while maintaining a strong sense of one's cultural self (cultural knowledge). However, science education studies (and multicultural education studies in general) often ignore Ladson-Billings' (1995) third tenet, critical consciousness (Johnson, 2010; Morrison, Robbins, & Rose, 2008), which has been described by Tsurusaki and colleagues (2013) as potentially *boundary transforming*. One of the few studies we found that paints a vivid picture of all three of Ladson-Billings' tenets of culturally relevant pedagogy in a *science* classroom (academic success, cultural competence, and critical consciousness) is Tsurusaki and colleagues' (2013) case study of a sixth-grade teacher using an equity-minded, reform-based curriculum (Choice, Control, and Change, or C3) focused on dynamic equilibrium in the human body. The curriculum (Koch, Contento, & Calabrese Barton, 2010) focused on promoting the use of scientific evidence to help students make healthful choices about their food and activity. Throughout the unit, students investigated factors from their biology and physical and social environments that influence their food and activity choices.

The teacher, Mrs. Hanson, was as committed to having her students learn science and engage in the practices of science (academic success) as she was to positioning students' everyday cultural practices around food as worthy of discussion and as significant aspects of their scientific meaning making (cultural competence). She engaged them in critical dialog about their lives and the role science could play in helping them make healthful decisions and prompted and celebrated students' critical thinking and questions about the relationships between their physical and social environments and their eating and activity practices (critical consciousness). One way she did this, the authors argue, was through her use of what they labeled "transformative boundary objects," which "coordinate activity and allow for knowledge integration across [cultural] worlds but also allow for the transformation of either the participating communities or the nature of the boundary itself" (Tsurusaki et al., 2013, p. 7). The paper describes four boundary objects Mrs. Hanson used—the bar graph, the science research question, nutrition labels, and public service announcements—that enabled a culturally relevant science. The boundary objects were tools that prompted discussions about social and environmental factors influencing food and activity practices, spurred students' critical analysis of their practices and science's practices, empowered students to make changes in their practices, and created new ways of participating in science.

As with funds-of-knowledge studies and cultural difference theory, most science education studies that use a culturally relevant pedagogy framework assume, *a priori*, that cultural worlds of students, science, and/or school science need bridging, and they frame scientific beliefs, worldviews, and practices as distinct from nondominant students' beliefs, worldviews, and practices (Warren, Ballenger, Ogonowski, Rosebery, & Hudicourt-Barnes, 2001). Studies that promote the dual purposes of academic/science learning and cultural competence often use an implicit definition of culture that assumes its internal coherence and its relative consistency or similarity across time and within similar racial and ethnic groups. On the one hand, these assumptions about culture lend themselves well to the development of curricular and pedagogical reforms that avoid deficit-based perspectives of culturally different learners. On the other hand, these approaches run the risk of essentializing culture, assuming homogeneity within ethnic and racial groups, and reproducing stereotypes about cultural and ethnic groups (Seiler, 2013).

We see these risks minimized in theoretical and pedagogical approaches that make explicit the issues of local and global power and inequity and provide inroads for using academic and cultural knowledge to destabilize borders between academic and home cultures. For instance, Tsurusaki and colleagues' (2013) approach to studying culturally relevant pedagogy privileged the teachers' everyday practices to understand how culturally relevant pedagogy unfolded and what it enabled rather than assuming an *a priori* definition. Similar to cultural difference theory, the "culture" of the students in that study was found in their everyday food and activity practices, which were partly *predictable responses to their positioning* amid larger social, economic, and cultural contexts. Still, the curriculum, teachers' practices, use of boundary objects, and students' engagement created *new meanings* of being a good participant in school science and *possibilities for changing* youths' food and activity practices in ways that blurred the boundaries between their home and school sciences' cultural practices.

Others have argued similarly—that what counts as "culture" in studies of culturally relevant science pedagogy sometimes suggests an overly bounded and tidy notion of culture. For instance, Carter (2010) argues that multicultural science education studies represent borders as "unproblematic lines between cultures and knowledges that need to be crossed" with "little discussion about the nature of borders themselves" (pp. 429–430). Quigley (2011) also pushes the field to move beyond "cultural congruence" frameworks toward a consideration of creating and studying "third spaces" in classrooms, which she describes as more fluid, student-initiated, less predictable spaces that do not frame students' cultural worlds and school science's cultural worlds in opposition to one another. Our discussion of culture in the next sections shifts from cultural difference perspectives to perspectives on cultural production and third space.

Cultural Production

Cultural production frames culture as a more dynamic, open-ended, and potentially transformative force than cultural difference, funds-of-knowledge, and culturally relevant pedagogy approaches. In this theoretical framework, culture is viewed as "a set of symbolic and material forms" or meanings. Eisenhart (2001a) defines culture as something that is "affected but not determined by history and structure, actively appropriated or 'produced' in groups to bring order and satisfaction to experiences" (p. 213). A cultural production view focuses on *local meanings produced by groups in everyday practice*, their connection to larger social structures, and the possibility, no matter how slim, of challenging the status quo (Levinson, Foley, & Holland, 1996). In this approach, culture is not a set of practices handed down across generations as a response to enduring social or environmental conditions, as is the case with cultural difference theory, "but a shared set of meanings, *continually produced* in everyday practice; new meanings can be congruent with what came before but also might have potential to alter what came before" (Carlone & Johnson, 2012, our emphasis, p. 157).

Cultural production maintains the primacy of *patterns* of behavior, taken-for-granted practices, and the meanings given to them that, in turn, organize future behavior. Cultural productions are not immediately evident in individual accomplishments or statements. "[T]o be indicative of cultural production, individual actions must reveal something about a group's shared meanings. Behaviour must be patterned, either in ways that align with local cultural meanings or contest them, to be of interest" (Carlone & Johnson, 2012, p. 157). Individual actions are interpreted "by patterns in the ways participants act in classrooms, label their own efforts, and describe themselves to others" (Eisenhart 2001a, 217). This distinction between collective and individual phenomena is important because, although a cultural production lens enables new understandings of *individuals* in practice (e.g., offering explanations for why they do what they do), these understandings hinge on understanding group-level processes and meanings that organize individuals' beliefs and actions; they also hinge on understanding the ways these local meanings are situated within macro-level contexts (e.g., larger social structures). With this lens, what individuals learn and know depends on how social practices enable and constrain participation, in what times and spaces, with what tools, with what goals and endpoints.

The difference between cultural production and cultural difference is that cultural production attends to the relationships between local practice and larger social structures in more fluid, dynamic ways. The local is shaped by and shapes (at least in the sense that it gives meaning to) larger social structures. The meaning of larger structures is not assumed *a priori* to be uniformly relevant to all members of a social group, as it is in cultural difference theory.[2] When one considers cultural production, the outcomes (meanings produced by groups) are always in question, thus leaving the possibility for changes to the status quo.

Applications of Cultural Production in Science Education Research

There has been a recent call for science education research to consider ways that cultural-production approaches can provide new insights for equitable science education (Carlone & Johnson, 2012; Seiler, 2013; Wood, Erichson, & Anicha, 2013). Seiler (2013), for example, critiques the prevalence and use of cultural difference approaches in science education research for their treatment of cultures as multiple, bounded, and reproducible ("pluralizable") and their emphasis on distinctions and differences (e.g., they are "discontinous"). Arguing that cultural difference approaches can lead to essentializing and stereotyping cultural groups, she argues for cultural production views that illuminate spaces of cultural overlap and/or the ways culture is shaped by larger social, political, and economic factors. In science education, cultural production approaches have not received widespread attention, but a few examples have appeared since the mid-1990s. The studies we outline use iterations of the original conception of cultural production, as outlined by Levinson, Foley, and Holland (1996).

Eisenhart (1996), for example, used the concept of cultural production to examine the way scientists were "produced" in a university biology program and a U.S. workplace employing biologists. She described how the opportunity structures at each site and individuals' responses to them created the conditions for new patterns of behavior and thinking to emerge. These new patterns were not completely different: They entailed older practices, but they were new enough to somewhat alter the context of practice.

Buxton (2001) used a cultural production lens to investigate how the everyday practices of two groups in a university science lab both reproduced and contested prototypical meanings of science as competitive and hierarchical. Buxton situates his work in the practice theory tradition, in which, he argues,

> culture is seen not as a set of characteristics as it is in older theories of culture, but rather as a process, continually being constructed in practice. Individuals are not seen as passively accepting the conditions in which they live and function. Instead, they are seen to have agency to counter the determining structures (although they must still do so while functioning within those structures).
>
> (p. 389)

Following Buxton (2001), practice theory is concerned with how "individual and group cultures are formed in practice, within and against larger societal forces and structures" (p. 389), and focuses both on individual agency and on the "pressures on the individual to conform to the culture as currently practiced" (p. 389). In Buxton's framing, cultural production takes place when people resist the status quo; when their practices are consistent with the status quo, they are engaging in cultural reproduction.

Buxton (2001) used this framework to examine a molecular biology laboratory at a large western university. The lab, headed by a woman, had a higher proportion of female postdoctoral researchers, graduate students, and undergraduates than other lab groups at the same university. His interest in studying this lab was to examine how science was practiced in this setting. Through his research, Buxton illuminated the ways in which "science practice, even in the most traditional settings, such as research labs, often does not look like the constrained image that we frequently present to students in K–16 science classes" (p. 405). For instance, he found that, counter to popular imagination,

> successful science practice, at least in the context of the research done in Sally's lab, was not just the result of raw intelligence. A good part of success in the lab came about as a result of hard work, dedication, and willingness to learn from others. Although intelligence was necessary, so, too, were intuition, dexterity, and skill at tool use.
>
> (p. 403)

This study uncovered examples of both what Buxton called cultural production and cultural reproduction. For example, the group in the lab who seemed most nonconformist was actually deeply involved in cultural reproduction, whereas a less ostentatious group turned out to be engaged in cultural production. One all-male group, who worked in the self-dubbed "Cool People's Bay," appeared to contest norms of science and meanings of scientist with their loud music and "wacky behavior." However, despite their outwardly rebellious appearance, this group was actually engaged in reproducing one of the norms of science practice: active competition for resources. For instance, an undergraduate research assistant was initially placed in this bay, but "after a time when she found how hard it was to keep any bench space for herself in that bay" (Buxton, 2001, p. 401), she gave up and moved to another space in the lab. The members of the Cool People's Bay had in effect driven a woman out of their group by not allowing her access to lab equipment. On the other hand, the all-female group who worked at the (also self-named) "Chick Bay" engaged in practices that were subtly resistant to science norms. They dedicated a larger space in their bay as a common area, meaning that the undergraduates who worked in this group had greater access to lab resources (in fact, it was to this space that the squeezed-out undergraduate moved). Two of the postdoctoral researchers in this group also tutored undergraduate women of color, an activity no one else in the lab carried out and one with obvious implications for opening up science to a wider variety of people. The women in the Chick Bay were producing a science culture characterized by sharing of resources and knowledge rather than competition.

Carlone (2004) used the cultural production framework to study the experiences of girls in physics. Following Eisenhart and Finkel (1998), she defined cultural production more widely than did Buxton (2001), as "meanings developed by groups in their everyday activities" that reproduce *and/or* contest prevailing meanings (of schooling, science, school science; Carlone, 2004, p. 44). She used this framing because

> cultural production enables us to account for how larger sociohistorical meanings shape participants' values, beliefs, and actions, but also the ways new meanings of science might emerge depending on the context in which

the classroom is positioned. It draws attention to the intersection of the local and global, the micro and macro.

> (Eisenhart & Finkel, 1998, p. 396)

Carlone (2004) laid out the cultural historical context and the science education practices that reproduce science as an "objective, privileged way of knowing pursued by an intellectual elite" (p. 394; e.g., direct instruction, technical-rationale discourse, narrow curriculum). She then studied what happened in a classroom using Active Physics, a curriculum specifically designed to contest traditional assumptions about physics by making it more relevant, centering it on themes rather than topics, and positioning "students as *producers* of scientific knowledge" (p. 395, italics in original). The impetus for the study was to see in what ways the cultural meanings of science produced in Active Physics were consistent with or contrary to prototypical meanings of science.

Using this lens, Carlone (2004) found that even in the context of the Active Physics classes she studied, hegemonic meanings of physics as "difficult" and of a scientist as someone with "raw ability" emerged. Despite the intention otherwise, hegemonic meanings of science and scientist prevailed. Furthermore, Carlone found that the teacher was one of the agents involved in this production; he found ways not related to the physics content to make the class difficult (e.g., not giving students enough time to complete their assignments). Thus, even the girls who did well in class "did not define themselves as 'science people' and opted not to pursue further study in physics" (p. 404).

Tonso (2006) used cultural production to analyze educational reforms at an engineering college. Her framing was consistent with that used by Carlone (2004), and, like Carlone, she used it as a tool to document how practices intended to produce new meanings instead reproduced the status quo. The engineering college she studied, in an attempt to bring engineering education more in alignment with the norms of engineering practice, complemented its traditional lecture-and-test classes with design classes in which students worked in groups to solve authentic engineering problems. Despite this new context, and despite many students (especially women students) performing well on these projects, the culture that was produced in this setting was congruent with larger cultural meanings of engineers as "overachievers" "whose test scores and grades ostensibly indicated being capable of doing engineering work at the highest levels" (Tonso, 2006, p. 302). The result was that some students, often women, were marginalized and dropped out of college even though they were competent engineers—simply because the engineering school failed to recognize them as such even with reforms intended to do the opposite. "Ultimately, in spite of enormous student agency constructing subjectivities as engineers and performing themselves as engineers, and at times doing so in resistance to campus culture, little cultural change seemed likely to result from their creative performances" (p. 301).

The cultural production lens frames culture as fluid and dynamic and produced by groups through practice in ways that contest and/or reproduce hegemonic practices and meanings. While cultural productions have been defined in the science education literature as meanings produced *against* (counter to) the status quo and cultural reproduction as meanings (re)produced *within* (as consistent with) it (e.g., Buxton, 2001), on a micro-level, both processes can happen concurrently. Especially important are the productions that have staying power (i.e., with a longer timescale and the ability to capture time, space, and people in counterhegemonic ways) and the (re)productions that shape-shift subtly to (re)organize time, space, and people in hegemonic ways. The cultural production lens offers insight into how science, in many settings and with many different actors across time, gets reproduced as elite and appropriate only for certain kinds of people. Similarly, the lens has the power to detect settings like the Chick Bay (Buxton, 2001) in which counterhegemonic meanings of science are produced. Cultural production analyses can lay bare the workings of cultural settings, revealing areas where reform is possible and where it is already taking place (and, as both Carlone [2004] and Tonso [2006] documented, areas where it appears to be taking place but is not).

Figured Worlds

In 1998, Holland and colleagues proposed a far-reaching "theory of identity and agency" that introduced the concept of figured worlds and linked it to ideas about social positioning ("positionality"), people's responses to their positioning ("spaces of authoring"), and social occasions to practice inhabiting possible or imaginary figured worlds ("serious play"). This theory elaborates processes for understanding cultural productions and reproductions in new ways, explicitly recognizing and working through tensions of "becoming somebody" amid on-the-ground cultural practices, existing and historically enduring larger social, economic, political contexts, and creative and transformative possibilities that emerge through creativity and imagination (Holland et al., 1998).

According to the theory, figured worlds are socially and culturally constructed realms of interpretation in which particular actors are recognized, certain acts judged significant, and specific trajectories and outcomes valued (Holland et al., 1998, p. 52). As Hatt (2007) explains, "Figured worlds represent the 'rules', 'guidelines', or social forces that influence (but do not completely dictate) the ways people speak, behave and 'practice' within social spaces" (pp. 149–150). Figured worlds circulate as ideological arenas for orchestrating identities and actions in both explicitly and implicitly structured contexts.

Holland and colleagues (1998) describe the "figured world of romance" borne out of a study of 23 female college students and their socially constructed romantic world (see also Holland & Eisenhart, 1990). The figured world of romance was organized by a logic of exchange in which women traded physical attractiveness and sexual favors for men's attention and gifts. The women used a gender-marked vocabulary to describe the actors in the world of romance (e.g., attractive women, unattractive women, boyfriends, lovers, hunks, dumb broads), acts associated with the world of romance (e.g., flirting, dumping, loving, having sex with), and the forces involved (attraction, love; Holland et al., 1998, p. 102). The authors argue that "the figured world of romance acquired motivating force as the women developed mastery of it, and their mastery, in turn, depended upon their development of a concept of themselves as actors in the world of romance" (p. 99).

People draw on figured worlds to think about and conjure identities, but they are not free to enact identities unchecked. Identities depend on one's positioning ("positional identity") in social status hierarchies, such as race, gender, or class, and in the imaginative system of figured worlds ("figurative identity"). Figurative identities have their source and are marked in an imaginative system, while "[p]ositional identities have to do with the day-to-day and on-the-ground [often unmarked] relations of power, deference and entitlement, social affiliation and distance . . . of the lived world" (Holland et al., 1998, p. 127). Positional aspects of identity overlap and interrelate with figurative identities in complicated ways.

People cannot always affect the way they are positioned, but they must "answer" or respond to that positioning in some way; this answering is referred to as a "space of authoring" (after Bakhtin). Although answers must be given, they are not predetermined, so the space of authoring is somewhat open ended and can include individual variations and improvisations, some of which may be taken up by others and stabilized into new "figured worlds of possibility" that sometimes lead to social changes (Holland et al., 1998; Monzó & Rueda 2009; Urrieta 2007), though stories of social change are few and far between in the literature.

Beth Hatt (2007) provided an example of creative authoring and the ways individual agency played into redefining or reimagining the rules of the game but ultimately did not lead to transforming youths' long-term social positioning. She described the "figured world of smartness" and how it plays out in schools to work against students of color and of low socioeconomic status. In the study, a group of typically marginalized students refigured the "world of smartness" as presented to them in school to accommodate a new imagery of "book smarts versus street smarts." "Book smarts" refers to the knowledge and attention to academic pursuits valued in school and gained by studying and working hard in school. "Street smarts" refers to the necessary know-how to navigate the poverty and street culture of the students' experiences outside of school. Students placed a higher value on street smarts as relevant to their lives and maligned "book smarts" as irrelevant. Thus, they actively disengaged from academic pursuits, with negative ramifications for their positioning within the school setting.

Application of Figured Worlds in Science Education Research

The science education literature has been rather slow to take up the concept of figured worlds in research studies and, to our knowledge, none have used the concept to enact science education reform. The scant bit of literature that uses this construct points to its explanatory potential in illuminating the multilevel influences on diverse youths' identity work. For example, Carlone, Scott, and Lowder (under review) conducted a critical ethnographic case study of three youths' identity work across fourth- through sixth-grade school science. To understand the enabling and constraining aspects of each year of school science on students' identity work, they conceptualized the science classroom not as its own figured world but as the *interweaving* of various figured worlds and identified different "figured worlds that influenced what counted as science and who got counted as a good science student in the different science classrooms the case study students . . . encountered." Though the figured world of traditional schooling was relevant in each science classroom to different degrees, the more progressive and inclusive fourth-grade classroom leveraged other figured worlds like family (emphasizing togetherness, nurturing, and collaboration) and childhood (privileging youth genres of "kidspeak" and kid humor). The more traditional sixth-grade classroom, on the other hand, leveraged, among others, the figured world of jock masculinity that encouraged forms of bullying, sarcasm, and jokes at the expense of those with less power. One of their arguments was that "a classroom rich and thick with threads from different (empowering and relevant) figured worlds . . . is a place where more students have greater opportunities to engage meaningfully in and to develop identities in science" (Carlone, et al., in press).

Following Holland and Lachicotte (2007), Carlone and colleagues (under review) used the construct of figured worlds to describe the identity work students had to do to be recognized as a competent participant in the setting, part of which had to do with positioning oneself in relation to the celebrated subject position:

> Becoming "scientific" meant positioning oneself (deliberately or not) and/or getting positioned as a "good" science participant and therefore aligned with being able to fit into and/or see oneself inhabiting the classroom's celebrated subject positions. This was easier for some students than others. When things went awry for students, we found it illuminating to understand their difficulties in light of the breadth of the available subject positions, their difficulties accessing the practices privileged within celebrated subject positions, and the sometimes problematic recognition work related to the raced, classed, and/or gendered nature of the celebrated subject positions.
>
> (Carlone, et al., in press)

The concepts of figured worlds and celebrated subject position allowed the authors to take seriously the power interwoven into and created within figured worlds and the positioning work involved in constructing identities within those worlds.

Their approach emphasized understanding the meaning of students' *individual identity work* (positioning and authoring) in the *cultural* context (figured worlds) of each year of school science, providing an explanation for the case study students' problematic science trajectories (declining interest and affiliation and decreased opportunities to engage in meaningful scientific practices) that went beyond typical descriptions of the "middle school science problem." In part, the case study students' difficulties arose from the fact that the celebrated subject positions were so narrowly constructed and heavily mediated by race, class, and gender that only two of the three scientifically talented students in the study were able and/or willing to do the identity work to align themselves with that space—work that had nothing to do with enriching their science selves and everything to do with playing the game of schooling. Aaliyah, an African American girl located deeper within the matrix of oppression (Johnson, Brown, Carlone, & Cuevas, 2011), had a more difficult time positioning herself as aligned with the celebrated subject position, despite her strong scientific and academic competence and interest. The study describes the increasingly limited subject positions available to students, the raced, classed, and gendered nature of those subject positions, and students' responses in light of those increasingly limited options. The authors admit to a more structuralist bent, in contrast to a more agentic view in Tan and Calabrese Barton's (2007) work described next. Carlone and colleagues' (in press) analysis demanded attention to multiple timescales (within and across years of school science) and levels of analysis (cultural, historical, individual, and across individuals).

Tan and Calabrese Barton (2007) similarly use the construct of figured worlds to highlight the structural, situated, and agentic aspect of identity work. Through ethnographic case studies of two Latina sixth-grade students (Amelia and Ginny) in a U.S. urban middle school in a low-income community, they highlight the dialogic nature of identity work, which involves being positioned by others and authoring oneself. Their take on figured worlds draws attention to the power dynamics inherent within them, and the ways individuals respond to those structures is constructed as a part of their agency:

> Novices gain social positions that are accorded by the established members of that world. How novices choose to accept, engage, resist or ignore such cues shape their developing identity-in-practice and determine the boundaries of their authoring space, which is driven by a sense of agency.
>
> (p. 49)

Tan and Calabrese Barton operationalized figured worlds as bounded spaces or arrangements of social activity (e.g., the whole-school context, group work, whole-class context) that were influenced by macro-level structures and global trends and enabled and constrained possible identities-in-practice for participants in those spaces. A further difference between Carlone and colleagues' (in press) use of figured worlds and Tan and Calabrese Barton's (2007) approach is that Tan and Calabrese Barton pay close attention to the *transformative possibilities* embedded in the girls' creative improvisations (i.e., *their agency*). In particular, the study demonstrated the way girls leveraged noncommodified forms of knowledge, relationships, and activities in ways to support their success in the class, transformed their identities-in-practice across the school year, and helped create "new worlds of school science which had shared characteristics of both their life-worlds and the world of school science" (Tan & Calabrese Barton, 2007, p. 64).

For example, Ginny, a shy girl whose participation aligned with a prototypical "good student" but who was hesitant to stand out, leveraged her "pop culture consumer" identity to write a song about bones and choreograph an accompanying dance to memorize a daunting amount of information about human anatomy. Her teacher (Mr. M.) liked it so much, he posted the song lyrics outside his classroom and made copies as a resource for her classmates. Amelia, on the other hand, was labeled a "problematic" student at the beginning of the year, but by the end of the year, her grades improved from 70s to a 100 on the final animal project. She was a regular participant in the school's weekend field trips that included overnight camping trips, fishing trips, and trips to museums. When she came back to the classroom, she shared stories with the class (unsolicited), but gradually Mr. M. began to elicit her stories as a way to increase the class's science interest and participation in the school's weekend field trips. Eventually, Amelia became the class's "spokesperson" for the field trips and a vocal and enthusiastic science participant. She did not tone down her outgoing and vocal participation to fit into the prototypical "good student" mode. Instead, she created her own rules and rituals to get recognized and participate in ways that allowed her to "be herself" and to be a good science student. In other words, these girls leveraged resources from their out-of-school worlds to transform their own and others' participation in the world of school science.

In a more recent article, Calabrese Barton and colleagues (2013) continue their exploration of figured worlds to illustrate the dynamic, intentional, cumulative, and contentious nature of identity work of middle school girls with nondominant backgrounds as they negotiate their possible futures in science. The authors focus on two girls' identity trajectories (Diane and Chantelle) across different figured worlds. The girls' histories, life experiences, talents, and recognition by others in various figured worlds provided resources and constraints that influenced their sense of future self in relationship to science. Furthermore, Chantelle's case demonstrated the fluidity of figured worlds in moments where she, a quiet and often "invisible" school science student, leveraged resources from her ongoing identity work in the Green Club (focusing on green energy technologies) to get recognized by her teachers and peers in her science classroom as an expert when she presented a documentary film she co-created and facilitated a workshop for them. Doing so reconfigured that figured world of school science, opening a space for Chantelle to get positioned differently—as an expert versus as an invisible, silent student. Chantelle's case illustrates that figured worlds can be perturbed, offering potential for new identities. However, Diane's case illustrates that when figured worlds are configured narrowly and in ways that are disconnected from an individual's cultural practices in other settings, it is difficult to sustain science interest and participation. The figured worlds of school science in which Diane participated (mostly traditional "school-type" science) were disconnected from her talents and identity work she did in other figured worlds and also were heavily mediated by race and class power dynamics in ways that compromised her science interest and participation.

Calabrese Barton and colleagues (2013) do an admirable job of using figured worlds to highlight structural *and* agentic aspects of identity work in ways previous work in science education has not been able to do. The girls' identity work was "intentional," drawing on available resources, but also "constrained by the historically, culturally, and socially legitimized norms, rules, and expectations that operate within the spaces in which such work takes place" (p. 38).

The science education literature using figured worlds does so for its explanatory potential. Figured worlds, like romance or smartness or jock masculinity, are fairly stable (though not fixed) "shared, idealized realms involving identifiable character types and actions. They are evoked by discourses and the cultural artifacts of those discourses, or objects and symbols inscribed by a collective attribution of meaning" (Michael, Andrade, & Bartlett, 2007, p. 168). Though they are "as-if realms," they affect behaviors, interactions, and identity work in real ways. They enable study of identities that encompasses structure and agency, multiple timescales, and micro-, meso-, and macro-level contexts.

Third Space

Another anthropological approach to science education research focuses on investigating third spaces and hybridity. The two terms are used in similar ways, and we will consider them together. In these frameworks, a third or hybrid space is created when students and teachers bring their home and community funds of knowledge into productive contact with the practices of school science. Ideally this will happen in a way that supports a nondominant perspective *and* advances science learning. Third space has been described as "a bridge, a navigational space, or a space for critical understandings of the relationship between science and students' 'everyday worlds'" (Moje et al, 2004, p. 54). Ideally, a third space will "integrate, rather than divide, everyday and academic knowledges" and "reshape how and why young people approach the content texts of their classrooms" (Moje et al., 2004, p. 54). In a third space, teachers and students "create opportunities to *collectively* generate new forms of joint activity to solve the double binds students encounter" (Gutiérrez, 2008, p. 160). Third space, in this framing of it, is not something a teacher creates on her own; it comes into existence through the interactions of all actors in a setting. Furthermore, third space draws on a definition of culture as "a set of symbolic and material forms, affected but not determined by history and structure, actively appropriated or 'produced' in groups to bring order and satisfaction to experiences" rather than something that is "coherent and coterminous with social background, language use, region, religion, or ethnicity" (Eisenhart 2001a, p. 212–213).

Researchers who make use of third space and hybridity refer to two different origins for their ideas, one derived from postcolonialism, the other within educational research. Richardson Bruna refers to these as "Third Space (Bhabha)/third space (Gutiérrez) hybridity" (2009, p. 225). Authors who invoke the postcolonial roots draw on the work of Homi Bhabha, who used the term in 1994 in his book *The Location of Culture*. The third space as described by Bhabha comes into being when colonized people inhabit spaces initially created by colonizers, and, in so doing, inevitably change the spaces, sometimes in ways that resist colonization. As Shumar (2010) describes it,

> Bhabha's postcolonial theory is about the complex and contradictory forms produced by the colonial situation itself and the specific ways in which a colonizer ideology is deployed to support the exploitation of a people and the ways in which that ideology has its own "cracks and fissures" which can be taken advantage of by a resistant and subordinate group.
>
> (p. 497)

The "hybridization" that can take place "both denies the binary reality and power of colonizer/colonized but also sets up possibilities for new social spaces for new discourses and new forms of subjectivities that potentially can be liberatory" (Shumar, 2010, p. 499). Thus, third space framings allow us to look for those spaces that allow for the transforming of power structures. Gonsalves, Seiler, and Salter (2011) describe this last aim as identifying "cracks in structure that may be taken advantage of by the subordinate group, in order to transform that structure" (p. 396).

Those who locate the origins of third space and hybridity within educational research typically refer to work by Gutiérrez and colleagues investigating literacy practices in educational contexts. Gutiérrez, Rymes, and Larson first

used the term "third space" in a 1995 article. They argued that classrooms are characterized by "scripts," which they define as "normative patterns of life within a classroom. These scripts, characterized by particular social, spatial, and language patterns, are resources that members use to interpret the activity of others and to guide their own participation" (p. 449). In the classroom the authors based their model on, the teacher's power in the classroom was maintained through using a "monologic script" that "attempts to stifle dialogue and interaction and the potential for taking up a critical stance" (p. 446). While some students were able to participate in this script, "those who do not comply with the teacher's rules for participation form their own *counterscript*" (p. 447). The third space, then, is where "these spaces might intersect and, thus, create the potential for more authentic interaction" (p. 446). The authors argue that classrooms in which communication can take place in the third space have "inherent cognitive and sociocultural benefits" (p. 447). Classrooms in which "participants construct classroom life within this third space" are

> classrooms where there has been a dramatic shift in the identity, roles, and scripts offered in the classroom. . . . The construction of such classrooms requires more than simply "adding-on" the student script; it requires jointly constructing a new sociocultural terrain in the classroom where both student and teacher not only actively resist the monologic transcendent script, but, more importantly, also create a meaningful context for learning.
>
> (p. 468)

In a later work, Gutiérrez (2008) describes the third space as a place where students can "reconceive who they are and what they might be able to accomplish academically and beyond" (p. 148). She argues that her

> use of the Third Space construct . . . has always been more than a celebration of the local literacies of students from nondominant groups. . . . [I]t is a transformative space where the potential for an expanded form of learning and the development of new knowledge are highlighted.
>
> (p. 152)

Moje and colleagues (2004) cite both Bhabha and Gutiérrez, as well as work in the funds-of-knowledge tradition, in their conceptualization of third space. They define third space as the merging of "the 'first space' of people's home, community, and peer networks with the 'second space' of the Discourses they encounter in more formalized institutions such as work, school, or church" (Moje et al., 2004, p. 41). Like Gutiérrez, they see the point of the third space as learning; they also see it as having value in preparing students for their lives beyond school: "supporting youth in learning how to navigate the texts and literate practices necessary for survival in secondary schools and in the 'complex, diverse and sometimes dangerous world' they will be part of beyond school" (Moje et al., 2004, p. 41, citing Moore, Bean, Birdyshaw, & Rycik, 1999).

Applications of Third Space in Science Education Research

Gutiérrez, Baquedano-Lopez, and Tejeda (1999), in an early example of the use of third space in science education, describe a unit on human reproduction in a second- and third-grade class that took place in the third space. Echoing work on funds of knowledge, the authors frame "diversity and difference and the resulting hybridity as resources for creating new learning spaces" (pp. 287–288) and then illustrate with a story. After some students in the class called others names, the teacher led a discussion of the repercussions of name calling. This led to the question of the worst thing they could think of to call one another. One student volunteered "homo" and suddenly, in the words of the classroom teacher, "something sparked that before I knew it they were talking about how a baby is made and how the sperm needs to reach the egg" (Gutiérrez et al., 1999, p. 292). This led the teacher and students to develop an extensive unit on human reproduction, a unit that was "neither part of the normative practice of the school nor of the home" (p. 292) and thus, in their framing, constituted a third space. As examples of hybridity, the authors cite the teacher allowing students to propose alternative classroom tasks, drawing on their knowledge of tadpoles to better understand sperm, affirming the words children's families use for breasts as an appropriate way to talk about human physiology, and bringing students' side comments into the classroom discussion. They describe children engaging in talk and activities involving scientific concepts (for instance, "students wiggled through cardboard fallopian tubes—simulating sperm traveling through a vagina to fertilize an egg," (p. 293) and argue for the value of using third spaces in the classroom: "Of importance here is not simply the recognition of hybridity and diversity in the activity and in the language practices, but rather how hybridity and diversity can be used to promote learning" (p. 301).

Rahm (2008) studies not hybrid spaces but hybrid identities. She describes the varied cultural and language backgrounds of schoolchildren in Montreal. Under these conditions,

> it is assumed that colonialism and globalization has brought together many cultures which has led to the emergence of hybrid cultural forms, identities and experiences. . . . Accordingly, the colonized appropriate the language and culture from their colonizers, yet also combine it with their own ways and hence, develop their own hybrid forms.
>
> (p. 101)

Citing Bhabha, Gutiérrez, and Moje and colleagues, Rahm argues that third space "presupposes the co-existence of multiple and diverse understandings" and allows hybrid social positionings to emerge (p. 102). She argues that studying the hybridized identities formed by schoolchildren in Montreal is important because "such hybridized identities need to be understood if we are to make sense of

students' engagement in science or lack thereof" (p. 101) and "[b]y focusing on such hybridity, we can learn much about developmental spaces that may have been ignored in the past" (p. 102). She looks for "in-between spaces" that "youth could claim their own, feel at ease in and be who they are" (p. 102). Finally, she assumes that for spaces to support "genuine learning, science literacy development and new positioning within as well as beyond the world of science," youth must, in an echo of cultural production, "take hold of them and populate them with their own meanings and make them their own" (p. 102). She calls this "thirding."

Rahm describes a scientist–museum–school partnership targeting low-achieving urban schools and an after-school science program for girls. She recounts five case studies about elementary-age students in these programs, including four "for whom hybridity was accepted and came to transform the activity into a third space or opportunity space and made possible the exploration of new possible selves and positions while acknowledging and respecting them for who they are" (Rahm, 2008, p. 117). The hybrid identity of one youth was rejected. "Instead, she was repositioned as somebody she could not identify with or that she resisted being. Given lack of recognition of her hybrid self, the educational opportunity did not become a space she could come to own" (117). For the four youth who successfully positioned themselves as "somebody who can do science and who enjoys science" (p. 116), Rahm recounts the benefits, including a student with learning problems coming to enjoy school, a girl who followed her own interests in both chemistry and the social implications of alcohol, and another girl who came to understand more about how telephones work. She concludes,

> [b]y creating opportunity spaces and places that build on youths' funds of knowledge and allow[ing] for the co-option of science between youth and adults, we could possibly turn youths' interest in science into genuine science literacy for many of them, irrespective of who they are or want to become.
>
> (p. 120)

Richardson Bruna (2009) envisions a third space dedicated to political change—to identifying and taking advantage of "cracks in the structure that advantage subordinate groups" (Gonsalves et al., 2011). She describes the lives and school science experiences of Jesús and María, who are both from Mexico and in the United States without documentation. They work the third shift (11:30 p.m.–6:30 a.m.) at a meatpacking plant; their job is to use powerful chemicals to clean up the plant after each day's slaughter of thousands of animals. Richardson Bruna (2009) describes the "tension between possibility and constraint" (p. 229) of María's experiences in her science class, which she attends every morning after working overnight. Her teacher works hard to help María master the science content; he works directly with her during class, he provides Spanish-language materials, he encourages students to translate for María, and he searches for metaphors that will be personally meaningful to her. But throughout, María struggles against her lack of mastery of instructional English and especially her exhaustion. Despite her teacher's efforts, María reached the end of a unit without mastering the topic.

Richardson Bruna (2009) then poses questions about what sort of science education might be useful to María and Jesús:

> Jesús and María, surely if they stay in the US and nearly just as surely if they return to Mexico, will not go on to study the sciences in college, and neither will they secure a science-based career. As long as "who they are" is "illegal" (here) and "poor" (there, as well as here), their opportunities for socioeconomic advancement are relegated to a market of low-wage labor. Where is the possible future for science education in this kind of constrained present?
>
> (p. 233)

Her answer is that science education needs to take up subject matter with political ends in mind.

Elmesky (2011), in an article that emerged from her collaborative work with urban high school students in a program designed to find ways to improve science education in urban schools, put forward a central obstacle:

> Students are expected to discount ways of being that are perceived as "nonscientific" (i.e., rap practices) in order to experience success in science classrooms. A lack of tolerance for hybridity within science classrooms limits the manners by which a student can experience a sense of belonging, and she/he may struggle to be their "own person."
>
> (p. 54)

One of the student researchers made the same point:

> I got so much stuff goin on outside of school that you have no idea about . . . teach me something—I'm gonna appreciate that. . . . Let this [school] be the place where I can do me. . . . I think that schools nowadays should tryda get the person who's actually being taught input because that's who it's about anyway, right? . . . I mean you're your own person.
>
> (p. 54)

In her article, she argues, as other third-space researchers do, for the inclusion of "heterogeneous cultural ways of being that would be typically considered as unscientific" (p. 56) to enrich and make more meaningful science, especially for marginalized African-American youth. Elmesky, like Rahm (2008), focuses on students' hybrid identities and argues that students need to find room for their complex identities in science settings. This is an urgent problem, she argues: "Students determine early on whether they belong or fit within a community" (Elmesky, 2011, p. 60), and these storylines of self form and re-form in practice.

She includes examples of both planned and freestyle student raps with science themes. She directly addresses the critique that there is not enough "real science" in the raps:

> Mainstream science teachers might argue that raps like Ivory's do not really address the science material deeply, and perhaps that is a viable perception. However, Shakeem [a student researcher] challenges such conclusions by asking, "Now if they say they can't see the science in it, then how come I could? . . . Maybe *you're* not thinkin wide enough. You know what I'm sayin? It's not *the way* [emphasis added] of learnin so it's like it's something new."
>
> (pp. 62–63)

Elmesky argues that when students rap about science and in science contexts, it not only gives them the opportunity to begin to work with science concepts, it also adds to their status ("Ivory's rap . . . helped her to achieve outcomes of respect or symbolic capital," [p. 63]) and helps "build solidarity with the group" (a benefit Elmesky saw after her own first rap attempt, which received student responses from "I'm sorry, but that sucked!" to "That was decent!" [p. 72]). Elmesky concludes with a call for "creolized forms of science" (p. 74) that embrace students' hybridization of their identities.

Despite the promise of these studies, a great deal of current writing on hybridity and third space seems to focus on how they should be used rather than using them *a priori* to frame research studies (see, for instance, Adams, Luitel, Afonso, & Taylor, 2008; Carter, 2006; Emdin, 2009; Gonsalves, Seiler, & Salter, 2011; Knain, 2006; Quigley, 2011; Richardson Bruna, 2009; Roth, 2008; Shumar, 2010). A notable exception is the collaboration of Calabrese Barton and Tan (see, for instance, Calabrese Barton & Tan, 2009; Calabrese Barton, Tan, & Rivet, 2008). Scholars are just beginning to explore this framework's potential to use hybridity and third space to "establish viable and consistent images of a science classroom that affords marginalized students the opportunity to be . . . one's 'own person' while simultaneously participating in the science discipline" (Elmesky, 2011, p. 54). Done well, third-space and hybridity work capitalizes on strengths from both the funds of knowledge research and cultural production. This approach lets us study how science settings can grow and change in response to what students bring with them to the setting, changes that are prompted not just by teachers or just by students but in the interaction between them.[3]

Conclusion

Culture has great "explanatory potential for the injustice and inequity tied up with science and science education's history and for science education's potential to use its power for the good of the people and the environment, and to challenge inequitable social structures" (Parsons & Carlone, 2013, p. 10). A cultural lens for science education can be a tool for counter-hegemony (Hammond & Brandt, 2004). As the scholarship reviewed in this chapter makes clear, both cultural anthropologists and science education researchers have made good use of culture. The classic definition of culture, with its implications for the meaning of cultural difference, has been used by many researchers in science education to identify, describe, and celebrate what nondominant students struggle with and what they can offer in formal education. Whether the focus is on the struggle or the offerings, science education researchers have used this knowledge to try and fashion classroom reforms that mitigate the difficulties and support the contributions of nondominant students and their communities. Many have been successful in the local contexts of their work.[4]

Over time, refinements and modifications to the classic definition of culture have been proposed and taken up by researchers. In science education, conceptions of funds of knowledge and culturally responsive pedagogy have led to closer ties between communities and local schools and to greater appreciation for the power dynamics that shape the lives of nondominant students. Concepts of cultural productions, figured worlds, and third space have pointed the way to the creative potential for innovation, transformation, and social change in the interactions of diverse children, their teachers and parents in classrooms.

What is most important about "culture" to many cultural anthropologists and science education researchers today is not the patterns of history, geography, ethnicity, or tradition but the actual enacted practices and negotiated meanings of people who interact together in groups. History, background, and tradition matter, of course; today's practices and meanings embed and draw on them, but they are not determined by them. Individuals and groups act in, with, and on practices and meanings in the local contexts of their lives that include multiple, diverse, and overlapping influences from school, family, community, and beyond. People's actions and interpretations in and of these contexts can be both reproductive and productive, both accepting and transgressive, with respect to history and structure.

Science education researchers who have relied on the concept of culture in its various versions have focused most of their attention on schools and classrooms—and understandably so. This is where individuals can have an immediate, direct impact on the lives of schoolchildren. Culture-oriented studies of local classrooms and the children in them give teachers, researchers, and others the context-sensitive tools to improve and expand educational opportunities.

But at the same time, the focus on diversity in local schools and classrooms—how to think about it, how to identify it, how to celebrate it, how to overcome or appreciate or learn from it—seems to have obscured the extraordinary power of hegemonic cultural forces in the wider society to shape what goes on in the name of education. Cultural forces driving increased standardized testing,

greater accountability, more market-driven reforms, and new forms of school segregation, ideological separation, and educational inequality are overwhelming the conscientious efforts of local school teachers, teacher educators, and reformers to improve education in ways consistent with ideas and commitments of researchers focused on (local) culture. These larger cultural forces have escaped all but the barest attention from science educational researchers. We must develop ways of thinking about culture beyond the local. This is not, in our view, a matter of scaling up what has been learned about culture locally. It is a matter of reconceptualizing culture for the purposes of equity-minded research and reform on a much larger scale.

There are other challenges. How do we take seriously the multicultural nature of classrooms, the changing nature of social life, unstable economic conditions, and increasing globalization? Where is "culture" amid the varied and diverse personal and social relationships and networks in which we participate? (Eisenhart, 2001b). These conditions make defining the group and the individual amid the group in science learning settings an incredibly complex endeavor. We need new thinking and new tools to research culture to understand its relevance for improving science education. While the articles in this chapter provide a start to this conversation, there is clearly more work to be done, theoretically, methodologically, and with regard to practice and policy. Science educators interested in culture and science education reform have major tasks ahead of them.

Notes

1. There are other important perspectives on culture that have informed science education research. Critical and poststructural approaches have been especially influential (e.g., Carter, 2006, 2006; Gough, 2010; Hodson, 2003; Roth & Calabrese Barton, 2004; Tan & Calabrese Barton, 2012).
2. For a comparison of the same data analyzed from a cultural difference perspective and from a cultural production perspective, and the benefits and insights possible from each approach, see Carlone and Johnson (2012).
3. The issues we cover in this chapter have been and continue to be salient in the U.S. context, where our own perspectives are rooted. As such, we have not discussed international or globalizing contexts. Nonetheless, we recognize that issues of cultural difference, cultural relevance, different levels of culture (micro and macro, local and global), and the functions of culture (hegemonic, counter-hegemonic) are likely to be even more complicated in international contexts.
4. Unfortunately, these efforts have usually been isolated and short term—dependent on the presence of innovative teachers or knowledgeable researchers.

References

Adams, J., Luitel, B. C., Afonso, E., & Taylor, P. C. (2008). A cogenerative inquiry using postcolonial theory to envisage culturally inclusive science education. *Cultural Studies of Science Education, 3*(4), 999–1019.

Aikenhead, G. S. (1996). Science education: Border crossing into the subculture of science. *Studies in Science Education, 27*, 1–52.

Aikenhead, G. S. (2006). *Science education for everyday life: Evidence-based practice.* New York: Teachers College Press.

Aikenhead, G. S., & Jegede, O. J. (1999). Cross-cultural science education: A cognitive explanation of a cultural phenomenon. *Journal of Research in Science Teaching, 36*(3), 269–287.

August, D., Branum-Martin, L., Cardenas-Hagan, E., & Francis, D. J. (2009). The impact of an instructional intervention on the science and language learning of middle grade English language learners. *Journal of Research on Educational Effectiveness, 2*(4), 345–376.

Barab, S. A., & Hay, K. E. (2001). Doing science at the elbows of experts: Issues related to the science apprenticeship camp. *Journal of Research in Science Teaching, 38*(1), 70–102.

Basu, S. J., & Calabrese Barton, A. (2007). Developing a sustained interest in science among urban minority youth. *Journal of Research in Science Teaching, 4*(3), 466–489.

Brandt, C., & Carlone, H. (2012). Ethnographies of science education: Situated practices of science learning for social/political transformation. *Ethnography and Education, 7*(2), 143–150.

Brown, J. S., Collins, A., & Duguid, P. (1989). Situated cognition and the culture of learning. *Educational Researcher, 18,* 32–42.

Buxton, C. A. (2001). Modeling science teaching on science practice? Painting a more accurate picture through an ethnographic lab study. *Journal of Research in Science Teaching, 38,* 387–407.

Buxton, C. A., Lee, O., & Santau. A. (2008). Promoting science among English language learners: Professional development for today's culturally and linguistically diverse classrooms. *Journal of Science Teacher Education, 19*(5), 495–511.

Buxton, C. A., Salinas, A., Mahotiere, M., Lee, O., & Secada, W. G. (2013). Leveraging cultural resources through teacher pedagogical reasoning: Elementary grade teachers analyze second language learners' science problem solving. *Teaching and Teacher Education, 32,* 31–42.

Calabrese Barton, A., Kang, H., Tan, E., O'Neill, T. B., Bautista-Guerra, J., & Brecklin, C. (2013). Crafting a future in science: Tracing middle school girls' identity work over time and space. *American Educational Research Journal, 50*(1), 37–75.

Calabrese Barton, A., & Osborne, M. D. (1998). Marginalized discourses and pedagogies: Constructively confronting science for all. *Journal of Research in Science Teaching, 35,* 339–340.

Calabrese Barton, A., & Tan, E. (2009). Funds of knowledge and discourses and hybrid space. *Journal of Research in Science Teaching, 46*(1), 50–73.

Calabrese Barton, A., Tan, E., & Rivet, A. (2008). Creating hybrid spaces for engaging school science among urban middle school girls. *American Educational Research Journal, 45*(1), 68–103.

Carlone, H., & Johnson, A. (2012). Unpacking "culture" in cultural studies of science education: Cultural difference vs. cultural production. *Ethnography and Education, 7*(2), 151–173.

Carlone, H. B. (2004). The cultural production of science in reform-based physics: Girls' access, participation, and resistance. *Journal of Research in Science Teaching, 41*(4), 392–414.

Carlone, H. B., Scott, C., & Lowder, C. (in press). Becoming (less) scientific in the figured worlds of school science learning: A longitudinal study of students' identity work.

Carter, L. (2006). Postcolonial interventions within science education: Using postcolonial ideas to reconsider cultural diversity scholarship. *Educational Philosophy and Theory, 38*(5), 677–691.

Carter, L. (2010). The armchair at the borders: The "messy" ideas of borders and border epistemologies within multicultural science education scholarship. *Science Education, 94,* 428–447.

Chaiklin, S., & Lave, J. (1993). *Understanding practice: Perspectives on activity and context.* Cambridge, UK: Cambridge University Press.

Chinn, C. A., & Malhotra, B. A. (2002). Epistemologically authentic inquiry in schools: A theoretical framework for evaluating inquiry tasks. *Science Education, 86,* 175–218.

Chinn, P. (2006). Preparing science teachers for culturally diverse students: Developing cultural literacy through cultural immersion, cultural translators and communities of practice. *Cultural Studies of Science Education, 1,* 367–402.

Chiu, M.-H., & Duit, R. (2011). Globalization: Science education from an international perspective. *Journal of Research in Science Teaching, 48*(6), 553–566.

Cobb, P. (1994). Where is the mind? Constructivist and sociocultural perspectives on mathematical development. *Educational Researcher, 23,* 13–20.

Cobern, W. W. (1996). Worldview theory and conceptual change in science education. *Science Education, 80,* 579–610.

Cobern, W., & Aikenhead, G. (1998). Cultural aspects of learning science. *International Handbook of Science Education, 2,* 39–52.

Collins, H. M. (1982). *Sociology of scientific knowledge.* Bath, UK: University Press.

Costa, V. B. (1995). When science is "another world": Relationships between worlds of family, friends, school, and science. *Science Education, 79*(3), 313–333.

Cowie, B., Jones, A., & Otrel-Cass, K. (2011). Re-engaging students in science: Issues of assessment, funds of knowledge and sites for learning. *International Journal of Science and Mathematics Education, 9*(2), 347–366.

Cunningham, C. M., & Helms, J. V. (1998). Sociology of science as a means to a more authentic, inclusive science education. *Journal of Research in Science Teaching, 35*(5), 483–499.

Eisenhart, M. (1996). The production of biologists at school and work: Making scientists, conservationists, or flowery bone-heads? In B. Levinson, D. Foley, & D. Holland (Eds.) *The cultural production of the educated person: Critical ethnographies of schooling and local practice* (pp. 169–185). Albany, NY: State University of New York Press.

Eisenhart, M. (2001a). Changing conceptions of culture and ethnographic methodology: Recent thematic shifts and their implications for research on teaching. In V. Richardson (Ed.), *Handbook of research on teaching* (4th ed.; pp. 209–225). Washington, DC: American Educational Research Association.

Eisenhart, M. (2001b). Educational ethnography past, present, and future: Ideas to think with. *Educational Researcher, 30*(8), 16–27.

Eisenhart, M., & Finkel, E. (1998). *Women's science: Learning and succeeding from the margins.* University of Chicago Press.

Eisenhart, M., Finkel, E., & Marion, S. F. (1996). Creating the conditions for scientific literacy: A re-examination. *American Educational Research Journal, 33,* 261–295.

Elmesky, R. (2011). Rap as a roadway: Creating creolized forms of science in an era of cultural globalization. *Cultural Studies of Science Education, 6*(1), 49–76.

Emdin, C. (2009). Urban science classrooms and new possibilities: On intersubjectivity and grammar in the third space. *Cultural Studies of Science Education, 4*(1), 239–254.

Gonsalves, A. J., Seiler, G., & Salter, D. E. (2011). Rethinking resources and hybridity. *Cultural Studies of Science Education, 6*(2), 389–399.

Gough, N. (2010). Thinking/acting locally/globally: Western science and environmental education in a global knowledge economy. *International Journal of Science Education, 11,* 1217–1237.

Grimberg, B. I., & Gummer, E. (2013). Teaching science from cultural points of intersection. *Journal of Research in Science Teaching, 50,* 12–32.

Gutiérrez, K., Rymes, B., & Larson, J. (1995). Script, counterscript, and underlife in the classroom: James Brown versus *Brown v. Board of Education. Harvard Educational Review, 65*(3), 445–472.

Gutiérrez, K. D. (2008). Developing a sociocritical literacy in the third space. *Reading Research Quarterly, 43*(2), 148–164.

Gutiérrez, K. D., Baquedano-Lopez, P., & Tejeda, C. (1999). Rethinking diversity: Hybridity and hybrid language practices in the third space. *Mind, Culture & Activity, 6*(4), 286.

Hammond, L., & Brandt, C. (2004). Science and cultural process: Defining an anthropological approach to science education. *Studies in Science Education, 1,* 1–47.

Hatt, B. (2007). Street smarts vs. book smarts: The figured world of smartness in the lives of marginalized, urban youth. *The Urban Review, 39*(2), 145–166.

Hawkins, J., & Pea, R. D. (1987). Tools for bridging the cultures of everyday and scientific thinking. *Journal of Research in Science Teaching, 24*(4), 291–307.

Heath, S. B. (1983). *Ways with words: Language, life, and work in communities.* Cambridge, MA: Harvard University Press.

Hodson, D. (2003). Time for action: Science education for an alternative future. *International Journal of Science Education*(6), 645–670.

Holland, D.C., & Eisenhart, M.A. (1990). *Educated in romance: Women, achievement, and college culture.* Chicago: University of Chicago Press.

Holland, D., & Lachicotte, W. (2007). Vygotsky, Mead and the new sociocultural studies of identity. In H. Daniels, M. Cole, & J. Wertsch (Eds.), *The Cambridge companion to Vygotsky* (pp. 101–135). Cambridge, UK: Cambridge University Press.

Holland, D., Lachicotte, W., Skinner, D., & Cain, C. (1998). *Identity and agency in cultural worlds.* Cambridge, MA: Harvard University Press.

Jegede, O. (1995). Collateral learning and the eco-cultural paradigm in science and mathematics education in Africa. *Studies in Science Education, 25,* 97–137.

Johnson, A., Brown, J., Carlone, H., & Cuevas, A. K. (2011). Authoring identity amidst the treacherous terrain of science: A multiracial feminist examination of the journeys of three women of color in science. *Journal of Research in Science Teaching, 48,* 339–366.

Johnson, C.C. (2011). The road to culturally relevant science: Exploring how teachers navigate change in pedagogy. *Journal of Research in Science Teaching, 48,* 170–198.

Johnson, C.C., & Fargo, J.D. (2010). Urban school reform enabled by transformative professional development: Impact on teacher change and student learning of science. *Urban Education, 45*(1), 4–29.

Kelly, G.J., & Chen, C. (2001). The sound of music: Constructing science as sociocultural practices through oral and written discourse. *Journal of Research in Science Teaching, 36,* 883–915.

Kelly, G.J., Chen, C., & Crawford, T. (1998). Methodological considerations for studying science-in-the-making in educational settings. *Research in Science Education, 28*(1), 23–49.

Knain, E. (2006). Achieving science literacy through transformation of multimodal textual resources. *Science Education, 90*(4), 656–659.

Koch, P.A., Contento, I.R., & Calabrese Barton, A. (2010). *Choice, control & change: Using science to make food and activity decisions: Linking food and the environment curriculum series.* South Burlington, VT: National Gardening Association.

Ladson-Billings, G. (1994). *The dreamkeepers: Successful teachers of African American children.* San Francisco: Jossey-Bass.

Ladson-Billings, G. (1995). Toward a theory of culturally relevant pedagogy. *American Educational Research Journal, 32,* 465–491.

Larson, J. (1995). *Fatima's Rules and other elements of an unintended chemistry curriculum.* Paper presented at the annual meeting of the American Educational Research Association, San Francisco, CA.

Latour, B., & Woolgar, S. (1986). *Laboratory life: The construction of scientific facts.* Princeton, NJ: Princeton University Press.

Lave, J., & E. Wenger (1991). *Situated learning: Legitimate peripheral participation.* Cambridge: Cambridge University Press.

Lee, O. (2001). Culture and language in science education: What do we know and what do we need to know? *Journal of Research in Science Teaching, 38*(5), 499–501.

Lee, O. (2005). Science Education and Student Diversity: Synthesis and Research Agenda. *Journal of Education for Students Placed at Risk (JESPAR), 10*(4), 431–440.

Lee, O., & Buxton, C. (2011). Engaging culturally and linguistically diverse students in learning science. *Theory Into Practice, 50,* 277–284.

Lee, O., Deaktor, R.A., Hart, J.E., Cuevas, P., & Enders, C. (2005). An instructional intervention's impact on the science and literacy achievement of culturally and linguistically diverse elementary students. *Journal of Research in Science Teaching, 42,* 857–887.

Lee, O., & Fradd, S. (1998). Science for all, including students from non-English-language backgrounds. *Educational Researcher, 27*(4), 12–21.

Lee, O., Lewis, S., Adamson, K., Maerten-Rivera, J., & Secada., W.G. (2008). Urban elementary school teachers' knowledge and practices in teaching science to English language learners. *Science Education, 92,* 733–758.

Lemke, J. L. (1990). *Talking science: Language, learning, and values.* Norwood, NJ: Ablex Publishing.

Lemke, J.L. (2001). Articulating communities: Sociocultural perspectives on science education. *Journal of Research in Science Teaching, 38*(3), 296–316.

Levinson, B.A., Foley, D.E., & Holland, D.C. (1996). *The cultural production of the educated person: Critical ethnographies of schooling and local practice.* New York: SUNY Press.

Mensah, F. M. (2011). A case for culturally relevant teaching in science education and lessons learned for teacher education. *The Journal of Negro Education, 80*(3), 296–309.

Michael, A., Andrade, N., & Bartlett, L. (2007). Figuring "success" in a bilingual high school. *The Urban Review, 39*(2), 167–189.

Moje, E.B., Ciechanowski, K.M., Kramer, K., Ellis, L., Carrillo, R., & Collazo, T. (2004). Working toward third space in content area literacy: An examination of everyday funds of knowledge and discourse. *Reading Research Quarterly, 39*(1), 38–70.

Moll, L.C., Amanti, C., Neff, D., & Gonzalez, N. (1992). Funds of knowledge for teaching: Using a qualitative approach to connect homes and classrooms. *Theory Into Practice, 31*(2), 132–141.

Monzó, L. D., & Rueda, R. (2009). Passing for English fluent: Latino immigrant children masking language proficiency. *Anthropology & Education Quarterly 40*(1), 20–40.

Moore, D. W., Bean, T. W., Birdyshaw, D., & Ryick, J. A. (1999). Adolescent literacy: A position statement. *Journal of Adolescent & Adult Literacy, 43,* 97–111.

Morrison, K.A., Robbins, H.H., & Rose, D.G. (2008). Operationalizing culturally relevant pedagogy: A synthesis of classroom-based research. *Equity and Excellence in Education, 41*(4), 433–452.

National Research Council. (1996). *National science education standards.* Washington, DC: National Academies Press.

Nieto, S. (2000). Placing equity front and center: Some thoughts on transforming teacher education for a new century. *Journal of Teacher Education, 51*(3), 180–187.

O'Loughlin, M. (1992). Rethinking science education: Beyond Piagetian constructivism toward a sociocultural model of teaching and learning. *Journal of Research in Science Teaching, 29,* 791–820.

Parsons, E.C., & Carlone, H. (2013). Culture and science education in the 21st century: Extending and making the cultural box more inclusive. *Journal of Research in Science Teaching, 50,* 1–11.

Parsons, E.C., Travis, C., & Simpson, J.S. (2005). The Black cultural ethos, students' instructional context preferences, and student achievement: An examination of culturally congruent science instruction in the eighth grade classes of one African American and one Euro-American teacher. *The Negro Educational Review, 56*(2 & 3), 183–204.

Patchen, T., & Cox-Petersen, A. (2008). Constructing cultural relevance in science: A case study of two elementary teachers. *Science Education, 92,* 994–1014.

Phelan, P., Davidson, A., & Cao, H. (1991). Students' multiple worlds: Negotiating the boundaries of family, peer, and school cultures. *Anthropology & Education Quarterly, 22,* 224–249.

Quigley, C. (2011). Pushing the boundaries of cultural congruence pedagogy in science education towards a third space. *Cultural Studies of Science Education, 6,* 549–557.

Rahm, J. (2008). Urban youths' hybrid positioning in science practices at the margin: A look inside a school–museum–scientist partnership project and an after-school science program. *Cultural Studies of Science Education, 3*(1), 97–121.

Richardson Bruna, K. (2009). Jesús and María in the jungle: An essay on possibility and constraint in the third-shift third space. *Cultural Studies of Science Education, 4*(1), 221–237.

Riojas-Cortez, M., Huerta, M.E., Flores, B.B., Perez, B., & Clark, E.R. (2008). Using cultural tools to develop scientific literacy of young Mexican American preschoolers. *Early Child Development and Care, 178*(5), 527–536.

Rodriguez, A.J. (1997). The dangerous discourse of invisibility: A critique of the National Research Council's National Science Education Standards. *Journal of Research in Science Teaching, 34,* 19–37.

Rosebery, A.S., Ogonowski, M., DiSchino, M., & Warren, B. (2010). "The coat traps all your body heat": Heterogeneity as fundamental to learning. *Journal of the Learning Sciences, 19*(3), 322–357.

Roth, W.-M. (2008). Bricolage, metissage, hybridity, heterogeneity, diaspora: Concepts for thinking science education in the 21st century. *Cultural Studies of Science Education, 3*(4), 891–916.

Roth, W.-M., & Calabrese Barton, A. (2004). *Rethinking scientific literacy.* New York: RoutledgeFalmer.

Seiler, G. (2013). New metaphors about culture: Implications for research in science teacher preparation. *Journal of Research in Science Teaching, 50*(1), 104–121.

Shumar, W. (2010). Homi Bhabha. *Cultural Studies of Science Education, 5*(2), 495–506.

Sikoyo, L. N., & Jacklin, H. (2009). Exploring the boundary between school science and everyday knowledge in primary school pedagogic practices. *British Journal of Sociology of Education, 30*(6), 713–726.

Tan, E., & Calabrese Barton, A. (2007). Unpacking science for all through the lens of identities-in-practice: The stories of Amelia and Ginny. *Cultural Studies of Science Education, 3,* 43–71.

Tan, E., & Calabrese Barton, A. (2012). *Empowering science and mathematics education in urban schools.* Chicago: University of Chicago Press.

Tobin, K., & Gallagher, J. J. (1987). What happens in high school science classrooms? *Journal of Curriculum Studies, 19,* 549–560.

Tonso, K. L. (2006). Student engineers and engineer identity: Campus engineer identities as figured world. *Cultural Studies of Science Education, 1*(2), 273–307.

Traweek, S. (1988). *Beamtimes and lifetimes: The world of high energy physicists.* Cambridge, MA: Harvard University Press.

Tsurusaki, B. K., Calabrese Barton, A., Tan, E., Koch, P., & Contento, I. (2013). Using transformative boundary objects to create critical engagement in science: A case study. *Science Education, 97,* 1–31.

Upadhyay, B. (2009). Teaching science for empowerment in an urban classroom: A case study of a Hmong teacher. *Equity & Excellence in Education, 42*(2), 217–232.

Urrieta, L. (2007). Identity production in figured worlds: How some Mexican Americans become Chicana/o activist educators. *The Urban Review, 39,* 117–144.

Vélez-Ibáñez, C. G., & Greenberg, J. B. (1992). Formation and transformation of funds of knowledge among U.S.-Mexican households. *Anthropology & Education Quarterly, 23*(4), 313–335.

Warren, B., Ballenger, C., Ogonowski, M., Rosebery, A. S., & Hudicourt-Barnes, J. (2001). Rethinking diversity in learning science: The logic of everyday sense-making. *Journal of Research in Science Teaching, 38,* 529–552.

Wood, N. B., Erichson, E. A., & Anicha, C. L. (2013). Cultural emergence: Theorizing culture in and from the margins of science education. *Journal of Research in Science Teaching, 50,* 122–136.

Xu, J., Coats, L. T., & Davidson, M. L. (2011). Promoting student interest in science: The perspectives of exemplary African American teachers. *American Educational Research Journal, 49*(1), 124–154.

33

Culturally Relevant Schooling in Science for Indigenous Learners Worldwide

Stressing the All *in Science Literacy for All*

ELEANOR ABRAMS, LARRY D. YORE, MEGAN BANG, BRYAN MCKINLEY JONES BRAYBOY, ANGELINA CASTAGNO, JOANNA KIDMAN, HUEI LEE, MARY GRACE VILLANUEVA, MING HUEY WANG, PAUL WEBB, AND CHIUNG-FEN YEN

Scientific literacy for ***all*** students (i.e., mainstream literacy for citizenship) has been the goal for many of the national and international reforms in science for more than 20 years. However, more recent efforts have been devoted to meeting global demands for a science, technology, engineering, and mathematics (STEM) workforce pipeline by increasing the number of students pursuing STEM degrees and careers. These efforts have focused on minorities, including indigenous people; but the focus on pipeline issues—rather than mainstream issues to grow the populations of qualified indigenous students interested in STEM careers—has left universities battling for a small number of qualified indigenous students and most countries striving to achieve mainstream and pipeline goals. We respectfully use the term *indigenous peoples* to refer to long-term inhabitants of a place with traditional knowledge of the place. We are aware that naming a large and diverse group also brings the "hue and connotation with which all attempts at labeling are imbued" (Carter & Walker, 2010, p. 343); therefore, when possible, we use specific proper names for specific places or peoples—American Native Indians, Australian Aboriginals, Canadian First Nations, Inuit, or Métis, Torres Strait Islanders, and so forth. For example, indigenous Australian students (Australian Aboriginals and Torres Strait Islanders) scored significantly lower in science than did other Australians on the 2009 Program of International Student Assessment (PISA), an established international test with nonindigenous foundations, reaffirming that trend of underachievement found in previous PISA tests (Thomson, De Bortoli, Nicholas, Hillman, & Buckley, 2010). The 2007 National Assessment of Educational Progress testing in the United States for science found fourth-grade White students scoring 163 and American Indians/Alaskan Natives scoring 135 out of a possible 300 points (Mead, Grigg, Moran, & Kuang, 2010). Likewise, in Canada, indigenous students consistently score lower than do nonindigenous students in reading, mathematics, and science. This gap in science

achievement continues through public secondary and postsecondary schooling. Indigenous high school students in Canada and the United States participate in advanced science courses at a much lower rate than do nonindigenous students, are less likely to pursue STEM majors in college, and are underrepresented in STEM careers (United States Department of Education, 2008; Yore et al., 2014). This gap negatively affects the economics, health, and well-being of indigenous communities as well as diminishes the vitality of the STEM disciplines. Such achievement gaps may lie in the inequalities of standardized testing—lack of authentic measures, inappropriate language demands, limited response modalities, and culturally sensitive administration conditions for indigenous students (Atkinson, 2010).

Several researchers have used secondary analyses of the PISA results from Aotearoa (New Zealand), Australia, and Canada to determine the differences in the reading, mathematics, and science literacies of 15-year-old indigenous and nonindigenous students (Anderson, Lin, Treagust, Ross, & Yore, 2007; McConney, Oliver, Woods-McConney, & Schibeci, 2013; Woods-McConney, Oliver, McConney, Major, & Schibeci, 2011; Yore et al., 2014). Likely, both reading and mathematics literacies served as gatekeepers or barriers for science literacy, as the correlations among these disciplinary literacies at the individual student level across the 2000 through 2009 international PISA results were extremely high (0.75–0.88; Yore et al., 2014). Woods-McConney and colleagues (2011) found that affective factors (i.e., enjoyment, interest, values, self-efficacy, and self-concept) were associated with participation in informal learning experiences and family and school factors (i.e., socioeconomic status, classroom teaching, time spent on science lessons) were associated with science literacy performance.

Research examining the teaching and learning of indigenous students in science classrooms has offered additional causes for their underperformance in science.

These include the differing epistemological and ontological underpinnings of indigenous knowledge and wisdom (IKW) when compared to the production of Western modern science (WMS; Snively & Williams, 2008; Yore, 2008); the manner of typical science instruction (Handa & Tippins, 2012); the nature of indigenous learners, and the potentially colonizing influence of schooling itself (Battiste, Kovach, & Balzer, 2010). There is also an ongoing debate about how scientific literacy is defined and by whom and whether a singular science literacy should be replaced by plural science literacies (Aikenhead & Ogawa, 2007).

The spectrum of solutions proposed ranges from "**Do not include IKW**" because it is a slippery slope to a post-modern view of science and the inclusion of creationist science, "**Infusing IKW into WMS**" on constructivist pedagogical grounds to engage indigenous students' prior knowledge and experiences, and "**Develop co-equal interpretations of IKW and WMS**" as multiple views of sciences and knowledge about nature and naturally occurring events. The first option, as evidenced from the PISA scores, has not worked at engaging indigenous students in science classrooms. This chapter will focus on the relative strengths and limitations of the second and third options as potential solutions. It is clear that any attempt to resolve the issues of indigenous engagement and achievement in science will likely be context specific and needs to consider the sociopolitical and sociocultural dimensions of the problem space, including cultural preservation, linguistic restoration, equity, social justice, economic prosperity, and identity as well as the content, pedagogical, and assessment dimensions normally considered in educational reforms. Colonization in the 16th to 19th centuries and movement of people between the continents and islands of the world in search of safety, survival, freedom, and economic advantages have led to mixtures of cultures within a given geographic place. Apparent monocultures (e.g., China, Japan, Sweden, Taiwan, etc.) are in fact multicultural countries. Some places (e.g., the United States) have adopted a *melting-pot* approach to assimilate the diversities into an ethnic and cultural alloy that establishes a national character aligned with the dominant culture. Canada, which originally enacted a similar assimilation approach to retain the dominant colonial English and French characteristics, has more recently enacted a multicultural mosaic that retains individual ethnic and cultural characteristics and acculturates diverse groups of people. Aotearoa New Zealand has implemented a bicultural approach by federal law, where the Treaty of Waitangi protects the rights of the Maori people (McKinley & Keegan, 2008).

In 2007, the United Nations (UN) supported the right of indigenous peoples to educate their children, understanding that each country and situation was different. The UN General Assembly's Article 14 (UN, 2007) declared that Indigenous peoples have the right, without discrimination, to establish and control their educational systems and institutions, provide education in their own languages, in a manner appropriate to their cultural methods of teaching and learning. Central governments shall, in partnership with indigenous peoples, support access for children to have an education in their own culture and language even. However, ensuring that indigenous students have access to culturally responsive education within the cultural institution that is science education has proven to be challenging.

Limitations to culturally responsive schooling (CRS) in science for indigenous students have been the lack of both indigenous perspectives and frank, honest, and fulsome considerations of knowledge about nature and naturally occurring events as part of science education reforms, curricula, and instruction.[1] A majority of researchers have conducted most of the research on the failure of indigenous learners to achieve and engage in science involving outdated interpretations of learning based on deficit models of learners and restricted to formal environments in schools (United States National Research Council [NRC], 2007, 2009). The lack of full participation by indigenous communities can lead to a skewed vision in which children of the majority society are whole and do not need to be fixed while children of the minority society are missing something and need to be fixed (Levinson, 2012).

The indigenous and nonindigenous authors of this chapter represent a small fraction of the international perspectives and diverse worldviews on how to support indigenous learners in science classrooms by design. This chapter is designed to complement the chapter on indigenous science education included in the last *Handbook on Research in Science Education* (McKinley, 2007) and focuses on post–2005 literature supporting indigenous learners in science classrooms. Tensions and conflicting viewpoints on what is CRS in science for indigenous learning globally are represented rather than resolved.

Making Sense of Nature and Naturally Occurring Events

People worldwide have attempted to explore, describe, and understand nature and naturally occurring events from the beginning of recorded history. Early wall paintings and petroglyphs have indicated people's interest in and attempts to record and describe things and events in their environments, while their ceremonies and spiritual traditions revealed beliefs about natural and supernatural causes. Each attempt reflected the people's cultural values, personal interests and priorities, intellectual resources, and available technologies and produced distinctive ways of thinking, truth-seeking procedures, knowledge claims, and reporting techniques. The understanding of the central intentions of this chapter requires a contextual overview of people's attempts to make sense of nature and naturally occurring events.

Cultural histories are rich with examples of common people trying to describe patterns of events in nature that focused on their survival. Many of these dealt with obtaining and preserving food, personal security, travel, games/contests, and weather conditions. These insights and technologies travelled with them as they moved from place to place. The usefulness of the insights and technologies may have changed as the biological, geographical, and meteorological features changed with their new location or as their understanding of nature and naturally occurring events changed. These insights and technologies were revised or replaced to meet new challenges and conditions and to take advantage of new knowledge and resources.

Stories About Nature and Naturally Occurring Events

Some historical efforts captured by stories, adages, or proverbs involve poetic descriptions and implied cause-effects in short, memorable verse. There is a tendency in modern societies to discount this place-based wisdom, without fully understanding or valuing its epistemic strength based on long-term observation and thinking. The most common stories are about the weather related to navigation, agriculture, and daily life, which used observable conditions of the environment and living things to forecast or predict upcoming weather conditions (Freier, 1989; Inwards, 1869). Both indigenous and nonindigenous peoples of North America, for example, could predictably forecast pending storms and winds and taught their children how to read the weather. First Nations peoples in Saskatchewan would watch the leaves of the ash tree or listen to the chatter of a squirrel to predict rain (Young, 2003). Most nonindigenous children in North America have learned the predictive adage: *Red sky at night, sailors' delight. Red sky at morning, sailors take warning.* Many readers will know of people who use their long-term residential experiences in a location and holistic knowledge of animal behaviors and climate conditions to predict short-term local weather better than the meteorologists do. Weather can also be explained scientifically by prevailing winds, high- and low-pressure cells, and movements of cold and warm air masses. Both knowledge sets are useful in daily living.

IKW and WMS regarding nature and naturally occurring events are similar to and different from one another. Understanding and addressing these similarities and differences are the central foci of this chapter, and some of our cultural and pedagogical findings may be applicable to engaging nonindigenous students with other traditional beliefs.

Indigenous Knowledge and Wisdom (IKW) and Science

The views of IKW and WMS vary across authors and philosophical perspectives (Horsthemke & Yore, 2014). Some people claim that various interpretations were merely views among several valid views of knowledge about nature and naturally occurring events. This postmodern position may or may not be true, but most scholars agree that it is worthwhile to know the similarities and differences among these knowledge systems.

IKW and WMS Stories

The following stories—the cause of wind or severe storms—from North American, Taiwanese, and WMS perspectives illustrate the similarities and differences in content and linguistic features; they continue the earlier theme established in weather lore.

Caduto and Bruchac (1991) retold the ancient Abenaki people's (People of the Dawn Land located along the eastern border of Canada and the United States) story about "Gluscabi and the Wind Eagle" (used here respecting the ownership of the Abenaki people):

> Long ago, Gluscabi lived with his grandmother, Woodchuck, in a small lodge beside the big water. . . . "Grandmother," Gluscabi said, "what makes the wind blow?"
>
> Grandmother Woodchuck looked up from her work. "Gluscabi," she said, "why do you want to know?" . . . "Because." he said. . . .
>
> [Gluscabi's grandmother told him:] "Far from here, on top of the tallest mountain, a great bird stands. This bird is named Wuchowsen, and when he flaps his wings he makes the wind blow."
>
> (pp. 41–42)

The story then describes Gluscabi's travel to Wuchowsen's home at the top of a mountain, how he tricks the Wind Eagle into being transported to a more advantageous mountain, and his ultimate entrapment in a crevice, resulting in no wind and very hot days. Gluscabi realizes his error and sets about to correct it. Caduto and Bruchac continued:

> Then Gluscabi climbed down into the crevice. He pulled the Wind Eagle free and placed him back on his mountain and untied his wings.
>
> "Uncle," Gluscabi said, "it is good that the wind should blow sometimes and other times it is good that it should be still."
>
> Wuchowsen, the Wind Eagle, agreed and said: "I hear what you say."
>
> So it is that sometimes there is wind and sometimes it is still to this very day. And so the story goes.
>
> (p. 49)

There are many similar IKW stories regarding rainbows, clouds, rain, and other weather events among the indigenous people worldwide, such as the Seediq and Bunun tribes in Taiwan (Lee, Chiang, & Lin, 2011). Seediq peoples treat rainbows as the bridge between ancestral spirits and living people. These stories say that men need to know hunting and women need to know weaving in order to walk across the Rainbow Bridge (*hakaw utux*) when they die to meet with ancestral spirits (*utux*). The Bunun peoples believe the rainbow (*hanivava*), like a wall, can separate the rain from good weather. Wherever rainbows are seen, it will not rain, while the places beyond the rainbows will still be raining. It is taboo in both tribes to point your finger toward rainbows, which represents irreverence.

The Bunun peoples have lived in the Wulu Gorge, Taitung county southeastern Taiwan, around a river terrace or tableland for a very long time. They have observed a "lift water" (literal translation) phenomenon in the fall near the mid-autumn festival, an established Bunun time marker, due to an airflow change that causes a particular phenomenon. The elders mentioned that rain happens after the cloud falls down and rises up again. Furthermore, according to the Bunun's long-time experience, before a typhoon, the clouds will float around because of the strong wind and concentrate toward the central mountain range. At dusk in the western sky, a flamboyant cloud (*sumbaiv*) will emerge. If the wind blows east to west, a typhoon will occur and cause it to rain very heavily, but it will not cause much damage. However, if the wind direction is north to south, it will be a strong typhoon and cause severe destruction.

Parallel WMS stories of what causes winds or severe storms would involve networks of claims and causal relationships among the rotation of the earth, solar radiation, differential heating and cooling, cold and hot air masses, pressure differences, and movement of air particles from areas of high concentration and high pressure to areas of low concentration and low pressure. Prevailing winds within 0 to 30 (easterlies), 30 to 60 (westerlies), 60 to 90 (easterlies) degrees north or south latitude from the equator are caused by the Coriolis effect, which involves the deflection of north-south or south-north surface movements of air and the rotation of the earth. Regional winds are caused by the Coriolis effect setting low- and high-pressure cells rotating and the serpentine movement of air particles along the high- to low-pressure gradient. Localized breezes (e.g., mountain, valley, land, ocean) are caused by the differential warming and cooling of land and water bodies that establish pressure differences and movement of air particles to balance the pressure differences. Severe storms (lightning-thunder, tornados, hurricanes, typhoons) result from (a) colliding cold and hot moist air masses that force the moist air to rise, cool, and condense, thereby releasing additional heat and causing static electricity and discharge and (b) rapidly rotating, super-strong low-pressure cells formed over heated land or ocean areas that move east-west in the tropics or west-east in the middle latitudes.

These IKW and WMS stories are different in their linguistic characteristics (e.g., terminology, causal linkages, logical connectives, terse style, personal voice, etc.), reporting genre (e.g., narrative story grammar, expository explanation), and ontological features (e.g., assumptions about reality, observer–observed relationships, generalized claims, cause–effect mechanisms). The question about which story is best should receive the relative response, *It depends*—since all of the stories have cultural value and personal importance to the peoples owning the stories and to outsiders who want to understand the

originators or specific events (Yore, Florence, Pearson, & Weaver, 2006).

Denying or ignoring the existence of alternative interpretations has the effect of shunning a knowledge system held by students, devaluing their prior knowledge, and disengaging them from considering any alternative view. These barriers to border crossing or bridge building between knowledge systems discount the fundamental principle of humanistic constructivism—assessing what people know and respectfully teaching them accordingly (Aikenhead, 2006). Effective science teachers have long respected religious interpretations of cosmology and developmental biology and have used weather lore to illustrate people's involvement in explaining naturally occurring events and connecting those explanations to WMS in their science classroom. Only recently have teachers in some schools been empowered to develop integrated IKW–WMS programs or infuse IKW into their science instruction (McKinley, 2007; McKinley & Stewart, 2012; Snively & Williams, 2008). Lack of engaging and authentic IKW appears to be the case for many peoples and students (indigenous and nonindigenous) in formal classrooms and informal environments, preventing them from crossing borders between IKW and WMS interpretations of and broadening their views of nature and naturally occurring events (George, 2013; Wright, Claxton, Williams, & Paul, 2011; Yore et al., 2014).

Characteristics of IKW

Scholars have provided summaries of the fundamental characteristics, attributes, and features of IKW (Aikenhead & Elliott, 2010; Aikenhead & Michell, 2012; Aikenhead & Ogawa; 2007; Fakudze & Rollnick, 2008; McKinley & Keegan, 2008; Rogers, 2007; Rose, 1996; Snively & Williams, 2008). Traditional IKW about nature and naturally occurring events are claims and explanations based on centuries of observations and descriptions within the oral traditions of the indigenous culture originating the knowledge. These place-based IKW claims are not static since they are verified with regular revisits to the place and are revised by those designated as knowledge keepers (Snively & Williams, 2008). The epistemic quality of the observations and thinking are not substantially different from that of formal scientists, although there may be less reliance on modern technologies. However, the ontological nature of explanations tended to be holistic and cyclic and a blend of spiritualism, mysticism, and physical causality (Yore, 2008). Aikenhead (2006) suggested that IKW was seen as knowledge that supports a way of living for survival and harmony; coexists with and celebrates mystery intimately and subordinately related over human actions; reflects a circular or cyclic conception of time; uses content validity on practical applications over thousands of years of survival as justification; and involves holistic, flexible, intuitive, and spiritual wisdom.

The Taiwanese Bunun people's worldview and their universal relationship were based on their sources of food and survival, which depended on millet planting and hunting. Central questions driving their knowledge system were: How can we grow good quality and quantity of millet? What is the best way to hunt the Formosan wild boar? (Lee et al., 2011). These knowledge quests and constructions used long-term observations of natural phenomena; their regularity and correlation with life events led to understandings of the basis for astronomical and meteorological knowledge that were deemed practical within tribal culture. These ideas' importance was illustrated when the Bunun people required two obligatory science courses in the school curriculum dealing with astronomical and meteorological events when consulted about the education of their children. When the tribal elders taught astronomical and meteorological knowledge, they stressed purpose and practicality, for example, observing wind direction, cloud layers, and local changes, and animal behaviors to avoid bad weather when hunting. They also stressed plant growth, seasonal changes, aspects of astrology (*bunuh*), and phases of the moon required to judge when to sow millet and to cultivate the seedlings and young plants. These ideas were directly connected to their core purposes of millet planting and hunting.

Apela Colorado, director of the Worldwide Indigenous Science Network (n.d.), pointed out that indigenous people do not separate the person from truth seeking and require close ownership of both the process and product to ensure validity and integrity of the knowledge. Her people, the Oneida tribe of the Iroquoian people, considered all things in nature to be intelligent and alive (animate) and that the purpose of IKW is to maintain balance concerned with understanding the relationships among all things; they collapse time and space, resulting in the overlap of past and present and limited separation—currency and closeness. She pointed out that IKW was holistic, including the spiritual and psychic senses; she suggested that this balance, which her people called the "Great Peace" (para. #7), was peaceful and electrifying; her people accept that they have not transcended nature as they remain embodied in the natural world.

Characteristics of WMS

History is replete with various and changing descriptions of science (Abd-El-Khalick, Chapter 31, this volume); some descriptions were romanticized views of truth-seeking processes that may have been idealized and may never have actually existed (Ziman, 2000). Philosophers who consider knowledge systems and knowledge production have frequently tried to define the ontological assumptions about reality on which the knowledge system is based and describe the epistemological beliefs and practices used to construct the knowledge claims. Yore, Hand, and Florence (2004) suggested that knowledge systems build on a realism assumption and stressed that the real world (reality) can be explored, described, and explained by people, these activities are within their capacities, and descriptive claims and representations of accurate depictions of

reality were independent of the observers. Naïve realism, a mid-continuum assumption, assumed that the claims and representations may not be actual one-to-one depictions of reality; but they are reasonable facsimiles of it and the progression toward more exacting depictions. Idealism, the extreme other end of the continuum, assumed that the observer observed and observations were inseparable. The epistemological considerations of the nature, source, and ways of knowing science involved inquiry, technological ways of knowing involved design, and both science and technology involved argument, critique, analysis, unique practices, and distinctive habits of mind (NRC, 2012; Yore, 2011).

Lederman and Lederman (2012; also Abd-El-Khalick, Chapter 31, this volume) pointed out the distinctions between the knowledge system (ontology) and the knowledge production (epistemology)—differences between observations and inferences and between laws and theories; the limitations of observations and need for creativity; realization that knowledge claims were subjective, tentative, and uncertain; and recognition of the cultural context and influences on knowledge production. Yore and colleagues (2004) used an epistemology–ontology map of the nature of science to identify and define three broad clusters of interpretations: traditional absolutist realist, modern evaluativist naïve realist, and postmodern multiplist idealist views. They interviewed university scientists and engineers about their views of science using these interpretations (brief description and percentage of scientists selecting each view follow):

- **Absolutist, Realist** (traditional view)—Discovery of truths about a real world (~13%)
- **Evaluativist, Naïve Realist** (modern view)—Proposal of best tentative ideas based on current evidence and understanding about a possible world that must be submitted to public evaluation (~81%)
- **Relativist, Idealist** (postmodern view)—Individual interpretations based on personal and lived experiences to be judged by the proposer (~6%)

They also found that university engineers did not view technology and engineering as applied sciences driven by inquiry but rather as driven by design and the desire to meet or alleviate people's needs. Yore (2011) considered WMS and technology/engineering as conjoined twins sharing some characteristics while having distinctive differences. The United States' framework for science education (NRC, 2012) has recognized these differences and identified engineering, technological design, and engineering practices integral to the K–12 science education goals.

WMS involves an epistemological–ontological knowledge production cycle. Good, Shymansky, and Yore (1999) provided an overview of the epistemological processes (*identified in italics*) and ontological constraints (**identified in boldface**) of WMS as **people's attempt** to *search out*, *describe*, and *explain* patterns of events occurring in the **natural world**, where claims are **generalized statements based on evidence** and explanations are **based on physical causality**, which must be submitted to *public evaluation*. Similarly, Ford (2008) described the epistemological and ontological features of the knowledge production cycle in science that included material aspects (*methods and accurate communications*) and social aspects (*peer review and critique*) of science where **Nature** is the *final and influential arbiter.*

Comparison of IKW and WMS

Clearly, there is some degree of similarity regarding the epistemological practices and beliefs of both IKW and WMS, since these knowledge systems involve sensory evidence and quality thinking. However, major differences are apparent in the ontological assumptions and requirements of the knowledge systems in terms of the underlying worldview, requirements for explanations, and generalized or place-based knowledge claims. Aikenhead (2006) stated:

> [IKW was] guided by the fact that the physical universe is mysterious but can be survived if one uses rational empirical means. [WMS was] guided by the fact that the physical universe is knowable through rational empirical means.
>
> (p. 133)

A synthesis of several views outlined dimensions upon which IKW and WMS differ: science and technology, social goals, intellectual goals, human actions, underlying logic, notion of time, and validity perspectives. There was not total agreement on the contrasting features among these authors, and their perspectives were dependent on the assumed views of IKW and WMS:

1. Science and Technology—WMS was seen as inquiry and different from technology, which was seen as design, not applied science, and as people's attempt to modify the environment to meet the needs of people or alleviate problems; this differentiation is not made for IKW, which assumed an integrated techno-science view.
2. Social Goals—WMS was driven by curiosity-based inquiry; technology was driven by mission-based design and innovation and by power over nature; IKW was about survival and harmony with nature.
3. Intellectual Goals—WMS eradicated spirituality in favor of physical causality and cause–effect mechanisms; technology was practical solutions to problems independent of cause; IKW stressed a wisdom dimension and coexisted with spirituality.
4. Human Actions—WMS was formal, objective, and decontextualized; technology was problem solving and invention; IKW was intimate, subjective, and interrelated.
5. Logical Assumptions—WMS was traditionally reductionist, aggressive, and manipulative and focused on analytical explanations; technology was traditionally based on the inventor's trial and error and judged on usability; IKW was holistic, gentle, accommodating, intuitive, and spiritual.
6. Time—WMS perceived time as a linear measure based on the beginning of the universe; technology was focused on the measurement of time; IKW perceived time as a cyclic occurrence.
7. Validity—WMS assumed the validity of knowledge claims by predictive power, strength of evidence, and theoretical coherence; technology judged innovations on practicality, cost, and safety; IKW based its validity on usability and effectiveness.

IKW supports a way of living for survival and harmony, coexists with and celebrates spirituality intimately and subordinately related over human actions, reflects a circular or cyclic conception of time, bases content validity on practical applications over thousands of years of survival, and wisdom (Aikenhead & Elliott, 2010; Lee, Yen, & Aikenhead, 2012, Little Bear, 2009). WMS values knowledge for its own sake, economic gains, and power over nature; eradicates mystery and spiritualism in favor of physical causality; disconnects and decouples claims from human action; promotes a rectilinear measure and conception of time; bases content validity on predictive accuracy and utility; and involves a cause-effect and mechanistic explanations.

Little Bear (2011), a Blackfoot person, focused on the convergence of IKW and WMS, limitations of English, and imposition of mathematics on nature. Culture and language cannot be disentangled from ways of doing and reporting claims about nature and naturally occurring events. He suggested that the search for regularity and patterns in WMS might be based on a false assumption and needs to consider the alternative assumption that there is no pattern, only chaos. Little Bear identified the fundamental tenets of IKW as dealing with flux, spirit, animate, renewal, land (space and place not time), and characteristics of language. The rhetorical powers of language in knowing (shaping what we know or can know—constructive function, epistemological features, and scientific metalanguage), sharing (communicative function), and persuading (argumentative function) are fundamental in doing and knowing about nature and naturally occurring events (Yore, 2012). Little Bear suggested that the nuanced terms for subtle differences in the Navajo and Blackfoot languages might be useful in achieving the resolution of the particle-motion difficulty in the Grand Unified Theory and advancements in String Theories.

Assumptions and beliefs vary between IKW and WMS, but they also vary within IKW (e.g., different subgroups within a larger group), within WMS (e.g., physics, chemistry, biology, earth and ocean sciences), and between topics within domains (e.g., classical/quantum mechanics, classical biology/ecology, meteorology/climate modeling, etc.). Researchers and teachers need to be aware and consider the nature of IKW and WMS knowledge systems—specifically, how ontology and epistemology influenced the traditions, conventions, and practices of knowledge communities; how language and mathematics might limit or expand knowledge about nature and naturally occurring events; how the knowledge was constructed and the roles of argumentation; what data were evidence for a knowledge claim; and what mechanisms were acceptable explanations for an event.

Controversies and conflicts are likely more critical within some topics in IKW and WMS because they were between fundamental religions and developmental biology (evolution) or cosmology (creation of the universe). Direct engagement of controversies before social capital and trust are established has been counterproductive. Therefore, technology as design and indigenous innovations may provide an effective initial bridge between IKW and WMS to build trust and common ground that is more fertile and may provide a transitional route for initial border crossings since the major difficulties involving *explanation* in WMS and IKW systems can be minimized in such an arena (Guo, Hsiung, Wang, & Yore, 2008). The lack of agreement and convergence in cultural studies of IKW and WMS has illustrated the barriers for two-way border crossings; they have focused primarily on scientific approaches rather than technological and humanistic constructivist approaches to facilitate border crossings (Aikenhead, 2006; Chinn, Hand, & Yore, 2008). If WMS was defined using a developmental definition of searching, describing, and explaining patterns of events in the natural universe (Good et al., 1999), then direct engagement of WMS and IKW approaches fails to produce agreement and consensus beyond the epistemological levels of searching and describing. Once the deliberations address the ontological dimensions of metaphysics, explanations, and fundamental elements of the knowledge domain, WMS, IKW, and other traditional forms of knowledge about nature and naturally occurring events clash on the fundamental elements (e.g., mass, length, time, and electronic or magnetic factors for physics) and explanations limited to physical causality and established mechanisms.

Technology as design that adapts the environment to alleviate or meet people's needs, on the other hand, has much more in common across cultures; and the ontological differences are not as pressing and obvious. In fact, modern technology represented by a range of practitioners (e.g., inventors, technicians, engineers, researchers) still values and recognizes trial-and-error design approaches found in most cultures; and every culture has examples of technologies that have helped them survive (Guo et al., 2008). The scientific inquiry and technology design (commonly known as R&D) epistemologies are similar across Western, Eastern, and traditional ways of knowing. The qualities of exploration, thinking, inquiry, description, and representation are similar across cultural attempts to search out and describe patterns of events in the natural universe.

Science Literacy for All

Science literacy for all has assumed an international cache without ever having a shared understanding of what it is and with little attention to the target audience—all people (Yore, 2012). Contemporary interpretations of science literacy have some agreement that it involves a fundamental sense of disciplinary literacy in science (e.g., cognitive and metacognitive factors, habits of mind, science and engineering practices, plausible thinking, languages, information communication technologies) and a derived sense of science understandings (e.g., big ideas, core concepts and cross-cutting themes, nature of science, scientific inquiry, technological design, socioscientific or science-technology-society-environment issues) that interact and allow global citizens to more fully participate in the public debate about issues resulting in informed decisions and sustainable solutions. This mainstream view of science literacy for citizenship broadly focuses on all students while providing a sound platform for some students' further study to address the pipeline issues—from pre-K through graduate school—of STEM careers. These efforts are often based in variety of *need* frameworks (e.g., socioenvironmental, economic, equity) that, without careful consideration, can serve to perpetuate neocolonial forms of science education (Aikenhead & Elliot, 2010). The authors of this section understand the desire for a common language around science that is accessible and inclusive, although we do not necessarily subscribe to the more dominant framing of science literacy. We have chosen to address the border crossings between IKW and WMS within the larger sociopolitical priorities, cultural and linguistic restoration, and the inclusive target of all citizens, especially indigenous people, who have been underserved and who are underrepresented in these debates and careers. Indeed, literature reporting the development of new forms of science instruction in indigenous communities across the globe has consistently reiterated the need for models of science education that support indigenous learners in successfully learning IKW and WMS (Aikenhead & Elliot, 2010; Barnhart, 2005; Lewthwaite & Renaud, 2009).

Considering the *All* and the *Science* in "Science Literacy for All"

Frankly, the notion of *science literacy for all* is a concept that is somewhat elusive when thinking about the ways that indigenous peoples, knowledge, and issues relate to science. This topic has been addressed in the literature (Bang & Medin, 2010; Brayboy & Maughan, 2009); however, some of the issues and questions raised have, largely, gone unaddressed for indigenous peoples regarding science. There appears to be incongruity between what is meant by *science* and the ways that indigenous peoples engage the world scientifically. Scholars have pointed to a tension that exists between perceptions of *real science* and other forms of science in school, where real science is narrowly conceived (Brayboy & Maughan, 2009; Eisen-hart, Finkel, & Marion, 1996; McConney et al., 2011). An overemphasis on science that is rooted in a sterile labora-tory and follows the scientific method narrowly conceived serves as a way to differentiate those who engage in *real science* and everyone else. Thus, the only apparent option for those who want to be *real scientists* is to take up partic-ular methods in particular places within specific contexts. Increasingly, indigenous communities and scholarship have been challenging and transforming notions of who does and teaches science in expansive ways (see Aiken-head & Ogawa, 2007; McKinley & Stewart, 2012). Indeed, the *all* and the *science* in science literacy for all requires flexibility, elasticity, and a rethinking of what science is, can be, and will be in the future. As it currently stands, the boundaries around the common notions of science are too rigid to enact the coequal option in science education and to allow underserved populations to consider being scientists, given the unique psychic costs associated with this move.

Ball and Osborne (1998) pointed to the ways that the consideration of science for all is problematic. They stated:

> Many schemes for educating "all" are little more than translations of the current curriculum and modal peda-gogy. "All" children are somehow benignly the same. "All" is not a word that carries heterogeneity. It suggests instead likeness and similarity. It implies children who are different slowly becoming more like all of us (whoever we are).
>
> (p. 395)

Their assessment rejects assimilation as a worthwhile model. Children, their culture, their belief system and concomitant value system, and their circumstances are different. Rather than assimilating these differences under the current monolithic notion of science, some indigenous communities and scholars have been working toward sig-nificant shifts in formal and informal settings to reconsider what is meant by science and the ways in which science education is conceived (Mack et al., 2012; Sutherland & Henning, 2009). The idea that underserved peoples and students take up the mores, values, policies, and practices of dominant cultures may result in the loss of the diver-sity of ideas, beliefs, ways of being and thinking, potential contributions to the scientific realm, and fresh perspec-tives to perplexing social and environmental issues. This is not to say that those members of underserved com-munities should not engage in the process of becoming professionals—particularly with an emphasis on thinking through the tried and true ways of engaging in science and in the ethics surrounding scientific inquiry—even though the notions of inquiry and some of the fundamental beliefs associated with being a scientist may be problematic for some communities and their belief systems. A form of scientific accommodation or acculturation wherein both underserved populations and science disciplines work toward cobuilding a system might serve all parties better

than calling for assimilation. Contemporary inquiries into the philosophy and history of WMS and IKW often view differences at the ontological level, but they also often take a historical lens of the development of WMS. It has not always been the case that the need for ontological coherence or exclusion of mystical realms was a neces-sary characteristic of science.

Specifically, science for all suggests there is a science that is universally applicable to and inclusive of all people. Indigenous peoples have not experienced a science like this. Instead, the science typically encountered in schools is a particular kind of school science—old WMS that pre-sumes universality, inclusivity, and neutrality—that is not the same as professional practicing science. However, the three dimensions of universality, inclusivity, and neutrality hold across both professional science and school science.

When placing the epistemological and ontological assumptions of native science (NS) and indigenous knowl-edge systems (IKS) alongside those of WMS, it becomes clear that WMS is not universal, inclusive, or neutral (Bang & Medin, 2010; Brayboy & Maughan, 2009; McConney et al., 2011). Indeed, only by drawing on NS, IKS, and culturally responsive schooling (CRS) can we begin to approximate what we would like to see as the goal of science for all— that is, a science that acknowledges, respects, and engages with indigenous knowledge as *real* and *scientific* and that ensures indigenous people's legitimate participation in sci-ence and science education in ways that do not infringe on indigenous sovereignty and self-determination.

When considering indigenous peoples and science, the *all* in science literacy for all must be expounded and expanded upon. To begin, from many indigenous perspec-tives, science is not something that happens in a labora-tory; instead, it is ubiquitous (Brayboy & Maughan, 2009; Kawagley, 2006). Indeed, science is so well integrated into day-to-day life that it falls under the rubric of daily practices and efforts of survival. For example, when indig-enous peoples read the weather (in ways that are more consistent and predictive than those of meteorologists), consider the migrating patterns (drawing on generations of knowledge passed down to them from their ancestors— none of which a zoologist might have), or understand the mating patterns of salmon (in ways that are consistent with—and in many ways more sophisticated than—what marine biologists do), they are engaging in the practice of sustenance and subsistence. In this notion, the stakes are considerably higher for reading the signs correctly to feed themselves, families, and communities than it might be for a scientist who may engage an incorrect calculation, faulty hypotheses, or inert data. The *all* then in science literacy for all should encompass the idea that science is ubiq-uitous. It should also note that science education is not exclusive to experiences in science classrooms; it happens outside of the brick and mortar called schools in interest-ing and powerful ways within informal environments.

The need for this sort of science for all becomes appar-ent when we consider the current state of indigenous involvement and lack of success in WMS. Studies have shown that indigenous students perform worse on standardized measures of science achievement than their peers do (Aikenhead & Elliott, 2010; Bang, 2009; McConney et al., 2011; Yore et al., 2014), that there is inadequate science instruction in most elementary schools and especially those serving students of color from low-income and rural areas, that many indigenous youth avoid science by the time they reach middle school (McKinley & Stewart, 2012), that many older indigenous students are counseled away from science courses (Sutherland & Henning, 2009), and that learning science can be especially challenging because of the specialized language involved (Chigeza, 2008).

Awareness of the need to improve science education for indigenous students is not new; according to Ovando (1992), the American Association for the Advancement of Science issued a number of useful recommendations in 1976 for improving science teaching and learning for indigenous youth. While these types of recommendations are important, the real change in the relationship between science and indigenous peoples will only result from a fundamental reconceptualization of what we mean by science (Brayboy & Maughan, 2009; McKinley & Stewart, 2012)—particularly in ways that recognize the colonial legacies and relationships to indigenous students and communities.

Next-Generation Science Literacy Education for All?

Many science educators have recognized that the narrowing and simplification of scientific subject matter taken up in schools and informal environments needs deep reconsideration (NRC, 2007, 2009). The interdisciplinarity, cross-cutting concepts, and practices dimensions of the new framework for science education recognize concepts across core domains and shift the engagement to science and engineering practices away from just subject matter (NRC, 2012). These changes reflect broader recognition of the role of epistemology in learning and science and a more holistic view of meaning making. The new framework focuses on three spheres of activities: investigating, evaluating, and developing explanations and solutions. These dimensions, though primarily defined within WMS, warrant cautious optimism for indigenous youth and communities because they help to shift the starting place for conversations about IKS and to move science education from codified exemplars of IKW to a view of competing knowledge systems and processes. What will be critical is the extent to which these new efforts do or do not reify the implicit and explicit positioning of Western epistemologies as superior to indigenous epistemologies.

There is a line of research concerned with students' epistemological beliefs about the nature of science itself. Researchers who are primarily interested in improving school science learning in its current form have addressed issues of epistemology in learning from the idea labeled *epistemological beliefs* (Hofer, 2008). There is a common assumption that there is an epistemological stance for science; when students' epistemologies match that of science, then they learn science more easily. In this scenario, the unspoken default rests on an assumption of the epistemic privilege of WMS. An alternative perspective is that students' epistemologies are contextualized and shift depending on the circumstances (Hofer, 2008) and that teachers must come to see student epistemologies as resources, not deficiencies, from which to draw in order to teach science more effectively—what some scholars have called a resources-based view of epistemology (Bang & Medin, 2010; Louca, Elby, Hammer, & Kagey, 2004).

Scholarship about indigenous communities, resources-based views of learners, and equity focused on learning and culture have proven to be helpful for improving science education in indigenous communities. These efforts have called for the explicit engagement and view of IKW and students' prior knowledge as valued resources in classroom learning. Although these efforts have been beneficial, they sometimes do not dig deeply enough into the sociopolitical, sociocultural, and philosophical dimensions of science education (McKinley & Stewart, 2012) and their implications for the future health and wellness of indigenous communities.

There have been two broad challenges as we moved forward. The first challenge was to ensure more indigenous students were participating and achieving in science. The second challenge was to find a place in the curricula and classrooms for indigenous knowledge that would lead to a decolonized science education. Indeed, development of a decolonized science education is beginning to emerge in some indigenous communities (Aikenhead & Elliot, 2010). While there is diversity in these burgeoning efforts, there have been some remarkable similarities in efforts and in the identification of key challenge areas (Bang & Medin, 2010; Keane, 2008; Richards & Scott, 2009; Wood & Lewthwaite, 2008). A central dimension has been the framework in which to engage in such a project: Is indigenous knowledge incorporated into the dominant models? Are IKW and WMS two paradigms? Is science seen as pluralistic? Is science viewed through a relativist lens? Are IKW and WMS complementary? While there has been some variation, there has been a resounding rejection of the strategy to have local exemplars of Western concepts that dominated cultural relevancy frameworks and have become viewed as the neocolonial trope in science education (Bazzul, 2012; C. Carter, 2010). Perhaps most encouragingly, the development of models for change in science education has emphasized a strategy in which reconfigured relationships among school leadership, teachers, and communities lead to the development of new curricular and pedagogical initiatives. McKinley and Stewart (2012) called for increased understanding of the complexity of these endeavors and noted the tendency of many stakeholders to hold inferiority assumptions about IKW.

The positioning of indigenous epistemologies as inferior to WMS epistemologies has created barriers for border crossings by indigenous students (Aikenhead & Ogawa, 2007), manifesting ethnic and academic identity conflicts (Nasir & Saxe, 2003), school push-out (Tuck, 2012), and other forms of passive resilience. When two different systems of knowledge, ways of knowing, or epistemologies interact, it can be difficult to make sense of the resulting conflict; however, scholars and communities are developing models and programs that work toward seeing complementarities and parallels as often as the conflicts (Barnhardt, 2005; Pierotti, 2010).

Rather than continue to leave students unsupported in this sense making, an equitable and successful science for all will need to elevate, engage, and support indigenous students utilizing both indigenous and Western epistemologies. Such pedagogical practices help to unearth the embedded assumptions of epistemological superiority often coded in value-judgment-laden discourses (Bang, Curley, Kessel, Marin, & Suzokovich, in press). Brayboy and Maughan (2009) suggested ways that teachers can merge indigenous epistemological, ontological, axiological, and pedagogical (what they frame as IKS) values with WMS so that students engage and are engaged by scientific concepts. What is important here is that CRS works at levels in which the normative assumptions typically coded *academic* are uprooted and all content and engagement becomes cultural. While there is a significant body of CRS work, there are far-reaching implications for the teaching of indigenous students, and significant work remains. The extent to which these possibilities are given time, space, and resources to develop will likely reflect the political will to reach more successful science education.

Culturally Responsive Schooling (CRS) for Indigenous Youth

Culturally responsive schooling is certainly not a new phenomenon; instead, it has been central to tribal nations' calls for improved schooling. CRS assumes

> that a firm grounding in the heritage language and culture indigenous to a particular place is a fundamental prerequisite for the development of culturally-healthy students and communities associated with that place. Attention to the local language, culture and place are essential ingredients for identifying the appropriate qualities and practices associated with culturally-responsive educators, curricula, and schools.
> (Standards for CRS, 1998, para. 2)

This educational approach requires shifts in teaching methods, curricular materials, teacher dispositions, and school–community relations.

The literature on CRS for indigenous youth comes out of other, even broader bodies of literature on multicultural education, cultural differences, and improving the academic achievement of youth who are not members of the dominant cultural group in the United States—African American, Hispanic, and Creole. One of the most general but direct definitions provided is that CRS "makes sense" to students who are not members of or assimilated into the dominant social group (Klug & Whitfield, 2003, p. 151) by building a bridge between a child's home culture and the school in order to effect improved learning and school achievement (Pewewardy & Hammer, 2003). Schools need to consider a number of important elements that relate to curriculum, pedagogy, school policy, student expectations, standards, assessment, teacher knowledge, and community involvement to support student learning. CRS in science education subsumes a number of dimensions, including but not exhaustive—culturally responsive curriculum, culturally relevant science, and culturally responsive pedagogy (Alaska Native Knowledge Network [ANKN], n.d.; Johnson, 2011; Stephens, 2003). Culturally responsive curriculum and relevant science have been or will be considered, but culturally responsive pedagogy (CRP) needs further consideration to expand beyond the idea that prior knowledge and experiences of all students should be viewed as intellectual resources not deficits.

Johnson (2011) built on earlier scholarship in the United States (meta-analysis and theoretical positions) to outline a CRP framework for teaching that involved academic success, cultural competence, and critical consciousness. She stated:

> Academic success refers to teachers having high expectations for their students and learning is not at the expense of losing cultural identity. . . . Cultural competence is achieved through teachers helping students to develop positive ethnic and cultural identities. . . . Critical consciousness is the ability for students to identify, understand, and critique societal issues and inequities.
> (p. 172)

Johnson and others believe that CRS must prepare teachers to teach in culturally diverse environments, since many teaching decisions are based on how they were taught at the same grade level (Moon, 2008), and that much more attention needs to be paid to these three dimensions, especially critical consciousness (Buxton, 2009). Furthermore, the progression of teachers' practices is influenced by their beliefs about learning, teaching, and their stage of development along a continuum of professional development—progressively focused on (a) self and survival, (b) content standards, and (c) students' learning and achievement. The case study of two middle school teachers (experienced male and novice female) working with predominately Hispanic student bodies revealed that they were able, with professional learning support, to develop conceptions and practices about self and others, structured social relationships, and knowledge to align more completely with Hispanic CRP (Johnson, 2011). However, three topics that are rarely included in discussions of CRS are sovereignty, racism, and epistemologies; any discussion of CRS for indigenous youth should take these issues into account (Castagno & Brayboy, 2008).

In general, scholars have found that efforts at CRS for indigenous youth result in students who have enhanced self-esteem (Agbo, 2004; Brayboy & Maughan, 2009; Glasson, Mhango, Phiri, & Lanier, 2010), develop healthy identity (McCarty, Romero, & Zepeda, 2006; Michell, Vizina, Augustus, & Sawyer, 2008; Trujillo, Viri, & Figueira, 2002), are more self-directed and politically active (Brayboy & Maughan, 2009; Glasson et al., 2010), give more respect to tribal elders (Agbo, 2004; McCarty et al., 2006), have a positive influence in their tribal community (Brayboy, 2005; Glasson et al., 2010; Richards, Hove, & Afolabi, 2008), exhibit more positive classroom behavior and engagement (Chinn, 2007; Lewthwaite & McMillan, 2007; Lipka, 1990), and achieve higher academic standings (Chinn et al., 2008; Klump & McNeir, 2005; Richards et al., 2008). A smaller body of scholarship points to the importance of recognizing all voices in the classroom and ensuring that indigenous students are not silenced in the schooling process (Aikenhead & Elliott, 2010; Belgarde, Mitchell, & Arquero, 2002; Chinn et al., 2008; Snively & Williams, 2008), which in turn leads to more meaningful educational experiences and student empowerment (Brayboy & Maughan, 2009; Lewthwaite & McMillan, 2007; Lewthwaite & Renaud, 2009).

The scholarship on CRS does not indicate that indigenous youth should learn tribal cultures and languages at the expense of learning mainstream culture and typical academic subjects. Most scholars, parents, and educational leaders believe that schools should facilitate the acquisition of all of this knowledge and skills. This both/and approach rather than an either/or approach would teach indigenous youth to become fluent in multiple ways of knowing and being. Schools that provide a challenging and high-quality education intimately connected and relevant to tribal communities will be far more likely to graduate youth who are academically prepared, connected to, and active members of their tribal community and knowledgeable about both the dominant and home cultures. Paris (2012) has called for a "culturally sustaining pedagogy" (p. 95) to "support young people in maintaining the cultural and linguistic competence of their communities while simultaneously offering access to dominant cultural competence" (Paris, 2012, p. 95). Recent literature on indigenous sciences and CRS has been arguing a similar point using different terminology (Aikenhead & Elliott, 2010; Bang & Medin, 2010; Brayboy & Castagno, 2009; Brayboy & Maughan, 2009; Castagno & Brayboy, 2008; McKinley, 2007). Honoring Paris's call to include explicitly the notion of sustainability in the process, the research cited in this chapter on indigenous science points to not only sustainability but also the strengthening of cultural and linguistic competence.

Because of the differences discussed and the deep tendency for schools to have limited views of science, for many indigenous students, learning science in school requires unidirectional crossing cultural borders and acquiring facility in another culture (Aikenhead & Elliott, 2010;

Brayboy & Maughan, 2009; Michell et al., 2008). Because of the potentially hazardous nature of these border crossings, scholars have recommended that science curricula be designed in culturally responsive ways and with practical, real-world applications in mind (Aikenhead & Elliott, 2010; McKinley & Stewart, 2009, 2012). It is also recommended that teachers adopt the role of cultural brokers in which they identify the culture of their students, introduce WMS as another cultural point of view imbued by society with power and prestige, and maintain explicit and clear communication about (a) which culture they are operating within and (b) that multiple cultures have value (Bang & Medin, 2010; Brayboy & Maughan, 2009; Castagno & Brayboy, 2008).

Scholars have called for science education that has direct relevance to the lives of indigenous students and tribal communities for more than 30 years (Aikenhead & Ogawa, 2007; Bang & Medin, 2010; McKinley, 2007). Effective curricula need to be connected and relevant to the local community and inclusive of community-based ways of knowing rather than some perceived unitary indigenous community. Educators can work toward this goal by seeking advice from tribal elders and other community members, commissioning local people to develop or codevelop curricular materials, and drawing on the local activities and resources.

Students' everyday lives are the starting point for humanistic constructivist approaches; this might mean integrating their worldviews and epistemologies into the curriculum, drawing on ecological themes, using oral stories and elders in the classroom, employing more naturalistic observations of nature, using authentic assessments of student knowledge, and adapting the classroom to look and feel more like the local community (Aikenhead & Elliott, 2010; Bang & Medin, 2010; Brayboy & Maughan, 2009; McKinley & Stewart, 2009, 2012). This work cannot be achieved through relying on textbooks alone; teachers need to cast a much wider net for learning materials and activities that relate to the local community. Other aspects of effective science education for indigenous youth include learning in an environment that is rich with the language of science and curricular content that is interesting and relevant, begins with the natural environment of the students, incorporates oral traditions as a source of knowledge about the natural world, and supplements textbooks with other instructive materials (Brayboy & Maughan, 2009; McKinley & Stewart, 2009, 2012; Stephens, 2003). This approach not only makes learning more relevant, responsive, and sustaining for students, but it also facilitates greater relationships between educators and community members and empowers students to be active members of their communities. Increasingly, there are models of science education and science curricula being developed in which youth and communities actively participate and construct the curricula used in schooling (ANKN, n.d.; Bang, Warren, Rosebery, & Medin, 2012; Michell et al., 2008).

Perhaps one of the most important questions in the discussion around effective science education for indigenous youth has been about how teachers enable all students to study WMS ways of knowing while respecting, accessing, and using indigenous ideas, beliefs, and values. Aikenhead and Ogawa (2007) provided one answer by proposing that effective science teaching should aim not at convincing students to accept the validity or legitimacy of the scientific information but rather at helping them understand the information and then consider the similarities and differences between the science information presented and their own epistemology and understanding of the world. In other words, science educators need to engage in pedagogy that presents science as one way of knowing (Bang & Medin, 2010; Bang, Warren et al., 2012). Brayboy and Maughan (2009) noted that science educators should first introduce students to the basic skills of science through familiar objects and events, then compare the ways science is employed in the mainstream culture and in their own culture before examining various and competing explanations for natural phenomena—all while not presenting any one way of knowing as superior. Such discussions about competing worldviews and epistemologies not only help students understand the nature of science but also draw on their previous knowledge, spark their interest, and encourage critical thinking (Aikenhead & Elliott, 2010; Bang & Medin, 2010; McKinley & Stewart, 2009, 2012).

An unfortunate finding in the scholarship is that many science teachers ignore the cultural backgrounds of students and the influence these backgrounds have on their participation in the schooling process (Aikenhead & Elliott, 2010; Aikenhead & Ogawa, 2007; McKinley, 2007). Students bring a wealth of knowledge and experience that relates to science; teachers should draw on this background and on students' strengths (resource-based view). Many indigenous students bring strengths to science learning, including knowledge about preserving and maintaining the environment (Kawagley, 2006), general knowledge of nature (Bang, Warren et al., 2012; Chinn et al., 2008), knowledge of technologies enabling survival in nature (Aikenhead & Michell, 2012), observation skills, and valuing the knowledge inherent in nature (Aikenhead & Michell, 2012; Chinn et al., 2008). However, issues of ownership of knowledge and how to engage in a CRS education without engaging in theft, exploitation, or distortion of indigenous knowledge need to be considered as curricula and instructional resources are developed for CRS.

Science Literacy for All: A Possibility of Equity for Indigenous Students and Communities

The re-envisioning of the dominant goals of science education to include NS and IKS should, first and foremost, "encourage students to learn both Aboriginal and Western Science and technology in a way that empowers them to make everyday choices between (1) participating in a First Nations cultural setting, and (2) participating in a

dominant . . . cultural setting" (Aikenhead, 1996, p. 17). This approach emphasizes heterogeneity in science sense making and establishes communication about nature between and among competing perspectives and the role of science in different cultural contexts. It requires establishing or maintaining a positive attitude toward WMS, NS, and other conceptions of science, acquiring an enlarged repertoire in the language of science, and understanding multiple and competing worldviews and epistemologies (Aikenhead, 2006).

Connected to these goals, however, is perhaps the most important goal of all: Science education cannot continue to operate under the assumption that all students must adopt the perspective of Westernized scientists. WMS presents a number of differences and conflicts for some indigenous students and tribal communities because of the assumptions, values, and hegemony it continues to perpetuate. Scholars have demonstrated that science learning, whether in formal or informal contexts, must aim to facilitate the learning of the culture of science without facilitating the assimilation of students into that culture. Further, a goal of science education for indigenous youth must be to assist in the goals of tribal communities' efforts toward economic development, environmental responsibility, cultural survival, and self-determination. Effectively exposing students to multiple worldviews without requiring the adoption of any particular view can aid in their acquisition of the knowledge and skills needed to better serve their communities and to move between communities.

Potential Buffers to and Supporters of Science Achievement by Indigenous Students

National and state curricula in South Africa (South Africa Department of Education, 2002), New Zealand (McKinley & Keegan, 2008), Hawaii (Chinn, 2007), Australia (Appanna, 2011), Papua New Guinea (Waldrip, Timothy, & Wilikai, 2007), and Canada (Aikenhead & Elliot, 2010) have called for science to be taught in the context of the social and cultural knowledge of the students. This section will consider how to use IKW and WMS such that they contribute to the progress and development of understanding both knowledge systems (Regmi & Fleming, 2012) and the cultural and national priorities of the indigenous and nonindigenous local and national governments.

Supporting Learning

Improving Language and Literacy Skills
Contemporary science literacy is considered composed of fundamental disciplinary literacy and understanding of the big ideas in science, leading to fuller participation in the public debate about socioscientific issues resulting in critical considerations, informed decisions, and sustainable solutions (Yore, 2012). Given that indigenous students may come from communities where language restoration

is a priority and from homes where English may be their second or third language (Warren & de Vries, 2009) and that conceptual ideas are inherently linked with language (Little Bear, 2011), using students' indigenous language and knowledge base may be helpful in strengthening students' general literacy skills in both the language of instruction and their home language as well as improving their scientific language and understandings (Webb, 2010). Border crossings have been used to describe students' internal and public negotiations of IKS and WMS domains (Aikenhead, 2006) and navigation to, from, and between cultures (indigenous, dominant, and scientific) and languages (home = L1, school = L2, school science = L3; Yore & Treagust, 2006). The three-language border-crossing process is real and difficult, and it is equally applicable even if L1, L2, and L3 are encountered in the same or different languages (Chinn et al., 2008). It can be disempowering for indigenous students when a science lesson burdens them with, first, a separate worldview that challenges their own, second, a language they do not relate to, and third, a context that has a history of discriminating against their ancestors (Appanna, 2011). Chigeza (2008) found that indigenous middle school students from Queensland and Torre Strait Islands with home languages of Aboriginal English or Creole needed to navigate language before negotiating the language challenges in science learning. Similar concerns were reported for indigenous students from Papua New Guinea (Pauka, Treagust, & Waldrip, 2005; Waldrip et al., 2007)

A quasi-experimental study on the effects of a pedagogical strategy that integrated the discursive practices of reading, writing, and engaging in argumentation and scientific inquiry with indigenous students in a rural area of South Africa revealed statistically significant improvements in students' reading skills in English (language of instruction), listening skills in both English and isiXhosa (dominant home language), and writing skills in isiXhosa (Webb & Mayaba, 2010). These findings are explained by the use and recognition of students' indigenous language in parallel with mediated use of English. Similarly, the use of a modified Science Notebooks strategy (Fulton & Campbell, 2004), affords the isiXhosa students the use of both print and visual components of their home language and language of instruction for learning science ideas and language, effective retrieval of their prior knowledge and experience, and more meaningful engagement with the concepts under investigation. The participating teachers believed that the practice not only promoted the students' language skills in isiXhosa and English but also strengthened their own pedagogical practices (Villanueva & Webb, 2008). Code-switching appeared to be a promising constructivist instructional strategy in multilingual environments where L2 was not the same as L1. Strategic code-switching allowed students to access and engage their prior knowledge and lived experiences, negotiate initial ideas, and construct understandings and conceptual networks in their fluent

language before developing the dominant and scientific discourses (Fakudze & Rollnick, 2008). Students' initial struggles and cognitive demand appeared to be reduced by their proficiency in their L1, allowing them to think first before developing the standard discourse in L2 and scientific terminology in L3.

Building, Enhancing, and Growing Networks of Ideas

Sutherland and Henning (2009) proposed a multicultural science education instructional approach that used certain aspects of indigenous knowledge to introduce topics and to explain and link important issues within and between IKW and WMS. They used alternative understandings of lightning in order to engage and then meet the needs, interests, aspirations, and values of diverse students. Other researchers have explored similar uses of indigenous conceptions of burning/combustion and time in the Atayal culture of Taiwan (Chang, Lee, & Yen, 2010; Lee et al., 2012). These researchers explored alternative conceptions in IKW to WMS and illustrated critical connections and contrasts to WMS using an infusion approach to support learning.

Teachers should recognize that, while students may have prior experiences that might relate to the science under consideration, they might not have sufficient language skills to explain their understandings using the canonical terminology and language of science. For example, many Xhosa students from the Eastern Cape of South Africa have experience carrying *umnquma* sticks and understand that they should not stand under trees during a storm (Meel, 2007); but they do not have the English language proficiency to express their ideas in order to provide a sufficient point of engagement for exploring and introducing scientific views of lightning and provide opportunities to move between *within-culture* and *between-culture* views of knowledge about the natural world (Chinn et al., 2008).

However, challenges still exist regarding how teachers use prior knowledge to guide instruction that changes or elaborates students' oral, written, and visual representations of concepts. One promising instructional approach, Science Writing Heuristic (SWH), has been effective across various science domains and topics, school levels, and students (Gunel, Hand, & Prain, 2007; McDermott & Hand, 2010). Using a modified version of the Reformed-Based Teaching Observation Protocol to measure teacher practices, Hand, Villanueva, and Yoon (in press) explored how expert-level and developing-level teachers used writing (print and visual representations) and argument-based inquiry (SWH) to address and develop students' understandings. The expert-level instructional practices were anchored in understanding students' frameworks and using those ideas to make meaning of the target topic (seasons). The students' writing demonstrated growth in their complexity of reasoning and use of diagrammatic representations over the instructional unit.

Critical Thinking

The application of within-culture and between-culture views of knowledge may have added benefits for indigenous students' higher-order thinking skills. Researchers contend that current understandings of cognition and learning—originating from distinctly different perspectives (philosophy, progressive education, and cognitive science), namely critical thinking, reflection, and metacognition (thinking about thinking as you are thinking to improve your thinking or personal accountability of our thoughts and judgments to decide what to believe or to do)—require a convergence of frameworks (Ford & Yore, 2012). Gleaning from the issues discussed in the previous section, human cognitive architecture recognizes that students bring an existing set of ideas to the classroom and that their prior knowledge serves as both an anchor and a starting point from which to consider, connect, and challenge new ideas. When students engage in self-regulated or self-directed reasoning, thinking critically, and reflecting on new understandings, research suggests that these processes and skills are not discrete but are interdependent constructs of learning. Ford and Yore (2012) argued that the convergence of these constructs takes into consideration the integration of "intellectual resources into planning, monitoring, and regulating thinking to improve grounds for a range of judgments about what to believe or what to do relevant to a critically reflective citizenry" (p. 266). In the context of using IKW in school science learning, engaging and comparing IKW and WMS frameworks may be useful for students to understand the goals of science education and explore ideas from their own cultural heritage (El-Hani & Souza de Ferreira Bandeira, 2008). As well, it may develop insights, appreciations, and values of IKW and WMS in both indigenous and nonindigenous students and develop their intellectual resources necessary for critical thinking, reflection, and metacognition.

Argument From Empirical Evidence

National science education frameworks and reforms have emphasized science as inquiry and as argumentation using empirical evidence; the new framework for K–12 science education identifies argument, critique, and evaluation as central practices for scientific inquiry and technological design (NRC, 2012; see Figure 3-1, p. 45). Villanueva and Hand (2011) asserted that argument-based approaches in the classroom should utilize the data and evidence produced from inquiry activities to help students formulate explanations as well as evaluate those explanations to develop strong conceptual understandings.

However, some researchers cautioned that argumentation—a Western construct—may be incompatible with traditional styles of indigenous people's deliberations, especially Asian or African discussion and debate. Gallard Martínez (2011) stated, "in many instances it is more culturally acceptable in South Africa to build consensus than to be confrontational" (p. 719). Yet, using Ford's (2008) description of the social aspect of the construction

and critique in science, it was understood that the analyses of data might yield different interpretations; he argued that these interpretations require evaluation, yet nature stands as the final arbiter, which may not be fully compatible with IKW views of knowledge production. The aim of argumentation is not a form of irreconcilable oppositions; rather, it is a process of building a body of knowledge through critical evaluation of ideas where multiple understandings are raised, evidence critiqued, and claims and counterclaims are evaluated (Nafukho, 2006). South African researchers (Ogunniyi, 2006; Ogunniyi & Hewson, 2008) have used argumentation based on both IKW and WMS issues to engage students in a type of dialogue that serves the rhetorical purpose of persuasion. Their practices used argumentation as having a claim, evidence for that claim, warrants that link the claim to the evidence, counterarguments, rebuttals, and conclusions. While researchers suggested that this dialogical model is useful for students' development of cognitive understandings, they claimed that interventions focused on argumentation might also be effective in promoting professional development, attitudes, knowledge, and skills (Langenhoven, Kwofie, & Ogunniyi, 2008).

Possible Challenges for Learning

The catalyst and potential improvement of indigenous students' engagement in school science, scientific literacy, and STEM–related careers are promising, but there are limiting factors. Possible buffers that moderate the interactive-constructive learning process or challenges to approaches that aim at supporting indigenous students' science achievement are perceived as hindrances to social mobility, unclear expectations of teachers, cultural collisions, and epistemological or ontological incompatibilities.

Hindrances to Social Mobility

Elliott (2011) suggested that limiting features to addressing the IKW–WMS issue by teachers were "that the topic of multicultural science education is too broad, unreferenced, undefined and too theoretical" (p. 4). George (1999) explored rural people's presuppositions about traditional knowledge about health and the marine environment in Trinidad and Tobago, West Indies, such as child rearing, menstruation, pregnancy, nutrition, herbal medicines, and marine technology; she found similarities and differences between IKW and WMS as people rework their knowledge stores to meet the current needs and to "function effectively in specific situations" (p. 92). Other studies (Gadicke, 2005; Lewthwaite & McMillan, 2007; Snively & Williams, 2008) have suggested that, before attempting to find specific solutions and materials to help facilitate cultural border crossings for indigenous students, one should be clear as to what knowledge groups these student belong and who owns the knowledge to be considered and explore the knowledge keepers' and students' views on the appropriateness for including such knowledge in the school curriculum. Gadicke (2005) found that knowledge keepers from nearby groups within the same First Nation in the Columbia River Valley in Canada had different place-based oral interpretations of creation and water-related stories. Snively and Williams (2008) proposed parallel systems or networks of IKW and WMS (*Two-Row Wampum* model or *Friendship Belt*) with cross-links to facilitate two-way border crossings; they stated,

> According to leading [indigenous] science scholars, the model for science education is that western science and [indigenous] science should co-exist and replace current efforts to incorporate or integrate [indigenous] knowledge into [nonindigenous] science programs. . . . The concept suggests a parallel model of complementary coexistence, which enables different worldviews to exist separately yet side by side.
>
> (p. 126)

The place-based nature of IKW and the need to cross between IKW and WMS as desired underpinned the rationale for a study that investigated isiXhosa mother-tongue-speaking pupils', teachers', and adult community members' awareness of Xhosa indigenous knowledge and their beliefs regarding its integration into the school science curriculum (Webb, 2012). The results suggested a shared awareness of IKW; the reasons for its inclusion in the school science curriculum were recognition of social justice, identity, cultural sensitivity, heritage, dignity, and perceived similarities, but not differences between IKW and WMS. However, reasons against inclusion were articulated and included: IKW was no longer relevant in the modern world, IKW will not help children learn new ways of understanding nature and naturally occurring events, and recognition that much of what is considered to be IKW was not scientific and would not help meet society's expectations of what was valuable to know in a global technoscientific society. However, a number of responses suggested that testing, explaining, and validating IKW might provide a useful point of engagement and departure when considering what constitutes scientific validation. Many of the arguments of the educational stakeholders suggested that issues of social mobility and access to societal goods and income were important to the respondents. These arguments were similar to those put forward for the use of the language of former colonial powers in Africa and Asia by indigenous home-language speakers (Setati, 2005).

Unclear Expectations of Teachers

Currently, many schools indigenous students attend have multicultural teaching staffs and student bodies composed of people from the dominant culture, recent immigrant cultures, and indigenous peoples. Even in indigenous-controlled or -governed schools in Canada, New Zealand, South Africa, and elsewhere, the lack of certified indigenous teachers requires the recruitment of nonindigenous teachers; frequently, the need for nonindigenous teachers

is in science and mathematics. The multicultural context has led to teachers teaching out of their certified disciplines and out of their cultures. Despite the best intentions and commitments of many nonindigenous teachers, most have inadequate understanding of appropriate pedagogies and the complexities of indigenous cultures, knowledge, and identities (Brayboy & Maughan, 2009; Santoro, Reid, Crawford, & Simpson, 2011; Villegas, Neugebauer, & Venegas, 2008). Even if teachers were prepared to teach indigenous learners, the larger world of science education, schooling, and assessment often does not support the strengths and learning resources of indigenous learners (Kidman, Abrams, & McRae, 2011).

Teacher education and professional development programs have only partially started to address these cross-cultural demands and opportunities. New Zealand teachers were urged to make science more relevant and more accessible to Māori students by acknowledging Māori culture beliefs and values (New Zealand Ministry of Education [NZMOE], 1993). Schools were encouraged, where appropriate, to teach science through the Māori language (NZMOE, 1993) and from a Māori perspective by adopting culturally relevant pedagogies (McKinley, 2007; McKinley & Keegan, 2008; Stewart, 2005; Wood & Lewthwaite, 2008). The British Columbia Ministry of Education (2011) made a similar declaration and provided partial instructional resources on its website. The ANKN (2006) has well-developed curriculum, resources, and professional development activities to provide CRS programs for indigenous students in Alaska. In Taiwan, recent efforts have attempted to engage indigenous students by using IKW and technologies and by infusing ideas (e.g., time, combustion) and innovations (e.g., clothing, house building, bamboo canons, animal traps, etc.) as springboards into scientific inquiry and technological design of the school science program (Chang et al., 2010; Guo et al., 2008; Lee et al., 2012).

Yet, despite political support, achievement of these political aims has not been without problems. In New Zealand, there are unresolved tensions between science in Māori and Māori science (Stewart, 2005) and continuing debates over terminology (McKinley & Keegan, 2008). In South Africa, the curriculum exhorts teachers to integrate IKW in their lessons. Ogunniyi (2007) noted that, while progress was encouraging in terms of integrating indigenous knowledge into the science and mathematics curricula, many teachers were uncertain about what was required and questioned their ability to respond to what appeared to be radically different teaching and learning pedagogies. In Canada, several researchers have taken on the challenges to teachers and teaching WMS in indigenous settings that consider IKW. Belczewski (2009) reported that an autobiographic inquiry into her attempts decolonized her "thinking and teaching practice in order to make science education relevant, meaningful, and respectful for [Mi'kmaq and Maliseet] students" (p. 191). Collaboration with students, parents, elders, and directors of indigenous education helped her gain insights into indigenous ways of being, knowing, and understanding nature and naturally occurring events, which required her to evaluate her established epistemic and ontological perspectives of the world. She believed that these new insights, beliefs, and appreciations changed her interactions with indigenous students. Hatcher, Bartlett, Marshall, and Marshall (2009) outlined concepts and approaches for teaching science in Mi'kmaq: *Toqwa'tu'kl Kjijitaqnn,* Cape Breton, Nova Scotia, Canada. Their approach used the guiding principle of *two-eyed seeing* and transdisciplinary integration of IKW and WMS that did not require students "to relinquish either position but can come to understand elements of both [IKW and WMS]" (Hatcher et al., 2009, p. 141). The resulting curriculum and instruction focused on place-based knowledge connected to culture and community, collaborative learning, supportive classroom environments, and indigenous pedagogy that promote coexistence of parallel knowledge systems.

Lewthwaite and McMillan (2007) and Lewthwaite and Renaud (2009) explored science education in Inuit schools of the Qikiqtani region, Nunavut, Canada. Lewthwaite and McMillan (2007) found negative differences between teachers' preferred and actual perceptions about resources, time, school ethos, and professional adequacy, knowledge, and attitudes. Lewthwaite and Renaud (2009) found a comparison of teachers' responses over 2 years revealed changes in all dimensions (except school priority, which was constant): cultural capacity, knowledge, general capacity, school-community cultural priority, and teacher interest decreased while instruction resources improved. The collective views and interactions of the factors explored in these studies illustrate the complexity of the issues and how environmental factors influenced teachers' and schools' ability to provide the desired program for indigenous learners in schools where there is turnover in leadership and teaching staffs. Sutherland and Henning (2009) described models for curriculum integration, reported results of an action-oriented conference of 50 indigenous and nonindigenous science teachers, consultants, and administrators in Manitoba, and discussed the implementations on science programs in indigenous contexts. The best practices that resulted from the conference involved considerations of elders, language, culture, and experiential learning that should guide the development and delivery of science education programs to instill a sense of place.

While there have been reports of successful attempts to infuse IKW ideas into science lessons in specific instances (Chang et al., 2010; Lee et al., 2012), there appears to be no systemic implementation of the process in national science curricula; teachers are generally left to fend for themselves (Ogunniyi, 2007). Until this situation is redressed, unclear expectations of teachers and a lack of support mechanisms will remain a buffer to the implementation strategies that effectively promote the achievement of indigenous students in science classrooms.

Building Ethical Research Relationships

Decolonizing Methodologies: Research and Indigenous Peoples (Tuhiwai Smith, 1999) provided groundbreaking insights into questions raised by indigenous scholars in different parts of the world about the ethics and protocols that need to be set in place when nonindigenous researchers and educators engage indigenous communities. These challenges in intercultural learning and research environments with indigenous learners have led to the establishment of a *decolonizing* research literature that calls upon nonindigenous scholars and educators to work in ways that actively prioritize indigenous self-determination, transformation, and healing (ANKN, 2006; Australian Institute of Aboriginal and Torres Strait Islander Studies, n.d.; Bishop, 2008; Hudson, Milne, Reynolds, Russell, & Smith, 2010; Social Sciences and Humanities Research Council of Canada, n.d.).

The emergence of decolonizing methodologies challenged, in part, the long history of scientific research conducted in colonial contexts during the 19th and early 20th centuries. The colonial landscapes provided the raw materials of field research that were later sent to imperial centers (e.g., London, Paris) for analysis. Scientific theories were generated at a distant place in metropolitan centers rather than in the locations and places from which raw materials were collected as data (Connell, 2007).

Similar tensions exist insofar as indigenous lands and communities are the location of a great deal of research activity conducted by nonindigenous researchers who have established research priorities and goals independently of the indigenous peoples who host their fieldwork. Once data are transported out of indigenous territories and analyzed in universities and research laboratories elsewhere, the data and resulting knowledge claims pass out of the control of the indigenous groups concerned. The ultimate benefits of research conducted in indigenous landscapes tend to go to nonindigenous stakeholders who have amassed financial, institutional, or political resources—not to people for whom the research results could do the most good (Castleden, Morgan, & Lamb, 2012; Muller, 2012). These contexts for data collection and interpretation and a pattern of knowledge production that favors Western academic protocols and procedures tend to reinforce the differences in the nature of IKW and WMS. The identification of IKW as local place-based knowledge in educational research situates that knowledge as culturally grounded with power for the originating location. Western knowledge is often characterized as generalizable, not possessing any cultural grounding and identification, and seen as the norm or as universal (Carjuzaa & Fenimore-Smith, 2010). This positioning of IKW has the potential to marginalize its usefulness or relevance for a modern society, thus causing teachers and communities to question whether IKW should be taught in a science classroom. However, highly regarded scientists believed that place-based knowledge were powerful resources when involved with research situated in indigenous settings (Yore et al., 2006).

Given that indigenous populations worldwide have different cultural priorities, histories, languages, systems of knowledge, aspirations, social systems, engagement with physical territories, and ways of engaging with the world, it simply has not been possible to formulate a one-size-fits-all approach to indigenous research. Thus, while mention was frequently made of indigenous students' underachievement in science across the world, the causes were likely to be found in local, as opposed to universal, circumstances relating to the particular histories of colonization, imperialism, and power of specific indigenous groups within a nation or region (Abrams, Yen, Blatt, & Ho, 2009; Middleton, Dupuis, & Tang, 2012).

In many industrialized nations, or in countries where indigenous groups have been dispossessed of ancestral lands or where a history of colonization has fractured the continuity of indigenous communities and their traditions, many indigenous learners are relocated into urban populations. These indigenous students find themselves without, or between, cultures and the normal support networks in their ancestral homelands (Chinn et al., 2008). Yet much research on classroom teaching persists in presenting tokenistic aspects of indigenous language or culture to increase student engagement and achievement in ways that assume that indigenous learners are actively involved in traditional and rural ways of life outside the classroom.

Research on short-term curricular units with embedded traditional crafts, games, and food taught in science classrooms parallels the much-criticized approach in multicultural education for other minorities where food, festivals, folklore, and fashions encouraged a tourist approach for both minority and majority students (Meyer & Rhoades, 2006). Some educational organizations have recommended infused *motivational hooks* consisting of cultural examples as a starting point for addressing IKW in science education. However, indigenous learners dispossessed of these ways of life through a history of colonization and relocation consider themselves to be active members of 21st-century multicultural urban communities rather than members of a primitivized or idealized pedagogical version of native culture. Interpreting outcomes of the inclusion of tokenistic bits of indigenous knowledge in the classroom needs to be done with caution because it creates a potential double-fail situation for these indigenous learners. First, they fail in science; then, because they may not necessarily feel connected to the way their culture was presented in the science classroom, they fail as indigenous people as well.

It is important that nonindigenous researchers and practitioners develop effective decolonizing strategies in their engagement with native communities. Since indigenous communities are so diverse, it is not possible to develop a simple checklist that will work every time in every situation. However, understanding how colonization has affected the lives of indigenous peoples both historically and in the present is a critical starting point for engaging with indigenous groups. Ways of bridging the divide between indigenous and nonindigenous groups can be formulated, but this is not always a straightforward process; there are, however, ethical principles that guide rather than techniques to be followed.

One commonsense underlying philosophical premise is that science education research be undertaken in strong, equal collaborations with indigenous partners rather than teams of nonindigenous researchers. Carjuzaa and Fenimore-Smith (2010) stated that such a community-based approach establishes a reciprocal relationship in which academic freedom and tribal sovereignty are honored. The partnership needs to be established, fostered, and maintained while recognizing and addressing the imbalance of power between the researcher and the researched community. We will explore only three of the important principles in guiding ethical science education research with indigenous communities: mutually beneficial relationships, participatory research orientation, and enhancing the self-determination of the indigenous communities. Tuhiwai Smith (1999, 2005), Cajete (2008), Grande (2008), and Wilson (2008), among other indigenous scholars, have laid extensive groundwork for critiquing dominant Eurocentric research methodologies and the principles to establishing an indigenous research agenda. Researchers must engage with that literature and reflect upon their own research culture, beliefs, and practices before engaging with indigenous schools, teachers, and learners.

Mutually Beneficial Relationships

Jacobs and colleagues (2010) argued that genuine research partnerships between indigenous groups and nonindigenous researchers need to be established, particularly in instances in which indigenous people are being asked to participate in research in which they have been subject to unethical practices or human rights violations in the past. There is a need to (a) cogenerate research questions of mutual interest, data collection, and interpretation procedures that reflect the cultural context and interpretative frameworks, (b) seek informed consent, and (c) ethically conduct the study (Cargo et al., 2008; Castleden et al., 2012). Therefore, researchers need to advise indigenous people affected by the study of the purpose, goals, and timeframe of the research, data gathering techniques, data verification and informant checks, positive and negative implications, and impact of the research and obtain informed consent of the appropriate indigenous governing bodies as well as the participants themselves, since some data may be community property. Consent may take months or even years to obtain, as indigenous communities often have reason to be suspicious of outside researchers and potential benefits of research; in addition, the authority may be composed of several indigenous agencies. The saying: *I am from the government or university, I am here to help you* does not always instill trust or confidence in many indigenous peoples. These negotiations are crucial in determining the nature of the mutually beneficial research to be undertaken. The questions that must be answered are:

- How will the research benefit both the researcher and the community?
- What methodologies will be used?
- Who owns the data?
- Who decides what, when, and where results are published?

These conversations allow the establishment of social capital and trust as well as the relationship to become more of *learning the meaning from* rather than *studied on, interpreted, and judged by.*

Partnerships, based on trusting relationships, can take a long time to develop social capital and trust and to articulate the problem space; this can pose problems for researchers who usually have funding schedules and deadlines to meet. Nevertheless, indigenous communities are not bound by external funding priorities; the development of ongoing relationships based on trust typically does not fit institutional schedules. Researchers need to develop generous and flexible timelines to accommodate the ebb and flow of the research process (Sarche, Novins, & Belcourt-Dittloff, 2010). For example, Hudson, Roberts, Smith, Tiakiwai, and Hemi (2012) took 2 years to build a relationship with an indigenous Māori community despite the fact that there were Māori researchers on the research team and the research partnership had originally been established at the behest of the Māori community. The dialogue developed during this period was critical in the formulation of new knowledge; it brought IKW and WMS together in a meaningful way for those community schools, likely avoided difficulties, and allowed maximum efficiency and effectiveness within the enacted inquiries.

The ANKN (2006) offers guidelines for ethical research *with* rather than *on* indigenous communities including schools. These guidelines are in addition to the requirements of institutional review boards (IRBs) and ethical regulations required by many funding agencies. IRB guidelines are typically designed to protect the individual, affiliated institutions, and funding agencies—not the collective community; some guidelines fail to acknowledge the unique cultures of indigenous peoples, the sovereignty of indigenous nations, and the historical position of indigenous peoples as objects of research (Carjuzaa & Fenimore-Smith, 2010). Therefore, ethical codes and rules set firmly with the research institution are designed to enhance awareness and avoid problems; however, professional conduct and ethical conduct are fundamental attributes of the researchers (Fine, Tuck, & Zeller-Berkman, 2008; Hansen & VanFleet, 2003; Lincoln & Cannella, 2009; Tuhiwai Smith, 1999). Indigenous peoples in some countries (e.g., Aotearoa New Zealand, Australia, Canada, and the United States) have developed research approaches and codes of ethical conduct that incorporate fundamental principles of respect for persons, beneficence, justice and indigenous ideas, knowledge ownership, values and beliefs. However, indigenous peoples in other countries are just starting to develop such ethical protocols. Nonindigenous and indigenous researchers need to hold themselves accountable to a strict ethical code of conduct in research and, as part of that code, may need to support financially the development of a research approach that supports an indigenous community's vitality, health, and sovereignty.

Mutually beneficial relationships imply trust, sharing of resources, co-ownership of the data and results, and a shared belief that the research will make a difference and result in good outcomes for all who are involved. To accomplish this goal, indigenous partners need to be involved in the research *at the beginning* of the research process (conception, planning, etc.) rather than when the research is ready to start (data collection). A community-based participatory research orientation supports such a process where stakeholders are involved in every aspect of the research from its conception to publication.

Community-Based Participatory Research (CBPR) Orientation

Indigenous and traditional populations (rural, reserve, remote, or urban) continue to seek ways to express their cultural sovereignty while solving community issues through education and science by establishing partnerships with institutions of higher education (Ferreira & Gendron, 2011). Community-based participatory research (CBPR) focuses on dialogical reflection, advocacy, and action as means to overcome relations of domination and subordination between oppressors and the oppressed, colonizers and the colonized. Within a CBPR orientation, research teams are developed that consist of both researchers and trained community stakeholders.

Membership on a CBPR cooperative requires sharing power, resources, credit, results, and knowledge as well as a reciprocal appreciation of each partner's knowledge and skills at each stage of the inquiry, including problem definition/issue selection, research design, conducting research, interpreting results, and determining how the results should be used for action. Indigenous peoples want their communities, knowledge, and heritage to be respected and valued; however, some indigenous communities want to share what they know but may limit what can be shared and the conditions for sharing (Battiste, 2008).

These kinds of partnerships require significant effort and planning for them to work in practice. Questions to be considered carefully by an intercultural team before they start to plan research would be:

- Does the project reflect the aspirations and priorities of the indigenous community?
- Who will gather the data—a cultural outsider or a trusted member of the local community? What language will be used?

- How will adequate rapport be established with respondents (especially children) to disclose their feelings and cultural beliefs?
- To what extent will the researcher be immersed as a participant-observer in indigenous children's classroom activities and perhaps out-of-school lives?
- How and whose culture, values, and beliefs will be represented in the results? (Abrams, Taylor, & Guo, 2013a, p. 16)

Lewthwaite and McMillian (2007) worked 4 years with three Inuit community schools to develop collaboratively with teachers (both Inuit and non–Inuit) and community members, especially elders knowledgeable in Inuit *Qaujimajatuqangit*, place-based learning materials that were consistent with the community's aspirations for science education and were aligned with the Pan-Canadian Science Protocol (Council of Ministers of Education, Canada, 1997). The first 2 years the research team focused on development of teaching principles. These principles had their origin in a variety of sources; the primary one was the knowledge and experience of all stakeholders (Inuit and non–Inuit teachers, science education professors, elders).

Linguistic competence by the researchers is a critical factor in the success of CBPR. Humans make meaning and determine relevance through language as part of their culture. Particular attention, therefore, must be paid to the use of language in all facets of the research to ensure that researchers do not continue to rely on colonial language to define indigenous reality (Battiste, 2008). The use of indigenous languages whenever the majority language is the second language, especially within the research instruments (surveys, focus groups, and interviews), underscores the important role indigenous knowledge plays in the beliefs, traditions, and values that permeate tribal communities. Intercultural research teams may need to set a priority to hire and train indigenous peoples to assist in all phases of the research project in order to ensure linguistic and cultural competence (ANKN, 2006).

Consideration must be given to the development of a genuine partnership that meets the needs of all partners and future partners. This is not an easy task because over time, the research cooperative will change its composition; with each new partner comes a new set of challenges to meet everyone's needs, which may mean revisiting earlier negotiations. CBPR involves an iterative process with constant open dialogue renewing each partner's commitment to the outcomes of the research.

Supporting the Self-Determination of the Education

Self-determination involves the sovereign right of indigenous communities to make and implement decisions, especially concerning the education of their children. Part of a community-based iterative process may involve building research capacity within indigenous communities or actively involving indigenous community researchers in the project. The ANKN (2006) encourages researchers who work with indigenous schools, teachers, or learners to address five things: (a) fund the support of an indigenous research committee appointed by the local community and charged with assessing and monitoring the research project and ensuring compliance with the expressed wishes of indigenous people; (b) hire and train indigenous people to assist in the study; (c) acknowledge the contributions of indigenous people; (d) inform relevant tribal governing bodies in nontechnical language of the major findings of the study; and (e) provide copies of the study for the local people. These steps help ensure a legacy of resource people and that the research supports indigenous people's sovereignty and enhances indigenous communities' ability to educate their children.

Kelly and associates (2012), for example, reported on academic researchers working alongside indigenous communities in rural New South Wales, Australia, to respond to indigenous concerns about the spread of influenza. After consultation with the communities involved, community members were recruited to conduct field research. The young indigenous people with a working knowledge of target health issues became involved with the study as field researchers; they had strong links to the communities and were able to negotiate a level of access, as trusted others, that was not available to outsiders. These researchers were able to combine academic knowledge with an in-depth sociocultural knowledge of their communities; as a result, the project was of ultimate benefit to the participating communities. In addition, a legacy upon the project's completion was that the research capacity was increased within these indigenous communities. Similar outcomes have been observed in science education projects where indigenous researchers from participating communities were recruited (Castleden et al., 2012; Kidman, 2007; Wright et al., 2011).

Moving Toward Antiracist Perspectives of Science Education for All

The central motive for considering IKW's role in science education has been social justice, economic opportunity, and equitable treatment of all people. This way of viewing IKW has been picked up in the Australian context by drawing on the insights of the Yolngu people of the Northern Territory, who have a long-established tradition of mixing knowledge from different sources in an equitable manner to achieve meaningful two-way collaborations (Muller, 2012). Muller argued that IKW and WMS can be viewed in a similar light and that worthwhile partnerships can be established between proponents of both knowledge systems in ways that acknowledge the aspirations of indigenous communities. This sort of *two tool boxes* approach makes possible the creation of a hybridized scientific domain whereby indigenous communities and credentialed scientists can work together to create new scientific knowledge and innovative classroom pedagogies (Kidman et al., 2011).

The recruitment of indigenous researchers also makes possible the development of place-based indigenous research methodologies and practices that fully reflect the sociopolitical and sociocultural perspectives. West, Stewart, Foster, and Usher (2012) worked in partnership with the Ngangikurungkurr people of Daly River in Northern Australia to establish a place-based indigenous methodology (the Dadirri Method) that promotes indigenous control of the research agenda and retains ownership of their knowledge. Indigenous methodologies drawn from the traditions of indigenous communities and geared toward self-determination, advocacy, and transformative and healing actions take the aspirations, histories, and priorities of particular indigenous communities into account (Evans, Hole, Berg, Hutchinson, & Sookraj, 2009). Reconciliation and redistribution of understanding are considered central and critical to resolving long-lasting controversies and social justice issues; education, teaching, and learning about nature and naturally occurring events are not exempt from these complex problems.

These new collaborations could create a *two-way street* that enhances the knowledge of both indigenous and nonindigenous students. Barnhardt (2008) stated:

> It is imperative, therefore, that we come at these issues on a two-way street, rather than view the problem as a one-way challenge to get indigenous people to buy into the western system. Indigenous people may need to understand western society, but not at the expense of what they already know and the way they have come to know it. Non-indigenous people, too, need to recognize the co-existence of multiple worldviews and knowledge systems, and find ways to understand and relate to the world in its multiple dimensions of diversity and complexity.
>
> (para. 3)

Universities in New Zealand, Canada, and Alaska have expanded or developed new doctoral programs in indigenous studies aimed at recruiting and preparing indigenous scholars to take on leadership roles and bring indigenous perspectives to research and policy makers, to realize this vision, and to support the self-determination of indigenous communities. Science education will expand as new researchers revisit and examine theoretical perspectives, research questions, and research methodologies from other worldviews.

Ethical science education research with indigenous communities has the potential for mutual benefit where indigenous communities can use the research data and results to understand better the education of their children, take control of the educational process, or work with researchers to develop better science classrooms. Individual community members can benefit from the training and employment opportunities as members of the research team and benefit from access to services and technology they might not have otherwise. Researchers

have the opportunity to truly understand and expand the ways they know and understand science education, gain a cultural-based understanding of their work, and know that their research had practical implications to make a difference. The achievement of these new perspectives is based on the internal desires, motives, and commitments of science education researchers and the science education community to help indigenous people achieve their science literacy goals, cultural and knowledge preservation, and language restoration and to ensure the acceptance and compliance of ethics principles—beneficence and nonmalfeasance, fidelity and responsibility, integrity, and respect for people's rights and dignity (www.apa.org/ethics/code/index.aspx).

Closing Remarks

The decades-old IKW–WMS debate has been unproductive in terms of better serving indigenous and nonindigenous peoples for a variety of reasons—not the least is the tremendous waste of human resources and effort and the continuation of intellectual apartheid, much like the artificial separation of the arts, humanities, and sciences in earlier centuries of Western cultures. Colonization of countries like the Philippines by various dominant countries (i.e., Spain, Japan, United States) has taken hundreds of years. It is likely to take a very long time to transform the disciplinary silos and decolonize these countries and indigenous peoples, but we must get started (personal communication with anonymous reviewer, February 2013). We believe that the options of infusing IKW into the WMS school curriculum and of developing a coequal parallel IKW–WMS curriculum are possible; we also believe that any disciplinary risks are manageable for the greater good within cultural preservation, linguistic restoration, equity, social justice, economic prosperity, and identity. We have viewed the issues of whether IKW is science or a valuable body of knowledge with the experience and progression of environmental studies and environmental education. Many universities refused to have environmental studies accepted as a department within the faculty of science because it was interdisciplinary, involving social sciences, sciences, and other disciplines. Today, many faculties of science and engineering offer programs in environmental studies and engineering. Environmental education was not fully accepted in either science or social sciences, but today it has a specific strand in the National Association for Research in Science Teaching and the American Education Research Association.

This rather large author team was recruited to bring together representatives of these diverse groups in a supportive environment without a fixed agenda other than to identify ideas and issues and to reveal common ground and unresolved issues within this complex problem space, while recognizing that indigenous people and indigenous knowledge stand as unique collections of peoples and knowledge systems rather than a single entity. These differences are apparent when reading the various sections of this chapter. But, most importantly, this author team attempted to identify potential solutions and productive research inquiries regarding how to help indigenous people realize their goals regarding science literacy for all at the mainstream citizenship level and the pipeline level for STEM career opportunities.

Border crossing or bridge building, like all metaphors, have strengths and limitations. L. Carter (2010) captured a weakness and limitation of the metaphor when she stated: "Borders have been typically represented within science education as unproblematic lines between cultures and knowledges that need to be crossed" (pp. 429–430). The assumption that these metaphors were not problematic needs consideration, but armchair IKW–WMS education also needs consideration. We have tried to describe IKW and WMS—although we pointed out that our visions were two of many possible visions of IKW and WMS (Footnote 1)—and the boundaries, borders, or demarcations could have been drawn in many different places to define the spaces. In fact, we have not disregarded that IKW and WMS may be the same space and our lines may be erased or changed drastically as science educators and teachers move toward Option #3—**Develop coequal interpretations of IKW and WMS.** Readers must realize that the identities ascribed to IKW and WMS are only valid at the most general level and that IKW and WMS are specific to individual ownership and discourse communities—indigenous and nonindigenous. The diversity across indigenous peoples and cultures and variance within indigenous groups were found worldwide. Similar diversity and variability were reported across views of science (i.e., tradition, modern, postmodern), science domains, and specific topics. We cannot make an airtight generalized statement about the IKW and WMS production enterprises. Other than technology and wisdom—arising from very long-term considerations—are integral parts of IKW, which means that technological design and indigenous technologies and innovations might be effective starting points in an infused or co-equal IKW–WMS curriculum. Furthermore, wisdom has critical potential for applying knowledge more successfully to science, technology, society, and environment issues, and an integrated IKW–WMS understanding brings new perspectives to other perplexing problems.

There are several case studies as positive examples of IKW being infused into the WMS school curriculum. The collaborative planning and delivery involved place-based topics, local resource people, and cultural and community resources; however, these case studies have not documented the long-term learning effects of these approaches (Handa & Tippins, 2012; Kidman, 2007; Lewthwaite & Renaud, 2009). Furthermore, several scholars encouraged the development and delivery of a coequal IKW and WMS curriculum, but there have been no evaluative studies to document the classroom implementation and learning effects of such a program (Aikenhead & Ogawa, 2007; Brayboy & Castagno, 2009; Kidman, Yen, & Abrams,

2012). There are needs for evidence-based best practices on how to have IKW and WMS coexist within a classroom rather than just an IKW–infused science curriculum. Teacher education programs need to prepare science teachers on how to create culturally relevant pedagogy based upon specific cultural strengths (funds of knowledge), learning theories, and innovative pedagogies (use of indigenous language and place-based teaching techniques) in order to meaningfully engage indigenous students. A focus should be on strengthening the pipeline of indigenous science teachers. Well-prepared indigenous and nonindigenous teachers are only one factor in CRS. High academic expectations for students in literacy and mathematics, access to advanced technologies and science opportunities, and a high level of community involvement have the potential to increase the high school graduation rate of indigenous students.

Regardless of the option selected, disciplinary and program integrity will be critical in that students exposed to any IKW–WMS program need to be taken seriously and their ideas accessed, engaged, and challenged to promote meaningful learning of both knowledge systems. As well, there needs to be a fulsome evaluation of the program's effectiveness and the students' learning in terms of achieving personal and professional goals. Saving the culture will be of little value if it means that the members of the culture are still left disadvantaged. There is a need to create items and response modes on the national/state assessments that reflect both IKW and WMS content/process/nature of knowledge and knowledge construction to support the inclusion of culturally relevant curricula in classrooms (Benson, 2012).

Future IKW–WMS education research needs to consider achievement, identity, and self-efficacy and needs to be long term. CBPR emphasizes mutually beneficial partnerships *with* rather than *on* indigenous learners, which might require changes in research questions, methodologies, and outcomes. Sharing of resources, especially financial, may enhance the self-determination of indigenous communities. There was a noticeable lack of literature on indigenous science education from certain parts of the world including South America, China, and North Africa. This paucity might be due to the lack of research in these areas or that many science education journals are published in English, silencing many indigenous voices. Some journals, namely, *L1–Educational Studies in Language and Literature* (Yore, Chinn, & Hand, 2008), *Canadian Journal of Science, Mathematics and Technology Education* (Michell, 2009), and *International Journal of Science and Mathematics Education* (Abrams et al., 2013b), have developed special issues to alleviate this scarcity.

WMS has been determined by national governments as a primary driver of economic growth, and STEM education policy is subsequently linked to achieving these economic goals. Many science education organizations are, therefore, focused on addressing the drastic need for STEM professionals in the 21st technoscientific economy (pipeline issue). An international mainstream–pipeline coordinated effort that increases the general STEM literacy level of all students, including indigenous citizens, and the pool of university/college/postsecondary qualified students will address the pipeline issue; it will achieve economic and employment opportunities and social justice lacking for many indigenous people as well as enhance the disciplines of science and science education.

Acknowledgments

The authors wish to thank Norman G. Lederman and Masakata Ogawa for reviewing this chapter and Shari Yore for the technical support in writing this chapter.

Note

1. *Disclaimer:* This chapter is addressing provocative, pressing, and passionate issues about underserved and underrepresented indigenous peoples and their traditional knowledge systems about nature and naturally occurring events. The multinational and multiethnic author team has tried to reveal some common issues while recognizing that the problem space is very diverse and the target indigenous knowledge stands as a unique collection of knowledge and production systems rather than a single entity. Therefore, readers must realize that the identity given to indigenous knowledge is only valid at the most general level and that indigenous knowledge is specific to individual ownership by indigenous groups.

References

Abrams, E., Taylor, P.C., & Guo, C.-J. (2013a). Contextualizing culturally relevant science and mathematics teaching for indigenous learning [Special issue]. *International Journal of Science and Mathematics Education, 11*(1), 1–21.

Abrams, E., Taylor, P.C., & Guo, C.-J. (Eds.). (2013b). Pedagogies of hope: Culturally relevant science and mathematics teaching for indigenous learners in science and mathematics [Special issue]. *International Journal of Science and Mathematics Education, 11*(1), 1–121.

Abrams, E., Yen, C.-F., Blatt, E., & Ho, L. (2009). Unpacking the complex influence of schooling, sense of place and culture on the motivation of Taiwanese elementary students to learn science in school: Using a socio-cultural approach with phenomenological research methodologies. In D.B. Zandvliet (Ed.), *Diversity in environmental education research* (pp. 103–129). Rotterdam, the Netherlands: Sense.

Agbo, S.A. (2004). First Nations perspectives on transforming the status of culture and language in schooling. *Journal of American Indian Education, 43*(1), 1–31.

Aikenhead, G. S. (1996). Science education: Border crossing into the subculture of science. *Studies in Science Education, 27*, 1–52.

Aikenhead, G.S. (2006). *Science education for everyday life: Evidence-based practice.* New York, NY: Teachers College Press.

Aikenhead, G.S., & Elliott, D. (2010). An emerging decolonizing science education in Canada. *Canadian Journal of Science, Mathematics and Technology Education, 10*(4), 321–338.

Aikenhead, G.S., & Michell, H. (2012). *Bridging cultures: Indigenous and scientific ways of knowing nature.* Toronto, ON: Pearson Education Canada.

Aikenhead, G.S., & Ogawa, M. (2007). Indigenous knowledge and science revisited. *Cultural Studies of Science Education, 2*(3), 539–620.

Alaska Native Knowledge Network. (n.d.). *Culturally-based curriculum resources.* Fairbanks, AK: University of Alaska Fairbanks. Retrieved from http://ankn.uaf.edu/Resources/course/view.php?id=2

Alaska Native Knowledge Network. (2006). *Alaska Federation of Natives guidelines for research.* Fairbanks, AK: University of Alaska Fairbanks. Retrieved from http://ankn.uaf.edu/IKS/afnguide.html

Anderson, J.O., Lin, H.-S., Treagust, D.F., Ross, S.P., & Yore, L.D. (2007). Using large-scale assessment datasets for research in science and mathematics education: Programme for International Student Assessment (PISA). *International Journal of Science and Mathematics Education, 5*(4), 591–614.

Appanna, S.D. (2011). Embedding indigenous perspectives in teaching school science. *Australian Journal of Indigenous Education, 40*, 18–22.

Atkinson, J.L. (2010). Are we creating the achievement gap? Examining how deficit mentalities influence indigenous science curriculum choices. In D.J. Tippins, M.P. Mueller, M. van Eijck, & J.D. Adams (Eds.), *Cultural studies and environmentalism: The confluence of eco-justice, place-based (science) education, and indigenous knowledge systems* (Vol. 3, pp. 439–446). Dordrecht, the Netherlands: Springer.

Australian Institute of Aboriginal and Torres Strait Islander Studies. (n.d.). *Research at AIATSIS.* Retrieved from www.aiatsis.gov.au/research/about.html

Ball, D.L., & Osborne, M.D. (1998). Teaching with difference: A response to Angela Calabrese Barton: Teaching science with homeless children: Pedagogy, representation, and identity. *Journal of Research in Science Teaching, 35*(4), 395–397.

Bang, M.E. (2009). *Understanding students' epistemologies: Examining practice and meaning in community contexts* (Doctoral dissertation). Northwestern University, Evanston, IL. Retrieved from ERIC (ED530427).

Bang, M.E., Curley, L., Kessel, A., Marin, A., & Suzokovich, E. (in press). Muskrat theories, tobacco in the streets, and living Chicago as indigenous lands. *Environmental Education Research.*

Bang, M.E., & Medin, D. (2010). Cultural processes in science education: Supporting the navigation of multiple epistemologies. *Science Education, 94*(6), 1008–1026.

Bang, M.E., Warren, B., Rosebery, A.S., & Medin, D. (2012). Desettling expectations in science education. *Human Development, 55*(5–6), 302–318.

Barnhardt, R. (2005). Indigenous knowledge systems and Alaska native ways of knowing. *Anthropology & Education Quarterly, 36*(1), 8–23.

Barnhardt, R. (2008). *Indigenous knowledge systems and higher education: Preparing Alaska Native PhD's for leadership roles in research.* Fairbanks, AK: Alaska Native Knowledge Network. Retrieved from www.ankn.uaf.edu/curriculum/Articles/RayBarnhardt/PreparingPhDs.html

Battiste, M. (2008). Research ethics for protecting indigenous knowledge and heritage: Institutional and researcher responsibilities. In N.K. Denzin, Y.S. Lincoln, & L. Tuhiwai Smith (Eds.), *Handbook of critical and indigenous methodologies* (pp. 497–510). Thousand Oaks, CA: Sage.

Battiste, M., Kovach, M., & Balzer, G. (2010). Celebrating the local, negotiating the school: Language and literacy in aboriginal communities. *Canadian Journal of Native Education, 32*, 4–12.

Bazzul, J. (2012). Neoliberal ideology, global capitalism, and science education: Engaging the question of subjectivity. *Cultural Studies of Science Education, 7*(4), 1001–1020.

Belczewski, A. (2009). Decolonizing science education and the science teacher: A White teacher's perspective. *Canadian Journal of Science, Mathematics and Technology Education, 9*(3), 191–202.

Belgarde, M.J., Mitchell, R.D., & Arquero, A. (2002). What do we have to do to create culturally responsive programs? The challenge of transforming American Indian teacher education. *Action in Teacher Education, 24*(2), 42–54.

Benson, J. (2012). *Student science achievement and the integration of indigenous knowledge in the classroom and on standardized tests* (Unpublished doctoral dissertation). University of New Hampshire, Durham, NH.

Bishop, R. (2008). Te Kotahitanga: Kaupapa Mâori in mainstream classrooms. In N. K. Denzin, Y. S. Lincoln, & L. Tuhiwai Smith (Eds.), *Handbook of critical and indigenous methodologies* (pp. 439–458). Thousand Oaks, CA: Sage.

Brayboy, B. M. J. (2005). Toward a tribal critical race theory in education. *The Urban Review, 37*(5), 425–446.

Brayboy, B. M. J., & Castagno, A. E. (2009). Self-determination through self-education: Culturally responsive schooling for Indigenous students in the USA. *Teaching Education, 20*(1), 31–53.

Brayboy, B. M. J., & Maughan, E. (2009). Indigenous knowledges and the story of the bean. *Harvard Educational Review, 79*(1), 1–21.

British Columbia Ministry of Education. (2011). *Aboriginal education resources: Learning resources.* Victoria, BC: Author. Retrieved from www.bced.gov.bc.ca/abed/documents.htm

Buxton, C. (2009). Science inquiry, academic language, and civic engagement. *Democracy in Education, 18*(3), 17–22.

Caduto, M. J., & Bruchac, J. (1991). *The native stories from keepers of the earth.* Calgary, AB: Fifth House.

Cajete, G. A. (2008). Sites of strength in indigenous research. In M. Villegas, S. R. Neugebauer, & K. R. Venegas (Eds.), *Indigenous knowledge and education: Sites of struggle, strength, and survivance* (pp. 204–210). Cambridge, MA: Harvard Education Publishing Group.

Cargo, M., Delormier, T., Lévesque, L., Horn-Miller, K., McComber, A., & Macaulay, A. C. (2008). Can the democratic ideal of participatory research be achieved? An inside look at an academic-indigenous community partnership. *Health Education Research, 23*(5), 904–914.

Carjuzaa, J., & Fenimore-Smith, K. (2010). The give away spirit: Reaching a shared vision of ethical indigenous research relationships. *Journal of Educational Controversy, 5*(2). Retrieved from www.wce.wwu.edu/Resources/CEP/eJournal/v005n002/a004.shtml

Carter, C. D. (2010). *Science and the near-death experience: How consciousness survives death.* Rochester, VT: Inner Traditions.

Carter, L. (2010). The armchair at the borders: The "messy" ideas of borders and border epistemologies within multicultural science education scholarship. *Science Education, 94*(3), 428–447.

Carter, L., & Walker, N. (2010). Traditional ecological knowledge, border theory and justice. In D. J. Tippins, M. P. Mueller, M. van Ejick, & J. D. Adams (Eds.), *Cultural studies and environmentalism: The confluence of ecojustice, place-based (science) education, and indigenous knowledge systems* (Vol. 3, pp. 337–348). Dordrecht, the Netherlands: Springer.

Castagno, A. E., & Brayboy, B. M. J. (2008). Culturally responsive schooling for indigenous youth: A review of the literature. *Review of Educational Research, 78*(4), 941–993.

Castleden, H., Morgan, V. S., & Lamb, C. (2012). "I spent the first year drinking tea": Exploring Canadian university researchers' perspectives on community-based participatory research involving indigenous peoples. *The Canadian Geographer/Le Géographe Canadien, 56*(2), 160–179.

Chang, J.-M., Lee, H., & Yen, C.-F. (2010). Alternative conceptions about burning held by Atayal Indigene students in Taiwan. *International Journal of Science and Mathematics Education, 8*(5), 911–935.

Chigeza, P. (2008). Language negotiations indigenous students navigate when learning science. *Australian Journal of Indigenous Education, 37,* 91–97.

Chinn, P. W. U. (2007). Decolonizing methodologies and indigenous knowledge: The role of culture, place and personal experience in professional development. *Journal of Research in Science Teaching, 44*(9), 1247–1268.

Chinn, P. W. U., Hand, B., & Yore, L. D. (2008). Culture, language, knowledge about nature and naturally occurring events, and science literacy for all: She says, he says, they say [Special issue]. *L1–Educational Studies in Language and Literature, 8*(1), 149–171. Retrieved from http://l1.publication-archive.com/show?repository=1&article=220

Connell, R. (2007). *Southern theory: The global dynamics of knowledge in social science.* Sydney, Australia: Allen & Unwin.

Council of Ministers of Education, Canada. (1997). *Common framework of science learning outcomes, K to 12: Pan-Canadian protocol for collaboration on school curriculum.* Retrieved from http://publications.cmec.ca/science/framework/

Eisenhart, M., Finkel, E., & Marion, S. F. (1996). Creating the conditions for scientific literacy: A re-examination. *American Educational Research Journal, 33*(2), 261–295.

El-Hani, C. N., & Souza de Ferreira Bandeira, F. P. (2008). Valuing indigenous knowledge: To call it "science" will not help. *Cultural Studies of Science Education, 3*(3), 751–779.

Elliott, F. (2011). From indigenous science examples to indigenous science perspectives. *Alberta Science Education Journal, 41*(1), 4–10.

Evans, M., Hole, R., Berg, L. D., Hutchinson, P., & Sookraj, D. (2009). Common insights, differing methodologies: Toward a fusion of indigenous methodologies, participatory action research, and White studies in an urban aboriginal research agenda. *Qualitative Inquiry, 15*(5), 893–910.

Fakudze, C., & Rollnick, M. (2008). Language, culture, ontological assumptions, epistemological beliefs, and knowledge about nature and naturally occurring events: Southern African perspective [Special issue]. *L1–Educational Studies in Language and Literature, 8*(1), 69–94. Retrieved from http://l1.publication-archive.com/publi c?fn=enter&repository=1&article=216

Ferreira, M. P., & Gendron, F. (2011). Community-based participatory research with traditional and indigenous communities of the Americas: Historical context and future directions. *International Journal of Critical Pedagogy, 3*(3), 153–168.

Fine, M., Tuck, E., & Zeller-Berkman, S. (2008). Do you believe in Geneva? Methods and ethics at the global-local nexus. In N. K. Denzin, Y. S. Lincoln, & L. Tuhiwai Smith (Eds.), *Handbook of critical and indigenous methodologies* (pp. 157–180). Thousand Oaks, CA: Sage.

Ford, C. L., & Yore, L. D. (2012). Toward convergence of critical thinking, metacognition, and reflection: Illustrations from natural and social sciences, teacher education, and classroom practice. In A. Zohar & Y. J. Dori (Eds.), *Metacognition in science education: Trends in current research* (pp. 251–271). Dordrecht, the Netherlands: Springer.

Ford, M. J. (2008). Disciplinary authority and accountability in scientific practice and learning. *Science Education, 92*(3), 404–423.

Freier, G. D. (1989). *Wonder of weather: 600 proverbs, sayings, facts & folklore about the always unpredictable weather.* Darby, PA: Diane.

Fulton, L., & Campbell, B. L. (2004). Student-centered notebooks. *Science and Children, 42*(3), 26–29.

Gadicke, J. M. (2005). *Integrating aboriginal knowledge into the elementary science curriculum* (Unpublished master's project). University of Victoria, Victoria, British Columbia, Canada.

Gallard Martínez, A. J. (2011). Argumentation and indigenous knowledge: Socio-historical influences in contextualizing an argumentation model in South African schools. *Cultural Studies of Science Education, 6*(3), 719–723.

George, J. (1999). Worldview analysis of knowledge in a rural village: Implications for science education. *Science Education, 83*(1), 77–95.

George, J. (2013). "Do you have to pack?" Preparing for culturally relevant science teaching in the Caribbean. *International Journal of Science Education, 35*(12), 2114–2131.

Glasson, G. E., Mhango, N., Phiri, A., & Lanier, M. (2010). Sustainability science education in Africa: Negotiating indigenous ways of living with nature in the third space. *International Journal of Science Education, 32*(1), 125–141.

Good, R. G., Shymansky, J. A., & Yore, L. D. (1999). Censorship in science and science education. In E. H. Brinkley (Ed.), *Caught off guard: Teachers rethinking censorship and controversy* (pp. 101–121). Boston, MA: Allyn & Bacon.

Grande, S. (2008). Red pedagogy: The un-methodology. In N. K. Denzin, Y. S. Lincoln, & L. Tuhiwai Smith (Eds.), *Handbook of critical and indigenous methodologies* (pp. 233–254). Thousand Oaks, CA: Sage.

Gunel, M., Hand, B., & Prain, V. (2007). Writing for learning in science: A secondary analysis of six studies. *International Journal of Science and Mathematics Education, 5*(4), 615–637.

Guo, C.-J., Hsiung, T.-H., Wang, C.-L., & Yore, L. D. (2008, March-April). *Border crossings: Bridging cultural perspectives with technology—Examples from Taiwan's indigenous people in the southeast area.* Paper presented at the annual meeting of the National Association for Research in Science Teaching, Baltimore, MD.

Hand, B., Villanueva, M. G., & Yoon, S. (in press). Moving from "fuzziness" to canonical knowledge: The role of writing in developing cognitive and representational resources. In P. D. Klein, P. Boscolo, L. Kirkpatrick, & C. Gelati (Eds.), *Writing as learning activity* (Vol. 17, pp. TBA). Dordrecht, the Netherlands: Springer.

Handa, V. C., & Tippins, D. J. (2012). Tensions in the third space: Locating relevancy in preservice science teacher preparation. *International Journal of Science and Mathematics Education. 11*(1), 237–265.

Hansen, S. A., & VanFleet, J. W. (2003). *Traditional knowledge and intellectual property: A handbook in issues and options for traditional knowledge holders in protecting their intellectual property and maintaining biological diversity.* Washington, DC: American Association for the Advancement of Science.

Hatcher, A., Bartlett, C., Marshall, A., & Marshall, M. (2009). Two-eyed seeing in the classroom environment: Concepts, approaches, and challenges. *Canadian Journal of Science, Mathematics and Technology Education, 9*(3), 141–153.

Hofer, B. K. (2008). Personal epistemology and culture. In M. S. Khine (Ed.), *Knowing, knowledge and beliefs: Epistemological studies across diverse culture* (pp. 3–22). Dordrecht, the Netherlands: Springer.

Horsthemke, K., & Yore, L. D. (2014). Challenges of multiculturalism in science education: Indigenisation, internationalisation, and *transkulturalät.* In M. R. Matthews (Ed.), *Handbook of history and philosophy of science and science teaching* (pp. 1759–1792). Dordrecht, the Netherlands: Springer.

Hudson, M., Milne, M., Reynolds, P., Russell, K., & Smith, B. (2010). *Te Ara Tika—Guidelines for Māori research ethics: A framework for researchers and ethics committee members.* Auckland, New Zealand: Health Research Council of New Zealand. Retrieved from www.hrc.govt.nz/sites/default/files/Te%20Ara%20Tika%20Guidelines%20for%20Maori%20Research%20Ethics.pdf

Hudson, M., Roberts, M., Smith, L., Tiakiwai, S.-J., & Hemi, M. (2012). The art of dialogue with indigenous communities in the new biotechnology world. *New Genetics and Society, 31*(1), 11–24.

Inwards, R. (1869). *Weather lore: A collection of proverbs, sayings, and rules concerning the weather.* London, UK: W. Tweedie.

Jacobs, B., Roffenbender, J., Collman, J., Cherry, K., Bitsòi, L. L., Bassett, K., & Evans, C. H., Jr. (2010). Bridging the divide between genomic science and indigenous peoples. *Journal of Law, Medicine & Ethics, 38*(3), 684–696.

Johnson, C. C. (2011). The road to culturally relevant science: Exploring how teachers navigate change in pedagogy. *Journal of Research in Science Teaching, 48*(2), 170–198.

Kawagley, A. O. (2006). *A Yupiaq worldview: A pathway to ecology and spirit* (2nd ed.). Long Grove, IL: Waveland Press.

Keane, M. (2008). Science education and worldview. *Cultural Studies of Science Education, 3*(3), 587–621.

Kelly, J., Saggers, S., Taylor, K., Pearce, G., Massey, P., Bull, J., Odo, T., Thomas, J., Billycan, R., Judd, J., Reilly, S., & Ahboo, S. (2012). "Makes you proud to be black eh?": Reflections on meaningful Indigenous research participation. *International Journal for Equity in Health, 11*(40): 1–8.

Kidman, J. (2007). *Engaging with Māori communities: An exploration of some tensions in the mediation of social sciences research* (Tihei Oreore Monograph Series). Auckland, New Zealand: Ngā Pae o te Māramatanga, University of Auckland.

Kidman, J., Abrams, E., & McRae, H. (2011). Imaginary subjects: School science, indigenous students, and knowledge–power relations. *British Journal of Sociology of Education, 32*(2), 203–220.

Kidman, J., Yen, C.-F., & Abrams, E. (2012). Indigenous students' experiences of the hidden curriculum in science education: A cross-national study in New Zealand and Taiwan. *International Journal of Science and Mathematics Education, 11*(1), 43–64.

Klug, B. J., & Whitfield, P. T. (2003). *Widening the circle: Culturally relevant pedagogy for American Indian children.* New York, NY: Routledge Falmer.

Klump, J., & McNeir, G. (2005). *Culturally responsive practices for student success: A regional sampler.* Portland, OR: Northwest Regional Educational Laboratory. Retrieved from http://educationnorthwest.org/webfm_send/296

Langenhoven, K., Kwofie, S., & Ogunniyi, M. B. (2008). *Science & indigenous knowledge systems project.* Unpublished study guides, School of Science & Mathematics Education, University of the Western Cape, Cape Town, South Africa.

Lederman, N. G., & Lederman, J. S. (2012). Nature of scientific knowledge and scientific inquiry: Building instructional capacity through professional development. In B. J. Fraser, K. Tobin, & C. J. McRobbie (Eds.), *Second international handbook of science education* (Vol. 24, pp. 335–359). Dordrecht, the Netherlands: Springer.

Lee, H., Chiang, C. L., & Lin, Y. C. (2011, July). *Bunun's worldview of nature and its influence on daily life.* Paper presented at 11th international IHPST & 6th Greek History, Philosophy and Science Teaching joint conference, Thessaloniki, Greece.

Lee, H., Yen, C.-F., & Aikenhead, G. S. (2012). Indigenous elementary students' science instruction in Taiwan: Indigenous knowledge and western science. *Research in Science Education, 42*(6), 1183–1199.

Levinson, M. (2012). *No citizen left behind.* Cambridge, MA: Harvard University Press.

Lewthwaite, B., & McMillan, B. (2007). Combining the views of both worlds: Perceived constraints and contributors to achieving aspirations for science education in Qikiqtani. *Canadian Journal of Science, Mathematics and Technology Education, 7*(4), 355–376.

Lewthwaite, B., & Renaud, R. (2009). Pilimmaksarniq: Working together for the common good in science curriculum development and delivery in Nunavut. *Canadian Journal of Science, Mathematics and Technology Education, 9*(3), 154–172.

Lincoln, Y. S., & Cannella, G. S. (2009). Ethics and the broader rethinking/reconceptualization of research as construct. *Cultural Studies ↔ Critical Methodologies, 9*(2), 273–285.

Lipka, J. (1990). Integrating cultural form and content in one Yup'ik Eskimo classroom: A case study. *Canadian Journal of Education, 17*(2), 18–32.

Little Bear, L. (2009). *Naturalizing indigenous knowledge* (Synthesis paper). Saskatoon, SK, & Calgary, AB: University of Saskatchewan Aboriginal Education Research Centre & First Nations and Adult Higher Education Consortium. Retrieved from www.ccl-cca.ca/pdfs/ablkc/naturalizeIndigenous_en.pdf

Little Bear, L. (2011, March 24). *Native science and Western science: Possibilities for a powerful collaboration.* The Simon Ortiz and Labriola Center Lecture on Indigenous Land, Culture, and Community [Video podcast]. Retrieved from www.youtube.com/watch?v=ycQtQZ9y3lc

Louca, L., Elby, A., Hammer, D., & Kagey, T. (2004). Epistemological resources: Applying a new epistemological framework to science instruction. *Educational Psychologist, 39*(1), 57–68.

Mack, E., Augare, H., Different Cloud-Jones, L., Davíd, D., Quiver Gaddie, H., Honey, R. E., . . . Wippert, R. (2012). Effective practices for creating transformative informal science education programs grounded in Native ways of knowing. *Cultural Studies of Science Education, 7*(1), 49–70.

McCarty, T. L., Romero, M. E., & Zepeda, O. (2006). Reclaiming the gift: Indigenous youth counter-narratives on native language loss and revitalization. *American Indian Quarterly, 30*(1), 28–48.

McConney, A., Oliver, M. C., Woods-McConney, A., & Schibeci, R. (2011). Bridging the gap? A comparative, retrospective analysis of science literacy and interest in science for Indigenous and non-Indigenous Australian students. *International Journal of Science Education, 33*(14), 2017–2035.

McDermott, M. A., & Hand, B. (2010). A secondary reanalysis of student perceptions of non-traditional writing tasks over a ten year period. *Journal of Research in Science Teaching, 47*(5), 518–539.

McKinley, E. (2007). Postcolonialism, indigenous students, and science education. In S. K. Abell & N. G. Lederman (Eds.), *Handbook of research on science education* (pp. 199–226). Mahwah, NJ: Lawrence Erlbaum.

McKinley, E., & Keegan, P.J. (2008). Curriculum and language in Aotearoa New Zealand: From science to Putaiao [Special issue]. *L1–Educational Studies in Language and Literature, 8*(1), 135–147. Retrieved from http://l1.publication-archive.com/public?fn=enter&repository=1&article=219

McKinley, E., & Stewart, G. (2009). Falling into place: Indigenous science education and research in the Pacific. In S.M. Ritchie (Ed.), *The world of science education: Handbook of research in Australasia* (pp. 49–66). Rotterdam, the Netherlands: Sense.

McKinley, E., & Stewart, G. (2012). Out of place: Indigenous knowledge in the science curriculum. In B.J. Fraser, K. Tobin, & C.J. McRobbie (Eds.), *Second international handbook of science education* (Vol. 24, pp. 541–554). Dordrecht, the Netherlands: Springer.

Mead, N., Grigg, W., Moran, R., & Kuang, M. (2010). *National Indian education study 2009—Part II: The educational experiences of American Indian and Alaska Native students in grades 4 and 8* (NCES 2010–463). Washington, DC: National Center for Education Statistics, Institute of Education Sciences, U.S. Department of Education. Retrieved from http://nces.ed.gov/nationsreportcard/pdf/studies/2010463.pdf

Meel, B.L. (2007). Lightning fatalities in the Transkei sub-region of South Africa. *Medicine, Science and the Law, 47*(2), 161–164.

Meyer, C.F., & Rhoades, E.K. (2006). Multiculturalism: Beyond food, festival, folklore, and fashion. *Kappa Delta Pi Record, 42*(2), 82–87.

Michell, H. (2009). Introduction to the Special Issue on indigenous science education from place: Best practices on Turtle Island. *Canadian Journal of Science, Mathematics and Technology Education, 9*(3), 137–140.

Michell, H., Vizina, Y., Augustus, C., & Sawyer, J. (2008). *Learning indigenous science from place: Research study examining indigenous-based science perspectives in Saskatchewan First Nations and Métis community contexts.* Saskatoon, SK: Aboriginal Education Research Centre. Retrieved from http://aerc.usask.ca/downloads/Learning%20Indigenous%20Science%20From%20Place.pdf

Middleton, M., Dupuis, J., & Tang, J. (2012). Classrooms and culture: The role of context in shaping motivation and identity for science learning in Indigenous adolescents. *International Journal of Science and Mathematics Education, 11*(1), 111–141.

Moon, F. (2008). Preparing elementary preservice teachers for urban elementary science classrooms: Challenging cultural biases toward diverse students. *Journal of Science Teacher Education, 19,* 85–109.

Muller, S. (2012). "Two ways": Bringing indigenous and non-indigenous knowledges together. In J.K. Weir (Ed.), *Country, native title and ecology* (pp. 57–79). Canberra, ACT, Australia: ANU E Press.

Nafukho, F.M. (2006). Ubuntu worldview: A traditional African view of adult learning in the workplace. *Advances in Developing Human Resources, 8*(3), 408–415.

Nasir, N.S., & Saxe, G.B. (2003). Ethnic and academic identities: A cultural practice perspective on emerging tensions and their management in the lives of minority students. *Educational Researcher, 32*(5), 14–18.

New Zealand Ministry of Education. (1993). *Science in the New Zealand curriculum.* Wellington, New Zealand: Learning Media.

Ogunniyi, M.B. (2006). Effects of a discursive course on two science teachers' perceptions of the nature of science. *African Journal of Research in Mathematics, Science and Technology Education, 10*(1), 93–102.

Ogunniyi, M.B. (2007). Teachers' stances and practical arguments regarding a science-indigenous knowledge curriculum: Part 1. *International Journal of Science Education, 29*(8), 963–986.

Ogunniyi, M.B., & Hewson, M.G. (2008). Effect of an argumentation-based course on teachers' disposition towards a science-indigenous knowledge curriculum. *International Journal of Environmental & Science Education, 3*(4), 159–177.

Ovando, C.J. (1992). Science. In J. Reyhner (Ed.), *Teaching American Indian students* (pp. 223–240). Norman, OK: University of Oklahoma Press.

Paris, D. (2012). Culturally sustaining pedagogy: A needed change in stance, terminology and practice. *Educational Researcher, 41*(3), 93–97.

Pauka, S., Treagust, D.F., & Waldrip, B.G. (2005). Village elders' and secondary school students' explanations of natural phenomena in Papua New Guinea. *International Journal of Science and Mathematics Education, 3*(2), 213–238.

Pewewardy, C., & Hammer, P.C. (2003). *Culturally responsive teaching for American Indian students. ERIC Digest.* Charleston, WV: ERIC Clearinghouse on Rural Education and Small Schools.

Pierotti, R.J. (2010). *Indigenous knowledge, ecology, and evolutionary biology.* New York, NY: Routledge.

Regmi, J., & Fleming, M. (2012). Indigenous knowledge and science in a globalized age. *Cultural Studies of Science Education, 7*(2), 479–484.

Richards, J., & Scott, M. (2009). *Aboriginal education: Strengthening the foundations.* Ottawa, ON: Canadian Policy Research Networks. Retrieved from http://cprn.org/documents/51984_FR.pdf

Richards, J., Hove, J., & Afolabi, K. (2008, June). *Explaining the Aboriginal–non-Aboriginal gap in student performance in BC schools.* Paper presented at the annual meeting of the Canadian Economics Association, Vancouver, BC. Available from www.csls.ca/events/cea2008/richards.pdf

Rogers, A. (2007). The making of *Cosmic Africa:* The research behind the film. *African Skies/Cieux Africains, 11*(July), 19–23.

Rose, D.B. (1996). *Nourishing terrains: Australian aboriginal views of landscape and wilderness.* Canberra, ACT, Australia: Australian Heritage Commission. Retrieved from www.environment.gov.au/resource/nourishing-terrains

Santoro, N., Reid, J.-A., Crawford, L., & Simpson, L. (2011). Teaching indigenous children: Listening to and learning from indigenous teachers. *Australian Journal of Teacher Education, 36*(10), 65–76.

Sarche, M., Novins, D., & Belcourt-Dittloff, A. (2010). Engaged scholarship with tribal communities. In H.E. Fitzgerald, C. Burack, & S. Seifer (Eds.), *Handbook of engaged scholarship: Contemporary landscapes, future directions* (Vol. 1, pp. 215–233). East Lansing, MI: Michigan State University Press.

Setati, M. (2005). Teaching mathematics in a primary multilingual classroom. *Journal for Research in Mathematics Education, 36*(5), 447–466.

Snively, G.J., & Williams, L.B. (2008). "Coming to know": Weaving Aboriginal and Western science knowledge, language, and literacy into the science classroom [Special issue]. *L1–Educational Studies in Language and Literature, 8*(1), 109–133. Retrieved from http://l1.publication-archive.com/public?fn=enter&repository=1&article=218

Social Sciences and Humanities Research Council of Canada. (n.d.). *Aboriginal research.* Retrieved from www.sshrc-crsh.gc.ca/funding-financement/programs-programmes/priority_areas-domaines_prioritaires/aboriginal_research-recherche_autochtone-eng.aspx

South Africa Department of Education. (2002). *Revised national curriculum statement for grades R–9 (schools) – Natural sciences* (Vol. 443, No. 23406). Pretoria, South Africa: Government Gazette.

Standards for Culturally-Responsive Schools Adopted by Native Educators. (Standards for CRS). (1998, March/April). *Sharing Our Pathways, 3*(2). Retrieved from www.ankn.uaf.edu/sop/sopv3i2.html#standard

Stephens, S. (2003). *Handbook for culturally responsive science curriculum* (2nd ed.). Fairbanks, AK: Alaska Native Knowledge Network.

Stewart, G. (2005). Māori in the science curriculum: Developments and possibilities. *Educational Philosophy and Theory, 37*(6), 851–870.

Sutherland, D., & Henning, D. (2009). Ininiwi-Kiskānītamowin: A framework for long-term science education. *Canadian Journal of Science, Mathematics and Technology Education, 9*(3), 173–190.

Thomson, S., De Bortoli, L., Nicholas, M., Hillman, K., & Buckley, S. (2010). *Challenges for Australian education: Results from PISA 2009: The PISA 2009 assessment of students' reading, mathematical and scientific literacy.* Retrieved from http://research.acer.edu.au/ozpisa/9

Trujillo, O.V., Viri, D., & Figueira, A. (2002, August). *The native educators research project.* Paper presented at the World Indigenous Peoples Conference on Education, Edmonton, Alberta, Canada.

Tuck, E. (2012). Repatriating the GED: Urban youth and the alternative to a high school diploma. *The High School Journal, 95*(4), 4–18.

Tuhiwai Smith, L. (1999). *Decolonizing methodologies: Research and indigenous peoples*. London, UK: Zed.

Tuhiwai Smith, L. (2005). On tricky ground: Researching the native in the age of uncertainty. In N. K. Denzin & Y. S. Lincoln (Eds.), *Sage handbook of qualitative research* (3rd ed., pp. 85–107). Thousand Oaks, CA: Sage.

United Nations. (2007). *United Nations declaration on the rights of indigenous peoples*. Resolution 61/295. New York, NY: UN General Assembly. Retrieved from www.un.org/esa/socdev/unpfii/documents/DRIPS_en.pdf

United States Department of Education. (2008). *Status and trends in the education of American Indians and Alaska Native: 2008* (NCES 2008–084). Washington, DC: National Center for Education Statistics. Retrieved from http://nces.ed.gov/pubs2008/nativetrends/index.asp

United States National Research Council. (2007). *Taking science to school: Learning and teaching science in grades K–8* (R. A. Duschl, H. A. Schweingruber, & A. W. Shouse, Eds.). Washington, DC: National Academies Press.

United States National Research Council. (2009). *Learning science in informal environments: People, places, and pursuits* (P. Bell, B. Lewenstein, A. W. Shouse, & M. A. Feder, Eds.). Washington, DC: National Academies Press.

United States National Research Council. (2012). *A framework for K–12 science education: Practices, crosscutting concepts, and core ideas* (H. Quinn, H. A. Schweingruber, & T. Keller, Eds.). Washington, DC: National Academies Press.

Villanueva, M. G., & Hand, B. (2011). Data versus evidence: Investigating the difference. *Science Scope, 35*(1), 42–45.

Villanueva, M. G., & Webb, P. (2008). Scientific investigations: The effect of the "Science Notebooks" approach in grade 6 classrooms in Port Elizabeth, South Africa. *African Journal of Research in Mathematics, Science and Technology Education, 12*(2), 3–16.

Villegas, M., Neugebauer, S. R., & Venegas, K. (Eds.). (2008). *Indigenous knowledge and education: Sites of struggle, strength, and survivance*. Cambridge, MA: Harvard Educational Publishing Group.

Waldrip, B. G., Timothy, J. T., & Wilikai, W. (2007). Pedagogic principles in negotiating cultural conflict: A Melanesian example. *International Journal of Science Education, 29*(1), 101–122.

Warren, E., & de Vries, E. (2009). Young Australian indigenous students' engagement with numeracy: Actions that assist to bridge the gap. *Australian Journal of Education, 53*(2), 159–175.

Webb, P. (2010). Science education and literacy: Imperatives for the developed and developing world [Special issue]. *Science, 328*(5977), 448–450.

Webb, P. (2012). Xhosa indigenous knowledge: Stakeholder awareness, value, and choice. *International Journal of Science and Mathematics Education, 11*(1), 89–110.

Webb, P., & Mayaba, N. (2010). The effect of an integrated strategies approach to promoting scientific literacy on grade 6 and 7 learners' general literacy skills. *African Journal of Research in Mathematics, Science and Technology Education, 14*(3), 34–49.

West, R., Stewart, L., Foster, K., & Usher, K. (2012). Through a critical lens: Indigenist research and the Dadirri method. *Qualitative Health Research, 22*(11), 1582–1590.

Wilson, S. (2008). *Research is ceremony: Indigenous research methods*. Black Point, NS, Canada: Fernwood.

Wood, A., & Lewthwaite, B. (2008). Māori science education in Aotearoa New Zealand. He pūtea whakarawe: Aspirations and realities. *Cultural Studies of Science Education, 3*(3), 625–662.

Woods-McConney, A., Oliver, M. C., McConney, A., Major, D., & Schibeci, R. (2013). Science engagement and literacy: A retrospective analysis for Indigenous and non-Indigenous students in Aotearoa New Zealand and Australia. *Research in Science Education, 43*, 233–252.

Worldwide Indigenous Science Network. (n.d.). *Distinctions of indigenous science*. Retrieved from www.wisn.org/what-is-indigenous-science.html

Wright, N., Claxton, E., Jr., Williams, L., & Paul, T. (2011). Giving voice to science from two perspectives: A case study. In L. D. Yore, E. Van der Flier-Keller, D. W. Blades, T. W. Pelton, & D. B. Zandvliet (Eds.), *Pacific CRYSTAL centre for science, mathematics, and technology literacy: Lessons learned* (pp. 67–82). Rotterdam, the Netherlands: Sense.

Yore, L. D. (2008). Science literacy for all students: Language, culture, and knowledge about nature and naturally occurring events [Special issue]. *L1–Educational Studies in Language and Literature, 8*(1), 5–21. Retrieved from http://l1.publication-archive.com/show?repository=1&article=213

Yore, L. D. (2011). Foundations of scientific, mathematical, and technological literacies—Common themes and theoretical frameworks. In L. D. Yore, E. Van der Flier-Keller, D. W. Blades, T. W. Pelton, & D. B. Zandvliet (Eds.), *Pacific CRYSTAL centre for science, mathematics, and technology literacy: Lessons learned* (pp. 23–44). Rotterdam, the Netherlands: Sense.

Yore, L. D. (2012). Science literacy for all—More than a slogan, logo, or rally flag! In K. C. D. Tan & M. Kim (Eds.), *Issues and challenges in science education research: Moving forward* (pp. 5–23). Dordrecht, the Netherlands: Springer.

Yore, L. D., Chinn, P. W. U., & Hand, B. (Eds.). (2008). Science literacy for all: Influences of culture, language, and knowledge about nature and naturally occurring events [Special issue]. *L1–Educational Studies in Language and Literature, 8*(1), 1–171. Retrieved from http://l1.publication-archive.com/public?fn=enter&repository=1&article=299

Yore, L. D., Florence, M. K., Pearson, T. W., & Weaver, A. J. (2006). Written discourse in scientific communities: A conversation with two scientists about their views of science, use of language, role of writing in doing science, and compatibility between their epistemic views and language [Special issue]. *International Journal of Science Education, 28*(2/3), 109–141.

Yore, L. D., Hand, B., & Florence, M. K. (2004). Scientists' views of science, models of writing, and science writing practices. *Journal of Research in Science Teaching, 41*(4), 338–369.

Yore, L. D., Neill, B. W., Francis-Pelton, L., Pelton, T., Milford, T., & Anderson, J. A. (2014). Closing the achievement gap from a Canadian perspective. In J. Clark (Ed.). *Closing the achievement gap from an international perspective: Transforming STEM for effective education* (pp. 73–104). Dordrecht, the Netherlands: Springer Publishers.

Yore, L. D., & Treagust, D. F. (2006). Current realities and future possibilities: Language and science literacy—empowering research and informing instruction [Special issue]. *International Journal of Science Education, 28*(2–3), 291–314.

Young, L. (2003). *First Nations weather*. Saskatoon, SK, Canada: Saskatchewan Indian Cultural Centre & Western Development Museum. Retrieved from www.wdm.ca/skteacherguide/SICCResearch/FNWeather_TeacherGuide.pdf

Ziman, J. (2000). *Real science: What it is, and what it means*. Cambridge, UK: Cambridge University Press.

34

Socioscientific Issues as a Curriculum Emphasis

Theory, Research, and Practice

Dana L. Zeidler

Introduction

Perspectives on Socioscientific Issues

Socioscientific issues (SSI) has proven to be a viable educational framework in recent years. References to SSI can be found in the literature as far back as the 1980s (e.g., Fleming, 1986a; 1986b), and certainly several seminal figures in the field of science education have advocated the importance of connecting science to matters of social importance, as some advocates of the science-technology-society (STS) movement did for many years before that (Aikenhead, 1980; Fensham, 1983; Gaskell, 1982; Orpwood & Roberts, 1980). However, in recent years, SSI has emerged as an educational construct influenced by ideologies embedded in the STS tradition but informed by theory and scholarship from philosophical, developmental, and sociological traditions that mark it off as distinct. My colleagues and I have been critical (perhaps to a fault) of STS (Sadler, 2004d; Zeidler & Keefer, 2003; Zeidler & Nichols, 2009; Zeidler, Sadler, Simmons, & Howes, 2005), likening it to an ideology in search of a theory. In contrast, we have offered a flexible framework that draws on bodies of scholarship that include but are not limited to cognitive and moral development, emotive reasoning, character education, sociomoral discourse, and the nature of science that situate SSI in a sociocultural perspective. Hence, while we offer an alternative ideology, ours is grounded in empirical research drawn from complementary fields. We have suggested "entry points" into science curricula that are of pedagogical importance to the larger science education community of researchers and practitioners that focus on nature of science issues, cultural issues, discourse issues and case-based issues as a means to developing a functional perspective of scientific literacy (SL). Such broad entry points in the SSI curriculum allow for the cultivation of scientific literacy by promoting the exercise of informal reasoning in which students are compelled to analyze, evaluate, discuss, and argue varied perspectives on complex issues that are ill structured but, precisely because they are context dependent, are fundamentally important to the quality of life in social and natural spheres (Kolstø, 2001a; Kuhn, 1993; Sadler, 2004a, 2004b; Zeidler 1984; Zeidler & Schafer, 1984).

Scientific literacy, in the broad "functional" sense that we understand it, necessarily includes the evaluation of moral and ethical factors in making judgments about both the validity and viability of situated scientific data and information relevant to the quality of public and environmental health (Sadler, 2011; Zeidler et al., 2005), extending Roberts' Vision II of SL (see Chapter 27 this volume). Thus, scientific literacy entails the ability to make informed decisions, analyze, synthesize, and evaluate varied sources of data and information, use moral reasoning to attend sensibly to ethical issues, and understand the complexity of connections inherent in SSI (Zeidler, 2001). Researchers like Hodson (2006), Kolstø (2001b), Saunders and Rennie (2013), and Wu and Tsai (2011) recognize the importance of the central claim that SSI necessarily taps into personal values and affective emotions, moral-ethical principles, and matters of social importance. Furthermore, others such as Hodson (2010), Levinson (2014), and Santos (2009) have rightly pointed out the need to harness those emotions and values and focus them on the implementation of social actions that can possibly reform and transform societal practices. And advocates of actor-network theory (Fioravanti & Velho, 2010; Latour, 2005) clearly emphasize that any attempt that privileges scientific reasoning on matters related to SSI but neglects to consider and attend to the normative factors (e.g., motivations, personal values, social milieu, Zeitgeist) that infiltrate these issues will likely fail. It is noteworthy that the United Nations Educational, Scientific and Cultural Organization (UNESCO) adopted a resolution in 2002 to advance a decade of educational effort, spanning from 2005 to 2014, for integrating principles, values, and practices that promote world sustainability and prudent development, rethinking all conventional aspects of teaching and learning (UNESCO, 2012). Central to the themes proposed in the resolution is an emphasis on curricula and teaching practices that promote values-based learning and interdisciplinary and holistic approaches (in contrast to only subject-specific learning) and emphasize critical reasoning over memorizing. Further, UNESCO's themes also encourage the use of multiple methods of instruction (e.g., writing, art, drama, debate, etc.), the practice of participatory decision making, and the use of information that is locally relevant to students. The SSI framework is, in fact, congruent with that vision.

To fully appreciate how SSI curriculum and SSI–based instruction differs from traditional (conventional) approaches and how SSI is properly contextualized as an instructional model, an illustration of "extreme" paradigms is helpful. While Figure 34.1 shows extreme endpoints along a teaching continuum, it is noted that actual classroom practices may entail movement along different dimensions between extremes. But a study in contrast is necessary to best situate SSI in the curriculum.

Traditional approaches tend to produce students whose epistemological beliefs and their justifications for those beliefs are derived through dogma or nonevidential (faith) methods of instruction. In the extreme case of this paradigm, students are taught in an autocratic fashion, where authority and text work against the development of reflective thinkers, and knowledge is seen as fixed and immutable. In contrast, the SSI framework is aligned with a progressive paradigm of instruction. Here, the justification of associated knowledge is derived through evidence-based reasoning, and challenging the assumptions of dominant knowledge claims is commonplace. SSI curriculum and associated pedagogy encourage students to prioritize methods of inquiry while interpreting issues, making decisions including moral judgments, solving problems, and engaging in various forms of discourse including argumentation and negotiation that are, in the long term, aimed at the development of character. Certainly, the focus tends to be more on the students than on the teacher, as well as on developing the most important habit of mind—a sense of open-mindedness, which is a prerequisite for the consideration, generation, and evaluation of new knowledge. The SSI framework is aligned with a progressive tradition that views social responsibility and social competence as forms of intelligence and, therefore, something that ought to be nurtured as an educational goal (Serpell, 2011).

Just as functional scientific literacy serves as the overarching concept connecting SSI to science education, a virtue ethic account of morality provides the overarching concept in which the practice of SSI is realized. Within this classical view, reasons can be distinguished from rules by evoking their applicability to practical rationality; that is, intentional actions are considered rational to the extent that they are responsive to reason. Hence, it is the value underlying the principles or moral action rather than the

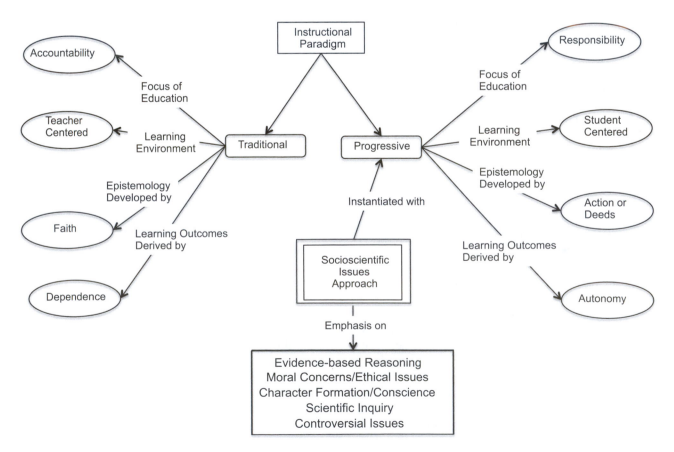

Figure 34.1 Continuum contrast of instructional paradigms. (From Zeidler, Applebaum, & Sadler, 2011)

principle in and of itself that provides the ultimate ground for its justification.

> How actions are understood as good or valuable derives from the value of the goal that is pursued and not the will or desires of the agent who pursues it. The fact that an action or behavior satisfies an agent's desire is not a reason for performing it; it is reason only that makes actions intelligible for practical deliberation and rational for us to perform. Classical theory is strongly committed to a value-centered as opposed to a hedonistic understanding of practical rationality. Close to a century of behaviorism makes this simple point both difficult to understand and difficult to grasp the extent of its radical implications.
>
> (Zeidler & Keefer, 2003, p. 27)

Therefore, under the SSI framework, justification of moral actions must be derived from discussion, rhetoric, and argument concerning the normativity of different values. Doing so resonates with eudaimonia—the Greek concept best conceived as "human flourishing." It encompasses both the ideas of phronesis—practical wisdom in action usually connected to moral intelligence—and arête—a type of civic virtue based on excellence derived from fulfilling one's potential in relation to one's participation in matters of public importance. While this all reeks of academic stuffiness, I do think that these ideas are critical to grasp in order to properly set the stage for "contemporary" classical virtue ethic accounts of key science education movements such as socioecological literacy, ecojustice, environmental literacy, and the like. Hence, SSI, understood in its idealized form, seeks to provide the academic and intellectual conditions necessary to achieve eudaimonia through the practice of practical wisdom and spread of virtue.

Socioscientific Issues or Socio-Scientific Issues?

The term "socioscientific issues" is sometimes written using a hyphen (i.e., "socio-scientific issues"). While this may be done to appeal to a sense of grammatical style, my use of the term sans hyphen has been quite deliberate. To my way of thinking, the unassuming hyphen cleaves the social context, where such issues reside, from the science that undergirds them. Some may suggest I am being overly academic, but I think the distinction is fundamentally important. My argument is a matter of perspective that views the bifurcation of science into nonnormative components (e.g., data gathering, observation, predictions, scientific methods and processes) and normative components (e.g., prescribing courses of action, choosing to create selected products, decisions about what *ought* to be done) as one that is fraught with peril. While such a distinction is, arguably, conceptually important, it can plausibly create a splintered view that allows for the abdication of any sense of responsibility during the practice of science. I simply do not wish to inadvertently drive a wedge cleaving science proper from the social milieu in which it operates. Doing so creates an artificial divorce compromising the conceptual integrity that bridges knowing with acting responsibly.

It is often dangerous to speak of any trend as if it were a uniform body of knowledge with all its associated conceptual components gathered tightly together under one common, collective theoretical framework. For example, researchers and educators having different epistemological perspectives may use the construct "nature of science" (NOS) but mean slightly different things by it. While SSI may also contain nuanced perspectives that carry a whole spectrum of possible interpretations, I assure the reader that my use of the term with broad brushstrokes is necessary in order to enter into a dialogue about trends, aims, and research unencumbered by messy qualifications each time the term is used.

In the case of SSI, for example, there are researchers who may not share the perspective I advocate, whereby the pedagogical practice of SSI is linked to the long-term goal of developing qualities of virtue and character. Certainly, SSI can be used as a means to provide a context for argumentation about the efficacy of scientific evidence without attention to moral reasoning. Likewise, SSI can be used as a context for developing argumentation skills without attention to the formation of character. Or perhaps SSI may be used as a context for developing more robust understanding of NOS but pay no attention toward developing the spread of eudaimonia. For this reason, I have chosen to use the term "socioscientific issues" rather than the hyphenated version of the phrase. Used in its ideal form, the SSI framework contains elements of the following principal characteristics, forming a sociocultural philosophy for developing scientific literacy:

- Utilize personally relevant, controversial, and ill-structured problems that require scientific, evidence-based reasoning to inform decisions about such topics.
- Employ the use of scientific topics with social ramifications that require students to engage in dialogue, discussion, debate, and argumentation.
- Integrate implicit and/or explicit ethical components that require some degree of moral reasoning.
- Emphasize the formation of virtue and character as long-range pedagogical goals.

SSI as curriculum practice, under the framework presented here, enacts these characteristics to varied degrees. But the important point is that this approach should not be confused with the mere implementation of a novel activity. The SSI framework exceeds the bounds of novelty in that it subsumes each of these principal characteristics and orchestrates them into a purposeful and cogent pedagogy flexible enough to meet the individual and contextual needs of our students and their learning environments. In some cases, resolution of issues in the science classroom may signify the end of that lesson. In other cases, SSI classroom lessons may serve as a springboard to social activism.

We now turn our attention to the research literature with the aim of providing deeper understandings of these curricula practices. I include here both conceptual and empirical scholarship. The former is necessary so as to build theory related to contextual reasoning, the formation of habits of mind, and the development of epistemological beliefs, while the latter is necessary to evaluate the merit of those claims. Utilizing and combining scholarship from both these areas aids in distinguishing ideology from empirical studies that support a theoretical framework drawn from progressive philosophy and contemporary sociology. I make no claims that this review provides an exhaustive account of all SSI literature. I have merely sought to present relatively current research that best fit aspects of key themes related to this framework, as I understand them, in terms of their centrality to SSI. Studies that are more central or are good "exemplars" relative to a selected theme are usually described in more detail, while others that support that theme tend to be clustered together. This was a decision aimed at helping the presentation of unifying ideas. There is no doubt that a case could be made for the presentation of alternative themes and different conceptualizations of those themes and therefore include or emphasize additional research and scholarship on SSI.

The four broad themes discussed in what follows include, by section:

I. Socioscientific Issues as Engagement of Curriculum Practice and Teachers' Pedagogical Beliefs—presents research that impacts the pedagogical application of classroom practice
II. Socioscientific Issues as Epistemological Development and Reasoning—reviews research on epistemological beliefs and the development of conceptual and psychological knowledge structures, including aspects of reflective judgment, discourse, and argumentation
III. Socioscientific Issues as Context for the Nature of Science—examines research on how SSI affords a contextualized setting of NOS
IV. Socioscientific Issues as Character Development and Citizenship Responsibility—considers how SSI serves to promote the development of morality

Following these themes, a summary of key ideas and suggestions for future research and practice is offered.

These themes were selected because of the significant degree to which they contribute to the overall impact SSI holds for curriculum and pedagogical practices, as well as for their important developmental outcomes that facilitate students' epistemological growth and conceptual understanding of scientific content. Finally, by its very nature, SSI is inherently interdisciplinary; hence, studies reported under one theme may very well have been reported under another heading. Again, the selection of a given study or argument for discussion under a particular theme is a matter of attuning to the features of scholarship that best resonate with the concept under consideration.

Theme I. Socioscientific Issues as Engagement of Curriculum Practice and Teachers' Pedagogical Beliefs

SSI and Teacher Practices

Teachers are central to the educational success of their students. Their pedagogical beliefs will tend to guide their craft. The research in this section focuses attention on how teachers' pedagogical beliefs connect to classroom practice and the implementation of curricula. Of particular interest is how ethical frameworks are viewed in relation to science teaching, available curriculum materials, and perceived obstacles to SSI implementation. Finally, the role of SSI in relation to ecological themes and informal science education is explored.

Some of the research on SSI has been focused on aspects of teachers' beliefs about practice, curriculum design, or engagement of issues meant to connect students with contemporary scientific content. In a study of how teachers conceptualize perspectives and strategies with respect to the explicit ethical focus of SSI, Sadler, Amirshokoohi, Kazempour, and Allspaw (2006) held focused semistructured interviews with 22 middle and high school teachers from three U.S. states. The authors hold the conviction that teacher beliefs do, to a degree, drive teaching practices (or are, at least, a precursor to pedagogical decisions and actions) and consequently affect the quality of student learning experiences (King, Shumow, & Lietz, 2001; Mueller & Zeidler, 2002; Zeidler, 2002). Therefore, it is important to understand the pedagogical orientations of teachers regarding how they perceive the significance of ethics in science. Based on their analyses, five profiles of teachers that typified different perspectives included: (A) viewing SSI as central to science education, understanding that ethics and values are necessarily part of instruction discourse and implementing these topics in their classroom practice regardless of perceived or real administrative constraints; (B) holding the same perspectives as (A) but perceived constraints as obstacles that limited their SSI instruction to less instructional time than they would otherwise prefer; (C) understood the link between ethics and science in the context of SSI but were ambivalent toward implementing SSI, relegating its appropriateness to other school areas like social science education—teachers with this profile might not exclude a conversation of ethics and science if it arose in class but did not purposely plan for such discussions; (D) rejecting the premise that science and ethics are interdependent (it should be noted that there was only one teacher expressing this viewpoint, but because this teacher's views were so disparate from any other profile, it had to be relegated to its own unique case); and, (E) holding similar views about the role of SSI in teaching ethics in science as in (A), but viewed the role of facilitating ethical values as a fundamental feature of education proper (not limited to science but relevant to all disciplines). The authors make clear that there was variation within profile perspectives and are hopeful that with proper emphasis in preservice teacher education and attention to working through impediments, the infusion of ethics via SSI can be realized for most potential teachers.

Using preservice teachers with physics and chemistry discipline backgrounds, Barrett and Nieswandt (2010) performed a qualitative analysis of 12 participants enrolled in a teacher education program to examine the beliefs they held about the importance of emphasizing ethics through an SSI teaching approach and connecting possible subject discipline identity to their views about the approach. A conceptual scheme was used to map students' conceptions of ethics along one axis that represented a continuum of moral responsibility and another axis that represented a continuum of ethical responsibility (toward an individual or a collective) to compare students' reasoning and justifications about their intended classroom SSI instruction (or lack of it). Similar to previous research (Sadler, 2004c; Sadler et al., 2006), some students relegated ethical aspects of science to the application of knowledge rather than to science's methodological features. The students also held varied beliefs between their personal sense of ethics and the use of ethics in science. For some, these beliefs were distinct and separate. For others, the beliefs were overlapping; and for a third group, these two beliefs were fully integrated. Not surprisingly, these views also reflected their purported views of science teaching practices ranging from focusing simply on subject matter knowledge for a given grade level with no attention to SSI to producing future scientists who are concerned about ethical issues to ensuring that citizens can employ critical thinking and be informed about SSI. The authors present the nuances of these positions as archetypes, each associated with particular science teaching goals and related to distinct pedagogical approaches characteristic of particular teacher identities.

Beyond teacher identity issues (see following section), part of the challenge of promoting ethical issues and citizenship responsibility in science education is attending to potential institutional obstructions (either real or perceived). The challenge of working through institutional impediments and related SSI implementation issues has not gone unnoticed by Saunders and Rennie (2011). They recognize that while recent international shifts in reform for scientific literacy necessitate an understanding of the SSI instructional model, many science teachers are ill prepared to face the challenges that such commitments to reform require. Teachers may lack institutional support and personal confidence to facilitate a framework for the exploration of ethical thinking in the science curricula, and the authors stress the need for more research on how SSI pedagogical content knowledge is effectively garnered and implemented by teachers (research by Levinson and Turner, 2001, also echoes this point). Since most secondary science teachers tend to rely on knowledge transmission approaches that fail to establish relevance, motivation, interest, or engagement for students (Lyons,

2006), Saunders and Rennie (2011) sought to implement an ethical framework for teachers (and their students) that coordinated a pluralistic approach to ethical decision making and justification for SSI. More specifically, the authors presented a cross-case analysis of four teachers examining the impact of a model for ethical inquiry and the response by their students to the units. In professional training seminars, teachers were immersed in SSI–based instruction while reviewing several existing ethical frameworks, which included consequentialism, rights and duties, autonomy, and virtue ethics approaches following a model suggested by Reiss (1999). A concerted emphasis was made to embed a framework of pluralism that included factors related to gender, developmental abilities, and ethnicity in an effort to develop respect toward a range of identities representing diverse and sometimes conflicting practices. Teachers had an opportunity to practice and model their SSI lessons before taking them out to their schools. Use of the ethical framework was modeled, and topics included global warming, genetic modification, euthanasia, prenatal genetic screening, and *in vitro* fertilization. Findings revealed four major themes: (1) usefulness of the model for ethical inquiry, (2) teacher knowledge and outcomes, (3) student knowledge and outcomes, and (4) unexpected learning. In summary, teachers found that this approach to ethical inquiry was quite doable and effective in their planning and teaching of SSI. The participating teachers all enjoyed learning about this SSI approach and increased their awareness of varied resources available that may be used to scaffold student learning. Further, evidence of robust student learning of scientific concepts and movement from poorly informed to well-informed positions of ethical decision making were reported. Finally, teachers were pleasantly surprised at the high level of student engagement and the demonstrated ability to work within the ethical SSI framework and think through multiple perspectives. This study clearly shows that with careful guidance and planning, teachers can develop skilled pedagogical content knowledge commensurate with effective SSI instruction. This research confirms prior research on SSI that maintains the degree of personal relevance for students is connected to the quality of learning science concepts and developing higher-order epistemological judgment (Barab, Sadler, Heiselt, Hicky, & Zuiker, 2007; Zeidler & Sadler, 2008b; Zeidler, Sadler, Applebaum, & Callahan, 2009).

An important study focusing on elementary preservice teachers' ability to adapt and navigate SSI curriculum materials was conducted by Forbes and Davis (2008). Recognizing the issue of teachers' access to existing materials that align with standards-based curriculum being limited, the authors noted the importance of teachers being able to adapt and modify existing curriculum materials. From a college methods class of 26 preservice teachers, 4 were selected and followed into their internship based on their expressed interest in teaching about SSI. Using interviews, journals, and online discussion threads, qualitative analyses produced emergent practices that were viewed as necessary to critique and adapt curriculum materials including but not limited to (1) understanding what constitutes worthwhile learning goals for science concepts and inquiry, (2) engaging students in meaningful learning, (3) modifications to activities that connected those lessons to students' lived experiences, and (4) the ability to assess if science content learning goals were met. Another important aspect of the study was the use of an informal reasoning framework (Sadler & Zeidler, 2005a) as an analytical tool that demonstrated patterns of reasoning about SSI in terms of rationalistic, intuitive, and emotive perspectives, as well as permutations of these perspectives. This framework allowed the interns to reflect on their own predispositions of the SSI under consideration for use in their classrooms. The authors point out that elementary teachers are in a unique position to draw on the wealth of multidisciplinary topics that SSI have to offer.

The potential to develop ecological themes through carefully crafted SSI curriculum has also been realized in recent studies. Calls for using ecojustice strategies have recently been more apparent in the literature (Bowers, 2001; Mueller, 2008, 2009; Mueller & Tippins, 2010; Mueller & Zeidler, 2010; Tippins, Mueller, van Eijck, & Adams, 2010; Zandvliet & Fisher, 2007) as a means to examine sustainability among animals and their natural systems as well a means to engage students in citizen science and youth activism. While much of the work in this area has been on developing a philosophy or theory base for ecojustice, there are some empirical studies to draw on as well (discussed next). From a conceptual basis, ecojustice includes communal activities embedded within indigenous knowledge systems (Mueller & Tippins, 2010) in that cultural traditions are factored into the broader spectrum of ecorelationships. Naturally, ecojustice is an overarching concept that subsumes social justice and environmental justice. This is where the connection between ecojustice and SSI becomes apparent: The SSI framework is inclusive in recognizing multiple perspectives and, subsequently, multiple knowledge systems. Hence, the moral-ethical considerations of the SSI approach easily allow for inquiry into policy making that considers the complexity of the confluence of living and nonliving interrelationships (Mueller & Zeidler, 2010).

One of the few studies to examine how SSI can impact young children engaged in informal science learning conditions sought to explore possible relationships between a socioscientific issues–embedded curriculum and outcome variables addressing environmental attitude and knowledge, oral and written argumentation, and critical-thinking skills (Burek & Zeidler, in-press). An all-day, informal, outdoor experience was provided to fourth-grade students by the county, where students took part in outdoor hikes to three different natural habitats, performed water quality sampling and testing, observed and examined the effects of water and wind erosion, and noted how the habitats within the preserve had been modified by human intervention. An environmental education instructor on site at the preserve conducted the field experiences. The excursion focused on water and land conservation, allowing for a 6- to 7-hour in-depth outdoor environmental exploration experience that provided students ample time to be immersed in the local habitats and make connections to their surroundings. The treatment classes were taught using a variety of SSI as the basis for learning environmental principles and content. Small-group discussions and debates and hands-on activities during outdoor excursions took place at the on-site preserve. The comparison group was not taught using those SSI strategies; however, they did participate in the in-depth informal outdoor experience at the preserve. Once the students returned to their regular classrooms, the conventional curriculum of life and physical science, including topics of erosion and human impact on different environments, was taught over a semester using traditional methods of teacher-lead and text-focused instruction such as worksheets and classroom presentations. Naturally, moral and ethical issues that arose during the small-group discussions and debates from the informal field center experience were revisited and easily integrated within the curriculum for the treatment group. Results indicated that the SSI approach assisted students in developing their critical-thinking skills and provided students the opportunity to experience, be exposed to, and participate in local and global environmental issues influencing their community. Statistical significance was found between groups in revealing a more positive attitude toward the environment for students in the treatment group. Qualitative interviews also indicated that some students in the treatment group provided more advanced argumentation skills by articulating alternate viewpoints on controversial environmental topics. Studies such as this provide evidence that environmentally-related SSI present opportunities to reconnect young students with science in real-world settings. The use of SSI has the potential to allow students to utilize their critical-thinking skills so they can better analyze and synthesize the scientific information needed to support arguments that have moral and ethical consequences (Dolan, Nichols, & Zeidler, 2009). Inasmuch as moral issues are an embedded part of most environmental and conservation topics, informal place-based education can provide effective and contextually reinforcing experiences when brought back into the classroom successfully (Falk, Dierking, & Storksdieck, 2007; Falk & Heimlich, 2009). It should be noted that some authors, like those just cited, prefer the term "free-choice learning" rather than informal learning in situations in which children can self-direct their own learning, as in the case of museums or aquariums. However, since the outdoor experiences the students in Burek and Zeidler's study had were structured to align with school curriculum, the authors chose to use "informal learning" to describe the experiences provided for the children. The larger point remains that such experiences may lead to an embedded sense of environmental stewardship by offering students a glimpse at how decisions and actions made today can have a lasting impact on their future.

Last, SSI–based instruction has also been viewed by numerous researchers as well as teachers as an opportunity for engagement of students, as citizens, to be a part of a collective pluralistic society who can not only make informed decisions about issues in general but become proactive in issues of environmental sustainability in particular (Bencze, Sperling, & Carter, 2012; Mueller, Zeidler, & Jenkins, 2011; Simonneaux & Simonneaux, 2012; Tytler, 2012). Bencze and colleagues (2012) stress that the problems associated with some issues, such as climate change, are so threatening that educators have an obligation to encourage students to become socially active in an effort to ameliorate such problems. Accordingly, the authors conceptualize SSI as a window into socioscientific activism using a pedagogical theoretical framework termed STEPWISE (Science & Technology Education Promoting Wellbeing for Individuals, Societies & Environments). This ambitious project begins with the assumption that students can be co-producers of knowledge and become an integral part of the political decision-making process. Accordingly, the authors explored the nature and extent of students' self-directed, research-informed activism and factors influencing their willingness to become socially engaged on important SSI through a focused case study of three teachers (who were part of a larger group undergoing the STEPWISE curriculum model) implementing SSI instruction with their students. Using semistructured interviews, artifacts of students' work, anecdotal records, and recordings of student interviews, six criteria were identified that were related to students' commitments toward activism: passionate indications of concern, clear indicators of intention to implement action, confidence in an action's effectiveness, self-efficacy, detailed analysis and planning of an action, and number and variety of actions. The findings provided strong evidence that secondary science students, in the context of their curriculum, can develop and implement with confidence research-based sociopolitical actions to tackle SSI. This research resonates with the stance that SSI–related curricula ought to allow for sociopolitical actions that can fundamentally transform policy (Hodson, 2010; Levinson, 2014).

SSI and Teacher Identity

Closely related to how teachers' pedagogical beliefs impact their classroom practice (discussed in the previous section) is how the development or expression of teachers' identity is congruent with progressive ideologies in general and SSI strategies in particular. This is also an important factor in the effective implementation of SSI, as such factors impact potential transformative pedagogical shifts. This section is aimed at bringing to light some of these issues.

SSI curriculum implementation may be a bit of a double-edged sword for some science educators who may be apprehensive about teaching scientific topics that are infused with moral and ethical perspectives. Of course, it is precisely the nature of well-placed topics that connect most significantly to students' developing sense of morality that allows students to identify with, analyze, and reflect on those issues. While most students seem to be immensely engaged and express increased confidence in their understanding of issues like cloning, euthanasia, genomics, and harvesting organs (Hanegan, Price, & Peterson, 2007; Sadler & Zeidler, 2005b), their instructors may be dissuaded from exploring such topics, ironically, because of the very controversy associated with them. The formation of a progressive teaching identity and associated pedagogical beliefs congruent with the SSI framework requires one to confront an array of possible obstacles. In their work in promoting issues-based science, technology, society, and environment (STSE) perspectives, Pedretti, Bencze, Hewitt, Romkey, and Jivraj (2007) confirm that on the one hand, teacher candidates express confidence in teaching controversial perspectives, but on the other hand, they are reluctant to do so, particularly during their early years of teaching. (It should be noted that Pedretti and her co-authors conceptualize STSE in a manner that shares many features of SSI education, particularly emphasizing the moral dimensions of socioscientific problems. Further conceptual similarities between STSE and SSI can be found in Pedretti, 2003.) The authors note that developing a sense of identity with this form of curriculum implementation is somewhat paradoxical for teachers in that while they find the experience engaging and interesting, they still question its place in the science curriculum. This result suggests that intellectually embracing SSI–type philosophy and implementing SSI–type teaching practices are not synonymous. No doubt, the marginalization of SSI curricula in both textbooks and school curriculum as well as failure of current curriculum reforms to connect with teachers' deeper values that actually do resonate with SSI initiatives help to explain the gap between perceived importance of the curriculum and its implementation (Hughes, 2000; Lee & Witz, 2009). Lee, Abd-El-Khalick, and Choi (2006) confirm that while teachers understand the need for and utility of incorporating SSI into their classrooms, concerns about the perceived lack of instructional time and unavailability of pertinent materials hinders their inclusion. However, such concerns can be addressed head-on by thoughtful models that scaffold materials as teachers explore SSI in a manner that addresses multiple ethical identities including cultural, ethnic, religious, and gender perspectives (Saunders & Renni, 2011).

It might even be the case that while a (practicing) teacher conceptualizes the significance of the SSI instructional model, the transformation to significantly move along a teaching continuum from more traditional approaches toward progressive postures (see Figure 34.1) requires deep structural shifts in both normative beliefs about the ends of education as well as epistemic shifts in its practice. For this to happen, consistent practice over longer periods of time is necessary. Consider, for example, an SSI framework developed by Zeidler, Applebaum, and Sadler (2011) for the implementation of a yearlong curriculum. The framework, though not necessarily prescribed as a fixed template, entailed eight major movements: (1) topic introduction—meant to hook and engage students and determine their preconceptions of subject matter; (2) challenge core beliefs with contentious questions—aimed at providing cognitive and moral dissonance to challenge prior beliefs about content and personal stances on issues; (3) formal instruction—to provide students with knowledge of fundamental vocabulary and knowledge of processes and functions to provide better comprehension of source material; (4) construct group investigations and presentations—focused on student inquiry of subject matter and engaging in socially shared group activities; (5) develop contextual questions directed toward content and concept discovery—so students may apply their informal reasoning skills and utilize newly acquired knowledge to evaluate evidence and make informed decisions in resolving contentious decisions; (6) class discussion, argumentation, and debate—to provide practice in character development by respecting the norms of classroom argumentation and discourse and developing an appreciation of multiple perspectives and evidence-based judgments; (7) clarification of concepts—allows the teacher to serve as a moderator and revisit key conceptual topics and themes of subject matter; and (8) knowledge and reasoning assessment—ensures that student learning and conceptual understanding could be documented by authentic and traditional means. The ability to transform one's teaching practice to ensure the kind of student outcomes associated with progressive ideology requires not only a conceptual shift in pedagogical orientations but also a commitment to overcome a multitude of challenging contextual factors residing in the students, administration, and oneself. While more work is no doubt needed to examine ways of surmounting such factors, there is a clear consensus that educational research has demonstrated the importance of connecting science teaching to contemporary relevance of students' worldviews (Fensham, 2009; Kincheloe & Tobin, 2009; Klosterman, Sadler, & Brown, 2012; Lemke, 2001; Matthews, 2009; Nuangchalerm, 2009; Ratcliffe & Millar, 2009; Sadler & Zeidler, 2009).

SSI and Web-Based Environments

Technology offers a viable tool to engage students in the exploration of SSI. In particular, a number of researchers have creatively used modifications of Web-based Inquiry Science Environment (WISE) to engage students in SSI inquiry. While there has been some work to systematically explore how other uses of technology may be applied within an SSI context (e.g., see Sadler, Klosterman, & Topcu's 2011 work on using a multi-user virtual environment, MUVE, created using current gaming principles in an SSI context), more SSI–related research, at this time,

has been focused on use of the WISE platform. This section presents some of the key studies in this area.

Some researchers have turned to the integration of Web-based technology into the SSI curriculum in an attempt to scaffold scientific concepts. This approach allows students to quickly move beyond the confines of the classroom and explore virtual discussion forums concerning the application of scientific ideas and their potential ethical consequences. One area that has shown a great range of diversity in its usefulness to teachers and students has been the adoption of the WISE curriculum that has demonstrated the ability to generate students' interest in SSI–related instruction (Linn, Clark, & Slotta, 2003; Linn, Lee, Tinker, Husic, & Chiu, 2006; Pea & Collins, 2008; Seethaler & Linn, 2004; Slotta & Linn, 2009) while supporting students' learning of both challenging science concepts and NOS.

Walker and Zeidler (2007) used a WISE template to promote student discourse on an inquiry-based SSI about genetically modified (GM) foods while examining their ability to utilize explicit NOS links and features of argumentation evoked during a class debate. Thirty-six science students from a vocational school, ranging from Grades 9 through 12 and representing diverse learning abilities, engaged in seven consecutive 1.5-hour periods of instructional time navigating the WISE framework. The WISE environment was modified by the authors to allow students to inquire about five stakeholder positions (commercial, government, special interest, media, and community advocates) representing diverse perspectives on GM foods. Questions were embedded in the SSI units to draw students' attention to NOS factors, and students were ultimately required to defend public policy positions in a debate activity. Students were not informed what position they would ultimately defend until the day of the debate and were required to organize sufficient evidence to support any of the three positions to which they might be assigned. In addition to NOS scales used for data collection, the WISE environment allowed for data to be collected via "chat rooms" where students' written responses to questions were recorded and questions concerning conceptual understanding of the genetics behind the controversy could be discussed. Results showed that students' responses reflected informed understanding of the subjective nature of science (e.g., personal motives, moral values) and an appreciation of experimental methods of research connected to the developmental and creative aspects of NOS. While NOS factors did not freely enter into the debate discussion, using a modified rating system for Toulmin's (1958) model of argumentation, it was found that students utilized more evidence-based content and recognized higher-order arguments, although some fallacious reasoning was also present. It was also clear that the WISE environment was able to focus students' attention on diverse perspectives and current scientific reports in a manner that scaffolded the development of curriculum.

In a related study, Tal, Kali, Magid, and Madhok (2011) also used the WISE environment to stimulate processes of negotiation and inquiry to engage 8th- and 10th-grade students in authentic decision making in the context of citizenship education for sustainable development. The WISE model allowed students to use interactive visualizations as they explored complex phenomena in an attempt to integrate varied knowledge sources. The authoring capability of WISE also allowed the researchers to adapt, revise, or refine existing modules. SSI issues (e.g., cystic fibrosis, dilemma of eradicating small pox virus, and debates about vaccination against West Nile virus) provided the sociocultural context for learning science outcomes associated with the modules. Previous research (Ben-Zvi Assaraf & Orion, 2005; Dori, Tal, & Tsaushu, 2003; Tal & Hochberg, 2003; Tal & Kedmi, 2006; Zeidler et al., 2005) helped inform the SSI curriculum and related pedagogy. A unique element to this study was the inclusion of an out-of-school (field trip) experience for one group of 10th graders that provided students with personal and meaningful authentic experiences. In this case, cystic fibrosis units in hospitals allowed students to meet with a social worker, a nurse, a physiotherapist, and a doctor and experience actual tests and exercises that patients undergo in their treatment. In addition, students were able to meet a patient close to their own age who described what everyday life entailed for them. For another group of 10th-grade students, in place of the field trip, additional authentic experiences were integrated with online environments that allowed for further interactions as students worked through modules. The authors found that students expressed their interest in and comfort level with the technology and were deeply engaged using the WISE platform. Of special interest was the fact that the complementarity of the WISE environments and the field trip provided students with relevance and the ability to understand multiple perspectives. Further, knowledge acquisition was demonstrated for both the online interaction and field trip conditions, with no significant difference in knowledge acquisition between these two experiences. It is evident that the design components implemented in this research provided personally relevant, contextualized experiences for students, thereby exemplifying one of the primary attributes of the SSI instructional model (Ratcliffe & Grace, 2003; Tal & Kedmi, 2006; Zeidler & Sadler, 2008a).

Evagorou (2011) also explored the use of the WISE online environment to facilitate discussion and argumentation on an SSI for primary students. Consistent with Aikenhead's (2006) definition, knowledge of content tempered with knowledge about the social processes of science supported the pursuit of SSI with the assistance of the WISE scaffolded online program congruent with several key principles: accessibility of science to all students, modeling the evaluation of ideas that can lead to new knowledge, learning vicariously and collaboratively, and developing a sense of autonomy and lifelong learning (Linn, Eylon, & Davis, 2004). The project, termed Technoskepsi (technology and thinking), allowed students to navigate the WISE environment that explored issues related to a local SSI on the effects of pig farms in the area surrounding where the students lived. (An additional SSI on building a zoo was used as an introduction to argumentation.) As with the Tal and colleagues (2011) study, an informal field trip component (a site visit to a working pig farm) was integrated with formal classroom instruction. Instructional objectives included developing an understanding of waste-management techniques and their environmental impact, understanding the systemic nature of their environment, inquiry into an authentic SSI, and evidence-based data collection and argumentation over the course of eight tightly integrated units that could last up to 80 minutes each. Data included students' written argumentation (captured from online artifacts), videos from whole-class discussions, and interviews. A modified version of Toulmin's (1958) Argumentation Pattern (TAP) created by Erduran and colleagues (2004) was used to assess the quality of students' arguments. Results indicated that the structure of students' arguments improved during and after the implementation of SSI curriculum materials and experiences. The students were able to identify and distinguish among different kinds of SSI arguments (e.g., social, environmental, financial, and moral factors). The findings also suggested that the WISE environment was successful in allowing students to collect evidence that they could integrate into their arguments. Additionally, students reported very positive affective experiences after reflecting on their participation in all aspects of the curriculum project.

Summary of Trends for Theme I: Socioscientific Issues as Engagement of Curriculum Practice and Teachers' Pedagogical Beliefs

The relationship between teachers' beliefs about pedagogical practices and perceived constraints concerning the implementation of SSI curriculum is an important area of concern. While most teachers generally accept the notion that ethical considerations do impact the practice of science, how to convey and express that in the context of day-to-day science teaching is not well understood, and the marginalization of SSI curricula in most standards-based movements exacerbates these concerns. However, SSI research has demonstrated the ability to connect contemporary science teaching and curricula to a good measure of relevance for students' worldviews. A focus on teacher identity shows promise in how teachers situate themselves as a conduit that connects science to larger sociocultural frameworks. What is clear to teachers is the general high level of student engagement when SSI inquiry is implemented in their classrooms. Research on how teachers can use and modify existing resources shows promise for allowing teachers to best match their curriculum to local needs and student interests. While research on SSI practice typically reports on middle and secondary school practices, far fewer studies examine how college and elementary students can benefit from SSI practices. Research has begun to explore how SSI may be useful in framing some of the underlying philosophy represented by eco-justice movement as well. More work of this kind should extend to how to reasonably involve students to engage in sociopolitical actions that extend beyond academic SSI discussions. The utilization of Web-based environments also shows promise to scaffold instruction of science content in well-designed instructional units that tap the SSI framework, but this work has yet to be fully explored.

Theme II. Socioscientific Issues as Epistemological Development and Reasoning

One of the appeals of the SSI instructional model is that it not only serves as a context for the delivery of content but also acts as a catalyst for various forms of epistemological beliefs and research into the development of conceptual and psychological knowledge structures. Studies that examine aspects of reflective judgment, discourse and argumentation, and the quality of reasoning about moral and ethical issues provide researchers insight into the developmental talents and capabilities of students, which, in turn, inform curriculum planning and related teaching practices. This section examines research that focuses on features of epistemological beliefs about science, their impact on thinking about ethical issues, as well as developmental aspects of reflective judgment in terms of how students reason about and evaluate evidence.

Liu, Lin, and Tsai (2011) investigated the assumption of relationships between scientific epistemological views (SEV) and how students tend to reason while making decisions on SSI. The conjecture that individuals who have varied conceptions of NOS may exhibit differential reasoning patterns when reasoning about SSI seems reasonable based on suggested inferences from previous research (Sadler, Chambers, & Zeidler, 2004; Schommer-Aikins & Hutter; 2002; Zeidler, Walker, Ackett, & Simmons, 2002). Using a mixed-methods approach with 177 college students (both science and nonscience majors), the SSI context consisted of environmental management of invasive species. The instrument for assessing SEV was developed by Tsai and Liu (2005) and consisted of five subscales that parsed beliefs about the nature of scientific knowledge into the role of social negotiations in science communities, invented and creative nature of science, theory-laden quality of scientific exploration, cultural impacts of science, and the changing and tentative features of science knowledge. The authors focused their attention on two dimensions of students' responses to the SSI environmental topics: reasoning modes of evidence students used to advance their arguments and their thinking disposition for developing criteria to evaluate those arguments. A coding scheme that distinguished between higher- and lower-order critical thinking skills was developed and entailed

the following contrasts: (a) recognizing the complexity of an issue (giving information irrelevant to decisions), (b) taking multiple perspectives (accepting single perspective), and (c) questioning omniscient authority (accepting authority). The results yielded categories of preferred reasoning modes including ecological, ethical-aesthetic, scientific-technological, and social-economic perspectives. The authors found statistical differences favoring nonscience majors adopting ecological, ethic-aesthetic, and social-economic reasoning modes. Science majors were also more likely to use only a single reasoning mode in their decision-making processes, while nonscience majors were more likely to reason from multiple perspectives. Further, it was also reported that students who held changing and tentative beliefs about the nature of scientific knowledge were more likely to acknowledge issues of complexity, multiple perspectives, and the importance of questioning authority in making decisions on SSI. The implications of these findings are quite interesting. While it may be the case that science majors, it can be argued, have higher levels of science content knowledge at their disposal, they have less sophisticated understandings about multiple modes of reasoning available to them (e.g., ethical-aesthetic, socio-economic, etc.) that can be used to justify stances on SSI. It may actually be the case that having a scientific background tends to inhibit one from being critical of issues related to that background.

Zeidler, Sadler, Applebaum, and Callahan (2009) explored the relationship between using an SSI year-long curriculum in anatomy and physiology (A&P) and advancing epistemological development (i.e., reflective judgment) in upper high school students. Following the SSI framework, students were exposed to moral problems that involve a number of discrepant scientific, social, or moral viewpoints, many of which conflicted with the students' own closely held beliefs. A concerted effort was made to devise a curriculum that was personally relevant to the students yet covered the underlying content and concepts for the course, providing opportunities for students to reflect on issues and evaluate claims, analyze evidence, and assess multiple viewpoints regarding ethical issues on scientific topics through social interaction and discourse. Two classes (one honors and one nonhonors class) were randomly selected to the treatment group, while the remaining two classes (one honors and one nonhonors) were placed in the comparison group. All groups received explicit NOS instruction that was integrated throughout the classes. The comparison groups were taught through traditional text, lecture, and laboratory investigations. The treatment group received the same NOS instruction, but in addition, NOS was embedded within an SSI framework that subsumed content-transcending themes (Kolstø, 2001b) commensurate with the approach of challenging core beliefs through all forms of discourse and argumentation. The SSI were developed in concert with the classroom teacher to assure that A&P content could be extracted from the SSI, which ranged in issues from marijuana and animal rights to organ allocation and stem cell research. The researchers used a mixed-methods strategy and obtained data on the Prototypic Reflective Judgment Interview (King & Kitchener, 1994, 2002, 2004) to assess reflective judgment developmental levels. Four independent raters were able to reach 100% agreement for coding the dominant stage of reflective reasoning and more than 90% for the less dominant stages. Quantitative results showed statistical significance from pre- to posttest within the SSI treatment group having a moderately large effect size, while no statistical differences were found within the comparison group. Qualitative data analysis clearly showed more nuanced differences in terms of epistemological development over the academic year. However, the data also revealed that students do not simply advance their epistemological reasoning uniformly across all contexts. While developmental increases may be had, for example, regarding chemical additives in food, a student may not make advances to higher levels of reasoning in the area of religion and science. This points to the clear effect of deeply entrenched core beliefs on students' evaluation of evidence and the highly contextualized nature of reasoning on SSI. The authors also drew comparisons between more advanced stages of reflective judgment and sophisticated views of NOS in that both require epistemological orientations that conceptualize and justify knowledge through processes of inquiry that are data driven, allow for the probabilistic nature of data, and are open to re-evaluation. This reciprocal relationship has also been noted by Abd-El-Khalick (2006). In earlier research, Zeidler (1985) had noted hierarchical relationships among formal cognitive structures and principled moral reasoning. In that study, the ability to exercise combinatorial and correlational reasoning in college students was found to significantly account for 22% of the variance of their principled (postconventional) moral reasoning competence. From an epistemological stance of reasoning about SSI, it makes theoretical sense that higher-order structures like the ability to think through multiple permutations of factors connected to an issue allow one to arrive at policy decisions in which the best composition of competing claims is derived in the course of resolving competing moral imperatives.

In a study that focused on high school students' scientific epistemological beliefs (SEB) and cognitive structures as applied to informal reasoning on a SSI concerning nuclear power, Wu and Tsai (2011) evoked dual process theory (Evans, 2003; Wu & Tsai, 2007) to contrast students' initial unconscious, pragmatic, and contextualized preliminary (intuitive) reactions from conscious and deliberative reasoning used to justify those initial reactions and formulate a final decision. The authors quantitatively assessed students' SEB using an instrument that consisted of four scales measuring source, certainty, development, and justification of knowledge. Qualitative sources of data to probe more deeply the structure of students' reasoning, as well as their modes of informal reasoning about the

issue, provided a well-developed integrated framework, allowing for multiple indicators of reasoning and argument. Findings included the fact that students' beliefs and justifications of scientific knowledge were significantly correlated with the quality of their informal reasoning. More specifically, the ability to make comparisons and the robustness of beliefs about the justification of scientific knowledge were the most important predictors of the quality of students' epistemological reasoning ability.

In an effort to promote effective citizenship, Sadler, Barab, and Scott (2007) suggested a theoretical construct termed socioscientific reasoning (SSR) to attend to the typical kinds of features of reasoning contained in most SSI. SSR was operationalized, based on a review of prior literature, to consist of four epistemological traits: (1) complexity—recognizing the inherent webs of connected intricacies of SSI; (2) perspectives—the ability to examine issues, competing claims, and interests from varied points of view; (3) inquiry—appreciating that issues are subject to ongoing examination; and (4) skepticism—possessing the posture to challenge potentially biased information. Using 24 middle school students engaged in socioscientific inquiry, the authors were able to evaluate students' reasoning on a SSI related to pollution and water quality following virtual exploration of a 10-day unit. More to the point under consideration, the authors were able to develop a rubric consisting of a scale of increasing robustness for each of the four traits comprising SSR. The use of this rubric offers a valid and reliable assessment scheme for the evaluation of SSR. Further research by Sadler and colleagues (2011) suggests that SSR is not a unitary construct but can best be thought of as an overarching construct in which component abilities work, to different extents, in concert while reasoning about SSI. Those authors also readily acknowledge that while these four abilities are important to reasoning about SSI, they may underrepresent the full range of reasoning strategies that allow for the full exploration of SSI.

Examination of cross-cultural epistemological orientations to SSI was conducted by Zeidler, Herman, Ruzek, Linder, and Lin (2013). This mixed-methods design allowed the authors to investigate how more than 300 high school–age students from Jamaica, South Africa, Sweden, Taiwan, and the United States conceptualized and justified their decisions related to distributive justice about the allocation of scarce medical resources. The authors focused on commonalities and unique differences among patterns of reasoning relative to distributive justice and normative views of fairness, the prioritization of scientific information related to the SSI, and relationships between cultural identity and students' epistemological beliefs about science. Students first responded to an open-ended instrument (Decisions about Socioscientific Issues) and next responded to the Epistemological Beliefs Assessment for Physical Science (EBAPS), both of which were translated into their native language by at least two native-speaking researchers. Responses were back-translated to English, and four researchers independently coded the data, modifying an *a priori* rubric through multiple iterations, reaching a 97% intercoder agreement. Potential conflicts were negotiated, resulting in virtually 100% agreement. The inductive analysis of students' justifications for the data from each country produced five major qualitative categories, consisting of (1) fairness, (2) pragmatism, (3) emotive reasoning, (4) utility, and (5) theological issues, as well as numerous subcategories. Quantitative analyses produced several significant differences, among which were student ranking preferences for distributive justice by country showing a moderately large effect size for the relationship between country and preference toward selecting criteria for allocating rare resources. A moderately large effect size was found for the variance of epistemological justification of their choices due to country of origin. Significant differences were also found in terms of the ability to raise scientifically relevant questions across countries. Finally, the results of students' responses on the EBAPS assessing epistemological beliefs over five dimensions related to scientific knowledge yielded significant differences on dimensions of structure of scientific knowledge and nature of knowing and learning. On the one hand, the qualitative findings show a degree of epistemological congruence among the samples of students from these countries. These findings add support to the claim that there are common underlying elements of socioscientific reasoning that either cut across or possibly transcend culture in terms of how individuals frame, justify, and reveal reasoning patterns on SSI and supporting the work of Sadler, Barab, and Scott (2007). On the other hand, the quantitative results did show some distinguishing features of scientific justification and epistemological orientations on SSI. Implications for a threshold model in terms of content knowledge transfer in the context of SSI supporting previous research (Sadler & Donnely, 2006; Sadler & Fowler, 2006) were advanced.

Yang (2005) studied 10th-grade students' personal epistemological orientations in terms of how they evaluate expert views and evidence on an SSI involving causes of flood disasters. What is important to note is that this particular issue was of great personal and cultural relevance for these particular students. This research utilized Perry's (1970) scheme of epistemological developmental perspectives that entailed four main forms of knowing: dualism, multiplicity, relativism, and contextual relativism. It is important to note that Perry's ideas gave rise to much of the later work on epistemological reasoning. Students' personal epistemology was identified using the Learning Environment Preference Questionnaire (LEP) constructed by Moore (1989, based on Perry's model), while an open-ended questionnaire was used to tap students' ability to evaluate the form and conclusions of data derived from an SSI. Content analysis of students' views with respect to examining evidence and expert opinion (intercoder agreement exceeding 90%) and a one-way ANOVA were used to demonstrate if an association existed between viewpoints about evidence and LEP scores. Students generally reflected early multiplicists' viewpoints, but between the positivist and constructivist ends of the continuum, they tended to reflect more positivist positions. Content analysis confirmed that while students seemed to realize the importance of scientific evidence as well as other forms of evidence, they did not understand how both could be integrated to advance scientific argumentation. They also tended to overweight expert opinion, equating that with being analogous to hard facts. Since the statistical analysis suggested that students' understanding of evidence and expert positions are associated with personal epistemology, the author stressed the importance of providing students practice in cultivating the ability to apply scientific reasoning to real-life issues. It is likely the case that, as Ratcliffe (1997) suggested, students need some degree of teacher intervention to cultivate metacognitive awareness of their own decision-making strategies.

SSI and Reasoning About Content Knowledge

SSI investigations have also yielded revealing insights as to how students frame knowledge of and about scientific content and how that knowledge may be realized through different modes of SSI instruction. This section considers research aimed at examining how students think about and conceptualize content knowledge during SSI negotiation and examines if gains in content knowledge are to be realized. Speculation about whether a certain threshold of content knowledge is necessary for the effective transfer of conceptual scientific understanding to varied contexts is discussed.

Nielsen (2012) examined how 16- to 18-year-old students reason about societal, ethical, and political issues, inferred or implied, by gene therapy topics. In particular, she was interested in how the use of scientific content contributes to the dialectics of group discussions. The lens used to examine student argumentation was "normative pragmatics," also known as design theory, and focuses on the practical significance of linguistic meanings where normative meaning is constructed and synergistically impacts group discourse (van Eemeren & Houtlosser, 2007). Nielsen found that students had three ways of representing science content: (1) explicit expressions of science content, (2) assertive expressions of science content, and (3) expressions with implicit science content. It appeared that students utilized science in the process of expressing ideas they deemed relevant. The content served as a means for establishing a normative factual baseline that provided a jumping-off place for subsequent socioscientific negotiations entailing explicit moral responsibilities. Yet the findings confirm previous research that shows how students, if not prompted to do differently, are reluctant to consider alternative positions and may focus more on persuasion than on making sense of alternative viewpoints or varied contexts (Grace & Ratcliffe, 2002; Sadler, 2004a).

Related to this, Kolstø and colleagues (2006) found that students tend to trust whatever scientific content is presented, without cross-checking the quality of the references or information provided in research articles. Further, students typically do not examine the connection between empirical evidence contained within various reports and the assertions made in the findings of those reports. This suggests some degree of epistemic dependence on experts. But it is also encouraging that students were, to some extent, able to evaluate the empirical adequacy of scientific content and the claims related to that content. Of course, the significance that conceptual understanding of science content has during the course of informal reasoning is certainly a relevant factor to consider in SSI research. Sadler and Zeidler (2005b) sought to investigate how differentiated content knowledge influenced college students' negotiation and resolution of complex SSI scenarios based on genetic engineering. SSI included both gene therapy concerns (e.g., increasing intelligence of potential offspring) and cloning disputes (e.g., producing a clone of a dying infant). In this study, participants were asked to offer arguments without the benefit of prompts specifying attention to argument structures such as counterpositions or rationales so the focus was on what they might offer during normal discourse rather than on argumentation proper. Students majoring in natural sciences (mostly biology) were compared to non–natural science majors (mostly psychology) on a measure of conceptual content understanding (Test of Basic Genetics Concepts), assuring that two distinct subsamples with differential understanding of the mechanisms of human heredity could be used. The criteria used for assessing the quality of informal reasoning ability included the examination of rationales for intrascenario coherence, interscenario noncontradiction, counterposition construction, and rebuttal construction. Two major results relevant to this section were found. First, no observable differences in rationalistic, emotive, or intuitive informal reasoning patterns were found between the two groups. However, the results did reveal that differences in students' content knowledge were related to variations in the quality of informal reasoning. Specifically, students with more advanced understandings of genetics expressed fewer instances of reasoning flaws, as defined by *a priori* criteria, and were more likely to incorporate the use of scientific content knowledge in their reasoning patterns than were students with less conceptual understandings of genetics. These findings added support to the work of Tytler, Duggan, and Gott (2001), who found that a lack of conceptual understanding of scientific content hindered students' ability to demonstrate high-quality reasoning, and Hogan (2002), who reported that higher understanding of content knowledge was associated with higher-quality argumentation and informal reasoning. Further, the results support the earlier work of Zeidler and Schafer (1984) that demonstrated a link between having richer conceptual understanding of scientific subject matter and the propensity to tap higher available levels of moral reasoning on SSI for college students.

Additional studies of the connection between SSI instruction and its impact on students' science content knowledge have been investigated, showing positive results for SSI–based instruction. Klosterman and Sadler (2010) used a multilevel assessment design to gain a comprehensive view of the impact of an SSI 3-week intervention on high school students enrolled in environmental science and chemistry classes. The assessments consisted of two measures: one of student content knowledge made using a standards-aligned content knowledge exam (distal assessment) and a curriculum-aligned exam (proximal assessment). The results showed that students' pre- to post-test science content scores significantly improved using the standards-aligned (distal) measure, while qualitative improvements, including students' ability to express more accurate, detailed and sophisticated understanding of SSI topics, were detected on the curriculum-aligned (proximal assessment) exam. Examining these results in concert with one another provides strong evidence for the effectiveness of using SSI to enhance gains in students' science content knowledge. Other work by Wongsri and Nuangchalerm (2010) also adds to our confidence that SSI instruction can lead to positive content knowledge learning outcomes. In this study, seventh-grade students in conventional learning activities were compared with students undergoing SSI–based learning activities. Each learning condition consisted of 12 lesson plans of instruction. Here, the authors found statistically significant differences between students in the two learning conditions (favoring SSI instruction) on measures of content achievement, analytical thinking, and moral reasoning.

A number of studies have examined related aspects of how the framing of content knowledge is realized to smaller or greater degrees in the SSI contexts. One pattern in the literature is that in the absence of guided instruction, students tend not to tap their content knowledge as they wrestle with ethical implications relevant to SSI (Albe, 2008a; Halverson, Siegel, & Freyermuth, 2009; Ratcliffe, 1997; Sadler, 2005; Sadler & Donnely, 2006; Simon & Amos, 2011; Walker & Zeidler, 2007). While these studies questioned students' propensity to utilize scientific concepts and terms during discourse on their own accord, these studies tended not to specifically focus on the learning of scientific content as a main outcome (other outcomes were generally the focus of the research; e.g., argumentation, nature of science understanding, fallacious reasoning, etc.). Moreover, a lack of observable indicators of the application of content knowledge during some SSI discussions does not mean this relationship is unimportant or ought not be pursued. Sadler and Donnely (2006) have suggested three possible reasons to account for the lack of the spontaneous use of content knowledge during SSI discourse: (1) Students simply fail to see the connection of school science to controversial issues (lack of content knowledge transfer), (2) students may not have a basic understanding of the context of the issue itself (lack of contextual understanding), and/or (3) a certain threshold of content knowledge must exist before its application can be realized (threshold model of knowledge transfer). Additional research from Sadler and Fowler (2006), Sadler and Zeidler (2005b), and Zeidler and colleagues (2013) offers supporting evidence of the threshold model. In the case of the latter study, it was inferred that a degree of epistemological sophistication was required for students to enact mature features of socioscientific reasoning. For these students, epistemological sophistication was beyond that of a certain qualitative threshold, allowing them to better assume utilitarian epistemological orientations across contexts and more holistically engage in SSI decisions that extended beyond immediate foreseeable consequences. In contrast, students below this threshold of epistemological sophistication were more likely to restrict their SSI decision making to the facts and consequences at hand. Regardless, most SSI researchers seem to be in agreement that students need explicit modeling and guidance in the use of supporting scientific evidence to internalize the critical role that conceptual understanding of scientific content has in informing moral judgments about SSI.

SSI and Patterns of Informal Reasoning, Argumentation, and Discourse

The use of SSI in classroom contexts is fundamentally a social endeavor requiring students to engage in many forms of informal reasoning and discourse. Important advances that add to our understanding of how students frame ideas and negotiate resolution to conflicting issues have been made in this area. Research included here focuses on understanding and facilitating the quality of students' reasoning, argument, and discourse experiences in the context of SSI instruction. These areas of research are seen as important contributing factors to students' epistemological development.

Some research (Zeidler, Lederman, & Taylor, 1992) has been focused on different forms of fallacious informal reasoning students may encounter while working their way through a given SSI. Some common problems associated with fallacies of relevance, where at least one premise is logically disconnected from its conclusion, are *ad hominem* arguments, appeal to popularity, false dilemma, begging the question, hasty generalization, and appeal to authority. Equally troublesome are fallacies of equivocation when key words in the argument have ambiguous meanings, or those words shift in meaning according to the context in which they are used. Other common forms of fallacious reasoning that mediate students' reasoning on SSI have been identified and include validity concerns, naïve conceptions of argument structure, effects of core beliefs on argumentation, inadequate sampling of evidence, and altering representation of argument and evidence (Zeidler, 1997; Zeidler, Osborne, Erduran, Simon, & Monk, 2003). While the value of argument in promoting dissonance, facilitating sociomoral discourse, and impacting moral development is well understood in the research

literature, the need for careful attention to possible faulty reasoning cannot be overstated. It is one thing for students to err in reasoning about SSI. It is quite another for individuals to be taken advantage of by others of dubious moral character who are well versed in sophist pursuits.

Exploring the decision making of 14-year-old students, Patronis, Potari, and Spiliotopoulou (1999) focused on how students justify developing arguments on an SSI and the kinds of arguments and values employed. This was an ethnographic study focusing on the dialogic pragmatics of classroom discourse. The authors noted that pragmatic arguments are often used as qualitative tools of thought as students consider contrasting values (e.g., personal happiness versus benefit for all) associated with social, ecological, economic, and practical aspects of the issues. In contrast, when students' thinking was focused on quantitative aspects of the issues (e.g., numbers, estimated calculations, school-based knowledge), the arguments appeared (or were presented) as value free. The authors point to the importance of engaging students to explore the interplay of different forms of argument as a critical precursor to becoming citizens capable of policy decisions.

Kolstø (2006) examined the patterns of student argumentation as 22 high school students reasoned informally about an SSI involving the proximity of power lines and increased risk of childhood leukemia. As with the study discussed earlier, Kolstø was interested in the interplay between scientific knowledge and personal values, as both are present in ethical and political issues involving many SSI. Using case study analysis, five main argument types were found and clearly presented: relative risk argument, precautionary argument, uncertainty argument, small risk argument, and pros-and-cons argument. The findings also point to the fact that while students used factual claims based on scientific information from expert sources of information provided in class in the formulation of their arguments, they did not integrate school science knowledge into their positions to any significant degree. Also of interest is Kolstø's own argument that since students evoke data as well as values to serve as warrants in claims about policy, science education has a role in helping to encourage students in the practice of thoughtful decision making, particularly when what constitutes relevant knowledge is determined, in part, by diverse people holding contrasting values. Kolstø built this work on prior research (2001b) using the same subjects. It is important to note that this SSI topic had been at the forefront of debates in the news, so students were familiar with the issue and it had direct relevance to their lives. In this earlier analysis, the focus was on students' perceived trustworthiness of expert knowledge claims. Through inductive analyses, four kinds of resolution strategies were revealed: (1) acceptance of knowledge claims, (2) evaluation of statements using reliability indicators and thinking for themselves, (3) acceptance of researchers and other authoritative sources, and (4) evaluation of sources in terms of interests, neutrality, or competence. When other experts did not question knowledge claims from one source, students accepted them as trustworthy. Further, students tended to have full trust in the researchers and their corresponding methods, even while questioning their neutrality and opinion about risks. This produced an interesting dual attitude of trust meshed with skepticism. Further, students could not suggest how they might judge the level of agreement among researchers about risk indicators and did not distinguish among researchers who might be more or less knowledgeable about the topic. Finally, most students evaluated the sources of knowledge more than the content of the statements advancing that knowledge.

Adding to the theoretical knowledge base, Sadler and Zeidler (2005a) were interested in discerning what patterns of informal reasoning college students use in response to SSI entailing six genetic engineering scenarios. The authors were informed by several trends in the research to help deal with the challenge of exploring and explaining how students think and feel as they engage in reasoning about such issues. These trends included the impact of personal experiences on the decision maker, emotive considerations, social considerations, morality, and perceptions of inherent complexity associated with SSI and helped shape construction of the moral dilemmas to best engage the students and tap their moral perceptions of problems associated with those issues. Two rounds of semistructured interviews were performed with the same students to allow them to take stances on the issues and ultimately provide detailed rationales, further justifications, and clarify positions on the issues. Analysis between the researchers was aimed at deriving meaning that typified the participants' reasoning patterns, but it is important to note that member checking was also used to enhance trustworthiness. The results revealed three main categories of informal reasoning evoked by students. First, *rationalistic informal reasoning* entailed the use of reason and logic to create supporting positions buttressed by the consideration of specific factors related to the problem. Second, *intuitive informal reasoning patterns* were observed when participants displayed immediate positive or negative affective feelings or reactions to an issue, and those feelings contributed to their reasoning and eventual resolution of the dilemmas. Third, *emotive reasoning patterns*, also affective in nature, were rooted in empathetic awareness toward the well-being of other people, real or fictitious, arising from the initial dilemmas. Further, the authors identified various modes of integrated informal reasoning patterns, where permutations of the three main types may either be at odds with one another (conflicting—usually producing more internal dissonance) or where two or more of the reasoning patterns were used in concert with each other (coordinated—usually producing internally consistent arguments). The findings also suggested that emotive and intuitive reasoning tended to be more aligned to the context of the SSI. Finally, while the majority of the participants perceived moral and ethical implications arising from the SSI, those concerns did not dominate

their informal reasoning; rather, moral and ethical issues contributed to an integrated response, along with other factors mentioned earlier, to the issues at hand. Dawson and Venville (2009) were able to confirm the appearance of rationalistic, intuitive, and emotive informal reasoning patterns in high school students ranging in ages from 12 to 17 from six metropolitan schools using the same SSI scenarios as Sadler and Zeidler (2005a). Additionally, arguments were also analyzed using Toulmin's (1958) argumentation patterns using a five-level analytical framework developed by Osborne, Erduran, and Simon (2004). They reported that most students used little to no data to support their claims and relied on intuitive and emotive informal reasoning more often than on rational patterns; however, rational patterns generally produced more robust arguments. The authors noted that the dispersion of informal argument patterns differed from Sadler and Zeidler's (2005a) study, with rational patterns appearing far less frequently in high school students than their college counterparts. Dawson and Venville (2009) surmised that the older college students may at first express intuitive responses but are able to maintain a sustained line of articulated reasoning, factoring in emotive and/or rationalistic reasoning prior to the formulation of a final conclusion. Finally, the authors noted that most of the high school students' arguments fell into the lower levels of the argumentation framework (level 2). And while rationalistic informal arguments were rare, they were the only type to reach into the higher level 4 (out of a possible 5). Lastly, Topcu, Sadler, and Yilmaz-Tuzun (2010) again examined the same SSI scenarios cited using preservice teachers, but with an eye toward observing the effect of issue context on the level of informal reasoning practices. The authors found a fairly uniform distribution of argument levels utilized over the six genetic engineering issues and concluded that the quality of informal reasoning practices might be more transferable across contexts than suggested by previous research (Sadler & Zeidler, 2005a). However, it should be kept in mind that the research by Sadler and Zeidler examined kinds of informal reasoning strategies but not the level of argumentation reached across different contexts. Furthermore, one might suggest that the six contexts used in these particular studies are not terribly disparate in that they all connect to some form of genetic engineering issue.

In contrast to using Toulmin's framework to examine argumentation, Chang and Chiu (2008) used a philosophical framework based on Lakatos' (1970, 1978) scientific research programs to evaluate informal argumentation about SSI. Whereas Toulmin's scheme typically evokes combinations of data, warrant, backing, qualifiers, claims, and rebuttals to examine levels of argumentation, the authors conceptualized Lakatos' philosophy as a framework providing coherence for a series of theories (rather than a single theory) that include the following components: hard-core, negative heuristic, positive heuristic, and protective belt. Each of these components was operationalized to a specific skill set of argument used in informal reasoning about SSI. Using 70 undergraduate science and nonscience majors, the authors found that science majors had greater use of analogies, whereas nonscience majors relied more on authority while framing arguments. Students also used a variety of resources to support their arguments about SSI, including general and scientific beliefs, nature of science, ethics, personal experience, analogy, and authority. Finally, the authors demonstrated that "hardcore" arguments about SSI do seem to be safeguarded by a "protective belt" rendering core beliefs challenging to alter. Their research supports the conceptualization of the coherence for arguments employed in informal reasoning of SSI found in Sadler (2004a) and Sadler and Zeidler (2004).

Other researchers have examined additional aspects of argumentation in SSI contexts. Dawson and Venville (2010) recommend that professional learning activities include designing purposeful argumentation strategies (e.g., the role of the teacher in whole-class discussion; the use of writing frames; the type of socioscientific issue; and the role of the students) that teachers can apply to their own unique circumstances so their students can benefit from SSI discourse. Lee (2007) stresses that an integrative SSI approach can guide students to engage in rational argumentation and promote conceptual understanding of subject matter, the process of scientific inquiry, and the development of values. Albe (2008a, 2008b) advocates for the development of teaching sequences on SSI that encourage students to examine the epistemological status of their knowledge by considering the way in which scientific knowledge is produced within a community and the role of controversy accompanying this process, including considerations of the nature and limitations of science, the status, role, and limits of evidence, possible competing interests involved, and the ways science communities establish knowledge. The role of epistemology in the formation of argument during SSI discourse may include tapping empirical scientific evidence as well as sociological elements that impact students' perceived actions of the agents. Confirming the reports of Zeidler and colleagues (2002), Albe (2008b) found that students tend to compartmentalize scientific evidence and personal knowledge in the process of deriving decisions about SSI. The integration of knowledge may reflect higher-order reasoning during argumentation on such issues.

Summary of Trends for Theme II.
Socioscientific Issues as Epistemological
Development and Reasoning

Research into aspects of epistemological beliefs, their development, and how these impact reasoning and argumentation concerning conceptual understanding of content knowledge is an area of great promise in science education. Studies examining features of informal reasoning in the context of SSI have furthered our understanding of how to structure pedagogy associated with SSI

curriculum. Further, the connections between epistemology and NOS understanding are realized in the general correspondence that exists between higher levels of epistemological sophistication and more robust understandings of the nature of science. It is also of interest to note that broader social science perspectives allow for multiple modes of reasoning about SSI. Carefully sequenced SSI curricula coupled with teaching strategies meant to induce cognitive and moral dissonance have been found to promote developmental changes in reflective judgment, supporting a generalized goal of development as an aim of education. Prior beliefs about the structure of scientific knowledge and core beliefs of students need to be consistently challenged to tap developmental structures and facilitate conceptual transfer of scientific content to appropriate contexts. Socioscientific reasoning, or the ability to evoke epistemological traits of consciousness that entail recognizing complexity and multiple perspectives and understanding inquiry and possessing skepticism, may very well represent a mode of universal reasoning useful across a plethora of contextualized SSI. While some cross-cultural data reveal nuanced differences in how groups of individuals may prioritize scientific information and implement elements of distributive justice in the context of SSI, cross-cultural congruity also exists with respect to how different national identities conceptualize, evaluate, and justify decisions of moral and ethical issues embedded in scientific contexts. More research is needed for both theory and practice to better connect how to scaffold science curriculum to ensure both the utilization and understanding of scientific knowledge helping to inform policy making and decisions about SSI and safeguard against core beliefs where they are found to produce fallacious reasoning or prevent conceptual understanding of arguments, discourse, and the co-construction of scientific knowledge.

Theme III. Socioscientific Issues as
Context for the Nature of Science

Working within the SSI framework is understood as a contextual-embedded undertaking. It has the potential to impact the daily lives of our students in both formal and informal settings and often blurs the sharp edges of both discipline-specific and cultural boundaries. Therefore, it should come as no surprise that SSI is aligned with other sociocultural perspectives in science education (Aikenhead, Orpwood, & Fensham, 2011; Gauch, 2009; Kincheloe & Tobin, 2009; Sadler, 2009). The research reviewed in this section considers these types of sociocultural viewpoints through the lens of the nature of science.

One area that has been the focus of several lines of research entails the relationship between the nature of science (NOS) and SSI. From one perspective, the relationship may be conceptualized as one in which NOS provides a context for the examination of SSI. Lederman, Antink, and Bartos (2014) clearly stress that a reflective, explicit approach to teaching NOS can be used with attention to appropriate SSI in order to enhance scientific literacy precisely because the complexity of certain scientific areas (e.g., genetics) is amenable to deeper epistemological meaning making during student discourse. Conversely, the relationship between these two constructs may be conceptualized as one in which SSI provides a context for understanding NOS. Zeidler, Applebaum, and Sadler (2011) conducted a longitudinal experiment in high school classes to understand how SSI could be leveraged to promote student learning of NOS and science content (among other outcomes). In this case, the SSI curriculum compelled both the teacher and the students to undergo a transformative process that included, among other things, discarding antiquated teaching methods and assuming responsibility for learning. Following a pedagogical focus that conveys how knowledge is generated and validated while exposing students to ethical problems that involve any number of discrepant scientific, social, or moral viewpoints, often conflicting with the students' own closely held beliefs, the studies reviewed next hold much promise for engaging students in science. And while academic arguments can rightfully be advanced for either perspective, the linkages between these two areas hold pedagogical importance in terms of advancing a sociocultural mindset for learning science. Inasmuch as this chapter is written through the lens of an SSI perspective, it may be helpful to think in terms of SSI providing a context for the practice of science in general and formation of NOS understanding in particular.

In one of the first studies to empirically explore the relationship between NOS and students' reactions to evidence that challenged their epistemological beliefs about SSI concerning research practices on animals, Zeidler, Walker, Ackett, and Simmons (2002) examined both high school and college-age students. A sample of 248 students from two diverse urban high school populations and two elementary science methods courses (senior college-level students) was selected, and students completed a written questionnaire aimed at revealing their views of NOS related to the tentativeness of science, the role of empirical evidence in science, the social and cultural factors in generating scientific knowledge, and the creative aspects of science. Student pairs were purposively selected based on the variation in their written responses to themes related to the SSI topic and interviewed using questions to elicit their epistemological reasoning on the issue. Through the process of discourse analysis, researchers found several interesting connections between students' beliefs about NOS and their decision making on the SSI. Many students purported an awareness of the role of social and cultural influences in scientific research. Further, students discussed the importance of scientific data in decision making. However, when researchers probed further concerning the justification of their decisions on the issue, personal opinions and core beliefs appeared to be the most prevalent guiding factors, suggesting that students' decision making is predominantly driven by the affective domain and not by

science content knowledge (including conceptions of the NOS). It was speculated that left to their own reasoning skills (i.e., without explicit instructional interventions), students tend to compartmentalize scientific evidence in a manner that meshes with personal core beliefs.

In a study conducted by Bell and Lederman (2003), 21 volunteer participants from higher education institutions were purposively selected to complete an open-ended questionnaire and a follow-up interview designed to examine their decision-making abilities for various SSI. The participants also completed a second open-ended questionnaire with follow-up interviews to assess their views of NOS, subsequently placing the participants into one of two groups reflecting either instrumental/dynamic or realist/static views of science. Profiles of characteristics related to each group's decision making on the SSI were formed and their decisions, decision-making factors, and decision-making strategies examined. Although the two groups possessed quite divergent views of NOS, there were no discernible differences detected in the analysis of factors related to their decision making. These findings, although specific to the studied population, still resonate with findings from other studies dealing with decision making on SSI. Sociocultural factors such as personal values, ethics, and social and political issues appear to mediate the decision-making process, as suggested in earlier work (Fleming, 1986a, 1986b; Zeidler & Schafer, 1984), where the integration of content knowledge and NOS was overshadowed by students' epistemological beliefs about personal and social moral norms.

More fine-grained relationships between NOS and SSI have been further explored in the literature. Based on the premise that the status of evidence is connected to typical NOS constructs (e.g., empirical, cultural-embeddedness, and tentative tenets), Sadler, Chambers, and Zeidler (2004) sought to investigate how students interpret and evaluate conflicting evidence embedded in an SSI. The researchers conducted an investigation of 84 high school students who reviewed two articles of equal scientific merit (constructed by the researchers to ensure the quality of evidence and arguments for each study were essentially equivalent) but offered opposing positions on the issue of global warming. A questionnaire designed to elicit their views about NOS in the context of the global warming debate was subsequently administered. A subset of 30 students was then interviewed to explore more deeply the connections between their conceptual NOS understandings and decision making on the global warming issue. Similar to the results of Bell and Lederman (2003), students displayed a range of views regarding the empirical, tentative, and social aspects of NOS. When it came to evaluating competing scientific claims, the researchers found that the students' prior beliefs and personal relevance were primary considerations in terms of judgments rendered as to the scientific merit contained in the two articles. The degree to which students associated more scientific merit between articles was essentially connected to their own conceptualizations of NOS. It would appear that where students need to negotiate conflicting evidence in SSI contexts, the understanding and reasoning of their views are mediated by a number of NOS–related factors along a continuum of naïve to sophisticated epistemological judgments.

In a review of the literature that examined informal reasoning in the context of SSI, Sadler (2004a) concluded that strategies developed in a manner consistent with the SSI conceptual framework can provide viable curriculum opportunities for developing informal reasoning strategies, argumentation skills, and conceptual understanding of content, as well NOS conceptualizations. Implying a synergistic relationship, he also suggested that research indicates that NOS appears to play some role in informal reasoning about SSI, although the precise nature of that relationship warranted further study. In two studies by Khishfe and Lederman (2006) and Walker and Zeidler (2007), it is interesting to note that NOS contextualized within SSI units produced gains in NOS understanding. However, in the case of the Khishfe and Lederman study, the gains were not significantly different from those of students in a decontextualized NOS class. And in the case of the Walker and Zeidler study, while students' answers to written questions related to the nature of science reflected enhanced conceptions of the tentative, creative, subjective, and social aspects of science, those aspects were not apparent later in a culminating debate and discussion that was held at the end of the SSI unit. In the Lederman and Khishfe study, it is important to remember that while SSI–contextualized NOS was not superior to gains in the decontextualized group, students still increased their NOS understanding. So the questions can still be raised as to the other possible benefits that could have resulted from the SSI–contextualized approach, such as student interest and engagement with subject matter and the possibility that scientific understanding was transferred to other learning situations. And in the Walker and Zeidler study, it may only mean that teachers might need to be more vigilant to draw out explicit connections to NOS conceptualizations with students and encourage them to reflect on how data-driven claims connect to the structure of scientific argumentation. The importance of fostering explicit-reflective NOS practice has, of course, been consistently put forward in the literature (Akerson, Abd-El-Khalick, & Lederman, 2000; Khishfe, & Lederman, 2007).

Ibáñez-Orcajo and Martínez-Aznar (2007) took into consideration the importance of explicitly building into learning unit objectives elements of NOS relative to problem solving in genetics for secondary students and doing so in conjunction with a contextualized view of how humanistic processes of science unfold via inquiry. Although they frame their investigation from an STS teaching approach, the authors clearly look to elements of SSI within that approach to overtly emphasize the social aspects of science informed by multiple perspectives from disciplines outside of science (e.g., philosophy, sociology, politics, etc.). The social context entailed topics of

human inheritance that have social implications. Characteristics of NOS, such as how science is done, what a theory is, perceptions of scientists, and the cultural context of science were thoughtfully integrated into a problem-solving pedagogical approach informed by many socio-cultural epistemological elements of science such as philosophical, historical, psychological, and sociological dimensions. The experimental group ($n = 30$) statistically exceeded the control group ($n = 19$) in terms of conceptual change about NOS and retained their new conceptual shifts in NOS understanding 5 months later. The findings support the "content-transcending knowledge" curriculum (Kolstø, 2001a) typified in SSI approaches where knowledge *about* science is weighted more heavily for students than knowledge within the specific domains *of* science (or where Vision II is preferred over Vision I; Roberts, 2007).

Several researchers have specifically advocated the position that SSI be used to engage students in central processes of science and that SSI provide numerous opportunities for explicit discussions of NOS through the lens of decisions formulated through discourse and inquiry (Abd-El-Khalick, 2006; Bell & Lederman, 2003; Bell, Matkins, & Gansneder, 2011; Matkins & Bell, 2007; Nuangchalerm, 2010; Sadler, 2009; Sadler, Chambers, & Zeidler, 2004; Walker & Zeidler, 2007; Zeidler, Sadler, Applebaum, & Callahan, 2009; Zeidler, Walker, Ackett, & Simmons, 2002). A direct comparison between teaching NOS explicitly and reflectively within a content-driven anatomy and physiology course and an SSI–driven A&P course among four classes of 11th- and 12th-grade students over the course of an academic school year was reported by Eastwood and colleagues (2012). Four classes were randomly assigned to either an SSI treatment group or a content comparison group, all taught by the same teacher who was well versed in both NOS and SSI instruction. It is important to note that for *both* groups, NOS instruction was implemented through explicit teaching, activities, and demonstrations coupled with making explicit connections between features of NOS and classroom content scaffolded over the academic year. The content group was taught using traditional content- and textbook-driven lecture and lab approaches. In contrast, the curriculum for the SSI group was driven by the SSI framework whereby 10 major SSI themes provided the scientific context for learning the major anatomy systems and the specific scientific concepts underpinning those systems over the school year. Hence, the SSI group situated its learning in contexts that tapped social, economic, ethical, and moral aspects underpinning the relevant science. Pretest and posttest comparisons were made using the Views of Nature of Science—Form C by multiple researchers blinded as to which responses belonged to a given group. An emergent coding scheme and taxonomy were established with high interrater reliability. The results were interesting in that SSI and content groups both produced significant gains in most NOS themes (e.g., empirical, tentative, creative, socially/culturally embedded, theory, and law). However, qualitative analyses revealed that students in the SSI group tended to use a greater number of examples to describe their views of the social/cultural NOS. The findings supported the claim that SSI can provide an effective sociocultural context for promoting gains in students' NOS conceptualizations.

Çalik and Coll (2012) argue that SSI provides a constructive way of exploring important features of NOS with students, thereby promoting scientific literacy. The authors also suggest that a science curriculum based on SSI provides a window through which students can view science as scientists do. Drawing on the work of Gauld (2005), who operationalizes scientific habits of mind (SHOM), to include aspects of mistrust of arguments from authority, open-mindedness, skepticism, rationality, objectivity, suspension of belief, and curiosity, they extend the argument that SHOM benefit all citizens who consider embedded aspects of science in their daily lives. While the main purpose of Çalik and Coll's research was to develop a valid and reliable instrument to measure SHOM through the construction of the Scientific Habits of Mind Survey, their work has significant implications particularly for SSI curriculum and research because of the clear linkages to contextualizing NOS within SSI frameworks. The survey they created appears to have excellent content, face, convergent, discriminant, concurrent, and predictive validity They conclude that SSI and SHOM show much promise conveying NOS through classroom discourse, argumentation, and case-based issues (as suggested by Zeidler et al., 2005).

Similarly, Lee (2008) explored a conceptual analysis using SSI as a context to understand aspects of the roles of science and their connection to NOS. The context was an actual case study of the SARS outbreak that originated in southern China and spread to Hong Kong and other countries by way of air travel. Roles of science, as conceptualized in this study, included understanding nature via discovery, using science for technological applications to solve problems, and using science to inform policy making on issues with scientific implications. These roles of science manifest themselves through aspects of NOS by revealing the epistemic values and practices present in sociocultural contexts. This particular case study illustrates how and where the social, political, and cultural contexts of those roles unfold. Lee contends that SSI case studies like this can further students' understanding of NOS and develop more informed conceptualizations of scientific literacy.

To further augment understanding of the relationship between the NOS and SSI, Khishfe (2012a) studied high school students' argumentation skills, response patterns, and epistemological understandings of NOS in two different SSI contexts. The premise was that since SSI impacts students' daily lives, it would provide a context of understanding for NOS and argumentation. Others do affirm that judicious use of SSI develops students' open-mindedness, ability to detect bias, and capacity to critically reflect on science-based issues (Ratcliffe & Grace, 2003; Simonneaux, 2008; Zeidler, et al., 2002; Zeidler, Sadler, Applebaum, & Callahan, 2009). Using SSI about genetically modified food and water fluoridation, Khishfe was able to provide two distinct contexts as a backdrop to ascertain differences in participants' views of NOS aspects and argumentation skills. NOS understandings were broken down into naïve, intermediary, and informed views, while argumentation components were parsed into responses that had no justification or invalid justification, valid justification supported by one reason, or valid justification supported by more than one reason. The students had no particular training in argumentation strategies prior to the study. Results from chi-square and qualitative analyses both showed significant and distinct differences in students' levels of epistemological understandings of NOS and quality of argumentation between these two SSI contexts. For example, a student could demonstrate varied NOS conceptions, arguing tentative aspects of NOS from a naïve view in the case of water fluoridation but informed views in the case of genetically modified food. Furthermore, students often used differential argumentation patterns in the justification of each SSI scenario. It was also noted that students with more informed views of NOS constructed stronger counterarguments. The results taken as a whole demonstrate that different SSI contexts have the potential to activate different epistemological representations of knowledge and influence how one reasons about that knowledge. While prior familiarity obviously plays a role, this work underscores the pedagogical importance of connecting scientific content to areas of personal relevance for students. Khishfe (2012b) again used SSI as a context to study students' decision-making factors as a result of explicit NOS instruction. Here, the context was a 4-week unit on genetic engineering for the treatment group, with opportunities to apply through discussion elements of NOS on issues like cloning and genetically modified food. And while the treatment group showed significant differences on several NOS factors from the control group, no differences were found between the groups' actual decisions. However, differences were in fact found within groups in decision-making factors (e.g., referring to more NOS factors, moral/ethical topics related to controversial SSI) from pre- to postintervention. Khishfe (2012b) suggested that certain NOS aspects (e.g., empirical, tentative, and subjective) might more closely align with decision making and argumentation in certain SSI contexts—that is, particular NOS aspects may be more conducive to reasoning about particular kinds of SSI. It seems clear, then, that SSI contexts may facilitate understandings of NOS. How this is further conceptualized and implemented in future research remains to be seen.

Summary of Trends for Theme III. Socioscientific Issues as Context for the Nature of Science

Numerous research studies have conceptualized SSI in a manner that provides a framework allowing for the expression of NOS elements. Through SSI scenarios, students can come to appreciate how concepts such as understanding tentativeness, the role of empirical evidence, sociocultural factors, and the like inform many of the inquiry processes associated with scientific discussions, decision making, and investigations. While research tends to support the assertion that properly implemented SSI curriculum can provide a sociocultural context for the facilitation of more robust NOS understanding, it cannot be assumed that students come to such realizations in the absence of explicit connections and examples. Hence, teachers' pedagogical skills play a critical role in teasing out many of the subtle examples of how NOS constructs come to be interwoven within SSI contexts. There are times when the negotiation of dissonant evidence is impacted by students' relative understanding of NOS–related factors. The extent to which SSI and NOS work in concert to mediate understandings of scientific content remains an open question for now. This is an exciting area of research with the potential to impact how science educators come to think about some of the most fundamental goals of science education. More studies are needed to determine alternative ways to leverage contextualized NOS during informal reasoning about moral and ethical issues and when applying that reasoning to the resolution of SSI.

Theme IV. Socioscientific Issues as Character Development and Citizenship Responsibility

Since the use of SSI can provide the opportunity for contextualized argumentation through the consideration of diverse viewpoints about how to achieve particular ethical ends, SSI may be leveraged in a manner aimed at contributing to the cultivation of character, citizenship, and social action. The research reviewed here stresses and explores these collective aims from different perspectives, emphasizing either a sense of personal responsibility, accountability, or empathy toward others as well as the environment. These traits are aligned with the development of virtue—generally understood as human excellence and, consequently, human flourishing.

Levinson (2008) stressed that the kind of reasoning employed during discussions of controversial issues cannot be disconnected from an awareness of others' perspectives; hence sensitivity is seen as a kind of communicative virtue that allows for an open exchange of ideas. Accordingly, he stresses the role of the personal narrative as a curricular tool that helps to situate the student in the issue, react to the issue, and evaluate the scientific and societal factors that undergird the issue. What is important here is the emphasis that Levinson and others (Aikenhead, 2005; Levinson, 2006; Tytler, Duggan, & Gott, 2001; Zeidler, Sadler, Simmons, & Howes, 2005) place on the use of scientific evidence to coordinate varied points of view on an issue. Levinson stresses that personal narratives of students and those with whom they identify can be used as a platform from which the experiences of other narratives (e.g., other people in disagreement, policy positions)

can be tapped and makes it clear that such exercises contribute to at least four interdependent pedagogical areas identified by Zeidler and colleagues (2005): nature of science, classroom discourse, cultural issues, and case-based issues. Levinson also presented examples of multiple levels of disagreement related to stem cell research based on McLaughlin's (2003) scheme for categorizing likely points of departure for consensus in a pluralistic society. These include (1) where insufficient evidence for reaching consensus exists at the moment but could be realized in the near future, (2) where evidence central to resolving an issue is conflicting, multifaceted, and hard to evaluate, (3) where the weights assigned to different criteria are challenged, (4) where desirable ends are agreed upon but the means to achieve them are at variance, (5) where the interpretation of agreed-upon criteria is questioned, (6) where there are competing normative expectations surrounding an issue, (7) where criteria connected to decisions are disputed, (8) where the lived experiences of individuals affect judgments among them in a conflicting manner, and (9) where there is no common understanding of the paradigm from which judgments are to be made. This framework can be used to inform curricular and pedagogical development of SSI, particularly where citizenship-related outcomes are emphasized.

In a study by Lee, Chang, Choi, Kim, and Zeidler (2012), 18 preservice teachers (PSTs) participated in an SSI program that focused on developing character and values through dialogical and reflective practices. The SSI context focused on nuclear power generation, climate change, and embryonic stem cell research. The authors examined the manner in which PSTs perceived such issues as fundamental moral problems, as well as the extent to which ecological worldviews, an indicator of global identity, and a sense of stewardship as a world citizen mediate reasoning on these kinds of issues. An interesting aspect of this research is the use of a coding frame and rubric based on prior research (Choi, Lee, Shin, Kim, & Krajcik, 2011) that contrasted personal, societal, and global claims from the perspectives of ecological worldviews, socioscientific accountability, and social and moral compassion. These three latter elements connect well to dimensions of character and values that global citizens ought to possess. Ecological worldviews situate an individual's personal values within the broader natural world (Colucci-Gray, Giuseppe Barbiero, & Gray, 2006; Mueller & Zeidler, 2010; Smith & Williams, 1999). Socioscientific accountability connects the individual to a sense of responsibility and his/her personal or collective actions in order that SSI are confronted (Hodson, 1999; Lee et al., 2012; Roth & Lee, 2004). Social and moral compassion enables the individual to be sensitive and empathetic to social justice concerns embedded in the environment, to value and respect multiple viewpoints, and to employ sociomoral reasoning across group norms (Fowler, Zeidler, & Sadler 2009; Sadler & Zeidler, 2005a; Zeidler et al. 2005; Zeidler & Sadler, 2008a). Lee and colleagues (2012) found that after dialogic discussions and reflective processes of SSI units over a 6-week period, while students did not consistently perceive themselves as moral change agents in relation to global SSI, they did approach SSI with empathy and caring. Further, the SSI curriculum was successful in engaging students in deep discussions about scientific concepts and enabled them to better understand the complexity of those issues. This study suggested that a carefully crafted SSI program could facilitate students' socioscientific reasoning (e.g., the recognition of the complexity of issues, examining issues from multiple perspectives, and the ability to invoke skepticism about information). The authors inferred that simply being exposed to SSI and participating in various classroom discourses could contribute to promoting feelings of responsibility and willingness to act—key precursors to effective action. Hence, this study shows much promise for the successful cultivation of character, compassion, and virtue within SSI–based curricula.

Building on the previous study, Lee and colleagues (2013) tapped into humanistic features of SSI to cultivate features of character and values from a global perspective using 132 middle school students enrolled in a general science course. The SSI context was genetic modification technology that was investigated over a 4-week period. As in the prior study, character and values in this context included three main elements: ecological worldview, social and moral compassion, and socioscientific accountability. Students received integrated instruction that combined both SSI instruction and regular science instruction, while homework assignments were aimed at encouraging self-reflection on the SSI issues. Quantitative and qualitative data were collected, including Likert items and videotapes of classroom discourse. The Likert scale produced a seven-factor model explaining 64.8 % of the total variance and included (1) interconnectedness and (2) sustainable development, both forming the ecological worldview construct; (3) moral and ethical sensitivity, (4) perspective and (5) empathic concern, all three comprising the social and moral compassion construct; and (6) feeling of responsibility and (7) willingness to act, both forming the socioscientific accountability construct. Among these three main constructs, significant differences were found for students' pre- to posttest scores on the social and moral compassion construct, indicating that the SSI program had a moderately large impact on the extent to which students became more sensitive and showed more compassion toward diverse cultures that may be affected by advances in technology. Significant differences were also shown for students on the socioscientific accountability construct, with a moderately large effect size representing a positive result for the degree to which they felt a sense of responsibility in terms of helping to mitigate SSI issues. Qualitative data reaffirmed these findings; however, more nuanced analysis also revealed that students tended to be anthropomorphic in their views about nature and somewhat reticent to actively participate within global communities to help alleviate problems. The reluctance of students to engage

in potentially sensitive issues has been reported elsewhere (Sternäng & Lundholm, 2011) and brings attention to the need for just-community approaches to scientific activism that may initially entail low individual personal cost and risk but shared satisfaction from the work of collective outcomes.

Reiss (2008) focused on the use of ethical frameworks contextualized in an advanced-level biology course for high school students. It is clear that the course was developed in response to the perception that much of school science was dull and irrelevant to most students. Rather than teach science from the privileged point of view of scientists, a concerted effort was made to embed the scientific concepts in an ethical framework that allowed the concepts to emerge from the contexts. Students were to engage in the issues (e.g., global climate change, genetic engineering, conservation biology, cystic fibrosis), critically evaluate those issues, and develop their own opinions as long as they were substantiated by evidence. Equally important, the driving force of these topics was an ethical framework that cloaked the issues in a relevant personal context for students, representative of an SSI approach. Hence, Reiss situated the conceptual model in an ethical framework based on Davis (1999) and a pluralistic approach as advocated by Zeidler and Lewis (2003). This entailed teaching science in a manner designed to heighten the ethical sensitivity of students, increase their ethical knowledge, improve associated ethical judgments, and allow students to exercise virtue. He used precepts of social justice techniques (see Reiss, 1999; 2003) to impress upon the students useful criteria for judging the efficacy of ethical conclusions, which included the degree to which those conclusions are supported by reason, deciding if the arguments and evidence supporting those conclusions were derived from a well-established ethical framework and if a reasonable degree of consensus was established supporting their validity following a process of negotiation and debate. At the end of the course, 17 student reports about biological issues were analyzed using four possible ethical frameworks representing themes embedded throughout the course: rights and duties, utilitarianism, autonomy, and/or virtue ethics. Out of these 17 student reports, 12 reflected the use of only a single framework of utilitarianism, while the remaining 5 contained two or more combinations of themes. The author also found that 16 of the 17 students employed anthropocentric arguments, 14 used egocentric arguments, and 13 offered biocentric ones. While Reiss cautions about the preliminary nature of the findings, it was clear that students could in fact utilize key features of ethical reasoning, and he has subsequently worked with large numbers of science teachers to more fully integrate ethical aspects into their science teaching.

Other studies have focused on, among other outcomes, qualities associated with citizenship and character such as moral sensitivity. Sadler (2004c) explored how moral sensitivity contributes to the resolution of SSI for college students. He found that students overtly expressed sensitivity to the moral features embedded within the SSI (genetic engineering in this case), and they also displayed empathy for the welfare of others. His qualitative analysis revealed the integration of moral and nonmoral concerns during socioscientific decision making. Clearly, students rely on emotive factors in calibrating their responses to socioscientific policy. Likewise, Fowler, Zeidler, and Sadler (2009) studied the effects of a yearlong SSI–based curriculum for high school students. Rather than SSI being an add-on to the anatomy and physiology course, SSI were infused, thereby driving the curriculum, while the scientific content was skillfully extracted from those issues by the teacher. The aim was to provide as many opportunities as possible for students to develop cohesive views of the social and moral context of science using both evidence and narrative and provide specific character-enhancing experiences that were connected to the content. Those experiences met the bar of being personally relevant to students, connecting to their sociocultural lives, and fostering dynamic contextualized argumentation skills. The researchers aimed to use this model in order to present unique opportunities for rethinking science education pedagogy and to contribute to an education in preparation for citizenship. Further, the researchers aligned the SSI program with an ethical framework that recognizes and taps the importance of moral emotions in formulating moral judgments, including (but not limited to) moral sensitivity, moral reasoning, moral commitment, and moral courage. Driving factors that helped to guide the course were also derived from Kolstø's (2001a) content-transcending themes for SSI instruction (e.g., the role of consensus in science, demands for underpinning evidence, scrutinizing science-related claims). Pre- to posttest comparisons between the SSI treatment group and the "traditional instruction" comparison group using ANCOVA indicated significant differences in favor of the SSI group on a measure of moral sensitivity. Contextual differences were noted, as one context appeared to produce greater gains and effect size than the other, but it was clear that these results confirmed the findings of earlier research whereby individuals tended to use higher and more robust levels of reasoning in contexts that matched their emotive sensibilities or affective beliefs (Zeidler & Schafer, 1984).

It has also been shown that SSI instruction ultimately provides opportunities for students to become involved as participatory citizens. A number of these studies are often situated in ecojustice-related movements. For example, Sperling and Bencze (2010) implemented an issue-based program for seventh-grade students with a focus on waste management and observed changes in the students' propensities toward active citizenship. Specifically, the students gained a sense of commitment toward issues connected to civic responsibilities and recognized a range of positive and negative impacts their actions produced on the well-being of themselves, society, and the environment. Further, evidence indicated that students were able

to retain these positive changes in their personal practices. Lewis and Leach (2006) maintain that school curriculum has the potential to play a useful preparatory role so that young students can gain more confidence and openness to partake in future consideration and engagement of scientific issues that have social consequences. Their research suggests that even a modest degree of scientific understanding will allow students to identify key relevant issues and engage in reasoned discussion. In related analytical work, Mueller and Zeidler (2010) advocate an ecojustice approach via SSI, suggesting that students' awareness of advanced technologies that de-emphasized or ignored potentially adverse impacts on the environment (e.g., the introduction of glofish—a genetically modified zebrafish) is critical to maintaining a just quality of life. Others agree that an ethic of care can perpetuate peaceful, responsible, sustainable actions that can be nurtured through citizen science and place-based ecojustice (Karrow & Fazio, 2010; Mueller, 2009; Sharma, 2010). And Roth and his colleagues (Lee & Roth, 2003; Roth & Désautels, 2004), examining the effects of student involvement in local community issues (e.g., various water projects), observed that students expressed a sense of responsibility while becoming part of a community through activism. Other researchers also advocate for science curricula that facilitate sociopolitical action and forms of social activism (Bencze, 2001; Hodson, 1999, 2003, 2010; Lester, Ma, Lee, & Lambert, 2006). Hence, this research has suggested the fruitfulness of developing character and values through using the SSI framework.

A theme running throughout these studies resides in the shared belief that the development of character, ethics, virtue, and the like is central to engaging our students, and the public at large, with public discourse about the role of science in our lives and the consequences our decisions may have for ourselves, our communities, nations beyond our borders, and our planet. A number of science educators have presented conceptual schemes for public understanding and engagement of science from ethical and sociocultural perspectives. The common philosophy underlying these schemes is the centrality of understanding that science education should be in the business of promoting tools for participatory citizenship (Aikenhead, 2007; Berkowitz & Simmons, 2003; Kolstø, 2000; Pouliot, 2009; Ratcliffe & Grace, 2003; Tal & Kedmi, 2006; Zeidler, in press ; Zeidler, Berkowitz, & Bennett, 2014). While some educators have discussed the socioethical dimension of science and the need for informed decision making on the basis of interdisciplinary ventures (Brown, 2002; Develaki, 2008; Östman & Almqvist, 2011), the studies reviewed here align more closely with the SSI framework as described in the introduction. It has been suggested that thinking in scientifically responsible ways requires features of character inasmuch as making informed judgments also needs to be tempered with compassion and caring—virtues of the scientifically literate individual. The SSI framework offers and invites students to dwell in the realm of intellectual independence and social interdependence as they assume shared responsibility for decisions and actions. Doing so requires the exercise of core virtues such as practical wisdom, justice as fairness, nonmaleficence, care, moral courage, and the like (Melville, Yaxley, & Wallace, 2007). Responsible scientific decision making requires the formation of conscience through the development of virtue and the practice of reflexive judgment (Zeidler & Sadler, 2008a, 2011). Students with experience in these matters, it is hoped, will become part of a global community having the inclination to function morally in the realm of worldly scientific matters.

Summary of Trends for Theme IV. Socioscientific Issues as Character Development and Citizenship Responsibility

In tasks that inherently contain competing positions, preferences, beliefs, and normative expectations that are informed by differential conceptual understandings of scientific content knowledge, it is clear that science educators need to turn an eye toward research that can add pedagogical value to classroom practice in terms of creating just communities for their resolution. In order to accomplish this large task, researchers have proposed methods and models for the facilitation of ecological and democratic stewardship. Accordingly, some have found it useful to break down competing interests from personal, societal, and global perspectives. Doing so helps to situate personal viewpoints on SSI into broader community perspectives, worldviews, and overarching ecological outlooks. Character traits like empathy, caring, responsibility, and willingness to take action on issues have been cultivated through SSI initiatives. Such traits help to nurture moral sensitivity and compassion and contribute to informing moral acts connected to the welfare of any polity. The incorporation of ethical frameworks into the study of science and science education has helped teachers and their students to feel accountable for actions that may ultimately lead toward a measure of environmental sustainability. Hence, research on SSI implementation has focused on means to enhance moral sensitivity by establishing a sense of community in the classroom and beyond its walls, thereby promoting participatory citizenship and democratic values.

Crossroads and Future Directions in SSI Research and Practice: Where to Go From Here? Overarching Core Questions

This is an exciting time for SSI research and practice, as the full potential of the SSI framework has yet to be tapped. I have presented elsewhere, along with my friend and colleague Troy Sadler, a list of core questions to promote scientific literacy through SSI with implications for theory and practice (Zeidler & Sadler, 2011). In light of this review of the literature, I would like to somewhat modify that original list. Of course, I make no claims that these are the most important or the only questions that should be raised. The intent is that their presentation offers to help frame just a few of the many areas awaiting further exploration and elaboration. I refer to these as overarching core questions in that these particular problems are extracted from the research reviewed and are presented in summary form in a manner that mirrors the four main themes presented in this chapter. Finally, the questions themselves may reside in one or more categories.

Socioscientific Issues as Engagement of Curriculum Practice and Teachers' Pedagogical Beliefs

- How can SSI best contribute to current and future understandings of scientific literacy?
- What does the full range of scientific inquiry (including the use of technology) look like in SSI contexts?
- How can preservice and inservice programs best develop teachers' identities toward SSI and related humanistic approaches to science education?
- How can SSI curricula be leveraged to facilitate environmental commitments and related sociopolitical action?

Socioscientific Issues as Epistemological Development and Reasoning

- How can cognitive, moral, and sociomoral frameworks inform our understanding of cultivating scientific literacy under the SSI framework?
- What methods ensure conceptual understanding and scaffolding of scientific content through all forms of SSI and SSR discourse?
- How might varied epistemic perspectives such as critical pedagogy, postcolonial, and feminist lenses, for example, empower research and practice in SSI?
- What intellectual and psychological constructs (e.g., cognitive, sociomoral, moral reasoning, perspective taking) contribute in fundamental and meaningful ways to SSR?

Socioscientific Issues as Context for the Nature of Science

- How can SSI contexts be leveraged to tap understandings of NOS?
- What explicit pedagogical strategies are effective to facilitate students' understandings of NOS within SSI strategies?
- What are the underlying connections between moral and ethical issues undergirding SSI and their impact on NOS conceptualizations?
- How can scientific inquiry in SSI contexts be used to promote and broaden students' understanding of NOS?

Socioscientific Issues as Character Development and Citizenship Responsibility

- How can sociocultural approaches and ethical frameworks contribute to the development of character and conscience in the context of SSI?
- How can the SSI framework be informed by related areas of research to develop students' sense of responsibility, civic obligation, and activism?
- How can features of prudence, conscience, and virtue be deliberately spread within SSI frameworks?
- How can cross-cultural research on SSI better inform conceptualizations of social, global, and environmental responsibility?

These questions tend to possess implications for the development and refinement of analytical, conceptual, and theoretical issues. They also have implications for the advancement of pedagogical, curricular, and policy issues. Science education scholars would do well to delve into relevant aspects of philosophy, sociology, psychology, and other disciplines outside our immediate areas of expertise to inform and guide their research programs. Adding breadth to our research base does not guarantee increased accuracy in our work. Done poorly, it might serve just to muddy the conceptual waters. Conversely, done well, with care and attention to underlying presuppositions, it does ensure a higher degree of potentiality for hitting the mark—to better unite the power of theory with philosophy through all forms of research. In turn, this will guide us in the design of curricula that are flexible and responsive to academic and developmental needs of our students. It will permit us to implement pedagogical practices that allow for the ecological community, school, and classroom conditions that serve our students' interests. Most importantly, we will be on a feasible trajectory toward securing scientific literacy for all.

Some Closing Thoughts on SSI and Science Education

> We call it "education," the "life of the mind," the "pursuit of the truth." But it is a matter of machine-tooling the young to the needs of our various baroque bureaucracies: corporate, governmental, military, trade union, educational. We call it "free enterprise." But it is a vastly restrictive system of oligopolistic market manipulation, tied by institutionalized corruption of the greatest munitions boondoggle in history and dedicated to infantilizing the public by turning it into a heard of compulsive consumers. We call it "pluralism." But it is a matter of the public authorities solemnly affirming everybody's right to his own opinion as an excuse for ignoring anybody's troubling challenge. In such pluralism, critical viewpoints become mere private prayers offered at the altar of an inconsequential conception of free speech. We call it "democracy." But it is a matter of public opinion polling in which a "random sample" is asked to nod or wag the head in response to a set of prefabricated alternatives,

> usually related to the *faits accompli* of decision makers, who can always construe the polls to serve their own ends.
>
> (Roszak, 1968, p. 16)

Decades ago, Roszak observed the coalescence of a "counterculture" concerned about the impact that technocratic societies imposed on our fragile world and who manifested their concern by choosing to exercise various modes of youthful opposition. The role of SSI in science education may also be observed in many forms and expressed in varied modalities. Certainly, it can play a role in students' conceptual understanding of scientific content. Guided by thoughtful and proper pedagogy, SSI can serve to form a foundation that allows students to scaffold and transfer that understanding to new contexts because they have socially and personally constructed their knowledge, own that knowledge, and have newfound confidence that future knowledge is within grasp—they need not wait on autocratic authorities to serve up the next helping of detached, factoid platters of mental mush. SSI can provide an engaging science curriculum by providing a personally relevant landscape on which to explore important scientific questions while contextualizing many elements of the nature of science. But perhaps most importantly, when the SSI framework is tapped to its optimal potential, it serves to democratize the formation of knowledge and level the playing field of political hegemony. SSI may contribute to the spread of virtue and the development of character. It can serve to arm our students with self-sustaining intellectual schemes to counter the perceived fait accompli of autocratic authority and policy makers.

Each of the four themes (Socioscientific Issues as Engagement of Curriculum Practice and Teachers' Pedagogical Beliefs, Socioscientific Issues as Epistemological Development and Reasoning, Socioscientific Issues as Context for the Nature of Science, and Socioscientific Issues as Character Development and Citizenship Responsibility) presented in this review impart implications for curriculum and pedagogical practices and offer a framework on which to cultivate epistemic understandings for children and young adults. The themes are clearly aligned with Roberts's (2007, 2011) notion of scientific literacy captured by Vision II and Aikenhead's (2006) humanistic perspective of school science. It is important to emphasize this point because of the implications it holds for the formation of policy. In a sense, the process of students' decision making about SSI is essentially an opportunity to practice the formation of collective policy judgments. It has been pointed out that policy making is fundamentally a moral activity (Zeidler, 1984). It entails the examination of competing claims, values, and evidence, thoughtful deliberation and negotiation, and the ability navigate the concept of optimality throughout this process. This concept is described well by Green (1975):

> By optimality, I mean to refer to the best composition of conflicting goals so that optimization of the whole set may require something less than the maximization of each

in order to get the greatest amount of them all in combination. . . . There is a kind of duality in its logic that may well mark it off as unique. On the one hand it has to do always with what can be chosen. Therefore, it is always related to the possible. "Optimal" means "feasible". But on the other hand, even etymologically, "optimality" relates to what is best. There is always that normative aspect to its logic. On the one hand, the concept of optimality deals always with what is possible, but on the other hand, it touches on what is ideal, which is best.

(p. 76)

Policy formation, then, should convey a sense of idealism tempered by the brute facts of imperfect people who must coexist in an imperfect world. Above all, it should be informed by a sense of conscience to guide the "formation of judgment in finding the fittingness of conduct to context" (Green, 1999, p. 195). Doing so would invoke a state of praxis, in Aristotle's (*Nichomachean Ethics*) sense of the word, connecting practical wisdom to moral virtue. It would entail the exercise of virtue—where policy is guided by the consideration of moral and ethical elements to achieve a perpetual state of human flourishing. Partaking in this venture, through all that the SSI framework has to offer, would be the model case of functional scientific literacy in action.

References

Abd-El-Khalick, F. (2006). Socioscientific issues in pre-college science classrooms. In D.L. Zeidler (Ed.), *The role of moral reasoning and discourse on socioscientific issues in science education* (pp. 41–61). Dordrecht, the Netherlands: Springer.

Aikenhead, G. S. (1980). *Science in social issues: Implications for teaching*. Ottawa, Canada: Science Council of Canada.

Aikenhead, G. S. (2005). Science-based occupations and the science curriculum: Concepts of evidence. *Science Education, 89,* 242–275.

Aikenhead, G. S. (2006). *Science education for everyday life: Evidence-based practice*. New York: Teachers College Press.

Aikenhead, G. S. (2007). Humanistic perspectives in the science curriculum. In S.K. Abell & N.G. Lederman (Eds.), *Handbook of research on science education* (pp. 881–910). London: Lawrence Erlbaum Associates.

Aikenhead, G. S., Orpwood, G., & Fensham, P. (2011). Scientific literacy for a knowledge society. In C. Linder, L. Östman, D.A. Roberts, P. Wickman, G. Erickson, & A. MacKinnon (Eds.), *Promoting scientific literacy: Science education research in transaction* (pp. 28–44). New York: Routledge/Taylor & Francis Group.

Akerson, V.L., Abd-El-Khalick, F.S., & Lederman, N.G. (2000). Influence of a reflective activity-based approach on elementary teachers' conceptions of the nature of science. *Journal of Research in Science Teaching, 37,* 295–317.

Albe, V. (2008a). Students' positions and considerations of scientific evidence about a controversial socioscientific issue. *Science & Education, 17*(8–9), 805–827.

Albe, V. (2008b). When scientific knowledge, daily life experience, epistemological and social considerations intersect: Students' argumentation in group discussions on a socio-scientific issue. *Research in Science Education, 38,* 67–90.

Barab, S. A., Sadler, T. D., Heiselt, C., Hickey, D., & Zuiker, S. (2010). Erratum to: Relating narrative, inquiry, and inscriptions: Supporting consequential play. *Journal of Science Education and Technology, 19*(4), 387–407.

Barrett, S.E., & Nieswandt, M. (2010). Teaching about ethics through socioscientific issues in physics and chemistry: Teacher candidates' beliefs. *Journal of Research in Science Teaching, 47,* 380–401.

Bell, R.L., & Lederman, N.G. (2003). Understandings of the nature of science and decision making on science- and technology-based issues. *Science Education, 87,* 352–377.

Bell, R.L., Matkins, J.J., & Gansneder, B.M. (2011). Impacts of contextual and explicit instruction on preservice elementary teachers' understandings of the nature of science. *Journal of Research in Science Teaching, 48,* 414–436.

Bencze, J.L. (2001). Subverting corporatism in school science. *Canadian Journal of Science, Mathematics and Technology Education, 1*(3), 349–355.

Bencze, J.L., Sperling, E., & Carter, L. (2012). Students' research-informed socio-scientific activism: Re/Visions for a sustainable future. *Research in Science Education, 42,* 129–148.

Ben-Zvi Assaraf, O., & Orion, N. (2005). Development of system thinking skills in the context of earth system education. *Journal of Research in Science Teaching, 42,* 518–560.

Berkowitz, M.W., & Simmons, P.E. (2003). Integrating science education and character education: The role of peer discussion. In D.L. Zeidler (Ed.), *The role of moral reasoning on socioscientific issues and discourse in science education* (pp. 117–138). Dordrecht, the Netherlands: Kluwer Academic Press.

Bowers, C.A. (2001). *Educating for eco-justice and community.* Athens: University of Georgia Press.

Brown, M.N. (2002). The mandate for interdisciplinarity in science education: The case of economic and environmental sciences. *Science & Education, 11,* 513–522.

Burek, K., & Zeidler, D.L. (in-press). Seeing the forest for the trees! Conservation and activism through socioscientific issues for young students. In M. Mueller & D.J. Tippins (Eds.), *Ecojustice, citizen science & youth activism: Situated tensions for science education.* Dordrecht, the Netherlands: Springer.

Çalik, M., & Coll, R.K. (2012). Investigating socioscientific issues via scientific habits of mind: Development and validation of the scientific habits of mind survey. *International Journal of Science Education, 34*(12), 1909–1930.

Chang, S.N., & Chiu, M.H. (2008). Lakatos' scientific research programmes as a framework for analysing informal argumentation about socio-scientific issues. *International Journal of Science Education, 30*(13), 1753–1773.

Choi, K., Lee, H., Shin, N., Kim, S., & Krajcik, J. (2011). Re-conceptualization of scientific literacy in South Korea for the 21st Century. *Journal of Research in Science Teaching, 48*(6), 670–697.

Colucci-Gray, L., Camino, E., Barbiero, G., & Gray, D. (2006). From scientific literacy to sustainability literacy: An ecological framework for education. *Science Education, 90,* 227–252.

Davis, M. (1999). *Ethics and the university.* London: Routledge.

Dawson, V., & Venville, G.J. (2009). High-school students' informal reasoning and argumentation about biotechnology: An indicator of scientific literacy? *International Journal of Science Education, 31,* 1421–1445.

Dawson, V.M., & Venville, G. (2010). Teaching strategies for developing students' argumentation skills about socioscientific issues in high school genetics. *Research in Science Education, 40*(2), 133–148.

Develaki, M. (2008). Social and ethical dimension of the natural sciences, complex problems of the age, interdisciplinarity, and the contribution of education. *Science & Education, 17,* 873–888.

Dolan, T.J., Nichols, B.H., & Zeidler, D.L. (2009). Using socioscientific issues in primary classrooms. *Journal of Elementary Science Teacher Education, 21*(3), 1–12.

Dori, Y.J., Tal, R.T., & Tsaushu, M. (2003). Learning and assessing biotechnology topics through case studies with built-in dilemmas. *Science Education, 87,* 767–793.

Eastwood, J.L., Sadler, T.D., Zeidler, D.L., Lewis, A., Amiri, L., & Applebaum, S. (2012). Contextualizing nature of science instruction in socioscientific issues. *International Journal of Science Education, 34*(15), 2289–2315.

Erduran, S., Simon, S., & Osborne, J. (2004). TAPping into argumentation: Developments in the application of Toulmin's argument pattern for studying science discourse. *Science & Education, 88*(6), 915–933.

Evagorou, M. (2011). Discussing a socioscientific issue in a primary school classroom: The case of using a technology-supported environment in formal and nonformal settings. In T.D. Sadler (Ed.), *Socio-scientific issues in science classrooms: Teaching, learning and research* (pp. 133–159). Dordrecht, the Netherlands: Springer.

Evans, J. St. B.T. (2003). Of two minds: Dual-process accounts of reasoning. *Trends in Cognitive Sciences, 7,* 454–459.

Falk, J. H., Storksdieck, M., & Dierking, L. D. (2007). Investigating public science interest and understanding: Evidence for the importance of free-choice learning. *Public Understanding of Science, 16*(4), 455–469.

Falk, J. H., & Heimlich, J. E. (2009). Who is the free-choice environmental education learner? In J. H. Falk, J. E. Heimlich, & S. Foutz (Ed.), *Free-choice learning and the environment* (pp. 23–38). Lanham MD, AltaMira Press.

Fensham, P.J. (1983). A research base for new objectives of science teaching. *Science Education, 67,* 3–12.

Fensham, P.J. (2009). Real world contexts in PISA science: Implications for context-based science education. *Journal of Research in Science Teaching, 46*(8), 884–896.

Fioravanti, C., & Velho, L. (2010). Let's follow the actors! Does actor-network theory have anything to contribute to science journalism? *Journal of Science Communication, 9*(4), 1–8.

Fischer-Mueller, J., & Zeidler, D.L. (2002). A case study of teacher beliefs in contemporary science education goals and classroom practices. *Science Educator, 11*(1), 46–57.

Fleming, R. (1986a). Adolescent reasoning in socio-scientific issues. Part I: Social cognition. *Journal of Research in Science Teaching, 23,* 677–687.

Fleming, R. (1986b). Adolescent reasoning in socio-scientific issues. Part II: Nonsocial cognition. *Journal of Research in Science Teaching, 23,* 689–698.

Forbes, C.T., & Davis, E.A. (2008). Exploring preservice elementary teachers' critique and adaptation of science curriculum materials in respect to socioscientific issues. *Science & Education, 17,* 829–854.

Fowler, S.R., Zeidler, D.L., & Sadler, T.D. (2009). Moral sensitivity in the context of socioscientific issues in high school science students. *International Journal of Science Teacher Education, 31*(2), 279–296.

Gaskell, P.J. (1982). Science, technology and society: Issues for science teachers. *Studies in Science Education, 9,* 33–46.

Gauch, Jr., H.G. (2009). Responses and clarification regarding science and worldviews. In Michael R. Matthews (Ed.), *Science, worldviews and education* (pp. 303–325). Dordrecht, the Netherlands: Springer.

Gauld, C.F. (2005). Habits of mind, scholarship and decision making in science and religion. *Science & Education, 14,* 291–308.

Grace, M.M., & Ratcliffe, M. (2002). The science and values that young people draw upon to make decisions about biological conservation issues. *International Journal of Science Education, 24*(11), 1157–1169.

Green, T.F. (1975). Perspectives on thinking about change: A study on the nature of policy thinking and the principles of moral education: Final report. Report for the Kettering Foundation Exploration Fund. Syracuse, NY: Center for Human Future.

Green, T.F. (1999). *Voices: The educational formation of conscience.* Notre Dame, IN: University of Notre Dame Press.

Halverson, K.L., Siegel, M.A., & Freyermuth, S.K. (2009). Lenses for framing decisions: Undergraduates' decision making about stem cell research. *International Journal of Science Education, 31*(9), 1249–1268.

Hanegan, N.L., Price, L., & Peterson, J. (2007). Disconnections between teacher expectations and students confidence in bioethics. *Science & Education, 17,* 921–940.

Hodson, D. (1999). Going beyond cultural pluralism: Science education for sociopolitical action. *Science Education, 83*(6), 775–796.

Hodson, D. (2003). Time for action: Science education for an alternative future. *International Journal of Science Education, 25*(6), 645–670.

Hodson, D. (2006). Why we should prioritize learning about science. *Canadian Journal of Science, Mathematics and Technology Education, 6*(3), 293–311.

Hodson, D. (2010). Science education as a call to action. *Canadian Journal of Science, Mathematics and Technology Education, 10*(3), 197–206.

Hogan, K. (2002). Small groups' ecological reasoning while making an environmental management decision. *Journal of Research in Science Teaching, 39,* 341–368.

Hughes, G. (2000). Marginalization of socioscientific material in science-technology-society science curricula: Some implications for gender inclusivity and curriculum reform. *Journal of Research in Science Teaching, 37*(5), 426–440.

Ibáñez-Orcajo, M. T., & Martínez-Aznar, M. M. (2007). Solving problems in genetics, part III: Change in the view of the nature of science. *International Journal of Science Education, 29*(6), 747–769.

Karrow, D., & Fazio, X. (2010). Educating-within-place: Care, citizen science, and ecojustice. In D. Tippins, M. Mueller, M. van Eijck, & J. Adams (Eds.), *Cultural studies and environmentalism: The confluence of ecojustice, place-based (science) education, and indigenous knowledge systems* (pp. 193–214). New York: Springer.

Khishfe, R. (2012a). Relationship between nature of science understandings and argumentation skills: A role for counterargument and contextual factors. *Journal of Research in Science Teaching, 49*(4), 489–514.

Khishfe, R. (2012b). Nature of science and decision-making. *International Journal of Science Education, 1*(1), 67–100.

Khishfe, R., & Lederman, N. (2006). Teaching nature of science within a controversial topic: Integrated versus non-integrated. *Journal of Research in Science Teaching, 43,* 395–318.

Khishfe, R., & Lederman, N. (2007). Relationship between instructional context and views of nature of science. *International Journal of Science Education, 29,* 939–961.

Kincheloe, J.L., & Tobin, K. (2009). The much exaggerated death of positivism. *Cultural Studies of Science Education, 4,* 513–528.

King, K., Shumow, L., & Lietz, S. (2001). Science education in an urban elementary school: Case studies of teacher beliefs and classroom practices. *Science Education, 85,* 89–110.

King, P.M., & Kitchener, K.S. (1994). *Developing reflective judgment: Understanding and promoting intellectual growth and critical thinking in adolescents and adults.* San Francisco: Jossey-Bass.

King, P.M., & Kitchener, K.S. (2002). The reflective judgment model: Twenty years of research on epistemic cognition. In B.K. Hofer & P.R. Pintrich (Eds.), *Personal epistemology: The psychology of beliefs about knowledge and knowing* (pp. 37–61). Mahwah, NJ: Lawrence Erlbaum Associates, Inc.

King, P.M., & Kitchener, K.S. (2004). Reflective judgment: Theory and research on the development of epistemic assumptions through adulthood. *Educational Psychologist, 39*(1), 5–18.

Klosterman, M.L., & Sadler, T.D. (2010). Multi-level assessment of scientific content knowledge gains associated with socioscientific issues-based instruction. *International Journal of Science Education, 32,* 1017–1043.

Klosterman, M.L., Sadler, T., & Brown, J. (2012). Science teachers' use of mass media to address socio-scientific and sustainability issues. *Research in Science Education, 42,* 51–74.

Kolstø, S.D. (2000). Consensus projects: Teaching science for citizenship. *International Journal of Science Education, 22*(6), 645–664.

Kolstø, S.D. (2001a). Scientific literacy for citizenship: Tools for dealing with the science dimension of controversial socioscientific issues. *Science Education, 85,* 291–310.

Kolstø, S.D. (2001b). "To trust or not to trust, . . ."—pupils' ways of judging information encountered in a socioscientific issue. *International Journal of Science Education, 23*(9), 877–901.

Kolstø, S.D. (2006). Patterns in students' argumentation confronted with a risk-focused socio-scientific issue. *International Journal of Science Education, 28,* 1689–1716.

Kolstø, S.D., Bungum, B., Arnesen, E., Isnes, A., Kristensen, T., Mathiassen, K., Mestad, I., Quale, A., Tonning, A.S.V., & Ulvik, M. (2006). Science students' critical examination of scientific information related to socioscientific issues. *Science Education, 90,* 632–655.

Kuhn, D. (1993). Science as argument: Implications for teaching and learning scientific thinking. *Science Education, 77,* 319–337.

Lakatos, I. (1970). The methodology of scientific research programmes. In I. Lakatos & A. Musgrave (Eds.), *Criticism and the growth of knowledge* (pp. 91–195). New York: Cambridge University Press.

Lakatos, I. (1978). *Falsification and the methodology of scientific research programmes.* New York: Cambridge University Press.

Latour, B. (2005). *Reassembling the social: An introduction to Actor-Network Theory.* Oxford, UK: Oxford University Press.

Lederman, N. G., Antink, A., & Bartos, S. (2014). Nature of science, scientific inquiry, and socio-scientific issues arising from genetics: A pathway to developing a scientifically literate citizenry. *Science & Education* 23(2), 285–302.

Lee, H., Abd-El-Khalick, F., & Choi, K. (2006). Korean science teachers' perceptions of the introduction of socioscientific issues into the science curriculum. *Canadian Journal of Science, Mathematics and Technology Education, 6*(2), 97–117.

Lee, H., Chang, H., Choi, K., Kim, S. W., & Zeidler, D. L. (2012). Developing character and values for global citizens: Analysis of pre-service science teachers' moral reasoning on socioscientific issues. *International Journal of Science Education, 34*(6), 925–953.

Lee, H., & Witz, K. G. (2009). Science teachers' inspiration for teaching socio-scientific issues: Disconnection with reform efforts. *International Journal of Science Education, 31,* 931–960.

Lee, H., Yoo, J., Choi, K., Kim, S., Krajcik, J., Herman, B., & Zeidler, D. L. (2013). Socioscientific issues as a vehicle for promoting character and values for global citizens. *International Journal of Science Education, 35*(12), 2079–2113.

Lee, S., & Roth, W. M. (2003). Of traversals and hybrid spaces: Science in the community. *Mind, Culture, & Activity, 10,* 120–142.

Lee, Y. C. (2007). Developing decision-making skills for socio-scientific issues. *Journal of Biological Education, 41,* 170–177.

Lee, Y. C. (2008). Exploring the roles and nature of science: A case study of severe acute respiratory syndrome. *International Journal of Science Education, 30*(4), 515–541.

Lemke, J. L. (2001). Articulating communities: Sociocultural perspectives on science education. *Journal of Research in Science Teaching, 38*(3), 296–316.

Lester, B. T., Ma, L., Lee, O., & Lambert J. (2006). Social activism in elementary science education: A science, technology, and society approach to teacher global warming. *International Journal of Science Education, 28*(4), 315–339.

Levinson, R. (2006). Towards a theoretical framework for teaching controversial socio-scientific issues. *International Journal of Science Education, 8,* 1201–1224.

Levinson, R. (2008). Promoting the role of the personal narrative in teaching controversial socio-scientific issues. *Science & Education, 17,* 855–871.

Levinson, R. (2013). Practice and theory of socio-scientific issues: An authentic model? *Studies in Science Education, 49*(1), 99–116.

Levinson, R., & Turner, S. (2001). *Valuable lessons: Engaging with the social context of science in schools.* London: The Wellcome Trust.

Lewis, J., & Leach, J. (2006). Discussion of socio-scientific issues: The role of science knowledge. *International Journal of Science Education, 28,* 1267–1287.

Linn, M. C., Clark, D., & Slotta, J. D. (2003). WISE design for knowledge integration. *Science Education, 87*(4), 517–538.

Linn, M. C., Eylon, B., & Davis, E. A. (2004). The knowledge integration perspective on learning. In M. Linn, E. Davis, & P. Bell (Eds.), *Internet environments for science education* (pp. 29–46). Hillsdale, NJ: Lawrence Erlbaum Associates.

Linn, M. C., Lee, H.-S., Tinker, R., Husic, F., & Chiu, J. L. (2006). Teaching and assessing knowledge integrations in science. *Science Education, 313,* 1049–1050.

Liu, S. Y., Lin, C. S., & Tsai, C. C. (2011). College students' scientific epistemological views and thinking patterns in socioscientific decision making. *Science Education, 95,* 497–517.

Lyons, T. (2006). Different countries, same science classes. Students' experiences of school science in their own words. *International Journal of Science Education, 28,* 591–613.

Matkins, J. J., & Bell, R. L. (2007). Awakening the scientist inside: Global climate change and the nature of science in an elementary science methods course. *Journal of Science Teacher Education, 18,* 137–163.

Matthews, M. R. (2009). Teaching the philosophical and worldview components of science. *Science & Education, 18*(6–7), 697–728.

McLaughlin, T. (2003). Teaching controversial issues in citizenship education. In A. Lockyer, B. Crick, & J. Annette (Eds.), *Education for democratic citizenship* (pp. 149–160). Ashgate, UK: Aldershot.

Melville, W., Yaxley, B., & Wallace, J. (2007). Virtues, teacher professional expertise, and socioscientific issues. *Canadian Journal of Environmental Education, 12,* 95–109.

Moore, W. S. (1989). The "learning environment preferences": Exploring the construct validity of an objective measure of the Perry scheme of intellectual development. *Journal of College Student Development, 30,* 504–514.

Mueller, M. (2008). EcoJustice as ecological literacy is much more than being "green!" *Educational Studies, 44,* 155–166.

Mueller, M. P. (2009). Educational reflections on the "ecological crisis": Ecojustice, environmentalism and sustainability. *Science & Education, 18,* 1031–1056.

Mueller, M. P., & Tippins, D. J. (2010). The need for confluence: Why a "river" runs through it. In D. Tippins, M. Mueller, M. van Eijck, & J. Adams (Eds.), *Cultural studies and environmentalism: The confluence of ecojustice, place-based (science) education, and indigenous knowledge systems* (pp. 1–4). New York: Springer.

Mueller, M. P., & Zeidler, D. L. (2010). Moral-ethical character and science education: Ecojustice ethics through socioscientific issues (SSI). In D. Tippins, M. Mueller, M. van Eijck, & J. Adams (Eds.), *Cultural studies and environmentalism: The confluence of ecojustice, place-based (science) education, and indigenous knowledge systems* (pp. 105–128). New York: Springer.

Mueller, M. P., Zeidler, D. L., & Jenkins, L. L. (2011). Earth's role in moral reasoning and functional scientific literacy. In J. L. DeVitis & T. Yu (Eds.), *Character and moral education: A reader* (pp. 382–391). New York: Peter Lang.

Nielsen, J. A. (2012). Science in discussions: An analysis of the use of science content in socioscientific discussions. *Science Education, 96,* 428–456.

Nuangchalerm, P. (2009). Development of socioscientific issues-base teaching for preservice teachers. *Journal of Social Sciences, 5*(3), 239–243.

Nuangchalerm, P. (2010). Engaging students to perceive nature of science through socioscientific issues-based instruction. *European Journal of Social Sciences, 13*(1), 34–37.

Orpwood, G. W. F., & Roberts, D. A. (1980). Science and society: Dimensions for science education for the '80s. *Orbit, 51,* 21–25.

Osborne, J., Erduran, S., & Simon, S. (2004). Enhancing the quality of argumentation in school science. *Journal or Research in Science Teaching, 41,* 994–1020.

Östman, L., & Almqvist, J. (2011). What do values and norms have to do with scientific literacy? In C. Linder, L. Östman, D. A., Roberts, P., Wickman, G., Erickson, & A. MacKinnon (Eds.), *Promoting scientific literacy: Science education research in transaction* (pp. 160–173). New York: Routledge/Taylor & Francis Group.

Patronis, T., Potari, D., & Spiliotopoulou, V. (1999). Students' argumentation in decision-making on a socio-scientific issue: Implications for teaching. *International Journal of Science Education, 21,* 745–754.

Pea, R., & Collins, A. (2008). Learning how to do science education: Four waves of reform. In Y. Kali, M. C. Linn, & J. E. Roseman (Eds.), *Designing coherent science education: Implications for curriculum, instruction, and policy* (pp. 3–12). New York: Teachers College Press.

Pedretti, E. (2003). Teaching science, technology, society and environment (STSE) education: Preservice teachers' philosophical and pedagogical landscapes. In D. L. Zeidler (Ed.), *The role of moral reasoning on socioscientific issues and discourse in science education* (pp. 219–239). Dordrecht, the Netherlands: Kluwer Academic Press.

Pedretti, E. G., Bencze, J. L., Hewitt, J., Romkey, L., & Jivraj, A. (2007). Promoting issues-based STSE perspectives in science teacher education: Problems of identity and ideology. *Science & Education, 17,* 941–960.

Perry, W. G. (1970). *Forms of intellectual and ethical development in the college years.* San Francisco: Jossey-Bass.

Pouliot, C. (2009). Using the deficit model, public debate model and co-production of knowledge models to interpret point of view of students concerning citizens' participation in socioscientific issues. *International Journal of Environmental & Science Education, 4*(1), 49–73.

Ratcliffe, M. (1997). Pupil decision-making about socio-scientific issues within the science curriculum. *International Journal of Science Education, 19*(2), 167–182.

Ratcliffe, M., & Grace, M. (2003). *Science education for citizenship: Teaching socio-scientific issues.* Buckingham, UK: Open University Press.

Ratcliffe, M., & Millar, R. (2009). Teaching for understanding of science in context: Evidence from the pilot trials of the twenty first century science courses. *Journal of Research in Science Teaching, 46*(8), 945–959.

Reiss, M. (1999). Teaching ethics in science. *Studies in Science Education, 34,* 115–140.

Reiss, M. (2003). Science education for social justice. In C. Vincent (Ed.), *Social justice education and identity* (pp. 153–164). London: RoutledgeFalmer.

Reiss, M. (2008). The use of ethical frameworks by students following a new science course for 16–18 year-olds. *Science & Education, 17,* 889–902.

Roberts, D. A. (2007). Scientific literacy/science literacy. In S. K. Abell & N. G. Lederman (Eds.), *Handbook of research on science education* (pp. 729–780). Mahwah, NJ: Lawrence Erlbaum Associates.

Roberts, D. A. (2011). Competing visions of scientific literacy: The influence of a science curriculum policy image. In C. Linder, L. Östman, D. A. Roberts, P. Wickman, G. Erickson, & A. MacKinnon (Eds.), *Promoting scientific literacy: Science education research in transaction* (pp. 11–27). New York: Routledge/Taylor & Francis Group.

Roszak, T. (1968). *The making of a counter culture: Reflection on the technocratic society and its youthful opposition.* New York: Anchor Books.

Roth, W.-M., & Désautels, J. (2004). Educating for citizenship: Reappraising the role of science education. *Canadian Journal of Science, Mathematics and Technology Education, 4*(2), 149–168.

Roth, W.-M., & Lee, S. (2004). Science education as/for participation in the community. *Science Education, 88*(2), 263–294.

Sadler, T. D. (2004a). Informal reasoning regarding socioscientific issues: A critical review of the research. *Journal of Research in Science Teaching, 41*(5), 513–536.

Sadler, T. D. (2004b). Moral and ethical dimensions of socioscientific decision-making as integral components of scientific literacy. *Science Educator, 13,* 39–48.

Sadler, T. D. (2004c). Moral sensitivity and its contribution to the resolution of socio-scientific issues. *Journal of Moral Education, 33*(3), 339–358.

Sadler, T. D. (2004d). Moral and ethical dimensions of socioscientific decision-making as integral components of scientific literacy. *The Science Educator, 13,* 39–48.

Sadler, T. D. (2005). Evolutionary theory as a guide to socioscientific decision-making. *Journal of Biological Education, 39*(2), 68–72.

Sadler, T. D. (2009). Situated learning in science education: Socio-scientific issues as contexts for practice. *Studies in Science Education, 45*(1), 1–42.

Sadler, T. D. (2011). Situating socio-scientific issues in classrooms as a means of achieving goals of science education. In T. D. Sadler (Ed.), *Socio-scientific issues in science classrooms: Teaching, learning and research* (pp. 1–9). Dordrecht, the Netherlands: Springer.

Sadler, T. D., Amirshokoohi, A., Kazempour, M., & Allspaw, K. M. (2006). Socioscience and ethics in science classrooms: Teacher perspectives and strategies. *Journal of Research in Science Teaching, 43,* 353–376.

Sadler, T. D., Barab, S. A., & Scott, B. (2007). What do students gain by engaging in socioscientific inquiry? *Research in Science Education, 37*(4), 371–391.

Sadler, T. D., Chambers, F. W., & Zeidler, D. L. (2004). Student conceptualizations of the nature of science in response to a socio-scientific issue. *International Journal of Science Education, 26,* 387–409.

Sadler, T. D., & Donnelly, L. A. (2006). Socioscientific argumentation: The effects of content knowledge and morality. *International Journal of Science Education, 28,* 1463–1488.

Sadler, T. D., & Fowler, S. R. (2006). A threshold model of content knowledge transfer for socioscientific argumentation. *Science Education, 90*(6), 986–1004.

Sadler, T. D., Klosterman, M. L., & Topcu, M. S. (2011). Learning science content and socio-scientific reasoning through classroom explorations of global climate change. In T. D. Sadler (Ed.), *Socio-scientific issues in science classrooms: Teaching, learning and research* (pp. 45–77). Dordrecht, the Netherlands: Springer.

Sadler, T. D., & Zeidler, D. L. (2004). The morality of socioscientific issues: Construal and resolution of genetic engineering dilemmas. *Science Education, 88*(1), 4–27.

Sadler, T. D., & Zeidler, D. L. (2005a). Patterns of informal reasoning in the context of socioscientific decision-making. *Journal of Research in Science Teaching, 42*(1), 112–138.

Sadler, T. D., & Zeidler, D. L. (2005b). The significance of content knowledge for informal reasoning regarding socioscientific issues: Applying genetics knowledge to genetic engineering issues. *Science Education, 89*(1), 71–93.

Sadler, T. D., & Zeidler, D. L. (2009). Scientific literacy, PISA, and socioscientific discourse: Assessment for progressive aims of science education. *Journal of Research in Science Teaching, 46*(8), 909–921.

Santos, W. L. P. dos. (2009). Scientific literacy: A Freirean perspective as a radical view of humanistic science Education. *Science Education, 93,* 361–382.

Saunders, K. J., & Rennie, L. J. (2013). A pedagogical model for ethical inquiry into socioscientific issues in science. *Research in Science Education, 43,* 253–274.

Schommer-Aikins, M., & Hutter, R. (2002). Epistemological beliefs and thinking about everyday controversial issues. *Journal of Psychology, 136*(1), 5–20.

Seethaler, S., & Linn, M. (2004). Genetically modified food in perspective: An inquiry-based curriculum to help middle school students make sense of tradeoffs. *International Journal of Science Education, 26*(14), 1765–1785.

Serpell, R. (2011). Social responsibility as a dimension of intelligence, and as an educational goal: Insights from programmatic research in an African society. *Child Development Perspectives, 5*(2), 126–133.

Sharma, A. (2010). Working for change: Reflections on the issue of sustainability and social change. In D. Tippins, M. Mueller, M. van Eijck, & J. Adams (Eds.), *Cultural studies and environmentalism: The confluence of ecojustice, place-based (science) education, and indigenous knowledge systems* (pp. 171–179). New York: Springer.

Simon, S., & Amos, R. (2011). Decision making and use of evidence in a socio-scientific problem on air quality. In T. D. Sadler (Ed.), *Socio-scientific issues in the classroom* (Vol. 39, pp. 167–192). Dordrecht, the Netherlands: Springer.

Simonneaux, L. (2008). Argumentation in socio-scientific contexts. In S. Erduran & M. P. Jiménez-Aleixandre (Eds.), *Argumentation in science education: Perspectives from classroom-based research* (pp. 179–199). Dordrecht, the Netherlands: Springer.

Simonneaux, J., & Simonneaux, L. (2012). Educational configurations for teaching environmental socioscientific issues within the perspective of sustainability. *Research in Science Education, 42,* 75–94.

Slotta, J.D., & Linn, M.C. (2009). *WISE science.* New York: Teachers' College Press.

Smith, G. A., & Williams, D. R. (Eds.). (1999). *Ecological education in action: On weaving education, culture, and the environment.* Albany: State University of New York Press.

Sperling, E., & Bencze, J.L. (2010). "More than particle theory": Citizenship through school science. *Canadian Journal of Science, Mathematics and Technology Education, 10*(3), 255–26.

Sternäng, L., & Lundholm, C. (2011). Climate change and morality: Students' perspectives on the individual and society. *International Journal of Science Education, 33*(8), 1131–1148.

Tal, R., & Hochberg, N. (2003). Reasoning, problem-solving and reflections: Participating in WISE project in Israel. *Science Education International, 14,* 3–19.

Tal, T., Kali, Y., Magid, M., & Madhok, J.J. (2011). Enhancing the authenticity of a web-based module for teaching simple inheritance. In T.D. Sadler (Ed.), *Socio-scientific issues in science classrooms: Teaching, learning and research* (pp. 11–38). Dordrecht, the Netherlands: Springer.

Tal, T., & Kedmi, Y. (2006). Teaching socioscientific issues: Classroom culture and students' performances. *Cultural Studies of Science Education, 1*(4), 615–644.

Tippins, D.J., Mueller, M.P., van Eijck, M., & Adams, J. (Eds.). (2010). *Cultural studies and environmentalism: The confluence of ecojustice, place-based (science) education, and indigenous knowledge systems.* Dordrecht, the Netherlands: Springer.

Topcu, M.S., Sadler, T.D., & Yilmaz-Tuzun, O. (2010). Preservice science teachers' informal reasoning about socioscientific issues: The influence of issue context. *International Journal of Science Education, 32,* 2475–2495.

Toulmin, S.E. (1958). *The uses of argument.* Cambridge, UK: Cambridge University Press.

Tsai, C.-C., & Liu, S.-Y. (2005). Developing a postdimensional instrument for assessing students' epistemological views toward science. *International Journal of Science Education, 27,* 1621–1638.

Tytler, R. (2012). Socio-scientific issues, sustainability and science education. *Research in Science Education, 42,* 155–163.

Tytler, R., Duggan, S., & Gott, R. (2001). Dimensions of evidence, the public understanding of science and science education. *International Journal of Science Education, 23,* 815–832.

UNESCO. (2012). Education for sustainable development (ESD). Retrieved December 6, 2012 from www.inruled.org/en/research/themes/a25999.html

van Eemeren, F.H., & Houtlosser, P. (2007). The study of argumentation as normative pragmatics. *Pragmatics: Quarterly Publication of the International Pragmatics Association, 15*(1), 161–177.

Walker, K.A., & Zeidler, D.L. (2007). Promoting discourse about socioscientific issues through scaffolded inquiry. *International Journal of Science Education, 29,* 1387–1410.

Wongsri, P., & Nuangchalerm, P. (2010). Learning outcomes between socioscientific issues-based learning and conventional learning activities. *Journal of Social Sciences, 6*(2), 240–243.

Wu, Y.T., & Tsai, C.C. (2007). High school students' informal reasoning on a socio-scientific issues: Qualitative and quantitative analyses. *International Journal of Science Education, 29,* 1163–1187.

Wu, Y.T., & Tsai, C.C. (2011). High school students' informal reasoning regarding a socio-scientific issue, with relation to scientific epistemological beliefs and cognitive structures. *International Journal of Science Education, 33*(3), 371–400.

Yang, F.-Y. (2005). Student views concerning evidence and the expert in reasoning a socio-scientific issue and personal epistemology. *Educational Studies, 31*(1), 65–84.

Zandvliet, D., & Fisher, D.L. (2007). *Sustainable communities, sustainable environments.* Rotterdam, the Netherlands: Sense Publishers.

Zeidler, D.L. (1984). Moral issues and social policy in science education: Closing the literacy gap. *Science Education, 68*(4), 411–419.

Zeidler, D.L. (1985). Hierarchical relationships among formal cognitive structures and their relationship to principled moral reasoning. *Journal of Research in Science Teaching, 22*(5), 461–471.

Zeidler, D.L. (1997). The central role of fallacious thinking in science education. *Science Education, 81*(4), 483–496.

Zeidler, D.L. (2001). Standard F: Participating in program development. In E. Siebert & W. McIntosh (Eds.), *Pathways to the science standards: College edition* (pp. 18–22). Arlington: VA National Science Teachers Association.

Zeidler, D.L. (2002). Dancing with maggots and saints: Past and future visions for subject matter knowledge, pedagogical knowledge, and pedagogical content knowledge in reform and science teacher education. *Journal of Science Teacher Education, 13*(1), 27–42.

Zeidler, D.L. (in-press). STEM education: A deficit framework for the 21st century? A sociocultural socioscientific response. *Cultural Studies in Science Education.*

Zeidler, D.L., Applebaum, S.M., & Sadler, T.D. (2011). Enacting a socioscientific issues classroom: Transformative transformations. In T.D. Sadler (Ed.), *Socio-scientific issues in science classrooms: Teaching, learning and research* (pp. 277–306). Dordrecht, the Netherlands: Springer.

Zeidler, D.L., Berkowitz, M., & Bennett, K. (2014). Thinking (scientifically) responsibly: The cultivation of character in a global science education community. In M.P. Mueller, D.J. Tippins, & A.J. Steward (Eds.), *Assessing schools for generation R (Responsibility): A guide to legislation and school policy in science education* (pp. 83–99). Dordrecht, the Netherlands: Springer.

Zeidler, D.L., Herman, B., Ruzek, M., Linder, A., & Lin, S.S. (2013). Cross-cultural epistemological orientations to socioscientific issues. *Journal of Research in Science Teaching, 50*(3), 251–283.

Zeidler, D.L., & Keefer, M. (2003). The role of moral reasoning and the status of socioscientific issues in science education: Philosophical, psychological and pedagogical considerations. In D.L. Zeidler (Ed.), *The role of moral reasoning on socioscientific issues and discourse in science education* (pp. 7–38). Dordrecht, the Netherlands: Kluwer Academic Press.

Zeidler, D.L., Lederman, N.G., & Taylor, S.C. (1992). Fallacies and student discourse: Conceptualizing the role of critical thinking in science education. *Science Education, 75*(4), 437–450.

Zeidler, D.L., & Lewis, J. (2003). Unifying themes in moral reasoning on socioscientific issues and discourse. In D.L. Zeidler (Ed.), *The role of moral reasoning on socioscientific issues and discourse in science education* (pp. 289–306). Dordrecht, the Netherlands: Kluwer Academic Press.

Zeidler, D.L., & Nichols, B.H. (2009). Socioscientific issues: Theory and practice. *Journal of Elementary Science Teacher Education, 21*(2), 49–58.

Zeidler, D.L., Osborne, J., Erduran, S., Simon, S., & Monk, M. (2003). The role of argument and fallacies during discourse about socioscientific issues. In D.L. Zeidler (Ed.), *The role of moral reasoning on socioscientific issues and discourse in science education* (pp. 97–116). Dordrecht, the Netherlands: Kluwer Academic Press.

Zeidler, D.L., & Sadler, T.D. (2008a). The role of moral reasoning in argumentation: Conscience, character and care. In S. Erduran & M. Pilar Jiménez-Aleixandre (Eds.), *Argumentation in science education: Perspectives from classroom-based research* (pp. 201–216). Dordrecht, the Netherlands: Springer Press.

Zeidler, D.L., & Sadler, T.D. (2008b). Social and ethical issues in science education: A prelude to action. *Science & Education, 17*(8, 9), 799–803.

Zeidler, D. L., & Sadler, D.L. (2011). An inclusive view of scientific literacy: Core issues and future directions of socioscientific reasoning. In C. Linder, L. Östman, D. A. Roberts, P. Wickman, G. Erickson, & A. MacKinnon (Eds.), *Promoting scientific literacy: Science education research in transaction* (pp. 176–192). New York: Routledge/Taylor & Francis Group.

Zeidler, D.L., Sadler, T.D., Applebaum, S., & Callahan, B.E. (2009). Advancing reflective judgment through socio-scientific issues. *Journal of Research in Science Teaching, 46,* 74–101.

Zeidler, D.L., Sadler, T.D., Simmons, M.L., & Howes, E.V. (2005). Beyond STS: A research-based framework for socioscientific issues education. *Science Education, 89*(3), 357–377.

Zeidler, D.L., & Schafer, L.E. (1984). Identifying mediating factors of moral reasoning in science education. *Journal of Research in Science Teaching, 21*(1), 1–15.

Zeidler, D.L., Walker, K.A., Ackett, W.A., & Simmons, M.L. (2002). Tangled up in views: Beliefs in the nature of science and responses to socio-scientific dilemmas. *Science Education, 86,* 343–367.

35

Project Assessment

Its History, Evolution, and Current Practice

SARAH BETH WOODRUFF AND JANE BUTLER KAHLE

Part 1: Reimagining the Evaluation and Assessment of Systemic Reform

Since the 1980s, systemic reform has been widely accepted as a meritorious approach to improving K–12 science education (Clune, Porter, & Raizen, 1999). Further, different waves of systemic reform have targeted particular aspects of the science education system that have had critical impact at each level—for example, assessment systems, accountability systems, systems of standards, and governance systems (Slavin, 2005). For this discussion, it will be helpful to conceive of the *system of science education* as both a horizontal and vertical arrangement of interconnected components and subsystems. For example, a horizontal systemic reform might address elementary science in all schools in a district. On the other hand, a vertical systemic effort might target teachers' knowledge of physical sciences in all school buildings and districts, within the purview of a state system of education. These systems are embedded in a national system of education that has increasingly influenced education policy and practice at all levels.

As noted by Supovitz and Taylor (2005), systemic education reform aims at broad-scale improvement in teaching and learning through the introduction of multifaceted, mutually reinforcing changes in the system. Elmore (1996) points out that the problem of systemic reform is primarily one of scale—in other words, the ability of systemic change to result in improved student performance ultimately is determined by the extent to which the reform reaches teachers' classrooms. While more than half a century of science education reform has resulted in greater coherence among system components and stronger alignment across levels of the education system—national, state, and local—improvement in student science performance has been less than satisfying.

Also at issue is how systemic education reform can be assessed at scale. As systemic reform efforts have proliferated, three general approaches to evaluating systemic initiatives have been applied (Chatterji, 2002; Supovitz & Taylor, 2005). Two of these three approaches, (a) examining a particular component of the system and (b) decomposing key components for individual examination, cannot capture the complexity and coherence of a systemic initiative. Further, Chatterji (2002) argues that these narrow and nonsystemic evaluation efforts have not provided schools, school systems, or states with information for strategic decision making. The third approach to systemic evaluation, which is closely associated with theory-based evaluation,[1] requires close examination of relevant components of the system simultaneously. Arguably, the capacity of evaluation to assess reform is greater in systems that are more local, though not necessarily less complex. For this reason and others, local assessment of projects has been encouraged and, in many cases, required by funders as a method to measure the impact of systemic reform.

Contributions of First Three Waves of Systemic Reform

Wave 1: Texts and Teaching. Although the term "systemic reform" was not used in the 1960s and 1970s, the United States embarked on large-scale reform efforts that addressed two major components of the education system, texts and teaching. These two aspects of the education system were viewed both educationally and politically as weaknesses (Dow, 1999; Nelkin, 1977; Office of Technology Assessment [OTA], 1988). Both reform efforts substantively changed science education, and the synergy between the two enhanced their separate effects. The reforms of the 1960s and 1970s were national in scope; they reflected a shared vision of improved science education, and they were driven by an urgent political need to educate a scientific and technical workforce. The curricular efforts focused on updating and improving the curricular materials used by students and resulted in improved content knowledge. The professional development for teachers also was focused on improving content knowledge and, to a lesser extent, enhancing instructional skills. One of the enduring effects of the teacher effort was enhanced teacher professionalism and autonomy (OTA, 1988; Sahlberg, 2006). Funding for curricular reform and teacher training continues today, with allocations consistently tied to political assessments of national, competitive science and technological advantage (Schneider & Keesler, 2007).

As research has documented (Dow, 1999; Nelkin, 1977; OTA, 1988), the vision of improved curricula in the first wave of reform was compromised by several political and educational realities. Research concerning the effectiveness of new curricula was seriously compromised by the lack of independent tests aligned with the goals of the curricula. Further, although the first wave of reform addressed two major components of the education system—texts and teaching—the politics of the day prevented articulation between those two massive efforts to improve science education systemically, and each effort was weakened by that reality. In retrospect, there is a considerable body of research suggesting that the new curricula improved both student attitudes and achievement (Kahle, 2004; Kahle & Woodruff, 2011). However, there is little evidence of the effect of the Teacher Training Institutes on either classroom practice or student achievement (OTA, 1988). As mentioned earlier, positive gains from the institutes were identified primarily by changes in the science teaching profession (OTA, 1988; Sahlberg, 2006).

Wave 2: Courses and Competencies. During the decade of the 1980s, U.S. schools embarked on one of the most widespread school reform efforts in history (Finn, 2002; Murphy, 1991 in Schneider & Keesler, 2007). For example, Toch (1991) estimated that more than 3,000 separate school reform measures were enacted during that decade. Efforts focused on raising achievement via more strict regulation, increasing science graduation requirements, and implementing standardized assessments.

Although it is arguable whether the second wave of reform was truly systemic, scholars have identified it as a time of major educational change. During the 1980s, two issues were paramount in affecting large-scale education reforms. First, states increased graduation requirements in mathematics and science while simultaneously limiting the types of courses that could be used to meet those requirements. Second, states began to institute high-stakes tests of students' skills and knowledge. However, as noted in one report, mandates of the 1980s did little

> to change the content of instruction (especially its focus on basic skills) or to alter the reigning notions of teaching and learning because, as some argued, fragmented and contradictory policies diverted teachers' attention and provided little or no support for the type of professional learning necessary.
>
> (Goertz, Floden, & O'Day, 1996, p. xi)

Further during this period, heightened external regulation of schools decreased the autonomy of teachers while increasing the influence of standards on teacher practice (Hargreaves & Goodson, 2006; Sahlberg, 2006).

As the decade drew to a close, the concept of a systemic approach to reforming science and mathematics education began to emerge in the literature (Horizon Research, Inc., 1994). Reform programs previously referred to as *comprehensive* were considered less extensive, and researchers and policy makers began to define ways in which reform could address an entire educational system.

Wave 3: Excellence and Equity. At the end of the 1980s, publication of standards in mathematics (National Council of Teachers of Mathematics [NCTA], 1989) and in science (American Association for the Advancement of Science [AAAS], 1993; National Research Council [NRC], 1996) required systemic reformers to balance the values of excellence and equity. Further, the decade of the 1990s introduced the nomenclature of systemic reform through broad and systematic programs initiated by the National Science Foundation (NSF). While Smith and O'Day (1991) described systemic reform as a state-level conceptual framework, the concept was applied to states, school districts, and individual school buildings, all of which represent systems of varying complexity. In its different iterations, systemic reform of science education targeted different levels of the education system as well as specific aspects of the system that intersect with each level. From 1991 to 2001, the NSF supported systemic reform of science and mathematics education at the state level (Statewide Systemic Initiatives, SSI), the school system level (Urban Systemic Initiatives, USI), the regional level (Rural Systemic Initiatives, RSI), and the school-building level (Local Systemic Change, LSC).[2] What these reforms had in common was the intent to affect everything influencing an educational *system*; however, the *system* was delimited (National Science Foundation [NSF], 2004).

As Heck (1998) notes, "Equity, as NSF has conceived it . . . is not a concept reserved for the traditionally underserved and underachieving groups" (p. 169). Rather, the entire system should change so that all children are able to reach their full potential. The NSF systemic initiatives were designed to improve all parts of the targeted education system; in so doing, it was assumed that changes would enhance student achievement in science and mathematics (Weiss & Webb, 2003). The proliferation of science courses in the 1980s may have contributed to academic tracking—the antithesis of equity. Therefore, the elimination of tracking was one of the goals of NSF's systemic initiative programs (i.e., SSI, USI, RSI, LSC), and it nearly single-handedly drove science education reform efforts in the 1990s (Kahle, 2007).

Concomitant with NSF's systemic reform efforts, the U.S. Department of Education proposed the No Child Left Behind (NCLB) legislation, which received bipartisan political support and which also focused on equity among schools and student groups. The No Child Left Behind Act of 2001 held public schools accountable for ensuring that all students met proficiency levels and made adequate yearly progress toward standardized learning goals (U.S. Department of Education [USDOE], 2002).

Although much can be learned from the multiple and broad-scale evaluations conducted during the third wave of reform, research concerning this wave is somewhat elusive. The published literature is mixed, concerning achievement of the dual goals of excellence and equity.[3] The extensive NSF evaluations of its systemic initiative programs as well as emerging research studies suggest that the overall goal of excellence (as defined by improved student achievement) largely was not reached (Laguarda, 1998; Zucker & Shields, 1997; Zucker, Shields, Adelman, & Powell, 1995). Individual research studies as well as case studies of selected systemic initiative projects, however, provide indications that the reforms of the 1990s strove for excellence and achieved it, albeit in small increments at various parts of the educational system (Kahle, Meece, & Scantlebury, 2000; Laguarda, 1998; Supovitz, 1996).

Education reforms of the last 20 years have increasingly emphasized the education system as the unit of change. Therefore, they have sought to align and promote coherence among components within the education system, though *system* has been defined at different grain sizes. Two lessons relevant to this chapter have been learned. First, local context is important. McLaughlin (1990) reviewed a RAND study of 293 projects conducted in 18 states, all of which received significant federal funds. He found that success depended primarily on local factors, not federal guidelines or funding levels. Second, he found that successful efforts shared a number of characteristics, such as commitment of district leadership, project's scope, and project's implementation strategy (McLaughlin, 1990). Those characteristics appeared to contribute to the success of initiatives as well as to their sustainability (Carpenter, et al., 2004; Goertz et al., 1996). Systemic reform across the last half century has focused on changes at both local and state levels. Success has come (in terms of student outcomes) when it has been guided by a vision and supported by politics of the day. Evaluation and research across the past 50 years have probed to understand systemic reform, to develop models to guide it, and to provide findings to support it.

Beyond Wave Three: What Is Systemic Reform Today?

Hargreaves and Goodson (2006) describe the current approach to systemic reform, taking hold in the late 1990s, as one of standardization and performance accountability. This phase of reform continues to be driven by NCLB mandates, but its target and associated rhetoric have shifted from arguments for equity to a central focus on economic competitiveness. Likewise, performance accountability, measured by scientific evidence, is touted to result in excellence (Sahlberg, 2006).

The vision of the current wave of systemic reform has been changed dramatically by the politics of the new century, which renewed the nation's focus on the contributions of science education to economic competitiveness (Bybee & Fuchs, 2006; Sahlberg, 2006). Science education is inescapably linked to the national need for education reform to serve an increasingly knowledge-based economy and to educate future innovators. Schneider and Keesler (2007) observe that the typical political response to strengthening U.S. competitiveness is to target resources for training the future science and technology workforce. What has changed over time is the extent to which the education system is held accountable for its contributions to U.S. economic competitiveness. That is, student performance and how to increase that performance are of paramount interest to policy makers and the public.

What Apple (2001) and Sahlberg (2006) described as the "marketization of education" theorizes that standardization and consequential accountability will improve the quality and effectiveness of teaching and learning, when productivity, effectiveness, accountability, and competitiveness are the drivers of education reform (Sahlberg, 2006, p. 262). At the national policy level, NCLB–initiated reforms aim to consolidate systemic alignment of state and federal education policies and standards. While its mechanisms are those of the economic market, its successful implementation depends nearly exclusively on local efforts to establish and achieve clear and compelling targets for improvement (Knapp, 2008 in Spicer, 2012). In order to merge these two seemingly incongruent ideas, education reform has shifted focus from Smith and O'Day's (1991) conceptualization of systemic reform as broad-scale change (i.e., changes in assessment, accountability, standards, and governance) to what Slavin (2005) describes as a bottom-up approach that involves designing ambitious models at the school level and building networks of technical assistance for schools undergoing reform. In addition, support is required in order to replicate effective models in other contexts. Five decades of systemic reform efforts have produced a number of positive outcomes for science teachers, their students, and schools largely through states establishing more clear policies to guide schools, including more rigorous expectations for students' performance and matriculation; aligned systems of assessments; uniform academic content standards; and higher standards for teacher licensure. Yet student science performance outcomes have improved very little given the investment of resources.[4] Of equal concern, U.S. schools have not succeeded in moving more students and a more diverse group of students into the scientific and technological workforce. NCLB supports standards-based education reform based on the premise that setting high standards and establishing measurable goals can improve individual outcomes in education. Most states have complied with NCLB mandates to develop and implement academic content standards, to measure student achievement through periodic testing and tracking yearly progress, and to require higher teacher qualifications. However, the quality of each state's implementation of NCLB provisions is variable, and results are not as positive as expected

(Dee & Jacob, 2011; Kroger, Campbell, Thacker, Becker, & Wise, 2007; Thomas B. Fordham Foundation, 2012). Sahlberg (2006), Hershberg (2005), and others observe that broad-scale education reforms, such as those promoted by NCLB, are insufficient to produce positive changes in what teachers and students do in schools. In fact, Anderson (2011) has found that test-based accountability policies, in particular, frequently correlate with negative changes in teacher instructional practice (i.e., discourage inquiry-based instruction), reduce the amount of science taught, and lessen teacher satisfaction with their instruction. The preponderance of evidence suggests that large-scale, systemic reform has little (positive) impact on teachers' classroom practice (Elmore, 1993, 1996; Hess, 1999). Even if impacts exist, large-scale evaluations of those reforms would likely fail to measure change in classroom practice or to establish a link between outcomes and reform efforts (Shavelson & Towne, 2002; Weiss, 2000).

Revisiting our representation of the system of science education as both a horizontal and a vertical arrangement of components and subsystems, we posit that the school or school district has become the new target of systemic reform. The remainder of this chapter will focus on the assessment of projects, generally involving small numbers of schools or school districts, and how these project-level assessments collectively might contribute to an understanding of systemic reform of science education.

Part 2: Changes in Policy Governing Project Assessment

Three associated changes in federal education policy caused a shift of attention from program-level evaluation to project-level assessment of federally funded science education reform initiatives. First, specific and consequential accountability mandates of No Child Left Behind largely are focused at the local level, requiring school districts and buildings to ensure the progress and achievement of students. Second, the requirement that research and evaluation of education reform efforts use scientifically based evidentiary models and approaches was not feasible to implement with rigor on a large scale. Third, federal policy focused almost exclusively on teacher content knowledge and instructional practice as the levers of improved student achievement. Measuring changes in these features and establishing a link between teacher content knowledge, teacher instructional practice, and improvement in students' science performance required proximal collection of data that were not typically a component of large-scale program evaluation.

Measuring Performance and Ensuring Accountability

In most states, sweeping policy changes followed on the heels of passage of the No Child Left Child Act of 2001. Accountability for performance drove the development of state academic content standards in science and mathematics, the implementation of new systems of high-stakes assessments as well as more rigorous requirements for high school graduation and teacher licensure. In many states, new science standards were based upon or developed from national science documents (i.e., Benchmarks for Science Literacy, AAAS, 1993; National Science Education Standards, NRC, 1996), and they provided frameworks for new assessments that required students to demonstrate their skills and understandings in a variety of ways. Forty-one states also adopted new graduation requirements for students, which specified more units of study and/or higher expectations for required units of science. These changes were aimed to address state-level system issues that might impede gains in students' achievement.

Issues underlying these changes in policy were not directly addressed by most states; that is, do schools have the capacity to ensure the achievement of all students in a more rigorous standards-based, academic environment? A 2007 National Research Council report argued that efforts to improve science education through standards-based reform would have limited impact if teacher preparation and professional development were not addressed.

Unfortunately, assessments of previous large-scale reform efforts provided very little direction regarding how to enhance schools' and teachers' capacity to improve science education. According to Kumar and Altschuld (2003), so little attention had been paid to systematically evaluating large-scale science education reform efforts that the condition of science education remained largely unchanged. Similarly, others noted that evaluations of science education projects, funded by various NSF programs, had been poorly implemented, leading to a dearth of information about improving science instruction and student achievement (Anderson, 2002; Government Accountability Office [GAO], 2003; Greene, DeStefano, Burgon, & Hall, 2006).

Typical program-level evaluations primarily provide quantitative information about participants served and outcomes that are directly measurable. However, as noted in one report on science, technology, engineering, and mathematics (STEM) education (GAO, 2012), federal agencies sponsoring STEM education programs "varied in their ability to provide reliable information on the numbers of students, teachers, or institutions served by their programs" (p. 23) and "did not use outcome measures in a way that is clearly reflected in their performance plans and performance reports" (p. 24).[5] This observation is supported by Katzenmeyer and Lawrenz (2006), who suggest that many large-scale science education reforms have not been evaluated well or that the evaluations have such a low priority (e.g., underfunded) that agencies such as the NSF have limited evidence of impacts and effects.

Other large-scale program evaluations collect and compile information from all funded projects under a programmatic umbrella. Each project is, in turn, conducting its own local assessment designed to address project information needs. Gullickson and Hanssen (2006) observe that although program evaluations are usually done by skilled evaluators, the collective quality of project assessments, typically conducted by lesser-skilled personnel, impacts the value of the program evaluation. They conclude that NSF and other federal funding agencies have not expended sufficient effort to determine the quality and usefulness of project-level assessments, nor have they sought to intervene with projects in order to improve the quality of their evaluation efforts.

Reliance on program-level evaluation to provide credible evidence that might add to the professional knowledge base of science educators and science education stakeholders is problematic for several reasons. First, program-level evaluations, even when conducted rigorously, rarely are comprehensive (Anderson, 2002; Chatterji, 2002). Most frequently, they measure the performance of each component of the system rather than assessing system performance (Chubin cited in Anderson, 2002). Second, program-level assessment cannot capture elements of context that impact outcomes of a program in different settings. According to Kumar and Altschuld (2003), substantive assessment of science education reform must consider the context (e.g., environment, resources, opportunities, and challenges) in which the reform operates. Third, the typical scale of program evaluation is grand, which, in turn, results in findings that are far removed from schools and classrooms. Last, seldom are the findings of program-level evaluation disseminated to practitioners (GAO, 2012).

Failure of program-level evaluations of systemic reform to inform practice has resulted in federal funders of science education initiatives (i.e., NSF, USDOE, National Institutes of Health [NIH]) shifting focus from broad evaluations of programs to building evaluation capacity by embedding requirements for project-level assessments into funding solicitations. Recently, the NSF has vigorously promoted evaluation as critical to ensure project and program credibility (Gullickson & Hanssen, 2006). Similarly, Schneider and Keesler (2007) observe that a primary goal of the USDOE, post–NCLB, is to encourage research studies that are designed to produce scientifically based evidence so that federal agencies, schools, and education reformers can make better decisions regarding programs and policies. The Interagency Education Research Initiative (IERI), a collaborative of NSF, USDOE, and NIH, funded 100 scientifically rigorous studies between 1999 and 2006 to develop and investigate the effectiveness of large-scale education interventions, such as increasing achievement in science, improving teacher professional development, and/or enhancing use of educational technology (Schneider & Keesler, 2007). Although this interagency initiative was short lived, current funding solicitations of these agencies strongly emphasize the requirement for projects to generate and rely upon scientifically based evidence of intervention efficacy.

Federal Guidance for Project Assessment

The No Child Left Behind stipulation that projects and programs receiving federal funds use scientifically

based research designs was immediately translated as a requirement for exclusive use of random assignment or, at least, quasi-experimental designs. Rigorous experimental research and evaluation designs were established as a priority for all USDOE programs, not just those funded by the Institute for Education Sciences (IES). Based upon the work of the Coalition for Evidence-Based Policy (2005), randomized controlled trials (RCT) became the *gold standard* for measuring an education intervention's impact. Schneider and Keesler (2007) observed that, following the lead of the USDOE, other federal agencies and private, nonprofit foundations began recommending the use of random assignment research designs in their subsequent solicitations as well. But federal legislation advocating a specific scientific approach to education research (USDOE, 2005) had implications for other types of research paradigms and was not without criticism.

The USDOE Institute of Education Sciences' What Works Clearinghouse (WWC) was established under the Education Sciences Reform Act of 2002. The WWC carries out IES's goal to use rigorous and relevant research, evaluation, and statistics to improve the U.S. education system. It provides assessments of scientific evidence on the effectiveness of education programs and policies and aims to be a central source for what works in education by systematically assessing the quality and findings of existing research.

While the What Works Clearinghouse reviews only randomized field trial experiments, a few initiatives are underway to provide systematic reviews of education studies that employ other designs (Schneider & Kessler, 2007). For example, the MSP-Knowledge Management and Dissemination (KMD) project, funded by the NSF and the USDOE and led by Horizon Research, aims to identify both research-based findings and practice-based insights on effective approaches to teacher professional development. MSP-KMD project leaders Weiss and Pasley (2008) propose a rigorous and systematic practice-based approach to research that might better address the complexity and diversity of education systems that often make experimental or quasi-experimental studies impossible. Similarly, in the November 2009 report of the GAO on program evaluation (GAO, 2009), the authors note, "[that] requiring evidence from randomized studies as sole proof of effectiveness will likely exclude many potentially effective and worthwhile practices" (p. 31). The GAO further recommends rigorous alternatives to random-assignment studies, including quasi-experimental comparison group studies, statistical analyses of observational or cross-sectional studies, and in-depth case studies. The report also makes general recommendations for strengthening evaluation effectiveness through measurement and design features.

Measuring What Counts

Teacher professional development has served as the primary vehicle for improving science teaching and learning, as demonstrated by the number and variety of programs and projects funded by federal and state agencies. A growing body of research suggests that this approach is effective. Banilower, Heck, and Weiss (2005) have concluded that the model of professional development utilized by NSF's Local Systemic Change projects has resulted in positive change in teachers' attitudes toward science instruction, their perceptions of pedagogical and content preparedness, and their self-reported use of standards-based instructional practices. They note, however, that although the impact of professional development is positive, the relationship between specific teacher practices and improvement in student learning remains undefined.

Partially due to NSF policies requiring research or evaluation of projects funded by the Foundation, research is available concerning the effectiveness of science teacher professional development from the 1990s. With its State-wide Systemic Initiative (SSI) program, NSF specifically targeted policies concerning teacher education at the state level. Although states were free to determine the focus of their respective SSIs, the majority focused on teacher professional development.[6] Another distinction of the SSI program was that both project and program evaluations were funded. As a consequence, studies were available during the course of the SSI projects concerning the effectiveness of different types of professional development for mathematics and science teachers.

In 2002, all states received new sources of federal monies for science and mathematics education. Monies were allocated to states through the Improving Teacher Quality (ITQ) Program. The purpose of the ITQ Program is to increase the academic achievement of all students by helping states and schools improve teacher quality. Funds received by states' education agencies are designated either as Mathematics and Science Partnership (MSP) Program monies or as ITQ funds. State agencies must offer competitive grants to colleges and universities to form partnerships between their schools/colleges of education and arts and sciences, and high-need schools. These programs support sustained and intensive high-quality science and mathematics professional development in order to ensure that teachers improve instruction and enhance student learning.

It might be assumed that projects designed and implemented by a single program to address the same programmatic goals would be similar and internally consistent, yet aspects of context, scale, and the potential for variability can undermine even the best-intentioned efforts at uniformity at the program level. So projects that appear to be similar may produce different results for subtle and unanticipated reasons. This situation poses a challenge, because traditional program evaluations are not designed to isolate key features that contribute to outcomes or to determine elements of effective program implementation. Similarly, within its education programs, the NSF approach to funding projects has reflected a fundamental belief that a project should have the flexibility to determine its own priorities (Katzenmeyer & Lawrenz, 2006).

Such flexibility results in great variability among funded projects within the same program, diminishing the capacity of program-level evaluation to inform improvement.

Nearly 50 years after Vannevar Bush's report to President Truman, *Science—The Endless Frontier* (Bush, 1960), indicated an urgent need to improve science and mathematics education, the emphasis on quality teaching reemerged as central to the No Child Left Behind Act of 2001. NCLB mandated that states ensure that all students are taught by *highly qualified* teachers[7] and that only evidence-based professional development programs receive federal funding. Federal policy and government agencies have chosen to emphasize content knowledge as the key measure of teacher quality and, until recently, have given less attention to teacher instructional practice despite policy language that stresses improving both the subject matter knowledge of teachers and how effectively they teach. The assumption made in the 1950s and again in 2001 was that teacher content knowledge would be directly related to student achievement in science; however, that assumption was not based on findings from research.

In a review of research commissioned by the U.S. Department of Education, Wilson, Floden, and Ferrini-Mundy (2001) suggested an absence of research connecting teacher knowledge to student learning. Their review included 57 (out of 313 identified) studies that met stringent criteria. They concluded that no research directly evaluated the relationship between teacher subject matter preparation and student learning. But, unlike the lack of research demonstrating a relationship between teacher content knowledge and student learning in science, there is a growing body of evidence that *how* science is taught does affect student achievement. Some research (e.g., Kahle, et al., 2000; Magnusson, Borko, Krajcik, & Layman, 1992; Sanders, Borko, & Lockard, 1993) suggests that differences in teacher instructional practices, partially resulting from differences in teachers' content knowledge, influence student learning.

Researchers in the 1980s and 1990s examined the effect of specific instructional strategies on student achievement. In 1996, Wise used a list of alternative strategies (i.e., questioning, focusing, manipulation, enhanced materials, testing, inquiry, enhanced context, and instructional media) to examine teaching. He then contrasted the effectiveness of alternative and traditional (e.g., textbooks, lectures, worksheets) teaching strategies. He concluded that the alternative strategies were fundamentally inquiry oriented and that they were more effective than traditional approaches in enhancing student achievement in science (Wise, 1996; Wise in Schroeder, Scott, Tolson, Huang, & Lee, 2007). A meta-analysis of U.S. research (1980 to 2004) done by Schroeder and colleagues (2007) studied the effect of specific science teaching strategies on student achievement. In the 61 studies that met their criteria for inclusion in the analysis, they identified eight alternative instructional strategies in science.[8] Using student performance as the dependent variable and the eight strategies as independent variables, they calculated effect sizes for each strategy, and all effect sizes were judged to be significant. The authors concluded: "The major implication of this research is that we have generated empirical evidence supporting the effectiveness of alternative teaching strategies in science" (p. 1436). The significance of this finding for science teacher content knowledge is that it indirectly impacts student achievement via pedagogical practice.

Part 3: Linking Project Effectiveness and Classroom Practice Through Project Assessment

Several conditions must be met in order to realize the full potential of project assessment to inform systemic science education reform as demonstrated by changes in teachers' classroom practice and improved student performance. First, project assessment must be explicitly described and promoted by funding agencies and valued by project personnel. Second, project assessment designs and approaches must be rooted in theoretical foundations and current literature that demonstrate an understanding of what is being assessed. Third, project assessment must be supported by development of the capacity of the field to conduct high-quality project assessments. Fourth, project assessments must be designed and implemented rigorously and purposefully with attention to project-level and programmatic goals and information needs. Fifth, a design-based approach to project assessment must provide, first, intermittent formative feedback so that project work can be retooled and implementation can be improved over time and, second, summative judgments regarding project impact and achievement of goals. Last, rigorous and high-quality project assessments must be synthesized using meta-analytic or other techniques in order to capitalize on the collective learning of individual projects within and across programs.

Valuing Project Assessment

Since the early 1990s, the NSF has provided general guidance regarding project assessment via its *User-Friendly Handbook for Project Evaluation: Science, Mathematics, Engineering, and Technology Education* (Fretchling, Stevens, Lawrenz, & Sharp, 1993). The handbook, which has been periodically updated, provides principal investigators and project evaluators with a basic understanding of recommended approaches to evaluation. Two important reasons for engaging in evaluation, noted in the *2002 User-Friendly Handbook for Project Evaluation* (Fretchling, Frierson, Hood, & Hughes, 2002), are "to provide information to improve the project; and to provide new insights or information that were not anticipated" (p. 3). In addition to these two reasons, demonstrating that project goals have been met is a primary measure of accountability.

Many programs of the NSF's Directorate for Education and Human Resources provide specific guidance regarding research and evaluation designs for funded projects.

For example, the Mathematics and Science Partnership (MSP) Program requires projects to use evidence-based research and evaluation designs that link current research to relevant questions about the strategies, goals, and outcomes of the project. Projects are required to employ credible quantitative and qualitative measures to document impact on student learning and teacher quality. Projects' evaluations are expected to guide project progress formatively and measure and report on the project's realization of improved student and teacher outcomes (NSF, 2012).

The U.S. Department of Education also provides specific guidance for its Title IIB Mathematics and Science Partnership Program, which is administered by state education agencies. The document, *How to Solicit Rigorous Evaluations of Mathematics and Science Partnerships (MSP) Projects: A User-Friendly Guide for MSP State Coordinators* (Coalition for Evidence-Based Policy, May 2005), was developed to "provide MSP state coordinators with a concrete, low-cost strategy to solicit rigorous evaluations of their state's MSP projects" (p. 3). This text identified randomized controlled trials (RCTs) as a method to produce valid evidence of impact over 1 to 2 years. In cases where RCTs are not feasible, the authors concede that a well-matched comparison-group study can establish possible evidence of intervention effectiveness, though their "estimates of the magnitude of an intervention's effect are often inaccurate" (p. 15).

Since the early 1990s, federal agencies, including the NSF and USDOE, have supported a range of education reform projects that are longer term (3 to 5 years) and more comprehensive (Kahle, 2007). Such projects are multiyear and multilayered. Increasing the length of time for a project to implement its intervention provides greater opportunity for project assessment to measure the intervention's impact and to report on its outcomes. These projects also receive substantial fiscal support. For example, between 2002 and 2003, federal Department of Education funding of states' MSP Programs has increased from $12.5 million to $100 million, and annually the NSF awards approximately $55 million to new and continuing MSP projects. Higher levels of funding facilitate the implementation of more rigorous and comprehensive project assessments. Because of the growing complexity, the DOE and the NSF require project evaluations to monitor ongoing activities formatively and to assess whether a project achieves its goals in a summative assessment. Further, project assessments help ensure both project and program credibility with policy makers and the public (Gullickson & Hanssen, 2006).

Although funding agencies emphasize the value of project assessment, project evaluators often serve as mediators among stakeholder groups that have different value preferences regarding the purposes and role of project assessment. For example, the value preferences of the project's principal investigators and team members sometimes conflict with those of federal and state funding agencies that set strict standards for project design and for evaluation methodology and rigor. Project assessment must balance the development of high-quality and useful evaluation plans with expectations for accountability and rigor in order to generate findings that are useful for informing state and local policy and practice. Ideally, project leaders engage project evaluators during proposal development. When evaluators become involved early in the process, they can promote project assessment as a lens for reflection and improvement and offer advice and suggestions concerning appropriate, valid, and reliable instruments and rigorous analyses to assess the project's goals. Still, tensions can develop between project personnel and project evaluators regarding consistent use of the same instruments and approaches to measure progress towards the project's goals over time. For example, project personnel may need to modify instruments to reflect changes in the project's professional development design or goals, while project evaluators hesitate to do so in order to preserve the rigor of the evaluation.

Assessment of Teacher Professional Development

Because recent reform efforts have focused squarely on improving science teachers' knowledge and practice, project effectiveness largely is measured by the extent to which the intervention impacts teachers' learning and performance directly and student learning and performance indirectly. The criteria by which teacher professional development is judged historically have been poorly defined. Recently, the literature on professional development is reaching some consensus on a set of features that contribute to impact on teachers' instructional behaviors and subsequent student learning (Yoon, Duncan, Lee, Scarloss, & Shapley, 2007). A few of these researchers also have provided empirical evidence regarding the impact of specific professional development features, such as content knowledge and pedagogical content knowledge (Cohen & Hill, 2000; Kennedy, 1999), active learning and coherence (Garet et al., 1999), and duration and frequency (Supovitz & Turner, 2000). Collectively, they identified the following features as integral to quality professional development: (a) content focus, (b) active learning, (c) coherence, (d) duration, and (e) collective participation[9] (Corcoran, 1995; Desimone, 2009; Desimone, Porter, Garet, Yoon, & Birman, 2002; Guskey & Yoon, 2009; Loucks-Horsley, Love, Stiles, Mundry, & Hewson, 2003; NRC, 1996).

A few studies of science teacher professional development have provided evidence regarding the link between teachers' professional learning and changes in their instructional practice. For example, Supovitz and Turner (2000) employed hierarchical linear modeling to study the relationship of teachers' participation in NSF's Local Systemic Change (LSC) professional development projects and their adoption of inquiry-based teaching practices. They reported two relevant findings: (a) The quantity of professional development in which teachers participate is strongly linked with both inquiry-based teaching practice

and investigative classroom culture, and (b) teachers' content preparation has a powerful influence on teaching practice and classroom culture. Similarly, Desimone and colleagues (2002) used a purposeful sample of 207 teachers in 30 schools, in 10 districts, and in 5 states to examine the characteristics of teacher professional development and the effect of professional development on teaching strategies in mathematics and science from 1996 to 1999.[10] The researchers identified six key features of professional development.[11] Desimone and colleagues (2002) reported that reform type, collective participation, active learning, and coherence led to changes in teaching practice.[12] Unlike Supovitz and Turner (2000), they found no effects for duration or for content focus. Given that findings regarding some components or features of professional development are inconclusive, further research is needed to investigate how interactions among features (e.g., duration, intensity, content) rather than how singular features impact teaching and learning outcomes.

Building Capacity for Project Assessment

Gullickson and Hanssen (2006) are not alone in their observation that the quality of many project evaluations is less than desirable despite guidance and recommendations provided by federal funding agencies. Government Performance and Results Act (GPRA) measures applied to the federal Mathematics and Science Partnership Program include the extent to which projects successfully utilized experimental or quasi-experimental evaluation designs. Early data suggested that MSP projects were meeting annual targets for increasing teacher content knowledge and improving student achievement, but those studies often did not use rigorous methodologies. In fact, all but a handful of projects struggled to comply with directives to implement evaluation designs that provided credible evidence regarding outcomes (USDOE, 2008). In a more recent review of DOE MSP projects' final evaluation reports, Abt Associates (2010) determined that only 4 projects out of 183 met the criteria for strong evaluation designs and implementation activities despite the DOE's stringent requirements for rigorous evaluations. While some lack of rigor in projects' assessments may be attributed to trade-offs that project evaluators must make in order to balance evaluation rigor and practicality, the consensus view is that the field is underprepared to develop and implement high-quality assessments of science and mathematics teaching and learning projects (Katzenmeyer & Lawrence, 2006; Kumar & Altschuld, 2003).

Many factors impact the quality of project assessment data and the potential usefulness of those data both to the project and to a large-scale program evaluation. Primary factors impacting the quality of the data are the rigor and appropriateness of project assessment methods, activities, and instruments. Katzenmeyer and Lawrenz (2006) summarize issues of quality in NSF project evaluations. They note that insufficient attention to alignment of methodology with evaluation questions, lack of the field's capacity to conduct assessment of STEM education projects, and few valid and reliable instruments for assessing important outcomes of STEM education initiatives are serious limitations to credible assessment of NSF projects.

One strategy for addressing the issue of quality assessment is for funding agencies, states, or knowledgeable others to provide explicit tools or templates to guide projects' assessment planning and technical assistance regarding selection of instrumentation and evaluation methods. While this intervention requires an initial input of resources, it builds and sustains capacity to plan and conduct high-quality project assessments, and it results in more efficient use of evaluation resources over time. The NSF's MSP Research, Evaluation, and Technical Assistance (RETA) projects are a large-scale example of how funders can implement programs of assistance for evaluators (NSF, 2012). Some states have replicated this approach by funding statewide evaluations of their MSP programs. For example, Ohio has addressed limitations in project assessment by contracting with an experienced external evaluation team to work closely and proactively with project evaluators to strengthen project assessments' capacity to produce defensible findings from the collection and analysis of project data. The external contractors' work included assisting with articulating projects' theories of change and interpreting the implications for evaluation; providing an explicit template for projects' evaluation planning, including explanations of federal criteria for rigor; technical assistance for identifying appropriate, valid, and reliable measurement instruments; identifying and developing self-assessment instruments for formative use in assessing aspects of the project; and implementing technical assistance for all of the above. Practical and higher-quality evaluation designs resulted from this intervention (Woodruff, Zorn, Raffle, & Oches, 2011).

Designing and Implementing Rigorous Project Assessments

Funding agencies, notably NSF, USDOE, and NIH, often describe rigorous requirements for evaluation and research in their requests for proposals. While expectations that projects' assessments will use experimental or quasi-experimental designs may be somewhat unrealistic, the collective knowledge emerging from implementation of well-conceived project assessments will increase knowledge of what works and local conditions that might facilitate or limit effective practices. For this reason, the quality of project assessments is of concern not only for projects and their funders but also for policy makers and education stakeholders. As described earlier in this chapter, federal agencies and other organizations have provided several important and helpful guidance documents and recommendations for improving the rigor and usefulness of project assessment. For this reason, we offer some broad observations about quality project assessment, including common issues and challenges of project assessment and how they can be addressed through appropriate assessment design and methods.

Based upon guidance provided by the U.S. Department of Education regarding MSP project evaluation (Abt Associates, Inc., 2010; Coalition for Evidence-Based Policy, 2005), state MSP Program evaluators assessed the likelihood that project evaluation plans of five Ohio MSP projects funded in 2010 would produce rigorous findings regarding their effect on student achievement and on teacher content knowledge. Each project was rated on six factors identified as critical to producing valid and defensible evaluation findings. Quality of evidence was determined by (a) alignment and appropriateness of instrument, metric, or evaluation approach with the outcome to be measured; (b) reliability and validity of instrument or metric used to measure the outcome; (c) sufficient and representative response rates to instruments and participation in evaluation activities; (d) triangulation of appropriate data sources used to build a body of evidence, particularly when alignment or validity of instruments used or response rates were less than optimal; and (e) consistency and rigor in the execution of evaluation activities, including administration of instruments, application of statistical procedures, and sufficient detail in reporting findings (Westat, 2002). All of the five Ohio MSP projects experienced similar though not insurmountable challenges in evaluation planning and implementation. Following the second year of project implementation, only one project's evaluation plan and activities resulted in findings of student and teacher impact that could be attributed to the project's intervention. A second project achieved a high level of evaluation rigor and could attribute some teacher and student impacts directly to the work of the project.

In this Ohio study, three challenges, commonly faced by most MSP projects, negatively impacted the quality of each project's assessment. First, due to a lack of comparison groups, most projects failed to demonstrate a relationship between student achievement gains and/or improvement in teacher content knowledge and project implementation, because they were unable to compare the results of the treatment group to a comparable, untreated group. Some projects used baseline student data, typically state assessment scores (required by USDOE Annual Performance Reports), to compensate for the lack of a comparison group, but similar trends in state data across years and the inability to directly connect the content of the projects' professional development to the content of the state assessments made this a tenuous approach. Only two of the five projects collected, analyzed, and reported comparison group student data using common and reasonably aligned instruments with both treatment and comparison groups. Second, due to the lack of alignment of instruments or metrics to outcomes, some projects did not choose valid, reliable, or appropriate instruments to measure intended outcomes. For example, self-report data were the most frequently used data source to measure increase in teacher content knowledge and pedagogical content knowledge. Projects also did not meet the expectation that they would triangulate data sources when appropriate instruments were either unavailable or insufficient to measure critical project outcomes. And, third, because of a lack of adequate participant sample size or retention rate, teacher-level data in most projects had less-than-adequate sample sizes, making the use of parametric (and, in some cases, nonparametric) statistical testing impossible. Further, some projects, due to the nature of their activities, intentionally planned for small groups of teacher participants but did not consider the implications of this decision for the project assessment (Woodruff, Zorn, Raffle, & Oches, 2012).

Common issues regarding evaluation rigor of these Ohio projects were primarily related to recruiting and retaining well-matched comparison groups, demonstrating equivalence (or correcting for pre-intervention differences), and maintaining adequate sample sizes. Gaps and errors in projects' assessments significantly impacted their ability to attribute outcomes to their professional development activities, though there was evidence that all projects had some measurable positive impact on teachers and their students (Woodruff et al., 2012). The researchers noted that these issues also were identified as problematic for most MSP projects by federal program evaluators and independent reviewers (i.e., Westat, Abt). One explanation for these findings is the lack of coordination of project design plans with project assessment plans. It is not unusual that project personnel, funding agencies, and other stakeholders have competing information needs, expectations, and values regarding an initiative and its assessment. Assessment plans should be integral to the development and management of a project, and project teams should include knowledgeable and experienced evaluators as key team members.

A rigorous project assessment must consider the projects' components both singularly and holistically in order to develop a sufficient body of evidence to demonstrate its impact. Such an approach includes concurrent collection of multiple sources of qualitative and quantitative data and an evaluation design that facilitates interaction among all qualitative and quantitative components and permits the close examination of process and impact. Utilizing multiple measures for collecting data is a form of triangulation, which contributes to the trustworthiness and rigor of the evaluation (Glesne, 2011). Defensibility of projects' claims of impact is directly based upon the quality of evidence generated by the project assessment and the project's ability to triangulate data sources to support claims. Another important aspect determining the rigor of a project's assessment is the extent to which the assessment can link outcomes, either directly or indirectly, to the work of the project. For example, typically it is necessary to compare the results of those who experienced an intervention (treatment group) with a well-matched group of those who did not (control/comparison group) in order to claim attribution of outcomes to the work of a project. In the absence of a comparison group, attribution cannot be claimed.

Many challenges to Ohio MSP projects' ability to provide adequate evidence of impact through their project assessments appeared to stem from one primary cause—lack of clear theories of change (Woodruff et al., 2012). In the absence of a clear understanding of the drivers at each stage of the process of teacher learning and change, projects were unable to connect their assessment plans to project plans, because they were unsure what to specifically measure, when to measure, and how best to measure. This observation is particularly critical if the potential of project assessment to inform science education reform is to be fully realized. Though project leaders generally understood their planned activities and provided rationales for employing project strategies and activities, many projects were not founded on coherent theories of the process by which teacher learning improves and translates into instructional change that leads to improved student achievement. In the absence of a clear understanding of the drivers at each stage of this complex process of teacher learning and change, projects will remain unable to explain and attribute their outcomes.

As noted earlier, sound assessment practice and a wealth of federal guidance has encouraged projects to develop logic models. The logic model should identify important, expected project outcomes as well as anticipated intermediate outcomes and determinants that should be measured by the project's assessment. An additional aspect of a project's logic model is that it restricts the range of objectives undertaken by a project and measured by its assessment. While projects' assessment plans should be comprehensive, assessments that are too broad in scope will not produce high-quality evidence of key outcomes, particularly when resources are limited.

Formative Project Assessment

Formative project assessment is a critical aspect of many federally funded projects. As noted in the NSF's 2012 solicitation for Mathematics and Science Partnership projects, "formative evaluation should provide evidence of the strengths and weaknesses of the project, informing the Partnership's understanding of what works and what does not in order to inform project progress and success" (p. 11). Formative evaluation should begin during project development and continue throughout the life of the project to assess ongoing project activities and provide information to inform and improve the project (NSF, 2010).

Formative project assessments may monitor a project's internal processes, intervention implementation, intermediate outcomes, or any combination of these aspects. Process or implementation evaluation assesses whether the project is being conducted as planned by looking at internal project processes as well as at the project's work with its constituents. An implementation evaluation provides opportunity for project personnel to check that project components are developed and operating as anticipated. It also provides project evaluators the opportunity to make early adjustments to assessment plans if critical data are not being captured, particularly if project components are modified or are not performing as expected.

Formative progress evaluation assesses progress toward meeting the goals of the project by reviewing evidence of expected intermediate outcomes. Progress evaluations generally involve collecting information relevant to a project's periodic benchmarks in order to determine the project's impact at various stages of implementation (NSF, 2010). Such data are useful for guiding modifications to improve the likelihood of the project achieving its long-term goals. Data collected as part of a progress evaluation also contribute to summative assessment of the project.

One project assessment strategy that effectively facilitates projects' use of formative feedback is the development, or articulation, of a conceptual model of a project's logic or theory of change (Chen, 1990). Evaluation, based on theory (W. K. Kellogg Foundation, 1998), is founded on the premise that every project is based on an implicit or explicit theory about how and why it will work. Generally, programs, such as the MSP Program, have a theory that has been explicated by the funder. Project evaluators and project personnel can build upon existing program theory to describe how their project will effect change and then develop key interim outcomes, which should be formatively measured. Documenting interim outcomes provides multiple opportunities to reflect on whether a project is on track and allows for modifications based on what has been learned. Those steps increase the potential for achieving long-term impacts. Ultimately, conceptual models facilitate the project team's reflection upon as well as their understanding and demonstration of effectiveness in ways that make sense for the project and for the funding program.

Summative Project Assessment

The purpose of summative assessment is to evaluate a project's success in reaching its stated goals and to determine its worth (NSF, 2010). The determination of worth or merit commonly must be substantiated by comparing the results of a particular intervention to other similar interventions or by judging the value of the project's outcomes relative to the investment of resources necessary to produce them. Summative assessment generally addresses many of the same questions as a progress evaluation, but it is conducted after the project is reasonably expected to produce outcomes. Summative project assessment should utilize data collected during the project's implementation as well as summative measures of impact in order to build an evidence base that renders a judgment relative to the outcomes and related processes, strategies, and activities of the project.

The quality of a summative assessment can be strengthened by ensuring the evaluation is conducted without bias, by triangulating results from multiple data sources, and by considering the purpose and use of the assessment report. The 2012 NSF MSP Program solicitation described summative evaluation in the following way: "summative evaluation should give an *objective analysis* of qualitative and quantitative data, thus demonstrating the effectiveness of the project on student and teacher outcomes and institutional change" (NSF, 2012, p. 11, italics added). Summative project assessments frequently are criticized, because they are conducted by internal personnel rather than personnel who are external to the project. When future funding or other high-stakes decisions rely upon a project's summative assessment, it is important to have an external evaluator who is knowledgeable, objective, and unbiased. When it is not possible to conduct an external project assessment, a reasonable approach is to conduct an internal evaluation and then contract with an outside evaluator to review the assessment design, instruments, and formative findings. In addition, the outside evaluator would assess the validity of the findings and conclusions. However, as the NSF and other federal funding agencies have revised their requirements for evaluation, many programs now require that project assessment be conducted by an individual or group external to the project and that the contracted evaluator be minimally qualified to do the work (NSF, 2010).

Summative project assessment should consider all valid sources of quantitative and qualitative data when arriving at conclusions. A number of rigorous analytical techniques to triangulate different data sources may be used by evaluators (Creswell, Plano Clark, Gutmann, & Hanson, 2003). Findings from different data sources may be incongruent, and it is the responsibility of an unbiased evaluator to consider and report on unanticipated findings or outcomes. By collecting and analyzing multiple sources of data, whether they be congruent or unanticipated, projects and funding programs can learn a great deal about a project's impact and its most critical components (Schorr & Kubisch, 1995).

Although the name implies differently, summative project assessments do not necessarily indicate that a project is complete. Patton (2006) argues that the concept of summative assessment is not meaningful for projects that are oriented toward change and continuous improvement and that operate within unstable environments. While a summative assessment may provide evidence of progress or describe an intervention's principles and outcomes, it may be inappropriate to assume that the project has reached a state of stabilization where it can be objectively and finally assessed. Ideally, summative assessment will go beyond describing a project's outcomes to provide it and funders with an understanding of *how* the project affected change in key outcomes. In addition, summative assessments have implications for the sustainability of projects, which is critical to funders. A summative assessment should provide information to make decisions about the future of a project's intervention. In this way, reports of a project's summative assessment contribute to the broader knowledge base by providing important information about how to implement similar interventions.

Capitalizing on Project Assessment

The potential of project assessment to achieve broad impact and to inform systemic science education reform lies in the collective synthesis of findings from rigorous, individual project assessments. Congruent findings from a number of large-scale project assessments may collectively lead to major policy implications and program improvement. While variability among projects is a concern to evaluators in making claims regarding program outcomes, Gullickson and Hanssen (2006) suggest that synthesizing individual project assessments is a viable way to address overarching programmatic or systemic questions. Conversely, synthesis of multiple project assessments under a single program umbrella may identify contextual conditions under which project interventions are most effective (Woodruff, Zorn, Noga, & Seabrook, 2009). Schneider and Keesler (2007) agree that what is "perhaps most important . . . is the focus on accumulating knowledge from different studies, which suggests an attempt to bring some coherence to a field that some have described as fragmented" (p. 212).

Planning for the synthesis of project-level assessments prior to project and assessment implementation can be an effective method for improving programmatic learning from projects' assessments. Several states have funded statewide evaluations of their respective MSP Programs. In some cases, these states (e.g., Wisconsin, Illinois, Pennsylvania) have implemented a large-scale project at multiple sites and contracted for the assessment of the project across sites. In other states—for example, Ohio—a longitudinal statewide evaluation has been conducted across a number of smaller, local projects. While the USDOE MSP Program requires that each funded project conduct an assessment to collect, analyze, and report on specific project outcomes, cross-project or cross-site evaluations typically utilize local project assessment data, recommend or require common cross-project instruments, and may provide technical assistance and guidance to local project assessment leaders and project teams in order to promote defensible project and program-level findings.

As described earlier, funding agencies can promote high-quality project assessment by describing clear expectations for assessment, specifying allocations of funds for assessment work, and setting up systems of support and technical assistance for projects. When external agencies or teams of skilled evaluators assume a consultative role, a number of positive outcomes may be expected. These outcomes include assessment capacity building within project teams, development of more rigorous and useful project assessment designs, and greater consistency and quality in reporting results across projects. This work also serves to inform states of what is reasonable to expect of project assessment and how to achieve high-quality evaluations that both meet expectations for accountability and are useful for informing state and local policies and practices. An interesting challenge to the cross-project program evaluation is significant diversity among funded projects, target schools and teachers, and professional development designs. A cross-project evaluation must balance the need for a reasonable degree of uniformity with flexibility that can accommodate variation in projects that are aligned with specific partner needs. If common measurement instruments are recommended or required, they should be purposefully selected to fit a variety of professional development content and to be appropriate for a range of local contexts. Cross-project evaluation efforts should merge with project assessment efforts so that value is added to both types of evaluations.

Cross-project, or multisite, evaluations of similar projects may be conducted as cluster evaluations. A cluster evaluation studies groups of projects demonstrating similar traits in order to learn more about policy and/or systemic change than would be possible from studying a single project (W. K. Kellogg Foundation, 1998). For example, a cluster evaluation could be used to look across a group of science teacher professional development projects in order to identify common threads and themes that, having cross-project confirmation, take on greater significance. Cluster evaluations also can determine how well a collection of projects fulfills the objectives of a program as well as measure variation in effectiveness across projects. Cluster evaluations typically rely heavily on local project assessment data, so conducting a cluster evaluation in tandem with providing a system of technical assistance for projects' own assessments will improve the quality of the data available. Cluster evaluations may be equally informative for projects as they are for funders. An important aspect of cluster evaluation is that each project can benefit from lessons learned by similar projects. Further, cluster evaluation can provide feedback to projects on commonalties and innovative strategies used by peer projects as well as inform the field regarding the implementation of projects' models in other schools.

One such example of a cross-project cluster evaluation was an exploratory cluster evaluation of Ohio's Mathematics and Science Partnership projects, conducted in 2009 (Woodruff, Hung, & Seabrook, 2009). This study explored the variability and commonality of implementation and impact of 15 3-year MSP projects administered by the Ohio Department of Education. Although projects shared common program goals of increasing teacher content knowledge, improving teaching practice, and improving student performance, considerable variability existed across projects. The evaluators' goal was to create clusters of project models to compare regarding implementation, programmatic changes over time, and impact. Cluster membership was assigned based on variability in program characteristics and contexts that were identified by the evaluators and project personnel. Such an approach was useful for reducing the number of cross-project comparisons (i.e., treating all 15 projects as unique cases) as well as for generating and operationalizing models that might be transferable or replicable in other sites. This approach also allowed for the identification of common themes that were critical to the success of particular programs and moved beyond case-based learning with heterogeneous projects with diverse participants.

Another effective method of synthesizing project assessments in ways that are useful, particularly to funders and policy makers, is to utilize a cross-project analysis framework theoretically rooted in program goals. The Public Value Model is one such framework that is applicable to reform of education systems. This model is based on Moore's (1995) Strategic Triangle Public Value Model, a framework for understanding the purpose of an organization through the lens of public value. The Public Value Model recognizes the constant interaction of the value provided by a program or project, its operational capacity or ability to provide public value, and its authorizing environment, which provides legitimacy and support. The model is particularly relevant to educational organizations in which change is inevitable and frequently unannounced, and projects' capacity and authorizing environments are often unstable. The Public Value Model analysis framework can provide a comprehensive picture of a program's broad impact by assessing the extent to which shared values contribute to individual project outcomes. Cross-project or cross-site evaluators may use the Strategic Triangle Public Value Model as a consistent lens to analyze project assessment data and information and to recognize common themes as well as disconnects that occur within projects. Such an approach also is useful in identifying contextual features of an individual project that may impact its outcomes.

Part 4: Do Project Assessments Help Change Classroom Practices and Enhance Student Learning?

Contributions of Project Assessment

As described earlier in this chapter, project assessment has emerged as a major component of federal- and state-funded efforts to improve science education in the United States. This section will review published findings from the most recent wave of large-scale reform projects of the Mathematics and Science Partnership (MSP) initiative, funded directly by National Science Foundation and by state departments of education with funds from the U.S. Department of Education (USDOE, 2008). The following goals, articulated in the initial NSF program solicitation, continue to drive the assessments of both NSF and USDOE MSP projects:

- Provide a challenging curriculum for every student;
- Enhance and sustain the number, quality, and diversity of K–12 mathematics and science teachers through professional development opportunities;
- Involve a network of researchers and practitioners; and
- Engage the learning community in the knowledge base being developed in current and future NSF Centers for Learning and Teaching of Science (NSF, 2002).

Although the goals of the MSP program have been refined by states through subsequent solicitations, the intent of the program to implement large-scale systemic reform that addresses the needs of all students, that facilitates partnerships among K–12 districts, higher education, and business and industry, and that results in sustainable change, has endured.

Ohio's MSP projects followed a decade of systemic reforms in Ohio in the 1990s[13] and together have produced a number of positive outcomes for mathematics and science teachers, their students, and the state. Findings from independent evaluations of Ohio's SSI (Discovery) and of Ohio's MSP projects suggest that teacher instructional practices were improved by teacher participation in the professional development experiences. In addition, findings from an NSF–funded research study (Kahle et al., 2000) indicate that student achievement was enhanced after teacher participation. This finding has been supported by research suggesting that the mathematics and science achievement of students is influenced by the content and pedagogical knowledge of their teachers (Monk, 1994; Schroeder, et al., 2007; Wise, 1996). Further, researchers (Desimone et al., 2002; Guyton, Fox, & Sisk, 1991; Lawrenz, 1975) generally concur that teacher attitudes regarding teaching and learning science impact the teacher's ability to teach standards-based science effectively. Teachers participating in three decades of Ohio's large-scale reform projects have reported significant positive changes in their expertise in teaching standards-based and inquiry science (Kahle et al., 2000; Woodruff, McCollum, Li, & Bautista, 2010).

Individual MSP project assessments have focused on identifying the project's progress and/or success in meeting its specific goals, which, in turn, reflect the MSP program's goals. In most cases, success has been measured by increased student achievement, which has previously been analyzed in terms of teacher participation in the professional development. However, few projects assessed changes in curricula or in classroom practices. Further, although sustainability of partnerships has been assessed, few projects included a rigorous assessment of changes in the collaborating IHEs or industrial/business partners. In spite of these limitations, the external assessments of many of the large-scale MSPs have provided evidence of various kinds of success, primarily changes in teacher content knowledge and in student achievement. The following review focuses on changes at the classroom level.

For example, Rand's evaluation of the Math Science Partnership of Southwest Pennsylvania analyzed progress in terms of student achievement, quality of the educator workforce, and sustainable partnerships (Pane et al., 2009). The evaluation reported that 58% of mathematics and science teachers (3,568 math and 1,321 science) in SW Pennsylvania were involved in the project. The mean number of hours of teacher participation was 25.1 for math teachers and 27.6 for science teachers. When teacher participation and student science achievement were analyzed at the district level,[14] findings showed no significant positive relationships between district-level leaders' or teachers' participation in the MSP and students' science achievement.

The assessment also analyzed changes in teacher quality and teachers' instructional practices pre- and post-participation in professional development activities. Teachers responded to a questionnaire that included four scales that assessed classroom instructional practices before they participated and 3 years afterward. Although math teachers' responses were significantly different on two of the four scales, no significant differences were found for science teachers on any of the scales.

Oyer's (2011) evaluation report of the Illinois Mathematics and Science Partnership provides an in-depth assessment of two models of professional development, one leading to a master's degree and one based on workshop institutes. The master's degree model involved 24 separate partnerships across 10 universities throughout the state, while the workshop institute model involved 10 partners in two cohorts.[15] Unfortunately, student outcome measures were not available, so there was no information concerning student achievement. However, the assessment concluded, "[T]here is no evidence that the two models (graduate versus workshop institute) are different in their student and teacher outcomes" (p. 51). After completing the professional development (either model), all but a few teachers responded *satisfied* or *very satisfied* on the following teacher questionnaire items: *improvement in their content knowledge, improvement in their access and use of new instructional resources,* and *improvement in their access and use of new STEM technologies.*[16] Although these are self-reported data, such responses suggest changes in instructional practices.

Another state that provided comprehensive evaluation and assessment of its MSP projects was Ohio. Ohio's Department of Education used its USDOE/MSP monies to fund 38 projects between 2006 and 2012 (USDOE, n.d.). In 2006, Ohio awarded its first MSP partnerships to nine projects, involving 29 Ohio colleges and universities and 147 school districts. Between 2007 and 2012, more than 330,400 Ohio students were instructed by teachers participating in the MSP projects. The state also funded an external program evaluation of its MSP projects. Data were collected from 15 Ohio MSP projects (funded in 2006 and 2007), which included more than 2,000 teacher participants. Elementary teachers comprised 65% of all participants. Large urban, suburban, and very small rural schools from all regions of the state were involved; further, 85% of the schools were identified as high need.[17] Components of the evaluation included a cluster analysis (Woodruff, et al., 2009), an instrument study, and an effect size study (Woodruff, Li, & Kao, 2010).

All 15 Ohio MSP projects, funded in 2006 and 2007, conducted individual project evaluations, and all claimed to have made measurable and valid improvements in teachers' content knowledge (using locally developed assessments). Similarly, all projects reported having achieved measurable improvements in pedagogy; however, for most projects this claim was not substantiated by classroom observation or by triangulation with other data. Four of the 15 projects reported measurable improvements in student performance on state assessments, with two projects reporting that the changes were statistically significant. However, none reported student data for a comparison or control group (Zorn et al., 2009).

While neither the local nor the state evaluations of these Ohio projects directly assessed the quality of the professional development, a cluster analysis performed as part of the 2007 to 2010 statewide evaluation provided insight into how aspects of the professional development were addressed by the projects. The cluster analysis collected data from each project regarding components of professional development. Researchers used hierarchical cluster analysis with Ward's clustering method (Ward, 1963) to group the 15 projects into five clusters. Each cluster differed on components that were uniquely important to that group of projects. The cluster data were used when reviewing projects' reports to determine if particular features of their professional development were related to their reported outcomes. Due to a lack of rigor in projects' assessment data, only tentative conclusions were reached. Researchers found that projects whose professional development involved teachers working together in groups, included STEM faculty in teacher content learning, and directly linked professional development content to teachers' grade level or classroom context reported more positive outcomes for teachers (i.e., perceptions of increased content knowledge, improved attitudes toward science instruction, more frequent use of standards-based teaching practices; Zorn et al., 2009).

In addition, the statewide evaluators analyzed data from a valid and reliable instrument, used by all projects, to measure change in classroom teaching. An effect size study, using data collected by the teacher instrument, found that the impact of the Ohio MSP professional development on self-reported teacher practices varied across projects and across program aspects. The largest programmatic effect sizes were found regarding teachers' preparedness to engage in standards-based instruction (pooled effect size, $(d) = .94$) and their expertise regarding the use of standards-based instruction ($d = 1.07$). Ohio's MSP program had a moderate impact on changing teachers' reported instructional practices and a small impact on teachers' perceptions of the importance of using standards-based instruction. Not surprisingly, some projects affected participating teachers more than did others (overall effect sizes (d) ranged from .02 to 1.77). All projects were at least moderately successful at helping teachers feel as though they had gained expertise in using standards-based instruction, yet none significantly changed teachers' attitudes about the importance of standards-based instruction (Woodruff et al., 2010).

Another large-scale project to improve mathematics and science education was the Western Wisconsin STEM Consortia Project (Mason, et al., 2012). This project, funded by an MSP grant from the Wisconsin Department of Public Instruction, provided professional development for 60 K–12 teachers in nine different school districts in western Wisconsin. Analyses of the responses of the 60 teacher participants indicated that 83% (50 of 60 participants) demonstrated significant gains in mathematics content knowledge, while 62% (37 of 60 participants) had significant gains in science content knowledge.[18] Only limited student achievement data were collected, which showed that the professional development of the teachers had some effect on student achievement.

Another MSP project, funded by the NSF, with rigorous external evaluation was the University of Pennsylvania's Science Teacher Institute project (Kahle & Woodruff, 2013). Although not statewide, it was based in a large urban city and its surrounding region, encompassing three states and serving more than 180 teachers and 12,000 students. The project targeted two groups of teachers, high school chemistry teachers and middle school science teachers. The professional development included both academic-year and summer courses and led to either master of science (chemistry teachers) or master of science education (middle school science teachers) degrees from the cooperating university. Five cohorts of teachers entered and progressed through the program. Changes in teaching practices were assessed by student and teacher questionnaires administered prior to the teachers' participation and after completion. Likewise, changes in student learning were assessed by content tests, pre– and post–teacher participation.

One of the goals of the project was to change classroom practices by increasing the frequency of teaching and learning by inquiry. Analyses of both teacher and student questionnaires indicated that teachers more frequently taught by inquiry and their students more often learned by inquiry after teachers had completed 2 to 3 years of professional development. This finding was reinforced by the lack of significant change among the last cohort of teachers that had only completed 1 year of professional development.[19] The findings strongly suggested that a lag exists between learning new content and new teaching strategies and implementation of those strategies in classrooms. Further, there were differences in the degree of change between the two teaching levels and subjects studied (middle school science and high school chemistry). Chemistry teachers and their students indicated significantly more frequent teaching and learning by inquiry after, compared to before, the professional development. Responses of middle school teachers and their students, however, suggested that the frequency of their use of inquiry did not increase after the professional development. They were rated high on the use of inquiry instruction before and after the professional development.[20] Evaluators of the project suggested that this finding might be due to the fact that chemistry, compared with middle school science, is a more traditional discipline. Therefore, students as well as teachers were more cognizant of changes in chemistry instruction.

Analyses of student achievement data, both in middle school science and in high school chemistry, indicated that significant improvement in achievement most often occurred 2 years after teachers began the professional development. Multiple regression analyses indicated that teacher content knowledge was predictive of student achievement in three middle school general science cohorts and in one high school chemistry cohort. These findings are supported by the studies of several other researchers (Cohen & Hill, 2000; Jacob & Lefgren, 2004; Jaquith, Mindich, Chung Wei, & Darling-Hammond, 2010; Lee, Deaktor, Enders, & Lambert, 2008).

Summary of Project Assessment Evidence

Although assessments of recent large-scale projects collected different information, most focused on the effect of teacher professional development, which stressed both content knowledge and standards-based pedagogy, on improved student learning. As indicated in this review, there is evidence that—in most cases—student achievement in science improved following teacher participation in mathematics and science professional development. Because of varying goals across the projects as well as difficulties in collecting comparison-group data, there is generally a lack of rigor in the data and the analyses. However, findings in the recent *Report of the 2012 National Survey of Science and Mathematics Education* (Banilower et al., 2013) support the findings of individual project assessments reviewed here. Banilower and colleagues (2013) indicate that the primary focus of the *National Survey* was on teachers and teaching. Items used by the *National Survey* to describe reform-oriented teaching[21] are similar, if not identical, to ones used in the assessments of MSP projects, discussed in this chapter.[22] Banilower and his colleagues concluded that there was essentially no difference in the frequency of use of reform-oriented instruction across the grade levels and that such strategies were most likely to be used in classes with high- compared to low-achieving students. One goal of the MSP projects was to enable all teachers, both those with high- and low-achieving students in their science classes, to implement inquiry. Participation in teacher professional development and changes in teaching and/or improved learning, assessed by the MSP projects, provide evidence that professional development focused on improved content knowledge and pedagogy can change classroom instruction and enhance student learning.

Recommendations to Improve the Impact of Project Assessment

During the last decade, there has been an increased interest in assessment (Darling-Hammond, 2010; Popham, 2008; Stobart, 2009). As shown from the review of evidence, assessments of teachers and teaching have been key to local and large-scale reform efforts. Data from the assessments of the science projects, discussed throughout this chapter, suggest that the projects met the goals of increasing teacher content knowledge and improving student achievement (using very broad achievement measures), but those assessments often did not use rigorous methodologies. In fact, projects have struggled to comply with directives to implement assessment designs that provide credible evidence regarding project outcomes (USDOE, 2008). In addition, science education researchers have argued that because large-scale reform efforts are both complex and integrated, it is nearly impossible to tease apart the effects of the components and attribute causality to one or the other (Cobb, Confrey, diSessa, Lehrer, & Schauble, 2003). Both issues have raised concerns about project assessments as well as with the implications of their findings. This section will suggest ways to refine project assessments in order to enhance both their impact and effectiveness to improve science education.

Recommendations concerning improving and expanding project assessment are varied and take different approaches. For example, Wieman (2012) claims that projects and their assessments rarely focus attention on learning, yet "there is an extensive body of recent research on how learning is accomplished with clear implications for what constitutes effective STEM teaching" (p. 25). He further states that failure to address this issue is "a root cause of the failures of many reform efforts" (p. 25). Other authors (Penuel & Fishman, 2012) posit that the implementation of the No Child Left Behind law, which required that states, districts, and schools receiving federal funding use programs that have evidence of results from scientifically based research, also have changed the nature of project assessment. Based on prior work, Penuel and Fishman propose that assessments or research of large-scale projects must include scientifically based research on innovations as well as *design-based implementation research* (DBIR; Penuel, Fishman, Cheng, & Sabelli, 2011). According to Penuel and Fishman (2012), DBIR "produces more scalable designs and a deeper understanding of the contexts of science education" (p. 282).

A study in Queensland, Australia, suggests a new framework for building assessment capabilities and promoting quality assurance (Colbert, Wyatt-Smith, & Klenowski, 2012). According to Colbert and his colleagues, there is a growing research and policy interest in how to build and sustain an assessment culture that supports quality teaching. Although the authors focus on teacher assessments of student learning, their recommendations are applicable to improving project assessments. For example, they propose that more rigorous assessment designs be used. Quoting Harlan (2004), they suggest that to preserve the validity of an assessment there must be "a clear definition of the domain assessed, evidence that in the assessment process the intended skills and knowledge are used by the learners" (Harlan, p. 25 in Colbert et al., 2012). They also recommend that assessments of student learning should not be viewed as end points, but rather assessments should lead to critical reflections on the evidence. Formative project assessments are often used to guide projects in ways to reach their goals; that is, they involve the principal investigators and the evaluators in reflection. Currently,

summative project assessments are viewed as end points, informing funders, principal investigators, and participants of whether the project met its goals, but as noted earlier, Patton (2006) suggests that the purpose of summative assessments be expanded as well.

The issue of improving assessments to impact teaching and learning in science is complicated by the fact that science education faces significant challenges in the coming decade. Yet assessments of large-scale projects clearly point to the efficacy of teacher professional development that is based in science content and promulgates inquiry instruction. Further, there are indications that several years of professional development are required before teachers fully integrate the new content and teaching techniques into their classrooms, a finding suggesting that expensive, long-term strategies are needed to achieve classroom impact. However, budget crises at the state and federal levels suggest the likelihood of threats to infrastructures in education that are essential to improvement, from professional development to curriculum research and development. Principal investigators and evaluators are likely to be asked to "do more with less" despite the significant time and resources that are required to bring about change (National Research Council, 2010).

As suggested throughout this chapter, assessments not only improve individual projects, but they also can lead to improved policies and contribute to the knowledge base of science teaching and learning. As more is learned about the potential impact of quality assessments, it is anticipated that rigorous and more detailed assessment guidelines will be incorporated into federal and state requests for proposals. Further, it is hoped that impediments to quality assessments, such as the lack of valid and reliable instruments, the identification of a control or comparison group, and rigorous analyses of the data, will be overcome. Only when those obstacles are removed will it be realistic to expect project assessments that change classroom practices.

Acknowledgments

We thank Catherine Milne and Debra Tomanek for their helpful reviews of this chapter.

Notes

1. Theory-based evaluation will be discussed in detail later in this chapter.
2. SSIs involved whole states, such as Maine; large cities such as Cleveland received USI funds; large, usually interstate rural areas with common educational issues formed RSIs, such as the Appalachian Rural Initiative, while LSCs were funded later and involved smaller urban areas such as Mesa Public Schools (Mesa Systemic Initiative) and the Oakland Unified School District.
3. It has been argued that NCLB's emphasis on equity may have contributed to diminished excellence in science and mathematics achievement.
4. U.S. students' average score in science literacy on PISA in 2009 was higher than the 2006 average. While U.S. students scored, on

average, below the OECD average in science literacy in 2006, the average score of U.S. students in 2009 was not measurably different from the 2009 OECD average (National Center for Education Statistics, 2009).

5. The outcome measures used were not identified prior to initiating the reform effort.

6. Twenty of the 25 states and territories primarily focused on teacher professional development.

7. Ingersoll (2007) noted that NCLB defines a *highly qualified* teacher as one who (a) has a bachelor's degree, (b) holds a regular or full state-approved teaching certificate or license, and (c) is competent in each of the academic subjects s/he teaches.

8. The authors updated the list developed by Wise (1996); however, several strategies are the same (i.e., questioning, enhanced material(s), inquiry, assessment (testing), and enhanced context). The strategies and their effect sizes were: Questioning Strategies (0.74), Enhanced Material Strategies (0.29), Assessment Strategies (0.51), Inquiry Strategies (0.65), Enhanced Context Strategies (1.48), Instructional Technology (IT) Strategies (0.48), and Collaborative Learning Strategies (0.95).

9. Features are defined as follows: (a) content focus—PD focuses on subject matter content and on how students learn knowledge and skills that comprise the content (i.e., pedagogical content knowledge); (b) active learning—PD is inquiry based, providing opportunities for teachers to experience the content as learners and adapt practices to classroom situations, with guidance; (c) coherence—PD is consistent with local reforms and policies; is based on an empirically validated theory of teacher learning and change; is consistent with and builds on teachers' current knowledge and beliefs; and complements, promotes, and extends effective curricula and instructional models; (d) duration—a sufficient amount of time is spent in each PD activity; time over which each activity is spread is sufficient for optimal learning; and the frequency of PD activities provides continuity; (e) collective participation—PD structures and activities promote interaction among teachers through ongoing collaboration and content experts help teachers facilitate implementation.

10. The study was conducted in the context of an evaluation of the Eisenhower Professional Development Program—Title II of the Elementary and Secondary Education Act (ESEA).

11. Three were structural features: (a) reform type (e.g., professional development provider), (b) duration, and (c) collective participation (e.g., teachers from same grade, school, or district). The other three features characterized the substance of the professional development. They were (a) active learning, (b) coherence, and (c) content focus. Using hierarchical linear modeling, they examined two levels of outcomes: the structural level and the teacher activity level.

12. It should be noted that this study used teacher self-report of teaching practices rather than independent observation of classrooms.

13. In addition to a Statewide Systemic Initiative, discussed earlier, Ohio received Urban Systemic Initiative grants in its three eligible cities (Cleveland, Cincinnati, and Columbus) and was part of the Appalachian Rural Systemic Initiative.

14. Student-level and statewide comparison analyses were not done because individual science achievement scores were not comparable, and comparison districts did not administer the same science achievement test as the MSP districts did.

15. A third cohort had not been identified for the 2011 evaluation report (Oyer, 2011).

16. The response rate was 64% for the teacher questionnaire.

17. Currently a high-need school is defined as one that (a) has student achievement scores below 75% on statewide assessments or (b) serves high numbers of students from families with incomes below the poverty line or (c) employs a high number of teachers who do not have "highly qualified" status in the academic area or subjects they are assigned to teach.

18. The project included 20 elementary teachers, 16 secondary math teachers, 11 secondary science teachers, 11 secondary career and technical education teachers, 1 math and science teacher, and 1 special education teacher. All responded to the same questionnaire.

19. The fifth cohort had only completed 1 year of the academic program when the paper was written. All cohorts completed the professional development during the period of the project.

20. These findings differ from those of other studies, which suggests that teachers in earlier grades are more likely to change their teaching strategies (Guskey & Yoon, 2009).

21. Three terms are frequently used to describe innovative science instruction. They are "inquiry," "standards based," and "reform oriented," and they are interchangeable.

22. These items have been used since the advent of the first round of science and mathematics standards in the mid-1990s. They include: students do hands-on laboratory activities, students must supply evidence for their claims, and students represent and/or analyze data using tables, charts, or graphs. In addition, the frequency of use of instructional technology was assessed in the National Survey.

References

Abt Associates, Inc. (2010). *Review of final MSP evaluations, performance period 2007: Analytic and technical support for mathematics and science partnerships.* Report to the U.S. Department of Education OESE/Mathematics and Science Partnerships,Washington, DC.

American Association for the Advancement of Science (AAAS). (1993). *Benchmarks for science literacy.* New York: Oxford University Press.

Anderson, B. (2002). Evaluating systemic reform: Evaluation needs, practices, and challenges. In J. W. Altschuld & D. D. Kumar (Eds.), *Evaluation of science and technology education at the dawn of a new millennium* (pp. 49–80). New York: Kluwer Academic/Plenum.

Anderson, K. (2011). Science education and test-based accountability: Reviewing their relationship and exploring implications for future policy. *Science Education, 96*(1), 104–129.

Apple, M. (2001). *Educating the "right" way: Markets, standards, God and inequality.* New York: Routledge.

Banilower, E.R., Heck, D.J., & Weiss, I.R. (2005). Can professional development make the vision of the standards a reality? The impact of the National Science Foundation's Local Systemic Change Through Teacher Enhancement Initiative. *Journal of Research in Science Teaching, 44*, 375–395.

Banilower, E.R., Smith, P.S., Weiss, I.R., Malzahn, K.A., Campell, K.A., & Weis, A.M. (2013). *Report of the 2012 national survey of science and mathematics education.* Chapel Hill, NC: Horizon Research, Inc.

Bush, V. (1960). *Science—the endless frontier.* Washington, DC: United States Government Printing Office.

Bybee, R.W., & Fuchs, B. (2006). Preparing the 21st century workforce: A new reform in science and technology education. *Journal of Research in Science Teaching, 43*, 349–352.

Carpenter, T.P., Blanton, M.L., Cobb, P., Franke, M.L., Kaput, J., & McClain, K. (2004). *Scaling up innovative practices in mathematics and science.* Research Report from National Center for Improving Student Learning and Achievement in Mathematics and Science. Madison: University of Wisconsin.

Chatterji, M. (2002). Models and methods for examining standards-based reforms and accountability initiatives: Have the tools of inquiry answered pressing questions on improving schools? *Review of Educational Research, 72*(3), 345–386.

Chen, H.-T. (1990). *Theory-driven evaluations.* Thousand Oaks, CA: Sage.

Clune, W.H., Porter, A.C., & Raizen, S.A. (1999, September 29). Systemic reform: What is it? How do we know? *Education Week, 19*(5), 31.

Coalition for Evidence-Based Policy. (2005). *How to solicit rigorous evaluations of mathematics and science partnerships (MSP) projects: A user-friendly guide for MSP state coordinators.* Chicago: National Opinion Research Center, University of Chicago.

Cobb, P., Confrey, J., diSessa, A., Lehrer, R., & Schauble, L. (2003). Design experiments in educational research. *Educational Researcher, 32*, 9–13.

Cohen, D. K., & Hill, H. C. (2000). Instructional policy and classroom performance: The mathematics reform in California. *Teachers College Record, 102,* 294–343.

Colbert, P., Wyatt-Smith, C., & Klenowski, V. (2012). A systems level approach to building sustainable assessment cultures: Moderation, quality task design and dependability of judgment. *Policy Futures in Education, 10*(4), 387–402.

Corcoran, T. B. (1995, June). Helping teachers teach well: Transforming professional development. *Consortium for Policy Research in Education Policy Briefs, 16,* 1–11.

Creswell, J. W., Plano Clark, V. L., Gutmann, M., & Hanson, W. (2003). Advanced mixed methods research designs. In A. Tashakkori & C. Teddlie (Eds.), *Handbook of mixed methods in social and behavioral research* (pp. 209–240). Thousand Oaks, CA: Sage.

Darling-Hammond, L. (2010). *The flat earth and education: How America's commitment to equity will determine our future.* New York: Teachers College Press.

Dee, T. S., & Jacob, B. (2011). The impact of No Child Left Behind on student achievement. *Journal of Policy Analysis and Management, 30*(3), 418–446.

Desimone, L. M. (2009). Improving impact studies of teachers' professional development: Toward better conceptualizations and measures. *Educational Researcher, 38*(3), 181–199.

Desimone, L. M., Porter, A. C., Garet, M. S., Yoon, K. S., & Birman, B. F. (2002). Effects of professional development on teachers' instruction: Results from a three-year longitudinal study. *Educational Evaluation and Policy Analysis, 24*(2), 81–112.

Dow, P. B. (1999). *Schoolhouse politics: Lessons from the* Sputnik *era.* Cambridge, MA: Harvard University Press.

Elmore, R. F. (1993). *The development and implementation of large-scale curriculum reforms.* Paper prepared for the American Association for the Advancement of Science. Cambridge, MA: Harvard Graduate School of Education, Center for Policy Research in Education.

Elmore, R. F. (1996). Getting to scale with good educational practice. *Harvard Educational Review, 66*(1), 1–26.

Finn, C. E. (2002). *No Child Left Behind: What will it take?* Washington, DC: Thomas B. Fordham Foundation.

Fretchling, J., Frierson, H., Hood, S., & Hughes, G. (2002). *The 2002 user-friendly handbook for project evaluation.* Arlington, VA: National Science Foundation.

Fretchling, J., Stevens, F., Lawrenze, F., & Sharp, L. (1993). *The user-friendly handbook for project evaluation: Science mathematics and technology education.* NSF 93–152. Arlington, VA: National Science Foundation.

Garet, M. S., Birman, B. F., Porter, A. C., Desimone, L., Herman, R., & Yoon, K. S. (1999). *Designing effective professional development: Lessons from the Eisenhower Program.* Washington, DC: U.S. Department of Education.

Glesne, C. (2011). *Becoming qualitative researchers: An introduction* (4th ed.). Boston: Allyn & Bacon.

Goertz, M. E., Floden, R. E., & O'Day, J. A. (1996). *Systemic reform. [Volume I: Findings and conclusions.] Studies of education reform.* East Lansing, MI: National Center for Research on Teacher Learning. (ERIC Document Reproduction Service No. ED397553)

Government Accountability Office (GAO). (2003). *Program evaluation: An evaluation culture and collaborative partnerships help build agency capacity.* GAO-03–454. Washington, DC: Author.

Government Accountability Office (GAO). (2009). *Program evaluation: A variety of rigorous methods can help identify effective interventions.* Report to Congressional Requesters, GAO-10–3. Washington, DC: Author.

Government Accountability Office (GAO). (2012). *Science, technology, engineering, and mathematics education: Strategic planning needed to better manage overlapping programs across multiple agencies.* GAO-12–108. Washington, DC: Author.

Greene, J. C., DeStefano, L., Burgon, H., & Hall, J. (2006). An educative, values-engaged approach to evaluating STEM educational programs. *New Directions for Evaluation, 2006*(109), 53–71.

Guskey, T. R., & Yoon, K. S. (2009). What works in professional development? *Phi Delta Kappan, 90*(7), 495–500.

Gullickson, A. R., & Hanssen, C. E. (2006). Local evaluation in multisite STEM programs: Relating evaluation use and program results. *New Directions for Evaluation, 109,* 97–103.

Guyton, E., Fox, M. C., & Sisk, K. A. (1991). Comparison of teacher attitudes, teacher efficacy, and teacher performance of first-year teachers prepared by alternative and traditional teacher education programs. *Action in Teacher Education, 13*(2), 1–9.

Hargreaves, A., & Goodson, I. (2006). Educational change over time? The sustainability and non-sustainability of three decades of secondary school change and continuity. *Educational Administration Quarterly, 42*(1), 3–41.

Heck, D. J. (1998). Evaluating equity in statewide systemic initiatives: Asking the right questions. *Journal of Women and Minorities in Science and Engineering, 4,* 161–181.

Hershberg, T. (2005). *Value-added assessment and systemic reform: Response to America's human capital development challenge.* Paper presented at the Challenge of Education Reform: Standards, Accountability, Resources and Policy, Cancun, Mexico.

Hess, F. (1999). *Spinning wheels: The politics of urban school reform.* Washington, DC: Brookings Intit. Press.

Horizon Research, Inc. (1994). *Reflections from Wingspread: Lessons learned about the National Science Foundation's Systemic Initiative.* A report on the March 1994 Wingspread conference. Chapel Hill, NC: Author.

Ingersoll, R. M. (2007, February). *Misdiagnosing the teacher quality problem.* (CPRE Policy Brief No. RB-49). Philadelphia: University of Pennsylvania, Consortium for Policy Research in Education.

Jacob, B. A., & Lefgren, L. (2004). The impact of teacher training on student achievement: Quasi-experimental evidence from school reform efforts in Chicago. *Journal of Human Resources, 39*(1), 50–79.

Jaquith, A., Mindich, D., Chung Wei, R., & Darling-Hammond, L. (2010). *Teacher professional learning in the United States: Case studies of state policies and strategies.* Dallas, TX: National Staff Development Council.

Kahle, J. B. (2004). Will girls be left behind? Gender differences and accountability. *Journal of Research in Science Teaching, 41,* 961–969.

Kahle, J. B. (2007). Systemic reform: Research, vision, and politics. In S. K. Abell & N. G. Lederman (Eds.), *The handbook of research on science education* (pp. 911–942). Mahwah, NJ: Erlbaum.

Kahle, J. B., Meece, J., & Scantlebury, K. (2000). Urban African-American middle school science students: Does standards-based teaching make a difference? *Journal of Research in Science Teaching, 37,* 1019–1041.

Kahle, J. B., & Woodruff, S. B. (2011). Science teacher education research and policy: Are they connected? In G. DeBoer (Ed.), *Research in science education: Vol. 5, The role of public policy in K–12 science education,* (pp. 47–75), Greenwich, CT: Information Age Publishing.

Kahle, J. B., & Woodruff, S. B. (2013). Ohio's 30 years of mathematics and science education reform: Practices, politics, and policies. In B. S. Wojnowski & C. Pea (Eds.), *Models and approaches to STEM professional development* (pp. 79–102). Arlington, VA: National Science Teachers Association Press.

Katzenmeyer, C., & Lawrenz, F. (2006). National science foundation perspectives on the nature of STEM program evaluation. *New Directions for Evaluation, 2006*(109), 7–18.

Kennedy, M. M. (1999). *Form and substance in mathematics and science professional development.* NISE brief (vol. 3, no. 2). Madison: University of Wisconsin–Madison, National Institute for Science Education.

Kroger, L. E., Campbell, H. L., Thacker, A. A., Becker, D. E., & Wise, L. L. (2007). *Behind the numbers: Interviews in 22 states about achievement data and the No Child Left Behind Act policies.* Retrieved from www.cep-dc.org/displayDocument.cfm?DocumentID=180

Kumar, D. D., & Altschuld, J. W. (2003). The need for comprehensive evaluation in science education. *Review of Policy Research, 20*(4), 603–615.

Laguarda, K. (1998). *Assessing the SSI's impacts on student achievement: An imperfect science.* Menlo Park, CA: SRI International.

Lawrenz, F. (1975). The relationship between teacher characteristics and student achievement and attitude. *Journal of Research in Science Teaching, 12,* 433–437.

Lee, O., Deaktor, R., Enders, C., & Lambert, J. (2008). Impact of a multi-year professional development intervention on science achievement of culturally and linguistically diverse elementary students. *Journal of Research in Science Teaching, 45,* 726–747.

Loucks-Horsley, S., Love, N., Stiles, K. E., Mundry, S., & Hewson, P. W. (2003). *Designing professional development for teachers of science and mathematics.* Thousand Oaks, CA: Corwin Press.

Magnusson, S., Borko, H., Krajcik, J. S., & Layman, J. W. (1992). *The relationship between teacher content and pedagogical content knowledge and student content knowledge of heat energy and temperature.* Paper presented at the annual meeting of the National American Association for Research in Science Teaching, Boston, MA.

Mason, K., Brewer, J., Redman, J., Bomar, C., Ghenciu, P., LeDocq, M., & Chapel, C. (2012). SySTEMically improving student academic achievement in mathematics and science. *Journal for Quality & Participation, 35*(2), 20–24.

McLaughlin, M. (1990). The RAND change agent study revisited: Macro perspectives and micro realities. *Educational Researcher, 19,* 11–16.

Monk, D. H. (1994). Subject area preparation of secondary mathematics and science teachers and student achievement. *Economics of Education Review, 13*(2), 125–145.

Moore, M. H. (1995). *Creating public value: Strategic management in government.* Cambridge, MA: Harvard University Press.

National Center for Education Statistics. (2009). *Science literacy performance of 15-year-olds.* Retrieved from http://nces.ed.gov/surveys/pisa/pisa2009highlights_4.asp

National Council of Teachers of Mathematics (NCTA). (1989). *Curriculum and evaluation standards for school mathematics.* Reston, VA: Author.

National Research Council (NRC). (1996). *National science education standards.* Washington, DC: National Academies Press.

National Research Council (NRC). (2007). *Taking science to school: Learning and teaching science in grades K–8.* Washington, DC: National Academies Press.

National Research Council (NRC). (2010). *Rising Above the Gathering Storm, revisited: Rapidly approaching category 5.* My Members of the 2005 "Rising Above the Gathering Storm" Committee; Prepared for the Presidents of the National Academy of Sciences, National Academy of Engineering and Institute of Medicine. Washington, DC: National Academies Press.

National Science Foundation (NSF). (2002). *Math and Science Partnership (MSP): Program solicitation.* NSF-02-061. Retrieved from www.nsf.gov/pubs/2002/nsf02061/nsf02061.htm

National Science Foundation (NSF). (2004). *A more synergistic whole: Education lessons about learning.* Retrieved from www.nsf.gov/about/history/nsf0050/education/moresynergistic.htm

National Science Foundation (NSF). (2010). *User-friendly handbook for project evaluation.* Retrieved from www.westat.com/pdf/projects/2010ufhb.pdf

National Science Foundation (NSF). (2012). *Math and Science Partnership (MSP): Program solicitation.* (NSF 12–518). Retrieved from www.nsf.gov/pubs/2012/nsf12518/nsf12518.htm

Nelkin, D. (1977). *Science textbook controversies and the politics of equal time.* Cambridge: MIT Press.

Office of Technology Assessment (OTA). (1988). *Elementary and secondary education for science and engineering—A technical memorandum* (OTA-TM-SET-41). Washington, DC: U.S. Government Printing Office.

Oyer, E. (2011). *Evaluation report: 2010–2011 Illinois Mathematics and Science Partnership.* Carmel, IN: EvalSolutions, Inc.

Pane, J. F., Williams, V. L., Olmsted, S. S., Yuan, K., Spindler, E., & Slaughter, M. E. (2009). *Math science partnership of southwest Pennsylvania: Measuring progress toward goals.* Santa Monica, CA: RAND Corporation.

Patton, M. Q. (2006). Evaluation for the way we work. *The Nonprofit Quarterly, 13*(1), 28–33.

Penuel, W. R., & Fishman, B. J. (2012). Large-scale science education intervention research we can use. *Journal of Research in Science Education, 49,* 281–304.

Penuel, W. R., Fishman, B. J., Cheng, B. H., & Sabelli, N. (2011). Organizing research and development at the intersection of learning, implementation, and design. *Educational Researcher, 40*(7), 331–337.

Popham, W. J. (2008). *Transformative assessment.* Alexandria, VA: Association for Supervision and Curriculum Development.

Sahlberg, P. (2006). Education reform for raising economic competitiveness. *Journal of Educational Change, 7*(4), 259–287.

Sanders, L. R., Borko, H., & Lockard, J. D. (1993). Secondary science teachers' knowledge base when teaching science courses in and out of their area of certification. *Journal of Research in Science Teaching, 30,* 723–736.

Schneider, B. L., & Keesler, V. A. (2007). School reform 2007: Transforming education into a scientific enterprise. *Annual Review of Sociology, 33,* 197–217.

Schorr, L. B., & Kubisch A. C. (1995, September). *New approaches to evaluation: Helping Sister Mary Paul, Geoff Canada, and Otis Johnson while convincing Pat Moynihan, Newt Gingrich, and the American public.* Presentation at Annie E. Casey Foundation Annual Research/Evaluation Conference, Baltimore, MD.

Schroeder, C. M., Scott, T. P., Tolson, H., Huang, T. Y., & Lee, Y. H. (2007). A meta-analysis of national research: Effects of teaching strategies on student achievement in science in the United States. *Journal of Research in Science Teaching, 44,* 1436–1460.

Shavelson, R. J., & Towne, L. (2002). *Scientific research in education.* Washington, DC: National Research Council, National Academies Press.

Slavin, R. E. (2005). Sand, bricks and seeds: School change strategies and readiness for reform. In D. Hopkins (Ed.), *The practice and theory of school improvement* (pp. 265–279). Dordrecht, the Netherlands: Springer.

Smith, M., & O'Day, J. (1991). Systemic school reform. In S. Fuhrman & B. Malen (Eds.), *The politics of curriculum and testing* (pp. 233–267). Bristol, PA: Falmer.

Spicer, D. E. (2012). Rhetoric, reality and research: The rhetoric of systemic reform, the reality of leadership development and current trends in school leadership research in the United States. *Italian Journal of Sociology of Education, 1,* 305–319.

Stobart, G. (2009). *Testing times: The uses and abuses of assessment.* London: Routledge.

Supovitz, J. (1996, December). *The impact over time of Project Discovery on teachers' attitudes, preparation, and teaching practice.* Final report. Chapel Hill, NC: Horizon Research, Inc.

Supovitz, J., & Taylor, B. S. (2005). Systemic education evaluation: Evaluating the impact of systemwide reform in education. *American Journal of Evaluation, 26*(2), 204–230.

Supovitz, J. A., & Turner, H. M. (2000). The effects of professional development on science teaching practices and classroom culture. *Journal of Research in Science Teaching, 37,* 963–980.

Thomas B. Fordham Foundation. (2012). *The state of state science standards.* Washington, DC: Author.

Toch, T. (1991). *In the name of excellence.* New York: Oxford University.

U.S. Department of Education (USDOE). (2002). *No Child Left Behind Act of 2001.* Washington, DC: Author.

U.S. Department of Education (USDOE). (2005). *Scientifically based evaluation methods* (FR Doc. 05–1317). Federal Register 70(Jan. 25):3586–89. Retrieved from www.gpo.gov/fdsys/pkg/FR-2005-01-25/pdf/05-1317.pdf

U.S. Department of Education (USDOE). (2008, September). *ESEA: Mathematics and science partnerships (OESE).* FY 2008 program performance report. Washington, DC: Author.

U.S. Department of Education (USDOE). (n.d.). *Mathematics and science partnerships program.* Retrieved from www.ed-msp.net/

W. K. Kellogg Foundation. (1998). *W. K. Kellogg Foundation evaluation handbook*. Battle Creek, MI: Author.

Ward, J. H. Jr. (1963), Hierarchical grouping to optimize an objective function. *Journal of the American Statistical Association, 58*, 236–244.

Weiss, C. H. (2000). Which links to which theories shall we evaluate? *New Directions for Evaluation, 87*, 35–45.

Weiss, I. R., & Pasley, J. D. (2008, March). *Using research findings and practice-based insights: Guidance for policy, practice, and future research*. Paper presented at the annual meeting of the American Educational Research Association, New York City.

Weiss, I. R., & Webb, N. (2003). *Study of the impact of the Statewide Systemic Initiatives program: Lessons learned*. Chapel Hill, NC: Horizon Research, Inc.

Westat. (2002). *Criteria for classifying designs of MSP evaluations*. Retrieved from http://ies.ed.gov/ncee/projects/evaluation/assistance_data.asp

Wieman, C. (2012). Applying new research to improve science education: Insights from several fields on how people learn to become experts can help us to dramatically enhance the effectiveness of science, technology, engineering, and mathematics education. *Issues in Science and Technology, 29*(1), 25–32.

Wilson, S., Floden, R., & Ferrini-Mundy, J. (2001). *Teacher preparation research: Current knowledge, gaps, and recommendations*. Seattle, WA: Center for the Study of Teaching and Policy.

Wise, K. C. (1996). Strategies for teaching science: What works? *Clearing House, 69*(6), 337–338.

Woodruff, S. B., Hung, H. L., & Seabrook, L. (2009, November). *Exploratory cluster analysis: Variability and commonality of the implementation and impact of Ohio Mathematics and Science Partnership (OMSP) projects*. Panel presentation at the Annual Conference of the American Evaluation Association, Orlando, FL.

Woodruff, S. B., Li, Y., & Kao, H. C. (2010). *Evaluation of Ohio Mathematics and Science Partnership program: Instrument validity and reliability study and study of programmatic and project-level effect size, June 2010*. Oxford, OH: Miami University, Ohio's Evaluation & Assessment Center for Mathematics and Science Education.

Woodruff, S. B., McCollum, T. L., Li, Y., & Bautista, N. U. (2010, March). *Enhancing elementary teachers' content and pedagogical knowledge through sustained professional development*. Paper presented at the Annual International Conference of the National Association for Research in Science Teaching, Philadelphia, PA.

Woodruff, S. B., Zorn, D., Noga, J., & Seabrook, L. (2009, April). *State-sponsored professional development: Lessons learned through dialogue across evaluation, theory, research, and practice*. Panel presentation at the Annual Meeting of the American Educational Research Association, San Diego, CA.

Woodruff, S. B., Zorn, D., Raffle, H., & Oches, B. (2011). *Ohio Mathematics and Science Partnership Program cross-project evaluation: Year 2 final report*. Oxford, OH: Miami University, Ohio's Evaluation & Assessment Center for Mathematics and Science Education.

Woodruff, S. B., Zorn, D., Raffle, H., & Oches, B. (2012). *Ohio Mathematics and Science Partnership Program cross-project evaluation: Final report*. Oxford, OH: Miami University, Ohio's Evaluation & Assessment Center for Mathematics and Science Education.

Yoon, K. S., Duncan, T., Lee, S. W., Scarloss, B., & Shapley, K. L. (2007). *Reviewing the evidence on how teacher professional development affects student achievement*. Issues and answers report, REL 2007 – No. 033. Washington, DC: U.S. Department of Education, Institute of Education Sciences, National Center for Education Evaluation and Regional Assistance, Regional Educational Laboratory Southwest.

Zorn, D., Seabrook, L., Marks, J., Chappell-Young, J., Hung, S., Marx, M., et al. (2009). *The Ohio Mathematics and Science Partnership program external evaluation: Year 2 report*. Oxford, OH: Miami University, Ohio's Evaluation & Assessment Center for Science and Mathematics Education.

Zucker, A. A., & Shields, P. M. (1997). *SSI strategies for reform: Preliminary findings from the evaluation of the National Science Foundation's Statewide Systemic Initiatives Program*. Menlo, Park, CA: SRI International.

Zucker, A. A., Shields, P. M., Adelman, N., & Powell, J. (1995). *Evaluation of the National Science Foundation's Statewide Systemic Initiatives Program: Second year report* (Report No. NSF 96–48). Arlington, VA: National Science Foundation.

36

Precollege Engineering Education

CHRISTINE M. CUNNINGHAM AND WILLIAM S. CARLSEN

Children are natural engineers. They tinker with the natural world and the designed world too: piling up sand or blocks to make dams and bridges; doodling wherever surfaces and media are available; taking things apart and putting them back together. They create forts out of blankets, cardboard, bushes, or wood. Their activities offer a foundation for future understandings: how technologies are designed, resourced, organized, and constructed; and how engineering affects people, society, and the environment. Children's natural interests create opportunities for the development of initial understandings about technology and engineering, and building upon those initial understandings is now an educational priority (e.g., American Association for the Advancement of Science [AAAS], 1993; National Research Council [NRC], 2012; Obama, 2009).

"Teaching engineering" is a common objective of technology education, taught in some countries as a distinct subject and emerging in others as a new curricular priority (Rasinen, 2003). Recent book-length reviews provide contemporary international perspectives on research and curriculum in technology education settings, settings that often trace their roots to industrial arts and vocational education (Benson & Lunt, 2011; Jones & De Vries, 2009) but increasingly also from other domains, such as the arts and the social sciences (Barlex, 2007). Given the goals of this volume, we have tried not to cover the same ground. For example, we consider studies of "teaching engineering" only where science learning was an explicit goal of instruction. Our primary concern in this chapter is not the *subject matter* of engineering but rather the implications of engineering education for the teaching and learning of science. For example, it has been suggested that when a young child engages in engineering activity, cognitive load may be reduced by operationalizing inchoate concepts or principles in physical objects, which enables the child to engage in problem solving and other productive activity that would not otherwise be possible (Levy, 2013). From a more sociocognitive perspective of learning, there is evidence that by emphasizing personal, real-world connections and constructing a need to know for related science, engineering design activities can enhance student motivation to learn science (Barron et al., 1998; Kolodner et al., 2003).

In colleges and universities, the formal study of engineering has typically followed and built upon years of prerequisite science studies. The emergence of engineering education as a goal for children's science study offers researchers today a laboratory for evaluating the logic of that sequence and an opportunity to consider fresh strategies for addressing perennial challenges in science education.

The first section of this chapter presents a contemporary view about how science and engineering should be represented in the precollege curriculum, drawing upon the U.S. *Framework for K–12 Science Education* (NRC, 2012), the policy context with which we are most familiar.[1] Science and engineering are related disciplines, but they are not identical. The U.S. efforts place particular emphasis on the practices of science and engineering—sometimes similar and sometimes different—and we use those practices to identify key findings from a number of engineering education research studies. Some of these studies have identified cognitive and sociocognitive elements (strategies, etc.) that may have the potential to improve science teaching and learning.

In the second section, we use the visual metaphor of cycles to further develop the idea of how science teaching might be informed and potentially reshaped by lessons from engineering. In Section 3, we review some miscellaneous (but intriguing) research findings, and finally, in Section 4, we identify some areas that appear to be promising for future research.

Section 1. Science and Engineering: Epistemic Practices

In the United States, there is growing consensus that science and engineering education for the 21st century should engage students in disciplinary practices (NRC, 2012).

Science and engineering are related disciplines, so it is not surprising that aspects of these features overlap. But by definition, they also diverge: what makes science and engineering distinct disciplines are the differences in their *epistemic practices* (Kelly, 2008, 2011): that is, how they (socially) achieve the solution of technical or theoretical problems. For example, a scientific problem might be "solved" through the publication of a general knowledge claim, after its evidence (e.g., description of an experiment, analysis of data) is subjected to evaluation by peers whose expertise closely resembles that of the author. An engineering problem, on the other hand, might be "solved" through the demonstration of a very specific solution—not a general knowledge claim—and its evaluation might include individuals with very different areas of expertise, such as economics, safety, and aesthetics.

Table 36.1 enumerates eight practices from *The Framework for K–12 Science Education* (NRC, 2012, pp. 50–53). Although the NRC document tabulates some discipline-specific differences for each practice, its emphasis is on the similarities. For our purposes here, we have added two new "relative emphasis" columns, with the goals of foregrounding the differences and reducing what we believe to be an overemphasis in the NRC document on academic engineering.[2]

1. Asking questions and defining problems. The *Framework* notes that whereas scientists ask questions about natural phenomena, with the goal of developing explanations and theories, engineers' work tends to be driven by real-world problems. Another way of looking at this difference is to contrast a scientist's goal of *progress* (in the development of theory and new explanations) with an engineer's goal of *product*: that is, concrete solutions to problems, like moving goods cost effectively while reducing carbon emissions.

From a pedagogical perspective, one perennial challenge of the scientific variant of this first practice is that the evaluation of *progress* requires disciplinary expertise, which novices lack, by definition! This conundrum may be one reason that an emphasis on "inquiry" has had mixed results in efforts to improve science teaching. Among the criteria for a good scientific question are that (a) the answer is not already known, (b) the question is suited for empirical study, and (c) success in answering the question would open new lines of inquiry. But evaluating each of those criteria requires deep disciplinary understanding. It should not be surprising that many student-initiated science investigations are confirmatory, inconclusive, or result in trivial conclusions.

One possible advantage of the engineering form of this first practice is developmental: Practical problems can be explicated without deep disciplinary understanding, certainly on the part of the student and potentially even on the part of the teacher. In other words, engineering problems can be formulated that are challenging and educationally productive yet accessible to novices. For example, Levy (2013) challenged 5- to 6-year-olds to solve four progressive engineering challenges: design and build a watering system for plants with different water needs; design and build a system to deliver equal amounts of water to two apartments, one higher than the other; design a machine to mix a variety of colored water samples; and design a "water garden" with pools and fountains. She found that, relative to children in a control group, children who engaged in engineering showed greatly increased understanding about relevant physical science concepts, such as the effects on flow rate of pipe resistance, occlusion diameter, and reservoir elevation.

2. Developing and using models. Modeling is used in varied ways in both science and engineering. The *Framework* notes that in science, models are commonly used to develop and refine explanations about the natural world, while in engineering, models serve to develop an understanding of design parameters and possible points of failure, to compare alternative solutions, and to advance the design process (NRC, 2012, p. 50). Put another way, scientific models emphasize explanatory and predictive functions; engineering models emphasize analytic and evaluative functions. Building models is not an easy task for students; novices tend to focus more on the appearance of models than on their functionality (Penner, Giles, Lehrer, & Schauble, 1997). However, in using models, students have the opportunity to learn to focus on and appreciate the behaviors of natural or technological systems—an appreciation that can be a foundation for more in-depth examination of function in the real world or in more advanced models (Penner, Lehrer, & Schauble, 1998).

One disciplinary difference with educational implications is the contrast between using models to construct an argument (scientific explanation) and using models to achieve a desired specific outcome (engineering optimization). In a study of upper elementary students, Schauble, Klopfer, and Raghavan (1991) compared the experiences of two groups of students whose work with the same models was sequenced differently. In both instances, students completed a science task (investigating the factors that affect spring length in a mechanical system) and an engineering task (improving the speed of boats in a canal system). Interestingly, the educational outcomes were superior for the engineering-first group. The authors noted John Dewey's (1913) observation that children benefit from ends-oriented, practical ("engineering") work as a predecessor to means-oriented science study. They also observed that several other studies have found that children, when asked to conduct scientific experiments to determine causes and effects, often instead focus on optimizing for a desirable outcome (e.g., Kuhn & Phelps, 1982).

One way of thinking about this difference is that in an engineering problem, a model is always a *product* of investigation. Even if it is not a physical object or system (which it often is), its components are likely to re-present an account of actual work: "We tried this, and we did this, and what we now show you includes specific features that incorporate our experiences." In science, models are

TABLE 36.1
Epistemic Practices and Goals of Science and Engineering

Practice (from NRC, 2012)	Relative emphasis in science	Relative emphasis in engineering
1. Asking questions and defining problems	Goals of theory development, empirical testability, and the development of general explanations: progress	Goal of explicating a practical problem to be resolved through the construction of a system or other technology: product
2. Developing and using models	Explanation and prediction	Analysis and evaluation
3. Planning and carrying out investigations	Systematic inquiry with the goals of testing hypotheses or otherwise evaluating and extending knowledge claims concerning the natural world	Acquiring data for use in generating new design specifications or evaluating a proposed design's fit to existing design specifications
4. Analyzing and interpreting data	Issues related to the global frame of the found, natural world (e.g., data representativeness, boundary conditions, external generalizability)	Attention to diverse multiple criteria: narrowly scientific (e.g., material properties) and other (e.g., cost, risk of failure)
5. Using mathematics and computational thinking	Tools: symbolic representations, transformations, simplification of complexity, noise reduction, hypothesis testing. Math is used to virtually test conceptual models, using real data.	Tools: stand-ins for real things and real phenomena. Math is used to virtually design concrete things, using both real and simulated data.
6. Constructing explanations and designing solutions	Logical accounts of observations, with attention to causality, uncertainty, further empirical testing, and conformance to current scientific understandings, with the objective a "best explanation," the culmination of Practices 1–5	"Design" is both the culmination of Practices 1–5 and a description of the process through which those practices are iterated, often many times. A preferred design is usually selected from among alternatives, considering tradeoffs among design specifications and constraints.
7. Engaging in argument from evidence	Goal is to persuade peers, as evidenced by their subsequent use of one's work in their own scientific activity	Goal is to persuade a client, as evidenced by the substantiation of the proposed solution in a technology or process.
8. Obtaining, evaluating, and communicating information	Free exchange of information is an important norm, with attribution; this exchange is a primary goal of science.	Products of engineering are generally legally proprietary, although they may be shared freely or in the civic realm.

more commonly used as a *prerequisite* of an investigation: one begins, for example, with a model of an ideal gas, a predator–prey cycle, or projectile motion, then engages in hands-on work to better understand an abstraction. Of course, inquiries in either discipline use models at different times and in different ways. Engineers often use models early in their work (e.g., finite element models) and scientific work often *yields* new models. But these variations don't contradict a core difference: Most science begins with conceptual models; most engineering ends with something real, concrete, instantiated.

In a physical model, students can use real-world objects and materials as cognitive resources that externalize aspects of a complex problem into something tangible. Students use models to gauge their own understandings, and teachers can use models as tools for assessment (NRC, 2012). Through modeling in engineering, students can develop skills in noticing and representing parts versus wholes and how parts connect, as well as skills in representing their ideas and plans (Fleer, 2000a). Research on children's drawing may be useful in further developing an understanding of how children make sense of the world through visual models (Anning, 1997). For example, even very young children can produce and label design drawings but may be limited to front-view representations (Fleer, 2000b).

Systems models and systems thinking are more important in some areas of science and engineering than others. Systems thinking entails understanding the relationship between micro- and macro-scales within a system, as well as understanding how behaviors at the subsystem level can differ from the emergent behaviors of the larger system (NRC, 2012). In engineering, systems thinking is a practice essential to the development of complex technologies, many with wide-reaching impacts on people, societies, and the environment.

In the engineered world, simple and readily accessible systems and subsystems abound. Children can begin to develop their skill with systems thinking even in elementary school by examining and reverse-engineering simple technologies such as retractable pens or by developing their own subsystems and systems within the classroom (Katehi, Pearson, & Feder, 2009). For example, Mehalik, Doppelt, and Schunn (2008) compared two curricular units designed to teach electricity to middle school students: One engaged students in systems design, while the other engaged students in scripted inquiry. The researchers later tested students individually on concepts common to both units, including resistance, voltage, and series and parallel circuits. They found that the students whose studies involved systems design showed more improvement than those who engaged in scripted inquiry; and the systems approach narrowed the achievement gap for African-American students. The researchers attributed the success of the approach in part to greater engagement by students and further argued that the design challenge strategy offered better opportunities for students to reason scientifically.

3. Planning and carrying out investigations. Engineers and scientists execute structured inquiries for different reasons: scientists "to test existing theories and explanations or revise and develop new ones" and engineers "to identify how effective, efficient, and durable their designs may be under a range of conditions" (NRC, 2012, p. 50). In other words, although the daily activities of many scientists and engineers may look identical, the intended outcome of science is mental and the intended outcome of engineering is material. From an epistemic perspective, science yields knowledge claims and engineering yields technologies, which are physical manifestations of engineering knowledge.

Engineering investigations often have multiple possible solutions. In contrast to scientific work, the solution to an engineering problem is often an array of alternatives that address problem criteria and balance tradeoffs in different ways. The ultimate decision about which solution is "best" requires human judgment: Are we willing to pay twice as much for a modest decrease in the risk of failure, for example? For students, the viability of diverse solutions and the validity of more varied values may enhance motivation and interest. Students are pushed to critically consider their solutions and defend the choices they make in their designs, not in terms of being the One Right Answer but as a sensible way to maximize positives and minimize negatives. Furthermore, because engineering problems tend to be situation dependent and engineering solutions evaluated with respect to the needs of a human client, engineering work in an educational setting may be perceived by students to be more authentic and socially beneficial. Research suggests that an emphasis on the social value of the object of student learning can be especially helpful for increasing the motivation of female students (Brotman & Moore, 2008). Addressing engineering's relevance to helping people may engage girls because they tend to have more interest in socially directed careers (Baker & Leary, 1995; Jones, Howe, & Rua, 2000; Miller, Blessing, & Schwartz, 2006).

4. Analyzing and interpreting data. Both scientists and engineers analyze and interpret data. However, scientists use data as persuasive evidence to support existing explanations or to advance new ones, whereas engineers embrace the more practical goal of comparing and evaluating solutions (NRC, 2012, p. 51). It should also be noted that science and engineering do not concern themselves with identical kinds of data. Scientific arguments use data to generalize empirical claims with respect to the found, natural world. Challenges to such arguments may center on questions about sampling, data representativeness, and natural boundary conditions, because these factors affect

generalizability, such as whether the conclusions of a lab experiment can plausibly predict similar outcomes in the field. Again, a degree of disciplinary perspective—or at least perspective about the world beyond the immediate study—is required. Engineers are more concerned with specifics: more "How will this bridge behave here?" than "How will this bridge behave anywhere?" Hence, the engineering form of this practice may offer some advantage to subject matter novices. Note that greater specificity of application doesn't make engineering problems easy: Because the products of engineering are tangible, engineering typically demands a much greater diversity of data types, not just scientific data (e.g., material properties) but also assessments of risk, cost, and other factors.

Engineering motivates students to collect and analyze data as they develop their own solutions, compare their solutions to those generated by others, and champion their designs to an audience, whether within or outside the classroom (Barron et al., 1998; Kolodner et al., 2003; Roth, 1995a). This puts children in the role of authorities about their own inventions: They collect and interpret their own data, exercise responsibility for deciding what is good enough and what needs improvement, and take ownership of their process and product (Silk, Schunn, & Cary, 2009). Ownership is a powerful and dynamic motivator in science (O'Neill, 2010; O'Neill & Calabrese Barton, 2005). Giving students authority to solve problems is potentially a strong precursor to productive disciplinary engagement, as is making students accountable to each other (Engle & Conant, 2002). For students who otherwise have difficulty with school and traditional learning structures, activity that promotes students' disciplinary "agency" may be especially beneficial, as it may offer students opportunities to develop new identities as competent and knowledgeable actors (Roth & Lee, 2007).

5. Mathematics and computational thinking are also integral to both disciplines. Mathematics is used to simulate, to analyze data, and to make predictions (NRC, 2012, p. 51). In science, mathematical tools simplify complexity and reduce noise, and math and inferential statistics offer well-understood ways of defining and testing conceptual models, with data from the real world. We may not be able to directly comprehend an ecosystem's biomass, but we can estimate that biomass by sampling and even use it as a variable in an experiment or a longitudinal study. Engineers use the same tools and more, with far greater use of computers to simulate *real things*. In fact, it is hard to envision much of modern engineering without computer simulations, which model and test structures, avionics systems, nuclear fuel rod assemblies, and traffic jams. Computers are used to design solid objects, then control machines that carve those objects out of solid metal or deposit them with 3D printing.

Until recently, the formal study of engineering content—even for engineering students—often did not begin in earnest until the second or third year of undergraduate study, because so much of the discipline builds on calculus, other advanced mathematics, and physics. Today, many colleges and universities offer freshman-level engineering design courses that precede or run concurrent with those prerequisites, often intended to give students earlier experiences with engineering, in an effort to reduce dropout from engineering majors. Authentic engineering experiences are possible earlier in part because computing devices offer powerful, inexpensive, easy-to-use tools. Such tools can make engineering experiences feasible for much younger learners. FIRST LEGO League is only one of many projects around the world in which elementary and middle school–age children learn to program microcontrollers and engage in technology design competitions, even before studying algebra.

Design challenges offer opportunities to apply mathematics in ways that children find compelling. Fifth graders who applied geometric principles to design blueprints and models of chairs, playhouses, and other objects in one study (SMART: Special Multimedia Arenas for Refining Thinking) were observed to engage eagerly in cycles of redesign, showed significant test gains in geometric understanding, and, when interviewed the following year, reported that they were proud of their accomplishments with the tasks (Barron et al., 1998).

6. Constructing explanations and designing solutions. While science focuses on constructing explanations of natural phenomena, engineering's primary emphasis is designing solutions to problems (NRC, 2012, p. 52). Levy (2013) points out that the latter aligns with children's natural interest in goal-oriented design activity. Engineering education engages students in designing solutions to real-world problems at an age-appropriate level. The practical context of these problems helps drive student interest and helps students build from concrete experiences to more abstract, generalizable understandings of engineering as a field (Fortus, Dershimer, Krajcik, Marx, & Mamlok-Naaman, 2004; Kolodner, 2006; McKay & McGrath, 2007).

A scientific explanation is a logical account of observations while attending to causality, uncertainty, replicability, and conformance to current scientific understandings; its objective is a "best" explanation, the culmination of Practices 1 through 5. Engineering design, on the other hand, is both the culmination of Practices 1 through 5 and a description of the process through which these practices are iteratively applied.

Although there are disciplinary differences between science and engineering with respect to this practice, compelling aspects of engineering practice can be exploited to teach disciplinary science. Several curriculum projects incorporating design have focused on methods for integrating engineering and science, with the aim of improving science learning. These projects use engineering challenges, often including a formal design cycle as a framework, to structure student exploration of scientific questions in K–12 classroom settings. Design-Based Science (DBS; Fortus et al., 2004), a curriculum for upper elementary school, and Learning by Design (LBD), a curriculum for middle school (Kolodner et al., 2003), are both structured by first presenting an engineering design task or challenge, followed by exploration of relevant scientific principles, then applying the science to design a solution for the challenge, repeating the steps in iterative loops that increase the complexity or scope of the questions being addressed. DBS student scores have shown significant improvement in understanding of science, as has an analysis of artifacts created by the students (Fortus et al., 2004). The DBS subject matter included concepts related to weather, density, heat exchange, and forces. LBD students have evidenced science content gains at least as good as or better than a comparison group; LBD also closed achievement gaps for low-income students and girls (Kolodner et al., 2003). In the LBD study, the science content included forces, motion, speed, collisions, and related topics.

7. Engaging in argument from evidence. Just as scientists engage in arguing from evidence as they propose or challenge theory, engineers argue from evidence as they advocate design decisions (NRC, 2012, p. 52). But there are more than functional differences: The goal of scientific argument is to persuade peers, and success is evidenced by peers' subsequent use of one's ideas in their own work. The goal of engineering argument is to persuade a client, as evidenced by the eventual substantiation of the proposed solution in a technology or process. These different audiences (and values) potentially matter, such as when a design challenge focuses on a social problem that community members and students care about. Curriculum units in the SMART and Jasper series require students to present design proposals to an outside-the-classroom audience (researchers, administrators, or others) to be evaluated; students' work is judged based on evidence and argument (Barron et al., 1998). External design boards were identified as a successful component of design projects in Engineering Concepts for the High School Classroom, where they were observed to be associated with positive changes in student perceptions of the role of the teacher as well (Carlsen, 1998). Other curricula also include activities in which students must present their solutions to the rest of the class and the teacher, providing students with opportunities to engage in this practice common to engineering and science (Fortus et al., 2004; Kolodner et al., 2003; Roth, Tobin, & Ritchie, 2001). Many of these projects note that engaging in argument from evidence is a practice that benefits from careful scaffolding by teachers and curriculum materials.

An aspect of engineering that inevitably surfaces in students' persuasive arguments is *balancing tradeoffs.* Engineering problems are defined by criteria, which designs must meet to be successful, and constraints, which limit the solution space. In almost all engineering problems, no perfect design exists in which all criteria can be fully satisfied. Criteria and constraints exist as variables; engineers balance the tradeoffs between these variables to optimize their designs. Students who engineer are thus exposed to complex problems in which the technologies they produce may all meet the definition for success but be very different. In the studies we reviewed, tradeoffs were featured prominently, with criteria and constraints explicitly noted or activities staged for student discovery; in most cases, projects direct students not just to make choices about these tradeoffs but to explain those choices to their peers (Barnett, 2005; Cunningham, 2009; Fortus et al., 2004; Kolodner et al., 2003; Mehalik et al., 2008). The existence of tradeoffs demands evaluation and discourages learners from prematurely closing down a problem.

Although some tradeoffs occur within the space of physical properties (e.g., reducing weight without overreducing strength), engineering problems usually include students' consideration of social criteria, such as ethics and economics. Designing solutions for clients (whether imaginary or real) and defending them encourages students to learn from each other and engage in external perspective taking (Brophy, Klein, Portsmore, & Rogers, 2008; Fortus et al., 2004). Asking students to consider the larger social ramifications of their engineering also helps prepare them to participate responsibly in the modern technological world.

8. Obtaining, evaluating, and communicating information. Scientists and engineers alike must communicate their findings clearly, in a variety of modes, using tools like mathematics, tables, graphs, drawings, models, and the written or spoken word (NRC, 2012, p. 53). The Learning By Design curriculum has focused on "ritualizing" a variety of communication practices so that students and teachers have repeated experiences with different means, modes, and motivations for communicating (Kolodner et al., 2003). In addition to written reports, students engage in three kinds of presentations. "Poster sessions" are used to have students report the methods and results of their investigations, "pin-up sessions" are used to present design briefs, including evidence-based justifications for any important decisions made by the team, and "gallery walks" are opportunities for student teams to show off the artifacts they have designed and gain feedback and ideas from others. Presentation rituals afford students opportunities to practice engaging in arguing from evidence, as well as using mathematical and computational thinking. They also structure the curriculum experience for students and teachers, providing important opportunities for students to synthesize and reflect on what they have learned and what they have yet to figure out.

Supporting collaboration is a key communication function for both scientists and engineers, who often work in teams made up of individuals who may have different expertise. Collaboration has been identified as an important element of "21st-century skills" (Partnership for 21st Century Skills, 2009); the benefits of giving students opportunities to formulate their ideas and place them in the public sphere for comment and reflection have been extensively documented (Hogan, Nastasi, & Pressley, 2000). In engineering education, collaborative work is frequently focused on having students share and sometimes co-opt techniques and ideas across groups (Roth, 1995b, 1997). Well-designed contexts for collaboration on design projects can afford collaborators rich opportunities to elaborate on scientific ideas (Kafai & Ching, 2001). Even beyond the benefits for learning, however, collaboration is an important skill in itself, highly sought after in the work world. In a study of engineering design in secondary chemistry instruction, Apedoe, Ellefson, & Schunn (2012) reported that collaboration led to cognitive gains for all members of a group composed heterogeneously and observed that high-ability students facilitated learning in lower-ability students. High-ability students also flourished from collaboration by taking on leadership and teaching roles within the group.

Despite their similarities, there are important disciplinary differences between science and engineering concerning information exchange. The free exchange of information—with attribution—is a sociological norm of science (Merton, 1973). The products of engineering, on the other hand, may be legally proprietary, although their owners may choose to license them or share them freely. The importance of students' "ownership of ideas" is often noted by engineering education (e.g., Silk et al., 2009) as one reason for students' enthusiastic engagement in design challenges.

Another important communication-related difference is the role of demonstration. Early in the history of science, demonstration was the principal way in which scientific findings were communicated to peers and attribution of discoveries established. Demonstrations in academies of natural science sometimes even included stagecraft to allow a natural philosopher to claim discovery without revealing details of potential financial value (Schaffer, 1989). Today, of course, publication in peer-reviewed journals is the gold standard for science, and public demonstrations of discoveries prior to such publication usually lead to questions about the validity of any claims (Park, 2003). But in engineering, demonstration remains a respected component of communication to clients and other audiences, and in much of engineering work, publication in peer-reviewed journals isn't even relevant. The reasons for these disciplinary differences are quite varied (for example, patent protections notwithstanding, inventors often have strong economic interests to keep proprietary details to themselves), but the educational implications merit consideration. Students may be able to solve problems before they fully understand the underlying science or before they can persuasively explain it. But they can still engage in meaningful work, and demonstration provides a way of decomposing such work into two sets of criteria that correspond to the different disciplinary emphases of engineering and science, as articulated in the Framework: Have you achieved a working *product?* To what extent do you understand the *process?*

Section 2. Praxis: Cycles of Practice

In working through the eight NRC practices, we described a number of differences between science and engineering, but an inventory of practices does not tell the whole story. The Framework's authors were careful not to suggest that the practices represent an orderly, chronological, linear "scientific method." Aspects of Practice 8, in particular, occur at multiple points in any inquiry, scientific or engineering. At the risk of oversimplifying, we offer Figure 36.1 as a general representation of scientific and engineering *praxis*, using the visual metaphor of cycles. The figure illustrates the following differences: (a) Science and engineering have different goals (Practices 1 and 6); (b) models inform investigations in science and result from investigations in engineering (Practice 2); and (c) engineering praxis is multi-iterative, with internal cycles of Practices 3, 8a, 4, and 5 (what might be called "Analysis" iterations) and larger cycles that include modeling and solution prototyping (adding Practices 2 and 6 to the Analysis cycles, in what might be called "Design" iterations).

Cycles are also often used to represent the flow of work in educational settings, for science (Lawson, 1985), engineering (Apedoe, Ellefson, & Schunn, 2012), and science-via-engineering-design (Kolodner, 2002). They are useful in curricular planning and, when generalized into a third dimension, become another curricular metaphor, the spiral curriculum. Besides their instrumental utility in planning, we believe that comparing these cycles can help us account for some other educational outcomes that have been reported in engineering education research.

Iteration. The process of engineering usually entails iteration: cycles of activity, testing, and analysis. As models and prototypes evolve, they are evaluated, improved, and re-evaluated. As with the systems approach, iteration offers advantages in tackling difficult problems. Instead of integrating subsystems, however, iteration entails sequential improvement. From a curricular perspective, iteration can be thought of as a structure for staging the demands of a task: A curriculum designer or teacher might require an initial cycle of student inquiry to examine systematically the properties of materials ("Analysis" iterations), then in a future lesson provide opportunities for students to develop and evaluate models of technologies that use those materials ("Design" iterations). A number of units in Engineering is Elementary are organized in just this way: Students first explore the properties of a number of materials (Analysis), then use those materials to create a technology to solve an assigned problem (Design; Cunningham, 2009). Improving design through iteration promotes cognitive gains because it compels students to confront their misunderstandings in order to improve (Capobianco, Diefes-Dux, Mena, & Weller, 2011) and because each iteration offers opportunities to strengthen students' understanding about the connections between models and real world (Hmelo, Holton, & Kolodner, 2000).

Although educators might anticipate student resistance to iteration ("Why do we have to do this again?"), iteration in engineering projects is often cited as having a positive motivational influence. Several curricula take advantage of this to build students' skills in investigation. The Learning By Design curriculum (Kolodner et al., 2003) was structured to have students move back and forth between an engineering design cycle and an inquiry cycle, as questions arise in design, are answered, and are implemented in redesign. Student interest is maintained in part because the students are personally engaged in the problems and they are able to monitor their own progress toward an ambitious goal. The Design-Based Science curriculum also includes embedded opportunities for investigation in their "learning cycle"—both in conducting "background research" after the initial step of defining the problem and in testing the artifacts that are developed (Fortus, Dershimer, Krajcik, Marx, & Mamlok-Naaman, 2004). When engineering projects require iteration, the

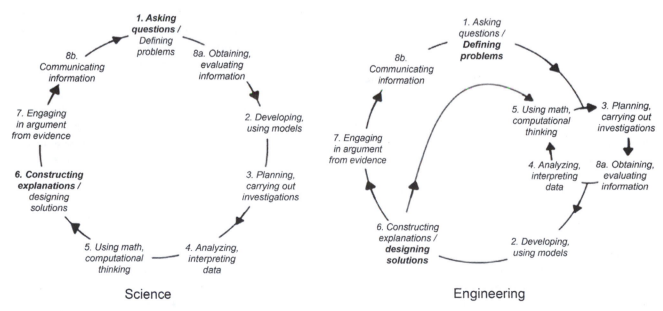

Figure 36.1 Cycles of epistemic practices in science and engineering.

process itself discourages students from prematurely closing down the consideration of alternative solutions, promoting creativity.

Failure. The expectation of iteration is related to the normative desirability of failure. Failure is a virtue in engineering (at least in the design phase!). The inevitability of tradeoffs means a quest for a balance: just enough but not too much of anything, because too much usually has consequences (excessive cost, weight, etc.). The test-and-improve cycle of engineering design assumes that designs will likely fail initially to meet the criteria and constraints of a problem and redesign will be necessary. It also assumes that even if a design is successful, there is likely room for further optimization; a successful design is often tested repeatedly to figure out at what point it fails. Fortus et al. (2004) and Kolodner (2006) both demonstrate the importance of the feedback that students receive from design failures and note that students are usually keen to investigate the reasons for failures. It is also relevant that designs fail (not students) and that the cause of failure is often quickly apparent and can be addressed, as when unbalanced forces cause a bridge model to collapse (Cajas, 2001). Failure is a signal to students that iteration is needed, often requiring no teacher intervention, and when students see failures as contributing to learning, they are more motivated to persist than if they see failures as errors (Blumenfeld et al., 1991). Obviously valuing and appreciating failure in this way is counter to major cultural trends in education. Appropriately scaffolded engineering experiences in school have the potential to transform classroom culture so that failure becomes a goal in educational design and a useful pedagogical tool (Fortus et al., 2004). Teachers' modeling of this cultural attitude can be meaningfully internalized by students (Barnett, 2005). As Rutland and Barlex (2008) note, teachers play a critical role in encouraging student risk taking and managing those risks.

Section 3. Other Factors

We next consider a handful of other findings that resist categorization as either practice or praxis.

Motivation. In addition to the importance of iteration and failure-as-virtue, researchers have identified aspects of engineering design as important student motivators, as evidenced by student reports (Barnett, 2005), classroom observations (Carlsen, 1998), and reduced student absenteeism (Barnett, 2005). Engineering design challenges support what Blumenfeld and colleagues (2006) identify as key determinants of student motivation: enhancing students' sense of their own competence and agency, encouraging students to take responsibility for their own learning (Fortus et al., 2005), making science more relevant by emphasizing the social and societal value of science and engineering (Brotman & Moore, 2008; Kolodner et al., 2003) and highlighting the instrumental value of science to engineering (Apedoe et al., 2008; Kanter, 2010). Several curricular projects have documented higher motivation

and engagement in engineering design tasks than for more traditional curriculum (e.g., Barron et al., 1998; Lachapelle et al., 2011), in addition to positive effects on student achievement. Engineering projects can make science content relevant to students, enhance students' sense of agency, and encourage students to take responsibility for their own learning (Barnett 2005; Blumenfeld et al., 2006, Fortus 2005; Kolodner 2003).

For the science classroom, a well-designed engineering task, like a well-designed laboratory exercise, should be more than just engaging; it should support the growth of conceptual understanding through purposeful activity. For math education, Ainley, Pratt, and Hansen (2006) define such support as *utility* and advocate its use in curricular planning. For science education, utility may function in two ways as a filter in selecting or designing hands-on work, like labs or design challenges: (1) Does the work solve a meaningful real-world problem (instrumental utility)? (2) Do students recognize that the work leads to better scientific understanding (conceptual utility)? These goals may be motivating to quite different students.

Problem solving. Engineering's emphasis on problem solving shapes students' scientific work in ways that differ from more conventional science instruction, with potentially positive and negative consequences. On the positive side, open-ended problems offer engagement and motivation for learning by providing students with opportunities for creative, active learning and choice (Bamberger, Cahill, Hagerty, Short, & Krajcik, 2010). Well-crafted design problems provide clear goals, which help students incrementally self-monitor their progress. They often offer significant autonomy for solution development rather than leading students step-by-step through a tightly defined "experiment." Problem solving in science focuses on developing theories and explanations; engineering problem solving is more focused on concrete solutions.

Engineering projects often address real-life problems with which students have experience, but less familiar problem-solving contexts can also be engaging if they are appropriately challenging. A nice example is described in Barnett's (2005) study of ninth-grade students who designed remotely operated vessels (ROVs). The project was created by researchers and local teachers for ninth-grade students from a low-income school enrolling 85% minority students. The researchers found that the "ROV design activity provided students with opportunities to naturally weave together skills, processes, and knowledge that are typically taught separately in the discrete subjects of traditional curricula, such as the relationship between the design of the ROV and the concepts of density and center of gravity" (p. 95). Remarkably, students described their experiences solving ROV–related problems as relevant to the real world and to their lives, and pre-post measures of students receiving the treatment showed improvement in understanding of physics concepts that were directly addressed through the design challenge, including density. However, despite significantly greater attendance rates in the treatment group than in comparison classrooms over the course of a year, there were no differences on end-of-year physics tests between treatment and comparison classrooms, which highlights two potentially negative consequences of a problem-solving approach: (1) There are opportunity costs associated with the time that must be invested, which may result in decreased instructional time devoted to teaching concepts and skills that "count" on standardized tests, and (2) students may fail to consolidate their understandings of relevant science concepts, even if they are used (perhaps only briefly) in their problem solving.

Cognitive load. Some researchers have argued that student learning in engineering design may result in reduced cognitive load as students externalize complex concepts or principles onto physical components (Levy, 2013; Roth, 1996). In some respects this strategy resembles that of systems modeling, where a complex problem is addressed by packaging complexity in smaller, comprehensible components, then connecting them. It has also been suggested that concepts or principles can be enacted in physical action. Citing the work of Vygotsky, Schon, and others, Levy (2013) argued that building artifacts entails "cycling between constructive action upon tangible objects and reflection upon its results" (p. 4) and often involves collaboration and assistance from others. With respect to cognitive load theory and the challenge of complexity, artifacts may function as external memory, the body and motor activity may serve as information structures, and the predetermined function of a design goal "lends coherence and meaning to the activity at hand, thus facilitating reasoning with a myriad of components and their interactions" (p. 6).

When children design, the physical artifacts they create actually structure subsequent design, because the shape of an emerging solution constrains the shape of subsequent work (Roth, 1996). Furthermore, "It is in building and playing with physical devices that the incompleteness of representations is exposed" (Roth, 1996, p. 160). Put another way, a material representation of an abstract conceptual model is experientially testable, and artifacts are concrete things that help to structure students' reflections and their discussion with others (Blumenfeld et al., 1991).

Narratives as cognitive scaffolds. Curriculum developers have devised methods to support students in both managing complexity and making connections to the real world (Barron et al., 1998; Kolodner et al., 2003; Krajcik & Blumenfeld, 2006). In programs that engaged upper elementary school students in science and mathematics through design and inquiry, Barron and colleagues (1998) introduced units with a video scenario for the design challenge: showing children (child actors in a video) walking through solving a similar problem, explaining their reasons, and making and overcoming common mistakes. This helped set the context for the challenge and engaged students in thinking about relevant issues, skills, and needed knowledge. Engineering is Elementary (EiE; Cunningham, 2009; Lachapelle & Cunningham, 2014 has

incorporated narrative "scaffolds" in all 20 of its engineering units, in the form of storybooks in which fictional children solve real-life design problems similar to the ones that students will later encounter. The EiE stories feature a diverse collection of child and adult characters, are set in international contexts, and include a number of other elements intended to capture children's imaginations. For example, in a unit on green engineering set in Botswana, a young girl named Lerato cares for her younger siblings and spends much of her time gathering firewood for cooking. With the help of an older, female college student from her village, Lerato learns about engineering and designs a solar oven, providing a model for young readers who go on to research and design ovens of their own. EiE students frequently refer to the fictional characters and their experiences during their subsequent work (and even a year later), providing evidence of the effectiveness of stories as maps for design activity.

Section 4. Future Directions

Researchers have recognized the possibility that science might "get lost" when it is taught via engineering design. Kanter (2010) developed strategies for ensuring that science learning remains a goal in design challenges and evaluated those strategies in a project-based science setting. He described approaches for stimulating students to seek new science knowledge that would subsequently help them, such as "unpacking a task." In another project-based study, Krajcik and colleagues (2008) described a "learning-goals-driven design model" that included curriculum features to ensure alignment among science standards, instructional activities, and assessment strategies. By moving back and forth between cycles of "design" and "investigation," Kolodner and colleagues (2003) strove to promote deep learning of science through student immersion in both engineering and science practices. Apedoe et al. (2008) decomposed a unit in chemistry into conceptual "subsystems," each featuring a cycle of student design and reconnection through an economical set of Big Ideas to explicitly foreground the science.

Engineering first? Given the cognitive and sociocultural features of engineering activity, it may be worth considering what a precollege "engineering first" approach might accomplish, especially for younger children. As science educators, it is certainly appropriate for us to ask how well science and science practices are taught through engineering activities in science classrooms. But consider the following potential advantages of an "engineering first" strategy:

1. Productive engagement in authentic work would be less reliant on students' and teachers' prior disciplinary knowledge.
2. It would focus on concrete models that are a physical manifestation of children's experience and action.
3. Its emphasis on optimization may be more natural than explanation for young learners.

4. Physical models and physical activity can reduce cognitive load by externalizing concepts and processes and may be useful even if the concepts or processes can't be described or explained.

5. The design approach provides "scaffolds" for making complex problems more cognitively accessible, such as system decomposition/integration and iteration.

6. Design encourages multiple solutions and there is rarely a single "right" answer, so children can be successful in different ways.

7. Engineering activity recognizes the importance of diverse skills and values and supports their use.

8. Student motivation and engagement are often very impressive for a number of reasons, including enhanced agency, ownership, opportunities for creativity, self-regulation, and feedback that doesn't require teacher intervention.

9. Engineering engagement takes advantage of children's natural interest in goal-oriented activity.

10. It shifts authority from the teacher to the students and other stakeholders.

11. Its emphasis on balancing tradeoffs invites higher-order thinking, such as evaluation.

12. It treats demonstration—a natural form of persuasion for children—as a legitimate epistemic practice.

13. It values failure and demonstrates its productivity.

From a policy perspective, the research at this time is much too thin to justify postponing science instruction until students have engineering experiences, but it does suggest a number of areas for future research and development.

Learning progressions. How might learning progressions research inform the sequencing of science and engineering subject matter? The growing number of STEM–themed schools may provide strategic settings to carry out components of such studies. For example, how do experiences with engineering design in the elementary grades impact students' understandings about systems in later grades? Do such experiences impede (or promote) the ability to understand and explain abstract concepts and models? Do design experiences result in differences in students' later creativity and open-mindedness or in greater difficulty accepting well-established knowledge?

For learning progressions research in settings in which engineering design is part of the curriculum, some special considerations are necessary. For example, in the early grades, it is important to assess knowledge in the context of activity. Young children are often able to *do* more than they can explain, and they may be better able to explain aloud *in* an activity setting than they can in interviews *outside* the activity context, in writing, or in drawings.

Prerequisites. Engineering requires skills and dispositions that are not normally considered goals of the science curriculum. If engineering is to be a significant part of science studies, how, where, and when will those skills be acquired? For example, planning an engineering solution often requires representing possible designs in drawings. This poses two obvious challenges. First, young children may be developmentally limited to creating two-dimensional, front-side representations at best (Fleer, 2000b), and they may be unwilling or cognitively unable to draw a design until *after* they have actually built it (Fleer & Sukroo, 1995). Second, for older students, the reality of curricular segregation becomes pronounced. Science is rarely taught by teachers who have been trained to provide instruction in technical drawing in two and three dimensions. Is facility with technical drawing a prerequisite skill, taught in technical courses, or will secondary education follow university engineering education in reducing its emphasis (Sorby, 1999)? With respect to the politics of the curriculum (more on that below), this is a charged question, but it is also one that offers opportunities for research. How do students experience engineering education if they cannot draw or use machine tools, or if they believe (due to lack of experience) that technical competence is somehow intellectually inferior to abstract knowledge?

Science education and technology education: Curricular politics? Or shared commitments? We began this chapter by demarcating our task to a relatively narrow focus on studies of engineering in and for science instruction. In doing this, we aspired to delimit the scope of our work and to skirt border disputes between science education and the other three STEM fields: technology, engineering, and mathematics. Bluntly, these fields include one (mathematics) that enjoys both societal status and security in the precollege curriculum, one (engineering) that is characterized by high status but has an almost negligible presence in the precollege curriculum, and one (technology) that, depending on the country of interest, varies widely around the world in status and curricular security (from ascendant to strong to threatened with extinction).

Although we've tried to avoid the border issues here, it is clear that they exist. The statements of policy makers notwithstanding, in most places STEM has an only aspirational curricular identity, and there will be many challenges in integrating what are currently disparate fields. We conclude by noting just one such challenge: teacher education. To date, there has been very little research on its role in preparing teachers who can teach both science and engineering. Capobianco (2010), in a case study of a single fifth-grade teacher, offered one early study that explored a number of relevant issues, with particular emphasis on the power (and peril) of uncertainty. Elsewhere, we have found some evidence that engineering can be introduced and sustained in middle and secondary classrooms with intensive professional development (Carlsen, 1998; Cunningham, Knight, Carlsen, & Kelly, 2007).

Very few precollege teachers have any formal training in engineering. This problem is especially acute at the elementary level. Collaborations between science and technology teachers are worth exploring—and studying carefully—but again, teacher education is a critical issue. A recent review of preservice technology teacher education programs in the United States reported that across

19 programs, a mean of only 7.6 credit hours of engineering coursework was required; even the mean for programs housed in colleges of engineering was less than three courses (Fantz & Katsioloudis, 2011). It will be essential to know much more about how experiences and training in engineering influence teachers' understandings, curricular planning, and classroom practices. Furthermore, the scope of research clearly needs to include interdisciplinary STEM education initiatives, because that is the direction that, through politics and policy, we are headed.

The NRC Framework has raised the profile of engineering in the precollege curriculum, and its effects are already being revealed through new science standards. Precollege engineering education is still in its infancy, and the role of science education going forward has yet to be written. But the possibilities are intriguing!

Acknowledgments

We wish to thank Stephen Petrina and David Barlex for their thoughtful reviews of an earlier draft of this chapter. We are also grateful to Cathy Lachapelle, Jonathan Hertel, Matthew Johnson, and Joseph Nichisti for assistance with the research and many useful suggestions.

Notes

1. Similar efforts have occurred in other countries, like Britain, and could be used to structure this first section. The U.S. example isn't unique, but it has several advantages here, including a well-documented and accessible paper trail of policy recommendations and research reports that are available online from the National Academy Press.

2. Almost 400 pages in length, the NRC (2012) *Framework* includes the word "client" only once, and terms like "patent," "intellectual property," and "secrecy" are completely absent. This isn't surprising—the *Framework* is an educational manifesto—but these omissions arguably reflect an overemphasis on academic engineering (and science!) and an underemphasis on engineering for corporations and other entities. According to the NSF, only 18% of employed U.S. scientists and engineers work in higher education. "Industry" is the largest employment sector (53%); the rest are self-employed (6%) or work for nonprofits (10%) or government (12%; Falkenheim & Burrelli, 2012).

References

Ainley, J., Pratt, D., & Hansen, A. (2006). Connecting engagement and focus in pedagogic task design. *British Educational Research Journal, 32*(1), 23–38.

American Association for the Advancement of Science (AAAS). (1993). *Benchmarks for science literacy.* Washington, DC: Author.

Anning, A. (1997). Drawing out ideas: Graphicacy and young children. *International Journal of Technology and Design Education, 7*(3), 219–239.

Apedoe, X., Ellefson, M., & Schunn, C. (2012). Learning together while designing: Does group size make a difference? *Journal of Science Education and Technology, 21*(1), 83–94.

Apedoe, X., Reynolds, B., Ellefson, M., & Schunn, C. (2008). Bringing engineering design into high school science classrooms: The heating/cooling unit. *Journal of Science Education and Technology, 17*(5), 454–465.

Baker, D., & Leary, R. (1995). Letting girls speak out about science. *Journal of Research in Science Teaching, 32*(1), 3–27.

Bamberger, Y., Cahill, C., Hagerty, J., Short, H., & Krajcik, J.S. (2010). Learning science by doing design: How can it work at the middle school level? *Journal of Education, Informatics and Cybernetics, 2*(2), 41–46.

Barlex, D. (Ed.). (2007). *Design and technology—for the next generation.* Whitchurch, UK: Cliffeco Communications.

Barnett, M. (2005). Engaging inner city students in learning through designing remote operated vehicles. *Journal of Science Education and Technology, 14*(1), 87–100.

Barron, B., Schwartz, D.L., Vye, N.J., Moore, A., Petrosino, A., Zech, L., & Bransford, J. D. (1998). Doing with understanding: Lessons from research on problem- and project-based learning. *Journal of the Learning Sciences, 7*(3 & 4), 271–311.

Benson, C., & Lunt, J. (Eds.). (2011). *International handbook of primary technology education: Reviewing the past twenty years* (Vol. 7). Rotterdam, the Netherlands: Sense.

Blumenfeld, P. C., Kempler, T. M., & Krajcik, J. S. (2006). Motivation and cognitive engagement in learning environments. In *The Cambridge handbook of the learning sciences* (pp. 475–488). New York, NY: Cambridge University Press.

Blumenfeld, P.C., Soloway, E., Marx, R., Krajcik, J.S., Guzdial, M., & Palincsar, A. (1991). Motivating project-based learning: Sustaining the doing, supporting the learning. *Educational Psychologist, 26*(3), 369–398.

Brophy, S., Klein, S., Portsmore, M., & Rogers, C. (2008). Advancing engineering education in P–12 classrooms. *Journal of Engineering Education, 97*(3), 369–387.

Brotman, J. S., & Moore, F. M. (2008). Girls and science: A review of four themes in the science education literature. *Journal of Research in Science Teaching, 45*(9), 971–1002.

Cajas, F. (2001). The science/technology interaction: Implications for science literacy. *Journal of Research in Science Teaching, 38*(7), 715–729.

Capobianco, B. M. (2010). Exploring a science teacher's uncertainty with integrating engineering design: An action research study. *Journal of Science Teacher Education, 22*(7), 645–660.

Capobianco, B.M., Diefes-Dux, H.A., Mena, I., & Weller, J. (2011). What is an engineer? Implications of elementary school student conceptions for engineering education. *Journal of Engineering Education, 100*(2), 304–328.

Carlsen, W.S. (1998). Engineering design in the classroom: Is it good science education or is it revolting? *Research in Science Education, 28*(1), 51–63.

Cunningham, C.M. (2009). Engineering is Elementary. *The Bridge, 30,* 11–17.

Cunningham, C.M., Knight, M.T., Carlsen, W.S., & Kelly, G. (2007). Integrating engineering in middle and high school classrooms. *International Journal of Engineering Education, 23*(1), 3.

Dewey, J. (1913). *Interest and effort in education.* Boston, MA: Houghton Mifflin.

Engle, R.A., & Conant, F.R. (2002). Guiding principles for fostering productive disciplinary engagement: Explaining an emergent argument in a community of learners classroom. *Cognition and Instruction, 20*(4), 399–483.

Falkenheim, J.C., & Burrelli, J.S. (2012, March). *Diversity in science and engineering employment in industry (NSF 12–311).* Arlington, VA: National Center for Science and Engineering Statistics.

Fantz, T.D., & Katsioloudis, P.J. (2011). Analysis of engineering content within technology education programs. *Journal of Technology Education, 23*(1), 19–31.

Fleer, M. (2000a). Interactive technology: Can children construct their own technological design briefs? *Research in Science Education, 30*(2), 241–253.

Fleer, M. (2000b). Working technologically: Investigations into how young children design and make during technology education. *International Journal of Technology & Design Education, 10*(1), 43–59.

Fleer, M., & Sukroo, J. (1995). *I can make my robot dance: Technology for 3–8 year olds.* Carlton, VIC: Curriculum Corporation.

Fortus, D., Dershimer, R.C., Krajcik, J.S., Marx, R.W., & Mamlok-Naaman, R. (2004). Design-based science and student learning. *Journal of Research in Science Teaching, 41*(10), 1081–1110.

Fortus, D., Krajcik, J. S., Dershimer, R. C., Marx, R. W., & Mamlok-Naaman, R. (2005). Design-based science and real-world problem-solving. *International Journal of Science Education, 27*(7), 855–879.

Hmelo, C. E., Holton, D. L., & Kolodner, J. L. (2000). Designing to learn about complex systems. *Journal of the Learning Sciences, 9*(3), 247–298.

Hogan, K., Nastasi, B. K., & Pressley, M. (2000). Discourse patterns and collaborative scientific reasoning in peer and teacher-guided discussions. *Cognition and Instruction, 17*(4), 379–432.

Jones, A., & De Vries, M. (2009). *International handbook of research and development in technology education* (Vol. 5). Rotterdam, the Netherlands: Sense Publishers.

Jones, M. G., Howe, A., & Rua, M. J. (2000). Gender differences in students' experiences, interests, and attitudes toward science and scientists. *Science Education, 84*(2), 180–192.

Kafai, Y. B., & Ching, C. C. (2001). Affordances of collaborative software design planning for elementary students' science talk. *Journal of the Learning Sciences, 10*(3), 323–363.

Kanter, D. E. (2010). Doing the project and learning the content: Designing project-based science curricula for meaningful understanding. *Science Education, 94*(3), 525–551.

Katehi, L., Pearson, G., & Feder, M. A. (2009). *Engineering in K–12 education: Understanding the status and improving the prospects.* Washington, DC: National Academies Press.

Kelly, G. J. (2008). Inquiry, activity, and epistemic practice. In R. A. Duschl & R. E. Grandy (Eds.), *Teaching scientific inquiry: Recommendations for research and implementation* (pp. 99–117; 288–291). Rotterdam, the Netherlands: Sense Publishers.

Kelly, G. J. (2011). Scientific literacy, discourse, and epistemic practices. In C. Linder, L. Ostman, D. A. Roberts, P.-O. Wickman, G. Erickson, & A. MacKinnon (Eds.), *Exploring the landscape of scientific literacy* (pp. 61–73). New York, NY: Routledge.

Kolodner, J. L. (2002). Facilitating the learning of design practices: Lessons learned from an inquiry into science education. *Journal of Industrial Teacher Education, 39*(3).

Kolodner, J. L. (2006). Case-based reasoning. In R. K. Sawyer (Ed.), *The Cambridge handbook of the learning sciences* (pp. 225–242). Cambridge, UK: Cambridge University Press.

Kolodner, J. L., Camp, P. J., Crismond, D., Fasse, B., Gray, J., Holbrook, J., Puntambekar, S., & Ryan, M. (2003). Problem-based learning meets case-based reasoning in the middle-school science classroom: Putting Learning by Design into practice. *Journal of the Learning Sciences, 12*(4), 495–547.

Krajcik, J. S., & Blumenfeld, P. C. (2006). Project-based learning. In R. K. Sawyer (Ed.), *The Cambridge handbook of the learning sciences* (pp. 317–334). New York, NY: Cambridge University Press.

Krajcik, J. S., McNeill, K. L., & Reiser, B. J. (2008). Learning-goals-driven design model: Developing curriculum materials that align with national standards and incorporate project-based pedagogy. *Science Education, 92*(1), 1–32.

Kuhn, D., & Phelps, E. (1982). The development of problem-solving strategies. In H. Reese (Ed.), *Advances in child development and behavior* (Vol. 17, pp. 1–44). New York, NY: Academic.

Lachapelle, C. P., & Cunningham, C. M. (2014). Engineering in elementary schools. In J. Strobel, S. Purzer, & M. Cardella (Eds.), *Engineering in pre-college settings: Synthesizing research, policy, and practices.* Lafayette, IN: Purdue University Press.

Lachapelle, C. P., Cunningham, C. M., Jocz, J., Kay, A. E., Phadnis, P., Wertheimer, J., & Arteaga, R. (2011). *Engineering is Elementary: An evaluation of years 4 through 6 field testing.* Boston: Museum of Science.

Lawson, A. E. (1985). *Science teaching and the development of thinking.* Belmont, CA: Wadsworth Publishing.

Levy, S. T. (2013). Young children's learning of water physics by constructing working systems. *International Journal of Technology and Design Education, 23*(3), 537–566.

McKay, M., & McGrath, B. (2007). Real-world problem-solving using real-time data. *International Journal of Engineering Education, 23*(1), 36–42.

Mehalik, M. M., Doppelt, Y., & Schunn, C. D. (2008). Middle-school science through design-based learning versus scripted inquiry: Better overall science concept learning and equity gap reduction. *Journal of Engineering Education, 97*(1), 1–15.

Merton, R. K. (1973). *The sociology of science: Theoretical and empirical investigations.* Chicago, IL: Chicago University Press.

Miller, P. H., Blessing, J. S., & Schwartz, S. (2006). Gender differences in high-school students' views about science. *International Journal of Science Education, 28*(4), 363–381.

National Research Council (NRC). (2012). *A framework for K–12 science education: Practices, crosscutting concepts, and core ideas.* Washington, DC: National Academies Press.

Obama, B. H. (2009, November 23). *Remarks on the "Educate to Innovate" Campaign.* Washington, DC: U.S. Government Printing Office. Retrieved from www.gpo.gov/fdsys/pkg/DCPD-200900940/content-detail.html

O'Neill, T. B. (2010). Fostering spaces of student ownership in middle school science. *Equity & Excellence in Education, 43*(1), 6–20.

O'Neill, T. B., & Calabrese Barton, A. (2005). Uncovering student ownership in science learning: The making of a student created mini-documentary. *School Science and Mathematics, 105*(6), 292–301.

Park, R. L. (2003). The seven warning signs of bogus science. *Chronicle of Higher Education, 49,* B20.

Partnership for 21st Century Skills. (2009). *Framework for 21st century learning.* Washington, DC: Author.

Penner, D. E., Giles, N. D., Lehrer, R., & Schauble, L. (1997). Building functional models: Designing an elbow. *Journal of Research in Science Teaching, 34*(2), 125–143.

Penner, D. E., Lehrer, R., & Schauble, L. (1998). From physical models to biomechanics: A design-based modeling approach. *Journal of the Learning Sciences, 7*(3/4), 429–449.

Rasinen, A. (2003). An analysis of the technology education curriculum of six countries. *Journal of Technology Education, 15*(1), 31–47.

Roth, W.-M. (1995a). From "wiggly structures" to "unshaky towers": Problem framing, solution finding, and negotiation of courses of actions during a civil engineering unit for elementary students. *Research in Science Education, 25*(4), 365–381.

Roth, W.-M. (1995b). Inventors, copycats, and everyone else: The emergence of shared resources and practices as defining aspects of classroom communities. *Science Education, 79*(5), 475–502.

Roth, W.-M. (1996). Art and artifact of children's designing: A situated cognition perspective. *Journal of the Learning Sciences, 5*(2), 129–166.

Roth, W.-M. (1997). Interactional structures during a Grade 4–5 open-design engineering unit. *Journal of Research in Science Teaching, 34*(3), 273–302.

Roth, W.-M., & Lee, Y.-J. (2007). "Vygotsky's neglected legacy": Cultural-historical activity theory. *Review of Educational Research, 77*(2), 186–232.

Roth, W.-M., Tobin, K., & Ritchie, S. (2001). *Re/constructing elementary science.* New York, NY: Peter Lang Publishing.

Rutland, M., & Barlex, D. (2008). Perspectives on pupil creativity in design and technology in the lower secondary education curriculum in England. *International Journal of Technology and Design Education, 18,* 139–165.

Schaffer, S. (1989). Glass works: Newton's prisms and the uses of experiment. In T. Pinch & S. Schaffer (Eds.), *The uses of experiment: Studies in the natural sciences* (pp. 67–104). New York, NY: Cambridge University Press.

Schauble, L., Klopfer, L. E., & Raghavan, K. (1991). Students' transition from engineering model to a science model of experimentation. *Journal of Research in Science Teaching, 28*(9), 859–882.

Silk, E. M., Schunn, C. D., & Cary, M. S. (2009). The impact of an engineering design curriculum on science reasoning in an urban setting. *Journal of Science Education and Technology, 18*(3), 209–223.

Sorby, S. A. (1999). Developing 3-D spatial visualization skills. *Engineering Design Graphics Journal, 63*(2), 21–32.

37

Review of Science Education Program Evaluation

Frances Lawrenz and Mao Thao

Introduction

This chapter provides an overview of science education program evaluation since the early 2000s, when the prior *Handbook of Research on Science Education* was published. It begins with an overview of current trends in science education programming followed by a presentation of evaluation definitions, philosophies, and developments. It then presents a description of selected models and guidelines for conducting science education program evaluations. Next, the chapter presents the U.S. perspective on funding science education programs and how funding patterns and accountability standards have influenced the evaluation of science education programs. A review of literature on science education evaluation and descriptions of evaluation instruments are then provided, followed by a concluding discussion providing implications for practice and suggestions for the future.

Overview of Trends in Science Education

Because evaluation is an applied science, science program evaluation is perforce intertwined with science education programming (Lawrenz, 2007a). Evaluations follow from what is being theorized and implemented by the science education community. Therefore, it is important to briefly consider what has been happening in science education.

In the past decade, science education has become more specifically interwoven with engineering, technology, and mathematics. This new conceptualization of science, technology, engineering, and mathematics is known as STEM. There is considerable discussion about the degree of integration versus separation that this conceptualization might imply (Moore, Stohlmann, Wang, Tank, & Roehrig, in press; Roehrig, Moore, Wang, & Park, 2012). The Next Generation Science Standards Framework (NRC, 2012a) clearly shows the addition of engineering to consideration of desired science education outcomes. Additionally,

the latest edition of the traditional United States (U.S.) national surveys of science education that have been conducted periodically, the 2012 National Survey of Science and Mathematics Education, includes new questions about technology and engineering (www.horizon-research.com/2012nssme/sample-page/instruments/).

Besides being more inclusive of mathematics, technology, and engineering, science education programming has moved in several directions. There is increased consideration of broader entities (e.g., nations, states, schools, communities, etc.; Fleischman, Hopstock, Pelczar, & Shelley, 2010; Provasnik et al., 2012) as mediating variables for science education outcomes. Science learning is being recognized as a lifelong endeavor (Falk, Dierking, & Storksdieck, 2005) and as something that often occurs outside of formal settings (NRC, 2010b). There is more emphasis on science learning in higher education and in disciplinary-specific settings (NRC, 2012b), as well as in consideration of workforce development (NRC, 2012c). There is increased emphasis on individualized, self-motivated learning rather than more group-delivered education (NRC, 2011). Finally, science education is becoming more global. Science education professional associations, journals, and conferences are generally considered to speak to international audiences (e.g., www.narst.org/, www.esera.org/, www.asera.org.au/, http://onlinelibrary.wiley.com/journal/10.1002/(ISSN)1098-2736, and www.tandfonline.com/toc/tsed20/current).

Review Methodology

An extensive review of the literature and available materials was conducted to provide the background for this chapter. There is a massive amount of material available because science education program evaluation crosses discipline areas and can include a range of considerations, from a teacher assessing students in the classroom to evaluations of international, multisite programs. There is a large amount of information available about government programming and evaluations, including assessment instruments, on the Web. The roles that the government plays in science program evaluation vary widely across countries. Because the authors of this chapter are most familiar with science education program evaluation in the United States, this chapter presents details on governmental roles in the United States as one example of the wide range of possibilities, acknowledging that this information is unique to the United States.

Detailed information on how the literature review of research on science program evaluation was conducted is presented in a later section. There was very little information related directly to research about science program evaluation. The literature search was restricted to sources in English and generally within the U.S. context. The references included in all sections are meant to be exemplary of the range of material available, not exhaustive.

What Is Evaluation?

Evaluation is a vibrant and rapidly evolving field of study undergirded by a range of philosophical stances mainly along two continua: objectivist-subjectivist epistemologies and utilitarian-pluralist values. The objectivists tend to rely on reproducible facts and a generalizable Truth (capital T), while the subjectivists depend upon accumulated experience and multiple truths (contextualized little Ts). Utilitarians generally assess overall impact nomothetically, while pluralists assess the impact on each individual in an ideographic way. In other words, pluralists are interested in what works uniquely for each individual while utilitarians are interested in what works for the most people. This difference in value structures supports different definitions and models for evaluation and the use of different evaluation methodologies. As a simplistic example, the use of change in mean scores implies a utilitarian, nomothetic approach, aiming for the most good for the most people, whereas separation of results into outcomes for different subgroups or individuals implies a pluralistic, ideographic approach, aiming for the most good for each individual.

These different stances are embodied in the variety of definitions about what constitutes evaluation. One of the first definitions of educational evaluation was provided by Stufflebeam and colleagues (1971) in *Educational Evaluation and Decision-Making*. This was a management approach to evaluation and more objectivist and utilitarian in its philosophy. In that book, the authors state, "the purpose of evaluation is not to prove but to improve" (p. v.). They defined evaluation as the systematic "process of delineating, obtaining and providing useful information for judging decision alternatives" (p. 36). Since then, that definition has been modified and others proposed.

The expansion of definitions is exemplified by the large number of evaluation textbooks, each with its own perspective. A recent Google search for "evaluation textbooks" brought back more than 16,000 hits. Rossi, Freeman, and Rosenbaum's (1979) *Evaluation: A Systematic Approach* is now in its seventh edition with an additional author (see Rossi, Freeman, & Lipsey, 2004). The original Worthen and Sanders (1973) text, *Educational Evaluation: Theory and Practice*, is now in a third rendition with an additional author as *Program Evaluation: Alternative Approaches and Practical Guidelines* (Fitzpatrick, Worthen, & Sanders, 2004). Michael Patton is a prolific writer, and his utilization-focused evaluation books continue to be popular (Patton, 1978, 2008, 2012).

The National Science Foundation (NSF) and its Education and Human Resources Directorate (EHR) have also provided an evolving set of "User-Friendly Handbooks" to explain what evaluation is to principal investigators and to help provide strong evaluations of their projects. These began with the Stevens, Lawrenz, Ely, and Huberman (1993) text, and the most recent example is Frechtling and colleagues (2010). NSF also produced the *Framework for Evaluating Impacts of Informal Science Education Projects* (Friedman, 2008). These tend to be objectivist and utilitarian in their approach, although the most recent user-friendly handbook has a more pluralist flavor.

Trends in Evaluation

Over the past years, three main trends in evaluation have been growth in cultural awareness, further professionalization of the field, and more proactive political activity. Several publications have contributed to this growth. One is the new, third edition of *The Program Evaluation Standards* (Yarborough, Shulha, Hopson, & Caruthers, 2011) and the development by the American Evaluation Association (AEA; 2004) of the *Guiding Principles for Evaluators* to make them more compatible with changing evaluation needs. The new edition of the standards is similar to prior editions in that it is organized into the same four dimensions of evaluation quality: utility, feasibility, propriety, and accuracy—but different in that it provides more connections among the dimensions, illustrations of the roles played by contexts and cultures in all dimensions, and a new chapter emphasizing meta-evaluation (Yarborough et al., 2011). The *Guiding Principles for Evaluators* include systematic inquiry, competence, integrity/honesty, respect for people, and responsibilities for general and public welfare (AEA, 2004). The emphasis on including diverse perspectives is reflected in the inclusion of the emerging critical interpretive approaches to science program evaluation, such as the approach proposed by Greene, DeStefano, Burgon, and Hall (2006) or the culturally responsive approach championed by Stafford Hood (see Hood, 2001; Hood, Hopson, & Frierson, 2005; Hood & Rosenstein, 2005), Rodney Hopson (see Hood et al., 2005; Mertens & Hopson, 2006; Thompson-Robinson, Hopson, & SenGupta, 2004), Donna Mertens (see Mertens, 2010; Mertens & Ginsberg, 2009; Mertens & Hopson, 2006), and the AEA diversity internship program (www.eval.org/GEDI).

Dunaway, Morrow, and Porter (2012) reported on the development and validation of a cultural competence scale for program evaluators. The 2011 statement from the AEA about cultural competence exemplifies the growth in both cultural awareness and political activity (AEA, 2011). The creation of the Evaluation Policy Task Force in 2007 and its several related public statements also highlight the growing work in the policy arena (AEA, 2007).

In addition to the trends mentioned, there has been increasing emphasis on evaluation capacity building (Huffman, Lawrenz, Thomas, & Clarkson, 2006; Stockdill, Baizerman, & Compton, 2002) and involvement in the evaluation process (Cousins et al., 2008; Huffman, Thomas, & Lawrenz, 2008), especially as it relates to increasing evaluation use and influence (King & Lawrenz, 2011). There has also been substantial growth in the use of mixed methods (Creswell & Plano Clark, 2011; Greene, 2007; Tashakkori & Teddlie, 2010).

Science program evaluation theory and practice must complement innovations in STEM education. Consequently, in parallel with science education, science program evaluation has moved toward the use of more careful consideration of contextual variables in sophisticated statistical models (Ingersoll & May, 2012; VanDerHeyden, McLaughlin, Algina, & Snyder, 2012; Zvoch, 2012). Science program evaluation has also focused on understanding how to assess scaling up of implementations (e.g., the recent requests for proposals from NSF's DRK-12 program www.nsf.gov/publications/pub_summ.jsp?WT.z_pims_id500047&ods_key=nsf11588 and the Institute for Education Sciences (IES; http://ies.ed.gov/funding/pdf/2013_84305A.pdf). Science education assessments, a form of evaluation, are conducted worldwide (see http://nces.ed.gov/surveys/pisa/ and http://nces.ed.gov/Timss/), and there is an emphasis on how to assess workforce and 21st-century skills for STEM careers (NRC, 2012c). In addition, there has been growth in the assessment of collaborations, innovations, and systems (Cronan, 2012). Finally, along with science education, science education evaluation is also becoming more global with international professional societies and journals (e.g., www.europeanevaluation.org/home.htm and www.aes.asn.au/).

Models for Evaluation

These recent trends in evaluation have given rise to the use of different models for evaluation, each of which has its own values perspectives. In the previous (Lawrenz, 2007a) handbook chapter, Stufflebeam's (2001) descriptive and evaluative review of 22 different evaluation models, which had been used over the previous 40 years, was presented. Building on this, Stufflebeam and Shinkfield (2007) more recently suggest five categories of program evaluation models or approaches: pseudo-evaluations, question- or methods-oriented, improvement and/or accountability, social agenda and advocacy, and eclectic. *The Sage Handbook of Evaluation* also presents several models (Shaw,

Greene, & Mark, 2006). In this wide array of models for evaluation, some have been linked specifically to science education program evaluation.

In the National Research Council's review (NRC, 2010a) of the educational programs of the National Oceanic and Atmospheric Administration (NOAA), the Targeting Outcomes of Programs (TOP) model for evaluation (Bennett & Rockwell, 1995, 2004) was discussed because it had been the model chosen by NOAA as a framework for evaluating all of its programs. The TOP model appears to fall into the Stufflebeam and Shinkfield (2007) improvement/accountability category, along with approaches such as the CIPP (context, input, process, and product) model (Cronbach, 1982; Stufflebeam, 2005). It is closer to the objectivist and utilitarian ends of the philosophical continua. The central thrust of this type of evaluation is to foster improvement and accountability through informing and assessing program decisions. The TOP model's connection between evaluation and programming is especially valuable for program development. It appears that for NOAA, at least, the model may not translate well to broader cross-program issues or to programs that are less participant development oriented.

Another recent model for STEM program evaluation that was proposed by Jennifer Greene and colleagues and researched through use with NSF projects is called an educative, values-engaged approach (Greene, Boyce, & Ahn, 2011; Greene, DeStefano, Burgon, & Hall, 2006). This model is closer to the pluralistic and subjective ends of the continua and probably fits in the Stufflebeam and Shinkfield's (2007) social agenda-advocacy category. The "educative" part of this evaluation approach means that it is intended to facilitate learning and better understanding about the program being evaluated. Its underlying logic, contextual appropriateness, potential power to effect change, connections to relevant standards and research evidence, and overall quality are all considered from diverse stakeholder perspectives. The idea of "values engagement" has two dimensions. First, it signals purposeful attention to the values that are intrinsic in STEM education programs, including value differences that may be present among key program stakeholders. Evaluators using this evaluation approach aspire to be inclusive in their engagement with varied value stances as part of assessing program quality and to promote stakeholder dialogue about them. Second, evaluators pay special attention to the values of diversity and equity. Diversity refers to the traditional sociodemographic markers such as class, gender, and race alongside the multiple other ways people are different from one another such as talents, humor, and learning styles. Equity in this approach is concerned with the access and the opportunity to participate and benefit from a program. Greene and colleagues (2011) suggest that this approach is best suited for evaluations that include assessments of program design and implementation, as well as program outcomes.

Another model for evaluation that is older but has moved to the fore recently and has been presented at the

NSF by Mel Mark is realist evaluation (Mark & Henry, 2013; Mark, Henry, & Julnes, 2000; Pawson & Tilley, 1997). Realist evaluation is grounded in the realism school of philosophy, which asserts that both the material and the social worlds are "real" and can have real effects and that it is possible to work toward a closer understanding of what causes change (Pawson & Tilley, 1997). Mark and Henry (2013) state that realist evaluation assumes the notion of evaluation as assisted sense making. This locates evaluation practice in the context of human judgment and action and can accommodate user-focused approaches. It also requires that the findings be accessible to relevant parties. The ultimate goal is social betterment, which is broad enough to encompass deliberate decision-making processes in a democratic society. Social betterment is distinct from social progress, is social and not individual, and implies equality of access. This model has aspects of both the utilitarian/pluralistic and the pluralistic/subjective ends of the continua and seems to fit into the Stufflebeam and Shinkfield's (2007) social agenda-advocacy category.

Another model of evaluation relevant to science education evaluation is culturally responsive evaluation (Hood et al., 2005; Hood & Rosenstein, 2005; Mertens & Hopson, 2006). The idea of integrating the cultural understanding of participants into evaluation is not new, but the emphasis on this in evaluation and especially science program evaluation is more recent. This model is important to science education program evaluation because it helps to address the broader impact of issues facing underrepresented groups and as such is more related to the advocacy agenda and pluralist and subjectivist values. Culturally responsive evaluation advocates a broad-scale, multidimensional, and multidisciplinary view of evaluation that requires practitioners with in-depth understanding of the cultures of the evaluation context and participants. Evaluators should be part of and responsive to the cultural milieu that is being evaluated. Hood, Hopson, and Frierson (2005) developed the culturally responsive evaluation (see also Hood, 2001), while other similar perspectives were also developed, including democratic evaluations (House & Howe, 2000) and inclusive evaluation (Mertens, 2005).

Appreciative inquiry is an evaluation approach as well as a philosophy from the field of organizational development that embraces a positive framework for evaluation (Coghlan, Preskill, & Catsambas, 2003; Preskill & Catsambas, 2006). Instead of adopting the focus on problems or on overcoming barriers that characterizes most deficit-related educational evaluation models, appreciative inquiry argues that organizations improve more effectively through identifying what they do well and focusing on how that can create a better future. It is a philosophy that focuses on identifying and emphasizing success factors or forces that can be used with other tools to improve the organization and its outcomes. As such, it is more subjective and would probably be in the eclectic or methodological category.

One final model, developmental evaluation, has been championed by Patton (2011). Developmental evaluation applies complexity concepts to enhance innovation and to support evaluation use. Innovations are different from standard projects and programs in that they are more a vision than a clearly specified approach and are quite likely to morph quickly as they move forward. Therefore, innovations need an evaluation approach attuned to complexity where how to achieve the desired results is not yet known. Developmental evaluation focuses on what is being developed through innovative engagement. It seems that this model might be more utilitarian but also subjective and perhaps fit into the methodological or eclectic category.

Conducting High-Quality Evaluations

Several steps can be taken to help ensure a high-quality evaluation. The new Evaluation Standards (Yarborough et al., 2011) and the *Guiding Principles for Evaluators* (AEA, 2004) provide excellent guidelines for conducting high-quality evaluations. The old definition provided by Stufflebeam and colleagues (1971), as mentioned earlier, can help to guide these considerations. Although this definition is management and decision-making focused, the key words can be applied to any type of evaluation. First and foremost, evaluation needs to be considered a process. Evaluation is ongoing, should be responsive to the program, and therefore should be changeable. Patton's (2011) developmental evaluation approach especially highlights this aspect of evaluation. Second, evaluations as applied research need to be useful. This usefulness is guaranteed through careful application of the delineate-obtain-provide trilogy of processes.

Delineation is a critical part of the evaluation process. Careful consideration needs to occur about the reasons for the evaluation—for example, what are the stakeholder needs and interests, what decisions will be made, what purpose does the evaluation serve, what variables are of interest, who will make the decisions, whose voices need to be heard, and what values are underlying the evaluation and its use. Consideration of these questions requires in-depth understanding of the program, the people involved, and the context. This understanding will allow the evaluator and the program to determine the most efficacious use of the evaluation budget. Is this a high-stakes summative evaluation in which the fate of the program will be decided by external sources, or is it more important to identify how to improve the program for local interests? The models discussed provide excellent organizational tools to support the delineation process. An additional component of delineation is a thorough exploration of what the program is intended to achieve and for whom. Stake's (1967) old ideas of anticipated and actual antecedents, transactions, and outcomes and examining the congruence and contingencies among them and to external standards is a comprehensive way for categorizing components to help with planning. The evaluator should also try to anticipate and have a plan to capture information about any unintended outcomes.

Although, as suggested in the view of evaluation as a process, delineation can take place continuously, in general the process of obtaining information occurs after the delineation phase. A wide range of information can be obtained through a variety of methodologies. There is much consideration in the literature about how best to employ different methodologies. For example, it may be important to understand the lived experiences of teachers undergoing a curriculum implementation project, which would lead to the use of phenomenological methods. Or as another example, it might be important to examine change in achievement test scores over time in different programs. The key is that whatever information is obtained should fit with the needs outlined in the delineation phase. The competent evaluator may not be an expert with all the methodologies but needs to know enough to know when an expert needs to be consulted. Different types of information fulfill different needs such as needs assessment, monitoring program operation, examining processes, and assessing outcomes. Obtaining information also requires the rigorous application of the selected methodologies, including the development and use of high-quality measures that capture the central goals of the program whatever they may be, such as motivation, identity development, affective disposition, or various levels of cognition. It is often important to examine subgroups within the populations—in other words, a more pluralistic than utilitarian perspective.

Once information is obtained and appropriately analyzed, it needs to be disseminated. Evaluations are conducted to serve specified needs not the inherent curiosity of a researcher. Generally evaluation results are of interest to any decision makers in the process and to the stakeholders of the program. Often the evaluation results are important for general social betterment and therefore of interest to the entire society. The needs and avenues for dissemination should be considered at the onset of the evaluation. The avenues should fit the audience and can include a variety of ideas ranging from the traditional reports to in-person discussions to putting on plays or developing poetry (Johnson, Hall, Greene, & Ahn, 2013 Lawrenz, Gullickson, & Toal, 2007).

The U.S. Federal Perspective

Because of its values orientation, evaluation is closely linked to decision making and policy development. Federal government policies, in particular, influence evaluation practice. This section presents information on how science education programs are funded, how the government approaches accountability for these programs, and how science education program evaluation is funded. The role a government plays in science program evaluation varies widely across countries. Because the authors of this chapter are most familiar with science program evaluation in the United States, this chapter presents details on governmental roles in the United States as one example of the wide range of possibilities, acknowledging that this information is unique to the United States.

Funding for Science Education Programs

Although the vast majority of funding for education in the United States, including science education, comes from state and local sources, the U.S. federal government plays a particularly important role in funding unique science education programs and in requiring accountability for the results of that funding. The two most important agencies for funding science education are the U.S. Department of Education (DOE) and the National Science Foundation (NSF). DOE supports research and evaluation though the IES, established in 2002 with a budget in 2012 of more than $200 million. It supports the National Assessment of Educational Progress (NAEP) continuous testing program. There are four centers: National Center for Educational Research (NCER), National Center for Special Education Research (NCSER), National Center for Education Statistics (NCES), and National Center for Education Evaluation and Regional Assistance (NCEE). It supports 10 Regional Educational Laboratories and the What Works Clearinghouse as well as the ERIC database.

The other major supporter of science education is NSF. All of its directorates support STEM education, but the primary support comes from the Education and Human Resources Directorate (EHR), which as of 2012 has four divisions: human resource development, research on learning in formal and informal settings, graduate education, and undergraduate education. STEM education, learning, and workforce development programs are rooting their approaches in the learning sciences, neuroscience, and other research literatures; investigating cognitive development, motivation, social interaction, and the nature of learning in diverse contexts; and utilizing cutting-edge, evidence-based approaches to engage the public and broaden the future scientific workforce at all levels of the STEM education enterprise (NRC, 1999, 2007, 2009). As pointed out in Lawrenz (2007a), EHR funding has moved through several stages since the 1960s: curriculum development, curriculum implementation, teacher inservice training, systemic initiatives, and partnerships. Presently, the emphasis is on research and evaluation to produce innovation and transformation.

Accountability for Science Programs

The field of evaluation and especially educational evaluation has exploded with the U.S. federal government's ever-increasing interest in accountability. The Lawrenz (2007a) chapter in the previous handbook documented how the growth in science education program evaluation mirrored NSF educational program funding. Although the National

Assessment of Educational Progress (NAEP; http://nces.ed.gov/nationsreportcard/), Trends in International Mathematics and Science (TIMSS; http://nces.ed.gov/timss/), and Program of International Science Assessment (PISA; http://nces.ed.gov/surveys/pisa/) programs have had and continue to have substantial effects on educational policies, the No Child Left Behind Act with its provision for data on the reading, mathematics, and science achievement of all U.S. K–12 students has had an enormous effect on educational policies and evaluation. The potential for linking program implementation to annually administered student achievement scores has opened up broad new avenues in science program evaluation. The requirements for the Math Science Partnership (MSP) to link their projects to students' outcomes are a prime example of this heightened level of accountability (NSF, 2012). Although there are well-reasoned objections to many of the components of the No Child Left Behind Act, there is no doubt that it heightened national interest in assessment of student achievement and in evaluation overall.

There is growing pressure on U.S. federal agencies to show that their funding priorities are evidence based and to provide plans for how both project and program evaluations demonstrate or validate impact and are used to support federal budget priorities (OMB, 2010). The Government Performance and Results Act (P.L. 103–62) was enacted in 1993 and was recently renewed as the GPRA Modernization Act of 2010. The GPRA requires agencies to engage in project-management tasks such as setting goals, measuring results, and reporting their progress (OMB, n.d.). In order to comply with the GPRA, agencies produce strategic plans and performance plans and conduct gap analysis of projects.

In 2007, OMB through the DOE and the Academic Competiveness Council (ACC) conducted a comprehensive investigation of all federal science education programs and the agencies that funded them in an attempt to promote collaboration and eliminate overlap. The investigation also made recommendations on the types of designs to use in conducting evaluations of science education programs (DOE, 2007). The report says that at that time, 12 federal agencies provided funding for STEM education, 8 of which provided funds specifically for K–12 STEM programs. The report goes on to say that in 2006, federal agencies spent $3.1 billion on STEM education, $574 million (18%) of which supported K–12 science education programs.

In addition to the findings of the federal Office of Management and Budget (OMB), the U.S. federal government also makes use of other evaluation mechanisms. For example, the National Academies and its National Research Council (NRC) provide advice on scientific and technical matters. The reviews conducted by the NRC involve the creation of committees of experts who volunteer their time to address a particular charge. Two such committees were charged to examine the educational programs in the National Aeronautics and Space Administration (NASA) (NRC, 2008) and National Oceanic and Atmospheric Administration (NOAA; NRC, 2010a) and the evaluations of these programs. Federal agencies also have a Committee of Visitors (COV) process through which a team of field-based experts comes into the agency, reviews the quality of the funded proposals, and produces a report. Finally, an agency may contract with an external evaluator to evaluate a particular program

Funding for Science Education Program Evaluation

Almost all funding for science education programs is accompanied by some accountability requirements even if it is only documenting how the money was spent. However, evaluation requirements for science education programs generally are much more comprehensive than simple accounting, and funding is provided to conduct these evaluations. Some examples serve to illustrate that point.

The Advancing Informal STEM Learning program at NSF invests in research and development of innovative and field-advancing out-of-school STEM learning and emerging STEM learning environments. In the program solicitation, it is suggested to proposers that they indicate an explicit conceptual framework or theory of action to guide the project and that rigorous evaluation appropriate to the project must be a part of the knowledge-building work.

The Louis Stokes Alliances for Minority Participation (LSAMP) program assists universities and colleges in diversifying the STEM workforce through their efforts at significantly increasing the numbers of students successfully completing high-quality degree programs in STEM disciplines. The 2012 solicitation states that NSF requires potential awardees to rigorously evaluate recruitment and retention programs and activities. It also states that a successful program-management practice would be developing specific evaluation plans and procedures for assessing qualitative and quantitative changes, including the definition of baseline of pre–LSAMP data that will be used to compare post–LSAMP retention, progression, and graduation rates in STEM fields.

The DOE supports science education through its research grants program and its IES. The mathematics and science education topic under this program supports research on the improvement of mathematics and science knowledge and skills of students from kindergarten through high school. DOE has a hierarchical approach to its research grants: the exploration goal, the development and innovation goal, the efficacy and replication goal, the effectiveness goal, and measurement. The final area, measurement, which is to develop, refine, or validate assessments, is the approach most directly related to evaluation, although all levels require evaluation to demonstrate achievement of the outcomes specific to that level.

In addition to supporting evaluation within funded projects, agencies also provide funds directly for evaluations. This direct support is provided through two mechanisms.

One is the direct funding of an evaluation that the agency wants either internally or externally conducted, such as the internally managed decadal review of the Centers for Ocean Science Education or the externally conducted Noyce program evaluation by Abt Associates.

The second mechanism for funding evaluation is providing a grants program that supports evaluation work. Three current examples of this are the NSF Promoting Research and Innovation in Methodologies for Evaluation (PRIME) program (www.nsf.gov/funding/pgm_summ.jsp?pims_id=503586&org=EHR), the American Educational Research Association (AERA) grants program (www.aera.net/Default.aspx?TabID=10242), and the measurement portion of the IES research grants program (http://ies.ed.gov/funding/). The PRIME program seeks to support research on evaluation with special emphasis on exploring innovative approaches for determining the impacts and usefulness of STEM education projects and programs. The AERA program provides small grants and training for researchers who conduct studies of education policy and practice using quantitative methods and including the analysis of data from the large-scale data sets sponsored by National Center for Education Statistics (NCES) and NSF. The IES measurement program is specifically designed to support the development of valid measures of science outcomes.

Research About Science Education Program Evaluation

A review of the literature was conducted to provide background on evaluation of science education programs. The literature search was restricted to publications between 2003 and 2013. Table 37.1 lists the relevant sources that were selected for inclusion. Additionally, it should be noted that this review of science education program evaluation literature is within the U.S. perspective; thus, it does not include international literature. We acknowledge that international trends in science education program evaluation may differ from those within the United States.

Relevant literature was found through searching the University of Minnesota book catalog (MNCAT) and journal databases, as well as top program evaluation and science education journals. Key search terms included "science curriculum evaluation," "evaluating science curriculum," "research on science curriculum evaluation," "physics curriculum evaluation," and "chemistry curriculum evaluation." Furthermore, the term "curriculum" was replaced with "education" for additional searches. Journal databases used include Google, Google Scholar, Academic Search Premier, and Education Resources Information Center (ERIC). Searches were also completed within the journals *New Directions for Evaluation*, *American Journal of Evaluation*, *Canadian Journal of Program Evaluation*, *Evaluation and Program Planning*, *Evaluation Review*, *Education Evaluation and Policy Analysis*, *Journal of Research in Science Teaching*, *Science Education*, *International Journal of Science Education*, and *International Journal of Science and Math Education*. In searches using the databases, the majority of the literature retrieved was on designing science curricula, evaluation reports of science education programs, the impact of science curricula, examples of science curricula or education programs, state standards for science curricula, science teacher training and professional development, and teacher or student classroom evaluations.

TABLE 37.1

List of Sources Included in the Review of Literature

Academic literature on science education evaluation

Altschuld, J. W., & Kumar, D. D. (Eds.). (2002a). *Evaluation of science and technology at the dawn of a new millennium.* New York, NY: Kluwer Academic/Plenum Publishers.
Relevant chapters:
- Chapter 1: Altschuld, J. W., & Kumar, D. D. What does the future have in store for the evaluation of science and technology education?
- Chapter 3: Anderson, B. Evaluating systemic reform: Evaluation needs, practices, and challenges
- Chapter 4: Cheek, D. W. Musings on science program evaluation in an era of educational accountability
- Chapter 7: Kumar, D. D., & Altschuld, J. A. Complementary approaches to evaluating technology in science teacher education
- Chapter 8: Tobin, K., & Roth, M. Evaluation of science teaching performance through co-teaching and co-generative dialoguing
- Chapter 9: Huffman, D. Evaluating science inquiry: A mixed-method approach
- Chapter 10: Cannon, J. R. Distance learning in science education: Practices and evaluation

Bimbaum, M., & Crohn, K. (Eds.). (2010). Challenges in evaluation of environmental education programs and policies. *Evaluation and Program Planning, 33.*
Relevant articles:
- Crohn, K., & Bimbaum, M. Environmental education evaluation: Time to reflect, time for change
- Carleton-Hug, A., & Hug, J. W. Challenges and opportunities for evaluating environmental education programs
- Flowers, A. B. Blazing an evaluation pathway: Lessons learned from applying utilization-focused evaluation to a conservation education program
- Fleming, M. L., & Easton, J. Building environmental education's evaluation capacity through distance education
- Zint, M. An introduction to *My Environmental Education Evaluation Resource Assistant* (MEERA), a web-based resource for self-directed learning about environmental education program evaluation
- Heimlich, J. E. Environmental education evaluation: Reinterpreting education as a strategy for meeting mission
- Monroe, M. C. Challenges for environmental education evaluation

(Continued)

TABLE 37.1
(Continued)

Academic literature on science education evaluation

Brandon, P. R., Taum, A. K., Young, D. B., Pottenger, F. M., & Speitel, T. W. (2008). The complexity of measuring the quality of program implementation with observations: the case of middle school inquiry-based science. *American Journal of Evaluation, 29*(3), 235–250.

Camargo, C., & Shavelson, R. (2009). Direct measures in environmental education evaluation: Behavioral intentions versus observable actions. *Applied Environmental Education and Communication, 8,* 165–173.

Hickey, D. T., & Zuiker, S. J. (2003). A new perspective for evaluating innovative science programs. *Science Education, 87*(4), 539–563.

Huffman, D., & Lawrenz, F. (Eds.). (2006). Critical issues in STEM evaluation. *New Directions for Evaluation, 109.*
Relevant articles:

- Katzenmeyer, C., & Lawrenz, F. National Science Foundation perspectives on the nature of STEM program evaluation
- Lawrenz, F., & Huffman, D. Methodological pluralism: The gold standard of STEM evaluation
- Mertens, D. M., & Hopson, R. K. Advancing evaluation of STEM efforts through attention to diversity and culture
- Greene, J. C., DeStefano, L., Burgon, H., & Hall, J. An educative, values-engaged approach to evaluating STEM educational programs
- Lawrenz, F., Huffman, D., & Thomas, K. Synthesis of STEM education evaluation ideas

King, J. A., & Lawrenz, F. (Eds.). (2011). Multisite evaluation practice: Lessons and reflections from four cases. *New Directions for Evaluation, 129.*
Relevant articles:

- Toal, S. A., & Gullickson, A. R. The upside of an annual survey in light of involvement and use: Evaluating the Advanced Technological Education program
- Johnson, K., & Weiss, I. R. Compulsory project-level involvement and the use of program-level evaluations: Evaluating the Local Systemic Change for Teacher Enhancement program
- Greenseid, L. O., & Lawrenz, F. Tensions and trade-offs in voluntary involvement: Evaluating the Collaboratives for Excellence Teacher Preparations
- Roseland, D., Volkov, B. B., & Callow-Heusser, C. The effect of technical assistance on involvement and use: The case of a research, evaluation, and technical assistance project
- Roseland, D., Greenseid, L. O., Volkov, B. B., & Lawrenz, F. Documenting the impact of multisite evaluations on the science, technology, engineering, and mathematics field

Lawrenz, F., & Desjardins, C. D. (2012). Trends in U.S. government-funded multisite K–12 science program evaluation. In B. J. Fraser, K. G. Tobin, & C. J. McRobbie (Eds.), *Second international handbook of science education* (Vol. 1, pp. 723–734). New York, NY: Springer.

Lee, Y. J., & Chue, S. (2011). The value of fidelity of implementation criteria to evaluate school-based science curriculum innovations. *International Journal of Science Education, 35*(15), 2508–2537.

Zint, M. (2013). Advancing environmental education program evaluation. In R. B. Stevenson, M. Brody, J. Dillon, & A. E. J. Wals (Eds.), *International handbook of research on environmental education* (pp. 298–309). New York, NY: Routledge.

Instruments

Brandon, P. R., Taum, A. K. H., Young, D. B., & Pottenger, F. M. (2008). The development and validation of the inquiry science observation coding sheet. *Evaluation and Program Planning, 31*(3), 247–258.

Lewthwaite, B., & Fisher, D. (2005). The development and validation of a primary science curriculum delivery evaluation questionnaire. *International Journal of Science Education, 27*(5), 593–606.

Minner, D., Ericson, E., Wu, S., & Martinez, A. (2012). *Compendium of research instruments for STEM education part 2: Measuring student's content knowledge, reasoning skills, and psychological attributes.* Cambridge, MA: Abt Associates. Retrieved from http://abtassociates.com/Reports/2012/Compendium-of-Research-Instruments-for-STEM-Ed-%281%29.aspx

Minner, D., Martinez, A., & Freeman, B. (2012). *Compendium of research instruments for STEM education part 1: Teacher practices, PCK, and content knowledge.* Cambridge, MA: Abt Associates. Retrieved from http://abtassociates.com/Reports/2012/Compendium-of-Research-Instruments-for-STEM-Educat.aspx

The Inquiring into Science Instruction Observation Protocol (ISIOP) (http://isiop.edc.org/)

The Reformed Teaching Observation Protocol (RTOP) (http://physicsed.buffalostate.edu/AZTEC/RTOP/RTOP_full/index.htm)

Turner, R. C., Keiffer, E. A., & Gitchel, W. D. (2010). *Observing inquiry-based learning environments: The scholastic inquiry observation (SIO) instrument.* Presented at the American Educational Research Association annual conference. Retrieved from http://gk12.uark.edu/programresults/SIO_Validation.pdf

Websites with resources and instruments for evaluation science education programs

Horizon Research, Inc. (www.horizon-research.com/instruments/)

My Environmental Education Evaluation Resource Assistant (MEERA) (http://meera.snre.umich.edu/links-resources/how-guides-conducting-ee-evaluation/ee-specific-evaluation-guides)

The Center for Advancement of Informal Science Education (http://informalscience.org/evaluation/evaluation-resources)

The Math and Science Partnership Network (MSPnet) (http://hub.mspnet.org/index.cfm/use_web/list/keyword_id-2715)

The National Institute of Health's Science Education Partnership Award (SEPA) (http://nihsepa.org/ed)

The Online Evaluation Resource Library (http://oerl.sri.com/instruments/cd/instrCD.html)

The Program in Education, Afterschool, and Resiliency (PEAR) (www.pearweb.org/atis/dashboard/index)

Academic Literature on Science Education Evaluation

While falling outside of the time restriction, an edited chapter book was particularly relevant and is included in this review because there are very few books focused on science education program evaluation specifically. This book was not included in the previous handbook chapter (Lawrenz, 2007a) due to the publication timeline of that handbook. The book, *Evaluation of Science and Technology Education at the Dawn of a New Millennium*, edited by Altschuld and Kumar (2002a), includes several relevant chapters on the evaluation of science education programs (see Anderson, 2002; Cannon, 2002; Cheek, 2002; Huffman, 2002; Kumar & Altschuld, 2002; Tobin & Roth, 2002). In their chapter, Atschuld and Kumar (2002b) projected a need for and growth of science and technology education evaluation. With this growth, they also saw a need for further training of evaluators in evaluating science and technology programs, as well as questioning what roles science and technology education evaluators play in the process. Furthermore, they felt that there would be new ways of thinking about evaluation in the science and technology education area. They cite the other chapters in the book as having contributed to such new ways of thinking—for example, the use of mixed methodology in science education evaluation (Huffman, 2002), evaluating educational reform (Anderson, 2002), evaluating technology use in science teacher education (Kumar & Altschuld, 2002), and others.

The literature review located a special volume issue focused on STEM–education–related evaluation, *Critical Issues in STEM Evaluation*, published in the *New Directions for Evaluation* series and edited by Huffman and Lawrenz (2006). This volume of articles addresses approaches and methodological considerations for evaluating STEM educational programs—for example, the importance of the use of mixed methodology in STEM evaluation (Lawrenz & Huffman, 2006), the aforementioned educative, values-engaged approach (Greene et al., 2006), or a cultural framework for evaluating STEM education with attention to culture, diversity, and power (Mertens & Hopson, 2006).

Several literature sources were found to have a specific focus on evaluating environmental education programs. A special issue of *Evaluation and Program Planning* titled *Challenges in Evaluation of Environmental Education Programs and Policies*, edited by Bimbaum and Crohn (2010), reviews challenges and methods for evaluating environmental education programs. For example, in their literature review, Carleton-Hug and Hug (2010) identify the lack of program objectives and lack of formative evaluations as key challenges for evaluating environmental education programs. Through examining these challenges, they suggest that there are opportunities for the growth of environmental education evaluation, citing increased interest in evaluation by environmental education practitioners, increased educational accountability, and the need

for an informed population. Also in the issue is Flowers's (2010) article on utilization-focused evaluation—a very common approach in environmental education evaluation. In her article, she uses a conservation education program as an example and discusses the experiences of conducting a utilization-focused evaluation with mixed methods that involved stakeholders in a participatory process. Flowers (2010) concludes with some recommendations and lessons learned in terms of the evaluation process that help to inform evaluation practices.

Additionally, in a review of evaluations of environmental science education programming, Camargo and Shavelson (2009) find that the majority of evaluations often assess participants' environmental attitudes through rating scales and environmental behaviors through self-report. They argue that direct measures of environmental knowledge and behavior are needed for programs to document observable change and that incorporation of direct measures is feasible. They suggest several direct measures of environmental knowledge and behavior, such as assessment of participant learning and observations of behaviors.

Zint (2013) also provides a synthesis of 10 published evaluations of environmental education programs specifically seeking to assess behavioral outcomes of participants, such as environmentally responsible behaviors. Zint (2013) outlines the aspects of the evaluations that may help inform future evaluation efforts of similar programs, including the evaluation approach, outcome measures, methods, involvement of stakeholders, and evaluation use. From the review, Zint (2013) provides recommendations on advancing evaluations of environmental evaluation programs, including using a specific evaluation approach (e.g., utilization-focused approach, theory-driven approach), using mixed methods, documenting program implementation, being thoughtful in measuring changes in behaviors, and having evaluators and researchers work together on future evaluations to appropriately measure environmental behavioral outcomes and assess long-term impacts of environmental education.

Science education programming is often spread across multiple sites. Thus, while not specifically focused on science education evaluation, multisite evaluations are important to consider. The special issue titled *Multi-Site Evaluation Practice: Lessons and Reflections From Four Cases*, edited by King and Lawrenz (2011) and published in the *New Directions for Evaluation* series, includes articles that use four NSF–funded multisite evaluations, including three STEM education and professional development programs and one technical assistance project, to examine patterns of involvement and evaluation use. The first four chapters examine the project-level involvement and evaluation use of primary investigators and evaluation staff in each of the four NSF–funded evaluations (Greenseid & Lawrenz, 2011; Johnson & Weiss, 2011; Roseland, Volkov, & Callow-Heusser, 2011; Toal & Gullickson, 2011). The remaining chapters are helpful for examining the impact and use of multisite evaluations on a broader level (e.g., Roseland, Greenseid, Volkov, & Lawrenz, 2011) and for thinking through multisite evaluations that are quite common within science education program evaluation (e.g., King et al., 2011).

In addition to the special issues, there were several other relevant articles. Lawrenz and Desjardins (2012) provide a thorough and historical review of government funding of K–12 science programs in the United States. They discuss the funding histories of three main science education funders: NSF, NASA, and NOAA. Funded programs often reflect the agencies' topical priorities and political agendas, which influence future science education programming and the ways in which programming is evaluated.

In another article, Hickey and Zuiker (2003) outline a sociocultural perspective for educational program evaluation that was developed from evaluations of innovative science programs. As new and innovative science educational curricula and programs are stressed to meet accountability demands, Hickey and Zuiker (2003) propose this sociocultural perspective as a way to evaluate innovative programs using externally developed performance assessments, a dialectical approach for connecting and making sense of individual-level and event-oriented learning, and comparisons of program outcomes across different implementations of the program. This approach measures learning and knowledge based on sociocultural theoretical views in which learning is described by participation in knowledge practices.

Some other articles discussed evaluating the fidelity of implementation in science education programming. Brandon, Taum, Young, Pottenger, and Speitel (2008) describe an observational method for evaluating the implementation of inquiry-science they called the Inquiry Science Questioning Quality (ISQQ) method. The ISQQ method involves trained expert judges who observe and evaluate teachers relative to each other using the "paired comparison method." In another article, Lee and Chue (2011) stress the importance of evaluating fidelity in science curriculum innovations and its benefits—for example, having better monitoring of accountability and improvement, as well as more confidence in program outcomes and causal associations. Using a science curriculum in Singapore as a case study, they demonstrate the evaluation of four implementation fidelity criteria, including dosage, adherence, quality of delivery, and participation responsiveness. They conclude that such an evaluation helps to provide important information on the progress of the program to stay on track, as well as teachers' ability to assess whether their delivery was consistent with how the curriculum is intended to be delivered and to assess the quality of their delivery.

Science Education Evaluation Resources and Instruments

In addition to a search for science education evaluation literature, a search was also conducted using Google and Google Scholar for science education evaluation instruments. Relevant instruments were generally classroom or teaching fidelity observational protocols, such as the Reformed Teaching Observation Protocol (RTOP; http://physicsed.buffalostate.edu/AZTEC/RTOP/RTOP_full/index.htm), Inquiry Science Observation Coding Sheet (Brandon, Taum, Young, & Pottenger, 2008), the Science Curriculum Implementation Questionnaire (SCIQ; Lewthwaite & Fisher, 2005), the Scholastic Inquiry Observation (SIO) Instrument (Turner, Keiffer, & Gitchel, 2010), and the Inquiring into Science Instruction Observation Protocol (ISIOP; http://isiop.edc.org/). In addition, researchers from Abt Associates compiled two compendiums of research instruments for STEM education (Minner, Ericson, Wu, & Martinez, 2012; Minner, Martinez, & Freeman, 2012). These compendiums provide detailed information on commonly used instruments in STEM research and evaluation.

Several websites also provided scales and questionnaires for science education evaluation. Horizon Research, Inc. (www.horizon-research.com/instruments/) has several observation and interview instruments available. The Program in Education, Afterschool, and Resiliency (PEAR) has a collection of many assessment tools for informal sciences, including scales and questionnaires (www.pearweb.org/atis/dashboard/index). While the Online Evaluation Resource Library is a broad collection of evaluation instruments, it includes some science education evaluation instruments (http://oerl.sri.com/instruments/cd/instrCD.html). Other websites have science education evaluation resources, such as the My Environmental Education Evaluation Resource Assistant (MEERA) website with its guides for environmental education evaluation (http://meera.snre.umich.edu/links-resources/how-guides-conducting-ee-evaluation/ee-specific-evaluation-guides); the Math and Science Partnership Network (MSPnet), which has general science resources but also lists some science education instruments and assessments (http://hub.mspnet.org/index.cfm/use_web/list/keyword_id-2715); the Center for Advancement of Informal Science Education with science evaluation resources (http://informalscience.org/evaluation/evaluation-resources); and the National Institutes of Health's Science Education Partnership Award (SEPA) website that lists evaluation tools and resources created or used by funded programs (http://nihsepa.org/ed).

Discussion and Implications

As suggested, a great deal of activity surrounds science education program evaluation. This is also true internationally, although this chapter focuses only on the United States. Science education program evaluation mirrors the trends and needs in science programming, especially in terms of externally funded science education programs, as they have the funds to support evaluations. There are many models for and definitions of evaluation structured to support the continua of values from objectivist-utilitarian-nomothetic to subjective-pluralist-ideographic. This diversity is validated by the varied value structures of the stakeholders commissioning evaluation studies.

The opportunities for evaluation in the United States are highlighted in this chapter as an example of a comprehensive support structure for science education and its evaluation. In the United States, federal agencies are subject to review by the federal Office of Management and Budget (OMB), and consequently federal funding is provided for evaluation of science education programs. Evaluations are mandated for national programs, resulting in significant funding for large-scale evaluation efforts of science education programs. Furthermore, individual projects are generally required to have their own evaluations. Funding to specifically improve the evaluation of science education is also provided; examples are the development of measurement instruments that could be used nationally and the development of new approaches to evaluation. Despite the frequency of science program evaluation, there has been only a small amount of research pertaining to it.

Areas for Growth

There are two main areas in which science education program evaluation could improve. These areas of concern include consideration of equity and diversity, as well as the various aspects of the quality of evaluations that are designed and carried out, including amount of effort, alignment with needs, and expertise. The equity and diversity concern is focused in terms of groups underrepresented in science and includes both achievement gap and workforce considerations. Equity in science is a continuing concern; as an example, in 1980 the Science and Engineering Equal Opportunity Act created the Committee on Equal Opportunity in Science and Engineering (CEOSE). Concomitantly, the program evaluation field has developed heightened awareness of the need for evaluations to be responsive to cultural diversity. As a consequence, it is critical that evaluations of science education programs be culturally responsive; framed in the existing context of culture, diversity, and power; and include consideration of cultural diversity at all stages of the evaluation process: selection of stakeholders, development of evaluation questions, design of the evaluation, data collection, and analysis and communication. This perspective may help to uncover basic but unstated assumptions about programming or evaluation findings. A related area for growth in the assessment of science education programming is in the inclusion of identity development as an important science education outcome variable. If the underrepresentation of some groups in STEM is to be ameliorated, learning how people come to identify themselves as scientists is critical.

The second area of concern in science program evaluation is the quality of the evaluations. Quality is highly embedded in the design of the evaluation—who and what is involved in the evaluation from both equity and generalizability standpoints, the effort expended in the evaluation, the degree of alignment with stakeholder needs, and the expertise of the evaluators.

The NRC–commissioned papers examining evaluations of NOAA and NASA science educational programs (Brackett, 2009; Lawrenz, 2007b) provide examples of how the designs of science program evaluations may not be as comprehensive as desirable. The reviews of these sets of science program evaluations had similar findings and in general describe the state of many science education program evaluations. Those papers suggested that the evaluations provided relevant descriptive information about the projects from the perspectives of those involved in them. The evaluations used mostly retrospective designs involving only the treatment group and self-report data, often asking participants to comment on how they had changed. Samples were often convenience samples, meaning people who were easy to obtain data from and who usually had a selection bias because they had chosen to participate. Although the data collection instruments used were appropriate, little information was provided on their construction or validity. There was only some use of pre- to postchange or comparison studies, although this is changing with the more recent emphasis on causality and large-scale, randomly controlled trials. These limitations in the designs of science education program evaluations are intertwined with the other aspects of quality—who is involved, the effort expended, and the evaluator's expertise.

Who should be involved in science program evaluation is somewhat addressed in the discussion about equity, but its importance cannot be overemphasized. In addition to equity concerns, however, are generalizability questions related to who should be included in the evaluation. Sampling techniques constrain the inferences that can be made about data. For example, the results of a randomized controlled trial of an intervention at one school may not generalize to other schools; generalizations can only be made to the population from which the sample was drawn. Sampling and inferences from qualitative work are equally constraining. Therefore it is critical for evaluation designers to carefully consider who should be included in a study and to whom inferences are to be made.

In addition to sampling concerns, there are questions about data-gathering methodologies. Although the use of mixed methods in evaluations is gaining popularity, there are still debates about the appropriateness of quantitative or qualitative techniques. The use of quantitative techniques, such as randomized controlled trials, over qualitative ones, such as case studies or phenomenology, is strongly supported by the U.S. Department of Education and societies such as the Society for Research on Educational Effectiveness (SREE). These techniques increase the ability to determine causality, but they also have flaws that have been outlined by several authors (Feuer, Towne, & Shavelson, 2002; Maxwell, 2004; NRC, 2002; Shavelson, Philips, Towne, & Feuer, 2003).

Some constraints in relation to randomized controlled trials relate specifically to evaluation. Randomized controlled trials tend to be very expensive in terms of both time and money, especially if you want to be able to generalize to a large population such as students in the United States. Among other issues in randomly controlled trials, there is the concern of how to persuade people who are not receiving the benefits of a program to participate in the evaluation as comparisons, although time-lag designs in which the comparison group participants receive the treatment at a later date help to alleviate some of that concern. Also, without some qualitative work identifying what is happening at the sites at which a randomly controlled trial of a program is being implemented, important information may be lost; the program is like a black box that produces an effect, but how that effect is produced may not always be clear. It is critical that evaluators carefully align their data-gathering methodologies to the specific questions being asked in the evaluation. For example, more quantitative designs might be used with mature programs to address summative questions, whereas more qualitative designs might be used to address formative or developmental questions.

Another consideration about quality is that the expectations for the outcomes of an evaluation may not be aligned with the resources provided. Often the specified and hoped-for outcomes of a science education program are very broad. An evaluation to determine achievement of these goals would be similarly broad and require substantial amounts of time and money. Generally, however, evaluation budgets are small. A contributing factor to limited evaluation budgets is that spending money on evaluation often means less money available for programming. Of course, evaluation can help projects be more efficient and effective, so the money is unlikely to be wasted, but how much to spend on evaluation may still be a difficult choice. Also, science education funders are often more interested in generic summative evaluations, which provide less input into improving programming and are generally more expensive than the smaller and more iterative formative evaluations. This can lead to evaluations that are not able to examine the more nuanced and unique aspects of a project or are less useful to project personnel.

The constraints on the quality of evaluation design imposed by resources may also lead to evaluations not being used as effectively as they could be because the evaluators cannot afford to provide information on the outcomes of interest in a manner that the project can use. For example, using an indicator of a valuable outcome (e.g., student self-report of desire to continue in college) rather than the outcome itself (e.g., college completion) requires less time and resources but can also be misleading. In addition, evaluation findings are often required within short time frames, which may affect the cost and the type of information gathered. Careful discussion of the level of effort in the evaluation and what can be reasonably expected from it is critical.

A final constraint on the quality of an evaluation is the expertise or experience of the evaluator. The evaluation standards (Yarborough et al., 2011), the Canadian evaluation system (www.avlic.ca/ces), AEA's emphasis on guiding principles for evaluators (AEA, 2004), essential competencies for program evaluators (Stevahn, King, Ghere, & Minnema, 2005), and evaluation-building capacity (Labin, Duffy, Meyers, Wandersman, & Lesesne, 2012) are responses to the need to raise the quality of evaluations. Sometimes experienced evaluators do not know enough about science education to conduct as focused an evaluation as is needed. In-depth understanding of science education in addition to knowledge of evaluation is a critical asset, somewhat akin to pedagogical content knowledge in addition to pedagogical knowledge. The work of science education program evaluators to bridge the two fields helps to improve both (Huffman & Lawrenz, 2006; King & Lawrenz, 2011).

Suggestions for the Future

Political will in the United States is presently focused on accountability, which can translate into evaluation. It would be sensible to respond to this desire for accountability in ways that lead to improvement in science education programs and their evaluations. One way to help would be to promote more sharing of science education evaluation results. There are some notable attempts at sharing such as MSPnet, Informal Science (http://informalscience.org), PEAR's Assessment Tools in Informal Science (ATIS), or the Innovative Technology Experiences for Students and Teachers' (ITEST) learning resource center STEM education instruments (http://itestlrc.edc.org/STEM_education_instruments). Additionally, many evaluation groups post their findings and their instruments, such as on the Horizon Research Inc. website cited earlier.

There should be a mechanism for publishing evaluation results so that the field could build on prior work both in terms of what works in different science education programs and what is the best way to evaluate them. This sharing might also help to address some of the evaluation resources issues. Presently much of the science education evaluation work is in reports held by the funders, not accessible to the general public. Evaluation results are often not publishable in traditional journals because they use confidential information about local settings, have small sample sizes, or are about specific projects. If these data were available, appropriate meta-analytic techniques might allow the development of more insights about the science education programming. If evaluation instruments and results were more readily accessible, it would be possible to improve the validity of the instruments, conduct more comparisons across programs, and have broad discussions on what should be considered measurable outcomes of science education programs (e.g., enjoyment of science or participation in lifelong learning, as well as content knowledge; Lin, Lawrenz, Lin, & Hong, 2012).

This increased sharing and discussion would allow science education program evaluation to move away from evaluations of single entities toward the evaluation of concepts, themes, and entire portfolios of programs.

As discussed, only some research has been conducted that is directly relevant to science education evaluation; therefore, more research is necessary. In particular, research about what can be accomplished at what cost and what skills are necessary for particular types of evaluation would be valuable. There is almost no information available on how best to research evaluation, although the work on meta-evaluation provides insights into how to evaluate evaluations (Hanssen, Lawrenz, & Dunet, 2008). Because science education will be continuously experiencing change, it will be important to determine how best to evaluate innovation and transformation. For example, what are the expected implications of innovations and how can they be identified, what makes one innovation better or worse than another, how can "big data" (collections of data sets so large and complex that it becomes difficult to process using traditional data processing applications), such as data from iPhones or Internet surfing, be incorporated into science education evaluations.

Another area of growth for research about science education evaluation centers around individuality. How should evaluation change as science education moves toward greater consideration of individual cognition and learning as opposed to more "delivered" education? How can evaluation move away from nomothetic approaches (which are more easily accepted in an accountability environment) toward ideographic approaches that are more individualized and much harder to generalize? This latter movement is mirrored in the medical field as more and more focus is placed on individual reactions to drugs than aggregated results from large clinical trials. How can science education evaluation inform science educators about individual learners? How can evaluation interface with new ideas of cognition and learning?

Another important area for research will be how to measure quality. How can evaluation better assess "value added" by science programs? How can science scores across years be validly constructed? What constitutes science growth? How can programs be evaluated against standards or ambitious outcomes rather than in a comparative sense? How should workforce development and 21st-century skills be assessed?

In summary, science education evaluation is a vibrant area that has seen much growth in the past decade. Evaluation has come to be viewed as critically important for the improvement of science education and is strongly supported by agencies that fund science education programs. New models, perspectives, and standards for conducting evaluations have been developed. The importance of value structures has been highlighted, stressing cultural relevance and individual worth. Despite the robust progress, research pertaining to different aspects of science education evaluation is sparse and it remains a rich field for the growth of future research.

Acknowledgments

We are grateful to Audrey Champagne and Terry Crooks for their helpful reviews of this chapter.

References

Altschuld, J. W., & Kumar, D. D. (Eds.). (2002a). *Evaluation of science and technology at the dawn of a new millennium.* New York, NY: Kluwer Academic/Plenum Publishers.

Altschuld, J. W., & Kumar, D. D. (2002b). What does the future have in store for the evaluation of science and technology education? In J. W. Altschuld & D. Kumar (Eds.), *Evaluation of science and technology education at the dawn of a new millennium* (pp. 1–22). New York, NY: Kluwer Academic/Plenum Publishers.

American Evaluation Association (AEA). (2004). *Guiding principles for evaluators.* Retrieved from www.eval.org/p/cm/ld/fid=51

American Evaluation Association (AEA). (2007). *AEA evaluation policy task force charge.* Retrieved from www.eval.org/p/cm/ld/fid=151

American Evaluation Association (AEA). (2011). *AEA statement on cultural competence in evaluation.* Retrieved from www.eval.org/p/cm/ld/fid=92

Anderson, B. (2002). Evaluating systemic reform: Evaluation needs, practices, and challenges. In J. W. Altschuld & D. Kumar (Eds.), *Evaluation of science and technology education at the dawn of a new millennium* (pp. 49–80). New York, NY: Kluwer Academic/Plenum Publishers.

Bennett, C., & Rockwell, K. (1995). *Targeting outcomes of programs (TOP): An integrated approach to planning and evaluation.* Unpublished manuscript. Lincoln: University of Nebraska.

Bennett, C., & Rockwell, K. (2004). *Targeting outcomes of programs (TOP): A hierarchy for targeting outcomes and evaluating their achievement.* Lincoln: University of Nebraska. Retrieved from http://digitalcommons.unl.edu/cgi/viewcontent.cgi?article=1047&context=aglecfacpub

Bimbaum, M., & Crohn, K. (Eds.). (2010). Challenges in evaluation of environmental education programs and policies. *Evaluation and Program Planning, 33*(2): 67–204.

Brackett, A. (2009). *Review of NOAA education program evaluation reports for the committee to review the NOAA Education Program.* Commissioned paper prepared for the National Academy of Sciences. April 17, 2009. Retrieved from www7.nationalacademies.org/bose/1NOAA%20Evaluation.pdf

Brandon, P. R., Taum, A. K. H., Young, D. B., & Pottenger, F. M. (2008). The development and validation of the inquiry science observation coding sheet. *Evaluation and Program Planning, 31*(3), 247–258.

Brandon, P. R., Taum, A. K., Young, D. B., Pottenger, F. M., & Speitel, T. W. (2008). The complexity of measuring the quality of program implementation with observations: the case of middle school inquiry-based science. *American Journal of Evaluation, 29*(3), 235–250.

Camargo, C., & Shavelson, R. (2009). Direct measures in environmental education evaluation: Behavioral intentions versus observable actions. *Applied Environmental Education and Communication, 8,* 165–173.

Cannon, J. R. (2002). Distance learning in science education: Practices and evaluation. In J. W. Altschuld & D. Kumar (Eds.), *Evaluation of science and technology education at the dawn of a new millennium* (pp. 243–266). New York, NY: Kluwer Academic/Plenum Publishers.

Carleton-Hug, A., & Hug, J. W. (2010). Challenges and opportunities for evaluating environmental education programs. *Evaluation and Program Planning, 33*(2), 159–164.

Cheek, D. W. (2002). Musings on science program evaluation in an era of educational accountability. In J. W. Altschuld & D. Kumar (Eds.), *Evaluation of science and technology education at the dawn of a new millennium* (pp. 81–104). New York, NY: Kluwer Academic/Plenum Publishers.

Coghlan, A. T., Preskill, H., & Catsambas, T. (2003). An overview of appreciative inquiry in evaluation. *New Directions for Evaluation, 2003*(100), 5–22.

Cousins, J. B., Elliott, C., Amo, C., Bourgeois, I., Chouinard, J., Goh, S. C., & Lahey, R. (2008). Organizational capacity to do and use evaluation: Results of a pan-Canadian survey of evaluators. *Canadian Journal of Program Evaluation, 23*(3), 1–35.

Creswell, J. W., & Plano Clark, V. L. (2011). *Designing and conducting mixed methods research* (2nd ed.). Los Angeles, CA: SAGE Publications, Inc.

Cronan, M. (2012). NSF industrial innovation and partnerships. *Research Development and Grant Writing News, 2*(11), 2–6.

Cronbach, L. J. (1982). *Designing evaluations of educational and social programs.* San Francisco, CA: Jossey-Bass.

Dunaway, K. E., Morrow, J. A., & Porter, B. E. (2012). Development and validation of the Cultural Competence of Program Evaluators (CCPE) self-report scale. *American Journal of Evaluation, 33*(4), 496–514.

Falk, J. H., Dierking, L. D., & Storksdieck, M. (2005). *A review of research on lifelong science learning.* Washington, DC: Board on Science Education, the National Academies.

Feuer, M. J., Towne, L., & Shavelson, R. J. (2002). Scientific culture and educational research. *Educational Researcher, 31*(8), 4–14.

Fitzpatrick, J. L., Worthen, B. R., & Sanders, J. R. (2004). *Program evaluation: Alternative approaches and practical guidelines* (3rd ed.). Boston, MA: Pearson Education Inc.

Fleischman, H. L., Hopstock, P. J., Pelczar, M. P., & Shelley, B. E. (2010). *Highlights from PISA 2009: Performance of U.S. 15-year-old students in reading, mathematics, and science literacy in an international context* (NCES 2011–004). Washington, DC: U.S. Department of Education, National Center for Education Statistics. U.S. Government Printing Office. Retrieved from http://nces.ed.gov/pubsearch/pubsinfo.asp?pubid=2011004

Flowers, A. B. (2010). Blazing an evaluation pathway: Lessons learned from applying utilization-focused evaluation to a conversation education program. *Evaluation and Program Planning, 33*(2), 165–171.

Frechtling, J., Mark. M. M., Rog, D. J., Thomas, V., Frierson, H., Hood, S., . . . & Johnson, E. (2010). *The 2010 user-friendly handbook for project evaluation.* Washington, DC: National Science Foundation. Retrieved from www.westat.com/Westat/expertise/evaluation/process.cfm

Friedman, A. J. (Ed.). (2008). *Framework for evaluating impacts of informal science education projects.* Washington, DC: National Science Foundation. Retrieved from www.aura-astronomy.org/news/EPO/eval_framework.pdf

Greene, J. C. (2007). *Mixed methodology in social inquiry.* San Francisco, CA: Jossey-Bass.

Greene, J. C., Boyce, A., & Ahn, J. (2011). *A values-engaged, educative approach for evaluating education programs: A guidebook for practice.* University of Illinois.

Greene, J. C., DeStefano, L., Burgon, H., & Hall, J. (2006). An educative, values-engaged approach to evaluating STEM educational programs. *New Directions for Evaluation, 2006*(109), 53–71.

Greenseid, L. O., & Lawrenz, F. (2011). Tensions and trade-offs in voluntary involvement: Evaluating the collaboratives for excellence in teacher preparation. *New Directions for Evaluation, 2011*(129), 25–31.

Hanssen, C. E., Lawrenz, F., & Dunet, D. O. (2008). Concurrent meta-evaluation: A critique. *American Journal of Evaluation, 29*(4), 572–582.

Hickey, D. T., & Zuiker, S. J. (2003). A new perspective for evaluating innovative science programs. *Science Education, 87*(4), 539–563.

Hood, S. (2001). Nobody knows my name: In praise of African American evaluators who were responsive. *New Directions for Evaluation, 2001*(92), 31–43.

Hood, S., Hopson, R. K., & Frierson, H. T. (2005). *The role of culture and cultural context: A mandate for inclusion, the discovery of truth and understanding in evaluative theory and practice.* Charlotte, NC: Information Age Publishing.

Hood, S., & Rosenstein, B. (2005). Culturally responsive evaluation. In S. Mathison (Ed.), *Encyclopedia of evaluation* (pp. 97–102). Thousand Oaks, CA: SAGE Publications, Inc.

House, E. R., & Howe, K. R. (2000). Deliberative democratic evaluation. *New Directions for Evaluation, 2000*(85), 3–23.

Huffman, D. (2002). Evaluating science inquiry: A mixed-method approach. In J. W. Altschuld & D. Kumar (Eds.), *Evaluation of science and technology education at the dawn of a new millennium* (pp. 219–242). New York, NY: Kluwer Academic/Plenum Publishers.

Huffman, D., & Lawrenz, F. (Eds). (2006). *Critical issues in STEM evaluation (No. 109).* San Francisco, CA: Jossey-Bass.

Huffman, D., Lawrenz, F., Thomas, K., & Clarkson, L. (2006). Collaborative evaluation communities in urban schools: A model of evaluation capacity building for STEM education. *New Directions for Evaluation, 2006*(109), 73–85.

Huffman, D., Thomas, K., & Lawrenz, F. (2008). A collaborative immersion approach to evaluation capacity building. *American Journal of Evaluation, 29*(3), 358–368.

Ingersoll, R. M., & May, H. (2012). The magnitude, destinations, and determinants of mathematics and science teacher turnover. *Educational Evaluation and Policy Analysis, 34*(4), 435–464.

Johnson, J., Hall, J., Greene, J. C., & Ahn, J. (2013). Exploring alternative approaches for presenting evaluation results. *American Journal of Evaluation.*

Johnson, K., & Weiss, I. R. (2011). Compulsory project-level involvement and the use of program-level evaluations: Evaluating the local systemic change for teacher enhancement program. *New Directions for Evaluation, 2011*(129), 17–23.

King, J. A., & Lawrenz, F. (Eds). (2011). *Multisite evaluation practice: Lessons and reflections from four cases (No. 129).* San Francisco, CA: Jossey-Bass.

King, J. A., Ross, P. A., Callow-Heusser, C., Gullickson, A. R., Lawrenz, F., & Weiss, I. R. (2011). Reflecting on multisite evaluation practice. *New Directions for Evaluation, 2011*(129), 59–71.

Kumar, D. D., & Altschuld, J. W. (2002). Complementary approaches to evaluating technology in science teacher education. In J. W. Altschuld & D. Kumar (Eds.), *Evaluation of science and technology education at the dawn of a new millennium* (pp. 165–186). New York, NY: Kluwer Academic/Plenum Publishers.

Labin, S. N., Duffy, J. L., Meyers, D. C., Wandersman, A., & Lesesne, C. A. (2012). A research synthesis of the evaluation capacity building literature. *American Journal of Evaluation, 33*(3), 307–338.

Lawrenz, F. (2007a). Review of science education program evaluation. In S. K. Abell & N. G. Lederman (Eds.), *Handbook of research on science education* (pp. 943–1006). Mahwah, NJ: Lawrence Erlbaum Associates.

Lawrenz, F. (2007b). *Summary and critique of selected evaluations of NASA educational programs.* Paper prepared for the National Research Council Committee for the Review and Evaluation of NASA's Pre-College Education Program, Washington, DC. Retrieved from http://sites.nationalacademies.org/DBASSE/BOSE/DBASSE_071087

Lawrenz, F., & Desjardins, C. D. (2012). Trends in U.S. government-funded multisite K–12 science program evaluation. In B. J. Fraser, K. G. Tobin, & C. J. McRobbie (Eds.), *Second international handbook of science education* (Vol. 1, pp. 723–734). New York, NY: Springer.

Lawrenz, F., Gullickson, A., & Toal, S. (2007). Dissemination: Handmaiden to evaluation use. *American Journal of Evaluation, 28*(3), 275–289.

Lawrenz, F., & Huffman, D. (2006). Methodological pluralism: The gold standard of STEM evaluation. *New Directions for Evaluation, 2006*(109), 19–34.

Lee, Y. J., & Chue, S. (2011). The value of fidelity of implementation criteria to evaluate school-based science curriculum innovations. *International Journal of Science Education, 35*(15), 2508–2537.

Lewthwaite, B., & Fisher, D. (2005). The development and validation of a primary science curriculum delivery evaluation questionnaire. *International Journal of Science Education, 27*(5), 593–606.

Lin, H., Lawrenz, F., Lin, S., & Hong, Z. (2012). Relationships among affective factors and preferred engagement in science-related activities. *Public Understanding of Science.* doi:10.1177/0963662511429412

Mark, M. M., & Henry, G. T. (2013). Multiple routes: Evaluation, assisted sense-making, and pathways to betterment. In M. C. Alkin

(Ed.), *Evaluation roots: A wider perspective of theorists' views and influences* (2nd ed., pp. 144–156). Thousand Oaks, CA: SAGE Publications, Inc.

Mark, M. M., Henry, G. T., & Julnes, G. (2000). *Evaluation: An integrated framework for understanding, guiding, and improving policies and programs.* San Francisco, CA: Jossey Bass.

Maxwell, J. A. (2004). Causal explanation, qualitative research, and scientific inquiry in education. *Educational Researcher, 33*(2), 3–11.

Mertens, D. M. (2005). Inclusive evaluation. In S. Mathison (Ed.), *Encyclopedia of evaluation* (pp. 248–249). Thousand Oaks, CA: SAGE Publications, Inc.

Mertens, D. M. (2010). *Research and evaluation in education and psychology: Integrating diversity with quantitative, qualitative, and mixed methods* (3rd ed.). Thousand Oaks, CA: SAGE Publications, Inc.

Mertens, D. M., & Ginsberg, P. E. (Eds.). (2009). *The handbook of social research ethics.* Thousand Oaks, CA: SAGE Publications, Inc.

Mertens, D. M., & Hopson, R. K. (2006). Advancing evaluation of STEM efforts through attention to diversity and culture. *New Directions for Evaluation, 2006*(109), 35–51.

Minner, D., Ericson, E., Wu, S., & Martinez, A. (2012). *Compendium of research instruments for STEM education part 2: Measuring students' content knowledge, reasoning skills, and psychological attributes.* Cambridge, MA: Abt Associates. Retrieved from http://abtassociates.com/Reports/2012/Compendium-of-Research-Instruments-for-STEM-Ed-%281%29.aspx

Minner, D., Martinez, A., & Freeman, B. (2012). *Compendium of research instruments for STEM education part 1: Teacher practices, PCK, and content knowledge.* Cambridge, MA: Abt Associates. Retrieved from http://abtassociates.com/Reports/2012/Compendium-of-Research-Instruments-for-STEM-Educat.aspx

Moore, T. J., Stohlmann, M. S., Wang, H. H., Tank, K. M., & Roehrig, G. H. (in press). Implementation and integration of engineering in K–12 STEM education. In J. Strobel, S. Purzer, & M. Cardella (Eds.), *Engineering in precollege settings: Research into practice.* Rotterdam, the Netherlands: Sense Publishers.

National Research Council (NRC). (1999). *How people learn: Brain, mind, experience and school.* Washington, DC: National Academies Press. Retrieved from www.nap.edu/catalog.php?record_id=9853

National Research Council (NRC). (2002). *Scientific research in education.* Washington, DC: National Academies Press. Retrieved from www.nap.edu/catalog.php?record_id=10236

National Research Council (NRC). (2007). *Taking science to school: Learning and teaching science in grades K–8.* Washington, DC: National Academies Press. Retrieved from www.nap.edu/catalog.php?record_id=11625

National Research Council (NRC). (2008). *NASA's elementary and secondary education program: Review and critique.* Washington, DC: National Academies Press. Retrieved from www.nap.edu/catalog.php?record_id=12081

National Research Council (NRC). (2009). *Learning science in informal environments: People, ideas, and pursuits.* Washington, DC: National Academies Press. Retrieved from www.nap.edu/catalog.php?record_id=12190

National Research Council (NRC). (2010a). *NOAA's education program: Review and critique.* Washington, DC: National Academies Press.

National Research Council (NRC). (2010b). *Surrounded by science: Learning science in informal environments.* Washington, DC: National Academies Press. Retrieved from www.nap.edu/catalog.php?record_id=12614

National Research Council (NRC). (2011). *Learning science through computer games and simulations.* Washington, DC: National Academies Press. Retrieved from www.nap.edu/catalog.php?record_id=13078

National Research Council (NRC). (2012a). *A framework for K–12 science education: Practices, crosscutting concepts, and core ideas.* Washington, DC: National Academies Press. Retrieved from www.nap.edu/catalog.php?record_id=13165

National Research Council (NRC). (2012b). *Discipline-based education research: Understanding and improving learning in undergraduate science and engineering.* Washington, DC: National Academies Press. Retrieved from www.nap.edu/catalog.php?record_id=13362

National Research Council (NRC). (2012c). *Education for life and work: Developing transferable knowledge and skills in the 21st Century.* Washington, DC: National Academies Press. Retrieved from www.nap.edu/catalog.php?record_id=13398

National Science Foundation (NSF). (2012). *Math and science partnership (MSP) program solicitation.* Retrieved from www.nsf.gov/pubs/2012/nsf12518/nsf12518.pdf

Patton, M. Q. (1978). *Utilization-focused evaluation* (1st ed.). Beverly Hills, CA: SAGE Publications, Inc.

Patton, M. Q. (2008). *Utilization-focused evaluation* (4th ed.). Thousand Oaks, CA: SAGE Publications, Inc.

Patton, M. Q. (2011). *Developmental evaluation applying complexity concepts to enhance evaluation.* New York, NY: Guildford Press.

Patton, M. Q. (2012). *Essentials of utilization-focused evaluation.* Thousand Oaks: CA: SAGE Publications, Inc.

Pawson, R., & Tilley, N. (1997). *Realistic evaluation.* Thousand Oaks, CA: SAGE Publications, Inc.

Preskil, H., & Catsambas, T. T. (2006). *Evaluation through appreciative inquiry.* Thousand Oaks, CA: SAGE Publications, Inc.

Provasnik, S., Kastberg, D., Ferraro, D., Lemanski, N., Roey, S., & Jenkins, F. (2012). *Highlights from TIMSS 2011: Mathematics and science achievement of U.S. fourth- and eighth-grade students in an international context* (NCES 2013–009). Washington, DC: National Center for Education Statistics, Institute of Education Sciences, U.S. Department of Education. Retrieved from http://nces.ed.gov/pubsearch/pubsinfo.asp?pubid=2013009

Roehrig, G. H., Moore, T. J., Wang, H. H., & Park, M. S. (2012). Is adding the E enough? Investigating the impact of K–12 engineering standards on the implementation of STEM integration. *School Science and Mathematics, 112*(1), 31–44.

Roseland, D., Greenseid, L. O., Volkov, B. B., & Lawrenz, F. (2011). Documenting the impact of multisite evaluations on the science, technology, engineering, and mathematics field. *New Directions for Evaluation, 2011*(129), 39–48.

Roseland, D., Volkov, B. B., & Callow-Heusser, C. (2011). The effect of technical assistance on involvement and use: The case of a research, evaluation, and technical assistance project. *New Directions for Evaluation, 2011*(129), 33–38.

Rossi, P. H., Freeman, H. E., & Lipsey, M. W. (2004). *Evaluation: A systematic approach* (7th ed.). Thousand Oaks, CA: SAGE Publications, Inc.

Rossi, P. H., Freeman, H. E., & Rosenbaum, S. (1979). *Evaluation: A systematic approach.* Thousand Oaks, CA: SAGE Publications, Inc.

Shavelson, R., Philips, D., Towne, L., & Feuer, M. J. (2003). On the science of education design studies. *Educational Researcher, 32*(1), 25–28.

Shaw, I., Greene, J. C., & Mark, M. M. (Eds.). (2006). *The SAGE handbook of evaluation.* Thousand Oaks, CA: SAGE Publications, Inc.

Stake, R. (1967). The countenance of educational evaluation. *Teachers College Record, 68*(7), 523–540.

Stevahn, L., King, J. A., Ghere, G., & Minnema, J. (2005). Establishing essential competencies for program evaluators. *American Journal of Evaluation, 26*(1), 43–59.

Stevens, F., Lawrenz, F., Ely, D., & Huberman, M. (1993). *The user-friendly handbook for project evaluation.* Washington, DC: National Science Foundation.

Stockdill, S. H., Baizerman, D., & Compton, D. (Eds.). (2002). Toward a definition of the ECB process: A conversation with the ECB literature. *New Directions for Evaluation, 2002*(93), 7–26.

Stufflebeam, D. L. (2001). Evaluation models. *New Directions for Evaluation, 2001*(89), 7–98.

Stufflebeam, D. L. (2005). CIPP model (context, input, process, product). In S. Mathison (Ed.), *International handbook of educational evaluation* (pp. 60–65). Thousand Oaks, CA: SAGE Publications, Inc.

Stufflebeam, D. L., Foley, W. J., Gephart, W. J., Guba, E. G., Hammond, R. L., Merriman, H. O., & Provus, M. M. (1971). *Educational evaluation and decision-making in education.* Itasca, IL: Peacock Publishers Incorporated.

Stufflebeam, D.L., & Shinkfield, A.J. (2007). *Evaluation theory, models, and applications.* San Francisco, CA: Wiley.

Tashakkori, A., & Teddlie, C (Eds.). (2010). *SAGE handbook of mixed methods in social and behavioral research.* Thousand Oaks, CA: SAGE Publications, Inc.

Thompson-Robinson, M., Hopson, R., & SenGupta, S. (Eds). (2004). *In search of cultural competence in evaluation: Toward principles and practices (No. 102).* San Francisco, CA: Jossey-Bass.

Toal, S.A., & Gullickson, A.R. (2011). The upside of an annual survey in light of involvement and use: Evaluating the advanced technological education program. *New Directions for Evaluation, 2011*(129), 9–15.

Tobin, K., & Roth, W. (2002). Evaluation of science teaching performance through coteaching and cogenerative dialoguing. In J.W. Altschuld & D. Kumar (Eds.), *Evaluation of science and technology education at the dawn of a new millennium* (pp. 187–218). New York, NY: Kluwer Academic/Plenum Publishers.

Turner, R.C., Keiffer, E.A., & Gitchel, W.D. (2010). *Observing inquiry-based learning environments: The scholastic inquiry observation (SIO) instrument.* Presented at the American Educational Research Association annual conference. Retrieved from http://gk12.uark.edu/programresults/SIO_Validation.pdf

U.S. Department of Education (DOE). (2007). *Report of the Academic Competitiveness Council.* Retrieved from http://ecommerce.nsta.org//nstaexpress/acc.pdf

U.S. Office of Management and Budget (OMB). (n.d.). *Government Performance and Results Act (GPRA) related materials.* Retrieved from www.whitehouse.gov/omb/mgmt-gpra/index-gpra

U.S. Office of Management and Budget (OMB). (2010). *Evaluating programs for efficacy and cost-efficiency [Memorandum: M-10–32].* Retrieved from www.whitehouse.gov/sites/default/files/omb/memoranda/2010/m10-32.pdf

Worthen, B.R., & Sanders, J.R. (1973). *Educational evaluation: Theory and practice.* Worthington, OH: C.A. Jones Publishing Company.

VanDerHeyden, A., McLaughlin, T., Algina, J., & Snyder, P. (2012). Randomized evaluation of a supplemental grade-wide mathematics intervention. *American Educational Research Journal, 49*(6), 1251–1284.

Yarbrough, D.B., Shulha, L.M., Hopson, R.K., & Caruthers, F.A. (2011). *The program evaluation standards: A guide for evaluators and evaluation users* (3rd ed.). Thousand Oaks, CA: SAGE Publications, Inc.

Zint, M. (2013). Advancing environmental education program evaluation. In R.B. Stevenson, M. Brody, J. Dillon, & A.E.J. Wals (Eds.), *International handbook of research on environmental education* (pp. 298–309). New York, NY: Routledge.

Zvoch, K. (2012). How does fidelity of implementation matter? Using multilevel models to detect relationships between participant outcomes and the delivery and receipt of treatment. *American Journal of Evaluation, 33*(4), 547–565.

38

The Central Role of Assessment in Pedagogy

Paul Black and J. Myron Atkin

Introduction

School governing boards at local and state levels in many countries long had the obligation of establishing the curriculum—by law, as in the United States, or by embedded practice, as in England, or by some combination of the two, as in Australia and Germany. These boards discussed and decided the subjects that should be taught and, not infrequently, determined the specific topics within each one that should be included.

Starting about 40 years ago, however, these discussions and decisions migrated to national levels (Atkin, 1980). Now the shift in authority is entrenched, and there is no realistic expectation of a reversion to more local control. Furthermore and of particular saliency for this chapter, decisions about the quality of learning and teaching are made increasingly on the basis of the published and publicized scores on mandatory assessments. Typically committees selected by the governing authority oversee the development of the frameworks, for which commercial test-construction companies then develop the assessments.

In the United States since the 1980s, the science frameworks have been developed by committees of the National Research Council, or NRC (NRC, 2011), and, separately, by many of the individual states. For international achievement—and comparison—the OECD has taken responsibility (OECD, 2013). In these and other cases, the frameworks have been a basis on which various national and international tests have been based.

The results of these tests, sometimes administered to virtually all students and sometimes to a carefully selected sample, are used to rank the quality of schools locally, nationally, and internationally. Education jurisdictions that stand high in the rankings celebrate and publicize their achievement. Those that do not usually take steps to "reform" their schools. In the United States, federal funding depends on the rise or fall of students' scores on the tests. But there is little public understanding of the tests themselves. Valid or not, they carry high-stakes consequences for students, teachers, and local governing boards. And they affect the curriculum profoundly.

It is clear that the influence of testing in general and its accountability function in particular have had damaging effects on the learning of students (Mansell, James, & the Assessment Reform Group, 2009). However, the problem is whether such deleterious effects are an inevitable effect of assessment in all its forms. A main theme of this chapter is to study this issue in the light of a broad view of the school curriculum, starting from consideration of the agency of the schools and their responsibility to society and to the students in their care. This will lead to considering a definition of pedagogy and using this basis to discuss the roles of assessment within this definition.

On the basis of these discussions, we advance the argument that the negative effects of assessment and testing are not inevitable and that within a redefinition of the role of assessment in pedagogy, it is possible to construct a positive relationship between accountability and effective schooling.

The Hidden Curriculum and the Agency of the School

The Social and Moral Responsibilities of the School

More than 35 years ago, Elliot Eisner (1978) used the term "hidden curriculum" to highlight the fact that schools teach much more than the syllabus, which is the printed list of facts, skills, and concepts prescribed or recommended for the various school subjects. Of particular importance, students learn about the behavior of adults in positions of responsibility. Does the teacher punish the entire class when a child or small group misbehaves? The hidden curriculum includes serious attention to personal and social behavior, such as taking turns and respecting the ideas of other students. It includes how *fair* teachers seem to be and whether they give even chances to all students. Do they humiliate those who misbehave? How do they handle situations in which a student accuses another of bullying or copying or lying? Does the teacher seem to have favorites?

Much of what students learn in school figures powerfully in their education and lies entirely outside the official syllabus. Such learning is rarely assessed, yet, arguably, it is one of the most important outcomes of the more than 15,000 hours spent in school during the most formative phase of a person's life.

Thus the influences on a student's development are both broader and deeper in range than might be implied in any curriculum document. A fundamental aspect of this range is expressed as follows by Milroy (1992), reacting to the first imposition of a National Curriculum in England:

> (Parents) know that, for the child, the encounter with the teacher is the first major step into outside society, the beginning of a long journey towards adulthood in which the role of the teacher is going to be decisive.
>
> (p. 57)

> Teachers are, therefore, not in the first instance agents either of the National Curriculum Council (or whatever follows it) or of the State. . . . The role of the teachers is to attract them progressively into the many realms of the culture to which they belong. This culture consists partly of a heritage, which links them to the past, and partly of a range of skills and opportunities, which links them to the future.
>
> (p. 59)

This view is focused on the role of the teacher, a focus that may be due in part to the author's role as head of an independent residential school in the U.K. A broader and more complex view is expressed by Greene (1983):

> Once children move from the intimacies of family life into the impersonality and organization associated with life in classrooms, they cannot help becoming subject to the prevailing ideology, to socialization in its varying forms. The norms are communicated by the hidden curriculum—because unacknowledged, often more powerful than what is explicitly taught—are in conflict with the values publicly affirmed.
>
> (p. 4)

This second quotation makes clear that Milroy's "culture" may be problematic—a contested area in which the school can choose to resist or reinforce the values and norms of the "prevailing ideology." Such choices are inevitably moral choices.

Education reformers of the past often couched their arguments in moral terms. From John Calvin to Jean-Jacques Rousseau to Matthew Arnold, the importance and quality of education was a passionate concern and was central to their conception of a just and humane society. Calvin advocated publicly supported schools to assure the proper relationship of young children to the deity. Rousseau saw in the young child the potential for understanding nature and to live in harmony with it by concrete, direct interaction in the outdoors: Such an association with the natural world would foster appreciation of the nonhuman forms of life that among which we all live.

Matthew Arnold, a poet, was one of Her Majesty's Inspectors of Schools and earned his livelihood by visiting classrooms and education administrators in all corners of England. His responsibility was to prepare reports for the London authorities and make suggestions for improvement. He was concerned that schooling was becoming too routinized. "Payment by results" was becoming popular in government circles. (It had uncanny similarities to the financial incentives embedded in the United States' No Child Left Behind Act about a century later whereby funding depends on the basis of the more concrete, quantifiable annual increases in test scores.)

With this late-19th-century development in education in England, Arnold feared for the future of the humanities in government-funded schools. He believed that more easily measureable and therefore more readily assessed subjects, like mathematics and the sciences, would crowd out poetry, the visual arts, music, and literature in the schools. He actively supported the teaching of these subjects, as he also fervently supported the teaching of mathematics and the sciences.

In the same volume of essays in which the quotation from Greene appeared, a Brazilian, Paulo Freire, one of the leading education reformers of the 1970s and 1980s, used a banking metaphor in his critique of schooling (Freire, 1983). His views reflected a form of liberation theology that was surfacing at the time, with a special focus on the poor. He wrote:

> Education becomes an act of depositing, in which the students are the depositories, and the teacher is the depositor. Instead of communicating, the teacher issues communiqués and makes deposits which the student patiently receives, memorizes, and repeats. The scope of action allowed to the student extends only as far as receiving, filing, and storing the deposits.
>
> (p. 284)

This quotation can be interpreted at two levels. One is about a society's intention that education limit the potential development of its citizens. The other assumes a more positive intention but a poverty of method in developing students' potential. If they are narrow in scope, assessment practices may help to realize the first; if they are broader, they may help to overcome the poverty of method in the second.

John Dewey and Broader Visions of School Education

In the early 1920s, Dewey's ideas about the most suitable education for children began to spread widely and rapidly. "Progressive" and "child centered" were often the labels used to underscore the view that schools are not solely for the purpose of preparing children for adult responsibilities and obligations. They are places where lives are lived, where learning is a full-time activity, where young people begin to find out more about the workings of the world into which they are born and that they will begin to shape. Such an education requires students to engage in a broader range of activities than solely preparing for the next test, then the next test after that, and so on. The quality of the education *experience* itself is what counts. In Dewey's philosophy, an educational experience should lead to pursuit of further educational experiences.

In the decades following the establishment of the Progressive Education Association in 1919, and building on the ideas of education reformers like Rousseau, Montessori, and many others, the operational meanings of these ideas were fleshed out for virtually all levels of education from preschool to colleges and universities. Examples of the latter in the United States are free-standing institutions like Antioch College, Bennington College (where Dewey was a trustee), and Sarah Lawrence College. There are also "colleges within colleges," like those at the University of California Davis and Tufts University.

Moral development was at the core of the interests of John Dewey, a philosopher and one of the main shapers of pragmatism, a set of ideas that started to develop in the United States in the late 19th century. At the core of the philosophy is an aversion to ideologies of any kind (Menand, 2001). He devoted much of his thought and writing to the education of school-age students.

Dewey in 1932 paid particular attention to the role of schools. He posited that a sense of morality is shaped first in group settings, beginning in the family (Dewey, 1985). It is here that a person begins to observe how parents and other relatives treat one another in a wide range of circumstances.

He elaborated this concept in a book thought to have been lost but recently published (2012). In it, he advances the view that a sense of what is moral develops further and, consequentially, in schools as children learn more deeply about a range of deeply held beliefs—especially when they observe rational discourse and begin to participate in it. Such activity is seldom found in the official curriculum, but it characterizes effective teaching in almost all subjects, including literature, music, the visual arts, science, history, and technology. Further, he suggests that such group participation is the seedbed for private and individual action—with respect to strangers, friends, animals, the environment, and a countless number of actions that one's friends and family will never know about.

Several creative innovators in science education were influenced strongly by Dewey. One was David Hawkins, a physicist and an historian of science (Hawkins, 1983): He tells us that children "should be led, not dragged" when they learn in school, and that their natural inquisitiveness should be the pivot. He wrote about children "messing about" in science, by which he meant building on their natural inquisitiveness to guide them, albeit subtly, to an understanding of the underlying science. Consider this case of "messing about" from Hawkins:

> Let me cite an example from my own recent experiences. Simple frames, each designed to support two or three weights on strings, were handed out one morning in a fifth-grade class. There was one such frame for each pair of children. In two earlier trial classes, we had introduced the same equipment with a much more "structured" beginning, demonstrating the striking phenomenon of coupled pendulums and raising questions about it before the laboratory work was allowed to begin. If there was guidance this time, however, it came only from the apparatus—a pendulum is to swing! In starting this way I, for one, naively assumed that a couple of hours of "Messing About" would suffice. After two hours, instead, we allowed two more and, in the end, a stretch of several weeks. In all this time, there was little or no evidence of boredom or confusion. Most of the questions we might have planned for came up unscheduled.
>
> (Hawkins, 1974, p. 4)

When Hawkins was invited to the University of Illinois at Champaign–Urbana to give a lecture in 1968 on the occasion of the celebration of the centennial celebration of the University's founding, he said that the title would be Not to Eat, Not for Love. Attendees learned that the reference was to the writing of Ralph Waldo Emerson, a New England Transcendentalist of the late 1800s:

> Four snakes gliding up and down a hollow for no purpose that I could see—not to eat, not for love, but only gliding.
>
> (Emerson, 1834, p. 1)

Another influential figure in science education strongly influenced by John Dewey was a friend and colleague of Hawkins at the University of Colorado: Frank Oppenheimer, a physicist, induced the City of San Francisco to permit the Palace of Fine Arts, built in 1915 for the Panama-Pacific Exposition, to be converted almost completely into a place for science learning. Tellingly, he did not call the institution he then created a museum. It was to be the Exploratorium, a place that is not primarily for exhibits to be seen and stimulate awe, but rather a place for children and adults to explore—to mess about with science—in a setting full of objects carefully chosen and designed to enable children to learn key concepts of science.

In his biography of Oppenheimer, *Something Incredibly Wonderful Happens: Frank Oppenheimer and the World He Made Up*, K. C. Cole writes of his first meeting with Oppenheimer at the Exploratorium:

> I introduced myself, and Frank took me on what amounted to a sightseeing trip . . . In fact, a place for sightseeing is exactly what Frank had in mind when he built the Exploratorium. Sightseeing, he liked to say, is the basis for all discovery. Marco Polo and Charles Darwin were both sightseers. "Individual sights combine to form patterns," he said, "which constitute a simple form of understanding."

The patterns that Darwin noticed changed the way people see themselves, their origins, their relationship with other living beings.

(Cole, 2009, p. 11)

In a section titled "A Decent Respect for Play," Cole writes:

The general unruliness of the place was amplified by the presence of a great number of dogs. Dogs slept next to staff members, followed people around the museum (sic), or waited for their walks tied to pieces of furniture. . . . So if you're trying to rip open the world to peek inside, the kids and dogs and everything are part of that.

(p. 17)

A footnote follows:

When I returned to the Exploratorium for a visit in 2005, I knocked on the door of a trailer only to have it opened by a dog who had been trained to pull on a rope and open the door when someone wanted entry.

(p. 17)

In the same section, Cole continues:

When Frank looked into the subject of play, he came to believe that it was much harder than it seemed, especially for adults. He asked his friend Bob Karplus, a physicist at the University of California at Berkeley, if he thought there was anything a young person should learn before it was too late, and Karplus's answer was "play."

(p. 19)

Implications for Effective Teaching

Dewey's arguments, and those of educators influenced strongly by his ideas, are rich in implications. It is clear that many of the most important results of schooling are informal and pervade all of its practices. However, for our present purpose, it is necessary to explore some of the characteristics of "effective teaching." To explore the meaning of this phrase could open up an agenda that would extend far beyond the limits of this chapter. For the present purpose, three main points will be presented. The first is expressed by the following argument by Thomas Groome, taken from his 1998 book *Educating for Life*:

Educators can take over functions that learners should be doing—learning how to learn, making up their own minds, reaching personal decisions. Such imbalance ill serves learners and can be destructive to educators. There is a fine line between empowering learners as their own people and overpowering them—making them too dependent or indebted to teacher or parent. Walking this tightrope is an aspect of the educator's spiritual discipline of a balanced life.

(p. 348)

This could be seen as a condemnation of the practice of "teaching to the test," but it goes far deeper in that it links together the long-term responsibility of the student's development to the teacher's own moral outlook.

The second point is also about the longer-term responsibility of the teacher to help the development of the student as a reflective and thereby independent learner. David Wood expresses this point, in his 1998 book on *How Children Think and Learn*, in the following way:

Vygotsky, as we have already seen, argues that such external and social activities are gradually internalized by the child as he comes to regulate his own internal activity. Such encounters are the source of experiences which eventually create the "inner dialogues" that form the process of mental self-regulation. Viewed in this way, learning is taking place on at least two levels: the child is learning about the task, developing "local expertise"; and he is also learning how to structure his own learning and reasoning.

(p. 98)

The third point takes further the arguments of the first two by considering one important component that can affect the power of the student as an independent learner— the link between each person's view of themselves and in particular of their power to engage effectively in a learning endeavor. The writings of Carol Dweck, in her 2006 book on *Mindsets*, highlight this issue by exploring the contrast between the *fixed* mindset and the *growth* mindset. The former she explains as follows:

I've seen so many people with one consuming goal of proving themselves—in the classroom, in their careers, and in their relationships. Every situation calls for a confirmation of their intelligence, personality or character. Every situation is evaluated: Will I succeed or fail? Will I look smart or dumb? Will I be accepted or rejected? Will I feel like a winner or a loser?

(p. 6)

What is at issue is not whether intelligence, personality, and character should be valued, but whether one believes they are fixed or believes that they can grow:

There's another mindset in which these traits are not simply a hand you're dealt with and have to live with, always trying to convince yourself and others that you have a royal flush when you're secretly worried it's a pair of tens. In this mindset, the hand you're dealt with is just the starting point for development. This growth mindset is based on the belief that your basic qualities are things you can cultivate through your own efforts. Although people may differ in every which way in their initial talents and aptitudes, interests or temperaments, every one can change and grow through application and experience.

(Dweck, 2006, pp. 6–7)

Explaining the perspective of people with this second mindset, she states:

[T]hey believe that a person's true potential is unknown (and unknowable); that it's impossible to foresee what can be accomplished with years of passion, toil and training.

(Dweck, 2006, p. 7)

Dweck's book illustrates the evidence about the effects of being guided by one mindset or the other with many individual examples, at many stages of people's careers both within and far beyond the years of schooling. However, one main basis for her arguments can be found in her detailed report on the 30 years of systematic research into school students' learning (Dweck, 2000). A key feature of these, and of related studies by other authors, is that the way in which students are given feedback about their work can influence their development of one mindset rather than the other. The competitive ethos, with its emphasis on improvement through regular testing and feedback of marks and grades, will develop the fixed mindset to the detriment of the growth mindset, with negative consequences for the development of the learner, consequences about which her research has established ample evidence.

The recurrent theme of this section is that the school influences the development of its students in many and various ways. Some of these are deep and all-pervasive effects that are difficult to reduce to issues of assessment and its place in pedagogy. What is salient is that in their work of nurturing the development of their students, schools and their teachers are engaged in a moral endeavor, and they cannot be relieved of this responsibility by external edicts. Furthermore, their teaching and learning work has to be assessed in the light of a view of their students' development that should have a strong focus on their development as independent and confident learners as well as on any measures of the particular knowledge and skills that characterize the several subjects of the school's curriculum. Thus, the next step in our argument is to explore how assessment can so function within a broader view of pedagogy that it supports rather than undermines these ideals.

The Role of Assessment in Teaching and Learning

In our introduction, we drew attention to the increasing influence of assessment, seen as the instrument for raising standards through the pressures of accountability. In the first main section, the argument was in sharp contrast, drawing attention to broader views of the central task of schools in fashioning the personal and social development of their students. There seems to be little by way of positive interplay between these two issues—indeed, the state testing fashions would seem to drive schools to adopt narrow and impoverished approaches to their central task. One could conclude that these two imperatives are hard to reconcile. In this section, we shall consider ways in which these two can be brought into harmony.

Our way of doing this will be to look again at the role of assessment within a theory of pedagogy, so we start with a brief discussion of the existing literature on pedagogy. Studies of teaching and learning in schools use the terms "pedagogy" and "instruction," but many do not define these precisely. "Pedagogy" is used by many as an inclusive term to cover all aspects of teaching and learning.

Such authors often focus on the exercise of power through curriculum and teaching: Examples would be the study by Paolo Freire (1992) and similar works that add such adjectives as "critical," "conflict," "liberatory," and "gender," all of which highlight the political function of pedagogy.

In these approaches, the term "instruction" represents one component of the broader realm of pedagogy. Examples are Shulman (1999) and Hallam and Ireson (1999). By contrast, Bruner (1966) used a broad definition of instruction in which it is seen as a guide to pedagogy, the latter being a collection of maxims. These contrasting definitions do not seem to reflect any fundamental difference between those who use these terms in these different ways. What is notable in much of this literature is that assessment receives scant attention.

However, Tyler devotes the last substantive chapter in his 1969 book on *Basic Principles of Curriculum and Instruction* to the problem of how the effectiveness of learning experiences can be evaluated, and Bruner devotes the last part of the last chapter in *Towards a Theory of Instruction* (1966) to the same topic. Tyler argues strongly that formal tests cannot on their own serve the purpose of evaluation: A wide range of measures, made and recorded at several stages during any teaching sequence and including measures of learners' attitudes and interests are required. It follows that if its findings are reduced to a single mark or grade, the evaluation cannot contribute to the development of effective instruction. Bruner (1966) makes similar points but gives more prominence to the role of evaluation in curriculum development: "Evaluation is best looked at as a form of educational intelligence for the guidance of curriculum construction and pedagogy" (p. 163).

He also draws attention to the culture of formal testing, which has given evaluation: "a history that is inappropriate to present practice of the kind being discussed here" (p. 165).

By contrast, Bruner emphasized its central role, stating, for example, that any curriculum-building team should include an evaluator, who must be involved from the outset and at all stages.

Since these writings were produced, the term "evaluation" has come to represent the scrutiny of the effects of particular innovations, being replaced by the term "assessment" to represent the everyday evaluation of the learning of students. This shift has been accompanied by a change of focus from Bruner's broad view toward a view that this aspect of a teacher's work is a marginal extra, thus separating it from a place in a unified theory of pedagogy. For example, Alexander (2008) stated that:

> Pedagogy is the act of teaching together with its attendant discourse of educational theories, values, evidence and justifications. It is what one needs to know, and the skills one needs to command, in order to make and justify the many different kinds of decision of which teaching is constituted. Curriculum is just one of its domains, albeit a central one.
>
> (p. 47)

However, while listing the core acts of teaching as "task, activity, interaction and assessment" (Alexander, 2008, p. 49), he subsequently gave the last of these very little attention.

It seems that existing work on pedagogy does not take us very far in the task of formulating positive links between the various roles of assessment and a model of pedagogy. New models of both pedagogy and assessment are needed—so composed that together they give assessment a more central and yet diverse role within the school's work of teaching and learning. Such models should be designed to help each school to ensure that its work serves the following aims:

- Nurture and build on students' natural appetites for curiosity and inquiry.
- Help the social development of all, including constructive involvement in social learning.
- Encourage students to express their thinking and to then reconstruct their ideas through dialogue with others.
- Guide students to take increasing responsibility for their own learning, thereby empowering them to develop as mature and reflective learners.

We shall explain, in the next few sections, how assessment can be given a central role in a model of pedagogy so that its role in achieving these aims may be more clearly understood. This will be done by examining in turn formative assessment, the links between formative and summative assessments, and the ways in which state frameworks could link these in frameworks that could actually enhance the validity of state assessments.

Formative Assessment: Learning Through Dialogue

In this section we start by an account of formative assessment, with a focus on the concept of dialogue as an essential feature of the school's work with and for its students. After this, we shall draw on this example to argue for a natural and close link between the formative and the summative and use this to expand the agenda in terms of a comprehensive framework of pedagogy within which assessment plays several important roles. This then leads to a full account of how several studies have explored the potential for enhancing the quality of teachers' own summative assessments. Consideration of the implication of such studies for the reform of state assessments systems follows, and so concludes the argument of this section.

A test as such may be either formative or summative or both—the distinction lies in the purpose for which information is interpreted and used, not in the means used to elicit that information (Wiliam & Black, 1996). The distinction is emphasized in the following definition:

> Assessment for learning is any assessment for which the first priority in its design and practice is to serve the purpose of promoting students' learning. It thus differs from assessment designed primarily to serve the purposes of accountability, or of ranking, or of certifying competence.
>
> An assessment activity can help learning if it provides information to be used as feedback, by teachers, and by their students, in assessing themselves and each other, to modify the teaching and learning activities in which they are engaged. Such assessment becomes "formative assessment" when the evidence is actually used to adapt the teaching to meet learning needs.
>
> (Black, Harrison, Lee, Marshall, & Wiliam, 2002, inside front cover)

This definition links the service of students' learning to dialogue, to carry out interactive exchanges between teacher and students and between students themselves. A teacher who had learned to use a formative approach summarized the changes she made in her use of questions in class as follows:

Questioning

- My whole teaching style has become more interactive. Instead of showing how to find solutions, a question is asked and students given time to explore answers together. My Year 8 target class is now well-used to this way of working. I find myself using this method more and more with other groups.

No hands

- Unless specifically asked students know not to put their hands up if they know the answer to a question. All students are expected to be able to answer at any time even if it is an "I don't know."

Supportive climate

- Students are comfortable with giving a wrong answer. They know that these can be as useful as correct ones. They are happy for other students to help explore their wrong answers further.

> (Black, Harrison, Lee, Marshall, & Wiliam, 2003, p. 40)

Research results on "wait time" (Rowe, 1974) have impressed many teachers with the need to give students time to think, leading them to encourage students to talk with one another before answers are called for, so that as many as possible will feel confident about expressing their ideas. The corollary of this approach is that each question has to be sufficiently open, from the learners' perspective, that it calls for thought and has to be sufficiently central to the learning aims that it justifies the time spent on discussing the ideas that ensue. It follows that closed questions, checking only on knowledge, would be seen to make little contribution to students' learning. If students have time to think, their wrong or partly right answers can give information about the students' understanding that will help the teacher to select the optimum way for the work to proceed.

The key issue is that the formative purpose of a question is achieved only if it elicits from students some significant indicator of their understanding and then enables the teacher or other students to respond by trying to correct or develop that understanding, and perhaps through listening to several responses lead the whole class to share in a discussion of the issue. Given that student participation is often unpredictable, the task of "steering" such dialogue is a delicate one. For example, a student's answer to a question can reveal how the student understands the issue, and the teacher can then respond to help develop that understanding. This is more difficult than it may seem. Consider this example (quoted by Black & Wiliam, 2009, from Fisher, 2005): a primary class had been drawing pictures of daffodils:

Teacher: "What is this flower called?"
Child: "I think it's called Betty."

The teacher might respond by asking other students the same question until someone produces the word "daffodil." All could then be told that this was the "right answer." However, an alternative response could be to ask the class whether "Betty" and "daffodil" are the same sort of answer, which could start a discussion of the difference between individual names and generic names. The first response would have missed the learning opportunity that would be exploited by the second. What the student understood by the terms "is . . . called" in the question was not the meaning that the teacher had in mind: It is commonplace that what is "heard" in any discussion is not what the speaker intended. However, the teacher, likewise, would have to pause and reflect on why the student might have given that answer before deciding how to respond.

In composing a useful response, the teacher has to interpret the thinking and the motivation that led the student to express the answer. It helps if the teacher first asks the student to explain how he or she arrived at that answer, then accepts any explanation without comment and asks others what they think. This gives value to the first answer and draws the class into a shared exploration of the issue. In doing this the teacher changes role, from being an interviewer of students on a one-to-one basis to being a conductor of dialogue in which all may be involved. This is challenging, in that the diverse inputs from several students will create a more complex task of interpretation; a more detailed examination of this problem is given in Black and Wiliam (2009). However, as student–student interactions are encouraged, the teacher will have time to reflect on how best to intervene. At the same time, students can be helping one another either to resolve or to express more clearly their difficulties.

Promoting a rich dialogue is a delicate task of teachers, for on the one hand tight control over the discussion can inhibit involvement of the learners, but on the other hand loose control can lead to digression so that the purpose of the learning is lost. Yet it is essential to strike this balance. The fundamental reason it is important to encourage the mutual involvement of as many students as possible in class dialogue is explained as follows:

> Children, we now know, need to talk, and to experience a rich diet of spoken language, in order to think and to learn. Reading, writing and number may be acknowledged curriculum "basics," but talk is arguably the true foundation of learning.
>
> (Alexander, 2006, p. 9)

In a more detailed exploration of this issue, Alexander states:

> Talk vitally mediates the cognitive and cultural spaces between adult and child, among children themselves, between teacher and learner, between society and the individual, between what the child knows and understands and what he or she has yet to know and understand.
>
> (Alexander, 2008, p. 92)

Research in many classrooms shows that such productive dialogue is rarely achieved (see, for example, Applebee, Langer, Nystrand, & Gamoran, 2003). The norm is the use of closed rather than open questions, very brief student responses, and a "dialogue" that is a sequence of teacher–student–teacher–student–teacher interactions, with few examples of student–student interactions, so that the teacher dominates the "discussion." However, teachers find it difficult to change from this pattern, for some fear that it will be difficult to deal with the unexpected in students' responses and that they may lose control of any free-ranging discussion. An example of a fragment of classroom dialogue in which a science teacher had begun to steer rather than control a classroom dialogue is given in Black and colleagues 2003 (pp. 37–39). A characteristic of this example is that every student contribution was expressed as a sentence, rather than as a single word or phrase, and that several students used the terms "because" and "think": These are significant as they are evidence that these students were engaged in thoughtful dialogue.

The discussion so far has focused on oral dialogue. Thoughtful dialogue can also be developed through written work if its main purpose is to provide feedback that helps learning. The difficulty with this aspect is that, for it to work well, teachers ought to stop giving marks or grades on written work. The research conclusions of Dweck (2000) are illustrated also by other research findings that written work is more likely to lead to improved learning if the teachers' feedback is in the form of comments and does not include marks or grades (Butler, 1988). In work that helped teachers to make such a change, those involved came to justify the new practice as follows:

- students rarely read comments preferring to compare marks with peers as their first reaction on getting work back;
- teachers rarely give students time in class to read comments that are written on work and probably few, if any students, return to consider these at home;

- often the comments are brief and/or not specific, for example "Details?";
- the same written comments frequently recur in a student's book, implying that students do not take note of, or act on, the comments

(Black et al., 2003, p. 43)

In consequence, teachers realized the need to spend more time on careful formulation of comments that would help students to understand their faults and to improve their work. Such comments as "Be more sensitive" and "You are mixing up the words 'solution' and 'mixture'" give the learner no useful guidance; however, if the latter comment were expanded to read, "This is generally fine but you are mixing up the words 'solution' and 'mixture'. Look up what we all wrote down about the difference and then check through this piece again" then the comment could guide the student to improve his understanding. The key point is that the written work is not to be treated as a terminal test, for which the marks produced are the end of the matter, but as an opportunity, through formative feedback, for improving learning. Simply giving a mark without such comments might take the teacher less time, but it will mean that the work will not achieve its purpose of improving students' learning.

One feature that distinguishes written from oral feedback is that there is time to frame comments that encourage further learning, with more opportunity for differentiation through separate interaction with individuals. The effects on motivation of the type of feedback are also important, as one teacher, involved in the work described by Black and colleagues (2003), discovered: "The results were especially noticeable in lower attainers since grades can often have a de-motivating effect with such students which can be extremely destructive to their self-esteem" (p. 85).

The teacher's task in promoting student learning through oral and written dialogue should be expanded further to include peer and self-assessment. This can be seen in terms of the overview scheme of Wiliam and Thompson (2007). They suggested that formative assessment can be conceptualized as consisting of five key strategies:

1. clarifying and sharing learning intentions and criteria for success
2. engineering effective classroom discussions and other learning tasks that elicit evidence of student understanding
3. providing feedback that moves learners forward
4. activating students as instructional resources for one another; and
5. activating students as the owners of their own learning

Developing Independent Learners: Self- and Peer Assessment

Involving as many students as possible in the last two of these cannot go as far, in whole-class dialogue, as involving all. So it is important to supplement such work with other means of developing the peer and self-assessment

that are required. Helping students collaborate effectively in groups is essential for achieving this aim. However, while there is strong evidence that collaborative groups can improve attainment (Johnson, Johnson, & Stanne, 2000), a survey of group work in U.K. classrooms (Blatchford, Baines, Rubie-Davies, Bassett, & Chowne, 2006) shows that the type of collaboration that can engage students in reasoned arguments about their own and one another's contributions is not often found. Intervention programs by Baines and colleagues (2009) and by Mercer and colleagues (2004) have demonstrated that students trained in such collaboration produce improved attainments, both in the quality of their arguments and in subsequent tests. The work of Dawes and colleagues (2004) is a good example of dissemination of the lessons learned about effective group work.

Such work can be a powerful tool in helping develop self-assessment by students. It can help meet this aim by giving them practice in assessing one another's work so that they might thereby develop the skills both of peer assessment and, by seeing their work through the eyes of their peers, of self-assessment also. To do this, students have to understand the aims of the work involved and the criteria by which this work should be assessed. In some topics in some subjects, the criteria might be well defined (e.g., calculating the value of a force in a physics problem); in others, there might be many different ways in which work could achieve excellence (e.g., comparing two different ways of exploring a novel phenomenon). Overall the aim should be to move students away from dependence on the teacher and toward independence in the power to guide their own learning. As one teacher expressed it:

> The kids are not skilled in what I am trying to get them to do. I think the process is more effective long term. If you invest time in it, it will pay off big dividends, this process of getting the students to be more independent in the way that they learn and taking the responsibility themselves.
>
> (Black et al., 2003, p. 52)

In helping students to develop their self-assessment, teachers must clearly specify aims so that students can both steer their work toward attaining them, which involves understanding what they mean, and develop understanding of the criteria by which the achievement of these aims can be judged. In many cases, such criteria are general and abstract, and understanding can only be attained through discussing particular and concrete examples. Students must be actively involved in such discussions if they are to achieve the understanding they need if they are to be able to guide their own learning in the future.

Formative and Summative Assessments: Their Role in Pedagogy

Up to this point in this section, the account has demonstrated the intertwining, within classroom practices, of formative assessment with a pedagogy that aims to develop the learning of students. However, the argument implies that there are three different phases of this activity, as follows:

A. *Making aims clear and explicit.* The teaching should be planned in the light of commitment to specific and clearly specified aims. An aim of teaching to achieve success in a forthcoming test would require a quite different plan of implementation than an aim of using a particular topic to develop students' skills of experimental inquiry.

B. *Designing effective activities.* A classroom activity, be it engaging in discussion based on responses to an open question or engaging in experimental work to display and then explore particular phenomena, has to be thought through by anticipating its potential value in promoting the overall aims. For example, an experiment demonstrated to a class may promote learning if it can present them with an engaging problem that could open up dialogue about an important concept.

C. *Formative implementation.* The planned activity has to be presented and the ensuing dialogue steered in ways that can realize, in and through the involvement of the students, the implementation of one or more of the main aims.

Within a precise definition of formative assessment, it occurs in phase C, but it is only effective as an aid to learning if there is coherence among all three steps.

This scheme would appear to have nothing to say about summative assessment, so the next step in the argument is to explore the links between assessment's formative and summative roles. At the beginning of the previous section, it was pointed out that a test as such may be either formative or summative or both—the distinction lies in the purpose for which information is interpreted and used, not in the means used to elicit that information. The term "test" would hardly be applied to the frequent formative interactions that may occur throughout classroom dialogue.

Summative Assessment by Teachers

The role of summative assessment within the teacher's pedagogy can be considered from two perspectives, the first being the more or less frequent use of tests to check on students' progress, while the second involves the use of summative tests for high-stakes testing.

For the first perspective, it is helpful to consider the formative use of summative tests. Students learn by marking one another's test responses, particularly if they have to develop the marking schemes in the light of their understanding of the criteria. Indeed, some have taken students' involvement further by asking them to compose questions they might expect to find in a test—a form of revision that has been shown to lead to enhanced achievements in the subsequent test (Foos, Mora, & Tkacz, 1994; King, 1995). Such work can be seen as an extension of the

task of making best use of written work generally: A test, while serving the summative function, might also be used, through formative feedback, as an opportunity for improving learning. Indeed, at the end of any learning episode, there should be a review that can serve as an overall check before moving on. It is here that tests, with formative use of their outcomes, can play a useful part. This point may be emphasized by pointing out that the conventional end-of-topic test is too late if it is at the end rather than scheduled within a plan that allows time for reworking any component of the planned learning for which the test has revealed significant weakness (Black & Dockrell, 1984). Further work by students to deal with problems revealed by a summative test can be a contribution to their learning.

Professional development work with teachers to help them incorporate these ideas into their practice has shown that they can forge a new and positive link in which summative assessment is seen as an integral and necessary part of effective pedagogy. This change of attitude can also extend to their students insofar as they are more directly involved in preparation for and assessment of their tests. As one teacher expressed it:

> They feel that the pressure to succeed in tests is being replaced by the need to understand the work that has been covered and the test is just an assessment along the way of what needs more work and what seems to be fine.
>
> (Black et al. 2003, pp. 56–57)

These conclusions can be taken further by adding a fourth phase to the scheme of three phases proposed as A, B, and C. The next phase would be:

D. *Informal summative assessment.* At the end of any learning episode, there should be review to check before moving on. It is here that tests, with formative use of their outcomes, can play a useful part.

The feedback provided in this phase may lead back to further work of type C. The findings might also lead the teacher to modify, in future, the planning involved in step B. The model does not specify a fixed sequence, for it is through the interactions, in both directions, between the component steps that pedagogy may be improved.

While the connection between formative and summative is represented by phase D, it does not go far enough. As pointed out in our introduction, teachers who have been committed to improving the learning experience of their students find that the pressures of accountability testing force them to teach to the test in ways that are in conflict with the aims that they value: The summative and the formative functions are seen, at worst, as irreconcilable and, at best, as uneasy bedfellows. The issue can be expressed by noting that the set of four phases, A to D, is incomplete, because phase D only goes as far as the relatively informal summative testing, which is usually within the control of the individual teacher. To complete the scheme, the following has to be added:

E. *Formal summative assessment*. The use of summative assessment becomes more formal when results are used to make decisions about each student's future work or career, to report progress to other teachers, school managements and parents, and to report the overall achievements more widely to satisfy the need for accountability.

While it cannot be argued that such a phase is unnecessary, there should be support for new ways to satisfy its legitimate aims without undermining the practices of effective pedagogy, and perhaps, more optimistically, by enhancing those practices. There are several reasons it is essential to seek these new ways.

Teachers' assessments of individual students are not just for external accountability—a student's year-on-year results are important both for the school management's assessment of each teacher's work and for every individual student. Advice to students and their parents about progress and about future choices among subjects and communication to the next teachers of the same students all depend on the summative assessments of their teachers. A notable example is the transition of students between any two institutions, whether from primary to middle or secondary school or between upper secondary stages or to college education.

More generally, it is important that students and their parents trust the judgments of their teachers: The distrust of politicians and others must be challenged. Such challenge will be effective if teachers and schools can be confident that the skills, practices, and policies underpinning the summative assessments for which they are responsible can be trusted as both fair to every student and comparable in standard within and between schools.

Improving Teachers' Summative Assessments: Benefits for Validity

The purpose of this section is to consider whether and how teachers' summative assessments can be developed to the point that they are and can be shown to be trustworthy. While, as argued earlier, this would be needed even in a context in which external accountability systems did not exist, our discussion will start by concentrating only on this context. It will then be extended, as it develops, to speak to the wider context of accountability.

In principle, a school's own assessments should be more helpful to students than their marks on an external test. Indeed, since the teacher has numerous opportunities over (say) a year's work with a class to observe the problems and achievements of every student, it seems ridiculous that the evidence of a few hours' work in the artificial conditions of the formal written test be preferred to any evidence that the teacher can produce. Indeed, because teachers are not subject to the same constraints of time and cost as external agencies, they ought to be able to take account of students' achievements in a range of contexts far broader than those of the formal written test. Thus,

teachers' assessments should, in principle, be better able to meet the criteria of reliability, validity, and dependability by which such agencies are themselves judged.

A particular aspect of this consideration of validity is raised by the following quotation from Harlen (2013):

> Recognising that, in the company of other learners, students can exceed what they can understand and do alone, throws into doubt what is their "true" level of performance. Is it the level of "independent performance" or the level of "assisted performance" in the social context? It has been argued that the level of performance when responding to assistance and the new tools provided by others gives a better assessment than administering tests of unassisted performance.
>
> (p. 32)

Thus, for example, if students work in groups to collect resources, exchange ideas, or consider alternative strategies in tackling a task and only work in independent isolation near the end or after completion of a task to produce material that can form part of each individual's portfolio, the outcomes may be better or at least different evidence of their capacity to achieve in the future than the results of formal tests. An argument similar to this is used in the literature that has developed the concept and application of dynamic assessment (Poehner & Lantolf, 2005).

Improving Teachers' Summative Assessments: Frameworks for Action

In order to consider how teachers' summative assessments can achieve their potential validity, we shall in this section consider published accounts of ways in which the summative assessments of teachers and their schools can be improved so that they can achieve the high standards required to secure the trust of all involved. Our ideas and recommendations are drawn from several sources. One source will be findings from a 2-year development study with three secondary schools in England (Black, Harrison, Hodgen, Marshall, & Serret, 2010, 2011). Further sources are the results of work reported in published studies, notably from Australia but also from the United States, Canada, and New Zealand. These studies show that the issues outlined have been a cause for concern in many different state systems. Moreover, the variety of the situations and of the innovations introduced in pursuit of reform described in these studies help to broaden understanding of the problems involved and to develop ways to tackle them.

The results of summative assessments are used by a range of stakeholders to inform decisions about the individuals. Their main concern should be that the use of the assessment evidence for their various purposes is justified by the quality of that evidence: This is the key concept of validity.

The following four features can undermine the validity of the results. The first is that the tasks or tests used may reflect only a fraction of all the aims and topics in the syllabus involved—it uses only a small sample of all of the tasks that could have been set, and a student might have performed differently with a different sample.

The second problem is that a student might have performed differently on the same tasks if they had been attempted on a different day.

The third problem is that a student might show a different performance with a different method of assessment—for example, in designing a science investigation with the real apparatus rather than with a paper exercise using only pictures of the apparatus.

The fourth problem is that there may be errors in the marking: These may be due to carelessness or to differences in the criteria used or in their interpretation by different markers.

All of these four can be classified as threats to the reliability of an assessment Enhancing reliability is an important requirement for enhancing validity, but it is not enough on its own. When all of the above have been separately tackled, the overall result may still be misleading because of a fifth limitation. A student may be very adept at tackling a range of the standard methods in a typical science test but be unable to deploy those methods in a problem that requires choice among several possible methods; or a student might be able to describe standard laboratory experiments but be unable to suggest an experimental method to check on a new hypothesis. In each of these cases, the inferences that can be made on the basis of the initial assessment might be seriously limited: The assessment is not valid, as it does not require students' use of their learning in an adequately wide range of contexts.

Finally, there is the need for comparability between the assessments of different teachers, both within any one school and between different schools. These different features—reliability, validity, comparability—all need attention if the overall aim, that the inferences users of the outcomes are likely to base on those outcomes will be justified, is to be achieved. It is also essential that the designers and the users of any assessment share the same understanding of the nature of the achievements that success with that assessment signifies.

It is hardly necessary to argue here that tests by agencies external to schools, who have to work within their limitations of cost and context, cannot meet all of these requirements—indeed it is because they cannot that any response to the demands of their tests may undermine the quality of the learning work of schools. The purpose of the argument here is to report in outline some of the practical steps that schools themselves can take to ensure that their own summative assessments can meet the criteria of reliability, validity, and comparability.

A *first* step is to audit existing practices, opening up exchanges between teachers about the ways in which they arrive at summative reports on their students. A *second* step is for teachers to consider together the concept of validity, which can de addressed by trying to answer the question "What does it mean to be good at our subject?", raising questions about the values to which teachers are

committed. A project in which these two steps were followed led the teachers involved to an acute awareness of the weakness of their current practices, setting the scene for a *third* step that involved investment of time in reform of those practices (Black et al., 2010).

Such reform naturally falls into two categories. One focuses on auditing and improving the conventional written tests teachers routinely use, often by adopting, uncritically, tests provided from outside the school. The other is to explore their own freedom to set assessment tasks in the less formal contexts of classroom and laboratory work. There are resources of ideas for such tasks, commonly called performance tasks, that can help develop new activities. It has been found that with teachers taking responsibility for their own tasks and involving their students more interactively in their production and their assessment, they developed new insights into their students' learning.

It follows naturally from such attempts that each student's end-of-year assessment should be based on a portfolio, a collection of diverse pieces of evidence, that may well include, among other evidence, the results of formal tests. The use of such portfolios has been explored in several countries. In the United States, some innovations of this type at state level have not worked well, while others have taken time to develop to acceptable levels (Koretz, 1998; Shapley & Bush, 1999; Simon & Forgette-Giroux, 2000). The main lessons are that the portfolio collections have to be planned through regular collaboration between groups of teachers who are required to and supported in working together to specify the samples of work produced by each student that will, taken as a whole, form the basis for valid assessment. This, as the *fourth* step in the process, both builds on the previous steps and looks forward to the next. It builds on the previous because the portfolio collection has to reflect their conclusions about validity.

However, it also has to look ahead, because the *fifth* step concerns the summary decisions about the levels of achievement that each portfolio reflects. If these results are to command public confidence, there has to be evidence that they are comparable across different teachers within a school and between different schools. This implies that there must be a degree of uniformity across the portfolios: For example, in the work reported by Black and colleagues (2011), teachers across three different schools agreed that every portfolio should contain six pieces of work, three of which would be identical tasks or tests for all involved in a given subject, while the other three could be left to the choice of each individual teacher, within the criterion that the six as a whole should constitute a valid collection.

The *sixth* and final step is to engage in a shared procedure to arrive at the final assessment decisions. For this to be workable, all teachers have to work to the same set of criteria, and then their personal decisions about each of their own students have to be checked. The checking procedure, described by the term "moderation," that has been found most effective involves an agreed-on process for drawing a sample from each group of students and having the collection of these samples assessed by all of the teachers involved. This can be a two-stage process, one for assuring comparability among all the teachers of a given subject within a school and then a second that establishes interschool alignment by moderation using selected results and samples from each school. A typical moderation meeting would involve a group of teachers reporting their independent gradings of each of the sample portfolios and then discussing the differences in judgment that inevitably arise, with the aim of arriving at a resolution of these differences. A possible consequence can be that some of the teachers may then revise all of their gradings. Many believe that prior to such meetings, there should be no comments on a sample circulated for moderation that might indicate the grading of any one teacher: The aim is to ensure the gradings that are reported at the start of a moderation meeting are strictly independent.

It is obvious that a procedure of the type described will be add to the existing workload of most teachers. Moreover, it will require organization of well-defined procedures, with the attendant dangers of bureaucratic imposition. Thus, the question that arises is whether the work and organized discipline involved are justified. One form of justification has been given in the introduction to this section: that the quality and comparability across the summative decisions of teachers and schools has to be assured and defensible if all the various groups that will be affected or influenced by the results are to have confidence in them. However, other benefits have been reported across several accounts coming from different states and systems. These we shall briefly summarize in three groups involving teachers, their reporting to parents, and the effects on their students.

Improving Teachers' Summative Assessments: Benefits for the Professional Development of Teachers

For teachers, one predictable effect has been their need to develop their assessment skills. In a project to improve the assessment practices of mathematics teachers in the United States, Webb described how he encountered this problem:

> Unfortunately, teachers often develop a set of classroom routines with little opportunity to examine and reflect on their concepts of classroom assessment and how this informs their decisions about the selection and design of questions and tasks, how they interpret student responses, and how to respond to students through instruction and feedback.
>
> (Webb, 2009, p. 11)

In a more comprehensive program in England to develop teachers' own summative assessment, a mathematics teacher who took the lead in the introduction of open-ended investigation tasks reported:

> Implementation of tasks—staff were a bit reluctant to do the projects, . . . but post projects their views changed and

this year development of investigation based tasks has become an issue that the KS3[1] staff have been keen to do and is being done as part of performance management.
>
> (Black et al., 2011, p. 461)

Less predictable were the positive effects of the debates that arise in moderation meetings. From the same project in England, one teacher noted the value of checking standards between schools:

> And we've had moderation meetings, we were together with the other schools, teachers in other schools looked at how rigorous our assessment would be and they criticised what, you know, our marking criteria (are). And we changed it, which is all been very positive.
>
> (Black et al., 2011, p. 459)

Another went further with the following reflection on the process:

> [T]hat the moderation and standardisation process was incredibly valuable in ensuring rigour, consistency and confidence with our approach to assessment; that teachers in school were highly motivated by being involved in the process that would impact on the achievement of students in their classes (like the moderation and standardisation at GCSE[2]).
>
> (Black et al., 2011, p. 459)

Similar benefit was reported from an evaluation in New Zealand of a national plan to develop the assessment practices of primary school teachers. The authors described the advantages of that process:

> [T]he introduction of standards requires primary teachers and schools to investigate the meaning of the work that students generate. Whilst teachers have always made judgments informally, moderation as an organised process requires making collaborative decisions to reach consensus agreements, and hence has become an important professional responsibility for all New Zealand's primary school teachers.
>
> (Hipkins & Robertson, 2011, p. 5)

One salient feature of moderation meetings arises when there is need to resolve uncertainty about borderline decisions when grades have to be assigned. The following characteristic incident was reported in a study in Queensland:

> When we were stuck whether to give them like a D or an E, or a C or a D, um, someone in the group was always able to pluck out, um. The pertinent point that could get us across the line one way or another and everyone else would just, would just go "yep, that's right, that's it" and so that was really good and I don't think you can come to that by yourself.
>
> (Wyatt-Smith, Klenowski, & Gunn, 2010, p. 66)

Those who would wish to assume that all criteria can be tightly defined within a detailed analytic scheme may find this unsatisfactory. However, when assessment involves more open-ended and creative work—such as reporting on one's investigation of a novel phenomenon in science or on a literature search leading to a report on controversy over the application of a discovery in medicine— such schemes may not be useful. The New Zealand study commented on this issue as follows: "Teachers bring their own working knowledge to the manner in which they draw on these referents during moderation and it is through the experience of sharing and negotiation that shared meanings and understandings can be created" (Hipkins & Robertson, 2011, p. 18–19).

This is a general issue that arises in many forms across the spectrum of assessment judgments. The underlying principle was set out clearly by Sadler as follows:

> Use of natural-language descriptions together with exemplars is unlikely to provide a complete substitute for, or render superfluous, the tacit knowledge of human appraisers, simply because external formulations cannot be exhaustive and cover every conceivable case (nor would we want them to).
>
> (Sadler, 1987, p. 201)

The effects of projects that have aimed to develop teachers' summative assessment practices are not confined to effects within the assessment processes themselves. It is only feasible here to convey the flavor of these by means of brief quotations from several studies. The first two are from separate evaluation reports on innovations, the first in Australia, the second in New Zealand:

> I just think the—it's the sharing with each other and that's professional, it's good professional development. . . . It was a really good process. I think the conversation bit of the process was the most valuable part.
>
> (Connolly, Klenowski, & Wyatt-Smith, 2011, p. 14)

> Similarly, teachers who examined student data together and worked out as a group what its implications were for deciding how best to help those under-achieving, difficult-to-move students, had higher achieving students than those schools where such a collective examination, diagnosis and problem-solving cycle did not operate.
>
> (Parr & Timperley, 2008, p. 69)

The development project in England by Black and colleagues (2011) reported similar benefits. One teacher involved in that work reported the positive effects as follows:

> I think it's quite a healthy thing for a department to be doing because I think it will encourage people to have conversations and it's about teaching and learning. . . . it really provides a discussion hopefully as well to talk about quality and you know what you think of was a success in English. Still really fundamental conversations.
>
> (Black et al., 2011, p. 461)

In reporting on his study with a group of mathematics teachers in the United States, Webb commented,

"Furthermore, as teachers adapted practices, they began to re-think the learning objectives of their curricula and the questions they used during instructional activities" (Webb, 2009, p. 14).

The specific point made there also arose in the following reflection on development work in Queensland:

> So basically once you have the assessment firmly in place the pedagogy becomes really clear because your pedagogy has to support that—that sort of quality assessment task. . . . that was a bit of a shift from what's usually done, usually assessment is that thing that you attach on the end of the unit whereas as opposed to sort of being the driver which it has now become.
>
> (Wyatt-Smith & Bridges, 2008, p. 48)

These last two quotations highlight a particular feature of the ways in which more is involved in the developments explored here than assessment practices themselves. These two are examples of an approach described, in the work of Wyatt-Smith and Bridges (2008), as "frontending" whereby, in the planning of teaching, the meaning of aims is explored by the discipline of formulating assessment activities that would provide evidence that students had achieved these aims. Such work explores the essential links between curriculum aims and summative assessment. In terms of the scheme of five phases, A to E, developed in the previous section, the fifth phase reacts back on the first. This could be seen as a description of the well-known negative effect whereby teachers interpret the aims of the curriculum by analysis of the final tests and plan their teaching accordingly, teaching to the test. However, the fault here does not lie in the interaction between aims and summative assessments—which is and has to be inescapable—but in the poor validity of the tests.

A bonus for teachers arising from their improved assessment practice and from their confidence therein was that it gave them a better basis for communicating with each student's parents. One issue here is teachers' enhanced confidence in their work, expressed by one teacher as follows:

> But I think if all the teachers had more, possibly more ownership of what we are actually doing in terms of summative assessment then you would have more confidence in saying to parents, which I think is one of the biggest things I find with lower school.
>
> (Black et al., 2011, p. 460)

An associated feature is that the individual student's portfolio is a more useful basis of evidence for engaging discussion with that student's parents:

> It provides you with convincing, comparative material and it's something that I have taken to meetings, with parents of students in classes other than my own. Being able to say, "well this is what John's been able to do and this is why he is still on a 5C and not a 6A." And parents seem to react well to that.
>
> (Black et al. 2011, p. 461)

A second associated feature is the effects of a reform of teachers' own summative assessments on their relationships with their students. One example of this type of outcome can be seen in this account by a teacher who took part in the work of Black and colleagues (2011) in England:

> [T]he kids felt it was the best piece of work they'd done. And a lot of teachers said "ok we're really pleased with how they've come out," it's seemed to really give kids the opportunity to do the best that they could have done. . . . Er, it just, the lower end kids it organises their work for them, it's basically a structured path for them to follow.
>
> (Black et al., 2011, p. 46)

What was happening here was that the tasks set in classroom conditions could be designed by the teachers to give the adequate degree of guidance. Indeed, one feature of that project was that teachers had to learn to "tune" the tasks that they were adapting or inventing so that they could give useful information about the achievement that the low attainers could display while at the same time giving opportunity for the high attainers to show how far they could go with the same task. A further benefit arose as teachers could observe the way in which students engaged in the classroom with tasks that they and their colleagues had designed, as the following example, from the same publication, shows:

> I think it changed the dynamics of the lesson a little bit, in terms of well, in terms of there being much more an element of them getting on trying to find out . . . they were trying to be more independent, I think, I think some of them struggled with that, and others . . . some of them, some still find it quite difficult if they are not hand held all the way through. When others were happier to sort of, go their own way.
>
> (Black et al., 2011, p. 460)

Further and more radical benefits have been reported, both for the work developed in New Zealand:

> [O]nce they understand that (shared assessment criteria) and they start applying it, then they've got that, "Oh, I can see where I have to go next. I don't have to have the teachers tell me." And that's what we've just started doing now is like, "You tell me what you want me to do with the lesson? What are your weak areas that you don't understand?" so they've just started doing that.
>
> (Harris & Brown, 2009, p. 376)

And, in similar vein, for the practices developed in Queensland:

> I think to a certain extent that we've empowered students in the learning process because there's not secret teacher's business anymore in terms of what the expectations are, that students are becoming very au fait with the criterion and being able to apply them in their own work.
>
> (Wyatt-Smith & Bridges, 2008, p. 61)

Improving Teachers' Summative Assessments: Implications for System Reform

The preceding section set out to describe ways in which attempts to improve the quality of teachers' summative assessments led to a need for new additional work, not only by teachers themselves but also by agencies that could support teachers through guidance and through providing occasions and contacts to facilitate them in the change process. However, it also showed the wide range of benefits, which can be summed up briefly by stating that to the extent to which they can take control of the process, teachers can achieve positive links between both formal and summative assessments. In consequence, these assessments not only cease to have negative effects on the schools' work but can actually produce positive interactions between summative assessments and pedagogy that can complement the positive links between formative assessment practices and pedagogy.

The difficult question that remains is whether this is merely a utopian dream. The demand of the public at large for evidence that can reassure them that schools are serving society in the best possible way is a legitimate one. The problem is that the methods that many state systems have adopted to meet that demand have been self-defeating in undermining the very qualities that the architects of these systems declare as their aims.

However, there exist examples of systems in which these difficulties have been tackled. The most comprehensive examples are the systems developed in the Australian states of New South Wales and Queensland. A useful account of these is given by Stanley and colleagues (2009) in their review of several national systems. What this account makes clear is that the systems developed and well-established in these Australian states specify procedures that assess a collection of a limited number of tasks (i.e., portfolios) from each student, with the state providing extensive resources for professional development, including resource materials of many kinds, to enhance the dependability of the summative assessment of teachers. Moderation procedures involve either scaling against external tests in New South Wales (where externally set tests and teachers' assessments each contribute 50% to the total) or joint work in school groups in Queensland, where outcomes, even for the school-leaving certification of students' achievements in their school subjects, are based entirely on teachers' assessments. However, these systems were developed over several years, and recently there has been dispute with the federal government, which wishes to introduce national assessments, a wish to be backed by making federal funding dependent on the results of such tests.

A system combining external tests with components assessed by schools seems more feasible than one wholly dependent on teachers' assessments, but to be set against the example of New South Wales is the fate of this type of solution, operated in England for more than 15 years, which failed to command respect for its validity and was abandoned for most school subjects. What is lacking in such examples is the commitment to build the infrastructure needed for supporting the development of teachers' practices and skills and an understanding among policy makers of the serious limitations of the externally set tests on which they place such reliance. Further analysis of these and other examples lies outside the scope of this chapter.

Closing Summary

The message of the first main section of this chapter may be summarized in the formulation that we used above when we proposed that the responsibility of the school should be to:

- Nurture and build on students' natural appetites for curiosity and inquiry
- Help the social development of all, including constructive involvement in social learning
- Encourage students to express their thinking and to then reconstruct their ideas through dialogue with others
- Guide students to take increasing responsibility for their own learning, thereby empowering them to develop as mature and reflective learners

Our discussion of the evidence about a variety of developments and insights helps to show how the different aspects of assessment fit naturally into a comprehensive model of pedagogy, thereby helping to establish how assessment can play an essential and positive role in helping to achieve all of these aims.

There are many obstacles to their achievement. One of the main hurdles is graphically described as follows:

Some students succeed in negotiating these, apparently drawing on resources other than those that the teachers provide. Others may spend the compulsory years (of schooling) in an environment that is essentially conducted in a foreign language in which they never gain sufficient proficiency. And students need to be fluent to negotiate the ever more demanding literacy-bound assessment requirements successfully. . . . Assumption of students' curriculum literacies is not sufficient. These need to be incorporated in direct instruction.

(Wyatt-Smith & Cumming, 2003, p. 58)

The problem depicted here is not a direct consequence of accountability testing. The causes of such difficulties are more subtle and more diverse; one general cause stems from an exclusive focus on a prescribed curriculum and a corresponding neglect of the hidden curriculum. Promoting involvement of all in social interactions through dialogue may be one key help in tackling the deeper obstacles involved.

If there is one feature that characterizes all of the positive outcomes for students that we have described above, it can be summed up in a final quotation:

Any change to assessment processes (or in fact any educational reform) hinges on support from teachers, and support for teachers, to ensure an ability to adapt at classroom level. . . . This requires theoretically-based yet practically-situated learning rather that decontextualised one-shot professional development.

(Gunn, 2007, p. 59)

In some state systems, this view has been a guiding principle. Sadly, in others, it has not been. In particular, the potential of the development of teachers' assessment skills to enrich their work has been ignored; invalid assessment tools have been used as a means to impose on and thereby undermine the professional development of teachers. In addition, such policies impoverish, both directly and indirectly, the education of students.

Acknowledgments

We are grateful to Wynne Harlen and Michael Reiss for their helpful reviews of our draft of this chapter.

Notes

1. KS3: Key Stage 3 is the 3 years of schooling between ages 11 and 14.
2. GCSE: General Certificate of Secondary Education: the national examination taken at about age 16.

References

Alexander, R. (2006). *Towards dialogic thinking: Rethinking classroom talk.* York, UK: Dialogos.

Alexander, R. (2008). *Essays in pedagogy.* Abingdon, UK: Routledge.

Applebee, A.N., Langer, J.A., Nystrand, M., & Gamoran, A. (2003). Discussion based approaches to developing understanding: Classroom instruction and student performance in middle and high school English. *American Educational Research Journal, 40*(3), 685–730.

Atkin, J. M. (1980). The government in the classroom. *Dædalus, 109*(3), 85–97.

Baines, E., Blatchford, P., & Kutnick, P. (2009). *Promoting effective group work in the primary classroom.* London, UK: Routledge.

Black, H.D., & Dockrell, W.B. (1984). *Criterion-referenced assessment in the classroom.* Edinburgh, UK: Scottish Council for Research in Education.

Black, P., Harrison, C., Hodgen, J., Marshall, M., & Serret, N. (2010). Validity in teachers' summative assessments. *Assessment in Education, 17*(2), 215–232.

Black, P., Harrison, C., Hodgen, J., Marshall, M., & Serret, N. (2011). Can teachers' summative assessments produce dependable results and also enhance classroom learning? *Assessment in Education, 18*(4), 451–469.

Black, P., Harrison, C., Lee, C., Marshall, B., & Wiliam, D. (2002). *Working inside the black box: Assessment for learning in the classroom.* London, UK: GL Assessment.

Black, P., Harrison, C., Lee, C., Marshall, B., & Wiliam, D. (2003). *Assessment for learning: putting it into practice.* Buckingham, UK: Open University Press.

Black, P., & Wiliam, D. (2009). Developing the theory of formative assessment. *Educational Assessment, Evaluation and Accountability, 21*(1), 5–31.

Blatchford, P., Baines, E., Rubie-Davies, C., Bassett, P., & Chowne, A. (2006). The effect of a new approach to group-work on pupil-pupil and teacher-pupil interaction. *Journal of Educational Psychology, 98,* 750–765.

Bruner, J. (1966). *Toward a theory of instruction*. New York: Norton for Harvard University Press.

Butler, R. (1988). Enhancing and undermining intrinsic motivation; the effects of task-involving and ego-involving evaluation on interest and performance. *British Journal of Educational Psychology, 58*(1), 1–14.

Cole, K.C. (2009). *Something incredibly wonderful happens: Frank Oppenheimer and the world he made up*. Boston: Houghton, Mifflin, Harcourt.

Connolly, C., Klenowski, V., & Wyatt-Smith, C.M. (2011). Moderation and consistency of teacher judgment: Teachers' views. *British Educational Research Journal, 1*, 1–22.

Dawes, L., Mercer, M., & Wegerif, R. (2004). *Thinking together*. Birmingham, UK: Imaginative Minds Ltd.

Dewey, J. (1985). *The later works, 1925–1953, Volume 7: 1932*. Carbondale: Southern Illinois Press.

Dewey, J. (2012). *Unmodern philosophy and modern philosophy*. Carbondale: Southern Illinois Press.

Dweck, C.S. (2000). *Self-theories: Their role in motivation, personality and development*. Philadelphia: Psychology Press.

Dweck, C.S. (2006). *Mindset: The new psychology of success*. New York: Random House.

Eisner, E. (1978). *The educational imagination*. New York: Macmillan.

Emerson, R.W. (1834). *Journal*, April 11.

Fisher R. (2005). *Teaching children to learn* (2nd ed.). Cheltenham, UK: Nelson Thornes.

Foos, P.W., Mora, J.J., & Tkacz, S. (1994). Student study techniques and the generation effect. *Journal of Educational Psychology, 86*(4), 567–576.

Freire, P. (1983). Banking education. In H. Giroux & D. Purpel (Eds.), *The hidden curriculum and moral education: Deception of discovery* (p. 284). Berkeley, CA: McCutchen.

Freire, P. (1992). *Pedagogy of hope*. New York: Continuum.

Greene, M. (1983). Introduction. In H. Giroux & D. Purpel (Eds.), *The hidden curriculum and moral education: Deception of discovery* (pp. 1–5). Berkeley, CA: McCutchen.

Groome, T.H. (1998). *Educating for life*. New York: Crossroad.

Gunn, S.J. (2007). Literature review. In C. Wyatt-Smith & G. Masters (Eds.), *Proposals for a new model of senior assessment: Realising potentials*. Unpublished report prepared for Queensland Studies Authority. Brisbane, Queensland, Australia.

Hallam, S., & Ireson, J. (1999). Pedagogy in the secondary school. In P. Mortimore (Ed.), *Understanding pedagogy and its impact on learning* (pp. 68–97). London, UK: Paul Chapman.

Harlen, W. (2013). *Assessment and inquiry-based science education*. Trieste, Italy: Global Network of Science Academies.

Harris, L.H., & Brown, G.T.L. (2009). The complexity of teachers' conceptions of assessment: tensions between the needs of schools and students. *Assessment in Education, 16*(3), 363–381.

Hawkins, D. (1974). *The informed vision: Essays on learning and human nature*. New York: Agathon Press.

Hawkins, D. (1983). Nature closely observed. *Daedalus, 112*(2), 65–89.

Hipkins, R., & Robertson, S. (2011). *Moderation and teacher learning: What can research tell us about their inter-relationships?* Wellington: New Zealand Council for Educational Research.

Johnson, D.W., Johnson, R.T., & Stanne, M.B. (2000). *Co-operative learning methods: A meta-analysis*. Retrieved from www.tablelearning.com/uploads/File/EXHIBIT-B.pdf

King, A. (1995). Inquiring minds really do want to know—using questioning to teach critical thinking. *Teaching of Psychology, 22*(1), 13–17.

Koretz, D. (1998). Large scale portfolio assessments in the US: Evidence pertaining to the quality of measurement. *Assessment in Education, 5*(3), 309–334.

Mansell, W., James, M., & the Assessment Reform Group. (2009). *Assessment in schools. Fit for purpose? A commentary by the Teaching and Learning Research Programme*. London, UK: ESRC TLRP, Institute of Education London. Retrieved from www.tlrp.org/pub/commentaries.html

Menand, L. (2001). *The metaphysical club: A story of ideas in America*. New York: Farrar, Straus, and Giroux.

Mercer, N., Dawes, L., Wegerif, R., & Sams, C. (2004). Reasoning as a scientist: Ways of helping children to use language to learn science. *British Educational Research Journal, 30*(3), 359–377.

Milroy, D. (1992). Teaching and learning: What a child expects from a good teacher. In *Education: Putting the Record Straight* (pp. 57–61). Stafford, UK: Network Educational Press.

National Research Council (NRC). (2011). *National science education standards*. Washington, DC: National Academies Press.

OECD. (2013). *Education at a Glance 2013: OECD indicators*. Paris, France: OECD. Retrieved from www.oecd.org/edu/eag2013%20%28eng%29--FINAL%2020%20June%202013.pdf

Parr, J.M., & Timperley, H.S. (2008). Teachers, schools and using evidence: Considerations of preparedness. *Assessment in Education, 15*(1), 57–71.

Poehner, M.E., & Lantolf, J.P. (2005). Dynamic assessment in the language classroom. *Language Teaching Research, 9*(3), 233–265.

Rowe, M.B. (1974). Wait time and rewards as instructional variables, their influence on language, logic and fate control. *Journal of Research in Science Teaching, 11*, 81–94.

Sadler, D.R. (1987). Specifying and promulgating achievement standards. *Oxford Review of Education, 13*(2), 191–209.

Shapley, K.S., & Bush, M.J. (1999). Developing a valid and reliable portfolio assessment in the primary grades: Building on practical experience. *Applied Measurement in Education, 12*(2), 111–132.

Shulman, L.S. (1999). Knowledge and teaching: Foundation of the new reform. In M.J. Leach & B. Moon (Eds.), *Learners and pedagogy* (pp. 61–71). London, UK: Chapman.

Simon, M. & Forgette-Giroux, R. (2000). Impact of a content selection framework on portfolio assessment at the classroom level. *Assessment in Education, 7*(1), 83–101.

Stanley, G., McCann, R., Gardner, J., Reynolds, L., & Wild, I. (2009). *Review of teacher assessment: What works best and issues for development*. Oxford, UK: Oxford University Centre for Educational Development—Report commissioned by the Qualifications and Curriculum Authority.

Tyler, R.W. (1969). *Basic principles of curriculum and instruction*. Chicago: University of Chicago Press.

Webb, D.C. (2009). Designing professional development for assessment. *Educational Designer, 1*(2). Retrieved from www.educationaldesigner.org/ed/volume1/issue2/article6/

Wiliam, D., & Black, P.J. (1996). Meanings and consequences: A basis for distinguishing formative and summative functions of assessment. *British Educational Research Journal, 22*(5), 537–548.

Wiliam, D., & Thompson, M. (2007). Integrating assessment with instruction: What will it take to make it work? In C.A. Dwyer (Ed.), *The future of assessment: Shaping teaching and learning* (pp. 53–82). Mahwah, NJ: Lawrence Erlbaum Associates.

Wood, D. (1998). *How children think and learn*. Oxford, UK: Blackwell.

Wyatt-Smith, C., Klenowski, V., & Gunn, S. (2010). The centrality of teachers' judgement practice in assessment: A study of standards in moderation. *Assessment in Education, 17*(1), 59–75.

Wyatt-Smith, C.M., & Bridges, S. (2008). *Meeting in the middle—assessment, pedagogy, learning and students at educational disadvantage*. Evaluation for the Literacy and Numeracy in the Middle Years of Schooling Initiative Strand A. Queensland Government Report. Retrieved from http://education.qld.gov.au/literacy/docs/deewr-myp-final-report.pdf

Wyatt-Smith, C.M., & Cumming, J.J. (2003). Curriculum literacies: Expanding domains of assessment. *Assessment in Education, 10*(1), 47–59.

39

Large-Scale Assessments in Science Education

Edward D. Britton and Steven A. Schneider

This chapter summarizes high-profile, large-scale assessments in science education at the international level and at the national and state levels within the United States. It builds upon the authors' prior handbook chapter on this same topic (Britton & Schneider, 2007). As is customary for a next edition, the following chapter first renders much of the same conceptual territory by removing some older material and providing updates. Further, in order to reflect changes in this field over the last decade, discussions are added about two new topics: (1) brief discussion of large-scale assessments for technology and engineering education and (2) discussion of new uses of technology in large-scale science assessments.

More education systems are seeking to attend more explicitly to technology and engineering education. One rationale for expanding the terrain of this chapter, which is charged with addressing science, is that the new or enhanced attention to technology and engineering often is being implemented within science classes (e.g., National Research Council [NRC], 2011), as described in an entirely new handbook chapter (36) by Cunningham and Carlsen; because these authors focus on curriculum and instruction rather than assessment, this chapter briefly discusses assessment in these subject areas. Regarding the second topic addition, technology is making possible different, more complex probing of what students know and can do in science; this is an exciting advance over technology merely serving as an alternative mode of executing the same kinds of assessment items that historically have been administered in paper-and-pencil tests.

The uses of large-scale assessments in science have grown substantially in the last 30 years. Early reviews could cover all of their uses within a single chapter (Doran, Lawrenz, & Helgeson, 1994; Tamir, 1988). Not long after those reviews, the variety and extent of their uses expanded considerably and has grown ever since (Kifer, 2000). Therefore, for this handbook, uses of large-scale assessments in science education are addressed among at least four chapters.

This chapter primarily focuses on two uses of large-scale assessment. First, the authors summarize internationally administered achievement tests. The authors describe the nature of different international comparisons and the contrasts among them. As an addition for this handbook edition, note that in recent years a few countries even have jurisdictions within them that are participating and reporting at their own level, that is, subnational jurisdictions. For example, specific Canadian provinces recently participated in and reported on their achievement in an international assessment, in addition to the fact that Canada as a country continued its regular national participation.

While the chapter points readers to seminal reports for each assessment, rendering the study results from each assessment is beyond the confines of this chapter, particularly because there now are so many of them. Further, the chapter generally cannot delve into the psychometric or other technical issues involved, even for those issues specific to science assessments (e.g., Quellmalz, Haertel, DeBarger, & Kreikemeier, 2005; Welch, Huffman, & Lawrenz, 1998).

The second use of large-scale assessments discussed here is national education systems' monitoring of student science achievement over time. This chapter focuses on the U.S. National Assessment of Educational Progress (NAEP) in science. Additionally, the authors describe NAEP's upcoming, first-ever national assessment of technology and engineering literacy, which will be prototyped at the eighth-grade level in 2014 (National Assessment Governing Board [NAGB], 2010). For jurisdictions within countries, assessments also can be designed for local or regional accountability or other forms of summative assessment for reporting to others outside the classroom; such assessments of student achievement generally are below the threshold that can be addressed within this chapter of an international handbook.

There are more uses of large-scale assessment in science, some of which are addressed in other handbook chapters: for evaluating science projects (Chapter 35, Woodruff & Kahle), for evaluating science programs (Chapter 37, Lawrenz & Thao), and for formative assessment purposes (Chapter 38, Black & Atkin). In many countries, large-scale assessments in specific science subjects (e.g., different exams for biology, chemistry, and physics) can be used in gauging qualification for entry to college (American Federation of Teachers [AFT] & National Center for Improving Science Education, 1994, 1996; Britton & Raizen, 1996; McIntosh, 2012). In some countries, qualification exams also can be used even earlier in schooling, such as for selection into different kinds of secondary schools (AFT, 1995). Some exams used for college entrance also can earn early college credit (e.g., Advanced Placement [AP] exams, International Baccalaureate [IB] exams).

Making room for new discussions in this handbook edition necessarily leads to letting go of some others. The authors' chapter in the prior handbook discussed in more detail the effects of large-scale assessment on science education. For example, that chapter considered whether the value of increased science instruction in elementary grades, which can be triggered by high-stakes science assessments, is offset by those assessments' possible narrowing influence on what science is taught and how it is taught. We note that, today, these potentially dampening effects of older test item formats and features may be decreasing through recent advances in item construction, instrument design, and uses of technology. The prior edition also pointed out then emerging attention in the United States to designing state science assessment systems, which clearly articulate curriculum, instruction, and assessment instead of being rife with disconnects that still were common within most states (Herman & Haertel, 2005; Herman, Webb, & Zuniga, 2005; Wilson & Bertenthal, 2005); the field has moved toward more articulated systems implementation in recent years.

International Science Assessments

The frequency of cross-national assessments in science has escalated over time to the point where it is now hard to keep track of them all. Table 39.1 provides a chronology of the major assessments conducted thus far or planned through 2015. This table only lists international publications of cross-national results for science achievement. The table does not list U.S. or other countries' reports that give a national perspective on cross-national achievement results.

TABLE 39.1
Chronology of International Large-Scale Assessments in Science

Year	Org.[1]	Short Name[2]	Subjects[4]	Ages/Grades[6]	Size[8]	Results & Select Publications[9]
1969–1970	IEA	FISS	S	10, 14, ES[7]	19	Comber & Keeves, 1973
1983–1986	IEA	SISS	S	10, 14, ES	17	IEA, 1988; Postlethwaite & Wiley, 1992
1988	ETS	IEAP	SM	13	6	LaPointe, Mead, & Phillips, 1989
1992	ETS	IEAP	SM	9, 13	20	LaPointe, Askew, & Mead, 1992
1994–1995	IEA	TIMSS[3]	SM	3–4, 7–8, ES	42	Beaton et al., 1996; Martin, et al., 1997, Mullis et al., 1998
1999	IEA	TIMSS-R[3]	SM	8	39	Martin et al., 2000
2000	OECD	PISA	R[5] (SM)	15	39	OECD, 2001, 2003
2003	IEA	TIMSS[3]	SM	4, 8	48	Martin, Mullis, Gonzalez, & Chrostowski, 2004
2003	OECD	PISA	M[5] (RS)	15	41	OECD, 2004
2006	OECD	PISA	S[5] (MR)	15	57	OECD, 2007a, 2007b
2007	IEA	TIMSS	SM	4, 8	50	Martin, Mullis, & Foy, 2008
2009	OECD	PISA	R[5] (SM)	15	75	OECD, 2010
2011	IEA	TIMSS	SM	4, 8	63	Martin, Mullis, Foy, & Stanco, 2012
2012	OECD	PISA	M[5] (RS)	15	64	
2015	IEA	TIMSS	SM	4, 8		
2015	OECD	PISA	S[5] (MR)	15		

[1] Sponsoring organizations: International Associations for the Evaluation of Educational Achievement (IEA); Educational Testing Service (ETS); Organization for Economic Co-Operation and Development (OECD)

[2] Short names of acronyms stand for the following full names of the studies: First International Science Study (FISS); Second International Science Study (SISS); International Assessment of Educational Progress (IAEP); Third International Mathematics and Science Study (TIMSS); Programme for International Student Assessment (PISA).

[3] The naming of the TIMSS evolved after the original TIMSS in 1995. The 1999 version become TIMSS-repeat, or TIMSS-R for short. Beginning in 2003, the full name was changed to Trends in Mathematics and Science Study, which still has the short name of TIMSS.

[4] S = science, M = mathematics, R = reading

[5] PISA assesses three subjects each time (reading, mathematics, science). In a given year, however, one subject is fully tested while only partial tests are given for the other two subjects. The lead subject has been rotated, and the first main administration of science was in 2006.

[6] International assessments have used two means of setting the target populations of students to be assessed. Some studies target students of a particular age, while others target students in a particular grade. These two strategies lead to different sampling strategies and have implications for study results.

[7] End Sec stands for End of Secondary. Since the last year of schooling varies among countries (e.g., some end at Grade 12, others at 13), the international study does not set a uniform age or grade level for the targeted secondary population.

[8] Size refers to number of participating countries. The number provided here is for the number of countries that participated in at least one test population (age/grade). Typically, a number of countries elect to participate in some rather than all populations.

[9] These sample reports are limited to those reporting international comparisons for international audiences versus U.S. or any other nation's perspective on its performance relative to other countries (e.g., Schmidt, McKnight, & Raizen, 1997). The reports selected also are limited to results of student achievement in science. Some studies report on other aspects of the study, such as accompanying analyses of the countries' science curricula (Schmidt et al., 1997).

Until 2000, the International Association for the Evaluation of Educational Achievement (IEA) had been the only main sponsor of cross-national comparisons. However, during 1988 through 1992, the Educational Testing Service (ETS) briefly entered the terrain during a time period between two testing administrations by the IEA. That is, the International Assessment of Educational Progress (IAEP), which borrows its name and some concepts from the ETS administration of the U.S. National Assessment of Educational Progress (NAEP), occurred between IEA's first and second international studies of science (LaPointe, Askew, & Mead, 1992; LaPointe, Mead, & Phillips, 1989).

The biggest acceleration in the frequency of international assessments occurred in 2000. In that year, the Paris-based Organisation for Economic Co-Operation and Development (OECD) launched a line of cross-national comparisons, the Programme for International Student Achievement (PISA). A later section contrasts the most notable differences in the nature of these two assessment lines. Since 2000, the IEA studies occur every 4 years while the OECD studies occur every 3 years.

Notice the following characteristics that can help distinguish among studies: (1) While all the listed studies assessed science, some studies assessed science only and others assessed both mathematics and science fairly equally. The PISA series emphasizes one of three subjects (reading, mathematics, science) in any given year, limiting the assessment of the other two subjects in that year. (2) The studies use either ages or grades for identifying target populations of students to be assessed. (3) Studies vary in the number of target populations they include. (4) There is considerable variation in the number of countries that participated, and a participating country may decide to assess only some of the target populations.

While these cross-national studies often are most known for comparisons of student achievement levels, they have important additional purposes and components. All studies include, in addition to achievement tests, some data collection from other sources such as national, school, teacher, or student questionnaires. These data yield systematic national and international characterizations of science education. Some tests offer additional student assessment options; for example, study organizations have at times offered a performance-based science assessment that countries can elect to add to their administration. Some studies go further and include an optional or required analysis of participating countries' science curricula, accompanying qualitative case studies of nations' science education, or video studies of classroom teaching in select countries. Using the above characteristics, the largest international science assessment to date remains the original 1995 administrations of the Third International Mathematics and Science Study (TIMSS).

Given the international audience of this handbook, the detailed Table 39.2 is a basic reference to enable readers in any country to readily identify the studies in which their nation participated, in which year(s), and for which target population(s).

What drove the growing interest in international studies? The most apparent rationale is national concerns about student achievement in a global context. Additionally, participation in these studies has built capacity within some countries for conducting large-scale assessments for their own national purposes. For many countries, these studies were first forays into large-scale assessments; countries learned about using such assessments as one tool in education policy and practice. What influences have studies had on countries' science education? The assessments have generated "world-class standards," and many nations have adjusted their curricula to be more internationally competitive.

IEA Studies

The International Association for the Evaluation of Educational Achievement (IEA), with administrative offices in Amsterdam and a technical data processing center in Hamburg, is an independent research organization composed of members from national and governmental research institutions and agencies. It began in 1958 at the UNESCO Institute for Education at Hamburg as a discussion and consultation among psychologists, sociologists, and psychometricians around issues of schools and student achievement and what constituted the proper evaluation of these. A Pilot Twelve-Country Study, conducted in 1959 to 1962, evaluated five areas: science, mathematics, reading comprehension, geography, and nonverbal ability. IEA studies are most widely known for assessing science content (including the nature of science), but they also are designed to assess students' performance expectations in science and perspectives toward science. As an example of the latter, the study framework for science in TIMSS called for investigation of students' understanding; theorizing, analyzing, and solving problems; use of tools, routine procedures, and science processes (performance expectations); and attitudes, careers, and participation by underrepresented groups (perspectives; Robitaille et al., 1993).

A hallmark of IEA studies has been placing an emphasis on students' opportunity to learn the subject matter. Opportunity to learn (OTL) has had a pragmatic focus on what is actually done in classrooms with respect to the subject assessed as opposed to what may be intended to occur in classrooms according to official standards or textbooks. This emphasis may also be seen as a natural development from the goal shared by all IEA studies to illuminate the factors that explain or cause differences in educational achievement (Postlethwaite, 1995). The IEA tripartite curriculum model defines curriculum at three different levels: the *intended*—what a system intends students to study and learn; the *implemented*—what is taught in classrooms; and the *attained*—what students are able to demonstrate that they know (Travers & Westbury, 1988).

First and Second International Science Studies

The First International Science Study (FISS) was conducted by the IEA from 1966 through 1973, part of a larger Six Subject Survey that was designed to apply what had been

TABLE 39.2
Countries Participating in International Assessments

Country	TIMSS 1995			TIMSS-R 1999	TIMSS 2003		TIMSS 2007		TIMSS Advanced 2008	TIMSS 2011		PISA (15-yr-olds)		
	4th	8th	ES[1]	8th	4th	8th	4th	8th	ES[1]	4th	8th	2006	2009	2012
Albania													x	x
Algeria							x	x						
Argentina		x		x		x						x	x	x
Armenia					x	x	x	x	x	x	x			
Australia	x	x	x	x	x	x	x	x		x	x	x	x	x
Austria	x	x	x				x			x		x	x	x
Azerbaijan										x		x	x	
Bahrain						x		x		x	x			
Belgium (Flemish)		x		x	x	x				x		x[2]	x[2]	x[2]
Belgium (French)		x												
Bosnia and Herzegovina								x						
Botswana						x		x						
Brazil												x	x	x
Bulgaria		x		x		x		x				x	x	x
Canada	x	x	x	x								x	x	x
Chile				x		x				x	x	x	x	x
Chinese Taipei				x	x	x	x	x		x	x	x	x	x
Colombia		x					x	x				x	x	x
Costa Rica													2010[3]	x
Croatia										x		x	x	x
Cyprus	x	x	x	x	x	x		x						
Czech Republic	x	x	x	x			x	x		x		x	x	x
Denmark		x	x				x			x		x	x	x
Egypt						x		x						
El Salvador							x	x						
England[4]	x	x		x	x	x	x	x		x	x			
Estonia						x						x	x	x
Finland				x						x	x	x	x	x
France		x	x									x	x	x
Georgia							x	x		x	x		2010[3]	
Germany		x	x				x			x		x	x	x
Ghana						x		x			x			
Greece	x	x	x									x	x	x
Hong Kong SAR	x	x		x	x	x	x	x		x	x	x	x	x
Hungary	x	x	x	x	x	x	x	x		x	x	x	x	x
Iceland	x	x	x									x	x	x
Indonesia				x		x		x			x	x	x	x
Iran, Islamic Republic of	x	x		x	x	x	x	x	x	x	x			
Ireland	x	x										x	x	x
Israel	x	x		x		x		x			x	x	x	x
Italy	x	x	x	x	x	x	x	x	x	x	x	x	x	x
Japan	x	x		x	x	x	x	x		x	x	x	x	x
Jordan				x		x		x			x	x	x	x
Kazakhstan							x			x	x		x	x
Korea, Republic of	x	x		x		x		x		x	x	x	x	x
Kyrgyz Republic												x	x	
Kuwait	x	x					x	x		x				
Latvia	x	x		x	x	x	x					x	x	x
Lebanon						x		x	x		x			

Liechtenstein												x	x	x
Lithuania		x	x	x	x	x	x	x		x	x	x	x	x
Luxembourg												x	x	x
Macau SAR												x	x	x
Macedonia, Republic of				x		x					x			
Malaysia				x		x		x			x		2010[3]	x
Malta								x		x			2010[3]	
Mauritius													2010[3]	
Mexico												x	x	x
Moldova				x	x	x							x	
Mongolia							x	x						
Montenegro												x	x	x
Morocco				x	x	x	x	x		x	x			
Netherlands	x	x	x	x	x	x	x		x	x		x	x	x
New Zealand	x	x	x	x	x	x	x			x	x	x	x	x
Northern Ireland[4]										x				
Norway	x	x	x		x	x	x	x	x	x	x	x	x	x
Oman								x		x	x			
Palestinian Nat'l Authority						x		x			x			
Panama													x	
Peru													x	x
Philippines				x	x	x			x					
Poland										x		x	x	x
Portugal	x	x								x		x	x	x
Qatar							x	x		x	x	x	x	x
Romania		x		x		x		x		x	x	x	x	x
Russian Federation		x	x	x	x	x	x	x	x	x	x	x	x	x
Saudi Arabia								x		x	x			
Scotland[4]	x	x			x	x	x	x						
Serbia						x		x		x		x	x	x
Singapore	x	x		x	x	x	x	x		x	x		x	x
Slovak Republic		x		x		x	x			x		x	x	x
Slovenia	x	x	x	x	x	x	x	x	x	x	x	x	x	x
South Africa		x	x	x		x								
Spain		x								x		x	x	x
Sweden		x	x		x	x	x		x	x	x	x	x	x
Switzerland		x	x									x	x	x
Syrian Arab Republic						x		x			x			
Thailand	x	x		x				x		x	x	x	x	x
Trinidad & Tobago													x	
Tunisia				x	x	x	x	x		x	x	x	x	x
Turkey				x				x		x	x	x	x	x
Ukraine							x	x			x			
United Arab Emirates										x	x		x[5]	x
United Kingdom[4]												x	x	x
United States	x	x	x	x	x	x	x	x		x	x	x	x	x
Uruguay												x	x	x
Vietnam														x
Yemen					x		x			x				
Total	27	43	22	39	26	48	37	50	10	50	42	57	70	63

[1] ES = End of Secondary

[2] OECD does not distinguish between Flemish Belgium and French Belgium.

[3] These countries took PISA 2009 in 2010.

[4] The countries of England, Scotland, and Northern Ireland participated in TIMSS, while PISA recognizes the United Kingdom as the unit of measure.

[5] Dubai did not participate in PISA in 2009.

learned in the First International Mathematics Study to other subjects. IEA studies routinely target one or more of three student populations: 10-year-olds, 14-year-olds, and those in the last year of secondary education. All three student populations were assessed in the areas of biology, chemistry, and physics; only 10-year-olds were assessed in earth science, whereas only the older two student populations were assessed in the areas of the nature and methods of science and understanding science. Nineteen national education systems participated in the assessments of the older two student populations; 17 participated in the study of 10-year-olds (Comber & Keeves, 1973).

The Second International Science Study (SISS), conducted in 1983 to 1986, sought to apply what had been learned from FISS as well as from the Second International Mathematics Study (SIMS), which had recently been conducted. There was an interest in examining achievement differences between countries and gathering some information that could suggest explanations for these differences as well as to make an attempt to explain the source of achievement differences *within* any one country. The number of countries that participated in SISS again varied according to the student population of interest. Fifteen national systems participated in the assessment of 10-year-olds (Grade 5 in the United States); 17 systems in the assessment of 14-year-olds (U.S. Grade 9); and 14 systems in the assessment of students in their last year of secondary education (U.S. Grade 12). For assessment purposes, four groups of students were defined for the oldest group: those who were studying biology, those studying chemistry, those studying physics, and those not studying any science at the time of assessment (IEA, 1988; Postlethwaite & Wiley, 1992). A report by Keeves (1992) discusses changes in achievement among the 10 countries that participated in both FISS and SISS over the 14 years between the two studies.

Third International Study of Science
The IEA's third foray into science assessment was done through a joint mathematics and science study. "The Third International Mathematics and Science Study is the largest, most comprehensive, and most rigorous study of schools and students ever." These remarks by Pascal Forgione, the Commissioner of Education Statistics, were the opening words in the first U.S. report coming from the U.S. participation in the TIMSS (National Center for Education Statistics [NCES], 1996, page 3). Subsequent versions of TIMSS have enlisted comparable or greater numbers of countries as the 1995 TIMSS. Table 39.2 shows the varying numbers of countries participating in versions of TIMSS over the years and within a given year. Note the large differences in numbers of countries participating at the various target grades.

What remains unprecedented today is the scope and depth of the information gathered in the first TIMSS. One of the goals of the original Third International Mathematics and Science Study (TIMSS), conducted in 1993 through 1995, was to collect data on mathematics and science education at the *same time* and with the *same students*

so that relationships between these two school subjects might be more easily explored. In addition to assessments in both mathematics and science, students completed a background survey. The teachers of the students participating in the assessments were also asked to complete an extensive survey, as was the principal (or other school official) in the schools where students were assessed.

Funded by the National Science Foundation of the United States, a pioneering in-depth analysis of curriculum standards and textbooks contributed a unique facet to the study and is likely to be one of the main reasons it will remain unparalleled (Schmidt, McKnight, Cogan, Jakwerth, & Houang, 1999; Schmidt, McKnight, & Raizen, 1997; Schmidt, Raizen, Britton, Bianchi, & Wolfe, 1997). Most of the countries were trained to analyze the science topics and student performance expectations found in their science textbooks, line by line, page by page (McKnight & Britton, 1992; Schmidt, Jakwerth, & McKnight, 1998). In contrast, most large-scale analyses of curriculum documents were limited to inspection at the more gross level of books' chapter titles. The very detailed TIMSS analysis required creation of document inspection procedures that were robust enough to use with very different kinds of textbooks; development of universal coding schema; multiday trainings of curriculum experts from participating countries; development of analytical frameworks and methods; and identification of reporting metrics along with new means of displaying and communicating them. Some prior IEA studies had curriculum analyses; for example, Rosier and Keeves (1991) reported the curriculum analysis in SISS. However, none of them employed such extensive data collection and analyses.

In collecting data from the three standard IEA student populations, TIMSS introduced a more complex and demanding means of sampling. It measured the two adjacent grade levels in which the most 9-year-olds were enrolled (Grades 3 and 4 in the United States), the two adjacent grade levels in which the most 13-year-olds were enrolled (U.S. Grades seven 7 and 8), and students in their last year of secondary school (U.S. Grade 12). A challenge for international comparative research is the differences among countries in the age at which students begin formal schooling. Does one want to study and compare students who are of a particular age but will have had varying numbers of years of formal schooling from one country to another, or does one want to study and compare students who have all had the same number of years of formal schooling but may differ in age by a year or more, thus confounding developmental maturity with educational exposure? In an attempt to proceed down a middle path, TIMSS defined the two younger student populations as the combination of both age and years of schooling: the two adjacent grades in which the majority of 9-year-olds (population 1) or 13-year-olds (population 2) were enrolled. Wiley and Wolfe (1992) discuss the additional kinds of analyses that such methods permit. Twenty-seven national systems participated in the assessment of 9-year-olds

(Grade 3 for the lower grade and Grade 4 for the upper grade in the United States and many other systems) and 43 systems in the assessment of 13-year-olds (Grade 7 for the lower grade and Grade 8 for the upper grade in the United States and many other countries). All but two countries (Israel and Kuwait) that assessed students in the upper of the two adjacent grades for 9- and 13-year-old students also assessed students in the lower grades (Beaton et al., 1996; Martin et al., 1997).

Two student populations were defined for assessment of the end-of-secondary student population: all students who were completing the last year of secondary education in their program and those students who were in their last year of secondary education and had specialized in science. Students in both populations took a science literacy assessment designed to measure what experts considered to be the level of scientific knowledge required to function as a science literate citizen of the 21st century. The science specialists were also given an assessment in physics. Twenty-two countries participated in the assessment of mathematics and science literacy, while only 16 countries participated in the physics assessment (Mullis et al., 1998).

Another aspect of TIMSS unique to the original 1995 study was the inclusion of an optional performance assessment component for both mathematics and science for students in fourth and eighth grade (Harmon et al., 1997). Far fewer countries participated in this aspect of the study (10 at fourth grade; 21 at eighth grade). These performance tasks required students to use materials and apparatus to solve a multistep practical problem such as designing and constructing a box to hold four plastic balls.

In conjunction with the U.S. participation in TIMSS 1995, the U.S. government through the National Center for Education Statistics funded two supplementary international projects: the videotape classroom study and three case studies (Stevenson, 1998; Stigler, Gonzales, Kwanaka, Knoll, & Serrano, 1999). Both kinds of studies focused on mathematics at the eighth-grade level in Germany, Japan, and the United States. For TIMSS 1999, a more extensive video study included science, and results were released early in 2006 (National Center for Education Statistics, 2006).

Recent Participation by Subnational Jurisdictions

Table 39.3 illustrates that, in recent years, the number of countries having participation by subnational jurisdictions has grown for both TIMSS and PISA. This phenomenon is particularly strong in Canada and the United States. In

TABLE 39.3
Subnational Jurisdictions Participating in International Assessments

Subnational Jurisdiction	TIMSS 2007		TIMSS 2011		PISA 2009	PISA 2012
	4th	8th	4th	8th	15 yrs	15 yrs
Canada						
Alberta	x		x	x		
British Columbia	x	x				
Ontario	x	x	x	x		
Quebec	x	x	x	x		
China						
Shanghai					x	x
India						
Himachal Pradesh					2010	
Tamil Nadu					2010	
Spain						
Basque Country		x				
United Arab Emirates						
Abu Dhabi			x	x		
Dubai	x	x	x	x	x	
United States						
Alabama				x		
California				x		
Colorado				x		
Connecticut				x		
Florida			x	x		
Indiana				x		
Massachusetts	x	x		x		
Minnesota	x	x		x		
North Carolina			x	x		
Venezuela						
Miranda					2010	

Note: 2010 = Administered PISA 2009 in 2010

the United States, the original TIMSS in 1995 garnered so much attention that states and consortia of school districts began to relate their local student science or mathematics performance to international results (e.g., Kimmelman et al., 1999). Such interested jurisdictions must go to additional effort and expense to participate. Using the United States as an example, the national study must have a certain number of students in a given state take the TIMSS test in order to construct a national sample. However, that number of students for a given state is not sufficient to be representative of that state's students. Strong reporting out at the state level necessitates that interested states have more students take the test.

OECD-PISA

The Organisation for Economic Co-operation and Development (OECD) launched a new cross-national assessment of science in 2000. The OECD is a Paris-based organization of industrialized countries that historically is most widely known for its cross-national reports on economics, such as comparisons of per capita spending on education. Within OECD, the Center for Education Research and Innovation (CERI) has since 1968 organized cross-national studies of education issues—for example, a qualitative study of innovations in science and mathematics education in participating countries (e.g., Black & Atkin, 1996; Raizen & Britton, 1997).

The regularly scheduled assessment by OECD is known as the Programme for International Student Achievement (PISA). It focuses only on 15-year-olds and includes assessment of three subject areas every year it is offered— literacy, mathematical literacy, and science literacy. In each cycle, however, one subject receives dominant attention (see Table 39.1). Science was emphasized for the first and only time thus far in 2006; it will be emphasized again in the 2015 administration. Like TIMSS, PISA has attracted strong international interest, as indicated by the participation of more than 40 countries in the first two administrations and considerably more since then.

PISA emphasizes students' application of science in real-life contexts. The PISA 2006 specification of scientific literacy had several interconnected aspects. *Context* involves recognizing life situations involving science and technology. *Knowledge* is understanding the natural world on the basis of scientific knowledge that includes both knowledge of the natural world as well as knowledge *about* science itself. The latter includes interactions among science and technology and the material, intellectual, and cultural environments. The *attitude* aspect includes interest in science, support for scientific inquiry, and motivation to act responsibly (e.g., toward natural resources and the environment). The PISA framework also gives priority to *competencies*: identifying scientific questions; describing, predicting, or explaining phenomena based on scientific knowledge; interpreting evidence and conclusions; and using scientific evidence to make and communicate decisions. In other words, solving science-based problems is a central student activity in PISA assessments.

Contrasting TIMSS and PISA Assessments

The TIMSS and PISA lines of assessment have similarities but also a number of significant contrasts (Hutchison & Schagen, 2006; Scott & Owen, 2005; Yee, de Lange, & Schmidt, 2006). They differ in their relative emphases among different science disciplines and technology and engineering; their relative balances between probing students' disciplinary content knowledge and applications of knowledge; and the kinds of item types used.

- The TIMSS and PISA test specifications give comparable emphasis to life sciences, whereas PISA has emphasized earth sciences more than TIMSS, and TIMSS has more strongly emphasized physical science.
- While the nominal content of the two science assessments is similar (life science, physical science), TIMSS primarily focuses on the formal content of the scientific disciplines, while PISA emphasizes students' application of science in real-life contexts. The first PISA criterion for choosing knowledge to be assessed is its relevance to real-life situations. The second criterion is that the selected knowledge should represent important scientific concepts. The TIMSS design typically reverses these priorities.
- The PISA emphasis on problem solving requires more open-ended than defined-response items than used in TIMSS (Nohara, 2001). Typical PISA items make more complex cognitive demands on students. Further, the kinds of knowledge probed by PISA required items involving significantly more reading, which has a general effect on students' willingness and ability to engage with questions on any test, including PISA (Ruddock, Clausen-May, Purple, & Ager, 2006).
- The PISA science framework gives significant attention to technology education. A number of countries have for more than 10 years included technology as an additional school subject, separate in the school day from science (Britton, De Long-Cotty, & Levenson, 2005).

Also, TIMSS sampling is classroom based while PISA sampling is school based. Given these differences, it is logical that students in a country may perform better on one test than on the other, depending upon the science curriculum and instructional practices in the country. Nevertheless, when PISA began, some countries having high prior performance on TIMSS were shocked that results were notably lower in PISA ("the PISA shock"; Yee, de Lange, & Schmidt, 2006). While the testing differences are better understood today, there still can be considerable confusion about why a country's results can differ and what those difference mean (Koretz, 2009).

Interpreting Results of International Comparisons

While the authors' earlier chapter gave a few summary country-specific results for the original TIMSS (Britton & Schneider, 2007), the fact that many more TIMSS and now PISA studies have transpired precludes having chapter space to render results in this edition. However, some key, first principles for attending to or interpreting international results are offered.

1. Discussion of results at the most summative level only indicates country rankings for science overall, such as country A scoring 2nd or country B scoring 37th. Note that overall science rankings by country can mask substantial differences among specific science areas. In addition to an overall scaled score for science, the TIMSS international science report included the average percentage correct in five broad science areas: earth science, life science, physics, chemistry, and environmental issues and the nature of science (Beaton et al., 1996). A later analysis of TIMSS Grade 8 data identified a group of "A+" countries as those countries significantly outperforming the majority of TIMSS countries (Valverde & Schmidt, 2000). However, even the highest overall performers had areas of science in which their performance was not as strong.

One of the books published by the U.S. National Research Center for TIMSS contained a more detailed analysis of student achievement that reflected even greater variation (Schmidt, McKnight, Cogan, Jakwerth, & Houang,1999). Among the five broad science areas, TIMSS could report on 15 to 17 subscales (the number depending upon the grade level); for example, life sciences included five subscales of plants and animals, organs and tissues, life processes and functions, life cycles and genetics, and human biology and health. The authors argued that the greater variation in achievement scores at the subscale level was a reflection of the variation in the science curricula among the participating countries. Considering the 17 eighth-grade curricular areas of science presented, one can see that each of the highest-performing countries ranked first in at least one of these categories. However, one country with overall high performance had the lowest rank in any one specific science area (21st in the area of life cycles and genetics), and each country had ranks of 10th or lower in 4 of the 17 curricular areas.

The extensive curriculum analysis, which was a unique aspect of TIMSS 1995, provided an in-depth analysis of these issues through an examination of official curriculum standards and textbooks (Schmidt, Raizen, Britton, Bianchi, & Wolfe, 1997). An examination of the curriculum in the highest-performing countries found that across these four countries (Singapore, the Czech Republic, Japan, and Korea), the five most emphasized science topics accounted for about 80% of the eighth-grade science textbook. These five most emphasized topics were electricity; chemical properties of matter; chemical changes; energy, types, sources, and conversions; and organs and tissues. This represents one biology topic, two physics topics, and two chemistry topics. Further, the Teacher Questionnaire in TIMSS provided two more indicators of the science curriculum in countries: the percentage of teachers who taught specific topics during the school year in which the student assessment was conducted and the relative proportion of instructional time devoted to specific topics. Several reports have combined these two

curricular indicators from teachers with the two curricular indicators of content standards and textbooks to provide a multifaceted perspective on what constitutes eighth-grade science across TIMSS countries (Cogan, Wang, & Schmidt, 2001; Schmidt et al., 2001). Comparing the five most emphasized eighth-grade science topics according these four indicators, only the topic of "human biology" is present in all four. Aspects of energy ("electricity," "energy processes," and "energy types, sources, conversions") also were well represented.

2. Results for Grade 4 are affected by the fact that not all countries intended to begin science instruction as soon as children enter school. In fact, three of the four top-performing countries at eighth grade—Singapore, Japan, and the Czech Republic—did not intend science instruction to begin until Grade 3 (see Schmidt, Raizen et al., 1997, pp. 83–84). The number of topics intended to be taught and learned at each grade, the emphasis afforded topics within a year, and the pattern of sequencing topics across the years of schooling have been identified as important indicators of the coherence, focus, and rigor of any country's curriculum (Schmidt, McKnight, & Raizen, 1997; Valverde & Schmidt, 2000).

3. Refer to the following different kinds of reports for different purposes: official international reporting of international results, official national reporting on international results, and discussions of results by many other groups. Sponsoring international organizations (IES and OECD) always release reports giving general comparisons or results across participating countries. Many countries also issue their own, official national reports that give the same international results, but display them in ways that indicate that nation's relative performance; provide more detailed national data than can be included in the international report; and may provide discussion of factors that could affect national performance (e.g., Schmidt et al., 1999). Finally, researchers beyond the study team, policy makers, and others may, with or without conducting additional analyses, provide additional interpretations of results and/or discussions of factors affecting the results (e.g., Carnoy & Rothstein, 2013; Phillips, 2010; Wang, 1998).

4. Caution must be taken when comparing results across different test administrations over the years. The number of countries involved in each assessment and the differences in the items comprising each assessment preclude drawing overly simplified conclusions from direct comparisons. Regarding the latter, for example, the relative amount of questioning among life science, physical science, and so forth can shift slightly from one administration to another. Further, because the scaled scores are formed each time on the basis of the participating students, the scaled scores for any two assessments, such as TIMSS 1995 and TIMSS 2003, are not directly comparable. On the other hand, international assessments do maintain some items in common across administrations. Marked advances in item response theory and Rasch measurement have enhanced equating of results over time. Therefore,

analysts can appropriately adjust scores for the different assessments to enable some appropriate comparisons.

National Assessment of Educational Progress

More than 40 years ago, the National Assessment of Educational Progress (NAEP) began gathering information on student achievement in selected academic subjects (Johnson, 1975). Each administration of NAEP has become an important and continuing source of information on what U.S. students know and are able to do at that time. The National Assessment Governing Board (NAGB) oversees the NAEP program.

NAEP Science 1975–2008

The first administration included practical skills tests in science (NAEP, 1975). It has grown in scope several times over the years. The third administration added items to assess student attitudes toward science (NAEP, 1978). The 1986 NAEP investigated students' home environments and the kinds of science instruction they received in school (Mullis & Jenkins, 1988). Also in 1986, an experimental assessment was developed to test higher-order thinking skills, and students interacted with a computer simulation for an item (NAEP, 1987). Originally, assessments were of students 9, 13, and 17 years old; beginning in 1983, the assessment has sampled students in Grades 4, 8, and 12. During the late 1980s, the Educational Testing Service (ETS), the contractor that conducts NAEP, made a brief, analogous foray into international assessments.

Since the mid-1990s, in addition to the national-level assessments, NAEP has conducted and reported state-level assessments at Grades 4 and 8 in science as well as reading, mathematics, and writing (Hudson, 1991). State-level science assessments, which are identical to the national assessments, are conducted every few years, most recently in 2009 (NCES, 2011) and 2011 (NCES, 2012). In accordance with the No Child Left Behind Act of 2001, schools receiving Title I funding are required to participate in NAEP math and reading; NAEP science participation at the state level is voluntary ("NAEP—About State NAEP," 2012b). Also prompted by the No Child Left Behind legislation, NAEP began a Trial Urban District Assessment (TUDA) in 2002 in which six large urban districts volunteered to administer NAEP reading and writing assessments (Lutkus, Weiner, Daane, & Jin, 2003). Twenty-one districts now participate in TUDA. NAEP science administrations occurred at the district level in 2005 and 2009, with 18 districts participating in the most recent exam ("NAEP—About the District Assessment," 2012a).

The resulting data on student knowledge and performance have been accompanied by background information that allows analyses of a number of student demographic and instructional factors related to achievement. The assessments have been designed to allow comparisons of student performance over time and among subgroups of students according to region, parental education, gender, and race/ethnicity (e.g., Campbell, Voelkl, & Donahue, 1998; NAEP, 1992). Researchers have conducted secondary analysis of the science assessment using NAEP data (e.g., Linn, De Benedictis, Delucchi, Harris, & Stage, 1987; Liu & Ruiz, 2008; Von Secker, 2004; Welch, Walberg, & Fraser, 1986). Selected items are also publically available, allowing researchers to evaluate questions (e.g., Abedi & Hejri, 2004) and conduct original research (e.g., Schneider, Krajcik, Marx, & Soloway, 2002).

The NAGB developed three levels of achievement for the assessment in 1990 (Vinovskis, 1998). *Basic* denotes partial mastery of prerequisite knowledge and skills that are fundamental for proficient work at each grade. *Proficient* represents solid academic performance for each grade assessed. Students reaching this level demonstrate subject-matter knowledge, application of such knowledge to real-world situations, and analytical skills appropriate to the subject matter. *Advanced* signifies superior performance. These levels are the primary means of reporting NAEP results to the general public and policy makers regarding what students should know and be able to do on NAEP assessments.

NAEP Science 2009–2021

In late 2005, NAGB approved a new framework to guide administrations of NAEP science from 2009 through 2021. The framework is a response to developments in science research and advances in science education around standards, cognition, international assessments, and assessment practices (NAGB, 2009). Results from the first administration of the new NAEP science in 2009 found 34%, 30%, and 21% of students at Grades 4, 8, and 12, respectively, performed at or above the Proficient level (NCES, 2011). In 2011, when the assessment was given only to eighth graders, 32% of students performed at or above the Proficient level and scores differences between White students and Black and Hispanic students decreased; gaps between male and female students and between private and public school students remained (NCES, 2012).

Science Content

The 2009 NAEP science content domain is defined by a series of content statements that describe key principles, concepts, and facts in three broad content areas: physical science, life science, and earth and space science (see Table 39.4). As measured by student response time, the distribution of items by content area should be as follows: roughly equal across physical, life, and earth and space science at Grade 4; more emphasis on earth and space science at Grade 8; a shift to more emphasis on physical and life science at Grade 12 (NAGB, 2009, p. viii). Some content cuts across the areas of physical, life, and earth and space science (NAGB, 2009, p. 24). Some instances of cross-cutting content are identified and described next.

Uses and transformations of energy and energy conservation. To demonstrate an understanding of energy uses, transformations, and conservation, students must be able to do so in the context of different types of systems. These systems include biological organisms, earth systems, ecosystems (combining both life forms and their physical environment), the solar system and other systems in the universe, and human-designed systems (NAGB, 2009, p. 42).

Biogeochemical cycles. To demonstrate an understanding of biogeochemical cycles, students must draw on their knowledge of matter and energy (physical science), structures and functions of living systems (life science), and

TABLE 39.4
Science Content for Grades 4, 8, and 12 in NAEP 2009–2021

Content	Major Topic	Minor Topics
Physical Science	Matter	Properties of matter
		Changes in matter
	Energy	Forms of energy
		Energy conversions and conservation
	Motion	Motion at the macroscopic and molecular levels
		Forces affecting motion
Life Science	Structures and functions of living systems	Organization and development of living system
		Matter and energy transformations in living systems
		Interdependence of living systems
	Changes in living systems	Heredity and reproduction of living systems
		Evolution and diversity of living systems
Earth and Space	Earth in space and time	Objects in the universe
		History of Earth
	Earth structures	Properties of Earth materials
		Tectonics
	Earth systems	Energy in Earth systems
		Climate and weather
		Biogeochemical cycles

Note: Adapted from "Science Framework for the 2009 National Assessment of Educational Progress," by NAGB, 2009.

Earth systems (earth and space science). Fixed amounts of chemical atoms or elements cycle within the Earth system; energy is transferred during this movement, which includes water and nutrient cycles; and human use of Earth's finite resources affects the land, oceans, and atmosphere, as well as plant and animal populations (NAGB, 2009, p. 56).

Science Practices

The second dimension of the framework is defined by four practices: identifying science principles, using science principles, using scientific inquiry, and using technological design (NAGB, 2009, p. 66). By crossing any science content statement above with the four practices, it is possible to generate specific performance expectations on which assessment items can be based. Therefore, neither content statements nor practice statements will be assessed in isolation; all assessment items will be derived from a combination of the two. Observed student responses to these items can then be compared with expected student responses in order to make inferences about what students know and can do.

Table 39.5 summarizes general performance expectations for each of the four practices. Certain ways of knowing and thinking—cognitive demands—underpin the four science practices. Four such cognitive demands are as follows: *knowing what, knowing how, knowing why,* and *knowing when and where to apply knowledge* (NAGB, 2009, p. 65). The set of four cognitive demands can be used as a lens to analyze student responses, thereby checking expectations regarding what content and practice(s) are being tapped by a given assessment item.

Science Item Formats

Item formats for the 2009 NAEP science assessment fall into two broad categories: selected-response items and constructed-response items. Selected-response items comprise individual multiple-choice items. Constructed-response items comprise short constructed-response items, extended constructed-response items, and concept maps. Other item types—cluster multiple-choice items, predict-observe-explain (POE) multiple-choice items, hands-on performance tasks, and interactive

TABLE 39.5
General Performance Expectations for Practices, NAEP Science 2009–2021

Identifying Science Principles	Using Science Principles	Using Scientific Inquiry	Using Technological Design
State correct science principles	Explain scientific observations or phenomena	Design and critique scientific investigations	Design and critique technological solutions to given problems
Connect different representations of science principles and patterns in data	Predict specific observations or phenomena	Conduct scientific investigations using appropriate tools and techniques	Identify scientific tradeoffs in design decisions and choose among alternative solutions
Make connections among closely related content statements	Propose, analyze, and evaluate alternative predictions or explanations	Find patters in data; relate patterns in data to theoretical models	Apply science principles or data to anticipate effects of technological design decisions
Describe, measure, or classify observations	Suggest example of observations that illustrate a science principle	Use empirical evidence to draw valid conclusions about explanations and predictions	
	←Communicate accurately and effectively→		

Note: Adapted from "Science Framework for the 2009 National Assessment of Educational Progress," by NAGB, 2009, p. 80.

computer tasks—may be used as either selected-response or constructed-response items (NAGB, 2009, p. 98).

As measured by student response time, roughly no more than 50% of the assessment items at each grade level should be selected-response items; the remainder should be made up of constructed-response items (NAGB, 2009, p. 97). In order to further probe students' abilities to combine their understandings with the investigative skills reflective of practices, a subsample of students should receive an additional 20 to 30 minutes of response time to complete hands-on performance and interactive computer tasks. There should be at least a total of four of these tasks at each grade; of these four tasks, there should be at least one hands-on *and* one interactive computer task per grade; the number of hands-on tasks should not exceed the number of interactive computer tasks (NAGB, 2009, p. 114).

In hands-on performance tasks, students manipulate selected physical objects and try to solve a scientific problem involving the objects (NAGB, 2009, p. 106). NAEP hands-on performance tasks should provide students with a concrete, well-contextualized task ·(problem) along with "laboratory" equipment and materials. However, the response format should give students the freedom to determine scientifically justifiable procedures for addressing the problem and arriving at a solution. Students' scores should be based on both the solution and the procedures created for carrying out the investigation and the solution.

Interactive computer tasks should be of four types: (1) information search and analysis, (2) empirical investigation, (3) simulation, and (4) concept maps (NAGB, 2009, p. 107). Information search and analysis items pose a scientific problem and ask students to query an information database to bring conceptual and empirical information to bear on the problem. Empirical investigation items put hands-on performance tasks on the computer and invite students to design and conduct a study to draw inferences and conclusions about a problem. Simulation items that model systems (e.g., food chains) pose problems of prediction and explanation about changes in the system and permit students to collect data and solve problems in the system. Concept map items probe aspects of the structure or organization of students' scientific knowledge by providing concept terms and having students build concept maps on the computer. A concept map is a network whose nodes are concept terms (e.g., density, buoyancy, mass). The nodes are connected by directed, labeled lines. A directed line shows the relationship between a pair of concept terms; the label on the line describes the relationship.

NAEP Technology and Engineering Literacy 2014+

More countries are adding more explicit attention to technology and engineering education in their national education systems, with that attention to date focusing more on technology than on engineering education. A number of countries have for more than 10 years included technology education as an additional school subject, separate in the school day from science (Britton, De Long-Cotty, & Levenson, 2005). Neither subject area has had a strong a foothold to date in the United States (Meade & Dugger, 2004). Standards for U.S. technology education were created some time ago (International Technology Education Association, 2000, renamed in recent years to International Technology and Engineering Education Association, or ITEEA). However, instruction on technology has mostly been enhanced within career and technical education (CTE) curricula rather than also gaining systemwide traction either through science classrooms and/or through having more students take technology courses. However, the U.S. situation is changing now. The next edition of national science standards contains some engineering, specifically engineering design, as elaborated by *The Framework for Science and Engineering Education* (NRC, 2011).

Given the scarcity of either technology or education in the United States, there is confusion about their terrains and the relationship between them and with science, as elaborated by Cunningham and Carlsen in Chapter 36 of this handbook. In brief, technology and engineering education for Grades 6 through 12 have a complementary relationship, with both emphasizing student hands-on investigation of solutions to human problems through use of an engineering design process and acquiring formal knowledge about the engineering design process. This is in contrast to using scientific inquiry into scientific phenomena. Technology education puts additional emphases on understanding and designing technologies and understanding the designed world, such as being literate in basic, contemporary content knowledge found in many fields such as transportation, the food industry, civil engineering, construction, or biomedical technology.

In preparation for measuring U.S. students' understanding of technology, NAGB commissioned the development of a Technology and Engineering Literacy (TEL) framework (NAGB, 2010). NAEP is now creating an assessment based on this framework, which will be piloted with eighth graders in 2014 ("More About the NAEP Technology and Engineering Literacy (TEL) Assessment," 2012). The content, practices, and item formats defined in both the science and technology and engineering literacy frameworks are discussed next.

Technology and Engineering Literacy Content

The TEL framework defines technology and engineering literacy as "the capacity to use, understand, and evaluate technology as well as to understand technological principles and strategies needed to develop solutions and achieve goals" (NAGB, 2010, p. xi). The focus of the framework is not mastery of specific tools but rather the knowledge and competencies all students need as citizens in a technology-driven society. Three content areas were identified as essential to technology and engineering literacy: technology and society, design and systems, and information and communication technology (ICT; see Table 39.6). These areas, although rooted in different domains (i.e., industrial arts, ICT, and science, technology, and society) are closely related, and proficiency

TABLE 39.6
Technology and Engineering Literacy Content for Grades 4, 8, and 12 in NAEP 2014

Content	Major Topics
Technology and Society	Interaction of Technology and Humans
	Effects of Technology on the Natural World
	Effects of Technology on the World of Information and Knowledge
	Ethics, Equality, & Responsibility
Design and Systems	Nature of Technology
	Engineering Design
	Systems Thinking
	Maintenance & Troubleshooting
Information and Communication Technology	Construction & Exchange of Ideas & Solutions
	Information Research
	Investigation of Problems
	Acknowledgement of Ideas & Information
	Selection and Use of Digital Tools

Note: Adapted from "Technology and Engineering Literacy Framework for the 2014 National Assessment of Educational Progress: Pre-Publication Edition," by NAGB, 2010, p. 2–2.

TABLE 39.7
General Performance Expectations for Practices, NAEP TEL 2014

Understanding Technological Principles	Developing Solutions and Achieving Goals	Communicating and Collaborating
Explain features and functions of technologies and systems	Apply simple steps and use technological tools to address authentic tasks	Communicate using contemporary technologies
Explain how components fit together	Analyze goals, plan, design, implement	Working individually or in teams
Make predictions, comparisons, and evaluations	Revise and evaluate possible solutions	Share ideas, designs, data, explanations, models, arguments, and presentations
		Develop representations

Note: Adapted from "Technology and Engineering Literacy Framework for the 2014 National Assessment of Educational Progress: Pre-Publication Edition," by NAGB, 2010, p. 3-2–3-3.

in one area supports understanding of another area. Technology and engineering literacy is viewed as cumulative, with experience in later years building upon knowledge gained in earlier years. As measured by student response time, the distribution of items by content area should be as follows: a strong emphasis on ICT at Grade 4; more emphasis on design and systems and less emphasis on ICT at Grade 8; roughly equal across technology and society, design and systems, and ICT at Grade 12 (NAGB, 2010, pp. 4–14).

Technology and Engineering Literacy Practices and Contexts

The TEL framework is also defined by three practices in which students are expected to apply knowledge from the three content areas: understanding technological principles, developing solutions and achieving goals, and communicating and collaborating (see Table 39.7). Crossing any content area with the three practices generates nine sets of performance expectations upon which assessment items will be based. The framework also emphasizes the importance of knowing how to apply technology and engineering literacy across different contexts, specifically, societal issues, design goals, and school and community problems (NAGB, 2010, pp. 3–23). Assessment items will be situated within one of these three context areas.

Technology and Engineering Literacy Item Formats

The NAEP TEL assessment will be completely computer based and consist of both scenario-based assessment sets and discrete item sets. Scenario-based sets, lasting between

12 and 25 minutes, present an overarching problem for students to solve through various interrelated tasks. Discrete item sets consist of 10 to 15 stand-alone items in both selected-response and short constructed-response formats. Twenty-five minutes will be allotted for discrete item sets. Given the nature of the NAEP TEL assessment, pattern tracking can be used to analyze students' performance in greater detail. For example, the computer-based assessment can capture the sequence of actions taken in solving a problem or the features of problems attended to by test takers.

State-Level Technology and Engineering Assessment

At the state level, science is tested through large-scale assessments in all U.S. states, at varying grade levels. In contrast, only Massachusetts currently has an assessment for technology and engineering that is separate from that state's science assessment; high school students can take this test as fulfillment of a graduation requirement to take and pass an end-of-course assessment either in technology/engineering or in one of three sciences. Further, the great majority of states do not contain any technology and/or engineering within their science tests (National Academy of Engineering, 2010). Many challenges lie ahead for creating state-level, large-scale assessments that address technology and engineering (Committee on Assessing Technological Literacy, 2006; Quellmalz, 2013).

Computer-Enhanced Science Assessment

The rapid implementation of new technologies to support assessment is profoundly changing what, how, when, and where science can be assessed. Contemporary science frameworks and standards are steering the nation toward more challenging, focused science goals. These documents advocate fewer, more integrated core disciplinary ideas, deeper understanding of dynamic science systems, and application of scientific understandings to real-world problems (College Board, 2009; NRC, 2011). A new generation of technology-powered assessment is developing to meet these challenges.

Limitations of Current Large-Scale Assessments

Technologies hold great promise for overcoming serious limitations of large-scale assessments. The preponderance of classroom, district, and state science tests remain disconnected, assessing discrete facts and few science practices (Quellmalz, DeBarger, Haertel, & Kreikemeier, 2005; Quellmalz, Timms, Silberglitt, & Buckley, 2012). State science tests are administered on demand, with federal regulations only requiring testing at the end of multiyear grade bands. Economical and logistical constraints on test length result in tests that cannot begin to measure even core concepts and practices, particularly not with the multiple-choice format.

The *Framework for K–12 Science Education* and the *Next Generation Science Standards (NGSS),* along with other national and international science frameworks and standards, advocate teaching and testing of deeper learning about systems in natural and designed worlds integrated with application of the practices used by scientists and engineers to study and design these systems (NRC, 2011). Assessments of the *Next Generation Science Standards* will require dynamic, richer, and more extended and complex representations of science phenomena along with ways for students to actively investigate and modify the interactions among system components and emergent system behaviors. In addition, there is an expectation that 21st-century skills such as communication and collaboration will be measured. These goals will require significant changes from current testing practices.

New Computer-Enhanced Assessment

Technologies offer numerous opportunities to reformulate science assessment. Support for the logistical functions of administration, scoring, and reporting can substantially reduce testing costs. Authoring systems and resource banks are streamlining test design and development. Digital collections of released items and tasks are allowing teachers to create classroom assessments aligned with state tests. Alignment tools can support searches for standards-based tasks and items. Online rater training and scoring systems support reliable application of rubrics. Annotated exemplars support interpretation of scores and implications for instruction. Social networking supports communities of practice and professional development on assessment literacy.

Perhaps the most transformative benefits of technologies are advances in the designs of the testing environments. Technologies can represent rich, authentic environments and complex problems to address. Problem-based scenarios can promote integration of science knowledge and practices

through the development, use, and investigation of system models. Multimedia displays can juxtapose multiple representations of science systems and overlay concrete depictions with abstract symbols. Assessment tasks can be in multiple static, active, or interactive modalities (Mayer & Johnson, 2008). Animations of dynamic, often invisible spatial, causal, and temporal science phenomena can be shown "in action." Students can control the pace and replay what they need to observe. Interactive features allow students to actively investigate science systems such that they can make predictions, run experiments, explain outcomes, and conduct multiple trials. Computer logs of these investigations allow measurement of pathways of science and engineering practices as they are being employed. In addition, response features such as drag and drop, drawing, and moving sliders to change variable values allow students to express their understandings in a range of formats beyond text. Such affordances can be particularly helpful for low-performing readers, English language learners, and students with disabilities (Dolan, Hall, Banerjee, Chun, & Strangman, 2005).

Forms of computer-based assessment are migrating from delivery on computers to other devices such as tablets, handheld devices, and tools not yet imagined. The increased mobility of assessment instruments will permit greater flexibility for where and when evidence of learning can be gathered. Flexible administration times and locales can shift annual, on-demand testing to curriculum-embedded and interim challenges that can be aggregated into cumulative reports of proficiency.

Computer-Based Examples

Large-scale computer-based testing now occurs in numerous international, national, and state assessment programs (Quellmalz & Pellegrino, 2009). In many of these programs, technologies are used not just to support testing logistics but to also design innovative tasks and items. For example, in the 2011 National Assessment of Educational Progress for writing, students used word processing and had access to spell checks. In 2006, the international PISA administration began piloting computer-based science assessments and in 2015 will administer simulation-based science tasks (OECD, 2010). The 2009 National Assessment of Educational Progress (NAEP) for science fielded interactive computer tasks to better assess science inquiry and will continue to administer these interactive investigations. The 2014 NAEP prototype for Technology and Engineering Literacy will be delivered online and include long and short scenario-based tasks to assess cross-cutting practices for understanding technological principles, developing solutions and achieving goals, and communicating and collaborating.

States are beginning to include simulations in their state science tests (Minnesota Department of Education, 2012; Silberglitt, Vineyard, King, & Bowler, 2011). The state assessment consortia developing tests for Common Core math and literacy standards will be computer delivered and scored. One of the consortia will employ computer-based adaptive testing. It is likely that similar state consortia will be formed to develop new assessments for the Next Generation Science Standards.

A number of research and development projects are exploring the affordances of technology for science assessment. For example, two aim at classroom assessment. The Diagnoser project includes question sets and activities targeted to address specific problematic ideas. Each component references a facet cluster (Minstrell, Anderson, Kraus, & Minstrell, 2008). The Science Assistments project has developed computerized microworlds aligned with Massachusetts science standards. The microworlds present tasks and questions on science inquiry supported with "widgets," or tools to scaffold inquiry (Gobert, Sao Pedro, Baker, Toto, & Montalvo, 2012). The Virtual Performance Assessment project is studying the potential of immersive virtual environments for assessing science inquiry assessments for summative and accountability purposes (Clarke-Midura, Code, Dede, Mayrath, & Zap, 2012).

A promising model is to build multilevel, balanced assessment systems based on common standards and design specifications. The SimScientists Assessment System is developing suites of simulation-based assessments that share science system model environments and task and item designs for sets of curriculum-embedded formative assessments and end-of-unit benchmark summative assessments that are require a class period to complete, and shorter NAEP-like 5- to 10-minute signature tasks that can be assembled into a year-end test (Quellmalz, Timms, Silberglitt, & Buckley, 2012; http://simscientists.org).

Figure 39.1 shows a screenshot of an excerpt from an end-of-unit benchmark assessment that tests students'

understanding of ecosystems and inquiry practices for investigating them. The screenshot is from a summative assessment scenario set in an Australian grassland. The overarching problem is that the ecosystem needs to be restored after a wildfire. In the first part of the scenario-based assessment, students observe the interactions of the organisms, identify the roles of the organisms and their interactions, then draw a food web representing the flow of energy and matter through the system. Then the students conduct a series of investigations about the consequences on population levels of varying numbers of predators and prey. In the Figure 39.1 screenshot, students' inquiry skills are assessed for using a simulation to conduct three investigations of what different numbers of organism populations would survive in a balanced ecosystem. Signature tasks developed for this suite that could be used in a year-end district or state test would be limited to just the construction of a food web (for a different ecosystem) and an investigation task like that in Figure 39.1 to build three balanced ecosystem models based on knowledge of the predator–prey relationships.

SimScientists projects have amassed evidence of the formative and summative assessments' technical quality, feasibility, and utility, thus demonstrating their great potential as a model for integrating simulations into balanced state assessment systems (Herman, Dai, Htut, Martinez, & Rivera, 2010; Pellegrino, Chudowsky, & Glaser, 2001; Quellmalz, et al., 2012). Coherence of the multilevel assessments would be forged by the linked set of simulation-based assessments in the form of curriculum-embedded modules for formative uses, unit benchmark assessments for summative

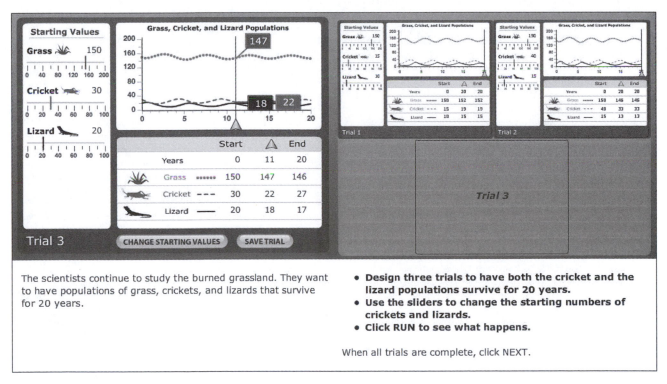

The scientists continue to study the burned grassland. They want to have populations of grass, crickets, and lizards that survive for 20 years.

- **Design three trials to have both the cricket and the lizard populations survive for 20 years.**
- **Use the sliders to change the starting numbers of crickets and lizards.**
- **Click RUN to see what happens.**

When all trials are complete, click NEXT.

Figure 39.1 Example of simulation-based science assessment, from SimScientists.

proficiencies, use of the unit benchmark data in district or state science reports, and use of signature tasks as components of district or state tests. Comprehensiveness would be achieved by adding measurements of science standards for cross-cutting system knowledge and core disciplinary ideas and active science and engineering practices. Continuity would be achieved by the multiple measures that unit benchmark assessments and sets of signature tasks would add to state science assessment reports.

Computer-enhanced assessment is rapidly evolving to support assessments of richer, deeper science learning. The capabilities of technologies will enable next-generation assessments to represent next-generation science learning.

Acknowledgments

Three colleagues in WestEd's STEM Program helped the authors in substantial ways: Research Associates Robert Allen and Aleata Hubbard pulled data and information to update the International and NAEP sections; Edys Quellmalz authored the new closing section on computer-enhanced and computer-based assessments. Three reviewers suggested very helpful enhancements and the authors are grateful for their assistance: Bill Schmidt, Peter Tymms, and Per Kind.

References

Abedi, J., & Hejri, F. (2004). Accommodations for students with limited English proficiency in the National Assessment of Educational Progress. *Applied Measurement in Education, 17*(4), 371–392.

American Federation of Teachers (AFT). (1995). *What secondary students abroad are expected to know: Gateway exams taken by average-achieving students in France, Germany, and Scotland.* Washington, DC: American Federation of Teachers.

American Federation of Teachers & National Center for Improving Science Education. (1994). *What college-bound students abroad are expected to know about biology: Exams from England, and Wales, France, Germany and Japan.* Washington, DC: American Federation of Teachers.

American Federation of Teachers & National Center for Improving Science Education. (1996). *What college-bound students abroad are expected to know about chemistry and physics: Exams from England, and Wales, France, Germany and Japan.* Washington, DC: American Federation of Teachers.

Beaton, A. E., Mullis, I. V. S., Martin, M. O., Gonzalez, E. J., Kelly, D. L., & Smith, T. A. (1996). *Science achievement in the middle school years: IEA's Third International Mathematics and Science Study.* Chestnut Hill, MA: Center for the Study of Testing, Evaluation, and Educational Policy, Boston College.

Black, P., & Atkin, J. M. (Eds.). (1996). *Changing the subject: Innovations in science, maths and technology education* (1st ed.). London: Routledge.

Britton, E. D., De Long-Cotty, B. D., & Levenson, T. (2005). *Bringing technology education into K–8 classrooms: A guide to curricular resources about the designed world.* Thousand Oaks, CA: Corwin Press.

Britton, E. D., & Raizen, S. A. (Eds.). (1996). *Examining the examinations: An international comparison of science and mathematics examinations for college-bound students.* Boston: Kluwer Academic.

Britton, E. D., & Schneider, S. A. (2007). Large-scale assessment in science education. In S. K. Abell & R. J. Larsen (Eds.), *Handbook of research in science education* (pp. 1007–1040). Mahwah, NJ: Lawrence Erlbaum Associates.

Campbell, J. R., Voelkl, K. E., & Donahue, P. L. (1998). *NAEP 1996 trends in academic progress. Addendum. Achievement of U.S. students in science, 1969 to 1996; mathematics, 1973 to 1996; reading, 1971 to 1996; writing, 1984 to 1996* (rev. ed.). Washington, DC: Office of Educational Research and Improvement, US Department of Education.

Carnoy, M., & Rothstein, R. (2013). *What do international tests really show about U.S. student performance?* Washington, DC: Economic Policy Institute. Retrieved from www.epi.org/publication/us-student-performance-testing/

Clarke-Midura, J., Code, J., Dede, C., Mayrath, M., & Zap, N. (2012). Thinking outside the bubble: Virtual performance assessments for measuring complex learning. In J. Clarke-Midura, M. Mayrath, & C. Dede (Eds.), *Technology-based assessments for 21st century skills: Theoretical and practical implications from modern research* (pp. 125–148). Charlotte, NC: Information Age.

Cogan, L. S., Wang, H. A., & Schmidt, W. H. (2001). Culturally specific patterns in the conceptualization of the school science curriculum: Insights from TIMSS. *Studies in Science Education, 36,* 105–133.

College Board. (2009). *Science: College Boards standards for college success.* Retrieved from http://professionals.collegeboard.com/prof-download/cbscs-science-standards-2009.pdf

Comber, L. C., & Keeves, J. P. (1973). *Science education in nineteen countries: An empirical study.* New York: Wiley.

Committee on Assessing Technological Literacy. (2006). *Tech tally: Approaches to assessing technological literacy.* Washington, DC: National Academies Press.

Dolan, R. P., Hall, T. E., Banerjee, M., Chun, E., & Strangman, N. (2005). Applying principles of universal design to test delivery: The effect of computer-based read-aloud on test performance of high school students with learning disabilities. *Journal of Technology, Learning & Assessment, 3*(7): 4–32.

Doran, R. L., Lawrenz, F., & Hegelson, S. (1994). Research on assessment in science. In D. L. Gabel (Ed.), *Handbook of research on science teaching and learning* (pp. 388–442). New York: Macmillan.

Gobert, J., Sao Pedro, M., Baker, R. S., Toto, E., & Montalvo, O. (2012). Leveraging educational data mining for real time performance assessment of scientific inquiry skills within microworlds. *Journal of Educational Data Mining, 4,* 153–185.

Harmon, M., Smith, T. A., Martin, M. O., Kelly, D. L., Beaton, A. E., Mullis, I. V. S., . . . Orpwood, G. (1997). *Performance assessment in IEA's Third International Mathematics and Science Study.* Chestnut Hill, MA: Center for the Study of Testing, Evaluation, and Educational Policy, Boston College.

Herman, J., Dai, Y., Htut, A. M., Martinez, M., & Rivera, N. (2010). *CRESST evaluation report: Evaluation of the Enhanced Assessment Grants (EAGs).* Los Angeles: CRESST.

Herman, J. L., & Haertel, H. (Eds.). (2005). Uses and misuses of data for educational accountability and improvement. *NSSE Yearbook, 104*(2).

Herman, J. L., Webb, N. M., & Zuniga, S. A. (2005, April). *Measurement issues in the alignment of standards and assessments: A case study.* Paper presented at the annual conference of the American Educational Research Association, Montreal, Canada.

Hudson, L. (1991). National initiatives for assessing science education. In A. Champagne, B. Lovitts, & B. Calinger (Eds.), *Assessment in the service of instruction* (p. 107). Washington, DC: American Association for the Advancement of Science.

Hutchison, D., & Schagen, I. (2006, November). *Comparisons between PISA and TIMSS: Are we the man with two watches?* Paper presented at the 2nd IEA International Research Conference, Washington, DC. Retrieved from www.iea.nl/fileadmin/user_upload/IRC/IRC_2006/Papers/IRC2006_Hutchison_Schagen.pdf

International Association for the Evaluation of Educational Achievement (IEA). (1988). *Science achievement in seventeen countries: A preliminary report* (1st ed.). Oxford, UK: Pergamon Press.

International Technology Education Association. (2000). *Standards for technological literacy: Content for the study of technology.* Reston, VA: International Technology Education Association.

Johnson, S. S. (1975). *Update on education: A digest of the National Assessment of Educational Progress.* Denver, CO: Education Commission of the States. Retrieved from www.eric.ed.gov/ERICWebPortal/detail?accno=ED113381

Keeves, J. P. (1992). *The IEA study of science III: Changes in science education and achievement, 1970 to 1984.* Oxford, UK: Pergamon Press.

Kifer, E. (2000). *Large-scale assessment: Dimensions, dilemmas, and policy.* Thousand Oaks, CA: Corwin Press.

Kimmelman, P., Kroeze, D., Schmidt, W., Van der Ploeg, A., McNeely, M., & Tan, A. (1999). *A first look at what we can learn from high performing school districts: An analysis of TIMSS data from the First in the World Consortium.* Washington, DC: National Center of Educational Statistics.

Koretz, D. (2009). How do American students measure up? Making sense of international comparisons. *Future of Children, 19*(1), 37–51.

LaPointe, A., Askew, J. M., & Mead, N. A. (1992). *Learning science.* Princeton, NJ: Educational Testing Service.

LaPointe, A., Mead, N. A., & Phillips, G. W. (1989). *A world of differences: An international assessment of mathematics and science.* Princeton, NJ: Educational Testing Service.

Linn, M. C., De Benedictis, T., Delucchi, K., Harris, A., & Stage, E. (1987). Gender differences in National Assessment of Educational Progress science items: What does "I don't know" really mean? *Journal of Research in Science Teaching, 24*(3), 267–278.

Liu, X., & Ruiz, M. E. (2008). Using data mining to predict K–12 students' performance on large-scale assessment items related to energy. *Journal of Research in Science Teaching, 45*(5), 554–573. doi:10.1002/tea.20232

Lutkus, A. D., Weiner, A. W., Daane, M. C., & Jin, Y. (2003). *The Nation's Report Card: Reading 2002, trial urban district assessment.* Washington, DC: National Center for Education Statistics. Retrieved from http://nces.ed.gov/pubsearch/pubsinfo.asp?pubid=2003523

Martin, M. O., Mullis, I. V. S., Beaton, A. E., Gonzalez, E. J., Kelly, D. L., & Smith, T. A. (1997). *Science achievement in the primary school years: IEA's Third International Mathematics and Science Study.* Chestnut Hill, MA: Center for the Study of Testing, Evaluation, and Educational Policy, Boston College.

Martin, M. O., Mullis, I. V. S., & Foy, P. (2008). *TIMSS 2007 international science report: Findings from IEA's Trends in International Mathematics and Science Study at the fourth and eighth grades.* Chestnut Hill, MA: TIMSS & PIRLS International Study Center, Boston College.

Martin, M. O., Mullis, I. V. S., Foy, P., & Stanco, G. M. (2012). *TIMSS 2011 international results in science.* Chestnut Hill, MA: TIMSS & PIRLS International Study Center, Boston College.

Martin, M. O., Mullis, I. V. S., Gonzalez, E. J., & Chrostowski, S. J. (2004). *TIMSS 2003: International science report: Findings from IEA's Trends in International Mathematics and Science Study at the fourth and eighth grades.* Chestnut Hill, MA: TIMSS & PIRLS International Study Center, Boston College.

Martin, M. O., Mullis, I. V. S., Gonzalez, E. J., Gregory, K. D., Smith, T. A., Chrostowski, S. J., … O'Connor, K. M. (2000). *TIMSS 1999: International science report: Findings from IEA's repeat of the Third International Mathematics and Science Study at the eighth grade.* Chestnut Hill, MA: International Study Center, Boston College.

Mayer, R. E., & Johnson, C. (2008). Revising the redundancy principle in multimedia learning. *Journal of Educational Psychology, 100,* 380–386.

McIntosh, S. (2012). *State high school exit exams: A policy in transition.* Washington, DC: Center on Education Policy.

McKnight, C., & Britton, E. (1992). *Methods for analyzing curricular materials.* East Lansing: Michigan State University, Survey of Mathematics and Science Opportunities, Technical Report Series.

Meade, S. D., & Dugger, W. E., Jr. (2004). Reporting on the status of technology education in the U.S. *Technology Teacher, 64*(2), 29–35.

Minnesota Department of Education. (2012). *Minnesota Comprehensive Assessments-Series III (MCA-III): Test specifications for science.* Retrieved from http://education.state.mn.us/mdeprod/idcplg?IdcService=GET_FIL E&dDocName=003177&RevisionSelectionMethod=latestReleased&Re ndition=primary

Minstrell, J. A., Anderson, R., Kraus, P., & Minstrell, J. E. (2008). Bridging from practice to research and back: Tools to support formative assessment. In J. Coffey, R. Douglas, & C. Sterns (Eds.), *Science assessment: Research and practical approaches* (pp. 39–56). Arlington, VA: NSTA Press.

More About the NAEP Technology and Engineering Literacy (TEL) Assessment. (2012). Retrieved from the National Center for Education Statistics website: http://nces.ed.gov/nationsreportcard/tel/moreabout.asp

Mullis, I. V. S., & Jenkins, L. B. (1988). *The science report card: Elements of risk and recovery. Trends and achievement based on the 1986 National Assessment.* Princeton, NJ: Educational Testing Service. Retrieved from www.eric.ed.gov/ERICWebPortal/detail?accno=ED300265

Mullis, I. V. S., Martin, M. O., Beaton, A. E., Gonzalez, E. J., Kelly, D. L., & Smith, T. A. (1998). *Mathematics and science achievement in the final year of secondary school: IEA's Third International Mathematics and Science Study.* Chestnut Hill, MA: Center for the Study of Testing, Evaluation, and Educational Policy, Boston College.

National Academy of Engineering. (2010). *Standards for K–12 engineering education?* Washington, DC: National Academies Press.

NAEP—About the District Assessment. (2012a). Retrieved from the National Center for Education Statistics website: http://nces.ed.gov/nationsreportcard/about/district.asp

NAEP—About State NAEP. (2012b). Retrieved from the National Center for Education Statistics website: http://nces.ed.gov/nationsreportcard/about/state.asp

National Assessment of Educational Progress (NAEP). (1975). *Selected results from the national assessments of science: scientific principles and procedures* (No. 04–5-02). Princeton, NJ: National Assessment of Educational Progress.

National Assessment of Educational Progress (NAEP). (1978). *The national assessment in sciences: Changes in achievement, 1969–72.* Denver, CO: Educational Commission of the States.

National Assessment of Educational Progress (NAEP). (1987). *Learning by doing—a manual for teaching and assessing higher order skills in science and mathematics* (No. 17, HOS-80). Princeton, NJ: National Assessment of Educational Progress.

National Assessment of Educational Progress (NAEP). (1992). *Trends in academic progress: Achievement of U.S. students in science 1969–70 to 1990, mathematics 1973 to 1990, reading 1971 to 1990, and writing 1984 to 1990.* Princeton, NJ: National Assessment of Educational Progress.

National Assessment Governing Board (NAGB). (2009). *Science framework for the 2009 national assessment of educational progress.* Washington, DC: Author. Retrieved from www.nagb.org/content/nagb/assets/documents/publications/frameworks/science-09.pdf

National Assessment Governing Board (NAGB). (2010). *Technology and engineering literacy framework for the 2014 National Assessment of Educational Progress: Pre-publication edition.* Retrieved from http://nagb.org/publications/frameworks.htm

National Center for Education Statistics (NCES). (1996). *Pursuing excellence: A study of U.S. eighth-grade mathematics and science teaching, learning, curriculum, and achievement in international context* (No. NCES 97–198). Washington, DC: U.S. Department of Education, National Center for Educational Statistics.

National Center for Education Statistics (NCES). (2006). *Highlights from the TIMSS 1999 video study of eighth-grade science teaching.* Washington, DC: Author.

National Center for Education Statistics (NCES). (2011). *The nation's report card: Science 2009* (No. 2011–451). Retrieved from http://nces.ed.gov/pubsearch/pubsinfo.asp?pubid=2011451

National Center for Education Statistics (NCES). (2012). *The nation's report card: Science 2011* (No. 2012–465). Retrieved from http://nces.ed.gov/pubsearch/pubsinfo.asp?pubid=2011451

National Research Council (NRC). (2011). *A framework for K–12 science education: Practices, crosscutting concepts, and core ideas.* Washington, DC: National Academies Press.

Nohara, D. (2001). *A comparison of the National Assessment of Educational Progress (NAEP), the Third International Mathematics and Science Study Repeat (TIMSS-R), and the Programme of International Student Assessment (PISA)* (Working Paper No. 2001–07). Washington, DC: National Center of Educational Statistics.

Organisation for Economic Co-operation and Development (OECD). (2001). *Knowledge and skills for life: First results from the OECD*

Programme for International Student Assessment (PISA), 2000. Education and skills. Paris: Author.

Organisation for Economic Co-operation and Development (OECD). (2003). *Literacy skills for the world of tomorrow. Further results from PISA 2000.* Paris: Author.

Organisation for Economic Co-operation and Development (OECD). (2004). *Learning for tomorrow's world: First results from PISA 2003.* Paris: Author.

Organisation for Economic Co-operation and Development (OECD). (2007a). *PISA 2006: Data* (Vol. 2). Paris: Author.

Organisation for Economic Co-operation and Development (OECD). (2007b). *PISA 2006: Science competencies for tomorrow's world* (Vol. 1). Paris: Author.

Organisation for Economic Co-operation and Development (OECD). (2010). *PISA computer-based assessment of student skills in science.* Paris: Author.

Pellegrino, J., Chudowsky, N., & Glaser, R. (2001). *Knowing what students know: The science and design of educational assessment.* Washington, DC: National Academies Press.

Phillips, G. W. (2010). *International benchmarking: State education performance standards.* Washington, DC: American Institutes for Research. Retrieved from www.air.org/files/AIR_Int_Benchmarking_State_Ed__Perf_Standards.pdf

Postlethwaite, T. N. (1995). International empirical research in comparative education: An example of the studies for the International Association for the Evaluation of Educational Achievement. *Journal für Internationale Bildungsforschung, 1*(1), 1–19.

Postlethwaite, T. N., & Wiley, D. E. (1992). *The IEA study of science II: Science achievement in twenty-three countries.* Oxford, UK: Pergamon Press.

Quellmalz, E. (2013). *Assessment of student learning in integrated science, technology, engineering, and mathematics (iSTEM).* Conference paper written at the request of the Committee on Integrated STEM Education, National Academy of Engineering, Washington, DC.

Quellmalz, E. S., DeBarger, A., Haertel, G., & Kreikemeier, P. (2005). *Validities of science inquiry assessments: Final report.* Menlo Park, CA: SRI International.

Quellmalz, E. S., Haertel, G. D., DeBarger, A., & Kreikemeier, P. (2005). *A study of evidence of the validities of assessments of science inquiry in the National Assessment of Educational Progress (NAEP), Trends in Mathematics and Science Survey (TIMSS), and the New Standards Science Reference Exam (NSSRE) in science* (Validities Technical Report no. 1). Menlo Park, CA: SRI International.

Quellmalz, E. S., & Pellegrino, J. W. (2009). Technology and testing. *Science, 323,* 75–79.

Quellmalz, E. S., Timms, M. J., Silberglitt, M. D., & Buckley, B. C. (2012). Science assessments for all: Integrating science simulations into balanced state science assessment systems. *Journal of Research in Science Teaching, 49,* 363–393. doi:10.1002/tea.21005

Raizen, S. A., & Britton, E. D. (Eds.). (1997). *Bold ventures: Patterns among innovations in science and mathematics education* (Vol. 1). Dordrecht, the Netherlands: Kluwer Academic Publishers.

Robitaille, D. F., Schmidt, W. H., Raizen, S., McKnight, C., Britton, E., & Nicol, C. (1993). *Curriculum frameworks for mathematics and science* (TIMSS Monograph No. 1.). Vancouver: Pacific Educational Press.

Rosier, M. J., & Keeves, J. P. (1991). *The IEA study of science I: Science education and curricula in twenty-three countries* (1st ed.). Oxford, UK: Pergamon Press.

Ruddock, G., Clausen-May, T., Purple, C., & Ager, R. (2006). *Validation study of the PISA 2000, PISA 2003 and TIMSS-2003 international studies of pupil attainment* (Research Report No. RR772). Retrieved from the United Kingdom Department of Education website: https://www.education.gov.uk/publications/eOrderingDownload/RR772.pdf

Schmidt, W. H., Jakwerth, P. M., & McKnight, C. C. (1998). Curriculum-sensitive assessment: Content does make a difference. *International Journal of Educational Research, 29,* 503–527.

Schmidt, W. H., McKnight, C. C., Cogan, L. S., Jakwerth, P. M., & Houang, R. T. (1999). *Facing the consequences: Using TIMSS for a closer look at U.S. mathematics and science education.* Dordrecht, the Netherlands: Kluwer Academic.

Schmidt, W. H., McKnight, C. C., Houang, R. T., Wang, H., Wiley, D. E., Cogan, L. S., & Wolfe, R. G. (2001). *Why schools matter: A cross-national comparison of curriculum and learning.* San Francisco: Jossey-Bass.

Schmidt, W. H., McKnight, C. C., & Raizen, S. (Eds.). (1997). *A splintered vision: An investigation of U.S. science and mathematics education.* New York: Springer.

Schmidt, W. H., Raizen, S., Britton, E. D., Bianchi, L. J., & Wolfe, R. G. (1997). *Many visions, many aims, volume II: A cross-national investigation of curricular intentions in school science.* Dordrecht, the Netherlands: Kluwer Academic.

Schneider, R. M., Krajcik, J., Marx, R. W., & Soloway, E. (2002). Performance of students in project-based science classrooms on a national measure of science achievement. *Journal of Research in Science Teaching, 39*(5), 410–422.

Scott, E., & Owen, E. (2005). *Brief: Comparing NAEP, TIMSS and PISA results.* Washington, DC: National Center of Educational Statistics. Retrieved from the National Center for Education Statistics website: http://nces.ed.gov/timss/pdf/naep_timss_pisa_comp.pdf

Silberglitt, M., Vineyard, R. N., King, K., & Bowler, K. (2011, June). *Balanced, multilevel science assessment systems.* Paper presented at the National Conference on Student Assessment, Orlando, FL.

Stevenson, H. W. (1998). A study of three cultures. *Phi Delta Kappan, 79*(7), 524–529.

Stigler, J. W., Gonzales, P., Kwanaka, T., Knoll, S., & Serrano, A. (1999). *The TIMSS videotape classroom study: Methods and findings from an exploratory research project on eighth-grade mathematics instruction in Germany, Japan, and the United States* (No. NCES 99–074). Washington, DC: U.S. Department of Education, National Center for Educational Statistics.

Tamir, P. (1988). Assessment and evaluation in science education: Opportunities to learn and outcomes. In B. J. Fraser & K. G. Tobin (Eds.), *International handbook of science education* (pp. 761–789). London: Kluwer Academic.

Travers, K. J., & Westbury, I. (1988). *The IEA study of mathematics I: Analysis of mathematics curricula* (Vol. 1). Oxford, UK: Pergamon Press.

Valverde, G. A., & Schmidt, W. H. (2000). Greater expectations: Learning from other nations in the quest for "world-class standards" in US school mathematics and science. *Journal of Curriculum Studies, 32*(5), 651–687.

Vinovskis, M. A. (1998). *Overseeing the Nation's Report Card: The creation and evolution of the National Assessment Governing Board (NAGB).* Retrieved from www.nagb.org/content/nagb/assets/documents/publications/95222.pdf

Von Secker, C. (2004). Science achievement in social contexts: Analysis from National Assessment of Educational Progress. *Journal of Educational Research, 98*(2), 67–78.

Wang, J. (1998). Comparative study of student science achievement between United States and China. *Journal of Research in Science Teaching, 35*(3), 329–336.

Welch, W. W., Huffman, D., & Lawrenz, F. (1998). The precision of data obtained in large-scale science assessments: An investigation of bootstrapping and half-sample replication methods. *Journal of Research in Science Teaching, 3,* 697–704.

Welch, W. W., Walberg, H. J., & Fraser, B. J. (1986). Predicting elementary science learning using national assessment data. *Journal of Research in Science Teaching, 23*(8), 699–706.

Wiley, D. E., & Wolfe, R. G. (1992). Major survey design issues for the IEA Third International Mathematics and Science Study. *Prospects, 22*(3), 297–304.

Wilson, M. R., & Bertenthal, M. W. (Eds.). (2005). *Systems for state science assessment.* Washington, DC: National Academies Press.

Yee, L., de Lange, J., & Schmidt, W. (2006). PISA: Promises, problems and possibilities. In M. Sanz-Solé, J. Soria, J. L. Varona, & J. Verdera (Eds.), *Proceedings of the International Congress of Mathematicians Vol. III* (pp. 1668–1672). Available at www.icm2006.org/proceedings/Vol_III/contents/ICM_Vol_3_80.pdf

Section VI

Science Teacher Education

Section Editor: J. John Loughran

40

Developing Understandings of Practice

Science Teacher Learning

J. John Loughran

[W]e have seen the evolution of teacher development from being seen as a curriculum problem (1920s–1950s) to a training problem (1960s–1980s) to a learning problem (1980s–2000s) to a policy problem (1990s to present) . . . there has also been a developing interest in the nexus between student learning and teacher learning . . . and the notion of teaching as a learning profession.

(Wallace & Loughran, 2012, p. 295)

Understanding how teaching has historically been positioned and repositioned is important when considering the notion of teacher learning. As the literature demonstrates, perceptions of teaching have consistently been challenged as the needs of and expectations for education have changed over time. Inevitably, those changes have impacted notions of the "development of professional practice" and so have been important in shaping not only what teachers do but also how they have been viewed as learners of teaching. As is clearly evident, there has been a major shift in views of teacher learning from a developmental model to those that align more closely with a professional learning model in which teachers are viewed as having more autonomy over their learning, and so are expected to be more responsible, informed, and active in relation to the development of their knowledge as professionals.

The development model began to be seriously challenged in the 1980s as research on teacher thinking (Clark & Peterson, 1986) became more prominent. The teacher thinking research drew attention to the complexity of teaching and, in so doing, questioned the nature of knowledge of teaching which, to that time, was largely based on studies by observers of practice with limited involvement from those actually responsible for that practice. At the same time as the teacher thinking research began to create new avenues of inquiry into practice, so too reflection re-emerged through the efforts of Donald Schön (1983, 1987) which immediately resonated with the teacher education community, igniting a great deal of interest and

further challenging traditional notions of learning to teach (Clift, Houston, & Pugach, 1990; Grimmett & Erickson, 1988). As new methods of research created new avenues for unpacking the complexity of teaching, teachers themselves became more actively involved in the process, and the teacher researcher movement (Cochran-Smith & Lytle, 1993) began to create a space for itself in the work of the academy.

At the same time as understandings of teaching evolved, so too the same was evident in views of school learning. As suggested by Clarke and Erickson (2004), constructivism reflected a shift in views of the nature of learning from a predominantly behaviorist model to more cognitivist and phenomenological models. In many ways, this coming together of developing views of teaching and learning created a situation through which transmissive teaching came under sustained scrutiny. As classroom teaching and learning attracted more and more attention (both from within and outside the profession), so too the notion of teacher learning came to the fore as expectations of that which comprised quality and expertise in (science) teaching and learning grew in importance.

The very use of the term "science teacher learning" (or "science teacher as learner") captures the essence of the hopes and expectations that science teaching as telling—transmissive practice—might be seriously challenged in ways that might prevent it from occurring in classrooms as a default teaching approach. The language of science teacher learning/science teacher as learner implies that quality practice is embedded in a science teacher's commitment to teaching for understanding in contrast to the delivery of propositional knowledge for students to absorb. Therefore, the very language of science teacher learning purposefully links expectations that it is not just students but also teachers who are active learners of science, congruent with the ideas of constructivism. As a consequence, developments pertaining to the nature of teaching and learning have combined in important ways to shape understandings of science practice—and are now reflected in the notion of teacher learning. The literature review that follows is based on this view of teacher learning/ teacher as learner through which teacher development and growth is a professional characteristic and is indicative of how the descriptor has come to characterize and impact science teachers' learning experiences.

Structure and Overview

The structure of this chapter is based around four areas in which science teaching is commonly conducted and, as such, influences the nature of school science: (1) preservice science teacher learning, (2) elementary science teacher learning, (3) secondary science teacher learning, and (4) science teacher educator learning. In the years since the last *Handbook of Science Education* (Abell & Lederman, 2007), in which "Science Teacher as Learner" was documented, the literature has expanded considerably. The literature now more fully demonstrates how science teacher learning has developed as a field by responding to the change in demands, expectations, and perceptions of the profession. In particular, the recent literature also illustrates a renewed emphasis on topics such as pedagogical content knowledge (PCK), reflective practice, and teachers' beliefs and practices, each of which is considered within the four major themes of teacher learning that serve as the structure for this chapter. The way in which the literature is organized and presented throughout the chapter is based not only on what the learning is but also how it was developed in order to open up for scrutiny what science teacher learning entails and how that learning might influence understandings of knowledge and practice as a science teacher.

Preservice Science Teacher Learning

It has long been recognized that student teachers' experiences of school science have a major impact on their expectations for and approaches to learning to teach. Lortie (1975) described the *Apprenticeship of Observation* as a powerful influence on students' perceptions of teaching, and there is little doubt that those experiences shape what a student teacher thinks it means to do teaching. Therefore, a great challenge for teacher education programs is to help student teachers see beyond their own experiences of teaching and find new ways to engage them in conceptualizing practice as something more than how they themselves were taught. Sarason (1990) noted the difficulty of seeing teaching as something more than that which individuals experienced as school students, so seeing beyond the "script" of their own classroom experiences is a major issue.

Despite the best efforts and intentions of all involved in the enterprise of teacher education, student teachers find it difficult to move beyond that which they have experienced, are comfortable with, and have been successful at

as students (Richardson, 1996). Thus student teachers may be inadvertently and subconsciously resistant to adopting approaches to teaching that are different from that which they experienced as students. Clearly, such a situation has a major impact on student teachers' developing views of science teaching and goes to the heart of what it means to challenge taken-for-granted assumptions and the deeply held beliefs of teaching that Pajares (1992) described as so difficult to change.

Much of the research into the relationship between beliefs and practice has highlighted the importance and value in challenging beliefs in productive ways in order to help restructure understandings of both learning and teaching (Bandura, 1986; Hashweh, 1996). Yet such challenges are central to creating an impetus for reconsidering and thus changing practice. Although challenging beliefs has been a common beginning point for attempting to reshape student teachers' views of and approaches to practice, detailed examples of preservice science teacher learning are not overly abundant in the research literature. Interestingly, with the development of self-study of teacher education practices (S-STEP), more attention has begun to be paid to ways of engaging student teachers in approaches to confronting their issues and concerns in order to open up new avenues for understanding how challenging existing beliefs can lead to new outcomes in science teacher education (Bullock, 2011). It is within the nature of the challenge to beliefs that change might be enacted; therefore, documenting and articulating such approaches might not only demonstrate how that might be facilitated but also what might be learned as a consequence.

Alternative Conceptions: Issues of Change

In a paper titled "Prognosis for Misconceptions Research," Settlage and Goldston (2007) offered a succinct and interesting study into the impact of alternative/misconceptions research. They highlighted how, in teacher education, it was important for student teachers to be confronted by their own misconceptions and for them to abstract from that what it might mean for science teaching and learning as a beginning science teacher because of the need to

> prepare teachers to challenge Rousseau's tabula rasa, reminding them that the learner's mind is not a blank slate; rather it is full of logical, systematically used ideas about the natural world and how it works that can pose barriers to learning science.
>
> (p. 798)

As they made clear, such understandings about misconceptions are built on research into children's science and conceptual change (Driver, Guesne, & Tiberghien, 1985; Hewson, Beeth, & Thorley, 1998; Osborne & Freyburg, 1985), which has, in one way or another, illustrated the value to learners in experiencing cognitive dissonance so that their existing conceptions might be not only personally apprehended but also restructured as a result of the experience. As the literature more than demonstrates, preservice science teachers' learning about teaching is clearly enhanced when they are confronted by situations in which their existing conceptions are challenged by situations that cause them to reconsider what they know and how they act (Pringle, 2006; Stump, 2010; Uzuntiryaki, Boz, & Kirbulut, 2010).

There are some who have argued that it is not clear whether eliciting students' alternative conceptions is an obstacle or a resource in relation to learning about science. However, Larkin (2012), in a study with preservice science student teachers, found that his participants saw value for their developing practice through an increased awareness and recognition of students' ideas. As a consequence, they also began to see how their beliefs about how learning occurs similarly impacted their understandings of practice. When they were confronted by alternative perspectives and saw into the dissonance of such situations, genuine learning resulted. Larkin's (2012) conclusions support the work of many others who have studied changes in conceptions and beliefs of prospective teachers. Such studies continually show how prospective science teachers see value for their learning through a focus on the notion of dissonance. However, dissonance alone is not sufficient to cause a change in thinking or views about science teaching and learning because the "apparent stability of misconceptions presents many challenges to teachers" (Burgoon, Heddle, & Duran, 2011, p. 102).

Isabelle and de Groot (2008) studied the use of the Itakura Method (hypothesis-experiment-instruction) with preservice elementary teachers ($N = 38$) and found statistically significant gains in their learning and retention as recorded in follow-up testing 1, 2, and 3 months after being taught through that method. Their findings are interesting, as it is not uncommon for student teachers to be aware of students' misconceptions but to have little understanding of how they develop or how to teach in ways that might address them (Gomez-Zwiep, 2008). Therefore, being placed in a learning situation that seriously influences understanding of scientific phenomena in meaningful ways offers insights into science teaching and learning that should not be ignored.

In studying dissonance, Dana and colleagues (1988) also highlighted the value of creating a *need to know* for student teachers. In so doing, they found that their participants were encouraged to reconsider the teacher-as-teller role, particularly when confronted by unanticipated classroom situations. Instances of how they were confronted by and responded to challenging situations offered insights into reasons for change in their views of teaching and learning that subsequently led to changes in practice. The teacher preparation program in which the study was conducted purposely created opportunities for student teacher participants to confront their taken-for-granted assumptions of teaching and learning, leading to a recognition that the "learning to teach process is generative" (p. 14).

At the heart of all of these studies is an implicit recognition that changing learners' conceptions involves much more than simple replacement; dissatisfaction alone

is not sufficient for reconstructing students' conceptual frameworks. Students tend to cling to their own conceptions even after experiencing events that directly challenge those conceptions . . . a new conception [needs to] be presented that the students see as intelligible, plausible, and fruitful.

(Burgoon et al., 2011, pp. 102–103)

One way of exploring such thinking is evident in many ways through the notion of pedagogical content knowledge (PCK; Shulman, 1986).

Pedagogical Content Knowledge: Learning About Teaching Science

Despite the diversity of interpretations and definitions of PCK that exist in the literature (Abell, 2008), PCK has been studied in considerable detail in preservice science education programs. It has been seen as one way of helping beginning science teachers see much more deeply into what it takes to teach science and how a vision for their ongoing professional learning might be viewed. In many ways, studies of PCK in preservice teacher education programs are indicative of the development of approaches to teaching and learning about science that build on the early work of the alternative conceptions research; it takes that learning and places it in the context of teaching.

Nilsson and Loughran (2012) used PCK as a focus for learning about teaching science and illustrated how instructive such an approach can be for student teachers. Nilsson's intensive efforts with her elementary student teachers show that by using PCK as a guide for what it means to develop knowledge of practice, student teachers begin to see beyond the technical-rational aspects of learning to teach. Using a pre- and posttest approach to studying the development of PCK, she was able to demonstrate that participants not only valued the development of a deeper thinking and questioning approach to teaching science, but they also became much more confident in confronting difficult aspects of practice that they previously either did not recognize or chose to avoid. However, research of this nature is highly dependent on listening carefully to and documenting student teachers' needs, issues, and concerns in learning about teaching science.

Van Driel and colleagues' (2002) investigation of preservice chemistry teachers' PCK is a case in point whereby the importance of listening to students created possibilities not only for recognizing but also responding to differences between beliefs and practices. Their participants learned a great deal by observing lessons taught by their mentor or peer, explaining that, "observing the students' responses to another teacher's approach had facilitated her understanding of students' learning difficulties much more than teaching her own lessons" (Van Driel et al., 2002, p. 583). In a similar vein, in working with student teachers on the particle model, De Jong and colleagues (2005) highlighted how their participants learned to see beyond recognizable issues in working with models to valuing the need to develop their teaching with models in order to better address their students' learning difficulties. Each of these studies highlights the place of experience in catalyzing participants' approaches to developing deeper understandings of their own practice and how listening to others' learning is instructive to learning about one's own practice.

As Lee and colleagues (2007) explained, experience helps beginning teachers become more aware of their learners' needs such that as their knowledge of learners increases, so too does their desire to respond in ways that further inform them about student learning. As a consequence, their knowledge of student learning is very closely tied to their ongoing development of instructional strategies. This point is clear in studies of both mathematics and science teacher education (Vail Lowery, 2002) and is strongly reinforced by an extensive study of one elementary teacher over a 10-year period by Mulholland and Wallace (2005) that offered insights into the development of a teacher's PCK over time. They do so using a tree metaphor as they illustrate how the initial (science) content knowledge base is shaped through experience to more fully encompass in-depth knowledge of student learning in concert with enhanced knowledge of practice, which they describe as an all-embracing view of PCK, something heavily dependent on learning through experience.

Veal (1999), another researcher interested in the PCK of preservice science teachers, also paid careful attention to student teachers' voices. Veal's participants questioned the use of language as an important shaping force in the implicit messages of teaching about science in ways that they had not previously recognized in their own learning of science. They also responded to their own sense of dissonance when confronted by difficulties in (re)learning chemistry and physics and began to make meaningful links to the ways in which they might then teach those concepts themselves. For example, one student teacher (Randi), in responding to a consideration of the abstract nature of chemistry, focused attention on the importance of concrete representations—a learning breakthrough that impacted Randi's view of teaching. However, Veal made clear that just because student teachers recognized the need for particular approaches to practice, it did not necessarily follow that changes were automatically implemented. This point is a reminder of the interplay between beliefs and practice and the role of dissonance as a catalyst for meaningful learning from experience for student teachers. He also noted how the influence of classroom teaching experience and participants' interactions with students tended to raise new issues for teaching and learning that could only really be apprehended through the experiences of student teachers. Therefore, Veal further supported the view that, to encourage student teachers' learning, their existing belief structures need to be sufficiently (and consistently) challenged in ways that will cause them to reconsider their taken-for-granted assumptions of science teaching and learning. Such challenges can be supported by placing them in positions where, for example, they need to

adapt and develop curriculum materials (Beyer & Davis, 2012), consider approaches to formative assessment (Falk, 2012), or teach using information and communications technology (ICT) (Angeli & Valanides, 2005). Regardless of approach, there is a constant sense of optimism in the literature about the nature of student teachers' learning about practice:

> The beginning teachers with whom we work do move beyond a focus on engaging, managing, and/or motivating their students, toward prioritizing learning goals . . . most do develop some PCK readiness while they are in our classes, and some . . . reflect sophisticated expertise with regard to finding out and working with their students' ideas.
>
> (Davis & Smithey, 2009, p. 764)

Learning Through Inquiry

The preservice education literature illustrates that inquiry-based teaching offers further possibilities for challenging student teachers' existing views and beliefs about teaching and learning science (Forbes, 2011). Duncan and colleagues (2010), for example, in researching student teachers' learning about implementing inquiry-based instruction, demonstrated that although it was a formidable learning task, their ability to critique their lesson plans became increasingly sophisticated over time. That finding is similarly supported by studies into student teachers' working with narratives of inquiry-based teaching in which their reflections on vignettes of practice were shown to be educative and helpful in shaping their developing PCK (Dietz & Davis, 2009). Further to this, through studying field-based experiences involving an inquiry approach, Bhattacharyya and colleagues (2009) highlighted how student teachers' personal agency beliefs were enhanced.

A cohering theme to all of these studies, however, is the problematic nature of the practicum, something that has been shown to be exacerbated by such things as associate teacher subjugation, availability of resources, time constraints, and the need to address curriculum standards (Fazio, Melville, & Bartley, 2010). More so, the complexity of learning about science teaching often means that student teachers need help and direction in developing and maintaining a concentrated and focused approach to their own learning intentions. In an in-depth study of teaching photosynthesis, it was shown that student teachers found it difficult to learn about teaching through an inquiry-based approach and to address alternative conceptions at the same time (Gunckel, 2011). Gunckel's findings have a bearing on understanding the multifaceted learning needs of preservice teachers and offer a reminder that not all inquiry is successful (Lustick, 2009).

In offering advice on learning to teach through standards, Allan and colleagues (2009) explored the complexity of learning about ethical and legal responsibilities in concert with safety in science. As a paper framed around advice, it has little to suggest about how student teachers learn when focused on managing the complexity of classroom practice. Clearly, alignment of theory and practice is not always deeply congruent when it comes to learning outcomes: "NSES (NRC, 1996) and *Science for All Americans* (AAAS, 1990) indicate . . . teaching and learning of science must go far beyond the simple transmittal of scientific facts, figures and processes" (Akcay & Yager, 2010, p. 644). Obviously it is challenging for student teachers to manage their learning at the same time as being expected to put that learning into practice.

Wagler (2010) makes a productive suggestion for another way of thinking about shaping student teacher learning with regard to standards. He advocates the use of well-constructed cases in teacher preparation programs because

> It is important to remember these processes [Standards] should not be interpreted as rigid, step-by-step formula, or single 'scientific method' . . . just as scientific inquiry processes used in studies conducted by professional scientists takes many forms, so too, the scientific studies children perform in their classrooms should take many forms.
>
> (p. 216)

His view is that cases allow student teachers to reflect upon and work with the ideas (in the cases) in ways that are not so readily available when working in the moment in a classroom, such that cases offer a vicarious experience with which they can identify. In so doing, he suggests that student teachers can learn about, reconsider, and factor into their practice what it might mean to use standards as a productive way of envisioning their overall teaching and learning expectations and goals, all of which is important in developing their confidence and ability to deal with science concepts and ideas in challenging and engaging ways (Gunning & Mensah, 2011; Howitt, 2007).

The Place of Experience in Learning to Teach Science

In conceptualizing learning about science teaching through reflection on experience, Eick and Dias (2005) constructed a community of practice using coteaching as a mechanism for supporting student teachers in building what Munby and Russell (1994) described as student teachers' *authority of experience*. Eick and Dias's (2005) study made clear how, through appropriate mechanisms, structures, opportunities and genuine mentor support, student teachers learned about practice in ways that impacted their teaching.

Munby and Russell's (1994) research into the authority of experience was driven by a desire to explicitly develop student teachers as learners through helping them to maintain a sustained concentration on and analysis of *their* teaching experiences. Two very strong examples of the impact of that work are in the work of Featherstone, Munby, and Russell (1997) and Bullock (Russell & Bullock, 1999) who, when they were student teachers, placed the authority of experience at the center of their learning

about teaching. Featherstone made clear how his views changed as he gathered feedback from his students about their learning and how he purposefully listened to his students to understand their perspectives on their learning. As a consequence, he worked to better align his teaching and learning intents so that what he was trying to do in the classroom was more closely allied with his actual practice. Following a series of lessons on "natural succession," he noted that

> I have been reminded just how important it is that one does not underestimate the value of creating a forum for listening to students' voices . . . there is something special about being able to say that my decision [about developing his teaching] is based on what I have learned from my students.
>
> (p. 136)

Bullock, another of Russell's student teachers, spent considerable time thinking about the differences between his views of science learning and his actual science teaching. Bullock was encouraged to take risks in his practice, and although his instincts told him to act differently, he soon experienced the value in allowing his students to explore science for themselves rather than being told about science by their teacher. His learning was important in shaping his ongoing approach to teaching, as it taught him to approach his students' learning from the basis of "experience first"; he learned to create experiences that invited his students to learn more meaningfully about science.

> [A]s educators [we] should remember that although it is apparent to us that, say, all objects undergo the same acceleration due to gravity near the Earth's surface, it remains a mystery to most high school students. "Experience first" allows people to discover science rather than be information sponges.
>
> (Bullock in Russell & Bullock, 1999, p. 137)

Eick (Eick & Dias, 2005; Eick, Ware, & Jones, 2004) pursued deeper understandings of the learning of student teachers through coteaching in a community of practice and illustrated the power of learning when reflection on experience is used as a productive way of catalyzing change. His work illustrates how important experience is in learning and how student teachers need real opportunities to learn from these experiences, not to just have experiences.

For a considerable period of time, there have been calls for teacher education programs to focus more on subject-specific pedagogy (Lederman, Gess-Newsome, & Latz, 1994). The outcomes of the student teacher learning research of Featherstone and Bullock most certainly highlight how their learning about teaching was deeply embedded in the subject matter knowledge they were teaching. As Eick and Dias (among others) have also demonstrated, preservice science teacher learning is considerably enhanced when teacher educators create conditions for effective reflective practice (Loughran, 2002). In so doing, student teachers are able to make their own decisions about that which is intelligible, plausible, and fruitful (Posner, Strike, Hewson, & Gertzog, 1982) and can therefore help build their own conceptual development in ways that make a difference for their practice. In genuinely focusing on learning about practice, student teachers are better able to see the value in attempting to align their learning with their actions in classrooms. As this section of the chapter more than demonstrates, when student teachers are given real opportunities to direct their own learning, the outcomes are very positive. That same lesson equally applies to experienced teachers.

Elementary Science Teacher Learning

It has been very well documented that elementary teachers' science knowledge base is not sufficiently deep or comprehensive (Appleton, 1992; Carr & Symington, 1991; Skamp, 1991). As a consequence, it is commonly suggested that the solution to the problem is to increase their science content knowledge. However, this solution is often misconstrued as a proxy for improving their science teaching more generally. Increasingly, that interpretation has been challenged (Bennett, Summers, & Askew, 1994).

Numerous studies have illustrated that addressing any one factor alone does not lead to enhanced confidence in the practice of elementary science teaching (Howitt, 2007; Ireland, Watters, Brownlee, & Lupton, 2012; Kang, 2007; Roychoudhury & Rice, 2010), but research into well-designed professional development programs demonstrates that participants' understanding of science concepts can be substantially enhanced.

Schibeci and Hickey (2000) took exception to the notion that increasing elementary teachers' science content knowledge was a panacea. They made their feelings known when they stated that "there is no place, in our view, for a 'cognitive deficit' model in providing assistance to elementary teachers to improve their content backgrounds" (p. 1168). Their view in this regard was linked to their experience in the development and delivery of professional development programs aimed at helping elementary science teachers become meaningful learners of science. Their combined experience as professional developers and researchers into elementary science education led them to conclude that genuine change was dependent on three salient dimensions: a scientific dimension—to promote change in teachers' concepts and support development of more sophisticated ideas, theories, and principles; a professional dimension—based on content to be taught in elementary classes, thus having high relevance and purpose to teachers; and a personal dimension—related to everyday life, providing a motivation for teachers to learn and understand.

Schibeci and Hickey (2000) concluded that content alone did not lead to more effective teaching of science in elementary classrooms. In fact, studies based on the nature of science (Posnanski, 2010), perceived roles and responsibilities (Smith & Jang, 2011), administrators' expectations (Milner, Sondergeld, Demir, Johnson, & Czerniak, 2012), and language (Vikström, 2008)—to name but a few—similarly highlight a diversity of issues that impact elementary teachers' science practice that are not necessarily solely subject matter knowledge based. Despite outcomes of this kind, the scientific dimension persists as the stereotypical response to concerns about science teaching and learning in elementary classrooms. The "content hurdle" can become an excuse for a lack of change in practice. In contrast, Appleton (Appleton, 2008; Koch & Appleton, 2007) studied mentoring as an approach to professional development to support change in elementary teachers' views of and practice in science teaching, while Solomon and Tresman (1999) advocated a model of professional development designed to support elementary teachers' identity formation and professional judgment:

> To be a professional is to hold values about the teaching to be done that transcend, but also inform the detailed items of daily practice . . . teaching is a kind of professional action that has to be built upon values, beliefs and knowledge. We also know that it is reflection on this action that slowly constructs a self-image based on reconstructions of previous episodes.
>
> (Solomon and Tresman, 1999, p. 315)

As these studies suggest, approaches to professional development that move beyond subject matter knowledge "upskilling" (or as Schibeci and Hickey, 2000, described it, the scientific dimension) appear to offer ways of supporting ongoing teacher change. However, to more fully respond to the myriad issues that lie at the heart of Schibeci and Hickey's (2000) other two dimensions—the professional and the personal—requires understanding barriers to change in ways that go beyond the "content excuse" in more sophisticated ways.

Seeing Beyond Activities That Work

In an interesting view of elementary teachers' need to engage students in science, Appleton (Appleton & Kindt, 2002) suggested that the overwhelming need for "science activities that work" can actually confound deeper understandings of the nature of classroom learning. Appleton explained how science content could be perceived as being well taught from a teacher's perspective if the activities used were viewed as being fun, hands on, and/or thematically developed. An extension of that perspective is that such measures of success similarly created greater confidence in teaching science but, paradoxically, might not really be developing students' understanding of the science concepts being explored through those activities.

Appleton's suggestion of the need to go beyond "activities that work" places a greater emphasis on the notion of science teachers as learners because it implies a need for them to learn to look below the surface of a busy classroom and to "unpack" the learning that is (or is not) occurring. How that might happen has been explored in a variety of ways.

Geddis (1996), in working with two experienced elementary teachers as they attempted to make science a more significant part of their teaching, drew attention to the fact that a concentration on teaching science disrupted their views of themselves as teachers. As was clearly the case with the research on student teachers in the previous section of this chapter, being confronted by an issue or creating a sense of dissonance is a meaningful way of encouraging a teacher to look again at what is happening in a pedagogical encounter.

Geddis's research involved two case studies conceptualized around Schön's (1983) notions of reflection on and reflection in action as well as that of reframing. His case studies demonstrated that his participants' actions created a sense of unease for them when "intervening in [their] students' learning" (p. 263). However, despite that unease, they viewed their interventions as necessary in order to pedagogically address their students' alternative conceptions.

Geddis's (1996) case studies highlighted how his participants constructed their identity, something that was largely based around "a variety of slogans whose central message is essentially, I teach *children, not subjects*" (p. 264). In beginning to see beyond activities that work, these elementary teachers' views of themselves as teachers, or their professional identities, were challenged and created an impetus for personal and professional change. Despite their efforts being framed by science subject matter knowledge, their learning outcomes extend beyond subject matter knowledge alone.

Geddis's participants' experiences of being confronted anew by their own practices harks back to the place of reflection as a catalyst for personal and professional change in ways advocated by researchers such as Russell (2000), Korthagen (1992), and Clarke (1994), something that has recently been revisited by Wieringa (2011) in the context of educational design. Building on the reflective processes to maintain productive pedagogical development, however, requires substantial support. Such support has been shown to be facilitated through the work of communities of practice (Wenger, 1998).

Communities of Practice: Supporting Learning

Putnam and Borko (1997) strongly argued that cognition and learning are, by nature, social, and so interactions with others are crucial not only to what is learned but also how that learning takes place. Their interest in professional development led them to a call for more sustained research into uncovering the elements that encourage teachers to change their practices and, more particularly, into the nature of teacher learning. Not surprisingly, such a call is closely tied to the need for understanding support structures for meaningful professional development, and so communities of practice (CoP) come to the fore in the research literature.

Fleer and Grace (2003) responded to this call through their study of a CoP. Their research highlighted the professional and personal dimensions of learning about practice, the subsequent changes in actions, and the ways in which they blossomed as a result of the collegial leadership available through the CoP. Their study illustrated how students' science experiences were deliberately broadened as more teachers joined in their quest for learning. By centering on children and their learning, participating teachers were drawn into an evolving community of science practice that reinforced and encouraged a teacher-as-learner stance. Interestingly, as the study was situated in an elementary setting, the integrated curriculum approach (so common in elementary schools) meant that approaches to science were holistic rather than focused solely on the science itself.

In a similar way, a CoP approach has been shown to make a major difference in the development of teaching for scientific literacy (Loughran, Smith, & Berry, 2011). The development of a CoP within an elementary school (as a consequence of that which participants described as professional development that fundamentally changed their views of science teaching and learning) led participants to elect to collaborate over a 2-year period to develop science literacy in their classes in an integrated and holistic fashion. Their CoP was based on trust, respect, and listening carefully to one another:

> To develop professional self-awareness requires trust and strong personal relationships . . . we spent a great deal of time listening . . . we deliberately attempted to encourage teachers to talk and take ownership of the planning process rather than sitting passively and expecting to have their problems solved.
>
> (Smith, 2011, p. 27)

A focus on the CoP as a unit of study frames the learning in terms of the social interactions and the communal support crucial to supporting learning and change. A very strong example of that research focus is evident in the study by Akerson and colleagues (2009). They were interested in working with elementary teachers to examine their developing understandings and practices of the nature of science (NoS). By situating their study within a CoP, they were able to develop what Wenger (1998) described as a shared repertoire built on mutual engagement in a joint enterprise by sharing knowledge, learning experiences, as well as resources and activities that were modeled for participants. Their research found that the interactions in the CoP reinforced changes in practice that were being modeled and encouraged through the associated professional development program. They also found that teachers more readily recognized and responded to NoS "teachable moments" and were excited to share their stories and experiences with one another about their learning.

> [T]he CoP provided a supportive element . . . many teachers stated how much they appreciated the ideas generated by the group and how critical this support was in helping

them grow as science teachers . . . As their knowledge increased, the teachers knew what questions to ask and how to make the change in their instruction . . . The CoP . . . provided a safe environment for teachers to verbalize their learning process and their internal struggles with new conceptions of how science works . . . Through the discussions teachers were able to identify elements of NOS embedded in their inquiries, and plan for teaching NOS to their students.

(Akerson, Cullen, & Hanson, 2009, p. 1110)

Secondary Science Teacher Learning

As the literature more than makes clear, preservice teacher education is a beginning, not an end unto itself (Northfield & Gunstone, 1997; Ritter, 2009). Therefore, what it means to begin a career as a science teacher is obviously different from what it means to be an experienced science teacher; the difference between them clearly has implications in terms of the nature of learning.

Within the literature, it is common for beginning teachers to be categorized according to the number of years they have been in the profession. The first 5 years of teaching are commonly considered to encompass the notion of beginning. Yet beginning does not necessarily need to be linked to time in the job. Studies by White, Russell, and Gunstone (2002) as well as Lockard (1993) illustrate how, in changing teaching allocations (i.e., teaching unfamiliar content or year levels) and, more particularly, when changing schools, experienced science teachers may be challenged in ways that are not all that different from being beginning science teachers again. With that caveat in place, the following section examines beginning science teachers' learning as captured through studies in which beginning is about the first few years in the profession.

Learning as a Beginning Science Teacher

Beginning teaching is challenging. Novice teachers are confronted by an array of situations, needs, and requirements, most of which they have little experience in navigating. There have been numerous studies into the issues associated with beginning science teaching (see, for example, Bianchini, Johnston, Oram, & Cavazos, 2003; Koballa, Glynn, & Upson, 2005; Luft et al., 2011), and at the heart of most is a recognition of the challenges associated with moving from being a preservice teacher to a beginning teacher. As Adams and Krockover (1997) illustrated in their research into that transition, reflection is a crucial component in learning about science teaching, especially in terms of moving from transmissive teaching to more student-centered approaches. In that shift, it also appears as though the seeds of PCK begin to be recognized as beginning science teachers search for a better alignment of their teaching and learning (Loughran, 1994).

In a year-long study of four new high school biology teachers, Carlsen (1991) attempted to quantify subject matter knowledge and how that knowledge affected novices' teaching. Carlsen's study offered insights into

the difficulties of coming to learn about teaching while at the same time learning about the "social and institutional concerns" of the workplace that actually "act[ed] at cross-purposes [to] goals like promoting inquiry through discourse" (p. 646). Inevitably, then, what Carlsen recognized as a sense of contradiction not only unsettled beginning teachers' developing understanding of their work but also impacted their approach to teaching. Munby, Cunningham, and Lock (2000), in a case study of a Year 9 science teacher, further highlighted the contradictions inherent in learning about "the system" and "learning about teaching" and described barriers that emerged as a consequence that limited opportunities for developing professional knowledge.

As longitudinal studies into the transition from student teacher to beginning teacher consistently demonstrate, managing the competing demands of the workplace as a whole in concert with developing more sophisticated approaches to and understandings of science teaching and learning is not easy. An excellent example of that transition appears in a study by Trumbull (1999) in which six beginning biology teachers' experiences are brought to life to give real access to their feelings, issues, concerns, and learning challenges. Trumbull (1999) followed her student teachers through their teacher preparation program and out into their first 3 years of teaching science. Based on extensive interview data, each teacher's story of her or his development and learning over time was told in ways that highlighted a number of issues across the cohort, which included:

- the contradiction between teaching for understanding and teaching to pass examinations
- the importance of a personal connection to content and how that helped in responding to the unexpected in classroom episodes
- coming to understand how taking risks in teaching requires a confidence to confront uncomfortable situations (for both teacher and learner)
- the challenges associated with learning how to support students to become more independent and responsible learners
- the frustration inherent in the perceived need to "cover the content" as opposed to learning concepts in depth

Across each of the case studies, one theme stands out above all others: that in beginning teaching, an awareness develops that content knowledge alone is not sufficient for good teaching. A strong content knowledge base is important, but in developing and refining practice, in becoming more understanding about the teaching–learning relationship, being more informed about and skillful in influencing student learning is crucial, and it is a steep learning curve.

The transition from preservice to inservice education has been described as an induction phase through which coming to understand the realities of science teaching not only becomes clearer to a teacher but also creates problems—some of which are not overcome. For example, as Anderson and Mitchener explained (1994), beginning teachers are confronted by the isolated nature of teaching, the abrupt nature of the transition into teaching, the well-recognized attrition rate of beginning teachers, and the personal and professional well-being struggles associated with being a beginning teacher. Across the literature on learning as a beginning science teacher, the transition into teaching (induction phase) challenges teachers to take seriously the issues by which they are confronted and to actively engage in responding in order to grow and develop as professionals. If that challenge is not accepted, then they very easily become another statistic that accounts for the well-documented attrition rate in the first 5 years of teaching.

Successfully traversing the terrain that encompasses the induction phase requires sharing of learning and serious mentoring by experienced colleagues so that professionalization rather than socialization is encouraged (Zeichner & Gore, 1990). That mentoring is most commonly successful when a "science teacher as learner" approach is modeled by experienced colleagues. Ensuring that approach is more often than not the norm of what matters for the teaching profession more generally (Wei, Darling-Hammond, Andree, Richardson, & Orphanos, 2009).

Experienced Science Teachers' Learning

The last decade of the last century marked a shift in the nature of research in science education and is documented in Klopfer's (1991) *A Summary of Science Education—1989*, which noted, to that point in time, that science education research was largely instrumental and generally involved studies that worked on teachers rather than with teachers. However, one of the major issues that began to emerge and that mirrored much of the research in teaching more generally was associated with the fact that "some researchers found that teachers had difficulty translating their knowledge into practice or that teachers believed that they had implemented more good practice into their classroom than observations supported" (p. 352). Klopfer's first point links to Polanyi's (1966) view about the tacit nature of teachers' knowledge. There have been many debates about what teachers' knowledge might look like and how it might be translated into practice, but typically the tacit nature of teachers' knowledge and how crucial it is that that knowledge be made explicit persists (Munby, Russell, & Martin, 2001).

Making the tacit explicit is not such a simple task, not least because there is little expectation in schools that such translation occur. However, one well-documented approach that has proved helpful has been when science teachers have worked together with science education researchers. That form of collaboration has acted as a catalyst for making the tacit nature of practice explicit and helped to illustrate the value of a language of teaching and learning. Geelan (1996) wrote about his "newfound"

need to read about educational theories and practices and described how important it was that he became more adept at reflecting on his own teaching; it helped him to grow and develop as a science teacher. Being placed in the position of a learner was important to Geelan as he became more articulate about and saw more deeply into his knowledge of teaching. Maor (1999) experienced similar outcomes as a consequence of being placed in the position of learner and was of the view that being confronted by one's own practice was important for reviewing and reflecting on teaching and learning. Science teacher as learner therefore created opportunities for constructivist views of learning to become more meaningful and applicable in their classroom teaching. Furthermore, it also led to more realistic views of the extent of change in practice (Klopfer's second point). When a teacher-as-learner stance is adopted, development and change are typically reported.

PEEL (Project for the Enhancement of Effective Learning; see Baird & Mitchell, 1986), a largely unfunded teacher initiative supported initially by science educators, was responsible for an ongoing teacher professional learning environment in which a language for learning (based on metacognition) had a major influence on teaching and student learning. Research reports from PEEL offer numerous examples of teachers as learners, generally driven by their need to articulate features of practice that needed to be explicit in order to better understand the impact on students' learning. While still working as a science teacher in a school, Mitchell found himself confronted by the difficulties of making the tacit parts of his practice explicit. When preparing a class on the topic of genetics for another teacher to take for him due to an impending absence from school, he offered a detailed description of how to teach the class. He was of the view that his students were at an important point in their learning about the topic and he had a number of "crucial pedagogical imperatives for the lesson" that were designed to consolidate students' learning. On his return to school, when speaking with the teacher who he had briefed to teach the lesson in his absence, he was surprised to hear that she had struggled with the class. However, as he discussed the situation with the teacher, it soon became apparent to him that "I did not 'forget' to mention these things . . . they were still tacit knowledge, in spite of all my experience in making skilled teaching explicit. They were so tacit that [they] only came out as I discussed [them with Debbie]" (Mitchell, 1999, p. 60). Making the tacit explicit is aided by the use of language, and PEEL teachers were at the forefront of illustrating how important a language of teaching and learning is to communicating knowledge of practice.

McMaster (1997) was a PEEL teacher who demonstrated how, through a concerted focus on students' learning, his language for discussing issues of teaching and learning led to deeper understandings of practice and changes in his science teaching. He described how he became more capable of aligning beliefs and practices about science teaching and, in so doing, became more able to discuss such efforts in ways that went beyond just "sharing activities that work."

As any reading of the PEEL literature illustrates, the project has had much to say about professional learning and the importance of encouraging teachers to become more articulate about their professional knowledge of practice. PEEL made clear that by placing the teacher at the center of learning, real change in school science can become a reality. A science-specific program that developed as a consequence of the learning outcomes of PEEL and was funded by an education system was that of STaL (Science Teaching and Learning; Lindsay, 2006).

STaL was organized in such a way as to purposely place science teachers in situations in which their science content knowledge could be challenged. Being confronted by phenomena that tested their own understanding of science helped participating teachers question and think more deeply about their teaching. (The shift in professional learning programs and the nature of texts for science teachers as a consequence of a focus on learning has developed considerably in recent times, as illustrated by the work of WestEd; see, for example, Daehler, Folsom, & Shinohara, 2011, and Biological Sciences Curriculum Studies, or BSCS.)

Building on a teacher-as-learner stance, STaL supported participants in making the tacit explicit by setting aside the final day of the year-long program for case writing (Shulman, 1992). All of the participants wrote cases based on a dilemma, issue, event, or critical incident that they determined had been important in helping them to articulate previously tacit aspects of their practice and that led them to gain new insights into science teaching and learning.

> Participating in the classes from a student perspective really provided a vital insight into the difficulties of expressing one's knowledge clearly . . . The internal conflicts that students face in developing their learning and the importance of extending their prior views were emphatically demonstrated and felt by all . . . writing [a case] has supported me in becoming more perceptive about the purpose and knowledge that underpins my teaching, to actively reflect on the learning taking place and to provide thought for improving my pedagogy . . . we need to celebrate our own teaching environment and provide depth of meaning to our personal curriculum delivery.
>
> (Colquhoun, 2006, pp. 11–13)

Making the tacit explicit through varying forms of academic support has had a noticeable impact on teachers' understanding of the complex nature of science teaching and learning. However, as Mitchell (2002) explained, "collaboration with academics can be very helpful, provided both groups [teachers and academics] recognize that they bring different and equally valuable expertise and ways of thinking to the partnership—that each has much to learn from the other" (p. 253). It is through this notion of partnership that science teacher learning stands out as defining new ways of recognizing, acknowledging, and building on teachers' professional knowledge of practice.

The Problematic Nature of Practice

If teaching is problematic, then there cannot be one correct and appropriate way to teach science. Finding ways to illustrate that teaching is problematic is a first step in highlighting the complexity of practice. One way of accessing the problematic is through the notion of dilemmas—the dilemmas that teachers face on a daily basis in working to teach their students science.

Dilemmas are often the starting point for cases (as briefly noted in the previous section), and what cases make abundantly clear is that to manage the dilemmas inherent in practice requires a thoughtful approach from a flexible and responsive teacher. Dilemmas cannot be managed by "sticking to a recipe" or following a training program. Teachers who communicate their responses to the dilemmas with which they are confronted offer windows into the thinking that underpins expertise and, in so doing, illustrate an approach to being a teacher that is based on valuing that which emerges when functioning as a learner (Aubusson, 2005).

Smith (2011) explained how, when working with teachers over an extended period of time, group discussions of pedagogy based on participants' sharing their dilemmas of practice were central to building teachers' confidence in risk taking, enhancing students' (and teachers') scientific literacy, and developing their professional knowledge of practice. She wanted to know what knowledge they called on when faced with dilemmas and how their reasoning and decisions in that process affected their thinking about their understanding of their students' learning. As she worked with the teachers in one particular school over a 2-year period, she noted how their understandings of practice developed and how their expertise stood out through the ways in which they developed a shared language of teaching and learning and carried that into the ways in which they constructed their teaching for scientific literacy.

As an education system–based approach to professional learning (funding was through the Catholic Education Office), Smith's work at the school level reflected the need for a school to function as a learning unit and to be capable of being reflective, flexible, and adaptable in ways similar to that expected of teachers. Lindsay (2011) captured the essence of that expectation when he noted that "the school [is] an entity in itself—a whole learning community . . . [and] there is acknowledgement of the interrelatedness of all elements of schooling and the often fickle balance which resides within a dynamic and ever-changing system" (p. 11). Just as teaching is problematic as it needs to be responsive to the dilemmas of practice, so too a school must be equally responsive if change is to be real and sustained.

This notion of dilemmas has proved to be an important "way in" to understanding the complexity of science teaching and learning at both the individual and collective levels. Wallace and Louden (2002), in their book *Dilemmas of Science Teaching: Perspectives on Problems in Practice*, offered teachers' accounts of explorations of practice that highlighted how framing teaching as problematic creates a learning-about-science-teaching agenda and leads experienced teachers to develop new insights into teaching and learning. As the accounts in their book make clear, when taken-for-granted assumptions of practice are challenged, the complexity of teaching quickly comes to the fore as dilemmas emerge in ways that would not have been recognized (or responded to) if teaching was based on what Schön (1983) described as a technical-rational approach. Some of the themes that are raised through Wallace and Louden's (2002) book include questioning the intent and approach to laboratory work and the value of the associated tasks, examination of group work and the exclusionary approaches of some students that limited the learning possibilities for others, and the use of questioning and how it influenced student learning and classroom discourse. Through a major focus on dilemmas, the literature illustrates time and time again that teaching is problematic, and placing teachers in the role of learner is central to shaping the development of their professional knowledge of practice.

Northfield's study of his classroom practice illustrated the close relationship between learning and teaching and how it impacts understanding of knowledge of teaching. When Northfield returned to classroom teaching, he captured his year-long examination of his teaching of a Year 7 class of high school students through the book *Opening the Classroom Door: Teacher, Researcher, Learner* (Loughran & Northfield, 1996). That book left no doubt that his stance was as a science teacher learner. Through extensive accounts of classroom situations, his reflections on practice through conversations with others, and his journal entries, he came to a point at which he was able to synthesize and categorize his learning in very powerful and insightful ways.

Northfield came to highlight the principles that shaped his approach to practice, but in so doing, he brought to the surface a major difference between his expectations for teaching and learning and those of his students. In trying to understand the differences, he explored how his teacher view that "learning requires learner consent" and his students' view that "learning is done to students and teachers have a major responsibility for achieving learning" (Loughran & Northfield, 1996, p. 137) impacted on his conceptualization of his role as a teacher. Northfield's account offered interesting insights into the world of the teacher as learner and highlighted the teacher as researcher as a crucial role in developing insights into practice.

Science Teacher as Researcher

Teacher research has become an increasingly important way of informing classroom practice (Clarke & Erickson, 2003; Cochran-Smith & Lytle, 1990) because it is directed by teachers—those who genuinely understand what it means to "do teaching" on a daily basis. Teacher research is driven by the pedagogical questions, issues, and concerns that arise for teachers in their classrooms with their students. Teacher research reports tend to be framed in ways that are relevant and of interest to other teachers, as opposed to the form traditional research by academics takes, which typically is not—not only because of the nature of the research itself but also because of the way it is reported.

McGoey and Ross (1999), in response to the lament about "the lack of teachers' application of research in informing their day-to-day practice" (p. 117), drew attention to the difference between that which many researchers might pursue and make available to practitioners and that which they, as teachers, actually choose to pursue. The difference between the two perspectives is explained by the fact that although many professional development projects attempt to support and are sympathetic to the work of science teachers (Johanna, Lavonen, Koponen, & Kurki-Suonio, 2002; Radford, 1998; Shymansky et al., 1993), teachers themselves have not necessarily been the initiators or sustainers of the research effort. Yet when teachers are the initiators and sustainers of the work, the focus and results are considerably different (Hoban, 2003).

There has been considerable research into the nature of science teachers' professional development and the conditions that support and sustain teachers interested in examining the teaching and learning in their own classrooms. Despite all that might be possible to refine continuing professional development programs and ways in which support and encouragement might be organized (Finegold, 2010), there remains little doubt that teacher research stands out as a most productive approach to teacher learning and pedagogical change, because

> [as] teachers begin to understand what they know from experience . . . they gain heightened awareness of how they can contribute to the research on education . . . they have access to understandings that go far beyond what the expert researchers have produced. In the new school culture teachers are viewed as learners . . . [they] are researchers and knowledge workers who reflect on their professional needs and current understandings . . . scholar teachers research their own professional practice.
>
> (Kincheloe, 2003, p. 18)

In her chapter on science teachers as researchers in Abell and Lederman's (2007) *Handbook of Research on Science Education*, Roth (2007) offered a compelling analysis of the role of teachers as researchers. Her analysis of the teacher researcher literature made clear that science teacher research supports teacher learning and that encouraging that process needs to begin in preservice education programs. She also made clear that science teacher research produces knowledge in ways that are important to teachers. For example, the overwhelming majority of studies she reviewed focused attention on developing and refining teaching strategies, the use of science inquiry strategies, and language-related strategies. Importantly, she concluded that "teacher research builds the bridge linking academic research and practice . . . [and] can extend academic research knowledge by exploring it in the context of real classrooms" (Roth, 2007, p. 1237). That is perhaps the reason teacher research has gained a foothold in the academic literature and what it is that encourages teachers to pursue such work despite it typically being an "additional extra" to their existing teaching role.

Fitzpatrick (1996), a science teacher and head of his school's science department, described what happened when he and his colleagues decided to "throw away" the existing Year 8 curriculum and replace it with a new course structure and new teaching and learning approaches, because "after years of stagnation . . . [he was] very quickly convinced of the benefits of adopting a constructivist philosophy" (p. 1). His report outlined their reasons for deciding to change and described how their work led to the development of new "pedagogical skills." Teacher research of this kind is typical of the majority of studies that Roth (2007) reviewed. However, teacher research of the form described by Dresner and Worley (2006) offers different insights and approaches into science teacher learning.

Dresner (2002) organized an ecology-based program (Teachers in the Woods—TIW) designed to link teachers with scientists for the purpose of conducting scientific research in national forests and parks over a 5-week summer institute as well as conducting collaborative ecological research at a site near their schools. This collaborative scientific research positioned these teacher researchers in a way different from that of teacher researchers of classroom practice. Dresner and Worley's (2006) report was designed as a follow-up with participating teachers from TIW to determine the impact over time of their research experiences on their practices. Dresner and Starvel (2004) initially reported on the mutual benefits of the scientific research collaboration, but the follow-up research (Dresner & Worley, 2006) interviews highlighted that over time,

> engaging teachers in real-world field science research is an effective way for teachers, and, consequently, their students, to learn ecological knowledge and skills [as such an] experience can lead to science teaching for greater conceptual understanding and increased motivation on the part of the students.
>
> (p. 12)

Another approach to teacher research was documented by Berry and Milroy (2002). Having decided to pay careful attention to their students' learning about atomic theory, Berry and Milroy were confronted by the realization that, having taken on board ideas about teaching for conceptual change, when they exposed their students' views about atomic theory, they were unsure of what to do next. What's more,

> when [they] turned to the research literature to find a context for teaching about atomic structure, or practical classroom assistance for dealing with the particular conceptions [they] had uncovered and wanted to challenge,

> [they] found little . . . [and nothing about] what to do with those students who already had a coherent view of the phenomenon.
>
> (pp. 200–201)

Because they were unable to find the research knowledge and help they required for the task they had set themselves, they became active science teacher learners, collaborating in a learning-about-science-teaching experience that was certainly much more demanding and challenging than they had anticipated. The nature of their work, the daily demands of teaching, and the need to make real progress (for their students and themselves) created a research agenda that they felt compelled to pursue. Their account was constructed around 10 powerful "snapshots" of their learning about science teaching, which, previous to their endeavors as teacher researchers, would not have been so readily obvious. Because they approached their work from a teacher research perspective, they recognized and responded to taken-for-granted aspects of their own practice in concert with the dilemmas, issues, and concerns made explicit through their pedagogical risk taking, which highlighted previously hidden aspects of their students' learning (or, in some instances, lack thereof).

The impetus for their teacher research was not to "set out to prove that our approach was a better way of teaching," but the consequence was that

> the learning felt better—there was much discussion and writing that questioned ideas and assumptions; students generally became better at explaining the reasons underpinning their responses; we understood concepts better ourselves and our students were demonstrating that they understood them too and were prepared to give reasons to support their answers.
>
> (p. 213)

Throughout the teacher-as-researcher literature, teachers' perceptions of enhanced quality of student learning as a consequence of their inquiries stand out as major reasons for not just beginning but also sustaining the research endeavor over time. Teacher research, therefore, illustrates how science teacher learning matters in the pursuit of educational change.

Science Teacher Educator Learning

From the mid-1990s, self-study of teacher education practices (Hamilton et al., 1998) has become increasingly influential in shaping approaches to teaching and research in teacher education. The impact has partly been as a result of a shift in focus toward teacher educators' desire to learn more about their own practices (Adler, 1993; Mueller, 2003; Nicol, 1997; Pereira, 2000) and partly in response to teacher educators' growing interest in the knowledge base of teaching and learning about teaching (Berry & Loughran, 2002; Richardson, 1997). Many science teacher educators have been engaged in self-study research because that work, in some part, mirrors the very concerns science educators have for their students' learning of science, such as confronting alternative conceptions, dealing with cognitive dissonance, and creating active and responsible learners.

Science teacher educator learning can therefore be seen in the ways in which science teacher educators have attempted to better understand the ways in which their teaching impacts their student teachers' learning. As a physics teacher educator, Russell (1997) was concerned to examine how his knowledge of practice could be made more accessible to his student teachers so that their learning of science teaching would encourage them to challenge the status quo of "science teaching as the delivery of facts." Russell challenged his student teachers to give honest feedback on his teaching and how it did (or did not) influence their learning about teaching and their thinking about their own practice. Through an explicit focus on a continued critique of his own practice, he was able to explore in detail aspects of his practice that were beneficial for his student teachers' learning and the pedagogic behaviors that were less helpful. He used "tickets out of class" as a way of creating a routine for regular feedback that some students carried further into extensive email correspondence after class to discuss their views, issues, and concerns with him.

In the context of chemistry teacher education, Chin (1997) sought to explore his practice and how his experiences of teaching prospective teachers shaped his thinking about being a science teacher educator. He was of the view that the experience helped him to "articulate some significant experiences that informed [his] beliefs about teaching and learning within the teacher education context" (p. 117). It is interesting that both of these teacher educators worked in the same institution and that around their work, for a period of time, a self-study group existed that met on a regular basis and shared their learning about teaching. Through that ongoing process, these teacher educators documented how their learning about their own science teaching informed their practice and what that meant for their students' learning about science teaching. (As noted earlier, some of their students also published their work (Featherstone, Munby, & Russell, 1997; Olmstead, 2007; Russell & Bullock, 1999; Smith, 1997) as a consequence of their involvement in a teacher education program that genuinely sought students teachers' active feedback and a sharing of their learning about teaching science.)

Some of the themes in the previous sections of this chapter recur in the learning of science teacher educators. PCK, for example, is a topic that continues to garner interest by science teacher educators in relation to their own knowledge of teaching about teaching science. Faikhamta and Clarke (2012) offered an extensive exploration of this topic, which was initiated because

> I wanted to inquire into whether I was successful as a teacher educator in supporting and developing PCK in my

students. I needed to articulate these ideas for myself, to clarify what I was attempting to do, to better support my student teachers' teaching approaches in the context of the field-based science methods course.

> (p. 3)

In terms of a science teacher educator as a learner, Faikhamta adopted the expectations of self-study research (e.g., the use of critical-friend, alternative perspectives on situations, a search for disconfirming data, public exploration of findings) and applied them in a challenging situation (as a beginning teacher educator). Examples of work like this illustrate the desire many science teacher educators have for pursuing their own learning about their own practices.

Garbett (2011, 2012) pursued her understanding of her teaching of science to preservice teachers and was confronted by that which Whitehead (1993) described as being a "living contradiction." Through her study of her practice, she came to see her teaching through her student teachers' eyes and, as a consequence, recognized that some of the things she was trying to do and the messages she was hoping to convey were actually being misinterpreted by her student teachers (in some ways echoing the work of Hoban, 1997). As someone concerned to develop her student teachers as independent and responsible learners, her decision to adopt a team teaching approach offered a new way of helping her to see that which was once not so apparent. Equally, in working with a valued other, she also became much more sensitive to, and aware of, the ways that teacher educators' practice impacts their student teachers' learning about teaching. Through changing the script for teaching about teaching (through, for example, team teaching and peer teaching), Garbett became a much more informed teacher educator and illustrated that her learning had been substantial. She concluded that

> modeling appropriate strategies for teaching science subject matter had unwittingly portrayed science teaching as facts and activities rather than a conduit to engagement in learning. I was preoccupied with demonstrating how to teach science content . . . I was not as confident in engaging student teachers in conversations about their understanding of learning to teach science.

> (Garbett, 2011. p. 13)

Another science teacher educator who learned from her student teachers was Segal (1999). She took on the challenge of placing herself in the position of being the learner and examined the difference between being a learner of science teaching and a learner of science learning. "I did not realise until I was a full participant in their [student-teachers'] explorations that my own understanding was tenuous" (Segal, 1999, p. 17). Her study showed how she came to better understand the dilemmas of practice (another theme that has been constant across the previous sections of this chapter) and what that meant in relation to her student teachers' learning about teaching science.

Segal also worked collaboratively with a colleague (see Schuck & Segal, 2002) to follow their student teachers into their first year of teaching. Again, their teacher education practices came into question as they learned a great deal about how their own assumptions about student teachers' learning of science were challenged when they sought evidence of meaningful change. Having specifically taught science in ways designed to create student-centered, activity-based small-group learning, it did not lead to student teachers using the same practices when they were full-time teachers. In many cases they found that their teaching to their student teachers had created an impression that such approaches were "seamless and unproblematic" (Schuck & Segal, 2002, p. 96). Therefore, when their student teachers were confronted by the reality of teaching in those ways themselves as full-time teachers, many retreated to the very teaching approaches they had experienced and been dissatisfied with as school students (teaching as telling). Following their student teachers out into the real world of practice had been an eye opener that challenged these teacher educators' views of science teaching and learning in teacher education programs.

As so many of the examples of science teacher educator learning illustrate, conditions for supporting inquiring into practice matter. That is especially evident in the recent book by Bullock and Russell (2012), *Self-Studies of Science Teacher Education Practices*, which captures the desire many science teacher educators have to better learn about their teaching of the teaching of science. Whether those conditions be through science educators as a community of practice (Schneider, 2007), a sustained focus on specific aspects of pedagogy (Lustick, 2010), or particular ways of "caring for and feeding" the professional development of science teacher educators (Johnston & Settlage, 2008), a focus on learning emerges as being just as important for teacher educators as it is for student teachers and teachers; but it does need to be recognized as risky business. Perhaps some of the most risky business in science teacher education is associated with accepting the learning challenge of teaching in the way that one expects of one's student teachers, and that becomes all the more challenging when conducted in real high school classes.

Russell (1995) chose to teach his physics methods class through modeling the teaching of physics in a high school class for his student teachers. That year-long experience highlighted a number of important issues for Russell that seriously impacted the way he conceptualized science teacher education from that point on. In a similar way, Tobin (2003) accepted the challenge of modeling teaching for his student teachers in an urban high school and was confronted by the fact that his previous science education knowledge and experiences proved to be less than helpful in a new and demanding situation. Just like Russell before him, so too Tobin questioned what it meant to be a science teacher educator and

how that influenced the learning about science teaching by his student teachers:

> I was to realize all too quickly that I needed to re-learn to teach in urban schools . . . For too long I had regarded teaching as knowledge that could be spoken, written, and thought. But words could not be turned into teaching to mediate the learning of students.
>
> (Tobin, 2003, p. 34)

Tobin's learning experiences echoed those noted earlier by Northfield, who accepted a half-time teaching allotment as a high school teacher while still working as a professor of teacher education. He also found that his academic knowledge of teaching was not all that helpful in the day-to-day busyness of teaching a Year 7 class.

As these accounts make clear, to "practice what we teach" (Dias, Eick, & Brantley-Dias, 2011) is perhaps the ultimate challenge for a teacher educator, and recently that challenge has again been taken up by Eick and reported in the academic literature (see, Dias et al., 2011). Going back to the classroom asks many things of a teacher educator. In Eick's case, it was as a consequence of his

> decision to engage in the teaching role [which] was motivated by the desire to test his conceptual knowledge of inquiry-based practice against the practical knowledge that could be learned through the daily work of teaching adolescents science using a reform-based curriculum.
>
> (p. 54)

Eick created a support group around his experience in order to research his experiences in a rigorous manner. His project aimed to determine what new personal practical knowledge on inquiry (another recurring theme) and its associated scientific practices might emerge from his teaching experience with this curriculum.

Through the range of experiences and challenges to understanding the nature of school science teaching and learning through inquiry, Eick's study illustrated that he did develop new insights into the practical knowledge of inquiry. However, the finding that stood out most for Eick and his collaborators was that "teacher education is most informed when our practices are driven by participation (not mere observation) in schools, grappling with issues that emerge and our efforts to resolve them" (Dias et al., 2011, p. 74). This finding creates one of the great tensions in teacher education: being able to draw on recent and relevant teaching experience while still maintaining scholarship in ways that are commensurate with the expectations of the academy.

Debates about the relative value and place of theoretical knowledge versus practical knowledge have been had for some time (see for example, Clandinin & Connelly, 1995; Fenstermacher, 1994; Munby et al., 2001) and indeed continue. There have been some notable attempts to bridge the divide in meaningful ways through carefully structured and thoughtfully planned teacher education programs (see, Korthagen et al., 2001). However, many such efforts are dependent on the work of individuals or small groups of teacher educators that choose to band together for some period of time to "make an effort" to create a more coherent and meaningful teacher education program. At the same time, alternative certification programs and their value and impact (Koballa, Upson Bradbury, Glynn, & Deaton, 2008; Upson Bradbury & Koballa, 2007), ebb and flow as arguments about teacher preparation in the hallowed halls of academia as opposed to the swampy lowlands of practice (Schön, 1983) lead to policy mandates and educational practices that are oftentimes beyond the control of teacher education per se. Hence, it is little wonder that calls for teacher educators to take more control of their own business and to develop a sustained research agenda that demonstrates that what they do makes a difference persist (Grossman & McDonald, 2008). It could well be argued that science teacher educator learning sits at the heart of what needs to be an empowered response.

Conclusion

The notion of teacher as learner is embedded in an expectation that pursuing deeper understandings of the relationship between teaching and learning must be real and meaningful in the work of teachers. Through exploring that relationship, teachers can become more informed and articulate about their professional knowledge of practice. As this review illustrates, it is a demanding task for a teacher (whether preservice, inservice, or teacher educator) to actively pursue the ideal of teaching science for enhanced student understanding because it is not as simple a task as it might initially appear.

The problematic nature of teaching means that it is not so easy to delineate cause and effect. Because teaching is problematic, managing the dilemmas, issues, and concerns that arise on a daily basis requires pedagogical expertise, and such expertise is something that must be developed and refined over time; it cannot be imposed. Learning (as this chapter shows) needs to be viewed as being in a synergistic relationship with teaching. When it is viewed that way, there can be no doubt that science teacher learning clearly matters, especially if, as a profession, we expect to be able to engender enhanced learning of science in our students.

Wallace (2003) outlined three conceptual themes that he considered crucial to understanding and creating conditions for teacher learning. They were that learning about teaching is:

1. situated, and as a consequence, the development of teachers' understanding and knowledge requires a focus on authentic activities
2. social and that "creating rich opportunities for diverse groups of teachers to participate in, and to shape, discourse communities" is critical (p. 10)
3. distributed; hence, collaboration is central to change

As Wallace illustrates, development hinges on learning, and learning tends to be more valuable when it is supported through collaboration. This then raises an interesting issue for progressing teacher learning in any formal or structured fashion. Teaching tends to be an isolated and individual enterprise and exists in an environment in which the time, space, and opportunity for learning may be limited because the imperative to "do teaching" can overwhelm the opportunities to genuinely reflect on learning about teaching.

At a time when teaching appears to be increasingly less valued as a career, when policy makers search for simple answers to complex questions, and when education bureaucracies lean toward technicist approaches to practice by placing greater emphasis on accountability and compliance and less on professional autonomy and responsibility, the notion of teacher as learner stands out as more important than ever.

Now is the time for science education research and practice to better demonstrate, articulate, and celebrate teachers' professional knowledge of practice and to highlight the place of science teacher learning in progressing the profession in positive and productive ways.

References

Abell, S. K. (2008). Twenty years later: Does pedagogical content knowledge remain a useful idea? *International Journal of Science Education 30*(10), 1405–1416.

Abell, S. K., & Lederman, N. G. (Eds.). (2007). *Handbook of science education.* Philadelphia: Erlbaum.

Adams, P. E., & Krockover, G. H. (1997). Beginning science teacher cognition and its origins in the preservice secondary science teacher program. *Journal of Research in Science Teaching, 34*(6), 633–653.

Adler, S. A. (1993). Teacher education: Research as reflective practice. *Teaching and Teacher Education, 9,* 159–167.

Akcay, H., & Yager, R. (2010). Accomplishing the Visions for Teacher Education programs advocated in the National Science Education Standards. *Journal of Science Teacher Education, 21*(6), 643–664.

Akerson, V. L., Cullen, T. A., & Hanson, D. L. (2009). Fostering a community of practice through a professional development program to improve elementary teachers' views of nature of science and teaching practice. *Journal of Research in Science Teaching, 46*(10), 1090–1113.

Allan, E., Shane, J., Brownstein, E., Ezrailson, C., Hagevik, R., & Veal, W. (2009). Using performance-based assessments to prepare safe science teachers. *Journal of Science Teacher Education, 20*(6), 495–500.

Anderson, R. D., & Mitchener, C. P. (1994). Research on science teacher education. In D. L. Gabel (Ed.), *Handbook of research on science teaching and learning* (pp. 3–44). New York: Macmillan.

Angeli, C., & Valanides, N. (2005). Preservice elementary teachers as information and communication technology designers: An instructional systems design model based on an expanded view of pedagogical content knowledge. *Journal of Computer Assisted Learning, 21*(4), 292–302.

Appleton, K. (1992). Discipline knowledge and confidence to teach science: Self-perceptions of primary teacher education students. *Research in Science Education, 22*(1), 11–19.

Appleton, K. (2008). Developing science pedagogical content knowledge through mentoring elementary teachers. *Journal of Science Teacher Education, 19*(6), 523–545.

Appleton, K., & Kindt, I. (2002). Beginning elementary teachers' development as teachers of science. *Journal of Science Teacher Education, 13*(1), 43–61.

Aubusson, P. (2005). Evolution from a problem-based to a project-based secondary teacher education program: Challenges, dilemmas and possibilities. In G. F. Hoban (Ed.), *The missing links in teacher education design: Developing a multi-linked conceptual framework* (pp. 37–55). Dordrecht, the Netherlands: Springer.

Baird, J. R., & Mitchell, I. J. (Eds.). (1986). *Improving the quality of teaching and learning: An Australian case study—the PEEL project.* Melbourne: Monash University Printing Service.

Bandura, A. (1986). *Social foundations of thought and action: A social cognitive theory.* Englewood Cliffs, NJ: Prentice-Hall.

Bennett, N., Summers, M., & Askew, M. (1994). Knowledge for teaching and teaching performance. In A. Pollard (Ed.), *Look before you leap? Research evidence for the curriculum at key stage two* (pp. 23–36). London: Tufnell Press.

Berry, A., & Loughran, J. J. (2002). Developing an understanding of learning to teach in teacher education. In J. Loughran & T. Russell (Eds.), *Improving teacher education practices through self-study* (pp. 13–29). London: RoutledgeFalmer.

Berry, A., & Milroy, P. (2002). Changes that matter. In J. Loughran, I. Mitchell, & J. Mitchell (Eds.), *Learning from teacher research* (pp. 196–221). New York: Teachers College Press.

Beyer, C. J., & Davis, E. A. (2012). Learning to critique and adapt science curriculum materials: Examining the development of preservice elementary teachers' pedagogical content knowledge. *Science Education, 96*(1), 130–157.

Bhattacharyya, S., Volk, T., & Lumpe, A. (2009). The influence of an extensive inquiry-based field experience on pre-service elementary student teachers' science teaching beliefs. *Journal of Science Teacher Education, 20*(3), 199–218.

Bianchini, J. A., Johnston, C. C., Oram, S. Y., & Cavazos, L. M. (2003). Learning to teach science in contemporary and equitable ways: The successes and struggles of first-year science teachers. *Science Education, 87*(3), 419–443.

Bullock, S. M. (2011). *Inside teacher education: Challenging prior views of teaching and learning.* Rotterdam, the Netherlands: Sense Publishers.

Bullock, S. M., & Russell, T. (Eds.). (2012). *Self-studies of science teacher education practices.* Dordrecht, the Netherlands: Springer.

Burgoon, J., Heddle, M., & Duran, E. (2011). Re-examining the similarities between teacher and student conceptions about physical science. *Journal of Science Teacher Education, 22*(2), 101–114.

Carlsen, W. S. (1991). Effects of new biology teachers' subject-matter knowledge on curricular planning. *Science Education, 75*(6), 631–647.

Carr, M., & Symington, D. (1991). The treatment of science discipline knowledge in primary teacher education. *Research in Science Education, 21*(1), 39–46.

Chin, P. (1997). Teaching and learning in teacher education: Who is carrying the ball? In J. Loughran & T. Russell (Eds.), *Teaching about teaching: Purpose, passion and pedagogy in teacher education* (pp. 117–129). London: Falmer Press.

Clandinin, D. J., & Connelly, F. M. (Eds.). (1995). *Teachers' professional knowledge landscapes.* New York: Teachers College Press.

Clark, C., & Peterson, P. (1986). Teachers' thought processes. In M. C. Wittrock (Ed.), *Handbook of research on teaching* (3rd ed., pp. 255–296). New York: MacMillan.

Clarke, A. (1994). Student-teacher reflection: Developing and defining a practice that is uniquely one's own. *International Journal of Science Education, 16*(5), 497–509.

Clarke, A., & Erickson, G. (Eds.). (2003). *Teacher research.* London: RoutledgeFalmer.

Clarke, A., & Erickson, G. (2004). Self-study: The fifth commonplace. *Australian Journal of Education, 48*(2), 199–211.

Clift, R., Houston, W., & Pugach, M. (Eds.). (1990). *Encouraging reflective practice in education.* New York: Teachers College Press.

Cochran-Smith, M., & Lytle, S. L. (1990). Research on teaching and teacher research: The issues that divide. *Educational Researcher, 19*(2), 2–11.

Cochran-Smith, M., & Lytle, S. L. (Eds.). (1993). *Inside/outside: Teacher research and knowledge.* New York: Teachers College Press.

Colquhoun, Y. (2006). Cases: A teacher's perspective. In J. Loughran & A. Berry (Eds.), *Looking into practice: Cases of science teaching and learning* (2nd ed., Vol. 1, pp. 11–14). Melbourne: Monash University and the Catholic Education Office Melbourne.

Daehler, K. R., Folsom, J., & Shinohara, M. (2011). *Making sense of science: Energy for teachers for Grades 6–8.* San Francisco: WestEd/NSTA press.

Dana, T. M., McLoughlin, A. S., & Freeman, T. B. (1988). *Creating dissonance in prospective teachers' conceptions of teaching and learning science.* Paper presented at the National Association for Research in Science Teaching, San Diego, CA.

Davis, E. A., & Smithey, J. (2009). Beginning teachers moving toward effective elementary science teaching. *Science Education, 93*(4), 745–770.

De Jong, O., Van Driel, J. H., & Verloop, N. (2005). Preservice teachers' pedagogical content knowledge of using particle models in teaching chemistry. *Journal of Research in Science Teaching, 42*(8), 947–964.

Dias, M., Eick, C., & Brantley-Dias, L. (2011). Practicing what we teach: A self-study in implementing an inquiry-based curriculum in a middle grades classroom. *Journal of Science Teacher Education, 22*(1), 53–78.

Dietz, C., & Davis, E. (2009). Preservice elementary teachers' reflection on narrative images of inquiry. *Journal of Science Teacher Education, 20*(3), 219–243.

Dresner, M. (2002). Monitoring forest biodiversity with teachers in the woods. *Journal of Environmental Education, 34*(1), 4–8.

Dresner, M., & Starvel, E. (2004). Mutual benefits of scientist/teacher partnerships. *Academic Exchange Quarterly, 8,* 252–256.

Dresner, M., & Worley, E. (2006). Teacher research experiences, partnerships with scientists, and teacher networks sustaining factors from professional development. *Journal of Science Teacher Education, 17*(1), 1–14.

Driver, R., Guesne, E., & Tiberghien, A. (Eds.). (1985). *Children's ideas in science.* Milton Keynes, UK: Open University Press.

Duncan, R., Pilitsis, V., & Piegaro, M. (2010). Development of preservice teachers' ability to critique and adapt inquiry-based instructional materials. *Journal of Science Teacher Education, 21*(1), 81–102.

Eick, C., & Dias, M. (2005). Building the authority of experience in communities of practice: The development of preservice teachers' practical knowledge through coteaching in inquiry classrooms. *Science Education, 89*(3), 470–491.

Eick, C. J., Ware, F. N., & Jones, M. T. (2004). Coteaching in a secondary science methods course: Learning through a coteaching model that supports early teacher practice. *Journal of Science Teacher Education, 15*(3), 197–209.

Faikhamta, C., & Clarke, A. (2012). A self-study of a Thai teacher educator developing a better understanding of PCK for teaching about teaching science. *Research in Science Education, 42,* 1–25.

Falk, A. (2012). Teachers learning from professional development in elementary science: Reciprocal relations between formative assessment and pedagogical content knowledge. *Science Education, 96*(2), 265–290.

Fazio, X., Melville, W., & Bartley, A. (2010). The problematic nature of the practicum: A key determinant of pre-service teachers' emerging inquiry-based science practices. *Journal of Science Teacher Education, 21*(6), 665–681.

Featherstone, D., Munby, H., & Russell, T. (Eds.). (1997). *Finding a voice while learning to teach.* London: Falmer Press.

Fenstermacher, G. D. (1994). The knower and the known: The nature of knowledge in research on teaching. In L. Darling-Hammond (Ed.), *Review of research in education* (Vol. 20, pp. 3–56). Washington DC: American Educational Research Association.

Finegold, P. (2010). *Professional reflections: International perspectives on science teachers' continuing professional development.* York, UK: National Science Learning Centre.

Fitzpatrick, B. (1996). *The application of constructivist learning strategies to the redesign of the lower secondary science curriculum.* Paper presented at the Proceedings of the 21st Annual Conference of the Western Australian Science Education Association, Perth, Western Australia.

Fleer, M., & Grace, T. (2003). Building a community of science learners through legitimate collegial participation. In J. Wallace & J. Loughran (Eds.), *Leadership and professional development in science education: New possibilities for enhancing teacher learning* (pp. 116–133). London: RoutledgeFalmer.

Forbes, C.T. (2011). Preservice elementary teachers' adaptation of science curriculum materials for inquiry-based elementary science. *Science Education, 95*(5), 927–955.

Garbett, D. (2011). Developing pedagogical practices to enhance confidence and competence in science teacher education. *Journal of Science Teacher Education, 22*(8), 729–743.

Garbett, D. (2012). The transformation from expert science teacher to science teacher educator. In S.M. Bullock & T. Russell (Eds.), *Self-studies of science teacher education practices* (Vol. 12, pp. 31–44). Dordrecht, the Netherlands: Springer.

Geddis, A.N. (1996). Science teaching and reflection: Incorporating new subject-matter into teachers' classroom frames. *International Journal of Science Education, 18*(2), 249–265.

Geelan, D.R. (1996). Learning to communicate: Developing as a science teacher. *Australian Science Teachers Journal, 42*(1), 30–43.

Gomez-Zwiep, S. (2008). Elementary teachers' understanding of students' science misconceptions: Implications for practice and teacher education. *Journal of Science Teacher Education, 19*(5), 437–454.

Grimmett, P.P., & Erickson, G. (1988). *Reflection in teacher education.* New York: Teachers College Press.

Grossman, P., & McDonald, M. (2008). Back to the future: Directions for research in teaching and teacher education. *American Educational Research Journal, 45*(1), 184–205.

Gunckel, K. (2011). Mediators of a preservice teacher's use of the inquiry-application instructional model. *Journal of Science Teacher Education, 22*(1), 79–100.

Gunning, A., & Mensah, F. (2011). Preservice elementary teachers' development of self-efficacy and confidence to teach science: A case study. *Journal of Science Teacher Education, 22*(2), 171–185.

Hamilton, M.L., Pinnegar, S., Russell, T., Loughran, J., & LaBoskey, V. (Eds.). (1998). *Reconceptualizing teaching practice: Self-study in teacher education.* London: Falmer Press.

Hashweh, M.Z. (1996). Effects of science teachers' epistemological beliefs in teaching. *Journal of Research in Science Teaching, 33*(1), 47–63.

Hewson, P.W., Beeth, M.E., & Thorley, R. (1998). Teaching for conceptual change. In B. Fraser & K. Tobin (Eds.), *International handbook of science education* (pp. 198–218). Dordrecht, the Netherlands: Kluwer.

Hoban, G. (2003). Changing the balance of a science teacher's belief system. In J. Wallace & J. Loughran (Eds.), *Leadership and professional development in science education: New possibilities for enhancing teacher learning* (pp. 19–33). London: RoutlegeFalmer.

Hoban, G.F. (1997). Learning about learning in the context of a science methods course. In J. Loughran & T. Russell (Eds.), *Teaching about teaching: Purpose, passion and pedagogy in teacher education* (pp. 133–149). London: Falmer Press.

Howitt, C. (2007). Pre-service elementary teachers' perceptions of factors in an holistic methods course influencing their confidence in teaching science. *Research in Science Education, 37*(1), 41–58.

Ireland, J., Watters, J., Brownlee, J., & Lupton, M. (2012). Elementary teachers' conceptions of inquiry teaching: Messages for teacher development. *Journal of Science Teacher Education, 23*(2), 159–175.

Isabelle, A., & de Groot, C. (2008). Alternate conceptions of preservice elementary teachers: The Itakura method. *Journal of Science Teacher Education, 19*(5), 417–435.

Johanna, J., Lavonen, J., Koponen, I., & Kurki-Suonio, K. (2002). Experiences from long-term in-service training for physics teachers in Finland. *Physics Education, 37*(2), 128–134.

Johnston, A., & Settlage, J. (2008). Framing the professional development of members of the science teacher education community. *Journal of Science Teacher Education, 19*(6), 513–521.

Kang, N.-H. (2007). Elementary teachers' teaching for conceptual understanding: Learning from action research. *Journal of Science Teacher Education, 18*(4), 469–495.

Kincheloe, J.L. (2003). *Teachers as researchers: Qualitative inquiry as a path to empowerment.* London: RoutledgeFalmer.

Klopfer, L.E. (1991). A summary of research in science education—1989. *Science Education, 75*, 255–402.

Koballa, T., Glynn, S., & Upson, L. (2005). Conceptions of teaching science held by novice teachers in an alternative certification program. *Journal of Science Teacher Education, 16*(4), 287–308.

Koballa, T., Upson Bradbury, L., Glynn, S., & Deaton, C. (2008). Conceptions of science teacher mentoring and mentoring practice in an alternative certification program. *Journal of Science Teacher Education, 19*(4), 391–411.

Koch, J., & Appleton, K. (2007). The effect of a mentoring model for elementary science professional development. *Journal of Science Teacher Education, 18*(2), 209–231.

Korthagen, F.A.J. (1992). Techniques for stimulating reflection in teacher education seminars. *Teaching and Teacher Education, 8*(3), 265–274.

Korthagen, F.A.J., Kessels, J., Koster, B., Langerwarf, B., & Wubbels, T. (Eds.). (2001). *Linking theory and practice: The pedagogy of realistic teacher education.* Mahwah, NJ: Lawrence Erlbaum Associates Publishers.

Larkin, D. (2012). Misconceptions about "misconceptions": Preservice secondary science teachers' views on the value and role of student ideas. *Science Education, 96*(5), 927–959.

Lederman, N.G., Gess-Newsome, J., & Latz, M.S. (1994). The nature and development of preservice science teachers' conceptions of subject matter and pedagogy. *Journal of Research in Science Teaching, 31*(2), 129–146.

Lee, E., Brown, M.N., Luft, J.A., & Roehrig, G.H. (2007). Assessing beginning secondary science teachers' PCK: Pilot year results. *School Science and Mathematics, 107*(2), 52–60.

Lindsay, S. (2006). Cases: Opening the classroom door. In J. Loughran & A. Berry (Eds.), *Looking into practice: Cases of science teaching and learning* (pp. 3–6). Melbourne: Catholic Education Office (Melbourne) and Monash University.

Lindsay, S. (2011). Scientific literacy: A symbol of change. In J. Loughran, K. Smith, & A. Berry (Eds.), *Scientific literacy under the microscope: A whole school approach to science teaching and learning* (pp. 3–15). Rotterdam, the Netherlands: Sense Publishers.

Lockard, D.L. (1993). Secondary science teachers' knowledge base when teaching science courses in and out of their area of certification. *Journal of Research in Science Teaching, 30*, 723–736.

Lortie, D.C. (1975). *Schoolteacher.* Chicago: Chicago University Press.

Loughran, J. (1994). Bridging the gap: An analysis of the needs of second-year science teachers. *Science Education, 78*(4), 365–386.

Loughran, J.J. (2002). Effective reflective practice: In search of meaning in learning about teaching. *Journal of Teacher Education, 53*(1), 33–43.

Loughran, J.J., & Northfield, J.R. (1996). *Opening the classroom door: Teacher, researcher, learner.* London: Falmer Press.

Loughran, J.J., Smith, K., & Berry, A. (2011). *Scientific literacy under the microscope: A whole school approach to science teaching and learning.* Rotterdam, the Netherlands: Sense Publishers.

Luft, J.A., Firestone, J.B., Wong, S.S., Ortega, I., Adams, K., & Bang, E. (2011). Beginning secondary science teacher induction: A two-year mixed methods study. *Journal of Research in Science Teaching, 48*(10), 1199–1224.

Lustick, D. (2009). The failure of inquiry: Preparing science teachers with an authentic investigation. *Journal of Science Teacher Education, 20*(6), 583–604.

Lustick, D. (2010). The priority of the question: Focus questions for sustained reasoning in science. *Journal of Science Teacher Education, 21*(5), 495–511.

Maor, D. (1999). Teachers-as-learners: The role of multimedia professional development program in changing classroom practice. *Australian Science Teachers Journal, 45*(3), 45–50.

McGoey, J., & Ross, J. (1999). Research, practice, and teacher internship. *Journal of Research in Science Teaching, 36*(2), 121–139.

McMaster, J. (1997). Theory into practice. In J. R. Baird & I. J. Mitchell (Eds.), *Improving the quality of teaching and learning: An Australian case study—the PEEL project* (3rd ed., pp. 135–143). Melbourne: Monash University.

Milner, A., Sondergeld, T., Demir, A., Johnson, C., & Czerniak, C. (2012). Elementary teachers' beliefs about teaching science and classroom practice: An examination of pre/post NCLB testing in science. *Journal of Science Teacher Education, 23*(2), 111–132.

Mitchell, I. J. (1999). Bridging the gulf between research and practice. In J. J. Loughran (Ed.), *Researching teaching: Methodologies and practices in understanding pedagogy* (pp. 44–64). London: Falmer Press.

Mitchell, I. J. (2002). Learning from teacher research for teacher research. In J. J. Loughran, I. Mitchell, & J. Mitchell (Eds.), *Learning from teacher research* (pp. 249–266). New York: Teachers College Press.

Mueller, A. (2003). Looking back and looking forward: Always becoming a teacher educator through self-study. *Reflective Practice, 4*(1), 67–84.

Mulholland, J., & Wallace, J. (2005). Growing the tree of teacher knowledge: Ten years of learning to teach elementary science. *Journal of Research in Science Teaching, 42*(7), 767–790.

Munby, H., Cunningham, M., & Lock, C. (2000). School science culture: A case study of barriers to developing professional knowledge. *Science Education, 84*(2), 193–211.

Munby, H., & Russell, T. (1994). The authority of experience in learning to teach: Messages from a physics methods class. *Journal of Teacher Education, 45*(2), 86–95.

Munby, H., Russell, T., & Martin, A. K. (2001). Teachers' knowledge and how it develops. In V. Richardson (Ed.), *Handbook of research on teaching* (4th ed., pp. 877–904). Washington, DC: American Educational Research Association.

Nicol, C. (1997). Learning to teach prospective teachers to teach mathematics: Struggles of a beginning teacher educator. In J. Loughran & T. Russell (Eds.), *Teaching about teaching: Purpose, passion and pedagogy in teacher education* (pp. 95–116). London: Falmer Press.

Nilsson, P., & Loughran, J. J. (2012). Understanding and assessing primary science student teachers' pedagogical content knowledge. *Journal of Science Teacher Education, 23*(7), 699–721.

Northfield, J. R., & Gunstone, R. F. (1997). Teacher education as a process of developing teacher knowledge. In J. Loughran & T. Russell (Eds.), *Teaching about teaching: Purpose, passion and pedagogy in teacher education* (pp. 48–56). London: Falmer Press.

Olmstead, M. (2007). Enacting a pedagogy of practicum supervision: One student teacher's experiences of powerful differences. In T. Russell & J. J. Loughran (Eds.), *Enacting a pedagogy of teacher education: Values, relationships and practices.* (pp. 138–148). London: Routledge.

Osborne, R. J., & Freyburg, P. (Eds.). (1985). *Learning in science: The implications of children's science.* Auckland: Heinemann.

Pajares, M. F. (1992). Teachers' beliefs and educational research: Cleaning up a messy construct. *Review of Educational Research, 62*(3), 307–332.

Pereira, P. (2000). Reconstructing oneself as a learner of mathematics. In J. Loughran & T. Russell (Eds.), *Exploring myths and legends of teacher education. Proceedings of the third international conference of the self-study of teacher education practices. Herstmonceux Castle, East Sussex, England* (pp. 204–207). Kingston, Ontario: Queen's University.

Polanyi, M. (1966). *The tacit dimension.* Garden City, NY: Doubleday.

Posnanski, T. (2010). Developing understanding of the nature of science within a professional development program for inservice elementary teachers: Project nature of elementary science teaching. *Journal of Science Teacher Education, 21*(5), 589–621.

Posner, G. J., Strike, K. A., Hewson, P. W., & Gertzog, W. A. (1982). Accommodation of a scientific conception: Toward a theory of conceptual change. *Science Education, 66*(2), 211–227.

Pringle, R. (2006). Preservice teachers' exploration of children's alternative conceptions: Cornerstone for planning to teach science. *Journal of Science Teacher Education, 17*(3), 291–307.

Putnam, R. T., & Borko, H. (1997). What do new views of knowledge and thinking have to say about research on teacher learning? *Educational Researcher, 29*(1), 4–15.

Radford, D. L. (1998). Transferring theory into practice: A model for professional development for science education reform. *Journal of Research in Science Teaching, 35*(1), 73–88.

Richardson, V. (1996). The role of attitudes and beliefs in learning to teach. In J. Sikula (Ed.), *Handbook of research on teacher education* (pp. 102–119). New York: Macmillan.

Richardson, V. (1997). Constructivist teaching and teacher education: Theory and practice. In V. Richardson (Ed.), *Constructivist teacher education: Building a world of new understandings* (pp. 3–14). London: Falmer Press.

Ritter, J. (2009). Developing a vision of teacher education: How my classroom teacher understandings evolved in the university environment. *Studying Teacher Education, 5*(1), 45–60.

Roth, K. (2007). Science teachers as researchers. In S. K. Abell & N. G. Lederman (Eds.), *Handbook of research on science education* (pp. 1203–1260). Mahwah, NJ: Lawrence Erlbaum Associates.

Roychoudhury, A., & Rice, D. (2010). Discourse of making sense of data: Implications for elementary teachers' science education. *Journal of Science Teacher Education, 21*(2), 181–203.

Russell, T. (1995). Returning to the physics classroom to re-think how one learns to teach physics. In T. Russell & F. A. J. Korthagen (Eds.), *Teachers who teach teachers: Reflections on teacher education* (pp. 95–109). London: Falmer Press.

Russell, T. (1997). Teaching teachers: How I teach IS the message. In J. Loughran & T. Russell (Eds.), *Teaching about teaching: Purpose, passion and pedagogy in teacher education* (pp. 32–47). London: Falmer Press.

Russell, T. (2000). Moving beyond 'default' teaching styles and programme structures: The rise, fall, and marginal persistence of reflective practice in pre-service teacher education in the period 1984–2000. Paper presented at the Making a difference through reflective practices: Values and actions. The first Carfax International Conference on Reflective Practice, University College Worcester, July 13–16, 2000.

Russell, T., & Bullock, S. (1999). Discovering our professional knowledge as teachers: Critical dialogues about learning from experience. In J. Loughran (Ed.), *Researching teaching: Methodologies and practices for understanding pedagogy* (pp. 132–151). London: Falmer Press.

Sarason, S. (1990). *The predictable failure of educational reform: Can we change course before it is too late?* San Francisco: Jossey-Bass.

Schibeci, R. A., & Hickey, R. (2000). Is it natural or processed? Elementary school teachers and conceptions about materials. *Journal of Research in Science Teaching, 37*(10), 1154–1170.

Schneider, R. (2007). Science teacher educators as a community of practice. *Journal of Science Teacher Education, 18*(5), 693–697.

Schön, D. A. (1983). *The reflective practitioner: How professionals think in action.* New York: Basic Books.

Schön, D. A. (1987). *Educating the reflective practitioner.* San Francisco: Jossey-Bass.

Schuck, S., & Segal, G. (2002). Learning about our teaching from our graduates, learning about our learning with critical friends. In J. Loughran & T. Russell (Eds.), *Improving teacher education practices through self-study* (pp. 88–101). London: RoutledgeFalmer.

Segal, G. (1999). *Collisions in a science education reform context: Anxieties, roles and power.* Paper presented at the American Educational Research Association, Montreal, Canada.

Settlage, J., & "Dee" Goldston, M. J. "Dee". (2007). Prognosis for science misconceptions research. *Journal of Science Teacher Education, 18*(6), 795–800.

Shulman, J. H. (1992). *Case methods in teacher education.* New York: Teachers College Press.

Shulman, L. S. (1986). Those who understand: Knowledge growth in teaching. *Educational Researcher, 15*(2), 4–14.

Shymansky, J. A., Woodworth, G., Norman, O., Dunkhase, J., Matthews, C., & Liu, C.-T. (1993). A study of changes in middle school teachers' understanding of selected ideas in science as a function of an in-service program focusing on student preconceptions. *Journal of Research in Science Teaching, 30*(7), 737–755.

Skamp, K. (1991). Primary science and technology: How confident are teachers? *Research in Science Education, 21*(1), 290–299.

Smith, D., & Jang, S. (2011). Pathways in learning to teach elementary science: Navigating contexts, roles, affordances and constraints. *Journal of Science Teacher Education, 22*(8), 745–768.

Smith, K. (1997). Learning to teach: A story of five crises. In D. Featherstone, H. Munby, & T. Russell (Eds.), *Finding a voice while learning to teach* (pp. 98–108). London: Falmer Press.

Smith, K. (2011). Learning from teacher thinking. In J. Loughran, K. Smith, & A. Berry (Eds.), *Scientific literacy under the microscope: A whole school approach to science teaching and learning* (pp. 25–36). Rotterdam, the Netherlands: Sense Publishers.

Solomon, J., & Tresman, S. (1999). A model for continued professional development: Knowledge, belief and action. *Journal of In-Service Education, 25*(2), 307–319.

Stump, S. L. (2010). Reflective tutoring: Insights into preservice teacher learning. *School Science and Mathematics, 110*(1), 47–54.

Tobin, K. (2003). The challenges of attaining a transformative science education in urban high schools. In J. Wallace & J. Loughran (Eds.), *Leadership and professional development in science education: New possibilities for enhancing teacher learning* (pp. 33–47). London: RoutledgeFalmer.

Trumbull, D. (1999). *The new science teacher: Cultivating good practice.* New York: Teachers College Press.

Upson Bradbury, L., & Koballa, T. (2007). Mentor advice giving in an alternative certification program for secondary science teaching: Opportunities and roadblocks in developing a knowledge base for teaching. *Journal of Science Teacher Education, 18*(6), 817–840.

Uzuntiryaki, E., Boz, Y., & Kirbulut, D. (2010). Do pre-service chemistry teachers reflect their beliefs about constructivism in their teaching practices? *Research in Science Education, 40*(3), 403–424.

Vail Lowery, N. (2002). Construction of teacher knowledge in context: Preparing elementary teachers to teach mathematics and science. *School Science and Mathematics, 102*(2), 68–83.

Van Driel, J. H., De Jong, O., & Verloop, N. (2002). The development of preservice chemistry teachers' pedagogical content knowledge. *Science Education, 86*(4), 572–590.

Veal, W. R. (1999, March). The TTF model to explain PCK in teacher development. Paper presented at the annual meeting of the National Association for Research in Science Teaching, Boston, MA. (Eric Document Reproduction Service No. ED 443690)

Vikström, A. (2008). What is intended, what is realized, and what is learned? Teaching and learning biology in the primary school classroom. *Journal of Science Teacher Education, 19*(3), 211–233.

Wagler, R. (2010). Using science teaching case narratives to evaluate the level of acceptance of scientific inquiry teaching in preservice elementary teachers. *Journal of Science Teacher Education, 21*(2), 215–226.

Wallace, J. (2003). Learning about teacher learning: Reflections of a science educator. In J. Wallace & J. Loughran (Eds.), *Leadership and professional development in science education* (pp. 1–16). London: RoutledgeFalmer.

Wallace, J., & Louden, W. (Eds.). (2002). *Dilemmas of science teaching: Perspectives on problems of practice.* London: RoutledgeFalmer.

Wallace, J., & Loughran, J. (2012). Science teacher learning. In B.J. Fraser, K. Tobin, & C.J. McRobbie (Eds.), *Second international handbook of science education* (Vol. 24, pp. 295–306). Dordrecht, the Netherlands: Springer.

Wei, R. C., Darling-Hammond, L., Andree, A., Richardson, N., & Orphanos, S. (2009). *Professional learning in the learning profession: A status report on teacher development in the U.S. and abroad.* Dallas, TX: National Staff Development Council.

Wenger, E. (1998). *Communities of practice: Learning, meaning, and identity.* Cambridge: Cambridge University Press.

White, G., Russell, T., & Gunstone, R. F. (2002). Curriculum change. In J. Wallace & W. Louden (Eds.), *Dilemmas of science teaching: Perspectives on problems of practice* (pp. 231–244). London: RoutledgeFalmer.

Whitehead, J. (1993). *The growth of educational knowledge: Creating your own living educational theories.* Bournemouth: Hyde Publications.

Wieringa, N. (2011). Teachers' educational design as a process of reflection-in-action: The lessons we can learn from Donald Schön's *The Reflective Practitioner* when studying the professional practice of teachers as educational designers. *Curriculum Inquiry, 41*(1), 167–174.

Zeichner, K. M., & Gore, J. M. (1990). Teacher socialization. In W. R. Houston (Ed.), *Handbook of research on teacher education* (pp. 329–348). New York: Macmillan.

41

Science Teacher Attitudes and Beliefs

Reforming Practice

M. Gail Jones and Megan Leagon

What accounts for well-meaning teachers' lack of implementation of . . . reform, even when they positively value the reform and believe they are implementing it in their classrooms?

(Gregoire, 2003, p. 148)

As new findings in scientific and educational research emerge, the need for science education reform remains constant. Perhaps the single most important factor in the quality of science education is the teacher. Teachers face a constantly changing landscape of standards, assessments, and curricula, and the beliefs and attitudes they hold shape the way they interpret and respond to changes and challenges. Science teacher beliefs and attitudes influence the interpretation of the curriculum, whether or not teachers use inquiry in their instruction, choices of assessments, and involvement in professional development.

Most models of professional development are designed to address the intersection of teacher knowledge, beliefs, attitudes, and ultimately teacher classroom practices. One of the powerful pitfalls that challenges the effectiveness of professional development is the failure to address teachers' attitudes and beliefs about their instructional practices. Providing teachers with new models of instruction or a new curriculum without addressing the underlying belief systems can lead to little meaningful change. But we know that constructing and changing teachers' attitudes and beliefs is dependent on an array of factors that include prior knowledge and experiences, self-efficacy, and epistemic beliefs, as well as the sociocultural context of the particular teacher and school. Research is beginning to unravel the complex relationships of these factors as we begin to model this process of teacher change.

In this chapter, we examine current research on teachers' beliefs and attitudes with a special focus on defining the myriad types of beliefs, examining the evidence for the influence of beliefs and attitudes on science instructional practices, and identifying new areas for future work. This review of research includes an overview of the historical research that has defined attitudes and beliefs and documented their influence on science teachers and their teaching. Studies were selected for review if they were published since the last edition of the *Handbook on Research in Science Teaching* was released. Studies selected for the review included research from science education research journals as well as studies from other journals that included an examination of science teacher attitudes and beliefs. Space does not allow us to discuss all the research on attitudes, beliefs, and associated factors, but instead we focused primarily on new trends and directions that have emerged over the last 5 years. Large numbers of studies in science teacher education acknowledge the impact of programs, curricula, instructional methods, and experiences on teachers, and these have been summarized or acknowledged. We sought here to move the research on science teacher attitudes and beliefs forward by delineating and modeling the factors that contribute to attitude and belief change. By understanding how beliefs and attitudes intersect with factors such as context, self-efficacy, or epistemic beliefs, we can better inform our approaches to reforming science education as well move toward new theoretical models of teaching and learning.

Defining Beliefs

In the section that follows, we describe teachers' beliefs from a philosophical and psychological perspective using research in personal epistemology and epistemic cognition. Understanding the foundations of epistemology and what constitutes as a belief or a belief system can provide a lens with which to view specific beliefs related to science, self (e.g., self-efficacy), and teaching.

Man is not logical and his intellectual history is a record of mental reserves and compromises. He hangs on to what he can in his old beliefs even when he is compelled to surrender their logical basis.

(Dewey, 1922, p. 224)

In this quote, Dewey addresses the continual, unavoidable interplay of knowledge and beliefs. There is an endless debate on the nature of knowing versus the nature of believing and how these two constructs impact work in science education, cognitive psychology, educational psychology, and instructional practice (Murphy & Mason, 2006). In order to more fully understand science teacher beliefs, it is important to distinguish what is meant by "knowledge" versus what is meant by "belief."

Some authors maintain that a belief is a particular type of knowledge (Nisbett & Ross, 1980), while others have argued that knowledge is a component of belief (Rokeach, 1968). Alexander and Dochy (1995) explored the dichotomy of knowledge and beliefs with an international study of adults' conceptions of these two components. In this study, adult participants of varying educational and cultural groups were presented five diagrams with an option to create a new diagram (as shown in Table 41.1). Participants were asked to choose which diagram best depicted their understanding of knowledge and beliefs.

TABLE 41.1
Graphic Representations of the Various Relationships of Knowledge and Beliefs

Representations of Possible Relations of Knowledge and Beliefs	Diagram Explanations
Diagram 1 (Independent)	Knowledge and beliefs are two separate, unrelated constructs.
Diagram 2 (Knowledge Subsumption)	Knowledge is one component of beliefs.
Diagram 3 (Belief Subsumption)	Beliefs are one component of knowledge.
Diagram 4 (Inseparable)	Knowledge and beliefs are overlapping and indistinguishable from one another.
Diagram 5 (Overlapping)	Knowledge and beliefs share integrated aspects while maintaining other distinct and separate constructs.
Diagram 6 (Other)	Participants may draw their own representation of knowledge and beliefs.
Diagram Key Knowledge Beliefs Knowledge + Beliefs	

Adapted from Alexander & Dochy (1995)

Alexander and Dochy (1995) found that 41% of American and European participants preferred Diagram 5, which acknowledges that knowledge and beliefs are simultaneously integrated and independent. With views of knowledge and beliefs as both interrelated and exclusive, attaching definitions to both constructs of knowledge and beliefs has proven to be a messy task (Boldrin & Mason, 2009). Southerland, Sinatra, and Mathews (2001) wrote,

> Thought cannot be considered scientific knowledge (as this is a third world entity). Instead individuals' thoughts are equated with beliefs. Using this framework, there is a fundamental distinction between scientific knowledge (a third world entity) and personal knowledge (clearly a second world entity). Although this is a clean distinction, this does not aid in understanding the nature of one's thoughts in terms of warrants, epistemological strengths, and the like. Thus, it fails to shed much light on the more commonplace distinctions between knowledge and beliefs. (pp. 331–332)

Southerland et al. (2001) described knowledge here as factual and justified according to objective criteria while acknowledging the distinction between scientific and personal knowledge. While both knowledge and beliefs have their roots in experience, knowledge is primarily a cognitive structure, while beliefs can have both cognitive and affective components. These two constructs are complex, and researchers are continuing to examine how they differ from one another as well as how they each contribute to learning and instruction.

Types of Beliefs

Beliefs About Knowledge

Traditionally, personal epistemology has been defined as beliefs about knowledge and the nature of knowing (Hofer & Pintrich, 1997; Sandoval, 2005). In addition to beliefs about knowledge, researchers also consider the justification of knowledge (King & Kitchener, 1994), beliefs about learning, and beliefs about knowing (Schommer-Aikins, 2004) to be tightly woven into one's epistemological beliefs. Examining personal epistemology has been of increasing interest in science education and psychology over the past decade (Hofer, 2001). By studying how one comes to know and how one perceives knowledge and knowing from an educational psychology perspective, we can begin to understand an individual's belief system, which can help frame further research in science teacher education. While providing a complete background of the field of personal epistemology and its early foundations would be extraordinarily fruitful, it is beyond the scope of this chapter (see Chandler, Hallett, & Sokol, 2002; Hofer & Pintrich, 1997).

Beliefs About Science

Research in personal epistemology and epistemic cognition has paved the way for researchers to begin considering beliefs about science from a more profound and dynamic perspective (Bell & Linn, 2002; Conley, Pintrich, Vekiri, & Harrison, 2004; Songer & Linn, 1991). Lederman (2007) noted that "NOS [Nature of Science] typically refers to the epistemology of science, science as a way of knowing, or the values and beliefs inherent to scientific knowledge and its development" (p. 833). How teachers view and understand this epistemological component of NOS may directly or indirectly influence their students' beliefs in the domain (Deniz, 2011; Eberle, 2008; Mansour, 2009).

In addition to the research being conducted with NOS, researchers are examining specific science epistemological beliefs held by teachers. Apostolou and Koulaidis (2010) conducted a study to assess the epistemological views of science teachers in regard to the scientific method, demarcation of science knowledge, change of scientific knowledge, and the status of scientific knowledge. These researchers posited four different positions for each of the previously mentioned aspects of science epistemology that were studied: empirico-inductive, hypothetico-deductive, contextualist,

TABLE 41.2
Synthesis of Science Teacher Epistemological Positions

Position	Scientific Method	Demarcation of Science Knowledge	Change of Scientific Knowledge	Status of Scientific Knowledge
Empirico-inductive	"Scientists accumulate initial observations and consequently construct theories (only one inductive scientific method exists)" (p. 150).	"Scientific knowledge which is constructed on the basis of the sound scientific method represents a good approximation of truth" (p. 151).	"This position holds that science progresses through the accumulation of new empirical data. This process can lead to a revision of an older theory or the construction of a new one. The older and the newer theories are compatible and comparable" (p. 152).	"Scientific knowledge has special status because it is an objective account of nature. This objectivity stems from the correct methodological choices" (p. 153).
Hypothetico-deductive	"Scientists devise hypotheses based on their theoretical constructs which are tested by observational and experimental data (only one scientific method exists)" (p. 150).	"Scientific knowledge which is constructed on the basis of the sound scientific method represents a good approximation of truth" (p. 151).	"Science progresses through the proliferation of theories and the competition between the theories. Certain of these theories are accepted (or rejected) by using rational criteria such as their scope, the multiplicity of empirical data which can be incorporated on them, etc. A certain theory is replaced when (and if) it contradicts a different theory which is better" (p. 152).	"Scientific knowledge has special status because it is an objective account of nature. This objectivity stems from the correct methodological choices" (p. 153). (Note that the empirioco-inductive and hypothetico-deductive positions were combined for this epistemological view.)
Contextualist	"There are a variety of scientific methods which are selected by the scientific community. In certain cases, rational criteria exist for selecting a scientific method" (p. 150).	"Rational criteria for the demarcation of the scientific knowledge exist for the most rational interpretation of this position. The criteria are selected by the scientific community" (p. 151).	"Science develops and progress in the interior of each paradigm with an accumulative way. However, the change of paradigm and the choice of a new paradigm create discontinuity in scientific development" (p. 152). "This reflects the position that during the development of science there are periods of continuity and periods of discontinuity (at the change of paradigms)" (p. 153).	"Scientific knowledge has particular status. This is true because it either constitutes a systematic and structured way of thought or because it has a particular usefulness" (p. 153).
Relativist	"According to this position, there are a variety of scientific methods. The scientific community selects the methods without the use of rational criteria" (p. 150).	"Demarcation between the scientific knowledge and the other forms of knowledge either does not exist or demarcation does not have a rational character of any type" (p. 151).	"Development of science and the change of theories do not occur according to some constant form" (p. 153).	"Scientific knowledge does not have any particular status. It is up to the individual to adhere to some ideology, which either accepts or rejects the existence of such a status" (p. 153).

From Apostolou & Koulaidis (2010, pp. 150–153)

and relativist. A synthesis of each position with its corresponding explanation can be found in Table 41.2. Using semistructured interviews addressing these four epistemological views, findings from this study indicated that of the experienced science teacher sample:

(a) 51.4% held eclectic[1] views regarding the scientific method
(b) 54.3% held empirico-inductive/hypothetico-deductive views in the demarcation of science knowledge
(c) 45.7% held empirico-inductive views on the change of scientific knowledge
(d) 34.4% held relativist views regarding the status of scientific knowledge

The science teacher's views on the scientific method have implications for the curricular decisions and instructional methods used. Apostolou and Koulaidis (2010) reported,

> 20% of the teachers consider that observations are not influenced by the theoretical frame but simultaneously consider that science follows a lot of different methods . . . it seems that they consider that two scientific methods exist, inductivism and deductivism.
>
> (p. 161)

This lack of continuity and discrepancy in science teacher beliefs concerning the scientific method may impact how students perceive science knowledge and science as an academic discipline (Apostolou & Koulaidis, 2010).

Other researchers have opted for another science epistemology framework altogether. Instead of thinking about epistemological beliefs in science as global justifications as outlined by NOS, Elby and Hammer (2010) suggested that epistemological beliefs should be viewed as "epistemological resources" (p. 4) that are "context-sensitive activation(s) of fine-grain knowledge elements (that) also described students' cognition concerning the nature of knowledge, knowing, and learning" (p. 3). Alternatively, Sandoval (2005) suggested that epistemological beliefs in science should be addressed using a "practical epistemologies" (p. 635) framework that integrates one's expressed beliefs about formal science with their practiced beliefs about science that develop by constructing knowledge through inquiry. Regardless of the framework used, there is often a discrepancy in the level of sophistication for similar constructs of epistemological beliefs regarding the nature of science. For instance, Elder (2002) found that students may report mature understandings of the changing nature of science (e.g., scientific knowledge derives from reasoning, thinking, and experimentation), but they may simultaneously believe that their role in science is passive and intended to complete projects and activities as opposed to being active and explaining observed phenomena. This discrepancy of understanding may be attributed to the teachers' epistemological beliefs in science and their influence on teacher practice (Conley et al., 2004; Elder, 2002).

Another interesting finding is that epistemological beliefs in science tend to differ based on specific disciplines (Schwartz & Lederman, 2008). Markic and Eilks (2012) examined preservice teachers' beliefs about classroom organization, teaching objectives, and epistemological beliefs. Markic and Eilks reported that the chemistry and physics preservice teachers held much more traditional beliefs about science teaching and learning than did the biology preservice teachers. Similarly, Rizk, Jaber, Halwany, and BouJaoude (2012) found that in comparison to other science disciplines, biology major students had more sophisticated epistemological beliefs regarding the certainty/simplicity of knowledge, source of knowledge, and attainability of knowledge. More research is needed to decipher why those in biology tend to hold more sophisticated beliefs in science teaching and learning than do those in other science disciplines.

Researchers continue to explore how teachers' beliefs about science knowledge and processes impact pedagogical and curricular decisions. It is becoming evident that one must consider not only science domains in regard to epistemological beliefs but also each specific discipline studied within the larger science umbrella (e.g., chemistry, biology, physics, etc.). We must also begin considering the disconnect and distinction between formal beliefs about science and practiced beliefs about science. Nevertheless, teacher beliefs in science are only one component of the larger belief system. Next we examine how beliefs about self (e.g., self-efficacy) impact the holistic belief system as well as science teacher practice.

Beliefs About Self: Self-Efficacy

Self-efficacy is emerging as a significant predictor of teacher behavior that influences instructional practice, motivation, the effectiveness of professional development and the success of educational reform. Bandura (1997) defined self-efficacy as "beliefs in one's capabilities to organize and execute the courses of action" (p. 3). Since Bandura first described self-efficacy, the construct has been widened to include more contextualized forms of efficacy that include science self-efficacy, teaching self-efficacy, and personal self-efficacy (Blonder, Benny, & Jones, in press). Self-efficacy is part of an individual's belief system and is influenced by prior experiences, successes, and failures, as well as feedback from others. Self-efficacy is also thought to influence cognitive processing and problem solving (Evans, 2011).

At the heart of the construct of self-efficacy is the theoretical position that maintains that individuals are self-regulating and will monitor and regulate their behavior (Bandura, 1982). Self-efficacy influences self-regulation as people make choices about how much time and effort to expend on a task and how long they will persist if presented with obstacles (Pajares, 1997). Furthermore, researchers are increasingly showing that self-efficacy is specific to particular skills, tasks, domains, and contexts (Bong, 2006).

Bandura (1997) made significant contributions to unpacking the elements of self-efficacy that influence teachers. He identified mastery experiences, vicarious experiences, and verbal persuasion as influential on the formation of self-efficacy. These factors have also been identified as critical components of successful professional development for teachers. Effective professional development programs build in opportunities for teachers to see successful teachers model new practices and experience success with the new practices.

Teaching efficacy, along with outcome expectancy, has been identified as part of the system of beliefs that influence teachers (Ashton & Webb, 1986; Gibson & Dembo, 1984). Outcome expectancy is defined as a teacher's belief that he or she can teach in such a way as to overcome factors that are not within the teacher's direct control (Gibson & Dembo, 1984; Tschannen-Moran, Woolfolk-Hoy, & Hoy, 1998). Angle and Moseley (2010) examined biology teachers' science teaching outcome expectancy scores and found that teachers whose students scored high on the biology achievement test also had high expectancy scores. These results suggested that the biology teachers' expectations for students contributed to their higher achievement.

Researchers have now documented the clear influence of self-efficacy on teachers' instructional practices. For example, teachers who have higher self-efficacy, content knowledge, and attitudes have students with higher achievement than do teachers who have lower levels of self-efficacy (Evans, 2011). Furthermore, teachers with higher self-efficacy have been shown to be more innovative (Berman, McLaughlin, Bass, Pauly, & Zellman, 1977; Guskey, 1988), put more effort into their teaching (Tschannen-Moran & Woolfolk-Hoy, 2001), and use more student-centered practices (Ramey-Gassert, Shroyer, & Staver, 1996). Researchers have also found differences in self-efficacy for pre- and inservice teachers (Appleton, 1995; Bleicher, 2007; Carleton, Fitch, & Krockover, 2008; Hartshorne, 2008; Harty, Samuel, & Anderson, 1991; Jarrett, 1999; Jarvis & Pell, 2004; McDevitt, Heikkinen, Alcorn, Ambrosio, & Gardner, 1993; Palmer, 2001, 2004; Pedersen & McCurdy, 1992; Scharmann & Hampton, 1995; Wenner, 1993). Other studies have established that there is a relationship between teachers' knowledge of science and their self-efficacy beliefs (Appleton, 1995; Harlen, 1997; Murphy, Neil, & Beggs, 2007; Schoon & Boone, 1998).

While recognizing the importance of teachers' self-efficacy, researchers have begun to design interventions to alter teachers' self-efficacy. Palmer (2011) provided 12 teachers with cognitive mastery, enactive mastery, modeling, and verbal persuasion experiences over a 2-year period and found that cognitive mastery or perceived success in understanding how to teach science and feedback after an observation contributed to increases in teachers' science teaching self-efficacy.

Within self-efficacy research, there is recognition that the culture of the school and the larger educational community influences teachers' self-efficacy. For example, when science teachers experience success working with other teachers in a professional learning community in which they plan, work, and assess their science education program together, their beliefs related to the capability of their colleagues promote a belief that, as individuals, they can be successful in future efforts to change their instructional practices. This type of interaction between self-efficacy and belief in the group's capability is known as group or collective efficacy (Bandura, 1982; Goddard, Hoy, & Woolfolk-Hoy, 2004; Tschannen-Moran, Woolfolk-Hoy, & Hoy, 1998). Research in self-efficacy continues to provide insight on how belief systems can influence both teacher practice and reform.

Beliefs About Teaching

> If student learning is facilitated by teachers' classroom practice, and teachers' classroom practice is, in part, a function of their beliefs as some research indicates . . . then one important goal of science education research is to study how ideas promoted in science teacher education become tools employed by practicing teachers.
> (Forbes & Davis, 2010, p. 383)

From the moment that teachers first step foot into a classroom as students until they day that they become the teachers, personal beliefs have been constructed regarding teaching practice. Teachers' perceptions and beliefs about science teaching are established and nurtured through their own experiences as learners. "Knowledge and beliefs about teaching are entangled, since what one believes about teaching necessarily hinges to a large extent, on one's knowledge of his or her discipline, as well as on one's beliefs about how children learn" (Crawford, 2007, p. 616). These personally constructed beliefs and knowledge about teaching influence the structure of the classroom, the way the science curriculum is interpreted, and how instructional practices are enacted.

> As teachers engage in their field of instruction, these beliefs expand in their epistemological orientation. Capturing the beliefs of teachers is important to those in science teacher education—ultimately, beliefs reveal how teachers view knowledge and learning, and suggest how they may enact their classroom practice.
> (Luft & Roehrig, 2007, p. 47)

Beliefs about teaching include but are not limited to beliefs about inquiry (Breslyn & McGinnis, 2011; Choi & Ramsey, 2009; Crawford, 2007; Saad & BouJaoude, 2012; Varma, Volkmann, & Hanuscin, 2009), fostering scientific argumentation and anchoring questions (Crippen, 2012; Forbes & Davis, 2009; Sandoval, 2005), and generalized beliefs about the nature of science knowledge and goals of teaching and learning (Friedrichsen, Van Driel, & Abell, 2011; Olafson & Schraw, 2006).

Beliefs About Students

Teachers' beliefs about their students also serve as a major component facilitating science curricular design and practice.

> A teacher's beliefs about how students learn can profoundly affect his or her design of instruction, as well as the role of the teacher in carrying out this instruction. If a teacher is concerned with how students make sense of science concepts, that teacher's goals may include how to promote students' deep thinking, rather than students memorizing factual and discrete information.
>
> (Crawford, 2007, p. 617)

Furthermore, teachers' beliefs about their students can impact behavior management decisions (Gibbs & Powell, 2012; Holt, Hargrove, & Harris, 2011), perceptions and responses to student motivational aspects (Maggioni & Parkinson, 2008), and student self-regulated learning (Elstad & Turmo, 2010). Beliefs about students can also range from cultural perceptions to assumptions about prior science knowledge to students' abilities in science (Otero & Nathan, 2008). The research on teachers' beliefs about students has tended to show that elementary, middle, and secondary teachers' beliefs have similar influences on their enacted classroom practice.

Teacher Beliefs and Inquiry

The United States National Science Education Standards (NSES) indicate that K–12 teachers should help foster the learning of scientific concepts and processes through inquiry techniques (National Research Council, 1996, 2000, 2012). A teacher's knowledge and beliefs regarding inquiry and science instruction are important factors in determining if inquiry techniques are used in the classroom and how inquiry techniques are then utilized. Sandoval (2005) noted that individuals with "more constructivist beliefs about scientific knowledge tend to learn more from inquiry-oriented instruction" (p. 646). However, even when a teacher holds a constructivist and inquiry-driven belief concerning ideal classroom instruction, oftentimes those beliefs do not translate into correlated practice. Crawford (2007) suggested that prospective teachers hold "complex, and sometimes conflicting beliefs" (p. 635) that can occasionally be represented as "competing belief sets" (p. 635). One teacher belief set includes personal beliefs about how instructional strategies should be implemented, which competes with a separate and distinct belief set of school culture expectations.

> There was tension between having a vision of teaching science as inquiry, and holding contradictory beliefs about schools, the role of the teacher, and the role of the student. . .These findings support those of McGinnis et al. (2004) pointing to novice teachers encountering affordances and constraints arising from the school culture, and these constraints can dissuade teachers from successfully carrying out reformed-based teaching strategies.
>
> (Crawford, 2007, p. 636)

While school culture greatly influences teacher beliefs on scientific inquiry practices, academic discipline may also actuate varying teacher beliefs regarding inquiry. Breslyn and McGinnis (2011) reported that the discipline area was a significant influence on exemplary science teachers' views and inquiry practices. These findings support the research on domain and academic discipline-specific belief sets described by Schwartz and Lederman (2008). Breslyn and McGinnis (2011) found that contrary to previous notions, the science curriculum and teacher's preservice experiences may not be the primary factors guiding teachers' use of inquiry. Instead, it is the underlying structure of their specific disciplines that facilitates teachers' perceptions and implementation of inquiry in the classroom. Thus, Breslyn and McGinnis (2011) suggest that "simply modifying the curriculum or providing additional preservice professional development will likely not result in changes in teaching with inquiry" (p. 73). Other researchers have found positive changes in beliefs about teaching and inquiry through preservice and inservice teacher development without regard to specific academic disciplines (Choi & Ramsey, 2009; Saad & BouJaoude, 2012; Varma, Volkmann, & Hanuscin, 2009).

Although similar patterns in beliefs about inquiry exist across elementary, middle, and high school teachers, different results are emerging from studies of college instructors. Until recently, research on postsecondary science teachers' beliefs, attitudes, and practices has been noticeably absent from the literature. In 2002, Harwood and colleagues examined college science instructors' beliefs about scientific inquiry and found that faculty defined inquiry as a process driven by questions and focusing on problem solving. Similarly, Brown, Abell, Demir, and Schmidt (2006) examined undergraduate college instructors' views of inquiry and found that the instructors held a narrow view of inquiry as open ended and student driven. As a result of these beliefs, the instructors believed inquiry was particularly time consuming and more appropriate for upper-level students. In a related study, Southerland, Gess-Newsome, and Johnston (2003) researched the collaboration among scientists as they worked together to teach a new course. The two physicists held very different views of inquiry than the ecologist did, and as a result, the collaborative instruction included little inquiry. Volkmann, Abell, and Zgagacz (2005) also looked at college instructors' collaboration while teaching inquiry to preservice teachers and found the instructors held different views of teaching and learning that resulted in conflict about the role of explanation in teaching science. Nonetheless, there is evidence to suggest that inquiry-based classrooms that focus on experimental design, data analysis, and argumentation promote epistemological thinking (Solomon, Scott, & Duveen, 1996) and may provide an avenue to examine changes in epistemological thinking over time (Conley et al., 2004).

Roles of Teacher Beliefs in Scientific Argumentation

"[I]n the area of science education, thinking about knowledge claims, use of evidence, and the justification of knowledge is often the explicit goal or focus of instruction in the curriculum" (Conley et al., 2004, p. 189). Since argumentation utilizes evidence to justify a claim or a way of knowing, scientific argumentation is fundamentally epistemological by nature. Two of the epistemological dimensions outlined by Schommer (1990) and Schraw and colleagues (1995) correspond seamlessly with aspects of argumentation: source of knowledge and omniscient authority, respectively.

Teachers' beliefs about scientific argumentation depend on teachers' epistemic beliefs. Teachers' justification of their knowledge in science (e.g., handed down by authority or derived from reason) can be a pivotal factor in making curricular decisions as well as potentially influencing their students' beliefs and justifications of knowledge in science. Crippen (2012) conducted a study with inservice high school teachers and the role of argumentation and justification of claims in science using a unique "argue-to-learn" intervention strategy. Results indicated that while teachers exhibited positive growth in science content knowledge, experimental results were not included in their final claim justifications. In a similar study, Schwartz and Glassner (2003) found that while learners frequently accept expert scientific opinion, they rarely use that knowledge in their justification process for proceeding argumentation activities.

Several other researchers have studied the role of evaluating scientific claims through argumentation (Berland & Hammer, 2012; Bottcher & Meisert, 2011; McDonald, 2010; Ogan-Bekiroglu & Eskin, 2012; Tippett, 2009), but there is little to be found concerning why learners (both students and teachers, alike) justify claims in a particular way. How do teachers decide what scientific data to analyze and, correspondingly, when the claim made is sufficient? Understanding teachers' beliefs about scientific argumentation is key to understanding how to promote classroom practices that require students to justify their claims in science investigations.

Science Teacher Beliefs, Attitudes, and Controversial Science Issues

Controversial issues bring to light the mismatch between teachers' knowledge (of science or science teaching), beliefs about the issue, and attitudes about teaching the topic. We now have a significant number of studies that have documented the failure of teachers to teach (or advocate for teaching) evolution even though they have been taught the topic in their teacher preparation program (Berkman & Plutzer, 2011; Leavy, McSorley, & Boté, 2007) or in professional development (Nehm, Kim, & Sheppard, 2009). These studies have shown the power of teachers' beliefs and attitudes as factors that highly influence teachers' decisions about *what* to teach in the area of evolution education and *how* to teach it. Furthermore, teacher education about teaching controversial issues tests our models about how to promote teacher change. In the United States, for example, evolution is part of the science curriculum across the country and is typically part of science education methods classes, but the research shows that more than 40% of science teachers report not teaching evolution or briefly mentioning it (Rutledge, & Mitchell, 2002). Climate change education is another controversial issue that is gaining attention. This topic, like evolution, is an area in which naïve conceptions exist (Cordero, Todd, & Abellera, 2008), and yet there is only limited research on attitudes and beliefs about teaching climate change (Begum, 2012; Lester, Ma, Lee, & Lambert, 2006; Papadimitriou, 2004).

New technologies such as genetically modified foods and nanotechnology have emerged as new controversial topics in science curricula. These topics present science teachers with new challenges about how to teach these topics and the degree to which they should confront the controversial issues that arise in the media (Cotton, 2006). In many cases, these topics, such as cloning or stem cell therapies, confront teachers' (and students') belief systems. Fonseca, Costa, Lencastre, and Tavares (2012) surveyed Portuguese teachers' beliefs about the importance of biotechnology and found that although the teachers thought biotechnology was interesting and important, they were uncertain about topics such as genetically modified foods. Fonseca and colleagues (2012) also examined teachers' beliefs about teaching biotechnology and found teachers were strongly supportive of biotechnology education. However, the participating teachers felt constrained by the limited time available to teach biotechnology and a lack of educational resources to teach the topic.

Similar topics such as environmental literacy and science, technology, and society (STS) issues continue to surface, yet there are still countless gaps in the literature. Amirshokoohi (2010) found that preservice elementary teachers exhibit low levels of both personal interest and environmental literacy yet maintain that it is important to teach students about these critical issues in STS. Other researchers have examined teacher beliefs in relation to technology integration (Ertmer, Ottenbreit-Leftwich, Sadik, Sendurer, & Sendurer, 2012) and evolution (Akyol, Tekkaya, Sungur, & Traynor, 2012; Blancke, De Smedt, De Cruz, Boudry, & Braeckman, 2012; Kim & Nehm, 2011). As these controversial issues in science education continue to arise, further research is needed to document how teacher beliefs and attitudes influence how these controversial topics are addressed in the classroom.

Teacher Attitudes

Turning the focus away from teacher beliefs to teacher attitudes, it becomes apparent that the terms "belief" and "attitude" continue to be loosely tossed around in research, with little effort made to more precisely define what these constructs represent. Often beliefs and attitudes are interchangeably used with terms such as "perception," "views," and "theories of action" (Kane, Sandretto, & Heath, 2002). Attitudes, unlike beliefs, are typically considered to be value laden. For example, Eagly and Chaiken (1993) described attitudes as "a psychological tendency that is expressed by evaluating a particular entity with some degree of favor or disfavor" (p. 1). Other definitions of attitude include "a predisposition to respond positively or negatively to things, people, places, events, or ideas" (Simpson, Koballa, Oliver, & Crawley, 1994, p. 212), "how favorable or unfavorable an individual feels about performing a behavior " (Jaccard, Litardo, & Wan, 1999, p. 103), and, more specifically for teachers, Ernest (1989) described attitudes as not including positive and negative affect but also other characteristics such as "liking, enjoyment and interest. . . teacher's confidence. . . the teachers' self-concept. . . valuing" (Ernest, 1989 p. 24). Attitudes are also considered to be a "state internal to the person" (Eagly, 1992, p. 694).

Much like the knowledge-and-belief dichotomy, distinguishing between attitudes and beliefs is also a befuddling endeavor. Traditionally, attitudes are considered to be affective, while beliefs are defined as cognitive constructs (Fishbein, 1967). However, researchers in different fields continue to define the constructs disparately. For example, van Aalderen-Smeets, Walma van der Molen, and Asma (2011) argue that attitudes consist of cognition, affect, and behavior. To these authors, the cognitive component of attitudes includes the "the evaluative thoughts and beliefs that a person has about the attitude object" (p. 162). The affective component they describe as moods and feelings and the behavioral component is described as the response individuals have when confronted with an attitude object. The attitude object is the entity (object or event) that elicits a response. Southerland et al. (2001) have also characterized beliefs as including both an affective and a cognitive component. Despite the lack of continuity in defining and distinguishing attitudes and beliefs, there is consensus that attitudes and beliefs have reciprocal influences on one another (Smith & Siegel, 2004).

Attitudes, Beliefs, and Behavior

The early research on attitudes focused on documenting the influence of attitudes on behavior (Maier, Greenfield, & Bulotsky-Shearer, in press). We know, for example, that negative attitudes are associated with teachers' tendencies to avoid teaching particular topics (Amato, 2004). More recent research has moved away from a view that attitudes predict behavior in a linear fashion to a more nuanced view that recognizes that attitudes may influence behavior differently depending on context (Eagley, 1992; van Aalderen-Smeets, Walma van der Molen, & Asma, 2011). Furthermore, we know that individuals may selectively attend to information that supports their attitudes but ignore information that does not (Eagley, 1992).

Affect, Teacher Attitudes, and Beliefs

One trend in the research on attitudes and beliefs has been the focus on the role of affect. Bandura (1997) identified affective state as one of the four primary sources of beliefs along with mastery experiences, vicarious experiences, and verbal persuasion. McCulloch (2009) argued that beliefs are a component of affect and that emotions, attitudes, beliefs, morals, values, and ethics are affective variables that interact with cognitive systems. Research on attitudes has focused on teachers' feelings about science (Harty et al., 1991; Haury, 1989; Koballa, 1986; Liang & Gabel, 2005; McDevitt et al., 1993; Mulholland & Wallace, 1996; Palmer, 2001, 2004; Pedersen & McCurdy, 1992; Ramey-Gassert et al., 1996; Young, 1998) as well as teachers' anxiety about science (Atwater, Gardner, & Kight, 1991; Bursal & Paznokas, 2006; Evans & Durant, 1995; Hartshorne, 2008; Haury, 1989; McDevitt et al., 1993; Palmer, 2004; Young, 1998).

In the past decade, there has been an increase in researchers' interest in understanding the role of teacher affect and emotion in defining teachers' attitudes. Emotion, like attitude, is a construct that suffers from being poorly defined. According to Schultz, Hong, Cross, and Osbon (2006), emotions are both conscious and unconscious judgments that are "socially constructed, personally enacted ways of being" (p. 344) that influence student–teacher relationships and teacher quality (Cross & Hong, 2012). Furthermore, emotions, according to Cross and Hong (2012), are the result of interactions of beliefs, goals, and identity that are context and incident dependent. The model that Cross and Hong (2012) have put forward to describe teachers' attitudes suggests that beliefs and identity overlap and collectively define emotions that subsequently influence teaching practices (see Figure 41.1).

The relationship between identity and belief systems has emerged as a major area of science education research conducted out of an interest in understanding how science teacher identity develops as well as how to shape and alter teacher identity. Furthermore, the movement of teachers and the globalization of education has highlighted the need to understand the contributions of culture, worldview, and contexts as factors that shape identity and associated belief systems.

Professional identity develops from science teachers' early personal experiences as students, with teacher role models, and through interactions with others who play a role in shaping teachers' views of themselves as teachers. These factors also play an important role in the development of a teacher's self-efficacy and motivation. Identity is believed to serve a role in helping teachers justify their professional choices and actions to themselves (Sutherland, Howard, & Markauskaite, 2010). Science teacher identity has been described as "an extension of past biography within contextual expectations" (Eick & Reed, 2002, p. 402). It has been argued that identity and the prior experiences that shape identity also define and contribute to belief systems just as belief systems likewise influence the

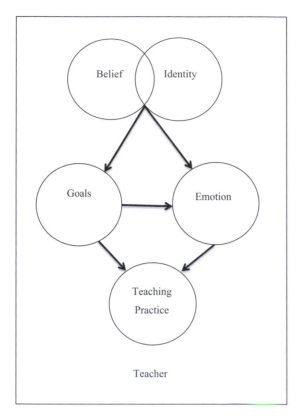

Figure 41.1 Relationships of beliefs, identity, goals, and emotion to teaching practices. (Modified from Cross and Hong, 2012)

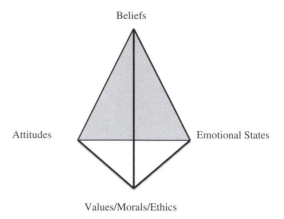

Figure 41.2 DeBellis and Goldin's (2006) framework for affect.

development of professional identity (Eick & Reed 2002; Fang, 1996; Kagan, 1992; Kane, Sandretto, & Heath, 2002; Pajares, 1992). Research in the area of identity and science teacher beliefs has included an examination of identity and beliefs as influences on classroom practices including inquiry (Eick & Reed, 2002; Luehmann, 2007) as well as teaching in culturally diverse settings (Settlage, Southerland, Smith, & Ceglie, 2009).

DeBellis and Goldin (2006) have proposed a model of affect that does not include identity but instead ties beliefs and attitudes to values/morals and ethics (see Figure 41.2). However, this model does not distinguish how the cognitive component of beliefs differs from the affective nature of attitudes. DeBellis and Goldin (2006) maintain that when individuals become frustrated with lack of success in learning, their negative affect becomes more influential, just as encouragement during problem solving can increase the gratification of successful problem solving, resulting in more positive affect in the learning context.

Understanding teacher affect is important as we try to map the relationships between affective experiences and instructional practices. This is particularly crucial for instruction-related controversial topics such as evolution, global warming, or sex education.

Theories of Attitude and Belief Change

Although the critical links between teachers' belief systems and practices have been documented, the mechanisms of belief change remain unclear. Several models

have been proposed to explain belief change, and some of the more promising models include dissonance theory, conceptual change, and dual process models (Gregoire, 2003). Dissonance theory emerged from research on attitude change and is based on the premise that when an individual experiences imbalanced cognitive positions, dissonance occurs and individuals are motivated to change their attitude. A key component of this view is whether the individual perceives that he or she has control over the dissonant event. If the dissonance is viewed as outside of the individual then this theory suggests little change will take place (Gregoire, 2003). The second theory of attitude change applies the same conditions to changes in attitudes that have been applied to conceptual change and include dissatisfaction with existing beliefs and finding new beliefs to be intelligible, plausible, and fruitful (Strike & Posner 1982).

For changes in beliefs, Gregoire (2003) proposed a cognitive-affective model to explain changes in beliefs that rests on the response the individual gives to an event— such as educational reform. Gregoire maintains that if the individual sees reform as a challenge and responds with intention then the result may be belief change. But if the individual sees the reform as a threat and responds with avoidance then the result is likely to be superficial or no change in beliefs. Gregoire further argues that self-efficacy is likely to mediate the avoidance or challenge response. An important component of Gregoire's theory is the role of mastery experiences that are likely to increase a teacher's efficacy and increase the likelihood that a teacher will embrace change. The implication here is that teachers need time to practice (master new skills) and get feedback on new instructional strategies if they are to implement new reforms.

Development of Attitudes and Beliefs

In general, researchers have found that attitudes improve with age and experience. But an exception to this was found in a study by Schwirian (1969), who reported that younger teachers are more positive than older teachers are. More recent research suggests that the development of beliefs is not necessarily linear and may be context dependent (Pilitsis & Duncan, 2012).

Forbes and Davis (2010) followed four beginning elementary teachers and examined their beliefs about the role of driving questions and investigation questions in teaching science. The teachers' beliefs about the role of questions changed over time but followed different trajectories depending on their knowledge and unique contexts. In a similar study, Crawford (2007) followed five prospective teachers and assessed their beliefs about teaching science. In this study, teachers' beliefs about teaching with inquiry influenced their decisions about planning instruction. Crawford found that the teachers held complex and at times conflicting beliefs.

One of the goals of attitude and belief research is to be able to predict and alter the development of teachers' beliefs. But it is becoming increasingly apparent that this process is more complex than originally thought. Recent research by Pilitsis and Duncan (2012) showed that preservice teachers' beliefs changed over the course of a methods class in ways that were not linear or consistent. These authors suggested that when a regression in beliefs occurs, it can signal a fundamental response to instruction about learning to teach. These results support a cognitive change model for beliefs such as the one discussed earlier by Gregoire (2003).

A 3-year study of teacher education conducted by Fletcher and Luft (2011) found that teachers' beliefs about teaching varied more across time than did teachers' beliefs about learning. Although the program emphasized reform-based teaching, by the end of the first year of teaching, these beginning teachers shifted back to a more traditional didactic orientation to teaching. Fletcher and Luft (2011) suggested that

> [o]ur research reminds science teacher educators that beliefs are personal constructions and that teacher preparation programs need to find new and different ways to challenge teachers to move toward the formation of reform-based beliefs. In essence, science teacher educators need to be as diligent in monitoring the teaching beliefs of their teachers are they are in monitoring content knowledge or instructional practices.
>
> (pp. 1144–1145)

Science Teacher Professional Development

As noted, one of the primary goals of professional development is to promote changes in teachers' attitudes and beliefs. Studies have documented this critical role of professional development in shaping attitudes toward teaching science (Moore, 1975), teaching science-technology-society topics (Kaya, Yager, & Dogan, 2009), and implementing innovative curricula (Ost, 1971). There is also evidence that teachers with more positive attitudes have students with higher achievement levels (Evans, 2011). Furthermore, professional development programs that do not take into account teachers' attitudes and beliefs have been found to be unsuccessful (Ryan, 2004; Stipek & Byler, 1997).

Martin-Dunlop and Fraser (2007) assessed preservice elementary teachers' perceptions of laboratory teaching and attitudes toward science before and after their educational program. The researchers found significant gains in the improvement of attitudes. Level of instructor support was found to predict student attitudes. Luft and Roehrig (2007) found that when preservice science teachers "display tendencies towards student-centered activities and instruction, [they] can develop more responsive ideologies with specialized support" (p. 48). Similarly, when preservice teachers are not afforded specialized support, the opposite holds true and their beliefs can move away from inquiry and more toward traditional practices. Preservice teachers' beliefs are most easily changed when they are provided with supportive parameters (Luft & Roehrig, 2007). Other research has shown that inservice teachers with more established teaching belief systems are most reluctant to change (Crawford, 2007).

Hutchins and Friedrichsen (2012) conducted one of the few studies that has looked at the impact of professional development on college teachers' views of inquiry. Hutchins and Friedrichsen applied the sociocultural model of embedded belief systems (Jones & Carter, 2007) to the analysis of the data and found that there was a differential impact of the program on instructors depending on their prior belief system. Participants who came into the program with a negative attitude toward the inquiry approach tended to maintain this attitude toward implementation of the professional development just as those participants who came into the program with positive attitudes maintained a positive stance and indicated interest in implementing the inquiry model in the future.

One of the strongest studies in the last 5 years related to changes in beliefs was conducted by Lumpe, Czerniak, Haney, and Beltyukova (2012). This study examined elementary teachers' teaching self-efficacy over an intensive professional development program and found that participating teachers experienced significant gains in teaching self-efficacy. Furthermore, teacher beliefs and the number of hours participating in professional development were significant predictors of students' science achievement.

Contexts, Culture, Conditions for Change

Science teachers' belief systems are clearly embedded in specific contexts, experiences, and cultural frameworks. These individual factors are often unique to the teacher and make trying to model and predict beliefs and attitudes a messy endeavor. As the teaching force is becoming increasingly diverse and student populations are more mobile, there is increased interest in understanding the intersections of culture, worldview, contexts (such as socioscientific issues and localized educational reforms), and belief systems.

It seems logical that the more a teacher learns about a particular topic (such as evolution or biotechnology), the more likely they would be to hold attitudes and beliefs similar to those of scientists. This is the basic premise of the knowledge deficit model that suggests that increased knowledge of a topic should predict a positive influence on attitudes (Prokop, Leskova, Kubiatko, & Diran, 2007), but this is not always the case. For example, Gardner and Jones (2011, 2013) examined preservice science and mathematics teachers' knowledge of, experiences with, and perceptions of biotechnology and nanotechnology and found that knowledge and experience with the topics did not predict perceptions of risk. Instead, perception of risk was linked to generalized perceptions of technological risks that included avoidance, awareness, and affinity. Allum, Sturgis, Tabourazi, and Brunton-Smith (2008) also reported in their meta-analysis that understandings of science were only loosely correlated with attitudes toward science.

Culture

Studies across different cultures have found that teachers' attitudes and beliefs toward specific topics may vary (Gardner & Jones, 2012). For example, studies of science teachers' views of biotechnology in India (Mohapatra, Priyadarshini, & Biswas, 2010) differed from the results obtained by researchers in the United States (Boone, Gartin, Boone, & Hughes, 2006) and Australia (Kidman, 2009). Culture, according to Nieto (1999), is "the ever changing values, traditions, social and political relationships, and worldview created, shared, and transformed by a group of people bound together by a combination of factors that include a common history, geographic location, language, social class, and religion" (p. 48). Given the importance of looking at the relationship between culture and attitudes, it is clear that the area is underresearched (Vedder, Horenczyk, Liebkind, & Nickmans, 2006).

Religion

Dagher and BouJaoude (1997) argue that in addition to culture, teachers' worldviews of science as well as religion are predictors of instructional practices. It has been argued that religious beliefs have perhaps been the most powerful motivator for human behavior (Katz, 2002). In recent years, there has been a growing interest among researchers to understand how an individual's religious beliefs intersect with their beliefs about science and science teaching (Colburn & Henriques, 2006; Deniz, Donnelly, & Yilmaz, 2008; Stolberg, 2007, 2008).

When confronted with science concepts that conflict with religious beliefs, Barbour (2000) suggested that the result can lead to conflict, independence, dialogue, or integration. Mansour (2011) studied Egyptian Muslim science teachers and applied Barbour's (2000) categorization of the relationship between science and religion (conflict, independence, dialogue, or integration) to the data analyses. Mansour (2011) reported that a majority of the teachers expressed an integrated view of science and religion. However, Mansour noted that teachers' personal religious beliefs shaped their views of science as well as of

Islam. Furthermore, Islamic beliefs informed the teachers' beliefs about the nature of science. For some teachers, religion left them feeling conflicted about scientific applications. For example, one of the teachers stated: "I do think, but I am not certain, that there are a lot of applications of genetic engineering that conflict with religion because it alters the creation of God in plants or animals" (Mansour, 2011, p. 297). Other teachers in the study held less absolutist views of science and religion, such as Dalia, who described science and religion as "two faces of one coin, as both of them give us different information. Science gives us scientific details and religion gives us values, morals, and ethical beliefs" (p. 297). In other cases, teachers believed that science can provide insight into religious views, as seen in this comment from one of the teachers in the study: "[t]he more mankind goes deeper into science, the more he grows aware of things around and the more he knows about the power of Allah" (p. 299). Mansour argues that science educators should strive to be aware of cultural differences that may exist among students that can lead to discomfort with Eurocentric science.

Another study by Mugaloglu and Bayram (2009) examined science teachers' attitudes toward science using a modified version of Science Teaching Attitudes Scales (STAS-II) and found that science teachers' attitudes about science teaching were not correlated with political, social, economic, or aesthetic values. They also reported that the teachers' religious values were negatively correlated with their attitudes toward teaching.

Measuring and Assessing Attitudes and Beliefs

The assessment of attitudes continues to be problematic due to the lack of psychometric information on validity and reliability of assessments as well as studies to replicate results (Appleton, 1995; Blalock et al., 2008; Coulson, 1992; Reid, 2006; Skamp, 1991). Often assessments are used for single studies and are underdeveloped to be useful to other researchers. Blalock, Lichtenstein, Owen, Pruski, Marshall, and Toepperwein (2008) reviewed attitude assessments of scientific attitudes and attitudes toward science, nature of science, and science career interests that had been published from 1935 through 2005. They found 42% of assessments lacked one or more fundamental psychometric measures and in general were undertheorized. The lack of adequate assessments makes it difficult to determine in many studies what was actually measured and how one study relates to another (Pardo & Calvo, 2002). Other researchers have criticized attitude and belief assessments for being designed to elicit desirable answers or failing to discriminate between positive and negative attitudes toward specific topics (van Aalderen-Smeets, Walma van der Molen, & Asma, 2011).

Early self-efficacy assessments have been criticized for being one dimensional and failing to be responsive to the particular aspects of the task or context being assessed

(Skaalvik & Skaalvik, 2007). An outgrowth of the original attempts to measure self-efficacy was an interest in examining collective or group efficacy. Skaalvik and Skaalvik (2007) created an assessment to measure collective teacher efficacy and used structural equation modeling to examine the relationships between the variables. They reported that collective teacher efficacy was related to teacher burnout and teacher self-efficacy. The researchers suggest that these two variables could have a reciprocal effect on each other. For example, if a teacher has low self-efficacy, they may feel stress when confronted with difficult tasks (such as inquiry) for which they feel ill prepared to tackle. Likewise, if a teacher experiences stress and burnout from challenging situations, their self-efficacy could decline. One important outcome of the Skaalvik and Skaalvik (2007) study was their success at examining self- and collective efficacy in a specific context (in this case, Norwegian schools) and their call for a closer look at the culture–education context and how it relates to measuring efficacy. Table 41.3 lists assessments used to measure beliefs, attitudes, and self-efficacy.

In 2007, Jones and Carter proposed a sociocultural model of the factors that contribute to beliefs and attitudes. In light of the research that has emerged over the last 5 years, we propose a revised model (Figure 41.3) that places greater emphasis on the roles of self-efficacy,

TABLE 41.3
Assessments of Science Teachers' Attitudes and Beliefs

Authors	Name of Assessment	Assessment Description
Shrigley (1974)	Science Attitude Scale (SAS)	Measures personal and professional attitudes
Enochs & Riggs (1990)	Science Teaching Efficacy Belief Instrument (STEBI)	Measures preservice teachers' science teaching self-efficacy and outcome expectancy
Martin-Dunlop & Fraser (2007)	Science Learning Environment and Attitude Scale	Measures science teacher attitudes
Lumpe, Haney, & Czerniak (2000)	The Context Beliefs About Teaching Science (CBATS)	Measures beliefs about teaching methods and curriculum, social support, resources, time within the curriculum, and preparation time
van Aalderen-Smeets, Walma van der Molen, & Asma (2011)	Dimensions of Attitude Towards Science Instrument	Assesses attitudes toward science
Barmby, Kind, & Jones (2008)	Attitudes Towards Science	Includes measures for attitudes towards learning science in school, practical work in science, science outside of school, importance of science, self-concept in science, and future participation in science
Adams, Perkins, Podolefsky, Dubson, Finkelstein, & Wieman (2006)	Colorado Attitudes About Learning Science Survey	Assesses student beliefs about physics and learning physics
Thomas, Pedersen, & Finson (2001)	DASTT-C	Uses drawings and a written component to elicit preservice teachers' perceptions of themselves as science teachers.
Lan (2012)	NAST-T Nanotechnology Attitude Scale for K–12 Teachers	Assesses K–12 teachers' attitudes related to the importance of nanotechnology, affective tendencies in science teaching, and behavioral tendencies to teach nanotechnology
Maier, Greenfield, & Bulotsky-Shearer (in press)	The Preschool Teacher Attitudes and Beliefs Toward Science Teaching questionnaire (P-TABS)	Measures early childhood teachers' attitudes and beliefs about science
Schommer (1990)	Epistemological Questionnaire (EQ)	Measures dimensions of epistemic beliefs: stability of knowledge, structure of knowledge, speed of learning, ability to learn, and source of knowledge

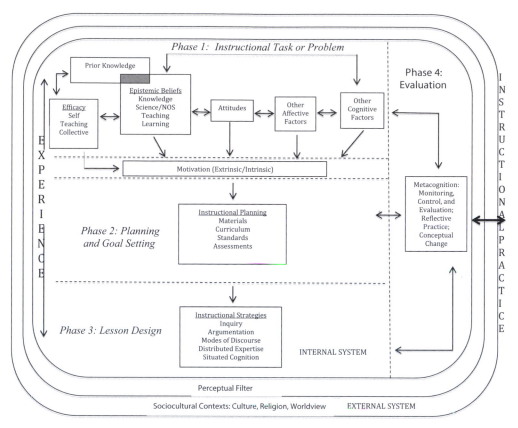

Figure 41.3 An integrated model of epistemic cognition, attitudes, and instructional practice. (Adapted from Muis, 2007, and Jones & Carter, 2007)

epistemic beliefs, self-regulated learning, and metacognition. This model is to be interpreted as a dynamic process versus a static product. Each phase of self-regulation is cyclic, with no definitive beginning or ending point.

To illustrate this model, consider a teacher confronted with a curricular standard to teach genetically modified foods. The teacher is faced with making a decision about whether to teach the topic and, if taught, what to teach (materials, curricula, standards, and assessments), as well as the instructional strategies to use (inquiry, argumentation, group work, case studies, etc.). The model presented here suggests that the experiences and prior knowledge that teachers bring to the instructional task will frame their epistemic beliefs, self-efficacy, attitudes, and other cognitive and affective factors. Each of these internal factors is influenced by the other factors, and all are embedded in the larger sociocultural context (religion, worldview, identity, and specific context) as well as the teacher's perceptual lens.

For example, if the teacher brings to the context strong religious convictions, authoritarian epistemic beliefs, and a cultural view of skepticism of science and technology, then the teacher may decide that the topic of genetically modified foods is not appropriate for students and may choose to ignore the curricular standard. On the other hand, if the teacher brings a relativist view of knowledge to the challenge of

teaching genetically modified foods, the teacher may decide that the topic is intricate as well as context dependent, and the teacher may be more likely to teach the complexities of genetic modification as outlined by the curricular standard. In the case of either teacher, the decision that is made about which curriculum to use, the strategies that will be used, and the assessments that will be implemented will be guided by the teacher's motivation, which is further informed by self-efficacy, prior knowledge, epistemic beliefs, attitudes, and other affective and cognitive factors. Furthermore, this model places emphasis on the metacognitive activity in which the teacher engages as he or she reflects on these decisions, works through cognitive conflicts, and implements the instruction. The model is designed to indicate that metacognition both influences and is influenced by the instructional practices. The model is considered to be active, continuous, and modified by feedback and metacognitive activity. As noted, the model is based on a foundation of sociocultural and individual contexts.

Research supports many of the relationships and influences between the different factors found in the model, but the overall system has yet to be fully tested. The weighting of the different factors and the pathways of influence are not known. Future research is needed to refine this model to more accurately reflect the complexity of self-regulating behavior and epistemic beliefs.

Summary and Future Research

Over the last 5 years, the research on attitudes and beliefs has continued to document the relationships between attitudes and beliefs of science teachers and instructional practices. Studies also continue to show the mismatch between teachers' knowledge and their teaching. In some cases, beliefs and attitudes take precedence over knowledge as influences on teachers' choices about teaching a particular topic (such as evolution). Recent research has also begun to unravel the complexities that exist about the factors that shape beliefs and attitudes. We know that in many cases, some factors affect and are affected by beliefs and attitudes. An example is that increases in knowledge contribute to changes in beliefs and attitudes, but reciprocally we know that beliefs and attitudes shape the development of knowledge.

One of the significant advancements that has taken place in science education research on attitudes and beliefs is the documentation of the influence that science teachers' epistemic beliefs have on teachers' planning and teaching with inquiry. Furthermore, researchers are unraveling the relationships between teachers' epistemic beliefs and their concepts of the nature of science. In addition, there has been an increase in the studies that document the influence of self-efficacy on science teachers' professional growth.

Only recently have researchers begun to integrate psychological models on the structure of beliefs and attitudes with research related to teachers' instructional practices. The work is increasing in sophistication and has the potential to provide more robust models to explain and predict science teachers' attitudes and beliefs.

Even with the large numbers of studies related to science teacher beliefs and attitudes, there are a number of holes and gaps in the literature. First, researchers need a clearer understanding of the relationships of worldview and culture on science teachers' beliefs and attitudes related to sociocultural issues. Second, we need to know more about how beliefs develop through time and across groups of people in particular contexts. There is a need to determine which beliefs contribute most strongly to science teachers' attitudes and how these beliefs form. Parallel to understanding how beliefs and attitudes form is a need to understand how beliefs and attitudes erode or decline over time. By understanding the formation and changes of attitudes and beliefs over the span of a teacher's career, we can design more effective professional education programs at the preservice and inservice levels. We need to learn how to support science teachers in ways that encourage resilience and increase teachers' self-efficacy to make changes in science programs. Finally, we need to know more about how epistemological beliefs are related to science teachers' planning and teaching as well as how metacognitive processes can promote or support epistemic cognition.

In summary, science teachers' beliefs and attitudes are part of a complex system that includes factors such as prior experiences, self-efficacy, epistemic beliefs, and affect that operate within specific sociocultural contexts. There is ample evidence of the powerful influence of science teachers' attitudes and beliefs on teaching science, and by helping teachers understand their beliefs, we can develop more reflective teachers who can not only grow professionally but who can also promote awareness and growth in their students.

Note

1. The authors used the term "eclectic" to describe views not strictly adhering to the four positions outlined (e.g., empirico-inductive, relativist, etc.).

References

Adams, W. K., Perkins, K. K., Podolefsky, N. S., Dubson, M., Finkelstein, N. D., & Wieman, C. E. (2006). New instrument for measuring student beliefs about physics and learning physics: The Colorado Learning Attitudes about Science Survey. *Physical Review Special Topics-Physics Education Research, 2*(1). doi:10.1103/PhysRevSTPER.2.010101

Akyol, G., Tekkaya, C., Sungur, S., & Traynor, A. (2012). Modeling the interrelationships among preservice science teachers' understanding and acceptance of evolution, their views on nature of science and self-efficacy beliefs regarding teaching evolution. *Journal of Science Teacher Education, 23*(8), 937–957.

Alexander, P. A., & Dochy, F. J. R. C. (1995). Conceptions of knowledge and beliefs: A comparison across varying cultural and educational communities. *American Educational Research Journal, 32*(2), 413–442.

Allum, N., Sturgis, P., Tabourazi, D., & Brunton-Smith, I. (2008). Science knowledge and attitudes across cultures: A meta-analysis. *Public Understanding of Science, 17,* 35–54.

Amato, S. A. (2004). Improving student teachers' mathematical knowledge. *Proceedings of the 10th International Congress on Mathematical Education.* Copenhagen, Denmark.

Amirshokoohi, A. (2010). Elementary preservice teachers' environmental literacy and views toward science, technology, and society (STS) issues. *Science Educator, 19*(1), 56–63.

Angle, J., & Moseley, C. (2010). Science teacher efficacy and outcome expectancy as predictors of students' end-of-instruction (EOI) biology I test scores. *School Science and Mathematics, 109*(8), 473–483.

Apostolou, A., & Koulaidis, V. (2010). Epistemology and science education: A study of epistemological views of teachers. *Research in Science & Technological Education, 28*(2), 149–166.

Appleton, K. (1995). Student teachers' confidence to teach science: Is more science knowledge necessary to improve self-confidence? *International Journal of Science Education, 17,* 357–369.

Ashton, P. T., & Webb, R. B. (1986). *Making a difference: Teachers' sense of efficacy and student achievement.* New York: Longman.

Atwater, M. M., Gardner, C., & Kight, C. R. (1991). Beliefs and attitudes of urban primary teachers toward physical science and teaching physical science. *Journal of Elementary Science Education, 3,* 3–12.

Bandura, A. (1982). Self-efficacy mechanism in human agency. *American Psychologist, 37*(2), 122–147.

Bandura, A. (1997). *Self-efficacy: The exercise of control.* New York: W. H. Freeman.

Barbour, I. A. (2000). *When science meets religion: Enemies, strangers or partners?* San Francisco: HarperCollins.

Barmby, P., Kind, P. M., & Jones, K. (2008). Examining changing attitudes in secondary school science. *International Journal of Science Education, 30*(8), 1075–1093.

Begum, S. (2012). A secondary science teacher's beliefs about environmental education and its relationship with the classroom practices. *International Journal of Social Sciences and Education, 2*(1), 10–29.

Bell, P., & Linn, M.C. (2002). Beliefs about science: How does science instruction contribute? In B.K. Hofer & P.R. Pintrich (Eds.), *Personal epistemology: The psychology of beliefs about knowledge and knowing* (pp. 321–346). Mahwah, NJ: Erlbaum.

Berkman, M.B., & Plutzer, E. (2011). Defeating creationism in the courtroom, but not in the classroom. *Science, 331*(6016), 404–405.

Berland, L.K., & Hammer, D. (2012). Framing for scientific argumentation. *Journal of Research in Science Teaching, 49*(1), 68–94.

Berman, P., McLaughlin, M., Bass, G., Pauly, E. & Zellman, G. (1977). *Federal programs supporting educational change. Vol VII: Factors affecting implementation and continuation (Report No. R-1589/7-HEW).* Santa Monica, CA: The Rand Corporation (Eric Document No. ED140-432).

Blalock, C., Lichtenstein, M., Owen, S., Pruski, L., Marshall, C., & Toepperwein, M. (2008). In pursuit of validity: A comprehensive review of science attitude instruments 1935–2005. *International Journal of Science Education, 30*(7), 961–977.

Blancke, S., De Smedt, J., De Cruz, H., Boudry, M., & Braeckman, J. (2012). The implications of the cognitive sciences for the relation between religion and science education: The case of evolutionary theory. *Science & Education, 21*(8), 1167–1184.

Bleicher, R.E. (2007). Nurturing confidence in preservice elementary science teachers. *Journal of Science Teacher Education, 18,* 841–860.

Blonder, R., Benny, N., & Jones, M.G. (in press). Teaching self-efficacy of science teachers. In C. Czerniak, R.H. Evans, & J. Luft (Eds.), *The role of science teachers' beliefs in international classrooms: From teacher actions to student learning.*

Boldrin, A., & Mason, L. (2009). Distinguishing between knowledge and beliefs: Students' epistemic criteria for differentiating. *Instructional Science: An International Journal of the Learning Sciences, 37*(2), 107–127.

Bong, M. (2006). Asking the right question. How confident are you that you could successfully perform these tasks? In F. Pajares & T. Urdan (Eds.), *Self-efficacy beliefs of adolescents* (pp. 287–305). Greenwich, CT: Information Age.

Boone, H.N., Gartin, S.A., Boone, D.A., & Hughes, J.E. (2006). Modernizing the agricultural education curriculum: An analysis of agricultural education teachers' attitudes, knowledge, and understanding of biotechnology. *Journal of Agricultural Education, 47*(1), 78–89.

Bottcher, F., & Meisert, A. (2011). Argumentation in science education: A model based framework. *Science & Education, 20*(2), 103–140.

Breslyn, W., & McGinnis, J.R. (2011). A comparison of exemplary biology, chemistry, earth science, and physics teachers' conceptions and enactment of inquiry. *Science Education, 96*(1), 48–77.

Brown, P.L., Abell, S.K., Demir, A., & Schmidt, F.J. (2006). College science teachers' views of classroom inquiry. *Science Education, 90,* 784–802.

Bursal, M., & Paznokas, L. (2006). Mathematics anxiety and preservice elementary teachers' confidence to teach mathematics and science. *School Science and Mathematics, 106,* 173–180.

Carleton, L.E., Fitch, J.C., & Krockover, G.H. (2008). An inservice teacher education program's effect on teacher efficacy and attitudes. *The Educational Forum, 72,* 46–62.

Chandler, M.J., Hallett, D., & Sokol, B.W. (2002). Competing claims about competing knowledge claims. In B.K. Hofer & P.R. Pintrich (Eds.), *Personal epistemology: The psychology of beliefs about knowledge and knowing* (pp. 145–168). Mahwah, NJ: Lawrence Erlbaum Associates.

Choi, S., & Ramsey, J. (2009). Constructing elementary teachers' beliefs, attitudes, and practical knowledge through an inquiry-based elementary science course. *School Science and Mathematics, 109*(6), 313–324.

Colburn, A., & Henriques, L. (2006). Clergy views on evolution, creationism, science, and religion. *Journal of Research in Science Teaching, 43*(4), 419–442.

Conley, A.M., Pintrich, P.R., Vekiri, I., & Harrison, D. (2004). Changes in epistemological beliefs in elementary science students. *Contemporary Educational Psychology, 29,* 186–204.

Cordero, E.C., Todd, A.M., & Abellera, D. (2008). Climate change education and the ecological footprint. *Bulletin of the American Meteorological Society, 89*(6), 865–872.

Cotton, D.R.E. (2006). Implementing curriculum guidance on environmental education: The importance of teachers' beliefs. *Journal of Curriculum Studies, 38*(1), 67–83.

Coulson, R. (1992). Development of an instrument for measuring attitudes of early childhood educators towards science. *Research in Science Education, 22,* 101–105.

Crawford, B. (2007). Learning to reach science as inquiry in the rough and tumble of practice. *Journal of Research in Science Teaching, 44*(4), 613–642.

Crippen, K.J. (2012). Argument as professional development: Impacting teacher knowledge and beliefs about science. *Journal of Science Teacher Education, 23*(8), 847–866.

Cross, D., & Hong, J. (2012). An examination of teachers' emotions in the school context. *Teaching and Teacher Education, 28,* 957–967.

Dagher, Z.R., & BouJaoude, S. (1997). Scientific views and religious beliefs of college students: The case of biological evolution. *Journal of Research in Science Teaching, 34*(5), 429–445.

DeBellis, V.A., & Goldin, G.A. (2006). Affect and meta-affect in mathematical problem solving: A representational perspective. *Educational Studies in Mathematics, 63,* 131–147.

Deniz, H. (2011). Examination of changes in prospective elementary teachers' epistemological beliefs in science and exploration of factors meditating that change. *Journal of Science Education and Technology, 20*(6), 750–760.

Deniz, H., Donnelly, L., & Yilmaz, I. (2008). Exploring the factors related to acceptance of evolutionary theory among Turkish preservice biology teachers: Toward a more informative conceptual ecology for biological evolution. *Journal of Research in Science Teaching, 45*(4), 420–443.

Dewey, J. (1922). *Human nature and conduct.* New York: Henry Holt.

Eagly, A., & Chaiken, S. (1993). *The psychology of attitudes.* Belmont, CA: Wadsworth Group/Thomson Learning.

Eagly, A.H. (1992). Uneven progress: Social psychology and the study of attitudes. *Journal of Personality and Social Psychology, 63,* 693–710.

Eberle, F. (2008). Teaching and coherent science: An investigation of teachers' beliefs about and practice of teaching science coherently. *School Science and Mathematics, 108*(3), 103–112.

Eick, C.J., & Reed, C.J. (2002), What makes an inquiry-oriented science teacher? The influence of learning histories on student teacher role identity and practice. *Science Education, 86,* 401–416.

Elby, A., & Hammer, D. (2010). Epistemological resources and framing: A cognitive framework for helping teachers interpret and respond to their students' epistemologies. In L.D. Bendixen & F.C. Feucht (Eds.), *Personal epistemology in the classroom: Theory, research, and implications for practice* (pp. 409–433). Cambridge, UK: Cambridge University Press.

Elder, A.D. (2002). Characterizing fifth grade students' epistemological beliefs in science. In B.K. Hofer & P.R. Pintrich (Eds.), *Personal epistemology: The psychology of beliefs about knowledge and knowing* (pp. 347–363). Mahwah, NJ: Lawrence Erlbaum Associates.

Elstad, E., & Turmo, A. (2010). Students' self-regulation and teachers' influences in science: Interplay between ethnicity and gender. *Research in Science & Technological Education, 28*(3), 249–260. doi: 10.1080/02635143.2010.501751

Enochs, L.G., & Riggs, I.M. (1990). Further development of an elementary science teaching efficacy belief instrument: A preservice elementary scale. *School Science and Mathematics, 90,* 694–706.

Ernest, P. (1989). The knowledge, beliefs and attitudes of the mathematics teacher: A model. *Journal of Education for Teaching, 15,* 13–34.

Ertmer, P.A., Ottenbreit-Leftwich, A.T., Sadik, O., Sendurer, E., & Sendurer, P. (2012). Teacher beliefs and technology integration practices: A critical relationship. *Computers & Education, 59,* 423–435.

Evans, B. (2011). Content knowledge, attitudes, and self-efficacy in the mathematics New York City Teaching Fellows (NYCTF) Program. *School Science and Mathematics, 111*(5), 225–235.

Evans, G., & Durant, J. (1995). The relationship between knowledge and attitudes in the public understanding of science in Britain. *Public Understanding of Science, 4*, 57–74.

Fang, Z. (1996). A review of research on teacher beliefs and practices. *Educational Research, 38*(1), 47–65.

Fishbein, M. (1967). A consideration of beliefs and their role in attitude measurement. In M. Fishbein (Ed.), *Readings in attitude theory and measurement.* (pp. 257–266). New York: John Wiley & Sons.

Fletcher, S., & Luft, J. (2011). Early career secondary science teachers: A longitudinal study of beliefs in relation to field experiences. *Science Education, 95*(6), 1124–1146.

Fonseca, M., Costa, P., Lencastre, L., & Tavares, F. (2012). Disclosing biology teachers' beliefs about biotechnology and biotechnology education. *Teaching and Teacher Education, 28*, 368–381.

Forbes, C.T., & Davis, E.A. (2010). Beginning elementary teachers' beliefs about the use of anchoring questions in science: A longitudinal study. *Science Education, 94*(2), 365–387.

Friedrichsen, P., Van Driel, J.H., & Abell, S.K. (2011). Taking a closer look at science teaching orientations. *Science Education, 95*(2), 358–376.

Gardner, G. E., & Jones, M. G. (2011). Science instructors' perceptions of the risks of biotechnology: Implications for science instruction. *Research in Science Education, 41*(5), 711–738.

Gardner, G. E., & Jones, M. G. (accepted March 28, 2013). Exploring pre-service teachers' perceptions of the risks of emergent technologies: Implications for teaching and learning. *Journal of Nano Education.*

Gibbs, S., & Powell, B. (2012). Teacher efficacy and pupil behaviour: The structure of teachers' individual and collective beliefs and their relationship with numbers of pupils excluded from school. *British Journal of Educational Psychology, 82*(4), 564–584.

Gibson, S., & Dembo, M. (1984). Teacher efficacy: A construct validation. *Journal of Educational Psychology, 76*, 569–582.

Goddard, R.D., Hoy, W.K., & Woolfolk-Hoy, A. (2004). Collective efficacy beliefs: Theoretical developments, empirical evidence, and future directions. *Educational Researcher, 33*, 3–13.

Gregoire, M. (2003). Is it a challenge or a threat? A dual-process model of teachers' cognition and appraisal processes during conceptual change. *Educational Psychology Review, 15*(2), 147–179.

Guskey, T. (1988). Teacher efficacy, self-concept, and attitudes toward the implementation of instructional innovation. *Teaching and Teacher Education, 4*(1), 63–69.

Harlen, W. (1997). Primary teachers' understanding in science and its impact in the classroom. *Research in Science Education, 27*(3), 323–337.

Hartshorne, R. (2008). Effects of hypermedia-infused professional development on attitudes toward teaching science. Journal of Educational Computing Research, 38, 333–351.

Harty, H., Samuel, J.V., & Anderson, H.O. (1991). Understanding the nature of science and attitudes towards science and science teaching of preservice elementary teachers in three preparation sequences. *Journal of Elementary Science Education, 3*, 13–22.

Harwood, W., Reiff, R., & Phillipson, T. (2002, January). *Scientists' conceptions of scientific inquiry: Voices from the front.* Paper presented at the meeting of the Association for the Education of Teachers in Science, Charlotte, NC.

Haury, D. (1989). The contribution of science locus of control orientation to expressions of attitude toward science teaching. *Journal of Research in Science Teaching, 26*, 503–517.

Hofer, B. K. (2001). Personal epistemology research: Implications for learning and instruction. *Educational Psychology Review, 13*(4): 353–382.

Hofer, B.K., & Pintrich, P.R. (1997). The development of epistemological theories: Beliefs about knowledge and knowing and their relation to learning. *Review of Educational Research, 67*(1), 88–140.

Holt, C., Hargrove, P., & Harris, S. (2011). An investigation into the life experiences and beliefs of teachers exhibiting highly effective classroom management behaviors. *Teacher Education and Practice, 24*(1), 96–113.

Hutchins, K., & Friedrichsen, P. (2012). Science faculty belief systems in a professional development program: Inquiry in college laboratories. *Journal of Science Teacher Education, 23*(8), 867–887.

Jaccard, J., Litardo, H., & Wan, C.K. (1999). Subjective culture: Social psychological models of behavior. In J. Adamopolis & Y. Kashima (Eds.), *Social psychology and cultural context.* Thousand Oaks, CA: Sage.

Jarrett, O. S. (1999). Science interest and confidence among preservice elementary teachers. *Journal of Elementary Science Education, 11*(1), 49–59.

Jarvis, T. & Pell, A. (2004). Primary teachers' changing attitudes and cognition during a two-year science in-service programme and their effect on pupils. *International Journal of Science Education 26*(14), 1787–1811.

Jones, M.G., & Carter, G. (2007). Science teacher attitudes and beliefs. *Handbook of research on science education,* 1067–1104.

Kagan, D.M. (1992). Implication of research on teacher belief. *Educational Psychologist, 27*, 65–90.

Kane, R.G., Sandretto, S., & Heath, C. (2002). Telling half the story: A critical review of the research into tertiary teachers' beliefs. *Review of Educational Research, 72*(2), 177–228.

Katz, S.H. (2002). Questions for a millennium: Religion and science from the perspective of a scientist. *Zygon, 37*(1), 45–54.

Kaya, O.N., Yager, R., Dogan, A. (2009). Changes in attitudes towards science–technology–society of preservice science teachers. *Research in Science Education, 39*(2), 257–279.

Kidman, G. (2009). Attitudes and interests towards biotechnology: The mismatch between students and teachers. *Eurasia Journal of Mathematics, Science and Technology, 5*(2), 135–143.

Kim, S.Y., & Nehm, R.H. (2011). A cross-cultural comparison of Korean and American science teachers' views of evolution and the nature of science. *International Journal of Science Education, 33*(2), 197–227.

King, P.M., & Kitchener, K.S. (1994). *Developing reflective judgment: Understanding and promoting intellectual growth and critical thinking in adolescents and adults.* San Francisco: Jossey-Bass Publishers.

Koballa, T.R., Jr. (1986). Teaching hands-on science activities: Variables that moderate attitude-behavior consistency. *Journal of Research in Science Teaching, 23*, 493–502.

Lan, Y. (2012). Development of an attitude scale to assess teachers' attitudes toward nanotechnology. *International Journal of Science Education, 34*(8), 1189–1210.

Leavy, A.M., McSorley, F.A., & Boté, L.A. (2007). An examination of what metaphor construction reveals about the evolution of preservice teachers' beliefs about teaching and learning. *Teaching and Teacher Education, 23*(7), 1217–1233.

Lederman, N.G. (2007). Nature of science: Past, present, and future. In S. K. Abell & N.G. Lederman (Eds.), *Handbook of research on science education* (pp. 831–880). Mahwah, NJ: Lawrence Erlbaum.

Lester, B.T., Ma, L., Lee, O., & Lambert, J. (2006). Social activism in elementary science education: A science, technology, and society approach to teach global warming. *International Journal of Science Education, 28*(4), 315–339.

Liang, L.L., & Gabel, D.L. (2005). Effectiveness of a constructivist approach to science instruction for prospective elementary teachers. *International Journal of Science Education, 27*, 1143–1162.

Luehmann, A.L. (2007). Identity development as a lens to science teacher preparation. *Science Education, 91*(5), 822–839.

Luft, J.A., & Roehrig, G.H. (2007). Capturing science teachers' epistemological beliefs: The development of the teacher beliefs interview. *Electronic Journal of Science Education, 11*(2).

Lumpe, A., Czerniak, C., Haney, J., & Beltyukova, S. (2012). Beliefs about teaching science: The relationship between elementary teachers' participation in professional development and student achievement. *International Journal of Science Education, 34*(2), 153–166.

Lumpe, A. T., Haney, J. J., & Czerniak, C. M. (2000). Assessing teachers' beliefs about their science teaching context. *Journal of Research in Science Teaching, 37,* 275–292.

Maggioni, L., & Parkinson, M. M. (2008). The role of teacher epistemic cognition, epistemic beliefs, and calibration in instruction. *Educational Psychology Review, 20*(4), 445–461.

Maier, M., Greenfield, D., & Bulotsky-Shearer, R. (in press). Development and validation of a preschool teachers' attitudes and beliefs toward teaching science questionnaire. *Early Childhood Research Quarterly.*

Mansour, N. (2009). Science teachers' beliefs and practices: Issues, implications and research agenda. *International Journal of Environmental and Science Education, 4*(1), 25–48.

Mansour, N. (2011), Science teachers' views of science and religion vs. the Islamic perspective: Conflicting or compatible? *Science Education, 95*(2), 281–309.

Markic, S., & Eilks, I. (2012). A comparison of student teachers' beliefs from four different science teaching domains using a mixed methods design. *International Journal of Science Education, 34*(4), 589–608.

Martin-Dunlop, C., & Fraser, B. J. (2007). Learning environment and attitudes associated with an innovative science course designed for prospective elementary teachers. *International Journal of Science and Mathematics Education, 6,* 163–190.

McCulloch, A. (2009). Insights into graphing calculator use: Methods for capturing activity and affect. *International Journal for Technology in Mathematics Education, 16*(2), 1–7.

McDevitt, T. M., Heikkinen, H. W., Alcorn, J. K., Ambrosio, A. L., & Gardner, A. L. (1993). Evaluation of the preparation of teachers in science and mathematics: Assessment of preservice teachers' attitudes and beliefs. *Science Education, 77,* 593–610.

McDonald, C. V. (2010). The influence of explicit nature of science and argumentation instruction on preservice primary teachers' views of nature of science. *Journal of Research in Science Teaching, 47*(9), 1137–1164.

McGinnis, R., Parker, P., & Graeber, A. (2004). A cultural perspective of the induction of five reform-minded beginning mathematics and science teachers. *Journal of Research in Science Teaching, 41,* 720–747.

Mohapatra, A. K., Priyadarshini, D., & Biswas, A. (2010). Genetically modified food: knowledge and attitude of teachers and students. *Journal of Science Education and Technology, 19*(5), 489–497.

Moore, R. (1975). A two-year study of a CCSS group's attitudes toward science and science teaching. *School Science and Mathematics, 75,* 288–290.

Mugaloglu, E., & Bayram, H. (2009). How are prospective science teachers' values and their attitudes towards science associated? Implications for science teacher training programs. *Procedia Social and Behavioral Sciences, 1,* 749–752.

Muis, K. R. (2007). The role of epistemic beliefs in self-regulated learning. *Educational Psychologist, 42,* 173–190.

Mulholland, J., & Wallace, J. (1996). Breaking the cycle: Preparing elementary teachers to teach science. *Journal of Elementary Science Education, 8,* 17–38.

Murphy, C., Neil, P., & Beggs, J. (2007). Primary science teacher confidence revisited: Ten years on. *Educational Research, 49,* 415–430.

Murphy, P. K., & Mason, L. (2006). Changing knowledge and changing beliefs. In P. A. Alexander & P. Winne (Eds.), *Handbook of educational psychology* (pp. 305–324). Mahwah, NJ: Lawrence Erlbaum Associates.

National Research Council. (1996). *National science education standards.* Washington, DC: National Academies Press.

National Research Council. (2000). *Inquiry and the national science education standards.* Washington, DC: National Academies Press.

National Research Council. (2012). *A framework for K–12 science education: Practices, cross-cutting concepts and core ideas.* Washington, DC: National Academies Press.

Nehm, R. H., Kim, S. Y., & Sheppard, K. (2009). Academic preparation in biology and advocacy for teaching evolution: Biology versus non-biology teachers. *Science Education, 93*(6), 1122–1146.

Nieto, S. (1999). *The light in their eyes: Creating multicultural learning communities.* New York: Teachers College Press.

Nisbett, R., & Ross, L. (1980). *Human inference: Strategies and shortcomings of social judgement.* Englewood Cliffs, NJ: Prentice-Hall.

Ogan-Bekiroglu, F., & Eskin, H. (2012). Examination of the relationship between engagement in scientific argumentation and conceptual knowledge. *International Journal of Science and Mathematics Education, 10*(6), 1415–1443.

Olafson, L., & Schraw, G. (2006). Teachers' beliefs and practices within and across domains. *International Journal of Educational Research, 45*(1–2), 71–84.

Ost, D. (1971). An evaluation of an institute for teachers of secondary-school biology. *American Biology Teacher, 33*(9), 546–548.

Otero, V. K., & Nathan, M. J. (2008). Preservice elementary teachers' views of their students' prior knowledge of science. *Journal of Research in Science Teaching, 45*(4), 497–523.

Pajares, F. (1997). Current directions in self-efficacy research. In H. W. Marsh, R. G. Craven, & D. M. McInerney (Eds.), *International advances in self research* (pp. 1–49). Greenwich, CT: Information Age.

Pajares, M. F. (1992). Teachers' beliefs and educational research: Cleaning up a messy construct. *Review of Educational Research, 62,* 307–332.

Palmer, D. (2011). Sources of efficacy information in an inservice program for elementary teachers. *Science Education, 95*(4), 577–600.

Palmer, D. H. (2001). Factors contributing to attitude exchange amongst preservice elementary teachers. *Science Education, 86,* 122–138.

Palmer, D. H. (2004). Situational interest and the attitudes towards science of primary teacher education students. *International Journal of Science Education, 26,* 895–908.

Papadimitriou, V. (2004). Prospective primary teachers' understanding of climate change, greenhouse effect, and ozone layer depletion. *Journal of Science Education and Technology, 13*(2), 299–307.

Pardo, R., & Calvo, F. (2002). Attitudes toward science among the European public: A methodological analysis. *Public Understanding of Science, 11,* 155–195.

Pedersen, J. E., & McCurdy, D. W. (1992). The effects of hands-on, minds-on teaching experiences on attitudes of preservice elementary teachers. *Science Education, 76,* 141–146.

Pilitsis, V., & Duncan, R. (2012). Changes in belief orientation of preservice teachers and their relation to inquiry activities. *Journal of Science Teacher Education, 23*(8), 909–936.

Prokop, P., Leskova, A., Kubiatko, M., & Diran, C. (2007). Slovakian students' knowledge of and attitudes toward biotechnology. *International Journal of Science Education, 29,* 895–907.

Ramey-Gassert, L., Shroyer, G., & Staver, J. (1996). A qualitative study of factors influencing science teaching self-efficacy of elementary level teachers. *Science Education, 80,* 283–315.

Reid, N. (2006). Thoughts on attitude measurement. *Research in Science & Technological Education, 24,* 3–27.

Rizk, N., Jaber, L., Halwany, S., & BouJaoude, S. (2012). Epistemological beliefs in science: An exploratory study of Lebanese university students' epistemologies. *International Journal of Science and Mathematics Education, 10*(3), 473–496.

Rokeach, M. (1968). *Beliefs, attitudes, and values: A theory of organization and change.* San Francisco: Jossey-Bass.

Rutledge, M. L., & Mitchell, M. A. (2002). High school biology teachers' knowledge structure, acceptance & teaching of evolution. *The American Biology Teacher, 64*(1), 21–28.

Ryan, S. (2004). Message in a model: Teachers' responses to a court-ordered mandate for curriculum reform. *Educational Policy, 18,* 661–685.

Saad, R., & BouJaoude, S. (2012). The relationship between teachers' knowledge and beliefs about science and inquiry and their classroom practices. *EURASIA Journal of Mathematics, Science & Technology Education, 8*(2), 113–128.

Sandoval, W.A. (2005). Understanding students' practical epistemologies and their influence on learning through inquiry. *Science Education, 89*(4), 634–656.

Scharmann, L. C., & Hampton, C. M. (1995). Cooperative learning and preservice elementary teacher science self efficacy. *Journal of Science Teacher Education, 6(3)*, 125–133.

Schommer, M. (1990). Effects of beliefs about the nature of knowledge on comprehension. *Journal of Educational Psychology, 82*(3), 498–504.

Schommer-Aikins, M. (2004). Explaining the epistemological belief system: Introducing the embedded systemic model and coordinated research approach. *Educational Psychologist, 39*(1), 19–29.

Schoon, K. J. & Boone, W. (1998). Self-efficacy and alternative conceptions of science preservice elementary teachers. *Science Education, 82*(5), 553–568.

Schraw, G., Dunkle, M.E., & Bendixen, L.D. (1995). Cognitive processes in well-defined and ill-defined problem solving. *Applied Cognitive Psychology, 9,* 523–538.

Schultz, P.A., Hong, J.Y., Cross, D.I., & Osbon, J.N. (2006). Reflections on investigating emotion in educational activity settings. *Educational Psychology Review, 18*(4), 343–360.

Schwartz, B., & Glassner, A. (2003). The blind and the paralytic: Supporting argumentation in every day and scientific issues. In J. Andriessen, M. Baker, & D. Suthers (Eds.), *Arguing to learn: Confronting cognitions in computer-supported collaborative learning environments* (pp. 227–260). Dordrecht, the Netherlands: Kluwer.

Schwartz, R., & Lederman, N. G. (2008). What scientists say: Scientists' views of nature of science and relation to science context. *International Journal of Science Education, 30*(6), 727–771.

Schwirian, P.M. (1969). Characteristics of elementary teachers related to attitudes toward science. *Journal of Research in Science Teaching, 6,* 203–213.

Settlage, J., Southerland, S.A., Smith, L.K., & Ceglie, R. (2009). Constructing a doubt-free teaching self: Self-efficacy, teacher identity, and science instruction within diverse settings. *Journal of Research in Science Teaching, 46*(1), 102–125.

Shrigley, R.L. (1974). The correlation of science attitude and science knowledge of preservice elementary teachers. *Science Education, 58*(2), 143–151.

Simpson, R.D., Koballa, T.R., Oliver, J.S., & Crawley, F. (1994). Research on the affective dimension of science learning. In D. Gable (Ed.), *Handbook of research on science teaching and learning* (pp. 211–234). New York: Macmillan.

Skaalvik, E.M., & Skaalvik, S. (2007). Dimensions of teacher self-efficacy and relations with strain factors, perceived collective teacher efficacy, and teacher burnout. *Journal of Educational Psychology, 99*(3), 611.

Skamp, K. (1991). Primary science and technology: How confident are teachers? *Research in Science Education, 21,* 290–299.

Smith, M.U., & Siegel, H. (2004). *Knowing, believing, and understanding: The goals of science education? Science and Education, 13,* 553–582.

Solomon, J., Scott, L., & Duveen, J. (1996). Large-scale exploration of pupils' understanding of the nature of science. *Science Education, 80*(5), 493–508.

Songer, N.B., & Linn, M.C. (1991). How do students' views of science influence knowledge integration? *Journal of Research in Science Teaching, 28,* 761–784.

Southerland, S., Sinatra, G., & Mathews, M. (2001). Beliefs, knowledge, and science education. *Educational Psychology Review, 13*(4), 325-351.

Southerland, S. A., Gess-Newsome, J., & Johnston, A. (2003). Portraying science in the classroom: The manifestation of scientists' beliefs in classroom practice. *Journal of Research in Science Teaching, 40,* 669–691.

Stipek, D., & Byler, P. (1997). Early childhood education teachers: Do they practice what they preach? *Childhood Research Quarterly, 12,* 305–325.

Stolberg, T. (2007). The religio-scientific frameworks of preservice primary teachers: An analysis of their influence on their teaching of science. *International Journal of Science Education, 29*(7), 909–930.

Stolberg, T.L. (2008). Understanding the approaches to the teaching of religious education of preservice primary teachers: The influence of religio-scientific frameworks. *Teaching and Teacher Education: An International Journal of Research and Studies, 24*(1), 190–203.

Strike, K.A., & Posner, G.J. (1982). Conceptual change and science teaching. *European Journal of Science Education, 4*(3), 231–240.

Sutherland, L., Howard, S., & Markauskaite, L. (2010). Professional identity creation: Examining the development of beginning preservice teachers' understanding of their work as teachers. *Teaching and Teacher Education, 26*(3), 455–465.

Thomas, J.A., Pedersen, J.E., & Finson, K. (2001). Validating the Draw-a-Science-Teacher-Test Checklist (DASTT-C): Exploring mental models and teacher beliefs. *Journal of Science Teacher Education, 12*(4), 295–310.

Tippett, C. (2009). Argumentation: The language of science. *Journal of Elementary Science Education, 21*(1), 17–25.

Tschannen-Moran, M. & Woolfolk-Hoy, A. (2001). Teacher efficacy: Capturing an elusive construct. *Teaching and Teacher Education, 17,* 783–805.

Tschannen-Moran, M., Woolfolk-Hoy, A., & Hoy, W. (1998). Teacher efficacy: Its meaning and measure. *Review of Educational Research, 68,* 202–248.

van Aalderen-Smeets, S.I., Walma van der Molen, J.H., & Asma, L.J. (2011). Primary teachers' attitudes toward science: A new theoretical framework. *Science Education, 96*(1), 158–182.

Varma, T., Volkmann, M., & Hanuscin, D. (2009). Preservice elementary teachers' perceptions of their understanding of inquiry and inquiry-based science pedagogy: Influence of an elementary science education methods course and a science field experience. *Journal of Elementary Science Education, 21*(4), 1–22.

Vedder, P., Horenczyk, G., Liebkind, K. & Nickmans, G. (2006). Problems in ethno-cultural diverse educational settings and strategies to cope with these challenges. *Educational Research Review, 1*(2): 157–168.

Volkmann, M.J., Abell, S.K., & Zgagacz, M. (2005). Teaching physics to preservice teachers: The challenges of inquiry. *Science Education, 89,* 847–869.

Wenner, G. J. (1993). Relationship between science knowledge levels and beliefs toward science instruction held by preservice elementary teachers. *Journal of Science Education and Technology, 2,* 461–468.

Young, T. (1998). Student teachers' attitudes towards science (STATS). *Evaluation and Research in Education, 12,* 96–111.

42

Research on Science Teacher Knowledge

Jan H. van Driel, Amanda Berry, and Jacobiene Meirink

ICLON-Leiden University Graduate School of Teaching, The Netherlands

In a very often-cited review of research on students' attitudes toward science, Osborne, Simon, and Collins (2003) conclude, "For the research evidence shows clearly that it is the teacher variables that are the most significant factor determining attitude, not curriculum variables" (p. 1070). The research contains a plethora of similar statements, all of which emphasize the central role of teachers in bringing about changes in students. Over the past 50 years, research on teachers and teaching has focused on different aspects to understand the role of teachers in educational processes: teachers' personality traits (e.g., being enthusiastic or having high expectations of students), teachers' behavior (e.g., being able to apply effective teaching behaviors and create a positive learning environment), teacher thinking (e.g., lesson planning and reflection), and teacher knowledge and beliefs.

This chapter focuses on science teacher knowledge. It begins with an overview of teacher knowledge research, briefly discussing some of the different strands in this research domain and some of the models that have been used to frame this research. This overview is used to situate the current review, also in relation to other reviews of the domain and to other chapters in this handbook. In the next part, findings of recent research on science teacher knowledge are discussed. Following this, some of the research approaches and instruments that have been developed and used in this research are reviewed. The chapter ends with a discussion of practical implications and suggestions for future research.

Situating This Review

The Nature of Teacher Knowledge

We view teacher knowledge as the total knowledge that a teacher has at his or her disposal at a particular moment that underlies his or her actions (Carter, 1990). This does not imply that all the knowledge a teacher has does actually play a role in his or her actions. Teachers can, either

consciously or not, refrain from using certain insights during their teaching. The basic idea is that a reciprocity exists between the whole of a teacher's cognition (in the broad sense) and his or her activities and that, consequently, it makes sense to investigate teachers' knowledge (Verloop, van Driel, & Meijer, 2001).

Teacher knowledge may have a variety of origins, including formal schooling in the past, that is, initial disciplinary training and teacher education, or continued professional training (cf. Calderhead, 1996), as well as practical experiences, occurring in day-to-day teaching practice. In this sense, teacher knowledge is not opposite to theoretical or academic knowledge. Obviously, teachers may differ enormously in the extent to which they have merged or integrated knowledge from different sources into conceptual frameworks that guide their actions in practice.

As Alexander, Schallert, and Hare (1991) noted, the term "knowledge" is mostly used to encompass "all that a person knows or believes to be true, whether or not it is verified as true in some sort of objective or external way" (p. 317). This is particularly relevant with respect to research on teacher knowledge. A recurring discussion in this research concerns the relation between teacher knowledge and beliefs. Like many others (e.g., Pajares, 1992), we view teacher knowledge and beliefs as strongly interconnected, although beliefs are seen as referring to personal values, attitudes, and ideologies, whereas knowledge refers to ideas derived through a teacher's practical experience and formal schooling (Calderhead, 1996). The latter is central in this chapter; research on science teachers' beliefs and attitudes is reviewed in Chapter 41 of this volume.

Whereas research on teacher knowledge initially aimed at the production of a "knowledge base" (Reynolds, 1989) of a rather static and prescriptive nature (cf. "knowledge *for* teachers," Fenstermacher, 1994), since the 1980s, the emphasis has shifted to investigating and appreciating the knowledge that teachers develop[1] in the course of their education and professional practice (cf. "knowledge *of* teachers"; Fenstermacher, 1994). However, since this shift, there have been discussions about the question of whether these studies should be confined to the description of the knowledge of individual teachers or very small groups of teachers in the form of narratives or biographies or whether attention should be focused on the more general characteristics of teacher knowledge. Many researchers contend that rather than describing individual manifestations of teacher knowledge, research should try to surpass the individual level. This implies that one should search for the "shared" components of teacher knowledge and attempt to find "certain overarching generalizable features which are common across teachers" (Brown & McIntyre, 1993, p. 19).

Underlying this discussion is the question about the aim of research on teacher knowledge: Should this research result in sets of rules that specify a direct tie between knowledge and practice that thus can be used as prescriptions for teachers (e.g., in teacher education programs), or should the resulting knowledge be seen as a source of schemata that can enhance teachers' "practical arguments" (Fenstermacher, 1986) and, subsequently, their options for action? In any case, research has not found shared features of teacher knowledge, valid for all teachers, at a large scale. Given the fact that teacher knowledge is by definition embedded in teachers' personal and professional contexts, it makes sense to focus the search for shared teacher knowledge on groups of teachers that are in similar situations with respect to variables such as subject matter, level of education, and age of students.

In the context of these discussions, Lee Shulman started a research program on teacher knowledge in the late 1980s that studied teachers from different subject domains, aiming to identify the knowledge that is essential for teaching. Importantly, this research program focused on what teachers know about teaching their subject to certain student groups, thus considering the teacher as a "knower" (Fenstermacher, 1994). The approach adopted in the Shulman program has had a very substantial and worldwide influence on research on science teacher knowledge in the last 25 years.

Models of Teacher Knowledge

In two highly influential publications, Shulman (1986, 1987) outlined a model for what he termed "the knowledge base for teaching." Central in this model was a new category of teacher knowledge called pedagogical content knowledge (PCK), described as "that special amalgam of content and pedagogy that is uniquely the province of teachers, their own special form of professional understanding" (Shulman, 1987, p. 8). Note how the idea of the teacher as "knower" is reflected in this description. In Shulman's model, PCK is shaped by teachers' knowledge of subject matter (substantive and syntactic) on the one hand and by their general pedagogical knowledge (e.g., about classroom management, instructional principles, learning theories) on the other hand. Moreover, the knowledge of their own professional context (school, students, community) impacts teachers' PCK (see Figure 42.1).

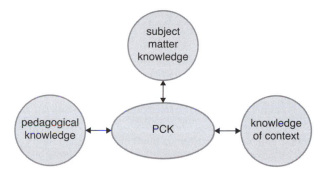

Figure 42.1 The Shulman model of teacher knowledge in which PCK is presented as a unique knowledge domain. (From Van Dijk & Kattman, 2007)

At the heart of PCK lies what teachers know about how their students learn specific subject matter or topics and the difficulties or misconceptions students may have regarding this topic related to the variety of representations (e.g., models, metaphors) and activities (e.g., explications, experiments) teachers know to teach this specific topic. These components are mutually related: The better teachers understand their students' learning difficulties with respect to a certain topic and the more representations and activities they have at their disposal, the more effectively they can teach about this topic. From this perspective, Loughran and colleagues defined PCK as "the knowledge that a teacher uses to provide teaching situations that help learners make sense of particular science content" (Loughran, Milroy, Berry, Mulhall, & Gunstone, 2001, p. 289).

Elaborating on Shulman's work, various scholars have proposed different definitions and conceptualizations of PCK in terms of the features included or integrated (an early overview can be found in van Driel, Verloop, & de Vos, 1998; for an updated version, see Kind, 2009a). Some described PCK as a "mixture" of several types of knowledge needed for teaching, while others explained PCK as the "synthesis" of all knowledge elements needed in order to be an effective teacher (cf. Cochran, DeRuiter, & King, 1993). Rather than representing PCK as a fixed or static body of knowledge, Mason (1999) defined PCK as an ability to combine content knowledge of a discipline with the teaching of that discipline. Adding to this, Hashweh (2005) proposed to consider PCK as a collection or repertoire of pedagogical constructions, which teachers acquire when repeatedly teaching a certain topic. Kansanen (2009) compared PCK to the broader concept of "subject-matter didactics," which stems from the German Didaktik tradition. Although it is beyond the scope of this chapter to discuss the Didaktik tradition, some studies have drawn from it in studying science teacher knowledge. For instance, Asikainen and Hirvonen (2010) used categories from Didaktik as well as the Shulman frameworks to analyze the perceptions of physics knowledge of experienced Finnish physics teachers. They found that the teachers strongly emphasized knowledge related to day-to-day teaching practice.

From the Didaktik perspective, this would be categorized as knowledge of the best instructional methods, while in Shulman's categorization it belongs to the category of representations and instructional strategies.

Several authors have pointed out that it is not always possible to make a clear distinction between PCK and subject matter knowledge (SMK; Kind, 2009a; Marks, 1990; Tobin, Tippins, & Gallard, 1994). However, studies on teaching of unfamiliar topics and studies in the context of preservice teacher education suggest that a thorough and coherent understanding of subject matter acts as a prerequisite to the development of PCK (van Driel, Verloop, & de Vos, 1998). At the same time, studies on preservice teachers have demonstrated how teaching experiences may stimulate the (further) development of teachers' SMK (e.g., Lederman, Gess-Newsome, & Latz, 1994).

Magnusson, Krajcik, and Borko (1999) presented a strong case for the existence of PCK as a separate and unique domain of knowledge related to teaching of specific topics. These authors conceptualized PCK as consisting of five components: (a) orientations toward science teaching, (b) knowledge of the curriculum, (c) knowledge of science assessment, (d) knowledge of science learners, and (e) knowledge of instructional strategies. This model of PCK has been particularly influential in research on science teacher knowledge since 2000 (Friedrichsen, van Driel, & Abell, 2011), and different versions of this model have been used by various scholars (e.g., Park & Oliver, 2008a, who extended the model with an affective component, that is, teacher efficacy, on the basis of their empirical research). It will be referred to hereafter as the Magnusson model.

In recent years, various modifications of Shulman's model and conceptualization have been published. For example, the complex relationship between teachers' SMK and their PCK has led researchers in the domain of mathematics education to develop the construct mathematical knowledge for teaching (MKT; Ball, Thames, & Phelps, 2008). This model is presented as a re-organization of the Shulman model, in particular reconsidering the role of content knowledge in the context of teaching and learning (see Figure 42.2). First, the authors distinguish between SMK and PCK. In the former, they separate common content knowledge (defined as "the mathematical knowledge and skill used in settings other than teaching," p. 399) from specialized content knowledge ("the mathematical knowledge and skill unique to teaching," p. 400). Within PCK, they redefine Shulman's abovementioned key elements (i.e., knowledge of student learning and knowledge of instructional strategies) as knowledge of content and students and knowledge of content and teaching, respectively. These domains combine teachers' knowing about mathematics with knowing about students (their misconceptions, mathematical thinking) and with knowing about teaching (e.g., choosing examples, sequencing). Although the MKT model is now used by several researchers in mathematics education, an adaptation by science education has, to our knowledge, not yet been published.

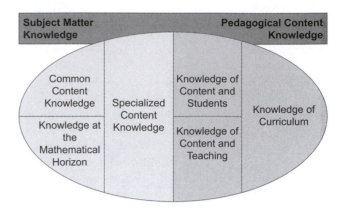

Figure 42.2 Domains of mathematical knowledge for teaching. (From Ball et al., 2008)

These modifications of the Shulman model are included here to demonstrate how some researchers have attempted to improve the original model, in particular by addressing what they saw as limitations. Typically, these researchers, as well as others, added knowledge categories to highlight the importance of certain aspects of teacher knowledge (i.e., specific forms of content knowledge in the MKT model). Clearly, other modifications and extensions are easy to imagine. This raises the question of what purpose these modifications serve. Adding new knowledge categories, unavoidably, creates a discussion of how each category relates to and is different from another (e.g., specialized content knowledge versus knowledge of content and teaching in the MKT model), and if, and how, these different categories can be distinguished in empirical research. This may be a challenge for educational researchers, however; for policy makers and administrators, models with different knowledge categories have the attraction of creating lists of knowledge components, or competencies, that may subsequently be used in teacher examination or accreditation procedures. The longer these lists are, the bigger the risk of "ticking off" becomes. Loughran and colleagues (2001), echoing criticisms of the process-product research of the 1960s and 1970s, argued that researchers often fail to acknowledge the complex relationships and interactions existing within a teacher's personal professional knowledge base and that investigations of PCK should avoid reducing teacher knowledge to a mechanistic, technical description of teaching, learning, and content.

For the purpose of this chapter, we have chosen to use a simple model of teacher knowledge (i.e., Figure 42.1). This model contains knowledge categories of which the importance for teaching practice has been well documented in research. In the following review, the emphasis will be on studies of science teachers' knowledge of subject matter and PCK and their mutual relationship. Science teachers' pedagogical knowledge and knowledge of context are sometimes part of these studies and will be included here when that is the case. Studies that focus solely on science teachers' pedagogical knowledge are rare, and the ones that we found were not specific to the teaching of science and thus will not be discussed here.

The Focus of This Chapter

This chapter replaces the one written by Sandra Abell in the first edition of this volume (Abell, 2007). In her chapter, Abell gave an extensive historical overview of research on science teacher knowledge between 1960 and the early 2000s. When it appeared, the Abell chapter was the most comprehensive review of research on science teacher knowledge ever published, and it will remain a valuable resource for anyone who is interested in this domain.

For the selection of studies to be included in this chapter, we applied the same criteria as Abell for her 2007 chapter. That is, we selected studies on both inservice and preservice science teachers at all levels of education. Furthermore, we included studies that were interesting from at least one perspective out of (a) conceptualization or model of science teacher knowledge, (b) research design or approach, and (c) findings regarding the content or structure of science teacher knowledge and its relation to teaching practice. Given the close relationship between teacher knowledge, thinking, and beliefs (see previous section), we included research on teacher thinking and beliefs only when these were studied as an integral part of teacher cognitions (in a broader sense). However, studies focusing on science teachers' beliefs, attitudes, or dispositions were excluded as these are reviewed in Chapter 41. We also avoided studies in which the *development* of science teacher knowledge was the central focus of attention unless they were interesting from the point of view of one of the three abovementioned perspectives. Other chapters in this volume include studies on teacher knowledge development as a result of participation in a preservice teacher education program (Chapter 43) or professional development (Chapter 44).

The literature search started with articles indexed in the Web of Science from January 2005 to November 2012, using the following combinations of keywords: "science" AND "teacher knowledge" and "science" AND "pedagogical content knowledge." This resulted in 220 unique hits. Additional searches were done in ERIC and in two journals, *Journal of Science Teacher Education* and *International Journal of Science and Mathematics Education*, also from January 2005 to November 2012 and using the same sets of keywords, resulting in an additional unique 249 hits. This number was reduced by excluding articles that were *not* about science teachers but on teachers of mathematics or technology or that seemed to fit better in one of the aforementioned chapters. Also, articles that were not written in English were excluded. Eventually, 119 articles have been included in the present review, including empirical studies, literature reviews, position papers, and articles on the testing and development of instruments and procedures.

In the following section, the findings of research on science teacher knowledge since 2005 will be reviewed.

We will start with studies that focus on subject matter knowledge, followed by research on pedagogical content knowledge. Next, we will address studies that have investigated subject matter knowledge and PCK in relation to each other and finish with research that aimed at relationships among various components of teacher knowledge, classroom practice, and student achievement.

Outcomes of Studies on Science Teacher Knowledge

Research on Science Teacher Subject Matter Knowledge

In her chapter in the first edition of this volume, Abell (2007) demonstrated that, in the course of time, science teacher subject matter knowledge (SMK) has been investigated with different methods and with different purposes. Whereas some studies focused on describing science teachers' SMK either in general or regarding specific topics, other studies attempted to relate teachers' SMK to other teacher characteristics or teaching practice. Methodologically, research became more sophisticated over time. Initially, numbers of courses or course hours taken or grade point averages on subject matter tests were used as indicators of teachers' SMK. In the 1980s, interest shifted toward studying teachers' conceptions of subject matter, whereas in later years teachers' SMK was more often studied *in situ*—for instance, while teaching a lesson. Most of the studies focused on elementary teachers and concerned specific aspects of their SMK, apparently because their background in science tends to be very limited. Moreover, elementary teachers often express a lack of confidence or anxiety when science is concerned. In terms of content, most studies on science teachers' SMK concerned the domain of physics, in particular topics such as force and motion, energy, and electricity.

The main findings of the research on science teachers' SMK until 2005 can be briefly summarized as follows:

(1) Teachers often demonstrate misunderstandings and misconceptions of science very similar to those of their students (Wandersee, Mintzes, & Novak, 1994). Whereas this may not be surprising for elementary teachers, studies of experienced secondary teachers (e.g., of chemistry or physics) often led to the same conclusion. Needless to say, this outcome is worrying in any case. The positive news is that some studies found that SMK improves through teaching, which is consistent with the ancient saying "While we teach, we learn" (Seneca).

(2) There is no clear relationship between science teachers' SMK and other teacher characteristics, such as attitude, confidence, or self-efficacy. The question of whether teachers with better or deeper subject matter knowledge perform better in practice also doesn't have a straightforward answer. However, studies that compared teaching in and out of one's certification

area revealed that teachers with low content knowledge tend to rely heavily on textbooks, talk a lot, ask few questions, and avoid cognitively challenging activities. This led Abell to conclude that "the evidence does support a positive relationship between SMK and teaching" (Abell, 2007, p. 1120).

The remainder of this section concentrates on studies on science teachers' SMK after 2005, focusing on studies that further contribute to this field of study either by challenging or by adding depth to what has been found earlier.

Recent Studies Focusing on Science Teachers' SMK

Adding to the research reviewed by Abell (2007), numerous studies have been published that focused on (inservice and, mostly, preservice) science teachers' SMK as such. Typically, these studies found weaknesses or misconceptions concerning teachers' understanding or mental models of specific science topics (e.g., electrical circuits, Shen, Gibbons, Wiegers, & McMahon, 2007; phases of the moon and lunar phenomena, Trundle, Atwood, & Christopher, 2006; ionization energy, Taber & Tan, 2011; distance force interactions, Kariotoglou, Spyrtou, & Tselfes, 2009; chemical equilibrium, Cheung, Ma, & Yang, 2009; body organs, Patrick & Tunnicliffe, 2010). Other studies reported teachers' limited abilities to define concepts (Galili & Lehavi, 2006), vocabulary (Carrier, 2013), or science processes (Emereole, 2009) correctly, leading to conclusions such as "subject knowledge remains a problematic issue in initial teacher education" (Waldron, Pike, Varley, Murphy, & Greenwood, 2007, p. 177). To give an example of this type of study, Burgoon, Heddle, and Duran (2010) explored the physical science conceptions of 103 elementary science teachers from the United States "to determine whether, after three decades of misconception research, teachers still possess conceptions similar to those held by students" (p. 859), and found, not surprisingly, that teachers expressed misconceptions regarding gravity, magnetism, gases, and temperature that were similar to common student misconceptions. As another example, Leite, Mendoza, and Borsese (2007) compared science teachers' explanations for liquid-state phenomena in three European countries. Data were collected by means of a questionnaire administered to 195 Italian, Portuguese, and Spanish inservice science teachers. On the whole, the authors found low percentages of correct answers. No systematic differences were found among participants from the three countries. However, teaching experience seemed to minimize some of the conceptual difficulties shown by inservice teachers. Compared to studies before 2005, more attention has been paid to new curricular topics, such as global warming and climate change (e.g., Bozdogan, Karsli, & Sahin, 2011; Crippen, 2012; Hayhoe, Bullock, & Hayhoe, 2011; Lambert, Lindgren, & Bleicher, 2012), but the conclusions tend to be similar—for instance, that teachers "had knowledge gaps and certain

misconceptions" (Bozdogan et al., 2011, p. 218) about the topic of the study.

Various studies focused on the development of SMK in the context of teacher education or professional development programs. Danusso, Testa, and Vicentini (2010) in a study of about 400 Italian preservice science teachers (PSTs) showed that their knowledge about models and modeling at the end of a 4- or 5-year degree diploma was still rather poor and confused. At the same time, a specifically designed intervention appeared to be effective in helping the preservice teachers to retain an informed knowledge about scientific models over a large time period. Schwartz-Bloom, Halpin, and Reiter (2011) developed a series of modules on pharmacology (i.e., drugs) for secondary schools in the United States, plus an accompanying professional development program. The teachers' self-reports, indicating that they learned something new in chemistry and biology, were supported by a quantitative assessment of SMK at several moments in time. The authors suggest that the long-term SMK retention was due to teachers' use of the modules in their classes, because those who actually used the modules had additional knowledge gains, and those who did not use the modules lost some of their initial knowledge gains. Papageorgiou, Stamovlasis, and Johnson (2013) aimed to improve the SMK of Greek primary school teachers ($n = 130$) about chemical change. After a specific intervention, the SMK of the participants, which was limited initially, had significantly improved. Among others, a relationship between teachers' particle ideas and their explanations was found. However, the authors concluded that even though "the present training course had a significant effectiveness on teachers' understanding of chemical changes [. . .] one 'shot' is not enough" (p. 23).

Several scholars investigated science teachers' SMK in the context of their participation in authentic research projects. In the United States in particular, this is a rather common form of professional development for science teachers. Some studies found mixed results of participants' experiences with such projects (e.g., Barnes, Hodge, Parker, & Koroly, 2006). Others (e.g., Morrison & Estes, 2007) applied an approach with research scientists and "real-world scenarios," which appeared to be an effective strategy to support middle school teachers "to teach science as a process and help them strengthen their science content understanding" (p. 165). Dresner and Worley (2006) interviewed 15 participants in a project called Teachers in the Woods, which provided ecology research experiences for science teachers in national forests and parks. The program consisted of a 5-week summer institute with additional academic-year workshops to ensure transfer of new skills to the classroom. The authors found engaging teachers in real-world field science research to be an effective way to gain SMK and skills (i.e., about ecology). The collegiality among teachers and scientists which was established during the period of field work impacted positively on the teachers' science learning.

Studies of Science Teachers' SMK in Relation to Other Teacher Variables

Several studies have focused on the relation between teachers' SMK and their confidence to teach science. In a case study of teaching within and outside specialism, Childs and McNicholl (2007) investigated the relationship between SMK and confidence. Basically, these authors confirmed the findings of previous studies (e.g., Sanders, Borko, & Lockard, 1993)—that is, within specialism, the teacher was more confident and taught more accurately and interactively, whereas outside specialism, her explanations were less clear, and students were forced to learn by recall of facts. Kind (2009b) investigated the use of sources of subject matter knowledge by preservice science teachers ($n = 71$) in the UK, within and outside their area of specialism, in relation to personal characteristics such as self-confidence and their sense of success. Interestingly, she found that some PSTs taught more successful lessons outside their specialism. These PSTs appeared to use a wider range of SMK sources, including, crucially, advice from experienced colleagues. On the other hand, within specialism, some PSTs reported an inability to select appropriate knowledge and/or strategies. In a follow-up study, Kind and Kind (2011) investigated misconceptions about basic chemical ideas taught at secondary school, such as particle theory and chemical bonding, in a sample of 150 PSTs. Not surprisingly, they found that biology and physics specialists have more extensive misconceptions in this domain than chemists do. Two personal characteristics—PSTs' preferences for teaching as a subject "specialist" or as a "generalist" teaching all sciences and their self-confidence—were assessed by responses to Likert-scale statements. No statistically significant relationships between personal characteristics and misconceptions were found, suggesting that chemistry may be being taught by PSTs who combine strong self-confidence with poor understandings of basic chemical ideas. Nugent and colleagues (2012) conducted a quasi-experimental study in the United States to determine the effects of a field-based, inquiry-focused course on PSTs' geoscience SMK, attitude toward science, confidence in teaching science, and inquiry understanding and skills. The results showed that the PSTs in the field-based condition ($n = 25$) outperformed the PSTs in the control group ($n = 37$) in terms of an increase of their conceptual knowledge, confidence in teaching science, attitude toward science, and inquiry skills.

Various studies have focused on the relation between teachers' SMK and affective variables, such as their self-efficacy beliefs. Bleicher and Lindgren (2005) studied a sample of U.S. preservice elementary teachers ($n = 49$) who learned science in a constructivist-oriented methods class. Analysis revealed that participants' increase of conceptual understanding was associated with an increase in self-efficacy and outcome expectancy beliefs. Nilsson and van Driel (2011) combined workshops with video seminars in a Swedish preservice elementary teacher education program aimed at the simultaneous development of the preservice teachers' knowledge of physics, their attitudes toward physics, and teaching it in elementary settings. Participants reported an increased understanding of physics concepts, but more significantly, they indicated that physics had become more meaningful to them and that their self-confidence toward teaching physics had developed. Nivalainen, Asikainen, and Nirvonen (2013) studied the effects of a guided inquiry laboratory course in a sample of 32 Finnish PSTs. On the basis of repeated interviews, they found that their approach helped PSTs to become aware of their misconceptions and limited understandings of subject matter knowledge and that the guided-inquiry environment subsequently encouraged them to construct SMK and helped them to understand the possibilities of practical work in teaching.

Another group of studies focused on science teachers' SMK in relation to their stances toward teaching certain controversial topics. In a U.S. study, Nehm, Kim, and Sheppard (2009; cf. Nehm & Schonfeld, 2007) measured certified biology and non–biology teachers' ($n = 167$) knowledge of evolution and the nature of science in relation to their stance toward teaching of creationism in schools. The authors found generally low levels of knowledge and many misconceptions about evolution and the nature of science in both biology and non–biology teachers. Moreover, they reported comparable anti-evolutionary positions in biology and non–biology teachers: Nearly half of the teachers in both groups advocated for the inclusion of creationism in school. SMK and teaching preference were only weakly associated, and there was no difference in preference for teaching creationism between those teachers who had taken an evolution course and those who had not. In another study on teaching evolution in a sample of inservice elementary teachers from the United States ($n = 64$), Nadelson and Nadelson (2010) found an association between familiarity with the topic and positions toward teaching it. In particular, some participants did not feel prepared or responsible for teaching evolution content. Akyol and colleagues (2012) also focused on the topic of evolution. In a sample of 415 Turkish PSTs, they found that a higher level of understanding of evolution was associated with a higher level of acceptance of evolution and with stronger self-efficacy beliefs for teaching evolution. Özden and colleagues (2008) investigated Turkish preservice teachers' ($n = 371$) attitudes to and knowledge of chemical hormone usage, a controversial topic in the field of modern biotechnology. They found the preservice teachers' SMK to be limited and reported "inadequate positive attitudes toward chemical hormone usage in daily life" (p. 3898), especially among male PSTs.

Summary

Much recent research on science teachers' SMK has followed the same "normal science" pattern that Abell (2007, p. 1133) observed. Although it may be important to investigate teachers' SMK in a certain context, as a scholarly community we haven't gained all that much from more studies that conclude that the participating teachers had limited knowledge of or misconceptions about the science topics under consideration. Studies that investigate science teachers' SMK in relation to other variables tend to be more interesting. Most of these studies seek to relate SMK (measured either by a content test or through teachers' self-reports) to affective variables, such as attitudes (e.g., preferences to teach), confidence, or self-efficacy (typically measured through questionnaires). In any case, these studies have shed more light on the relationships between SMK and these affective variables compared to the Abell review. Several studies (e.g., Kind & Kind, 2011; Nehm et al., 2009) demonstrate that these relationships are not straightforward but may depend on the context of the study or the topic under consideration (e.g., evolution). However, there still have been relatively few studies on the development of SMK in the context of teaching (cf. Abell, 2007, p. 1134). Basically, the studies reviewed here seem to confirm that teachers' SMK increases with teaching experience and that a higher level of SMK is typically associated with more confidence and more interactive and adventurous ways of teaching. These findings, however, are not new. In the next section, we shift our attention to research on science teachers' PCK before considering studies that relate SMK and its development to PCK and teaching practice.

Research on Science Teacher Pedagogical Content Knowledge

In her review, Abell (2007) observed that compared with research on teacher SMK in science, research on PCK was still very much in its infancy. She organized her analysis of PCK studies according to the five components of the Magnusson model. The main findings according to each of these components can be briefly summarized as follows:

(1) *Orientations toward science teaching:* Similar to PCK research generally, research in this domain is characterized by a lack of clarity about what is being studied. This seems to be a consequence of several factors, including few studies that explicitly focus on the concept of orientations, different theoretical perspectives adopted by individual researchers, and the introduction of new terms (e.g., "functional paradigm," "approaches to teaching," "values orientation") rather than building on existing terminology. Nevertheless, some conclusions about research on orientations are possible: (i) Orientations influence teachers' learning and practice, although this influence appears to be indirect, (ii) orientations are much less coherently held and much more context specific than previous research led us to believe, (iii) although teachers have a range of orientations that guide their practice, their set of teaching strategies is far more narrow, and (iv) orientations can change (Abell, 2007, p. 1126). This led Abell to conclude,

"Much more work is needed to understand the frameworks that guide science teachers in their planning and enactment of instruction" (p. 1126).

(2) *Knowledge of science learners:* Research in this area focuses on knowledge that teachers have about student science learning and includes studies examining teacher knowledge of students' science ideas, both descriptive studies and studies conducted within the context of teaching. Abell (2007) summarized work in this field as "lack[ing] cohesion in terms of the research questions addressed . . . Overall it appears that teachers lack knowledge of student science conceptions, but this knowledge improves with teaching experience" (p. 1128).

(3) *Knowledge of science curriculum:* This component includes teachers' knowledge of required goals and objectives and knowledge of specific programs and resources. Few studies specifically focused on this component, leading Abell to conclude that little is known about science teachers' knowledge about selection, design, and analysis of science curriculum materials. This seems surprising and problematic, for instance, in the context of curriculum reform efforts.

(4) *Knowledge of science instructional strategies:* This component includes teachers' knowledge of subject- and topic-specific teaching methods and strategies. Research in this category reveals that knowledge of instructional strategies is linked to SMK and knowledge of learners but also requires more complex knowledge of the selected strategy in use. Studies of the development of teacher knowledge of instructional strategies demonstrate the complexity of science teaching in terms of SMK and PCK interplay and the influences of experience and context.

(5) *Knowledge of science assessment:* This component includes what is assessed as well as teachers' approaches to assessment. Research outcomes indicate that how and what teachers choose to assess appears to be mediated by their beliefs and values and that, typically, there are contradictions between teachers' goals for assessment and their assessment practices. However, Abell concluded that more studies in this domain are needed to better understand what science teachers know about assessment and how they enact their knowledge in assessment practices.

In recent years, several publications reviewing research on science teachers' PCK have been published. A special issue of the *International Journal of Science Education* contained reports of six empirical studies from five different continents, bookended by an editorial based on an interview with Lee Shulman reflecting on the origins of PCK (Berry, Loughran, & van Driel, 2008) and a concluding piece by Sandra Abell reflecting on 20 years of PCK research (Abell, 2008). Schneider and Plasman (2011) reviewed research from 1986 through 2010 on science teachers' PCK to explore possible sequences in the ways science teachers' knowledge becomes more sophisticated, using the idea of learning progressions to frame their review. The authors conclude it to be helpful for teachers to focus on student learning before developing their ideas about teaching and stressed the importance of reflection in the process of PCK development. In a recent handbook chapter on the development of science teachers' PCK, Chinn (2012) focused on teacher education programs that situate teachers' learning of PCK in learners' communities, cultures, and experiences and that address goals spanning universal scientific literacy, equity, and sustainable socio-ecological systems. In an extensive review of research on science teachers' PCK, Kind (2009a) discusses several models of PCK, outcomes of empirical research on preservice and inservice science teachers' PCK, its development in practice, and ways to elicit PCK. Kind pays particular attention to the relationship between SMK and PCK, concluding that "it remains unclear whether or not SMK is part of PCK" (Kind, 2009a, p. 192) while pointing out that SMK as teachers learn it during their disciplinary schooling is different from "school-SMK" (cf. Deng, 2007).

In organizing this review, we first consider studies that specifically examine one (or more) of the Magnusson components. Next, we examine studies within an emerging line of research that seeks to relate several of the PCK components.

Recent Studies That Focus on Components of PCK

Following up on Abell's (2007) conclusion that science teaching orientations is "a messy construct" (p. 1126) and that more research in this area is needed, Friedrichsen and colleagues (2011) reviewed the research literature on science teaching orientations, tracing back to its origins in the 1980s. These authors identified several problematic issues regarding the way science teaching orientations have been used in research. First, researchers have used the concept in different or unclear ways. Some (e.g., Park & Oliver, 2008a; Schwarz & Gwekwerere, 2007) have followed the Anderson and Smith (1987) interpretation of orientations in terms of general views of or beliefs about science and teaching (e.g., didactic or activity-driven), whereas others have followed the Magnusson and colleagues (1999) interpretation of orientations as knowledge of purposes and goals of teaching science (e.g., Cohen & Yarden, 2009). Second, many studies have focused on orientations as an isolated construct, unrelated to other PCK components (e.g., Avraamidou & Zembal-Saul, 2005; Volkman & Zgagacz, 2004). This approach contrasts with the Magnusson model, in which orientation is an overarching construct that shapes the various components of PCK. Third, since Magnusson and colleagues (1999) listed nine possible orientations, several authors have chosen to label teachers as holding only one of these (Schwarz & Gwekwerere, 2007, or have reduced the list to two or three (Käpylä, Heikkinen, & Asunta, 2009; Roehrig & Luft, 2006). Others, however, acknowledged that teachers can hold several orientations (Volkman & Zgagacz,

2004). As an outcome of their review, Friedrichsen and colleagues (2011) recommend that future studies in this field investigate science teaching orientations in relation to other knowledge components, in particular studies "that focus on how science teaching orientations impact science teachers' emerging or developing PCK" (p. 373).

The remainder of this section focuses on individual studies of science teachers' PCK. Some researchers used the Magnusson model but ignored science teaching orientations, focusing on one or more of the other PCK components instead, such as knowledge of instructional strategies (e.g., to introduce particulate theory; Boz & Boz, 2008), knowledge of assessment (e.g., to investigate science teachers' tools and reasons for using assessment; Siegel & Wissehr, 2011), or knowledge of science learners (e.g., Kang, 2007, in which teachers used action research, or Harlow, Swanson, & Otero, 2012, who asked PSTs to analyze children's ideas through videos). Park and Oliver (2009) focused on two components, knowledge of science learners and knowledge of instructional strategies, to investigate how science teachers translated their knowledge of gifted students into instructional strategies for teaching science.

Several studies focused on teachers' knowledge of students' ideas about particular science topics. For example, Kellner and colleagues (2011) investigated beginning Swedish PSTs' ($n = 32$) knowledge of junior high school student difficulties in four science and mathematics topics (plant growth, gases, equations, and heat and temperature). While PSTs claimed no prior knowledge of specific student difficulties, the study revealed that collectively, PSTs were able to identify many student difficulties described in earlier research. Making explicit the range of conceptions appeared to be useful in promoting knowledge development among these PSTs. In a study on teaching acid-base chemistry, Dreschler and van Driel (2008) investigated experienced Swedish chemistry teachers' ($n = 9$) knowledge of student learning difficulties in this area. The authors used authentic student work (i.e., student responses to test questions) in an interview setting to probe teachers' understanding. All teachers recognized at least some of the preconceptions and learning problems of the students, in particular confusion among students between different models of acids and bases and confusion between the phenomenological and the particle levels. Within their sample, the authors distinguished two groups of teachers: One group showed a greater awareness of student learning difficulties and planned their teaching explicitly to address these difficulties, using different models of acids and bases for this purpose, whereas the other group was less focused on student learning and thought it was sufficient to distinguish in their teaching between the phenomenological and the particle level.

Summary

Studies investigating specific components of science teachers' PCK have continued to accumulate over the past years. Mostly, research interest has focused on science teaching orientations and knowledge of student learning. The general conclusions tend to be similar to those of Abell (2007), such as that science teachers often have limited knowledge of how their students understand and learn science content. However, teaching experience tends to improve teachers' knowledge of student difficulties in science. Also, specific interventions in teacher education programs may be effective (Kellner et al., 2011). Another conclusion is that these studies typically do not investigate PCK in the context of teaching practice, although several studies use artifacts from practice to elicit components of teachers' PCK (e.g., Dreschler & van Driel, 2008).

Studies of PCK That Seek to Relate Several PCK Components

While the studies mentioned focus on the study of one component of PCK, a developing line of research operates from a more holistic perspective, with researchers investigating the relationship among different PCK components and how these components become integrated for and within science teachers' practice. Such studies work from the idea that developing an understanding of the nature of the integration of different PCK components will help to shed more light on the process of PCK development. The following section summarizes research on PCK that attempts to investigate PCK from this more integrated or holistic perspective. Studies belonging to this category include two main groups: those that seek to document the PCK of science teachers "as it is" and those that focus on the development of science teachers' PCK through the use of specific interventions.

STUDIES OF SCIENCE TEACHER PCK "AS IT IS" USING THE
MAGNUSSON MODEL

The following examples illustrate research investigating science teachers' PCK at a particular point in time, or "as it is," viewed through the perspective of the Magnusson model. Studies in this area include research focusing on preservice, inservice, and university-level teachers of science.

In a study of experienced science teachers, Park and Chen (2012) sought to understand the nature of the interaction among different PCK components and how they were integrated into PCK that guided teachers' practice. They investigated the PCK of four teachers working in the same U.S. high school and using the same curriculum materials, teaching the topics of photosynthesis and heredity. The researchers constructed PCK maps for each teacher for each topic to illustrate the connections among different PCK components and the relative strength of these connections. Analysis of the maps and their patterns led the researchers to identify five particular features of the integration of PCK components:

> a) integration of components was idiosyncratic and topic specific; b) knowledge of student understanding and knowledge of instructional strategies and representations were central in the integration, c) knowledge of science curriculum and knowledge of science assessment of science learning had most limited connections with other components, d) knowledge of assessment of science learning was more often connected with knowledge of student understanding and knowledge of instructional strategies and representations than with other components, e) didactic orientations toward teaching science directed knowledge of instructional strategies and representations inhibiting its connection with other components.
>
> (Park & Chen, 2012, p. 930)

Overall, the study highlighted that the quality of PCK depends on the coherence among the components as well as the strength of individual components and demonstrated a way of making PCK visible through the use of a PCK map.

Padilla and van Driel (2011) also explored the relationship among PCK components in a study of five experienced Dutch university teachers of quantum chemistry. Relationships were found to exist among certain components, in particular between specific orientations to teaching science and knowledge of instructional strategies and between teachers' knowledge of student learning and their curriculum. Outcomes also revealed that while the teachers held different "pictures" of their PCK for this topic, there were some parallels between them (for example, in terms of what they considered important and unimportant in the teaching of the topic). Finally, the researchers found that these teachers built their PCK quite differently from each other. Kaya (2009) reported similar findings in a study of the relationships among PCK components (excluding science teaching orientations) of Turkish PSTs about the ozone layer. The authors found relationships to exist among knowledge of student learning, knowledge of curriculum, and knowledge of instructional strategies, with low correlations between knowledge of assessment and the other components.

As a final example of a study on relationships between PCK components, Friedrichsen and colleagues (2009) examined the effect of prior teaching experience on PSTs' PCK development related to the topic of genetic variation. The researchers constructed PCK profiles of a sample of PSTs entering a U.S. alternative certification teaching program, comparing two PSTs with 2 years of prior teaching experience with two PSTs without experience. The study revealed that prior teaching experience made little difference to participants' PCK for teaching this topic. Both groups drew on general pedagogical knowledge and possessed little PCK for the topic. Teaching orientations acted as a filter for participants' knowledge of learners, instructional strategies, curriculum, and assessment. The researchers asserted that teaching experience, in the absence of teacher education, did not appear to contribute to the development of PCK. However, teaching experience did seem to lead to more integration among PCK components.

STUDIES OF SCIENCE TEACHER PCK "AS IT IS" USING OTHER
CONCEPTUALIZATIONS

Several researchers developed their own forms for documenting teachers' PCK based on frameworks other than the Magnusson model. For example, Loughran and colleagues (2004) developed a unique two-part representation of science teachers' PCK, which they called CoRes (content representations) and PaP-eRs (pedagogical and professional-experience repertoire). A CoRe is a framework that is structured around questions related to some of the elements of Shulman's knowledge base, in particular teachers' understandings of specific aspects that represent and shape the content for teaching. PaP-eRs are short narratives that provide insights into teachers' pedagogical reasoning and judgment in teaching a specific aspect of science content. Together, these representations are used to depict teachers' PCK for specific science topics. These researchers developed CoRes and PaP-eRs from working with experienced Australian science teachers for a range of commonly taught Australian high school science topics (Loughran, Berry, & Mulhall, 2012). The work of these researchers reveals individual variation among teachers with respect to their PCK for the same topic, yet at the same time commonalities among teachers with respect to aspects such as what is important to teach for particular topics, specific difficulties encountered by learners, and teachers' instructional approaches.

Several researchers have utilized the CoRes and PaP-eRs tools in their own research contexts (e.g., Davidowitz & Rollnick, 2011). Padilla and colleagues (2008) combined the development of a CoRe with the application of a conceptual profile model to explore the nature and structure of the PCK of four Mexican university chemistry professors for the topic "amount of substance." The researchers developed "conceptual profiles" for each of the four professors to characterize their PCK based on their particular ways of thinking about the topic. The study revealed two frames for thinking about teaching among the four professors, one centered in an empiricist frame and the other in a formal rationalist frame. The researchers propose that the dichotomy reflects a historical division in chemistry. Bindernagel and Eilks (2009) developed a similar tool to CoRes, which they called Roadmaps, that they used to portray the PCK of 28 German chemistry teachers for the topic of submicroscopic models. Roadmaps illustrate the various pathways that teachers use in developing student understanding of the topic. The researchers found a range of different pathways based on teachers' reasoning about curricular goals and student difficulties, as well as teachers' different orientations toward the topic.

Summary

Studies seeking to capture science teachers' PCK "as it is" represent a growing line of research. Since this research is still in its early stages, most studies are descriptive rather than explanatory. Among other things, these studies highlighted considerable differences in the PCK of experienced teachers for the same topic, even when subject matter knowledge is similar and they teach the same content. Broadly, these studies can be divided into two main groups: those that represent teachers' PCK as viewed through the Magnusson perspective and those that seek to develop their own PCK representations. Studies in the former category provide some evidence that relationships exist among some PCK components (e.g., between knowledge of student learning and knowledge of instructional strategies) and that the strength of relationships between various components differs. A worrying and perhaps surprising aspect emerging from studies in this category is the limited integration of teachers' knowledge of assessment with other knowledge components, given the role that assessment typically plays in driving instruction. Furthermore, studies in this category indicate that teachers' science teaching orientations seem to influence their choice of instructional strategies. Studies in the latter category succeeded in describing PCK in a holistic way, illustrating the complexity of individual teachers' PCK as well as identifying shared aspects of teachers' PCK for the teaching of particular content.

Studies of Inservice Science Teacher PCK Over Time

The following studies concerned inservice science teachers and focused on the process of the development of their PCK over time. In particular, the studies attempted to capture the interaction and integration of PCK components with each other and with other knowledge components.

A number of studies focused on the development of inservice secondary teachers' PCK in the context of an external change, such as curriculum innovation. For example, Henze, van Driel, and Verloop (2008) studied a group of nine inservice science teachers over 3 years while they were implementing a new syllabus in the Netherlands. In this context, the researchers aimed to identify the content and structure of the teachers' PCK for a specific topic, models of the solar system and the universe. PCK development was described in terms of relations among four different components derived from the Magnusson model: knowledge about instructional strategies, knowledge about students' understanding, knowledge about assessment of students, and knowledge about goals and objectives of the topic in the curriculum. From the analysis of the data, two qualitatively different types of PCK emerged. Type A was described as oriented toward model content, while Type B was typified as oriented toward model content, model production, and thinking about the nature of models. The results also indicated that these two types of PCK developed in qualitatively different ways. For Type A, PCK development was found to be related to teachers' limited subject matter knowledge and their mainly positivist view on models and modeling. In contrast, PCK development of teachers representing Type B was connected to their more comprehensive subject matter knowledge and a more relativist view on models and modeling in science.

In another study of experienced science teachers in the context of curriculum reform, Cohen and Yarden (2009) investigated the PCK of six Israeli junior high school science and technology teachers for the topic of cells and the macro–micro relationship after the introduction of a new syllabus. The study was conducted with experienced teachers following their participation in a long-term professional development (PD) program related to the new syllabus. From the study, researchers identified two types of factors that influenced PCK development: internal (that originate from the teacher) and external (from the educational system). Additionally, the researchers concluded that the PCK of the participating teachers had both individual and shared aspects (cf. Loughran et al., 2012). In another study of PCK in the context of curriculum change, Coenders and colleagues (2010) studied three inservice Dutch chemistry teachers, focusing on their design and subsequent use of curricular materials. The researchers found gains in all five categories of the Magnusson model for each teacher during the cycle of developing the new materials and using them in class.

As an alternative to curriculum reform, teacher certification may also act as a stimulus to PCK development. Park and Oliver (2008b) investigated the PCK development of three chemistry teachers working in the same U.S. high school in the context of the National Board Certification (NBC) process. The authors found that the NBC process "pushed the teachers to not only add to but also integrate the five components of this [Magnusson] model in ways they had not done previously" (Park & Oliver, 2008b, p. 828). An important factor in stimulating the integration of different knowledge components was the NBC requirement that teachers analyze and articulate their pedagogical decisions and actions.

Other studies focused on PCK development in the context of PD programs. Falk (2012) investigated how a group of U.S. fourth-grade elementary teachers "both used and built different components of PCK as they engaged in collaborative formative assessment" (p. 269) of their students' work in the context of a science PD program on the topic of electricity and electrical circuits. Teachers taught the unit concurrently with their participation in the PD, and, for each of the sessions, teachers brought selected samples of student work for collective deliberation. Findings both supported the notion of PCK as a resource for teachers' formative assessment practice as well as provided empirical support for the reciprocal relationship, "where teachers' engagement in formative assessment created opportunities for them to construct new PCK" (Falk, 2012, p. 285). However, the author found that not all PCK components were built and used in this reciprocal way; for example, teachers used but did not build knowledge of instructional strategies and knowledge of local curriculum.

A few longitudinal studies focused on PCK development of elementary teachers. For example, Mulholland and Wallace (2005) reported the growth of one elementary teacher's science PCK over 10 years, from her preservice years through to the ninth year of her practice. The study showed that for this teacher, while SMK begins as the major component of PCK, "it is soon overshadowed by general teaching and interactive knowledge" (Mulholland

& Wallace, 2005, p. 785). As other knowledge bases become stronger, science SMK bases began to grow again. The study highlights "the interactiveness of the knowledge bases and how these bases are situated around the teaching of science to particular groups of children" (Mulholland & Wallace, 2005, p. 787). Further, the study highlighted the importance of curriculum materials as a "major source of new subject matter knowledge" (Mulholland & Wallace, 2005, p. 787). In another example of a longitudinal case study with one elementary teacher, Schneider (2013) focused on the role of curriculum materials as a resource to develop the teacher's PCK about teaching science as inquiry. The author found that interacting with the materials provided important "educative support" for the teacher in anticipating, understanding, and guiding students' science learning and managing a balance between supporting student participation and achieving curricular goals and led to the refinement of her PCK.

Studies of Preservice Science Teacher PCK in the Context of a Teacher Education Program

Various studies have been conducted on ways of enhancing the PCK of PSTs through the use of specific tools, approaches, and methods in the context of a teacher education program. For example, De Jong and colleagues (2005) used a workshop format in which Dutch chemistry PSTs ($n = 12$) were asked to prepare and teach a series of lessons on the topic of particle models to secondary school students. Following the workshop, all participants could describe specific learning difficulties of secondary students in relating properties of substances to constituent particles. PSTs also developed their knowledge of instructional strategies about particle models, although development varied among the PSTs. Reflecting on and discussing teaching experiences appeared to be crucial for this development. Significant gains in the growth of PCK through short-term, intensive, skills-oriented workshops were also found by Justi and van Driel (2006), who incorporated the design of a lesson series in an action research project that was a requirement for preservice Dutch secondary science teachers as part of their teacher education program. It was found that, in particular, reflective activities (such as writing reports and sharing experiences in collective meetings) stimulated the development of subject matter knowledge and PCK of these preservice teachers. In a similar study, Beyer and Davis (2012) investigated how elementary PSTs ($n = 24$) in a U.S. science methods course developed and used their PCK to identify strengths and weaknesses in science curriculum materials and whether they were able to make productive adaptations in planning for instruction. The researchers provided two different scaffolds to the PSTs: a criterion-based approach to analysis of the lesson materials and a set of criteria representing key ideas about effective science teaching. Results showed that the PSTs' PCK improved significantly over time when they had multiple opportunities to practice applying the same criterion in their planning.

Other studies on PCK development of PSTs include one by Brown, Friedrichsen, and Abell (2013), who investigated the development and interaction of three components of the Magnusson model (science teaching orientations, knowledge of science learners, and knowledge of instructional sequence) for four secondary biology PSTs during a 1-year teacher education program in the United States. The researchers found that during their preservice program, as PSTs' knowledge and experience increased, the interaction between their knowledge of learners and knowledge of instructional sequences became more integrated.

Research using CoRes and PaP-eRs has also been conducted in the context of science teacher education programs, where researchers have sought to stimulate the development of PSTs' PCK and promote their awareness of PCK as a meaningful construct for teachers. Loughran, Mulhall, and Berry (2008) employed a modified version of their CoRe and PaP-eRs framework in a preservice science teacher education program, whereby secondary PSTs developed their own CoRes and PaP-eRs based on their learning about PCK at university and from their experiences of teaching science in schools. A science teacher educator worked with PSTs during the final year of their teacher education program in Australia. The teacher educator combined the structured framework of the CoRes and PaP-eRs with ongoing reflective activities to sensitize PSTs to the notion of PCK and what it might mean for their practice. In this way, PSTs developed more sophisticated ways to think about and conceptualize their understanding of teaching science. Similar studies using adapted versions of CoRes and/or PaP-eRs have been reported by Hume and Berry (2011, 2013) and Nilsson and Loughran (2012). For example, in a study by Hume and Berry (2013), chemistry PSTs in New Zealand designed CoRes in negotiation with their school-based mentor teachers on topics they were teaching in practicum. PSTs refined their CoRes based on their teaching experiences and through ongoing discussions with their mentors. Findings indicated that the CoRe task improved PSTs' awareness of the different PCK components and provided a useful framework for focused conversations about chemistry teaching between PSTs and their mentor teachers.

Summary

Studies investigating the development of science teachers' PCK are beginning to accumulate. As with studies investigating PCK at one point in time, researchers have either used the Magnusson model in order to examine PCK development as a change in the nature and interaction of its various components or they employed their own models or representations to capture and portray change in teachers' PCK. A common context for studies of inservice teachers' PCK development appears to be in terms of a curriculum intervention or reform, with or without related professional development activities. Researchers have identified relationships between the interaction and growth of (at least some of the) different PCK components, along with further empirical evidence of the important role of reflection in the process of PCK development. Some researchers, such as Brown and colleagues (2013), have pointed to limitations of the Magnusson model for representing the dynamics of PCK development. Given the early stage of research in this area, questions related to what PSTs do with their PCK and how practice interacts with PCK so far remain largely unexplored.

Research on Relations Among Science Teacher Subject Matter Knowledge, Pedagogical Content Knowledge, and General Pedagogical Knowledge

In her review of research on PCK in science education, Kind (2009a) distinguishes three strands of research on the relationship between PCK and SMK: research that sees PCK and SMK as separate types of knowledge, research that sees no difference between the two, and research that considers the boundary between PCK and SMK to be blurred. Kind discusses many studies from the "separate" strand that demonstrate how SMK is transformed into PCK, especially in the context of learning to teach or when teaching unfamiliar topics. Interestingly, she suggests that

> [a] pre-service teacher with no prior PCK on which to draw is more open to developing PCK across science specialist subjects. Pedagogical content knowledge for outside specialism teaching may be easier to develop initially, as s/he is in the process of interpreting academic SMK for school purposes.
>
> (Kind, 2009a, p. 191)

However, Kind (2009a) concludes that "it remains unclear whether or not SMK is part of PCK" (p. 192). In this section, we address recent studies that have investigated PCK and SMK and their development in relation to each other.

Starting with studies on inservice science teachers, Kirschner, Borowksi, and Fischer (2011) investigated the relationship among the SMK, PCK, and pedagogical knowledge of German physics teachers ($n = 279$). For this purpose, a PCK paper-and-pencil test was developed consisting of 17 open-ended and multiple-choice items, with a focus on teaching mechanics. The PCK test had a good Rasch item reliability (.80). Tests for SMK and pedagogical knowledge were also developed. Multidimensional Rasch modeling revealed that SMK and PCK were different dimensions of teacher knowledge, although they were strongly correlated (.66). Correlations of SMK and PCK, respectively, with pedagogical knowledge were substantially weaker (between 0.1 and 0.4).

Other studies applied a qualitative approach. Henze, van Driel, and Verloop (2007) studied the relations among SMK, PCK, and general pedagogical knowledge in a group of experienced Dutch science teachers ($n = 9$), focusing on models and modeling in science. The authors found that PCK and general pedagogical knowledge were related in a consistent way. In particular, teachers whose pedagogical knowledge was dominated by behaviorist/cognitive ideas held PCK with a focus on knowledge of instructional strategies aimed at science content. On the other hand, the PCK of teachers with more constructivist pedagogical knowledge appeared to be more integrated, including knowledge of students' learning, and aimed at a more diverse set of learning objectives. However, teachers' SMK of models and modeling in science seemed unrelated to their PCK and pedagogical knowledge. In two case studies, Rollnick and colleagues (2008) focused on the PCK of inservice South African teachers about the mole and chemical equilibrium, respectively, in relation to the teachers' SMK and their context. The authors concluded that SMK is one of four "fundamental domains of knowledge for teaching" (Rollnick et al., 2008, p. 1380), together with knowledge of students, context, and general pedagogy. PCK is considered "an amalgam of these domains that, when combined, produce directly observable products in the classroom, which we refer to as 'manifestations'" (Rollnick et al., 2008, p. 1380), such as the representations of subject matter and instructional strategies they use. The authors demonstrated that even if teachers have similar SMK, their PCK may be quite different in terms of its manifestations, in particular if they work in different contexts.

Halai (2012) examined relations among SMK, PCK, and pedagogical knowledge through the perspective of teacher participation in action research projects. Halai performed a metasynthesis of 20 action research studies undertaken in the classroom by Pakistani inservice science teachers to develop their understanding of an innovative strategy for teaching science. Findings from this study revealed that action research contributed to developing understanding in all three domains of teacher knowledge: SMK, PCK, and pedagogical knowledge. Teachers developed an understanding of the theory and practice of the innovative strategy they implemented and found that the transformation of their SMK into PCK that "fit" the new ways of teaching was the most challenging and rewarding part of their action research.

Several studies investigated the development of SMK and PCK and their relationship in the context of preservice science teacher education. Johnston and Ahtee (2006) investigated elementary PSTs' attitudes, SMK, and PCK in physics in two institutions in England ($n = 98$) and Finland ($n = 89$), using a practical physics activity and a questionnaire. The authors found that unless PSTs had developed sound SMK, PCK was bound to be minimal. They advocate that teacher education programs in physics should particularly concentrate on helping PSTs to teach difficult concepts in a meaningful and accessible way, developing positive attitudes alongside understanding and pedagogical skills. Similarly, Usak, Özden, and Eilks (2011) conducted a study of Turkish PSTs ($n = 30$), focusing on their SMK, PCK, and beliefs about science teaching on the topic of chemical reactions. The authors

reported deficits in the PSTs' SMK, who also appeared to hold very traditional and teacher-centered beliefs about chemistry teaching at the secondary level. Apparently these beliefs plus the limited SMK hindered the formation of PCK.

Kaya (2009) studied the PCK of Turkish PSTs about ozone layer depletion, combining the results of a survey on content knowledge ($n = 216$) with interviews with three groups of 25 PSTs, identified as having high, average and low ability in the domain. The interviews were structured according to the PCK components from the Magnusson model, excluding science teaching orientations. The authors found medium to strong correlations between SMK and the various PCK components (between .32 and .77). However, knowledge of assessment was not correlated to the other three PCK components. The authors concluded that "for the PSTs with strong subject matter knowledge, there was more appropriate pedagogical knowledge, whereas there was more naïve pedagogical knowledge for those with low subject matter knowledge" (Kaya, 2009, p. 979). Käplyä, Heikkinen, and Asunta (2009) investigated the effect of the amount and the quality of SMK on PCK, comparing 10 elementary and 10 secondary Finnish PSTs on the topics of photosynthesis and plant growth. Questionnaires, a lesson-preparation task, and an interview were used to collect data. Elementary PSTs appeared not to be aware of students' conceptual difficulties and had problems in choosing the most important content. Secondary PSTs had much better SMK, which had a positive influence on their PCK and, subsequently, on effective teaching. However, neither of the groups had knowledge of suitable experiments and demonstrations, which limited the development of their PCK. The authors conclude that PCK should be explicitly taught in teacher education programs.

Other studies reported more success in developing PCK alongside SMK in the course of a teacher education program. Nilsson (2008) studied PSTs ($n = 4$) in Sweden who taught physics over a year to students aged 9 to 11 years. The study portrayed the complex nature of the development of PCK as a transformative process based on PSTs' existing SMK and pedagogical knowledge. The role of teaching experience and reflection in public was crucial in this development. Davis and Petish (2005) studied two pairs of elementary PSTs in the United States, focusing on the relationship between their SMK and emerging PCK and, in particular, their knowledge of instructional representations. The authors stressed the use of real-world applications to mediate the development of SMK and PCK. Nelson and Davis (2012) incorporated a unit in their methods course to support PSTs in evaluating elementary student–generated scientific models. To effectively engage in evaluation of students' scientific models, elementary PSTs needed to develop SMK about the science represented in the model, as well as knowledge of scientific models and modeling practices, including knowledge of relevant model evaluation criteria. With appropriate supports in place, the program was successful in developing these forms of modeling-related knowledge, as well as promoting PSTs' self-efficacy in this domain. In addition, PSTs were able to adopt criterion-based approaches to evaluating students' scientific models, which was seen as indicative of their emerging PCK about scientific modeling. Sperandeo-Mineo, Fazio, and Tarantino (2006), in a study of Italian PSTs ($n = 28$), reported gains in SMK, which in turn helped the PSTs "towards the construction of an appropriate PCK" (p. 260).

Summary

These studies further support the evidence that PCK and SMK are separate categories of teacher knowledge that can be empirically distinguished (cf. Baumert et al., 2010). Typically, SMK continues to be seen to act as a source or basis for the development of PCK, suggesting that a thorough knowledge of subject matter is necessary but not sufficient as a requisite for the formation of PCK. For instance, Anderson and Clark (2012) concluded that PCK develops in context on the basis of other knowledge areas (in particular, SMK), but, once formed, becomes a knowledge domain in its own right from which teachers can draw. An older study by Sanders, Borko, and Lockard (1993), however, demonstrated that experienced science teachers, when teaching a topic out of their area of certification, can quickly learn the new content as well as adequate content-specific instructional strategies while relying on their knowledge of general pedagogy. The latter helps them to maintain the flow in their classes. This finding seems consistent with Kind's idea that PCK may be *easier* to develop when teachers teach outside their area of specialization and are in a process of understanding academic SMK for school purposes (Kind, 2009b, p. 191). This suggests that PCK development doesn't have to "wait" for SMK to be developed but rather that both can be developed simultaneously. Unfortunately, recent studies have not focused on this particular interaction among science teachers' SMK, PCK, and general pedagogical knowledge. Consequently, the mechanisms by which various components of science teacher knowledge impact on each other remain mostly unclear.

Research on Science Teacher Knowledge in Relation to Student Learning

Abell (2007) concluded her chapter by stating,

> The research in both SMK and PCK has predominantly been at the level of description . . . The ultimate goal of science teacher knowledge research must be not only to understand teacher knowledge, but also to improve practice, thereby improving student learning.
>
> (p. 1134)

Five years later, in their handbook chapter, Fischer, Borowski, and Tepner (2012) concluded, "Most of the research on CK and PCK [. . .] still remains on a descriptive level" (p. 443). These authors also advocate studies that correlate science teacher knowledge to classroom interaction and student learning outcomes. Such studies have been done in the domain of mathematics education (e.g., Baumert et al., 2010; Hill, Rowan, & Ball, 2005) and are beginning to appear in the domain of science education.

Some studies have explored the relationship between science teacher knowledge and student learning in the context of professional development programs. Kanter and Konstantopoulos (2010) used video recordings of teachers' lessons in a study that sought to relate aspects of teacher knowledge to student variables (i.e., achievement and attitudes toward science). Studying participants ($n = 9$) in a PD program that was geared toward implementing a project-based science curriculum for minority students in the United States, the authors reported gains in the teachers' SMK and PCK that were significantly correlated to gains in student achievement but not, however, to students' attitudes. Roth and colleagues (2011) developed a video-based professional development program aimed at improving teacher and student learning at the upper elementary level. They found that the program resulted in gains in teachers' SMK and PCK about student thinking (based on an analysis of teachers' comments to video recordings of science classroom teaching), which were found to be significantly correlated to changes in teaching practices and student learning gains. Both these studies assessed PCK through converting teachers' analyses of video recordings (of their own or somebody else's lessons) into numerical scores so that statistical analyses (e.g., relations of PCK with student learning) were made possible.

In an ongoing U.S. project, Gardner and Gess-Newsome (2011) developed a rubric to capture biology teachers' PCK. The ultimate goal of the studies was to explore relationships of teachers' PCK, SMK, and general pedagogical knowledge with each other and with teaching practice and student learning. The Reformed Teaching Observation Protocol (RTOP; Sawada et al., 2002) was used to score teaching practice and general pedagogical knowledge. For teachers' SMK and student achievement, biology content tests were used. Applying these instruments, Gess-Newsome and colleagues (2011) reported the results of a study on secondary biology teachers ($n = 35$), who participated in a 2-year project in which they selected and implemented educative curriculum materials supported by transformative professional development. Data were collected two to five times across the project. The analysis of the data revealed several interesting outcomes. First, confirmatory factor analysis demonstrated a two-component model of PCK, including a PCK content knowledge and a PCK pedagogical knowledge component. Second, all teacher knowledge and practice variables increased significantly as a result of the intervention. Student achievement scores also improved significantly from the beginning to the end of the academic year. Next, exploring relationships, the authors found that PCK content knowledge and SMK were strongly correlated (.67; i.e., very similar to the abovementioned study by Kirschner et al., 2011).

Multiple regression analysis showed that only PCK content knowledge and general pedagogical knowledge were related to teaching practice: Teachers with higher scores on these types of knowledge applied more inquiry-based teaching practices. Using hierarchical linear modeling to explore relationships between student learning and teacher variables, it turned out that only teachers' SMK explained a significant amount of variance in student achievement. However, neither the other knowledge types nor teaching practice were statistically significant related to student learning outcomes. This result contrasts, for instance, with the Baumert and colleagues (2010) study in mathematics education. To account for these differences, the authors point at different definitions of teacher knowledge and of PCK in particular, plus differences in ways of testing PCK (rubrics versus paper-and-pencil tests). Moreover, situational characteristics (e.g., available time or materials) may have obscured the relationships among teacher variables and student achievement (cf. attribution error; Kennedy, 2010).

To investigate how teachers use content knowledge in interaction with students, Alonzo, Kobarg, and Seidel (2012) used video recordings of two German physics teachers who taught about optics. The students in these teachers' classes performed a pre- and a posttest on knowledge and interest in optics, showing that in one class, knowledge gains were substantially larger. The authors identified three types of use of content in which the two teachers differed. Acknowledging the problem of inferring teachers' knowledge from their behavior, these could be related to core components of PCK: *flexible* use of content, which is related to knowledge of student learning difficulties, *rich* use of content, which connects to teachers' knowledge of instructional representations, and *learner-centeredness*, which indicates an interplay between these two components. Anderson and Clark (2012) also conducted an in-depth study of the interaction between teacher knowledge and student learning. In a longitudinal case study of a New Zealand elementary teacher and her class, these researchers described the nature and development of syntactic aspects of the teacher's SMK and PCK (i.e., about the nature of science) as she planned and taught a unit on science investigation. Analysis of student learning indicated that the teacher's syntactic PCK was effective in that the ideas and processes she made most explicit through repeated practice were among those most commonly noted by her students. Reflection on the effectiveness of these experiences appeared to enhance the teacher's PCK. The authors concluded that their findings support the idea that PCK develops in context on the basis of other knowledge areas (in particular, SMK) but, once formed, becomes a knowledge domain in its own right from which teachers can draw.

Summary

Research that relates science teacher knowledge to student learning is just beginning to emerge. Most of these studies adopt a statistical approach: Measures of teacher knowledge are, somehow, quantified and correlated to student variables, such as achievement or interest. So far, these studies seem to have in common that gains in teachers' SMK (as a result of participating in a certain intervention) are accompanied by gains in student learning of science content. Typically, similar instruments were used to measure teachers' and students' understanding of content, which may explain at least some of the correlation between these two variables. However, the results of these studies are mixed as far as PCK and teaching practice are included. Studies applied different approaches to investigating science teachers' PCK, such as analyzing teachers' comments on videos (Roth et al., 2011), rubrics based on teachers' (oral and written) reflections (Gardner & Gess-Newsome, 2011), or scoring teachers' use of content during teaching (Alonzo et al., 2012). All these approaches, obviously, are quite different from the more or less standardized content tests that were used to measure teachers' SMK. Also, it is not always clear whether the PCK under consideration referred to the same topics that were central in the SMK measures. As Gess-Newsome and colleagues (2011) suggested, the way in which PCK is conceptualized and subsequently studied impacts strongly on the way teachers' PCK is scored or valued. Thus, there may be substantial gaps between measures of teachers' PCK and student achievement, explaining why some studies failed to find a relationship between these variables. This issue will be elaborated in the Discussion section.

Methodological Aspects of Research on Science Teacher Knowledge

In the previous sections, we only paid marginal attention to the research designs and instruments that are used in research on science teacher knowledge. However, there is quite a debate about methodological issues in this type of research. In her closing comments about recommendations for future studies, Abell (2007) stated that in research on science teacher SMK, research approaches have been used in a fairly consistent manner. However, she also concluded that more consensus is needed on the methodologies for studying science teachers' PCK, specifically to understand how teachers transform SMK into viable classroom instruction. Finally, Abell advocated to perform studies in which different aspects of teacher knowledge are connected to each other and to classroom practice and student learning, which will require more complex research designs and fitting data collection instruments. In this section, we explore how research on science teacher knowledge since 2005 has addressed these methodological issues, focusing on instruments that have been developed to investigate science teacher SMK and PCK.

Measuring Science Teachers' SMK

Studies on science teacher knowledge from the last 10 years show that, on the whole, "classical" data collection instruments have continued to be used, mostly questionnaires, interviews, and classroom observations. To measure SMK, questionnaires and standard validated science achievement tests (e.g., Heller, Daehler, Wong, Shinohara, & Miratrix, 2012) are most commonly employed. In addition to existing and validated questionnaires and achievement tests, new questionnaires have been developed, in particular to measure teachers' SMK of new curricular topics. A recent example is Lambert, Lindgren, and Bleicher's study (2012) on preservice and inservice teachers' knowledge about global climate change. The authors argue that teachers, for example, need to understand which nature- or human-induced factors influence the climate. To investigate teachers' SMK in this domain, they developed the Knowledge of Global Climate Change (KGCC) instrument, which consists of both multiple-choice items and extensive-responsive items. To develop the instrument, the constructive modeling approach framework (Wilson, 2005) was used, which distinguishes four components (construct map, item design, outcome space, and measurement model). Hayhoe, Bullock, and Hayhoe (2011) also developed a questionnaire to measure science teachers' SMK about climate change. They used a binary-choice format to avoid the "positive statement bias" of the Likert scale and the superfluous distracters in multiple-choice tests. Besides studies on teachers' SMK of climate change, other topics such as air pollution (Cibik & Darcin, 2009) and chemical hormone usage (Özden, Usak, Prokop, Turkoglu, & Bahar, 2008) have been studied by means of questionnaires. Tretter and colleagues (2013) developed assessments of teacher knowledge in the domains of physical, life, and earth/space science as part of the Diagnostic Teacher Assessments of Mathematics and Science (DTAMS) project. The assessment consists of a blend of multiple-choice as well as open-response questions in a questionnaire, thus aiming to measure both the depth and the breadth of teachers' SMK. As a final example, Everett, Otto, and Luera (2009) used four different data collection instruments to assess PSTs' knowledge of models to examine which instrument is most suitable to determine PSTs' growth in knowledge of models and their use of this knowledge in classrooms. The four instruments included a Y/N questionnaire for identification of models, concept maps, open-ended questions, and the questionnaire Students' Understanding of Models in Science (SUMS). It appeared that all instruments measured growth of SMK. The authors considered the instruments unsuitable, however, to measure how PSTs used their knowledge in practice to teach about models or how models can be used to teach science concepts.

Eliciting Science Teachers' PCK

In contrast to studies on SMK, research on science teachers' PCK tends to use a broader variety of instruments in which usually the "local" context of teachers' knowledge is acknowledged. Often a combination of different methods is used to understand teachers' PCK in its full complexity. Kind (2009a) distinguished two categories within research methods to elicit PCK: studies exploring PCK *in situ*, focusing on how teachers actually teach science in classroom and laboratory settings, versus those using "prompts" as elicitation tasks as an approximation of the teaching context. *In situ* studies may collect data over a longer period of time rather than capturing teachers' PCK at an instant. Typically, these studies are characterized by the use of multiple data collection instruments, such as interviews and observation protocols, and combine the collected data in a triangulation procedure. Finally, many of these studies are small scale and tend to focus on the PCK of beginning teachers. The second category refers to studies that developed specific prompts as elicitation tasks, such as confronting teachers with students' answers to questions in a standardized student achievement test or vignettes of typical classroom situations. In the next section, we discuss examples of various approaches to eliciting PCK. As we will see, most studies combine different methods of data collection to capture the complexity of PCK, some of which are more *in situ* than others.

Some studies investigated PCK with specially designed rubrics, using *in situ* data (i.e., classroom observations) in combination with other types of data. For example, Park, Jang, Chen, and Jung (2011) assessed teachers' levels of PCK using a rubric that was based on observations of teaching practice and pre/post observation interviews. The rubric focused on the two components from the Magnusson model that are most prominently featured in classroom situations, such as knowledge of student understanding and knowledge of instructional strategies and representations. Gardner and Gess-Newsome (2011) also developed a PCK rubric based on a combination of video tapes of teachers' classroom instruction, teacher interviews, plus teachers' written reflections, focusing on various biology topics. The rubric aimed to capture aspects of content knowledge, pedagogical knowledge, and contextual knowledge within individual teachers' PCK. For each aspect, criteria were described that were scored with 0, 1, 2, and 3 (corresponding to limited, basic, proficient, or advanced teacher knowledge). This way of scoring teachers' PCK allowed researchers to determine possible growth in teachers' levels of PCK.

Loughran, Mulhall, and Berry (2004) developed a specific approach to address the problems of capturing and portraying PCK in a holistic, integrated manner. As mentioned earlier, these authors developed CoRes and PaP-eRs. The CoRe framework was developed as an interview tool, to be used with individual science teachers or small groups of teachers, to elicit teachers' understanding of important aspects of teaching specific content using prompts to elicit the pedagogical reasoning behind their decision making. The outcomes of these interviews were used as the representation itself. PaP-eRs are closely connected to CoRes and are meant to provide additional insight into the various interacting elements that constitute a teacher's PCK. PaP-eRs include a variety of narrative representations of classroom teaching, such as a teacher's reflection on a teaching situation, a teacher's annotated curriculum document, or a description of a student's perspective on science learning.

Other studies used authentic artifacts from science teaching as probes to elicit teachers' PCK. For instance, video fragments (Kanter & Konstantopoulos, 2010) or scenario questions (e.g., Van Dijk, 2009) have been used for this purpose. Cohen and Yarden (2009) employed various techniques to examine teachers' PCK about assessment, focusing on the topic of cells. In addition to confronting teachers with students' answers to certain tasks, the authors used visual illustrations of how the cell could be taught in conjunction with other topics. The teachers were asked to choose the illustration that fitted best with their understanding of the guideline. Also, teachers were asked to discuss and classify unfamiliar test questions for students from different grades and to eliminate questions they considered not suitable.

Several studies used lesson plans to examine teachers' PCK and its development. For example, Gullberg and colleagues (2008), Kellner and colleagues (2011), Käpylä and colleagues (2009), and Friedrichsen and colleagues (2009) used the lesson preparation method (van der Valk & Broekman, 1999). In this method, teachers are asked to design one or more lessons as if they have to teach that lesson the next day. During the preparation of the lesson, teachers are not allowed to use resources such as textbooks for pupils, since this is considered to hinder the creativity of teachers. Based on their lesson design, the teachers are interviewed to elicit their knowledge of instructional strategies and assessment. Orleans (2010) also used a lesson-planning task in which PSTs were asked to make a lesson plan in 30 minutes. The pre- and posttest design of this study made it possible to look for progress in PSTs' knowledge about assessment and knowledge of instructional strategies.

Finally, standardized ways to investigate science teachers' PCK are beginning to emerge in the literature. These studies depart from the *in situ* approach in trying to develop measures of PCK that can be administered among large samples of teachers. For example, Schmelzing and colleagues (2013) described the development of a labor-efficient paper-and-pencil test to measure biology teachers' "declarative PCK" about the cardiovascular system. The development of the test was mainly based on a literature review and an analysis of videotaped biology lessons. The test consisted of 15 open-ended items across two scales: PCK of student learning and conceptions and of representations and strategies, respectively. To explore the validity of the instrument, it was demonstrated that inservice biology teachers scored higher on the test than did preservice teachers and biologists. Similar to this paper-and-pencil test, also in Germany, Jüttner and Neuhaus (2012) created a PCK test to measure teachers' knowledge of students' errors and ways to deal with them. The items of this test were based on students' erroneous answers in an achievement test about the knee jerk in biology and

were divided into three knowledge dimensions: declarative knowledge, procedural knowledge, and conditional knowledge. The validity of the items was checked by means of qualitative think-aloud interviews with teachers taking the test. The authors concluded that the test requires more detailed statistical analysis in a next study with a larger sample of teachers.

Summary

Based on the number of recent studies that specifically focus on how to study science teachers' SMK and PCK, it appears that measuring teacher knowledge (and beliefs) is a recurring theme in research in science education. It seems that science teachers' SMK is mostly investigated with standardized tests, such as questionnaires and achievement tests. New questionnaires have been developed to measure teachers' SMK of new curricular topics. With respect to eliciting science teachers' PCK, the studies described in this review show that there is still a huge variety in methods and instruments used. The various methods can be represented along a spectrum that ranges from a focus on how science is actually taught in practice (*in situ*) to the use of standardized written tests with open-ended or multiple-choice items. Whereas the former methods aim to capture "PCK-in-action" (Alonzo et al., 2012), the latter target "declarative PCK" (Schmelzing et al., 2013). Most studies, however, combine methods that are more or less distant to classroom teaching. Finally, it should be noted that many authors tend to rely on previous studies and adapt or refine data collection instruments for their own specific context.

Discussion

Since the first edition of this handbook appeared in 2007, research on science teacher knowledge has continued to attract attention from scholars around the globe. Many of these studies take place in the context of preparing new science teachers (i.e., in a preservice program). Also, much research on science teacher knowledge is done in the context of reform of science education, which is ongoing across the globe and is typically accompanied by programs of professional development. Usually, these studies are informed by an interest to monitor what teachers know or need to know to teach science effectively and to explore how science teacher knowledge can be enhanced. As for research on SMK, Abell's conclusion still seems to stand: "The research on SMK is cohesive, partly because definitions of SMK are commonly shared even when research methods differ" (Abell, 2007, p. 1133). Reflecting on research in recent years, this also implies that, as a scholarly community, we haven't seen too many new insights emerging from research that focused exclusively on science teachers' SMK. Studies in this domain seem to be inspired mostly by concerns about a sound understanding of science content by teachers, especially beginning and elementary teachers. Therefore, such studies seem mostly relevant for policy makers and educators in the context of designing programs to strengthen the SMK of certain groups of (aspiring) teachers.

As for PCK, Abell (2007) stated that research in this domain was "less cohesive" (p. 1133) or even "pre-science" (p. 1134), mainly because of disagreement among scholars about conceptualizations of PCK and, consequently, ways to investigate it. Recently, Settlage (2013) stated that in most PCK research, a static conception of knowledge as something that is stored in teachers' minds is applied. Settlage argued that many studies have been limited to investigating or portraying what teachers know or think without relating this to what teachers actually do in classroom practice, let alone what their students gain from it. Although we agree that there is still controversy about the nature and the status of PCK, we think that the current review demonstrates that research on science teacher PCK has made substantial progress in recent years. Whereas earlier research indeed was often limited to descriptive studies of certain aspects or components of the PCK of a small number of science teachers at a certain moment in time, recent research includes studies of larger samples and studies that seek relationships within components of PCK, as well as among PCK, SMK, and other variables, at both teacher and student level. Also, recent PCK studies have begun to explore the effects of specific interventions, either in preservice teacher education or professional development programs, on the development of science teachers' PCK. We notice in recent PCK research, roughly, a dichotomy between studies that seek to understand why teachers teach certain subject matter in the way they do and how their approach is aimed at promoting student learning versus studies that try to establish quantitative relationships between teacher and student variables. The former type of studies typically acknowledge the contextual characteristics and personal experiences that shape teachers' understanding of how their students learn or fail to learn specific content and what they can do to promote their students' understanding and appreciation of science content. These studies usually concern small numbers of science teachers and apply designs including multiple methods of data collection, such as teacher self-reports, as well as artifacts from teaching practice (e.g., student work and video recordings of lessons). Studies such as the one by Alonzo and colleagues (2012) nicely illustrate this strand of research. These authors related the flexibility and richness of teachers' use of content during science lessons to core components of PCK. We would argue that such studies regard PCK as "knowledge *of* teachers" (Fenstermacher, 1994).

On the other hand, studies aimed at investigating teacher knowledge through measures such as paper-and-pencil tests or rubrics seem to be based on a "knowledge *for* teachers" idea. That is, in such studies, teacher knowledge is perceived as standardized and thus measurable, making it possible to distinguish between teachers with "strong" and "weak" knowledge. Although this may be a valid and useful way to look at teachers' SMK, we think

that this stance is problematic when PCK is concerned. Given the notion of flexibility mentioned earlier, we would argue that high-quality PCK is *not* characterized by knowing as many strategies as possible to teach a certain topic plus all the misconceptions students may have about it but by knowing when to apply a certain strategy in recognition of students' actual learning needs and understanding why a certain teaching approach may be useful in one situation (i.e., a particular class of students at a certain moment) but may not work the next day with a different group of students. It seems hard to capture this kind of knowledge that is "uniquely the province of teachers, their own special form of professional understanding" (Shulman, 1987, p. 8) through some standardized measure that does justice to the situational and personal aspects that are, inherently, part of a teacher's PCK.

To frame the current review, we used a rather simple model of teacher knowledge (i.e., Figure 42.1). In effect, we mainly considered studies focusing on science teachers' SMK, PCK, or both. In some of these studies, science teachers' pedagogical and contextual knowledge was included, but typically in relation to SMK or PCK. We found very few studies focusing exclusively on science teachers' pedagogical or contextual knowledge. In the light of the ongoing debate about the relationship between SMK and PCK, we think that recent studies in science education, both small scale and large scale, provide support for the idea that SMK and PCK are separate types of teacher knowledge, that both exist in their own right. However, an interesting point emerges about the very different ways in which SMK and PCK are determined across various studies (e.g., standardized test versus *in situ*). One could reason that these methodological differences necessarily lead to finding different types of knowledge. On the other hand, the reverse argument, that is, that SMK and PCK are investigated differently *because* they are different types of knowledge, might also apply. Nevertheless, almost every study in this domain points at relationships between SMK and PCK, either statistical or conceptual. However, this relationship is not straightforward. Studies on the development of science teacher knowledge, in particular, have revealed different mechanisms of how SMK and PCK may impact on each other. It seems safe to say that teachers who have a thorough understanding of the science content *before* they start to teach this content develop PCK on the basis of their SMK. Strong SMK tends to be associated with strong confidence to teach. However, there is evidence that this may hinder the development of PCK, for instance, because teachers who understand the content thoroughly and teach it confidently may be unaware of the problems that many of their students have in making sense of this content (cf. Kind & Kind, 2011). On the other hand, teachers who begin to teach certain content without solid SMK have a chance to develop SMK and PCK simultaneously. For example, being confronted with questions of their students, these teachers may become aware of the gaps in their own SMK while at the same time learning how their students perceive the content at hand. In situations like this, teachers' general pedagogical knowledge may play a supportive role in the development of both PCK and SMK. Another truism, which is neither new nor controversial, is that the development of PCK is bound to be limited within the context of preservice teacher education and needs to be continued during teachers' professional practice as teachers build their experience of teaching specific topics. In this way, they may expand their knowledge of how students come to understand these topics and what they can do to promote their students' learning. However, for this development of PCK to take place, reflection on teaching is necessary. This may be done informally and spontaneously, but programs for professional development can direct and promote this development.

Implications for Science Teacher Education and Professional Development

Overlooking the studies in this review, several implications for the design of programs for science teacher education and professional development may be derived. Specific strategies seem to be potentially powerful to further the development of science teacher knowledge. First and most importantly, programs need to have a focus on student learning of science content. The studies reviewed here contain various examples of how this can be put into practice. For example, science teachers, both prospective and experienced, can benefit from studying authentic student work (e.g., Heller et al., 2012), collecting data from students in their own classes (e.g., Justi & van Driel, 2006), or analyzing videos of classroom situations, preferably taught by the teacher (e.g., Kanter & Konstantopoulos, 2010). Second, programs need to include opportunities for science teachers to plan and design ways to teach certain science content and try at least some of these ways out in their own practice. Analyzing existing or innovative curricular materials may be part of this strategy (see e.g., Beyer & Davis, 2012; Schneider, 2013). During these activities, support from and collaboration with peers and mentors as well as facilitators can be particularly useful (see e.g., Appleton, 2008; Hume & Berry, 2013)—for instance, through observing each other's lessons and discussing them afterward. To specifically promote the development of both SMK and PCK, the use of real-world applications of science seems beneficial (see e.g., Davis & Petish, 2005; Dresner & Worley, 2006). Preferably, these strategies are combined, for example, in a project-based approach in which teachers do (collaborative) action research.

We suggest that programs for science teacher education and professional development, rather than targeting specific aspects of science teacher knowledge (e.g., knowledge of assessment or knowledge of student learning), aim at the development of science teacher knowledge in relation to the practice of teaching or learning to teach science. Ultimately, such programs should contribute to establishing science teaching practices that promote students' understanding of and interest in science.

Recommendations for Future Research

We think it is fair to conclude the current review by stating that researchers between 2007 and 2012 have made progress in response to this repeated call. In our view, studies on science teacher knowledge since 2007 have addressed more complex research questions and, consequently, have become more sophisticated in terms of their methodologies. Nevertheless, we would advocate research programs to continue work in this domain. In particular, we would suggest the following lines of research. First, in future research, the relationship between SMK and PCK needs more attention, preferably in association with pedagogical knowledge. Studies need to have a classroom teaching component to investigate how teachers use their SMK in interaction with students and how both SMK and PCK develop in such a context, possibly mediated by teachers' pedagogical knowledge. Next, we would advocate both qualitative and quantitative studies that relate science teacher knowledge to student learning. The former could relate classroom interactions about subject matter (e.g., recorded on video) to teacher knowledge (e.g., elicited by stimulated-recall interviews) and student understanding (e.g., by a specific task students perform at the end of an observed classroom situation or shortly afterward). Such studies would contribute to our understanding of how processes of teaching and learning of subject matter may impact each other.

Studies that aim to relate science teacher knowledge to student learning in a statistical way need to deal with several challenges. First, such studies need labor-efficient ways to investigate science teacher knowledge, including PCK, in large-scale projects. For this purpose, we would advocate the use of a combination of instruments that capture not only what is in a teacher's mind (SMK and "declarative PCK"; cf. Schmelzing et al. 2013) but also how teachers enact their understanding in classroom situations in a way that does justice to their consideration of personal and contextual aspects. Rubrics, based on teachers' written reflections (cf. Gardner & Gess-Newsome, 2011), seem potentially useful to serve this goal. Moreover, it is crucial to take mediating factors into account to avoid attribution error (cf. Kennedy, 2010) and to align measures of teacher knowledge, in particular PCK, with measures of student learning. For instance, a test of student understanding should be consistent with the learning objectives teachers explicitly aim to achieve among their students.

So far, research has paid very little attention to the role and the expertise of the people who play a pivotal role in promoting the development of science teacher knowledge, that is, science teacher educators and facilitators. Several science teacher educators have conducted self-studies (for a review, see Loughran & Berry, 2012). As an example, Goodnough (2006) conducted a self-study on the implementation of a problem-based learning approach to her teaching of PSTs and found that many aspects of her own PCK were developed as a consequence of the innovation.

Berry and van Driel (2012) conducted an exploratory study on a sample of science teacher educators from Australia and the Netherlands that demonstrated that although these teacher educators shared similar concerns, they had very diverse approaches to preparing science teachers in terms of promoting PSTs' knowledge and emerging practice. We would welcome studies that document the expertise of science teacher educators and facilitators and that investigate their interaction with the participants in their programs, taking into account contextual aspects of these programs, to increase our understanding of the knowledge development of preservice and inservice science teachers.

Acknowledgments

We would like to acknowledge Patricia Friedrichsen and Peter Hewson, who reviewed this chapter.

Note

1. Throughout this chapter we use the phrase "knowledge development" instead of "learning." The teacher as learner and the process of learning to teach science are the focus of Chapters 40 and 43, respectively. Our use of the phrase "knowledge development" typically refers to studies that compare data at different points in time and make inferences from the differences. We considered "knowledge growth" or "knowledge change" as alternatives but chose "knowledge development," as this phrase is most commonly used in the studies we reviewed.

References

Abell, S. (2008). Twenty years later: Does pedagogical content knowledge remain a useful idea? *International Journal of Science Education, 30,* 1405–1416.

Abell, S. K. (2007). Research on science teacher knowledge. In S. Abell & N. G. Lederman (Eds.), *Handbook of research on science education* (pp. 1105–1149). Mahwah, NJ: Lawrence Erlbaum Associates.

Akyol, G., Tekkaya, C., Sungur, S., & Traynor, A. (2012). Modeling the interrelationships among pre-service science teachers' understanding and acceptance of evolution, their views on nature of science and self-efficacy beliefs regarding teaching evolution. *Journal of Science Teacher Education, 23,* 937–957. doi:10.1007/s10972-012-9296-x

Alexander, P. A., Schallert, D. L., & Hare, V. C. (1991). Coming to terms: How researchers in learning and literacy talk about knowledge. *Review of Educational Research, 61,* 315–343.

Alonzo, A. C., Kobarg, M., & Seidel, T. (2012). Pedagogical content knowledge as reflected in teacher–student interactions: Analysis of two video cases. *Journal of Research in Science Teaching, 49,* 1211–1239.

Anderson, C. W., & Smith, E. L. (1987). Teaching science. In V. Richardson-Koehler (Ed.), *Educators' handbook: A research perspective* (pp. 84–111). New York: Longman.

Anderson, D., & Clark, M. (2012). Development of syntactic subject matter knowledge and pedagogical content knowledge for science by a generalist elementary teacher. *Teachers and Teaching: Theory & Practice, 18,* 315–330. doi:10.1080/13540602.2012.629838

Appleton, K. (2008). Developing science pedagogical content knowledge through mentoring elementary teachers. *Journal of Science Teacher Education, 19,* 523–545.

Asikainen, M. A., & Hirvonen, P. E. (2010). Finnish cooperating physics teachers' conceptions of physics teachers' teacher knowledge. *Journal of Science Teacher Education, 21,* 431–450.

Avraamidou, L., & Zembal-Saul, C. (2005). Giving priority to evidence in science teaching: A first-year elementary teacher's specialized practices and knowledge. *Journal of Research in Science Teaching, 42,* 965–986.

Ball, D., Thames, M. H., & Phelps, G. (2008). Content knowledge for teaching: What makes it special? *Journal of Teacher Education, 59,* 389–407. doi:10.1177/0022487108324554

Barnes, M. B., Hodge, E. M., Parker, M., & Koroly, M. J. (2006). The teacher research update experience: Perceptions of practicing science, mathematics, and technology teachers. *Journal of Science Teacher Education, 17,* 243–263. doi:10.1007/s10972-006-9007-6

Baumert, J., Kunter, M., Blum, W., Brunner, M., Voss, T., Jordan, A., et al. (2010). Teachers' mathematical knowledge, cognitive activation in the classroom, and student progress. *American Educational Research Journal, 47,* 133–180.

Berry, A., Loughran, J., & van Driel, J. H. (2008). Revisiting the roots of pedagogical content knowledge. *International Journal of Science Education, 30,* 1271–1280.

Berry, A., & van Driel, J. H. (2012). Teaching about teaching science: Aims, strategies and backgrounds of science teacher educators. *Journal of Teacher Education, 64,* 117–128.

Beyer, C. J., & Davis, E. A. (2012). Learning to critique and adapt science curriculum materials: Examining the development of pre-service elementary teachers' pedagogical content knowledge. *Science Education, 96,* 130–157.

Bindernagel, J. A., & Eilks, I. (2009). Evaluating roadmaps to portray and develop chemistry teachers' PCK about curricular structures concerning sub-microscopic models. *Chemistry Education Research and Practice, 10,* 77–85.

Bleicher, R. E., & Lindgren, J. (2005). Success in science learning and preservice science teaching self-efficacy. *Journal of Science Teacher Education, 16,* 205–225.

Boz, N., & Boz, Y. (2008). A qualitative case study of prospective chemistry teachers' knowledge about instructional strategies: Introducing particulate theory. *Journal of Science Teacher Education, 19,* 135–156.

Bozdogan, A. E., Karsli, F., & Sahin, C. (2011). A study on the prospective teachers' knowledge, teaching methods and attitudes towards global warming with respect to different variables. *Energy Education Science and Technology. Part B: Social and Educational Studies, 3,* 315–330.

Brown, P., Friedrichsen, P., & Abell, S. K. (2013). The development of prospective secondary biology teachers' PCK. *Journal of Science Teacher Education, 24,* 133–155. doi:10.1007/s10972-012-9312-1

Brown, S., & McIntyre, D. (1993). *Making sense of teaching.* Buckingham, UK: Open University Press.

Burgoon, J. N., Heddle, M. L., & Duran, E. (2010). Re-examining the similarities between teacher and student conceptions. *Journal of Science Teacher Education, 21,* 859–872. doi:10.1007/s10972-009-9177-0

Calderhead, J. (1996). Teachers: Beliefs and knowledge. In D. Berliner & R. Calfee (Eds.), *Handbook of educational psychology* (pp. 709–725). New York: Macmillan.

Carrier, S. J. (2013). Elementary pre-service teachers' science vocabulary: Knowledge and application. *Journal of Science Teacher Education, 24,* 405–425. doi:10.1007/s10972-012-9270-7

Carter, K. (1990). Teachers' knowledge and learning to teach. In W. R. Houston (Ed.), *Handbook of research on teacher education* (pp. 291–310). New York: Macmillan.

Cheung, D., Ma, H. J., & Yang, J. (2009). Teachers' misconceptions about the effects of addition of more reactants or products on chemical equilibrium. *International Journal of Science and Mathematics Education, 7,* 1111–1133.

Childs, A., & McNicholl, J. (2007). Science teachers teaching outside of subject specialism: Challenges, strategies adopted and implications for initial teacher education. *Teacher Development, 11,* 1–20.

Chinn, P. W. U. (2012). Developing teachers' place-based and culture-based pedagogical content knowledge and agency. In B. J. Fraser, K. Tobin, & C. J. McRobbie (Eds.), *Second international handbook of science education* (pp. 323–334). Dordrecht, the Netherlands: Springer. doi:10.1007/978-1-4020-9041-7_30

Cibik, A. S., & Darcin, E. S. (2009). Pre-service science teachers' knowledge level about some basic air pollutants. *Journal of Baltic Science Education, 8,* 22–34.

Cochran, K. F., DeRuiter, J. A., & King, R. A. (1993). Pedagogical content knowing: An integrative model for teacher preparation. *Journal of Teacher Education, 44,* 263–272.

Coenders, F., Terlouw, C., Dijkstra, S., & Pieters, J. (2010). The effects of the design and development of a chemistry curriculum reform on teachers' professional growth: A case study. *Journal of Science Teacher Education, 21,* 535–557. doi:10.1007/s10972-010-9194-z

Cohen, R., & Yarden, A. (2009). Experienced junior-high-school teachers' PCK in light of a curriculum change: "The cell is to be studied longitudinally." *Research in Science Education, 39,* 131–155. doi:10.1007/s11165-008-9088-7

Crippen, K. J. (2012). Argument as professional development: Impacting teacher knowledge and beliefs about science. *Journal of Science Teacher Education, 23,* 847–866. doi:10.1007/s10972-012-9282-3

Danusso, L., Testa, I., & Vicentini, M. (2010). Improving prospective teachers' knowledge about scientific models and modelling: Design and evaluation of a teacher education intervention. *International Journal of Science Education, 32,* 871–905.

Davidowitz, B., & Rollnick, M. (2011). What lies at the heart of good undergraduate teaching? A case study in organic chemistry. *Chemistry Education Research and Practice, 12,* 355–366.

Davis, E. A., & Petish, D. (2005). Real-world applications and instructional representations among prospective elementary science teachers. *Journal of Science Teacher Education, 16,* 263–286.

De Jong., O., van Driel, J. H., & Verloop, N. (2005). Preservice teachers' pedagogical content knowledge of using particle models in teaching chemistry. *Journal of Research in Science Teaching, 42,* 947–964.

Deng, Z. (2007). Transforming the subject matter: Examining the intellectual roots of pedagogical content knowledge. *Curriculum Inquiry, 37,* 279–295.

Dreschler, M., & van Driel, J. H. (2008). Experienced teachers' pedagogical content knowledge of teaching acid–base chemistry. *Research in Science Education, 38,* 611–631.

Dresner, M., & Worley, E. (2006). Teacher research experiences, partnerships with scientists, and teacher networks sustaining factors from professional development. *Journal of Science Teacher Education, 17,* 1–14.

Emereole, H. U. (2009). Learners' and teachers' conceptual knowledge of science processes: The case of Botswana. *International Journal of Science and Mathematics Education, 7,* 1033–1056.

Everett, S. A., Otto, C. A., & Luera, G. R. (2009). Preservice elementary teachers' growth in knowledge of models in a science capstone course. *International Journal of Science and Mathematics Education, 7,* 1201–1225.

Falk, A. (2012). Teachers learning from professional development in elementary science: Reciprocal relations between formative assessment and pedagogical content knowledge. *Science Education, 96,* 265–290.

Fenstermacher, G. D. (1986). Philosophy of research on teaching: Three aspects. In M. C. Wittrock (Ed.), *Handbook of research on teaching* (3rd ed., pp. 37–49). New York: Macmillan.

Fenstermacher, G. D. (1994). The knower and the known: The nature of knowledge in research on teaching. In L. Darling-Hammond (Ed.), *Review of research in education* (pp. 3–56). Washington, DC: American Educational Research Association.

Fischer, H. E., Borowksi, A., & Tepner, O. (2012). Professional knowledge of science teachers. In B. J. Fraser, K. Tobin, & C. J. McRobbie (Eds.), *Second international handbook of science education* (pp. 435–448). Dordrecht, the Netherlands: Springer. doi:10.1007/978-1-4020-9041-7_30

Friedrichsen, P., van Driel, J., & Abell, S. (2011). Taking a closer look at science teaching orientations. *Science Education, 95,* 358–376.

Friedrichsen, P. J., Abell, S. K., Pareja, E. M., Brown P. L., Lankford, D. M., & Volkmann, M. J. (2009). Does teaching experience matter?

Examining biology teachers' prior knowledge for teaching in an alternative certification program. *Journal of Research in Science Teaching, 46,* 357–383.

Galili, I., & Lehavi, Y. (2006). Definitions of physical concepts: A study of physics teachers' knowledge and views. *International Journal of Science Education, 28,* 521–541.

Gardner, A. L., & Gess-Newsome, J. (2011, April). *A PCK rubric to measure teachers' knowledge of inquiry based instruction using three data sources.* Paper presented at the Annual Meeting of the National Association for Research in Science Teaching, Orlando, FL.

Gess-Newsome, J., Cardenas, S., Austin, B. A., Carlson, J., Gardner, A. L., Stuhlsatz, M. A. M., Taylor, J. A., & Wilson, C. D. (2011, April). *Impact of educative materials and transformative professional development on teachers' PCK, practice, and student achievement.* Paper presented at the Annual Meeting of the National Association for Research in Science Teaching, Orlando, FL.

Goodnough, K. (2006). Enhancing pedagogical content knowledge through self-study: An exploration of problem-based learning. *Teaching in Higher Education, 11,* 301–318.

Gullberg, A., Kellner, E., Attorps, I., Thoren, I., & Tarneberg, R. (2008). Prospective teachers' initial conceptions about pupils' understanding of science and mathematics. *European Journal of Teacher Education, 31,* 257–278.

Halai, N. (2012). Developing understanding of innovative strategies of teaching science through action research: A qualitative meta-synthesis from Pakistan. *International Journal of Science and Mathematics Education, 10,* 387–415.

Harlow, D. B., Swanson, L. H., & Otero, V. K. (2012). Prospective elementary teachers' analysis of children's science talk in an undergraduate physics course. *Journal of Science Teacher Education.* doi:10.1007/s10972-012-9319-7

Hashweh, M. Z. (2005). Teacher pedagogical constructions: A reconfiguration of pedagogical content knowledge. *Teachers and Teaching: Theory and Practice, 11,* 273–292.

Hayhoe, D., Bullock, S., & Hayhoe, K. (2011). A kaleidoscope of understanding: Comparing real with random data, using binary-choice items, to study preservice elementary teachers' knowledge of climate change. *Weather, Climate and Society, 3,* 254–260.

Heller, J., Daehler, K. R., Wong, N., Shinohara, M., & Miratrix, L. W. (2012). Differential effects of three professional development models on teacher knowledge and student achievement in elementary science. *Journal of Research in Science Teaching, 49,* 333–362.

Henze, I., van Driel, J. H., & Verloop, N. (2007). The change of science teachers' personal knowledge about teaching models and modelling in the context of science education reform. *International Journal of Science Education, 29,* 1819–1846.

Henze, I., van Driel, J. H., & Verloop, N. (2008). Development of experienced science teachers' pedagogical content knowledge of models of the solar system and the universe. *International Journal of Science Education, 30,* 1321–1342.

Hill, H. C., Rowan, B., & Ball, D. L. (2005). Effects of teachers' mathematical knowledge for teaching on student achievement. *American Educational Research Journal, 42,* 371–406.

Hume, A., & Berry, A. (2011). Constructing CoRes—a strategy for building PCK in pre-service science teacher education. *Research in Science Education, 41,* 341–355. doi:10.1007/s11165-010-9168-3

Hume, A., & Berry, A. (2013). Enhancing the practicum experience for pre-service chemistry teachers through collaborative CoRe design with mentor teachers. *Research in Science Education, 43,* 2107–2136. doi:10.1007/s11165-012-9346-6.

Johnston, J., & Ahtee, M. (2006). Comparing primary student teachers' attitudes, subject knowledge and pedagogical content knowledge needs in a physics activity. *Teaching and Teacher Education, 22,* 503–512.

Justi, R., & van Driel, J. H. (2006). The use of the Interconnected Model of Teacher Professional Growth for understanding the development of science teachers' knowledge on models and modelling. *Teaching and Teacher Education, 22,* 437–450.

Jüttner, M., & Neuhaus, B. (2012). Development of items for a pedagogical content knowledge-test based on empirical analysis of pupils' errors. *International Journal of Science Education, 34*, 1125–1143.

Kang, N. H. (2007). Elementary teachers' teaching for conceptual understanding: Learning from action research. *Journal of Science Teacher Education, 18*, 469–495. doi:10.1007/s10972-007-9050-y

Kansanen, P. (2009). Subject-matter didactics as a central knowledge base for teachers, or should it be called pedagogical content knowledge? *Pedagogy, Culture & Society, 17*, 29–39.

Kanter, D., & Konstantopoulos, S. (2010). The impact of project-based science on minority student achievement, attitudes, and career plans: An examination of the effects of teacher content knowledge, pedagogical content knowledge, and inquiry-based practices. *Science Education, 94*, 855–887.

Käpylä, M., Heikkinen, J., & Asunta, T. (2009). Influence of content knowledge on pedagogical content knowledge: The case of teaching photosynthesis and plant growth. *International Journal of Science Education, 31*, 1395–1415.

Kariotoglou, P., Spyrtou, A., & Tselfes, V. (2009). How student teachers understand distance force interactions in different contexts. *International Journal of Science and Mathematics Education, 7*, 851–873.

Kaya, O. N. (2009). The nature of relationships among the components of pedagogical content knowledge of preservice science teachers: "Ozone layer depletion" as an example. *International Journal of Science Education, 31*, 961–988.

Kellner, E., Gullberg, A., Attorps, I., Thoren, I., & Tarneberg, R. (2011). Prospective teachers' initial conceptions about pupils' difficulties in science and mathematics: A potential resource in teacher education. *International Journal of Science and Mathematics Education, 9*, 843–866.

Kennedy, M. M. (2010). Attribution error and the quest for teacher quality. *Educational Researcher, 39*, 591–598.

Kind, V. (2009a). Pedagogical content knowledge in science education: Perspectives and potential for progress. *Studies in Science Education, 45*, 169–204.

Kind, V. (2009b). A conflict in your head: An exploration of trainee science teachers' subject matter knowledge development and its impact on teacher self-confidence. *International Journal of Science Education, 31*, 1529–1562.

Kind, V., & Kind, P. M. (2011). Beginning to teach chemistry: How personal and academic characteristics of pre-service science teachers compare with their understandings of basic chemical ideas. *International Journal of Science Education, 33*, 2123–2158.

Kirschner, S., Borowksi, A., & Fischer, H. E. (2011, September). *measuring physics teachers' pedagogical content knowledge.* Paper presented at the biannual conference of the European Science Education Research Association, Lyon, France.

Lambert, J. L., Lindgren, J., & Bleicher, R. (2012). Assessing elementary science methods students' understanding about global climate change. *International Journal of Science Education, 34*, 1167–1187.

Lederman, N. G., Gess-Newsome, J., & Latz, M. S. (1994). The nature and development of preservice science teachers' conceptions of subject matter and pedagogy. *Journal of Research in Science Teaching, 31*, 129–146.

Leite, L., Mendoza, J., & Borsese, A. (2007). Teachers' and prospective teachers' explanations of liquid-state phenomena: A comparative study involving three European countries. *Journal of Research in Science Teaching, 44*, 349–374.

Loughran, J., Milroy, P., Berry, A., Mulhall, P., & Gunstone, R. (2001). Science cases in action: Documenting science teachers' pedagogical content knowledge through PaP-eRs. *Research in Science Education, 31*, 289–307.

Loughran, J., Mulhall, P., & Berry, A. (2008). Exploring pedagogical content knowledge in science teacher education: A case study. *International Journal of Science Education, 30*, 1301–1320.

Loughran, J. J., & Berry, A. (2012). Developing science teacher educators' pedagogy of teacher education. In B. J. Fraser, K. Tobin, & C. J. McRobbie (Eds.), *Second international handbook of science education* (pp. 401–415). Dordrecht, the Netherlands: Springer.

Loughran, J. J., Berry, A., & Mulhall, P. (2012). *Understanding and developing science teachers' pedagogical content knowledge* (2nd ed.). Rotterdam, the Netherlands: Sense Publishers.

Loughran, J. J., Mulhall, P., &. Berry, A. (2004). In search of pedagogical content knowledge in science: Developing ways of articulating and documenting professional practice. *Journal of Research in Science Teaching, 41*, 370–391.

Magnusson, S., Krajcik, J., & Borko, H. (1999). Nature, sources and development of pedagogical content knowledge. In J. Gess-Newsome & N. G. Lederman (Eds.), *Examining pedagogical content knowledge* (pp. 95–132). Dordrecht, the Netherlands: Kluwer Academic.

Marks, R. (1990). Pedagogical content knowledge: From a mathematical case to a modified conception. *Journal of Teacher Education, 41*, 3–11.

Mason, C. L. (1999). The triad approach: A consensus for science teaching and learning. In J. Gess-Newsome & N. G. Lederman (Eds.), *Examining pedagogical content knowledge: The construct and its implications for science education* (pp. 277–292). Dordrecht, the Netherlands: Kluwer.

Morrison, J. A., & Estes, J. C. (2007). Using scientists and real-world scenarios in professional development for middle school science teachers. *Journal of Science Teacher Education, 18*, 165–184. doi:10.1007/s10972-006-9034-3

Mulholland, J., & Wallace, J. (2005). Growing the tree of teacher knowledge: Ten years of learning to teach elementary science. *Journal of Research in Science Teaching, 42*, 767–790.

Nadelson, L. S., & Nadelson, S. (2010). K–8 educators perceptions and preparedness for teaching evolution topics. *Journal of Science Teacher Education, 21*, 843–858.

Nehm, R. H., Kim, S. Y., & Sheppard, K. (2009). Academic preparation in biology and advocacy for teaching evolution: Biology versus non-biology teachers. *Science Education, 93*, 1122–1146.

Nehm, R. H., & Schonfeld, I. S. (2007). Does increasing biology teacher knowledge of evolution and the nature of science lead to greater preference for the teaching of evolution in schools? *Journal of Science Teacher Education, 18*, 699–723.

Nelson, M. M., & Davis, E. A. (2012). Preservice elementary teachers' evaluations of elementary students' scientific models: An aspect of pedagogical content knowledge for scientific modeling. *International Journal of Science Education, 34*, 1931–1959.

Nilsson, P. (2008). Teaching for understanding: The complex nature of pedagogical content knowledge in pre-service education. *International Journal of Science Education, 30*, 1281–1299.

Nilsson, P., & Loughran, J. J. (2012). Exploring the development of pre-service science elementary teachers' pedagogical content knowledge. *Journal of Science Teacher Education, 23*, 699–721.

Nilsson, P., & van Driel, J. H. (2011). How will we understand what we teach?—Primary student teachers' perceptions of their development of knowledge and attitudes towards physics. *Research in Science Education, 41*, 541–560.

Nivalainen, V., Asikainen, M. A., & Nirvonen, P. E. (2013). Open guided inquiry laboratory in physics teacher education. *Journal of Science Teacher Education, 24*, 449–474. doi:10.1007/s10972-012-9316-x

Nugent, G., Toland, M. D., Levy, R., Kunz, G., Harwood, D., Green, D., & Kitts, K. (2012). The impact of an inquiry-based geoscience field course on pre-service teachers. *Journal of Science Teacher Education, 23*, 503–529.

Orleans, A. V. (2010). Enhancing teacher competence through online training. *Asia Pacific Education Researcher, 19*, 371–386.

Osborne, J., Simon, S., & Collins, S. (2003). Attitudes towards science: A review of the literature and its implications. *International Journal of Science Education, 25*, 1049–1079.

Özden, M., Usak, M., Prokop, P., Turkoglu, T., & Bahar, C. (2008). Student teachers' knowledge of and attitudes toward chemical hormone usage in biotechnology. *African Journal of Biotechnology, 7*, 3892–3899.

Padilla, K., Ponce-de-Léon, A. M., Rembado, F. M., & Garritz, A. (2008). Undergraduate professors' pedagogical content knowledge: The case of "amount of substance." *International Journal of Science Education, 30*, 1389–1404.

Padilla, K., & van Driel, J. H. (2011). The relationships between PCK components: The case of quantum chemistry professors. *Chemistry Education Research and Practice, 12,* 367–378.

Pajares, M. F. (1992). Teachers' beliefs and educational research. Cleaning up a messy construct. *Review of Educational Research, 62,* 307–332.

Papageorgiou, G., Stamovlasis, D., & Johnson, P. (2013). Primary teachers' understanding of four chemical phenomena: Effect of an in-service training course. *Journal of Science Teacher Education, 24,* 763–787. doi:10.1007/s10972-012-9295-y

Park, S., & Chen, Y. C. (2012). Mapping out the integration of the components of pedagogical content knowledge (PCK): Examples from high school biology classroom. *Journal of Research in Science Teaching, 49,* 922–941.

Park, S., Jang, J. Y., Chen, Y. C., & Jung, J. (2011). Is pedagogical content knowledge (PCK) necessary for reformed science teaching? Evidence from an empirical study. *Research in Science Education, 41,* 245–260.

Park, S., & Oliver, J. S. (2008a). Revisiting the conceptualisation of pedagogical content knowledge (PCK): PCK as a conceptual tool to understand teachers as professionals. *Research in Science Education, 38,* 261–284.

Park, S., & Oliver, J. S. (2008b). National board certification (NBC) as a catalyst for teachers' learning about teaching: The effects of the NBC process on candidate teachers' PCK development. *Journal of Research in Science Teaching, 45,* 812–834.

Park, S., & Oliver, J. S. (2009). The translation of teachers' understanding of gifted students into instructional strategies for teaching science. *Journal of Science Teacher Education, 20,* 333–351.

Patrick, P. G., & Tunnicliffe, S. D. (2010). Science teachers' drawings of what is inside the human body. *Journal of Biological Education, 44,* 81–87.

Reynolds, M. C. (Ed.). (1989). *The knowledge base for the beginning teacher.* Oxford: Pergamon Press.

Roehrig, G. H., & Luft, J. (2006). Does one size fit all? The induction experience of beginning science teachers from different teacher-preparation programs. *Journal of Research in Science Teaching, 43,* 963–985.

Rollnick, M., Bennett, J., Rhemtula, M., Dharsey, N., & Ndlovu, T. (2008). The place of subject matter knowledge in pedagogical content knowledge: A case study of South African teachers teaching the amount of substance and chemical equilibrium. *International Journal of Science Education, 30,* 1365–1388.

Roth, K. J., Garnier, H. E., Chen, C., Lemmens, M., Schwille, K., & Wickler, N. I. Z. (2011). Videobased lesson analysis: Effective science PD for teacher and student learning. *Journal of Research in Science Teaching, 48,* 117–148.

Sanders, L. R., Borko, H., & Lockard, J. D. (1993). Secondary science teachers' knowledge base when teaching science courses in and out of their area of certification. *Journal of Research in Science Teaching, 30,* 723–736.

Sawada, D., Piburn, M., Judson, E., Turley, J., Falconer, K., Benford, R., & Bloom, I. (2002). Measuring reform practices in science and mathematics classrooms: The Reformed Teaching Observation Protocol. *School Science and Mathematics, 102,* 245–253.

Schmelzing, S., van Driel, J. H., Jüttner, M., Brandenbusch, S., Sandmann, A., & Neuhaus, B. J. (2013). Development, evaluation, and validation of a paper-and-pencil test for measuring two components of biology teachers' pedagogical content knowledge concerning the "cardiovascular system." *International Journal of Science and Mathematics Education, 11,* 1369–1390. doi:10.1007/s10763-012-9384-6

Schneider, R. M. (2013). Opportunities for teacher learning during enactment of inquiry science curriculum materials: Exploring the potential for teacher educative materials. *Journal of Science Teacher Education, 24,* 323–346. doi:10.1007/s10972-012-9309-9

Schneider, R. M., & Plasman, K. (2011). Science teacher learning progressions: A review of science teachers' pedagogical content knowledge development. *Review of Educational Research, 81,* 530–565.

Schwartz-Bloom, M. D., Halpin, M. J., & Reiter, J. P. (2011). Teaching high school chemistry in the context of pharmacology helps both teachers and students learn. *Journal of Chemical Education, 88,* 744–750.

Schwarz, C., & Gwekwerere, Y. (2007). Using a guided inquiry and modeling instructional framework (EIMA) to support pre-service K–8 science teaching. *Science Education, 91,* 158–186.

Settlage, J. (2013). On acknowledging PCK's shortcomings. *Journal of Science Teacher Education, 24,* 1–12.

Shen, J., Gibbons, P. C., Wiegers, J. F., & McMahon, A. P. (2007). Using research based assessment tools in professional development in current electricity. *Journal of Science Teacher Education, 18,* 431–459. doi:10.1007/s10972-007-9061-8

Shulman, L. S. (1986). Those who understand: Knowledge growth in teaching. *Educational Researcher, 15,* 4–14.

Shulman, L. S. (1987). Knowledge and teaching: Foundations of the new reform. *Harvard Educational Review, 57,* 1–22.

Siegel, M. A., & Wissehr, C. (2011). Preparing for the plunge: Preservice teachers' assessment literacy. *Journal of Science Teacher Education, 22,* 371–391.

Sperandeo-Mineo, R. M., Fazio, C., & Tarantino, G. (2006). Pedagogical content knowledge development and pre-service physics teacher education: A case study. *Research in Science Education, 36,* 235–268.

Taber, K., & Tan, K. C. D. (2011). The insidious nature of "hard-core" alternative conceptions: Implications for the constructivist research programme of patterns in high school students' and pre-service teachers' thinking about ionisation energy. *International Journal of Science Education, 33,* 259–297.

Tobin, K., Tippins, D. J., & Gallard, A. J. (1994). Research on instructional strategies for teaching science. In D. L. Gabel (Ed.), *Handbook of research on science teaching and learning* (pp. 45–93). New York: Macmillan.

Tretter, T. R., Brown, S. L., Bush, W. S., Saderholm, J. C., & Holmes, V. L. (2013). Valid and reliable science content assessments for science teachers. *Journal of Science Teacher Education, 24,* 269–295. doi:10.1007/s10972-012-9299-7

Trundle, K. C., Atwood, R. K., & Christopher, J. E. (2006). Preservice elementary teachers' knowledge of observable moon phases and pattern of change in phases. *Journal of Science Teacher Education, 17,* 87–101. doi:10.1007/s10972-006-9006-7

Usak, M., Özden, M., & Eilks, I. (2011). A case study of beginning science teachers' subject matter (SMK) and pedagogical content knowledge (PCK) of teaching chemical reaction in Turkey. *European Journal of Teacher Education, 34,* 407–429.

van der Valk, T., & Broekman, H. (1999). The lesson preparation method: A way of investigating pre-service teachers' pedagogical content knowledge. *European Journal of Teacher Education, 22,* 11–22.

Van Dijk, E. M. (2009). Teachers' views on understanding evolutionary theory: A PCK-study in the framework of the ERTE-model. *Teaching and Teacher Education, 25,* 259–267.

Van Dijk, E. M., & Kattman, U. (2007). A research model for the study of science teachers' PCK and improving teacher education. *Teaching and Teacher Education, 23,* 885–897.

van Driel, J. H., Verloop, N., & de Vos, W. (1998). Developing science teachers' pedagogical content knowledge. *Journal of Research in Science Teaching, 35,* 673–695.

Verloop, N., van Driel, J., & Meijer, P. (2001). Teacher knowledge and the knowledge base of teaching. *International Journal of Educational Research, 35,* 441–461.

Volkmann, M., & Zgagacz, M. (2004). Learning to teach physics through inquiry: The lived experiences of a graduate teaching assistant. *Journal of Research in Science Teaching, 41,* 584–602.

Waldron, F., Pike, S., Varley, J., Murphy, C., & Greenwood, R. (2007). Student teachers' prior experiences of history, geography and science: Initial findings of an all-Ireland survey. *Irish Educational Studies, 26,* 177–194.

Wandersee, J. H., Mintzes, J. J., & Novak, J. D. (1994). Research on alternative conceptions in science. In D. L. Gabel (Ed.), *Handbook of research on science teaching and learning* (pp. 177–210). New York: Macmillan.

Wilson, M. (2005). *Constructing measures: An item response modeling approach.* Mahwah, NJ: Erlbaum.

43

Learning to Teach Science

Tom Russell and Andrea K. Martin

Consider the proposition that teacher educators could overestimate what they can teach new teachers, while also underestimating their ability to provide appropriate conditions for them to learn about teaching. Such a proposition serves to shift the teacher education task (at both preservice and inservice levels) from one of delivering what has to be known by teachers to one of providing better conditions for learning about teaching.

(Northfield, 1998, p. 698)

We write as teacher educators who are passionate about improving science education and teacher education in general and the experience of learning to teach science in particular. In this chapter we permit our experiences as teacher educators to inform and shape our accounts and interpretations of research related to learning to teach science. One of the most striking observations we can offer about research related to learning to teach science is the extent to which science education research appears *not* to be extended and extrapolated to programs of science teacher education. Research appears to confirm what our own experiences as teacher educators tell us: *A fundamental challenge resides in the prior teaching and learning beliefs and experiences of those learning to teach, just as a fundamental challenge of teaching science resides in students' prior beliefs about phenomena.* The research associated with constructivism and conceptual change reminds us that beliefs and experiences are deeply intertwined (see Özdemir & Clark, 2007; Pelech & Pieper, 2010; Vosniadou, 1994, 2008). Just as children in elementary, middle, and secondary schools tend to be unaware of their initial beliefs about phenomena and unaware of how personal experiences shape and constrain those beliefs, so those who are learning to teach science tend to be unaware of their initial beliefs about what and how they will learn in a program of science teacher education.

In our experience, many prospective teachers assume that they know very little about teaching, that they will learn teaching ideas in university classes, and that they will apply what they learn in classes during their school practicum experiences. Is this really very different from children's assumptions in a science class? Do they not assume that they know little about science, that they will be taught science concepts, and that they will apply what they learn when given opportunities by their teachers? "*Science separates knowledge from experience*" (Franklin, 1994). Similarly, school and university alike often treat students in ways that imply that experience has little to do with knowledge. Those learning to teach tend to be unaware that they were learning a great deal about *how* to teach science as they were learning scientific concepts while studying science in school and university classes.

Northfield (1998) tackles this theme in a discussion of how science teacher education is *practiced*. He begins by quoting an unnamed individual with a provocative comment about teacher education: "Teacher preparation is necessary and worthwhile, but it is generally conducted in the wrong place, at the wrong time, for too little time" (p. 695). Northfield draws on the work of Farnham-Diggory (1994) to introduce three models of how novices become experts—behavior, apprenticeship, and development. His concern is one that we share: *How does school experience influence an individual's learning to teach?* He then immediately offers a challenging answer:

If experience is seen as a place to *apply* the ideas and theories of the course, then the campus program could be seen to be out of step with the demands and concerns of the new teacher (the wrong time, the wrong place and too little time).

(p. 696)

Much the same conclusion could be drawn about how we view experience in the context of children's learning in science classrooms. Northfield's statement at the opening of this chapter helps us frame our approach in this chapter: Whether in the science classroom or in the science teacher education program, how individuals learn from experience remains a poorly understood phenomenon. Here we focus less on what knowledge can be taught to teacher candidates in propositional form and more on providing better learning conditions for those who are learning to teach science.

Chapters in research handbooks often attempt to provide comprehensive surveys of published research. While we are attentive to such research, our major goal in this chapter is to stimulate new perspectives for thinking about the values and actions that occur in preservice programs for those who are learning to teach science. Driving this chapter is our concern for understanding and promoting better conditions for learning about teaching and better conditions for learning about teaching science. Our premise is that science teaching and learning will only move forward if reform initiatives move beyond rhetoric to achieve what will amount to epistemological and conceptual revolutions in how we think and act as science teachers and science teacher educators.

We summarize our overall argument in the following points:

1. Calls for change to how science is taught in schools and universities can be traced to the 1960s and even earlier in the 20th century. Dewey's (1938) contrast between traditional and progressive education shows just how little the fundamentals of school culture (Sarason, 1996) have changed.

2. Teaching for conceptual development and change has been a dominant theme in the science education research literature for several decades (e.g., Hewson, Beeth, & Thorley, 1998; Vosniadou, 2008), but only a small fraction of that research considers how individuals learn to teach science in preservice programs.

3. Teaching practices are far more stable (Sarason, 1996) than those who call for change seem to realize (see Handelsman et al., 2004). Logic alone cannot change teaching practices that were initially learned indirectly and unintentionally from one's own teachers.

4. Learning from experience (Munby & Russell, 1994) is an undervalued and neglected aspect of science teaching and learning that is similarly undervalued in programs in which individuals learn to teach science. This undervaluation is rooted in the value that the university associates with rigorous argument and positivist epistemology. While learning from experience is being recognized as an element of teachers' professional development as attention is given to teacher research and action research, these tend to be undervalued as inferior forms of research.

5. Research on conceptual change now offers a broad range of suggestions for teaching that supports inquiry learning, deeper learning, and metacognition (Linn, 2006). Conceptual change research indicates that achieving more complete conceptual understanding does not necessarily achieve the significant epistemological change that must accompany that understanding (Elby, 2001).

6. Learning to teach science needs to attend not only to conceptual change approaches for teaching fundamental concepts of science but also to conceptual change approaches to teaching fundamental concepts of teaching and learning (Linn, 2006).

7. There is a need for explicit attention to epistemological issues associated with teaching science and learning to teach science. So long as the dominant epistemology of the university is essentially positivistic and closely linked to how we know in the various disciplines of science, we submit that the long-sought breakthroughs in how science is taught and learned cannot be achieved (see Schön, 1995).

Learning From Experience and the Authority of Experience

In our culture, we speak easily of "learning from experience" in everyday life and yet we also hear many stories in which people seem not to have learned from experience. Just as propositional knowledge claims are easily forgotten and links are not always made from one context to another, so it is with learning from experience, which seems to be a marginal feature of many classrooms in the formal learning contexts of schools and universities. Science teachers are often credited with an advantage of being able to work with everyday materials, yet laboratory experiences are rarely described by students as major contributing activities in their learning of concepts. Because learning from experience is not a significant feature of many classrooms, when those learning to teach science begin a professional preparation program, the role of learning from experience may never have been considered. Quite universally, student teachers report that the practicum is the most significant element of their preparation for teaching, yet this does not mean that new science teachers understand how they learn from experience or that they are proficient in learning from experience. Munby and Russell (1994) addressed this issue when they introduced the term "authority of experience."

> Listening to one's own experience is not the same as listening to the experience of others, and the [physics method] students seem to indicate that they still place much more authority with those who have experience and with those who speak with confidence about how teaching should be done. They seem reluctant to listen to or to trust their own experiences as an authoritative source of knowledge about teaching. We wonder how and to what extent they will begin to hear the voice of their own experiences as they begin their teaching careers.
>
> The basic tension in teacher education derives for us from preservice students wanting to move from being under authority to being in authority, without appreciating the potential that the authority of experience can give to their learning to teach. The challenge for teacher education is to help new teachers recognize and identify the place and function of the authority of experience. If this is not done, the authority of experience can fall victim to the danger that accompanies all versions of authority: mere possession is not enough because authority can be abused.
>
> (Munby & Russell, 1994, pp. 93–94)

One of Dewey's points is that familiar educational patterns persist as tradition, not on the basis of their rationale (Dewey, 1938, pp. 28–29). Bringing the authority of experience into programs for learning to teach science will involve all the familiar challenges of learning from experience.

> There is no discipline in the world so severe as the discipline of experience subjected to the tests of intelligent development and direction. . . . The road of the new education is not an easier one to follow than the old road but a more strenuous and difficult one. . . . The greatest danger that attends its future is, I believe, the idea that it is an easy way to follow.
>
> (Dewey, 1938, p. 90)

We find it interesting that the issue of learning from experience and the associated epistemological issues tend not to be raised in the conceptual change literature, and here we call attention to the issue of learning from experience because it represents an important, perhaps essential, perspective for helping individuals learn to teach science.

A strong case for recognizing the authority of experience in the science classroom appears in the findings and recommendations reported in a book intended for those who teach first-year undergraduate courses in physics. Knight (2004) summarizes 25 years of physics education research on students' concepts and problem-solving strategies with three conclusions that have direct implications not only for teaching science *but also for learning to teach science.*

- Students enter our classroom not as "blank slates," *tabula rasa*, but filled with many prior concepts.
- Students' prior concepts are remarkably resistant to change.
- Students' knowledge is not organized in any coherent framework (Knight, 2004, p. 25).

These statements remind us that, in contrast to what is learned from textbooks, that which is learned from experience can be very powerful without being coherently organized. Knight (2004) closes his analysis with the report that "the results of physics education research can be sliced and rearranged in many patterns, but I see Five Lessons for teachers."

1. Keep students actively engaged and provide rapid feedback. (p. 42)
2. Focus on phenomena rather than abstractions. (p. 42)
3. Deal explicitly with students' alternative conceptions. (p. 43)
4. Teach and use explicit problem-solving skills and strategies. (p. 44)
5. Write homework and exam problems that go beyond symbol manipulation to engage students in the qualitative and conceptual analysis of physical phenomena. (p. 44)

The first four lessons can be translated directly from teaching science to learning to teach science. The fifth lesson could easily be reshaped to "engage students in the qualitative and conceptual analysis of educational phenomena." In traditional preservice teacher education programs, one might view these as research findings to include in a "knowledge base" to be transmitted to preservice science teachers. Our analysis of the research literature confirms that it is *entirely counterproductive* to simply transmit such lessons to teachers as content. Rather, preservice science teacher education programs must explore the implications of these lessons through all the learning experiences created in teacher education classrooms.

To remind us of the importance of attending to narrative knowledge as well as to propositional knowledge, we include in this chapter a number of Narrative Boxes that document some of chapter author Russell's personal learning from experience over a quarter century of trying to improve his ways of teaching individuals how to teach science. An additional Narrative Box illustrates a teacher candidate's account of the impact of practicum experiences on his learning to teach science. Each Narrative Box ends with an italicized question related to learning from our own teaching and learning experiences.

Narrative Box 1 **Is experience important for learning?**

I began teaching as an untrained volunteer teacher in northern Nigeria. For 2 years, with help from my students, I taught myself to teach—learning from experience as best I could. During a master's program in which I gained certification as a physics teacher, I noticed that I had many more questions than most of the others in my classes. Experience generates questions, both for teachers and for students. Science teachers could probably provide their students with much more in the way of direct experience of phenomena of science, should they wish to increase the number of "real questions" that their students ask in science classes.

Were your own science classes rich in hands-on experiences that stimulated your personal interest in understanding science concepts? How important is experience for motivating you to understand a topic more fully and completely?

To illustrate learning from experience in the context of preservice science teacher education, we next recount briefly Russell's personal learning from experience as a teacher educator trying to understand how experience helps those learning to teach.

Narrative Box 2 **A new experience inspires new frames for a teacher educator's work**

In both 1991 and 1992, I arranged to teach one class of physics in a local high school and, in return, the school's regular physics teacher helped teach the physics method course at Queen's. Building on the 1991 experience, I arranged for one of my physics method classes in 1992 to be held each week in the room where I taught physics earlier in the day, with an invitation to preservice teachers to observe my class if they wished. Despite being in the physics classroom myself and holding some of my classes in the school rather than at the university, the impact on the preservice teachers seemed minimal. A series of interviews with some of the preservice teachers led me to develop a list of potential barriers to learning from experience that the preservice teachers seemed to bring to their efforts to learn to teach. Just as Knight (2004) reports, the future physics teachers certainly did not arrive as blank slates; rather, they had strong views that did not change easily.

Do teacher educators at times treat teacher candidates as blank slates? Is it important for teacher educators to occasionally return to the school classroom?

Five years later, when the preservice program at Queen's changed dramatically to begin with 14 weeks of teaching experience, the barriers implicit in the 1993 candidates seemed to have vanished, replaced by frames for learning from experience, as Table 43.1 indicates. Russell (2000) provides a more detailed account from which this summary is constructed.

Reflection by Those Learning to Teach

Bryan and Abell (1999) provide a case study of a student teacher named Barbara. Early in their argument, the authors declare their perspectives on the role of experience in learning to teach:

> The heart of knowing how to teach cannot be learned from coursework alone. The construction of professional knowledge requires experience. . . . Experience influences the frames that teachers employ in identifying problems of practice, in approaching those problems and implementing solutions, and in making sense of the outcomes of their actions.
>
> (pp. 121–122)

The case of Barbara begins with an account of what Barbara believed about science teaching and learning and moves on to describe her vision for teaching elementary science as well as the tensions within her thinking about her professional responsibilities. Of particular interest is Barbara's initial premise that a teacher should continue to teach a scientific concept until all children show that they understand it. Once the process of reflection became apparent, "Barbara began to shift her perspective and reframe the tension between her vision and practice. Her professional experience provided feedback that forced her to confront the idea that in teaching science, teachers need to consider more than students getting it" (Bryan & Abell, 1999, p. 131). This case study of Barbara is one that could help new science teachers anticipate the challenges and prospects of student teaching, although the real help would probably be realized *during* rather than *before* the student teacher assignment. The implications for further study of learning from experience are clear:

> Barbara's case implicitly underscores the fallacy of certain assumptions underlying traditional teacher education programs: (a) that propositional knowledge from course readings and lectures can be translated directly into practice, and (b) that prospective teachers develop professional knowledge before experience rather than in conjunction with experience. . . . Teacher educators are challenged to coach prospective teachers to purposefully and systematically inquire into their own practices, encouraging them to make such inquiry a habit.
>
> (Bryan & Abell, 1999, p. 136)

Just as a conceptual change approach to teaching science begins with students' experiences, so Abell and Bryan conclude that "the genesis of the process of developing professional knowledge should be seen as inherent in experience" (Bryan & Abell, 1999, p. 136). "A preeminent goal of science teacher education should be to help prospective teachers challenge and refine their ideas about teaching and learning science and learn how to learn from experience" (Bryan & Abell, 1999, p. 137).

TABLE 43.1

Barriers to Learning to Teach and Frames for Learning to Teach

Barriers to Learning to Teach	Frames for Learning to Teach
Prior views of preservice science teachers who gained teaching experience very gradually during an 8-month program.	Views of preservice science teachers who began a 9-month program with 14 weeks of teaching experience.
Teaching can be told.	Teaching cannot be told.
Learning to teach is passive.	Learning to teach is active.
Discussion and opinion are irrelevant.	Discussion, opinion, and sharing of experiences are crucial.
Personal reactions to teaching are irrelevant.	Personal reactions to teaching are the starting point.
Goals for future students do not apply personally.	Goals for future students definitely must apply personally.
Theory is largely irrelevant.	Theory is relevant.
Experience cannot be analyzed or understood.	Experience can be analyzed and understood.

(Russell, 2000, 231–232, 238–239)

Narrative Box 3 Narrowing the gap between practice and theory, actions and values

In 1983, in my sixth year of teaching a preservice science course and visiting candidates in their practicum classrooms, I was feeling acutely aware of the gaps between educational theory and practice. Many of the strategies I promoted in my classes could not be observed in my students' classes in the practicum setting. A colleague loaned me a copy of a new book by Donald Schön (1983) with the title *The Reflective Practitioner: How Professionals Think in Action*. My first sabbatical leave later that year provided an opportunity to study this book and prepare a research proposal that would let me explore this new perspective in the context of preservice teacher education. Years of work with the ideas have led me to conclude that Schön's terminology is more readily adopted than it is understood. I see Schön arguing two main points:

(1) Learning from teaching experience involves finding new frames or perspectives (perhaps from the research literature) to better understand surprising and puzzling events of practice.
(2) Improving as a teacher involves deliberately narrowing the inevitable gaps between our values as teachers and the effects of our teaching actions on those we teach.

How do you react when asked to "reflect"? Do you have enough experiences to reflect about? Would it help if someone undertook to teach you how to reflect?

Zembel-Saul, Krajcik, and Blumenfeld (2002) build on the conclusion by Bryan and Abell (1999, p. 121) that "experience plays a significant role in developing professional knowledge." To this they add their own conclusion that "what we do know . . . is that experience alone is not enough. It needs to be coupled with thoughtful reflection on action" (p. 460). Their overall conclusions make important points that remind science teacher educators yet again of the importance of the cooperating teacher in supporting the student teacher's professional learning.

There is evidence that cooperating teachers who facilitate students' meaningful learning in general and support student teachers in their efforts to continue to emphasize science content representation can positively influence the territory student teachers attempt to master. Conversely, cooperating teachers who fail to support student teachers in continuing the process of planning, teaching, and reflection on substantive issues of content representation are likely to reroute the entire process of learning to teach.
(Zembel-Saul et al., 2002, p. 460)

They also remind us that our collective understanding of how experience contributes to learning to teach still requires attention and development.

There is an urgent need to understand better the role of experience in learning to teach, in particular the aspects of

teaching experiences that support or hinder new teachers' continuing development in the often fragile domain of science content knowledge and its representations.
(Zembel-Saul et al., 2002, p. 461)

As Narrative Box 3 suggests, understanding and attending to the role of experience involves far more than asking would-be science teachers to "reflect" on their experiences.

Narrative Box 4 Can reflection be taught?

In 2001, one of my classes included an individual who knew that he would never be a teacher. He had to wait 18 months to begin a training program, and his future employers were willing to support his time in a preservice education program. As a result, he had more time than most to critique the various elements of the program. At the end of the year, we revisited a series of weekly practicum reports that he had volunteered to send me (and to which I replied quickly). He suggested that our corresponding about his practicum experiences had done more than any other program element to teach him how to reflect. He offered advice to my colleagues and me: "Don't tell people to reflect. Instead, teach them how to reflect and then show them that that is what you have done." My subsequent attempts to follow this advice have paid positive dividends.

What specific meanings do you associate with the words "reflect" and "reflection"? Do you see reflection as something that can be taught? Is it possible to reflect during teaching as well as after?

We turn next to the extensive and ever-growing literature of research on conceptual change.

The Complex Challenge of Conceptual Change

Venturing into the literature of conceptual change is daunting; the sheer volume of research is overwhelming. Pfundt and Duit (1994) refer to approximately 3,500 studies related to students' alternative conceptions in science. White (2001) tracks shifts in researchers' foci, reporting that earlier studies concentrated on identification of conceptual change while later studies attended to efforts to bring students' beliefs more in line with those of scientists. Recently, attention has been directed to mapping how conceptions are developed. The nomenclature itself is varied and, contingent on researchers' predilections, the labels used could be *misconceptions, alternative conceptions, preconceptions, naïve conceptions, intuitive science*, or *alternative frameworks* (Guzzetti, Snyder, Glass, & Gamas, 1993).

Conceptual change is central to learning and teaching science. Duschl and Hamilton (1998) describe science learning as a process of conceptual change that is concerned with issues about the development of scientific knowledge. This entails understanding how learners decide among competing or alternative views, models, or theories of the natural world. Because students build conceptions from their everyday experiences and carry these with them into the classroom, they often conflict with science conceptions presented in school.

> Learning science is especially difficult in fields in which students' preinstructional conceptions are deeply rooted in daily life experiences. Conceptions that are based on empirical evidence through sense experiences (like the process of seeing, thermal phenomena, and conceptions of forces and motions) fall into this category as do everyday ways of speaking about natural and technical phenomena.
>
> (Duit & Treagust, 1998, p. 15)

As Duschl and Hamilton (1998) point out, conceptual change involves the restructuring of both declarative and procedural knowledge. They contend that too often science education research is focused on the nature and organization of relevant declarative knowledge and the necessary changes that take place or need to take place in that knowledge or its organization. More attention and study needs to be directed toward the changes in or attempts to change the strategic use of restructured knowledge. Prospective teachers need to reframe their understanding of science learning to recognize the inherent challenges attached when prevailing concepts are subjected to scrutiny and validation. Unless new teachers understand why conceptual change is so complex, they are unlikely to be able to effect changes and grasp why those changes may be delimited and constrained.

Teaching Conceptual Change

Research on conceptual change is providing evidence of the need for change in how science is taught. Linn and Eylon (2011) framed the issue in these terms:

> Our goal . . . is to make it feasible for all students to become autonomous learners who view scientific evidence critically and endeavor to develop a coherent view of scientific phenomena. We also seek to help teachers adopt a role of intelligent facilitator of discourse and inquiry, rather than all knowing disseminator of facts. . . . There is a wealth of evidence from the research literature in education and the broader learning sciences that the absorption model is antiquated and insufficient.
>
> (p. 6)

The extensive work of Novak (e.g., Novak, 1987, 1989, 1993) provides a useful framework both for understanding why conceptual change is so critical if students are to *learn how to learn* in science and for understanding why instruction often fails. Novak builds on Ausubel's (1968) hypothesis that the single most important factor influencing learning is prior knowledge and Kelly's (1955) personal construct theory that emphasizes the view that knowledge is constructed and is highly personal, idiosyncratic, and socially negotiated.

Novak and Gowin (1984) advance a set of three knowledge claims about students' preconceptions that are carried into their science classes, with subsequent effects on their learning (Wandersee, Mintzes, & Novak, 1994). The first claim suggests that learners are not "empty vessels" but bring with them a finite but diverse set of ideas about natural objects and events. These notions are often inconsistent with scientists' and science teachers' explanations. The second claim proposes that students' alternative conceptions cut across age, ability, gender, and cultural boundaries, and these ideas are tenacious and resistant to extinction by conventional teaching strategies. The third claim is broad based and engages the sociocultural context, viewing alternative conceptions as the product of a diverse set of personal experiences that include direct observation of natural objects and events, peer culture, everyday language, the mass media, as well as teachers' explanations and instructional materials. As a postscript, they suggest that teachers often subscribe to the same alternative conceptions as their students do (Mintzes, Wandersee, & Novak, 1997).

Novak and his group have also advanced three claims regarding successful science learners: (1) The process of constructing meanings relies on the development of elaborate, strongly hierarchical, well-differentiated, and highly integrated frameworks of related concepts; (2) conceptual change requires that knowledge is restructured by making and breaking interconnections between concepts and replacing or substituting one concept with another; and (3) successful science learners regularly use strategies that enable them to plan, monitor, control, and regulate their own learning (Mintzes, Wandersee, & Novak, 1997).

Posner, Strike, Hewson, and Gertzog's (1982) theory of conceptual change makes a valuable contribution to understanding its complexity and the conditions necessary for change to occur. Indeed, Duit and Treagust (1998) describe it as the most influential theory on conceptual change in science education, with wide-ranging applications in other fields as well. Posner and colleagues (1982) propose that conceptual change will not occur unless learners experience some level of dissatisfaction with their current beliefs or understandings. As long as an existing conception has a successful explanatory track record, learners will hold fast to their initial conception and be satisfied with it. Complicating matters is the impact of prior knowledge. Insufficient prior knowledge means that a new concept may be misunderstood or poorly understood. Therefore prior knowledge is a necessary but not sufficient condition for conceptual change. For a new idea to be accepted, it must meet three conditions: *intelligibility* (understandable), *plausibility* (reasonable), and *fruitfulness* (useful). Learners need to understand what an idea means, what its potential or actual utility is, and why scientists are concerned with coherence and internal consistency. If an idea is plausible, then learners need to be able to reconcile the idea with their own beliefs and be able to make sense of it. Hodson (1998) points out that "making sense" in scientific terms may be very different from commonsense views. If an idea is fruitful, then learners will gain something of value as a result: assistance in problem solving, predicting, or arriving at new insights, as well as direction toward new areas for further study and inquiry.

Kagan (1992) neatly summarizes the recommendations by Posner and colleagues (1982) for what teachers can do to promote students' conceptual change. Teachers must (a) help students to make their implicit beliefs explicit; (b) confront students with the inadequacies and inconsistencies of their beliefs; and (c) provide extended opportunities for integrating and differentiating old and new knowledge, eliminating brittle preconceptions that impede learning, and elaborating anchors that facilitate learning.

Any discussion of conceptual change must include Piagetian ideas, specifically *assimilation, accommodation, disequilibrium*, and *equilibration* (Duit & Treagust, 1998). When new events do not fit with existing schemes, then a state of disequilibrium or "mental discomfort" exists that propels efforts to make sense of observations and puzzling events (McDevitt & Ormrod, 2002). Through accommodation— replacing, reorganizing, or more effectively integrating their schemes—learners can resolve the discordances and return to a state of equilibrium. Thus equilibration is the movement from equilibrium to disequilibrium and back to equilibrium. In essence, this process necessitates the active involvement of the learner and is premised on learners' developing increasingly complex understandings. These understandings do not occur in isolation but require interaction with one's environment.

Vygotsky's work also must be acknowledged, given its impact on conceptual change and the development of constructivist ideas as well as its contrast to Piagetian theory. Central to Vygotskyian theory is the influence of sociocultural factors on cognitive development. Where Piaget saw the social environment as another source of information or experience that generated conflict and adaptation for the child, Vygotsky saw the sociocultural environment as not just the trigger but the source of the child's higher cognitive processes (Duschl & Hamilton, 1998). Therefore, knowledge acquisition, use, and change are contingent upon children's social activities and interactions (e.g., conversations, disagreements, etc.), as well as on the merging of thought and language during their early years and the acculturation provided by parents, other adults, and formal schooling (McDevitt & Ormrod, 2002). The coparticipation of the student and the teacher and the dialogical relationship that should be fostered while negotiating the zone of proximal development is embedded in Vygotskyian theory. The often-used metaphor of scaffolding to capture the teacher– child interaction has tended to downplay that the more competent as well as the less competent individual can profit from the interaction (Tudge & Scrimsher, 2003).

Duschl and Hamilton (1998) credit Vygotsky's work as having stimulated research that addresses the social context of cognition and learning. This includes work in the areas of reciprocal teaching, collaborative learning, guided participation, and authentic approaches to teaching, learning, and assessment. In addition, constructs like situated cognition, apprenticeships, cognitive apprenticeships, and the social construction of meaning can be linked to Vygotskyian theory. Each of these involves the contextual nature of learning and the interrelation of individual, interpersonal, and cultural-historical factors in development (Tudge & Scrimsher, 2003). Overall, they point to the confluence of factors impacting conceptual change and the imperative of considering the range of experiences students bring with them into the classroom, the dynamics and discourse of the classroom context, and the cultural-historical imprint on schooling itself.

Teaching for Conceptual Change

A few cautionary notes are in order: Misconceptions are persistent and highly resistant to change (Duit & Treagust, 1998; Guzetti, Snyder, Glass, & Gamas, 1993; Mintzes, Wandersee, & Novak, 1997). During the late 1970s and into the 1980s, the predominant assumption was that students' misconceptions had to be extinguished before they could be replaced by the correct scientific view; however, there appears to be no study that confirms that a particular student's conception could be totally extinguished and then replaced (Duit & Treagust, 1998). Rather, most studies reveal that the preexisting idea stays "alive" in particular contexts (Duit & Treagust, 1998), what diSessa (1993) describes as refinement rather than replacement of concepts. As previously noted, Chinn and Brewer (1998) address the question of the fate of the old knowledge and the new information after knowledge change takes place. They suggest that there are significant instructional implications. If a teacher believes that the old knowledge is simply replaced by the new, then there is no cause for concern about the old interfering with subsequent learning. However, if the old knowledge coexists with and influences understanding of new knowledge, then instruction must be designed to gradually reduce the potency of the old knowledge.

The essence of teaching for conceptual change is restructuring of knowledge (Mintzes, Wandersee, & Novak, 1997). Yet this is far easier said than done when the range and variability of students' responses to cognitive restructuring are reviewed. Hodson (1998) provides a helpful overview of students' resistant responses. If an idea(s) has been useful in the past, then there will be little, if any, need to replace it. Therefore rather than replacement, students may hold onto their views by denying the efficacy or accuracy of the new data, or they may rework the data so that it meshes with their existing beliefs. A variation of this is to distort the new idea until it is compatible with the old. Some students look for evidence to confirm their ideas rather than disconfirm. In this case, their original notion prevails, rather like selective perception, in which one sees only what one chooses to see. Hodson (1998) also points to variations in personality traits that may make some students more receptive to new ideas. Others, however, may adopt a more cavalier attitude and disengage from efforts to resolve discordances, essentially the "I don't care and can't be bothered" stance. And some students may be reluctant to pursue alternatives because what they know (or think that they know) is consistent with their own cognitive schema. Therefore if they hold onto what they know, they do not have the anxiety and stress that can accompany what is unknown, uncertain, or unfamiliar.

The work of the Children's Learning in Science (CLIS) group at the University of Leeds (e.g., Driver, 1989; Scott, Asoko, & Driver, 1992; Scott & Driver, 1998) is seminal in the area of constructivist approaches to conceptual change. They suggest that there are certain commonalities that extend across scientific disciplines and that support reconceptualizations. These can be characterized as instructional activities/sequences that involve a teaching approach designed to address a particular learning demand (Scott, Asoko, & Driver, 1992; Scott & Driver, 1998). These are sequenced as follows: (a) orientation or "messing about," which uses students' prior knowledge and existing conceptions as a starting point that can then be extended in the process of working towards a scientific point of view; (b) an externalizing or elicitation phase in which conceptions that are global and ill defined are differentiated (e.g., heat and temperature, weight and mass); (c) modification or restructuring, in which experiential bridges are built to a new conception; and (d) the construction of new conceptions through practice or application. At this point, students' preconceptions may be incommensurate with scientific conceptions. If so, Scott and Driver's (1998) recommendation is for the teacher to acknowledge and discuss the students' ideas and then indicate that scientists hold an alternate view and present that model. The students can subsequently revisit the scientific model in relation to their own prior ideas.

Creating conditions for cognitive conflict in which teachers challenge students to look for limitations in their views or deliberately provide examples of discrepant or surprising events, often through hands-on demonstrations or activities, can spur reconceptualization (Hodson, 1998). We question the extent to which preservice teacher education anchors science courses within a conceptual change framework, explores conceptual change theory, probes the concepts that teacher candidates hold about science and learning science, provokes cognitive conflict, and exposes candidates to instructional approaches and strategies to support conceptual change. Unless prospective teachers are directly challenged to confront their own alternative conceptions and work through the process of conceptual change, it is highly unlikely that they will be able to support their own students in doing so.

Narrative Box 5 **Identifying one's default teaching style**

In 1997 to 1998, the preservice program at Queen's University changed dramatically. After registration and brief introductions to professors and fellow students, candidates began their practicum experiences on the first day of school. Only during a 2-week return to the university after 8 weeks of teaching did individuals begin to get to know each other. The intensity of discussions was unlike anything I had ever experienced. I was challenged to assist people who would be returning to the same classes in the same schools and who sought answers and insights appropriate to very pressing questions of engagement, motivation, planning, and discipline. For the first time I began speaking of "default" teaching styles—the teaching moves we make based on reflex and habit, not on frames of mind. These are the teaching moves we make that are comfortable and familiar because our own teachers used them when teaching us. This prompted the insight that each new teacher needs to identify and understand her or his own default teaching style before being able to modify that style to include new teaching behaviors selected deliberately on the basis of frames of mind.

Do you find it interesting or productive to think of your own teaching behaviors in terms of default styles and deliberate efforts to modify them to enact teaching moves that will enhance the quality of student learning?

Teaching for Conceptual Change in Preservice Science Teacher Education

Our sense of the research is that there is little explicit attention to conceptual change with respect to teaching and learning when science teacher educators raise the topic of teaching for conceptual change with respect to science topics. A paper by Elby (2001) signals the potential significance of epistemological issues when teaching for conceptual change in physics, and we extend Elby's insights to the significance of epistemological issues associated with concepts of teaching and learning. The following excerpts from Elby's report point to a way forward. The crucial feature is the view that attention to epistemological development must be explicit.

> Many of the best research-based reformed physics curricula, ones that help students obtain a measurably deeper conceptual understanding, generally fail to spur significant epistemological development. Apparently, students can participate in activities that help them learn more effectively *without* reflecting upon and changing their beliefs about how to learn effectively. These students may revert to their old learning strategies in subsequent courses.
>
> In this paper, I show that instructional practices and curricular elements explicitly intended to foster epistemological development can lead to significant improvement in students' views about knowledge and learning.
>
> (Elby, 2001, p. S54)

In concluding his paper, Elby summarizes his reasoning as follows:

> Here's the argument. First, the fact that so many excellent physics courses fail to foster significant epistemological change. . . . suggests that isolated pieces of epistemologically focused curriculum aren't enough. Instead, the epistemological focus must suffuse every aspect of the course.

Second, the classroom atmosphere created by the instructor, and the way he/she interacts with individual students, undoubtedly plays a large role in fostering reflection about learning.

(Elby, 2001, p. S63)

Students' epistemological beliefs—their views about the nature of knowledge and learning—affect their mindset, metacognitive practices, and study habits in a physics course. Even the best reform curricula, however, have not been very successful at helping students develop more sophisticated epistemological beliefs.

(Elby, 2001, p. S64)

We would immediately apply this conclusion to the context of learning to teach science by suggesting that significant attention needs to be given to the epistemological beliefs of prospective science teachers, both in terms of the science concepts they will teach and in terms of the educational concepts they bring to a preservice program.

To give a modest level of plausibility to this extension, we draw on an argument by McGoey and Ross (1999), both secondary science teachers, in which they provide a vivid account of student resistance to conceptual change and the complex teaching skills needed to negotiate it.

We suspect that almost every teacher who has used a CC [conceptual change] model in the classroom has borne the brunt of student anger, frustration, and criticism. Students do not like having their ideas elicited in a nonjudgmental manner, only to have those ideas revealed as inadequate (whether it be mere seconds or days later). Some students eventually just stop giving their ideas. "Don't express your thoughts, wait until someone else does, wait for the right answer to be transmitted and memorize it." Dealing with this without disaffecting students emotionally and intellectually requires delicate, precise, and theoretically sound skills of the teacher.

(McGoey & Ross, 1999, p. 118)

As if this were not difficult enough, the challenges continue when students respond in ways that indicate they do hold significant epistemological beliefs:

The really messy stuff appears when the teacher gets a range of different (though adequate) models from the students. Now the fat is really in the fire. If the teacher refuses to give a single answer, positivist-minded students demand the right answer. Give a single answer and you may promote positivism. Give them a few rules (beware logical empiricism!) and the students interpret it as carte blanche for relativism or conventionalism. Another response of students is to challenge the teacher's practice outright. These attacks assert that since everybody knows that science is simply a universal body of facts and methods, just give us the recipe and tell us the answer so we can study for the test.

(McGoey & Ross, 1999, pp. 118–119)

These two teachers then extend their discussion to teacher education and to the stress that candidates experience when they experience cognitive conflict associated

with relying extensively on content knowledge. Again, we see that epistemological assumptions about teaching and learning are implicit.

Teacher interns are often deeply troubled to have their content knowledge questioned. They are already nervous enough about whether they can get in front of 30 adolescents for 80 minutes. . . . Content knowledge is often their major life-saving device. When student teachers engage in action research activities that undermine overreliance upon content knowledge, they experience considerable distress. The experience is extremely unsettling.

(McGoey & Ross, 1999, p. 119).

Here we draw to a close this extended discussion of conceptual change in the context of learning to teach science. We have provided an extensive overview of major arguments with respect to conceptual change in science teaching as a prelude to extending the topic of conceptual change to learning to teach science. In both contexts we believe that Elby's (2001) attention to epistemological beliefs is essential for progress beyond numerous but largely unproductive calls for changes to how science is taught.

To remind readers of the present reality of science teaching in many jurisdictions, we cite conclusions reported by the National Research Council (2006) and interpreted by Linn (2008, p. 696):

In order to fit the curriculum into the instructional time, districts or states provide pacing guides that allocate instructional time to chapters in the science text with little time for review. California seventh-grade life-science standards, for example, include 40 disciplinary topics and five investigation and experimentation standards. . . . Each of these 40 topics and accompanying inquiry activities receive[s] 3–4 days of instruction. This limited time deters teachers from revisiting ideas or even emphasizing connections among ideas.

We turn next to consideration of research that proposes a knowledge integration framework to guide the learning of science.

Conceptual Change in a Knowledge Integration Framework

Sawyer sets the stage for the knowledge integration perspective with a statement about the importance of articulating the knowledge an individual is developing:

One of the reasons that articulation [of one's developing knowledge] is so helpful to learning is that it makes possible *reflection* or *metacognition*—thinking about the process of learning and thinking about knowledge. Learning scientists have repeatedly demonstrated the importance of reflection in learning for deeper understanding. Many learning sciences classrooms are designed to foster reflection, and most of them foster reflection by providing students with tools that make it easier for them to articulate their developing understandings. Once students have articulated their developing understandings, learning environments should support them in reflecting on what they have just articulated. One of the most central topics in learning sciences research is how to support students in educationally beneficial reflection.

(Sawyer, 2006, p. 12)

Linn and her colleagues (Linn, 2006, 2008; Linn & Eylon, 2006, 2011; Linn, Kali, Davis, & Horwitz, 2008) have synthesized a great deal of research on conceptual change by building a knowledge integration framework that yields important recommendations both for the teaching of science and for learning to teach science. Linn (2008) introduces knowledge integration in the following way:

An emerging group of researchers advocates a "knowledge in pieces" or "knowledge integration" view. This group suggests that students build individual ideas in various ways and that these ideas may exist alongside each other in a repertoire. . . . This group generally respects the intellectual work that produced the ideas and argues that the goal of instruction is to introduce more powerful ideas, as well as to encourage students to inspect, distinguish, and evaluate the ideas in a way that leads to some form of reconciliation or coherence.

(Linn, 2008, p. 695)

The knowledge integration framework calls for capitalizing on students' ability to make sense of scientific phenomena by empowering them to distinguish among ideas, consider new ideas, and promote the most promising ones.

(Linn, 2008, p. 702)

Linn and Eylon (2006) describe 10 "design patterns," each of which is based on "four interrelated processes of knowledge integration. . . . Instruction typically interleaves the four processes, moving among them rather than following a linear sequence" (p. 523). The four processes are: "elicit or generate ideas from repertoire of ideas, add new ideas to help distinguish or link ideas, evaluate ideas and identify criteria [and] sort out ideas by promoting, demoting, merging, and reorganizing" (Linn & Eylon, 2006, p. 526). They then proceed to list 10 design patterns "that best represent current research on instruction" (Linn & Eylon, 2006, p. 525). The 10 patterns for instruction are "orient, diagnose, and guide; predict, observe, explain; illustrate ideas; experiment; explore a simulation; create an artifact; construct an argument; critique; collaborate; reflect" (Linn & Eylon, 2006, pp. 525–534).

Research points to four main processes that work together to promote knowledge integration: eliciting ideas, adding ideas, developing criteria, and sorting out ideas. Instruction often neglects the processes of developing criteria and sorting out ideas. . . . The activity sequences making up the design patterns represent essential elements in successful instruction. Design patterns transcend disciplinary knowledge, but raise questions about which design patterns are successful for which disciplinary topics.

(Linn & Eylon, 2006, p. 536).

When the four processes and 10 design patterns are set out in a 4 × 10 table (Linn & Eylon, 2006, p. 526) that makes explicit how each of the four knowledge integration processes contributes to each of the 10 design patterns, teachers are provided with a robust guide to the knowledge integration approach.

Linn and Eylon (2011) also list four principles that promote knowledge integration: "make science accessible, make thinking visible, help students learn from others, [and] promote autonomy" (p. 109):

The knowledge integration perspective connects conceptual change and effective instruction. . . . Variability in student ideas is [seen as] fundamentally a valuable feature and . . . instruction designed to capitalize on the variability and the creativity of student ideas has potential for facilitating conceptual change. The knowledge integration framework does not advocate unguided discovery or radical constructivism, but rather argues that understanding that students generate new ideas to make sense of science leads to important and essential design decisions.

(Linn, 2008, p. 715)

In our interpretation of the work of Linn and her colleagues, principles and patterns for learning to teach science can and should also serve as *principles for learning to teach people how to teach*. The knowledge integration framework can guide teacher education itself just as powerfully as it can guide the teaching of science. Recalling Northfield's (1998, p. 698) comments about providing "appropriate conditions for [new teachers] to learn about teaching," we see the four processes and 10 patterns of the knowledge integration framework as an excellent basis for providing appropriate conditions for learning about teaching and learning.

Persistent Themes in Research on Learning to Teach Science

Anderson and Mitchener's (1996) extensive review of research on science teacher education provides a strong foundation for the issues of learning to teach science that are explored and developed in this chapter. They describe a "traditional model" of preservice science teacher education that has three elements—educational foundations, methods courses, and field experiences and student teaching. Anderson and Mitchener conclude their review with statements that bear repeating:

Looking back, this three-pronged traditional model of preservice teacher education has survived relatively intact since its birth in the normal school. . . . The challenge facing science teacher educators today is this: how will you address in a coherent, comprehensive manner such emerging issues as new views of content knowledge, constructivist approaches to teaching and learning, and a reflective disposition to educating teachers. In addition, thoughtful science teacher educators need to attend to the theoretical orientation of their programs and how important professional issues are addressed within these orientations.

(Anderson & Mitchener, 1996, p. 19)

These reviewers went on to identify six dominant themes in research on the preservice curriculum in the 20th century: an "established preservice model," "inadequate subject matter preparation," "haphazard education preparation," the "importance of inquiry," "reliance on the laboratory," and "valued educational technologies" (Anderson & Mitchener, 1996, pp. 21–22). We find little to indicate that these dominant themes have changed. Anderson and Mitchener (1996) describe criticisms directed at the traditional model and then offer important conclusions:

> Considering the longevity and volume of such efforts, one would expect a review of preservice science teacher education programs to portray a rich landscape, complete with diverse views, cohesive images, and defined detail. Research on these programs, however, is neither accessible nor diverse.
>
> Indeed, there is a dearth of literature describing preservice science teacher education programs. . . . Actual portrayals of comprehensive programs—including conceptual and structural components—are rare.
>
> Differences that do exist among programs are most often found at the course level. Innovative efforts in reforming science teacher preparation usually are directed at changing one or two isolated components within a program, as opposed to the program as a whole.
>
> (Anderson & Mitchener, 1996, p. 23)

Our review of literature available since Anderson and Mitchener's review leads us to the conclusion that the six dominant themes they identified continue to appear in research related to learning to teach science, despite repeated calls for change and reform in science education and in preservice teacher education.

The Project for Enhancing Effective Learning

The Project for Enhancing Effective Learning (PEEL) is a unique example of teacher-directed, teacher-sustained collaborative action research. PEEL is a comprehensive school-based program for improving the quality of teaching in schools. With supportive links to nearby universities, PEEL began in 1985 in one school in the western suburbs of Melbourne, Australia. The key issues were deceptively simple:

> The major aim of PEEL is to improve the quality of school learning and teaching. Training for this improvement is centred on having students become more willing and able to accept responsibility and control for their own learning. Training has three aspects: increasing students' knowledge of what learning is and how it works; enhancing students' awareness of learning progress and outcome; improving students' control of learning through more purposeful decision making.
>
> (Baird & Mitchell, 1986, p. iii)

Overtly, PEEL aims to improve the quality of both learning and teaching. Thus it is a comprehensive program of inservice professional development for teachers as well as a project for enhancing effective student learning and metacognition (White & Mitchell, 1994).

Our interpretation of the initial approach taken by PEEL is this: Rather than criticize students for their *poor learning tendencies*, teachers can reward students for *good learning behaviors*, and thus help students develop from being passive to being metacognitive in their stance toward their own learning. One of the earliest activities within PEEL was the development of two lists of student behaviors. The list of Poor Learning Tendencies would be familiar to any teacher and could be generated readily by any group of teachers asked to list the various ways in which students wittingly and unwittingly make their own learning more difficult. A list of Good Learning Behaviors soon followed. One example involves the contrast between the poor learning tendency, "Staying Stuck," in which a student sees no alternative but to ask for and wait for help from the teacher, and the good learning behavior, "Refers to earlier work before asking for help." How many students use "waiting for the teacher's help" as an excuse to do nothing but wait? The shift in perspective for both teacher and student is positive when students are taught that there are constructive alternatives to "staying stuck."

Notice, in this interpretation of PEEL, that a central element involves *reframing* the activities of teachers *and* the activities of students within the classroom context. Most teachers are aware of numerous "reform" efforts that seek to change, in various ways, how teacher and students interact, usually with a view to improve educational results for students. The power of PEEL is that it provides an extensive and thoughtfully organized array of specific and practical procedures (Mitchell, 2009) for the various small steps that are inevitably involved in working to a larger goal. The PEEL list of Principles of Teaching for Quality Learning illustrates what those larger goals might be:

1. Share intellectual control with students.
2. Look for occasions when students can work out part (or all) of the content or instructions.
3. Provide opportunities for choice and independent decision making.
4. Provide a diverse range of ways of experiencing success.
5. Promote talk that is exploratory, tentative, and hypothetical.
6. Encourage students to learn from other students' questions and comments.
7. Build a classroom environment that supports risk taking.
8. Use a wide variety of intellectually challenging teaching procedures.
9. Use teaching procedures that are designed to promote specific aspects of quality learning.
10. Develop students' awareness of the big picture: how the various activities fit together and link to the big ideas.
11. Regularly raise students' awareness of the nature of different aspects of quality learning.
12. Promote assessment as part of the learning process. (Mitchell, Mitchell, McKinnon, & Scheele, 2004).

As attractive as these principles appear to the professional eye of the experienced teacher, they are very broad principles that emerged within PEEL only after years of work developing and sharing collections of specific practical teaching procedures. To present such a list to a beginning teacher with no teaching experience is to accomplish nothing at all. To use such a list to help beginning teachers interpret early teaching experiences in relation to their own goals and beliefs is to facilitate conceptual change. To apply these principles to teacher education classrooms as well as to classrooms in schools is to begin to realize the need for epistemological reframing in both contexts. These principles have been constructed from the vast array of experiences within PEEL since its inception.

Narrative Box 6 Do students notice your major goals for teaching?

When I began teaching preservice candidates in 1977, my 3 years of work with experienced teachers had a major impact. I had just finished working with a group of history teachers in a program that taught them how to analyze their own teaching. As a group, their overall reactions to their analysis can be summarized in two conclusions: 1. "We talk far more than we realized we did," and 2. "It is extremely difficult to change how much talking we do." Imagine how confused my first teacher education classes were when I tried to teach by talking less than most of my colleagues, a strategy that I attempted because I wanted to try for myself the challenge that the history teachers had identified. One early issue became "How do I model doing LESS of something?"

What major values do you hold for your teaching that will require you, as a teacher, to act in ways that differ from the norms of teacher behavior?

To extend our earlier references to the importance of epistemological considerations both in teaching science and in learning to teach science, we turn now to perspectives on knowledge acquisition and on knowledge construction in learning to teach.

White and Gunstone (2008) have contributed to the conceptual change literature from the perspective of the teaching of science. Their analysis of the development of research on alternative conceptions and conceptual change indicates that some of the latest research "implies that it is inevitable that for many phenomena people will acquire a primitive model, which is not totally discarded on later learning of the scientific explanation" (White & Gunstone, 2008, p. 627). We believe that much the same could be true of beginning teachers, who enter an initial teacher education program with a primitive model of how teaching and learning occur and relate to each other. "One approach to alternative conceptions and conceptual change would be to get learners to be reflective, open to new beliefs, and able to recognize contradictions between beliefs and resolve them" (White & Gunstone, 2008, p. 627). Schön

(1983) gave considerable impetus to the "teacher as reflective practitioner" movement with his distinction between problem solving and problem setting (pp. 39–42). His point is that we often focus solely on problem solving without taking time to analyze a situation in terms of problem setting—how we are conceptualizing the problem we wish to solve. Reframing problems to develop and enact new approaches became an attractive image for teachers thinking professionally about their work. The argument has intrinsic appeal in the context of teacher education and learning to teach, and it readily extends to the conceptual change approaches so often advocated in the science education community. We suggest that it is the context in which an individual confronts a problem that will determine whether a primitive model or a more complex and robust model will be used to guide problem setting and problem solving.

Linn (2008, pp. 694–695) has also drawn a contrast between "extinguishing" and "distinguishing" students' beliefs, pointing out that some researchers suggest that students can replace one set of beliefs with another, thereby "extinguishing" the primitive beliefs, while other researchers (herself included) prefer to assume that the introduction of new ideas can enable students to analyze conflicting ideas, "distinguishing" them from one another with a view to achieving coherence. The knowledge integration framework clearly focuses on the much richer and more complex task of teaching students how to identify, evaluate, and distinguish beliefs.

While Linn and colleagues do not address explicitly the place of laboratory or practical work in science teaching, Abrahams and Millar (2008, p. 1967) explored the issue of the effectiveness of practical work and drew conclusions that fit well with a knowledge integration perspective.

> Given the clear importance in any practical task of helping the students to do what the teacher intends with objects and materials in the limited time available, "recipes" are likely to continue to have a significant role in science practical work. If, however, the scale of the cognitive challenge for students in linking their actions and observations to a framework of ideas were recognized, teachers might then divide practical lesson time more equitably between "doing" and "learning." These do not, of course, have to be rigidly separated, but teachers need, on the basis of our data in this study, to devote a greater proportion of the lesson time to helping students use ideas associated with the phenomena they have produced, rather than seeing the successful production of the phenomenon as an end in itself.

We draw several conclusions about learning to teach science that are important to our overall argument.

1. The learning processes of students, new teachers, and experienced teachers have much in common.
2. Conceptual change, or reframing, is central for both the student of science and the future teacher of science. Science educators continue to seek ways to help more teachers enact teaching that fosters conceptual change,

while teacher educators continue to seek ways to help more new teachers enact learning strategies that will lead to professional awareness and confidence.

3. Reframing, or conceptual change, involves processes that cannot be made deliberate or sequenced in a time-table. Reframing appears to occur for individuals who have the confidence to actively seek new ways of seeing their learning, be it learning of science or learning how to teach science.

This concludes our account of important arguments about acquiring and constructing knowledge in the context of learning to teach. Programs for learning to teach science continue to operate on patterns guided more by tradition than by arguments such as these.

The Bigger Picture: Learning as Absorption or Knowledge Integration

Early in the 20th century, when schools as we know them today were first established and all children were expected to attend school, society appears to have been satisfied with approaches that are today characterized by terms such as transmission, absorption, and instructionism. As Hoetker and Ahlbrand (1969) concluded in their article about "the persistence of the recitation," teacher–student patterns of interaction have been highly stable and often expect students to be passive. Those who would improve the quality of learning in school classrooms often use terms such as "metacognition," "active learning," "engagement," "deep learning," "transformative learning," and, most recently, "knowledge integration." Linn and Eylon (2011) suggest that a traditional teaching approach that settles for absorption is inadequate and

> fails to meet the needs of students or their teachers. Expecting students to absorb information implies that their pre-existing ideas are of limited value. Furthermore, most students are cognitive economists, seeking to use their cognitive resources economically. When instruction emphasizes absorption, it sends the message that students do not need to evaluate evidence critically or attempt to reconcile apparent contradictions. Indeed, the absorption approach may convince students to avoid making sense of science at all.
>
> (p. 7)

They set out their argument in favor of knowledge integration in these terms:

> When absorption fails, it is common to argue that (a) students are not sufficiently motivated or do not work hard enough, (b) students need to develop a larger vocabulary, master some set of facts or details, or develop more powerful reasoning skills before they can understand the material, or (c) students are inhibited by misconceptions or naïve ideas that interfere with their ability to absorb the new knowledge. The absorption approach guides the design of most textbooks, lectures, and even laboratory experiences. In this book we argue that instruction should

be designed using a knowledge integration (KI) approach that involves building on personal ideas, using evidence to distinguish alternatives, and reflecting on alternative accounts of scientific phenomena.

> (Linn & Eylon, 2011, p. 4)

As Linn and Eylon (2011, p. 10) point out, their knowledge integration framework builds on the large body of research on the topic of learning by inquiry. In "inquiry-rich environments, students often participate in the full inquiry cycle including posing their own questions, gathering and analyzing data, and evaluating evidence against hypotheses and theories" (Jeong & Songer, 2008, p. 180).

The stance toward teaching taken by Linn and colleagues seems highly compatible with perspectives in the recent work of Hattie (2008, 2012), in which he makes a strong, research-driven appeal to teachers to focus first and foremost on their impact on the learning of their students. Where Linn and colleagues describe 10 design patterns, Hattie argues for "multiple ways of knowing" "multiple ways of interacting," "multiple opportunities for practicing," and "knowing that we are learning" (Hattie, 2012, pp. 101–102). Hattie summarizes his analysis of teachers' work by presenting eight mind frames (Hattie, 2012, pp. 160–168). "The claim is that teachers and school leaders who develop these ways of thinking are more likely to have major impacts on student learning" (Hattie, 2012, p. 160).

"Frames of mind," "mind frames," or "ways of thinking" are three phrases calling attention to the importance of how teachers think about their work from a big-picture perspective. "Frames" is a potentially useful term because it fits well with Schön's (1983) term, "reframing," whereby an unexpected or puzzling student response might trigger a new way of thinking that in turn suggests a possible new response to a student or situation; Schön called this "reflection-in-action," where the crucial phrase is "in action." Reframing seems much more likely to occur in the context of classroom action than in a lecture or reading *about* classroom action. When a new action meets up with teachers' and students' existing, well-established patterns of classroom behavior, the potential for conflict and tension is obvious. If we remind ourselves that these typical patterns of behavior are habits, habits that were learned originally by observing teachers during many years as a student, then what we know about the difficulties of changing habits (Duhigg, 2012) tells us that both frames and habits must be considered in any attempt to develop the professional skills of a teacher. Narrative Box 6 illustrates how one individual learning to teach science is simultaneously linking and developing habits and frames of mind for teaching.

Narrative Box 7 **Professional learning described by a teacher candidate in science**

The following is a metacognitive analysis of my personal and teaching habits as well as my mind frames *regarding how students learn*. It is intended to provide deeper insight into my development over the past 2 months, as my analyses of my own teaching and learning have led me to discover some of the profound lessons that all teachers should know. Firstly, I learned that teachers need to have their cake and eat it too. Secondly, I realized that rewards can actually hurt students.

During my first practicum I really embraced active learning (Knight, 2004). I did lots of POEs (predict-observe-explain) and I incorporated several PEEL (Project for Enhancing Effective Learning) procedures into my lesson plans. Sadly, when I got back to classes at Queen's I couldn't say how much my students had actually learned. That insight was very disorienting. What grounded me again was a connection to Hattie's (2012) description of how a "passionate, inspired teacher" (p. 24) plans lessons: by focusing on the learning that needs to happen before thinking about how to conduct the lesson. Accordingly, for my next practicum I consulted the science curriculum document (Ontario Ministry of Education, 2008) to find the expectations that I would be responsible for teaching. Then I focused on having "the mind frame to foster intellectual demand, challenge, and learning" (Hattie, 2012, p. 35). And . . . it worked! Students learned relativity well. I became a focused, determined, exhausted teacher. With all my focus on the learning, I had lost sight of the various methods of teaching. Still I had made tremendous strides towards connecting with the students. As Alfie Kohn would put it, I had begun "working with" students rather than "doing to" students. Pedagogically, however, I was a one-trick pony: talking and then helping the students solve problems.

To address my methodlessness, I revisited the PEEL procedures and discovered a whole new world of pedagogical insights. No longer was this just a database of different teaching methods; it was a tool box with various procedures to fix learning problems. Then Ian Mitchell showed me the menu option where I can browse the procedures according to learning requirements. Now I know that I need to have a wide repertoire of teaching methods so that I can better facilitate the LEARNING that needs to happen. Another, more academic, way of putting it would be: I need to develop my technological pedagogical content knowledge (Mishra & Koehler, 2006). Yet another, more creative, way of putting it would be: I need to have my cake and eat it too.

The idea of "working with" students aligned seamlessly with Ian Mitchell's talk about sharing intellectual control with students. This idea also extends beyond teaching content, even though it has content-learning implications . . . implications that I have felt, myself, when I was given trust and decision-making power over my own learning. The most important effect was on HOW I learn. Under such conditions, not only was my learning more enjoyable, but also the intrinsic value was amplified by the fact that I wanted the learning that I had decided to pursue to be valid. I want my students to have that kind of enjoyment—the pleasure of finding things out. Rather than appealing to their hedonistic faculties with bribes and threats (I mean positive reinforcement and inevitable consequences), now I realize that the curriculum may not always afford me much latitude regarding content. However, I'm sure that if I can present any content as an interesting problem, then students can have choices by being given autonomy over how to solve the problem. That way they can learn more than

what's on the page; they can learn why it's worth being on the page in the first place.

The effects of my having intellectual control over my learning can be seen in the one-page poster I prepared. As a teacher, I need to remember why I love physics and math. If I don't see the value in what I'm teaching then my students NEVER will. We may get through the curriculum, but what a pointless endeavor it would be! I know that I can't teach everything to students, nor can I expect them to like everything that I like. Also, I need to give them freedom to decide where they see potential value. Nevertheless, I am a leader in the classroom and my attitude towards what they are learning will affect their interest as well as the value they place in the subject. So, if I can focus on the learning as well as on how to teach, afford students the respect and choices necessary to encourage vulnerability and risk-taking, and also set an example for the kind of person I want students to be, then I can discover more ways of helping students learn.

Matthew Brown, Queen's University, 12 February 2013

Bullock's (2011) detailed analysis of the professional learning of five science teacher candidates as they moved between a science methods class and various practicum experiences gives further insight into the complex interaction of prior views of teaching and learning, new frames of mind, and the development of productive habits for science teaching. A series of case studies of science teacher educators analyzing their own teacher education practices (Bullock & Russell, 2012) sheds further light on the complex interaction between frames and habits.

As both Hattie and Linn suggest, one of the major differences between absorption and knowledge integration as frames for thinking about learning is the demand that knowledge integration places on teachers; making student learning visible means that teachers must do far more listening to students than is required by an absorption mindset. Cook-Sather (2002) put the issues very clearly:

> The work of authorizing student perspectives is essential because of the various ways that it can improve current educational practice, re-inform existing conversations about educational reform, and point to the discussions and reform efforts yet to be undertaken. Authorizing student perspectives can directly improve educational practice because when teachers listen to and learn from students, they can begin to see the world from those students' perspectives.
>
> (p. 3)

Listening to students' voices may be one of the most challenging new habits required of those learning to teach science; they have neither the mindset nor the experiences of being listened to by their former teachers.

> The authorizing of student perspectives for which I am arguing here is not simply about including students as a gesture. It is about including students to change the terms and the outcomes of the conversations about educational policy and practice. Such a reform cannot take place

within the dominant and persistent ways of thinking or the old structures for participation.

(Cook-Sather, 2002, p. 12)

From the arguments presented, we conclude that creating contexts for the development of new habits and mind frames, in part by giving voice to students (Featherstone & Grade 10 students, 1997), is essential if we are to create better conditions for learning to teach science.

Creating Better Conditions for Learning to Teach Science

White (2001) suggests that the two decades from 1980 to 2000 produced a revolution in research on science teaching: "The change in the amount of research is sufficient alone to warrant the term *revolution*, but even more significant is its nature" (p. 457). Against a background of revolution, the foreground offers clarion calls for reform and the improvement of science education (e.g., American Association for the Advancement of Science, 1989, 1993, 2001; Council of Ministers of Education, Canada, 1997; Curriculum Corporation, 1994a, 1994b; National Research Council, 1996, 2006). Prominent among the recommendations are changes in science classrooms whereby instruction is situated in a context that supports students' explorations of questions that develop deeper understandings of science content and processes and encourages learners to share developing ideas and information (Crawford, Krajcik, & Marx, 1999; Krajcik & Blumenfeld, 2006). More broadly, reform efforts urge closer attention to students' conceptions of the nature of science and scientific inquiry (Lederman, 1992, 1998). Lederman (1998) makes the case that, unless teachers have a functional understanding of these concepts, there is little hope of achieving the vision of science teaching and learning that is detailed in the reform literature. It is but a small step to argue that these types of understandings must be embedded in teacher education programs if prospective teachers are to move beyond the rhetoric of reform and become scientifically capable themselves and enable their students to do likewise. Hodson (1998), building on the discussion document of the Scottish Consultative Council on the Curriculum (1996), describes scientific capability as far more than the acquisition of scientific knowledge, understanding, and skills. "It also involves the development of personal qualities and attitudes, the formulation of one's own views on a wide range of issues that have a scientific and/or technological dimension and the establishment of an underlying value position" (p. 3).

Learning Science as a Discipline

Duit and Treagust (1998) relate learning science to the conceptions held by students and teachers of science content, conceptions of the nature of science, the aims of science instruction, the purpose of teaching events, and the nature of the learning process. The complexity of the construct "learning science," with its multiple components, points to many of the issues that confound science teacher education. These include the tenacity of students' conceptions about science and scientific inquiry as well as the tenacity of their experiences learning science—the procedural aspects in addition to the propositional, the pedagogy they were exposed to in their science classes and the (subconscious) interpretation they attached to it.

Lederman (1998) contends that science education reforms have presented an ambiguous picture when it comes to scientific inquiry. Inquiry can be perceived as (a) a set of skills that students learn and combine when they undertake scientific investigation, (b) a cognitive outcome that students should achieve that involves not just "doing" but "knowing why they are doing," or (c) a pedagogy scaffolded on the belief that students need to *do* science as opposed to learning about science and learning how to do science. Too often it is only the pedagogical aspect of inquiry that science teachers glean from the reform documents, "with the two former senses lost in the shuffle" (Lederman, 1998). Here then is an avenue that science teacher educators need to pursue. Unless prospective teachers can discriminate between and among these perspectives, they will be hard pressed to effect inquiry in their own classrooms that does little more than reproduce THE METHOD, at worst, or that absents *knowing* from *doing,* at best.

Seeing science as a discipline that is continually questioning itself is predicated on justification of knowledge claims. When students develop and cling to a final-form view of science, it becomes clear that the tentative nature of scientific knowledge claims is poorly understood, and authoritarian views of science as absolute truth and final form prevail (Duschl, 1990). This raises the question of how teacher educators challenge their students' conceptions of science and the extent to which prospective teachers have been schooled in final-form science.

The Significance of the Discourse of Science

Without careful attention to the particular language of science that is used to understand the world, scientific understanding cannot be had. Without the particular and technical language that science uses to constructs its worldview, "science is unthinkable without the technical language it has developed to construct its world view" (Martin, 1990, p. 115). Wildy and Wallace (1995) see good science teachers as valuing the structures and conventions of the discipline and as teaching for understanding by helping students to accept and use scientific language and protocols. This entails identifying how scientific language is used to "classify, decompose, and explain; its protocols and conventions are used to define and structure the discipline. This technical language involves generic structures, like reports, explanations, definitions and experiments, to construct the content of science and a scientific world view" (Wildy & Wallace, 1995, p. 153). Costa (1993) likens school science to a rite of passage where students are inducted into membership of a scientific community by virtue of familiarity with and understanding of its specialized language and agreed-upon procedures. Two points arise: (1) There is some debate about whether school science can claim to approach induction into a scientific community:

> When science is removed from contexts that match and support its goals of inquiry and experiment, its character can change. School science is distinct from experimental science because it is practiced in an institution whose goals are not the goals of science, and so school science becomes an inauthentic representation of experimental science.
> (Munby, Cunningham, & Lock, 2000, p. 208)

and (2) for some students, the actual experience of science classrooms seems a long way from coming to understand much at all about science:

> We hardly do anything except copy notes that the teacher has written (not our own words) and do experiments that the teacher does for us. In other words we aren't given any real work. . . . All we do is sit there and watch demonstrations and listen to the teacher talk. Everyone just sits there and looks like they're listening. I hate science.
> (Baird, Gunstone, Penna, Fensham, & White, 1990, p. 13)

Put most simply, science cannot be learned—or taught—in the absence of its discourse. Similarly, we contend, how we teach science cannot be learned—or taught—in the absence of educational discourse. Programs of science teacher education must always struggle to avoid the criticism that its version of learning to teach science has become an inauthentic representation of the teaching of science in schools.

Finally, the knowledge integration framework is a powerful support for those who would create better conditions for learning to teach science. Linn (2008) identified five central issues of conceptual change that need to be considered collectively: memory and forgetting as influences on the trajectory of understanding, factors affecting rate of student development, the significance of the learning context, distinguishing types of explanations of scientific phenomena, and explaining student responses to instructional activities that promote understanding and self-monitoring (Linn, 2008, pp. 695–702).

> The knowledge integration perspective connects conceptual change and effective instruction. It suggests that research on conceptual change will be most informative when combined with instructional investigations. . . . Variability in student ideas is fundamentally a valuable feature and . . . instruction designed to capitalize on the variability and the creativity of student ideas has potential for facilitating conceptual change. The knowledge integration framework does not advocate unguided discovery or radical constructivism, but rather argues that understanding that students generate new ideas to make sense of science leads to important and essential design decisions.
> (Linn, 2008, p. 715)

In the context of learning to teach science, we must acknowledge that future science teachers also generate new ideas, this time in the context of making sense of how science is and could be taught. Exploring those ideas within instruction guided by the knowledge integration framework will help to create better conditions for learning to teach science.

Conclusion

Although it continues to be easy to pin the hopes for improved teaching of science on those who are just entering the teaching profession, research on conceptual change suggests that this approach is fundamentally flawed. Experienced teachers and teacher educators who ask of new teachers what they have not attempted themselves are ignoring the reality that we learn to teach more by what is modeled than by what is told. Our review of literature about learning to teach science suggests that, in general, science teacher educators continue to be reluctant to practice in their own teaching the procedures and strategies that research suggests. Teachers are learning that action research is a way to explore in practice the challenges of teaching for conceptual change. Similarly, teacher educators must explore the same challenges of teaching for conceptual change in their own practice as they work with those learning to teach science. The growing literature of self-study of teacher education practices offers both guidance and illustration (Loughran, Hamilton, LaBoskey, & Russell, 2004).

Many people are pessimistic about the prospect of actually moving beyond the rhetoric of reform. In this chapter we have endeavored to show that moving forward requires epistemological and conceptual revolutions, reframing not only how we think about teaching science but also how we think about learning to teach science. Changes in our thinking must be accompanied by corresponding changes in our actions. Progress requires and demands that perspectives that move us forward in teaching science be extended to the context of learning to teach science. The two contexts may seem to proceed independently because of the university's implicit epistemology that suggests that research findings can and should be passed on to practitioners. This implicit epistemology fails to acknowledge how practitioners learn, as it also fails to acknowledge that those who teach in universities are practitioners as well as researchers. We concur with Schön's (1995) much-neglected call for a new epistemology that must be explored and developed both in universities and in schools. Thus we must consider conceptual change not just as change in how students—and prospective teachers—think about phenomena but also as change in how students—and prospective teachers—think about education. Similarly, conceptual changes happen not just to students but also to prospective teachers, experienced teachers, and teacher educators—to teachers in schools and also to teachers in universities. The knowledge integration framework represents a significant step forward in scaffolding an epistemological and conceptual revolution. The entire argument for better conditions for learning to teach science always needs to complete the circle of reasoning about theory and practice.

Acknowledgments

We would like to thank J. John Loughran and M. Gail Jones for providing reviews for this chapter.

References

Abrahams, I., & Millar, R. (2008). Does practical work really work? A study of the effectiveness of practical work as a teaching and learning method in school science. *International Journal of Science Education, 30*(14), 1945–1969.

American Association for the Advancement of Science. (1989). *Science for all Americans.* New York, NY: Oxford University Press.

American Association for the Advancement of Science. (1993). *Benchmarks for science literacy.* New York, NY: Oxford University Press.

American Association for the Advancement of Science. (2001). *Designs for science literacy.* New York, NY: Oxford University Press.

Anderson, R. D., & Mitchener, C. P. (1996). Research on science teacher education. In D. Gabel (Ed.), *Handbook of research on science teaching and learning* (pp. 3–44). New York, NY: Macmillan.

Ausubel, D. (1968). *Educational psychology: A cognitive view.* New York, NY: Holt, Rinehart & Winston.

Baird, J. R., Gunstone, R. F., Penna, C., Fensham, P. J., & White, R. T. (1990). Researching balance between cognition and affect in science teaching and learning. *Research in Science Education, 20,* 11–20.

Baird, J. R., & Mitchell, I. M. (Eds.). (1986). *Improving the quality of teaching and learning: An Australian Case Study—The PEEL Project.* Melbourne, VIC, Australia: Monash University.

Bullock, S. M. (2011). *Inside teacher education: Challenging prior views of teaching and learning.* Rotterdam, the Netherlands: Sense Publishers.

Bullock, S. M., & Russell, T. (Eds.). (2012). *Self-studies of science teacher education practices.* Dordrecht, the Netherlands: Springer.

Bryan, L. A., & Abell, S. K. (1999). The development of professional knowledge in learning to teach elementary science. *Journal of Research in Science Teaching, 36,* 121–139.

Chinn, C. A., & Brewer, W. F. (1998). Theories of knowledge acquisition. In B. J. Fraser & K. G. Tobin (Eds.), *International handbook of science education, Part one* (pp. 97–113). Dordrecht, the Netherlands: Kluwer Academic Publishers.

Cook-Sather, A. (2002). Authorizing students' perspectives: Toward trust, dialogue, and change in education. *Educational Researcher, 31*(4), 3–14.

Costa, V. B. (1993). School science as a rite of passage: A new frame for familiar problems. *Journal of Research in Science Teaching, 30,* 649–668.

Council of Ministers of Education, Canada. (1997). *Pan-Canadian protocol for collaboration on school curriculum: Common framework of science learning outcomes K–12 (draft).* Toronto, ON: Author.

Crawford, B. A., Krajcik, J. S., & Marx, R. W. (1999). Elements of a community of learners in a middle school science classroom. *Science Education, 83,* 701–723.

Curriculum Corporation. (1994a). *Science—a curriculum profile for Australian schools.* Carlton, VIC, Australia: Curriculum Corporation.

Curriculum Corporation. (1994b). *A statement on science for Australian schools.* Carlton, VIC, Australia: Curriculum Corporation.

Dewey, J. (1938). *Experience and education.* New York, NY: Macmillan.

DiSessa, A. (1993). Toward an epistemology of physics. *Cognition and Instruction, 10,* 105–225.

Driver, R. (1989). Changing conceptions. In P. Adey, J. Bliss, J. Head, & M. Shayer (Eds.), *Adolescent development and school science* (pp. 79–99). Lewes, UK: Falmer Press.

Duhigg, C. (2012). *The power of habit: Why we do what we do in life and business.* Toronto, ON: Doubleday Canada.

Duit, R., & Treagust, D. F. (1998). Learning in science—from behaviourism towards social constructivism and beyond. In B. J. Fraser & K. G. Tobin (Eds.), *International handbook of science education, Part one* (pp. 3–26). Dordrecht, the Netherlands: Kluwer Academic Publishers.

Duschl, R. A. (1990). *Restructuring science education: The importance of theories and their development.* New York, NY: Teachers College Press.

Duschl, R. A., & Hamilton, R. J. (1998). Conceptual change in science and in the learning of science. In B. J. Fraser & K. G. Tobin (Eds.), *International handbook of science education, Part two* (pp. 1047–1065). Dordrecht, the Netherlands: Kluwer Academic Publishers.

Elby, A. (2001). Helping physics students learn how to learn. *American Journal of Physics, Physics Education Research Supplement, 69*(7), S54–S64.

Farnham-Diggory, S. (1994). Paradigms of knowledge and instruction. *Review of Educational Research, 64,* 463–477.

Featherstone, D., & Grade 10 science students. (1997). Students as critical friends: Helping students find voices. In D. Featherstone, H. Munby, & T. Russell (Eds.), *Finding a voice while learning to teach* (pp. 120–136). London, UK: Falmer Press.

Franklin, U. (1994). *Making connections: Science and the future of citizenship.* Paper presented at the meeting of the Science Teachers Association of Ontario, Toronto.

Guzzetti, B. J., Snyder, T. E., Glass, G. V., & Gamas, W. S. (1993). Promoting conceptual change in science: A comparative meta-analysis of instructional interventions from reading education and science education. *Reading Research Quarterly, 28*(2), 117–154.

Handelsman, J., Ebert-May, D., Beichner, R., Bruns, P., Chang, A., DeHaan, R., et al. (2004). Scientific teaching. *Science, 304,* 521–522.

Hattie, J. (2008). *Visible learning: A synthesis of over 800 meta-analyses relating to achievement.* London, UK: Routledge.

Hattie, J. (2012). *Visible learning for teachers: Maximizing impact on learning.* London, UK: Routledge.

Hewson, P. W., Beeth, M. E., & Thorley, N. R. (1998). Teaching for conceptual change. In B. J. Fraser & K. G. Tobin (Eds.), *International handbook of science education* (pp. 199–218). Dordrecht, the Netherlands: Kluwer Academic Publishers.

Hodson, D. (1998). *Teaching and learning science: Towards a personalized approach.* Buckingham, UK: Open University Press.

Hoetker, J., & Ahlbrand, W. P. (1969). The persistence of the recitation. *American Educational Research Journal, 6*(2), 145–167.

Jeong, H., & Songer, N. B. (2008). Understanding scientific evidence and the data collection process: Explorations of why, who, when, what, and how. In C. L. Petroselli (Ed.), *Science education issues and developments* (pp. 169–200). New York, NY: Nova Science Publishers.

Kagan, D. M. (1992). Implications of research on teacher belief. *Educational Psychologist, 27*(1), 65–90.

Kelly, G. (1955). *The psychology of personal constructs.* New York, NY: Norton.

Knight, R. D. (2004). *Five easy lessons: Strategies for successful physics teaching.* San Francisco, CA: Addison-Wesley.

Krajcik, J. S., & Blumenfeld, P. C. (2006). Project-based learning. In R. K. Sawyer (Ed.), *The Cambridge handbook of the learning sciences* (pp. 317–333). Cambridge, UK: Cambridge University Press.

Lederman, N. G. (1992). Students' and teachers' conceptions of the nature of science: A review of the research. *Journal of Research in Science Teaching, 29,* 331–359.

Lederman, N. G. (1998). The state of science education: Subject matter without context. *Electronic Journal of Science Education, 3*(2). Retrieved from http://wolfweb.unr.edu/homepage/jcannon/ejse/lederman.html

Linn, M. C. (2006). The knowledge integration perspective on learning and instruction. In R. K. Sawyer (Ed.), *The Cambridge handbook of the learning sciences* (pp. 243–264). Cambridge, UK: Cambridge University Press.

Linn, M. C. (2008). Teaching for conceptual change: Distinguish or extinguish ideas. In S. Vosniadou (Ed.), *International handbook of research on conceptual change* (pp. 694–722). London, UK: Routledge.

Linn, M.C., & Eylon, B.-S. (2006). Science education: Integrating views of learning and instruction. In P.A. Alexander & P.H. Winne (Eds.), *Handbook of educational psychology* (2nd ed., pp. 511–544). Mahwah, NJ: Lawrence Erlbaum Associates.

Linn, M.C., & Eylon, B.-S. (2011). *Science learning and instruction: Taking advantage of technology to promote knowledge integration.* London, UK: Routledge.

Linn, M.C., Kali, Y., Davis, E.A., & Horwitz, P. (2008). Policies to promote coherence. In Y. Kali, M.C. Linn, & J.E. Roseman (Eds.), *Designing coherent science education: Implications for curriculum, instruction, and policy* (pp. 201–210). New York, NY: Teachers College Press.

Loughran, J.J., Hamilton, M.L., LaBoskey, V.K., & Russell, T. (Eds.). (2004). *International handbook of self-study of teaching and teacher education practices.* Dordrecht, the Netherlands: Kluwer Academic Publishers.

Martin, J.R. (1990). Literacy in science: Learning to handle text as technology. In R. Christie (Ed.), *Literacy for a changing world* (pp. 79–117). Hawthorn, VIC, Australia: Australian Council for Educational Research.

McDevitt, T.M., & Ormrod, J.E. (2002). *Child development and education.* Upper Saddle River, NJ: Merrill Prentice Hall.

McGoey, J., & Ross, J. (1999). Research, practice, and teacher internship. *Journal of Research in Science Teaching, 36*(2), 117–120.

Mintzes, J.J., Wandersee, J.H., & Novak, J.D. (1997). Meaningful learning in science: The human constructivist perspective. In G.D. Phye (Ed.), *Handbook of academic learning: Construction of knowledge* (pp. 404–447). San Diego, CA: Academic Press.

Mishra, P., & Koehler, M. (2006). Technological pedagogical content knowledge: A framework for teacher knowledge. *Teachers College Record, 108*(6), 1017–1054.

Mitchell, I. (2009). *Teaching for effective learning: The complete book of PEEL teaching procedures* (4th ed.). Melbourne, VIC, Australia: PEEL Publishing (see also http://peelweb.org).

Mitchell, I., Mitchell, J., McKinnon, R., & Scheele, S. (2004). *PEEL in practice: 1100 ideas for quality teaching.* Melbourne, VIC, Australia: PEEL Publishing.

Munby, H., Cunningham, M., & Lock, C. (2000). School science culture: A case study of barriers to developing professional knowledge. *Science Education, 84*(2), 193–211.

Munby, H., & Russell, T. (1994). The authority of experience in learning to teach: Messages from a physics method class. *Journal of Teacher Education, 45*(2), 86–95.

National Research Council. (1996). *National science education standards.* Washington, DC: National Academies Press.

National Research Council. (2006). *Learning to think spatially.* Washington, DC: National Academies Press.

Northfield, J. (1998). Teacher education and the practice of science teacher education. In B.J. Fraser & K.G. Tobin (Eds.), *International handbook of science teacher education* (pp. 695–706). Dordrecht, the Netherlands: Kluwer.

Novak, J. (1987). Human constructivism: Toward a unity of psychological and epistemological meaning making. In J.D. Novak (Ed.), *Proceedings of the second international seminar on misconceptions and educational strategies in science and mathematics* (Vol. 1, pp. 349–360). Ithaca, NY: Cornell University Department of Education.

Novak, J. (1989). The use of metacognitive tools to facilitate meaningful learning. In P. Adey (Ed.), *Adolescent development and school science* (pp. 227–239). London, UK: Falmer Press.

Novak, J. (1993). Human constructivism: A unification of psychological and epistemological phenomena in meaning making. *International Journal of Personal Construct Psychology, 6,* 167–193.

Novak, J., & Gowin, D.B. (1984). *Learning how to learn.* Cambridge, UK: Cambridge University Press.

Ontario Ministry of Education. (2008). *The Ontario curriculum grades 11 and 12: Science.* Toronto, ON: Queen's Printer.

Özdemir, G., & Clark, D.B. (2007). An overview of conceptual change theories. *Eurasia Journal of Mathematics, Science & Technology Education, 3*(4), 351–361.

Pelech, J., & Pieper, G. (Ed.). (2010). *The comprehensive handbook of constructivist teaching: From theory to practice.* Charlotte, NC: Information Age Publishing.

Pfundt, H., & Duit, R. (1994). *Students' alternative frameworks and science education.* Kiel, Germany: Institute for Science Education, University of Kiel.

Posner, G.J., Strike, K.A., Hewson, P.W., & Gertzog, W.A. (1982). Accommodation of a scientific conception: Toward a theory of conceptual change. *Science Education, 66,* 211–227.

Russell, T. (2000). Teaching to build on school experiences. In R. Upitis (Ed.), *Who will teach? A case study of teacher education reform* (pp. 227–240). San Francisco, CA: Caddo Gap Press.

Sarason, S.B. (1996). *Revisiting "the culture of the school and the problem of change."* New York, NY: Teachers College Press.

Sawyer, R.K. (2006). Introduction: The new science of learning. In R.K. Sawyer (Ed.), *The Cambridge handbook of the learning sciences* (pp. 1–16). Cambridge, UK: Cambridge University Press.

Schön, D.A. (1983). *The reflective practitioner: How professionals think in action.* New York, NY: Basic Books.

Schön, D.A. (1995). The new scholarship requires a new epistemology. *Change, 27,* 27–34.

Scott, P., Asoko, H., & Driver, R. (1992). Teaching for conceptual change: A review of strategies. In R. Duit, F. Goldberg, & H. Neidderer (Eds.), *Research in physics learning: Theoretical issues and empirical studies* (pp. 310–329). Kiel, Germany: Schmidt & Klannig.

Scott, P.H., & Driver, R.H. (1998). Learning about science teaching: Perspectives from an action research project. In B.J. Fraser & K.G. Tobin (Eds.), *International handbook of science education* (pp. 67–80). Dordrecht, the Netherlands: Kluwer Academic Publishers.

Scottish Consultative Council on the Curriculum. (1996). *Science education in Scottish schools: Looking to the future.* Broughty Ferry, Scotland: Author.

Tudge, J., & Scrimsher, S. (2003). Lev S. Vygotsky on education: A cultural-historical, interpersonal, and individual approach to development. In B.J. Zimmerman & D.H. Schunk (Eds.), *Educational psychology, a century of contributions* (pp. 207–228). Mahwah, NJ: Lawrence Erlbaum Associates.

Vosniadou, S. (1994). Capturing and modeling the process of conceptual change. *Learning and Instruction, 4,* 45–69.

Vosniadou, S. (Ed.). (2008). *International handbook of research on conceptual change.* London: Routledge.

Wandersee, J., Mintzes, J., & Novak, J. (1994). Research on alternative conceptions in science. In D. Gabel (Ed.), *Handbook of research on science teaching and learning* (pp. 177–210). New York: Macmillan.

White, R. (2001). The revolution in research on science teaching. In V. Richardson (Ed.), *Handbook of research on teaching* (4th ed., pp. 457–471). Washington, DC: American Educational Research Association.

White, R.T., & Gunstone, R.F. (2008). The conceptual change approach and the teaching of science. In S. Vosniadou (Ed.), *International handbook of research on conceptual change* (pp. 619–628). London, UK: Routledge.

White, R.T., & Mitchell, I.J. (1994). Metacognition and the quality of learning. *Studies in Science Education, 23,* 21–37.

Wildy, H., & Wallace, J. (1995). Understanding teaching or teaching for understanding: Alternative frameworks for science classrooms. *Journal of Research in Science Teaching, 32,* 143–156.

Zembel-Saul, C., Krajcik, J., & Blumenfeld, P. (2002). Elementary student teachers' science content representations. *Journal of Research in Science Teaching, 39,* 443–463.

44

Research on Teacher Professional Development Programs in Science

Julie A. Luft and Peter W. Hewson

Science teachers are an essential link between the scientifically oriented citizens of the present and the future. In order to prepare students for the scientific and technological changes of the 21st century, teachers will need ongoing science professional development opportunities. Educational programs that are as dynamic as the societies in which teachers and students live will require new approaches—and research—on professional development. This research should suggest powerful and purposeful ways in which science teachers can enhance, refine, or reconstruct their practice.

A goal of this chapter is to guide science teacher educators who are involved in developing, enacting, and studying professional development programs (PDPs). In order to accomplish this, we review recent research on teacher PDPs in science. Based on this review, we outline a model that links policy, PDPs, teachers, and students and suggests areas in which research should and could be conducted in order to advance teacher professional development. This model recognizes not only the relationships among these key components, but also that PDPs are situated within dynamic contexts.

There are several key sections in this chapter, beginning with a discussion of the most important characteristics of PDPs in science. Next, we discuss prior research on PDPs in general and PDPs in science, studies of PDPs, and the process of finding studies for this review. After this overview, there is a discussion of the reviewed research in light of the Policy, PDPs, Teachers, and Students model. Within each section, salient articles are discussed and approaches to further avenues of study are offered. This chapter concludes with a discussion of the "wicked problems" (Rittel & Webber, 1973) in PDPs for science teachers, as well as suggestions for conducting and sharing future research.

Teacher PDPs in Science

Professional development can be viewed as the ongoing learning experience of a teacher. It can begin prior to working in a classroom and continue until the final year of one's career in education. For science teachers, the specific character of science is an essential ingredient of teacher practice, of teacher learning, and thus of programs designed to facilitate these outcomes. The entire process of professional development is ultimately influenced by policy and concerned with student learning.

Among those who engage in PDPs, there is an emphasis on professional learning. This emphasis strives to eliminate the unidirectional notion that PDPs provide teachers with skills and knowledge. Early definitions of professional learning suggested that teachers learned as they worked alone or in collective groups and that their learning was directed by the context in which they worked. Lieberman (1995), as an early advocate of professional learning, suggested that learning "is both personal and professional, individual and collective, inquiry based and technical (p. 592)." More recently, the notion of professional learning is being advanced as a complex and iterative interaction of the teacher, the school, and the learning activity (Opfer & Pedder, 2011). Professional learning provides an important framework for conceptualization and enactment of PDPs.

In this review, we focus on an area of the professional learning process: *PDPs for science teachers*. As an important component of a teacher's career, PDPs are purposefully constructed learning opportunities for science teachers that follow initial teacher preparation programs. These programs are focused on important content, attend to the context that supports and guides teacher learning, and consist of a process that supports teacher learning (Darling-Hammond, Chung Wei, Andree, Richardson, & Orphanos, 2009). As we discuss later in the review, PDPs are influenced by policy and concerned with the learning of students.

When focusing on PDPs, it is important to reject the notion that these programs and the developers who run them are active providers, while the teachers are passive recipients. On the contrary, it is of the utmost importance to recognize that teachers themselves are responsible for their own professional development (Kennedy,

1999; Shapiro & Last, 2002; Wilson & Berne, 1999). Any activity should have the purpose of supporting teachers to take responsibility for their own learning and to be active learners.

Science PDPs have unique requirements. The content, context, and process of the program should be clearly defined. The content of PDPs for science teachers should focus on a discipline and consist of domains and knowledge. According to Gardner (1972), disciplines are specialized areas of study that "span the alphabet from aerodynamics to zoology" (p. 26), while domains consist of the objects that are studied or explored, such as living things or elements. Subject matter knowledge is produced by the discipline and can sometimes cross disciplines.

Subject matter knowledge has a substantive structure, which is an "interrelated collection of powerful ideas that guide research in a discipline" (Gardner, 1972; p. 27). In science, this consists of theories, laws, facts, and concepts that are important in studies in the discipline. Subject matter knowledge also consists of syntactical structure (Schwab, 1964), the way in which knowledge is generated by the discipline (Gardner, 1972). In science, this consists of the logic and reasoning used by scientists in the process of inquiry.

The context of PDPs for science teachers can range from the school environment to national policies. At the school level, context decisions relate to supporting the learning of science teachers. This can connect to the design of the PDP, which can consist of teachers in a school participating in a learning community (Darling-Hammond et al., 2009). Local contextual elements should also be considered in the design of a PDP, which may include the cultural background of the students, the language needs of the students, or the content knowledge of the teachers.

National context is also important to consider, as there is a global call for scientifically oriented citizens in our ever-changing world (e.g., National Research Council, 2007). For policy makers, the professional learning of science teachers has become increasingly important. Emerging policy documents across the globe articulate the need for science teachers to receive ample professional development opportunities in order to enhance and improve their knowledge and practices (e.g., Eurydice, 2011; National Research Council, 2009; National Science Board, 2012). Often the national context is influenced by a nation's orientation toward science. National contexts may emphasize the applied side of science knowledge, the social implications of science, or scientific practices.

The process within a PDP for science teachers includes setting goals, planning, enacting, looking at outcomes, and reflecting on the entire process (Loucks-Horsley, Stiles, Mundry, Love, & Hewson, 2010). Goals may vary in a PDP for science teachers. For instance, science teachers can look at student learning, revise curriculum, learn to use curriculum, or refine instructional practices (Loucks-Horsley et al., 2010). Throughout the PDP, the collection of data is essential in order to revise the program. This results in an adaptive PDP that ultimately supports teacher and student learning.

It is not clear how PDPs for science teachers are enacted across the globe. However, in general, the access that teachers have to such programs is uneven and the programs vary in their structure (Darling-Hammond et al., 2009; Hendriks, Luyten, Scheerens, Sleegers, & Steen, 2010). Teachers from the United States have fewer opportunities to participate in extended PDPs and fewer opportunities to work together than do some of their international peers (Darling-Hammond et al., 2009; National Science Board, 2012).

Research in this Review of Teacher PDPs in Science

Most Recent Review of Research

Our review of recent research on teacher professional development in science is based on Hewson's (2007) chapter in the first edition of this handbook (Abell & Lederman, 2007). That review only included studies with an explicit focus on the two central elements: a comprehensive description of the PDP and a focus on practicing teachers of science. A subset of these studies also included students. Since the publication of the first edition, the field has progressed in various ways. Some research areas are now saturated, while others, not considered in the previous review, hold out exciting and challenging possibilities.

Hewson's (2007) review was guided by three focal points. The first addressed how teachers developed professionally. The Learning in Science Project (Teacher Development) in New Zealand (Bell & Gilbert, 1996) served as the basis for this discussion. Researchers Bell and Gilbert (1996) identified the personal development, social development, and professional development of science teachers as they worked with 48 teachers over 3 years. This description of how teachers developed professionally has served as a theoretical framework for researchers exploring the professional development process.

The second focal point addressed how successful professional developers plan and implement PDPs. The books by Loucks-Horsley and her colleagues (1998, 2003) guided this discussion. These books drew on the practice of experienced professional developers to conceptualize a model PDP. The model offered specific suggestions about the process of planning PDPs, the knowledge and beliefs underlying effective PDPs, the context in which PDPs can exist, the critical issues that need to be considered in the professional development process, and the strategies that can be used in the professional development process. For those interested in planning PDPs, these books, now in a third edition (Loucks-Horsley et al., 2010), are essential guides.

The final focal point addressed the relationship between teachers and PDPs. The section drew upon the work of Fishman, Marx, Best, and Tal (2003) to explore the relationship between PDPs and science teachers' practice. Their process of PDP design had much in common with Loucks-Horsley, Love, Stiles, Mundry, and Hewson

(2003), but it went further in its explicit focus on teacher enactment in the classroom and the resulting student learning and performance.

The remainder of the chapter explored different studies in the midst of these focal points. These studies were grouped in two ways: studies that only considered the influence of PDPs on the teachers who participated in them and studies that included student outcomes from classes taught by teachers who participated in PDPs. After reviewing these studies, several conclusions were reached and suggestions were offered about how to better understand the field of science teacher professional development. One major conclusion was the need to consider not only the people and programs involved in science teacher professional development, but also the systems in which these programs are embedded.

Types of Studies Informing PDP Research

Several types of studies provide direction for those involved in PDPs for teachers. Synthesis studies, for example, draw upon the work of others in order to draw compelling conclusions about PDP structure and function (e.g., Capps, Crawford, & Constas, 2012; Gerard, Varma, Corliss, & Linn, 2011). Capps and colleagues (2012), for example, specifically examined research on PDPs that supported the use of inquiry instruction among science teachers. From their review, they concluded that few empirical studies looked at PDPs focused on inquiry instruction and that more empirical studies were needed in this area. They also suggested that more research programs should study the connections between the PDP supporting the use of inquiry and teacher knowledge, practices, and beliefs.

Another type of study in the area of professional development draws upon the analysis of large sets of teacher data in order to make important conclusions about the professional development process (e.g., Banilower, Heck, & Weiss, 2007; Garet, Porter, Desimone, Birman, & Yoon, 2001; Supovitz & Turner, 2000). Banilower and colleagues (2007), in a study of 42 projects associated with the U.S. National Science Foundation's Local Systemic Change through Teacher Enhancement Initiative, concluded that high-quality K–8 PDPs resulted in teachers developing positive attitudes toward science and feeling more prepared in terms of pedagogical skills and content knowledge. They also reported that the longer the PDP, the more likely teachers were to implement the associated instructional materials.

A third type of study that contributes to our knowledge of professional development is one that carefully examines various aspects of the teacher professional development process. These types of studies vary greatly and utilize quantitative, qualitative, and mixed methodologies. Each study is designed to answer a specific question or to highlight a certain aspect of professional development. For instance, Penuel, Gallagher, and Moorthy (2011) studied 53 middle school earth science teachers who were randomly assigned to different PDPs. They used hierarchical linear modeling to determine the impact of the PDP on teachers and students. They concluded that explicit instruction and effective modeling played an important role in the learning of the students and the teacher. In contrast, Watson, Steele, Vozzo, and Aubusson (2007) captured the experiences of 12 teachers through interviews and artifacts during a PDP. The program was designed to help non–physics teachers learn to teach physics. In this study, the well-intentioned and well-configured PDP was no match for the lack of discipline knowledge of the teacher and the teacher's school community.

Certainly there are other forms of research conducted on PDPs. For this chapter, however, these general categorizations were important in our contemplation of the research involving PDPs. Synthesis studies, the analysis of data sets, and small-scale studies each provided different insights into the professional development process.

Studies Examined in this Review

There were numerous steps involved in conducting this research review. First, parameters were articulated in order to identify potential studies. One parameter was the focus of the articles. We considered only studies that described or were situated within a PDP for science teachers. Lengthy descriptions of the PDP were not necessary, but the program's inclusion in the study was a key factor. As a result, we excluded studies that only considered teacher learning or that considered teachers who crafted their own professional development experiences outside of a structured program. Both of these categories of study are considered elsewhere in this handbook.

Another parameter was that only research studies focusing on practicing teachers, as distinct from studies of initial teacher education, were considered for this review. Studies of prospective teachers involved in initial teacher education are discussed elsewhere in this volume. While this convenient division reflects the reality that initial teacher education and inservice teacher PDPs are different enterprises, it is still acknowledged that teacher learning should continue throughout the professional life of a teacher (Feiman-Nemser, 2001). Certainly, the emphasis and intensity of teacher learning changes as teachers move from initial certification to being experienced professionals in the field.

A third parameter involved selection of studies that had an explicit focus on teachers of science. This requirement arises from the nature of the present volume. While science may appear to be a straightforward concept, it varied among the different studies. Science could exist as learning about the nature of science, learning key concepts in the different disciplines, or even learning how students learned about various aspects of science. These dimensions and many more were accounted for in this review. Additionally, the focus on science had the practical effect of limiting the number of reviewed studies.

To find these studies, we searched a number of science education and education journals that use a peer-review process. Most of the journals were in the field of science education, while a few journals were focused on the broad field of education. The *Journal of Research in Science Teaching, Research in Science Education, Journal of Science Teacher Education,* the *International Journal of Science Education, Science Education,* and the *American Educational Research Journal* were the primary journals of interest in this review. Since this review complements Hewson's (2007) review, articles between 2002 and 2012 were of interest.

Our initial search by hand resulted in more than 200 potential articles. Each article was read to assess the rationale of the study, the research methods, and the stated conclusions. These three areas were accounted for concurrently, as they are often relate to each other in published research. This approach did not favor qualitative or quantitative methods, but instead identified studies that were aligned with the American Educational Research Association (AERA) standards for empirical research (American Educational Research Association, 2006).

The rationale for the study was important because it situated the study within some area related to a PDP. Studies that did not have a clear connection to PDPs were eliminated. In examining the study methods, evidence was required suggesting that the appropriate data collection methods were used in reference to the study question and that the analyses of data were complete and aligned with the methods selected in the study. Studies with limited or incorrect descriptions of the data collection and analysis methods were eliminated. In terms of stated conclusions, it was important that the findings did not overstep the collected data. Conclusions that reached beyond the data were not eliminated, but the appropriate conclusions were noted.

In the remaining studies, we looked for research groups or authors who used the same data set in several publications and that arrived at similar conclusions. For instance, a large-scale PDP may have resulted in multiple publications over several years that addressed the same topic, or the data from a small PDP may have been examined differently and still had similar findings. These studies were examined side by side, and the most salient study of the collection was included in this review. By being selective, it was possible to highlight the most representative study within a group of studies.

By the end of the review process, more than 50 research studies were selected for inclusion in this chapter review. During article selection, an attempt was made to include research from around the world. Unfortunately, the number of studies about PDPs in science outside the United States (U.S.) was limited. This is likely the result of the significant amount of local/national funding sources for PDPs in science and mathematics in the U.S. This funding can also support the reporting of research on PDPs. It is also possible that PDPs in science outside the U.S. were published in local/national journals we didn't consider or in languages other than English.

Guiding Work in Teacher PDPs in Science

What is Known

Research studies in the field of science education reveal several important qualities pertaining to the design, enactment, and need for PDPs. These qualities are often the result of findings from studies that draw upon existing data sets, studies that examine a group of individuals, or studies that synthesize published research articles. The conclusions reached from these studies can guide those who are crafting PDPs and those who are designing research programs in the field of professional development.

Teachers experience different degrees of change in the midst of PDPs. It is widely accepted that teachers need to engage in professional development activities in order to improve their instructional practice and student learning. This is evident in numerous policy documents about teacher professional development and in the many professional development activities that exist for science teachers. With a view toward teacher growth, there are compelling discussions about how teachers can change (e.g., Banilower et al., 2007; Garet et al., 2001; Supovitz & Turner, 2000). For example, Supovitz and Turner (2000), in an analysis of the U.S. National Science Foundation's Local Systemic Change through Teacher Enhancement Initiative data, concluded that the quality of teacher instruction is related to the number of hours of professional development. Specifically, in order for teachers to achieve the level of investigative culture desired by professional developers, they reported that teachers needed more than 160 hours of professional development programming.

In another study focused on teacher change, Dori and Herscovitz (2005) followed and documented the change experienced by 50 science teachers over 3 years as they participated in a PDP in Israel. The teachers drew upon different program attributes in order to support their different instructional needs. While this study revealed the impact of the program on the teachers, its underlying contribution was the portrayal of how the teachers changed in different ways over time.

These findings, along with the research of others, suggest that more difficult changes in practice take additional professional development time. In addition, these findings suggest that teachers change in different ways over time and need different forms of instructional support in order to modify their instruction. Attending to the individual instructional requirements of teachers, including the context in which they work, is essential throughout a PDP.

Collaboration is important in supporting teacher growth. When teachers work collaboratively, they reinforce, build, expand, and challenge their notions about teaching science. Wilson and Berne (1999), in their review of professional development research, found that successfully supporting the use of new practices among teachers required collaboration among peers and within educational communities. Similarly, in a later analysis of science and mathematics teacher data from the U.S. Eisenhower Mathematics and Science Education program, Garet and colleagues (2001) found that collective participation within a school, grade level, or subject was an important supporting feature of PDPs. They stressed that collective participation was a necessary but not sufficient feature in PDPs in order for teachers to change their classroom practices.

The notion that collaboration is conducive to professional growth is worthy of further investigation. Nelson (2009), for instance, in a study of U.S. science teachers involved in a professional learning community (PLC), reported on the complexity of working collaboratively in order to enhance teacher learning. In her study, sustained dialogue helped teachers move toward the instruction valued in the PDP, but the process of having teachers hold professional discussions about practice was both challenging and rewarding. Similarly, Richmond and Manokore (2011) explored the dialogue of U.S. science teachers who were involved in a PLC. They found that the dialogue within the PLC was important as teachers negotiated external constraints; dialogue enhanced their knowledge and confidence.

Coherency is important in science teacher PDPs. The coherency of a PDP is essential for supporting teacher learning. Coherency is often considered to be the way in which PDPs offer focused learning opportunities related to local or national standards. The studies by Garet and colleagues (2001) and Supovitz and Turner (2000) demonstrate the importance of coherence in a PDP in order to support teacher learning. Both of these studies concluded that teachers who experienced a coherent program, along with other factors, were more likely to improve their instruction.

The support for creating coherency in teacher learning has continued over the years. In one study, attention to coherence was important within the PDP and between the PDP and preservice coursework. In a small-scale study of beginning U.S. science teachers, Roehrig and Luft (2006) followed 16 secondary science teachers from a preservice program into their first years of teaching. They found that when a coherent focus on reform-based instruction existed between a teacher's preservice program and induction support program, the new teachers were likely to enact reform-based instruction in their classrooms.

Content knowledge is an important component of a PDP. Over time, there has been a notable shift in the importance of content knowledge in a PDP. Early PDPs focused on helping teachers learn scientific processes or general instructional practices. More recent studies by Garet and colleagues (2001) and Supovitz and Turner (2000) reinforce the importance of science content knowledge in PDPs for science teachers. Supovitz and Turner (2000) even suggested that the content knowledge of a teacher

was a powerful predictor of the use of investigation-oriented instruction.

Capps and colleagues (2012), in an empirical review of inquiry PDPs, also concluded that content knowledge should be a core feature in PDP design. They further suggested that a focus within the PDP on the content knowledge that a teacher will need to teach or the content knowledge the student should learn enhances the content knowledge of a science teacher. In their review, they included the nature of science and science as inquiry as separate forms of content knowledge.

Summary. These four areas should guide the planning and enactment of PDPs: (1) incorporating adequate support for teacher change, (2) opportunities for collaboration, (3) a coherent program, and (4) a focus on content knowledge. For those involved in the research of PDPs, these areas should not be the focus of a study. However, carefully reasoned and supported explorations into the nuances within these areas may be fruitful.

Examining the Research in Science Teacher PDPs

In the examination of PDP studies in science, four organizing components emerged: policy, PDPs, teachers, and students. Policy includes federal, regional, state, local, and school policies and standards that help determine the quantity and quality of the PDPs. PDPs include, among other areas, those who offer the program, the process within the program, and the content within the program. Teachers are the participants in the programs, with most research examining teacher learning, teacher change, or teacher practice. Students are the ultimate beneficiaries of any PDP for teachers, and student learning outcomes are an important measure of success. Figure 44.1 is a graphical representation of the four organizing components, with the lines representing existing and potential research between them.

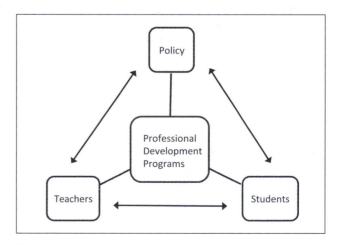

Figure 44.1 A model to guide the research on professional development programs for science teachers.

Policy, in the model, is an anchoring component and was found in several of the studies on PDPs. Often this orientation emphasizes student learning, since it is the intended outcome of science teachers engaged in PDPs. Policy documents from several countries articulate the need for science teachers to receive ample professional development opportunities in order to enhance and improve their instructional knowledge and practices (e.g., Eurydice, 2011; National Research Council, 2009). With additional learning opportunities, according to policy makers, science teachers will successfully prepare their students for the 21st century.

PDPs, in the model, refers to the content within the program, the context that supports and guides teacher learning, and the process that supports teacher development (National Staff Development Council, 2001). These elements are situated in a professional development process that generally includes setting goals, planning, enacting, looking at outcomes, and reflecting on the entire process (Loucks et al., 2010).

This is an important area of study, as the current state of science teacher PDPs can be improved across the globe. The access that teachers have to PDPs is currently uneven and the programs differ greatly in their structure (Darling-Hammond et al., 2009; Hendriks et al., 2010). Furthermore, science teachers participate in professional development activities in varying degrees. For example, in a survey of 3,000 science educators conducted by the U.S. National Science Teachers Association, a majority of science teachers reported having more opportunities for nonscience PDPs than they did for science PDPs (Luft, Wong, & Ortega, 2009). Additionally, an analysis of the 2007–2008 U.S. Schools and Staffing Survey data revealed that when science teachers did participate in PDPs, only 29% engaged in more than 33 hours (National Science Board, 2012).

Science teachers, in this model, are the beneficiaries of PDPs. They are professionals who have an extensive knowledge base of conceptions, beliefs, and practices that they bring to bear on the unique complexities of their daily work lives, a knowledge base that is shared within a professional community. They are also adult learners who have an interest in and control over the continuing development of their professional practice. As such, they come into PDPs with the intent of integrating their new learning into their practice in order to be more effective teachers of their students.

Students, who have equal importance to teachers in this model, are the ultimate recipients of science teacher PDPs. In some instances, student learning is mediated through their teachers, who are transforming their own learning into a revised teaching practice. In other instances, teacher and student learning are mutualistic and dependent upon each other. The position of teachers and student learning in a PDP is dependent upon the assumptions and design of the PDP.

Within the model there are different characterizations of the connections. For instance, between policy and PDPs, there is a directive or influential character. Policy with respect to science teacher education is about setting goals, creating incentives, providing resources, and establishing accountability measures. Illustrations of the influential or directive impact of policy are found in this chapter. The connections among PDPs, teachers, and students are characterized differently. In considering what it means to teach and learn science, there are different orientations toward the research, focusing on exploring how programs support the teaching and learning of science instruction and of science itself. Illustrations of different teaching and learning characterizations are also found in this chapter.

This model is important because it can guide the exploration of the components (policy, PDPs, teachers, students) and of the connections between them. In following this model, all research on PDPs should address two or more of these components, which should be evident in the research report. By acknowledging components, researchers will gain greater clarity into which lines of research have developed over time and thus contribute to our fund of knowledge. For instance, with extensive research in an identified area, researchers may realize the need to conduct synthesis studies. Additionally, by clearly emphasizing what type of research exists in science teacher PDPs, researchers will be able to identify the research questions that need to be pursued in order to contribute to the field.

This model will be used to guide the discussion of research conducted over the last 10 years in the area of science teacher PDPs.

Components: Policy, PDPs, and Teachers

Few studies explore the connection among policy, PDPs, and teachers. However, a study by Penuel, Fishman, Yamaguchi, and Gallagher (2007) recognized policy makers' concerns about the effectiveness of government- or state-funded PDPs. In this study, more than 450 teachers participated in a 2-year PDP at 28 different locations in the U.S. The authors wanted to identify the types of professional development activities associated with increased program implementation and to determine if teacher knowledge and practices improved with PDP participation and if the follow-up component of a PDP influenced teacher knowledge and practice. Data in the study were drawn from the existing database of a large-scale project in the U.S. consisting of self-reported data by the teachers and information from the different school sites.

When the quantitative data analysis was completed, the authors concluded that the success of the PDP depended upon how the program was structured and implemented by the coordinators. That is, the PDP had a significant impact on the teachers when there was an alignment with state, regional, or national standards and the school curriculum. In addition to this finding, they also reported that the program made a significant impact on the teachers when there was a threshold amount of time, a focus on content and science as inquiry, and opportunities for collective participation and reform-like experiences. Penuel and colleagues (2007) also named important factors that contributed to the implementation of the program by the teachers, including professional development opportunities after the initial session, classroom supplies, and technological support. Policy implications enter the discussion when the authors call for more studies in this area, which would require government funding.

Summary. Studies that recognize the relationship among policy, PDPs, and teachers have the potential to explore the impact of policy on teachers. In Penuel and colleagues (2007), the program was aligned with policy goals and their research shed light on how to better support teacher learning through PDPs. They pointed out the boundary between policy and school culture and how it can influence teachers involved in a PDP. This study also reinforced previous findings about how the structure and enactment of PDPs affect teacher learning.

Studies that link policy, PDPs, and teachers are most often carried out at several locations. The unique nature of a multisite study (scale-up program) allows for a general understanding of program structure in relationship to teacher learning. However, there are limitations to what can be learned in a scale-up setting, as site-specific program configurations can impact the fidelity of implementation. In addition, when considering science teachers, the focus of PDPs in this review, the unique nature of science knowledge may not be amenable to a generalized implementation in different sites. In exploring this connection, we need to examine the programs enacted at the different sites, as well as the representation and learning of content knowledge. These types of studies will reveal the promise and constraints of scaling up PDPs for science teacher learning and can potentially provide guidance to policy makers.

Components: Policy, PDPs, and Students

In the last few years, there has been an increase in the amount of research that connects policy, PDPs, and students. These types of studies often link student achievement to the process of professional development, with the goal of discussing policy implications (e.g., Geier et al., 2008; Lee, Deaktor, Enders, & Lambert, 2008; Pruitt & Wallace, 2012). In 2008, for example, Geier and colleagues (2008) reported on student achievement in an urban district as a result of a districtwide PDP that was aligned with the project-based inquiry model in the district curriculum. This research project responded to the No Child Left Behind Act of 2001, a national policy in the U.S. that mandates the testing of students in order to ensure accountability in different content areas. Often, students in urban areas or students who are linguistically and culturally diverse do not perform at the level of their nonurban and nondiverse peers on state tests. Geier and colleagues (2008) sought to study the effectiveness of a coherent professional development and curriculum program on roughly 5,000 middle school students in an urban area. The results of this study, which uses state science test scores as the assessment, revealed that students

whose teachers were involved in the districtwide PDP had significant standardized test gains when compared to students of teachers not involved in the program. In their conclusion, the authors make policy recommendations about the alignment of best practices in professional development and curriculum in order to achieve better results on state assessments.

Lee and colleagues (2008) completed a similar study to that of Geier and colleagues (2008) but instead focused on linguistically and culturally diverse students in the U.S. In their study, third-, fourth-, and fifth-grade teachers in 6 elementary schools participated in a multiyear PDP that focused on cultivating inquiry instruction and positive beliefs about science and literacy among diverse students. This was completed by coordinating district curriculum use with a PDP. The study itself focused on how the students of the teachers performed on a researcher-created science test over 3 years. The quantitative analysis of data from this study revealed that *all* students had significant gains at the end of 3 years but that third-grade students demonstrated the largest gains. In conclusion, the authors offered general suggestions related to conducting research in the midst of accountability policy.

More recently, Lara-Alecio and colleagues (2012) focused on the effect of a PDP on middle school English language learners' (ELLs') knowledge of science and English language literacy. The policy component of this study is related to the increase in ELLs in science classrooms in the U.S. and the need to make science instruction conducive to the learning of ELLs. Their study used a randomized experiment with state science and language assessments, while the professional development component focused on having teachers integrate language and science instruction. They found a significant and positive effect of the PDP on ELLs. At the conclusion of their article, they offer specific suggestions to policy makers about the amount of time needed to support language development and the importance of integrating science and literacy instruction to support the learning of ELLs.

Pruitt and Wallace (2012), in a more state policy–focused study, examined how a state-required mentoring program for science teachers improved student achievement. The mentoring program in this study was for new teachers at low-performing schools and was sponsored by a U.S. state education agency. The authors wanted to know if the students of teachers with mentors had improved their test performance and graduation rates. The results from the study revealed that overall there was no significant difference between students whose teachers did or did not participate in mentoring programs. When the data were further examined, however, some of the lowest-achieving schools had reached parity with mainstream schools. At the conclusion of the study, the authors offered recommendations for policy makers, including better research on practices associated with state-level programs, and they suggested broad guidelines for the structure of the mentoring program.

Summary. These studies reveal the different types of policy that can influence PDPs, with the goal of improving student learning. While all of these enacted studies were influenced by a national policy, they also were influenced by policies on local curriculum and local policies about expected outcomes. The nested nature of policy in these studies may be unique to countries that do not have nationalized curricula. However, in countries with national curricula, other nested policies may impact the design of PDPs that strive to promote student learning. In this area of research, we should consider the nested nature of policies and their impact on student learning.

Future investigations that link policy, PDPs, and students should provide ample detail about each component. The policies, the program design, and the student outcomes should all be adequately described. The added detail will help characterize the connection among these components. For instance, additional detail could result in a better understanding of the transformation of a policy into a PDP, or information could be gleaned about how the PDP structure impacts student learning.

Among these components, there are several areas worth further investigation. For instance, metrics assessing student learning could be used that emphasize the logic and reasoning in a science field, as well as conceptual understanding. Future studies could also explore the retention or transfer of student knowledge or abilities (a result of the PDP) as they move on to different grade levels or different courses. Furthermore, future studies could look at students across different grades in order to help build knowledge about student learning over time, in the context of teachers who are active in PDPs.

Components: Policy, PDPs, Teachers, and Students

Studies that bridged all four components—policy, PDPs, teachers, and students—were difficult to find for this review. One such study, by Ostermeier, Prenzel, and Duit (2010), could be viewed as having a national and international policy orientation, as the study encompassed a national response to the results of an international assessment. Their research looks at a PDP that was created after German students earned a low ranking on the Third International Mathematics and Science Study (TIMSS). After the PDP had been in place for a few years, teachers and students were studied in order to determine teacher and student improvement and involvement in science.

The data from the teachers and students in the PDP were compared to a representative sample of German schools tested in Program for International Student Assessment (PISA), a later study with a different sample pool than TIMSS. The research report of Ostermeier and colleagues (2010) discussed how teachers engaged in the PDP, the type of support the teachers wanted, the products and understandings of the teachers as a result of the program, and the learning of the students. After analyzing the data, they concluded that professional development was

important for teachers and students and that there was a need to conduct research on large-scale PDPs. The authors recommended the program as a model for improving science education in Europe. This conclusion, along with the purpose of the study, places this study in the realm of national and international policy.

Summary. Among the policy-oriented studies, this study has a unique design and orientation toward PISA and TIMSS. By discussing and evaluating the different components of the professional development process, this study is able to provide a new perspective—one that accounts for policy, teachers, and students. Ostermeier and colleagues (2010) reinforce the idea that PDPs are essential in improving classroom instruction. They also present a problem-oriented model program that can be used in different countries. The level of detail they provide about the program further contributes to an international discussion about preparing scientifically oriented citizens. This study provides guidance to those interested in professional development research or evaluation on how to contribute to the international discussion about professional development while examining the impact of a large-scale program.

The constraint associated with this type of study, however, pertains to the sheer amount of data needed in order to suggest consistency and coherence from the program to the teacher to the students. Furthermore, the collected data need to align between areas and should be comprehensive enough to allow for the appropriate connections. Although this is a difficult and ambitious type of study, it has potential to move the field of professional development forward on multiple levels. Developing ways to present these types of studies in a concise yet comprehensive manner will certainly be a formidable task for those engaged in this type of work.

Components: PDPs and Teachers

The majority of research in the field of science teacher professional development focuses on aspects of PDPs and their impact on teachers. Studies in this domain explore the structure of the PDP, the practices used within the PDPs, and the change in science teacher knowledge or practice as a result of the program. Often these studies connect the program process to teacher learning, with the intention of clarifying the connection of teacher learning and PDPs. In reviewing studies in this area, it was not uncommon for studies to straddle different topics, such as PDP strategies, teacher knowledge, or teacher instructional practice.

The research articles in this section are grouped according to focus, or the area most salient in the study. After a discussion of each group of studies, a summary emphasizes current and future directions. In this way, emerging and potential areas of research can be addressed that encompass PDPs and teachers.

PDPs, science teachers, and school culture. It is frequently noted that the culture of a school has more influence than a

PDP does on a teacher. This is often discussed in the conclusion of a PDP study, as school culture is rarely the direct object of study in PDP research. Khourey-Bowers, Dinko, and Hart (2005), however, present one of the few studies to explore U.S. school culture in the midst of a PDP. They examined the beliefs and practices of secondary science teachers engaged in the second year of a 5-year PDP. The program created school district cohorts as a way to support the change and growth of the teachers within schools. To document the change among the 216 teachers, the authors designed a quantitative study that used (a) surveys that captured the perceptions of the teacher leaders and the teacher groups about their participation, (b) reputable questionnaires that captured the teachers' demographics, beliefs, attitudes, practices, and community involvement, and (c) recognized observational protocols to document the quality of classroom instruction. They ultimately found that creating learning communities within schools supported change in teachers' beliefs, practices, and knowledge and that it helped to foster a more collegial learning community.

PDPs and e-learning. An emerging area of research is the use of technology within PDPs. Research in this area explores how PDPs can be offered using various e-learning innovations. These studies range from examinations of the use of online learning programs to teachers blogging in learning communities.

An example of a study that examined online learning can be found in the work of Harlen and Doubler (2004). Harlen is from the United Kingdom, while Doubler is from the U.S. They conducted a 2-year study about teacher learning of inquiry in an online program and on-campus program. Using a collection of pre- and post-program interviews, reports of classroom practice, lesson plans, and a time log, they descriptively and qualitatively analyzed the data in order to understand the experiences of the teachers in both programs. Their 2-year study with elementary and middle school teachers revealed the advantages and disadvantages of the online environment to support teacher learning. Overall, they found the online environment to be supportive of reflection, yet they suggested that more support in the form of written communication may be needed.

Counter to Harlen and Doubler's (2004) findings are Elster's (2010) findings about teachers involved in online learning communities. In Elster's (2010) study, biology teachers collaborated with researchers to improve their instruction of biology at several German school sites. The communities were configured to support teacher reflection and the instruction of the Biology in Context program. Extensive interviews with teachers and their students throughout the program revealed that the online system was best for collaboration, and it was less useful for instruction, learning, and reflection. However, similar to Harlen and Doubler (2004), Elster (2010) suggested that a hybrid learning system may be more supportive of teacher learning.

In an examination of different learning environments, Annetta and Shymansky (2008) explored the attitudes of U.S. elementary school teachers as they engaged in different distance education configurations of a PDP. One configuration used live, interactive television in which a presenter broadcasted to up to eight remote sites of teachers. Another configuration used video tapes of the live session and a facilitator-led discussion with remote sites of teachers. The final configuration allowed for individuals to stream the video of the live session and then discuss the video with other teachers through a discussion board. The teachers in this group had 1 week to view the video and interact in the discussion board. A survey of participating elementary teachers revealed that the type of delivery mechanism played an important role in their attitudes toward the program, with the teachers in the live setting reporting much greater interaction than the other groups. The Web-based group reported the least amount of interaction. They concluded from their quantitative analysis that the live programs best supported the teachers, but they added that teacher experience in the use of technology may have been a factor in this result.

In a unique study on blogging, Luehmann and Tinelli (2012) explored how 15 secondary science teachers built a student-centered, inquiry identity over a year. These teachers enrolled in a year-long course offered at U.S. university that was focused on curricular reform in science education. In addition to meeting in person, the teachers were required to maintain a personal and professional blog. They had to post at least 28 times, with only 4 assigned post topics. The blogs and a survey were collected from the teachers. Luehmann and Tinelli (2012) qualitatively examined the blogs and the responses of the teachers to open-ended questions and a survey. They found that blogging offered unique opportunities to the science teachers and could support their professional learning to varying degrees. However, they suggested that consideration be given to the composition of the group involved in the blogging community.

PDPs and early-career teachers. Most professional development studies involve groups of teachers specifically targeted by the PDP. In the design and development of such programs, early career content specialists are often overlooked. One mixed-methods study by Luft and colleagues (2011) focused on newly qualified U.S. secondary science teachers. More than 100 first-year teachers participated in one of four different induction programs. Two of the induction programs focused on providing science-specific induction support, while the other two programs had limited opportunities for science teachers to improve their instructional practice and knowledge. After their first year, the teachers in the science-specific induction programs enacted more inquiry-based lessons and held views more consistent with student-centered instruction. However, by the second year, school culture was more prevalent in the lives of the newly qualified science teachers and constrained the reform-based orientations of the teachers in the science induction program. Only some of the instructional approaches persisted in the teachers receiving science-specific support. This study revealed that science-specific induction programs may provide reform-based instructional support to teachers in different school settings in their first year, which may last into the second year of teaching.

PDPs to support teacher leadership.   A new form of research in the area of professional development explores how teachers learn to become leaders in their fields. There are two studies in this area, and each explores the formation of leadership skills through a PDP in different ways. The study by Hofstein, Carmeli, and Shore (2004) followed 18 chemistry coordinators in Israel as they developed their leadership abilities at their school, as well as their content and pedagogical knowledge. The goal of the program was multifaceted, but it targeted school-based leaders with the intention of changing the teaching of science at the school level. During the program, the chemistry coordinators had opportunities to adapt and design classroom lessons and units, create assessments, and prepare and present on topics relevant to the school site. Both qualitative and quantitative data were collected. These data sources revealed that the teachers recognized their new roles, adopted new leadership and team management skills, and were able to carry out some of the envisioned leadership activities.

Howe and Stubbs (2003) examined how individual science teachers developed into leaders. In their study, they followed three experienced U.S. middle school science teachers as they participated in a PDP that was designed to build leadership capacity. Interviews, observations, and documents were the data sources for the three case studies. These data were examined within a model of teacher leadership in order to understand the process of development among the teachers. The analyzed data revealed how the teachers evolved as leaders and what constrained or supported their development. All of the teachers identified key components that were important in their development as leaders: mutual respect between teachers and scientists, opportunities for teachers to assume leadership, the development of a community of practice, and challenging tasks. Howe and Stubbs (2003) ultimately suggested that in order for teachers to have access to these new roles, schools need to consider how to remove organizational constraints that limit opportunities to learn and practice leadership skills.

Teacher change in PDPs.   Studies in this area examine different models that explain how science teachers change as they are involved in a PDP, or they determine which factors support teacher change during a PDP. Ebert and Crippen (2010), for instance, evaluated a model of belief change that allowed for both the prediction and assessment of teacher change. The model had a conceptual change orientation and was originally used in the area of mathematics. Three high school biology teachers involved in a long-term PDP in the U.S. were the subjects

in the study. In order to determine the adequacy of the model, the authors created case studies from observational and instructional data of the subjects. At the conclusion of the study, the authors felt their proposed cognitive affective model of conceptual change accurately described the change process of the three teachers. The implications of this study may be useful for those involved in PDPs. However, given the small sample size, further research is needed to examine the adequacy of the model.

In a study on teacher change, Freeman, Marx, and Cimellaro (2004) sought to identify factors that are important in successful PDPs. Questionnaires, reflections, and focus group interviews were collected from more than 50 U.S. science teachers. These data were qualitatively analyzed in order to determine what factors supported teachers during a problem-based PDP. Their data revealed that teachers needed to be both physically and psychologically comfortable, teachers' prior experience with technology determined how technology was used, and the program needed to have a balance between formal instruction and informal interactions. The authors concluded that these factors should be taken into account when designing PDPs in order to support teacher change.

PDP strategies and teacher learning.   Several studies focus on the various strategies that exist within PDPs (e.g., Dori & Herscovitz, 2005; van der Valk & de Jong, 2009). These studies look at specific ways in which a PDP in science supports teacher learning, the building of teacher knowledge, or the enactment of various instructional practices by a teacher. Dori and Herscovitz (2005) explored how a 3-year case-based PDP in Israel influenced the instruction and development of the participating middle school science teachers. The cases integrated into the program often posed problems and that dealt with social issues. The authors collected both qualitative and quantitative data as the teachers engaged in case discussions and as teachers created cases to use with their students. In analyzing the data, Dori and Herscovitz (2005) concluded that the teachers implemented the case discussion strategies in their classrooms because they became active learners and designers in the PDP.

The Dutch team of van der Valk and de Jong (2009) examined a year-long PDP that focused on scaffolding to support the use of open inquiry among secondary science teachers. Over the course of a year, seven teachers experienced scaffolding techniques as they designed, discussed, and implemented scaffolding tools in their classrooms. Both qualitative and quantitative data were collected and analyzed in this multimethod study. The results indicated that the scaffolding tools allowed the teachers to utilize more inquiry instruction with their students. The authors concluded that a scaffolding orientation for teachers was as important as scaffolding for students.

Falik, Eylon, and Rosenfeld (2008), of Israel, also explored a long-term PDP that supported the use of problem-based learning. Closed- and open-response questionnaires were collected from novice and experienced teachers. From the quantitative and qualitative analysis, the authors found support for their PDP model. They also gained an understanding of how the school, teacher, and students influenced the teachers as they engaged in the PDP. Their discussion of these areas reinforced the role of context in supporting teacher change.

PDPs, curriculum, and teachers. Supporting teachers in their use of curriculum is an ongoing focus for those who conduct PDPs and study teachers. Stolk, De Jong, Bulte, and Pilot (2011), for example, explored how to support chemistry teachers in the Netherlands to use context-based curriculum. In their PDP, teachers enacted a context-based unit with their students and then designed a new context-based unit to use in their classes. Six teachers were involved in this study, and the data consisted of documents from the program and observations. All of the teachers found the first curriculum unit useful in terms of understanding context-based curriculum. However, when it came to designing a new unit, the teachers faced several constraints and struggled with enacting a context-based unit. The authors concluded that more support was needed to develop and enact the advocated context-based curriculum.

In a different view of the implementation, Jeanpierre, Oberhauser, and Freeman (2005) examined how an inquiry-based curriculum was utilized in the classrooms of teachers participating in a PDP. In the program, teachers were immersed in an inquiry experience that involved monarch butterflies in the U.S. The teachers worked closely with scientists on all aspects of data collection and analysis pertaining to the breeding or migration of the monarch butterflies. An analysis of observations and interviews from the PDP revealed that almost all of the teachers in the PDP did incorporate some aspect of monarch ecology into their classroom; however, the use of inquiry practices that were embedded in the program did not transfer readily to the classroom. In this study, certain parts of the curriculum were enacted in the classroom, yet the authentic science experiences that the teachers had did not transfer to the classroom.

Instructional practices as a result of PDPs. An important outcome of PDPs is the science teacher's classroom instructional practice. Studies that explore the instruction of science teachers as a result of a PDP often examine mediating factors such as beliefs or self-efficacy. Mediating factors are those factors that relate to enhanced instructional practice. Johnson (2007), for instance, explored how a 2-year PDP in the U.S. made an impact on the instruction of 6 middle school science teachers. Data included observations and interviews of the science teachers while they were involved in either a 1- or 2-year PDP. Johnson (2007) concluded that the teachers were able to implement standards-based instruction, yet each teacher implemented the instruction differently and the beliefs of

the teacher contributed to the implemented instruction. An additional finding of this study was the important role of the school environment in terms of supporting a teacher's use of the instructional strategies emphasized in the PDP.

Scherz, Bialer, and Eylon (2008), of Israel, presented a unique perspective on the relationship between professional development and the teacher. In their study, they used evidence-based portfolios created by teachers in order to assess their levels of practice related to the implementation of science skills. The teachers in this study had some experience in using science skills in the classroom. The PDP was designed to support their ongoing use of these skills. From the collected data found in the portfolios, the authors identified an implementation progression of science skills related to instruction. They suggested using this information to design a better program, thereby "customizing" the professional development experience.

Huffman (2006) explored how 13 physics teachers in the U.S. used new pedagogical approaches in their science classrooms as a result of a PDP. Three groups of teachers were examined: experienced users of the new pedagogy, beginning users of the new pedagogy, and a group of comparison teachers who used traditional instructional methods. Qualitative and quantitative results suggested that the PDP increased the teachers' use of experiments with students and alternative assessment methods. Huffman (2006), however, also found it was more difficult for teachers to increase their use of constructivist discussion methods and discussion regarding the nature of scientific inquiry.

In a unique study of practices and beliefs, Lavonen, Jauhiainen, Koponen, and Kurki-Suonio (2004) created a PDP to support physics teachers' use of experiments. The 98 Finnish teachers in this study participated in an 18-month PDP that engaged them in physics experiments. Throughout the program, the teachers were prompted to consider the important role of experiments in physics in order to challenge their beliefs about using experiments. Survey data and emails were analyzed to determine if the beliefs of the teachers changed, along with their use of experiments. From the data, there was not a significant change in either the beliefs of the teachers or their use of experiments. The study by Lavonen and colleagues (2004) reveals the importance of specifically targeting beliefs and practices in order to impact the practice of teachers.

PDPs and teacher self-efficacy. Monitoring the change of science teachers' self-efficacy has been a long-standing area of interest among researchers in professional development. Self-efficacy has often been considered essential in the instructional practices promoted by PDPs. That is, without good self-efficacy, important instructional practices will not be adopted by a science teacher. In the studies in examined in this review, self-efficacy was often monitored through the Science Teaching Efficacy Belief Instrument (STEBI; Enochs & Riggs, 1990). The STEBI is a 23-item instrument that uses a rating scale from strongly agree to strongly disagree, and is developed for elementary teachers.

Palmer (2011) studied the self-efficacy of 12 Australian elementary teachers who participated in a PDP. Data were collected through interviews and the STEBI prior to, during, after, and 2 years after the program. The data were analyzed in order to understand the improvement of the teachers' self-efficacy. The author concluded that the teachers' self-efficacy improved as they engaged in a PDP that targeted his/her perceived ability to teach science. In addition, the self-efficacy improved as teachers were provided feedback about their teaching.

In another study using the STEBI, Lakshmanan, Heath, Perlmutter, and Elder (2011) explored how PLCs supported teacher self-efficacy. In addition to the STEBI, data were also collected through observations of practice. In this study, the self-efficacy of the elementary and middle school U.S. teachers did not significantly increase by the end of the program. However, teachers with higher self-efficacy tended to use practices advocated by the PDP, while teachers with lower self-efficacy struggled to adopt the practices advocated by the PDP. The authors concluded that those conducting PDPs needed to take into account the self-efficacy of teachers.

Teacher knowledge and PDPs.   The development of teacher knowledge has been a long-standing area of interest to those involved in PDP research. Studies in this area focus on the knowledge that teachers develop as a result of a PDP. This knowledge can be as specific as improving teachers' understanding of the nature of science, content knowledge, or pedagogical content knowledge or as broad as improving the knowledge of science teachers in general.

In the content area of the nature of science (NoS), Posnanski (2010) and Akerson, Cullen, and Hanson (2009) have explored how U.S. elementary teachers improved their understanding of the NoS in the midst of a PDP. Both of these studies used the Views of the Nature of Science questionnaire (VNOS; Lederman, Abd-El-Khalick, Bell, & Schwartz, 2002) in order to monitor how the teachers changed their understanding of NoS. Posnanski (2010) administered the VNOS before and after the PDP and collected additional interviews and observational data. The analysis of data revealed that an explicit focus on the teaching of NoS in the PDP did improve the knowledge of the participating teachers. Similarly, Akerson and colleagues (2009) concluded that PDPs that incorporated opportunities for teachers to learn in communities did improve the teachers' understanding of NoS.

In a unique PDP in Australia, Berry, Loughran, Smith, and Lindsay (2009) developed a program in which teachers worked with academics over the course of a year as teacher researchers. As the teachers and researchers worked together, they contemplated the professional knowledge of the teachers. This PDP focused on understanding the knowledge of the teachers, as well as finding ways in which to capture the tacit knowledge of a science teacher. Through the use of cases, the authors were able to document how teachers improved their professional knowledge. In looking at the data from the teachers, Berry and colleagues (2009) concluded that the cases provided a venue in which to improve the professional knowledge of the participating teachers.

In a more targeted approach to develop knowledge, Bertram and Loughran (2012) used explicit discussion of content knowledge and pedagogical decisions in order to enhance the pedagogical content knowledge of teachers. Their study reported on 6 teachers in Australia who participated in a program for 2 years that involved explicit discussions between teachers and educational researchers. The teachers also participated in interviews during the PDP, and they provided various documents associated with the program. The analyzed data revealed that the teachers found value in focusing on content knowledge and instruction, and they improved in certain areas of their pedagogical content knowledge. However, the science teachers were hesitant to adopt the process of explicit discussions in their practice due to limitations of time.

Seeking to build science teachers' metastrategic knowledge, Zohar (2006) created a PDP in Israel that met for 56 hours over 6 months. The program had three phases. In the first phase, the 14 junior high and high school science teachers learned about thinking skills in science and were asked to develop higher-order thinking-skill tasks for the students in their classes. In the second and third phases, the teachers implemented their developed higher-order thinking tasks. Interviews, observations, and artifacts were collected from teachers throughout the program and analyzed qualitatively in order to understand changes in their use of metastrategic knowledge. The results of the analysis revealed that the teachers were able to develop their metastrategic knowledge, but only about a third of the teachers could consistently use the instructional practices associated with metastrategic knowledge in their classrooms. Zohar (2006) concluded that the teachers had variable forms of metastrategic knowledge, which in turn affected the implementation of higher-order thinking-skill tasks.

Conceptions are similar to knowledge, and Lotter, Harwood, and Bonner's (2007) research revealed the importance of conceptions of inquiry when teachers learned to use the inquiry strategies promoted in a PDP. Their study followed 3 U.S. secondary science teachers as they participated in a PDP that involved working with their peers and students and testing their own lesson plans. Observations and interviews were used to document the teachers' conceptions of inquiry. An analysis of the data showed how different conceptions of inquiry influenced the teachers' use of reform-based instruction. The authors concluded that the teachers' conceptions of inquiry interacted with their professional development experience, which resulted in each teacher enacting reform-based instruction in a different way with their classes.

An area that has gained more attention in the last few years is argumentation. Simon and Johnson (2008), of the

United Kingdom, developed a PDP that helped teachers build their abilities to support argumentation in the classroom. In this study, they had teachers create portfolios in order to help teachers apply their learning, to document the evidence regarding their learning, and to facilitate a reflective analysis of learning to use argumentation. The portfolios of just two teachers who participated in their PDP formed the basis of this study. By examining the portfolios, Simon and Johnson (2008) found that the portfolio process was a positive experience for these teachers as they developed their skills of supporting argumentation among their students. The authors concluded, however, that portfolios were difficult and time consuming for some teachers and that the portfolios may not be the best way to support the development of knowledge pertaining to argumentation.

PDP scientists and science teachers. PDPs in science education can involve scientists as well as science educators. The research shows that for a variety of reasons, scientists have mixed success in working with teachers. Drayton and Falk (2006), for instance, worked with more than 20 teams consisting of an ecologist (scientist) and teachers in the U.S. Over the course of 1 year, teachers and scientists worked closely together in order to learn about ecological research and inquiry in science. The goal of the partnership was to have teachers build a partnership with an ecologist rather than classroom applications. The authors collected questionnaires and portfolios from the team members. They descriptively and qualitatively analyzed the data on the teams throughout the project. Findings were based on the entire group, along with selected case studies. The authors concluded that there were uneven collaborations between the teams; only some of the teams were productive and focused on learning inquiry in an ecological setting. They attributed the uneven collaborations to several factors, including the scientists' knowledge of classroom realities and content, different professional cultures between the scientists and teachers, and perceived power and status of scientists by teachers.

Similarly, Hughes, Molyneaux, and Dixon (2012) conducted a qualitative study of 3 teachers working with scientists in a U.S.-based Research Experience for Teachers program. This 6-week program was designed to allow teachers to work with scientists in the morning and then in teacher cohorts in the afternoon. Scientists volunteered to work with teachers. The data collection in this study consisted of interviews with teachers, observations of teachers in laboratories, written learning evaluations of teachers by scientists, and postprogram classroom observations and interviews with teachers. These data were crafted into cases. They found that teachers enjoyed several benefits as they worked closely with scientists over a year. The teachers improved their understanding of inquiry, felt they were part of a community, and received valuable information from the scientists. The authors, however, stated that the

mentoring style of the scientist did make a difference in the learning of the teacher and how the information gained was translated to the students of the teacher.

In looking at the knowledge and skills of scientists in PDPs, there is evidence that scientists struggle to communicate about science to science teachers. Schuster and Carlsen (2009), for instance, studied science doctoral students in the U.S. who worked with teachers over the course of the 5 days. The topics of the different programs consisted of astronomy, meteorology, microbiology, astrobiology, and materials science. The data sources in this study were comprised of observations of the workshops and interviews with instructors and participants. The analysis of the data was done qualitatively and revealed the scientists' pedagogical orientations. Shuster and Carlsen (2009) reported that research scientists were limited in their abilities to translate practices in science into learning experiences for science teachers.

Similarly, Bell and Odom (2012) explored how education and science professors and a science educator engaged in a PDP targeting middle level teachers. The PDP was held at a U.S. university, lasted 2 weeks, and was focused on inquiry-based science. The program was collaboratively planned among the professors. Using inquiry-based instruction, they took turns in leading different lessons. The data sources consisted of observations and interviews, which were analyzed qualitatively. The results of the analysis revealed that professors valued reform-based instruction but did not enact this type of instruction consistently. Furthermore, the professors' views about their field and the teachers colored their presentation of the program content.

Summary. The research that connects PDPs and teachers is quite diverse. Some researchers emphasize a program's structure, while others may prioritize how a teacher's knowledge, beliefs, and practices develop over time in response to particular strategies. Capturing the professional learning of teachers in the midst of PDPs and exploring the impact of different program formats is, however, a changing research emphasis.

In terms of different formats, PDP providers now utilize different approaches and venues in which to support science teacher learning. A rapidly expanding orientation is toward e-learning opportunities. Within the e-learning community, hybrid models of professional development appear to have promise. The opportunity for communication in an e-learning community can be purposeful for some teachers, but there is an ongoing need of teachers to connect in person with each other.

Another emerging area has science teachers involved in the design and enactment of their own PDPs in order to support their learning. One way to involve teachers entails embedding the PDP in their daily work and utilizing their daily experiences in order to modify the program. Another approach is to have teachers collaborate with PDP directors in order to support their own learning of the advocated strategies. When science teachers can guide their own professional development, they can better meet their own and their students' learning needs.

From these studies, it is also evident that there is an interaction between context and the outcomes of PDPs. For science teachers, a school context can encourage or inhibit the use of a desired PDP outcome. Principals, existing curriculum, and colleagues are just a few contextual factors that can thwart or support a science teacher's use of new instructional approaches or development as a teacher leader. It is important to attend to context when developing PDPs.

There is also evidence that PDPs must be strategically configured in order to build self-efficacy or target the beliefs, knowledge, or practices of science teachers. Achieving improved self-efficacy, inquiry-oriented beliefs, or the specific use of an instructional practice requires carefully planned PDPs that take into account the knowledge and learning experiences of the participating teachers. While there are different ways to support teacher learning in a PDP, it is important to monitor the learning of the teacher in terms of PDP goals. We should add, in designing carefully planned PDPs, Loucks-Horsley and colleagues' (2010) conceptualizations of different professional development approaches (Immersion in Content, Standards and Research, Examining Teaching and Learning, Aligning and Implementing Curriculum, and Professional Development Structures) and PDP design are still useful.

From this review, it is clear that the professional development process for a teacher is complex and that there is a need for a model to describe the teacher learning process

in the midst of professional development opportunities. We suggest one potential model that draws upon the work of Schwab (1978), Fenstermacher (1986), and others.

Within this model (see Figure 44.2), Schwab's (1978) four commonplaces of schooling—teaching, learning, subject matter, and context—are important. Teaching is ontologically related to learning and therefore without meaning in its absence (Fenstermacher, 1986). Subject matter is both syntactical and substantive (Gardner, 1972; Schwab, 1964). Context is guided by the physical and social environment in which teachers work (Schwab, 1978).

This model is based on the work of Borko (2004), Short (2006), and Lauffer and Lauffer (2009) and reveals the nested, complex nature of PDPs. There are three domains, which consist of relationships between teaching and learning within and between each domain. The *School* domain, influenced by Schwab (1978) and Fenstermacher (1986), focuses on work in classrooms. The *Professional Development* domain addresses the learning of the teacher. The third domain, *Leadership Development*, concentrates on preparing professional development specialists. Between the different participants there are interactions, and across all domains is the influence of content and context. There is certainly a need for research that explores teaching and learning in and between the different domains.

Figure 44.2 and this review of research reinforce the importance of the structure and process of PDPs and the learning and teaching of teachers. However, the varied

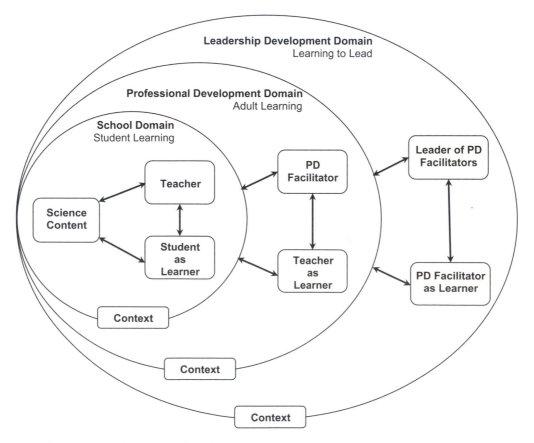

Figure 44.2 Teaching–learning domains in professional development.

nature of the studies that bridge PDPs and teachers do suggest more specific areas of research. Specific areas that are worthy of additional examination are:

- *Exploring different approaches to professional development that support teacher learning.* There should be well-reasoned approaches to professional development that support teacher learning. That is, teachers should have opportunities to learn in ways that transcend the traditional PDP designs. For instance, technology (as mentioned earlier) offers science teachers new ways to collaborate with their peers and it provides a new venue in which to learn about science. The potential of alternative PDP delivery systems that are responsive to the knowledge of teachers is unexplored. This is the next generation of PDPs for science teachers, and they have promise in providing personalized teacher learning.

- *Studying how teachers learn in the midst of PDPs.* Most studies provide pre- and postevent data pertaining to teachers in the professional development process. With the development of new PDPs, more will need to be done to understand how teachers learn as they are engaged in different learning opportunities. Current studies on teacher learning reveal a complex process that interacts with information, experiences, and students. Understanding how PDPs specifically support the process of teacher learning is essential research that will ultimately benefit science teachers.

- *Studying how teachers put their learning into practice.* Teachers take on different roles as they participate in different domains in Figure 44.2. A teacher who has the role of a *learner* in the professional development domain when he or she engages in a PDP takes on the role of a *science teacher* in the school domain. There is a need to explore how teachers engage in the complex process of connecting these two roles and understanding how they integrate their science teaching practice in the school domain while they learn in the professional development domain.

- *Examining how to support those who provide and engage in PDPs.* There is little research that studies those who work with teachers to facilitate their professional learning. These individuals have come from the ranks of scientists, teacher leaders, PDP coordinators, doctoral students, and science teachers. Research in this area could explore, for instance, how scientists build their knowledge to work with science teachers in different PDPs or how science coordinators guide teacher learning in the midst of PDPs. Understanding how to prepare and support those who work with science teachers is an important line of work to continue.

- *Exploring how teachers adapt or translate the curriculum or instructional approaches advocated in the PDP.* Most researchers document the change that teachers make as the result of a PDP and then report if the change made by teachers aligns with the goal of the program.

This simple model negates the complexity of learning and the knowledge of the teacher. Understanding how a teacher adapts curriculum or instructional approaches associated with the PDP is certainly a worthwhile area of study. This area will increase with importance as more learning opportunities are offered to teachers in the online environment and through programs that require shorter periods of involvement. With the knowledge of how curriculum or instructional approaches are adapted, all forms of PDPs could be modified in order to better support their translation into the classroom.

- *Understanding career-specific professional development.* Most PDPs focus on a group or cluster of teachers with different backgrounds and different years of experience. In these programs, they are learning to implement new curriculum, learning about a new instructional approach, or building specific practices, knowledge, or cognitive orientations. There is a significant need to understand how science teachers progress throughout their careers and how to support their development. Studies, for instance, could be conducted to understand how to better support early-career teachers, developing teacher leaders, or the unique professional needs of mid-career science teachers. The information that could be gained from such studies has the potential to result in PDPs that consider a professional progression of teacher opportunity and capacity.

Components: PDPs and Students

Research in this area explores how a PDP influences some aspect of student learning without explicitly considering the role of teachers. Cuevas, Lee, Hart, and Deaktor (2005), for example, studied how 25 elementary students of 7 teachers improved their inquiry abilities as their teachers participated in an inquiry-oriented PDP and used supporting curriculum. Initially, the PDP and curriculum materials were developed to support low-achieving, low-socioeconomic-status, and English-as-a-second-language students in the United States. The materials were provided to all teachers, and all teachers participated in 4 days of a PDP. Even though the program targeted specific students, the quantitative results of the study found that all students improved in their inquiry ability. The authors concluded, as have other researchers, that good instructional materials and professional development opportunities can improve student learning.

Venville and Dawson (2010) reported on the results of a short-term PDP in Australia that focused on improving students' ability to engage in argumentation about socioscientific issues in the area of genetics. In this case study, teachers participated in a short-term PDP that focused on improving students' skills in the use argumentation, informal reasoning, and conceptual understanding of science. After the short intervention, the teachers taught argumentation to their students during a class period. In the following class periods, students used their newly acquired skills. The quantitative results from this study indicated that the students of the teachers participating in the professional learning event significantly improved in their use of argumentation, informal reasoning, and conceptual understanding.

Summary. The ultimate intended outcome of any PDP is student learning. Studies that focus on PDPs and student learning outcomes can provide comprehensive views of student learning related to the goals of a PDP. In the studies in this section, student learning was assessed with different measures, which portrayed various ways in which students learned about science. By understanding how students learn science from measures outside of achievement scores, teachers engaged in and those directing PDPs can acquire a different understanding of the impact of a PDP on students. When data transcend standardized test measurements on student learning, the complex nature of student learning as a result of teacher professional development is revealed.

Two observations can be made about future studies in this area. First, studies that explore PDPs and student learning tend to provide limited information about the involvement and role of the teacher. This should be acknowledged by the authors when they disseminate their studies. Second, studies in this area should continue to look at the complex nature of student learning as a result of PDPs. Understanding how different aspects of a PDP can result in student learning will be important as new models of PDPs are studied and tested. In fact, it is likely that these studies are necessary before large-scale studies are conducted that involve policy, teachers, or students.

Components: PDPs, Teachers, and Students

An emerging area of study in PDPs connects PDPs, teachers, and students. Roth and colleagues (2011) studied how a coherent content story line and student thinking approach supported teacher and student learning. In their study, they divided more than 40 U.S. elementary teachers and their students into two groups: One group focused on student learning in the midst of the instructional goals of the lesson (coherent story line) and content knowledge, and one group focused on just content knowledge. Observational data were collected in addition to measures of content and pedagogical knowledge. The authors found that a PDP with a coherent study line and content knowledge instruction resulted in significant teacher and student gains, more than when there was just a focus on content knowledge. This quantitative study highlighted the importance of having teachers consider the overall instructional goals, along with student learning and the necessary content. The authors also concluded that connecting to the overall goals or storyline is something that is unique to PDPs.

Similarly, Heller, Daehler, Wong, Shinohara, and Miratrix (2012) explored how different professional development interventions influenced teacher and student outcomes. In this project, the authors compared the use of teaching cases, the examination of student work, and metacognitive analysis with a no-treatment control on more than 270 U.S. elementary teachers and 7,000 students. They used a random assignment process and developed instruments to measure teacher and student knowledge. They found that when teachers engaged in teaching cases and the examination of student work, their students improved in their accuracy and written justifications.

Research in this area also examines how PDPs can support the use of technological practices in the classroom. Gerard, Varma, Corliss, and Linn (2011), for instance, synthesized professional development research that explored the use of technology-enhanced practices in the science classroom and their effect on students' inquiry learning experiences. They concluded that teachers benefited most from long-term support and constructivist orientations when learning how to use technology-enhanced inquiry science in the classroom. Not surprisingly, they found that PDPs varied considerably in terms of how they supported science teachers in their use of technology.

Summary. These studies highlight major shifts in the design of PDPs. One shift recognizes the importance of incorporating an understanding of student thinking in the design of PDPs. Programs in this area illustrate important forms of research that consider the program configuration, the learning of the teacher about the content and about students, and the learning of the student. Another shift pertains to the inclusion of technology in the professional development enterprise. As technology becomes more ubiquitous in learning and teaching, there is a need to understand how PDPs with different forms of communication technology can support teacher and student learning. These are the most important shifts in PDP design for science teachers in the last 10 years.

As additional studies are conducted on PDPs and teacher and student learning, scholars should consider the fact that most of the research in this area has been done with elementary or middle school teachers and students. Secondary teachers and students have a different orientation toward science, and the very nature of their learning may be different than that of elementary or middle school teachers or students.

Another aspect of this research pertains to understanding the relationship of how teachers learn from their students, how students are learning, and how the PDP connects to the learning of both teacher and student. This type of research will help clarify how PDPs can be modified in order to respond to both teachers and students. In addition, this type of research can clarify how such programs can be configured in order optimize their impact on science teachers and students. This type of research moves the professional development community one step further in understanding and enacting personalized PDPs.

The Present and Future of Research in PDPs in Science

In this review, it is evident that there are enduring and emerging lines of research in the field of PDPs. Enduring lines of research, such as the change in teacher knowledge as a result of a PDP or the inclusion of an authentic science experience during a PDP, will continue to refine our knowledge in these areas. This will be done through new approaches to data collection and analysis and through ongoing contemplation of presented findings. Emerging lines of research, such as the use of e-learning approaches in PDPs or the connection of student and teacher learning, are the result of new tools that can be used to support learning and our changing knowledge base about learning. Exploring these areas will require the use of standardized and new approaches to research. Both enduring and emerging lines of research have the potential to impact the content, the context, and the process of PDPs.

In order to guide those who are involved in research on PDPs in science, there are several points to be made as a result of this review. Some points are more specific and target a unique problem that calls for investigation. The points have been listed throughout this review and are found in the summary sections. Other points are general and are meant to guide the field as a whole. These points are the result of a broader view of the research, and they are meant to orient researchers to potentially important areas of study. The following paragraphs will address these more general points.

First, we must be more strategic in our research endeavors. There are clearly some forms of research in the field that are no longer useful. For instance, there is no need for additional research that touts the importance of teachers working together, nor do we need research indicating the general success of PDPs. There are, however, areas of study within these topics that bear examination. For instance, it would be useful to know how teachers learn about a concept as they engage in a PDP and how specific strategies best support teacher learning and student learning. As PDP researchers move forward, they must clarify how the proposed research addresses some problem. In addition, those who review these studies must push researchers to move beyond "known conclusions."

In terms of looking at PDPs broadly, it will be important to understand the connections among policy, PDPs, teachers, and students. There are, of course, many ways to expand upon the connections. For instance, if the study is broad, attuned to national policy, and explores the learning of teachers, then the policy and the learning outcome should be clearly articulated as they pertain to teachers. If the study explores a more specific area, then an orienting statement should be provided that shares the connection and then the specific topic of study. For instance, a study that bridges PDPs and teachers should state this connection but also add that the study seeks to explore the construct of teacher knowledge in biology. By clearly stating connections, it will be easier to identify collections of studies that can be used in research syntheses.

When conducting studies that explore policy and PDPs with teachers and students or just teachers or students, researchers should consider the sample of students. Several of the policy-oriented studies targeted students in poverty or who were linguistically and culturally diverse. While these are important populations to study and populations deserving of our utmost attention, it is also important to consider the efficacy of the PDP among a variety of students, including those who are very young or those with disabilities. One immediate step, however, would be better descriptions of the student populations involved in the studies.

An enduring line of research exists with elementary teachers who are involved in PDPs. Over time, studies have focused on their efficacy to teach science, as well as building their knowledge and practices for teaching. In the upcoming years, middle-level science teachers and science faculty in higher education will be important populations to examine as they engage in PDPs. After all, it is these teachers who can initiate and cultivate an interest and passion in science. But with the shift to a more global scientific society (viewed through PISA and TIMSS), secondary science teachers will not only need deep content knowledge, they will also need to learn how to enact the emerging reforms that require socioscientific or integrated science approaches. Understanding how PDPs can better support secondary science teachers in the midst of these changes calls for essential research.

An emerging area of study in coming years will pertain to the incorporation of e-learning approaches into PDPs. Connecting these studies to the components of policy, teachers, or students will be a greater challenge, but essential. Within the studies reviewed in the chapter, the use of e-learning approaches to support teacher learning was preliminary. There is a need to explore how these environments can support teacher and student learning in new ways, and there is a need to consider how to maximize teacher learning through various e-learning opportunities. Even more elusive is the connection among policy, PDPs, and the e-learning environment. Understanding this connection will be essential. Clearly, this area of research has the most potential in the upcoming years to redefine the process of professional development.

Finally, the use of different research methods is an emerging area. To begin with, there is a need to conduct more synthesis studies of PDP research. Small-scale studies are essential; they provide important insights into aspects of PDPs. Synthesis studies, which examine sets of similarly oriented areas, can provide important information for those who are engaged in both the research and enactment of PDPs. However, one of the greatest challenges in crafting synthesis studies will be finding studies that have adequate methodological details.

There is also a need for additional comparison studies that explore aspects of PDPs. The studies should be used to understand how different PDP components contribute to teacher or student learning. Crafting these studies requires attention to various methodological decisions and a well-conceived theoretical and conceptual orientation about teacher learning.

Wicked Problems

Even with the plethora of research in professional development, there are problems that will haunt science education researchers for years. As these problems won't be solved quickly, they could be ignored by those involved in PDP research. However, these problems deserve the ongoing attention of the research community—which means tackling these problems in small steps. These are "wicked problems" (Rittel & Webber, 1973); the solutions are not easy, there may be multiple explanations, and the problem has a great deal of complexity. However, discussing and exploring these problems will provide opportunities to redefine how teachers experience PDPs. Wicked problems pertaining to PDPs for science teachers include:

- *Understanding the promise and pitfalls involved in scaling up PDPs.* Research in the field of PDPs should examine the reality of scaling up a program. When a small-scale PDP has produced promising results, there is often enthusiasm for expanding a program. This process of scaling up could mean reaching more teachers by broadening different grade levels, school districts, content topics, or teaching approaches. Doing so, however, raises various issues that can compromise the integrity and fidelity of the innovation that is being scaled up. Some of these issues include the need to work with nonvolunteer teachers, to increase the number of professional developers and their institutional homes, to work across different contexts, and to find the necessary financial and community resources to support scaling up. In other words, while the idea of scaling up is alluring and promising, its reality is unknown. The impact of context and the nature of teacher learning suggest that scaling up may be an elusive construct.

- *Understanding how to provide relevant information to policy makers and professional development specialists regarding PDPs.* It is important that research guide PDPs in science education. This occurs when research reaches professional development providers and those who make policy. Unfortunately, most research pertaining to PDPs in science rarely reaches these audiences. This may be attributed to the lack of desire of policy makers and professional development providers to acquire this research or the lack of clear suggestions offered by the research, or it may be that there are just too many articles to read. Bridging research to policy and practice is a persistent problem that certainly needs the attention of researchers. Solving this problem may require new forms of presenting and disseminating research, as well as working more closely with policy makers and professional development providers to understand their needs.

- *Understanding how to create high-impact PDPs that meet the needs of all teachers and all their students.*

With this knowledge, traditional configurations or orientations of PDPs would be challenged, and teacher and student learning would be enhanced. Pursuing research in this area may entail starting with teacher and student learning in science and working backward to consider the configuration of a PDP. Of course, it could also start with novel PDP formats and exploring the learning of teachers and then students. No matter how studies proceed, there is a great need to develop PDPs that can be rapidly personalized in order to maximize the learning of all teachers and their students. Characterizing the process of this program will usher in new models of PDPs, which may be shorter in duration, be diagnostic, or bypass or attend to school culture.

- *Understanding the boundaries of context associated with PDPs.* An enticing research problem in PDPs pertains to understanding the boundaries of context and how context can impact teacher learning. For instance, the context in which a teacher works is certainly important in terms of his/her instruction, yet collaborative and targeted professional development methods may override the impact of context. A political context can also affect the design and enactment of a PDP and result in different forms of teacher learning. Context is a broad construct that can range from national policy to the school or from the current value of science within a community to the very nature of science pursuits. By understanding the boundaries of context and teacher learning, we gain the potential to design PDPs that better support teacher learning in science.

- *Understanding the professional development process as it pertains to policy, the program, the teachers, and the students.* PDPs for science teachers have weak and strong connections to policy, teachers, and students. The strength of these connections depends upon the design and enactment of the program. Understanding the potential impact of each component upon the process of a program can ultimately guide those who are providing or studying PDPs. For instance, some policies may have more impact on potential PDPs than will the learning of science among students. Conversely, learning science in fundamentally new ways may have a potential impact on policy. These directions and magnitude of impact among these different connections are worth questioning and exploring.

Final Comments

Even though several different directions can be pursued by those involved in professional development research, it is clear that research reporting standards are needed in the area of PDP research. The standards that are proposed are in addition to accepted practices in reporting research. All studies in this area should still share, for instance, a theoretical orientation, a literature review, and description of the population of the participants in the study. There should also be clarifying details about the program under study.

Standards for research involving PDPs should include a clear statement about the orientation of the research as associated with the PDP. This would be, for example, a statement about the study connecting the components discussed previously, which would include policy, PDPs, teachers, or students. A specific statement might clarify that "this study looks at the connection of policy to PDPs to teachers" or that "the conducted research adds to studies in the PDP and teacher domain." By including this information, those who conduct syntheses of research in this field will also have a better understanding of the intention of the researchers.

Standards for research involving PDPs should also require clear statements about the PDP. They should include at least the amount of time teachers are engaged in the program, the credentials/background/experience of the instructors, the goals of the program, and the process and strategies used in the program. If appropriate, there should be a discussion about the unique aspects of the PDP.

Standards in professional development research should also include suggestions or implications that have some pragmatic value. The conclusions offered in a research report should not be limited to an audience of other researchers—especially when they relate to PDPs. Professional development providers could benefit from specific suggestions arising from the study data. Teachers could find information that would help them to identify programs best suited to their needs. While there are several target audiences, the information should be always be presented simply and within the bounds of the data in the study.

Clearly, these are initial standards for reporting PDP research. In the upcoming years, there may be more. But for now, these standards will increase the impact of research in this area.

Authors' Note

We would like to thank the reviewers of this chapter for their thoughtful comments. In addition, we appreciate all of the comments provided by those people who discussed this chapter with us during the writing process. We would also like to acknowledge the assistance of two graduate students at the University of Georgia: Celestin Ntemngwa in retrieving several of these studies for us and Shannon Dubois for her extensive comments on this chapter.

References

Abell, S. K., & Lederman, N. G (Eds.). (2007). *Handbook of research on science education.* Mahwah, NJ: Lawrence Erlbaum Associates.

Akerson, V. A., Cullen, T., & Hanson, D. L. (2009). Fostering a community of practice through a professional development program to improve elementary teachers' views of nature of science and teaching practice. *Journal of Research in Science Teaching, 46,* 1090–1113.

American Educational Research Association. (2006). Standards for reporting on empirical social science research in AERA publications. *Educational Researcher, 35*(6), 33–40.

Annetta, L., & Shymansky, J. A. (2008). A comparison of rural elementary school teacher attitudes toward three modes of distance education for science professional development. *Journal of Science Teacher Education, 19,* 255–267.

Banilower, E. R., Heck, D. J., & Weiss, I. R. (2007). Can professional development make the vision of the standards a reality? The impact of the National Science Foundation's local systemic change through teacher enhancement initiative. *Journal of Research in Science Teaching, 44,* 375–395.

Bell, B., & Gilbert, J. (1996). *Teacher development: A model from science education.* London: Falmer Press.

Bell, C. V., & Odom. A. L. (2012). Reflections on discourse practices during professional development on the learning cycle. *Journal of Science Teacher Education, 23,* 601–620.

Berry, A., Loughran, J., Smith, K., & Lindsay, S. (2009). Capturing and enhancing science teachers' professional knowledge. *Research in Science Education, 39,* 575–594.

Bertram, A., & Loughran, J. (2012). Science teachers' views on CoRes and PaP-eRs as a framework for articulating and developing pedagogical content knowledge. *Research in Science Education, 42,* 1027–1047.

Borko, H. (2004). Professional development and teacher learning: Mapping the terrain. *Educational Researcher, 33,* 3–15.

Capps, D. K., Crawford, B. A., & Constas, M. A. (2012). A review of empirical literature on inquiry professional development: Alignment with best practices and a critique of the findings. *Journal of Science Teacher Education, 23,* 291–318.

Cuevas, P., Lee, O., Hart, J., & Deaktor, R. (2005). Improving science inquiry with elementary students of diverse backgrounds. *Journal of Research in Science Teaching, 42,* 337–357.

Darling-Hammond, L., Chung Wei, R., Andree, A., Richardson, N., & Orphanos, S. (2009). *Professional learning in the learning profession: A status report on teacher development in the United States and abroad.* Oxford, OH: National Staff Development Council.

Drayton, B., & Falk, J. (2006). Dimensions that shape teacher–scientist collaborations for teacher enhancement. *Science Education, 90*(4), 734–761.

Dori, Y. J., & Herscovitz, O. (2005). Case-based long-term professional development of science teachers. *International Journal of Science Education, 27,* 1413–1446.

Ebert, E. K., & Crippen, K. J. (2010). Applying a cognitive-affective model of conceptual change to professional development. *Journal of Science Teacher Education, 21,* 371–388.

Elster, D. (2010). Learning communities in teacher education: The impact of e-competence. *International Journal of Science Education, 32,* 2185–2216.

Enochs, L., & Riggs, I. (1990). Further development of an elementary science teaching efficacy belief instrument: A preservice elementary scale. *School Science and Mathematics, 90,* 694–706.

Eurydice. (2011). *Science education in Europe: National policies, practices and research.* Brussels: Eurydice. Retrieved from http://eacea.ec.europa.eu/education

Falik, O., Eylon, B.-S., & Rosenfeld, S (2008). Motivating teachers to enact free-choice project-based learning in science and technology (PBLSAT): Effects of a professional development model. *Journal of Science Teacher Education, 19,* 565–591.

Feiman-Nemser, S. (2001). From preparation to practice: Designing a continuum to strengthen and sustain teaching. *Teachers College Record, 103,* 1013–1055.

Fenstermacher, G. D. (1986). Philosophy of research on teaching: Three aspects. In M. C. Wittrock (Ed.), *Handbook of research on teaching* (3rd ed.; pp. 37–49). New York, NY: Macmillan.

Fishman, B. J., Marx, R. W., Best, S., & Tal, R. T. (2003). Linking teacher and student learning to improve professional development in systemic reform. *Teaching and Teacher Education, 19,* 643–658.

Freeman, J. G., Marx, R. W., & Cimellaro, L. (2004). Emerging considerations for professional development institutes for science teachers. *Journal of Science Teacher Education, 15*(2), 111–131.

Gardner, P. L. (1972). Structure-of-knowledge theory and science education. *Educational Philosophy and Theory, 4*(2), 25–46.

Garet, M.S., Porter, A.C., Desimone, L., Birman, B., & Yoon, K.S. (2001). What makes professional development effective? Results from a national sample of teachers. *American Educational Research Journal, 38,* 915–945.

Geier, R., Blumenfeld, P.C., Marx, R.W., Krajcik, J.S., Fishman, B., Soloway, E., & Clay-Chambers, J. (2008). Standardized test outcomes for students engaged in inquiry-based science curricula in the context of urban reform. *Journal of Research in Science Teaching, 45,* 922–939.

Gerard, L.F., Varma, K., Corliss, S.B., & Linn, M.C. (2011). Professional development for technologically enhanced inquiry science. *Review of Educational Research, 81,* 408–448.

Harlen, W., & Doubler, S.J. (2004). Can teachers learn through enquiry on-line? Studying professional development in science delivered online and on-campus. *International Journal of Science Education, 26,* 1247–1267.

Heller, J.I., Daehler, K.R., Wong, N., Shinohara, M., & Miratrix, L.W. (2012). Differential effects of three professional development models on teacher knowledge and student achievement in elementary science. *Journal of Research in Science Teaching, 49,* 333–362.

Hendriks, M., Luyten, H., Scheerens, J., Sleegers, P., & Steen, R. (Eds.). (2010). *Teachers' professional development: Europe in international comparison: An analysis of teachers' professional development based on the OECD's Teaching and Learning International Survey* (TALIS). Office for Official Publications of the European Union, Luxembourg, viewed Oct. 17, 2012, at http://hdl.voced.edu.au/10707/176573

Hewson, P.W. (2007). Teacher professional development in science. In S.K. Abell & N.G. Lederman (Eds.), *Handbook of research on science education* (pp. 1105–1150). Mahwah, NJ: Lawrence Erlbaum Associates.

Hofstein, A., Carmeli, M., & Shore, R. (2004). The professional development of high school chemistry coordinators. *Journal of Science Teacher Education, 15,* 3–24.

Howe, A.C., & Stubbs, H.S. (2003). From science teacher to teacher leader: Leadership development as meaning making in a community of practice. *Science Education, 87,* 281–297.

Huffman, D. (2006). Reforming pedagogy: Inservice teacher education and instructional reform. *Journal of Science Teacher Education, 17,* 121–136.

Hughes, R., Molyneaux, K., & Dixon, P. (2012). The role of scientist mentors on teacher's perceptions of the community of science during a summer research experience. *Research in Science Education, 42,* 915–941.

Jeanpierre, B., Oberhauser, K., & Freeman, C. (2005). Characteristics of professional development that effect change in secondary science teachers' classroom practices. *Journal of Research in Science Teaching, 42,* 668–690.

Johnson, C.C. (2007). Whole school collaborative sustained professional development and science teacher change: Signs of progress. *Journal of Science Teacher Education, 18,* 629–661.

Kennedy, M.M. (1999). Form and substance in mathematics and science professional development. *NISE Brief, 3*(2), 1–8.

Khourey-Bowers, C., Dinko, R.L., & Hart, R. (2005). Influence of a shared leadership model in creating a school culture of inquiry and collegiality. *Journal of Research in Science Teaching, 42,* 3–24.

Lakshmanan, A., Heath, B.P., Perlmutter, A., & Elder, M. (2011). The impact of science content and professional learning communities on science teaching efficacy and standards-based instruction. *Journal of Research in Science Teaching, 48,* 534–551.

Lara-Alecio, R., Tong, F., Irby, B.J., Guerrero, C., Huerta, M., & Fan, Y. (2012). The effect of an instruction intervention on middle school English learners' science and English reading achievement. *Journal of Research in Science Teaching, 49,* 987–1011.

Lauffer, H.B., & Lauffer, D.W. (2009). Building professional development cadres. In S. Mundry & K.E. Stiles (Eds.), Professional learning communities for science teaching: Lessons from research and practice (pp. 55–72). Arlington, VA: NSTA Press.

Lavonen, J., Jauhiainen, J., Koponen, I.T., & Kurki-Suonio, K. (2004). Effect of a long-term in-service training program on teachers' beliefs about the role of experiments in physics education. *International Journal of Science Education, 26,* 309–328.

Lederman, N.G., Abd-El-Khalick, F., Bell, R., & Schwartz, R. (2002). Views of nature of science questionnaire: Toward valid and meaningful assessment of learners' conceptions of nature of science. *Journal of Research in Science Teaching, 39,* 497–521.

Lee, O., Deaktor, R., Enders, C., & Lambert, J. (2008). Impact of a multiyear professional development intervention on science achievement of culturally and linguistically diverse elementary students. *Journal of Research in Science Teaching, 45,* 726–747.

Lieberman, A. (1995). Practices that support teacher development: Transforming conceptions of professional learning. *Phi Delta Kappan, 76,* 591–596.

Lotter, C., Harwood, W.S., & Bonner, J.J. (2007). The influence of core teaching conceptions on teachers' use of inquiry practices. *Journal of Research in Science Teaching, 9,* 1318–1347.

Loucks-Horsley, S., Hewson, P.W., Love, N., & Stiles, K.E. (1998). *Designing professional development for teachers of science and mathematics.* Thousand Oaks, CA: Corwin.

Loucks-Horsley, S., Love, N., Stiles, K.E., Mundry, S., & Hewson, P.W. (2003). *Designing professional development for teachers of science and mathematics* (2nd ed.). Thousand Oaks, CA: Corwin.

Loucks-Horsley, S., Stiles, K., Mundry, S.E., Love, N.B., & Hewson, P.W. (2010). *Designing professional development for teachers of science and mathematics* (3rd ed.). Thousand Oaks, CA: Corwin.

Luehmann, A.L., & Tinelli, L. (2012). Teacher professional identity development with social networking technologies; learning reform through blogging. *Educational Media International, 45,* 323–333.

Luft, J.A., Firestone, J., Wong, S., Adams, K., & Ortega, I. (2011). Beginning secondary science teacher induction: A two-year mixed methods study. *Journal of Research in Science Teaching, 48*(10), 1199–1224.

Luft, J.A., Wong, S., & Ortega, I. (2009). *The NSTA state of science education survey—2009, full report.* Arlington, VA: National Science Teacher Association.

National Research Council. (2007). *Rising above the gathering storm: Energizing and employing America for a brighter economic future.* Washington, DC: National Academies Press.

National Research Council. (2009). *Strengthening high school chemistry education through teacher outreach programs: A workshop summary to the chemical sciences roundtable.* Washington, DC: National Academies Press.

National Science Board. (2012). *Science and engineering indicators 2012.* Arlington VA: National Science Foundation (NSB 12–01).

National Staff Development Council. (2001). *Standards for staff development* (rev. ed.). Oxford, OH: NSDC.

Nelson, T.H. (2009). Teachers' collaborative inquiry and professional growth: Should we be optimistic? *Science Education, 93,* 548–580.

No Child Left Behind Act of 2001, 20 U.S.C. § 6319 (2008).

Opfer, V.D., & Pedder, D. (2011). Conceptualizing teacher professional learning. *Review of Educational Research, 81,* 367–407. doi:10.3102/0034654311413609

Ostermeier, C., Prenzel, M., & Duit, R. (2010). Improving science and mathematics instruction: The SINUS Project as an example for reform as teacher professional development. *International Journal of Science Education, 32,* 303–327.

Palmer, D. (2011). Sources of efficacy information in an inservice program for elementary teachers. *Science Education, 95,* 577–600.

Penuel, W.R., Fishman, B.J., Yamaguchi, R., & Gallagher, L.P. (2007). What makes professional development effective? Strategies that foster curriculum implementation. *American Education Research Journal, 44,* 921–958.

Penuel, W.R., Gallagher, L.P., & Moorthy, S. (2011). Preparing teachers to design sequences of instruction in Earth systems science: A comparison of three professional development programs. *American Educational Research Journal, 48,* 996–1025.

Posnanski, T. (2010). Developing understanding of the nature of science within a professional development program for inservice elementary teachers: Project nature of elementary science teaching. *Journal of Science Teacher Education, 21,* 589–621.

Pruitt, S.L., & Wallace, C. S (2012). The effect of a state department of education teacher mentor initiative on science achievement. *Journal of Science Teacher Education, 23,* 367–385. doi:10.1007/s10972-012-9280-5

Richmond, G., & Manokore, V. (2011). Identifying elements critical for functional and sustainable professional learning communities. *Science Education, 95,* 543–570.

Rittel, H.W.J., & Webber, M.M. (1973). Dilemmas in a general theory of planning. *Policy Sciences, 4*(2), 155–169.

Roehrig, G.H., & Luft, J.A. (2006). Does one size fit all? The experiences of beginning teachers from different teacher preparation programs during an induction program. *Journal of Research in Science Teaching, 43,* 963–985.

Roth, K., Garnier, H.E., Chen, K., Lemmens, M., Schwille, K., & Wickler, N.I.Z. (2011). Video lesson analysis: Effective science PD for teacher and student learning. *Journal of Research in Science Teaching, 48,* 117–148.

Scherz, Z., Bialer, L., & Eylon, B.-S. (2008). Learning about teachers' accomplishment in "learning skills for science" practice: The use of portfolios in an evidence-based continuous professional development program. *International Journal of Science Education, 30,* 643–667.

Schuster, D.A., & Carlsen, W.S. (2009). Scientists' teaching orientations in the context of teacher professional development. *Science Education, 93,* 635–655.

Schwab, J.J. (1964). Structure of the disciplines: Meanings and significances. In G.W. Ford & L. Pugno (Eds.), *The structure of knowledge and the curriculum* (pp. 6–30). Chicago: Rand McNally.

Schwab, J.J. (1978). The practical: Translation into curriculum. In I. Westbury & N.J. Wilkoff (Eds.), *Science curriculum and liberal education: Selected essays of Joseph J. Schwab* (pp. 365–383). Chicago: University of Chicago Press.

Shapiro, B.L., & Last, S. (2002). Starting points for transformation: Resources to craft a philosophy to guide professional development in elementary science. In P. Fraser-Abder (Ed.), *Professional development of science teachers: Local insights with lessons for the global community* (pp. 1–20). New York: Routledge Falmer.

Short, J. B. (2006). Leading professional development for curriculum reform. In J. Rhoton and P. Shane (Eds.),*Teaching science in the 21st century* (pp. 85–99). Arlington: NSTA Press.

Simon, S., & Johnson, S. (2008). Professional learning portfolios for argumentation in school science. *International Journal of Science Education, 30,* 669–688.

Stolk, M.J., De Jong, O., Bulte, A.M., & Pilot, A. (2011). Exploring a framework for professional development in curriculum innovation: Empowering teachers for designing context-based chemistry education. *Research in Science Education, 41*(3), 369–388.

Supovitz, J., & Turner, H. M. (2000). The effects of professional development on science teaching practices and classroom culture. *Journal of Research in Science Teaching, 37,* 963–980.

van der Valk, T., & de Jong, O. (2009). Scaffolding science teachers in the open-inquiry teaching. *International Journal of Science Education, 31,* 829–850.

Venville, G. I., & Dawson, V.M. (2010). The impact of a classroom intervention on Grade 10 students' argumentation skills, informal reasoning, and conceptual understanding of science. *Journal of Research in Science Teaching, 47,* 952–977.

Watson, K., Steele, F., Vozzo, L., & Aubusson, P. (2007). Changing the subject: Retraining teachers to teach science. *Research in Science Education, 37,* 141–154.

Wilson, S., & Berne, J. (1999). Teacher learning and the acquisition of professional knowledge: An examination of the research on contemporary professional development. *Review of Research in Education, 24,* 173–209.

Zohar, A. (2006): The nature and development of teachers' metastrategic knowledge in the context of teaching higher order thinking. *Journal of the Learning Sciences, 15*(3), 331–377.

Contributors

Fouad Abd-El-Khalick, University of Illinois at Urbana-Champaign, USA

Eleanor Abrams, University of New Hampshire, USA

Tamer G. Amin, American University of Beirut, Lebanon

J. Myron Atkin, Stanford University, USA

Megan Bang, University of Washington, USA

Angela Calabrese Barton, Michigan State University, USA

Amanda Berry, ICLON-Leiden University, Netherlands

Paul Black, King's College London, UK

William J. Boone, Miami University, USA

Bryan McKinley Jones Brayboy, Arizona State University, USA

Edward D. Britton, WestEd, USA

Cory A. Buxton, The University of Georgia, USA

Rodger W. Bybee, Biological Sciences Curriculum Study (Retired), USA

Heidi B. Carlone, The University of North Carolina at Greensboro, USA

William S. Carlsen, The Pennsylvania State University, USA

Angelina Castagno, Northern Arizona University, USA

Barbara A. Crawford, The University of Georgia, USA

Christine M. Cunningham, Museum of Science, Boston, USA

Charlene M. Czerniak, University of Toledo, USA

George E. DeBoer, American Association for the Advancement of Science, USA

Onno De Jong, Utrecht University, Netherlands

Justin Dillon, King's College London, UK

Reinders Duit, IPN–Leibniz Institute for Science and Mathematics Education, Germany

Margaret Eisenhart, University of Colorado Boulder, USA

Hans E. Fischer, University Duisburg-Essen, Germany

Barry J. Fraser, Curtin University, Australia

Mark J. S. Gan, University of Auckland, New Zealand

Peter W. Hewson, University of Wisconsin–Madison, USA

Georgia W. Hodges, The University of Georgia, USA

Dietmar Höttecke, University of Hamburg, Germany

Angela Johnson, St. Mary's College of Maryland, USA

Carla C. Johnson, Purdue University, USA

M. Gail Jones, North Carolina State University, USA

Jane Butler Kahle, Miami University, USA

Sami Kahn, University of South Florida, USA

Gregory J. Kelly, The Pennsylvania State University, USA

Joanna Kidman, Victoria University of Wellington, New Zealand

Joseph S. Krajcik, Michigan State University, USA

Frances Lawrenz, University of Minnesota, USA

Reuven Lazarowitz, Israel Institute of Technology, IIT TECHNION, Israel

Megan Leagon, North Carolina State University, USA

Judith S. Lederman, Illinois Institute of Technology, USA

Norman G. Lederman, Illinois Institute of Technology, USA

Huei Lee, National Dong Hwa University, Taiwan.

Okhee Lee, New York University, USA

Richard Lehrer, Vanderbilt University, USA

Julie Libarkin, Michigan State University, USA

J. John Loughran, Monash University, Australia

Julie A. Luft, The University of Georgia, USA

Andrea K. Martin, Queen's University, Canada

J. Randy McGinnis, University of Maryland, College Park, USA

Elizabeth McKinley, University of Auckland, New Zealand

Jacobiene Meirink, ICLON–Leiden University, Netherlands

Kongju Mun, Michigan State University, USA

Knut Neumann, IPN–Leibniz Institute for Science and Mathematics Education, Germany

Hans Niedderer, Mälardalens University, Sweden

J. Steve Oliver, The University of Georgia, USA

Tara O'Neill, University of Hawaii at Manoa, USA

Nir Orion, Weizmann Institute of Science, Israel

Jonathan Osborne, Stanford University, USA

Eileen Carlton Parsons, University of North Carolina at Chapel Hill, USA

Léonie J. Rennie, Curtin University, Australia

Douglas A. Roberts, University of Calgary, Canada

Kathleen J. Roth, Biological Sciences Curriculum Study (BSCS), USA

Tom Russell, Queen's University, Canada

Kathryn Scantlebury, University of Delaware, USA

Horst Schecker, University of Bremen, Institute of Science Education, Germany

Steven A. Schneider, WestEd, USA

Carol L. Smith, University of Massachusetts at Boston, USA

Keith S. Taber, University of Cambridge, UK

Edna Tan, The University of North Carolina at Greensboro, USA

Peter Charles Taylor, Curtin University, Australia

Mao Thao, University of Minnesota, USA

David F. Treagust, Curtin University, Australia

Chi-Yan Tsui, Curtin University, Australia

Russell Tytler, Deakin University, Australia

Jan H. van Driel, ICLON–Leiden University, Netherlands

Mary Grace Villanueva, Nelson Mandela Metropolitan University, South Africa

Ming Huey Wang, National Taiwan Normal University, Taiwan

Paul Webb, Nelson Mandela Metropolitan University, South Africa

Per-Olof Wickman, Stockholm University, Sweden

Marianne Wiser, Clark University, USA

Mihye Won, Curtin University, Australia

Sarah Beth Woodruff, Miami University, USA

Chiung-Fen Yen, Providence University, Taiwan

Larry D. Yore, University of Victoria, Canada

Dana L. Zeidler, University of South Florida, USA

Subject Index

Note: page numbers in *italics* indicate figures or tables.

Author Index